STRONG'S

HANDI-REFERENCE

CONCORDANCE

Advancing the Ministries of the Gospel
AMG Publishers
God's Word to you is our highest calling.

JAMES STRONG, LL.D, S.T.D.
EDITOR: WARREN BAKER

Strong's Handi-Reference Concordance

Edited by Warren Baker

Published by AMG Publishers
6815 Shallowford Rd.
Chattanooga, TN 37421

ISBN 978-0–89957–119–5

First printing—June 2006

Cover designed by Market Street Design, Chattanooga, Tennessee
Interior design by Warren Baker
Typesetting by Warren Baker and Jennifer Ross
Proofreading by Cheri Mullins, Trevor and Lori Overcash, Dan and Gloria Penwell, and Rick Steele.

Printed in Canada
11 10 –T– 10 9 8 7 6 5 4

Table of Contents

Books of the Bible

Genesis	Ge	Isaiah	Isa	Romans	Ro
Exodus	Ex	Jeremiah	Jer	1 Corinthians	1Co
Leviticus	Le	Lamentations	La	2 Corinthians	2Co
Numbers	Nu	Ezekiel	Eze	Galatians	Gal
Deuteronomy	Dt	Daniel	Da	Ephesians	Eph
Joshua	Jos	Hosea	Hos	Philippians	Php
Judges	Jgs	Joel	Joel	Colossians	Col
Ruth	Ru	Amos	Am	1 Thessalonians	1Th
1 Samuel	1Sa	Obadiah	Ob	2 Thessalonians	2Th
2 Samuel	2Sa	Jonah	Jnh	1 Timothy	1Ti
1 Kings	1Ki	Micah	Mic	2 Timothy	2Ti
2 Kings	2Ki	Nahum	Na	Titus	Tit
1 Chronicles	1Ch	Habakkuk	Hab	Philemon	Phm
2 Chronicles	2Ch	Zephaniah	Zep	Hebrews	Heb
Ezra	Ezr	Haggai	Hag	James	Jas
Nehemiah	Ne	Zechariah	Zec	1 Peter	1Pe
Esther	Est	Malachi	Mal	2 Peter	2Pe
Job	Job	Matthew	Mt	1 John	1Jn
Psalms	Ps	Mark	Mk	2 John	2Jn
Proverbs	Pr	Luke	Lk	3 John	3Jn
Ecclesiastes	Ecc	John	Jn	Jude	Jude
Song of Songs	SS	Acts	Ac	Revelation	Rev

A

ABASE

Job 40:11	every one that is proud, and **a**	8213
Isa 31:4	nor **a** himself for the noise of	6031
Eze 21:26	is low, and **a** him that is high,	8213
Da 4:37	that walk in pride he is able to **a**	8214

ABASED

Mt 23:12	**shall exalt himself shall be a,**	*5013*
Lk 14:11	**that exalteth himself shall be a:**	*5013*
Lk 18:14	**exalteth himself shall be a;**	*5013*
Php 4:12	I know both how to be **a**, and I	*5013*

ABATED

Ge 8:3	and fifty days the waters were **a**	2637
Le 27:18	shall be **a** from thy estimation	1639
Dt 34:7	not dim, nor his natural force **a**	5127

ABBA

Mk 14:36	And he said, **A**, Father, all things	*5*
Ro 8:15	of adoption, whereby we cry, **A**	*5*
Gal 4:6	into your hearts, crying, **A**, Father.	*5*

ABHOR

Le 26:15	if your soul **a** my judgments, so	1602
Le 26:30	your idols, and my soul shall **a** you	1602
Dt 7:26	thou shalt utterly **a** it; for it is a	8581
Dt 23:7	Thou shalt not **a** an Edomite;	8581
Dt 23:7	thou shalt not **a** an Egyptian:	8581
Job 42:6	Wherefore I **a** myself, and repent	3988
Ps 5:6	the Lord will **a** the bloody and	8581
Ps 119:163	I hate and **a** lying: but thy	8581
Jer 14:21	Do not **a** us, for thy name's sake,	5006
Am 6:8	I **a** the excellency of Jacob, and	8374
Ro 12:9	**A** that which is evil; cleave to	*655*

ABHORRED

Ex 5:21	ye have made our savour to be **a**	887
Le 26:43	because their soul **a** my statutes	1602
1Sa 2:17	men **a** the offering of the Lord	5006
2Sa 16:21	shall hear that thou art **a** of thy	887
1Ki 11:25	and he **a** Israel, and reigned	6973
Job 19:19	All my inward friends **a** me:	8581
Ps 22:24	he hath not despised nor **a** the	8262
Pro 22:14	he that is **a** of the Lord shall fall	2194
La 2:7	he hath **a** his sanctuary, he hath	5010
Eze 16:25	hast made thy beauty to be **a**,	8581
Zec 11:8	and their soul also **a** me	973

ABHORREST

Ro 2:22	thou that **a** idols, dost thou commit	*948*

ABHORRETH

Job 33:20	So that his life **a** bread, and	2092
Ps 10:3	the covetous, whom the Lord **a**	5006
Isa 49:7	to him whom the nation **a**, to a	8581

ABIDE See also ABODE.

Ge 19:2	we will **a** in the street all night	3885
Ge 44:33	let thy servant **a** instead of the lad	3427
Ex 16:29	**a** ye every man in his place,	3427
Le 19:13	shall not **a** with thee all night	3885
Nu 31:19	**a** without the camp seven days:	2583
Nu 35:25	he shall **a** in it unto the death of	3427
Dt 3:19	**a** in your cities which I have	3427
Ru 2:8	**a** here fast by my maidens:	1692
1Sa 5:7	God of Israel shall not **a** with us:	3427
1Sa 22:23	**A** thou with me, fear not:	3427
2Sa 11:11	the ark, and Israel, and Judah, **a**	3427
2Sa 16:18	with him will I **a**	3427
1Ki 8:13	a settled place for thee to **a** in	3427
2Ch 32:10	ye **a** in the siege in Jerusalem?	3427
Ps 15:1	who shall **a** in thy tabernacle?	1481
Ps 61:4	I will **a** in thy tabernacle	1481
Ps 61:7	He shall **a** before God for ever:	3427
Ps 91:1	shall **a** under the shadow	3885
Pr 19:23	he that hath it shall **a** satisfied;	3885
Ecc 8:15	shall **a** with him of his labour	3867
Jer 10:10	the nations shall not be able to **a**	3557
Jer 49:18	no man shall **a** there	3427
Jer 49:33	there shall no man **a** there,	3427
Jer 50:40	so shall no man **a** there	3427
Hos 3:4	children of Israel shall **a** many	3427
Joel 2:11	and who can **a** it?	3557
Na 1:6	who can **a** in the fierceness of his	6965
Mal 3:2	may **a** the day of his coming?	3557
Lk 19:5	**for today I must a at thy house.**	*3306*
Lk 24:29	constrained him, saying, **A** with	*3306*
Jn 12:46	**believeth on me should not a in**	*3306*
Jn 14:16	**that he may a with you for ever:**	*3306*
Jn 15:4	**A in me, and I in you**	*3306*
Jn 15:4	**except it a in the vine;**	*3306*
Jn 15:4	**no more can ye, except ye a in me**	*3306*
Jn 15:6	**If a man a not in me, he is cast**	*3306*
Jn 15:7	**If ye a in me, and my words a in**	*3306*
Jn 15:10	**ye shall a in my love**	*3306*
Ac 27:31	Except these **a** in the ship,	*3306*
Ro 11:23	if they **a** not still in unbelief,	*1961*
1Co 3:14	any man's work **a** which he hath	*3306*
1Co 7:8	if they **a** even as I.	*3306*
1Co 7:20	every man **a** in the same calling	*3306*
1Co 7:40	she is happier if she so **a**,	*3306*
Php 1:24	to **a** in the flesh is more needful	*1961*
1Jn 2:28	little children, **a** in him;	*3306*

ABIDETH

Nu 31:23	all that **a** not the fire ye shall	935
Ps 49:12	man being in honour **a** not:	3885
Ps 55:19	even he that **a** of old	3427
Ps 119:90	established the earth, and it **a**	5975
Pr 15:31	reproof of life **a** among the wise	3885
Ecc 1:4	the earth **a** for ever	5975
Jer 21:9	He that **a** in this city shall die	3427
Jn 3:36	the wrath of God **a** on him	3306
Jn 8:35	**but the Son a ever**	*3306*
Jn 12:24	**ground and die, it a alone:**	*3306*
Jn 12:34	of the law that Christ **a** for ever:	*3306*
Jn 15:5	**He that a in me, and I in him,**	*3306*
1Co 13:13	now **a** faith, hope, charity	*3306*
2Ti 2:13	he **a** faithful: he cannot deny	*3306*
Heb 7:3	**a** a priest continually	*3306*
1Pe 1:23	which liveth and **a** for ever.	*3306*
1Jn 2:6	He that saith he **a** in him	*3306*
1Jn 2:14	the word of God **a** in you	*3306*
1Jn 2:17	doeth the will of God **a** for ever	*3306*
1Jn 3:6	Whosoever **a** in him sinneth not:	*3306*
1Jn 3:14	He that loveth not his brother **a** in	*3306*
1Jn 3:24	hereby we know that he **a** in us,	*3306*
2Jn 1:9	**a** not in the doctrine of Christ	*3306*

ABIDING

Nu	24:2	he saw Israel **a** in his tents	7931
Jgs	16:9	**a** with her in the chamber	3427
Lk	2:8	shepherds **a** in the field,	*63*
Jn	5:38	ye have not his word **a** in you:	*3306*
1Jn	3:15	no murderer hath eternal life **a**	3306

ABILITY

Le	27:8	according to his **a** that vowed	5381
Ezr	2:69	They gave after their **a**	3581
Ne	5:8	We after our **a** have redeemed	1767
Da	1:4	such as had **a** in them	3581
Mt	25:15	according to his several **a**;	*1411*
Ac	11:29	every man according to his **a**,	*2141*
1Pe	4:11	as of the **a** which God giveth;	*2479*

ABLE

Ge	13:6	the land was not **a** to bear them,	5375
Ge	15:5	if thou be **a** to number them	3201
Ex	18:25	Moses chose **a** men out of all	2428
Ex	40:35	Moses was not **a** to enter into the	3201
Le	5:7	be not **a** to bring a lamb,	5060, 1767
Le	5:11	he be not **a**	5381
Le	12:8	be not **a** to bring a lamb,	4672, 1767
Le	25:26	himself be **a** to redeem it;	5381
Nu	1:3	all that are **a** to go forth to war	3318
Nu	11:14	I am not **a** to bear all this people	3201
Nu	13:30	we are well **a** to overcome it.	3201
Nu	13:31	not **a** to go up against the people;	3201
Nu	14:16	the Lord was not **a** to bring this	3201
Dt	16:17	man shall give as he is **a**,	4979, 3027
Jos	1:5	There shall not any man be **a** to	3320
1Sa	17:9	If he be **a** to fight with me,	3201
1Ch	9:13	**a** men for the work of the service	2428
1Ch	29:14	that we should be **a** to offer	6113, 3581
2Ch	2:6	who is **a** to build him an house,	3581
2Ch	32:14	your God should be **a** to deliver	3201
Ne	4:10	we are not **a** to build the wall.	3201
Job	41:10	who then is **a** to stand before me?	
Pr	27:4	who is **a** to stand before envy?	
Ecc	8:17	yet shall he not be **a** to find it.	3201
Jer	10:10	the nations shall not be **a** to abide	3201
Jer	49:10	he shall not be **a** to hide himself:	3201
La	1:14	I am not **a** to rise up.	3201
Eze	7:19	their gold shall not be **a** to deliver	3201
Eze	33:12	shall the righteous be **a** to live	3201
Da	2:26	Art thou **a** to make known unto	3546
Da	3:17	God whom we serve is **a** to deliver	3202
Da	4:18	but thou art **a**; for the spirit of	3546
Da	4:37	walk in pride he is **a** to abase	3202
Da	6:20	**a** to deliver thee from the lions?	3202
Am	7:10	land is not **a** to bear all his words.	3201
Zep	1:18	nor their gold shall be **a** to deliver	3201
Mt	3:9	God is **a** of these stone to raise	*1410*
Mt	9:28	Believe ye that I am **a** to do this?	*1410*
Mt	10:28	but are not **a** to kill the soul;	*1410*
Mt	10:28	fear him which is **a** to destroy	*1410*
Mt	19:12	He that is **a** to receive it, let him.	*1410*
Mt	20:22	Are ye **a** to drink of the cup that I	*1410*
Mt	22:46	no man was **a** to answer him	*1410*
Mt	26:61	am **a** to destroy the temple of God,	*1410*
Mt	4:33	as they were **a** to hear	*1410*
Mt	22:46	no man was **a** to answer him	*1410*
Mt	26:61	am **a** to destroy the temple of God,	*1410*
Mk	4:33	as they were **a** to hear	*1410*
Lk	3:8	God is **a** of these stones to raise	*1410*
Lk	13:24	to enter in, and shall not be **a**	*2480*
Lk	14:30	began to build, and was not **a** to	*2480*
Lk	21:15	not be **a** to gainsay nor resist	*1410*
Jn	10:29	no man is **a** to pluck them out of	*1410*
Jn	21:6	now they were not **a** to draw it	*2480*
Ac	6:10	were not **a** to resist the wisdom	*2480*
Ac	15:10	neither our fathers nor we were **a**	*2480*
Ac	20:32	the word of his grace, which is **a**	*1410*
Ro	4:21	what he had promised, he was **a**	*1415*
Ro	8:39	shall be **a** to separate us from the	*1410*
Ro	11:23	God is **a** to graff them in again.	*1415*
Ro	14:4	for God is **a** to make him stand.	*1415*
Ro	15:14	**a** also to admonish one another	*1410*
1Co	3:2	hitherto ye were not **a** to bear it,	*1410*
1Co	10:13	to be tempted above that ye are **a**;	*1410*
2Co	1:4	may be **a** to comfort them which	*1410*
2Co	9:8	God is **a** to make all grace abound	*1415*
Eph	3:18	**a** to comprehend with all saints	*1840*
Eph	3:20	Now unto him that is **a** to do	*1410*
Eph	6:16	ye shall be **a** to quench all the	*1410*
Php	3:21	he is **a** even to subdue all things	*1410*
2Ti	1:12	persuaded that he is **a** to keep	*1415*
2Ti	2:2	shall be **a** to teach others also.	*2425*
2Ti	3:7	never **a** to come to the knowledge	*1410*
2Ti	3:15	scriptures, which are **a** to make	*1410*
Tit	1:9	he may be **a** by sound doctrine	*1415*
Heb	2:18	he is **a** to succour them that are	*1410*
Heb	5:7	was **a** to save him from death,	*1410*
Heb	7:25	Wherefore he is **a** also to save	*1410*
Heb	11:19	that God was **a** to raise him up,	*1415*
Jas	1:21	which is **a** to save your souls.	*1410*
Jas	3:2	**a** also to bridle the whole body	*1415*
Jas	4:12	lawgiver, who is **a** to save and to	*1410*
2Pe	1:15	ye may be **a** after my decease to	*2192*
Jude	24	Now unto him that is **a** to keep	*1410*
Rev	5:3	was **a** to open the book, neither	*1410*
Rev	6:17	who shall be **a** to stand?	*1410*
Rev	13:4	who is **a** to make war with him?	*1410*
Rev	15:8	was **a** to enter into the temple	*1410*

ABODE See also ABIDE.

Ge	29:14	**a** with him the space of a month,	3427
Ge	49:24	But his bow **a** in strength, and	3427
Ex	24:16	glory of the Lord **a** upon mount	7931
Ex	40:35	because the cloud **a** thereon	7931
Nu	9:17	the place where the cloud **a**, there	7931
Dt	9:9	then I **a** in the mount forty days	3427
Jgs	21:2	and **a** there till even before God.	3427
1Sa	7:2	while the ark **a** in Kirjath-jearim,	3427
1Sa	23:14	David **a** in the wilderness	3427
1Sa	26:3	David **a** in the wilderness, and he	3427
Jer	38:28	So Jeremiah **a** in the court of the	3427
Mt	17:22	while they **a** in Galilee, Jesus	*390*
Jn	1:32	like a dove, and it **a** upon him.	*3306*
Jn	8:44	**a** not in the truth, because there	*2476*
Jn	14:23	and make our **a** with him.	3438

ABOLISH

Isa	2:18	the idols he shall utterly **a**.	2498

ABOLISHED

Isa	51:6	my righteousness shall not be **a**.	2865
Eze	6:6	and your works may be **a**.	4229
2Co	3:13	to the end of that which is **a**:	*2673*
Eph	2:15	Having **a** in his flesh the enmity	*2673*
2Ti	1:10	Christ, who hath **a** death,	*2673*

ABOMINABLE

Le	18:30	not any one of these **a** customs,	8441
Le	20:25	ye shall not make your souls **a**	8262
1Ch	21:6	the king's word was **a** to Joab.	8581
2Ch	15:8	put away the **a** idols out of all	8251
Job	15:16	How much more **a** and filthy is	8581
Ps	14:1	they have done **a** works,	8581
Ps	53:1	and have done **a** iniquity:	8581
Jer	44:4	do not this **a** thing that I hate	8441
Eze	16:52	thou hast committed more **a** than	8581
Na	3:6	I will cast **a** filth upon thee,	8251
Tit	1:16	him, being **a**, and disobedient,	*947*
Rev	21:8	unbelieving, and the **a**, and	*948*

ABOMINATION

Ge	46:34	every shepherd is an **a** unto the	8441
Le	7:18	it shall be an **a**,	6292
Le	18:22	as with womankind; it is **a**,	8441
Le	20:13	of them have committed an **a**:	8441
Dt	7:25	for it is an **a** to the Lord thy God.	8441
Dt	7:26	shalt thou bring an **a** into thine	8441
Dt	17:4	such **a** is wrought in Israel:	8441
Dt	22:5	all that do so are **a** unto the	8441
Dt	23:18	both these are **a** unto the Lord	8441
Dt	24:4	that is **a** before the Lord;	8441
Dt	25:16	unrighteously, are an **a** unto	8441
Pr	6:16	seven are an **a** unto him:	8441
Pr	8:7	and wickedness is an **a** to my lips	8441
Pr	11:1	false balance is **a** to the Lord:	8441
Pr	11:20	are of a froward heart are **a** to	8441
Pr	12:22	Lying lips are **a** to the Lord:	8441
Pr	13:19	it is **a** to fools to depart from evil.	8441
Pr	15:8	wicked is an **a** to the Lord:	8441
Pr	15:9	way of the wicked is an **a** unto the	8441
Pr	15:26	thoughts of the wicked are an **a** to	8441
Pr	16:5	proud in heart is an **a** to	8441
Pr	16:12	**a** to kings to commit wickedness:	8441
Pr	17:15	both are **a** to the Lord	8441
Pr	20:10	both of them are alike **a** to the	8441
Pr	20:23	Divers weights are an **a** unto	8441
Pr	21:27	sacrifice of the wicked is **a**:	8441
Pr	24:9	and the scorner is an **a** to men	8441
Pr	28:9	even his prayer shall be **a**.	8441
Pr	29:27	an unjust man is an **a** to the just:	8441
Pr	29:27	is upright in the way is **a** to the	8441
Isa	1:13	incense is an **a** unto me;	8441
Jer	2:7	made mine heritage an **a**.	8441
Jer	6:15	when they had committed **a**?	8441
Jer	8:12	when they had committed **a**?	8441
Eze	22:11	**a** with his neighbour's wife;	8441
Eze	33:26	ye work **a**, and ye defile every	8441
Da	11:31	place the **a** that maketh desolate.	8251
Da	12:11	the **a** that maketh desolate set up,	8251
Mal	2:11	and an **a** is committed in Israel	8441
Mt	24:15	**see the a of desolation,**	*946*
Mk	13:14	**shall see the a of desolation,**	*946*
Lk	16:15	**is a in the sight of God.**	*946*
Rev	21:27	worketh **a**, or maketh a lie:	*946*

ABOMINATIONS

Le	18:27	all these **a** have the men of the	8441
Le	18:29	shall commit any of these **a**,	8441
Dt	18:12	and because of these **a** the Lord	8441
2Ki	16:3	according to the **a** of the heathen,	8441
2Ki	21:2	after the **a** of the heathen,	8441
2Ch	33:2	like unto the **a** of the heathen	8441
2Ch	34:33	Josiah took away all the **a** out of	8441
2Ch	36:8	and his **a** which he did,	8441
2Ch	36:14	after all the **a** of the heathen;	8441
Ezr	9:1	according to their **a**,	8441
Pr	26:25	for there are seven **a** in his heart	8441
Isa	66:3	their soul delighteth in their **a**	8251
Jer	4:1	put away thine **a** out of my sight	8251
Eze	5:11	and with all thine **a** therefore	8441
Eze	7:3	recompense upon thee all thine **a**,	8441
Eze	7:9	according to thy ways and thine **a**	8441
Eze	8:15	thou shalt see greater **a**	8441
Eze	9:4	that cry for all the **a** that be done	8441
Eze	11:21	detestable things and their **a**,	8441
Eze	16:2	cause Jerusalem to know her **a**,	8441
Eze	20:4	cause them to know the **a** of their	8441
Eze	20:7	Cast ye away every man the **a** of	8251
Eze	20:8	cast away the **a** of their eyes,	8251
Eze	36:31	iniquities and for your **a**	8441
Eze	43:8	defiled my holy name by their **a**	8441
Hos	9:10	**a** were according as they loved.	8251
Rev	17:4	full of **a** and filthiness of	*946*
Rev	17:5	mother of harlots and **a** of the	*946*

ABOUND

Pr	28:20	A faithful man shall **a** with	7227
Mt	24:12	**because iniquity shall a,**	*4129*
Ro	5:20	grace did much more **a**:	*5248*
Ro	6:1	that grace may **a**?	*4121*
Ro	15:13	that ye may **a** in hope, through	*4052*
2Co	1:5	sufferings of Christ **a** in us, so our	*4052*
2Co	8:7	that ye **a** in this grace also	*4052*
2Co	9:8	to make all grace **a** toward you:	*4052*
Php	1:9	that your love may **a** yet more	*4052*
Php	4:12	both to **a** and to suffer need.	*4052*
Php	4:17	that may **a** to your account.	*4121*
1Th	3:12	make you to increase and **a** in	*4052*
1Th	4:1	so ye would **a** more and more	*4052*
2Pe	1:8	if these things be in you, and **a**,	*4121*

ABOUNDED

Ro	3:7	hath more **a** through my lie unto	*4052*
Ro	5:15	hath **a** unto many	*4052*
Ro	5:20	But where sin **a**, grace did much	*4121*
2Co	8:2	**a** unto the riches of their liberality	*4052*

ABOUNDETH

Pr	29:22	a furious man **a** in transgression.	7227
2Co	1:5	consolation also **a** by Christ.	*4052*
2Th	1:3	all toward each other **a**;	*4121*

ABOUNDING

1Co	15:58	always **a** in the work of the Lord,	*4052*
Col	2:7	**a** therein with thanksgiving.	*4052*

ABROAD

Ge	11:4	lest we be scattered **a** upon the	6527
Ge	11:8	the Lord scattered them **a** from	6527
Ge	28:14	and thou shalt spread **a** to the	6555
Ex	9:33	from Pharaoh, and spread **a** his	6566
Dt	32:11	spreadeth **a** her wings, taketh	6566
2Ki	4:3	vessels **a** of all thy neighbours,	2351
2Ch	26:8	Uzziah: and his name spread **a**	
Ne	1:8	I will scatter you **a** among the	6327
Job	15:23	wandereth **a** for bread, saying,	5074
Job	40:11	Cast **a** the rage of thy wrath	6327
Isa	24:1	**a** the inhabitants thereof.	6327
Isa	44:24	spreadeth **a** the earth by myself;	7554

Eze 34:21 till ye have scattered them **a**; 2351
Zec 2:6 spread you **a** as the four winds 6566
Mt 9:31 **a** his fame in all that country. *1310*
Mt 9:36 scattered **a**, as sheep having no *4496*
Mt 26:31 **the flock shall be scattered a** *1287*
Mk 1:28 fame spread **a** throughout all *1831*
Mk 4:22 **but that it should come a** *1519, 5318*
Mk 6:14 (for his name was spread **a**:) *1519, 1096*
Lk 1:65 these sayings were noised **a** *1255*
Lk 5:15 more went there a fame **a** of him: *1330*
Jn 21:23 went this saying **a** among the *1831*
Ac 2:6 when this was noised **a**, ... *1096, 5456*
Ac 8:4 they that were scattered **a** went *1289*
Ac 11:19 scattered **a** upon the persecution *1289*
Ro 5:5 love of God is shed **a** in our hearts *1632*
Ro 16:19 your obedience is come **a** unto all *864*
2Co 9:9 He hath dispersed **a**; he hath *4650*
1Th 1:8 faith to God-ward is spread **a**; *1831*
Jas 1:1 tribes which are scattered **a**, ... *1290*

ABSENCE

Lk 22:6 in the **a** of the multitude. *817*
Php 2:12 now much more in my **a**, ... *666*

ABSENT

Ge 31:49 when we are **a** one from another. 5641
2Co 5:8 rather to be **a** from the body, ... *1553*
2Co 5:9 that, whether present or **a**, ... *1553*
2Co 10:1 being **a** am bold toward you: *548*
2Co 13:10 write these things being **a**, ... *548*
Php 1:27 come and see you, or else be **a**, ... *548*
Col 2:5 though I be **a** in the flesh, ... *548*

ABSTAIN

Ac 15:20 they **a** from pollutions of idols, ... *567*
Ac 15:29 ye **a** from meats offered to idols, ... *567*
1Th 4:3 that ye should **a** from fornication: *567*
1Th 5:22 **A** from all appearance of evil. *567*
1Ti 4:3 commanding to **a** from meats, ... *567*
1Pe 2:11 **a** from fleshly lusts, which war *567*

ABUNDANCE

Dt 28:47 for the **a** of all things; 7230
2Sa 12:30 the spoil of the city in great **a**. 7235
1Ki 1:25 fat cattle and sheep in **a**, ... 7230
1Ki 10:10 came no more such **a** of spices 7230
1Ki 18:41 there is a sound of **a** of rain. 1995
1Ch 22:3 David prepared iron in **a** for the 7230
1Ch 22:3 brass in **a** without weight; 7230
1Ch 22:4 Also cedar trees in **a** 369, 4557
1Ch 22:14 iron without weight; for it is in **a**, ... 7230
1Ch 22:15 workmen with thee in **a**, ... 7230
1Ch 29:2 marble stones in **a**. 7230
2Ch 9:1 spices, and gold in **a**, ... 7230
2Ch 17:5 he had riches and honour in **a** 7230
2Ch 18:2 killed sheep and oxen for him in **a**, ... 7230
2Ch 24:11 gathered money in **a**. 7230
2Ch 29:35 the burnt offerings were in **a**, ... 7230
Job 22:11 and **a** of waters cover thee 8229
Job 38:34 that **a** of waters may cover 8229
Ps 37:11 delight themselves in the **a** of 7230
Ps 52:7 trusted in the **a** of his riches, ... 7230
Ecc 5:10 he that loveth **a** with increase: 1995
Ecc 5:12 but the **a** of the rich will not 7647
Isa 15:7 the **a** they have gotten, ... 3502
Isa 47:9 great **a** of thine enchantments 6109
Jer 33:6 reveal unto them the **a** of peace 6283
Eze 16:49 and **a** of idleness was in her 7962
Eze 26:10 By reason of the **a** of his horses 8229
Zec 14:14 silver, and apparel, in great **a**. 7230
Mt 12:34 **out of the a of the heart the** *4051*
Lk 6:45 **of the a of the heart his mouth** *4051*
Lk 12:15 **consisteth not in the a of the** *4052*
Lk 21:4 **these have of their a cast in unto.** *4052*
Ro 5:17 they which receive **a** of grace *4050*
2Co 12:7 through the **a** of the revelations, ... *5236*
Rev 18:3 the **a** of her delicacies *1411*

ABUNDANT

Ex 34:6 and **a** in goodness and truth, ... 7227
Isa 56:12 much more **a**. 1419
Jer 51:13 many waters, **a** in treasures, ... 7227
1Co 12:23 have more **a** comeliness. *4055*
2Co 11:23 in labours more **a**, in stripes *4056*
Php 1:26 may be more **a** in Jesus Christ *4052*
1Pe 1:3 according to his **a** mercy hath *4183*

ABUNDANTLY

Ge 1:20 Let the waters bring forth **a** 8317
Ge 8:17 they may breed **a** in the earth, ... 8317
Ge 9:7 bring forth **a** in the earth, and 8317
Ex 1:7 fruitful, and increased **a**, and 8317
1Ch 22:5 David prepared **a** before his death 7230
1Ch 22:8 Thou has shed blood **a**, ... 7230
Ps 36:8 They shall be **a** satisfied with 7301
Ps 132:15 I will **a** bless her provision: 1288
Ps 145:7 They shall **a** utter the memory 5042
SS 5:1 drink, yea, drink **a**. O beloved 7937
Isa 55:7 for he will **a** pardon. 7235
Jn 10:10 **might have it more a** *4053*
1Co 15:10 I laboured more **a** than they all; *4054*
2Co 12:15 the more **a** I love you, the less I *4056*
Eph 3:20 able to do exceeding **a** above *1537, 4053*
Tit 3:6 Which he shed on us **a** through *4146*
2Pe 1:11 shall be ministered unto you **a** *4146*

ABUSE

1Sa 31:4 thrust me through, and **a** me. 5953
1Ch 10:4 these uncircumcised come and **a** 5953
1Co 9:18 I **a** not my power in the gospel *2710*

ABUSED

Jgs 19:25 they knew her, and **a** her 5953

ABUSERS

1Co 6:9 **a** of themselves with mankind, ... *733*

ABUSING

1Co 7:31 that use this world, as not **a** it: *2710*

ACCEPT

Ge 32:20 peradventure he will **a** of me. 5375
Le 26:43 they shall **a** of the punishment 7521
Job 13:8 Will ye **a** his person? will ye 5375
Job 13:10 if ye do secretly **a** persons 5375
Job 32:21 Let me not, I pray you, **a** any 5375
Job 42:8 for him will I **a**: 5375
Ps 20:3 **a** thy burnt sacrifice; 1878
Ps 82:2 **a** the persons of the wicked? 5375
Ps 119:108 **A**, I beseech thee, the freewill 7521
Pr 18:5 to **a** the person of the wicked, ... 5375
Jer 14:10 the Lord doth not **a** them; 7521
Eze 20:41 will **a** you with your sweet savour, ... 7521
Eze 43:27 I will **a** you, saith the Lord God. 7521
Am 5:22 meat offerings, I will not **a** them; 7521

Mal 1:8 pleased with thee, or **a** thy ... 5375
Mal 1:10 neither will I **a** an offering at ... 7521

ACCEPTABLE
Le 22:20 it shall not be **a** for you. ... 7522
Ps 19:14 be **a** in thy sight, O Lord, ... 7522
Ps 69:13 is unto thee, O Lord, in an **a** time: ... 7522
Pr 10:32 of the righteous know what is **a** ... 7522
Pr 21:3 justice and judgment is more **a** ... 977
Ecc 12:10 preacher sought to find out **a** ... 2656
Isa 49:8 In an **a** time have I heard thee, ... 7522
Isa 61:2 proclaim the **a** year of the Lord, ... 7522
Jer 6:20 your burnt offerings are not **a**, ... 7522
Da 4:27 O king, let my counsel be **a** unto ... 8232
Lk 4:19 **To preach the a year of the Lord.** ... *1184*
Ro 12:1 living sacrifice, holy, **a** unto God, ... *2101*
Ro 12:2 and **a**, and perfect, will of God. ... *2101*
Eph 5:10 Proving what is **a** unto the Lord ... *2101*
Php 4:18 a sweet smell, a sacrifice **a**, ... *1184*
1Ti 2:3 this is good and **a** in the sight of ... *587*
1Ti 5:4 good and **a** before God. ... *587*
1Pe 2:5 **a** to God by Jesus Christ. ... *2144*
1Pe 2:20 this is **a** with God. ... *5485*

ACCEPTABLY
Heb 12:28 serve God **a** with reverence and ... *2102*

ACCEPTATION
1Ti 1:15 worthy of all **a**, that ... *594*
1Ti 4:9 saying and worthy of all **a**. ... *594*

ACCEPTED
Ge 4:7 doest well, shalt thou not be **a**? ... 7613
Ge 19:21 I have **a** thee concerning this ... 5375
Le 22:21 shall be perfect to be **a**; ... 7522
1Sa 18:5 and he was **a** in the sight of all ... 3190
Job 42:9 the Lord also **a** Job. ... 5375
Isa 56:7 their sacrifices shall be **a** upon ... 7522
Lk 4:24 **No prophet is a in his own** ... *1184*
2Co 5:9 we may be **a** of him. ... *2101*
2Co 6:2 behold, now is the **a** time; ... *2144*
2Co 8:12 it is **a** according to that a man ... *2144*
Eph 1:6 wherein he hath made us **a** in ... *5487*

ACCEPTEST
Lk 20:21 neither **a** thou the person of any ... *2983*

ACCEPTETH
Job 34:19 him that **a** not the persons of ... 5375
Ecc 9:7 God now **a** thy works. ... 7521
Hos 8:13 the Lord **a** them not; ... 7521
Gal 2:6 God **a** no man's person: ... *2983*

ACCESS
Ro 5:2 we have **a** by faith into this grace ... *4318*
Eph 2:18 we both have **a** by one Spirit ... *4318*
Eph 3:12 **a** with confidence by the faith of ... *4318*

ACCOMPANY
Heb 6:9 things that **a** salvation, ... *2192*

ACCOMPLISH
Le 22:21 to **a** his vow, ... 6381
Ps 64:6 they **a** a diligent search: ... 8552
Isa 55:11 it shall **a** that which I please, ... 6213
Jer 44:25 ye will surely **a** your vows, ... 6965
Eze 7:8 and **a** mine anger upon thee: ... 3615
Da 9:2 that he would **a** seventy years in ... 4390
Lk 9:31 which he should **a** at Jerusalem ... *4137*

ACCOMPLISHED
2Ch 36:22 word of the Lord ... might be **a**, ... 3615
Est 2:12 days of their purifications **a**, ... 4390
Pr 13:19 The desire **a** is sweet to the soul: ... 1961
Isa 40:2 her warfare is **a**, that her ... 4390
Jer 25:12 when seventy years are **a**, that I ... 4390
Jer 29:10 after seventy years be **a** at ... 4390
La 4:11 The Lord hath **a** his fury; ... 3615
La 4:22 punishment of thine iniquity is **a**, ... 8552
Eze 5:13 Thus shall mine anger be **a**, ... 3615
Da 12:7 and when he shall have **a** to ... 3615
Lk 1:23 days of his ministration were **a**, ... *4130*
Lk 2:6 the days were **a** that she should ... *4130*
Lk 2:21 when eight days were **a** ... *4130*
Lk 18:31 the Son of man shall be **a**. ... *5055*
Lk 22:37 **must yet be a in me,** ... *5055*
Jn 19:28 knowing that all things were now **a**, ... *5055*
1Pe 5:9 afflictions are **a** in your brethren ... *2005*

ACCOMPLISHING
Heb 9:6 **a** the service of God. ... *2005*

ACCOMPLISHMENT
Ac 21:26 the **a** of the days of purification, ... *1604*

ACCORD
Le 25:5 which groweth of its own **a** ... 5599
Ac 1:14 continued with one **a** in prayer ... *3661*
Ac 2:1 were all with one **a** in one place ... *3661*
Ac 2:46 daily with one **a** in the temple, ... *3661*
Ac 4:24 up their voice to God with one **a**, ... *3661*
Ac 5:12 they were all with one **a** in ... *3661*
Ac 7:57 and ran upon him with one **a**, ... *3661*
Ac 8:6 the people with one **a** gave heed ... *3661*
Ac 12:10 opened to them of his own **a**: ... *844*
Ac 12:20 but they came with one **a** to him, ... *3661*
Ac 15:25 being assembled with one **a**, to ... *3661*
Ac 18:12 made insurrection with one **a** ... *3661*
Ac 19:29 rushed with one **a** into the ... *3661*
2Co 8:17 of his own **a** he went unto you. ... *830*
Php 2:2 love, being of one **a**, of one mind. ... *4861*

ACCOUNT
Job 33:13 he giveth not **a** of any of his ... 6030
Ps 144:3 son of man, that thou makest **a** ... 2803
Ecc 7:27 one by one, to find out the **a**; ... 2808
Mt 12:36 **they shall give a thereof in the** ... *3056*
Mt 18:23 **would take a of his servants** ... *5056*
Lk 16:2 **give an a of thy stewardship;** ... *3056*
Ac 19:40 whereby we may give an **a** of this ... *3056*
Ro 14:12 every one of us shall give **a** of ... *3056*
1Co 4:1 Let a man so **a** of us, as of the ... *3049*
Php 4:17 fruit that may abound to your **a**. ... *3056*
Phm 4:18 put that on mine **a**; ... *1677*
Heb 13:17 as they that must give **a**, ... *3056*
1Pe 4:5 shall give **a** to him that is ready ... *3056*

ACCOUNTED
Dt 2:11 Which also were **a** giants, as the ... 2803
Dt 2:20 (That also was **a** a land of giants: ... 2803
1Ki 10:21 it was nothing **a** of in the days ... 2803
2Ch 9:20 of silver; it was not any thing **a** ... 2803
Ps 22:30 it shall be **a** to the Lord for a ... 5608
Isa 2:22 wherein is he to be **a** of? ... 2803
Mk 10:42 **they which are a to rule over** ... *1380*
Lk 20:35 **which shall be a worthy to** ... *2661*
Lk 21:36 **that ye may be a worthy to** ... *2661*

Lk 22:24 which of them should be **a** the *1380*
Ro 8:36 we are **a** as sheep for the *3049*
Gal 3:6 it was **a** to him for righteousness. *3049*

ACCOUNTING
Heb 11:19 **A** that God was able to raise *3049*

ACCOUNTS
Da 6:2 that the princes might give **a** 2941

ACCURSED
Dt 21:23 he that is hanged is **a** of God 7045
Jos 6:18 keep yourselves from the **a** 2764
Jos 7:1 took of the **a** thing: 2764
Jos 7:13 until ye take away the **a** thing 2764
Jos 7:15 taken with the **a** thing shall be 2764
1Ch 2:7 who transgressed in the thing **a** 2764
Isa 65:20 an hundred years old shall be **a** 7043
Ro 9:3 that myself were **a** from Christ *331*
1Co 12:3 calleth Jesus **a**: and that no man *331*
Gal 1:8 preached unto you, let him be **a**. *331*
Gal 1:9 have received, let him be **a** *331*

ACCUSATION
Mt 27:37 over his head his **a** written, ...*156*
Mk 15:26 his **a** was written over, ...*156*
Lk 6:7 might find an **a** against him. *2724*
Lk 19:8 by false **a**, I restore him fourfold *4811*
Jn 18:29 What **a** bring ye against this *2724*
Ac 25:18 they brought none **a** of such *156*
1Ti 5:19 receive not an **a**, but before two *2724*
2Pe 2:11 bring not railing **a** against them *2920*
Jud 9 a railing **a**, but said, The Lord *2920*

ACCUSE
Pr 30:10 **A** not a servant unto his master, ...3960
Mt 12:10 that they might **a** him. *2723*
Mk 3:2 sabbath day; that they might **a** *2723*
Lk 3:14 neither **a** any falsely; and be *4811*
Lk 11:54 his mouth, that they might **a** *2723*
Lk 23:2 they began to **a** him, ...*2723*
Lk 23:14 whereof ye **a** him: *2723*
Jn 5:45 **Do not think that I will a you to** *2723*
Jn 8:6 that they might have to **a** him. *2723*
Ac 24:2 Tertullus began to **a** him, ...*2723*
Ac 24:8 these things, whereof we **a** him. *2723*
Ac 14:13 whereof they now **a** me. *2723*
Ac 25:5 go down with me, and **a** this man, ...*2723*
Ac 25:11 whereof these **a** me, no man may *2723*
Ac 28:19 ought to **a** my nation of *2723*
1Pe 3:16 ashamed that falsely **a** your *1908*

ACCUSED
Da 3:8 Chaldeans came near, and **a** 399, 7170
Da 6:24 those men which had **a** 399, 7170
Mt 27:12 he was **a** of the chief priests *2723*
Mk 15:3 the chief priests **a** him of many *2723*
Lk 16:1 **the same was a unto him that he** *1225*
Lk 23:10 scribes stood and vehemently **a** *2723*
Ac 22:30 wherefore he was **a** of the Jews, ...*2723*
Ac 23:28 the cause wherefore they **a** him, ...*1458*
Ac 23:29 be **a** of questions of their law, ...*1458*
Ac 25:16 before that he which is **a** have *2723*
Ac 26:2 things whereof I am **a** of the *1458*
Ac 26:7 king Agrippa, I am **a** of the Jews *1458*
Tit 1:6 children not **a** of riot, or *1722, 2724*
Rev 12:10 which **a** them before our God *2723*

ACCUSER
Rev 12:10 for the **a** of our brethren is cast *2725*

ACCUSERS
Jn 8:10 **where are those thine a?** *2725*
Ac 23:30 gave commandment to his **a** *2725*
Ac 23:35 when thine **a** are also come. *2725*
Ac 24:8 Commanding his **a** to come unto *2725*
Ac 25:16 have the **a** face to face, ...*2725*
Ac 25:18 when the **a** stood up, ...*2725*
2Ti 3:3 trucebreakers, false **a**, ...*1228*
Tit 2:3 not false **a**, not given to much *1228*

ACCUSETH
Jn 5:45 there is one that **a** you, even *2723*

ACCUSING
Ro 2:15 their thoughts the mean while **a** *2723*

ACCUSTOMED See also UNACCUSTOMED.
Jer 13:23 that are **a** to do evil. 3928

ACKNOWLEDGE
Dt 21:17 he shall **a** the son of the hated 5234
Dt 33:9 neither did he **a** his brethren, ...5234
Ps 51:3 I **a** my transgressions: 3045
Pr 3:6 In all thy ways **a** him, ...3045
Isa 33:13 ye that are near, **a** my might. 3045
Jer 3:13 Only **a** thine iniquity, ...3045
Jer 14:20 We **a**, O Lord, our wickedness, ...3045
Hos 5:15 till they **a** their offence,

ACKNOWLEDGED
Ps 32:5 I **a** my sin unto thee, and mine 3045
2Co 1:14 ye have **a** us in part. *1922*

ACKNOWLEDGETH
1Jn 2:23 he that **a** the Son hath the Father

ACKNOWLEDGING
2Ti 2:25 repentance to the **a** of the truth; *1922*
Tit 1:1 and the **a** of the truth which is *1922*
Phm 6 by the **a** of every good thing *1922*

ACKNOWLEDGMENT
Col 2:2 to the **a** of the mystery of God, ...*1922*

ACQUAINT
Job 22:21 **A** now thyself with him, ...5532

ACQUAINTANCE
2Ki 12:5 it to them, every man of his **a**: 4378
2Ki 12:7 receive no more money of your **a**, ...4378
Job 19:13 and mine **a** are verily estranged 3045
Job 42:11 all they that had been of his **a** 3045
Ps 55:13 my guide, and mine **a**. 3045
Lk 2:44 among their kinsfolk and **a**. *1110*
Lk 23:49 all his **a**, and the women that *1110*
Ac 24:23 he should forbid none of his **a** *2398*

ACQUAINTED
Ps 139:3 and art **a** with all my ways 5532
Isa 53:3 man of sorrows, and **a** with grief: 3045

ACQUAINTING
Ecc 2:3 **a** mine heart with wisdom; 5090

ACQUIT
Job 10:14 thou wilt not **a** me from mine 5352
Na 1:3 will not at all **a** the wicked: 5352

ACTIONS
1Sa 2:3 by him **a** are weighed. 5949

ACTS
Dt 11:3 his **a**, which he did in the midst 4639
Dt 11:7 seen all the great **a** of the Lord 4639
Jgs 5:11 the righteous **a** of the Lord,
1Sa 12:7 all the righteous **a** of the Lord,
Est 10:2 all the **a** of his power and of his 4640
Ps 103:7 his **a** unto the children of Israel. 5949
Ps 106:2 Who can utter the mighty **a** of
Ps 145:12 to the sons of men his mighty **a**
Ps 150:2 Praise him for his mighty **a**

ADD
Ge 30:24 Lord shall **a** to me another son. 3254
Dt 4:2 Ye shall not **a** unto the word 3254
Dt 12:32 thou shalt not **a** thereto, nor 3254
Dt 19:9 then shalt thou **a** three cities 3254
Dt 29:19 to **a** drunkenness to thirst: 5595
1Ki 12:14 heavy, and I will **a** to your yoke: 3254
2Ki 20:6 And I will **a** unto thy days fifteen 3254
2Ch 10:14 I will **a** thereto: my father 3254
2Ch 28:13 ye intend to **a** more to our sins 3254
Ps 69:27 **A** iniquity unto their iniquity: 5414
Pr 3:2 peace, shall they **a** to thee 3254
Pr 30:6 **A** thou not unto his words, lest he 3254
Isa 30:1 that they may **a** sin to sin: 5595
Isa 38:5 I will **a** unto thy days fifteen 3254
Mt 6:27 **can a one cubit unto his stature?** *4369*
Lk 12:25 **can a to his stature one cubit?** *4369*
Php 1:16 to **a** affliction to my bonds: *2018*
2Pe 1:5 **a** to your faith virtue; *2023*
Rev 22:18 If any man shall **a** unto these, *2007*
Rev 22:18 God shall **a** unto him the plagues *2007*

ADDED
Dt 5:22 great voice: and he **a** no more 3254
1Sa 12:19 we have **a** unto all our sins this 3254
Jer 36:32 there were **a** besides unto them 3254
Jer 45:3 Lord hath **a** grief to my sorrow; 3254
Da 4:36 excellent majesty was **a** unto me 3255
Mt 6:33 **these things shall be a unto you** *4369*
Lk 12:31 **these things shall be a unto you** *4369*
Ac 2:41 there were **a** unto them about *4369*
Ac 2:47 the Lord **a** to the church daily *4369*
Ac 5:14 believers were the more **a** to the *4369*
Ac 11:24 much people was **a** unto the Lord. *4369*
Gal 3:19 was **a** because of transgressions, *4369*

ADDER
Ge 49:17 serpent by the way, an **a** in the 8207
Ps 58:4 the deaf **a** that stoppeth her ear; 6620
Ps 91:13 shall tread upon the lion and **a** 6620
Pr 23:32 a serpent, and stingeth like an **a**. 6848

ADDERS'
Ps 140:3 **a** poison is under their lips 5919

ADDETH
Job 34:37 he **a** rebellion unto his sin, 3254
Pr 10:22 he **a** no sorrow with it. 3254
Pr 16:23 **a** learning to his lips. 3254
Gal 3:15 no man disannulled, or **a** *1928*

ADDICTED
1Co 16:15 they have **a** themselves to the *5021*

ADJURE
1Ki 22:16 How many times shall I **a** thee 7650
2Ch 18:15 How many times shall I **a** thee 7650
Mt 26:63 I **a** thee by the living God, *1844*
Mk 5:7 I **a** thee by God, that thou *3726*
Ac 19:13 We **a** you by Jesus whom Paul *3726*

ADJURED
Jos 6:26 Joshua **a** them at that time, 7650
1Sa 14:24 for Saul had **a** the people, 422

ADMINISTERED See also MINISTERED.
2Co 8:19 which is **a** by us to the glory of *1247*
2Co 8:20 abundance which is **a** by us: *1247*

ADMIRATION
Jude 16 having men's persons in **a** *2296*
Rev 17:6 her, I wondered with great **a**. *2295*

ADMIRED
2Th 1:10 to be **a** in all them that believe *2296*

ADMONISH
Ro 15:14 able also to **a** one another. *3560*
1Th 5:12 over you in the Lord, and **a** you; *3560*
2Th 3:15 but **a** him as a brother. *3560*

ADMONISHED
Ecc 4:13 who will no more be **a**. 2094
Ecc 12:12 by these, my son, be **a**: 2094
Jer 42:19 know certainly that I have **a** 5749
Ac 27:9 already past, Paul **a** them, *3867*
Heb 8:5 as Moses was **a** of God when *5537*

ADMONISHING
Col 3:16 **a** one another in psalms and *3560*

ADMONITION
1Co 10:11 they are written for our **a**, *3559*
Eph 6:4 the nurture and **a** of the Lord. *3559*
Tit 3:10 after the first and second **a** reject; *3559*

ADOPTION
Ro 8:15 ye have received the Spirit of **a**, *5206*
Ro 8:23 waiting for the **a**, to wit, the *5206*
Ro 9:4 to whom pertaineth the **a**, and *5206*
Gal 4:5 we might receive the **a** of sons *5206*
Eph 1:5 unto the **a** of children by Jesus *5206*

ADORN
1Ti 2:9 that women **a** themselves in *2885*
Tit 2:10 they may **a** the doctrine of God *2885*

ADORNED
Jer 31:4 thou shalt again be **a** with thy 5710
Lk 21:5 how it was **a** with goodly stones *2885*
1Pe 3:5 **a** themselves, being in subjection *2885*
Rev 21:2 as a bride **a** for her husband *2885*

ADORNETH
Isa 61:10 a bride **a** herself with her jewels. 5710

ADORNING
1Pe 3:3 **a** let it not be that outward **a** *2889*

ADULTERER
Le 20:10 the **a** and the adulteress shall 5003
Job 24:15 the eye also of the **a** waiteth for 5003
Isa 57:3 the seed of the **a** 5003

ADULTERERS

Ps	50:18	hast been partaker with **a**.	5003
Jer	9:2	they be all **a**,	5003
Jer	23:10	the land is full of **a**;	5003
Hos	7:4	They are all **a**,	5003
Mal	3:5	the sorcerers, and against the **a**,	5003
Lk	18:11	**extortioners, unjust, a,**	*3432*
1Co	6:9	nor idolaters, nor **a**,	*3432*
Heb	13:4	whoremongers and **a** God will	*3432*
Jas	4:4	Ye **a** and adulteresses,	*3432*

ADULTERESS

Le	20:10	adulterer and the **a** shall surely	5003
Pr	6:26	and the **a** will hunt for the	802, 376
Hos	3:1	beloved of her friend, yet an **a**,	5003
Ro	7:3	she shall be called an **a**:	*3428*
Ro	7:3	so that she is no **a**,	*3428*

ADULTERESSES

Eze	23:45	after the manner of **a**,	5003
Eze	23:45	because they are **a**,	5003
Jas	4:4	Ye adulterers and **a**,	*3428*

ADULTERIES

Jer	13:27	I have seen thine **a**,	5004
Eze	23:43	her that was old in **a**,	5004
Hos	2:2	out of her sight, and her **a**	5005
Mt	15:19	**murders, a, fornications,**	*3430*
Mk	7:21	evil thoughts, **a**, fornications,	*3430*

ADULTEROUS

Pr	30:20	such is the way of an **a** woman;	5003
Mt	12:39	**An evil and a generation seeketh**	*3428*
Mt	16:4	**A wicked and a generation**	*3428*
Mk	8:38	**in this a and sinful generation;**	*3428*

ADULTERY

Ex	20:14	Thou shalt not commit **a**	5003
Le	20:10	the man that committeth **a**	5003
Dt	5:18	Neither shalt thou commit **a**	5003
Pr	6:32	committeth **a** with a woman	5003
Jer	3:8	backsliding Israel committed **a**	5003
Jer	3:9	and committed **a** with stones	5003
Jer	5:7	they then committed **a**, and	5003
Jer	7:9	ye steal, murder, and commit **a**,	5003
Jer	23:14	they commit **a**, and walk in lies:	5003
Jer	29:23	in Israel, and have committed **a**	5003
Eze	16:32	a wife that committeth **a**,	5003
Eze	23:37	they have committed **a**, and blood	5003
Eze	23:37	their idols have they committed **a**,	5003
Hos	4:2	stealing, and committing **a**,	5003
Hos	4:13	your spouses shall commit **a**	5003
Hos	4:14	when they commit **a**:	5003
Mt	5:27	**Thou shalt not commit a:**	*3431*
Mt	5:28	**hath committed a with her**	*3431*
Mt	5:32	**causeth her to commit a:**	*3429*
Mt	5:32	**that is divorced committeth a.**	*3429*
Mt	19:9	**marry another, committeth a**	*3429*
Mt	19:9	**is put away doth commit a**	*3429*
Mt	19:18	**Thou shalt not commit a**	*3431*
Mk	10:11	**committeth a against her.**	*3429*
Mk	10:12	**to another, she committeth a**	*3429*
Mk	10:19	**Do not commit a,**	*3431*
Lk	16:18	**marrieth another, committeth a:**	*3431*
Lk	16:18	**from her husband committeth a**	*3431*
Lk	18:20	**Do not commit a, Do not kill,**	*3431*
Jn	8:3	unto him a woman taken in **a**;	*3430*
Jn	8:4	was taken in **a**, in the very act.	*3431*
Ro	2:22	dost thou commit **a**?	*3431*
Ro	13:9	Thou shalt not commit **a**, Thou	*3431*
Gal	5:19	**A**, fornication, uncleanness,	*3430*
Jas	2:11	Do not commit **a**, said also	*3431*
2Pe	2:14	Having eyes full of **a**,	*3428*
Rev	2:22	**and them that commit a with her.**	*3431*

ADVANTAGE

Job	35:3	thou saidst, What **a** will it be	5532
Ro	3:1	What **a** then hath the Jew?	*4053*
2Co	2:11	Lest Satan should get an **a** of us:	*4122*
Jude	16	in admiration because of **a**	*5622*

ADVANTAGED

Lk	9:25	**For what is a man a,**	*5623*

ADVANTAGETH

1Co	15:32	what **a** it me, if the dead rise.	*3786*

ADVERSARIES

Ex	23:22	and an adversary unto thine **a**.	6696
Dt	32:43	render vengeance to his **a**,	6862
Jos	5:13	Art thou for us, or for our **a**?	6862
1Sa	2:10	**a** of the Lord shall be broken to	7378
2Sa	19:22	should this day be **a** unto me?	7854
Ps	38:20	render evil for good are mine **a**;	7853
Ps	69:19	mine **a** are all before thee	6887
Ps	71:13	**a** to my soul;	7853
Ps	81:14	turned my hand against their **a**.	6862
Ps	89:42	hast set the right hand of his **a**;	6862
Ps	109:4	For my love they are my **a**:	7853
Ps	109:20	the reward of mine **a**	7853
Ps	109:29	Let mine **a** be clothed with	7853
Isa	1:24	I will ease me of mine **a**,	6862
Isa	59:18	he will repay, fury to his **a**,	6862
Isa	63:18	our **a** have trodden down thy	6862
Isa	64:2	make thy name known to thine **a**,	6862
Jer	30:16	devoured; and all thine **a**,	6862
Jer	46:10	avenge him of his **a**:	6862
La	1:5	Her **a** are the chief,	6862
La	1:7	the **a** saw her, and did mock	6862
La	1:17	his **a** should be round about him:	6862
La	2:17	set up the horn of thine **a**.	6862
Mic	5:9	lifted up upon thine **a**,	6862
Na	1:2	Lord will take vengeance on his **a**,	6862
Lk	13:17	all his **a** were ashamed;	*480*
Lk	21:15	**your a shall not be able to gainsay**	*480*
1Co	16:9	unto me, and there are many **a**.	*480*
Php	1:28	in nothing terrified by your **a**:	*480*
Heb	10:27	which shall devour the **a**.	*5227*

ADVERSARY

Ex	23:22	and an **a** unto thine adversaries	6887
Nu	22:22	stood in the way for an **a** against	7854
1Sa	1:6	her **a** also provoked her sore.	6869
1Sa	29:4	lest in the battle he be an **a**	7854
1Ki	5:4	is neither **a** nor evil occurrent	7854
1Ki	11:14	the Lord stirred up an **a** unto	7854
1Ki	11:23	God stirred him up another **a**,	7854
1Ki	11:25	he was an **a** to Israel all the days	7854
Est	7:6	The **a** and enemy is this wicked	6862
Job	31:35	mine **a** had written a book	376, 7379
Ps	74:10	how long shall the **a** reproach?	6862
Isa	50:8	who is mine **a**?	1166, 4941
La	1:10	The **a** hath spread out his hand	6862
La	2:4	with his right hand as an **a**,	6862

La 4:12 have believed that the **a** and the 6862
Mt 5:25 **Agree with thine a quickly,** *476*
Lk 12:58 **with thine a to the magistrate,** *476*
Lk 18:3 **saying, Avenge me of mine a** *476*
1Ti 5:14 give none occasion to the **a** *480*
1Pe 5:8 because your **a** the devil, ...*476*

ADVERSITIES
1Sa 10:19 saved you out of all your **a** 7451
Ps 31:7 hast known my soul in **a**; 6869

ADVERSITY
2Sa 4:9 redeemed my soul out of all **a**, ...6869
2Ch 15:6 God did vex them with all **a**. 6869
Ps 10:6 I shall never be in **a**. 7451
Ps 35:51 But in mine **a** they rejoiced, ...6761
Ps 94:13 give him rest from the days of **a**, ...7451
Pr 17:17 a brother is born for **a**. 6869
Pr 24:10 If thou faint in the day of **a**, ...6869
Ecc 7:14 in the day of **a** consider: 7451
Isa 30:20 the Lord give you the bread of **a**, ...6862
Heb 13:3 and them which suffer **a**, ...*2558*

ADVICE
Jgs 19:30 consider of it, take **a**, and speak 5779
Jgs 20:7 give here your **a** and counsel. 1697
1Sa 25:33 blessed be thy **a**, and blessed be 2940
2Sa 19:43 that our **a** should not be first had 1697
2Ch 10:9 What **a** give ye that we may 3289
2Ch 10:14 answered them after the **a** of 6098
2Ch 25:17 Amaziah king of Judah took **a**, ...3289
Pr 20:18 and with good **a** make war 8458
2Co 8:10 herein I give my **a**: for this is *1106*

ADVISE
2Sa 24:13 **a**, and see what answer I shall 3045
1Ki 12:6 How do ye **a** that I may answer 3289
1Ch 21:12 **a** thyself what word I shall 7200

ADVISED
Pr 13:10 with the well **a** is wisdom. 3289
Ac 27:12 the more part **a** to depart *1012, 5087*

ADVOCATE
1Jn 2:1 **a** with the Father, Jesus Christ *3875*

AFFAIRS
1Ch 26:32 pertaining to God, and **a** of the 1697
Ps 112:5 he will guide his **a** 1697
Da 2:49 the **a** of the province of Babylon: 5673
Da 3:12 whom thou hast set over the **a** of 5673
Eph 6:21 also may know my **a**, ...*2596*
Eph 6:22 ye might know our **a**, ...*4012*
Php 1:27 I may hear of your **a**, that ye *4012*
2Ti 2:4 entangleth himself with the **a** of *4230*

AFFECTION
1Ch 29:3 because I have set my **a** to the 7521
Ro 1:31 without natural **a**, implacable, ...*794*
Col 3:2 Set your **a** on things above, ...*5426*
Col 3:5 uncleanness, inordinate **a**, ...*3806*
2Ti 3:3 Without natural **a**, trucebreakers *794*

AFFECTIONS
Ro 1:26 God gave them up unto vile **a**: *3806*
Gal 5:24 crucified the flesh with the **a** *3804*

AFFINITY
1Ki 3:1 Solomon made **a** with Pharaoh 2859
2Ch 18:1 and joined **a** with Ahab. 2859
Ezr 9:14 and join in **a** with the people 2859

AFFIRM
1Ti 1:7 what they say, nor whereof they **a**. *1226*
Tit 3:8 I will that thou **a** constantly, ...*1226*

AFFIRMED
Lk 22:59 another confidently **a**, saying, ...*1340*
Ac 12:15 she constantly **a** that it was even *1340*
Ac 25:19 whom Paul **a** to be alive. *5335*

AFFLICT
Ge 15:13 they shall **a** them four hundred 6031
Ge 31:50 If thou shalt **a** my daughters, ...6031
Ex 1:11 over them taskmasters to **a** them 6031
Ex 22:22 Ye shall not **a** any widow, ...6031
Ex 22:23 If thou **a** them in any wise, ...6031
Le 16:29 ye shall **a** your souls, ...6031
Le 16:31 you, and ye shall **a** your souls, ...6031
Le 23:27 ye shall **a** your souls, and offer an 6031
Le 23:32 ye shall **a** your souls: in the ninth 6031
Nu 30:13 every binding oath to **a** the soul, ...6031
Jgs 16:6 thou mightest be bound to **a** thee 6031
Jgs 16:19 and she began to **a** him, ...6031
2Sa 7:10 shall the children of wickedness **a** 6031
1Ki 11:39 I will for this **a** the seed of David, ...6031
2Ch 6:26 when thou dost **a** them; 6031
Ezr 8:21 **a** ourselves before our God, ...6031
Job 37:23 plenty of justice: he will not **a**. 6031
Ps 44:2 how thou didst **a** the people, ...7489
Ps 55:19 God shall hear, and **a** them, ...6031
Ps 89:22 nor the son of wickedness **a** him. 6031
Ps 94:5 and **a** thine heritage 6031
Ps 143:12 destroy all them that **a** my soul: 6887
Isa 58:5 a day for a man to **a** his soul? 6031
Isa 64:12 hold thy peace, and **a** us very sore? 6031
Jer 31:28 down, and to destroy, and to **a**; 7489
La 3:33 For he doth not **a** willingly 6031
Am 5:12 they **a** the just, they take a bribe, ...6887
Na 1:12 I will **a** thee no more 6031
Zep 3:19 I will undo all that **a** thee: 6031

AFFLICTED
Ex 1:12 But the more they **a** them, the 6031
Le 23:29 shall not be **a** in that same day, ...6031
Nu 11:11 Wherefore hast thou **a** thy 7489
Dt 26:6 evil entreated us, and **a** us, ...6031
Ru 1:21 the Almighty hath **a** me? 7489
2Sa 22:28 the **a** people thou wilt save: 6041
Job 6:14 To him that is **a** pity should be 4523
Job 34:28 and he heareth the cry of the **a**. 6041
Ps 22:24 abhorred the affliction of the **a**; 6041
Ps 25:16 me; for I am desolate and **a**. 6041
Ps 82:3 do justice to the **a** and needy. 6041
Ps 88:15 I am **a** and ready to die from my 6041
Ps 107:17 because of their iniquities, are **a** 6031
Ps 116:10 I was greatly **a**: 6031
Ps 119:67 Before I was **a** I went astray: 6031
Ps 119:75 thou in faithfulness hast **a** me. 6031
Ps 129:1, 2 Many a time have they **a** me. 6887
Ps 140:12 maintain the cause of the **a**, and 6041
Pr 15:15 All the days of the **a** are evil: 6041
Pr 22:22 neither oppress the **a** in the gate: 6041
Pr 26:28 hateth those that are **a** by it; 1790
Pr 31:5 the judgment of any of the **a**. 6040
Isa 49:13 and will have mercy upon his **a**. 6041

Isa	51:21	Therefore hear now this, thou **a**,	6041
Isa	53:4	smitten of God, and **a**.	6031
Isa	53:7	He was oppressed, and he was **a**,	6031
Isa	54:11	O thou **a**, tossed with tempest, and	6041
Isa	58:3	wherefore have we **a** our soul,	6031
Isa	58:10	satisfy the **a** soul;	6031
Isa	60:14	The sons also of them that **a** thee	6031
Isa	63:9	In all their affliction he was **a**,	6862
La	1:4	priests sigh, her virgins are **a**,	3013
La	1:5	for the Lord hath **a** her for the	3013
La	1:12	wherewith the Lord hath **a** me	3013
Mic	4:6	her that I have **a**;	7489
Na	1:12	Though I have **a** thee,	6031
Zep	3:12	of thee an **a** and poor people,	6041
Mt	24:9	**they deliver you up to be a,**	*2347*
2Co	1:6	And whether we be **a**,	*2346*
1Ti	5:10	if she have relieved the **a**,	*2346*
Heb	11:37	being destitute, **a**, tormented;	*2346*
Jas	4:9	Be **a**, and mourn, and weep:	*5003*
Jas	5:13	Is any among you **a**?	*2553*

AFFLICTION

Ge	16:11	the Lord hath heard thy **a**	6040
Ge	29:32	the Lord hath looked upon my **a**;	6040
Ge	31:42	God hath seen mine **a**	6040
Ge	41:52	in the land of my **a**	6040
Ex	3:7	surely seen the **a** of my people	6040
Ex	3:17	bring you up out of the **a** of Egypt	6040
Ex	4:31	he had looked upon their **a**,	6040
Dt	16:3	the bread of **a**;	6040
1Sa	1:11	look on the **a** of thine handmaid,	6040
2Sa	16:12	the Lord will look on mine **a**,	5869
1Ki	22:27	feed him with bread of **a**	3905
1Ki	22:27	and with water of **a**,	3905
2Ki	14:26	the Lord saw the **a** of Israel,	6040
2Ch	20:9	and cry unto thee in our **a**,	6869
Ne	9:9	didst see the **a** of our fathers	6040
Job	5:6	**a** cometh not forth of the dust,	205
Job	30:16	days of **a** have taken hold upon	6040
Job	36:15	He delivereth the poor in his **a**,	6040
Ps	25:18	Look upon mine **a** and my pain;	6040
Ps	88:9	eye mourneth by reason of **a**:	6040
Ps	106:44	he regarded their **a**	6862
Ps	107:10	bound in **a** and iron;	6040
Ps	119:92	then have perished in mine **a**,	6040
Ps	119:153	Consider mine **a**,	6040
Isa	30:20	water of **a**, yet shall not	3905
Isa	48:10	in the furnace of **a**	6040
Jer	15:11	of evil and in the time of **a**	6869
Jer	16:19	my refuge in the day of **a**,	6869
Jer	30:15	Why criest thou for thine **a**?	7667
La	1:3	gone into captivity because of **a**,	6040
La	1:9	O Lord, behold my **a**:	6040
La	3:1	I am the man that hath seen **a**	6040
Hos	5:15	in their **a** they will seek me early	6862
Jnh	2:2	reason of mine **a** unto the Lord,	6869
Na	1:9	**a** shall not rise up the second time	6869
Mk	4:17	**when a or persecution ariseth**	*2347*
Mk	13:19	**in those days shall be a,**	*2347*
2Co	2:4	out of much **a** and anguish of	*2347*
2Co	4:17	light **a**, which is but for a moment,	*2347*
2Co	8:2	How that in a great trial of **a**	*2347*
Php	4:14	ye did communicate with my **a**.	*2347*
Heb	11:25	Choosing rather to suffer **a** with	*4797*
Jas	1:27	and widows in their **a**,	*2347*
Jas	5:10	an example of suffering **a**, and	*2552*

AFFLICTIONS

Ps	34:19	Many are the **a** of the righteous:	7451
Ac	7:10	delivered him out of all his **a**,	*2347*
2Co	6:4	in **a**, in necessities, in distresses,	*2347*
Col	1:24	which is behind of the **a** of Christ	*2347*
2Ti	1:8	partaker of the **a** of the gospel	*4777*
2Ti	4:5	**a**, do the work of an evangelist,	*2553*
Heb	10:33	both by reproaches and **a**;	*2347*
1Pe	5:9	the same **a** are accomplished	*3804*

AFRAID

Ge	3:10	I was **a**, because I was naked;	3372
Ge	18:15	I laughed not; for she was **a**.	3372
Ge	43:18	And the men were **a**, because	3372
Ex	3:6	he was **a** to look upon God.	3372
Ex	15:14	people shall hear, and be **a**:	7264
Ex	34:30	they were **a** to come nigh him.	3372
Dt	1:17	ye shall not be **a** of the face of man;	1481
Dt	5:5	ye were **a** by reason of the fire,	3372
Dt	7:19	all the people of whom thou art **a**.	3373
Dt	20:1	be not **a** of them: for the Lord	3372
Jos	1:9	not **a**, neither be thou dismayed	6206
Jgs	7:3	Whosoever is fearful and **a**,	2730
Ru	3:8	that the man was **a**, and turned	2729
1Sa	18:12	And Saul was **a** of David,	3372
1Sa	18:29	Saul was yet the more **a** of David;	3372
1Sa	28:13	the king said unto her, Be not **a**:	3372
1Sa	31:4	would not: for he was sore **a**.	3372
2Sa	1:14	How wast thou not **a** to stretch	3372
2Sa	6:9	David was **a** of the Lord that day,	3372
2Sa	22:5	of ungodly men made me **a**;	1204
Est	7:6	Haman was **a** before the king	1204
Job	3:25	which I was **a** of is come unto me	3025
Job	9:28	I am **a** of all my sorrows, I	3025
Job	13:11	not his excellency make you **a**?	1204
Job	23:15	when I consider, I am **a** of him	6342
Ps	3:6	I will not be **a** of ten thousands	3372
Ps	27:1	of whom shall I be **a**?	6342
Ps	56:3	time I am **a**, I will trust in thee	3372
Ps	91:5	Thou shalt not be **a** for the	3372
Ps	112:8	is established, he shall not be **a**,	3372
Pr	3:24	thou shalt not be **a**:	6342
Pr	3:25	Be not **a** of sudden fear,	3372
Isa	13:8	And they shall be **a**: pangs and	926
Isa	37:6	Be not **a** of the words	3372
Isa	51:12	that thou shouldest be **a** of a man	3372
Isa	57:11	of whom hast thou been **a** or	1672
Jer	1:8	Be not **a** of their faces:	3372
Jer	2:12	be horribly **a**, be ye very desolate,	8175
Jer	10:5	Be not **a** of them; for they cannot	3372
Jer	30:10	none shall make him **a**.	2729
Jer	36:16	heard all the words, they were **a**	6342
Jer	36:24	Yet they were not **a**,	6342
Jer	42:11	Be not **a** of the king of Babylon.	3372
Eze	2:6	son of man, be not **a** of them,	3372
Da	4:5	I saw a dream which made me **a**,	1763
Da	8:17	when he came, I was **a**,	1204
Am	3:6	the people not be **a**?	2729
Jnh	1:5	Then the mariners were **a**,	3372
Jnh	1:10	Then were the men exceedingly **a**,	3372
Mt	14:27	**it is I; be not a**	*5399*
Mt	14:30	the wind boisterous, he was **a**;	*5399*
Mt	17:7	**Arise, and be not a**	*5399*
Mt	25:25	**And I was a, and went and hid**	*5399*
Mt	28:10	**Be not a: go tell my brethren.**	*5399*
Mk	5:15	his right mind: and they were **a**.	*5399*

Mk 5:36	**Be not a, only believe.**	*5399*
Mk 6:50	**it is I; be not a**	*5399*
Mk 9:32	and were **a** to ask him.	*5399*
Mk 16:8	any man; for they were **a**	*5399*
Lk 2:9	and they were sore **a**.	*5399*
Lk 12:4	**Be not a of them that kill.**	*5399*
Jn 6:20	**It is I; be not a,**	*5399*
Jn 14:27	**be troubled, neither let it be a**	*1168*
Jn 19:8	he was the more **a**;	*5399*
Ac 18:9	**Be not a, but speak, and hold**	*5399*
Ac 22:9	saw indeed the light, and were **a**;	*1719*
Ro 13:3	Wilt thou then not be **a** of the	*5399*
Heb 11:23	and they were not **a** of the king's	*5399*

AFRESH

Heb 6:6	to themselves the Son of God **a**,	*388*

AFTERWARD

Ge 32:20	and **a** I will see his face;	310, 3651
Ge 38:30	And **a** came out his brother,	310
Ex 34:32	**a** all the children of Israel	310, 3651
Le 14:19	**a** he shall kill the burnt offering:	310
Le 16:28	**a** he shall come into the camp	310, 3651
Le 22:7	and shall **a** eat of the holy things;	310
Dt 24:21	thou shalt not glean it **a**:	310
Jgs 16:4	came to pass **a**, that he loved	310, 3651
1Sa 24:5	**a**, that David's heart smote	310, 3651
Ps 73:24	and **a** receive me to glory,	310
Isa 1:26	**a** thou shalt be called,	310, 3651
Eze 41:1	**A** he brought me to the temple,	
Joel 2:28	come to pass **a**, that I will	310, 3651
Mt 4:2	he was **a** an hungred	*5305*
Mt 21:29	**but a he repented, and went**	*5305*
Mt 21:32	**ye had seen it, repented not a,**	*5305*
Mt 25:11	**A came also the other virgins,**	*5305*
Mk 4:17	**a, when affliction or persecution**	*1534*
Mk 16:14	**A** he appeared unto the eleven	*5305*
Lk 17:8	**a thou shalt eat and drink?**	*3326, 5023*
Lk 18:4	**but a he said within himself,**	*3326, 5023*
Jn 5:14	**A** Jesus findeth him in the	*3326, 5023*
Ac 13:21	And **a** they desired a king:	*2547*
1Co 15:23	**a** they that are Christ's at his	*1899*
Jude 5	**a** destroyed them that believed not	*1208*

AFTERWARDS

Ex 11:1	**a** he will let you go hence:	310, 3651
Pr 24:27	**a** build thine house.	310
Pr 29:11	a wise man keepeth it in till **a**	268
Eze 11:24	**A** the spirit took me up, and	
Jn 13:36	**but thou shalt follow me a**	*5305*

AGATE

Ex 28:19	the third row a ligure, a **a**, and	7618
Eze 27:16	fine linen, and coral, and **a**	3539

AGE

Ge 15:15	shalt be buried in a good old **a**	7872
Ge 18:11	well stricken in **a**; and it ceased	3117
Ge 21:2	bare Abraham a son in his old **a**,	
Ge 25:8	Abraham … died in a good old **a**,	7872
Jos 23:2	I am old and stricken in **a**:	3117
Ru 4:15	and a nourisher of thine old **a**:	7872
1Sa 2:33	shall die in the flower of their **a**	582
1Ch 29:28	died in a good old **a**, full of days,	7872
Job 5:26	come to thy grave in a full **a**,	3624
Ps 39:5	mine **a** is as nothing before thee:	2465
Ps 71:9	me not off in the time of old **a**;	
Ps 92:14	still bring forth fruit in old **a**;	7872
Lk 3:23	about thirty years of **a**, being (as	
Lk 8:42	twelve years of **a**, and she lay a dying	
John 9:21	we know not: he is of **a**; ask him:	*2244*
1Co 7:36	she pass the flower of her **a**	*5230*
Heb 11:11	when she was past **a**, because she	*2244*

AGES

Eph 2:7	That in the **a** to come he might	*165*
Eph 3:5	Which in other **a** was not made	*1074*
Eph 3:21	throughout all **a**, world without	*1074*
Col 1:26	hid from **a** and from generations,	*165*

AGONY

Lk 22:44	being in an **a** he prayed more	*74*

AGREE

Mt 5:25	**A with thine adversary quickly,**	*2132*
Mt 18:19	**That if two of you shall a on**	*4856*
Mt 20:13	**didst not thou a with me for a**	*4856*
Mk 14:59	neither so did their witness **a**	*2470*
Ac 15:15	**a** the words of the prophets;	*4856*
1Jn 5:8	blood: and these three **a** in one	*1526*
Rev 17:17	fulfil his will, and to **a**,	*4160, 3391, 1106*

AGREED

Am 3:3	walk together, except they be **a**?	3259
Mt 20:2	**And when he had a with the**	*4856*
Mk 14:56	their witness **a** not together	*2470*
John 9:22	for the Jews had **a** already	*4934*
Ac 5:9	ye have **a** together to tempt the spirit	*4856*

AGREEMENT

Isa 28:18	and your **a** with hell shall not	2380
2Co 6:16	what **a** hath the temple of God	*4783*

AGREETH

Mk 14:70	and thy speech **a** thereto	*3662*
Lk 5:36	**out of the new a not with the old**	*4856*

AILETH

Ge 21:17	said unto her, What **a** thee, Hagar?	
2Sa 14:5	king said unto her, What **a** thee?	
2Ki 6:28	king said unto her, What **a** thee	

AIR

Ge 1:26	the fowl of the **a**, and over	8064
Ge 2:20	gave names … to the fowl of the **a**,	8064
Ge 6:7	fowls of the **a**; for it repenteth me	8064
Ge 7:3	Of fowls also of the **a** by sevens,	8064
1Sa 17:44	thy flesh unto the fowls of the **a**,	8064
Job 41:16	no **a** can come between them	7307
Ps 8:8	The fowls of the **a**, and the fish of	8064
Pr 30:19	The way of an eagle in the **a**;	8064
Ecc 10:20	bird of the **a** shall carry the voice	8064
Mt 6:26	**Behold the fowls of the a:**	*3772*
Mt 8:20	**the birds of the a have nests;**	*3772*
Mk 4:32	**fowls of the a may lodge under**	*3772*
Lk 8:5	**the fowls of the a devoured it**	*3772*
Lk 9:58	**and birds of the a have nests;**	*3772*
Lk 13:19	**the fowls of the a lodged in the**	*3772*
1Co 9:26	not as one that beateth the **a**:	*109*
1Co 14:9	for ye shall speak into the **a**	*109*
Eph 2:2	prince of the power of the **a**,	*109*
1Th 4:17	to meet the Lord in the **a**: and	*109*
Rev 9:2	the sun and the **a** were darkened	*109*
Rev 16:17	poured out his vial into the **a**;	*109*

ALABASTER

Mt	26:7	having an **a** box of very precious	*211*
Mk	14:3	having an **a** box of ointment	*211*
Lk	7:37	brought an **a** box of ointment	*211*

ALARM

Nu	10:9	blow an **a** with the trumpets;	7321
2Ch	13:12	with sounding trumpets to cry **a**	7321
Jer	4:19	sound of the trumpet, the **a** of war	8643
Joel	2:1	sound of **a** in my holy mountain:	7321

ALIEN

Dt	14:21	thou mayest sell it unto an **a**:	5237
Job	19:15	I am an **a** in their sight	5237
Ps	69:8	an **a** unto my mother's children	5237
Isa	61:5	the **a** shall be your ploughmen	5236

ALIENATED

Eze	23:18	then my mind was **a** from her	3363
Eze	23:28	them from whom thy mind is **a**:	5361
Eph	4:18	being **a** from the life of God	*526*
Col	1:21	that were sometime **a** and enemies	*526*

ALIENS

La	5:2	our houses to **a**	5237
Eph	2:12	being **a** from the commonwealth	*526*
Heb	11:34	to flight the armies of the **a**	*245*

ALIVE See also QUICK

Ge	6:19	to keep them **a** with thee;	2421
Ge	7:23	and Noah only remained **a**, and	
Ge	43:7	Is your father yet **a**?	2416
Ge	45:28	Joseph my son is yet **a**:	2416
Ge	50:20	to save much people **a**	2421
Le	10:16	sons of Aaron which were left **a**,	
Le	16:10	be presented **a** before the Lord,	2416
Nu	16:33	went down **a** into the pit, and the	2416
Nu	31:15	Have ye saved all the women **a**?	2421
Dt	4:4	**a** every one of you this day	2416
Dt	6:24	that he might preserve us **a**	2421
Dt	20:16	save **a** nothing that breatheth:	2421
Dt	32:39	I kill, and I make **a**; I wound	2421
Jos	6:25	Joshua saved Rahab the harlot **a**	2421
Jos	14:10	the Lord hath kept me **a**	2421
Jgs	8:19	if ye had saved them **a**, I would	2421
1Sa	2:6	The Lord killeth, and maketh **a**:	2421
1Sa	27:9	left neither man nor woman **a**,	2421
2Sa	12:22	While the child was yet **a**, I fasted	2416
1Ki	21:15	for Naboth is not **a**, but dead	2416
2Ki	5:7	Am I God, to kill and to make **a**,	2421
Ps	22:29	none can keep **a** his own soul	2421
Ps	30:3	thou hast kept me **a**,	2421
Pr	1:12	swallow them up **a** as the grave;	2416
Ecc	4:2	than the living which are yet **a**	2416
Jer	49:11	I will preserve them **a**;	2421
Eze	18:27	he shall save his soul **a**	2421
Da	5:19	whom he would he kept **a**;	2418
Mk	16:11	when they had heard that he was **a**,	*2198*
Lk	15:24	**my son was dead, and is a again;**	*326*
Lk	24:23	angels, which said that he was **a**	*2198*
Ac	1:3	he shewed himself **a** after his	*2198*
Ac	25:19	whom Paul affirmed to be **a**	*2198*
Ro	6:11	dead indeed unto sin, but **a** unto	*2198*
Ro	7:9	I was **a** without the law once:	*2198*
1Co	15:22	so in Christ shall all be made **a**	*2227*
1Th	4:15	we which are **a** and remain	*2198*
1Th	4:17	are **a** and remain shall be caught	*2198*
Rev	1:18	**behold, I am a for evermore,**	*2198*
Rev	2:8	**which was dead, and is a;**	*2198*
Rev	19:20	both were cast **a** into a lake of fire	*2198*

ALL See also ALWAY.

Ge	2:2	the seventh day from **a** his work	3605
Ge	3:14	thou art cursed above **a** cattle	3605
Ge	3:17	eat of it **a** the days of thy life;	3605
Ge	3:20	she was the mother of **a** living	3605
Ge	6:13	end of **a** flesh is come before me;	3605
Ge	6:17	upon the earth, to destroy **a** flesh	3605
Ge	7:15	the ark, two and two of **a** flesh,	3605
Ge	7:22	**A** in whose nostrils was the	3605
Ge	9:11	neither shall **a** flesh be cut off any	3605
Ge	11:6	and they have **a** one language;	3605
Ge	17:8	**a** the land of Canaan, for an	
Ge	18:18	and **a** the nations of the earth	3605
Ge	18:25	Shall not the Judge of **a** the earth	3605
Ge	19:31	after the manner of **a** the earth:	3605
Ge	22:18	**a** the nations of the earth be blessed	3605
Ge	24:1	had blessed Abraham in **a** things	3605
Ge	25:5	gave **a** that he had unto Isaac	3605
Ge	26:4	**a** the nations of the earth be	3605
Ge	37:3	loved Joseph more than **a** his	3605
Ge	39:6	he left **a** that he had in Joseph's	3605
Ge	39:22	to Joseph's hand **a** the prisoners	3605
Ge	41:43	ruler over **a** the land of Egypt	3605
Ge	41:55	**a** the land of Egypt was famished	3605
Ge	41:56	Joseph opened **a** the storehouses	3605
Ge	42:11	We are **a** one man's sons; we are	3605
Ge	45:9	hath made me lord of **a** Egypt:	3605
Ge	45:15	kissed **a** his brethren, and wept	3605
Ge	46:26	**A** the souls that came with Jacob	3605
Ge	49:28	**A** these are the twelve tribes of	3605
Ex	9:14	is none like me in **a** the earth	3605
Ex	11:5	And **a** the firstborn in the land	3605
Ex	13:2	Sanctify unto me **a** the firstborn	3605
Ex	19:5	for **a** the earth is mine:	3605
Ex	19:8	**A** that the Lord hath spoken we	3605
Le	9:23	Lord appeared unto **a** the people	3605
Le	17:14	life of **a** flesh is the blood thereof:	3605
Le	25:10	liberty throughout **a** the land	
Nu	8:18	Levites for **a** the firstborn of the	3605
Nu	33:52	shall drive out **a** the inhabitants	3605
Dt	5:26	For who is there of **a** flesh, that	3605
Dt	6:2	thy God, to keep **a** his statutes	3605
Dt	10:12	Lord thy God with **a** thy heart	3605
Dt	11:22	your God, to walk in **a** his ways	3605
Dt	12:10	you rest from **a** your enemies	3605
Dt	13:3	God with **a** your heart	3605
Dt	15:10	God shall bless thee in **a** thy works	3605
Dt	18:12	For **a** that do these things are	3605
Dt	26:12	**a** the tithes of thine increase	3605
Dt	26:16	thine heart, and with **a** thy soul	3605
Dt	29:20	**a** the curses that are written in	3605
Dt	30:3	gather thee from **a** the nations,	3605
Dt	30:6	Lord thy God with **a** thine heart,	3605
Jos	6:23	brought out **a** her kindred, and	3605
Jos	22:5	**a** your heart and with **a** your soul	3605
Jos	23:14	I am going the way of **a** the earth:	3605
Ru	3:5	**A** that thou sayest unto me I will	3605
1Sa	7:3	unto the Lord with **a** your hearts	3605
1Sa	12:20	serve the Lord with **a** your heart;	3605
1Sa	12:24	him in truth with **a** your heart	3605
1Sa	18:30	himself more wisely than **a**	3605
2Sa	8:15	And David reigned over **a** Israel;	3605

2Sa 12:12 I will do this thing before **a** Israel, ...3605
2Sa 23:5 **a** my salvation, and **a** my desire 3605
1Ki 1:20 the eyes of **a** Israel are upon thee, ...3605
1Ki 2:4 in truth with **a** their heart 3605
1Ki 4:21 Solomon reigned over **a** kingdoms 3605
1Ki 4:31 For he was wiser than **a** men; 3605
1Ki 8:23 before thee with **a** their heart: 3605
1Ki 8:48 unto thee with **a** their heart 3605
1Ki 8:56 hath not failed one word of **a** 3605
1Ki 8:59 of his people Israel at **a** times
1Ki 9:6 at **a** turn from following me,
1Ki 10:23 exceeded **a** the kings of the earth 3605
1Ki 11:13 will not rend away **a** the kingdom; 3605
1Ki 14:8 who followed me with **a** his heart, ...3605
1Ki 14:9 evil above **a** that were before thee: 3605
1Ki 14:26 he took away **a** the shields of gold 3605
1Ki 15:3 walked in **a** the sins of his father 3605
1Ki 15:14 perfect with the Lord **a** his days 3605
1Ki 16:7 for **a** the evil that he did in the 3605
1Ki 16:25 did worse than **a** that were before 3605
1Ki 16:33 Lord God of Israel to anger than **a** 3605
1Ki 19:18 **a** the knees which have not bowed 3605
2Ki 5:15 no God in **a** the earth, but in Israel 3605
2Ki 13:11 he departed not from **a** the sins of 3605
2Ki 14:24 he departed not from **a** the sins 3605
2Ki 15:18 be departed not **a** his days from 3605
2Ki 17:16 worshipped **a** the host of heaven, ...3605
2Ki 17:20 Lord rejected **a** the seed of Israel, ...3605
2Ki 18:5 was none like him among **a** the 3605
2Ki 21:5 altars for **a** the host of heaven 3605
2Ki 22:2 in **a** the way of David his father, ...3605
2Ki 23:3 and his statutes with **a** their heart 3605
2Ki 23:25 to the Lord with **a** his heart, ...3605
2Ki 24:13 carried out thence **a** the treasures 3605
2Ki 24:14 And he carried away **a** Jerusalem 3605
1Ch 12:38 make David king over **a** Israel: 3605
1Ch 13:8 and **a** Israel played before God 3605
1Ch 15:28 Thus **a** Israel brought up the ark 3605
1Ch 16:9 talk ye of **a** his wondrous works 3605
1Ch 16:25 also is to be feared above **a** gods 3605
1Ch 17:2 David, Do **a** that is in thine heart; 3605
1Ch 18:14 So David reigned over **a** Israel, ...3605
1Ch 28:19 **A** this, said David, the Lord made 3605
2Ch 2:5 for great is our God above **a** gods 3605
2Ch 6:38 return to thee with **a** their heart 3605
2Ch 9:2 Solomon told her **a** her questions: 3605
2Ch 10:16 when **a** Israel saw that the king 3605
2Ch 12:13 chosen out of **a** the tribes of Israel, ...3605
2Ch 15:12 their fathers with **a** their heart 3605
2Ch 15:15 And **a** Judah rejoiced at the oath: 3605
2Ch 15:17 of Asa was perfect **a** his days 3605
2Ch 18:16 I did see **a** Israel scattered upon 3605
2Ch 22:9 sought the Lord with **a** his heart 3605
2Ch 22:10 destroyed **a** the seed royal of the 3605
2Ch 25:24 he took **a** the gold and the silver, ...3605
2Ch 29:24 make an atonement for **a** Israel 3605
2Ch 29:28 **a** the congregation worshipped 3605
2Ch 32:30 Hezekiah prospered in **a** his works 3605
2Ch 33:3 worshipped **a** the host of heaven 3605
2Ch 34:30 he read in their ears **a** the words 3605
2Ch 35:18 neither did **a** the kings of Israel 3605
2Ch 36:18 **a** these he brought to Babylon 3605
Ezr 1:2 hath given me **a** the kingdoms 3605
Ezr 1:11 **A** the vessels of gold and of silver 3605
Ezr 7:6 king granted him **a** his request, ...3605
Ezr 7:16 **a** the silver and gold that thou 3606
Ezr 7:21 decree to **a** the treasurers which 3606
Ezr 7:25 river, **a** such as know the laws 3606
Ezr 7:28 before **a** the king's mighty princes 3605
Ezr 8:22 hand of our God is upon **a** them 3605
Ezr 8:22 power and his wrath is against **a** 3605
Ezr 10:3 our God to put away **a** the wives 3605
Ne 5:19 my God, for good, according to **a** 3605
Ne 6:16 when **a** our enemies heard thereof, ...3605
Ne 8:5 book in the sight of **a** the people; 3605
Ne 8:9 For **a** the people wept, when they 3605
Ne 8:12 And **a** the people went their way 3605
Ne 13:26 God made him king over **a** Israel: 3605
Ne 13:27 unto you to do **a** this great evil 3605
Est 2:17 loved Esther above **a** the women, ...3605
Est 3:6 sought to destroy **a** the Jews that 3605
Est 5:13 Yet **a** this availeth me nothing 3605
Est 9:24 enemy of **a** the Jews, had devised 3605
Est 10:3 and speaking peace to **a** his seed 3605
Job 1:12 **a** that he hath is in thy power; 3605
Job 1:22 In **a** this Job sinned not, ...3605
Job 2:4 yea, **a** that a man hath will he give 3605
Job 2:10 In **a** this did not Job sin with his 3605
Job 4:14 which made **a** my bones to shake 7230
Job 13:4 ye are **a** physicians of no value 3605
Job 16:2 miserable comforters are ye **a** 3605
Job 33:29 Lo, **a** these things worketh God 3605
Job 34:15 **A** flesh shall perish together 3605
Job 34:19 they **a** are the work of his hands 3605
Job 38:18 earth? declare if thou knowest it **a** 3605
Ps 2:12 Blessed are **a** they that put their 3605
Ps 8:1 is thy name in **a** the earth! 3605
Ps 8:6 hast put **a** things under his feet: 3605
Ps 9:17 and **a** the nations that forget God 3605
Ps 10:4 God is not in **a** his thoughts 3605
Ps 16:3 in whom is **a** my delight 3605
Ps 18:30 he is a buckler to **a** those that 3605
Ps 19:4 is gone out through **a** the earth, ...3605
Ps 22:7 **A** they that see me laugh me to 3605
Ps 22:14 out like water, and **a** my bones 3605
Ps 22:17 I may tell **a** my bones: they look 3605
Ps 23:6 mercy shall follow me **a** the days 3605
Ps 25:22 O God, out of **a** his troubles 3605
Ps 31:23 O love the Lord, **a** ye his saints: 3605
Ps 33:8 Let **a** the earth fear the Lord: 3605
Ps 33:13 from heaven; he beholdeth **a** the 3605
Ps 34:6 saved him out of **a** his troubles 3605
Ps 34:20 He keepeth **a** his bones: not one 3605
Ps 38:9 Lord, **a** my desire is before thee; 3605
Ps 39:8 me from **a** my transgressions: 3605
Ps 40:16 Let **a** those that seek thee rejoice 3605
Ps 51:9 from my sins, and blot out **a** mine 3605
Ps 62:8 Trust in him at **a** times; 3605
Ps 67:3 let **a** the people praise thee 3605
Ps 76:9 to save **a** the meek of the earth 3605
Ps 78:32 For **a** this they sinned still, and 3605
Ps 86:12 Lord my God, with **a** my heart: 3605
Ps 96:4 he is to be feared above **a** gods 3605
Ps 103:1 **a** that is within me, bless his holy 3605
Ps 103:3 Who forgiveth **a** thine iniquities; 3605
Ps 103:19 and his kingdom ruleth over **a** 3605
Ps 104:24 in wisdom hast thou made them **a**: 3605
Ps 111:7 **a** his commandments are sure 3605
Ps 119:86 **A** thy commandments are faithful: 3605
Ps 119:151 **a** thy commandments are truth 3605
Ps 119:172 **a** thy commandments are righteous 3605
Ps 121:7 shall preserve thee from **a** evil: 3605

A

Ps	135:5	that our Lord is above **a** gods	3605
Ps	139:3	art acquainted with **a** my ways	3605
Ps	139:16	in thy book **a** my members were	3605
Ps	145:20	preserveth **a** them that love him:	3605
Pr	1:14	us; let us **a** have one purse:	3605
Pr	3:5	in the Lord with **a** thine heart;	3605
Pr	3:6	In **a** thy ways acknowledge him	3605
Pr	4:23	Keep thy heart with **a** diligence;	3605
Pr	5:19	her breasts satisfy thee at **a** times	3605
Pr	8:9	**a** plain to him that understandeth	3605
Pr	14:23	In **a** labour there is profit: but	3605
Pr	16:2	**A** the ways of a man are clean in	3605
Pr	17:17	A friend loveth at **a** times, and a	3605
Pr	22:2	the Lord is the maker of them **a**	3605
Pr	26:10	great God that formed **a** things	3605
Pr	29:11	A fool uttereth **a** his mind: but a	3605
Ecc	1:2	vanity of vanities; **a** is vanity	3605
Ecc	1:8	**A** things are full of labour; man	3605
Ecc	1:14	**a** is vanity and vexation of spirit	3605
Ecc	3:20	**A** go unto one place;	3605
Ecc	6:7	**A** the labour of man is for his	3605
Ecc	7:23	**A** this have I proved by wisdom:	3605
Ecc	8:17	Then I beheld **a** the work of God,	3605
Ecc	9:1	**a** this I considered in my heart	3605
Ecc	9:2	**A** things come alike to **a**: there	3605
Ecc	9:11	and chance happeneth to them **a**	3605
Isa	5:25	For **a** this his anger is not turned	3605
Isa	14:26	stretched out upon **a** the nations	3605
Isa	22:3	**A** thy rulers are fled together	3605
Isa	25:8	wipe away tears from off **a** faces;	3605
Isa	34:2	and his fury upon **a** their armies:	3605
Isa	38:17	cast **a** my sins behind thy back	3605
Isa	39:2	**a** that was found in his treasures:	3605
Isa	39:4	**A** that is in mine house have they	3605
Isa	40:6	What shall I cry? **A** flesh is grass,	3605
Isa	45:13	and I will direct **a** his ways:	3605
Isa	46:10	and I will do **a** my pleasure:	3605
Isa	49:26	**a** flesh shall know that I the Lord	3605
Isa	50:11	Behold, **a** ye that kindle a fire	3605
Isa	53:6	**A** we like sheep have gone astray;	3605
Isa	53:6	laid on him the iniquity of us **a**	3605
Isa	61:2	our God; to comfort **a** that mourn;	3605,
Isa	63:9	In **a** their affliction he was afflicted	3605
Isa	64:6	**a** our righteousnesses are as filthy	3605
Jer	1:7	go to **a** that I shall send thee,	3605
Jer	1:15	and against **a** the cities of Judah	3605
Jer	4:25	**a** the birds of the heavens were	3605
Jer	7:23	walk ye in **a** the ways that I have	3605
Jer	11:8	them **a** the words of this covenant	3605
Jer	17:9	heart is deceitful above **a** things,	3605
Jer	22:20	for **a** thy lovers are destroyed	3605
Jer	23:14	are **a** of them unto me as Sodom,	3605
Jer	25:13	prophesied against **a** the nations	3605
Jer	27:7	And **a** nations shall serve him, and	3605
Jer	28:3	**a** the vessels of the Lord's house	3605
Jer	29:4	**a** that are carried away captives,	3605
Jer	29:13	search for me with **a** your heart	3605
Jer	29:14	will gather you from **a** the nations	3605
Jer	30:11	I make a full end of **a** nations	3605
Jer	32:27	I am the Lord, the God of **a** flesh:	3605
Jer	33:8	I will pardon **a** their iniquities	3605
Jer	35:17	of Jerusalem **a** the evil that I have	3605
Jer	36:6	read them in the ears of **a** Judah	3605
Jer	37:21	**a** the bread in the city was spent	3605
Jer	38:9	**a** that they have done to Jeremiah	3605
Jer	39:1	king of Babylon and **a** his army	3605
Jer	39:6	king of Babylon slew **a** the nobles	3605
Jer	40:4	behold, **a** the land is before thee:	3605
Jer	42:2	thy God, even for **a** this remnant;	3605
Jer	44:8	a curse and a reproach among **a**	3605
Jer	45:5	I will bring evil upon **a** flesh,	3605
Jer	46:28	make a full end of **a** the nations	3605
Jer	50:30	**a** her men of war shall be cut off	3605
Jer	51:7	that made **a** the earth drunken:	3605
Jer	51:19	for he is the former of **a** things:	3605
Jer	51:47	**a** her slain shall fall in the midst	3605
Jer	52:10	slew also **a** the princes of Judah	3605
La	1:2	among **a** her lovers she hath none	3605
La	1:8	**a** that honoured her despise her,	3605
La	1:10	hath spread out his hand upon **a**	3605
La	2:2	The Lord hath swallowed up **a**	3605
La	2:15	**A** that pass by clap their hands at	3605
Eze	7:17	**A** hands shall be feeble,	3605
Eze	16:33	givest thy gifts to **a** thy lovers,	3605
Eze	18:4	Behold, **a** souls are mine; as the	3605
Eze	20:40	there shall **a** the house of Israel,	3605
Eze	20:43	for **a** your evils that ye have	3605
Eze	21:5	That **a** flesh may know that I	3605
Eze	25:8	Judah is like unto **a** the heathen;	3605
Eze	31:12	**a** the people of the earth are gone	3605
Eze	37:24	they **a** shall have one shepherd:	3650
Eze	39:23	so fell they **a** by the sword.	3650
Eze	47:12	shall grow **a** trees for meat,	3650
Da	1:4	skilful in **a** wisdom, and cunning	3650
Da	1:17	knowledge and skill in **a** learning	3650
Da	1:17	understanding in **a** visions and	3650
Da	1:19	among them **a** was found none like	3650
Da	9:14	God is righteous in **a** his works	3605
Hos	2:11	sabbaths, and **a** her solemn feasts	3605
Hos	7:2	I remember **a** their wickedness:	3605
Hos	14:2	take away **a** iniquity, and receive	3605
Joel	2:12	ye even to me with **a** your heart	3605
Joel	2:28	pour out my spirit upon **a** flesh;	3605
Am	3:2	punish you for **a** your iniquities.	3605
Am	5:16	Wailing shall be in **a** streets;	3605
Am	9:5	**a** that dwell therein shall mourn:	3605
Mic	7:19	cast **a** their sins into the depths	3605
Na	1:3	will not at **a** acquit the wicked:	
Na	3:1	city! it is **a** full of lies and	3605
Hab	2:8	**a** the remnant of the people shall	3605
Hab	2:20	let **a** the earth keep silence	3605
Zep	3:14	glad and rejoice with **a** the heart,	3605
Hag	1:14	the spirit of **a** the remnant of the	3605
Hag	2:7	And I will shake **a** nations,	3605
Zec	2:13	Be silent, O **a** flesh, before the	3605
Zec	9:1	of man, as of **a** the tribes of Israel,	3605
Zec	14:2	**a** nations against Jerusalem to	3605
Mal	2:10	Have we not **a** one father? hath	3605
Mal	3:10	**a** the tithes into the storehouse,	3605
Mt	3:15	**us to fulfil a righteousness.**	*3956*
Mt	5:18	**till a be fulfilled**	*3956*
Mt	6:33	**a these things shall be added**	*3956*
Mt	11:27	**A things are delivered unto me**	*3956*
Mt	12:15	and he healed them **a**;	*3956*
Mt	13:32	**indeed is the least of a seeds:**	*3956*
Mt	19:11	**A men cannot receive this saying,**	*3956*
Mt	19:26	**with God a things are possible.**	*3956*
Mt	21:4	**A** this was done, that it might	*3650*
Mt	21:22	**a things, whatsoever ye shall ask,**	*3956*
Mt	22:37	**the Lord thy God with a thy heart,**	*3650*
Mt	23:36	**A these things shall come upon**	*3956*
Mt	24:6	**for a these things must come to.**	*3956*

Mt	24:34	**till a these things be fulfilled**	3956
Mt	26:27	**saying, Drink ye a of it;**	3956
Mt	28:18	**A power is given unto me in**	3956
Mt	28:19	**and teach a nations, baptising**	3956
Mt	28:20	**to observe a things whatsoever**	3956
Mk	1:5	out unto him **a** the land of Judaea,	3956
Mk	1:37	**A** men seek for thee.	3956
Mk	3:28	**A sins shall be forgiven unto**	3956
Mk	9:23	**a things are possible to him that**	3956
Mk	10:27	**with God a things are possible.**	3956
Mk	10:44	**chiefest, shall be servant of a**	3956
Mk	12:29	**The first of a the commandments**	3956
Mk	12:30	**Lord thy God with a thy heart,**	3650
Mk	13:23	**I have foretold you a things.**	3956
Mk	13:30	**till a these things be done.**	3956
Mk	14:36	**a things are possible unto thee;**	3956
Mk	14:50	And they **a** forsook him, and fled.	3956
Mk	16:15	**Go ye into a the world,**	537
Lk	1:3	perfect understanding of **a** things	3956
Lk	1:6	walking in **a** the commandments	3956
Lk	2:19	But Mary kept **a** these things,	3956
Lk	2:51	kept **a** these sayings in her heart	3956
Lk	3:6	And **a** flesh shall see the salvation	3956
Lk	10:22	**A things are delivered to me of**	3956
Lk	10:27	Lord thy God with **a** thy heart,	3650
Lk	11:41	**a things are clean unto you**	3956
Lk	14:17	**for a things are now ready**	3956
Lk	15:14	**And when he had spent a,**	3956
Lk	18:12	**I give tithes of a that I possess.**	3956
Lk	18:31	**and a things that are written**	3956
Lk	20:38	**for a live unto him**	3956
Lk	21:32	**not pass away, till a be fulfilled**	3956
Lk	24:44	**that a things must be fulfilled**	3956
Jn	1:3	**A** things were made by him;	3956
Jn	3:35	given **a** things into his hand	3956
Jn	4:39	He told me **a** that ever I did:	3956
Jn	5:20	**and sheweth him a things**	3956
Jn	5:23	**a men should honour the Son,**	3956
Jn	6:37	**A that the Father giveth me shall**	3956
Jn	6:39	**of a which he hath given me**	3956
Jn	10:8	**A that ever came before me**	3956
Jn	16:13	**he will guide you into a truth:**	3956
Jn	17:2	**given him power over a flesh,**	3956
Jn	17:21	**That they a may be one;**	3956
Jn	21:17	Lord, thou knowest **a** things;	3956
Ac	1:8	**and in a Judaea, and in Samaria,**	3956
Ac	3:21	times of restitution of **a** things	3956
Ac	5:20	**a** the words of this life	3956
Ac	7:10	delivered him out of **a** his afflictions	3956
Ac	7:50	my hands made **a** these things?	3956
Ac	9:21	**a** that heard him were amazed	3956
Ac	10:2	feared God with **a** his house	3956
Ac	10:36	(he is Lord of **a**:)	3956
Ac	13:10	thou enemy of **a** righteousness	5956
Ac	15:18	Known unto God are **a** his works	5956
Ac	16:34	believing in God with **a** his house	3832
Ac	20:18	I have been with you at **a** seasons	5956
Ac	20:27	**a** the counsel of God	3956
Ac	21:30	And **a** the city was moved	5650
Ac	23:1	I have lived in **a** good conscience	5956
Ac	26:3	expert in **a** customs and questions	3956
Ac	27:44	they escaped **a** safe to land	3956
Ro	3:9	that they are **a** under sin;	3956
Ro	3:12	They are **a** gone out of the way	3956
Ro	3:19	**a** the world may become guilty	3956
Ro	3:23	For **a** have sinned, and come short	3956
Ro	5:12	and so death passed upon **a** men	3956
Ro	5:18	upon **a** men unto justification of	3956
Ro	9:5	who is over **a**, God blessed for ever	3956
Ro	9:6	For they are not **a** Israel	3956
Ro	11:26	And so **a** Israel shall be saved:	3956
Ro	12:17	honest in the sight of **a** men	3956
Ro	12:18	live peaceably with **a** men	3956
Ro	13:7	Render therefore to **a** their dues:	3956
1Co	2:10	the Spirit searcheth **a** things	3956
1Co	6:12	but **a** things are not expedient:	3956
1Co	8:6	by whom are **a** things, and we by	3956
1Co	9:22	I am made **a** things to **a** men,	3956
1Co	10:23	**A** things are lawful for me	3956
1Co	10:23	**a** things are lawful for me,	3956
1Co	10:31	do **a** to the glory of God	3956
1Co	10:33	I please **a** men in **a** things,	3956
1Co	12:26	**a** the members suffer with it;	3956
1Co	12:26	**a** the members rejoice with it	3956
1Co	13:3	though I bestow **a** my goods to	3956
1Co	13:7	Beareth **a** things, believeth **a**	3956
1Co	13:7	hopeth **a** things, endureth **a**	3956
1Co	14:40	Let **a** things be done decently and	3956
1Co	15:8	And last of **a** he was seen of me	3956
1Co	15:19	we are of **a** men most miserable	3956
1Co	15:22	For as in Adam **a** die,	3956
1Co	15:22	in Christ shall **a** be made alive	3956
1Co	15:28	that God may be **a** in **a**	3956
1Co	15:39	**A** flesh is not the same flesh:	4561
2Co	1:3	the God of **a** comfort;	3650
2Co	5:14	then were **a** dead:	3956
2Co	5:15	And that he died for **a**	3956
2Co	5:17	behold, **a** things are become new	3956
2Co	11:28	the care of **a** the churches	3956
Gal	3:8	In thee shall **a** nations be blessed	3956
Gal	3:22	hath concluded **a** under sin	3956
Gal	4:1	though he be lord of **a**;	3956
Gal	5:14	For **a** the law is fulfilled in one	3956
Gal	6:10	let us do good unto **a** men,	3956
Eph	1:22	to be the head over **a** things	3956
Eph	1:23	of him that filleth **a** in **a**	3956
Eph	3:9	created **a** things by Jesus Christ:	3956
Eph	3:19	with **a** the fulness of God.	3956
Eph	3:20	above **a** that we ask or think,	3956
Eph	4:6	and Father of **a**, who is above **a**	3956
Eph	6:16	to quench **a** the fiery darts	3956
Php	2:14	Do **a** things without murmurings	3956
Php	2:21	For **a** seek their own	3956
Php	3:8	I count **a** things but loss	3956
Php	4:7	which passeth **a** understanding	3956
Php	4:13	I can do **a** things through Christ	3956
Php	4:18	But I have **a**, and abound:	3956
Col	1:16	**a** things were created by him,	3956
Col	1:17	he is before **a** things,	3956
Col	1:17	and by him **a** things consist	3956
Col	1:18	that in **a** things he might have	3956
Col	1:19	in him should **a** fulness dwell;	3956
Col	1:20	to reconcile **a** things unto himself;	3956
Col	2:9	dwelleth **a** the fulness of the	3956
Col	2:13	forgiven you **a** trespasses;	3956
Col	3:11	but Christ is **a**, and in **a**	3956
Col	3:16	dwell in you richly in **a** wisdom;	3956
Col	3:17	do **a** in the name of the Lord	3956
Col	3:20	obey your parents in **a** things:	3956
Col	4:12	complete in **a** the will of God	3956
1Th	5:21	Prove **a** things; hold fast that	3956
1Th	5:22	Abstain from **a** appearance of	3956

A

1Ti 1:15 worthy of **a** acceptation, *3956*
1Ti 4:9 worthy of **a** acceptation *3956*
1Ti 4:10 who is the Saviour of **a** men *3956*
1Ti 6:10 love of money is the root of **a** evil: *3956*
1Ti 6:17 giveth us richly **a** things to enjoy; *3956*
2Ti 3:16 **A** scripture is given by *3956*
Heb 2:10 for whom are **a** things, *3956*
Heb 2:10 and by whom are **a** things *3956*
Heb 3:2 Moses was faithful in **a** his house. *3650*
Heb 3:4 but he that built **a** things is God *3956*
Heb 11:13 these **a** died in faith, not having *3956*
Heb 12:14 Follow peace with **a** men *3956*
Heb 12:23 to God the Judge of **a**, *3956*
Heb 13:4 marriage is honourable in **a** *3956*
Jas 1:2 count it **a** joy when ye fall *3955*
Jas 1:8 unstable in **a** his ways *3955*
Jas 1:21 lay apart **a** filthiness *3956*
Jas 2:10 he is guilty of **a** *3955*
Jas 4:16 **a** such rejoicing is evil *3955*
1Pe 1:24 For **a** flesh is as grass *3955*
1Pe 4:7 the end of **a** things is at hand: *3956*
1Pe 5:7 Casting **a** your care upon him; *3956*
2Pe 1:3 **a** things that pertain unto life *3956*
1Jn 1:5 and in him is no darkness at **a** *3762*
1Jn 1:7 cleanseth us from **a** sin *3956*
1Jn 1:9 cleanse us from **a** unrighteousness *3956*
1Jn 5:17 **A** unrighteousness is sin: *3956*
Rev 4:11 for thou hast created **a** things, *3956*
Rev 7:17 away **a** tears from their eyes *3956*
Rev 8:3 with the prayers of **a** saints *3956*
Rev 21:4 God shall wipe away **a** tears *3956*
Rev 21:5 Behold, I make **a** things new *3956*
Rev 21:8 and **a** liars, shall have their part *3956*

ALLEGORY

Gal 4:24 Which things are an **a**: for these *238*

ALLELUIA (al-le-loo´-yah)

Rev 19:1 people in heaven, saying, **A**; *239*
Rev 19:3 they said, **A**. And her *239*
Rev 19:4 the throne, saying, Amen; **A** *239*
Rev 19:6 mighty thunderings, saying, **A** *239*

ALLOW See also DISALLOWED.

Lk 11:48 ye a the deeds of your fathers: *4989*
Ac 24:15 which they themselves also **a** *4327*
Ro 7:15 that which I do I **a** not: *1097*

ALLOWED See also DISALLOWED.

1Th 2:4 But as we were **a** of God to be *1381*

ALLURE

Hos 2:14 I will **a** her, and bring her into 6601
2Pe 2:18 **a** through the lusts of the flesh *1185*

ALMIGHTY

Ge 17:1 said unto him, I am the **A** God; 7706
Ge 35:11 God said unto him, I am God **A** 7706
Job 8:3 doth the **A** pervert justice? 7706
Job 33:4 breath of the **A** hath given me life 7706
Job 34:12 will the **A** pervert judgment 7706
Job 35:13 neither will the **A** regard it 7706
Job 37:23 the **A**, we cannot find him out: 7706
Job 40:2 he that contendeth with the **A** 7706
Ps 91:1 under the shadow of the **A** 7706
Rev 4:8 Holy, holy, holy, Lord God **A** *3841*

ALMOND

Ecc 12:5 the **a** tree shall flourish, 8247
Jer 1:11 I see a rod of an **a** tree 8247

ALMS

Mt 6:1 do not your a before men, *7554*
Mt 6:4 That thine a may be in secret: *1654*
Lk 11:41 give a of such things as ye have; *1654*
Lk 12:33 Sell that ye have, and give a; *1654*
Ac 3:10 it was he which sat for **a** *1654*

ALPHA (al´-fah)

Rev 1:8 I am A and Omega, the *1*
Rev 1:11 I am A and Omega, the first and *1*
Rev 21:6 I am **A** and Omega, the beginning *1*
Rev 22:13 I am A and Omega, the beginning *1*

ALTAR

Ge 8:20 Noah builded an **a** unto the Lord 4196
Ge 22:9 his son, and laid him on the **a** 4196
Ex 17:15 And Moses built an **a**, 4196
Ex 24:6 the blood he sprinkled on the **a** 4196
Ex 29:37 an atonement for the **a**, and 4196
Ex 30:27 and the **a** of incense, 4196
Ex 40:10 and it shall be an **a** most holy 4196
Le 1:15 the priest shall bring it unto the **a**, 4196
Le 3:11 the priest shall burn it upon the **a**: 4196
Le 8:16 Moses burnt it upon the **a** 4196
Nu 7:84 This was the dedication of the **a** 4196
Jos 22:23 That we have built us an **a** to turn 4196
Jos 22:34 called the **a** Ed: 4196
Jgs 6:24 Then Gideon built an **a** there 4196
Jgs 6:28 the **a** of Baal was cast down 4196
1Sa 14:35 And Saul built an **a** 4196
1Sa 14:35 the same was the first **a** 4196
2Sa 24:25 David built there an **a** 4196
1Ki 1:50 caught hold on the horns of the **a**: 4196
1Ki 3:4 did Solomon offer upon that **a** 4196
1Ki 13:2 and said, O **a**, **a**, 4196
1Ki 13:3 the **a** shall be rent 4196
2Ch 7:7 brasen **a** which Solomon had made 4196
Ezr 3:2 builded the **a** of the God of Israel, 4196
Ps 43:4 Then will I go unto the **a** of God, 4196
Isa 60:7 with acceptance on mine **a** 4196
La 2:7 The Lord hath cast off his **a** 4196
Eze 43:15 So the **a** shall be four cubits: 741
Eze 43:26 Seven days shall they purge the **a** 4196
Am 3:14 the horns of the **a** shall be cut off, 4196
Am 9:1 the Lord standing upon the **a**: 4196
Mal 1:7 offer polluted bread upon mine **a**; 4196
Mal 1:10 kindle fire on mine **a** for nought 4196
Mal 2:13 covering the **a** of the Lord with tears 4196
Mt 5:23 bring thy gift to the a, *2379*
Ac 17:23 I found an **a** with this inscription *1041*
Heb 7:13 no man gave attendance at the **a** *2379*
Jas 2:21 offered Isaac his son upon the **a**? *2379*
Rev 6:9 under the **a** the souls *2379*
Rev 8:3 of all saints upon the golden **a** *2379*

ALTARS

Ex 34:13 But ye shall destroy their **a**, 4196
Nu 23:1 Build me here seven **a**, 4196
Dt 7:5 ye shall destroy their **a**, 4196
2Ki 21:4 he built **a** in the house of the Lord, 4196
2Ki 21:5 built **a** for all the host of heaven 4196
Isa 17:8 he shall not look to the **a** 4196
Jer 11:13 even **a** to burn incense unto Baal 4196

Jer	17:2	their children remember their **a**	4196
Eze	6:4	your **a** shall be desolate	4196
Hos	8:11	Ephraim hath made many **a** to sin,	4196
Ro	11:3	and digged down thine **a**;	*2379*

ALTER

Le	27:10	He shall not **a** it, nor change it,	2498
Ezr	6:11	that whosoever shall **a** this word	8133
Ezr	6:12	that shall put to their hand to **a**	8133
Ps	89:34	covenant will I not break, nor **a**	8138

ALTERED

Est	1:19	it be not **a**, That Vashti come	5674
Lk	9:29	of his countenance was **a**,	*1096, 2087*

ALTERETH

Da	6:8, 12	and Persians, which **a** not	5709

ALWAY

Ex	25:30	the table shewbread before me **a**	8548
Nu	9:16	So it was **a**: the cloud covered it	8548
1Ki	11:36	have a light **a** before me	3605, 3117
Pr	28:14	Happy is the man that feareth **a**:	8548
Mt	28:20	**I am with you a, even unto.**	*3956, 2250*
Jn	7:6	**but your time is a ready**	*3842*
2Co	6:10	As sorrowful, yet **a** rejoicing;	*104*
Php	4:4	Rejoice in the Lord **a**:	*104*
Col	4:6	Let your speech be **a** with grace,	*104*
1Th	2:16	to fill up their sins **a**;	*104*
2Th	2:13	bound to give thanks **a** to God	*104*
Tit	1:12	the Cretians are **a** liars	*104*
Heb	3:10	They do **a** err in their heart:	*104*

ALWAYS

Ge	6:3	My spirit shall not **a** strive with	5769
1Ch	16:15	Be ye mindful **a** of his covenant;	5769
Job	32:9	Great men are not **a** wise:	
Ps	16:8	I have set the Lord **a** before me:	8548
Ps	103:9	He will not **a** chide:	5331
Pr	5:19	be thou ravished **a** with her love	8548
Pr	8:30	rejoicing **a** before him;	3605, 6256
Ecc	9:8	Let thy garments be **a** white;	3605, 6256
Mt	18:10	**their angels do a behold the**	*1223, 3956*
Mt	26:11	**ye have the poor a with you;**	*3842*
Mk	14:7	**but me ye have not a**	*3842*
Lk	18:1	that men ought **a** to pray,	*3842*
Lk	21:36	**pray a, that ye may be**	*1722, 3956, 2540*
Jn	8:29	**I do a those things that please**	*3842*
Jn	11:42	**I knew that thou hearest me a:**	*3842*
Jn	12:8	**the poor a ye have with you;**	*3842*
1Co	15:58	**a** abounding in the work of the	*3842*
2Co	4:10	**A** bearing about in the body	*3842*
2Co	5:6	Therefore we are **a** confident	*3842*
Eph	5:20	Giving thanks **a** for all things	*3842*
Eph	6:18	Praying **a** with all	*1722, 3956, 2540*
Php	1:4	**A** in every prayer of mine for you	*3842*
Php	2:12	my beloved, as ye have **a** obeyed	*3842*
Col	1:3	praying **a** for you	*3842*
1Th	1:2	We give thanks to God **a** for you	*3842*
2Pe	1:12	**a** in remembrance of these things,	*104*
2Pe	1:15	these things **a** in remembrance	*1539*

AM

Ex	3:14	said unto Moses, I **A** that I **A**:	1961
Ex	3:14	Israel, I **A** hath sent me unto you	1961
Le	19:18	neighbour as thyself: I **a** the Lord	3605
Ps	88:4	I **a** as a man that hath no strength:	1961
Ps	139:21	**a** not I grieved with those that rise	3605
Job	12:3	I **a** not inferior to you: yea, who	1961
Jer	50:31	Behold, I **a** against thee	3605
Mt	3:11	whose shoes I **a** not worthy to	*1510*
Mt	3:17	my beloved Son, in whom I **a** well	
Mt	8:8	I **a** not worthy	*1510*
Mt	8:9	For I **a** a man under authority,	*1510*
Mt	11:29	**for I a meek and lowly in heart:**	*1510*
Mt	16:13	**that I the Son of man a?**	*1511*
Mt	16:15	**But whom say ye that I a?**	*1511*
Mt	18:20	**there a I in the midst of them.**	*1510*
Mt	20:15	**Is thine eye evil, because I a good**	*1510*
Mt	22:32	**I a the God of Abraham, and the**	*1510*
Mt	24:5	**saying, I a Christ; and shall**	*1510*
Mt	27:24	I **a** innocent of the blood of this	*1510*
Mt	27:43	for he said, I **a** the Son of God	*1510*
Mt	28:20	**and, lo, I a with you alway, even.**	*1510*
Mk	1:7	whose shoes I **a** not worthy to	*1510*
Mk	8:27	**Whom do men say that I a?**	*1511*
Mk	8:29	**But whom say ye that I a?** And	*1511*
Mk	13:6	**in my name, saying, I a Christ;**	*1510*
Mk	14:62	And Jesus said, **I a: and ye shall**	*1510*
Lk	1:19	I **a** Gabriel, that stand in the	*1510*
Lk	3:16	whose shoes I **a** not worthy to	*1510*
Lk	5:8	for I **a** a sinful man, O Lord	*1510*
Lk	7:6	for I **a** not worthy that thou	*1510*
Lk	9:18	**Whom say the people that I a?**	*1511*
Lk	9:20	**But whom say ye that I a?** Peter	*1511*
Lk	15:19	**a no more worthy to be called**	*1510*
Lk	21:8	**saying, I a Christ; and the time**	*1510*
Lk	22:70	he said unto them, **Ye say that I a.**	*1510*
Jn	1:20	but confessed, I **a** not the Christ	*1510*
Jn	3:28	I **a** not the Christ	*1510*
Jn	4:26	I that speak to thee **a** he	*1510*
Jn	6:35	said unto them, **I a the bread of**	*1510*
Jn	6:48	**I a that bread of life.**	*1510*
Jn	6:51	**I a the living bread which came**	*1510*
Jn	7:34	**where I a, thither ye cannot**	*1510*
Jn	8:12	**I a the light of the world: he that**	*1510*
Jn	8:16	**for I a not alone, but I and the**	*1510*
Jn	8:23	**I a from above: ye are of this**	*1510*
Jn	8:23	**I a not of this world.**	*1510*
Jn	8:24	**believe not that I a he, ye shall**	*1510*
Jn	8:28	**ye know that I a he, and that I do**	*1510*
Jn	8:58	**Before Abraham was, I a.**	*1510*
Jn	9:5	**I a the light of the world.**	*1510*
Jn	10:7	**I a the door of the sheep**	*1510*
Jn	10:9	**I a the door: by me if any man**	*1510*
Jn	10:11	**I a the good shepherd: the good**	*1510*
Jn	10:14	**I a the good shepherd, and know**	*1510*
Jn	11:25	**I a the resurrection, and the life:**	*1510*
Jn	12:26	**and where I a, there shall also my**	*1510*
Jn	12:46	**I a come a light into the world,**	
Jn	13:13	**and ye say well; for so I a.**	*1510*
Jn	14:3	**that where I a, there ye may be**	*1510*
Jn	14:6	**I a the way, the truth, and the life:**	*1510*
Jn	15:1	**I a the true vine, and my Father**	*1510*
Jn	15:5	**I a the vine, ye are the branches:**	*1510*
Jn	17:11	**now I a no more in the world,**	*1510*
Jn	17:14	**even as I a not of the world**	*1510*
Jn	17:16	**even as I a not of the world**	*1510*
Jn	18:5	Jesus saith unto them, **I a he**	*1510*
Jn	18:6	he said unto them, **I a he,** they	*1510*
Jn	18:8	**I have told you that I a he: if**	*1510*
Jn	18:17	man's disciples? He saith, I **a** not	*1510*
Jn	18:25	He denied it, and said, I **a** not	*1510*
Jn	18:35	**A** I a Jew? Thine own nation	*1510*

A

Jn	18:37	**Thou sayest that I a a king.**	*1510*
Jn	19:21	but that he said, I **a** King of the	*1510*
Ac	9:5	**I a Jesus whom thou persecutest:**	*1510*
Ac	10:21	Behold, I **a** he whom ye seek:	*1510*
Ac	18:10	**For I a with thee, and no man**	*1510*
Ac	22:8	**I a Jesus of Nazareth, whom thou**	*1510*
Ac	26:15	**I a Jesus whom thou persecutest.**	*1510*
1Co	3:4	For while one saith, I **a** of Paul;	*1510*
1Co	9:1	**A** I not an apostle?	*1510*
1Co	15:10	the grace of God I **a** what I **a**:	*1510*
2Co	12:10	for when I **a** weak,	*1510*
Php	4:11	in whatsoever state I **a**,	*1510*
1Ti	1:15	to save sinners; of whom I **a**	*1510*
1Pe	1:16	Be ye holy; for I **a** holy	*1510*
Rev	1:8	**I a Alpha and Omega, the**	*1510*
Rev	1:11	**I a Alpha and Omega, the first**	*1510*
Rev	1:17	**Fear not; I a the first and the last:**	*1510*
Rev	1:18	**I a he that liveth, and was dead;**	*1510*
Rev	1:18	**I a alive for evermore, Amen;**	*1510*
Rev	2:23	**I a he which searcheth the reins**	*1510*
Rev	3:17	**Because thou sayest, I a rich,**	*1510*
Rev	22:13	**I a Alpha and Omega, the**	*1510*
Rev	22:16	**I a the root and the offspring**	*1510*

AMAZED

Job	32:15	They were **a**, they answered no	2865
Eze	32:10	will make many people **a** at thee	8074
Mt	12:23	all the people were **a**,	*1839*
Mt	19:25	they were exceedingly **a**,	*1605*
Mk	1:27	And they were all **a**	*2284*
Mk	2:12	insomuch that they were all **a**,	*1839*
Mk	6:51	they were sore **a** in themselves,	*1839*
Mk	9:15	they beheld him, were greatly **a**	*1568*
Mk	10:32	and they were **a**;	*2284*
Mk	14:33	began to be sore **a**	*1568*
Mk	16:8	for they trembled and were **a**:	*1611*
Lk	2:48	they saw him, they were **a**:	*1605*
Lk	4:36	And they were all **a**	*1096, 2285*
Lk	5:26	And they were all **a**	*1611, 2983*
Lk	9:43	**a** at the mighty power of God	*1605*
Ac	2:7	they were all **a** and marvelled,	*1839*
Ac	2:12	were all **a**, and were in doubt,	*1839*
Ac	9:21	all that heard him were **a**	*1839*

AMBASSADOR

Pr	13:17	but a faithful **a** is health	6735
Jer	49:14	an **a** is sent unto the heathen,	6735
Ob	1	an **a** is sent among the heathen,	6735
Eph	6:20	For which I am an **a** in bonds:	*4243*

AMBASSADORS

Jos	9:4	and made as if they had been **a**,	6735
Isa	33:7	the **a** of peace shall weep bitterly	4397
2Co	5:20	we are **a** for Christ,	*4243*

AMBUSH

Jos	8:2	lay thee an **a** for the city	693
Jos	8:21	saw that the **a** had taken the city,	693

AMBUSHES

Jer	51:12	set up the watchmen, prepare the **a**:	693

AMEN

Nu	5:22	And the woman shall say, **A, a.**	543
Ps	41:13	to everlasting. **A**, and **A**.	543
Ps	72:19	filled with his glory; **A**, and **A**.	543
Ps	89:52	for evermore. **A**, and **A**.	543
Mt	6:13	**and the glory, for ever. A.**	*281*
Mt	28:20	**unto the end of the world. A**	*281*
1Co	14:16	unlearned say **A** at thy giving of	*281*
2Co	1:20	yea, and in him **A**, unto the glory	*281*
Rev	1:18	**I am alive for evermore, A;**	*281*
Rev	3:14	**These things saith the A**	*281*
Rev	5:14	And the four beasts said, **A**.	*281*
Rev	7:12	unto our God for ever and ever. **A**.	*281*
Rev	19:4	Sat on the throne, saying, **A**;	*281*

AMEND

Jer	7:3	**A** your ways and your doings	3190
Jer	26:13	**a** your ways and your doings,	3190
Jer	35:15	and **a** your doings	3190

AMENDS

Le	5:16	he shall make **a** for the harm	*7999*

AMISS

2Ch	6:37	We have sinned, we have done **a**,	5753
Da	3:29	speak anything **a** against the God	7955
Lk	23:41	this man hath done nothing **a**	*824*
Jas	4:3	receive not, because ye ask **a**	*2560*

ANCESTORS

Le	26:45	remember the covenant of their **a**,	7223

ANCHOR

Heb	6:19	hope we have as an **a** of the soul,	*45*

ANCHORS

Ac	27:29	they cast four **a** out of the stern	*45*
Ac	27:40	they had taken up the **a**,	*45*

ANCIENT

2Ki	19:25	Hast thou not heard ... of **a** times	6924
Pr	22:28	Remove not the **a** landmark	5769
Isa	37:26	Hast thou not heard ... of **a** times	6924
Da	7:9	**A** of days did sit, whose garment	6268
Da	7:13	and came to the **A** of days	6268
Da	7:22	**A** of days came, and judgment	6268

ANCIENTS

Ps	119:100	I understand more than the **a**,	2204
Eze	8:11	seventy men of the **a** of the	2204

ANGEL See also ARCHANGEL.

Ge	16:7	the **a** of the Lord found her by a	4397
Ge	22:15	**a** of the Lord called unto Abraham	4397
Ge	24:7	he shall send his **a** before thee	4397
Nu	22:22	the **a** of the Lord stood in the way	4397
Nu	22:24	the **a** of the Lord stood in a path	4397
Jgs	6:22	perceived that he was an **a**	4397
Jgs	13:21	**a** of the Lord did no more appear	4397
2Sa	19:27	the king is as an **a** of God:	4397
2Sa	24:16	to the **a** that destroyed the people,	4397
2Sa	24:16	**a** of the Lord was by the threshing	4397
1Ki	19:5	an **a** touched him, and said unto	4397
1Ch	21:15	**a** that destroyed, It is enough	4397
Hos	12:4	he had power over the **a**,	4397
Zec	1:9	the **a** that talked with me	4397
La	1:13	the **a** said unto him, Fear not,	*32*
Lk	1:30	**a** said unto her, Fear not, Mary:	*32*
Lk	2:10	the **a** said unto them, Fear not:	*32*
Ac	10:22	warned from God by an holy **a**	*32*
Ac	12:23	the **a** of the Lord smote him,	*32*
2Co	11:14	transformed into an **a** of light	*32*
Rev	2:1	**the a of the church of Ephesus**	*32*
Rev	2:8	**the a of the church in Smyrna**	*32*
Rev	2:12	**to the a of the church in Pergamos.**	*32*

Rev	2:18	**the a of the church in Thyatira**	*32*
Rev	3:1	**unto the a of the church in Sardis**	*32*
Rev	3:7	**the a of the church in Philadelphia.**	*32*
Rev	3:14	**unto the a of the church of the**	*32*
Rev	8:7	The first **a** sounded, and there	*32*
Rev	8:8	the second **a** sounded, and as it	*32*
Rev	8:10	the third **a** sounded, and there fell	*32*
Rev	8:12	the fourth **a** sounded, and the	*32*
Rev	9:1	the fifth **a** sounded, and I saw	*32*
Rev	9:13	and the sixth **a** sounded.	*32*
Rev	10:7	of the voice of the seventh **a**,	*32*
Rev	11:15	and the seventh **a** sounded;	*32*
Rev	14:6	I saw another **a** fly in the midst	*32*
Rev	14:8	and there followed another **a**,	*32*
Rev	14:9	the third **a** followed them	*32*
Rev	14:19	**a** thrust in his sickle into the earth,	*32*
Rev	16:3	the second **a** poured out his vial	*32*
Rev	16:4	the third **a** poured out his vial	*32*
Rev	16:8	the fourth **a** poured out his vial	*32*
Rev	16:10	the fifth **a** poured out his vial	*32*
Rev	16:12	the sixth **a** poured out his vial	*32*
Rev	16:17	the seventh **a** poured out his vial	*32*
Rev	22:16	**have sent mine a to testify unto**	*32*

ANGEL'S

Rev	10:10	the little book out of the **a** hand,	*32*

ANGELS

Ge	19:1	there came two **a** to Sodom	4397
Ge	19:15	then the **a** hastened Lot,	4397
Ps	8:5	him a little lower than the **a**,	430
Ps	91:11	shall give his **a** charge over thee,	4397
Mt	13:41	**Son of man shall send forth his a,**	*32*
Lk	20:36	**for they are equal unto the a;**	*2465*
Jn	1:51	**the a of God ascending and**	*32*
Jn	20:12	seeth two **a** in white sitting, the	*32*
1Co	4:9	world, and to **a**, and to men	*32*
1Co	6:3	Know ye not that we shall judge **a**?	*32*
2Th	1:7	from heaven with his mighty **a**,	*32*
1Ti	3:16	in the Spirit, seen of **a**, preached	*32*
1Ti	5:21	Jesus Christ, and the elect **a**,	*32*
Heb	1:4	made so much better than the **a**,	*32*
Heb	1:5	unto which of the **a** said he at	*32*
Heb	1:6	let all the **a** of God worship him.	*32*
Heb	2:7	a little lower than the **a**;	*32*
Rev	1:20	**the a of the seven churches:**	*32*
Rev	3:5	**my Father, and before his a.**	*32*
Rev	14:10	in the presence of the holy **a**,	*32*

ANGELS'

Ps	78:25	Man did eat **a** food:	47

ANGER

Ge	27:45	Until thy brother's **a** turn away	639
Ge	30:2	Jacob's **a** was kindled against	639
Ex	32:19	Moses' **a** waxed hot, and he cast	639
Dt	4:25	Lord thy God, to provoke him to **a**	3707
2Sa	12:5	David's **a** was greatly kindled	639
1Ki	16:2	provoke me to **a** with their sins;	*3707*
Ne	9:17	merciful, slow to **a**, and of great	639
Job	9:13	If God will not withdraw his **a**	639
Ps	6:1	O Lord, rebuke me not in thine **a**	639
Ps	37:8	Cease from **a**, and forsake wrath:	639
Ps	145:8	slow to **a**, and of great mercy	639
Pr	15:1	grievous words stir up **a**	639
Pr	15:18	that is slow to **a** appeaseth strife	639
Pr	16:32	slow to **a** is better than the mighty,	639
Pr	19:11	discretion of a man deferreth his **a**;	639
Pr	20:2	whoso provoketh him to **a** sinneth	5674
Pr	21:14	A gift in secret pacifieth **a**	639
Pr	22:8	the rod of his **a** shall fail	5678
Pr	27:4	is cruel, and **a** is outrageous;	639
Ecc	7:9	**a** resteth in the bosom of fools	3708
Isa	1:4	the Holy One of Israel unto **a**	5006
Jer	3:12	and I will not keep **a** forever	
Jer	7:19	Do they provoke me to **a**?	*3707*
Jer	32:32	provoke me to **a**, they, their kings,	*3707*
Jer	52:3	through the **a** of the Lord it came	639
La	1:12	in the day of his fierce **a**	639
La	2:22	day of the Lord's **a** none escaped	639
Joel	2:13	slow to **a**, and of great kindness,	639
Jnh	4:2	slow to **a**, and of great kindness,	639
Mic	7:18	he retaineth not his **a** for ever	639
Na	1:3	The Lord is slow to **a**, and great	639
Na	1:6	abide in the fierceness of his **a**?	639
Col	3:8	put off all these; **a**, wrath, malice	*3709*
Col	3:21	provoke not your children to **a**	

ANGRY

Ge	18:30	Oh let not the Lord be **a**, and	2734
Ge	45:5	grieved, nor **a** with yourselves	2734
1Ki	11:9	And the Lord was **a** with Solomon,	599
Ps	2:12	Kiss the Son, lest he be **a**, and	599
Ps	7:11	God is **a** with the wicked every	2194
Ps	76:7	in thy sight when once thou art **a**?	639
Ps	79:5	wilt thou be **a** for ever? shall thy	599
Ps	85:5	Wilt thou be **a** with us for ever?	599
Pr	14:17	that is soon **a** dealeth foolishly:	639
Pr	21:19	a contentious and an **a** woman.	3708
Pr	22:24	no friendship with an **a** man;	639
Pr	29:22	An **a** man stirreth up strife	639
Ecc	5:6	should God be **a** at thy voice,	7107
Ecc	7:9	Be not hasty in thy spirit to be **a**:	3707
SS	1:6	my mother's children were **a**	2734
Da	2:12	the king was **a** and very furious,	1149
Jnh	4:4	Lord, Doest thou well to be **a**?	2734
Jnh	4:9	I do well to be **a**, even unto death.	2734
Mt	5:22	**whosoever is a with his brother**	*3710*
Lk	14:21	**the master of the house being a**	*3710*
Lk	15:28	**he was a, and would not go in:**	*3710*
Jn	7:23	**are ye a at me, because I have**	*5520*
Eph	4:26	Be ye **a**, and sin not: let not the	*3710*
Tit	1:7	not soon **a**, not given to wine,	*3711*

ANGUISH

Ge	42:21	we saw the **a** of his soul, when	6869
Ex	6:9	hearkened not ... for **a** of spirit,	7115
2Sa	1:9	**a** is come upon me, because my	7661
Job	7:11	I will speak in the **a** of my spirit;	6862
Pr	1:27	distress and **a** cometh upon you	6695
Jn	16:21	**she remembereth no more the a,**	*2347*
Ro	2:9	and **a**, upon every soul of man.	*4730*
2Co	2:4	of much affliction and **a** of heart	*4928*

ANOINT

Ex	30:26	And thou shalt **a** the tabernacle.	4886
Ex	30:30	thou shalt **a** Aaron and his sons,	4886
Ex	40:10	**a** the altar of the burnt offering,	4886
Jgs	9:15	If in truth ye **a** me king over you,	4886
Ru	3:3	Wash thyself therefore, and **a**	5480
1Sa	15:1	The Lord sent me to **a** thee to be	4886
Da	9:24	and to **a** the most Holy.	4886
Mt	6:17	**a thine head, and wash thy face;**	*218*
Mk	14:8	**to a my body to the burying.**	*3462*

Mk	16:1	they might come and **a** him.	*218*
Lk	7:46	**My head with oil thou didst not a:**	*218*
Rev	3:18	**a thine eyes with eyesalve, that**	*1472*

ANOINTED

Ex	29:2	wafers unleavened **a** with oil:	4886
Le	4:3	If the priest that is **a** do sin	4899
Le	7:36	in the day that he **a** them,	4886
1Sa	10:1	Lord hath **a** thee to be captain	4886
1Sa	12:3	before the Lord, and before his **a**:	4899
1Sa	15:17	the Lord **a** thee king over Israel?	4886
1Sa	16:6	Surely the Lord's **a** is before him	4899
2Sa	5:3	they **a** David king over Israel.	4886
2Sa	19:10	Absalom, whom we **a** over us,	4886
2Sa	19:21	because he cursed the Lord's **a**?	4899
1Ch	16:22	Touch not mine **a**, and do my	4899
Ps	105:15	Touch not mine **a**,	4899
Isa	61:1	the Lord hath **a** me to preach	4886
Lk	4:18	**hath a me to preach the gospel**	*5548*
Lk	7:46	**hath a my feet with ointment.**	*218*
Jn	9:6	**a** the eyes of the blind man	*2025, 1909*
Jn	12:3	**a** the feet of Jesus, and wiped	*218*
Heb	1:9	**a** thee with the oil of gladness	*5548*

ANOINTEST

Ps	23:5	thou **a** my head with oil; my	1878

ANOINTING

Ex	25:6	spices for **a** oil, and for sweet	4888
Ex	30:25	it shall be an holy **a** oil.	4888
Ex	40:15	**a** shall surely be an everlasting	4888
1Jn	2:27	But the **a** which ye have received	*5545*

ANSWER

Ge	30:33	shall my righteousness **a** for me	6030
Ge	41:16	God shall give Pharaoh an **a** of	6030
2Sa	3:11	he could not **a** Abner a word	7725
1Ki	12:9	that we may **a** this people	7725, 1697
Job	9:3	cannot **a** him one of a thousand	6030
Job	9:14	How much less shall I **a** him,	6030
Job	19:16	servant, and he gave me no **a**;	6030
Job	31:35	that the Almighty would **a** me,	6030
Job	40:2	he that reproveth God, let him **a**	6030
Job	40:5	have I spoken; but I will not **a**:	6030
Pr	1:28	call upon me, but I will not **a**;	6030
Pr	15:1	A soft **a** turneth away wrath:	4617
Pr	16:1	**a** of the tongue, is from the Lord	4617
Pr	26:4	**A** not a fool according to his	6030
Pr	26:5	**A** a fool according to his folly,	6030
Isa	50:2	I called, was there none to **a**?	6030
Isa	58:9	thou call, and the Lord shall **a**;	6030
Isa	65:12	when I called, ye did not answer;	6030
Isa	65:24	before they call, I will **a**;	6030
Isa	66:4	when I called, none did **a**;	6030
Jer	33:3	Call unto me, and I will **a** thee,	6030
Eze	14:4	I the Lord will **a** him that cometh	6030
Da	3:16	careful to **a** thee in this matter	8421
Mic	3:7	for there is no **a** of God	4617
Mt	22:46	no man was able to **a** him a word	*611*
Mt	25:37	**Then shall the righteous a him,**	*611*
Mk	11:29	**ask of you one question, and a me**	*611*
Mk	11:30	**from heaven, or of men? a me.**	*611*
Lk	11:7	**shall a and say, Trouble me not:**	*611*
Lk	14:6	could not **a** him again to these.	*470*
Lk	20:3	**ask you one thing; and a me:**	*2036*
Lk	20:26	they marvelled at his **a**, and held	*612*
Lk	21:14	**meditate before what ye shall a:**	*626*
Lk	22:68	**ye will not a me, nor let me go.**	*611*
Jn	19:9	Jesus gave him no **a**	*612*
Ac	25:16	have licence to **a** for himself	*627*
Col	4:6	how ye ought to **a** every man.	*611*
2Ti	4:16	first **a** no man stood with me,	*627*
1Pe	3:15	**a** to every man that asketh you	*627*
1Pe	3:21	**a** of a good conscience toward	*1906*

ANSWERED

Ex	19:19	and God **a** him by a voice.	6030
Ex	24:3	and all the people **a** with one voice,	6030
1Sa	3:4	and he **a**, Here am I.	559
1Sa	28:6	the Lord **a** him not, neither by	6030
1Ki	12:13	the king **a** the people roughly,	6030
2Ki	18:36	and **a** him not a word:	6030
2Ch	10:13	And the king **a** them roughly;	6030
Job	32:12	convinced Job, or that **a** his words:	6030
Job	32:15	were amazed they **a** no more:	6030
Job	32:16	stood still, and **a** no more,	6030
Job	38:1	Lord **a** Job out of the whirlwind,	6030
Ps	18:41	the Lord, but he **a** them not.	6030
Ps	81:7	I **a** thee in the secret place of	6030
Isa	36:21	peace, and **a** him not a word:	6030
Mt	27:14	he **a** him to never a word;	*611*
Mk	12:28	perceiving that he had **a** them well,	*611*
Mk	12:34	saw that he **a** discreetly,	*611*
Mk	14:61	held his peace and **a** nothing.	*611*
Mk	15:3	many things: but he **a** nothing.	*611*
Mk	15:5	Jesus yet **a** nothing; so that Pilate	*611*
Lk	10:28	unto him, **Thou hast a right:**	*611*
Ac	11:9	the voice **a** me again from heaven,	*611*
Ac	19:15	the evil spirit **a** and said	*611*

ANSWEREST

Mt	26:62	unto him, **A** thou nothing?	*611*
Mk	14:60	saying, **A** thou nothing?	*611*
Mk	15:4	him, saying, **a** thou nothing?	*611*
Jn	18:22	**A** thou the high priest so?	*611*

ANSWERETH

1Sa	28:15	and **a** me no more, neither by	6030
1Ki	18:24	the God that **a** by fire, let him	6030
Pr	18:13	He that **a** a matter before	7725
Pr	18:23	intreaties; but the rich **a** roughly	6030
Pr	27:19	As in water face **a** to face, so	
Ecc	5:20	God **a** him in the joy of his	6030
Ecc	10:19	but money **a** all things	6030

ANSWERING

Tit	2:9	well in all things; not **a** again:	*488*

ANSWERS

Job	21:34	**a** there remaineth falsehood?	8666
Job	34:36	of his **a** for wicked men.	8666
Lk	2:47	at his understanding and **a**	*612*

ANT

Pro	6:6	Go to the **a**, thou sluggard;	5244

ANTICHRIST

1Jn	2:18	ye have heard that **a** shall come	*500*
1Jn	2:22	He is **a**, that denieth the Father	*500*
1Jn	4:3	this is that spirit of **a**, whereof	*500*
2Jn	7	This is a deceiver and an **a**	*500*

ANTICHRISTS

1Jn	2:18	come, even now are there many **a**	*500*

ANTS

Pr	30:25	The **a** are a people not strong,	5244

APART

Ex	13:12	thou shalt set **a** unto the Lord	5674
Le	15:19	she shall be put **a** seven days;	5079
Le	18:19	as long as she is put **a** for her	5079
Ps	4:3	the Lord hath set **a** him that is	6395
Eze	22:10	they humbled her that was set **a**	5079
Mt	14:13	into a desert place **a**	*2596, 2398*
Mt	14:23	into a mountain **a** to pray:	*2596, 2398*
Mt	17:1	into an high mountain **a**,	*2596, 2398*
Mt	17:19	the disciples to Jesus **a**,	*2596, 2398*
Mt	20:17	took the twelve disciples **a** in	*2596, 2398*
Mk	6:31	**ye yourselves a into a desert**	*2596, 2398*
Mk	9:2	mountain **a** by themselves:	*2596, 2398*
Jas	1:21	Wherefore lay **a** all filthiness	*659*

APOSTLE

Ro	1:1	called to be an **a**, separated unto	*652*
Ro	11:13	as I am the **a** of the Gentiles	*652*
1Co	1:1	called to be an **a** of Jesus Christ	*652*
1Co	9:1	Am I not an **a**? am I not free?	*652*
1Co	9:2	If I be not an **a** unto others,	*652*
1Co	15:9	not meet to be called an **a**,	*652*
2Co	12:12	the signs of an **a** were wrought	*652*
1Ti	2:7	am ordained a preacher, and an **a**,	*652*
2Ti	1:11	appointed a preacher, and an **a**,	*652*
Heb	3:1	consider the **A** and High Priest	*652*
2Pe	1:1	a servant and an **a** of Jesus	*652*

APOSTLES

Mt	10:2	names of the twelve **a** are these;	*652*
Ac	1:26	numbered with the eleven **a**	*652*
Ac	2:43	and signs were done by the **a**	*652*
Ac	4:33	the **a** witness of the resurrection	*652*
Ac	4:36	by the **a** was surnamed Barnabas	*652*
Ac	5:12	hands of the **a** were many signs	*652*
Ac	5:18	laid their hands on the **a**	*652*
Ac	5:34	to put the **a** forth a little space;	*652*
Ac	5:40	called the **a**, and beaten them	*652*
Ac	8:1	Judea and Samaria, except the **a**	*652*
Ac	8:14	the **a** which were at Jerusalem	*652*
Ac	14:4	with the Jews, and part with the **a**,	*652*
Ac	14:14	when the **a**, Barnabas and Paul,	*652*
Ac	15:6	the **a** and elders came together	*652*
Ro	16:7	who are of note among the **a**,	*652*
1Co	4:9	God hath set forth us the **a** last	*652*
1Co	12:29	Are all **a**? are all prophets?	*652*
1Co	15:7	of James; then of all the **a**	*652*
1Co	15:9	I am the least of the **a**, that am	*652*
2Co	11:5	a whit behind the very chiefest **a**	*652*
2Co	11:13	are false **a**, deceitful workers	*5570*
2Co	11:13	themselves into the **a** of Christ	*652*
2Co	12:11	the very chiefest **a**, though I be	*652*
Gal	1:17	to them which were **a** before me;	*652*
Gal	1:19	other of the **a** saw I none, save	*652*
Eph	2:20	foundation of the **a** and prophets,	*652*
Eph	3:5	revealed unto his holy **a**	*652*
Eph	4:11	gave some, **a**; and some, prophets;	*652*
1Th	2:6	burdensome, as the **a** of Christ	*652*
2Pe	3:2	the **a** of the Lord and Saviour:	*652*
Rev	2:2	**them which say they are a,**	*652*
Rev	18:20	ye holy **a** and prophets;	*652*
Rev	21:14	names of the twelve **a** of the Lamb	*652*

APOSTLES'

Ac	2:42	in the **a** doctrine and fellowship	*652*
Ac	4:35	laid them down at the **a** feet:	*652*
Ac	8:18	through laying on of the **a** hands	*652*

APOSTLESHIP

1Co	9:2	seal of mine **a** are ye in the Lord	*651*
Gal	2:8	to the **a** of the circumcision,	*651*

APPEAL

Ac	25:11	I **a** unto Caesar	*1941*
Ac	28:19	constrained to **a** unto Caesar:	*1941*

APPEALED

Ac	25:12	Hast thou **a** unto Caesar?	*1941*
Ac	26:32	if he had not **a** unto Caesar	*1941*

APPEAR

Ge	1:9	let the dry land **a**: and it was so	7200
Ex	23:17	all thy males shall **a** before	7200
Dt	16:16	they shall not **a** ... empty:	7200
Jgs	13:21	angel of the Lord did no more **a**	7200
2Ch	1:7	night did God **a** unto Solomon,	7200
Mt	6:16	**they may a unto men to fast**	*5316*
Mt	23:27	**which indeed a beautiful outward,**	*5316*
Mt	23:28	**ye also outwardly a righteous**	*5316*
Mt	24:30	**shall a the sign of the Son of man**	*5316*
Ac	26:16	**in the which I will a unto thee;**	*3700*
Ro	7:13	But sin, that it might **a** sin,	*5316*
2Co	5:10	all **a** before the judgment seat	*5319*
Col	3:4	Christ, who is our life, shall **a**,	*5319*
Heb	9:24	**a** in the presence of God for us	*1718*
Heb	9:28	them that look for him shall he **a**	*3700*
Heb	11:3	not made of things which do **a**	*5316*
1Pe	4:18	the ungodly and the sinner **a**?	*5316*
1Pe	5:4	when the chief Shepherd shall **a**,	*5319*
1Jn	2:28	when he shall **a**, we may have	*5319*
1Jn	3:2	when he shall **a**, we shall be like him,	*5319*
Rev	3:18	**of thy nakedness do not a;**	*5319*

APPEARANCE

Nu	9:16	and the **a** of fire by night	4758
1Sa	16:7	man looketh on the outward **a**,	5869
Eze	1:13	their **a** was like burning coals	4758
Eze	1:16	The **a** of the wheels	4758
Eze	1:26	as the **a** of a man above it	4758
Eze	40:3	whose **a** was like the **a** of brass	4758
Da	10:6	his face as the **a** of lightning	4758
Joel	2:4	**a** of them is as the **a** of horses;	4758
Jn	7:24	**Judge not according to the a,**	*3799*
2Co	5:12	glory in **a**, and not in heart	*4383*
2Co	10:7	on things after the outward **a**?	*4383*
1Th	5:22	Abstain from all **a** of evil	*1491*

APPEARED

Ge	12:7	And the Lord **a** unto Abram	7200
Ge	17:1	And when ... the Lord **a** to Abram	7200
Ge	26:24	**a** unto him the same night	7200
Ge	35:7	because there God **a** unto him,	1540
Ex	16:10	glory of the Lord **a** in the cloud	7200
1Ki	3:5	In Gibeon the Lord **a** to Solomon	7200
1Ki	9:2	the Lord **a** to Solomon the second	7200
2Ch	3:1	where the Lord **a** unto David	7200
2Ch	7:12	the Lord **a** to Solomon by night,	7200
Ne	4:21	of the morning till the stars **a**	3318
Eze	10:1	there **a** over them as it were a	7200
Eze	10:8	And there **a** in the cherubims	7200
Da	1:15	countenances **a** fairer and fatter	7200

Mt 2:7 what time the star **a** ... *5316*
Mt 13:26 **then a the tares also.** ... *5316*
Mk 16:9 he **a** first to Mary Magdalene ... *5316*
Mk 16:12 **a** in another form unto two of ... *5319*
Mk 16:14 Afterward he **a** unto the eleven ... *5319*
Ac 2:3 there **a** unto them cloven tongues ... *3700*
Ac 7:35 angel which **a** to him in the bush ... *3700*
Ac 9:17 Jesus, that **a** unto thee in the way ... *3700*
Ac 16:9 a vision **a** to Paul in the night; ... *3700*
Ac 26:16 **I a unto thee for this purpose,** ... *3700*
Tit 2:11 salvation hath **a** to all men ... *2014*
Heb 9:26 hath he **a** to put away sin by ... *5319*

APPEARETH

Jer 6:1 evil **a** out of the north, ... 8259
Mal 3:2 who shall stand when he **a**? ... 7200
Mt 2:13 angel of the Lord **a** to Joseph in ... 5316
Jas 4:14 a vapour, that **a** for a little time, ... 5316

APPEARING

1Ti 6:14 the **a** of our Lord Jesus Christ: ... *2015*
2Ti 1:10 the **a** of our Saviour Jesus Christ, ... *2015*
2Ti 4:1 at his **a** and his kingdom; ... *2015*
2Ti 4:8 them also that love his **a** ... *2015*
Tit 2:13 the glorious **a** of the great God ... *2015*
1Pe 1:7 glory at the **a** of Jesus Christ: ... *602*

APPETITE

Job 38:39 or fill the **a** of the young lions ... 2416
Pr 23:2 if thou be a man given to **a** ... 5315
Ecc 6:7 yet the **a** is not filled. ... 5315
Isa 29:8 he is faint, and his soul hath **a** ... 8264

APPLE

Dt 32:10 he kept him as the **a** of his eye. ... 380
Ps 17:8 Keep me as the **a** of the eye ... 380, 1323
Pr 7:2 my law as the **a** of thine eye ... 380
La 2:18 not the **a** of thine eye cease ... 1323
Zec 2:8 toucheth the **a** of his eye. ... 892

APPLES

Pr 25:11 A word fitly spoken is like **a** of ... 8598
SS 2:5 flagons, comfort me with **a** ... 8598

APPLIED

Ecc 7:25 I **a** mine heart to know, and ... 5437
Ecc 8:9 and **a** my heart unto every work ... 5414
Ecc 8:16 I **a** mine heart to know wisdom, ... 5414

APPLY

Ps 90:12 may **a** our hearts unto wisdom. ... 935
Pr 2:2 **a** thine heart to understanding; ... 5186
Pr 22:17 **a** thine heart unto my knowledge ... 7896
Pr 23:12 **A** thine heart unto instruction ... 935

APPOINT See also **APPOINTETH.**

Ge 30:28 **A** me thy wages, and I will give. ... 5344
Ge 41:34 him **a** officers over the land, ... 6485
Ex 21:13 then I will **a** thee a place, ... 7760
Ex 30:16 and shall **a** it for the service of ... 5414
Nu 3:10 And thou shalt **a** Aaron ... 6485
Jos 20:2 **A** out for you cities of refuge, ... 5414
1Sa 8:12 And he will **a** him captains ... 7760
2Sa 6:21 to **a** me ruler over the people ... 6680
2Sa 7:10 I will **a** a place for my people ... 7760
Est 2:3 And let the king **a** officers ... 6485
Job 14:13 **a** me a set time, and remember me ... 7896
Isa 26:1 salvation will God **a** for walls ... 7896
Jer 15:3 I will **a** over them four kinds, ... 6485
Eze 21:19 son of man, **a** thee two ways, ... 7760
Mt 24:51 **and a him his portion with** ... *5087*
Lk 12:46 **and will a him his portion with** ... *5087*
Lk 22:29 **I a unto you a kingdom, as my** ... *1303*

APPOINTED See also **DISAPPOINTED.**

Ge 4:25 said she, hath **a** me another seed ... 7896
Ge 18:14 At the time **a** I will return ... 4150
Ge 24:44 woman whom the Lord hath **a** ... 3198
Ex 9:5 And the Lord **a** a set time, ... 7760
Nu 9:2 keep the passover at his **a** season ... 4150
Jgs 18:17 men that were **a** with weapons ... 2296
Jgs 20:38 there was an **a** sign between ... 4150
1Sa 13:11 camest not within the days **a**, ... 4150
1Sa 20:35 field at the time **a** with David, ... 4150
1Sa 29:4 his place which thou hast **a** him, ... 6485
2Sa 17:14 Lord had **a** to defeat the good ... 6680
2Sa 20:5 the set time which he had **a** him, ... 3259
2Sa 24:15 the morning even to the time **a** ... 4150
1Ch 6:48 Levites were **a** unto all manner ... 5414
2Ch 31:2 And Hezekiah **a** the courses ... 5975
Ezr 3:8 and **a** the Levites, from twenty ... 5975
Ne 5:14 I was **a** to be their governor ... 6680
Ne 9:17 in their rebellion **a** a capatin ... 5414
Est 1:8 king had **a** to all the officers ... 3245
Job 7:1 **a** time to man upon the earth? ... 6635
Job 7:3 wearisome nights are **a** to me ... 4487
Job 14:5 thou hast **a** his bounds that he ... 6213
Job 14:14 days of my **a** time will I wait, ... 6635
Job 20:29 the heritage **a** unto him by God ... 561
Job 30:23 the house **a** for all living ... 4150
Ps 78:5 **a** a law in Israel, which he ... 7760
Ps 79:11 preserve thou those that are **a** ... 1121
Ps 81:3 in the new moon, in the time **a**, ... 3677
Ps 102:20 loose those that are **a** to death; ... 1121
Ps 104:19 He **a** the moon for seasons: ... 6213
Pr 7:20 will come home at the day **a** ... 3677
Pr 8:29 when he **a** the foundations of ... 2710
Pr 31:8 all such as are **a** to destruction ... 1121
Isa 44:7 since I **a** the ancient people? ... 7760
Jer 8:7 the stork … knoweth her **a** times; ... 4150
Jer 33:25 if I have not **a** the ordinances ... 7760
Jer 46:17 he hath passed the time **a** ... 4150
Eze 43:21 he shall burn it in the **a** place ... 4662
Da 1:5 And the king **a** them a daily ... 4487
Da 11:29 At the time **a** he shall return, ... 4150
Mic 6:9 the rod, and who hath **a** it ... 3259
Hab 2:3 the vision is yet for an **a** time, ... 4150
Lk 3:13 than that which is **a** you ... *1299*
Lk 10:1 the Lord **a** other seventy also ... *322*
Lk 22:29 **as my Father hath a unto me;** ... *1303*
Ac 1:23 **a** two, Joseph called Barsabas, ... *2476*
Ac 7:44 as he had **a**, speaking unto Moses, ... *1299*
Ac 17:26 determined the times before **a**, ... *4384*
Ac 17:31 Because he hath **a** a day, ... *2476*
Ac 20:13 for so he had **a**, minding himself ... *1299*
Ac 22:10 **which are a for thee to do.** ... *5021*
Ac 28:23 And when they had **a** him a day ... *5021*
1Co 4:9 as it were **a** to death; ... *1935*
Gal 4:2 until the time **a** of the father ... *4287*
1Th 3:3 know that we are **a** thereunto ... *2749*
1Th 5:9 God hath not **a** us to wrath, ... *5087*
Heb 1:2 he hath **a** heir of all things ... *5087*
Heb 9:27 as it is **a** unto men once to die, ... *606*
1Pe 2:8 whereunto also they were **a** ... *5087*

APPOINTETH

Da	5:21	he **a** over it whomsoever he will.	6966

APPOINTMENT

Nu	4:27	At the **a** of Aaron and his sons	6310
2Sa	13:32	by the **a** of Absalom this hath	6310
Ezr	6:9	according to the **a** of the priests	3983
Job	2:11	for they had made an **a** together	3259

APPREHEND

2Co	11:32	desirous to **a** me:	4084
Php	3:12	if that I may **a** that for which.	2638

APPREHENDED

Ac	12:4	when he had **a** him,	4084
Php	3:12	for which also I am **a** for Christ	*2638*
Php	3:13	I count not myself to have **a**:	*2638*

APPROACH

Le	18:6	None of you shall **a** to any that	7126
Le	18:14	thou shalt not **a** to his wife:	7126
Le	18:19	thou shalt not **a** unto a woman	7126
Le	20:16	if a woman **a** unto any beast,	7126
Le	21:18	hath a blemish, he shall not **a**:	7126
Nu	4:19	they **a** unto the most holy things:	5066
Dt	20:3	Israel, ye **a** this day unto battle	7126
Dt	31:14	thy days **a** that thou must die:	7126
Jos	8:5	people that are with me will **a**	7126
Jer	30:21	engaged his heart to **a** unto me?	5066
Eze	42:13	the priests that **a** unto the Lord	7138
Eze	42:14	shall **a** to those things which are	7126
1Ti	6:16	in the light which no man can **a**	*676*

APPROACHETH

Lk	12:33	where no thief **a**, neither moth	*1448*

APPROACHING

Isa	58:2	they take delight in **a** to God	7132
Heb	10:25	the more, as ye see the day **a**	*1448*

APPROVE

1Co	16:3	whosoever ye shall **a** by ... letters	*1381*
Php	1:10	may **a** things that are excellent;	*1381*

APPROVED

Ac	2:22	a man **a** of God among you by	*584*
Ro	14:18	acceptable to God, and **a** of men	*1384*
1Co	11:19	which are **a** may be made manifest	*1384*
2Co	7:11	ye have **a** yourselves to be clear	*4921*
2Co	10:18	not he that commendeth himself is **a**,	*1384*
2Co	13:7	not that we should appear **a**,	*1384*
2Ti	2:15	Study to shew thyself **a** unto God	*1384*

APPROVING

2Co	6:4	**a** ourselves as the ministers of	*4921*

ARCHANGEL See also ANGEL.

1Th	4:16	with the voice of the **a**,	*743*
Jude	9	Michael the **a**, when contending	*743*

ARCHER

Ge	21:20	he grew ... and became an **a**	7198
Jer	51:3	let the **a** bend his bow	1869

ARCHERS

Ge	49:23	**a** have sorely grieved him,	1167, 2671
Jgs	5:11	are delivered from the noise of **a**	2686
1Sa	31:3	the **a** hit him, and he	3384, 376, 7198
1Ch	10:3	he was wounded of the **a**	3384
2Ch	35:23	the **a** shot at king Josiah;	3384
Job	16:13	His **a** compass me round about,	7228
Isa	22:3	they are bound by the **a**	7198
Jer	50:29	Call together the **a** against	7228

ARCHES

Eze	40:30	**a** round about were five and twenty	361
Eze	40:34	the **a** thereof were toward the	361

ARISE See also AROSE; RISE.

Ge	13:17	**A**, walk through the land	6965
Ge	19:15	**A**, take thy wife, and thy two	6965
Ge	27:43	**a**, flee thou to Laban my brother	6965
Ge	35:1	**A**, go up to Beth-el, and dwell	6965
Ge	43:13	Take also your brother, and **a**,	6965
Dt	9:12	**A**, get thee down quickly from	6965
Dt	17:8	there **a** a matter too hard for thee	
Jos	1:2	therefore **a**, go over this Jordan,	6965
1Sa	16:12	**A**, anoint him: for this is he	6965
2Sa	3:21	Abner said unto David, I will **a**	6965
2Sa	13:15	Ammon said unto her, **A**, be gone.	6965
2Sa	15:14	**A**, and let us flee;	6965
1Ki	19:5	said unto him, **A** and eat	6965
1Ki	19:7	**A** and eat; because the journey is	6965
1Ch	22:19	**a** therefore, and build ye the	6965
2Ch	6:41	Now therefore **a**, O Lord God,	6965
Ne	2:20	we his servants will **a** and build:	6965
Est	4:14	and deliverance **a** to the Jews	5975
Job	7:4	When shall I **a**, and the night	6965
Ps	3:7	**A**, O Lord; save me, O my God:	6965
Ps	9:19	**A**, O Lord; let not man prevail:	6965
Ps	44:23	why sleepest thou, O Lord? **a**	6974
Ps	44:26	**a** for our help, and redeem us	6965
Ps	74:22	**A**, O God, plead thine own cause:	6965
Ps	78:6	who should **a** and declare them to	6965
Ps	82:8	**A**, O God, judge the earth:	6965
Ps	88:10	shall the dead **a** and praise thee?	6965
Ps	89:9	when the waves thereof **a**, thou	7721
Ps	109:28	they **a**, let them be ashamed;	6965
Ps	132:8	**A**, O Lord, into thy rest;	6965
Pr	6:9	when wilt thou **a** out of thy sleep?	6965
Pr	31:28	Her children **a** up, and call her	6965
SS	2:13	**A**, my love, my fair one, and	6965
Isa	26:19	with my dead body shall they **a**	6965
Isa	49:7	Kings shall see and **a**,	6965
Isa	52:2	**a**, and sit down, O Jerusalem:	6965
Isa	60:1	**A**, shine; for thy light is come,	6965
Isa	60:2	but the Lord shall **a** upon thee,	2224
Jer	1:17	gird up thy loins, and **a**	6965
Jer	2:27	they will say, **A**, and save us	6965
Jer	2:28	let them **a**, if they can save thee	6965
Jer	18:2	**A**, and go down to the potter's	6965
La	2:19	**A**, cry out in the night:	6965
Eze	3:22	**A**, go forth into the plain,	6965
Da	2:39	And after thee shall **a** another	6966
Da	7:5	**A**, devour much flesh	6966
Da	7:17	which shall **a** out of the earth	6966
Da	7:24	ten kings that shall **a**:	6966
Hos	10:14	a tumult **a** among thy people	6965
Am	7:2, 5	by whom shall Jacob **a**? for	6965
Jnh	1:2	**A**, go to Nineveh, that great city	6965
Jnh	1:6	**a**, call upon thy God,	6965
Jnh	3:2	**A**, go unto Nineveh	6965
Jnh	4:8	when the sun did **a**,	2224
Mic	2:10	**A** ye, and depart, for this is not	6965
Mic	4:13	**A** and thresh, O daughter of	6965
Mic	7:8	enemy: when I fall, I shall **a**;	6965

A

A

Hab	2:19	**A**, it shall teach! Behold, it is	5782
Mal	4:2	shall the Sun of righteousness **a**	2224
Mt	2:13	**A**, and take the young child	*1453*
Mt	2:20	**A**, and take the young child	*7453*
Mt	9:6	**A, take up thy bed, and go unto**	*1453*
Mt	24:24	**For there shall a false Christs,**	*1453*
Mk	2:9	**or to say, A, and take up thy bed,**	*1453*
Mk	5:41	Damsel, I say unto thee, **a**	*1453*
Lk	5:24	**I say unto thee, A, and take up**	*1453*
Lk	7:14	**Young man, I say unto thee, A.**	*1453*
Lk	8:54	called, saying, **Maid, a**	*1453*
Lk	15:18	**I will a and go to my father,**	*450*
Lk	17:19	he said unto him, **A, go thy way:**	*450*
Lk	24:38	**why do thoughts a in your hearts?**	*305*
Ac	8:26	**A**, and go toward the south.	*450*
Ac	9:6	**A, and go into the city, and it**	*450*
Ac	9:11	**A, and go into the street which**	*450*
Ac	9:34	**a**, and make thy bed. And he	*450*
Ac	9:40	him to the body said, Tabitha, **a**	*450*
Ac	10:20	**A** therefore, and get thee down	*450*
Ac	11:7	**A**, Peter; slay and eat	*450*
Ac	12:7	raised him up, saying, **A** up	*450*
Ac	22:10	me, **A, and go into Damascus;**	*450*
Ac	22:16	**a**, and be baptized, and wash away	*450*
Eph	5:14	**a** from the dead, and Christ shall	*450*
2Pe	1:19	the day star **a** in your hearts:	*393*

ARISETH See also **RISETH.**

1Ki	18:44	**a** a little cloud out of the sea	5927
Ps	112:4	Unto the upright there **a** light	2224
Ecc	1:5	The sun also **a**, and the sun	2224
Isa	2:19	when he **a** to shake terribly	6965
Isa	2:21	when he **a** to shake terribly	6965
Nah	3:17	when the sun **a** they flee away	2224
Mt	13:21	**tribulation or persecution a**	*1096*
Mk	4:17	**affliction or persecution a for**	*1096*
Jn	7:52	for out of Galilee **a** no prophet	*1453*
Heb	7:15	there **a** another priest,	*450*

ARK

Ge	6:14	Make thee an **a** of gopher wood;	8392
Ge	6:15	the length of the **a** shall be three	8392
Ge	6:18	thou shalt come into the **a**,	8392
Ge	6:19	shalt thou bring into the **a**,	8392
Ge	7:1	thou and all thy house into the **a**;	8392
Ge	7:7	sons wives with him, into the **a**,	8392
Ge	7:9	two and two unto Noah into the **a**	8392
Ge	7:15	went in unto Noah into the **a**,	8392
Ge	7:17	increased, and bare up the **a**	8392
Ge	7:18	the **a** went upon the face of the	8392
Ge	7:23	that were with him in the **a**	8392
Ge	8:4	the **a** rested in the seventh month,	8392
Ge	8:6	Noah opened the window of the **a**	8392
Ge	8:9	she returned unto him into the **a**	8392
Ge	8:10	sent forth the dove out of the **a**;	8392
Ge	8:13	removed the covering of the **a**,	8392
Ge	8:16	Go forth of the **a**,	8392
Ex	2:3	she look for him an **a** for bulrushes,	8392
Ex	25:10	shall make an **a** of shittim wood:	*727*
Ex	25:14	into the rings by the sides of the **a**,	*727*
Ex	25:16	shalt put into the **a** the testimony	*727*
Ex	25:21	the mercy seat above upon the **a**	*727*
Ex	25:22	are upon the **a** of the testimony	*727*
Ex	26:33	within the vail the **a** of the	*727*
Ex	37:1	Bezaleel made the **a** of shittim	*727*
Ex	40:3	and cover the **a** with the vail	*727*
Ex	40:20	put the testimony into the **a**	*727*
Ex	40:21	brought the **a** into the tabernacle,	*727*
Le	16:2	which is upon the **a**	*727*
Nu	4:5	cover the **a** of testimony with it:	*727*
Nu	10:35	when the **a** set forward,	*727*
Nu	14:44	nevertheless the **a** of the covenant	*727*
Dt	10:1	make thee an **a** of wood	*727*
Dt	10:3	made an **a** of shittim wood	*727*
Dt	10:5	put the tables into the **a** which.	*727*
Dt	31:9	the sons of Levi which bear the **a**	*727*
Jos	3:3	When ye see the **a** of the covenant	*727*
Jos	3:11	Behold, the **a** of the covenant	*727*
Jos	3:13	that bear the **a** of the Lord	*727*
Jos	4:5	Pass over before the **a** of the Lord	*727*
Jos	4:11	that the **a** of the Lord passed over	*727*
Jgs	20:27	the **a** of the covenant of God was	727
1Sa	3:3	where the **a** of God was,	727
1Sa	4:4	bring from thence the **a** of	727
1Sa	4:5	when the **a** of the covenant	727
1Sa	4:11	And the **a** of God was taken;	727
1Sa	4:13	his heart trembled for the **a** of God	727
1Sa	4:17	and the **a** of God is taken	727
1Sa	4:19	that the **a** of God was taken,	727
1Sa	4:21	because the **a** of God was taken,	727
1Sa	5:2	When the Philistines took the **a**	727
1Sa	5:4	the ground before the **a** of the Lord;	
1Sa	5:7	The **a** of the God of Israel	727
1Sa	5:8	What shall we do with the **a** of	727
1Sa	5:10	Therefore they sent the **a** of God	727
1Sa	5:10	They have brought about the **a** of	727
1Sa	5:11	Send away the **a** of the God of	727
1Sa	6:3	If ye send away the **a** of	727
1Sa	6:19	because they had looked into the **a**	727
1Sa	7:1	Eleazar his son to keep the **a** of	727
1Sa	14:18	Bring hither the **a** of God	727
2Sa	6:2	bring up from thence the **a** of God,	727
2Sa	6:3	they set the **a** of God upon a new	727
2Sa	6:6	put forth his hand to the **a** of God,	727
2Sa	6:7	there he died by the **a** of God	727
2Sa	6:10	David would not remove the **a** of	727
2Sa	6:12	went and brought up the **a** of	727
2Sa	6:16	as the **a** of the Lord came into the	727
2Sa	7:2	but the **a** of God dwelleth within	727
2Sa	15:25	Carry back the **a** of God into the	727
1Ki	2:26	because thou barest the **a** of	727
1Ki	3:15	stood before the **a** of the covenant	727
1Ki	8:4	they brought up the **a** of the Lord,	727
1Ki	8:6	the priests brought in the **a** of the	727
1Ki	8:9	nothing in the **a** save the two	727
1Ch	6:31	after that the **a** had rest	727
1Ch	13:3	let us bring again the **a** of our God	727
1Ch	13:9	put forth his hand to hold the **a**;	727
1Ch	13:14	the **a** of God remained	727
1Ch	15:2	None ought to carry the **a** of God	727
1Ch	15:15	the Levites bare the **a** of God	727
1Ch	15:23	doorkeepers for the **a**	727
1Ch	15:26	helped the Levites that bare the **a**	727
1Ch	15:28	Thus all Israel brought up the **a**	727
1Ch	16:4	Levites to minister before the **a**	727
1Ch	28:2	an house of rest for the **a** of	727
2Ch	1:4	But the **a** of God had David	727
2Ch	5:2	to bring up the **a** of the covenant	727
2Ch	5:8	their wings over the place of the **a**,	727
2Ch	5:8	and the cherubims covered the **a**,	727
2Ch	5:10	nothing in the **a** save the two	727
2Ch	35:3	Put the holy **a** in the house	727

Jer	3:16	The **a** of the covenant of the Lord:	727
Mt	24:38	**day that Noe entered into the a,**	*2787*
Lk	17:27	Noe entered into the **a**, and the	*2787*
Heb	9:4	censer, and the **a** of the covenant	*2787*
Heb	11:7	prepared an **a** to the saving of	*2787*
1Pe	3:20	while the **a** was a preparing	*2787*
Rev	11:19	was seen in his temple the **a** of	*2787*

ARM

Ex	6:6	you with a stretched out **a**,	2220
Ex	15:16	thine **a** they shall be as still as stone	2220
Dt	4:34	and by a stretched out **a**, and by	2220
Dt	7:19	and the stretched out **a**,	2220
2Sa	1:10	the bracelet that was on his **a**,	2220
1Ki	8:42	hand, and of thy stretched out **a**;)	2220
2Ch	6:32	and thy stretched out **a**;	2220
Job	40:9	Hast thou an **a** like God?	2220
Ps	10:15	Break thou the **a** of the wicked	2220
Ps	44:3	neither did their own **a** save them:	2220
Ps	77:15	with thine **a** redeemed thy people,	2220
Ps	136:12	and with a stretched out **a**:)	2220
SS	8:6	thine heart, as a seal upon thine **a**	2220
Isa	9:20	every man the flesh of his own **a**	2220
Isa	33:2	be thou their **a** every morning,	2220
Isa	40:10	and his **a** shall rule for him:	2220
Isa	40:11	shall gather the lambs with his **a**,	2220
Isa	52:10	Lord hath made bare his holy **a**	2220
Isa	53:1	to whom is the **a** of the Lord	2220
Isa	59:16	his **a** brought salvation unto him;	2220
Isa	63:12	Moses with his glorious **a**, dividing	2220
Jer	32:17	great power and stretched out **a**,	2220
Jer	32:21	and with a stretched out **a**,	248
Eze	4:7	and thine **a** shall be uncovered,	2220
Eze	20:33	with a stretched out **a**, and with	2220
Da	11:6	not retain the power of the **a**;	2220
Zec	11:17	the sword shall be upon his **a**,	2220
Lk	1:51	hath shewed strength with his **a**;	1023
Jn	12:38	to whom hath the **a** of the Lord	*1023*
Ac	13:17	with an high **a** brought he them.	*1023*
1Pe	4:1	**a** yourselves likewise with the	*3695*

ARMED

Ge	14:14	when … he **a** his trained servants,	7324
Nu	31:5	twelve thousand **a** for war	2502
Nu	32:27	every man **a** for war,	2502
Nu	32:32	will pass over **a** before the Lord	2502
Dt	3:18	pass over **a** before your brethren.	2502
Jos	1:14	pass before your brethren **a**,	2571
Jos	6:7	that is **a** pass on before the ark	2502
Jos	6:9	the **a** men went before the priests	2502
1Sa	17:5	he was **a** with a coat of mail;	3847
1Sa	17:38	Saul **a** David with his armour,	3847
1Sa	17:38	also he **a** him with a coat of mail	3847
Job	39:21	he goeth on to meet the **a** men	5402
Pr	6:11	and thy want as an **a** man	4043
Pr	24:34	and thy want as an **a** man	4043
Lk	11:21	**strong man a keepeth his palace.**	*2528*

ARMIES

Ex	6:26	from … Egypt according to their **a**	6635
Ex	12:17	your **a** out of the land of Egypt:	6635
Nu	1:3	number them by their **a**.	6635
Nu	2:3	pitch throughout their **a**: and	6635
Nu	10:28	of Israel according to their **a**	6635
Nu	33:1	their **a** under the hand of Moses	6635
1Sa	17:10	I defy the **a** of Israel this day;	4634
1Sa	17:26	defy the **a** of the living God?	4634
1Sa	17:45	the God of the **a** of Israel,	4634
1Sa	28:1	the Philistines gathered their **a**	4264
Job	25:3	Is there any number of his **a**?	1416
Isa	34:2	his fury upon all their **a**: he	6635
Mt	22:7	**he sent forth his a, and destroyed**	*4753*
Lk	21:20	**Jerusalem compassed with a,**	*4760*
Heb	11:34	turned to flight the **a** of the aliens	*3925*
Rev	19:14	And the **a** which were in heaven	*4753*

ARMOUR

1Sa	17:38	Saul armed David with his **a**,	4055
1Sa	17:39	girded his sword upon his **a**,	4055
1Sa	17:54	he put his **a** in his tent	3627
1Ki	22:38	they washed his **a**; according	2185
2Ki	3:21	all that were able to put on **a**,	2290
1Ch	10:9	they took his head, and his **a**,	3627
Isa	22:8	the **a** of the house of the forest.	5402
Isa	39:2	the house of his **a**, and all that	3627
Lk	11:22	**him all his a wherein he trusted,**	*3833*
Ro	13:12	let us put on the **a** of light	*3696*
2Co	6:7	by the **a** of righteousness on the	*3696*
Eph	6:11	Put on the whole **a** of God, that	*3833*
Eph	6:13	take unto you the whole **a** of God,	*3833*

ARMOURBEARER

Jgs	9:54	the young man his **a**,	5375, 3627
1Sa	31:4	Then said Saul unto his **a**,	5375, 3627
1Sa	31:4	his **a** would not; for he was	5375, 3627
1Sa	31:5	**a** saw that Saul was dead,	5375, 3627
1Ch	10:4	Then said Saul to his **a**,	5375, 3627
1Ch	10:4	his **a** would not;	5375, 3627
1Ch	10:5	his **a** saw that Saul was dead,	5375, 3627

ARMS

Dt	33:27	underneath are the everlasting **a**	2220
Jgs	15:14	the cords that were upon his **a**	2220
Jgs	16:12	he brake them from off his **a** like	2220
2Ki	9:24	smote Jehoram between his **a**,	2220
Job	22:9	the **a** of the fatherless have been	2220
Ps	18:34	bow of steel is broken by mine **a**.	2220
Ps	37:17	For the **a** of the wicked shall be	2220
Pr	31:17	strength, and strengtheneth her **a**.	2220
Isa	51:5	mine **a** shall judge the people:	2220
Eze	13:20	I will tear them from your **a**,	2220
Eze	30:24	but I will break Pharaoh's **a**,	2220
Da	2:32	his breast and his **a** of silver,	1872
Da	10:6	his **a** and his feet like in colour	2220
Mk	9:36	when he had taken him in his **a**,	*1723*
Mk	10:16	he took them up in his **a**, put his	*1723*
Lk	2:28	took he him up in his **a**,	*43*

ARMY

Dt	11:4	what he did unto the **a** of Egypt,	2428
1Sa	4:16	I fled to day out of the **a**.	4634
1Sa	17:21	battle in array, **a** against **a**	4634
1Ki	20:25	number thee an **a**	2428
2Ki	25:5	the **a** of the Chaldees pursued	2428
1Ch	20:1	Joab led forth the power of the **a**,	6635
2Ch	13:3	in array with an **a** of valiant	2438
2Ch	25:7	let not the **a** of Israel go with	6635
2Ch	25:9	I have given to the **a** of Israel?	1416
2Ch	25:10	the **a** that was come to him out of	1416
2Ch	25:13	But the soldiers of the **a** which	1416
Jer	32:2	Babylon's **a** besieged Jerusalem:	2428
Jer	34:7	the king of Babylon's **a** fought	2428
Jer	35:11	for fear of the **a** of the Chaldeans,	2428
Jer	37:11	for fear of Pharaoh's **a**,	2428

A

Jer	39:5	Chaldeans' **a** pursued after them,	2428
Jer	52:4	he and all his **a**, against Jerusalem	2428
Jer	52:8	all his **a** was scattered from him	2428
Eze	17:17	Pharaoh with his mighty **a**	2428
Eze	29:18	caused his **a** to serve a great service	2428
Eze	29:19	and it shall be the wages for his **a**,	2428
Eze	32:31	Pharaoh and all his **a** slain by	2428
Eze	37:10	an exceeding great **a**	2428
Da	3:20	mighty men that were in his **a**	2429
Da	4:35	according to his will in the **a** of	2429
Da	11:7	which shall come with an **a**,	2428
Da	11:25	of the south with a great **a**;	2428
Joel	2:25	my great **a** which I sent among	2428
Zec	9:8	mine house because of the **a**,	4675
Ac	23:27	then came I with an **a**, and	*4753*
Rev	9:16	number of the **a** of the horsemen	*4753*
Rev	19:19	sat on the horse, and against his **a**.	*4753*

AROSE See also ARISE.

Ge	19:15	when the morning **a**, then the	5927
Ge	19:33	she lay down, nor when she **a**	6965
Ge	19:35	and the younger **a**, and lay with	6965
Ge	19:35	she lay down, nor when she **a**	6965
Ge	24:61	And Rebekah **a**, and her damsels,	6965
Ex	1:8	there **a** up a new king over Egypt,	6965
Dt	34:10	there **a** not a prophet since in	6965
Jgs	2:10	**a** another generation after them,	6965
Jgs	19:3	her husband **a**, and went after her,	6965
Jgs	20:8	And all the people **a** as one man,	6965
Ru	1:6	she **a** with her daughters in law,	6965
1Sa	17:35	he **a** against me, I caught him	6965
1Sa	20:34	**a** from the table in fierce anger,	6965
1Sa	20:41	soon as the lad was gone, David **a**	6965
1Sa	24:4	Then David **a**, and cut off the skirt	6965
1Sa	25:41	And she **a**, and bowed herself.	6965
1Sa	25:42	Abigail hasted, and **a**,	6965
1Sa	26:5	David **a**, and came to the place	6965
1Sa	27:2	David **a**, and he passed over with	6965
1Sa	28:23	hearkened unto their voice. So he **a**	6965
1Sa	31:12	All the valiant men **a**,	6965
2Sa	2:15	Then there **a** and went over by	6965
2Sa	6:2	And David **a**, and went with all	6965
2Sa	11:2	that David **a** from off his bed,	6965
2Sa	12:17	And the elders of his house **a**,	6965
2Sa	13:29	Then all the king's sons **a**,	6965
2Sa	13:31	the king **a**, and tare his garments,	6965
1Ki	8:54	he **a** from before the altar of the	6965
1Ki	19:8	And he **a**, and did eat and drink,	6965
2Ch	22:10	she **a** and destroyed all the seed	6965
Ezr	9:5	I **a** up from my heaviness;	6965
Job	1:20	Then Job **a**, and rent his mantle,	6965
Ecc	1:5	hasteth to his place where he **a**	2224
Da	6:19	king **a** very early in the morning,	6966
Jnh	3:3	Jonah **a**, and went unto Nineveh,	6965
Jnh	3:6	and he **a** from his throne,	6965
Mt	2:14	he **a** he took the young child and	*1453*
Mt	8:26	he **a**, and rebuked the winds	*1453*
Mt	25:7	**all those virgins a, and trimmed**	*1453*
Mk	2:12	immediately he **a**, took up the bed	*1453*
Mk	4:39	he **a**, and rebuked the wind,	*1326*
Mk	5:42	the damsel **a**, and walked;	*450*
Mk	9:27	lifted him up; and he **a**	*450*
Lk	6:48	**a, the stream beat vehemently**	*1096*
Lk	8:24	he **a**, and rebuked the wind	*1453*
Lk	15:14	**a a mighty famine in that land;**	*1096*
Lk	15:20	**he a, and came to his father.**	*450*
Lk	24:12	**a** Peter, and ran unto the sepulchre;	*450*
Jn	6:18	sea **a** by reason of a great wind	*1326*
Jn	11:29	she **a** quickly, and came unto him	*1453*
Ac	6:1	**a** a murmuring of the Grecians	*1096*
Ac	6:9	there **a** certain of the synagogue,	*450*
Ac	9:8	Saul **a** from the earth; and when	*1453*
Ac	9:34	thy bed. And he **a** immediately	*450*
Ac	19:23	same time there **a** no small stir,	*1096*
Ac	23:7	there **a** a dissension between the	*1096*
Ac	23:9	**a** a great cry: and the scribes	*1096*
Ac	23:10	when there **a** a great dissension	*1096*
Ac	27:14	**a** against it a tempestuous wind	*906*
Rev	9:2	there **a** a smoke out of the pit,	*305*

ARRAY

Jgs	20:20	men of Israel put themselves in **a**	6186
1Sa	4:2	Philistines put themselves in **a**	6186
1Sa	17:8	come out to set your battle in **a**?	6186
1Sa	17:21	Philistines had put the battle in **a**	6186
2Sa	10:17	the Syrians set themselves in **a**	6186
1Ch	19:17	when David had put the battle in **a**	6186
2Ch	13:3	And Abijah set the battle in **a**	631
2Ch	13:3	Jeroboam also set the battle in **a**	6186
Est	6:9	**a** the man withal whom the king	3847
Job	6:4	set themselves in **a** against me	6186
Job	40:10	**a** thyself with glory and beauty	3847
Isa	22:7	set themselves in **a** at the gate	7896
Jer	6:23	they ride upon horses, set in **a**	6186
Jer	50:14	yourselves in **a** against Babylon	6186
Joel	2:5	a strong people set in battle **a**	6186
1Ti	2:9	or gold, or pearls, or costly **a**;	*2441*

ARRAYED

Ge	41:42	**a** him in vestures of fine linen,	3847
2Ch	5:12	**a** in white linen, having cymbals	3847
Est	6:11	**a** Mordecai, and brought him on	3847
Mt	6:29	**was not a like one of these.**	*4016*
Lk	12:27	**was not a like one of these.**	*4016*
Lk	23:11	**a** him in a gorgeous robe, and	*4016*
Ac	12:21	Herod, **a** in royal apparel,	*1746*
Rev	7:13	these which are **a** in white robes?	*4016*
Rev	17:4	And the woman was **a** in purple	*4016*
Rev	19:8	she should be **a** in fine linen,	*4016*

ARROGANCY

1Sa	2:3	not **a** come out of your mouth:	6277
Pr	8:13	pride, and **a**, and the evil way,	1347
Isa	13:11	the **a** of the proud to cease,	1347
Jer	48:29	his **a**, and his pride	1347

ARROW

1Sa	20:36	he shot an **a** beyond him	2678
1Sa	20:37	is not the **a** beyond thee?	2678
2Ki	9:24	the **a** went out at his heart,	2678
2Ki	13:17	The **a** of the Lord's deliverance,	2671
2Ki	19:32	nor shoot an **a** there	2671
Job	41:28	**a** cannot make him flee:	1121, 7198
Ps	11:2	they make ready their **a**	2671
Ps	64:7	God shall shoot at them with an **a**;	2671
Ps	91:5	for the **a** that flieth by day;	2671
Pr	25:18	a sword, and a sharp **a**.	2671
Isa	37:33	nor shoot an **a** there,	2671
Jer	9:8	Their tongue is as an **a**	2671
La	3:12	set me as a mark for the **a**.	2671
Zec	9:14	his **a** shall go forth	2671

ARROWS

Nu	24:8	pierce them through with his **a**.	2671
Dt	32:42	make mine **a** drunk with blood	2671
1Sa	20:20	I will shoot three **a** on the side	2671
1Sa	20:22	the **a** are beyond thee;	2671
1Sa	20:38	Jonathan's lad gathered up the **a**,	2678
2Sa	22:15	he sent out **a**, and scattered them;	2671
2Ki	13:15	And he took unto him bow and **a**.	2671
1Ch	12:12	in hurling stones and shooting **a**	2671
2Ch	26:15	to shoot **a** and great stones	2671
Job	6:4	For the **a** of the Almighty are	2671
Ps	7:13	he ordaineth his **a** against the	2671
Ps	18:14	Yea, he sent out his **a**,	2671
Ps	38:2	For thine **a** stick fast in me,	2671
Ps	45:5	Thine **a** are sharp in the heart	2671
Ps	58:7	bendeth his bow to shoot his **a**,	2671
Ps	64:3	bend their bows to shoot their **a**,	2671
Ps	76:3	brake he the **a** of the bow,	7565
Ps	77:17	thine **a** also went abroad	2687
Ps	120:4	Sharp **a** of the mighty,	2671
Ps	127:4	As **a** are in the hand of a mighty	2671
Ps	144:6	shoot out thine **a**, and destroy	2671
Pr	26:18	casteth firebrands, **a**, and death,	2671
Isa	5:28	Whose **a** are sharp,	2671
Isa	7:24	With **a** and with bows shall men	2671
Jer	50:9	their **a** shall be as of a mighty	2671
Jer	50:14	shoot at her, spare no **a**	2671
Jer	51:11	Make bright the **a**	2671
La	3:13	hath caused the **a** of his quiver	1121
Eze	5:16	send upon them the evil **a** of	2671
Eze	21:21	he made his **a** bright, he	2671
Eze	39:3	and will cause thine **a** to fall	2671
Eze	39:9	the bows and the **a**, and the	2671
Hab	3:11	at the light of thine **a** they went,	2671

ARTS

Ac	19:19	them also which used curious **a**	*4021*

ASCEND

Ps	24:3	Who shall **a** into the hill of the	5927
Ps	139:8	If I **a** up into heaven,	5927
Isa	14:13	I will **a** into heaven,	5927
Eze	38:9	Thou shalt **a** and come like a	5927
Jn	6:62	**ye shall see the Son of man a up**	*305*
Jn	20:17	**I a unto my Father, and your**	*305*
Ro	10:6	Who shall **a** into heaven?	*305*
Rev	17:8	shall **a** out of the bottomless pit,	*305*

ASCENDED

Ex	19:18	and the smoke thereof **a**	5927
Jos	8:20	the smoke of the city **a** up	5927
Jgs	13:20	that the angel of the Lord **a** in	5927
Jgs	20:40	flame of the city **a** up to heaven,	5927
Ps	68:18	Thou hast **a** on high,	5927
Pr	30:4	Who hath **a** up into heaven,	5927
Jn	3:13	**no man hath a up to heaven,**	*305*
Jn	20:17	**for I am not yet a to my Father:**	*305*
Ac	2:34	David is not **a** into the heavens:	*305*
Eph	4:8	When he **a** up on high,	*305*
Eph	4:9	(Now that he **a**, what is it	*305*
Eph	4:10	is the same also that **a** up	*305*
Rev	8:4	**a** up before God out of the angel's	*305*
Rev	11:12	they **a** up to heaven in a cloud;	*305*

ASCENDETH

Rev	11:7	that **a** out of the bottomless pit	*305*
Rev	14:11	their torment **a** up for ever	*305*

ASCENDING

Ge	28:12	angels of God **a** and descending	5927
1Sa	28:13	I saw gods **a** out of the earth.	5927
Jn	1:51	**the angels of God a and**	*305*
Rev	7:2	another angel **a** from the east,	*305*

ASCRIBE

Dt	32:3	**a** ye greatness unto our God.	3051
Job	36:3	**a** righteousness to my Maker	5414
Ps	68:34	**A** ye strength unto God:	5414

ASCRIBED

1Sa	18:8	to me they have **a** but thousands:	5414

ASHAMED

Ge	2:25	and were not **a**	954
Nu	12:14	should she not be **a** seven days?	3637
Jgs	3:25	they tarried till they were **a**	954
2Sa	10:5	because the men were greatly **a**	3637
2Sa	19:3	as people being **a** steal away	3637
2Ki	2:17	they urged him till he was **a**,	954
2Ki	8:11	until he was **a**: and the man of	954
2Ch	30:15	and the Levites were **a**,	3637
Ezr	8:22	I was **a** to require of the king	954
Ezr	9:6	I am **a** and blush to lift up my face	954
Job	6:20	they came thither, and were **a**	2659
Job	11:3	shall no man make thee **a**?	3637
Job	19:3	ye are not **a** that ye make	954
Ps	6:10	Let all mine enemies be **a**	954
Ps	25:2	I trust in thee: let me not be **a**,	954
Ps	25:3	let none that wait on thee be **a**,	954
Ps	25:20	let me not be **a**; for I put	954
Ps	34:5	their faces were not **a**	2659
Ps	35:26	be **a** and brought to confusion	954
Ps	37:19	shall not be **a** in the evil time:	954
Ps	40:14	Let them be **a** and confounded	954
Ps	70:2	Let them be **a** and confounded	954
Ps	74:21	let not the oppressed return **a**	3637
Ps	86:17	may see it, and be **a**	954
Ps	109:28	them be **a**; but let thy servant	954
Ps	119:78	Let the proud be **a**;	954
Pr	12:4	she that maketh **a** is as rottenness	954
Isa	1:29	For they shall be **a** of the oaks	954
Isa	24:23	and the sun **a**, when the LORD	954
Isa	26:11	be **a** for their envy at the people;	954
Isa	29:22	Jacob shall not now be **a**,	954
Isa	30:5	They were all **a** of a people	954
Isa	44:9	nor know; that they may be **a**.	954
Isa	45:17	shall not be **a** nor confounded	954
Isa	49:23	shall not be **a** that wait for me	954
Jer	2:26	the thief is **a** when he is found.	1322
Jer	3:3	thou refusedst to be **a**.	3637
Jer	6:15	Were they **a** when they had	954
Jer	8:9	The wise men are **a**,	954
Jer	8:12	were they **a** when they	954
Jer	14:4	the plowmen were **a**,	954
Jer	22:22	surely then shalt thou be **a**	954
Jer	31:19	I was **a**, yea, even confounded	954
Jer	50:12	she that bare you shall be **a**	2659
Eze	16:61	remember thy ways, and be **a**,	3637
Eze	36:32	be **a** and confounded for your own	954
Eze	43:11	they be **a** of all that	3637
Hos	10:6	Israel shall be **a** of his own counsel	954
Joel	2:26	My people shall never be **a**.	954
Joel	2:27	My people shall never be **a**.	954
Mic	3:7	the seers be **a**, and the diviners	954
Zep	3:11	In that day shalt thou not be **a**	954

Zec 13:4 the prophets shall be **a** every one .954
Mk 8:38 **therefore shall be a of me** *1870*
Mk 8:38 **shall the Son of man be a,** *1870*
Lk 9:26 **whosoever shall be a of me** *1870*
Lk 9:26 **of him shall the Son of man be a,** *1870*
Lk 13:17 all his adversaries were **a** *2617*
Lk 16:3 **I cannot dig; to beg I am a.** *153*
Ro 1:16 am not **a** of the gospel of Christ: *1870*
Ro 5:5 hope maketh not **a**; because *2617*
Ro 6:21 whereof ye are now **a**? *7870*
Ro 9:33 believeth on him shall not be **a**. *2617*
Ro 10:11 on him shall not be **a** *2617*
Php 1:20 in nothing I shall be **a**, .153
2Th 3:14 with him, that he may be **a**, 1788
2Ti 1:8 thou therefore **a** of the testimony *1870*
2Ti 1:12 nevertheless I am not **a** 1870
2Ti 1:16 and was not **a** of my chain: *1870*
2Ti 2:15 workman that needeth not to be **a**, *422*
Tit 2:8 the contrary part may be **a**, *1788*
Heb 2:11 is not **a** to call them brethren, *1870*
Heb 11:16 is not **a** to be called their God; *1870*
1Pe 3:16 as of evildoers, they may be **a** *2617*
1Pe 4:16 a Christian, let him not be **a**; *153*
1Jn 2:28 not be **a** before him. *153*

ASHES

Ge 18:27 which am but dust and **a** .665
Ex 9:8 you handfuls of **a** of the furnace, 6368
Le 4:12 where the **a** are poured out, and 1880
Nu 19:9 the **a** of the heifer, .665
2Sa 13:19 Tamar put **a** on her head, .665
1Ki 13:5 the **a** poured out from the altar, 1880
1Ki 20:38 disguised himself with **a** upon .665
Est 4:1 put on sackcloth with **a**, .665
Est 4:3 many lay in sackcloth and **a**. .665
Job 2:8 he sat down among the **a** .665
Job 13:12 remembrances are like unto **a**. .665
Job 30:19 I am become like dust and **a**, .665
Job 42:6 repent in dust and **a** .665
Isa 44:20 He feedeth on **a** .665
Isa 58:5 spread sackcloth and **a** under him? .665
Isa 61:3 to give unto them beauty for **a**, .665
Jer 31:40 and of the **a**, and all the fields 1880
La 3:16 he hath covered me with **a** .665
Eze 28:18 I will bring thee to **a**, .665
Da 9:3 with fasting, and sackcloth, and **a** .665
Jnh 3:6 him with sackcloth, and sat in **a**. .665
Mal 4:3 for they shall be **a** .665
Mt 11:21 **long ago in sackcloth and a.** *4700*
Lk 10:13 **sitting in sackcloth and a.** *4700*
Heb 9:13 the **a** of an heifer sprinkling the *4700*
2Pe 2:6 Sodom and Gomorrha into **a** *5077*

ASIDE

Ex 3:3 I will now turn **a**, and see this
Nu 5:12 If any man's wife go **a**, .7847
Nu 5:20 if thou hast gone **a** .7847
Nu 5:29 when a wife goeth **a** .7847
Nu 22:23 and the ass turned **a** .5186
Dt 11:16 ye turn **a**, and serve other gods,
Jgs 14:8 he turned **a** to see the carcase
Ru 4:1 Ho, such a one! turn **a**, sit down
1Sa 8:3 but turned **a** after lucre, .5186
2Sa 2:21 Turn thee **a** to thy right hand, or .5186
2Sa 3:27 And when … Joab took him **a** in .5186
2Sa 6:10 but David carried it **a** .5186
2Sa 18:30 Turn **a**, and stand here .5437
2Ki 22:2 turned not **a** to the right hand .5493
Ps 14:3 They are all gone **a**, .5493
Ps 40:4 nor such as turn **a** to lies .7847
Ps 78:57 were turned **a** like a deceitful .2015
Ps 101:3 the work of them that turn **a** .7750
Ps 125:5 As for such as turn **a** unto their .5186
SS 1:7 should I be as one that turneth **a** .5844
SS 6:1 whither is thy beloved turned **a**? .6437
Isa 10:2 To turn **a** the needy from .5186
Isa 29:21 and turn **a** the just for a thing of .5186
Isa 30:11 turn **a** out of the path, .5186
Isa 44:20 heart hath turned him **a**, .5186
Jer 14:8 a wayfaring man that turneth **a** .5186
Jer 15:5 who shall go **a** to ask how thou .5493
Am 2:7 and turn **a** the way of the meek: .5186
Am 5:12 they turn **a** the poor .5186
Mal 3:5 and that turn **a** the stranger .5186
Mk 7:8 **laying a the commandment of** *.863*
Mk 7:33 **a** from the multitude, *.2596, 2398*
Jn 13:4 and laid **a** his garments; *.5087*
1Ti 1:6 turned **a** into vain jangling; *.1824*
1Ti 5:15 some are already turned **a** after *.1824*
Heb 12:1 let us lay **a** every weight, and *.659*
1Pe 2:1 Wherefore laying **a** all malice, *.659*

ASK

Ge 32:29 thou dost **a** after my name? .7592
Dt 4:32 **a** now of the days that are past, .7592
Dt 13:14 enquire, and make search, and **a** .7592
Jos 4:21 When your children shall **a** .7592
Jos 15:18 she moved him to **a** of her .7592
Jgs 1:14 she moved him to **a** of her .7592
Jgs 18:5 **A** counsel, we pray thee, of God, .7592
1Sa 12:19 our sins this evil, to **a** us a king .7592
1Sa 28:16 Wherefore then dost thou **a** of me, .7592
1Ki 2:22 **a** for him the kingdom also; .7592
1Ki 3:5 God said, **A** what I shall give thee .7592
2Ki 2:9 **A** what I shall do for thee .7592
2Ch 1:7 **A** what I shall give thee .7592
2Ch 20:4 to **a** help of the Lord: .1245
Ps 2:8 **A** of me, and I shall give thee .7592
Isa 7:11 **A** thee a sign of the Lord .7592
Isa 58:2 **a** of me the ordinances of justice; .7592
Jer 6:16 and **a** for the old paths, .7592
Jer 18:13 **A** ye now among the heathen, .7592
Jer 50:5 They shall **a** the way to Zion .7592
La 4:4 the young children **a** bread, .7592
Da 6:7 whosoever shall **a** a petition of .1156
Hos 4:12 My people **a** counsel at their .7592
Zec 10:1 **A** ye of the Lord rain .7592
Mt 6:8 **have need of, before ye a him.** *.154*
Mt 7:7 **A, and it shall be given you;** *.154*
Mt 7:9 **if his son a bread, will he give** *.154*
Mt 18:19 **anything that they shall a,** *.154*
Mt 20:22 **said, Ye know not what ye a.** *.154*
Mt 21:22 **whatsoever ye shall a in prayer** *.154*
Mt 21:24 **I also will a you one thing,** *.2065*
Mt 22:46 **a** him any more questions *.1905*
Mk 6:24 unto her mother, What shall I **a**? *.154*
Mk 10:38 **Ye know not what ye a:** *.154*
Mk 11:29 **I will also a of you one question,** *.1905*
Mk 12:34 And no man after that durst **a** *.1905*
Lk 6:9 **I will a you one thing; Is it** *.1905*
Lk 6:30 **away thy goods a them not** *.523*
Lk 11:9 **A, and it shall be given you;** *.154*

Lk 11:11 If a son shall **a** bread of any 154
Lk 11:13 Holy Spirit to them that **a** him? 154
Lk 12:48 of him they will **a** the more. 154
Lk 19:31 if any man **a** you, ...2065
Lk 20:3 I will also **a** you one thing; 2065
Lk 20:40 they durst not **a** him any 1905
Lk 22:68 And if I also **a** you, ...2065
Jn 9:23 his parents, He is of age: **a** him 2055
Jn 11:22 whatsoever thou wilt **a** of God, ...154
Jn 14:13 whatsoever ye shall **a** in my 154
Jn 14:14 If ye shall **a** any thing in my 154
Jn 15:7 abide in you, ye shall **a** what 154
Jn 15:16 whatsoever ye shall **a** of the 154
Jn 16:23 ye shall **a** me nothing 2065
Jn 16:24 **a**, and ye shall receive, that your 154
Jn 16:26 At that day ye shall **a** in my name: 154
Jn 18:21 Why askest thou me? **a** them 1905
Jn 21:12 none of the disciples durst **a** 1833
1Co 14:35 let them **a** their husbands at 1905
Eph 3:20 above all that we **a** or think, ...154
Jas 1:5 you lack wisdom, let him **a** of 154
Jas 1:6 But let him **a** in faith, nothing 154
Jas 4:2 ye have not, because ye **a** not 154
Jas 4:3 Ye **a**, and receive not, because 154
1Jn 3:22 whatsoever we **a**, we receive 154
1Jn 5:14 if we **a** any thing according to his 154
1Jn 5:16 not unto death, he shall **a**, and 154

ASKED

Ex 18:7 they **a** each other of their welfare; 7592
Jos 9:14 **a** not counsel at the mouth of the 7592
Jos 19:50 gave him the city which he **a**. 7592
Jgs 20:18 and **a** counsel of God, ...7592
Jgs 20:23 and **a** counsel of the Lord, ...7592
1Sa 1:27 my petition which I **a** of him: 7592
1Sa 8:10 the people that **a** of him a king. 7592
1Sa 14:37 And Saul **a** counsel of God, ...7592
1Ki 3:11 Because thou hast **a** this thing 7592
1Ki 3:11 hast **a** for thyself understanding 7592
1Ki 3:13 thee that which thou hast not **a**, ...7592
2Ch 1:11 thou hast not **a** riches, ...7592
2Ch 1:11 neither yet hast **a** long life; 7592
2Ch 1:11 hast **a** wisdom and knowledge 7592
2Ch 9:12 all her desire, whatsoever she **a**, ...7592
Ne 1:2 and I **a** them concerning the Jews 7592
Ps 21:4 He **a** life of thee, ...7592
Isa 65:1 I am sought of them that **a** not 7592
Jer 37:17 the king **a** him secretly in his 7592
Jer 38:27 the princes unto Jeremiah, and **a** 7592
Da 2:10 **a** such things at any magician, ...7593
Mk 5:9 And he **a** him, What is thy name? 1905
Mk 7:5 Pharisees and scribes **a** him, ...1905
Mk 8:5 he **a** them, How many loaves 1905
Mk 10:2 Pharisees came to him, and **a** him, ...1905
Mk 14:61 Again the high priest **a** him, and 1905
Mk 15:2 And Pilate **a** him, Art thou the 1905
Mk 15:4 And Pilate **a** him again, saying, ...1905
Lk 1:63 he **a** for a writing table, and wrote, ...154
Lk 9:18 and he **a** them, saying, Whom say 1905
Lk 15:26 and **a** what these things meant. 4441
Lk 22:64 **a** him, saying, Prophesy, who is it 1905
Lk 23:3 And Pilate **a** him, saying, Art 1905
Jn 4:10 thou wouldest have **a** of him, ...154
Jn 16:24 have ye **a** nothing in my name: 154
Jn 18:19 The high priest then **a** Jesus of 2065
Ro 10:20 unto them that **a** not after me. 1905

ASKETH

Ex 13:14 when thy son **a** thee 7592
Dt 6:20 thy son **a** thee in time to come, ...7592
Mic 7:3 and the judge **a** for a reward; 7592
Mt 5:42 Give to him that **a** thee, and 154
Mt 7:8 every one that **a** receiveth; 154
Lk 6:30 Give to every man that **a** of thee; 154
Lk 11:10 every one that **a** receiveth; 154
Jn 16:5 none of you **a** me, ...2065
1Pe 3:15 every man that **a** you a reason 154

ASKING

1Sa 12:17 in **a** you a king. 7592
Ps 78:18 tempted God in their heart by **a** 7592
Lk 2:46 them, and **a** them questions. 1905
1Co 10:27 eat, **a** no question for conscience 350

ASLEEP

Jgs 4:21 he was fast **a** and weary 7290
1Sa 26:12 for they were all **a**; 3463
Jnh 1:5 and he lay, and was fast **a**. 7290
Mt 8:24 but he was **a** 2518
Mt 26:40 and findeth them **a**, ...2518
Mt 26:43 came and found them **a** again; 2518
Mk 4:38 **a** on a pillow: and they awake 2518
Mk 14:40 he found them **a** again, ...2518
Lk 8:23 as they sailed he fell **a**, ...879
Ac 7:60 when he had said this, he fell **a**, ...2837
1Co 15:6 but some are fallen **a**. 2837
1Co 15:18 also which are fallen **a** in Christ 2837
1Th 4:13 concerning them which are **a**, ...2837
1Th 4:15 not prevent them which are **a** 2837
2Pe 3:4 since the fathers fell **a**, all things 2837

ASPS

Dt 32:33 and the cruel venom of **a**, ...6620
Ro 3:13 poison of **a** is under their lips: 785

ASS

Ge 22:5 abide ye here with the **a**; 2543
Ge 49:14 Issachar is a strong **a** couching 2543
Ex 13:13 every firstling, of an **a** thou shalt 2543
Ex 20:17 nor his ox, nor his **a**, nor anything 2543
Ex 21:33 an ox or an **a** fall therein; 2543
Ex 22:10 deliver unto his neighbour an **a**, ...2543
Ex 23:5 If thou see the **a** of him that 2543
Nu 22:23 the **a** saw the angel of the Lord 860
Nu 22:25 the **a** saw the angel of the Lord, ...860
Nu 22:27 the **a** saw the angel of the Lord, ...860
Nu 22:28 Lord opened the mouth of the **a** 860
Dt 22:4 see thy brother's **a** or his ox fall 2543
Dt 22:10 plow with an ox and an **a** together 2543
Jgs 1:14 she lighted from off her **a**; 2543
Jgs 15:16 With the jawbone of an **a**, ...2543
1Sa 12:3 or whose **a** have I taken? 2543
1Sa 16:20 Jesse took an **a** laden with bread, ...2543
1Sa 25:23 hasted, and lighted off the **a**, ...2543
1Ki 13:28 and the **a** and the lion standing 2543
Job 6:5 Doth the wild **a** bray 6501
Pr 26:3 a bridle for the **a**. 2543
Zec 9:9 lowly, and riding upon an **a**, ...2543
Zec 9:9 and upon a colt and foal of an **a**. 860
Mt 21:2 ye shall find an **a** tied, ...3688
Mt 21:5 meek, and sitting upon an **a**, ...3688
Mt 21:5 and a colt and foal of an **a**, ...5268
Lk 13:15 loose his ox or his **a** from the 3688
Lk 14:5 Which of you shall have an **a** or 3688

Jn 12:14 when he had found a young **a**, ...*3678*
2Pe 2:16 **a** speaking with man's voice *5268*

ASSEMBLE
Isa 11:12 shall **a** the outcasts of Israel, ...622
Eze 11:17 and **a** you out of the countries 622
Da 11:10 **a** a multitude of great forces: 622
Joel 2:16 Gather the people, ... **a** the elders, ...6908

ASSEMBLED
Nu 1:18 they **a** all the congregation 6950
1Sa 2:22 **a** at the door of the tabernacle 6633
1Ki 8:1 Solomon **a** the elders of Israel, ...6950
1Ch 28:1 David **a** all the princes of Israel, ...6950
2Ch 5:6 were **a** unto him before the ark, ...3259
Ezr 9:4 Then were **a** unto me every one 622
Da 6:11 these men **a**, and found Daniel 7284
Da 6:15 Then these men **a** unto the king, ...7284
Mt 26:3 **a** together the chief priests, ...*4863*
Mt 28:12 they were **a** with the elders, ...*4863*
Jn 20:19 where the disciples were **a** *4863*
Ac 15:25 being **a** with one accord, ...*1096*

ASSEMBLIES
Ps 86:14 and the **a** of violent men 5712
Isa 1:13 railing of **a**, I cannot away with; 4744
Am 5:21 not smell in your solemn **a** 6116

ASSEMBLING
Heb 10:25 the **a** of ourselves together, ...*1997*

ASSEMBLY
Ge 49:6 into their secret; unto their **a**, ...6951
Le 23:36 it is a solemn **a**; 6116
Nu 14:5 on their faces before all the **a** 6951
Nu 20:6 went from the presence of the **a** 6951
Nu 29:35 ye shall have a solemn **a** 6116
Dt 16:8 a solemn **a** to the Lord thy God 6116
1Sa 17:47 this **a** shall know that the Lord 6951
2Ki 10:20 Proclaim a solemn **a** for Baal 6116
2Ch 7:9 they made a solemn **a**: 6116
Ne 8:18 the eighth day was solemn **a**, ...6116
Jer 15:17 I sat not in the **a** of the mockers, ...5475
Jer 50:9 Babylon an **a** of great nations, ...6951
La 2:6 destroyed his places of the **a** 4150
Joel 1:14 call a solemn **a**, gather the elders 6116
Joel 2:15 sanctify a fast, call a solemn **a** 6116
Zep 3:18 are sorrowful for the solemn **a**, ...4150
Ac 19:39 determined in a lawful **a**. *1577*
Heb 12:23 **a** and church of the firstborn, ...*3831*
Jas 2:2 there come unto your **a** a man *4864*

ASSES
Ge 43:24 he gave their **a** provender 2543
1Sa 9:20 And as for thine **a** that were lost 860
1Sa 10:16 plainly that the **a** were found. 860
2Sa 16:2 The **a** be for the king's household 2543

ASSIGNED
Jos 20:8 they **a** Bezer in the wilderness 5414
2Sa 11:16 that he **a** Uriah unto a place 5414

ASSURANCE
Isa 32:17 quietness and **a** for ever. 983
Ac 17:31 he hath given **a** unto all men, ...*4102*
Col 2:2 of the full **a** of understanding, ...*4136*
1Th 1:5 and in much **a**; as ye know *4136*
He 6:11 the full **a** of hope unto the end: *4136*
He 10:22 in full **a** of faith, having our *4136*

ASSURED
Jer 14:13 **a** peace in this place. 571
2Ti 3:14 and hast been **a** of, ...*4104*

ASSUREDLY
1Ki 1:13 **A** Solomon thy son shall reign 3588
Jer 32:41 **a** with my whole heart 571
Ac 2:36 house of Israel know **a**, ...*806*

ASTONISHED
1Ki 9:8 passeth by it shall be **a**, ...8074
Job 21:5 Mark me, and be **a**, and lay your 8074
Jer 2:12 Be **a**, O ye heavens, at this, ...8074
Jer 18:16 that passeth thereby shall be **a**, ...8074
Jer 19:8 that passeth thereby shall be **a** 8074
Mt 7:28 the people were **a** at his doctrine: *1605*
Mt 22:33 they were **a** at his doctrine *1605*
Mk 1:22 they were **a** at his doctrine: *1605*
Mk 5:42 **a** with a great astonishment *1839*
Mk 6:2 many hearing him were **a**, ...*1605*
Mk 7:37 were beyond measure **a**, ...*1605*
Mk 10:24 disciples were **a** at his words. *2284*
Mk 10:26 they were **a** out of measure, ...*1605*
Mk 11:18 the people was **a** at his doctrine *1605*
Lk 2:47 were **a** at his understanding *1839*
Lk 4:32 they were **a** at his doctrine: *1605*
Lk 5:9 For he was **a**, and all that *4023, 2285*
Lk 24:22 made us **a**, which were early *1839*
Ac 9:6 And he trembling and **a** said, ...*2284*
Ac 10:45 were **a**, as many as came with *1839*
Ac 12:16 saw him, they were **a**. *1839*
Ac 13:12 **a** at the doctrine of the Lord. *1605*

ASTONISHMENT
Dt 28:28 and **a** of heart: 8541
Dt 28:37 thou shalt become an **a**, ...8047
2Ch 29:8 to trouble, to **a**, and to hissing, ...8047
Ps 60:3 made us to drink the wine of **a** 8653
Jer 25:9 make them an **a**, and an hissing, ...8047
Jer 25:11 desolation, and an **a**; 8047
Jer 25:18 a desolation, an **a**, an hissing, ...8047
Jer 29:18 a curse, and an **a**, ...8047
Jer 42:18 execration, and an **a**, ...8047
Jer 44:12 an **a**, and a curse, ...8047
Jer 44:22 desolation, and an **a**, ...8047
Jer 51:37 an **a**, and an hissing, ...8047
Eze 4:16 water by measure, and with **a** 8078
Eze 5:15 instruction and an **a**: 8047
Eze 12:19 and drink their water with **a**, ...8078
Eze 23:33 with the cup of **a** and desolation, ...8047
Zec 12:4 smite every horse with **a**, ...8541
Mk 5:42 astonished with a great **a** *1611*

ASTRAY
Ex 23:4 enemy's ox or his ass going **a**, ...8582
Ps 58:3 they go **a** as soon as they be born, ...8582
Ps 119:67 Before I was afflicted I went **a**: 7683
Ps 119:176 I have gone **a** like a lost sheep: 8582
Pr 5:23 of his folly he shall go **a** 7686
Pr 7:25 go not **a** in her paths 8582
Pr 28:10 causeth the righteous to go **a** 7686
Isa 53:6 All we like sheep have gone **a**; 8582
Jer 50:6 have caused them to go **a**, ...8582
Eze 14:11 Israel may go no more **a** from me, ...8582
Eze 44:10 when Israel went **a**, ...8582
Eze 48:11 which went not **a** 8582
Mt 18:12 and one of them be gone **a**, ...*4105*

Mt	18:12	**and seeketh that which is gone a?**	*4105*
Mt	18:13	**ninety and nine which went not a.**	*4105*
1Pe	2:25	ye were as sheep going **a**;	*4105*
2Pe	2:15	and are gone **a**, following the way	*4105*

ASTROLOGER

Da	2:10	things at any magician, or **a**,	826

ASTROLOGERS

Isa	47:13	now the **a**, the stargazers,	1895, 8064
Da	1:20	**a** that were in all his realm	825
Da	2:2	the magicians, and the **a**,	825
Da	2:27	cannot the wise men, the **a**	826
Da	5:7	cried aloud to bring in the **a**,	826
Da	5:11	master of the magicians, **a**,	826

ASUNDER

Nu	16:31	the ground clave **a** that was	
2Ki	2:11	and parted them both **a**;	996
Mt	19:6	**together, let not man put a.**	*5563*
Mt	24:51	**shall cut him a, and appoint him**	*1371*
Mk	10:9	**let not man put a.**	*5562*
Ac	1:18	he burst **a** in the midst,	*2977*
Ac	15:39	they departed **a** one from the	*673*
Heb	11:37	they were sawn **a**, were tempted,	*4249*

ATE

Ps	106:28	and **a** the sacrifices of the dead.	398
Da	10:3	I **a** no pleasant bread, neither	398
Rev	10:10	of the angel's hand, and **a** it up;	*2719*

ATHIRST

Mt	25:44	**saw we thee an hungred, or a,**	*1372*
Rev	21:6	I will give to him that is **a**	*1372*
Rev	22:17	let him that is **a** come	*1372*

ATONEMENT

Ex	29:37	shall make an **a** for the altar,	3722
Ex	30:10	once in the year shall he make **a**	3722
Ex	30:15	to make **a** for your souls.	3722
Le	4:20	priest shall make an **a** for them,	3722
Le	4:31	priest shall make an **a** for him	3722
Le	4:35	shall make an **a** for his sin	3722
Le	5:18	an **a** for him concerning his	3722
Le	12:8	priest shall make an **a** for her,	3722
Le	14:20	and the priest shall make an **a**	3722
Le	16:11	and shall make an **a** for himself,	3722
Le	16:16	shall make an **a** for the holy place,	3722
Le	16:17	to make an **a** in the holy place,	3722
Le	16:33	make an **a** for the holy sanctuary,	3722
Le	16:33	shall make an **a** for the tabernacle	3722
Le	16:33	and he shall make an **a** for the	3722
Le	23:27	there shall be a day of **a**:	3725
Nu	6:11	and make an **a** for him,	3722
Nu	16:46	and make an **a** for them:	3722
Nu	25:13	an **a** for the children of Israel.	3722
Nu	29:11	the sin offering of **a**,	3725
2Ch	29:24	to make an **a** for all Israel:	3722
Ne	10:33	to make an **a** for Israel,	3722
Ro	5:11	we have now received the **a**.	*2643*

ATTAIN

Ps	139:6	it is high, I cannot **a** unto it.	
Pr	1:5	a man of understanding shall **a**	7069
Php	3:11	I might **a** unto the resurrection	*2658*

ATTAINED

Ge	47:9	not **a** unto the days of the years	5381
1Ch	11:21	howbeit he **a** not to the first three.	935
1Ch	11:25	but **a** not to the first three	935
Ro	9:30	have **a** to righteousness	*2638*
Ro	9:31	not **a** to the law of righteousness	*5348*
Php	3:12	Not as though I had already **a**,	*2983*
Php	3:16	whereto we have already **a**,	*5348*
1Ti	4:6	whereunto: thou hast **a**.	*3877*

ATTEND

Ps	86:6	**a** to the voice of my supplications	7181
Ps	142:6	**A** unto my cry: for I am brought	7181
Pr	4:1	and **a** to know understanding.	7181
Pr	4:20	My son, **a** to my words:	7181
Pr	5:1	My son, **a** unto my wisdom,	7181
Pr	7:24	and **a** to the words of my mouth.	7181
1Co	7:35	that ye may **a** upon the Lord	*2145*

ATTENDANCE

1Ti	4:13	Till I come, give **a** to reading,	*4337*
Heb	7:13	no man gave **a** at the altar	*4337*

ATTENTIVE

Ne	1:6	let now thine ear be **a**,	7183
Ne	8:3	were **a** unto the book of the law.	
Lk	9:48	were very **a** to hear him.	*1582*

ATTIRE

Pr	7:10	the **a** of an harlot,	7897

AUDIENCE

Ex	24:7	read in the **a** of the people:	241
1Ch	28:8	and in the **a** of our God,	241
Ne	13:1	in the **a** of the people;	241
Ac	13:16	ye that fear God, give **a**.	*191*
Ac	22:22	they gave him **a** unto this word	*191*

AUSTERE

Lk	19:21	**because thou art an a man:**	*840*
Lk	19:22	**that I was an a man,**	*840*

AUTHOR

1Co	14:33	God is not the **a** of confusion, but	
Heb	5:9	became the **a** of eternal salvation	*159*
Heb	12:2	the **a** and finisher of our faith;	*747*

AUTHORITIES

1Pe	3:22	**a** and powers being made subject	*1849*

AUTHORITY

Est	9:29	Mordecai the Jew, ... with all **a**,	8633
Pr	29:2	When the righteous are in **a**, the	7235
Mt	7:29	taught them as one having **a**,	*1849*
Mt	8:9	For I am a man under **a**,	*1849*
Mt	21:23	what **a** doest thou these things?	*1849*
Mt	21:24	by what **a** I do these things.	*1849*
Mt	21:27	by what **a** I do these things.	*1849*
Mk	1:22	as one that had **a**,	*1849*
Mk	1:27	for with **a** commandeth he even	*1849*
Mk	11:28	and who gave thee this **a**	*1849*
Mk	11:29	by what **a** I do these things,	*1849*
Mk	11:33	by what **a** I do these things,	*1849*
Mk	13:34	gave **a** to his servants,	*1849*
Lk	4:36	with **a** and power he commandeth	*1849*
Lk	7:8	am a man set under **a**,	1849
Lk	9:1	gave them power and **a** over all	*1849*
Lk	19:17	**have thou a over ten cities.**	*1849*
Lk	20:2	who is he that gave thee this **a**?	*1849*
Lk	20:8	**by what a I do these things.**	*1849*
Jn	5:27	**hath given him a to execute**	*1849*
Ac	9:14	he hath **a** from the chief priests	*1849*

Ac 26:12 went to Damascus with **a** and *1849*
1Co 15:24 all rule and all **a** and power............*1849*
1Ti 2:2 and for all that are in **a**; *5247*
1Ti 2:12 nor to usurp **a** over the man, but *831*
Tit 2:15 exhort, and rebuke with all **a**. *2003*
Rev 13:2 power, and his seat, and great **a**. *1849*

AVAILETH
Est 5:13 all this **a** me nothing, ...7737
Gal 5:6 neither circumcision **a** any thing, ...*2480*
Gal 6:15 neither circumcision **a** any thing, ...*2480*
Jas 5:16 prayer of a righteous man **a** much......*2480*

AVENGE
Le 19:18 Thou shalt not **a**, nor bear any 5358
Le 26:25 a sword ... that shall **a** the quarrel 5358
Dt 32:43 will **a** the blood of his servants, ...5358
1Sa 24:12 and the Lord **a** me of thee: 5358
Est 8:13 to **a** themselves on their enemies 5358
Isa 1:24 and **a** me of mine enemies: 5358
Jer 46:10 he may **a** him of his adversaries:.......5358
Lk 18:3 **saying, A me of mine adversary.**........*1556*
Lk 18:7 **not God a his own elect,** ...*4160, 3588, 1557*
Lk 18:8 **he will a them speedily.** *4160, 3588, 1557*
Ro 12:19 Dearly beloved, **a** not yourselves, ...*1556*
Rev 6:10 dost thou not judge and **a** our *1556*

AVENGED
Ge 4:24 If Cain shall be **a** sevenfold, ...5358
Jos 10:13 the people had **a** themselves 5358
Jgs 16:28 that I may be at once **a** of the 5358
1Sa 14:24 that I may be **a** on mine enemies 5358
2Sa 4:8 the Lord hath **a** my lord 5414, 5360
Jer 5:9 shall not my soul be **a** on such 5358
Jer 5:29 shall not my soul be **a** on such 5358
Jer 9:9 shall not my soul be **a** on such 5358
Rev 18:20 God hath **a** you on her *2919, 3588, 2917*
Rev 19:2 hath **a** the blood of his servants *1556*

AVENGER
Nu 35:12 for refuge from the **a**; that the 1350
Dt 19:6 Lest the **a** of the blood pursue the 1350
Jos 20:3 your refuge from the **a** of blood 1350
Ps 44:16 by reason of the enemy and **a**. 5358
1Th 4:6 the Lord is the **a** of all such,...........*1558*

AVENGETH
2Sa 22:48 It is God that **a** me,.............5414, 5360
Ps 18:47 It is God that **a** me,.............5414, 5360

AVENGING
Jgs 5:2 Praise ye the Lord for the **a** 6544, 6546
1Sa 25:26 from **a** thyself with thine own 3467

AVOID
Pr 4:15 **A** it, pass not by it, turn from it, ...6544
Ro 16:17 which ye have learned; and **a** *1578*
1Co 7:2 Nevertheless, to **a** fornication, ...*1223*
2Ti 2:23 and unlearned question **a**, ...*3868*
Tit 3:9 But **a** foolish questions, and *4026*

AVOIDING
1Ti 6:20 **a** profane and vain babblings, ...*1624*

AVOUCHED
Dt 26:17 thou hast **a** the Lord this day to 559
Dt 26:18 the Lord hath **a** thee this day 559

AWAKE See also AWOKE.
Job 8:6 surely now he would **a** for thee, ...5782
Job 14:12 they shall not **a**, nor be raised 6974
Ps 17:15 I shall be satisfied, when I **a**, with 6974
Ps 44:23 **A**, why sleepest thou, O Lord? 5782
Ps 59:5 **a** to visit all the heathen: 6974
Ps 139:18 when I **a**, I am still with thee. 6974
Pr 23:35 when shall I **a**? I will seek it yet 6974
SS 2:7 nor **a** my love, till he please 5782
SS 3:5 not up, nor **a** my love, till he 5782
SS 8:4 ye stir not up, nor **a** my love,..........5782
Isa 26:19 **A** and sing, ye that dwell in dust: 6974
Isa 51:9 **A, a**, put on strength, O arm of 5782
Isa 51:17 **A, a**; stand up, O Jerusalem, ...5782
Joel 1:5 **A**, ye drunkards, and weep; 6974
Hab 2:19 him that saith to the wood, **A**;.........6974
Zec 13:7 **A**, O sword, against my shepherd, ...5782
Mk 4:38 they **a** him, and say unto him *1326*
Jn 11:11 **that I may a him out of sleep.** *1852*
Ro 13:11 it is high time to **a** out of sleep:........*1453*
1Co 15:34 **A** to righteousness, and sin not; *1594*
Eph 5:14 **A** thou that sleepest, and arise *1453*

AWAKED
1Sa 26:12 saw it, nor knew it, neither **a** 6974
1Ki 18:27 he sleepeth, and must be **a**. 3364
Jer 31:26, Upon this I **a**, and beheld; 6974

AWAKEST
Ps 73:20 when thou **a**, thou shalt despise 5782
Pr 6:22 when thou **a**, it shall talk with 6974

AWAKETH
Ps 73:20 As a dream when one **a**; 6974
Isa 29:8 but he **a**, and his soul is empty:........6974

AWARE See also WARE.
Mt 24:50 **in an hour that he is not a of,** *1097*
Lk 11:44 **over them are not a of them.**..........*1492*
Lk 12:46 **and at an hour when he is not a,** *1097*

AWE
Ps 4:4 Stand in **a**, and sin not: 7264
Ps 33:8 of the world stand in **a** of him. 1481
Ps 119:161 heart standeth in **a** of thy word 6342

AWOKE
Ge 9:24 And Noah **a** from his wine, ...3364
Jgs 16:20 And he **a** out of his sleep,.............3364
1Ki 3:15 And Solomon **a**; and, behold, it 3364
Mt 8:25 **a** him, saying, Lord, save us: *1453*
Lk 8:24 they came to him, and **a** him, ...*1326*

AX
Dt 19:5 with the **a** to cut down the tree, ...1631
Jgs 9:48 Abimelech took an **a** in his hand, ...7134
1Ki 6:7 neither hammer nor **a** nor any 1631
2Ki 6:5 the **a** head fell into the water: 1270
Isa 10:15 Shall the **a** boast itself 1631
Mt 3:10 now also the **a** is laid unto the *513*

AXE
Lk 3:9 now also the **a** is laid unto the *573*

AXES
Eze 26:9 with his **a** he shall break down 2719

B

BABBLER

Ecc 10:11 and a **b** is no better 1167, 3956
Ac 17:18 said, What will this **b** say? *4691*

BABBLING

Pr 23:29 who hath **b**? who hath wounds 7879

BABBLINGS

1Ti 6:20 avoiding profane and vain **b**, *2757*
2Ti 2:16 shun profane and vain **b**: for *2757*

BABE

Lk 1:41 the **b** leaped in her womb; *1025*
Lk 2:12 the **b** wrapped in swaddling clothes *1025*
Lk 2:16 Mary, and Joseph, and the **b** lying *1025*
Heb 5:13 of righteousness: for he is a **b** *3516*

BABES

Ps 8:2 of the mouth of **b** and sucklings 5768
Ps 17:14 rest of their substance to their **b** 5768
Isa 3:4 and **b** shall rule over them 8586
Mt 11:25 **hast revealed them unto b** *3516*
Mt 21:16 **Out of the mouth of b** *3516*
Lk 10:21 **hast revealed them unto b:** *3516*
Ro 2:20 teacher of **b**, which hast the form *3516*
1Co 3:1 as unto **b** in Christ *3516*
1Pe 2:2 As newborn **b**, desire the sincere *1025*

BACK

Ge 19:26 his wife looked **b** from behind
Ex 33:23 thou shalt see my **b** parts: 268
Nu 24:11 hath kept thee **b** from honour 4513
Jos 23:12 if ye do in any wise go **b** 7725
Jgs 11:35 the Lord, and I cannot go **b** 7725
1Sa 15:11 he is turned **b** from following me, 7725
2Sa 1:22 the bow of Jonathan turned not **b**, 268
2Sa 12:23 can I bring him **b** again? I 7725
2Sa 15:25 Carry **b** the ark of God into the 7725
1Ki 13:19 So he went **b** with him, and did eat 7725
1Ki 13:23 prophet whom he had brought **b** 7725
1Ki 18:37 hast turned their heart **b** again 322
2Ki 2:24 And he turned **b**, and looked on 310
2Ki 20:9 ten degrees, or go **b** ten degrees? 7725
1Ch 21:20 And Oman turned **b**, and saw the 7725
Job 23:12 I gone **b** from the commandment 4185
Ps 14:7 the Lord bringeth **b** the captivity 7725
Ps 19:13 Keep **b** thy servant also from 2820
Ps 44:18 Our heart is not turned **b**, neither 268
Ps 53:6 God bringeth **b** the captivity of 7725
Pr 10:13 a rod is for the **b** of him that is 1458
Pr 19:29 and stripes for the **b** of fools 1458
Pr 26:3 a rod for the fool's **b** 1458
Isa 14:27 out, and who shall turn it **b**? 7725
Isa 38:17 cast all my sins behind thy **b** 1458
Isa 42:17 They shall be turned **b**, they shall 268
Isa 50:5 neither turned away **b** 268
Isa 50:6 I gave my **b** to the smiters, and 1458
Jer 2:27 have turned their **b** unto me 6203
Jer 32:33 they have turned unto me the **b**, 6203
Jer 42:4 I will keep nothing **b** from you 4513
Eze 23:35 me behind thy **b**, therefore bear 1458
Eze 44:1 Then he brought me **b** the way of 7725
Zep 3:20 when I turn **b** your captivity 7725
Mt 24:18 **return b to take his clothes** *3694*
Mt 28:2 came and rolled **b** the stone *617*
Mk 13:16 **that is in the field not turn b** *617*
Lk 2:45 turned **b** again to Jerusalem, *5290*
Lk 9:62 **looking b, is fit for the kingdom** *3694*
Lk 17:15 turned **b**, and with a loud voice *5290*
Lk 17:31 **let him likewise not return b** *3694*
Jn 6:66 many of his disciples went **b**, *3694*
Jn 20:14 turned herself **b**, and saw Jesus *3694*
Ac 5:2 And kept **b** part of the price, *3557*
Ac 7:39 hearts turned **b** again into Egypt *4762*
Ac 20:20 how I kept **b** nothing that was *5288*
Ro 11:10 and bow down their **b** alway *3577*
Heb 10:38 but if any man draw **b**, my soul *5288*
Jas 5:4 is of you kept **b** by fraud, *650*

BACKBITERS

Ro 1:30 **B**, haters of God, despiteful, *2637*

BACKBITETH

Ps 15:3 He that **b** not with his tongue, 7270

BACKBITING

Pr 25:23 angry countenance a **b** tongue 5643

BACKBITINGS

2Co 12:20 strifes, **b**, whisperings, *2636*

BACKS

Ex 23:27 all thine enemies turn their **b** 6203
Jos 7:8 when Israel turneth their **b** 6203
Ne 9:26 cast thy law behind their **b**, 1458
Eze 8:16 with their **b** toward the temple 268
Eze 10:12 and their **b**, and their hands 1354

BACKSLIDER

Pr 14:14 The **b** in heart shall be filled 5472

BACKSLIDING

Jer 3:6 that which **b** Israel hath done? 4878
Jer 3:8 **b** Israel committed adultery 4878
Jer 3:12 Return, thou **b** Israel, saith the 4878
Jer 8:5 slidden back by a perpetual **b**? 4878
Jer 31:22 O thou **b** daughter? 7728
Jer 49:4 thy flowing valley, O **b** daughter? 7728
Hos 4:16 Israel slideth back as a **b** heifer 5637
Hos 11:7 my people are bent to **b** from me: 4878
Hos 14:4 I will heal their **b** 4878

BACKSLIDINGS

Jer 3:22 and I will heal your **b** 4878
Jer 5:6 their **b** are increased 4878
Jer 14:7 our **b** are many; 4878

BAD See also WORSE.

Ge 24:50 cannot speak unto thee **b** or good 7451
Ge 31:24 not to Jacob either good or **b** 7451
Le 27:10 nor change it, a good for a **b** 7451
Le 27:14 estimate it, whether it be good or **b**, 7451
2Sa 13:22 brother Amnon neither good nor **b** 7451
1Ki 3:9 discern between good and **b** 7451
Mt 13:48 **into vessels, but cast the b away** *4550*
Mt 22:10 **as they found, both b and good:** *4190*
2Co 5:10 done, whether it be good or **b** *2556*

BADE See also BID; FORBAD.

Ge 43:17 did as Joseph **b**; and the man 559
Ex 16:24 up till the morning, as Moses **b** 6680
Nu 14:10 congregation **b** stone them with 559

B

Ru 3:6 all that her mother in law **b** her 6680
1Sa 24:10 and some **b** me kill thee: but 559
Lk 14:10 **when he that b thee cometh, he** *2564*
Lk 14:16 **made a great supper, and b many:** *2564*
Ac 11:12 the Spirit **b** me go with them, ...*2036*
Ac 18:21 **b** them farewell, saying, I must *657*
Ac 22:24 **b** that he should be examined *2036*

BAG
Dt 25:13 not have in thy **b** divers weights, ...3599
1Sa 17:49 David put his hand in his **b**, ...3627
Mic 6:11 with the **b** of deceitful weights? 3599
Hag 1:6 to put it into a **b** with holes 6872
Jn 12:6 he was a thief, and had the **b** *1101*
Jn 13:29 thought, because Judas had the **b** *1101*

BAKE
Ge 19:3 did **b** unleavened bread, and they 644
Ex 16:23 **b** that which ye will **b** 644
2Sa 13:8 in his sight, and did **b** the cakes 1310

BAKED
Ex 12:39 And they **b** unleavened cakes 644
Isa 44:19 I have **b** bread upon the coals 644

BAKETH
Isa 44:15 he kindleth it, and **b** bread; 644

BAKER
Ge 40:1 and his **b** had offended their lord 644
Ge 40:16 When the chief **b** saw that the 644
Ge 40:22 But he hanged the chief **b**: 644
Ge 41:10 both me and the chief **b**: 644
Hos 7:4 as an oven heated by the **b**, ...644
Hos 7:6 their **b** sleepeth all the night; 644

BALANCE
Job 31:6 Let me be weighed in an even **b** 3976
Pr 11:1 false **b** is abomination to the 3976
Pr 16:11 just weight and **b** are the Lord's: 3976
Isa 40:12 and the hills in a **b**? 3976
Isa 40:15 count as the small dust of the **b** 3976

BALANCES
Le 19:36 Just **b**, just weights, a just 3976
Jer 32:10 weighed him the money in the **b** 3976
Eze 45:10 Ye shall have just **b** 3976
Da 5:27 Thou art weighed in the **b** 3976
Hos 12:7 the **b** of deceit are in his hand: 3976
Am 8:5 falsifying the **b** by deceit? 3976
Mic 6:11 pure with the wicked **b**, ...3976
Rev 6:5 had a pair of **b** in his hand

BALANCINGS
Job 37:16 thou know the **b** of the clouds, ...4657

BALD
Le 13:40 he is **b**; yet is he clean 7142
Le 13:41 he is forehead **b**: yet is he clean 1371
2Ki 2:23 **b** head; go up, thou **b** head 7142

BALDNESS
Le 21:5 They shall not make **b** upon their 7144
Dt 14:1 nor make any **b** between your 7144
Isa 22:12 to mourning, and to **b**, ...7144
Eze 7:18 **b** upon all their heads 7144
Am 8:10 **b** upon every head; and I will 7144
Mic 1:16 enlarge thy **b** as the eagle; 7144

BALL
Isa 22:18 and toss thee like a **b** into a 1754

BALM
Jer 8:22 Is there no **b** in Gilead; 6875
Jer 46:11 Go up into Gilead, and take **b** 6875
Jer 51:8 take **b** for her pain, if so be she 6875

BAND
1Sa 10:26 him a **b** of men, whose hearts 2428
2Ki 13:21 they spied a **b** of men; and they 1416
Ezr 8:22 the king a **b** of soldiers and 2428
Da 4:23 in the earth, even with a **b** of iron 613
Mt 27:27 gathered unto him the whole **b** 4686
Mk 15:16 they call together the whole **b** 4686
Jn 18:3 having received a **b** of men and *4686*
Jn 18:12 Then the **b** and the captain and *4686*
Ac 27:1 Julius, a centurion of Augustus' **b** *4686*

BANDED
Ac 23:12 of the Jews **b** together, ...*4160, 4963*

BANDS
Ge 32:10 and now I am become two **b** 4264
Jgs 15:14 his **b** loosed from off his hands 612
1Ch 12:23 of the **b**, that were ready armed 7218
2Ch 26:11 went out to war by **b**, according 1416
Job 1:17 Chaldeans made out three **b**, and 7218
Job 38:31 Pleiades, or loose the **b** of Orion? 4189
Ps 2:3 break their **b** asunder, and cast 4147
Ps 107:14 and break their **b** in sunder 4147
Isa 52:2 loose thyself from the **b** of thy 4147
Eze 3:25 they shall put **b** upon thee, and 5688
Zec 11:7 Beauty, the other I called **B**; 2256
Zec 11:14 asunder mine other staff, even **B** 2256
Ac 16:26 and every one's **b** were loosed *1199*
Ac 22:30 he loosed him from his **b**, and *1199*

BANISHED
2Sa 14:14 that his **b** be not expelled 5080

BANISHMENT
Ezr 7:26 it be unto death, or to **b**, ...8331
La 2:14 false burdens and causes of **b** 4065

BANK
Ge 41:17 I stood upon the **b** of the river: 8193
2Ki 2:13 and stood by the **b** of Jordan; 8193
2Ki 19:32 shield, nor cast a **b** against it 5550
Isa 37:33 shields, nor cast a **b** against it 5550
Lk 19:23 **money into the b, that at my** *5132*

BANKS
Jos 4:18 flowed over all his **b**, as they did 1415
1Ch 12:15 it had overflown all his **b**; 1428

BANNER
Ps 60:4 given a **b** to them that fear 5251
SS 2:4 and his **b** over me was love 1714

BANNERS
Ps 20:5 set up our **b**: the Lord fulfil all 1713
SS 6:10 and terrible as an army with **b**? 1713

BANQUET
Est 5:5 the king and Haman came to the **b** 4960
Est 5:12 come in with the king unto the **b** 4960
Est 7:8 into the place of the **b** of wine; 4960
Da 5:10 his lord, came into the **b** house: 4961
Am 6:7 the **b** of them that stretched 4797

BAPTISM

Mt	3:7	and Sadducees come to his **b**,	*908*
Mt	20:22	**the b that I am baptized with?**	*908*
Mt	21:25	**The b of John, whence was it?**	*908*
Mk	1:4	preach the **b** of repentance for	*908*
Mk	10:38	**the b that I am baptized with?**	*908*
Mk	11:30	**The b of John, was it from heaven,**	*908*
Lk	3:3	preaching the **b** of repentance	*908*
Lk	12:50	**I have a b to be baptized with,**	*908*
Lk	20:4	**The b of John, was it from heaven,**	*908*
Ac	1:22	Beginning from the **b** of John,	*908*
Ac	13:24	the **b** of repentance to all the people	*908*
Ac	19:4	with the **b** of repentance, saying	*908*
Ro	6:4	buried with him by **b** into death:	*908*
Eph	4:5	One Lord, one faith, one **b**,	*908*
Col	2:12	Buried with him in **b**, wherein	*908*
1Pe	3:21	even **b** doth also now save us	*908*

BAPTISMS

Heb	6:2	Of the doctrine of **b**, and of laying	*909*

BAPTIST (bap´-tist)

Mt	3:1	In those days came John the **B**,	*910*
Mt	11:11	**risen a greater than John the B**	*910*
Mt	11:12	**from the days of John the B until**	*910*
Mt	16:14	Some say that thou art John the **B**	*910*
Mk	6:24	she said, The head of John the **B**	*910*
Lk	7:28	**greater prophet than John the B**	*910*
Lk	7:33	**John the B came neither eating**	*910*

BAPTIST'S (bap´-tists)

Mt	14:8	Give me here John **B** head in	*910*

BAPTIZE

Mt	3:11	I indeed **b** you with water	*907*
Mk	1:8	he shall **b** you with the Holy Ghost,	*907*
Lk	3:16	he shall **b** you with the Holy Ghost	*907*
Jn	1:33	he that sent me to **b** with water,	*907*
1Co	1:17	Christ sent me not to **b**, but to	*907*

BAPTIZED

Mt	3:14	I have need to be **b** of thee, and	*907*
Mt	20:22	**the baptism that I am b with?**	*907*
Mt	20:23	**and be b with the baptism**	*907*
Mk	1:8	I indeed have **b** you with water:	*907*
Mk	10:38	**and be b with the baptism**	*907*
Mk	10:39	**and with the baptism that I am b**	*907*
Mk	16:16	**believeth and is b shall be saved;**	*907*
Lk	3:12	Then came also publicans to be **b**,	*907*
Lk	3:21	that Jesus also being **b**,	*907*
Lk	7:29	being **b** with the baptism of John	*907*
Lk	12:50	**I have a baptism to be b with:**	*907*
Jn	4:1	Jesus made and **b** more disciples	*907*
Jn	4:2	(Though Jesus himself **b** not,	*907*
Ac	1:5	**John truly b with water;**	*907*
Ac	1:5	**ye shall be b with the Holy Ghost.**	*907*
Ac	2:38	Repent, and be **b** every one of you	*907*
Ac	8:12	were **b**, both men and women	*907*
Ac	8:36	what doth hinder me to be **b**?	*907*
Ac	9:18	forthwith, and arose, and was **b**	*907*
Ac	10:47	water, that these should not be **b**	*907*
Ac	11:16	**John indeed b with water;**	*907*
Ac	11:16	**ye shall be b with the Holy Ghost**	*907*
Ac	16:33	was **b**, he and all his, straightway	*907*
Ac	19:3	Unto what then were ye **b**?	*907*
Ac	19:5	heard this, they were **b** in the name	*907*
Ac	22:16	and be **b**, and wash away thy sins	*907*
Ro	6:3	were **b** into his death?	*907*
1Co	1:14	I thank God that I **b** none of you,	*907*
1Co	10:2	were all **b** unto Moses in the cloud	*907*
1Co	12:13	For by one Spirit are we all **b** into	*907*
1Co	15:29	why are they then **b** for the dead?	*907*
Gal	3:27	as have been **b** into Christ have put	*907*

BAPTIZING

Mt	28:19	**b them in the name of the Father**	*907*
Jn	1:28	Jordan, where John was **b**	*907*

BAR

Jgs	16:3	away with them, **b** and all, and	1280
Ne	7:3	them shut the doors, and **b** them:	270

BARBARIAN

1Co	14:11	unto him that speaketh a **b**	*915*
Col	3:11	**B**, Scythian, bond nor free:	*915*

BARBARIANS

Ac	28:4	when the **b** saw the venomous	*915*
Ro	1:14	to the Greeks, and to the **B**;	*915*

BARBAROUS

Ac	28:2	the **b** people shewed us no little	*915*

BARBED

Job	41:7	thou fill his skin with **b** irons?	7905

BARBER'S

Eze	5:1	sharp knife, take thee a **b** razor,	1532

BARE See also FORBARE.

Ge	4:1	she conceived, and **b** Cain, and	3205
Ge	4:2	she again **b** his brother Abel	3205
Ge	7:17	increased, and **b** up the ark,	5375
Ge	16:16	when Hagar **b** Ishmael to Abram	3205
Ge	21:2	Sarah conceived, and **b** Abraham a	3205
Ex	6:20	and she **b** him Aaron and Moses:	3205
Ex	19:4	and how I **b** you on eagles' wings	5375
Dt	31:9	the sons of Levi, which **b** the ark	5375
Jos	3:15	and the feet of the priests that **b**	5375
1Ch	2:4	Tamar, his daughter in law, **b** him	3205
Isa	52:10	Lord hath made **b** his holy arm	2834
Isa	53:12	and he **b** the sin of many, and	5375
Mt	8:17	our infirmities, and **b** our	*941*
Mk	14:56	For many **b** false witness against	*5575*
Lk	4:22	all **b** him witness, and wondered	*3140*
Lk	8:8	**and sprang up, and b fruit an**	*4160*
Lk	11:27	Blessed is the womb that **b** thee	*941*
Lk	23:29	**and the wombs that never b**	*1080*
Jn	1:15	John **b** witness of him, and cried,	*3140*
Jn	1:32	And John **b** record, saying, I saw	*3140*
Jn	5:33	**and he b witness unto the truth**	*3140*
Jn	12:6	had the bag, and **b** what was put	*941*
1Pe	2:24	who his own self **b** our sins in his	*399*
Rev	1:2	Who **b** record of the word of God,	*3140*
Rev	22:2	which **b** twelve manner of fruits,	*4160*

BAREFOOT

Isa	20:3	Isaiah hath walked naked and **b**	3182
Isa	20:4	young and old, naked and **b**,	3182

BARK

Isa	56:10	all dumb dogs, they cannot **b**;	5024

BARLEY

Ex	9:31	the flax and the **b** was smitten:	8184
Dt	8:8	A land of wheat, and **b**, and vines	8184
Jgs	7:13	and, lo, a cake of **b** bread tumbled	8184

Ru 1:22 in the beginning of **b** harvest....8184
Ru 2:23 to glean unto the end of **b** harvest....8184
2Ki 7:1 two measures of **b** for a shekel,....8184
2Ki 7:18 saying, Two measures of **b** for a....8184
Jn 6:9 which hath five **b** loaves and two....*2916*
Jn 6:13 the fragments of the five **b** loaves,....*2916*
Rev 6:6 three measures of **b** for a penny;....*2915*

BARN
Hag 2:19 Is the seed yet in the **b**....4035
Mt 13:30 **but gather the wheat into my b**....*596*
Lk 12:24 **neither have storehouse nor b;**....*596*

BARNS
Pr 3:10 shall thy **b** be filled with plenty,....618
Joel 1:17 the **b** are broken down;....4460
Mt 6:26 **do they reap, nor gather into b;**....*596*
Lk 12:18 **I will pull down my b, and build**....*596*

BARREL
1Ki 17:14 The **b** of meal shall not waste,....3537

BARRELS
1Ki 18:33 Fill four **b** with water, and pour....3537

BARREN
Ge 11:30 Sarai was **b**; she had no child....6135
Ge 29:31 but Rachel was **b**....6135
Ps 113:9 maketh the **b** woman to keep....6135
Pr 30:16 The grave; and the **b** womb;....6115
Lk 1:7 because that Elisabeth was **b**,....*4723*
Lk 23:29 **Blessed are the b, and the wombs**....4723
Gal 4:27 Rejoice, thou **b** that bearest not;....*4723*
2Pe 1:8 neither be **b** nor unfruitful in the....*692*

BARS
Ex 26:26 shall make **b** of shittim wood;....1280
1Sa 23:7 a town that hath gates and **b**....1280
2Ch 14:7 walls, and towers, gates, and **b**....1280
Job 17:16 shall go down to the **b** of the pit,....905
Job 40:18 his bones are like **b** of iron....4300
Ps 107:16 and cut the **b** of iron in sunder....1280
Ps 147:16 strengthened the **b** of thy gates;....1280
Pr 18:19 are like the **b** of a castle....1280
Isa 45:2 and cut in sunder the **b** of iron:....1280
La 2:9 hath destroyed and broken her **b**....1280

BASE See also ABASE; DEBASE.
2Sa 6:22 will be **b** in mine own sight:....8217
Job 30:8 yea, children of **b** men:....1097, 8034
Isa 3:5 the **b** against the honourable....7034
Mal 2:9 and **b** before all the people,....8217
1Co 1:28 And **b** things of the world....36
2Co 10:1 who in presence am **b** among....*5011*

BASER
Ac 17:5 lewd fellows of the **b** sort,....*60*

BASES
2Ki 25:13 and the **b**, and the brasen sea....4350
Ezr 3:3 they set the altar upon his **b**;....4350
Jer 52:17 and the **b**, and the brasen sea....4350

BASEST
Eze 29:15 shall be the **b** of the kingdoms;....8217
Da 4:17 setteth up over it the **b** of men....8215

BASKET
Ge 40:17 birds did eat them out of the **b**....5536
Ex 29:32 and the bread that is in the **b**,....5536
Dt 28:5 Blessed shall be thy **b** and thy....2935
Dt 28:17 Cursed shall be thy **b** and thy....2935
Jer 24:2 One **b** had very good figs,....1731
Ac 9:25 let him down by the wall in a **b**....*4711*
2Co 11:33 in a **b** was I let down by the wall,....*4553*

BASKETS
Ge 40:18 The three **b** are three days:....5536
Mt 14:20 that remained twelve **b** full....*2894*
Mt 15:37 meat that was left seven **b** full....*4711*
Mt 16:9 **and how many b ye took up?**....*2894*
Mk 6:43 twelve **b** full of the fragments,....*2894*
Mk 8:8 meat that was left seven **b**....*4711*
Mk 8:19 **how many b full of fragments**....*2894*
Lk 9:17 remained to them twelve **b**....*2894*
Jn 6:13 and filled twelve **b** with the....*2894*

BASON
Ex 12:22 with the blood that is in the **b**;....5592
Jn 13:5 that he poureth water into a **b**,....*3537*

BASONS
Ex 24:6 half of the blood, and put it in **b**;....101
1Ki 7:40 the shovels, and the **b**, So Hiram....4219
2Ch 4:8 he made an hundred **b** of gold....4219
Ezr 1:10 Thirty **b** of gold,....3713

BAT
Le 11:19 kind, and the lapwing, and the **b**....5847
Dt 14:18 the lapwing, and the **b**....5847

BATH
Isa 5:10 of vineyard shall yield one **b**,....1324
Eze 45:10 a just ephah, and a just **b**....1324
Eze 45:14 offer the tenth part of a **b**....1324

BATHE
Le 15:7 **b** himself in water, and be unclean....7364
Le 15:18 shall both **b** themselves in water....7364
Nu 19:19 clothes, and **b** himself in water,....7364

BATHED
Isa 34:5 my sword shall be **b** in heaven:....7301

BATHS
1Ki 7:26 it contained two thousand **b**....1324
1Ki 7:38 one laver contained forty **b**:....1324
2Ch 4:5 received and held three thousand **b**....1324
Eze 45:14 for ten **b** are an homer....1324

BATTERED
2Sa 20:15 **b** the wall, to throw it down....7843

BATTERING
Eze 4:2 set **b** rams against it
Eze 21:22 appoint **b** rams against the gates

BATTLE
Nu 31:14 which came from the **b**....6635, 4421
Nu 31:27 upon them who went out to **b**,....6635
Nu 31:28 men of war which went out to **b**,....6635
Dt 20:1 When thou goest out to **b** against....4421
Dt 20:3 ye approach this day unto **b**,....4421
Dt 20:7 lest he die in the **b**, and another....4421
Jos 11:19 of Gibeon: all other they took in **b**....4421
Jgs 20:18 of us shall go up first to the **b**....4421
1Sa 13:22 So it came to pass in the day of **b**....4421
1Sa 17:8 come out to set your **b** in array?....4421
1Sa 17:28 that thou mightest see the **b**,....4421
1Sa 17:47 for the **b** is the Lord's and he....4421

1Sa	26:10	he shall descend into **b**, and perish	4421
1Sa	31:3	the **b** went sore against Saul	4421
2Sa	1:25	fallen in the midst of the **b**!	4421
2Sa	11:1	the time when kings go forth to **b**,	
2Sa	11:15	in the forefront of the hottest **b**,	4421
2Sa	11:25	make thy **b** more strong against	4421
2Sa	19:3	steal away when they flee in **b**	4421
2Sa	19:10	anointed over us, is dead in **b**	4421
1Ki	22:30	enter into the **b**; but put thou on	4421
1Ki	22:35	the **b** increased that day: and the	4421
1Ch	10:3	the **b** went sore against Saul	4421
1Ch	12:33	Zebulun, such as went forth to **b**,	6635
1Ch	12:36	of Asher, such as went forth to **b**,	6635
1Ch	20:1	the time that kings go out to **b**,	
2Ch	20:15	for the **b** is not yours, but God's	4421
2Ch	20:17	shall not need to fight in this **b**	
Job	15:24	him, as a king ready to the **b**	3593
Job	38:23	against the day of **b** and war?	7128
Job	39:25	he smelleth the **b** afar off,	4421
Job	41:8	remember the **b**, do no more	4421
Ps	24:8	mighty, the Lord mighty in **b**	4421
Ps	55:18	my soul in peace from the **b**	7128
Ps	140:7	covered my head in the day of **b**	5402
Pr	21:31	is prepared against the day of **b**	4421
Ecc	9:11	nor the **b** to the strong, neither	4421
Isa	9:5	For every **b** of the warrior is	5430
Isa	28:6	strength to them that turn the **b**	4421
Isa	42:25	the strength of **b**: and it hath set	4421
Jer	8:6	as the horse rusheth into the **b**	4421
Jer	18:21	men be slain by the sword in **b**	4421
Jer	50:22	A sound of **b** is in the land,	4421
Jer	51:20	Thou art my **b** axe and weapons	4661
Eze	7:14	none goeth to the **b**: for my	4421
Eze	13:5	to stand in the **b** in the day	4421
Da	11:20	neither in anger, nor in **b**	4421
Hos	1:7	by bow, nor by sword, nor by **b**	4421
Hos	2:18	the bow and the sword and the **b**	4421
Am	1:14	with shouting in the day of **b**	4421
Ob	1	let us rise up against her in **b**	4421
Zec	10:5	in the mire of the streets in the **b**	4421
Zec	14:2	nations against Jerusalem to **b**;	4421
1Co	14:8	who shall prepare himself to the **b**?	*4171*
Rev	9:9	of many horses running to **b**	*4171*
Rev	16:14	to the **b** of that great day of God	*4171*
Rev	20:8	to gather them together to **b**:	*4171*

BATTLEMENTS

Jer	5:10	take away her **b**; for they are	5189

BATTLES

1Sa	8:20	go out before us, and fight our **b**	4421
1Sa	18:17	fight the Lord's **b**. For Saul	4421
1Sa	25:28	my lord fighteth the **b** of the Lord	4421
1Ch	26:27	spoils won in **b** did they dedicate	4421
2Ch	32:8	and to fight our **b**. And the people	4421

BAY

Zec	6:3	fourth chariot grisled and **b** horses	554
Zec	6:7	And the **b** went forth, and sought	554

BDELLIUM (del´-le-um)

Ge	2:12	there is **b** and the onyx stone	916
Nu	11:7	colour thereof as the colour of **b**	916

BEACON

Isa	30:17	left as a **b** upon the top of a	8650

BEAM

Jgs	16:14	went away with the pin of the **b**,	708
1Sa	17:7	of his spear was like a weaver's **b**;	4500
2Ki	6:5	as one was felling a **b**, the axe head	6982
Hab	2:11	**b** out of the timber shall answer	3714
Mt	7:4	**behold, a b is in thine own eye?**	*1385*
Lk	6:42	**cast out first the b out of thine**	*1385*

BEAMS

1Ki	6:9	covered the house with **b** and	1356
1Ki	7:12	a row of cedar **b**, both for the	3773
2Ch	3:7	the **b**, the posts, and the walls	6982
Ne	2:8	give me timber to make **b** for the	7136

BEAR See also BARE; FORBEAR.

Ge	4:13	is greater than I can **b**	5375
Ge	13:6	the land was not able to **b** them	5375
Ge	17:17	Sarah, that is ninety years old, **b**?	3205
Ge	18:13	Shall I of a surety **b** a child,	3205
Ge	43:9	then let me **b** the blame forever:	2398
Ex	18:22	shall **b** the burden with thee	5375
Ex	20:16	Thou shalt not **b** false witness	6030
Le	5:1	it, then he shall **b** his iniquity	5375
Le	5:17	guilty, and shall **b** his iniquity.	5375
Le	22:9	lest they **b** sin for it, and die	5375
Le	24:15	curseth his God shall **b** his sin	5375
Nu	11:14	I am not able to **b** all this people	5375
Nu	18:1	**b** the iniquity of your priesthood	5375
Nu	18:22	congregation, lest they **b** sin, and	5375
1Sa	17:36	slew both the lion and the **b**	1677
2Sa	18:20	thou shalt **b** no tidings, because	1319
Est	1:22	every man should **b** rule in his	8323
Pr	17:12	Let a **b** robbed of her whelps	1677
Pr	18:14	but a wounded spirit who can **b**?	5375
Pr	28:15	roaring lion, and a ranging **b**;	1677
Pr	30:21	and for four which it cannot **b**	5375
Isa	7:14	virgin shall conceive, and **b** a son,	3205
Jer	17:21	**b** no burden on the sabbath day,	5375
Jer	31:19	I did **b** the reproach of my youth	5375
La	3:10	He was unto me as a **b** lying in	1677
La	3:27	good for a man that he **b** the yoke	5375
Eze	16:52	**b** thine own shame for thy sins	5375
Eze	18:20	The son shall not **b** the iniquity	5375
Eze	18:20	neither shall the father **b**	5375
Da	7:5	beast, a second, like to a **b**,	1678
Hos	13:18	I will meet them as a **b** that is	1677
Am	7:10	land is not able to **b** all his words	3557
Mic	7:9	I will **b** the indignation of the	5375
Zec	6:13	he shall **b** the glory, and sit and	5375
Mt	3:11	whose shoes I am not worthy to **b**	*941*
Mt	4:6	their hands they shall **b** thee up	*142*
Mt	19:18	**Thou shalt not b false witness**	*5576*
Mt	27:32	him they compelled to **b** his cross	*142*
Mk	10:19	**Do not b false witness, Defraud**	*5575*
Mk	15:21	Alexander and Rufus, to **b** his	*142*
Lk	1:13	wife Elisabeth shall **b** thee a son	*1080*
Lk	4:11	their hands they shall **b** thee up	*142*
Lk	11:48	**Truly ye b witness that ye allow**	*3140*
Lk	13:9	**And if it b fruit, well: and if not,**	*4160*
Lk	14:27	**whosoever doth not b his cross,**	*941*
Lk	18:7	**though he b long with them?**	*3114*
Lk	18:20	**Do not b false witness, Honour**	*5576*
Lk	23:26	that he might **b** it after Jesus	*5342*
Jn	1:7	to **b** witness of the Light, that all	*3140*
Jn	2:8	**b unto the governor of the feast**	*5342*
Jn	3:28	yourselves **b** me witness, that I	*3140*

Jn 5:31 If I **b** witness of myself, my *3140*
Jn 5:36 works that I do, **b** witness of me *3140*
Jn 8:14 Though I **b** record of myself, *3140*
Jn 8:18 I am one that **b** witness of myself, *3140*
Jn 10:25 Father's name, they **b** witness of *3140*
Jn 15:4 the branch cannot **b** fruit of itself, *5342*
Jn 15:8 that ye **b** much fruit; so shall ye *5342*
Jn 15:27 ye also shall **b** witness, because, *3140*
Jn 16:12 but ye cannot **b** them now *941*
Jn 18:23 **b** witness of the evil: but if well, *3140*
Jn 18:37 I should **b** witness unto the truth. *3140*
Ac 9:15 to **b** my name before the Gentiles, *941*
Ac 23:11 must thou **b** witness also at Rome *3140*
Ro 10:2 For I **b** them record that they *3140*
Ro 13:9 Thou shalt not **b** false witness *5576*
Ro 15:1 to **b** the infirmities of the weak *941*
1Co 10:13 that ye may be able to **b** it *5297*
1Co 15:49 also **b** the image of the heavenly *5409*
2Co 11:1 **b** with me a little in my folly: *430*
2Co 11:4 ye might well **b** with him *430*
Gal 5:10 shall **b** his judgment, whosoever *941*
Gal 6:2 **B** ye one another's burdens *941*
Gal 6:5 every man shall **b** his own burden *941*
Gal 6:17 for I **b** on my body the marks of *941*
Heb 9:28 offered to **b** the sins of many *399*
Jas 3:12 my brethren, **b** olive berries? *4160*
1Jn 1:2 and **b** witness and shew unto you *3140*
Rev 2:2 canst not **b** them which are evil: *941*
Rev 13:2 his feet were as the feet of a **b**, *715*

BEARD
1Sa 17:35 him by his **b**, and smote him 2206
2Sa 19:24 his feet, nor trimmed his **b**, 8222
2Sa 20:9 And Joab took Amasa by the **b** 2206
Ezr 9:3 of my **b**, and sat down astonied 2206
Jer 48:37 shall be bald and every **b** clipped: 2206
Eze 5:1 upon thine head and upon thy **b** 2206

BEARDS
2Sa 10:4 shaved off the one half of the **b**, 2206
Jer 41:5 **b** shaven, and their clothes rent, 2206

BEARERS
2Ch 2:18 of them to be **b** of burdens, 5449
2Ch 34:13 they were over the **b** of burdens 5449
Ne 4:10 of the **b** of burdens is decayed, 5449

BEAREST
Jn 8:13 Thou **b** record of thyself; thy *3140*
Gal 4:27 Rejoice, thou barren that **b** not; *5088*

BEARETH See also FORBEARETH.
Joel 2:22 tree that **b** her fruit, the fig tree 5375
Mt 13:23 also **b** fruit, and bringeth forth, *2592*
Jn 5:32 another that **b** witness of me: *3140*
Jn 8:18 that sent me **b** witness of me *3140*
Jn 15:2 branch in me that **b** not fruit *5342*
Ro 8:16 The Spirit itself **b** witness with *4828*
Ro 13:4 for he **b** not the sword in vain: *5409*
1Co 13:7 **B** all things, believeth all things *4722*
1Jn 5:6 it is the Spirit that **b** witness, *3140*

BEARING See also FORBEARING.
Ge 1:29 given you every herb **b** seed, 2232
Jos 3:14 priests **b** the ark of the covenant 5375
2Sa 15:24 **b** the ark of the covenant of God: 5375
Mk 14:13 a man **b** a pitcher of water: *941*
Lk 22:10 meet you, **b** a pitcher of water; *941*
Jn 19:17 **b** his cross went forth *941*
Ro 2:15 conscience also **b** witness, and *4828*
Ro 9:1 conscience also **b** me witness *4828*
2Co 4:10 Always **b** about in the body the *4064*
Heb 2:4 God also **b** them witness both *4901*
Heb 13:13 without the camp, **b** his reproach. *5342*

BEARS
2Ki 2:24 forth two she **b** out of the wood, 1677
Isa 59:11 We roar all like **b**, and mourn 1677

BEAST
Ge 1:24 and **b** of the earth after his kind: 2416
Ge 1:25 God made the **b** of the earth 2416
Ge 2:19 God formed every **b** of the field, 2416
Ge 2:20 every **b** of the field; but for Adam 2416
Ge 3:1 subtil than any **b** of the field 2416
Ge 6:7 man, and **b**, and the creeping 929
Ge 7:2 Of every clean **b** thou shalt take 929
Ge 37:20 Some evil **b** hath devoured him: 2416
Ex 12:12 land of Egypt, both man and **b**; 929
Ex 13:15 of man; and the firstborn of **b**; 929
Ex 22:19 lieth with a **b** shall surely 929
Le 20:15 And if a man lie with a **b** 929
Le 20:16 if a woman approach unto any **b**, 929
Le 24:18 **b** for **b** 5315
Ne 2:12 save the **b** that I rode upon 929
Ps 50:10 every **b** of the forest is mine 2416
Pr 12:10 regardeth the life of his **b**: 929
Ecc 3:21 the spirit of the **b** that goeth 929
Jer 27:5 the **b** that are upon the ground, 929
Eze 14:13 will cut off man and **b** from it: 929
Da 7:5 And behold another **b**, a second, 2423
Da 7:7 behold a fourth **b**, dreadful and 2423
Da 7:19 know the truth of the fourth **b**, 2423
Jnh 3:8 But let man and **b** be covered 929
Lk 10:34 and set him on his own **b**, and *2934*
Heb 12:20 And if so much as a **b** touch the *2342*
Rev 4:7 the first **b** was like a lion, *2226*
Rev 13:1 saw a **b** rise up out of the sea *2342*
Rev 13:3 the world wondered after the **b** *2342*
Rev 13:4 worshipped the **b**, saying *2342*
Rev 13:11 I beheld another **b** coming up *2342*
Rev 13:12 therein to worship the first **b**, *2342*
Rev 14:9 If any man worship the **b** and his *2342*
Rev 16:2 the mark of the **b**, and upon them *2342*
Rev 17:12 as kings one hour with the **b** *2342*
Rev 19:20 And the **b** was taken, *2342*
Rev 20:4 had not worshipped the **b**, *2342*
Rev 20:10 where the **b** and the false prophet *2342*

BEAST'S
Da 4:16 and let a **b** heart be given unto 2423

BEASTS
Ge 7:2 of **b** that are not clean by two, 929
Ex 11:5 and all the firstborn of **b** 929
Le 11:46 This is the law of the **b**, and of 929
Dt 14:4 These are the **b** which ye shall 929
Dt 14:6 cheweth the cud among the **b**, 929
1Sa 17:44 of the air, and to the **b** of the field 929
1Sa 17:46 and to the wild **b** of the earth; 2416
Ps 8:7 oxen, yea, and the **b** of the field; 929
Ps 49:12 he is like the **b** that perish. 929
Ps 49:20 is like the **b** that perish. 929
Ps 50:11 the wild **b** of the field are mine 2123
Pr 30:30 lion which is strongest among **b**, 929

Jer 28:14 given him the **b** of the field also ... 2416
Jer 34:20 heaven, and to the **b** of the earth ... 929
Da 2:38 the **b** of the field and the fowls ... 2423
Da 4:15 let his portion be with the **b**. ... 2423
Da 4:32 shall be with the **b** of the field: ... 2423
Da 5:21 his heart was made like the **b**, ... 2423
Da 7:3 four great **b** came up from the sea, ... 2423
Da 7:17 These great **b**, which are four, ... 2423
Hos 2:18 a covenant for them with the **b** of ... 2416
Joel 1:18 How do the **b** groan! the herds of ... 929
Joel 1:20 The **b** of the field cry also ... 929
Am 5:22 the peace offerings of your fat **b** ... 4806
Zep 2:15 a place for **b** to lie down in! ... 2416
Ac 10:12 all manner of fourfooted **b** ... *5074*
Ac 11:6 and saw fourfooted **b** of the earth ... *5074*
Ro 1:23 fourfooted **b**, and creeping things ... *5074*
Heb 13:11 of those **b**, whose blood is brought ... *2226*
Jas 3:7 Every kind of **b**, and of birds ... *2342*
Rev 4:6 were four **b** full of eyes ... *2226*
Rev 4:8 And the four **b** had each of them ... *2226*
Rev 5:8 the four **b** and four and twenty ... *2226*
Rev 7:11 about the elders and the four **b** ... *2226*
Rev 15:7 one of the four **b** gave unto the ... *2226*
Rev 19:4 elders and the four **b** fell down ... *2226*

BEAT

Ex 39:3 did **b** the gold into thin plates, ... 7554
Jgs 19:22 **b** at the door, and spake to the ... 1849
Ru 2:17 and **b** out that she had gleaned: ... 2251
Ps 18:42 did I **b** them small as the dust ... 7833
Pr 23:14 Thou shalt **b** him with the rod, ... 5221
Isa 2:4 **b** their swords into plowshares, ... 3807
Joel 3:10 **B** your plowshares into swords, ... 3807
Mic 4:3 **b** their swords into plowshares, ... 3807
Mt 7:27 **b upon that house; and it fell:** ... *4350*
Mk 12:3 **they caught him, and b him** ... *1194*
Lk 6:48 **stream b vehemently upon that** ... *4366*
Lk 12:45 **shall begin to b the menservants** ... *5180*
Lk 20:11 **servant: and they b him also,** ... *1194*
Ac 18:17 **b** him before the judgment seat ... *5180*
Ac 22:19 and **b** in every synagogue ... *1194*

BEATEN

Ex 5:16 and, behold, thy servants are **b**; ... 5221
Ex 37:7 of gold, **b** out of one piece ... 4749
Ex 37:17 **b** work made he the candlestick; ... 4749
Dt 25:2 the wicked man be worthy to be **b**, ... 5221
1Ki 10:16 two hundred targets of **b** gold: ... 7820
1Ki 10:17 three hundred shields of **b** gold; ... 7820
2Ch 34:7 **b** the graven images into powder, ... 3807
Mic 1:7 images thereof shall be **b** to pieces, ... 3807
Mk 13:9 **in the synagogues ye shall be b** ... *1194*
Lk 12:47 **shall be b with many stripes** ... *1194*
Lk 12:48 **shall be b with few stripes** ... *1194*
Ac 5:40 called the apostles, and **b** them, ... *1194*
Ac 16:37 have **b** us openly uncondemned ... *1194*
2Co 11:25 Thrice was I **b** with rods, once ... *4463*

BEATEST

Pr 23:13 if thou **b** him with the rod, ... 5221

BEATETH

1Co 9:26 not as one that **b** the air: ... *1194*

BEAUTIFUL

Ge 29:17 Rachel was **b** and well ... 3303, 8389
Dt 21:11 among the captives a **b** woman, ... 3303, 8389
2Sa 11:2 was very **b** to look upon ... 2896
Est 2:7 the maid was fair and **b**; ... 2896, 4758
Ps 48:2 **B** for situation, the joy of the ... 3303
Ecc 3:11 made every thing **b** in his time: ... 3303
SS 6:4 Thou art **b**, O my love, ... 3303
Isa 52:7 How **b** upon the mountains are ... 4998
Eze 16:13 thou wast exceeding **b**, and thou ... 3303
Mt 23:27 **which indeed appear b outward,** ... *5611*
Ac 3:2 the temple which is called **B**, ... *5611*
Ac 3:10 sat for alms at the **B** gate ... *5611*
Ro 10:15 How **b** are the feet of them that ... *5611*

BEAUTIFY

Ezr 7:27 to **b** the house of the Lord ... 6286
Ps 149:4 he will **b** the meek with salvation, ... 6286
Isa 60:13 to **b** the place of my sanctuary; ... 6286

BEAUTY

2Sa 1:19 The **b** of Israel is slain upon thy ... 6643
2Sa 14:25 praised as Absalom for his **b** ... 3303
1Ch 16:29 the Lord in the **b** of holiness ... 1927
2Ch 20:21 should praise the **b** of holiness ... 1927
Ps 27:4 to behold the **b** of the Lord ... 5278
Ps 29:2 the Lord in the **b** of holiness ... 1927
Ps 45:11 the king greatly desire thy **b** ... 3308
Ps 50:2 out of Zion, the perfection of **b**, ... 3308
Ps 90:17 let the **b** of the Lord our God ... 5278
Ps 96:9 the Lord in the **b** of holiness: ... 1927
Pr 6:25 Lust not after her **b** in thine ... 3308
Pr 31:30 Favour is deceitful, and **b** is vain: ... 3308
Isa 33:17 eyes shall see the king in his **b**. ... 3308
Isa 53:2 no **b** that we should desire him ... 4758
Isa 61:3 to give unto them **b** for ashes, ... 6287
La 2:15 the perfection of **b**, The joy of ... 3308
Eze 16:15 thou didst trust in thine own **b**, ... 3308
Zec 11:7 the one I called **B**, and the other ... 5278

BECKONED

Lk 5:7 they **b** unto their partners ... *2656*

BECOME

Ge 3:22 Behold, the man is **b** as one of us ... 1961
Ge 18:18 Abraham shall surely **b** a great ... 1961
Ge 37:20 We shall see what will **b** of his ... 1961
Ex 15:6 **b** glorious in power: thy right ... 142
Ex 32:23 we wot not what is **b** of him ... 1961
1Sa 28:16 from thee, and is **b** thine enemy? ... 1961
2Sa 7:24 and thou, Lord, art **b** their God ... 1961
Est 2:11 what should **b** of her ... 6213
Job 7:5 skin is broken, and **b** loathsome ... 3988
Job 30:19 and I am **b** like dust and ashes ... 4911
Job 30:21 Thou art **b** cruel to me: with ... 2015
Ps 118:22 is **b** the head stone of the corner ... 1961
Pr 29:21 have him **b** his son at the length ... 1961
Isa 1:21 the faithful city **b** an harlot! ... 1961
Isa 60:22 A little one shall **b** a thousand, ... 1961
Jer 3:1 from him, and **b** another man's ... 1961
Jer 5:13 And the prophets shall **b** wind, ... 1961
La 1:1 how is she **b** as a widow! she ... 1961
La 4:1 How is the gold **b** dim! how is ... 6004
Jnh 4:5 see what would **b** of the city ... 1961
Zep 2:15 is she **b** a desolation, a place for ... 1961
Mt 18:3 **converted, and b as little children,** ... *1096*
Mt 21:42 **is b the head of the corner** ... *1096, 1519*
Mk 1:17 **make you to b fishers of men** ... *1096*
Mk 12:10 **is b the head of the corner:** ... *1096, 1519*
Lk 20:17 **is b the head of the corner?** ... *1096, 1519*

Jn	1:12	he power to **b** the sons of God,	*1096*
Ac	4:11	is **b** the head of the corner	*1096, 1519*
Ro	3:19	world may **b** guilty before God	*1096*
Ro	4:18	he might **b** the father of many	*1096*
Ro	7:13	might **b** exceeding sinful	*1096*
1Co	3:18	**b** a fool, that he may be wise	*1096*
1Co	8:9	**b** a stumblingblock to them that	*1096*
1Co	13:1	I am **b** as sounding brass, or a	*1096*
1Co	15:20	**b** the first-fruits of them that slept	*1096*
2Co	5:17	behold, all things are **b** new	*1096*
Gal	5:4	Christ is **b** of no effect unto you	*2673*
Tit	2:1	things which **b** sound doctrine:	*4241*
Rev	11:15	The kingdoms of this world are **b**	*1096*
Rev	18:2	is **b** the habitation of devils, and	*1096*

BECOMETH

Ps	93:5	holiness **b** thine house, O Lord	4998
Pr	17:7	Excellent speech **b** not a fool	5000
Pr	17:18	**b** surety in the presence of his	6148
Mt	3:15	**for thus it b us to fulfil all**	*4241*
Mt	13:22	**the word, and he b unfruitful**	*1096*
Mk	4:19	**the word, and it b unfruitful**	*1096*
1Ti	2:10	**b** women professing godliness)	*526*
Tit	2:3	be in behaviour as **b** holiness,	*2412*

BED

Ge	49:33	gathered up his feet into the **b**	4296
2Ki	1:16	shalt not come down off that **b**	4296
Est	7:8	Haman was fallen upon the **b**	4296
Job	17:13	made my **b** in the darkness	3326
Ps	4:4	with your own heart upon your **b**,	4904
Ps	139:8	if I make my **b** in hell, behold,	3331
Pr	26:14	So doth the slothful upon his **b**	4296
SS	3:1	By night on my **b** I sought him	4904
Eze	23:17	came to her into the **b** of love,	4904
Da	4:13	the visions of my head upon my **b**,	4903
Da	7:1	visions of his head upon his **b**	4903
Mt	9:6	**take up thy b, and go unto thine**	*2825*
Mk	2:4	they let down the **b** wherein	*2895*
Mk	2:9	**Arise, and take up thy b,**	*2895*
Mk	2:11	**Arise, and take up thy b, and go**	*2895*
Lk	11:7	**my children are with me in b;**	*2845*
Lk	17:34	**there shall be two men in one b;**	*2825*
Jn	5:8	**Rise, take up thy b, and walk**	*2895*
Jn	5:12	Take up thy bed, and walk?	*2895*
Heb	13:4	**b** undefiled: but whoremongers	*2845*
Rev	2:22	Behold, I will cast her into a **b**	*2825*

BEDCHAMBER

Ecc	10:20	curse not the rich in thy **b**;	2315, 4296

BED'S

Ge	47:31	bowed himself upon the **b** head	4296

BEDS

Isa	57:2	they shall rest in their **b**, each	4904
Mic	2:1	and work evil upon their **b**!	4904

BEDSTEAD

Dt	3:11	his **b** was a **b** of iron;	6210

BEES

Jgs	14:8	of **b** and honey in the carcase	1682

BEFALL

Ge	42:38	if mischief **b** him by the way	1241
Nu	49:1	tell you that which shall **b** you	7122
Ps	91:10	There shall be no evil **b** thee,	579
Ac	20:22	the things that shall **b** me	*4876*

BEFALLEN

Le	10:19	and such things have **b** me:	7122
Dt	31:21	many evils and troubles are **b**	4672
Jgs	6:13	why then is all this **b** us?	4672

BEFELL

2Sa	19:7	evil that **b** thee from thy youth	935
Ac	20:19	and temptations, which **b** me by	*4819*

BEFOREHAND See also AFOREHAND.

Mk	13:11	**take no thought b what ye shall**	*4305*
1Ti	5:24	Some men's sins are open **b**,	*4271*
1Pe	1:11	testified **b** the sufferings of Christ,	*4303*

BEFORETIME See also AFORETIME.

Jos	20:5	and hated him not **b**	8543, 8032
1Sa	9:9	a Prophet was **b** called a Seer.)	6440
Ac	8:9	called Simon, which **b** in the same	*4391*

BEG

Pr	20:4	therefore shall he **b** in the harvest,	7592
Lk	16:3	**cannot dig; to b I am ashamed**	*1871*

BEGGAR

Lk	16:20	**was a certain b named Lazarus,**	*4434*
Lk	16:22	**that the b died, and was carried**	*4434*

BEGGED

Mt	27:58	Pilate, and **b** the body of Jesus	*154*
Lk	23:52	Pilate, and **b** the body of Jesus	*154*
Jn	9:8	Is not this he that sat and **b**?	*4319*

BEGGING

Ps	37:25	forsaken, nor his seed **b** bread	1245

BEGIN

Ge	11:6	this they **b** to do: and now	2490
Dt	2:25	will I **b** to put the dread of thee	2490
Dt	16:9	**b** to number the seven weeks	2490
1Sa	3:12	when I **b**, I will also make an end	2490
1Sa	22:15	Did I then **b** to enquire of God	2490
Mt	24:49	**b to smite his fellow servants,**	*756*
Lk	3:8	**b** not to say within yourselves,	*756*
Lk	14:9	**thou b with shame to take the**	*756*
Lk	14:29	**behold it b to mock him,**	*756*
Lk	21:28	**these things b to come to pass**	*756*
Lk	23:30	**they b to say to the mountains**	*756*
1Pe	4:17	must **b** at the house of God:	*756*
Rev	10:7	he shall **b** to sound, the mystery	*3295*

BEGINNING

Ge	1:1	In the **b** God created the heaven	7225
Ge	10:10	the **b** of his kingdom was Babel,	7225
Ex	12:2	the **b** of months: it shall be the	7218
Dt	11:12	the **b** of the year even unto the	7225
Dt	21:17	for he is the **b** of his strength;	7225
Job	8:7	Though thy **b** was small, yet thy	7225
Job	42:12	end of Job more than his **b**	7225
Ps	111:10	of the Lord is the **b** of wisdom:	7225
Pr	1:7	the **b** of knowledge: but fools	7225
Pr	8:22	possessed me in the **b** of his	7225
Pr	8:23	up from everlasting, from the **b**,	7218
Pr	9:10	fear of the Lord is the **b** of	8462
Pr	17:14	The **b** of strife is as when	7225
Pr	20:21	hastily at the **b**; but the end	7223
Ecc	3:11	that God maketh from the **b**	7218
Ecc	7:8	end of a thing than the **b** thereof:	7225
Ecc	10:13	The **b** of the words of his mouth	8462
Isa	41:26	Who hath declared from the **b**,	7218

Isa 46:10 Declaring the end from the **b**,..................7225
Isa 48:16 not spoken in secret from the **b**;..............7218
Isa 64:4 For since the **b** of the world men 5769
Da 9:21 seen in the vision at the **b**........................8462
Mt 14:30 **b** to sink, he cried, saying, ...*756*
Mt 19:8 **from the b it was not so** *746*
Mk 10:6 **from the b of the creation**..........................*746*
Mk 13:19 **such as was not from the b** *746*
Lk 24:27 **b** at Moses and all the prophets, ...*756*
Jn 1:1 In the **b** was the Word, and the.................*746*
Jn 1:2 The same was in the **b** with God *746*
Jn 2:11 This **b** of miracles did Jesus.......................*746*
Jn 6:64 Jesus knew from the **b** who *746*
Jn 8:25 **I said unto you from the b**..........................*746*
Jn 8:44 **was a murderer from the b**, ...*746*
Jn 15:27 **ye have been with me from the b**..............*746*
Jn 16:4 **not unto you at the b, because I**................*746*
Ac 15:18 his works from the **b** of the
Eph 3:9 which from the **b** of the world
Col 1:18 who is the **b**, the firstborn *746*
2Th 2:13 God hath from the **b** chosen you...............*746*
Heb 1:10 Thou, Lord, in the **b** hast laid *746*
Heb 3:14 if we hold the **b** of our confidence *746*
Heb 7:3 having neither **b** of days, nor end..............*746*
2Pe 2:20 is worse with them than the **b**.................*4423*
2Pe 3:4 were from the **b** of the creation *746*
1Jn 1:1 That which was from the **b**, ...*746*
1Jn 2:7 which ye had from the **b**.............................*746*
1Jn 2:13 him that is from the **b**.................................*746*
1Jn 2:24 which ye have heard from the **b**................*746*
1Jn 3:8 the devil sinneth from the **b**.......................*746*
1Jn 3:11 that ye heard from the **b**.............................*746*
2Jn 5 which we had from the **b**............................*746*
2Jn 6 as ye have heard from the **b**.......................*746*
Rev 1:8 **the b and the ending,**..................................*746*
Rev 3:14 **the b of the creation of God;** *746*
Rev 21:6 the **b** and the end. I will.............................*746*
Rev 22:13 **Alpha and Omega, the b and the** *746*

BEGINNINGS
Mk 13:8 **these are the b of sorrows** *746*

BEGOTTEN See also FIRSTBEGOTTEN.
Ps 2:7 my son; this day have I **b** thee..................3205
Jn 1:14 as of the only **b** of the Father,)..................*3439*
Jn 1:18 the only **b** Son, which is...........................*3439*
Jn 3:16 **his only b Son, that whosoever**................*3439*
Jn 3:18 **name of the only b Son of God**...............*3439*
Ac 13:33 my Son, this day have I **b** thee..................*2090*
1Co 4:15 I have **b** you through the gospel *1080*
Phm 10 whom I have **b** in my bonds: *2050*
Heb 1:5 my Son, this day have I **b** thee? *1080*
Heb 5:5 my Son, to day have I **b** thee *1080*
Heb 11:17 offered up his only **b** son..........................*3459*
1Pe 1:3 **b** us again unto a lively hope......................*313*
1Jn 4:9 God sent his only **b** Son...........................*3439*
1Jn 5:1 loveth him also that is **b** of him...............*1080*
1Jn 5:18 but he that is **b** of God keepeth *1080*
Rev 1:5 first **b** of the dead, and the prince............*4416*

BEGUILE
Col 2:4 lest any man should **b** you with...............*3884*
Col 2:18 Let no man **b** you of your reward............*2603*

BEGUILED
Ge 3:13 The serpent **b** me, and I did eat...............5377
Ge 29:25 wherefore then hast thou **b** me? 7411
Jos 9:22 Wherefore have ye **b** us, saying................7411
2Co 11:3 as the serpent **b** Eve through his..............*1818*

BEGUILING
2Pe 2:14 **b** unstable souls: an heart they.................*1185*

BEGUN
Nu 16:46 from the Lord; the plague is **b** 2490
Dt 3:24 thou hast **b** to shew thy servant...............2490
Est 6:13 before whom thou hast **b** to fall, ...2490
Est 9:23 undertook to do as they had **b**,................2490
Mt 18:24 **when he had b to reckon, one was** *756*
2Co 8:10 who have **b** before, not only to do...........*4278*
Gal 3:3 having **b** in the Spirit, are ye now *1728*
Php 1:6 that he which hath **b** a good *1728*

BEHALF
Ex 27:21 on the **b** of the children of Israel...............854
2Sa 3:12 messengers to David on his **b**, ...8478
2Ch 16:9 to shew himself strong in the **b** 5973
Job 36:2 I have yet to speak on God's **b**
1Co 1:4 thank my God always on your **b**,.............*4012*
Php 1:29 it is given in the **b** of Christ......................*5228*
1Pe 4:16 let him glorify God on this **b** *3313*

BEHAVE
Ps 101:2 I will **b** myself wisely in a perfect.............7919
1Co 13:5 Doth not **b** itself unseemly.........................*807*
1Ti 3:15 to **b** thyself in the house of God, ...*390*

BEHAVED
1Sa 18:14 David **b** himself wisely in all his..............7919
1Sa 18:30 David **b** himself more wisely than...........7919
2Th 3:7 for we **b** not ourselves disorderly...............*312*

BEHAVETH
1Co 7:36 think that he **b** himself uncomely *807*

BEHAVIOUR
1Sa 21:13 he changed his **b** before them,.................2940
1Ti 3:2 vigilant, sober, of good **b**, ...*2887*
Tit 2:3 that they be in **b** as becometh *2688*

BEHEADED
Mt 14:10 he sent, and **b** John in the prison,..............*607*
Mk 6:16 It is John, whom I **b** *607*
Lk 9:9 Herod said, John have I **b**; *607*
Rev 20:4 the souls of them that were **b**...................*3990*

BEHELD See also BEHOLD.
Nu 21:9 when he **b** the serpent of brass 5027
Nu 23:21 He hath not **b** iniquity in Jacob 5027
Job 31:26 If I **b** the sun when it shined....................7200
Ps 119:158 I **b** the transgressors, and was grieved.....7200
Ps 142:4 and **b**, but there was no man 7200
Ecc 8:17 Then I **b** all the work of God,..................7200
Isa 41:28 For I **b**, and there was no man;................7200
Jer 4:25 I **b**, and, lo, there was no man..................7200
Eze 1:15 Now as I **b** the living creatures,.................7200
Da 7:9 **b** till the thrones were cast 2370, 934
Hab 3:6 he **b**, and drove asunder the.....................7200
Mk 12:41 **b** how the people cast money...................*2334*
Lk 10:18 **I b Satan as lightning fall from**................*2334*
Lk 19:41 **b** the city, and wept over it *1492*
Lk 20:17 **b** them, and said, **What is this** *1689*
Lk 22:56 a certain maid **b** him as he sat *1492*
Lk 24:12 he **b** the linen clothes laid by.......................*991*
Jn 1:14 we **b** his glory, the glory as of...................*2300*
Ac 1:9 while they **b**, he was taken up; *991*

Rev	7:9	After this I **b**, and lo, a great	*1492*
Rev	13:11	I **b** another beast coming up out	*1492*

BEHEMOTH (be´-he-moth)

Job	40:15	Behold now **b**, which I made	930

BEHOLD See also **BEHELD.**

Ge	1:29	God said, **B**, I have given you	2009
Ge	1:31	had made, and, **b**, it was very good	2009
Ge	3:22	**B**, the man is become as one of	2005
Ge	6:17	And, **b**, I, even I, do bring a flood	2005
Ge	9:9	And I, **b**, I establish my covenant	2005
Ge	15:17	the sun went down, **b** a smoking	2009
Ge	17:4	As for me, **b**, my covenant is	2009
Ge	19:2	**B**, now, my lords, turn in, I pray	2009
Ge	19:8	**B** now, I have two daughters	2009
Ge	19:20	**B** now, this city is near to flee	2009
Ge	22:1	And he said, **B**, here I am	2009
Ge	28:12	**b** the angels of God ascending	2009
Ge	28:13	And, **b**, the Lord stood above it	2009
Ge	29:25	in the morning, **b**, it was Leah:	2009
Ge	37:19	another, **B**, this dreamer cometh	2009
Ge	37:25	and, **b**, a company of Ishmeelites	2009
Ge	41:1	that Pharaoh dreamed: and, **b**,	2009
Ex	3:2	looked, and, **b**, the bush burned	2009
Ex	3:9	**b**, the cry of the children of Israel	2009
Ex	16:10	**b**, the glory of the Lord	2009
Ex	24:8	**B** the blood of the covenant	2009
Ex	34:30	**b**, the skin of his face shone;	2009
Nu	12:10	**b**, Miriam became leprous	2009
Nu	22:11	**B**, there is a people come out	2009
Nu	25:12	**B**, I give unto him my covenant	2005
Nu	32:23	**b**, ye have sinned	2009
Dt	9:16	I looked, and, **b**, ye had sinned	2009
Dt	10:14	**B**, the heaven and the heaven	2005
Dt	11:26	**B**, I set before you this day a	7200
Dt	32:49	and **b** the land of Canaan, which	7200
Jos	3:11	**B**, the ark of the covenant	2009
Jos	5:13	**b**, there stood a man	2009
Jos	23:4	**B**, I have divided unto you by lot	7200
Jos	23:14	And, **b**, this day I am going	2009
Jos	24:27	**B**, this stone shall be a witness	2009
Jgs	6:37	**B**, I will put a fleece of wool	2009
Jgs	11:34	**b**, his daughter came out	2009
Ru	3:8	**b**, a woman lay at his feet	2009
1Sa	3:11	to Samuel, **B**, I will do a thing in	2009
1Sa	5:34	**b**, Dagon was fallen upon his	2009
1Sa	12:13	Now therefore **b** the king	2009
1Sa	15:22	**B**, to obey is better than sacrifice,	2009
1Sa	16:15	**B** now, an evil spirit from God	2009
1Sa	20:23	**b**, the Lord be between	2009
1Sa	26:7	**b**, Saul lay sleeping within	2009
1Sa	26:21	**b**, I have played the fool,	2009
1Sa	26:22	**B** the king's spear!	2009
2Sa	4:10	**B**, Saul is dead	2009
2Sa	12:18	**B**, while the child was yet alive	2009
2Sa	15:26	**b**, here am I, let him do	2005
1Ki	5:5	And, **b**, I purpose to build	2005
1Ki	10:7	**b**, the half was not told me:	2009
1Ki	11:31	**B**, I will rend the kingdom	2005
1Ki	22:23	**b**, the Lord hath put a lying	2009
2Ki	2:11	**b**, there appeared a chariot	2009
2Ki	4:32	**b**, the child was dead,	2009
2Ki	5:15	**B**, now I know that there is	2009
2Ki	7:2	**B**, thou shalt see it with thine	2009
2Ch	2:4	**B**, I build an house	2009
2Ch	6:18	**b**, heaven and the heaven of	2009
2Ch	9:6	**b**, the one half of the greatness	2009
2Ch	13:12	**b**, God himself is with us	2009
2Ch	34:24	**B**, I will bring evil upon this	2005
Job	1:12	**B**, all that he hath is in thy	2009
Job	2:6	**B**, he is in thine hand;	2009
Job	4:3	**B**, thou hast instructed many,	2009
Job	28:28	**B**, the fear of the Lord	2005
Job	32:11	**B**, I waited for your words;	2005
Job	33:12	**B**, in this thou art not just:	2005
Job	36:5	**B**, God is mighty,	2005
Job	36:22	**B**, God exalteth by his power:	2005
Job	36:26	**B**, God is great, and we know	2005
Job	36:30	**B**, he spreadeth his light	2005
Job	39:29	her eyes **b** afar off	5027
Job	40:11	and **b** every one that is proud,	7200
Job	40:15	**B** now behemoth, which I made	2009
Ps	27:4	to **b** the beauty of the Lord, and	2372
Ps	51:5	**B**, I was shapen in iniquity;	2005
Ps	51:6	**B**, thou desirest truth in the	2005
Ps	119:18	that I may **b** wondrous things	5027
Ps	121:4	**B**, he that keepeth Israel shall	2009
Ps	133:1	**B**, how good and how pleasant	2009
Pr	1:23	**B**, I will pour out my spirit unto	2009
Pr	11:31	**B**, the righteous shall be	2005
Ecc	1:14	**b**, all is vanity and vexation of	2009
Ecc	2:1	**b**, this also is vanity	2009
Ecc	2:11	**b**, all was vanity and vexation of	2009
Ecc	2:12	I turned myself to **b** wisdom	7200
Ecc	4:1	**B** the tears of such as were	2009
Ecc	5:18	**B** that which I have seen: good	2009
Ecc	7:27	**B**, this have I found, saith the	7200
Ecc	11:7	it is for the eyes to **b** the sun:	7200
SS	1:15	**B**, thou art fair, my love;	2009
SS	1:15	**b**, thou art fair;	2009
SS	1:16	**B**, thou art fair, my beloved	2009
SS	4:1	**B**, thou art fair, my love;	2009
SS	4:1	**b**, thou art fair;	2009
Isa	3:1	**B**, the Lord, the Lord of hosts	2009
Isa	7:14	**B**, a virgin shall conceive	2009
Isa	12:2	**B**, God is my salvation;	2009
Isa	13:9	**B**, the day of the Lord cometh	2009
Isa	22:17	**B**, the Lord will carry thee	2009
Isa	28:16	**B**, I lay in Zion for a foundation	2005
Isa	29:14	**b**, I will proceed to do a marvelous	2005
Isa	30:27	**B**, the name of the Lord cometh	2009
Isa	38:5	**b**, I will add unto thy days	2005
Isa	38:8	**B**, I will bring again the shadow	2005
Isa	39:6	**B**, the days come,	2009
Isa	40:9	**B** your God!	2009
Isa	42:1	**B** my servant, whom I upheld;	2005
Isa	43:19	**B**, I will do a new thing;	2005
Isa	49:16	**B**, I have graven thee upon	2005
Isa	50:9	**B**, the Lord God will help me;	2005
Isa	55:5	**B**, thou shalt call a nation	2005
Isa	59:1	**B**, the Lord's hand is not	2005
Isa	60:2	**b**, the darkness shall cover	2009
Isa	62:11	**B**, the Lord hath proclaimed	2009
Isa	62:11	**b**, his reward is with him	2009
Isa	65:17	**B**, I create new heavens and a new	2005
Isa	65:18	**b**, I create Jerusalem a rejoicing	2005
Isa	66:12	**B**, I will extend peace to her	2005
Isa	66:15	**b**, the Lord will come with fire	2009
Jer	1:6	**B**, I cannot speak:	2009
Jer	1:9	**B**, I have put my words in thy	2009

Jer	3:22	**B**, we come unto thee;	2005
Jer	6:22	**B**, a people cometh from the	2009
Jer	7:8	**B**, ye trust in lying words	2009
Jer	9:7	**B**, I will melt them, and try them;	2005
Jer	9:15	**B**, I will feed them, even this	2005
Jer	9:25	**B**, the days come, saith the Lord,	2009
Jer	12:14	**B**, I will pluck them out of their	2005
Jer	16:14	**b**, the days come, saith the Lord,	2009
Jer	18:6	**B**, as the clay is in the potter's	2009
Jer	23:5	**B**, the days come,	2009
Jer	23:30	**B**, I am against the prophets,	2005
Jer	23:39	**b**, I, even I, will utterly forget	2005
Jer	26:14	**b**, I am in your hand:	2005
Jer	30:18	**B**, I will bring again the captivity	2005
Jer	31:8	**B**, I will bring them from the north	2005
Jer	31:31	**B**, the days come,	2009
Jer	32:17	**b**, thou hast made the heaven	2009
Jer	32:27	**B**, I am the Lord,	2009
Jer	33:14	**B**, the days come,	2009
Jer	42:4	**b**, I will pray unto the Lord	2005
Jer	50:31	**B**, I am against thee	2005
Jer	50:41	**B**, a people shall come from the	2009
La	1:9	O Lord, **b** my affliction: for the	7200
La	1:12	**b**, and see if there be any sorrow	5027
La	5:1	consider, and **b** our reproach	7200
Eze	1:4	And I looked, and, **b**, a whirlwind	2009
Eze	3:23	**b**, the glory of the Lord stood there,	2009
Eze	5:8	**B**, I, even I, am against	2005
Eze	7:10	**B** the day, **b**, it is come:	2009
Eze	8:16	**b**, at the door of the temple	2009
Eze	10:9	**b** the four wheels by the	2009
Eze	15:4	**B**, it is cast into the fire for fuel;	2009
Eze	16:8	**b**, thy time was the time of love;	2009
Eze	18:4	**B**, all souls are mine;	2005
Eze	24:16	**b**, I take away from thee the	2005
Eze	24:21	**B**, I will profane my sanctuary,	2005
Eze	28:3	**B**, thou art wiser than Daniel;	2009
Eze	28:7	**B**, therefore I will bring strangers	2005
Eze	34:10	**B**, I am against the shepherds;	2005
Eze	34:11	**B**, I, even I, will both search my	2005
Eze	36:9	**b**, I am for you, and I will	2005
Eze	37:7	and **b** a shaking, and the bones	2009
Eze	40:3	**b**, there was a man,	2009
Eze	40:4	Son of man, **b** with thine eyes,	7200
Eze	44:4	and, **b**, the glory of the Lord filled	2009
Da	7:2	**b**, the four winds of the heaven	718
Da	7:7	and **b** a fourth beast, dreadful and	718
Da	8:15	**b**, there stood before me	2009
Hos	2:6	**b**, I will hedge up thy way	2005
Joel	3:1	For, **b**, in those days, and in that	2009
Am	6:14	**b**, I will raise up against you	2005
Am	7:8	**B**, I will set a plumbline	2005
Ob	2	**B**, I have made thee small	2009
Mic	7:9	and I shall **b** his righteousness	7200
Na	1:15	**B** upon the mountains the	2209
Zep	3:19	**B**, at that time I will undo all	2005
Zec	3:8	**b**, I will bring forth my servant	2005
Zec	3:9	For **b** the stone that I have laid	2009
Zec	6:12	**B**, the man whose name is The	2009
Zec	8:7	**B**, I will save my people	2005
Zec	9:9	**b**, thy king cometh unto thee:	2009
Mal	3:1	**B**, I will send my messenger	2005
Mal	4:5	**B**, I will send you Elijah the	2009
Mt	1:23	**B**, a virgin shall be with child,	*2400*
Mt	2:1	**b**, there came wise men from the	*2400*
Mt	6:26	**B the fowls of the air: for they**	*1689*
Mt	7:4	**b, a beam is in thine own eye?**	*2400*
Mt	10:16	**B, I send you forth as sheep**	*2400*
Mt	11:10	**B, I send my messenger before**	*2400*
Mt	12:41	**b, a greater than Jonas is here**	*2400*
Mt	12:42	**b, a greater than Solomon is here**	*2400*
Mt	12:49	**B, my mother and my brethren!**	*2400*
Mt	18:10	**do always b the face of my Father**	*991*
Mt	19:27	**B**, we have forsaken all, and	*2400*
Mt	21:5	**B**, thy King cometh unto thee,	*2400*
Mt	23:38	**B, your house is left unto you**	*2400*
Mt	26:45	**b, the hour is at hand, and the**	*2400*
Mt	26:46	**b, he is at hand that doth betray**	*2400*
Mt	27:51	**b**, the veil of the temple was rent	*2400*
Mt	28:2	**b**, there was a great earthquake:	*2400*
Mk	1:2	**B**, I send my messenger before	*2400*
Mk	3:34	**B my mother and my brethren!**	*2396*
Mk	13:23	**b, I have foretold you all things**	*2400*
Mk	14:41	**b, the Son of man is betrayed**	*2400*
Mk	15:35	heard it, said, **B**, he calleth Elias	*2400*
Lk	2:10	for, **b**, I bring you good tidings of	*2400*
Lk	2:34	**B**, this child is set for the fall	*2400*
Lk	6:23	**for, b, your reward is great**	*2400*
Lk	7:27	**B, I send my messenger before**	*2400*
Lk	10:3	**b, I send you forth as lambs**	*2400*
Lk	11:31	**and, b, a greater than Solomon**	*2400*
Lk	11:32	**and, b, a greater than Jonas**	*2400*
Lk	13:32	**B, I cast out devils, and I do**	*2400*
Lk	17:21	**for, b, the kingdom of God**	*2400*
Lk	22:31	**b, Satan hath desired to have you,**	*2400*
Lk	24:39	**B my hands and my feet, that it**	*1492*
Jn	1:29	**B** the Lamb of God, which taketh	*2396*
Jn	1:36	**B** the Lamb of God!	*2396*
Jn	1:47	**B an Israelite indeed, in whom**	*2396*
Jn	5:14	**B, thou art made whole: sin no**	*2396*
Jn	11:36	the Jews, **B** how he loved him!	*2396*
Jn	12:15	**b**, thy King cometh, sitting on an	*2400*
Jn	16:32	**B, the hour cometh, yea, is now**	*2400*
Jn	19:14	unto the Jews, **B** your king!	*2396*
Jn	19:26	unto his mother, **Woman, b thy**	*2400*
Jn	19:27	**B thy mother!** And from that	*2400*
Jn	20:27	**hither thy finger, and b my**	*2396*
Ac	5:28	and, **b**, ye have filled Jerusalem	*2400*
Ac	7:56	**B**, I see the heavens opened,	*2400*
Ac	9:10	And he said, **B**, I am here, Lord	*2400*
Ac	20:22	And now, **b**, I go bound in the	*2400*
Ro	9:33	**B**, I lay in Sion a stumblingstone	*2400*
1Co	15:51	**B**, I shew you a mystery; We	*2400*
2Co	5:17	**b**, all things are become new	*2400*
2Co	6:2	**b**, now is the accepted time;	*2400*
2Co	6:2	**b**, now is the day of salvation.)	*2400*
Heb	8:8	**B**, the days come, saith the Lord	*2400*
Jas	3:5	**B**, how great a matter a little fire	*2400*
Jas	5:9	**b**, the judge standeth before the	*2400*
Jas	5:11	**B**, we count them happy which	*2400*
1Pe	2:6	**B**, I lay in Sion a chief corner	*2400*
1Pe	3:2	they **b** your chaste conversation	*2029*
1Jn	3:1	**B**, what manner of love the	*1492*
Jude	14	**B**, the Lord cometh with ten	*2400*
Rev	1:7	**B**, he cometh with clouds; and	*2400*
Rev	1:18	**and, b, I am alive for evermore,**	*2400*
Rev	5:5	**b**, the Lion of the tribe of Judah	*2400*
Rev	16:15	**B**, I come as a thief. Blessed	*2400*
Rev	21:3	**B**, the tabernacle of God is with	*2400*
Rev	21:5	said, **B**, I make all things new	*2400*

B

Rev	22:7	**B, I come quickly:** blessed is he	*2400*
Rev	22:12	**And, b, I come quickly; and my**	*2400*

BEHOLDEST

Mt	7:3	why, **b** thou the mote that is in thy	*991*
Lk	6:41	And why **b** thou the mote that is	*991*

BEHOLDING

Ps	119:37	Turn away mine eyes from **b**	7200
Pr	15:3	every place, **b** the evil and the	6822
Ecc	5:11	the **b** of them with their eyes?	7200
Mk	10:21	Jesus **b** him loved him, and said	*1689*
Lk	23:49	stood afar off **b** these things,	*3708*
2Co	3:18	**b** as in a glass the glory of the	*2734*
Jas	1:23	like unto a man **b** his natural	*2657*

BEHOVED

Lk	24:46	thus it **b** Christ to suffer, and	*1163*
Heb	2:17	in all things it **b** him to be made	*3784*

BELIEF See also UNBELIEF.

2Th	2:13	of the Spirit and **b** of the truth:	*4102*

BELIEVE

Ex	4:1	they will not **b** me, nor hearken	539
Dt	1:32	ye did not **b** the Lord your God	539
2Ch	20:20	**b** his prophets, so shall ye prosper	539
Pr	26:25	When he speaketh fair, **b** him not:	539
Isa	43:10	that ye may know and **b** me, and	539
Hab	1:5	ye will not **b**, though it be told	539
Mt	9:28	**B ye that I am able to do this?**	*4100*
Mk	1:15	**repent ye, and b the gospel**	*4100, 1722*
Mk	5:36	**Be not afraid, only b**	*4100*
Mk	9:23	**If thou canst b, all things are**	*4100*
Mk	9:24	Lord, I **b**; help thou mine	*4100*
Mk	13:21	**or, lo, he is there; b him not:**	*4100*
Lk	8:12	**lest they should b and be saved**	*4100*
Lk	24:25	**fools, and slow of heart to b**	*4100, 1909*
Jn	1:7	all men through him might **b**	*4100*
Jn	1:12	even to them that **b** on his name:	*4100*
Jn	5:38	**whom he hath sent, him ye b not**	*4100*
Jn	5:47	**but if ye b not his writings**	*4100*
Jn	8:24	**if ye b not that I am he, ye shall**	*4100*
Jn	9:35	**Dost thou b on the Son of God?**	*4100*
Jn	9:36	Who is he, Lord, that I might **b**	*4100*
Jn	11:27	I **b** that thou art the Christ, the	*4100*
Jn	12:36	**b in the light, that ye may be**	*4100*
Jn	14:1	**ye b in God, b also in me**	*4100*
Jn	14:11	**B me that I am in the Father,**	*4100*
Jn	16:31	answered them, **Do ye now b?**	*4100*
Jn	17:21	**that the world may b that thou**	*4100*
Jn	20:25	my hand into his side, I will not **b**	*4100*
Ac	8:37	I **b** that Jesus Christ is the Son of	*4100*
Ac	13:39	by him all that **b** are justified	*4100*
Ro	3:3	For what if some did not **b**?	*569*
Ro	4:11	be the father of all them that **b**,	*4100*
Ro	6:8	we **b** that we shall also live with	*4100*
Ro	10:9	shalt **b** in thine heart that God	*4100*
Ro	10:14	not believed? and how shall they **b**	*4100*
1Co	14:22	not to them that **b**,	*4100*
Php	1:29	not only to **b** on him, but also to	*4100*
1Th	4:14	if we **b** that Jesus died and rose	*4100*
2Th	2:11	delusion, that they should **b** a lie:	*4100*
2Ti	2:13	If we **b** not, yet he abideth	*569*
Heb	11:6	must **b** that he is, and that he is	*4100*
Jas	2:19	the devils also **b**, and tremble	*4100*
1Pe	2:7	Unto you therefore which **b** he is	*4100*
1Jn	3:23	That we should **b** on the name of	*4100*
1Jn	4:1	Beloved, **b** not every spirit, but	*4100*
1Jn	5:13	ye may **b** on the name of the Son	*4100*

BELIEVED

Ge	15:6	And he **b** in the Lord; and he	539
Ps	27:13	unless I had **b** to see the goodness	539
Ps	116:10	I **b**, therefore have I spoken: I	539
Isa	53:1	Who hath **b** our report? and to	539
Jnh	3:5	So the people of Nineveh **b** God,	539
Mt	8:13	**and as thou hast b, so be it**	*4100*
Mt	21:32	**publicans and the harlots b him:**	*4100*
Lk	1:1	things which are most surely **b**	*4135*
Jn	2:22	and they **b** the scripture, and the	*4100*
Jn	2:23	many **b** in his name, when they	*4100*
Jn	3:18	**already, because he hath not b**	*4100*
Jn	4:53	himself **b**, and his whole house	*4100*
Jn	5:46	**had ye b Moses,**	*4100*
Jn	10:42	And many **b** on him there	*4100*
Jn	11:45	things which Jesus did, **b** on him	*4100*
Jn	12:38	Lord, who hath **b** our report?	*4100*
Jn	16:27	**have b that I came out from God**	*4100*
Jn	17:8	**and they have b that thou didst**	*4100*
Jn	20:29	**have not seen, and yet have b**	*4100*
Ac	2:44	And all that **b** were together	*4100*
Ac	4:32	of them that **b** were of one heart	*4100*
Ac	11:17	who **b** on the Lord Jesus Christ;	*4100*
Ac	13:48	as were ordained to eternal life **b**	*4100*
Ac	14:23	them to the Lord, on whom they **b**	*4100*
Ac	17:5	the Jews which **b** not, moved	*544*
Ac	18:27	helped them much which had **b**	*4100*
Ac	19:2	received the Holy Ghost since ye **b**?	*4100*
Ro	4:3	Abraham **b** God, and it was	*569, 4100*
Ro	4:18	who against hope **b** in hope,	*4100*
Ro	10:14	on him in whom they have not **b**?	*4100*
Ro	10:16	saith, Lord, who hath **b** our report?	*4100*
Ro	13:11	salvation nearer than when we **b**	*4100*
1Co	15:2	unless ye have **b** in vain	*4100*
Gal	3:6	as Abraham **b** God, and it was	*4100*
2Th	2:12	who **b** not the truth, but had	*4100*
2Ti	1:12	I know whom I have **b**, and am	*4100*
Tit	3:8	that they which have **b** in God	*4100*
Heb	4:3	which have **b** do enter into rest,	*4100*
Heb	11:31	perished not with them that **b**	*544*
Jas	2:23	Abraham **b** God, and it was	*4100*
1Jn	4:16	we have known and **b** the love	*4100*
Jude	5	destroyed them that **b** not	*4100*

BELIEVERS See also UNBELIEVERS.

Ac	5:14	And **b** were the more added	*4100*
1Ti	4:12	be thou an example of the **b**, in	*4103*

BELIEVEST

Jn	1:50	**thee under the fig tree, b thou?**	*4100*
Jn	11:26	**in me shall never die. B thou**	*4100*
Ac	8:37	If thou **b** with all thine heart,	*4100*
Ac	26:27	King Agrippa, **b** thou the prophets?	*4100*
Jas	2:19	Thou **b** that there is one God;	*4100*

BELIEVETH

Pr	14:15	The simple **b** every word:	539
Mk	9:23	**are possible to him that b**	*4100*
Mk	16:16	**He that b and is baptized shall**	*4100*
Jn	3:15	**whosoever b in him should**	*4100*
Jn	3:16	**whosoever b in him should**	*4100*
Jn	3:18	**but he that b not is condemned**	*4100*
Jn	3:36	He that **b** on the Son hath	*4100*

Jn	6:35	**he that b on me shall never thirst.**	*4100*
Jn	6:47	**He that b on me hath everlasting**	*4100*
Jn	11:25	**he that b in me, though he were**	*4100*
Jn	11:26	**and b in me shall never die**	*4100*
Jn	12:44	**He that b on me, b not on me,**	*4100*
Jn	14:12	**He that b on me, the works that I**	*4100*
Ac	10:43	whosoever **b** in him shall receive	*4100*
Ro	1:16	unto salvation to every one that **b**;	*4100*
Ro	9:33	whosoever **b** on him shall not be	*4100*
Ro	10:4	righteousness to every one that **b**	*4100*
Ro	10:10	For with the heart man **b** unto	*4100*
Ro	14:2	For one **b** that he may eat all	*4100*
1Co	7:12	hath a wife, that **b** not, and she	*571*
1Co	7:13	hath an husband that **b** not, and	*571*
1Co	13:7	**b** all things, hopeth all things	*4100*
1Co	14:24	there come in one that **b** not, or	*571*
2Co	6:15	hath he that **b** with an infidel?	*4103*
1Jn	5:1	Whosoever **b** that Jesus is the	*4100*
1Jn	5:10	he that **b** not God hath made	*4100*
1Jn	5:10	because he **b** not the record	*4100*

BELIEVING See also UNBELIEVING.

Jn	20:27	**and be not faithless, but b**	*4103*
Jn	20:31	and that **b** ye might have life	*4100*
Ac	16:34	rejoiced, **b** in God with all his	*4100*
Ac	24:14	**b** all things which are written	*4100*
1Ti	6:2	And they that have **b** masters	*4103*
1Pe	1:8	yet **b**, ye rejoice with joy	*4100*

BELLS

Ex	39:25	**b** of pure gold, and put the **b**	6472
Zec	14:20	there be upon the **b** of the horses	4698

BELLY

Ge	3:14	upon thy **b** shalt thou go, and	1512
Le	11:42	goeth upon the **b**, and whatsoever	1512
Nu	5:21	thy thigh to rot, and thy **b** to	990
Jgs	3:22	not draw the dagger out of his **b**,	990
Job	20:15	God shall cast them out of his **b**,	990
Job	32:19	**b** is as wine which hath no vent;	990
Job	40:16	his force is in the navel of his **b**	990
Ps	22:10	art my God from my mother's **b**	990
Pr	18:20	A man's **b** shall be satisfied with	990
Pr	20:27	searching all the inward parts of the **b**	990
Pr	26:22	into the innermost parts of the **b**	990
SS	5:14	his **b** is as bright ivory, overlaid	4578
SS	7:2	thy **b** is like an heap of wheat set	990
Jer	1:5	Before I formed thee in the **b** I	990
Eze	3:3	cause thy **b** to eat, and fill thy	990
Jnh	1:17	in the **b** of the fish three days	4578
Jnh	2:2	out of the **b** of hell cried I, and	990
Mt	12:40	**three nights in the whale's b;**	*2836*
Mt	15:17	**in at the mouth goeth into the b,**	*2836*
Mk	7:19	**but into the b, and goeth out into**	*2836*
Lk	15:16	**he would fain have filled his b**	*2836*
Jn	7:38	**out of his b shall flow rivers of**	*2836*
Ro	16:18	Jesus Christ, but their own **b**;	*2836*
1Co	6:13	Meats for the **b**	2836
1Co	6:13	and the **b** for meats:	*2836*
Php	3:19	whose God is their **b**, and whose	*2836*
Rev	10:10	as I had eaten it, my **b** was bitter	*2836*

BELONG

Ge	40:8	Do not interpretations **b** to God?	
Dt	29:29	The secret things **b** unto the Lord	
Ps	47:9	shields of the earth **b** unto God	
Pr	24:23	These things also **b** to the wise	
Mk	9:41	**because ye b to Christ, verily I**	*1510*
Lk	19:42	**things which b unto thy peace!**	

BELONGED

1Ki	1:8	mighty men which **b** to David	
Est	1:9	house which **b** to king Ahasuerus	
Est	2:9	things as **b** to her, and seven	4490
Lk	23:7	he **b** unto Herod's jurisdiction	*1510*

BELONGEST

1Sa	30:13	unto him, To whom **b** thou?	

BELONGETH

Dt	32:35	To me **b** vengeance, and	
Ezr	10:4	for this matter **b** unto thee:	
Ps	3:8	Salvation **b** unto the Lord: thy	
Ps	62:11	heard this; that power **b** unto God	
Ps	94:1	O Lord God, to whom vengeance **b**;	
Ps	94:1	O God, to whom vengeance **b**, shew	
Da	9:7	O Lord, righteousness **b** unto thee	
Heb	5:14	But strong meat **b** to them that	*1510*
Heb	10:30	Vengeance **b** unto me, I will	

BELONGING

Ru	2:3	a part of the field **b** unto Boaz	
Pr	26:17	with strife **b** not to him, is like	

BELOVED See also WELL BELOVED.

Dt	21:15	wives, one **b**, and another hated,	157
Ne	13:26	was **b** of his God, and God made	157
Ps	127:2	for so he giveth his **b** sleep	3039
SS	1:16	Behold, thou art fair, my **b**,	157
SS	2:8	The voice of my **b**! behold, he	1730
SS	2:9	My **b** is like a roe or a young hart:	1730
SS	2:16	My **b** is mine, and I am his:	1730
SS	5:2	the voice of my **b** that knocketh,	1730
SS	5:8	if ye find my **b**, that ye tell him	1730
SS	6:1	Whither is thy **b** gone, O thou	1730
SS	8:14	Make haste, my **b**, and be thou like	1730
Jer	12:7	dearly **b** of my soul into the hand	3033
Da	10:19	said, O man greatly **b**, fear not:	2530
Mt	3:17	saying, This is my **b** Son, in whom	*27*
Mt	17:5	which said, This is my **b** Son	*27*
Mk	1:11	Thou art my **b** Son, in whom	*27*
Mk	9:7	saying, This is my **b** Son: hear him	*27*
Lk	3:22	which said, Thou art my **b** Son;	*27*
Lk	9:35	saying, This is my **b** Son: hear	*27*
Lk	20:13	**shall I do? I will send my b son:**	*27*
Ro	12:19	Dearly **b**, avenge not yourselves,	*27*
1Co	4:17	who is my **b** son, and faithful in the	*27*
1Co	15:58	Therefore, my **b** brethren, be ye	*27*
Eph	1:6	he hath made us accepted in the **b**	*25*
Col	4:14	Luke, the **b** physician, and Demas,	*27*
2Ti	1:2	To Timothy, my dearly **b** son:	*27*
Jas	1:16	Do not err, my **b** brethren	*27*
2Pe	1:17	This is my **b** Son, in whom I am	*27*
2Pe	3:8	But, **b**, be not ignorant of this	*27*
2Pe	3:14	Wherefore, **b**, seeing that ye look	*27*
2Pe	3:15	our **b** brother Paul also according	*27*
2Pe	3:17	Ye therefore, **b**, seeing ye know	*27*
1Jn	3:2	**B**, now are we the sons of God,	*27*
1Jn	3:21	**B**, if our heart condemn us not,	*27*
1Jn	4:1	**B**, believe not every spirit, but try	*27*
1Jn	4:11	**B**, if God so loved us, we ought also	*27*

BEMOAN

Jer	15:5	O Jerusalem? or who shall **b** thee?	5110
Jer	16:5	neither go to lament nor **b** them:	5110

Jer 22:10 not for the dead, neither **b** him: ... 5110
Na 3:7 is laid waste: who will **b** her? ... 5110

BEMOANED
Job 42:11 they **b** him, and comforted him ... 5110

BEND
Ps 11:2 the wicked **b** their bow, they ... 1869
Jer 9:3 they **b** their tongues like their ... 1869
Jer 48:17 All ye that are about him **b** him ... 5110
Na 3:7 is laid waste: who will **b** her ... 5110
Jer 50:14 all ye that **b** the bow, ... 1869
Eze 17:7 vine did **b** her roots toward him, ... 3719

BENDETH
Ps 58:7 he **b** his bow to shoot his arrows, ... 1869
Jer 51:3 Against him that **b** let the archer ... 1869

BENDING
Isa 60:14 thee shall come **b** unto thee; ... 7817

BENEATH
Ex 20:4 or that is in the earth **b**, or that ... 8478
Ex 32:19 and brake them **b** the mount ... 8478
Dt 4:18 that is in the waters **b** the earth: ... 8478
Dt 4:39 upon the earth **b**: there is none ... 8478
Dt 5:8 or that is in the waters **b**, ... 8478
Jos 2:11 in heaven above, and in earth **b** ... 8478
1Ki 8:23 in heaven above, or on earth **b**, ... 8478
Pr 15:24 that he may depart from hell **b** ... 4295
Isa 14:9 Hell from **b** is moved for thee to ... 8478
Isa 51:6 and look upon the earth **b** ... 8478
Jn 8:23 **Ye are from b; I am from above:** ... *2736*
Ac 2:19 and signs in the earth **b**; blood ... 2736

BENEFACTORS
Lk 22:25 **authority upon them are called b** ... *2110*

BENEFIT
2Ch 32:25 according to the **b** done unto ... 1576
Jer 18:10 wherewith I said I would **b** them ... 3190
2Co 1:15 that ye might have a second **b**; ... *5485*
Phm 14 that thy **b** should not be as it ... *18*

BENEFITS
Ps 103:2 and forget not all his **b**: ... 1576
Ps 116:12 Lord for all his **b** toward me? ... 8408

BENEVOLENCE
1Co 7:3 render unto the wife due **b** ... *2133*

BENT
Ps 7:12 he hath **b** his bow, and made it ... 1869
Isa 5:28 all their bows **b**, their horses' ... 1869
La 2:4 He hath **b** his bow like an enemy: ... 1869
La 3:12 He hath **b** his bow, and set me as ... 1869
Hos 11:7 my people are **b** to backsliding ... 8511

BEREAVE
Ecc 4:8 I labour and **b** my soul of good? ... 2637
Eze 5:17 beasts, and they shall **b** thee: ... 7921
Hos 9:12 yet will I **b** them, that there shall ... 7921

BEREAVED
Ge 42:36 Me have ye **b** of my children: ... 7921
Ge 43:14 I be **b** of my children, I am **b** ... 7921

BERRIES
Isa 17:6 two or three **b** in the top of the ... 1620
Jas 3:12 tree, by brethren, bear olive **b**? ... *1636*

BERYL (ber´-il)
Eze 1:16 was like unto the colour of a **b** ... 8658
Eze 10:9 was as the colour of a **b** stone ... 8658
Rev 21:20 seventh, chrysolyte; the eighth, **b**; ... 969

BESEECH
Ex 3:18 and now let us go, we **b** thee ... 4994
Nu 12:11 I **b** thee, lay not the sin upon us, ... 4994
2Sa 24:10 and now I **b** thee, O Lord, take ... 4994
2Ki 19:19 I **b** thee, save thou us out of his ... 4994
2Ki 20:3 I **b** thee, O Lord, remember now ... 577
Ne 1:5 And said, I **b** thee, O Lord God ... 577
Job 42:4 Hear, I **b** thee, and I will speak: ... 4994
Ps 80:14 Return, we **b** thee, O God of hosts: ... 4994
Ps 119:108 Accept, I **b** thee, the freewill ... 4994
Jer 38:4 We **b** thee, let this man be put to ... 4994
Da 1:12 Prove thy servants, I **b** thee, ten ... 4994
Am 7:5 O Lord God, cease, I **b** thee: by ... 4994
Jnh 4:3 take, I **b** thee, my life from me: ... 4994
Ro 12:1 I **b** you therefore, brethren, by ... *3870*
Ro 15:30 Now I **b** you, brethren, for the ... *3870*
Ro 16:17 Now I **b** you, brethren, mark ... *3870*
1Co 1:10 Now I **b** you, brethren, by the ... *3870*
2Co 2:8 Wherefore I **b** you that ye would ... *3870*
Gal 4:12 Brethren, I **b** you, be as I am: ... *1189*
Eph 4:1 **b** you that ye walk worthy of the ... *3870*
Heb 13:22 I **b** you, brethren, suffer the ... *3870*

BESET
Ps 22:12 of Bashan have **b** me round ... 3803
Ps 139:5 hast **b** me behind and before, ... 6696
Heb 12:1 the sin which doth so easily **b** us, ... *2139*

BESIEGE
Dt 20:12 thee, then thou shalt **b** it: ... 6696
Dt 28:52 And he shall **b** thee in all thy ... 6887
Dt 28:52 **b** thee in all thy gates ... 6887
1Sa 23:8 to **b** David and his men ... 6696
2Ki 24:11 city, and his servants did **b** ... 6696
2Ch 6:28 if their enemies **b** them in the ... 6696

BESIEGED
2Ki 17:5 Samaria, and **b** it three years ... 6696
2Ki 18:9 came up against Samaria, and **b** it ... 6696
2Ki 24:10 and the city was **b** ... 935, 4692
Ecc 9:14 and **b** it, and built great ... 5437
Da 1:1 unto Jerusalem, and **b** it ... 6696

BESOUGHT
Ge 42:21 when he **b** us, and we would not ... 2603
2Sa 12:16 David therefore **b** God for the ... 1245
1Ki 13:6 And the man of God **b** the Lord, ... 2470
2Ch 33:12 he **b** the Lord his God, ... 2470
Ezr 8:23 fasted and **b** our God for this: ... 1245
Est 8:3 and **b** him with tears to put ... 2603
Mt 8:31 the devils **b** him, saying, If thou ... *3870*
Mt 8:34 they **b** him that he would depart ... *3870*
Mt 14:36 And **b** him that they might only ... *3870*
Mk 6:56 streets, and **b** him that they ... *3870*
Lk 8:31 And they **b** him that he would ... *3870*
Lk 9:40 I **b** thy disciples to cast him out; ... *1189*
Lk 11:37 certain Pharisee **b** him to dine ... *2065*
Jn 4:40 they **b** him that he would tarry ... *2065*
Jn 19:31 **b** Pilate that their legs might ... *2065*
Jn 19:38 **b** Pilate that he might take ... *2065*
Ac 16:15 she **b** us, saying, If ye have ... *3870*
2Co 12:8 I **b** the Lord thrice, that it might ... *3870*

BEST

Ge	43:11	take of the **b** fruits in the land in	2173
Ge	47:6	in the **b** of the land make thy	4315
Nu	36:6	marry to whom they think **b**;	2896
Dt	23:16	where it liketh him **b**: thou	2896
2Sa	18:4	What seemeth you **b** I will do	3190
1Ki	10:18	and overlaid it with the **b** gold	6338
Est	2:9	her maids unto the **b** place of the	2896
Ps	39:5	man at his **b** state is altogether	5324
Lk	15:22	Bring forth the **b** robe, and put	*4413*
1Co	12:31	but covet earnestly the **b** gifts:	*2909*

BESTOW

Dt	14:26	And thou shalt **b** that money for	5414
Lk	12:17	**I have no room where to b**	*4863*
1Co	12:23	upon these we **b** more abundant	*4060*
1Co	13:3	And though I **b** all my goods to	*5595*

BESTOWED

1Ki	10:26	horsemen, whom he **b** in the	3240
2Ki	5:24	their hand, and **b** them in the	6485
2Ki	12:15	the money to be **b** on workmen:	5414
1Ch	29:25	**b** upon him such royal majesty	5414
Isa	63:7	to all that the Lord hath **b** on us	1580
Jn	4:38	**whereon ye b no labour: other**	*2872*
2Co	8:1	grace of God **b** on the churches	*1325*
Gal	4:11	lest I have **b** upon you labour in	*2872*
1Jn	3:1	of love the Father hath **b** on us,	*1325*

BETRAY

1Ch	12:17	but if ye be come to **b** me to	7411
Mt	24:10	**and shall b one another, and**	*3860*
Mt	26:16	he sought opportunity to **b** him	*3860*
Mt	26:21	**one of you shall b me**	*3860*
Mt	26:23	**in the dish, the same shall b me**	*3860*
Mt	26:46	**he is at hand that doth b me**	*3860*
Mk	13:12	**the brother shall b the brother**	*3860*
Mk	14:10	the chief priests, to **b** him unto	*3860*
Mk	14:11	he might conveniently **b** him	*3860*
Mk	14:18	**eateth with me shall b me**	*3860*
Lk	22:4	how he might **b** him unto them	*3860*
Lk	22:6	sought opportunity to **b** him	*3860*
Jn	6:64	not, and who should **b** him	*3860*
Jn	6:71	he it was that should **b** him, being	*3860*
Jn	13:2	Iscariot, Simon's son, to **b** him;	*3860*
Jn	13:11	For he knew who should **b** him;	*3860*
Jn	13:21	**you, that one of you shall b me**	*3860*

BETRAYED

Mt	17:22	**The Son of man shall be b into**	*3860*
Mt	20:18	**The Son of man shall be b unto**	*3860*
Mt	26:2	**Son of man is b to be crucified**	*3860*
Mt	26:24	**by whom the Son of man is b!**	*3860*
Mt	26:25	Then Judas, which **b** him	*3860*
Mt	26:45	**Son of man is b into the hands of**	*3860*
Mt	26:48	Now he that **b** him gave them a	*3860*
Mt	27:3	Then Judas, which had **b** him	*3860*
Mt	27:4	I have sinned in that I have **b**	*3860*
Mk	3:19	Judas Iscariot, which also **b** him:	*3860*
Mk	14:21	**by whom the Son of man is b!**	*3860*
Mk	14:41	**Son of man is b into the hands**	*3860*
Mk	14:44	And he that **b** him had given them	*3860*
Lk	21:16	**And ye shall be b both by**	*3860*
Lk	22:22	**unto that man by whom he is b!**	*3860*
Jn	18:2	And Judas also, which **b** him,	*3860*
Jn	18:5	Judas also, which **b** him, stood	*3860*
1Co	11:23	night in which he was **b** took	*3860*

BETRAYERS

Ac	7:52	ye have been now the **b** and	*4273*

BETRAYEST

Lk	22:48	**b thou the Son of man with a**	*3860*

BETRAYETH

Mk	14:42	**lo, he that b me is at hand**	*3860*
Lk	22:21	**the hand of him that b me is with**	*3860*
Jn	21:20	Lord, which is he that **b** thee?	*3860*

BETROTH

Dt	28:30	Thou shalt **b** a wife, and another	781
Hos	2:19	And I will **b** thee unto me for ever;	781

BETROTHED

Ex	21:8	who hath **b** her to himself,	3259
Ex	22:16	maid that is not **b**, and lie with	781
Le	19:20	that is a bondmaid, **b** to an	2778
Dt	20:7	that hath **b** a wife, and hath not	781
Dt	22:25	But if a man find a **b** damsel in the	781
Dt	22:27	the **b** damsel cried, and there was	781

BETTER

Ge	29:19	**b** that I give her to thee, than	2896
Ex	14:12	**b** for us to serve the Egyptians	2896
Nu	14:3	not **b** for us to return into Egypt?	2896
Jgs	18:19	is it **b** for thee to be a priest unto	2896
Ru	4:15	which is **b** to thee than seven sons,	2896
1Sa	1:8	am not I **b** to thee than ten sons?	2896
1Sa	15:22	Behold, to obey is **b** than sacrifice,	2896
1Sa	15:28	neighbour of thine, that is **b** than	2896
2Sa	17:14	**b** than the counsel of Ahithophel.	2896
1Ki	1:47	God make the name of Solomon **b**	3190
1Ki	21:2	I will give thee for it a **b** vineyard	2896
Ps	37:16	**b** than the riches of many wicked	2896
Ps	84:10	a day in thy courts is **b** than a	2896
Ps	118:8	**b** to trust in the Lord than to	2896
Pr	8:11	For wisdom is **b** than rubies;	2896
Pr	15:16	**B** is little with the fear of the	2896
Pr	15:17	**B** is a dinner of herbs where love is,	2896
Pr	16:8	**B** is a little with righteousness	2896
Pr	16:19	**B** it is to be of an humble spirit	2896
Pr	16:32	slow to anger is **b** than the mighty	2896
Pr	17:1	**B** is a dry morsel, and quietness	2896
Pr	19:1	**B** is the poor that walketh in his	2896
Pr	19:22	and a poor man is **b** than a liar	2896
Pr	21:9	**b** to dwell in a corner of the	2896
Pr	21:19	**b** to dwell in the wilderness	2896
Pr	25:7	**b** it is that it be said unto thee,	2896
Pr	25:24	It is **b** to dwell in the corner	2896
Pr	27:5	Open rebuke is **b** than secret love	2896
Pr	27:10	**b** is a neighbour that is near than	2896
Pr	28:6	**B** is the poor that walketh in his	2896
Ecc	2:24	nothing **b** for a man, than that he	2896
Ecc	3:22	I perceive that there is nothing **b**,	2896
Ecc	4:6	**B** is an handful with quietness	2896
Ecc	4:9	Two are **b** than one; because they	2896
Ecc	4:13	**B** is a poor and a wise child than	2896
Ecc	5:5	**B** is it that thou shouldest not	2896
Ecc	6:3	an untimely birth is **b** than he	2896
Ecc	6:9	**B** is the sight of the eyes than the	2896
Ecc	6:11	what is man the **b**?	3148
Ecc	7:1	A good name is **b** than	2896
Ecc	7:2	**b** to go to the house of mourning,	2896
Ecc	7:3	Sorrow is **b** than laughter: for by	2896
Ecc	7:5	**b** to hear the rebuke of the wise,	2896

Ecc	7:8	**B** is the end of a thing than the	2896
Ecc	7:10	cause that the former days were **b**	2896
Ecc	8:15	hath no **b** thing under the sun,	2896
Ecc	9:4	a living dog is **b** than a dead lion	2896
Ecc	9:16	said I, Wisdom is **b** than strength:	2896
Ecc	9:18	Wisdom is **b** than weapons of war:	2896
Ecc	10:11	and a babbler is no **b**	3504
SS	1:2	for thy love is **b** than wine	2896
La	4:9	**b** than they that be slain with	2896
Eze	36:11	will do **b** unto you than at your	2896
Da	1:20	ten times **b** than all the magicians	3027
Hos	2:7	then it was **b** with me than now	2896
Jnh	4:3	it is **b** for me to die than to live	2896
Mt	6:26	Are ye not much **b** than they?	*1308*
Mt	12:12	then is a man **b** than a sheep?	*1308*
Mt	18:6	it were **b** for him that a millstone	*4851*
Mt	18:8	it is **b** for thee to enter into life	*2570*
Mk	9:42	is **b** for him that a millstone	*2570, 3123*
Mk	9:43	it is **b** for thee to enter into life	*2570*
Mk	9:45	it is **b** for thee to enter halt	*2570*
Mk	9:47	it is **b** for thee to enter into the	*2570*
Lk	5:39	for he saith, The old is **b**	*5543*
Lk	12:24	more are ye **b** than the fowls?	*1308*
Lk	17:2	were **b** for him that a millstone	*3081*
Ro	3:9	What then? are we **b** than they?	*4284*
1Co	7:9	it is **b** to marry than to burn	*2909*
1Co	9:15	it were **b** for me to die,	*2570, 3123*
1Co	11:17	not for the **b**, but for the worse	*2909*
Php	1:23	to be with Christ; which is far **b**	*2909*
Php	2:3	esteem other **b** than themselves	*5242*
Heb	1:4	made so much **b** than the angels,	*2909*
Heb	6:9	we are persuaded **b** things of you,	*2909*
Heb	7:19	but the bringing in of a **b** hope	*2909*
Heb	7:22	made a surety of a **b** testament	*2909*
Heb	8:6	the mediator of a **b** covenant	*2909*
Heb	8:6	was established upon **b** promises	*2909*
Heb	9:23	with **b** sacrifices than these	*2909*
Heb	10:34	in heaven a **b** and an enduring	*2909*
Heb	11:16	But now they desire a **b** country	*2909*
Heb	11:35	they might obtain a **b** resurrection:	*2909*
Heb	11:40	provided some **b** thing for us,	*2909*
Heb	12:24	**b** things than that of Abel	*2909*
1Pe	3:17	it is **b**, if the will of God be so,	*2909*
2Pe	2:21	For it had been **b** for them not to	*2909*

BEWAIL

Dt	21:13	and **b** her father and her mother	1058
Jgs	11:37	and **b** my virginity, I and my	1058
2Co	12:21	and that I shall **b** many which	*3996*
Rev	18:9	shall **b** her, and lament for her	*2799*

BEWAILED

Lk	8:52	And all wept, and **b** her: but he	*2875*
Lk	23:27	which also **b** and lamented	*2875*

BEWARE

Ge	24:6	**B** thou that thou bring not my	8104
Ex	23:21	**B** of him, and obey his voice,	8104
Dt	6:12	Then **b** lest thou forget the Lord,	8104
Dt	8:11	**B** that thou forget not the Lord	8104
Dt	15:9	**B** that there be not a thought in	8104
Jgs	13:4	Now therefore **b**, I pray thee,	8104
2Sa	18:12	**B** that none touch the young man	8104
Mt	7:15	**B** of false prophets, which come	*4337*
Mt	10:17	But **b** of men: for they will	*4337*
Mt	16:6	Take heed and **b** of the leaven	*4337*
Mt	16:11	that ye should **b** of the leaven	*4337*
Mk	8:15	Take heed, **b** of the leaven of the	*991*
Mk	12:38	**B** of the scribes, which love to go	*991*
Lk	12:1	**B** ye of the leaven of the	*4337*
Lk	12:15	heed, and **b** of covetousness:	*5442*
Lk	20:46	**B** of the scribes, which desire	*4337*
Ac	13:40	**B** therefore, lest that come	*991*
Php	3:2	**B** of dogs, **b** of evilworkers	*991*
Col	2:8	**B** lest any man spoil you	*991*
2Pe	3:17	**b** lest ye also, being led away	*5442*

BEWITCHED

Ac	8:9	used sorcery, and **b** the people	
Ac	8:11	he had **b** them with sorceries	*1839*
Gal	3:1	foolish Galatians, who hath **b**	*940*

BID See also BADE; FORBID.

1Sa	9:27	**B** the servant pass on before us.	559
2Ki	5:13	if the prophet had **b** thee do	1696
Jnh	3:2	the preaching that I **b** thee	1696
Zep	1:7	prepared a sacrifice, he hath **b**	6942
Mt	14:28	**b** me come unto thee on the	*2753*
Lk	9:61	let me first go **b** them farewell,	*657*
Lk	10:40	**b** her therefore that she help me	*2036*
1Co	10:27	any of them that believe not **b**	*2564*
2Jn	10	house, neither **b** him God speed:	*3004*

BIDDEN See also FORBIDDEN.

2Sa	16:11	for the Lord hath **b** him	559
Mt	22:4	Tell them which are **b**, Behold, I	*2564*
Mt	22:8	which were **b** were not worthy	*2564*
Lk	14:8	When thou art **b** of any man	*2564*
Lk	14:10	when thou art **b**, go and sit down	*2564*
Lk	14:24	none of those men which were **b**	*2564*

BIDDETH See also FORBIDDETH.

2Jn	11	For he that **b** him God speed	*3004*

BIER

2Sa	3:31	king David himself followed the **b**	4296
Lk	7:14	And he came and touched the **b**	*4673*

BILL

Dt	24:1	write her a **b** of divorcement,	5612
Isa	50:1	Where is the **b** of your mother's	5612
Jer	3:8	and given her a **b** of divorce;	5612
Mk	10:4	to write a **b** of divorcement,	*975*

BIND See also BOUND.

Nu	30:2	swear an oath to **b** his soul	631
Nu	30:3	Lord, and **b** herself by a bond	631
Jgs	15:10	To **b** Samson are we come up	631
Jgs	15:12	We are come down to **b** thee,	631
Jgs	16:5	that we may **b** him to afflict him:	631
Job	38:31	Canst thou **b** the sweet	7194
Job	39:10	Canst thou **b** the unicorn with	7194
Pr	3:3	**b** them about thy neck; write	7194
Pr	6:21	**B** them continually upon thine	7194
Pr	7:3	**B** them upon thy fingers, write	7194
Isa	61:1	to **b** up the brokenhearted,	2280
Eze	34:16	**b** up that which was broken,	2280
Hos	6:1	smitten, and he will **b** us up	2280
Mt	12:29	except he first **b** the strong man?	*1210*
Mt	13:30	**b** them in bundles to burn them:	*1210*
Mt	16:19	whatsoever thou shalt **b** on earth	*1210*
Mt	18:18	shall **b** on earth shall be bound in	*1210*
Mt	22:13	**B** him hand and foot, and take	*1210*
Mt	23:4	For they **b** heavy burdens and	*1195*
Mk	3:27	he will first **b** the strong man;	*1210*

Mk 5:3 no man could **b** him, no, not with ... *1210*
Ac 9:14 to **b** all that call on thy name. ... *1210*

BINDETH
Job 5:18 For he maketh sore, and **b** up: ... 2280
Job 26:8 He **b** up the waters in his thick ... 6887
Job 28:11 **b** the floods from overflowing; ... 2280
Ps 147:3 in heart, and **b** up their wounds ... 2280
Pr 26:8 As he that **b** a stone in a sling ... 6887
Isa 30:26 that the Lord **b** up the breach ... 2280

BINDING
Nu 30:13 every **b** oath to afflict the soul ... 632
Ac 22:4 **b** and delivering into prisons ... *1195*

BIRD
Ge 7:14 his kind, every **b** of every sort ... 6833
Ps 124:7 **b** out of the snare of the fowlers: ... 6833
Pr 1:17 spread in the sight of any **b** ... 1167, 3671
Pr 7:23 as a **b** hasteth to the snare, and ... 6833
Pr 26:2 As the **b** by wandering, as the ... 6833
Pr 27:8 As a **b** that wandereth from ... 6833
Ecc 10:20 **b** of the air shall carry the voice ... 5775
La 3:52 enemies chased me sore, like a **b**, ... 6833
Am 3:5 Can a **b** fall in a snare upon the ... 6833

BIRDS
Ge 40:17 and the **b** did eat them out of the ... 5775
Ge 40:19 **b** shall eat thy flesh from off thee ... 5775
Ecc 9:12 and as the **b** that are caught in ... 6833
SS 2:12 time of the singing of **b** is come,
Jer 4:25 the **b** of the heavens were fled ... 5775
Jer 5:27 As a cage is full of **b**, so are their ... 5775
Mt 8:20 **and the b of the air have nests;** ... *4071*
Mt 13:32 **so that the b of the air come** ... *4071*
Lk 9:58 **holes, and b of the air have nests;** ... *4071*

BIRTH
Job 3:16 untimely **b** I had not been; ... 5309
Ps 58:8 like the untimely **b** of a woman, ... 5309
Ecc 6:3 an untimely **b** is better than he ... 5309
Ecc 7:1 of death than the day of one's **b** ... 3205
Eze 16:3 Thy **b** and thy nativity is of the ... 4351
Mt 1:18 the **b** of Jesus Christ was on this ... 1083
Lk 1:14 and many shall rejoice at his **b** ... *1083*
Jn 9:1 man which was blind from his **b** ... *1079*
Gal 4:19 I travail in **b** again until Christ ... *5605*
Rev 12:2 cried, travailing in **b**, and pained ... *5605*

BIRTHRIGHT
Ge 25:31 Jacob said, Sell me this day thy **b**. ... 1062
Ge 25:33 and he sold his **b** unto Jacob ... 1062
Ge 27:36 he took away my **b**; and, behold ... 1062
1Ch 5:1 his **b** was given unto the sons ... 1062
1Ch 5:2 ruler; but the **b** was Joseph's:) ... 1062
Heb 12:16 for one morsel of meat sold his **b** ... *4415*

BISHOP
1Ti 3:1 If a man desire the office of a **b**, ... *1984*
1Ti 3:2 A **b** then must be blameless, the ... *1985*
Tit 1:7 For a **b** must be blameless, as the ... *1985*
1Pe 2:25 Shepherd and **B** of your souls ... *1985*

BISHOPRICK
Ac 1:20 therein: and his **b** let another ... *1984*

BITE
Ecc 10:8 an hedge, a serpent shall **b** him ... 5391
Ecc 10:11 will **b** without enchantment; ... 5391
Mic 3:5 that **b** with their teeth, and cry, ... 5391
Gal 5:15 if ye **b** and devour one another, ... *1148*

BITETH See also BACKBITETH.
Ge 49:17 the path, that **b** the horse heels, ... 5391
Pr 23:32 it **b** like a serpent, and stingeth ... 5391

BITS
Jas 3:3 we put **b** in the horses mouths, ... *5469*

BITTEN
Nu 21:9 if a serpent had **b** any man, when ... 5391

BITTER
Ge 27:34 with a great and exceeding **b** cry, ... 4751
Ex 12:8 with **b** herbs they shall eat it ... 4844
Ex 15:23 waters of Marah, for they were **b** ... 4751
Nu 5:18 **b** water that causeth the curse: ... 4751
Nu 9:11 unleavened bread and **b** herbs ... 4844
2Ki 14:26 of Israel, that it was very **b** ... 4784
Est 4:1 cried with a loud and a **b** cry; ... 4751
Job 3:20 and life unto the **b** in soul; ... 4751
Pr 5:4 her end is **b** as wormwood, sharp ... 4751
Pr 27:7 to the hungry soul every **b** thing ... 4751
Ecc 7:26 more **b** than death the woman ... 4751
Isa 5:20 put **b** for sweet, and sweet for **b**! ... 4751
Jer 4:18 is thy wickedness, because it is **b**, ... 4751
Eze 27:31 bitterness of heart and **b** wailing ... 4751
Am 8:10 and the end thereof as a **b** day ... 4751
Col 3:19 wives, and be not **b** against them ... *4087*
Jas 3:11 same place sweet water and **b**? ... *4089*
Jas 3:14 If ye have **b** envying and strife ... *4089*
Rev 10:9 it shall make thy belly **b**, but it ... *4087*

BITTERLY
Ru 1:20 Almighty hath dealt very **b** with ... 4843
Isa 22:4 I will weep **b**, labor not to comfort ... 4843
Zep 1:14 the mighty man shall cry there **b** ... 4751
Mt 26:75 And he went out, and wept **b** ... *4090*
Lk 22:62 Peter went out, and wept **b** ... *4090*

BITTERNESS
1Sa 1:10 she was in **b** of soul, and prayed ... 4751
Job 7:11 I will complain in the **b** of my ... 4751
Job 10:1 I will speak in the **b** of my soul, ... 4751
Job 21:25 another dieth in the **b** of his soul, ... 4751
Pr 14:10 The heart knoweth his own **b**; ... 4751
Isa 38:17 Behold, for peace I had great **b**: ... 4843
La 3:15 He hath filled me with **b**, ... 4844
Eze 3:14 took me away, and I went in **b** ... 4751
Zec 12:10 as one that is in **b** ... 4843
Ac 8:23 thou art in the gall of **b**, and in ... *4088*
Ro 3:14 mouth is full of cursing and **b**: ... *4088*
Eph 4:31 Let all **b**, and wrath, and anger ... *4088*
Heb 12:15 lest any root of **b** springing up ... *4088*

BLACK
Job 30:30 My skin is **b** upon me, and my ... 7835
SS 1:6 not upon me, because I am **b**, ... 7840
Jer 4:28 and the heavens above be **b**: ... 6937
La 5:10 Our skin was **b** like an oven ... 3648
Mt 5:36 canst not make one hair white or **b** ... *3189*
Rev 6:5 And I beheld, and lo a **b** horse; ... *3189*
Rev 6:12 sun became **b** as sackcloth of ... *3189*

BLACKNESS
Job 3:5 let the **b** of the day terrify it. ... 3650
Isa 50:3 I clothe the heavens with **b**, ... 6940
Jude 13 to whom is reserved the **b** of ... *2217*

BLADE

Jgs 3:22 the haft also went in after the **b**; 3851
Mt 13:26 **But when the b was sprung up** *5528*
Mk 4:28 **first the b, then the ear, after** *5528*

BLAME See also **UNBLAMEABLE.**

Ge 43:9 then let me bear the **b** for ever: 2398
Ge 44:32 then I shall bear the **b** to my 2398
2Co 8:20 that no man should **b** us in this *3469*
Eph 1:4 be holy and without **b**.................................*299*

BLAMED

2Co 6:3 that the ministry be not **b**: *3469*
Gal 2:11 the face, because he was to be **b** *2607*

BLAMELESS

Jos 2:17 We will be **b** of this thine oath.................5355
Mt 12:5 **profane the sabbath, and are b?**.................*338*
1Co 1:8 that ye may be **b** in the day of....................*410*
Php 2:15 that ye may be **b** and harmless...................*273*
Php 3:6 which is in the law, **b**.................................*273*
1Th 5:23 be preserved **b** unto the coming *274*
1Ti 3:2 a bishop then must be **b**, the......................*423*
1Ti 3:10 office of a deacon, being found **b** *410*
1Ti 5:7 in charge, that they may be **b** *423*
Tit 1:6 if any be **b**, the husband of one *410*
Tit 1:7 For a bishop must be **b**, as the *410*
2Pe 3:14 in peace, without spot, and **b** 298

BLASPHEME

1Ki 21:13 Naboth did **b** God and the king 1288
Mk 3:28 **wherewith soever they shall b** *987*
Mk 3:29 **he that shall b against the Holy**.................*987*
Ac 26:11 and compelled them to **b**; *987*
1Ti 1:20 that they may learn not to **b**.......................*987*
Jas 2:7 Do not they **b** that worthy name *987*
Rev 13:6 to **b** his name, and his tabernacle, ...*987*

BLASPHEMED

Isa 37:23 Whom hast thou reproached and **b**?.......1442
Eze 20:27 in this your fathers have **b** me..................1442
Ac 18:6 they opposed themselves, and **b**,................*987*
Ro 2:24 the name of God is **b** among the *987*
1Ti 6:1 God and his doctrine be not **b**...................*987*
Tit 2:5 that the word of God be not **b**...................*987*
Rev 16:9 heat, and **b** the name of God *987*
Rev 16:11 **b** the God of heaven because of.................*987*
Rev 16:21 men **b** God because of the plague *987*

BLASPHEMER

1Ti 1:13 Who was before a **b**, and a *989*

BLASPHEMERS

Ac 19:37 churches, nor yet **b** of your *987*
2Ti 3:2 covetous, boasters, proud, **b** *989*

BLASPHEMEST

Jn 10:36 **Thou b; because I said, I am the** *987*

BLASPHEMETH

Le 24:16 he that **b** the name of the Lord,...............5344
Mt 9:3 within themselves, This man **b** *987*
Lk 12:10 **unto him that b against the Holy**.............*987*

BLASPHEMIES

Eze 35:12 I have heard all thy **b** which thou 5007
Mt 15:19 **thefts, false witness, b:** *988*
Mk 2:7 Why doth this man thus speak **b**?..............*988*
Mk 3:28 **b wherewith soever they shall** *988*
Lk 5:21 Who is this which speaketh **b**? *988*
Rev 13:5 mouth speaking great things and **b**; *988*

BLASPHEMOUS

Ac 6:11 we have heard him speak **b** words *989*
Ac 6:13 ceaseth not to speak **b** words......................*989*

BLASPHEMOUSLY

Lk 22:65 things **b** spake they against him.................*987*

BLASPHEMY

Isa 37:3 trouble, and of rebuke, and of **b**: 5007
Mt 12:31 **the b against the Holy Ghost** *988*
Mt 26:65 behold, now ye have heard his **b** *988*
Mk 7:22 **an evil eye, b, pride, foolishness:** *988*
Mk 14:64 Ye have heard the **b**: what think................*988*
Jn 10:33 for **b**; and because that thou, ...*988*
Col 3:8 anger, wrath, malice, **b**, filthy *988*
Rev 2:9 **I know the b of them which say** *988*
Rev 13:1 and upon his heads the name of **b** *988*
Rev 13:6 And he opened his mouth in **b**.................*988*
Rev 17:3 full of names of **b**, having seven *988*

BLAST

Ex 15:8 And with the **b** of thy nostrils..................7307
2Sa 22:16 at the **b** of the breath of his......................5397
Job 4:9 By the **b** of God they perish, and.............5397
Isa 25:4 when the **b** of the terrible ones................7307

BLEMISH

Ex 12:5 Your lamb shall be without **b**, ...8549
Le 3:6 he shall offer it without **b**.........................8549
Le 6:6 a ram without **b** out of the flock, ...8549
Le 21:21 No man that hath a **b** of the seed............3971
Le 24:20 as he hath caused a **b** in a..........................3971
Nu 19:2 without spot, wherein is no **b**, ...3971
Dt 15:21 be any **b** therein, as if it be lame, ...3971
2Sa 14:25 head there was no **b** in him.......................3971
Eze 46:13 lamb of the first year without **b**:..............8549
Da 1:4 Children in whom was no **b**, but.............3971
Eph 5:27 it should be holy and without **b** *299*
1Pe 1:19 as of a lamb without **b** and without..........*299*

BLESS

Ge 12:2 and I will **b** thee, and make thy 1288
Ge 12:3 And I will **b** them that **b** thee,..................1288
Ge 22:17 in blessing I will **b** thee, and in 1288
Ge 26:24 for I am with thee, and will **b** thee, ...1288
Ge 27:38 **b** me, even me also, O my father 1288
Ge 28:3 God Almighty **b** thee, and make.............1288
Ge 32:26 let thee go, except thou **b** me 1288
Nu 6:24 The Lord **b** thee, and keep thee: 1288
Dt 8:10 then thou shalt **b** the Lord thy.................1288
Dt 24:19 thy God may **b** thee in all the work.........1288
Dt 28:12 and to **b** all the work of thine 1288
Dt 29:19 that he **b** himself in his heart...................1288
2Sa 7:29 let it please thee to **b** the house of...........1288
1Ch 4:10 Oh that thou wouldest **b** me.....................1288
Ne 9:5 **b** the Lord your God forever and 1288
Ps 16:7 I will **b** the Lord, who hath given 1288
Ps 34:1 I will **b** the Lord at all times: his 1288
Ps 62:4 they **b** with their mouth, but they 1288
Ps 67:1 God be merciful unto us and **b** us;..........1288
Ps 103:1 **B** the Lord, O my soul, and all.................1288
Ps 103:2 **B** the Lord, O my soul, and forget...........1288
Ps 103:20 **B** the Lord, ye his angels, that 1288
Ps 104:1 **B** the Lord, O my soul. O Lord.................1288
Ps 135:20 ye that fear the Lord, **b** the Lord.............1288

Ps	145:21	and let all flesh **b** his holy name	1288
Pr	30:11	and doth not **b** their mother	1288
Jer	31:23	The Lord **b** thee, O habitation of	1288
Mt	5:44	**b** them that curse you, do good	*2127*
Lk	6:28	**B** them that curse you, and pray	*2127*
Ro	12:14	**B** them which persecute you: **b**,	*2127*
1Co	4:12	being reviled, we **b**; being	*2127*
1Co	10:16	The cup of blessing which we **b**,	*2127*
1Co	14:16	Else when thou shalt **b** with the	*2127*
Heb	6:14	Surely blessing I will **b** thee, and	*2127*
Jas	3:9	Therewith **b** we God, even the	*2127*

BLESSED

Ge	1:22	And God **b** them, saying	1288
Ge	2:3	And God **b** the seventh day, and	1288
Ge	9:1	And God **b** Noah and his sons,	1288
Ge	12:3	shall all families of the earth be **b**	1288
Ge	18:18	the nations of the earth shall be **b**	1288
Ge	27:29	and **b** be he that blesseth thee	1288
Ge	30:27	that the Lord hath **b** me for thy	1288
Ge	47:10	Jacob **b** Pharaoh, and went out	1288
Ex	20:11	the Lord **b** the sabbath day, and	1288
Nu	24:9	**B** is he that blesseth thee, and	1288
Dt	2:7	the Lord thy God hath **b** thee in	1288
Jgs	5:24	**B** above women shall Jael the wife	1288
1Sa	25:39	**B** be the Lord, that hath pleaded	1288
2Sa	6:11	and the Lord **b** Obed-edom, and	1288
2Ch	2:12	**B** be the Lord God of Israel, that	1288
Ezr	7:27	**B** be the Lord God of our fathers	1288
Ne	8:6	Ezra **b** the Lord, the great God	1288
Job	1:10	hast **b** the work of his hands,	1288
Job	42:12	So the Lord **b** the latter end of	1288
Ps	1:1	**B** is the man that walketh not	835
Ps	2:12	**B** are all they that put their	835
Ps	32:1	**B** is he whose transgression is	835
Ps	33:12	**B** is the nation whose God is the	835
Ps	34:8	**b** is the man that trusteth in him	835
Ps	40:4	**B** is that man that maketh the	835
Ps	41:1	**B** is he that considereth the poor:	835
Ps	65:4	**B** is the man whom thou choosest,	835
Ps	89:15	**B** is the people that know the	835
Ps	118:26	**B** be he that cometh in the name	1288
Ps	128:1	**B** is every one that feareth the	835
Isa	56:2	**B** is the man that doeth this	835
Mal	3:12	And all nations shall call you **b**	833
Mt	5:3	**B are the poor in spirit:**	*3107*
Mt	5:4	**B, are they that mourn: for they**	*3107*
Mt	5:5	**B are the meek: for they shall**	*3707*
Mt	5:6	**B are they which do hunger and**	*3107*
Mt	5:7	**B are the merciful: for they shall**	*3107*
Mt	5:8	**B are the pure in heart: for they**	*3107*
Mt	5:9	**B are the peacemakers: for they**	*3107*
Mt	5:10	**B are they which are persecuted**	*3107*
Mt	5:11	**B are ye, when men shall revile**	*3107*
Mt	11:6	**And b is he, whosoever shall not**	*3107*
Mt	13:16	**But b are your eyes, for they see:**	*3107*
Mt	16:17	said unto him, **B art thou, Simon**	*3107*
Mt	23:39	**B is he that cometh in the name**	*2127*
Mt	24:46	**B is that servant, whom his lord**	*3107*
Mt	25:34	**ye b of my Father, inherit the**	*2127*
Mk	6:41	he looked up to heaven, and **b**,	*2127*
Mk	11:9	**B** is he that cometh in the name	*2127*
Mk	14:61	thou the Christ, the Son of the **B**?	*2128*
Lk	1:42	**B** art thou among women,	*2127*
Lk	1:42	and **b** is the fruit of thy womb.	*2127*
Lk	1:48	all generations shall call me **b**	*3106*
Lk	1:68	**B** be the Lord God of Israel;	*2128*
Lk	2:28	him up in his arms, and **b** God,	*2127*
Lk	6:20	disciples, and said, **B be ye poor:**	*3107*
Lk	6:21	**B are ye that hunger now: for ye**	*3107*
Lk	6:21	**B are ye that weep now: for ye**	*3107*
Lk	6:22	**B are ye, when men shall hate**	*3107*
Lk	7:23	**And b is he, whosoever shall not**	
Lk	10:23	**B are the eyes which see the**	*3107*
Lk	11:28	**Yea rather, b are they that hear**	*3107*
Lk	12:37	**B are those servants, whom the**	*3107*
Lk	12:38	**b are those servants**	*3107*
Lk	12:43	**B is that servant, whom his lord**	*3107*
Lk	13:35	**B is he that cometh in the name**	*2127*
Lk	14:14	**thou shalt be b; for they cannot**	*3107*
Jn	12:13	**B** is the King of Israel that	*2127*
Jn	20:29	**b are they that have not seen**	*3107*
Ac	3:25	all the kindreds of the earth be **b**	*1757*
Ac	20:35	**more b to give than to receive**	*3107*
Ro	1:25	the Creator, who is **b** for ever	*2128*
Ro	4:7	**B** are they whose iniquities are	*3707*
2Co	1:3	**B** be God, even the Father of our	*2128*
2Co	11:31	Jesus Christ, which is **b** for	*2128*
Gal	3:9	are **b** with faithful Abraham	*2727*
Eph	1:3	**b** us with all spiritual blessings	*2127*
1Ti	6:15	**b** and only Potentate, the King	*3107*
Tit	2:13	Looking for that **b** hope, and the	*3107*
Heb	7:6	**b** him that had the promises	*2127*
Heb	11:21	Jacob, when he was a dying, **b**	*2127*
Jas	1:12	**B** is the man that endureth	*3107*
Jas	1:25	this man shall be **b** in his deed	*3707*
Rev	1:3	**B** is he that readeth, and they	*3707*
Rev	14:13	**B** are the dead which die in the	*3707*
Rev	16:15	**B** is he that watcheth, and	*3707*
Rev	19:9	**B** are they which are called	*3707*
Rev	20:6	**B** and holy is he that hath part	*3707*
Rev	22:7	**b** is he that keepeth the sayings	*3707*
Rev	22:14	**B** are they that do his	*3707*

BLESSETH

Ge	27:29	thee, and blessed be he that **b** thee.	1288
Nu	24:9	Blessed is he that **b** thee, and	1288
Dt	15:6	the Lord thy God **b** thee, as he	1288

BLESSING

Ge	22:17	That in **b** I will bless thee, and in	1288
Ge	27:38	Hast thou but one **b**, my father?	1293
Dt	11:26	you this day a **b** and a curse;	1293
Dt	11:27	A **b** if ye obey the commandments	1293
Dt	23:5	thy God turned the curse into a **b**	1293
Dt	28:8	The Lord shall command the **b**	1293
Dt	33:1	this is the **b** wherewith Moses	1293
Dt	33:7	And this is the **b** of Judah:	
Jos	15:19	Who answereth, Give me a **b**;	1293
Ne	13:2	God turned the curse into a **b**.	1293
Job	29:13	**b** of him that was ready to perish	1293
Pr	10:22	The **b** of the Lord, it maketh rich	1293
Pr	11:11	By the **b** of the upright the city is	1293
Isa	65:8	Destroy it not; for a **b** is in it:	1293
Eze	34:26	there shall be showers of **b**	1293
Joel	2:14	repent, and leave a **b** behind him;	1293
Zec	8:13	I save you, and ye shall be a **b**:	1293
Mal	3:10	pour you out a **b**, that there shall	1293
1Co	10:16	The cup of **b** which we bless,	*2129*
Gal	3:14	the **b** of Abraham might come	*2129*
Heb	6:14	Saying, Surely **b** I will bless thee,	*2129*
Heb	12:17	would have inherited the **b**,	*2129*

Jas	3:10	mouth proceedeth **b** and cursing	*2129*
Rev	5:12	and honour, and glory, and **b**.	*2129*
Rev	5:13	**B**, and honour, and glory,	*2129*
Rev	7:12	**B**, and glory, and wisdom,	*2129*

BLESSINGS

Ge	49:25	bless thee with **b** of heaven above,	1293
Dt	28:2	all these **b** shall come on thee,	1293
Jos	8:34	the **b** and cursings, according to	1293
Pr	10:6	**B** are upon the head of the just:	1293
Pr	28:20	faithful man shall abound with **b**:	1293
Mal	2:2	I will curse your **b**: yea, I have	1293
Eph	1:3	with all spiritual **b** in heavenly	*2129*

BLEW

Jos	6:8	Lord, and **b** with the trumpets:	8628
Jgs	7:19	they **b** the trumpets, and brake	8628
2Sa	2:28	So Joab **b** a trumpet, and all	8628
2Sa	18:16	And Joab **b** the trumpet, and the	8628
1Ki	1:39	And they **b** the trumpet; and all	8628
Mt	7:25	**winds b, and beat upon that**	*4154*
Mt	7:27	**b, and beat upon that house;**	*4154*
Jn	6:18	by reason of a great wind that **b**	*4154*
Ac	27:13	south wind **b** softly, supposing	*5285*

BLIND

Le	22:22	**B**, or broken, or maimed, or	5788
Dt	16:19	a gift doth **b** the eyes of the wise,	5786
Job	29:15	I was eyes to the **b**, and feet was I	5787
Isa	35:5	eyes of the **b** shall be opened	5787
Isa	56:10	His watchmen are **b**: they are all	5787
Isa	59:10	for the wall like the **b**, and we	5787
La	4:14	wandered as **b** men in the streets,	5787
Mal	1:8	the **b** for sacrifice, is it not evil?	5787
Mt	11:5	**The b receive their sight, and the**	*5185*
Mt	12:22	one possessed with a devil, **b**,	*5185*
Mt	15:14	**if the b lead the b,**	*5185*
Mt	21:14	the **b** and the lame came to him	*5185*
Mt	23:16	**Woe unto you, ye b guides,**	*5185*
Mt	23:17	**Ye fools and b: for whether is**	*5185*
Mt	23:19	**Ye fools and b: for whether is**	*5185*
Mt	23:24	**Ye b guides, which strain at a**	*5185*
Mt	23:26	**Thou b Pharisee, cleanse first**	*5185*
Mk	8:22	and they bring a **b** man unto him,	*5155*
Mk	10:51	The **b** man said unto him, Lord,	*5185*
Lk	4:18	**and recovering of sight to the b,**	*5185*
Lk	6:39	**Can the b lead the b?**	*5185*
Lk	7:21	many that were **b** he gave sight	*5185*
Lk	14:21	**maimed, and the halt, and the b**	*5155*
Jn	9:2	his parents, that he was born **b**?	*5185*
Jn	9:8	had seen him that he was **b**,	*5185*
Jn	9:19	your son, who ye say was born **b**?	*5185*
Jn	9:25	whereas I was **b**, now I see.	*5185*
Jn	9:39	**they which see might be made b**	*5185*
Jn	9:40	and said unto him, Are we **b** also	*5185*
Jn	9:41	**If ye were b, ye should have no**	*5185*
Jn	10:21	a devil open the eyes of the **b**?	*5185*
Jn	11:37	opened the eyes of the **b**, have	*5185*
Ac	13:11	shalt be **b**, not seeing the sun	*5185*
Ro	2:19	thou thyself art a guide of the **b**,	*5185*
2Pe	1:9	he that lacketh these things is **b**	*5185*
Rev	3:17	**and poor, and b, and naked:**	*5185*

BLINDED

Jn	12:40	He hath **b** their eyes, and	*5186*
Ro	11:7	obtained it, and the rest were **b**.	*4456*
2Co	3:14	But their minds were **b**: for until	*4456*
2Co	4:4	of this world hath **b** the minds	*5156*
1Jn	2:11	that darkness hath **b** his eyes	*5156*

BLINDETH

Ex	23:8	**b** the wise, and perverteth the	5786

BLINDNESS

Ge	19:11	at the door of the house with **b**,	5575
2Ki	6:18	And he smote them with **b**	5575
Ro	11:25	**b** in part is happened to Israel	*4457*
Eph	4:18	because of the **b** of their heart:	*4457*

BLOOD See also BLOODGUILTINESS.

Ge	4:10	of thy brother's **b** crieth unto me	1818
Ge	9:6	sheddeth man's **b**, … his **b** be shed:	1818
Ge	37:31	goats, and dipped the coat in the **b**;	1818
Ex	7:20	in the river were turned to **b**	1818
Ex	12:7	shall take of the **b**, and strike it	1818
Ex	12:13	when I see the **b**, I will pass over	1818
Ex	12:23	he seeth the **b** upon the lintel,	1818
Ex	22:2	shall no **b** be shed for him.	1818
Ex	24:8	Behold the **b** of the covenant,	1818
Ex	29:20	sprinkle the **b** upon the altar	1818
Le	3:2	sprinkle the **b** upon the altar	1818
Le	4:6	dip his finger in the **b**, and	1818
Le	4:34	shall pour out all the **b** thereof	1818
Le	6:30	whereof any of the **b** is brought	1818
Le	7:26	ye shall eat no manner of **b**,	1818
Le	8:23	and Moses took of the **b** of it, and	1818
Le	16:15	bring his **b** within the vail,	1818
Le	17:4	**b** shall be imputed unto that man;	1818
Le	17:10	that eateth any manner of **b**:	1818
Le	17:11	the life of the flesh is in the **b**:	1818
Le	17:14	the life of all flesh is the **b** thereof:	1818
Le	19:26	shall not eat anything with the **b**:	1818
Le	20:9	his **b** shall be upon him	1818
Le	20:11	their **b** shall be upon them.	1818
Le	20:12	wrought confusion; their **b** shall	1818
Le	20:16	put to death; their **b** shall be	1818
Nu	35:21	the revenger of **b** shall slay	1818
Nu	35:25	of the hand of the revenger of **b**,	1818
Nu	35:27	And the revenger of **b** find him	1818
Dt	19:12	into the hand of the avenger of **b**,	1818
Dt	19:13	of innocent **b** from Israel	1818
Jos	20:3	refuge from the avenger of **b**	1818
1Sa	19:5	wilt thou sin against innocent **b**,	1818
2Sa	3:28	from the **b** of Abner the son	1818
2Sa	4:11	therefore now require his **b**	1818
1Ki	2:32	the Lord shall return his **b**.	1818
1Ki	2:33	Their **b** shall therefore return	1818
1Ki	18:28	lancets, till the **b** gushed out	1818
1Ki	21:19	dogs licked the **b** of Naboth	1818
2Ki	24:4	filled Jerusalem with innocent **b**	1818
1Ch	11:19	shall I drink the **b** of these men	1818
1Ch	22:8	Thou hast shed **b** abundantly,	1818
1Ch	28:3	man of war, and hast shed **b**	1818
2Ch	24:25	conspired against him for the **b**	1818
Job	16:18	O earth, cover not thou my **b**,	1818
Ps	30:9	What profit is their in my **b**, when	1818
Ps	50:13	of bulls, or drink the **b** of goats?	1818
Ps	58:10	his feet in the **b** of the wicked.	1818
Ps	72:14	precious shall their **b** be in his	1818
Ps	79:3	Their **b** have they shed like water	1818
Ps	94:21	and condemn the innocent **b**.	1818
Ps	105:29	turned their waters into **b**, and	1818
Ps	106:38	the land was polluted with **b**.	1818
Pr	1:11	let us lay wait for **b**, let us look	1818

Pr	1:16	evil, and make haste to shed **b**	1818
Pr	1:18	they lay wait for their own **b**;	1818
Pr	6:17	and hands that shed innocent **b**,	1818
Pr	12:6	to lie in wait for **b**: but the mouth	1818
Pr	28:17	violence to the **b** of any person	1818
Pr	30:33	of the nose bringeth forth **b**:	1818
Isa	1:11	I delight not in the **b** of bullocks	1818
Isa	4:4	have purged the **b** of Jerusalem	1818
Isa	9:5	noise, and garments rolled in **b**;	1818
Isa	26:21	the earth also shall disclose her **b**,	1818
Isa	33:15	his ears from hearing of **b**,	1818
Isa	34:3	shall be melted with their **b**	1818
Isa	34:6	sword of the Lord is filled with **b**,	1818
Isa	34:7	their land shall be soaked with **b**,	1818
Isa	59:7	make haste to shed innocent **b**	1818
Jer	7:6	shed not innocent **b** in this place,	1818
Jer	22:17	and for to shed innocent **b**, and	1818
Jer	48:10	keepeth back his sword from **b**	1818
La	4:13	that have shed the **b** of the just	1818
La	4:14	polluted themselves with **b**, so	1818
Eze	3:18	but his **b** will I require at thine	1818
Eze	3:20	but his **b** will I require at thine	1818
Eze	9:9	the land is full of **b**, and the city	1818
Eze	22:4	Thou art become guilty in thy **b**	1818
Eze	33:4	his **b** shall be upon his own head	1818
Eze	33:5	warning; his **b** shall be upon him	1818
Eze	33:6	but his **b** will I require at the	1818
Eze	33:8	but his **b** will I require at thine	1818
Eze	39:19	and drink **b** till ye be drunken, of	1818
Hos	4:2	they break out, and **b** toucheth **b**	1818
Joel	2:31	darkness, and the moon into **b**,	1818
Joel	3:19	they have shed innocent **b** in their	1818
Jnh	1:14	and lay not upon us innocent **b**:	1818
Mic	7:2	they all lie in wait for **b**; they	1818
Hab	2:12	him that buildeth a town with **b**,	1818
Zec	9:11	by the **b** of thy covenant I have	1818
Mt	9:20	diseased with an issue of **b** twelve	*131*
Mt	16:17	**for flesh and b hath not revealed**	*129*
Mt	23:30	**with them in the b of the prophets**	*129*
Mt	23:35	**from the b of righteous Abel**	*129*
Mt	23:35	**unto the b of Zacharias son of**	*129*
Mt	26:28	**For this is my b of the new**	*129*
Mt	27:4	**I have betrayed the innocent b**	*129*
Mt	27:6	because it is the price of **b**	*129*
Mt	27:8	was called, The field of **b**, unto this	*129*
Mt	27:24	I am innocent of the **b** of this just	*129*
Mt	27:25	His **b** be on us, and on our children	*129*
Mk	5:25	which had an issue of **b** twelve	*129*
Mk	5:29	the fountain of her **b** was dried up;	*129*
Mk	14:24	**This is my b of the new testament,**	*129*
Lk	8:43	having an issue of **b** twelve years,	*129*
Lk	11:51	**From the b of Abel**	*129*
Lk	13:1	whose **b** Pilate had mingled with	*129*
Lk	22:20	**new testament in my b, which is**	*129*
Lk	22:44	great drops of **b** falling down to	*129*
Jn	1:13	Which were born, not of **b**, nor of	*129*
Jn	6:53	**Son of man, and drink his b, he**	*129*
Jn	6:54	**my flesh, and drinketh my b,**	*129*
Jn	6:55	**is meat indeed, and my b is drink**	*129*
Jn	6:56	**my flesh, and drinketh my b,**	*129*
Jn	19:34	forthwith came there out **b** and	*129*
Ac	1:19	that is to say, The field of **b**.	*129*
Ac	2:20	into darkness, and the moon into **b**,	*129*
Ac	5:28	intend to bring this man's **b** upon	*129*
Ac	18:6	Your **b** be upon your own heads; I	*129*
Ac	20:26	that I am pure from the **b** of all	*129*
Ac	22:20	the **b** of thy martyr Stephen was	*129*
Ro	3:15	Their feet are swift to shed **b**:	*129*
Ro	3:25	through faith in his **b**, to declare	*129*
Ro	5:9	then, being now justified by his **b**,	*129*
1Co	10:16	the communion of the **b** of Christ?	*129*
1Co	11:25	**the new testament in my b:**	*129*
1Co	11:27	of the body and **b** of the Lord	*129*
Eph	1:7	have redemption through his **b**, the	*129*
Eph	2:13	are made nigh by the **b** of Christ	*129*
Eph	6:12	wrestle not against flesh and **b**	*129*
Col	1:14	redemption through his **b**, even	*129*
Col	1:20	made peace through the **b** of his	*129*
Heb	2:14	partakers of flesh and **b**, he also	*129*
Heb	9:7	once every year, not without **b**,	*129*
Heb	9:12	calves, but by his own **b** he	*129*
Heb	9:13	For if the **b** of bulls and of goats,	*129*
Heb	9:18	testament was dedicated without **b**	*129*
Heb	9:20	Saying, this is the **b** of the	*129*
Heb	9:21	sprinkled with **b** both the	*129*
Heb	9:22	are by the law purged with **b**; and	*129*
Heb	9:22	without shedding of **b** is no	*130*
Heb	10:4	that the **b** of bulls and of goats	*129*
Heb	10:19	to enter into the holiest by the **b** of	*129*
Heb	10:29	and hath counted the **b** of the	*129*
Heb	11:28	passover, and the sprinkling of **b**,	*129*
Heb	12:4	not yet resisted unto **b**, striving	*129*
Heb	12:24	to the **b** of sprinkling, that	*129*
Heb	13:20	through the **b** of the everlasting	*129*
1Pe	1:2	sprinkling of the **b** of Jesus Christ:	*129*
1Pe	1:19	with the precious **b** of Christ, as of	*129*
1Jn	1:7	the **b** of Jesus Christ his Son	*129*
Rev	1:5	us from our sins in his own **b**,	*129*
Rev	5:9	redeemed us to God by thy **b** out of	*129*
Rev	6:10	thou not judge and avenge our **b**	*129*
Rev	6:12	of hair, and the moon became as **b**;	*129*
Rev	7:14	them white in the **b** of the Lamb	*129*
Rev	8:7	hail and fire mingled with **b**, and	*129*
Rev	8:8	third part of the sea became **b**	*129*
Rev	11:6	over waters to turn them to **b**, and	*129*
Rev	12:11	by the **b** of the Lamb, and by the	*129*
Rev	14:20	the city, and **b** came out of the	*129*
Rev	16:3	it became as the **b** of a dead man:	*129*
Rev	16:6	shed the **b** of saints and prophets,	*129*
Rev	17:6	drunken with the **b** of the saints	*129*
Rev	18:24	And in her was found the **b** of	*129*
Rev	19:2	avenged the **b** of his servants at	*129*
Rev	19:13	clothed with a vesture dipped in **b**	*129*

BLOODGUILTINESS

Ps	51:14	Deliver me from **b**, O God	1818

BLOODY

Ex	4:25	Surely a **b** husband art thou to	1818
2Sa	16:8	because thou art a **b** man	1818
2Sa	21:1	for Saul, and for his **b** house,	1818
Na	3:1	Woe to the **b** city! it is all full	1818

BLOSSOM

Nu	17:5	whom I shall choose, shall **b**	6524
Hab	3:17	Although the fig tree shall not **b**,	6524

BLOT

Ex	32:32	**b** me, I pray thee, out of thy book	4229
Nu	5:23	and he shall **b** them out with the	4229
Dt	9:14	and **b** out their name from under	4229
Dt	25:19	**b** out the remembrance of Amalek	4229

Dt 29:20 the Lord shall **b** out his name 4229
2Ki 14:27 he would **b** out the name of Israel 4229
Ps 51:9 sins, and **b** out all mine iniquities 4229
Rev 3:5 **I will not b out his name out of** *1813*

BLOTTED
Ne 4:5 let not their sin be **b** out from 4229
Ps 69:28 Let them be **b** out of the book....4229
Ps 109:13 following let their name be **b** out....4229
Ac 3:19 your sins may be **b** out, when *1813*

BLOTTETH
Isa 43:25 he that **b** out thy transgressions....4229

BLOW
Ex 15:10 Thou didst **b** with thy wind, the....5398
Nu 10:10 ye shall **b** with the trumpets over 8628
Jgs 7:18 When I **b** with the trumpet, I 8628
Ps 39:10 I am consumed by the **b** of thine 8409
Ps 147:18 he causeth his wind to **b**, and 5380
SS 4:16 **b** upon my garden, that the....6315
Jer 4:5 **B** ye the trumpet in the land:....8628
Eze 21:31 I will **b** against thee in the fire 6315
Joel 2:1 **B** ye the trumpet in Zion, ...8628
Joel 2:15 **B** the trumpet in Zion, sanctify 8628
Lk 12:55 **when ye see the south wind b,**....*4154*
Rev 7:1 wind should not **b** on the earth,....*4164*

BLOWETH
Isa 40:7 the spirit of the Lord **b** upon it:....5380
Jn 3:8 **The wind b where it listeth,**....*4154*

BLOWING
Nu 29:1 a day of **b** the trumpets unto you,....8643
Jos 6:9 on and **b** with the trumpets,....8628

BLOWN
Eze 7:14 They have **b** the trumpet, even 8628
Am 3:6 Shall a trumpet be **b** in the city,....8628

BLUE
Ex 26:31 shalt make a vail of **b**, and purple, ...8504
Ex 26:36 for the door of the tent, of **b**,....8504
Ex 28:5 shall take gold, and **b**, and purple,....8504
Ex 28:15 thou shalt make it; of gold, of **b**,....8504
Ex 36:35 he made a vail of **b**, and purple, ...8504
Ex 36:37 for the tabernacle door of **b**,....8504
Ex 38:18 the court was needlework, of **b**,....8504
Ex 39:1 of the **b**, and purple, and scarlet, ...8504
Ex 39:2 the ephod of gold, **b**, and purple, ...8504
Ex 39:3 it into wires, to work it in the **b**,....8504
Ex 39:5 thereof; of gold, **b**, and purple, ...8504
Ex 39:8 of gold, **b**, and purple, and scarlet, ...8504
Ex 39:21 the ephod with a lace of **b**, that it....8504
Ex 39:22 ephod of woven work, all of **b**, ...8504
Ex 39:24 of the robe pomegranates of **b**....8504
Ex 39:29 twined linen, and **b**, and purple, ...8504
Ex 39:31 they tied unto it a lace of **b**, to 8504
Nu 4:6 spread over it a cloth wholly of **b**, ...8504
Nu 4:7 they shall spread a cloth of **b**, ...8504
Nu 4:9 they shall take a cloth of **b**, and 8504
Nu 4:11 spread a cloth of **b**, and cover it....8504
Nu 4:12 and put them in a cloth of **b**,....8504
2Ch 2:7 in purple, and crimson, and **b**, ...8504
Est 8:15 the king in royal apparel of **b**....8504
Eze 23:6 were clothed with **b**, captains....8504
Eze 27:7 **b** and purple from the isles 8504
Eze 27:24 in **b** clothes, and broidered work,....8504

BLUSH
Ezr 9:6 I am ashamed and **b** to lift 3637
Jer 6:15 ashamed, neither could they **b**....3637
Jer 8:12 neither could they **b**: therefore 3637

BOAST
2Ch 25:19 thine heart lifteth thee up to **b**....3513
Ps 44:8 In God we **b** all the day long,....1984
Ps 94:4 workers of iniquity **b** themselves?....559
Pr 27:1 **B** not thyself of to morrow; for 1984
Isa 10:15 Shall the ax **b** itself against him 6286
Ro 11:18 **B** not against the branches. But....*2620*
Eph 2:9 not of works, lest any man should **b** *2744*

BOASTERS
Ro 1:30 despiteful, proud, **b**, inventors....*213*
2Ti 3:2 covetous, **b**, proud, blasphemers,....*213*

BOASTEST
Ps 52:1 Why **b** thou thyself in mischief,....1984

BOASTETH
Ps 10:3 wicked **b** of his heart's desire, ...1984
Pr 20:14 he is gone his way, then he **b**....1984
Pr 25:14 Whoso **b** himself of a false gift 1984
Jas 3:5 little member, and **b** great things....*3166*

BOASTING
Ro 3:27 Where is **b** then? It is excluded *2746*
2Co 10:15 Not **b** of things without our....*2744*

BOASTINGS
Jas 4:16 now ye rejoice in your **b**: all *212*

BODIES
1Sa 31:12 body of Saul and the **b** of his....1472
2Ch 20:25 riches with the dead **b**, and 6297
Ne 9:37 they have dominion over our **b**, ...1472
Jer 31:40 the whole valley of the dead **b**, ...6297
Eze 1:11 another, and two covered their **b**....1472
Eze 1:23 covered on that side, their **b**....1472
Da 3:27 upon whose **b** the fire had no....1655
Da 3:28 and yielded their **b**, that they....1655
Am 8:3 there shall be many dead **b** in 6297
Mt 27:52 and many **b** of the saints which....*4983*
Jn 19:31 the **b** should not remain upon....*4983*
Ro 1:24 to dishonour their own **b** between *4983*
Ro 8:11 shall also quicken your mortal **b**....*4983*
Ro 12:1 ye present your **b** a living sacrifice....*4983*
1Co 6:15 your **b** are the members of Christ *4983*
1Co 15:40 also celestial **b**, and **b** terrestrial:....*4983*
Eph 5:28 to love their wives as their own **b** *4983*
Heb 10:22 and our **b** washed with pure *4983*
Heb 13:11 For the **b** of those beasts, whose *4983*
Rev 11:8 And their dead **b** shall lie in the....*4430*
Rev 11:9 shall see their dead **b** three days....*4430*

BODILY
Lk 3:22 Holy Ghost descended in a **b** *4984*
2Co 10:10 but his **b** presence is weak, and....*4983*
Col 2:9 all the fulness of the Godhead **b** *4985*
1Ti 4:8 For **b** exercise profiteth little: *4984*

BODY See also BUSYBODY; SOMEBODY.
Le 21:11 any dead **b**, nor defile himself....5315
Nu 9:7 we are denied by the dead **b** of a 5315
Nu 9:10 unclean by reason of a dead **b**, ...5315
Nu 19:13 Whosoever toucheth the dead **b** of 5315
Dt 21:23 His **b** shall not remain all....5038

1Sa 31:10 they fastened his **b** to the wall of 1472
1Sa 31:12 took the **b** of Saul and the bodies 1472
1Ch 10:12 took away the **b** of Saul, and the 1480
Job 19:26 worms destroy this **b**, yet in
Pr 5:11 when thy flesh and thy **b** are 7607
Isa 26:19 with my dead **b** shall they arise 5038
Jer 26:23 and cast his dead **b** into the 5038
Jer 36:30 and his dead **b** shall be cast out 5038
Eze 10:12 And their whole **b**, and their 1320
Da 5:21 his **b** was wet with the dew of 1655
Da 7:11 and his **b**: destroyed, and given to 1655
Da 10:6 His **b** also was like the beryl, 1472
Mic 6:7 the fruit of my **b** for the sin of 990
Hag 2:13 unclean by a dead **b** touch any 5315
Mt 5:29 not that thy whole **b** should be *4983*
Mt 6:22 The light of the **b** is the eye: if *4983*
Mt 6:25 nor yet for your **b**, what ye shall *4983*
Mt 10:28 able to destroy both soul and **b** in *4983*
Mt 26:12 poured this ointment on my **b**, *4983*
Mt 26:26 and said, Take, eat; this is my **b** *4983*
Mt 27:58 begged the **b** of Jesus. Then *4983*
Mk 14:8 aforehand to anoint my **b** to the *4983*
Mk 14:22 and said, Take, eat: this is my **b** *4983*
Mk 14:51 cloth cast about his naked **b**; *4983*
Mk 15:43 unto Pilate, and craved the **b** of *4983*
Lk 11:34 The light of the **b** is the eye: *4983*
Lk 11:36 If thy whole **b** therefore be full of *4983*
Lk 12:4 not afraid of them that kill the **b**, *4983*
Lk 12:22 neither for the **b**, what ye shall *4983*
Lk 17:37 Wheresoever the **b** is, thither will *4983*
Lk 22:19 This is my **b** which is given for *4983*
Lk 24:23 when they found not his **b**, they *4983*
Jn 2:21 he spake of the temple of his **b** *4983*
Jn 19:38 came therefore, and took the **b** *4983*
Jn 19:40 Then took they the **b** of Jesus, *4983*
Jn 20:12 the feet, where the **b** of Jesus had *4983*
Ro 4:19 he considered not his own **b** now *4983*
Ro 6:6 the **b** of sin might be destroyed, *4983*
Ro 6:12 reign in your mortal **b**, that ye *4983*
Ro 7:4 dead to the law by the **b** of Christ; *4983*
Ro 7:24 shall deliver me from the **b** of this *4983*
Ro 8:13 do mortify the deeds of the **b**, ye *4983*
Ro 8:23 to wit, the redemption of our **b** *4983*
Ro 12:5 being many, are one **b** in Christ *4983*
1Co 5:3 For I verily, as absent in **b**, but *4983*
1Co 6:13 Now the **b** is not for fornication, *4983*
1Co 6:16 is joined to an harlot is one **b**? *4983*
1Co 6:18 sinneth against his own **b** *4983*
1Co 6:19 your **b** is the temple of the Holy *4983*
1Co 7:4 wife hath not power of her own **b**, *4983*
1Co 7:4 hath not power of his own **b**, *4983*
1Co 7:34 she may be holy both in **b** and in *4983*
1Co 9:27 But I keep under my **b**, and bring *4983*
1Co 10:16 is it not the communion of the **b** *4983*
1Co 11:24 Take, eat: this is my **b**, which is *4983*
1Co 11:27 shall be guilty of the **b** and blood *4983*
1Co 12:12 For as the **b** is one, and hath many *4983*
1Co 12:13 are we all baptized into one **b**, *4983*
1Co 12:15 I am not of the **b**; is it *4983*
1Co 12:19 all one member, where were the **b**? *4983*
1Co 12:20 many members, yet but one **b** *4983*
1Co 12:27 Now ye are the **b** of Christ, and *4983*
1Co 13:3 though I give my **b** to be burned, *4983*
1Co 15:38 But God giveth it a **b** as it hath *4983*
1Co 15:44 it is raised a spiritual **b** *4983*
2Co 4:10 bearing about in the **b** the dying *4983*
2Co 5:8 rather to be absent from the **b** *4983*
2Co 5:10 receive the things done in his **b**, *4983*
2Co 12:3 in the **b**, or out of the **b**, I cannot *4983*
Gal 6:17 I bear in my **b** the marks of the *4983*
Eph 1:23 Which is his **b**, the fulness of him *4983*
Eph 3:6 fellow heirs, and of the same **b**, *4954*
Eph 4:4 There is one **b**, and one Spirit *4983*
Eph 4:12 ministry, for the edifying of the **b** *4983*
Eph 4:16 From whom the whole **b** fitly *4983*
Eph 5:23 and he is the saviour of the **b** *4983*
Eph 5:30 For we are members of his **b**, of *4983*
Php 1:20 Christ shall be magnified in my **b**, *4983*
Php 3:21 Who shall change our vile **b**, that *4983*
Col 1:18 And he is the head of the **b**, the *4983*
Col 2:11 putting off the **b** of the sins of the *4983*
Col 2:17 of things to come; but the **b** is of *4983*
Col 2:23 humility, and neglecting of the **b**; *4983*
Col 3:15 which also ye are called in one **b**; *4983*
1Th 5:23 and **b** be preserved blameless *4983*
Heb 10:5 but a **b** hast thou prepared me: *4983*
Heb 10:10 through the offering of the **b** of *4983*
Heb 13:3 as being yourselves also in the **b** *4983*
Jas 2:16 things which are needful to the **b**; *4983*
Jas 3:2 able also to bridle the whole **b** *4983*
Jas 3:6 that it defileth the whole **b**, and *4983*
1Pe 2:24 bare our sins in his own **b** on the *4983*
Jude 9 he disputed about the **b** of Moses, *4983*

BOIL
Ex 9:11 because of the boils; for the **b** 7822
Job 41:31 He maketh the deep to **b** like a 7570
Isa 64:2 the fire causeth the waters to **b** 1158

BOILED
2Ki 6:29 So we **b** my son, and did eat him: 1310
Job 30:27 My bowels **b**, and rested not: 7570

BOILS
Ex 9:11 before Moses because of the **b**; 7822
Job 2:7 smote Job with sore **b** from the 7822

BOISTEROUS
Mt 14:30 when he saw the wind **b**, he was *2478*

BOLD
Pr 28:1 but the righteous are **b** as a lion 982
Ro 10:20 Esaias is very **b**, and saith, I was *662*
2Co 10:1 being absent am **b** toward you: *2292*
Php 1:14 much more **b** to speak the word *5111*

BOLDLY
Mk 15:43 and went in **b** unto Pilate, and *5111*
Jn 7:26 But, lo, he speaketh **b**, and they *3954*
Ac 9:27 he had preached **b** at Damascus *3955*
Eph 6:20 may speak **b**, as I ought to speak *3955*
Heb 4:16 Let us therefore come **b** unto *3954*
Heb 13:6 So that we may **b** say, The Lord *2292*

BOLDNESS
Ecc 8:1 the **b** of his face shall be changed 5797
Ac 4:13 they saw the **b** of Peter and John, *3954*
2Co 7:4 Great is my **b** of speech toward *3954*
Php 1:20 but that with all **b**, as always *3954*

BOND See also BONDWOMAN; BOUND.
Nu 30:2 an oath to bind his soul with a **b**; 632
Nu 30:3 bind herself by a **b**, being in her 632
Eze 20:37 I will bring you into the **b** of the 4562

Lk	13:16	**be loosed from this b on the**	*1199*
Ac	8:23	bitterness, and in the **b** of	*4886*
Eph	4:3	of the Spirit in the **b** of peace	*4886*
Col	3:14	which is the **b** of perfectness	*4886*
Rev	13:16	rich and poor, free and **b**, to	*1401*

BONDAGE

Ex	1:14	their lives bitter with hard **b**,	5656
Ex	20:2	of Egypt, out of the house of **b**	5650
Dt	6:12	of Egypt, from the house of **b**	5650
Dt	13:5	you out of the house of **b**,	5650
Ezr	9:9	hath not forsaken us in our **b**,	5659
Jn	8:33	and were never in **b** to any man:	*1398*
Ro	8:15	received the spirit of **b** again to	*1397*
Gal	2:4	that they might bring us into **b**:	*2615*
Gal	5:1	again with the yoke of **b**	*1397*
Heb	2:15	all their lifetime subject to **b**	*1397*
2Pe	2:19	of the same is he brought in **b**	*1402*

BONDMEN

Dt	6:21	We were Pharaoh's **b** in Egypt;	5650
1Ki	9:22	Israel did Solomon make no **b**:	5650
2Ki	4:1	unto him my two sons to be **b**	5650

BONDS

Ps	116:16	handmaid: thou hast loosed my **b**	4147
Na	1:13	and will burst thy **b** in sunder	4147
Ac	26:31	nothing worthy of death or of **b**	*1199*
Eph	6:20	which I am an ambassador in **b**:	*254*
Php	1:16	to add affliction to my **b**:	*1199*
Col	4:3	for which I am also in **b**:	*1210*
2Ti	2:9	as an evil doer, even unto **b**;	*1199*
Phm	10	whom I have begotten in my **b**	*1199*
Heb	10:34	had compassion of me in my **b**,	*1199*

BONDWOMAN

Ge	21:10	Cast out this **b** and her son: for	519
Ge	21:12	because of thy **b**; in all that Sarah	519
Gal	4:30	Cast out the **b** and her son:	*3814*

BONDWOMEN

Est	7:4	bondmen and **b**, I had held my	8198

BONE See JAWBONE.

Ge	2:23	This is now **b** of my bones, and	6106
Nu	9:12	nor break any **b** of it:	6106
Job	2:5	touch his **b** and his flesh, and he	6106
Job	19:20	My **b** cleaveth to my skin and to	6106
Pr	25:15	a soft tongue breaketh the **b**	1634
Eze	37:7	bones came together, **b** to his **b**	6106
Jn	19:36	A **b** of him shall not be broken	*3747*

BONES

Ge	2:23	bone of my **b**, and flesh of my	6106
Ex	13:19	took the **b** of Joseph with him:	6106
2Sa	21:12	went and took the **b** of Saul	6106
2Ki	13:21	and touched the **b** of Elisha,	6106
2Ch	34:5	**b** of the priests upon their altars	6106
Job	4:14	which made all my **b** to shake	6106
Job	30:17	My **b** are pierced in me in the	6106
Job	40:18	his **b** are like bars of iron.	1634
Ps	22:14	all my **b** are out of joint:	6106
Ps	34:20	He keepeth all his **b**: not one of	6106
Ps	38:3	neither is there any rest in my **b**	6106
Ps	51:8	the **b** which thou hast broken	6106
Ps	102:5	my **b** cleave to my skin	6106
Pr	12:4	is as rottenness in his **b**	6106
Pr	14:30	but envy the rottenness of the **b**	6106
Pr	16:24	to the soul and health to the **b**	6106
Pr	17:23	a broken spirit drieth the **b**	1634
Ecc	11:5	how the **b** do grow in the womb	6106
Jer	23:9	all my **b** shake; I am like a	6106
La	1:13	he sent fire into my **b**, and it	6106
La	4:8	their skin cleaveth to their **b**;	6106
Eze	37:1	the valley which was full of **b**,	6106
Eze	37:3	Son of man, can these **b** live?	6106
Eze	37:4	O ye dry **b**, hear the word	6106
Eze	37:11	these **b** are the whole house of	6106
Da	6:24	and brake all their **b** in pieces or	1635
Am	6:10	to bring out the **b** out of the house,	6106
Mt	23:27	**full of dead men's b, and of all**	*3747*
Lk	24:39	**hath not flesh and b, as ye see**	*3747*
Eph	5:30	body, of his flesh, and of his **b**	*3747*
Heb	11:22	commandment concerning his **b**	*3747*

BOOK

Ge	5:1	This is the **b** of the generations of	5612
Ex	24:7	he took the **b** of the covenant, and	5612
Ex	32:33	me, him will I blot out of my **b**	5612
Dt	28:58	this law that are written in this **b**,	5612
Dt	31:26	Take this **b** of the law and put it	5612
Jos	1:8	This **b** of the law shall not depart	5612
Jos	23:6	all that is written in the **b** of the	5612
2Ki	14:6	which is written in the **b** of the law	5612
2Ki	22:8	I have found the **b** of the law in	5612
2Ki	22:11	king had heard the words of the **b**	5612
2Ki	23:2	all the words of the **b** of the	5612
2Ki	23:21	written in the **b** of this covenant	5612
Ezr	4:15	search may be made in the **b** of	5609
Ne	8:3	people were attentive unto the **b**	5612
Ne	8:8	they read in the **b** in the law of	5612
Est	10:2	in the **b** of the chronicles of the	5612
Job	19:23	oh that they were printed in a **b**!	5612
Ps	40:7	in the volume of the **b** it is	5612
Ps	56:8	thy bottle: are they not in thy **b**?	5612
Ps	69:28	Let them be blotted out of the **b** of	5612
Ps	139:16	in thy **b** all my members were	5612
Isa	29:11	the words of a **b** that is sealed,	5612
Jer	36:2	Take thee a roll of a **b**, and write	5612
Jer	36:10	Then read Baruch in the **b** the	5612
Da	12:1	shall be found written in the **b**	5612
Da	12:4	shut up the words, and seal the **b**	5612
Lk	4:20	he closed the **b**, and he gave it	*975*
Jn	20:30	which are not written in this **b**:	*975*
Php	4:3	whose names are in the **b** of life	*976*
Heb	10:7	(in the volume of the **b** it is	*975*
Rev	1:11	**What thou seest, write in a b, and**	*975*
Rev	3:5	**blot out his name out of the b of**	*976*
Rev	5:2	Who is worthy to open the **b**, and	*975*
Rev	5:4	worthy to open and to read the **b**,	*975*
Rev	5:5	hath prevailed to open the **b**, and	*975*
Rev	13:8	not written in the **b** of life of the	*976*
Rev	17:8	names were not written in the **b**	*976*
Rev	20:12	which is the **b** of life:	*976*
Rev	20:15	was not found written in the **b**	*976*
Rev	21:27	written in the Lamb's **b** of life	*975*
Rev	22:7	sayings of the prophecy of this **b**	*975*
Rev	22:10	sayings of the prophecy of this **b**:	*975*
Rev	22:18	plagues that are written in this **b**:	*975*
Rev	22:19	take away his part out of the **b** of	*976*

BOOKS

Ecc	12:12	making many **b** there is no end;	5612
Da	7:10	judgment was set, and the **b**	5609

Da	9:2	I Daniel understood by **b** the	5612
Jn	21:25	could not contain the **b** that	*975*
Ac	19:19	brought their **b** together, and	*976*
Rev	20:12	the **b** were opened: and another	*975*

BOOTH

Jnh	4:5	and there made him a **b**, and sat	5521

BOOTHS

Le	23:42	Ye shall dwell in **b** seven days;	5521
Ne	8:14	children of Israel should dwell in **b**	5521

BOOTY

Nu	31:32	the **b**, being the rest of the prey	4455
Zep	1:13	their goods shall become a **b**,	4933

BORDER

Ge	10:19	the **b** of the Canaanites was	1366
Ex	19:12	or touch the **b** of it: whosoever	7097
Ex	25:25	a golden crown to the **b** thereof	4526
Nu	20:21	passage through his **b**:	1366
Nu	21:23	Israel to pass through his **b**:	1366
Nu	35:26	the **b** of the city of his refuge,	1366
Dt	12:20	God shall enlarge thy **b**, as he	1366
Jos	15:1	to the **b** of Edom the wilderness	1366
Jos	22:25	the Lord hath made Jordan a **b**	1366
1Sa	10:2	in the **b** of Benjamin at Zelzah;	1366
2Sa	8:3	to recover his **b** at the river	3027
1Ki	4:21	and unto the **b** of Egypt:	1366
2Ch	9:26	Philistines, and to the **b** of Egypt	1366
Pr	15:25	will establish the **b** of the widow	1366
Jer	31:17	shall come again to their own **b**	1366
Jer	50:26	from the utmost **b**, open her	7093
Eze	11:10	will judge you in the **b** of Israel;	1366
Eze	47:13	This shall be the **b**, whereby ye	1366
Joel	3:6	remove them far from their **b**	1366
Am	1:13	that they might enlarge their **b**:	1366
Ob	7	have brought thee even to the **b**:	1366
Mal	1:4	The **b** of wickedness, and, The	1366
Mal	1:5	magnified from the **b** of Israel	1366
Lk	8:44	touched the **b** of his garment;	*2899*

BORDERS

Ex	8:2	I will smite all thy **b** with frogs:	1366
Ex	16:35	unto the **b** of the land of Canaan.	7097
Ex	34:24	before thee, and enlarge thy **b**:	1366
Nu	20:17	until we have passed thy **b**	1366
Nu	21:22	until we be passed thy **b**	1366
Nu	35:27	him without the **b** of the city of	1366
Jos	13:2	all the **b** of the Philistines,	1552
Jos	22:11	the **b** of Jordan, at the passage	1552
1Ki	7:36	**b** thereof, he graved cherubim,	4526
2Ki	16:17	Ahaz cut off the **b** of the bases,	4526
Ps	74:17	hast set all the **b** of the earth:	1367
Isa	60:18	nor destruction within thy **b**;	1366
Jer	15:13	all thy sins, even in all thy **b**	1366
Eze	27:4	Thy **b** are in the midst of the seas,	1366
Mt	23:5	**enlarge the b of their garments,**	*2899*

BORE See also **BARE.**

Ex	21:6	master shall **b** his ear through	7527
Job	41:2	**b** his jaw through with a thorn?	5344

BORED

2Ki	12:9	and **b** a hole in the lid of it,	5344

BORN See also **FIRSTBORN; FORBORN; NEWBORN.**

Ge	6:1	and daughters were **b** unto them,	3205
Ge	10:1	them were sons **b** after the flood.	3205
Ge	15:3	one **b** in my house is mine heir	1121
Ge	17:17	Shall a child be **b** unto him that	3205
Ge	21:5	his son Isaac was **b** unto him.	3205
Ge	30:20	I have **b** him six sons: and she	3205
Ge	30:25	Rachel had **b** Joseph, that Jacob	3205
Ex	1:22	Every son that is **b** ye shall cast	3209
Ex	12:19	be a stranger, or **b** in the land.	249
Ex	12:48	be as one that is **b** in the land:	249
Le	19:34	unto you as one **b** among you	249
Nu	15:30	be **b** in the land, or a stranger,	249
Dt	21:15	and they have **b** him children,	3205
Ru	4:15	than seven sons, hath **b** him	3205
2Sa	12:14	the child also that is **b** unto thee	3209
2Sa	21:20	and he also was **b** to the giant	3205
2Sa	21:22	four were **b** to the giant in Gath,	3205
1Ch	22:9	a son shall be **b** to thee, who shall	3205
Ezr	10:3	such as are **b** of them, according	3205
Job	3:3	the day perish wherein I was **b**,	3205
Job	5:7	man is **b** unto trouble, as the	3205
Job	14:1	Man that is **b** of a woman is of	3205
Job	15:7	Art thou the first man that was **b**?	3205
Job	15:14	he which is **b** of a woman, that he	3205
Job	25:4	he be clean that is **b** of a woman?	3205
Ps	22:31	a people that shall be **b**, that he	3205
Ps	58:3	go astray as soon as they be **b**,	990
Pr	17:17	and a brother is **b** for adversity	3205
Ecc	3:2	A time to be **b**, and a time to die;	3205
Ecc	4:14	is **b** in his kingdom becometh	3205
Isa	9:6	unto us a child is **b**, unto us a son	3205
Jer	20:14	be the day wherein I was **b**:	3205
Jer	20:15	A man child is **b** unto thee;	3205
Jer	22:26	country where ye were not **b**;	3205
Hos	2:3	her as in the day that she was **b**	3205
Mt	1:16	of whom was **b** Jesus, who is	*1080*
Mt	2:2	is he that is **b** King of the Jews?	*5088*
Mt	2:4	of them where Christ should be **b**	*1080*
Mt	11:11	**Among them that are b of women**	*1084*
Mt	26:24	**that man if he had not been b**	*1080*
Mk	14:21	**that man if he had never been b**	*1080*
Lk	1:35	that holy thing which shall be **b**	*1080*
Lk	2:11	For unto you is **b** this day in the	*5088*
Lk	7:28	**Among those that are b of women**	*1084*
Jn	1:13	Which were **b**, not of blood, nor	*1080*
Jn	3:3	**Except a man be b again, he**	*1080*
Jn	3:4	can a man be **b** when he is old?	*1080*
Jn	3:4	into his mother's womb, and be **b**?	*1080*
Jn	3:5	**Except a man be b of water and**	*1080*
Jn	3:6	**which is b of the flesh is flesh;**	*1080*
Jn	3:6	**which is b of the Spirit is spirit**	*1080*
Jn	3:7	**unto thee, Ye must be b again**	*1080*
Jn	3:8	**every one that is b of the Spirit**	*1080*
Jn	8:41	We be not **b** of fornication; we	*1080*
Jn	9:2	or his parents, that he was **b** blind?	*1080*
Jn	9:20	our son, and that he was **b** blind:	*1080*
Jn	9:32	the eyes of one that was **b** blind	*1080*
Jn	9:34	Thou wast altogether **b** in sins,	*1080*
Jn	16:21	**joy that a man is b into the world.**	*1080*
Jn	18:37	**To this end was I b, and for this**	*1080*
Ac	2:8	own tongue, wherein we were **b**?	*1080*
Ro	9:11	(For the children being not yet **b**	*1080*
1Co	15:8	also, as of one **b** out of due time	*1626*
Gal	4:29	he that was **b** after the flesh	*1080*
Heb	11:23	By faith Moses, when he was **b**,	*1080*
1Pe	1:23	**b** again not of corruptible seed,	*313*
1Jn	2:29	doeth righteousness is **b** of him	*1080*

1Jn	3:9	Whosoever is **b** of God doth not	*1080*
1Jn	4:7	every one that loveth is **b** of God,	*1080*
1Jn	5:1	Jesus is the Christ is **b** of God:	*1080*
1Jn	5:4	For whatsoever is **b** of God	*1080*
1Jn	5:18	whosoever is **b** of God sinneth not;	*1080*
Rev	12:4	her child as soon as it was **b**	*5088*

BORNE

Ex	25:14	the ark may be **b** with them.	5375
Ex	25:28	the table may be **b** with them.	5375
Job	34:31	I have **b** chastisement, I will not	5375
Ps	55:12	then I could have **b** it: neither	5375
Ps	69:7	I have **b** reproach; shame hath	5375
Isa	53:4	Surely he hath **b** our griefs,	5375
Jer	10:5	they must needs be **b**, because	5375
Jer	15:10	thou hast **b** me a man of strife	3205
La	5:7	and we have **b** their iniquities.	5445
Eze	32:25	yet have they **b** their shame	5375
Eze	36:6	ye have **b** the shame of the	5375
Am	5:26	**b** the tabernacle of your Moloch	5375
Mt	20:12	**which have b the burden and heat**	*941*
Mt	23:4	**burdens and grievous to be b,**	*1418*
Lk	11:46	**with burdens grievous to be b,**	*1418*
Jn	20:15	Sir, if thou have **b** him hence,	*941*
Rev	2:3	**And hast b, and hast patience,**	*941*

BORROW

Ex	11:2	every man **b** of his neighbour,	7592
Ex	22:14	**b** ought of his neighbour,	7592
Dt	28:12	nations, and thou shalt not **b**	3867
2Ki	4:3	**b** thee vessels abroad of all thy	7592
2Ki	4:3	even empty vessels; **b** not a few	
Mt	5:42	**from him that would b of thee**	*1155*

BORROWED

Ex	12:35	they **b** of the Egyptians jewels	7592
2Ki	6:5	Alas, master! for it was **b**	7592
Ne	5:4	We have **b** money for the king's	3867

BORROWER

Pr	22:7	the **b** is servant to the lender	3867
Isa	24:2	so with the **b**; as with the taker	3867

BORROWETH

Ps	37:21	The wicked **b**, and payeth not	3867

BOSOM

Ge	16:5	I have given my maid into thy **b**;	2436
Ex	4:7	Put thine hand into thy **b** again	2436
2Sa	12:8	thy master's wives into thy **b**,	2436
1Ki	3:20	and laid her dead child in my **b**	2436
Pr	5:20	and embrace the **b** of a stranger?	2436
Pr	6:27	Can a man take fire in his **b**, and	2436
Pr	17:23	man taketh a gift out of the **b** to	2436
Pr	19:24	man hideth his hand in his **b**,	6747
Pr	21:14	a reward in the **b** strong wrath.	2436
Pr	26:15	slothful hideth his hand in his **b**;	6747
Ecc	7:9	anger resteth in the **b** of fools.	2436
Isa	40:11	and carry them in his **b**, and shall	2436
Mic	7:5	from her that lieth in thy **b**	2436
Lk	6:38	**shall men give into your b**	*2859*
Lk	16:22	**by the angels into Abraham's b:**	*2859*
Jn	1:18	which is in the **b** of the Father,	*2859*
Jn	13:23	leaning on Jesus' **b** one of his	*2859*

BOTTLE

Ge	21:14	took bread, and a **b** of water,	2573
Ge	21:19	filled the **b** with water, and gave	2573
1Sa	10:3	another carrying a **b** of wine:	5035
1Sa	16:20	and a **b** of wine, and a kid, and	4997
Ps	56:8	put thou my tears into thy **b**:	4997
Jer	13:12	Every **b** shall be filled with wine:	5035
Jer	19:10	Then shalt thou break the **b** in	1228

BOTTLES

Jos	9:13	these **b** of wine, which we filled,	4997
Job	32:19	it is ready to burst like new **b**	178
Job	38:37	or who can stay the **b** of heaven,	5035
Hos	7:5	have made him sick with **b** of	2573
Mt	9:17	**put new wine into old b:**	*779*
Mk	2:22	**new wine doth burst the b,**	*779*
Lk	5:38	**new wine must be put into new b;**	*779*

BOTTOM

Ex	15:5	they sank into the **b** as a stone	4688
Le	4:18	blood at the **b** of the altar of the	3247
Job	36:30	and covereth the **b** of the sea,	8328
SS	3:10	**b** thereof of gold, the covering	7507
Da	6:24	or ever they came at the **b** of the	773
Mt	27:51	from the top to the **b**; and the	*2736*
Mk	15:38	in twain from the top to the **b**	*2736*

BOTTOMLESS

Rev	9:1	was given the key of the **b** pit	*12*
Rev	9:11	the angel of the **b** pit, whose	*12*
Rev	11:7	that ascendeth out of the **b** pit	*12*
Rev	17:8	and shall ascend out of the **b** pit,	*12*
Rev	20:1	having the key of the **b** pit and a	*12*
Rev	20:3	cast him into the **b** pit, and shut	*12*

BOUGH

Ge	49:22	Joseph is a fruitful **b**,	1121
Jgs	9:49	cut down every man his **b**, and	7754
Isa	10:33	the Lord of hosts, shall lop the **b**	6288

BOUGHS

2Sa	18:9	the thick **b** of a great oak, and	7730
Ps	80:10	and the **b** thereof were like the	6057
Isa	27:11	When the **b** thereof are	7105
Eze	17:23	it shall bring forth **b**, and bear	6057
Eze	31:8	the fir trees were not like his **b**	5589
Eze	31:12	his **b** are broken by all the rivers	6288
Da	4:12	of the heaven dwelt in the **b**	6056

BOUGHT

Ge	17:13	and he that is **b** with thy money,	4736
Ge	39:1	**b** him of the hands of the	7069
Ge	47:20	And Joseph **b** all the land of	7069
Ge	47:23	Behold, I have **b** you this day and	7069
Le	25:28	hand of him that hath **b** it until	7069
Le	27:24	unto him of whom it was **b**, even	7069
Dt	32:6	he thy father that hath **b** thee?	7069
2Sa	24:24	So David **b** the threshingfloor and	7069
Jer	32:43	And fields shall be **b** in this land,	7069
Hos	3:2	So I **b** her to me for fifteen pieces	3739
Mt	13:46	**and sold all that he had, and b it.**	*59*
Mt	21:12	sold and **b** in the temple, and	*59*
Mt	27:7	**b** with them the potter's field, to	*59*
Mk	11:15	cast out them that sold and **b** in	*59*
Lk	14:18	**I have b a piece of ground, and I**	*59*
Lk	17:28	**they did eat, they drank, they b,**	*59*
Lk	19:45	that sold therein, and them that **b**;	*59*
1Co	6:20	For ye are **b** with a price:	*59*
1Co	7:23	Ye are **b** with a price; be not ye	*59*
2Pe	2:1	denying the Lord that **b** them, and	*59*

BOUND

Ge 22:9 and **b** Isaac his son, and laid 6123
Ge 38:28 and **b** upon his hand a scarlet 7194
Ge 39:20 where the king's prisoners were **b**: 631
Ge 42:19 let one of your brethren be b 631
Ge 42:24 Simeon, and **b** him before their 631
Ge 44:30 seeing that his life is **b** up in the 7194
Nu 30:4 wherewith she hath **b** her soul 631
Jos 2:21 and she **b** the scarlet line in the 7194
Jgs 16:6 wherewith thou mightest be **b** to 631
Jgs 16:13 me wherewith thou mightest be **b** 631
Jgs 16:21 and **b** him with fetters of brass; 631
2Ki 25:7 and **b** him with fetters of brass, ...631
Ps 104:9 Thou hast set a **b** that they may 1366
Pr 22:15 Foolishness is **b** in the heart of a 7194
Pr 30:4 who hath **b** the waters in a 6887
Isa 61:1 of the prison to them that are **b**; 631
Jer 5:22 the **b** of the sea by a perpetual 1366
Jer 52:11 and the king of Babylon **b** him 631
Eze 34:4 neither have ye **b** up that which 2280
Da 3:24 Did not we cast three men **b** into 3729
Hos 4:19 The wind hath **b** her up in her 6887
Hos 13:12 The iniquity of Ephraim is **b** up; 6887
Na 3:10 and all her great men were **b** in 7576
Mt 14:3 laid hold on John, and **b** him, ...*1210*
Mt 16:19 on earth shall be **b** in heaven; *1210*
Mt 18:18 on earth shall be **b** in heaven; *1210*
Mt 27:2 when they had **b** him, they led him *1210*
Mk 5:4 had been often **b** with fetters and *1210*
Mk 6:17 laid hold upon John, and **b** him in *1210*
Mk 15:1 and **b** Jesus, and carried him *1210*
Lk 8:29 he was kept **b** with chains and in *1196*
Lk 10:34 **And went to him, and b up his** *2611*
Lk 13:16 **whom Satan hath b, lo, these** *1210*
Jn 11:44 his face was **b** about with a *4019*
Jn 18:12 the Jews took Jesus and **b** him *1210*
Jn 18:24 Now Annas had sent him **b** unto *1210*
Ac 9:2 he might bring them **b** unto *1210*
Ac 12:6 **b** with two chains: and the *1210*
Ac 20:22 I go **b** in the spirit unto *1210*
Ac 21:13 I am ready not to be **b** only, but *1210*
Ac 22:5 **b** unto Jerusalem, for to be *1210*
Ac 22:25 as they **b** him with thongs, Paul *4385*
Ac 23:12 and **b** themselves under a curse, ...*332*
Ac 23:21 have **b** themselves with an oath, ...*332*
Ac 24:27 the Jews a pleasure, left Paul **b** *1210*
Ac 28:20 hope of Israel I am **b** with this *4029*
Ro 7:2 which hath an husband is **b** by *1210*
1Co 7:27 Art thou **b** unto a wife? seek not *1210*
1Co 7:39 The wife is **b** by the law as long as *1210*
2Ti 2:9 but the word of God is not **b** *1210*
Heb 13:3 them that are in bonds, as **b** *4887*
Rev 9:14 Loose the four angels which are **b** *1210*
Rev 20:2 Satan, and **b** him a thousand *1210*

BOUNDS

Ex 19:12 thou shalt set **b** unto the people 1379
Ex 23:31 set thy **b** from the Red sea even 1366
Job 14:5 hast appointed his **b** that he 2706
Job 26:10 waters with **b**, until the day 2706
Isa 10:13 removed the **b** of the people 1367
Ac 17:26 and the **b** of their habitation; *3734*

BOUNTIFUL

Pr 22:9 hath a **b** eye shall be blessed; 2896

BOUNTIFULLY

Ps 13:6 he hath dealt **b** with me 1580
Ps 119:17 Deal **b** with thy servant, that I 1580
2Co 9:6 which soweth **b** shall reap also **b** *2129*

BOUNTY

1Ki 10:13 Solomon gave her of his royal **b** 3027

BOW See also BOWSHOT.

Ge 9:13 I do set my **b** in the cloud, and it 7198
Ge 27:29 and nations **b** down to thee: 7812
Ge 37:10 come to **b** down ourselves to thee 7812
Ge 41:43 cried before him, **B** the knee: 86
Ge 49:8 children shall **b** down before thee. 7812
Ex 11:8 and **b** down themselves unto me, ...7812
Ex 20:5 Thou shalt not **b** down thyself 7812
Dt 5:9 Thou shalt not **b** down thyself 7812
Jgs 2:19 them, and to **b** down unto them; 7812
2Sa 1:22 the **b** of Jonathan turned not back, ...7198
1Ki 22:34 certain man drew a **b** at a venture, ...7198
2Ki 13:16 Put thine hand upon the **b**. And 7198
2Ki 17:35 other gods, nor **b** yourselves to 7812
Job 31:10 and let others **b** down upon her 3766
Ps 22:29 go down to the dust shall **b** 3766
Ps 31:2 **B** down thine ear to me; deliver 5186
Ps 44:6 I will not trust in my **b**, neither 7198
Ps 78:57 turned aside like a deceitful **b**: 7198
Ps 86:1 **B** down thine ear, O Lord, hear 5186
Pr 5:1 **b** thine ear to my understanding: 5186
Pr 14:19 The evil **b** before the good; and 7817
Pr 22:17 **B** down thine ear, and hear the 5186
Isa 45:23 unto me every knee shall **b**, every 3766
Isa 60:14 shall **b** themselves down at the 7812
Jer 9:3 bend their tongues like their **b** 7198
La 3:12 He hath bent his **b**, and set me as 7198
Eze 1:28 As the appearance of the **b** that is 7198
Hos 1:5 I will break the **b** of Israel 7198
Hos 7:16 they are like a deceitful **b**: 7198
Hab 3:6 the perpetual hills did **b**: 7817
Ro 11:10 and **b** down their back alway *4781*
Ro 14:11 every knee shall **b** to me, and *2578*
Eph 3:14 I **b** my knees unto the Father *2578*
Php 2:10 of Jesus every knee should **b**, ...*2578*
Rev 6:2 he that sat on him had a **b**; *5115*

BOWED

Ge 18:2 and **b** himself toward the ground, ...7812
Ge 19:1 **b** himself with his face toward 7812
Ge 24:48 **b** down my head, and worshipped 6915
Ge 42:6 and **b** down themselves before 7812
Ex 4:31 **b** their heads and worshipped 6915
Ex 12:27 **b** the head and worshipped 6915
Ex 34:8 Moses made haste, and **b** his head 6915
Nu 22:31 he **b** down his head, and fell flat 6915
Jgs 16:30 he **b** himself with all his might; 5186
Ru 2:10 and **b** herself to the ground, and 7812
1Sa 20:41 and **b** himself three times: 7812
1Sa 28:14 to the ground, and **b** himself. 7812
2Sa 9:8 And he **b** himself, and said, ...7812
2Sa 22:10 He **b** the heavens also, and 5186
1Ki 1:47 the king **b** himself upon the bed. 7813
1Ki 2:19 to meet her, and **b** himself unto 7812
1Ki 19:18 which have not **b** unto Baal, ...3766
2Ch 20:18 Jehoshaphat **b** his head with his 6915
2Ch 29:30 **b** their heads and worshipped 6915
Ne 8:6 **b** their heads, and worshipped 6915
Est 3:2 Mordecai **b** not, nor did him 3766

Ps 35:14 I **b** down heavily, as one that....7817
Ps 145:14 all those that be **b** down....3721
Ps 146:8 raiseth them that are **b** down:....3721
Isa 2:17 loftiness of man shall be **b** down,....7817
Mt 27:29 and they **b** the knee before him....*1120*
Lk 24:5 afraid, and **b** down their faces....*2827*
Jn 19:30 **b** his head, and gave up the ghost....*2827*
Ro 11:4 have not **b** the knee to the image....*2578*

BOWELS

Ge 15:4 of thine own **b** shall be thine....4578
Ge 43:30 his **b** did yearn upon his brother:....7358
1Ki 3:26 her **b** yearned upon her son,....7358
2Ch 21:19 his **b** fell out by reason of his....4578
2Ch 32:21 they that came forth of his own **b**....4578
Job 30:27 My **b** boiled, and rested not:....4578
Ps 22:14 it is melted in the midst of my **b**....4578
Ps 109:18 into his **b** like water, and like....7130
SS 5:4 and my **b** were moved for him.....4578
Jer 4:19 My **b**, my **b**! I am pained at my....4578
La 1:20 my **b** are troubled; mine heart....4578
La 2:11 my **b** are troubled, my liver is....4578
Eze 3:3 and fill thy **b** with this roll that....4578
Ac 1:18 and all his **b** gushed out....*4698*
2Co 6:12 are straightened in your own **b**....*4698*
Php 1:8 you all in the **b** of Jesus Christ....*4698*
Php 2:1 Spirit, if any **b** and mercies,....*4698*
Col 3:12 **b** of mercies, kindness....*4698*
Phm 7 the **b** of the saints are refreshed....*4698*
1Jn 3:17 shutteth up his **b** of compassion....*4698*

BOWETH

Jgs 7:5 every one that **b** down upon....3766
Isa 2:9 And the mean man **b** down,....7817

BOWING

Mk 15:19 **b** their knees worshipped him....*5087*

BOWL

Jgs 6:38 of the fleece, a **b** full of water....5602
Ecc 12:6 or the golden **b** be broken,....1543
Zec 4:2 with a **b** upon the top of it, and his....1543

BOWLS

Ex 25:33 Three **b** made like unto almonds,....1375
Ex 25:34 four **b** made like unto almonds,....1375
1Ki 7:50 And the **b**, and the snuffers,....5592
Am 6:6 that drink wine in **b**, and anoint....4219
Zec 9:15 they shall be filled like **b**, and as....4219
Zec 14:20 shall be like **b** before the altar.....4219

BOWS

1Sa 2:4 **b** of the mighty men are broken,....7198
Ne 4:16 spears, the shields, and the **b**....7198
Ps 37:15 and their **b** shall be broken....7198
Ps 78:9 being armed, and carrying **b**,....7198
Isa 13:18 Their **b** also shall dash the young....7198
Jer 51:56 every one of their **b** is broken:....7198

BOWSHOT

Ge 21:16 way off, as it were a **b**:....2909, 7198

BOX

2Ki 9:3 Then take the **b** of oil, and pour....6378
Mt 26:7 having an alabaster **b** of very....*211*
Mk 14:3 having an alabaster **b** of....*211*
Lk 7:37 brought an alabaster **b** of....*211*

BOY

Joel 3:3 given a **b** for an harlot, and....3206

BOYS

Ge 25:27 And the **b** grew: and Esau was....5288
Zec 8:5 **b** and girls playing in the streets....3206

BRACELET

2Sa 1:10 and the **b** that was on his arm,....685

BRACELETS

Ge 24:22 two **b** for her hands of ten....6781
Ge 38:18 Thy signet, and thy **b**, and thy....6616
Eze 23:42 **b** upon their hands, and....6781

BRAKE See also BREAK; BROKEN.

Ex 32:19 and **b** them beneath the mount....7665
Dt 9:17 and **b** them before your eyes....7665
Jgs 7:20 the trumpets, and **b** the pitchers....7665
Jgs 9:53 head, and all to **b** his skull....7533
1Sa 4:18 and his neck **b**, and he died:....7665
1Ki 19:11 and **b** in pieces the rocks before....7665
2Ki 11:18 house of Baal, and **b** it down;....5422
2Ki 11:18 his images **b** they in pieces....7665
2Ki 14:13 **b** down the wall of Jerusalem....6555
2Ki 18:4 **b** in pieces the brasen serpent....3807
2Ki 25:10 **b** down the walls of Jerusalem....5422
2Ch 21:17 and **b** into it, and carried away....1234
2Ch 25:23 **b** down the wall of Jerusalem....6555
2Ch 36:19 **b** down the wall of Jerusalem....5422
Job 38:8 when it **b** forth, as if it had....1518
Ps 107:14 and **b** their bands in sunder....5423
Jer 39:8 **b** down the walls of Jerusalem.....5422
Jer 52:14 **b** down all the walls of Jerusalem....5422
Jer 52:17 the Chaldeans **b**, and carried....7665
Eze 17:16 whose covenant he **b**, even with....6565
Da 6:24 and **b** all their bones in pieces....1855
Da 7:7 it devoured and **b** in pieces,....1855
Mt 14:19 he blessed, and **b**, and gave....*2806*
Mt 15:36 and gave thanks, and **b** them....*2806*
Mt 26:26 bread, and blessed it, and **b**....*2806*
Mk 6:41 and **b** the loaves, and gave them....*2622*
Mk 8:6 and gave thanks, and **b**, and....*2806*
Mk 8:19 **When I b the five loaves among**....*2806*
Mk 14:3 and she **b** the box, and poured....*4937*
Mk 14:22 took bread, and blessed, and **b**....*2806*
Lk 8:29 he **b** the bands, and was....*1284*
Lk 9:16 he blessed them, and **b**, and....*2622*
Lk 22:19 and gave thanks and **b** it....*2806*
Lk 24:30 and blessed it, and **b**, and gave....*2806*
Jn 19:33 already, they **b** not his legs:....*2608*
1Co 11:24 he **b** it, and said, **Take, eat:**....2806

BRAKEST

Ex 34:1 the first tables, which thou **b**....7665
Dt 10:2 the first tables which thou **b**,....7665

BRANCH

Job 29:19 dew lay all night upon my **b**....7105
Ps 80:15 the **b** that thou madest strong....1121
Pr 11:28 righteous shall flourish as a **b**....5929
Isa 4:2 day shall the **b** of the Lord....6780
Isa 11:1 **B** shall grow out of his roots:....5342
Isa 60:21 the **b** of my planting, the work of....5342
Jer 23:5 raise unto David a righteous **B**,....6780
Jer 33:15 at that time, will I cause the **B** of....6780
Zec 3:8 bring forth my servant the **B**....6780
Zec 6:12 the man whose name is The **B**:....6780

Mal 4:1 leave them neither root nor **b** ... 6057
Mt 24:32 **When his b is yet tender, and** ... *2798*
Mk 13:28 **When her b is yet tender, and** ... *2798*
Jn 15:2 **Every b in me that beareth not** ... *2814*
Jn 15:4 As the **b** cannot bear fruit of ... *2814*
Jn 15:6 he is cast forth as a **b**, and is ... *2814*

BRANCHES
Ge 40:12 The three **b** are three days: ... 8299
Ge 49:22 a well; whose **b** run over the ... 1121
Ne 8:15 and fetch olive **b**, and pine **b**, ... 5929
Eze 17:23 the shadow of the **b** thereof shall ... 1808
Eze 19:10 fruitful and full of **b** by reason ... 6058
Eze 31:9 fair by the multitude of his **b**: ... 1808
Eze 31:12 in all the valleys his **b** are fallen, ... 1808
Da 4:21 and upon whose **b** the fowls of ... 6056
Zec 4:12 these two olive **b** which through ... 7641
Mt 13:32 **come and lodge in the b thereof** ... *2798*
Mt 21:8 others cut down **b** from the trees, ... *2798*
Mk 4:32 **shooteth out great b; so that** ... *2798*
Mk 11:8 others cut down **b** off the trees, ... *4746*
Lk 13:19 **fowls of the air lodged in the b** ... *2798*
Jn 12:13 Took **b** of palm trees, and went ... *902*
Jn 15:5 **I am the vine, ye are the b** ... *2814*
Ro 11:16 if the root be holy so are the **b** ... *2798*
Ro 11:21 if God spared not the natural **b**, ... *2798*

BRAND See also FIREBRAND.
Zec 3:2 is not this a **b** plucked out of the ... 181

BRANDISH
Eze 32:10 I shall **b** my sword before them; ... 5774

BRASEN
Ex 38:4 he made for the altar a **b** grate ... 5178
Ex 38:30 and the **b** altar, and the **b** grate ... 5178
Nu 16:39 the priest took the **b** censers, ... 5178
1Ki 8:64 **b** altar that was before the Lord ... 5178
2Ki 16:17 down the sea from off the **b** oxen ... 5178
2Ki 18:4 brake in pieces the **b** serpent that ... 5178
1Ch 18:8 wherewith Solomon made the **b** ... 5178
2Ch 7:7 **b** altar which Solomon had made ... 5178
Jer 52:17 the **b** sea that was in the house of ... 5178

BRASS
Ex 27:3 thereof thou shalt make of **b** ... 5178
Ex 27:19 the pins of the court, shall be of **b**, ... 5178
Ex 30:18 Thou shalt also make a laver of **b** ... 5178
Ex 31:4 in gold, and in silver, and in **b**, ... 5178
Ex 35:5 the Lord; gold, and silver, and **b**, ... 5178
Le 26:19 as iron, and your earth as **b**: ... 5158
Nu 21:9 Moses made a serpent of **b**, and ... 5178
Dt 8:9 of whose hills thou mayest dig **b** ... 5178
Jos 6:19 vessels of **b** and iron, are ... 5178
Jgs 16:21 bound him with fetters of **b**; and ... 5178
1Sa 17:5 had an helmet of **b** upon his head ... 5178
2Sa 21:16 three hundred shekels of **b** in ... 5178
1Ki 7:14 cunning to work all works in **b** ... 5178
1Ki 7:45 of the Lord, were of bright **b** ... 5178
1Ki 7:47 the weight of the **b** found out, ... 5178
2Ki 25:7 bound him with fetters of **b**, and ... 5178
2Ki 25:13 carried the **b** of them to Babylon. ... 5178
1Ch 18:8 brought David very much **b**, ... 5178
1Ch 22:14 and of **b** and iron without weight; ... 5178
1Ch 22:16 the gold, the silver, and the **b**, ... 5178
1Ch 29:2 the **b** for things of **b**, the iron for ... 5178
2Ch 2:7 in silver, and in **b**, and in iron, ... 5178
2Ch 2:14 in gold, and in silver, and in **b** ... 5178
2Ch 4:9 overlaid the doors of them with **b** ... 5178
2Ch 4:16 house of the Lord, of bright **b** ... 5178
2Ch 4:18 the weight of the **b** could not be ... 5178
2Ch 12:10 king Rehoboam made shields of **b** ... 5178
Job 40:18 bones are as strong pieces of **b**; ... 5154
Job 41:27 as straw, and **b** as rotten wood ... 5154
Isa 45:2 break in pieces the gates of **b**, ... 5154
Isa 60:17 For **b** I will bring gold, and for ... 5178
Jer 52:17 and carried all the **b** of them to ... 5178
Eze 1:7 like the colour of burnished **b** ... 5178
Eze 22:18 all they are **b**, and tin, and iron, ... 5178
Eze 22:20 they gather silver, and **b**, and iron, ... 5178
Eze 24:11 that the **b** of it may be hot, and ... 5178
Eze 40:3 was like the appearance of **b**, ... 5178
Da 2:32 his belly and his thighs of **b** ... 5174
Da 2:35 the clay, the **b**, the silver, and ... 5174
Da 2:39 another third kingdom of **b**, ... 5174
Da 2:45 the iron, the **b**, the clay, the ... 5174
Da 4:23 with a band of iron and **b**, ... 5174
Da 5:23 the gods of silver, and gold, of **b**, ... 5174
Da 7:19 were of iron, and his nails of **b**; ... 5174
Da 10:6 feet like in colour to polished **b** ... 5174
Mt 10:9 **nor silver, nor b in your purses,** ... *5475*
1Co 13:1 I am become as sounding **b**, ... *5475*
Rev 1:15 and his feet like unto fine **b**, as ... *5474*
Rev 2:18 **and his feet are like fine b** ... *5474*
Rev 9:20 idols of gold, and silver, and **b**, ... *5470*

BRAWLER
1Ti 3:3 patient, not a **b**, not covetous; ... *269*

BRAWLERS
Tit 3:2 evil of no man, to be no **b**, but ... *269*

BRAWLING
Pr 21:9 with a **b** woman in a wide house ... 4090
Pr 25:24 with a **b** woman in a wide house ... 4090

BRAY
Job 6:5 Doth the wild ass **b** when he ... 5101
Pr 27:22 shouldest **b** a fool in a mortar ... 3806

BREACH
Le 24:20 **B** for **b**, eye for eye, tooth for ... 7667
Nu 14:34 ye shall know my **b** of promise ... 8569
2Sa 5:20 before me, as the **b** of waters ... 6556
2Sa 6:8 Lord had made a **b** upon Uzzah: ... 6556
Job 16:14 He breaketh me with **b** upon **b**, ... 6556
Ps 106:23 chosen stood before him in the **b** ... 6556
Pr 15:4 therein is a **b** in the spirit ... 7667
Isa 30:26 bindeth up the **b** of his people, ... 7667
Jer 14:17 people is broken with a great **b**, ... 7667
La 2:13 thy **b** is great like the sea: ... 7667

BREACHES
1Ki 11:27 repaired the **b** of the city of ... 6556
2Ki 12:7 repair ye not the **b** of the house? ... 919
Ne 4:7 the **b** began to be stopped, then ... 6555
Ps 60:2 heal the **b** thereof; for it shaketh. ... 7667
Isa 22:9 **b** of the city of David, that they ... 1233
Am 9:11 and close up the **b** thereof; ... 6556

BREAD See also SHEWBREAD.
Ge 3:19 sweat of thy face shalt thou eat **b**, ... 3899
Ge 25:34 Jacob gave Esau **b** and pottage ... 3899
Ge 27:17 gave the savoury meat and the **b**, ... 3899
Ge 28:20 and will give me **b** to eat, ... 3899

Ge	39:6	save the **b** which he did eat.	3899
Ge	41:54	all the land of Egypt there was **b**	3899
Ge	41:55	the people cried to Pharaoh for **b**:	3899
Ge	43:32	the Egyptians might not eat **b**	3899
Ge	47:13	And there was no **b** in all the land;	3899
Ge	47:17	Joseph gave them **b** in exchange	3899
Ge	47:19	buy us and our land for **b**, and we	3899
Ex	12:15	whosoever eateth leavened **b**	
Ex	12:17	observe the feast of unleavened **b**;	
Ex	13:6	thou shalt eat unleavened **b**,	
Ex	16:4	I will rain **b** from heaven for you;	3899
Ex	16:12	morning ye shall be filled with **b**;	3899
Ex	16:15	the **b** which the Lord hath given	3899
Ex	16:29	on the sixth day the **b** of two days;	3899
Ex	23:15	the feast of unleavened **b**:	
Ex	34:18	The feast of unleavened **b** shalt	
Ex	34:28	he did neither eat **b**, nor drink	3899
Ex	40:23	he set the **b** in order upon it	3899
Le	8:31	the **b** that is in the basket of	3899
Le	21:8	for he offereth the **b** of thy God:	3899
Le	26:26	ten women shall bake your **b**	3899
Nu	4:7	the continual **b** shall be thereon:	3899
Nu	9:11	eat it with unleavened **b** and bitter	
Nu	14:9	they are **b** for us: their defence	3899
Nu	21:5	our soul loatheth this light **b**	3899
Dt	8:3	man doth not live by **b** only,	3899
Dt	8:9	A land wherein thou shalt eat **b**	3899
Dt	9:9	I neither did eat **b** nor drink	3899
Dt	23:4	they met you not with **b** and with	3899
Jgs	8:6	should give **b** unto thine army?	3899
Jgs	19:5	thine heart with a morsel of **b**,	3899
Ru	1:6	visited his people in giving them **b**	3899
1Sa	2:36	that I may eat a piece of **b**	3899
1Sa	9:7	the **b** is spent in our vessels,	3899
1Sa	21:6	the priest gave him hallowed **b**:	
1Sa	22:13	in that thou hast given him **b**,	3899
2Sa	3:35	if I taste **b**, or ought else, till the	3899
2Sa	9:10	thy master's son shall eat **b** always	3899
1Ki	13:22	Eat no **b**, and drink no water;	3899
1Ki	17:6	ravens brought him **b** and flesh	3899
1Ki	21:5	so sad that thou eatest no **b**?	3899
1Ki	22:27	feed him with **b** of affliction and	3899
2Ki	4:8	and she constrained him to eat **b**	3899
1Ch	16:3	to every one a loaf of **b**, and a	3899
2Ch	30:13	the feast of unleavened **b** in the	
Ezr	6:22	feast of unleavened **b** seven days	
Ezr	10:6	he did eat no **b**, nor drink water:	3899
Ne	5:14	brethren have not eaten the **b** of	3899
Ne	9:15	And gavest them **b** from heaven	3899
Job	33:20	his life abhorreth **b**, and his soul	3899
Job	42:11	and did eat **b** with him in his	3899
Ps	14:4	up my people as they eat **b**, and	3899
Ps	37:25	forsaken, nor his seed begging **b**	3899
Ps	53:4	eat up my people as they eat **b**:	3899
Ps	78:20	he give **b** also? can he provide	3899
Ps	80:5	feedest them with the **b** of tears;	3899
Ps	102:4	grass; so that I forget to eat my **b**	3899
Ps	102:9	I have eaten ashes like **b**, and	3899
Ps	105:40	and satisfied them with the **b** of	3899
Ps	127:2	to eat the **b** of sorrows: for so	3899
Pr	4:17	they eat the **b** of wickedness, and	3899
Pr	6:26	a man is brought to a piece of **b**:	3899
Pr	9:5	Come, eat of my **b**, and drink of	3899
Pr	9:17	are sweet, and **b** eaten in secret is	3899
Pr	12:9	honoureth himself, and lacketh **b**	3899
Pr	12:11	his land shall be satisfied with **b**:	3899
Pr	20:13	and thou shalt be satisfied with **b**	3899
Pr	20:17	**B** of deceit is sweet to a man;	3899
Pr	22:9	for he giveth of his **b** to the poor	3899
Pr	23:6	the **b** of him that hath an evil eye,	3899
Pr	25:21	enemy be hungry, give him **b** to	3899
Pr	28:19	his land shall have plenty of **b**:	3899
Pr	28:21	For a piece of **b** that man will	3899
Pr	31:27	and eateth not the **b** of idleness	3899
Ecc	9:7	eat thy **b** with joy, and drink	3899
Ecc	9:11	neither yet **b** to the wise, nor	3899
Ecc	11:1	Cast thy **b** upon the waters: for	3899
Isa	3:7	house is neither **b** nor clothing:	3899
Isa	30:20	the **b** of adversity, and the water	3899
Isa	30:23	and **b** of the increase of the earth,	3899
Isa	55:2	money for that which is not **b**?	3899
Isa	55:10	seed to the sower, and **b** to the	3899
Jer	37:21	the bakers' street, until all the **b**	3899
Jer	38:9	for there is no more **b** in the city	3899
Jer	42:14	nor have hunger of **b**; and there	3899
Jer	52:6	there was no **b** for the people of	3899
La	1:11	All her people sigh, they seek **b**;	3899
La	4:4	the young children ask **b**, and no	3899
Eze	12:18	of man, eat thy **b** with quaking,	3899
Eze	12:19	shall eat their **b** with carefulness,	3899
Eze	18:7	given his **b** to the hungry, and	3899
Eze	24:17	thy lips, and eat not the **b** of men	3899
Eze	44:7	when ye offer my **b**, the fat and	3899
Da	10:3	I ate no pleasant **b**, neither	3899
Hos	2:5	give me my **b** and my water,	3899
Am	7:12	and there eat **b**, and prophesy	3899
Am	8:11	not a famine of **b**, nor a thirst for	3899
Ob	7	they that eat thy **b** laid a	3899
Hag	2:12	and with his skirt do touch **b**,	3899
Mt	4:3	that these stones be made **b**	*740*
Mt	4:4	**Man shall not live by b alone,**	*740*
Mt	6:11	**Give us this day our daily b**	*740*
Mt	7:9	**whom if his son ask b, will he**	*740*
Mt	15:2	not their hands, when they eat **b**	*740*
Mt	15:26	**not meet to take the children's b,**	*740*
Mt	16:8	**because ye have brought no b?**	*740*
Mt	26:26	Jesus took **b**, and blessed it, and	*740*
Mk	3:20	could not so much as eat **b**.	*740*
Mk	6:8	no scrip, no **b**, no money in their	*740*
Mk	6:37	two hundred pennyworth of **b**,	*740*
Mk	7:5	but eat **b** with unwashen hands?	*740*
Mk	7:27	**not meet to take the children's b,**	*740*
Mk	8:17	**reason ye, because ye have no b?**	*740*
Mk	14:22	Jesus took **b**, and blessed, and	*740*
Lk	4:3	this stone that it be made **b**	*740*
Lk	4:4	**man shall not live by b alone, but**	*740*
Lk	7:33	**neither eating b nor drinking**	*740*
Lk	9:3	**scrip, neither b, neither money;**	*740*
Lk	11:3	**Give us day by day our daily b**	*740*
Lk	11:11	**If a son shall ask b of any of you**	*740*
Lk	14:1	to eat **b** on the sabbath day, that	*740*
Lk	14:15	he that shall eat **b** in the kingdom	*740*
Lk	15:17	**servants of my father's have b**	*740*
Lk	22:19	he took **b**, and gave thanks, and	*740*
Lk	24:35	known of them in breaking of **b**	*740*
Jn	6:5	**Whence shall we buy b, that these**	*740*
Jn	6:32	**my Father giveth you the true b**	*740*
Jn	6:35	**I am the b of life: he that cometh**	*740*
Jn	6:48	**I am that b of life**	*740*
Jn	6:51	**the b that I will give is my flesh,**	*740*

Jn	6:58	**he that eateth of this b shall live**	*740*
Jn	13:18	**He that eateth b with me hath**	*740*
Jn	21:9	there, and fish laid thereon, and **b**	*740*
1Co	5:8	unleavened **b** of sincerity and	
1Co	10:16	The **b** which we break, it is not	*740*
1Co	10:17	are all partakers of that one **b**,	*740*
1Co	11:26	as often as ye eat this **b**, and drink	*740*
2Th	3:8	Neither did we eat any man's **b**	*740*
2Th	3:12	they work, and eat their own **b**	*740*

BREADTH See also HANDBREADTH.

Ge	6:15	the **b** of it fifty cubits, and the	7341
Dt	2:5	not so much as a foot **b**;	4096
Jgs	20:16	could sling stones at an hair **b**,	
Job	37:10	and the **b** of the waters is	7341
Job	38:18	Hast thou perceived the **b** of the	7338
Isa	8:8	shall fill the **b** of thy land, O	7341
Eze	40:5	he measured the **b** of the	7341
Hab	1:6	through the **b** of the land, to	4800
Zec	2:2	to see what is the **b** thereof, and	7341
Eph	3:18	what is the **b**, and length, and	*4174*
Rev	20:9	they went up on the **b** of the	*4114*
Rev	21:16	and the **b** and the height of it are	*4114*

BREAK See also BRAKE; BROKEN.

Ge	19:9	even Lot, came near to **b** the	7665
Ge	27:40	that thou shalt **b** his yoke from	6561
Ex	12:46	neither shall ye **b** a bone	7665
Ex	19:24	the people **b** through to come up	2040
Ex	34:13	**b** their images, and cut down	7665
Le	26:15	but that ye **b** my covenant:	6565
Le	26:19	I will **b** the pride of your power;	7665
Le	26:44	to **b** my covenant with them: for	6565
Dt	7:5	**b** down their images, and cut	7665
Dt	31:20	provoke me, and **b** my covenant	6565
Jgs	2:1	I will never **b** my covenant with	6565
Jgs	8:9	again in peace, I will **b** down this	5422
2Ki	25:13	did the Chaldees **b** in pieces, and	7665
Ps	2:3	Let us **b** their bands asunder,	5423
Ps	2:9	Thou shalt **b** them with a rod of	7489
Ps	89:34	My covenant will I not **b**, nor	2490
Ecc	3:3	a time to **b** down, and a time to	6555
SS	2:17	Until the day **b**, and the	6315
SS	4:6	day **b**, and the shadows flee	6315
Isa	14:7	and is quiet: they **b** forth into	6476
Isa	28:24	doth he open and **b** the clods of	7702
Isa	28:28	nor **b** it with the wheel of his	2000
Isa	30:14	And he shall **b** it as the breaking	7665
Isa	35:6	in the wilderness shall waters **b**	1234
Isa	42:3	A bruised reed shall he not **b**	7665
Isa	45:2	I will **b** in pieces the gates of	7665
Isa	49:13	and **b** forth into singing, O	6476
Isa	52:9	**B** forth into joy, sing together,	6476
Isa	54:1	**b** forth into singing, and cry	6476
Isa	58:8	Then shall thy light **b** forth as	1234
Jer	4:3	**B** up your fallow ground, and	5214
Jer	14:21	remember, **b** not thy covenant	6565
Jer	19:10	Then shalt thou **b** the bottle in	7665
Jer	28:11	Even so will I **b** the yoke of	7665
Jer	30:8	I will **b** his yoke from off thy	7665
Jer	33:20	If ye can **b** my covenant of the	6565
Jer	45:4	which I have built will I **b** down,	2040
Jer	51:20	for with thee will I **b** in pieces	5310
Eze	16:38	women that **b** wedlock and shed	5003
Eze	17:15	or shall he **b** the covenant, and	6565
Eze	30:24	but I will **b** Pharaoh's arms, and	7665
Da	2:44	it shall **b** in pieces and consume	1854
Da	4:27	**b** off thy sins by righteousness,	6562
Da	7:23	shall tread it down, and **b** it in	1854
Hos	10:2	he shall **b** down their altars, he	6202
Hos	10:12	mercy; **b** up your fallow ground:	5214
Joel	2:7	and they shall not **b** their ranks:	5670
Am	5:6	lest he **b** out like fire in the	6743
Zec	11:10	that I might **b** my covenant	6565
Mt	5:19	**shall b one of these least**	*3089*
Mt	6:19	**where thieves b through and**	*1358*
Mt	9:17	**else the bottles b, and the wine**	*4486*
Mt	12:20	A bruised reed shall he not **b**,	*2608*
1Co	10:16	The bread which we **b**, is it not	*2806*
Gal	4:27	**b** forth and cry, thou that	*4486*

BREAKER See also COVENANTBREAKERS; TRUCE-BREAKERS.

Ro	2:25	but if thou be a **b** of the law,	*3848*

BREAKETH

Ge	32:26	he said, Let me go, for the day **b**,	5927
Job	12:14	Behold, he **b** down, and it	2040
Ps	29:5	yea, the Lord **b** the cedars	7665
Pr	25:15	and a soft tongue **b** the bone	7665
Ecc	10:8	whoso **b** an hedge, a serpent	6555
Jer	19:11	as one **b** a potter's vessel, that	7665
Jer	23:29	like a hammer that **b** the rock in	6327
Da	2:40	as iron that **b** all these, shall it	7940

BREAKING

Ge	32:24	a man with him until the **b** of	5927
Ex	22:2	If a thief be found **b** up, and be	4290
Isa	22:5	**b** down the walls, and of crying	6979
Eze	16:59	despised the oath in **b** the	6565
Lk	24:35	known of them in **b** of bread.	*2800*
Ro	2:23	**b** the law dishonourest thou	*3847*

BREAST

Ex	29:26	thou shalt take the **b** of the	2373
Ex	29:27	sanctify the **b** of the wave	2373
Le	7:30	the fat with the **b**, it shall he	2373
Le	7:31	but the **b** shall be Aaron's and his	2373
Nu	6:20	priest, with the wave **b** and heave	2373
Job	24:9	pluck the fatherless from the **b**,	7699
Da	2:32	his **b** and his arms of silver, his	2306
Lk	18:13	**but smote upon his b, saying,**	*4738*
Jn	13:25	He then lying on Jesus' **b** saith	*4738*
Jn	21:20	which also leaned on his **b** at	*4738*

BREASTPLATE

Ex	25:7	be set in the ephod, and in the **b**,	2833
Ex	28:29	the children of Israel in the **b** of	2833
Ex	28:30	put in the **b** of judgment the	2833
Le	8:8	he put the **b** upon him:	2833
Isa	59:17	put on righteousness as a **b**,	8302
Eph	6:14	having on the **b** of righteousness;	*2382*
1Th	5:8	putting on the **b** of faith and love;	*2382*

BREASTPLATES

Rev	9:9	**b**, as it were **b** of iron;	*2382*
Rev	9:17	**b** of fire, and of jacinth, and	*2382*

BREASTS

Le	9:21	the **b** and the right shoulder	2373
Job	3:12	or why the **b** that I should suck?	7699
Ps	22:9	when I was upon my mother's **b**	7699
Pr	5:19	let her **b** satisfy thee at all times;	1717
SS	1:13	shall lie all night betwixt my **b**	7699

SS 4:5 Thy two **b** are like two young roes ... 7699
SS 7:3 thy two **b** are like two young roes ... 7699
Isa 28:9 the milk, and drawn from the **b** ... 7699
Isa 66:11 satisfied with the **b** of her ... 7699
Eze 16:7 thy **b** are fashioned, and thine ... 7699
Hos 2:2 adulteries from between her **b**; ... 7699
Joel 2:16 and those that suck the **b**: ... 7699
Lk 23:48 smote their **b**, and returned. ... *4738*
Rev 15:6 their **b** girded with golden girdles ... *4738*

BREATH

Ge 2:7 into his nostrils the **b** of life; ... 5397
Ge 6:17 wherein is the **b** of life, from ... 7307
Ge 7:15 flesh, wherein is the **b** of life ... 7307
2Sa 22:16 at the blast of the **b** of his nostrils ... 7307
Job 4:9 and by the **b** of his nostrils are ... 7307
Job 9:18 will not suffer me to take my **b** ... 7307
Job 12:10 and the **b** of all mankind. ... 7307
Job 19:17 My **b** is strange to my wife, ... 7307
Job 33:4 and the **b** of the Almighty hath ... 5397
Job 34:14 unto himself his spirit and his **b**; ... 5397
Job 37:10 By the **b** of God frost is given: ... 5397
Job 41:21 His **b** kindleth coals, and a flame ... 5315
Ps 18:15 the blast of the **b** of thy nostrils. ... 7307
Ps 33:6 the host of them by the **b** of his ... 7307
Ps 104:29 thou takest away their **b**, they ... 7307
Ps 146:4 His **b** goeth forth, he returneth ... 7307
Ps 150:6 every thing that hath **b** praise ... 5397
Ecc 3:19 yea, they have all one **b**; so that ... 7307
Isa 2:22 from man, whose **b** is in his ... 5397
Isa 30:33 the **b** of the Lord, like a stream ... 5397
Isa 33:11 your **b**, as fire, shall devour you. ... 7307
Isa 42:5 he that giveth **b** unto the people ... 5397
Jer 10:14 falsehood, and there is no **b** in ... 7307
Jer 51:17 falsehood, and there is no **b** in ... 7307
La 4:20 **b** of our nostrils, the anointed ... 7307
Eze 37:6 and put **b** in you, and ye shall ... 7307
Eze 37:10 the **b** came into them, and they ... 7307
Da 5:23 God in whose hand thy **b** is, and ... 5396
Da 10:17 me, neither is there **b** left in me. ... 5397
Hab 2:19 there is no **b** at all in the midst ... 7307
Ac 17:25 he giveth to all life, and **b**, and ... *4157*

BREATHE

Jos 11:11 there was not any left to **b**: and ... 5397
Ps 27:12 me, and such as **b** out cruelty, ... 3307
Eze 37:9 and **b** upon these slain, that ... 5301

BREATHED

Ge 2:7 and **b** into his nostrils the breath ... 5301
Jn 20:22 said this, he **b** on them, and said ... *1720*

BREECHES

Ex 28:42 thou shalt make them linen **b** to ... 4370
Le 6:10 and his linen **b** shall he put upon ... 4370

BREED

Ge 8:17 that they may **b** abundantly in ... 8317

BRETHREN See also **BROTHER.**

Ge 9:22 his father, and told his two **b** ... 251
Ge 13:8 and thy herdmen; for we be **b** ... 251
Ge 19:7 pray you, **b**, do not so wickedly ... 251
Ge 37:4 loved him more than all his **b**, ... 251
Ge 37:9 another dream, and told it his **b**, ... 251
Ge 37:11 his **b** envied him; but his father ... 251
Ge 37:23 when Joseph was come unto his **b**, ... 251
Ge 42:6 Joseph's **b** came, and bowed ... 251
Ge 42:8 Joseph knew his **b**, but they knew ... 251
Ge 45:3 Joseph said unto his **b**, I am Joseph ... 251
Ex 2:11 smiting an Hebrew, one of his **b** ... 251
Le 21:10 the high priest among his **b**, ... 251
Le 25:46 over your **b** the children of Israel, ... 251
Le 25:48 one of his **b** may redeem him: ... 251
Nu 27:4 possession among the **b** of our ... 251
Nu 32:6 Shall your **b** go to war, and shall ... 251
Dt 1:16 Hear the causes between your **b**, ... 251
Dt 10:9 no part nor inheritance with his **b**; ... 251
Dt 17:15 from among thy **b** shalt thou set ... 251
Dt 17:20 heart be not lifted up above his **b**, ... 251
Dt 18:18 a Prophet from among their **b**, ... 251
Dt 25:5 If **b** dwell together, and one of ... 251
Jos 1:15 Until the Lord have given your **b** ... 251
Jos 14:8 Nevertheless my **b** that went up ... 251
Jos 22:4 God hath given rest unto your **b**, ... 251
Jgs 9:24 aided him in the killing of his **b** ... 251
Jgs 19:23 said unto them, Nay, my **b**, nay, ... 251
Jgs 20:13 hearken to the voice of their **b** ... 251
Ru 4:10 not cut off from among his **b**, ... 251
1Sa 16:13 anointed him in the midst of his **b**: ... 251
1Sa 22:1 his **b** and all his father's house ... 251
2Sa 15:20 take back thy **b**: mercy and truth ... 251
2Sa 19:12 Ye are my **b**, ye are my bones ... 251
1Ch 15:16 appoint their **b** to be the singers ... 251
1Ch 16:7 into the hand of Asaph and his **b** ... 251
1Ch 16:37 Asaph and his **b**, to minister before ... 251
1Ch 28:2 Hear me, my **b**, and my people: ... 251
2Ch 11:4 go up, nor fight against your **b**: ... 251
2Ch 19:10 come upon you, and upon your **b**: ... 251
2Ch 28:8 carried away captive of their **b** ... 251
2Ch 29:34 their **b** the Levites did help ... 251
Ezr 6:20 for their **b** the priests, and for ... 251
Ezr 7:18 seem good to thee, and to thy **b**, ... 252
Ne 1:2 That Hanani, one of my **b**, came, ... 251
Ne 5:8 and will ye even sell your **b**? ... 251
Ne 13:13 was to distribute unto their **b** ... 251
Est 10:3 accepted of the multitude of his **b** ... 251
Job 6:15 My **b** have dealt deceitfully as a ... 251
Job 19:13 He hath put my **b** far from me, ... 251
Job 42:11 came there unto him all his **b**, ... 251
Ps 69:8 become a stranger unto my **b**, ... 251
Ps 133:1 is for **b** to dwell together in unity! ... 251
Pr 6:19 he that soweth discord among **b**. ... 251
Pr 17:2 of the inheritance among the **b** ... 251
Pr 19:7 All the **b** of the poor do hate him: ... 251
Isa 66:5 Your **b** that hated you, that cast ... 251
Jer 29:16 of your **b** that are not gone forth ... 251
Eze 11:15 Son of man, thy **b**, even thy ... 251
Mic 5:3 the remnant of his **b** shall return ... 251
Mt 5:47 **if ye salute your b only, what do ye** ... *80*
Mt 12:48 **my mother? and who are my b?** ... *80*
Mt 12:49 **said, Behold my mother and my b!** ... *80*
Mt 13:55 **b, James, and Joses, and Simon,** ... *80*
Mt 19:29 **b, or sisters, or father, or mother,** ... *80*
Mt 23:8 **even Christ; and all ye are b** ... *80*
Mt 25:40 **the least of these my b, ye have** ... *80*
Mt 28:10 **tell my b that they go into Galilee,** ... *80*
Mk 3:34 **Behold my mother and my b!** ... *80*
Mk 10:29 **left house, or b, or sisters,** ... *80*
Lk 8:21 **My mother and my b are these** ... *80*
Lk 14:12 **not thy friends, nor thy b, neither** ... *80*
Lk 14:26 **children, and b, and sisters, yea,** ... *80*
Lk 16:28 **I have five b; that he may testify** ... *80*

Lk	18:29	**parents, or b, or wife, or children,**	*80*
Lk	21:16	**by parents, and b, and kinsfolks,**	*80*
Lk	22:32	**art converted, strengthen thy b**	*80*
Jn	7:5	neither did his **b** believe in him.	*80*
Jn	7:10	But when his **b** were gone up,	*80*
Jn	20:17	**go to my b, and say unto them,**	*80*
Jn	21:23	saying abroad among the **b**,	*80*
Ac	2:37	Men and **b**, what shall we do?	*80*
Ac	7:13	Joseph was made known to his **b**;	*80*
Ac	11:29	send relief unto the **b** which dwelt	*80*
Ac	14:2	minds evil affected against the **b**	*80*
Ac	15:32	exhorted the **b** with many words	*80*
Ac	15:40	being recommended by the **b** unto	*80*
Ac	23:1	Men and **b**, I have lived in all good	*80*
Ac	23:6	Men and **b**, I am a Pharisee,	*80*
Ro	1:13	you ignorant, **b**, that oftentimes I	*80*
Ro	8:12	Therefore, **b**, we are debtors,	*80*
Ro	8:29	be the firstborn among many **b**	*80*
Ro	9:3	accursed from Christ for my **b**,	*80*
Ro	10:1	**B**, my heart's desire and prayer to	*80*
Ro	11:25	not, **b**, that ye should be ignorant	*80*
Ro	12:1	I beseech you therefore, **b**, by the	*80*
Ro	15:30	Now I beseech you, **b**, for the Lord	*80*
Ro	16:17	I beseech you, **b**, mark them which	*80*
1Co	3:1	I, **b**, could not speak unto you as	*80*
1Co	6:5	be able to judge between his **b**?	*80*
1Co	7:24	**B**, let every man, wherein he is	*80*
1Co	8:12	ye sin so against the **b**, and wound	*80*
1Co	15:6	of above five hundred **b** at once;	*80*
2Co	11:26	the sea, in perils among false **b**:	*5569*
Gal	2:4	that because of false **b** unawares	*5569*
Gal	4:28	Now we, **b**, as Isaac was, are the	*80*
Gal	5:13	**b**, ye have been called unto liberty;	*80*
Gal	6:1	**B**, if a man be overtaken in a fault,	*80*
Eph	6:10	Finally, my **b**, be strong in the	*80*
Php	4:1	my **b** dearly beloved and longed	*80*
Php	4:8	Finally, **b**, whatsoever things are	*80*
1Th	1:4	Knowing, **b** beloved, your election	*80*
1Ti	4:6	put the **b** in remembrance of these	*80*
1Ti	6:2	not despise them, because they are **b**;	*80*
Heb	2:11	he is not ashamed to call them **b**,	*80*
Jas	1:2	My **b**, count it all joy when ye fall	*80*
Jas	1:16	Do not err, my beloved **b**.	*80*
Jas	2:1	My **b**, have not the faith of our	*80*
Jas	4:11	Speak not evil one of another, **b**	*80*
Jas	5:9	Grudge not one against another, **b**	*80*
1Pe	1:22	unto unfeigned love of the **b**, see	*5360*
1Pe	3:8	love as **b**, be pitiful, be courteous:	*5361*
1Jn	3:14	because we love the **b**. He that	*80*
1Jn	3:16	to lay down our lives for the **b**	*80*
3Jn	5	thou doest to the **b**, and to	*80*
3Jn	10	he himself receive the **b**, and	*80*
Rev	12:10	the accuser of our **b** is cast down,	*80*
Rev	19:10	of thy **b** that have the testimony	*80*
Rev	22:9	of thy **b** the prophets, and of them	*80*

BRETHREN'S

Dt	20:8	lest his **b** heart faint as well as	251

BRIBE

1Sa	12:3	hand have I received any **b**	3724
Am	5:12	they take a **b**, and they turn aside	3724

BRIBES

1Sa	8:3	aside after lucre, and took **b**,	7810
Ps	26:10	and their right hand is full of **b**,	7810
Isa	33:15	his hands from holding of **b**	7810

BRICK

Ge	11:3	Go to, let us make **b**, and burn	3835
Ex	5:7	give the people straw to make **b**,	3835
Isa	65:3	burneth incense upon altars of **b**;	3843

B

BRICKKILN

2Sa	12:31	made them pass through the **b**:	4404

BRICKS

Ex	5:8	the tale of the **b**, which they did	3843

BRIDE

Isa	61:10	a **b** adorneth herself with jewels	3618
Isa	62:5	bridegroom rejoiceth over the **b**,	3618
Jn	3:29	that hath the **b** is the bridegroom:	*3565*
Rev	21:2	prepared as a **b** adorned for her	*3565*
Rev	21:9	shew thee the **b**, the Lamb's wife	*3565*
Rev	22:17	the Spirit and the **b** say, Come.	*3565*

BRIDECHAMBER

Mt	9:15	**Can the children of the b mourn,**	*3567*
Mk	2:19	**Can the children of the b fast,**	*3567*
Lk	5:34	**make the children of the b fast,**	*3567*

BRIDEGROOM

Ps	19:5	a **b** coming out of his chamber,	2860
Mt	9:15	**as long as the b is with them?**	*3566*
Mt	25:1	**and went forth to meet the b**	*3566*
Mt	25:6	**Behold, the b cometh; go ye out**	*3566*
Mk	2:19	**while the b is with them?**	*3566*
Mk	2:19	**as long as they have the b**	*3566*
Mk	2:20	**when the b shall be taken away**	*3566*
Lk	5:34	**fast, while the b is with them?**	*3566*
Jn	2:9	governor of the feast called the **b**,	*3566*
Jn	3:29	that hath the bride is the **b**:	*3566*

BRIDLE

2Ki	19:28	my **b** in thy lips, and I will turn	4964
Job	41:13	come to him with his double **b**?	7448
Ps	39:1	I will keep my mouth with a **b**,	4269
Pr	26:3	a **b** for the ass, and a rod for the	4964
Jas	3:2	able also to **b** the whole body.	*5469*

BRIER

Isa	55:13	instead of the **b** shall come up	5636
Eze	28:24	shall be no more a pricking **b**	5544
Mic	7:4	The best of them is as a **b**: the	2312

BRIERS

Isa	5:6	but there shall come up **b** and	8068
Isa	7:24	all the land shall become **b** and	8068
Isa	9:18	it shall devour the **b** and thorns,	8068
Isa	10:17	and devour his thorns and his **b**	8068
Isa	27:4	who would set the **b** and thorns	8068

BRIGHT

Le	13:4	If the **b** spot be white in the skin	934
Le	13:25	the hair in the **b** spot be turned	934
Le	13:28	if the **b** spot stay in his place, and	934
1Ki	7:45	of the Lord, were of **b** brass	4803
Eze	1:13	and the fire was **b**, and out of	5051
Lk	11:36	**as when the b shining of a candle**	*796*
Ac	10:30	stood before me in **b** clothing,	2986
Rev	22:16	**and the b and morning star**	*2986*

BRIGHTNESS

2Sa	22:13	Through the **b** before him were	5051
Ps	18:12	At the **b** that was before him his	5051
Isa	59:9	for **b**, but we walk in darkness.	5054

Isa 60:3 and kings to the **b** of thy rising................5051
Eze 10:4 the court was full of the **b** of the 5051
Da 4:36 mine honour and **b** returned...................2122
Am 5:20 even very dark, and no **b** in it?.................5051
Hab 3:4 And his **b** was as the light;........................5051
Ac 26:13 light from heaven, above the **b** of............*2987*
2Th 2:8 with the **b** of his coming;.........................*2015*
Heb 1:3 Who being the **b** of his glory *541*

BRIM

Jos 3:15 were dipped in the **b** of the......................7097
1Ki 7:26 and the **b** thereof was wrought................8193
2Ch 4:2 from **b** to **b**, round in compass,...............8193
Jn 2:7 And they filled them up to the **b** 507

BRIMSTONE

Ge 19:24 Sodom and upon Gomorrah **b**................1614
Dt 29:23 the whole land thereof is **b**, and 1614
Ps 11:6 he shall rain snares, fire and **b**, ...1614
Isa 30:33 like a stream of **b**, doth kindle it.............1614
Isa 34:9 the dust thereof into **b**, and the 1614
Eze 38:22 and great hail stones, fire and **b**..............1614
Lk 17:29 **fire and b from heaven, and**....................*2303*
Rev 9:17 issued fire and smoke and **b**....................*2303*
Rev 9:18 the smoke, and by the **b**, which *2303*
Rev 14:10 with fire and **b** in the presence of............*2303*
Rev 19:20 a lake of fire burning with **b**,...................*2303*
Rev 20:10 the lake of fire and **b**, where the..............*2303*
Rev 21:8 lake which burneth with fire and **b**: *2303*

BRING See also **BROUGHT.**

Ge 1:11 Let the earth **b** forth grass, the.................1876
Ge 1:20 the waters **b** forth abundantly..................8317
Ge 1:24 Let the earth **b** forth the living.................3318
Ge 3:16 in sorrow thou shalt **b** forth....................3205
Ge 6:19 two of every sort shalt thou **b** into 935
Ge 8:17 **B** forth with thee every living 3318
Ge 19:5 **b** them out unto us, that we may 3318
Ge 27:7 **B** me venison, and make me......................935
Ge 41:32 and God will shortly **b** it to pass.............6213
Ge 50:20 to, **b** to pass, as it is this day, to 6213
Ex 3:17 I will **b** you up out of the 5927
Ex 12:51 the Lord did **b** the children of..................3318
Ex 13:5 the Lord shall **b** thee into the.....................935
Le 24:14 **B** forth him that hath cursed 3318
Nu 17:10 **B** Aaron's rod again before the.................7725
Dt 22:14 and **b** up an evil name upon her, ...3318
Dt 28:49 shall **b** a nation against thee.....................5375
Dt 30:5 And the Lord thy God will **b** thee.............935
Jgs 6:30 **B** out thy son, that he may die:................3318
Jgs 19:22 **B** forth the man that came into...............3318
1Sa 11:12 **b** the men, that we may put them 5414
1Sa 13:9 **B** hither a burnt offering to me, ...5066
1Sa 14:18 **B** hither the ark of God. For the.............5066
1Sa 15:32 **B** ye hither to me Agag the king 5066
1Sa 23:9 priest, **B** hither the ephod. 5066
1Sa 28:11 And he said, **B** me up Samuel..................5927
2Sa 12:23 can I **b** him back again? I shall.................7725
2Sa 13:10 **B** the meat into the chamber, ...935
2Sa 14:21 **b** the young man Absalom 7725
2Sa 17:13 then shall all Israel **b** ropes.......................5375
1Ch 13:12 How shall I **b** the ark of God 935
2Ch 34:24 I will **b** evil upon this place, and................935
Ne 10:34 to **b** it into the house of our God, ...935
Ne 13:18 **b** more wrath upon Israel by 935
Est 6:1 to **b** the book of records of the 935
Est 6:9 **b** him on horseback through 7392
Job 14:4 Who can **b** a clean thing out of 5414
Job 30:23 thou wilt **b** me to death, and the 7725
Job 33:30 To **b** back his soul from the pit................7725
Job 40:20 the mountains **b** him forth food, ...5375
Ps 25:17 O **b** thou me out of my distresses. 3318
Ps 43:3 let them **b** me unto thy holy hill,...............935
Ps 59:11 and **b** them down, O Lord our 3381
Ps 71:20 **b** me up again from the depths 5927
Ps 72:3 The mountains shall **b** peace to...............5375
Ps 92:14 They shall still **b** forth fruit in..................5107
Ps 94:23 And he shall **b** upon them their 7725
Ps 96:8 **b** an offering, and come into his.............5375
Ps 142:7 **B** my soul out of prison, that I 3318
Pr 4:8 she shall **b** thee to honour, when.............3513
Pr 27:1 knowest not what a day may **b** 3205
Pr 29:8 Scornful men **b** a city into a.....................6315
Pr 29:23 A man's pride shall **b** him low: 8213
Ecc 3:22 for who shall **b** him to see what.................935
Ecc 11:9 God will **b** thee into judgment. 935
Ecc 12:14 God shall **b** every work into........................935
Isa 1:13 **B** no more vain oblations; incense 935
Isa 31:2 and will **b** evil, and will not call.................935
Isa 38:8 I will **b** again the shadow of the..............7725
Isa 42:1 he shall **b** forth judgment to the.............3318
Isa 42:3 he shall **b** forth judgment unto................3318
Isa 42:7 to **b** out the prisoners from the 3318
Isa 42:16 And I will **b** the blind by a way................3212
Isa 46:13 I **b** near my righteousness; it....................7126
Isa 63:6 and I will **b** down their strength.............3381
Isa 65:9 And I will **b** forth a seed out of................3318
Isa 66:4 will **b** their fears upon them;......................935
Isa 66:20 And they shall **b** all your brethren............935
Jer 4:6 for I will **b** evil from the north, ...935
Jer 5:15 I will **b** a nation upon you from 935
Jer 6:19 I will **b** evil upon this people, ...935
Jer 8:1 they shall **b** out the bones of the 3318
Jer 10:24 anger, lest thou **b** me to nothing.
Jer 11:8 therefore I will **b** upon them all.................935
Jer 11:11 I will **b** evil upon them, which....................935
Jer 19:3 I will **b** evil upon this place, the.................935
Jer 19:15 I will **b** upon this city and upon all...........935
Jer 23:12 for I will **b** evil upon them, even 935
Jer 23:40 I will **b** an everlasting reproach................5414
Jer 24:6 And will **b** them again to this 7725
Jer 28:6 to **b** again the vessels of the......................7725
Jer 30:3 that I will **b** again the captivity 7725
Jer 30:18 I will **b** again the captivity of 7725
Jer 31:8 I will **b** them from the north......................935
Jer 31:23 I shall **b** again their captivity....................7725
Jer 31:32 **b** them out of the land of Egypt;.............3318
Jer 32:42 so will I **b** unto them all the.......................935
Jer 33:6 I will **b** it health and cure, and.................4608
Jer 35:17 I will **b** upon Judah and upon all 935
Jer 38:23 they shall **b** out all thy wives 4672
Jer 39:16 I will **b** my words upon this city................935
Jer 42:17 the evil that I will **b** upon them. 935
Jer 45:5 I will **b** evil upon all flesh, saith 935
Jer 48:47 Yet will I **b** again the captivity..................7725
Jer 49:36 And upon Elam will I **b** the four 935
Jer 51:40 I will **b** them down like lambs to.............3381
Eze 7:24 Wherefore I will **b** the worst of..................935
Eze 12:13 and I will **b** him to Babylon to the 935
Eze 20:15 I would not **b** them into the land..............935
Eze 20:42 when I shall **b** you into the land................935
Eze 28:7 I will **b** strangers upon thee, the 935

Eze 28:8 They shall **b** thee down to the....3381
Eze 28:18 and I will **b** thee to ashes upon....5414
Eze 34:16 and **b** again that which was....7725
Eze 36:24 and will **b** you into your own land....935
Eze 37:6 and will **b** up flesh upon you,....5927
Eze 39:25 Now will I **b** again the captivity....7725
Da 3:13 his rage and fury commanded to **b**....858
Da 5:2 commanded to **b** the golden and....858
Da 9:24 **b** in everlasting righteousness,....935
Hos 9:12 Though they **b** up their children,....1431
Joel 3:1 I shall **b** again the captivity of....7725
Am 4:1 masters, **B**, and let us drink....935
Am 9:2 heaven, thence will I **b** them....3381
Ob 4 thence will I **b** thee down, saith....3381
Jnh 1:13 the men rowed hard to **b** it to....7725
Mic 7:9 he will **b** me forth to the light,....3318
Zep 3:5 doth he **b** his judgment to light....5414
Hag 1:6 and **b** in little; yet eat, but ye....935
Zec 3:8 I will **b** forth my servant the....935
Zec 5:4 I will **b** it forth, saith the Lord of....3318
Zec 13:9 And I will **b** the third part....935
Mal 3:10 **B** ye all the tithes into the....935
Mt 1:23 and shall **b** forth a son, and they....*5088*
Mt 2:8 **b** me word again, that I may....*518*
Mt 3:8 **B** forth therefore fruits meet for....*4160*
Mt 5:23 **if thou b thy gift to the altar,**....*4374*
Mt 7:18 **A good tree cannot b forth evil**....*4160*
Mt 14:18 He said, **B them hither to me.**....*5342*
Mt 17:17 **suffer you? b him hither to me**....*5342*
Mt 21:2 **loose them, and b them unto me.**....*71*
Mk 4:20 **b forth fruit, some thirtyfold,**....*2592*
Mk 9:19 **shall I suffer you? b him unto me.**....*5342*
Mk 11:2 **never man sat; loose him, and b.**....*71*
Mk 12:15 **tempt ye me? b me a penny,**....*5342*
Lk 1:31 and **b** forth a son, and shall call....*5088*
Lk 2:10 I **b** you good tidings of great joy,....*2097*
Lk 6:43 **neither doth a corrupt tree b**....*4160*
Lk 8:14 **pleasures of this life, and b no**....*5062*
Lk 9:41 **suffer you? B thy son hither.**....*4317*
Lk 12:11 **when they b you unto the**....*4574*
Lk 14:21 **b in hither the poor, and the**....*1521*
La 15:22 **B forth the best robe, and put it**....*1627*
Lk 15:23 **b hither the fatted calf, and kill**....*5542*
Jn 15:2 **that it may b forth more fruit**....*5542*
Jn 21:10 **B of the fish which ye have now**....*5542*
Ac 9:2 he might **b** them bound unto....*71*
Ac 22:5 to **b** them which were there bound....*71*
Ro 7:4 we should **b** forth fruit unto God....*2592*
Ro 10:6 (that is, to **b** Christ down from....*2609*
Ro 10:7 to **b** up Christ again from the....*321*
Ro 10:15 and **b** glad tidings of good things!....*2097*
1Co 1:19 **b** to nothing the understanding....*114*
1Co 1:28 to **b** to nought things that are:....*2675*
1Co 9:27 under my body, and **b** it into....*1596*
Gal 3:24 schoolmaster to **b** us unto Christ,
Eph 6:4 **b** them up in the nurture and....*1625*
1Th 4:14 sleep in Jesus will God **b** with him....*71*
2Ti 4:11 Take Mark, and **b** him with thee:....*71*
1Pe 3:18 that he might **b** us to God, being....*4317*
2Pe 2:11 **b** not railing accusation against....*5342*
Jude 9 durst not **b** against him a railing....*2018*

BRINGETH

1Sa 2:7 rich: he **b** low, and lifteth up....8213
Ps 1:3 **b** forth his fruit in his season:....5414
Pr 21:27 he **b** it with a wicked mind?....935
Pr 29:25 The fear of man **b** a snare: but....5414
Pr 30:33 churning of milk **b** forth butter,....3318
Pr 30:33 wringing of the nose **b** forth....3318
Isa 52:7 the feet of him that **b** good....1319
Hos 10:1 he **b** forth fruit unto himself:....7737
Na 1:15 feet of him that **b** good tidings,....1319
Mt 3:20 tree which **b** not forth good fruit....*4160*
Mt 7:17 **good tree b forth good fruit;**....*4160*
Mt 7:19 **tree that b not forth good fruit is**....*4160*
Mt 12:35 **of the heart b forth good things:**....*1544*
Lk 6:43 **b not forth corrupt fruit; neither**....*4160*
Lk 6:45 **his heart b forth that which is evil:**....*4595*
Jn 12:24 **if it die, it b forth much fruit.**....*5542*
Jn 15:5 **the same b forth much fruit:**....*5542*
Tit 2:11 grace of God that **b** salvation....*4992*
Heb 1:6 when he **b** in the first begotton....*1521*
Jas 1:15 when lust hath conceived, it **b**....*616*
Jas 1:15 when it is finished, **b** forth death....*5088*

BRINGING

Ex 12:42 for **b** them out from the land of....3318
Nu 5:15 **b** iniquity to remembrance....2142
2Ki 21:12 am **b** such evil upon Jerusalem....935
Da 9:12 by **b** upon us a great evil:....935
Mt 21:43 **a nation b forth the fruits thereof.**....*4160*
Ro 7:23 **b** me into captivity to the law of....*163*
2Co 10:5 **b** into captivity every thought to....*163*
Heb 2:10 **b** many sons unto glory, to make....*71*

BROAD See also ABROAD.

Nu 16:38 let them make them **b** plates for....7555
Ps 119:96 commandment is exceeding **b**....7342
Jer 51:58 The **b** walls of Babylon shall be....7342
Na 2:4 against another in the **b** ways:....7339
Mt 7:13 **b is the way, that leadeth to**....*2149*
Mt 23:5 **they make b their phylacteries,**....*4115*

BROIDED

1Ti 2:9 not with **b** hair, or gold, or....*4117*

BROIDERED

Eze 16:10 I clothed thee also with **b** work,....7553
Eze 16:13 fine linen, and silk, and **b** work;....7553

BROILED

Lk 24:42 they gave him a piece of a **b** fish,....*3702*

BROKEN See also BROKENHEARTED.

Ge 7:11 fountains of the great deep **b** up,....1234
Le 22:24 bruised, or crushed, or **b**, or cut;....5423
Nu 15:31 and hath **b** his commandment,....6565
1Sa 2:10 shall be **b** to pieces; out of....2865
2Sa 22:35 a bow of steel is **b** by mine arms....5181
1Ki 18:30 altar of the Lord that was **b**....2040
1Ki 22:48 the ships were **b** at Ezion-geber....7665
2Ki 11:6 the house, that it be not **b** down....4535
2Ki 25:4 And the city was **b** up, and all....1234
1Ch 14:11 God hath **b** in upon mine enemies....6555
2Ch 20:37 the Lord hath **b** thy works....6555
2Ch 24:7 that wicked woman, had **b** up....6555
Ne 1:3 wall of Jerusalem also is **b** down,....6555
Job 7:5 my skin is **b**, and become....7280
Ps 3:7 hast **b** the teeth of the ungodly....7665
Ps 31:12 of mind: I am like a **b** vessel....6
Ps 34:18 unto them that are of a **b** heart;....7665
Ps 34:20 his bones: not one of them is **b**....7665
Ps 37:17 the arms of the wicked shall be **b**;....7665
Ps 51:8 the bones which thou hast **b** may....1794

Ps	51:17	sacrifices of God are a **b** spirit:	7665
Ps	55:20	him: he hath **b** his covenant.	2490
Ps	69:20	Reproach hath **b** my heart;	7665
Ps	147:3	He healeth the **b** in heart,	7665
Pr	3:20	knowledge the depths are **b** up,	1234
Pr	6:15	suddenly shall he be **b** without	7665
Pr	15:13	sorrow of the heart the spirit is **b**,	5218
Pr	17:22	but a **b** spirit drieth the bones.	5218
Pr	24:31	stone wall thereof was **b** down	2040
Ecc	4:12	a threefold cord is not quickly **b**	5423
Ecc	12:6	or the golden bowl be **b**,	7533
Isa	8:9	and ye shall be **b** in pieces.	2844
Isa	14:29	rod of him that smote thee is **b**:	7665
Isa	16:8	the heathen have **b** down the	1986
Isa	21:9	images of her gods he hath **b**	7665
Isa	24:5	**b** the everlasting covenant.	6565
Isa	24:19	The earth is utterly **b** down	7489
Isa	28:13	and fall backward, and be **b**,	7665
Isa	30:14	potter's vessel that is **b** in pieces;	3807
Isa	33:8	he hath **b** the covenant, he hath	6565
Jer	11:10	of Judah have **b** my covenant	6565
Jer	14:17	virgin daughter of my people is **b**	7665
Jer	23:9	Mine heart within me is **b**	7665
Jer	28:2	**b** the yoke of the king of Babylon.	7665
Jer	33:21	Then may also my covenant be **b**	6565
Jer	48:38	I have **b** Moab like a vessel	7665
Jer	50:17	king of Babylon hath **b** his bones	6105
Eze	6:9	I am **b** with their whorish heart,	7665
Eze	17:19	and my covenant that he hath **b**,	6331
Eze	30:21	I have **b** the arm of Pharaoh	7665
Eze	44:7	and they have **b** my covenant	6565
Da	2:35	silver, and the gold, **b** to pieces	1854
Da	11:4	his kingdom shall be **b**, and shall	7665
Joel	1:17	the barns are **b** down; for the	2040
Jnh	1:4	that the ship was like to be **b**	7665
Mt	21:44	**fall on this stone shall be b:**	*4917*
Mt	24:43	**suffered his house to be b up.**	*1358*
Lk	12:39	**suffered his house to be b**	*1358*
Lk	20:18	**fall upon that stone shall be b;**	*4917*
Jn	7:23	**law of Moses should not be b;**	*3089*
Jn	10:35	**and the scripture cannot be b;**	*3089*
Jn	19:31	that their legs might be **b**,	*2608*
Jn	19:36	A bone of him shall not be **b**	*4937*
Ac	13:43	when the congregation was **b**	*3089*
Ac	20:11	and had **b** bread, and eaten,	*2805*
Ac	27:44	some on **b** pieces of the ship.	*3089*
Ro	11:20	because of unbelief they were **b** off,	*1575*
1Co	11:24	**is my body, which is b for you:**	*2806*
Eph	2:14	hath **b** down the middle wall	*3089*
Rev	2:27	**of a potter shall they be b**	*4937*

BROKENHEARTED

Isa	61:1	bind up the **b**, to proclaim	7665, 3820
Lk	4:18	**hath sent me to heal the b,**	*4937, 2588*

BROOD

Lk	13:34	**as a hen doth gather her b**	*3555*

BROOK

1Sa	17:40	five smooth stones out of the **b**,	5158
1Ki	2:37	out and passest over the **b** Kidron,	5158
1Ki	17:7	the **b** dried up, because there	5158
2Ki	23:6	burned it at the **b** Kidron.	5158
Job	6:15	have dealt deceitfully as a **b**,	5158
Pr	18:4	of wisdom as a flowing **b**	5158

BROOKS

Dt	8:7	good land, a land of **b** of water,	5158
Job	6:15	and as a stream of **b** they pass	5158
Ps	42:1	hart panteth after the water **b**	650

BROTH

Jgs	6:20	this rock, and pour out the **b**	4839
Isa	65:4	and **b** of abominable things	6564

BROTHER See also BRETHREN.

Ge	4:8	Cain rose up against Abel his **b**,	251
Ge	4:9	Where is Abel thy **b**?	251
Ge	9:5	at the hand of every man's **b**	251
Ge	14:14	Abram heard that his **b** was taken	251
Ge	27:11	Esau my **b** is a hairy man, and	251
Ge	27:35	Thy **b** came with subtilty,	251
Ge	27:41	then will I slay my **b** Jacob.	251
Ge	27:43	flee thou to Laban my **b** to Haran;	251
Ge	37:26	is it if we slay our **b**, and conceal	251
Ge	45:4	he said, I am Joseph your **b**, whom	251
Ex	7:1	Aaron thy **b** shall be thy prophet.	251
Ex	32:27	slay every man his **b**, and every	251
Le	25:36	God; that thy **b** may live with thee	251
Dt	15:12	if thy **b**, an Hebrew man, or an	251
Dt	23:19	not lend upon usury to thy **b**;	251
Dt	25:7	My husband's **b** refuseth to raise	2993
Jgs	20:28	of Benjamin my **b**, or shall I cease?	251
2Sa	1:26	distressed for thee, my **b** Jonathan:	251
2Sa	3:30	because he had slain their **b**	251
2Sa	13:12	she answered him, Nay, my **b**, do	251
2Sa	21:19	slew the **b** of Goliath the Gittite,	
1Ki	2:7	I fled because of Absalom thy **b**	251
1Ki	20:32	said, Is he yet alive? he is my **b**	251
Job	30:29	I am a **b** to dragons, and a	251
Ps	35:14	though he had been my friend or **b**:	251
Ps	49:7	can by any means redeem his **b**,	251
Pr	17:17	times, and a **b** is born for adversity	251
Pr	18:9	is **b** to him that is a great waster	251
Pr	18:19	A **b** offended is harder to be won	251
Pr	18:24	friend that sticketh closer than a **b**	251
Pr	27:10	that is near than a **b** far off.	251
Isa	19:2	fight every one against his **b**, and	251
Jer	9:4	trust ye not in any **b**: for	251
Jer	34:17	liberty, every one to his **b**,	251
Eze	33:30	every one to his **b**, saying, Come,	251
Eze	38:21	man's sword shall be against his **b**,	251
Ob	10	thy violence against thy **b** Jacob,	251
Zec	7:9	compassions every man to his **b**:	251
Mal	1:2	Was not Esau Jacob's **b**? saith	251
Mt	5:22	**whosoever shall say to his b, Raca,**	*80*
Mt	5:23	**thy b hath ought against thee;**	*80*
Mt	5:24	**first be reconciled to thy b, and**	*80*
Mt	7:4	**wilt thou say to thy b, Let me**	*80*
Mt	10:21	**b shall deliver up the b to death,**	*80*
Mt	12:50	**the same is my b, and sister, and**	*80*
Mt	18:15	**thy b shall trespass against thee,**	*80*
Mt	18:15	**hear thee, thou hast gained thy b**	*80*
Mt	18:35	**every one his b their trespasses.**	*80*
Mt	22:24	his **b** shall marry his wife,	*80*
Mk	3:35	**will of God, the same is my b, and**	*80*
Mk	12:19	If a man's **b** die, and leave his wife	*80*
Mk	13:12	**the b shall betray the b to death,**	*80*
Lk	6:42	**say to thy b, B, let me pull out the**	*80*
Lk	12:13	Master, speak to my **b**, that he	*80*
Lk	15:27	**said unto him, Thy b is come;**	*80*
Lk	15:32	**for this thy b was dead, and is alive**	*80*

Lk	17:3	**If thy b trespass against thee,**	*80*
Lk	20:28	that his **b** should take his wife,	*80*
Jn	11:23	unto her, **Thy b shall rise again**	*80*
Jn	11:32	hadst been here, my **b** had not died.	*80*
Ac	12:2	he killed James the **b** of John with	*80*
Ro	14:10	why dost thou judge thy **b**? or why	*80*
Ro	14:21	thing whereby thy **b** stumbleth,	*80*
1Co	5:11	that is called a **b** be a fornicator,	*80*
1Co	6:6	**b** goeth to law with **b**, and that	*80*
Eph	6:21	a beloved **b** and faithful minister	*80*
1Th	4:6	and defraud his **b** in any matter:	*80*
2Th	3:6	from every **b** that walketh	*80*
2Th	3:15	but admonish him as a **b**	*80*
Jas	1:9	Let the **b** of low degree rejoice	*80*
Jas	2:15	If a **b** or sister be naked, and	*80*
Jas	4:11	evil of his **b**, and judgeth his **b**	*80*
1Jn	2:10	He that loveth his **b** abideth in the	*80*
1Jn	2:11	he that hateth his **b** is in darkness,	*80*
1Jn	3:10	neither he that loveth not his **b**	*80*
1Jn	3:12	wicked one, and slew his **b**	*80*
1Jn	3:17	seeth his **b** have need, and	*80*
1Jn	4:20	hateth his **b**, he is a liar: for he	*80*
1Jn	4:21	who loveth God love his **b** also.	*80*
1Jn	5:16	any man see his **b** sin a sin which	*80*
Jude	1	of Jesus Christ, and **b** of James,	*80*
Rev	1:9	I John who also am your **b**, and	*80*

BROTHERHOOD

Zec	11:14	the **b** between Judah and Israel.	264
1Pe	2:17	Love the **b**. Fear God. Honour	*81*

BROTHERLY

Am	1:9	remembered not the **b** covenant:	251
Ro	12:10	one to another with **b** love;	*5360*
1Th	4:9	But as touching **b** love ye need	*5360*
Heb	13:1	Let **b** love continue.	*5360*
2Pe	1:7	godliness **b** kindness; and to **b**	*5360*

BROTHER'S

Ge	4:9	I know not: Am I my **b** keeper?	251
Ge	4:10	the voice of thy **b** blood crieth	251
Ge	12:5	Sarah his wife, and Lot his **b** son,	251
Ge	27:44	until thy **b** fury turn away;	251
Ge	38:8	in unto thy **b** wife, and marry her,	251
Ge	38:9	he went in unto his **b** wife, that he	251
Le	18:16	it is thy **b** nakedness.	251
Le	20:21	if a man shall take his **b** wife,	251
Dt	25:7	then let his **b** wife go up to the	2994
Dt	25:9	Then shall his **b** wife come unto	2994
1Ki	2:15	turned about, and is become my **b**:	251
Job	1:13	drinking wine in their eldest **b**	251
Mt	7:3	**the mote that is in thy b eye,**	*80*
Mt	7:5	**out the mote out of thy b eye.**	*80*
Mk	6:18	lawful for thee to have thy **b** wife	*80*
Lk	6:41	**mote that is in thy b eye,**	*80*
Lk	6:42	**out the mote that is in thy b eye**	*80*
Ro	14:13	an occasion to fall in his **b** way	*80*
1Jn	3:12	were evil, and his **b** righteous	*80*

BROUGHT

Ge	2:19	and **b** them unto Adam to see	935
Ge	2:22	and **b** her unto the man.	935
Ge	4:3	that Cain **b** of the fruit of the	935
Ge	14:16	**b** again his brother Lot,	7725
Ge	14:18	King of Salem **b** forth bread and	3318
Ge	15:7	I am the Lord that **b** thee out of	3318
Ge	19:17	when they had **b** them forth	3318
Ge	24:53	And the servant **b** forth jewels	3318
Ge	37:28	and they **b** Joseph into Egypt.	935
Ge	39:14	he hath **b** in an Hebrew unto us	935
Ge	41:14	**b** him hastily out of the dungeon:	7323
Ge	41:47	the earth **b** forth by handfuls	6213
Ex	18:26	the hard causes they **b** unto	935
Ex	20:2	have **b** thee out of the land of	3318
Ex	32:21	hast **b** so great a sin upon them?	935
Ex	32:23	the man that **b** us up out of the	5927
Ex	35:29	Israel **b** a willing offering	935
Ex	40:21	he **b** the ark into the tabernacle,	935
Le	19:36	which **b** you out of the land of	3318
Le	25:38	which **b** you forth out of the land	3318
Nu	6:13	he shall be **b** unto the door of	935
Nu	9:13	he **b** not the offering of the Lord	7126
Nu	12:15	not till Miriam was **b** in again.	622
Nu	13:32	And they **b** up an evil report of	3318
Nu	16:14	thou hast not **b** us into a land	935
Nu	27:5	And Moses **b** their cause before	7126
Dt	1:25	unto us, and **b** us word again,	7725
Dt	6:12	which **b** thee forth out of the	3318
Dt	9:26	which thou hast **b** forth out of	3318
Dt	9:28	he hath **b** them out to slay them	3318
Dt	26:13	I have **b** away the hallowed	1197
Dt	31:20	For when I shall have **b** them	935
Jos	6:23	and **b** out Rahab, and her father,	3318
Jos	14:7	and I **b** him word again as it was	7725
Jos	24:7	and **b** the sea upon them, and	935
Jgs	5:25	she **b** forth butter in a lordly dish	7126
Jgs	11:35	thou hast **b** me very low, and	3766
Jgs	16:18	her, and **b** money in their hand	5927
Jgs	19:25	took his concubine, and **b** her	3318
Ru	1:21	the Lord hath **b** me home again	7725
1Sa	18:27	David **b** their foreskins, and they	935
1Sa	21:15	**b** this fellow to play the mad man	935
1Sa	30:16	And when he had **b** him down,	3381
2Sa	1:10	have **b** them thither unto my Lord.	935
2Sa	4:8	**b** the head of Ish-bosheth unto	935
2Sa	4:10	thinking to have **b** good tidings,	1319
2Sa	6:12	David went and **b** up the ark	5927
2Sa	7:18	that thou hast **b** me hitherto?	935
2Sa	8:2	became David's servants, and **b**	5375
2Sa	8:6	servants to David, and **b** gifts	5375
2Sa	8:7	of Hadadezer, and **b** them to	935
2Sa	8:10	Joram **b** with him vessels of	1961
2Sa	23:16	and **b** it to David: nevertheless	935
1Ki	5:17	and they **b** great stones, costly	5265
1Ki	6:7	made ready before it was **b**	4551
1Ki	8:6	And the priests **b** in the ark of	935
1Ki	10:25	they **b** every man his present,	935
1Ki	17:6	the ravens **b** him bread and flesh,	935
2Ki	4:42	and **b** the man of God bread of	935
2Ki	5:6	And he **b** the letter to the king	935
2Ki	10:8	They have **b** the heads of the	935
2Ki	17:4	and **b** no present to the king of	5927
2Ki	20:11	and he **b** the shadow ten degrees	7725
2Ki	23:6	And he **b** out the grove from the	3318
2Ki	23:8	And he **b** all the priests out of the	935
2Ki	24:16	the king of Babylon **b** captive to	935
1Ch	11:18	and **b** it to David; but David	935
1Ch	14:17	and the Lord **b** the fear of him	5414
1Ch	20:3	he **b** out the people that were in	3318
2Ch	5:1	and Solomon **b** in all the things	935
2Ch	8:11	Solomon **b** up the daughter of	5927
2Ch	15:18	And he **b** into the house of God	935

2Ch	17:5	and all Judah **b** to Jehoshaphat	5414
2Ch	25:12	and **b** them unto the top of the	935
2Ch	28:19	the Lord **b** Judah low because	3665
2Ch	28:27	they **b** him not into the sepulchres	935
2Ch	29:16	and **b** out all the uncleanness	3318
2Ch	33:13	and **b** him again to Jerusalem	7725
2Ch	36:17	Therefore he **b** upon them the	5927
2Ch	36:18	all these he **b** to Babylon	935
Ezr	1:7	the king **b** forth the vessels of the	3318
Ezr	6:5	and **b** again unto the temple	1946
Ne	4:15	and God had **b** their counsel	6565
Ne	9:33	just in all that is **b** upon us; for	935
Ne	13:19	there should no burden be **b** in	935
Est	1:17	Vashti the queen to be **b** in before	935
Est	2:8	that Esther was **b** also unto the	3947
Est	6:8	Let the royal apparel be **b** which	935
Job	4:12	a thing was secretly **b** to me,	1589
Job	21:32	Yet shall he be **b** to the grave,	2986
Job	42:11	evil the Lord had **b** upon him:	935
Ps	7:14	mischief, and **b** forth falsehood	3205
Ps	30:3	thou hast **b** up my soul from	5927
Ps	71:24	for they are **b** unto shame,	2659
Ps	78:16	**b** streams also out of the rock,	3318
Ps	79:8	us: for we are **b** very low	1809
Ps	90:2	Before the mountains were **b**	3205
Ps	106:43	and were **b** low for their iniquity	4355
Ps	116:6	I was **b** low, and he helped me	1809
Ps	142:6	for I am **b** very low; deliver me	1809
Pr	6:26	a man is **b** to a piece of bread:	
SS	1:4	the king hath **b** me into his	935
Isa	5:15	the mean man shall be **b** down,	7817
Isa	14:15	thou shalt be **b** down to hell,	3381
Isa	25:5	the terrible ones shall be **b** low	6030
Isa	29:4	And thou shalt be **b** down,	8213
Isa	29:20	the terrible one is **b** to nought,	656
Isa	37:26	now have I **b** it to pass, that thou	935
Isa	48:15	I have **b** him, and he shall make	935
Isa	53:7	is **b** as a lamb to the slaughter,	2986
Isa	59:16	therefore his arm **b** salvation	3467
Isa	63:11	Where is he that **b** them up out	5927
Jer	2:6	where is the Lord that **b** us up	5927
Jer	2:7	**b** you into a plentiful country,	935
Jer	11:4	the day that I **b** them forth out	3318
Jer	16:15	liveth, that **b** up the children	5927
Jer	23:8	The Lord liveth, which **b** up	5927
Jer	32:42	Like as I have **b** all this great	935
Jer	39:5	they **b** him up to Nebuchadnezzar	5927
Jer	40:3	Now the Lord hath **b** it, and done	935
La	2:2	hath **b** them down to the ground:	5060
La	4:5	they that were **b** up in scarlet	539
Eze	8:3	and **b** me in the visions of God	935
Eze	8:16	And he **b** me into the inner court	935
Eze	11:24	and **b** me in a vision by the Spirit	935
Eze	14:22	remnant that shall be **b** forth,	3318
Eze	17:24	I the Lord have **b** down the high	8213
Eze	19:4	and they **b** him with chains	935
Eze	30:11	shall be **b** to destroy the land:	935
Eze	37:13	**b** you up out of your graves,	5927
Eze	40:2	In the visions of God **b** he me	935
Eze	40:4	art thou **b** hither: declare all	935
Eze	41:1	Afterward he **b** me to the temple,	935
Eze	44:7	that ye have **b** into my sanctuary	935
Da	1:2	**b** the vessels into the treasure	935
Da	1:9	God had **b** Daniel into favour	5414
Da	6:16	and they **b** Daniel, and cast him	858
Da	9:14	upon the evil, and **b** it upon us:	935
Hos	12:13	the Lord **b** Israel out of Egypt,	5927
Am	3:1	I **b** up from the land of Egypt,	5927
Hag	1:9	and when ye **b** it home, I did	935
Mal	1:13	and ye **b** that which was torn,	935
Mt	1:25	**b** forth her firstborn son:	*5088*
Mt	4:24	they **b** unto him all sick people	*4374*
Mt	10:18	**ye shall be b before governors**	*71*
Mt	11:23	**heaven, shalt be b down to hell:**	*2601*
Mt	12:25	**is b to desolation; and every city**	*2049*
Mt	13:26	**and b forth fruit, then appeared**	*4160*
Mt	16:8	**because ye have b no bread?**	*2989*
Mt	18:24	**one was b unto him, which owed**	*4374*
Mk	4:8	**and b forth, some thirty, and**	*5342*
Mk	4:29	**when the fruit is b forth,**	*3860*
Mk	10:13	they **b** young children to him,	*4374*
Mk	13:9	**ye shall be b before rulers and**	*2476*
Lk	2:7	she **b** forth her firstborn son,	*5088*
Lk	4:16	Nazareth, where he had been **b** up:	*5742*
Lk	7:37	**b** an alabaster box of ointment,	*2865*
Lk	10:34	**b him to an inn, and took care**	*71*
Lk	11:17	**against itself is b to desolation;**	*2049*
Lk	18:15	they **b** unto him also infants,	*4374*
Lk	21:12	**being b before kings and rulers**	*71*
Lk	22:54	**b** him into the high priest's	*1521*
Jn	18:16	kept the door, and **b** in Peter,	*1521*
Jn	19:13	he **b** Jesus forth, and sat down	*71*
Ac	7:40	Moses, which **b** us out of the	*1806*
Ac	7:45	**b** in with Jesus into the	*1521*
Ac	12:6	Herod would have **b** him forth,	*4254*
Ac	16:16	which **b** her masters much gain	*3930*
Ac	19:24	**b** no small gain unto the	*3930*
Ac	20:12	they **b** the young man alive, and	*71*
Ac	21:28	**b** Greeks also into the temple,	*1521*
Ac	25:18	they **b** none accusation of such	*2018*
Ac	27:24	thou must be **b** before Caesar	*3936*
1Co	15:54	then shall be **b** to pass the	*1096*
1Ti	6:7	we **b** nothing into this world,	*1533*
2Ti	1:10	and hath **b** life and immortality	*5461*
Heb	13:20	that **b** again from the dead our	*321*
Rev	12:5	And she **b** forth a man child,	*5088*

BROUGHTEST

Ex	32:7	thy people, which thou **b** out of	5927
Dt	9:28	land whence thou **b** us out say,	3318
Ne	9:15	**b** forth water for them out of	3318

BROW

Lk	4:29	and led him unto the **b** of the hill	*3790*

BRUISE

Ge	3:15	it shall **b** thy head,	7779
Ge	3:15	and thou shalt **b** his heel	7779
Isa	53:10	Yet it pleased the Lord to **b** him;	1792
Jer	30:12	Thy **b** is incurable, and thy	7667
Ro	16:20	**b** Satan under your feet shortly	*4937*

BRUISED

Le	22:24	unto the Lord that which is **b**,	4600
Isa	42:3	A **b** reed shall he not break, and	7533
Isa	53:5	he was **b** for our iniquities: the	1792
Mt	12:20	A **b** reed shall he not break, and	*4937*
Lk	4:18	set at liberty them that are **b**,	*2352*

BRUTE

2Pe	2:12	these, as natural **b** beasts, made	*249*
Jude	10	know naturally, as **b** beasts, in	*249*

BRUTISH
Ps 49:10 the fool and the **b** person perish, 1197
Ps 92:6 a **b** man knoweth not; neither 1197
Pr 12:1 but he that hateth reproof is **b** 1197
Pr 30:2 Surely I am more **b** than any 1197
Jer 10:8 they are altogether **b** and foolish: 1197
Jer 10:14 Every man is **b** in his knowledge: 1197
Jer 10:21 the pastors are become **b**, and 1197
Jer 51:17 Every man is **b** by his knowledge; 1197

BUCKET
Isa 40:15 the nations are as a drop of a **b**, 1805

BUCKLER
2Sa 22:31 a **b** to all them that trust in him. 4043
Ps 18:30 he is a **b** to all those that trust 4043
Pr 2:7 a **b** to them that walk uprightly 4043
Eze 23:24 set against thee **b** and shield 6793

BUCKLERS
SS 4:4 there hang a thousand **b**, all 4043
Eze 39:9 the shields and the **b**, the bows 6793

BUD
Ps 132:17 I make the horn of David to **b**: 6779

Isa 18:5 when the **b** is perfect, and the 6525
Isa 27:6 Israel shall blossom and **b**, and 6524
Isa 55:10 maketh it bring forth and **b**, that 6779
Isa 61:11 the earth bringeth forth her **b**, 6779
Eze 29:21 of the house of Israel to **b** forth, 6779

BUDDED
Nu 17:8 Aaron for the house of Levi was **b**, 6524
Eze 7:10 hath blossomed, pride hath **b** 6524
Heb 9:4 Aaron's rod that **b**, and the tables *985*

BUFFET
Mk 14:65 to cover his face, and to **b** him *2852*
2Co 12:7 messenger of Satan to **b** me, lest *2852*

BUFFETED
Mt 26:67 they spit in his face and **b** him; *2852*
1Co 4:11 and are **b**, and have no certain *2852*
1Pe 2:20 when ye be **b** for your faults, ye *2852*

BUILD
Ge 11:4 Go to, let us **b** us a city and 1129
Ge 11:8 and they left off to **b** the city 1129
Nu 23:1 **B** me here seven altars, and 1129
Nu 32:24 **B** you cities for your little ones, 1129
Ru 4:11 two did **b** the house of Israel: 1129
2Sa 7:5 Shalt thou **b** me an house for me 1129
1Ki 5:3 my father could not **b** an house 1129
1Ki 5:5 shall **b** an house unto my name 1129
1Ki 8:19 thou shalt not **b** the house; but 1129
1Ki 11:7 Then did Solomon **b** an high place 1129
1Ch 17:12 He shall **b** me an house, and I will 1129
1Ch 22:7 it was in my mind to **b** an house 1129
1Ch 22:11 **b** the house of the Lord thy God, 1129
1Ch 29:19 and to **b** the palace, for the which 1129
2Ch 2:5 the house which I **b** is great: for 1129
2Ch 14:7 Let us **b** these cities, and make 1129
2Ch 36:23 to **b** him an house in Jerusalem, 1129
Ezr 1:2 to **b** him an house at Jerusalem, 1129
Ezr 4:3 but we ourselves together will **b** 1129
Ezr 5:17 was made of Cyrus the king to **b** 1124
Ne 2:17 let us **b** up the wall of Jerusalem, 1129
Ps 51:18 **b** thou the walls of Jerusalem 1129
Ps 102:16 the Lord shall **b** up Zion, he shall 1129
Ps 127:1 Except the Lord **b** the house, they 1129
Pr 24:27 and afterwards **b** thine house 1129
Ecc 3:3 break down, and a time to **b** up; 1129
Isa 45:13 he shall **b** my city, and he shall 1129
Isa 65:22 shall not **b**, and another inhabit; 1129
Isa 66:1 where is the house that ye **b** unto 1129
Jer 1:10 to throw down, to **b**, and to plant 1129
Jer 18:9 concerning a kingdom, to **b** and 1129
Jer 29:28 **B** ye houses, and dwell in them; 1129
Jer 35:7 Neither shall ye **b** house, nor sow 1129
Eze 11:3 let us **b** houses: this city is the 1129
Eze 36:36 that I the Lord **b** the ruined 1129
Da 9:25 to restore and to **b** Jerusalem 1129
Mic 3:10 They **b** up Zion with blood, and 1129
Hag 1:8 and **b** the house; and I will take 1129
Zec 6:12 and he shall **b** the temple of the 1129
Mt 16:18 **upon this rock I will b my** *3618*
Mt 23:29 **because ye b the tombs of the** *3618*
Mt 26:61 God, and to **b** it in three days *3618*
Mk 14:58 within three days I will **b** another *3618*
Lk 11:48 **them, and ye b their sepulchres** *3618*
Lk 12:18 **I will pull down my barns, and b** *3618*
Lk 14:30 **This man began to b, and was not** *3618*
Ac 7:49 what house will ye **b** me? saith *3618*
Ac 15:16 **b** again the tabernacle of David, *456*
Ac 20:32 to **b** you up, and to give you an *2026*
Ro 15:20 lest I should **b** upon another *3618*
1Co 3:12 Now if any man **b** upon this *2026*
Gal 2:18 if I **b** again the things which I *3618*

BUILDED
Ge 10:11 and **b** Nineveh, and the city 1129
Ge 12:7 there **b** he an altar unto the Lord, 1129
Jos 22:16 in that ye have **b** you an altar, 1129
1Ki 8:27 less this house that I have **b**? 1129
2Ki 23:13 Solomon the king of Israel had **b** 1129
Ezr 3:2 and **b** the altar of the God of Israel, 1129
Ezr 4:13 if this city be **b**, and the walls set 1124
Ezr 5:11 which a great king of Israel **b** and 1124
Ezr 6:14 And they **b**, and finished it, 1124
Ne 4:17 They which **b** on the wall, and 1129
Ne 6:1 heard that I had **b** the wall, and 1129
Pr 9:1 Wisdom hath **b** her house, she 1129
Pr 24:3 Through wisdom is an house **b**; 1129
Ecc 2:4 I **b** me houses; I planted me 1129
Lk 17:28 **they sold, they planted, they b;** *3618*
Eph 2:22 In whom ye also are **b** together *4925*
Heb 3:4 every house is **b** by some man; *2680*

BUILDER See also MASTERBUILDER.
Heb 11:10 whose **b** and maker is God. *5079*

BUILDERS
1Ki 5:18 Solomon's **b** and Hiram's **b** 1129
Ezr 3:10 when the **b** laid the foundation 1129
Ps 118:22 the stone which the **b** refused 1129
Mt 21:42 **The stone which the b rejected,** *3618*
Mk 12:10 **The stone which the b rejected** *3618*
Lk 20:17 **The stone which the b rejected,** *3618*
Ac 4:11 which was set at nought of you **b**, *3618*
1Pe 2:7 the stone which the **b** disallowed, *3618*

BUILDEST
Ne 6:6 which cause thou **b** the wall, 1129
Mt 27:40 temple, and **b** it in three days, *3618*
Mk 15:29 temple, and **b** it in three days, *3618*

BUILDETH

Pr	14:1	Every wise woman **b** her house:	1129
Jer	22:13	Woe unto him that **b** his house	1129
Hos	8:14	and **b** temples; and Judah	1129
Am	9:6	that **b** his stories in the heaven,	1129
Hab	2:12	Woe to him that **b** a town with	1129
1Co	3:10	take heed how he **b** thereupon.	*2026*

BUILDING

Jos	22:19	in **b** you an altar beside the	1129
1Ki	3:1	made an end of **b** his own house,	1129
1Ki	6:7	when it was in **b**, was built of	1129
1Ki	6:38	So was he seven years in **b** it	1129
1Ki	7:1	Solomon was **b** his own house	1129
Ezr	4:4	Judah, and troubled them in **b**,	1129
Ezr	6:8	for the **b** of this house of God:	1124
Ecc	10:18	By much slothfulness the **b**	4746
Jn	2:20	was this temple in **b**, and wilt	*3618*
1Co	3:9	husbandry, ye are God's **b**	*3619*
2Co	5:1	we have a **b** of God, an house	*3619*
Eph	2:21	In whom all the **b** fitly framed	*3619*
Heb	9:11	that is to say, not of this **b**;	*2937*
Jude	20	**b** up yourselves on your most	*2026*
Rev	21:18	the **b** of the wall of it was of	*1759*

BUILDINGS

Mt	24:1	to shew him the **b** of the temple.	*3619*
Mk	13:2	him, **Seest thou these great b?**	*3619*

BUILT

Ge	22:9	and Abraham **b** an altar there,	1129
Ex	1:11	**b** for Pharaoh treasure cities,	1129
Dt	13:16	for ever; it shall not be **b** again.	1129
2Sa	5:11	and they **b** David an house	1129
1Ki	6:14	So Solomon **b** the house, and	1129
1Ki	9:10	Solomon had **b** the two houses	1129
1Ki	9:24	house which Solomon had **b** for	1129
1Ki	18:32	And with the stones he **b** an altar	1129
2Ki	21:4	And he **b** altars in the house of	1129
2Ki	21:5	And he **b** altars for all the host of	1129
2Ch	6:18	less this house which I have **b**!	1129
2Ch	11:5	**b** cities for defence in Judah,	1129
2Ch	26:10	Also he **b** towers in the desert,	1129
2Ch	27:4	and in the forests he **b** castles	1129
2Ch	33:4	Also he **b** altars in the house of	1129
Ne	4:6	So **b** we the wall; and all the wall	1129
Ps	89:2	Mercy shall be **b** up for ever: thy	1129
Ecc	9:14	and **b** great bulwarks against it:	1129
Jer	19:5	They have **b** also the high places	1129
Jer	31:4	thou shalt be **b**, O virgin of Israel:	1129
Jer	45:4	which I have **b** will I break down,	1129
Eze	16:24	also **b** unto thee an eminent place,	1129
Da	4:30	I have **b** for the house of the	1124
Hag	1:2	that the Lord's house should be **b**	1129
Mt	7:24	**which b his house upon a rock:**	*3618*
Mt	21:33	**winepress in it, and b a tower,**	*3618*
Lk	6:49	**a foundation b an house upon**	*3618*
Lk	7:5	and he hath **b** us a synagogue	*3618*
Ac	7:47	But Solomon **b** him an house.	*3618*
1Co	3:14	abide which he hath **b** thereupon,	*2026*
Eph	2:20	And are **b** upon the foundation	*2026*
Col	2:7	Rooted and **b** up in him, and	*2026*
Heb	3:4	but he that **b** all things is God.	*2680*
1Pe	2:5	are **b** up a spiritual house,	*3618*

BULL

Isa	51:20	as a wild **b** in a net: they are	8377

BULLOCK

Ex	29:10	hands upon the head of the **b**	6499
Ex	29:11	shalt kill the **b** before the Lord,	6499
Ex	29:12	take of the blood of the **b**, and	6499
Ex	29:14	the flesh of the **b**, and his skin,	6499
Ex	29:36	And thou shalt offer every day a **b**	6499
Le	8:2	a **b** for the sin offering, and two	6499
Le	8:14	hands upon the head of the **b** for	6499
Le	9:4	Also a **b** and a ram for peace	7794
Le	16:3	a young **b** for a sin offering, and	6499
Le	22:23	Either a **b** or a lamb, that hath	7794
Le	22:27	When a **b**, or a sheep, or a goat	7794
Nu	15:8	when thou preparest a **b** for	1121, 1241
Nu	29:36	one **b**, one ram, seven lambs of	6499
1Ki	18:23	and let them choose one **b** for	6499
1Ki	18:23	and I will dress the other **b**,	6499
1Ki	18:33	and cut the **b** in pieces; and laid	6499
Isa	65:25	lion shall eat straw like the **b**:	1241
Eze	45:22	for all the people of the land a **b**	6499

BULLOCK'S

Le	4:4	his hand upon the **b** head,	6499
Le	4:16	anointed, shall bring of the **b**	6499

BULLOCKS

Nu	7:87	were twelve **b**, the rams twelve,	6499
Nu	7:88	were twenty and four **b**, the rams	6499
Nu	29:13	thirteen young **b**, two rams,	6499
Nu	29:17	ye shall offer twelve young **b**,	6499
Nu	29:20	the third day eleven **b**, two rams,	6499
Nu	29:23	on the fourth day ten **b**, two rams,	6499
Nu	29:26	And on the fifth day nine **b**, two	6499
Nu	29:29	on the sixth day eight **b**, two	6499
Nu	29:32	And on the seventh day seven **b**,	6499
1Ch	29:21	a thousand **b**, a thousand rams,	6499
2Ch	29:32	threescore and ten **b**, an hundred	1241
2Ch	30:24	thousand **b** and seven thousand	6499
2Ch	35:7	three thousand **b**: these were	1241
Ezr	6:17	an hundred **b**, two hundred rams,	8450
Ezr	7:17	buy speedily with this money **b**,	8450
Ezr	8:35	twelve **b** for all Israel, ninety	6499
Job	42:8	take unto you now seven **b** and	6499
Ps	51:19	then shall they offer **b** upon thine	6499
Isa	1:11	I delight not in the blood of **b**,	6499
Jer	50:27	Slay all her **b**; let them go down	6499
Eze	45:23	seven **b** and seven rams without	6499

BULLS

Ps	22:12	Many **b** have compassed me:	6499
Ps	50:13	Will I eat the flesh of **b**, or drink	47
Jer	50:11	heifer at grass, and bellow as **b**;	47
Jer	52:20	and twelve brasen **b** that were	1241
Heb	9:13	if the blood of **b** and of goats,	*5022*
Heb	10:4	not possible that the blood of **b**	*5022*

BULRUSH

Isa	58:5	bow down his head as a **b**,	100

BULRUSHES

Ex	2:3	took for him an ark of **b**,	1573
Isa	18:2	in vessels of **b** upon the waters,	1573

BULWARKS

Dt	20:20	shall build **b** against the city	4692
Ps	48:13	Mark ye well her **b**, consider her	2430
Ecc	9:14	and built great **b** against it:	4685

BUNDLE

Ge 42:35 every man's **b** of money was in 6872
1Sa 25:29 bound in the **b** of life with the 6872
SS 1:13 a **b** of myrrh is my wellbeloved 6872

BUNDLES

Ge 42:35 their father saw the **b** of money, ...6872
Mt 13:30 **bind them in b to burn them:** *1197*

BURDEN

Ex 18:22 and they shall bear the **b** with thee.
Ex 23:5 lying under his **b**, and wouldest 4853
Nu 4:19 one to his service and to his **b**: 4853
Nu 4:47 service of the **b** in the tabernacle 4853
Nu 4:49 according to his **b**: thus were they 4853
Nu 11:17 they shall bear the **b** of the people 4853
Dt 1:12 and your **b**, and your strife? 4853
2Ch 35:3 not be a **b** upon your shoulders: 4853
Ne 13:19 no **b** be brought in on the sabbath 4853
Job 7:20 so that I am a **b** to myself? 4853
Ps 38:4 as an heavy **b** they are too heavy 4853
Ps 55:22 Cast thy **b** upon the Lord, and he 3053
Isa 13:1 The **b** of Babylon, which Isaiah 4853
Isa 15:1 The **b** of Moab. Because in the 4853
Isa 19:1 The **b** of Egypt. Behold, the Lord 4853
Isa 22:1 The **b** of the valley of vision 4853
Isa 30:27 the **b** thereof is heavy: his lips 4858
Isa 46:2 they could not deliver the **b**, but 4853
Jer 17:21 bear no **b** on the sabbath day, ...4853
Jer 23:33 saying, What is the **b** of the Lord? 4853
Jer 23:34 that shall say, The **b** of the Lord, ...4853
Jer 23:36 every man's word shall be his **b** 4853
Jer 23:38 ye say, The **b** of the Lord; 4853
Na 1:1 The **b** of Nineveh. The book of 4853
Hab 1:1 **b** which Habakkuk the prophet 4853
Zec 12:1 The **b** of the word of the Lord 4853
Mal 1:1 The **b** of the word of the Lord to 4853
Mt 11:30 **yoke is easy, and my b is light** *5413*
Mt 20:12 **which have borne the b and heat** *922*
Ac 15:28 upon you no greater **b** than these *922*
Gal 6:5 every man shall bear his own **b**. *5413*
Rev 2:24 **will put upon you none other b** *922*

BURDENED

2Co 5:4 do groan, being **b**: not for that *916*
2Co 8:13 other men be eased, and ye **b**: *2347*

BURDENS

Ex 1:11 to afflict them with their **b** 5450
Ex 6:7 bringeth you out from under the **b** 5450
2Ch 2:18 to be bearers of **b**, and fourscore 5449
Ne 4:17 and they that bare **b**, with those 5447
Ne 13:15 all manner of **b**, which they 4853
Isa 58:6 to undo the heavy **b**, and to 92
La 2:14 false **b** and causes of banishment. 4864
Mt 23:4 **For they bind heavy b and** *5413*
Lk 11:46 **with b grievous to be borne, and** *5413*
Lk 11:46 **ye yourselves touch not the b** *5413*
Gal 6:2 Bear ye one another's **b**, and *922*

BURDENSOME

Zec 12:3 will I make Jerusalem a **b** stone 4614
2Co 11:9 kept myself from being **b** unto *4*
2Co 12:13 I myself was not **b** to you? *2655*
2Co 12:14 I will not be **b** to you: for I seek *2655*
1Th 2:6 we might have been **b**, as the *1722, 922*

BURIAL

Ecc 6:3 good, and also that ye have no **b**; 6900
Isa 14:20 not be joined with them in **b**, ...6900
Mt 26:12 **my body, she did it for my b** *1779*

BURIED See also BURYINGPLACE.

Ge 15:15 thou shalt be **b** in a good old age 6912
Ge 49:31 There they **b** Abraham and Sarah 6912
Ge 50:13 and **b** him in the cave of the field 6912
Nu 33:4 For the Egyptians **b** all their 6912
Ru 1:17 and there will I be **b**: the Lord 6912
1Ki 2:10 slept with his fathers, and was **b** 6912
1Ki 13:31 wherein the man of God is **b**; 6912
1Ch 10:12 and **b** their bones under the oak 6912
2Ch 21:20 Howbeit they **b** him in the city of 6912
Ecc 8:10 And so I saw the wicked **b**, who 6912
Jer 8:2 shall not be gathered, nor be **b**; 6912
Jer 16:4 lamented; neither shall they be **b**; 6912
Jer 20:6 thou shalt die, and shalt be **b** 6912
Jer 25:33 lamented, neither gathered, nor **b**; 6912
Eze 39:15 till the buriers have **b** it in the 6912
Lk 16:22 **rich man also died, and was b;** *2290*
Ac 2:29 he is both dead and **b**, and his *2290*
Ac 5:9 the feet of them which have **b** thy *2290*
Ro 6:4 we are **b** with him by baptism *4916*
1Co 15:4 And that he was **b**, and that he *2290*
Col 2:12 **B** with him in baptism, wherein *4916*

BURN

Ge 44:18 let not thine anger **b** against thy 2734
Ex 29:18 And thou shalt **b** the whole ram 6999
Ex 29:34 then thou shalt **b** the remainder 8313
Ex 30:1 make an altar to **b** incense upon: 4729
Le 1:9 the priest shall **b** all on the altar, ...6999
Le 1:15 **b** it on the altar; and the blood 6999
Le 6:12 and the priest shall **b** wood on it 1197
Le 13:52 He shall therefore **b** that garment, ...8313
Dt 5:23 the mountain did **b** with fire,) 1197
Dt 13:16 and shalt **b** with fire the city, ...8313
Dt 32:22 and shall **b** unto the lowest hell, ...3344
Jgs 14:15 lest we **b** thee and thy father's 8313
1Ki 13:2 the high places that **b** incense 6999
2Ki 16:15 Upon the great altar **b** the morning 6999
2Ki 18:4 children of Israel did **b** incense 6699
2Ki 23:5 ordained to **b** incense in the 6699
2Ch 26:16 the temple of the Lord to **b** 6999
2Ch 28:25 places to **b** incense unto other 6999
Ps 79:5 shall thy jealousy **b** like fire? 1197
Ps 89:46 shall thy wrath **b** like fire? 1197
Isa 1:31 and they shall both **b** together, ...1197
Isa 44:15 shall it be for a man to **b**: for he 1197
Jer 4:4 and **b** that none can quench it, ...1197
Jer 7:31 **b** their sons and their daughters 8313
Jer 15:14 anger, which shall **b** upon you 3344
Jer 17:4 anger, which shall **b** for ever 3344
Jer 19:5 to **b** their sons with fire for 8313
Jer 21:12 and **b** that none can quench it, ...1197
Jer 36:25 that he would not **b** the roll: 8313
Jer 44:17 to **b** incense unto the queen of 6999
Jer 44:25 **b** incense to the queen of heaven, ...6999
Eze 5:2 Thou shalt **b** with fire a third 1197
Eze 39:9 and they shall **b** them with fire 1197
Hos 4:13 **b** incense upon the hills, ...6999
Mal 4:1 that shall **b** as an oven; and all 1197
Mt 3:12 but he will **b** up the chaff with *2618*
Mt 13:30 **bind them in bundles to b** *2618*

Lk 1:9 his lot was to **b** incense when... *2370*
Lk 3:17 but the chaff he will **b** with fire... *2618*
Lk 24:32 Did not our heart **b** within us,... *2545*
1Co 7:9 it is better to marry than to **b**... *4448*
2Co 11:29 who is offended, and I **b** not?... *4448*
Rev 17:16 and **b** her with fire... *2618*

BURNED See also BURNT.
Ex 3:2 the bush **b** with fire, and the... 1197
Le 8:16 and Moses **b** it upon the altar... 6999
Dt 4:11 the mountain **b** with fire unto... 1197
Dt 9:15 and the mount **b** with fire:... 1197
2Sa 5:21 and David and his men **b** them... 5375
2Ki 23:4 he **b** them without Jerusalem... 8313
2Ki 23:11 and **b** the chariots of the sun... 8313
2Ki 23:15 to powder, and **b** the grove... 8313
2Ki 23:20 and **b** men's bones upon them,... 8313
2Ch 29:7 have not **b** incense nor offered... 6999
Ne 1:3 gates thereof are **b** with fire... 3341
Est 1:12 wroth, and his anger **b** in him... 1197
Job 30:30 and my bones are **b** with heat... 2787
Ps 39:3 while I was musing the fire **b**:... 1197
Pr 6:27 and his clothes not be **b**?... 8313
Pr 6:28 hot coals, and his feet not be **b**?... 3554
Isa 42:25 and it **b** him, yet he laid it not... 1197
Isa 43:2 thou shalt not be **b**; neither... 3554
Isa 64:11 is **b** up with fire: and all our... 8316
Jer 1:16 have **b** incense unto other gods,... 6999
Jer 9:10 they are **b** up, so that none can... 3341
Jer 18:15 they have **b** incense to vanity,... 6999
Jer 19:4 **b** incense in it unto other gods,... 6999
Jer 36:29 Thou hast **b** this roll, saying... 8313
Jer 44:23 Because ye have **b** incense, and... 6999
Jer 52:13 And **b** the house of the Lord,... 8313
La 2:3 he **b** against Jacob like a flaming... 1197
Eze 15:5 fire hath devoured it, and it is **b**?... 2787
Eze 24:10 it well, and let the bones be **b**... 2787
Hos 2:13 wherein she **b** incense to them,... 6999
Joel 1:19 the flame hath **b** all the trees of... 3857
Na 1:5 the earth is **b** at his presence,... 5375
Mt 13:40 **the tares are gathered and b in**... *2618*
Mt 22:7 **murderers, and b up their city**... *1714*
Jn 15:6 **into the fire, and they are b.**... *2545*
Ac 19:19 and **b** them before all men: and... *2618*
Ro 1:27 **b** in their lust one toward... *1572*
1Co 3:15 If any man's work shall be **b**, he... *2618*
1Co 13:3 I give my body to be **b**, and have... *2545*
Heb 6:8 cursing, whose end is to be **b**... *2740*
Heb 12:18 and that **b** with fire, nor unto... *2545*
Heb 13:11 high priest for sin, are **b** without... *2618*
2Pe 3:10 works that are therein shall be **b**... *2618*
Rev 1:15 as if they **b** in a furnace; and his... *4448*
Rev 18:8 she shall be utterly **b** with fire:... *2618*

BURNETH
Ps 83:14 As the fire **b** a wood, and as the... 1197
Ps 97:3 A fire goeth before him, and **b** up... 3857
Isa 62:1 thereof as a lamp that **b**... 1197
Isa 64:2 As when the melting fire **b**, the... 6919
Isa 65:5 nose, a fire that **b** all the day... 3344
Am 6:10 that **b** him, to bring out the bones... 5635
Rev 21:8 in the lake which **b** with fire and... *2545*

BURNING
Ex 21:25 **B** for **b**, wound for wound,... 3555
Le 6:13 The fire shall ever be **b** upon... 3344
Le 16:12 shall take a censer full of **b** coals... 784
Nu 19:6 cast it into the midst of the **b** of... 8316
Dt 29:23 brimstone, and salt, and **b**, that... 8316
2Ch 16:14 they made a very great **b** for him... 8316
2Ch 21:19 his people made no **b** for him,... 8316
Job 41:19 Out of his mouth go **b** lamps,... 3940
Pr 16:27 in his lips there is as a **b** fire... 6867
Pr 26:21 As coals are to **b** coals, and... 1513
Pr 26:23 **B** lips and a wicked heart are... 1814
Isa 4:4 and by the spirit of **b**... 1197
Isa 30:27 **b** with his anger, and the burden... 1197
Jer 20:9 was in mine heart as a **b** fire... 1197
Eze 1:13 like **b** coals of fire, and like the... 1197
Da 3:17 able to deliver us from the **b** fiery... 3345
Da 3:20 cast them into the **b** fiery furnace... 3345
Da 7:9 flame, and his wheels as **b** fire... 1815
Da 7:11 and given to the **b** flame... 3346
Am 4:11 firebrand plucked out of the **b**:... 8316
Lk 12:35 **girded about, and your lights b;**... *2545*
Jn 5:35 **He was a b and a shining light:**... *2545*
Rev 4:5 lamps of fire **b** before the throne,... *2545*
Rev 8:8 a great mountain **b** with fire was... *2545*
Rev 8:10 **b** as it were a lamp, and it fell... *2545*
Rev 18:9 they shall see the smoke of her **b**,... *4451*
Rev 19:20 a lake of fire **b** with brimstone... *2545*

BURNINGS
Isa 33:12 people shall be as the **b** of lime... 4955
Isa 33:14 us shall dwell with everlasting **b**?... 4168
Jer 34:5 and with the **b** of thy fathers,... 4955

BURNT See also BURNED.
Ge 8:20 offered **b** offerings on the altar... 5930
Ge 22:2 offer him there for a **b** offering... 5930
Ge 22:7 where is the lamb for a **b** offering?... 5930
Ge 38:24 Bring her forth, and let her be **b**... 8313
Ex 3:3 sight, why the bush is not **b**... 1197
Ex 10:25 **b** offerings, that we may sacrifice... 5930
Ex 20:24 sacrifice thereon thy **b** offerings... 5930
Ex 29:42 continual **b** offering throughout... 5930
Ex 40:10 anoint the altar of the **b** offering,... 5930
Le 1:4 upon the head of the **b** offering;... 5930
Le 2:12 they shall not be **b** on the altar... 5927
Le 4:30 horns of the altar of **b** offering,... 5930
Le 6:9 the law of the **b** offering:... 5930
Le 6:23 shall be wholly **b**: it shall not... 6999
Le 7:17 the third day shall be **b** with fire... 8313
Le 7:37 This is the law of the **b** offering,... 5930
Le 9:7 sin offering, and thy **b** offering,... 5930
Le 9:11 he **b** with fire without the camp... 8313
Le 10:16 it was **b**: and he was angry with... 8313
Le 10:19 sin offering and their **b** offering... 5930
Le 12:8 the one for the **b** offering, and the... 5930
Le 17:8 offereth a **b** offering or sacrifice,... 5930
Le 23:37 a **b** offering, and a meat offering,... 5930
Nu 6:14 without blemish for a **b** offering:... 5930
Nu 10:10 over your **b** offerings, and over... 5930
Nu 23:15 Stand here by thy **b** offering,... 5930
Nu 28:6 a continual **b** offering, which was... 5930
Nu 28:10 the **b** offering of every Sabbath,... 5930
Nu 28:14 the **b** offering of every month... 5930
Nu 28:23 the **b** offering in the morning... 5930
Nu 28:24 the continual **b** offering, and his... 5930
Nu 29:38 **b** offering, and his meat offering,... 5930
Dt 9:21 and **b** it with fire, and stamped it,... 8313
Dt 12:11 **b** offerings, and your sacrifices,... 5930
Dt 12:31 daughters they have **b** in the fire... 8313

Jos	6:24	they **b** the city with fire, and	8313
Jos	22:29	to build an altar for **b** offerings,	5930
Jgs	15:6	**b** her and her father with fire.	8313
2Sa	24:24	neither will I offer **b** offerings	5930
1Ki	3:3	and **b** incense in high places.	6999
1Ki	9:25	did Solomon offer **b** offerings	5930
1Ki	13:2	bones shall be **b** upon thee	8313
1Ki	15:13	her idol, and **b** it by the brook	8313
1Ki	18:38	fell, and consumed the **b** sacrifice,	5930
2Ki	17:31	Sepharvites **b** their children	8313
2Ki	25:9	And he **b** the house of the Lord,	8313
2Ki	25:9	every great man's house **b** he	8313
1Ch	21:24	nor offer **b** offerings without cost.	5930
1Ch	21:26	offered **b** offerings and peace	5930
2Ch	1:6	offered a thousand **b** offerings	5930
2Ch	7:1	and consumed the **b** offering	5930
2Ch	23:18	the **b** offerings of the Lord, as it	5930
2Ch	28:3	and **b** his children in the fire,	1197
2Ch	29:24	the **b** offering and the sin	5930
2Ch	29:31	as were of a free heart **b** offerings.	5930
2Ch	31:2	priests and Levites for **b** offerings	5930
2Ch	31:3	his substance for the **b** offerings,	5930
2Ch	34:5	he **b** the bones of the priests,	8313
Ezr	3:4	and offered the daily **b** offerings	5930
Ne	10:33	and for the continual **b** offering,	5930
Job	1:5	and offered **b** offerings according	5930
Job	42:8	up for yourselves a **b** offering;	5930
Ps	20:3	and accept thy **b** sacrifice;	5930
Ps	40:6	**b** offering and sin offering hast	5930
Ps	51:16	thou delightest not in **b** offering	5930
Ps	51:19	**b** offering and whole **b** offering:	5930
Isa	1:11	I am full of the **b** offerings of	5930
Isa	61:8	I hate robbery for **b** offering;	5930
Jer	6:20	your **b** offerings are not acceptable,	5930
Jer	19:5	burn their sons with fire for **b**	5930
Jer	51:25	will make thee a **b** mountain.	8316
Eze	43:27	priests shall make your **b** offerings	5930
Eze	45:17	prince's part to give **b** offerings,	5930
Eze	46:12	prepare a voluntary **b** offering	5930
Hos	6:6	of God more than **b** offerings.	5930
Am	5:22	ye offer me **b** offerings and your	5930
Mic	6:6	come before him with **b** offerings,	5930
Mk	12:33	more than all whole **b** offerings	*3646*
Heb	10:6	In **b** offerings and sacrifices for	*3646*
Heb	10:8	and **b** offerings and offering for	*3646*
Rev	8:7	the third part of trees was **b** up,	*2618*

BURNT-OFFERING See BURNT and OFFERING.

BURNT-SACRIFICE See BURNT and SACRIFICE.

BURST

Jer	2:20	thy yoke, and **b** thy bands;	5423
Jer	5:5	broken the yoke, and **b** the bonds.	5423
Na	1:13	and will **b** thy bonds in sunder.	5423
Mk	2:22	**doth b the battles, and the wine**	*4486*
Lk	5:37	**new wine will b the bottles,**	*4486*
Ac	1:18	he **b** asunder in the midst,	*2297*

BURSTING

Isa	30:14	shall not be found in the **b** of it	4386

BURY See also BURIED; BURYING.

Ge	23:4	I may **b** my dead out of my sight	6912
Ge	47:29	**b** me not, I pray thee, in Egypt:	6912
Ge	50:14	went up with him to **b** his father,	6912
Dt	21:23	shall in any wise **b** him that day;	6912
1Ki	2:31	and fall upon him, and **b** him;	6912
1Ki	13:31	When I am dead, then **b** me in	6912
2Ki	9:10	and there shall be none to **b** her.	6912
2Ki	9:35	they went to **b** her: but they	6912
Ps	79:3	and there was none to **b** them.	6912
Jer	14:16	they shall have none to **b** them,	6912
Jer	19:11	till there be no place to **b**	6912
Eze	39:11	and there shall they **b** Gog and	6912
Mt	8:21	me first to go and **b** my father	*2290*
Mt	8:22	**and let the dead b their dead.**	*2290*
Mt	27:7	potter's field, to **b** strangers in	*5027*
Lk	9:59	me first to go and **b** my father	*2290*
Lk	9:60	**Let the dead b their dead:**	*2290*
Jn	19:40	the manner of the Jews is to **b**	*1779*

BURYING

2Ki	13:21	as they were **b** a man, that,	6912
Mk	14:8	**to anoint my body to the b.**	*1780*
Jn	12:7	**against the day of my b hath she**	*1780*

BURYINGPLACE

Ge	23:4	give me a possession of a **b**	6913
Ge	47:30	bury me in their **b**. And he said,	6913

BUSH

Ex	3:2	and the **b** was not consumed.	5572
Ex	3:4	him out of the midst of the **b**,	5572
Dt	33:16	will of him that dwelt in the **b**:	5572
Mk	12:26	**how in the b God spake unto him**	*942*
Lk	20:37	**even Moses shewed at the b,**	*942*
Ac	7:30	Lord in a flame of fire in a **b**	*942*

BUSHEL

Mt	5:15	**a candle, and put it under a b,**	*3426*
Mk	4:21	**brought to be put under a b,**	*3426*
Lk	11:33	**neither under a b, but on a**	*3426*

BUSINESS

Ge	39:11	went into the house to do his **b**;	4399
Jos	2:14	yours, if ye utter not this our **b**	1697
Jos	2:20	if thou utter this our **b**, then we	1697
1Sa	21:2	man know anything of the **b**	1697
2Ch	13:10	the Levites wait upon their **b**:	4399
Ne	11:22	over the **b** of the house of God	4399
Ne	13:30	Levites, every one in his **b**;	4399
Est	3:9	that have the charge of the **b**,	4399
Ps	107:23	ships, that do **b** in great waters;	4399
Pr	22:29	thou a man diligent in his **b**?	4399
Ecc	5:3	through the multitude of **b**;	6045
Ecc	8:16	the **b** that is done upon the earth:	6045
Da	8:27	rose up, and did the king's **b**;	4399
Lk	2:49	**must be about my father's b?**	
Ac	6:3	we may appoint over this **b**	*5532*
Ro	12:11	Not slothful in **b**; fervent in	*4710*
1Th	4:11	to do your own **b**, and to work	*2398*

BUSYBODIES

2Th	3:11	working not at all, but are **b**	*4020*
1Ti	5:13	but tattlers also and **b**, speaking	*4021*

BUSYBODY

1Pe	4:15	or as a **b** in other men's matters	*244*

BUTLER

Ge	40:5	the **b** and the baker of the king of	4945
Ge	40:9	chief **b** told his dream to Joseph	4945
Ge	40:23	Yet did not the chief **b** remember	4945
Ge	41:9	spake the chief **b** unto Pharaoh,	4945

BUTTER

Jgs	5:25	brought forth **b** in a lordly dish	2529
Ps	55:21	his mouth were smoother than **b**,	4260
Pr	30:33	of milk bringeth forth **b**, and the	2529
Isa	7:15	**B** and honey shall he eat, that he	2529
Isa	7:22	for **b** and honey shall every one	2529

BUY See also BOUGHT.

Ge	41:57	Egypt to Joseph for to **b** corn;	7666
Ge	42:7	From the land of Canaan to **b** food.	7666
Ge	44:25	Go again, and **b** us a little food.	7666
Ex	21:2	If thou **b** an Hebrew servant	7069
Le	22:11	But if the priest **b** any soul with	7069
Dt	2:6	Ye shall **b** meat of them for money,	7666
Ru	4:5	**b** it also of Ruth the Moabitess,	7069
Ru	4:8	kinsman said unto Boaz, **b** it for thee	7069
1Ch	21:24	I will verily **b** it for the full price:	7069
Ezr	7:17	**b** speedily with this money	7066
Ne	10:31	not **b** it of them on the sabbath	3947
Pr	23:23	**B** the truth, and sell it not;	7069
Isa	55:1	come ye, **b**, and eat;	7666
Jer	32:7	**B** thee my field that is in	7069
Am	8:6	That we may **b** the poor for silver	7069
Mt	14:15	villages, and **b** themselves victuals	*59*
Mt	25:10	**while they went to b, the**	*59*
Mk	6:36	villages, and **b** themselves bread:	*59*
Lk	9:13	go and **b** meat for all this people	*59*
Lk	22:36	**let him sell his garment, and b one.**	*59*
Jn	6:5	**Whence shall we b bread, that**	*59*
Jn	13:29	**B** those things that we have need	*59*
Jas	4:13	a year, and **b** and sell, and get gain:	*1710*
Rev	3:18	**I counsel thee to b of me gold**	*59*
Rev	13:17	that no man might **b** or sell,	*59*

BUYER

Pr	20:14	it is naught, saith the **b**: but	7069
Isa	24:2	as with the **b**, so with the seller;	7069
Eze	7:12	let not the **b** rejoice, nor the seller	7069

BUYEST

Le	25:14	**b** ought of thy neighbour's hand,	7069
Ru	4:5	What day thou **b** the field of the	7069

BUYETH

Pr	31:16	She considereth a field, and **b** it:	3947
Mt	13:44	**all that he hath, and b that field**	*59*
Rev	18:11	for no man **b** their merchandise	*59*

BYWORD

Dt	28:37	a **b**, among all nations whither	8148
1Ki	9:7	and a **b** among all people:	8148
2Ch	7:20	and a **b** among all nations	8148
Job	17:6	made me also a **b** of the people	4914
Job	30:9	their song, yea, I am their **b**.	4405
Ps	44:14	us a **b** among the heathen,	4912

C

CAESAR (se´-zur) See also CAESAR'S.

Mt	22:17	to give tribute unto **C**, or not?	*2541*
Mt	22:21	**unto C the things which are**	*2541*
Mk	12:17	**C the things that are Caesar's,**	*2541*
Lk	2:1	a decree from **C** Augustus,	*2541*
Lk	20:25	**C the things which be Caesar's,**	*2541*
Jn	19:15	answered, We have no king but **C**	*2541*
Ac	11:28	pass in the days of Claudius **C**	*2541*
Ac	25:8	nor yet against **C**, have I offended	*2541*
Ac	25:11	unto them. I appeal unto **C**	*2541*
Ac	25:21	be kept till I might send him to **C**	*2541*
Ac	26:32	if he had not appealed unto **C**	*2541*
Ac	28:19	constrained to appeal unto **C**;	*2541*

CAESAR'S (se´-zurs)

Mt	22:21	**Caesar the things which are C;**	*2541*
Mk	12:17	**to Caesar the things that are C,**	*2542*
Lk	20:25	**Caesar the things which be C,**	*2542*
Ac	25:10	I stand at **C** judgment seat,	*2541*

CAGE

Jer	5:27	As a **c** is full of birds, so are their	3619
Rev	18:2	a **c** of every unclean and hateful	*5438*

CAKE

Ex	29:23	and one **c** of oiled bread, and one	2471
Nu	15:20	Ye shall offer up a **c** of the first	2471
Jgs	7:13	a **c** of barley bread tumbled into	6742
1Sa	30:12	gave him a piece of a **c** of figs	1690
1Ki	17:12	I have not a **c**, but an handful of	4580
Hos	7:8	Ephraim is a **c** not turned	5692

CAKES

Ge	18:6	it, and make **c** upon the hearth	5692
Ex	29:2	bread, and **c** unleavened	2471
Le	24:5	bake twelve **c** thereof: two tenth	2471
Nu	6:15	**c** of fine flour mingled with oil	2471
Nu	11:8	baked it in pans, and make **c** of it:	5692
1Sa	25:18	two hundred **c** of figs, and laid	1690
2Sa	13:10	and Tamar took the **c** which she had	3834
Jer	7:18	make **c** to the queen of heaven,	3561
Eze	4:12	And thou shalt eat it as barley **c**,	5692

CALAMITIES

Ps	57:1	refuge, until these **c** be overpast	1942
Pr	17:5	he that is glad at **c** shall not be	343

CALAMITY

Dt	32:35	the day of their **c** is at hand, and	343
Job	30:13	they set forward my **c**, they have	1942
Ps	18:18	prevented me in the day of my **c**:	343
Pr	19:13	foolish son is the **c** of his father:	1942
Pr	27:10	brother's house in the day of thy **c**:	343
Jer	49:8	will bring the **c** of Esau upon him,	343
Eze	35:5	the sword in the time of their **c**,	343
Ob	13	in the day of their **c**; yea, thou	343

CALDRON

1Sa	2:14	the pan, or kettle, or **c**, or pot;	7037
Job	41:20	as out of a seething pot or **c**	100
Mic	3:3	the pot, and as flesh within the **c**	7037

CALF

Ge	18:7	fetcht a **c** tender and good,	1121, 1241
Ge	18:8	the **c** which he had dressed,	1121, 1241
Ex	32:4	after he had made it a molten **c**:	5695
Ex	32:8	they have made them a molten **c**,	5695
Ex	32:19	he saw the **c**, and the dancing:	5695
Ex	32:20	took the **c** which they had made,	5695
Ex	32:24	fire, and there came out this **c**.	5695
Ex	32:35	made the **c**, which Aaron made.	5695
Le	9:8	slew the **c** of the sin offering	5695
Dt	9:16	and had made you a molten **c**:	5695
Ne	9:18	They had made them a molten **c**,	5695
Ps	29:6	maketh them also to skip like a **c**;	5695
Ps	106:19	They made a **c** in Horeb, and	5695
Jer	34:18	when they cut the **c** in twain, and	5695
Jer	34:19	passed between the parts of the **c**;	5695
Hos	8:6	the **c** of Samaria shall be broken	5695
Lk	15:23	**bring hither the fatted c, and kill**	*3448*
Lk	15:27	**thy father hath killed the fatted c,**	*3448*
Rev	4:7	the second beast like a **c**, and the	*3448*

CALL

Ge	4:26	began men to **c** upon the name	7121
Ge	17:19	and thou shalt **c** his name Isaac:	7121
Ge	30:13	the daughters will **c** me blessed:	833
Dt	4:26	I **c** heaven and earth to witness	5749
Dt	30:19	I **c** heaven and earth to record	5749
Jgs	16:25	**C** for Samson, that he may make	7121
Ru	1:20	**C** me not Naomi, **c** me Mara: for	7121
1Sa	3:6	Here am I; for thou didst **c** me	7121
1Sa	16:3	And **c** Jesse to the sacrifice, and I	7121
2Sa	22:4	I will **c** on the Lord, who is worthy	7121
1Ki	1:28	**C** me Bath-sheba. And she came	7121
1Ki	18:24	**c** ye on the name of your gods,	7121
1Ki	18:24	I will **c** on the name of the Lord:	7121
2Ki	5:11	**c** on the name of the Lord his	7121
2Ki	10:19	**c** unto me all the prophets of Baal,	7121
Job	27:10	will he always **c** upon God?	7121
Ps	4:1	Hear me when I **c**, O God of my	7121
Ps	4:3	the Lord will hear when I **c** unto	7121
Ps	14:4	bread, and **c** not upon the Lord	7121
Ps	18:3	I will **c** upon the Lord, who is	7121
Ps	50:15	**c** upon me in the day of trouble:	7121
Ps	55:16	I will **c** upon God; and the Lord	7121
Ps	72:17	all nations shall **c** him blessed	833
Ps	86:7	In the day of my trouble I will **c**	7121
Ps	91:15	He shall **c** upon me, and I will	7121
Ps	105:1	**c** upon his name: make known his	7121
Ps	116:2	therefore will I **c** upon him as long	7121
Ps	116:13	and **c** upon the name of the Lord.	7121
Pr	7:4	**c** understanding thy kinswoman:	7121
Pr	31:28	arise up, and **c** her blessed;	833
Isa	5:20	that **c** evil good, and good evil;	559
Isa	7:14	and shall **c** his name Immanuel.	7121
Isa	12:4	Praise the Lord, **c** upon his name,	7121
Isa	31:2	will not **c** back his words: but	5493
Isa	44:7	And who, as I, shall **c**, and shall	7121
Isa	45:3	the Lord, which **c** thee by thy name,	7121
Isa	58:9	thou **c**, and the Lord shall answer;	7121
Isa	60:14	shall **c** thee, The city of the Lord,	7121
Isa	60:18	thou shalt **c** thy walls Salvation,	7121
Isa	61:6	**c** you the Ministers of our God:	7121
Jer	3:17	**c** Jerusalem the throne of the Lord;	7121
Jer	6:30	Reprobate silver shall men **c**	7121
Jer	25:29	I will call for a sword upon all the	7121
Jer	29:12	Then shall ye **c** upon me, and ye	7121
Jer	33:3	**C** unto me, and I will answer	7121
La	2:15	city that men **c** The perfection of	559

Eze	38:21	And I will c for a sword against	7121
Da	2:2	commanded to c the magicians,	7121
Hos	7:11	they c to Egypt, they go to Assyria.	7121
Joel	2:32	whosoever shall c on the name of	7121
Joel	2:32	remnant whom the Lord shall c	7121
Jnh	1:6	arise, c upon thy God, if so be	7121
Zep	3:9	all c upon the name of the Lord	7121
Mal	3:12	all nations shall c you blessed:	833
Mt	1:21	thou shalt c his name Jesus:	*2564*
Mt	1:23	shall call his name Emmanuel,	*2564*
Mt	9:13	**I am not come to c the righteous,**	*2564*
Mt	20:8	**C the labourers, and give them**	*2564*
Mt	22:43	**doth David in spirit c him Lord,**	*2564*
Mt	22:45	**If David then c him Lord, how is**	*2564*
Mk	2:17	**came not to c the righteous, but**	*2564*
Mk	15:12	whom ye c the King of the Jews?	*3004*
Lk	1:13	thou shalt c his name John	*2564*
Lk	1:31	son, and shalt c his name Jesus	*2564*
Lk	1:48	generations shall c me blessed.	*3106*
Lk	6:46	**And why c ye me, Lord, Lord,**	*2564*
Jn	4:16	**Go, c thy husband, and come**	*5455*
Jn	13:13	**Ye c me Master and Lord: and ye**	*5455*
Ac	2:21	whosoever shall c on the name of	*1941*
Ac	2:39	many as the Lord our God shall c.	*4341*
Ac	10:28	I should not c any man common	*3004*
Ac	24:14	c heresy, so worship I the God	*3004*
Ro	10:13	whosoever shall c upon the name	*1941*
Ro	10:14	How then shall they c on him in	*1941*
2Ti	1:5	When I c to remembrance the	*2983*
Heb	10:32	c to remembrance the former days,	*363*
Jas	5:14	c for the elders of the church;	*4341*

CALLED

Ge	1:5	And God c the light Day,	7121
Ge	1:5	and the darkness he c Night.	7121
Ge	1:8	God c the firmament Heaven.	7121
Ge	1:10	and God c the dry land Earth;	7121
Ge	1:10	together of the waters c he Seas:	7121
Ge	2:19	Adam c every living creature,	7121
Ge	2:23	she shall be c Woman, because	7121
Ge	3:9	And the Lord God c unto Adam,	7121
Ge	3:20	And Adam c his wife's name Eve;	7121
Ge	11:9	therefore is the name of it c Babel;	7121
Ge	12:8	and c upon the name of the Lord.	7121
Ge	13:4	Abram c on the name of the Lord.	7121
Ge	16:13	And she c the name of the Lord	7121
Ge	17:5	thy name any more be c Abram,	7121
Ge	21:12	in Isaac shall thy seed be c.	7121
Ge	32:28	name shall be c no more Jacob.	559
Ge	35:10	shall not be c any more Jacob	7121
Ge	35:10	and he c his name Israel	7121
Ex	2:10	And she c his name Moses:	7121
Ex	3:4	God c unto him out of the midst	7121
Ex	16:31	c the name thereof Manna:	7121
Ex	17:15	c the name of it Jehovah-nissi:	7121
Ex	33:7	and c it the Tabernacle of the	7121
Dt	3:13	which was c the land of giants	7121
Dt	15:2	because it is c the Lord's release	7121
Jos	24:9	sent and c Balaam the son of Beor	7121
Jgs	6:24	and c it Jehovah-shalom:	7121
Jgs	13:24	and c his name Samson:	7121
Jgs	16:28	And Samson c unto the Lord,	7121
1Sa	1:20	a son, and c his name Samuel	7121
1Sa	3:4	That the Lord c Samuel:	7121
1Sa	3:6	the Lord c yet again, Samuel	7121
1Sa	3:6	I c not, my son; lie down again	7121
1Sa	3:8	Lord c Samuel again the third	7121
1Sa	3:8	that the Lord had c the child	7121
1Sa	3:10	the Lord came, and stood, and c	7121
2Sa	5:9	and c it the city of David	7121
2Sa	12:24	and he c his name Solomon:	7121
2Sa	22:7	In my distress I c upon the Lord,	7121
1Ki	1:10	Solomon his brother, he c not	7121
1Ki	18:26	and c on the name of Baal	7121
1Ch	4:10	And Jabez c on the God of Israel	7121
1Ch	13:6	cherubims, whose name is c on it	7121
2Ch	7:14	people, which are c by thy name	7121
Est	4:11	who is not c, there is one law	7121
Est	4:11	I have not been c to come in	7121
Est	9:26	they c these days Purim after	7121
Job	9:16	I had c, and he had answered me;	7121
Ps	18:6	In my distress I c upon the Lord	7121
Ps	31:17	O Lord; for I have c upon thee:	7121
Ps	79:6	kingdoms that have not c upon	7121
Ps	88:9	Lord, I have c daily upon thee	7121
Ps	118:5	I c upon the Lord in distress: the	7121
Pr	1:24	I have c, and ye refused; I have	7121
Pr	16:21	wise in heart shall be c prudent:	7121
Pr	24:8	be c a mischievous person.	7121
SS	5:6	c him, but he gave me no answer	7121
Isa	4:1	only let us be c by thy name,	7121
Isa	9:6	his name shall be c Wonderful	7121
Isa	32:5	person shall be no more c liberal	7121
Isa	35:8	it shall be c The way of holiness;	7121
Isa	42:6	I the Lord have c thee	7121
Isa	43:1	I have c thee by thy name;	7121
Isa	43:7	every one that is c by my name:	7121
Isa	43:22	thou hast not c upon me, O Jacob	7121
Isa	47:1	thou shalt no more be c tender	7121
Isa	48:12	O Jacob and Israel, my c; I am he;	7121
Isa	48:15	yea, I have c him: I have	7121
Isa	49:1	The Lord hath c me from the	7121
Isa	50:2	I c, was there none to answer?	7121
Isa	56:7	mine house shall be c an house of	7121
Isa	58:12	and thou shalt be c, The repairer	7121
Isa	62:2	thou shalt be c by a new name	7121
Isa	65:12	when I c, ye did not answer;	7121
Isa	66:4	when I c, none did answer;	7121
Jer	30:17	they c thee an Outcast, saying,	7121
La	1:15	he hath c an assembly against me	7121
La	1:21	bring the day that thou hast c,	7121
Da	5:12	now let Daniel be c, and he will	7123
Da	8:16	which c, and said, Gabriel, make	7121
Da	9:19	thy people are c by thy name	7121
Da	10:1	whose name was c Belteshazzar;	7121
Hos	11:1	him, and c my son out of Egypt	7121
Am	7:4	Lord God c to contend by fire	7121
Zec	8:3	Jerusalem shall be c a city of	7121
Zec	11:7	the one I c Beauty,	7121
Zec	11:7	and the other I c Bands;	7121
Mt	1:16	born Jesus, who is c Christ	*3004*
Mt	1:25	and he c his name Jesus	*2564*
Mt	2:7	privily c the wise men, enquired	*2564*
Mt	2:15	Out of Egypt have I c my son	*2564*
Mt	2:23	He shall be c a Nazarene	*2564*
Mt	4:18	Simon c Peter, and Andrew his	*3004*
Mt	5:9	**shall be c the children of God**	*2564*
Mt	5:19	**he shall be c the least in the**	*2564*
Mt	5:19	**the same shall be c great in the**	*2564*
Mt	10:2	The first, Simon, who is c Peter,	*3004*
Mt	10:25	**If they have c the master of the**	*2564*
Mt	13:55	is not his mother c Mary? and	*3004*

Mt	18:2	Jesus **c** a little child unto him,	*4341*
Mt	20:16	**for many be c, but few chosen.**	*2822*
Mt	21:13	**My house shall be c the house of**	*2564*
Mt	22:14	**many are c, but few are chosen**	*2822*
Mt	23:7	**and to be c of men, Rabbi, Rabbi**	*2564*
Mt	23:8	**be not ye c Rabbi: for one is your**	*2564*
Mt	23:10	**Neither be ye c masters: for one**	*2564*
Mt	25:14	**c his own servants, and delivered,**	*2564*
Mt	26:14	Then one of the twelve, **c** Judas	*3004*
Mt	26:36	unto a place **c** Gethsemane, and	*3004*
Mt	27:8	that field was **c**, The field of	*2564*
Mt	27:16	a notable prisoner, **c** Barabbas	*3004*
Mt	27:17	or Jesus which is **c** Christ?	*3004*
Mt	27:22	do then with Jesus which is **c**	*3004*
Mt	27:33	unto a place **c** Golgotha, that is	*3004*
Mk	6:7	And he **c** unto him the twelve	*4341*
Mk	11:17	**My house shall be c of all nations**	*2564*
Mk	14:72	Peter **c** to mind the word that	*365*
Lk	1:32	shall be **c** the Son of the Highest:	*2564*
Lk	1:35	shall be **c** the Son of God	*2564*
Lk	1:36	with her, who was **c** barren	*2564*
Lk	1:60	Not so, but he shall be **c** John	*2564*
Lk	1:76	shall be **c** the prophet of the	*2564*
Lk	2:4	of David, which is **c** Bethlehem;	*2564*
Lk	2:21	his name was **c** Jesus, which was	*2564*
Lk	2:23	shall be **c** holy to the Lord;)	*2564*
Lk	8:2	Mary **c** Magdalene, out of whom	*2564*
Lk	15:19	**no more worthy to be c thy son:**	*2564*
Lk	15:21	**no more worthy to be c thy son.**	*2564*
Lk	19:29	the mount **c** the mount of Olives,	*2564*
Lk	22:1	which is **c** the Passover.	*3004*
Lk	22:47	he that was **c** Judas, one of the	*3004*
Lk	23:33	to the place which is **c** Calvary	*2564*
Lk	24:13	to a village **c** Emmaus, which	*3686*
Jn	1:42	**thou shalt be c Cephas,** which	*2564*
Jn	1:48	**Before that Philip c thee, when**	*5455*
Jn	4:25	Messias cometh, which is **c** Christ:	*3004*
Jn	9:11	A man that is **c** Jesus made clay	*3004*
Jn	12:17	when he **c** Lazarus out of his	*5455*
Jn	15:15	**but I have c you friends;**	*2046*
Jn	18:33	**c** Jesus, and said unto him, Art	*5455*
Jn	19:13	in a place that is **c** the Pavement,	*3004*
Jn	19:17	a place **c** the place of a skull,	*3004*
Jn	19:17	is **c** in the Hebrew Golgotha:	*3004*
Ac	1:12	from the mount **c** Olivet, which	*2564*
Ac	3:11	the porch that is **c** Solomon's	*2564*
Ac	9:11	**the street which is c Straight**	*2564*
Ac	9:11	**for one c Saul of Tarsus: for**	*3686*
Ac	9:36	by interpretation is **c** Dorcas:	*3004*
Ac	10:1	of the band **c** the Italian band,	*2564*
Ac	11:26	the disciples were **c** Christians	*5537*
Ac	13:9	Then Saul, (who also is **c** Paul,)	*4341*
Ac	14:12	they **c** Barnabas, Jupiter; and	*2564*
Ac	23:6	I am **c** in question	*2919*
Ac	27:8	which is **c** The fair havens;	*2564*
Ac	27:14	tempestuous wind, **c** Euroclydon.	*2564*
Ac	28:17	Paul **c** the chief of the Jews	*4779*
Ro	1:1	**c** to be an apostle, separated	*2822*
Ro	1:6	are ye also the **c** of Jesus Christ:	*2822*
Ro	2:17	Behold, thou art **c** a Jew, and	*2028*
Ro	8:28	to them who are the **c** according	*2822*
Ro	8:30	them he also **c**: and whom he **c**	*2564*
Ro	9:7	In Isaac shall thy seed be **c**	*2564*
1Co	1:1	**c** to be an apostle of Jesus Christ	*2822*
1Co	1:2	in Christ Jesus, **c** to be saints,	*2522*
1Co	1:9	by whom ye were **c** unto the	*2564*
1Co	1:26	mighty, not many noble, are **c**:	
1Co	7:15	but God hath **c** us to peace	*2564*
1Co	7:22	he that is **c**, being free, is	*2564*
1Co	8:5	though there be that are **c** gods,	*3004*
1Co	15:9	am not meet to be **c** an apostle,	*2564*
Gal	1:15	and **c** me by his grace	*2564*
Gal	5:13	ye have been **c** unto liberty;	*2564*
Eph	4:4	even as ye are **c** in one hope	*2564*
Col	3:15	to the which also ye are **c**	*2564*
1Th	2:12	worthy of God, who hath **c** you	*2564*
2Th	2:4	himself above all that is **c** God,	*3004*
1Ti	6:12	life, whereunto thou art also **c**,	*2564*
1Ti	6:20	oppositions of science falsely so **c**	*5581*
2Ti	1:9	and **c** us with an holy calling,	*2564*
Heb	3:13	while it is **c** Today; lest any	*2564*
Heb	5:10	**C** of God an high priest after	*4316*
Heb	7:11	not be **c** after the order of Aaron?	*3004*
Heb	9:3	tabernacle which is **c** the Holiest	*3004*
Heb	9:15	are **c** might receive the promise	*2564*
Heb	11:8	Abraham, when he was **c** to go	*2564*
Heb	11:16	not ashamed to be **c** their God:	*1941*
Heb	11:18	in Isaac shall thy seed be **c**:	*2564*
Heb	11:24	refused to be **c** the son of	*3004*
Jas	2:23	he was **c** the Friend of God	*2564*
1Pe	1:15	as he which hath **c** you is holy	*2564*
1Pe	2:9	who hath **c** you out of darkness	*2564*
1Pe	5:10	the God of all grace, who hath **c** us	*2564*
2Pe	1:3	of him that hath **c** us to glory	*2564*
1Jn	3:1	we should be **c** the sons of God:	*2564*
Jude	1	preserved in Jesus Christ, and **c**	*2822*
Rev	1:9	was in the isle that is **c** Patmos	*2564*
Rev	8:11	name of the star is **c** Wormwood:	*3004*
Rev	11:8	spiritually is **c** Sodom and Egypt	*2564*
Rev	12:9	serpent, **c** the Devil, and Satan	*2564*
Rev	19:9	which are **c** unto the marriage	*2564*
Rev	19:11	him was **c** Faithful and True,	*2564*
Rev	19:13	his name is **c** The Word of God	*2564*

CALLEST

Mt	19:17	**Why c thou me good? there is**	*3004*
Mk	10:18	unto him, **Why c thou me good?**	*3004*
Lk	18:19	**Why c thou me good? none is**	*3004*

CALLETH

Ps	42:7	Deep **c** unto deep at the noise	7121
Pro	18:6	and his mouth **c** for strokes	7121
Isa	21:11	He **c** to me out of Seir, Watchman,	7121
Isa	59:4	None **c** for justice, nor any	7121
Am	9:6	he that **c** for the waters of the sea,	7121
Mt	27:47	that, said, This man **c** for Elias	*5455*
Mk	12:37	**therefore himself c him Lord;**	*3004*
Mk	15:35	heard it, said Behold, he **c** Elias	*5455*
Lk	20:37	**c the Lord the God of Abraham,**	*3004*
Lk	20:44	**David therefore c him Lord, how**	*2564*
Jn	10:3	**and he c his own sheep by name,**	*2564*
Jn	11:28	The Master is come, and **c** for thee	*5455*
1Co	12:3	**c** Jesus accursed: and that no	*3004*
1Th	5:24	Faithful is he that **c** you, who	*2564*
Rev	2:20	**which c herself a prophetess, to**	*3004*

CALLING

Isa	46:11	**C** a ravenous bird from the east,	7121
Mk	11:21	Peter **c** to remembrance saith	*363*
Lk	7:19	And John **c** unto him two of his	*4341*
Ac	7:59	stoned Stephen, **c** upon God, and	*1941*
Ac	22:16	sins, **c** on the name of the Lord	*1941*
Ro	11:29	gifts and **c** of God are without	*2821*

1Co	1:26	For ye see your **c**, brethren, how	*2821*
1Co	7:20	abide in the same **c** wherein he	*2821*
Eph	1:18	what is the hope of his **c**, and	*2821*
Eph	4:4	are called in one hope of your **c**;	*2821*
Php	3:14	for the prize of the high **c** of	*2821*
2Th	1:11	would count you worthy of this **c**	*2821*
2Ti	1:9	us, and called us with an holy **c**	*2821*
Heb	3:1	partakers of the heavenly **c**,	*2821*
2Pe	1:10	give diligence to make your **c**	*2821*

CALM

Ps	107:29	He maketh the storm a **c**, so that	1827
Mt	8:26	the sea; and there was a great **c**	*1055*
Mk	4:39	ceased, and there was a great **c**	*1055*
Lk	8:24	they ceased, and there was a **c**	*1055*

CALVARY (cal´-va-ry)

Lk	23:33	which is called **C**, there they	*2898*

CALVES

1Ki	12:28	made two **c** of gold, and said	5695
2Ki	10:29	golden **c** that were in Beth-el,	5695
2Ki	17:16	them molten images, even two **c**,	5695
2Ch	11:15	and for the **c** which he had made	5695
2Ch	13:8	there are with you golden **c**, which	5695
Heb	9:12	by the blood of goats and **c**, but	*3448*
Heb	9:19	took the blood of **c** and of goats,	*3448*

CAME

Ge	6:4	sons of God **c** in unto the daughters	935
Ge	11:5	the Lord **c** down to see the city	3381
Ge	15:1	word of the Lord **c** unto Abram	1961
Ge	19:1	And there **c** two angels to Sodom	935
Ge	19:9	Lot, and **c** near to break the door	5066
Ge	25:25	And the first **c** out red, all over	3318
Ge	25:26	after that **c** his brother out,	3318
Ge	39:17	us, **c** in unto me to mock me:	935
Ge	41:18	there **c** up out of the river seven	5927
Ge	41:19	seven other kine **c** up after them,	5927
Ge	41:22	seven ears **c** up in one stalk,	5927
Ge	41:27	ill favoured kine that **c** up	5927
Ge	42:6	and Joseph's brethren **c**, and	935
Ge	43:26	And when Joseph **c** home, they	935
Ge	44:14	And Judah and his brethren **c**	935
Ge	46:28	they **c** into the land of Goshen	935
Ex	2:5	And the daughter of Pharaoh **c**	3381
Ex	2:17	shepherds **c** and drove them away	935
Ex	2:23	and their cry **c** up unto God	5927
Ex	3:1	and **c** to the mountain of God	935
Ex	8:6	and the frogs **c** up, and covered	5927
Ex	8:24	there **c** a grievous swarm of flies	935
Ex	12:29	it **c** to pass, that at midnight	1961
Ex	12:41	the selfsame day it **c** to pass,	1961
Ex	12:51	And it **c** to pass the selfsame day	1961
Ex	13:3	ye **c** out from Egypt, out of the	3318
Ex	16:13	that at even the quails **c** up,	5927
Ex	19:20	Lord **c** down upon mount Sinai,	3381
Ex	32:24	fire, and there **c** out this calf	3318
Ex	34:29	Moses **c** down from mount Sinai	3381
Ex	34:34	took the vail off, until he **c** out	3318
Le	9:24	And there **c** a fire out from before	3318
Nu	11:25	And the Lord **c** down in a cloud,	3381
Nu	12:5	And the Lord **c** down in the pillar	3381
Nu	16:35	there **c** out a fire from the Lord,	3318
Nu	19:2	and upon which never **c** yoke	5927
Nu	20:11	and the water **c** out abundantly,	3318
Nu	22:9	And God **c** unto Balaam, and said,	935
Nu	22:20	And God **c** unto Balaam at night,	935
Nu	24:2	the spirit of God **c** upon him	1961
Dt	4:45	after they **c** forth out of Egypt,	3318
Dt	23:4	when ye **c** forth out of Egypt;	3318
Dt	32:17	to new gods that **c** newly up,	935
Dt	33:2	The Lord **c** from Sinai, and	935
Jos	2:1	and **c** into an harlot's house	935
Jos	2:4	There **c** men unto me, but I	935
Jos	3:16	waters which **c** down from above	3381
Jos	4:22	Israel **c** over this Jordan on dry	5674
Jos	6:16	it **c** to pass, at the seventh time	1961
Jgs	1:28	**c** to pass, when Israel was strong,	1961
Jgs	2:1	an angel of the Lord **c** up from	5927
Jgs	3:10	the Spirit of the Lord **c** upon him,	1961
Jgs	3:22	of his belly: and the dirt **c** out	3318
Jgs	6:11	And there **c** an angel of the Lord,	935
Jgs	6:34	Spirit of the Lord **c** upon Gideon,	3847
Jgs	9:25	they robbed all that **c** along that	5674
Jgs	11:16	when Israel **c** up from Egypt,	5927
Jgs	11:29	Spirit of the Lord **c** upon	1961
Jgs	13:6	A man of God **c** unto me	935
Jgs	13:9	the angel of God **c** again unto the	935
Jgs	14:6	Spirit of the Lord **c** mightily	6743
Jgs	14:14	Out of the eater **c** forth meat,	3318
Jgs	14:14	out of the strong **c** forth sweetness.	3318
Jgs	14:19	Spirit of the Lord **c** upon him,	6743
Jgs	15:14	Spirit of the Lord **c** mightily	6743, 935
Jgs	15:19	there **c** water thereout: and when	3318
Jgs	15:19	spirit **c** again, and he revived;	7725
Jgs	16:16	**c** to pass, when she pressed him	1961
Jgs	21:2	the people **c** to the house of God,	935
Jgs	21:5	him that **c** not up to the Lord	5927
Ru	2:6	the Moabitish damsel that **c** back	7725
Ru	3:7	she **c** softly, and uncovered his feet	935
Ru	3:8	it **c** to pass at midnight, that the	1961
Ru	3:14	known that a woman **c** into the floor	935
Ru	3:16	when she **c** to her mother in law,	935
Ru	4:1	kinsman of whom Boaz spake **c** by;	5674
1Sa	2:27	there **c** a man of God unto Eli,	935
1Sa	3:10	the Lord **c**, and stood, and called	935
1Sa	4:5	ark of the covenant of the Lord **c** into	935
1Sa	4:16	I am he that **c** out of the army,	935
1Sa	4:18	**c** to pass, when he made mention	1961
1Sa	5:10	as the ark of God **c** to Ekron,	935
1Sa	6:14	the cart **c** into the field of Joshua,	935
1Sa	7:2	it **c** to pass, while the ark abode	1961
1Sa	7:13	**c** no more into the coast of Israel:	935
1Sa	8:1	**c** to pass, when Samuel was old,	1961
1Sa	9:26	**c** to pass about the spring of the	1961
1Sa	10:10	the Spirit of God **c** upon him	6743
1Sa	10:13	made an end of prophesying, he **c**	935
1Sa	11:6	the Spirit of God **c** upon Saul	6743
1Sa	13:8	Samuel **c** not to Gilgal; and the	935
1Sa	14:19	it **c** to pass, while Saul talked	1961
1Sa	14:20	they **c** to the battle: and, behold,	935
1Sa	15:13	Samuel **c** to Saul: and Saul said	935
1Sa	15:35	Samuel **c** no more to see Saul	
1Sa	16:13	Spirit of the Lord **c** upon David	6743
1Sa	16:21	David **c** to Saul, and stood before	935
1Sa	16:23	it **c** to pass, when the evil spirit	1961
1Sa	17:23	there **c** up the champion, the	5927
1Sa	17:34	and there **c** a lion, and a bear,	935
1Sa	18:6	the women **c** out of all cities	3318
1Sa	18:10	spirit from God **c** upon Saul,	6473
1Sa	28:8	they **c** to the woman by night:	935
1Sa	30:12	when he had eaten, his spirit **c** again	7725

1Sa	31:8	Philistines **c** to strip the slain,	935
2Sa	1:1	**c** to pass after the death of Saul,	1961
2Sa	1:2	a man **c** out of the camp from Saul	935
2Sa	2:23	that the spear **c** out behind	3318
2Sa	3:25	he **c** to deceive thee, and to know	935
2Sa	3:35	all the people **c** to cause David to	935
2Sa	4:5	**c** about the heat of the day to the	935
2Sa	5:17	Philistines **c** up to seek David;	5927
2Sa	6:16	the ark of the Lord **c** into the city	935
2Sa	7:4	word of the Lord **c** unto Nathan,	1961
2Sa	11:2	it **c** to pass in an evening tide,	1961
2Sa	11:4	and she **c** in unto him, and he lay	935
2Sa	12:4	And there **c** a traveller unto the	935
2Sa	12:20	and **c** into the house of the Lord,	935
2Sa	12:20	then he **c** to his own house;	935
2Sa	15:6	all Israel that **c** to the king for	935
2Sa	15:7	And it **c** to pass after forty years,	1961
2Sa	15:18	six hundred men which **c** after	935
2Sa	16:11	my son, which **c** forth of my bowels	3318
2Sa	18:4	all the people **c** out by hundreds	3318
2Sa	19:24	the son of Saul **c** down to meet	3381
1Ki	1:22	Nathan the prophet also **c** in	935
1Ki	1:28	And she **c** into the king's presence	935
1Ki	1:53	he **c** and bowed himself to king	7126
1Ki	2:7	so they **c** to me when I fled because	935
1Ki	4:27	that **c** unto king Solomon's table,	7131
1Ki	6:11	word of the Lord **c** to Solomon,	1961
1Ki	8:9	they **c** out of the land of Egypt	3318
1Ki	10:1	**c** to prove him with hard questions.	935
1Ki	10:14	gold that **c** to Solomon in one year	935
1Ki	11:4	**c** to pass, when Solomon was old,	1961
1Ki	13:1	there **c** a man of God out of Judah	935
1Ki	13:10	returned not by the way that he **c**	935
1Ki	13:12	man of God went, which **c** from	935
1Ki	13:29	and the old prophet **c** to the city,	935
1Ki	17:2	the word of the Lord **c** unto him	1961
1Ki	17:22	soul of the child **c** into him again,	7725
1Ki	18:1	the word of the Lord **c** to Elijah	1961
1Ki	19:4	**c** and sat down under a juniper tree:	935
1Ki	20:28	there **c** a man of God, and spake	5066
1Ki	21:4	Ahab **c** into his house heavy and	935
1Ki	21:5	But Jezebel his wife **c** to him, and	935
1Ki	21:17	word of the Lord **c** to Elijah	1961
1Ki	22:21	there **c** forth a spirit, and stood	3318
2Ki	1:10	there **c** down fire from heaven	3381
2Ki	1:12	fire of God **c** down from heaven,	3381
2Ki	1:14	there **c** fire down from heaven	3381
2Ki	2:23	there **c** forth little children out	3318
2Ki	2:24	there **c** forth two she bears out	3318
2Ki	4:27	Gehazi **c** near to thrust her away	5066
2Ki	5:14	his flesh **c** again like unto the	7725
2Ki	9:11	wherefore **c** this mad fellow to	935
2Ki	10:21	and all the worshippers of Baal **c**,	935
2Ki	10:21	there was not a man left that **c** not	935
2Ki	11:16	way by the which the horses **c**	3996
2Ki	24:11	Nebuchadnezzar king of Babylon **c**	935
1Ch	12:38	**c** with a perfect heart to Hebron	935
1Ch	17:3	that the word of God **c** to Nathan,	1961
2Ch	7:1	the fire **c** down from heaven, and	3381
2Ch	7:11	all that **c** into Solomon's heart to	935
2Ch	9:1	she **c** to prove Solomon with hard	935
2Ch	9:6	believed not their words, until I **c**	935
2Ch	9:13	gold that **c** to Solomon in one year	935
2Ch	14:14	the fear of the Lord **c** upon them:	1961
2Ch	15:1	the Spirit of God **c** upon Azariah	1961
2Ch	18:20	Then there **c** out a spirit, and	3318
2Ch	24:20	the Spirit of God **c** upon Zechariah	3847
2Ch	25:7	But there **c** a man of God to him	935
2Ch	30:27	their prayer **c** up to his holy dwelling	935
2Ch	32:26	the wrath of the Lord **c** not upon	935
2Ch	36:6	**c** up Nebuchadnezzar king of	5927
Ezr	2:68	they **c** to the house of the Lord	935
Ne	13:21	**c** they no more on the sabbath	935
Est	2:14	she **c** in unto the king no more,	935
Est	6:12	Mordecai **c** again to the king's	7725
Est	7:1	king and Haman **c** to banquet	935
Est	8:1	Mordecai **c** before the king;	935
Est	9:25	when Esther **c** before the king;	935
Job	1:6	and Satan **c** also among them	935
Job	1:21	Naked **c** I out of my mother's womb,	3318
Job	2:1	and Satan **c** also among them	935
Job	3:26	neither was I quiet; yet trouble **c**	935
Job	4:14	Fear **c** upon me, and trembling	7122
Job	26:4	and whose spirit **c** from thee?	3318
Job	29:13	was ready to perish **c** upon me:	935
Job	30:26	looked for good, then evil **c** unto me:	935
Job	30:26	I waited for light, there **c** darkness	935
Job	38:29	Out of whose womb **c** the ice?	3318
Ps	18:6	and my cry **c** before him, even	935
Ps	27:2	**c** upon me to eat up my flesh	7126
Ps	105:19	Until the time that his word **c**:	935
Ps	105:23	Israel also **c** into Egypt; and	935
Ps	105:31	and there **c** divers sorts of flies	935
Ps	105:34	He spake, and the locusts **c**,	935
Ecc	5:15	shall he return to go as he **c**	935
Ecc	5:16	in all points as he **c**, so shall he go:	935
Isa	50:2	when I **c**, was there no man?	935
Jer	7:31	them not, neither **c** it into my heart	5927
Jer	14:3	they **c** to the pits, and found no water	935
Jer	19:5	spake it, neither **c** it into my mind:	5927
Jer	44:21	them, and **c** it not into his mind?	5927
Eze	1:4	whirlwind **c** out of the north	935
Eze	33:22	he that was escaped **c**; and ... opened	935
Eze	37:7	the bones **c** together, bone to his	7126
Eze	37:10	the breath **c** into them, and they	935
Eze	43:4	the glory of the Lord **c** into the	935
Eze	47:1	the waters **c** down from under	3381
Da	2:29	O king, thy thoughts **c** into thy	5559
Da	3:26	**c** forth of the midst of the fire	5312
Da	4:8	at the last Daniel **c** in before me,	5954
Da	4:13	an holy one **c** down from heaven;	5182
Da	4:28	All this **c** upon the king	4291
Da	5:5	In the same hour **c** forth fingers	5312
Da	5:8	Then **c** in all the king's wise men:	5954
Da	6:20	when he **c** to the den, he cried	7127
Da	6:24	ever they **c** at the bottom of the den	4291
Da	7:3	great beasts **c** up from the sea,	5559
Da	7:8	**c** up among them another little	5559
Da	7:13	one like the Son of man **c**	858, 1934
Da	7:13	and **c** to the Ancient of days,	4291
Da	7:22	Until the Ancient of days **c**, and	858
Da	7:22	time **c** that the saints possessed	4291
Da	8:9	one of them **c** forth a little horn,	3318
Da	10:3	neither **c** flesh nor wine in my mouth	935
Am	6:1	to whom the house of Israel **c**!	935
Ob	5	If thieves **c** to thee, if robbers	935
Jnh	1:6	So the shipmaster **c** to him, and	7126
Jnh	4:8	it **c** to pass, when the sun did arise	1961
Jnh	4:10	**c** up in a night, and perished in a	1961
Mic	1:12	evil **c** down from the Lord unto	3381
Hab	3:14	they **c** out as a whirlwind to	
Hag	1:9	looked for much, and, lo, it **c** to little;	

Zec	4:1	angel that talked with me c again,	7725
Zec	6:1	there c four chariots out from	3318
Zec	7:12	therefore c a great wrath from the	1961
Zec	14:16	nations which c against Jerusalem	935
Mt	1:18	before they c together, she was	4905
Mt	2:1	there c wise men from the east	3854
Mt	2:9	till it c and stood over where the	2064
Mt	3:1	those days c John the Baptist	3854
Mt	4:3	when the tempter c to him,	4334
Mt	4:11	angels c and ministered unto him,	4334
Mt	7:25	the floods c, and the winds blew	2064
Mt	8:34	whole city c out to meet Jesus:	1831
Mt	9:10	sinners c and sat down with him	2064
Mt	9:14	c to him the disciples of John	4334
Mt	9:20	c behind him, and touched the hem	4334
Mt	10:34	I c not to send peace, but a sword.	2064
Mt	11:18	John c neither eating nor drinking	2064
Mt	11:19	The Son of man c eating and	2064
Mt	12:42	c from the uttermost parts to hear	2064
Mt	13:4	fowls c and devoured them up:	2064
Mt	13:25	his enemy c and sowed tares	2064
Mt	14:33	c and worshipped him, saying,	2064
Mt	16:1	Sadducees c, and tempting desired	4334
Mt	17:7	Jesus c and touched them, and	4334
Mt	17:19	c the disciples to Jesus apart,	4334
Mt	20:9	when they c that were hired	2064
Mt	20:28	c not to be ministered unto,	2064
Mt	21:32	For John c unto you in the way	2064
Mt	24:39	until the flood c, and took them	2064
Mt	25:10	went to buy, the bridegroom c;	2064
Mt	25:36	in prison, and ye c unto me.	2064
Mt	25:39	or in prison, and c unto thee?	2064
Mt	26:43	he c and found them asleep	2064
Mt	26:60	though many false witnesses c,	4334
Mt	26:60	At the last c two false witnesses	4334
Mt	27:53	c out of the graves after his	1831
Mt	27:57	there c a rich man of Arimathaea,	2064
Mt	28:1	c Mary Magdalene and the other	2064
Mt	28:2	and c and rolled back the stone	4334
Mt	28:9	they c and held him by the feet	4334
Mt	28:13	c by night, and stole him away	2064
Mk	1:11	And there c a voice from heaven,	1096
Mk	1:38	preach … for therefore c I forth.	1831
Mk	2:17	I c not to call the righteous, but	2064
Mk	4:4	fowls of the air c and devoured it	2064
Mk	8:3	for divers of them c from far.	2240
Mk	9:7	a voice c out of the cloud, saying,	2064
Mk	9:26	rent him sore, and c out of him:	1831
Mk	10:45	c not to be ministered unto, but	2064
Mk	11:13	when he c to it, he found nothing	2064
Mk	14:3	c a woman having an alabaster	2064
Mk	15:43	waited for the kingdom of God, c,	2064
Mk	16:2	they c unto the sepulchre at the	2064
Lk	1:28	the angel c in unto her, and said	1525
Lk	1:57	Now Elisabeth's full time c that	4130
Lk	1:59	they c to circumcise the child;	2064
Lk	1:65	fear c on all that dwelt round	1096
Lk	2:1	it c to pass … world should be taxed	1096
Lk	2:9	the angel of the Lord c upon	2186
Lk	2:15	it c to pass, as the angels were	1096
Lk	2:16	they c with haste, and found	2064
Lk	2:27	he c by the Spirit into the temple:	2064
Lk	3:2	the word of God c unto John the	1096
Lk	3:12	c also publicans to be baptized,	2064
Lk	3:22	a voice c from heaven, which said,	1096
Lk	4:41	devils also c out of many, crying	1831
Lk	7:14	And he c and touched the bier:	4334
Lk	7:33	John the Baptist c neither eating	2064
Lk	7:45	since the time I c in hath not	1525
Lk	8:23	there c down a storm of wind on	2597
Lk	8:41	there c a man named Jairus, and	2064
Lk	8:55	her spirit c again, and she arose	1994
Lk	9:34	c a cloud, and overshadowed	1096
Lk	9:35	there c a voice out of the cloud	1096
Lk	10:31	by chance there c down a certain	2597
Lk	13:6	he c and sought fruit thereon,	2064
Lk	15:17	And when he c to himself, he	2064
Lk	15:20	he arose, and c to his father.	2064
Lk	15:25	c and drew nigh to the house, he	2064
Lk	15:28	therefore c his father out, and	1831
Lk	16:21	the dogs c and licked his sores.	2064
Lk	16:22	it c to pass that the beggar died,	1096
Lk	17:27	and the flood c, and destroyed	2064
Lk	22:7	c the day of unleavened bread,	2064
Lk	24:23	they found not his body, they c,	2064
Lk	24:51	it c to pass, while he blessed	2096
Jn	1:7	The same c for a witness, to bear	2064
Jn	1:11	He c unto his own, and his own	2064
Jn	1:17	grace and truth c by Jesus Christ	1096
Jn	3:2	The same c to Jesus by night, and	2064
Jn	3:13	but he that c down from heaven,	2597
Jn	6:38	For I c down from heaven, not to	2597
Jn	6:51	bread which c down from heaven:	2597
Jn	6:58	This is that bread which c down	2597
Jn	8:42	from God; neither c I of myself,	2064
Jn	10:8	All that ever c before me are	2064
Jn	10:35	unto whom the word of God c,	1096
Jn	11:44	he that was dead c forth, bound	1831
Jn	12:1	before the passover c to Bethany,	2064
Jn	12:27	for this cause c I unto this hour.	2064
Jn	12:28	Then c there a voice from heaven	2064
Jn	12:30	This voice c not because of me,	1096
Jn	12:47	for I c not to judge the world,	2064
Jn	16:27	believed that I c out from God.	1831
Jn	16:28	I c forth from the Father, and am	1831
Jn	17:8	that I c out from thee, and they	1831
Jn	18:37	for this cause c I into the world,	2064
Jn	19:5	then c Jesus forth, wearing the	1831
Jn	19:32	c the soldiers, and brake the legs of	2064
Jn	19:34	forthwith c there out blood and	1831
Jn	19:39	And there c also Nicodemus,	2064
Jn	19:39	at the first c to Jesus by night,	2064
Jn	20:3	disciple, and c to the sepulchre	2064
Jn	20:4	did outrun Peter, and c first to the	2064
Jn	20:18	Mary Magdalene c and told the	2064
Jn	20:19	c Jesus and stood in the midst,	2064
Jn	20:26	c Jesus, the doors being shut,	2064
Ac	2:43	And fear c upon every soul:	1096
Ac	5:5	great fear c on all them that	1096
Ac	5:11	great fear c upon all the church,	1096
Ac	7:23	it c into his heart to visit his	305
Ac	8:7	c out of many that were possessed	1831
Ac	10:13	there c a voice to him, Rise, Peter;	1096
Ac	11:5	four corners; and it c even to me:	2064
Ac	11:27	c prophets from Jerusalem unto	2718
Ac	12:7	angel of the Lord c upon him	2186
Ac	12:13	damsel c to hearken, named Rhoda.	4334
Ac	15:6	apostles and elders c together	4863
Ac	19:6	the Holy Ghost c on them;	2064
Ac	19:18	many that believed c, and confessed,	2064
Ac	24:24	Felix c with his wife Drusilla,	3854
Ro	5:18	one judgment c upon all men to	

Ro	5:18	the free gift **c** upon all men unto	
Ro	7:9	the commandment **c**, sin revived	*2064*
Ro	9:5	as concerning the flesh Christ **c**,	
1Co	2:1	**c** not with excellency of speech	*2064*
1Co	15:21	since by man **c** death, by man **c** also	
Gal	2:4	**c** in privily to spy out our liberty	*3922*
Gal	3:23	But before faith **c**, we were kept	*2064*
Eph	2:17	And **c** and preached peace to you	*2064*
1Th	1:5	gospel **c** not unto you in word only	*1096*
1Ti	1:15	Christ Jesus **c** into the world to	*2064*
Heb	3:16	not all that **c** out of Egypt by	*1831*
2Pe	1:18	this voice which **c** from heaven	*5342*
2Pe	1:21	the prophecy **c** not in old time	*5342*
1Jn	5:6	he that **c** by water and blood,	*2064*
Rev	5:7	And he **c** and took the book out	*2064*
Rev	7:14	These are they which **c** out of	*2064*
Rev	8:3	angel **c** and stood at the altar,	*2064*
Rev	9:3	there **c** out of the smoke locusts	*1831*
Rev	14:20	blood **c** out of the winepress	*1831*
Rev	15:6	seven angels **c** out of the temple,	*1831*
Rev	16:17	**c** a great voice out of the temple	*1831*
Rev	16:19	Babylon **c** in remembrance	*3415*
Rev	19:5	And a voice **c** out of the throne	*1881*
Rev	20:9	and fire **c** down from God out of	*2597*
Rev	21:9	**c** unto me one of the seven angels	*2064*

CAMEL

Ge	24:64	saw Isaac, she lighted off the **c**	1581
Le	11:4	**c**, because he cheweth the cud,	1581
Mt	19:24	easier for a **c** to go through the	*2574*
Mt	23:24	at a gnat, and swallow a **c**	*2574*
Mk	10:25	easier for a **c** to go through the	*2574*
Lk	18:25	easier for a **c** to go through a	*2574*

CAMELS

Ge	24:10	took ten **c** of the **c** of his master,	1581
Ge	24:11	he made his **c** to kneel down	1581
Ge	24:14	I will give thy **c** drink also: let	1581
Ge	24:19	draw water for thy **c** also, until	1581
Ge	24:32	and provender for the **c**,	1581
Ge	24:44	I will also draw for thy **c**: let the	1581
Jgs	7:12	and their **c** were without number,	1581
1Ki	10:2	with **c** that bare spices, and very	1581
1Ch	5:21	cattle; of their **c** fifty thousand,	1581
Ezr	2:67	Their **c**, four hundred thirty and	1581
Job	1:17	fell upon the **c**, and have carried	1581
Job	42:12	six thousand **c**, and a thousand	1581
Isa	60:6	The multitude of **c** shall cover	1581
Jer	49:32	And their **c** shall be a booty, and	1581

CAMEST

Ge	24:5	into the land from whence thou **c**?	3318
Ex	23:15	for in it thou **c** out from Egypt:	3318
1Sa	13:11	and that thou **c** not within the days	935
1Ki	13:14	the man of God that **c** from Judah?	935
Mt	22:12	**Friend, how c thou in hither not**	*1525*
Jn	16:30	believe that thou **c** forth from God	*1831*

CAMP

Ex	16:13	quails came up, and covered the **c**	4264
Ex	29:14	burn with fire without the **c**:	4264
Ex	32:17	There is a noise of war in the **c**	4264
Le	4:21	forth the bullock without the **c**	4264
Le	6:11	the ashes without the **c** unto a	4264
Le	13:46	without the **c** shall his habitation	4264
Nu	5:2	put out of the **c** every leper,	4264
Nu	11:9	dew fell upon the **c** in the night,	4264
Nu	11:26	remained two of the men in the **c**,	4264
Nu	12:15	Miriam was shut out from the **c**	4264
Nu	15:35	him with stones without the **c**	4264
Dt	23:14	God walketh in the midst of thy **c**,	4264
1Sa	4:5	of the Lord came into the **c**,	4264
1Sa	4:6	noise of this great shout in the **c**	4264
1Sa	4:7	they said, God is come into the **c**	4264
Ps	106:16	They envied Moses also in the **c**,	4264
Isa	29:3	And I will **c** against thee round	2583
Joel	2:11	for his **c** is very great: for he is	4264
Na	3:17	**c** in the hedges in the cold day,	2583
Heb	13:11	sin, are burned without the **c**	*3925*
Heb	13:13	unto him without the **c**, bearing	*3925*
Rev	20:9	compassed the **c** of the saints	*3925*

CAMPS

Nu	5:3	that they defile not their **c**, in	4264
Nu	10:25	the rereward of all the **c**	4264
Am	4:10	the stink of your **c** to come up	4264

CANDLE

Job	18:6	and his **c** shall be put out with	5216
Job	21:17	oft is the **c** of the wicked put out!	5216
Ps	18:28	For thou wilt light my **c**:	5216
Pr	20:27	the **c** of the Lord, searching	5216
Pr	31:18	her **c** goeth not out by night	5216
Jer	25:10	millstones, and the light of the **c**	5216
Mt	5:15	**men light a c, and put it under**	*3088*
Mk	4:21	**Is a c brought to be put under**	*3088*
Lk	11:33	**No man, when he hath lighted a c,**	*3088*
Lk	15:8	**doth not light a c, and sweep**	*3088*
Rev	18:23	the light of a **c** shall shine no more	*3088*
Rev	22:5	they need no **c**, neither light of the	*3088*

CANDLES

Zep	1:12	I will search Jerusalem with **c**	5216

CANDLESTICK

Ex	25:31	thou shalt make a **c** of pure gold:	4501
Ex	35:14	The **c** also for the light, and his	4501
Ex	37:19	six branches going out of the **c**	4501
Ex	40:24	he put the **c** in the tent of the	4501
Nu	8:3	over against the **c**, as the Lord	4501
2Ki	4:10	bed, and a table, and a stool, and a **c**:	4501
1Ch	28:15	by weight for every **c**, and for the	4501
2Ch	13:11	and the **c** of gold with the lamps	4501
Zec	4:11	upon the right side of the **c**	4501
Mt	5:15	**but on a c; and it giveth light**	*3087*
Mk	4:21	**a bed? and not to be set on a c?**	*3087*
Lk	8:16	**but setteth it on a c, that they**	*3087*
Rev	2:5	**remove thy c out of his place,**	*3087*

CANDLESTICKS

1Ki	7:49	the **c** of pure gold, five on the right	4501
1Ch	28:15	the weight for the **c** of gold, and	4501
Rev	1:12	turned, I saw seven golden **c**;	*3087*
Rev	1:20	**hand, and the seven golden c**	*3087*
Rev	2:1	**midst of the seven golden c;**	*3087*

CANE

Isa	43:24	Thou hast bought me no sweet **c**	7070
Jer	6:20	Sheba, and the sweet **c** from a far	7070

CANKER

2Ti	2:17	their word will eat as doth a **c**	*1044*

CANKERED

Jas	5:3	Your gold and silver is **c**: and	*2728*

CANKERWORM

Joel	1:4	and that which the **c** hath left	3218
Joel	2:25	the **c**, and the caterpillar, and the	3218
Na	3:15	it shall eat thee up like the **c**:	3218
Na	3:15	make thyself many as the **c**,	3218
Na	3:16	the **c** spoileth, and flieth away	3218

CANNOT

Ge	24:50	we **c** speak unto thee bad or	3808, 3201
Ge	32:12	the sand of the sea, which **c** be	3808
Ge	34:14	We **c** do this thing, to give	3808, 3201
Ge	43:22	**c** tell who put our money	3808
Le	14:21	be poor, and **c** get so much;	369, 3027
Nu	22:18	I **c** go beyond the word of	3808, 3201
Nu	23:20	he hath blessed; and I **c** reverse	3808
Jos	24:19	Ye **c** serve the Lord: for he is	3808, 3201
Ru	4:6	I **c** redeem it for myself, lest	3808, 3201
Ru	4:6	my right to thyself; for I **c**	3808, 3201
1Sa	17:39	I **c** go with these; for I	3808
1Sa	17:55	As thy soul liveth, O king, I **c** tell	518
1Ki	3:8	that **c** be numbered nor counted	3808
1Ki	8:27	heaven of heavens **c** contain	3808
2Ch	24:20	of the Lord, that ye **c** prosper?	3808
Job	6:30	**c** my taste discern perverse things?	3808
Job	9:3	**c** answer him one of a thousand	3808
Job	17:10	**c** find one wise man among you	3808
Job	19:8	fenced up my way that I **c** pass	3808
Job	31:31	had of his flesh! we **c** be satisfied.	3808
Job	36:18	then a great ransom **c** deliver thee.	3808
Job	37:5	doeth he, which we **c** comprehend.	408
Job	37:19	we **c** order our speech by reason	3808
Job	37:23	Almighty, we **c** find him out:	3808
Ps	77:4	I am so troubled that I **c** speak	3808
Ps	125:1	mount Zion, which **c** be removed,	3808
Ps	139:6	for me; it is high, I **c** attain	3808, 3201
Ecc	1:15	crooked **c** be made straight:	3808, 3201
SS	8:7	Many waters **c** quench love,	3808, 3201
Isa	38:18	For the grave **c** praise thee,	3808
Isa	45:20	and pray unto a god that **c** save	3808
Isa	50:2	hand shortened at all, that it **c**	3808
Isa	56:10	all dumb dogs, they **c** bark;	3808, 3201
Isa	59:1	is not shortened, that it **c** save;	3808
Isa	59:1	his ear heavy, that it **c** hear:	3808
Jer	1:6	Ah, Lord God! behold, I **c** speak;	3808
Jer	7:8	trust in lying words, that **c** profit	1115
Jer	24:8	evil figs, which **c** be eaten, they	3808
Jer	33:22	host of heaven **c** be numbered	3808
Da	2:27	demanded **c** the wise men,	3809, 3202
Hos	1:10	the sea, which **c** be measured nor	3808
Jnh	4:11	that **c** discern between their right	3808
Mt	5:14	**city that is set on an hill c**	*3756, 1410*
Mt	6:24	**c serve God and mammon**	*3756, 1410*
Mt	7:18	**good tree c bring forth evil**	*3756, 1410*
Mt	27:42	saved others; himself he **c** save	*3756, 1410*
Mk	3:24	**itself, that kingdom c stand**	*3756, 1410*
Mk	15:31	others; himself he **c** save	*3756, 1410*
Lk	14:26	**life also, he c be my disciple.**	*3756, 1410*
Lk	14:27	**after me, c be my disciple**	*3756, 1410*
Lk	14:33	**he hath, he c be my disciple.**	*3756, 1410*
Lk	16:13	**Ye c serve God and mammon.**	*3756, 1410*
Jn	3:3	**c see the kingdom of God**	*3756, 1410*
Jn	3:5	**c enter into the kingdom of**	*3756, 1410*
Jn	7:7	**world c hate you; but me it**	*3756, 1410*
Jn	8:21	**whither I go, ye c come.**	*3756, 1410*
Jn	10:35	**the scripture c be broken;**	*3756, 1410*
Jn	14:17	**whom the world c receive**	*3756, 1410*
Jn	15:4	**As the branch c bear fruit**	*3756, 1410*
Jn	16:12	**but ye c bear them now**	*3756, 1410*
Ac	4:20	we **c** but speak the things	*3756, 1410*
Ro	8:8	are in the flesh **c** please God	*3756, 1410*
Ro	8:26	groanings which **c** be uttered	*215*
1Co	10:21	**c** drink the cup of the Lord	*3756, 1410*
1Co	12:21	the eye **c** say unto the hand,	*3756, 1410*
1Co	15:50	flesh and blood **c** inherit the	*3756, 1410*
2Co	12:2	out of the body, I **c** tell:	*3756, 1492*
2Ti	2:13	abideth faithful: he **c** deny	*3756, 1410*
Tit	1:2	which God, that **c** lie, promised	*893*
Heb	4:15	priest which **c** be touched	*3361, 1410*
Heb	12:28	a kingdom which **c** be moved,	*761*
Jas	1:13	for God **c** be tempted with evil	*551*
1Jn	3:9	he **c** sin, because he is born	*3756, 1410*

CANST

Ge	41:15	that thou **c** understand a dream to	
Job	11:7	**C** thou by searching find out God?	
Job	11:8	deeper than hell; what **c** thou know?	
Job	38:32	or **c** thou guide Arcturus with his	
Job	38:35	**C** thou send lightnings, that they	
Job	40:9	or **c** thou thunder with a voice	
Job	41:1	**C** thou draw out leviathan with an	
Job	42:2	I know that thou **c** do every	3201
Jer	12:5	how **c** thou contend with horses?	
Da	5:16	that thou **c** make interpretations,	3202
Mt	8:2	if thou wilt, thou **c** make me clean	*1410*
Mk	9:23	**If thou c believe, all things are**	*1410*
Jn	13:36	**Whither I go, thou c not follow**	*1410*
Ac	21:37	Who said, **C** thou speak Greek?	*1097*

CAPTAIN

Ge	40:4	**c** of the guard charged Joseph	8269
Jos	5:14	but as **c** of the host of the Lord	8269
Jos	5:15	**c** of the Lord's host said unto	8269
Jgs	11:6	and be our **c**, that we may fight	7101
1Sa	9:16	to be **c** over my people Israel,	5057
2Sa	5:8	David's soul, he shall be chief and **c**	
1Ki	11:21	Joab the **c** of the host was dead,	8269
2Ki	1:9	unto him a **c** of fifty with his fifty	8269
2Ki	20:5	tell Hezekiah the **c** of my people,	5057
Ne	9:17	in their rebellion appointed a **c**	7218
Jer	40:2	**c** of the guard took Jeremiah,	7227
Jn	18:12	band and the **c** and officers	*5506*
Ac	21:31	tidings came unto the chief **c**	*5506*
Ac	23:10	chief **c**, fearing lest Paul should	*5506*
Ac	28:16	delivered the prisoners to the **c**	*4759*
Heb	2:10	make the **c** of their salvation perfect	*747*

CAPTAINS

Ex	15:4	his chosen **c** also are drowned	7991
2Sa	18:5	the king gave all the **c** charge	8269
2Ch	32:6	set **c** of war over the people,	8269
Job	39:25	the thunder of the **c**, and the	8269
Jer	51:23	with thee will I break in pieces **c**	6346
Eze	21:22	to appoint **c**, to open the mouth	3733
Da	3:3	the governors, and **c**, the judges,	6347
Da	3:27	**c**, and the king's counsellers,	6347
Ac	25:23	with the chief **c**, and principal	*5506*
Rev	6:15	the rich men, and the chief **c**,	*5506*

CAPTIVE

Ge	34:29	their wives took they **c**, and	7617
Ex	12:29	unto the firstborn of the **c** that was	7628
2Ki	15:29	and carried them **c** to Assyria	1540
2Ki	24:16	king of Babylon brought **c** to	1473

1Ch	5:6	king of Assyria carried away **c**:	1540
2Ch	25:12	children of Judah carry away **c**,	7617
Ps	68:18	thou hast led captivity **c**: thou	7617
Isa	49:21	am desolate, a **c**, and removing	1473
Isa	51:14	The **c** exile hasteneth that he	6808
Isa	52:2	thy neck, O **c** daughter of Zion.	7628
Jer	1:3	carrying away of Jerusalem **c**	1540
Jer	13:17	Lord's flock is carried away **c**	7617
Jer	24:5	are carried away **c** of Judah,	1546
Jer	29:14	I caused you to be carried away **c**	1540
Jer	39:9	carried away **c** into Babylon the	1540
Jer	41:10	Then Ishmael carried away **c**	7617
Jer	52:27	Thus Judah was carried away **c**	1540
Jer	52:28	Nebuchadrezzar carried away **c**	1540
Jer	52:30	carried away **c** of the Jews seven	1540
Am	7:11	Israel shall surely be led away **c**	1540
Lk	21:24	**shall be led away c into all**	*163*
Eph	4:8	upon high, he led captivity **c**, and	*162*
2Ti	3:6	lead **c** silly women laden with	*162*

CAPTIVES

Dt	21:11	And seest among the **c** a beautiful	7633
1Sa	30:5	David's two wives were taken **c**,	7617
2Ch	28:5	away a great multitude of them **c**	7633
2Ch	28:11	deliver the **c** again, which ye	7633
Ps	106:46	of all those that carried them **c**	7617
Isa	45:13	and he shall let go my **c**, not	1546
Isa	49:25	the **c** of the mighty shall be taken	7628
Isa	61:1	to proclaim liberty to the **c**, and	7628
Jer	28:4	with all the **c** of Judah, that went	1546
Eze	1:1	I was among the **c** by the river	1473
Da	2:25	found a man of the **c** of Judah	1123, 1547
Da	11:8	shall also carry **c** into Egypt	7628
Lk	4:18	**to preach deliverance to the c**	*164*

CAPTIVITY

Dt	21:13	the raiment of her **c** from off	7633
Dt	28:41	them; for they shall go into **c**	7628
Dt	30:3	the Lord thy God will turn thy **c**,	7622
Jgs	5:12	and lead thy **c** captive, thou son	7628
2Ki	24:15	carried he into **c** from Jerusalem	1473
2Ki	25:27	thirtieth year of the **c** of	1546
2Ch	29:9	daughters and our wives are in **c**	7628
Ezr	1:11	bring up with them of the **c** that	1473
Ezr	9:7	to the sword, to **c**, and to a spoil,	7628
Ezr	10:16	the children of the **c** did so. And	1473
Ne	1:3	remnant that are left of the **c**	7628
Est	2:6	from Jerusalem with the **c**,	1473
Job	42:10	Lord turned the **c** of Job when	7622
Ps	14:7	Lord bringeth back the **c** of his	7622
Ps	53:6	God bringeth back the **c** of his	7622
Ps	68:18	high, thou hast led **c** captive:	7628
Ps	78:61	delivered his strength into **c**, and	7628
Ps	85:1	brought back the **c** of Jacob	7622
Ps	126:1	the Lord turned again the **c** of	7622
Ps	126:4	Turn again our **c**, O Lord, as the	7622
Isa	5:13	my people are gone into **c**,	1540
Jer	15:2	such as are for the **c**, to the **c**	7628
Jer	29:14	and I will turn away your **c**	7622
Jer	29:20	word of the Lord, all ye of the **c**,	1473
Jer	29:28	This **c** is long: build ye houses	
Jer	32:44	I will cause their **c** to return,	7622
Jer	33:7	I will cause the **c** of Judah and the	7622
Jer	33:7	and the **c** of Israel to return,	7622
Jer	43:11	and such as are for **c** to **c**;	7628
Jer	46:19	furnish thyself to go into **c**:	1473
Jer	49:39	I will bring again the **c** of Elam	7622
La	1:3	Judah is gone into **c** because	1540
La	1:5	her children are gone into **c**	7628
La	2:14	thine iniquity to turn away thy **c**;	7622
La	4:22	no more carry thee away into **c**:	1540
Eze	11:24	Spirit of God ... to them of the **c**	1473
Eze	16:53	the **c** of Sodom and her daughters,	7622
Eze	33:21	in the twelfth year of our **c**, in the	1546
Eze	39:23	Israel went into **c** for their iniquity	1540
Da	5:13	art of the children of the **c** of	1547
Da	6:13	which is of the children of the **c**	1547
Da	11:33	by the sword, and by flame, by **c**,	7628
Hos	6:11	when I returned the **c** of my	7622
Joel	3:1	shall bring again the **c** of Judah	7622
Am	7:17	Israel shall surely go into **c**	1540
Ob	20	And the **c** of this host of the	1546
Mic	1:16	for they are gone into **c** from	1540
Na	3:10	she went into **c**: her young	7628
Zep	2:7	them, and turn away their **c**	7622
Ro	7:23	bringing me into **c** to the law of	*163*
2Co	10:5	bringing into **c** every thought to	*163*
Eph	4:8	he led **c** captive, and gave gifts	*161*
Rev	13:10	that leadeth into **c** shall go into **c**:	*161*

CARCASE

Le	11:8	and their **c** shall ye not touch;	5038
Le	11:24	whosoever toucheth the **c** of them	5038
Le	11:40	he that eateth of the **c** of it shall	5038
Dt	14:8	flesh, nor touch their dead **c**	5038
Jgs	14:8	aside to see the **c** of the lion:	4658
Jgs	14:8	and honey in the **c** of the lion	1472
Jgs	14:9	honey out of the **c** of the lion	1472
1Ki	13:24	the lion also stood by the **c**	5038
1Ki	13:28	and found his **c** cast in the way	5038
1Ki	13:28	the lion had not eaten the **c**	5038
1Ki	13:29	prophet took up the **c** of the man	5038
2Ki	9:37	the **c** of Jezebel shall be as dung	5038
Mt	24:28	**For wheresoever the c is, there**	*4430*

CARCASES

Ge	15:11	the fowls came down upon the **c**,	6297
Le	11:11	shall have their **c** in abomination	5038
Le	26:30	cast your **c** upon the **c** of your	6297
Nu	14:33	your **c** be wasted in the wilderness	6297
Isa	5:25	their **c** were torn in the midst of	5038
Isa	34:3	stink shall come up out of their **c**,	6297
Jer	7:33	the **c** of this people shall be meat	5038
Eze	43:9	the **c** of their kings, far from me	6297
Na	3:3	slain, and a great number of **c**;	6297
Heb	3:17	whose **c** fell in the wilderness?	2966

CARE

Jer	49:31	nation, that dwelleth without **c**	983
Mt	13:22	**the c of this world, and the**	*3308*
Lk	10:34	**to an inn, and took c of him**	*1959*
Lk	10:35	**Take c of him; and whatsoever**	*1959*
1Co	7:21	being a servant? **c** not for it;	*3199*
1Co	9:9	Doth God take **c** for oxen?	*3199*
2Co	7:12	or **c** for you in the sight of God	*4710*
2Co	11:28	daily, the **c** of all the churches	*3308*
Php	2:20	will naturally **c** for your state	*3309*
1Ti	3:5	shall he take **c** of the church of	*1959*
1Pe	5:7	Casting all your **c** upon him;	*3308*

CARED

Ps	142:4	failed me; no man **c** for my soul	1875
Jn	12:6	not that he **c** for the poor;	*3199*
Ac	18:17	Gallio **c** for none of those things	*3199*

CAREFUL

Da 3:16 we are not **c** to answer thee in …2818
Lk 10:41 **Martha, thou art c and troubled** …*3309*
Php 4:6 Be **c** for nothing; but in …*3309*
Tit 3:8 be **c** to maintain good works …*5431*

CAREFULLY

Heb 12:17 though he sought it **c** with tears …*1567*

CAREFULNESS

Eze 12:19 eat their bread with **c**, and drink …1674
2Co 7:11 sort, what **c** it wrought in you …*4710*

CARELESS

Isa 32:9 ye **c** daughters; give ear unto my …982
Isa 32:11 at ease; be troubled, ye **c** ones: …982

CARELESSLY

Isa 47:8 that dwellest **c**, that sayest in …983
Zep 2:15 is the rejoicing city that dwelt **c**, …983

CARES

Mk 4:19 **the c of this world, and the** …*3308*
Lk 8:14 **are choked with c and riches and** …*3308*
Lk 21:34 **and c of this life, and so that day** …*3308*

CAREST

Mt 22:16 neither **c** thou for any man: for …*3199*
Mk 4:38 Master, **c** thou not that we perish? …*3199*
Mk 12:14 thou art true, and **c** for no man: …*3199*

CARETH

Jn 10:13 **hireling, and c not for the sheep.** …*3199*
1Co 7:32 He that is unmarried **c** for the …*3309*
1Co 7:33 he that is married **c** for the …*3309*
1Pe 5:7 upon him, for he **c** for you …*3199*

CARNAL

Ro 7:14 but I am **c**, sold under sin …*4559*
1Co 3:3 For ye are yet **c**: for whereas …*4559*
1Co 3:4 I am of Apollos; are ye not **c**? …*4559*
2Co 10:4 weapons of our warfare are not **c**, …*4559*
Heb 7:16 the law of a **c** commandment, …*4559*

CARNALLY

Le 18:20 thou shalt not lie **c** with thy …7903, 2233
Ro 8:6 to be **c** minded is death; but to …*4561*

CARPENTER

Isa 44:13 The **c** stretched out his rule; …2796, 6086
Mk 6:3 Is not this the **c**, the son of …*5045*

CARPENTER'S

Mt 13:55 Is not this the **c** son? is not his …*5045*

CARPENTERS

2Sa 5:11 **c**, and masons: and they …2796, 6086
1Ch 14:1 with masons and **c**, to build …2796, 6086
Ezr 3:7 unto the masons, and to the **c**; …2796
Jer 24:1 with the **c** and smiths, from …2796
Zec 1:20 And the Lord shewed me four **c** …2796

CARRIAGE

Jgs 18:21 the cattle and the **c** before them, …3520
1Sa 17:22 the hand of the keeper of the **c**, …3627

CARRIAGES

Isa 46:1 your **c** were heavy loaden; …5385
Ac 21:15 we took up our **c**, and went up …*643*

CARRIED

Ge 46:5 of Israel **c** Jacob their father, …5375
Ge 50:13 For his sons **c** him into the land …5375
1Sa 5:8 ark of the God of Israel be **c** …5437
1Sa 5:8 **c** the ark of the God of Israel …5437
2Sa 6:10 David **c** it aside into the house …5186
2Sa 15:29 and Abiathar **c** the ark of God …7725
1Ki 8:47 whither they were **c** captives, …7617
1Ki 17:19 and **c** him up into a loft, …5927
2Ki 15:29 and **c** them captive to Assyria …1540
2Ki 17:11 the Lord **c** away before them; …1540
2Ki 17:23 So was Israel **c** away out of their …1540
2Ki 20:17 shall be **c** unto Babylon: …5375
2Ki 23:4 **c** the ashes of them unto Beth-el …5375
1Ch 5:6 king of Assyria **c** away captive: …1540
1Ch 6:15 when the Lord **c** away Judah …1540
1Ch 13:7 And they **c** the ark of God …7392
2Ch 28:15 and **c** all the feeble of them …5095
2Ch 33:11 fetters, and **c** him to Babylon. …3212
2Ch 36:20 sword **c** he away to Babylon; …1473
Ezr 5:12 **c** the people away into Bablyon. …1541
Est 2:6 king of Babylon had **c** away …1540
Job 10:19 I should have been **c** from the …2986
Isa 46:3 are **c** from the womb: …5375
Isa 53:4 our grief, and **c** our sorrows: …5445
Jer 13:19 shall be wholly **c** away captive …1540
Eze 37:1 and **c** me out in the spirit …3318
Da 2:35 and the wind **c** them away, …5376
Joel 3:5 have **c** into your temples …935
Am 1:6 because they **c** away captive …1540
Mk 15:1 bound Jesus, and **c** him away …*667*
Lk 16:22 **was c by the angels into** …*667*
Lk 24:51 them, and **c** up into heaven …*399*
Ac 8:2 **c** Stephen to his burial, …*4792*
1Co 12:2 **c** away unto these dumb idols, …*520*
Eph 4:14 and **c** about with every wind …*4064*
Heb 13:9 Be not **c** about with divers …*4064*
Jude 12 without water, **c** about of winds; …*4064*
Rev 17:3 So he **c** me away in the spirit …*667*
Rev 21:10 **c** me away in the spirit to a great …*667*

CARRIETH

Job 21:18 chaff that the storm **c** away …1589
Job 27:21 The east wind **c** him away …5375
Rev 17:7 and of the beast that **c** her …*941*

CARRY

Ge 43:12 sacks, **c** it again in your hand; …7725
Ge 44:1 as much as they can **c**, and put …5375
Ge 50:25 shall **c** up my bones from hence …5927
Ex 13:19 ye shall **c** up my bones away …5927
Jos 4:3 ye shall **c** them over with you, …5674
1Sa 17:18 And **c** these ten cheeses unto …935
2Sa 15:25 **C** back the ark of God into the …7725
1Ki 18:12 the Spirit of the Lord shall **c** thee …5375
2Ki 18:11 the king of Assyria did **c** away …1540
1Ch 15:2 None ought to **c** the ark of God …5375
1Ch 15:2 the Lord chosen to **c** the ark …5375
Job 15:12 Why doth thine heart **c** thee …3947
Ps 49:17 he shall **c** nothing away: his glory …3947
Ecc 10:20 a bird of the air shall **c** the voice …3212
Jer 20:4 shall **c** them captive into Babylon, …1540
Jer 39:7 with chains, to **c** him to Babylon …935
Eze 22:9 In thee are men that **c** tales to …7400
Eze 38:13 to **c** away silver and gold, to …5375
Da 11:8 And shall also **c** captives into …935
Lk 10:4 **C neither purse, nor scrip, nor** …*941*

Jn	21:18	**gird thee, and c thee whither**	*5342*
1Ti	6:7	is certain we can **c** nothing out	*1627*

CARRYING

Ps	78:9	**c** bows, turned back in the day	7411
Jer	1:3	**c** away of Jerusalem captive	1540
Mt	1:17	from David until the **c** away	*3350*
Ac	5:10	**c** her forth, buried her by her	*1627*

CART

1Sa	6:8	the Lord, and lay it upon the **c**;	5699
1Sa	6:11	the ark of the Lord upon the **c**	5699
2Sa	6:3	set the ark of God upon a new **c**,	5699
Isa	28:27	neither is a **c** wheel turned about	5699

CARVED

Jgs	18:18	fetched the **c** image, the ephod,	6459
1Ki	6:29	**c** figures of cherubims and palm	6603
2Ch	33:7	he set a **c** image, the idol which	6459
2Ch	34:3	the **c** images, and the molten	6456
Ps	74:6	now they break down the **c** work	6603
Pr	7:16	with **c** works, with fine linen of	2405

CARVING

Ex	31:5	and in **c** of timber, to work in all	2799
Ex	35:33	and in **c** of wood, to make any	2799

CARVINGS

1Ki	6:32	**c** of cherubims and palm trees	4734

CASE

Ps	144:15	that people, that is in such a **c**:	3602
Mt	5:20	**ye shall in no c enter into the**	*3364*
Mt	19:10	If the **c** of the man be so with his	*156*

CASEMENT

Pr	7:6	I looked through my **c**,	822

CAST

Ge	21:10	**C** out this bondwoman and her	1644
Ge	21:15	and she **c** the child under one of	7993
Ge	37:24	took him, and **c** him into a pit:	7993
Ex	1:22	is born ye shall **c** into the river	7993
Ex	4:3	And he said, **C** it on the ground	7993
Ex	7:9	Take thy rod, and **c** it before	7993
Ex	7:10	and Aaron **c** down his rod before	7993
Ex	10:19	locusts, and **c** them into the Red	8628
Ex	32:19	he **c** the tables out of his hands	7993
Ex	32:24	then I **c** it into the fire, and	7993
Le	16:8	Aaron shall **c** lots upon the two	5414
Dt	9:4	Lord thy God hath **c** them out	1920
Jos	10:11	the Lord **c** down great stones	7993
Jos	18:10	And Joshua **c** lots for them	7993
Jgs	6:28	the altar of Baal was **c** down	5422
Jgs	15:17	that he **c** away the jawbone out	7993
1Sa	20:33	And Saul **c** a javelin at him to	2904
2Sa	16:6	And he **c** stones at David, and at	5619
1Ki	19:19	and **c** his mantle upon him	7993
1Ch	26:14	they **c** lots; and his lot came out	5307
Ne	9:26	and **c** thy law behind their backs	7993
Est	9:24	and had **c** Pur, that is, the lot,	5307
Job	8:20	God will not **c** away a perfect	3988
Job	41:9	shall not one be **c** down even	2904
Ps	22:10	I was **c** upon thee from the womb:	7993
Ps	22:18	and **c** lots upon my vesture	5307
Ps	37:24	he shall not be utterly **c** down:	2904
Ps	42:5	Why art thou **c** down, O my soul?	7817
Ps	51:11	**C** me not away from thy presence;	7993
Ps	55:3	they **c** iniquity upon me, and in	4131
Ps	55:22	**C** thy burden upon the Lord,	7993
Ps	77:7	Will the Lord **c** off for ever?	2186
Ps	94:14	Lord will not **c** off his people	5203
Ps	140:10	let them be **c** into the fire;	5307
Ps	144:6	**C** forth lightning, and scatter	1299
Pr	1:14	**C** in thy lot among us; let us all	5307
Pr	16:33	The lot is **c** into the lap; but	2904
Pr	22:10	**C** out the scorner, and contention	1644
Ecc	3:5	A time to **c** away stones, and a	7993
Ecc	3:6	and a time to **c** away;	7993
Ecc	11:1	**C** thy bread upon the waters:	7971
Isa	2:20	a man shall **c** his idols of silver,	7993
Isa	16:2	wandering bird **c** out of the nest	7971
Isa	57:14	**C** ye up, **c** ye up, prepare the	5549
Jer	6:6	**c** a mount against Jerusalem:	8210
Jer	8:12	visitation, they shall be **c** down	3782
La	2:7	The Lord hath **c** off his altar, he	2186
La	3:31	the Lord will not **c** off for ever	2186
Eze	31:16	when I **c** him down to hell with	3381
Eze	43:24	and the priests shall **c** salt upon	7993
Da	3:15	ye shall be **c** the same hour into	7412
Da	3:24	Did not we **c** three men bound	7412
Da	6:7	he shall be **c** into the den of lions	7412
Da	6:24	they **c** them into the den of lions,	7412
Ob	11	and **c** lots upon Jerusalem,	3032
Jnh	1:15	and **c** him forth into the sea:	2904
Mic	2:5	none that shall **c** a cord by lot	7993
Mic	7:19	and thou wilt **c** all their sins	7993
Na	3:10	they **c** lots for her honourable	3032
Zec	11:13	**C** it unto the potter a goodly	7993
Mt	4:6	the Son of God, **c** thyself down:	*906*
Mt	5:13	**good for nothing, but to be c out,**	*906*
Mt	5:29	**pluck it out, and c it from thee:**	*906*
Mt	5:29	**thy whole body should be c into**	*906*
Mt	7:5	**first c out the beam out of thine**	*1544*
Mt	7:5	**see clearly to c out the mote out**	*1544*
Mt	7:6	**neither c ye your pearls before**	*906*
Mt	7:22	**in thy name have c out devils?**	*1544*
Mt	8:12	**shall be c out into outer darkness:**	*1544*
Mt	8:16	he **c** out the spirits with his word,	*1544*
Mt	10:8	**lepers, raise the dead, c out devils:**	*1544*
Mt	12:26	**if Satan c out Satan, he is divided.**	*1544*
Mt	12:27	**And if I by Beelzebub c out devils,**	*1544*
Mt	12:28	**if I c out devils by the Spirit**	*1544*
Mt	17:27	**go thou to the sea, and c an hook,**	*906*
Mt	22:13	**and c him into outer darkness;**	*1544*
Mt	25:30	**And c ye the unprofitable servant**	*1544*
Mt	27:35	upon my vesture did they **c** lots	*906*
Mk	3:23	**How can Satan c out Satan?**	*1544*
Mk	9:42	**his neck, and he were c into the**	*906*
Mk	11:7	and **c** their garments on him;	*1911*
Mk	12:4	**at him they c stones, and**	*3036*
Lk	4:9	Son of God, **c** thyself down from	*906*
Lk	11:20	**if I with the finger of God c out**	*1544*
Lk	12:5	**hath power to c into hell; yea, I**	*1685*
Lk	23:34	parted his raiment, and **c** lots	*906*
Jn	6:37	**to me I will in no wise c out.**	*1544*
Jn	8:7	**let him first c a stone at her.**	*906*
Jn	15:6	**he is c forth as a branch, and is**	*906*
Jn	19:24	Let us not rend it, but **c** lots for it,	*2975*
Jn	19:24	and for my vesture they did **c** lots	*906*
Jn	21:6	**C the net on the right side of the**	*906*
Ac	7:58	**c** him out of the city, and stoned	*1544*
Ac	16:23	they **c** them into prison, charging	*906*
Ro	11:2	God hath not **c** away his people	*683*
2Co	7:6	comforteth those that are **c** down	*5011*

1Ti 5:12 they have **c** off their first faith *114*
Heb 10:35 **C** not away therefore your confidence ... *577*
2Pe 2:4 but **c** them down to hell, and *5020*
Rev 2:10 **the devil shall c some of you into** *906*
Rev 2:14 **Balac to c a stumblingblock** *906*
Rev 4:10 and **c** their crowns before the *906*
Rev 12:9 the great dragon was **c** out, that *906*
Rev 12:9 and his angels were **c** out with *906*
Rev 12:15 the serpent **c** out of his mouth *906*
Rev 12:16 the dragon **c** out of his mouth. *906*
Rev 14:19 **c** it into the great winepress of *906*
Rev 18:21 millstone, and **c** it into the sea *906*
Rev 19:20 These both were **c** alive into a *906*
Rev 20:3 **c** him into the bottomless pit, and *906*
Rev 20:10 was **c** into the lake of fire and *906*
Rev 20:14 death and hell were **c** into the *906*
Rev 20:15 was **c** into the lake of fire *906*

CASTAWAY
1Co 9:27 to others, I myself should be a **c** *96*

CASTEST
Ps 88:14 Lord, why **c** thou off my soul? 2186

CASTETH
Ps 147:17 He **c** forth his ice like morsels: 7993
Pr 19:15 Slothfulness **c** into a deep sleep; 5307
Mt 9:34 He **c** out devils through the prince *1544*
1Jn 4:18 perfect love **c** out fear: because *906*
3Jn 10 and **c** them out of the church. *1544*
Rev 6:13 as a fig tree **c** her untimely figs, ... *906*

CASTING
Mt 27:35 parted his garments, **c** lots: that *906*
Mk 1:16 Andrew his brother **c** a net into *906*
Mk 15:24 parted his garments, **c** lots upon *906*
Lk 9:49 we saw one **c** out devils in thy *1544*
Lk 21:1 the rich men **c** their gifts into the *906*
Lk 21:2 a certain poor widow **c** in thither *906*
Ro 11:15 For if the **c** away of them be the *580*
2Co 10:5 **C** down imaginations, and every *2507*
1Pe 5:7 **C** all your care upon him; for he *1977*

CASTLE
1Ch 11:5 David took the **c** of Zion, which 4686
1Ch 11:7 David dwelt in the **c**; therefore 4679
Pr 18:19 contentions are like the bars of a **c** 759
Ac 21:37 Paul was to be led into the **c**, he *3925*

CASTLES
Nu 31:10 they dwelt, and all their goodly **c**, ...2918
2Ch 17:12 he built in Judah **c**, and cities 1003
2Ch 27:4 and in the forests he built **c** and 1003

CATCH
2Ki 7:12 we shall **c** them alive, and get 8610
Ps 10:9 in wait to **c** the poor he doth **c** 2414
Hab 1:15 they **c** them in their net, and 1641
Lk 5:10 **henceforth thou shalt c men** *2221*

CATERPILLER
Ps 78:46 their increase unto the **c**, and 2625
Isa 33:4 the gathering of the **c**: as the 2625
Joel 1:4 cankerworm hath left hath the **c** 2625

CATERPILLERS
2Ch 6:28 mildew, locusts, or **c**; if their 2625
Ps 105:34 the locusts came, and **c**, and 3218
Jer 51:27 horses to come up as the rough **c** 3218

CATTLE
Ge 1:24 **c**, and creeping thing, and beast 929
Ge 2:20 Adam gave names to all **c**, and to 929
Ge 3:14 thou art cursed above all **c**, and 929
Ge 13:2 Abram was very rich in **c**, in 4735
Ge 30:32 all the speckled and spotted **c**, ...7716
Ge 30:32 and all the brown **c** among the 7716
Ge 30:39 and brought forth **c** ringstraked, ...6629
Ge 30:41 the rods before the eyes of the **c** 6629
Ge 31:8 all the **c** bare speckled: and if 6629
Ge 31:8 then bare all the **c** ringstraked 6629
Ge 47:16 Joseph said, Give your **c**; and I 4735
Ex 9:6 all the **c** of Egypt died: 4735
Ex 9:7 not one of the **c** of the Israelites 4735
Nu 3:41 all the firstlings among the **c** of the 929
Dt 28:51 he shall eat the fruit of thy **c**, and 929
Jos 8:27 Only the **c** and the spoil of that 929
Jos 11:14 these cities, and the **c**, the children 929
Jos 14:4 with their suburbs for their **c** and 4735
1Ki 1:25 fat **c** in abundance, and hath 4806
Ps 50:10 the **c** upon a thousand hills 929
Isa 7:25 for the treading of lesser **c** 7716
Jnh 4:11 left hand; and also much **c**? 929
Zec 13:5 to keep **c** from my youth. 7069
Lk 17:7 **a servant plowing or feeding c,** *4165*

CAUGHT
Ge 22:13 ram **c** in a thicket by his horns: 270
Ge 39:12 And she **c** him by his garment, ...8610
Jgs 15:4 went and **c** three hundred foxes, ...3920
2Sa 18:9 and his head **c** hold of the oak, ...2388
1Ki 2:28 and **c** hold on the horns of the 2388
2Ki 4:27 she **c** him by the feet: but 2388
Pr 7:13 So she **c** him, and kissed him, ...2388
Mt 21:39 **they c him, and cast him out** *2983*
Mk 12:3 **And they c him and beat him,** *2983*
Jn 21:3 and that night they **c** nothing *4084*
Jn 21:10 **the fish which we have now c** *4084*
Ac 8:39 Spirit of the Lord **c** away Philip, ... *726*
Ac 16:19 they **c** Paul and Silas, and drew *1949*
2Co 12:2 one **c** up to the third heaven. *726*
2Co 12:4 he was **c** up into paradise *726*
1Th 4:17 shall be **c** up together with *726*
Rev 12:5 her child was **c** up unto God, ... *726*

CAUL
Ex 29:13 the **c** that is above the liver, ...3508
Le 3:4 **c** above the liver, with the kidneys, ...3508
Le 9:10 and the **c** above the liver of the 3508
Hos 13:8 and will rend the **c** of their heart, ...5458

CAUSE
Ge 7:4 I will **c** it to rain upon the earth
Ex 8:5 and **c** frogs to come up upon
Ex 27:20 to **c** the lamp to burn always
Nu 27:5 brought their **c** before the Lord 4941
Dt 1:17 the **c** that is too hard for you 1697
Dt 24:4 thou shalt not **c** the land to sin,
1Sa 17:29 now done? Is there not a **c**? 1697
1Sa 19:5 blood, to slay David without a **c**? 2600
2Sa 15:4 suit or **c** might come unto me, ...4941
1Ki 12:15 the **c** was from the Lord 5438
2Ki 19:7 **c** him to fall by the sword
2Ch 10:15 for the **c** was of God, that the 5252
Ezr 4:15 which **c** was this city destroyed.
Ne 6:6 for which **c** thou buildest the wall,
Ne 13:26 did outlandish women **c** to sin.

Est 5:5 **C** Haman to make haste,
Job 2:3 him, to destroy him without **c** 2600
Job 13:18 I have ordered my **c**; I know 4941
Job 38:27 and to **c** the bud of the tender
Ps 35:1 Plead my **c**, O Lord, with them
Ps 35:19 the eye that hate me without a **c** 2600
Ps 67:1 bless us; and **c** his face to shine
Ps 74:22 Arise, O God, plead thine own **c**: 7379
Ps 80:3 and **c** thy face to shine; and we
Ps 80:19 God of hosts, **c** thy face to shine;
Ps 143:8 **C** me to hear thy lovingkindness
Pr 1:11 for the innocent without **c**: 2600
Pr 4:16 away, unless they **c** some to fall
Pr 22:23 the Lord will plead their **c**, and 7379
Pr 25:9 Debate thy **c** with thy neighbour 7379
Isa 1:23 neither doth the **c** of the widow 7379
Isa 30:11 **c** the Holy One of Israel to cease
Isa 30:30 And the Lord shall **c** his glorious
Jer 3:12 and I will not **c** mine anger to
Jer 14:22 of the Gentiles that can **c** rain?
Jer 16:21 I will **c** them to know mine hand
Jer 33:11 I will **c** to return the captivity of
Jer 33:15 **c** the Branch of righteousness
La 3:59 seen my wrong: judge thou my **c** 4941
Eze 14:23 that I have not done without **c** all 2600
Eze 29:4 I will **c** the fish of thy rivers to stick
Eze 29:21 I **c** the horn of the house of Israel
Eze 32:14 **c** their rivers to run like oil, saith the
Eze 36:12 Yea, I will **c** men to walk upon
Eze 39:3 and will **c** thine arrows to fall out of
Da 9:17 and **c** thy face to shine upon thy
Da 9:27 shall **c** the sacrifice and the oblation
Hos 2:11 I will also **c** all her mirth to cease,
Am 8:9 I will **c** the sun to go down at noon,
Jnh 1:7 may know for whose **c** this evil is 7945
Zec 13:2 I will **c** the prophets and the unclean
Mt 19:5 **For this c shall a man leave** *1752*
Mk 13:12 **shall c them to be put to death** *2289*
Lk 23:22 I have found no **c** of death in him: *158*
Jn 12:27 **for this c came I unto this hour** *1223*
Jn 18:37 **this c came I into the world,**
Ac 13:28 though they found no **c** of death *156*
Ac 28:18 there was no **c** of death in me *156*
Ro 1:26 For this **c** God gave them *1223*
Ro 16:17 mark them which **c** divisions *4160*
1Co 11:30 For this **c** many are weak *1223*
2Co 4:16 For which **c** we faint not; but *1352*
Eph 3:14 For this **c** I bow my knees unto *5484*
Eph 5:31 For this **c** shall a man leave his *873*
Heb 9:15 for this **c** he is the mediator *1223*
Rev 12:15 he might **c** her to be carried *4160*

CAUSED
Ge 2:5 the Lord God had not **c** it to rain
Ge 2:21 And the Lord God **c** a deep sleep to
Ex 14:21 and the Lord **c** the sea to go
Jgs 16:19 she **c** him to shave off the seven
1Sa 20:17 Jonathan **c** David to swear again,
Est 5:14 and he **c** the gallows to be made
Job 29:13 I **c** the widow's heart to sing for joy
Ps 78:26 He **c** an east wind to blow
Pr 7:21 With her much fair speech she **c**
Isa 63:14 the Spirit of the Lord **c** him to rest:
Jer 12:14 I have **c** my people Israel to inherit;
Jer 29:14 I **c** you to be carried away captive
Jer 29:31 him not, and he **c** you to trust in a lie:
Jer 50:6 shepherds have **c** them to go astray,
La 3:13 He hath **c** the arrows of his quiver
Eze 20:26 in that they **c** to pass through the fire
Am 4:7 **c** it not to rain upon another city:
Mal 2:8 ye have **c** many to stumble at the law;
Ac 15:3 they **c** great joy unto all the *4160*

CAUSES
Ex 18:26 hard **c** they brought unto Moses, ...1697
La 3:58 O Lord, thou hast pleaded the **c** 7379
Ac 26:21 For these **c** the Jews caught me *1752*

CAUSETH
Ps 104:14 He **c** the grass to grow for the cattle,
Ps 107:40 **c** them to wander in the wilderness
Ps 147:18 he **c** his wind to blow, and the
Pr 10:10 winketh with the eye **c** sorrow: 5414
Pr 19:26 a son that **c** shame, and bringeth
Eze 26:3 as the sea **c** his waves to come up
Mt 5:32 **c her to commit adultery: and** *4160*
2Co 9:11 **c** through us thanksgiving to *2716*
Rev 13:16 he **c** all, both small and great, ...*4160*

CAUSING
SS 7:9 **c** the lips of those that are asleep
Isa 30:28 in the jaws of the people, **c** them to
Jer 33:12 of shepherds, **c** their flocks to lie

CAVE
Ge 19:30 and he dwelt in a **c**, he and his two 4631
Ge 25:9 buried him in the **c** of Machpelah 4631
Jos 10:17 five kings are found hid in a **c** 4631
Jos 10:18 stones upon the mouth of the **c** 4631
1Sa 22:1 and escaped to the **c** Adullam: 4631
1Sa 24:3 where was a **c**; and Saul went in 4631
1Sa 24:7 Saul rose up out of the **c**, and 4631
1Sa 24:10 today into mine hand in the **c**: 4631
Jn 11:38 It was a **c**, and a stone lay upon *4693*

CAVES
Jgs 6:2 in the mountains, and **c**, and 4631
1Sa 13:6 people did hide themselves in **c**, ...4631
Isa 2:19 into the **c** of the earth, for fear 4247
Heb 11:38 mountains, and in dens and **c** *3692*

CEASE
Ge 8:22 and day and night shall not **c** 7673
1Sa 7:8 **C** not to cry unto the Lord our 2790
Ne 6:3 why should the work **c**, whilst I 7673
Job 10:20 **C** then, and let me alone, that I 2308
Job 14:7 tender branch thereof will not **c** 2308
Ps 46:9 He maketh wars to **c** unto the 7673
Ps 89:44 Thou hast made his glory to **c** 7673
Pr 19:27 **C**, my son, to hear the instruction 2308
Pr 23:4 **c** from thine own wisdom 2308
Ecc 12:3 and the grinders **c** because they 988
Isa 1:16 before mine eyes; **c** to do evil: 2308
Isa 13:11 the arrogancy of the proud to **c**, ...7673
Isa 30:11 cause the Holy One of Israel to **c** 7673
Jer 7:34 Then will I cause to **c** from the 7673
La 2:18 let not the apple of thine eye **c** 1826
Eze 6:6 your idols may be broken and **c**, ...7673
Eze 26:13 cause the noise of thy songs to **c**; 7673
Da 9:27 sacrifice and the oblation to **c**, ...7673
Hos 2:11 will also cause all her mirth to **c**, ...7673
1Co 13:8 there be tongues, they shall **c**; *3973*
Eph 1:16 **C** not to give thanks for you *3973*
Col 1:9 do not **c** to pray for you, and to *3973*

CEASED

Ge	18:11	it **c** to be with Sarah after the	2308
Jos	5:12	and the manna **c** on the morrow	7673
Ezr	4:24	Then **c** the work of the house of	989
Job	32:1	these three men **c** to answer Job,	7673
Ps	35:15	they did tear me, and **c** not:	1826
La	5:15	The joy of our heart is **c**; our	7673
Jnh	1:15	and the sea **c** from her raging	5975
Mk	4:39	the wind **c**, and there was a great	*2869*
Lk	7:45	**came in hath not c to kiss my**	*1257*
Lk	8:24	they **c**, and there was a calm	*3973*
Lk	11:1	when he **c**, one of his disciples	*3973*
Ac	5:42	they **c** not to teach and preach	*3973*
Gal	5:11	then is the offence of the cross **c**	*2673*
1Pe	4:1	suffered in the flesh hath **c** from	*3973*

CEASETH

Ps	12:1	Help, Lord, for the godly man **c**;	1584
Pr	26:20	there is no talebearer, the strife **c**	8367
Isa	24:8	The mirth of tabrets **c**, the noise	7673
La	3:49	eye trickleth down, and **c** not	1820
Ac	6:13	This man **c** not to speak	*3973*

CEASING

1Sa	12:23	the Lord in **c** to pray for you:	2308
Ro	1:9	that without **c** I make mention of	*89*
1Th	1:3	Remembering without **c** your	*89*
1Th	2:13	also thank we God without **c**	*89*
1Th	5:17	Pray without **c**	*89*

CEDAR

Nu	19:6	the priest shall take **c** wood,	730
2Sa	7:2	I dwell in an house of **c**, but the	730
1Ki	6:9	house with beams and boards of **c**	730
2Ki	14:9	sent to the **c** that was in Lebanon,	730
2Ki	19:23	and will cut down the tall **c** trees	730
1Ch	22:4	they of Tyre brought much **c** wood	730
Ezr	3:7	to bring **c** trees from Lebanon	730
Job	40:17	He moveth his tail like a **c**: the	730
Ps	92:12	he shall grow like a **c** in Lebanon	730
SS	1:17	The beams of our house are **c**,	730
Jer	22:14	cieled with **c**, and painted with	730
Zep	2:14	for he shall uncover the **c** work	731
Zec	11:2	for the **c** is fallen; because the	730

CEDARS

Jgs	9:15	and devour the **c** of Lebanon	730
1Ch	17:1	I dwell in an house of **c**, but the	730
2Ch	2:3	send him **c** to build him an house	730
Ps	104:16	**c** of Lebanon, which he hath	730
Eze	31:8	The **c** in the garden of God could	730
Am	2:9	like the height of the **c**, and he	730
Zec	11:1	that the fire may devour thy **c**	730

CELEBRATE

Le	23:32	even, shall ye **c** your sabbath	7673
Le	23:41	shall **c** it in the seventh month.	2287

CELESTIAL

1Co	15:40	There are also **c** bodies, and	*2032*
1Co	15:40	but the glory of the **c** is one,	*2032*

CELLARS

1Ch	27:27	for the wine **c** was Zabdi the	214
1Ch	27:28	and over the **c** of oil was Joash:	214

CENSER

Le	16:12	shall take a **c** full of burning coals	4289
Nu	16:17	and Aaron, each of you his **c**	4289
Heb	9:4	Which had the golden **c**, and the	*2369*
Rev	8:3	at the altar, having a golden **c**;	*3031*

CENSERS

Nu	4:14	the **c**, the fleshhooks, and the	4289
Nu	16:6	This do; Take you **c**, Korah, and	4289
1Ki	7:50	spoons, and the **c** of pure gold;	4289

CENTURION (sen-too´-ree-un)

Mt	8:13	Jesus said unto the **c**, **Go thy way;**	*1543*
Mk	15:39	**c**, which stood over against him,	*2760*
Ac	10:1	**c** of the band called the Italian	*1543*
Ac	10:22	they said, Cornelius the **c**, a just	*1543*
Ac	27:1	Julius, a **c** of Augustus' band	*1543*
Ac	27:6	there the **c** found a ship of	*1543*
Ac	27:43	the **c**, willing to save Paul, kept	*1543*

CENTURIONS (sen-too´-ree-uns)

Ac	21:32	immediately took soldiers and **c**	*1543*
Ac	23:17	Paul called one of the **c** unto him	*1543*

CERTAIN

Ge	38:1	turned in to a **c** Adullamite,	376
Dt	13:13	**C** men, the children of Belial,	
Dt	13:14	thing **c**, that such abomination	3559
Jgs	9:53	a **c** woman cast a piece of a	259
1Sa	21:7	a **c** man of the servants of Saul	
1Ki	2:42	Know for a **c**, on the day thou	
1Ki	20:35	**c** man of the sons of the prophets	259
1Ki	22:34	And a **c** man drew a bow at a	
2Ki	4:1	Now there cried a **c** woman of the	259
Ne	11:23	that a **c** portion should be for	
Est	2:5	**c** Jew whose name was Mordecai	376
Da	2:45	and the dream is **c**, and the	3330
Da	8:13	another saint said unto that **c**	6422
Da	8:27	Daniel fainted, and was sick **c** days;	
Da	10:5	behold a **c** man clothed in linen	259
Mt	8:19	a **c** scribe came, and said unto	*1520*
Mt	17:14	came to him a **c** man, kneeling	
Mt	18:23	**heaven likened unto a c king,**	*444*
Mt	21:28	**A c man had two sons; and he**	
Mk	5:25	a **c** woman, which had an issue	
Mk	5:35	**c** which said, Thy daughter is	
Mk	12:1	**A c man planted a vineyard**	
Lk	1:5	a **c** priest named Zacharias, of the	*5100*
Lk	7:41	**There was a c creditor which had**	*5100*
Lk	8:2	**c** women, which had been healed	*5100*
Lk	10:25	a **c** lawyer stood up, and tempted	*5100*
Lk	10:30	**A c man went down from**	*5100*
Lk	10:31	**came down a c priest that way:**	*5100*
Lk	10:33	**a c Samaritan, as he journeyed,**	*5100*
Lk	10:38	and a **c** woman named Martha	*5100*
Lk	13:6	**A c man had a fig tree planted**	*5100*
Lk	14:16	**A c man made a great supper,**	*5100*
Lk	15:11	**A c man had two sons:**	*5100*
Lk	16:1	**There was a c rich man, which**	*5100*
Lk	16:19	**a c rich man, which was clothed**	*5100*
Lk	16:20	**was a c beggar named Lazarus,**	*5100*
Lk	20:9	**A c man planted a vineyard,**	*5100*
Lk	21:2	saw also a **c** poor widow casting	*5100*
Jn	12:20	there were **c** Greeks among them	*5100*
Ac	3:2	And a **c** man lame from his	*5100*
Ac	5:1	But a **c** man named Ananias,	*5100*
Ac	5:2	brought a **c** part, and laid it at	*5100*
Ac	13:6	a **c** sorcerer, a false prophet	*5100*
Ac	15:5	up **c** of the sect of the Pharisees	*5100*
Ac	16:1	Timotheus, the son of a **c** woman,	*5100*

Ac 16:14 a **c** woman named Lydia, a seller *5100*
Ac 16:16 a **c** damsel possessed with a spirit *5100*
Ac 17:18 **c** philosophers of the Epicureans, ... *5100*
Ac 18:2 a **c** Jew named Aquila, born in *5100*
Ac 18:24 And a **c** Jew named Apollos, born *5100*
Ac 19:24 a **c** man named Demetrius, a *5100*
Ac 23:12 **c** of the Jews banded together, ... *5100*
Ac 24:1 with a **c** orator named Tertullus, ... *5100*
Ac 25:13 **c** days king Agrippa and Bernice *5100*
Ac 27:1 Paul and **c** other prisoners *5100*
Ro 15:26 a **c** contribution for the poor *5100*
1Co 4:11 and have no **c** dwellingplace; *790*
1Ti 6:7 it is **c** we can carry nothing out *1212*
Jude 4 For there are **c** men crept in *5100*

CERTAINLY
Ge 18:10 I will **c** return unto thee 7725
Ge 26:28 We saw **c** that the Lord was with
Ex 3:12 he said, **C** I will be with thee; 3588
1Sa 25:28 the Lord will **c** make my lord a sure
2Ch 18:27 If thou **c** return in peace,
Jer 44:17 we will **c** do whatsoever thing goeth
La 2:16 **c** this is the day that we looked 389
Lk 23:47 **C** this was a righteous man *3689*

CERTAINTY
Jos 23:13 Know for a **c** that the Lord your God
Pr 22:21 the **c** of the words of truth; that 7189
Ac 21:34 not know the **c** for the tumult, ... *804*

CERTIFIED
Ezr 4:14 have we sent and **c** the king; 3046
Est 2:22 and Esther **c** the king thereof in 559

CERTIFY
Ezr 4:16 We **c** the king that, if this city 3046
Ezr 5:10 asked their names also, to **c** thee 3046
Gal 1:11 But I **c** you, brethren, that the *1107*

CHAFF
Job 21:18 **c** that the storm carrieth away 4671
Ps 1:4 **c** which the wind driveth away 4671
Jer 23:28 What is the **c** to the wheat? 8401
Mt 3:12 burn up the **c** with unquenchable *892*
Lk 3:17 the **c** he will burn with fire *891*

CHAIN
Ge 41:42 put a gold **c** about his neck; 7242
Ps 73:6 compasseth them about as a **c**; 6059
SS 4:9 eyes, with one **c** of thy neck. 6060
Da 5:7 have a **c** of gold about his neck, ... 2002
Ac 28:20 of Israel I am bound with this **c** *254*
2Ti 1:16 and was not ashamed of my **c** *254*
Rev 20:1 pit and a great **c** in his hand *254*

CHAINS
Ex 39:17 **c** of gold in the two rings 5688
Pr 1:9 thy head, and **c** about thy neck 6060
SS 1:10 jewels, thy neck with **c** of gold 2737
Jer 52:11 king of Babylon bound him in **c** 5178
Mk 5:4 the **c** had been plucked asunder *254*
Ac 12:6 two soldiers, bound with two **c**: *254*
Ac 12:7 And his **c** fell off from his hands *254*
2Pe 2:4 delivered them into **c** of darkness, ... *4577*
Jude 6 hath reserved in everlasting **c** *1199*

CHAMBER
Jgs 3:24 covereth his feet in his summer **c** 2315
2Sa 18:33 the **c** over the gate, and wept: 5944
Ne 13:4 of the **c** of the house of our God, ... 3957
Ne 13:5 had prepared for him a great **c**, ... 3957
Ps 19:5 bridegroom coming out of his **c**, ... 2646
SS 3:4 the **c** of her that conceived me 2315
Da 6:10 windows being open in his **c** 5952
Joel 2:16 the bridegroom go forth of his **c**, ... 2315
Ac 9:37 they laid her in an upper **c**: *5253*

CHAMBERLAIN
Est 2:3 custody of Hege the king's **c**, ... 5631
Est 2:14 of Shaashgaz, the king's **c**, which 5631
Ac 12:20 Blastus the king's **c** *1909, 2846, 3588*
Ro 16:23 Erastus the **c** of the city saluteth *3623*

CHAMBERLAINS
Est 1:15 of the king Ahasuerus by the **c**? 5631

CHAMBERS
2Ch 31:11 to prepare **c** in the house of the 3957
Ezr 8:29 the **c** of the house of the Lord. 3957
Ne 10:37 to the **c** of the house of our God; 3957
Ps 104:3 Who layeth the beams of his **c** 5944
Pr 7:27 going down to the **c** of death. 2315
SS 1:4 king hath brought me into his **c** 2315
Mt 24:26 **behold, he is in the secret c;** *5009*

CHAMPION
1Sa 17:4 went out a **c** out of the camp 376, 1143
1Sa 17:23 the **c**, the Philistine of Gath, ... 376, 1143

CHANCE
Dt 22:6 If a bird's nest **c** to be before thee 7122
1Sa 6:9 it was a **c** that happened to us 4745
Ecc 9:11 time and **c** happened! to them 6294
Lk 10:31 **by c there came down a certain** *4795*

CHANCELLOR
Ezr 4:9 Then wrote Rehum the **c**, ... 1169, 2942
Ezr 4:17 an answer unto Rehum the **c** 1169, 2942

CHANGE
Ge 35:2 be clean, and **c** your garments: 2498
Le 27:10 nor **c** it, a good for a bad, or a 4171
Jgs 14:19 gave **c** of garments unto them 2487
Job 17:12 They **c** the night into day: and 7760
Ps 102:26 as a vesture shalt thou **c** them 2498
Pr 24:21 with them that are given to **c**: 8138
Jer 13:23 Can the Ethiopian **c** his skin, or 2015
Da 7:25 and think to **c** times and laws: 8133
Mal 3:6 I am the Lord, I **c** not; therefore 8138
Ro 1:26 their women did **c** the natural *3337*
Php 3:21 Who shall **c** our vile body, that it *3345*

CHANGED
Ge 31:7 and **c** my wages ten times; but 2498
Le 13:16 turn again, and be **c** unto white, ... 2015
1Sa 21:13 he **c** his behaviour before them, ... 8138
Job 30:18 of my disease is my raiment **c**; 2664
Ps 106:20 Thus they **c** their glory into the 4171
Ecc 8:1 boldness of his face shall be **c** 8132
Jer 2:11 Hath a nation **c** their gods 4171
Jer 2:11 my people have **c** their glory for 4171
Da 3:19 the form of his visage was **c** 8133
Da 5:6 the king's countenance was **c**, and 8133
Da 7:28 my countenance **c** in me: but I 8133
Mk 2:4 hath **c** the portion of my people: *4171*
Ro 1:23 **c** the glory of the uncorruptible *236*
Ro 1:25 Who **c** the truth of God into a *3337*
1Co 15:51 all sleep, but we shall all be **c**, ... *236*

1Co 15:52 incorruptible, and we shall be **c** *236*
2Co 3:18 are **c** into the same image from *3339*
Heb 7:12 priesthood being **c**, there is made *3346*

CHANGES

2Ki 5:5 of gold, and ten **c** of raiment 2487
2Ki 5:23 two bags, with two **c** of garments 2487
Job 10:17 me; **c** and war are against me 2487
Ps 55:19 Because they have no **c**, therefore 2487

CHANGETH

Ps 15:4 to his own hurt, and **c** not 4171
Da 2:21 he **c** the times and the seasons: 8133

CHANNEL

Isa 27:12 from the **c** of the river unto the 7641

CHANNELS

2Sa 22:16 the **c** of the sea appeared, the 650
Ps 18:15 Then the **c** of waters were seen 650

CHARGE

Ge 28:6 he blessed him he gave him a **c**, ...6680
Nu 3:31 And their **c** shall be the ark 4931
Nu 5:19 the priest shall **c** her by an oath, ...7650
Nu 18:8 I also have given thee the **c** of 4931
Nu 27:23 and gave him a **c**, as the Lord 6680
Dt 3:28 **c** Joshua, and encourage him..........6680
2Sa 14:8 I will give **c** concerning thee 6680
Ne 10:32 to **c** ourselves yearly with the..........5414
Est 3:9 that have the **c** of the business.........6213
Est 4:8 to **c** her that she should go in 6680
Job 34:13 Who hath given him a **c** over 6485
Ps 91:11 shall give his angels **c** over thee 6680
Zec 3:7 keep my **c**, then thou shalt also 4931
Mt 4:6 give his angels **c** concerning *1781*
Mk 9:25 **I c thee, come out of him, and** *2004*
Lk 4:10 shall give his angels **c** over thee, ...*1781*
Ac 7:60 Lord, lay not this sin to their **c** *2476*
Ac 23:29 to have nothing laid to his **c** *1462*
1Co 9:18 the gospel of Christ without **c**, ...*77*
1Ti 5:21 I **c** thee before God, and the Lord *1263*
2Ti 4:16 it may not be laid to their **c** *3049*

CHARGEABLE

Ne 5:15 before me were **c** unto the people, ...3513
2Co 11:9 I was **c** to no man: for that............*2655*
2Th 3:8 that we might not be **c** to any *1912*

CHARGED

Ge 40:4 the captain of the guard **c** Joseph 6485
Ex 1:22 Pharaoh **c** all his people, saying 6680
Dt 27:11 Moses **c** the people the same day 6680
Jos 18:8 and Joshua **c** them that went 6680
1Ki 2:1 he **c** Solomon his son, saying, ...6680
2Ch 36:23 hath **c** me to build him an house 6485
Ezr 1:2 and he hath **c** me to build him 6485
Est 2:20 Mordecai had **c** her: for Esther 6680
Job 1:22 sinned not, nor **c** God foolishly 5414
Mt 9:30 Jesus straitly **c** them, saying *1690*
Mt 16:20 Then **c** he his disciples that they *1291*
Lk 5:14 And he **c** him to **tell no man:** *3853*
Ac 23:22 **c** him, See thou tell no man *3853*
1Ti 5:16 and let not the church be **c**; *916*

CHARGER

Nu 7:13 And his offering was one silver **c**, ...7086
Mt 14:8 here John Baptist's head in a **c**.........*4094*
Mk 6:25 by and by in a **c** the head of John *4094*

CHARGES

2Ch 8:14 the Levites to their **c**, to praise.........4931
2Ch 31:17 in their **c** by their courses: 4931
Ac 21:24 **c** with them, that they may shave *1159*
1Co 9:7 warfare any time at his own **c**? *3800*

CHARGING

Ac 16:23 **c** the jailor to keep them safely: *3853*
2Ti 2:14 **c** them before the Lord that they *1263*

CHARIOT

Ge 46:29 Joseph made ready his **c**, and 4818
Jgs 4:15 Sisera lighted down off his **c**, and 4818
1Ki 12:18 speed to get him up to his **c**...........4818
1Ki 22:38 the **c** in the pool of Samaria; 7393
2Ki 2:11 appeared a **c** of fire, and horses 7393
2Ki 9:16 Jehu rode in a **c**, and went to Jezreel; ...7393
2Ki 9:24 heart, and he sunk down in his **c** 7393
Ps 46:9 he burneth the **c** in the fire 5699
Ps 104:3 who maketh the clouds his **c**: 7398
SS 3:9 King Solomon made himself a **c** 668
Jer 51:21 thee will I break in pieces the **c** 7393
Ac 8:28 and sitting in his **c** read Esaias *716*
Ac 8:29 Go near, and join thyself to this **c** *716*
Ac 8:38 he commanded the **c** to stand still: *716*

CHARIOTS

Ex 14:7 and all the **c** of Egypt 7393
Ex 14:9 **c** of Pharaoh, and his horsemen 7393
Ex 14:17 upon all his host, upon his **c**, ...7393
Ex 14:23 even all Pharaoh's horses, his **c**, ...7393
Ex 14:26 the Egyptians, upon their **c**, ...7393
Jos 11:6 and burn their **c** with fire.............4818
Jos 17:16 have **c** of iron, both they who are 7393
Jos 24:6 **c** and horsemen unto the Red sea 7393
Jgs 4:15 discomfited Sisera, and all his **c**........7393
Jgs 4:16 Barak pursued after the **c**, and 7393
2Ki 6:17 mountain was full of horses and **c** 7393
2Ki 23:11 burned the **c** of the sun with fire 7393
Ps 20:7 trust in **c**, and some in horses: 7393
SS 1:9 company of horses in Pharaoh's **c** 7393
Isa 22:18 **c** of thy glory shall be the shame.......4818
Jer 4:13 his **c** shall be as a whirlwind: 4818
Joel 2:5 Like the noise of **c** on the tops of 4818
Na 2:3 **c** shall be with flaming torches 7393
Zec 6:1 came four **c** out from between 4818
Rev 9:9 as the sound of **c** of many horses *716*

CHARITY

1Cor 8:1 Knowledge puffeth up, but **c** *26*
1Cor 13:1 of angels, and have not **c**, I am *26*
1Cor 13:2 mountains, and have not **c**, ...*26*
1Cor 13:3 to be burned, and have not **c** *26*
1Cor 13:4 **C** suffereth long, and is kind; *26*
1Cor 13:4 **c** envieth not; **c** vaunteth not *26*
1Cor 13:8 **C** never faileth: but whether *26*
1Cor13:13 now abideth faith, hope, **c**, these *26*
1Cor13:13 the greatest of these is **c** *26*
1Cor 14:1 Follow after **c**, and desire *26*
1Cor16:14 all your things be done with **c** *26*
Col 3:14 above all these things put on **c**, ...*26*
1Ti 2:15 in faith and **c** and holiness with *26*
2Ti 2:22 follow righteousness, faith, **c**, ...*26*
1Pe 5:14 ye one another with a kiss of **c** *26*
2Pe 1:7 and to brotherly kindness **c** *26*
Jude 12 spots in your feasts of **c**, when *26*
Rev 2:19 **I know thy works, and c, and** *26*

CHARMERS
Ps 58:5 hearken to the voice of **c**, 3907
Isa 19:3 seek to the idols, and to the **c**, 328

CHASE
Le 26:7 And ye shall **c** your enemies, and 7291
Le 26:36 the sound of a shaken leaf shall **c** 7291
Dt 32:30 How should one **c** a thousand 7291
Ps 35:5 and let the angel of the Lord **c** 1760

CHASED
Jos 7:5 for they **c** them from before the 7291
Jgs 9:40 And Abimelech **c** him, and he 7291
Jgs 20:43 **c** them, and trode them down 7291
Job 20:8 he shall be **c** away as a vision of 5074
Isa 13:14 it shall be as the **c** roe, and as a 5080
Isa 17:13 and shall be **c** as the chaff of the 7291

CHASTE
2Co 11:2 present you as a **c** virgin to *53*
Tit 2:5 discreet, **c**, keepers at home, *53*
1Pe 3:2 they behold your **c** conversation *53*

CHASTEN
2Sa 7:14 I will **c** him with the rod of men, 3198
Ps 38:1 **c** me in thy hot displeasure 3256
Pr 19:18 **C** thy son while there is hope, 3256
Rev 3:19 **many as I love, I rebuke and c** *3811*

CHASTENED
Job 33:19 He is **c** also with pain upon his 3198
Ps 118:18 The Lord hath **c** me sore: but he 3256
1Co 11:32 we are **c** of the Lord, that we *3811*
2Co 6:9 as **c**, and not killed; *3811*
Heb 12:10 for a few days **c** us after their own *3811*

CHASTENETH
Dt 8:5 as a man **c** his son, so 3256
Dt 8:5 the Lord thy God **c** thee 3256
Pr 13:24 he that loveth him **c** him 4148
Heb 12:6 For whom the Lord loveth he **c** *3811*

CHASTENING
Pr 3:11 despise not the **c** of the Lord; 4148
Heb 12:5 despise not thou the **c** of the *3809*
Heb 12:7 If ye endure **c**, God dealeth with *3809*

CHASTISE
1Ki 12:11 but I will **c** you with scorpions 3256
1Ki 12:14 with whips, but I will **c** you with 3256
Lk 23:16 I will therefore **c** him, and release *3811*

CHASTISED
1Ki 12:14 my father also **c** you with whips 3256
Jer 31:18 Thou hast **c** me, and I was **c**, 3256

CHASTISEMENT
Dt 11:2 not seen the **c** of the Lord your 4148
Isa 53:5 the **c** of our peace was upon 4148
Heb 12:8 But if ye be without **c**, whereof *3309*

CHEEK
Ps 3:7 all mine enemies upon the **c** bone; 3895
Joel 1:6 hath the **c** teeth of a great lion 4973
Mt 5:39 **smite thee upon thy right c**, *4600*

CHEEKS
SS 1:10 Thy **c** are comely with rows of 3895
SS 5:13 His **c** are as a bed of spices, as 3895
La 1:2 and her tears are on her **c** 3895

CHEER
Ecc 11:9 and let thy heart **c** thee in the 3190
Mt 9:2 **be of good c; thy sins be forgiven** *2293*
Jn 16:33 **but be of good c; I have overcome** *2293*
Ac 23:11 **Be of good c, Paul: for as thou** *2293*

CHEERFUL
Pr 15:13 A merry heart maketh a **c** 3190
2Co 9:7 for God loveth a **c** giver *2431*

CHEESE
2Sa 17:29 sheep, and **c** of kine, for David, 8194
Job 10:10 as milk, and curdled me like **c**? 1385

CHERISHETH
Eph 5:29 but nourished and **c** it, even *2282*
1Th 2:7 even as a nurse **c** her children: *2282*

CHERUB (cher´-ub)
Ex 25:19 one **c** on the one end, 3742
Ex 25:19 and the other **c** on the other end: 3742
2Sa 22:11 he rode upon a **c**, and did fly: 3742
1Ki 6:27 of the other **c** touched the wall; 3742
Ps 18:10 he rode upon a **c**, and did fly: 3742
Eze 10:9 one wheel by one **c**, and another 3742
Eze 10:9 another wheel by another **c** 3742
Eze 28:16 I will destroy thee, O covering **c**, 3742

CHERUBIMS (cher´-u-bims)
Ge 3:24 of the garden of Eden **C** and 3742
Ex 25:19 mercy seat shall ye make the **c** 3742
Ex 25:20 **c** shall stretch forth their wings 3742
Ex 25:20 seat shall the faces of the **c** 3742
Ex 26:1 **c** of cunning work shalt thou 3742
Ex 37:8 the mercy seat made he the **c** 3742
Ex 37:9 the **c** spread out their wings on 3742
Ex 37:9 seatward were the faces of the **c** 3742
1Ki 8:7 **c** spread forth their two wings 3742
1Ki 8:7 ark, and the **c** covered the ark 3742
2Ch 5:8 the **c** spread forth their wings 3742
2Ch 5:8 **c** covered the ark and the staves 3742
Ps 80:1 that dwellest between the **c** 3742
Ps 99:1 he sitteth between the **c**; let 3742
Eze 10:2 coals of fire from between the **c** 3742
Eze 10:3 **c** stood on the right side of the 3742
Eze 10:6 the wheels, from between the **c** 3742
Eze 10:9 behold the four wheels by the **c**, 3742
Eze 11:22 the **c** lift up their wings, and the 3742
Heb 9:5 **c** of glory shadowing the *5502*

CHESNUT
Eze 31:8 and the **c** trees were not like 6196

CHEST
2Ki 12:10 much money in the **c**, that the 727
2Ch 24:11 **c** was brought unto the king's 727
2Ch 24:11 came and emptied the **c**, and took 727

CHEW
Le 11:4 shall ye not eat of them that **c** 5927
Dt 14:7 **c** the cud, but divide not the hoof; 5927

CHEWETH
Le 11:7 he **c** not the cud; he is unclean 1641
Le 11:26 not clovenfooted, nor **c** the cud 5927

CHIDE
Ex 17:2 Wherefore the people did **c** with 7378
Jgs 8:1 they did **c** with him sharply 7378
Ps 103:9 He will not always **c**: neither will 7378

CHIEF

Ge	40:2	against the **c** of the butlers,	8269
Ge	40:2	and against the **c** of the bakers	8269
Ge	40:9	**c** butler told his dream to Joseph,	8269
Ge	40:16	When the **c** baker saw that the	8269
Ge	40:21	he restored the **c** butler unto his	8269
Ge	40:22	he hanged the **c** baker: as Joseph	8269
Ge	40:23	Yet did not the **c** butler remember	8269
Ge	41:9	spake the **c** butler unto Pharaoh	8269
Ezr	10:5	Ezra, and made the **c** priests	8269
Ps	78:51	the **c** of their strength in the	7225
Pr	16:28	a whisperer separateth **c** friends	441
Jer	20:1	**c** governor in the house of the	5057
Da	2:48	and **c** of the governors over all	7229
Da	10:13	lo, Michael, one of the **c** princes	7223
Mt	20:18	**be betrayed unto the c priests**	*749*
Mt	20:27	**whosoever will be c among you,**	*4413*
Mt	23:6	**the c seats in the synagogues**	*4410*
Mt	27:3	silver to the **c** priests and elders	*749*
Mt	27:6	the **c** priests took the silver pieces	*749*
Mt	27:41	also the **c** priests mocking him	*749*
Mk	10:33	**be delivered unto the c priests,**	*749*
Mk	12:39	**the c seats in the synagogues,**	*4410*
Lk	11:15	devils through Beelzebub the **c**	*758*
Lk	19:2	was the **c** among the publicans	*754*
Lk	22:26	**that is c, as he that doth serve**	*2283*
Ac	14:12	because he was the **c** speaker	*2288*
Ac	17:4	and of the **c** women not a few	*4413*
Ac	23:10	the **c** captain, fearing lest Paul	*5506*
Eph	2:20	himself being the **c** corner stone;	*204*
1Ti	1:15	to save sinners; of whom I am **c**	*4413*
1Pe	2:6	I lay in Sion a **c** corner stone,	*204*
1Pe	5:4	when the **c** Shepherd shall appear,	*750*
Rev	6:15	**c** captains, and the mighty men,	*5506*

CHIEFEST

SS	5:10	ruddy, the **c** among ten thousand	1713
Mk	10:44	**the c shall be servant of all**	*4413*
2Co	12:11	behind the very **c** apostles	*5228, 3029*

CHIEFLY

Php	4:22	**c** they that are of Caesar's	*3122*
2Pe	2:10	**c** them that walk after the flesh	*3122*

CHILD

Ge	11:30	Sarai was barren; she had no **c**	2056
Ge	16:11	her, Behold, thou art with **c**,	2030
Ge	18:13	Shall I of a surety bear a **c**	
Ge	21:15	cast the **c** under one of the shrubs	3206
Ge	21:16	Let me not see the death of the **c**	3206
Ge	44:20	and a **c** of his old age, a little one;	3206
Ex	2:2	saw him that he was a goodly **c**,	3206
Ex	2:3	and put the **c** therein; and she	3206
Ex	2:6	had opened it, she saw the **c**	3206
Ex	2:9	Take this **c** away, and nurse it	3206
Ex	2:9	the woman took the **c**, and nursed	3206
Jgs	11:34	she was his only **c**; beside her he	3173
Jgs	13:7	the **c** shall be Nazarite to God	5288
Ru	4:16	Naomi took the **c**, and laid it in	3206
1Sa	1:22	I will not go up until the **c** be	5288
1Sa	1:25	and brought the **c** to Eli	5288
1Sa	1:27	For this **c** I prayed; and the	5288
1Sa	2:11	the **c** did minister unto the Lord	5288
1Sa	2:21	**c** Samuel grew before the Lord	5288
1Sa	2:25	And the **c** Samuel grew on, and	5288
1Sa	3:1	And the **c** Samuel ministered	5288
1Sa	4:21	she named the **c** Ichabod,	5288
2Sa	12:15	And the Lord struck the **c** that	3206
2Sa	12:16	therefore besought God for the **c**;	5288
2Sa	12:18	the seventh day, that the **c** died	3206
2Sa	12:18	to tell him that the **c** was dead:	3206
2Sa	12:22	While the **c** was yet alive, I fasted	3206
2Sa	12:22	gracious to me, that the **c** may live?	3206
1Ki	3:19	this woman's **c** died in the night;	1121
1Ki	3:20	and laid her dead **c** in my bosom	1121
1Ki	3:25	Divide the living **c** in two, and	3206
1Ki	3:26	the woman whose the living **c** was	1121
1Ki	3:27	Give her the living **c**, and in no	3205
1Ki	17:21	he stretched himself upon the **c**	3206
1Ki	17:22	the soul of the **c** came into him	3206
1Ki	17:23	Elijah took the **c**, and brought	3206
2Ki	4:29	my staff upon the face of the **c**	5288
2Ki	4:31	laid the staff on the face of the **c**;	5288
2Ki	4:31	him, saying, The **c** is not awaked	5288
2Ki	4:32	the **c** was dead and laid upon his	5288
2Ki	4:34	he went up, and lay upon the **c**,	3206
2Ki	4:34	stretched himself upon the **c**;	
2Ki	4:34	the flesh of the **c** waxed warm	3206
2Ki	4:35	the **c** sneezed seven times	5288
2Ki	4:35	and the **c** opened his eyes	5288
Pr	20:11	a **c** is known by his doings,	5288
Pr	22:6	Train up a **c** in the way he	5288
Pr	22:15	is bound in the heart of a **c**;	5288
Pr	23:13	Withhold not correction from the **c**	5288
Pr	29:15	but a **c** left to himself bringeth	5288
Ecc	4:13	Better is a poor and a wise **c**	3206
Isa	9:6	unto us a **c** is born, unto us a	3206
Isa	11:6	and a little **c** shall lead them	5288
Isa	65:20	the **c** shall die an hundred years	5288
Jer	1:6	I cannot speak: for I am a **c**	5288
Jer	1:7	Say not, I am a **c**: for thou shalt	5288
Mt	1:18	with **c** of the Holy Ghost	*1722, 1064, 2192*
Mt	1:23	a virgin shall be with **c**,	*1722, 1064, 2192*
Mt	2:8	search diligently for the young **c**;	*3813*
Mt	2:9	stood over where the young **c** was	*3813*
Mt	2:13	Herod will seek the young **c** to	*3813*
Mt	2:14	took the young **c** and his mother	*3813*
Mt	2:20	Arise, and take the young **c** and	*3813*
Mt	18:2	And Jesus called a little **c** unto	*3813*
Mt	18:4	**humble himself as this little c,**	*3813*
Mt	18:5	**shall receive one such little c**	*3813*
Mk	10:15	**the kingdom of God as a little c,**	*3813*
Lk	1:7	And they had no **c**, because that	*5043*
Lk	1:76	And thou, **c**, shalt be called the	*3813*
Lk	1:80	the **c** grew, and waxed strong	*3813*
Lk	2:5	wife, being great with **c**	*1471*
Lk	2:17	was told them concerning this **c**	*3813*
Lk	2:27	parents brought in the **c** Jesus,	*3813*
Lk	2:43	the **c** Jesus tarried behind	*3816*
Lk	9:38	my son: for he is mine only **c**	*3439*
Lk	9:48	**Whosoever shall receive this c**	*3813*
Lk	18:17	**the kingdom of God as a little c**	*3813*
Jn	4:49	Sir, come down ere my **c** die	*3813*
Ac	4:27	against thy holy **c** Jesus, whom	*3816*
Ac	4:30	by the name of thy holy **c** Jesus	*3816*
1Co	13:11	When I was a **c**, I spake as a **c**,	3516
1Co	13:11	I understood as a **c**,	*3516*
1Co	13:11	I thought as a **c**:	*3516*
2Ti	3:15	from a **c** thou hast known the	*1025*
Heb	11:23	they saw he was a proper **c**;	*3813*
Rev	12:4	to devour her **c** as soon as it	*5043*
Rev	12:5	she brought forth a man **c**, who	*5297*
Rev	12:5	her **c** was caught up unto God	*5043*

CHILDHOOD

1Sa	12:2	walked before you from my **c**	5271
Ecc	11:10	evil from thy flesh: for **c** and	3208

CHILDISH

1Co	13:11	a man, I put away **c** things	*3516*

CHILDLESS

Ge	15:2	wilt thou give me, seeing I go **c**,	6185
1Sa	15:33	thy sword hath made women **c**,	7921
1Sa	15:33	so shall thy mother be **c**,	7921
Lk	20:30	took her to wife, and he died **c**,	*815*

CHILDREN

Ge	3:16	sorrow thou shalt bring forth **c**;	1121
Ge	11:5	which the **c** of men builded	1121
Ge	16:1	Sarai Abram's wife bare him no **c**	
Ge	25:22	**c** struggled together within her;	1121
Ge	30:1	Give me **c**, or else I die,	1121
Ge	30:26	Give me my wives and my **c**,	3206
Ge	32:32	Therefore the **c** of Israel eat not	1121
Ge	36:31	any king over the **c** of Israel	1121
Ge	37:3	loved Joseph more than all his **c**,	1121
Ge	45:10	and thy **c**, and thy children's **c**,	1121
Ex	1:7	And the **c** of Israel were fruitful,	1121
Ex	2:25	God looked upon the **c** of Israel,	1121
Ex	3:10	the **c** of Israel out of Egypt	1121
Ex	3:14	thou say unto the **c** of Israel, I AM	1121
Ex	4:31	Lord had visited the **c** of Israel,	1121
Ex	10:20	would not let the **c** of Israel go	1121
Ex	13:15	the firstborn of my **c** I redeem	1121
Ex	14:8	pursued after the **c** of Israel: and	1121
Ex	14:16	**c** of Israel shall go on dry ground	1121
Ex	14:22	the **c** of Israel went into the midst	1121
Ex	16:2	the **c** of Israel murmured against	1121
Ex	16:35	And the **c** of Israel did eat manna	1121
Ex	25:22	commandment unto the **c** of Israel	1121
Ex	28:12	stones of memorial unto the **c** of	1121
Ex	28:21	the **c** of Israel, twelve, according	1121
Ex	29:43	I will meet with the **c** of Israel	1121
Ex	29:45	I will dwell among the **c** of Israel	1121
Ex	30:16	memorial unto the **c** of Israel	1121
Ex	31:16	**c** of Israel shall keep the sabbath,	1121
Ex	39:7	for a memorial to the **c** of Israel;	1121
Le	16:19	from the uncleanness of the **c** of	1121
Le	16:21	the iniquities of the **c** of Israel,	1121
Le	16:34	an atonement for the **c** of Israel	1121
Le	22:3	**c** of Israel hallow unto the Lord	1121
Le	23:43	the **c** of Israel to dwell in booths,	1121
Nu	9:2	**c** of Israel also keep the passover	1121
Nu	31:18	But all the women **c**, that have	2945
Dt	2:9	unto the **c** of Lot for a possession	1121
Dt	34:8	the **c** of Israel wept for Moses	1121
Jos	4:6	your **c** ask their fathers in time	1121
Jos	4:7	a memorial unto the **c** of Israel	1121
Jos	7:1	**c** of Israel committed a trespass	1121
Jos	7:1	kindled against the **c** of Israel	1121
Jos	10:4	peace with Joshua and with the **c**	1121
Jos	14:4	the **c** of Joseph were two tribes,	1121
Jos	22:27	your **c** may not say to our **c** in time	1121
Jgs	2:11	the **c** of Israel did evil in the sight	1121
Jgs	3:7	And the **c** of Israel did evil	1121
Jgs	3:8	and the **c** of Israel served	1121
Jgs	3:9	up a deliverer to the **c** of Israel	1121
Jgs	3:12	the **c** of Israel did evil again	1121
Jgs	3:15	**c** of Israel cried unto the Lord,	1121
Jgs	4:1	the **c** of Israel again did evil	1121
Jgs	4:3	**c** of Israel cried unto the Lord:	1121
Jgs	4:3	oppressed the **c** of Israel	1121
Jgs	4:24	hand of the **c** of Israel prospered,	1121
Jgs	6:1	**c** of Israel did evil in the sight of	1121
Jgs	6:6	**c** of Israel cried unto the Lord	1121
Jgs	6:8	sent a prophet unto the **c** of Israel,	1121
Jgs	8:33	the **c** of Israel turned again, and	1121
Jgs	8:34	**c** of Israel remembered not the	1121
Jgs	10:6	the **c** of Israel did evil again	1121
Jgs	10:8	and oppressed the **c** of Israel:	1121
Jgs	10:10	the **c** of Israel cried unto the Lord,	1121
Jgs	10:11	Lord said unto the **c** of Israel,	1121
Jgs	13:1	the **c** of Israel did evil again	1121
Jgs	14:16	a riddle unto the **c** of my people	1121
Jgs	14:17	the riddle to the **c** of her people	1121
Jgs	20:18	battle against the **c** of Benjamin?	1121
Jgs	20:27	**c** of Israel enquired of the Lord	1121
Jgs	21:6	the **c** of Israel repented them for	1121
1Sa	1:2	but Hannah had no **c**	3206
1Sa	16:11	unto Jesse, Are here all thy **c**?	5288
2Sa	1:18	bade them teach the **c** of Judah	1121
2Sa	7:10	the **c** of wickedness afflict them	1121
1Ki	2:4	If thy **c** take heed to their way	1121
1Ki	8:39	the hearts of all the **c** of men;	1121
1Ki	21:13	came in two men, **c** of Belial,	1121
2Ki	2:23	came forth little **c** out of the city,	5288
2Ki	2:24	and tare forty and two **c** of them	3206
2Ki	8:12	and wilt dash their **c**, and rip	6768
2Ki	17:31	Sepharvites burnt their **c** in fire	1121
1Ch	20:4	that was of the **c** of the giant:	3211
2Ch	7:3	all the **c** of Israel saw how the fire	1121
2Ch	25:12	the **c** of Judah carry away captive,	1121
Ezr	2:41	The singers: the **c** of Asaph, an	1121
Ezr	4:1	heard that the **c** of the captivity	1121
Ezr	8:35	**c** of those that had been carried	1121
Ezr	9:12	an inheritance to your **c** forever	1121
Ne	1:6	confess the sins of the **c** of Israel	1121
Ne	2:10	seek the welfare of the **c** of Israel	1121
Est	3:13	and old, little **c** and women	2945
Job	8:4	If thy **c** have sinned against him	1121
Job	20:10	his **c** shall seek to please the poor	1121
Job	30:8	**c** of fools, yea, **c** of base men:	1121
Ps	14:2	from heaven upon the **c** of men, to	1121
Ps	36:7	the **c** of men put their trust	1121
Ps	72:4	he shall save the **c** of the needy	1121
Ps	89:30	If his **c** forsake my law, and walk	1121
Ps	102:28	**c** of thy servants shall continue	1121
Ps	103:13	Like as a father pitieth his **c**, so	1121
Ps	103:17	righteousness unto children's **c**;	1121
Ps	109:10	Let his **c** be continually vagabonds,	1121
Ps	127:3	Lo, **c** are an heritage of the Lord:	1121
Ps	127:4	so are the **c** of the youth	1121
Ps	132:12	If thy **c** will keep my covenant	1121
Ps	149:2	**c** of Zion be joyful in their king	1121
Pr	4:1	Hear, ye **c**, the instruction of a	1121
Pr	14:26	his **c** shall have a place of refuge	1121
Pr	15:11	the hearts of the **c** of men?	1121
Pr	17:6	Children's **c** are the crown of old	1121
Pr	31:28	her **c** arise up and call her blessed;	1121
Isa	1:2	I have nourished and brought up **c**,	1121
Isa	3:4	I will give **c** to be their princes,	5288
Isa	8:18	**c** whom the Lord hath given me	3206
Isa	13:16	**c** also shall be dashed to pieces	5768
Isa	38:19	the **c** shall make known thy truth	1121
Isa	47:9	day, the loss of **c**, and widowhood:	
Isa	54:1	than the **c** of the married wife	1121

Isa	54:13	thy c shall be taught of the Lord;	1121
Isa	54:13	great shall be the peace of thy c	1121
Isa	63:8	my people, c that will not lie:	1121
Isa	66:20	the c of Israel bring an offering	1121
Jer	3:14	O backsliding c, saith the Lord;	1121
Jer	3:22	Return, ye backsliding c, and I	1121
Jer	7:30	c of Judah have done evil in my	1121
Jer	31:15	Rahel weeping for her c refused	1121
Jer	31:15	to be comforted for her c,	1121
La	1:5	her c are gone into captivity	5768
La	1:16	my c are desolate, because the	1121
La	2:20	their fruit, and c of a span long?	5768
La	4:4	young c ask bread, and no man	5768
Eze	2:4	are impudent c and stiffhearted	1121
Da	1:4	C in whom was no blemish, but	3206
Da	1:6	c of Judah, Daniel, Hananiah	1121
Da	1:10	the c which are of your sort?	3206
Da	1:15	the c which did eat the portion	3206
Da	1:17	for these four c, God gave them	3206
Da	2:38	wheresoever the c of men dwell,	1123
Da	5:13	which art of the c of the captivity	1123
Da	6:13	Daniel, which is of the c of the	1123
Da	6:24	the den of lions, them, their c,	1123
Da	12:1	great prince which standeth for the c	1121
Hos	2:4	will not have mercy upon her c;	1121
Hos	4:6	I will also forget thy c	1121
Joel	1:3	Tell ye your c of it, and	1121
Joel	1:3	let your c tell their c	1121
Joel	1:3	and their c another generation	1121
Am	9:7	Are ye not as c of the Ethiopians	1121
Mic	2:9	c have ye taken away my glory	5768
Na	3:10	young c also were dashed in pieces	5768
Zec	10:7	their c shall see it, and be glad;	1121
Mt	2:16	and slew all the c that were in	*3816*
Mt	2:18	Rachel weeping for her c, and	*5043*
Mt	3:9	to raise up c unto Abraham	*5043*
Mt	5:9	**they shall be called the c of God.**	*5207*
Mt	7:11	**to give good gifts unto your c,**	*5043*
Mt	10:21	**and the c shall rise up against**	*5045*
Mt	12:27	**by whom do your c cast them**	*5207*
Mt	18:3	**and become as little c, ye shall**	*3813*
Mt	19:13	brought unto him little c, that	*3813*
Mt	19:14	said, **Suffer little c, and forbid**	*3813*
Mt	21:15	and the c crying in the temple,	*3816*
Mt	23:37	**would I have gathered thy c**	*5043*
Mt	27:25	His blood be on us, and on our c	*5049*
Mk	9:37	**receive one of such c in my**	*3813*
Mk	10:14	**Suffer the little c to come unto**	*3813*
Mk	13:12	**and c shall rise up against their**	*5043*
Lk	11:13	**to give good gifts unto your c**	*5043*
Lk	18:16	**Suffer little c to come unto me,**	*3813*
Lk	20:34	**The c of this world marry, and**	*5207*
Lk	20:36	**the c of the resurrection.**	*5207*
Jn	8:39	**If ye were Abraham's c, ye would**	*5043*
Jn	12:36	**that ye may be the c of light.**	*5207*
Jn	13:33	**Little c, yet a little while I am**	*5040*
Ro	8:16	spirit, that we are the c of God:	*5043*
Ro	8:17	And if c, then heirs; heirs of God,	*5043*
Ro	8:21	the glorious liberty of the c of God.	*5043*
Ro	9:8	They which are the c of the flesh,	*5043*
Ro	9:8	the c of the promise are counted	*5043*
Ro	9:26	be called the c of the living God.	*5207*
2Co	6:13	(I speak as unto my c,) be ye also	*5043*
2Co	12:14	the c ought not to lay up for the	*5043*
Gal	3:26	ye are all the c of God by faith	*5207*
Gal	4:19	My little c, of whom I travail	*5040*
Gal	4:28	as Isaac was, are the c of promise.	*5043*
Eph	1:5	us unto the adoption of c by	*5206*
Eph	2:2	worketh in the c of disobedience:	*5207*
Eph	2:3	were by nature the c of wrath,	*5043*
Eph	4:14	be no more c, tossed to and fro,	*3516*
Eph	5:1	followers of God, as dear c;	*5043*
Eph	5:6	God upon the c of disobedience.	*5207*
Eph	5:8	in the Lord: walk as c of light:	*5043*
Eph	6:1	C, obey your parents in the Lord:	*5043*
Eph	6:4	provoke not your c to wrath,	*5043*
Col	3:20	C, obey your parents in all	*5043*
Col	3:21	provoke not your c to anger,	*5043*
1Th	5:5	Ye are all the c of light,	*5207*
1Ti	3:4	having his c in subjection with	*5043*
1Ti	3:12	ruling their c and their own	*5043*
1Ti	5:14	younger women marry, bear c,	*5041*
Tit	2:4	their husbands, to love their c,	*5388*
Heb	2:14	then as the c are partakers	*3813*
Heb	12:5	speaketh unto you as unto c	*5027*
1Pet	1:14	As obedient c, not fashioning	*5043*
1Jn	2:18	Little c, it is the last time: and	*3813*
1Jn	2:28	And now, little c, abide in him;	*5040*
1Jn	3:7	Little c, let no man deceive you:	*5040*
1Jn	4:4	Ye are of God, little c, and have	*5040*
1Jn	5:21	Little c, keep yourselves from	*5040*
2Jn	4	that I found of thy c walking in	*5043*
3Jn	4	joy I have to hear that my c walk	*5043*
Rev	2:23	**And I will kill her c with death;**	*5043*

CHILDREN'S

Ps	103:17	righteousness unto c children;	1121
Pr	13:22	leaveth an inheritance to his c	1121
Pr	17:6	C children are the crown of old men;	1121
Jer	31:29	and the c teeth are set on edge.	1121
Eze	18:2	the c teeth are set on edge?	1121
Mk	7:27	**it is not meet to take the c bread,**	*5043*
Mk	7:28	the table eat of the c crumbs	*3813*

CHILD'S

Ex	2:8	went and called the c mother.	3206
1Ki	17:21	let this c soul come into him again.	3206
Mt	2:20	which sought the young c life	*3813*

CHOICE

Ge	23:6	c of our sepulchres bury thy dead;	4005
Dt	12:11	your c vows which ye vow unto	4005
1Ch	7:40	c and mighty men of valour,	1305
Pr	8:10	knowledge rather than c gold.	977
Jer	22:7	shall cut down thy c cedars,	4005
Eze	24:5	Take the c of the flock, and burn	4005
Ac	15:7	God made c among us, that the	*1586*

CHOICEST

Isa	5:2	planted it with the c vine,	8321
Isa	22:7	c valleys shall be full of chariots,	4005

CHOKE

Mt	13:22	**deceitfulness of riches, c the**	*4846*
Mk	4:19	**entering in, c the word, and it**	*4846*

CHOKED

Mt	13:7	**thorns sprung up, and c them:**	*638*
Mk	4:7	**c it, and it yielded no fruit.**	*4846*
Lk	8:7	**sprang up with it and c it.**	*635*
Lk	8:14	**and are c with cares and riches**	*4846*

CHOOSE

Ex	17:9	C us out men, and go out,	977
Nu	16:7	the man whom the Lord doth c,	977

Dt	12:11	God shall **c** to cause his name	.977
Dt	15:20	the place which the Lord shall **c**,	.977
Dt	26:2	God shall **c** to place his name	.977
Jos	24:15	**c** you this day whom ye will serve;	.977
1Sa	17:8	**c** you a man for you, and let	.1262
2Sa	21:6	of Saul, whom the Lord did **c**	.972
Ne	9:7	the God, who didst **c** Abram,	.977
Job	9:14	and **c** out my words to reason	.977
Isa	7:15	refuse the evil, and **c** the good,	.977
Isa	56:4	and **c** the things that please me,	.977
Isa	65:12	**c** that wherein I delighted not.	.977
Isa	66:4	I also will **c** their delusions,	.977
Zec	1:17	Zion, and shall yet **c** Jerusalem.	.977
Php	1:22	yet what I shall **c** I wot not.	*.138*

CHOOSEST

Job	15:5	thou **c** the tongue of the crafty	.977
Ps	65:4	Blessed is the man whom thou **c**,	.977

CHOOSETH

Job	7:15	So that my soul **c** strangling,	.977
Isa	40:20	he hath no oblation **c** a tree that	.977

CHOSE

Ge	6:2	them wives of all which they **c**,	.977
Ge	13:11	Lot **c** him all the plain of Jordan;	.977
Ex	18:25	Moses **c** able men out of all Israel,	.977
1Sa	17:40	and **c** him five smooth stones out	.977
2Sa	10:9	behind, he **c** of all the choice men	.977
1Ki	8:16	but I **c** David to be over my people	.977
1Ki	11:34	David my servant's sake whom I **c**,	.977
1Ch	28:4	the Lord God of Israel **c** me before	.977
Ps	78:68	But **c** the tribe of Judah, the	.977
Ps	78:70	He **c** David also his servant,	.977
Eze	20:5	In the day when I **c** Israel,	.977
Lk	6:13	of them he **c** twelve, whom also	*.1586*
Lk	14:7	they **c** out the chief rooms; saying	*.1586*
Ac	6:5	they **c** Stephen, a man full of faith	*.1586*
Ac	15:40	And Paul **c** Silas, and departed,	*.1951*

CHOSEN

Dt	7:6	the Lord thy God hath **c** thee to be	.977
Dt	21:5	Lord thy God hath **c** to minister	.977
Jos	24:22	that ye have **c** you the Lord to	.977
1Sa	10:24	See ye him whom the Lord hath **c**,	.977
1Sa	12:13	the king whom ye have **c**, and	.977
1Sa	16:10	Jesse, The Lord hath not **c** these.	.977
1Sa	20:30	that thou hast **c** the son of Jesse	.977
1Ki	11:13	Jerusalem's sake which I have **c**	.977
1Ch	16:13	ye children of Jacob, his **c** ones.	.972
1Ch	28:4	he hath **c** Judah to be the ruler:	.977
1Ch	28:5	he hath **c** Solomon my son to sit	.977
2Ch	6:6	and have **c** David to be over my	.977
2Ch	29:11	Lord hath **c** you to stand before	.970
Ps	89:3	I have made a covenant with my **c**,	.972
Ps	89:19	exalted one **c** out of the people.	.970
Ps	105:26	and Aaron whom he had **c**,	.977
Ps	105:43	with joy, and his **c** with gladness:	.972
Ps	106:5	That I may see the good of thy **c**,	.972
Ps	119:30	I have **c** the way of truth: thy	.977
Ps	119:173	help me; for I have **c** thy precepts.	.977
Pr	16:16	rather to be **c** than silver!	.977
Pr	22:1	A good name is rather to be **c**	.977
Isa	41:9	I have **c** thee, and not cast thee	.977
Isa	48:10	**c** thee in the furnace of affliction.	.977
Jer	8:3	death shall be **c** rather than life	.977
Hag	2:23	for I have **c** thee, saith the Lord	.977
Zec	3:2	the Lord that hath **c** Jerusalem	.977
Mt	20:16	**for many be called, but few c**	*.1588*
Mt	22:14	**many are called, but few are c**	*.1588*
Lk	10:42	**Mary hath c that good part**	*.1586*
Jn	6:70	**Have not I c you twelve, and one**	*.1586*
Jn	15:16	**Ye have not c me,**	*.1586*
Jn	15:16	**but I have c you, and**	*.1586*
Jn	15:19	**I have c you out of the world,**	*.1586*
Ac	1:2	the apostles whom he had **c**	*.1586*
Ac	1:24	whether of these two thou hast **c**,	*.1586*
1Co	1:27	God hath **c** the foolish things of	*.1586*
1Co	1:27	God hath **c** the weak things of	*.1586*
Eph	1:4	as he hath **c** us in him before the	*.1586*
2Ti	2:4	he may please him who hath **c**	*.4758*
Jas	2:5	Hath not God **c** the poor of this	*.1586*
1Pe	2:9	ye are a **c** generation, a royal	*.1588*
Rev	17:14	him are called, and **c**, and faithful.	*.1588*

CHRIST (krist)

Mt	1:16	was born Jesus, who is called **C**,	*.5547*
Mt	1:18	the birth of Jesus **C** was on this	*.5547*
Mt	2:4	of them where **C** should be born	*.5547*
Mt	16:16	Thou art the **C**, the Son of the	*.5547*
Mt	16:20	no man that he was Jesus the **C**,	*.5547*
Mt	22:42	**What think ye of C? whose son**	*.5547*
Mt	24:5	**my name, saying, I am C; and**	*.5547*
Mt	26:63	whether thou be the **C**, the Son	*.5547*
Mt	26:68	Prophesy unto us, thou **C**, Who is	*.5547*
Mt	27:17	or Jesus which is called **C**?	*.5547*
Mk	1:1	of the gospel of Jesus **C**,	*.5547*
Mk	8:29	saith unto him, Thou art the **C**,	*.5547*
Mk	14:61	Art thou the **C**, the Son of the	*.5547*
Mk	15:32	Let **C** the King of Israel descend	*.5547*
Lk	2:11	a Saviour, which is **C** the Lord.	*.5547*
Lk	2:26	before he had seen the Lord's **C**,	*.5547*
Lk	4:41	Thou art **C** the Son of God.	*.5547*
Lk	20:41	**say they that C is David's son?**	*.5547*
Lk	22:67	Art thou the **C**? tell us. And he	*.5547*
Lk	23:39	saying, If thou be **C**, save thyself	*.5547*
Lk	24:26	**Ought not C to have suffered**	*.5547*
Lk	24:46	**thus it behoved C to suffer, and to**	*.5547*
Jn	1:17	grace and truth came by Jesus **C**	*.5547*
Jn	1:41	which is, being interpreted, the **C**,	*.5547*
Jn	4:25	Messias cometh, which is called **C**	*.5547*
Jn	4:29	that even I did: is not this the **C**?	*.5547*
Jn	7:26	indeed that this is the very **C**?	*.5547*
Jn	7:41	Shall **C** come out of Galilee?	*.5547*
Jn	7:42	**C** cometh of the seed of David, and	*.5547*
Jn	10:24	If thou be the **C**, tell us plainly	*.5547*
Jn	11:27	I believe that thou art the **C**,	*.5547*
Jn	17:3	**Jesus C, whom thou hast sent.**	*.5547*
Jn	20:31	might believe that Jesus is the **C**,	*.5547*
Ac	2:30	raise up **C** to sit on his throne;	*.5547*
Ac	2:36	ye have crucified, both Lord and **C**.	*.5547*
Ac	3:18	prophets, that **C** should suffer, he	*.5547*
Ac	4:26	the Lord, and against his **C**.	*.5547*
Ac	8:12	and the name of Jesus **C**, they were	*.5547*
Ac	8:37	that Jesus **C** is the Son of God.	*.5547*
Ac	11:17	believed on the Lord Jesus **C**;	*.5547*
Ac	16:31	Believe on the Lord Jesus **C**, and	*.5547*
Ac	17:3	**C** must needs have suffered, and	*.5547*
Ac	18:28	the scriptures that Jesus was **C**	*.5547*
Ac	26:23	That **C** should suffer, and that	*.5547*
Ro	1:16	not ashamed of the gospel of **C**	*.5547*
Ro	3:22	is by faith of Jesus **C** unto all	*.5547*
Ro	3:24	redemption that is in **C** Jesus:	*.5547*

Ro	5:6	in due time **C** died for the ungodly.	*5547*
Ro	5:8	were yet sinners, **C** died for us.	*5547*
Ro	5:17	shall reign in life by one, Jesus **C**.)	*5547*
Ro	5:21	eternal life by Jesus **C** our Lord.	*5547*
Ro	6:3	were baptized into Jesus **C** were	*5547*
Ro	6:4	as **C** was raised up from the dead	*5547*
Ro	6:8	if we be dead with **C**, we believe	*5547*
Ro	6:23	eternal life through Jesus **C** our	*5547*
Ro	7:4	dead to the law by the body of **C**;	*5547*
Ro	8:2	Spirit of life in **C** Jesus hath	*5547*
Ro	8:10	if **C** be in you, the body is dead	*5547*
Ro	8:11	that raised up **C** from the dead	*5547*
Ro	8:17	of God, and joint-heirs with **C**;	*5547*
Ro	8:35	separate us from the love of **C**?	*5547*
Ro	8:39	love of God, which is in **C** Jesus	*5547*
Ro	10:4	**C** is the end of the law for	*5547*
Ro	12:5	being many, are one body in **C**,	*5547*
Ro	13:14	But put ye on the Lord Jesus **C**,	*5547*
Ro	14:9	**C** both died, and rose, and revived,	*5547*
Ro	14:10	before the judgment seat of **C**.	*5547*
Ro	14:15	with thy meat, for whom **C** died.	*5547*
Ro	15:3	For even **C** pleased not himself;	*5547*
Ro	15:19	fully preached the gospel of **C**.	*5547*
Ro	15:20	not where **C** was named, lest I	*5547*
Ro	15:29	the blessing of the gospel of **C**.	*5547*
1Co	1:2	them that are sanctified in **C** Jesus,	*5547*
1Co	1:8	in the day of our Lord Jesus **C**.	*5547*
1Co	1:9	of his Son Jesus **C** our Lord.	*5547*
1Co	1:12	and I of Cephas; and I of **C**.	*5547*
1Co	1:13	Is **C** divided? was Paul crucified	*5547*
1Co	1:17	**C** sent me not to baptize, but to	*5547*
1Co	1:23	But we preach **C** crucified,	*5547*
1Co	2:16	But we have the mind of **C**.	*5547*
1Co	3:1	even as unto babes in **C**.	*5547*
1Co	3:23	ye are Christ's; and **C** is God's.	*5547*
1Co	4:1	ministers of **C**, and stewards of	*5547*
1Co	4:10	sake, but ye are wise in **C**;	*5547*
1Co	5:7	**C** our passover is sacrificed for	*5547*
1Co	6:15	bodies are the members of **C**?	*5547*
1Co	8:6	Jesus **C**, by whom are all things,	*5547*
1Co	8:11	brother perish, for whom **C** died?	*5547*
1Co	8:12	conscience, ye sin against **C**.	*5547*
1Co	9:18	the gospel of **C** without charge,	*5547*
1Co	10:4	and that rock was **C**.	*5547*
1Co	10:9	neither let us tempt **C**, as some	*5547*
1Co	10:16	communion of the blood of **C**?	*5547*
1Co	10:16	communion of the body of **C**?	*5547*
1Co	11:3	that the head of every man is **C**;	*5547*
1Co	11:3	man; and the head of **C** is God.	*5547*
1Co	15:3	**C** died for our sins according to	*5547*
1Co	15:13	of the dead, then is **C** not risen:	*5547*
1Co	15:14	if **C** be not risen, then is our	*5547*
1Co	15:15	of God that he raised up **C**	*5547*
1Co	15:16	rise not, then is not **C** raised:	*5547*
1Co	15:17	**C** be not raised, your faith is vain;	*5547*
1Co	15:19	this life only we have hope in **C**,	*5547*
1Co	15:20	now is **C** risen from the dead,	*5547*
1Co	15:22	in **C** shall all be made alive	*5547*
1Co	15:57	victory through our Lord Jesus **C**	*5547*
2Co	2:10	forgave I it in the person of **C**;	*5547*
2Co	2:14	always causeth us to triumph in **C**,	*5547*
2Co	3:14	which vail is done away in **C**.	*5547*
2Co	4:4	light of the glorious gospel of **C**,	*5547*
2Co	5:10	judgment seat of **C**; that every	*5547*
2Co	5:14	For the love of **C** constraineth us;	*5547*
2Co	5:17	if any man be in **C**, he is a new	*5547*
2Co	5:19	God was in **C**, reconciling the	*5547*
2Co	5:20	we are ambassadors for **C**, as	*5547*
2Co	6:15	what concord hath **C** with Belial?	*5547*
2Co	10:1	meekness and gentleness of **C**,	*5547*
2Co	10:14	in preaching the gospel of **C**	*5547*
2Co	11:10	truth of **C** is in me, no man shall	*5547*
2Co	12:9	power of **C** may rest upon me.	*5547*
2Co	12:19	we speak before God in **C**: but	*5547*
2Co	13:3	seek a proof of **C** speaking in me,	*5547*
Gal	1:1	neither by man, but by Jesus **C**,	*5547*
Gal	1:6	grace of **C** unto another gospel:	*5547*
Gal	1:7	would pervert the gospel of **C**.	*5547*
Gal	1:12	but by the revelation of Jesus **C**.	*5547*
Gal	2:16	law, but by the faith of Jesus **C**,	*5547*
Gal	2:17	we seek to be justified by **C**,	*5547*
Gal	2:17	is therefore **C** the minister of sin?	*5547*
Gal	2:20	I am crucified with **C**	*5547*
Gal	2:20	yet not I, but **C** liveth in me:	*5547*
Gal	2:21	by the law, then **C** is dead in vain.	*5547*
Gal	3:13	**C** hath redeemed us from the	*5547*
Gal	3:24	schoolmaster to bring us unto **C**,	*5547*
Gal	3:27	baptized into **C** have put on **C**	*5547*
Gal	3:28	for ye are all one in **C** Jesus	*5547*
Gal	4:7	then an heir of God through **C**.	*5547*
Gal	4:14	angel of God, even as **C** Jesus.	*5547*
Gal	5:1	wherewith **C** hath made us free,	*5547*
Gal	6:2	burdens, and so fulfil the law of **C**.	*5547*
Gal	6:12	persecution for the cross of **C**.	*5547*
Gal	6:14	cross of our Lord Jesus **C**, by	*5547*
Eph	1:10	all things in **C**, both which are in	*5547*
Eph	1:12	his glory, who first trusted in **C**.	*5547*
Eph	1:20	Which he wrought it **C**, when he	*5547*
Eph	2:5	quickened us together with **C**,	*5547*
Eph	2:6	in heavenly places in **C** Jesus	*5547*
Eph	2:10	in **C** Jesus unto good works,	*5547*
Eph	2:13	are made nigh by the blood of **C**.	*5547*
Eph	2:20	**C** himself being the chief corner	*5547*
Eph	3:1	prisoner of Jesus **C** for you	*5547*
Eph	3:8	the unsearchable riches of **C**;	*5547*
Eph	3:9	created all things by Jesus **C**	*5547*
Eph	3:11	which he purposed in **C** Jesus	*5547*
Eph	3:17	**C** may dwell in your hearts by	*5547*
Eph	3:19	the love of **C**, which passeth	*5547*
Eph	4:7	to the measure of the gift of **C**.	*5547*
Eph	4:12	for the edifying of the body of **C**	*5547*
Eph	4:15	which is the head, even **C**	*5547*
Eph	5:2	as **C** also hath loved us, and hath	*5547*
Eph	5:5	in the kingdom of **C** and of God.	*5547*
Eph	5:14	dead, and **C** shall give thee light.	*5547*
Eph	5:23	**C** is the head of the church:	*5547*
Eph	5:25	even as **C** also loved the church,	*5547*
Eph	6:6	the servants of **C**, doing the will	*5547*
Php	1:6	perform it until the day of Jesus C.	*5547*
Php	1:10	without offence till the day of **C**;	*5547*
Php	1:13	my bonds in **C** are manifest in all	*5547*
Php	1:15	indeed preach **C** even of envy and	*5547*
Php	1:16	The one preach **C** of contention,	*5547*
Php	1:18	or in truth, **C** is preached;	*5547*
Php	1:20	**C** shall be magnified in my body,	*5547*
Php	1:21	For me to live is **C**, and to die is	*5547*
Php	2:1	be therefore any consolation in **C**,	*5547*
Php	2:5	you, which was also in **C** Jesus:	*5547*
Php	2:11	Jesus **C** is Lord, to the glory of God	*5547*
Php	2:16	I may rejoice in the day of **C**,	*5547*
Php	3:7	those I counted loss for **C**.	*5547*
Php	3:8	knowledge of **C** Jesus my Lord:	*5547*

Php	3:12	I am apprehended of **C** Jesus.	5547
Php	3:14	the high calling of God in **C** Jesus	5547
Php	3:18	are the enemies of the cross of **C**	5547
Php	4:7	hearts and minds through **C** Jesus.	5547
Php	4:13	**C** which strengtheneth me.	5547
Php	4:19	to his riches in glory by **C** Jesus.	5547
Col	1:4	we heard of your faith in **C** Jesus,	5547
Col	1:27	is **C** in you, the hope of glory:	5547
Col	1:28	every man perfect in **C** Jesus:	5547
Col	2:5	stedfastness of your faith in **C**.	5547
Col	2:6	therefore received **C** Jesus the	5547
Col	2:20	dead with **C** from the rudiments	5547
Col	3:1	If ye then be risen with **C**,	5547
Col	3:1	where **C** sitteth on the right hand	5547
Col	3:3	your life is hid with **C** in God.	5547
Col	3:4	**C**, who is our life, shall appear,	5547
Col	3:11	but **C** is all, and in all.	5547
Col	3:13	as **C** forgave you, so also do ye	5547
Col	3:16	the word of **C** dwell in you richly	5547
Col	4:3	speak the mystery of **C**, for which	5547
1Th	2:19	our Lord Jesus **C** at his coming?	5547
1Th	3:2	fellowlabourer in the gospel of **C**,	5547
1Th	3:11	Lord Jesus **C**, direct our way	5547
1Th	3:13	the coming of our Lord Jesus **C**	5547
1Th	4:16	the dead in **C** shall rise first:	5547
1Th	5:9	salvation by our Lord Jesus **C**,	5547
1Th	5:18	this is the will of God in **C** Jesus	5547
2Th	2:1	the coming of our Lord Jesus **C**,	5547
2Th	2:2	as that the day of **C** is at hand	5547
2Th	3:5	into the patient waiting for **C**.	5547
1Ti	1:12	thank **C** Jesus our Lord, who hath	5547
1Ti	1:14	and love which is in **C** Jesus.	5547
1Ti	1:15	that **C** Jesus came into the world	5547
1Ti	3:13	in the faith which is in **C** Jesus.	5547
1Ti	4:6	be a good minister of Jesus **C**,	5547
1Ti	5:11	begun to wax wanton against **C**,	5547
1Ti	6:13	**C** Jesus, who before Pontius Pilate	5547
2Ti	1:1	promise of life which is in **C** Jesus,	5547
2Ti	1:9	in **C** Jesus before the world began,	5547
2Ti	1:10	appearing of our Saviour Jesus **C**,	5547
2Ti	2:3	as a good soldier of Jesus **C**	5547
2Ti	3:12	live godly in **C** Jesus shall suffer	5547
2Ti	4:1	Lord Jesus **C**, who shall judge	5547
Tit	2:13	great God and our Saviour Jesus **C**;	5547
Phm	23	my fellowprisoner in **C** Jesus;	5547
Heb	3:6	**C** as a son over his own house;	5547
Heb	3:14	For we are made partakers of **C**,	5547
Heb	6:1	the principles of the doctrine of **C**,	5547
Heb	9:11	But **C** being come an high priest	5547
Heb	9:24	**C** is not entered in to the holy places	5547
Heb	9:28	**C** was once offered to bear the sins	5547
Heb	10:10	of the body of Jesus **C** once for all.	5547
Heb	11:26	the reproach of **C** greater riches	5547
Heb	13:8	Jesus **C** the same yesterday, and	5547
1Pe	1:3	resurrection of Jesus **C** from the	5547
1Pe	1:7	glory at the appearing of Jesus **C**	5547
1Pe	1:19	precious blood of **C**, as of a lamb	5547
1Pe	3:16	your good conversation in **C**.	5547
2Pe	1:8	knowledge of our Lord Jesus **C**	5547
2Pe	1:16	and coming of our Lord Jesus **C**,	5547
1Jn	2:1	the Father, Jesus C the righteous	5547
1Jn	2:22	that denieth that Jesus is the **C**?	5547
1Jn	4:2	that Jesus **C** is come in the flesh	5547
1Jn	4:3	confesseth not that Jesus **C** is	5547
1Jn	5:1	believeth that Jesus is the **C** is	5547
2Jn	7	that Jesus **C** is come in the flesh.	5547
2Jn	9	abideth not in the doctrine of **C**,	5547
Jude	1	preserved in Jesus **C**, and called:	5547
Jude	21	the mercy of our Lord Jesus **C**	5547
Rev	1:1	Revelation of Jesus **C**, which God	5547
Rev	1:2	testimony of Jesus **C**, and of all	5547
Rev	1:5	from Jesus **C**, who is the faithful	5547
Rev	1:9	kingdom and patience of Jesus **C**,	5547
Rev	11:15	of our Lord, and of his **C**;	5547
Rev	20:4	reigned with **C** a thousand years.	5547
Rev	20:6	shall be priests of God and of **C**,	5547
Rev	22:21	Lord Jesus **C** be with you all.	5547

CHRIST'S (krists)

1Co	3:23	ye are **C**; and Christ is God's	5547
1Co	7:22	is called, being free, is **C** servant	5547
2Co	5:20	in **C** stead, be ye reconciled to	5547
2Co	10:7	man trust to himself that he is **C**,	5547
2Co	12:10	in distresses for **C** sake:	5547
Gal	3:29	if ye be **C**, then are ye Abraham's	5547
Gal	5:24	are **C** have crucified the flesh	5547
Eph	4:32	God for **C** sake hath forgiven	5547
Php	2:21	not the things which are Jesus **C**	5547
1Pe	4:13	as ye are partakers of **C**	5547

CHRISTS (krists)

Mt	24:24	**For there shall arise false C, and**	5580
Mk	13:22	**For false C and false prophets**	5580

CHRISTIAN (kris´-tyan)

Ac	26:28	thou persuadest me to be a **C**	5546
1Pe	4:16	if any man suffer as a **C**, let him	5546

CHRISTIANS (kris´-tyans)

Ac	11:26	disciples were called **C** first in	5546

CHRONICLES

1Ki	14:19	**c** of the kings of Israel.	1697, 3117
1Ch	27:24	**c** of King David.	1697, 3117
Ne	12:23	book of the **c**, even until	1697, 3117
Est	2:23	book of the **c** before the king	1697, 3117
Est	10:2	**c** of the kings of Media and	1697, 3117

CHURCH

Mt	16:18	**upon this rock I will build my c**	1577
Mt	18:17	**tell it unto the c**	1577
Mt	18:17	**but if he neglect to hear the c,**	1577
Ac	2:47	the Lord added to the **c** daily	1577
Ac	5:11	fear came upon all the **c**, and	1577
Ac	8:3	he made havoc of the **c**,	1577
Ac	11:22	the **c** which was in Jerusalem:	1577
Ac	12:1	his hands to vex certain of the **c**.	1577
Ac	14:23	ordained them elders in every **c**,	1577
Ac	15:3	brought on their way by the **c**,	1577
Ac	15:22	and elders, with the whole **c**,	1577
Ac	20:28	overseers, to feed the **c** of God,	1577
Ro	16:6	greet the **c** that is in their house	1577
1Co	1:2	Unto the **c** of God which is at	1577
1Co	10:32	Gentiles; nor to the **c** of God:	1577
1Co	11:18	when ye come together in the **c**,	1577
1Co	11:22	or despise ye the **c** of God, and	1577
1Co	14:4	that prophesieth edifieth the **c**.	1577
1Co	14:5	interpret, that the **c** may receive	1577
1Co	14:12	excel to the edifying of the **c**.	1577
1Co	14:28	let him keep silence in the **c**;	1577
1Co	14:35	for women to speak in the **c**	1577
1Co	15:9	I persecuted the **c** of God.	1577
Eph	1:22	the head over all things to the **c**,	1577
Eph	5:23	Christ is the head of the **c**	1577

Eph	5:24	Therefore as the **c** is subject unto	*1577*
Eph	5:25	as Christ also loved the **c**, and	*1577*
Eph	5:27	present it to himself a glorious **c**,	*1577*
Php	3:6	Concerning zeal, persecuting the **c**;	*1577*
Col	1:18	the head of the body, the **c**	*1577*
1Ti	3:15	the **c** of the living God, the pillar	*1577*
Heb	2:12	in the midst of the **c** will I sing	*1577*
1Pe	5:13	The **c** that is at Babylon, elected	*1577*
3Jn	10	and casteth them out of the **c**	*1577*
Rev	2:1	**the angel of the c of Ephesus**	*1577*
Rev	2:8	**the angel of the c in Smyrna**	*1577*
Rev	2:12	**to the angel of the c in Pergamos**	*1577*
Rev	2:18	**the angel of the c in Thyatira**	*1577*
Rev	3:1	**the angel of the c in Sardis write;**	*1577*
Rev	3:7	**the angel of the c in Philadelphia**	*1577*
Rev	3:14	**angel of the c of the Laodiceans**	*1577*

CHURCHES

Ac	9:31	Then had the **c** rest throughout	*1577*
Ac	19:37	which are neither robbers of **c**,	*2477*
1Co	7:17	And so ordain I in all **c**.	*1577*
1Co	14:33	of peace, as in all **c** of the saints	*1577*
1Co	14:34	your women keep silence in the **c**	*1577*
2Co	8:1	bestowed on the **c** of Macedonia;	*1577*
2Co	8:18	gospel throughout all the **c**;	*1577*
2Co	8:19	was also chosen of the **c** to travel	*1577*
2Co	11:8	I robbed other **c**, taking wages of	*1577*
2Co	11:28	me daily, the care of all the **c**.	*1577*
2Co	12:13	ye were inferior to other **c**,	*1577*
1Th	2:14	became followers of the **c** of God	*1577*
Rev	1:4	John to the seven **c** which are in	*1577*
Rev	1:11	**and send it unto the seven c**	*1577*
Rev	1:20	**are the angels of the seven c**	*1577*
Rev	2:7	**what the Spirit saith unto the c;**	*1577*
Rev	2:11	**the Spirit saith unto the c; He**	*1577*
Rev	2:17	**the Spirit saith unto the c; To**	*1577*
Rev	2:23	**all the c shall know that I am he**	*1577*
Rev	22:16	**unto you these things in the c**	*1577*

CINNAMON

Ex	30:23	and of sweet **c** half so much	7076
SS	4:14	calamus and **c**, with all trees of	7076
Rev	18:13	**c**, and odours, and ointments	*2792*

CIRCUIT

Job	22:14	he walketh in the **c** of heaven.	2329
Ps	19:6	and his **c** unto the ends of it:	8622

CIRCUMCISE

Dt	10:16	**C** therefore the foreskin of your	4135
Lk	1:59	day they came to **c** the child;	*4059*
Jn	7:22	**ye on the sabbath day c a man**	*4059*
Ac	15:5	That it was needful to **c** them,	*4059*
Ac	21:21	saying that they ought not to **c**	*4059*

CIRCUMCISED

Ge	17:12	that is eight days old shall be **c**	4135
Ge	17:25	when he was **c** in the flesh of his	4135
Ge	17:26	the selfsame day was Abraham **c**,	4135
Ge	21:4	And Abraham **c** his son Isaac	4135
Ge	34:15	that every male of you be **c**;	4135
Ex	12:48	let all his males be **c**, and then let	4135
Jos	5:3	**c** the children of Israel at the hill	4135
Jos	5:5	of Egypt, them they had not **c**.	4135
Ac	7:8	Isaac, and **c** him the eighth day;	*4059*
Ac	15:1	be **c** after the manner of Moses,	*4059*
Ac	15:24	Ye must be **c**, and keep the law:	*4059*
Ac	16:3	and took and **c** him because of	*4059*
Ro	4:11	believe, though they be not **c**;	*203*
1Co	7:18	Is any man called being **c**?	*4059*
Gal	5:2	if ye be **c**, Christ shall profit you	*4059*
Gal	5:3	again to every man that is **c**,	*4059*
Gal	6:12	they constrain you to be **c**; only	*4059*
Php	3:5	**C** the eighth day, of the stock of	*4061*

CIRCUMCISION See also UNCIRCUMCISION.

Ex	4:26	husband thou art, because of the **c**.	4139
Jn	7:22	**Moses therefore gave unto you c;**	*4061*
Ac	10:45	they of the **c** which believed	*4061*
Ro	2:25	For **c** verily profiteth, if thou keep	*4061*
Ro	2:25	thy **c** is made uncircumcision.	*4061*
Ro	2:28	is that **c**, which is outward in the	*4061*
Ro	2:29	**c** is that of the heart, in the spirit,	*4061*
Ro	3:30	shall justify the **c** by faith, and	*4061*
Ro	4:9	blessedness then upon the **c** only,	*4061*
Ro	4:11	And he received the sign of **c**,	*4061*
Ro	15:8	a minister of the **c** for the truth	*4061*
1Co	7:19	**C** is nothing, and uncircumcision	*4061*
Gal	2:12	fearing them which were of the **c**.	*4061*
Gal	5:6	neither **c** availeth any thing,	*4061*
Eph	2:11	**C** in the flesh made by hands;	*4061*
Php	3:3	For we are the **c**, which worship	*4061*
Col	2:11	with the **c** made without hands,	*4061*
Col	2:11	sins of the flesh by the **c** of Christ:	*4061*
Col	3:11	**c** nor uncircumcision, Barbarian,	*4061*

CISTERN

Pr	5:15	Drink waters out of thine own **c**,	953
Ecc	12:6	or the wheel broken at the **c**.	953

CITIES

Ge	13:12	Lot dwelled in the **c** of the plain,	5892
Ge	19:29	God destroyed the **c** of the plain,	5892
Ex	1:11	built for Pharaoh treasure **c**,	5892
Nu	13:28	and the **c** are walled, and very	5892
Nu	32:17	ones shall dwell in the fenced **c**	5892
Nu	35:6	there shall be six **c** for refuge,	5892
Nu	35:12	they shall be unto you **c** for refuge	5892
Nu	35:14	give three **c** on this side Jordan,	5892
Dt	1:28	the **c** are great and walled up	5892
Dt	9:1	**c** great and fenced up to heaven,	5892
Dt	19:11	and fleeth into one of these **c**;	5892
Jos	10:2	a great city, as one of the royal **c**,	5892
Jos	11:13	**c** that stood still in their strength,	5892
Jos	20:2	Appoint out for you **c** of refuge	5892
2Ki	23:8	all the priests out of the **c** of Judah,	5892
2Ki	23:19	the high places that were in the **c**	5892
1Ch	13:2	Levites which are in their **c** and	5892
1Ch	19:13	people, and for the **c** of our God:	5892
2Ch	11:5	in Jerusalem, and built **c** for	5892
2Ch	11:10	Judah and in Benjamin fenced **c**	5892
Ne	9:25	took strong **c**, and fat land,	5892
Ne	10:37	tithes in all the **c** of our tillage	5892
Job	15:28	he dwelleth in desolate **c**, and in	5892
Ps	69:35	and will build the **c** of Judah:	5892
Isa	17:9	strong **c** be as a forsaken bough,	5892
Jer	2:28	the number of thy **c** are thy gods	5892
Jer	5:6	leopard shall watch over their **c**	5892
Jer	13:19	**c** of the south shall be shut up,	5892
Jer	25:18	Jerusalem, and the **c** of Judah,	5892
Eze	36:10	the **c** shall be inhabited, and the	5892
Hos	8:14	but I will send a fire upon his **c**	5892
Hos	11:6	the sword shall abide on his **c**	5892
Ob	20	shall possess the **c** of the south	5892
Mt	10:23	**over the c of Israel, till the Son**	*4172*

Mt	11:1	to teach and to preach in their **c**	*4172*
Lk	4:43	**kingdom of God to other c also:**	*4172*
Lk	19:17	**have thou authority over ten c**	*4172*
Lk	19:19	**to him, Be thou also over five c**	*4172*
Ac	8:40	he preached in all the **c**, till he	*4172*
2Pe	2:6	**c** of Sodom and Gomorrha into	*4172*
Jude	7	Gomorrha, and the **c** about them	*4172*
Rev	16:19	parts, and the **c** of the nations	*4172*

CITY

Ge	11:4	let us build us a **c** and a tower,	5892
Ge	11:5	the Lord came down to see the **c**	5892
Ge	11:8	and they left off to build the **c**	5892
Ge	18:24	be fifty righteous within the **c**	5892
Ge	18:28	destroy all the **c** for lack of five?	5892
Ge	19:20	this **c** is near to flee unto, and it	5892
Le	14:40	an unclean place without the **c**	5892
Le	14:53	let go the living bird out of the **c**	5892
Le	25:29	a dwelling house in a walled **c**	5892
Nu	35:26	the border of the **c** of his refuge,	5892
Nu	35:32	that is fled to the **c** of his refuge	5892
Dt	13:16	and shalt burn with fire the **c**	5892
Dt	20:19	When thou shalt besiege a **c** a long	5892
Dt	22:21	the men of her **c** shall stone her	5892
Jos	6:3	And ye shall compass the **c**, all ye	5892
Jos	6:3	go round about the **c** once. Thus	5892
Jos	6:4	seventh day ye shall compass the **c**	5892
Jos	6:5	wall of the **c** shall fall down flat,	5892
Jos	6:11	ark of the Lord compassed the **c**	5892
Jos	6:14	second day they compassed the **c**	5892
Jos	6:15	day they compassed the **c** seven	5892
Jos	6:17	the **c** shall be accursed, even it,	5892
Jos	6:24	And they burnt the **c** with fire,	5892
Jos	8:1	king of Ai, and his people, and his **c**,	5892
Jos	8:17	and they left the **c** open, and	5892
Jos	19:29	the strong **c** Tyre; and the coast	5892
Jos	19:50	gave him the **c** which he asked,	5892
Jos	21:13	**c** of refuge for the slayer;	5892
Jgs	1:16	out of the **c** of palm trees with	5892
Jgs	1:24	saw a man come forth out of the **c**	5892
Jgs	16:3	took the doors of the gate of the **c**	5892
Ru	4:2	took ten men of the elders of the **c**	5892
1Sa	5:12	cry of the **c** went up to heaven,	5892
1Sa	9:6	there is in this **c** a man of God,	5892
1Sa	9:10	the **c** where the man of God was	5892
1Sa	28:3	him in Ramah, even in his own **c**	5892
2Sa	5:7	Zion: the same is the **c** of David	5892
2Sa	6:10	unto him into the **c** of David: but	5892
2Sa	10:3	to search the **c**, and to spy it out	5892
2Sa	15:25	back the ark of God into the **c**	5892
2Sa	19:37	die in mine own **c**, and be buried	5892
2Sa	20:16	cried a wise woman out of the **c**,	5892
1Ki	2:10	and was buried in the **c** of David.	5892
1Ki	8:44	pray unto the Lord toward the **c**	5892
1Ki	15:8	they buried him in the **c** of David:	5892
2Ki	10:25	went to the **c** of the house of Baal	5892
2Ki	23:27	and will cast off this **c** Jerusalem	5892
1Ch	11:7	they called it the **c** of David	5892
2Ch	24:16	in the **c** of David among the kings	5892
2Ch	24:25	they buried him in the **c** of David,	5892
2Ch	32:30	to the west side of the **c** of David	5892
2Ch	33:14	built a wall without the **c** of David	5892
Ezr	4:16	if this **c** be builded again, and the	7149
Ne	2:5	the **c** of my father's sepulchres	5892
Ne	2:8	house, and for the wall of the **c**,	5892
Ne	11:1	to dwell in Jerusalem the holy **c**,	5892
Est	8:11	the Jews which were in every **c**	5892
Ps	46:4	shall make glad the **c** of God,	5892
Ps	48:1	the **c** of our God, in the mountain	5892
Ps	48:2	north, the **c** of the great King	7151
Ps	48:8	in the **c** of our God:	5892
Ps	87:3	are spoken of thee, O **c** of God	5892
Ps	107:36	may prepare a **c** for habitation;	5892
Ps	127:1	except the Lord keep the **c**	5892
Pr	10:15	rich man's wealth is his strong **c**	7151
Pr	11:10	the righteous, the **c** rejoiceth:	7151
Pr	11:11	of the upright the **c** is exalted:	7176
Pr	18:11	rich man's wealth is his strong **c**	7151
Pr	18:19	harder to be won than a strong **c**	7151
Pr	21:22	man scaleth the **c** of the mighty	5892
Ecc	9:15	he by his wisdom delivered the **c**;	5892
Isa	1:26	be called, The **c** of righteousness	5892
Isa	14:31	Howl, O gate; cry, O **c**;	5892
Isa	19:18	The **c** of destruction	5892
Isa	24:12	In the **c** is left desolation,	5892
Isa	26:1	We have a strong **c**; salvation	5892
Isa	45:13	he shall build my **c**, and he	5892
Isa	48:2	they call themselves of the holy **c**,	5892
Isa	52:1	O Jerusalem, the holy **c**	5892
Jer	31:38	the **c** shall be built to the Lord	5892
Jer	37:10	tent; and burn this **c** with fire	5892
Jer	38:17	and this **c** shall not be burned	5892
Jer	48:8	and no **c** shall escape:	5892
Jer	49:25	is the **c** of praise not left,	5892
Jer	49:25	the **c** of my joy	7151
La	1:1	How doth the **c** sit solitary,	5892
La	1:19	elders gave up the ghost in the **c**,	5892
La	2:15	**c** that men call The perfection of	5892
Eze	11:3	this **c** is the caldron, and we be the	
Eze	22:2	wilt thou judge the bloody **c**?	5892
Eze	22:3	The **c** sheddeth blood in the midst	5892
Da	9:16	away from thy **c** Jerusalem,	5892
Da	9:18	**c** which is called by thy name:	5892
Da	9:24	thy people and upon thy holy **c**	5892
Am	4:7	I caused it to rain upon one **c**,	5892
Am	4:7	it not to rain upon another **c**,	5892
Jnh	1:2	go to Nineveh, that great **c**, and	5892
Jnh	3:3	Nineveh was an exceeding great **c**	5892
Jnh	4:5	see what would become of the **c**	5892
Jnh	4:11	not I spare Nineveh, that great **c**	5892
Na	3:1	Woe to the bloody **c**! it is all full	5892
Zec	8:3	shall be called a **c** of truth;	5892
Mt	2:23	and dwelt in a **c** called Nazareth:	4172
Mt	5:14	**A c that is set on an hill cannot**	*4172*
Mt	5:35	**for it is the c of the great King**	*4172*
Mt	8:34	whole **c** came out to meet Jesus:	*4172*
Mt	12:25	**c or house divided against itself**	*4172*
Mt	26:18	**Go into the c to such a man, and**	*4172*
Lk	1:26	a **c** of Galilee, named Nazareth,	*4172*
Lk	1:39	with haste, into a **c** of Juda;	*4172*
Lk	2:3	taxed, every one into his own **c**	*4172*
Lk	2:4	out of the **c** of Nazareth, into	*4172*
Lk	2:4	Judaea, unto the **c** of David,	*4172*
Lk	2:11	day in the **c** of David a Saviour,	*4172*
Lk	8:39	published throughout the whole **c**	*4172*
Lk	9:5	**when ye go out of that c, shake**	*4172*
Lk	10:10	**whatsoever c ye enter, and**	*4172*
Lk	10:11	**Even the very dust of your c,**	*4172*
Lk	24:49	**tarry ye in the c of Jerusalem,**	*4172*
Jn	19:20	was crucified was nigh to the **c**	*4172*
Ac	8:8	And there was great joy in that **c**	*4172*
Ac	9:6	**Arise, and go into the c, and it**	*4172*

Ac 11:5 I was in the **c** of Joppa praying: *4172*
Ac 16:14 of purple, of the **c** of Thyatira, ...*4172*
Ac 17:5 set all the **c** on an uproar *4172*
Ac 17:16 the **c** wholly given to idolatry *4172*
Ac 18:10 **for I have much people in this c** *4172*
Ac 20:23 Holy Ghost witnesseth in every **c**, ...*4172*
2Co 11:26 in perils in the **c**, in perils in *4172*
Tit 1:5 ordain elders in every **c**, as I had *4172*
Heb 11:10 For he looked for a **c** which hath *4172*
Heb 12:22 **c** of the living God, the heavenly *4172*
Rev 3:12 **the name of the c of my God,** *4172*
Rev 11:2 holy **c** shall they tread under foot *4172*
Rev 11:13 and the tenth part of the **c** fell *4172*
Rev 14:8 is fallen, is fallen, that great **c** *4172*
Rev 18:10 great **c** Babylon, that mighty **c**! *4172*
Rev 21:2 saw the holy **c**, new Jerusalem, ...*4172*
Rev 21:10 and shewed me that great **c**, the *4172*
Rev 21:14 of the **c** had twelve foundations, ...*4172*
Rev 21:18 the **c** was pure gold, like unto *4172*
Rev 21:19 the foundations of the wall of the **c** *4172*
Rev 21:21 the street of the **c** was pure gold, ...*4172*
Rev 21:23 the **c** had no need of the sun, ...*4172*
Rev 22:14 in through the gates into the **c** *4172*
Rev 22:19 out of the holy **c**, and from the *4172*

CLAP

Job 27:23 Men shall **c** their hands at him, ...5606
Ps 47:1 O **c** your hands, all ye people; 8628
Ps 98:8 Let the floods **c** their hands: let 4222
Isa 55:12 of the field shall **c** their hands. 4222
Na 3:19 shall **c** the hands over thee: 8628

CLAVE

Ge 22:3 and **c** the wood for the burnt 1234
Ge 34:3 And his soul **c** unto Dinah the 1692
Jgs 15:19 But God **c** an hollow place that 1234
Ru 1:14 but Ruth **c** unto her. 1692
1Sa 6:14 and they **c** the wood of the cart, ...1234
1Ki 11:2 Solomon **c** unto these in love 1692
Ps 78:15 He **c** the rocks in the wilderness, ...1234
Isa 48:21 he **c** the rock also, and the 1234
Ac 17:34 men **c** unto him, and believed: *2853*

CLAWS

Da 4:33 feathers, and his nails like birds' **c**
Zec 11:16 fat, and tear their **c** in pieces. 6541

CLAY

Job 10:9 thou hast made me as the **c**; and 2563
Job 33:6 I also am formed out of the **c** 2563
Ps 40:2 out of the miry **c**, and set my feet 2916
Isa 29:16 be esteemed as the potter's **c** 2563
Jer 18:4 that he made of **c** was marred 2563
Jer 18:6 as the **c** is in the potter's hand, so 2563
Da 2:33 feet part of iron and part of **c** 2635
Da 2:34 were of iron and **c**, and brake them 2635
Da 2:41 part of potter's **c**, and part of iron, ...2635
Da 2:41 sawest the iron mixed with miry **c**, ...2635
Jn 9:6 and made **c** of the spittle, and he *4081*
Jn 9:11 man that is called Jesus made **c**, ...*4081*
Jn 9:14 when Jesus made the **c**, and *4081*
Ro 9:21 not the potter power over the **c**, ...*4081*

CLEAN

Ge 7:2 Of every **c** beast thou shalt take 2889
Ge 7:2 of beasts that are not **c** by two, ...2889
Ge 8:20 every **c** beast, and of every **c** fowl, ...2889
Le 6:11 without the camp unto a **c** place 2889
Le 7:19 all that be **c** shall eat thereof. 2889
Le 13:6 the priest shall pronounce him **c** 2891
Le 14:4 be cleansed two birds alive and **c**, ...2889
Le 16:30 ye may be **c** from all your sins 2891
Nu 19:18 a **c** person shall take hyssop, and 2889
Dt 14:11 Of all **c** birds ye shall eat 2889
Dt 14:20 But of all **c** fowls ye may eat 2889
2Ki 5:13 he saith to thee, Wash, and be **c**? 2891
2Ki 5:14 of a little child, and he was **c** 2891
Job 9:30 and make my hands never so **c**; 2141
Job 11:4 doctrine is pure, and I am **c** in 1249
Job 33:9 I am **c** without transgression, I 2134
Ps 19:9 The fear of the Lord is **c**, ...2889
Ps 24:4 He that hath **c** hands, and a pure 5355
Ps 51:7 me with hyssop, and I shall be **c** 2891
Ps 51:10 Create in me a **c** heart, O God; 2889
Ps 73:1 even to such as are of a **c** heart 1249
Pr 14:4 Where no oxen are, the crib is **c** 1249
Pr 16:2 ways of a man are **c** in his own 2134
Pr 20:9 can say, I have made my heart **c** 2135
Isa 1:16 Wash you, make you **c**; put away 2135
Isa 66:20 bring an offering in a **c** vessel 2889
Zec 11:17 his arm shall be **c** dried up, and 2889
Mt 8:2 thou wilt, thou canst make me **c** *2513*
Mt 8:3 him, saying, **I will; be thou c** *2513*
Mt 27:59 the body, he wrapped it in a **c** *2513*
Mk 1:40 wilt, thou canst make me **c** *2511*
Lk 11:39 **Now do ye Pharisees make c** *2511*
Jn 13:10 **and ye are c, but not all** *2513*
Jn 15:3 **Now ye are c through the word** *2513*
Ac 18:6 upon your own heads; I am **c** *2513*
Rev 19:8 arrayed in fine linen, **c** and white *2513*
Rev 19:14 clothed in fine linen, white and **c** *2573*

CLEANNESS

2Sa 22:25 according to my **c** in his eye sight 1252
Ps 18:24 the **c** of my hands in his eyesight 1252
Am 4:6 I also have given you **c** of teeth 5356

CLEANSE

Ex 29:36 and thou shalt **c** the altar, when 2398
Le 16:19 seven times, and **c** it, and hallow 2891
2Ch 29:16 house of the Lord, to **c** it, ...2891
Ps 19:12 **c** thou me from secret faults 5352
Ps 51:2 mine iniquity, and **c** me from my 5352
Ps 119:9 Wherewithal shall a young man **c** 2135
Eze 36:25 from all your idols, will I **c** you 2891
Joel 3:21 For I will **c** their blood that I 5352
Mt 10:8 **c the lepers, raise the dead, cast** *2511*
Mt 23:26 **c first that which is within the** *2511*
Eph 5:26 That he might sanctify and **c** it *2511*
Jas 4:8 **C** your hands, ye sinners; and *2511*
1Jn 1:9 to **c** us from all unrighteousness *2511*

CLEANSED

Nu 35:33 the land cannot be **c** of the blood 3722
Jos 22:17 which we are not **c** until this day 2891
2Ch 29:18 have **c** all the house of the Lord, ...2891
Job 35:3 I have, if I be **c** from my sin?
Ps 73:13 Verily I have **c** my heart in vain 2135
Mt 8:3 immediately his leprosy was **c** *2511*
Mt 11:5 **lepers are c, and the deaf hear,** *2511*
Mk 1:42 departed from him and he was **c** *2511*
Lk 7:22 **the lepers are c, the deaf hear,** *2511*
Lk 17:17 **Were there not ten c? but where** *2511*
Ac 10:15 What God hath **c**, that call not thou *2511*

CLEANSETH
Pr 20:30 blueness of a wound **c** away evil: 8562
1Jn 1:7 blood of Jesus Christ his Son **c** us *2511*

CLEANSING
Le 14:2 law of the leper in the day of his **c** 2893
Le 14:23 them on the eighth day for his **c** 2893
Nu 6:9 shave his head in the day of his **c**, 2893
Mk 1:44 **and offer for thy c those things** *2512*
Lk 5:14 **and offer for thy c, according as** *2512*

CLEAR
Ge 24:8 shalt be **c** from this my oath: 5352
Ex 34:7 will by no means **c** the guilty; 5352
Isa 18:4 like a **c** heat upon herbs, and like 6703
Am 8:9 will darken the earth in the **c** day: 216
Zec 14:6 the light shall not be **c**, nor dark 3368
Rev 21:11 like a jasper stone, **c** as crystal; *2929*
Rev 21:18 was pure gold, like unto **c** glass *2513*
Rev 22:1 river of water of life, **c** as crystal, *2986*

CLEARLY
Job 33:3 my lips shall utter knowledge **c** 1305
Mt 7:5 **then shalt thou see c to cast out** *1227*
Ro 1:20 are **c** seen, being understood by *2529*

CLEAVE
Ge 2:24 shall **c** unto his wife: and they 1692
Dt 4:4 But ye that did **c** unto the Lord 1695
Jos 22:5 to **c** unto him and to serve him, 1692
Jos 23:8 But **c** unto the Lord your God, as 1692
Ps 102:5 groaning my bones **c** to my skin 1692
Zec 14:4 of Olives shall **c** in the midst 1234
Mt 19:5 **c to his wife: and they twain** *4347*
Mk 10:7 **and mother, and c to his wife;** *4347*
Ro 12:9 **c** to that which is good *2853*

CLEAVETH
Dt 14:6 and **c** the cleft into two claws, 8157
Job 16:13 he **c** my reins asunder, and doth 6398
Job 19:20 My bone **c** to my skin and to my 1692
Ps 22:15 and my tongue **c** to my jaws; 1692
Ps 119:25 My soul **c** unto the dust: quicken 1692
Ps 141:7 when one cutteth and **c** wood 1234
Jer 13:11 the girdle **c** to the loins of a man, 1692
La 4:4 The tongue of the sucking child **c** 1692
La 4:8 their skin **c** to their bones; it is 6821
Lk 10:11 **dust of your city, which c on us,** *2853*

CLEFTS
SS 2:14 in the **c** of the rock, in the secret 2288
Isa 2:21 To go into the **c** of the rocks, 5366
Ob 3 that dwellest in the **c** of the rock, 2288

CLIFT
Ex 33:22 put thee in a **c** of the rock, 5366

CLIMBED
1Sa 14:13 Jonathan **c** up upon his hands 5927
Lk 19:4 **c** up into a sycomore tree to see *305*

CLODS
Hos 10:11 and Jacob shall break his **c** 7702
Joel 1:17 seed is rotten under their **c**, 4053

CLOKE
Mt 5:40 **thy coat, let him have thy c also** *2440*
1Th 2:5 nor a **c** of covetousness; God is *4392*
2Ti 4:13 The **c** that I left at Troas with *5341*
1Pe 2:16 liberty for a **c** of maliciousness *1942*

CLOSE
2Sa 22:46 be afraid out of their **c** places. 4526
Job 28:21 kept **c** from the fowls of the air 5641
Da 8:7 saw him come **c** unto the ram, 681

CLOSED
Ge 2:21 **c** up the flesh instead thereof; 5462
Ge 20:18 the Lord had fast **c** up all the 6113
Nu 16:33 and the earth **c** upon them: 3680
Da 12:9 the words are **c** up and sealed 5640
Mt 13:15 **their eyes they have c; lest at** *2576*
Lk 4:20 **c** the book, and he gave it again *4428*

CLOSET
Joel 2:16 and the bride out of her **c** 2646
Mt 6:6 **thou prayest, enter into thy c** *5009*

CLOTH
Nu 4:6 spread over it a **c** wholly of blue 899
Nu 4:8 spread upon them a **c** of scarlet, 899
1Sa 21:9 wrapped in a **c** behind the ephod: 8071
2Sa 20:12 cast a **c** upon him, when he saw 899
Mt 9:16 **of new c unto an old garment,** *4470*
Mk 14:51 linen **c** cast about his naked body; *4616*

CLOTHE
Ex 40:14 his sons, and **c** them with coats: 3847
Est 4:4 she sent raiment to **c** Mordecai, 3847
Ps 132:18 His enemies will **c** with shame: 3847
Isa 50:3 I **c** the heavens with blackness 3847
Mt 6:30 **if God so c the grass of the field,** *294*
Lk 12:28 **If then God so c the grass, which** *294*

CLOTHED
Ge 3:21 make coats of skins, and **c** them 3847
2Sa 1:24 over Saul, who **c** you in scarlet, 3847
2Ch 6:41 O Lord God, be **c** with salvation, 3847
Est 4:2 the king's gate **c** with sackcloth. 3830
Job 7:5 My flesh is **c** with worms and 3847
Job 10:11 hast **c** me with skin and flesh, 3847
Ps 93:1 he is **c** with majesty; 3847
Ps 93:1 the Lord is **c** with strength, 3847
Ps 104:1 art **c** with honour and majesty. 3847
Pr 31:21 her household are **c** with scarlet 3847
Da 5:29 and they **c** Daniel with scarlet, 3848
Zec 3:3 Joshua was **c** with filthy garments, 3847
Mt 6:31 **or, Wherewithal shall we be c?** *4016*
Mt 11:8 **A man c in soft raiment?** *294*
Mt 25:36 **Naked, and ye c me: I was sick,** *4016*
Mt 25:38 **thee in? or naked, and c thee?** *4016*
Mt 25:43 **naked, and ye c me not: sick,** *4016*
Mk 1:6 And John was **c** with camel's hair *1746*
Mk 5:15 and **c**, and in his right mind: *2439*
Mk 15:17 **c** him with purple, and platted *1746*
Lk 16:19 **was c in purple and fine linen,** *1737*
2Co 5:2 earnestly desiring to be **c** upon *1902*
1Pe 5:5 be **c** with humility: for God *1463*
Rev 3:5 **shall be c in white raiment;** *4016*
Rev 7:9 **c** with white robes, and palms in *4016*
Rev 12:1 a woman **c** with the sun, and the *4016*
Rev 15:6 **c** in pure and white linen, and *1746*
Rev 18:16 city, that was **c** in fine linen *4016*
Rev 19:13 **c** with a vesture dipped in blood: *4016*

CLOTHES
Ge 37:29 in the pit; and he rent his **c** 899
Ge 37:34 And Jacob rent his **c**, and put 8071
Ge 49:11 in wine, and his **c** in the blood 5497

Le 13:6 shall wash his **c**, and be clean. 899
Dt 29:5 **c** are not waxen old upon you, ...8008
Jos 7:6 Joshua rent his **c**, and fell to the 8071
2Sa 1:11 David took hold on his **c**, and rent, ...899
2Ki 22:11 book of the law, that he rent his **c**. 899
2Ki 22:19 hast rent thy **c**, and wept before 899
2Ch 34:19 words of the law, that he rent his **c** 899
Ne 9:21 their **c** waxed not old, and their 8008
Est 4:1 Mordecai rent his **c**, and put on 899
Eze 27:24 in blue **c**, and broidered work, ...1545
Mt 26:65 Then the high priest rent his **c**, ...*2440*
Mk 5:28 If I may but touch his **c**, I shall *2440*
Mk 5:30 and said, **Who touched my c?** *2440*
Lk 2:7 and wrapped him in swaddling **c**, ...*4683*
Lk 2:12 the babe wrapped in swaddling **c**, ...*4633*
Lk 19:36 they spread their **c** in the way. *2440*
Jn 19:40 and wound it in linen **c** with the *3608*
Jn 20:5 looking in, saw the linen **c** lying; *3608*
Jn 20:6 and seeth the linen **c** lie, ...*3608*
Ac 22:23 cast off their **c**, and threw dust *2440*

CLOTHING

Job 22:6 and stripped the naked of their **c**. 899
Pr 27:26 lambs are for thy **c**, and the goats 3830
Pr 31:22 her **c** is silk and purple 3830
Pr 31:25 Strength and honour are her **c**; 3830
Mt 7:15 **come to you in sheep's c, but** *1742*
Mk 12:38 **which love to go in long c, and** *4749*
Ac 10:30 stood before me in bright **c**, ...*2066*

CLOUD

Ge 9:13 I do set my bow in the **c**, and it 6051
Ge 9:14 when I bring a **c** over the earth, ...6051
Ge 9:14 the bow shall be seen in the **c** 6051
Ge 9:16 And the bow shall be in the **c**; 6051
Ex 13:21 them by day in a pillar of a **c**, ...6051
Ex 13:22 took not away the pillar of the **c** 6051
Ex 14:24 the pillar of fire and of the **c**, ...6051
Ex 16:10 of the Lord appeared in the **c**. 6051
Ex 19:9 I come unto thee in a thick **c**, ...6051
Ex 24:15 a **c** covered the mount. 6051
Ex 24:16 Moses out of the midst of the **c** 6051
Ex 34:5 And the Lord descended in the **c**, ...6051
Ex 40:34 a **c** covered the tent of the 6051
Le 16:13 that the **c** of the incense may 6051
Nu 9:16 the **c** covered it by day, and the 6051
Nu 9:19 **c** tarried long upon the tabernacle 6051
Nu 9:21 **c** was taken up in the morning, ...6051
Nu 11:25 And the Lord came down in a **c**, ...6051
1Ki 8:10 the **c** filled the house of the Lord, ...6051
1Ki 18:44 ariseth a little **c** out of the sea, ...5645
Ps 78:14 daytime also he led them with a **c**, ...6051
Ps 105:39 He spread a **c** for a covering; and 6051
Pr 16:15 favour is as a **c** of the latter rain. 5645
Isa 4:5 a **c** and smoke by day, and the 6051
Isa 19:1 the Lord rideth upon a swift **c**, ...5645
Mt 17:5 and behold a voice out of the **c**, ...*3507*
Lk 12:54 **ye see a c rise out of the west** *3507*
Lk 21:27 **in a c with power and great glory.** *3507*
Ac 1:9 a **c** received him out of their sight. *3507*
1Co 10:1 all our fathers were under the **c**, ...*3507*
1Co 10:2 Moses in the **c** and in the sea; *3507*
Heb 12:1 with so great a **c** of witnesses, ...*3509*
Rev 11:12 ascended up to heaven in a **c**; *3507*
Rev 14:14 upon the **c** one sat like unto the Son ...*3507*

CLOUDS

Jgs 5:4 the **c** also dropped water. 5645
1Ki 18:45 was black with **c** and wind, ...5645
Job 35:5 **c** which are higher than thou. 7834
Ps 68:34 and his strength is in the **c**. 7834
Ps 104:3 who maketh the **c** his chariot: 5645
Ps 147:8 Who covereth the heaven with **c**, ...5645
Pr 25:14 is like **c** and wind without rain. 5387
Ecc 11:3 If the **c** be full of rain, they empty 5645
Ecc 12:2 nor the **c** return after the rain: 5645
Da 7:13 of man came with the **c** of heaven 6050
Mt 24:30 **in the c of heaven with power** *3507*
Mt 26:64 **and coming in the c of heaven.** *3507*
Mk 13:26 **the Son of man coming in the c** *3507*
1Th 4:17 up together with them in the **c**, ...*3507*
Jude 12 **c** they are without water, carried *3507*
Rev 1:7 Behold he cometh with **c**; and *3507*

CLOUDY

Ex 33:9 **c** pillar descended, and stood 6051
Ex 33:10 the people saw the **c** pillar stand 6051
Ps 99:7 spake unto them in the **c** pillar: 6051
Eze 34:12 scattered in the **c** and dark day 6051

CLUSTER

Nu 13:23 a branch with one **c** of grapes, ...811
Nu 13:24 the **c** of grapes which the children 811
SS 1:14 My beloved is unto me as a **c** of 811

CLUSTERS

Ge 40:10 the **c** thereof brought forth ripe 811
1Sa 25:18 and an hundred **c** of raisins, ...6778
1Sa 30:12 cake of figs, and two **c** of raisins: 6778

COAL

2Sa 14:7 so they shall quench my **c** which 1513
Isa 6:6 having a live **c** in his hand, ...7531
La 4:8 Their visage is blacker than a **c**; 7815

COALS

Le 16:12 take a censer full of burning **c** 1513
2Sa 22:13 before him were **c** of fire 1513
1Ki 19:6 there was a cake baken on the **c**, ...7529
Pr 25:22 thou shalt heap **c** of fire upon his 1513
SS 8:6 the **c** thereof are **c** of fire, which 7565
Jn 21:9 they saw a fire of **c** there, and fish *439*
Ro 12:20 thou shalt heap **c** of fire on his *440*

COAST

Ex 10:4 I bring the locusts into thy **c** 1366
Nu 13:29 the sea, and by the **c** of Jordan 3027
Nu 34:3 the outmost **c** of the salt sea 7097
Dt 11:24 uttermost sea shall your **c** be. 1366
Dt 19:8 the Lord thy God enlarge thy **c**, ...1366
Jos 1:4 down of the sun, shall be your **c**. 1366
1Ch 4:10 bless me indeed, and enlarge my **c**, ...1366
Lk 6:17 from the sea **c** of Tyre and Sidon, ...*3882*

COASTS

Ex 10:19 one locust in all the **c** of Egypt. 1366
Jgs 19:29 sent her into all the **c** of Israel. 1366
Ps 105:31 flies, and lice in all their **c** 1366
Joel 3:4 Zidon, and all the **c** of Palestine? 1552
Mt 8:34 he would depart out of their **c**. *3725*
Mk 5:17 pray him to depart out of their **c** *3725*
Ac 13:50 and expelled them out of their **c** *3725*
Ac 27:2 meaning to sail by the **c** of Asia; *5777*

COAT

Ge	37:3	made him a **c** of many colours.	3801
Ge	37:23	out of his **c**, his **c** of many colours	3801
Ge	37:31	they took Joseph's **c**, and killed	3801
Ge	37:31	and dipped the **c** in the blood;	3801
Ge	37:32	whether it be thy son's **c** or no	3801
Ge	37:33	it, and said, It is my son's **c**;	3801
1Sa	2:19	his mother made him a little **c**,	4598
1Sa	17:5	he was armed with a **c** of mail;	8302
1Sa	17:38	he armed him with a **c** of mail	8302
Lk	6:29	**forbid not to take thy c also.**	*5509*

COATS

Ge	3:21	did the Lord God make **c** of skins,	3801
Da	3:27	neither were their **c** changed,	5622
Mt	10:10	**neither two c, neither shoes,**	*5509*
Lk	3:11	He that hath two **c**, let him	*5509*
Lk	9:3	**money; neither have two c apiece.**	*5509*

COCK

Mt	26:34	**this night, before the c crow, thou**	*220*
Mt	26:74	and immediately the **c** crew.	*220*
Mt	26:75	Before the **c** crow, thou shalt deny	*220*
Mk	14:72	the second time the **c** crew.	*220*
Lk	22:34	**the c shall not crow this day,**	*220*
Jn	13:38	**The c shall not crow, till thou hast**	*220*
Jn	18:27	and immediately the **c** crew.	*220*

COFFER

1Sa	6:8	a trespass offering, in a **c** by the	712
1Sa	6:11	the **c** with the mice of gold and	712

COLD

Job	37:9	whirlwind: and **c** out of the north.	7135
Ps	147:17	who can stand before his **c**?	7135
Pr	20:4	will not plow by reason of the **c**;	2779
Pr	25:13	As the **c** of snow in the time of	6793
Pr	25:25	**c** waters to a thirsty soul, so is	7119
Mt	10:42	**these little ones a cup of c water**	*5593*
Mt	24:12	**the love of many shall wax c**	*5594*
Jn	18:18	made a fire of coals; for it was **c**:	*5592*
2Co	11:27	in fastings often, in **c** and	*5592*
Rev	3:15	**that thou art neither c nor hot:**	*5593*
Rev	3:15	**I would thou wert c or hot.**	*5593*
Rev	3:16	**and neither c nor hot, I will spue**	*5593*

COLLECTION

2Ch	24:9	to the Lord the **c** that Moses	4864
1Co	16:1	concerning the **c** for the saints,	*3048*

COLOUR

Nu	11:7	**c** thereof as the **c** of bdellium.	5869
Eze	1:4	midst thereof as the **c** of amber,	5869
Eze	1:7	like the **c** of burnished brass.	5869
Eze	10:9	wheels was as the **c** of a beryl	5869
Rev	17:4	arrayed in purple and scarlet **c**,	*4392*

COLOURS

Ge	37:3	he made him a coat of many **c**.	6446
Ge	37:23	coat of many **c** that was on him;	6446
Ge	37:32	And they sent the coat of many **c**,	6446

COLT

Mk	11:2	**ye shall find a c tied, whereon**	*4454*
Mk	11:4	and found the **c** tied by the door	*4454*
Mk	11:5	them, What do ye, loosing the **c**?	*4454*
Mk	11:7	brought the **c** to Jesus, and cast	*4454*
Lk	19:35	cast their garments upon the **c**,	*4454*

COME

Ge	6:13	end of all flesh is **c** before me;	935
Ge	6:18	and thou shalt **c** into the ark, thou,	935
Ge	41:29	there **c** seven years of great plenty	935
Ge	42:10	but to buy food are thy servants **c**.	935
Ge	44:23	Except your youngest brother **c**	3381
Ge	45:4	**C** near to me, I pray you. And	5066
Ge	45:16	Joseph's brethren are **c**: and it	935
Ge	47:4	to sojourn in the land are we **c**;	935
Ge	50:5	my father, and I will **c** again.	7725
Ex	3:8	And I am **c** down to deliver them	3381
Ex	3:9	children of Israel is **c** unto me:	935
Ex	8:4	the frogs shall **c** up both on thee,	5927
Ex	9:19	the hail shall **c** down upon them,	3381
Ex	12:23	not suffer the destroyer to **c** in	935
Ex	14:26	may **c** again upon the Egyptians,	7725
Ex	17:6	and there shall **c** water out of it,	3318
Ex	18:15	the people **c** unto me to enquire	935
Ex	19:9	**c** unto thee in a thick cloud,	935
Ex	19:11	third day the Lord will **c** down	3381
Ex	19:23	cannot **c** up to mount Sinai:	5927
Ex	24:2	Moses alone shall **c** near the Lord:	5066
Ex	24:12	Lord said unto Moses, **C** up to me	5927
Ex	28:43	when they **c** in unto the tabernacle	935
Ex	28:43	when they **c** near unto the altar	5066
Ex	30:20	**c** near to the altar to minister,	5066
Ex	35:10	wise hearted among you shall **c**,	935
Le	14:8	that he shall **c** into the camp	935
Le	14:43	if the plague **c** again, and break	7725
Le	16:23	Aaron shall **c** into the tabernacle	935
Le	21:23	nor **c** nigh unto the altar, because	5066
Nu	5:14	spirit of jealousy **c** upon him,	5674
Nu	6:5	shall no razor **c** upon his head:	5674
Nu	6:6	he shall **c** at no dead body	935
Nu	22:14	Balaam refuseth to **c** with us	1980
Nu	22:36	Balak heard that Balaam was **c**,	935
Nu	24:17	there shall **c** a Star out of Jacob,	1869
Nu	35:10	When ye be **c** over Jordan into	5674
Dt	6:20	thy son asketh thee in time to **c**,	4279
Dt	28:2	these blessings shall **c** on thee,	935
Dt	28:15	all these curses shall **c** upon thee,	935
Dt	29:22	So that the generation to **c** of	314
Dt	31:11	When all Israel is **c** to appear	935
Jos	2:3	**c** to search out all the country	935
Jos	2:18	Behold, when we **c** into the land,	935
Jos	3:13	waters that **c** down from above;	3381
Jos	3:15	as they that bare the ark were **c**	935
Jos	6:19	**c** into the treasury of the Lord	935
Jos	10:6	**c** up to us quickly, and save us,	5927
Jos	22:27	say to our children in time to **c**,	4279
Jgs	1:24	the spies saw a man **c** forth out	3318
Jgs	9:10	tree, **C** thou, and reign over us	3212
Jgs	9:14	bramble, **C** thou, and reign over us	3212
Jgs	9:15	let fire **c** out of the bramble, and	3318
Jgs	11:6	**C**, and be our captain, that we	3212
Jgs	13:5	and no razor shall **c** on his head:	5927
Jgs	15:10	To bind Samson are we **c**	5927
Jgs	15:12	We are **c** down to bind thee, that	3381
Jgs	16:2	saying, Samson is **c** hither	935
Jgs	16:17	There hath not **c** a razor upon	5927
Ru	2:12	under whose wings thou art **c** to trust	935
1Sa	1:11	shall no razor **c** upon his head	5927
1Sa	2:3	arrogancy **c** out of your mouth:	3318
1Sa	5:5	nor any that **c** into Dagon's house,	935
1Sa	6:7	on which there hath **c** no yoke,	5927
1Sa	10:5	that thou shalt **c** to the hill of God,	935

1Sa	11:10	To morrow we will **c** out unto you,	3318
1Sa	14:11	Hebrews **c** forth out of the holes	3318
1Sa	16:2	say, I am **c** to sacrifice to the Lord.	935
1Sa	16:5	and **c** with me to the sacrifice.	935
1Sa	16:11	will not sit down till he **c** hither.	935
1Sa	16:16	**c** to pass, when the evil spirit	1961
1Sa	17:25	surely to defy Israel is he **c** up:	5927
1Sa	17:44	**C** to me, and I will give thy flesh	3212
1Sa	17:45	but I **c** to thee in the name of the	935
1Sa	25:8	we **c** in a good day: give, I pray	935
1Sa	26:10	him; or his day shall **c** to die;	935
2Sa	5:8	the lame shall not **c** into the house	935
2Sa	11:7	And when Uriah was **c** unto him,	935
2Sa	16:7	**C** out, **c** out, thou bloody man.	3318
2Sa	24:13	Shall seven years of famine **c** unto	935
1Ki	13:22	thy carcase shall not **c** unto the	935
1Ki	15:19	**c** and break thy league with	3212
1Ki	17:18	art thou **c** unto me to call my sin	935
1Ki	17:21	let this child's soul **c** into him	7725
2Ki	1:10	then let fire **c** down from heaven	3381
2Ki	4:36	And when she was **c** in unto him,	935
2Ki	5:10	and thy flesh shall **c** again to thee,	7725
2Ki	5:11	He will surely **c** out to me,	3318
2Ki	8:7	saying, The man of God is **c** hither	935
2Ki	19:9	he is **c** out to fight against thee:	3318
1Ch	16:29	**c** before him: worship the Lord	935
2Ch	5:11	were **c** out of the holy place:	3318
2Ch	6:32	if they **c** and pray in this house;	935
2Ch	8:11	the ark of the Lord hath **c**	935
Ezr	3:8	that were **c** out of the captivity	935
Ezr	4:12	are **c** unto Jerusalem, building	858
Est	2:12	when every maid's turn was **c**	5060
Est	4:14	thou art **c** to the kingdom	5060
Est	8:6	evil that shall **c** unto my people?	4672
Job	2:11	heard of all this evil that was **c**	935
Job	23:10	tried me, I shall **c** forth as gold	3318
Ps	24:7	and the King of glory shall **c** in	935
Ps	24:9	and the King of glory shall **c** in	935
Ps	42:2	shall I **c** and appear before God?	935
Ps	50:3	Our God shall **c**, and shall not	935
Ps	65:2	prayer, unto thee shall all flesh **c**.	935
Ps	88:2	Let my prayer **c** before thee:	935
Ps	95:6	O **c**, let us worship and bow down:	935
Ps	100:2	**c** before his presence with singing	935
Ps	102:18	be written for the generation to **c**	314
Ps	126:6	doubtless **c** again with rejoicing,	935
Pr	1:11	**C** with us, let us lay wait for	3212
Pr	5:8	**c** not nigh the door of her house:	7126
Pr	7:18	**C**, let us take our fill of love until	3212
Pr	7:20	will **c** home at the day appointed	935
Pr	25:4	shall **c** forth a vessel for the finer	3318
Pr	31:25	she shall rejoice in time to **c**.	314
Ecc	1:11	remembrance of things that are to **c**	314
Ecc	2:16	the days to **c** shall all be forgotten.	935
Ecc	7:18	he that feareth God shall **c** forth	3318
Ecc	12:1	while the evil days **c** not, nor	935
Isa	1:18	**C** now, and let us reason	3212
Isa	11:1	And there shall **c** forth a rod out	3318
Isa	31:4	so shall the Lord of hosts **c** down	3381
Isa	35:4	God will **c** with vengeance,	935
Isa	35:4	he will **c** and save you.	935
Isa	40:10	Lord God will **c** with strong hand,	935
Isa	55:1	**c** ye to the waters, and he that	3212
Isa	55:1	hath no money; **c** ye, buy, and eat;	3212
Isa	55:1	yea, **c**, buy wine and milk	3212
Isa	55:3	Incline your ear, and **c** unto me:	3212
Isa	59:19	the enemy shall **c** in like a flood,	935
Isa	59:20	And the Redeemer shall **c** to Zion,	935
Isa	60:1	Arise, shine; for thy light is **c**,	935
Isa	63:4	and the year of my redeemed is **c**	935
Jer	4:4	lest my fury **c** forth like fire	3318
Jer	4:13	he shall **c** up as clouds,	5927
Jer	6:26	spoiler shall suddenly **c** upon us	935
Jer	25:12	**c** to pass, when seventy years	1961
Jer	26:2	**c** to worship in the Lord's house	935
Jer	49:19	he shall **c** up like a lion from the	5927
Jer	49:22	he shall **c** up and fly as the eagle,	5927
La	4:18	days are fulfilled; for our end is **c**	935
Eze	7:2	the end is **c** upon the four corners	935
Eze	7:6	An end is **c**, the end is **c**: it	935
Eze	7:7	the time is **c**, the day of trouble is	935
Eze	7:10	Behold the day, behold, it is **c**	935
Eze	38:18	time when Gog shall **c** against the	935
Da	3:2	to **c** to the dedication of the	858
Da	8:7	I saw him **c** close unto the ram,	5060
Da	9:22	I am now **c** forth to give thee	3318
Da	9:23	I am **c** to shew thee; for thou art	935
Da	10:20	lo, the prince of Grecia shall **c**	935
Da	11:6	shall **c** to the king of the north to	935
Da	11:9	So the king of the south shall **c**	935
Da	11:15	So the king of the north shall **c**	935
Da	11:21	but he shall **c** in peaceably, and	935
Hos	1:11	they shall **c** up out of the land:	5927
Hos	6:3	and he shall **c** unto us as the rain,	935
Hos	9:7	The days of visitation are **c**,	935
Hos	9:7	the days of recompence are **c**;	935
Joel	2:20	and his stink shall **c** up,	5927
Joel	2:20	and his ill savour shall **c** up	5927
Joel	2:31	and the terrible day of the Lord **c**	635
Joel	2:32	**c** to pass, that whosoever shall	1961
Joel	3:12	**c** up to the valley of Jehoshaphat:	5927
Joel	3:18	a fountain shall **c** forth out of the	3318
Am	4:10	the stink of your camps to **c** up	5927
Ob	21	saviours shall **c** up on mount	5927
Jnh	1:2	wickedness is **c** up before me	5927
Jnh	1:7	**C**, and let us cast lots, that we	3212
Mic	5:2	out of thee shall he **c** forth unto	3318
Zep	1:8	**c** to pass in the day of the Lord's	1961
Zep	2:2	the day of the Lord's anger **c**	935
Hag	2:7	the desire of all nations shall **c**	935
Zec	14:5	my God shall **c**, and all the saints	935
Mal	3:1	shall suddenly **c** to his temple	935
Mal	3:1	behold, he shall **c**, saith the Lord	935
Mal	4:6	lest I **c** and smite the earth	935
Mt	2:2	east, and are **c** to worship him	*2064*
Mt	2:6	out of thee shall **c** a Governor,	*1831*
Mt	2:8	I may **c** and worship him also	*2064*
Mt	5:17	**that I am c to destroy the law**	*2064*
Mt	5:17	**I am not c to destroy, but to**	*2064*
Mt	6:10	**Thy kingdom c. Thy will be done**	*2064*
Mt	7:15	**c to you in sheep's clothing,**	*2064*
Mt	9:13	**I am not c to call the righteous,**	*2064*
Mt	9:15	**days will c, when the bridegroom**	*2064*
Mt	10:12	**ye c into an house, salute it**	*1525*
Mt	10:34	**I am c to send peace on earth:**	*2064*
Mt	11:3	Art thou he that should **c**, or do	*2064*
Mt	11:28	**C unto me, all ye that labour**	*1205*
Mt	12:28	**kingdom of God is c unto you**	*5348*
Mt	12:44	**when he is c, he findeth it empty,**	*2064*
Mt	14:28	bid me **c** unto thee on the water	*2064*
Mt	14:29	And he said, **C.** And when	*2064*
Mt	16:24	**If any man will c after me**	*2064*

Mt	16:27	Son of man shall c in the glory	2064
Mt	17:10	scribes that Elias must first c?	2064
Mt	17:11	Elias truly shall first c, and	2064
Mt	17:12	unto you, That Elias is c already,	2064
Mt	18:11	For the Son of man is c to save	2064
Mt	19:21	in heaven: and c and follow me	1204
Mt	21:38	c, let us kill him, and let us seize	2205
Mt	24:5	For many shall c in my name	2064
Mt	24:6	all these things must c to pass,	1096
Mt	24:42	not what hour your Lord doth c	2064
Mt	25:31	When the Son of man shall c in	2064
Mt	25:34	C, ye blessed of my Father,	1205
Mt	26:55	Are ye c out as against a thief	1831
Mt	27:40	of God, c down from the cross	2597
Mt	27:42	let him now c down from the cross,	2597
Mt	27:49	whether Elias will c to save him	2064
Mt	27:64	lest his disciples c by night	2064
Mt	28:6	C, see the place where the Lord	1205
Mk	1:17	C ye after me, and I will make	1205
Mk	4:29	sickle, because the harvest is c	3936
Mk	6:31	C ye yourselves apart into a	1205
Mk	8:34	Whosoever will c after me, let	2064
Mk	9:1	kingdom of God c with power	2064
Mk	10:14	Suffer the little children to c	2064
Mk	10:21	c, take up the cross, and follow	1204
Mk	13:6	For many shall c in my name,	2064
Mk	14:41	it is enough, the hour is c;	2064
Mk	15:30	Save thyself, and c down from	2597
Lk	1:35	Holy Ghost shall c upon thee,	1904
Lk	7:19	Art thou he that should c?	2064
Lk	9:23	If any man will c after me,	2064
Lk	9:54	that we command fire to c down	2597
Lk	10:9	The kingdom of God is c nigh	1448
Lk	10:35	when I c again, I will repay thee	1880
Lk	11:2	Thy kingdom c. Thy will be	2064
Lk	12:49	I am c to send fire on the earth;	2064
Lk	13:7	I c seeking fruit on this fig tree,	2064
Lk	14:26	If any man c to me, and hate not	2064
Lk	14:27	bear his cross, and c after me,	2064
Lk	18:30	in the world to c life everlasting	2064
Lk	19:5	make haste, and c down; for	2597
Lk	19:9	day is salvation c to this house,	1096
Lk	19:10	For the Son of man is c to seek	2064
Lk	19:13	said unto them, Occupy till I c	2064
Lk	21:8	for many shall c in my name	2064
Lk	21:9	these things must first c to pass;	1096
Lk	21:34	that day c upon you unawares	2186
Lk	21:35	as a snare shall it c on all them	1904
Lk	24:12	at that which was c to pass	1096
Jn	1:39	He saith unto them, C and see	2064
Jn	1:46	good thing c out of Nazareth?	1511
Jn	2:4	with thee? mine hour is not yet c	2240
Jn	3:2	thou art a teacher c from God:	2064
Jn	3:19	light is c into the world, and men	2064
Jn	4:16	call thy husband, and c hither	2064
Jn	4:25	is called Christ: when he is c,	2064
Jn	4:29	C, see a man, which told me all	1205
Jn	4:49	Sir, c down ere my child die	2597
Jn	5:43	I am c in my Father's name, and	2064
Jn	5:43	another shall c in his own name,	2064
Jn	6:14	a truth that prophet that should c	2064
Jn	6:37	Father giveth me shall c to me;	2240
Jn	6:44	No man can c to me, except the	2064
Jn	6:65	c unto me, except it were given	2064
Jn	7:6	My time is not yet c: but your	3918
Jn	7:28	I am not c of myself, but he that	2064
Jn	7:34	where I am, thither ye cannot c	2064
Jn	7:37	let him c unto me, and drink.	2064
Jn	7:41	Shall Christ c out of Galilee?	2064
Jn	8:21	sins: whither I go, ye cannot c	2064
Jn	9:39	I am c into this world, that they	2064
Jn	10:10	I am c that they might have life,	2064
Jn	11:43	a loud voice, Lazarus, c forth	1204
Jn	12:23	hour is c, that the Son of man	2064
Jn	12:46	I am c a light into the world,	2064
Jn	13:33	Whither I go, ye cannot c; so	2064
Jn	14:3	I will c again, and receive you	2064
Jn	14:18	you comfortless: I will c to you	2064
Jn	14:28	I go away, and c again unto you	2064
Jn	15:26	But when the Comforter is c,	2064
Jn	16:7	Comforter will not c unto you;	2064
Jn	16:8	when he is c, he will reprove	2064
Jn	16:13	when he, the Spirit of truth, is c,	2064
Jn	16:13	he will shew you things to c	2064
Jn	17:1	Father, the hour is c; glorify thy.	2064
Jn	21:12	Jesus saith unto them, C and dine	1205
Jn	21:22	he tarry till I c, what is that	2064
Ac	1:8	the Holy Ghost is c upon you:	1904
Ac	1:11	shall so c in like manner as ye	2064
Ac	2:1	the day of Pentecost was fully c,	4545
Ac	2:20	and notable day of the Lord c	2064
Ac	3:19	the times of refreshing shall c	2064
Ac	8:27	c to Jerusalem for to worship	2064
Ac	8:39	they were c up out of the water,	305
Ac	10:4	c up for a memorial before God	305
Ac	12:11	Peter was c to himself, he said	1096
Ac	14:11	The gods are c down to us in the	2597
Ac	16:9	saying, C over into Macedonia	1224
Ac	26:22	and Moses did say should c	1096
Ac	28:6	no harm c to him, they changed	1096
Ro	3:8	Let us do evil, that good may c?	2064
Ro	3:23	For all have sinned, and c short	5302
Ro	5:14	the figure of him that was to c	3195
Ro	8:38	things present, nor things to c,	3195
Ro	11:11	salvation is c unto the Gentiles	
Ro	16:19	obedience is c abroad unto all men	864
1Co	11:18	when ye c together in the church	4905
1Co	11:26	shew the Lord's death till he c	2064
1Co	11:33	when ye c together to eat, tarry	4905
1Co	13:10	when that which is perfect is c,	2064
2Co	6:17	c out from among them, and be	1831
2Co	12:14	third time I am ready to c to you:	2064
2Co	12:20	lest, when I c, I shall not find you	2064
Gal	2:21	for if righteousness c by the law	
Gal	3:25	But after that faith is c, we are	2064
Gal	4:4	the fulness of the time was c	2064
Eph	2:7	that in the ages to c he might	1904
Eph	4:13	Till we all c in the unity of the	2658
Col	2:17	are a shadow of things to c;	3195
1Th	1:10	delivered us from the wrath to c	2064
2Th	1:10	When he shall c to be glorified in	2064
2Th	2:3	except there c a falling away	2064
1Ti	2:4	c unto the knowledge of the truth	2064
2Ti	3:1	last days perilous times shall c	1764
2Ti	3:7	never able to c to the knowledge	2064
Heb	2:5	put in subjection the world to c	3195
Heb	4:16	Let us therefore c boldly unto	4334
Heb	9:11	But Christ being c an high priest	3854
Heb	10:1	a shadow of good things to c,	3195
Heb	10:9	Then said he, Lo, I c to do thy	2240
Heb	11:24	Moses, when he was c to years	1096
Heb	13:14	city, but we seek one to c	3195

Jas	2:2	if there c unto your assembly a	1525
1Pe	1:10	the grace that should c unto you:	
2Pe	3:3	there shall c in the last days	2064
2Pe	3:9	that all should c to repentance	5562
2Pe	3:10	But the day of the Lord will c as	2240
1Jn	2:18	heard that antichrist shall c	2064
1Jn	4:2	that Jesus Christ is c in the flesh	2064
2Jn	7	confess not that Jesus Christ is c	2064
Rev	1:4	and which was, and which is to c;	2064
Rev	1:8	and which was, and which is to c	2064
Rev	2:16	I will c unto thee quickly, and	2064
Rev	2:25	ye have already hold fast till I c	2240
Rev	3:3	I will c on thee as a thief, and	2240
Rev	3:3	shalt not know what hour I will c	2240
Rev	3:10	of temptation, which shall c upon	2064
Rev	3:20	open the door, I will c into him,	1525
Rev	4:1	which said, C up hither, and I	305
Rev	6:17	the great day of his wrath is c;	2064
Rev	9:12	and, behold, there c two woes	2064
Rev	10:1	I saw another mighty angel c	2597
Rev	11:17	which art, and wast, and art to c;	2064
Rev	12:10	Now is c salvation, and strength,	1096
Rev	15:4	all nations shall c and worship	2240
Rev	16:13	unclean spirits like frogs c out	
Rev	16:15	I c as a thief. Blessed is he that	2064
Rev	19:7	the marriage of the Lamb is c,	2064
Rev	19:17	C and gather yourselves together	1205
Rev	22:7	Behold, I c quickly: blessed is he	2064
Rev	22:12	behold, I c quickly; and my	2064
Rev	22:17	the Spirit and the bride say, C	2064
Rev	22:17	And let him that heareth say, C	2064
Rev	22:17	And let him that is athirst c	2064
Rev	22:20	Surely I c quickly. Amen	2064
Rev	22:20	Even so, c, Lord Jesus	2064

COMELINESS

Isa	53:2	he hath no form nor c; and when	1926
1Co	12:23	parts have more abundant c	2157

COMELY

Ps	33:1	for praise is c for the upright	5000
Ps	147:1	for it is pleasant; and praise is c	5000
SS	1:10	Thy cheeks are c with rows of	4998
SS	2:14	voice, and thy countenance is c	5000
1Co	7:35	you, but for that which is c	2155
1Co	11:13	is it c that a woman pray unto	4241

COMEST

Jgs	19:17	goest thou? and whence c thou?	935
1Sa	16:4	C thou peaceably?	935
1Sa	17:43	Am I a dog, that thou c to me	935
1Sa	17:45	Thou c to me with a sword, and	935
Job	1:7	said unto Satan, Whence c thou?	935
Job	2:2	From whence c thou? And Satan	935
Jnh	1:8	and whence c thou? What is thy	935
2Ti	4:13	when thou c, bring with thee, and	2064

COMETH

Ge	24:43	when the virgin c forth to draw	3318
Ge	37:19	Behold, this dreamer c	935
Nu	3:10	stranger that c nigh shall be	7131
Nu	5:30	the spirit of jealousy c upon him,	5674
Jgs	13:14	eat of any thing that c of the vine,	3318
1Sa	9:6	all that he saith c surely to pass:	935
1Sa	20:27	Wherefore c not the son of Jesse	935
2Ki	12:4	all the money that c into any	5927
Job	14:2	He c forth like a flower, and is	3318
Job	37:9	Out of the south c the whirlwind:	935
Job	37:22	Fair weather c out of the north:	857
Ps	98:9	Lord; for he c to judge the earth:	935
Ps	118:26	Blessed be he that c in the name	935
Ps	121:1	the hills, from whence c my help	935
Ps	121:2	My help c from the Lord, which	
Pr	2:6	out of his mouth c knowledge and	
Pr	13:10	by pride c contention: but with	5414
Pr	18:3	When the wicked c, then c also	935
Pr	29:26	every man's judgment c from the Lord	
Ecc	6:4	For he c in with vanity, and	935
Ecc	11:8	All that c is vanity	935
SS	2:8	he c leaping upon the mountains,	935
Isa	13:9	Behold, the day of the Lord c,	935
Isa	26:21	Lord c out of his place to punish	3318
Isa	30:27	the name of the Lord c from far	935
Isa	62:11	salvation c; behold, his reward is	935
Da	12:12	waiteth, and c to the thousand	5060
Joel	2:1	for the day of the Lord c, for it is	935
Mic	1:3	the Lord c forth out of his place,	3318
Mic	5:6	when he c into our land, and when.	935
Mic	7:4	watchmen and thy visitation c;	935
Zec	9:9	thy King c unto thee: he is just,	935
Zec	14:1	day of the Lord c, and thy spoil	935
Mal	4:1	the day c, that shall burn as an	935
Mt	3:11	but he that c after me is mightier	2064
Mt	13:19	then c the wicked one, and	2064
Mt	15:11	that which c out of the mouth,	1607
Mt	18:7	that man by whom the offence c	2064
Mt	21:9	Blessed is he that c in the name of	2064
Mt	23:39	Blessed is he that c in the name	2064
Mt	24:44	as ye think not the Son of man c	2064
Mt	25:6	made, Behold, the bridegroom c	2064
Mt	25:13	hour wherein the Son of man c	2064
Mk	1:7	There c one mightier than I	2064
Mk	4:15	Satan c immediately, and taketh	2064
Mk	7:20	That which c out of the man,	1607
Mk	9:12	Elias verily c first, and restoreth	2064
Mk	11:9	he that c in the name of the Lord:	2064
Mk	14:37	he c, and findeth them sleeping	2064
Mk	14:41	And he c the third time, and saith	2064
Lk	3:16	but one mightier than I c,	2064
Lk	6:47	c to me, and heareth my sayings,	2064
Lk	11:25	when he c, he findeth it swept	2064
Lk	12:40	Son of man c at an hour when	2064
Lk	12:43	when he c shall find so doing	2064
Lk	17:20	of God c not with observation:	2064
Lk	18:8	Son of man c, shall he find faith	2064
Jn	1:9	every man that c into the world	2064
Jn	1:15	c after me is preferred before me:	2064
Jn	1:30	me c a man which is preferred	2064
Jn	3:20	c to the light, lest his deeds	2064
Jn	3:21	he that doeth truth c to the light,	2064
Jn	3:31	He that c from above is above all:	2064
Jn	4:21	the hour c, when ye shall neither	2064
Jn	4:23	the hour c, and now is, when	2064
Jn	4:25	Messias c, which is called Christ:	2064
Jn	4:35	four months, and then c harvest?	2064
Jn	6:35	that c to me shall never hunger;	2064
Jn	6:37	c to me I will in no wise cast out.	2064
Jn	7:31	Christ c, will he do more miracles	2064
Jn	7:42	Christ c of the seed of David	2064
Jn	9:4	night c, when no man can work	2064
Jn	14:6	c unto the Father, but by me.	2064
Jn	14:30	the prince of this world c, and	2064
Jn	20:1	c Mary Magdalene early, when it	2064

Jn	20:2	she runneth, and **c** to Simon Peter,	*2064*
Jn	21:13	Jesus then **c**, and taketh bread,	*2064*
Ac	13:25	there **c** one after me, whose shoes	*2064*
Ro	10:17	So then faith **c** by hearing, and	
2Co	11:4	For if he that **c** preacheth another	*2064*
Eph	5:6	of these things **c** the wrath of God	*2064*
Col	3:6	the wrath of God **c** on the children	*2064*
1Th	5:2	the day of the Lord so **c** as a thief	*2064*
Heb	11:6	for he that **c** to God must believe	*4334*
Jas	1:17	**c** down from the Father of lights,	*2591*
Jude	14	the Lord **c** with ten thousands of	*2064*
Rev	1:7	Behold, he **c** with clouds; and	*2064*
Rev	3:12	**new Jerusalem, which c down**	*2597*
Rev	11:14	behold, the third woe **c** quickly	*2064*
Rev	17:10	when he **c**, he must continue a	*2064*

COMFORT

Ge	18:5	and **c** ye your hearts; after that	5582
Ge	37:35	all his daughters rose up to **c** him;	5162
2Sa	10:2	David sent to **c** him by the hand	5162
Job	7:13	My bed shall **c** me, my couch	5162
Ps	23:4	thy rod and thy staff they **c** me	5162
Ps	71:21	and **c** me on every side	5162
Ps	119:76	merciful kindness be for my **c**	5162
SS	2:5	with flagons, **c** me with apples:	7502
Isa	40:1	**C** ye, **c** ye my people, saith your	5162
Zec	1:17	and the Lord shall yet **c** Zion,	5162
Mt	9:22	**Daughter, be of good c; thy faith**	*2293*
Mk	10:49	of good **c**, rise; he calleth thee	*2293*
Lk	8:48	**Daughter, be of good c; thy faith**	*2293*
Ac	9:31	and in the **c** of the Holy Ghost	*3874*
Ro	15:4	patience and **c** of the scriptures	*3874*
2Co	1:3	of mercies, and the God of all **c**;	*3874*
2Co	1:4	by the **c** wherewith we ourselves	*3874*
2Co	7:13	we were comforted in your **c**	*3874*
2Co	13:11	Be perfect, be of good **c**, be of	*3870*
Eph	6:22	and that he might **c** your hearts	*3870*
Php	2:1	if any **c** of love, if any fellowship	*3890*
1Th	4:18	**c** one another with these words	*3870*
2Th	2:17	**C** your hearts, and stablish you	*3870*

COMFORTED

Ge	24:67	Isaac was **c** after his mother's	5162
Ge	38:12	wife died; and Judah was **c**,	5162
Ru	2:13	for that thou hast **c** me, and for	5162
2Sa	12:24	And David **c** Bath-sheba his wife,	5162
Ps	77:2	not: my soul refused to be **c**	5162
Ps	119:52	of old, O Lord; and have **c** myself.	5162
Isa	66:13	ye shall be **c** in Jerusalem	5162
Eze	5:13	rest upon them, and I will be **c**:	5162
Mt	5:4	**that mourn: for they shall be c**	*3870*
Lk	16:25	**but now he is c, and thou art**	*3870*
Ac	20:12	alive, and were not a little **c**	*3870*
Ro	1:12	that I may be **c** together with you	*4837*
2Co	1:4	wherewith we ourselves are **c**	*3870*
2Co	1:6	or whether we be **c**, it is for your	*3870*
Col	2:2	That their hearts might be **c**	*3870*

COMFORTER

La	1:9	down wonderfully: she had no **c**	5162
La	1:16	the **c** that should relieve my soul	5162
Jn	14:16	**and he shall give you another C,**	*3875*
Jn	14:26	**the C, which is the Holy Ghost,**	*3875*
Jn	15:26	**But when the C is come, whom I**	*3875*
Jn	16:7	**the C will not come unto you;**	*3875*

COMFORTERS

Job	16:2	miserable **c** are ye all	5162
Ps	69:20	none; and for **c**, but I found none	5162
Na	3:7	whence shall I seek **c** for thee?	5162

COMFORTETH

Isa	51:12	I, even I, am he that **c** you:	5162
2Co	1:4	Who **c** us in all our tribulation,	*3870*
2Co	7:6	that **c** those that are cast down,	*3870*

C

COMFORTS

Ps	94:19	within me thy **c** delight my soul	8575
Isa	57:18	and restore **c** unto him and to	5150

COMING

Ge	30:30	hath blessed thee since my **c**	7272
2Sa	3:25	know thy going out and thy **c** in,	4126
Ps	19:5	bridegroom **c** out of his chamber	3318
Ps	37:13	for he seeth that his day is **c**	935
Ps	121:8	and thy **c** in from this time forth,	935
Da	4:23	watcher and an holy one **c** down	5182
Mal	3:2	who may abide the day of his **c**?	935
Mt	16:28	**the Son of man c in his kingdom.**	*2064*
Mt	24:3	what shall be the sign of the **c**	*3952*
Mt	24:27	**also the c of the Son of man be,**	*3952*
Mt	26:64	**and c in the clouds of heaven.**	*2064*
Mk	1:10	straightway **c** up out of the water	*305*
Mk	13:26	**the Son of man c in the clouds**	*2064*
Mk	13:36	**c suddenly he find you sleeping**	*2064*
Lk	18:5	**by her continual c she weary me.**	*2064*
Lk	21:27	**shall they see the Son of man c**	*2064*
Jn	1:27	**c** after me is preferred before me,	*2064*
Jn	5:7	but while I am **c**, another steppeth	*2064*
Jn	5:25	**The hour is c, and now is, when**	*2064*
Jn	5:28	**for the hour is c, in the which all**	*2064*
Jn	10:12	**seeth the wolf c, and leaveth the**	*2064*
Ac	7:52	before of the **c** of the Just One;	*1660*
Ac	10:3	an angel of God **c** in to him,	*1525*
1Co	1:7	waiting for the **c** of our Lord	*602*
1Co	15:23	they that are Christ's at his **c**	*3952*
2Co	13:1	This is the third time I am **c**	*2064*
1Th	4:15	remain unto the **c** of the Lord	*3952*
1Th	5:23	the **c** of our Lord Jesus Christ	*3952*
2Th	2:8	with the brightness of his **c**	*3952*
Jas	5:8	the **c** of the Lord draweth nigh	*3952*
2Pe	1:16	power and **c** of our Lord Jesus	*3952*
1Jn	2:28	be ashamed before him at his **c**	*3952*
Rev	13:11	beast **c** up out of the earth;	*305*
Rev	21:2	new Jerusalem, **c** down from God	*2597*

COMMAND

Ge	50:16	Thy father did **c** before he died,	6680
Ex	8:27	Lord our God, as he shall **c** us.	559
Ex	34:11	thou that which I **c** thee this day:	6680
Le	25:21	I will **c** my blessing upon you	6680
Nu	5:2	**C** the children of Israel, that they	6680
Dt	6:6	words, which I **c** thee this day	6680
Dt	8:11	statutes, which I **c** thee this day:	6680
Dt	27:4	set up these stones, which I **c** you	6680
Jos	4:16	**C** the priests that bear the ark	6680
Jos	11:15	so did Moses **c** Joshua, and so did	6680
Job	39:27	the eagle mount up at thy **c**,	6310
Isa	5:6	also **c** the clouds that they rain	6680
Mt	4:3	**c** that these stones be made bread.	*2036*
Mt	27:64	**C** therefore that the sepulchre be	*2753*
Mk	10:3	unto them, **What did Moses c you?**	*1781*
Jn	15:14	**if ye do whatsoever I c you,**	*1781*

Jn 15:17 **These things I c you, that ye love** *1781*
Ac 5:28 Did not we straitly **c** you that ye *3853*
Ac 16:18 I **c** thee in the name of Jesus *3853*
1Co 7:10 unto the married I **c**, yet not I, ...*3583*
1Ti 4:11 These things **c** and teach. *3853*

COMMANDED

Ge 2:16 And the Lord God **c** the man, ...6680
Ge 3:11 the tree, whereof I **c** thee that 6680
Ge 3:17 the tree, of which I **c** thee, saying, ...6680
Ge 7:16 of all flesh, as God had **c** him: 6680
Ge 21:4 eight days old, as God had **c** him. 6680
Ge 42:25 Then Joseph **c** to fill their sacks, ...6680
Ex 7:6 as the Lord **c** them, so did they 6680
Ex 40:32 they washed; as the Lord **c** Moses. 6680
Le 7:38 the Lord **c** Moses in mount Sinai, ...6680
Le 8:9 holy crown; as the Lord **c** Moses 6680
Le 8:35 that ye die not: for so I am **c** 6680
Le 9:6 the Lord **c** that ye should do: 6680
Nu 1:19 the Lord **c** Moses, so he numbered 6680
Nu 34:13 Lord **c** to give unto the nine tribes, ...6680
Nu 34:29 Lord **c** to divide the inheritance 6680
Dt 4:5 even as the Lord my God **c** me, ...6680
Dt 6:1 the Lord your God **c** to teach 6680
Dt 6:17 statues, which he hath **c** thee 6680
Dt 13:5 the Lord thy God **c** thee to walk 6680
Dt 33:4 Moses **c** us a law, even the 6680
Jos 1:9 Have not I **c** thee? Be strong 6680
Jos 4:8 as Joshua **c**, and took up twelve 6680
Jos 14:2 as the Lord **c** by the hand of Moses, ...6680
Ru 2:15 Boaz **c** his young men, saying, ...6680
1Sa 17:20 and went, as Jesse had **c** him; 6680
2Sa 7:7 whom I **c** to feed my people 6680
1Ki 17:4 I have **c** the ravens to feed thee 6680
1Ki 17:9 I have **c** a widow woman there to 6680
1Ch 14:16 David therefore did as God **c** him: 6680
Ezr 5:3 Who hath **c** you to build 7761, 2942
Ezr 5:9 Who **c** you to build this 7761, 2942
Ne 13:19 I **c** that the gates should be shut, ...559
Est 4:13 Mordecai **c** to answer Esther, ...559
Est 4:17 according to all that Esther had **c** 6680
Est 6:1 he **c** to bring the book of records 559
Est 8:9 that Mordecai **c** unto the Jews, ...6680
Ps 78:23 Though he had **c** the clouds from 6680
Ps 119:4 hast **c** us to keep thy precepts 6680
Ps 119:138 testimonies that thou hast **c** are 6680
Ps 148:5 for he **c**, and they were created 6680
La 1:17 the Lord hath **c** concerning Jacob, ...6680
Eze 37:7 I prophesied as I was **c**: and as I 6680
Da 2:2 the king **c** to call the magicians, ...559
Da 2:12 and **c** to destroy all the wise men 560
Da 3:20 And he **c** the most mighty men 560
Da 5:2 **c** to bring the golden and silver 560
Da 6:23 and **c** that they should take Daniel 560
Am 2:12 **c** the prophets, saying, Prophesy 6680
Mt 8:4 **offer the gift that Moses c, for a** *4367*
Mt 14:19 he **c** the multitude to sit down on *2753*
Mt 15:4 **For God c, saying, Honour thy** *1781*
Mt 27:58 Pilate **c** the body to be delivered *2753*
Mt 28:20 **whatsoever I have c you: and, lo,** *1781*
Mk 6:27 and **c** his head to be brought *2004*
Lk 9:21 and **c** them to tell no man *3853*
Jn 8:5 Now Moses in the law **c** us, ...*1781*
Ac 4:18 and **c** them not to speak at all nor *3853*
Ac 10:42 he **c** us to preach unto the people, ...*3853*
Ac 10:48 he **c** them to be baptized in the *4367*
Ac 21:33 and **c** him to be bound with two *2753*
2Co 4:6 For God, who **c** the light to shine *2036*

COMMANDEDST

Ne 9:14 **c** them precepts, statutes, and laws, ...6680
Jer 32:23 of all that thou **c** them to do: 6680

COMMANDEST

Jos 1:16 All that thou **c** us we will do, ...6680
Ac 23:3 and **c** me to be smitten contrary *2753*

COMMANDETH

Job 9:7 Which **c** the sun, and it riseth not; 559
Job 36:32 and **c** it not to shine by the cloud 6680
Ps 107:25 For he **c**, and raiseth the stormy 559
Mk 1:27 **c** he even the unclean spirits, ...*2004*
Lk 4:36 power he **c** the unclean spirits *2004*
Lk 8:25 he **c** even the winds and water, ...*2004*

COMMANDING

Ge 49:33 Jacob had made an end of **c** his 6680
Mt 11:1 an end of **c** his twelve disciples, ...*1299*
1Ti 4:3 **c** to abstain from meats, which

COMMANDMENT

Ex 36:6 Moses gave **c**, and they caused 6680
Nu 15:31 hath broken his **c**, that soul shall 4687
Jos 1:18 be that doth rebel against thy **c**, ...6310
2Sa 12:9 despised the **c** of the Lord, to do 1697
2Ki 17:37 the law, and the **c**, which he wrote 4687
1Ch 28:21 people will be wholly at thy **c** 1697
Ezr 10:3 that tremble at the **c** of our God; 4687
Ne 12:24 the **c** of David the man of God, ...4687
Est 1:12 refused to come at the king's **c** 1697
Est 2:20 for Esther did the **c** of Mordecai, ...3982
Est 4:5 and gave him a **c** to Mordecai, ...6680
Est 8:17 the king's **c** and his decree came, ...1697
Ps 19:8 **c** of the Lord is pure, enlightening 4687
Pr 6:23 **c** is a lamp: and the law is light; 4687
Pr 13:13 feareth the **c** shall be rewarded 4687
Pr 19:16 keepeth the **c** keepeth his own 4687
Ecc 8:5 keepeth the **c** shall feel no evil 4687
Hos 5:11 he willingly walked after the **c** 6673
Mt 15:3 **Why do ye also transgress the c** *1785*
Mt 15:6 **made the c of God of none effect** *1785*
Mt 22:36 which is the great **c** in the law? *1785*
Mt 22:38 **This is the first and great c** *1785*
Mk 12:30 **strength: this is the first c** *1785*
Mk 12:31 **there is none other c greater than** *1785*
Jn 10:18 **This c have I received of my** *1785*
Jn 12:50 **And I know that his c is life** *1785*
Jn 13:34 **A new c I give unto you, That ye** *1785*
Jn 14:31 **as the Father gave me c, even so** *1781*
Jn 15:12 **This is my c, That ye love** *1785*
Ro 7:9 but when the **c** came, sin revived *1785*
Ro 7:12 the **c** holy, and just, and good *1785*
Ro 16:26 the **c** of the everlasting God, ...*2003*
Eph 6:2 which is the first **c** with promise; *1785*
1Ti 1:5 Now the end of the **c** is charity *3852*
Heb 7:16 not after the law of a carnal **c**, ...*1785*
Heb 11:22 and gave **c** concerning his bones *1781*
Heb 11:23 were not afraid of the king's **c** *1297*
1Jn 2:7 I write no new **c** unto you, ...*1785*
1Jn 2:7 but an old **c** which ye had from the *1785*
1Jn 2:7 The old **c** is the word which ye *1785*
1Jn 3:23 love one another, as he gave us **c** *1785*
2Jn 4 have received a **c** from the Father *1785*
2Jn 6 This is the **c**, That, as ye have *1785*

COMMANDMENTS

Ge	26:5	my **c**, my statutes, and my laws	4687
Ex	20:6	them that love me, and keep my **c**	4687
Ex	34:28	words of the covenant, the ten **c**	1697
Dt	4:13	to perform, even ten **c**: and he	1697
Dt	10:4	the ten **c**, which the Lord spake	1697
Dt	13:18	Lord thy God, to keep all his **c**	4687
Dt	15:5	observe to do all these **c** which I	4687
Ne	10:29	do all the **c** of the Lord our God,	4687
Ps	119:10	O let me not wander from thy **c**	4687
Ps	119:19	hide not thy **c** from me	4687
Ps	119:47	I will delight myself in thy **c**	4687
Ps	119:86	All thy **c** are faithful: they	4687
Ps	119:127	I love thy **c** above gold; yea	4687
Pr	4:4	my words: keep my **c**, and live	4687
Pr	10:8	The wise in heart will receive **c**	4687
Ecc	12:13	Fear God, and keep his **c** for this	4687
Mt	5:19	**shall break one of these least c,**	*1785*
Mt	22:40	**On these two c hang all the law**	*1785*
Mk	10:19	**Thou knowest the c, Do not commit**	*1785*
Lk	18:20	**Thou knowest the c, Do not**	*1785*
Jn	14:15	**If ye love me, keep my c**	*1785*
Jn	15:10	**If ye keep my c, ye shall abide in**	*1785*
Jn	15:10	**kept my Father's c, and abide in**	*1785*
Ac	1:2	had given **c** unto the apostles	*1781*
Col	2:22	after the **c** and doctrines of men?	*1778*
1Jn	2:4	and keepeth not his **c**, is a liar	*1785*
1Jn	5:2	when we love God, and keep his **c**	*1785*
1Jn	5:3	love of God, that we keep his **c**	*1785*
1Jn	5:3	and his **c** are not grievous	*1785*
2Jn	6	this is love, that we walk after his **c**	*1785*
Rev	22:14	Blessed are they that do his **c**	*1785*

COMMEND

Lk	23:46	**into thy hands I c my spirit:**	*3908*
Ac	20:32	brethren, I **c** you to God, and to	*3908*

COMMENDED

Pr	12:8	be **c** according to his wisdom:	1984
Lk	16:8	**the lord c the unjust steward,**	*1867*
Ac	14:23	they **c** them to the Lord, on whom	*3908*

COMMENDETH

Ro	5:8	But God **c** his love toward us,	*4921*
1Co	8:8	But meat **c** us not to God:	*3936*

COMMIT

Ex	20:14	thou shalt not **c** adultery	5003
Le	6:2	If a soul sin, and **c** a trespass	4600
Dt	5:18	Neither shalt thou **c** adultery	5003
Dt	19:20	**c** no more any such evil among	6213
2Sa	7:14	If he **c** iniquity, I will chasten	5753
Ps	31:5	Into thine hand I **c** my spirit:	6485
Ps	37:5	**C** thy way unto the Lord; trust	1556
Pr	16:3	**C** thy works unto the Lord,	1556
Mt	5:27	**Thou shalt not c adultery:**	*3431*
Mk	10:19	**Do not c adultery,**	*3431*
Lk	12:48	**did c things worthy of stripes,**	*4160*
Lk	16:11	**c to your trust the true riches?**	*4100*
Jn	2:24	Jesus did not **c** himself unto	*4100*
Ro	2:22	a man should not **c** adultery,	*3431*
2Ti	2:2	the same **c** thou to faithful men,	*3908*
Jas	2:9	ye **c** sin, and are convinced of the	*2038*
1Jn	3:9	is born of God doth not **c** sin;	*4160*
Rev	2:20	**to c fornication, and to eat things**	*4203*

COMMITTED

Ge	39:8	he hath **c** all that he hath to my	5414
Ge	39:22	of the prison **c** to Joseph's hand	5414
Dt	21:22	man have **c** a sin worthy of death,	1961
Jgs	20:6	**c** lewdness and folly in Israel	6213
Ps	106:6	we have **c** iniquity, we have done	5753
Jer	2:13	For my people have **c** two evils;	6213
Eze	16:52	**c** more abominable than they:	8581
Eze	23:37	their idols have they **c** adultery	5003
Da	9:5	sinned, and have **c** iniquity,	5753
Mal	2:11	an abomination is **c** in Israel	6213
Mt	5:28	**hath c adultery with her already**	*3431*
Mk	15:7	**c** murder in the insurrection.	*4160*
Lk	12:48	**to whom men have c much, of**	*3908*
Ac	8:3	men and women **c** them to prison	*3860*
Ac	25:11	or have **c** any thing worthy of	*4238*
Ac	27:40	they **c** themselves unto the sea,	*1439*
Ro	3:2	them were **c** the oracles of God	*4100*
2Co	5:19	and hath **c** unto us the word of	*5087*
1Ti	1:11	which was **c** to my trust	*4100*
2Ti	1:12	able to keep that which I have **c**	*3866*
Jas	5:15	if he have **c** sins, they shall be	*4160*

COMMITTETH

Le	20:10	man that **c** adultery with another	5003
Eze	8:6	that the house of Israel **c** here,	6213
Mt	5:32	**her that is divorced c adultery**	*3429*
Mt	19:9	**marry another, c adultery: and**	*3429*
Jn	8:34	**c sin is the servant of sin**	*4160*
1Jn	3:4	Whosoever **c** sin transgresseth	*4160*
1Jn	3:8	He that **c** sin is of the devil; for	*4160*

COMMON

Le	4:27	**c** people sin through ignorance,	776
1Sa	21:4	is no **c** bread under mine hand,	2455
Jer	31:5	and shall eat them as **c** things	2490
Mt	27:27	took Jesus into the **c** hall, and	*4232*
Ac	2:44	and had all things **c**;	*2839*
Ac	4:32	but they had all things **c**	*2839*
Ac	5:18	put them in the **c** prison.	*1219*
Ac	10:14	any thing that is **c** or unclean.	*2839*
1Co	10:13	you but such as is **c** to man:	*442*
Jude	3	write unto you of the **c** salvation,	*2839*

COMMONLY

Mt	28:15	is **c** reported among the Jews	*1310*
1Co	5:1	It is reported **c** that there is	*3654*

COMMUNE

Ge	34:6	out unto Jacob to **c** with him	1696
Ex	25:22	and I will **c** with thee from above	1696
1Sa	19:3	I will **c** with my father of thee;	1696
Ps	4:4	**c** with your own heart upon your	559

COMMUNED

Ge	23:8	And he **c** with them, saying, If it	1696
1Sa	9:25	Samuel **c** with Saul upon the top	1696
1Sa	25:39	David sent and **c** with Abigail	1696
1Ki	10:2	she was come to Solomon, she **c**	1696
Lk	24:15	they **c** together and reasoned,	*3656*
Ac	24:26	him the oftener, and **c** with him	*3656*

COMMUNICATE

Php	4:14	that ye did **c** with my affliction.	*4790*
Heb	13:16	to do good and to **c** forget not:	*2842*

COMMUNICATED

Gal	2:2	**c** unto them that gospel which I	*394*
Php	4:15	church **c** with me as concerning	*2841*

COMMUNICATION

2Sa	3:17	And Abner had **c** with the elders	1697
Mt	5:37	**your c be, Yea, yea; Nay, nay:**	*3056*
Eph	4:29	Let no corrupt **c** proceed out of	*3056*
Col	3:8	filthy **c** out of your mouth	*148*
Phm	6	The **c** of thy faith may become	*2842*

COMMUNION

1Co	10:16	not the **c** of the blood of Christ?	*2842*
2Co	6:14	what **c** hath light with darkness?	*2842*
2Co	13:14	the **c** of the Holy Ghost, be with	*2842*

COMPANIES

Jgs	7:16	three hundred men into three **c**,	7218
1Sa	11:11	Saul put the people in three **c**;	7218
Ne	12:31	two great **c** of them that gave thanks,	4256
Isa	57:13	criest, let thy **c** deliver thee	736
Mk	6:39	sat down by **c** upon the green	*4849*

COMPANION

Jgs	14:20	Samson's wife was given to his **c**,	4828
Jgs	15:2	I gave her to thy **c**: is not her	4828
Jgs	15:6	his wife, and given her to his **c**	4828
Ps	119:63	am a **c** of all them that fear thee,	2270
Pr	13:20	but a **c** of fools shall be destroyed.	7462
Pr	28:7	but he that is a **c** of riotous men	7462
Mal	2:14	yet is she thy **c**, and the wife of	2278
Php	2:25	my brother, and **c** in labour,	*4904*
Rev	1:9	and **c** in tribulation, and in the	*4791*

COMPANIONS

Jgs	14:11	they brought thirty **c** to be with	4828
SS	8:13	the **c** hearken to thy voice:	2270
Isa	1:23	are rebellious, and **c** of thieves:	2270
Ac	19:29	of Macedonia, Paul's **c** in travel,	*4898*

COMPANY

Ge	32:8	If Esau come to the one **c**,	4264
Ge	35:11	a **c** of nations shall be of thee,	6951
Ge	37:25	a **c** of Ishmeelites came from	736
Nu	26:9	in the **c** of Korah, when they	5712
Nu	26:10	when that **c** died, what time the	5712
Ps	55:14	unto the house of God in **c**	7285
Ps	106:18	And a fire was kindled in their **c**;	5712
Pr	29:3	he that keepeth **c** with harlots	7462
SS	6:13	As it were the **c** of two armies.	4246
Eze	38:15	horses, a great **c**, and a mighty	6951
Lk	5:29	**c** of publicans and of others that	*3793*
Lk	6:17	and the **c** of his disciples, and a	*3793*
Lk	9:14	**them sit down by fifties in a c**	*2828*
Lk	23:27	great **c** of people, and of women,	*4128*
Ac	10:28	is a Jew to keep **c**, or come unto	*2853*
Ac	13:13	when Paul and his **c** loosed	*3588, 4012*
Ac	21:8	day we that were of Paul's **c**	*4012*
1Co	5:11	written unto you not to keep **c**,	*4874*
2Th	3:14	that man, and have no **c** with him,	*4874*
Heb	12:22	to an innumerable **c** of angels,	*3461*
Rev	18:17	all the **c** in ships, and sailors,	*3658*

COMPARE

Isa	46:5	and **c** me, that we may be like?	4911
Mk	4:30	**what comparison shall we c it?**	*3846*

COMPARED

Ps	89:6	who in the heaven can be **c** unto	6186
Pr	8:11	may be desired are not to be **c** to	7737
SS	1:9	I have **c** thee, O my love, to a	1819

COMPARING

1Co	2:13	**c** spiritual things with spiritual	*4793*
2Co	10:12	**c** themselves among themselves,	*4793*

COMPARISON

Hag	2:3	is it not in your eyes in **c** of it as	3644
Mk	4:30	**or with what c shall we compare**	*3850*

COMPASS

Ex	27:5	put it under the **c** of the altar	3749
Nu	21:4	way of the Red sea, to **c** the land	5437
Jos	6:4	ye shall **c** the city seven times,	5437
Job	16:13	His archers **c** me round about,	5437
Job	40:22	willows of the brook **c** him about	5437
Ps	32:7	thou shalt **c** me about with songs	5437
Ps	32:10	Lord, mercy shall **c** him about.	5437
Mt	23:15	**ye c sea and land to make one**	*4013*
Lk	19:43	**a trench about thee, and c thee**	*4033*
Ac	28:13	thence we fetched a **c**, and came	*4022*

COMPASSED

Ge	19:4	**c** the house round, both old and	5437
Jos	6:11	So the ark of the Lord **c** the city,	5437
Jos	6:14	the second day they **c** the city once,	5437
Jos	6:15	on that day they **c** the city seven	5437
2Sa	22:5	waves of death **c** me, the floods	661
2Sa	22:6	The sorrows of hell **c** me about;	5437
Job	19:6	and hath **c** me with his net.	5362
Job	26:10	hath **c** the waters with bounds,	2328
Ps	18:4	The sorrows of death **c** me, and	661
Ps	18:5	The sorrows of hell **c** me about:	5437
Ps	116:3	The sorrows of death **c** me, and	661
Ps	118:12	They **c** me about like bees; they	5437
La	3:5	me, and **c** me with gall and travail.	5362
Lk	21:20	**shall see Jerusalem c with armies,**	*2944*
Heb	5:2	himself also is **c** with infirmity	*4029*
Heb	12:1	are **c** about with so great a cloud	*4029*
Rev	20:9	and **c** the camp of the saints about,	*2944*

COMPASSETH

Ps	73:6	pride **c** them about as a chain:	6059
Hos	11:12	Ephraim **c** me about with lies,	37

COMPASSION

Ex	2:6	And she had **c** on him, and said,	2550
Ps	78:38	he, being full of **c**, forgave their	7349
Ps	86:15	a God full of **c**, and gracious,	7349
Ps	111:4	Lord is gracious and full of **c**.	7349
Ps	112:4	and full of **c** and nghteous,	7349
Ps	145:8	Lord is gracious, and full of **c**;	7349
Jer	12:15	I will return, and have **c** on them,	7355
Mt	9:36	he was moved with **c** on them,	*4697*
Mt	14:14	was moved with **c** toward them,	*4697*
Mt	20:34	Jesus had **c** on them, and touched	*4697*
Mk	1:41	Jesus, moved with **c**, put forth	*4697*
Mk	6:34	was moved with **c** toward them	*4697*
Mk	8:2	**have c on the multitude, because**	*4697*
Lk	10:33	**he saw him, he had c on him,**	*4697*
Lk	15:20	**his father saw him, and had c,**	*4697*
Ro	9:15	will have **c** on whom I will have **c**	*3627*
Heb	10:34	For ye had **c** of me in my bonds,	*4834*
1Pe	3:8	having **c** one of another, love	*4835*
Jude	22	have **c** making a difference:	*1653*

COMPASSIONS

La	3:22	consumed, because his **c** fail not	7355
Zec	7:9	shew mercy and **c** every man to	7356

COMPEL
Est 1:8 none did **c**: for so the king had 597
Mt 5:41 **shall c thee to go a mile, go with** *29*
Lk 14:23 **c them to come in, that my house** *315*

COMPELLED
1Sa 28:23 together with the woman, **c** him; 6555
Mt 27:32 him they **c** to bear his cross. *29*
2Co 12:11 a fool in glorying; ye have **c** me: *315*
Gal 2:3 a Greek, was **c** to be circumcised: *315*

COMPLAIN
Job 7:11 **c** in the bitterness of my soul. 7878
Job 31:38 the furrows likewise thereof **c**; 1058
La 3:39 Wherefore doth a living man **c**, ...596

COMPLAINT
Job 21:4 is my **c** to man? And if it were so, ...7879
Job 23:2 today is my **c** bitter: my stroke is 7879

COMPLETE
Col 2:10 are **c** in him, which is the head *4137*
Col 4:12 perfect and **c** in all the will of God. *4137*

COMPREHEND
Job 37:5 doeth he, which we cannot **c**. 3045
Eph 3:18 able to **c** with all saints what is *2638*

CONCEAL
Ge 37:26 slay our brother, and **c** his blood? 3680
Job 27:11 is with the Almighty will I not **c** 3582
Pr 25:2 It is the glory of God to **c** a thing: 5641

CONCEALED
Job 6:10 not **c** the words of the Holy One 3582
Ps 40:10 I have not **c** thy lovingkindness 3582

CONCEALETH
Pr 11:13 is of a faithful spirit **c** the matter 3680
Pr 12:23 A prudent man **c** knowledge: but 3680

CONCEIT
Pr 26:12 thou a man wise in his own **c**? 5869
Pr 26:16 The sluggard is wiser in his own **c** 5869
Pr 28:11 The rich man is wise in his own **c**; 5869

CONCEITS
Ro 11:25 be wise in your own **c**; *3844, 1438*
Ro 12:16 Be not wise in your own **c**. *3844, 1438*

CONCEIVE
Ge 30:38 should **c** when they came to drink 3179
Ge 30:41 that they might **c** among the rods 3179
Jgs 13:3 but thou shalt **c**, and bear a son 2029
Ps 51:5 and in sin did my mother **c** me 3179
Isa 7:14 a virgin shall **c**, and bear a son 2030
Lk 1:31 thou shalt **c** in thy womb, and *4815*
Heb 11:11 received strength to **c** seed, ...*2602*

CONCEIVED
Ge 21:2 Sarah **c**, and bare Abraham a son 2029
Ge 25:21 and Rebekah his wife **c** 2029
Ge 30:39 And the flocks **c** before the rods, ...3179
1Sa 1:20 after Hannah had **c**, that she bare 2029
Job 3:3 was said, There is a man child **c**. 2029
Isa 8:3 and she **c**, and bare a son. 2029
Hos 1:3 which **c**, and bare him a son. 2029
Mt 1:20 that which is **c** in her is of the *1080*
Lk 1:24 his wife Elisabeth **c**, and hid *4815*
Lk 1:36 hath also **c** a son in her old age: *4815*
Lk 2:21 before he was **c** in the womb. *4815*
Ac 5:4 why hast thou **c** this thing in *5087*
Jas 1:15 Then when lust hath **c**, it bringeth *4815*

CONCEPTION
Ge 3:16 multiply thy sorrow and thy **c**; 2032
Ru 4:13 the Lord gave her **c**, and she bare 2032
Hos 9:11 from the womb, and from the **c**. 2032

CONCERN
Ac 28:31 things which **c** the Lord Jesus *4012*
2Co 11:30 glory of the things which **c** mine *4012*

CONCERNING
Nu 8:22 commanded Moses **c** the Levites, ...5921
Nu 10:29 Lord hath spoken good **c** Israel 5921
Ru 4:7 **c** redeeming and **c** changing, ...5921
1Sa 3:12 which I have spoken **c** his house: 413
1Ki 8:41 Moreover **c** a stranger, that is 413
Ezr 5:5 answer by letter **c** this matter. 5922
Ne 13:14 Remember me, O my God, **c** this, ...5921
Ecc 3:18 I said in mine heart **c** the estate 5921
Mt 4:6 give his angels charge **c** thee: *4012*
Mt 16:11 **I spake it not to you c bread,** *4012*
Lk 2:17 which was told them **c** this child *4012*
Lk 18:31 **by the prophets c the Son of man**
Lk 22:37 **for the things c me have an end** *4012*
Lk 24:19 **C** Jesus of Nazareth, which was *4012*
Lk 24:27 scriptures the things **c** himself. *4012*
Lk 24:44 **and in the psalms, c me** *4012*
Ac 1:16 **c** Judas, which was guide to them *4012*
Ac 2:25 David speaketh **c** him, I foresaw *1519*
Ac 13:34 And as **c** that he raised him up *3754*
Ac 22:18 **not receive thy testimony c me** *4012*
Ro 1:3 **C** his son Jesus Christ our Lord, ...*4012*
Ro 9:27 Esaias also crieth **c** Israel, ...*5228*
Ro 11:28 As **c** the gospel, they are enemies *2596*
Ro 16:19 which is good, and simple **c** evil. *1519*
Eph 4:22 **c** the former conversation the old *2596*
Eph 5:32 I speak **c** Christ and the church. *1519*
Php 3:6 **C** zeal, persecuting the church: *2596*
1Th 5:18 will of God in Christ Jesus **c** you, ...*1519*
2Ti 3:8 minds, reprobate **c** the faith. *4012*
Heb 7:14 Moses spake nothing **c** priesthood. *4012*
Heb 11:22 gave commandment **c** his bones *4012*
1Pe 4:12 **c** the fiery trial which is to try you, ...*4012*
2Pe 3:9 Lord is not slack **c** his promise, ...*4314*

CONCLUDED
Ro 11:32 For God hath **c** them all in *4788*
Gal 3:22 the scripture hath **c** all under *4788*

CONCLUSION
Ecc 12:13 Let us hear the **c** of the whole 5490

CONCORD
2Co 6:15 And what **c** hath Christ with *4857*

CONCUBINE
Ge 35:22 Bilhah his father's **c**: and Israel 6370
Jgs 20:6 And I took my **c**, and cut her in 6370
2Sa 3:7 And Saul had a **c**, whose name was 6370

CONCUBINES
Ge 25:6 the sons of the **c**, which Abraham 6370
2Sa 5:13 David took him more **c** and wives 6370
1Ki 11:3 and three hundred **c**: and his 6370
Est 2:14 chamberlain, which kept the **c**: 6370
SS 6:9 the, queens and the **c**, and they 6370

CONCUPISCENCE

Ro 7:8 wrought in me all manner of c *1939*
1Th 4:5 Not in the lust of c, even as the *1939*

CONDEMN

Job 9:20 mine own mouth shall c me: 7561
Job 34:17 wilt thou c him that is most just? 7561
Ps 109:31 him from those that c his soul. 8199
Pr 12:2 a man of wicked devices will he c 7561
Mt 12:41 and shall c it: because they *2632*
Mt 12:42 and shall c it: for she came from *2632*
Mt 20:18 they shall c him to death, ...*2632*
Lk 6:37 c not, and ye shall not be *2613*
Jn 3:17 Son into the world to c the world *2919*
Jn 8:11 Neither do I c thee: go, and sin no *2632*
1Jn 3:20 For if our heart c us, God is *2607*
1Jn 3:21 if our heart c us not, then have *2607*

CONDEMNATION

Jn 3:19 And this is the c, that light is *2920*
Jn 5:24 shall not come into c; but is *2920*
Ro 5:16 for the judgment was by one to c, ...*2631*
Ro 5:18 judgment came upon all men to c; *2631*
Ro 8:1 now no c to them which are in *2631*
Jas 3:1 we shall receive the greater c. *2917*
Jas 5:12 your nay, nay; lest ye fall into c. *5272*

CONDEMNED

Job 32:3 no answer, and yet had c Job. 7561
Mt 12:7 ye would not have c the guiltless. *2613*
Mt 12:37 and by thy words thou shalt be c *2613*
Mk 14:64 they all c him to be guilty of death. *2632*
Lk 6:37 and ye shall not be c: forgive, ...*2613*
Jn 3:18 believeth on him is not c: but he *2919*
Jn 3:18 that believeth not is c already, ...*2919*
Tit 2:8 Sound speech, that cannot be c; *176*
Heb 11:7 by the which he c the world, and *2632*

CONDEMNETH

Job 15:6 Thine own mouth c thee, and 7561
Ro 8:34 Who is he that c? It is Christ *2632*
Ro 14:22 Happy is he that c not himself *4314*

CONDUCT

2Sa 19:15 king, to c the king over Jordan. 5674
2Sa 19:31 the king, to c him over Jordan. 7971
1Co 16:11 but c him forth in peace, that he *4311*

CONFEDERACY

Isa 8:12 Say ye not, A c, to all them to 7195
Ob 7 All the men of thy c have brought 1285

CONFEDERATE

Ge 14:13 these were c with Abram. 1167, 1285
Ps 83:5 they are c against thee: 1285, 3772

CONFERRED

1Ki 1:7 And he c with Joab the son 1961, 1697
Gal 1:16 I c not with flesh and blood: *4323*

CONFESS

Le 5:5 he shall c that he hath sinned 3034
Nu 5:7 c their sin which they have done: 3034
Ps 32:5 I will c my transgressions unto 3034
Mt 10:32 shall c me before men, him will *3670*
Lk 12:8 shall the Son of man also c *3670*
Ro 10:9 c with thy mouth the Lord Jesus *3670*
Ro 14:11 and every tongue shall c to God *1843*
Ro 15:9 c to thee among the Gentiles, ...*1843*
Php 2:11 should c that Jesus Christ is Lord, ...*1843*
Jas 5:16 C your faults one to another, and *1843*
1Jn 1:9 If we c our sins, he is faithful and *3670*
1Jn 4:15 c that Jesus is the Son of God, ...*3670*
Rev 3:5 will c his name before my Father, ...*1843*

CONFESSED

Ne 9:2 stood and c their sins, and the 3034
Jn 1:20 he c, and denied not; but *3670*
Jn 1:20 c, I am not the Christ *3670*
Heb 11:13 and c that they were strangers *3670*

CONFESSETH

Pr 28:13 c and forsaketh them shall have 3034
1Jn 4:2 Every spirit that c that Jesus *3670*
1Jn 4:3 every spirit that c not that Jesus *3670*

CONFESSING

Da 9:20 praying, and c my sin and the 3034
Mt 3:6 of him in Jordan, c their sins. *1843*
Mk 1:5 in the river of Jordan, c their sins. *1843*

CONFESSION

Ezr 10:11 make c unto the Lord God of 8426
Da 9:4 Lord my God, and made my c, ...3034
Ro 10:10 mouth c is made unto salvation; *3670*

CONFIDENCE

Job 4:6 not this thy fear, thy c, thy hope, ...3690
Ps 118:8 in the Lord than to put c in man. 982
Pr 3:26 the Lord shall be thy c, and 3689
Pr 14:26 the fear of the Lord is strong c: 4009
Mic 7:5 a friend, put ye not c in a guide: 982
2Co 1:15 in this c I was minded to come *4006*
2Co 2:3 having c in you all, that my joy *3982*
Gal 5:10 have c in you through the Lord, ...*3982*
Eph 3:12 and access with c by the faith *4006*
Php 3:3 and have no c in the flesh. *3982*
Php 3:4 might also have c in the flesh. *4006*
Heb 3:14 if we hold the beginning of our c *5287*
1Jn 3:21 then have we c toward God. *3954*

CONFIDENT

Ps 27:3 against me, in this will I be c 982
Pr 14:16 but the fool rageth, and is c 982
2Co 5:8 are c, I say, and willing rather *2292*
Php 1:6 Being c of this very thing, that *3982*
Php 1:14 waxing c by my bonds, are much *3982*

CONFIRM

Ps 68:9 thou didst c thine inheritance, ...3559
Da 9:27 And he shall c the convenant 1396
Ro 15:8 to c the promises made unto the *950*
2Co 2:8 would c your love toward him *2964*

CONFIRMED

Est 9:32 Esther c these matters of Purim; 6965
1Co 1:6 testimony of Christ was c in you: *950*
Gal 3:17 that was c before of God in Christ, ...*4300*
Heb 6:17 of his counsel, c it by an oath: *3315*

CONFORMED

Ro 8:29 to be c to the image of his Son *4832*
Ro 12:2 And be not c to this world: but *4964*

CONFOUND

Ge 11:7 and there c their language, ...1101
Ge 11:9 the Lord did there c the language 1101
1Co 1:27 things of the world to c the wise; *2617*
1Co 1:27 c the things which are mighty; *2617*

CONFOUNDED
Job 6:20 were **c** because they had hoped; 954
Ps 22:5 trusted in thee, and were not **c** 954
Ps 35:4 Let them be **c** and put to shame 954
Isa 24:23 Then the moon shall be **c**, ...2659
Mic 3:7 ashamed, and the diviners **c**: 2659
Zec 10:5 the riders on horses shall be **c** 3001
1Pe 2:6 believeth on him shall not be **c** *2617*

CONFUSION
Job 10:15 I am full of **c**; therefore see 7036
Ps 44:15 My **c** is continually before me, ...3639
Da 9:8 Lord, to us belongeth **c** of face, ...1322
Ac 19:29 the whole city was filled with **c**: *4799*
1Co 14:33 For God is not the author of **c**, ...*181*

CONGREGATION
Ex 12:19 be cut off from the **c** of Israel, ...5712
Ex 27:21 the tabernacle of the **c** without 4150
Le 4:13 And if the whole **c** of Israel sin 5712
Nu 1:2 Take ye the sum of all the **c** 5712
Nu 1:16 were the renowned of the **c**, ...5712
Nu 35:25 the **c** shall restore him to the city 5712
Dt 31:30 spake in the ears of all the **c** of 4150
Jos 8:35 Joshua read not before all the **c** 6951
2Ch 1:3 Solomon, and all the **c** with him, ...6951
2Ch 29:28 all the **c** worshipped, and the 6951
Ezr 2:64 whole **c** together was forty and two 6951
Ne 8:2 brought the law before the **c** both 6951
Ps 1:5 sinners in the **c** of the righteous 5712
Ps 26:5 have hated the **c** of evil doers; 6951
Ps 149:1 and his praise in the **c** of saints 6951
Isa 14:13 sit also upon the mount of the **c**, ...4150
La 1:10 they should not enter into thy **c** 6951
Joel 2:16 Gather the people, sanctify the **c** 6951
Ac 13:43 Now when the **c** was broken up *4864*

CONGREGATIONS
Ps 26:12 in the **c**, will I bless the Lord. 4721
Ps 74:4 roar in the midst of thy **c**; 4150

CONQUERORS
Ro 8:37 we are more than **c** through him *5245*

CONSCIENCE
Ac 23:1 have lived in all good **c** before God *4893*
Ac 24:16 to have always a **c** void of offence *4893*
Ro 2:15 their **c** also bearing witness, and *4893*
1Co 8:7 and their **c** being weak is defiled. *4893*
1Co 8:10 shall not the **c** of him which is weak ...*4893*
1Co 10:29 liberty judged of another man's **c**? *4893*
2Co 1:12 is this, the testimony of our **c**, ...*4893*
1Ti 1:19 Holding faith, and a good **c**; *4893*
1Ti 3:9 mystery of the faith in a pure **c** *4893*
1Ti 4:2 their **c** seared with a hot iron; *4893*
Heb 9:14 purge your **c** from dead works *4893*
Heb 10:2 should have had no more **c** of sins *4893*
Heb 10:22 hearts sprinkled from an evil **c**, ...*4893*
1Pe 2:19 if a man for **c** toward God endure *4883*

CONSECRATE
Ex 29:9 shalt **c** Aaron and his sons. 3027
Ex 32:39 **C** yourselves today to the 4390, 3027
Mic 4:13 and I will **c** their gain unto the 2763

CONSECRATED
Ex 29:29 anointed therein, and to be **c** 4390, 3027
2Ch 26:18 Aaron, that are **c** to burn incense: 6942
Ezr 3:5 set feasts of the Lord that were **c**, ...6942
Heb 7:28 the Son, who is **c** for evermore *5048*
Heb 10:20 way, which he hath **c** for us, ...*1457*

CONSECRATION
Ex 29:22 for it is a ram of **c**: 4394
Ex 29:31 thou shalt take the ram of the **c**, ...4394
Nu 6:7 because the **c** of his God is upon 5145

CONSECRATIONS
Le 8:28 they were **c** for a sweet savour: 4394
Le 8:31 bread that is in the basket of **c** 4394

CONSENT
Ge 34:15 But in this will we **c** unto you: 225
1Sa 11:7 and they came out with one **c** 376
1Ki 20:8 him, Hearken not unto him, nor **c** 14
Pr 1:10 if sinners entice thee, **c** thou not 14
Zep 3:9 the Lord, to serve him with one **c** 7926
1Ti 6:3 and **c** not to wholesome words, ...4334

CONSENTED
Da 1:14 So he **c** to them in this matter, ...8085
Ac 18:20 longer time with them, he **c** not; *1962*

CONSENTING
Ac 8:1 And Saul was **c** unto his death *4909*
Ac 22:20 standing by, and **c** unto his death, ...*4909*

CONSIDER
Dt 4:39 Know therefore this day, and **c** 7725
Dt 8:5 Thou shalt also **c** in thine heart 3045
Job 37:14 and **c** the wondrous works of God 995
Ps 5:1 O Lord, **c** my mediation. 995
Ps 8:3 When I **c** thy heavens, the work 7200
Ps 50:22 Now **c** this, ye that forget God, ...995
Ps 119:153 **C** mine affliction, and deliver me: 7200
Ps 119:159 **C** how I love thy precepts: 7200
Pr 6:6 the ant, thou sluggard; **c** her ways, ...7200
Ecc 7:13 **C** the work of God: for who 7200
La 1:11 see, O Lord, and **c**; for I am 5027
Mt 6:28 **C the lilies of the field, how they.** *2648*
Lk 12:24 **C the ravens: for they neither** *2657*
2Ti 2:7 **C** what I say; and the Lord give *3539*
Heb 3:1 **c** the Apostle and High Priest *2657*
Heb 7:4 Now **c** how great this man was, ...*2334*
Heb 10:24 let us **c** one another to provoke *2657*
Heb 12:3 For **c** him that endured such *357*

CONSIDERED
Job 1:8 Hast thou **c** my servant Job, ...7760, 3820
Job 2:3 Hast thou **c** my servant Job, ...3820
Ps 31:7 thou hast **c** my trouble; thou 7200
Ecc 4:15 I **c** all the living which walk 7200
Ro 4:19 he **c** not his own body now dead, ...*2657*

CONSIDEREST
Jer 33:24 **C** thou not what this people have 7200
Mt 7:3 **but c not the beam that is in** *2657*

CONSIDERETH
Ps 41:1 Blessed is he that **c** the poor: 7919
Pr 21:12 wisely **c** the house of the wicked: 7919
Pr 29:7 The righteous **c** the cause of the 3045
Pr 31:16 She **c** a field, and buyeth it: 2161

CONSIDERING
Da 8:5 I was **c**, behold, an he goat came 995
Gal 6:1 **c** thyself, lest thou also be *4648*
Heb 13:7 **c** the end of their conversation *333*

CONSIST

Col 1:17	things, and by him all things **c**	*4921*

CONSOLATION

Jer 16:7	give them the cup of **c** to drink	8575
Lk 2:25	waiting for the **c** of Israel:	*3874*
Lk 6:24	for ye have received your **c**	*3874*
Ac 4:36	being interpreted, The son of **c**,)	*3874*
2Co 1:6	it is for your **c** and salvation	*3874*
Php 2:1	any **c** in Christ, if any comfort	*3874*
Phm 7	we have great joy and **c** in thy	*3874*

CONSPIRACY

2Ki 12:20	servants arose, and made a **c**, and	7195
2Ki 14:19	Now they made a **c** against	7195
Jer 11:9	the Lord said unto me, A **c** is	7195
Ac 23:13	than forty which had made this **c**	4945

CONSPIRED

Ge 37:18	they **c** against him to slay him.	5230
Ne 4:8	**c** all of them together to come	7194
Am 7:10	Amos hath **c** against thee in the	7194

CONSTANTLY

Pr 21:28	man that heareth speaketh **c**	5331
Ac 12:15	she **c** affirmed that it was even	*1340*
Tit 3:8	things I will that thou affirm **c**,	*1226*

CONSTRAIN

Gal 6:12	they **c** you to be circumcised;	*315*

CONSTRAINED

2Ki 4:8	she **c** him to eat bread. And so	2388
Mt 14:22	Jesus **c** his disciples to get into a	*315*
Mk 6:45	straightway he **c** his disciples to	*315*
Ac 28:19	I was **c** to appeal unto Caesar;	*315*

CONSTRAINETH

Job 32:18	the spirit within me **c** me,	6693
2Co 5:14	the love of Christ **c** us; because	*4912*

CONSULTED

1Ki 12:6	Rehoboam **c** with the old men,	3289
1Ki 12:8	and **c** with the young men that	3289
Ne 5:7	Then I **c** with myself, and I	4427
Ps 83:5	have **c** together with one consent:	3289
Mt 26:4	**c** that they might take Jesus by	*4823*
Jn 12:10	the chief priests **c** that they	*1011*

CONSUME

Ge 41:30	and the famine shall **c** the land;	3615
Dt 5:25	this great fire will **c** us: if we	398
Dt 28:38	for the locust shall **c** it	2628
Est 9:24	to **c** them, and to destroy them;	2000
Job 24:19	and heat **c** the snow waters:	1497
Ps 37:20	**c**; into smoke shall they **c** away	3615
Ps 59:13	**C** them in wrath, **c** them, that	3615
Da 7:26	**c** and to destroy it unto the end	8046
Lk 9:54	down from heaven, and **c** them,	*355*
2Th 2:8	the Lord shall **c** with the spirit	*355*
Jas 4:3	that ye may **c** it upon your lusts	*1159*

CONSUMED

Ex 3:2	with fire, and the bush was not **c**	398
Le 9:24	and **c** upon the altar the burnt	398
Nu 16:26	lest ye be **c** in all their sins	5595
Jos 10:20	great slaughter, till they were **c**	8552
Ezr 9:14	till thou hadst **c** us, so that	3615
Ne 2:3	the gates thereof are **c** with fire?	398
Job 4:9	breath of his nostrils are they **c**	3615
Job 7:9	cloud is **c** and vanisheth away:	3615
Ps 6:7	Mine eye is **c** because of grief:	6244
Ps 31:10	iniquity, and my bones are **c**	6244
Ps 119:139	My zeal hath **c** me, because mine	6789
Isa 1:28	that forsake the Lord shall be **c**	3615
La 3:22	Lord's mercies that we are not **c**	8552
Da 11:16	which by his hand shall be **c**	3615
Gal 5:15	take heed that ye be not **c** one of	*355*

CONSUMING

Dt 4:24	the Lord thy God is a **c** fire,	398
Dt 9:3	as a **c** fire he shall destroy them,	398
Heb 12:29	For our God is a **c** fire	*2654*

CONSUMPTION

Le 26:16	terror, **c**, and the burning ague,	7829
Dt 28:22	The Lord shall smite thee with a **c**,	7829
Isa 10:23	God of hosts shall make a **c**,	3617

CONTAIN

1Ki 8:27	heaven of heavens cannot **c** thee;	3557
Jn 21:25	even the world itself could not **c**	*5562*
1Co 7:9	if they cannot **c**, let them marry:	*1467*

CONTEMNED

Ps 15:4	In whose eyes a vile person is **c**;	959
Ps 107:11	**c** the council of the most High:	5006
SS 8:7	for love, it would utterly be **c**	936

CONTEMPT

Ps 119:22	Remove from me reproach and **c**;	937
Isa 23:9	to bring into **c** all the honourable	7043
Da 12:2	some to shame and everlasting **c**	1860

CONTEMPTIBLE

Mal 1:7	ye say. The table of the Lord is **c**	959
2Co 10:10	is weak, and his speech **c**	*1848*

CONTEND

Dt 2:9	neither **c** with them in battle:	1624
Job 13:8	his person? will ye **c** for God?	7378
Pr 28:4	such as keep the law **c** with them.	1624
Isa 57:16	I will not **c** for ever, neither will I	7378
Am 7:4	the Lord God called to **c** by fire,	7378
Jude 3	ye should earnestly **c** for the faith	*1864*

CONTENDETH

Job 40:2	Shall he that **c** with the Almighty	7378
Pr 29:9	If a wise man **c** with a foolish	8199

CONTENT

Ex 2:21	And Moses was **c** to dwell with	2974
Jos 7:7	would to God we had been **c**, and	2974
2Ki 5:23	Naaman said, Be **c**, take two	2974
Pr 6:35	neither will he rest **c**, though thou	14
Mk 15:15	Pilate, willing to **c** the	*2425, 3588, 4160*
Php 4:11	state I am, therewith to be **c**	*842*
Heb 13:5	be **c** with such things as ye have:	*714*

CONTENTION

Pr 13:10	by pride cometh **c**: but with the	4683
Pr 18:6	A fool's lips enter into **c**, and his	7379
Pr 22:10	out the scorner, and **c** shall go out;	4066
Php 1:16	The one preach Christ of **c**, not	*2052*
1Th 2:2	the gospel of God with much **c**	*73*

CONTENTIONS

Pr 19:13	the **c** of a wife are a continual	4079
1Co 1:11	that there are **c** among you	*2504*
Tit 3:9	genealogies, and **c**, and strivings	*2504*

CONTENTIOUS
Pr 21:29 with a **c** and an angry woman 4066
Pr 27:15 rainy day and a **c** woman are alike......4066
1Co 11:16 But if any man seem to be **c**, ...*5380*

CONTENTMENT
1Ti 6:6 godliness with **c** is great gain. *841*

CONTINUAL
Ex 29:42 a **c** burnt offering throughout 8548
Nu 28:3 day by day, for a **c** burnt offering.......8548
2Ki 25:30 his allowance was a **c** allowance 8548
2Ch 2:4 for the **c** shewbread, and for the 8548
Pr 15:15 of a merry heart hath a **c** feast 8548
Pr 19:13 of a wife are a **c** dropping. 2956
Pr 27:15 A **c** dropping in a very rainy day 2956
Jer 52:34 a **c** diet given him of the king 8548
Lk 18:5 **lest by her c coming** *1519, 5056*
Ro 9:2 great heaviness and **c** sorrow *88*

CONTINUALLY
Ge 6:5 of his heart was only evil **c** 3605, 3117
Ge 8:3 returned from off the earth **c**: 1980, 7725
Le 24:2 to cause the lamps to burn **c** 8548
2Sa 9:7 shalt eat bread at my table **c** 8548
1Ch 16:11 his strength, seek his face **c** 8548
Job 1:5 Thus did Job **c** 3605, 3117
Ps 34:1 praise shall **c** be in my mouth. 8548
Ps 40:11 and thy truth **c** preserve me 8548
Ps 52:1 goodness of God endureth **c** 3605, 3117
Ps 71:14 I will hope **c**, and will yet praise 8548
Ps 109:15 Let them be before the Lord **c** 8548
Ps 119:44 So shall I keep thy law **c** for ever 8548
Ps 119:109 My soul is **c** in my hand: 8548
Pr 6:14 he deviseth mischief **c**; 6256
Pr 6:21 Bind them **c** upon thine heart 8548
Isa 21:8 I stand **c** upon the watchtower 8548
Isa 65:3 that provoketh me to anger **c** 8548
Eze 46:14 offering **c** by a perpetual ordinance 8548
Da 6:16 Thy God whom thou servest **c** 8411
Da 6:20 is thy God, whom thou servest **c** 8411
Lk 24:53 And were **c** in the temple *1725*
Ac 6:4 will give ourselves **c** to prayer *4342*
Heb 7:3 of God; abideth a priest **c** *1519, 1336*
Heb 10:1 offered year by year **c** make *1519, 1336*
Heb 13:15 the sacrifice of praise to God **c** *1275*

CONTINUE
1Sa 12:14 **c** following the Lord your God: 1961
1Sa 13:14 now thy kingdom shall not **c**: 6965
1Ki 2:4 That the Lord may **c** his word 6965
Ps 36:10 **c** thy lovingkindness unto them 4900
Da 11:8 shall **c** more years than the king 5975
Mt 15:32 **they c with me now three days** *4357*
Jn 8:31 **If ye c in my word, then are ye** *3306*
Jn 15:9 **I loved you: c ye in my love** *3306*
Ro 6:1 Shall we **c** in sin, that grace *1961*
Gal 2:5 of the gospel might **c** with you *1265*
Col 4:2 **C** in prayer, and watch in the *4342*
1Ti 2:15 if they **c** in faith and charity *3306*
1Ti 4:16 **c** in them: for in doing this thou *1961*
Heb 13:1 Let brotherly love **c** *3306*
1Jn 2:24 remain in you, ye also shall **c** *3306*

CONTINUED
1Sa 1:12 she **c** praying before the Lord, ...7235
2Sa 6:11 ark of the Lord **c** in the house 3427
Ne 5:16 also I **c** in the work of this wall, ...2388
Ps 72:17 shall be **c** as long as the sun: 5125
Lk 22:28 **c with me in my temptations** *1265*
Ac 1:14 all **c** with one accord in prayer *4342*
Ac 2:42 they **c** steadfastly in the apostles *4342*
Ac 12:16 But Peter **c** knocking, and when *1961*
Heb 8:9 they **c** not in my covenant *1696*

C

CONTINUETH
1Ti 5:5 **c** in supplications and prayers *4357*
Heb 7:24 this man, because he **c** ever, ...*3306*
Jas 1:25 law of liberty, and **c** therein, ...*3887*

CONTINUING
Ac 2:46 And they, **c** daily with one accord *4342*
Ro 12:12 tribulations; **c** instant in prayer; *4342*

CONTRADICTION
Heb 7:7 without all **c** the less is blessed *485*
Heb 12:3 **c** of sinners against himself, ...*485*

CONTRARY
Le 26:24 Then will I also walk **c** unto you 7147
Mk 6:48 for the wind was **c** unto them: *1727*
Ac 18:13 men to worship God **c** to the law *3844*
Gal 5:17 these are **c** the one to the other: *480*
1Th 2:15 not God, and are **c** to all men: *1727*
1Ti 1:10 thing that is **c** to sound doctrine; *480*
Tit 2:8 is of the **c** part may be ashamed, ...*1727*

CONTRITE
Ps 34:18 saveth such as be of a **c** spirit..........1793
Ps 51:17 a broken and a **c** heart, O God 1794
Isa 66:2 him that is poor and of a **c** spirit, ...5223

CONTROVERSY
Jer 25:31 Lord hath a **c** with the nations, ...7379
Eze 44:24 in **c** they shall stand in judgment; 7379
Mic 6:2 the Lord hath a **c** with his people, ...7379
1Ti 3:16 without **c** great is the mystery *3672*

CONVENIENT
Pr 30:8 feed me with food **c** for me: 2706
Mk 6:21 And when a **c** day was come, ...*2121*
Ac 24:25 when I have a **c** season, I will call *2540*

CONVERSATION
Ps 37:14 to slay such as be of upright **c** 1870
2Co 1:12 we have had our **c** in the world, ...*390*
Eph 2:3 we all had our **c** in times past *390*
Eph 4:22 put off concerning the former **c** *391*
Php 1:27 let your **c** be as it becometh the *4176*
1Ti 4:12 in word, in **c**, in charity, in spirit, ...*391*
Heb 13:5 your **c** be without covetousness; *5158*
1Pe 1:15 so be ye holy in all manner of **c**; *391*
1Pe 3:1 be won by the **c** of the wives; *391*

CONVERT
Isa 6:10 with their heart, and **c**, and be 7725
Jas 5:19 from the truth, and one **c** him; *1994*

CONVERTED
Ps 51:13 and sinners shall be **c** unto thee 7725
Mt 13:15 **and should be c, and I should** *1994*
Mk 4:12 **they should be c, and their sins** *1994*
Lk 22:32 **and when thou art c, strengthen** *1994*
Ac 3:19 Repent ye therefore, and be **c**, ...*1994*

CONVERTING
Ps 19:7 of the Lord is perfect, **c** the soul: 7725

CONVEY
Ne 2:7 river, that they may **c** me over 5674

CONVINCE
Tit 1:9 exhort and to **c** the gainsayers. *1651*
Jude 15 to **c** all that are ungodly among *1827*

CONVINCED
Job 38:12 there was none of you that **c** Job, ...3198
Ac 18:28 For he mightily **c** the Jews, ...*1246*

CONVINCETH
Jn 8:46 **Which of you c me of sin?** *1651*

CONVOCATION
Nu 28:26 be out, ye shall have an holy **c**; 4744
Nu 29:1 the month, ye shall have an holy **c**; 4744

COOL
Ge 3:8 in the garden in the **c** of the day; 7307
Lk 16:24 **finger in water, and c my tongue;** *2711*

COPY
Dt 17:18 he shall write him a **c** of this law 4932
Jos 8:32 a **c** of the law of Moses, which he 4932
Ezr 4:11 This is the **c** of the letter that 6573
Est 4:8 the **c** of the writing of the decree 6572

CORBAN (cor´-ban)
Mk 7:11 **It is C, that is to say, a gift,** *2878*

CORD
Jos 2:15 down by a **c** through the window: 2256
Ecc 4:12 threefold **c** is not quickly broken 2339
Ecc 12:6 Or ever the silver **c** be loosed, or 2256

CORDS
Nu 3:26 **c** of it for all the service thereof. 4340
Nu 3:37 sockets, their pins, and their **c** 4340
Jgs 15:13 they bound him with two new **c**, ...5688
Jgs 15:14 the **c** that were upon his arms 5688
Pr 5:22 be holden with the **c** of his sins. 2256
Hos 11:4 I drew them with **c** of a man, with 2256
Jn 2:15 he had made a scourge of small **c**, ...*4979*

CORN
Ge 27:28 earth, and plenty of **c** and wine: 1715
Ge 42:1 saw that there was **c** in Egypt 7668
Ge 42:25 to fill their sacks with **c**, and to 1250
Dt 16:9 to put the sickle to the **c** 7054
Jos 5:12 eaten of the old **c** of the land; 5669
Ru 3:7 down at the end of the heap of **c**: 6194
Ne 10:39 offering of the **c**, of the new wine, ...1715
Ps 78:24 given them of the **c** of heaven 1715
Pr 11:26 He that withholdeth **c**, the 1250
Mt 12:1 the sabbath day through the **c**; *4702*
Lk 6:1 disciples plucked the ears of **c**, ...*4719*
Jn 12:24 **Except a c of wheat fall into the** *2848*
1Co 9:9 of the ox that treadeth out the **c**
1Ti 5:18 muzzle the ox that treadeth out the **c**

CORNER
Le 21:5 shave off the **c** of their beard, ...6285
2Ki 11:11 from the right **c** of the temple 3802
2Ch 28:24 altars in every **c** of Jerusalem. 6438
Job 38:6 or who laid the **c** stone thereof; 6438
Ps 118:22 become the head stone of the **c** 6438
Pr 21:9 to dwell in a **c** of the housetop, ...6438
Pr 25:24 to dwell in the **c** of the housetop 6438
Isa 28:16 precious **c** stone, a sure foundation: 6438
Zec 10:4 Out of him came forth the **c**, ...6438
Mt 21:42 **same is become the head of the c:** *1137*
Mk 12:10 **is become the head of the c:** *1137*
Lk 20:17 **same is become the head of the c?** *1137*
Ac 4:11 which is become the head of the **c**: *1137*
Eph 2:20 Christ himself being the chief **c** *204*
1Pe 2:6 I lay in Sion a chief **c** stone, elect, ...*204*

CORNERS
Ex 25:12 put them in the four **c** thereof; 6471
Ex 26:23 make for the **c** of the tabernacle 4742
Le 19:9 not wholly reap the **c** of thy field, ...6285
Le 19:27 shalt thou mar the **c** of thy beard 6285
Dt 32:26 said, I would scatter them into **c**, ...6284
Job 1:19 smote the four **c** of the house 6438
Mt 6:5 **in the c of the streets, that they** *1137*
Rev 7:1 standing on the four **c** of the earth, ...1137

CORNET
Ps 98:6 With trumpets and sound of **c** 7782
Da 3:7 people heard the sound of the **c**, ...7162
Hos 5:8 Blow ye the **c** in Gilbeah, and the 7782

CORRECT
Ps 39:11 thou with rebukes dost **c** man 3256
Pr 29:17 **C** thy son, and he shall give thee 3256
Jer 30:11 I will **c** thee in measure, and will 3256

CORRECTED
Pr 29:19 A servant will not be **c** by words: 3256
Heb 12:9 fathers of our flesh which **c** us *3810*

CORRECTETH
Job 5:17 happy is the man whom God **c**: 3198
Pr 3:12 For whom the Lord loveth he **c**; 3198

CORRECTION
Pr 3:11 neither be weary of his **c**: 8433
Pr 7:22 as a fool to the **c** of the stocks; 4148
Pr 15:10 **C** is grievous unto him that 4148
Pr 22:15 rod of **c** shall drive it far from him 4148
Pr 23:13 Withhold not **c** from the child: 4148
2Ti 3:16 for reproof, for **c**, for instruction *1882*

CORRUPT
Ge 6:11 The earth also was **c** before God, ...7843
Ge 6:12 it was **c**; for all flesh had corrupted 7843
Ps 53:1 **C** are they, and have done 7843
Ps 73:8 They are **c**, and speak wickedly 4167
Pr 25:26 troubled fountain, and a **c** spring 7843
Da 2:9 have prepared lying and **c** words 7844
Da 11:32 shall he **c** by flatteries: but the 2610
Mt 6:20 **neither moth nor dust doth c,** *853*
Mt 7:17 **a c tree bringeth forth evil fruit** *4550*
Mt 12:33 **make the tree c, and his fruit c:** *4550*
Eph 4:22 old man, which is **c** according to *5351*
Eph 4:29 Let no **c** communication proceed *4550*
2Ti 3:8 men of **c** minds, reprobate *2704*
Jude 10 those things they **c** themselves *5351*

CORRUPTED
Ex 8:24 land was **c** by reason of the swarm 7843
Eze 28:17 thou hast **c** thy wisdom by reason 7843
2Co 7:2 we have **c** no man, we have *5351*
2Co 11:3 your minds should be **c** from the *5351*

CORRUPTIBLE
1Co 9:25 they do it to obtain a **c** crown; *5349*
1Co 15:53 this **c** must put on incorruption, ...*5349*

1Co 15:54	So when this **c** shall have put on	*5349*
1Pe 1:18	were not redeemed with **c** things,	*5349*
1Pe 1:23	not of **c** seed, but of incorruptible,	*5349*

CORRUPTION

Ps 16:10	suffer thine Holy One to see **c**	7845
Jnh 2:6	thou brought up my life from **c**	7845
Ac 2:27	suffer thine Holy One to see **c**	*1312*
Ac 2:31	in hell, neither his flesh did see **c**	*1312*
Ac 13:35	not suffer thine Holy One to see **c**	*1312*
1Co 15:50	neither doth **c** inherit incorruption	*5356*
Gal 6:8	shall of the flesh reap **c**; but he	*5356*
2Pe 1:4	escaped the **c** that is in the world	*5356*

COST

2Sa 24:24	of that which doth **c** me nothing	2600
1Ch 21:24	nor offer burnt offerings without **c**	2600
Lk 14:28	**down first, and counteth the c**	*1160*

COSTLY

1Ki 5:17	**c** stones, and hewed stones,	3368
Jn 12:3	of ointment of spikenard, very **c**,	*4186*
1Ti 2:9	or gold, or pearls, or **c** array:	*4185*

COUCH

Ps 6:6	I water my **c** with my tears	6210
Lk 5:24	**take up thy c, and go unto thine**	*2826*

COULD

Ex 2:3	when she **c** not longer hide him,	3201
Ex 9:11	magicians **c** not stand before Moses	3201
Ex 15:23	**c** not drink of the waters of Marah	3201
1Sa 3:2	to wax dim, that he **c** not see;	3201
1Sa 4:15	eyes were dim, that he **c** not see	3201
Ne 13:24	**c** not speak in the Jews' language	5234
Est 6:1	that night **c** not the king sleep	5074
Da 5:8	but they **c** not read the writing	3546
Da 5:15	they **c** not shew the interpretation	3546
Jnh 1:13	they **c** not: for the sea wrought,	3201
Mt 17:16	and they **c** not cure him	*1410*
Mt 26:40	**What, c ye not watch with me**	*2480*
Mk 9:18	cast him out; and they **c** not	*2489*
Mk 14:8	**She hath done what she c: she is**	*2192*
Ac 25:7	Paul, which they **c** not prove	*2480*
2Co 3:7	Israel **c** not stedfastly behold	*1410*
Gal 3:21	a law given which **c** have given	*1410*
Rev 14:3	and no man **c** learn that song but	*1410*

COULDEST

Mk 14:37	**c not thou watch one hour?**	*2480*

COUNCIL

Mt 5:22	**Raca, shall be in danger of the c:**	*4892*
Mt 12:14	Pharisees went out, and held a **c**	*4824*
Jn 11:47	chief priests and the Pharisees a **c**,	*4892*
Ac 23:1	Paul, earnestly beholding the **c**,	*4892*

COUNSEL

Ex 18:19	I will give thee **c**, and God shall	3289
Nu 31:16	through the **c** of Balaam, to	1697
Dt 32:28	For they are a nation void of **c**,	6098
1Sa 14:37	And Saul asked **c** of God, Shall I	
2Sa 17:23	saw that his **c** was not followed	6098
1Ki 12:8	he forsook the **c** of the old men,	6098
1Ki 12:9	What **c** give ye that we may	3289
1Ki 12:13	forsook the old men's **c** that they	6098
Ne 6:7	and let us take **c** together	3289
Job 10:3	shine upon the **c** of the wicked?	6098
Ps 1:1	walketh not in the **c** of the ungodly,	6098
Ps 2:2	the rulers take **c** together,	3245
Ps 33:11	The **c** of the Lord standeth for	6098
Ps 64:2	Hide me from the secret **c** of the	5475
Ps 71:10	that lay wait for my soul take **c**	3289
Pr 8:14	**C** is mine, and sound wisdom:	6098
Pr 11:14	Where no **c** is, the people fall:	8458
Pr 12:15	that hearkeneth unto **c** is wise	6098
Pr 19:20	Hear **c**, and receive instruction	6098
Pr 20:5	**C** in the heart of man is like deep	6098
Pr 20:18	Every purpose is established by **c**:	6098
Pr 24:6	wise **c** thou shalt make thy war	8458
Pr 27:9	of a man's friend by hearty **c**	6098
Isa 5:19	the **c** of the Holy One of Israel	6098
Jer 23:18	hath stood in the **c** of the Lord,	5475
Jer 32:19	Great in **c**, and mighty in work:	6098
Da 4:27	let my **c** be acceptable unto thee,	4431
Mt 22:15	took **c** how they might entangle	*4824*
Mt 27:1	and elders of the people took **c**	*4824*
Lk 7:30	lawyers rejected the **c** of God	*1012*
Ac 2:23	determinate **c** and foreknowledge	*1012*
Ac 5:33	heart, and took **c** to slay them	*1011*
Ac 9:23	the Jews took **c** to kill him:	*4823*
Eph 1:11	after the **c** of his own will:	*1012*

COUNSELLER

1Ch 27:32	Jonathan David's uncle was a **c**,	3289
2Ch 22:3	mother was his **c** to do wickedly	3289
Isa 9:6	shall be called Wonderful, **C**,	3289

COUNSELLERS

2Ch 22:4	they were his **c** after the death	3289
Ezr 4:5	hired **c** against them, to frustrate	3289
Ps 119:24	also are my delight and my **c**	6098
Pr 11:14	multitude of **c** there is safety	3289
Pr 12:20	but to the **c** of peace is joy	3289
Pr 24:6	multitude of **c** there is safety	3289
Da 3:27	king's **c**, being gathered together,	1907

COUNSELLOR

Mk 15:43	of Arimathaea, an honourable **c**,	*1010*
Ro 11:34	or who hath been his **c**?	*4825*

COUNSELS

Ps 5:10	let them fall by their own **c**;	4156
Pr 1:5	shall attain unto wise **c**:	8458
Pr 12:5	the **c** of the wicked are deceit	8458
Pr 22:20	things in **c** and knowledge	4156
Mic 6:16	ye walk in their **c**: that I should	4156
1Co 4:5	manifest the **c** of the hearts:	*1012*

COUNT

Le 25:27	**c** the years of the sale thereof,	2803
Nu 23:10	Who can **c** the dust of Jacob,	4487
Job 31:4	see my ways, and **c** all my steps?	5608
Ps 87:6	The Lord shall **c**, when he writeth	5608
Ps 139:18	If I should **c** them, they are more	5608
Ac 20:24	neither **c** I my life dear unto	*2192*
Php 3:8	I **c** all things but loss for the	*2233*
Php 3:8	do **c** them but dung, that I may	*2233*
Jas 1:2	**c** it all joy when ye fall into	*2233*
Jas 5:11	we **c** them happy which endure	*3106*
2Pe 3:9	as some men **c** slackness; but is	*2233*

COUNTED

Ge 15:6	he **c** it to him for righteousness	2803
1Ki 3:8	be numbered nor **c** for multitude	5608
Ps 44:22	we are **c** as sheep for the slaughter	2803
Ps 106:31	was **c** unto him for righteousness	2803

C

Pr	17:28	he holdeth his peace, is **c** wise:	2803
Isa	33:18	where is he that **c** the towers?	5608
Mt	14:5	because they **c** him as a prophet	*2192*
Ac	5:41	that they were **c** worthy to suffer	*2661*
Ro	4:3	**c** unto him for righteousness	*3049*
Ro	4:5	his faith is **c** for righteousness	*3049*
Php	3:7	gain to me, those I **c** loss for	*2233*
2Th	1:5	may be **c** worthy of the kingdom	*2661*
1Ti	1:12	that he **c** me faithful, putting me	*2233*
1Ti	5:17	well be **c** worthy of double honour	*515*
Heb	10:29	hath **c** the blood of the covenant,	*2233*

COUNTENANCE

Ge	4:5	Cain was very wroth, and his **c** fell	6440
Ge	4:6	why is thy **c** fallen?	6440
Nu	6:26	The Lord lift up his **c** upon thee	6440
Jgs	13:6	his **c** was like the **c** of an angel	4758
1Sa	16:7	Look not on his **c**, or on the	4758
1Sa	17:42	youth, and ruddy, and of a fair **c**	4758
Ne	2:2	Why is thy **c** sad, seeing thou art	6440
Ne	2:3	why should not thy **c** be sad	6440
Job	29:24	light of my **c** they cast not down	6440
Ps	4:6	lift thou up the light of thy **c**	6440
Ps	43:5	health of my **c**, and my God	6440
Ps	89:15	walk, O Lord, in the light of **c**:	6440
Pr	15:13	merry heart maketh a cheerful **c**:	6440
Pr	25:23	an angry **c** a backbiting tongue	6440
Pr	27:17	sharpeneth the **c** of his friend	6440
SS	2:14	is thy voice, and thy **c** is comely	4758
Da	5:6	the king's **c** was changed, and	2122
Mt	28:3	His **c** was like lightning, and his	*2397*
Lk	9:29	his **c** was altered, and	*4383*
2Co	3:7	of Moses for the glory of his **c**;	*4383*
Rev	1:16	and his **c** was as the sun shineth	*3799*

COUNTENANCES

Da	1:13	Then let our **c** be looked upon	4758
Da	1:15	their **c** appeared fairer and	4758

COUNTETH

Job	19:11	he **c** me unto him as one of his	2803
Lk	14:28	**and c the cost, whether he have**	*5585*

COUNTRIES

Ge	10:20	after their tongues, in their **c**,	776
Ge	41:57	all **c** came into Egypt to Joseph	776
Eze	36:19	were dispersed through the **c**,	776
Lk	21:21	**that are in the c enter thereinto**	*5562*

COUNTRY

Ge	12:1	Get thee out of thy **c**, and from thy	776
Ge	14:7	smote all the **c** of the Amalekites,	7704
Ge	29:26	It must not be so done in our **c**	4725
Le	24:22	stranger, as for one of your own **c**:	249
Jos	2:24	the inhabitants of the **c** do faint	776
Jos	6:22	men that had spied out the **c**,	776
Jgs	8:28	**c** was in quietness forty years	776
Ru	1:1	to sojourn in the **c** of Moab, he,	7704
1Sa	27:7	the time that David dwelt in the **c**	7704
1Sa	27:11	dwelleth in the **c** of the Philistines	7704
Pr	25:25	soul, so is good news from a far **c**	776
Jnh	1:8	what is thy **c**? and of what people	776
Mt	2:12	into their own **c** another way	*5561*
Mt	13:54	he was come into his own **c**, he	*3968*
Mt	13:57	**without honour, save in his own c,**	*3968*
Mt	25:14	**a man travelling into a far c, who**	*589*
Lk	2:8	were in the same **c** shepherds	*5561*
Lk	4:24	**prophet is accepted in his own c**	*3968*
Lk	15:13	**took his journey into a far c, and**	*5561*
Lk	15:15	**himself to a citizen of that c;**	*5561*
Jn	4:44	hath no honour in his own **c**	*3968*
Ac	7:3	Get thee out of thy **c**, and from	*1093*
Heb	11:14	declare plainly that they seek a **c**	*3968*

COUNTRYMEN

2Co	11:26	in perils by mine own **c**, in perils	*1085*
1Th	2:14	suffered like things of your own **c**,	*4853*

COUPLE

Ex	26:6	and **c** the curtains together with	2266
Ex	36:18	of brass to **c** the tent together	2266

COUPLED

1Pe	3:2	chaste conversation **c** with fear	

COURAGE

Dt	31:6	Be strong and of a good **c**, fear not	553
Dt	31:7	Be strong and of a good **c**: for	553
Dt	31:23	Be strong and of a good **c**: for	553
Jos	1:6	Be strong and of a good **c**: for unto	553
Jos	1:9	Be strong and of a good **c**; be not	553
Jos	1:18	only be strong and of a good **c**	553
Jos	10:25	be strong and of good **c**: for thus	553
Ps	27:14	Wait on the Lord: be of good **c**	2388
Ps	31:24	Be of good **c**, and he shall	2388
Ac	28:15	saw, he thanked God, and took **c**	*2294*

COURAGEOUS

Jos	1:7	Only be thou strong and very **c**,	553
2Sa	13:28	I commanded you? be **c**, and be	2388
2Ch	32:7	Be strong and **c**, be not afraid	553

COURSE

Ps	82:5	of the earth are out of **c**	4131
Jer	23:10	their **c** is evil, and their force is	4794
Ac	13:25	as John fulfilled his **c**, he said	*1408*
Ac	20:24	that I might finish my **c** with joy,	*1408*
Eph	2:2	according to the **c** of this world,	*165*
2Th	3:1	word of the Lord may have free **c**,	*5143*
2Ti	4:7	I have finished my **c**, I have kept	*1408*
Jas	3:6	setteth on fire the **c** of nature;	*5164*

COURSES

2Ch	31:2	appointed the **c** of the priests and	4256
2Ch	31:2	and the Levites after their **c**,	4256
Isa	44:4	as willows by the water **c**	2988

COURT

Le	6:16	place; in the **c** of the tabernacle	2691
2Ki	20:4	was gone out into the middle **c**,	5892
2Ch	20:5	house of the Lord, before the new **c**,	2691
Est	5:2	Esther the queen standing in the **c**	2691
Est	6:5	Behold, Haman standeth in the **c**	2691
Isa	34:13	of dragons, and a **c** for owls	2681
Jer	32:2	was shut up in the **c** of the prison,	2691
Eze	10:3	and the cloud filled the inner **c**	2691
Rev	11:2	the **c** which is without the temple	*833*

COURTS

1Ch	28:6	he shall build my house and my **c**:	2691
Ne	8:16	and in the **c** of the house of God	2691
Ps	65:4	thee, that he may dwell in thy **c**:	2691
Ps	84:2	even fainteth for the **c** of the Lord:	2691
Ps	84:10	For a day in thy **c** is better than	2691
Ps	96:8	an offering, and come into his **c**	2691
Ps	100:4	into his **c** with praise: be thankful	2691

COVENANT

Ge	6:18	with thee will I establish my **c**;	1285
Ge	9:9	behold, I establish my **c** with you,	1285
Ge	9:11	I will establish my **c** with you;	1285
Ge	9:12	This is the token of the **c** which	1285
Ge	9:16	the everlasting **c** between God	1285
Ge	15:18	the Lord made a **c** with Abram	1285
Ge	17:7	for an everlasting **c**, to be a God	1285
Ge	17:21	my **c** will I establish with Isaac	1285
Ex	24:7	And he took the book of the **c**,	1285
Ex	34:28	upon the tables the words of the **c**	1285
Le	26:42	will I remember my **c** with Jacob,	1285
Le	26:42	and also my **c** with Isaac,	1285
Le	26:42	and also my **c** with Abraham	1285
Nu	18:19	it is a **c** of salt for ever before the	1285
Nu	25:13	the **c** of an everlasting priesthood;	1285
Dt	9:11	stone, even the tables of the **c**	1285
Dt	10:8	to bear the ark of the **c** of the Lord	1285
Jos	3:3	When ye see the ark of the **c** of	1285
Jos	3:6	Take up the ark of the **c**, and pass	1285
Jos	3:17	priests that bare the ark of the **c**	1285
Jos	6:8	and the ark of the **c** of the Lord	1285
Jos	24:25	Joshua made a **c** with the people	1285
Jgs	2:1	I will never break my **c** with you	1285
Jgs	2:20	people hath transgressed my **c**	1285
1Sa	4:3	Let us fetch the ark of the **c** of the	1285
1Sa	11:1	Make a **c** with us, and we will	1285
1Sa	18:3	Jonathan and David made a **c**	1285
2Ki	13:23	because of his **c** with Abraham	1285
2Ki	23:21	it is written in the book of this **c**	1285
1Ch	11:3	David made a **c** with them in	1285
1Ch	16:15	Be ye mindful always of his **c**;	1285
1Ch	16:17	to Israel for an everlasting **c**	1285
1Ch	28:2	house of rest for the ark of the **c**	1285
Ezr	10:3	let us make a **c** with our God	1285
Ne	9:8	madest a **c** with him to give the land	1285
Ne	9:32	God, who keepest **c** and mercy	1285
Job	31:1	I made a **c** with mine eyes; why	1285
Ps	25:10	as keep his **c** and his testimonies	1285
Ps	50:5	made a **c** with me by sacrifice	1285
Ps	89:3	I have made a **c** with my chosen,	1285
Ps	89:34	My **c** will I not break, nor alter	1285
Ps	105:8	hath remembered his **c** for ever,	1285
Ps	105:10	and to Israel for an everlasting **c**:	1285
Ps	132:12	If thy children will keep my **c** and	1285
Pr	2:17	and forgetteth the **c** of her God	1285
Isa	28:18	**c** with death shall be disannulled,	1285
Isa	54:10	neither shall the **c** of my peace be	1285
Isa	55:3	make an everlasting **c** with you	1285
Jer	3:16	The ark of the **c** of the Lord:	1285
Jer	11:6	Hear ye the words of this **c**, and do	1285
Jer	33:21	also my **c** be broken with David	1285
Jer	50:5	to the Lord in a perpetual **c** that	1285
Eze	16:60	I will remember my **c** with thee in	1285
Eze	16:60	establish unto thee an everlasting **c**	1285
Eze	17:14	by keeping of his **c** it might stand	1285
Eze	37:26	will make a **c** of peace with them:	1285
Eze	37:26	shall be an everlasting **c** with them:	1285
Da	9:27	he shall confirm the **c** with many	1285
Da	11:28	heart shall be against the holy **c**;	1285
Hos	2:18	in that day will I make a **c** for them	1285
Am	1:9	remembered not the brotherly **c**:	1285
Zec	9:11	by the blood of thy **c** I have sent	1285
Mal	2:14	companion, and the wife of thy **c**	1285
Mal	3:1	the messenger of the **c**, whom ye	1285
Lk	1:72	to remember his holy **c**;	*1242*
Ac	3:25	**c** which God made with our fathers,	*1242*
Heb	8:6	he is the mediator of a better **c**,	*1242*
Heb	8:10	this is the **c** that I will make with	*1242*
Heb	8:13	In that he saith, A new **c**, he	
Heb	9:1	Then verily the first **c** had also	
Heb	12:24	Jesus the mediator of the new **c**,	*1242*
Heb	13:20	the blood of the everlasting **c**,	*1242*

C

COVENANTBREAKERS See also BREAKER.

Ro	1:31	**c**, without natural affection.	*802*

COVENANTED

2Ch	7:18	as, I have **c** with David thy father	3772
Mt	26:15	they **c** with him for thirty pieces	*2476*
Lk	22:5	glad, and **c** to give him money	*4934*

COVENANTS

Gal	4:24	for these are the two **c**; the one	*1242*
Eph	2:12	strangers from the **c** of promise,	*1242*

COVER

Ex	10:5	they shall **c** the face of the earth,	3680
Ex	33:22	and will **c** thee with my hand while	5526
Ex	40:3	and **c** the ark with the vail	5526
Nu	4:5	**c** the ark of testimony with it:	3680
1Sa	24:3	Saul went in to **c** his feet: and	5526
Job	16:18	**c** not thou my blood, and let my	3680
Ps	91:4	He shall **c** thee with his feathers,	5526
Ps	139:11	Surely the darkness shall **c** me;	7779
Isa	14:11	under thee, and the worms **c** thee	4374
Isa	22:17	captivity, and will surely **c** thee	5844
Eze	32:7	I will **c** the sun with a cloud,	3680
Hos	10:8	shall say to the mountains, **C** us;	3680
Hab	2:14	glory of the Lord, as the waters **c**	3680
Mk	14:65	spit on him, and to **c** his face	*4028*
Lk	23:30	**Fall on us; and to the hills, C us**	*2572*
1Pe	4:8	charity shall **c** the multitude of	*2572*

COVERED

Ge	7:19	under the whole heaven, were **c**	3680
Ge	7:20	and the mountains were **c**	3680
Ge	9:23	**c** the nakedness of their father;	3680
Ex	8:6	the frogs came up, and **c** the land	3680
Ex	14:28	waters returned, and **c** the chariots	3680
Ex	15:10	the sea **c** them: they sank as lead	3680
Ex	16:13	quails came up, and **c** the camp:	3680
Ex	24:15	and a cloud **c** the mount	3680
Ex	40:21	and **c** the ark of the testimony;	5526
Ex	40:34	Then a cloud **c** the tent of the	3680
Nu	16:42	the cloud **c** it, and the glory of	3680
Jgs	4:18	she **c** him with a mantle	3680
Jgs	4:19	and give him drink, and **c** him	3680
1Ki	6:9	and **c** the house with beams and	5603
1Ki	8:7	and the cherubims **c** the ark and	5526
2Ki	19:1	and **c** himself with sackcloth,	3680
Est	7:8	mouth, they **c** Haman's face	2645
Job	31:33	If I **c** my transgressions as Adam,	3680
Ps	32:1	is forgiven, whose sin is **c**	3680
Ps	69:7	reproach; shame hath **c** my face	3680
Ps	139:13	thou hast **c** me in my mother's	5526
Pr	26:26	Whose hatred is **c** by deceit	3680
Isa	6:2	with twain he **c** his face,	3680
Isa	6:2	and with twain he **c** his feet	3680
Isa	51:16	I have **c** thee in the shadow of mine	3680
La	3:44	Thou hast **c** thyself with a cloud	5526
Jnh	3:6	and **c** him with sackcloth, and sat	3680
Jnh	3:8	man and beast be **c** with sackcloth	3680
Hab	3:3	His glory **c** the heavens, and the	3680

Lk 12:2 **there is nothing c, that shall not** *4780*
Ro 4:7 forgiven, and whose sins are **c** *1943*
1Co 11:4 having his head **c**, dishonoureth *2596*
1Co 11:6 shorn or shaven, let her be **c** *2619*

COVERETH

Nu 22:11 which **c** the face of the earth: 3680
Jgs 3:24 he **c** his feet in his summer 5526
Job 36:32 With clouds he **c** the light; 3680
Ps 73:6 violence **c** them as a garment 5848
Ps 147:8 Who **c** the heaven with clouds 3680
Pr 10:12 up strifes: but love **c** all sins 3680
Pr 12:16 but a prudent man **c** shame 3680
Pr 28:13 that **c** his sins shall not prosper: 3680
Lk 8:16 **a candle, c it with a vessel,** *2572*

COVERING

Ge 8:13 Noah removed the **c** of the ark 4372
Ex 25:20 **c** the mercy seat with their wings, ...5526
Ex 26:7 to be a **c** upon the tabernacle: 168
Ex 26:14 a **c** for the tent of rams' skins, ...4372
Ex 26:14 and a **c** above of badgers' skins 4372
Ex 35:12 mercy seat, and the vail of the **c**, ...4539
Ex 40:19 the **c** of the tent above upon it; 4372
2Sa 17:19 spread a **c** over the well's mouth, ...4539
Job 24:7 that they have no **c** in the cold 3682
Ps 105:39 He spread a cloud for a **c**; and 4539
1Co 11:15 for her hair is given her for a **c** *4018*

COVERT

Ps 61:4 I will trust in the **c** of thy wings, ...5643
Isa 4:16 a **c** from storm and from rain 5643

COVET

Ex 20:17 shalt not **c** thy neighbour's house, ...2530
Dt 5:21 shalt thou **c** thy neighbour's house, ...183
Ro 7:7 law had said, thou shalt not **c**. *1937*
1Co 12:31 But **c** earnestly the best gifts: *2206*
1Co 14:39 **c** to prophesy, and forbid not to *2206*

COVETED

Jos 7:21 then I **c** them, and took them; 2530
Ac 20:33 I have **c** no man's silver, or gold, ... *1937*

COVETOUS

Ps 10:3 blesseth the **c**, whom the Lord 1214
Lk 16:14 the Pharisees also, who were **c**, ... *5366*
1Co 5:10 or with the **c**, or extortioners, or *4123*
Eph 5:5 nor **c** man, who is an idolater, ... *4123*
1Ti 3:3 patient, not a brawler, not **c**; *866*

COVETOUSNESS

Ex 18:21 fear God, men of truth, hating **c**; 1215
Pr 28:16 hateth **c** shall prolong his days. 1215
Mk 7:22 **Thefts, c, wickedness, deceit,** *4124*
Lk 12:15 **Take heed, and beware of c:** *4124*
Ro 1:29 wickedness, **c**, maliciousness; *4124*
Col 3:5 and **c**, which is idolatry: *4124*
1Th 2:5 as ye know, nor a cloke of **c**; *4124*
Heb 13:5 your conversation be without **c**; *866*

COW

Le 22:28 And whether it be **c** or ewe, ye 7794
Isa 11:7 And the **c** and the bear shall feed; 6510

CRAFT

Da 8:25 cause **c** to prosper in his hand; 4820
Mk 14:1 how they might take him by **c**, ... *1388*
Ac 18:3 because he was of the same **c**, ... *3673*

CRAFTINESS

Job 5:13 taketh the wise in their own **c**: 6193
Lk 20:23 But he perceived their **c**, and *3834*
2Co 4:2 not walking in **c**, nor handling the *3834*
Eph 4:14 the sleight of men, and cunning, **c** *3834*

CRAFTSMEN

2Ki 24:14 and all the **c** and smiths: none 2796
2Ki 24:16 and **c** and smiths a thousand, all 2796
Ac 19:24 brought no small gain unto the **c**; *5079*
Ac 19:38 and the **c** which are with him, ... *5079*

CRAFTY

Job 15:5 thou choosest the tongue of the **c**. 6175
2Co 12:16 being **c**, I caught you with guile. *3835*

CREATE

Ps 51:10 **C** in me a clean heart, O God; 1254
Isa 45:7 I form the light, and **c** darkness: 1254
Isa 57:19 I **c** the fruit of the lips; Peace, ...1254
Isa 65:17 I **c** new heavens and a new earth: 1254

CREATED

Ge 1:1 God **c** the heaven and the earth. 1254
Ge 1:21 And God **c** great whales, and every 1254
Ge 1:27 So God **c** man in his own image, ...1254
Ge 1:27 in the image of God **c** he him; 1254
Ge 1:27 male and female **c** he them. 1254
Ge 5:1 In the day that God **c** man, in the 1254
Ge 5:2 Male and female **c** he them; and 1254
Ge 6:7 I will destroy man whom I have **c** 1254
Ps 148:5 he commanded, and they were **c** 1254
Isa 41:20 the Holy One of Israel hath **c** it. 1254
Isa 42:5 he that **c** the heavens, and 1254
Isa 43:7 I have **c** him for my glory, I have 1254
Isa 45:8 I the Lord have **c** it. 1254
Mal 2:10 hath not one God **c** us? why do we 1254
Mk 13:19 **which God c unto this time,** *2936*
Eph 2:10 **c** in Christ Jesus unto good works, ... *2936*
Eph 3:9 in God, who **c** all things by Jesus *2936*
Col 1:16 by him were things **c**, that are in *2936*
Col 1:16 all things were **c** by him, and for *2936*
Col 3:10 after the image of him that **c** him: *2936*
Rev 4:11 for thou hast **c** all things, and for *2936*
Rev 4:11 thy pleasure they are and were **c**. *2936*
Rev 10:6 who **c** heaven, and the things that *2936*

CREATION

Mk 10:6 **But from the beginning of the c** *2937*
Ro 1:20 from the **c** of the world are clearly *2937*
Ro 8:22 that the whole **c** groaneth and *2937*
Rev 3:14 the beginning of the **c** of God; *2937*

CREATOR

Ecc 12:1 Remember now thy **C** in the days 1254
Isa 40:28 the **C** of the ends of the earth, ...1254
Ro 1:25 more than the **C**, who is blessed *2936*
1Pe 4:19 well doing, as unto a faithful **C**, ... *2939*

CREATURE

Ge 1:20 the moving **c** that hath life, and 8318
Ge 1:24 the earth bring forth the living **c** 5315
Ge 2:19 called every living **c**, that was the 5315
Ge 9:15 and every living **c** of all flesh; 5315
Ge 9:16 between God and every living **c** 5315
Eze 1:20 spirit of the living **c** was in the 2416
Mk 16:15 **and preach the gospel to every c** *2937*
Ro 1:25 and served the **c** more than the *2937*

Ro	8:39	nor any other **c**, shall be able to	*2937*
2Co	5:17	he is a new **c**; old things are	*2937*
Col	1:15	God, the firstborn of every **c**:	*2937*
1Ti	4:4	For every **c** of God is good and	*2938*
Rev	5:13	And every **c** which is in heaven,	*2938*

CREATURES

Isa	13:21	houses shall be full of doleful **c**;	255
Eze	1:5	came the likeness of four living **c**.	2416
Eze	1:19	when the living **c** went, the wheels	2416
Jas	1:18	be a kind of firstfruits of his **c**.	*2938*
Rev	8:9	third part of the **c** which were in	*2938*

CREDITOR

Dt	15:2	Every **c** that lendeth	1167, 4874, 3027
Lk	7:41	**There was a certain c which had**	*1157*

CREEP

Le	11:20	All fowls that **c**, going upon all	8318
Le	11:31	unclean to you among all that **c**:	8318
2Ti	3:6	are they which **c** into houses,	*1744, 1519*

CREEPETH

Ge	1:25	and every thing that **c** upon the	7431
Ge	7:21	and of every creeping thing that **c**	8317
Ge	8:17	and of every creeping thing that **c**	7430
Ge	8:19	fowl, and whatsoever **c** upon the	7430
Dt	4:18	The likeness of any thing that **c**	7430

CREEPING

Ge	1:24	cattle, and **c** thing, and beast of	7431
Ge	1:26	over every **c** thing that creepeth	7431
Le	5:2	carcase of unclean **c** things, and	8318
Ps	104:25	things **c** innumerable, both small	7431
Ac	10:12	and wild beasts, and **c** things, and	*2062*
Ro	1:23	fourfooted beasts, and **c** things.	*2052*

CREW

Mt	26:74	And immediately the cock **c**.	*5455*
Jn	18:27	again: and immediately the cock **c**	*5455*

CRIED

Ge	39:14	me, and I **c** with a loud voice:	7121
Ge	41:55	people **c** to Pharaoh for bread:	6817
Ex	2:23	and they **c**, and their cry came up	2199
Ex	14:10	and the children of Israel **c** out	6817
Nu	14:1	lifted up their voice, and **c**;	5414
Jgs	7:20	they **c**, The sword of the Lord,	7121
Jgs	7:21	all the host ran, and **c**, and fled.	7321
1Sa	7:9	and Samuel **c** unto the Lord for	2199
1Sa	15:11	and he **c** unto the Lord all night	2199
1Sa	24:8	out of the cave, and **c** after Saul,	7121
1Ki	17:21	the child three times, and **c** unto	7121
1Ki	18:28	they **c** aloud, and cut themselves	7121
Est	4:1	and **c** with a loud and a bitter cry;	2199
Ps	18:6	and **c** unto my God: he heard	7768
Ps	34:6	This poor man **c**, and the Lord	7121
Ps	119:145	I **c** with my whole heart;	7121
Ps	119:146	I **c** unto thee; save me, and I	7121
Ps	120:1	In my distress I **c** unto the Lord	7121
Jer	20:8	I **c** violence and spoil;	7121
Eze	10:13	As for the wheels, it was **c** unto	7121
Da	5:7	The king **c** aloud to bring in the	7123
Jnh	1:5	and **c** every man unto his god,	2199
Jnh	1:14	they **c** unto the Lord, and said,	7121
Jnh	2:2	out of the belly of hell **c** I, and	7768
Mt	14:30	beginning to sink, he **c**, saying,	*2896*
Mt	20:30	**c** out, saying, Have mercy on us,	*2896*
Mt	20:31	but they **c** the more, saying,	*2896*
Mt	21:9	**c**, saying, Hosanna to the son of	*2896*
Mt	27:46	Jesus **c** with a loud voice, saying,	*310*
Mt	27:50	Jesus, when he had **c** again with	*2896*
Mk	3:11	**c**, saying, Thou art the Son of God	*2896*
Mk	15:13	they **c** out again, Crucify him.	*2896*
Mk	15:37	And Jesus **c** with a loud voice,	*863*
Lk	16:24	**he c and said, Father Abraham,**	*5455*
Lk	18:38	he **c**, saying, Jesus, thou son of	*994*
Lk	23:21	But they **c**, saying, Crucify him,	*2019*
Lk	23:46	when Jesus had **c** with a loud	*5455*
Jn	1:15	and **c**, saying, This was he of	*2896*
Jn	7:37	Jesus stood and **c**, saying, **If any**	*2896*
Jn	11:43	he **c** with a loud voice, **Lazarus,**	*2905*
Jn	12:13	to meet him, and **c**, Hosanna:	*2905*
Ac	7:60	and **c** with a loud voice, Lord,	*2896*
Ac	19:28	and **c** out, saying, Great is Diana	*2896*
Rev	10:3	when he had **c**, seven thunders	*2896*
Rev	12:2	And she being with child **c**,	*2896*
Rev	18:18	And **c** when they saw the smoke	*2896*
Rev	18:19	and **c**, weeping and wailing,	*2896*
Rev	19:17	and he **c** with a loud voice,	*2896*

CRIEST

Ex	14:15	Wherefore **c** thou unto me?	6817
Pr	2:3	Yea, if thou **c** after knowledge,	7121
Jer	30:15	Why **c** thou for thine affliction?	2199

CRIETH

Ge	4:10	the voice of thy brother's blood **c**	6817
Ps	84:2	my heart and my flesh **c** out for	7442
Pr	1:20	Wisdom **c** without; she uttereth	7442
Isa	40:3	of him that **c** in the wilderness,	7121
Mt	15:23	Send her away; for she **c** after us	*2896*

CRIMSON

2Ch	2:7	in purple, and **c**, and blue,	3758
Isa	1:18	though they be red like **c**,	8438
Jer	4:30	thou clothest thyself with **c**,	8144

CROOKED

Dt	32:5	are a perverse and **c** generation	6618
Ps	125:5	turn aside unto their **c** ways,	6128
Ecc	1:15	is **c** cannot be made straight:	5791
Isa	40:4	and the **c** shall be made straight,	6121
Isa	45:2	and make the **c** places straight:	1921
Lk	3:5	the **c** shall be made straight,	*4646*
Php	2:15	midst of a **c** and perverse nation,	*4646*

CROSS

Mt	10:38	**And he that taketh not his c,**	*4716*
Mt	16:24	**deny himself, and take up his c,**	*4716*
Mt	27:32	him they compelled to bear his **c**	*4716*
Mt	27:40	Son of God, come down from the **c**,	*4716*
Mt	27:42	let him now come down from the **c**,	*4716*
Mk	15:21	and Rufus, to bear his **c**.	*4716*
Lk	14:27	**whosoever doth not bear his c,**	*4716*
Jn	19:19	wrote a title, and put it on the **c**.	*4716*
Jn	19:25	stood by the **c** of Jesus his mother,	*4716*
Jn	19:31	should not remain upon the **c** on	*4716*
1Co	1:17	lest the **c** of Christ should be made	*4716*
1Co	1:18	the preaching of the **c** is to them	*4716*
Gal	6:12	should suffer persecution for the **c**	*4716*
Gal	6:14	save in the **c** of our Lord Jesus	*4716*
Php	2:8	death, even the death of the **c**	*4716*
Php	3:18	are the enemies of the **c** of Christ:	*4716*
Col	1:20	peace through the blood of his **c**,	*4716*
Col	2:14	out of the way, nailing it to his **c**;	*4716*
Heb	12:2	endured the **c**, despising the shame.	*4716*

CROW

Mt	26:34	**this night, before the cock c,**	*5455*
Mt	26:75	Before the cock **c**, thou shalt deny	*5455*
Mk	14:30	**before the cock c twice, thou**	*5455*
Mk	14:72	him, Before the **c** crow twice, thou	*5455*

CROWN

Ex	25:11	make upon it a **c** of gold round	2213
Le	21:12	**c** of the anointing oil of his God	5145
2Sa	1:10	took the **c** that was upon his head,	5145
2Sa	12:30	And he took their king's **c** from	5850
Est	8:15	and with a great **c** of gold,	5850
Job	19:9	and taken the **c** from my head.	5850
Ps	89:39	hast profaned his **c** by casting it	5145
Ps	132:18	upon himself shall his **c** flourish.	5145
Pr	12:4	woman is a **c** to her husband:	5850
Pr	17:6	Children's children are the **c** of	5850
Isa	28:5	Lord of hosts be for a **c** of glory,	5850
La	5:16	The **c** is fallen from our head:	5850
Mt	27:29	they had platted a **c** of thorns,	*4735*
Mk	15:17	and platted a **c** of thorns,	*4735*
Jn	19:2	the soldiers platted a **c** of thorns,	*4735*
Jn	19:5	wearing the **c** of thorns, and the	*4735*
1Co	9:25	to obtain a corruptible **c**; but we	*4735*
Php	4:1	and longed for, my joy and **c**,	*4735*
2Ti	4:8	up for me a **c** of righteousness,	*4735*
Jas	1:12	he shall receive the **c** of life,	*4735*
1Pe	5:4	a **c** of glory that fadeth not away	*4735*
Rev	2:10	**and I will give thee a c of life.**	*4735*
Rev	6:2	and a **c** was given unto him:	*4735*
Rev	12:1	upon her head a **c** of twelve stars:	*4735*

CROWNED

Ps	8:5	**c** him with glory and honour	5849
Pr	14:18	prudent are **c** with knowledge	3803
Heb	2:9	death, **c** with glory and honour;	*4737*

CROWNS

Rev	4:4	they had on their heads **c** of gold	*4735*
Rev	4:10	and cast their **c** before the throne,	*4735*
Rev	9:7	heads were as it were **c** like gold,	*4735*
Rev	12:3	and seven **c** upon his heads.	*1238*
Rev	13:1	and upon his horns ten **c**, and	*1238*
Rev	19:12	and on his head were many **c**;	*1238*

CRUCIFIED

Mt	26:2	**Son of man is betrayed to be c**	*4717*
Mt	27:22	all say unto him, Let him be **c**.	*4717*
Mt	27:35	And they **c** him, and parted his	*4717*
Mt	27:38	were there two thieves **c** with him,	*4717*
Mt	28:5	that ye seek Jesus, which was **c**.	*4717*
Mk	15:25	was the third hour, and they **c** him.	*4717*
Mk	15:32	that were **c** with him reviled him	*4957*
Mk	16:6	Jesus of Nazareth, which was **c**:	*4717*
Lk	23:33	called Calvary, there they **c** him	*4717*
Lk	24:7	and be **c**, and the third day rise	*4717*
Lk	24:20	to death, and have **c** him.	*4717*
Jn	19:18	Where they **c** him, and two others	*4717*
Jn	19:32	the other which was **c** with him.	*4957*
Ac	2:23	wicked hands have **c** and slain:	*4362*
Ac	2:36	same Jesus, whom ye have **c**,	*4717*
Ac	4:10	Christ of Nazareth, whom ye **c**,	*4717*
Ro	6:6	that our old man is **c** with him,	*4957*
1Co	1:23	we preach Christ **c**, unto the Jews	*4717*
1Co	2:2	you, save Jesus Christ, and him **c**.	*4717*
1Co	2:8	would not have **c** the Lord of glory	*4717*
Gal	2:20	I am **c** with Christ: nevertheless	*4957*
Gal	6:14	by whom the world is **c** unto me,	*4717*

CRUCIFY

Mt	20:19	**and to scourge, and to c him:**	*4717*
Mt	23:34	**some of them ye shall kill and c;**	*4717*
Mt	27:31	and led him away to **c** him.	*4717*
Mk	15:13	they cried out again, **C** him.	*4717*
Mk	15:14	out the more exceedingly, **C** him.	*4717*
Mk	15:27	And with him they **c** two thieves;	4717
Lk	23:21	they cried, saying, **C** him, **c** him.	4717
Jn	19:6	Take ye him, and **c** him: for I find	4717
Jn	19:15	Shall I **c** your King? The chief	4717
Heb	6:6	they **c** to themselves the Son of God	*388*

CRUEL

Dt	32:33	dragons, and the **c** venom of asps	393
Pr	11:17	he that is **c** troubleth his own flesh.	394
Jer	50:42	they are **c**, and will not shew mercy:	394
La	4:3	daughter of my people is become **c**,	393

CRUELTY

Ge	49:5	instruments of **c** are in their	2555
Eze	34:4	and with **c** have ye ruled them	6531

CRUMBS

Mt	15:27	dogs eat of the **c** which fell from	*5589*
Lk	16:21	**to be fed with the c which fell**	*5589*

CRUSE

1Ki	17:14	waste, neither shall the **c** of oil fail,	6835

CRUSH

Job	39:15	that the foot may **c** them, or that	2115
La	3:34	**c** under his feet all the prisoners	1792

CRUSHED

Le	22:24	bruised, or **c**, or broken, or cut:	3807
Nu	22:25	**c** Balaam's foot against the wall:	3905
Job	5:4	they are **c** in the gate, neither is	1792

CRY

Ge	18:20	**c** of Sodom and Gomorrah is	2201
Ex	2:23	their **c** came up unto God by	7775
Ex	3:9	**c** of the children of Israel is come	6818
Ex	12:30	there was a great **c** in Egypt;	6818
Le	13:45	and shall **c**, Unclean, unclean.	7121
Jgs	10:14	Go and **c** unto the gods which ye	2199
1Sa	7:8	Cease not to **c** unto the Lord our	2199
1Ki	18:27	**C** aloud: for he is a god; either	7121
Ne	9:9	heardest their **c** by the Red sea;	2201
Job	27:9	Will God hear his **c** when trouble	6818
Ps	9:12	forgetteth not the **c** of the humble	6818
Ps	17:1	attend unto my **c**, give ear unto	7440
Ps	22:2	O my God, I **c** in the daytime,	7121
Ps	34:15	his ears are open unto their **c**	7775
Ps	55:17	at noon; will I pray, and **c** aloud:	1993
Ps	86:3	O Lord: for I **c** unto thee daily.	7121
Pr	21:13	his ears at the **c** of the poor,	2201
Isa	14:31	Howl, O gate; **c**, O city; thou,	2199
Isa	42:14	will I **c** like a travailing woman;	6463
Jer	2:2	and **c** in the ears of Jerusalem,	7121
Jer	14:2	the **c** of Jerusalem is gone up.	6682
Joel	1:19	O Lord, to thee will I **c**: for the	7121
Mic	3:5	with their teeth, and **c**, Peace:	7121
Mt	25:6	**at midnight there was a c made,**	*2906*
Lk	19:40	**stones would immediately c out.**	*2896*
Ro	8:15	whereby we **c**, Abba, Father.	*2896*

CRYING

1Sa	4:14	Eli heard the noise of the **c**,	6818
Ps	69:3	I am weary of my **c**: my throat	7121
Mt	3:3	voice of one **c** in the wilderness,	*994*
Mk	1:3	voice of one **c** in the wilderness,	*994*
Lk	3:4	voice of one **c** in the wilderness,	*994*
Ac	21:28	**C** out, Men of Israel, help: This	*2896*
Ac	21:36	followed after, **c**, Away with him.	*2896*
Gal	4:6	into your hearts, **c**, Abba, Father	*2896*
Rev	14:15	**c** with a loud voice to him that	*2896*
Rev	21:4	neither sorrow, nor **c**, neither	*2906*

CRYSTAL

Rev	4:6	was a sea of glass like unto **c**:	*2930*
Rev	21:11	like a jasper stone, clear as **c**;	*2929*
Rev	22:1	river of water of life, clear as **c**,	*2930*

CUBIT

Ge	6:16	a **c** shalt thou finish it above;	520
Jgs	3:16	had two edges, of a **c** length;	1574
Eze	40:5	six cubits long by the **c** and an hand	520
Mt	6:27	**can add one c unto his stature?**	*4083*
Lk	12:25	**can add to his stature one c?**	*4083*

CUBITS

Ge	6:15	the ark shall be three hundred **c**,	520
Ge	6:15	the breadth of it fifty **c**,	520
Ge	6:15	and the height of it thirty **c**	520
Ge	7:20	Fifteen **c** upward did the waters	520
1Sa	17:4	whose height was six **c** and a span	520
1Ki	6:23	cherubims of olive tree, each ten **c**	520
1Ch	11:23	a man of great stature, five **c** high;	520
Neh	3:13	and a thousand **c** on the wall unto	520
Est	5:14	Let a gallows be made of fifty **c**	520
Est	7:9	Behold also, the gallows fifty **c** high,	520
Da	3:1	whose height was threescore **c**,	521
Da	3:1	and the breadth thereof six **c**:	521
Rev	21:17	an hundred and forty and four **c**,	*4088*

CUD

Le	11:3	cheweth the **c**, among the beasts,	1625
Dt	14:6	cheweth the **c** among the beasts,	1625
Dt	14:7	for they chew the **c**, but divide	1625

CUMI (coo´-mi)

Mk	5:41	unto her, **Talitha c;** which is,	*2891*

CUNNING

Ge	25:27	Esau was a **c** hunter, a man of	3045
Ex	36:35	cherubims made he it of **c** work.	2803
1Sa	16:16	seek out a man, who is a **c** player	3045
1Sa	16:18	that is **c** in playing, and a mighty	3045
Da	1:4	and **c** in knowledge, and	3045
Eph	4:14	sleight of men, and **c** craftiness,	

CUP

Ge	40:11	and Pharaoh's **c** was in my hand:	3563
Ge	44:2	And put my **c**, the silver **c**, in the	1375
Ge	44:12	**c** was found in Benjamin's sack	1375
1Ki	7:26	was wrought like the brim of a **c**,	3563
Ps	23:5	head with oil; my **c** runneth over	3563
Ps	116:13	I will take the **c** of salvation, and	3563
Isa	51:17	of the Lord the **c** of his fury;	3563
Jer	49:12	judgment was not to drink of the **c**	3563
La	4:21	the **c** also shall pass through unto	3563
Zec	12:2	make Jerusalem a **c** of trembling	5592
Mt	10:42	**c of cold water only in the name**	*4221*
Mt	20:22	**drink of the c that I shall drink**	*4221*
Mt	20:23	**Ye shall drink indeed of my c,**	*4221*
Mt	26:27	he took the **c**, and gave thanks,	*4221*
Mt	26:39	**possible, let this c pass from me:**	*4221*
Mt	26:42	**c may not pass away from me,**	*4221*
Mk	14:36	**take away this c from me:**	*4221*
Lk	22:17	he took the **c**, and gave thanks,	*4221*
Lk	22:20	Likewise also the **c** after supper,	*4221*
Lk	22:20	**This c is the new testament in my**	*4221*
Lk	22:42	**if thou be willing, remove this c**	*4221*
Jn	18:11	**c which my Father hath given me,**	*4221*
1Co	10:21	Ye cannot drink the **c** of the Lord,	*4221*
1Co	11:25	same manner also he took the **c**,	*4221*
1Co	11:25	**This c is the new testament in my**	*4221*
1Co	11:26	and drink this **c**, ye do show	*4221*
1Co	11:27	drink this **c** of the Lord, unworthily,	*4221*
Rev	17:4	having a golden **c** in her hand full	*4221*

CURE

Jer	33:6	I will bring it health and **c**,	4832
Mt	17:16	and they could not **c** him.	*2323*
Lk	9:1	over all devils, and to **c** diseases	*2323*

CURED

Mt	17:18	child was **c** from that very hour.	*2323*
Lk	7:21	he **c** many of their infirmities and	*2323*
Jn	5:10	said unto him that was **c**. It is the	*2323*

CURIOUS

Ex	35:32	devise **c** works, to work in gold,	4284
Ac	19:19	used **c** arts brought their books	*4021*

CURSE

Ge	8:21	I will not again **c** the ground any	7043
Ge	27:13	Upon me be thy **c**, my son:	7045
Nu	22:17	I pray thee, **c** me this people.	6895
Dt	23:5	God turned the **c** into a blessing	7045
Jos	24:9	Balaam the son of Beor to **c** you:	7043
2Sa	16:9	should this dead dog **c** my lord	7043
Ne	13:2	God turned the **c** into a blessing	7045
Job	1:11	and he will **c** thee to thy face	1288
Job	2:5	and he will **c** thee to thy face	1288
Job	2:9	**c** God, and die	1288
Job	3:8	that **c** the day, who are	779
Ps	62:4	their mouth, but they **c** inwardly	7043
Pr	30:10	lest he **c** thee, and thou be found	7043
Jer	24:9	and a proverb, a taunt and a **c**,	7045
Da	9:11	the **c** is poured upon us, and the	423
Mal	2:2	and I will **c** your blessings:	779
Mt	5:44	**bless them that c you, do good to**	*2672*
Mk	14:71	But he began to **c** and to swear	*332*
Lk	6:28	**Bless them that c you, and pray**	*2672*
Ac	23:12	and bound themselves under a **c**,	*332*
Gal	3:13	redeemed us from the **c** of the	*2671*
Gal	3:13	law, being made a **c** for us:	*2671*

CURSED

Ge	3:14	thou art **c** above all cattle, and	779
Ge	3:17	**c** is the ground for thy sake; in	779
Ge	4:11	now art thou **c** from the earth,	779
Ge	9:25	he said, **C** be Canaan; a servant of	779
Le	20:9	hath **c** his father or his mother;	7043
Nu	23:8	I curse, whom God hath not **c**?	6895
Jgs	21:18	**C** be he that giveth a wife to	779
1Sa	17:43	Philistine **c** David by his gods:	7043
Job	1:5	sinned, and **c** God in their hearts	1288
Job	3:1	Job his mouth, and **c** his day	7043
Mt	25:41	**Depart from me, ye c, into**	*2672*
Jn	7:49	who knoweth not the law are **c**	*1944*

Gal 3:10 **C is every one that continueth** *1944*
Gal 3:13 **C is every one that hangeth on a** *1944*

CURSES
Nu 5:23 the priest shall write these **c** in 423
Dt 28:15 these **c** shall come upon thee 7045
2Ch 34:24 all the **c** that are written in the 423

CURSETH
Ge 12:3 and curse him that **c** thee: and in 7043
Ge 27:29 cursed be every one that **c** thee 779
Pr 20:20 Whoso **c** his father or his mother 7043
Pr 30:11 There is a generation that **c** their 7043
Mt 15:4 **He that c father or mother, let** *2551*
Mk 7:10 **Whoso c father or mother, let** *2551*

CURSING
Dt 30:19 life and death, blessing and **c**: 7045
Ps 10:7 His mouth is full of **c** and deceit 423
Ps 109:18 he clothed himself with **c** like as 7045
Ro 3:14 Whose mouth is full of **c** and *685*
Jas 3:10 mouth proceedeth blessing and **c** *2671*

CURTAIN
Ex 26:2 The length of one **c** shall be eight 3407
Nu 3:26 the **c** for the door of the court, ...4539
Ps 104:2 out the heavens like a **c**: 3407
Isa 40:22 stretcheth out the heavens as a **c**, ...1852

CURTAINS
Ex 26:1 ten **c** of fine twined linen, and 3407
Nu 4:25 shall bear the **c** of the tabernacle, ...3407
2Sa 7:2 the ark of God dwelleth within **c** 3407

CUSTODY
Nu 3:36 under the **c** and charge of the 6486
Est 2:8 the palace, to the **c** of Hegai, that 3027
Est 2:8 the king's house, to the **c** of Hegai, ...3027

CUSTOM
Ge 31:35 for the **c** of women is upon me 1870
1Sa 2:13 priest's **c** with the people was, ...4941
Ezr 4:13 they not pay toll, tribute, and **c**, ...1983
Mt 9:9 sitting at the receipt of **c**: *5058*
Mt 17:25 **of the earth take c or tribute?** *5056*
Lk 1:9 to the **c** of the priest's office, his *1485*
Jn 18:39 ye have a **c**, that I should release *4914*
Ro 13:7 is due; **c** to whom **c**; fear to whom *5056*
1Co 11:16 we have no such **c**, neither the *4914*

CUSTOMS
Jer 10:3 the **c** of the people are vain:...........2708
Ac 6:14 the **c** which Moses delivered us *1485*
Ac 16:21 teach **c** which are not lawful for us *1485*
Ac 21:21 neither to walk after the **c** *1485*

CUT
Ge 9:11 neither shall all flesh be **c** off any 3772
Ex 9:15 shalt be **c** off from the earth 3582
Ex 12:19 be **c** off from the congregation 3772
Ex 29:17 thou shalt **c** the ram in pieces, ...5408
Dt 12:29 thy God shall **c** off the nations 3772
Jos 3:13 the waters of Jordan shall be **c** off 3772
Jos 3:16 salt sea, failed, and were **c** off: 3772
Jos 4:7 of Jordan were **c** off before the ark 3772
Jgs 1:6 **c** off his thumbs and his great toes, ...7112
Jgs 1:7 thumbs and their great toes **c** off 7112
Jgs 20:6 and **c** her in pieces, and sent her 5408
Ru 4:10 the name of the dead be not **c** off 3772
1Sa 17:51 him, and **c** off his head therewith 3772
1Sa 24:4 and **c** off the skirt of Saul's robe 3772
1Sa 24:5 because he had **c** off Saul's skirt 3772
1Sa 24:11 that I **c** off the skirt of thy robe 3772
1Sa 24:21 thou wilt not **c** off my seed after 3772
2Ki 6:6 he **c** down a stick, and cast it in 7094
2Ki 19:23 will **c** down the tall cedar trees 3772
Job 4:7 where were the righteous **c** off? 3582
Job 14:2 flower, and is **c** down: he fleeth 5243
Job 24:24 and **c** off as the tops of the ears 5243
Ps 12:3 Lord shall **c** off all flattering lips 3772
Ps 37:34 when the wicked are **c** off, thou 3772
Ps 90:10 it is soon **c** off, and we fly away 1504
Ps 109:15 he may **c** off the memory of them 3772
Pr 10:31 the froward tongue shall be **c** out. 3772
Isa 53:8 **c** off out of the land of the living: 1504
Jer 7:29 **C** off thine hair, O Jerusalem, ...1494
Jer 11:19 and let us **c** him off from the land 3772
La 3:53 have **c** off my life in the dungeon, ...6789
Da 2:5 ye shall be **c** in pieces, and your 5648
Da 2:34 a stone was **c** out without hands 1505
Da 9:26 shall Messiah be **c** off, but not for 3772
Hos 10:7 her king is **c** off as the foam upon 1820
Joel 1:5 for it is **c** off from your mouth 3772
Joel 1:9 the drink offering is **c** off from the 3772
Am 3:14 horns of the altar shall be **c** off, ...1438
Ob 9 Esau may be **c** off by slaughter 3772
Ob 10 and thou shalt be **c** off for ever 3772
Hab 3:17 flock shall be **c** off from the fold 1504
Mal 2:12 The Lord will **c** off the man that 3772
Mt 5:30 **c it off, and cast it from thee:** *1581*
Mt 18:8 **c them off, and cast them from** *1581*
Mt 24:51 **shall c him asunder, and appoint** *1371*
Mk 9:43 **if thy hand offend thee, c it off:** *609*
Mk 9:45 **if thy foot offend thee, c it off:** *609*
Mk 11:8 **c** down branches of the trees, ...*2875*
Lk 13:7 **c it down; why cumbereth it the** *1581*
Lk 13:9 **after that thou shalt c it down** *1581*
Lk 22:50 priest, and **c** off his right ear *851*
Jn 18:10 servant, and **c** off his right ear *609*
Jn 18:26 kinsman whose ear Peter **c** off *609*
Ac 5:33 that, they were **c** to the heart, ...*1282*
Ac 7:54 they were **c** to the heart, and they *1282*
Ro 11:22 otherwise thou also shalt be **c** off. *1581*
Ro 11:24 thou wert **c** out of the olive tree *1581*

CUTTETH
Job 28:10 **c** out rivers among the rocks; 1234
Ps 46:9 bow, and **c** the spear in sunder; 7112
Pr 26:6 hand of the fool **c** off the feet, ...7096

CUTTING
Ex 31:5 And in **c** of stones, to set them 2799
Mk 5:5 crying, and **c** himself with stones 2629

CYMBALS
2Sa 6:5 and on cornets, and on **c** 6767
1Ch 13:8 with timbrels, and with **c**, ...4700
1Ch 15:16 psalteries and harps and **c**, ...4700
Ne 12:27 with singing, with **c**, psalteries 4700
Ps 150:5 Praise him upon the loud **c**: 6767
Ps 150:5 him upon the high sounding **c** 6767

D

DAGGER
Jgs 3:16 Ehud made him a **d** which had two 2719

DAILY
Ex 5:19 your bricks of your **d** tasks 3117
Ex 16:5 twice as much as they gather **d** 3117
Nu 28:24 this manner ye shall offer **d**, ...3117
Jgs 16:16 pressed him **d** with her words 3117
2Ki 25:30 a **d** rate for every day, ...3117
Ezr 3:4 the **d** burnt offerings by number 3117
Ps 13:2 having sorrow in my heart **d**? 3119
Ps 42:10 while they say **d** unto me 3605, 3117
Ps 61:8 I may **d** perform my vows 3117
Ps 72:15 and **d** shall he be praised 3605, 3117
Ps 88:9 I have called **d** upon thee 3605, 3117
Pr 8:30 and I was **d** his delight, ...3117
Isa 58:2 Yet they seek me **d**, and delight 3117
Jer 20:7 I am in derision **d**, every one 3605, 3117
Eze 45:23 without blemish **d** the seven days; 3117
Eze 46:13 shalt **d** prepare a burnt offering 3117
Da 1:5 appointed them a **d** provision 3117
Da 8:13 vision concerning the **d** sacrifice, ...8548
Da 11:31 shall take away the **d** sacrifice, ...8548
Da 12:11 **d** sacrifice shall be taken away 8548
Mt 6:11 **Give us this day our d bread** *1967*
Mt 26:55 **I sat d with you teaching** *2596, 2250*
Mk 14:49 **d with you in the temple** *2596, 2250*
Lk 9:23 **and take up his cross d,** *2596, 2250*
Lk 11:3 **us day by day our d bread** *1967*
Lk 22:53 **d with you in the temple,** *2596, 2250*
Ac 2:46 continuing **d** with one accord *2596, 2250*
Ac 2:47 Lord added to the church **d** *2596, 2250*
Ac 3:2 whom they laid **d** at the gate *2596, 2250*
Ac 6:1 neglected in the **d** ministration *2522*
Ac 16:5 increased in number **d** *2596, 2250*
Ac 17:11 searched the scriptures **d** *2596, 2250*
1Co 15:31 Jesus our Lord, I die **d** *2596, 2250*
Heb 3:13 exhort one another **d**, ...*2596, 1538, 2250*
Heb 7:27 Who needeth not **d**, as *2596, 2250*
Heb 10:11 priest standeth **d** ministering *2596, 2250*
Jas 2:15 naked, and destitute of **d** food, ...*2184*

DAINTIES
Ps 141:4 and let me not eat of their **d** 4516
Pr 23:3 not desirous of his **d**: for they 4303

DAINTY
Pr 23:6 neither desire thou his **d** meats: 4303
Rev 18:14 things which were **d** and goodly *3045*

DAMAGE
Est 7:4 not countervail the king's **d** 5143
Da 6:2 and the king should have no **d** 5142
2Co 7:9 that ye might receive **d** by us in *2210*

DAMNABLE
2Pe 2:1 privily shall bring in **d** heresies, ...*684*

DAMNATION
Mt 23:14 **ye shall receive the greater d** *2917*
Mt 23:33 **how can ye escape the d of hell?** *2920*
Mk 3:29 **but is in danger of eternal d:** *2920*
Mk 12:40 **these shall receive greater d** *2917*
Lk 20:47 **the same shall receive greater d** *2917*
Jn 5:29 **unto the resurrection of d** *2920*
Ro 3:8 good may come? whose **d** is just *2917*
Ro 13:2 shall receive to themselves **d** *2927*
1Co 11:29 eateth and drinketh **d** to himself, ...*2917*
1Ti 5:12 Having **d**, because they have cast *2917*
2Pe 2:3 not, and their **d** slumbereth not *684*

DAMNED
Mk 16:16 **he that believeth not shall be d** *2632*
Ro 14:23 he that doubteth is **d** if he eat, ...*2632*
2Th 2:12 That they all might be **d** who *2919*

DAMSEL
Ge 24:16 And the **d** was very fair to look 5291
Ge 34:12 unto me: but give me the **d** to 5291
Dt 22:20 of virginity be not found for the **d**: 5291
Dt 22:24 the **d**, because she cried not 5291
Dt 22:26 unto the **d** thou shalt do nothing; 5291
Dt 22:28 If a man find a **d** that is a virgin 5291
Ru 2:5 over the reapers, Whose **d** is this? 5291
1Ki 1:4 And the **d** was very fair 5291
Mt 14:11 in a charger, and given to the **d**: *2877*
Mk 5:39 **the d is not dead, but sleepeth** *3813*
Mk 5:41 interpreted, **D**, I say unto thee *2877*
Mk 6:22 the king said unto the **d**, Ask of *2877*
Jn 18:17 Then saith the **d** that kept the *3814*

DAMSEL'S
Dt 22:15 bring forth the tokens of the **d** 5291
Dt 22:29 shall give unto the **d** father fifty 5291
Jgs 19:8 and the **d** father said, Comfort 5291

DANCE
Ps 150:4 Praise him with the timbrel and **d**: 4234
Ecc 3:4 a time to mourn, and a time to **d**; 7540
Jer 31:13 shall the virgin rejoice in the **d** 4234
La 5:15 our **d** is turned into mourning 4234

DANCED
2Sa 6:14 David **d** before the Lord with all 3769
Mt 11:17 **unto you, and ye have not d;** *3738*
Mt 14:6 the daughter of Herodias **d** before *3738*
Mk 6:22 the said Herodias came in, and **d**, ...*3738*
Lk 7:32 **unto you, and ye have not d;** *3738*

DANCES
Ex 15:20 her with timbrels and with **d** 4246
Jgs 21:21 of Shiloh come out to dance in **d**, ...4246
1Sa 21:11 sing one to another of him in **d**, ...4246
1Sa 29:5 they sang one to another in **d**, ...4246

DANCING
Ex 32:19 that he saw the calf, and the **d** 4246
2Sa 6:16 saw king David leaping and **d** 3769
1Ch 15:29 saw king David **d** and playing: 7540
Ps 30:11 for me my mourning into **d**: 4234
Lk 15:25 **the house, he heard musick and d** *5525*

DANGER
Mt 5:21 **shall be in d of the judgment:** *1777*
Mt 5:22 **fool, shall be in d of hell fire** *1777*
Mk 3:29 **is in d of eternal damnation:** *1777*

DARE
Job 41:10 None is so fierce that **d** stir him
Ro 5:7 man some would even **d** to die *5111*
1Co 6:1 **D** any of you, having a matter *5111*

DARK

Ge 15:17 the sun went down, and it was **d**, ...5939
Le 13:6 if the plague be somewhat **d**, ...3544
Ne 13:19 gates of Jerusalem began to be **d** 6751
Ps 18:11 round about him were **d** waters...............2824
Ps 74:20 the **d** places of the earth are full 4285
Ps 78:2 I will utter **d** sayings of old:......................2420
Ps 88:12 thy wonders be known in the **d**?.............2822
Pr 1:6 of the wise, and their **d** sayings................2420
Pr 7:9 evening, in the black and **d** night: 653
Isa 29:15 their works are in the **d**, and they...........4285
Jer 13:16 stumble upon the **d** mountains, ...5399
Eze 8:12 the house of Israel do in the **d**, ...2822
Eze 32:7 and make the stars thereof **d**;..................6937
Eze 34:12 scattered in the cloudy and **d** day............6205
Da 8:23 and understanding **d** sentences,...............2420
Joel 2:10 the sun and the moon shall be **d**, ...6937
Am 5:8 maketh the day **d** with night:....................2821
Am 5:20 very **d**, and no brightness in it?..................651
Mic 3:6 and it shall be **d** unto you, that................2821
Zec 14:6 light shall not be clear, nor **d**:...................7087
Lk 11:36 **full of light, having no part d**, ...*4652*
Jn 20:1 Magdalene early, when it was yet **d**,.........*4653*
2Pe 1:19 light that shineth in a **d** place,....................*850*

DARKENED

Ex 10:15 earth, so that the land was **d**; 2821
Ps 69:23 Let their eyes be **d**, that they see 2821
Ecc 12:2 stars, be not **d**, nor the clouds..................2821
Isa 5:30 light is **d** in the heavens thereof...............2821
Isa 9:19 the Lord of hosts is the land **d**, ...6272
Isa 13:10 sun shall be **d** in his going forth, ...2821
Isa 24:11 all joy is **d**, the mirth of the......................6150
Joel 3:15 sun and the moon shall be **d**,...................6937
Zec 11:17 his right eye shall be utterly **d**..................3543
Mt 24:29 **of those days shall the sun be d**,.............*4654*
Mk 13:24 **the sun shall be d, and the moon** *4654*
Lk 23:45 And the sun was **d**, and the veil *4654*
Ro 1:21 and their foolish heart was **d**....................*4654*
Ro 11:10 Let their eyes be **d**, that they may *4654*
Eph 4:18 Having the understanding **d**, ...*4654*
Rev 8:12 so as the third part of them was **d** *4654*
Rev 9:2 and the sun and the air were **d**.................*4654*

DARKENETH

Job 38:2 Who is this that **d** counsel by...................2821

DARKLY

1Co 13:12 we see through a glass, **d**;..................*1722, 135*

DARKNESS

Ge 1:2 **d** was upon the face of the deep 2822
Ge 1:4 God divided the light from the **d** 2822
Ge 1:5 Day, and the **d** he called Night.................2822
Ge 1:18 and to divide the light from the **d**: 2822
Ge 15:12 horror of great **d** fell upon him 2825
Ex 10:21 even **d** which may be felt..........................2822
Ex 14:20 it was a cloud and **d** to them,...................2822
Ex 20:21 drew near unto the thick **d**.......................6205
Dt 4:11 unto the midst of heaven, with **d**,............2822
Dt 5:23 voice out of the midst of the **d**,................2822
Dt 28:29 as the blind gropeth in **d**, ...653
1Sa 2:9 the wicked shall be silent in **d**; 2822
2Sa 22:29 and the Lord will lighten my **d** 2822
1Ki 8:12 he would dwell in the thick **d**..................6205
Job 3:4 Let that day be **d**; let not God 2822
Job 30:26 I waited for light, there came **d**. 652
Job 34:22 There is no **d**, nor shadow of...................2822
Job 37:19 order our speech by reason of **d** 2822
Job 38:19 and as for **d**, where is the place................2822
Ps 18:28 my God will enlighten my **d**. 2822
Ps 82:5 understand; they walk on in **d**: 2825
Ps 91:6 the pestilence that walketh in **d**; 652
Ps 97:2 and **d** are round about him:......................6205
Ps 107:14 He brought them out of **d** and the..........2822
Ps 139:11 I say, Surely the **d** shall cover me; 2822
Ps 139:12 **d** and the light are both alike to...............2825
Pr 2:13 to walk in the ways of **d**;..........................2822
Pr 4:19 The way of the wicked is as **d**.....................653
Pr 20:20 shall be put out in obscure **d**....................2822
Ecc 2:13 folly, as far as light excelleth **d**..................2822
Ecc 5:17 All his days also he eateth in **d**.................2822
Ecc 11:8 let him remember the days of **d**;..............2822
Isa 5:20 put **d** for light, and light for **d**;.................2822
Isa 8:22 behold trouble and **d**, dimness of............2825
Isa 9:2 The people that walked in **d** have............2822
Isa 42:7 them that sit in **d** out of the prison.........2822
Isa 45:7 I form the light, and create **d**: 2822
Isa 50:10 walketh in **d**, and hath no light? 2825
Isa 59:9 for brightness, but we walk in **d**. 653
Isa 60:2 the **d** shall cover the earth 2822
Isa 60:2 and gross **d** the people:............................6205
Jer 13:16 of death, and make it gross **d**. 6205
Da 2:22 he knoweth what is in the **d**,....................2816
Joel 2:2 a day of clouds and of thick **d**,.................6205
Joel 2:31 The sun shall be turned into **d**,................2822
Am 5:18 the day of the Lord is **d**, and not 2822
Am 5:20 shall not the day of the Lord be **d**,...........2822
Zep 1:15 a day of clouds and thick **d** 6205
Mt 4:16 The people which sat in **d** saw *4655*
Mt 6:23 **thy whole body shall be full of d**.............*4652*
Mt 6:23 **in thee be d, how great is that d!** *4655*
Mt 8:12 **shall be cast out into outer d:** *4655*
Mt 10:27 **What I tell you in d, that speak** *4653*
Mt 22:13 **away, and cast him into outer d;** *4655*
Mt 25:30 **unprofitable servant into outer d:**...........*4655*
Mt 27:45 there was **d** over all the land.....................*4655*
Mk 15:33 there was **d** over the whole land *4655*
Lk 1:79 To give light to them that sit in **d** *4655*
Lk 11:35 **light which is in thee be not d** *4655*
Lk 22:53 **is your hour, and the power of d**............*4655*
Lk 23:44 there was a **d** over all the earth *4655*
Jn 1:5 And the light shineth in **d**; and................*4653*
Jn 1:5 and the **d** comprehended it not *4653*
Jn 3:19 **men loved d rather than light,**..................*4655*
Jn 8:12 **followeth me shall not walk in d,** *4653*
Jn 12:35 **the light, lest d come upon you:** *4655*
Jn 12:46 **on me should not abide in d**....................*4653*
Ac 2:20 The sun shall be turned into **d**,................*4655*
Ro 13:12 cast off the works of **d**, and let us *4655*
1Co 4:5 to light the hidden things of **d**, ...*4655*
2Co 4:6 the light to shine out of **d**, hath *4655*
2Co 6:14 communion hath light with **d**? *4655*
Eph 5:11 with the unfruitful works of **d**, ...*4655*
Eph 6:12 the rulers of the **d** of this world,.............*4655*
Col 1:13 delivered us from the power of **d**,............*4655*
1Th 5:5 we are not of the night, nor of **d**.............*4655*
Heb 12:18 nor unto blackness, and **d**, and *4655*
1Pe 2:9 hath called you out of **d** into his..............*4655*
2Pe 2:17 the mist of **d** is reserved for ever..............*4655*
1Jn 1:5 light, and in him is no **d** at all. *4653*
1Jn 1:6 and walk in **d**, we lie, and do not.............*4655*
1Jn 2:9 brother, is in **d** even until now *4653*

1Jn	2:11	goeth, because that **d** hath blinded	*4653*
Jude	6	in everlasting chains under **d**	*2217*
Jude	13	the blackness of **d** for ever.	*4655*
Rev	16:10	and his kingdom was full of **d**;	*4656*

DART

Pr	7:23	Till a **d** strike through his liver;	2671
Heb	12:20	or thrust through with a **d**:	*1002*

DARTS

2Sa	18:14	he took three **d** in his hand	7626
Eph	6:16	all the fiery **d** of the wicked	*956*

DASH

Ps	2:9	thou shalt **d** them in pieces like	5310
Ps	91:12	thou **d** thy foot against a stone	5062
Mt	4:6	thou **d** thy foot against a stone	*4350*
Lk	4:11	thou **d** thy foot against a stone	*4350*

DASHED

Isa	13:16	children also shall be **d** to pieces	7376
Hos	13:16	their infants shall be **d** in pieces,	7376
Na	3:10	children also were **d** in pieces	7376

DAUGHTER

Ge	29:28	gave him Rachel his **d** to wife also	1328
Ge	34:5	that he had defiled Dinah his **d**:	1328
Ge	38:11	said Judah to Tamar his **d** in law	3618
Ge	38:24	Tamar thy **d** in law hath played	3618
Ex	1:16	but if it be a **d**, then she shall live	1323
Ex	2:5	And the **d** of Pharaoh came down	1323
Le	18:9	**d** of thy father, or **d** of thy mother,	1323
Le	19:29	Do not prostitute thy **d**, to cause	1323
Nu	27:8	his inheritance to pass unto his **d**	1323
Dt	18:10	his son or his **d** to pass through	1323
Dt	22:17	I found not thy **d** a maid; and yet	1323
Jgs	11:34	his **d** came out to meet him	1323
Ru	3:10	Blessed be thou of the Lord, my **d**:	1323
Ru	4:15	thy **d** in law, which loveth thee	3618
1Sa	18:20	And Michal Saul's **d** loved David:	1323
2Ki	8:18	for the **d** of Ahab was his wife:	1323
1Ch	2:4	Tamar his **d** in law bare him	3618
Est	2:7	that is, Esther, his uncle's **d**:	1323
Ps	45:13	The king's **d** is all glorious within:	1323
Isa	22:4	the spoiling of the **d** of my people	1323
Jer	8:19	the cry of the **d** of my people	1323
Jer	9:1	the slain of the **d** of my people!	1323
Jer	14:17	for the virgin **d** of my people is	1323
La	1:6	from the **d** of Zion all her beauty	1323
La	2:4	the tabernacle of the **d** of Zion:	1323
La	2:10	The elders of the **d** of Zion sit	1323
La	2:11	destruction of the **d** of my people;	1323
La	3:48	destruction of the **d** of my people	1323
La	4:6	the iniquity of the **d** of my people	1323
Eze	14:20	shall deliver neither son nor **d**;	1323
Eze	16:44	As is the mother, so is her **d**	1323
Da	11:6	for the king's **d** of the south	1323
Mic	4:10	O **d** of Zion, like a woman in travail:	1323
Mic	7:6	**d** riseth up against her mother,	1323
Zec	2:10	Sing and rejoice, O **d** of Zion:	1323
Zec	9:9	Rejoice greatly, O **d** of Zion;	1323
Mal	2:11	hath married the **d** of a strange god	1323
Mt	9:22	**D, be of good comfort; thy faith**	*2364*
Mt	10:35	**and the d against her mother,**	*2364*
Mt	10:37	**loveth son or d more than me**	*2364*
Mt	14:6	the **d** of Herodias danced before	*2364*
Mt	15:28	And her **d** was made whole from	*2364*
Mt	21:5	Tell ye the **d** of Sion, Behold	*2364*
Mk	5:34	**D, thy faith hath made thee**	*2364*
Mk	5:35	Thy **d** is dead: why troublest thou	*2364*
Mk	6:22	the **d** of the said Herodias came	*2364*
Mk	7:29	**the devil is gone out of thy d**	*2364*
Lk	8:48	**D, be of good comfort: thy faith**	*2364*
Lk	8:49	Thy **d** is dead; trouble not the	*2364*
Lk	12:53	**against the d, and the d against**	*2364*
Lk	13:16	**a d of Abraham, whom Satan**	*2364*
Jn	12:15	Fear not, **d** of Sion: behold, thy	*2364*
Heb	11:24	be called the son of Pharaoh's **d**;	*2364*

DAUGHTER IN LAW See DAUGHTER and LAW.

DAUGHTER'S

Le	18:17	or her **d** daughter, to uncover her	1323
Dt	22:17	are the tokens of my **d** virginity	1323

DAUGHTERS

Ge	6:1	earth, and **d** were born unto them	1121
Ge	6:2	the sons of God saw the **d** of men	1121
Ge	19:8	have two **d** which have not known	1121
Ge	19:15	and thy two **d**, which are here;	1121
Ge	19:30	dwelt in a cave, he and his two **d**,	1121
Ge	29:16	Laban had two **d**: the name of the	1121
Ge	31:26	carried away my **d**, as captives	1121
Ge	34:1	went out to see the **d** of the land,	1121
Le	26:29	the flesh of your **d** shall ye eat	1121
Nu	25:1	whoredom with the **d** of Moab	1121
Nu	27:7	The **d** of Zelophehad speak right:	1121
Nu	36:6	concerning the **d** of Zelophehad	1121
Dt	12:31	sons and their **d** they have burnt	1121
Dt	23:17	be no whore of the **d** of Israel	1121
Jgs	11:40	**d** of Israel went yearly to lament	1121
Jgs	21:21	the **d** of Shiloh come out to dance	1121
1Sa	8:13	And he will take your **d** to be	1121
2Sa	1:24	Ye **d** of Israel, weep over Saul,	1121
2Ki	17:17	their **d** to pass through the fire,	1121
Ezr	9:2	taken of their **d** for themselves,	1121
Ne	5:5	our **d** are brought unto bondage	1121
Job	1:18	Thy sons and thy **d** were eating	1121
Job	42:15	found so fair as the **d** of Job:	1121
Ps	48:11	let the **d** of Judah be glad,	1121
Ps	97:8	the **d** of Judah rejoiced because of	1121
Ps	106:37	sacrificed their sons and their **d**	1121
Pr	30:15	horseleach hath two **d**, crying,	1121
Pr	31:29	Many **d** have done virtuously, but	1121
Ecc	12:4	**d** of musick shall be brought low;	1121
SS	2:7	I charge you, O ye **d** of Jerusalem,	1121
SS	3:5	I charge you, O ye **d** of Jerusalem,	1121
SS	5:8	I charge you, O **d** of Jerusalem,	1121
SS	8:4	I charge you, O **d** of Jerusalem,	1121
Isa	3:16	Because the **d** of Zion are haughty,	1121
Isa	4:4	away the filth of the **d** of Zion,	1121
Isa	32:9	hear my voice, ye careless **d**;	1121
Isa	43:6	and my **d** from the ends of the earth;	1121
Jer	7:31	their sons and their **d** in the fire;	1121
Jer	9:20	teach your **d** wailing, and every	1121
Jer	16:3	concerning the **d** that are born in	1121
Jer	19:9	flesh of their **d**, and they shall eat	1121
Jer	32:35	their **d** to pass through the fire	1121
Jer	48:46	taken captives, and thy **d** captives	1121
La	3:51	because of all the **d** of my city	1121
Eze	13:17	against the **d** of thy people, which	1121
Eze	16:46	thy right hand, is Sodom and her **d**	1121
Eze	16:55	When thy sisters, Sodom and her **d**,	1121
Eze	16:55	Samaria and her **d**, shall return	1121

Eze 26:8 He shall slay with the sword thy **d**...........1121
Eze 32:16 the **d** of the nations shall lament.............1121
Hos 4:13 your **d** shall commit whoredom..............1121
Joel 2:28 sons and your **d** shall prophesy...............1121
Am 7:17 and thy **d** shall fall by the sword,.............1121
Lk 1:5 his wife was of the **d** of Aaron.................*2364*
Lk 23:28 **D of Jerusalem, weep not for me,**............*2364*
Ac 2:17 sons and your **d** shall prophesy................*2364*
2Co 6:18 ye shall be my sons and **d**, saith...............*2364*
1Pe 3:6 whose **d** ye are, as long as ye do..............*5043*

DAWN

Mt 28:1 began to **d** toward the first day................*2020*
2Pe 1:19 until the day **d**, and the day star...............*1306*

DAWNING

Job 3:9 neither let it see the **d** of the day: 6079
Ps 119:147 prevented the **d** of the morning...............5399

DAY

Ge 1:5 God called the light **D**, and the................3117
Ge 1:14 to divide the **d** from the night; 3117
Ge 1:16 the greater light to rule the **d**...................3117
Ge 2:2 the seventh **d** God ended his work..........3117
Ge 2:3 God blessed the seventh **d**, and................3117
Ge 3:5 in the **d** ye eat thereof, then your.............3117
Ge 3:8 the garden in the cool of the **d**:................3117
Ge 5:1 In the **d** that God created man 3117
Ge 7:13 In the selfsame **d** entered Noah 3117
Ge 25:31 said, Sell me this **d** thy birthright 3117
Ge 27:45 deprived also of you both in one **d**?........3117
Ge 40:7 Wherefore look ye so sadly to **d**? 3117
Ge 47:26 over the land of Egypt unto this **d**...........3117
Ex 10:28 in that **d** thou seest my face thou 3117
Ex 12:14 **d** shall be unto you for a memorial;........3117
Ex 12:17 observe this **d** in your generations 3117
Ex 13:22 the pillar of the cloud by **d**, nor...............3119
Ex 20:8 Remember the sabbath **d**, to keep 3117
Ex 20:11 the Lord blessed the sabbath **d**,................3117
Ex 35:2 to you an holy **d**, a sabbath of
Le 23:27 there shall be a **d** of atonement: 3117
Nu 3:13 the **d** that I smote all the firstborn 3117
Nu 11:19 Ye shall not eat one **d**, nor two.................3117
Nu 14:34 each **d** for a year, shall ye bear..................3117
Nu 30:14 hold his peace at her from **d** to **d**; 3117
Dt 4:26 earth to witness against you this **d**, ...3117
Dt 4:32 since the **d** that God created man............3117
Dt 9:1 art to pass over Jordan this **d**, ...3117
Dt 11:26 I set before you this **d** a blessing.............3117
Dt 19:9 command thee this **d**, to love the 3117
Dt 29:12 thy God maketh with thee this **d**:............3117
Dt 30:19 heaven and earth to record this **d**............3117
Jos 6:25 even unto this **d**; because she hid 3117
Jos 10:13 not to go down about a whole **d** 3117
Jos 10:14 no **d** like that before it or after it 3117
Jos 24:15 choose you this **d** whom ye will..............3117
Jgs 11:27 the Judge be judge this **d** between...........3117
Jgs 21:3 should be to **d** one tribe lacking.............3117
Ru 2:19 Where hast thou gleaned to **d**? 3117
1Sa 10:19 ye have this **d** rejected your God, ...3117
1Sa 15:35 to see Saul until the **d** of his death: 3117
1Sa 23:14 Saul sought him every **d**, but God...........3117
1Sa 26:10 his **d** shall come to die;............................3117
2Sa 13:37 David mourned for his son every **d** 3117
2Sa 20:3 shut up unto the **d** of their death 3117
1Ki 3:6 to sit on his throne, as it is this **d**............3117
1Ki 4:22 Solomon's provision for one **d** was 3117
1Ki 18:36 known this **d** that thou art God 3117
1Ch 11:22 slew a lion in a pit in a snowy **d**...............3117
1Ch 13:12 David was afraid of God that **d**, ...3117
Ezr 3:4 as the duty of every **d** required;...............3117
Ne 9:12 them in the **d** by a cloudy pillar;..............3119
Ne 13:1 On that **d** they read in the book.............3117
Est 2:11 Mordecai walked every **d** before..............3117
Job 1:6 Now there was a **d** when the sons of.......3117
Job 1:13 there was a **d** when his sons and.............3117
Job 2:1 Again there was a **d** when the sons..........3117
Job 3:1 Job his mouth, and cursed his **d**.............3117
Job 19:25 stand at the latter **d** upon the
Ps 1:2 in his law doth he meditate **d** and...........3119
Ps 2:7 Son; this **d** have I begotten thee...............3117
Ps 19:2 **D** unto **d** uttereth speech, and 3117
Ps 25:5 on thee do I wait all the **d** 3117
Ps 32:3 through my roaring all the **d** long...........3117
Ps 44:22 For thy sake are we killed all the **d**...........3117
Ps 50:15 call upon me in the **d** of trouble:.............3117
Ps 59:16 and refuge in the **d** of my trouble............3117
Ps 74:16 The **d** is thine, the night also is................3117
Ps 84:10 a **d** in thy courts is better than a 3117
Ps 91:5 for the arrow that flieth by **d**;...................3119
Ps 95:7 To **d** if ye will hear his voice....................3117
Ps 119:164 Seven times a **d** do I praise thee..............3117
Ps 146:4 in that very **d** his thoughts perish............3117
Pr 4:18 more and more unto the perfect **d**..........3117
Pr 7:14 this **d** have I payed my vows....................3117
Pr 11:4 Riches profit not in the **d** of wrath:.........3117
Pr 16:4 the wicked for the **d** of evil 3117
Pr 24:10 If thou faint in the **d** of adversity 3117
Pr 27:1 for thou knowest not what a **d** may........3117
Ecc 7:1 the **d** of death than the **d** of one's...........3117
Ecc 8:16 there is that neither **d** nor night 3117
SS 2:17 Until the **d** break, and the shadows.........3117
SS 4:6 Until the **d** break, and the shadows.........3117
Isa 2:12 the **d** of the Lord of hosts shall be...........3117
Isa 4:1 In that **d** seven women shall take 3117
Isa 10:3 will ye do in the **d** of visitation 3117
Isa 13:6 the **d** of the Lord is at hand;....................3117
Isa 13:9 the **d** of the Lord cometh, cruel...............3117
Isa 22:5 it is a **d** of trouble, and of treading..........3117
Isa 30:25 in the **d** of the great slaughter, ...3117
Isa 34:8 is the **d** of the Lord's vengeance,.............3117
Isa 34:10 not be quenched night nor **d**; 3119
Isa 47:9 come to thee in a moment in one **d**,.......3117
Isa 56:12 to morrow shall be as this **d**....................3117
Isa 58:13 doing thy pleasure on my holy **d**; 3117
Isa 65:5 a fire that burneth all the **d** 3117
Isa 66:8 be made to bring forth in one **d**?.............3117
Jer 1:10 I have this **d** set thee over the...................3117
Jer 1:18 I have made thee this **d** a defenced..........3117
Jer 3:25 from our youth even unto this **d**, ...3117
Jer 4:9 it shall come to pass at that **d**,..................3117
Jer 6:4 the **d** goeth away, for the shadows...........3117
Jer 7:22 in the **d** that I brought them out 3117
Jer 7:25 Since the **d** that your fathers came 3117
Jer 7:25 of the land of Egypt unto this **d** 3117
Jer 9:1 that I might weep **d** and night for...........3119
Jer 11:4 in the **d** that I brought them....................3117
Jer 11:5 milk and honey, as it is this **d**..................3117
Jer 11:7 in the **d** that I brought them up 3117
Jer 11:7 in the land of Egypt even unto this **d**, ...3117
Jer 14:17 run down with tears night and **d**.............3119
Jer 33:25 covenant be not with **d** and night 3119
Jer 46:10 For this is the **d** of the Lord God.............3117

Jer	46:21	**d** of their calamity was come upon	3117
Jer	52:11	in prison till the **d** of his death	3117
La	1:12	me in the **d** of his fierce anger	3117
La	3:14	people; and their song all the **d**.	3117
Eze	7:10	Behold, the **d**, behold, it is come:	3117
Eze	23:38	defiled my sanctuary in the same **d**	3117
Eze	28:15	from the **d** that thou wast created,	3117
Eze	33:12	in the **d** that he sinneth	3117
Da	6:10	upon his knees three times a **d**,	3118
Da	6:13	maketh his petition three times a **d**,	3118
Joel	1:15	for the **d**! for the **d** of the Lord	3117
Joel	2:2	**d** of clouds and of thick darkness	3117
Joel	2:11	the **d** of the Lord is great and very	3117
Joel	2:31	and the terrible **d** of the Lord come	3117
Joel	3:14	**d** of the Lord is near in the valley	3117
Am	5:18	you that desire the **d** of the Lord!	3117
Am	5:18	the **d** of the Lord is darkness,	3117
Ob	15	the **d** of the Lord is near upon all	3117
Na	1:7	a strong hold in the **d** of trouble;	3117
Na	2:3	in the **d** of his preparation, and	3117
Zep	1:7	the **d** of the Lord is at hand:	3117
Zep	1:14	The great **d** of the Lord is near	3117
Zep	1:15	That **d** is a **d** of wrath	3117
Zep	1:15	a **d** of darkness and gloominess,	3117
Zep	2:3	hid in the **d** of the Lord's anger	3117
Zec	4:10	despised the **d** of small things?	3117
Zec	12:3	in that **d** will I make Jerusalem	3117
Zec	13:1	In that **d** there shall be a fountain	3117
Zec	13:4	in that **d**, that the prophets shall	3117
Zec	14:1	**d** of the Lord cometh, and thy	3117
Zec	14:4	his feet shall stand in that **d**	3117
Zec	14:8	be in that **d**, that living waters	3117
Mal	3:2	who may abide the **d** of his coming?	3117
Mal	4:5	great and dreadful **d** of the Lord:	3117
Mt	6:11	**Give us this d our daily bread**	*4594*
Mt	6:30	**grass of the field, which to d is,**	*4594*
Mt	6:34	**Sufficient unto this d is the evil**	*2250*
Mt	7:22	**Many will say to me in that d**	*2250*
Mt	10:15	**in the d of judgment, than for**	*2250*
Mt	11:24	**of Sodom, in the d of judgment,**	*2250*
Mt	12:8	**is Lord even of the sabbath d**	
Mt	12:11	**fall into a pit on the sabbath d**	
Mt	12:36	**thereof in the d of judgment**	*2250*
Mt	17:23	**third d he shall be raised again**	*2250*
Mt	20:6	**Why stand ye here all the d idle?**	*2250*
Mt	20:19	**the third d he shall rise again**	*2250*
Mt	24:36	**d and hour knoweth no man,**	*2250*
Mt	24:50	**a d when he looketh not for him,**	*2250*
Mt	25:13	**know neither the d nor the hour**	*2250*
Mt	26:29	**d when I drink it new with you**	*2250*
Mk	3:2	would heal him on the sabbath **d**;	
Mk	6:11	**Gomorrha in the d of judgment,**	*2250*
Mk	9:31	**killed, he shall rise the third d.**	*2250*
Mk	10:34	**the third d he shall rise again**	*2250*
Mk	13:32	**of that d and that hour knoweth**	*2250*
Mk	14:25	**until that d that I drink it new**	*2250*
Mk	16:2	first **d** of the week, they came unto	
Lk	2:11	unto you is born this **d** in the city	*4594*
Lk	4:21	**This d is this scripture fulfilled**	*4594*
Lk	6:7	he would heal on the sabbath **d**;	
Lk	6:23	**Rejoice ye in that d, and leap for**	*2250*
Lk	9:22	**slain, and be raised the third d**	*2250*
Lk	13:14	healed on the sabbath **d**, and	
Lk	13:32	**the third d I shall be perfected**	
Lk	14:3	**lawful to heal on the sabbath d?**	
Lk	16:19	**fared sumptuously every d:**	*2250*
Lk	17:4	**seven times in a d, and seven**	*2250*
Lk	17:24	**also the Son of man be in his d**	*2250*
Lk	17:27	**d that Noe entered into the ark,**	*2250*
Lk	17:29	**d that Lot went out of Sodom**	*2250*
Lk	17:30	**d when the Son of man is**	*2250*
Lk	18:33	**the third d he shall rise again**	*2250*
Lk	19:5	**to d I must abide at thy house**	*4594*
Lk	19:9	**d is salvation come to this house,**	*4594*
Lk	19:42	**at least in this thy d, the things**	*2250*
Lk	21:34	**that d come upon you unawares.**	*2250*
Lk	22:34	**the cock shall not crow this d,**	*4594*
Lk	23:43	**I say unto thee, To d shalt thou**	*4594*
Lk	24:1	Now upon the first **d** of the week,	
Lk	24:7	and the third **d** rise again	*2250*
Lk	24:21	is the third **d** since these things	*2250*
Lk	24:46	**rise from the dead the third d:**	*2250*
Jn	1:29	next **d** John seeth Jesus coming	*1887*
Jn	6:39	**raise it up again at the last d**	*2250*
Jn	6:40	**raise him up at the last d**	*2250*
Jn	6:44	**raise him up at the last d**	*2250*
Jn	6:54	**raise him up at the last d**	*2250*
Jn	7:23	**If a man on the sabbath d receive**	
Jn	8:56	**Abraham rejoiced to see my d:**	*2250*
Jn	9:4	**him that sent me, while it is d:**	*2250*
Jn	11:9	**there not twelve hours in the d?**	*2250*
Jn	11:24	in the resurrection at the last **d**.	*2250*
Jn	12:7	**against the d of my burying hath**	*2250*
Jn	14:20	**At that d ye shall know that I**	*2250*
Jn	16:23	**in that d ye shall ask me nothing**	*2250*
Jn	19:31	upon the cross on the sabbath **d**,	
Jn	20:19	first **d** of the week, when the doors	*2250*
Ac	1:2	Until the **d** in which he was taken	*2250*
Ac	2:1	the **d** of Pentecost was fully come,	*2250*
Ac	2:20	before that great and notable **d** of	*2250*
Ac	10:40	Him God raised up the third **d**,	*2250*
Ac	13:33	Son, this **d** have I begotten thee.	*4594*
Ac	15:21	the synagogues every sabbath **d**.	
Ac	17:31	Because he hath appointed a **d**, in	*2250*
Ro	2:5	the **d** of wrath and revelation	*2250*
Ro	2:16	In the **d** when God shall judge	*2250*
Ro	8:36	we are killed all the **d** long;	*2250*
Ro	13:12	the **d** is at hand: let us therefore	*2250*
Ro	13:13	Let us walk honestly, as in the **d**;	*2250*
Ro	14:5	esteemeth one **d** above another:	*2250*
Ro	14:5	another esteemeth every **d** alike.	*2250*
1Co	1:8	blameless in the **d** of our Lord	*2250*
1Co	15:4	he rose again the third **d** according	*2250*
2Co	4:16	inward man is renewed **d** by **d**	*2250*
2Co	6:2	behold, now is the **d** of salvation.)	*2250*
Eph	4:30	sealed unto the **d** of redemption	*2250*
Php	1:6	it until the **d** of Jesus Christ:	*2250*
Php	1:10	without offence till the **d** of Christ;	*2250*
Php	3:5	Circumcised the eighth **d**, of the	*2250*
1Th	5:2	**d** of the Lord so cometh as a thief	*2250*
1Th	5:4	that that **d** should overtake you	*2250*
2Th	2:3	for that **d** shall not come, except	
2Ti	1:18	find mercy of the Lord in that **d**:	*2250*
2Ti	4:8	judge, shall give me at that **d**:	*2250*
Heb	1:5	this **d** have I begotten thee?	*4594*
Heb	3:7	saith, To **d** if ye will hear his voice,	*4594*
Heb	3:15	While it is said, To **d** if ye will hear	*4594*
Heb	4:4	And God did rest the seventh **d**	*2250*
Heb	5:5	my Son, to **d** have I begotten thee.	*4594*
Heb	13:8	yesterday, and to **d**, and for ever	*4594*
Jas	4:13	ye that say, To **d** or to morrow we	*4594*
Jas	5:5	hearts, as in a **d** of slaughter	*2250*

1Pe	2:12	glorify God in the **d** of visitation.	*2250*
2Pe	1:19	the **d** star arise in your hearts:	*5459*
2Pe	2:8	his righteous soul from **d** to **d**.	*2250*
2Pe	3:8	**d** is with the Lord as a thousand	*2250*
2Pe	3:8	and a thousand years as one **d**.	*2250*
2Pe	3:10	But the **d** of the Lord will come	*2250*
1Jn	4:17	boldness in the **d** of judgment:	*2250*
Jude	6	unto the judgment of the great **d**	*2250*
Rev	1:10	I was in the Spirit on the Lord's **d**	*2250*
Rev	4:8	and they rest not **d** and night,	*2250*
Rev	6:17	the great **d** of his wrath is come;	*2250*
Rev	7:15	him **d** and night in his temple:	*2250*
Rev	9:15	for an hour, and a **d**, and a month,	*2250*
Rev	12:10	them before our God **d** and night.	*2250*
Rev	14:11	and they have no rest **d** nor night,	*2250*
Rev	16:14	of that great **d** of God Almighty	*2250*
Rev	20:10	**d** and night for ever and ever	*2250*

DAYS

Ge	1:14	for seasons, and for **d**, and years:	3117
Ge	6:4	giants in the earth in those **d**;	3117
Ge	7:4	to rain upon the earth forty **d**.	3117
Ge	17:12	he that is eight **d** old shall be	3117
Ge	40:12	The three branches are three **d**:	3117
Ge	47:9	few and evil have the **d** of the years	3117
Ex	12:19	Seven **d** shall there be no leaven	3117
Ex	16:29	the sixth day the bread of two **d**;	3117
Ex	20:9	Six **d** shalt thou labour, and do all	3117
Ex	20:12	thy **d** may be long upon the land	3117
Ex	24:18	Moses was in the mount forty **d**.	3117
Ex	31:17	in six **d** the Lord made heaven and	3117
Le	8:35	congregation day and night seven **d**,	3117
Le	12:2	she shall be unclean seven **d**;	3117
Le	12:4	her purifying three and thirty **d**;	3117
Nu	6:5	the **d** of the vow of his separation	3117
Nu	9:22	whether it were two **d**, or a month,	3117
Nu	12:14	shut out from the camp seven **d**,	3117
Nu	13:25	searching of the land after forty **d**	3117
Nu	14:34	even forty **d**, each day for a year,	3117
Dt	4:9	from thy heart all the **d** of thy life:	3117
Dt	4:32	ask now of the **d** that are past,	3117
Dt	5:13	Six **d** thou shalt labour, and do all	3117
Dt	5:16	that thy **d** may be prolonged, and	3117
Dt	9:9	I abode in the mount forty **d**	3117
Dt	9:18	the Lord, as at the first, forty **d**	3117
Dt	22:19	may not put her away all his **d**.	3117
Dt	22:29	may not put her away all his **d**.	3117
Dt	32:7	Remember the **d** of old, consider	3117
Jos	1:5	before thee all the **d** of thy life:	3117
Jos	1:11	within three **d** ye shall pass over	3117
Jgs	14:14	in three **d** expound the riddle	3117
Jgs	17:6	In those **d** there was no king in	3117
Jgs	18:1	those **d** there was no king in Israel:	3117
Jgs	21:25	those **d** there was no king in Israel:	3117
Ru	1:1	in the **d** when the judges ruled,	3117
1Ki	12:5	Depart yet for three **d**, then come	3117
1Ki	15:14	perfect with the Lord all his **d**.	3117
1Ki	19:8	the strength of that meat forty **d**	3117
2Ki	20:6	I will add unto thy **d** fifteen years:	3117
1Ch	13:3	enquired not at it in the **d** of Saul	3117
Ezr	6:22	feast of unleavened bread seven **d**	3117
Est	1:5	both unto great and small, seven **d**,	3117
Est	2:12	so were the **d** of their purifications	3117
Est	9:26	they called these **d** Purim after	3117
Ps	21:4	length of **d** for ever and ever.	3117
Ps	23:6	shall follow me all the **d** of my life:	3117
Ps	37:18	The Lord knoweth the **d** of the	3117
Ps	39:4	the measure of my **d**, what it is;	3117
Ps	89:29	his throne as the **d** of heaven.	3117
Ps	90:10	The **d** of our years are threescore	3117
Ps	90:12	So teach us to number our **d**,	3117
Ps	103:15	As for man, his **d** are as grass:	3117
Pr	3:2	For length of **d**, and long life,	3117
Pr	10:27	The fear of the Lord prolongeth **d**:	3117
Pr	15:15	All the **d** of the afflicted are evil:	3117
Pr	31:12	and not evil all the **d** of her life	3117
Ecc	2:16	**d** to come shall all be forgotten	3117
Ecc	5:18	all the **d** of his life, which God	3117
Ecc	6:3	the **d** of his years be many,	3117
Ecc	6:12	all the **d** of his vain life which he	3117
Ecc	9:9	the **d** of the life of thy vanity,	3117
Ecc	11:1	thou shalt find it after many **d**	3117
Ecc	12:1	now thy Creator in the **d** of thy	3117
Isa	2:2	it shall come to pass in the last **d**,	3117
Isa	38:5	I will add unto thy **d** fifteen years	3117
Jer	2:32	forgotten me **d** without number	3117
La	4:18	end is near, our **d** are fulfilled;	3117
La	5:21	be turned; renew our **d** as of old	3117
Eze	3:15	astonished among them seven **d**.	3117
Eze	43:26	Seven **d** shall they purge the altar	3117
Eze	46:1	six working **d**; but on the sabbath	3117
Da	1:15	end of ten **d** their countenances	3117
Da	6:7	of any God or man for thirty **d**,	3118
Da	7:9	and the Ancient of **d** did sit,	3118
Da	7:22	Until the Ancient of **d** came, and	3118
Da	8:14	and three hundred **d**;	6153, 1242
Da	10:14	for yet the vision is for many **d**	3117
Da	12:11	thousand two hundred and ninety **d**	3117
Da	12:12	hundred and five and thirty **d**.	3117
Hos	2:11	her feast **d**, her new moons,	
Joel	2:29	those **d** will I pour out my spirit	3117
Am	5:21	I hate, I despise your feast **d**,	
Jnh	1:17	was in the belly of the fish three **d**	3117
Jnh	3:4	Yet forty **d**, and Nineveh shall be	3117
Hab	1:5	I will work a work in your **d**	3117
Mt	4:2	when he had fasted forty **d**	*2250*
Mt	12:12	**lawful to do well on the sabbath d**	
Mt	12:40	**as Jonas was three d and three nights**	*2250*
Mt	12:40	**so shall the son of man be three d**	*2250*
Mt	24:22	**except those d should be**	*2250*
Mt	24:37	**But as the d of Noe were,**	*2250*
Mt	24:38	**For as in the d that were before**	*2250*
Mt	26:61	and to build it in three **d**	*2250*
Mt	27:40	and buildest it in three **d**, save	*2250*
Mt	27:63	After three **d** I will rise again	*2250*
Mk	1:13	there in the wilderness forty **d**,	*2250*
Mk	3:4	**to do good on the sabbath d,**	
Mk	8:2	**have now been with me three d**	*2250*
Mk	8:31	killed, and after three **d** rise again	*2250*
Mk	13:20	**had shortened those d, no flesh**	*2250*
Mk	13:24	**in those d, after that tribulation**	*2250*
Mk	14:58	within three **d** I will build another	*2250*
Mk	15:29	temple, and buildest it in three **d**,	*2250*
Lk	2:22	when the **d** of her purification	*2250*
Lk	2:46	that after three **d** they found him	*2250*
Lk	4:2	forty **d** tempted of the devil. And	*2250*
Lk	6:9	**lawful on the sabbath d to do good,**	
Lk	17:26	**as it was in the d of Noe, so shall**	*2250*
Lk	17:26	**be also in the d of the Son of**	*2250*
Lk	17:28	**as it was in the d of Lot;**	*2250*
Lk	21:22	**For these be the d of vengeance,**	*2250*
Lk	23:29	**behold, the d are coming, in the**	*2250*

Jn	2:19	**in three d I will raise it up**	*2250*
Jn	11:17	he had lain in the grave four **d**	*2250*
Ac	1:3	being seen of them forty **d**, and	*2250*
Ac	1:5	**the Holy Ghost not many d hence**	*2250*
Ac	2:18	pour out in those **d** of my Spirit;	*2250*
Gal	4:10	Ye observe **d**, and months,	*2250*
Eph	5:16	the time, because the **d** are evil	*2250*
Col	2:16	the new moon, or of the sabbath **d**:	
2Ti	3:1	last **d** perilous times shall come	*2250*
Heb	1:2	in these last **d** spoken unto us	*2250*
Heb	7:3	beginning of **d**, nor end of life;	*2250*
Heb	8:10	the house of Israel after those **d**,	*2250*
Heb	10:32	call to remembrance the former **d**,	*2250*
Heb	11:30	were compassed about seven **d**	*2250*
Heb	12:10	they verily for a few **d** chastened	*2250*
Jas	5:3	treasure together for the last **d**	*2250*
1Pe	3:10	that will love life, and see good **d**,	*2250*
1Pe	3:20	of God waited in the **d** of Noah,	*2250*
2Pe	3:3	shall come in the last **d** scoffers,	*2250*
Rev	2:10	**ye shall have tribulation ten d:**	*2250*
Rev	9:6	in those **d** shall men seek death,	*2250*
Rev	11:3	two hundred and threescore **d**,	*2250*
Rev	11:6	rain not in the **d** of their prophecy:	*2250*
Rev	11:9	dead bodies three **d** and a half,	*2250*
Rev	11:11	three **d** and a half the Spirit of life	*2250*
Rev	12:6	two hundred and threescore **d**.	*2250*

DAYS'

Ex	3:18	we beseech thee, three **d** journey	3117
Ex	5:3	we pray thee, three **d** journey into	3117
Ex	8:27	**d** journey into the wilderness,	3117
1Sa	11:3	Give us seven **d** respite, that we	3117
2Sa	24:13	three **d** pestilence in thy land?	3117
Jnh	3:3	great city of three **d** journey.	3117

DAYSMAN

Job	9:33	Neither is there any **d** betwixt us,	3198

DAYSPRING

Lk	1:78	**d** from on high hath visited us,	*395*

DAYSTAR See DAY and STAR.

DAYTIME

Ps	22:2	O my God, I cry in the **d**, but thou	3119
Ps	78:14	**d** also he led them with a cloud,	3119
Isa	4:6	a shadow in the **d** from the heat,	3119

DEACON

1Ti	3:10	let them use the office of a **d**,	*1247*
1Ti	3:13	that have used the office of a **d**,	*1247*

DEACONS

1Ti	3:8	Likewise must the **d** be grave,	*1249*
1Ti	3:12	the **d** be the husbands of one wife,	*1249*

DEAD

Ge	20:3	art but a **d** man, for the woman	4191
Ge	23:4	that I may bury my **d** out of my	4191
Ge	44:20	and his brother is **d**, and he alone	4191
Ex	4:19	men are **d** which sought thy life	4191
Ex	12:30	a house where there was not one **d**	4191
Ex	12:33	for they said, We be all **d** men.	4191
Ex	14:30	Israel saw the Egyptians **d** upon	4191
Dt	25:6	the name of his brother which is **d**,	4191
Jgs	2:19	the judge was **d**, that they returned,	4191
Jgs	16:30	the **d** which he slew at his death	4191
Ru	4:5	the **d**, to raise up the name of the **d**	4191
2Sa	1:4	Saul and Jonathan his son are **d**	4191
2Sa	4:10	Saul is **d**, thinking to have brought	4191
2Sa	11:21	Thy servant Uriah the Hittite is **d**	4191
2Sa	11:26	Uriah her husband was **d**, she	4191
2Sa	12:18	if we tell him that the child is **d**?	4191
2Sa	12:23	he is **d**, wherefore should I fast?	4191
2Sa	13:33	for Amnon only is **d**	4191
2Sa	16:9	this **d** dog curse my lord the king?	4191
1Ki	3:20	laid her **d** child in my bosom	4191
2Ki	4:32	child was **d**, and laid upon his bed	4191
2Ki	8:5	he had restored a **d** body to life	4191
Ps	31:12	I am forgotten as a **d** man	4191
Ps	88:10	shall the **d** arise and praise thee?	7496
Ps	110:6	fill the places with the **d** bodies;	1472
Pr	2:18	death, and her paths unto the **d**.	7496
Pr	9:18	knoweth not that the **d** are there;	7496
Pr	21:16	in the congregation of the **d**.	7496
Ecc	4:2	praised the **d** which are already **d**	4191
Ecc	9:4	a living dog is better than a **d** lion.	4191
Ecc	9:5	but the **d** know not any thing,	4191
Ecc	10:1	**D** flies cause the ointment of the	4194
Isa	14:9	it stirreth up the **d** for thee,	7496
Isa	26:19	with my **d** body shall they arise	5038
Jer	22:10	Weep ye not for the **d**, neither	4191
Jer	31:40	the whole valley of the **d** bodies,	6297
Am	8:3	there shall be many **d** bodies	6297
Mt	2:19	But when Herod was **d**, behold,	*5053*
Mt	2:20	for they are **d** which sought the	*2348*
Mt	8:22	**me; and let the d bury their d.**	*3498*
Mt	9:24	**for the maid is not d, but sleepeth.**	*599*
Mt	11:5	**the d are raised up, and the poor**	*3498*
Mt	17:9	**of man be risen again from the d.**	*3498*
Mt	22:31	**touching the resurrection of the d,**	*3498*
Mt	22:32	**God is not the God of the d, but**	*3498*
Mt	23:27	**within full of d men's bones, and**	*3498*
Mt	27:64	He is risen from the **d**: so the last	*3498*
Mt	28:7	that he is risen from the **d**;	*3498*
Mk	5:39	**the damsel is not d, but sleepeth**	*599*
Mk	9:9	Son of man were risen from the **d**	*3498*
Mk	12:25	**when they shall rise from the d**	*3498*
Mk	12:26	**as touching the d, that they rise:**	*3498*
Mk	12:27	**He is not the God of the d**	*3498*
Lk	7:22	**the deaf hear, the d are raised**	*3498*
Lk	8:52	**not; she is not d, but sleepeth**	*599*
Lk	9:60	unto him, **Let the d bury their d:**	*3498*
Lk	10:30	**and departed, leaving him half d**	*2258*
Lk	15:24	**For this my son was d, and is**	*3498*
Lk	15:32	**for this thy brother was d, and is**	*3498*
Lk	16:31	**though one rose from the d**	*3498*
Lk	20:35	**and the resurrection from the d,**	*3498*
Lk	20:37	**Now that the d are raised, even**	*3498*
Lk	20:38	**For he is not a God of the d,**	*3498*
Lk	24:5	seek ye the living among the **d**?	*3498*
Lk	24:46	**to rise from the d the third day:**	*3498*
Jn	2:22	therefore he was risen from the **d**,	*3498*
Jn	5:21	**as the Father raiseth up the d**	*3498*
Jn	6:58	**fathers did eat manna, and are d:**	*599*
Jn	11:14	unto them plainly, **Lazarus is d.**	*599*
Jn	11:25	**though he were d, yet shall he live:**	*599*
Jn	19:33	that he was **d** already, they brake	*2348*
Jn	20:9	he must rise again from the **d**	*3498*
Jn	21:14	after that he was risen from the **d**	*3498*
Ac	3:15	God hath raised from the **d**;	*3498*
Ac	4:10	whom God raised from the **d**, even	*3498*
Ac	10:42	to be the Judge of quick and **d**	*3498*
Ac	13:30	But God raised him from the **d**:	*3498*
Ac	17:3	and risen again from the **d**;	*3498*

Ac	17:31	he hath raised him from the **d**	*3498*
Ac	26:8	you, that God should raise the **d**?	*3498*
Ro	1:4	by the resurrection from the **d**:	*3498*
Ro	5:15	the offence of one many be **d**,	*599*
Ro	6:2	How shall we, that are **d** to sin,	*599*
Ro	6:4	Christ was raised up from the **d**	*3498*
Ro	6:8	if we be **d** with Christ, we believe	*599*
Ro	6:11	to be **d** indeed unto sin, but alive	*3498*
Ro	7:2	if the husband be **d**, she is loosed	*599*
Ro	7:8	For without the law sin was **d**	*3498*
Ro	8:10	the body is **d** because of sin;	*3498*
Ro	8:11	that raised up Christ from the **d**	*3498*
Ro	10:7	bring up Christ again from the **d**.	*3498*
Ro	10:9	hath raised him from the **d**, thou	*3498*
Ro	14:9	be Lord both of the **d** and living	*3494*
1Co	7:39	but if her husband be **d**, she is at	*2837*
1Co	15:13	if there be no resurrection of the **d**	*3498*
1Co	15:16	For if the **d** rise not, then is not	*3498*
1Co	15:20	now is Christ risen from the **d**	*3498*
1Co	15:21	came also the resurrection of the **d**,	*3498*
1Co	15:29	why are they then baptized for the **d**?	*3498*
1Co	15:52	the **d** shall be raised incorruptible	*3498*
2Co	5:14	one died for all, then were all **d**:	*599*
Gal	2:19	I through the law am **d** to the	*599*
Gal	2:21	the law, then Christ is **d** in vain	*599*
Eph	2:1	were **d** in trespasses and sins;	*3498*
Php	3:11	unto the resurrection of the **d**.	*3498*
Col	1:18	the firstborn from the **d**;	*3498*
Col	2:13	And you, being **d** in your sins	*3498*
Col	2:20	if ye be **d** with Christ from the	*599*
Col	3:3	For ye are **d**, and your life is hid	*599*
1Th	1:10	whom he raised from the **d**, even	*3498*
1Th	4:16	the **d** in Christ shall rise first:	*3498*
1Ti	5:6	in pleasure is **d** while she liveth	*2348*
2Ti	2:11	For if we be **d** with him, we shall	*4880*
2Ti	4:1	shall judge the quick and the **d**	*3498*
Heb	9:14	your conscience from **d** works to	*3498*
Heb	9:17	of force after men are **d**:	*3498*
Heb	11:19	to raise him up, even from the **d**;	*3498*
Heb	11:35	received their **d** raised to life	*3498*
Heb	13:20	brought again from the **d** our Lord	*3498*
Jas	2:20	that faith without works is **d**?	*3498*
Jas	2:26	so faith without works is **d** also	*3498*
1Pe	1:21	that raised him up from the **d**, and	*3498*
1Pe	2:24	that we, being **d** to sins, should	*581*
1Pe	4:5	to judge the quick and the **d**	*3498*
1Pe	4:6	preached also to them that are **d**,	*3498*
Rev	1:5	the first begotten of the **d**, and	*3498*
Rev	1:17	saw him, I fell at his feet as **d**.	*3498*
Rev	1:18	**I am he that liveth, and was d;**	*3498*
Rev	2:8	**last, which was d, and is alive;**	*3498*
Rev	3:1	**a name that thou livest, and art d**	*3498*
Rev	11:8	**d** bodies shall lie in the streets	*4430*
Rev	14:13	Blessed are the **d** which die in the	*3498*
Rev	20:5	the rest of the **d** lived not again	*3498*
Rev	20:12	And I saw the **d**, small and great	*3498*
Rev	20:12	and the **d** were judged out of	*3498*
Rev	20:13	gave up the **d** which were in it,	*3498*
Rev	20:13	death and hell delivered up the **d**	*3498*

DEADLY

Mk	16:18	**and if they drink any d thing,**	*2286*
Jas	3:8	an unruly evil, full of **d** poison	*2287*
Rev	13:3	**d** wound was healed; and all	*2288*
Rev	13:12	whose **d** wound was healed	*2288*

DEAF

Ex	4:11	who maketh the dumb, or **d**, or	2795
Le	19:14	Thou shalt not curse the **d**, nor	2795
Isa	35:5	ears of the **d** shall be unstopped	2795
Isa	42:18	Hear, ye **d**; and look, ye blind,	2795
Mic	7:16	their mouth, their ears shall be **d**.	2790
Mt	11:5	**and the d hear, the dead are**	*2974*
Mk	7:37	he maketh both the **d** to hear, and	*2974*
Mk	9:25	**Thou dumb and d spirit, I charge**	*2974*
Lk	7:22	**the d hear, the dead are raised,**	*2974*

DEAL

Ge	19:9	now will we **d** worse with thee,	
Ge	21:23	thou wilt not **d** falsely with me,	
Ge	24:49	if ye will **d** kindly and truly with	6213
Ge	34:31	Should he **d** with our sister as	6213
Ge	47:29	and **d** kindly and truly with me;	6213
Le	19:11	shall not steal, neither **d** falsely	
Dt	7:5	thus shall ye **d** with them; ye shall	6213
Jos	2:14	will **d** kindly and truly with thee.	6213
Job	42:8	lest I **d** with you after your folly	6213
Ps	75:4	**D** not foolishly: and to the	
Ps	119:17	**D** bountifully with thy servant	1580
Ps	119:124	**D** with thy servant according	6213
Pr	12:22	they that **d** truly are his delight	6213
Isa	58:7	to **d** thy bread to the hungry	6536
Jer	21:2	Lord will **d** with us according to	6213
Eze	8:18	Therefore will I also **d** in fury:	6213
Eze	18:9	kept my judgments, to **d** truly;	6213
Eze	23:25	they shall **d** furiously with thee:	6213
Eze	23:29	they shall **d** with thee hatefully	6213
Da	1:13	as thou seest, **d** with thy servants	6213
Hab	1:13	upon them that **d** treacherously	
Mal	2:10	why do we **d** treacherously every	
Mal	2:15	let none **d** treacherously against	
Mal	2:16	spirit, that ye **d** not treacherously	
Mk	7:36	so much the more a great **d**.	*4054*

DEALETH

Pr	10:4	He becometh poor that **d** with	6213
Pr	13:16	prudent man **d** with knowledge:	6213
Pr	14:17	He that is soon angry **d** foolishly:	6213
Pr	21:24	his name, who **d** in proud wrath	6213
Jer	8:10	unto the priest every one **d** falsely.	6213
Heb	12:7	God **d** with you as with sons;	*4374*

DEALINGS

Jn	4:9	have no **d** with the Samaritans.	*4798*

DEALT

Ge	16:6	when Sarai **d** hardly with her	
Ge	33:11	God hath **d** graciously with me	
Ex	1:20	God **d** well with the midwives:	
Ex	14:11	wherefore hast thou **d** thus with	6213
Ex	21:8	seeing he hath **d** deceitfully with	
Ru	1:20	the Almighty hath **d** very bitterly	
2Ki	12:15	workmen: for they **d** faithfully	6213
2Ki	21:6	and **d** with familiar spirits and	6213
2Ki	22:7	hand, because they **d** faithfully	6213
2Ch	6:37	done amiss, and have **d** wickedly;	
2Ch	33:6	**d** with a familiar spirit, and with	6213
Ne	1:7	**d** very corruptly against thee	
Ps	13:6	he hath **d** bountifully with me	1580
Ps	44:17	have we **d** falsely in thy covenant	
Ps	103:10	hath not **d** with us after our sins;	6213
Ps	119:78	for they **d** perversely with me	
Ps	147:20	He hath not **d** so with any nation:	6213

Jer 3:20 have ye **d** treacherously with me,
La 1:2 have **d** treacherously with her
Eze 22:7 of thee have they **d** by oppression 6213
Hos 5:7 **d** treacherously against the Lord:
Joel 2:26 your God that hath **d** wondrously...........6213
Zec 1:6 our doings, so hath he **d** with us 6213
Lk 2:48 why hast thou thus **d** with us? *4160*
Ro 12:3 as God hath **d** to every man....................*3307*

DEAR
Lk 7:2 who was **d** unto him, was sick *1784*
Ac 20:24 count I my life **d** unto myself,..................*5093*
Eph 5:1 followers of God, as **d** children;..................*27*
Col 1:13 into the kingdom of his **d** Son:....................*26*

DEARTH
Ge 41:54 seven years of **d** began to come, ...7458
2Ki 4:38 and there was a **d** in the land;..................7458
Ne 5:3 might buy corn, because of the **d**. 7458
Ac 7:11 there came a **d** over all the land..............*3042*
Ac 11:28 be great **d** throughout all the *3042*

DEATH
Ge 21:16 Let me not see the **d** of the child 4194
Ge 24:67 was comforted after his mother's **d**
Ex 10:17 take away from me this **d** only.................4194
Ex 19:12 mount shall be surely put to **d**:................4191
Ex 21:12 he die, shall be surely put to **d** 4191
Ex 21:15 his mother, shall be surely put to **d**. 4191
Ex 31:14 defileth it shall surely be put to **d**: 4191
Ex 35:2 work therein shall be put to **d**.................4191
Le 20:15 he shall surely be put to **d**: and ye 4191
Le 20:27 a wizard, shall surely be put to **d**: 4191
Le 24:17 any man shall surely be put to **d**.............4191
Le 27:29 but shall surely be put to **d**.......................4191
Nu 3:10 cometh nigh shall be put to **d**. 4191
Nu 15:35 The man shall be surely put to **d**: 4191
Nu 16:29 these men die the common **d** of all.........4194
Nu 23:10 Let me die the **d** of the righteous 4194
Nu 35:16 murderer shall surely be put to **d** 4191
Nu 35:28 until the **d** of the high priest:...................4194
Dt 13:5 of dreams, shall be put to **d**;.....................4191
Dt 17:6 witness he shall not be put to **d**..............4191
Dt 24:16 shall be put to **d** for his own sin 4191
Jgs 13:7 the womb to the day of his **d**. 4194
Jgs 16:16 his soul was vexed unto **d**;.......................4191
Jgs 16:30 the dead which he slew at his **d** 4194
Ru 1:17 if ought but **d** part thee and me 4194
1Sa 20:3 but a step between me and **d** 4194
1Sa 22:22 I have occasioned the **d** of all the
1Ki 2:26 not at this time put thee to **d** 4191
1Ki 11:40 in Egypt until the **d** of Solomon.............4194
2Ki 4:40 man of God, there is **d** in the pot 4194
Est 4:11 one law of his to put him to **d**, ...4191
Job 3:21 long for **d**, but it cometh not; 4194
Job 34:22 is no darkness, nor shadow of **d**, ...6757
Ps 6:5 in **d** there is no remembrance of 4194
Ps 13:3 lest I sleep the sleep of **d**;.........................4194
Ps 23:4 the valley of the shadow of **d** 6757
Ps 33:19 To deliver their soul from **d**, and 4194
Ps 56:13 hast delivered my soul from **d**: 4194
Ps 68:20 the Lord belong the issues from **d**...........4194
Ps 89:48 he that liveth, and shall not see **d**? 4194
Pr 2:18 her house inclineth unto **d**, and...............4194
Pr 5:5 Her feet go down to **d**; her steps..............4194
Pr 8:36 all they that hate me love **d** 4194
Pr 10:2 righteousness delivereth from **d** 4194
Pr 11:4 righteousness delivereth from **d** 4194
Pr 14:12 the end thereof are the ways of **d**.............4194
Pr 14:32 the righteous hath hope in his **d**.............4194
Pr 16:14 of a king is as messengers of **d**: 4194
Pr 16:25 the end thereof are the ways of **d**............4194
Pr 18:21 **D** and life are in the power of the...........4194
Pr 26:18 casteth firebrands, arrows, and **d**, ...4194
Ecc 7:1 day of **d** than the day of one's birth 4194
Ecc 7:26 more bitter than **d** the woman.................4194
Ecc 8:8 power in the day of **d**: and there is..........4194
SS 8:6 love is strong as **d**; jealousy is..................4194
Isa 25:8 He will swallow up **d** in victory;..............4194
Isa 28:15 We have made a covenant with **d** 4194
Isa 53:9 wicked, and with the rich in his **d**; 4194
Isa 53:12 hath poured out his soul unto **d**:.............4194
Jer 15:2 Such as are for **d**, to **d**; and such.............4194
Jer 21:8 the way of life, and the way of **d**.............4194
Jer 43:11 such as are for **d** to **d**; and such 4194
Jer 52:11 in prison till the day of his **d**...................4194
Eze 18:32 pleasure in the **d** of him that dieth..........4194
Eze 33:11 no pleasure in the **d** of the wicked; 4194
Am 5:8 turneth the shadow of **d** into the............6757
Jnh 4:9 well to be angry, even unto **d** 4194
Hab 2:5 his desire as hell, and is as **d**....................4194
Mt 2:15 was there until the **d** of Herod:...............*5054*
Mt 10:21 **deliver up the brother to d,**.....................*2288*
Mt 15:4 **or mother, let him die the d**....................*2288*
Mt 16:28 **shall not taste of d, till they see** *2288*
Mt 20:18 **and they shall condemn him to d,** *2288*
Mt 26:38 **exceeding sorrowful, even unto d:** *2288*
Mt 26:59 against Jesus, to put him to **d**;.................*2289*
Mt 26:66 and said, He is guilty of **d**.........................*2288*
Mk 5:23 daughter lieth at the point of **d**:..............*2079*
Mk 9:1 **shall not taste of d, till they have**............*2288*
Mk 13:12 **shall betray the brother to d,**...................*2288*
Mk 14:34 **is exceeding sorrowful unto d:** *2288*
Mk 14:55 against Jesus to put him to **d**; and *2289*
Mk 14:64 condemned him to be guilty of **d**...........*2288*
Lk 18:33 **scourge him, and put him to d:**..................*615*
Lk 23:15 nothing worthy of **d** is done unto *2288*
Lk 23:22 found no cause of **d** in him: I will *2288*
Jn 5:24 **but is passed from d unto life**.................*2288*
Jn 8:51 **my saying, he shall never see d**...............*2288*
Jn 11:4 **This sickness is not unto d, but**..............*2288*
Jn 12:33 signifying what **d** he should die.............*2288*
Jn 18:32 signifying what **d** he should die..............*2288*
Jn 21:19 by what **d** he should glorify God *2288*
Ac 8:1 Saul was consenting unto his **d**..................*336*
Ac 13:28 they found no cause of **d** in him *2288*
Ac 22:4 I persecuted this way unto the **d**,............*2288*
Ac 22:20 by, and consenting unto his **d**, ...*336*
Ac 26:10 when they were put to **d**, I gave *337*
Ro 1:32 such things are worthy of **d**,.....................*2288*
Ro 5:10 by the **d** of his Son, much more,.................*2288*
Ro 5:14 **d** reigned from Adam to Moses *2288*
Ro 6:5 in the likeness of his **d**, we shall be *2288*
Ro 6:16 of sin unto **d**, or of obedience..................*2288*
Ro 6:23 For the wages of sin is **d**; but the *2288*
Ro 7:24 me from the body of this **d**?.....................*2288*
Ro 8:6 to be carnally minded is **d**; *2288*
Ro 8:38 neither **d**, nor life, nor angels, nor *2288*
1Co 3:22 or life, or **d**, or things present....................*2288*
1Co 15:21 by man came **d**, by man came *2288*
1Co 15:54 **D** is swallowed up in victory....................*2288*
1Co 15:55 O **d**, where is thy sting? O grave...............*2288*
1Co 15:56 sting of **d** is sin; and the strength.............*2288*

D

2Co 1:9 had the sentence of **d** in ourselves *2288*
2Co 1:10 delivered us from so great a **d**, *2288*
2Co 2:16 one we are the savour of **d** unto **d**; *2288*
Php 2:8 and became obedient unto **d** *2288*
Php 2:8 even the **d** of the cross *2288*
Php 3:10 made conformable unto his **d**; *2288*
Heb 2:9 God should taste **d** for every man *2288*
Heb 2:14 him that had the power of **d** *2288*
Heb 9:16 must also of necessity be the **d** *2288*
Heb 11:5 that he should not see **d**; *2288*
Jas 1:15 it is finished, bringeth forth **d** *2288*
Jas 5:20 save a soul from **d**, and shall hide *2288*
1Jn 3:14 we have passed from **d** unto life, *2288*
1Jn 5:16 a sin which is not unto **d**, he shall *2288*
1Jn 5:16 There is a sin unto **d**: I do not *2288*
Rev 1:18 **the keys of hell and of d** *2288*
Rev 2:10 **be thou faithful unto d, and I will** *2288*
Rev 2:11 **shall not be hurt of the second d** *2288*
Rev 6:8 his name that sat on him was **D**, *2288*
Rev 9:6 men seek **d**, and shall not find it; *2288*
Rev 12:11 loved not their lives unto the **d** *2288*
Rev 20:6 the second **d** hath no power, but *2288*
Rev 20:13 **d** and hell delivered up the dead *2288*
Rev 20:14 **d** and hell were cast into the *2288*
Rev 20:14 lake of fire. This is the second **d**, *2288*
Rev 21:4 be no more **d**, neither sorrow, *2288*
Rev 21:8 brimstone: which is the second **d** *2288*

DEBASE
Isa 57:9 didst **d** thyself even unto hell 8213

DEBATE
Pr 25:9 **D** thy cause with thy neighbour 7378

DEBT
Mt 18:27 **him, and forgave him the d** *1156*
Mt 18:30 **prison, till he should pay the d** *3784*
Mt 18:32 **I forgave thee all that d, because** *3782*

DEBTOR
Mt 23:16 **the gold of the temple, he is a d!** *3784*
Ro 1:14 I am **d** both to the Greeks, and *3781*

DEBTORS
Mt 6:12 **our debts, as we forgive our d** *3781*
Lk 7:41 **certain creditor which had two d:** *5533*
Lk 16:5 **called every one of his lord's d** *5533*
Ro 8:12 we are **d**, not to the flesh, *3781*

DEBTS
Mt 6:12 **forgive us our d, as we forgive** *3783*

DECAYETH
Ecc 10:18 slothfulness the building **d**; 4355
Heb 8:13 that which **d** and waxeth old *3822*

DECEASE
Lk 9:31 spake of his **d** which he should *1841*

DECEIT
Ps 10:7 His mouth is full of cursing and **d** 4820
Ps 36:3 of his mouth are iniquity and **d**: 4820
Ps 72:14 shall redeem their soul from **d** 8496
Ps 101:7 **d** shall not dwell within my 7423
Pr 12:5 the counsels of the wicked are **d** 4820
Pr 12:20 **D** is in the heart of them that 4820
Pr 14:8 but the folly of fools is **d** 4820
Pr 20:17 Bread of **d** is sweet to a man; 8267
Pr 26:26 Whose hatred is covered by **d**, 4860
Jer 9:6 through **d** they refuse to know me, 4820
Jer 14:14 nought, and the **d** of their heart. 8649
Jer 23:26 of the **d** of their own heart; 8649
Hos 12:7 the balances of **d** are in his hand: 4820
Am 8:5 and falsifying the balances by **d**? 4820
Mk 7:22 **wickedness, d, lasciviousness, an** *1388*
Ro 1:29 full of envy, murder, debate, **d**, *1388*
Ro 3:13 their tongues they have used **d**; *1387*
Col 2:8 through philosophy and vain **d**, *539*
1Th 2:3 our exhortation was not of **d**, *4106*

DECEITFUL
Ps 43:1 me from the **d** and unjust man 4820
Ps 55:23 bloody and **d** men shall not live 4820
Ps 78:57 were turned aside like a **d** bow 7423
Pr 11:18 The wicked worketh a **d** work: 8267
Pr 14:25 but a **d** witness speaketh lies 4820
Pr 23:3 his dainties: for they are **d** meat 3577
Pr 27:6 but the kisses of an enemy are **d** 6280
Pr 31:30 Favour is **d**, and beauty is vain: 8267
Jer 17:9 The heart is **d** above all things 6121
Hos 7:16 High: they are like a **d** bow: 7423
Mic 6:12 their tongue is **d** in their mouth 7423
Zep 3:13 **d** tongue be found in their mouth: 8649
2Co 11:13 false apostles, **d** workers, *1386*
Eph 4:22 corrupt according to the **d** lusts; *539*

DECEITFULLY
Ex 8:29 let not Pharaoh deal **d** any more 2048
Ex 21:8 seeing he hath dealt **d** with her 898
Le 6:4 thing which he hath **d** gotten 6231
Ps 24:4 his soul unto vanity, nor sworn **d** 4820
Jer 48:10 doeth the work of the Lord **d**, 7423
2Co 4:2 nor handling the word of God **d**, *1389*

DECEITFULNESS
Mt 13:22 **the d of riches, choke the word,** *539*
Mk 4:19 **the d of riches, and the lusts of** *539*
Heb 3:13 be hardened through the **d** of sin *539*

DECEIVE
2Sa 3:25 that he came to **d** thee, and to 6601
2Ki 19:10 God in whom thou trustest **d** thee 5377
2Ch 32:15 let not Hezekiah **d** you, nor 5377
Pr 24:28 cause; and **d** not with thy lips 6601
Jer 9:5 will **d** every one his neighbour, 2048
Jer 37:9 **D** not yourselves, saying, The 5377
Mt 24:4 **Take heed that no man d you.** *4105*
Mt 24:11 **shall rise, and shall d many.** *4105*
Mt 24:24 **they shall d the very elect.** *4105*
Mk 13:5 **Take heed lest any man d you:** *4105*
Mk 13:6 **I am Christ; and shall d many.** *4105*
1Co 3:18 Let no man **d** himself. If any *1818*
Eph 4:14 whereby they lie in wait to **d**; *4106*
Eph 5:6 Let no man **d** you with vain words: *538*
2Th 2:3 Let no man **d** you by any means: *1818*
1Jn 1:8 we **d** ourselves, and the truth *4105*
1Jn 3:7 let no man **d** you: he that doeth *4105*
Rev 20:3 that he should **d** the nations no *4105*

DECEIVED
Ge 31:7 your father hath **d** me, and 2048
Dt 11:16 that your heart be not **d**, 6601
1Sa 19:17 Why hast thou **d** me so, and sent 7411
1Sa 28:12 Why hast thou **d** me? for thou art 7411
Pr 20:1 whosoever is **d** thereby is not 7686
Isa 44:20 a **d** heart had turned him aside, 2048

Jer 4:10 thou hast greatly **d** this people 5377
Jer 20:7 thou hast **d** me, and I was **d**: 6601
La 1:19 I called for my lovers, but they **d** 7411
Eze 14:9 if the prophet be **d** when he hath 6601
Ob 3 pride of thine heart hath **d** thee, 5377
Lk 21:8 **Take heed that ye be not d** *4105*
Jn 7:47 the Pharisees, Are ye also **d**? *4105*
Ro 7:11 **d** me, and by it slew me *1818*
1Co 6:9 Be not **d**: neither fornicators, nor *4105*
1Co 15:33 Be not **d**; evil communications *4105*
Gal 6:7 Be not **d**; God is not mocked: *4105*
1Ti 2:14 Adam was not **d**, but the woman *538*
2Ti 3:13 worse, deceiving, and being **d** *4105*
Tit 3:3 **d**, serving divers lusts and *4105*
Rev 18:23 thy sorceries were all nations **d** *4105*
Rev 19:20 with which he **d** them that had *4105*
Rev 20:10 the devil that **d** them was cast *4105*

DECEIVER

Ge 27:12 I shall seem to him as a **d**; 8591
Mal 1:14 cursed be the **d**, which hath in 5230
Mt 27:63 we remember that that **d** said, *4108*
2Jn 7 This is a **d** and an antichrist. *4108*

DECEIVERS

Tit 1:10 unruly and vain talkers and **d**, *5423*
2Jn 7 For many **d** are entered into the *4108*

DECEIVETH

Pr 26:19 the man that **d** his neighbour, 7411
Jn 7:12 said, Nay; but he **d** the people *4105*
Gal 6:3 when he is nothing, he **d** himself. *5422*
Jas 1:26 his tongue, but **d** his own heart, *538*
Rev 12:9 Satan, which **d** the whole world: *4105*
Rev 13:14 **d** them that dwell on the earth *4105*

DECEIVING

2Ti 3:13 worse and worse, **d**, and being *4105*
Jas 1:22 hearers only, **d** your own selves. *3884*

DECENTLY

1Co 14:40 all things be done **d** and in order *2156*

DECIDED

1Ki 20:40 judgment be; thyself hast **d** it. 2782

DECISION

Joel 3:14 multitudes in the valley of **d**: for 2742
Joel 3:14 the Lord is near in the valley of **d** 2742

DECK

Jer 10:4 **d** it with silver and with gold; 3302

DECKED

Pr 7:16 I have **d** my bed with coverings 7234
Eze 16:13 wast thou **d** with gold and silver; 5710
Rev 17:4 **d** with gold and precious stones *5558*
Rev 18:16 **d** with gold, and precious stones, *5558*

DECKETH

Isa 61:10 as a bridegroom **d** himself with 3547

DECLARE

Jos 20:4 and shall **d** his cause in the ears 1696
1Ki 22:13 prophets **d** good unto the king
1Ch 16:24 **D** his glory among the heathen; 5608
Job 38:4 **d**, if thou hast understanding. 5046
Job 38:18 earth? **d** if thou knowest it all. 5046
Job 40:7 of thee, and **d** thou unto me 3045
Job 42:4 of thee, and **d** thou unto me 3045
Ps 2:7 I will **d** the decree: the Lord 5608
Ps 19:1 The heavens **d** the glory of God; 5608
Ps 22:31 **d** his righteousness unto a people 5046
Ps 30:9 praise thee? shall it **d** thy truth? 5046
Ps 38:18 For I will **d** mine iniquity; 5046
Ps 40:5 if I would **d** and speak of them, 5046
Ps 50:6 heavens shall **d** his righteousness: 5046
Ps 73:28 that I may **d** all thy works. 5608
Ps 78:6 and **d** them to their children: 5608
Ps 96:3 **D** his glory among the heathen, 5608
Ps 97:6 The heavens **d** his righteousness, 5046
Ps 145:8 acts: and I will **d** thy greatness. 5608
Isa 3:9 they **d** their sin as Sodom, they 5046
Isa 21:6 let him **d** what he seeth. 5046
Isa 42:9 new things do I **d**: before they 5046
Isa 43:9 who among them can **d** this, 5046
Isa 45:19 I **d** things that are right. 5046
Isa 53:8 and who shall **d** his generation? 7878
Isa 66:19 and they shall **d** my glory among 5046
Jer 38:15 If I **d** it unto thee, wilt thou not 5046
Jer 38:25 **D** unto us now what thou hast 5046
Jer 42:20 **d** unto us, and we will do it. 5046
Jer 50:28 to **d** in Zion the vengeance of the 5046
Eze 12:16 they may **d** all their abominations; 5608
Da 4:18 **d** the interpretation thereof, 560
Mic 3:8 to **d** unto Jacob his transgression, 5046
Mt 13:36 **D** unto us the parable of the *5419*
Mt 15:15 unto him, **D** unto us this parable *5419*
Jn 17:26 **them thy name, and will d it:** *1107*
Ac 13:32 we **d** unto you glad tidings, how *2097*
Ac 13:41 though a man **d** it unto you *1555*
Ac 17:23 worship, him **d** I unto you *2605*
Ac 20:27 **d** unto you all the counsel of God *312*
Ro 3:25 to **d** his righteousness for the *1732*
1Co 3:13 for the day shall **d** it, because *1213*
Heb 11:14 **d** plainly that they seek a *1718*
1Jn 1:3 seen and heard **d** we unto you, *518*
1Jn 1:5 **d** unto you, that God is light *312*

DECLARED

Ex 9:16 my name may be **d** throughout 5608
Dt 4:13 And he **d** unto you his covenant 5046
Ps 40:10 I have **d** thy faithfulness and thy 559
Ps 71:17 have I **d** thy wondrous works. 5046
Ps 88:11 Shall thy lovingkindness be **d** 5608
Ps 119:13 With my lips have I **d** all the 5608
Isa 21:2 A grievous vision is **d** unto me; 5046
Isa 43:12 I have **d**, and have saved, and I 5046
Isa 45:21 who hath **d** this from ancient 8085
Isa 48:3 I have **d** the former things from 5046
Isa 48:5 from the beginning **d** it to thee; 5046
Lk 8:47 **d** unto him before all the people *518*
Jn 1:18 the Father, he hath **d** him: *1834*
Jn 17:26 **I have d unto them thy name,** *1107*
Ac 12:17 **d** unto them how the Lord had *1334*
Ac 15:4 **d** all things that God had done *312*
Ac 21:19 **d** particularly what things God *1834*
Ro 1:4 **d** to be the Son of God with power, *3724*
Ro 9:17 my name might be **d** throughout *1229*
Col 1:3 Who also **d** unto us your love *1213*
Rev 10:7 **d** to his servants the prophets *2097*

DECLARETH

Isa 41:26 there is none that **d**, yea, there is 5046
Hos 4:12 and their staff **d** unto them for 5046
Am 4:13 **d** unto man what is his thought 5046

DECLARING

Isa	46:10	**D** the end from the beginning	5046
Ac	15:12	**d** what miracles and wonders	*1834*

DECLINE

Ex	23:2	**d** after many to wrest judgment:	5186
Dt	17:11	shall not **d** from the sentence	5493
Pr	4:5	neither **d** from the words of my	5186
Pr	7:25	Let not thine heart **d** to her ways	7847

DECLINED

2Ch	34:2	**d** neither to the right hand, nor	5493
Ps	119:51	yet have I not **d** from thy law.	5186

DECLINETH

Ps	102:11	days are like a shadow that **d**;	5186
Ps	109:23	gone like the shadow when it **d**:	5186

DECREASE

Jn	3:30	He must increase, but I must **d**.	*1642*

DECREE

2Ch	30:5	So they established a **d** to make	1697
Ezr	5:13	Cyrus made a **d** to build this	2942
Ezr	6:1	Darius the king made a **d**, and	2942
Ezr	6:8	I make a **d** what ye shall do to	2942
Ezr	6:12	I Darius have made a **d**: let it	2942
Ezr	7:21	I Artaxerxes the king, do make a **d**	2942
Est	1:20	the king's **d** which he shall make	6599
Est	4:3	commandment and his **d** came,	1881
Est	8:17	commandment and his **d** came,	1881
Est	9:13	according unto this day's **d**, and let	1881
Est	9:32	And the **d** of Esther confirmed	3982
Ps	2:7	I will declare the **d**: the Lord hath	2706
Ps	148:6	made a **d** which shall not pass	2706
Pr	8:15	reign, and princes **d** justice	2710
Pr	8:29	When he gave to the sea his **d**,	2706
Isa	10:1	unto them that **d** unrighteous	2710
Jer	5:22	of the sea by a perpetual **d**,	2706
Da	2:9	there is but one **d** for you:	1882
Da	2:13	And the **d** went forth that wise men	1882
Da	3:10	Thou, O king, hast made a **d**,	2942
Da	3:29	I make a **d**, That every people,	2942
Da	6:7	to make a firm **d**, that whosoever	633
Da	6:15	no **d** nor statute which the king	633
Da	6:26	I make a **d**, That in every	2942
Jnh	3:7	the **d** of the king and his nobles,	2940
Mic	7:11	day shall the **d** be far removed.	2706
Zep	2:2	Before the **d** bring forth, before	2706
Lk	2:1	there went out a **d** from Caesar	*1378*

DECREED

Est	9:31	and as they had **d** for themselves	6965
1Co	7:37	hath so **d** in his heart that he	*2919*

DECREES

Isa	10:1	that decree unrighteous **d**, and	2711

DEDICATE

Dt	20:5	battle, and another man **d** it.	2596
2Sa	8:11	Which also king David did **d**	6942
1Ch	26:27	did they **d** to maintain the house	6942
2Ch	2:4	to **d** it to him, and to burn	6942

DEDICATED

Dt	20:5	new house, and hath not **d** it?	2596
2Sa	8:11	the silver and gold that he had **d**	6942
1Ki	7:51	which David his father had **d**;	6944
1Ki	8:63	and all the children of Israel **d**	2596
2Ki	12:4	money of the **d** things that is	6944
2Ki	12:18	kings of Judah, had **d**, and his	6942
2Ch	7:5	and all the people **d** the house	2596
2Ch	24:7	**d** things of the house of the Lord	6944
Eze	44:29	every **d** thing in Israel shall be	2764
Heb	9:18	testament was **d** without blood	*1457*

DEDICATION

Nu	7:88	This was the **d** of the altar,	2598
2Ch	7:9	they kept the **d** of the altar	2598
Ezr	6:16	kept the **d** of this house of God	2597
Ne	12:27	at the **d** of the wall of Jerusalem	2598
Da	3:2	come to the **d** of the image	2597
Jn	10:22	at Jerusalem the feast of the **d**,	*1456*

DEED

Ge	44:15	What **d** is this that ye have done?	4639
Jgs	19:30	There was no such **d** done nor	
1Sa	26:4	that Saul was come in very **d**	3559
2Sa	12:14	by this **d** thou hast given great	1697
2Ch	6:18	But will God in very **d** dwell with men	
Lk	23:51	to the counsel and **d** of them;	*4234*
Lk	24:19	mighty in **d** and word before God	*2041*
Ro	15:18	Gentiles obedient, by word and **d**,	*2041*
1Co	5:2	hath done this **d** might be taken	*2041*
Col	3:17	ye do in word or **d**, do all in the	*2041*
Jas	1:25	man shall be blessed in his **d**.	*4162*
1Jn	3:18	tongue; but in **d** and in truth	*2041*

DEEDS

Ge	20:9	thou hast done **d** unto me that	4639
Ezr	9:13	for our evil **d**, and for our	4639
Ps	28:4	Give them according to their **d**,	6467
Ps	105:1	make known his **d** among the	5949
Isa	59:18	According to their **d**,	1578
Jer	25:14	them according to their **d**, and	6467
Lk	11:48	**ye allow the d of your fathers:**	*2041*
Lk	23:41	the due reward of our **d**	*3739, 4238*
Jn	3:19	**because their d were evil**	*2041*
Jn	3:20	**lest his d should be reproved**	*2041*
Jn	8:41	**Ye do the d of your father**	*2041*
Ac	7:22	was mighty in words and in **d**.	*2041*
Ac	19:18	confessed, and shewed their **d**.	*4234*
Ro	2:6	to every man according to his **d**:	*2041*
Ro	3:20	by the **d** of the law there shall no	*2041*
Ro	3:28	faith without the **d** of the law	*2041*
Ro	8:13	do mortify the **d** of the body,	*4234*
2Co	12:12	and wonders, and mighty **d**.	*1411*
Col	3:9	put off the old man with his **d**;	*4234*
2Pe	2:8	today with their unlawful **d**;	*2041*
2Jn	11	speed is partaker of his evil **d**	*2041*
Jude	15	of all their ungodly **d** which	*2041*
Rev	2:6	**hatest the d of the Nicolaitanes**	*2041*
Rev	2:22	**except they repent of their d**	*2041*
Rev	16:11	and repented not of their **d**	*2041*

DEEP

Ge	1:2	was upon the face of the **d**	8415
Ge	2:21	God caused a **d** sleep to fall upon	8639
Ge	7:11	fountains of the great **d** broken	8415
Ge	8:2	The fountains also of the **d** and	8415
Ge	15:12	down, a **d** sleep fell upon Abram;	8639
1Sa	26:12	**d** sleep from the Lord was fallen	8639
Job	4:13	when **d** sleep falleth on men	8639
Job	33:15	when **d** sleep falleth upon men	8639
Job	41:31	maketh the **d** to boil like a pot:	4688
Ps	42:7	**D** calleth unto **d** at the noise of	8415

Ps 64:6 one of them, and the heart, is **d**. 6013
Ps 69:15 neither let the **d** swallow me up 4688
Ps 92:5 and thy thoughts are very **d** 6009
Ps 95:4 In his hand are the **d** places of the 4278
Ps 104:6 Thou coveredst it with the **d** as 8415
Ps 135:6 in the seas, and all **d** places. 8415
Pr 8:28 the fountains of the **d**: 8415
Pr 18:4 of a man's mouth are as **d** waters 6013
Pr 19:15 casteth into a **d** sleep: and an 8639
Pr 20:5 in the heart of man is like **d** water; 6013
Pr 22:14 mouth of strange women is a **d** pit; 6013
Pr 23:27 whore is a **d** ditch; and a strange 6013
Ecc 7:24 far off, and exceeding **d**, who can 6013
Isa 29:10 the spirit of **d** sleep, and hath 8639
Isa 44:27 That saith to the **d**, Be dry, 6683
Isa 63:13 That led them through the **d**, as 8415
Eze 23:32 shalt drink of thy sister's cup **d** 6013
Eze 34:18 to have drunk of the **d** waters 4950
Da 2:22 revealeth the **d** and secret things: 5994
Da 8:18 I was in a **d** sleep on my face 7290
Da 10:9 then was I in a **d** sleep on my face 7290
Jnh 2:3 thou hadst cast me into the **d**, 4688
Lk 5:4 **Launch out into the d, and let** *899*
Lk 6:48 **built an house, and digged d,** *2532, 900*
Jn 4:11 to draw with, and the well is **d**: *901*
Ac 20:9 being fallen into a **d** sleep: *901*
Ro 10:7 Who shall descend into the **d**? *12*
1Co 2:10 things, yea, the **d** things of God *899*
2Co 8:2 their **d** poverty abounded unto the *899*
2Co 11:25 and a day I have been in the **d**; *1037*

DEEPER
Le 13:3 plague in sight be **d** than the skin 6013
Isa 33:19 a people of **d** speech than thou 6012

DEEPLY
Isa 31:6 children of Israel have **d** revolted 6009
Hos 9:9 They have **d** corrupted themselves, 6009
Mk 8:12 he sighed **d** in his spirit, and saith, *389*

DEEPNESS
Mt 13:5 **because they had no d of earth:** *899*

DEFAMED
1Co 4:13 Being **d**, we intreat: we are made *987*

DEFAMING
Jer 20:10 For I heard the **d** of many, fear 1681

DEFEAT
2Sa 15:34 me **d** the counsel of Ahithophel. 6565
2Sa 17:14 **d** the good counsel of Ahithophel, 6565

DEFENCE
Nu 14:9 their **d** is departed from them 6738
2Ch 11:5 Jerusalem, and built cities for **d** 4692
Ps 7:10 My **d** is of God, which saveth 4043
Ps 59:9 wait upon thee: for God is my **d** 4869
Ps 59:17 God is my **d**, and the God of my 4869
Ps 62:2 and my salvation; he is my **d**; 4869
Ps 89:18 For the Lord is our **d**: and the 4043
Ps 94:22 the Lord is my **d**; and my God 4869
Ecc 7:12 wisdom is a **d**, and money is a **d**: 6738
Isa 4:5 upon all the glory shall be a **d** 2646
Ac 19:33 have made his **d** unto the people *626*
Ac 22:1 hear ye my **d**, which I make *627*
Php 1:7 **d** and confirmation of the gospel, *627*
Php 1:17 I am set for the **d** of the gospel *627*

DEFENCED
Isa 36:1 against all the **d** cities of Judah, 1219
Jer 8:14 and let us enter into the **d** cities 4013
Eze 21:20 and to Judah in Jerusalem the **d**. 1219

DEFEND
2Ki 19:34 For I will **d** this city, to save it 1598
2Ki 20:6 will **d** this city for mine own sake, 1598
Ps 20:1 name of the God of Jacob **d** thee; 7682
Ps 82:3 **D** the poor and fatherless: do 8199
Isa 31:5 the Lord of hosts **d** Jerusalem; 1598
Isa 37:35 For I will **d** this city to save it 1598
Zec 9:15 The Lord of hosts shall **d** them; 1598
Zec 12:8 In that day shall the Lord **d** the 1598

DEFENDED
Ac 7:24 suffer wrong, he **d** him; and smote *292*

DEFER
Ecc 5:4 **d** not to pay it; for he hath no 309
Isa 48:9 will I **d** mine anger, and for my 748

DEFERRED
Ge 34:19 young man **d** not to do the thing, 309
Pr 13:12 Hope **d** maketh the heart sick: 4900

DEFERRETH
Pr 19:11 discretion of a man **d** his anger; 748

DEFIED
Nu 23:8 defy, whom the Lord hath not **d**? 2194
1Sa 17:36 seeing he hath **d** the armies of 2778
2Sa 21:21 And when he **d** Israel, Jonathan 2778

DEFILE
Le 11:44 neither shall ye **d** yourselves 2930
Le 15:31 when they **d** my tabernacle that is 2930
Le 18:20 neighbour's wife, to **d** thyself with 2930
Le 18:23 thou lie with any beast to **d** thyself 2930
Le 20:3 to **d** my sanctuary, and to profane 2930
Le 22:8 not eat to **d** himself therewith: 2930
Nu 5:3 that they **d** not their camps, in the 2930
Nu 35:34 **D** not therefore the land which ye 2930
SS 5:3 my feet; how shall I **d** them? 2936
Isa 30:22 Ye shall **d** also the covering of thy 2930
Jer 32:34 called by my name, to **d** it 2930
Eze 7:22 robbers shall enter into it, and **d**. 2490
Eze 9:7 he said unto them, **D** the house 2930
Eze 20:18 nor **d** yourselves with their idols: 2930
Eze 33:26 ye **d** every one his neighbour's 2930
Eze 43:7 shall the house of Israel no more **d**, 2930
Eze 44:25 husband, they may **d** themselves 2930
Da 1:8 he would not **d** himself with the 1351
Mt 15:18 **the heart; and they d the man.** *2840*
Mk 7:15 **entering into him can d him: but** *2840*
Mk 7:23 **come from within, and d the man.** *2840*
1Co 3:17 If any man **d** the temple of God, *5351*
1Ti 1:10 that **d** themselves with mankind, *733*
Jude 8 these filthy dreamers **d** the flesh, *3392*

DEFILED
Ge 34:13 he had **d** Dinah their sister: 2930
Le 18:24 all these the nations are **d** which 2930
Le 18:25 the land is **d**: therefore I do visit 2930
Le 19:31 wizards, to be **d** by them: I am the 2930
Le 21:3 no husband; for her may he be **d**. 2930
Nu 5:2 and whosoever is **d** by the dead: 2931
Nu 5:14 jealous of his wife, and she be **d** 2930
Nu 5:28 if the woman be not **d**, but be 2930

D

Nu 6:12 lost, because his separation was **d**............2930
Nu 9:7 We are **d** by the dead body of a 2931
Nu 19:20 hath **d** the sanctuary of the Lord:............2930
Dt 21:23 that thy land be not **d**, which the............2930
Dt 24:4 after that she is **d**; for that is.....................2930
2Ki 23:8 and **d** the high places where the 2930
Neh 13:29 they have **d** the priesthood,......................1351
Ps 79:1 thy holy temple have they **d**; 2930
Ps 106:39 Thus were they **d** with their own.............2930
Isa 24:5 The earth also is **d** under the 2610
Isa 59:3 your hands are **d** with blood, and 1351
Jer 2:7 when ye entered, ye **d** my land.................2930
Jer 16:18 because they have **d** my land....................2490
Eze 5:11 thou hast **d** my sanctuary with 2930
Eze 22:4 and hast **d** thyself in thine idols...............2930
Eze 23:17 they **d** her with their whoredom 2930
Eze 23:38 they have **d** my sanctuary in the..............2930
Eze 43:8 they have even **d** my holy name...............2930
Mic 4:11 that say, Let her be **d**, and let our.............2610
Mk 7:2 eat bread with **d**, that is to say..................*2839*
Jn 18:28 lest they should be **d**; but that..................*3392*
1Co 8:7 their conscience being weak is **d**.............*3435*
Tit 1:15 their mind and conscience is **d**................*3392*
Heb 12:15 you, and thereby many be **d**;....................*3392*
Rev 14:4 which were not **d** with women; *3435*

DEFILETH

Ex 31:14 every one that **d** it shall surely 2490
Nu 19:13 **d** the tabernacle of the Lord:....................2930
Nu 35:33 for blood it **d** the land: and the................2610
Mt 15:11 **out of the mouth, this d a man.** *2840*
Mt 15:20 **with unwashen hands d not a man**.........*2840*
Jas 3:6 members, that it **d** the whole body,.........*4695*
Rev 21:27 enter into it any thing that **d**,..................*2840*

DEFRAUD

Le 19:13 Thou shalt not **d** thy neighbour,..............6231
Mt 10:19 **D not, Honour thy father and**...................*650*
1Co 7:5 **D** ye not one the other, except it................*650*
1Th 4:6 and **d** his brother in any matter...............*4122*

DEFRAUDED

1Sa 12:3 I taken? or whom have I **d**? 6231
1Co 6:7 rather suffer yourselves to be **d**?................*650*
2Co 7:2 no man, we have **d** no man......................*4122*

DEFY

Nu 23:8 hath not cursed? or how shall I **d**, ...2194
1Sa 17:10 I **d** the armies of Israel this day; 2778

DEGREE

Ps 62:9 **d** are vanity, and men of high **d**
Lk 1:52 seats, and exalted them of low **d**.............*5011*
1Ti 3:13 purchase to themselves a good **d**, ...*898*
Jas 1:9 Let the brother of low **d** rejoice *5071*

DEGREES

2Ki 20:9 the shadow go forward ten **d**, ...4609
Isa 38:8 Ahaz, ten **d** backward. So the sun............4609

DELAY

Ex 22:29 Thou shalt not **d** to offer the......................309

DELAYED

Ex 32:1 Moses **d** to come down out of the............954

DELAYETH

Mt 24:48 **My lord d his coming;** *5549*
Lk 12:45 **My lord d his coming; and shall**.............*5549*

DELECTABLE

Isa 44:9 their **d** things shall not profit;..................2530

DELICACIES

Rev 18:3 through the abundance of her **d**.............*4764*

DELICATE

Dt 28:54 is tender among you, and very **d** 6028
Dt 28:56 The tender and **d** woman among............6028
Jer 6:2 to a comely and **d** woman........................6026

DELICATELY

Pr 29:21 He that **d** bringeth up his servant............6445
La 4:5 They that did feed **d** are desolate.............4574
Lk 7:25 **and live d, are in king's courts**................*5172*

DELICATES

Jer 51:34 he hath filled his belly with my **d**, ...5730

DELICIOUSLY

Rev 18:7 glorified herself, and lived **d**, ...*4763*

DELIGHT

Ge 34:19 he had **d** in Jacob's daughter:...................2654
Nu 14:8 If the Lord **d** in us, then he will...............2654
Dt 21:14 if thou have no **d** in her, then 2654
2Sa 15:26 I have no **d** in thee; behold, here 2654
2Sa 24:3 doth my lord the king **d** in this................2654
Est 6:6 To whom would the king **d** to do...........2654
Job 34:9 that he should **d** himself with God 7521
Ps 1:2 But his **d** is in the law of the Lord; 2656
Ps 37:4 **D** thyself also in the Lord; and.................6026
Ps 40:8 I **d** to do thy will, O my God:...................2654
Ps 62:4 they **d** in lies: they bless with 7521
Ps 94:19 me thy comforts **d** my soul. 8173
Ps 119:16 I will **d** myself in thy statutes: 8173
Ps 119:174 O Lord; and thy law is my **d**.....................8191
Pr 1:22 the scorners **d** in their scorning,..............2531
Pr 2:14 and **d** in the frowardness of the...............1523
Pr 11:1 but a just weight is his **d**,..........................7522
Pr 11:20 but such as are upright are his **d**.............7522
Pr 12:22 but they that deal truly are his **d**..............7522
Pr 15:8 the prayer of the upright is his **d** 7522
Pr 16:13 Righteous lips are the **d** of kings;.............7522
Pr 18:2 fool hath no **d** in understanding 2654
Pr 19:10 **D** is not seemly for a fool; 8588
Pr 24:25 them that rebuke him shall be **d**.............5276
Pr 29:17 he shall give **d** unto thy soul.....................4574
SS 2:3 under his shadow with great **d**,................2530
Isa 1:11 I **d** not in the blood of bullocks...............2654
Isa 13:17 as for gold, they shall not **d** in it 2654
Isa 58:2 me daily, and **d** to know my ways,...........2654
Isa 58:13 call the sabbath a **d**, the holy of 6027
Jer 6:10 reproach; they have no **d** in it. 2654
Jer 9:24 in these things I **d**, saith the Lord............2654
Mal 3:1 of the covenant, whom ye **d** in: 2655
Ro 7:22 For I **d** in the law of God after *4913*

DELIGHTED

1Sa 19:2 Saul's son **d** much in David:.....................2654
1Ki 10:9 which **d** in thee, to set thee on the...........2654
Est 2:14 no more, except the king **d** in her............2654
Ps 18:19 delivered me, because he **d** in me............2654
Ps 22:8 deliver him, seeing he **d** in him................2654
Ps 109:17 as he **d** not in blessing, so let it be 2654
Isa 65:12 did choose that wherein I **d** not...............2654
Isa 66:4 and chose that in which I **d** not...............2654

DELIGHTEST

Ps	51:16	thou **d** not in burnt offering	7521

DELIGHTETH

Est	6:6	man whom the king **d** to honour?	2654
Ps	37:23	Lord: and he **d** in his way	2654
Ps	112:1	**d** greatly in his commandments	2654
Pr	3:12	a father the son in whom he **d**	7521
Isa	42:1	mine elect, in whom my soul **d**;	7521
Mic	7:18	for ever, because he **d** in mercy.	2654
Mal	2:17	and he **d** in them; or, Where is the	2654

DELIGHTS

2Sa	1:24	you in scarlet, with other **d**,	5730
Ps	119:92	Unless thy law had been my **d**,	8191
Pr	8:31	my **d** were with the sons of men	8191
SS	7:6	pleasant art thou, O love, for **d**!	8588

DELIVER

Ge	32:11	**D** me, I pray thee, from the hand	5337
Ge	37:22	to **d** him to his father again	7725
Ge	42:34	will I **d** you your brother, and ye	5414
Ex	3:8	I am come down to **d** them	5337
Ex	5:18	yet shall ye **d** the tale of bricks	5414
Ex	21:13	but God **d** him into his hand;	579
Ex	22:10	If a man **d** unto his neighbour	5414
Nu	35:25	congregation shall **d** the slayer	5337
Dt	7:2	Lord thy God shall **d** them before	5414
Dt	7:24	shall **d** their kings into thine hand	5414
Dt	19:12	**d** him into the hand of the avenger	5414
Dt	23:15	not **d** unto his master the servant	5462
Dt	25:11	to **d** her husband out of the hand	5337
Dt	32:39	any that can **d** out of my hand.	5337
Jos	2:13	have, and **d** our lives from death.	5337
Jos	7:7	to **d** us into the hand of the	5414
Jos	11:6	about this time will I **d** them up	5414
Jos	20:5	not **d** the slayer up into his hand;	5462
Jgs	10:13	wherefore I will **d** you no more	3467
Jgs	10:14	let them **d** you in the time of	3467
1Sa	4:8	who shall **d** us out of the hand of	5337
1Sa	7:3	he will **d** you out of the hand of the	5337
1Sa	12:21	things, which cannot profit nor **d**;	5337
1Sa	17:46	the Lord **d** thee into mine hand;	5462
1Sa	24:4	I will **d** thine enemy into thine	5414
1Sa	26:24	him **d** me out of all tribulation	5337
2Sa	3:14	**D** me my wife Michal, which I	5414
2Sa	20:21	**d** him only, and I will depart	5414
1Ki	8:46	**d** them to the enemy, so that they	5414
2Ki	18:29	he shall not be able to **d** you	5337
2Ki	18:30	The Lord will surely **d** us, and this	5337
1Ch	14:10	for I will **d** them into thine hand	5414
2Ch	25:20	that he might **d** them into the	5414
2Ch	32:11	The Lord our God shall **d** us out	5337
2Ch	32:13	**d** their lands out of mine hand?	5337
Ezr	7:19	those **d** thou before the God of	8000
Ps	7:2	in pieces, while there is none to **d**	5337
Ps	22:4	trusted, and thou didst **d** them	6403
Ps	22:8	on the Lord that he would **d** him:	6403
Ps	22:8	**d** him, seeing he delighted in	5337
Ps	27:12	**D** me not over unto the will of	5414
Ps	31:1	**d** me in thy righteousness	6403
Ps	33:19	To **d** their soul from death, and	5337
Ps	39:8	**D** me from all my transgressions:	5337
Ps	40:13	Be pleased, O Lord, to **d** me:	5337
Ps	41:1	Lord will **d** him in time of trouble.	4422
Ps	43:1	O **d** me from the deceitful and	6403
Ps	50:22	in pieces, and there be none to **d**	5337
Ps	51:14	**D** me from bloodguiltiness, O God	5337
Ps	59:1	**D** me from mine enemies, O my	5337
Ps	70:1	Make haste, O God, to **d** me:	5337
Ps	71:2	**D** me in thy righteousness, and	5337
Ps	72:12	shall **d** the needy when he crieth;	5337
Ps	79:9	**d** us, and purge away our sins	5337
Ps	106:43	Many times did he **d** them; but	5337
Ps	109:21	thy mercy is good, **d** thou me	5337
Ps	119:134	**D** me from the oppression of	6299
Ps	120:2	**D** my soul, O Lord, from lying	5337
Ps	140:1	**D** me, O Lord, from the evil man:	2502
Pr	2:12	To **d** thee from the way of the evil	5337
Pr	2:16	To **d** thee from the strange woman	5337
Pr	4:9	a crown of glory shall she **d** to	4042
Pr	6:3	this now, my son, and **d** thyself,	5337
Pr	11:6	of the upright shall **d** them:	5337
Pr	12:6	mouth of the upright shall **d** them	5337
Pr	19:19	if thou **d** him, yet thou must	5337
Pr	23:14	and shall **d** his soul from hell	5337
Pr	24:11	If thou forbear to **d** them that are	5337
Ecc	8:8	neither shall wickedness **d** those	4422
Isa	19:20	a great one, and he shall **d** them.	5337
Isa	29:11	men **d** to one that is learned,	5414
Isa	36:15	The Lord will surely **d** us: this city	5337
Isa	43:13	there is none that can **d** out of my	5337
Isa	44:17	**D** me; for thou art my god.	5337
Isa	47:14	they shall not **d** themselves from	5337
Isa	50:2	or have I no power to **d**?	5337
Jer	1:8	I am with thee to **d** thee, saith	5337
Jer	18:21	**d** up their children to the famine,	5414
Jer	21:7	I will **d** Zedekiah king of Judah,	5414
Jer	38:20	They shall not **d** thee. Obey, I	5414
Jer	39:17	But I will **d** thee in that day,	5337
Jer	43:11	and **d** such as are for death to	
Jer	51:45	and **d** ye every man his soul	4422
La	5:8	there is none that doth **d** us out	6561
Eze	7:19	gold shall not be able to **d** them	5337
Eze	14:14	they should **d** but their own souls	5337
Eze	14:20	shall **d** neither son nor daughter;	5337
Eze	23:28	I will **d** thee into the hand of them	5414
Eze	25:7	and will **d** thee for a spoil to the	5414
Eze	33:5	taketh warning shall **d** his soul	4422
Eze	33:12	of the righteous shall not **d** him	5337
Eze	34:12	and will **d** them out of all places	5337
Da	3:15	who is that God that shall **d** you	7804
Da	3:17	is able to **d** us from the burning	7804
Da	3:29	God that can **d** after this sort.	5338
Da	6:14	set his heart on Daniel to **d** him:	7804
Da	6:20	able to **d** thee from the lions?	7804
Hos	2:10	shall **d** her out of mine hand	5337
Am	2:15	swift of foot shall not **d** himself:	4422
Am	6:8	therefore will I **d** up the city	5462
Jnh	4:6	head, to **d** him from his grief	5337
Mic	5:8	teareth in pieces, and none can **d**	5337
Zep	1:18	shall be able to **d** them in the day	5337
Zec	11:6	I will **d** the men every one	4672
Mt	5:25	**adversary d thee to the judge,**	*3860*
Mt	6:13	**temptation, but d us from evil:**	*4506*
Mt	10:17	**will d you up to the councils,**	*3860*
Mt	10:21	**the brother shall d up the brother**	*3860*
Mt	20:19	**And shall d him to the Gentiles**	*3860*
Mt	24:9	**Then shall they d you up to be**	*3860*
Mt	27:43	let him **d** him now, if he will have	*4506*
Mk	10:33	**and shall d him to the Gentiles:**	*3860*
Mk	13:11	**and d you up, take no thought**	*3860*
Lk	11:4	**temptation; but d us from evil**	*4506*

Lk 12:58 **the judge d thee to the officer** ... *3860*
Ac 7:34 and am come down to **d** them ... *1807*
Ac 25:16 to **d** any man to die, before that ... *5483*
Ro 7:24 who shall **d** me from the body of ... *4506*
1Co 5:5 To **d** such an one unto Satan ... *3860*
2Co 1:10 we trust that he will yet **d** us; ... *4506*
Gal 1:4 that he might **d** us from this ... *1807*
2Ti 4:18 the Lord shall **d** me from every ... *4506*
Heb 2:15 and **d** them who through fear of ... *525*
2Pe 2:9 The Lord knoweth how to **d** the ... *4506*

DELIVERANCE

Ge 45:7 save your lives by a great **d** ... 6413
1Ch 11:14 Lord saved them by a great **d** ... 8668
2Ch 12:7 but I will grant them some **d**; ... 6413
Ezr 9:13 hast given us such **d** as this; ... 6413
Est 4:14 enlargement and **d** arise to the ... 2020
Ps 32:7 me about with the songs of **d** ... 6405
Joel 2:32 and in Jerusalem shall be **d** ... 6413
Ob 17 upon Mount Zion shall be **d** ... 6413
Lk 4:18 **to preach d to the captives, and** ... *859*
Heb 11:35 were tortured, not accepting **d**; ... *629*

DELIVERED

Ge 9:2 sea; into your hand are they **d** ... 5414
Ge 25:24 her days to be **d** were fulfilled, ... 3205
Ge 37:21 and he **d** him out of their hands; ... 5337
Ex 1:19 and are **d** ere the midwives come ... 3205
Ex 18:8 way, and how the Lord **d** them. ... 5337
Ex 18:10 of Pharaoh, who hath **d** the people ... 5337
Le 6:4 which was **d** him to keep, or the ... 6487
Le 26:25 and ye shall be **d** into the ... 5414
Dt 2:36 the Lord our God **d** all unto us: ... 5414
Dt 5:22 of stone, and **d** them unto me. ... 5414
Dt 9:10 And the Lord **d** unto me two tables ... 5414
Dt 31:9 and **d** it unto the priests the sons ... 5414
Jos 2:24 the Lord hath **d** into our hands ... 5414
Jos 10:8 I have **d** them into thine hand; ... 5414
Jos 21:44 the Lord **d** all their enemies into ... 5414
Jos 24:10 so I **d** you out of his hand ... 5337
Jgs 2:14 and he **d** them into the hands of ... 5414
Jgs 2:16 which **d** them out of the hand of ... 3467
Jgs 3:10 the Lord **d** Chushan-rishathaim ... 5414
Jgs 4:14 hath **d** Sisera into thine hand: ... 5414
Jgs 16:23 hath **d** Samson our enemy into our ... 5414
1Sa 17:35 and **d** it out of his mouth: ... 5337
1Sa 17:37 **d** me out of the paw of the lion ... 5337
2Sa 12:7 I **d** thee out of the hand of Saul; ... 5337
2Sa 16:8 and the Lord hath **d** the kingdom ... 5414
2Sa 21:6 Let seven men of his sons be **d** ... 5414
2Sa 22:20 he **d** me, because he delighted in ... 2502
1Ki 13:26 Lord hath **d** him unto the lion, ... 5414
2Ki 18:33 any of the gods of the nations, **d** ... 5337
2Ki 19:10 Jerusalem shall not be **d** into ... 5414
2Ki 19:12 the gods of the nation **d** them ... 5337
Ps 7:4 have **d** him that without cause ... 2502
Ps 18:17 He **d** me from my strong enemy, ... 5337
Ps 22:5 They cried unto thee and were **d**: ... 4422
Ps 33:16 a mighty man is not **d** by much ... 5337
Ps 34:4 and **d** me from all my fears ... 5337
Ps 55:18 He hath **d** my soul in peace ... 6299
Ps 56:13 thou hast **d** my soul from death: ... 5337
Ps 78:61 And **d** his strength into captivity ... 5414
Ps 116:8 thou hast **d** my soul from death, ... 2502
Pr 11:8 The righteous is **d** out of trouble, ... 2502
Pr 11:9 knowledge shall the just be **d** ... 2502
Pr 11:21 seed of the righteous shall be **d** ... 4422
Pr 28:26 walketh wisely, he shall be **d** ... 4422
Ecc 9:15 and he by his wisdom **d** the city; ... 4422
Isa 36:18 the gods of the nations **d** his land ... 5337
Isa 38:17 hast in love to my soul **d** it from the
Jer 7:10 are **d** to do all these abominations? ... 5337
Jer 20:13 he hath **d** the soul of the poor ... 5337
Eze 3:19 iniquity; but thou hast **d** thy soul ... 5337
Eze 3:21 warned; also thou hast **d** thy soul ... 5337
Eze 31:14 they are all **d** unto death, to the ... 5414
Eze 33:9 iniquity; but thou hast **d** thy soul ... 5337
Da 3:28 hath sent his angel, and **d** his ... 7804
Da 6:27 who hath **d** Daniel from the power ... 7804
Da 12:1 thy people shall be **d**, every one ... 4422
Joel 2:32 the name of the Lord shall be **d**: ... 4422
Am 9:1 escapeth of them shall not be **d** ... 4422
Mal 3:15 they that tempt God are even **d** ... 4422
Mt 11:27 **All things are d unto me of my** ... *3860*
Mt 18:34 **and d him to the tormentors, till** ... *3860*
Mt 27:2 and **d** him to Pontius Pilate the ... *3860*
Mt 27:18 that for envy they had **d** him ... *3860*
Mt 27:26 Jesus, he **d** him to be crucified ... *3860*
Mt 27:58 commanded the body to be **d** ... *591*
Mk 7:13 **your tradition, which ye have d:** ... *3860*
Mk 9:31 **is d into the hands of men, and** ... *3860*
Mk 10:33 **the Son of man shall be d unto** ... *3860*
Mk 15:1 him away, and **d** him to Pilate ... *3860*
Mk 15:10 chief priests had **d** him for envy ... *3860*
Lk 1:57 time came that she should be **d**; ... *5088*
Lk 2:6 accomplished that she should be **d** ... *5088*
Lk 4:17 was **d** unto him the book of the ... *1929*
Lk 7:15 And he **d** him to his mother ... *1325*
Lk 9:44 **Son of man shall be d into the** ... *3860*
Lk 10:22 **things are d to me of my Father:** ... *3860*
Lk 18:32 **he shall be d unto the Gentiles,** ... *3860*
Lk 23:25 but he **d** Jesus to their will ... *3860*
Lk 24:7 must be **d** into the hands of sinful ... *3860*
Lk 24:20 and our rulers **d** him to be ... *3860*
Jn 16:21 **as soon as she is d of the child,** ... *1080*
Jn 18:36 **that I should not be d to the Jews:** ... *3860*
Jn 19:11 **therefore he that d me unto thee** ... *3860*
Ac 3:13 whom ye **d** up, and denied him ... *3860*
Ac 7:10 And **d** him out of all his afflictions, ... *1807*
Ro 4:25 Who was **d** for our offences, and ... *3860*
Ro 7:6 now we are **d** from the law, ... *2673*
Ro 8:21 shall be **d** from the bondage of ... *1659*
Ro 8:32 own Son, but **d** him up for us all, ... *3860*
1Co 11:23 which also I **d** unto you, that the ... *3860*
1Co 15:3 For I **d** unto you first of all that ... *3860*
1Co 15:24 shall have **d** up the kingdom ... *3860*
2Co 1:10 Who **d** us from so great a death, ... *4506*
Col 1:13 **d** us from the power of darkness, ... *4506*
1Th 1:10 Jesus which **d** us from the wrath ... *4506*
2Th 3:2 we may be **d** from unreasonable ... *4506*
1Ti 1:20 whom I have **d** unto Satan, that ... *3860*
2Ti 4:17 was **d** out of the mouth of the lion ... *4506*
Heb 11:11 and was **d** of a child when she ... *5088*
2Pe 2:4 **d** them into chains of darkness, ... *3860*
2Pe 2:7 And **d** just Lot, vexed with the ... *4506*
Jude 3 faith which was once **d** unto the ... *3860*
Rev 12:4 woman which was ready to be **d** ... *5088*
Rev 20:13 death and hell **d** up the dead ... *1325*

DELIVEREDST

Mt 25:20 **Lord, thou d unto me five talents:** ... *3860*
Mt 25:22 **Lord, thou d unto me two talents:** ... *3860*

DELIVERER

Jgs	3:9	the Lord raised up a **d** to the	3467
Jgs	3:15	the Lord raised them up a **d**,	3467
Jgs	18:28	there was no **d**, because it was	5337
Ps	18:2	my fortress, and my **d**; my God,	6403
Ps	70:5	thou art my help and my **d**; O Lord,	6403
Ac	7:35	God send to be a ruler and a **d** by	*3086*
Ro	11:26	shall come out of Sion the **D**,	*4506*

DELIVERETH

Job	36:15	He **d** the poor in his affliction,	2502
Ps	34:17	**d** them out of all their troubles	5337
Ps	144:10	who **d** David his servant from	6475
Pr	10:2	but righteousness **d** from death.	5337
Pr	11:4	but righteousness **d** from death.	5337
Pr	14:25	A true witness **d** souls: but a	5337
Isa	42:22	for a prey, and none **d**; for a spoil,	5337
Da	6:27	He **d** and rescueth, and he	7804

DELIVERING

Lk	21:12	**d you up to the synagogues, and**	*3860*
Ac	22:4	and **d** into prisons both men and	*3860*

DELIVERY

Isa	26:17	draweth near the time of her **d**,	3205

DELUSION

2Th	2:11	God shall send them strong **d**	*4106*

DELUSIONS

Isa	66:4	I also will choose their **d**,	8586

DEMAND

Job	38:3	for I will **d** of thee, and answer	7592
Job	40:7	like a man: I will **d** of thee, and	7592
Job	42:4	will speak: I will **d** of thee, and	7592

DEMANDED

Ex	5:14	were beaten, and **d**, Wherefore	559
2Sa	11:7	David **d** of him how Joab did	7592
Da	2:27	The secret which the king hath **d**	7593
Mt	2:4	he **d** of them where Christ should	*4441*
Lk	3:14	soldiers likewise **d** of him, saying	*1905*
Lk	17:20	when he was **d** of the Pharisees,	*1905*
Ac	21:33	and **d** who he was, and what	*4441*

DEMONSTRATION

1Co	2:4	in **d** of the Spirit and of power:	*585*

DEN See also DENS.

Ps	10:9	in wait secretly as a lion in his **d**:	5520
Jer	7:11	a **d** of robbers in your eyes?	4631
Jer	9:11	heaps, and a **d** of dragons; and I	4583
Da	6:7	shall be cast into the **d** of lions	1358
Da	6:24	they cast them into the **d** of lions,	1358
Am	3:4	will a young lion cry out of his **d**,	4585
Mt	21:13	**but ye have made it a d of thieves.**	*4693*
Mk	11:17	**but ye have made it a d of thieves.**	*4693*
Lk	19:46	**but ye have made it a d of thieves.**	*4693*

DENIED

Ge	18:15	Sarah **d**, saying, I laughed not;	3584
1Ki	20:7	my gold, and I **d** him not.	4513
Mt	26:70	he **d** before them all, saying	*720*
Mt	26:72	again he **d** with an oath, I do not	*720*
Mk	14:68	But he **d**, saying, I know not	*726*
Mk	14:70	And he **d** it again. And a little after	*720*
Lk	8:45	When all **d**, Peter and they that	*720*
Lk	12:9	**be d before the angels of God.**	*533*
Lk	22:57	he **d** him, saying, Woman, I know	*720*
Jn	13:38	**crow, till thou hast d me thrice.**	*533*
Jn	18:25	He **d** it, and said, I am not,	*720*
Jn	18:27	Peter then **d** again: and	*720*
Ac	3:13	**d** him in the presence of Pilate,	*720*
Ac	3:14	ye **d** the Holy One and the Just	*720*
1Ti	5:8	he hath **d** the faith, and is worse	*720*
Rev	2:13	**hast not d my faith, even in those**	*720*
Rev	3:8	**word, and hast not d my name.**	*720*

DENIETH

Lk	12:9	**he that d me before men shall be**	*720*
1Jn	2:22	he that **d** that Jesus is the Christ?	*720*
1Jn	2:23	Whosoever **d** the Son, the same	*720*

DENS

Jgs	6:2	of Israel made them the **d** which	4492
Heb	11:38	and in **d** and caves of the earth	*4693*
Rev	6:15	hid themselves in the **d** and in	*4693*

DENY

Jos	24:27	unto you, lest ye **d** your God.	3584
1Ki	2:16	one petition of thee, **d** me not	7725
Pr	30:7	**d** me them not before I die:	4513
Pr	30:9	be full, and **d** thee, and say, Who	3584
Mt	10:33	**whosoever shall d me before men,**	*720*
Mt	10:33	**him will I also d before my Father**	*720*
Mt	16:24	**come after me, let him d himself,**	*533*
Mt	26:34	**cock crow, thou shalt d me thrice**	*533*
Mk	8:34	**let him d himself, and take up**	*533*
Mk	14:30	**crow twice, thou shalt d me thrice**	*533*
Mk	14:72	twice, thou shalt **d** me thrice	*533*
Lk	9:23	**come after me, let him d himself,**	*533*
Lk	20:27	**d** that there is any resurrection;	*483*
Lk	22:34	**thrice d that thou knowest me**	*533*
Lk	22:61	**cock crow, thou shalt d me thrice**	*533*
2Ti	2:12	if we **d** him, he also will **d** us:	*720*
2Ti	2:13	faithful: he cannot **d** himself.	*720*
Tit	1:16	but in works they **d** him, being	*720*

DENYING

2Ti	3:5	of godliness, but **d** the power	*720*
Tit	2:12	**d** ungodliness and worldly lusts,	*720*
2Pe	2:1	**d** the Lord that bought them,	*720*
Jude	4	**d** the only Lord God, and our Lord	*720*

DEPART

Ge	49:10	sceptre shall not **d** from Judah,	5493
Ex	21:22	so that her fruit **d** from her,	3318
Ex	33:1	**D**, and go up hence, thou and	3212
Dt	4:9	lest they **d** from thy heart all the	5493
Jos	1:8	This book of the law shall not **d**	4185
2Sa	7:15	mercy shall not **d** away from him,	5493
1Ki	12:5	unto them, **D** yet for three days,	3212
Ps	6:8	**D** from me, all ye workers of	5493
Ps	34:14	**D** from evil, and do good; seek	5493
Ps	37:27	**D** from evil, and do good; and	5493
Ps	55:11	and guile **d** not from her streets	4185
Ps	119:115	**D** from me, ye evildoers: for I	5493
Pr	3:7	fear the Lord, and **d** from evil.	5493
Pr	3:21	let not them **d** from thine eyes:	3868
Pr	4:21	Let them not **d** from thine eyes;	3868
Pr	5:7	**d** not from the words of my	5493
Pr	13:14	to **d** from the snares of death	5493
Pr	13:19	abomination to fools to **d** from	5493
Pr	14:27	to **d** from the snares of death	5493
Pr	15:24	that he may **d** from hell beneath.	5493

Pr 16:6	fear of the Lord men **d** from evil.	5493
Pr 16:17	of the upright is to **d** from evil	5493
Pr 17:13	evil shall not **d** from his house.	4185
Pr 22:6	he is old, he will not **d** from it	5493
Pr 27:22	not his foolishness **d** from him.	5493
Isa 52:11	**D** ye, **d** ye, go ye out from thence,	5493
Isa 54:10	the mountains shall **d**, and the	4185
Isa 54:10	but my kindness shall not **d** from	4185
Jer 6:8	lest my soul **d** from thee; lest	3363
Jer 37:9	from us: for they shall not **d**.	1980
La 4:15	it is unclean; **d**, **d**, touch not:	5493
Hos 9:12	woe also to them when I **d** from	5493
Mic 2:10	Arise ye, and **d**; for this is not	3212
Mt 7:23	**d from me, ye that work iniquity**	*672*
Mt 10:14	**When ye d out of that house**	*1831*
Mt 25:41	**D from me, ye cursed, into**	*4198*
Mk 6:11	**ye d thence, shake off the dust**	*1607*
Lk 2:29	lettest thou thy servant **d** in peace,	*630*
Lk 5:8	**D** from me; for I am a sinful man	*1831*
Lk 12:59	**thou shalt not d thence, till thou**	*1831*
Lk 13:27	**d from me, all ye workers of**	*868*
Lk 13:31	Get thee out, and **d** hence: for	*4198*
Jn 13:1	that he should **d** out of this world	*3327*
Jn 16:7	**but if I d, I will send him unto**	*4198*
Ac 1:4	they should not **d** from Jerusalem	*5562*
Ac 22:21	**D: for I will send thee far hence**	*4198*
1Co 7:10	not the wife **d** from her husband	*5562*
1Co 7:11	she **d**, let her remain unmarried,	*5562*
1Co 7:15	if the unbelieving **d**, let him **d**.	*5562*
2Co 12:8	thrice, that it might **d** from me	*868*
Php 1:23	having a desire to **d**, and to be	*360*
1Ti 4:1	some shall **d** from the faith,	*868*
2Ti 2:19	name of Christ **d** from iniquity	*868*
Jas 2:16	say unto them, **D** in peace, be ye	*5217*

DEPARTED

Ge 31:40	and my sleep **d** from mine eyes	5074
Ex 33:11	**d** not out of the tabernacle	4185
Nu 10:33	**d** from the mount of the Lord	5265
Nu 12:10	cloud **d** from off the tabernacle;	5493
Dt 24:2	when she is **d** out of his house,	3318
1Sa 4:21	saying, The glory is **d** from Israel:	1540
1Sa 16:14	the Spirit of the Lord **d** from Saul,	5493
1Sa 16:23	and the evil spirit **d** from him	5493
1Sa 28:15	God is **d** from me, and answereth	5493
1Sa 28:16	seeing the Lord is **d** from thee,	5493
1Ki 20:36	as thou art **d** from me a lion shall	1980
2Ki 10:31	**d** not from the sins of Jeroboam,	5493
2Ki 13:2	Israel to sin; he **d** not therefrom.	5493
2Ki 13:6	They **d** not from the sins of the	5493
2Ki 13:11	**d** not from all the sins of Jeroboam	5493
2Ki 14:24	**d** not from all the sins of Jeroboam	5493
2Ki 15:9	he **d** not from the sins of Jeroboam	5493
2Ki 15:18	he **d** not all his days from the sins	5493
2Ki 15:24	**d** not from the sins of Jeroboam	5493
2Ki 15:28	**d** not from the sins of Jeroboam	5493
2Ki 19:36	So Sennacherib king of Assyria **d**,	5265
Ne 9:19	cloud **d** not from them by day,	5493
Isa 37:37	So Sennacherib king of Assyria **d**,	5265
La 1:6	of Zion all her beauty is **d**:	3318
Eze 6:9	their whorish heart, which hath **d**	5493
Eze 10:18	the glory of the Lord **d** from off	3318
Da 4:31	The kingdom is **d** from thee	5709
Mt 2:12	**d** into their own country another	*402*
Mt 2:14	mother by night, and **d** into Egypt:	*402*
Mt 17:18	he **d** out of him: and the child	*1831*
Lk 1:38	word. And the angel **d** from her.	*565*
Lk 2:37	which **d** not from the temple	*868*
Lk 8:38	out of whom the devils were **d**	*1831*
Lk 10:30	**him, d, leaving him half dead.**	*565*
Jn 6:15	**d** again into a mountain himself	*402*
Ac 12:10	forthwith the angel **d** from him.	*868*
Ac 19:12	and the diseases **d** from them	*525*
Rev 6:14	the heaven **d** as a scroll when it is	*673*
Rev 18:14	lusted after are **d** from thee, and	*565*
Rev 18:14	and goodly are **d** from thee, and	*565*

DEPARTETH

Pr 14:16	A wise man feareth, and **d** from	5493
Ecc 6:4	and **d** in darkness, and his name	3212
Isa 59:15	and he that **d** from evil maketh	5493
Jer 3:20	a wife treacherously **d** from her	
Jer 17:5	and whose heart **d** from the Lord,	5493
Lk 9:30	bruising him hardly **d** from him,	*672*

DEPARTING

Ge 35:18	her soul was in **d** (for she died),	3318
Isa 59:13	**d** away from our God, speaking	5253
Da 9:5	even by **d** from thy precepts and	5493
Da 9:11	transgressed thy law, even by **d**,	5493
Ac 20:29	I know this, that after my **d**	*867*
Heb 3:12	unbelief, in **d** from the living God	*868*
Heb 11:22	the **d** of the children of Israel	*1841*

DEPARTURE

Eze 26:18	the sea shall be troubled at thy **d**	3318
2Ti 4:6	and the time of my **d** is at hand	*359*

DEPOSED

Da 5:20	he was **d** from his kingly throne,	5182

DEPRIVED

Ge 27:45	why should I be **d** also of you	7921
Job 39:17	God hath **d** her of wisdom,	5382

DEPTH

Job 38:16	walked in the search of the **d**?	8415
Ps 33:7	layeth up the **d** in storehouses	8415
Pr 25:3	for height, and the earth for **d**,	6012
Isa 7:11	ask it either in the **d** or in the	6009
Jnh 2:5	the **d** closed me round about, the	8415
Mt 18:6	**were drowned in the d of the sea**	*3989*
Mk 4:5	**because it had no d of earth:**	*899*
Ro 8:39	Nor height, nor **d**, nor any other	*899*
Ro 11:33	O the **d** of the riches both of the	*899*
Eph 3:18	the breadth, and length, and **d**, and	*899*

DEPTHS

Ex 15:5	The **d** have covered them; they	8415
Ex 15:8	**d** were congealed in the heart	8415
Ps 68:22	again from the **d** of the sea:	4688
Ps 71:20	up, again from the **d** of the earth	8415
Ps 106:9	so he led them through the **d**,	8415
Ps 107:26	they go down again to the **d**:	8415
Ps 130:1	Out of the **d** have I cried unto thee,	4615
Pr 3:20	By his knowledge the **d** are	8415
Pr 8:24	When there were no **d**, I was	8415
Pr 9:18	her guests are in the **d** of hell.	6010
Isa 51:10	that hath made the **d** of the sea	4615
Eze 27:34	by the seas in the **d** of the waters	4615
Mic 7:19	their sins into the **d** of the sea.	4688
Rev 2:24	**have not known the d of Satan,**	*899*

DERIDE

Hab 1:10	they shall **d** every strong hold;	7832

DERIDED

Lk	16:14	all these things: and they **d** him	*1592*
Lk	23:35	the rulers also with them **d** him	*1592*

DERISION

Ps	2:4	the Lord shall have them in **d**	3932
Ps	44:13	a scorn and a **d** to them that are	7047
Ps	59:8	shalt have all the heathen in **d**	3932
Ps	79:4	a scorn and **d** to them that are	7047
Jer	20:7	am in **d** daily, every one mocketh	7814
La	3:14	I was a **d** to all my people;	7814
Eze	23:32	laughed to scorn and had in **d**;	3932
Eze	36:4	which became a prey and **d** to the	3932
Hos	7:16	shall be their **d** in the land of Egypt.	3932

DESCEND

1Sa	26:10	he shall **d** into battle, and perish	3381
Ps	49:17	his glory shall not **d** after him	3381
Eze	26:20	them that **d** into the pit, with the	3381
Eze	31:16	them that **d** into the pit: and all	3381
Mk	15:32	Let Christ the king of Israel **d**	*2597*
Ro	10:7	Or, Who shall **d** into the deep?	*2597*
1Th	4:16	Lord himself shall **d** from heaven	*2597*

DESCENDED

Ex	19:18	the Lord **d** upon it in fire: and	3381
Ex	33:9	the cloudy pillar **d**, and stood at	3381
Ex	34:5	And the Lord **d** in the cloud	3381
Dt	9:21	the brook that **d** out of the mount	3381
Ps	133:3	**d** upon the mountains of Zion:	3381
Pr	30:4	ascended up into heaven, or **d**?	3381
Mt	7:25	**And the rain d, and the floods**	*2597*
Mt	28:2	for the angel of the Lord **d** from	*2597*
Lk	3:22	the Holy Ghost **d** in a bodily shape	*2597*
Eph	4:9	but that he also **d** first into the	*2597*
Eph	4:10	He that **d** is the same also that	*2597*

DESCENDETH

Jas	3:15	This wisdom **d** not from above	*2718*

DESCENDING

Ge	28:12	angels of God ascending and **d**	3381
Mt	3:16	Spirit of God **d** like a dove,	*2597*
Mk	1:10	the Spirit like a dove **d** upon him	*2597*
Jn	1:32	I saw the Spirit **d** from heaven	*2597*
Jn	1:33	whom thou shalt see the Spirit **d**,	*2597*
Jn	1:51	**angels of God ascending and d**	*2597*
Rev	21:10	Jerusalem, **d** out of heaven from	*2597*

DESCENT

Lk	19:37	at the **d** of the mount of Olives,	*2600*
Heb	7:3	without mother, without **d**,	*35*

DESCRIBE

Jos	18:4	and go through the land, and **d** it	3789

DESCRIBETH

Ro	4:6	as David also **d** the blessedness	*3004*
Ro	10:5	Moses **d** the righteousness which	*1125*

DESERT

Ex	3:1	to the backside of the **d**, and	4057
Ex	5:3	three days journey into the **d**,	4057
Dt	32:10	He found him in a **d** land, and	4057
2Ch	26:10	he built towers in the **d**, and	4057
Ps	106:14	and tempted God in the **d**	3452
Isa	35:1	the **d** shall rejoice, and blossom	6160
Isa	35:6	break out, and streams in the **d**	6160
Isa	40:3	make straight in the **d** a highway	6160
Isa	43:20	rivers in the **d**, to give drink to my	3452
Mt	24:26	**Behold, he is in the d; go not**	*2048*
Mk	6:31	**yourselves apart into a d place,**	*2048*
Jn	6:31	fathers did eat manna in the **d**;	*2048*

DESERTS

Isa	48:21	he led them through the **d**: he	2723
Lk	1:80	and was in the **d** till the day of	*2048*
Heb	11:38	wandered in **d**, and in mountains,	*2047*

DESERVE

Ezr	9:13	us less than our iniquities **d**, and	

DESERVETH

Job	11:6	of thee less than thine iniquity **d**	

DESIRE

Ge	3:16	thy **d** shall be to thy husband	8669
Ge	4:7	unto thee shall be his **d**, and thou	8669
Dt	5:21	shalt thou **d** thy neighbour's wife	2530
Dt	7:25	shalt not **d** the silver or gold	2530
Dt	21:11	and hast a **d** unto her, that thou	2836
1Sa	9:20	on whom is all the **d** of Israel?	2532
2Sa	23:5	all my salvation, and all my **d**,	2656
2Ch	15:15	sought him with their whole **d**;	7522
Ne	1:11	who **d** to fear thy name: and	2655
Job	13:3	and I **d** to reason with God	2654
Job	33:32	speak, for I **d** to justify thee	2654
Job	34:36	My **d** is that Job may be tried	15
Ps	10:3	wicked boasteth of his heart's **d**,	8378
Ps	10:17	hast heard the **d** of the humble:	8378
Ps	21:2	Thou hast given him his heart's **d**	8378
Ps	38:9	Lord, all my **d** is before thee;	8378
Ps	40:6	and offering thou didst not **d**;	2654
Ps	70:2	put to confusion, that **d** my hurt.	2655
Ps	73:25	upon earth that I **d** beside thee	2654
Ps	78:29	for he gave them their own **d**;	8378
Ps	145:16	satisfiest the **d** of every living	7522
Pr	3:15	all the things thou canst **d** are	2656
Pr	10:24	but the **d** of the righteous shall	8378
Pr	11:23	The **d** of the righteous is only good:	8378
Pr	13:12	when the **d** cometh, it is a tree of	8378
Pr	13:19	The **d** accomplished is sweet to	8378
Pr	18:1	Through **d** a man, having separated	8378
Pr	19:22	The **d** of a man is his kindness:	8378
Pr	21:25	The **d** of the slothful killeth him;	8378
Pr	23:6	neither **d** thou his dainty meats:	183
Pr	24:1	men, neither **d** to be with them	183
Ecc	6:9	eyes than the wandering of the **d**:	5315
Ecc	12:5	be a burden, and **d** shall fail:	35
SS	7:10	beloved's, and his **d** is toward me	8669
Isa	26:8	the **d** of our soul is to thy name,	8378
Isa	53:2	no beauty that we should **d** him	2530
Eze	24:16	away from thee the **d** of thine	4261
Eze	24:21	strength, the **d** of your eyes,	4261
Da	2:18	That they would **d** mercies of the	1156
Da	11:37	nor the **d** of women, nor regard	2532
Am	5:18	Woe unto you that **d** the day of	183
Hab	2:5	who enlargeth his **d** as hell, and	5315
Hag	2:7	the **d** of all nations shall come:	2532
Mk	9:35	**If any man d to be first,**	*2309*
Mk	10:35	do for us whatsoever we shall **d**	*154*
Mk	11:24	**What things soever ye d, when**	*154*
Lk	17:22	**ye shall d to see one of the days**	*1937*
Lk	20:46	**the scribes, which d to walk in**	*2309*
Ro	10:1	Brethren my heart's **d** and prayer	*2107*
1Co	14:1	and **d** spiritual gifts, but rather	*2206*

2Co 7:11 yea, what vehement **d**, yea, what *1972*
2Co 12:6 For though I would **d** to glory, *2309*
Gal 4:9 ye **d** again to be in bondage? *2309*
Gal 4:21 Tell me, ye that **d** to be under the *2309*
Php 1:23 having a **d** to depart, and to be *1939*
Php 4:17 Not because I **d** a gift: *1934*
1Ti 3:1 If a man **d** the office of a bishop, *3713*
Heb 11:16 But now they **d** a better country, *3713*
Jas 4:2 kill, and **d** to have, and cannot *2206*
1Pe 1:12 which things the angels **d** to look *1937*
1Pe 2:2 **d** the sincere milk of the word, *1971*
Rev 9:6 shall **d** to die, and death shall flee *1937*

DESIRED
Ge 3:6 and a tree to be **d** to make one 2530
1Ki 9:19 that which Solomon **d** to build in 2836
2Ch 11:23 And he **d** many wives 7592
2Ch 21:20 and departed without being **d** 2532
Est 2:13 whatsoever she **d** was given her 559
Ps 19:10 More to be **d** are they than gold, 2530
Ps 27:4 One thing have I **d** of the Lord, 7592
Pr 8:11 all the things that may be **d** are 2656
Pr 21:20 There is treasure to be **d** and oil 2530
Ecc 2:10 whatsoever mine eyes **d** I kept 7592
Isa 1:29 the oaks which ye have **d**, and ye 2530
Isa 26:9 With my soul have I **d** thee 183
Da 2:16 Daniel went in, and **d** of the king 1156
Hos 6:6 For I **d** mercy, and not sacrifice 2654
Mt 13:17 **righteous men have d to see those** *1939*
Mt 16:1 **d** him that he would shew them *1905*
Lk 10:24 **prophets and kings have d to see** *2309*
Lk 22:31 **Satan hath d to have you, that** *1809*
Jn 12:21 **d** him, saying, Sir, we would see *2065*
Ac 3:14 the Just, and **d** a murderer to *154*
Ac 7:46 **d** to find a tabernacle for the God *154*
1Jn 5:15 the petitions that we **d** of him *154*

DESIRES
Ps 37:4 give thee the **d** of thine heart. 4862
Ps 140:8 Grant not, O Lord, the **d** of the 3970
Eph 2:3 fulfilling the **d** of the flesh and of *2307*

DESIREST
Ps 51:6 thou **d** truth in the inward parts: 2654
Ps 51:16 For thou **d** not sacrifice; else 2654

DESIRETH
1Sa 2:16 take as much as thy soul **d**; 8378
1Sa 18:25 The king **d** not any dowry, 2656
1Sa 20:4 Whatsoever thy soul **d**, 559
2Sa 3:21 reign over all that thine heart **d**. 8378
1Ki 11:37 according to all that thy soul **d**, 8378
Ps 34:12 What man is he that **d** life, 2655
Pr 12:12 The wicked **d** the net of evil men: 2530
Pr 13:4 The soul of the sluggard **d**, and 183
Pr 21:10 The soul of the wicked **d** evil: 183
Ecc 6:2 nothing for his soul of all that he **d**, 183
Lk 5:39 **drunk old wine straightway d** *2309*
Lk 14:32 **and d conditions of peace.** *2065*
1Ti 3:1 of a bishop, he **d** a good work. *1937*

DESIRING
Mt 12:46 without, **d** to speak with him. *2212*
Mt 20:20 and **d** a certain thing of him. *154*
Lk 16:21 **d to be fed with the crumbs** *1937*
2Co 5:2 earnestly **d** to be clothed upon *1971*
1Ti 1:7 **D** to be teachers of the law; *2309*

DESIROUS
Pr 23:3 Be not **d** of his dainties: for they 183
Lk 23:8 for he was **d** to see him a long *2309*
Gal 5:26 Let us not be **d** of vain glory, *2755*

DESOLATE
Ge 47:19 not die, that the land be not **d** 3456
Ex 23:29 lest the land become **d** and the 8077
Le 26:33 your land shall be **d**, and your 8077
Le 26:35 As long as it lieth **d**, it shall rest; 8074
2Sa 13:20 Tamar remained **d** in her brother 8076
2Ch 36:21 as long as she lay **d**, she kept 8074
Ps 25:16 upon me; for I am **d** and afflicted. 3173
Ps 34:21 they that hate the righteous shall be **d**. 816
Ps 143:4 me; my heart within me is **d**. 8074
Isa 1:7 Your country is **d**, your cities are 8077
Isa 5:9 many houses shall be **d**, even 8047
Isa 13:9 fierce anger, to lay the land **d** 8047
Isa 27:10 the defenced city shall be **d**, 910
Jer 4:27 The whole land shall be **d**; yet 8077
Jer 6:8 lest I make thee **d**, a land not 8077
Jer 7:34 of the bride: for the land shall be **d**. 2723
Jer 12:11 the whole land is made **d**, because 8074
Jer 33:10 streets of Jerusalem, that are **d**, 8074
Jer 50:13 but it shall be wholly **d** 8077
Jer 51:26 but thou shalt be **d** for ever, 8077
La 1:4 feasts: all her gates are **d**: and 8076
La 1:16 my children are **d**, because the 8076
La 4:5 They that did feed delicately are **d** 8074
Eze 6:4 And your altars shall be **d**, and 8074
Eze 12:19 that her land may be **d** from all 3456
Eze 14:16 delivered, but the land shall be **d** 8077
Eze 15:8 I will make the land **d**, because 8077
Eze 26:20 of the earth, in places **d** of old, 2723
Eze 35:14 rejoiceth, I will make thee **d** 8077
Eze 36:35 This land that was **d** is become 8074
Da 9:27 he shall make it **d**, even until the 8074
Da 11:31 the abomination that maketh **d** 8074
Da 12:11 abomination that maketh **d** set up, 8074
Joel 1:18 the flocks of sheep are made **d** 816
Joel 2:3 behind them a **d** wilderness; 8077
Mic 1:7 the idols thereof will I lay **d**: 8077
Mic 6:13 making thee **d** because of thy sins 8074
Mic 7:13 land shall be **d** because of them 8077
Mal 1:4 return and build the **d** places: 2723
Mt 23:38 **your house is left unto you d** *2048*
Lk 13:35 **your house is left unto you d:** *2048*
Ac 1:20 Let his habitation be **d**, and let *2048*
Gal 4:27 the **d** hath many more children *2048*
1Ti 5:5 that is a widow indeed, and **d**, *3443*
Rev 17:16 shall make her **d** and naked, *2049*
Rev 18:19 for in one hour is she made **d**. *2049*

DESOLATION
Le 26:31 bring your sanctuaries unto **d**, 8074
Le 26:32 And I will bring the land into **d**: 8074
Jos 8:28 for ever, even a **d** unto this day 8077
2Ki 22:19 should become a **d** and a curse, 8047
Ps 73:19 How are they brought into **d**, 8047
Pr 1:27 When your fear cometh as **d**, 7584
Pr 3:25 neither of the **d** of the wicked, 7722
Isa 64:10 is a wilderness, Jerusalem a **d**. 8077
Jer 22:5 that this house shall become a **d**, 2723
Jer 25:11 this whole land shall be a **d**, 2723
Jer 34:22 Judah a **d** without an inhabitant 8077
Jer 44:22 therefore is your land a **d**, and an 2723

Jer	51:29	Babylon a **d** without an inhabitant	8047
La	3:47	come upon us, **d** and destruction	7612
Eze	7:27	prince shall be clothed with **d**,	8077
Eze	23:33	the cup of astonishment and **d**,	8077
Da	8:13	transgression of **d**, to give both	8074
Zep	1:15	a day of wasteness and **d**, a day	4875
Zep	2:15	how is she become a **d**, a place	8047
Mt	12:25	**against itself is brought to d;**	*2049*
Mt	24:15	**the abomination of d, spoken of**	*2050*
Mk	13:14	**ye shall see the abomination of d,**	*2050*
Lk	11:17	**against itself is brought to d;**	*2049*
Lk	21:20	**know that the d thereof is nigh.**	*2050*

DESOLATIONS

Isa	61:4	cities, the **d** of many generations	8074
Eze	35:9	I will make thee perpetual **d**, and	8077
Da	9:2	seventy years in the **d** of Jerusalem	2723
Da	9:26	end of the war **d** are determined.	8074

DESPAIR

Ecc	2:20	my heart to **d** of all the labour	2976
2Co	4:8	we are perplexed, but not in **d**;	*1820*

DESPAIRED

2Co	1:8	insomuch that we **d** even of life:	*1820*

DESPERATE

Isa	17:11	the day of grief and of **d** sorrow.	605

DESPERATELY

Jer	17:9	above all things, and **d** wicked: who	605

DESPISE

Le	26:15	if ye shall **d** my statues, or if	3988
1Sa	2:30	and they that **d** me shall be lightly	959
Est	1:17	that they shall **d** their husbands	959
Ps	51:17	heart, O God, thou wilt not **d**.	959
Ps	102:17	destitute, and not **d** their prayer	959
Pr	1:7	fools **d** wisdom and instruction	936
Pr	3:11	**d** not the chastening of the Lord;	3988
Pr	6:30	Men do not **d** a thief, if he steal	936
Pr	23:9	he will **d** the wisdom of thy words	936
Pr	23:22	**d** not thy mother when she is old	936
Jer	4:30	thy lovers will **d** thee, they	3988
La	1:8	all that honoured her **d** her,	2107
Am	5:21	I hate, I **d** your feast days, and I	3988
Mal	1:6	you, O priests, that **d** my name	959
Mt	6:24	**hold to the one, and d the other**	*2706*
Mt	18:10	**ye d not one of these little ones;**	*2706*
Lk	16:13	**hold to the one, and d the other**	*2706*
Ro	14:3	Let not him that eateth **d** him	*1848*
1Co	11:22	or **d** ye the church of God,	*2706*
1Co	16:11	Let no man therefore **d** him:	*1848*
1Th	5:20	**D** not prophesyings. Prove all	*1848*
1Ti	4:12	Let no man **d** thy youth: but be	*2706*
Tit	2:15	authority. Let no man **d** thee	*4065*
Heb	12:5	**d** not thou the chastening of	*3643*
2Pe	2:10	uncleanness, and **d** government	*2706*
Jude	8	**d** dominion, and speak evil	*114*

DESPISED

Ge	16:4	her mistress was **d** in her eyes.	7043
Ge	25:34	way: thus Esau **d** his birthright	959
Le	26:43	because they **d** my judgments,	3988
Nu	11:20	ye have **d** the Lord which is	3988
1Sa	10:27	And they **d** him, and brought him	959
2Sa	6:16	and she **d** him in her heart	959
2Sa	12:9	**d** the commandment of the Lord,	959
2Ch	36:16	and **d** his words, and misused his	959
Ne	2:19	and **d** us, and said, What is this	959
Ps	22:6	of men, and **d** of the people	959
Ps	22:24	not **d** nor abhorred the afflictions	959
Ps	106:24	Yea, they **d** the pleasant land,	3988
Pr	1:30	counsel: they **d** all my reproof.	5006
Pr	5:12	and my heart **d** reproof;	5006
Pr	12:8	is of a perverse heart shall be **d**	937
Pr	12:9	He that is **d**, and hath a servant,	7034
Ecc	9:16	the poor man's wisdom is **d**,	959
Isa	5:24	**d** the word of the Holy One of	5006
Isa	53:3	He is **d** and rejected of men; a	959
Isa	53:3	he was **d**, and we esteemed him not.	959
Isa	60:14	all they that **d** thee shall bow	5006
La	2:6	**d** in the indignation of his anger	5006
Eze	17:18	Seeing he **d** the oath by breaking	959
Eze	20:13	they **d** my judgments, which if	3988
Eze	20:16	they **d** my judgments, and walked	3988
Eze	22:8	Thou hast **d** mine holy things,	959
Am	2:4	they have **d** the law of the Lord,	3988
Ob	2	the heathen: thou art greatly **d**.	959
Zec	4:10	hath **d** the day of small things?	937
Mal	1:6	Wherein have we **d** thy name?	959
Lk	18:9	were righteous, and **d** others:	*1848*
Ac	19:27	Diana should be **d**,	*1519, 3762, 3049*
1Co	1:28	things which are **d** hath God	*1848*
1Co	4:10	ye are honourable, but we are **d**.	*820*
Heb	10:28	He that **d** Moses' law died without	*114*
Jas	2:6	But ye have **d** the poor. Do not	*818*

DESPISERS

2Ti	3:3	fierce, **d** of those that are good,	*865*

DESPISEST

Ro	2:4	**d** thou the riches of his goodness	*2706*

DESPISETH

Pr	11:12	void of wisdom **d** his neighbour:	936
Pr	13:13	Whoso **d** the word shall be	936
Pr	14:2	that is perverse in his ways **d** him.	959
Pr	14:21	He that **d** his neighbour sinneth:	936
Pr	15:5	A fool **d** his father's instruction:	5006
Pr	15:20	but a foolish man **d** his mother	959
Pr	15:32	refuseth instruction **d** his own	3988
Pr	19:16	but he that **d** his ways shall die	959
Pr	30:17	father, and **d** to obey his mother,	936
Isa	49:7	to him whom man **d**, to him whom	960
Lk	10:16	**he that d you d me;**	*114*
Lk	10:16	**and he that d me d him that sent.**	*114*
1Th	4:8	He therefore that **d**, **d** not man,	*114*

DESPISING

Heb	12:2	the cross, **d** the shame, and is	*2706*

DESPITE

Heb	10:29	and hath done **d** unto the Spirit	*1796*

DESPITEFUL

Eze	25:15	taken vengeance with a **d** heart,	7589
Eze	36:5	with **d** minds, to cast it out for	7589
Ro	1:30	Backbiters, haters of God, **d**,	*5197*

DESPITEFULLY

Mt	5:44	**pray for them which d use you,**	*1908*
Lk	6:28	**pray for them which d use you**	*1908*

DESTITUTE

Ps	102:17	will regard the prayer of the **d**,	6199
Pr	15:21	joy to him that is **d** of wisdom:	2638

1Ti	6:5	corrupt minds and **d** of the truth,	*650*
Heb	11:37	being **d**, afflicted, tormented;	*5302*
Jas	2:15	or sister be naked, and **d** of daily food,	*3007*

DESTROY

Ge	6:7	And the Lord said, I will **d** man	4229
Ge	6:17	to **d** all flesh, wherein is the breath	7843
Ge	7:4	that I have made will I **d** from off	4229
Ge	9:11	more be a flood to **d** the earth.	7843
Ge	18:23	**d** the righteous with the wicked?	5595
Ge	18:32	I will not **d** it for ten's sake	7843
Ex	34:13	But ye shall **d** their altars,	5422
Nu	33:52	and **d** all their molten images,	6
Dt	6:15	and **d** thee from off the face of	8045
Dt	9:3	a consuming fire he shall **d** them,	8045
Dt	9:14	Let me alone, that I may **d** them,	8045
Dt	9:26	God, **d** not thy people and thine	7843
Dt	20:19	shalt not **d** the trees thereof by	7843
Dt	28:63	Lord will rejoice over you to **d** you,	6
Dt	33:27	thee; and shall say, **D** them.	8045
Jos	7:12	**d** the accursed from among you.	8045
Jos	11:20	that he might **d** them utterly,	2763
Jgs	21:11	Ye shall utterly **d** every male,	2763
1Sa	15:9	and would not utterly **d** them:	2763
1Sa	24:21	that thou wilt not **d** my name	8045
1Sa	26:9	**D** him not: for who can stretch	7843
2Sa	24:16	his hand upon Jerusalem to **d** it,	7843
2Ki	10:19	he might **d** the worshippers of Baal	6
2Ch	12:7	I will not **d** them, but I will grant	7843
2Ch	21:7	would not **d** the house of David,	7843
2Ch	25:16	God hath determined to **d** thee,	7843
Ezr	6:12	to alter and to **d** this house of God	2255
Est	3:6	Haman sought to **d** all the Jews	8045
Job	2:3	him, to **d** him without cause	1104
Job	19:26	after my skin worms **d** this body,	5362
Ps	18:40	I might **d** them that hate me.	6789
Ps	40:14	that seek after my soul to **d** it;	5595
Ps	52:5	God shall likewise **d** thee for ever,	5422
Ps	63:9	those that seek my soul, to **d** it,	7722
Ps	69:4	they that would **d** me, being	6789
Ps	106:23	he would **d** them, had not Moses	8045
Ps	106:34	They did not **d** the nations,	8045
Ps	118:10	name of the Lord will I **d** them	4135
Pr	1:32	the prosperity of fools shall **d** them	6
Pr	11:3	of transgressors shall **d** them.	7703
Pr	15:25	will **d** the house of the proud:	5255
Pr	21:7	of the wicked shall **d** them;	1641
Ecc	5:6	and **d** the work of thine hands?	2254
Ecc	7:16	why shouldest thou **d** thyself?	8074
Isa	10:7	**d** and cut off nations not a few.	8045
Isa	13:9	**d** the sinners thereof out of it	8045
Isa	19:3	and I will **d** the counsel thereof:	1104
Isa	25:7	And he will **d** in this mountain	1104
Isa	51:13	as if he were ready to **d**?	7843
Jer	1:10	to pull down, and to **d**, and to	6
Jer	13:14	nor have mercy, but **d** them	7843
Jer	15:7	I will **d** my people, since they return	6
Jer	17:18	**d** them with double destruction.	7665
Jer	23:1	Woe be unto the pastors that **d** and	6
Jer	25:9	will utterly **d** them, and make them	2763
Jer	36:29	certainly come and **d** this land,	7843
Jer	49:9	they will **d** till they have enough	7843
La	2:8	Lord hath purposed to **d** the wall	7843
Eze	6:3	and I will **d** your high places.	6
Eze	9:8	wilt thou **d** all the residue of Israel	7843
Eze	22:30	the land, that I should not **d** it;	7843
Eze	26:12	walls, and **d** thy pleasant houses:	5422
Eze	30:13	I will also **d** the idols, and I will	6
Da	2:24	**D** not the wise men of Babylon:	7
Da	8:24	**d** the mighty and the holy people	7843
Da	8:25	heart, and by peace shall **d** many:	7843
Am	9:8	I will not utterly **d** the house of	8045
Mic	2:10	it is polluted, it shall **d** you,	2254
Mt	2:13	seek the young child to **d** him.	*622*
Mt	5:17	**I am not come to d, but to fulfil**	*2647*
Mt	10:28	**able to d both soul and body in hell**	*622*
Mt	12:14	against him, how they might **d** him.	*622*
Mt	26:61	said, I am able to **d** the temple	*2647*
Mt	27:20	should ask Barabbas, and **d** Jesus	*522*
Mk	3:6	against him, how they might **d** him.	*622*
Mk	11:18	sought how they might **d** him:	*622*
Mk	12:9	**he will come and d the husbandmen**	*622*
Mk	14:58	I will **d** this temple that is made	*2647*
Lk	6:9	**to save life, or to d it?**	*622*
Lk	9:56	**not come to d men's lives, but**	*622*
Lk	20:16	**He shall come and d these**	*622*
Jn	2:19	**D this temple, and in three days**	*3089*
Jn	10:10	**to steal, and to kill, and to d**	*622*
Ac	6:14	Jesus of Nazareth shall **d** this place,	2647
Ro	14:20	For meat **d** not the work of God.	*2647*
1Co	1:19	I will **d** the wisdom of the wise,	*622*
1Co	3:17	temple of God, him shall God **d**;	*5351*
1Co	6:13	God shall **d** both it and them.	*2673*
2Th	2:8	and shall **d** with the brightness	*2673*
Heb	2:14	through death he might **d** him	*2673*
Jas	4:12	who is able to save and to **d**:	*622*
1Jn	3:8	that he might **d** the works of the	*3089*
Rev	11:18	**d** them which **d** the earth	*1311*

DESTROYED

Ge	7:23	And every living substance was **d**	4229
Ge	13:10	before the Lord **d** Sodom and	7843
Ge	19:29	when God **d** the cities of the plain,	7843
Ex	10:7	knowest thou not yet that Egypt is **d**?	6
Ex	22:20	Lord only, he shall be utterly **d**	2763
Dt	4:26	days upon it, but shall utterly be **d**	8045
Dt	9:8	was angry with you to have **d** you.	8045
Dt	9:20	angry with Aaron to have **d** him:	8045
Jos	10:1	taken Ai, and utterly **d** it;	2763
Jos	10:40	but utterly **d** all that breathed,	2763
Jos	23:15	until he have **d** you from off this	8045
1Sa	15:21	which should have been utterly **d**,	2764
2Sa	24:16	the angel that **d** the people,	7843
1Ki	15:29	that breathed, until he had **d** him,	8045
2Ki	11:1	she arose and **d** all the seed royal.	6
1Ch	21:12	three months to be **d** before thy	5595
1Ch	21:15	and said to the angel that **d**,	7843
2Ch	15:6	And nation was **d** of nation,	3807
2Ch	32:14	nations that my fathers utterly **d**,	2763
2Ch	36:19	**d** all the goodly vessels thereof.	7843
Ezr	4:15	for which cause was this city **d**.	2718
Ezr	5:12	who **d** this house, and carried the	5642
Est	3:9	it be written that they may be **d**:	6
Est	9:12	Jews have slain and **d** five hundred	6
Ps	9:5	thou hast **d** the wicked, thou hast	6
Ps	11:3	If the foundations be **d**, what can	2040
Ps	37:38	transgressors shall be **d** together:	8045
Ps	137:8	of Babylon, who art to be **d**;	7703
Pr	13:13	despiseth the word shall be **d**:	2254
Pr	13:20	a companion of fools shall be **d**.	7321
Pr	13:23	is that is **d** for want of judgment.	5595
Pr	29:1	shall suddenly be **d**, and that	7665

Isa	9:16	they that are led of them are **d**.	1104
Isa	34:2	he hath utterly **d** them, he hath	2763
Isa	37:19	stone: therefore they have **d** them.	6
Jer	12:10	Many pastors have **d** my vineyard,	7843
Jer	22:20	passages: for all thy lovers are **d**	7665
Jer	51:8	Babylon is suddenly fallen and **d**:	7665
La	2:5	he hath **d** his strong holds, and	7843
Da	2:44	kingdom, which shall never be **d**:	2255
Da	6:26	kingdom that which shall not be **d**,	2255
Da	7:11	the beast was slain, and his body **d**,	7
Da	7:14	kingdom that which shall not be **d**.	2255
Da	11:20	but within few days he shall be **d**,	7665
Hos	4:6	My people are **d** for lack of	1820
Mt	22:7	**and d those murderers, and burned**	*622*
Lk	17:27	**the flood came, and d them all.**	*622*
Lk	17:29	**from heaven, and d them all.**	*622*
Ac	3:23	shall be **d** from among the people.	*1842*
Ac	9:21	Is not this he that **d** them which	*4199*
Ro	6:6	that the body of sin might be **d**,	*2673*
1Co	10:9	tempted and were **d** of serpents.	*622*
1Co	15:26	The last enemy that shall be **d**.	*2673*
2Co	4:9	forsaken; cast down, but not **d**;	*622*
Gal	1:23	the faith which once he **d**	*4199*
Gal	2:18	build again the things which I **d**,	*2647*
Heb	11:28	lest he that **d** the first born	*3645*
2Pe	2:12	beasts, made to be taken and **d**,	*5356*
Jude	5	afterward **d** them that believed not	*622*
Rev	8:9	the third part of the ships were **d**	*1311*

DESTROYER

Ex	12:23	will not suffer the **d** to come in	7843
Pr	28:24	the same is the companion of a **d**.	7843
Jer	4:7	and the **d** of the Gentiles is on his	7843

DESTROYEST

Mt	27:40	thou that **d** the temple, and	*2647*
Mk	15:29	Ah, thou that **d** the temple, and	*2647*

DESTROYETH

Pr	6:32	he that doeth it **d** his own soul.	7843
Pr	11:9	with his mouth **d** his neighbour:	7843
Pr	31:3	thy ways to that which **d** kings.	4229
Ecc	7:7	man mad; and a gift **d** the heart	6
Ecc	9:18	war: but one sinner **d** much good	6

DESTROYING

Jos	11:11	edge of the sword, utterly **d** them:	2763
1Ch	21:12	angel of the Lord **d** throughout	7843
Isa	37:11	by **d** them utterly; and shalt thou	2763
Jer	2:30	your prophets, like a **d** lion	7843
La	2:8	not withdrawn his hand from **d**:	1104

DESTRUCTION

Dt	7:23	destroy them with a mighty **d**,	4103
Dt	32:34	burning heat, and with bitter **d**:	6986
1Sa	5:11	there was a deadly **d** throughout	4103
1Ki	20:42	whom I appointed to utter **d**,	2764
2Ch	22:4	the death of his father to his **d**	4889
2Ch	26:16	his heart was lifted up to his **d**:	7843
Est	8:6	how can I endure to see the **d** of my	13
Job	31:29	If I rejoiced at the **d** of him that	6365
Ps	35:8	**d** come upon him at unawares;	7722
Ps	55:23	bring them down into the pit of **d**:	7845
Ps	88:11	grave? or thy faithfulness in **d**?	11
Ps	91:6	the **d** that wasteth at noonday.	6986
Ps	103:4	Who redeemeth thy life from **d**:	7845
Pr	1:27	your **d** cometh as a whirlwind;	343
Pr	10:14	the mouth of the foolish is near **d**.	4288
Pr	10:15	the **d** of the poor is their poverty.	4288
Pr	13:3	openeth wide his lips shall have **d**	4288
Pr	15:11	Hell and **d** are before the Lord:	11
Pr	16:18	Pride goeth before **d**, and an	7667
Pr	18:7	A fools mouth is his **d**, and his	4288
Pr	18:12	Before **d** the heart of man is haughty,	7667
Pr	24:2	their heart studieth **d**, and their	7701
Pr	27:20	Hell and **d** are never full;	10
Pr	31:8	all such as are appointed to **d**.	2475
Isa	13:6	come as a **d** from the Almighty	7701
Isa	19:18	one shall be called, The city of **d**	2041
Jer	4:6	evil from the north and a great **d**.	7667
Jer	4:20	**D** upon **d** is cried: for the whole	7667
Jer	6:1	out of the north, and great **d**	7667
Jer	17:18	and destroy them with double **d**.	7670
Jer	48:5	the enemies have heard a cry of **d**	7667
La	3:47	come upon us, desolation and **d**.	7667
La	3:48	**d** of the daughter of my people.	7667
Eze	5:16	which shall be for their **d**,	4889
Eze	7:25	**D** cometh; and they shall seek	7089
Hos	7:13	**d** unto them! because they have	7701
Hos	13:14	O grave, I will be thy **d**:	6987
Joel	1:15	and as a **d** from the Almighty	7701
Ob	12	of Judah in the day of their **d**;	6
Zec	14:11	there shall be no more utter **d**;	2764
Mt	7:13	**broad is the way, that leadeth to d,**	*684*
Ro	3:16	**D** and misery are in their ways:	*4938*
Ro	9:22	vessels of wrath fitted to **d**.	*684*
1Co	5:5	unto Satan for the **d** of the flesh,	*3639*
2Co	10:8	edification, and not for your **d**,	*2506*
Php	3:19	Whose end is **d**, whose God is	*684*
1Th	5:3	sudden **d** cometh upon them,	*3639*
2Th	1:9	be punished with everlasting **d**	*3639*
1Ti	6:9	drown men in **d** and perdition.	*3639*
2Pe	2:1	bring upon themselves swift **d**	*684*
2Pe	3:16	other scriptures, unto their own **d**.	*684*

DETERMINATE

Ac	2:23	delivered by the **d** counsel and	*3724*

DETERMINATION

Zep	3:8	for my **d** is to gather the nations,	4941

DETERMINE

Ex	21:22	and he shall pay as the judges **d**	

DETERMINED

1Sa	20:7	be sure that evil is **d** by him.	3615
1Sa	20:9	evil were **d** by my father to come.	3615
1Sa	20:33	Jonathan knew that it was **d** of his	3615
1Sa	25:17	evil is **d** against our master,	3615
2Sa	13:32	this hath been **d** from the day	7760
2Ch	2:1	Solomon **d** to build an house for	559
2Ch	25:16	know that God hath **d** to destroy	3289
Est	7:7	there was evil **d** against him by	3615
Job	14:5	Seeing his days are **d**, the number	2782
Isa	19:17	hosts, which he hath **d** against it.	3289
Da	9:24	Seventy weeks are **d** upon thy	2852
Da	9:26	end of the war desolations are **d**.	2782
Da	11:36	for that that is **d** shall be done	2782
Lk	22:22	**Son of man goeth, as it was d**	*3724*
Ac	3:13	Pilate, when he was **d** to let him	*2919*
Ac	11:29	**d** to send relief unto the brethren	*3724*
Ac	15:2	they **d** that Paul and Barnabas,	*5021*
Ac	19:39	shall be **d** in a lawful assembly	*1956*
1Co	2:2	For I **d** not to know any thing	*2919*

D

DETEST

Dt	7:26	thou shalt utterly **d** it, and thou	8262

DETESTABLE

Eze	5:11	sanctuary with all thy **d** things,	8251
Eze	7:20	and of their **d** things therein:	8251
Eze	11:21	**d** things and their abominations,	8251
Eze	37:23	idols, nor with their **d** things,	8251

DEVICE

2Ch	2:14	to find out every **d** which shall	4284
Est	8:3	his **d** that he had devised against	4284
Ecc	9:10	for there is no work, nor **d**, nor	2808
Jer	18:11	and devise a **d** against you:	4284
La	3:62	their **d** against me all the day.	1902
Ac	17:29	stone, graven by art and man's **d**.	*1761*

DEVICES

Ps	10:2	let them be taken in the **d** that	4209
Pr	1:31	and be filled with their own **d**.	4156
Pr	12:2	man of wicked **d** will he condemn.	4209
Pr	14:17	a man of wicked **d** is hated	4209
Pr	19:21	are many **d** in a man's heart;	4284
Isa	32:7	wicked **d** to destroy the poor	2154
Jer	18:12	we will walk after our own **d**,	4284
Jer	18:18	let us devise **d** against Jeremiah;	4284
Da	11:24	forecast his **d** against the strong	4284
2Co	2:11	we are not ignorant of his **d**.	*3540*

DEVIL

Mt	4:1	wilderness to be tempted of the **d**	*1228*
Mt	11:18	**and they say, He hath a d**	*1140*
Mt	12:22	one possessed with a **d**, blind,	*1139*
Mt	13:39	**enemy that sowed them is the d;**	*1228*
Mt	15:22	is grievously vexed with a **d**.	*1139*
Mt	17:18	Jesus rebuked the **d**; and he	*1140*
Mt	25:41	**prepared for the d and his angels:**	*1228*
Mk	7:29	**d is gone out of thy daughter**	*1140*
Lk	4:2	Being forty days tempted of the **d**	*1228*
Lk	7:33	**wine; and ye say, He hath a d**	*1140*
Lk	8:12	**cometh the d, and taketh away**	*1228*
Lk	9:42	**d** threw him down, and tare him.	*1140*
Jn	6:70	**twelve, and one of you is a d?**	*1228*
Jn	8:44	**Ye are of your father the d,**	*1228*
Jn	8:49	Jesus answered, **I have not a d;**	*1140*
Jn	10:20	many of them said, He hath a **d**;	*1140*
Jn	10:21	Can a **d** open the eyes of the blind?	*1140*
Jn	13:2	**d** having now put into the heart	*1228*
Ac	13:10	thou child of the **d**, thou enemy	*1228*
Eph	4:27	Neither give place to the **d**.	*1228*
Eph	6:11	stand against the wiles of the **d**	*1228*
1Ti	3:7	reproach and the snare of the **d**	*1228*
2Ti	2:26	out of the snare of the **d**, who	*1228*
Heb	2:14	power of death, that is, the **d**;	*1228*
Jas	4:7	Resist the **d**, and he will flee from	*1228*
1Pe	5:8	because your adversary the **d**,	*1228*
1Jn	3:8	that committeth sin is of the **d**;	*1228*
1Jn	3:8	**d** sinneth from the beginning.	*1228*
1Jn	3:10	manifest, and the children of the **d**:	*1228*
Jude	9	when contending with the **d** be	*1228*
Rev	2:10	**the d shall cast some of you into**	*1228*
Rev	12:9	that old serpent, called the **D**, and	*1228*
Rev	12:12	the **d** is come down unto you,	*1228*
Rev	20:2	that old serpent, which is the **D**,	*1228*
Rev	20:10	the **d** that deceived them was cast	*1228*

DEVILISH

Jas	3:15	above, but is earthly, sensual, **d**	*1141*

DEVILS

Le	17:7	offer their sacrifices unto **d**, after	8163
Dt	32:17	sacrificed unto **d**, not to God;	7700
Ps	106:37	sons and their daughters unto **d**,	7700
Mt	4:24	which were possessed with **d**,	*1139*
Mt	7:22	**in thy name have cast out d?**	*1140*
Mt	8:28	met him two possessed with **d**,	*1139*
Mt	9:34	Pharisees said, He casteth out **d**	*1140*
Mt	10:8	**lepers, raise the dead, cast out d:**	*1140*
Mt	12:27	**if I by Beelzebub cast out d,**	*1140*
Mt	12:28	**if I cast out d by the Spirit of**	*1140*
Mk	1:34	and suffered not the **d** to speak,	*1140*
Mk	16:9	out of whom he had cast seven **d**,	*1140*
Mk	16:17	**my name shall they cast out d;**	*1140*
Lk	8:2	out of whom went seven **d**,	*1140*
Lk	8:30	because many **d** were entered	*1140*
Lk	9:49	Master, we saw one casting out **d**	*1140*
Lk	10:17	even the **d** are subject unto us	*1140*
Lk	11:18	**I cast out d through Beelzebub**	*1140*
Lk	11:20	**with the finger of God cast out d**	*1140*
Lk	13:32	**I cast out d, and I do cures**	*1140*
1Co	10:20	sacrifice to **d**, and not to God:	*1140*
1Co	10:21	Lord's table, and of the table of **d**.	*1140*
1Ti	4:1	spirits, and doctrines of **d**;	*1140*
Jas	2:19	the **d** also believe, and tremble	*1140*
Rev	9:20	that they should not worship **d**	*1140*
Rev	16:14	For they are the spirits of **d**,	*1142*
Rev	18:2	is become the habitation of **d**,	*1142*

DEVISE

Ex	31:4	To **d** cunning works, to work in	2803
2Sa	14:14	person: yet doth he **d** means, that his	2803
Ps	35:4	to confusion that **d** my hurt.	2803
Pr	3:29	**D** not evil against thy neighbour,	2790
Pr	14:22	Do they not err that **d** evil? but	2790
Pr	16:30	shutteth his eyes to **d** froward	2803
Jer	18:18	let us **d** devices against Jeremiah;	2803
Mic	2:1	Woe to them that **d** iniquity, and	2803

DEVISED

2Sa	21:5	that **d** against us that we should	1819
1Ki	12:33	in the month which he had **d**	908
Est	8:5	reverse the letters **d** by Haman	4284
Ps	31:13	they **d** to take away my life	2161
Jer	11:19	they had **d** devices against me,	2803
La	2:17	hath done that which he had **d**;	2161
2Pe	1:16	not followed cunningly **d** fables,	*4679*

DEVISETH

Ps	36:4	He **d** mischief upon his bed; he	2803
Ps	52:2	tongue **d** mischiefs; like a sharp	2803
Pr	6:14	heart, he **d** mischief continually;	2790
Pr	6:18	heart that **d** wicked imaginations,	2790
Pr	16:9	A man's heart **d** his ways; but the	2803
Pr	24:8	He that **d** to do evil shall be	2803
Isa	32:8	But the liberal **d** liberal things;	3289

DEVOTED

Le	27:28	every **d** thing is most holy unto	2764
Nu	18:14	Every thing **d** in Israel shall be	2764

DEVOTIONS

Ac	17:23	I passed by, and beheld your **d**,	*4574*

DEVOUR

Ge	49:27	the morning he shall **d** the prey,	398
Jgs	9:15	and **d** the cedars of Lebanon	398
2Sa	2:26	Shall the sword **d** for ever?	398
Ps	50:3	silence: a fire shall **d** before him,	398
Pr	30:14	to **d** the poor from off the earth,	398
Isa	33:11	your breath, as fire, shall **d** you	398
Isa	42:14	I will destroy and **d** at once	7602
Jer	2:3	all that **d** him shall offend:	398
Jer	17:27	shall **d** the palaces of Jerusalem,	398
Jer	30:16	Therefore all they that **d** shall be	398
Eze	15:7	fire, and another fire shall **d** them;	398
Eze	20:47	it shall **d** every green tree in thee,	398
Eze	23:37	them through the fire, to **d** them.	402
Da	7:5	thus unto it, Arise, **d** much flesh	399
Da	7:23	and shall **d** the whole earth,	399
Hos	5:7	now shall a month **d** them with	398
Hos	8:14	and it shall **d** the palaces thereof.	398
Am	2:5	shall **d** the palaces of Jerusalem.	398
Am	5:6	in the house of Joseph, and **d** it,	398
Na	2:13	the sword shall **d** thy young lions:	398
Hab	3:14	was as to **d** the poor secretly	398
Zec	9:15	and they shall **d**, and subdue with	398
Mt	23:14	**ye d widows' houses, and for**	*2719*
Mk	12:40	**Which d widows' houses, and for**	*2719*
Lk	20:47	**Which d widows' houses, and for**	*2719*
2Co	11:20	if a man **d** you, if a man take	*2719*
Gal	5:15	if ye bite and **d** one another,	*2719*
Heb	10:27	which shall **d** the adversaries	*2068*
1Pe	5:8	about, seeking whom he may **d**:	*2666*
Rev	12:4	for to **d** her child as soon as	*2719*

DEVOURED

Ge	31:15	and hath quite **d** also our money.	398
Ge	37:33	an evil beast hath **d** him: Joseph	398
Ge	41:7	And the seven thin ears **d** the	1104
Le	10:2	and **d** them, and they died before	398
Nu	26:10	the fire **d** two hundred and fifty	398
Dt	31:17	and they shall be **d**, and many evils	398
Dt	32:24	and **d** with burning heat, and	3898
2Sa	18:8	and the wood **d** more people that	398
2Sa	18:8	that day than the sword **d**.	398
2Sa	22:9	and fire out of his mouth **d**:	398
Ps	79:7	For they have **d** Jacob, and laid	398
Jer	2:30	own sword hath **d** your prophets,	398
Jer	3:24	shame hath **d** the labour of our	398
Jer	50:7	All that found them have **d** them:	398
La	4:11	it hath **d** the foundations thereof.	398
Eze	15:5	when the fire hath **d** it, and it is	398
Eze	16:20	thou sacrificed unto them to be **d**	398
Eze	22:25	they have **d** souls; they have taken	398
Eze	23:25	thy residue shall be **d** by the fire	398
Eze	39:4	to the beasts of the field to be **d**.	402
Da	7:7	teeth: it **d** and brake in pieces,	399
Hos	7:7	an oven, and have **d** their judges;	398
Hos	7:9	Strangers have **d** his strength, and	398
Joel	1:19	to thee will I cry for the fire hath **d**	398
Am	7:4	and it **d** the great deep, and did eat	398
Zep	1:18	shall be **d** by the fire of his jealousy:	398
Zep	3:8	be **d** with the fire of my jealousy	398
Mt	13:4	**the fowls came and d them up:**	*2719*
Mk	4:4	**fowls of the air came and d it up.**	*2719*
Lk	8:5	**and the fowls of the air d it.**	*2719*
Lk	15:30	**hath d thy living with harlots,**	*2719*
Rev	20:9	out of heaven, and **d** them	*2719*

DEVOURER

Mal	3:11	I will rebuke the **d** for your sakes,	398

DEVOURETH

2Sa	11:25	sword **d** one as well as another:	398
Pr	19:28	mouth of the wicked **d** iniquity	1104
Pr	20:25	man who **d** that which is holy,	3216
La	2:3	a flaming fire, which **d** round about	398
Joel	2:3	A fire **d** before them; and behind	398
Hab	1:13	when the wicked **d** the man that	1104

DEVOURING

Ex	24:17	like **d** fire on the top of the mount	398
Isa	29:6	tempest, and the flame of **d** fire.	398
Isa	30:27	and his tongue as a **d** fire:	398

DEVOUT

Lk	2:25	the same man was just and **d**,	*2126*
Ac	2:5	Jews, **d** men, out of every nation	*2126*
Ac	8:2	And **d** men carried Stephen to his	*2126*
Ac	10:2	A **d** man, and one that feared God	*2152*
Ac	13:50	stirred up the **d** and honourable	*4576*
Ac	22:12	a **d** man according to the law,	*2152*

DEW

Ge	27:28	God give thee of the **d** of heaven,	2919
Nu	11:9	when the **d** fell upon the camp	2919
Dt	33:28	also his heavens shall drop down **d**	2919
Jgs	6:37	if the **d** be on the fleece only,	2919
2Sa	17:12	light upon him as the **d** falleth	2919
1Ki	17:1	there shall not be **d** nor rain	2919
Job	38:28	who hath begotten the drops of **d**?	2919
Pr	3:20	and the clouds drop down the **d**.	2919
Pr	19:12	his favour is as **d** upon the grass.	2919
Isa	18:4	like a cloud of **d** in the heart of	2919
Da	4:15	let it be wet with the **d** of heaven,	2920
Da	4:33	and his body was wet with the **d** of	2920
Da	5:21	body was wet with the **d** of heaven;	2920
Hos	6:4	and as the early **d** it goeth away	2919
Hos	13:3	and as the early **d** that passeth	2919
Hag	1:10	heaven over you is stayed from **d**,	2919

DIADEM

Isa	28:5	and for a **d** of beauty, unto the	6843
Isa	62:3	a royal **d** in the hand of thy God.	6797
Eze	21:26	Remove the **d**, and take off the	4701

DIAL

Isa	38:8	which is; gone down in the sun **d**	4609

DIAMOND

Ex	28:18	an emerald, a sapphire, and a **d**	3095
Jer	17:1	and with the point of a **d**:	8068
Eze	28:13	the sardius, topaz, and the **d**,	3095

DIE

Ge	2:17	eatest thereof thou shalt surely **d**	4191
Ge	3:3	neither shall ye touch it, lest ye **d**.	4191
Ge	6:17	thing that is in the earth shall **d**.	1478
Ge	30:1	Give me children, or else I **d**	4191
Ge	42:2	thence; that we may live, and not **d**	4191
Ge	45:28	I will go and see him before I **d**	4191
Ge	47:15	why should we **d** in thy presence?	4191
Ex	14:11	us away to **d** in the wilderness?	4191
Ex	20:19	not God speak with us, lest we **d**	4191
Ex	21:12	that smiteth a man, so that he **d**,	4191
Ex	28:35	he cometh out, that he **d** not	4191
Le	16:2	is upon the ark; that he **d** not:	4191
Nu	4:15	touch any holy thing, lest they **d**,	4191

Nu	16:29	If these men **d** the common death	4191
Nu	18:22	lest they bear sin, and **d**	4191
Nu	21:5	of Egypt to **d** in the wilderness?	4191
Nu	23:10	me **d** the death of the righteous,	4191
Nu	27:8	If a man **d**, and have no son	4191
Dt	19:11	smite him mortally that he **d**,	4191
Dt	19:12	avenger of blood, that he may **d**	4191
Dt	22:22	then they shall both of them **d**	4191
Dt	22:25	man only that lay with her shall **d**:	4191
Dt	24:7	that thief shall **d**; and thou shalt	4191
Dt	32:50	And **d** in the mount whither thou	4191
Jos	20:9	not **d** by the hand of the avenger	4191
Ru	1:17	Where thou diest, will I **d**, and	4191
1Sa	14:45	Shall Jonathan **d**, who hath	4191
1Sa	26:16	ye are worthy to **d**, because ye	4194
2Sa	12:14	is born unto thee shall surely **d**	4191
1Ki	19:4	for himself that he might **d**;	4191
Job	2:9	thine integrity? curse God, and **d**	4191
Job	36:12	they shall **d** without knowledge	1478
Ps	41:5	When shall he **d**, and his name	4191
Ps	104:29	they **d**, and return to their dust	1478
Pr	5:23	He shall **d** without instruction;	4191
Pr	10:21	but fools **d** for want of wisdom	4191
Pr	15:10	he that hateth reproof shall **d**	4191
Pr	19:16	he that despiseth his ways shall **d**	4191
Pr	23:13	him with the rod, he shall not **d**	4191
Pr	30:7	deny me them not before I **d**	4191
Ecc	3:2	A time to be born, and a time to **d**;	4191
Ecc	7:17	why shouldest thou **d** before thy	4191
Ecc	9:5	the living know that they shall **d**:	4191
Isa	22:13	drink; for to-morrow we shall **d**	4191
Isa	65:20	the child shall **d** an hundred years	4191
Jer	16:4	They shall **d** of grievous deaths;	4191
Jer	26:11	This man is worthy to **d**; for he	4194
Jer	26:16	This man is not worthy to **d**:	4194
Jer	31:30	But every one shall **d** for his own	4191
Jer	42:16	in Egypt; and there ye shall **d**	4191
Eze	3:18	Thou shalt surely **d**; and thou	4191
Eze	3:19	way, he shall **d** in his iniquity;	4191
Eze	17:16	in the midst of Babylon he shall **d**	4191
Eze	18:17	he shall not **d** for the iniquity of	4191
Eze	18:20	The soul that sinneth, it shall **d**	4191
Eze	18:28	he shall surely live, he shall not **d**	4191
Eze	33:14	Thou shalt surely **d**; if he turn	4191
Am	7:11	Jeroboam shall **d** by the sword	4191
Jnh	4:3	is better for me to **d** than to live	4194
Jnh	4:8	wished in himself to **d**, and said	4191
Jnh	4:8	It is better for me to **d** than to live	4191
Hab	1:12	mine Holy One? we shall not **d**	4191
Mt	15:4	**or mother, let him d the death**	*5053*
Mk	7:10	**let him d the death:**	*5053*
Mk	12:19	If a man's brother **d**, and leave	*599*
Lk	7:2	him, was sick, and ready to **d**	*5053*
Lk	20:28	If any man's brother **d**, having a	*599*
Lk	20:36	**Neither can they d any more: for**	*599*
Jn	6:50	**a man may eat thereof, and not d**	*599*
Jn	8:24	**that ye shall d in your sins: for if**	*599*
Jn	11:26	**and believeth in me shall never d**	*599*
Jn	11:51	that Jesus should **d** for that nation;	*599*
Jn	12:24	**it abideth alone: but if it d, it**	*599*
Jn	19:7	and by our law he ought to **d**,	*599*
Ro	5:7	for a righteous man will one **d**	*599*
Ro	14:8	whether we **d**, we **d** unto the Lord:	*599*
1Co	9:15	better for me to **d**, than that any	*599*
1Co	15:22	For as in Adam all **d**, even so	*599*
1Co	15:31	in Christ Jesus our Lord, I **d** daily	*599*
1Co	15:32	eat and drink; for to morrow we **d**	*599*
1Co	15:36	sowest is not quickened, except it **d**:	*599*
2Co	7:3	our hearts to **d** and live with you	*4880*
Php	1:21	to live is Christ, and to **d** is gain	*599*
Heb	9:27	it is appointed unto men once to **d**,	*599*
Rev	3:2	**which remain that are ready to d**	*599*
Rev	9:6	not find it; and shall desire to **d**,	*599*
Rev	14:13	are the dead which **d** in the Lord	*599*

DIED

Ge	7:21	And all flesh **d** that moved upon	1478
Ex	9:6	of the children of Israel **d** not one	4191
Ex	16:3	Would to God we had **d** by the	4191
Nu	14:2	God we had **d** in this wilderness!	4191
Nu	20:3	Would God that we had **d** when	1478
Nu	27:3	Our father **d** in the wilderness, and	4191
1Sa	4:18	and his neck brake, and he **d**	4191
1Sa	31:6	So Saul **d**, and his three sons	4191
2Sa	3:33	said, **D** Abner as a fool dieth?	4191
2Sa	6:7	and there he **d** by the ark of God	4191
2Sa	17:23	and hanged himself, and **d**, and	4191
2Sa	18:33	would God I had **d** for thee	4191
1Ki	14:17	threshold of the door, the child **d**:	4191
2Ki	1:17	So he **d** according to the word of	4191
2Ki	7:20	upon him in the gate, and he **d**	4191
1Ch	10:5	fell likewise on the sword, and **d**	4191
1Ch	10:13	So Saul **d** for his transgression	4191
2Ch	13:20	the Lord struck him, and he **d**	4191
2Ch	24:15	and was full of days when he **d**;	4191
Job	3:11	Why **d** I not from the womb?	4191
Isa	6:1	In the year that king Uzziah **d**	4194
Eze	24:18	and at even my wife **d**; and I did	4191
Lk	16:22	**it came to pass, that the beggar d,**	*599*
Lk	16:22	**rich man also d, and was buried;**	*599*
Jn	11:21	here, my brother had not **d**	*599*
Ro	5:6	time Christ **d** for the ungodly	*599*
Ro	5:8	were yet sinners, Christ **d** for us	*599*
Ro	6:10	in that he **d**, he **d** unto sin once:	*599*
Ro	8:34	It is Christ that **d**, yea rather	*599*
Ro	14:9	To this end Christ both **d**, and rose,	*599*
1Co	15:3	how that Christ **d** for our sins	*599*
2Co	5:14	one **d** for all, then were all dead:	*599*
1Th	4:14	that Jesus **d** and rose again, even	*599*
1Th	5:10	Who **d** for us, that, whether we	*599*
Heb	10:28	Moses' law **d** without mercy under	*599*
Heb	11:13	These all **d** in faith, not having	*599*
Heb	11:22	By faith Joseph when he **d**, made	*5053*
Rev	8:11	many men **d** of the waters,	*599*
Rev	16:3	every living soul **d** in the sea.	*599*

DIEST

Ru	1:17	Where thou **d**, will I die, and	4191

DIETH

Le	22:8	That which **d** of itself, or is torn	5038
2Sa	3:33	said, Died Abner as a fool **d**?	4194
Ps	49:17	when he **d** he shall carry nothing	4194
Pr	11:7	a wicked man **d**, his expectation	4194
Ecc	2:16	And how **d** the wise man? as the	4191
Ecc	3:19	as the one **d**, so **d** the other;	4194
Eze	18:32	pleasure in the death of him that **d**,	4191
Mk	9:44	**Where their worm d not, and**	*5053*
Mk	9:46	**Where their worm d not, and**	*5053*
Mk	9:48	**Where their worm d not, and**	*5053*
Ro	6:9	raised from the dead, **d** no more;	*599*
Ro	14:7	himself, and no man **d** to himself	*599*

DIFFER
1Co 4:7 maketh thee to **d** from another? ... *1252*

DIFFERENCE
Ex 11:7 the Lord doth put a **d** between ... 6395
Le 10:10 And that ye may put **d** between holy ... 914
Le 11:47 **d** between the unclean and the ... 914
Ro 3:22 that believe: for there is no **d** ... *1293*
Ro 10:12 no **d** between the Jew and the ... *1293*
1Co 7:34 There is **d** also between a wife ... *3307*
Jude 22 have compassion, making a **d**: ... *1252*

DIFFERENCES
1Co 12:5 there are **d** of administrations ... *1243*

DIFFERETH
1Co 15:41 for one star **d** from another star ... *1308*

DIFFERING
Ro 12:6 gifts **d** according to the grace ... *1313*

DIG
Ex 21:33 if a man shall **d** a pit, and not ... 3738
Eze 8:8 Son of man, **d** now in the wall: ... 2864
Eze 12:5 **D** thou through the wall in their ... 2864
Am 9:2 Though they **d** into hell, thence ... 2864
Lk 13:8 **I shall d about it, and dung it:** ... *4626*
Lk 16:3 **I cannot d; to beg I am ashamed** ... *4626*

DIGGED
Ge 21:30 unto me, that I have **d** this well ... 2658
Ex 7:24 the Egyptians **d** round about the ... 2658
2Ch 26:10 in the desert, and **d** many wells: ... 2672
Ps 7:15 He made a pit, and **d** it, and is ... 2658
Ps 35:7 cause they have **d** for my soul ... 2658
Ps 57:6 they have **d** a pit before me, into ... 3738
Ps 119:85 The proud have **d** pits for me, ... 3738
Jer 18:20 they have **d** a pit for my soul ... 3738
Mt 21:33 **and d a winepress in it, and built** ... *3736*
Mt 25:18 **and d in the earth, and hid his** ... *3736*
Mk 12:1 **and d a place for the winefat** ... *3736*
Lk 6:48 **d deep, and laid the foundation** ... *4626*
Ro 11:3 and **d** down thine altars; ... *2679*

DIGGETH
Pr 16:27 An ungodly man **d** up evil: and ... 3738
Pr 26:27 Whoso **d** a pit shall fall therein: ... 3738
Ecc 10:8 He that **d** a pit shall fall into it; ... 2658

DIGNITIES
2Pe 2:10 are not afraid to speak evil of **d** ... *1391*
Jude 8 dominion, and speak evil of **d** ... *1391*

DIGNITY
Est 6:3 What honour and **d** has been done ... 1420
Ecc 10:6 Folly is set in great **d**, and the ... 4791

DILIGENCE
Pr 4:23 Keep thy heart with all **d**; for out ... 4929
Lk 12:58 **way, give d that thou mayest be** ... *2039*
2Ti 4:21 Do thy **d** to come before winter ... *4704*
2Pe 1:5 giving all **d**, add to your faith ... *4710*
2Pe 1:10 give **d** to make your calling and ... *4710*

DILIGENT
Dt 19:18 judges shall make **d** inquisition: ... 3190
Jos 22:5 **d** heed to do the commandment ... 3966
Ps 64:6 they accomplish a **d** search:
Ps 77:6 heart: and my spirit made **d** search
Pr 10:4 the hand of the **d** maketh rich ... 2742
Pr 12:24 The hand of the **d** shall bear rule: ... 2742
Pr 12:27 substance of a **d** man is precious ... 2742
Pr 13:4 the soul of the **d** shall be made fat ... 2742
Pr 21:5 The thoughts of the **d** tend only to ... 2742
Pr 22:29 thou a man **d** in his business? ... 4106
Pr 27:23 **d** to know the state of they flocks, ... 3045
2Pe 3:14 **d** that ye may be found of him in ... *4704*

DILIGENTLY
Dt 4:9 keep thy soul **d**, lest thou forget ... 3966
Dt 6:7 teach them **d** unto thy children ... 8150
Dt 6:17 Ye shall **d** keep the commandments
Dt 13:14 make search, and ask **d**; and ... 3190
Ezr 7:23 let it be **d** done for the house of ... 149
Job 13:17 Hear **d** my speech, and my
Ps 37:10 thou shalt **d** consider his place ... 995
Ps 119:4 us to keep thy precepts **d** ... 3966
Pr 7:15 **d** to seek thy face, and I have ... 7836
Pr 11:27 He that **d** seeketh good procureth ... 7836
Pr 23:1 ruler, consider **d** what is before thee:
Mt 2:7 of them **d** what time the star
Mt 2:8 search **d** for the young child; ... *199*
Mt 2:16 had **d** enquired of the wise men.
Lk 15:8 **house, and seek d till she find it?** ... *1960*
Heb 11:6 reward of them that **d** seek him ... *1567*
Heb 12:15 Looking **d** lest any man fail of
1Pe 1:10 have enquired and searched **d**,

DIM
Ge 27:1 was old, and his eyes were **d**, ... 3543
Ge 48:10 the eyes of Israel were **d** for age, ... 3513
La 4:1 How is the gold become **d**! how ... 6044

DIMINISH
Ex 5:8 ye shall not **d** ought thereof: for ... 1639
Le 25:16 thou shalt **d** the price of it: ... 4591
Jer 26:2 speak unto them; **d** not a word: ... 1639

DIMINISHED
Ex 5:11 ought of your work shall be **d**. ... 1639
Pr 13:11 gotten by vanity shall be **d**: ... 4591
Eze 16:27 and have **d** thine ordinary food, ... 1639

DINE
Ge 43:16 these men shall **d** with me at noon ... 398
Lk 11:37 besought him to **d** with him: ... *709*
Jn 21:12 saith unto them, **Come and d** ... *709*

DINNER
Pr 15:17 is a **d** of herbs where love is ... 737
Mt 22:4 **Behold, I have prepared my d:** ... *712*
Lk 14:12 **When thou makest a d or a supper,** ... *712*

DIP
Ex 12:22 **d** it in the blood that is in the ... 2881
Le 14:16 the priest shall **d** his right finger ... 2881
Dt 33:24 and let him **d** his foot in oil ... 2881
Ru 2:14 and **d** thy morsel in the vinegar ... 2881
Lk 16:24 **that he may d the tip of his finger** ... *911*

DIPPED
Ge 37:31 and **d** the coat in the blood; ... 2881
Le 9:9 and he **d** his finger in the blood ... 2881
2Ki 5:14 **d** himself seven times in Jordan, ... 2881
Ps 68:23 thy foot may be **d** in the blood ... 4272
Jn 13:26 **give a sop, when I have d it** ... *911*
Jn 13:26 had **d** the sop, he gave it to Judas ... *1686*
Rev 19:13 with a vesture **d** in blood: ... *911*

DIRECT
Ps 5:3 will I **d** my prayer unto thee....6186
Pr 3:6 him, and he shall **d** thy paths....3474
Pr 11:5 of the perfect shall **d** his way:....3474
Ecc 10:10 but wisdom is profitable to **d**....3787
Isa 45:13 and I will **d** all his ways:....3474
Jer 10:23 man that walketh to **d** his steps....3559
2Th 3:5 **d** your hearts into the love of God....*2720*

D

DIRECTED
Isa 40:13 Who hath **d** the spirit of the Lord....8505

DIRECTETH
Pr 16:9 way: but the Lord **d** his steps....3559
Pr 21:29 as for the upright, he **d** his way....3559

DISALLOWED
Nu 30:5 her, because her father **d** her....5106
Nu 30:8 her husband **d** her on the day that....5106
1Pe 2:4 **d** indeed of men, but chosen of....*593*
1Pe 2:7 the stone which the builders **d**,....*593*

DISAPPOINTED
Pr 15:22 Without counsel purposes are **d**:....6565

DISCERN
Ge 31:32 **d** thou what is thine with me,....5234
Ge 38:25 **D**, I pray thee, whose are these....5234
2Sa 14:17 lord the king to **d** good and bad:....8085
2Sa 19:35 can I **d** between good and evil?....3045
1Ki 3:9 I may **d** between good and bad:....995
Ezr 3:13 the people could not **d** the noise....5234
Eze 44:23 them to **d** between the unclean....3045
Jnh 4:11 that cannot **d** between their right....3045
Mal 3:18 and **d** between the righteous and....7200
Mt 16:3 **ye can d the face of the sky;**....*1252*
Mt 16:3 **but can ye not d the signs of the**
Heb 5:14 exercised to **d** both good and evil....*1253*

DISCERNED
Ge 27:23 he **d** him not, because his hands....5234
Pr 7:7 I **d** among the youths, a young....995
1Co 2:14 because they are spiritually **d**....*350*

DISCERNER
Heb 4:12 and is a **d** of the thoughts and....*2924*

DISCERNETH
Ecc 8:5 and a wise man's heart **d** both....3045

DISCERNING
1Co 11:29 himself, not **d** the Lord's body....*1252*
1Co 12:10 to another **d** of spirits; to another....*1253*

DISCHARGE
Ecc 8:8 and there is no **d** in that war;....4917

DISCIPLE
Mt 10:42 **water only in the name of a d,**....*3101*
Lk 6:40 **The d is not above his master:**....*3101*
Lk 14:26 **own life also, he cannot be my d**....*3101*
Lk 14:27 **come after me, cannot be my d**....*3101*
Lk 14:33 **that he hath, he cannot be my d,**....*3101*
Jn 9:28 Thou art his **d**; but we are Moses'....*3101*
Jn 19:27 Then saith he to the **d**, **Behold thy**....*3101*
Jn 19:27 from that hour that **d** took her....*3101*
Jn 20:2 to the other **d**, whom Jesus loved....*3101*
Jn 20:4 and the other **d** did outrun Peter....*3101*
Jn 21:20 seeth the **d** whom Jesus loved....*3101*
Jn 21:23 that that **d** should not die;....*3101*

DISCIPLES
Isa 8:16 seal the law among my **d**....3928
Mt 9:14 came to him the **d** of John, saying....*3101*
Mt 12:2 thy **d** do that which is not lawful....*3101*
Mt 14:26 the **d** saw him walking on the sea....*3101*
Mt 17:6 when the **d** heard it, they fell....*3101*
Mt 19:13 and pray: and the **d** rebuked them....*3101*
Mt 26:8 his **d** saw it, they had indignation....*3101*
Mt 26:18 **passover at thy house with my d**....*3101*
Mt 26:56 Then all the **d** forsook him, and....*3101*
Mt 27:64 lest his **d** come by night, and steal....*3101*
Mt 28:13 Say ye, His **d** came by night,....*3101*
Mk 2:18 Pharisees fast, but thy **d** fast not?....*3101*
Mk 10:24 the **d** were astonished at his words....*3101*
Mk 14:14 **shall eat the passover with my d?**....*3101*
Mk 14:32 and he saith to his **d**, **Sit ye here**....*3101*
Mk 16:7 tell his **d** and Peter that he goeth....*3101*
Lk 6:1 his **d** plucked the ears of corn....*3101*
Lk 18:15 his **d** saw it, they rebuked them....*3101*
Lk 19:39 unto him, Master, rebuke thy **d**....*3101*
Lk 22:11 **eat the passover with my d?**....*3101*
Lk 22:45 his **d**, he found them sleeping....*3101*
Jn 2:2 called, and his **d**, to the marriage....*3101*
Jn 2:17 his **d** remembered that it was....*3101*
Jn 2:22 his **d** remembered that he had said....*3101*
Jn 6:22 that his **d** were gone away alone;....*3101*
Jn 6:66 many of his **d** went back, and....*3101*
Jn 8:31 **word, then are ye my d indeed;**....*3101*
Jn 9:27 it again? will ye also be his **d**?....*3101*
Jn 13:23 one of his **d**, whom Jesus loved....*3101*
Jn 13:35 **know that ye are my d, if ye have**....*3101*
Jn 15:8 **much fruit; so shall ye be my d**....*3101*
Jn 18:17 not thou also one of this man's **d**?....*3101*
Jn 18:25 Art not thou also one of his **d**?....*3101*
Jn 20:19 shut where the **d** were assembled....*3101*
Jn 20:26 his **d** were within, and Thomas....*3101*
Jn 20:30 did Jesus in the presence of his **d**....*3101*
Jn 21:4 the **d** knew not that it was Jesus....*3101*
Jn 21:14 Jesus shewed himself to his **d**....*3101*
Ac 9:1 and slaughter against the **d** of the....*3101*
Ac 11:26 the **d** were called Christians first in....*3101*
Ac 14:22 Confirming the souls of the **d**, and....*3101*
Ac 15:10 to put a yoke upon the neck of the **d**,....*3101*

DISCIPLES'
Jn 13:5 to wash the **d** feet, and to wipe....*3101*

DISCLOSE
Isa 26:21 the earth also shall **d** her blood,....1540

DISCOMFITED
Ex 17:13 And Joshua **d** Amalek and his....2522
Nu 14:45 smote them, and **d** them, even....3807
Jgs 4:15 And the Lord **d** Sisera, and all his....2000
Ps 18:14 shot out lightnings, and **d** them....1949

DISCONTENTED
1Sa 22:2 every one that was **d**,....4751, 5315

DISCORD
Pr 6:14 continually; he soweth **d**....4066
Pr 6:19 that soweth **d** among brethren....4090

DISCOURAGED
Nu 21:4 the soul of the people was much **d**....7114
Nu 32:9 they **d** the heart of the children....5106
Dt 1:28 our brethren have **d** our heart....4549
Col 3:21 children to anger, lest they be **d**....*120*

DISCOVER
Pr 18:2 but that his heart may **d** itself. 1540
Pr 25:9 and **d** not a secret to another: 1540
Isa 3:17 Lord will **d** their secret parts 6168
Eze 16:37 will **d** thy nakedness unto them 1540
Hos 2:10 now will I **d** her lewdness in the 1540
Na 3:5 will **d** thy skirts upon thy face, ... 1540

DISCOVERED
Ex 20:26 that thy nakedness be not **d** 1540
Le 20:18 he hath **d** her fountain, and she 6168
Ps 18:15 foundations of the world were **d** 1540
Isa 57:8 thou hast **d** thyself to another 1540
La 2:14 they have not **d** thine iniquity 1540
Eze 16:36 thy nakedness **d** through thy 1540
Eze 21:24 that your transgressions are **d** 1540
Eze 23:18 she **d** her whoredoms, and **d** her 1540

DISCREET
Ge 41:39 none so **d** and wise as thou art: 995
Tit 2:5 To be **d**, chaste, keepers at home *4998*

DISCRETION
Ps 112:5 he will guide his affairs with **d** 4941
Pr 1:4 the young man knowledge and **d** 4209
Pr 3:21 eyes: keep sound wisdom and **d**: 4209
Pr 5:2 That thou mayest regard **d**, and 4209
Pr 11:22 a fair woman which is without **d** 2940
Pr 19:11 **d** of a man deferreth his anger; 7922
Isa 28:26 his God doth instruct him to **d**, ... 4941
Jer 10:12 out the heavens by his **d**. 8394

DISEASE
2Ki 1:2 whether I shall recover of this **d**. 2483
2Ki 8:9 Shall I recover of this **d**? 2483
2Ch 16:12 yet in his **d** he sought not to the 2483
Ps 38:7 are filled with a loathsome **d**:
Ecc 6:2 this is vanity, and it is an evil **d** 2483
Jn 5:4 whole of whatsoever **d** he had *3553*

DISEASED
1Ki 15:23 his old age he was **d** in his feet 2470
Eze 34:4 The **d** have ye not strengthened 2456
Mt 9:20 was **d** with an issue of blood

DISEASES
Ex 15:26 put none of these **d** upon thee, ... 4245
Dt 28:60 bring upon thee all the **d** of Egypt, ... 4064
Ps 103:3 iniquities: who healeth all thy **d**; 8463
Mk 1:34 many that were sick of divers **d** *3554*
Lk 6:17 him; and to be healed of their **d**; *3554*
Lk 9:1 over all devils, and to cure **d** *3554*

DISFIGURE
Mt 6:16 **for they d their faces, that they** *853*

DISGRACE
Jer 14:21 do not **d** the throne of thy glory: 5034

DISGUISE
1Ki 14:2 Arise, I pray thee, and **d** thyself, ... 8138
1Ki 22:30 I will **d** myself and enter into the 2664

DISGUISED
1Sa 28:8 And Saul **d** himself, and put on 2664
1Ki 20:38 and **d** himself with ashes upon 2664
1Ki 22:30 And the king of Israel **d** himself, ... 2664
2Ch 35:22 but **d** himself, that he might fight 2664

DISH
Jgs 5:25 brought forth butter in a lordly **d** 5602
2Ki 21:13 as a man wipeth a **d**, wiping it 6747
Mt 26:23 **dippeth his hand with me in the d,** *5165*
Mk 14:20 **that dippeth with me in the d,** *5165*

DISHONEST
Eze 22:27 to destroy souls, to get **d** gain 1215

DISHONESTY
2Co 4:2 renounced the hidden things of **d**, ... *152*

DISHONOUR
Ezr 4:14 meet for us to see the king's **d**, ... 6173
Ps 35:26 be clothed with shame and **d** that 3639
Ps 71:13 be covered with reproach and **d** 3639
Pr 6:33 A wound and **d** shall he get; 7036
Jn 8:49 **honour my Father, and ye do d me.** *818*
Ro 1:24 to **d** their own bodies between *818*
Ro 9:21 unto honour, and another unto **d**? *819*
1Co 15:43 It is sown in **d**; it is raised in *819*
2Ti 2:20 some to honour, and some to **d** *819*

DISHONOUREST
Ro 2:23 breaking the law **d** thou God? *818*

DISHONOURETH
1Co 11:4 his head covered, **d** his head *2617*
1Co 11:5 her head uncovered **d** her head: *2617*

DISMAYED
Dt 31:8 thee: fear not, neither be **d** 2865
Jos 1:9 neither be thou **d**: for the Lord 2865
Jos 10:25 Fear not, nor be **d**, be strong and 2865
1Sa 17:11 Philistine, they were **d**, and greatly 2865
1Ch 28:20 fear not, nor be **d**: for the Lord 2865
2Ch 20:15 Be not afraid nor **d** by reason of 2865
2Ch 32:7 be not afraid nor **d** for the king of 2865
Isa 21:3 of it; I was **d** at the seeing of it 926
Isa 41:10 be not **d**; for I am thy God: 8159
Jer 8:9 ashamed, they are **d** and taken: 2865
Jer 10:2 be not **d** at the signs of heaven; 2865
Jer 23:4 they shall fear no more, nor be **d** 2865
Jer 30:10 neither be **d**, O Israel: for, lo, ... 2865
Jer 50:36 mighty men; and they shall be **d** 2865
Eze 2:6 of their words, nor be **d** at their 2865

DISOBEDIENCE See also **OBEDIENCE.**
Ro 5:19 by one man's **d** many were made *3876*
2Co 10:6 to revenge all **d**, when your *3876*
Eph 2:2 now worketh in the children of **d**: *543*
Eph 5:6 of God upon the children of **d** *543*
Col 3:6 of God cometh on the children of **d**; *543*
Heb 2:2 transgression and **d** received a *3876*

DISOBEDIENT See also **OBEDIENT.**
1Ki 13:26 the man of God, who was **d** unto 4784
Ne 9:26 Nevertheless they were **d**, and 4784
Ac 26:19 was not **d** unto the heavenly vision: *545*
Ro 1:30 of evil things, **d** to parents *545*
Ro 10:21 unto a **d** and gainsaying people *544*
1Ti 1:9 but for the lawless and **d**, for the *506*
2Ti 3:2 blasphemers, **d** to parents *545*
Tit 1:16 being abominable, and **d**, and unto *545*
Tit 3:3 sometimes foolish, **d**, deceived *545*
1Pe 2:7 but unto them which be **d**, ... *544*
1Pe 2:8 stumble at the word, being **d**: *544*
1Pe 3:20 Which sometime were **d**, when *544*

DISORDERLY
2Th 3:6 every brother that walketh **d** ... *814*
2Th 3:11 some which walk among you **d**, ... *814*

DISPENSATION
1Co 9:17 a **d** of the gospel is committed ... *3622*
Eph 1:10 That in the **d** of the fulness of ... *3622*
Eph 3:2 heard of the **d** of the grace of God ... *3622*
Col 1:25 according to the **d** of God which ... *3622*

DISPERSE
1Sa 14:34 **D** yourselves among the people, ... 6327
Pr 15:7 The lips of the wise **d** knowledge: ... 2219
Eze 22:15 and **d** thee in the countries, and ... 2219

DISPERSED
2Ch 11:23 **d** of all his children throughout ... 6555
Est 3:8 and **d** among the people in all ... 6504
Ps 112:9 He hath **d**, he hath given to the ... 6340
Pr 5:16 Let thy fountains be **d** abroad ... 6327
Isa 11:12 gather together the **d** of Judah ... 5310
Eze 36:19 were **d** through the countries: ... 2219
Jn 7:35 unto the **d** among the Gentiles? ... *1290*
2Co 9:9 He hath **d** abroad; he hath given ... *4650*

DISPLAYED
Ps 60:4 may be **d** because of the truth ... 5127

DISPLEASE
Ge 31:35 Let it not **d** my lord that I cannot ... 2734
Nu 22:34 **d** thee, I will get me back ... 7489, 5869
2Sa 11:25 Let not this thing **d** thee, for ... 7489, 5869
Pr 24:18 the Lord see it, and it **d** him ... 7489, 5869

DISPLEASED
Ge 38:10 which he did **d** the Lord: ... 7489, 5869
Ge 48:17 head of Ephraim, it **d** him: ... 7489, 5869
Nu 11:1 complained, it **d** the Lord: ... 7451, 241
1Sa 8:6 But the thing **d** Samuel ... 7489, 5869
1Sa 18:8 and the saying **d** him; and he ... 7489, 5869
2Sa 11:27 thing that David had done **d** ... 7489, 5869
1Ki 1:6 his father had not **d** him at any ... 6087
1Ki 21:4 came into his house heavy and **d** ... 2198
1Ch 21:7 God was **d** with this thing; ... 3415, 5869
Isa 59:15 it **d** him that there was no ... 7489, 5869
Da 6:14 was sore **d** with himself, and set ... 888
Jnh 4:1 But it **d** Jonah exceedingly ... 7489, 5869
Hab 3:8 the Lord **d** against the rivers? ... 2734
Zec 1:2 The Lord hath been sore **d** with ... 7107
Zec 1:15 at ease: for I was but a little **d** ... 7107
Mt 21:15 son of David; they were sore **d** ... *23*
Mk 10:14 Jesus saw it, he was much **d** ... *23*
Mk 10:41 began to be much **d** with James ... *23*

DISPLEASURE
Dt 9:19 was afraid of the anger and hot **d**, ... 2534
Jgs 15:3 though I do them a **d** ... 7451
Ps 2:5 and vex them in his sore **d** ... 2740

DISPOSED
1Co 10:27 you to a feast, and ye be **d** to go; ... *2309*

DISPOSING
Pr 16:33 the whole **d** thereof is of the Lord ... 4941

DISPOSSESS
Nu 33:53 And ye shall **d** the inhabitants ... 3423
Dt 7:17 more than I; how can I **d** them? ... 3423

DISPUTATIONS
Ro 14:1 receive ye, but not to doubtful **d** ... *1253*

DISPUTED
Mk 9:34 they had **d** among themselves, ... *1256*
Ac 17:17 **d** he in the synagogue with the ... *1256*
Jude 9 he **d** about the body of Moses, ... *1256*

DISPUTER
1Co 1:20 where is the **d** of this world? ... *4804*

DISPUTING
Ac 6:9 and of Asia, **d** with Stephen ... *4802*
Ac 15:7 when there had been much **d** ... *4803*
Ac 19:8 three months, **d** and persuading ... *1256*

DISPUTINGS
Php 2:14 without murmurings and **d**: ... *1261*
1Ti 6:5 Perverse **d** of men of corrupt ... *3859*

DISQUIETED
1Sa 28:15 Why hast thou **d** me, to bring me ... 7264
Ps 42:5 and why art thou **d** in me? hope ... 1993
Ps 42:11 why art thou **d** within me? hope ... 1993
Ps 43:5 why art thou **d** within me? hope ... 1993
Pr 30:21 For three things the earth is **d**, ... 7264

DISSEMBLED
Jos 7:11 and have also stolen, and **d** also ... 3584
Jer 42:20 For ye **d** in your hearts, when ye ... 8582
Gal 2:13 other Jews **d** likewise with him; ... *4942*

DISSENSION
Ac 15:2 had no small **d** and disputation ... *4714*
Ac 23:7 a **d** between the Pharisees and the ... *4714*
Ac 23:10 And when there arose a great **d**, ... *4714*

DISSIMULATION
Ro 12:9 Let love be without **d**. Abhor ... *505*
Gal 2:13 was carried away with their **d** ... *5272*

DISSOLVE
Da 5:16 interpretations, and **d** doubts: ... 8271

DISSOLVED
Ps 75:3 the inhabitants therefore are **d**: ... 4127
Isa 24:19 the earth is clean **d**, the earth ... 6565
Isa 34:4 all the host of heaven shall be **d**, ... 4743
Na 2:6 and the palace shall be **d** ... 4127
2Co 5:1 house of this tabernacle were **d**, ... *2647*
2Pe 3:11 that all things shall be **d**, ... *3089*
2Pe 3:12 heavens being on fire shall be **d**, ... *3089*

DISTAFF
Pr 31:19 and her hands hold the **d** ... 6418

DISTIL
Dt 32:2 my speech shall **d** as the dew ... 5140

DISTINCTION
1Co 14:7 except they give a **d** in the sounds, ... *1293*

DISTINCTLY
Ne 8:8 law of God **d**, and gave the sense ... 6567

DISTRESS
Ge 42:21 therefore is this **d** come upon us ... 6869
Dt 2:9 **D** not the Moabites, neither ... 6696
Dt 2:19 Ammon, **d** them not, nor meddle ... 6696
Dt 28:57 enemy shall **d** thee in thy gates ... 6693
Jgs 11:7 unto me now when ye are in **d**? ... 6887

1Sa 22:2 And every one that was in **d**,....................4689
2Sa 22:7 In my **d** I called upon the Lord,...............6862
1Ki 1:29 redeemed my soul out of all **d**, ...6869
2Ch 28:22 And in the time of his **d** did he 6887
Ne 2:17 Ye see the **d** that we are in, ...7451
Ne 9:37 pleasure, and we are in great **d**................6869
Ps 4:1 enlarged me when I was in **d**; 6862
Ps 18:6 In my **d** I called upon the Lord...............6862
Ps 120:1 In my **d** I cried unto the Lord..................6869
Pr 1:27 **d** and anguish cometh upon you............6869
Isa 25:4 a strength to the needy in his **d**,...............6862
Isa 29:7 and her munition, and that **d** her...........6693
Ob 12 spoken proudly in the day of **d**,..............6869
Ob 14 that did remain in the day of **d**,..............6869
Zep 1:15 a day of trouble and **d**, a day of...............4691
Zep 1:17 And I will bring **d** upon men,..................6887
Lk 21:23 **there shall be great d in the land,**..............*318*
Lk 21:25 **and upon the earth d of nations,** *4928*
Ro 8:35 tribulation, or **d**, or persecution, ...*4730*

DISTRESSED

Ge 32:7 Jacob was greatly afraid and **d**: 3334
Jgs 2:15 them: and they were greatly **d**..................3334
1Sa 13:6 (for the people were **d**,) then the.............5065
1Sa 14:24 the men of Israel were **d** that day: 5065
1Sa 28:15 And Saul answered, I am sore **d**;.............6887
1Sa 30:6 And David was greatly **d**; for the 3334
2Sa 1:26 I am **d** for thee, my brother......................6887
2Co 4:8 troubled on every side, yet not **d**; *4729*

DISTRESSES

Ps 25:17 O bring thou me out of my **d**.................4691
Ps 107:6 he delivered them out of their **d**.............4691
2Co 12:10 persecutions, in **d** for Christ's sake: *4730*

DISTRIBUTE

Ne 13:13 was to **d** unto their brethren 2505
Lk 18:22 **d unto the poor, and thou shalt**...............*1239*
1Ti 6:18 works, ready to **d**, willing to *2130*

DISTRIBUTED

Jn 6:11 he **d** to the disciples, and the....................*1239*
1Co 7:17 as God hath **d** to every man,.....................*3307*
2Co 10:13 rule which God hath **d** to us *3307*

DISTRIBUTING

Ro 12:13 **D** to the necessity of saints;......................*2841*

DISTRIBUTION

Ac 4:35 feet: and **d** was made unto every *1239*
2Co 9:13 and for your liberal **d** unto them,............*2842*

DITCH

Ps 7:15 is fallen into the **d** which he.....................7845
Pr 23:27 For a whore is a deep **d**; and a 7745
Isa 22:11 Ye made also a **d** between the 4724
Mt 15:14 **blind, both shall fall into the d**..................*999*
Lk 6:39 **they not both fall into the d?**.....................*999*

DIVERS See also DIVERSE.

Dt 22:9 sow thy vineyard with **d** seeds: 3610
Dt 22:11 a garment of **d** sorts, as of........................8162
Dt 25:14 not have in thine house **d** measures,
2Sa 13:19 rent her garment of **d** colours..................6446
1Ch 29:2 glistering stones, and of **d** colours...........7553
2Ch 16:14 filled with sweet odours and **d** kinds
2Ch 30:11 **d** of Asher and Manasseh and....................582
Pr 20:10 **D** weights, and **d** measures
Pr 20:23 **D** weights are an abomination
Ecc 5:7 words there are also **d** vanities:
Mt 4:24 with **d** diseases and torments,..................*4164*
Mt 24:7 **and earthquakes, in d places**
Mk 8:3 **for d of them came from far**....................*5100*
Mk 13:8 **shall be earthquakes in d places,**
Lk 21:11 **great earthquakes shall be in d**
1Co 12:10 to another **d** kinds of tongues;
2Ti 3:6 with sins, led away with **d** lusts, ...*4164*
Tit 3:3 serving **d** lusts and pleasures....................*4164*
Heb 1:1 times and in **d** manners spake in............*4187*
Heb 2:4 and with **d** miracles, and gifts of.............*4164*
Heb 13:9 with **d** and strange doctrines....................*4164*
Jas 1:2 when ye fall into **d** temptations; *4164*

DIVERSE See also DIVERS.

Est 3:8 their laws are **d** from all people; 8138
Da 7:7 and it was **d** from all the beasts 8133
Da 7:23 which shall be **d** from all kingdoms, ...8133

DIVERSITIES

1Co 12:4 Now there are **d** of gifts, but the *1243*
1Co 12:6 there are **d** of operations, but it *1243*

DIVIDE

Ge 1:6 let it **d** the waters from the waters 914
Ge 1:14 to **d** the day from the night;.......................914
Ge 1:18 to **d** the light from the darkness: 914
Ex 14:16 thine hand over the sea, and **d** it: 1234
Ex 26:33 the vail shall **d** unto you between 914
Le 1:17 thereof, but shall not **d** it asunder: 914
Le 11:4 cud, or of them that **d** the hoof: 6536
Le 11:7 the swine, though he **d** the hoof,.............6536
Nu 31:27 And **d** the prey into two parts;.................2673
Nu 33:54 And ye shall **d** the land by lot for 5157
Jos 1:6 shalt thou **d** for an inheritance
1Ki 3:25 **D** the living child in two, and 1504
1Ki 3:26 be neither mine nor thine, but **d** it..........1504
Ne 9:11 thou didst **d** the sea before them, ...1234
Ps 74:13 Thou didst **d** the sea by thy.......................6565
Pr 16:19 than to **d** the spoil with the proud 2505
Isa 9:3 rejoice when they **d** the spoil 2505
Isa 53:12 Therefore will I **d** him a portion..............5312
Eze 45:1 Moreover, when ye shall **d** by lot.............5307
Da 11:39 and shall **d** the land for gain 2505
Lk 12:13 that he **d** the inheritance with me *3307*
Lk 22:17 **Take this, and d it among**.........................*1266*

DIVIDED

Ge 1:4 God **d** the light from the darkness 914
Ge 1:7 and **d** the waters which were under...........914
Ge 10:5 were the isles of the Gentiles **d**................6504
Ge 10:32 by these were the nations **d** in the 5504
Ge 15:10 another: but the birds **d** he not................1334
Ge 32:7 and he **d** the people that was with...........2673
Ex 14:21 dry land, and the waters were **d**...............1234
Nu 26:55 the land shall be **d** by lot: 2505
Dt 4:19 which the Lord thy God hath **d**...............2505
Dt 32:8 **d** to the nations their inheritance
Jos 18:10 there Joshua **d** the land unto the 2505
Jgs 7:16 And he **d** the three hundred men............2673
2Sa 1:23 in their death they were not **d**:.................6504
1Ki 16:21 Then were the people of Israel **d** 2505
2Ki 2:8 they were **d** hither and thither 2673
1Ch 1:19 in his days the earth was **d**: 6385
1Ch 23:6 And David **d** them into courses.................2505
Job 38:25 Who hath **d** a watercourse for the...........6385
Ps 68:12 that tarried at home **d** the spoil...............2505

Ps 78:13 He **d** the sea, and caused them 1234
Ps 78:55 and **d** them an inheritance by....5307
Ps 136:13 To him which **d** the Red sea into....1504
Isa 34:17 his hand hath **d** it unto them by....2505
Isa 51:15 the Lord thy God, that **d** the sea,....7280
La 4:16 anger of the Lord hath **d** them;....2505
Eze 37:22 neither shall they be **d** into two....2673
Da 5:28 Thy kingdom is **d**, and given....6537
Da 11:4 and shall be **d** toward the four....2673
Hos 10:2 Their heart is **d**; now shall they....2505
Zec 14:1 and thy spoil shall be **d** in the....2505
Mt 12:25 **Every kingdom d against itself is .**....*3307*
Mt 12:26 **Satan, he is d against himself;**....*3307*
Mk 3:25 **if a house be d against itself,**....*3307*
Mk 6:41 the two fishes **d** he among them all....*3307*
Lk 11:17 **Every kingdom d against itself is.**....*1266*
Lk 12:52 **there shall be five in one house d,**....*1266*
Lk 12:53 **father shall be d against the son,**....*1266*
Lk 15:12 **And he d unto them his living**....*1244*
Ac 13:19 he **d** their land to them by lot....*2624*
1Co 1:13 Is Christ **d**? was Paul crucified....*3307*
Rev 16:19 the great city was **d** into three....*1096*

DIVIDER
Lk 12:14 **made me a judge or a d over you?**....*3312*

DIVIDETH
Le 11:4 the cud; but **d** not the hoof;....6536
Jer 31:35 which **d** the sea when the waves....7280
Mt 25:32 **as a shepherd d his sheep from**....*575*
Lk 11:22 **he trusted, and d his spoils**....*1239*

DIVIDING
Da 7:25 a time and times and the **d** of....6387
1Co 12:11 **d** to every man severally as he....*1244*
2Ti 2:15 rightly **d** the word of truth....*3718*
Heb 4:12 even to the **d** asunder of soul and....*3311*

DIVINATION
Nu 23:23 is there any **d** against Israel:....7081
Dt 18:10 or that useth **d**, or an observer....7081
2Ki 17:17 used **d** and enchantments, and....7081
Jer 14:14 a false vision and **d**, and a thing....7081
Eze 13:6 vanity and lying **d**, saying, The....7081
Eze 21:21 head of the two ways, to use **d**:....7081
Eze 21:22 hand was the **d** for Jerusalem,....7081
Ac 16:16 possessed with a spirit of **d** met us,....*4436*

DIVINE
Ge 44:15 such a man as I can certainly **d**?....5172
1Sa 28:8 **d** unto me by the familiar spirit,....7080
Pr 16:10 A **d** sentence is in the lips of the....7081
Eze 13:9 that see vanity, and that **d** lies:....7080
Eze 21:29 whiles they **d** a lie unto thee....7080
Mic 3:6 unto you, that ye shall not **d**;....7080
Mic 3:11 the prophets thereof **d** for money:....7080
Heb 9:1 had also ordinances of **d** service....*2999*
2Pe 1:3 According as his **d** power hath....*2304*
2Pe 1:4 might be partakers of the **d** nature,....*2304*

DIVINERS
Dt 18:14 observers of times, and unto **d**:....7080
1Sa 6:2 called for the priests, and the **d**,....7080
Isa 44:25 of the liars, and maketh **d** mad;....7080
Jer 27:9 to your **d**, nor to your dreamers,....7080
Jer 29:8 Let not your prophets and your **d**,....7080
Mic 3:7 ashamed, and the **d** confounded:....7080
Zec 10:2 and the **d** have seen a lie,....7080

DIVINING
Eze 22:28 seeing vanity, and **d** lies unto....7080

DIVISION
Lk 12:51 **I tell you, Nay; but rather d**....*1267*
Jn 7:43 there was a **d** among the people....*4978*
Jn 9:16 there was a **d** among them.....*4978*
Jn 10:19 There was a **d** therefore again....*4978*

DIVISIONS
Jos 11:23 to their **d** by their tribes....4256
Jos 18:10 of Israel according to their **d**.....4256
Ezr 6:18 they set the priests in their **d**,....6392
Ro 16:17 them which cause **d** and offences....*1370*
1Co 1:10 that there be no **d** among you;....*4978*
1Co 3:3 you envying, and strife, and **d**,....*1370*
1Co 11:18 hear that there be **d** among you;....*4978*

DIVORCE
Jer 3:8 away, and given her a bill of **d**;....3748

DIVORCED
Le 21:14 widow, or a **d** woman, or profane,....1644
Le 22:13 priest's daughter be a widow, or **d**,....1644
Nu 30:9 of a widow, and of her that is **d**,....1644
Mt 5:32 **her that is d committeth adultery.**....*630*

DIVORCEMENT
Dt 24:1 then let him write her a bill of **d**,....3748
Isa 50:1 Where is the bill of your mother's **d**,....3748
Mt 5:31 **let him give her a writing of d**....*647*
Mt 19:7 command to give a writing of **d**,....*647*
Mk 10:4 Moses suffered to write a bill of **d**,....*647*

DOCTOR
Ac 5:34 named Gamaliel, a **d** of the law,....*3547*

DOCTORS
Lk 2:46 sitting in the midst of the **d**,....*1320*

DOCTRINE
Dt 32:2 My **d** shall drop as the rain,....3948
Job 11:4 My **d** is pure, and I am clean in....3948
Pr 4:2 I give you good **d**, forsake ye not....3948
Isa 28:9 shall he make to understand **d**?....8052
Jer 10:8 the stock is a **d** of vanities.....4148
Mt 7:28 people were astonished at his **d**:....*1322*
Mt 16:12 but of the **d** of the Pharisees and....*1322*
Mt 22:33 they were astonished at his **d**.....*1322*
Mk 1:27 what new **d** is this? for with....*1322*
Jn 7:16 **My d is not mine, but his that**....*1322*
Jn 7:17 **he shall know of the d, whether**....*1322*
Jn 18:19 of his disciples, and of his **d**....*1322*
Ac 2:42 in the apostles' **d** and fellowship,....*1322*
Ac 5:28 filled Jerusalem with your **d**,....*1322*
Ac 17:19 what this new **d**, whereof thou....*1322*
Ro 6:17 form of **d** which was delivered....*1322*
Ro 16:17 offences contrary to the **d** which....*1322*
1Co 14:6 or by prophesying, or by **d**?....*1322*
1Co 14:26 of you hath a psalm, hath a **d**,....*1322*
Eph 4:14 about with every wind of **d**,....*1319*
1Ti 1:3 some that they teach no other **d**,
1Ti 1:10 that is contrary to sound **d**;....*1319*
1Ti 4:6 up in words of faith and of good **d**,....*1319*
1Ti 5:17 who labour in the word and **d**,....*1319*
1Ti 6:1 God and his **d** be not blasphemed....*1319*
1Ti 6:3 **d** which is according to godliness....*1319*
2Ti 3:16 is profitable for **d**, for reproof,....*1319*
2Ti 4:2 with all longsuffering and **d**....*1322*

2Ti 4:3 they will not endure sound **d**; *1319*
Tit 1:9 able by sound **d** both to exhort *1319*
Tit 2:1 things which become sound **d**: *1319*
Tit 2:7 in **d** shewing uncorruptness, *1319*
Tit 2:10 adorn the **d** of God our Saviour *1319*
Heb 6:1 leaving the principles of the **d** *3056*
Heb 6:2 Of the **d** of baptisms, and of *1322*
2Jn 9 abideth not in the **d** of Christ, *1322*
2Jn 9 that abideth in the **d** of Christ, *1322*
Rev 2:14 **that hold the d of Balaam, who** *1322*
Rev 2:15 **hold the d of the Nicolaitanes,** *1322*
Rev 2:24 **as many as have not this d,** *1322*

DOCTRINES
Mt 15:9 **for d the commandments of men.** *1319*
Mk 7:7 **for d the commandments of men.** *1319*
Col 2:22 the commandments and **d** of men? *1319*
1Ti 4:1 seducing spirits, and **d** of devils; *1319*
Heb 13:9 about with divers and strange **d**. *1322*

DOER See also EVILDOER.
Ge 39:22 did there, he was the **d** of it 6213
2Sa 3:39 Lord shall reward the **d** of evil 6213
Ps 31:23 plentifully rewardeth the proud **d** 6213
Pr 17:4 wicked **d** giveth heed to false lips;
2Ti 2:9 as an evil **d**, even unto bonds; *2557*
Jas 1:23 hearer of the word, and not a **d**, *4163*
Jas 1:25 hearer, but a **d** of the work, *4163*
Jas 4:11 not a **d** of the law, but a judge *4163*

DOERS
2Ki 22:5 the hand of the **d** of the work, 6213
Job 8:20 neither will he help the evil **d**:
Ro 2:13 **d** of the law shall be justified. *4163*
Jas 1:22 be ye **d** of the word, and not *4163*

DOG
Ex 11:7 shall not a **d** move his tongue 3611
Dt 23:18 the price of a **d**, into the house 3611
Jgs 7:5 with his tongue, as a **d** lappeth, 3611
1Sa 17:43 Am I a **d**, that thou comest to me 3611
1Sa 24:14 pursue? after a dead **d**, after a flea. 3611
2Sa 16:9 Why should this dead **d** curse my 3611
2Ki 8:13 is thy servant a **d**, that he should 3611
Ps 22:20 darling from the power of the **d** 3611
Pr 26:11 As a **d** returneth to his vomit, 3611
Pr 26:17 one that taketh a **d** by the ears 3611
Ecc 9:4 living **d** is better than a dead lion 3611
2Pe 2:22 The **d** is turned to his own vomit *2965*

DOG'S
2Sa 3:8 Am I a **d** head, which against 3611
Isa 66:3 a lamb, as if he cut off a **d** neck; 3611

DOGS
Ex 22:31 the field; ye shall cast it to the **d**. 3611
1Ki 14:11 in the city shall the **d** eat; and him 3611
1Ki 21:19 place where **d** licked the blood of 3611
1Ki 21:23 The **d** shall eat Jezebel by the wall 3611
1Ki 22:38 and the **d** licked up his blood; 3611
2Ki 9:10 the **d** shall eat Jezebel in the 3611
2Ki 9:36 shall **d** eat the flesh of Jezebel: 3611
Ps 22:16 For **d** have compassed me: the 3611
Isa 56:10 all ignorant, they are all dumb **d**, 3611
Isa 56:11 Yea, they are greedy **d** which can 3611
Mt 7:6 **not that which is holy unto the d,** *2965*
Mt 15:26 **bread, and to cast it to d.** *2952*
Mt 15:27 yet the **d** eat of the crumbs which *2952*
Mk 7:27 **bread, and to cast it unto the d.** *2952*
Mk 7:28 yet the **d** under the table eat of the *2952*
Lk 16:21 **the d came and licked his sores** *2965*
Php 3:2 Beware of **d**, beware of evil *2965*
Rev 22:15 For without are **d**, and sorcerers *2965*

DOLEFUL
Isa 13:21 houses shall be full of **d** creatures; 255
Mic 2:4 and lament with a **d** lamentation, 5093

D

DOMINION
Ge 1:26 and let them have **d** over the fish 7287
Ge 1:28 and have **d** over the fish of the sea, 7287
Ge 37:8 shalt thou indeed have **d** over us? 4910
1Ki 4:24 he had **d** over all the region on 7287
Ne 9:37 also they have **d** over our bodies 4910
Job 38:33 canst thou set the **d** thereof in 4896
Ps 8:6 Thou madest him to have **d** over 4910
Ps 72:8 He shall have **d** also from sea to 7287
Ps 103:22 his works in all places of his **d**: 4475
Ps 119:133 let not iniquity have **d** over me 7980
Ps 145:13 and thy **d** endureth throughout 4475
Jer 34:1 the kingdoms of the earth of his **d**, 4475
Da 4:3 and his **d** is from generation to 7985
Da 4:34 whose **d** is an everlasting **d**, 7985
Da 6:26 That in every **d** of my kingdom 7985
Da 6:26 his **d** shall be even unto the end 7985
Da 7:14 his **d** is an everlasting **d**, 7985
Da 11:3 up, that shall rule with great **d** 4474
Da 11:4 according to his **d** which he ruled: 4915
Zec 9:10 and his **d** shall be from sea to 4915
Mt 20:25 **princes of the Gentiles exercise d** *2634*
Ro 6:9 death hath no more **d** over him *2961*
Ro 6:14 sin shall not have **d** over you: *2961*
Ro 7:1 the law hath **d** over a man as long *2961*
2Co 1:24 that we have **d** over your faith, *2961*
Eph 1:21 might, and **d**, and every name that *2963*
1Pe 4:11 be praise and **d** for ever and ever *2904*
1Pe 5:11 To him be glory and **d** for ever *2904*
Jude 8 despise **d**, and speak evil of *2963*
Jude 25 **d** and power, both now and ever *2904*
Rev 1:6 to him be glory and **d** for ever *2904*

DOMINIONS
Da 7:27 all **d** shall serve and obey him 7985
Col 1:16 or **d**, or principalities, or powers: *2963*

DOOR
Ge 4:7 doest not well, sin lieth at the **d** 6607
Ge 6:16 and the **d** of the ark shalt thou set 6607
Ge 18:10 Sarah heard it in the tent **d** 6607
Ge 19:11 wearied themselves to find the **d** 6607
Ex 12:7 on the **d** post of the houses 4947
Ex 12:23 the Lord will pass over the **d**, 6607
Ex 21:6 unto the **d** post; and his master 4201
Ex 29:42 at the **d** of the tabernacle of the 6607
Ex 33:8 and stood every man at his tent **d**, 6607
Ex 33:9 stood at the **d** of the tabernacle, 6607
Ex 40:6 before the **d** of the tabernacle of 6607
Le 3:2 kill it at the **d** of the tabernacle 6607
Le 8:33 And ye shall not go out of the **d** 6607
Le 17:4 And bringeth it not unto the **d** of 6607
Nu 6:18 his separation at the **d** of the 6607
Nu 16:27 and stood in the **d** of their tents 6607
Dt 11:20 write them upon the **d** posts 4201
Dt 15:17 it through his ear unto the **d**, 1817
Jgs 4:20 Stand in the **d** of the tent, and it 6607

Jgs 9:52 went hard unto the **d** of the tower 6607
Jgs 19:26 down at the **d** of the man's house............6607
2Sa 11:9 Uriah slept at the **d** of the king's..............6607
2Sa 13:17 from me, and bolt the **d** after her 1817
1Ki 14:6 her feet, as she came in at the **d**...............6607
1Ki 14:17 threshold of the **d**, the child died; 1004
1Ki 14:27 kept the **d** of the king's house 6607
2Ki 4:5 shut the **d** upon her and upon her 1817
2Ki 6:32 the **d**, and hold him fast at the **d**: 1817
2Ki 9:10 And he opened the **d**, and fled.................1817
Est 2:21 which kept the **d**, were wroth...................5592
Est 6:2 the keepers of the **d**, who sought.............5592
Ps 141:3 my mouth; keep the **d** of my lips.............1817
Pr 5:8 come not nigh the **d** of her house: 6607
Pr 9:14 she sitteth at the **d** of her house...............6607
Pr 26:14 As the **d** turneth upon his hinges 1817
Isa 6:4 posts of the **d** moved at the voice 5592
Eze 8:8 had digged in the wall, behold a **d**...........6607
Eze 8:16 at the **d** of the temple of the Lord 6607
Eze 41:16 The **d** posts, and the narrow 5592
Eze 46:3 shall worship at the **d** of this gate............6607
Am 9:1 he said, Smite the lintel of the **d**,
Mt 6:6 **when thou hast shut thy d** *2374*
Mt 25:10 **marriage: and the d was shut**...................*2374*
Mt 27:60 stone to the **d** of the sepulchre,................*2374*
Mt 28:2 rolled back the stone from the **d**,.............*2374*
Mk 11:4 colt tied by the **d** without in a place *2374*
Mk 16:3 stone from the **d** of the sepulchre? *2374*
Lk 11:7 **the d is now shut, and my** *2374*
Lk 13:25 **to knock at the d, saying, Lord,** *2374*
Jn 10:1 **by the d into the sheepfold, but**..............*2374*
Jn 10:2 **the d is the shepherd of the sheep**...........*2374*
Jn 10:7 **unto you, I am the d of the sheep** *2374*
Jn 10:9 **I am the d: by me if any man**...................*2374*
Jn 18:16 Peter stood at the **d** without.....................*2374*
Jn 18:17 the damsel that kept the **d**........................*2377*
Ac 5:9 at the **d**, and shall carry thee out *2374*
Ac 14:27 the **d** of faith unto the Gentiles................*2374*
1Co 16:9 a great **d** and effectual is opened.............*2374*
2Co 2:12 and a **d** was opened unto me *2374*
Col 4:3 open unto us a **d** of utterance,.................*2374*
Jas 5:9 the judge standeth before the **d**................*2374*
Rev 3:8 **set before thee an open d,** *2374*
Rev 3:20 **I stand at the d, and knock: if**.................*2374*
Rev 3:20 **hear my voice, and open the d,**................*2374*
Rev 4:1 a **d** was opened in heaven:........................*2374*

DOORKEEPER
Ps 84:10 I had rather be a **d** in the house...............5605

DOOR-POST See DOOR and POST.

DOORS
Jos 2:19 shall go out of the **d** of thy house............1817
Jgs 11:31 cometh forth of the **d** of my house 1817
Jgs 16:3 took the **d** of the gate of the city,.............1817
2Ki 18:16 did cut off the gold from the **d** of............1817
2Ch 3:7 and the **d** thereof, with gold;....................1817
2Ch 4:9 and overlaid the **d** of them with 1817
2Ch 28:24 shut up the **d** of the house of the 1817
2Ch 29:3 the **d** of the house of the Lord 1817
2Ch 29:7 have shut up the **d** of the porch...............1817
2Ch 34:9 the Levites that kept the **d** had.................5592
Ne 3:1 set up the **d** of it; even unto the...............1817
Ne 6:10 let us shut the **d** of the temple: 1817
Ne 7:1 was built, and I had set up the **d**,.............1817
Job 3:10 not up the **d** of my mother's womb 1817
Job 38:8 Or who shut up the sea with **d**, ...1817
Ps 24:7 be ye lift up, ye everlasting **d**; 6607
Ps 24:9 lift them up, ye everlasting **d**; 6607
Ps 78:23 and opened the **d** of heaven,....................1817
Pr 8:34 waiting at the posts of my **d**.....................6607
Ecc 12:4 the **d** shall be shut in the streets,..............1817
Isa 26:20 shut thy **d** about thee: hide.......................1817
Eze 41:25 on the **d** of the temple, cherubims 1817
Mic 7:5 keep the **d** of my mouth from her...........6607
Mt 24:33 **it is near, even at the d**.............................*2374*
Mk 13:29 **it is nigh, even at the d** *2374*
Jn 20:26 the **d** being shut, and stood in the *2374*
Ac 5:19 opened the prison **d**, and brought...........*2374*
Ac 16:27 seeing the prison **d** open, he drew *2374*

DOTED
Eze 23:5 and she **d** on her lovers, on the................5689

DOTING
1Ti 6:4 but **d** about questions and strifes.............*3552*

DOUBLE
Ge 43:12 take **d** money in your hand;.....................4932
Ex 22:7 the thief be found, let him pay **d** 8147
2Ki 2:9 **d** portion of thy spirit be upon me 8147
Ps 12:2 and with a **d** heart do they speak
Isa 40:2 received of the Lord's hand **d** for.............3718
Jer 16:18 their iniquity and their sin **d**;...................4932
Jer 17:18 destroy them with **d** destruction 4932
1Ti 5:17 be counted worthy of **d** honour...............*1362*
Jas 1:8 A **d** minded man is unstable in all...........*1374*
Jas 4:8 purify your hearts, ye **d** minded *1374*
Rev 18:6 **d** according to her works:...............*3588, 1362*

DOUBLED
Ge 41:32 for that the dream was **d** unto 8138
Eze 21:14 and let the sword be **d** the third...............3717

DOUBLE-MINDED See DOUBLE and MINDED.

DOUBLETONGUED
1Ti 3:8 not **d**, not given to much wine.................*1351*

DOUBT
Ge 37:33 Joseph is without **d** rent in pieces
Dt 28:66 thy life shall hang in **d** before thee:
Mt 14:31 **little faith, wherefore didst thou d?**.........*1365*
Mt 21:21 **If ye have faith, and d not, ye**...................*1252*
Mk 11:23 **shall not d in his heart, but shall**.............*1252*
Lk 11:20 **no d the kingdom of God is come** *686*
Jn 10:24 long dost thou make us to **d**? *142, 5590*
Ac 28:4 No **d** this man is a murderer.....................*3843*
1Co 9:10 For our sakes, no **d**, this is written:..........*1063*
Gal 4:20 voice; for I stand in **d** of you.....................*639*
1Jn 2:19 they would no **d** have continued *639*

DOUBTED
Mt 28:17 worshipped him: but some **d**..................*1365*
Ac 10:17 while Peter **d** in himself what...................*1280*

DOUBTETH
Ro 14:23 he that **d** is damned if he eat....................*1252*

DOUBTFUL
Lk 12:29 **drink, neither be ye of d mind**.................*3349*
Ro 14:1 ye, but not to **d** disputations *1261*

DOUBTING
Ac 11:12 bade me go with them, nothing **d** *1252*
1Ti 2:8 holy hands, without wrath and **d** *1261*

DOUBTLESS
Nu 14:30 **D** ye shall not come into the ...518
Ps 126:6 **d** come again with rejoicing,
Isa 63:16 **D** thou art our Father, though ...3588
1Co 9:2 unto others, yet **d** I am to you: ...*1065*

DOVE
Ge 8:9 the **d** found no rest for the sole of ...3123
Ge 8:12 seven days; and sent forth the **d**; ...3123
Ps 55:6 O that I had wings like a **d**! for ...3123
Ps 68:13 ye be as the wings of a **d** covered ...3123
SS 6:9 My **d**, my undefiled is but one; ...3123
Isa 38:14 I did mourn as a **d**: mine eyes fail ...3123
Hos 7:11 Ephraim also is like a silly **d** ...3123
Mt 3:16 Spirit of God descending like a **d**, ...*4058*
Mk 1:10 and the Spirit like a **d** descending ...*4058*
Lk 3:22 in a bodily shape like a **d** upon ...*4058*
Jn 1:32 descending from heaven like a **d** ...*4058*

DOVES
SS 5:12 His eyes are as the eyes of **d** ...3123
Isa 59:11 like bears, and mourn sore like **d**: ...3123
Eze 7:16 shall be on the mountains like **d** ...3123
Mt 10:16 **as serpents, and harmless as d** ...*4058*
Mt 21:12 the seats of them that sold **d**, ...*4058*
Mk 11:15 the seats of them that sold **d**; ...*4058*
Jn 2:16 said unto them that sold **d**, **Take** ...*4058*

DOWNSITTING
Ps 139:2 Thou knowest my **d** and mine ...3427

DOWNWARD
Ecc 3:21 the spirit of the beast that goeth **d** ...4295
Isa 37:31 shall again take root **d**, and bear ...4295
Eze 1:27 appearance of his loins even **d**, I saw ...4295
Eze 8:2 appearance of his loins even **d**, fire ...4295

DOWRY
Ge 34:12 Ask me never so much **d** and gift, ...4119
1Sa 18:25 The king desireth not any **d**, but ...4119

DRAGON
Isa 27:1 he shall slay the **d** that is in the ...8577
Jer 51:34 hath swallowed me up like a **d**, ...8577
Eze 29:3 the great **d** that lieth in the midst ...8577
Rev 12:3 behold a great red **d**, having ...*1404*
Rev 12:7 his angels fought against the **d**; ...*1404*
Rev 12:9 the great **d** was cast out, that ...*1404*
Rev 12:13 when the **d** saw that he was cast ...*1404*
Rev 13:2 and the **d** gave him his power ...*1404*
Rev 13:4 they worshipped the **d** which gave ...*1404*
Rev 16:13 out of the mouth of the **d**, ...*1404*
Rev 20:2 he laid hold on the **d**, that old ...*1404*

DRAGONS
Dt 32:23 Their wine is the poison of **d**, ...8577
Job 30:29 I am a brother to **d**, and a ...8577
Isa 34:13 it shall be an habitation of **d**, ...8577
Jer 14:6 they snuffed up the wind like **d**; ...8577
Jer 51:37 a dwellingplace for **d**, an ...8577
Mic 1:8 make a wailing like the **d**, and ...8577

DRANK
Ge 9:21 And he **d** of the wine, and was ...8354
Ge 43:34 they **d**, and were merry with him ...8354
2Sa 12:3 and **d** of his own cup, and lay in ...8354
1Ki 17:6 evening; and he **d** of the brook
Da 1:8 nor with the wine which he **d**: ...4960
Da 5:4 They **d** wine, and praised the gods ...8355
Mk 14:23 it to them; and they all **d** of it ...*4095*
Lk 17:27 **They did eat, they d, they married** ...*4095*
Lk 17:28 **they did eat, they d, they bought,** ...*4095*
1Co 10:4 for they **d** of that spiritual Rock ...*4095*

DRAUGHT
Mt 15:17 **and is cast out into the d?** ...*856*
Mk 7:19 **goeth out into the d, purging** ...*856*
Lk 5:4 **and let down your nets for a d** ...*61*

D

DRAVE See also DROVE.
Ex 14:25 that they **d** them heavily: so that ...5090
Jos 16:10 they **d** not out the Canaanites ...3423
Jos 24:12 **d** them out from before you ...1644
Jos 24:18 the Lord **d** out from before us ...1644
Jgs 1:19 he **d** out the inhabitants of the ...3423
Jgs 6:9 and **d** them out from before you, ...1644
1Sa 30:20 and the herds, which they **d** ...5090
2Sa 6:3 sons of Abinadab, **d** the new cart ...5090
2Ki 16:6 and **d** the Jews from Elath: ...5394
2Ki 17:21 **d** Israel from following the Lord, ...5071
1Ch 13:7 and Uzza and Ahio **d** the cart ...5090
Ac 7:45 whom God **d** out before the face ...*1856*
Ac 18:16 **d** them from the judgment seat ...*556*

DRAW
Ge 24:44 I will also **d** for thy camels: ...7579
Ex 3:5 **D** not nigh hither: put off thy
Le 26:33 and will **d** out a sword after you; ...7324
Jgs 3:22 he could not **d** the dagger out ...8025
Jgs 9:54 **D** thy sword, and slay me, that ...8025
1Sa 14:38 **D** ye near hither, all the chief of
1Sa 31:4 his armourbearer, **D** thy sword ...8025
Job 41:1 Canst thou **d** out leviathan with ...4900
Ps 28:3 **D** me not away with the wicked, ...4900
Ps 69:18 **D** nigh unto my soul, and redeem
Ps 73:28 is good for me to **d** near to God:
Pr 20:5 of understanding will **d** it out ...1802
Ecc 12:1 **d** nigh, when thou shalt say,
Isa 5:18 **d** iniquity with cords of vanity, ...4900
Isa 5:19 of the Holy One of Israel **d** nigh
Isa 29:13 people **d** near me with their mouth,
Isa 58:10 **d** out thy soul to the hungry ...6329
La 4:3 sea monsters **d** out the breast, ...2502
Eze 5:12 I will **d** out a sword after them. ...7324
Eze 28:7 **d** their swords against the beauty ...7324
Joel 3:9 let all the men of war **d** near;
Jn 4:11 Sir, thou hast nothing to **d** with, ...*502*
Jn 6:44 **Father which hath sent me d him:** ...*1670*
Jn 12:32 **the earth, will d all men unto me** ...*1670*
Jn 21:6 now they were not able to **d** it for ...*1670*
Heb 7:19 by the which we **d** nigh unto God
Heb 10:22 Let us **d** near with a true heart ...*4334*
Heb 10:38 but if any man **d** back, my soul ...*5288*
Heb 10:39 we are not of them who **d** back ...*5289*
Jas 2:6 rich men oppress you, and **d** you ...*1670*
Jas 4:8 **D** nigh to God, and he will **d** nigh

DRAWETH
Dt 25:11 and the wife of the one **d** near
Ps 10:9 when he **d** him into his net ...4900
Ps 88:3 my life **d** nigh unto the grave
Isa 26:17 as a **d** near the time of her delivery,
Mt 15:8 **This people d nigh unto me with**
Lk 21:8 **the time d near: go ye not**
Lk 21:28 **for your redemption d nigh**
Jas 5:8 the coming of the Lord **d** nigh

DRAWING
Jn 6:19 the sea, and **d** nigh unto the ship; *1096*

DRAWN
Nu 22:23 and his sword **d** in his hand: 8025
Nu 22:31 and his sword **d** in his hand: 8025
Dt 30:17 but shall be **d** away, and worship 5080
Jos 5:13 against him with his sword **d** 8025
Jos 8:6 till we have **d** them from the city; 5423
Jgs 20:31 were **d** away from the city; and 5423
1Ch 21:16 having a **d** sword in his hand 8025
Ps 37:14 The wicked have **d** out the sword, 6605
Pr 24:11 them that are **d** unto death, 3947
Jer 22:19 burial of an ass, **d** and cast forth 5498
Jer 31:3 lovingkindness have I **d** thee 4900
Eze 21:5 I the Lord have **d** forth my sword 3318
Ac 11:10 all were **d** up again into heaven *385*
Jas 1:14 when he is **d** away of his own lust, *1828*

DREAD
Ge 9:2 the fear of you and the **d** of you 2844
Ex 15:16 Fear and **d** shall fall upon them; 6343
Dt 1:29 **D** not, neither be afraid of them 6206
Dt 2:25 the **d** of thee and the fear of thee 6343
Dt 11:25 and the **d** of you upon all the land 4172
1Ch 22:13 courage; **d** not, nor be dismayed. 3372
Isa 8:13 fear, and let him be your **d** 6206

DREADFUL
Ge 28:17 How **d** is this place! this is none 3372
Eze 1:18 were so high that they were **d**; 3374
Da 7:7 a fourth beast, **d** and terrible, 1763
Da 9:4 O Lord, the great and **d** God, 3372
Mal 1:14 name is **d** among the heathen 3372
Mal 4:5 the great and **d** day of the Lord: 3372

DREAM
Ge 37:5 Joseph dreamed a **d**, and he told 2472
Ge 37:9 he dreamed yet another **d**, and 2472
Ge 40:5 they dreamed a **d** both of them, 2472
Ge 41:15 that thou canst understand a **d** 2472
Ge 41:25 The **d** of Pharaoh is one: God 2472
Ge 41:32 for that the **d** was double unto 2472
Jgs 7:15 Gideon heard the telling of the **d**, 2472
1Ki 3:5 Lord appeared to Solomon in a **d**, 2472
Ps 73:20 As a **d** when one awaketh; 2472
Ps 126:1 Zion, we were like them that **d** 2472
Jer 23:28 The prophet that hath a **d**, let him 2472
Da 2:3 I have dreamed a **d**, and my spirit 2472
Da 2:28 Thy **d**, and the visions of thy head 2493
Da 4:5 saw a **d** which made me afraid 2493
Da 4:18 This **d** I king Nebuchadnezzar 2493
Da 4:19 the **d** be to them that hate thee, 2493
Da 7:1 Daniel had a **d** and visions of his 2493
Joel 2:28 your old men shall **d** dreams, your 2492
Mt 1:20 Lord appeared unto him in a **d**, *3677*
Mt 2:12 being warned of God in a **d** that *3677*
Mt 2:13 Lord appeareth to Joseph in a **d**, *3677*
Mt 2:22 being warned of God in a **d**, he *3677*
Mt 27:19 this day in a **d** because of him *3677*
Ac 2:17 and your old men shall **d** dreams: *1798*

DREAMED
Ge 28:12 And he **d**, and behold a ladder set 2492
Ge 37:5 And Joseph **d** a dream, and he told 2492
Ge 37:10 is this dream that thou hast **d**? 2492
Ge 40:5 And they **d** a dream both of them 2492
Ge 41:1 of two full years, that Pharaoh **d**: 2492
Ge 41:15 unto Joseph, I have **d** a dream 2492
Ge 42:9 the dreams which he **d** of them, 2492
Jer 23:25 name, saying, I have **d**, I have **d** 2492
Jer 29:8 dreams, which ye cause to be **d** 2492
Da 2:1 Nebuchadnezzar **d** dreams 2492

DREAMER
Ge 37:19 Behold, this **d** cometh 1167, 2472
Dt 13:1 you a prophet, or a **d** of dreams, 2492

DREAMERS
Jude 8 Likewise also these filthy **d** defile *1797*

DREAMETH
Isa 29:8 as when an hungry man **d**, and 2492
Isa 29:8 as when a thirsty man **d**, 2492

DREAMS
Ge 37:8 hated him yet the more for his **d**, 2472
Ge 37:20 see what will become of his **d** 2472
Ge 42:9 Joseph remembered the **d** which 2472
Dt 13:1 or a dreamer of **d**, and giveth thee 2472
1Sa 28:6 neither by **d**, nor by Urim, nor by 2472
1Sa 28:15 neither by prophets, nor by **d**: 2472
Ecc 5:7 in the multitude of **d** and many 2472
Jer 23:27 to forget my name by their **d** 2472
Jer 23:32 against them that prophesy false **d** 2472
Jer 29:8 neither hearken to your **d** which 2472
Da 1:17 understanding in all visions and **d** 2472
Da 5:12 interpreting of **d**, and shewing of 2493
Joel 2:28 your old men shall dream **d**, your 2472
Zec 10:2 seen a lie, and have told false **d**; 2472
Ac 2:17 and your old men shall dream **d**: *1797*

DRESS
Ge 2:15 of Eden to **d** it and to keep it 5647
Dt 28:39 shalt plant vineyards, and **d** them 5647
2Sa 12:4 to **d** for the wayfaring man that 6213
2Sa 13:7 Amnon's house, and **d** him meat 6213
1Ki 17:12 that I may go in and **d** it for me 6213
1Ki 18:23 I will **d** the other bullock, and lay 6213

DRESSED
2Sa 12:4 and **d** it for the man that was come 6213
1Ki 18:26 which was given them, and they **d** 6213

DREW
Ge 37:28 and they **d** and lifted up Joseph 4900
Ex 2:10 Because I **d** him out of the water 4871
Ex 20:21 **d** near unto the thick darkness
Jgs 8:20 But the youth **d** not his sword: 8025
Ru 4:8 for thee. So he **d** off his shoe 8025
1Sa 17:40 and he **d** near to the Philistine.
1Ki 22:34 certain man **d** a bow at a venture, 4900
Est 5:2 So Esther **d** near, and touched
Ps 18:16 he **d** me out of many waters 4871
Jer 38:13 they **d** up Jeremiah with cords, 4900
Zep 3:2 Lord; she **d** not near to her God
Mt 21:34 **when the time of the fruit d near,**
Lk 22:47 **d** near unto Jesus to kiss him.
Jn 18:10 Peter having a sword **d** it, and *1670*
Ac 16:27 he **d** out his sword, and would have *4685*
Rev 12:4 **d** the third part of the stars *4951*

DRIED
Ge 8:13 waters were **d** up from off the earth: 2717
Nu 6:3 nor eat moist grapes, or **d** 3002
Jos 2:10 **d** up the water of the Red sea 3001

Jos 4:23 God **d** up the waters of Jordan ... 3001
Jgs 16:7 green withs that were never **d**, ... 2717
1Ki 17:7 that the brook **d** up, because ... 3001
Ps 22:15 strength is **d** up like a potsherd; ... 3001
Ps 69:3 my throat is **d**: mine eyes fail ... 2787
Ps 106:9 Red sea also, and it was **d** up: ... 2717
Isa 19:5 river shall be wasted and **d** up ... 3001
Isa 51:10 thou not it which hath **d** the sea ... 2717
Eze 37:11 they say, Our bones are **d**, and ... 3001
Hos 9:16 their root is **d** up, they shall bear ... 3001
Joel 1:12 The vine is **d** up, and the fig tree ... 3001
Mk 5:29 fountain of her blood was **d** up; ... *3583*
Mk 11:20 the fig tree **d** up from the roots ... *3583*
Rev 16:12 and the water thereof was **d** up ... *3583*

DRIETH

Pr 17:22 but a broken spirit **d** the bones ... 3001
Na 1:4 it dry, and **d** up all the rivers: ... 2717

DRINK

Ge 19:32 let us make our father **d** wine ... 8248
Ge 24:14 I will give thy camels **d** also: ... 8248
Ge 24:46 I will give thy camels **d** also: ... 8248
Ex 7:21 the Egyptians could not **d** of the ... 8354
Ex 15:24 Moses, saying, What shall we **d**? ... 8354
Ex 17:2 Give us water that we may **d**. ... 8354
Ex 29:41 according to the **d** offering thereof ... 5262
Ex 30:9 shall ye pour **d** offering thereon. ... 5262
Ex 32:20 and made the children of Israel **d** ... 8248
Le 10:9 wine nor strong **d**, thou, nor thy ... 7941
Le 23:37 a sacrifice, and **d** offerings, every ... 5262
Nu 5:24 cause the woman to **d** the bitter ... 8248
Nu 6:3 himself from wine and strong **d** ... 7941
Nu 6:20 that the Nazarite may **d** wine ... 8354
Nu 15:7 for a **d** offering thou shalt offer ... 5262
Nu 20:17 neither will we **d** of the water of ... 8354
Nu 28:10 burnt offering, and his **d** offering ... 5262
Dt 2:6 them for money, that ye may **d** ... 8354
Dt 32:38 the wine of their **d** offerings? ... 5257
Jgs 4:19 I pray thee, a little water to **d**; ... 8248
Jgs 7:6 bowed down upon their knees to **d** ... 8354
Jgs 13:7 and now **d** no wine nor strong ... 8354
Jgs 13:7 no wine nor strong **d**, neither ... 7941
1Sa 1:15 drunk neither wine nor strong **d** ... 7941
2Sa 11:11 to eat and to **d**, and to lie with my ... 8354
2Sa 23:15 one would give me **d** of the water ... 8248
2Sa 23:17 lives? therefore he would not **d** it ... 8354
1Ki 13:9 Eat no bread, nor **d** water, nor turn ... 8354
1Ki 13:18 he may eat bread and **d** water ... 8354
1Ki 17:4 be, that thou shalt **d** of the brook; ... 8354
1Ki 19:8 eat and **d**, and went in the strength ... 8354
1Ch 11:17 would give me **d** of the water ... 8248
1Ch 11:18 David would not **d** of it, but poured ... 8354
1Ch 11:19 shall I **d** the blood of these men ... 8354
Ezr 10:6 he did eat no bread, nor **d** water: ... 8354
Est 1:7 gave them **d** in vessels of gold ... 8248
Est 4:16 neither eat nor **d** three days, night ... 8354
Job 1:4 sisters to eat and to **d** with them ... 8354
Ps 16:4 **d** offerings of blood will I not ... 5262
Ps 50:13 of bulls, or **d** the blood of goats? ... 8354
Ps 60:3 to **d** the wine of astonishment ... 8248
Ps 69:21 thirst they gave me vinegar to **d** ... 8248
Ps 80:5 tears to **d** in great measure ... 8248
Ps 102:9 and mingled my **d** with weeping ... 8249
Pr 4:17 and **d** the wine of violence ... 8354
Pr 5:15 **D** waters out of thine own cistern ... 8354
Pr 9:5 eat of my bread, and **d** of the wine ... 8354
Pr 20:1 is a mocker, strong **d** is raging: ... 7941
Pr 23:7 Eat and **d**, saith he to thee; ... 8354
Pr 25:21 be thirsty, give him water to **d** ... 8248
Pr 31:4 it is not for kings to **d** wine; ... 8354
Pr 31:5 Lest they **d**, and forget the law ... 8354
Pr 31:6 Give strong **d** unto him that is ... 7941
Pr 31:7 Let him **d**, and forget his ... 8354
Ecc 2:24 than that he should eat and **d**, ... 8354
Ecc 3:13 every man should eat and **d**, and ... 8354
Ecc 5:18 comely for one to eat and to **d** ... 8354
Ecc 8:15 to eat, and to **d**, and to be merry: ... 8354
Ecc 9:7 **d** thy wine with a merry heart; ... 8354
Isa 22:13 let us eat and **d**; for tomorrow ... 8354
Isa 24:9 They shall not **d** wine with a song; ... 8354
Isa 28:7 have erred through strong **d** ... 7941
Isa 29:9 stagger, but not with strong **d** ... 7941
Isa 51:22 thou shalt no more **d** it again: ... 8354
Isa 56:12 will fill ourselves with strong **d**; ... 7941
Jer 7:18 **d** offerings unto other gods, that ... 5262
Jer 8:14 and given us water of gall to **d** ... 8248
Jer 16:7 them the cup of consolation to **d** ... 8248
Jer 23:15 make them **d** the water of gall: ... 8248
Jer 25:28 Lord of hosts; Ye shall certainly **d** ... 8354
Jer 32:29 out **d** offerings unto other gods ... 5262
Jer 35:14 commanded his sons not to **d** wine, ... 8354
Jer 44:17 pour out **d** offerings unto her ... 5262
Jer 44:25 to pour out **d** offerings unto her ... 5262
Jer 49:12 but thou shalt surely **d** of it ... 8354
Eze 12:18 and **d** thy water with trembling ... 8354
Eze 23:32 Thou shalt **d** of thy sister's cup ... 8354
Eze 34:19 they **d** that which ye have fouled ... 8354
Eze 39:17 that ye may eat flesh, and **d** blood ... 8354
Eze 39:19 and **d** blood till ye be drunken ... 8354
Eze 44:21 Neither shall any priest **d** wine ... 8354
Da 1:12 pulse to eat, and water to **d** ... 8354
Hos 4:18 Their **d** is sour: they have ... 5435
Joel 1:13 and the **d** offering is withholden ... 5262
Joel 3:3 sold a girl for wine, that they might **d** ... 8354
Am 2:8 they **d** the wine of the condemned ... 8354
Am 2:12 ye gave the Nazarites wine to **d**; ... 8248
Am 5:11 but ye shall not **d** wine of them ... 8354
Am 9:14 vineyards, and **d** the wine thereof; ... 8354
Ob 16 all the heathen **d** continually ... 8354
Jnh 3:7 let them not feed, nor **d** water: ... 8354
Mic 2:11 thee of wine and of strong **d**; ... 7941
Hab 2:15 him that giveth his neighbour **d** ... 8248
Zep 1:13 but not **d** the wine thereof. ... 8354
Hag 1:6 ye **d**, but ye are not filled ... 8354
Zec 7:6 yourselves, and **d** for yourselves? ... 8354
Mt 6:31 **What shall we d? or, Wherewithal** ... *4095*
Mt 10:42 **d unto one of these little ones** ... *4222*
Mt 20:22 **to d of the cup that I shall d of,** ... *4095*
Mt 20:23 **Ye shall d indeed of my cup,** ... *4095*
Mt 24:49 **to eat and d with the drunken;** ... *4095*
Mt 25:35 **I was thirsty, and ye gave me d:** ... *4222*
Mt 25:42 **I was thirsty and ye gave me no d:** ... *4222*
Mt 26:27 **to them, saying, D ye all of it;** ... *4095*
Mt 26:29 **I will not d henceforth of this** ... *4095*
Mt 26:29 **day when I d it new with you** ... *4095*
Mt 26:42 **except I d it, thy will be done** ... *4095*
Mt 27:34 vinegar to **d** mingled with gall: ... *4095*
Mk 9:41 **shall give you a cup of water to d** ... *4222*
Mk 10:38 **can ye d of the cup that I d of?** ... *4095*
Mk 10:39 **indeed d of the cup that I d of;** ... *4095*
Mk 14:25 **vine, until that day that I d it** ... *4095*

Mk	15:36	gave him to **d**, saying, Let alone;	*4222*
Mk	16:18	and if they **d** any deadly thing,	*4095*
Lk	1:15	shall **d** neither wine nor strong	*4095*
Lk	5:30	do ye eat and **d** with publicans	*4095*
Lk	12:19	thine ease, eat, **d**, and be merry	*4095*
Lk	12:29	ye shall eat or what ye shall **d**	*4095*
Lk	12:45	to eat and **d**, and to be drunken;	*4095*
Lk	17:8	afterward thou shalt eat and **d**?	*4095*
Lk	22:18	will not **d** of the fruit of the vine,	*4095*
Lk	22:30	ye may eat and **d** at my table	*4095*
Jn	4:7	Jesus saith unto her, Give me to **d**.	*4095*
Jn	4:9	askest **d** of me, which am a woman	*4095*
Jn	4:10	Give me to **d**; thou wouldest	*4095*
Jn	6:53	and **d** his blood, ye have no life	*4095*
Jn	6:55	and my blood is **d** indeed	*4215*
Jn	7:37	let him come unto me, and **d**.	*4095*
Jn	18:11	hath given me, shall I not **d** it?	*4095*
Ac	9:9	sight, and neither did eat nor **d**.	*4095*
Ac	23:12	they would neither eat nor **d** till	*4095*
Ro	12:20	if he thirst, give him **d**: for in so	*4222*
Ro	14:17	kingdom of God is not meat and **d**;	*4213*
Ro	14:21	nor to **d** wine, nor any thing	*4095*
1Co	9:4	Have we not power to eat and to **d**?	*4095*
1Co	10:4	And did all **d** the same spiritual	*4095*
1Co	10:7	The people sat down to eat and **d**.	*4095*
1Co	10:21	Ye cannot **d** the cup of the Lord	*4095*
1Co	10:31	Whether therefore ye eat, or **d**, or	*4095*
1Co	11:22	ye not houses to eat and to **d** in?	*4095*
1Co	11:25	this do ye, as oft as ye **d** it,	*4095*
1Co	11:26	ye eat this bread, and **d** this cup	*4095*
1Co	11:27	**d** this cup of the Lord, unworthily	*4095*
1Co	11:28	of that bread, and **d** of that cup	*4095*
1Co	12:13	all made to **d** into one Spirit	*4222*
1Co	15:32	let us eat and **d**; for to morrow	*4095*
Col	2:16	judge you in meat, or in **d**,	*4213*
1Ti	5:23	**D** no longer water, but use a	*5202*
Rev	14:8	because she made all nations **d**	*4222*
Rev	14:10	The same shall **d** of the wine	*4095*
Rev	16:6	thou hast given them blood to **d**;	*4095*

DRINKETH

Ge	44:5	Is not this it in which my lord **d**,	8354
Job	6:4	poison whereof **d** up my spirit:	8354
Job	15:16	man, which **d** iniquity like water?	8354
Job	34:7	Job, who **d** up scorning like water?	8354
Job	40:23	Behold, he **d** up a river, and	6231
Isa	29:8	behold, he **d**; but he awaketh,	8354
Mk	2:16	**d** with publicans and sinners?	*4095*
Jn	4:13	**d** of this water shall thirst again:	*4095*
Jn	4:14	But whosoever **d** of the water	*4095*
Jn	6:54	and **d** my blood, hath eternal life;	*4095*
Jn	6:56	eateth my flesh, and **d** my blood,	*4095*
1Co	11:29	unworthily, eateth and **d** damnation	*4095*
Heb	6:7	the earth which **d** in the rain	*4095*

DRINKING

Ge	24:19	also, until they have done **d**.	8354
1Sa	30:16	earth, eating and **d**, and dancing	8354
1Ki	10:21	king Solomon's **d** vessels were of gold,	4945
1Ki	20:16	Ben-hadad was **d** himself drunk in	8354
Job	1:13	his daughters were eating and **d**	8354
Mt	11:18	John came neither eating nor **d**,	*4095*
Mt	11:19	Son of man came eating and **d**,	*4095*
Mt	24:38	they were eating and **d**, marrying.	*4095*
Lk	10:7	eating and **d** such things as they	*4095*

DRINK-OFFERING See DRINK and OFFERING.

DRIVE See also DRAVE; DROVE.

Ex	6:1	with a strong hand shall he **d** them	1644
Ex	23:29	I will not **d** them out from before	1644
Ex	23:30	By little and little I will **d** them	1644
Nu	22:11	to overcome them, and **d** them out	1644
Nu	33:55	if ye will not **d** out the inhabitants	3423
Dt	4:38	To **d** out nations from before thee	3423
Dt	9:3	so shalt thou **d** them out, and	3423
Dt	9:4	the Lord doth **d** them out from	3423
Dt	9:5	the Lord thy God doth **d** them out	3423
Jos	15:63	children of Judah could not **d** them	3423
Jos	17:12	children of Manasseh could not **d**	3423
Jos	23:13	your God will no more **d** out any	3423
Jgs	1:19	could not **d** out the inhabitants of	3423
Jgs	2:3	I will not **d** them out from before	1644
Ps	44:2	thou didst **d** out the heathen with	3423
Pr	22:15	the rod of correction shall **d** it far	
Jer	24:9	all places whither I shall **d** them	5080
Jer	27:15	that I might **d** you out, and that	5080
Jer	46:15	not, because the Lord did **d** them	1920
Da	4:25	they shall **d** thee from men, and	2957
Hos	9:15	I will **d** them out of mine house,	1644

DRIVEN

Ge	4:14	thou hast **d** me out this day from	1644
Ex	10:11	they were **d** out from Pharaoh's	1644
Dt	4:19	shouldest be **d** to worship them	5080
Dt	30:1	whither the Lord thy God hath **d**	5080
Dt	30:4	If any of thine be **d** out unto the	5080
Jos	23:9	the Lord hath **d** out from before	3423
1Sa	26:19	for they have **d** me out this day	1644
Ps	40:14	let them be **d** backward and put	5472
Ps	68:2	As smoke is **d** away, so drive	5086
Ps	114:3	it, and fled: Jordan was **d** back	5437
Pr	14:32	The wicked is **d** away in his	1760
Isa	8:22	they shall be **d** to darkness	5080
Jer	16:15	the lands whither he had **d** them:	5080
Jer	23:2	scattered my flock, and **d** them	5080
Jer	23:3	all countries whither I have **d** them	5080
Jer	29:18	the nations whither I have **d** them:	5080
Jer	32:37	all countries, whither I have **d**.	5080
Jer	46:28	the nations whither I have **d** thee:	5080
Jer	50:17	the lions have **d** him away:	5080
Eze	34:16	bring again that which was **d** away,	5080
Da	4:33	he was **d** from men, and did eat	2957
Da	5:21	he was **d** from the sons of men;	2957
Da	9:7	countries whither thou hast **d**.	5080
Hos	13:3	chaff that is **d** with the whirlwind	5590
Lk	8:29	**d** of the devil into the wilderness.)	*1643*
Jas	1:6	the sea **d** with the wind and tossed	*416*
Jas	3:4	are **d** of fierce winds, yet are they	*1643*

DRIVER

1Ki	22:34	he said unto the **d** of his chariot,	7395

DRIVETH

Ps	1:4	the chaff which the wind **d** away	5086
Pr	25:23	The north wind **d** away rain: so	2342
Mk	1:12	spirit **d** him into the wilderness	*1544*

DRIVING

2Ki	9:20	and the **d** is like the **d** of Jehu	4491

DROP

Dt	32:2	My doctrine shall **d** as the rain,	6201
Dt	33:28	also his heaven shall **d** down dew	6201
Pr	3:20	and the clouds **d** down the dew	7491

Pr 5:3 woman **d** as an honeycomb, ...5197
Isa 40:15 a **d** of a bucket, and are counted..............4752
Isa 45:8 **D** down, ye heavens, from above 7491
Am 7:16 **d** not thy word against the house 5197
Am 9:13 and the mountains shall **d** sweet 5197

DROPPED
Jgs 5:4 the heavens **d**, the clouds also **d**...............5197
1Sa 14:26 behold, the honey **d**; but no man 1982
Ps 68:8 heavens also **d** at the presence of.............5197

DROPPING
Pr 19:13 of a wife are a continual **d**........................1812
Pr 27:15 A continual **d** in a very rainy day 1812

DROPS
Lk 22:44 as it were great **d** of blood falling *2361*

DROSS
Pr 25:4 Take away the **d** from the silver,...............5509
Pr 26:23 a potsherd covered with silver **d** 5509
Isa 1:25 purely purge away thy **d**, and take...........5509
Eze 22:18 house of Israel is to me become **d**; 5509

DROUGHT
Dt 8:15 serpents, and scorpions, and **d**,................6774
Isa 58:11 and satisfy thy soul in **d**, and....................6710
Jer 2:6 through a land of **d**, and of the................6723
Jer 17:8 not be careful in the year of **d**..................1226
Hos 13:5 wilderness, in the land of great **d**.............8514
Hag 1:11 I called for a **d** upon the land...................2721

DROVE See also DRAVE.
Ge 3:24 So he **d** out the man; and he....................1644
Ge 33:8 What meanest thou by all this **d**..............4264
Hab 3:6 and **d** asunder the nations; and 5425
Jn 2:15 he **d** them all out of the temple *1544*

DROWN
1Ti 6:9 which **d** men in destruction and *1036*

DROWNED
Ex 15:4 his chosen captains also are **d** 2883
Am 8:8 and it shall be cast out and **d**, as 8248
Am 9:5 and shall be **d**, as by the flood of 8248
Mt 18:6 **he were d in the depth of the sea**.............*2670*
Heb 11:29 Egyptians assaying to do were **d** *2666*

DROWSINESS
Pr 23:21 **d** shall clothe a man with rags 5124

DRUNK
Dt 29:6 neither have ye **d** wine or strong 8354
Dt 32:42 make mine arrows **d** with blood,.............7937
1Sa 1:15 I have **d** neither wine nor strong 8354
2Sa 11:13 and he made him **d**: and at even 7937
1Ki 16:9 drinking himself **d** in the house of..........7910
1Ki 20:16 drinking himself **d** in the pavilions, ...7910
SS 5:1 I have **d** my wine with my milk: 8354
Isa 51:17 hast **d** at the hand of the Lord 8354
Isa 63:6 and make them **d** in my fury 7937
Jer 46:10 and made **d** with their blood: 7301
Jer 51:57 And I will make **d** her princes,..................7937
Da 5:23 have **d** wine in them; and thou.................8355
Lk 5:39 **No man also having d old wine**...............*4095*
Jn 2:10 when men have well **d**, then......................*3184*
Eph 5:18 And be not **d** with wine, wherein *3182*
Rev 17:2 have been made **d** with the wine *3182*
Rev 18:3 all nations have **d** of the wine

DRUNKARD
Dt 21:20 voice; he is a glutton, and a **d**...................5435
Pr 23:21 the **d** and the glutton shall come 5435
Pr 26:9 goeth up into the hand of a **d**, ...7910
Isa 24:20 shall reel to and fro like a **d**, ...7910
1Co 5:11 railer, or a **d**, or an extortioner;................*3183*

DRUNKARDS
Ps 69:12 and I was the song of the **d**............8354, 7941
Joel 1:5 Awake, ye **d**, and weep; and howl 7910
Na 1:10 while they are drunken as **d**, ...5435
1Co 6:10 nor **d**, nor revilers, nor.............................*3183*

DRUNKEN
Ge 9:21 he drank of the wine, and was **d**;.............7943
1Sa 1:13 Eli thought she had been **d** 7910
1Sa 25:36 within him, for he was very **d** 7910
Ps 107:27 and stagger like a **d** man,..........................7910
Isa 19:14 a **d** man staggereth in his vomit 7910
Isa 29:9 they are **d**, but not with wine;..................7937
Isa 49:26 shall be **d** with their own blood...............7937
Isa 51:21 and **d**, but not with wine:.........................7937
Jer 23:9 I am like a **d** man, and like a 7910
Jer 25:27 Drink ye, and be **d**, and spue, ...7937
Jer 51:7 the nations have **d** of her wine;................8354
La 3:15 hath made me **d** with wormwood...........7301
La 5:4 We have **d** our water for money; 8354
Eze 39:19 and drink blood till ye be **d**,......................7943
Na 1:10 while they are **d** as drunkards...................5435
Hab 2:15 to him, and makest him **d** also, ...7937
Mt 24:49 **and to eat and drink with the d**;..............*3184*
Lk 12:45 **eat and drink, and to be d**;........................*3182*
Lk 17:8 **till I have eaten and d; and**.......................*4095*
Ac 2:15 For these are not **d**, as ye suppose,...........*3184*
1Co 11:21 one is hungry, and another is **d** *3184*
1Th 5:7 they that be **d** are **d** in the night *3184*
Rev 17:6 **d** with the blood of the saints, ...*3184*

DRUNKENNESS
Dt 29:19 mine heart, to add **d** to thirst...................7302
Ecc 10:17 for strength, and not for **d**! 8358
Jer 13:13 inhabitants of Jerusalem, with **d**.............7943
Eze 23:33 shall be filled with **d** and sorrow,.............7943
Lk 21:34 **and d, and cares of this life**, ...*3178*
Ro 13:13 **rioting and d, not in chambering**............*3178*
Gal 5:21 Envyings, murders, **d**, revellings,..............*3178*

DRY
Ge 1:10 And God called the **d** land Earth;............3004
Ge 7:22 of all that was in the **d** land, died 2724
Ex 4:9 become blood upon the **d** land;...............3006
Ex 14:29 of Israel walked upon **d** land 3004
Jos 3:17 Israelites passed over on **d** ground, ...2724
Jos 4:22 came over this Jordan on **d** land...............3004
Jos 9:5 their provision was **d** and mouldy...........3001
Jgs 6:37 and it be **d** upon all the earth beside,.......2721
Jgs 6:39 it now be **d** only upon the fleece, ...2721
2Ki 2:8 they two went over on **d** ground 2724
Ps 63:1 for thee in a **d** and thirsty land 6723
Ps 66:6 He turned the sea into **d** land; 3004
Ps 95:5 and his hands formed the **d** land.............3006
Pr 17:1 Better is a **d** morsel, and quietness 2720
Isa 32:2 as rivers of water in a **d** place, ...6724
Isa 44:3 and floods upon the **d** ground:................3004
Isa 44:27 saith to the deep, Be **d**,..............................2717
Isa 50:2 at my rebuke I **d** up the sea, ...2717
Isa 56:3 say, Behold, I am a **d** tree...........................3002

Eze	30:12	I will make the rivers **d**, and sell	2724
Eze	37:4	O ye **d** bones, hear the word of	3002
Hos	9:14	miscarrying womb and **d** breasts	6784
Jnh	1:9	hath made the sea and the **d** land	3004
Jnh	2:10	vomited out Jonah upon the **d** land	3004
Na	1:4	rebuketh the sea, and maketh it **d**,	3001
Lk	11:24	**he walketh through d places,**	*504*
Lk	23:31	**what shall be done in the d?**	*3584*
Heb	11:29	through the Red sea as by **d** land:	*3584*

D

DUE

Le	10:13	for they be thy **d** and thy sons' **d**	2706
Le	26:4	I will give thee rain in **d** season	
Nu	28:2	offer unto me in their **d** season	
Dt	18:3	be the priest's **d** from the people,	4941
Dt	32:35	their foot shall slide in **d** time:	
1Ch	16:29	Give unto the Lord the glory **d**	
Ps	29:2	Lord the glory **d** unto his name;	
Ps	96:8	the Lord the glory **d** unto his name:	
Pr	3:27	not good from them to whom it is **d**,	1167
Pr	15:23	a word spoken in **d** season, how	
Mt	18:34	**pay all that was d unto him**	*3784*
Lk	12:42	**their portion of meat in d season?**	
Lk	23:41	we receive the **d** reward of our deeds;	*514*
Ro	5:6	in **d** time Christ died for the ungodly.	*514*
Ro	13:7	dues: tribute to whom tribute is **d**;	*514*
1Co	7:3	unto the wife **d** benevolence:	*3784*
1Co	15:8	as of one born out of **d** time.	
Gal	6:9	for in **d** season we shall reap	*2398*
1Ti	2:6	for all, to be testified in **d** time	*2398*
Tit	1:3	in **d** time manifested his word	*2398*
1Pe	5:6	that he may exalt you in **d** time:	*2398*

DUES

Ro	13:7	Render therefore to all their **d**	*3782*

DULL

Mt	13:15	**their ears are d of hearing, and**	*917*
Ac	28:27	their ears are **d** of hearing, and	*917*
Heb	5:11	seeing ye are **d** of hearing	*3576*

DUMB

Ex	4:11	or who maketh the **d**, or deaf, or the	483
Ps	39:2	I was **d** with silence, I held my	481
Pr	31:8	Open thy mouth for the **d** in the	483
Isa	53:7	a sheep before her shearers is **d**,	481
Isa	56:10	they are all **d** dogs, they cannot	483
Eze	24:27	shalt speak, and be no more **d**:	481
Eze	33:22	was opened, and I was no more **d**	481
Da	10:15	toward the ground, and I became **d**	481
Hab	2:19	Awake; to the **d** stone, Arise,	1748
Mt	9:33	devil was cast out, the **d** spake:	*2974*
Mt	12:22	with a devil, blind, and **d**: and he	*2974*
Mt	15:31	when they saw the **d** to speak	*2974*
Mk	7:37	deaf to hear, and the **d** to speak	*216*
Mk	9:25	**Thou d and deaf spirit, I charge**	*216*
Lk	1:20	shalt be **d**, and not able to speak	*4623*
Ac	8:32	like a lamb **d** before his shearer	*880*
1Co	12:2	carried away unto these **d** idols,	*880*
2Pe	2:16	**d** ass speaking with man's voice	*880*

DUNG See also DUNGHILL.

Le	8:17	and his hide, his flesh, and his **d**,	6569
1Ki	14:10	as a man taketh away **d**, till it be	1557
2Ki	9:37	Jezebel shall be as **d** upon the face	1828
Job	20:7	shall perish for ever like his own **d**:	1561
Ps	83:10	they became as **d** for the earth.	1828
Isa	36:12	may eat their own **d**	2716(6675)
Jer	8:2	they shall be for **d** upon the face	1828
Jer	16:4	they shall be as **d** upon the face of	1828
Jer	25:33	they shall be **d** upon the ground	1828
Eze	4:15	Lo I have given thee cow's **d**	6832
Mal	2:3	spread **d** upon your faces, even	6569
Lk	13:8	**I shall dig about it, and d it:**	*906, 2874*
Php	3:8	and do count them but **d**, that I	*4657*

DUNGEON

Ge	40:15	that they should put me into the **d**	953
Ge	41:14	brought him hastily out of the **d**:	953
Ex	12:29	the captive that was in the **d**;	1004, 953
Jer	38:6	And in the **d** there was no water, but	953
Jer	38:10	Jeremiah the prophet out of the **d**	953
La	3:53	They have cut off my life in the **d**	953

DUNGHILL See also DUNG.

1Sa	2:8	lifted up the beggar from the **d**,	830
Ezr	6:11	his house be made a **d** for this	5122
Da	2:5	your houses shall be made a **d**	5122
Lk	14:35	**for the land, nor yet for the d;**	*2874*

DUNGHILLS

La	4:5	brought up in scarlet embrace **d**	830

DUST

Ge	2:7	Lord God formed man of the **d** of	6083
Ge	3:14	and **d** shalt thou eat all the days of	6083
Ge	3:19	and unto **d** shalt thou return	6083
Ge	13:16	man can number the **d** of the earth,	6083
Ge	18:27	Lord, which am but **d** and ashes:	6083
Ex	8:17	and smote the **d** of the earth,	6083
Le	14:41	they shall pour out the **d** that	6083
Le	17:13	blood thereof, and cover it with **d**	6083
Nu	23:10	Who can count the **d** of Jacob,	6083
Dt	9:21	I cast the **d** thereof into the brook	6083
Dt	32:24	the poison of serpents of the **d**	6083
Jos	7:6	and put **d** upon their heads	6083
2Sa	16:13	threw stones at him, and cast **d**	6083
1Ki	16:2	I exalted thee out of the **d**,	6083
1Ki	18:38	the wood, and the stones, and the **d**,	6083
Job	2:12	sprinkled **d** upon their heads	6083
Job	10:9	wilt thou bring me into **d** again?	6083
Job	30:19	I am become like **d** and ashes	6083
Job	34:15	man shall turn again unto **d**	6083
Job	39:14	earth, and warmeth them in **d**,	6083
Job	42:6	and repent in **d** and ashes	6083
Ps	22:29	they that go down to the **d** shall	6083
Ps	30:9	Shall the **d** praise thee? shall it	6083
Ps	72:9	and his enemies shall lick the **d**	6083
Ps	103:14	he remembereth that we are **d**	6083
Ps	104:29	they die, and return to their **d**	6083
Ecc	3:20	all are of the **d**, and all turn to **d**	6083
Ecc	12:7	Then shall the **d** return to the earth	6083
Isa	40:12	comprehended the **d** of the earth	6083
Isa	40:15	as the small **d** of the balance:	7834
Isa	65:25	and **d** shall be the serpent's meat	6083
La	2:10	have cast up **d** upon their heads;	6083
La	3:29	He putteth his mouth in the **d**;	6083
Eze	27:30	shall cast up **d** upon their heads	6083
Da	12:2	many of them that sleep in the **d**	6083
Mic	7:17	shall lick the **d** like a serpent,	6083
Na	1:3	the clouds are the **d** of his feet.	80
Na	3:18	thy nobles shall dwell in the **d**:	
Zep	1:17	blood shall be poured out as **d**,	6083
Zec	9:3	heaped up silver as the **d**, and fine	6083

Mk	6:11	**shake off the d under your feet**	*5522*
Lk	10:11	**Even the very d of your city,**	*2868*
Ac	13:51	they shook off the **d** of their feet	*2868*
Ac	22:23	clothes, and threw **d** into the air	*2868*
Rev	18:19	And they cast **d** on their heads,	*5522*

DUTY

Ex	21:10	and her **d** of marriage, shall he not	
Dt	25:5	**d** of an husband's brother unto her	
2Ch	8:14	as the **d** of every day required:	1697
Ezr	3:4	as the **d** of every day required;	1697
Ecc	12:13	for this is the whole **d** of man	1697
Lk	17:10	**done that which was our d to do.**	*3784*

DWELL

Ge	4:20	the father of such as **d** in tents,	3427
Ge	13:6	so that they could not **d** together,	3427
Ge	26:2	**d** in the land which I shall tell	7931
Ge	30:20	now will my husband **d** with me,	2082
Ge	34:22	consent unto us for to **d** with us	3427
Ge	47:6	in the land of Goshen let them **d**:	3427
Ex	15:17	thou hast made for thee to **d** in	3427
Ex	25:8	that I may **d** among them	7931
Le	23:42	Ye shall **d** in booths seven days;	3427
Nu	13:28	people be strong that **d** in the land,	3427
Nu	14:30	make you **d** therein, save Caleb	7931
Nu	35:32	should come again to **d** in the land	3427
Dt	12:11	to cause his name to **d** there;	7931
Dt	25:5	If brethren **d** together, and one of	3427
Dt	30:20	that thou mayest **d** in the land	3427
Jos	20:6	he shall **d** in that city, until he stand	3427
2Sa	7:2	I **d** in an house of cedar, but the ark	3427
2Sa	7:5	build me an house for me to **d** in?	3427
1Ki	3:17	I and this woman **d** in one house;	3427
1Ki	8:12	The Lord said that he would **d** in	7931
1Ki	8:13	built thee an house to **d** in, a	2073
1Ki	8:27	will God indeed **d** on the earth?	3427
1Ch	17:4	not build me an house to **d** in:	3427
1Ch	23:25	may **d** in Jerusalem for ever:	7931
2Ch	6:18	will God in very deed **d** with men	3427
2Ch	8:11	shall not **d** in the house of David	3427
Ezr	6:12	hath caused his name to **d** there	7932
Ne	8:14	children of Israel should **d** in booths	3427
Job	4:19	in them that **d** in houses of clay,	7931
Ps	4:8	Lord, only makest me **d** in safety	3427
Ps	5:4	neither shall evil **d** with thee	1481
Ps	23:6	I will **d** in the house of the Lord	3427
Ps	24:1	world, and they that **d** therein	3427
Ps	27:4	I may **d** in the house of the Lord	3427
Ps	65:4	that he may **d** in thy courts:	7931
Ps	68:16	hill which God desireth to **d** in;	3427
Ps	69:36	they that love his name shall **d**.	7931
Ps	84:10	to **d** in the tents of wickedness	1752
Ps	98:7	world, and they that **d** therein	3427
Ps	132:14	here will I **d**; for I have desired it	3427
Ps	133:1	brethren to **d** together in unity!	3427
Ps	139:9	and **d** in the uttermost parts of the	7931
Pr	1:33	hearkeneth unto me shall **d** safely	7931
Pr	2:21	the upright shall **d** in the land	7931
Pr	8:12	I wisdom **d** with prudence, and	7931
Pr	21:19	It is better to **d** in the wilderness	3427
Pr	25:24	to **d** in the corner of the housetop	3427
Isa	6:5	I **d** in the midst of a people of	3427
Isa	9:2	that **d** in the land of the shadow	3427
Isa	11:6	wolf also shall **d** with the lamb,	1481
Isa	33:14	shall **d** with everlasting burnings?	1481
Isa	33:24	that **d** therein shall be forgiven	3427
Isa	51:6	**d** therein shall die in like manner:	3427
Isa	57:15	I **d** in the high and holy place	7931
Jer	23:6	Israel shall **d** safely: and this	7931
Jer	23:8	they shall **d** in their own land	3427
Jer	33:16	and Jerusalem shall **d** safely:	7931
Jer	40:9	**d** in the land, and serve the king	3427
Jer	42:13	We will not **d** in this land, neither	3427
Jer	48:28	leave the cities, and **d** in the rock	7931
Jer	49:18	neither shall a son of man **d** in it	1481
Jer	50:40	shall any son of man **d** therein	1481
Eze	2:6	thou dost **d** among scorpions:	3427
Eze	16:46	daughters that **d** at thy left hand:	3427
Eze	34:28	but they shall **d** safely, and none	3427
Eze	39:9	they that **d** in the cities of Israel	3427
Da	2:38	wheresoever the children of men **d**,	1753
Joel	3:20	Judah shall **d** for ever, and	3427
Am	5:11	but ye shall not **d** in them;	3427
Am	9:5	all that **d** therein shall mourn:	3427
Na	1:5	the world, and all that **d** therein	3427
Na	3:18	thy nobles shall **d** in the dust:	7931
Zep	1:18	of all them that **d** in the land	3427
Hag	1:4	to **d** in your cieled houses, and	3427
Zec	2:11	people: and I will **d** in the midst	7931
Zec	8:3	will **d** in the midst of Jerusalem:	7931
Zec	8:8	shall **d** in the midst of Jerusalem:	7931
Mt	12:45	**and they enter in and d there:**	*2730*
Lk	11:26	**and they enter in, and d there:**	*2730*
Lk	21:35	**all them that d on the face of the**	*2521*
Ac	13:27	For they that **d** at Jerusalem, and	*2730*
Ac	17:26	to **d** on all the face of the earth,	*2730*
Ro	8:9	that the Spirit of God **d** in you	*3611*
Ro	8:11	raised up Jesus from the dead **d**.	*3611*
1Co	7:12	and she be pleased to **d** with him,	*3611*
1Co	7:13	if he be pleased to **d** with her	*3611*
2Co	6:16	God hath said, I will **d** in them	*1774*
Eph	3:17	That Christ may **d** in your hearts	*2730*
Col	1:19	that in him should all fulness **d**;	*2730*
Col	3:16	Let the word of Christ **d** in you	*1774*
1Pe	3:7	husbands **d** with them according	*4924*
1Jn	4:13	know we that we **d** in him	*3306*
Rev	3:10	**try them that d upon the earth**	*2730*
Rev	6:10	blood on them that **d** on the earth?	*2730*
Rev	7:15	on the throne shall **d** among them.	*4637*
Rev	11:10	that **d** upon the earth shall rejoice	*2730*
Rev	13:8	all that **d** upon the earth shall	*2730*
Rev	13:12	which **d** therein to worship the	*2730*
Rev	14:6	to preach unto them that **d** on	*2730*
Rev	17:8	they that **d** on the earth shall wonder	*2730*
Rev	21:3	and he will **d** with them, and they	*4637*

DWELLEST

2Ki	19:15	which **d** between the cherubims	3427
Ps	80:1	that **d** between the cherubims	3427
Ps	123:1	O thou that **d** in the heavens	3427
Isa	37:16	that **d** between the cherubims	3427
Isa	47:8	to pleasures, that **d** carelessly	3427
Jer	51:13	O thou that **d** upon many waters	7931
Eze	7:7	O thou that **d** in the land:	3427
Eze	12:2	thou **d** in the midst of a rebellious	3427
Jn	1:38	Master,) where **d** thou?	*3306*
Rev	2:13	**and where thou d, even where**	*2730*

DWELLETH

Le	19:34	the stranger that **d** with you	1481
Jos	22:19	wherein the Lord's tabernacle **d**.	7931

1Sa	4:4	which **d** between the cherubims:	3427
2Sa	6:2	that **d** between the cherubims	3427
Ps	9:11	to the Lord, which **d** in Zion:	3427
Ps	91:1	He that **d** in the secret place of the	3427
Ps	113:5	the Lord our God, who **d** on high,	3427
Pr	3:29	seeing he **d** securely by thee	3427
Isa	33:5	for he **d** on high: he hath filled	7931
Jer	44:2	desolation, and no man **d** therein,	3427
Jer	51:43	a land wherein no man **d**, neither	3427
La	1:3	she **d** among the heathen, she	3427
Eze	16:46	that **d** at thy right hand, is Sodom	3427
Eze	38:14	when my people of Israel **d** safely,	3427
Da	2:22	darkness, and the light **d** with	8271
Joel	3:21	cleansed: for the Lord **d** in Zion.	7931
Am	8:8	every one mourn that **d** therein?	3427
Mt	23:21	**by it, and by him that d therein**	*2730*
Jn	6:56	**my blood, d in me, and I in him.**	*3306*
Jn	14:10	**the Father that d in me, he doeth**	*3306*
Jn	14:17	**for he d with you, and shall be**	*3306*
Ac	7:48	the most High **d** not in temples	*2730*
Ac	17:24	of heaven and earth, **d** not in temples	*2730*
Ro	7:17	that do it, but sin that **d** in me	*3611*
Ro	7:18	is, in my flesh,) **d** no good thing:	*3611*
Ro	7:20	I that do it, but sin that **d** in me	*3611*
Ro	8:11	bodies by his Spirit that **d** in you.	*1774*
1Co	3:16	and that the Spirit of God **d** in you?	*3611*
Col	2:9	in him **d** all the fulness of the	*2730*
2Ti	1:14	the Holy Ghost which **d** in us.	*1774*
Jas	4:5	The spirit that **d** in us lusteth	*2730*
2Pe	3:13	earth, wherein **d** righteousness.	*2730*
1Jn	3:17	how **d** the love of God in him?	*3306*
1Jn	4:12	God **d** in us, and his love is	*3306*
1Jn	4:15	God **d** in him, and he in God	*3306*
1Jn	4:16	he that **d** in love **d** in God, and	*3306*
2Jn	2	the truth's sake, which **d** in us,	*3306*
Rev	2:13	**slain among you, where Satan d**	*2730*

DWELLING

Ge	25:27	Jacob was a plain man, **d** in tents.	3427
Le	25:29	if a man sell a **d** house in a walled	4186
1Ki	8:30	and hear thou in heaven thy **d**	3427
1Ki	8:39	Then hear thou in heaven thy **d**	3427
2Ch	6:2	a place for thy **d** for ever.	3427
2Ch	6:39	even from thy **d** place, their prayer,	3427
2Ch	30:27	came up to his holy **d** place,	4583
Ps	49:11	their **d** places to all generations;	4908
Ps	90:1	Lord, thou hast been our **d** place	4583
Pr	21:20	and oil in the **d** of the wise;	5116
Pr	24:15	against the **d** of the righteous;	5116
Isa	4:5	every **d** place of mount Zion,	4349
Eze	38:11	all of them **d** without walls, and	3427
Da	2:11	gods, whose **d** is not with flesh	4070
Da	4:25	thy **d** shall be with the beasts	4070
Joel	3:17	the Lord your God **d** in Zion,	7931
Mk	5:3	Who had his **d** among the tombs;	*2731*
1Ti	6:16	**d** in the light which no man can	*3611*
Heb	11:9	**d** in tabernacles with Isaac and	*2730*
2Pe	2:8	righteous man **d** among them,	*1460*

DWELLINGPLACE

1Co	4:11	are buffeted, have no certain **d**;	*790*

DWELLINGPLACES

Jer	30:18	tents, and have mercy on his **d**;	4908
Jer	51:30	women: they have burned her **d**;	4908
Eze	37:23	I will save them out of all their **d**,	4186
Hab	1:6	possess the **d** that are not theirs	4908

DWELLINGS

Ex	10:23	of Israel had light in their **d**	4186
Le	3:17	all your **d**, that ye eat neither fat	4186
Le	23:3	sabbath of the Lord in all your **d**	4186
Ps	55:15	wickedness is in their **d**, and	4033
Ps	87:2	Zion more than all the **d** of Jacob	4908
Isa	32:18	and in sure **d**, and in quiet resting	4908
Jer	9:19	because our **d** have cast us out	4908

DWELT

Ge	4:16	the Lord, and **d** in the land of Nod,	3427
Ge	13:18	and **d** in the plain of Mamre,	3427
Ge	14:12	who **d** in Sodom, and his goods,	3427
Ge	19:30	and he **d** in a cave, he and his two	3427
Ge	47:27	And Israel **d** in the land of Egypt,	3427
Ex	2:15	and **d** in the land of Midian:	3427
Le	26:35	sabbaths, when ye **d** upon it	3427
Dt	1:6	have **d** long enough in this mount:	3427
Dt	2:20	giants **d** therein in old time;	3427
Dt	8:12	built goodly houses, and **d** therein;	3427
Dt	33:16	will of him that **d** in the bush:	7931
Jos	2:15	and she **d** upon the wall.	3427
Jos	24:2	**d** on the other side of the flood	3427
Jos	24:7	**d** in the wilderness a long season.	3427
Jgs	4:5	**d** under the palm tree of Deborah	3427
Jgs	18:7	they **d** careless, after the manner	3427
1Sa	27:3	And David **d** with Achish at Gath,	3427
2Sa	7:6	I have not **d** in any house since	3427
2Sa	14:28	So Absalom **d** two full years in	3427
1Ki	4:25	And Judah and Israel **d** safely,	3427
1Ch	10:7	Philistines came and **d** in them.	3427
1Ch	11:7	And David **d** in the castle;	3427
1Ch	17:5	I have not **d** in an house since the	3427
2Ch	34:22	she **d** in Jerusalem in the college:)	3427
Ne	4:12	the Jews which **d** by them came,	3427
Ne	11:1	of the people **d** at Jerusalem:	3427
Est	9:19	that **d** in the unwalled towns,	3427
Ps	74:2	mount Zion, wherein thou hast **d**.	7931
Pa	94:17	my soul had almost **d** in silence	7931
Ps	120:6	My soul hath long **d** with him	7931
Isa	13:20	neither shall it be **d** in from	7931
Isa	37:37	and returned, and **d** at Nineveh	3427
Jer	2:6	through, and where no man **d**?	3427
Jer	50:39	neither shall it be **d** in from	7931
Eze	3:15	that **d** by the river of Chebar, and	3427
Eze	31:6	and under his shadow **d** all great	3427
Eze	36:17	the house of Israel **d** in their own	3427
Da	4:12	the fowls of the heaven **d** in the	1753
Zep	2:15	rejoicing city that **d** carelessly,	3427
Mt	2:23	and **d** in a city called Nazareth:	*2730*
Lk	1:65	on all that **d** round about them:	*4039*
Lk	13:4	**all men that d in Jerusalem?**	*2730*
Jn	1:14	and **d** among us, (and we beheld	*4637*
Jn	1:39	They came and saw where he **d**,	*3306*
Ac	28:30	Paul **d** two whole years in his	*3306*
2Ti	1:5	which **d** first in thy grandmother	*1774*
Rev	11:10	them that **d** on the earth.	*2730*

DYED

Ex	25:5	rams' skins **d** red, and badgers'	
Ex	36:19	rams' skins **d** red, and a covering	
Isa	63:1	with **d** garments from Bozrah?	2556

DYING

Mk	12:20	first took a wife, and **d** left no	*599*
2Co	4:10	bearing about in the body the **d**	*3500*
2Co	6:9	known; as **d**, and, behold, we live;	*599*

E

EACH

Ps	85:10	and peace have kissed **e** other.	
Isa	57:2	**e** one walking in his uprightness	
Lk	13:15	**doth not e one of you on the**	*1538*
Php	2:3	let **e** esteem other better than	*240*

EAGLE

Le	11:13	the **e**, and the ossifrage, and the	5404
Job	39:27	Doth the **e** mount up at thy	5404
Pr	23:5	fly away as an **e** toward heaven.	5404
Pr	30:19	The way of an **e** in the air;	5404
Jer	49:16	make thy nest as high as the **e**,	5404
Eze	1:10	they four also had the face of an **e**	5404
Eze	17:3	A great **e** with great wings, long	5404
Hos	8:1	He shall come as an **e** against the	5404
Ob	4	Though thou exalt thyself as the **e**,	5404
Mic	1:16	enlarge thy baldness as the **e**;	5404
Hab	1:8	they shall fly as the **e** that hasteth	5404
Rev	4:7	the fourth beast was like a flying **e**	*105*
Rev	12:14	were given two wings of a great **e**,	*105*

EAGLE'S

Ps	103:5	thy youth is renewed like the **e**	5404
Da	7:4	was like a lion, and had **e** wings;	5403

EAGLES

2Sa	1:23	they were swifter than **e**, they	5404
Pr	30:17	and the young **e** shall eat it	5404
Isa	40:31	shall mount up with wings as **e**;	5404
Jer	4:13	his horses are swifter than **e**.	5404
La	4:19	swifter than the **e** of the heaven:	5404
Mt	24:28	**is, there will the e be gathered**	*105*
Lk	17:37	**is, thither will the e be gathered**	*105*

EAGLES'

Ex	19:4	and how I bare you on **e** wings,	5404
Da	4:33	his hairs were grown like **e**	5403

EAR

Ex	21:6	his master shall bore his **e** through	241
Ex	29:20	upon the tip of the right **e** of Aaron,	241
Le	14:25	tip of the right **e** of him	241
2Ki	19:16	Lord, bow down thine **e**, and hear:	241
2Ch	24:19	them: but they would not give **e**	238
Job	42:5	of thee by the hearing of the **e**	241
Ps	39:12	give **e** unto my cry; hold not thy	238
Ps	94:9	planted the **e**, shall he not hear?	241
Pr	2:2	thou incline thine **e** unto wisdom,	241
Pr	5:13	mine **e** to them that instructed me!	241
Pr	15:31	The **e** that heareth the reproof of	241
Pr	17:4	liar giveth **e** to a naughty tongue	238
Pr	18:15	**e** of the wise seeketh knowledge.	241
Pr	20:12	The hearing **e**, and the seeing eye,	241
Pr	25:12	a wise reprover upon an obedient **e**	241
Pr	28:9	away his **e** from hearing the law,	241
Ecc	1:8	nor the **e** filled with hearing	241
Isa	50:4	wakeneth mine **e** to hear as the	241
Isa	59:1	his **e** heavy, that it cannot hear:	241
Isa	64:4	not heard, nor perceived by the **e**,	238
Jer	6:10	behold, their **e** is uncircumcised,	241
La	3:56	hide not thine **e** at my breathing,	241
Da	9:18	O my God, incline thine **e**, and hear;	241
Mt	10:27	**what ye hear in the e, that preach**	*3775*
Mk	4:28	**first the blade, then the e, after**	*4719*
Lk	12:3	**which ye have spoken in the e**	*3775*
Lk	22:50	high priest, and cut off his right **e**	*3775*
Lk	22:51	he touched his **e**, and healed him.	*5621*
Jn	18:26	his kinsman whose **e** Peter cut off,	*5621*
1Co	2:9	nor **e** heard, neither have entered	*3775*
1Co	12:16	And if the **e** shall say, Because I	*3775*
Rev	2:7	He that hath an **e**, let him	*3775*
Rev	13:9	If any man have an **e**, let him hear.	*3775*

EARLY

Ex	9:13	Moses, Rise up **e** in the morning,	7925
Ex	34:4	Moses rose up **e** in the morning,	7925
1Sa	17:20	David rose up **e** in the morning,	7925
Ps	63:1	art my God; **e** will I seek thee:	7836
Ps	127:2	It is vain for you to rise up **e**,	7925
Pr	1:28	they shall seek me **e**, but they	7836
Pr	8:17	that seek me **e** shall find me	7836
Pr	27:14	voice, rising **e** in the morning,	7925
Isa	5:11	Woe unto them that rise up **e**	7925
Isa	26:9	within me will I seek thee **e**:	7836
Da	6:19	king arose very **e** in the morning,	8238
Hos	5:15	affliction they will seek me **e**	7836
Hos	6:4	as the **e** dew it goeth away	7925
Hos	13:3	as the **e** dew that passeth away	7925
Mk	16:9	risen **e** the first day of the week,	*260, 4404*
Lk	24:22	which were **e** at the sepulchre;	*3721*
Jn	20:1	cometh Mary Magdalene **e**, when	*4404*
Jas	5:7	he receive the **e** and latter rain.	*4406*

EARNEST

Ro	8:19	the **e** expectation of the creature	*603*
2Co	1:22	the **e** of the Spirit in our hearts.	*728*
2Co	5:5	given unto us the **e** of the Spirit.	*728*
Eph	1:14	Which is the **e** of our inheritance	*728*
Php	1:20	to my **e** expectation and my hope,	*603*
Heb	2:1	we ought to give the more **e** heed	*4056*

EARNESTLY

Jer	11:7	For I **e** protested unto your fathers	
Mic	7:3	may do evil with both hands **e**,	3190
Lk	22:44	in an agony he prayed more **e**:	*1617*
Lk	22:56	and **e** looked upon him, and said,	*816*
1Co	12:31	But covet **e** the best gifts:	*2206*
2Co	5:2	**e** desiring to be clothed upon	*1971*
Jas	5:17	prayed **e** that it might not rain:	*4335*
Jude	3	ye should **e** contend for the faith	*1864*

EARNETH

Hag	1:6	he that **e** wages, **e** wages to put it	7936

EARRINGS

Ex	32:3	people brake off the golden **e**	5141
Eze	16:12	**e** in thine ears, and a beautiful	5694
Hos	2:13	herself with her **e** and her jewels,	5141

EARS

Ge	41:24	thin **e** devoured the seven good **e**:	7641
Ge	41:26	the seven good **e** are seven years:	7641
Nu	11:18	ye have wept in the **e** of the Lord,	241
1Sa	15:14	bleating of the sheep in mine **e**,	241
2Sa	22:7	my cry did enter into his **e**	241
2Ki	23:2	read in their **e** all the words of the	241
Pr	21:13	Whoso stoppeth his **e** at the cry	241
Pr	23:9	Speak not in the **e** of a fool:	241
Pr	23:12	thine **e** to the words of knowledge.	241
Pr	26:17	one that taketh a dog by the **e**	241

Isa	22:14	revealed in mine **e** by the Lord	241
Isa	35:5	**e** of the deaf shall be unstopped.	241
Isa	42:20	opening the **e**, but he heareth not.	241
Isa	49:20	other, shall say again in thine **e**,	241
Jer	2:2	Go and cry in the **e** of Jerusalem,	241
Zec	7:11	and stopped their **e**, that they	241
Mt	11:15	**He that hath e to hear, let him**	*3775*
Mt	13:9	**Who hath e to hear, let him hear**	*3775*
Mt	13:15	**and their e are dull of hearing,**	*3775*
Mt	13:43	**Who hath e to hear, let him hear.**	*3775*
Mk	4:9	**He that hath e to hear, let him**	*3775*
Mk	4:23	**If any man have e to hear,**	*3775*
Mk	7:16	**If any man have e to hear, let**	*3775*
Mk	8:18	**and having e, hear ye not?**	*3775*
Lk	4:21	**this scripture fulfilled in your e**	*3775*
Lk	8:8	**He that hath e to hear, let him**	*3775*
Lk	9:44	**sayings sink down into your e**	*3775*
Lk	14:35	**He that hath e to hear, let him**	*3775*
Ac	17:20	certain strange things to our **e**:	*189*
Ro	11:8	and **e** that they should not hear;)	*3775*
2Ti	4:3	teachers, having itching **e**;	*189*
2Ti	4:4	turn away their **e** from the truth,	*189*
Jas	5:4	entered into the **e** of the Lord	*3775*
1Pe	3:12	his **e** are open unto their prayers:	*3775*

EARTH

Ge	1:1	God created the heaven and the **e**	776
Ge	1:2	And the **e** was without form, and	776
Ge	1:10	And God called the dry land **E**;	776
Ge	1:28	multiply, and replenish the **e**, and	776
Ge	2:1	the heavens and the **e** were finished	776
Ge	2:5	had not caused it to rain upon the **e**,	776
Ge	4:11	now art thou cursed from the **e**,	127
Ge	6:6	that he had made man on the **e**,	776
Ge	6:11	**e** also was corrupt before God,	776
Ge	6:11	the **e** was filled with violence.	776
Ge	8:17	be fruitful, and multiply upon the **e**	776
Ge	10:25	in his days was the **e** divided;	776
Ge	11:1	the whole **e** was of one language,	776
Ge	13:16	make thy seed as the dust of the **e**:	776
Ge	18:25	not the Judge of all the **e** do right?	776
Ge	41:47	the **e** brought forth by handfuls	776
Ge	42:6	before him with their faces to the **e**	776
Ge	43:26	bowed themselves to him to the **e**,	776
Ge	45:7	to preserve you a posterity in the **e**	776
Ge	48:16	a multitude in the midst of the **e**	776
Ex	8:17	and smote the dust of the **e**,	776
Ex	9:14	there is none like me in all the **e**	776
Ex	20:4	or that is in the **e** beneath, or	776
Ex	20:4	that is in the water under the **e**	776
Nu	16:34	Lest the **e** swallow us up also	776
Nu	26:10	And the **e** opened her mouth, and	776
Dt	3:24	what God is there in heaven or in **e**,	776
Dt	4:32	that God created man upon the **e**,	776
Dt	4:40	mayest prolong thy days upon the **e**	127
Dt	11:6	now the **e** opened her mouth, and	776
Dt	28:23	**e** that is under thee shall be brass	776
Jgs	5:4	the **e** trembled, and the heavens	776
1Sa	2:8	the pillars of the **e** are the Lord's,	776
1Sa	28:13	I saw gods ascending out of the **e**	776
2Sa	22:8	Then the **e** shook and trembled:	776
1Ki	8:23	in heaven above, or on **e** beneath,	776
1Ki	8:27	will God indeed dwell on the **e**?	776
2Ki	5:15	that there is no God in all the **e**	776
2Ki	19:15	thou hast made heaven and **e**	776
1Ch	1:19	in his days the **e** was divided:	776
1Ch	29:11	in the heaven and in the **e** is thine;	776
2Ch	2:12	that made heaven and **e**, who hath	776
Job	1:7	From going to and fro in the **e**,	776
Job	2:2	From going to and fro in the **e**,	776
Job	26:7	and hangeth the **e** upon nothing	776
Job	38:4	when I laid the foundations of the **e**?	776
Ps	8:1	excellent is thy name in all the **e**!	776
Ps	8:9	excellent is thy name in all the **e**!	776
Ps	19:4	line is gone out through all the **e**,	776
Ps	24:1	The **e** is the Lord's, and the	776
Ps	37:11	But the meek shall inherit the **e**;	776
Ps	46:2	we fear, though the **e** be removed,	776
Ps	46:10	am God: I will be exalted in the **e**	776
Ps	47:7	For God is the King of all the **e**:	776
Ps	68:8	The **e** shook, the heavens also	776
Ps	73:25	there is none upon **e** that I desire	776
Ps	104:5	Who laid the foundations of the **e**	776
Ps	114:7	Tremble, thou **e**, at the presence	776
Ps	115:15	the Lord, which made heaven and **e**	776
Ps	121:2	the Lord, which made heaven and **e**	776
Ps	124:8	the Lord, who made heaven and **e**	776
Ps	134:3	The Lord that made heaven and **e**	776
Pr	30:21	For three things the **e** is disquieted,	776
Pr	30:24	things which are little upon the **e**,	776
Ecc	1:4	but the **e** abideth for ever	776
Ecc	5:2	God is in heaven, and thou upon **e**	776
Isa	6:3	the whole **e** is full of his glory	776
Isa	11:4	with equity for the meek of the **e**:	776
Isa	11:4	and he shall smite the **e** with the rod	776
Isa	11:12	from the four corners of the **e**	776
Isa	13:13	and the **e** shall remove out of her	776
Isa	37:16	thou hast made heaven and **e**	776
Isa	40:28	the Creator of the ends of the **e**,	776
Isa	48:13	hath laid the foundation of the **e**,	776
Isa	51:6	the e shall wax old like a garment	776
Isa	51:13	and laid the foundations of the **e**;	776
Isa	51:16	and lay the foundations of the **e**	776
Isa	60:2	the darkness shall cover the **e**	776
Isa	65:17	I create new heavens and a new **e**:	776
Isa	66:1	throne, and the **e** is my footstool:	776
Isa	66:22	as the new heavens and the new **e**	776
Jer	10:10	at his wrath the **e** shall tremble,	776
Jer	10:11	not made the heavens and the **e**,	778
Jer	23:24	Do not I fill heaven and **e**? saith the	776
Jer	31:22	hath created a new thing in the **e**,	776
Jer	31:37	foundations of the **e** searched out	776
Jer	32:17	made the heaven and the **e** by thy	776
La	2:1	cast down from heaven unto the **e**	776
La	2:15	of beauty, The joy of the whole **e**?	776
Joel	2:10	The **e** shall quake before them;	776
Joel	3:16	the heavens and the **e** shall shake:	776
Mic	6:2	ye strong foundations of the **e**:	776
Hag	2:21	I will shake the heavens and the **e**;	776
Zec	1:10	to walk to and fro through the **e**	776
Zec	4:10	run to and fro through the whole **e**	776
Zec	12:1	and layeth the foundation of the **e**,	776
Mt	5:18	**Till heaven and e pass, one jot or**	*1093*
Mt	6:10	**will be done in e, as it is in**	*1093*
Mt	11:25	**O Father, Lord of heaven and e,**	*1093*
Mt	24:35	**Heaven and e shall pass away, but**	*1093*
Mt	27:51	**e** did quake, and the rocks rent;	*1093*
Mt	28:18	**given unto me in heaven and in e,**	*1093*
Mk	2:10	**Son of man hath power on e to**	*1093*
Mk	13:31	**Heaven and e shall pass away:**	*1093*
Lk	2:14	on **e** peace, good will toward men	*1093*
Lk	10:21	**O Father, Lord of heaven and e,**	*1093*

Lk 18:8 **shall he find faith on the e?** *1093*
Lk 21:33 **Heaven and e shall pass away:** *1093*
Jn 12:32 **if I be lifted up from the e,** *1093*
Ac 4:24 which hast made heaven, and **e**, *1093*
Ac 7:49 my throne, and **e** is my footstool: *1093*
Ac 14:15 God, which made heaven, and **e**, *1093*
Ac 17:24 is Lord of heaven and **e**, dwelleth *1093*
Ro 10:18 their sound went into all the **e**, *1093*
1Co 10:26 For the **e** is the Lord's, and the *1093*
1Co 10:28 for the **e** is the Lord's, and the *1093*
1Co 15:47 The first man is of the **e**, earthy: *1093*
Heb 1:10 hast laid the foundation of the **e**; *1093*
Heb 12:26 once more I shake not the **e** only *1093*
2Pe 3:7 heavens and the **e**, which are now *1093*
1Jn 5:8 are three that bear witness in **e**, *1093*
Rev 3:10 **to try them that dwell upon the e.** *1093*
Rev 5:3 nor in **e**, neither under the **e**, *1093*
Rev 6:13 the stars of heaven fell unto the **e** *1093*
Rev 7:1 on the four corners of the **e**, *1093*
Rev 7:1 holding the four winds of the **e**, *1093*
Rev 17:18 reigneth over the kings of the **e** *1093*
Rev 20:8 in the four quarters of the **e**, *1093*
Rev 20:11 the **e** and the heaven fled away; *1093*
Rev 21:1 I saw a new heaven and a new **e**: *1093*
Rev 21:1 and first **e** were passed away; *1093*

EARTHEN
Nu 5:17 take holy water in an **e** vessel; 2789
Jer 19:1 Go and get a potter's **e** bottle, 2789
Jer 32:14 and put them in an **e** vessel, 2789
La 4:2 are they esteemed as **e** pitchers, 2789
2Co 4:7 have this treasure in **e** vessels, *3749*

EARTHLY
Jn 3:12 **If I have told you e things,** *1919*
Jn 3:31 that is of the earth is **e**, *1537, 3588, 1093*
2Co 5:1 if our **e** house of this tabernacle *1919*
Php 3:19 their shame, who mind **e** things.) *1919*
Jas 3:15 above, but is **e**, sensual, devilish. *1919*

EARTHQUAKE
1Ki 19:11 but the Lord was not in the **e**: 7494
Am 1:1 two years before the **e** 7494
Zec 14:5 the **e** in the days of Uzziah 7494
Mt 28:2 behold, there was a great **e**: *4578*
Ac 16:26 And suddenly there was a great **e**, *4578*
Rev 6:12 lo, there was a great **e**; *4578*
Rev 8:5 and lightnings, and an **e**, *4578*
Rev 11:13 same hour was there a great **e**, *4578*

EARTHQUAKES
Mt 24:7 **and e, in divers places** *4578*
Mk 13:8 **there shall be e in divers places,** *4578*
Lk 21:11 **great e shall be in divers places,** *4578*

EASE
Dt 28:65 these nations shalt thou find no **e**, 7280
Am 6:1 Woe to them that are at **e** in Zion, 7600
Lk 12:19 **take thine e, eat, drink, and be** *373*

EASIER
Mt 9:5 **whether is e, to say, Thy sins be** *2123*
Mt 19:24 **It is e for a camel to go through** *2123*
Mk 2:9 **Whether it is e to say to the sick** *2123*
Mk 10:25 **It is e for a camel to go through** *2123*
Lk 5:23 **Whether is e, to say, Thy sins be** *2123*
Lk 16:17 **it is e for heaven and earth to** *2123*
Lk 18:25 **For it is e for a camel to go** *2123*

EASILY
Heb 12:1 the sin which doth so **e** beset us

EAST
Ge 3:24 at the **e** of the garden of Eden 6924
Job 1:3 greatest of all the men of the **e** 6924
Eze 8:16 worshipped the sun toward the **e**, 6924
Eze 48:21 the oblation toward the **e** border, 6921
Jnh 4:8 God prepared a vehement **e** wind; 6921
Mt 2:1 men from the **e** to Jerusalem, *395*
Mt 2:2 we have seen his star in the **e** *395*
Mt 8:11 **shall come from the e and west** *395*
Mt 24:27 **the lightning cometh out of the e,** *395*
Lk 13:29 **they shall come from the e, and** *395*
Rev 7:2 angel ascending from the **e**, *395*
Rev 16:12 the way of the kings of the **e** *395*

EASTER
Ac 12:4 intending after **E** to bring him *3957*

EASTWARD
Ge 2:8 God planted a garden **e** of Eden; 6924

EASY
Pr 14:6 knowledge is **e** unto him that 7043
Mt 11:30 **For my yoke is e, and my burden** *5543*
Jas 3:17 **e** to be intreated, full of mercy *2138*

EAT
Ge 2:17 thou shalt not **e** of it: for in the 398
Ge 3:1 not **e** of every tree of the garden? 398
Ge 3:5 know that in the day ye **e** thereof, 398
Ge 3:6 husband with her; and he did **e** 398
Ge 3:12 she gave me of the tree, and I did **e** 398
Ge 3:13 serpent beguiled me, and I did **e** 398
Ge 3:14 dust shalt thou **e** all the days of thy 398
Ge 3:17 thou **e** of it all the days of thy life; 398
Ge 27:25 and I will **e** of my son's venison 398
Ge 43:32 not **e** bread with the Hebrews; 398
Ex 12:15 days shall ye **e** unleavened bread; 398
Ex 16:35 they did **e** manna, until they came 398
Le 6:26 that offereth it for sin shall **e** it: 398
Le 17:12 No soul of you shall **e** blood 398
Le 21:22 He shall **e** the bread of his God 398
Le 22:4 he shall not **e** of the holy things, 398
Nu 11:18 will give you flesh, and ye shall **e** 398
Nu 18:10 most holy place shalt thou **e** it; 398
Dt 12:16 Only ye shall not **e** the blood; 398
Dt 14:4 are the beasts which ye shall **e**: 398
Dt 14:7 Nevertheless these ye shall not **e** 398
Dt 16:8 Six days shalt thou **e** unleavened 398
1Ki 18:41 Get thee up, **e** and drink; for there 398
2Ki 6:28 and we will **e** my son tomorrow 398
Ezr 2:63 should not **e** of the most holy things, 398
Ps 78:25 Man did **e** angels' food: he sent 398
Pr 4:17 they **e** the bread of wickedness 3898
Pr 23:1 thou sittest to **e** with a ruler, 3898
Pr 24:13 **e** thou honey, because it is good; 398
Pr 25:27 It is not good to **e** much honey: 398
Ecc 5:12 sweet, whether he **e** little or much: 398
Isa 11:7 the lion shall **e** straw like the ox 398
Isa 22:13 drinking wine: let us **e** and drink; 398
Jer 15:16 were found, and I did **e** them; 398
Jer 19:9 I will cause them to **e** the flesh of 398
Eze 3:1 Son of man, **e** that thou findest; 398
Da 1:12 let them give us pulse to **e** 398
Hos 4:8 They **e** up the sin of my people, 398

Zec	11:9	**e** every one the flesh of another	398
Mt	6:31	What shall we **e**? or, What	*5315*
Mt	15:20	but to **e** with unwashen hands	*5315*
Mt	15:27	the dogs **e** of the crumbs which	*2068*
Mt	15:38	did **e** were four thousand men	*2068*
Mt	26:26	said, Take, **e**; this is my body	*5315*
Mk	2:26	and did **e** the shewbread, which is	*5315*
Mk	14:14	where I shall **e** the passover with	*5315*
Mk	14:22	said, Take, **e**; this is my body	*5315*
Lk	10:8	**e** such things as are set before	*2068*
Lk	12:29	seek not ye what ye shall **e**,	*5315*
Lk	14:1	to **e** bread on the sabbath day,	*5315*
Lk	15:23	and let us **e**, and be merry:	*5315*
Lk	22:15	I have desired to **e** this passover	*5315*
Lk	24:43	he took it, and did **e** before them	*5315*
Jn	4:32	I have meat to **e** that ye know not	*5315*
Jn	6:5	we buy bread, that these may **e**?	*5315*
Jn	6:49	Your fathers did **e** manna in the	*5315*
Jn	6:51	if any man **e** of this bread,	*5315*
Jn	6:53	Except ye **e** the flesh of the Son of	*5315*
Ro	14:23	that doubteth is damned if he **e**,	*5315*
1Co	5:11	with such an one no not to **e**	*4906*
1Co	8:13	I will **e** no flesh while the world	*5315*
1Co	11:24	Take, **e**; this is my body, which	*5315*
1Co	11:26	as often as ye **e** this bread,	*2068*
1Co	11:27	whosoever shall **e** this bread, and	*2068*
1Co	11:34	man hunger, let him **e** at home;	*2068*
1Co	15:32	let us **e** and drink; for tomorrow	*5315*
2Th	3:10	not work, neither should he **e**	*2068*
2Ti	2:17	word will **e** as doth a canker	*3542, 2192*
Jas	5:3	and shall **e** your flesh as it were	*5315*
Rev	2:7	will I give to **e** of the tree of life,	*5315*
Rev	2:20	to **e** things sacrificed unto idols	*5315*
Rev	10:9	Take it, and **e** it up; and it shall	*2719*
Rev	17:16	and shall **e** her flesh, and burn her	*5315*
Rev	19:18	That ye may **e** the flesh of kings	*5315*

EATEN

Ge	3:11	Hast thou **e** of the tree, whereof I	398
Ex	29:34	it shall not be **e**, because it is holy	398
Le	19:7	if it be **e** at all on the third day	398
1Sa	30:12	and when he had **e**, his spirit came	398
Ps	69:9	the zeal of thine house hath **e** me	398
Pr	9:17	and bread **e** in secret is pleasant	398
Pr	23:8	The morsel which thou hast **e**	398
Hos	10:13	ye have **e** the fruit of lies:	398
Jn	2:17	zeal of thine house hath **e** me up	*2719*
Jn	6:13	and above unto them that had **e**	*977*
Rev	10:10	as soon as I had **e** it	*5315*

EATETH

Ex	12:15	whosoever **e** leavened bread from	398
Le	7:18	the soul that **e** of it shall bear his	398
Le	17:10	that **e** any manner of blood; I will	398
Le	17:14	whosoever **e** it shall be cut off	398
Pr	13:25	The righteous **e** to the satisfying of	398
Pr	30:20	she **e**, and wipeth her mouth	398
Pr	31:27	and **e** not the bread of idleness	398
Ecc	5:17	All his days also he **e** in darkness	398
Mk	14:18	you, One of you which **e** with me	*2068*
Lk	15:2	receiveth sinners, and **e** with them	*4906*
Jn	6:54	Whoso **e** my flesh, and drinketh.	*5176*
Jn	13:18	He that **e** bread with me hath	*5176*
Ro	14:6	He that **e**, **e** to the Lord, for he	*2068*
Ro	14:23	because he **e** not of faith:	*2068*
1Co	11:29	he that **e** and drinketh unworthily	*2068*

EATING

1Sa	14:34	sin not against the Lord in **e**	398
1Ki	4:20	**e** and drinking, and making merry	398
2Ki	4:40	as they were **e** of the pottage	398
Job	1:13	his sons and his daughters were **e**	398
Mt	11:19	Son of man came **e** and drinking,	*2068*
Mt	24:38	were **e** and drinking, marrying	*5176*
Lk	7:34	The Son of man is come **e** and	*2068*

EDGE See also TWO-EDGED.

Jgs	4:16	Sisera fell upon the **e** of the sword;	6310
Job	1:15	servants with the **e** of the sword;	6310
Ecc	10:10	and he do not whet the **e**,	6440
Jer	31:29	the children's teeth are set on **e**	6949
Eze	18:2	the children's teeth are set on **e**?	6949
Lk	21:24	shall fall by the **e** of the sword,	*4750*
Heb	11:34	escaped the **e** of the sword, out of	*4750*

EDGES

Rev	2:12	hath the sharp sword with two **e**;	*1366*

EDIFICATION

Ro	15:2	his neighbour for his good to **e**	*3619*
1Co	14:3	speaketh unto men to **e**	*3619*

EDIFIETH

1Co	8:1	puffeth up, but charity **e**	*3618*
1Co	14:4	an unknown tongue **e** himself;	*3618*

EDIFY

Ro	14:19	wherewith one may **e** another	*3619*
1Co	10:23	lawful for me, but all things **e** not	*3618*
1Th	5:11	together, and **e** one another,	*3618*

EDIFYING

1Co	14:5	that the church may receive **e**	*3619*
1Co	14:12	may excel to the **e** of the church	*3619*
1Co	14:26	Let all things be done unto **e**	*3619*
2Co	12:19	things, dearly beloved, for your **e**	*3619*
Eph	4:12	for the **e** of the body of Christ:	*3619*
Eph	4:16	unto the **e** of itself in love	*3619*
Eph	4:29	which is good to the use of **e**,	*3619*
1Ti	1:4	than godly **e** which is in faith:	*3618*

EFFECT

Nu	30:8	shall make her vow … of none **e**:	6565
Isa	32:17	the **e** of righteousness quietness	5656
Eze	12:23	hand, and the **e** of every vision	1697
Mt	15:6	commandment of God of none **e**	*208*
Mk	7:13	the word of God of none **e**	*208*
Ro	3:3	make the faith of God without **e**?	*2673*
Ro	4:14	and the promise made of none **e**:	*2673*
Ro	9:6	word of God hath taken none **e**	*1601*
1Co	1:17	Christ should be made of none **e**	*2758*
Gal	3:17	make the promise of none **e**	*2673*
Gal	5:4	Christ is become of no **e** unto	*2673*

EFFECTUAL

1Co	16:9	a great door and **e** is opened	*1756*
2Co	1:6	which is **e** in the enduring of the	*1754*
Eph	3:7	by the **e** working of his power	*1753*
Eph	4:16	the **e** working in the measure of	*1753*
Phm	6	become **e** by the acknowledging	*1756*
Jas	5:16	**e** fervent prayer of a righteous	*1754*

EFFECTUALLY

Gal	2:8	(For he that wrought **e** in Peter	*2754*
1Th	2:13	which **e** worketh also in you	*1754*

EFFEMINATE
1Co 6:9 adulterers, nor **e**, nor abusers of *3120*

EGG
Lk 11:12 **Or if he shall ask an e, will he** *5609*

EIGHT See also EIGHTEEN.
Ge 17:12 is **e** days old shall be circumcised 8083
Nu 35:7 Levites shall be forty and **e** cities: 8083
Ecc 11:2 a portion to seven, and also to **e**; 8083
Lk 2:21 when **e** days were accomplished *3638*
Lk 9:28 about **e** days after these sayings, ...*3638*
1Pe 3:20 is, **e** souls were saved by water *3638*

EIGHTEEN
Lk 13:4 **Or those e, upon whom** *1176, 2532, 3638*

EIGHTH
Le 12:3 the **e** day the flesh of his foreskin 8066
Lk 1:59 **e** day they came to circumcise *3590*

EITHER See also NEITHER.
Nu 24:13 **e** good or bad of mine own mind;
Dt 17:3 **e** the sun, or moon, or any of
1Sa 20:2 will do nothing **e** great or small,
1Ki 18:27 **e** he is talking, or he is pursuing, ...3588
Ecc 9:1 man knoweth **e** love or hatred 1571
Ecc 11:6 not whether shall prosper, **e** this
Mt 6:24 **for e he will hate the one, and** *2228*
Mt 12:33 **E make the tree good, and his** *2228*
Lk 16:13 **two masters: for e he will hate** *2228*

ELDER
Ge 25:23 and the **e** shall serve the younger 7227
Lk 15:25 **Now his e son was in the field:** *4245*
Ro 9:12 The **e** shall serve the younger *3187*
1Ti 5:1 Rebuke not an **e**, but entreat him *4245*
1Ti 5:2 **e** women as mothers; the younger *4245*
1Ti 5:19 an **e** receive not an accusation, ...*4245*
1Pe 5:5 submit yourselves unto the **e** *4245*

ELDERS
Le 4:15 the **e** of the congregation shall 2205
Dt 25:9 unto him in the presence of the **e**, ...2205
Jos 20:4 his cause in the ears of the **e** of 2205
Ru 4:11 and the **e**, said, We are witnesses. 2205
1Sa 16:4 the **e** of the town trembled at his 2205
Ezr 6:14 And the **e** of the Jews builded, ...7868
Ps 107:32 praise him in the assembly of the **e** 2205
Pr 31:23 when he sitteth among the **e** of the 2205
La 1:19 my priests and mine **e** gave up the 2205
La 2:10 The **e** of the daughter of Zion 2205
La 4:16 priests, they favoured not the **e**, ...2205
La 5:12 the faces of **e** were not honoured 2205
La 5:14 The **e** have ceased from the gate, ...2205
Eze 8:1 and the **e** of Judah sat before me, ...2205
Mt 15:2 transgress the tradition of the **e**? *4245*
Mt 16:21 suffer many things of the **e** and *4245*
Mt 27:3 silver to the chief priests and **e**, ...*4245*
Mt 27:12 accused of the chief priests and **e**, ...*4245*
Mk 8:31 and be rejected of the **e**, and of the *4245*
Lk 7:3 he sent unto him the **e** of the Jews, ...*4245*
Lk 9:22 **and be rejected of the e and chief** *4245*
Ac 11:30 and sent it to the **e** by the hands *4245*
Ac 14:23 ordained them **e** in every church, ...*4245*
1Ti 5:17 Let the **e** that rule well be counted *4245*
Tit 1:5 ordain **e** in every city, as I had *4245*
Heb 11:2 For by it the **e** obtained a good *4245*
Jas 5:14 let him call for the **e** of the church; *4245*
Rev 4:4 I saw four and twenty **e** sitting *4245*
Rev 5:8 and four and twenty **e** fell down *4245*
Rev 7:11 and about the **e** and the four beasts, ...*4245*
Rev 11:16 the four and twenty **e**, which sat *4245*
Rev 14:3 before the four beasts, and the **e**: *4245*
Rev 19:4 the four and twenty **e** and the four *4245*

ELDEST
2Ch 22:1 of men ... had slain all the **e** 7223
Job 1:13 wine in their **e** brother's 1060
Jn 8:9 beginning at the **e**, even unto the *4245*

ELECT
Isa 42:1 **e**, in whom my soul delighteth; 972
Isa 45:4 sake, and Israel mine **e** 972
Isa 65:9 mine **e** shall inherit it, and my 972
Isa 65:22 mine **e** shall long enjoy the work 972
Mt 24:24 **they shall deceive the very e** *1588*
Mt 24:31 **and they shall gather together his e** *1588*
Mk 13:22 **if it were possible, even the e** *1588*
Lk 18:7 **shall not God avenge his own e,** *1588*
Ro 8:33 any thing to the charge of God's **e**? *1588*
Col 3:12 Put on therefore, as the **e** of God, ...*1588*
1Ti 5:21 Lord Jesus Christ, and the **e** angels, ...*1588*
Tit 1:1 according to the faith of God's **e**, ...*1588*
1Pe 1:2 **E** according to the foreknowledge *1588*
1Pe 2:6 a chief corner stone, **e**, precious: *1588*
2Jn 1 The elder unto the **e** lady and her *1588*

ELECTION
Ro 9:11 the purpose of God according to **e** *1589*
Ro 11:5 according to the **e** of grace *1589*
Ro 11:7 the **e** hath obtained it, and the rest *1589*
Ro 11:28 as touching the **e**, they are beloved *1589*
1Th 1:4 brethren beloved, your **e** of God. *1589*
2Pe 1:10 make your calling and **e** sure: *1589*

ELECT'S
Mt 24:22 **for the e sake those days shall be** *1588*
Mk 13:20 **for the e sake, whom he hath** *1588*
2Ti 2:10 endure all things for the **e** sakes, ...*1588*

ELEMENTS
Gal 4:3 in bondage under the **e** of the *4747*
2Pe 3:10 the **e** shall melt with fervent heat, ...*4747*

ELEVEN
Ge 37:9 and the moon and the **e** stars 259, 6240
Mt 28:16 Then the **e** disciples went away *1733*
Mk 16:14 he appeared unto the **e** as they *1733*
Lk 24:9 told all these things unto the **e** 1733
Lk 24:33 found the **e** gathered together *1733*

ELEVENTH
Mt 20:6 **about the e hour he went out,** *1734*
Mt 20:9 **that were hired about the e hour,** *1734*

ELOQUENT
Ex 4:10 O my Lord, I am not **e**, ...376, 1697
Isa 3:3 artificer, and the **e** orator. 995
Ac 18:24 an **e** man, and mighty in the *3052*

ELSE
Ge 30:1 Give me children, or **e** I die 369
Ex 8:21 **E**, if thou wilt not let my people 3588
Ex 10:4 **E**, if thou refuse to let my people 3588
Dt 4:35 he is God; there is none **e** beside 5750
Dt 4:39 the earth beneath: there is none **e**. 5750

1Ki 8:60 is God, and that there is none **e** 5750
Ne 2:2 this is nothing **e** but sorrow of
Ps 51:16 thou desirest not sacrifice; **e** would I
Isa 45:5 am the Lord, and there is none **e**, ...5750
Isa 45:6 I am the Lord, and there is none **e** 5750
Isa 45:14 and there is none **e**, there is no God. ...5750
Isa 45:18 I am the Lord; and there is none **e** 5750
Isa 45:21 and there is no God **e** beside me; a 5750
Isa 45:22 for I am God, and there is none **e** 5750
Isa 46:9 I am God, and there is none **e**: I 5750
Isa 47:8 I am, and none **e** beside me; I shall 5750
Isa 47:10 I am, and none **e** beside me 5750
Joel 2:27 am the Lord your God, and none **e**: 5750
Mt 6:24 **he will hate the one. ... or e he**
Lk 16:13 **or e he will hold to the one,**
Jn 14:11 **e believe me for the very works'** *1490*
Ro 2:15 accusing or **e** excusing one *2532*
Rev 2:5 **or e I will come unto thee** *1490*
Rev 2:16 **Repent; or e I will come unto** *1490*

EMBALMED
Ge 50:2 and the physicians **e** Israel 2590

EMBRACE
2Ki 4:16 time of life, thou shalt **e** a son. 2263
Job 24:8 **e** the rock for want of a shelter. 2263
Pr 4:8 to honour when thou dost **e** her. 2263
Pr 5:20 and **e** the bosom of a stranger? 2263
Ecc 3:5 a time to **e**, and a time to refrain 2263
La 4:5 brought up in scarlet **e** dunghills. 2263

EMBRACED
Ge 33:4 Esau ran to meet him, and **e** him, ...2263
Heb 11:13 **e** them, and confessed that they *782*

EMBRACING
Ecc 3:5 a time to refrain from **e**; 2263

EMMANUEL See also IMMANUEL.
Mt 1:23 they shall call his name **E**, ...*1694*

EMPTIED
2Ch 24:11 officer came and **e** the chest, ...6168
Isa 24:3 The land shall be utterly **e**, and 1238

EMPTY
Ge 37:24 the pit was **e**; there was no water 7386
Ge 41:27 the seven **e** ears blasted with the 7386
Ex 3:21 when ye go, ye shall not go **e**: 7387
Ex 34:20 And none shall appear before me **e** 7387
Dt 16:16 shall not appear before the Lord **e**: 7387
2Sa 1:22 the sword of Saul returned not **e** 7387
2Ki 4:3 borrow thee vessels ... **e** vessels; 7385
Ecc 11:3 they **e** themselves upon the earth; 7324
Isa 24:1 the Lord maketh the earth **e** 1238
Isa 29:8 he awaketh, and his soul is **e**: 7385
Isa 32:6 to make **e** the soul of the hungry, ...7324
Jer 14:3 returned with their vessels **e**; 7387
Jer 48:12 shall **e** his vessels, and break 7324
Jer 51:2 shall fan her, and shall **e** her land: 1238
Jer 51:34 he hath made me an **e** vessel, ...7385
Hab 1:17 Shall they therefore **e** their net, ...7324
Mt 12:44 **he findeth it e, swept, and** *4980*
Mk 12:3 **beat him, and sent him away e** *2756*
Lk 20:10 **beat him, and sent him away e** *2755*

ENABLED
1Ti 1:12 Jesus our Lord, who hath **e** me, ...*1743*

ENCAMP
Nu 10:31 how we are to **e** in the wilderness, ...2583
Ps 27:3 Though an host should **e** against 2583

ENCAMPED
Ex 18:5 where he **e** at the mount of God: 2583
Nu 33:10 and **e** by the Red sea. 2583
2Ch 32:1 and **e** against the fenced cities, ...2583

ENCAMPETH
Ps 34:7 The angel of the Lord **e** round 2583
Ps 53:5 the bones of him that **e** against 2583

ENCHANTER
Dt 18:10 spirits, or an **e**, or a witch, ...5172

ENCHANTERS
Jer 27:9 your **e**, nor to your sorcerers, ...6049

ENCHANTMENT
Le 19:26 neither shall ye use **e**, ...5172
Nu 23:23 there is no **e** against Jacob, ...5172
Ecc 10:11 the serpent will bite without **e**; 3908

ENCHANTMENTS
Ex 7:22 of Egypt did so with their **e**: 3909
Ex 8:7 the magicians did so with their **e**, ...3909
Nu 24:1 to seek for **e**, but he set his face 5172
2Ki 17:17 and used divination and **e**, and 5172
2Ki 21:6 and observed times, and used **e**, ...5172
2Ch 33:6 also he observed times, and used **e**, ...5172
Isa 47:9 the great abundance of thine **e** 2267
Isa 47:12 Stand now with thine **e**, and with 2267

ENCOURAGE
Dt 1:38 he shall go in thither **e**: him: 2388
Ps 64:5 They **e** themselves in an evil 2388

ENCOURAGED
Jgs 20:22 the men of Israel **e** themselves, ...2388
1Sa 30:6 but David **e** himself in the Lord 2388
2Ch 31:4 that they might be **e** in the law of 2388
2Ch 35:2 and **e** them to the service of the 2388

END
Ge 6:13 The **e** of all flesh is come before 7093
Ex 8:22 to the **e** thou mayest know that I 4616
Nu 24:20 but his latter **e** shall be that he perish
Dt 15:1 At the **e** of every seven years thou 7093
Dt 32:29 they would consider their latter **e**!
1Sa 3:12 I begin, I will also make an **e** 3615
2Ch 7:1 Solomon had made an **e** of praying, ...3615
Job 34:36 that Job may be tried unto the **e** 5331
Job 42:12 the Lord blessed the latter **e** of Job
Ps 19:4 their words to the **e** of the world. 7097
Ps 19:6 forth is from the **e** of the heaven, ...7097
Ps 39:4 Lord, make me to know mine **e**, ...7093
Pr 5:4 But her **e** is bitter as wormwood, ...319
Pr 14:12 **e** thereof are the ways of death. 319
Pr 14:13 the **e** of that mirth is heaviness. 319
Pr 16:25 the **e** thereof are the ways of death. 319
Pr 19:20 thou mayest be wise in thy latter **e**
Pr 20:21 the **e** thereof shall not be blessed. 319
Pr 23:18 For surely there is an **e**; and 319
Ecc 3:11 from the beginning to the **e** 5490
Ecc 4:8 yet is there no **e** of all his labour; 7093
Ecc 4:16 There is no **e** of all the people, ...7093
Ecc 7:2 for that is the **e** of all men; 5490
Ecc 7:8 Better is the **e** of a thing than the 319

Ecc 7:14	**e** that man should find nothing	1700
Ecc 12:12	making many books there is no **e**;	7093
Isa 2:7	is there any **e** of their treasures;	7097
Isa 9:7	and peace there shall be no **e**,	7093
Isa 23:17	pass after the **e** of seventy years,	7093
Isa 45:17	world without **e**.	5704, 5769, 5703
Isa 46:10	the **e** from the beginning,	319
Jer 29:11	of evil, to give you an expected **e**	319
Jer 30:11	I make a full **e** of all nations	3615
Jer 30:11	yet will I not make a full **e** of thee:	3615
La 4:18	our **e** is near, our days are fulfilled;	7093
Eze 20:26	to the **e** that they might know	4616
Da 4:34	the **e** of the days I Nebuchadnezzar	7118
Da 8:17	time of the **e** shall be the vision.	7093
Da 12:8	shall be the **e** of these things?	319
Da 12:9	and sealed till the time of the **e**	7093
Na 1:9	the Lord? he will make an utter **e**:	3615
Mt 10:22	**endureth to the e shall be saved.**	*5056*
Mt 24:13	**he that shall endure unto the e,**	*5056*
Mt 24:31	**from one e of heaven to the other**	*206*
Mt 28:20	**even unto the e of the world**	*4930*
Lk 1:33	of his kingdom there shall be no **e**	*5056*
Lk 21:9	**but the e is not by and by**	*5056*
Jn 18:37	**To this e was I born, and for this**	
Ro 6:21	for the **e** of those things is death.	*5056*
Ro 10:4	For Christ is the **e** of the law	*5056*
Ro 14:9	to this **e** Christ both died, and rose	
Eph 3:21	ages, world without **e**	*165, 3588, 165*
Php 3:19	Whose **e** is destruction, whose God	*5056*
Heb 7:3	beginning of days, nor **e** of life;	*5056*
Heb 13:7	the **e** of their conversation.	*1545*
Jas 5:11	and have seen the **e** of the Lord;	*5056*
1Pe 1:9	Receiving the **e** of your faith,	*5056*
1Pe 1:13	and hope to the **e** for the grace	*5049*
1Pe 4:7	But the **e** of all things is at hand:	*5056*
2Pe 2:20	the latter **e** is worse with them	*2078*
Rev 2:26	**and keepeth my works unto the e,**	*5056*
Rev 21:6	the beginning and the **e**, I will give	*5056*
Rev 22:13	**Omega, the beginning and the e,**	*5056*

ENDEAVOURING

Eph 4:3	**E** to keep the unity of the Spirit	*4704*

ENDED

Ge 2:2	And on the seventh day God **e**	3615
Job 31:40	The words of Job are **e**.	8552
Ps 72:20	of David the son of Jesse are **e**	3615
Jn 13:2	supper being **e**, the devil having	*1096*

ENDING

Rev 1:8	**Omega, the beginning and the e,**	*5056*

ENDLESS

1Ti 1:4	to fables and **e** genealogies, which	*562*
Heb 7:16	but after the power of an **e** life	*179*

ENDS

1Sa 2:10	Lord shall judge the **e** of the earth;	657
Job 28:24	he looketh to the **e** of the earth,	7098
Ps 19:6	and his circuit unto the **e** of it:	7098
Ps 22:27	All the **e** of the world shall	657
Ps 65:5	confidence of all the **e** of the earth,	7099
Ps 67:7	all the **e** of the earth shall fear	657
Ps 98:3	all the **e** of the earth have seen the	657
Pr 17:24	of a fool are in the **e** of the earth.	7097
Pr 30:4	established all the **e** of the earth?	657
Isa 40:28	the Creator of the **e** of the earth,	7098
Isa 41:5	the **e** of the earth were afraid,	7098
Isa 45:22	saved, all the **e** of the earth:	657
Isa 52:10	all the **e** of the earth shall see the	657
Jer 16:19	shall come unto thee from the **e** of	657
Eze 15:4	the fire devoureth both the **e** of it,	7098
Ac 13:47	salvation unto the **e** of the earth	*2078*
Ro 10:18	their words unto the **e** of the world.	*4009*

ENDUED

2Ch 2:12	a wise son, **e** with prudence and	3045
Lk 24:49	**until ye be e with power from on**	*1746*
Jas 3:13	**e** with knowledge among you?	*1990*

ENDURE

Ex 18:23	then thou shalt be able to **e**,	5975
Est 8:6	how can I **e** to see the destruction	3201
Ps 9:7	But the Lord shall **e** for ever:	3427
Ps 30:5	weeping may **e** for a night, but	3885
Ps 72:5	as long as the sun and moon **e**,	6440
Ps 102:12	thou, O Lord, shalt **e** for ever;	3427
Ps 102:26	shall perish, but thou shalt **e**:	5975
Ps 104:31	glory of the Lord shall **e** for ever:	1961
Pr 27:24	ever: and doth the crown **e** to every	
Mt 24:13	**But he that shall e unto the end,**	*5278*
Mk 4:17	**and so e but for a time:**	*2076*
Mk 13:13	**but he that shall e unto the end,**	*5278*
2Th 1:4	and tribulations that ye **e**:	*430*
2Ti 2:3	therefore **e** hardness, as a good	*2553*
2Ti 2:10	Therefore I **e** all things for the	*5278*
2Ti 4:3	they will not **e** sound doctrine;	*430*
2Ti 4:5	**e** afflictions, do the work of an	*2553*
Heb 12:7	If ye **e** chastening, God dealeth	*5278*
Heb 12:20	(For they could not **e** that which	*5342*
Jas 5:11	we count them happy which **e**	*5278*
1Pe 2:19	conscience toward God **e** grief,	*5297*

ENDURED

Ro 9:22	**e** with much longsuffering the	*5342*
Heb 6:15	And so, after he had patiently **e**,	*3114*
Heb 10:32	ye **e** a great fight of afflictions;	*5274*
Heb 11:27	for he **e**, as seeing him who is	*2594*
Heb 12:2	**e** the cross, despising the shame,	*5278*
Heb 12:3	him that **e** such contradiction	*5278*

ENDURETH

1Ch 16:34	he is good; for his mercy **e** for ever.	
Ps 30:5	For his anger **e** but a moment;	
Ps 72:7	peace so long as the moon **e**	1097
Ps 100:5	and his truth **e** to all generations	
Ps 106:1	he is good: for his mercy **e** for ever.	
Ps 107:1	he is good: for his mercy **e** for ever.	
Ps 111:3	and his righteousness **e** for ever	5975
Ps 112:3	and his righteousness **e** for ever	5975
Ps 118:2	Israel now say, that his mercy **e** for	
Ps 119:160	thy righteous judgments **e** for ever.	
Ps 135:13	Thy name, O Lord, **e** for ever;	
Ps 136:1	he is good: for his mercy **e** for ever.	
Ps 136:15	the Red sea: for his mercy **e** for ever.	
Ps 136:17	great kings: for his mercy **e** for ever:	
Ps 145:13	and thy dominion **e** throughout all	
Jer 33:11	for his mercy **e** for ever and of them	
Mt 10:22	**that e to the end shall be saved**	*5278*
Jn 6:27	**which e unto everlasting life,**	*3306*
1Co 13:7	hopeth all things, **e** all things.	*5278*
Jas 1:12	is the man that **e** temptation:	*5278*
1Pe 1:25	the word of the Lord **e** for ever	*3306*

E

ENDURING

Ps 19:9 of the Lord is clean, **e** for ever: 5975
Heb 10:34 a better and an **e** substance. *3306*

ENEMIES

Ge 14:20 delivered thine **e** into thy hand. 6862
Ex 23:22 I will be an enemy unto thine **e**, ...341
Le 26:37 no power to stand before your **e** 341
Nu 24:10 I called thee to curse mine **e**, ...341
Dt 20:1 goest out to battle against thine **e**, ...341
Dt 20:4 to fight for you against your **e**, ...341
Dt 28:25 thee to be smitten before thine **e**: 341
Dt 28:48 Therefore shalt thou serve thine **e** 341
Jos 7:12 Israel could not stand before their **e** 341
Jos 23:1 rest unto Israel from all their **e** 341
Jgs 2:14 sold them into the hands of their **e** 341
Jgs 5:31 So let all thine **e** perish, ...341
1Sa 14:47 against all his **e** on every side 341
2Sa 12:14 great occasion to the **e** of the Lord 341
2Sa 24:13 flee three months before thine **e**, ...6862
1Ki 3:11 nor hast asked the life of thine **e**; 341
2Ch 1:11 or honour, nor the life of thine **e**, ...8130
Ne 4:15 our **e** heard that it was known 341
Est 9:22 the Jews rested from their **e**, ...341
Ps 6:10 Let all mine **e** be ashamed and 341
Ps 18:48 He delivereth me from mine **e**: 341
Ps 23:5 me in the presence of mine **e**: 6887
Ps 25:2 let not mine **e** triumph over me 341
Ps 59:1 Deliver me from mine **e**, O my God: 341
Ps 71:10 For mine **e** speak against me; 341
Ps 78:53 but the sea overwhelmed their **e** 341
Ps 92:9 for, lo, thine **e** shall perish; 341
Ps 102:8 Mine **e** reproach me all the day; 341
Ps 110:1 until I make thine **e** thy footstool 341
Ps 119:98 hast made me wiser than mine **e**: 341
Ps 119:139 mine **e** have forgotten thy words 6862
Ps 143:9 Deliver me, O Lord, from mine **e**: 341
Pr 16:7 maketh even his **e** to be at peace 341
Jer 12:7 my soul into the hand of her **e** 341
La 1:21 mine **e** have heard of my trouble; 341
Am 9:4 go into captivity before their **e** 341
Mic 7:6 a man's **e** are the men of his own 341
Mt 5:44 **Love your e, bless them that curse** *2190*
Mt 22:44 **till I make thine e thy footstool?** *2190*
Mk 12:36 **till I make thine e thy footstool** *2190*
Lk 6:27 **Love your e, do good to them that** *2190*
Lk 19:43 **thine e shall cast a trench about** *2190*
Lk 20:43 **Till I make thine e thy footstool** *2190*
Ro 5:10 when we were **e**, we were reconciled *2190*
1Co 15:25 till he hath put all **e** under his feet *2190*
Php 3:18 that they are the **e** of the cross of *2190*
Heb 1:13 until I make thine **e** thy footstool? *2190*
Heb 10:13 till his **e** be made his footstool *2190*
Rev 11:5 their mouth and devoureth their **e**: *2190*
Rev 11:12 and their **e** beheld them. *2190*

ENEMY

Ex 15:9 The **e** said, I will pursue, I will 341
Ex 23:22 I will be an **e** unto thine enemies 340
Jgs 16:23 hath delivered Samson our **e** into 341
1Sa 18:29 Saul became David's **e** continually 341
2Ch 6:24 be put to the worse before the **e**, ...341
Est 7:6 adversary and **e** is this wicked Haman ...341
Ps 13:2 how long shall mine **e** be exalted 341
Ps 74:10 shall the **e** blaspheme thy name 341
Pr 24:17 Rejoice not when thine **e** falleth, ...341
Pr 25:21 If thine **e** be hungry, give him 8130
Pr 27:6 the kisses of an **e** are deceitful 8130
Isa 59:19 the **e** shall come in like a flood, ...6862
Jer 30:14 thee with the wound of an **e**, ...341
La 1:5 gone into captivity before the **e** 6862
La 2:5 The Lord was as an **e**: he hath 341
Mic 7:8 Rejoice not against me, O mine **e**: 341
Mt 5:43 **thy neighbour, and hate thine e** *2190*
Mt 13:39 **The e that sowed them is the** *2190*
Lk 10:19 **and over all the power of the e** *2190*
Ac 13:10 devil, thou **e** of all righteousness, ...*2190*
Ro 12:20 Therefore if thine **e** hunger, feed *2190*
1Co 15:26 The last **e** that shall be destroyed *2190*
Gal 4:16 Am I therefore become your **e**, ...*2190*
2Th 3:15 Yet count him not as an **e**, ...*2190*
Jas 4:4 friend of the world is the **e** of God *2190*

ENEMY'S

Ex 23:4 If thou meet thine **e** ox or his ass 341

ENGINES

2Ch 26:15 And he made in Jerusalem **e**, ...2810
Eze 26:9 he shall set **e** of war against thy 4239

ENGRAFTED

Jas 1:21 with meekness the **e** word, which *1721*

ENJOY

Le 26:43 shall **e** her sabbaths, while she 7521
Jos 1:15 land of your possession, and **e** it 3423
Ecc 2:1 with mirth, therefore **e** pleasure: 7200
Ecc 3:13 and **e** the good of all his labour, ...7200
Ecc 5:18 eat and drink, and to **e** the good 7200
1Ti 6:17 giveth us richly all things to **e**; *619*
Heb 11:25 than to **e** the pleasures of sin *2192, 619*

ENJOYED

2Ch 36:21 until the land had **e** her sabbaths: 7521

ENLARGE

Ex 34:24 before thee, and **e** thy borders: 7337
Dt 12:20 When the Lord thy God shall **e** thy 7337
1Ch 4:10 wouldest bless .... and **e** my coast 7235
Ps 119:32 when thou shalt **e** my heart 7337
Am 1:13 that they might **e** their border: 7337
Mt 23:5 **e the borders of their garments,** *3170*

ENLARGED

2Sa 22:37 Thou hast **e** my steps under me; 7337
Ps 25:17 The troubles of my heart are **e**: 7337
Isa 57:8 gone up; thou hast **e** thy bed, ...7337
2Co 6:11 is open unto you, our heart is **e** *4115*

ENLARGETH

Hab 2:5 who **e** his desire as hell, and is 7337

ENLIGHTENED See also LIGHTENED.

Job 33:30 to be **e** with the light of the living 215
Ps 97:4 His lightnings **e** the world: 215
Eph 1:18 of your understanding being **e**; *5461*
Heb 6:4 those who were once **e**, and have *5461*

ENLIGHTENING

Ps 19:8 of the Lord is pure, **e** the eyes 215

ENMITY

Ge 3:15 put **e** between thee and the woman, ...342
Nu 35:21 Or in **e** smite him with his hand 342
Nu 35:22 thrust him suddenly without **e**,
Lk 23:12 were at **e** between themselves *2189*

Ro	8:7	the carnal mind is **e** against God:	*2189*
Eph	2:15	abolished in his flesh the **e**,	*2189*
Jas	4:4	friendship of the world is **e** with	*2189*

ENOUGH

Ge	45:28	Israel said, It is **e**; Joseph my	7227
2Sa	24:16	It is **e**: stay now thine hand. And	7227
1Ki	19:4	It is **e**; now, O Lord, take away	7227
1Ch	21:15	It is **e**, stay now thine hand. And	7227
Pr	28:19	persons shall have poverty **e**	7644
Pr	30:15	yea, four things say not, It is **e**	1952
Pr	30:16	and the fire that saith not, It is **e**	1952
Isa	56:11	dogs which can never have **e**,	7654
Hos	4:10	they shall eat, and not have **e**:	7644
Ob	5	not have stolen till they had **e**?	1767
Mal	3:10	that there shall not be room **e**	1767
Mt	10:25	**It is e for the disciple that he be**	*713*
Mk	14:41	**your rest; it is e, the hour is come;**	*566*
Lk	15:17	**have bread e and to spare, and I**	*4052*
Lk	22:38	he said unto them, It is **e**	*2425*

ENQUIRE

Ex	18:15	people come unto me to **e** of God:	1875
Dt	12:30	that thou **e** not after their gods,	1875
1Sa	9:9	when a man went to **e** of God,	1875
1Ki	22:5	**E**, I pray thee, at the word of the	1875
2Ki	1:2	**e** of Baal-zebub the god of Ekron	1875
2Ki	1:16	no God in Israel to **e** of his word?	1875
2Ki	22:13	Go ye, **e** of the Lord for me	1875
1Ch	10:13	had a familiar spirit, to **e** of it:	1875
2Ch	34:26	who sent you to **e** of the Lord,	1875
Ps	27:4	the Lord, and to **e** in his temple	1239
Ecc	7:10	dost not **e** wisely concerning this	7592
Jer	21:2	**E**, I pray thee, of the Lord for us;	1875
Eze	14:7	prophet to **e** of him concerning	1875
Eze	20:3	Are ye come to **e** of me?	1875
Mt	10:11	**e who in it is worthy; and there**	*1833*
Lk	22:23	began to **e** among themselves	*4802*
Jn	16:19	**Do ye e among yourselves of that**	*2212*

ENQUIRED

Dt	17:4	**e** diligently, and, behold, it be	1875
Jgs	20:27	children of Israel **e** of the Lord	7592
1Sa	22:10	And he **e** of the Lord for him	7592
1Sa	23:4	David **e** of the Lord yet again	7592
1Sa	28:6	And when Saul **e** of the Lord	7592
2Sa	11:3	David sent and **e** after the woman	1875
2Sa	16:23	as if a man had **e** at the oracle	7592
1Ch	10:14	And **e** not of the Lord: therefore	1875
1Ch	13:3	we **e** not at it in the days of Saul	1875
Eze	14:3	should I be **e** of at all by them?	1875
Eze	20:3	Lord God, I will not be **e** of by you	1875
Eze	36:37	I will yet for this be **e** of by the	1875
Da	1:20	king **e** of them, he found them	1245
Zep	1:6	sought the Lord, nor **e** for him	1875
Mt	2:7	**e** of them diligently what time the	*198*
Mt	2:16	had diligently **e** of the wise men	*198*
Jn	4:52	Then **e** he of them the hour	*4441*
1Pe	1:10	have **e** and searched diligently	*1567*

ENRICH See also RICH.

1Sa	17:25	king will **e** him with great riches	6238
Eze	27:33	thou didst **e** the kings of the earth	6238

ENRICHED

1Co	1:5	in every thing ye are **e** by him,	*4148*
2Co	9:11	**e** in every thing to all bountifulness,	*4148*

ENSIGN

Nu	2:2	the **e** of their father's house:	226
Isa	5:26	he will lift up an **e** to the nations	5251
Isa	11:12	he shall set up an **e** for the nations,	5251
Isa	18:3	lifteth up an **e** on the mountains;	5251
Isa	30:17	and as an **e** on an hill	5251
Isa	31:9	his princes shall be afraid of the **e**,	5251
Zec	9:16	lifted up as an **e** upon his land	5264

ENSUE

1Pe	3:11	let him seek peace, and **e** it	*1377*

ENTANGLE

Mt	22:15	how they might **e** him in his talk	*3802*

ENTANGLED

Gal	5:1	**e** again with the yoke of bondage	*1758*
2Pe	2:20	they are again **e** therein, and	*1707*

ENTANGLETH

2Ti	2:4	**e** himself with the affairs of the	*1707*

ENTER

Ex	40:35	Moses was not able to **e** into the	935
Nu	20:24	for he shall not **e** into the land	935
Dt	29:12	thou shouldest **e** into covenant	5674
2Ch	7:2	priests could not **e** into the house	935
Est	4:2	none might **e** into the king's gate	935
Ps	37:15	sword shall **e** into their own heart	935
Ps	95:11	that they should not **e** into my rest	935
Ps	100:4	**E** into his gates with thanksgiving	935
Ps	118:20	into which the righteous shall **e**	935
Pr	4:14	**E** not into the path of the wicked	935
Pr	18:6	A fool's lips **e** into contention	935
Pr	23:10	and **e** not into the fields of the	935
Isa	2:10	**E** into the rock, and hide thee in	935
Isa	26:2	which keepeth the truth may **e** in	935
Isa	59:14	in the street, and equity cannot **e**	935
Jer	16:5	**E** not into the house of mourning,	935
La	1:10	should not **e** into thy congregation	935
Eze	7:22	for the robbers shall **e** into it	935
Eze	37:5	I will cause breath to **e** into you	935
Eze	42:14	When the priests **e** therein, then	935
Eze	44:2	and no man shall **e** in by it;	935
Eze	46:2	And the prince shall **e** by the way	935
Hos	11:9	and I will not **e** into the city	935
Joel	2:9	they shall **e** in at the windows	935
Mt	5:20	**e into the kingdom of heaven**	*1525*
Mt	7:13	**E ye in at the strait gate:**	*1525*
Mt	12:29	**one e into a strong man's house**	*1525*
Mt	18:3	**not e into the kingdom of heaven**	*1525*
Mt	18:9	**thee to e into life with one eye,**	*1525*
Mt	19:17	**if thou wilt e into life, keep the**	*1525*
Mt	19:23	**shall hardly e into the kingdom of**	*1525*
Mt	19:24	**to e into the kingdom of God**	*1525*
Mt	25:21	**e thou into the joy of thy lord**	*1525*
Mt	26:41	**that ye e not into temptation:**	*1525*
Mk	3:27	**can e into a strong man's house,**	*1525*
Mk	9:47	**thee to e into the kingdom of God**	*1525*
Mk	10:15	**little child, he shall not e therein**	*1525*
Mk	10:23	**riches e into the kingdom of God!**	*1525*
Mk	14:38	**pray, lest ye e into temptation**	*1525*
Lk	8:16	**they which e in may see the light**	*1531*
Lk	10:5	**whatsoever house ye e, first say,**	*1525*
Lk	13:24	**Strive to e in at the strait gate:**	*1525*
Lk	18:17	**child shall in no wise e therein**	*1525*
Lk	18:24	**riches e into the kingdom of God!**	*1525*

Lk 22:40 **that ye e not into temptation** *1525*
Lk 22:46 **pray, lest ye e into temptation** *1525*
Lk 24:26 **things, and to e into his glory?** *1525*
Jn 3:4 can he **e** the second time into his *1525*
Jn 3:5 **cannot e into the kingdom of God** *1525*
Jn 10:9 **if any man e in, he shall be saved,** *1525*
Heb 3:11 They shall not **e** into my rest.) *1525*
Heb 3:19 that they could not **e** in because *1525*
Heb 4:11 therefore to **e** into that rest, lest *1525*
Heb 10:19 boldness to **e** into the holiest by *1529*
Rev 15:8 was able to **e** into the temple, ... *1525*
Rev 21:27 there shall in no wise **e** into it *1525*
Rev 22:14 **E** in through the gates into the city *1525*

ENTERED
Ge 7:13 In the selfsame day **e** Noah, and 935
Ex 33:9 as Moses **e** into the tabernacle, ...935
2Ch 12:11 king **e** into the house of the Lord 935
2Ch 15:12 **e** into a covenant to seek the Lord 935
2Ch 27:2 howbeit he **e** not into the temple 935
Jer 34:10 which had **e** into the covenant, ...935
Jer 37:16 was **e** into the dungeon, and into 935
La 1:10 the heathen **e** into her sanctuary, ...935
Eze 2:2 the spirit **e** into me when he spake 935
Eze 3:24 Then the spirit **e** into me, and set 935
Eze 16:8 and **e** into a covenant with thee 935
Eze 44:2 the God of Israel, hath **e** in by it, ...935
Ob 11 and foreigners **e** into his gates 935
Mt 12:4 **How he e into the house of God,** *1525*
Mt 24:38 **the day that Noe e into the ark,** *1525*
Lk 6:6 **e** into the synagogue and taught: *1525*
Lk 8:30 many devils were **e** into him *1525*
Lk 17:27 **day that Noe e into the ark,** *1525*
Lk 22:3 Then **e** Satan into Judas surnamed *1525*
Lk 24:3 they **e** in, and found not the body *1525*
Jn 4:38 **and ye are e into their labours** *1525*
Jn 6:17 **e** into a ship, and went over the *1694*
Jn 13:27 after the sop Satan **e** into him *1525*
Ro 5:12 sin **e** into the world, and death by *1525*
Ro 5:20 Moreover the law **e**, that the *3922*
1Co 2:9 neither have **e** into the heart of *305*
Heb 4:6 **e** not in because of unbelief: *1525*
Heb 6:20 Whither the forerunner is for us **e**, ... *1525*
Heb 9:12 he **e** in once into the holy place *1525*
Heb 9:24 For Christ is not **e** into the holy *1525*
Jas 5:4 are **e** into the ears of the Lord *1525*
2Jn 7 deceivers are **e** into the world *1525*
Rev 11:11 spirit of life from God **e** into them *1525*

ENTERETH
Nu 4:30 that **e** into the service, to do the 935
Pr 2:10 When wisdom **e** into thine heart, ...935
Pr 17:10 A reproof **e** more into a wise man 5181
Mt 15:17 **whatsoever e in at the mouth** *1531*
Mk 7:18 **from without e into the man** *1531*
Mk 7:19 **Because it e not into his heart,** *1531*
Jn 10:2 **But he that e in by the door is** *1535*
Heb 6:19 which **e** into that within the veil; *1535*
Heb 9:25 as the high priest **e** into the holy *1535*

ENTERING See also ENTRANCE; ENTRY.
Mk 4:19 **the lusts of other things e in,** *1531*
Mk 7:15 **that e into him can defile him;** *1531*
1Th 1:9 what manner of **e** in we had unto *1529*

ENTERTAIN
Heb 13:2 Be not forgetful to **e** strangers: *5381*

ENTERTAINED
Heb 13:2 some have **e** angels unawares *3579*

ENTICE
Ex 22:16 if a man **e** a maid that is not 6601
Dt 13:6 **e** thee secretly, saying, Let us go 5496
Jgs 14:15 **E** thy husband, that he may 6601
Jgs 16:5 **E** him, and see wherein his great 6601
2Ch 18:19 Who shall **e** Ahab king of Israel 6601
Pr 1:10 My son, if sinners **e** thee, consent 6601

ENTICED
Job 31:27 my heart hath been secretly **e**, ...6601
Jer 20:10 Peradventure he will be **e**, and 6601
Jas 1:14 drawn away of his own lust, and **e** *1185*

ENTICETH
Pr 16:29 A violent man **e** his neighbour 6601

ENTICING
1Co 2:4 with **e** words of man's wisdom *3981*
Col 2:4 should beguile you with **e** words *4086*

ENTIRE
Jas 1:4 that ye may be perfect and **e** *3648*

ENTRANCE See also ENTERING; ENTRY.
1Ki 18:46 ran before Ahab to the **e** of Jezreel 935
Ps 119:130 The **e** of thy words giveth light; 6608
1Th 2:1 know our **e** in unto you, that it *1529*
2Pe 1:11 an **e** shall be ministered unto you *1529*

ENTREATED See also INTREATED.
Ex 5:22 hast thou so evil **e** this people?
Mt 22:6 **e them spitefully, and slew them** *5295*
Lk 18:32 **shall be mocked, and spitefully e,** *5195*
Lk 20:11 **e him shamefully, and sent him** *818*
Ac 7:19 evil **e** our fathers, so that they *2559*

ENTRY See also ENTERING; ENTRANCE
Pr 8:3 at the **e** of the city, at the coming 6310
Jer 43:9 is at the **e** of Pharaoh's house 6607
Eze 8:5 this image of jealousy in the **e** 872

ENVIED
Ge 30:1 no children, Rachel **e** her sister; 7065
Ge 37:11 his brethren **e** him; but his father 7065
Ps 106:16 They **e** Moses also in the camp 7065

ENVIETH
1Co 13:4 charity **e** not; charity vaunteth *2206*

ENVIOUS
Ps 37:1 neither be thou **e** against the 7065
Ps 73:3 For I was **e** at the foolish, when 7065
Pr 24:1 Be not thou **e** against evil men, ...7065
Pr 24:19 neither be thou **e** at the wicked; 7065

ENVY
Pr 3:31 **E** thou not the oppressor, and 7065
Pr 14:30 but **e** the rottenness of the bones 7068
Pr 23:17 Let not thine heart **e** sinners: but 7065
Pr 27:4 who is able to stand before **e**? 7068
Ecc 9:6 their hatred, and their **e**, is now 7068
Mt 27:18 that for **e** they had delivered him *5355*
Mk 15:10 priests had delivered him for **e** *5355*
Ac 7:9 patriarchs, moved with **e**, sold *2206*
Ac 13:45 were filled with **e**, and spake *2205*
Ac 17:5 which believed not, moved with **e** *2206*
Ro 1:29 full of **e**, murder, debate, deceit *5355*

Php	1:15	preach Christ even of **e** and strife;	*5355*
1Ti	6:4	whereof cometh **e**, strife, railings,	*5355*
Tit	3:3	living in malice and **e**, hateful,	*5355*
Jas	4:5	that dwelleth in us lusteth to **e**?	*5355*

ENVYING

Ro	13:13	wantonness, not in strife and **e**	*2205*
1Co	3:3	**e**, and strife, and divisions, are	*2205*
Gal	5:26	one another, **e** one another	*5354*
Jas	3:14	But if ye have bitter **e** and strife	*2205*
Jas	3:16	For where **e** and strife is, there	*2205*

EPHOD (e´-fod)

Ex	28:4	a breastplate, and an **e**, and a robe	646
Ex	28:6	they shall make the **e** of gold	646
1Sa	2:28	to wear an **e** before me? and did	646
1Sa	23:9	the priest, Bring hither the **e**	646
1Sa	30:7	I pray thee, bring me hither the **e**	646

EPISTLE

2Co	3:3	the **e** of Christ ministered by us,	*1992*
2Th	3:17	which is the token in every **e**:	*1992*

EQUAL See also UNEQUAL.

Ps	17:2	behold the things that are **e**	4339
Ps	55:13	it was thou, a man mine **e**	6187
Pr	26:7	The legs of the lame are not **e**:	1809
Isa	40:25	will ye liken me, or shall I be **e**?	7737
Isa	46:5	will ye liken me, and make me **e**	7737
Eze	33:20	The way of the Lord is not **e**	8505
Mt	20:12	**thou hast made them e unto us,**	*2470*
Lk	20:36	**for they are e unto the angels;**	*2465*
Jn	5:18	making himself **e** with God	*2470*
Php	2:6	it not robbery to be **e** with God:	*2470*
Col	4:1	servants that which is just and **e**;	*2471*
Rev	21:16	breadth and the height of it are **e**	*2470*

EQUITY

Ps	98:9	the world, and the people with **e**	4339
Pr	2:9	and judgment, and **e**; yea, every	4339
Pr	17:26	good, nor to strike princes for **e**	3476
Ecc	2:21	and in knowledge, and in **e**;	3788
Isa	59:14	in the street, and **e** cannot enter	5229
Mic	3:9	abhor judgment, pervert all **e**	3477
Mal	2:6	walked with me in peace and **e**,	4334

ERR

Ps	95:10	is a people that do **e** in their heart,	8582
Ps	119:21	rebuked the proud … which do **e**	7686
Ps	119:118	hast trodden down all them that **e**	7686
Pr	14:22	Do they not **e** that devise evil?	8582
Pr	19:27	the instruction that causeth to **e**	7686
Isa	3:12	which lead thee cause thee to **e**	8582
Isa	9:16	of this people cause them to **e**;	8582
Isa	28:7	they **e** in vision, they stumble in	7686
Isa	63:17	why hast thou made us to **e** from	8582
Jer	23:13	and caused my people Israel to **e**,	8582
Jer	23:32	cause my people to **e** by their lies	8582
Hos	4:12	whoredoms hath caused them to **e**,	8582
Am	2:4	and their lies caused them to **e**,	8582
Mic	3:5	prophets that make my people **e**,	8582
Mt	22:29	**Ye do e, not knowing the**	*4105*
Mk	12:24	**Do ye not therefore e, because**	*4105*
Mk	12:27	**ye therefore do greatly e**	*4105*
Heb	3:10	They do alway **e** in their heart;	*4105*
Jas	1:16	Do not **e**, my beloved brethren	*4105*
Jas	5:19	Brethren, if any of you do **e** from	*4105*

ERRAND

Ge	24:33	not eat, until I have told mine **e**	1697
Jgs	3:19	I have a secret **e** unto thee	1697

ERRED

Le	5:18	his ignorance wherein he **e** and	7683
Nu	15:22	if ye have **e**, and not observed all	7683
1Sa	26:21	the fool, and have **e** exceedingly	7683
Job	6:24	me to understand wherein I have **e**	7683
Ps	119:110	I have **e** not from thy precepts	8582
Isa	28:7	priest and the prophet have **e**	7686
Isa	29:24	They also that **e** in spirit shall	8582
1Ti	6:10	they have **e** from the faith, and	*635*
1Ti	6:21	have **e** concerning the faith	*795*
2Ti	2:18	Who concerning the truth have **e**,	*795*

ERRETH

Pr	10:17	but he that refuseth reproof **e**	8582
Eze	45:20	every one that **e** and for him that	7686

ERROR

2Sa	6:7	God smote him there for his **e**;	7944
Ecc	5:6	neither say thou … it was an **e**:	7684
Isa	32:6	and to utter **e** against the Lord,	8432
Da	6:4	neither was there any **e** or fault	7960
Mt	27:64	so the last **e** shall be worse than	*4106*
Ro	1:27	that recompence of their **e** which	*4106*
Jas	5:20	the sinner from the **e** of his way	*4106*
2Pe	2:18	escaped from them who live in **e**	*4106*
2Pe	3:17	being led away with the **e** of the	*4106*
1Jn	4:6	spirit of truth, and the spirit of **e**	*4106*
Jude	11	ran greedily after the **e** of Balaam	*4106*

ERRORS

Ps	19:12	Who can understand his **e**?	7691
Jer	10:15	are vanity, and the work of **e**	8595
Jer	51:18	They are vanity, the work of **e**	8595
Heb	9:7	himself, and for the **e** of the people	*51*

ESCAPE

Ge	19:17	**E** for thy life; look not behind	4422
Ge	19:22	Haste thee, **e** thither; for I can not	4422
Ge	32:8	other company which is left shall **e**	6413
Jos	8:22	let none of them remain or **e**	6412
1Sa	27:1	so shall I **e** out of his hand	4422
2Sa	15:14	we shall not else **e** from Absalom:	6413
1Ki	18:40	let not one of them **e**. And they	4422
2Ki	10:24	If any of the men … **e**	4422
2Ki	19:31	and they that **e** out of mount Zion:	6413
Ezr	9:8	to leave us a remnant to **e**	6413
Est	4:13	thou shalt **e** in the king's house,	4422
Ps	56:7	Shall they **e** by iniquity? in thine	6405
Ps	71:2	cause me to **e**: incline thine ear	6403
Ps	141:10	own nets, whilst that I withal **e**	5674
Pr	19:5	he that speaketh lies shall not **e**	4422
Ecc	7:26	pleaseth God shall **e** from her;	4422
Isa	37:32	and they that **e** out of mount Zion:	6413
Isa	66:19	I will send those that **e** of them	6412
Jer	11:11	they shall not be able to **e**;	3318
Jer	32:4	shall not **e** out of the hand of the	4422
Jer	38:18	shalt not **e** out of their hand	4422
Jer	42:17	none of them shall remain or **e**	6412
Jer	44:28	a small number that **e** the sword	6412
Jer	46:6	flee away, nor the mighty man **e**;	4422
Jer	48:8	no city shall **e**: the valley also	4422
Jer	50:29	let none thereof **e**: recompense	6413
Eze	6:9	they that **e** of you shall remember	6412

Eze	17:15	shall he **e** that doeth such things?	4422
Joel	2:3	yea, and nothing shall **e** them	6413
Ob	14	to cut off those of his that did **e**;	6412
Mt	23:33	**ye e the damnation of hell?**	*5343, 575*
Lk	21:36	**worthy to e all these things**	*1628*
Ac	27:42	of them should swim out, and **e**	*1309*
Ro	2:3	thou shalt **e** the judgment of God?	*1628*
1Co	10:13	temptation also make a way to **e**,	*1545*
1Th	5:3	with child; and they shall not **e**	*1628*
Heb	2:3	How shall we **e**, if we neglect so	*1628*
Heb	12:25	earth, much more shall not we **e**	*5343*

ESCAPED

Ge	14:13	And there came one that had **e**,	6412
Dt	23:15	servant which is **e** from his master	5337
Jgs	3:29	of valour; and there **e** not a man	4422
1Sa	19:10	and David fled, and **e** that night	4422
1Sa	19:12	and he went, and fled, and **e**	4422
1Sa	19:17	away mine enemy, that he is **e**?	4422
1Sa	22:1	thence, and **e** to the cave Adullam:	4422
1Sa	22:20	sons of Ahimelech … **e**, and fled	4422
1Sa	30:17	and there **e** not a man of them	4422
2Sa	1:3	Out of the camp of Israel am I **e**	4422
2Sa	4:6	Rechab and Baanah his brother **e**	4422
1Ki	20:20	Ben-hadad the king of Syria **e**	4422
2Ki	19:30	that is **e** of the house of Judah	6413
2Ki	19:37	they **e** into the land of Armenia	4422
1Ch	4:43	of the Amalekites that were **e**	6413
2Ch	20:24	fallen to the earth, and none **e**	6413
2Ch	30:6	the remnant of you, that are **e**	6413
2Ch	36:20	them that had **e** from the sword	7611
Ezr	9:15	we remain yet **e**, as it is this day:	6413
Ne	1:2	concerning the Jews that had **e**	6413
Job	1:15	I only am **e** alone to tell	4422
Job	1:16	I only am **e** alone to tell	4422
Job	1:17	I only am **e** alone to tell	4422
Job	1:19	I only am **e** alone to tell	4422
Ps	124:7	Our soul is **e** as a bird out of the	4422
Isa	4:2	for them that are **e** of Israel	6413
Isa	10:20	such as are **e** of the house of Jacob,	6413
Isa	37:31	that is **e** of the house of Judah	6413
Jer	51:50	Ye that have **e** the sword	6412
La	2:22	the day of the Lord's anger none **e**	6412
Eze	24:27	mouth be opened to him which is **e**	6412
Eze	33:21	one that had **e** out of Jerusalem	6412
Eze	33:22	evening, afore he that was **e** came;	6412
Jn	10:39	him: but he **e** out of their hand	*1831*
Ac	28:4	whom, though he hath **e** the sea,	*1295*
2Co	11:33	was I let down by the wall, and **e**	*1628*
Heb	11:34	of fire, **e** the edge of the sword	*5343*
Heb	12:25	For if they **e** not who refused him	*5343*
2Pe	1:4	having **e** the corruption that is in	*668*
2Pe	2:18	those that were clean **e** from them	*668*
2Pe	2:20	For if after they have **e** the	*668*

ESCAPETH

1Ki	19:17	him that **e** from the sword of Jehu	4422
Am	9:1	he that **e** of them shall not be	6412

ESCAPING

Ezr	9:14	should be no remnant nor **e**?	6413

ESCHEW

1Pe	3:11	Let him **e** evil, and do good;	*1578*

ESCHEWED

Job	1:1	one that feared God, and **e** evil	5493

ESCHEWETH

Job	1:8	son that feareth God and **e** evil?	5493
Job	2:3	one that feareth God, and **e** evil?	5493

ESPECIALLY

Gal	6:10	men, **e** unto them who are of the	*3122*
1Ti	5:17	**e** they who labour in the word and	*3122*

ESPIED See also ESPY; SPY.

Ge	42:27	provender in the inn, he **e**	7200
Eze	20:6	into a land that I had **e** for them,	8446

ESPOUSALS

SS	3:11	crowned him in the day of his **e**,	2861
Jer	2:2	of thy youth, the love of thine **e**,	3623

ESPOUSED

Mt	1:18	When as his mother Mary was **e**	*3423*
Lk	1:27	To a virgin **e** to a man whose	*3423*
Lk	2:5	To be taxed with Mary his **e** wife,	*3423*
2Co	11:2	For I have **e** you to one husband	*718*

ESPY See also ESPIED; SPY.

Jos	14:7	sent me ... to **e** out the land	7270

ESTABLISH See also STABLISH.

Ge	6:18	with thee will I **e** my covenant;	6965
Ge	9:11	And I will **e** my covenant with you;	6965
Ge	17:7	And I will **e** my covenant between	6965
Ge	17:19	and I will **e** my covenant with him	6965
Nu	30:13	her husband may **e** it or her	6965
Dt	8:18	that he may **e** his covenant which	6965
Dt	28:9	The Lord shall **e** thee an holy people	6965
1Ki	9:5	Then I will **e** the throne of thy	6965
1Ki	15:4	after him, and to **e** Jerusalem	5975
1Ch	22:10	and I will **e** the throne of his	3559
1Ch	28:7	Moreover I will **e** his kingdom	3559
2Ch	9:8	loved Israel, to **e** them for ever	5975
Ps	7:9	but **e** the just: for the righteous	3559
Ps	89:4	Thy seed will I **e** for ever	3559
Ps	90:17	and **e** thou the work of our hands	3559
Pr	15:25	he will **e** the border of the widow	5324
Isa	9:7	and to **e** it with judgment and	5582
Isa	49:8	of the people, to **e** the earth, to	6965
Jer	33:2	the Lord that formed it, to **e** it;	3559
Eze	16:62	And I will **e** my covenant with thee;	6965
Da	6:8	Now, O king, **e** the decree	6966
Am	5:15	and **e** judgment in the gate:	3322
Ro	3:31	God forbid: yea, we **e** the law	*2476*
Ro	10:3	about to **e** their own righteousness,	*2476*
1Th	3:2	to **e** you, and to comfort you	*4741*
Heb	10:9	the first, that he may **e** the second	*2476*

ESTABLISHED See also STABLISHED.

Ge	9:17	the covenant, which I have **e**	6965
Ge	41:32	because the thing is **e** by God	3559
Ex	6:4	I have also **e** my covenant with	6965
Ex	15:17	O Lord, which thy hands have **e**	3559
Dt	19:15	witnesses, shall the matter be **e**	6965
Dt	32:6	hath he not made thee, and **e** thee?	3559
1Sa	3:20	knew that Samuel was **e** to be a	539
1Sa	13:13	the Lord have **e** thy kingdom	3559
1Sa	20:31	shalt not be **e**, nor thy kingdom	3559
2Sa	7:26	house of thy servant David be **e**	3559
1Ki	2:12	and his kingdom was **e** greatly	3559
1Ch	17:24	let the house of David … be **e**	3559
2Ch	20:20	so shall ye be **e**; believe his	539
2Ch	30:5	So they **e** a decree to make	5975

Ps	24:2	and **e** it upon the floods	3559
Ps	40:2	feet upon a rock, and **e** my goings	3559
Ps	89:37	It shall be **e** for ever as the moon,	3559
Ps	93:2	Thy throne is **e** of old: thou art	3559
Ps	96:10	the world also shall be **e** that it	3559
Ps	119:90	thou hast **e** the earth, and it	3559
Ps	140:11	Let not an evil speaker be **e**	3559
Pr	3:19	by understanding hath he **e** the	3559
Pr	4:26	and let all thy ways be **e**	3559
Pr	12:3	man shall not be **e** by wickedness:	3559
Pr	15:22	of counsellors they are **e**	6965
Pr	16:3	and thy thoughts shall be **e**	3559
Pr	16:12	the throne is **e** by righteousness	3559
Pr	20:18	Every purpose is **e** by counsel:	3559
Pr	24:3	and by understanding it is **e**:	3559
Pr	25:5	and his throne shall be **e** in	3559
Pr	29:14	his throne shall be **e** for ever	3559
Pr	30:4	hath **e** all the ends of the earth?	6965
Isa	16:5	in mercy shall the throne be **e**:	3559
Isa	45:18	he hath **e** it, he created it	3559
Isa	54:14	In righteousness shalt thou be **e**:	3559
Jer	10:12	hath **e** the world by his wisdom,	3559
Jer	51:15	by his power, he hath **e** the world	3559
Da	4:36	I was **e** in my kingdom,	8627
Mic	4:1	be **e** in the top of the mountains,	3559
Hab	1:12	thou hast **e** them for correction	3245
Mt	18:16	**witnesses every word may be e**	*2476*
Ac	16:5	were the churches **e** in the faith,	*4732*
Ro	1:11	to the end ye may be **e**;	*4741*
2Co	13:1	witnesses shall every word be **e**	*2476*
Heb	8:6	was **e** upon better promises	*3549*
Heb	13:9	that the heart be **e** with grace;	*950*
2Pe	1:12	and be **e** in the present truth	*4741*

ESTABLISHETH See also STABLISHETH.

Pr	29:4	The king by judgment **e** the land:	5975
Da	6:15	nor statute which the king **e**	6966

ESTATE See also STATE.

1Ch	17:17	regarded me according to the **e**	8448
Est	1:19	king give her royal **e** unto another	
Ps	136:23	Who remembered us in our low **e**:	
Ecc	1:16	Lo, I am come to great **e**,	
Ecc	3:18	concerning the **e** of the sons of	1700
Da	11:21	And in his **e** shall stand up a vile	3653
Da	11:38	in his **e** shall he honour the God	3653
Lk	1:48	the low **e** of his handmaiden:	
Ro	12:16	condescend to men of low **e**,	
Col	4:8	he might know your **e**, and	*3588, 4012*
Jude	6	which kept not their first **e**,	

ESTEEM

Job	36:19	Will he **e** thy riches? no, not	6186
Isa	53:4	yet we did **e** him stricken,	2803
Php	2:3	**e** other better than themselves.	*2233*
1Th	5:13	And to **e** them very highly in love	*2233*

ESTEEMED

Dt	32:15	lightly **e** the Rock of his salvation.	5034
1Sa	2:30	despise me shall be lightly **e**	7043
Job	23:12	I have **e** the words of his mouth	6845
Pr	17:28	shutteth his lips is **e** a man of	
Isa	29:16	shall be **e** as the potter's clay	2803
Isa	53:3	was despised, and we **e** him not	2803
La	4:2	are they **e** as earthen pitchers,	2803
Lk	16:15	**which is highly e among men**	
1Co	6:4	them to judge who are least **e**	*1848*

ESTEEMETH

Ro	14:5	One man **e** one day above another:	*2919*
Ro	14:5	another **e** every day alike	*2919*
Ro	14:14	but to him that **e** any thing to be	*3049*

ESTEEMING

Heb	11:26	**E** the reproach of Christ greater	*2233*

ESTIMATE

Le	27:14	as the priest shall **e** it, so shall	6186

ESTIMATION

Le	27:8	But if he be poorer than thy **e**,	6187
Le	27:17	year of jubile, according to thy **e**	6187

ESTRANGED

Ps	58:3	The wicked are **e** from the womb:	2114
Ps	78:30	They were not **e** from their lust	2114
Jer	19:4	and have **e** this place, and have	5234

ETERNAL

Dt	33:27	The **e** God is thy refuge, and	6924
Mt	19:16	shall I do, that I may have **e** life?	*166*
Mt	25:46	**but the righteous into life e**	*166*
Mk	3:29	**in danger of e damnation:**	*166*
Mk	10:17	I do that I may inherit **e** life?	*166*
Mk	10:30	**and in the world to come e life.**	*166*
Lk	10:25	what shall I do to inherit **e** life?	*166*
Lk	18:18	what shall I do to inherit **e** life?	*166*
Jn	3:15	**should not perish, but have e life.**	*166*
Jn	4:36	**and gathereth fruit unto life e:**	*166*
Jn	5:39	**for in them ye think ye have e life:**	*166*
Jn	6:54	**and drinketh my blood, hath e life;**	*266*
Jn	6:68	thou hast the words of **e** life	*166*
Jn	10:28	**And I give unto them e life;**	*166*
Jn	12:25	**this world shall keep it unto life e**	*166*
Jn	17:2	**he should give e life to as many as**	*166*
Jn	17:3	**this is life e, that they might know**	*166*
Ac	13:48	many as were ordained to **e** life	*166*
Ro	1:20	even his **e** power and Godhead;	*126*
Ro	2:7	honour and immortality, **e** life:	*166*
Ro	5:21	through righteousness unto **e** life	*166*
Ro	6:23	but the gift of God is **e** life through	*166*
2Co	4:17	exceeding and **e** weight of glory;	*166*
2Co	4:18	the things which are not seen are **e**	*166*
2Co	5:1	made with hands, **e** in the heavens	*166*
Eph	3:11	According the **e** purpose which	*165*
1Ti	1:17	Now unto the King **e**, immortal,	*165*
1Ti	6:12	lay hold on **e** life, whereunto thou	*166*
1Ti	6:19	that they may lay hold on **e** life	*166*
2Ti	2:10	is in Christ Jesus with **e** glory	*166*
Tit	1:2	In hope of **e** life, which God, that	*166*
Tit	3:7	according to the hope of **e** life	*166*
Heb	5:9	became the author of **e** salvation	*166*
Heb	6:2	of the dead, and of **e** judgment	*166*
Heb	9:12	having obtained **e** redemption	*166*
Heb	9:14	who through the **e** Spirit offered	*166*
Heb	9:15	the promise of **e** redemption	*166*
1Pe	5:10	who hath called us unto his **e** glory	*166*
1Jn	1:2	shew unto you that **e** life, which	*166*
1Jn	2:25	he hath promised us, even **e** life	*166*
1Jn	3:15	no murderer hath **e** life abiding in	*166*
1Jn	5:11	that God hath given to us **e** life	*166*
1Jn	5:13	ye may know that ye have **e** life	*166*
1Jn	5:20	This is the true God, and **e** life	*166*
Jude	7	suffering the vengeance of **e** fire	*166*
Jude	21	of our Lord Jesus Christ unto **e** life	*166*

ETERNITY

Isa	57:15	and lofty One that inhabiteth **e**,	5703

EUNUCH

Ac	8:34	the **e** answered Philip, and said	*2135*
Ac	8:39	that the **e** saw him no more:	*2135*

EUNUCHS

Isa	39:7	and they shall be **e** in the palace of	5631
Isa	56:4	unto the **e** that keep my sabbaths	5631
Da	1:7	the prince of the **e** gave names:	5631
Da	1:18	prince of the **e** brought them in	5631
Mt	19:12	**For there are some e, which were**	*2135*

EVANGELIST

Ac	21:8	entered the house of Philip the **e**,	*2099*
2Ti	4:5	afflictions, do the work of an **e**,	*2099*

EVANGELISTS

Eph	4:11	and some, **e**; and some, pastors	*2099*

EVEN

Ge	27:38	bless me, **e** me also, O my father	1571
Ex	16:12	At **e** ye shall eat flesh, and in the	6153
Le	17:15	and be unclean until the **e**:	6153
Le	23:5	day of the first month at **e**	6153
Le	23:32	the ninth day of the month at **e**,	6153
Nu	9:15	and at **e** there was upon the	6153
Nu	9:21	abode from **e** unto the morning,	6153
Nu	19:10	and be unclean until the **e**:	6153
Nu	28:4	other lamb shalt thou offer at **e**;	6153
Dt	12:31	for **e** their sons and their	1571
Dt	16:6	sacrifice the passover at **e**,	6153
Dt	18:20	**e** that prophet shall die	
Dt	28:67	Would God it were **e** and at **e**	6153
Dt	32:39	that I, **e** I, am he, and there is	
Jgs	20:23	wept before the Lord until **e**	6153
Jgs	21:2	abode there till **e** before God	6153
Ru	2:17	she gleaned in the field until **e**,	6153
2Sa	1:12	and fasted until **e**, for Saul, and	6153
1Ki	18:22	I, **e** I only, remain a prophet of the	
1Ki	19:14	and I, **e** I only, am left: and they	
1Ch	21:17	**e** I it is that have sinned and done evil	
Ezr	4:5	**e** until the reign of Darius king	
Ezr	7:21	And I, **e** I Artaxerxes the king,	
Job	31:6	me be weighed in an **e** balance,	6664
Ps	26:12	My foot standeth in an **e** place:	4334
Ps	139:10	**E** there shall thy hand lead me,	1571
Pr	14:13	**E** in laughter the heart is	1571
Pr	14:20	is hated **e** of his own neighbour:	1571
Pr	16:4	**e** the wicked for the day of evil.	1571
Pr	16:7	he maketh **e** his enemies to be at	1571
Pr	17:28	**E** a fool, when he holdeth his	1571
Pr	20:11	**E** a child is known by his doings,	1571
Pr	28:9	**e** his prayer shall be abomination.	1571
Ecc	2:12	**e** that which hath been already	853
Ecc	2:15	so it happeneth **e** to me;	1571
Ecc	11:5	**e** so thou knowest not the works	3602
Isa	37:16	thou art the God, **e** thou alone	
Isa	37:20	thou art the Lord, **e** thou only	
Isa	43:11	I, **e** I, am the Lord;	
Isa	43:25	I, **e** I, am he that blotteth out	
Isa	51:12	I, **e** I, am he that comforteth you:	
Jer	6:11	**e** the husband with the wife	1571
Jer	23:39	behold, I, **e** I, will utterly forget	
Jer	49:37	evil upon them, **e** my fierce anger,	853
Eze	5:8	Behold, I, **e** I, am against thee,	1571
Eze	6:3	Behold, I, **e** I, will bring a sword	
Eze	12:7	in the **e** I digged through the wall	6153
Eze	24:18	and at **e** my wife died;	6153
Eze	34:11	Behold, I, **e** I, will both search	
Eze	34:20	Behold, I, **e** I, will judge between the	
Da	5:14	I have **e** heard of thee,	
Da	8:15	when I, **e** I Daniel, had seen	
Da	11:1	Darius the Mede, **e** I, stood to	
Hos	5:14	I, **e** I, will tear and go away;	
Mt	5:48	**perfect, e as your Father**	*5618*
Mk	13:22	**if it were possible, e the elect**	*2532*
Mk	13:35	**at e, or at midnight, or at the**	*3796*
Lk	18:11	**or e as this publican**	*2532*
Jn	17:16	**They are not of the world, e as I**	*2532*
Jn	20:21	**hath sent me, e so send I you**	*2504*
Ro	1:20	**e** his eternal power and Godhead;	
Ro	1:26	for **e** their women did change the	*5037*
Ro	5:7	a good man some would **e** dare to die.	
Ro	8:34	who is **e** at the right hand of God,	*2532*
Ro	15:3	For **e** Christ pleased not himself;	*2532*
1Co	11:14	Doth not **e** nature itself teach you,	*3762*
1Co	15:22	**e** so in Christ shall all be made	*2532*
2Co	1:8	that we despaired **e** of life:	*2532*
Php	2:8	obedient unto death, **e** the death	*1161*
Php	3:18	now tell you **e** weeping	*2532*
Col	1:14	**e** the forgiveness of sins:	
Col	3:13	**e** as Christ forgave you, so also do	*2532*
Jas	2:17	**E** so faith, if it hath not works,	*2532*
Jas	3:5	**E** so the tongue is a little member	*2532*
1Jn	3:3	purifieth himself, **e** as he is pure	*2531*
1Jn	3:7	is righteous, **e** as he is righteous	*2531*
Rev	22:20	**E** so, come, Lord Jesus	*3483*

EVENING

Ge	1:5	**e** and the morning were the first	6153
Ge	1:8	**e** and the morning were the second	6153
Ge	1:13	**e** and the morning were the third	6153
Ge	1:19	**e** and the morning were the fourth	6153
Ge	1:23	**e** and the morning were the fifth	6153
Ge	1:31	**e** and the morning were the sixth	6153
Ex	12:6	Israel shall kill it in the **e**	6153
Ex	16:8	shall give you in the **e** flesh to eat,	6153
1Ki	18:36	the offering of the **e** sacrifice	
Ezr	9:4	I sat astonished until the **e** sacrifice.	6153
Ps	55:17	**E**, and morning, and at noon	6153
Ecc	11:6	in the **e** withhold not thine hand:	6153
Jer	6:4	shadows of the **e** are stretched out	6153
Eze	46:2	gate shall not be shut until the **e**	6153
Da	8:26	vision of the **e** and the morning	6153
Mt	16:2	**When it is e, ye say, It will be fair**	*3798*
Lk	24:29	toward **e**, and the day is far spent,	*2073*
Jn	20:19	same day at **e**, being the first	*3798*

EVENT

Ecc	2:14	one **e** happeneth to them all	4745
Ecc	9:2	one **e** to the righteous, and to the	4745
Ecc	9:3	that there is one **e** unto all:	4745

EVER See also EVERMORE.

Ge	3:22	life, and eat, and live for **e**:	5769
Ge	13:15	I give it, and to thy seed for **e**	5769
Ge	43:9	let me bear the blame for **e**:	3605, 3117
Ge	44:32	the blame to my father for **e**	3605, 3117
Ex	3:15	this is my name for **e**, and	5769
Ex	12:14	a feast by an ordinance for **e**	5769
Ex	28:43	it shall be a statute for **e** unto him	5769
Ex	31:17	the children of Israel for **e**:	5769

Le	16:31	afflict your souls, by a statute for **e**	5769
Le	25:23	The land shall not be sold for **e**:	6783
Dt	4:33	Did **e** people hear the voice of God	
Dt	12:28	with thy children after thee for **e**,	5769
Jos	4:24	fear the Lord your God for **e**	3605, 3117
1Sa	3:13	I will judge his house for **e**	5769
2Sa	7:13	the throne of his kingdom for **e**	5769
1Ki	10:9	the Lord loved Israel for **e**,	5769
1Ki	11:39	seed of David, but not for **e**	3605, 3117
2Ki	21:7	will I put my name for **e**:	5769
1Ch	28:9	he will cast thee off for **e**	5703
Ps	10:16	The Lord is King for **e**	5769
Ps	22:26	him: your heart shall live for **e**	5703
Ps	23:6	the house of the Lord for **e**,	753, 3117
Ps	33:11	counsel of the Lord standeth for **e**,	5769
Ps	45:6	Thy throne, O God, is for **e**	5769
Ps	51:3	and my sin is **e** before me.	8548
Ps	73:26	heart, and my portion for **e**.	5769
Ps	79:5	Lord? wilt thou be angry for **e**?	5331
Ps	103:9	neither will he keep his anger for **e**.	5769
Ps	110:4	Thou art a priest for **e** after the	5769
Ps	119:89	For **e**, O Lord, thy word is settled	5769
Ps	125:2	people from henceforth even for **e**.	5769
Ps	136:1	his mercy endureth for **e**	5769
Ps	136:26	his mercy endureth for **e**	5769
Pr	8:23	the beginning, or **e** the earth	6924
Pr	12:19	truth shall be established for **e**	5703
Pr	27:24	for riches are not for **e**	5769
Ecc	2:16	more than of the fool for **e**;	5769
Ecc	3:14	God doeth, it shall be for **e**	5769
Ecc	12:6	Or **e** the silver cord be loosed,	
Isa	40:8	word of our God shall stand for **e**	5769
La	3:31	For the Lord will not cast off for **e**	5769
La	5:19	Thou O Lord, remainest for **e**;	5769
Eze	43:7	midst of the children of Israel for **e**,	5769
Da	4:34	and honoured him that liveth for **e**,	5957
Da	6:26	the living God, and stedfast for **e**,	5957
Da	12:3	righteousness as the stars for **e**	5769
Mic	7:18	he retaineth not his anger for **e**,	5703
Zec	1:5	prophets, do they live for **e**?	5769
Mt	6:13	**power, and the glory, for e**	*165*
Lk	15:31	**Son, thou art e with me, and all**	*3842*
Jn	4:29	told me all things that **e** I did:	*3745*
Jn	6:58	**of this bread shall live for e**	*165*
Jn	8:35	**but the Son abideth e**	*165*
Jn	10:8	**All that e came before me are**	*3745*
Ro	1:25	Creator, who is blessed for **e**	*165*
Heb	1:8	thy throne, O God, is for **e** and **e**:	*165*
Heb	7:21	Thou art a priest for **e** after the	*165*
Heb	7:25	he **e** liveth to make intercession	*3842*
Heb	13:8	yesterday, and to day, and for **e**	*165*
1Jn	2:17	doeth the will of God abideth for **e**.	*165*
Jude	25	and power, both now and **e**.	*3956, 165*
Rev	5:13	and unto the Lamb for **e** and **e**	*165*
Rev	11:15	and he shall reign for **e** and **e**	*165*
Rev	14:11	torment ascendeth up for **e** and **e**:	*165*
Rev	20:10	tormented day and night for **e** and **e**.	*165*
Rev	22:5	and they shall reign for **e** and **e**.	*165*

EVERLASTING

Ge	9:16	I may remember the **e** covenant	5769
Ge	17:7	an **e** covenant, to be a God unto	5769
Ge	17:8	for an **e** possession; and I will be	5769
Ge	17:13	be in your flesh for an **e** covenant.	5769
Ge	49:26	the utmost bound of the **e** hills:	5769
Ex	40:15	an **e** priesthood throughout their	5769
Le	16:34	this shall be an **e** statute unto you,	5769
Dt	33:27	and underneath are the **e** arms:	5769
Ps	24:7	be ye lift up, ye **e** doors;	5769
Ps	24:9	even lift them up, ye **e** doors;	5769
Ps	100:5	the Lord is good; his mercy is **e**;	5769
Ps	139:24	and lead me in the way **e**	5769
Ps	145:13	Thy kingdom is an **e** kingdom,	5769
Pr	8:23	I was set up from **e**, from the	5769
Isa	9:6	The **e** Father, The Prince of Peace	5703
Isa	33:14	us shall dwell with **e** burnings?	5769
Isa	40:28	not heard, that the **e** God, the Lord,	5769
Isa	55:3	I will make an **e** covenant with you,	5769
Jer	10:10	the living God, and an **e** king:	5769
Jer	31:3	I have loved thee with an **e** love:	5769
Eze	37:26	shall be an **e** covenant with them:	5769
Da	4:34	whose dominion is an **e** dominion,	5957
Da	7:27	whose kingdom is an **e** kingdom,	5957
Da	9:24	and to bring in **e** righteousness,	5769
Da	12:2	some to **e** life, and some to shame	5769
Mic	5:2	forth have been from of old, from **e**	5769
Mt	19:29	**and shall inherit e life.**	*166*
Mt	25:41	**from me, ye cursed, into e fire,**	*166*
Mt	25:46	**shall go away into e punishment:**	*166*
Lk	18:30	**and in the world to come life e**	*166*
Jn	3:16	**should not perish, but have e life**	*166*
Jn	4:14	**of water springing up into e life.**	*166*
Jn	5:24	**on him that sent me, hath e life,**	*166*
Jn	6:47	**believeth on me hath e life.**	*166*
Jn	12:50	**that his commandment is life e:**	*166*
Ro	16:26	the commandment of the **e** God,	*166*
Gal	6:8	shall of the spirit reap life **e**	*166*
2Th	1:9	be punished with **e** destruction	*166*
2Th	2:16	and hath given us **e** consolation	*166*
1Ti	1:16	believe on him to life **e**	*166*
1Ti	6:16	to whom be honour and power **e**	*166*
Heb	13:20	the blood of the **e** covenant,	*166*
2Pe	1:11	to the **e** kingdom of our Lord and	*166*
Jude	6	he hath reserved in **e** chains	*126*
Rev	14:6	having the **e** gospel to preach	*166*

EVERMORE

2Sa	22:51	unto David, and to his seed for **e**	5769
Ps	16:11	hand there are pleasures for **e**	5331
Ps	37:27	and do good; and dwell for **e**	5769
Ps	121:8	from this time forth, and even for **e**	5769
Ps	133:3	the blessing, even life for **e**	5769
Eze	37:28	shall be in the midst of them for **e**	5769
Jn	6:34	Lord, **e** give us this bread	*3842*
2Co	11:31	Christ, which is blessed for **e**,	*3588, 165*
1Th	5:16	Rejoice **e**	*3842*
Heb	7:28	Son, who is consecrated for **e**	*3588, 165*
Rev	1:18	**I am alive for e,**	*3588, 165*

EVERY

Ge	1:31	God saw **e** thing that he had made,	3605
Ge	2:16	**e** tree of the garden thou mayest	3605
Ge	6:5	**e** imagination of the thoughts	3605
Ge	6:20	two of **e** sort shall come unto thee,	3605
Ge	17:10	**E** man child among you shall be	3605
Ge	45:1	Cause **e** man to go out from me	3605
Ex	1:22	**E** son that is born ye shall cast	3605
Le	20:9	**e** one that curseth his father or	376
Nu	21:8	**E** one that is bitten, when he	3605
Dt	8:3	but by **e** word that proceedeth	3605
Dt	11:24	**E** place whereon the soles of your	3605
Jgs	21:25	**e** man did that which was right in	

1Ki	5:4	God hath given me rest on **e** side,	5437
2Ki	17:29	Howbeit **e** nation made gods	
Job	42:2	I know that thou canst do **e** thing,	3605
Ps	39:5	**e** man at his best state is altogether	3605
Ps	39:6	**e** man walketh in a vain shew:	
Ps	115:8	so is **e** one that trusteth in them.	3605
Ps	119:104	therefore I hate **e** false way.	3605
Ps	145:16	the desire of **e** living thing.	3605
Ps	150:6	Let **e** thing that hath breath	3605
Pr	14:1	**E** wise woman buildeth her house:	
Pr	14:15	The simple believeth **e** word:	3605
Pr	15:3	The eyes of the Lord are in **e** place,	3605
Pr	16:5	**E** one that is proud in heart	3605
Pr	21:2	**E** way of a man is right in his	3605
Pr	30:5	**E** word of God is pure:	3605
Ecc	3:1	To **e** thing there is a season,	3605
Ecc	3:1	to **e** purpose under the heaven:	3605
Ecc	3:11	**e** thing beautiful in his time:	3605
Ecc	12:14	God shall bring **e** work into	3605
Ecc	12:14	with **e** secret thing, whether it be	3605
Isa	40:4	**E** valley shall be exalted	3605
Isa	40:4	**e** mountain and hill shall be made	3605
Isa	45:23	unto me **e** knee shall bow,	3605
Isa	55:1	Ho, **e** one that thirsteth,	3605
La	3:23	They are new **e** morning: great is	
La	4:1	poured out in the top of **e** street.	3605
Jnh	1:5	and cried **e** man unto his god,	
Mal	2:17	**E** one that doeth evil is good in	3605
Mt	4:4	**but by e word that proceedeth out**	*3956*
Mt	7:8	**For e one that asketh receiveth;**	*3956*
Mt	12:36	**e idle word that men shall speak**	*3956*
Mk	16:15	**preach the gospel to e creature**	*3956*
Lk	2:41	**e** year at the feast of the passover	*2596*
Lk	3:5	**E** valley shall be filled,	*3956*
Lk	4:4	**but by e word of God.**	*3956*
Lk	11:10	**For e one that asketh receiveth;**	*3956*
Lk	11:17	**E kingdom divided against itself**	*3956*
Lk	18:14	**e one that exalteth himself shall**	*3956*
Jn	3:8	**e one that is born of the Spirit**	*3956*
Ac	2:8	hear we **e** man in our own tongue,	*1538*
Ac	17:27	he be not far from **e** one of us:	*1538*
Ac	18:4	in the synagogue **e** sabbath,	*3956*
Ac	20:23	Holy Ghost witnesseth in **e** city,	*2596*
Ac	20:31	to warn **e** one night and day,	*1538*
Ac	21:26	be offered for **e** one of them.	*1538*
Ac	21:28	that teacheth all men **e** where	*3837*
Ac	22:19	beat in **e** synagogue them that	*2596*
Ac	26:11	them oft in **e** synagogue,	*3956*
Ro	1:16	salvation to **e** one that believeth;	*3956*
Ro	2:6	to **e** man according to his deeds:	1538
Ro	3:4	God be true, but **e** man a liar	*3956*
Ro	14:5	another esteemeth **e** day alike	*3956*
Ro	14:5	Let **e** man be fully persuaded	*1538*
Ro	14:11	**e** knee shall bow to me,	*3956*
Ro	14:12	**e** one of us shall give account	*1538*
1Co	3:13	the fire shall try **e** man's work	*1538*
1Co	11:3	the head of **e** man is Christ;	*3956*
2Co	4:8	We are troubled on **e** side,	*1722, 3956*
Gal	3:13	is **e** one that hangeth on a tree:	*3956*
Gal	6:5	**e** man shall bear his own burden	*1538*
Eph	4:14	about with **e** wind of doctrine,	*3596*
Php	1:3	upon **e** remembrance of you,	*3956*
Php	2:10	name of Jesus **e** knee should bow,	*3596*
Php	2:11	And that **e** tongue should confess	*3596*
1Th	5:18	In **e** thing give thanks: for this	*3956*
2Ti	2:19	Let **e** one that nameth the name	*3956*
Heb	2:9	God should taste death for **e** man	*3956*
Heb	12:1	let us lay aside **e** weight, and the	*3956*
Heb	12:6	and scourgeth **e** son whom he	*3956*
Jas	1:14	**e** man is tempted, when he is	*2535*
Jas	1:17	**E** good gift and **e** perfect gift	*3956*
Jas	1:19	let **e** man be swift to hear, slow to	*3956*
Jas	3:16	there is confusion and **e** evil work.	*3956*
1Jn	2:29	**e** one that doeth righteousness is	*3956*
1Jn	3:3	And **e** man that hath this hope	*3956*
1Jn	4:1	believe not **e** spirit, but try the	*3956*
Rev	1:7	**e** eye shall see him, and they also	*3956*
Rev	5:13	And **e** creature which is in heaven	*3956*
Rev	16:3	and **e** living soul died in the sea	*3956*
Rev	20:13	were judged **e** man according to	*1538*
Rev	21:21	**e** several gate was of one pearl:	*1538*
Rev	22:2	yielded her fruit **e** month:	*2596, 1520, 1538*
Rev	22:12	**to give e man according as his**	*1538*
Rev	22:18	I testify unto **e** man that heareth	*3956*

EVIDENCE

Jer	32:14	this **e** of the purchase,	5612
Heb	11:1	the **e** of things not seen	*1650*

EVIDENT

Gal	3:11	in the sight of God, it is **e**: for	*1212*
Php	1:28	is to them an **e** token of perdition,	*1732*
Heb	7:14	For it is **e** that our Lord sprang	*4271*

EVIL

Ge	2:9	tree of knowledge of good and **e**	7451
Ge	3:5	be as gods, knowing good and **e**	7451
Ge	6:5	of his heart was only **e** continually	7451
Ge	8:21	imagination of man's heart is **e**	7451
Ge	37:20	Some **e** beast hath devoured him:	7451
Ge	47:9	few and **e** have the days of the	7451
Ge	48:16	which redeemed me from all **e**,	7451
Ge	50:20	for you, ye thought **e** against me;	7451
Ex	10:10	look to it; for **e** is before you	7451
Ex	23:2	not follow a multitude to do **e**;	7451
Ex	32:14	**e** which he thought to do unto his	7451
Nu	13:32	they brought up an **e** report of	1681
Nu	14:35	do it unto all this **e** congregation,	7451
Nu	14:37	that did bring up the **e** report	7451
Dt	13:5	So shalt thou put the **e** away	7451
Dt	15:9	thine eye be **e** against thy poor	7489
Dt	19:19	put the **e** away from among you	7451
Dt	30:15	life and good, and death and **e**;	7451
Jos	24:15	if it seem **e** unto you to serve the	7489
Jgs	20:13	death, and put away **e** from Israel.	7451
1Sa	12:19	have added unto all our sins this **e**:	7451
1Sa	16:14	an **e** spirit from the Lord troubled	7451
1Sa	16:16	the **e** spirit from God is upon thee	7451
1Sa	16:23	it came to pass, when the **e** spirit	7451
1Sa	25:21	he hath requited me **e** for good	7451
2Sa	13:16	**e** in sending me away is greater	7451
2Sa	19:35	I discern between good and **e**?	7451
2Sa	24:16	the Lord repented him of the **e**,	7451
1Ki	11:6	Solomon did **e** in the sight of the	7451
2Ki	8:12	I know the **e** that thou wilt do	7451
2Ki	17:17	to do **e** in the sight of the Lord,	7451
2Ki	21:9	seduced them to do more **e** than	7451
1Ch	21:15	and he repented him of the **e**	7451
2Ch	18:17	prophesy good unto me, but **e**?	7451
Ne	13:18	our God bring all this **e** upon us	7451
Est	8:6	**e** that shall come unto my people?	7451
Job	1:1	that feared God, and eschewed **e**	7451
Job	2:10	God, and shall we not receive **e**?	7451

Ps 23:4 I will fear no **e**: for thou art 7451
Ps 34:14 Depart from **e**, and do good; seek 7451
Ps 35:12 They rewarded me **e** for good to 7451
Ps 37:27 Depart from **e**, and do good; and 7451
Ps 51:4 and done this **e** in thy sight: 7451
Ps 56:5 their thoughts are against me for **e**. 7451
Ps 97:10 Ye that love the Lord, hate **e**: 7451
Ps 109:5 have rewarded me **e** for good 7451
Pr 1:16 their feet run to **e**, and make haste 7451
Pr 3:7 fear the Lord, and depart from **e** 7451
Pr 3:29 not **e** against thy neighbour 7451
Pr 6:24 To keep thee from the **e** woman, ... 7451
Pr 8:13 The fear of the Lord is to hate **e**: 7451
Pr 14:16 man feareth, and departeth from **e**: 7451
Pr 15:3 eyes of the Lord … beholding the **e** 7451
Pr 16:4 even the wicked for the day of **e** 7451
Pr 16:6 of the Lord men depart from **e** 7451
Pr 16:27 An ungodly man diggeth up **e**: 7451
Pr 17:13 Whoso rewardeth **e** for good 7451
Pr 20:8 A king … scattereth away all **e** with 7451
Pr 20:22 Say not thou I will recompense **e**; 7451
Pr 21:10 The soul of the wicked desireth **e**; 7451
Pr 24:19 Fret not thyself because of **e** men, ... 7489
Pr 28:5 **E** men understand not judgment: 7451
Pr 31:12 She will do him good and not **e** 7451
Ecc 2:21 This also is vanity and a great **e** 7451
Ecc 4:3 **e** work that is done under the sun 7451
Ecc 5:1 they consider not that they do **e** 7451
Ecc 8:11 sentence against an **e** work is not 7451
Ecc 8:11 men is fully set in them to do **e** 7451
Ecc 8:12 a sinner do **e** an hundred times, ... 7451
Ecc 12:1 while the **e** days come not, nor the 7451
Ecc 12:14 it be good, or whether it be **e** 7451
Isa 5:20 them that call **e** good, and good **e**; 7451
Isa 41:23 do good, nor do **e**, that we may be 7489
Isa 45:7 I make peace, and create **e**: I 7451
Isa 59:7 Their feet run to **e**, and they 7451
Jer 3:17 the imagination of their **e** heart 7451
Jer 4:6 I will bring **e** from the north, ... 7451
Jer 4:22 they are wise to do **e**, but to 7489
Jer 7:24 in the imagination of their **e** heart 7451
Jer 11:8 the imagination of their **e** heart: 7451
Jer 16:12 the imagination of his **e** heart 7451
Jer 18:8 If that nation, … turn from their **e** 7451
Jer 18:12 do the imagination of his **e** heart 7451
Jer 42:6 it be good, or whether it be **e**, ... 7451
Eze 33:11 turn ye from your **e** ways; for 7451
Eze 36:31 ye remember your own **e** ways, ... 7451
Da 9:12 by bringing upon us a great **e**: 7451
Am 5:14 Seek good, and not **e**, that ye may 7451
Am 5:15 Hate the **e**, and love the good, ... 7451
Jnh 1:7 for whose cause that **e** is upon us. 7451
Jnh 4:2 and repentest thee of the **e** 7451
Mic 2:1 and work **e** upon their beds! 7451
Mic 3:2 Who hate the good, and love the **e**; 7451
Hab 1:13 art of purer eyes than to behold **e**, ... 7451
Mal 1:8 offer the lame and sick, is it not **e**? 7451
Mal 2:17 Every one that doeth **e** is good 7451
Mt 5:11 **shall say all manner of e** *4190, 4487*
Mt 5:45 **maketh his sun to rise on the e** *4190*
Mt 6:13 **but deliver us from e:** *4190*
Mt 6:23 **if thine eye be e, thy whole body** *4190*
Mt 6:34 **Sufficient unto the day is the e** *2549*
Mt 7:11 **If ye then, being e, know how to** *4190*
Mt 7:17 **corrupt tree bringeth forth e fruit.** *4190*
Mt 20:15 **Is thine eye e, because I am good?** *4190*
Mt 27:23 Why, what **e** hath he done? *2556*
Mk 15:14 Why, what **e** hath he done? *2556*
Lk 6:45 **and an e man out of the e** *4190*
Lk 11:4 **but deliver us from e** *4190*
Lk 11:13 **If ye then, being e, know how to** *4190*
Lk 11:34 **when thine eye is e, thy body also** *4190*
Lk 23:22 Why, what **e** hath he done? *2556*
Jn 3:19 **light, because their deeds were e** *4190*
Jn 3:20 **every one that doeth e hateth the** *5337*
Ac 23:9 We find no **e** in this man: *2556*
Ro 1:30 inventors of **e** things, disobedient *2556*
Ro 3:8 that we say,) Let us do **e**, that good *2556*
Ro 7:19 but the **e** which I would not *2556*
Ro 7:21 do good, **e** is present with me *2556*
Ro 12:9 Abhor that which is **e**; cleave to *4190*
Ro 12:17 Recompense to no man **e** for **e** *2556*
Ro 12:21 but overcome **e** with good *2556*
Ro 14:16 Let not then your good be **e** spoken of:
1Co 13:5 easily provoked, thinketh no **e**; *2556*
1Co 15:33 **e** communications corrupt good *2556*
Gal 1:4 deliver us from this present **e** *4190*
Eph 5:16 the time, because the days are **e** *4190*
Eph 6:13 be able to withstand in the **e** day *4190*
1Th 5:15 See that none render **e** for **e** *2556*
1Th 5:22 Abstain from all appearance of **e** *4190*
1Ti 6:10 love of money is the root of all **e**: *2556*
Tit 3:2 speak **e** of no man, to be no *987*
Heb 10:22 sprinkled from an **e** conscience *4190*
Jas 1:13 God cannot be tempted with **e** *2556*
Jas 3:8 an unruly **e**, full of deadly poison *2556*
Jas 4:16 boastings: all such rejoicing is **e** *4190*
1Pe 3:9 Not rendering **e** for **e**, or railing *2556*
1Pe 3:11 let him eschew **e**, and do good; *2556*
1Pe 3:12 Lord is against them that do **e** *2556*
3Jn 11 that doeth **e** hath not seen God *2554*
Rev 2:2 **canst not bear them which are e:** *2556*

EVILDOER See also EVIL and DOER
Isa 9:17 every one is a hypocrite and an **e** 7489
1Pe 4:15 or as an **e**, or as a busybody *2555*

EVILDOERS
Ps 37:1 Fret not thyself because of **e** 7489
Jer 20:13 soul of the poor from the hand of **e** 7489
1Pe 3:16 speak evil of you, as of **e** 2555

EVILS
Dt 31:17 Are not these **e** come upon us, ... 7451
Ps 40:12 innumerable **e** have compassed me 7451
Lk 3:19 all the **e** which Herod had done *4190*

EWE
Ge 21:29 What mean these seven **e** lambs 3535
Le 22:28 cow or **e**, ye shall not kill it and 7716
2Sa 12:3 one little **e** lamb, which had had 3535

EXACT
Dt 15:2 shall not **e** it of his neighbour 5065
Dt 15:3 foreigner thou mayest **e** it again: 5065
Lk 3:13 **E** no more than that which is 4238

EXACTETH
Job 11:6 God **e** of thee less than thine 5382

EXALT
Ps 34:3 and let us **e** his name together 7311
Ps 99:9 **E** the Lord our God, and worship 7311
Ps 118:28 thou art my God, I will **e** thee 7311

Pr 4:8 E her, and she shall promote thee: 5549
Isa 14:13 I will e my throne above the stars 7311
Isa 25:1 thou art my God; I will e thee 7311
Eze 21:26 e him that is low, and abase him 1361
Ob 4 Though thou e thyself as the eagle 1361
Mt 23:12 And whosoever shall e himself 5312
1Pe 5:6 that he may e you in due time: 5312

EXALTED

2Sa 22:47 and e be the God of the rock of 7311
1Ch 29:11 thou art e as head above all 5375
Ne 9:5 name, which is e above all 7311
Ps 13:2 how long shall mine enemy be e 7311
Ps 18:46 let the God of my salvation be e 7311
Ps 46:10 I will be e among the heathen 7311
Ps 57:5 thou e, O God, above the heavens; 7311
Ps 97:9 thou art e far above all gods 5927
Ps 108:5 thou e, O God, above the heavens: 7311
Pr 11:11 of the upright the city is e: 7311
Isa 2:11 Lord alone shall be e in that day. 7682
Isa 33:5 The Lord is e, for he dwelleth on 7682
Isa 40:4 Every valley shall be e, and every 5375
Hos 13:6 filled, and their heart was e; 7311
Mt 11:23 which art e unto heaven, shall be 5312
Mt 23:12 shall humble himself shall be e 5312
Lk 1:52 seats, and e them of low degree 5312
Lk 10:15 which art e to heaven, shalt be 5312
Lk 14:11 that humbleth himself shall be e 5312
La 18:14 that humbleth himself shall be e 5312
Ac 2:33 being by the right hand of God e, ...5312
Ac 5:31 Him hath God e with his right 5312
2Co 11:7 abasing myself that ye might be e 5312
2Co 12:7 lest I should be e above measure 5229
Php 2:9 God also hath highly e him, ...5251
Jas 1:9 low degree rejoice in that he is e 5311

EXALTETH

Pr 14:29 he that is hasty of spirit e folly. 7311
Pr 14:34 Righteousness e a nation: but sin 7311
Pr 17:19 e his gate seeketh destruction. 1361
Lk 14:11 e himself shall be abased; 5312
Lk 18:14 that e himself shall be abased; 5312
2Co 10:5 every high thing that e itself 1869
2Th 2:4 Who opposeth and e himself 5229

EXAMINE

Ps 26:2 E me, O Lord, and prove me; 974
1Co 11:28 let a man e himself, and so let 1381
2Co 13:5 E yourselves, whether ye be in 3985

EXAMINED

Lk 23:14 I, having e him before you, ...350
Ac 12:19 found him not, he e the keepers, ...350

EXAMPLE

Mt 1:19 make her a public e, was minded 3856
Jn 13:15 For I have given you an e, that 5262
Heb 4:11 fall after the same e of unbelief, ...5262
Heb 8:5 serve unto the e and shadow 5262
Jas 5:10 for an e of suffering affliction 5262
1Pe 2:21 leaving us an e, that ye should 5261
Jude 7 for an e, suffering the vengeance 1164

EXAMPLES

1Co 10:6 Now these things were our e, ...5179

EXCEED

Mt 5:20 your righteouness shall e the 4052

EXCEEDED

1Sa 20:41 one with another, until David e 1431
1Ki 10:23 So king Solomon e all the kings 1431

EXCEEDEST

2Ch 9:6 thou e the fame that I heard 3254

EXCEEDETH

1Ki 10:7 thy wisdom and prosperity e the 3254

EXCEEDING

Ge 15:1 shield, and thy e great reward 3966
Ge 27:34 with a great and e bitter cry, ...3966
1Sa 2:3 Talk no more so e proudly;
Pr 30:24 the earth, but they are e wise:
Da 3:22 and the furnace e hot, the flame 3493
Da 6:23 was the king e glad for him 7689
Jnh 3:3 Nineveh was an e great city 430
Jnh 4:6 Jonah was e glad of the gourd 1419
Mt 2:10 they rejoiced with e great joy 4970
Mt 2:16 of the wise men, was e wroth, ...3029
Mt 4:8 him up into an e high mountain, ...3029
Mt 5:12 Rejoice, and be e glad; for great
Mt 17:23 And they were e sorry 4970
Mt 26:22 And they were e sorrowful, and 4970
Mt 26:38 soul is e sorrowful, even unto 4036
Mk 9:3 became shining, e white as snow; 3029
Mk 14:34 soul is e sorrowful unto death: 4036
Lk 23:8 when Herod saw Jesus, he was e glad: ...3029
Ro 7:13 sin ... might become e sinful 2596, 5236
2Co 4:17 a far more e and eternal 1519, 5236
Eph 1:19 the e greatness of his power 5235
Eph 3:20 e abundantly above all that we 5228
2Pe 1:4 us e great and precious promises:
Jude 24 the presence of his glory with e joy,
Rev 16:21 the plague thereof was e great 4970

EXCEEDINGLY

Ge 13:13 and sinners before the Lord e 3966
1Sa 26:21 the fool, and have erred e 7235, 3966
2Sa 13:15 Then Amnon hated her e; 1419, 3966
1Ch 29:25 the Lord magnified Solomon e 4605
Est 4:4 Then was the queen e grieved; 3966
Ps 106:14 But lusted e in the wilderness,
Ps 119:167 testimonies; and I love them e. 3966
Ps 123:3 for we are e filled with contempt 7227
Da 7:7 strong e; and it had great iron 3493
Jnh 1:16 Then the men feared the Lord e, ...1419
Jnh 4:1 it displeased Jonah e, and he was 1419
Mt 19:25 e amazed, saying, Who then can 4970
Mk 4:41 they feared e, and said one 5401, 3173
Mk 15:14 cried out the more e, Crucify him. 4056
Ac 26:11 and being e mad against them, ...4057
Gal 1:14 more e zealous of the traditions 4056
2Th 1:3 your faith groweth e, and the charity
Heb 12:21 Moses said, I e fear and quake:) 1630

EXCELLED

1Ki 4:30 Solomon's wisdom e the wisdom 7227

EXCELLENCY

Ps 47:4 the e of Jacob whom he loved 1347
Ps 62:4 to cast him down from his e: 7613
Ecc 7:12 but the e of knowledge is, that 3504
Eze 24:21 the e of your strength, the desire 1347
Am 6:8 I abhor the e of Jacob, and hate 1347
Am 8:7 hath sworn by the e of Jacob, ...1347
Na 2:2 turned away the e of Jacob, ...1347

2Co 4:7 the **e** of the power may be of God *5236*
Php 3:8 the **e** of the knowledge of Christ *5242*

EXCELLENT
Job 37:23 he is **e** in power, and in judgment, ... 7689
Ps 8:1 **e** is thy name in all the earth! 117
Ps 36:7 **e** is thy loving kindness, O God! 3368
Ps 148:13 his name alone is **e**; his glory is 7682
Ps 150:2 him according to his **e** greatness. 7230
Pr 12:26 The righteous is more **e** than his 8446
Pr 17:7 **E** speech becometh not a fool; 3499
Pr 17:27 of understanding is of an **e** spirit. 7119
Pr 22:20 not I written to thee **e** things in 7991
Isa 12:5 for he hath done **e** things: 1348
Da 4:36 and **e** majesty was added unto me, ... 3493
Da 5:12 Forasmuch as an **e** spirit, and 3493
Da 6:3 because an **e** spirit was in him; 3493
1Co 12:31 shew I unto you a more **e** way. ... *2596, 5236*
Php 1:10 ye may approve things that are **e**; *1308*
Heb 1:4 obtained a more **e** name than they *1313*
Heb 8:6 hath he obtained a more **e** ministry, ... *1313*
Heb 11:4 a more **e** sacrifice than Cain, ... *4119*
2Pe 1:17 a voice to him from the **e** glory *3169*

EXCELLEST
Pr 31:29 virtuously, but thou **e** them all. 5927

EXCELLETH
Ecc 2:13 Then I saw that wisdom **e** folly 3504
2Co 3:10 by reason of the glory that **e** *5235*

EXCEPT
Ge 31:42 **E** the God of my father, the God 3884
Ge 43:5 not see my face, **e** your brother 1115
Dt 32:30 **e** their Rock had sold 518, 3808, 3588
Est 2:14 **e** the king delighted in her 3588, 518
Ps 127:1 **E** the Lord build the house 518, 3808
Pr 4:16 sleep not, **e** they have done 3808
Da 3:28 nor any god, **e** their own God 3861
Am 3:3 walk together, **e** they be agreed? 1115
Mt 5:20 **e your righteousness shall exceed** *3362*
Mt 12:29 **e he first bind the strong man?** *3362*
Mt 18:3 **E ye be converted, and become** *3362*
Mt 26:42 **e I drink it, thy will be done** *3362*
Lk 13:3 **e ye repent, ye shall all** *3362*
Jn 3:3 **E a man be born again, he cannot** *3362*
Jn 3:5 **E a man be born of water and of** *3362*
Jn 4:48 **E ye see signs and wonders, ye** *3362*
Jn 6:44 **e the Father which hath sent me** *3362*
Jn 6:53 **E ye eat the flesh of the Son of** *3362*
Jn 20:25 **E** I shall see in his hands the print *3362*
Ac 8:31 How can I, **e** some man should *3362*
Ro 7:7 **e** the law had said, Thou shalt not *1508*
Ro 9:29 **E** the Lord of Sabaoth had left us *1508*
Ro 10:15 **e** they be sent, as it is written *3362*
1Co 15:36 sowest is not quickened, **e** it die: *3362*
2Co 13:5 is in you, **e** ye be reprobates? *1509*
2Th 2:3 **e** there come a falling away first, ... *3362*
2Ti 2:5 not crowned, **e** he strive lawfully *3362*
Rev 2:5 **out of his place, e thou repent** *3362*
Rev 2:22 **e they repent of their deeds.** *3362*

EXCESS
Mt 23:25 **they are full of extortion and e** *192*
Eph 5:18 drunk with wine, wherein is **e**; *810*
1Pe 4:3 **e** of wine, revellings *3632*
1Pe 4:4 **e** of riot, speaking evil of you: *401*

EXCHANGE
Ge 47:17 them bread in **e** for horses, and
Le 27:10 and the **e** thereof shall be holy 8545
Mt 16:26 **shall a man give in e for his soul?.** *465*
Mk 8:37 **shall a man give in e for his soul?.** *465*

EXCHANGERS
Mt 25:27 **to have put my money to the e,** *5133*

EXCLUDED
Ro 3:27 Where is boasting then? It is **e** *1576*

EXCUSE
Lk 14:18 **with one consent began to make e** *3868*
Ro 1:20 so that they are without **e**: *379*

EXCUSED
Lk 14:18 **and see it: I pray thee have me e** *3868*

EXCUSING
Ro 2:15 accusing or else **e** one another;) *626*

EXECUTE
Ex 12:12 will **e** judgment: I am the Lord. 6213
Nu 5:30 priest shall **e** upon her all this law. 6213
Dt 10:18 **e** the judgment of the fatherless 6213
Ps 119:84 when wilt thou **e** judgment on 6213
Ps 149:7 To **e** vengeance upon the heathen, ... 6213
Jer 7:5 thoroughly **e** judgment between 6213
Jer 21:12 **E** judgment in the morning, and 1777
Jer 23:5 and prosper, and shall **e** judgment 6213
Jer 33:15 and he shall **e** judgment and 6213
Eze 5:10 and I will **e** judgments in thee, ... 6213
Hos 11:9 not **e** the fierceness of mine anger 6213
Mic 5:15 And I will **e** vengeance in anger, ... 6213
Mic 7:9 my cause, and **e** judgment for me: 6213
Zec 7:9 **E** true judgment, and shew 8199
Zec 8:16 **e** the judgment of truth and peace 8199
Jn 5:27 **authority to e judgment also,** *4160*
Ro 13:4 a revenger to **e** wrath upon him
Jude 15 To **e** judgment upon all, and to *4160*

EXECUTED
Nu 33:4 gods also the Lord **e** judgments 6213
2Sa 8:15 David **e** judgment and justice 6213
Ezr 7:26 judgment be **e** speedily upon him, ... 5648
Ecc 8:11 an evil work is not **e** speedily, ... 6213
Jer 23:20 until he have **e**, and till he have 6213
Eze 11:12 neither **e** my judgments, but have 6213
Eze 20:24 they had not **e** my judgments, ... 6213
Eze 23:10 for they had **e** judgment upon her 6213
Eze 39:21 see my judgment that I have **e**, ... 6213
Lk 1:8 that while he **e** the priest's office *2407*

EXECUTETH
Ps 9:16 by the judgment which he **e**: 6213
Ps 103:6 The Lord **e** righteousness and 6213
Jer 5:1 if there be any that **e** judgment, ... 6213
Joel 2:11 for he is strong that **e** his word: 6213

EXECUTIONER
Mk 6:27 king sent an **e**, and commanded *4688*

EXERCISE
Ps 131:1 do I **e** myself in great matters, ... 1980
Jer 9:24 the Lord which **e** lovingkindness, ... 6213
Mk 10:42 **the Gentiles e lordship over them;** *2634*
1Ti 4:7 **e** thyself rather unto godliness *1128*
1Ti 4:8 For bodily **e** profiteth little: but *1129*

EXERCISED
Ecc 1:13 sons of man to be **e** therewith. 6031
Ecc 3:10 to the sons of men to be **e** in it. 6031
Heb 5:14 **e** to discern both good and evil. *1128*
Heb 12:11 unto them which are **e** thereby.........*1128*
2Pe 2:14 have **e** with covetous practices; *1128*

EXERCISETH
Rev 13:12 **e** all the power of the first beast *4160*

EXHORT
1Th 4:1 and **e** you by the Lord Jesus, ...*3870*
1Th 5:14 we **e** you, brethren, warn them *3870*
2Th 3:12 and **e** by our Lord Jesus Christ, ...*3870*
1Ti 2:1 I **e** therefore, that, first of all, ...*3870*
1Ti 6:2 These things teach and **e** *3870*
2Ti 4:2 rebuke, **e** with all long suffering *3870*
Tit 1:9 to **e** and to convince the gainsayers. *3870*
Tit 2:6 likewise **e** to be sober minded. *3870*
Tit 2:9 **E** servants to be obedient unto their
Tit 2:15 speak, and **e**, and rebuke with all *3870*
Heb 3:13 But **e** one another daily, while it *3870*
1Pe 5:1 I **e**, who am also an elder, ...*3870*
Jude 3 me to write unto you, and **e** you *3870*

EXHORTATION
Lk 3:18 **e** preached he unto the people *3870*
Ac 13:15 any word of **e** for the people, ...*3874*
1Co 14:3 edification, and **e**, and comfort *3874*
1Th 2:3 For our **e** was not of deceit, ...*3874*
1Ti 4:13 to reading, to **e**, to doctrine. *3874*
Heb 12:5 forgotten the **e** which speaketh *3874*

EXHORTED
Ac 11:23 and **e** them all, that with purpose *3870*

EXHORTING
Ac 14:22 **e** them to continue in the faith,........*3870*
Heb 10:25 but **e** one another: and so much *3870*

EXILE
2Sa 15:19 art a stranger, and also an **e** 1540
Isa 51:14 The captive **e** hasteneth that he 6808

EXORCISTS
Ac 19:13 vagabond Jews, **e**, took upon them *1845*

EXPECTATION
Ps 62:5 upon God; for my **e** is from him. 8615
Pr 10:28 the **e** of the wicked shall perish 8615
Pr 11:7 man dieth, his **e** shall perish: 8615
Pr 11:23 the **e** of the wicked is wrath. 8615
Pr 23:18 and thine **e** shall not be cut off. 8615
Pr 24:14 and thy **e** shall not be cut off. 8615
Isa 20:6 such is our **e** whither we flee 4007
Ro 8:19 the earnest **e** of the creature *603*
Php 1:20 to my earnest **e** and my hope, ...*603*

EXPECTED
Jer 29:11 not of evil, to give you an **e** end 8615

EXPECTING
Ac 3:5 **e** to receive something of them *4328*
Heb 10:13 **e** till his enemies be made his *1551*

EXPEDIENT
Jn 11:50 Nor consider that it is **e** for us, ...*4851*
Jn 16:7 **It is e for you that I go away:**..........*4851*
Jn 18:14 it was **e** that one man should die *4851*
1Co 6:12 unto me, but all things are not **e**: *4851*
1Co 10:23 but all things are not **e**:...............*4851*
2Co 12:1 not **e** for me doubtless to glory *4851*

EXPEL
Jos 23:5 shall **e** them from before you, ...1920
Jgs 11:7 Did not ye hate me, and **e** me 1644

EXPELLED
Jos 13:13 of Israel **e** not the Geshurites, ...3423
2Sa 14:14 his banished be not **e** from him. 5080
Ac 13:50 and **e** them out of their coasts. *1544*

EXPERIENCE
Ge 30:27 by **e** that the Lord hath blessed 5172
Ecc 1:16 my heart had great **e** of wisdom 7200
Ro 5:4 And patience, **e**; and **e**, hope: *1382*

EXPERT
1Ch 12:33 **e** in war, with all instruments of 6186
SS 3:8 being **e** in war: every man hath 3925
Jer 50:9 shall be as of a mighty **e** man; 7919
Ac 26:3 be **e** in all customs and questions *1109*

EXPIRED
1Sa 18:26 and the days were not **e**...............4390
2Sa 11:1 after the year was **e**, at the time 8666
1Ch 17:11 when thy days be **e** that thou 4390
1Ch 20:1 after the year was **e**, at the time 8666
2Ch 36:10 was **e**, king Nebuchadnezzar 8666
Est 1:5 And when these days were **e**, ...4390
Eze 43:27 these days are **e**, it shall be, ...3615
Ac 7:30 And when forty years were **e**, ...*4137*
Rev 20:7 when the thousand years are **e**, ...*5055*

EXPLOITS
Da 11:28 and he shall do **e**, and return to
Da 11:32 God shall be strong, and do **e**

EXPOUND
Jgs 14:14 not in three days **e** the riddle 5046

EXPOUNDED
Jgs 14:19 unto them which **e** the riddle..........5046
Mk 4:34 he **e** all things to his disciples. *1956*
Lk 24:27 he **e** unto them in all the scriptures *1329*
Ac 18:26 and **e** unto him the way of God *1620*
Ac 28:23 to whom he **e** and testified the *1620*

EXPRESS
Heb 1:3 and the **e** image of his person *5481*

EXPRESSED
1Ch 12:31 which were **e** by name, to come 5344
1Ch 16:41 were **e** by name, to give thanks 5344
2Ch 28:15 which were **e** by name rose up, ...5344

EXPRESSLY
1Sa 20:21 If I **e** say unto the lad, Behold, ...559
Eze 1:3 word of the Lord came **e** unto Ezekiel
1Ti 4:1 Now the Spirit speaketh **e**, ...*4490*

EXTEND
Ps 109:12 Let there be none to **e** mercy 4900
Isa 66:12 I will **e** peace to her like a river, ...5186

EXTENDED
Ezr 7:28 **e** mercy unto me before the king, ...5186

EXTINCT
Job 17:1 breath is corrupt, my days are **e**, ...2193

EXTOL
Ps 30:1 I will **e** thee, O Lord; for thou 7311
Ps 68:4 **e** him that rideth upon the 5549
Ps 145:1 I will **e** thee, my God, O king; 7311
Da 4:37 I Nebuchadnezzar praise and **e** 7313

EXTOLLED
Isa 52:13 he shall be exalted and **e**, and be 5375

EXTORTION
Eze 22:12 gained of thy neighbours by **e**, ...6233
Mt 23:25 **they are full of e and excess.** *724*

EXTORTIONER
1Co 5:11 a railer, or a drunkard, or an **e**; *727*

EXTORTIONERS
Lk 18:11 **not as other men are, e, unjust,** *727*
1Co 5:10 covetous, or **e**, or with idolaters; *727*
1Co 6:10 revilers, nor **e**, shall inherit the *727*

EXTREMITY
Job 35:15 he knoweth it not in great **e** 6580

EYE
Ex 21:24 **E** for **e**, tooth for tooth, hand for 5869
Le 24:20 **e** for **e**, tooth for tooth: as he 5869
Dt 7:16 **e** shall have no pity upon them: 5869
Dt 15:9 thine **e** be evil against thy poor 5869
Dt 19:13 Thine **e** shall not pity him, but 5869
Dt 19:21 but life shall go for life, **e** for **e**, ...5869
Dt 25:12 hand, thine **e** shall not pity her. 5869
Dt 32:10 he kept him as the apple of his **e** 5869
Dt 34:7 his **e** was not dim, nor his natural 5869
Job 16:20 mine **e** poureth out tears unto God 5869
Job 17:7 **e** also is dim by reason of sorrow, ...5869
Job 42:5 but now mine **e** seeth thee 5869
Ps 17:8 Keep me as the apple of the **e**, ...5869
Ps 32:8 I will guide thee with mine **e** 5869
Ps 33:18 the **e** of the Lord is upon them 5869
Ps 88:9 **e** mourneth by reason of affliction: 5869
Ps 94:9 he that formed the **e**, shall he not 5869
Pr 7:2 my law as the apple of thine **e** 5869
Pr 10:10 that winketh with the **e** causeth 5869
Pr 20:12 The hearing ear, and the seeing **e**, ...5869
Pr 28:22 hasteth to be rich hath an evil **e**, ...5869
Pr 30:17 The **e** that mocketh at his father, ...5869
Ecc 1:8 the **e** is not satisfied with seeing, ...5869
Ecc 4:8 is his **e** satisfied with riches; 5869
Isa 13:18 their **e** shall not spare children 5869
Isa 64:4 neither hath the **e** seen, O God, ...5869
Jer 13:17 mine **e** shall weep sore, and run 5869
La 1:16 mine **e**, mine **e** runneth down with 5869
La 2:18 let not the apple of thine **e** cease 5869
La 3:48 Mine **e** runneth down with rivers of ...5869
Eze 7:9 And mine **e** shall not spare, neither 5869
Eze 8:18 mine **e** shall not spare, neither 5869
Zec 2:8 you toucheth the apple of his **e** 5869
Mt 5:29 **if thy right e offend thee, pluck** *3788*
Mt 5:38 **e for an e, and a tooth for a** *3788*
Mt 6:22 **The light of the body is the e:** *3788*
Mt 6:23 **But if thine e be evil, thy whole** *3788*
Mt 7:4 **behold, a beam is in thine own e?** *3788*
Mt 18:9 **if thine e offend thee, pluck it** *3788*
Mt 19:24 **to go through the e of a needle,** *5169*
Mt 20:15 **thine e evil, because I am good?** *3788*
Lk 6:41 **the beam that is in thine own e?** *3788*
Lk 11:34 **The light of the body is the e:** *3788*
Lk 18:25 **camel to go through a needle's e,** *5168*
1Co 2:9 **E** hath not seen, nor ear heard *3788*
1Co 12:16 Because I am not the **e**, I am not *3788*
1Co 12:17 If the whole body were an **e**, where *3788*
1Co 12:21 the **e** cannot say unto the hand, ...*3788*
1Co 15:52 in the twinkling of an **e**, at the *3788*
Rev 1:7 every **e** shall see him, and they *3788*

EYED
Ge 29:17 Leah was tender **e**; but Rachel 5869
1Sa 18:9 Saul **e** David from that day 5770

EYELIDS
Job 16:16 on my **e** is the shadow of death; 6079
Ps 11:4 his **e** try, the children of men 6079
Pr 4:25 thine **e** look straight before thee 6079
Pr 6:4 thine eyes, nor slumber to thine **e** 6079
Pr 6:25 neither let her take thee with her **e** 6079
Pr 30:13 and their **e** are lifted up 6079

EYE'S
Ex 21:26 let him go free for his **e** sake 5869

EYES
Ge 3:5 then your **e** shall be opened, and 5869
Ge 3:6 and that it was pleasant to the **e**, ...5869
Ge 6:8 found grace in the **e** of the Lord 5869
Ge 16:4 her mistress was despised in her **e** 5869
Ge 18:2 And he lifted up his **e** and looked 5869
Ge 19:8 do ye to them as is good in your **e**: 5869
Ge 21:19 God opened her **e**, and she saw a 5869
Ge 22:13 Abraham lifted up his **e**, and looked ...5869
Ge 24:64 Rebekah lifted up her **e**, and when 5869
Ge 39:7 his master's wife cast her **e** upon 5869
Ex 24:17 in the **e** of the children of Israel 5869
Nu 5:13 be hid from the **e** of her husband, ...5869
Nu 10:31 thou mayest be to us instead of **e** 5869
Nu 15:39 your own heart and your own **e**, ...5869
Nu 22:31 the Lord opened the **e** of Balaam, ...5869
Nu 24:16 a trance, but having his **e** open: 5869
Dt 4:19 And lest thou lift up thine **e** unto 5869
Dt 9:17 and brake them before your **e** 5869
Dt 11:7 your **e** have seen all the great acts 5869
Dt 12:8 whatsoever is right in his own **e** 5869
Dt 13:18 which is right in the **e** of the Lord 5869
Dt 29:4 a heart to perceive, and **e** to see, ...5869
Dt 34:4 caused thee to see it with thine **e**, ...5869
Jos 5:13 he lifted up his **e** and looked, ...5869
Jgs 16:21 took him, and put out his **e**, ...5869
Jgs 16:28 of the Philistines for my two **e** 5869
Jgs 17:6 that which was right in his own **e** 5869
Jgs 21:25 that which was right in his own **e** 5869
1Sa 6:13 lifted up their **e**, and saw the ark, ...5869
1Sa 26:21 my soul was precious in thine **e** 5869
1Ki 9:3 **e** and mine heart shall be there 5869
1Ki 11:33 do that which is right in mine **e** 5869
1Ki 15:5 was right in the **e** of the Lord 5869
2Ki 4:34 and his **e** upon his **e**, and his hands 5869
2Ki 6:17 Lord, I pray thee, open his **e**, ...5869
2Ki 22:20 thine **e** shall not see all the evil 5869
2Ki 25:7 the sons of Zedekiah before his **e**, ...5869
2Ki 25:7 and put out the **e** of Zedekiah 5869
1Ch 13:4 was right in the **e** of all the people 5869
1Ch 21:16 And David lifted up his **e**, and saw 5869
2Ch 16:9 the **e** of the Lord run to and fro 5869
2Ch 20:12 but our **e** are upon thee 5869
2Ch 34:28 neither shall thine **e** see all the evil 5869

Ne	6:16	much cast down in their own **e**:	5869
Est	1:17	despise their husbands in their **e**,	5869
Job	2:12	they lifted up their **e** afar off,	5869
Job	32:1	he was righteous in his own **e**	5869
Job	34:21	his **e** are upon the ways of man,	5869
Ps	19:8	Lord is pure, enlightening the **e**	5869
Ps	25:15	Mine **e** are ever toward the Lord;	5869
Ps	36:1	there is no fear of God before his **e**	5869
Ps	66:7	his **e** behold the nations: let not	5869
Ps	101:3	set no wicked thing before mine **e**:	5869
Ps	115:5	**e** have they, but they see not:	5869
Ps	118:23	doing; it is marvellous in our **e**	5869
Ps	119:18	Open thou mine **e**, that I may	5869
Ps	119:37	mine **e** from beholding vanity;	5869
Ps	121:1	I will lift up mine **e** unto the hills,	5869
Ps	135:16	**e** have they, but they see not;	5869
Ps	145:15	The **e** of all wait upon thee:	5869
Pr	3:7	Be not wise in thine own **e**:	5869
Pr	3:21	let not them depart from thine **e**:	5869
Pr	4:21	Let them not depart from thine **e**;	5869
Pr	5:21	man are before the **e** of the Lord	5869
Pr	10:26	smoke to the **e**, so is the sluggard	5869
Pr	12:15	way of a fool is right in his own **e**:	5869
Pr	15:3	**e** of the Lord are in every place,	5869
Pr	16:2	of a man are clean in his own **e**;	5869
Pr	17:8	as a precious stone in the **e** of him	5869
Pr	20:8	scattereth away all evil with his **e**	5869
Pr	21:2	way of a man is right in his own **e**:	5869
Pr	23:5	thine **e** upon that which is not?	5869
Pr	23:29	cause? who hath redness of **e**?	5869
Pr	23:33	Thine **e** shall behold strange	5869
Pr	27:20	so the **e** of man are never satisfied	5869
Pr	29:13	the Lord lighteneth both their **e**	5869
Pr	30:12	that are pure in their own **e**,	5869
Ecc	2:10	**e** desired I kept not from them	5869
Ecc	2:14	The wise man's **e** are in his head;	5869
Ecc	5:11	beholding of them with their **e**?	5869
Ecc	6:9	Better is the sight of the **e** than	5869
Ecc	11:7	thing it is for the **e** to behold the	5869
Ecc	11:9	heart, and in the sight of thine **e**:	5869
Isa	5:21	them that are wise in their own **e**,	5869
Isa	6:5	for mine **e** have seen the King,	5869
Isa	6:10	lest they see with their **e**,	5869
Isa	11:3	not judge after the sight of his **e**	5869
Isa	17:7	and his **e** shall have respect to the	5869
Isa	33:15	and shutteth his **e** from seeing evil;	5869
Isa	35:5	the **e** of the blind shall be opened,	5869
Isa	42:7	To open the blind **e**, to bring out	5869
Isa	44:18	he hath shut their **e**, that they	5869
Isa	51:6	Lift up your **e** to the heavens,	5869
Isa	59:10	we grope as if we had no **e**:	5869
Jer	5:21	which have **e**, and see not;	5869
Jer	9:1	and mine **e** a fountain of tears	5869
Jer	14:17	Let mine **e** run down with tears	5869
Jer	16:17	mine **e** are upon all their ways:	5869
Jer	29:21	he shall slay them before your **e**;	5869
Jer	32:19	thine **e** are open upon all the ways	5869
Jer	52:11	Then he put out the **e** of Zedekiah;	5869
La	2:11	Mine **e** do fail with tears,	5869
Eze	6:9	their **e**, which go a whoring after	5869
Eze	10:12	wheels, were full of **e** round about	5869
Eze	18:12	and hath lifted up his **e** to the idols	5869
Eze	20:8	away the abominations of their **e**,	5869
Eze	22:26	hid their **e** from my sabbaths	5869
Eze	24:21	the desire of your **e**, and that which	5869
Eze	36:23	be sanctified in you before their **e**	5869
Eze	40:4	Son of man, behold with thine **e**,	5869
Eze	44:5	mark well, and behold with thine **e**,	5869
Da	4:34	Nebuchadnezzar lifted up mine **e**	5870
Da	8:21	great horn that is between his **e**	5869
Da	10:6	his **e** as lamps of fire, and his arms	5869
Am	9:4	will set mine **e** upon them for evil,	5869
Am	9:8	the **e** of the Lord God are upon	5869
Hab	1:13	Thou art of purer **e** than to behold	5869
Hag	2:3	not in your **e** in comparison of it	5869
Zec	3:9	upon one stone shall be seven **e**:	5869
Zec	4:10	they are the **e** of the Lord, which	5869
Zec	8:6	it also be marvellous in mine **e**?	5869
Mt	9:29	Then touched he their **e**, saying	*3788*
Mt	13:15	**time they should see with their e,**	*3788*
Mt	13:16	**blessed are your e, for they see:**	*3788*
Mt	20:34	their **e** received sight, and they	*3788*
Mt	21:42	**and it is marvellous in our e?**	*3788*
Mk	8:18	**Having e, see ye not? and having**	*3788*
Mk	8:23	and when he had spit on his **e**,	*3659*
Mk	9:47	**having two e to be cast into hell**	*3788*
Mk	12:11	**and it is marvellous in our e?**	*3788*
Lk	2:30	For mine **e** have seen thy salvation,	*3788*
Lk	10:23	**Blessed are the e which see the**	*3788*
Lk	16:23	**And in hell he lifted up his e,**	*3788*
Lk	18:13	**up so much as his e unto heaven,**	*3788*
Lk	19:42	**but now they are hid from thine e**	*3788*
Lk	24:16	**e** were holden that they should	*3788*
Jn	4:35	**Lift up your e, and look on the**	*3788*
Jn	9:6	he anointed the **e** of the blind man	*3788*
Jn	10:21	Can a devil open the **e** of the blind?	*3788*
Jn	11:41	Jesus lifted up his **e**, and said,	*3788*
Jn	12:40	He hath blinded their **e**, and	*3788*
Jn	17:1	and lifted up his **e** to heaven, and	*3788*
Ac	9:8	his **e** were opened, he saw no man:	*3788*
Ac	26:18	**To open their e, and to turn them**	*3788*
Ac	28:27	lest they should see with their **e**,	*3788*
Ro	3:18	is not fear of God before their **e**	*3788*
Ro	11:8	**e** that they should not see, and	*3788*
Gal	3:1	before whose **e** Jesus Christ hath	*3788*
Gal	4:15	have plucked out your own **e**,	*3788*
Eph	1:18	The **e** of your understanding being	*3788*
Heb	4:13	and opened unto the **e** of him with	*3788*
1Pe	3:12	For the **e** of the Lord are over the	*3788*
2Pe	2:14	Having **e** full of adultery, and that	*3788*
1Jn	1:1	which we have seen with our **e**,	*3788*
1Jn	2:11	that darkness hath blinded his **e**,	*3788*
1Jn	2:16	lust of the **e**, and the pride of life,	*3788*
Rev	1:14	and his **e** were as a flame of fire;	*3788*
Rev	2:18	**hath his e like unto a flame of**	*3788*
Rev	3:18	**and anoint thine e with eyesalve,**	*3788*
Rev	4:6	there four beasts full of **e** before	*3788*
Rev	4:8	and they were full of **e** within:	*3788*
Rev	5:6	seven **e**, which are the seven spirits	*3788*
Rev	7:17	wipe away all tears from their **e**	*3788*
Rev	19:12	His **e** were as a flame of fire,	*3788*
Rev	21:4	wipe away all tears from their **e**;	*3788*

EYESALVE

Rev	3:18	**and anoint thine eyes with e, that**	*2854*

EYESERVICE

Eph	6:6	Not with **e**, as menpleasers; but as	*3787*
Col	3:22	not with **e**, as menpleasers; but in	*3787*

EYEWITNESSES

Lk	1:2	which from the beginning were **e**,	*845*
2Pe	1:16	but were **e** of his majesty	*2030*

F

FABLES

1Ti	1:4	Neither give heed to **f** and endless	*3454*
1Ti	4:7	refuse profane and old wives' **f**	*3454*
2Pe	1:16	not followed cunningly devised **f**	*3454*

FACE

Ge	1:2	Spirit of God moved upon the **f** of	6440
Ge	3:19	In the sweat of thy **f** shalt thou eat	639
Ge	7:18	ark went upon the **f** of the waters	6440
Ge	17:17	Then Abraham fell upon his **f**	6440
Ge	32:30	for I have seen God **f** to **f**	6440
Ge	38:15	because she had covered her **f**	6440
Ge	48:11	I had not thought to see thy **f**:	6440
Ex	2:15	Moses fled from the **f** of Pharaoh,	6440
Ex	3:6	Moses hid his **f**; for he was afraid	6440
Ex	14:19	cloud went from before their **f**	
Ex	34:29	wist not that the skin of his **f** shone	6440
Nu	6:25	Lord make his **f** shine upon thee,	6440
Dt	5:4	Lord talked with you **f** to **f** in the	6440
Dt	34:10	whom the Lord knew **f** to **f**	6440
Jgs	6:22	seen an angel of the Lord **f** to **f**	6440
1Sa	24:8	David stooped with his **f** to the	639
1Ki	19:13	he wrapped his **f** in his mantle	6440
2Ki	4:29	lay my staff upon the **f** of the child	6440
2Ch	6:42	not away the **f** of thine anointed:	6440
2Ch	7:14	and pray, and seek my **f**,	6440
Est	7:8	mouth, they covered Haman's **f**	6440
Job	1:11	and he will curse thee to thy **f**	6440
Job	38:30	and the **f** of the deep is frozen	6440
Ps	27:9	Hide not thy **f** far from me;	6440
Ps	51:9	Hide thy **f** from my sins,	6440
Ps	69:17	hide not thy **f** from thy servant;	6440
Ps	80:7	of hosts, and cause thy **f** to shine;	6440
Pr	21:29	A wicked man hardeneth his **f**:	6440
Ecc	8:1	wisdom maketh his **f** to shine	6440
Isa	6:2	with twain he covered his **f**,	6440
Isa	50:7	have I set my **f** like a flint	6440
Jer	4:30	thou rentest thy **f** with painting	5869
Eze	1:10	the **f** of a man, and the **f** of a lion,	6440
Eze	10:14	the first **f** was the **f** of a cherub	6440
Eze	41:19	**f** of a young lion toward the palm	6440
Da	2:46	Nebuchadnezzar fell upon his **f**,	600
Da	8:18	I was in a deep sleep on my **f**	6440
Da	10:6	**f** as the appearance of lightning,	6440
Na	2:1	in pieces is come up before thy **f**:	6440
Mt	16:3	**ye can discern the f of the sky;**	*4383*
Mt	17:2	and his **f** did shine as the sun,	*4383*
Mt	18:10	**always behold the f of my Father**	*4383*
Mt	26:67	Then did they spit in his **f**,	*4383*
Lk	9:51	set his **f** to go to Jerusalem,	*4383*
Lk	22:64	struck him on the **f**, and asked	*4383*
Ac	6:15	saw his **f** as it had been the **f** of	*4383*
1Co	13:12	a glass, darkly; but then **f** to **f**:	*4383*
2Co	3:18	with open **f** beholding as in a glass	*4383*
Jas	1:23	beholding his natural **f** in a glass:	*4383*
3Jn	14	see thee, and we shall speak **f** to **f**	*4750*
Rev	4:7	the third beast had a **f** as a man	*4383*
Rev	10:1	and his **f** was as it were the sun	*4383*

FACES

Ge	9:23	and their **f** were backward, and	6440
Ex	37:9	were the **f** of the cherubims	6440
Nu	14:5	Moses and Aaron fell on their **f**	6440
1Ch	12:8	whose **f** were like the **f** of lions	6440
Isa	25:8	wipe away tears from off all **f**;	6440
Isa	53:3	we hid as it were our **f** from him;	6440
Jer	5:3	made their **f** harder than a rock;	6440
Jer	30:6	all **f** are turned into palenesss?	6440
Eze	1:6	And every one had four **f**,	6440
Eze	41:18	and every cherub had two **f**;	6440
Da	1:10	why should he see your **f** worse	6440
Na	2:10	**f** of them shall gather blackness	6440
Mt	6:16	**for they disfigure their f, that**	*4383*
Rev	11:16	upon their **f**, and worshipped God	*4383*

FADE

2Sa	22:46	Strangers shall **f** away, and they	5034
Isa	64:6	and we all do **f** as a leaf;	5034
Eze	47:12	whose leaf shall not **f**, neither	5034
Jas	1:11	so also shall the rich man **f** away	*3138*

FADETH

Isa	24:4	The earth mourneth and **f** away,	5034
Isa	40:8	the flower **f**: but the word of	5034
1Pe	5:4	a crown of glory that **f** not away	*262*

FADING

Isa	28:1	glorious beauty is a **f** flower,	5034
Isa	28:4	shall be a **f** flower, and as the	5034

FAIL

Ge	47:16	you for your cattle, if money **f**	656
Jos	1:5	I will not **f** thee, nor forsake thee	7503
1Ki	17:14	neither shall the cruse of oil **f**,	2637
Ezr	6:9	given them day by day without **f**:	7960
Est	9:28	should not **f** from among the Jews,	5674
Ps	69:3	eyes **f** while I wait for my God	3615
Ps	119:123	Mine eyes **f** for thy salvation	3615
Pr	22:8	and the rod of his anger shall **f**	3615
Isa	51:14	nor that his bread should **f**	2637
Jer	48:33	and I have caused wine to **f** from	7673
La	3:22	because his compassions **f** not	3615
Lk	16:17	**than one tittle of the law to f**	*4098*
Lk	22:32	**for thee, that thy faith f not:**	*1587*
1Co	13:8	there be prophecies, they shall **f**;	*2673*
Heb	12:15	any man **f** of the grace of God;	*5302*

FAILED

Ge	47:15	And when money **f** in the land	8552
Jos	3:16	the plain, even the salt sea, **f**,	8552
Ps	142:4	refuge **f** me; no man cared for my	6
Jer	51:30	their might hath **f**; they became	5405

FAILETH

Ps	38:10	heart panteth, my strength **f** me:	5800
Isa	15:6	grass **f**, there is no green thing	3615
Isa	41:17	and their tongue **f** for thirst, I the	5405
Zep	3:5	his judgment to light, he **f** not;	5737
Lk	12:33	**treasure in the heavens that f not,**	*413*
1Co	13:8	Charity never **f**: but whether	*1601*

FAILING

Dt	28:65	a trembling heart, and **f** of eyes	3631
Lk	21:26	**Men's hearts f them for fear,**	*574*

FAIN

Job	27:22	he would **f** flee out of his hand	1272
Lk	15:16	**he would f have filled his belly**	*1987*

FAINT

Ge	25:30	that same red pottage; for I am **f**:	5889
Dt	20:3	let not your hearts **f**, fear not,	7401
Pr	24:10	If thou **f** in the day of adversity	7503
Isa	40:30	Even the youths shall **f** and be	3286
Isa	40:31	and they shall walk, and not **f**	3286
La	1:22	sighs are many, and my heart is **f**	1742
Eze	21:7	and every spirit shall **f**, and all	3543
Mt	15:32	**lest they f in the way**	*1590*
Lk	18:1	always to pray, and not to **f**;	*1573*
Gal	6:9	we shall reap, if we **f** not	*1590*
Heb	12:5	**f** when thou art rebuked of him:	*1590*

FAINTED

Ge	45:26	Jacob's heart **f**, for he believed	6313
Ps	27:13	I had **f**, unless I had believed	
Jnh	2:7	When my soul **f** within me I	5848
Rev	2:3	**hast laboured, and hast not f**	*2577*

FAINTEST

Job	4:5	it is come upon thee, and thou **f**;	3811

FAINTETH

Ps	119:81	My soul **f** for thy salvation:	3615
Isa	10:18	be as when a standardbearer **f**	4549

FAINTHEARTED

Dt	20:8	there that is fearful and **f**?	7390, 3824
Isa	7:4	quiet; fear not, neither be **f**	3824, 7401

FAINTNESS

Le	26:36	I will send a **f** into their hearts	4816

FAIR

Ge	6:2	daughters of men that they were **f**;	2896
1Sa	17:42	ruddy, and of a **f** countenance	3303
Est	2:3	together all the **f** young virgins	2896, 4758
Job	37:22	**F** weather cometh out of the	2091
Pr	7:21	With her much **f** speech she	3948
SS	1:15	Behold, thou art **f**, my love;	3302
SS	6:10	**f** as the moon, clear as the sun,	3303
Isa	54:11	will lay thy stones with **f** colours	6320
Eze	31:3	cedar in Lebanon with **f** branches,	3303
Da	4:21	Whose leaves were **f**, and the fruit	8209
Zec	3:5	them set a **f** mitre upon his head,	2889
Mt	16:2	**ye say, It will be f weather:**	*2105*
Ac	27:8	which is called The **f** havens;	*2568*

FAIRER

Jgs	15:2	her younger sister **f** than she?	2896
Da	1:15	appeared **f** and fatter in flesh	2896

FAIREST

SS	1:8	O thou **f** among women, go thy	3303
SS	5:9	thou **f** among women? what is thy	3303
SS	6:1	O thou **f** among women? whither	3303

FAIR-HAVENS See FAIR and HAVENS.

FAITH

Hab	2:4	but the just shall live by his **f**	530
Mt	6:30	**more clothe you, O ye of little f?**	*3640*
Mt	8:10	**I have not found so great f, no,**	*4102*
Mt	14:31	**O thou of little f, wherefore didst**	*3640*
Mt	17:20	**If ye have f as a grain of mustard**	*4102*
Mk	5:34	**Daughter, thy f hath made thee**	*4102*
Mk	11:22	saith unto them, **Have f in God**	*4102*
Lk	22:32	**prayed for thee, that thy f fail**	*4102*
Ac	6:5	a man full of **f** and of the Holy	*4102*
Ac	6:8	Stephen, full of **f** and power	*4102*
Ac	11:24	full of the Holy Ghost and of **f**:	*4102*
Ac	26:18	**are sanctified by f that is in me**	*4102*
Ro	1:17	God revealed from **f** to **f**: as it is	*4102*
Ro	1:17	written, The just shall live by **f**	*4102*
Ro	3:28	a man is justified by **f** without the	*4102*
Ro	4:5	his **f** is counted for righteousness	*4102*
Ro	5:1	being justified by **f**, we have peace	*4102*
Ro	10:8	is, the word of **f**, which we preach;	*4102*
Ro	10:17	So then **f** cometh by hearing,	*4102*
Ro	12:3	to every man the measure of **f**	*4102*
Ro	14:23	whatsoever is not of **f** is sin	*4102*
1Co	13:2	though I have all **f**, so that I could	*4102*
1Co	13:13	And now abideth **f**, hope, charity	*4102*
1Co	16:13	Watch ye, stand fast in the **f**	*4102*
2Co	5:7	(For we walk by **f**, not by sight)	*4102*
Gal	2:20	I live by the **f** of the Son of God,	*4102*
Gal	3:11	for, The just shall live by **f**.	*4102*
Gal	5:22	gentleness, goodness, **f**,	*4102*
Gal	6:10	who are of the household of **f**.	*4102*
Eph	2:8	by grace are ye saved through **f**;	*4102*
Eph	4:5	One Lord, one **f**, one baptism	*4102*
Eph	6:16	Above all, taking the shield of **f**.	*4102*
Col	2:7	stablished in the **f**, as ye have been	*4102*
1Th	1:3	your work of **f**, and labour of love,	*4102*
1Th	5:8	the breastplate of **f** and love;	*4102*
1Ti	1:5	conscience, and of **f** unfeigned:	*4102*
1Ti	3:9	Holding the mystery of the **f** in a	*4102*
1Ti	4:12	in charity, in spirit, in **f**, in purity	*4102*
1Ti	5:8	he hath denied the **f**, and is worse	*4102*
1Ti	6:11	godliness, **f**, love, patience	*4102*
2Ti	1:5	the unfeigned **f** that is in thee,	*4102*
2Ti	4:7	my course, I have kept the **f**:	*4102*
Tit	1:4	mine own son after the common **f**;	*4102*
Heb	10:22	a true heart in full assurance of **f**,	*4102*
Heb	10:38	Now the just shall live by **f**:	*4102*
Heb	11:1	Now **f** is the substance of things	*4102*
Heb	11:6	without **f** it is impossible to please	*4102*
Heb	11:13	These all died in **f**, not having	*4102*
Heb	11:29	by **f** he passed through the Red	*4102*
Heb	12:2	the author and finisher of our **f**;	*4102*
Jas	1:3	trying of your **f** worketh patience	*4102*
Jas	1:6	let him ask in **f**, nothing wavering	*4102*
Jas	2:18	Thou hast **f**, and I have works:	*4102*
Jas	2:22	and by works was **f** made perfect?	*4102*
Jas	2:24	man is justified, and not by **f** only	*4102*
Jas	5:15	the prayer of **f** shall save the sick,	*4102*
1Pe	1:7	That the trial of your **f**, being much	*4102*
2Pe	1:5	add to your **f** virtue: and to virtue	*4102*
1Jn	5:4	overcometh the world, even our **f**.	*4102*
Jude	3	for the **f** which was once delivered	*4102*
Jude	20	up yourselves on your most holy **f**,	*4102*
Rev	2:19	**and charity, and service, and f,**	*4102*
Rev	14:12	of God, and the **f** of Jesus	*4102*

FAITHFUL See also UNFAITHFUL.

Dt	7:9	thy God, he is God, the **f** God,	539
1Sa	2:35	I will raise me up a **f** priest,	539
Ne	7:2	he was a **f** man, and feared God	571
Ps	119:86	All thy commandments are **f**:	530
Pr	14:5	A **f** witness will not lie: but a false	529
Pr	27:6	**F** are the wounds of a friend;	539
Isa	49:7	because of the Lord that is **f**.	539
Jer	42:5	a true and **f** witness between us	539
Mt	25:23	**Well done, good and f servant:**	*4103*
Lk	12:42	**then is that f and wise steward,**	*4103*

Lk 19:17 **thou hast been f in a very little,** ... *4103*
Ac 16:15 have judged me to be **f** to the Lord, ... *4103*
1Co 4:2 stewards, that a man be found **f**. ... *4103*
1Co 10:13 but God is **f**, who will not suffer ... *4103*
1Th 5:24 **F** is he that calleth you, ... *4103*
2Th 3:3 Lord is **f**, who shall stablish you, ... *4103*
2Ti 2:2 the same commit thou to **f** men ... *4103*
2Ti 2:13 yet he abideth **f**: he cannot deny ... *4103*
Tit 3:8 This is a **f** saying, and these things ... *4103*
Heb 11:11 judged him **f** who had promised ... *4103*
1Pe 4:19 in well doing, as unto a **f** Creator ... *4103*
1Jn 1:9 he is **f** and just to forgive us our ... *4103*
Rev 1:5 Jesus Christ who is the **f** witness, ... *4103*
Rev 2:13 **Antipas was my f martyr, who** ... *4103*
Rev 3:14 **the Amen, the f and true witness,** ... *4103*
Rev 19:11 upon him was called **F** and True, ... *4103*
Rev 22:6 These saying are **f** and true: ... *4103*

FAITHFULLY See also UNFAITHFULLY.

2Ki 22:7 their hand, because they dealt **f** ... 530
2Ch 19:9 Lord, **f**, and with a perfect heart ... 530
Pr 29:14 The king that **f** judgeth the poor ... 571
3Jn 5 doest **f** whatsoever thou doest ... *4103*

FAITHFULNESS

1Sa 26:23 man his righteousness and his **f**: ... 530
Ps 36:5 thy **f** reacheth unto the clouds. ... 530
Ps 89:24 But my **f** and my mercy shall be with ... 530
Ps 119:90 Thy **f** is unto all generations: ... 530
La 3:23 every morning: great is thy **f** ... 530
Hos 2:20 will even betroth thee unto me in **f**: ... 530

FAITHLESS

Mt 17:17 said, **O f and perverse generation,** ... *571*
Jn 20:27 **and be not f, but believing.** ... *571*

FALL

Ge 2:21 a deep sleep to **f** upon Adam ... 5370
Nu 14:29 carcases shall **f** in this wilderness; ... 5307
Jos 6:5 the wall of the city shall **f** down ... 5307
Jgs 8:21 Rise thou, and **f** upon us: ... 6293
Ru 2:16 let **f** also some of the handfuls ... 7997
1Sa 3:19 and did let none of his words **f** to ... 5307
1Sa 14:45 shall not one hair of his head **f** to ... 5307
2Sa 24:14 us **f** now into the hand of the Lord; ... 5307
1Ch 21:13 let me not **f** into the hand of man ... 5307
Est 6:13 but shalt surely **f** before him ... 5307
Job 31:22 arm **f** from my shoulder blade, ... 5307
Ps 37:24 Though he **f**, he shall not be ... 5307
Ps 91:7 A thousand shall **f** at thy side, ... 5307
Ps 140:10 Let burning coals **f** upon them: ... 4131
Pr 10:8 but a prating fool shall **f** ... 3832
Pr 11:28 that trusteth in his riches shall **f**: ... 5307
Pr 16:18 and an haughty spirit before a **f**. ... 3783
Pr 26:27 diggeth a pit shall **f** therein: ... 5307
Ecc 10:8 that diggeth a pit shall **f** into it; ... 5307
Isa 24:18 noise of the fear shall **f** into the pit; ... 5307
Isa 46:6 they **f** down, yea, they worship ... 5456
Jer 8:4 Shall they **f**, and not arise? shall ... 5307
Jer 50:32 most proud shall stumble and **f**, ... 5307
Jer 51:44 yea, the wall of Babylon shall **f**. ... 5307
La 1:14 he hath made my strength to **f**, ... 3782
Eze 5:12 a third part shall **f** by the sword ... 5307
Eze 13:11 ye, O great hailstones, shall **f**; ... 5307
Eze 26:15 isles shake at the sound of thy **f**, ... 4658
Eze 30:25 the arms of Pharaoh shall **f** down; ... 5307
Eze 39:3 will cause thine arrows to **f** out of ... 5307
Da 3:5 ye **f** down and worship the golden ... 5308
Hos 10:8 and to the hills, **F** on us ... 5307
Am 3:5 Can a bird **f** in a snare upon the ... 5307
Mic 7:8 enemy: when I **f**, I shall arise; ... 5307
Mt 4:9 wilt **f** down and worship me ... *4098*
Mt 7:27 **and great was the f of it** ... *4431*
Mt 15:14 **blind, both shall f into the ditch.** ... *409*
Mt 15:27 which **f** from their masters' table ... *409*
Mt 24:29 **and the stars shall f from heaven,** ... *409*
Lk 8:13 **and in time of temptation f away** ... *868*
Lk 23:30 **F on us; and to the hills, Cover** ... *4098*
Jn 12:24 **wheat f into the ground and die,** ... *4098*
1Co 10:12 he standeth take heed lest he **f** ... *4098*
1Ti 3:6 pride he **f** into the condemnation ... *1706*
Heb 6:6 If they shall **f** away, to renew ... *3895*
Jas 1:2 when ye **f** into divers temptations; ... *4045*
Rev 4:10 four and twenty elders **f** down ... *4098*
Rev 6:16 mountains and rocks, **F** on us, ... *4098*
Rev 9:1 and I saw a star **f** from heaven ... *4098*

FALLEN

Ge 4:6 and why is thy countenance **f**? ... 5307
Jgs 3:25 their lord was **f** down dead on the ... 5307
1Sa 5:3 was **f** upon his face to the earth ... 5307
2Sa 1:19 high places: how are the mighty **f**! ... 5307
Est 7:8 Haman was **f** upon the bed where ... 5307
Job 1:16 The fire of God is **f** from heaven, ... 5307
Ps 7:15 is **f** into the ditch which he made. ... 5307
Isa 3:8 is ruined, and Judah is **f**: ... 5307
Isa 21:9 and said, Babylon is **f**, is **f**; ... 5307
Jer 51:8 Babylon is suddenly **f** and ... 5307
La 5:16 The crown is **f** from our head: ... 5307
Am 5:2 The virgin of Israel is **f**; she ... 5307
Am 9:11 the tabernacle of David that is **f**. ... 5307
Lk 14:5 **have an ass or an ox f into a pit,** ... *1706*
Ac 20:9 being **f** into a deep sleep: ... *2702*
1Co 15:6 but some are **f** asleep ... *2837*
1Co 15:18 also which are **f** asleep in Christ ... *2837*
Gal 5:4 by the law; ye are **f** from grace ... *1601*
Rev 2:5 **from whence thou art f** ... *1601*
Rev 14:8 Babylon is **f**, is **f**, that great city ... *4098*
Rev 17:10 five are **f**, and one is, and the ... *4098*

FALLETH

Nu 33:54 in the place where his lot **f**; ... 3318
2Sa 17:12 as the dew **f** on the ground: ... 5307
Job 4:13 when deep sleep **f** on men, ... 5307
Pr 24:16 For a just man **f** seven times, ... 5307
Pr 24:17 Rejoice not when thine enemy **f**, ... 5307
Isa 44:17 he **f** down unto it, and worshippeth ... 5456
Da 3:6 **f** not down and worshippeth shall ... 5308
Mt 17:15 for ofttimes he **f** into the fire, ... *4098*
Lk 11:17 **a house divided against a house f.** ... *4098*
Lk 15:12 **the portion of goods that f to me.** ... *1911*
Jas 1:11 the grass, and the flower thereof **f**, ... *1601*
1Pe 1:24 and the flower thereof **f** away: ... *1601*

FALLING

Nu 24:4 **f** into a trance, but having his ... 5307
Ps 56:13 not thou deliver my feet from **f**, ... 1762
Pr 25:26 A righteous man **f** down before ... 4131
Lk 22:44 of blood **f** down to the ground ... *2597*
Ac 1:18 **f** headlong, he burst asunder ... *4248, 1096*
2Th 2:3 except there come a **f** away first, ... *646*
Jude 24 that is able to keep you from **f**, ... *679*

FALLOW

Jer	4:3	Break up your **f** ground, and sow	5215
Hos	10:12	break up your **f** ground: for it is	5215

FALSE

Ex	20:16	Thou shalt not bear **f** witness	8267
Dt	19:16	If a **f** witness rise up against any	2555
Job	36:4	truly my words shall not be **f**:	8267
Ps	27:12	**f** witnesses are risen up against	8267
Ps	35:11	**F** witnesses did rise up; they	2555
Pr	6:19	A **f** witness that speaketh lies,	8267
Pr	11:1	A **f** balance is abomination to	4820
Pr	21:28	A **f** witness shall perish: but the	3577
Jer	23:32	them that prophesy **f** dreams,	8267
Eze	21:23	as a **f** divination in their sight,	7723
Zec	10:2	a lie, and have told **f** dreams;	7723
Mal	3:5	and against **f** swearers, and	8267
Mt	7:15	**Beware of f prophets, which come**	*5578*
Mt	19:18	**Thou shalt not bear f witness,**	*5576*
Mt	24:24	**For there shall arise f Christs,**	
Mt	26:59	sought **f** witness against Jesus,	*5580*
Mk	10:19	**Do not bear f witness, Defraud**	*5576*
Lk	6:26	**their fathers to the f prophets.**	*5575*
Lk	18:20	**Do not bear f witness, Honour**	*5576*
Ac	13:6	sorcerer, a **f** prophet, a Jew,	*5571*
Ro	13:9	Thou shalt not bear **f** witness,	*5576*
2Co	11:26	sea, in perils among **f** brethren;	*5569*
2Ti	3:3	trucebreakers, **f** accusers,	*1228*
2Pe	2:1	there were **f** prophets also among	*5578*
1Jn	4:1	because many **f** prophets are gone	*5578*
Rev	16:13	out of the mouth of the **f** prophet	*5578*
Rev	19:20	**f** prophet that wrought miracles	*5578*
Rev	20:10	the beast and the **f** prophet are	*5578*

FALSEHOOD

2Sa	18:13	wrought **f** against mine own life:	8267
Job	21:34	your answers there remaineth **f**?	4604
Ps	114:8	their right hand is a right hand of **f**	8267
Isa	57:4	of transgression, a seed of **f**,	8267
Jer	13:25	hast forgotten me, and trusted in **f**.	8267
Mic	2:11	walking in the spirit and **f** do lie,	8267

FALSELY

Ge	21:23	that thou wilt not deal **f** with me,	8266
Le	19:11	Ye shall not steal, neither deal **f**.	3584
Le	19:12	ye shall not swear by my name **f**.	8267
Jer	5:31	prophets prophesy **f**, and the	8267
Jer	7:9	and commit adultery, and swear **f**	8267
Hos	10:4	swearing **f** in making a covenant:	7723
Mt	5:11	**all manner of evil against you f,**	*5574*
1Ti	6:20	oppositions of science **f** so called:	*5581*

FALSE-PROPHET See FALSE and PROPHET.

FALSIFYING

Am	8:5	and **f** the balances by deceit?	5791

FAME

Ge	45:16	**f** thereof was heard in Pharaoh's	6963
Jos	6:27	his **f** was noised throughout all	8089
1Ki	10:1	of Sheba heard of the **f** of Solomon	8088
1Ch	14:17	the **f** of David went out into all	8034
Est	9:4	his **f** went out throughout all the	8089
Isa	66:19	afar off, that have not heard my **f**	8088
Mt	4:24	his **f** went throughout all Syria:	*189*
Mt	14:1	tetrarch heard of the **f** of Jesus,	*189*
Lk	5:15	went there a **f** abroad of him	*3056*

FAMILIAR

Dt	18:11	or a consulter with **f** spirits, or	
1Sa	28:7	woman that hath a **f** spirit at En-dor.	
Job	19:14	my **f** friends have forgotten me	3045

FAMILIARS

Jer	20:10	all my **f** watched for my halting.	7965

FAMILIAR-SPIRIT See FAMILIAR and SPIRIT.

FAMILIES

Ge	12:3	shall all **f** of the earth be blessed	4940
Nu	1:2	the children of Israel, after their **f**,	4940
Nu	11:10	people weep throughout their **f**,	4940
Nu	36:12	married into the **f** of the sons of	4940
1Sa	9:21	and my family the least of all the **f**	4940
Ne	4:13	after their **f** with their swords,	4940
Ps	107:41	and maketh him **f** like a flock.	4940
Jer	10:25	the **f** that call not on thy name:	4940
Jer	31:1	the God of all the **f** of Israel,	4940
Zec	12:14	**f** that remain, every family apart,	4940

FAMILY

Le	25:49	is nigh of kin unto him of his **f**.	4940
Dt	29:18	in **f**, or tribe, whose heart turneth	4940
Jos	7:14	the **f** which the Lord shall take	4940
Jos	7:17	And he brought the **f** of Judah;	4940
Jgs	6:15	behold, my **f** is poor in Manasseh,	504
1Sa	9:21	my **f** the least of all the families	4940
2Sa	16:5	a man of the **f** of the house of Saul,	4940
1Ch	6:70	the **f** of the remnant of the sons	4940
1Ch	13:14	ark of God remained with the **f** of	1004
Est	9:28	every **f**, every province, and every	4940
Jer	8:3	of them that remain of this evil **f**,	4940
Mic	2:3	against this **f** do I devise an evil,	4940
Eph	3:15	**f** in heaven and earth is named	*3965*

FAMINE

Ge	12:10	And there was a **f** in the land:	7458
Ge	41:27	east wind shall be seven years of **f**	7458
Ge	41:56	And the **f** was over all the face of	7458
Ge	42:5	the **f** was in the land of Canaan.	7458
Ge	45:11	yet there are five years of **f**;	7458
Ru	1:1	that there was a **f** in the land	7458
2Sa	21:1	there was a **f** in the days of David	7458
2Sa	24:13	Shall seven years of **f** come unto	7458
2Ki	8:1	the Lord hath called for a **f**;	7458
1Ch	21:12	Either three years' **f**; or three	7458
Job	5:20	In **f** he shall redeem thee from	7458
Ps	37:19	days of **f** they shall be satisfied	7459
Isa	14:30	I will kill thy root with **f**,	7458
Jer	5:12	neither shall we see sword nor **f**:	7458
Jer	14:18	behold them that are sick with **f**!	7458
Jer	24:10	I will send the sword, the **f**,	7458
Jer	52:6	month the **f** was sore in the city,	7458
Eze	5:16	upon them the evil arrows of **f**,	7458
Eze	14:21	and the **f**, and the noisome beast,	7458
Am	8:11	not a **f** of bread, nor a thirst of	7458
Lk	4:25	**when great f was throughout all**	*3042*
Lk	15:14	**there arose a mighty f in that**	*3042*
Ro	8:35	or **f**, or nakedness, or peril, or	*3042*
Rev	18:8	day, death, and mourning, and **f**;	*3042*

FAMINES

Mt	24:7	**there shall be f, and pestilences,**	*3042*
Mk	13:8	**and there shall be f and troubles:**	*3042*

FAMISH
Pr 10:3 the soul of the righteous to **f**:....................7456
Zep 2:11 will **f** all the gods of the earth; 7329

FAMISHED
Ge 41:55 when all the land of Egypt was **f**,.............7456
Isa 5:13 and their honourable men are **f**,..............7458

FAMOUS
Nu 16:2 assembly, **f** in the congregation,...............7148
Ru 4:11 Ephratah … **f** in Beth-lehem: 7121, 8034
1Ch 5:24 mighty men of valour, **f** men,..................8034
Ps 74:5 A man was **f** according as he had 3045
Eze 23:10 she became **f** among women....................8034

FAN
Isa 41:16 Thou shalt **f** them, and the wind.............2219
Jer 15:7 And I will **f** them … in the gates.............2219
Jer 51:2 Babylon fanners, that shall **f** her, ...2219
Mt 3:12 Whose **f** is in his hand, and he.................*4425*

FARE
1Sa 17:18 and look how thy brethren **f**, ...7965
Jnh 1:3 he paid the **f** thereof, and went................7939
Ac 15:29 ye shall do well. **F** ye well..........................*4517*

FARED
Lk 16:19 **and f sumptuously every day:** *2165*

FAREWELL
Lk 9:61 but let me first go bid them **f**, ...*657*
Ac 23:30 what they had against him. **F**...................*4517*

FARTHER See also FURTHER.
Mt 26:39 And he went a little **f**, and fell..................*4281*
Mk 1:19 And when he had gone a little **f**..............*4260*

FARTHING
Mt 5:26 **thou hast paid the uttermost f** *2835*
Mt 10:29 **not two sparrows sold for a f?**....................*787*
Mk 12:42 in two mites, which make a **f** *2835*

FARTHINGS
Lk 12:6 **not five sparrows sold for two f,**................*787*

FASHION
Ge 6:15 **f** which thou shalt make it of:
2Ki 16:10 the **f** of the altar, and the pattern.............1823
Job 31:15 did not one **f** us in the womb?.................3559
Lk 9:29 the **f** of his countenance was....................*1491*
1Co 7:31 for the **f** of this world passeth *4976*
Php 2:8 And being found in **f** as a man, ...*4976*

FASHIONED
Ex 32:4 and **f** it with a graving tool,.......................3335
Job 10:8 hands have made me and **f** me 6213
Ps 119:73 hands have made me and **f** me: 3559
Php 3:21 be **f** like unto his glorious body,...............*4832*

FASHIONETH
Ps 33:15 He **f** their hearts alike; he 3335
Isa 44:12 the coals, and **f** it with hammers, ...3335
Isa 45:9 Shall the clay say to him that **f** it,.............3335

FASHIONING
1Pe 1:14 not **f** yourselves according to the *4964*

FAST
Ge 20:18 Lord had **f** closed up all the wombs
Jgs 16:11 they bind me **f** with new ropes
Ru 2:23 So she kept **f** by the maidens of Boaz
2Sa 12:21 didst **f** and weep for the child, ...6684
Est 4:16 and **f** ye for me, and neither eat...............6684
Job 27:6 My righteousness I hold **f**, and will
Ps 38:2 For thine arrows stick **f** in me,
Ps 111:8 They stand **f** for ever and ever
Pr 4:13 Take **f** hold of instruction; let her not
Isa 58:3 Behold, in the day of your **f** ye.................6685
Jer 14:12 When they **f**, I will not hear their 6684
Jer 36:9 proclaimed a **f** before the Lord 6685
Jnh 1:5 and he lay, and was **f** asleep
Jnh 3:5 and proclaimed a **f**, and put on 6685
Mt 6:16 **Moreover when ye f, be not, as**................*3522*
Mt 9:14 Why do we and the Pharisees **f** oft, ...*3522*
Mk 2:18 of John and of the Pharisees **f**,.................*3522*
Lk 18:12 **I f twice in the week,**................................*3522*
Ac 16:24 made their feet **f** in the stocks *805*
Gal 5:1 Stand **f** therefore in the liberty
Php 1:27 that ye stand **f** in one spirit, with one
1Th 5:21 hold **f** that which is good..........................*2722*
Heb 4:14 let us hold **f** our profession
Heb 10:23 Let us hold **f** the profession of our *2722*
Rev 2:13 **and thou holdest f my name,**

FASTED
Jgs 20:26 **f** that day until even, and offered.............6684
2Sa 12:22 child was yet alive, I **f** and wept: 6684
Ezr 8:23 So we **f** and besought our God................6684
Ne 1:4 and **f**, and prayed before the God of.......6684
Mt 4:2 when he had **f** forty days *3522*
Ac 13:3 when they had **f** and prayed,....................*3522*

FASTEN
Ex 28:14 and **f** the wreathen chains to the 5414
Isa 22:23 And I will **f** him as a nail..........................8628
Jer 10:4 they **f** it with nails and with 2388

FASTENED
Ex 40:18 and **f** his sockets, and set up the 5414
Jgs 16:14 And she **f** it with the pin,...........................8628
1Sa 31:10 and they **f** his body to the wall of............8628
Est 1:6 **f** with cords of fine linen and purple 270
Job 38:6 are the foundations thereof **f**? 2883
Isa 41:7 **f** it with nails, that it should not 2388
Lk 4:20 in the synagogue were **f** on him.................*816*
Ac 11:6 which when I had **f** mine eyes, I *816*

FASTENING
Ac 3:4 Peter, **f** his eyes upon him with *816*

FASTEST
Mt 6:17 **when thou f, anoint thine head,**..............*3522*

FASTING
Ne 9:1 of Israel were assembled with **f**,...............6685
Est 4:3 and **f**, and weeping, and wailing; 6685
Ps 35:13 I humbled my soul with **f**;........................6685
Ps 109:24 My knees are weak through **f**;..................6685
Da 9:3 with **f**, and sackcloth, and ashes:..............6685
Mt 17:21 **not out but by prayer and f** *3521*
Mk 9:29 **by nothing, but by prayer and f** *3521*
Ac 10:30 Four days ago I was **f** until this................*3522*
1Co 7:5 give yourselves to **f** and prayer;................*3521*

FASTINGS
Est 9:31 the matters of the **f** and their cry.............6685
Lk 2:37 with **f** and prayers night and day.............*3521*
2Co 6:5 in labours, in watchings, in **f**; *3521*
2Co 11:27 in **f** often, in cold and nakedness. *3521*

FAT See also **PRESSFAT; WINEFAT.**

Ge 4:4 his flock and of the **f** thereof. 2459
Ge 41:4 seven well favoured and **f** kine 1277
Ex 23:18 shall the **f** of my sacrifice remain 2459
Le 3:16 savour: all the **f** is the Lord's 2459
Le 3:17 that ye eat neither **f** nor blood. 2459
Le 4:35 as the **f** of the lamb is taken away 2459
Le 7:23 Ye shall eat no manner of **f**, 2459
Le 17:6 and burn the **f** for a sweet savour 2459
Nu 13:20 land is, whether it be **f** or lean, 8082
Dt 31:20 filled themselves, and waxen **f**; 1878
Jgs 3:17 and Eglon was a very **f** man. 1277
Jgs 3:22 and the **f** closed upon the blade, 2459
1Sa 15:22 and to hearken than the **f** of rams 2459
Ne 8:10 eat the **f**, and drink the sweet, 4924
Ne 9:25 and were filled, and became **f**, and 8082
Ps 17:10 They are inclosed in their own **f**: 2459
Ps 119:70 Their heart is as **f** as grease; 2954
Pr 11:25 The liberal soul shall be made **f**: 1878
Pr 28:25 trust in the Lord shall be made **f** 1878
Isa 6:10 Make the heart of this people **f**, 8082
Isa 30:23 and it shall be **f** and plenteous: 1879
Jer 50:11 ye are grown **f** as the heifer 6335
Eze 44:7 my bread, the **f** and the blood, 2459
Hab 1:16 by them their portion is **f**, 8082
Zec 11:16 but he shall eat the flesh of the **f**, 1277

FATFLESHED

Ge 41:2 seven well favoured kine and **f**; 1277
Ge 41:18 seven kine, **f** and well favoured; 1277

FATHER

Ge 2:24 a man leave his **f** and his mother, 1
Ge 9:22 saw the nakedness of his **f**, 1
Ge 10:21 Shem also, the **f** of all the children 1
Ge 17:4 thou shalt be a **f** of many nations. 1
Ge 19:36 of Lot with child by their **f** 1
Ge 22:7 Abraham his **f**, and said, My **f**: 1
Ge 26:24 I am the God of Abraham thy **f**; 1
Ge 27:18 came unto his **f**, and said, My **f**: 1
Ge 28:7 Jacob obeyed his **f** and his mother, 1
Ge 31:29 but the God of your **f** spake unto me 1
Ge 32:9 and God of my **f** Isaac, the Lord 1
Ge 36:9 of Esau the **f** of the Edomites in 1
Ge 37:4 saw that their **f** loved him more than 1
Ge 37:35 Thus his **f** wept for him 1
Ge 43:7 Is your **f** yet alive? have ye another 1
Ge 44:20 my lord, We have a **f**, an old man, 1
Ge 45:3 I am Joseph; doth my **f** yet live? 1
Ge 46:3 I am God, the God of thy **f**: 1
Ge 48:1 told Joseph, Behold, thy **f** is sick: 1
Ge 50:2 the physicians to embalm his **f**: 1
Ge 50:6 Pharaoh said, Go up, and bury thy **f**, 1
Ex 3:1 the flock of Jethro his **f** in law, 2859
Ex 3:6 I am the God of thy **f**, 1
Ex 18:4 God of my **f**, said he, was mine help, 1
Ex 20:12 Honour thy **f** and thy mother: 1
Ex 21:15 he that smiteth his **f**, or his mother 1
Ex 21:17 he that curseth his **f**, or his mother 1
Le 18:11 begotten of thy **f**, she is thy sister 1
Nu 27:3 Our **f** died in the wilderness, 1
Nu 30:4 her **f** shall hold his peace at her: 1
Dt 5:16 Honour thy **f** and thy mother, 1
Jos 2:13 that ye will save alive my **f**, 1
Jos 6:23 brought out Rahab, and her **f**, and 1
Jgs 14:3 Samson said unto his **f**, Get her for 1
Jgs 17:10 and be unto me a **f** and a priest, 1
Ru 4:17 he is the **f** of Jesse, the **f** of David 1
1Sa 19:2 Saul my **f** seeketh to kill thee: 1
1Sa 20:6 If thy **f** at all miss me, then say, 1
2Sa 7:14 I will be his **f**, and he shall be my 1
2Sa 17:8 and thy **f** is a man of war, and will 1
2Sa 17:10 knoweth that thy **f** is a mighty man 1
1Ki 2:24 set me on the throne of David my **f**, 1
1Ki 2:26 ark of the Lord before David my **f** 1
1Ki 8:17 And it was in the heart of David my **f** 1
1Ki 9:4 before me, as David thy **f** walked, 1
1Ki 12:4 Thy **f** made our yoke grievous: 1
1Ki 12:10 saying, Thy **f** made our yoke heavy, 1
1Ki 15:3 he walked in all the sins of his **f** 1
1Ki 15:15 things which his **f** had dedicated, 1
1Ki 19:20 thee, kiss my **f** and my mother, 1
2Ki 2:12 My **f**, my **f**, the chariot of Israel, 1
2Ki 3:2 image of Baal that his **f** had made 1
2Ki 4:19 he said unto his **f**, My head, my head 1
2Ki 21:21 served the idols that his **f** served, 1
1Ch 19:2 because his **f** shewed kindness to me 25
1Ch 24:2 Nadab and Abihu died before their **f**, 25
2Ch 7:18 I have covenanted with David thy **f**, 25
2Ch 10:4 the grievous servitude of thy **f**, 25
2Ch 17:4 sought to the Lord God of his **f** 25
Est 2:7 for she had neither **f** nor mother, 1
Job 29:16 I was a **f** to the poor: and the cause 1
Job 38:28 Hath the rain a **f**? or who hath 1
Ps 68:5 A **f** of the fatherless, and a judge of 1
Ps 103:13 Like as a **f** pitieth his children, so 1
Pr 1:8 My son, hear the instruction of thy **f**, 1
Pr 3:12 as a **f** the son in whom he delighteth 1
Pr 10:1 A wise son maketh a glad **f**: but a 1
Pr 17:25 A foolish son is a grief to his **f**, and 1
Pr 23:24 The **f** of the righteous shall greatly 1
Pr 28:24 Whoso robbeth his **f** or his mother, 1
Pr 29:3 loveth wisdom rejoiceth his **f**: but he 1
Isa 9:6 everlasting **F**, The Prince of Peace 1
Jer 2:27 Saying to a stock, Thou art my **f**; 1
Eze 18:4 souls are mine; as the soul of the **f**, 1
Eze 18:17 shall not die for the iniquity of his **f**, 1
Da 5:13 the king my **f** brought out of Jewry? 2
Mal 2:10 Have we not all one **f**? hath not one 2
Mt 3:9 We have Abraham to our **f**: for I *3962*
Mt 5:16 **glorify your F which is in heaven.** *3962*
Mt 5:45 **ye may be the children of your F** *3962*
Mt 6:1 **of your F which is in heaven.** *3962*
Mt 6:6 **pray to thy F which is in secret;** *3962*
Mt 6:9 **F which are in heaven, Hallowed** *3962*
Mt 6:14 **your heavenly F will also forgive** *3962*
Mt 6:18 **but unto thy F which is in secret:** *3962*
Mt 8:21 suffer me first to go and bury my **f**. *3962*
Mt 10:20 **Spirit of your F which speaketh** *3962*
Mt 10:32 **will I confess also before my F.** *3962*
Mt 10:33 **him will I also deny before my F.** *3962*
Mt 11:25 **I thank thee, O F, Lord of heaven** *3962*
Mt 15:4 **He that curseth f or mother, let** *3962*
Mt 16:17 **but my F which is in heaven.** *3962*
Mt 16:27 **shall come in the glory of his F** *3962*
Mt 19:5 **shall a man leave f and mother,** *3962*
Mt 19:19 **Honour thy f and thy mother:** *3962*
Mt 20:23 **for whom it is prepared of my F** *3962*
Mt 25:34 **Come, ye blessed of my F, inherit** *3962*
Mt 26:39 **O my F, if it be possible, let this** *3962*
Mt 26:42 **O my F, if this cup may not pass** *3962*
Mt 28:19 **them in the name of the F,** *3962*

Mk	14:36	he said, Abba, **F**, all things are	3962
Lk	2:48	behold, thy **f** and I have sought thee	3962
Lk	10:21	I thank thee, O **F**, Lord of heaven	3962
Lk	11:2	say, Our **F** which art in heaven,	3962
Lk	12:30	your **F** knoweth that ye have need	3962
Lk	15:12	of them said to his **f**, **F**, give me	3962
Lk	15:21	**F**, I have sinned against heaven,	3962
Lk	22:42	Saying, **F**, if thou be willing	3962
Lk	23:34	**F**, forgive them; for they know	3962
Lk	23:46	**F**, into thy hands I commend my	3962
Jn	1:14	as of the only begotten of the **F**,)	3962
Jn	4:12	Art thou greater than our **f** Jacob,	3962
Jn	4:23	shall worship the **F** in spirit and	3962
Jn	5:18	but said also that God was his **F**,	3962
Jn	5:20	For the **F** loveth the Son, and	3962
Jn	5:23	Son, even as they honour the **F**	3962
Jn	5:26	For as the **F** hath life in himself;	3962
Jn	6:27	for him hath God the **F** sealed.	3962
Jn	6:37	All that the **F** giveth me shall	3962
Jn	6:44	except the **F** which hath sent me	3962
Jn	6:46	is of God, he hath seen the **F**	3962
Jn	8:19	ye should have known my **F** also.	3962
Jn	8:28	as my **F** hath taught me, I speak	3962
Jn	8:41	Ye do the deeds of your **f**.	3962
Jn	8:41	we have one **F**, even God	3962
Jn	8:42	God were your **F**, ye would love	3962
Jn	8:49	but I honour my **F**, and ye do	3962
Jn	8:56	Your **f** Abraham rejoiced to see	3962
Jn	10:15	even so know I the **F**:	3962
Jn	10:30	I and my **F** are one	3962
Jn	10:38	that the **F** is in me, and I in him.	3962
Jn	11:41	**F**, I thank thee that thou hast	3962
Jn	12:27	**F**, save me from this hour; but	3962
Jn	12:28	**F**, glorify thy name. Then came	3962
Jn	14:6	cometh unto the **F**, but by me.	3962
Jn	14:7	ye should have known my **F** also:	3962
Jn	14:8	Lord, shew us the **F**, and it	3962
Jn	14:11	Believe me that I am in the **F**,	3962
Jn	14:12	he do; because I go unto my **F**.	3962
Jn	14:16	And I will pray the **F**, and he	3962
Jn	14:28	because I said, I go unto the **F**:	3962
Jn	15:1	and my **F** is the husbandman.	3962
Jn	15:8	Herein is my **F** glorified, that ye	3962
Jn	15:16	ye shall ask of the **F** in my name,	3962
Jn	15:23	that hateth me hateth my **F** also.	3962
Jn	15:26	which proceedeth from the **F**,	3962
Jn	16:10	because I go to my **F**, and ye see	3962
Jn	16:23	ye shall ask the **F** in my name,	3962
Jn	16:25	shall shew you plainly of the **F**	3962
Jn	16:28	I came forth from the **F**, and am	3962
Jn	17:1	**F**, the hour is come; glorify thy	3962
Jn	17:5	And now, O **F**, glorify thou me	3962
Jn	17:11	Holy **F**, keep through thine own	3962
Jn	17:21	as thou, **F**, art in me, and I in	3962
Jn	18:11	cup which my **F** hath given me,	3962
Jn	20:17	I ascend unto my **F**, and your **F**,	3962
Jn	20:21	as my **F** hath sent me, even so	3962
Ac	1:4	but wait for the promise of the **F**,	3962
Ac	1:7	the **F** hath put in his own power.	3962
Ac	2:33	received of the **F** the promise of	3962
Ro	4:11	be the **f** of all them that believe,	3962
Ro	4:16	Abraham, who is the **f** of us all,	3962
Ro	8:15	adoption, whereby we cry, Abba, **F**,	3962
Ro	15:6	God, even the **F** of our Lord Jesus	3962
2Co	1:3	the **F** of mercies, and the God of	3962
Gal	1:3	peace from God the **F**, and from	3962
Gal	4:6	unto your hearts, crying, Abba, **F**	3962
Eph	2:18	access by one Spirit unto the **F**	3962
Eph	4:6	One God and **F** of all, who is above	3962
Eph	5:31	a man leave his **f** and mother,	3962
Eph	6:2	Honour thy **f** and mother; which	3962
Col	1:19	For it pleased the **F** that in him	
1Ti	5:1	an elder, but intreat him as a **f**;	3962
Heb	1:5	And again, I will be to him a **F**,	3962
Heb	7:3	Without **f**, without mother,	540
Heb	7:10	he was yet in the loins of his **f**,	3962
Jas	1:17	cometh down from the **F** of lights,	3962
1Pe	1:2	the foreknowledge of God the **F**,	3962
1Jn	1:3	our fellowship is with the **F**, and	3962
1Jn	2:1	we have an advocate with the **F**,	3962
1Jn	2:13	because ye have known the **F**	3962
1Jn	2:15	the love of the **F** is not in him.	3962
1Jn	2:16	is not the **F**, but is of the world.	3962
1Jn	2:24	continue in the Son, and in the **F**	3962
1Jn	3:1	of love the **F** hath bestowed upon	3962
1Jn	4:14	**F** sent the Son to the Saviour	3962
1Jn	5:7	**F**, the Word, and the Holy Ghost:	3962
2Jn	9	he hath both the **F** and the Son.	3962
Rev	2:27	even as I received of my **F**	3962
Rev	3:21	set down with my **F** in his throne.	3962

FATHER IN LAW See FATHER.

FATHERLESS

Ex	22:24	be widows, and your children **f**.	3490
Job	22:9	arms of the **f** have been broken.	3490
Ps	10:18	to judge the **f** and the oppressed,	3490
Ps	82:3	Defend the poor and **f**: do justice	3490
Ps	109:9	Let his children be **f**, and his wife	3490
Ps	146:9	he relieveth the **f** and widow: but	3490
Isa	1:17	judge the **f**, plead for the widow.	3490
Isa	10:2	and that they may rob the **f**!	3490
Jer	49:11	Leave thy **f** children, I will preserve	3490
La	5:3	We are orphans and **f**, our	369, 1
Mal	3:5	in his wages, the widow, and the **f**,	3490
Jas	1:27	To visit the **f** and widows in their	3737

FATHER'S

Ge	9:23	and they saw not their **f** nakedness.	1
Ge	29:9	Rachel came with her **f** sheep: for	1
Ge	48:17	and he held up his **f** hand,	1
Ge	49:8	thy **f** children shall bow down before	1
Ex	15:2	my **f** God, and I will exalt him	1
Le	16:32	in the priest's office in his **f** stead,	1
Le	18:12	she is thy **f** near kinswoman.	1
Dt	22:30	A man shall not take his **f** wife,	1
Jos	2:12	shew kindness unto my **f** house,	1
Jos	6:25	the harlot alive, and her **f** household,	1
Jgs	14:15	lest we burn thee and thy **f** house	1
1Sa	17:15	to feed his **f** sheep at Beth-lehem.	1
2Sa	3:7	thou gone in unto my **f** concubine?	1
2Sa	9:7	kindness for Jonathan thy **f** sake,	1
1Ch	5:1	forasmuch as he defiled his **f** bed,	1
Ne	1:6	both I and my **f** house have sinned	1
Est	4:14	and thy **f** house shall be destroyed:	1
Pr	6:20	My son, keep thy **f** commandment,	1
Pr	13:1	A wise son heareth his **f** instruction:	1
Pr	15:5	A fool despiseth his **f** instruction:	1
Isa	22:23	for a glorious throne to his **f** house.	1
Jer	35:14	but obey their **f** commandment:	1
Eze	18:14	a son, that seeth all his **f** sins which	1
Mt	26:29	new with you in my **F** kingdom.	3962
Lk	2:49	I must be about my **F** business?	3962

Lk 15:17 **hired servants of my f have bread** *3962*
Jn 2:16 **make not my F house an house of** *3962*
Jn 5:43 **I am come in my F name, and ye** *3962*
Jn 6:39 **And this is the F will which hath** *3962*
Jn 10:29 **to pluck them out of my F hand.** *3962*
Jn 14:2 **In my F house are many** *3962*
Rev 14:1 having his **F** name written in *3962*

FATHERS See also FOREFATHERS.

Ge 15:15 And thou shalt go to thy **f** in peace; 1
Ge 31:3 Return unto the land of thy **f**, ...1
Ge 48:15 my **f** Abraham and Isaac did walk, ...1
Ge 49:29 bury me with my **f** in the cave that is............1
Ex 3:13 The God of your **f** hath sent me unto 1
Ex 20:5 visiting the iniquity of the **f** upon the 1
Nu 20:15 the Egyptians vexed us, and our **f**: 1
Dt 1:21 the Lord God of thy **f** hath said 1
Dt 4:31 nor forget the covenant of thy **f** which..........1
Dt 5:9 visiting the iniquity of the **f** upon the 1
Dt 6:3 the Lord God of thy **f** hath promised............1
Dt 10:15 the Lord had a delight in thy **f** 1
Dt 24:16 The **f** shall not be put to death for................1
Dt 29:25 covenant of the Lord God of their **f**, ...1
Dt 31:16 Behold, thou shalt sleep with thy **f**; 1
Jos 4:6 children ask their **f** in time to
Jos 24:2 Your **f** dwelt on the other side of the.............1
Jos 24:14 the gods which your **f** served on the 1
Jgs 2:1 the land which I sware unto your **f**; 1
Jgs 2:12 they forsook the Lord God of their **f**,............1
Jgs 6:13 his miracles which our **f** told us of, ...1
1Sa 12:6 brought your **f** up out of the land 1
1Sa 12:8 and your **f** cried unto the Lord, ...1
1Ki 19:4 for I am not better than my **f**.........................1
2Ki 17:15 covenant that he made with their **f**, ...1
1Ch 12:17 the God of our **f** look thereon, and 1
1Ch 26:32 and seven hundred chief **f**, ...1
1Ch 29:18 Abraham, Isaac, and of Israel, our **f**,.............1
1Ch 29:20 blessed the Lord God of their **f**, ...1
2Ch 14:4 to seek the Lord God of their **f**, and 1
2Ch 30:8 be ye not stiffnecked, as your **f** were,.............1
Ezr 7:27 Blessed be the Lord God of our **f**,..................1
Ne 7:70 chief of the **f** gave unto the work...................1
Ne 7:71 the chief of the **f** gave to the treasure 1
Ne 9:34 our priests, nor our **f**, kept thy law, ...1
Ps 22:4 Our **f** trusted in thee; they trusted,................1
Ps 106:6 We have sinned with our **f**, we have 1
Pr 22:28 ancient landmark, which thy **f** have set.........1
Isa 64:11 house, where our **f** praised thee, ...1
Jer 6:21 the **f** and the sons together shall fall 1
Jer 16:11 Because your **f** have forsaken me, ...1
Jer 31:29 The **f** have eaten a sour grape, ...1
Jer 47:3 the **f** shall not look back to their....................1
La 5:7 Our **f** have sinned, and are not; 1
Eze 18:2 saying, The **f** have eaten sour grapes, ...1
Eze 20:36 Like as I pleaded with your **f** in the...............1
Da 2:23 praise thee, O thou God of my **f**, ...2
Hos 9:10 I saw your **f** as the firstripe in the fig............1
Mal 4:6 the heart of the **f** to the children, ...1
Mt 23:30 **we had been in the days of our f**, ...*3962*
Lk 1:17 to turn the hearts of the **f** to the *3962*
Lk 11:47 **prophets, and your f killed them**............*3962*
Jn 4:20 **f** worshipped in this mountain; *3962*
Jn 6:49 **f did eat manna in the wilderness**, ...*3962*
Ac 5:30 The God of our **f** raised up Jesus, ...*3962*
Ac 7:32 Saying, I am the God of thy **f**, ...*3962*
1Co 10:1 all our **f** were under the cloud, ...*3962*
Eph 6:4 ye **f**, provoke not your children to *3962*
Col 3:21 **F**, provoke not your children to *3962*
1Ti 1:9 for murderers of **f** and murderers.............*3964*
1Pe 1:18 received by tradition from your **f**;.............*3970*
1Jn 2:13 I write unto you, **f**, because ye..................*3962*

FATHERS'

Ex 6:14 These be the heads of their **f** houses:.............1
Nu 32:14 ye are risen up in your **f** stead, an..................1
Ne 2:5 the city of my **f** sepulchres, that I 1
Eze 20:24 their eyes were after their **f** idols. 1
Eze 22:10 they discovered their **f** nakedness: 1
Ro 11:28 they are beloved for the **f** sakes *3962*

FATHOMS

Ac 27:28 sounded, and found it twenty **f**:...............*3712*
Ac 27:28 again, and found it fifteen **f**.......................*3712*

FATLING

Isa 11:6 young lion and the **f** together; 4806

FATLINGS

1Sa 15:9 and of the **f**, and the lambs, ...4932
Ps 66:15 unto thee burnt sacrifices of **f**,.................4220
Mt 22:4 **my oxen and my f are killed**, ...*4619*

FATNESS

Ge 27:28 of heaven, and the **f** of the earth,.............4924
Jgs 9:9 Should I leave my **f**, wherewith................1880
Job 15:27 he covereth his face with his **f**, ...2459
Ps 36:8 satisfied with the **f** of thy house;..............1880
Ps 63:5 be satisfied as with marrow and **f**;...........1880
Isa 17:4 the **f** of his flesh shall wax lean. 4924
IIsa 55:2 let your soul delight itself in **f**..................1880
Ro 11:17 the root and **f** of the olive tree; *4096*

FATS

Joel 3:13 the press is full, the **f** overflow; 3342

FATTED

1Ki 4:23 and fallowdeer, and **f** fowl. 75
Lk 15:23 **And bring hither the f calf, and**..............*4618*
Lk 15:27 **thy father hath killed the f calf**, ...*4618*
Lk 15:30 **thou hast killed for him the f calf**...........*4618*

FATTER

Da 1:15 appeared fairer and **f** in flesh 1277

FATTEST

Ps 78:31 upon them, and slew the **f** of them, ...4924
Da 11:24 upon the **f** places of the province; 4924

FAULT

Ex 5:16 but the **f** is in thine own people...............2398
1Sa 29:3 I have found no **f** in him since.................3972
Da 6:4 could find none occasion nor **f**;...............7844
Mt 18:15 **and tell him his f between thee**...............*1651*
Lk 23:4 I find no **f** in this man. *158*
Lk 23:14 have found no **f** in this man........................*158*
Jn 18:38 I find in him no **f** at all. *156*
Jn 19:4 know that I find no **f** in him. *156*
Jn 19:6 for I find no **f** in him. *156*
Gal 6:1 if a man be overtaken in a **f**,.....................*3900*
Heb 8:8 For finding **f** with them, he saith,............*3201*
Rev 14:5 are without **f** before the throne.................*299*

FAULTLESS

Heb 8:7 if that first covenant had been **f**, ...*273*
Jude 24 and to present you **f** before the..................*299*

FAULTS

Ge 41:9 I do remember my **f** this day: 2399
Ps 19:12 cleanse thou me from secret **f**
Jas 5:16 Confess your **f** one to another, ...*3900*

FAULTY

2Sa 14:13 this thing as one which is **f**, ...818
Hos 10:2 now shall they be found **f**: 816

FAVOUR

Ge 18:3 now I have found **f** in thy sight, ...2580
Ge 39:21 him **f** in the sight of the keeper 2580
Ex 12:36 Lord gave the people **f** in the sight 2580
Ru 2:13 Let me find **f** in thy sight, ...2580
1Sa 2:26 and was in **f** both with the Lord, ...2896
1Sa 16:22 for he hath found **f** in my sight. 2580
Est 2:15 Esther obtained **f** in the sight of 2580
Ps 30:5 his **f** is life: weeping may endure 7522
Pr 8:35 and shall obtain **f** of the Lord. 7522
Pr 12:2 good man obtaineth **f** of the Lord: 7522
Pr 13:15 Good understanding giveth **f**: 2580
Pr 14:35 king's **f** is toward a wise servant: 7522
Pr 16:15 **f** is as a cloud of the latter rain. 7522
Pr 19:12 his **f** is as dew upon the grass. 7522
Pr 22:1 **f** rather than silver and gold. 2580
Pr 31:30 **F** is deceitful, and beauty is vain: 2580
Da 1:9 God had brought Daniel into **f** 2617
Lk 1:30 for thou hast found **f** with God *5485*
Lk 2:52 and in **f** with God and man *5485*

FAVOURABLE

Jgs 21:22 Be **f** unto them for our sakes: 2603
Ps 85:1 thou hast been **f** unto thy land: 7520

FAVOURED

Ge 29:17 Rachel was beautiful and well **f** 4758
Ge 41:2 out of the river seven well **f** kine 4758
Ge 41:18 kine, fatfleshed and well **f**; 8389
Ge 41:19 poor and very ill **f** and leanfleshed, ...8389
La 4:16 priests, and **f** not the elders 2603
Da 1:4 was no blemish, but well **f**, ...4758
Lk 1:28 Hail, thou that art highly **f**, ...*5487*

FAVOUREST

Ps 41:11 By this I know that thou **f** me, ...2654

FAVOURETH

2Sa 20:11 He that **f** Joab, and he that is for 2654

FEAR

Ge 15:1 **F** not, Abram: I am thy shield, ...3372
Ge 26:24 **f** not, for I am with thee, and will 3372
Ge 35:17 **F** not; thou shalt have this son 3372
Ex 14:13 **F** ye not, stand still, and see the 3372
Ex 15:16 **F** and dread shall fall upon them; 367
Nu 14:9 neither **f** ye the people of the land; 3372
Dt 6:2 That thou mightest **f** the Lord thy 3372
Dt 6:13 Thou shalt **f** the Lord thy God, ...3372
Dt 10:20 Thou shalt **f** the Lord thy God; 3372
Dt 19:20 which remain shall hear, and **f**, ...3372
Jos 8:1 **F** not, neither be thou dismayed: 3372
Jos 24:14 Now therefore **f** the Lord, and 3372
Ru 3:11 my daughter, **f** not; I will do to 3372
1Sa 4:20 **F** not; for thou hast born a son 3372
1Sa 12:14 If ye will **f** the Lord, and serve 3372
1Ki 17:13 Elijah said unto her, **F** not; 3372
1Ch 16:30 **F** before him, all the earth: 2342
Ezr 3:3 **f** was upon them because of the 367
Ne 5:9 ought ye not to walk in the **f** of 3374
Est 8:17 the **f** of the Jews fell upon them 6343
Est 9:3 the **f** of Mordecai fell upon them 6343
Job 1:9 said, Doth Job **f** God for nought? 3372
Job 28:28 the **f** of the Lord, that is wisdom; 3374
Job 41:33 his like, who is made without **f** 2844
Ps 2:11 Serve the Lord with **f**, and rejoice 3374
Ps 19:9 The **f** of the Lord is clean, ...3374
Ps 23:4 I will **f** no evil: for thou art with 3372
Ps 27:1 whom shall I **f**? the Lord is the 3372
Ps 33:8 Let all the earth **f** the Lord: 3372
Ps 52:6 The righteous also shall see, and **f** 3372
Ps 56:4 I will not **f** what flesh can do unto 3372
Ps 111:10 The **f** of the Lord is the beginning 3374
Ps 118:6 Lord is on my side; I will not **f**: 3372
Pr 1:7 The **f** of the Lord is the beginning 3374
Pr 14:26 In the **f** of the Lord is strong 3374
Ecc 12:13 matter: **F** God, and keep his 3372
Isa 33:6 the **f** of the Lord is his treasure 3374
Isa 41:10 **F** thou not; for I am with thee: 3372
Jer 5:24 Let us now **f** the Lord our God, ...3372
Jer 49:29 unto them, **F** is on every side. 4032
Da 6:26 and **f** before the God of Daniel: 1763
Jnh 1:9 I **f** the Lord, the God of heaven 3373
Mal 4:2 But unto you that **f** my name 3373
Mt 1:20 **f** not to take unto thee Mary *5399*
Mt 10:28 **f not them which kill the body,** *5399*
Lk 1:12 was troubled, and **f** fell upon him *5401*
Lk 1:13 **F** not, Zacharias: for thy prayer *5399*
Lk 1:30 **F** not, Mary: for thou hast found *5399*
Lk 2:10 **F** not: for, behold, I bring you *5399*
Lk 8:50 **F not: believe only, and she shall** *5399*
Lk 12:32 **F not, little flock; for it is your** *5399*
Jn 7:13 openly of him for **f** of the Jews *5401*
Ac 5:11 great **f** came upon all the church *5401*
Ro 3:18 There is no **f** of God before their *5401*
Ro 13:7 **f** to whom **f**; honour to whom *5401*
Php 2:12 salvation with **f** and trembling *5401*
2Ti 1:7 hath not given us the spirit of **f**; *1167*
Heb 11:7 moved with **f**, prepared an ark *2125*
1Pe 2:17 **F** God. Honour the king. *5399*
1Jn 4:18 There is no **f** in love; but perfect *5401*
1Jn 4:18 love casteth out **f**: because **f** hath *5401*
Jude 23 others save with **f**, pulling them *5401*
Rev 1:17 saying unto me, **F not; I am the** *5399*
Rev 2:10 **F none of those things which** *5399*
Rev 11:11 great **f** fell upon them which saw *5401*
Rev 14:7 **F** God, and give glory to him; *5399*
Rev 19:5 that **f** him, both small and great. *5399*

FEARED

Ge 26:7 for he **f** to say, She is my wife; 3372
Ex 2:14 And Moses **f**, and said, Surely this 3372
Jos 4:14 they **f** Moses, all the days of his life. 3372
1Sa 3:15 Samuel **f** to shew Eli the vision 3372
1Sa 15:24 because I **f** the people, and obeyed 3372
1Ki 18:3 Obadiah **f** the Lord greatly: 3373
Job 1:1 and one that **f** God, and eschewed 3373
Ps 96:4 he is to be **f** above all gods 3372
Jnh 1:16 the men **f** the Lord exceedingly, ...3372
Mt 27:54 **f** greatly, saying, Truly this was *5399*
Mk 6:20 For Herod **f** John, knowing that *5399*
Lk 18:2 **judge, which f not God, neither** *5399*
Lk 22:2 kill him; for they **f** the people *5399*
Jn 9:22 because they **f** the Jews: for the *5399*
Ac 10:2 one that **f** God with all his house *5399*

FEAREST

Ge 22:12	now I know that thou **f** God,	3373
Isa 57:11	even of old, and thou **f** me not?	3372
Jer 22:25	hand of them whose face thou **f**,	1481

FEARETH

Job 1:8	an upright man, one that **f** God,	3373
Job 2:3	an upright man, one that **f** God,	3373
Ps 25:12	What man is he that **f** the Lord?	3373
Pr 31:30	but a woman that **f** the Lord	3373
Isa 50:10	Who is among you that **f** the Lord,	3373
Ac 10:22	a just man, and one that **f** God,	*5399*
1Jn 4:18	He that **f** is not made perfect in	*5399*

FEARFUL

Ex 15:11	**f** in praises, doing wonders?	3372
Dt 28:58	fear this glorious and **f** name,	3372
Jgs 7:3	Whosoever is **f** and afraid, let	3373
Mt 8:26	**Why are ye f, O ye of little faith?**	*1169*
Mk 4:40	said unto them, **Why are ye so f?**	*1169*
Heb 10:31	It is a **f** thing to fall into the hands	*5398*
Rev 21:8	the **f**, and unbelieving, and the	*1169*

FEARFULLY

Ps 139:14	I am **f** and wonderfully made:	3372

FEARFULNESS

Ps 55:5	**F** and trembling are come upon	3374
Isa 21:4	heart panted, **f** affrighted me:	6427
Isa 33:14	**f** hath surprised the hypocrites.	7461

FEARING

Jos 22:25	children cease from **f** the Lord	3372
Mk 5:33	But the woman **f** and trembling	*5399*
Gal 2:12	himself, **f** them which were of the	*5399*
Col 3:22	but in singleness of heart, **f** God:	*5399*

FEARS

Ps 34:4	and delivered me from all my **f**	4035
Ecc 12:5	and **f** shall be in the way,	2849
2Co 7:5	were fightings, within were **f**	*5401*

FEAST

Ge 19:3	he made them a **f**, and did bake	4960
Ex 12:14	ye shall keep it a **f** to the Lord	2282
Ex 12:17	observe the **f** of unleavened bread;	
Ex 23:16	And the **f** of harvest, the firstfruits	2282
Ex 34:25	sacrifice of the **f** of the passover	2282
Le 23:34	the **f** of tabernacles for seven days	2282
Dt 16:15	days shalt thou keep a solemn **f**	2287
2Ch 7:8	Solomon kept the **f** seven days	2282
2Ch 8:13	even in the **f** of unleavened bread,	2282
Ezr 6:22	kept the **f** of unleavened bread	2282
Est 8:17	and gladness, a **f** and a good day	4960
Pr 15:15	a merry heart hath a continual **f**	4960
Hos 2:11	her **f** days, her new moons, and	2282
Am 5:21	I hate, I despise your **f** days,	2282
Mt 26:2	**two days is the f of the passover,**	
Lk 2:41	every year at the **f** of the passover.	*1859*
Lk 22:1	the **f** of unleavened bread drew	*1859*
Lk 23:17	release one unto them at the **f**	*1859*
Jn 2:9	When the ruler of the **f** had tasted	*755*
Jn 7:8	**Go ye up unto this f;**	*1859*
Jn 13:1	Now before the **f** of the passover	*1859*
1Co 5:8	let us keep the **f**, not with old leaven,	*1858*
1Co 10:27	them that believe not bid you to a **f**	
2Pe 2:13	deceivings while they **f** with you;	*4910*
Jude 12	of charity, when they **f** with you,	*4910*

FEAST-DAY See FEAST.

FEASTED

Job 1:4	his sons went and **f** in their	6213, 4960

FEASTING

Est 9:17	and made it a day of **f** and	4960
Job 1:5	when the days of their **f** were	4960
Ecc 7:2	than to go to the house of **f**:	4960
Jer 16:8	not also go into the house of **f**,	4960

FEASTS

Le 23:2	Concerning the **f** of the Lord,	4150
Le 23:2	convocations, even these are my **f**	4150
Nu 15:3	in your solemn **f**, to make a sweet	4150
2Ch 2:4	and on the solemn **f** of the Lord	4150
2Ch 8:13	new moons, and on the solemn **f**	4150
Ezr 3:5	and of all the set **f** of the Lord	4150
Ne 10:33	the set **f**, and for the holy things,	4150
Ps 35:16	With hypocritical mockers in **f**	4580
Jer 51:39	In their heat I will make their **f**	4960
La 2:6	caused the solemn **f** and sabbaths	4150
Eze 46:11	And in the **f** and in the solemnities	2282
Am 8:10	I will turn your **f** into mourning	2282
Zec 8:19	joy and gladness, and cheerful **f**;	4150
Mt 23:6	**love the uppermost rooms at f**	*1173*
Mk 12:39	**and the uppermost rooms at f:**	*1173*
Lk 20:46	**and the chief rooms at f;**	*1173*
Jude 12	are spots in your **f** of charity.	

FEATHERED

Ps 78:27	and **f** fowls like as the sand	3671
Eze 39:17	Speak unto every **f** fowl, and to	3671

FEATHERS

Le 1:16	pluck away his crop with his **f**,	5133
Job 39:13	wings and **f** unto the ostrich?	2624
Ps 91:4	He shall cover thee with his **f**,	84
Eze 17:3	great wings, long winged, full of **f**,	5133
Da 4:33	hairs were grown like eagles' **f**,	

FED

Ge 30:36	Jacob **f** the rest of Laban's flocks	7462
Ge 48:15	the God which **f** me all my life	7462
Ex 16:32	I have **f** you in the wilderness	398
Dt 8:3	to hunger, and **f** thee with manna,	398
2Sa 20:3	put them in ward, and **f** them	3557
1Ki 18:13	and **f** them with bread and water?	3557
Ps 37:3	and verily thou shalt be **f**	7462
Eze 16:19	and honey, wherewith I **f** thee,	398
Da 5:21	they **f** him with grass like oxen,	2939
Zec 11:7	called Bands; and I **f** the flock.	7462
Mt 25:37	**thee an hungered, and f thee?**	*5142*
Mk 5:14	they that **f** the swine fled, and	*1006*
Lk 16:21	**desiring to be f with the crumbs**	*5526*
1Co 3:2	I have **f** you with milk, and not	*4222*

FEEBLE

Ge 30:42	But when the cattle were **f**, he	5848
1Sa 2:5	hath many children is waxed **f**	535
Ne 4:2	What do these **f** Jews? will they	537
Job 4:4	hast strengthened the **f** knees,	3766
Ps 38:8	I am **f** and sore broken:	6313
Pr 30:26	The conies are but a **f** folk,	3808, 6099
Jer 6:24	our hands wax **f**: anguish hath	7503
Eze 7:17	All hands shall be **f**, and all knees	7503
1Co 12:22	which seem to be more **f**, are	*772*
Heb 12:12	hang down, and the **f** knees;	*3886*

FEEBLEMINDED See also MINDED.
1Th 5:14 comfort the **f**, support the weak, ... *3642*

FEEBLENESS
Jer 47:3 to their children for **f** of hands; ... 7510

FEEBLER
Ge 30:42 so the **f** were Laban's, and the ... 5848

FEED
Ge 25:30 **F** me, I pray thee, with that same ... 3938
Ge 37:12 went to **f** their father's flock in ... 7462
Ge 37:13 Do not thy brethren **f** the flock in ... 7462
Ge 37:16 tell me, I pray thee, where they **f** ... 7462
Ex 34:3 neither let the flocks nor herds **f** ... 7462
1Ki 17:4 commanded the ravens to **f** thee ... 3557
1Ki 22:27 and **f** him with bread of affliction ... 398
Job 24:20 the worm shall **f** sweetly on him;
Pr 10:21 The lips of the righteous **f** many: ... 7462
Pr 30:8 **f** me with food convenient for me: ... 2963
Isa 11:7 And the cow and the bear shall **f**; ... 7462
Isa 65:25 wolf and the lamb shall **f** together, ... 7462
Jer 23:2 the pastors that **f** my people; ... 7462
Jer 23:15 I will **f** them with wormwood, and ... 398
Da 11:26 that **f** the portion of his meat ... 398
Mic 5:4 and **f** in the strength of the Lord ... 7462
Zec 11:4 **F** the flock of the slaughter; ... 7462
Lk 15:15 **him into his fields to f swine** ... *1006*
Jn 21:15 He saith unto him, **F my lambs** ... *1006*
Jn 21:16 He saith unto him, **F my sheep** ... *4165*
Jn 21:17 Jesus saith unto him, **F my sheep.** ... *1006*
Ac 20:28 overseers, to **f** the church of God ... *4165*
Ro 12:20 if thine enemy hunger, **f** him; if ... *5595*
1Co 13:3 bestow all my goods to **f** the poor, ... *5595*
1Pe 5:2 **F** the flock of God which is ... *4165*

FEEDEST
Ps 80:5 **f** them with the bread of tears; ... 398
SS 1:7 my soul loveth, where thou **f**, ... 7462

FEEDETH
Pr 15:14 mouth of fools **f** on foolishness. ... 7462
Isa 44:20 He **f** on ashes: a deceived heart ... 7462
Mt 6:26 **yet your heavenly Father f them** ... *5142*
Lk 12:24 **and God f them: how much more** ... *5142*
1Co 9:7 who **f** a flock, and eateth not ... *4165*

FEEDING See also FEEDINGPLACE.
Ge 37:2 was **f** the flock with his brethren; ... 7462
Mt 8:30 them an herd of many swine **f** ... *1006*
Mk 5:11 mountains a great herd of swine **f** ... *1006*
Lk 17:7 **a servant plowing or f cattle,** ... *4165*
Jude 12 you, **f** themselves without fear: ... *4165*

FEEDINGPLACE
Na 2:11 and the **f** of the young lions, ... 4829

FEEL See also FELT.
Ge 27:12 will **f** me, and I shall seem to him ... 4959
Jgs 16:26 Suffer me that I may **f** the pillars ... 4184
Job 20:20 shall not **f** quietness in his belly, ... 3045
Ps 58:9 Before your pots can **f** the thorns, ... 995
Ecc 8:5 the commandment shall **f** no evil ... 3045
Ac 17:27 if haply they might **f** after him, ... *5554*

FEELING
Eph 4:19 Who being past **f** have given ... *524*
Heb 4:15 cannot be touched with the **f** of our ... *4834*

FEET
Ge 18:4 wash your **f**, and rest yourselves ... 7272
Ge 24:32 and water to wash his **f**, and the ... 7272
Ex 3:5 put off thy shoes from off thy **f**, ... 7272
Dt 11:24 the soles of your **f** shall tread ... 7272
Jos 4:18 soles of the priests' **f** were lifted ... 7272
Jos 10:24 put your **f** upon the necks of these ... 7272
Jgs 3:24 he covereth his **f** in his summer ... 7272
Ru 3:4 uncover his **f**, and lay thee down; ... 4772
1Sa 24:3 and Saul went in to cover his **f**: ... 7272
2Sa 4:4 had a son that was lame of his **f**. ... 7272
2Sa 22:34 He maketh my **f** like hind's **f**: ... 7272
1Ki 15:23 old age he was diseased in his **f**. ... 7272
2Ki 4:27 she caught him by the **f**: but ... 7272
2Ki 9:35 the skull, and the **f**, and the palms ... 7272
2Ch 3:13 they stood on their **f**, and their ... 7272
Ne 9:21 not old, and their **f** swelled not. ... 7272
Job 13:27 puttest my **f** also in the stocks, ... 7272
Ps 8:6 hast put all things under his **f**: ... 7272
Ps 18:33 He maketh my **f** like hinds' **f**, ... 7272
Ps 22:16 they pierced my hands and my **f** ... 7272
Ps 40:2 and set my **f** upon a rock, ... 7272
Ps 56:13 not thou deliver my **f** from falling, ... 7272
Ps 66:9 suffereth not our **f** to be moved. ... 7272
Ps 119:105 Thy word is a lamp unto my **f**, ... 7272
Pr 19:2 he that hasteth with his **f** sinneth. ... 7272
SS 7:1 How beautiful are thy **f** with ... 6471
Isa 6:2 with twain he covered his **f**, and ... 7272
Isa 52:7 the **f** of him that bringeth good ... 7272
Eze 2:1 Son of man, stand upon my **f**, ... 7272
Da 2:33 his **f** part of iron and part of clay ... 7271
Da 7:4 made stand upon the **f** as a man ... 7271
Na 1:15 the **f** of him that bringeth good ... 7272
Hab 3:19 he will make my **f** like hinds' **f** ... 7272
Mt 7:6 **they trample them under their f,** ... 4228
Mt 10:14 **city, shake off the dust of your f** ... *4228*
Mt 18:8 **than having two hands or two f** ... *4228*
Mt 28:9 they came and held him by the **f** ... *4228*
Mk 6:11 **dust under your f for a testimony** ... *4228*
Lk 7:38 and began to wash his **f** with tears, ... *4228*
Lk 7:45 **hath not ceased to kiss my f** ... *4228*
Lk 15:22 **on his hand, and shoes on his f:** ... *4228*
Lk 24:39 **Behold my hands and my f,** ... *4228*
Jn 11:2 and wiped his **f** with her hair ... *4228*
Jn 13:5 and began to wash the disciples' **f**, ... *4228*
Jn 13:8 Thou shalt never wash my **f** ... *4228*
Jn 13:10 **needeth not save to wash his f** ... *4228*
Jn 20:12 at the head, and the other at the **f**, ... *4228*
Ac 5:2 part, and laid it at the apostles' **f** ... *4228*
Ac 5:9 the **f** of them which have buried ... *4228*
Ac 7:58 their clothes at a young man's **f**, ... *4228*
Ac 13:25 of his **f** I am not worthy to loose ... *4228*
Ac 13:51 they shook off the dust of their **f** ... *4228*
Ro 10:15 How beautiful are the **f** of them ... *4228*
1Co 15:25 hath put all enemies under his **f** ... *4228*
Eph 1:22 And hath put all things under his **f** ... *4228*
Eph 6:15 your **f** shod with the preparation ... *4228*
Rev 1:17 I saw him, I fell at his **f** as dead. ... *4228*
Rev 2:18 **and his f are like fine brass;** ... *4228*
Rev 13:2 and his **f** were as the **f** of a bear, ... *4228*

FEIGN
2Sa 14:2 thee, **f** thyself to be a mourner,
1Ki 14:5 **f** herself to be another woman. ... 5234
Lk 20:20 sent forth spies which would **f** ... *5271*

FEIGNED See also UNFEIGNED.
1Sa 21:13 and **f** himself mad in their hands,
Ps 17:1 that goeth not out of **f** lips 4820
2Pe 2:3 with **f** words make merchandise.............*4112*

FEIGNEDLY
Jer 3:10 me with her whole heart, but **f**, ...8267

FEIGNEST
1Ki 14:6 why **f** thou thyself to be another? 5234
Ne 6:8 thou **f** them out of thine own heart. 908

FELL
Ge 4:5 very wroth, and his countenance **f** 5307
Ge 15:12 a deep sleep **f** upon Abram; and, ...5307
Ge 33:4 and **f** on his neck, and kissed him: 5307
Nu 11:9 in the night, the manna **f** upon it. 3381
Nu 22:27 angel of the Lord, she **f** down 7257
Jos 5:14 Joshua **f** on his face to the earth, ...5307
Jos 6:20 shout, that the wall **f** down flat, ...5307
Jgs 7:13 unto a tent, and smote it that it **f**.............5307
Jgs 16:30 and the house **f** upon the lords,...............5307
Ru 2:10 Then she **f** on her face, and bowed..........5307
1Sa 4:18 he **f** from off the seat backward 5307
1Sa 31:4 Saul took a sword, and **f** upon it..............5307
1Ki 18:38 Then the fire of the Lord **f** 5307
2Ki 2:13 mantle of Elijah that **f** from him 5307
2Ki 6:5 the axe head **f** into the water:...................5307
Ezr 9:5 I **f** upon my knees, and spread.................3766
Est 9:3 the fear of Mordecai **f** upon them 5307
Ps 107:12 they **f** down, and there was none.............3782
Eze 11:5 the Spirit of the Lord **f** upon me, ...5307
Da 2:46 Nebuchadnezzar **f** upon his face,.............5308
Da 3:7 **f** down and worshipped the golden.........5308
Da 4:31 there **f** a voice from heaven, saying,.........5308
Da 7:20 came up, and before whom three **f**;.........5308
Jnh 1:7 lots, and the lot **f** upon Jonah 5307
Mt 7:25 **and it f not: for it was founded**...............*4098*
Mt 13:4 **some seeds f by the way side**...................*4098*
Mt 13:5 **Some f upon stony places, where** *4098*
Mk 4:7 **And some f among thorns, and**..............*4098*
Mk 4:8 **And other f on good ground, and**...........*4098*
Lk 6:49 **immediately it f; and the ruin** *4098*
Lk 8:7 **And some f among thorns; and**..............*4098*
Lk 8:8 **And other f on good ground, and**...........*4098*
Lk 8:14 **which f among thorns are they,**..............*4098*
Lk 10:30 **f among thieves, which stripped** *4045*
Lk 16:21 **f from the rich man's table:**......................*4098*
Ac 1:25 from which Judas by transgression **f**
Ac 1:26 and the lot **f** upon Matthias; *4098*
Ac 5:5 **f** down, and gave up the ghost: *4098*
Ac 5:10 Then **f** she down straightway at...............*4098*
Ac 9:18 there **f** from his eyes as it had been *634*
Ac 10:44 the Holy Ghost **f** on all them which........*1968*
Ac 12:7 his chains **f** off from his hands................*1601*
Ac 20:9 and **f** down from the third loft,................*4098*
Heb 11:30 faith the walls of Jericho **f** down.............*4098*
Rev 5:8 elders **f** down before the Lamb *4098*
Rev 5:14 **f** down and worshipped him that...........*4098*
Rev 6:13 stars of heaven **f** unto the earth, ...*4098*
Rev 8:10 there **f** a great star from heaven, ...*4098*
Rev 11:13 and the tenth part of the city **f**................*4098*
Rev 16:21 there **f** upon men a great hail...................*2597*
Rev 22:8 I **f** down to worship before the feet *4098*

FELLED
2Ki 3:25 and **f** all the good trees: only in 5307

FELLEST
2Sa 3:34 before wicked men, so **f** thou...................5307

FELLING
2Ki 6:5 But as one was **f** a beam, ...5307

FELLOW
Ex 2:13 Wherefore smitest thou thy **f**?..................7453
Jgs 7:22 every man's sword against his **f**,...............7453
1Sa 21:15 have brought this **f** to play the mad
2Sa 2:16 caught every one his **f** by the head, ...7453
Mt 26:71 This **f** was also with Jesus of
Jn 9:29 as for this **f**, we know not from
Ac 18:13 Saying, This **f** persuadeth men
Ac 24:5 found this man a pestilent **f**, and

FELLOWCITIZENS
Eph 2:19 but **f** with the saints, and of the *4847*

FELLOWDISCIPLES
Jn 11:16 Didymus, unto his **f**, Let us also *4827*

FELLOWHEIRS
Eph 3:6 That the Gentiles should be **f**,.................*4789*

FELLOWHELPER
2Co 8:23 partner and **f** concerning you: *4904*

FELLOWHELPERS
3Jn 8 that we might be **f** to the truth. *4904*

FELLOWLABOURER
1Th 3:2 our **f** in the gospel of Christ.....................*4904*
Phm 1 our dearly beloved, and **f**..........................*4904*

FELLOWLABOURERS
Php 4:3 also, and with other my **f**,.........................*4904*
Phm 24 Demas, Lucas, my **f** *4904*

FELLOWPRISONER
Col 4:10 Aristarchus my **f** saluteth you, ...*4869*
Phm 23 Epaphras, my **f** in Christ Jesus; *4869*

FELLOWPRISONERS
Ro 16:7 and Junia, my kinsmen, and my **f**,...........*4869*

FELLOW'S
2Sa 2:16 thrust his sword in his **f** side;...................7453

FELLOWS
Jgs 18:25 lest angry **f** run upon thee, and 582
Ps 45:7 the oil of gladness above thy **f**..................2270
Isa 44:11 Behold, all his **f** shall be ashamed:...........2270
Da 2:13 they sought Daniel and his **f**....................2269
Da 7:20 look was more stout than his **f**.................2273
Mt 11:16 **markets, and calling unto their f,**............*2083*
Ac 17:5 certain lewd **f** of the baser sort,..................*435*

FELLOWSERVANT
Mt 18:29 **And his f fell down at his feet,**.................*4889*
Col 1:7 Epaphras our dear **f**, who is for *4889*
Col 4:7 minister and **f** in the Lord: *4889*
Rev 19:10 do it not: I am thy **f**, and of thy *4889*
Rev 22:9 do it not: for I am thy **f**, and of thy *4889*

FELLOWSERVANTS
Mt 18:28 **went out, and found one of his f,**............*4889*
Mt 18:31 **So when his f saw what was done,**...........*4889*
Mt 24:49 **And shall begin to smite his f,**.................*4889*
Rev 6:11 their **f** also and their brethren, ...*4889*

FELLOWSHIP

Ps	94:20	of iniquity have **f** with thee,	2266
Ac	2:42	and **f**, and in breaking of bread,	*2842*
1Co	1:9	were called unto the **f** of his Son	*2842*
2Co	6:14	what **f** hath righteousness with	*3352*
Gal	2:9	and Barnabas the right hands of **f**;	*2842*
Eph	5:11	And have no **f** with the unfruitful	*4790*
Php	1:5	your **f** in the gospel from the first	*2842*
Php	2:1	of love, if any **f** of the Spirit,	*2842*
Php	3:10	and the **f** of his sufferings,	*2842*
1Jn	1:3	ye also may have **f** with us: and	*2842*
1Jn	1:6	If we say that we have **f** with him	*2842*

FELLOWSOLDIER

Php	2:25	and companion in labour, and **f**,	*4961*
Phm	2	and Archippus our **f**, and to the	*4961*

FELT

Ge	27:22	and he **f** him, and said, the voice	4959
Ex	10:21	even darkness which may be **f**.	4959
Pr	23:35	I **f** it not: when shall I awake?	3045
Mk	5:29	**f** in her body that she was healed	*1097*
Ac	28:5	beast into the fire, and **f** no harm.	*3958*

FEMALE

Ge	1:27	him; male and **f** created he them	5347
Ge	5:2	Male and **f** created he them; and	5347
Ge	7:2	thee by sevens, the male and his **f**:	802
Ge	7:3	air by sevens, the male and the **f**;	5347
Ge	7:16	went in male and **f** of all flesh	5347
Le	4:28	of the goats, a **f** without blemish,	5347
Le	12:7	her that hath born a male or a **f**	5347
Nu	5:3	Both male and **f** shall ye put out,	5347
Mt	19:4	**beginning made them male and f,**	*2338*
Mk	10:6	**God made them male and f**	*2338*
Gal	3:28	there is neither male nor **f**: for	*2358*

FENCED

Nu	32:36	**f** cities: and folds for sheep	4013
Dt	3:5	cities were **f** with high walls,	1219
Jos	14:12	that the cities were great and **f**:	1219
2Ki	3:19	And ye shall smite every **f** city	4013
2Ch	8:5	**f** cities, with walls, gates, and	4692
Job	10:11	**f** me with bones and sinews	7753
Eze	36:35	and ruined cities are become **f**,	1219
Hos	8:14	Judah had multiplied **f** cities:	1219

FERVENT

Ac	18:25	being **f** in the spirit, he spake	*2204*
Ro	12:11	**f** in spirit; serving the Lord;	*2204*
Jas	5:16	**f** prayer of a righteous man	
1Pe	4:8	have **f** charity among yourselves:	*1618*
2Pe	3:10	the elements shall melt with **f** heat,	

FERVENTLY

Col	4:12	labouring **f** for you in prayers,	
1Pe	1:22	one another with a pure heart **f**:	*1619*

FETCH

Ge	18:5	And I will **f** a morsel of bread,	3947
Ex	2:5	she sent her maid to **f** it	3947
Nu	20:10	we **f** you water out of this rock?	3318
1Sa	4:3	Let us **f** the ark of the covenant	3947
1Sa	16:11	Send and **f** him: for we will not	3947
1Ki	17:10	**F** me, I pray thee, a little water	3947
Job	36:3	I will **f** my knowledge from afar,	5375
Isa	56:12	I will **f** wine, and we will fill	3947
Ac	16:37	come themselves and **f** us out	*1806*

FETCHED

Ge	18:4	Let a little water, I pray you, be **f**,	3947
Jgs	18:18	**f** the carved image, the ephod	3947
1Sa	7:1	and **f** up the ark of the Lord	5927
2Ch	12:11	the guard came and **f** them, and	5375

FETTERS

Jgs	16:21	and bound him with **f** of brass;	5178
Ps	149:8	and their nobles with **f** of iron;	3525
Mk	5:4	often bound with **f** and chains,	*3976*
Mk	5:4	and the **f** broken in pieces:	*3976*
Lk	8:29	kept bound with chains and in **f**;	*3976*

FEVER

Dt	28:22	with a consumption, and with a **f**	6920
Mt	8:14	wife's mother laid, and sick of a **f**	*4445*
Mk	1:30	wife's mother lay sick of a **f**,	*4445*
Lk	4:38	mother was taken with a great **f**;	*4446*
Jn	4:52	at the seventh hour the **f** left him	*4446*
Ac	28:8	lay sick of a **f** and of a bloody flux:	*4446*

FEW

Ge	47:9	**f** and evil have the days of the	4592
Nu	9:20	when the cloud was a **f** days upon	4557
2Ki	4:3	empty vessels; borrow not a **f**.	4591
Ne	2:12	I and some **f** men with me;	4592
Job	10:20	Are not my days **f**? cease then,	4592
Ps	109:8	Let his days be **f**: and let another	4592
Ecc	5:2	therefore let thy words be **f**	4592
Da	11:20	**f** days he shall be destroyed	259
Mt	7:14	**and f there be that find it.**	*3641*
Mt	9:37	**but the labourers are f;**	*3641*
Mt	15:34	Seven, and a **f** little fishes	*3641*
Mt	20:16	**for many be called, but f chosen**	*3641*
Mt	25:21	**thou hast been faithful over a f**	*3641*
Lk	10:2	**is great, but the labourers are f:**	*3641*
Lk	12:48	**shall be beaten with f stripes.**	*3641*
Heb	13:22	a letter unto you in **f** words	*1024*
1Pe	3:20	wherein **f**, that is, eight souls	*3641*
Rev	2:14	**But I have a f things against thee,**	*3641*

FEWER

Nu	33:54	and to the **f** ye shall give the less	4592

FEWEST

Dt	7:7	ye were the **f** of all people:	4592

FIDELITY

Tit	2:10	but shewing all good **f**; that they	*4102*

FIELD

Ge	2:5	every plant of the **f** before it was	7704
Ge	2:19	God formed every beast of the **f**	7704
Ge	3:1	than any beast of the **f** which the	7704
Ge	3:18	and thou shalt eat the herb of the **f**;	7704
Ge	23:19	the cave of the **f** of Machpelah	7704
Ge	25:27	a cunning hunter, a man of the **f**;	7704
Ge	27:27	my son is as the smell of a **f** which	7704
Ge	37:7	we were binding sheaves in the **f**,	7704
Ge	50:13	the cave of the **f** of Machpelah,	7704
Ex	9:25	the hail smote every herb of the **f**,	7704
Le	25:3	Six years thou shalt sow thy **f**,	7704
Le	27:18	he sanctify his **f** after the jubile	7704
Dt	20:19	the tree of the **f** is man's life)	7704
Ru	2:3	gleaned in the **f** after the reapers:	7704
Ru	4:5	buyest the **f** of the hand of Naomi,	7704
1Sa	20:24	So David hid himself in the **f**:	7704
2Ki	19:26	they were as the grass of the **f**,	7704

Job 5:23 beasts of the **f** shall be at peace................7704
Job 40:20 where all the beasts of the **f** play..............7704
Ps 103:15 flower of the **f**, so he flourisheth..............7704
Pr 31:16 She considereth a **f**, and buyeth it:...........7704
Isa 5:8 join house to house, that lay **f** to **f**,..........7704
Isa 40:6 thereof is as the flower of the **f**: 7704
Isa 55:12 and all the trees of the **f** shall clap...........7704
Jer 26:18 Zion shall be plowed like a **f**, ...7704
Da 4:23 portion be with the beasts of the **f**, ...1251
Joel 2:22 Be not afraid, ye beasts of the **f**:...............7704
Mic 3:12 Zion for your sake be plowed as a **f**,........7704
Mt 6:28 **Consider the lilies of the f, how**...................*68*
Mt 6:30 **so clothe the grass of the f, which**...............*68*
Mt 13:24 **which sowed good seed in his f:**...................*68*
Mt 13:38 **The f is the world; the good seed**................*68*
Mt 13:44 **is like unto treasure hid in a f;**....................*68*
Mt 24:40 **Then shall two be in the f;**...........................*68*
Mt 27:8 that **f** was called, The **f** of blood, ...*68*
Mt 27:10 And gave them for the potter's **f**,.................*68*
Mk 13:16 **him that is in the f not turn back**................*68*
Lk 2:8 shepherds abiding in the **f**, keeping.............*68*
Lk 15:25 **Now his elder son was in the f**.....................*68*
Ac 1:19 that is to say, The **f** of blood......................*5564*

FIELDS
Nu 19:16 slain with a sword in the open **f**, ...7704
Dt 32:32 Sodom, and of the **f** of Gomorrah: 7709
1Sa 8:14 take your **f**, and your vineyards, ...7704
1Sa 22:7 Jesse give every one of you good **f**...........7704
Ps 107:37 sow the **f**, and plant vineyards, ...7704
Pr 23:10 not into the **f** of the fatherless:.................7704
Jer 32:15 Houses and **f** and vineyards shall 7704
Mic 2:2 covet **f**, and take them by violence;..........7704
Hab 3:17 and the **f** shall yield no meat;...................7709
Lk 15:15 **sent him into his f to feed swine**..................*68*
Jn 4:35 **look on the f; for they are white**.............*5561*
Jas 5:4 who have reaped down your **f**,.................*5561*

FIERCE
Ex 32:12 Turn from thy **f** wrath, and repent..........2740
Nu 25:4 **f** anger of the Lord may be turned..........2740
1Sa 20:34 arose from the table in **f** anger.................2750
2Ch 28:11 **f** wrath of the Lord is upon you 2740
Job 10:16 Thou huntest me as a **f** lion: 7826
Isa 13:13 and in the day of his **f** anger 2740
Jer 4:8 **f** anger of the Lord is not turned.............2740
Da 8:23 a king of **f** countenance, and....................5794
Hab 1:8 more **f** than the evening wolves: 2300
Mt 8:28 exceeding **f**, so that no man might *5467*
Lk 23:5 they were the more **f**, saying.....................*2001*
2Ti 3:3 false accusers, incontinent, **f**,......................*434*
Jas 3:4 driven of **f** winds, yet are they..................*4642*

FIERCENESS
Dt 13:17 turn from the **f** of his anger 2740
Jos 7:26 turned from the **f** of his anger 2740
Job 39:24 He swalloweth the ground with **f**............7494
Ps 85:3 thyself from the **f** of thine anger..............2740
Jer 28:38 because of the **f** of the oppressor.............2740
Rev 19:15 the **f** and wrath of Almighty God............*2572*

FIERCER
2Sa 19:43 words of the men of Judah were **f**...........7185

FIERY
Nu 21:6 the Lord sent **f** serpents among 8314
Nu 21:8 a **f** serpent, and set it upon a pole: 8314
Dt 33:2 right hand went a **f** law for them...............799
Ps 21:9 Thou shalt make them as a **f** oven.............784
Isa 14:29 fruit shall be a **f** flying serpent 8314
Da 3:6 midst of a burning **f** furnace.....................5135
Da 3:20 to cast them into the burning **f**................5135
Da 7:10 A **f** stream issued and came forth............5135
Eph 6:16 all the **f** darts of the wicked......................*4448*
1Pe 4:12 the **f** trial which is to try you...................*4451*

FIFTEEN
Ge 5:10 eight hundred and **f** years, ...2568, 6240
Ge 7:20 **F** cubits upward did the...........................6240
Ex 38:15 were hangings of **f** cubits;...............2568, 6240
Le 27:7 estimation shall be **f** shekels...........2568, 6240
2Sa 19:17 house of Saul, and his **f** sons..........2568, 6240
2Ki 20:6 will add unto thy days **f** years; 2568, 6240
Isa 38:5 will add unto thy days **f** years 2568, 6240
Ac 7:14 threescore and **f** souls......................*1440, 4002*
Gal 1:18 Peter, and abode with him **f** days.............*1178*

FIFTEENTH
Est 9:18 **f** day of the same they rested,.........2568, 6240
Lk 3:1 Now in the **f** year of the reign *4003*

FIFTH
Ge 1:23 and the morning were the **f** day...............2549
Ge 30:17 conceived, and bare Jacob the **f**...............2549
Ge 47:24 that ye shall give the **f** part unto 2549
Le 19:25 And in the **f** year shall ye eat of the.........2549
Nu 33:38 in the first day of the **f** month 2549
Jos 19:24 the **f** lot came out for the tribe 2549
2Sa 2:23 spear smote him under the **f** rib.............2570
Ezr 7:8 came to Jerusalem in the **f** month,..........2549
Ne 6:15 finished in the twenty and **f** day 2568
Rev 6:9 when he had opened the **f** seal.................*3991*
Rev 9:1 And the **f** angel sounded, and I saw.........*3991*
Rev 16:10 And the **f** angel poured out his vial.........*3991*
Rev 21:20 The **f**, sardonyx; the sixth, sardius; *3991*

FIFTIES
Ex 18:21 rulers of **f**, and rulers of tens:..................2572
Dt 1:15 captains over **f**, and captains over............2572
Mk 6:40 in ranks, by hundreds, and by **f** *4004*
Lk 9:14 **them sit down by f in a company**............*4004*

FIFTIETH
Le 25:10 And ye shall hallow the **f** year 2572
Le 25:11 A jubile shall that **f** year be unto.............2572

FIFTY
Ge 6:15 the breadth of it **f** cubits, and..................2572
Ge 7:24 the earth an hundred and **f** days..............2572
Ge 9:23 flood three hundred and **f** years 2572
Ge 18:24 Peradventure there be **f** righteous 2572
Ge 18:28 there shall lack five of the **f**......................2572
Le 23:16 sabbath shall ye number **f** days;...............2572
Nu 4:3 even until **f** years old, all that...................2572
Nu 4:23 until **f** years old shalt thou number.........2572
Nu 8:25 the age of **f** years they shall cease.............2572
Nu 16:35 consumed the two hundred and **f**...........2572
Nu 26:10 devoured two hundred and **f** men:...........2572
Jos 7:21 and a wedge of gold of **f** shekels..............2572
1Ki 18:4 and hid them by **f** in a cave,.....................2572
1Ki 18:13 the Lord's prophets by **f** in a cave, ...2572
1Ki 18:19 prophets of Baal four hundred and **f**......2572
2Ki 2:7 **f** men of the sons of the prophets 2572
Ne 5:17 an hundred and **f** of the Jews and 2572
Est 5:14 gallows be made of **f** cubits high, ...2572

Est 7:9 also, the gallows **f** cubits high, 2572
Lk 7:41 **hundred pence, and the other f.** *4004*
Lk 16:6 **and sit down quickly, and write f** *4004*
Jn 8:57 Thou art not yet **f** years old *4004*
Jn 21:11 an hundred and **f** and three: *4004*
Ac 13:20 of four hundred and **f** years *4004*
Ac 19:19 found it **f** thousand pieces of *4002, 3461*

FIG
Ge 3:7 and they sewed **f** leaves together 8384
Jgs 9:10 the trees said to the **f** tree, 8384
Pr 27:18 Whoso keepeth the **f** tree shall eat 8384
SS 2:13 **f** tree putteth forth her green figs, 8384
Na 3:12 strong holds shall be like **f** trees 8384
Mt 21:19 when he saw a **f** tree in the way, *4808*
Mt 21:21 **this which is done to the f tree,** *4808*
Mt 24:32 **learn a parable of the f tree;** *4808*
Mk 11:13 a **f** tree afar off having leaves, *4808*
Mk 11:20 they saw the **f** tree dried up *4808*
Mk 13:28 **learn a parable of the f tree;** *4808*
Lk 13:6 **certain man had a f tree planted** *4808*
Lk 21:29 **Behold the f tree, and all the** *4808*
Jn 1:48 **when thou wast under the f tree,** *4808*
Jn 1:50 I saw thee under the **f** tree, *4808*
Jas 3:12 Can the **f** tree, my brethren, bear *4808*
Rev 6:13 a **f** tree casteth her untimely figs, *4808*

FIGHT See also FOUGHT.
Ex 14:14 The Lord shall **f** for you, and ye 3898
Dt 1:30 he shall go **f** for you according to all 3898
Dt 3:22 your God he shall **f** for you 3898
Jos 9:2 to **f** with Joshua and with Israel, 3898
1Sa 15:18 and **f** against them until they be 3898
1Sa 17:9 If he be able to **f** with me, 3898
1Sa 17:10 man, that we may **f** together 3898
1Sa 17:32 go and **f** with this Philistine 3898
1Sa 18:17 for me, and **f** the Lord's battles 3898
1Ki 22:31 **F** neither with small nor great, 3898
2Ch 13:12 **f** ye not against the Lord God 3898
Ne 4:8 to **f** against Jerusalem, and to 3898
Ne 4:20 our God shall **f** for us 3898
Ps 35:1 **f** against them that **f** against me 3898
Isa 31:4 to **f** for mount Zion, and for the 6633
Jn 18:36 **then would my servants f,** *75*
Ac 5:39 be found even to **f** against God *2314*
Ac 23:9 let us not **f** against God *2313*
1Co 9:26 so **f** I, not as one that beateth *4438*
1Ti 6:12 **F** the good … of faith, lay hold on *75*
1Ti 6:12 the good **f** of faith, lay hold on *73*
2Ti 4:7 a good **f**, I have finished my course *73*
Heb 10:32 endured a great **f** of afflictions; *119*
Rev 2:16 **f against them with the sword** *4170*

FIGHTETH
Ex 14:25 the Lord **f** for them against the 3898
Jos 23:10 he it is that **f** for you, as he hath 3898
1Sa 25:28 my lord **f** the battles of the Lord, 3898

FIGHTING
1Sa 17:19 of Elah, **f** with the Philistines 3898
2Ch 26:11 host of **f** men, that went 6213, 4421
Ps 56:1 me up; he **f** daily oppresseth me 3898

FIGHTINGS
2Co 7:5 without were **f**, within were fears *3163*
Jas 4:1 come wars and **f** among you? *3163*

FIGS
Nu 13:23 the pomegranates, and of the **f** 8384
2Ki 20:7 Isaiah said, Take a lump of **f**. 8384
SS 2:13 fig tree putteth forth her green **f**, 6291
Jer 24:3 I said, **F**; the good **f**, very good; 8384
Mt 7:16 **grapes of thorns, or f of thistles?** *4810*
Mk 11:13 for the time of **f** was not yet *4810*
Lk 6:44 **of thorns men do not gather f,** *4810*
Jas 3:12 either a vine, **f**? so can no fountain *4810*
Rev 6:13 a fig tree casteth her untimely **f**, *3653*

FIGURE See also DISFIGURE; TRANSFIGURED.
Dt 4:16 image, the similitude of any **f**, 5566
Isa 44:13 maketh it after the **f** of a man, 8403
Ro 5:14 is the **f** of him that was to come *5179*
1Co 4:6 I have in a **f** transferred to myself *3345*
Heb 9:9 was a **f** for the time then present *3850*
Heb 11:19 also he received him in a **f**. *3850*
1Pe 3:21 like **f** whereunto even baptism *499*

FIGURES
1Ki 6:29 carved **f** of cherubims and palm *4734*
Ac 7:43 **f** which ye made to worship *5179*
Heb 9:24 which are the **f** of the true; *499*

FILL
Ge 1:22 and **f** the waters in the seas 4390
Ge 44:1 **F** the men's sacks with food, as 4390
Ex 16:32 **F** an omer of it to be kept 4393
1Sa 16:1 **f** thine horn with oil, and go, 4390
1Ki 18:33 **F** four barrels with water, and 4390
Job 23:4 and **f** my mouth with arguments 4390
Ps 83:16 **F** their faces with shame; that 4390
Pr 7:18 Come, let us take our **f** of love 7301
Isa 56:12 **f** ourselves with strong drink; 5433
Jer 23:24 Do not I **f** heaven and earth? 4390
Hag 2:7 and I will **f** this house with glory, 4390
Mt 9:16 **which is put in to f it up taketh** *4138*
Mt 23:32 **F ye up then the measure of** *4137*
Jn 2:7 **F the water pots with water** *1072*
1Th 2:16 to **f** up their sins alway: for the *378*

FILLED
Ge 6:11 the earth was **f** with violence 4390
Ge 21:19 went, and **f** the bottle with water 4390
Ge 24:16 and **f** her pitcher, and came up 4390
Ex 1:7 and the land was **f** with them 4390
Ex 28:3 whom I have **f** with the spirit 4390
Ex 40:34 and the glory of the Lord **f** the 4390
Nu 14:21 the earth shall be **f** with the glory 4390
1Ki 7:14 and he was **f** with wisdom, and 4390
1Ki 8:10 the cloud **f** the house of the Lord, 4390
2Ki 3:25 cast every man his stone, and **f** it; 4390
2Ch 5:13 the house was **f** with a cloud 4390
Job 16:8 thou hast **f** me with wrinkles, 7059
Ps 71:8 Let my mouth be **f** with thy praise 4390
Ps 72:19 the whole earth be **f** with his glory; 4390
Ps 126:2 was our mouth **f** with laughter 4390
Pr 3:10 shall thy barns be **f** with plenty 4390
Pr 20:17 his mouth shall be **f** with gravel 4390
Isa 6:1 up, and his train **f** the temple 4390
Isa 6:4 and the house was **f** with smoke 4390
Isa 34:6 sword of the Lord is **f** with blood 4390
La 3:15 He hath **f** me with bitterness 7646
Eze 10:3 and the cloud **f** the inner court 4390
Eze 43:5 the glory of the Lord **f** the house 4390
Eze 44:4 the Lord **f** the house of the Lord: 4390

F

Hab 2:14	shall be **f** with the knowledge	4390
Mt 5:6	**righteousness: for they shall be f.**	*5526*
Mt 27:48	a spunge, and **f** it with vinegar	*4130*
Mk 7:27	**Let the children first be f:**	*5526*
Lk 1:15	he shall be **f** with the Holy Ghost	*4130*
Lk 1:41	Elisabeth was **f** with the Holy	*4130*
Lk 1:67	Zacharias was **f** with the Holy	*4130*
Lk 2:40	strong in spirit, **f** with wisdom:	*4137*
Lk 3:5	Every valley shall be **f**, and every	*4137*
Lk 14:23	**come in, that my house may be f:**	*1072*
Jn 2:7	And they **f** them up to the brim	*2072*
Jn 6:13	and **f** twelve baskets with the	*2072*
Jn 6:26	**ye did eat the loaves, and were f**	*5526*
Jn 16:6	**sorrow hath f your heart**	*4137*
Ac 2:4	were all **f** with the Holy Ghost,	*4130*
Ac 3:10	and they were **f** with wonder and	*4130*
Ac 5:3	hath Satan **f** thine heart to lie	*4237*
Ac 9:17	and be **f** with the Holy Ghost,	*4130*
Ac 13:52	And the disciples were **f** with joy,	*4137*
Ac 19:29	whole city was **f** with confusion:	*4230*
2Co 7:4	**f** with comfort, I am exceeding	*4237*
Eph 5:18	but be **f** with the Spirit;	*4237*
Jas 2:16	in peace, be ye warmed and **f**;	*5526*
Rev 15:8	the temple was **f** with smoke	*1072*
Rev 18:6	she hath **f** fill to her double	*2767*

FILLEDST

Dt 6:11	all good things, which thou **f** not,	4390
Eze 27:33	thou **f** many people: thou didst	7646

FILLEST

Ps 17:14	whose belly thou **f** with thy hid	4390

FILLETED

Ex 38:17	all the pillars of the court were **f**.	2836

FILLETH

Job 9:18	but **f** me with bitterness	7646
Ps 84:6	the rain also **f** the pools	5844
Ps 107:9	**f** the hungry soul with goodness	4390
Ps 129:7	Wherewith the mower **f** not his	4390
Ps 147:14	**f** thee with the finest of the wheat	7646
Eph 1:23	the fulness of him that **f** all in all	*4237*

FILLETS

Ex 27:10	and their **f** shall be of silver	2838
Ex 36:38	chapiters and their **f** with gold	2838
Ex 38:17	of the pillars and their **f** of silver;	2838

FILLING See also FULFILLING.

Ac 14:17	**f** our hearts with food and	*1705*

FILTH

Isa 4:4	the **f** of the daughters of Zion,	6675
Na 3:6	I will cast abominable **f** upon thee	
1Co 4:13	are made as the **f** of the world	*4027*
1Pe 3:21	putting away of the **f** of the flesh	*4589*

FILTHINESS

2Ch 29:5	forth the **f** out of the holy place	5079
Ezr 6:21	them from the **f** of the heathen of	2932
Pr 30:12	yet is not washed from their **f**	6675
Eze 22:15	will consume thy **f** out of thee	2932
Eze 36:25	ye shall be clean: from all your **f**,	2932
2Cor 7:1	from all **f** of the flesh and spirit	*3436*
Eph 5:4	Neither **f**, nor foolish talking, nor	*252*
Jas 1:21	lay apart all **f** and superfluity	*4507*
Rev 17:4	full of abominations and **f** of her	*168*

FILTHY

Job 15:16	more abominable and **f** is man	444
Ps 14:3	aside, they are altogether become **f**:	444
Isa 64:6	righteousness are as **f** rags;	5708
Zec 3:3	was clothed with **f** garments,	6674
Col 3:8	**f** communication out of your	*148*
1Ti 3:3	no striker, not greedy of **f** lucre;	
Tit 1:11	they ought not, for **f** lucre's sake	*150*
1Pe 5:2	not for **f** lucre, but of a ready mind;	*147*
Jude 8	also these **f** dreamers defile	
Rev 22:11	he which is **f**, let him be **f** still:	*4520*

FINALLY

2Co 13:11	**F**, brethren, farewell. Be perfect,	*3063*
Eph 6:10	**F**, my brethren, be strong in the	*3063*
Php 3:1	**F**, my brethren, rejoice in the Lord	*3063*
Php 4:8	**F**, brethren, whatsoever things are	*3063*
2Th 3:1	**F**, brethren, pray for us, that the	*3063*
1Pe 3:8	**F**, be ye all of one mind, having	*5056*

FIND See also FOUND.

Ge 18:26	If I **f** in Sodom fifty righteous	4672
Ge 19:11	wearied themselves to **f** the door	4672
Ge 33:8	to **f** grace in the sight of my lord	4672
Ex 5:11	get you straw where ye can **f** it:	4672
Nu 32:23	be sure your sin will **f** you out	4672
Ru 2:13	Let me **f** favour in thy sight	4672
1Sa 1:18	handmaid **f** grace in thy sight	4672
1Sa 20:21	saying, Go **f** out the arrows	4672
Ezr 4:15	thou **f** in the book of the records,	7912
Job 11:7	Canst thou by searching **f** out God?	4672
Ps 132:5	Until I **f** out a place for the Lord	4672
Pr 2:5	Lord, and **f** the knowledge of God	4672
Pr 8:17	that seek me early shall **f** me	4672
Pr 31:10	Who can **f** a virtuous woman?	4672
Ecc 3:11	no man can **f** out the work that God	4672
Jer 6:16	and ye shall **f** rest for your souls	4672
Jer 29:13	And ye shall seek me, and **f** me,	4672
Da 6:4	to **f** occasion against Daniel	7912
Mt 7:7	**seek, and ye shall f; knock, and**	*2247*
Mt 10:39	**his life for my sake shall f it**	*2247*
Mt 11:29	**ye shall f rest unto your souls**	*2247*
Mt 16:25	**lose his life for my sake shall f it**	*2247*
Mt 24:46	**when he cometh shall f so doing,**	*2247*
Mk 11:2	**ye shall f a colt tied, whereon**	*2247*
Mk 13:36	**suddenly he f you sleeping**	*2247*
Lk 2:12	Ye shall **f** the babe wrapped in	*2247*
Lk 12:37	**when he cometh shall f watching:**	*2147*
Lk 12:43	**when he cometh shall f so doing**	*2147*
Lk 13:7	**fruit on this fig tree, and f none:**	*2147*
Lk 15:4	**that which is lost, until he f it?**	*2147*
Lk 18:8	**shall he f faith on the earth?**	*2147*
Lk 23:4	I **f** no fault in this man	*2147*
Jn 10:9	**shall go in and out, and f pasture**	*2147*
Jn 18:38	I **f** in him no fault at all,	*2147*
Jn 21:6	**side of the ship, and ye shall f.**	*2147*
Ac 23:9	We **f** no evil in this man:	*2147*
2Co 9:4	with me, and **f** you unprepared,	*2147*
2Ti 1:18	that he may **f** mercy of the Lord	*2147*
Heb 4:16	we may obtain mercy, and **f** grace	*2147*
Rev 9:6	seek death, and shall not **f** it;	*2147*

FINDEST

Ge 31:32	with whomsoever thou **f** thy gods,	4672
Eze 3:1	Son of man, eat that thou **f**;	4672

FINDETH

Ge 4:14	every one that **f** me shall slay me	4672
Ps 119:162	thy word as one that **f** great spoil	4672
Pr 3:13	Happy is the man that **f** wisdom,	4672
Pr 18:22	Whoso **f** a wife **f** a good thing,	4672
Ecc 9:10	Whatsoever thy hand **f** to do, do it	4672
Mt 7:8	**he that seeketh f; and to him**	*2147*
Mt 10:39	**He that f his life shall lose it:**	*2147*
Mt 12:43	**places, seeking rest, and f none**	*2147*
Mk 14:37	he cometh, and **f** them sleeping,	*2147*
Lk 11:10	**receiveth; and he that seeketh f;**	*2147*
Jn 1:41	He first **f** his own brother Simon	*2147*
Jn 1:43	and **f** Philip, and saith unto him,	*2147*
Jn 1:45	Philip **f** Nathanael, and saith unto	*2147*

FINDING

Ge 4:15	lest any **f** him should kill him	4672
Job 9:10	doeth great things past **f** out;	2714
Lk 11:24	**and f none, he saith, I will return**	*2147*
Ac 4:21	**f** nothing how they might punish	*2147*
Ac 21:2	And **f** a ship sailing over unto	*2147*
Ro 11:33	and his ways past **f** out!	*421*

FINE

Ge 18:6	quickly three measures of **f** meal,	5560
Ge 41:42	and arrayed him in vestures of **f** linen,	
Ex 25:4	scarlet, and **f** linen, and goats' hair,	
Ex 26:1	with ten curtains of **f** twined linen,	
Le 2:4	shall be unleavened cakes of **f** flour	
2Ch 3:5	which he overlaid with **f** gold,	2896
Ezr 8:27	two vessels of **f** copper, precious	6668
Est 1:6	fastened with cords of **f** linen and	
Ps 19:10	yea, than much **f** gold: sweeter also	
Pr 8:19	is better than gold, yea, than **f** gold;	
Pr 31:24	She maketh **f** linen, and selleth	
SS 5:11	His head is as the most **f** gold,	
Da 2:32	This image's head was of **f** gold,	2869
Lk 16:19	**was clothed in purple and f linen,**	
Rev 2:18	**and his feet are like f brass;**	
Rev 18:13	and **f** flour, and wheat, and	4585
Rev 18:16	great city, that was clothed in **f** linen	
Rev 19:8	the **f** linen is the righteousness of	

FINER

Pr 25:4	come forth a vessel for the **f**	6884

FINEST

Ps 81:16	them also with the **f** of the wheat:	2459
Ps 147:14	filleth thee with the **f** of the wheat	2459

FINGER

Ex 8:19	Pharaoh, This is the **f** of God:	676
Ex 31:18	stone, written with the **f** of God	676
Le 4:6	priest shall dip his **f** in the blood	676
Le 14:16	sprinkle of the oil with his **f** seven	676
Dt 9:10	them was written with the **f** of God;	676
1Ki 12:10	My little **f** shall be thicker than	
Lk 11:20	**with the f of God cast out devils,**	*1147*
Lk 16:24	**may dip the tip of his f in water,**	*1147*
Jn 8:6	with his **f** wrote on the ground,	*1147*
Jn 20:25	put my **f** into the print of the nails,	*1147*
Jn 20:27	**Reach hither thy f, and behold**	*1147*

FINGERS

2Sa 21:20	that had on every hand six **f**,	676
1Ch 20:6	**f** and toes were four and twenty,	676
Ps 8:3	thy heavens, the work of thy **f**,	676
Pr 7:3	Bind them upon thy **f**, write them	676
Da 5:5	In the same hour came forth **f** of a	677
Mt 23:4	**move them with one of their f**	*1147*
Mk 7:33	put his **f** into his ears, and he spit,	*1147*
Lk 11:46	**the burdens with one of your f**	*1147*

FINING

Pr 17:3	The **f** pot is for silver, and the	4715
Pr 27:21	As the **f** pot for silver, and the	4715

FINISH

Ge 6:16	in a cubit shalt thou **f** it above;	3615
Da 9:24	to **f** the transgression, and to	3607
Zec 4:9	his hands shall also **f** it;	1214
Lk 14:28	**whether he have sufficient to f it?**	*535*
Jn 4:34	**that sent me, and to f his work**	*5048*
Jn 5:36	**the Father hath given me to f,**	*5048*
Ac 20:24	I might **f** my course with joy	*5048*
2Co 8:6	he would also **f** in you the same	*2005*

FINISHED

Ge 2:1	the heavens and the earth were **f**	3615
Ex 39:32	of the tent of the congregation **f**:	3615
Dt 31:24	law in a book, until they were **f**,	8552
Ru 3:18	until he have **f** the thing this day	3615
1Ki 6:14	Solomon built the house, and **f** it	3615
1Ki 6:38	eighth month, was the house **f**	3615
1Ki 9:1	when Solomon had **f** the building	3615
1Ki 9:25	the Lord. So he **f** the house	7999
Ezr 6:15	this house was **f** on the third day	3319
Ne 6:15	So the wall was **f** in the twenty	7999
Jn 17:4	**I have f the work which thou**	*5048*
Jn 19:30	he said, **It is f:** and he bowed	*5055*
2Ti 4:7	I have **f** my course, I have kept	*5055*
Heb 4:3	works were **f** from the foundation	*1096*
Jas 1:15	sin, when it is **f**, bringeth forth	*658*
Rev 10:7	the mystery of God should be **f**,	*5055*
Rev 20:5	until the thousand years were **f**	*5055*

FINISHER

Heb 12:2	Jesus the author and **f** of our	*5047*

FINS

Le 11:12	Whatsoever hath no **f** nor scales	5579
Dt 14:9	have **f** and scales shall ye eat:	5579

FIR

2Sa 6:5	of instruments made of **f** wood,	1265
1Ki 5:10	gave Solomon cedar trees and **f**	1265
Ps 104:17	stork, the **f** trees are her house	1265
Isa 41:19	I will set in the desert the **f** tree,	1265
Hos 14:8	I am like a green **f** tree	1265
Na 2:3	**f** trees shall be terribly shaken	1265

FIRE

Ge 19:24	brimstone and **f** from the Lord out	784
Ge 22:6	and he took the **f** in his hand, and a	784
Ex 3:2	appeared unto him in a flame of **f**	784
Ex 9:24	and **f** mingled with the hail, very	784
Ex 13:21	and by night in a pillar of **f**	784
Ex 14:24	the pillar of **f** and of the cloud,	784
Ex 19:18	the Lord descended upon it in **f**:	784
Ex 29:18	offering made by **f** unto the Lord	
Le 1:7	the priest shall put **f** upon the altar	784
Le 4:12	burn him on the wood with **f**:	784
Le 6:13	The **f** shall ever be burning upon	784
Le 18:21	seed pass through the **f** to Molech,	
Nu 3:4	offered strange **f** before the Lord,	784
Nu 11:1	**f** of the Lord burnt among them,	784

Nu	16:35	there came out a **f** from the Lord,	784
Nu	26:61	offered strange **f** before the Lord.	784
Nu	31:23	Every thing that may abide the **f**.	784
Dt	1:33	in **f** by night, to shew you by what	784
Dt	4:24	the Lord thy God is a consuming **f**,	784
Dt	4:33	speaking out of the midst of the **f**,	784
Dt	7:5	burn their graven images with **f**.	784
Dt	32:22	For a **f** is kindled in mine anger,	784
Jos	7:15	accursed thing shall be burnt with **f**,	784
Jos	11:6	and burn their chariots with **f**.	784
Jgs	6:21	there rose up **f** out of the rock,	784
Jgs	15:14	as flax that was burnt with **f**,	784
1Ki	18:23	lay it on wood, and put no **f** under:	784
1Ki	18:24	and the God that answereth by **f**,	784
1Ki	18:38	Then the **f** of the Lord fell,	784
1Ki	19:12	a **f**; but the Lord was not in the **f**:	784
2Ki	1:10	then let **f** come down from heaven,	784
2Ki	1:12	**f** of God came down from heaven,	784
2Ki	2:11	a chariot of **f**, and horses of **f**, and	784
2Ki	6:17	was full of horses and chariots of **f**.	784
1Ch	21:26	he answered him from heaven by **f**	784
2Ch	7:3	Israel saw how the **f** came down,	784
Ne	1:3	the gates thereof are burned with **f**	784
Ne	9:12	and in the night by a pillar of **f**.	784
Job	1:16	The **f** of God is fallen from heaven,	784
Job	41:19	and sparks of **f** leap out	784
Ps	104:4	spirits; his ministers a flaming **f**:	784
Ps	105:39	and **f** to give light in the night.	784
Pr	6:27	Can a man take **f** in his bosom,	784
Pr	25:22	shalt heap coals of **f** upon his head,	
Pr	26:20	no wood is, there the **f** goeth out:	784
Isa	9:19	people shall be as the fuel of the **f**:	784
Isa	10:17	the light of Israel shall be for a **f**,	784
Isa	43:2	when thou walkest through the **f**.	784
Isa	66:15	behold, the Lord will come with **f**,	784
Jer	4:4	lest my fury come forth like **f**.	784
Jer	17:4	ye have kindled a **f** in mine anger,	784
Jer	23:29	Is not my word like as a **f**?	784
La	4:11	and hath kindled a **f** in Zion	784
Eze	10:6	Take **f** from between the wheels,	784
Eze	10:7	**f** that was between the cherubims,	784
Eze	36:5	Surely in the **f** of my jealousy have	784
Da	3:22	the flame of the **f** slew those men	5135
Da	3:24	bound into the midst of the **f**?	5135
Da	3:26	came forth of the midst of the **f**	5135
Da	3:27	whose bodies the **f** had no power,	5135
Da	10:6	and his eyes as lamps of **f**,	784
Am	7:4	Lord God called to contend by **f**.	784
Mal	3:2	for he is like a refiner's **f**,	784
Mt	3:11	with the Holy Ghost, and with **f**:	*4442*
Mt	5:22	**fool, shall be in danger of hell f.**	*4442*
Mt	7:19	**is hewn down, and cast into the f.**	*4442*
Mt	18:8	**feet to be cast into everlasting f.**	*4442*
Mt	18:9	**two eyes to be cast into hell f.**	*4442*
Mt	25:41	**into everlasting f, prepared for**	*4442*
Mk	9:43	**f that never shall be quenched:**	*4442*
Mk	14:54	and warmed himself at the **f**.	*5457*
Lk	3:16	with the Holy Ghost and with **f**:	*4442*
Lk	9:54	that we command **f** to come down	*4442*
Lk	12:49	**I am come to send f on the earth;**	*4442*
Lk	17:29	**it rained f and brimstone from**	*4442*
Jn	15:6	**them, and cast them into the f,**	*4442*
Ac	2:3	them cloven tongues like as of **f**,	*4442*
Ac	7:30	the Lord in a flame of **f** in a bush	*4442*
Ro	12:20	shalt heap coals of **f** on his head	*4442*
1Co	3:15	shall be saved; yet so as by **f**.	*4442*
Heb	1:7	and his ministers a flame of **f**.	*4442*
Heb	12:29	For our God is a consuming **f**.	*4442*
Jas	3:5	great a matter a little **f** kindleth!	*4442*
Jas	3:6	tongue is a **f**, a world of iniquity:	*4442*
1Pe	1:7	though it be tried with **f**, might	*4442*
2Pe	3:7	reserved unto **f** against the day of	*4442*
Jude	7	the vengeance of eternal **f**.	*4442*
Jude	23	fear, pulling them out of the **f**;	*4442*
Rev	2:18	**his eyes like unto a flame of f,**	*4442*
Rev	3:18	**to buy of me gold tried in the f,**	*4442*
Rev	4:5	seven lamps of **f** burning before	*4442*
Rev	8:7	hail and **f** mingled with blood,	*4442*
Rev	9:17	having breastplates of **f**, and of	*4447*
Rev	11:5	**f** proceedeth out of their mouth,	*4442*
Rev	14:10	tormented with **f** and brimstone	*4442*
Rev	14:18	which had power over **f**; and cried	*4442*
Rev	15:2	were a sea of glass mingled with **f**:	*4442*
Rev	16:8	unto him to scorch men with **f**.	*4442*
Rev	19:12	His eyes were as a flame of **f**,	*4442*
Rev	19:20	lake of **f** burning with brimstone.	*4442*
Rev	20:9	and **f** came down from God out of	*4442*
Rev	20:10	into the lake of **f** and brimstone,	*4442*
Rev	20:14	hell were cast into the lake of **f**.	*4442*
Rev	21:8	burneth with **f** and brimstone:	*4442*

FIREBRAND See also BRAND.

Jgs	15:4	turned tail to tail, and put a **f**	3940
Am	4:11	ye were as a **f** plucked out of the	181

FIREBRANDS

Jgs	15:4	and took **f** and turned tail to tail,	3940
Pr	26:18	As a mad man who casteth **f**,	2131
Isa	7:4	for the two tails of these smoking **f**,	181

FIREPANS

Ex	27:3	and his fleshhooks, and his **f**;	4289
Ex	38:3	and the fleshhooks, and the **f**:	4289
2Ki	25:15	And the **f**, and the bowls, and such	4289
Jer	52:19	the basons, and the **f**, and the bowls,	4289

FIRES

Isa	24:15	glorify ye the Lord in the **f**, even	217

FIRM

Jos	3:17	the covenant of the Lord stood **f**	3559
Jos	4:3	where the priests' feet stood **f**,	3559
Job	41:23	they are **f** in themselves; they	3332
Job	41:24	His heart is as **f** as a stone; they	3332
Ps	73:4	their death; but their strength is **f**.	1277
Da	6:7	and to make a **f** decree,	8631
Heb	3:6	rejoicing of the hope **f** unto the end	*949*

FIRMAMENT

Ge	1:6	Let there be a **f** in the midst of	7549
Ge	1:7	God made the **f**, and divided the	7549
Ge	1:8	And God called the **f** Heaven.	7549
Ge	1:14	Let there be lights in the **f** of the	7549
Ge	1:17	God set them in the **f** of heaven to	7549
Ps	19:1	and the **f** sheweth his handywork	7549
Ps	150:1	praise him in the **f** of his power.	7549
Eze	1:25	And there was a voice from the **f**	7549
Da	12:3	shine as the brightness of the **f**;	7549

FIRST See also FIRSTBEGOTTEN; FIRSTBORN; FIRSTFRUIT.

Ge	1:5	and the morning were the **f** day.	259
Ge	25:25	And the **f** came out red, all over	7223
Ex	4:8	hearken to the voice of the **f** sign,	7223

Ex	12:5	blemish, a male of the **f** year;	1121
Ex	22:29	to offer the **f** of thy ripe fruits,	4395
Ex	34:1	tables of stone like unto the **f**:	7223
Le	23:39	on the **f** day shall be a sabbath,	7223
Nu	28:18	**f** day shall be an holy convocation;	7223
Dt	11:14	the **f** rain and the latter rain,	3138
1Ki	17:13	make me thereof a little cake **f**,	7223
1Ch	16:7	David delivered **f** this psalm to	7218
Ezr	1:1	the **f** year of Cyrus king of Persia,	259
Ne	8:18	from the **f** day unto the last day,	7223
Job	15:7	Art thou the **f** man that was born?	7223
Isa	41:4	the Lord, the **f**, and with the last;	7223
Isa	44:6	I am the **f**, and I am the last; and	7223
Jer	36:28	words that were in the **f** roll,	7223
Da	1:21	even unto the **f** year of king Cyrus.	259
Da	6:2	presidents of whom Daniel was **f**:	2298
Da	7:4	The **f** was like a lion, and had	6933
Da	9:2	In the **f** year of his reign I Daniel	259
Hos	2:7	go and return to my **f** husband:	7223
Zec	6:2	In the **f** chariot were red horses:	7223
Mt	6:33	**But seek ye f the kingdom of God,**	*4412*
Mt	7:5	**f cast out the beam out of thine**	*4412*
Mt	8:21	suffer me **f** to go and bury my	*4412*
Mt	12:29	**except he f bind the strong man?**	*4412*
Mt	13:30	**Gather ye together f the tares,**	*4412*
Mt	17:11	**Elias truly shall f come, and**	*4412*
Mt	17:27	**take up the fish that f cometh up;**	*4413*
Mt	19:30	**But many that are f shall be last;**	*4413*
Mt	20:10	**when the f came, they supposed**	*4413*
Mt	20:16	**the last shall be f, and the f last:**	*4413*
Mt	22:38	**is the f and great commandment.**	*4413*
Mt	28:1	toward the **f** day of the week,	*3391*
Mk	4:28	**f the blade, then the ear,**	*4412*
Mk	9:35	**man desire to be f, the same shall**	*4413*
Mk	10:31	**But many that are f shall be last;**	*4413*
Mk	12:28	Which is the **f** commandment of	*4413*
Mk	12:29	**The f of all the commandments**	*4413*
Mk	13:10	**the gospel must f be published**	*4412*
Mk	16:2	morning the **f** day of the week,	*3391*
Mk	16:9	early the **f** day of the week,	*4415*
Lk	2:2	taxing was **f** made when Cyrenius	*4413*
Lk	6:42	**hypocrite, cast out f the beam**	*4412*
Lk	11:26	**of that man is worse than the f.**	*4413*
Lk	14:28	**sitteth not down f, and counteth**	*4412*
Lk	16:5	**and said unto the f, How much**	*4413*
Lk	17:25	**But f must he suffer many things,**	*4412*
Lk	21:9	**these things must f come to pass;**	*4412*
Lk	24:1	Now upon the **f** day of the week,	*3391*
Jn	1:41	**f** findeth his own brother Simon,	*4413*
Jn	8:7	**let him f cast a stone at her.**	*4413*
Jn	19:32	and brake the legs of the **f**, and of	*4413*
Jn	20:1	**f** day of the week cometh Mary	*3391*
Jn	20:4	Peter, and came **f** to the sepulchre	*4413*
Jn	20:8	which came **f** to the sepulchre, and	*4413*
Jn	20:19	being the **f** day of the week,	*3391*
Ac	11:26	were called Christians **f** in Antioch	*4412*
Ac	20:7	And upon the **f** day of the week,	*3391*
Ac	26:4	at the **f** among mine own nation	*746*
Ro	1:16	to the Jew **f**, and also to the Greek.	*4412*
Ro	2:9	the Jew **f**, and also of the Gentile;	*4412*
1Co	12:28	**f** apostles, secondarily prophets,	*4412*
1Co	14:30	sitteth by, let the **f** hold his peace	*4413*
1Co	15:3	I delivered unto you **f** of all	*1722, 4413*
1Co	15:45	**f** man Adam was made a living	*4413*
1Co	16:2	Upon the **f** day of the week let	*3391*
2Co	8:12	if there be **f** a willing mind,	*4295*
Eph	1:12	who **f** trusted in Christ	*4276*
Eph	4:9	also descended **f** into the lower	*4412*
Eph	6:2	**f** commandment with promise;	*4413*
1Th	4:16	the dead in Christ shall rise **f**	*4412*
2Th	2:3	except there come a falling away **f**,	*4412*
1Ti	2:13	Adam was **f** formed, then Eve	*4413*
1Ti	5:12	they have cast off their **f** faith	*4413*
2Ti	4:16	At my **f** answer no man stood with	*4413*
Tit	3:10	after the **f** and second admonition	*3391*
Heb	7:27	**f** for his own sins, and then for	*4386*
Heb	8:7	that **f** covenant had been faultless,	*4413*
Heb	9:1	Then verily the **f** covenant had	*4413*
Heb	9:6	went always into the **f** tabernacle	*4413*
Heb	9:15	that were under the **f** testament,	*4413*
Heb	10:9	He taketh away the **f**, that he may	*4413*
Jas	3:17	is **f** pure, then peaceable, gentle,	*4412*
2Pe	1:20	Knowing this **f**, that no prophecy	*4412*
1Jn	4:19	love him, because he **f** loved us	*4413*
Jude	6	which kept not their **f** estate,	*746*
Rev	1:11	**Alpha and Omega, the f and the**	*4413*
Rev	1:17	**Fear not; I am the f and the last:**	*4413*
Rev	2:4	**because thou hast left thy f love**	*4413*
Rev	2:8	**saith the f and the last, which**	*4413*
Rev	2:19	**the last to be more than the f.**	*4413*
Rev	8:7	The **f** angel sounded, and there	*4413*
Rev	13:12	therein to worship the **f** beast,	*4413*
Rev	16:2	the **f** went, and poured out his vial	*4413*
Rev	20:5	This is the **f** resurrection	*4413*
Rev	21:1	the **f** heaven and the **f** earth were	*4413*
Rev	21:19	the **f** foundation was jasper; the	*4413*
Rev	22:13	**and the end, the f and the last**	*4413*

FIRSTBEGOTTEN See also FIRST and BEGOTTEN.

Heb	1:6	bringeth in the **f** into the world,	*4416*

FIRSTBORN See also BORN.

Ge	19:31	And the **f** said unto the younger,	1067
Ge	27:19	I am Esau thy **f**; I have done	1060
Ge	35:23	Reuben, Jacob's **f**, and Simeon,	1060
Ex	4:22	Israel is my son, even my **f**:	1060
Ex	11:5	all the **f** in the land of Egypt shall	1060
Ex	12:12	and will smite all the **f** in the land	1060
Ex	12:29	Lord smote all the **f** in the land of	1060
Ex	13:2	Sanctify unto me all the **f**,	1060
Ex	13:15	the Lord slew all the **f** in the land	1060
Ex	34:20	the **f** of thy sons thou shalt redeem,	1060
Nu	3:12	all the **f** that openeth the matrix	1060
Nu	3:40	Number all the **f** of the males of the	1060
Nu	18:15	**f** of man shalt thou surely redeem,	1060
Nu	33:4	the Egyptians buried all their **f**,	1060
Jos	17:1	for he was the **f** of Joseph;	1060
1Ch	5:1	the sons of Reuben the **f** of Israel,	1060
1Ch	6:28	the sons of Samuel; the **f** Vashni,	1060
1Ch	26:10	not the **f**, yet his father made him	1060
Job	18:13	the **f** of death shall devour his	1060
Ps	89:27	Also I will make him my **f**	1060
Ps	135:8	Who smote the **f** of Egypt,	1060
Mic	6:7	I give my **f** for my transgression	1060
Mt	1:25	she had brought forth her **f** son:	*4416*
Ro	8:29	be the **f** among many brethren	*4416*
Col	1:15	God, the **f** of every creature:	*4416*
Col	1:18	the beginning, the **f** from the dead;	*4116*
Heb	12:23	assembly and church of the **f**,	*4416*

FIRSTFRUIT

Dt	18:4	**f** also of thy corn, of thy wine,	7225
Ro	11:16	if the **f** be holy, the lump is also	*536*

FIRSTFRUITS

Ex	23:16	the **f** of thy labours, which thou	1061
Ex	34:26	first of the **f** of thy land thou shalt	1061
Le	2:14	offer a meat offering of thy **f**	1061
Le	23:17	they are the **f** unto the Lord.	1061
Nu	28:26	Also in the day of the **f**, when ye	1061
Ne	10:35	And to bring the **f** of our ground,	1061
Ne	12:44	for the **f**, and for the tithes, to	7225
Eze	20:40	I require your offerings, and the **f**	7225
Eze	48:14	neither exchange, nor alienate the **f**	7225
Pr	3:9	with the **f** of all thine increase:	7225
Ro	8:23	which have the **f** of the Spirit,	*536*
1Co	15:23	Christ the **f**; afterward they that	*536*
Jas	1:18	be a kind of **f** of his creatures,	*536*
Rev	14:4	the **f** unto God and to the Lamb	*536*

F

FIRSTLING

Ex	13:13	every **f** of an ass thou shalt redeem	6363
Ex	34:19	and every **f** among thy cattle,	6363
Le	27:26	which should be the Lord's **f**, no	1069
Nu	18:17	But the **f** of a cow, or the **f** of a	1060
Dt	15:19	All the **f** males that come of thy	1060
Dt	33:17	glory is like the **f** of his bullock,	1060

FIRSTLINGS

Ge	4:4	also brought of the **f** of his flock	1062
Dt	12:6	and the **f** of your herds	1062
Ne	10:36	**f** of our herds and of our flocks,	1062

FIRSTRIPE See also RIPE.

Nu	13:20	was the time of the **f** grapes.	1061
Na	3:12	be like fig trees with the **f** figs:	1063

FISH See also FISHERMEN; FISHERS; FISHING.

Ge	1:26	dominion over the **f** of the sea	1710
Ex	7:18	And the **f** that is in the river shall	1710
Nu	11:5	remember the **f**, which we did eat	1710
Ne	12:39	above the **f** gate, and the tower	1709
Job	41:7	irons or his head with **f** spears?	1709
Isa	19:10	make sluices and ponds for **f**.	5315
Jer	16:16	and they shall **f** them; and after	1770
Eze	47:10	as the **f** of the great sea,	1710
Jnh	1:17	Jonah was in the belly of the **f**.	1709
Jnh	2:10	And the Lord spake unto the **f**,	1709
Mt	7:10	**Or if he ask a f, will he give him**	*2486*
Lk	11:11	**or if he ask a f, will he for a f**	*2486*
Lk	24:42	gave him a piece of a broiled **f**,	*2486*
Jn	21:13	and giveth them, and **f** likewise	*3795*

FISHERMEN

Lk	5:2	but the **f** were gone out of them,	*231*

FISHER'S

Jn	21:7	he grit his **f** coat unto him, (for	*1908*

FISHERS

Isa	19:8	The **f** also shall mourn, and all	1771
Eze	47:10	that the **f** shall stand upon it	1728
Mt	4:19	**I will make you f of men**	*231*
Mk	1:17	**I will make you to become f of**	*231*

FISHES

Ge	9:2	shall be upon all the **f** of the sea;	1709
Job	12:8	the **f** of the sea shall declare unto	1709
Eze	38:20	So that the **f** of the sea, and the	1709
Hab	1:14	makest men as the **f** of the sea,	1709
Mt	14:17	here but five loaves, and two **f**.	*2486*
Mt	15:34	said, Seven and a few little **f**	*2485*
Mk	6:38	they say, Five, and two **f**.	*2486*
Mk	6:41	the two **f** divided he among them	*2486*
Lk	9:13	no more but five loaves and two **f**;	*2486*
Jn	6:9	barley loaves, and two small **f**:	*3795*
Jn	21:11	drew the net to land full of great **f**,	*2486*

FISHHOOKS

Am	4:2	and your posterity with **f**,	5518, 1729

FISHING

Jn	21:3	Peter saith unto them, I go a **f**.	*239*

FIST

Ex	21:18	or with his **f**, and he die not,	106
Isa	58:4	to smite with the **f** of wickedness:	106

FISTS

Pr	30:4	hath gathered the wind in his **f**?	2651

FIT

Le	16:21	by the hand of a **f** man into the	6261
Pr	24:27	make it **f** for thyself in the field:	6257
Lk	9:62	**is f for the kingdom of God**	*2111*
Ac	22:22	it is not **f** that he should live	*2520*
Col	3:18	husbands, as it is **f** in the Lord	*433*

FITLY

Eph	2:21	all the building **f** framed together	*4883*
Eph	4:16	the whole body **f** joined together	*4883*

FITTED

1Ki	6:35	with gold **f** upon the carved work	3474
Ro	9:22	vessels of wrath **f** to destruction:	*2675*

FIVE

Ge	5:11	nine hundred and **f** years: and	2568
Ge	5:21	Enoch lived sixty and **f** years	2568
Ge	5:32	Noah was **f** hundred years old:	2568
Ge	12:4	Abram was seventy and **f** years old	2568
Ge	18:28	Peradventure there shall lack **f** of	2568
Ge	45:11	yet there are **f** years of famine;	2568
Ex	22:1	he shall restore **f** oxen for an ox,	2568
Ex	36:38	**f** pillars of it with their hooks:	2568
Le	27:6	a month old even unto **f** years old,	2568
Nu	7:23	**f** rams, **f** he goats, **f** lambs of the	2568
Nu	11:19	two days, nor **f** days, neither ten	2568
Nu	31:8	**f** kings of Midian: Balaam also	2568
Jos	8:12	he look about **f** thousand men,	2568
Jos	10:17	**f** kings are found hid in a cave	2568
Jos	13:3	**f** lords of the Philistines; the	2568
Jgs	18:17	**f** men that went to spy out the land	2568
1Sa	6:18	of the Philistines belonging to the **f**	2568
1Sa	17:40	**f** smooth stones out of the brook,	2568
1Sa	22:18	fourscore and **f** persons that did	2568
2Sa	4:4	He was **f** years old when the	2568
2Sa	21:8	**f** sons of Michal the daughter of	2568
1Ki	4:32	his songs were a thousand and **f**.	2568
1Ki	6:24	and **f** cubits the other wing	2568
1Ki	7:23	and his height was **f** cubits: and	2568
1Ki	7:39	**f** on the left side of the house:	2568
1Ki	7:49	of pure gold, **f** on the right side,	2568
1Ki	9:23	over Solomon's work, **f** hundred and	2568
2Ki	7:13	**f** of the horses that remain,	2568
2Ki	14:2	twenty and **f** years old when he	2568
1Ch	11:23	of great stature, **f** cubits high;	2568
2Ch	3:11	one wing of the one cherub was **f**	2568
2Ch	3:12	of the other cherub was **f** cubits	2568
2Ch	6:13	and **f** cubits broad, and three cubits	2568
2Ch	35:9	small cattle, and **f** hundred oxen	2568
Ezr	2:69	and **f** thousand pound of silver,	2568

Ne 7:68 mules, two hundred forty and f: 2568
Ne 7:70 f hundred and thirty priests' 2568
Est 9:12 and destroyed f hundred men in 2568
Job 1:3 camels, and f hundred yoke of oxen, 2568
Isa 30:17 at the rebuke of f shall ye flee: 2568
Eze 45:2 sanctuary f hundred in length, 2568
Mt 14:17 here but f loaves, and two fishes. *4002*
Mt 14:21 were about f thousand men, *4000*
Mt 16:9 of the f thousand, and how many *4000*
Mt 25:2 And f of them were wise, *4000*
Mt 25:15 And unto one he gave f talents, *4000*
Mt 25:20 so he that had received f talents *4000*
Mk 6:41 when he had taken the f loaves *4000*
Mk 8:19 When I brake the f loaves among *4002*
Lk 1:24 hid herself f months, saying, *4002*
Lk 7:41 one owed f hundred pence, and *4001*
Lk 9:13 more but f loaves and two fishes; *4002*
Lk 12:6 f sparrows sold for two farthings, *4002*
Lk 12:52 there shall be f in one house *4002*
Lk 16:28 For I have f brethren; that he *4002*
Lk 19:18 thy pound hath gained f pounds *4002*
Jn 4:18 For thou hast had f husbands; *4002*
Jn 6:9 which hath f barley loaves, and two *4002*
Jn 6:10 in number about f thousand. *4000*
Ac 24:1 And after f days Ananias the *4002*
1Co 14:19 church I had rather speak f words *4002*
1Co 15:6 seen of above f hundred brethren *4001*
2Co 11:24 f times received I forty stripes *3999*
Rev 9:5 should be tormented f months: *4002*
Rev 9:10 power was to hurt men f months. *4002*
Rev 17:10 f are fallen, and one is, and the *4002*

FIVE HUNDRED See FIVE and HUNDRED.

FIVE THOUSAND See FIVE and THOUSAND.

FIXED
Ps 57:7 My heart is f, O God, my heart 3559
Ps 108:1 O God, my heart is f; I will sing 3559
Ps 112:7 his heart is f, trusting in the Lord 3559
Lk 16:26 us and you there is a great gulf f: *4741*

FLAGON
2Sa 6:19 piece of flesh, and a f of wine 809

FLAGONS
SS 2:5 Stay me with f, comfort me with 809
Isa 22:24 even to all the vessels of f 5035

FLAGS
Ex 2:3 laid it in the f by the river's brink 5488
Ex 2:5 when she saw the ark among the f 5488
Isa 19:6 the reeds and f shall wither. 5488

FLAME
Ex 3:2 the Lord appeared unto him in a f 3827
Jgs 13:20 when the f went up toward heaven 3851
Job 41:21 and a f goeth out of his mouth. 3851
Ps 106:18 the f burned up the wicked. 3852
Isa 5:24 and the f consumeth the chaff, so 3852
Isa 10:17 and his Holy One for a f: 3852
Isa 43:2 neither shall the f kindle upon 3852
Eze 20:47 flaming f shall not be quenched, 7957
Da 3:22 the f of the fire slew those men 7631
Lk 16:24 for I am tormented in this f *5395*
Ac 7:30 in a f of fire in a bush *5395*
Heb 1:7 and his ministers a f of fire. *5595*
Rev 2:18 hath his eyes like unto a f of fire, *5395*

FLAMES
Ps 29:7 voice of the Lord divideth the f 3852
Isa 13:8 their faces shall be as f 3851
Isa 66:15 and his rebuke with f of fire. 3851

FLAMING See also ENFLAMING.
Ge 3:24 f sword which turned every way, 3858
Ps 105:32 and f fire in their land 3852
La 2:3 burned against Jacob like a f fire, 3852
Eze 20:47 the f flame shall not be quenched, 3852
Na 2:3 shall be with f torches in the day 784

FLASH
Eze 1:14 the appearance of a f of lightning 965

FLAT
Nu 22:31 bowed down his head, and fell f
Jos 6:5 wall of the city shall fall down f, 8478

FLATTER
Ps 5:9 they f with their tongue. 2505
Ps 78:36 Nevertheless they did f him with 6601

FLATTERETH
Ps 36:2 For he f himself in his own eyes, 2505
Pr 7:5 stranger which f with her words. 2505
Pr 28:23 than he that f with the tongue. 2505

FLATTERIES
Da 11:32 covenant shall he corrupt by f: 2514

FLATTERING
Ps 12:2 f lips and with a double heart 2513
Pr 7:21 the f of her lips she forced him. 2506
Pr 26:28 and a f mouth worketh ruin. 2509
1Th 2:5 used we f words, as ye know, *2850*

FLATTERY
Job 17:5 that speaketh f to his friends, 2506
Pr 6:24 from the f of the tongue of a 2513

FLAX
Ex 9:31 the f and the barley was smitten: 6594
Jos 2:6 and hid them with the stalks of f 6593
Pr 31:13 seeketh wool, and f, and worketh 6593
Isa 42:3 smoking f shall he not quench: 6594
Hos 2:5 my wool and my f, mine oil and 6593
Mt 12:20 smoking f shall he not quench, *3043*

FLAY
2Ch 29:34 could not f all the burnt offerings: 6584

FLEA
1Sa 24:14 after a dead dog, after a f 6550
1Sa 26:20 of Israel is come out to seek a f, 6550

FLED
Ge 14:10 kings of Sodom and Gomorrah f, 5127
Ge 16:6 Sarai dealt hardly with her, she f 1272
Ge 35:7 he f from the face of his brother. 1272
Ge 39:13 his garment in her hand, and was f 5127
Ex 2:15 Moses f from the face of Pharaoh, 1272
Jos 7:4 and they f before the men of Ai. 5127
Jos 10:16 But these five kings f, and hid 5127
Jgs 4:15 his chariot, and f away on his feet. 5127
1Sa 4:17 Israel is f before the Philistines, 5127
1Sa 19:18 So David f, and escaped, and came 1272
1Sa 21:10 and f that day for fear of Saul, 1272
1Sa 27:4 it was told Saul that David was f 1272
2Sa 4:4 and his nurse took him up, and f: 5127

F

2Sa	13:34	Absalom **f**. And the young man	1272
1Ki	2:7	**f** because of Absalom thy brother	1272
1Ki	2:28	And Joab **f** unto the tabernacle	5127
1Ki	11:40	Jeroboam arose, and **f** into Egypt,	1272
2Ki	7:7	they arose and **f** in the twilight,	5127
2Ki	25:4	and all the men of war **f** by night	
2Ch	10:2	**f** from the presence of Solomon	1272
Ps	3:*title*	he **f** from Absalom his son.	1272
Ps	57:*title*	he **f** from Saul in the cave.	1272
Ps	114:3	the sea saw it, and **f**: Jordan was	5127
Isa	33:3	noise of the tumult the people **f**;	5074
Jer	9:10	the heavens and the beast are **f**;	5074
Jer	52:7	all the men of war **f**, and went	1272
Da	10:7	so that they **f** to hide themselves	1272
Zec	14:5	ye **f** from before the earthquake	5127
Mt	26:56	the disciples forsook him, and **f**.	*5343*
Mk	14:50	And they all forsook him, and **f**.	*5343*
Mk	16:8	quickly, and **f** from the sepulchre;	*5343*
Ac	16:27	that the prisoners had been **f**	*1628*
Heb	6:18	who have **f** for refuge to lay hold	*2703*
Rev	12:6	the woman **f** into the wilderness,	*5343*
Rev	16:20	And every island **f** away, and the	*5343*
Rev	20:11	the earth and the heaven **f** away;	*5343*

FLEE

Ge	16:8	**f** from the face of my mistress	1272
Ge	27:43	arise, **f** thou to Laban my brother	1272
Ex	21:13	thee a place whither he shall **f**.	5127
Nu	35:11	that the slayer may **f** thither,	5127
Dt	19:5	he shall **f** unto one of those cities,	5127
Dt	28:25	and **f** seven ways before them:	5127
Jos	8:6	They **f** before us, as at the first:	5127
Jgs	20:32	Let us **f**, and draw them from the	5127
2Sa	15:14	and let us **f**: for we shall not else	1227
1Ki	12:18	up to his chariot, to **f** to Jerusalem.	5127
Ne	6:11	Should such a man as I **f**?	1272
Job	30:10	abhor me, they **f** far from me,	7368
Ps	11:1	**F** as a bird to your mountain?	5110
Ps	139:7	shall I **f** from thy presence?	1272
Pr	28:1	wicked **f** when no man pursueth:	5127
Isa	13:14	**f** every one into his own land.	5127
Isa	35:10	sorrow and sighing shall **f** away	5127
Isa	51:11	sorrow and mourning shall **f**	5127
Jer	4:29	whole city shall **f** for the noise	1272
Jer	49:8	**F** ye, turn back, dwell deep,	5127
Am	2:16	the mighty shall **f** away naked	5127
Jnh	1:3	Jonah rose up to **f** unto Tarshish	1272
Na	3:17	when the sun ariseth they **f** away,	5074
Zec	14:5	And ye shall **f** to the valley of the	5127
Mt	3:7	you to **f** from the wrath to come?	*5343*
Mt	10:23	**f ye into another: for verily I say**	*5343*
Lk	3:7	you to **f** from the wrath to come?	*5343*
Jn	10:5	**will f from him: for they know**	*5343*
1Co	6:18	**F** fornication. Every sin that a	*5343*
1Co	10:14	my dearly beloved, **f** from idolatry	*5343*
1Ti	6:11	O man of God, **f** these things;	*5343*
2Ti	2:22	**F** also youthful lusts: but follow	*5343*
Jas	4:7	the devil, and he will **f** from you.	*5343*
Rev	9:6	and death shall **f** from them.	*5343*

FLEECE

Dt	18:4	the first of the **f** of thy sheep,	1488
Jgs	6:37	and if the dew be on the **f** only,	1492
Jgs	6:38	and wringed the dew out of the **f**	1492
Jgs	6:40	for it was dry upon the **f** only,	1492

FLEEING

Le	26:36	they shall flee, as **f** from a sword;	4499
Dt	4:42	and that **f** unto one of these cities	5127
Job	30:3	**f** into the wilderness in former	6207

FLEETH

Dt	19:11	and **f** into one of these cities:	5127
Isa	24:18	who **f** from the noise of the fear	5127
Jn	10:12	**leaveth the sheep, and f: and the**	*5343*
Jn	10:13	**The hireling f, because he is an**	*5343*

FLESH

Ge	2:21	closed up the **f** instead thereof;	1320
Ge	2:23	bone of my bones, and **f** of my **f**;	1320
Ge	2:24	and they shall be one **f**.	1320
Ge	6:3	with man, for that he also is **f**:	1320
Ge	6:13	The end of all **f** is come before me;	1320
Ge	7:15	two of all **f**, wherein is the breath	1320
Ge	7:21	all **f** died that moved upon the	1320
Ge	9:15	and every living creature of all **f**;	1320
Ge	17:11	circumcise the **f** of your foreskin;	1320
Ge	17:23	circumcised the **f** of their foreskin	1320
Ge	29:14	Surely thou art my bone and my **f**	1320
Ex	16:8	give you in the evening **f** to eat,	1320
Ex	29:14	the **f** of the bullock, and his skin,	1320
Ex	29:31	and seethe his **f** in the holy place	1320
Ex	29:34	ought of the **f** of the consecrations,	1320
Le	7:18	And if any of the **f** of the sacrifice	1320
Le	7:20	But the soul that eateth of the **f**	1320
Le	8:31	Boil the **f** at the door of the	1320
Le	11:8	Of their **f** shall ye not eat, and their	1320
Le	12:3	the eighth day the **f** of his foreskin	1320
Le	13:14	But when raw **f** appeareth in him,	1320
Le	14:9	also he shall wash his **f** in water,	1320
Le	15:13	and bathe his **f** in running water,	1320
Le	15:19	and her issue in her **f** be blood,	1320
Le	17:14	For it is the life of all **f**;	1320
Le	21:5	nor make any cuttings in their **f**	1320
Nu	11:18	tomorrow, and ye shall eat **f**: for	1320
Nu	16:22	the God of the spirits of all **f**,	1320
Nu	19:5	her skin, and her **f**, and her blood,	1320
Dt	12:23	mayest not eat the life with the **f**	1320
Dt	28:53	**f** of thy sons and of thy daughters,	1320
Dt	32:42	and my sword shall devour **f**;	1320
1Sa	2:15	Give **f** to roast for the priest; for	1320
1 Sa	17:44	and I will give thy **f** unto the fowls	1320
2Sa	5:1	Behold, we are thy bone and thy **f**.	1320
1Ki	17:6	him bread and **f** in the morning,	1320
2Ki	4:34	and the **f** of the child waxed warm	1320
2Ki	5:14	his **f** came again like unto the **f** of	1320
2Ki	9:36	shall dogs eat the **f** of Jezebel:	1320
Ne	5:5	Yet now our **f** is as the **f** of our	1320
Job	4:15	my face; the hair of my **f** stood up:	1320
Job	7:5	My **f** is clothed with worms and	1320
Job	19:26	yet in my **f** shall I see God:	1320
Ps	16:9	my **f** also shall rest in hope.	1320
Ps	56:4	I will not fear what **f** can do unto	1320
Ps	63:1	my **f** longeth for thee in a dry and	1320
Ps	73:26	My **f** and my heart faileth: but	7607
Ps	84:2	my heart and my **f** crieth out for	1320
Ps	109:24	fasting; and my **f** faileth of fatness.	1320
Ps	145:21	and let all **f** bless his holy name	1320
Pr	5:11	thy **f** and thy body are consumed,	1320
Pr	14:30	a sound heart is the life of the **f**:	1320
Ecc	11:10	and put away evil from thy **f**:	1320
Ecc	12:12	much study is a weariness of the **f**.	1320

Isa 40:6 What shall I cry? All **f** is grass, ... 1320
Isa 49:26 and all **f** shall know that I the Lord ... 1320
Isa 66:16 will the Lord plead with all **f**: ... 1320
Jer 11:15 and the holy **f** is passed from thee? ... 1320
Jer 12:12 the land: no **f** shall have peace ... 1320
Jer 19:9 cause them to eat the **f** of their sons ... 1320
Jer 32:27 I am the Lord, the God of all **f**: ... 1320
La 3:4 My **f** and my skin hath he made ... 1320
Eze 11:19 take the stony heart out of their **f**, ... 1320
Eze 20:48 And all **f** shall see that I the Lord ... 1320
Eze 24:10 consume the **f**, and spice it well, ... 1320
Eze 39:18 Ye shall eat the **f** of the mighty, ... 1320
Eze 44:7 and uncircumcised in **f**, to be in my ... 1320
Da 1:15 appeared fairer and fatter in **f** ... 1320
Joel 2:28 will pour out my spirit upon all **f**: ... 1320
Hag 2:12 If one bear holy **f** in the skirt of ... 1320
Zec 2:13 Be silent, O all **f**, before the Lord: ... 1320
Mt 16:17 **f and blood hath not revealed it** ... *4561*
Mt 19:5 **and they twain shall be one f?** ... *4561*
Mt 26:41 **indeed is willing, but the f is** ... *4561*
Lk 24:39 **for a spirit hath not f and bones,** ... *4561*
Jn 1:13 nor of the will of the **f**, nor of the ... *4561*
Jn 1:14 And the Word was made **f**, and ... *4561*
Jn 3:6 **That which is born of the f is f;** ... *4561*
Jn 6:51 **the bread that I will give is my f,** ... *4561*
Jn 6:53 **Except ye eat the f of the Son of** ... *4561*
Jn 6:63 **quickeneth; the f profiteth** ... *4561*
Ac 2:17 pour out of my Spirit upon all **f**: ... *4561*
Ro 3:20 shall no **f** be justified in his sight: ... *4561*
Ro 8:1 after the **f**, but after the Spirit ... *4561*
Ro 8:4 in us, who walk not after the **f**, ... *4561*
Ro 8:8 that are in the **f** cannot please God ... *4561*
Ro 8:13 For if ye live after the **f**, ye shall ... *4561*
Ro 13:14 and make not provision for the **f** ... *4561*
1Co 1:29 no **f** should glory in his presence ... *4561*
1Co 5:5 Satan for the destruction of the **f**, ... *4561*
1Co 6:16 for two, saith he, shall be one **f** ... *4561*
1Co 15:50 that **f** and blood cannot inherit the ... *4561*
2Co 10:2 as if we walked according to the **f** ... *4561*
2Co 12:7 a thorn in the **f**, the messenger of ... *4561*
Gal 2:16 of the law shall no **f** be justified. ... *4561*
Gal 2:20 the life which I now live in the **f** ... *4561*
Gal 4:29 as then he that was born after the **f** ... *4561*
Gal 5:16 ye shall not fulfil the lust of the **f** ... *4561*
Gal 5:17 the **f** lusteth against the Spirit, ... *4561*
Gal 5:24 crucified the **f** with the affections ... *4561*
Gal 6:8 soweth to his **f** shall of the **f** reap ... *4561*
Eph 2:3 in the lusts of our **f**, fulfilling the ... *4561*
Eph 5:29 no man ever yet hated his own **f**; ... *4561*
Eph 5:31 and they two shall be one **f** ... *4561*
Eph 6:12 we wrestle not against **f** and blood, ... *4561*
Col 2:5 For though I be absent in the **f**, ... *4561*
Col 2:13 and the uncircumcision of your **f** ... *4561*
1Ti 3:16 God was manifest in the **f**, justified ... *4561*
1Pe 1:24 For all **f** is grass, and all the glory ... *4561*
1Pe 3:18 to death in the **f**, but quickened ... *4561*
1Pe 4:1 Christ hath suffered for us in the **f**, ... *4561*
2Pe 2:10 that walk after the **f** in the lust of ... *4561*
1Jn 2:16 the lust of the **f**, and the lust of the ... *4561*
1Jn 4:2 that Jesus Christ is come in the **f** ... *4561*
2Jn 7 that Jesus Christ is come in the **f** ... *4561*
Jude 23 even the garment spotted by the **f** ... *4561*
Rev 17:16 and shall eat her **f**, and burn her ... *4561*
Rev 19:18 captains, and the **f** of mighty men, ... *4561*
Rev 19:21 the fowls were filled with their **f** ... *4561*

FLESHHOOKS
Ex 27:3 and his **f**, and his firepans: all the ... 4207
Nu 4:14 the censers, the **f**, and the shovels, ... 4207
1Ch 28:17 pure gold for the **f**, and the bowls, ... 4207
2Ch 4:16 and the shovels, and the **f**, and all ... 4207

FLESHLY
2Co 1:12 not with **f** wisdom, but by the ... *4559*
2Co 3:3 but in **f** tables of the heart. ... *4560*
Col 2:18 vainly puffed up by his **f** mind,
1Pe 2:11 abstain from **f** lusts, which war ... *4559*

FLESH-POTS See FLESH and POTS.

FLEW
1Sa 14:32 And the people **f** upon the spoil, ... 6213
Isa 6:6 Then **f** one of the seraphims unto ... 5774

FLIES
Ex 8:21 I will send swarms of **f** upon thee, and
Ex 8:24 there came a grievous swarm of **f** into
Ex 8:29 that the swarms of **f** may depart from
Ex 8:31 and he removed the swarms of **f** from
Ps 78:45 He sent divers sorts of **f** among ... 6157
Ps 105:31 there came divers sorts of **f**, and ... 6157
Ecc 10:1 Dead **f** cause the ointment of the ... 2070

FLIETH
Dt 4:17 likeness of any winged fowl that **f** ... 5774
Dt 14:19 creeping thing that **f** is unclean ... 5775
Dt 28:49 the earth as swift as the eagle **f**; ... 1675
Ps 91:5 nor for the arrow that **f** by day; ... 5774

FLIGHT
Le 26:8 you shall put ten thousand to **f** ... 7291
1Ch 12:15 and they put to **f** all them of the ... 1272
Isa 52:12 not go out with haste, nor go by **f**: ... 4499
Am 2:14 The **f** shall perish from the swift ... 4498
Mt 24:20 **But pray ye that your f be not in** ... *5457*
Heb 11:34 turned to **f** the armies of the aliens ... *5457*

FLINT
Dt 8:15 forth water out of the rock of **f**; ... 2496
Ps 114:8 the **f** into a fountain of waters. ... 2496
Isa 50:7 have I set my face like a **f**, ... 2496

FLOCK
Ge 4:4 the firstlings of his **f** and the fat ... 6629
Ge 29:10 and watered the **f** of Laban his ... 6629
Ge 30:32 I will pass through all thy **f** to day, ... 6629
Ge 33:13 them one day, all the **f** will die. ... 6629
Ex 2:19 enough for us, and watered the **f** ... 6629
Ex 3:1 kept the **f** of Jethro his father in ... 6629
Le 5:6 female from the **f**, a lamb or a kid ... 6629
Le 6:6 ram without blemish out of the **f** ... 6629
Dt 12:17 firstlings of thy herds or of thy **f**, ... 6629
1Sa 17:34 and took a lamb out of the **f**: ... 5739
2Ch 35:7 Josiah gave to the people, of the **f**, ... 6629
Ezr 10:19 they offered a ram of the **f** for their ... 6629
Job 21:11 send forth their little ones like a **f**, ... 6629
Ps 77:20 Thou leddest thy people like a **f** by ... 6629
Ps 107:41 and maketh him families like a **f** ... 6629
SS 4:1 thy hair is as a **f** of goats, that ... 5739
Isa 40:11 He shall feed his **f** like a shepherd: ... 5739
Jer 13:17 Lord's **f** is carried away captive ... 5739
Jer 23:3 I will gather the remnant of my **f** ... 6629
Jer 31:10 him, as a shepherd doth his **f** ... 5739
Eze 24:5 Take the choice of the **f**, and ... 6629
Eze 34:6 my **f** was scattered upon all the ... 6629

Eze	34:10	I will require my **f** at their hand,	6629
Eze	34:12	As a shepherd seeketh out his **f**	5739
Eze	34:22	Therefore will I save my **f**, and	6629
Eze	36:38	the holy **f**, as the **f** of Jerusalem	6629
Eze	45:15	And one lamb out of the **f**, out of	6629
Am	7:15	Lord took me as I followed the **f**	6629
Mic	4:8	And thou, O tower of the **f**, the	5739
Hab	3:17	the **f** shall be cut off from the fold,	6629
Zec	10:3	Lord of hosts hath visited his **f**	5739
Zec	11:17	idol shepherd that leaveth the **f**!	6629
Mt	26:31	**sheep of the f shall be scattered**	*4167*
Lk	2:8	watch over their **f** by night.	*4167*
Lk	12:32	**Fear not, little f; for it is your**	*4168*
Ac	20:29	in among you, not sparing the **f**	*4168*
1Co	9:7	who feedeth a **f**, and eateth not of	*4167*
1Pe	5:2	the **f** of God which is among you,	*4168*

FLOCKS

Ge	13:5	with Abram, had **f**, and herds,	6629
Ge	30:36	Jacob fed the rest of Laban's **f**	6629
Ge	30:40	of the **f** toward the ringstraked,	6629
Ge	47:17	exchange for horses, and for the **f**,	6629
Ge	50:8	only their little ones, and their **f**,	6629
Ex	12:38	and **f**, and herds, even very much	6629
Le	5:15	ram without blemish out of the **f**,	6629
Nu	32:36	Our little ones, our wives, our **f**,	4735
Dt	8:13	thy herds and thy **f** multiply,	6629
1Sa	30:20	David took all the **f** and the herds,	6629
2Ch	17:11	the Arabians brought him **f**, seven	6629
Job	24:2	they violently take away **f**, and	5739
Ps	78:48	and their **f** to hot thunderbolts	4735
Isa	65:10	And Sharon shall be a fold of **f**	6629
Jer	5:17	shall eat up thy **f** and thine herds:	6629
Jer	10:21	and all their **f** shall be scattered.	4830
Eze	34:2	not the shepherds feed the **f**?	6629
Joel	1:18	the **f** of sheep are made desolate.	5739
Mic	5:8	young lion among the **f** of sheep:	5739
Zep	2:14	And **f** shall lie down in the midst	5739

FLOOD

Ge	6:17	I do bring a **f** of waters upon the	3999
Ge	7:7	because of the waters of the **f**	3999
Ge	7:17	**f** was forty days upon the earth;	3999
Ge	9:11	off any more by the waters of a **f**;	3999
Ge	10:32	divided in the earth after the **f**	3999
Jos	24:2	dwelt on the other side of the **f**	5104
Jos	24:14	served on the other side of the **f**,	5104
Ps	29:10	The Lord sitteth upon the **f**; yea,	3999
Isa	59:19	the enemy shall come in like a **f**,	5104
Da	9:26	The end thereof shall be with a **f**,	7858
Am	8:8	drowned, as by the **f** of Egypt.	2975
Mt	24:38	**f they were eating and drinking,**	*2627*
Mt	24:39	**until the f came, and took them**	*2627*
Lk	6:48	**when the f arose, the stream beat**	*4132*
2Pe	2:5	bringing in the **f** upon the world	*2627*
Rev	12:15	her to be carried away of the **f**	*4216*

FLOODS

Ex	15:8	the **f** stood upright as an heap,	5140
2Sa	22:5	**f** of ungodly men made me afraid;	5158
Ps	18:4	**f** of ungodly men made me afraid	5158
Ps	78:44	rivers into blood; and their **f**,	5140
Ps	98:8	the **f** clap their hands: let the hills	5104
Isa	44:3	and **f** upon the dry ground:	5140
Jnh	2:3	and the **f** compassed me about:	5104
Mt	7:27	**and the f came, and the winds**	*4215*

FLOOR See also THRESHINGFLOOR.

Ru	3:3	and get thee down to the **f**:	1637
Ru	3:14	that a woman came unto the **f**	1637
1Ki	6:15	the **f** of the house, and the walls	7172
1Ki	6:30	And the **f** of the house he overlaid	7172
Hos	9:2	The **f** and the winepress shall	1637
Mic	4:12	them as the sheaves into the **f**	1637
Lk	3:17	and he will throughly purge his **f**,	*257*

FLOORS See also THRESHINGFLOORS.

Joel	2:24	And the **f** shall be full of wheat,	1637

FLOUR

Ex	29:2	wheaten **f** shalt thou make them.	5560
Le	2:1	his offering shall be of fine **f**;	5560
Le	2:7	it shall be made of fine **f** with oil.	5560
Le	14:21	and one tenth deal of fine **f**	5560
Le	23:17	tenth deals: they shall be of fine **f**;	5560
Nu	6:15	cakes of fine **f** mingled with oil,	5560
Nu	7:19	full of fine **f** mingled with oil for a	5560
Nu	15:4	meal offering of a tenth deal of **f**	5560
Nu	15:9	offering of three tenth deals of **f**	5560
Nu	28:12	two tenth deals of **f** for a meat	5560
Nu	28:20	shall be of **f** mingled with oil:	5560
1Sa	1:24	bullocks, and one ephah of **f**,	7058
2Sa	13:8	And she took **f**, and kneaded it,	1217
1Ki	4:22	was thirty measures of fine **f**,	5560
1Ch	9:29	the fine **f**, and the wine, and the	5560
Eze	16:13	thou didst eat fine **f**, and honey,	5560
Rev	18:13	fine **f**, and wheat, and beasts,	*4585*

FLOURISH

Ps	72:7	In his days shall the righteous **f**;	6524
Ps	92:12	The righteous shall **f** like the	6524
Ps	92:13	lord shall f in the courts of our God	6524
Pr	11:28	the righteous shall **f** as a branch,	6524
Ecc	12:5	and the almond tree shall **f**,	5006
Isa	17:11	shalt thou make thy seed to **f**:	6524
Eze	17:24	and have made the dry tree to **f**:	6524

FLOURISHED

SS	6:11	and to see whether the vine **f**,	6524
Php	4:10	your care of me hath **f** again;	*330*

FLOURISHING

Ps	92:14	they shall be fat and **f**;	7488
Da	4:4	mine house, and **f** in my palace:	7487

FLOW See also OVERFLOW.

Job	20:28	his goods shall **f** away in the day	5064
Isa	2:2	and all nations shall **f** unto it.	5102
Isa	48:21	the waters to **f** out of the rock	5140
Jer	31:12	shall **f** together to the goodness	5102
Joel	3:18	the hills shall **f** with milk, and	3212
Jn	7:38	**belly shall f rivers of living water.**	*4482*

FLOWED See also OVERFLOWED.

Jos	4:18	and **f** over all his banks, as they	3212
Isa	64:3	mountains **f** down at thy presence	2151
La	3:54	Waters **f** over mine head; then	6687

FLOWER

Ex	25:33	a knop and a **f** in one branch;	6525
1Sa	2:33	shall die in the **f** of their age	582
Job	14:2	He cometh forth like a **f**, and is cut	6731
Isa	18:5	sour grape is ripening in the **f**,	5328
Isa	40:8	**f** fadeth: but the word of our God	6731
1Co	7:36	if she pass the **f** of her age,	*5230*
Jas	1:11	the grass, and the **f** thereof falleth,	*438*

FLOWERS
Ex 37:20 like almonds, his knops, and his **f**: 6525
Le 15:24 her **f** be upon him, he shall be 5079
1Ki 7:26 the brim of a cup, with **f** of lilies: 6525
2Ch 4:5 brim of a cup, and **f** of lilies; 6525
SS 5:13 as a bed of spices, as sweet **f**: 4026

FLOWETH See also OVERFLOWETH.
Le 20:24 land that **f** with milk and honey: 2100
Dt 6:3 land that **f** with milk and honey. 2100

FLOWING See also OVERFLOWING.
Ex 3:8 a land **f** with milk and honey; 2100
Pr 18:4 wellspring of wisdom as a **f** brook 5042
Isa 66:12 the glory of the Gentiles like a **f** 7857
Jer 18:14 the cold **f** waters that come from 5140
Jer 49:4 **f** valley, O backsliding daughter? 2100

FLUTE
Da 3:5 ye hear the sound of the cornet, **f**, 4953

FLUTTERETH
Dt 32:11 up her nest, **f** over her young, 7363

FLY See also FLEW; FLIES; FLYING.
Ge 1:20 fowl that may **f** above the earth 5774
2Sa 22:11 he rode upon a cherub, and did **f**: 5774
Job 5:7 trouble, as the sparks **f** upward. 5774
Ps 18:10 rode upon a cherub, and did **f**: 5774
Ps 55:6 would I **f** away, and be at rest. 5774
Pr 23:5 they **f** away as an eagle toward 5774
Isa 6:2 his feet, and with twain he did **f** 5774
Jer 48:40 Behold, he shall **f** as an eagle, 1675
Eze 13:20 hunt the souls to make them **f**, 6524
Rev 14:6 saw another angel **f** in the midst *4072*

FLYING
Le 11:21 ye eat of every **f** creeping thing 5775
Ps 148:10 creeping things, and **f** fowl: 3671
Isa 14:29 his fruit shall be a fiery **f** serpent. 5774
Isa 31:5 birds **f**, so will the Lord of hosts 5774
Zec 5:2 And I answered, I see a **f** roll; 5774
Rev 8:13 **f** through the midst of heaven, *4072*

FOAL
Ge 49:11 Binding his **f** unto the vine, and 5895
Zec 9:9 and upon a colt the **f** of an ass 1121
Mt 21:5 and a colt the **f** of an ass. *5207*

FOAMETH
Mk 9:18 he **f**, and gnashed with his teeth, *875*
Lk 9:39 and it teareth him that he **f** again, *876*

FOES
1Ch 21:12 to be destroyed before thy **f**, 6862
Ps 27:2 even mine enemies and my **f**, 341
Ps 89:23 beat down his **f** before his face, 6862
Ac 2:35 Until I make thy **f** thy footstool. *2190*

FOLD See also SHEEPFOLD.
Isa 65:10 And Sharon shall be a **f** of flocks 5116
Hab 3:17 flock shall be cut off from the **f** 4356
Jn 10:16 **I have, which are not of this f:** *833*

FOLDING
Pr 6:10 a little **f** of the hands to sleep: 2264

FOLDS See also SHEEPFOLDS.
Nu 32:36 fenced cities: and **f** for sheep. 1448
Jer 23:3 will bring them again to their **f**; 5116

FOLK See also FOLKS; KINSFOLK.
Mk 6:5 laid his hands upon a few sick **f**
Jn 5:3 a great multitude of impotent **f**,

FOLLOW
Ge 24:5 not be willing to **f** me unto 3212, 310
Ex 11:8 and all the people that **f** thee: 7272
Ex 23:2 not **f** a multitude to do evil; 1961, 310
Jgs 3:28 he said unto them, **F** after me: 7291
1Sa 30:21 so faint that they could not **f** 3212, 310
1Ki 18:21 God, **f** him: but if Baal, then **f** 3212, 310
Ps 23:6 goodness and mercy shall **f** me 7291
Ps 119:150 draw nigh that **f** after mischief: 7291
Isa 51:1 me, ye that **f** after righteousness 7291
Jer 17:16 from being a pastor to **f** thee: 310
Hos 6:3 if we **f** on to know the Lord: 7291
Mt 4:19 he saith unto them, **F** me, *1205, 3694*
Mt 8:22 And Jesus said unto him, **F me;** *190*
Mt 16:24 **and take up his cross, and f me.** *190*
Mt 19:21 **in heaven: and come and f me.** *190*
Mk 2:14 and said unto him, **F me.** And he *190*
Mk 8:34 **and take up his cross, and f me.** *190*
Mk 14:13 **bearing a pitcher of water: f him.** *190*
Lk 5:27 and he said unto him, **F me** *190*
Lk 9:59 And he said unto another, **F me.** *190*
Lk 18:22 **in heaven: and come, f me.** *190*
Jn 1:43 Philip, and saith unto him, **F me.** *190*
Jn 10:5 **And a stranger will they not f,** *190*
Jn 10:27 **and I know them, and they f me:** *190*
Jn 13:36 **not f me now; but thou shalt f me** *190*
Jn 21:22 **what is that to thee? f thou me** *190*
1Co 14:1 **F** after charity, and desire *1377*
1Th 5:15 but ever **f** that which is good *1377*
1Ti 6:11 **f** after righteousness, godliness *1377*
2Ti 2:22 **f** righteousness, faith, charity, *1377*
Heb 12:14 **F** peace with all men, and *1377*
3Jn 11 Beloved, **f** not that which is evil, *3401*
Rev 14:4 These are they which **f** the Lamb *190*

FOLLOWED
Nu 14:24 hath **f** me fully, him will I bring 310
Nu 32:12 for they have wholly **f** the Lord 310
Jos 14:8 but I wholly **f** the Lord my God 310
Jgs 2:12 and **f** other gods, of the gods 3212, 310
1Sa 17:14 and the three eldest **f** Saul 1980, 310
2Sa 2:10 the house of Judah **f** David 1961, 310
1Ki 12:20 none that **f** the house of David 310
1Ki 14:8 who **f** me with all his heart 1980, 310
1Ki 18:18 Lord, and thou hast **f** Baalim 3212, 310
2Ki 5:21 So Gehazi **f** after Naaman 7291
2Ki 17:15 they **f** vanity, and became vain 3212, 310
Ps 68:25 the players on instruments **f** after;
Am 7:15 the Lord took me as I **f** the flock, 310
Mt 4:20 straightway left their nets, and **f**. *190*
Mt 8:10 and said to them that **f**, **Verily I say** *190*
Mt 9:27 two blind men **f** him, crying, and *190*
Mt 19:27 we have forsaken all, and **f** thee; *190*
Mt 19:28 **That ye which have f me, in the** *190*
Mt 20:34 received sight, and they **f** him *190*
Mt 26:58 Peter **f** him afar off unto the high *190*
Mt 27:55 **f** Jesus from Galilee, ministering *190*
Mk 2:14 **Follow me.** And he arose and **f** him *190*
Mk 3:7 great multitude from Galilee **f** him, *190*
Mk 10:28 have left all, and have **f** thee *190*
Mk 14:54 Peter **f** him afar off, even into the *190*
Lk 5:11 they forsook all, and **f** him *190*

F

Lk 23:49 and the women that **f** him from *4870*
Lk 23:55 **f** after, and beheld the sepulchre, ... *2628*
Jn 1:37 heard him speak, and they **f** Jesus *190*
Jn 1:40 which heard John speak, and **f** him, ... *190*
Jn 18:15 And Simon Peter **f** Jesus, and so did *190*
Ac 13:43 proselytes **f** Paul and Barnabas: *190*
Ro 9:30 which **f** not after righteousness *1377*
1Co 10:4 of that spiritual Rock that **f** them: *190*
1Ti 5:10 have diligently **f** every good work. *1872*
Rev 6:8 was Death, and Hell **f** with him. *190*
Rev 14:8 and there **f** another angel, saying, ... *190*
Rev 19:14 armies which were in heaven **f** him *190*

FOLLOWERS

1Co 4:16 I beseech you, be ye **f** of me *3402*
Php 3:17 be **f** together of me, and mark *4831*
1Th 2:14 became **f** of the churches of God *3402*
Heb 6:12 but **f** of them who through faith *3432*

FOLLOWETH

2Ki 11:15 that **f** her kill with the sword 935, 310
Ps 63:8 My soul **f** hard after thee: 1692
Pr 15:9 him that **f** after righteousness. 7291
Pr 28:19 but he that **f** after vain persons 7291
Eze 16:34 none **f** thee to commit whoredoms: 310
Mt 10:38 **and f after me, is not worthy of** *190*
Mk 9:38 we forbad him, because he **f** not *190*
Jn 8:12 **he that f me shall not walk in** *190*

FOLLOWING

Ge 41:31 by reason of that famine **f**; 310, 3651
Jos 22:18 must turn away this day from **f** the 310
Ru 1:16 or to return from **f** after thee:
1Sa 12:14 continue **f** the Lord your God: 310
1Sa 12:20 yet turn not aside from **f** the Lord 310
2Sa 2:21 would not turn aside from **f** of him 310
2Ki 17:21 drave Israel from **f** the Lord 310
2Ch 25:27 did turn away from **f** the Lord 310
Ps 109:13 in the generation **f** let their name 312
Lk 13:33 **and tomorrow, and the day f:** *2192*
Jn 1:38 Jesus turned, and saw them **f** *190*
Jn 20:6 Then cometh Simon Peter **f** him, ... *190*
Jn 21:20 the disciple whom Jesus loved **f**; *190*
Ac 23:11 And the night **f** the Lord stood

FOLLY

Ge 34:7 he had wrought **f** in Israel 5039
Jos 7:15 and because he hath wrought **f** 5039
1Sa 25:25 Nabal is his name, and **f** is with 5039
Job 4:18 his angels he charged with **f**: 8417
Ps 85:8 but let them not turn again to **f** 3690
Pr 13:16 but a fool layeth open his **f** 200
Pr 14:18 The simple inherit **f**: but the 200
Pr 14:29 he that is hasty of spirit exalteth **f** 200
Pr 16:22 but the instruction of fools is **f** 200
Pr 26:4 Answer not a fool according to his **f**, ... 200
Pr 26:11 so a fool returneth to his **f** 200
Ecc 2:12 wisdom, and madness, and **f**: 5531
Ecc 2:13 I saw that wisdom excelleth **f** 5531
Ecc 10:6 **F** is set in great dignity, and the 5529
2Co 11:1 bear with me a little in my **f**: *877*
2Ti 3:9 their **f** shall be manifest unto all *454*

FOOD

Ge 2:9 to the sight, and good for **f**; 3978
Ge 3:6 saw that the tree was good for **f**, ... 3978
Ge 6:21 and it shall be for **f** for thee, ... 402
Ge 41:35 And let them gather all the **f** 400
Ge 42:7 From the land of Canaan to buy **f** 400
Ge 42:33 and take **f** for the famine of your
Ge 43:4 we will go down and buy thee **f**: 400
Ge 44:1 Fill the men's sacks with **f**, ... 400
Ge 47:24 seed of the field, and for your **f** 400
Le 3:11 it is the **f** of the offering made 3899
Le 19:23 planted all manner of trees for **f**, ... 3978
1Sa 14:24 be the man that eateth any **f** until 3899
1Sa 14:28 be the man that eateth any **f** this 3899
1Ki 5:11 thousand measures of wheat for **f** 4361
Job 38:41 provideth for the raven his **f**? 6718
Ps 78:25 man did eat angels' **f** he sent 3899
Ps 136:25 Who giveth **f** to all flesh: for his 3899
Ps 147:9 He giveth to the beast his **f**, ... 3899
Pr 27:27 have goats' milk enough for thy **f**, ... 3899
Pr 31:14 she bringeth her **f** from afar 3899
2Co 9:10 both minister bread for your **f**, ... *1035*
1Ti 6:8 having **f** and raiment let us be *1304*

FOOL

1Sa 26:21 behold, I have played the **f**, and 5528
Ps 14:1 The **f** hath said in his heart, ... 5036
Ps 92:6 neither doth a **f** understand this 3684
Pr 10:8 commandments: but a prating **f** 191
Pr 10:23 It is as sport to a **f** to do mischief: 3684
Pr 11:29 **f** shall be servant to the wise 191
Pr 15:5 **f** despiseth his father's instruction: 191
Pr 17:10 than an hundred stripes into a **f** 3684
Pr 17:16 in the hand of a **f** to get wisdom, ... 3684
Pr 17:21 and the father of a **f** hath no joy. 5036
Pr 17:28 a **f**, when he holdeth his peace, ... 191
Pr 19:1 is perverse in his lips, and is a **f** 3684
Pr 20:3 but every **f** will be meddling 191
Pr 26:1 So honour is not seemly for a **f** 3684
Pr 26:5 Answer a **f** according to his folly, ... 3684
Pr 26:10 rewardeth the **f**, and rewardeth 3684
Pr 28:26 trusteth in his own heart is a **f**: 3684
Pr 29:11 A **f** uttereth all his mind: 3684
Ecc 2:14 but the **f** walketh in darkness: 3684
Ecc 4:3 The **f** foldeth his hands together, ... 3684
Ecc 10:3 he that is a **f** walketh by the way, ... 5530
Ecc 10:12 but the lips of a **f** will swallow up 3684
Ecc 10:14 A **f** also is full of words: 5530
Mt 5:22 **but whosoever shall say, Thou f,** *3474*
Lk 12:20 **Thou f, this night thy soul shall** *876*
1Co 3:18 become a **f**, that he may be wise *3474*
2Co 11:16 Let no man think me a **f**; *876*
2Co 11:23 (I speak as a **f**) I am more; *3912*
2Co 12:11 I am become a **f** in glorying; *876*

FOOLISH

Dt 32:6 O **f** people and unwise? is not he 5036
Job 2:10 speakest as one of the **f** women 5039
Ps 39:8 me not the reproach of the **f** 5036
Ps 74:22 the **f** man reproacheth thee daily 5036
Pr 9:6 Forsake the **f**, and live; and go 6612
Pr 10:1 a **f** son is the heaviness of his 3684
Pr 14:7 Go from the presence of a **f** man, ... 3684
Pr 17:25 A **f** son is grief to his father, ... 3684
Pr 21:20 but a **f** man spendeth it up. 3684
Ecc 7:17 neither be thou **f**: why shouldest 5530
Jer 4:22 For my people is **f**, they have not 191
La 2:14 seen vain and **f** things for thee; 8602
Zec 11:15 the instruments of a **f** shepherd 196
Mt 25:2 **them were wise, and five were f** *3474*

Mt 25:3 **They that were f took their lamps,** *3474*
Mt 25:8 **And the f said unto the wise,** *3474*
Ro 2:20 An instructor of the **f**, a teacher *878*
1Co 1:27 God hath chosen the **f** things of *3474*
Gal 3:1 O **f** Galatians, who hath bewitched *453*
1Ti 6:9 into many **f** and hurtful lusts, *453*
Tit 3:3 ourselves also were sometimes **f**, *453*
1Pe 2:15 to silence the ignorance of **f** men: *878*

FOOLISHLY
Nu 12:11 wherein we have done **f**, and 2973
Job 1:22 sinned not, nor charged God **f**. 8604
Pr 14:17 He that is soon angry dealeth **f**: 200
2Co 11:17 but as it were **f**, in this 1722, 877

FOOLISHNESS
Ps 69:5 O God, thou knowest my **f**; 200
Pr 15:2 mouth of fools poureth out **f**. 200
Pr 22:15 **F** is bound in the heart of a child; 200
Mk 7:22 **an evil eye, blasphemy, pride, f:** *877*
1Co 1:18 the cross is to them that perish, **f**; *3472*
1Co 1:21 the **f** of preaching to save them *3472*
1Co 1:25 the **f** of God is wiser than men; *3474*
1Co 3:19 wisdom of this world is **f** with God. *3472*

FOOL'S
Pr 18:7 A **f** mouth is his destruction, 3684
Pr 27:3 a **f** wrath is heavier than them 191
Ecc 5:3 a **f** voice is known by multitude 3684

FOOLS
Job 12:17 and maketh the judges **f** 1984
Ps 94:8 and ye **f**, when will ye be wise? 3684
Ps 107:17 **F**, because of their transgression, 191
Pr 1:7 **f** despise wisdom and instruction 191
Pr 10:21 but **f** die for want of wisdom 191
Pr 13:20 companion of **f** shall be destroyed. 3684
Pr 14:9 **F** make a mock at sin: but 191
Pr 26:9 is a parable in the mouth of **f** 3684
Ecc 5:1 than to give the sacrifice of **f**: 3684
Ecc 7:9 for anger resteth in the bosom of **f**. 3684
Mt 23:17 **Ye f and blind: for whether is** *3474*
Lk 11:40 **Ye f, did not he that made that** *878*
Lk 24:25 **O f, and slow of heart to believe** *453*
Ro 1:22 to be wise, they became **f**, *3471*
1Co 4:10 We are **f** for Christ's sake, but ye *3474*
Eph 5:15 circumspectly, not as **f**, but as *781*

FOOT See also FEET.
Ge 41:44 shall no man lift up his hand or **f** 7272
Ex 21:24 for tooth, hand for hand, **f** for **f**, 7272
Le 8:11 laver and his **f**, to sanctify them 3653
Nu 22:25 crushed Balaam's **f** against the 7272
Dt 8:4 did thy **f** swell, these forty years. 7272
Dt 19:21 for tooth, hand for hand, **f** for **f** 7272
Dt 25:9 and loose his shoe from off his **f** 7272
Dt 28:65 shall the sole of thy **f** have rest: 7272
Dt 33:24 and let him dip his **f** in oil 7272
Jos 5:15 Loose thy shoe from off thy **f**; 7272
2Sa 2:18 was as light of **f** as a wild roe 7272
2Ki 9:33 the horses: and he trode her under **f**
Job 23:11 My **f** hath held his steps, his way 7272
Job 39:15 forgetteth that the **f** may crush 7272
Ps 26:12 My **f** standeth in an even place: 7272
Ps 36:11 Let not the **f** of pride come against 7272
Ps 66:6 they went through the flood on **f** 7272
Ps 91:12 thou dash thy **f** against a stone. 7272
Ps 121:3 will not suffer thy **f** to be moved: 7272
Pr 3:23 and thy **f** shall not stumble 7272
Pr 25:17 thy **f** from thy neighbour's house; 7272
Isa 14:25 my mountains tread him under **f** 947
Isa 20:2 and put off thy shoe from thy **f** 7272
Isa 58:13 turn away thy **f** from the sabbath, 7272
Jer 12:10 have trodden my portion under **f**, 947
La 1:15 Lord hath trodden under **f** all 5541
Eze 29:11 No **f** of man shall pass through it, 7272
Mt 4:6 lest at any time thou dash thy **f**. *4228*
Mt 5:13 **and to be trodden under f of men.** *2662*
Mt 18:8 **if thy hand or thy f offend thee,** *4228*
Mk 9:45 **if thy f offend thee, cut it off:** *4228*
Lk 4:11 thou dash thy **f** against a stone. *4228*
Jn 11:44 hand and **f** with graveclothes: *4228*
1Co 12:15 If the **f** shall say, Because I am not *4228*
Heb 10:29 trodden under **f** the Son of God, *2662*
Rev 10:2 and he set his right **f** upon the *4228*
Rev 11:2 the holy city shall they tread under **f**

FOOT-BREADTH See FOOT and BREADTH.

FOOTSTEPS
Ps 17:5 in thy paths, that my **f** slip not. 6471
Ps 89:51 reproached the **f** of thine anointed. 6119
SS 1:8 thy way forth by the **f** of the flock, 6119

FOOTSTOOL
1Ch 28:2 and for the **f** of our God, 1916, 7272
Ps 110:1 I make thine enemies thy **f**. 1916, 7272
Ps 132:7 we will worship at his **f**. 1916, 7272
Isa 66:1 and the earth is my **f**: where 1916, 7272
Mt 5:35 **earth; for it is his f:** *5286, 3588, 4228*
Mt 22:44 **thine enemies thy f?** *5286, 3588, 4228*
Ac 2:35 make thy foes thy **f**. *5286, 3588, 4228*
Ac 7:49 and earth is my **f**: *5286, 3588, 4228*
Heb 10:13 enemies be made his **f**. *5286, 3588, 4228*

FORASMUCH
Ge 41:39 **F** as God hath shewed thee all 310
Jos 17:14 **f** as the Lord hath blessed me 5704
1Sa 24:18 **f** as when the Lord had 854, 834
1Ki 13:21 **F** as thou hast disobeyed the 3282, 834
2Ch 6:8 **F** as it was in thine heart to
Isa 29:13 **F** as this people draw near me 3282, 365
Da 4:18 **f** as all the wise men of 3606, 6903, 1768
Da 5:12 **F** as an excellent spirit 3606, 6903, 1768
Da 6:4 **f** as he was faithful, 3606, 6903, 1768
Mt 18:25 **But f as he had not to pay,**
Ac 11:17 **F** then as God gave them the *1487*
Ac 17:29 **F** then as we are the offspring of
1Co 11:7 **f** as he is the image and glory of God:
1Co 14:12 **f** as ye are zealous of spiritual *1893*
1Pe 4:1 **F** then as Christ hath suffered for us

FORBEAR See also BEAR.
1Ki 22:6 battle, or shall I **f**? And they said, 2308
2Ch 18:5 or shall I **f**? And they said 2308
2Ch 35:21 **f** thee from meddling with God 2308
Job 16:6 and though I **f**, what am I eased? 2308
Eze 24:17 **F** to cry, make no mourning 1826
1Co 9:6 have not we power to **f** working? *3361*
1Th 3:1 when we could no longer **f**, we *4722*

FORBEARING See also BEARING.
Eph 4:2 **f** one another in love; *430*
Eph 6:9 things unto them, **f** threatening: *447*
Col 3:13 **F** one another, and forgiving one *430*

FORBID See also BID; FORBAD.

Ge	44:7	God **f** that thy servants should	2486
1Sa	12:23	God **f** that I should sin against	2486
1Sa	14:45	God **f**: as the Lord liveth	2486
1Sa	24:6	he said unto his men, The Lord **f**	2486
Mt	19:14	**and f them not, to come unto me:**	*2967*
Mk	9:39	But Jesus said, **F him not:**	*2967*
Mk	10:14	**to come unto me, and f them not:**	*2967*
Lk	6:29	**f not to take thy coat also**	*2967*
Lk	18:16	**and f them not: for of such is the**	*2967*
Ac	10:47	Can any man **f** water, that these	*2967*
Ro	3:4	God **f**: let God be true, but	*3361, 1096*
Ro	6:15	law, but under grace? God **f**	*3361, 1096*
Ro	11:1	cast away his people? God **f**	*3361, 1096*
1Co	14:39	and **f** not to speak with tongues	*2967*
Gal	3:21	the promises of God? God **f**:	*3361, 1096*
Gal	6:14	God **f** that I should glory	*3361, 1096*

FORBIDDEN See also BIDDEN.

Le	5:17	things which are **f** to be done by	3808
Dt	4:23	the Lord thy God hath **f** thee	6680
Ac	16:6	**f** of the Holy Ghost to preach	*2967*

FORBIDDING

Lk	23:2	**f** to give tribute to Caesar, saying	*2967*
1Th	2:16	**F** us to speak to the Gentiles	*2967*
1Ti	4:3	**F** to marry, and commanding to	*2967*

FORCE

Ge	31:31	wouldest take by **f** thy daughters	1497
2Sa	13:12	Nay, my brother, do not **f** me;	6031
Est	7:8	he **f** the queen also before me	3533
Job	30:18	By the great **f** of my disease	3581
Jer	18:21	their blood by the **f** of the sword	3027
Eze	34:4	but with **f** and with cruelty have	2394
Mt	11:12	**and the violent take it by f**	*726*
Jn	6:15	take him by **f**, to make him a king	*726*

FORCED

Jgs	1:34	Amorites **f** the children of Dan	3905
1Sa	13:12	I **f** myself therefore, and offered a	662
2Sa	13:14	than she, **f** her, and lay with her	6031
2Sa	13:22	because he had **f** his sister	6031
Pr	7:21	the flattering of her lips she **f** him	5080

FORCES

Job	36:19	nor all the **f** of strength	3981
Isa	60:11	unto thee the **f** of the Gentiles	2428
Jer	40:13	and all the captains of the **f** that	2428
Da	11:10	assemble a multitude of great **f**:	2428
Da	11:38	shall he honour the God of **f**:	4581

FOREFRONT

Ex	26:9	in the **f** of the tabernacle	4136, 6440
Ex	28:37	upon the **f** of the mitre it shall	4136, 6440
2Sa	11:15	in the **f** of the hottest battle	4136, 6440
2Ch	20:27	Jehoshaphat in the **f** of them,	7218
Eze	40:19	from the **f** of the lower gate unto	6440

FOREHEAD

Ex	28:38	And it shall be upon Aaron's **f**,	4696
Le	13:42	or bald **f**, a white reddish sore;	1372
Le	13:43	or in his bald **f**, as the leprosy	1372
1Sa	17:49	that the stone sunk into his **f**;	4696
2Ch	26:20	behold, he was leprous in his **f**,	4696
Eze	3:8	**f** strong against their foreheads	4696
Eze	16:12	And I put jewel on thy **f**	639
Rev	17:5	upon her **f** was a name written,	*3359*

FOREHEADS

Rev	7:3	servants of our God in their **f**	*3359*
Rev	13:16	in their right hand, or in their **f**:	*3359*
Rev	14:1	Father's name written in their **f**	*3359*
Rev	22:4	and his name shall be in their **f**	*3359*

FOREKNEW

Ro	11:2	cast away his people which he **f**	*4267*

FOREKNOW

Ro	8:29	For whom he did **f**, he also did	*4267*

FOREKNOWLEDGE

Ac	2:23	and **f** of God, ye have taken, and	*4268*
1Pe	1:2	Elect according to the **f** of God	*4268*

FOREORDAINED

1Pe	1:20	Who verily was **f** before the	*4267*

FORERUNNER

Heb	6:20	Whither the **f** is for us entered	*4274*

FORESAW

Ac	2:25	I **f** the Lord always before my	*4308*

FORESEEING

Gal	3:8	the scripture, **f** that God would	*4275*

FORESKIN

Ge	17:11	circumcise the flesh of your **f**;	6190
Ge	17:23	circumcised the flesh of their **f**	6190
Ex	4:25	stone, and cut off the **f** of her son,	6190
Dt	10:16	Circumcise therefore the **f** of your	6190

FORESKINS

1Sa	18:25	an hundred **f** of the Philistines,	6190
1Sa	18:27	David brought their **f**, and they	6190
Jer	4:4	and take away the **f** of your heart,	6190

FOREST

1Ki	10:21	of the house of the **f** of Lebanon	3293
2Ki	19:23	and into the **f** of his Carmel	3293
Ne	2:8	Asaph the keeper of the king's **f**	6508
Ps	50:10	For every beast of the **f** is mine,	3293
Isa	10:34	shall cut down the thickets of the **f**	3293
Isa	32:15	fruitful field be counted for a **f**	3293
Isa	44:14	himself among the trees of the **f**;	3293
Jer	5:6	a lion out of the **f** shall slay them,	3293
Jer	21:14	I will kindle a fire in the **f** thereof,	3293
Eze	15:2	which is among the trees of the **f**?	3293
Eze	20:46	prophesy against the **f** of the south	3293
Am	3:4	Will a lion rear in the **f**, when he	3293
Zec	11:2	the **f** of the vintage is come down.	3293

FORESTS

2Ch	27:4	and in the **f** he built castles and	2793
Ps	29:9	to calve, and discovereth the **f**:	3295
Eze	39:10	neither cut down any out of the **f**;	3293

FORETELL See also FORETOLD.

2Co	13:2	and **f** you, as if I were present,	*4302*

FORETOLD

Mt	13:23	**behold, I have f you all things.**	*4280*
Ac	3:24	have likewise **f** of these days	*4293*

FOREVER See EVER.

FOREWARN

Lk	12:5	**I will f you whom ye shall fear:**	*5263*

FOREWARNED
1Th 4:6 all such as we also have **f** you and ... *4277*

FORFEITED
Ezr 10:8 all his substance should be **f**, and ... 2763

FORGAT See also **FORGOT.**
Jgs 3:7 and **f** the Lord their God, and ... 7911
Ps 78:11 And **f** his works, and his wonders ... 7911
Ps 106:21 They **f** God their saviour, which ... 7911
Hos 2:13 went after her lovers, and **f** me, ... 7911

FORGAVE
Ps 78:38 **f** their iniquity, and destroyed ... 3722
Mt 18:27 **loosed him, and f him the debt.** ... *863*
Mt 18:32 **I f thee all that debt, because thou** ... *863*
Lk 7:42 **to pay, he frankly f them both.** ... *5483*
Lk 7:43 that he, to whom he **f** most ... *5483*
2Co 2:10 if I **f** any thing, to whom I **f** it, ... *5483*
2Co 2:10 for your sakes **f** I it in the person
Col 3:13 even as Christ **f** you, so also do ye.

FORGET See also **FORGAT; FORGOT; FORGOTTEN.**
Ge 41:51 hath made me **f** all my toil, ... 5382
Dt 4:23 lest ye **f** the covenant of the Lord ... 7911
Dt 6:12 Then beware lest thou **f** the Lord, ... 7911
Dt 8:14 and thou **f** the Lord thy God, ... 7911
Dt 25:19 under heaven; thou shalt not **f** it. ... 7911
Job 8:13 So are the paths of all that **f** God; ... 7911
Ps 9:17 and all the nations that **f** God. ... 7913
Ps 13:1 How long wilt thou **f** me, O Lord? ... 7911
Ps 50:22 ye that **f** God, lest I tear you in ... 7911
Ps 78:7 and not **f** the works of God, ... 7911
Ps 119:16 thy statutes: I will not **f** thy word. ... 7911
Ps 119:93 I will never **f** thy precepts: for ... 7911
Ps 119:109 in my hand: yet do I not **f** thy law ... 7911
Ps 137:5 If I **f** thee, O Jerusalem, ... 7911
Pr 3:1 My son, **f** not my law; but let thine ... 7911
Pr 4:5 get understanding: **f** it not; ... 7911
Isa 65:11 forsake the Lord, that **f** my holy ... 7913
Jer 23:39 I, even I, will utterly **f** you ... 5382
Hos 4:6 thy God, I will also **f** thy children. ... 7911
Heb 6:10 to **f** your work and labour of love ... *1950*

FORGETFUL
Heb 13:2 Be not **f** to entertain strangers; ... *1950*
Jas 1:25 being not a **f** hearer, but a doer ... *1953*

FORGETFULNESS
Ps 88:12 righteousness in the land of **f**? ... 5388

FORGETTING
Php 3:13 **f** those things which are behind ... *1950*

FORGIVE See also **FORGAVE.**
Ge 50:17 **F**, I pray thee now the trespass, ... 5375
Ex 10:17 Now therefore **f**, I pray thee, my ... 5375
Nu 30:5 the Lord shall **f** her, because her ... 5545
Nu 30:12 void; and the Lord shall **f** her. ... 5545
1Sa 25:28 I pray thee, **f** the trespass of thine ... 5375
1Ki 8:34 and **f** the sin of thy people Israel, ... 5545
1Ki 8:50 And **f** thy people that have sinned ... 5545
2Ch 6:25 hear thou from the heavens, and **f** ... 5545
2Ch 7:14 and will **f** their sin, and will heal ... 5545
Ps 25:18 my pain; and **f** all my sins ... 5375
Jer 31:34 I will **f** their iniquity, and I will ... 5545
Da 9:19 O Lord, hear; O Lord, **f**; ... 5545
Am 7:2 O Lord God, **f**, I beseech thee: ... 5545
Mt 6:12 **f us our debts, as we f our** ... *863*
Mt 6:14 **For if ye f men their trespasses,** ... *863*
Mt 9:6 **hath power on earth to f sins,** ... *863*
Mt 18:21 my brother sin against me, and I **f**. ... *863*
Mt 18:35 **f not every one his brother their** ... *863*
Mk 2:7 who can **f** sins but God only? ... *863*
Mk 2:10 **man hath power on earth to f sins,** ... *863*
Mk 11:25 **may f you your trespasses.** ... *863*
Lk 5:21 Who can **f** sins, but God alone? ... *863*
Lk 5:24 **hath power upon earth to f sins,** ... *863*
Lk 6:37 **f and ye shall be forgiven:** ... *630*
Lk 11:4 **f us our sins; for we also f every** ... *863*
Lk 17:3 **and if he repent, f him.** ... *863*
Lk 23:34 Then said Jesus, Father, **f** them; ... *863*
2Co 2:10 To whom ye **f** any thing, I **f** also: ... *5483*
1Jn 1:9 faithful and just to **f** us our sins, ... *863*

FORGIVEN
Le 4:26 concerning his sin, and it shall be **f** ... 5545
Le 5:13 of these, and it shall be **f** him: ... 5545
Le 6:7 shall be **f** him for any thing of all ... 5545
Nu 14:19 and as thou hast **f** this people, ... 5375
Mt 9:2 **be of good cheer; thy sins be f** ... *863*
Mt 12:31 **and blasphemy shall be f unto** ... *863*
Mk 2:5 the palsy, **Son, thy sins be f thee.** ... *863*
Mk 3:28 **All sins shall be f unto the sons of** ... *863*
Mk 4:12 **and their sins should be f them.** ... *863*
Lk 5:23 **Thy sins be f thee; or to say, Rise** ... *863*
Lk 7:47 **Her sins, which are many, are f;** ... *863*
Lk 7:48 he said unto her, Thy sins are **f** ... *863*
Lk 12:10 **the Son of man, it shall be f him:** ... *863*
Ac 8:22 thought of thine heart may be **f** thee. ... *863*
Eph 4:32 God for Christ's sake hath **f** you ... *5483*
Jas 5:15 sins, they shall be **f** him ... *863*

FORGIVENESS
Mk 3:29 **the Holy Ghost hath never f,** ... *859*
Ac 13:38 preached unto you the **f** of sins: ... *859*
Ac 26:18 **that they may receive f of sins,** ... *859*
Col 1:14 through his blood, even the **f** of sins: ... *859*

FORGIVETH
Ps 103:8 Who **f** all thine iniquities; who ... 5545
Lk 7:49 Who is this that **f** sins also? ... *863*

FORGIVING
Ex 34:7 for thousands, **f** iniquity and ... 5375
Eph 4:32 **f** one another, even as God for ... *5483*

FORGOTTEN
Dt 26:13 neither have I **f** them; ... 7911
Dt 32:18 and hast **f** God that formed thee. ... 7911
Ps 9:18 the needy shall not always be **f**; ... 7911
Ps 44:20 If we have **f** the name of our God, ... 7911
Ps 77:9 Hath God **f** to be gracious? hath ... 7911
Ecc 2:16 in the days to come shall all be **f**. ... 7911
Isa 17:10 Because thou hast **f** the God of thy ... 7911
Isa 44:21 Israel, thou shalt not be **f** of me ... 5382
Isa 49:14 and my Lord hath **f** me ... 7913
Jer 3:21 they have **f** the Lord their God. ... 7911
Jer 18:15 my people hath **f** me, they have ... 7911
Jer 23:27 their fathers have **f** my name ... 7911
Jer 50:5 covenant that shall not be **f** ... 7911
Eze 22:12 and hast **f** me, saith the Lord God ... 7911
Hos 4:6 thou hast **f** the law of thy God, ... 7911
Hos 8:14 For Israel hath **f** his Maker, ... 7911
Lk 12:6 **not one of them is f before God?** ... *1950*
Heb 12:5 And ye have **f** the exhortation ... *1585*

FORM

Ge	1:2	And the earth was without **f**,	8414
2Ch	4:7	of gold according to their **f**, and	4941
Isa	45:7	I **f** the light, and create darkness:	3335
Isa	53:2	he hath no **f** nor comeliness;	8389
Jer	4:23	earth, and, lo, it was without **f**	8414
Eze	10:8	the **f** of a man's hand under their	8403
Da	3:25	**f** of the fourth is like the Son of	7299
Ro	6:17	that **f** of doctrine which was	*5179*
Php	2:6	Who, being in the **f** of God,	*3444*
Php	2:7	took upon him the **f** of a servant,	*3444*
2Ti	3:5	Having a **f** of godliness, but	*3446*

FORMED See also CONFORMED; TRANSFORMED.

Ge	2:7	And the Lord God **f** man of the	3335
Ge	2:19	the ground the Lord **f** every beast	3335
2Ki	19:25	of ancient times that I have **f** it?	3335
Job	33:6	I also am **f** out of the clay	7169
Ps	95:5	and his hands **f** the dry land.	3335
Pr	26:10	The great God that **f** all things	2342
Isa	43:1	and he that **f** thee, O Israel,	3335
Isa	44:24	and he that **f** thee from the womb,	3335
Isa	45:18	God himself that **f** the earth and	3335
Isa	54:17	No weapon that is **f** against thee	3335
Jer	33:2	the Lord that **f** it, to establish it;	3335
Gal	4:19	until Christ be **f** in you,	*3445*
1Ti	2:13	Adam was first **f**, then Eve	*4111*

FORMER

Nu	21:26	fought against the **f** king Moab,	7223
Ru	4:7	this was the manner in **f** time	6440
Ne	5:15	the **f** governors that had been	7223
Job	8:8	enquire, I pray thee, of the **f** age,	7223
Ps	89:49	where are thy **f** lovingkindnesses,	7223
Ecc	7:10	the **f** days were better than these?	7223
Isa	42:9	the **f** things are come to pass,	7223
Isa	61:4	shall raise up the **f** desolations,	7223
Isa	65:17	and the **f** shall not be remembered,	7223
Jer	5:24	rain, both the **f** and the latter,	3138
Jer	34:5	**f** kings which were before thee,	7223
Eze	16:55	shall return to their **f** estate, and	6927
Da	11:13	a multitude greater than the **f**,	7223
Hos	6:3	latter and **f** rain unto the earth.	3138
Joel	2:23	the **f** rain, and the latter rain	4175
Zec	7:7	Lord hath cried by the **f** prophets,	7223
Ac	1:1	The **f** treatise have I made, O	*4413*
1Pe	1:14	according to the **f** lusts in your	*4386*
Rev	21:4	for the **f** things are passed away,	*4413*

FORNICATION

2Ch	21:11	of Jerusalem to commit **f**, and	2181
Eze	16:26	Thou hast also committed **f** with	2181
Mt	5:32	**his wife, saving for the cause of f,**	*4202*
Jn	8:41	We be not born of **f**, we have one	*4202*
Ac	15:29	from things strangled, and from **f**:	*4202*
Ro	1:29	**f** wickedness, covetousness,	*4202*
1Co	6:13	Now the body is not for **f**,	*4202*
1Co	6:18	Flee **f**. Every sin that a man doeth	*4202*
1Co	7:2	to avoid **f**, let every man have	*4202*
2Co	12:21	and **f** and lasciviousness which	*4202*
Eph	5:3	But **f**, and all uncleanness, or	*4202*
1Th	4:3	that ye should abstain from **f**	*4202*
Rev	2:14	**unto idols, and to commit f**	*4203*
Rev	2:20	**to commit f, and to eat things**	*4203*
Rev	2:21	**gave her space to repent of her f;**	*4202*
Rev	14:8	the wine of the wrath of her **f**	*4202*
Rev	17:2	drunk with the wine of her **f**	*4202*
Rev	18:3	of the wine of the wrath of her **f**,	*4202*
Rev	19:2	did corrupt the earth with her **f**,	*4202*

FORNICATIONS

Mt	15:19	**thoughts, murders, adulteries, f,**	*4202*
Mk	7:21	**evil thoughts, adulteries, f,**	*4202*

FORNICATOR

1Co	5:11	Man that is called a brother be a **f**,	*4205*
Heb	12:16	Lest there be any **f**, or profane	*4205*

FORNICATORS

1Co	5:10	altogether with the **f** of this world	*4205*
1Co	6:9	neither **f**, nor idolaters, nor	*4205*

FORSAKE See also FORSOOK.

Dt	14:27	thou shalt not **f** him; for he hath	5800
Dt	31:8	will not fail thee, neither **f** thee:	5800
Dt	31:17	and I will **f** them, and I will hide	5800
Jos	24:16	forbid that we should **f** the Lord,	5800
Jos	24:20	If ye **f** the Lord, and serve strange	5800
1Sa	12:22	the Lord will not **f** his people for	5203
2Ch	15:2	but if ye **f** him, he will **f** you	5800
Ps	27:9	leave me not, neither **f** me, O God	5800
Ps	38:21	**F** me not, O Lord: O my God,	5800
Ps	71:18	O God, **f** me not; until I have	5800
Ps	89:30	If his children **f** my law, and walk	5800
Ps	119:8	will keep thy statutes: O **f** me not	5800
Pr	1:8	and **f** not the law of thy mother:	5203
Pr	4:6	**F** her not, and she shall preserve	5800
Isa	1:28	that **f** the Lord shall be consumed	5800
Isa	41:17	the God of Israel will not **f** them	5800
Isa	65:11	But ye are they that **f** the Lord	5800
Jer	23:33	I will even **f** you, saith the Lord	5203
Da	11:30	them that **f** the holy covenant	5800
Heb	13:5	I will never leave thee, nor **f** thee	*1459*

FORSAKEN

Dt	28:20	doings, whereby thou hast **f** me	5800
Jgs	6:13	but now the Lord hath **f** us	5203
Jgs	10:10	have **f** our God, and also served	5800
1Ki	18:18	**f** the commandments of the Lord,	5800
1Ki	19:14	of Israel have **f** thy covenant	5800
2Ch	12:5	thus saith the Lord, Ye have **f** me	5800
2Ch	13:11	Lord our God, but ye have **f** him	5800
2Ch	24:20	have **f** the Lord, he hath also **f** you	5800
2Ch	28:6	men; because they had **f** the Lord	5800
2Ch	34:25	**f** me, and have burned incense	5800
Ezr	9:9	yet our God hath not **f** us	5800
Ne	13:11	Why is the house of God **f**?	5800
Job	20:19	oppressed and hath **f** the poor;	5800
Ps	22:1	my God, why hast thou **f** me?	5800
Ps	37:25	have I not seen the righteous **f**,	5800
Isa	1:4	they have **f** the Lord, they have	5800
Isa	2:6	thou hast **f** thy people the house	5203
Isa	49:14	Zion said, The Lord hath **f** me,	5800
Jer	2:13	have **f** me the fountain of living	5800
Jer	2:17	in that thou hast **f** the Lord thy	5800
Jer	4:29	every city shall be **f**, and not a man	5800
Jer	9:13	they have **f** my law which I set	5800
Jer	15:6	thou hast **f** me, saith the lord,	5203
Jer	16:11	fathers have **f** me, saith the Lord,	5800
Jer	17:13	they have **f** the Lord, the fountain	5800
Jer	19:4	have **f** me, and have estranged	5800
Jer	22:9	have **f** the covenant of the Lord	5800
Jer	51:5	Israel hath not been **f**, nor Judah	488
Eze	9:9	say, The Lord hath **f** the earth	5800

Mt	19:29	**every one that hath f houses**	*863*
Mt	27:46	my God, why hast thou **f** me?	*1459*
Mk	15:34	God, my God, why hast thou **f** me?	*1459*
2Co	4:9	persecuted, but not **f**; cast down	*1459*
2Ti	4:10	Demas hath **f** me, having loved	*1459*
2Pe	2:15	Which have **f** the right way, and	*2641*

FORSAKING

Heb	10:25	Not **f** the assembling of ourselves	*1459*

FORSOOK

Dt	32:15	then he **f** God which made him,	5203
Jgs	2:12	**f** the Lord God of their fathers,	5800
Jgs	2:13	they **f** the Lord, and served Baal	5800
1Ki	9:9	Because they **f** the Lord their God,	5800
1Ki	12:8	he **f** the counsel of the old men	5800
2Ki	21:22	he **f** the Lord God of his fathers	5800
2Ch	7:22	they **f** the Lord God of their fathers,	5800
2Ch	10:13	Rehoboam **f** the counsel of the old	5800
2Ch	12:1	he **f** the law of the Lord, and all	5800
Ps	119:87	earth; but I **f** not thy precepts	5800
Isa	58:2	**f** not the ordinance of their God;	5800
Mt	26:56	all the disciples **f** him, and fled	*863*
Mk	1:18	they **f** their nets, and followed	*863*
Mk	14:50	And they all **f** him, and fled	*863*
2Ti	4:16	stood with me, but all men **f** me;	*1459*

FORTH

Ge	1:11	said, Let the earth bring **f** grass,	1876
Ge	1:20	God said, Let the waters bring **f**	8317
Ge	1:24	earth bring **f** the living creature	3318
Ge	3:16	thou shalt bring **f** children; and	3205
Ge	8:7	a raven, which went **f** to and fro,	3318
Ge	8:12	sent **f** the dove; which returned not	
Ge	8:16	Go **f** of the ark, thou, and thy wife,	3318
Ge	9:7	bring **f** abundantly in the earth,	8317
Ge	9:18	of Noah, that went **f** of the ark,	3318
Ge	41:47	the earth brought **f** by handfuls	6213
Ex	4:4	he put **f** his hand and caught it	7971
Ex	8:3	shall bring **f** frogs abundantly,	8317
Ex	9:22	Stretch **f** thine hand toward heaven	
Ex	9:23	And Moses stretched **f** his rod toward	
Ex	10:13	Moses stretched **f** his rod over the land	
Ex	12:39	which they brought **f** out of Egypt,	3318
Ex	14:27	stretched **f** his hand over the sea	
Ex	19:17	Moses brought **f** the people out of	3318
Nu	1:3	are able to go **f** to war in Israel:	3318
Nu	11:20	Why came we **f** out of Egypt?	3318
Nu	17:8	was budded, and brought **f** buds	3318
Nu	20:8	rock, and it shall give **f** his water,	
Nu	20:16	hath brought us **f** out of Egypt;	3318
Nu	24:8	God brought him **f** out of Egypt;	4161
Dt	16:1	brought thee **f** out of the land of	3318
Dt	21:10	thou goest **f** to war against thine	3318
Dt	25:11	putteth **f** her hand, and taketh	7971
Dt	29:25	he brought them **f** out of the land	3318
Jgs	3:21	Ehud put **f** his left hand, and took	7971
Jgs	5:25	brought **f** water in a lordly dish	7126
Jgs	6:21	the Lord put **f** the end of the staff	7971
Jgs	14:13	put **f** thy riddle, that we may hear	2330
Jgs	14:14	Out of the eater came **f** meat	3318
1Sa	24:10	will not put **f** mine hand against	7971
2Sa	6:6	Uzzah put **f** his hand to the ark	7971
2Sa	11:1	at the time when kings go **f** to war	3318
2Sa	19:7	swear by the Lord, if thou go not **f**,	3318
2Sa	20:8	and as he went **f** it fell out	3318
2Sa	22:20	He brought me **f** also into a large	3318
1Ki	8:7	For the cherubims spread **f** their	
1Ki	8:16	I brought **f** my people Israel out	3318
1Ki	8:19	thy son that shall come **f** out of	3318
1Ki	8:22	spread **f** his hands toward heaven:	
1Ki	19:11	And he said, Go **f**, and stand upon	3318
1Ki	22:21	there came **f** a spirit and stood	3318
2Ki	9:15	let none go **f** nor escape out of the	3318
2Ki	11:7	of all you that go **f** on the sabbath,	3318
2Ki	19:31	Jerusalem shall go **f** a remnant,	3318
1Ch	13:9	Uzzah put **f** his hand to hold the	7971
1Ch	14:15	for God is gone **f** before thee to	3318
1Ch	16:23	shew **f** from day to day his	1319
2Ch	5:8	For the cherubims spread **f** their	
2Ch	6:9	but thy son which shall come **f** out	3318
2Ch	25:9	able to go **f** to war, that could	3318
Est	5:9	went Haman **f** that day joyful and	3318
Job	1:11	But put **f** thine hand now, and	7971
Job	2:5	But put **f** thine hand now, and	7971
Job	23:10	he hath tried me, I shall come **f** as	3318
Ps	1:3	that bringeth **f** his fruit in his	5414
Ps	7:14	mischief, and brought **f** falsehood	3205
Ps	19:6	His going **f** is from the end of the	4161
Ps	55:20	He hath put **f** his hands against	7971
Ps	79:13	we will shew **f** thy praise to all	5608
Ps	90:2	the mountains were brought **f**	3205
Ps	92:14	still bring **f** fruit in old age;	5107
Ps	96:2	shew **f** his salvation from day to	
Ps	105:30	brought **f** frogs in abundance,	8317
Ps	106:2	who can shew **f** all his praise?	
Ps	113:2	from this time **f** and for evermore	
Ps	125:3	the righteous put **f** their hands	7971
Ps	126:6	He that goeth **f** and weepeth	
Ps	147:15	He sendeth **f** his commandment	
Pr	8:25	before the hills was I brought **f**:	2342
Pr	30:33	churning of milk bringeth **f** butter,	3318
Ecc	5:15	he came **f** of his mother's womb,	3318
SS	1:3	thy name is as ointment poured **f**	
SS	8:5	she brought thee **f** that bare thee,	2254
Isa	1:15	And when ye spread **f** your hands	
Isa	2:3	for out of Zion shall go **f** the law,	3318
Isa	5:2	that it should bring **f** grapes,	6213
Isa	23:4	travail not, nor bring **f** children,	3205
Isa	33:11	chaff, ye shall bring **f** stubble:	3205
Isa	37:36	Then the angel of the Lord went **f**	3318
Isa	42:3	bring **f** judgment unto truth	3318
Isa	42:13	Lord shall go **f** as a mighty man	3318
Isa	43:17	bringeth **f** the chariot and horse,	4161
Isa	45:8	and let them bring **f** salvation	6509
Isa	51:13	that hath stretched **f** the heavens	
Isa	51:18	sons whom she hath brought **f**;	3205
Isa	55:11	So shall my word be that goeth **f**	3318
Isa	58:8	Then shall the light break **f** as	
Isa	58:9	the putting **f** of the finger, and	7971
Isa	61:11	as the earth bringeth **f** her bud	3318
Isa	65:9	I will bring **f** a seed out of Jacob	3318
Isa	66:7	she travailed, she brought **f**;	3205
Jer	4:4	lest my fury come **f** like fire	3318
Jer	15:2	Whither shall ye go **f**? then thou	3318
Jer	17:22	carry **f** a burden out of your houses	3318
Jer	25:32	shall go **f** from nation to nation	3318
Jer	29:16	not gone **f** with you into captivity;	3318
Jer	30:23	the Lord goeth **f** with fury, a	3318
Jer	37:12	Jeremiah went **f** out of Jerusalem	3318
Jer	50:25	and hath brought **f** the weapons of	3318
Jer	51:16	and bringeth **f** the wind out of his	3318
Jer	52:31	and brought him **f** out of prison,	3318

F

Eze	1:13	out of the fire went **f** lightning	3318
Eze	10:7	cherub stretched **f** his hand from	
Eze	12:4	as they that go **f** into captivity	4161
Eze	17:2	Son of man, put **f** a riddle, and	2330
Eze	17:6	a vine and brought **f** branches,	6213
Eze	21:4	shall my sword go **f** out of his	3318
Eze	21:19	twain shall come **f** out of one land:	3318
Eze	30:9	shall messengers go **f** from me	3318
Eze	42:15	he brought me **f** toward the gate	3318
Eze	47:10	shall be a place to spread **f** nets;	
Da	2:13	decree went **f** that the wise men	5312
Da	5:5	In the same hour came **f** fingers	5312
Da	8:9	out of one of them came **f** a little	3318
Da	9:22	I am now come **f** to give thee skill	3318
Da	11:11	shall set **f** a great multitude;	5975
Hos	9:13	shall bring **f** his children to the	3318
Hos	10:1	he bringeth **f** fruit unto himself:	7737
Joel	2:16	bridegroom go **f** of his chamber	3318
Jnh	1:5	cast **f** the wares that were in the	2904
Jnh	1:12	and cast me **f** into the sea: so	2904
Mic	1:3	Lord cometh **f** out of his place	3318
Mic	4:2	for the law shall go **f** of Zion, and	3318
Hab	1:4	and judgment doth never go **f**: for	3318
Hab	3:5	burning coals went **f** at his feet	3318
Zep	2:2	Before the decree bring **f**, before	3205
Zec	2:3	angel that talked with me went **f**,	3318
Zec	3:8	bring **f** my servant the Branch	935
Zec	5:5	angel that talked with me went **f**,	3318
Zec	9:14	arrow shall go **f** as the lightning:	3318
Zec	14:3	Then shall the Lord go **f**, and fight	3318
Mt	1:21	And she shall bring **f** a son, and	*5088*
Mt	1:25	till she had brought **f** her firstborn	*5088*
Mt	7:17	**good tree bringeth f good fruit;**	*4160*
Mt	7:18	**good tree cannot bring f evil fruit,**	*4160*
Mt	10:16	**Behold, I send you f as sheep**	*649*
Mt	12:13	**Stretch f thine hand**	*1614*
Mt	12:35	**of the heart bringeth f good**	*1544*
Mt	13:3	**Behold a sower went f to sow;**	*1831*
Mt	13:23	**beareth fruit, and bringeth f,**	*4160*
Mt	13:49	**the angels shall come f,**	*3318*
Mt	13:52	**bringeth f out of his treasure**	*1544*
Mt	15:18	**mouth came f from the heart;**	*3318*
Mt	21:43	**to a nation bringing f the fruits**	*4160*
Mt	22:4	**he sent f other servants, saying,**	*649*
Mt	25:1	**went f to meet the bridegroom,**	*1831*
Mk	1:41	put **f** his hand, and touched him,	*1614*
Mk	3:5	the man, **Stretch f thine hand.**	*1614*
Mk	4:20	**and bring f fruit, some thirtyfold,**	*2592*
Mk	6:7	to send them **f** by two and two;	*1614*
Mk	9:29	**This kind can come f by nothing,**	*1831*
Mk	11:1	sendeth **f** two of his disciples	*1614*
Lk	1:31	bring **f** a son, and shalt call his	*5088*
Lk	1:57	be delivered; and she brought **f**.	*1080*
Lk	2:7	she brought **f** her firstborn son	*5088*
Lk	3:8	Bring **f** therefore fruits worthy of	*4160*
Lk	6:10	unto the man, **Stretch f thy hand**	*1614*
Lk	6:43	**a corrupt tree bring f good fruit**	*4160*
Lk	6:45	**bringeth f that which is good;**	*4393*
Lk	8:15	**and bring f fruit with patience.**	
Lk	10:2	**that he would send f labourers**	*1544*
Lk	10:3	**I send you f as lambs among**	*649*
Lk	12:16	**rich man brought f plentifully;**	*2164*
Lk	15:22	**Bring f the best robe, and put it**	*1627*
Lk	20:20	sent **f** spies, which should feign	*649*
Jn	2:10	doth set **f** good wine; and when	*5087*
Jn	2:11	and manifested **f** his glory;	*5319*
Jn	10:4	**when he putteth f his own sheep,**	*1544*
Jn	11:43	a loud voice, **Lazarus, come f.**	*1854*
Jn	12:24	**if it die, it bringeth f much fruit**	
Jn	15:2	**that it may bring f more fruit,**	
Jn	15:6	**he is cast f as a branch, and is**	*1854*
Jn	16:28	**I came f from the Father, and**	*1831*
Jn	16:30	that thou camest **f** from God	*1831*
Jn	19:4	Pilate therefore went **f** again,	*1854*
Jn	19:5	came Jesus **f**, wearing the crown	*1854*
Jn	19:17	went **f** into a place called the	*1831*
Jn	21:18	**thou shalt stretch f thy hands,**	*1614*
Ac	4:30	By stretching **f** thine hand to heal;	*1614*
Ac	13:4	being sent **f** by the Holy Ghost	*1599*
Ac	23:28	brought him **f** into their council:	*2609*
Ac	26:1	Then Paul stretched **f** the hand,	*1614*
Ro	3:25	Whom God hath set **f** to be a	*4388*
Ro	7:4	that we should bring **f** fruit unto	
Gal	4:4	God sent **f** his son, made of a	*1821*
Gal	4:6	God hath sent **f** the Spirit of his	*1821*
Php	2:16	Holding **f** the word of life; that I	*1907*
Col	1:6	and bringeth **f** fruit, as it doth	*1901*
Heb	1:14	sent **f** to minister for them who	*649*
Jas	1:15	lust hath conceived, it bringeth **f**	*616*
Jas	3:11	Doth a fountain send **f** at the same	*1032*
Jas	5:18	and the earth brought **f** her fruit	*985*
1Pe	2:9	that ye should shew **f** the praises	*1804*
Rev	6:2	went **f** conquering, and to conquer	*1831*
Rev	12:5	And she brought **f** a man child	*5088*
Rev	12:13	woman which brought **f** the man	*5088*

FORTIFY

Jgs	9:31	they **f** the city against thee	6696
Ne	4:2	Jews? will they **f** themselves?	5800
Isa	22:10	ye broken down to **f** the wall	1219
Na	2:1	loins strong, **f** thy power mightily	553

FORTRESS

2Sa	22:2	The Lord is my rock, and my **f**,	4686
Ps	18:2	rock, and my **f**, and my deliverer;	4686
Ps	31:3	For thou art my rock and my **f**;	4686
Ps	71:3	for thou art my rock and my **f**	4686
Ps	91:2	He is my refuge and my **f**:	4686
Jer	6:27	a tower and a **f** among my people,	4013
Jer	16:19	O Lord, my strength, and my **f**,	4581
Da	11:7	shall enter into the **f** of the king	4581

FORTS

2Ki	25:1	they built **f** against it round about	1785
Isa	29:3	and I will raise **f** against thee	4694
Isa	32:14	**f** and towers shall be for dens	6076
Eze	33:27	that be in the **f** and in the caves	4679

FORTY

Ge	7:4	upon the earth **f** days and **f** nights;	705
Ge	7:17	flood was **f** days upon the earth;	705
Ge	8:6	it came to pass at the end of **f** days,	705
Ge	18:28	he said, If I find there **f** and five,	705
Ge	25:20	Isaac was **f** years old when he took	705
Ge	26:34	Esau was **f** years old when he took	705
Ex	16:35	of Israel did eat manna **f** years,	705
Ex	24:18	in the mount **f** days and **f** nights	705
Ex	34:28	with the Lord **f** days and **f** nights;	705
Nu	14:33	wander in the wilderness **f** years,	705
Nu	32:13	wander in the wilderness **f** years,	705
Dt	2:7	these **f** years the Lord thy God	705
Dt	8:2	these **f** years in the wilderness,	705
Dt	9:9	in the mount **f** days and **f** nights	705

Dt	9:25	before the Lord **f** days and **f** nights,	705
Dt	10:10	the first time, **f** days and **f** nights;	705
Dt	25:3	**F** stripes he may give him, and	705
Dt	29:5	led you **f** years in the wilderness:	705
Jos	5:6	walked **f** years in the wilderness,	705
Jos	14:7	**F** years old was I when Moses the	705
Jgs	3:11	And the land had rest **f** years	705
Jgs	8:28	country was in quietness **f** years	705
1Sa	4:18	And he had judged Israel **f** years	705
2Sa	5:4	to reign, and he reigned **f** years	705
1Ki	4:26	Solomon had **f** thousand stalls of	705
1Ki	19:8	of that meat **f** days and **f** nights	705
Job	42:16	lived Job an hundred and **f** years	705
Ps	95:10	**F** years long was I grieved with	705
Jnh	3:4	yet **f** days, and Nineveh shall be	705
Mt	4:2	he had fasted **f** days and **f** nights	*5062*
Mk	1:13	was there in the wilderness **f** days,	*5062*
Lk	4:2	Being **f** days tempted of the devil	*5062*
Ac	1:3	proofs, being seen of them **f** days,	*5062*
Ac	4:22	For the man was above **f** years old,	*5062*
Ac	7:23	And when he was full **f** years old	*5063*
Ac	7:36	sea, and in the wilderness **f** years	*5062*
2Co	11:24	times received I **f** stripes save one	*5062*
Heb	3:9	me, and saw my works **f** years	*5062*
Heb	3:17	with whom was he grieved **f** years?	*5062*
Rev	14:1	with him an hundred **f** and four	*5062*

FORWARD See also HENCEFORWARD.

Ex	14:15	children of Israel, that they go **f**	5265
Nu	1:51	And when the tabernacle setteth **f**,	5265
1Sa	10:3	Then shalt thou go on **f** from	1973
1Sa	16:13	upon David from that day **f**	4605
1Sa	30:25	And it was so from that day **f**,	4605
2Ki	20:9	shall the shadow go **f** ten degrees	
Eze	43:27	and so **f**, the priests shall make	1973
Zec	1:15	and they helped **f** the affliction	
Mk	14:35	And he went **f** a little, and fell on	*4281*
Ac	19:33	the Jews putting him **f**	*4261*
2Co	8:17	but being more **f**, of his own	*4707*

FOUGHT

Ex	17:8	came Amalek, and **f** with Israel	3898
Nu	21:1	then he **f** against Israel, and took	3898
Jos	10:14	the Lord **f** for Israel	3898
Jos	10:42	the Lord God of Israel **f** for Israel	3898
Jos	23:3	your God is he that hath **f** for you	3898
Jos	24:8	and they **f** with you: and I gave	3898
Jgs	5:20	They **f** from heaven;	3898
Jgs	9:17	(For my father **f** for you, and	3898
1Sa	14:47	and **f** against all his enemies on	3898
1Sa	19:8	went out, and **f** with the Philistines,	3898
1Sa	31:1	the Philistines **f** against Israel:	3898
2Sa	10:17	in array against David, and **f** with	3898
2Sa	12:26	And Joab **f** against Rabbah of the	3898
Ps	109:3	and **f** against me without a cause	3898
Isa	20:1	and **f** against Ashdod, and took it;	3898
Jer	34:1	the people, **f** against Jerusalem	3898
Zec	14:12	that have **f** against Jerusalem;	6633
1Co	15:32	I have **f** with beasts at Ephesus,	*2341*
2Ti	4:7	I have **f** a good fight, I have	*75*
Rev	12:7	his angels **f** against the dragon;	*4170*

FOUL

Job	16:16	My face is **f** with weeping, and	2560
Mt	16:3	**It will be f weather to day: for**	*5494*
Mk	9:25	he rebuked the **f** spirit, saying	*169*
Rev	18:2	hold of every **f** spirit, and a cage	*169*

FOUND

Ge	2:20	there was not **f** an help meet	4672
Ge	6:8	Noah **f** grace in the eyes of the	4672
Ge	8:9	**f** no rest for the sole of her foot,	4672
Ge	16:7	And the angel of the Lord **f** her	4672
Ge	18:3	now I have **f** favour in thy sight,	4672
Ge	18:29	Peradventure there shall be forty **f**	4672
Ge	19:19	servant hath **f** grace in thy sight	4672
Ge	26:19	**f** there a well of springing water	4672
Ge	26:32	said unto him, We have **f** water	4672
Ge	30:27	if I have **f** favour in thine eyes,	4672
Ge	31:35	he searched, but **f** not the images	4672
Ge	39:4	And Joseph **f** grace in his sight	4672
Ge	44:8	which we **f** in our sacks' mouths	4672
Ge	44:12	the cup was **f** in Benjamin's sack.	4672
Ge	47:14	the money that was **f** in the land	4672
Ge	47:29	If now I have **f** grace in thy sight	4672
Ex	12:19	days shall there be no leaven **f** in	4672
Ex	15:22	in the wilderness, and **f** no water	4672
Ex	16:27	for to gather, and they **f** none	4672
Ex	22:4	If the theft be certainly **f** in his	4672
Ex	22:7	if the thief be **f**, let him pay	4672
Ex	33:12	thou hast also **f** grace in my sight	4672
Ex	34:9	now I have **f** grace in thy sight,	4672
Le	6:3	Or have **f** that which was lost	4672
Nu	15:32	they **f** a man that gathered sticks	4672
Dt	17:2	If there be **f** among you, within	4672
Dt	22:22	If a man be **f** lying with a woman	4672
Dt	24:7	If a man be **f** stealing any of his	4672
Jgs	6:17	If now I have **f** grace in thy sight,	4672
Jgs	15:15	he **f** a new jawbone of an ass,	4672
Ru	2:10	Why have I **f** grace in thine eyes,	4672
1Sa	13:22	was neither sword nor spear **f** in	4672
1Sa	16:22	for he hath **f** favour in my sight	4672
1Sa	20:3	that I have **f** grace in thine eyes;	4672
1Sa	27:5	If I have now **f** grace in thine eyes,	4672
1Sa	29:3	and I have **f** no fault in him since	4672
1Sa	31:8	that they **f** Saul and his three sons	4672
2Sa	14:22	that I have **f** grace in thy sight,	4672
2Sa	17:13	be not one small stone **f** there	
1Ki	13:14	and **f** him sitting under an oak:	467
1Ki	13:28	he went and **f** his carcase cast in	467
1Ki	19:19	and **f** Elisha the son of Shaphat	467
1Ki	20:36	him, a lion **f** him, and slew him	467
2Ki	2:17	sought three days, but **f** him not	467
2Ki	4:39	and **f** a wild vine, and gathered	467
2Ki	9:35	**f** no more of her than the skull	467
2Ki	12:18	gold that was **f** in the treasures	467
2Ki	22:8	I have **f** the book of the law in the	467
2Ki	22:13	the words of this book that is **f**:	467
2Ki	23:2	book of the covenant which was **f**	467
1Ch	10:8	they **f** Saul and his sons fallen	467
1Ch	26:31	were **f** among them mighty men	467
2Ch	29:16	they **f** in the temple of the Lord	4672
2Ch	34:30	book of the covenant that was **f** in	4672
Ezr	10:18	priests there were **f** that had taken	4672
Ne	2:5	and if thy servant have **f** favour in	
Ne	5:8	peace, and **f** nothing to answer	4672
Ne	7:5	And I **f** a register of the genealogy	4672
Ne	8:14	And they **f** written in the law	4672
Est	6:2	it was **f** written, that Mordecai	4672
Est	8:5	if I have **f** favour in his sight,	4672
Job	28:12	But where shall wisdom be **f**? and	4672
Job	42:15	were no women **f** so fair as the	4672
Ps	37:36	sought him, but he could not be **f**	4672
Ps	84:3	yea, the sparrow hath **f** an house,	4672

Ps 107:4 way; they **f** no city to dwell in. 4672
Pr 7:15 to seek thy face, and I have **f** thee 4672
Pr 10:13 hath understanding wisdom is **f**: 4672
Pr 16:31 it be **f** in the way of righteousness. 4672
Pr 25:16 Hast thou **f** honey? eat so much 4672
Pr 30:10 curse thee, and thou be **f** guilty.
Ecc 7:28 man among a thousand have I **f**; 4672
Ecc 9:15 Now there was **f** in it a poor wise 4672
SS 3:1 I sought him, but I **f** him not 4672
SS 3:4 but I **f** him whom my soul loveth: 4672
Isa 10:10 As my hand hath **f** the kingdoms 4672
Isa 51:3 joy and gladness shall be **f** therein, 4672
Isa 55:6 ye the Lord while he may be **f**, 4672
Isa 57:10 thou hast **f** the life of thine hand; 4672
Isa 65:8 As the new wine is **f** in the cluster, 4672
Jer 15:16 Thy words were **f**, and I did eat 4672
Jer 31:2 were left of the sword **f** grace in 4672
Jer 41:8 But ten men were **f** among them 4672
Jer 41:12 and **f** him by the great waters that 4672
Jer 50:20 shall not be **f**: for I will pardon 4672
Eze 22:30 not destroy it: but I **f** none. 4672
Eze 28:15 created, till iniquity was **f** in thee 4672
Da 1:19 them all was **f** none like Daniel, 4672
Da 1:20 he **f** them ten times better than all 4672
Da 5:11 wisdom of the gods, was **f** in him; 7912
Da 5:27 in the balances, and art **f** wanting 7912
Da 6:11 and **f** Daniel praying and making 7912
Da 6:23 no manner of hurt was **f** upon him, 7912
Da 11:19 stumble and fall, and not be **f** 4672
Hos 9:10 I **f** Israel like grapes in the 4672
Jnh 1:3 and he **f** a ship going to Tarshish: 4672
Zep 3:13 shall a deceitful tongue be **f** in 4672
Mt 1:18 she was **f** with child of the Holy *2147*
Mt 2:8 child; and when ye have **f** him *2147*
Mt 8:10 **I have not f so great faith, no,** *2147*
Mt 13:46 **he had f one pearl of great price,** *2147*
Mt 21:19 **f** nothing thereon, but leaves only, *2147*
Mt 26:43 he came and **f** them asleep again: *2147*
Mt 27:32 they **f** a man of Cyrene, Simon by *2147*
Mk 11:4 and **f** the colt tied by the door *2147*
Mk 14:55 to put him to death; and **f** none. *2147*
Lk 1:30 Mary: for thou hast **f** favour *2147*
Lk 2:16 came with haste, and **f** Mary, and 429
Lk 2:46 they **f** him in the temple, sitting *2147*
Lk 7:9 **I have not f so great faith, no,** *2147*
Lk 13:6 **sought fruit thereon, and f none.** *2147*
Lk 15:6 **I have f my sheep which was lost.** *2147*
Lk 15:32 **alive again; and was lost, and is f.** *2147*
Lk 23:2 We **f** this fellow perverting the *2147*
Lk 23:14 you, have **f** no fault in this man *2147*
Lk 24:2 And they **f** the stone rolled away *2147*
Lk 24:3 and **f** not the body of the Lord *2147*
Lk 24:23 And when they **f** not his body, they *2147*
Jn 1:41 We have **f** the Messias, which is *2147*
Jn 2:14 And **f** in the temple those that sold *2147*
Jn 9:35 and when he had **f** him, he said *2147*
Jn 11:17 he **f** that he had lain in the grave *2147*
Ac 5:10 young men came in, and **f** her dead, *2147*
Ac 7:11 and our fathers **f** no sustenance, *2147*
Ac 7:46 Who **f** favour before God, and *2147*
Ac 10:27 **f** many that were come together *2147*
Ac 13:6 **f** a certain sorcerer, a false prophet, *2147*
Ac 13:22 I have **f** David the son of Jesse, *2147*
Ac 17:23 I **f** an altar with this inscription, *2147*
Ac 18:2 And **f** a certain Jew named Aquila, *2147*
Ac 24:5 we have **f** this man a pestilent *2147*
Ac 24:12 they neither **f** me in the temple *2147*
Ac 28:14 Where we **f** brethren, and were *2147*
Ro 7:10 to life, I **f** to be unto death *2147*
1Co 4:2 stewards, that a man be **f** faithful *2147*
1Co 15:15 Yea, and we are **f** false witnesses *2147*
Gal 2:17 we ourselves also are **f** sinners, *2147*
Php 2:8 And being **f** in fashion as a man, *2147*
Php 3:9 And be **f** in him, not having mine *2147*
Heb 11:5 and was not **f**, because God had *2147*
1Pe 1:7 might be **f** unto praise and honour *2147*
1Pe 2:22 neither was guile **f** in his mouth: *2147*
2Jn 4 **f** of thy children walking in truth, *2147*
Rev 3:2 **for I nave not f thy works perfect** *2147*
Rev 5:4 no man was **f** worthy to open and *2147*
Rev 14:5 And in their mouth was **f** no guile: *2147*
Rev 18:24 in her was **f** the blood of prophets, *2147*
Rev 20:15 And whosoever was not **f** written *2147*

FOUNDATION

Ex 9:18 the **f** thereof even until now 3245
1Ki 5:17 stones, to lay the **f** of the house 3245
1Ki 6:37 In the fourth year was the **f** of the 3245
2Ch 23:5 a third part at the gate of the **f**. 3247
Ezr 3:6 **f** of the temple of the Lord was not 3245
Ezr 3:10 when the builders laid the **f** of the 3245
Ezr 5:16 and laid the **f** of the house of God 787
Job 4:19 whose **f** is in the dust, which are 3247
Ps 102:25 Of old hast thou laid the **f** of the 3245
Isa 28:16 I lay in Zion for a **f** a stone, 3248
Eze 13:14 the **f** thereof shall be discovered, 3247
Hag 2:18 **f** of the Lord's temple was laid 3245
Mt 25:34 **for you from the f of the world:** *2602*
Lk 6:48 **deep, and laid the f on a rock:** *2310*
Lk 11:50 **shed from the f of the world,** *2602*
Lk 14:29 **after he hath laid the f, and is** *2310*
Jn 17:24 **lovest me before the f of the** *2602*
Ro 15:20 build upon anothers man's **f** *2310*
1Co 3:11 For other **f** can no man lay than *2310*
Eph 2:20 built upon the **f** of the apostles *2310*
2Ti 2:19 the **f** of God standeth sure, having *2310*
Heb 6:1 laying again the **f** of repentance *2310*
1Pe 1:20 before the **f** of the world, but was *2602*
Rev 13:8 Lamb slain from the **f** of the world. *2602*
Rev 21:19 The first **f** was jasper; the second, *2310*

FOUNDATIONS

2Sa 22:8 the **f** of heaven moved and shook, 4146
Ezr 6:3 let the **f** thereof be strongly laid; 787
Job 38:4 thou when I laid the **f** of the earth? 3245
Ps 18:15 the **f** of the world were discovered 4146
Pr 8:29 he appointed the **f** of the earth: 4146
Isa 51:16 and lay the **f** of the earth, 3245
Jer 31:37 and the **f** of the earth searched out 4146
Eze 30:4 and her **f** shall be broken down. 3247
Heb 11:10 he looked for a city which hath **f** *2310*
Rev 21:14 the wall of the city had twelve **f** *2310*

FOUNDED

Ps 24:2 For he hath **f** it upon the seas, 3245
Pr 3:19 Lord by wisdom hath **f** the earth; 3245
Isa 14:32 the Lord hath **f** Zion, and the poor 3245
Mt 7:25 **fell not: for it was f upon a rock** *2311*

FOUNTAIN

Ge 16:7 found her by a **f** of water in the 5869
Le 11:36 nevertheless a **f** or pit, wherein 4599
Dt 33:28 **f** of Jacob shall be upon a land 5869

1Sa 29:1 Israelites pitched by a **f** which 5869
Ps 36:9 For with thee is the **f** of life: 4726
Pr 13:14 The law of the wise is a **f** of life, ...4726
Pr 14:27 The fear of the Lord is a **f** of life, ...4726
SS 4:12 a spring shut up, a **f** sealed 4599
Jer 2:13 forsaken me the **f** of living waters, ...4726
Jer 9:1 waters, and mine eyes a **f** of tears, ...4726
Hos 13:15 and his **f** shall be dried up: 4599
Jas 3:11 Doth a **f** send forth at the same *4077*
Rev 21:6 that is athirst of the **f** of the water *4077*

FOUNTAINS
Ge 7:11 were all the **f** of the great deep 4599
Ge 8:2 **f** also of the deep and the windows 4599
1Ki 18:5 unto all **f** of water, and unto all 4599
2Ch 32:4 stopped all the **f**, and the brook 4599
Isa 41:18 and **f** in the midst of the valleys: 4599
Rev 7:17 shall lead them unto living **f** of *4077*
Rev 14:7 the sea, and the **f** of waters *4077*

FOUR
Ge 2:10 parted, and became into **f** heads. 702
Ge 15:13 shall afflict them **f** hundred years; 702
Ge 33:1 and with him **f** hundred men. 702
Ex 12:41 the **f** hundred and thirty years, ...702
Ex 27:4 net shalt thou make **f** brasen rings 702
Ex 28:17 even **f** rows of stones: the first row 702
Ex 37:20 were **f** bowls made like almonds, ...702
Ex 39:10 they set in it **f** rows of stones: 702
Le 11:21 creeping thing that goeth upon all **f**, ...702
Nu 7:7 Two wagons and **f** oxen he gave 702
Nu 25:9 plague were twenty and **f** thousand 702
Dt 22:12 upon the **f** quarters of thy vesture, ...702
Jgs 9:34 against Shechem in **f** companies 702
Jgs 19:2 and was there **f** whole months. 702
Jgs 20:17 **f** hundred thousand men that drew 702
1Sa 25:13 after David about **f** hundred men; 702
2Sa 21:20 six toes, **f** and twenty in number; 702
1Ki 6:1 in the **f** hundred and eightieth year 702
1Ki 7:19 lily work in the porch, **f** cubits. 702
1Ki 7:30 **f** corners thereof had undersetters; 702
1Ki 10:26 thousand and **f** hundred chariots, ...702
1Ki 18:19 the prophets of Baal **f** hundred and 702
1Ki 18:22 Baal's prophets are **f** hundred and 702
1Ch 12:26 Levi **f** thousand and six hundred 702
1Ch 23:5 and **f** thousand praised the Lord 702
1Ch 26:17 northward **f** a day, southward **f** a 702
2Ch 9:25 Solomon had **f** thousand stalls for 702
2Ch 18:5 of prophets **f** hundred men, and 702
Ne 7:43 children of Hodevah, seventy and **f** 702
Pr 30:15 **f** things say not, It is enough: 702
Pr 30:24 **f** things which are little upon the 702
Isa 11:12 from the **f** corners of the earth. 702
Jer 49:36 the **f** winds from the **f** quarters 702
Eze 1:6 And every one had **f** faces, ...702
Eze 1:15 living creatures, with his **f** faces 702
Eze 7:2 upon the **f** corners of the land 702
Eze 10:10 they **f** had one likeness, as if a 702
Eze 37:9 come from the **f** winds, O breath, ...702
Eze 40:41 and **f** tables on that side, ...702
Eze 43:14 the greater settle shall be **f** cubits, ...702
Eze 45:19 upon the **f** corners of the settle 702
Eze 46:22 In the **f** corners of the court were 702
Eze 48:16 the west side **f** thousand and five 702
Da 3:25 Lo, I see **f** men loose, walking 703
Da 7:3 And **f** great beasts came up from 703
Da 7:6 the beast had also **f** heads; 703
Da 8:8 and for it came up **f** notable ones 702
Da 8:22 **f** stood up for it, **f** kingdoms shall 702
Da 11:4 be divided toward the **f** winds of 702
Zec 1:20 the Lord shewed me **f** carpenters 702
Zec 6:1 there came **f** chariots out from 702
Mt 15:38 **f** thousand men, beside women *5070*
Mt 16:10 **seven loaves of the f thousand,** *5070*
Mt 24:31 **together his elect from the f** *5064*
Lk 2:37 of about fourscore and **f** years, ...*5064*
Jn 4:35 **not ye, There are yet f months,** *5072*
Jn 11:17 lain in the grave **f** days already *5064*
Ac 5:36 number of men about **f** hundred *6071*
Ac 10:11 great sheet knit at the **f** corners *5064*
Ac 21:23 We have **f** men which have a vow *5064*
Rev 4:4 throne were **f** and twenty seats: *5064*
Rev 4:8 And the **f** beasts had each of them *5064*
Rev 5:6 of the throne and of the **f** beasts, ...*5064*
Rev 5:14 And the **f** beasts said, Amen *5064*
Rev 6:1 one of the **f** beasts saying, Come *5064*
Rev 7:1 after these things I saw **f** angels *5064*
Rev 7:11 about the elders and the **f** beasts, ...*5064*
Rev 9:14 Loose the **f** angels which are *5064*
Rev 14:1 and hundred forty and **f** thousand, ...*5064*
Rev 15:7 And one of the **f** beasts gave *5064*
Rev 20:8 are in the **f** quarters of the earth, ...*5064*

FOURFOLD
2Sa 12:6 And he shall restore the lamb **f** 706
Lk 19:8 false accusation, I restore him **f** *5073*

FOURFOOTED
Ac 11:6 and saw **f** beasts of the earth, ...*5074*
Ro 1:23 **f** beasts, and creeping things. *5074*

FOUR HUNDRED See FOUR and HUNDRED.

FOURSCORE
Ge 16:16 Abram was **f** and six years old 8084
Ex 7:7 And Moses was **f** years old 8084
Jgs 3:30 And the land had rest **f** years. 8084
2Sa 19:32 a very aged man, even **f** years old: 8084
1Ki 5:15 and **f** thousand hewers in the 8084
2Ch 11:1 an hundred and **f** thousand chosen 8084
Ezr 8:8 Michael, and with him **f** males. 8084
Ps 90:10 if by reason of strength they be **f** 8084
Isa 37:36 a hundred and **f** and five thousand: 8084
Lk 2:37 widow of about **f** and four years *3589*

FOURSQUARE
Ex 27:1 the altar shall be **f**: and the height 7251
Ex 30:2 **f** shall it be: and two cubits shall 7251
Ex 38:1 it was **f**; and three cubits the 7251
1Ki 7:31 with their borders, **f**, not round, ...7251
Eze 48:20 ye shall offer the holy oblation **f** 7243

FOURTEEN
Ge 31:41 I served thee **f** years for thy 702, 6240
Nu 1:27 **f** thousand and six hundred. 702, 7657
Nu 29:13 and **f** lambs of the first year; 702, 6240
Nu 29:32 and **f** lambs of the 702, 6240
2Ch 13:21 mighty, and married **f** wives 702, 6240
Eze 43:17 **f** broad in the four squares 702, 6240
Mt 1:17 Abraham to David are **f** generations *1180*
Mt 1:17 in to Babylon are **f** generations; *1180*
Mt 1:17 unto Christ are **f** generations *1180*

FOURTEENTH

Ex	12:6	shall keep it up until the **f** day	702, 6240
Le	23:5	In the **f** day of the first month	702, 6240
Nu	9:5	the passover on the **f** day of	702, 6240
Nu	28:16	in the **f** day of the first month	702, 6240
2Ki	18:13	in the **f** year of king Hezekiah	702, 6240
Ezr	6:19	the passover upon the **f** day	702, 6240
Est	9:19	the **f** day of the month Adar	702, 6240
Isa	36:1	in the **f** year of king Hezekiah,	702, 6240
Eze	45:21	first month, in the **f** day of the	702, 6240

FOURTH

Ge	1:19	and the morning were the **f** day	7243
Ge	15:16	the **f** generation they shall come	7243
Ex	28:20	the **f** row a beryl, and an onyx,	7243
Ex	29:40	and the **f** part of an hin of wine	7243
Le	23:13	of wine, the **f** part of an hin	7243
Nu	14:18	unto the third and **f** generation.	7256
Nu	15:5	And the **f** part of an hin of wine	7243
Nu	28:5	the **f** part of an hin of beaten oil	7243
Dt	5:9	unto the third and **f** generation	7256
Jgs	19:5	And it came to pass on the **f** day,	7243
1Ki	6:37	In the **f** year was the foundation	7243
2Ki	6:25	the **f** part of a cab of dove's dung	7255
2Ki	15:12	of Israel unto the **f** generation	7243
2Ki	25:3	of the **f** month the famine prevailed	
1Ch	12:10	Mishmannah the **f**, Jeremiah the	7243
1Ch	27:7	The **f** captain for the **f** month was	7243
Ezr	8:33	Now on the **f** day was the silver	7243
Ne	9:3	their God one **f** part of the day; of	7243
Jer	51:59	Babylon in the **f** year of his reign.	7243
Eze	1:1	in the **f** month, in the fifth day of	7243
Da	2:40	And the **f** kingdom shall be strong	7244
Da	7:7	and behold a **f** beast, dreadful and	7244
Da	7:23	The **f** beast shall be the **f** kingdom	7244
Zec	6:3	the **f** chariot grisled and bay horses	7243
Mk	6:48	and about the **f** watch of the night	*5067*
Rev	6:7	And when he had opened the **f** seal,	*5067*
Rev	6:8	them over the **f** part of the earth,	*5067*
Rev	16:8	And the **f** angel poured out his vial	*5067*

FOWL

Ge	1:20	and **f** that may fly above the earth	5775
Ge	1:22	and let **f** multiply in the earth.	5775
Ge	1:28	and over the **f** of the air, and over	5775
Ge	2:19	and every **f** of the air; and brought	5775
Ge	7:14	every **f** after his kind, every bird	5775
Ge	7:23	the **f** of the heaven; and they were	5775
Ge	8:19	every creeping thing, and every **f**,	5775
Ge	9:2	and upon every **f** of the air,	5775
Ge	9:10	creature that is with you, of the **f**,	5775
Le	11:46	the law of the beasts, and of the **f**	5775
Le	20:25	souls abominable by beast, or by **f**	5775
1Ki	4:23	and fallowdeer, and fatted **f**	1257
Job	28:7	is a path which no **f** knoweth,	5861
Ps	148:10	creeping things, and flying **f**:	6833
Eze	17:23	shall dwell all **f** of every wing;	6833
Eze	44:31	or torn, whether it be **f** or beast	5775

FOWLER

Ps	91:3	thee from the snare of the **f**, and	3353
Hos	9:8	but the prophet is a snare of a **f**	3353

FOWLS

Ge	6:20	**f** after their kind, and of cattle	5775
Ge	7:8	**f**, and of every thing that creepeth	5775
Le	1:14	his offering to the Lord be of **f**,	5775
Dt	14:20	But of all clean **f** ye may eat.	5775
1Sa	17:44	and I will give thy flesh unto the **f**	5775
1Ki	21:24	the field shall the **f** of the air eat	5775
Job	28:21	kept close from the **f** of the air	5775
Ps	50:11	I know all the **f** of the mountains:	5775
Isa	18:6	the **f** shall summer upon them,	5861
Jer	16:4	shall be meat for the **f** of heaven,	5775
Eze	31:6	the **f** of heaven made their nests	5775
Da	2:38	and the **f** of the heaven hath he	5776
Da	4:14	it, and the **f** from his branches:	6853
Hos	2:18	with the **f** of the heaven, and with	5775
Mt	6:26	**Behold the f of the air: for they**	*4071*
Mt	13:4	**the f came and devoured them**	*4071*
Mk	4:32	**the f of the air my lodge under**	*4071*
Lk	12:24	**more are ye better than the f?**	*4071*
Ac	10:12	creeping things, and **f** of the air	*4071*
Rev	19:17	saying to all the **f** that fly in the	*3732*
Rev	19:21	the **f** were filled with their flesh.	*3732*

FOX

Lk	13:32	**Go ye, and tell that f, Behold, I**	*258*

FOXES

Jgs	15:4	went and caught three hundred **f**,	7776
SS	2:15	Take us the **f**, the little **f**, that	7776
Lk	9:58	**F have holes, and birds of the air**	*258*

FRAGMENTS

Mt	14:20	took up of the **f** that remained	*2801*
Mk	6:43	up twelve baskets full of the **f**	*2801*
Mk	8:20	**baskets full of f took ye up?**	*2801*
Jn	6:13	filled twelve baskets with the **f**	*2801*

FRANKINCENSE

Ex	30:34	these sweet spices with pure **f**:	3828
Le	2:2	with all the **f** there of; and the	3828
Le	2:16	with all the **f** thereof: it is an	3828
Le	6:15	all the **f** which is upon the meat	3828
1Ch	9:29	the oil, and the **f**, and the spices	3828
Ne	13:9	with the meat offering and the **f**	3828
SS	4:6	of myrrh, and to the hill of **f**	3828
Mt	2:11	gifts; gold, and **f**, and myrrh	*3030*

FRANKLY

Lk	7:42	**to pay, he f forgave them both**	*5435*

FRAUD See also DEFRAUD.

Ps	10:7	full of cursing and deceit and **f**	8496
Jas	5:4	which is of you kept back by **f**,	*650*

FRECKLED

Le	13:39	it is a **f** spot that groweth in the	933

FREE See also FREEMAN; FREEWILL; FREEWOMAN.

Ex	21:2	in the seventh he shall go out **f**	2670
Ex	21:11	shall she go out **f** without money	2600
Ex	36:3	brought yet unto him **f** offerings	5071
Nu	5:19	be thou **f** from this bitter water	5352
Dt	15:12	thou shalt let him go **f** from thee	2670
1Sa	17:25	his father's house **f** in Israel	2670
2Ch	29:31	and as many as were of a **f** heart	5081
Job	39:5	Who hath sent out the wild ass **f**?	2670
Ps	88:5	**F** among the dead, like the slain	2670
Isa	58:6	and to let the oppressed go **f**,	2670
Jer	34:10	every one his maidservant, go **f**,	2670
Mt	15:6	**or his mother, he shall be f.**	
Jn	8:32	**and the truth shall make you f**	*1659*
Jn	8:36	**Son therefore shall make you f**	*1659*
Ac	22:28	And Paul said, But I was **f** born.	

Ro	6:18	Being then made **f** from sin, ye	*1659*
Ro	8:2	hath made me **f** from the law of	*1659*
1Co	7:22	that is called, being **f**, is Christ's	*1658*
1Co	12:13	whether we be bond or **f**; and have	*1658*
Gal	4:26	But Jerusalem which is above is **f**,	*1658*
Gal	5:1	wherewith Christ hath made us **f**	*1659*
Col	3:11	Barbarian, Scythian, bond nor **f**:	*1658*
1Pe	2:16	As **f**, and not using your liberty	*1658*
Rev	6:15	every bondman, and every **f** man	*1658*
Rev	19:18	all men, both **f** and bond, both	*1658*

FREED

Ro	6:7	For he that is dead is **f** from sin	*1344*

FREEDOM

Le	19:20	at all redeemed, nor **f** given her;	2668
Ac	22:28	a great sum obtained I this **f**	*4174*

FREELY

Ge	2:16	tree of the garden thou mayest **f** eat:	
Ezr	2:68	offered **f** for the house of God to	
Ps	54:6	I will **f** sacrifice unto thee: I	5071
Mt	10:8	**f ye have received, f give**	*1432*
Ro	3:24	Being justified **f** by his grace	*1432*
1Co	2:12	we might know the things that are **f**	
2Co	11:7	to you the gospel of God **f**?	*1432*
Rev	21:6	the fountain of the water of life **f**.	*1432*

FREEWILL See also FREE and WILL.

Le	22:18	all his **f** offerings, which they	5071
Le	22:23	mayest thou offer for a **f** offering;	5071
Nu	15:3	a vow, or in a **f** offering, or in your	5071
Dt	12:6	your vows, and your **f** offerings, and	5071
Dt	16:10	of a **f** offering of thine hand, which	5071
2Ch	31:14	the **f** offerings of God, to distribute	5071
Ezr	3:5	offered a **f** offering unto the Lord	5071
Ezr	7:16	with the **f** offering of the people,	5069
Ps	119:108	the **f** offerings of my mouth, O	5071

FREEWOMAN

Gal	4:22	by a bondmaid, the other by a **f**.	*1658*
Gal	4:30	not be heir with the son of the **f**	*1658*

FRESH See also AFRESH; REFRESH.

Ps	92:10	I shall be anointed with **f** oil	7488
Jas	3:12	both yield salt water and **f**.	*1099*

FRIEND

Ex	33:11	face, as a man speaketh unto his **f**	7453
Dt	13:6	or the wife of thy bosom, or thy **f**,	7453
2Sa	16:16	Hushai the Archite, David's **f**	7463
2Ch	20:7	seed of Abraham thy **f** for ever?	157
Job	6:27	and ye dig a pit for your **f**.	7451
Ps	41:9	mine own familiar **f** in whom I trusted	
Pr	6:1	son, if thou be surety for thy **f**,	7453
Pr	17:17	A **f** loveth at all times, and a	7453
Pr	18:24	and there is a **f** that sticketh closer	157
Pr	27:6	Faithful are the wounds of a **f**;	157
Pr	27:9	doth the sweetness of a man's **f** by	7453
Pr	27:14	blesseth his **f** with a loud voice	7453
SS	5:16	my **f**, O daughters of Jerusalem	7453
Isa	41:8	chosen, the seed of Abraham my **f**	157
Hos	3:1	yet, love a woman beloved of her **f**,	7453
Mt	11:19	**a f of publicans and sinners**	*5384*
Mt	22:12	**F, how camest thou in hither not**	*2083*
Lk	7:34	**a f of publicans and sinners!**	*5384*
Lk	11:5	**Which of you shall have a f, and**	*5384*
Lk	14:10	**F, go up higher: then shalt thou**	*5384*
Jn	11:11	**Our f Lazarus sleepeth; but I go,**	*5384*
Jas	2:23	and he was called the **F** of God	*5384*
Jas	4:4	**f** of the world is the enemy of God	*5384*

FRIENDS

1Sa	30:26	to his **f**, saying, Behold a present	7453
2Sa	19:6	thine enemies, and hatest thy **f**	157
Est	5:10	he sent and called for his **f**,	157
Job	2:11	when Job's three **f** heard of all	7453
Job	16:20	My **f** scorn me: but mine eye	7453
Job	19:14	and my familiar **f** have forgotten me.	
Job	42:7	thee, and against thy two **f**: for ye	7453
Ps	38:11	My lovers and my **f** stand aloof	7453
Pr	16:28	and a whisperer separateth chief **f**.	441
Pr	18:24	A man that hath **f** must shew	7453
Jer	20:4	terror to thyself, and to all thy **f**:	157
La	1:2	her **f** have dealt treacherously	7453
Mk	3:21	when his **f** heard of it, they	*3588, 3844*
Mk	5:19	**Go home to thy f, and tell them**	*4674*
Lk	12:4	**And I say unto you my f, Be not**	*5384*
Lk	14:12	**call not thy f, nor thy brethren**	*5384*
Lk	15:29	**I might make merry with my f:**	*5384*
Jn	15:13	**a man lay down his life for his f**	*5384*
Jn	15:14	**Ye are my f, if ye do whatsoever**	*5384*
Jn	15:15	**I have called you f; for all things**	*5384*
Ac	27:3	to go unto his **f** to refresh himself	*5384*
3Jn	14	Our **f** salute thee	*5384*

FRIENDSHIP

Pr	22:24	Make no **f** with an angry man;	7462
Jas	4:4	**f** of the world is enmity with God?	*5373*

FRO See also FROWARD.

Ge	8:7	raven, which went forth to and **f**,	7725
2Ch	16:9	the eyes of the Lord run to and **f**	7751
Job	2:2	From going to and **f** in the earth,	7751
Job	13:25	break a leaf driven to and **f**?	
Pr	21:6	a vanity tossed to and **f** of them	
Isa	33:4	as the running to and **f** of locusts	
Jer	5:1	ye to and **f** through the streets	7751
Eze	27:19	Dan also and Javan going to and **f**.	235
Am	8:12	they shall run to and **f** to seed the	7751
Zec	1:11	We have walked to and **f** through the	
Zec	6:7	Get you hence, walk to and **f** through	
Eph	4:14	tossed to and **f**, and carried about	*2831*

FROGS

Ex	8:2	will smite all thy borders with **f**:	6854
Ex	8:4	the **f** shall come up both on thee	6854
Ex	8:6	the **f** came up, and covered the land	6854
Ex	8:7	and brought up **f** upon the land of	6854
Ex	8:9	the **f** from thee and thy houses,	6854
Ex	8:11	And the **f** shall depart from thee,	6854
Ex	8:13	and the **f** died out of the houses,	6854
Rev	16:13	I saw three unclean spirits like **f**	*944*

FROST

Ge	31:40	consumed me, and the **f** by night;	7140
Job	37:10	By the breath of God **f** is given:	7140
Ps	78:47	and their sycamore trees with **f**.	2602

FROWARD

Dt	32:20	for they are a very **f** generation,	8419
Ps	18:26	and with the **f** thou wilt shew	6141
Ps	101:4	A **f** heart shall depart from me:	6141
Pr	2:12	the man that speaketh **f** things;	8419
Pr	3:32	the **f** is abomination to the Lord:	3868
Pr	4:24	Put away from thee a **f** mouth,	6143

Pr	8:13	and the **f** mouth, do I hate	8419
Pr	11:20	are of a **f** heart are abomination	6141
Pr	16:28	A **f** man soweth strife: and a	8419
Pr	22:5	snares are in the way of the **f**:	6141

FRUIT See also **FIRSTFRUIT.**

Ge	1:11	**f** tree yielding **f** after his kind,	6529
Ge	1:29	is the **f** of a tree yielding seed;	6529
Ge	3:3	**f** of the tree which is in the midst	6529
Ge	4:3	Cain brought of the **f** of the ground	6529
Ex	21:22	so that her **f** depart from her,	3206
Le	19:24	year all the **f** thereof shall be holy	6529
Le	27:30	the **f** of the tree, is the Lord's:	6529
Nu	13:27	and honey; and this is the **f** of it	6529
Dt	7:13	**f** of thy womb, and the **f** of thy	6529
Dt	26:2	the first of all the **f** of the earth	6529
Dt	28:11	in the **f** of thy body, and in the **f** of	6529
Dt	28:51	the **f** of thy cattle, and the **f** of thy	6529
Dt	30:9	thy cattle, and in the **f** of thy land,	6529
Jgs	9:11	my sweetness, and my good **f**,	8270
Ne	10:35	the firstfruits of all **f** of all trees,	6529
Ps	1:3	bringeth forth his **f** in his season;	6529
Ps	92:14	shall still bring forth **f** in old age;	5107
Ps	127:3	the **f** of the womb is his reward.	6529
Pr	8:19	My **f** is better than gold, yea, than	6529
Pr	11:30	The **f** of the righteous is a tree	6529
Pr	12:14	with good by the **f** of his mouth:	6529
Pr	31:16	the **f** of her hands she planteth	6529
SS	2:3	and his **f** was sweet to my taste	6529
Isa	4:2	the **f** of the earth shall be excellent	6529
Isa	13:18	have no pity on the **f** of the womb;	6529
Isa	27:9	is all the **f** to take away his sin;	6529
Isa	57:19	I create the **f** of the lips;	5108
Jer	2:7	eat the **f** thereof and the goodness	6529
Jer	11:19	Let us destroy the tree with the **f**	3899
Jer	17:8	neither shall cease from yielding **f**	6529
Jer	21:14	according to the **f** of your doings,	6529
La	2:20	Shall the women eat their **f**, and	6529
Eze	19:12	and the east wind dried up her **f**:	6529
Eze	36:8	and yield your **f** to my people	6529
Eze	36:30	I will multiply the **f** of the tree,	6529
Da	4:12	the **f** thereof much, and it was meat	4
Hos	9:16	yet will I slay even the beloved **f**	
Hos	14:8	From me is thy **f** found	6529
Am	2:9	I destroyed his **f** from above,	6529
Am	8:2	And I said, A basket of summer **f**	
Mic	6:7	**f** of my body for the sin of my soul?	6529
Mic	7:1	my soul desired the first ripe **f**	
Hab	3:17	neither shall **f** be in the vines;	2981
Mal	3:11	your vine cast her **f** before the	7920
Mt	7:17	**tree bringeth forth good f;**	*2590*
Mt	12:33	**the tree good, and his f good;**	*2590*
Mt	13:8	**and brought forth f, some an**	*2590*
Mt	13:23	**also beareth f, and bringeth forth,**	*2592*
Mt	21:19	**no f grow on thee henceforward**	*2590*
Mt	26:29	**henceforth of this f of the vine,**	*1081*
Mk	4:7	**and choked it, and it yielded no f**	*2590*
Mk	4:20	**and bring forth f, some thirtyfold,**	*2592*
Mk	11:14	**No man eat f of thee hereafter**	*2590*
Mk	12:2	**from the husbandmen of the f of**	*2590*
Mk	14:25	**drink no more of the f of the**	*1081*
Lk	1:42	blessed is the **f** of thy womb.	*2590*
Lk	3:9	bringeth not forth good **f** is hewn	*2590*
Lk	6:43	**tree bringeth not forth corrupt f;**	*2590*
Lk	8:14	**and bring no f to perfection**	*5062*
Lk	13:7	**these three years I come seeking f**	*2590*
Lk	20:10	**that they should give him of the f**	*2590*
Lk	22:18	**will not drink of the f of the vine,**	*1081*
Jn	4:36	**and gathereth f unto life eternal:**	*2590*
Jn	12:24	**if it die, it bringeth forth much f**	*2590*
Jn	15:2	**that beareth f, he purgeth it,**	*2590*
Jn	15:4	**the branch cannot bear f of**	*2590*
Jn	15:8	**glorified, that ye bear much f;**	*2590*
Jn	15:16	**ye should go and bring forth f,**	*2590*
Ac	2:30	that of the **f** of his loins, he would	*2590*
Ro	6:22	ye have your **f** unto holiness,	*2590*
Ro	7:4	we should bring forth **f** unto God.	*2592*
Gal	5:22	But the **f** of the Spirit is love,	*2590*
Eph	5:9	**f** of the Spirit is in all goodness	*2590*
Php	4:17	but I desire **f** that may abound	*2590*
Heb	12:11	it yieldeth the peaceable **f** of	*2590*
Heb	13:15	the f of our lips giving thanks to his	*2590*
Jas	3:18	And the **f** of righteouness is sown	*2590*
Jude	12	without **f**, twice dead,	*175*
Rev	22:2	yielded her **f** every month: and the	*175*

FRUITFUL See also **UNFRUITFUL**

Ge	1:22	Be **f**, and multiply, and fill the	6509
Ge	8:17	be **f**, and multiply upon the earth.	6509
Ge	17:6	And I will make thee exceeding **f**,	6509
Ge	35:11	be **f** and multiply; a nation	6509
Ge	48:4	Behold, I will make thee **f**, and	6509
Ex	1:7	the children of Israel were **f**, and	6509
Ps	128:3	Thy wife shall be as a **f** vine	6509
Isa	5:1	a vineyard in a very **f** hill:	1121, 8081
Isa	17:6	the outmost **f** branches thereof,	6509
Isa	29:17	field, and the **f** field shall be	3759
Isa	32:15	wilderness be a **f** field, and the	3759
Jer	23:3	and they shall be **f** and increase.	6509
Eze	19:10	she was **f** and full of branches	6509
Ac	14:17	and **f** seasons, filling our hearts	*2593*

FRUITS

Ge	43:11	take of the best **f** in the land	2173
Ex	23:10	shall gather in the **f** thereof:	8393
Le	25:16	the **f** doth he sell unto thee	8393
2Sa	16:1	hundred of summer **f**, and a bottle	
2Ki	19:29	vineyards, and eat the **f** thereof	6529
Ps	107:37	which may yield **f** of increase	6529
SS	4:13	with pleasant **f**; camphire, with	6529
Isa	16:9	for the shouting for thy summer **f**	
Jer	40:10	gather ye wine, and summer **f**, and	
Jer	48:32	spoiler is fallen upon they summer **f**	
Mic	7:1	they have gathered the summer **f**,	
Mt	3:8	therefore **f** meet for repentance:	*2590*
Mt	7:16	**Ye shall know them by their f**	*2590*
Mt	21:34	**they might receive the f of it.**	*2590*
Lk	3:8	therefore **f** worthy of repentance;	*2590*
Lk	12:18	**I bestow all my f and my goods,**	*1081*
Php	1:11	with the **f** of righteousness,	*2590*
Jas	3:17	full of mercy and good **f**,	*2590*
Rev	22:2	which bare twelve manner of **f**,	*2590*

FULFIL

Ge	29:27	**F** her week, and we will give thee	4390
1Ki	2:27	he might **f** the word of the Lord,	4390
2Ch	36:21	To **f** the word of the Lord by the	4390
Ps	20:4	and **f** all thy counsel.	4390
Ps	145:19	He will **f** the desire of them that	6213
Mt	3:15	**us to f all righteousness.**	*4137*
Mt	5:17	**not come to destroy, but to f.**	*4137*
Ro	2:27	it it **f** the law, judge thee,	*5055*
Gal	6:2	and so **f** the law of Christ,	*378*

Col 1:25 for you, to **f** the word of God; *4137*
Col 4:17 in the Lord, that thou **f** it. *4137*
Jas 2:8 If ye **f** the royal law according to *5055*

FULFILLED

Ge 25:24 her days to be delivered were **f**, 4390
Ge 29:28 Jacob did so, and **f** her week: 4390
Ge 50:3 for so are **f** the days of those 4390
Ex 7:25 And seven days were **f**, after that 4390
Le 12:6 the days of her purifying are **f**, 4390
Nu 6:13 the days of his separation are **f**: 4390
2Sa 14:22 hath **f** the request of his servant 6213
1Ki 8:24 and hasts **f** it with thine hand, 4390
Job 36:17 **f** the judgment of the wicked: 4390
La 2:17 he hath **f** his word that he had 1214
Da 10:3 till three whole weeks were **f** 4390
Mt 2:15 it might be **f** which was spoken *4137*
Mt 2:23 that it might be **f** which was *4137*
Mt 5:18 **from the law, till all be f.** *1096*
Mt 13:14 **And in them is f the prophecy** *378*
Mt 24:34 **pass, till all these things be f** *1096*
Mt 26:54 **then shall the scriptures be f** *4137*
Mt 26:56 **of the prophets might be f** *4137*
Mt 27:9 was **f** that which was spoken *4137*
Mk 1:15 **The time is f, and the Kingdom** *4137*
Mk 14:49 **but the scriptures must be f.** *4137*
Lk 1:20 which shall be **f** in their season. *4137*
Lk 4:21 **is this scripture f in your ears** *4137*
Lk 21:24 **times of the Gentiles be f** *4137*
Lk 22:16 **until it be f in the kingdom** *4137*
Jn 3:29 this my joy therefore is **f** *4137*
Jn 13:18 **but that the scripture may be f,** *4137*
Jn 17:13 **that they might have my joy f** *4137*
Jn 18:32 the saying of Jesus might be **f**, *4137*
Ac 3:18 should suffer, he hath so **f** *4137*
Ac 12:25 when they had **f** their ministry, *4137*
Ac 13:33 God hath **f** the same unto us *1603*
Ro 8:4 of the law might be **f** in us, *4137*
Ro 13:8 loveth another hath **f** the law *4137*
Gal 5:14 all the law is **f** in one word, *4137*
Rev 6:11 killed as they were, should be **f** *4137*
Rev 17:17 until the words of God shall be **f** *5055*

FULFILLING

Ps 148:8 vapours; stormy wind **f** his word: 6213
Eph 2:3 **f** the desires of the flesh and of *4160*

FULL

Ge 14:10 the vale of Siddim was **f** of slimepits;
Ge 25:8 an old man, and **f** of years; 7649
Ge 41:22 came up in one stalk, **f** and good: 4392
Ex 16:33 put an omer **f** of manna therein, 4393
Le 2:14 even corn beaten out of **f** ears 3759
Le 25:29 within a **f** year may he redeem it. 3117
Nu 7:13 both of them were **f** of fine flour 4392
Nu 7:19 **f** of fine flour mingled with oil 4392
Nu 7:56 spoon of ten shekels, **f** of incense: 4392
Nu 7:86 spoons were twelve, **f** of incense 4392
Nu 24:13 give me his house **f** of silver 4393
Dt 6:11 thou shalt have eaten and be **f**; 7646
Dt 8:12 when thou hast eaten and art **f** 7646
Dt 34:9 Nun was **f** of the spirit of wisdom; 4392
Jgs 16:27 house was **f** of men and women; 4390
Ru 2:12 and a **f** reward be given thee 8003
1Sa 18:27 gave them in **f** tale to the king, 4390
2Sa 8:2 and with one **f** line to keep alive. 4393
2Ki 3:16 Lord, Make this valley **f** of ditches.
2Ki 4:6 when the vessels were **f**, that she 4390
2Ki 7:15 was **f** of garments and vessels, 4392
2Ki 10:21 of Baal was **f** from one end 4390
1Ch 11:13 a parcel of ground **f** of barley; 4392
1Ch 29:28 **f** of days, riches, and honour: 7646
Ne 9:25 possessed houses **f** of all goods, 4392
Job 5:26 shalt come to thy grave in a **f** age, 3624
Job 10:15 I am **f** of confusion; therefore see 7646
Job 14:1 is of few days, and **f** of trouble 7646
Job 21:23 One dieth in his **f** strength, being 8537
Job 42:17 Job died, being old and **f** of days 7646
Ps 17:14 they are **f** of children, and leave 7646
Ps 29:4 voice of the Lord is **f** of majesty
Ps 69:20 and I am **f** of heaviness: and I looked
Ps 78:25 he sent them meat to the **f** 7648
Ps 86:15 a God **f** of compassion, and gracious
Ps 111:4 Lord is gracious and **f** of compassion.
Ps 119:64 earth, O Lord, is **f** of thy mercy: 4390
Ps 144:13 That our garners may be **f**, 4392
Pr 17:1 than an house **f** of sacrifices 4392
Pr 27:20 Hell and destruction are never **f**; 7646
Ecc 1:7 yet the sea is not **f**; unto the 4392
Ecc 10:14 A fool also is **f** of words: 7235
Isa 1:11 I am **f** of the burnt offerings of 7646
Isa 2:7 their land is also **f** of horses, 4390
Isa 6:3 the whole earth is **f** of his glory. 4393
Isa 22:2 art **f** of stirs, a tumultuous city, 4392
Isa 30:27 his lips are **f** of indignation, and 4390
Jer 4:12 a **f** wind from those places shall 4392
Jer 5:18 I will not make a **f** end with you.
Jer 5:27 so are their houses **f** of deceit: 4392
Jer 6:11 aged with him that is **f** of days. 4390
Jer 30:11 though I make a **f** end of all nations
Jer 35:5 pots **f** of wine, and cups, and I 4392
La 3:30 he is filled **f** with reproach. 7646
Eze 7:23 the land is **f** of bloody crimes, 4390
Eze 10:4 the court was **f** of the brightness 4390
Eze 11:13 Lord God! wilt thou make a **f** end
Eze 28:12 **f** of wisdom, and perfect in 4392
Eze 39:19 ye shall eat fat till ye be **f**. 7654
Da 3:19 Was Nebuchadnezzar **f** of fury, 4391
Joel 2:24 And the floors shall be **f** of wheat, 4390
Mic 6:12 rich men thereof are **f** of violence, 4390
Hab 3:3 the earth was **f** of his praise, 4390
Mt 6:22 **the whole body shall be f of light.** *5460*
Mt 15:37 that was left seven baskets **f** *4134*
Mt 23:25 **within they are f of extortion** *1073*
Mt 23:27 **are within f of dead men's bones,** *1073*
Mt 23:28 **are f of hypocrisy and iniquity** *3324*
Mk 8:19 **many baskets f of fragments** *4134*
Mk 15:36 And one ran and filled a spunge **f**
Lk 4:1 Jesus being **f** of the Holy Ghost *4134*
Lk 6:25 **Woe unto you that are f! for ye** *1705*
Lk 11:36 **whole body therefore be f of light,** *5460*
Lk 11:39 **your inward part is f of ravening** *1073*
Lk 16:20 **laid at his gate, f of sores,**
Jn 1:14 the Father,) **f** of grace and truth. *4134*
Jn 7:8 **my time is not yet f come.** *4137*
Jn 15:11 **and that your joy might be f.** *4137*
Jn 16:24 **receive, that your joy may be f.** *4137*
Ac 2:13 These men are **f** of new wine *3325*
Ac 6:3 **f** of the Holy Ghost and wisdom, *4134*
Ac 6:8 Stephen, **f** of faith and power, *4134*
Ac 7:55 he, being **f** of the Holy Ghost, *4134*
Ac 11:24 **f** of the Holy Ghost and of faith: *4134*
Ro 3:14 is **f** of cursing and bitterness: *1073*

Ro 15:14 that ye are also **f** of goodness, ...*3324*
Php 2:26 you all, and was **f** of heaviness,
Col 2:2 the **f** assurance of understanding,............*4136*
Heb 6:11 **f** assurance of hope unto the end: *4136*
Heb 10:22 in **f** assurance of faith, having *4136*
Jas 3:17 **f** of mercy and good fruits, without *3324*
1Pe 1:8 with joy unspeakable and **f** of glory:
1Jn 1:4 you, that your joy may be **f**......................*4137*
2Jn 12 to face, that our joy may be **f**....................*4137*
Rev 5:8 harps, and golden vials **f** of odours, ...*1073*
Rev 15:7 **f** of the wrath of God, who liveth *1073*
Rev 16:10 his kingdom was **f** of darkness;
Rev 17:4 cup in her hand **f** of abominations..........*1073*
Rev 21:9 vials **f** of the seven last plagues,................*1073*

FULLY
Nu 7:1 had **f** set up the tabernacle, ...3615
Ru 2:11 It hath **f** been shewed me, all 5046
Ecc 8:11 heart of the sons of men is **f** set..............4390
Ac 2:1 the day of Pentecost was **f** come, ...*4545*
Ro 14:5 Let every man be **f** persuaded *4135*
Ro 15:19 I have **f** preached the gospel of.................*4137*
2Ti 3:10 thou hast **f** known my doctrine, ...*3877*

FULNESS See also THANKFULNESS.
Nu 18:27 and as the **f** of the winepress....................4395
1Ch 16:32 Let the sea roar, and the **f** thereof: 4393
Ps 16:11 in thy presence is **f** of joy;.........................7648
Ps 98:7 Let the sea roar, and the **f** thereof; 4393
Jn 1:16 of his **f** have all we received *4138*
Ro 15:29 come in the **f** of the blessing *4135*
1Co 10:28 is the Lord's and the **f** thereof; *4138*
Gal 4:4 when the **f** of the time was come.............*4138*
Eph 1:10 dispensation of the **f** of times *4138*
Eph 3:19 be filled with all the **f** of God. *4138*
Eph 4:13 the stature of the **f** of Christ:....................*4138*
Col 2:9 all the **f** of the Godhead bodily................*4138*

FURIOUS
Pr 29:22 and a **f** man aboundeth in........................2534
Eze 25:17 upon them with **f** rebukes;.......................2534
Na 1:2 Lord revengeth, and is **f**;................1167, 2534

FURNACE
Ge 15:17 behold a smoking **f**, and a 8574
Ex 9:8 to you handfuls of ashes of the **f**, ...3536
Ex 19:18 ascended as the smoke of a **f**....................3536
1Ki 8:51 from the midst of the **f** of iron: 3564
Ps 12:6 as silver tried in a **f** of earth,.....................5948
Pr 27:21 and the **f** for gold: so is a man 3564
Isa 48:10 I have chosen thee in the **f** of...................3564
Eze 22:18 and lead, in the midst of the **f**;..................3564
Da 3:11 the midst of a burning fiery **f**.....................861
Da 3:19 heat the **f** one seven times more 861
Da 3:21 the midst of the burning fiery **f**.................861
Da 3:26 to the mouth of the burning fiery **f**...........861
Mt 13:42 **shall cast them into a f of fire:** *2575*
Rev 1:15 as if they burned in a **f**;............................*2575*

FURNISH
Ps 78:19 God **f** a table in the wilderness?...............6186
Jer 46:19 **f** thyself to go into captivity: 6213, 3627

FURNISHED
Mt 22:10 **the wedding was f with guests.** *4130*
Mk 14:15 **large upper room f and prepared:**...........*4766*
Lk 22:12 **shew you a large upper room f:**...............*4768*
2Ti 3:17 throughly **f** unto all good works *1822*

FURNITURE
Ex 31:7 and all the **f** of the tabernacle, ...3627
Ex 31:8 the table and his **f**, and the.......................3627
Ex 31:8 pure candlestick with all his **f**, ...3627

FURTHER See also FARTHER.
Nu 22:26 the angel of the Lord went **f**.....................3254
1Sa 10:22 enquired of the Lord **f**, if the man...........5750
Job 38:11 shalt thou come, but no **f**: 3254
Ps 140:8 **f** not his wicked device; lest they 6329
Mt 26:65 what **f** need have we of witnesses?...........*2089*
Mk 14:63 What need we any **f** witnesses? *2089*
Lk 24:28 as though he would have gone **f**.............*4206*
Ac 4:21 when they had **f** threatened them,
Ac 12:3 he proceeded **f** to take Peter also.
Ac 24:4 I be not **f** tedious unto thee............*1909, 4118*
2Ti 3:9 proceed no **f**: for their folly *1909, 4118*

FURTHERANCE
Php 1:12 rather unto the **f** of the gospel; *4297*
Php 1:25 for your **f** and joy of faith;........................*4297*

FURTHERMORE See also MORE; MOREOVER.
Ex 4:6 And the Lord said **f** unto him,.................5750
Dt 4:21 **F** the Lord was angry with me for
Dt 9:13 **F** the Lord spake unto me,
1Ch 17:10 **F** I tell thee that the Lord will build
1Ch 29:1 **F** David the king said unto the
Eze 8:6 He said **f** unto me, Son of man, seest
Eze 23:40 And **f**, that ye have sent for men................637
1Th 4:1 **F** then we beseech you, brethren,.............*3063*
Heb 12:9 **F** we have had fathers of our flesh *1534*

FURY
Ge 27:44 until thy brother's **f** turn away;................2534
Job 20:23 God shall cast the **f** of his wrath 2740
Isa 34:2 and his **f** upon all their armies:................2534
Isa 51:13 because of the **f** of the oppressor, ...2534
Isa 51:22 the dregs of the cup of my **f**;....................2534
Isa 63:3 anger, and trample them in my **f**; 2534
Jer 4:4 lest my **f** come forth like fire, ...2534
Jer 7:20 mine anger and my **f** shall be...................2534
Jer 21:5 and in **f**, and in great wrath. 2534
Jer 23:19 the Lord is gone forth in **f**, ...2534
Jer 30:23 of the Lord goeth forth with **f**,..................2534
Jer 32:37 and in my **f**, and in great wrath; 2534
Jer 36:7 **f** that the Lord hath pronounced.............2534
Jer 42:18 and my **f** hath been poured forth 2534
La 2:4 he poured out his **f** like fire 2534
Eze 5:15 in **f** and in furious rebukes. 2534
Eze 6:12 I accomplish my **f** upon them..................2534
Eze 13:13 with a stormy wind in my **f**;.....................2534
Eze 14:19 pour out my **f** upon it in blood, ...2534
Eze 20:8 I will pour out my **f** upon them, ...2534
Eze 21:17 and I will cause my **f** to rest: 2534
Eze 24:8 That it might cause **f** to come up 2534
Eze 36:18 my **f** upon them for the blood.................2534
Da 3:13 rage and **f** commanded to bring..............2528
Da 9:16 thine anger and thy **f** be turned...............2534
Mic 5:15 in anger and **f** upon the heathen, ...2534
Zec 8:2 I was jealous for her with great **f** 2534

G

GAIN

Pr	1:19	every one that is greedy of **g**;	1214
Pr	3:14	and the **g** thereof than fine gold.	8393
Pr	15:27	He that is greedy of **g** troubleth	1214
Pr	28:8	by usury and unjust **g** increaseth	8636
Eze	22:27	destroy souls, to get dishonest **g**	1214
Da	11:39	and shall divide the land for **g**.	4242
Mt	16:26	**if he shall g the whole world,**	*2770*
Lk	9:25	**if he g the whole world, and lose**	*2770*
Ac	16:16	brought her masters much **g** by	*2039*
Ac	19:24	brought no small **g** unto the	*2039*
1Co	9:19	unto all, that I might **g** the more.	*2770*
1Co	9:22	that I might **g** the weak:	*2770*
2Co	12:17	Did I make a **g** of you by any	*4122*
Php	1:21	to live is Christ, and to die is **g**	*2771*
Php	3:7	But what things were **g** to me,	*2771*
1Ti	6:5	supposing that **g** is godliness:	*4200*
1Ti	6:6	godliness with contentment is great **g**.	*4200*
Jas	4:13	and buy and sell, and get **g**:	*2770*

GAINED

Mt	18:15	**thee, thou hast g thy brother.**	*2770*
Mt	25:20	**I have g beside them five talents.**	*2770*
Lk	19:15	**every man had g by trading.**	*1281*

GAINS

Ac	16:19	the hope of their **g** was gone,	*2089*

GAINSAY

Lk	21:15	**shall not be able to g nor resist**	*471*

GAINSAYERS

Tit	1:9	to exhort and to convince the **g**	*483*

GAINSAYING

Ro	10:21	a disobedient and **g** people	*483*

GALL

Ps	69:21	gave me also **g** for my meat;	7219
Jer	8:14	given us water of **g** to drink,	7219
Jer	23:15	make them drink the water of **g**	7219
La	3:19	misery, the wormwood and the **g**	7219
Am	6:12	ye have turned judgment into **g**,	7219
Mt	27:34	vinegar to drink mingled with **g**:	*5521*
Ac	8:23	thou art in the **g** of bitterness,	*5521*

GALLERIES

SS	7:5	the king is held in the **g**	7298
Eze	41:15	and the **g** thereof on the one side	862
Eze	41:16	windows, and the **g** round about	862
Eze	42:5	for the **g** were higher than these,	862

GALLERY

Eze	42:3	**g** against **g** in the three stories.	862

GALLEY

Isa	33:21	wherein shall go no **g** with oars,	590

GALLOWS

Est	5:14	a **g** be made of fifty cubits high,	6086
Est	6:4	to hang Mordecai on the **g** that he	6086
Est	7:10	So they hanged Haman on the **g**.	6086
Est	9:13	ten sons be hanged upon the **g**	6086

GAP

Eze	22:30	and stand in the **g** before me.	6556

GAPED

Job	16:10	**g** upon me with their mouth;	6473
Ps	22:13	**g** upon me with their mouths,	6475

GAPS

Eze	13:5	Ye have not gone up into the **g**,	6556

GARDEN

Ge	2:8	And the Lord God planted a **g**	1588
Ge	2:9	of life also in the midst of the **g**,	1588
Ge	2:10	out of Eden to water the **g**;	1588
Ge	2:15	him into the **g** of Eden to dress it	1588
Ge	2:16	of the **g** thou mayest freely eat:	1588
Ge	3:1	shall not eat of every tree of the **g**?	1588
Ge	3:8	the Lord God walking in the **g**	1588
Ge	3:10	I heard thy voice in the **g**,	1588
Ge	3:23	sent him forth from the **g** of Eden,	1588
Ge	13:10	even as the **g** of the Lord,	1588
1Ki	21:2	that I may have it for a **g** of herbs,	1588
2Ki	21:18	buried in the **g** of his own house,	1588
Est	1:5	court of the **g** of the king's palace;	1594
Est	7:8	king returned out of the palace **g**	1594
SS	4:12	A **g** inclosed is my sister, my	1588
SS	5:1	I am come into my **g**, my sister,	1588
Isa	1:30	and as a **g** that hath no water	1593
Isa	51:3	her desert like the **g** of the Lord;	1588
Isa	61:11	and as the **g** causeth the things	1593
Jer	31:12	their soul shall be as a watered **g**;	1588
Jer	39:4	by the way of the king's **g**,	1588
Eze	28:13	been in Eden the **g** of God;	1588
Eze	31:8	The cedars in the **g** of God	1588
Eze	31:8	nor any tree in the **g** of God	1588
Eze	36:35	is become like the **g** of Eden;	1588
Joel	2:3	the land is as the **g** of Eden	1588
Lk	13:19	**a man took, and cast into his g;**	*2779*
Jn	18:26	Did not I see thee in the **g**	*2779*
Jn	19:41	a **g**; and in the **g** a new sepulchre,	*2779*

GARDENER

Jn	20:15	She, supposing him to be the **g**,	*2780*

GARDENS

Ecc	2:5	I made me **g** and orchards,	1593
SS	8:13	Thou that dwellest in the **g**,	1588
Isa	65:3	that sacrificeth in **g**, and burneth	1593
Isa	66:17	the **g** behind one tree in the midst,	1593
Jer	29:28	plant **g**, and eat the fruit of them.	1593
Am	4:9	when your **g** and your vineyards	1593
Am	9:14	make **g**, and eat the fruit of them.	1593

GARLICK

Nu	11:5	leeks, and the onions, and the **g**	7762

GARMENT

Ge	9:23	And Shem and Japheth took a **g**,	8071
Ge	25:25	red, all over like an hairy **g**;	155
Ge	39:12	he left his **g** in her hand,	899
Ge	39:18	he left his **g** with me, and fled	899
Le	6:10	the priest shall put on his linen **g**,	4055
Le	13:47	**g** also that the plague of leprosy	899
Le	13:52	He shall therefore burn that **g**,	899
Le	15:17	And every **g**, and every skin,	899
Le	19:19	neither shall a **g** mingled of linen	899
Dt	22:5	shall a man put on a woman's **g**	8071
Jos	7:21	Babylonish **g**, and two hundred	155

Ezr	9:3	I rent my **g** and my mantle,	899
Job	38:9	I made the cloud the **g** thereof,	3830
Ps	69:11	I made sackcloth also my **g**;	3830
Ps	73:6	violence covereth them as a **g**	7897
Ps	102:26	all of them shall wax old like a **g**;	899
Ps	104:2	thyself with light as with a **g**:	8008
Ps	104:6	it with the deep as with a **g**:	3830
Pr	20:16	his **g** that is surety for a stranger:	899
Pr	25:20	that taketh away a **g** in cold weather.	899
Pr	27:13	Take his **g** that is surety	899
Pr	30:4	who hath bound the waters in a **g**?	8071
Isa	50:9	they all shall wax old as a **g**;	899
Isa	51:6	the earth shall wax old like a **g**,	899
Isa	51:8	shall eat them up like a **g**	899
Isa	61:3	the **g** of praise for the spirit of	4594
Jer	43:12	as a shepherd putteth on his **g**;	899
Eze	18:7	hath covered the naked with a **g**;	899
Da	7:9	whose **g** was white as snow,	3831
Zec	13:4	wear a rough **g** to deceive:	155
Mal	2:16	one covereth violence with his **g**,	3830
Mt	9:16	**piece of new cloth unto an old g,**	*2440*
Mt	22:11	**which had not on a wedding g**	*1742*
Mk	13:16	**back again for to take up his g**	*2440*
Mk	16:5	clothed in a long white **g**: and	*4749*
Lk	22:36	**let him sell his g, and buy one.**	*2440*
Ac	12:8	Cast thy **g** about thee, and follow	*2440*
Heb	1:11	all shall wax old as doth a **g**;	*2440*
Jude	23	hating even the **g** spotted by the	*5509*
Rev	1:13	clothed with a **g** down to the foot,	*4158*

GARMENTS

Ge	38:14	she put her widow's **g** off from	899
Ge	49:11	he washed his **g** in wine, and his	3830
Ex	28:2	thou shalt make holy **g** for Aaron	899
Ex	29:21	and upon his **g** and upon his sons,	899
Le	16:4	these are holy **g**; therefore shall	899
Le	16:23	and shall put off the linen **g**,	899
Le	21:10	is consecrated to put on the **g**,	899
Nu	20:28	And Moses stripped Aaron of his **g**,	899
Jgs	14:13	sheets and thirty changes of **g**	899
2Sa	10:4	cut off their **g** in the middle,	4063
2Sa	13:31	the king arose, and tare his **g**,	899
2Ki	5:23	two bags, with two changes of **g**	899
2Ki	7:15	all the way was full of **g** and vessels	899
2Ki	25:29	And changed his prison **g**: and he	899
Ps	22:18	They part my **g** among them,	899
Ps	45:8	All thy **g** smell of myrrh, and aloes,	899
Ecc	9:8	Let thy **g** be always white;	899
Isa	9:5	noise, and **g** rolled in blood;	8071
Isa	59:17	he put on the **g** of vengeance	899
Isa	61:10	clothed me with the **g** of salvation,	899
Isa	63:3	shall be sprinkled upon my **g**,	899
Jer	36:24	were not afraid, nor rent their **g**,	899
Jer	52:33	And changed his prison **g**: and he	899
La	4:14	that men could not touch their **g**	3830
Eze	42:14	but there they shall lay their **g**	899
Eze	44:19	they shall put off their **g** wherein	899
Joel	2:13	rend your heart, and not your **g**,	899
Zec	3:4	Take away the filthy **g** from him.	899
Mt	21:8	spread their **g** in the way;	*2440*
Mt	23:5	**enlarge the borders of their g,**	*2440*
Mt	27:35	and parted his **g**, casting lots:	*2440*
Mt	27:35	They parted my **g** among them,	*2440*
Lk	19:35	they cast their **g** upon the colt,	*2440*
Lk	24:4	men stood by them in shining **g**	*2067*
Jn	13:4	from supper, and laid aside his **g**;	*2440*
Jn	19:23	took his **g** and made four parts,	*2440*
Ac	9:39	the coats and **g** which Dorcas made	*2440*
Jas	5:2	and your **g** are motheaten.	*2440*
Rev	3:4	**which have not defiled their g.**	*2440*
Rev	16:15	**that watcheth, and keepeth his g,**	*2440*

GARNERS

Ps	144:13	That our **g** may be full, affording	4200
Joel	1:17	the **g** are laid desolate, the barns	214

GARNISHED

2Ch	3:6.	And he **g** the house with precious	6823
Mt	12:44	**he findeth it empty, swept, and g**	*2885*
Rev	21:19	of the wall of the city were **g**	*2885*

GARRISON

1Sa	13:3	Jonathan smote the **g** of the	5333
1Sa	14:6	Come, and let us go over unto the **g**	4673
1Sa	14:12	men of the **g** answered Jonathan	4675

GARRISONS

2Ch	17:2	and set **g** in the land of Judah,	5333
Eze	26:11	and thy strong **g** shall go down	4676

GATE

Ge	19:1	Lot sat in the **g** of Sodom:	8179
Ge	22:17	possess the **g** of his enemies;	8179
Ge	23:18	that went in at the **g** of his city,	8179
Ge	28:17	and this is the **g** of heaven.	8179
Ex	32:26	Moses stood in the **g** of the camp,	8179
Ex	40:33	set up the hanging of the court **g**	8179
Dt	22:15	unto the elders of the city in the **g**	8179
Dt	25:7	go up to the **g** unto the elders,	8179
Jos	2:5	about the time of shutting of the **g**,	8179
Jos	8:29	cast it at the entering of the **g**	8179
Jgs	16:3	took the doors of the **g** of the city,	8179
Ru	4:1	Then went Boaz up to the **g**,	8179
1Sa	4:18	seat backward by the side of the **g**,	8179
2Sa	3:27	Joab took him aside in the **g**	8179
2Sa	15:2	stood beside the way of the **g**:	8179
2Sa	18:33	up to the chamber over the **g**,	8179
2Sa	19:8	the king doth sit in the **g**	8179
1Ki	17:10	when he came to the **g** of the city,	6607
2Ki	7:1	for a shekel, in the **g** of Samaria;	8179
2Ki	7:17	the people trode upon him in the **g**,	8179
2Ki	11:19	the way of the **g** of the guard.	8179
2Ki	25:4	way of the **g** between two walls,	8179
1Ch	11:17	well of Beth-lehem, that is at the **g**!	8179
2Ch	18:9	the entering in of the **g** of Samaria;	8179
2Ch	35:15	and the porters waited at every **g**	8179
Ne	2:13	by night by the **g** of the valley,	8179
Ne	12:39	they stood still in the prison **g**.	8179
Est	2:21	while Mordecai sat in the king's **g**.	8179
Est	3:2	servants, that were in the king's **g**,	8179
Est	4:2	none might enter into the king's **g**	8179
Est	5:9	saw Mordecai in the king's **g**,	8179
Est	6:10	Jew, that sitteth at the king's **g**.	8179
Job	5:4	and they are crushed in the **g**,	8179
Ps	69:12	They that sit in the **g** speak	8179
Ps	118:20	This **g** of the Lord, into which the	8179
Ps	127:5	speak with the enemies in the **g**	8179
Pr	17:19	he that exalteth his **g** seeketh	6607
Pr	22:22	oppress the afflicted in the **g**;	8179
Pr	24:7	he openeth not his mouth in the **g**.	8179
Isa	22:7	set themselves in array at the **g**	8179
Isa	24:12	the **g** is smitten with destruction.	8179
Isa	28:6	them that turn the battle to the **g**	8179
Isa	29:21	for him that reproveth in the **g**,	8179

Jer	7:2	Stand in the **g** of the Lord's house,	8179
Jer	38:7	the king then sitting in the **g**	8179
Jer	39:4	by the **g** betwixt the two walls:	8179
Jer	52:7	of the **g** between the two walls,	8179
La	5:14	elders have ceased from the **g**,	8179
Eze	8:3	to the door of the inner **g** that	8179
Eze	8:5	at the **g** of the altar this image	8179
Eze	8:14	brought me to the door of the **g** of	8179
Eze	40:3	measuring reed; he stood in the **g**	8179
Eze	44:2	This **g** shall be shut, it shall not	8179
Eze	46:2	but the **g** shall not be shut until	8179
Eze	46:3	shall worship at the door of this **g**	8179
Da	2:49	Daniel sat in the **g** of the king	8651
Am	5:10	hate him that rebuketh in the **g**	8179
Am	5:12	they turn aside the poor in the **g**	8179
Am	5:15	and establish judgment in the **g**:	8179
Mic	1:9	he is come unto the **g** of my people,	8179
Mic	1:12	the Lord unto the **g** of Jerusalem	8179
Zep	1:10	the noise of a cry from the fish **g**,	8179
Mt	7:13	**Enter ye in at the strait g**	*4439*
Mt	7:13	**for wide is the g, and broad is**	*4439*
Mt	7:14	**Because strait is the g, and**	*4439*
Lk	13:24	**Strive to enter in at the strait g**	*4439*
Lk	16:20	**which was laid at his g, full of**	*4440*
Ac	3:2	the **g** of the temple which is called	*2374*
Ac	3:10	at the Beautiful **g** of the temple:	*4439*
Ac	12:14	she opened not the **g** for gladness,	*4440*
Ac	12:14	told how Peter stood before the **g**	*4440*
Heb	13:12	own blood, suffered without the **g**	*4439*
Rev	21:21	every ... **g** was of one pearl:	*3588, 4440*

GATES

Ex	20:10	thy stranger that is within thy **g**	8179
Dt	3:5	with high walls, **g**, and bars;	1817
Dt	5:14	thy stranger that is within thy **g**;	8179
Dt	6:9	posts of thy house, and on thy **g**	8179
Dt	12:12	the Levite that is within your **g**;	8179
Dt	12:15	kill and eat flesh in all thy **g**,	8179
Dt	12:17	Thou mayest not eat within thy **g**	8179
Dt	12:18	and the Levite that is within thy **g**:	8179
Dt	14:21	unto the stranger that is in thy **g**,	8179
Dt	14:29	which are within thy **g**, shall come,	8179
Dt	15:22	Thou shalt eat it within thy **g**	8179
Dt	16:5	the passover within any of thy **g**,	8179
Dt	16:11	and the Levite that is within thy **g**,	8179
Dt	16:14	widow, that are within thy **g**	8179
Dt	17:5	that wicked thing, unto thy **g**,	8179
Dt	17:8	of controversy within thy **g**:	8179
Dt	18:6	if a Levite come from any of thy **g**	8179
Dt	24:14	that are in thy land within thy **g**	8179
Dt	26:12	that they may eat within thy **g**,	8179
Dt	28:52	he shall besiege thee in all thy **g**,	8179
Dt	28:57	enemy shall distress thee in thy **g**	8179
Dt	31:12	thy stranger that is within thy **g**,	8179
Jos	6:26	son shall he set up the **g** of it	1817
Jgs	5:8	then was war in the **g**: was there	8179
Jgs	5:11	people of the Lord go down to the **g**	8179
1Sa	23:7	into a town that hath **g** and bars	1817
2Sa	18:24	David sat between the two **g**: and	8179
1Ki	16:34	up the **g** thereof in his youngest son	1817
2Ki	23:8	down the high places of the **g**	8179
1Ch	9:19	keepers of the **g** of the tabernacle:	5592
2Ch	31:2	to praise in the **g** of the tents	8179
Ne	2:3	**g** thereof are consumed with fire?	8179
Ne	2:17	the **g** thereof are burned with fire:	8179
Ne	7:3	Let not the **g** of Jerusalem be opened	8179
Ne	13:19	that the **g** should be shut,	1817
Job	38:17	Have the **g** of death been opened	8179
Ps	9:13	liftest me up from the **g** of death:	8179
Ps	24:7	your heads, O ye **g**; and be ye lift up	8179
Ps	24:9	your heads, O ye **g**; even lift them	8179
Ps	87:2	The Lord loveth the **g** of Zion	8179
Ps	100:4	Enter into his **g** with thanksgiving,	8179
Ps	107:18	draw near unto the **g** of death	8179
Ps	118:19	Open to me the **g** of righteousness:	8179
Ps	122:2	Our feet shall stand within thy **g**,	8179
Pr	1:21	in the openings of the **g**: in the	8179
Pr	8:3	She crieth at the **g**, at the entry of	8179
Pr	8:34	watching daily at my **g**, wailing	1817
Pr	14:19	wicked at the **g** of the righteous	8179
Pr	31:23	Her husband is known in the **g**,	8179
Pr	31:31	her own works praise her in the **g**	8179
SS	7:13	at our **g** are all manner of pleasant	6607
Isa	3:26	her **g** shall lament and mourn;	6607
Isa	13:2	go into the **g** of the nobles	6607
Isa	26:2	Open ye the **g**, that the righteous	8179
Isa	38:10	I shall go to the **g** of the grave:	8179
Isa	45:1	and the **g** shall not be shut;	8179
Isa	45:2	break in pieces the **g** of brass,	1817
Isa	60:11	thy **g** shall be open continually;	8179
Isa	60:18	walls Salvation, and thy **g** Praise.	8179
Isa	62:10	through the **g**; prepare ye the way	8179
Jer	7:2	that enter in at these **g** to worship	8179
Jer	17:24	bring in no burden through the **g**	8179
Jer	17:27	I kindle a fire in the **g** thereof,	8179
Jer	49:31	which have neither **g** nor bar	1817
Jer	51:58	and her high **g** shall be burned	8179
La	1:4	**g** are desolate: her priests sigh	8179
La	2:9	Her **g** are sunk into the ground;	8179
La	4:12	entered into the **g** of Jerusalem.	8179
Eze	26:10	when he shall enter into thy **g**,	8179
Eze	38:11	and having neither bars nor **g**,	1817
Ob	11	foreigners entered into his **g**,	8179
Na	2:6	**g** of the rivers shall be opened,	8179
Na	3:13	**g** of thy land shall be set wide open	8179
Zec	8:16	truth and peace in your **g**	8179
Mt	16:18	**the g of hell shall not prevail**	*4439*
Ac	9:24	they watched the **g** day and night	*4439*
Rev	21:12	and had twelve **g**,	*4440*
Rev	21:12	and at the **g** twelve angels,	*4440*
Rev	21:13	On the east three **g**;	*4440*
Rev	21:13	on the north three **g**,	*4440*
Rev	21:13	on the south three **g**;	*4440*
Rev	21:13	and on the west three **g**	*4440*
Rev	21:15	and the **g** thereof, and the wall	*4440*
Rev	21:21	the twelve **g** were twelve pearls;	*4440*
Rev	21:25	And the **g** of it shall not be shut	*4440*
Rev	22:14	enter in through the **g** into the city,	*4440*

GATHER

Ge	6:21	and thou shalt **g** it to thee;	622
Ge	31:46	said unto his brethren, **G** stones;	3950
Ge	49:2	**G** yourselves together, and hear,	6908
Ex	5:12	to **g** stubble instead of straw	7197
Ex	16:5	twice as much as they **g** daily	3950
Ex	16:16	**G** of it every man according to his	3950
Ex	16:26	Six days ye shall **g** it; but on the	3950
Le	19:10	neither shalt thou **g** every grape	3950
Le	25:11	nor **g** the grapes in it of thy vine	1219
Le	25:20	not sow, nor **g** in our increase:	622
Nu	11:16	**G** unto me seventy men of the	622
Dt	28:38	Shalt **g** but little in; for the locust	622

Dt	30:3	and **g** thee from all the nations,	6908
Ru	2:7	me glean and **g** after the reapers	622
2Sa	3:21	and will **g** all Israel unto my lord	6908
1Ki	18:19	**g** to me all Israel unto mount	6908
2Ki	22:20	I will **g** thee unto thy fathers,.	622
2Ch	24:5	**g** of all Israel money to repair	6908
Ne	1:9	yet will I **g** them from thence,.	6908
Est	2:3	may **g** together all the fair young	6908
Est	4:16	**g** together all the Jews that are	3664
Job	34:14	if he **g** unto himself his spirit	622
Ps	26:9	**G** not my soul with sinners	622
Ps	39:6	and knoweth not who shall **g** them	622
Ps	50:5	**G** my saints together unto me;	622
Ps	94:21	**g** themselves together against	1413
Ps	104:28	That thou givest them they **g**:	3950
Pr	28:8	**g** it for him that will pity the poor	6908
Ecc	2:26	to **g** and to heap up, that he may	622
Ecc	3:5	and a time to **g** stones together;	3664
Isa	11:12	**g** together the dispersed of Judah	6908
Isa	40:11	shall **g** the lambs with his arm,	6908
Isa	54:7	with great mercies will I **g** thee	6908
Isa	54:15	whosoever shall **g** together against	1481
Isa	56:8	Yet will I **g** others to him,.	6908
Isa	66:18	I will **g** all nations and tongues;	6908
Jer	4:5	the trumpet in the land: cry, **g**.	4390
Jer	7:18	children **g** wood, and the fathers	3950
Jer	9:22	and none shall **g** them	622
Jer	23:3	I will **g** the remnant of my flock	6908
Jer	29:14	I will **g** you from all the nations,.	6908
Jer	31:10	He that scattered Israel will **g** him,	6908
Jer	32:37	I will **g** them out of all countries,	6908
Eze	11:17	I will even **g** you from the people,	6908
Eze	16:37	therefore I will **g** all thy lovers,	6908
Eze	20:34	and will **g** you out of the countries	6908
Eze	29:13	At the end of forty years will I **g**.	6908
Eze	37:21	and will **g** them on every side,.	6908
Da	3:2	sent to **g** together the princes,	3673
Hos	8:10	now will I **g** them, and they shall	6908
Joel	1:14	**g** the elders and all the	622
Joel	2:16	**G** the people, sanctify the.	622
Joel	2:16	assemble the elders, **g** the children,.	622
Joel	3:2	I will also **g** all nations, and will	6908
Mic	2:12	surely **g** the remnant of Israel;.	6908
Na	2:10	the faces of them all **g** blackness	6908
Hab	1:9	shall **g** the captivity as the sand.	622
Zep	2:1	**g** together, O nation not desired;	7197
Zep	3:18	I will **g** them that are sorrowful	622
Zec	10:10	and **g** them out of Assyria; and I	6908
Zec	14:2	**g** all nations against Jerusalem.	622
Mt	6:26	**do they reap, nor g into barns;**	*4863*
Mt	7:14	**Do men g grapes of thorns,**	*4816*
Mt	13:30	**G ye together first the tares,**	*4816*
Mt	13:30	**but g the wheat into my barn.**	*4863*
Mt	13:41	**they shall g out of his kingdom**	*4816*
Mt	24:13	**they shall g together his elect**	*1996*
Mk	13:27	**and shall g together his elect.**	*1996*
Lk	6:44	**of thorns men do not g figs,**	*4816*
Lk	6:44	**of a bramble bush g they grapes,**	*5166*
Lk	13:34	**as a hen doth g her brood under**	
Jn	6:12	**G up the fragments that remain,**	*4863*
Jn	15:6	**and men g them, and cast them**	*4863*
Eph	1:10	he might **g** together in one all	*346*
Rev	14:18	**g** the clusters of the vine of the	*5166*
Rev	16:14	to **g** them to battle of that great	*4863*
Rev	19:17	Come and **g** yourselves together	*4863*
Rev	20:8	to **g** them together to battle:	*4863*

GATHERED

Ge	1:9	be **g** together unto one place,	6960
Ge	12:5	their substance that they had **g**.	7408
Ge	25:8	of years; and was **g** to his people.	622
Ge	41:49	And Joseph **g** corn as the sand	6651
Ge	47:14	And Joseph **g** up all the money.	3950
Ex	15:8	the waters were **g** together, the	6192
Ex	16:17	and **g**, some more, some less	3950
Ex	16:18	he that **g** much had nothing over,	
Ex	16:18	and he that **g** little had no lack;	
Ex	16:22	the sixth day they **g** twice as much	3950
Ex	32:1	**g** themselves together unto Aaron,	6950
Nu	11:22	all the fish of the sea be **g** together	622
Nu	11:24	and **g** the seventy men of the elders	622
Nu	11:32	and they **g** the quails:	622
Nu	15:32	they found a man that **g** sticks	7197
Nu	16:19	And Korah **g** all the congregation.	6950
Jos	24:1	Joshua **g** all the tribes of Israel	622
Jgs	4:13	Sisera **g** together all his chariots,.	2199
Jgs	7:23	the men of Israel **g** themselves	6817
Jgs	9:6	the men of Shechem **g** together,	622
Jgs	11:3	were **g** vain men to Jephthah,	3950
Jgs	16:23	of the Philistines **g** them together.	6908
Jgs	20:14	children of Benjamin **g** themselves.	622
1Sa	7:7	children of Israel were **g** together	6908
1Sa	17:1	Philistines **g** together their armies	622
1Sa	20:38	Jonathan's lad **g** up the arrows,	3950
1Sa	25:1	all the Israelites were **g** together	6908
1Sa	28:1	that the Philistines **g** their armies	6908
1Sa	28:4	and Saul **g** all Israel together, and	6908
2Sa	17:11	all Israel be generally **g** unto thee,.	622
2Sa	21:13	and they **g** the bones of them	622
2Sa	23:9	that were there **g** together to battle,	622
1Ki	10:26	And Solomon **g** together chariots.	622
1Ki	22:6	of Israel **g** the prophets together,	6908
2Ki	3:21	they **g** all that were able to put on	6817
2Ki	23:1	and they **g** unto him all the elders	622
1Ch	11:1	all Israel **g** themselves to David	6908
1Ch	19:17	and he **g** all Israel, and passed over.	622
2Ch	13:7	there are **g** unto him vain men,.	6908
2Ch	23:2	**g** the Levites out of all the cities	6908
2Ch	24:5	And he **g** together the priests	6908
2Ch	24:11	day, and **g** money in abundance	622
2Ch	34:17	they have **g** together the money	5413
Ezr	7:28	and I **g** together out of Israel.	6908
Ezr	8:15	And I **g** them together to the river	6908
Est	2:19	when the virgins were **g** together	6908
Est	9:2	The Jews **g** themselves together.	6950
Ps	47:9	The princes of the people are **g**.	622
Ps	59:3	the mighty are **g** against me;	1481
Ps	140:2	are they **g** together for war.	1481
Pr	27:25	and herbs of the mountains are **g**.	622
Pr	30:4	who hath **g** the winds in his fists?	622
Ecc	2:8	I **g** me also silver and gold,	3664
SS	5:1	I have **g** my myrrh with my spice;	717
Isa	10:14	are left, have I **g** all the earth;.	622
Isa	13:4	kingdoms of nations **g** together:	622
Isa	24:22	as prisoners are **g** in the pit,.	626
Isa	27:12	ye shall be **g** one by one,	3950
Isa	34:16	and his spirit it hath **g** them.	6908
Isa	43:9	Let all the nations be **g** together	6908
Isa	49:5	Though Israel be not **g**, yet shall.	622
Jer	8:2	they shall not be **g**, nor be buried;	622
Jer	25:33	shall not be lamented, neither **g**,.	622
Jer	26:9	people were **g** against Jeremiah	6950
Eze	39:28	have **g** them unto their own land,	3664

Mic 4:11 many nations are **g** against thee,... 622
Zec 12:3 people of the earth be **g** together... 622
Mt 13:2 great multitudes were g together... *4863*
Mt 13:40 As therefore the tares are g and... *4816*
Mt 13:47 into the sea, and g of every kind:... *4863*
Mt 13:48 and g the good into vessels,... *4816*
Mt 18:20 three are g together in my name,... *4863*
Mt 22:34 to silence, they were **g** together... *4863*
Mt 23:37 often would I have g thy children... *1996*
Mt 24:28 will the eagles be g together... *4863*
Mt 25:32 before him shall be g all nations:... *4863*
Mk 1:33 city was **g** together at the door... *1996*
Mk 5:21 much people **g** unto him: and he... *4863*
Mk 6:30 the apostles **g** themselves together... *4863*
Lk 11:29 people were **g** thick together,... 1865
Lk 13:34 how often would I have g thy... *1996*
Lk 17:37 will the eagles be g together... *4863*
Lk 24:33 and found the eleven **g** together... *4867*
Jn 11:47 Then **g** the chief priests and the... *4863*
Ac 4:26 rulers were **g** together against the... *4863*
Ac 12:12 many were **g** together praying... *4863*
Ac 14:27 and had **g** the church together,... *4863*
Ac 17:5 **g** a company, and set all the city... *3792*
2Co 8:15 He that had **g** much had nothing
2Co 8:15 and he that had **g** little had no lack.
Rev 14:19 and **g** the vine of the earth,... *5166*
Rev 16:16 And he **g** them together into a... *4863*
Rev 19:19 and their armies, **g** together to... *4863*

GATHERER

Am 7:14 and a **g** of sycomore fruit:... 1103

GATHERETH

Ps 33:7 he **g** the waters of the sea... 3664
Ps 41:6 his heart **g** iniquity to itself;... 6908
Pr 6:8 and **g** her food in the harvest... 103
Pr 10:5 He that **g** in summer is a wise son:... 103
Pr 13:11 but he that **g** by labour shall... 6908
Na 3:18 mountains, and no man **g** them.... 6908
Hab 2:5 but **g** unto him all nations... 622
Mt 12:30 he that g not with me scattereth... *4863*
Mt 23:37 even as a hen g her chickens... *1996*
Jn 4:36 and g fruit unto life eternal:... *4863*

GATHERING

Ge 1:10 and the **g** together of the waters... 4723
Nu 15:33 they that found him **g** sticks... 7197
1Ki 17:10 widow woman was there **g** of sticks:... 7197
2Ch 20:25 were three days in **g** of the spoil,... 962
Mt 25:24 g where thou hast not strawed:... *4863*
2Th 2:1 by our **g** together unto him,... *1997*

GAVE

Ge 2:20 And Adam **g** names to all cattle,... 7121
Ge 3:6 and **g** also unto her husband... 5414
Ge 3:12 to be with me, she **g** me of the tree,... 5414
Ge 14:20 And he **g** him tithes of all... 5414
Ge 25:5 And Abraham **g** all that he had... 5414
Ge 25:8 Then Abraham **g** up the ghost, and
Ge 25:34 Jacob **g** Esau bread and pottage... 5414
Ge 28:4 which God **g** unto Abraham... 5414
Ge 29:28 and he **g** him Rachel his daughter... 5414
Ge 35:12 the land which I **g** Abraham and... 5414
Ge 38:26 I **g** her not to Shelah my son... 5414
Ge 47:17 Joseph **g** them bread in exchange... 5414
Nu 11:25 and **g** it unto the seventy elders:... 5414
Dt 2:12 this possession, which the Lord **g**... 5414
Dt 9:11 the Lord **g** me the two tables... 5414
Dt 22:16 I **g** my daughter unto this man... 5414
Jos 1:14 the land which Moses **g** you on... 5414
Jos 11:23 and Joshua **g** it for an inheritance... 5414
Jos 13:14 tribe of Levi he **g** none inheritance;... 5414
Jos 14:13 and **g** unto Caleb the son of... 5414
Jos 17:4 he **g** them an inheritance among... 5414
Jos 19:50 they **g** him the city which he asked,... 5414
Jos 21:12 villages thereof, **g** they to Caleb... 5414
Jos 24:4 I **g** unto Isaac, Jacob and Esau;... 5414
Jgs 15:2 I **g** her to thy companion:... 5414
Jgs 20:36 for the men of Israel **g** place to... 5414
Ru 4:13 the Lord **g** her conception, and she... 5414
1Sa 1:5 Hannah he **g** a worthy portion;... 5414
1Sa 10:9 Samuel, God **g** him another heart:
1Sa 18:27 Saul **g** him Michal his daughter... 5414
2Sa 12:8 And I **g** thee thy master's house,... 5414
1Ki 4:29 And God **g** Solomon wisdom and... 5414
1Ki 5:10 Hiram **g** Solomon cedar trees and... 5414
1Ki 9:11 Solomon **g** Hiram twenty cities... 5414
1Ki 10:10 queen of Sheba **g** to king Solomon... 5414
1Ki 10:13 king Solomon **g** unto the queen of... 5414
2Ki 13:5 (And the Lord **g** Israel a saviour,... 5414
2Ki 18:15 And Hezekiah **g** him all the silver... 5414
2Ki 21:8 land which I **g** their fathers;... 5414
1Ch 28:11 Then David **g** to Solomon his son... 5414
2Ch 10:8 counsel which the old men **g** him,... 3289
2Ch 15:15 and the Lord **g** them rest round about.
2Ch 20:30 for his God **g** him rest round about
2Ch 26:8 the Ammonites **g** gifts to Uzziah:... 5414
2Ch 32:24 unto him, and he **g** him a sign... 5414
2Ch 35:8 **g** unto the priests for the passover... 5414
Ezr 2:69 They **g** after their ability unto... 5414
Ezr 7:11 the king Artaxerxes **g** unto Ezra... 5414
Ne 2:9 river, and **g** them the king's letters... 5414
Ne 8:8 of God distinctly, and **g** the sense,... 7760
Ne 12:40 companies of them that **g** thanks
Est 4:8 he **g** him the copy of the writing... 5414
Est 8:2 Haman, and **g** it unto Mordecai.... 5414
Job 1:21 the Lord **g**, and the Lord hath taken.... 5414
Job 42:10 also the Lord **g** Job twice as much... 3254
Ps 18:13 and the Highest **g** his voice;... 5414
Ps 68:11 The Lord **g** the word: great was... 5414
Ps 69:21 in my thirst they **g** me vinegar to drink.
Ps 78:29 for he **g** them their own desire;... 935
Ps 81:12 So I **g** them up unto their own... 7971
Ps 105:32 **g** them hail for rain, and flaming... 5414
Ps 105:44 **g** them the lands of the heathen:... 5414
Ps 106:15 And he **g** them their request;... 5414
Ps 136:21 And **g** their land for an heritage:... 5414
Pr 8:29 When he **g** to the sea his decree,... 7760
Ecc 1:13 **g** my heart to seek and search... 5414
Ecc 1:17 I **g** my heart to know wisdom,... 5414
Ecc 12:7 spirit shall return unto God who **g**.... 5414
Isa 41:2 **g** them as the dust to his sword,... 5414
Isa 42:24 Who **g** Jacob for a spoil, and... 5414
Isa 50:6 I **g** my back to the smiters, and my.... 5414
Jer 7:7 the land that I **g** to your fathers,... 5414
Jer 32:12 I **g** the evidence of the purchase... 5414
Jer 40:5 captain of the guard **g** him victuals... 5414
La 1:19 and mine elders **g** up the ghost
Eze 20:11 And I **g** them my statutes, and... 5414
Eze 36:28 the land that I **g** to your fathers;... 5414
Da 1:7 prince of the eunuchs **g** names:... 7760
Da 1:16 should drink; and **g** them pulse... 5414
Da 1:17 God **g** them knowledge and skill... 5414

Da	2:48	and **g** him many great gifts, and	3052
Da	5:18	most high God **g** Nebuchadnezzar	3052
Da	6:10	and **g** thanks before his God, as he did	
Hos	13:11	I **g** thee a king in mine anger,	5414
Am	2:12	ye **g** the Nazarites wine to drink;	
Mt	10:1	**g** them power against unclean	*1325*
Mt	15:36	and **g** thanks, and brake them,	*1325*
Mt	21:23	who **g** thee this authority?	*1325*
Mt	25:15	**unto one he g five talents, to**	*1325*
Mt	25:35	**an hungred, and ye g me meat:**	*1325*
Mt	25:37	**or thirsty, and g thee drink?**	*4222*
Mt	25:42	**an hungred, and ye g me no meat:**	*1325*
Mt	26:26	brake it, and **g** it to the disciples,	*1325*
Mt	26:48	that betrayed him **g** them a sign,	*1325*
Mt	27:34	**g** him vinegar to drink mingled	*1325*
Mt	28:12	**g** large money unto the soldiers,	*1325*
Mk	5:13	forthwith Jesus **g** them leave	*2010*
Mk	6:28	and the damsel **g** it to her mother	*1325*
Mk	13:34	**and g authority to his servants,**	*1325*
Mk	14:23	had given thanks, he **g** it to them:	*1325*
Mk	15:37	with a loud voice, and **g** up the ghost,	
Lk	2:38	**g** thanks likewise unto the Lord,	*437*
Lk	7:21	many that were blind he **g** sight	*5453*
Lk	9:1	**g** them power and authority over	*1325*
Lk	18:43	they saw it, **g** praise unto God	*1325*
Lk	20:2	who is he that **g** thee this authority?	*1325*
Lk	22:19	and **g** thanks, and brake it,	
Lk	23:24	Pilate **g** sentence that it should be	
Lk	23:29	**and the paps which never g suck**	
Lk	24:30	blessed it, and brake and **g** to them,	*1929*
Lk	24:42	they **g** him a piece of a broiled fish,	*1929*
Jn	1:12	**g** he power to become the sons	*1325*
Jn	3:16	**that he g his only begotten Son,**	*1325*
Jn	6:31	**g** them bread from heaven to eat	*1325*
Jn	6:32	**Moses g you not that bread from**	*1325*
Jn	7:22	**Moses … g unto you circumcision;**	*1325*
Jn	13:26	the sop, he **g** it to Judas Iscariot,	*1325*
Jn	19:9	thou? But Jesus **g** him no answer	*1325*
Jn	19:30	his head, and **g** up the ghost	*3860*
Jn	19:38	and Pilate **g** him leave. He came	*2010*
Ac	2:4	as the Spirit **g** them utterance	*1325*
Ac	7:8	**g** him the covenant of circumcision:	*1325*
Ac	7:42	**g** them up to worship the host of	*3860*
Ac	12:23	because he **g** not God the glory:	*1325*
Ac	13:20	after that he **g** unto them judges	*1325*
Ac	14:17	and **g** us rain from heaven, and	*1325*
Ac	26:10	I **g** my voice against them	*2702*
Ro	1:24	Wherefore God also **g** them up to	*3860*
Ro	1:28	God **g** them over to a reprobate	*3860*
1Co	3:5	even as the Lord **g** to every man?	*1325*
1Co	3:6	watered; but God **g** the increase	
Gal	1:4	Who **g** himself for our sins, that	*1325*
Gal	2:20	loved me, and **g** himself for me	*3860*
Gal	3:18	God **g** it to Abraham by promise	*5483*
Eph	1:22	**g** him to be the head over all	*1325*
Eph	4:8	captive, and **g** gifts unto men	*1325*
Eph	4:11	he **g** some, apostles: and some	*1325*
Eph	5:25	the church, and **g** himself for it;	*3860*
1Ti	2:6	Who **g** himself a ransom for all,	*1325*
Tit	2:14	Who **g** himself for us, that he might	*1325*
Heb	7:2	Abraham **g** a tenth part of all;	
Heb	12:9	we **g** them reverence: shall we not	*1788*
Jas	5:18	the heaven **g** rain, and the earth.	*1325*
1Jn	5:10	the record that God **g** of his Son.	*3140*
Rev	2:21	**I g her space to repent of her**	*1325*
Rev	11:13	and **g** glory to the God of heaven	*1325*
Rev	13:2	the dragon **g** him his power,	*1325*
Rev	13:4	which **g** power unto the beast:	*1325*
Rev	15:7	**g** unto the seven angels seven	*1325*
Rev	20:13	sea **g** up the dead which were in it;	*1325*

GAVEST See also FORGAVEST.

Ge	3:12	woman whom thou **g** to be with	5414
1Ki	8:34	unto the land which thou **g** unto	5414
2Ch	6:38	toward their land, which thou **g**	5414
Ne	9:20	**g** also thy good spirit to instruct	5414
Ne	9:27	**g** them saviours, who saved them	5414
Ne	9:36	land that thou **g** unto our fathers	5414
Lk	7:44	**g me no water for my feet:**	*1325*
Lk	7:45	**Thou g me no kiss: but this**	*1325*
Lk	15:29	**and yet thou never g me a kid,**	*1325*
Jn	17:4	**the work which thou g me to do.**	*1325*
Jn	17:6	**which thou g me out of the world:**	*1325*
Jn	17:8	**them the words which thou g me;**	*1325*
Jn	17:12	**those that thou g me I have kept,**	*1325*
Jn	17:22	**glory which thou g me I have**	*1325*
Jn	18:9	which thou **g** me have I lost none	*1325*

GAZE

Ex	19:21	break through unto the Lord to **g**,	7200

GAZING

Ac	1:11	why stand ye **g** up into heaven?	*1689*

GAZINGSTOCK

Na	3:6	and will set thee as a **g**	7210
Heb	10:33	whilst ye were made a **g** both by	*2301*

GENDER

2Ti	2:23	knowing that they do **g** strifes	*1080*

GENEALOGIES

1Ch	5:17	All these were reckoned by **g** in	3187
1Ch	9:1	all Israel were reckoned by **g**;	3187
2Ch	31:19	to all that were reckoned by **g**	3187
1Ti	1:4	give heed to fables and endless **g**	*1076*
Tit	3:9	But avoid foolish questions, and **g**	*1076*

GENEALOGY

1Ch	4:33	their habitations, and their **g**	3188
1Ch	5:1	and the **g** is not to be reckoned	3188
1Ch	7:9	after their **g** by their generations,	3188
2Ch	31:17	the **g** of the priests by the house	3188
Ezr	2:62	those that were reckoned by **g**,	3188
Ezr	8:3	were reckoned by **g** of the males	3188
Ne	7:5	that they might be reckoned by **g**	3188

GENERAL

1Ch	27:34	and the **g** of the king's army	8269
Heb	12:23	to the **g** assembly and church of	*3831*

GENERATION

Ge	7:1	righteous before me in this **g**.	1755
Ge	15:16	But in the fourth **g** they shall come	1755
Ex	17:16	war with Amalek from **g** to **g**	1755
Ex	20:5	unto the third and fourth **g** of them	
Ex	34:7	unto the third and to the fourth **g**	
Nu	14:18	children unto the third and fourth **g**	
Nu	32:13	until all the **g**, that had done evil	1755
Dt	5:9	unto the third and fourth **g** of them	
Dt	23:3	even to their tenth **g** shall they not	1755
Dt	32:5	they are a perverse and crooked **g**.	1755
Jgs	2:10	there arose another **g** after them,	1755
2Ki	15:12	throne of Israel unto the fourth **g**	
Est	9:28	kept throughout every **g**, every	1755

Ps	12:7	preserve them from this **g** for ever	1755
Ps	14:5	God is in the **g** of the righteous	1755
Ps	24:6	is the **g** of them that seek him,	1755
Ps	48:13	ye may tell it to the **g** following.	1755
Ps	78:6	That the **g** to come might know	1755
Ps	78:8	a **g** that set not their heart aright,	1755
Ps	102:18	shall be written for the **g** to come:	1755
Ps	109:13	in the **g** following let their name.	1755
Ps	145:4	One **g** shall praise thy works to	1755
Pr	27:24	doth the crown endure to every **g**?	1755
Pr	30:11	is a **g** that curseth their father,	1755
Pr	30:12	a **g** that are pure in their own eyes,	1755
Ecc	1:4	One **g** passeth away, and another **g**.	1755
Isa	34:10	from **g** to **g** it shall lie waste;	1755
Isa	51:8	my salvation from **g** to **g**	1755
Isa	53:8	and who shall declare his **g**? for he	1755
Jer	7:29	and forsaken the **g** of his wrath.	1755
La	5:19	thy throne from **g** to **g**	1755
Da	4:3	his dominion is from **g** to **g**.	1859
Mt	1:1	the book of the **g** of Jesus Christ,	*1078*
Mt	3:7	O **g** of vipers, who hath warned	*1081*
Mt	11:16	**whereunto shall I liken this g?**	*1074*
Mt	12:34	**O g of vipers, how can ye,**	*1081*
Mt	12:39	**An evil and adulterous g seeketh**	*1074*
Mt	12:45	**shall it be also unto this wicked g,**	*1074*
Mt	16:4	**wicked and adulterous g seeketh**	*1074*
Mt	17:17	**O faithless and perverse g, how**	*1074*
Mt	23:33	**Ye serpents, ye g of vipers, how**	*1081*
Mt	23:36	**things shall come upon this g.**	*1074*
Mt	24:34	**This g shall not pass, till all these.**	*1074*
Mk	8:12	**Why doth this g seek after a sign?**	*1074*
Mk	9:19	**O faithless g, how long shall I be**	*1074*
Lk	1:50	on them that fear him from **g** to **g**	*1074*
Lk	3:7	O **g** of vipers, who hath warned	*1081*
Lk	7:31	**shall I liken the men of this g?**	*1074*
Lk	9:41	**O faithless and perverse g, how**	*1074*
Lk	11:30	**also the Son of man be to this g**	*1074*
Lk	11:31	**the men of this g, and condemn**	*1074*
Lk	11:51	**It shall be required of this g**	*1074*
Lk	16:8	**in their g wiser than the children.**	*1074*
Lk	21:32	**This g shall not pass away, till**	*1074*
Ac	8:33	who shall declare his **g**? for his	*1074*
Heb	3:10	I was grieved with that **g**,	*1074*
1Pe	2:9	a chosen **g**, a royal priesthood,	*1085*

GENERATIONS

Ge	2:4	These are the **g** of the heavens.	8435
Ge	5:1	This is the book of the **g** of Adam.	8435
Ge	6:9	These are the **g** of Noah: Noah was	8435
Ge	6:9	a just man and perfect in his **g**,	8435
Ge	17:9	and thy seed after thee in their **g**.	1755
Ge	17:12	every man child in your **g**, he that	1755
Ge	25:19	And these are the **g** of Isaac,	8435
Ge	37:2	These are the **g** of Jacob	8435
Ex	3:15	this is my memorial unto all **g**	1755
Ex	12:17	ye observe this day in your **g**.	1755
Ex	27:21	a statute for ever unto their **g**	1755
Ex	29:42	burnt offering throughout your **g**.	1755
Ex	30:8	before the Lord throughout your **g**	1755
Ex	31:16	the sabbath throughout their **g**.	1755
Ex	40:15	priesthood throughout their **g**	1755
Le	3:17	perpetual statute for your **g**.	1755
Le	23:31	for ever throughout your **g**	1755
Le	24:3	a statute for ever in your **g**.	1755
Nu	15:15	an ordinance for ever in your **g**.	1755
Nu	35:29	throughout your **g** in all your	1755
Dt	7:9	commandments to a thousand **g**;	1755
Jos	22:28	to us or to our **g** in time to come,	1755
1Ch	7:2	valiant men of might in their **g**;	8435
1Ch	16:15	he commanded to a thousand **g**;	1755
Job	42:16	and his sons' sons, even four **g**	1755
Ps	33:11	the thoughts of his heart to all **g**.	1755
Ps	49:11	and their dwelling places to all **g**;	1755
Ps	79:13	will shew forth thy praise to all **g**	1755
Ps	85:5	draw out thine anger to all **g**?	1755
Ps	89:4	and build up thy throne to all **g**	1755
Ps	90:1	been our dwelling place in all **g**.	1755
Ps	100:5	and his truth endureth to all **g**	1755
Ps	102:12	and thy remembrance unto all **g**.	1755
Ps	105:8	he commanded to a thousand **g**	1755
Ps	119:90	Thy faithfulness is unto all **g**:	1755
Ps	135:13	memorial, O Lord, throughout all **g**.	1755
Isa	51:9	in the ancient days, in the **g** of old	1755
Isa	60:15	excellency, a joy of many **g**.	1755
Joel	2:2	even to the years of many **g**.	1755
Mt	1:17	Abraham to David are fourteen **g**;	*1074*
Mt	1:17	away into Babylon are fourteen **g**;	*1074*
Mt	1:17	Babylon unto Christ are fourteen **g**	*1074*
Lk	1:48	all **g** shall call me blessed	*1074*

GENTLE

2Ti	2:24	not strive; but be **g** unto all men,	*2261*
Tit	3:2	to be no brawlers, but **g**, shewing	*1933*
Jas	3:17	**g**, and easy to be intreated,	*1933*
1Pe	2:18	not only to the good and **g**, but also.	*1933*

GENTLENESS

2Sa	22:36	and thy **g** hath made me great.	6031
2Co	10:1	by the meekness and **g** of Christ,	*1932*
Gal	5:22	longsuffering, **g**, goodness, faith,	*5544*

GENTLY

2Sa	18:5	Deal **g** for my sake with the	3814
Isa	40:11	**g** lead those that are with young	

GET See also GAT; GOT.

Ge	12:1	**G** thee out of thy country, and	3212
Ge	19:14	said, Up, **g** you out of this place;	3318
Ge	45:17	**g** you unto the land of Canaan;	935
Ex	5:11	**g** you straw where ye can find it:	3947
Ex	14:17	I will **g** me honour upon Pharaoh,	3513
Ex	32:7	Go, **g** thee down; for thy people,	3381
Nu	27:12	**G** thee up into this mount	5927
Dt	3:27	**G** thee up into the top of Pisgah,	5927
Dt	8:18	that giveth the power to **g** wealth,	6213
Dt	32:49	**G** thee up into this mountain	5927
Jgs	14:3	**G** her for me; for she pleaseth me.	3947
1Sa	22:5	and **g** thee into the land of Judah	935
2Sa	20:6	lest he **g** him fenced cities, and	4672
1Ki	18:41	**G** thee up, eat and drink; for	5927
2Ki	3:13	**g** thee to the prophets of thy	3212
Ne	9:10	So didst thou **g** thee a name, as it	6213
Pr	4:5	**G** wisdom, **g** understanding:	7069
Pr	6:33	wound and dishonour shall he **g**;	4672
Pr	16:16	better is it to **g** wisdom than gold!	7069
Pr	17:16	the hand of a fool to **g** wisdom	7069
Ecc	3:6	A time to **g**, and a time to lose;	1245
Isa	40:9	**g** thee up into the high mountain;	5927
Jer	5:5	I will **g** me unto the great men	3212
Jer	19:1	and **g** a potter's earthen bottle,	7069
Jer	49:30	Flee, **g** you far off, dwell deep,	5110
Jer	49:31	Arise, **g** you up unto the wealthy	5927
La	3:7	me about, that I cannot **g** out:	3318

Eze	3:11	go, **g** thee to them of the captivity,	935
Eze	22:27	to destroy souls, to **g** dishonest	1214
Zec	6:7	**G** you hence, walk to and fro.	3212
Mt	4:10	**G thee hence, Satan: for it is**	*5217*
Mt	16:23	unto Peter, **G thee behind me,**.	*5217*
Lk	4:8	**G thee behind me, Satan: for it**.	*5217*
Ac	7:3	**G** thee out of thy country, and	*1831*
Ac	22:18	**g thee quickly out of Jerusalem:**	*1831*
2Co	2:11	Lest Satan should **g** an advantage	*4122*

GETTETH See also **BEGETTETH; FORGETTETH.**

Pr	3:13	the man that **g** understanding.	6329
Pr	9:7	a scorner **g** to himself shame:	3947
Pr	15:32	heareth reproof **g** understanding	7069
Pr	18:15	heart of the prudent **g** knowledge;	7069
Pr	19:8	He that **g** wisdom loveth his own	7069
Jer	48:44	and he that **g** up out of the pit	5927

GETTING See also **FORGETTING.**

Pr	4:7	with all thy **g** get understanding	7069
Pr	21:6	**g** of treasures by a lying tongue.	6467

GHOST

Ge	25:8	Then Abraham gave up the **g**,	1478
Ge	35:29	And Isaac gave up the **g**, and died,	1478
Job	3:11	why did I not give up the **g** when	1478
Job	10:18	Oh that I had given up the **g**,	1478
Job	14:10	yea, man giveth up the **g**, and	1478
La	1:19	mine elders gave up the **g** in the	1478
Mt	1:18	found with child of the Holy **G**.	*4151*
Mt	3:11	with the Holy **G**, and with fire:	*4151*
Mt	12:31	**blasphemy against the Holy G**	*4151*
Mt	27:50	yielded up the **g**.	*4151*
Mt	28:19	of the Son, and of the Holy **G**:	*4151*
Mk	1:8	baptize you with the Holy **G**	*4151*
Mk	3:29	**blaspheme against the Holy G**	*4151*
Mk	13:11	**ye that speak, but the Holy G**	*4151*
Mk	15:37	a loud voice, and gave up the **g**	*1606*
Lk	1:15	be filled with the Holy **G**,	*4151*
Lk	1:35	Holy **G** shall come upon thee,	*4151*
Lk	1:41	was filled with the Holy **G**	*4151*
Lk	1:67	was filled with the Holy **G**,	*4151*
Lk	2:25	and the Holy **G** was upon him,	*4151*
Lk	3:16	baptize you with the Holy **G**	*4151*
Lk	3:22	And the Holy **G** descended in	*4151*
Lk	4:1	Jesus being full of the Holy **G**	*4151*
Lk	12:10	**against the Holy G**	*4151*
Lk	12:12	**For the Holy G shall teach**.	*4151*
Lk	23:46	said thus, he gave up the **g**	*1606*
Jn	7:39	for the Holy **G** was not yet.	*4151*
Jn	14:26	**Holy G, whom the Father**	*4151*
Jn	19:30	his head, and gave up the **g**	*4151*
Jn	20:22	them, **Receive ye the Holy G:**	*4151*
Ac	1:2	he through the Holy **G** had	*4151*
Ac	1:5	**be baptized with the Holy G**.	*4151*
Ac	1:8	**after that the Holy G is come**	*4151*
Ac	2:4	were all filled with the Holy **G**,	*4151*
Ac	2:38	receive the gift of the Holy **G**,	*4151*
Ac	4:8	Peter, filled with the Holy **G**,	*4151*
Ac	4:31	were all filled with the Holy **G**,	*4151*
Ac	5:3	to lie to the Holy **G**, and to keep	*4151*
Ac	5:5	fell down, and gave up the **g**:	*1634*
Ac	5:10	at his feet and yielded up the **g**:	*1634*
Ac	5:32	and so is also the Holy **G**,	*4151*
Ac	6:3	full of the Holy **G** and wisdom,	*4151*
Ac	6:5	of faith and of the Holy **G**,	*4151*
Ac	7:51	do always resist the Holy **G**:	*4151*
Ac	7:55	he, being full of the Holy **G**,	*4151*
Ac	8:17	they received the Holy **G**	*4151*
Ac	8:18	Holy **G** was given, he offered them.	*4151*
Ac	9:17	and be filled with the Holy **G**	*4151*
Ac	9:31	in the comfort of the Holy **G**,	*4151*
Ac	10:38	the Holy **G** and with power:	*4151*
Ac	10:44	the Holy **G** fell on all them	*4151*
Ac	10:45	poured out the gift of the Holy **G**.	*4151*
Ac	10:47	have received the Holy **G** as	*4151*
Ac	11:15	the Holy **G** fell on them, as on	*4151*
Ac	11:16	**be baptized with the Holy G**.	*4151*
Ac	11:24	man, and full of the Holy **G**.	*4151*
Ac	13:2	the Holy **G** said, Separate me.	*4151*
Ac	13:4	being sent forth by the Holy **G**,	*4151*
Ac	13:9	Paul,) filled with the Holy **G**,	*4151*
Ac	13:52	with joy, and with the Holy **G**,	*4151*
Ac	15:28	it seemed good to the Holy **G**,	*4151*
Ac	16:6	were forbidden of the Holy **G**	*4151*
Ac	19:2	Have ye received the Holy **G**	*4151*
Ac	19:2	whether there be any Holy **G**.	*4151*
Ac	20:23	that the Holy **G** witnesseth	*4151*
Ac	20:28	Holy **G** hath made you overseers,	*4151*
Ac	28:25	spake the Holy **G** by Esaias	*4151*
Ro	5:5	by the Holy **G** which is given.	*4151*
Ro	9:1	me witness in the Holy **G**,	*4151*
Ro	14:17	peace, and joy in the Holy **G**	*4151*
Ro	15:13	the power of the Holy **G**.	*4151*
Ro	15:16	being sanctified by the Holy **G**	*4151*
1Co	2:13	the Holy **G** teacheth; comparing	*4151*
1Co	6:19	the temple of the Holy **G**	*4151*
1Co	12:3	the Lord, but by the Holy **G**.	*4151*
2Co	6:6	the Holy **G**, by love unfeigned,	*4151*
2Co	13:14	the communion of the Holy **G**,	*4151*
1Th	1:5	in power, and in the Holy **G**,	*4151*
1Th	1:6	with joy of the Holy **G**:	*4151*
2Ti	1:14	by the Holy **G** which dwelleth	*4151*
Tit	3:5	and renewing of the Holy **G**;	*4151*
Heb	2:4	gifts of the Holy **G**, according	*4151*
Heb	6:4	made partakers of the Holy **G**,	*4151*
Heb	9:8	The Holy **G** this signifying,	*4151*
Heb	10:15	Holy **G** also is a witness to us:	*4151*
1Pe	1:12	Holy **G** sent down from heaven;	*4151*
2Pe	1:21	were moved by the Holy **G**	*4151*
1Jn	5:7	Holy **G**: and these three are one	*4151*
Jude	20	holy faith, praying in the Holy **G**,	*4151*

GIANT

2Sa	21:20	and he also was born to the **g**	7497
2Sa	21:22	four were born to the **g** in Gath	7497
1Ch	20:4	that was of the children of the **g**:	7497
Job	16:14	he runneth upon me like a **g**,	1368

GIANTS

Ge	6:4	were **g** in the earth in those days;	5303
Nu	13:33	And there we saw the **g**, the sons	5303
Dt	2:11	accounted **g**, as the Anakims;	7497
Dt	2:20	accounted a land of **g**: **g** dwelt.	7497
Dt	3:11	remained of the remnant of **g**;	7497
Jos	12:4	was of the remnants of the **g**,	7497
Jos	13:12	remained of the remnant of the **g**.	7497
Jos	18:16	which is in the valley of the **g**	7497

GIFT

Ge	34:12	me never so much dowry and **g**,	4976
Ex	23:8	And thou shalt take no **g**:	7810
Ex	23:8	for the **g** blindeth the wise	7810
Nu	18:6	are given as a **g** for the Lord	4979

Dt 16:19 neither take a **g**: for a **g** doth 7810
Ps 45:12 of Tyre shall be there with a **g**; 4503
Pr 17:8 A **g** is as a precious stone in the 7810
Pr 17:23 A wicked man taketh a **g** out of 7810
Pr 18:16 A man's **g** maketh room for him, ... 4976
Pr 21:14 A **g** in secret pacifieth anger: 4976
Pr 25:14 boasteth himself of a false **g** 4991
Ecc 3:13 of all his labour, it is the **g** of God 4991
Ecc 5:19 in his labour; this is the **g** of God...... 4991
Ecc 7:7 and a **g** destroyeth the heart 4979
Eze 46:16 prince give a **g** unto any of his sons,.... 4979
Mt 5:23 **if thou bring thy g to the altar** *1435*
Mt 5:24 **leave there thy g before the altar,** *1435*
Mt 5:24 **and then come and offer thy g** *1435*
Mt 15:5 **It is a g, by whatsoever thou** *1435*
Mt 23:18 **sweareth by the g that is upon it** *1435*
Mt 23:19 **or the altar that sanctifieth the g?**...... *1435*
Mk 7:11 **Corban, that is to say, a g, by** *1435*
Jn 4:10 **If thou knewest the g of God** *1431*
Ac 2:38 receive the **g** of the Holy Ghost........ *1431*
Ac 8:20 hast thought that the **g** of God *1431*
Ac 10:45 poured out the **g** of the Holy Ghost.... *1431*
Ro 1:11 impart unto you some spiritual **g**, ... *5486*
Ro 5:15 as the offence, so also is the free **g**...... *5486*
Ro 5:16 the free **g** is of many offences *5486*
Ro 5:17 the **g** of righteousness shall reign *1431*
Ro 5:18 the free **g** came upon all men unto
Ro 6:23 but the **g** of God is eternal life......... *5486*
1Co 1:7 So that ye come behind in no **g**; *5486*
1Co 7:7 every man hath his proper **g** of God, ... *5486*
1Co 13:2 though I have the **g** of prophecy
2Co 9:15 unto God for his unspeakable **g** *1431*
Eph 2:8 of yourselves: it is the **g** of God: *1435*
Eph 3:7 according to the **g** of the grace of...... *1431*
Eph 4:7 the measure of the **g** of Christ......... *1431*
Ph 4:17 Not because I desire a **g**: but I......... *1390*
1Ti 4:14 Neglect not the **g** that is in thee *5486*
2Ti 1:6 stir up the **g** of God, which is in *5486*
Heb 6:4 have tasted of the heavenly **g**, ... *1431*
Jas 1:17 Every good **g** and every perfect **g** *1394*
1Pe 4:10 As every man hath received the **g**, ... *5486*

GIFTS

Ge 25:6 Abraham gave **g**, and sent them 4979
Ex 28:38 Israel shall hallow all their holy **g**; 4979
Le 23:38 beside your **g**, and beside all your...... 4979
Nu 18:29 Out of all your **g** ye shall offer......... 4979
2Sa 8:6 to David, and brought **g**.............. 4503
2Ch 21:3 their father gave them great **g**......... 4979
2Ch 26:8 Ammonites gave **g** to Uzziah: 4503
2Ch 32:23 many brought **g** unto the Lord 4503
Est 9:22 portions one to another, and **g**........ 4979
Ps 68:18 thou hast received **g** for men; 4979
Pr 6:35 though thou givest many **g** 7810
Pr 15:27 but he that hateth **g** shall live 4979
Pr 19:6 is a friend to him that giveth **g** 4976
Pr 29:4 that receiveth **g** overthroweth it 8641
Isa 1:23 every one loveth **g**, and followeth...... 7810
Eze 16:33 They give **g** to all whores:............ 5078
Eze 16:33 but thou givest thy **g** to all thy......... 5083
Eze 20:26 I polluted them in their own **g**,........ 4979
Eze 20:39 holy name no more with your **g**, ... 4979
Eze 22:12 have they taken **g** to shed blood;....... 7810
Da 2:6 shall receive of me **g** and rewards...... 4978
Da 2:48 and gave him many great **g**, and....... 4978
Da 5:17 Let thy **g** be to thyself, and give........ 4978
Mt 2:11 they presented unto him **g**; gold....... *1435*
Mt 7:11 **give good g unto your children,** *1435*
Lk 11:13 **give good g unto your children:** *1390*
Lk 21:1 casting their **g** into the treasury........ *1435*
Ro 11:29 For the **g** and calling of God are *5486*
Ro 12:6 Having then **g** differing according *5486*
1Co 12:1 concerning spiritual **g**, brethren
1Co 12:4 there are diversities of **g**, but the....... *5486*
1Co 12:9 to another the **g** of healing by the...... *5486*
1Co 12:30 Have all the **g** of healing? do all........ *5486*
1Co 12:31 covet earnestly the best **g**: and......... *5486*
1Co 14:1 desire spiritual **g**, but rather that
Eph 4:8 captive, and gave **g** unto men *1390*
Heb 2:4 miracles, and **g** of the Holy Ghost,..... *3311*
Heb 8:3 ordained to offer **g** and sacrifices:...... *1435*
Heb 11:4 God testifying of his **g**: and by it....... *1435*
Rev 11:10 shall send **g** one to another;........... *1435*

GIRD See also **GIRT.**

Ex 29:5 and **g** him with the curious girdle 640
Jgs 3:16 he did **g** it under his raiment.......... 2296
1Sa 25:13 **G** ye on every man his sword 2296
2Sa 3:31 **g** you with sackcloth, and mourn...... 2296
2Ki 4:29 **G** up thy loins, and take my staff 2296
2Ki 9:1 **G** up thy loins, and take this box 2296
Job 38:3 **G** up now thy loins like a man;......... 247
Job 40:7 **G** up thy loins now like a man:......... 247
Ps 45:3 **G** thy sword upon thy thigh, O........ 2296
Isa 15:3 **g** themselves with sackcloth: 2296
Jer 4:8 For this **g** you with sackcloth.......... 2296
Jer 6:26 **g** thee with sackcloth, and wallow 2296
Jer 49:3 **g** you with sackcloth; lament, and 2296
Eze 27:31 and **g** them with sackcloth, and 2296
Joel 1:13 **G** yourselves, and lament, ye 2296
Lk 12:37 **that he shall g himself, and make**...... *4024*
Lk 17:8 **and g thyself, and serve me, till**........ *4024*
Jn 21:18 **another shall g thee, and carry**........ *2224*
1Pe 1:13 Wherefore **g** up the loins of your *328*

GIRDED See also **GIRT; UNGIRDED.**

Ex 12:11 shall ye eat it; with your loins **g**, ... 2296
Le 8:13 them, and **g** them with girdles,........ 2296
Le 16:4 and shall be **g** with a linen girdle,...... 2296
1Sa 2:4 stumbled are **g** with strength........... 247
1Sa 2:18 a child, **g** with a linen ephod.......... 2296
1Sa 17:39 And David **g** his sword upon his 2296
1Sa 25:13 and David also **g** on his sword:........ 2296
2Sa 6:14 David was **g** with a linen ephod 2296
2Sa 21:16 he being **g** with a new sword.......... 2296
2Sa 22:40 For thou hast **g** me with strength 247
1Ki 18:46 and he **g** up his loins, and ran......... 8151
1Ki 20:32 So they **g** sackcloth on their loins, ... 2296
Ne 4:18 one had his sword **g** by his side, ... 631
Ps 18:39 For thou hast **g** me with strength 247
Ps 30:11 sackcloth, and **g** me with gladness;...... 247
Ps 65:6 mountains; being **g** with power:......... 247
Ps 93:1 wherewith he hath **g** himself: 247
Ps 109:19 wherewith he is **g** continually 2296
Isa 45:5 I **g** thee, though thou hast not.......... 247
La 2:10 they have **g** themselves with 2296
Da 10:5 whose loins were **g** with fine gold...... 2296
Joel 1:8 like a virgin **g** with sackcloth.......... 2296
Lk 12:35 **Let your loins be g about,** *4024*
Jn 13:4 and took a towel, and **g** himself *1241*
Jn 13:5 the towel wherewith he was **g** *1241*
Rev 15:6 breasts **g** with golden girdles *4024*

GIRDETH
Ps 18:32 It is God that **g** me with strength 247
Pr 31:17 She **g** her loins with strength, ... 2296

GIRDING See also UNDERGIRDING.
Isa 3:24 of a stomacher a **g** of sackcloth; 4228
Isa 22:12 baldness, and to **g** with sackcloth:. 2296

GIRDLE
Ex 28:8 And the curious **g** of the ephod,. 2805
Ex 39:20 above the curious **g** of the ephod 2805
Ex 39:29 a **g** of fine twined linen, and blue, ... 73
Le 8:7 and girded him with the **g**, and. 73
2Sa 20:8 upon it a **g** with a sword fastened. 2290
1Ki 2:5 put the blood of war upon his **g**. 2290
2Ki 1:8 girt with a **g** of leather about his. 232
Isa 5:27 shall the **g** of their loins be loosed,. 232
Isa 11:5 righteousness shall be the **g** of his 232
Isa 11:5 loins, and faithfulness the **g** of his 232
Jer 13:7 **g** was marred, it was profitable for 232
Jer 13:10 as this **g**, which is good for nothing 232
Jer 13:11 For as the **g** cleaveth to the loins. 232
Mt 3:4 and a leathern **g** about his loins;. *2223*
Mk 1:6 with a **g** of a skin about his loins;. *2225*
Ac 21:11 bind the man that owneth this **g**, ... *2223*
Rev 1:13 about the paps with a golden **g**, ... *2223*

GIRDLES
Pr 31:24 delivereth **g** unto the merchant. 2289
Eze 23:15 with **g** upon their loins, exceeding 232
Rev 15:6 breasts girded with golden **g** *2223*

GIRL
Joel 3:3 and sold a **g** for wine, that they. 3207

GIRLS
Zec 8:5 boys and **g** playing in the streets. 3207

GIRT See also GIRD.
2Ki 1:8 and **g** with a girdle of leather about 247
Eph 6:14 your loins **g** about with truth,. *4024*
Rev 1:13 and **g** about the paps with a golden *4024*

GIVE See also FORGIVE; GAVE.
Ge 1:15 heaven to **g** light upon the earth,
Ge 12:7 Unto thy seed will I **g** this land; 5414
Ge 13:15 to thee will I **g** it, and to thy seed 5414
Ge 15:2 what wilt thou **g** me, seeing I go. 5414
Ge 15:7 to **g** thee this land to inherit it. 5414
Ge 17:16 I will bless her, and **g** thee a son 5414
Ge 23:13 I will **g** thee money for the field;. 5414
Ge 24:7 Unto thy seed will I **g** this land; 5414
Ge 27:28 God **g** thee of the dew of heaven 5414
Ge 28:4 **g** thee the blessing of Abraham, ... 5414
Ge 29:21 **G** me my wife, for my days are 3051
Ge 29:26 **g** the younger before the firstborn 5414
Ge 30:1 **G** me children, or else I die 3051
Ge 30:26 **G** me my wives and my children. 5414
Ge 34:14 this thing, to **g** our sister to one that . . . 5414
Ge 34:21 and let us **g** them our daughters. 5414
Ge 38:9 he should **g** seed to his brother. 5414
Ge 38:18 What pledge shall I **g** thee? And 5414
Ge 47:15 Joseph, and said, **G** us bread:. 3051
Ge 47:16 And Joseph said, **G** your cattle;. 3051
Ge 47:19 and **g** us seed, that we may live, ... 5414
Ge 47:24 shall **g** the fifth part unto Pharaoh, ... 5414
Ex 5:10 Pharaoh, I will not **g** you straw. 5414
Ex 6:4 to **g** them the land of Canaan 5414
Ex 12:25 the land which the Lord will **g** you, ... 5414
Ex 13:21 a pillar of fire, to **g** them light;
Ex 17:2 **G** us water that we may drink. 5414
Ex 21:23 then thou shalt **g** life for life 5414
Ex 24:12 and I will **g** thee tables of stone. 5414
Ex 30:12 shall they **g** every man a ransom. 5414
Ex 30:15 The rich shall not **g** more,
Le 20:24 I will **g** it unto you to possess it, ... 5414
Le 25:2 come into the land which I **g** you, ... 5414
Le 26:4 I will **g** you rain in due season 5414
Nu 11:13 **G** us flesh, that we may eat 5414
Nu 22:13 the Lord refuseth to **g** me leave. 5414
Nu 24:13 If Balak would **g** me his house full 5414
Nu 25:12 I **g** unto him my covenant of peace:. . . . 5414
Nu 35:13 cities which ye shall **g** six cities 5414
Nu 35:14 Ye shall **g** three cities on this side 5414
Dt 1:8 to **g** unto them and to their seed 5414
Dt 1:35 I sware to **g** unto your fathers, ... 5414
Dt 2:5 I will not **g** you of their land, ... 5414
Dt 2:28 **g** me water for money, that I may. 5414
Dt 5:31 the land which I **g** them to possess. 5414
Dt 7:13 he sware unto thy fathers to **g**. 5414
Dt 10:11 I sware unto their fathers to **g**. 5414
Dt 16:17 Every man shall **g** as he is able,
Dt 19:8 the land which he promised to **g** 5414
Dt 24:1 her a bill of divorcement, and **g** it. 5414
Jos 14:12 **g** me this mountain, whereof the 5414
Jos 15:19 **G** me a blessing; for thou hast. 5414
Jos 17:4 to **g** us an inheritance among our. 5414
Jgs 1:15 **G** me a blessing: for thou hast. 3051
Jgs 21:1 shall not any of us **g** his daughters 5414
Ru 4:12 seed which the Lord shall **g** thee. 5414
1Sa 1:11 then I will **g** him unto the Lord 5414
1Sa 2:32 wealth which God shall **g** Israel:. 3190
1Sa 6:5 **g** glory unto the God of Israel: 5414
1Sa 8:6 said, **G** us a king to judge us 5414
1Sa 14:41 **G** a perfect lot. And Saul and 3051
1Sa 17:44 I will **g** thy flesh unto the fowls. 5414
1Ki 3:5 God said, Ask what I shall **g** thee 5414
1Ki 3:27 **G** her the living child, and in no. 5414
1Ki 11:13 **g** one tribe to thy son for David 5414
1Ki 11:31 and will **g** ten tribes to thee: 5414
1Ki 13:8 If thou wilt **g** me half thine house,. 5414
1Ki 21:7 will **g** thee the vineyard of Naboth 5414
2Ki 6:28 **G** thy son, that we may eat him to 5414
2Ki 14:9 **G** thy daughter to my son to wife: 5414
1Ch 16:28 **g** unto the Lord glory and strength 3051
1Ch 16:29 **G** unto the Lord the glory due 3051
1Ch 22:12 the Lord **g** thee wisdom and 5414
1Ch 29:19 **g** unto Solomon my son a perfect. 5414
2Ch 1:7 Ask what I shall **g** thee 5414
2Ch 1:10 **G** me now wisdom and knowledge,. . . . 5414
2Ch 1:12 I will **g** thee riches, and wealth,. 5414
2Ch 30:12 to **g** them one heart to do the. 5414
2Ch 32:11 **g** over yourselves to die by famine 5414
Ezr 9:12 **g** not your daughters unto their 5414
Ne 4:4 and **g** them for a prey in the land. 5414
Ne 13:25 Ye shall not **g** your daughters 5414
Job 2:4 all that a man hath will he **g** for 5414
Job 3:11 why did I not **g** up the ghost. 1478
Ps 2:8 and I shall **g** thee the heathen for. 5415
Ps 6:5 in the grave who shall **g** thee thanks?
Ps 28:4 **G** them according to their deeds, ... 5414
Ps 29:1 **g** unto the Lord glory and strength 3051
Ps 29:2 **G** unto the Lord the glory due 3051
Ps 30:12 I will **g** thanks unto thee for ever.

Ps	37:4	and he shall **g** thee the desires of	5414
Ps	49:7	nor **g** to God a ransom for him:	5414
Ps	51:16	not sacrifice; else would I **g** it:	5414
Ps	84:11	the Lord will **g** grace and glory:	5414
Ps	91:11	he shall **g** his angels charge over thee	
Ps	96:7	**g** unto the Lord glory and strength.	3051
Ps	96:8	**G** unto the Lord the glory due	3051
Ps	115:1	but unto thy name **g** glory, for thy	
Ps	118:1	O **g** thanks unto the Lord; for he	
Ps	119:125	**g** me understanding, that I may know	
Ps	119:144	**g** me understanding, and I shall live	
Ps	132:4	I will not **g** sleep to mine eyes	5414
Ps	136:26	O **g** thanks unto the God of heaven:	
Pr	4:2	I **g** you good doctrine, forsake ye	5414
Pr	5:9	thou **g** thine honour unto others,	5414
Pr	6:4	**G** not sleep to thine eyes, nor	5414
Pr	6:31	he shall **g** all the substance of his	5414
Pr	9:9	**G** instruction to a wise man and	5414
Pr	23:26	My son, **g** me thine heart, and let	5414
Pr	25:21	enemy be hungry, **g** him bread to	
Pr	25:21	if he be thirsty, **g** him water to drink:	
Pr	30:8	**g** me neither poverty nor riches;	5414
Pr	30:15	hath two daughters, crying, **G**, **g**.	3051
Pr	31:3	**G** not thy strength unto women,	5414
Pr	31:6	**G** strong drink unto him that is	5414
Pr	31:31	**G** her of the fruit of her hands;	5414
Ecc	2:3	heart to **g** myself unto wine	4900
Ecc	5:1	to hear, than to **g** the sacrifice of	5414
Ecc	11:2	**G** a portion to seven, and also to	5414
SS	8:7	if a man would **g** all the substance	5414
Isa	7:14	Lord himself shall **g** you a sign,	5414
Isa	42:6	and **g** thee for a covenant of the	5414
Isa	42:8	my glory will I not **g** to another,	5414
Isa	42:12	Let them **g** glory unto the Lord,	7760
Isa	48:11	I will not **g** my glory unto another	5414
Isa	55:10	that it may **g** seed to the sower,	5414
Isa	56:5	I will **g** them an everlasting name,	5414
Isa	61:3	to **g** unto them beauty for ashes,	5414
Jer	3:15	And I will **g** you pastors according	5414
Jer	8:10	will I **g** their wives unto others,	5414
Jer	13:16	**G** glory to the Lord your God,	5414
Jer	14:22	or can the heavens **g** showers?	5414
Jer	17:10	**g** every man according to his ways,	5414
Jer	24:7	will **g** them an heart to know me,	5414
Jer	29:11	not of evil, to **g** you an expected end.	5414
Jer	32:19	to **g** every one according to his	5414
Jer	32:39	And I will **g** them one heart, and	5414
Jer	37:21	**g** him daily a piece of bread out	5414
La	3:65	**G** them sorrow of heart, thy	5414
La	4:3	they **g** suck to their young ones: the	
Eze	11:2	and **g** wicked counsel in this city:	
Eze	11:19	And I will **g** them one heart,	5414
Eze	21:11	to **g** it into the hand of the slayer.	5414
Eze	23:31	will I **g** her cup into thine hand.	5414
Eze	36:26	A new heart also will I **g** you,	5414
Eze	36:26	and I will **g** you an heart of flesh.	5414
Eze	39:11	I will **g** unto Gog a place there	5414
Eze	44:28	**g** them no possession in Israel:	5414
Eze	46:16	If the prince **g** a gift unto any of	5414
Da	1:12	let them **g** us pulse to eat, and	5414
Hos	9:14	**g** them a miscarrying womb	5414
Zec	8:12	the heavens shall **g** their dew;	5414
Zec	10:1	and **g** them showers of rain, to	5414
Mt	4:6	He shall **g** his angels charge	
Mt	5:31	**g** her a writing of divorcement:	*1325*
Mt	5:42	**G** to him that asketh thee, and	*1325*
Mt	6:11	**G** us this day our daily bread.	*1325*
Mt	7:6	**G** not that which is holy unto the	*1325*
Mt	7:9	ask bread, will he **g** him a stone?	*1929*
Mt	7:10	a fish, will he **g** him a serpent?	*1929*
Mt	7:11	**g** good gifts unto your children,	*1325*
Mt	10:8	freely ye have received, freely **g**.	*1325*
Mt	16:19	I will **g** unto thee the keys of the	*1325*
Mt	16:26	a man **g** in exchange for his soul?	*1325*
Mt	19:7	to **g** a writing of divorcement,	*1325*
Mt	19:21	**g** to the poor, and thou shalt	*1325*
Mt	20:23	and on my left, is not mine to **g**,	*1325*
Mt	20:28	to **g** his life a ransom for many	*1325*
Mt	24:19	them that **g** suck in those days!	
Mt	24:29	the moon shall not **g** her light,	*1325*
Mt	24:45	to **g** them meat in due season?	*1325*
Mk	8:37	what shall a man **g** in exchange	*1325*
Mk	10:40	on my left hand is not mine to **g**;	*1325*
Mk	10:45	to **g** his life a ransom for many	*1325*
Mk	12:14	Is it lawful to **g** tribute to Caesar,	*1325*
Mk	13:24	the moon shall not **g** her light,	*1325*
Lk	1:79	To **g** light to them that sit in	*2014*
Lk	4:10	shall **g** his angels charge over thee,	
Lk	6:30	**G** to every man that asketh of	*1325*
Lk	6:38	**G**, and it shall be given unto you;	*1325*
Lk	11:3	**G** us day by day our daily bread	*1325*
Lk	11:11	will he **g** him a stone? or if he	*1929*
Lk	11:11	will he for a fish **g** him a serpent?	*1929*
Lk	11:13	your heavenly Father **g** the Holy	*1325*
Lk	12:33	Sell that ye have, and **g** alms;	*1325*
Lk	12:51	I am come to **g** peace on earth?	*1325*
Lk	14:9	say to thee, **G** this man place;	*1325*
Lk	15:12	Father, **g** me the portion of goods.	*1325*
Lk	17:18	that returned to **g** glory to God,	*1325*
Lk	18:12	I **g** tithes of all that I possess.	
Lk	19:24	**g** it to him that hath ten pounds	*1325*
Lk	21:23	to them that **g** suck, in those days!	
Jn	4:10	saith to thee, **G** me to drink;	*1325*
Jn	4:14	the water that I shall **g** him shall	*1325*
Jn	6:27	the Son of man shall **g** unto you:	*1325*
Jn	6:34	Lord, evermore **g** us this bread	*1325*
Jn	6:51	I will **g** for the life of the world.	*1325*
Jn	6:52	How can this man **g** us his flesh	*1325*
Jn	9:24	said unto him, **G** God the praise:	*1325*
Jn	10:28	And I **g** unto them eternal life;	*1325*
Jn	13:26	to whom I shall **g** a sop, when I.	*1929*
Jn	13:34	A new commandment I **g** unto.	*1325*
Jn	14:16	shall **g** you another Comforter,	*1325*
Jn	14:27	my peace I **g** unto you: not as the.	*1325*
Jn	14:27	as the world giveth, **g** I unto you.	*1325*
Jn	15:16	in my name, he may **g** it you	*1325*
Jn	16:23	in my name, he will **g** it you	*1325*
Jn	17:2	he should **g** eternal life to as many.	*1325*
Ac	3:6	but such as I have **g** I thee: In the	*1325*
Ac	6:4	**g** ourselves continually to prayer,	*4342*
Ac	8:19	Saying, **G** me also this power, that	*1325*
Ac	20:35	more blessed to **g** than to receive.	*1325*
Ro	8:32	him also freely **g** us all things?	*5483*
Ro	12:20	if he thirst, **g** him drink: for in so	*4222*
Ro	14:12	shall **g** account of himself to God.	*1325*
1Co	7:5	ye may **g** yourselves to fasting	*4980*
1Co	10:32	**G** none offence, neither to the	*1096*
1Co	13:3	though I **g** my body to be burned,	*3860*
1Co	14:8	the trumpet **g** an uncertain sound	*1325*
2Co	8:10	herein I **g** my advice: for this is	*1325*
Eph	4:27	Neither **g** place to the devil	*1325*
Eph	4:28	have to **g** to him that needeth.	*3330*

1Th 5:18 In everything **g** thanks: for this is the
1Ti 1:4 Neither **g** heed to fables and endless
1Ti 5:14 **g** none occasion to the adversary *1325*
2Ti 4:8 judge, shall **g** me at that day: *591*
Heb 13:17 they that must **g** account, that *591*
1Pe 3:15 be ready always to **g** an answer
Rev 2:7 **will I g to eat of the tree of life,** *1325*
Rev 2:10 **and I will g thee a crown of life** *1325*
Rev 2:17 **that overcometh will I g to eat** *1325*
Rev 2:17 **and will g him a white stone,** *1325*
Rev 2:26 **to him will I g power over the.** *1325*
Rev 2:28 **And I will g him the morning star.** *1325*
Rev 10:9 said unto him, **G** me the little book *1325*
Rev 11:3 will **g** power unto my two witnesses, *1325*
Rev 13:15 **g** life unto the image of the beast, *1325*
Rev 16:9 they repented not to **g** him glory *1325*
Rev 16:19 to **g** unto her the cup of the wine, *1325*
Rev 17:17 **g** their kingdom unto the beast, *1325*
Rev 21:6 I will **g** unto him that is athirst *1325*
Rev 22:12 **g every man according as his work** *591*

GIVEN See also FORGIVEN.
Ge 1:29 **g** you every herb bearing seed, 5414
Ge 15:3 Behold, to me thou hast **g** no seed: 5414
Ge 15:18 Unto thy seed have I **g** this land, 5414
Ge 27:37 all his brethren have I **g** to him 5414
Ge 29:33 he hath therefore **g** me this son. 5414
Ge 38:14 she was not **g** unto him to wife 5414
Ge 48:22 I have **g** to thee one portion above 5414
Ex 5:18 for there shall no straw be **g** you, 5414
Ex 16:29 the Lord hath **g** you the sabbath, 5414
Ex 21:4 If his master have **g** him a wife, 5414
Le 19:20 not at all redeemed, nor freedom **g** 5414
Le 20:3 he hath **g** of his seed unto Molech, 5414
Nu 8:19 And I have **g** the Levites as a gift 5414
Nu 18:11 I have **g** them unto thee, and to thy 5414
Nu 18:24 I have **g** the Levites to inherit: 5414
Nu 33:53 I have **g** you the land to possess it. 5414
Dt 8:10 good land which he hath **g** thee 5414
Dt 22:17 **g** occasions of speech against 7760
Dt 25:19 the Lord thy God hath **g** thee rest
Dt 26:14 nor **g** ought thereof for the dead: 5414
Dt 28:31 shall be **g** unto thine enemies, 5414
Dt 28:32 daughters shall be **g** unto another 5414
Dt 29:4 the Lord hath not **g** you an heart 5414
Jos 1:13 Lord your God hath **g** you rest,
Jos 6:2 I have **g** into thine hand Jericho, 5414
Jos 17:14 Why hast thou **g** me but one lot 5414
Jgs 14:20 Samson's wife was **g** to his companion
Jgs 18:10 God hath **g** it into your hands; 5414
1Sa 1:27 the Lord hath **g** me my petition 5414
1Sa 15:28 hath **g** it to a neighbour of thine 5414
1Sa 18:19 Saul's daughter should have been **g** 5414
1Sa 22:13 in that thou hast **g** him bread, 5414
1Sa 25:44 Saul had **g** Michal his daughter, 5414
2Sa 4:10 I would have **g** him a reward 5414
2Sa 12:14 hast **g** great occasion to the enemies
2Sa 19:42 or hath he **g** us any gift? 5375
1Ki 1:48 hath **g** one to sit on my throne 5414
1Ki 3:6 **g** him a son to sit on his throne 5414
1Ki 3:12 I have **g** thee a wise and an 5414
1Ki 9:12 cities which Solomon had **g** him; 5414
1Ki 13:5 sign which the man of God had **g** 5414
2Ki 25:30 allowance **g** him of the king, 5414
1Ch 22:18 hath he not **g** you rest on every side?
1Ch 28:5 the Lord hath **g** me many sons,) 5414
1Ch 29:14 and of thine own have we **g** thee 5414
2Ch 2:12 **g** to David the king a wise son, 5414
2Ch 22:6 of the wounds which were **g** him 5221
2Ch 34:18 the priest hath **g** me a book. 5414
2Ch 36:23 hath the Lord God of heaven **g** me; 5414
Ezr 1:2 The Lord God of heaven hath **g** me 5414
Ezr 6:4 expences be **g** out of the king's 3052
Ezr 6:9 be **g** them day by day without fail: 3052
Ne 2:7 letters be **g** me to the governors 5414
Ne 10:29 God's law, which was **g** by Moses 5414
Est 2:13 whatsoever she desired was **g** her 5414
Est 5:3 it shall be even **g** thee to the half 5414
Est 7:3 let my life be **g** me at my petition, 5414
Job 15:19 unto whom alone the earth was **g**, 5414
Job 33:4 breath of the Almighty hath **g** me life
Job 38:36 hath **g** understanding to the heart? 5414
Job 39:19 Hast thou **g** the horse strength? 5414
Ps 16:7 the Lord, who hath **g** me counsel:
Ps 21:2 hast **g** him his heart's desire 5414
Ps 44:11 **g** us like sheep appointed for 5414
Ps 71:3 hast **g** commandment to save me;
Ps 115:16 earth hath he **g** to the children 5414
Ps 118:18 he hath not **g** me over unto death, 5414
Ps 120:3 What shall be **g** unto thee? or what 5414
Pr 19:17 that which he hath **g** will he pay 1576
Pr 23:2 if thou be a man **g** to appetite 1167
Pr 24:21 not with them that are **g** to change:
Ecc 1:13 sore travail hath God **g** to the sons 5414
Ecc 6:2 man to whom God hath **g** riches, 5414
Ecc 12:11 which are **g** from one shepherd 5414
Isa 9:6 a child is born, unto us a son is **g**: 5414
Isa 23:11 the Lord hath **g** a commandment
Isa 47:8 thou that art **g** to pleasures, that
Isa 55:4 Behold, I have **g** him for a witness 5414
Jer 11:18 the Lord hath **g** me knowledge
Jer 15:9 she hath **g** up the ghost; her sun 5301
Jer 25:5 land that the Lord hath **g** unto you 5414
Jer 27:5 **g** it unto whom it seemed meet 5414
Jer 28:14 **g** him the beasts of the field also 5414
Jer 35:15 the land which I have **g** to you 5414
La 1:11 **g** their pleasant things for meat 5414
La 2:7 **g** up into the hand of the enemy 5462
Eze 3:20 because thou hast not **g** him warning,
Eze 16:34 and no reward is **g** unto thee 5414
Eze 18:7 hath **g** his bread to the hungry, 5414
Eze 18:16 hath **g** his bread to the hungry, 5414
Da 2:37 for the God of heaven hath **g** thee 3052
Da 4:16 let a beast's heart be **g** unto him; 3052
Da 5:28 and **g** to the Medes and Persians 3052
Da 7:4 and a man's heart was **g** to it. 3052
Da 7:6 and dominion was **g** to it. 3052
Da 7:22 and judgment was **g** to the saints 3052
Hos 2:12 rewards that my lovers have **g** me: 5414
Joel 2:23 he hath **g** you the former rain 5414
Joel 3:3 and have **g** a boy for an harlot, 5414
Mt 7:7 **Ask, and it shall be g you: seek,** *1325*
Mt 12:39 **and there shall no sign be g to it,** *1325*
Mt 13:11 **g unto you to know the mysteries.** *1325*
Mt 13:12 **whosoever hath, to him shall be g** *1325*
Mt 14:11 in a charger, and **g** to the damsel; *1325*
Mt 16:4 **there shall no sign be g unto it,** *1325*
Mt 22:30 **marry, nor are g in marriage,** *1547*
Mt 25:29 **every one that hath shall be g,** *1325*
Mt 26:9 sold for much, and **g** to the poor *1325*
Mt 28:18 **All power is g unto me in heaven.** *1325*
Mk 4:25 **he that hath, to him shall be g:** *1325*

Mk 8:12 no sign be **g** unto this generation. *1325*
Mk 13:11 shall be **g** you in that hour, ... *1325*
Mk 14:23 cup, and when he had **g** thanks,
Lk 6:38 Give, and it shall be **g** unto you; *1325*
Lk 8:10 you it is **g** to know the mysteries *1325*
Lk 8:18 whosoever hath, to him shall be **g**;. *1325*
Lk 11:29 there shall no sign be **g** it, but the *1325*
Lk 12:48 unto whomsoever much is **g**, of *1325*
Lk 17:27 they were **g** in marriage, until the
Lk 19:15 whom he had **g** the money, that. *1325*
Lk 20:34 marry, and are **g** in marriage; but
Lk 20:35 neither marry, nor are **g** in
Lk 22:19 This is my body which is **g** for *1325*
Jn 3:27 except it be **g** him from heaven *1325*
Jn 4:10 he would have **g** thee living water. *1325*
Jn 5:26 so hath he **g** to the Son to have. *1325*
Jn 5:36 which the Father hath **g** me. *1325*
Jn 6:11 when he had **g** thanks, he distributed
Jn 7:39 for the Holy Ghost was not yet **g**;
Jn 11:57 Pharisees had **g** a commandment, ... *1325*
Jn 12:5 hundred pence, and **g** to the poor?. *1325*
Jn 13:15 For I have **g** you an example *1325*
Jn 17:2 thou hast **g** him power over all. *1325*
Jn 17:7 whatsoever thou hast **g** me are of. *1325*
Jn 17:9 for them which thou hast **g** me; *1325*
Jn 17:11 those whom thou hast **g** me, that. *1325*
Jn 17:14 I have **g** them thy word; and the. *1325*
Jn 17:24 my glory, which thou hast **g** me: *1325*
Jn 19:11 except it were **g** thee from above: *1325*
Ac 1:2 Holy Ghost had **g** commandments
Ac 3:16 hath **g** him this perfect soundness *1325*
Ac 4:12 name under heaven **g** among men, ... *1325*
Ac 17:16 saw the city wholly **g** to idolatry
Ro 5:5 by the Holy Ghost which is **g** unto *1325*
Ro 11:8 hath **g** them the spirit of slumber, ... *1325*
Ro 11:35 Or who hath first **g** to him, and it. *4272*
Ro 12:6 the grace that is **g** to us, whether. *1325*
Ro 12:13 necessity of saints; **g** to hospitality *1377*
Ro 15:15 the grace that is **g** to me of God,. *1325*
1Co 1:4 the grace of God which is **g** you by *1325*
1Co 11:15 for her hair is **g** her for a covering *1325*
1Co 11:24 And when he had **g** thanks, he
1Co 12:7 manifestation of the Spirit is **g** *1325*
1Co 16:1 as I have **g** order to the churches
2Co 1:22 and **g** the earnest of the Spirit. *1325*
2Co 5:18 **g** to us the ministry of reconciliation . . . *1325*
2Co 9:9 **g** to the poor: his righteousness *1325*
2Co 10:8 the Lord hath **g** us for edification, ... *1325*
2Co 12:7 there was **g** to me a thorn in the. *1325*
Gal 3:21 for if there had been a law **g** *1325*
Gal 3:21 which could have **g** life, verily *2227*
Gal 3:22 might be **g** to them that believe *1325*
Eph 3:8 is this grace **g**, that I should preach *1325*
Eph 4:7 unto every one of us is **g** grace *1325*
Php 1:29 you it is **g** in the behalf of Christ, ... *5483*
Php 2:9 and **g** him a name which is above. *5483*
1Th 4:8 also **g** unto us his holy Spirit *1325*
1Ti 3:2 **g** to hospitality, apt to teach;
1Ti 3:3 Not **g** to wine, no striker, not greedy . . . *3943*
1Ti 3:8 not **g** to much wine, not greedy *4337*
1Ti 4:14 which was **g** thee by prophecy. *1325*
2Ti 1:7 For God hath not **g** us the spirit *1325*
2Ti 3:16 All scripture is **g** by inspiration
Tit 1:7 not soon angry, not **g** to wine *3943*
Tit 1:7 not **g** to filthy lucre;
Tit 2:3 not **g** to much wine, teachers of *1402*
Heb 2:13 the children which God hath **g** *1325*
Heb 4:8 For if Jesus had **g** them rest, then
Jas 1:5 upbraideth not; and it shall be **g**. *1325*
2Pe 1:4 Whereby are **g** unto us exceeding *1433*
Hos 3:24 by the Spirit which he hath **g** us *1325*
1Jn 4:13 because he hath **g** us of his Spirit *1325*
1Jn 5:11 that God hath **g** to us eternal life, ... *1325*
1Jn 5:20 and hath **g** us an understanding, ... *1325*
Rev 6:2 and a crown was **g** unto him: *1325*
Rev 6:4 power was **g** to him that sat thereon . . . *1325*
Rev 6:8 power was **g** unto them over the. *1325*
Rev 6:11 white robes were **g** unto every one *1325*
Rev 7:2 to whom it was **g** to hurt the earth. *1325*
Rev 8:2 to them were **g** seven trumpets *1325*
Rev 8:3 there was **g** unto him much incense, . . . *1325*
Rev 9:1 was **g** the key of the bottomless pit. *1325*
Rev 9:5 to them it was **g** that they should *1325*
Rev 11:1 there was **g** me a reed like unto a *1325*
Rev 11:2 for it is **g** unto the Gentiles:. *1325*
Rev 12:14 to the woman were **g** two wings *1325*
Rev 13:5 there was **g** unto him a mouth *1325*
Rev 13:5 power was **g** unto him to continue. *1325*
Rev 13:7 it was **g** unto him to make war *1325*
Rev 16:6 thou hast **g** them blood to drink; *1325*
Rev 16:8 power was **g** unto him to scorch. *1325*
Rev 20:4 and judgment was **g** unto them:. *1325*

GIVER See also LAWGIVER.

2Co 9:7 for God loveth a cheerful **g** *1395*

GIVEST

Dt 15:9 thou **g** him nought; and he cry. 5414
Job 35:7 what **g** thou him? or what 5414
Ps 50:19 thou **g** thy mouth to evil, and 7971
Ps 80:5 and **g** them tears to drink in great
Ps 145:15 thou **g** them their meat in due 5414
Pr 6:35 content, though thou **g** many gifts.
Eze 3:18 thou **g** him not warning, nor speakest.
Eze 16:33 thou **g** thy gifts to all thy lovers, ... 5414

GIVETH See also FORGIVETH.

Ge 49:21 hind let loose: he **g** goodly words. 5414
Ex 20:12 the land which the Lord thy God **g** 5414
Le 20:4 when he **g** of his seed unto Molech,. . . . 5414
Nu 5:10 whatsoever any man **g** the priest, ... 5414
Dt 4:40 the land which the Lord thy God **g** 5414
Dt 5:16 the land which the Lord thy God **g** 5414
Dt 8:18 it is he that **g** thee power to get. 5414
Dt 12:9 which the Lord your God **g** you.. 5414
Dt 12:10 and when he **g** you rest from all
Dt 13:1 and **g** thee a sign or a wonder,. 5414
Dt 16:20 the land which the Lord thy God **g** 5414
Dt 19:10 thy God **g** thee for an inheritance, ... 5414
Dt 24:3 a bill of divorcement, and **g** it 5414
Dt 27:3 thy God **g** thee, a land that floweth., . . . 5414
Jos 1:11 which the Lord your God **g** you 5414
Jgs 21:18 Cursed be he that **g** a wife to. 5414
Job 5:10 Who **g** rain upon the earth, and 5414
Job 32:8 the Almighty **g** them understanding.
Job 34:29 When he **g** queitness, who then
Job 35:10 who **g** songs in the night;. 5414
Job 35:12 There they cry, but none **g** answer,
Ps 68:35 he that **g** strength and power. 5414
Ps 119:130 The entrance of thy words **g** light;
Ps 119:130 it **g** understanding unto the simple
Ps 127:2 for so he **g** his beloved sleep 5414
Ps 136:25 Who **g** food to all flesh: for his 5414

Ps 144:10 is he that **g** salvation unto kings:....... 5414
Ps 147:9 He **g** to the beast his food,............ 5414
Ps 147:16 He **g** snow like wool: he.............. 5414
Pr 2:6 For the Lord **g** wisdom: out of his 5414
Pr 3:34 but he **g** grace unto the lowly 5414
Pr 17:4 A wicked doer **g** heed to false lips;
Pr 17:4 and a liar **g** ear to a naughty tongue
Pr 19:6 is a friend to him that **g** gifts
Pr 21:26 the righteous **g** and spareth not 5414
Pr 22:9 he **g** of his bread to the poor.......... 5414
Pr 22:16 he that **g** to the rich, shall surely....... 5414
Pr 23:31 when it **g** his colour in the cup, ... 5414
Pr 24:26 kiss his lips that **g** a right answer
Pr 26:8 so is he that **g** honour to a fool........ 5414
Pr 28:27 that **g** unto the poor shall not lack: 5414
Ecc 2:26 For God **g** to a man that is good....... 5414
Ecc 5:18 days of his life, which God **g** him: 5414
Ecc 6:2 God **g** him not power to eat thereof,
Ecc 8:15 which God **g** him under the sun....... 5414
Isa 40:29 He **g** power to the faint; and to........ 5414
Jer 5:24 the Lord our God, that **g** rain,......... 5414
Jer 31:35 Lord, which **g** the sun for a light....... 5414
La 3:30 **g** his cheek to him that smiteth........ 5414
Da 2:21 he **g** wisdom unto the wise, and....... 3052
Da 4:25 and **g** it to whomsoever he will........ 5415
Da 4:32 and **g** it to whomsoever he will........ 5415
Hab 2:15 him that **g** his neighbour drink,
Mt 5:15 **and it g light unto all that are in**
Jn 3:34 God **g** not the Spirit by measure....... *1325*
Jn 6:32 **my Father g you the true bread** *1325*
Jn 6:33 **and g life unto the world**............. *1325*
Jn 6:37 **All that the Father g me shall** *1325*
Jn 10:11 **good shepherd g his life for the** *5087*
Jn 14:27 **not as the world g, give I unto** *1325*
Ac 17:25 seeing he **g** to all life, and breath, ... *1325*
1Co 3:7 but God that **g** the increase.
1Co 7:38 he that **g** her in marriage doeth well;
1Co 15:57 God which **g** us the victory through ... *1325*
2Co 3:6 letter killeth, but the Spirit **g** life.
1Ti 6:17 **g** us richly all things to enjoy;......... *3930*
Jas 1:5 ask of God, that **g** to all men. *1325*
Jas 4:6 But he **g** more grace. Wherefore *1325*
Jas 4:6 but **g** grace unto the humble.......... *1325*
1Pe 4:11 it as of the ability which God **g**: *5524*
1Pe 5:5 proud, and **g** grace to the humble...... *1325*

GIVING See also FORGIVING; THANKSGIVING.

Dt 21:17 by **g** him a double portion of all. 5414
Ru 1:6 visited his people in **g** them bread...... 5414
1Ki 5:9 in **g** food for my household........... 5414
Job 11:20 shall be as the **g** up of the ghost 4646
Mt 24:38 **marrying and g in marriage,**
Lk 17:16 at his feet, **g** him thanks: and he was
Ac 15:8 **g** them the Holy Ghost, even as *1325*
Ro 4:20 strong in faith, **g** glory to God;
Ro 9:4 covenants, and the **g** of the law........ *3548*
2Co 6:3 **G** no offence in any thing, that *1325*
Eph 5:20 **G** thanks always for all things
Php 4:15 concerning **g** and receiving, but *1394*
Col 1:12 **G** thanks unto the Father, which
Col 3:17 **g** thanks to God and the Father
1Ti 4:1 **g** heed to seducing spirits, and
Tit 1:14 Not **g** heed to Jewish fables, and
1Pe 3:7 **g** honour unto the wife, as unto *632*
2Pe 1:5 **g** all diligence, add to your faith *3923*
Jude 7 **g** themselves over to fornication....... *3923*

GLAD

Ex 4:14 thee, he will be **g** in his heart.......... 8056
Jgs 18:20 And the priest's heart was **g**, ... 3190
1Ki 8:66 joyful and **g** of heart for all the........ 2896
1Ch 16:31 Let the heavens be **g**, and let 8056
2Ch 7:10 **g** and merry in heart for the 8056
Job 3:22 rejoice exceedingly, and are **g**,......... 7797
Job 22:19 The righteous see it, and are **g**......... 8056
Ps 21:6 thou hast made him exceeding **g** 2302
Ps 31:7 be **g** and rejoice in thy mercy:......... 1523
Ps 32:11 Be **g** in the Lord, and rejoice, ... 8056
Ps 34:2 humble shall hear thereof, and be **g** 8056
Ps 35:27 Let them shout for joy, and be **g**, ... 8056
Ps 40:16 seek thee rejoice and be **g** in thee:...... 8055
Ps 46:4 shall make **g** the city of God,.......... 8056
Ps 48:11 let the daughters of Judah be **g**........ 1523
Ps 64:10 righteous shall be **g** in the Lord,....... 8056
Ps 67:4 O let the nations be **g** and sing........ 8056
Ps 68:3 But let the righteous be **g**; let.......... 8056
Ps 69:32 humble shall see this, and be **g**:........ 8056
Ps 70:4 seek thee rejoice and be **g** in thee:...... 8056
Ps 96:11 and let the earth be **g**; let the sea....... 1523
Ps 104:15 wine that maketh **g** the heart of 8056
Ps 118:24 made; we will rejoice and be **g** in it 8056
Ps 119:74 They that fear thee will be **g** 8056
Ps 122:1 I was **g** when they said unto me,....... 8056
Ps 126:3 things for us; whereof we are **g**........ 8056
Pr 10:1 A wise son maketh a **g** father:......... 8056
Pr 12:25 but a good word maketh it **g**.......... 8056
Pr 15:20 A wise son maketh a **g** father:......... 8056
Pr 17:5 and he that is **g** at calamities 8056
Pr 23:25 father and thy mother shall be **g**, ... 8056
Pr 24:17 let not thine heart be **g** when he....... 1523
Pr 27:11 be wise, and make my heart **g**, ... 8056
Isa 65:18 be ye **g** and rejoice for ever 7796
Isa 66:10 and be **g** with her, all ye that love 1523
La 4:21 Rejoice and be **g**, O daughter of 8056
Da 6:23 was the king exceeding **g** for him,...... 2868
Hos 7:3 They make the king **g** with their....... 8056
Joel 2:23 Be **g** then, ye children of Zion, ... 1523
Jnh 4:6 so Jonah was exceeding **g** of the 8056
Hab 1:15 therefore they rejoice and are **g**........ 1523
Zec 10:7 shall see it, and be **g**; their heart 8056
Mt 5:12 Rejoice, and be exceedingly **g** *21*
Mk 14:11 when they heard it, they were **g**, ... *5463*
Lk 1:19 to shew thee these **g** tidings........... *2097*
Lk 8:1 the **g** tidings of the kingdom.......... *2097*
Lk 15:32 **we should make merry, and be g** *5463*
Lk 23:8 saw Jesus, he was exceeding **g** *5453*
Jn 8:56 **and he saw it, and was g**.............. *5463*
Jn 11:15 **And I am g for your sakes that**........ *5463*
Jn 20:20 Then were the disciples **g**, when *5463*
Ac 13:32 we declare unto you **g** tidings,......... *2097*
Ac 13:48 Gentiles heard this, they were **g**, ... *5463*
Ro 10:15 of peace, and bring **g** tidings *2097*
2Co 2:2 who is he then that maketh me **g**,...... *2165*
1Pe 4:13 be **g** also with exceeding joy........... *5463*
Rev 19:7 Let us be **g** and rejoice, and we *5463*

GLADLY

Mk 6:20 many things, and heard him **g**......... *2234*
Mk 12:37 the common people heard him **g** *2234*
Lk 8:40 the people **g** received him:............ *2234*
2Co 11:19 For ye suffer fools **g**, seeing ye......... *2234*
2Co 12:9 Most **g** therefore will I rather *2236*
2Co 12:15 I will very **g** spend and be spent *2236*

GLADNESS

Nu	10:10	Also in the day of your **g**,	8057
Dt	28:47	joyfulness, and with **g** of heart,	2898
2Ch	29:30	they sang praises with **g**, and	8057
2Ch	30:21	bread seven days with great **g**:	8057
2Ch	30:23	kept over seven days with **g**	8057
Ne	8:17	And there was very great **g**.	8057
Ne	12:27	to keep the dedication with **g**,	8057
Est	8:16	The Jews had light, and **g**, and joy,	8057
Est	9:18	made it a day of feasting and **g**	8057
Ps	4:7	Thou hast put **g** in my heart,	8057
Ps	30:11	sackcloth, and girded me with **g**;	8057
Ps	45:7	anointed thee with the oil of **g**	8342
Ps	51:8	Make me to hear joy and **g**;	8057
Ps	97:11	and **g** for the upright in heart	8057
Ps	100:2	Serve the Lord with **g**: come	8057
Pr	10:28	hope of the righteous shall be **g**:	8057
Isa	30:29	and **g** of heart, as when one goeth	8057
Isa	35:10	they shall obtain joy and **g**, and	8057
Isa	51:3	joy and **g** shall be found therein,	8057
Jer	16:9	voice of mirth, and the voice of **g**,	8057
Jer	33:11	The voice of joy, and the voice of **g**,	8057
Jer	48:33	And joy and **g** is taken from the	8057
Joel	1:16	and **g** from the house of our God?	1524
Zec	8:19	to the house of Judah joy and **g**,	8057
Mk	4:16	**immediately receive it with g;**	*5479*
Lk	1:14	And thou shalt have joy and **g**;	*20*
Ac	2:46	with **g** and singleness of heart,	*20*
Ac	12:14	she opened not the gate for **g**,	*5479*
Heb	1:9	hath anointed thee with the oil of **g**	*20*

GLASS

Job	37:18	and as a molten looking **g**?	7209
1Co	13:12	now we see through a **g** darkly;	*2072*
2Co	3:18	beholding as in a **g** the glory of	*2734*
Jas	1:23	beholding his natural face in a **g**:	*2072*
Rev	4:6	was a sea of **g** like unto crystal:	*5193*
Rev	15:2	a sea of **g** mingled with fire:	*5193*
Rev	21:18	was pure gold, like unto clear **g**.	*5194*
Rev	21:21	gold, as it were transparent **g**.	*5194*

GLEAN

Le	19:10	thou shalt not **g** thy vineyard,	5953
Dt	24:21	thou shalt not **g** it afterward:	5953
Ru	2:2	and **g** ears of corn after him	3950
Ru	2:8	Go not to **g** in another field,	3950
Ru	2:15	Let her **g** even among the sheaves,	3950
Jer	6:9	shall thoroughly **g** the remnant.	5953

GLEANED

Jgs	20:45	they **g** of them in the highways	5953
Ru	2:17	So she **g** in the field until even,	3950
Ru	2:19	Where hast thou **g** to day?	3950

GLEANING

Le	23:22	shalt thou gather any **g** of thy	3951
Isa	17:6	Yet **g** grapes shall be left in it,	5955
Jer	49:9	they not leave some **g** grapes?	5955

GLEANINGS

Le	19:9	neither shalt thou gather the **g** of thy	3951

GLISTERING See also GLITTERING.

1Ch	29:2	**g** stones, and of divers colours,	6320
Lk	9:29	his raiment was white and **g**	*1823*

GLITTER

Eze	21:10	it is furbished that it may **g**	1300

GLITTERING See also GLISTERING.

Dt	32:41	If I whet my **g** sword, and mine	1300
Na	3:3	the bright sword and the **g** spear:	1300
Hab	3:11	at the shining of thy **g** spear	1300

GLOOMINESS

Joel	2:2	A day of darkness and of **g**, a day	653
Zep	1:15	a day of darkness and **g**, a day of	653

GLORIETH

Jer	9:24	But let him that **g** glory in this,	1984
1Co	1:31	that **g**, let him glory in the Lord.	*2744*
2Co	10:17	that **g**, let him glory in the Lord.	*2744*

GLORIFIED

Le	10:3	before all the people I will be **g**.	3513
Isa	44:23	Jacob, and **g** himself in Israel.	6286
Isa	49:3	O Israel, in whom I will be **g**.	6286
Isa	55:5	One of Israel; for he hath **g** thee	6286
Isa	60:9	of Israel, because he hath **g** thee	6286
Isa	66:5	Let the Lord be **g**: but he shall	3513
Eze	28:22	I will be **g** in the midst of thee:	3513
Hag	1:8	and I will be **g**, saith the Lord.	3513
Mt	9:8	they marvelled, and **g** God, which	*1392*
Mt	15:31	and they **g** the God of Israel.	*1392*
Lk	5:26	were all amazed, and they **g** God,	*1392*
Lk	13:13	she was made straight, and **g** God	*1392*
Lk	17:15	and with a loud voice **g** God.	*1392*
Lk	23:47	saw what was done, he **g** God,	*1392*
Jn	7:39	because that Jesus was not yet **g**.)	*1392*
Jn	11:4	**Son of God might be g thereby**	*1392*
Jn	12:23	**that the Son of man should be g**	*1392*
Jn	12:28	I have both **g** it, and will glorify	*1392*
Jn	13:31	**Now is the Son of man g,**	*1392*
Jn	13:32	**If God be g in him, God shall**	*1392*
Jn	14:13	**the Father may be g in the Son.**	*1392*
Jn	15:8	**Herein is my Father g, that ye**	*1392*
Jn	17:4	**I have g thee on the earth: I**	*1392*
Jn	17:10	**and am g in them**	*1392*
Ac	3:13	hath **g** His Son Jesus;	*1392*
Ac	4:21	for all men **g** God for that which	*1392*
Ac	11:18	they held their peace, and **g** God,	*1392*
Ro	1:21	they **g** him not as God, neither	*1392*
Ro	8:30	whom he justified, them he also **g**,	*1392*
2Th	3:1	may have free course and be **g**,	*1392*
Heb	5:5	Christ **g** not himself to be made	*1392*
1Pe	4:11	may be **g** through Jesus Christ,	*1392*
Rev	18:7	How much she hath **g** herself,	*1392*

GLORIFIETH

Ps	50:23	Whoso offereth praise **g** me: and	3513

GLORIFY

Ps	22:23	all ye the seed of Jacob, **g** him;	3513
Ps	50:15	deliver thee, and thou shalt **g** me.	3513
Ps	86:12	I will **g** thy name for evermore	3513
Isa	24:15	**g** ye the Lord in the fires, even the	3513
Isa	25:3	shall the strong people **g** thee,	3513
Isa	60:7	I will **g** the house of my glory.	6286
Mt	5:16	**see your good works, and g your**	*1392*
Jn	12:28	**Father, g thy name. Then came**	*1392*
Jn	12:28	have both glorified it, and will **g** it	*1392*
Jn	13:32	**and shall straightway g him.**	*1392*
Jn	16:14	**He shall g me: for he shall receive**	*1392*
Jn	17:1	**g thy Son, that thy Son also**	*1392*
Jn	17:1	**that thy Son also may g thee:**	*1392*
Jn	17:5	**O Father, g thou me with thine**	*1392*
Jn	21:19	by what death he should **g** God	*1392*

Ro 15:4 fear thee, O Lord, and **g** thy name?..... *1392*
Ro 15:9 the Gentiles might **g** God for his....... *1392*
1Co 6:20 therefore **g** God in your body,.......... *1392*
2Co 9:13 they **g** God for your professed......... *1392*
1Pe 2:12 **g** God in the day of visitation.......... *1392*
1Pe 4:16 let him **g** God on this behalf........... *1392*

GLORIFYING
Lk 2:20 **g** and praising God for all things *1392*
Lk 5:25 departed to his own house, **g** God...... *1392*

GLORIOUS
Ex 15:6 O Lord, is become **g** in power: 142
Ex 15:11 who is like thee, **g** in holiness,........... 142
Dt 28:58 fear this **g** and fearful name........... 3513
2Sa 6:20 How **g** was the king of Israel to day,.... 3513
Ne 9:5 blessed be thy **g** name, which is 3519
Est 1:4 shewed the riches of his **g** kingdom 3519
Ps 45:13 king's daughter is all **g** within:......... 3520
Ps 66:2 of his name: make his praise **g** 3519
Ps 72:19 And blessed be his **g** name for ever:.... 3519
Ps 76:4 Thou art more **g** and excellent 215
Ps 87:3 **G** things are spoken of thee, O 3513
Ps 111:3 His work is honourable and **g**: 1926
Ps 145:5 I will speak of the **g** honour of thy..... 3519
Ps 145:12 and the **g** majesty of his kingdom...... 3519
Isa 4:2 of the Lord be beautiful and **g**, ... 3519
Isa 22:23 and he shall be for a **g** throne 3519
Isa 28:1 whose **g** beauty is a fading flower, ... 6643
Isa 30:30 the Lord shall cause his **g** voice........ 1935
Isa 33:21 But there the **g** Lord will be........... 117
Isa 60:13 I will make the place of my feet **g**...... 3513
Isa 63:1 **g** in his apparel, travelling in the....... 1921
Isa 63:12 with his **g** arm, dividing the water 8597
Isa 63:14 people, to make thyself a **g** name....... 8597
Jer 17:12 A **g** high throne from the............. 3519
Da 11:16 and he shall stand in the **g** land,....... 6643
Da 11:41 He shall enter also into the **g** land 6643
Lk 13:17 **g** things that were done by him........ *1741*
Ro 8:21 **g** liberty of the children of God. *1391*
2Co 3:8 of the spirit be rather **g**?......... *1722, 1391*
2Co 3:11 which is done away was **g**,....... *1223, 1391*
2Co 3:11 that which remaineth is **g** *1722, 1391*
2Co 4:4 the light of the **g** gospel of Christ, ... *1391*
Eph 5:27 present it to himself a **g** church,....... *1741*
Php 3:21 fashioned like unto his **g** body,........ *1391*
Col 1:11 according to his **g** power, unto......... *1391*
1Ti 1:11 the **g** gospel of the blessed God,....... *1391*
Tit 2:13 the **g** appearing of the great God *1391*

GLORIOUSLY
Ex 15:21 to the Lord, for he hath triumphed **g**
Isa 24:23 and before his ancients **g**............. 3519

GLORY See also VAINGLORY.
Ex 16:7 ye shall see the **g** of the Lord; 3519
Ex 16:10 **g** of the Lord appeared in a cloud...... 3519
Ex 24:16 **g** of the Lord abode upon mount...... 3519
Ex 24:17 **g** of the Lord was like devouring 3519
Ex 33:22 while my **g** passeth by, I will put....... 3519
Ex 40:34 **g** of the Lord filled the tabernacle...... 3519
Le 9:6 **g** of the Lord shall appear unto you. ... 3519
Nu 14:21 be filled with the **g** of the Lord........ 3519
Nu 14:22 those men which have seen my **g**,...... 3519
Nu 20:6 **g** of the Lord appeared unto them. 3519
Dt 5:24 Lord our God hath shewed us his **g**.... 3519
Jos 7:19 thee, **g** to the Lord God of Israel, ... 3519
1Sa 2:8 make them inherit the throne of **g**: 3519
1Sa 4:21 The **g** is departed from Israel:......... 3519
1Sa 4:22 The **g** is departed from Israel:......... 3519
1Sa 6:5 shall give **g** unto the God of Israel:..... 3519
1Ki 8:11 **g** of the Lord had filled the house...... 3519
1Ch 16:10 **G** ye in his holy name: let the 1984
1Ch 16:24 Declare his **g** among the heathen;...... 3519
1Ch 16:27 **G** and honour are in his presence; 1935
1Ch 16:28 give unto the Lord **g** and strength...... 3519
1Ch 16:29 the Lord the **g** due unto his name:..... 3519
1Ch 16:35 holy name, and **g** in thy praise......... 7623
2Ch 5:14 **g** of the Lord had filled the house...... 3519
2Ch 7:1 the **g** of the Lord filled the house....... 3519
2Ch 7:3 the **g** of the Lord upon the house, ... 3519
Job 19:9 He hath stripped me of my **g**,......... 3519
Job 40:10 array thyself with **g** and beauty. 1935
Ps 4:2 long will ye turn my **g** into shame? 3519
Ps 8:1 hast set thy **g** above the heavens........ 1935
Ps 8:5 crowned him with **g** and honour....... 3519
Ps 19:1 The heavens declare the **g** of God; 3519
Ps 21:5 His **g** is great in thy salvation:......... 3519
Ps 24:7 and the King of **g** shall come in. 3519
Ps 24:8 Who is this King of **g**? The Lord....... 3519
Ps 24:9 and the King of **g** shall come in. 3519
Ps 24:10 Who is this King of **g**? The Lord....... 3519
Ps 24:10 of hosts, he is the King of **g**........... 3519
Ps 29:1 give unto the Lord **g** and strength...... 3519
Ps 29:2 the Lord the **g** due unto his name;..... 3519
Ps 29:3 the God of **g** thundereth: the Lord..... 3519
Ps 49:17 his **g** shall not descend after him. 3519
Ps 57:5 let thy **g** be above all the earth......... 3519
Ps 57:11 let thy **g** be above all the earth......... 3519
Ps 63:2 To see thy power and thy **g**,........... 3519
Ps 64:10 all the upright in heart shall **g**......... 1984
Ps 72:19 whole earth be filled with his **g**; 3519
Ps 73:24 and afterward receive me to **g**......... 3519
Ps 79:9 Help us ... for the **g** of thy name:...... 3519
Ps 84:11 the Lord will give grace and **g**: 3519
Ps 89:17 thou art the **g** of their strength: 8597
Ps 89:44 Thou hast made his **g** to cease,........ 2892
Ps 96:3 Declare his **g** among the heathen,...... 3519
Ps 96:7 give unto the Lord **g** and strength 3519
Ps 96:8 the Lord the **g** due unto his name:..... 3519
Ps 102:15 and all the kings of the earth thy **g**. 3519
Ps 104:31 **g** of the Lord shall endure for ever: 3519
Ps 105:3 **G** ye in his holy name: let the 1984
Ps 106:20 Thus they changed their **g** into........ 3519
Ps 108:5 and thy **g** above all the earth; 3519
Ps 113:4 and his **g** above the heavens........... 3519
Ps 115:1 but unto thy name give **g**, for thy...... 3519
Ps 138:5 for great is the **g** of the Lord........... 3519
Pr 3:35 The wise shall inherit **g**: but 3519
Pr 4:9 a crown of **g** shall she deliver.......... 8597
Pr 16:31 The hoary head is a crown of **g**, ... 8597
Pr 17:6 the **g** of children are their fathers....... 8597
Pr 19:11 his **g** to pass over a transgression....... 8597
Pr 20:29 **g** of young men is their strength: 8597
Pr 25:2 the **g** of God to conceal a thing: 3519
Pr 25:27 to search their own **g** is not **g**.......... 3519
Pr 28:12 men do rejoice, there is great **g**: 8597
Isa 2:19 and for the **g** of his majesty, ... 1926
Isa 2:21 and for the **g** of his majesty, ... 1926
Isa 3:8 to provoke the eyes of his **g**........... 3519
Isa 6:3 the whole earth is full of his **g**......... 3519
Isa 10:3 and where will ye leave your **g**?........ 3519
Isa 13:19 Babylon, the **g** of kingdoms, the....... 6643

Isa	23:9	to stain the pride of all **g**, and to	6643
Isa	28:5	Lord of hosts be for a crown of **g**,	6643
Isa	35:2	they shall see the **g** of the Lord,	3519
Isa	40:5	the **g** of the Lord shall be revealed,	3519
Isa	41:16	shalt **g** in the Holy One of Israel.	1984
Isa	42:8	my **g** will I not give to another,	3519
Isa	43:7	for I have created him for my **g**,	3519
Isa	48:11	I will not give my **g** unto another.	3519
Isa	59:19	his **g** from the rising of the sun.	3519
Isa	62:3	Thou shalt also be a crown of **g**	8597
Isa	63:15	of thy holiness and of thy **g**:	8597
Isa	66:18	they shall come, and see my **g**	3519
Isa	66:19	declare my **g** among the Gentiles	3519
Jer	9:23	Let not the wise man **g** in his	1984
Jer	9:23	let the mighty man **g** in his might,	1984
Jer	9:23	let not the rich man **g** in his riches:	1984
Jer	9:24	But let him that glorieth **g** in this,	1984
Jer	13:16	Give **g** to the Lord your God,	3519
Jer	14:21	not disgrace the throne of thy **g**:	3519
Eze	1:28	the likeness of the **g** of the Lord.	3519
Eze	8:4	the **g** of the God of Israel was there,	3519
Eze	10:4	of the brightness of the Lord's **g**	3519
Eze	10:18	the **g** of the Lord departed from off	3519
Eze	11:23	the **g** of the Lord went up from the	3519
Eze	39:21	I will set my **g** among the heathen,	3519
Eze	43:5	the **g** of the Lord filled the house.	3519
Eze	44:4	the **g** of the Lord filled the house	3519
Da	2:37	power, and strength, and **g**.	3367
Da	4:36	and for the **g** of my kingdom,	3367
Da	5:20	and they took his **g** from him:	3367
Da	7:14	was given him dominion, and **g**,	3367
Hos	4:7	therefore will I change their **g**	3519
Hos	9:11	their **g** shall fly away like a bird,	3519
Mic	2:9	have ye taken away my **g** for ever.	1926
Hab	2:16	thou art filled with shame for **g**:	3519
Hab	3:3	His **g** covered the heavens, and	1935
Hag	2:3	that saw this house in her first **g**?	3519
Hag	2:9	The **g** of this latter house shall be	3519
Zec	11:3	for their **g** is spoiled: a voice of	155
Zec	12:7	that the **g** of the house of David	8597
Mt	6:2	**that they may have g of men.**	*1392*
Mt	6:29	**even Solomon in all his g was not.**	*1391*
Mt	16:27	**come in the g of his Father with**	*1391*
Mt	19:28	**shall sit in the throne of his g,**	*1391*
Mt	24:30	**with power and great g**	*1391*
Mt	25:31	**Son of man shall come in his g,**	*1391*
Mt	25:31	**he sit upon the throne of his g:**	*1391*
Mk	8:38	**Cometh in the g of his Father with**	*1391*
Lk	2:14	**G** to God in the highest, and on	*1391*
Lk	9:26	**when he shall come in his own g,**	*1391*
Lk	12:27	**that Solomon in all his g was not**	*1391*
Lk	17:18	**returned to give g to God, save**	*1391*
Lk	21:27	**in a cloud with power and great g**	*1391*
Lk	24:26	**things, and to enter into his g?**	*1391*
Jn	1:14	we beheld his **g**, the **g** as of the	*1391*
Jn	7:18	**of himself seeketh his own g: but**	*1391*
Jn	8:50	**I seek not mine own g: there is**	*1391*
Jn	11:40	**thou shouldest see the g of God?**	*1391*
Jn	17:5	**with the g which I had with thee**	*1391*
Jn	17:22	**And the g which thou gavest me**	*1391*
Jn	17:24	**that they may behold my g,**	*1391*
Ac	7:2	The God of **g** appeared unto our	*1391*
Ac	12:23	because he gave not God the **g**:	*1391*
Ro	1:23	the **g** of the uncorruptible God into	*1391*
Ro	2:10	**g**, honour, and peace, to every man	*1391*
Ro	3:23	and come short of the **g** of God;	*1391*
Ro	4:2	he hath whereof to **g**: but not	*2745*
Ro	4:20	strong in faith, giving **g** to God;	*1391*
Ro	5:2	and rejoice in hope of the **g** of God	*1391*
Ro	8:18	the **g** which shall be revealed in us.	*1391*
Ro	9:23	make known the riches of his **g** on	*1391*
Ro	11:36	to whom be **g** for ever. Amen.	*1391*
Ro	15:17	I have therefore whereof I may **g**	*2746*
Ro	16:27	To God only wise, be **g** through	*1391*
1Co	1:29	no flesh should **g** in his presence.	*2744*
1Co	1:31	that glorieth, let him **g** in the Lord.	*2744*
1Co	2:8	not have crucified the Lord of **g**	*1391*
1Co	3:21	Therefore let no man **g** in men.	*2744*
1Co	9:16	I have nothing to **g** of: for	*2745*
1Co	10:31	ye do, do all to the **g** of God	*1391*
1Co	11:7	as he is the image and **g** of God:	*1391*
1Co	11:7	but the woman is the **g** of the man.	*1391*
1Co	11:15	have long hair, it is a **g** to her:	*1391*
1Co	15:40	but the **g** of the celestial is one,	*1391*
1Co	15:41	There is one **g** of the sun, and	*1391*
1Co	15:41	and another **g** of the moon, and	*1391*
1Co	15:41	and another **g** of the stars: for	*1391*
1Co	15:41	differeth from another star in **g**.	*1391*
1Co	15:43	sown in dishonour; it is raised in **g**:	*1391*
2Co	3:10	which was made glorious had no **g**	*1392*
2Co	3:10	by reason of the **g** that excelleth.	*1391*
2Co	3:18	into the same image from **g** to **g**,	*1391*
2Co	4:6	the knowledge of the **g** of God	*1391*
2Co	4:17	exceeding and eternal weight of **g**;	*1391*
2Co	8:23	the churches, and the **g** of Christ.	*1391*
2Co	10:17	glorieth, let him **g** in the Lord.	*2744*
2Co	11:30	If I must needs **g**, I will **g** of the	*2744*
2Co	12:9	will I rather **g** in my infirmities,	*2744*
Gal	5:26	Let us not be desirous of vain **g**,	*2755*
Gal	6:14	But God forbid that I should **g**,	*2744*
Eph	1:17	the Father of **g**, may give unto you	*1391*
Eph	3:21	Unto him be **g** in the church by	*1391*
Php	3:19	and whose **g** is in their shame,	*1391*
Col	1:27	the riches of the **g** of this mystery	*1391*
Col	1:27	is Christ in you, the hope of **g**.	*1391*
Col	3:4	shall ye also appear with him in **g**.	*1391*
1Th	2:6	Nor of men sought we **g**, neither	*1391*
1Th	2:12	called you unto his kingdom and **g**	*1391*
2Th	1:9	and from the **g** of his power;	*1391*
1Ti	1:17	be honour and **g** for ever and ever.	*1391*
1Ti	3:16	in the world, received up into **g**.	*1391*
2Ti	2:10	is in Christ Jesus with eternal **g**.	*1391*
2Ti	4:18	to whom be **g** for ever and ever.	*1391*
Heb	1:3	Who being the brightness of his **g**,	*1391*
Heb	2:7	crownedst him with **g** and honour,	*1391*
Heb	2:10	in bringing many sons unto **g**,	*1391*
Heb	3:3	worthy of more **g** than Moses,	*1391*
Heb	13:21	to whom be **g** for ever and ever.	*1391*
Jas	2:1	Lord Jesus Christ, the Lord of **g**,	*1391*
Jas	3:14	**g** not, and lie not against the truth	*2620*
1Pe	1:7	honour and **g** at the appearing of	*1391*
1Pe	1:8	joy unspeakable and full of **g**:	*1392*
1Pe	1:24	the **g** of man as the flower of grass.	*1391*
1Pe	2:20	For what **g** is it, if, when ye be	*2811*
1Pe	4:14	the spirit of **g** and of God resteth	*1391*
1Pe	5:4	ye shall receive a crown of **g** that.	*1391*
1Pe	5:10	hath called us unto his eternal **g**	*1391*
1Pe	5:11	him be **g** and dominion for ever	*1391*
2Pe	1:17	voice to him from the excellent **g**,	*1391*
2Pe	3:18	To him be **g** both now and for ever.	*1391*
Jude	25	our Saviour, be **g** and majesty,	*1391*
Rev	4:9	those beasts give **g** and honour	*1391*

Rev 4:11 receive **g** and honour and power. *1391*
Rev 5:12 and honour, and **g**, and blessing, *1391*
Rev 5:13 Blessing, and honour, and **g**, and *1391*
Rev 7:12 Saying, Amen: Blessing, and **g**, *1391*
Rev 11:13 and gave **g** to the God of heaven. *1391*
Rev 14:7 Fear God, and give **g** to him; *1391*
Rev 15:8 with smoke from the **g** of God, *1391*
Rev 16:9 they repented not to give him **g**. *1391*
Rev 18:1 the earth was lightened with his **g**. *1391*
Rev 19:1 Salvation, and **g**, and honour, and *1391*
Rev 21:11 Having the **g** of God: and her light. *1391*
Rev 21:23 for the **g** of God did lighten it, and. *1391*
Rev 21:24 bring their **g** and honour into it. *1391*
Rev 21:26 they shall bring the **g** and honour *1391*

GLORYING

1Co 5:6 Your **g** is not good. Know ye not. *2745*
1Co 9:15 any man should make my **g** void *2745*
2Co 12:11 I am become a fool in **g**; ye have. *2744*

GLUTTON

Dt 21:20 he is a **g**, and a drunkard. 2151
Pr 23:21 the drunkard and the **g** shall come. 2151

GLUTTONOUS

Mt 11:19 **a man g, and a winebibber, a.** *5314*
Lk 7:34 **a g man, and a winebibber,** *5314*

GNASH

Ps 112:10 he shall **g** with his teeth, and 2786
La 2:16 they hiss and **g** the teeth: they 2786

GNASHED

Ps 35:16 they **g** upon me with their teeth 2786
Ac 7:54 they **g** on him with their teeth. *1031*

GNASHETH

Job 16:9 he **g** upon me with his teeth; 2786
Ps 37:12 and **g** upon him with his teeth. 2786
Mk 9:18 foameth, and **g** with his teeth, *5149*

GNASHING

Mt 8:12 **shall be weeping and g of teeth.** *1030*
Mt 13:42 **shall be wailing and g of teeth.** *1030*
Mt 13:50 **shall be wailing and g of teeth.** *1030*
Mt 22:13 **shall be weeping and g of teeth.** *1030*
Mt 24:51 **shall be weeping and g of teeth.** *1030*
Mt 25:30 **shall be weeping and g of teeth.** *1030*

GNAT

Mt 23:24 **which strain at a g, and swallow** *2971*

GNAWED

Rev 16:10 and they **g** their tongues for pain, *3145*

GO See also AGO; WENT.

Ge 3:14 upon thy belly shalt thou **g**, and 3212
Ge 11:7 let us **g** down, and there confound 3381
Ge 15:15 Shalt **g** to thy fathers in peace; 935
Ge 24:58 Wilt thou **g** with this man? 3212
Ge 27:9 **G** now to the flock, and fetch me 3212
Ge 32:26 not let thee **g**, except thou bless me 7971
Ge 37:30 child is not; and I, whither shall I **g**? 935
Ge 37:35 I will **g** down into the grave unto 3381
Ge 38:8 **G** in unto thy brother's wife, and 935
Ge 44:34 For how shall I **g** up to my father, 5927
Ge 46:3 fear not to **g** down into Egypt; 3381
Ex 3:11 am I, that I should **g** unto Pharaoh, 3212
Ex 3:19 king of Egypt will not let you **g**, 1980
Ex 3:20 and after that he will let you **g**. 7971
Ex 5:1 Let my people **g**, that they may 7971
Ex 5:2 obey his voice to let Israel **g**? 7971
Ex 5:11 **G** ye, get you straw where ye can 3212
Ex 6:1 a strong hand shall he let them **g**, 7971
Ex 8:2 if thou refuse to let them **g**, 7971
Ex 11:4 About midnight will I **g** out into 3318
Ex 12:22 none of you shall **g** out at the 3318
Ex 12:31 and **g**, serve the Lord, as ye have 3212
Ex 14:5 that we have let Israel **g** from 7971
Ex 14:21 Lord caused the sea to **g** back. 3212
Ex 19:12 that ye **g** not up into the mount, 5927
Ex 19:21 **G** down, charge the people, lest 3381
Ex 21:2 he shall **g** out free for nothing. 3318
Ex 23:23 mine Angel shall **g** before thee, 3212
Ex 32:34 mine Angel shall **g** before thee: 3212
Le 6:13 on the altar; it shall never **g** out 3518
Le 14:53 But he shall let **g** the living bird. 7971
Le 16:10 to let him **g** for a scapegoat 7971
Le 21:23 he shall not **g** in unto the vail, 935
Le 25:31 and they shall **g** out in the jubile. 3318
Le 25:54 he shall **g** out in the year of jubile, 3318
Nu 1:3 all that are able to **g** forth to war 3318
Nu 10:9 And if ye **g** to war in your land 935
Nu 13:30 Let us **g** up at once, and possess it: 5927
Nu 21:22 **g** along by the king's high way, 3212
Nu 32:6 Shall your brethren **g** to war, 935
Dt 3:27 thou shalt not **g** over this Jordan 5674
Dt 4:5 the land whither ye **g** to possess it. 935
Dt 6:14 Ye shall not **g** after other gods 3212
Dt 11:28 to **g** after other gods, which ye 3212
Dt 12:25 that it may **g** well with thee, and with
Dt 13:13 **g** and serve other gods, which ye 3212
Dt 19:21 life shall **g** for life, eye for eye, tooth
Dt 22:13 and **g** in unto her, and hate her, 935
Dt 24:5 he shall not **g** out to war, neither 3318
Dt 24:19 thou shalt not **g** again to fetch it: 7725
Dt 25:5 brother shall **g** in unto her, and. 935
Dt 28:41 for they shall **g** into captivity, 3212
Dt 30:12 Who shall **g** up for us to heaven 5927
Dt 30:13 Who shall **g** over the sea for us, 5674
Jos 1:11 to **g** in to possess the land, which 935
Jos 6:22 **G** into the harlot's house, and 935
Jos 18:8 **G** and walk through the land, 3212
Jos 23:12 if ye do in any wise **g** back, and. 7725
Jgs 10:14 **G** and cry unto the gods which. 3212
Jgs 18:2 **G**, search the land: who when. 3212
Jgs 20:23 Shall I **g** up again to battle 5066
Ru 1:16 for whither thou goest, I will **g**; 3212
Ru 2:8 **G** not to glean in another field, 3212
Ru 3:4 shalt **g** in, and uncover his feet, 935
1Sa 9:9 Come, and let us **g** to the seer: 3212
1Sa 9:19 and to morrow I will let thee **g**, 7971
1Sa 17:32 **g** and fight with this Philistine 3212
1Sa 17:39 I cannot **g** with these; for I have 3212
1Sa 20:21 saying, **G**, find out the arrows 3212
1Sa 26:19 saying, **G**, serve other gods. 3212
2Sa 5:19 Shall I **g** up to the Philistines? 5927
2Sa 7:3 **G**, do all that is in thine heart; 3212
2Sa 11:1 time when kings **g** forth to battle, 3318
2Sa 12:23 I shall **g** to him, but he shall not 1980
2Sa 13:39 longed to **g** forth unto Absalom: 3318
2Sa 15:9 the king said unto him, **G** in peace 3212
2Sa 16:21 **G** in unto thy father's concubines, 935
1Ki 2:6 let not his hoar head **g** down to 3381
1Ki 3:7 know not how to **g** out or come in. 3318

1Ki	9:6	but **g** and serve other gods,	1980
1Ki	17:13	Fear not; **g** and do as thou hast	935
1Ki	18:1	**G**, show thyself unto Ahab; and	3212
1Ki	18:43	**G** up now, look toward the sea	5927
1Ki	18:43	he said, **G** again seven times	7725
2Ki	2:23	**G** up, thou bald head; **g** up, thou	5927
2Ki	5:10	**G** and wash in Jordan seven	1980
2Ki	10:25	**G** in, and slay them; let none	935
2Ki	20:5	on the third day thou shalt **g** up	5927
2Ki	20:9	shall the shadow **g** forward ten	1980
2Ki	20:9	degrees, or **g** back ten degrees?	7725
2Ki	22:13	**G** ye, enquire of the Lord for me,	3212
2Ch	18:21	I will **g** out, and be a lying spirit	3318
Ne	9:19	the way wherein they should **g**	3212
Est	2:12	maid's turn was come to **g** into	935
Est	4:8	that she should **g** in unto the king,	935
Est	4:16	**G**, gather together all the Jews	3212
Job	23:8	I **g** forward, but he is not there;	1980
Ps	22:29	all they that **g** down to the dust	3381
Ps	28:1	them that **g** down into the pit	3381
Ps	30:9	when I **g** down to the pit? shall	3381
Ps	32:8	the way which thou shalt **g**?	3212
Ps	39:13	before I **g** hence, and be no more.	3212
Ps	42:9	why **g** I mourning because of the	3212
Ps	43:2	why **g** I mourning because of the	1980
Ps	55:15	let them **g** down quick into hell:	3381
Ps	88:4	them that **g** down into the pit:	3381
Ps	139:7	Whither shall I **g** from thy spirit?	3212
Pr	1:12	as those that **g** down into the pit:	3381
Pr	2:19	None that **g** unto her return again,	935
Pr	3:28	not unto thy neighbour, **G**, and come	3212
Pr	4:14	**g** not in the way of evil men	833
Pr	5:5	Her feet **g** down to death; her	3381
Pr	6:3	**g**, humble thyself, and make sure	3212
Pr	6:6	**G** to the ant, thou sluggard;	3212
Pr	6:28	Can one **g** upon hot coals, and	1980
Pr	7:25	**g** not astray in her paths	8582
Pr	9:6	**g** in the way of understanding	833
Pr	14:7	**G** from the presence of a foolish man	3212
Pr	15:12	neither will he **g** unto the wise	3212
Pr	22:6	a child in the way he should **g**:	6310
Pr	22:24	with a furious man thou shalt not **g**:	935
Pr	25:8	**G** not forth hastily to strive,	3318
Pr	27:10	neither **g** into thy brother's house	935
Pr	28:10	causeth the righteous to **g** astray	7686
Pr	30:29	three things which **g** well, yea,	6806
Ecc	2:1	I said in mine heart, **G** to now,	3212
Ecc	6:6	no good: do not all **g** to one place?	1980
Ecc	7:2	to **g** to the house of mourning,	3212
Ecc	7:2	than to **g** to the house of feasting:	3212
Ecc	9:7	**G** thy way, eat thy bread with	3212
Isa	2:3	out of Zion shall **g** forth the law,	3318
Isa	6:8	who will **g** for us? Then said I,	3212
Isa	6:9	he said, **G**, and tell this people,	3212
Isa	21:6	**G**, set a watchman, let him	3212
Isa	38:15	I shall **g** softly all my years in	1718
Isa	38:18	they that **g** down into the pit	3381
Isa	38:22	What is the sign that I shall **g** up	5927
Isa	49:9	say to the prisoners, **G** forth;	3318
Isa	55:12	For ye shall **g** out with joy, and	3318
Jer	21:12	lest my fury **g** out like fire, and	3318
Jer	22:22	thy lovers shall **g** into captivity:	3212
Jer	25:6	**g** not after other gods to serve	3212
Jer	35:15	**g** not after other gods to serve	3212
Jer	48:5	continual weeping shall **g** up;	5927
Jer	49:3	their king shall **g** into captivity,	3212
Eze	1:20	Whithersoever the spirit was to **g**,	3212
Eze	1:20	thither was their spirit to **g**;	3212
Eze	10:2	**G** in between the wheels, even	935
Eze	12:4	as they that **g** forth into captivity	4161
Eze	13:20	and will let the souls **g**, even the	7971
Eze	14:11	Israel may **g** no more astray from	8582
Eze	20:39	**G** ye, serve ye every one his idols,	3212
Eze	26:20	with them that **g** down to the pit,	3381
Eze	30:17	these cities shall **g** into captivity	3212
Eze	32:25	with them that **g** down to the pit:	3381
Da	12:9	he said, **G** thy way, Daniel: for	3212
Hos	1:2	**G** take unto thee a wife of	3212
Hos	2:5	I will **g** after my lovers, that give	3212
Hos	2:7	**g** and return to my first husband;	3212
Joel	2:16	let the bridegroom **g** forth of his	3318
Am	1:15	their king shall **g** into captivity,	1980
Am	7:15	**G**, prophesy unto my people Israel.	3212
Am	7:17	Israel shall surely **g** into captivity	3212
Am	8:9	cause the sun to **g** down at noon	935
Jnh	1:2	Arise, **g** to Nineveh, that great city,	3212
Jnh	3:2	Arise, **g** unto Nineveh, that great	3312
Zec	14:16	shall even **g** up from year to year	5927
Mt	2:8	**G** and search diligently for the	*4198*
Mt	5:24	**before the altar, and g thy way;**	*5217*
Mt	5:41	**a mile, g with him twain.**	*5217*
Mt	8:9	I say to this man, **G** and he goeth;	*4198*
Mt	8:21	suffer me first to **g** and bury my	*565*
Mt	8:31	suffer us to **g** away into the herd	*565*
Mt	8:32	And he said unto them, **G**. And	*5217*
Mt	10:6	**But g rather to the lost sheep**	*4198*
Mt	16:21	that he must **g** unto Jerusalem,	*565*
Mt	18:15	**g and tell him his fault between**	*5217*
Mt	19:24	**for a camel to g through the eye**	*1330*
Mt	21:28	**g work to day in my vineyard.**	*5217*
Mt	21:30	**And he answered and said I g, sir:**	*565*
Mt	25:46	**these shall g away into everlasting**	*565*
Mt	28:7	**g** quickly, and tell his disciples	*4198*
Mt	28:10	**Be not afraid: g tell my brethren**	*565*
Mt	28:19	**G ye therefore, and teach all**	*4198*
Mk	9:43	**having two hands to g into hell,**	*565*
Mk	10:21	**g thy way, sell whatsoever thou**	*5217*
Mk	10:25	**to g through the eye of a needle,**	*1525*
Mk	10:33	**Behold, we g up to Jerusalem;**	*305*
Mk	10:52	**G thy way; thy faith hath made**	*5217*
Mk	12:38	**which love to g in long clothing,**	*4043*
Mk	14:42	**Rise up, let us g: lo, he that**	*71*
Mk	16:7	But **g** your way, tell his disciples:	*5217*
Mk	16:15	he said unto them, **G ye into all**	*4198*
Lk	7:50	**faith hath saved thee; g in peace**	*4198*
Lk	8:48	**made thee whole; g in peace**	*4198*
Lk	8:51	he suffered no man to **g** in, save	*1525*
Lk	9:51	set his face to **g** to Jerusalem,	*4198*
Lk	9:59	me first to **g** and bury my father.	*565*
Lk	10:7	**G not from house to house.**	*3327*
Lk	10:37	unto him, **G, and do thou likewise.**	*4198*
Lk	14:10	**g and sit down in the lowest**	*4198*
Lk	14:10	**Friend, g up higher: then shalt**	*4320*
Lk	15:18	**I will arise and g to my father,**	*4198*
Lk	17:7	**G and sit down to meat?**	*3928*
Lk	17:19	**Arise, g thy way: thy faith hath**	*4198*
Lk	18:25	**camel to g through a needle's eye,**	*1525*
Jn	4:4	must needs **g** through Samaria.	*1330*
Jn	4:16	**G, call thy husband, and come**	*5217*
Jn	4:50	**G thy way; thy son liveth.** And	*4198*
Jn	6:67	**Will ye also g away?**	*5217*
Jn	6:68	Lord, to whom shall we **g**? thou	*565*

Jn 7:19 Why g ye about to kill me? 2212
Jn 8:11 do I condemn thee: g, and sin no 4198
Jn 8:14 whence I came, and whither I g; 5217
Jn 8:21 I g my way, and ye shall seek me, 5217
Jn 8:21 whither I g, ye cannot come. 5227
Jn 9:7 G, wash in the pool on Siloam, 5227
Jn 13:33 Whither I g, ye cannot come; so 5217
Jn 13:36 Whither I g, thou canst not follow 5217
Jn 14:2 I g to prepare a place for you. 4198
Jn 14:3 if I g and prepare a place for you, 4198
Jn 14:4 whither I g ye know, and the way 5217
Jn 14:12 do; because I g unto my Father. 4198
Jn 14:28 I said, I g unto the Father: 4198
Jn 16:5 I g my way to him that sent me; 5227
Jn 16:7 expedient for you that I g away: 565
Jn 16:7 for if I g not away, the Comforter 565
Jn 16:10 because I g to my Father, and ye 5227
Jn 16:16 see me, because I g to my Father. 5227
Jn 18:8 ye seek me, let these g their way: 5227
Jn 19:12 thou let this man g, thou art not 630
Jn 20:17 but g to my brethren, and say 4198
Jn 21:3 Peter saith unto them, I g a fishing. 5227
Jn 21:3 unto him, We also g with thee. 2064
Ac 1:11 ye have seen him g into heaven. 4198
Ac 4:21 they let them g, finding nothing 630
Ac 5:40 name of Jesus, and let them g 630
Ac 9:15 G thy way: for he is a chosen. 4198
Ac 11:12 the spirit bade me g with them, 4905
Ac 20:22 behold, I g bound in the spirit 4198
Ac 22:10 Arise, and g into Damascus; and 4198
Ac 24:25 G thy way for this time; when I. 4198
Ac 25:9 said, Wilt thou g up to Jerusalem, 305
Ac 25:12 Caesar? unto Caesar shalt thou g 4198
Eph 4:26 let not the sun g down upon your 1931
1Th 4:6 no man g beyond and defraud 5233
Heb 6:1 let us g on unto perfection; not. 5342
Jas 4:13 G to now, ye that say, To day or. 33
Jas 4:13 we will g into such a city, 4198
Jas 5:1 G to now, ye rich men, weep and 33
Rev 3:12 and he shall g no more out:. 1831
Rev 10:8 G and take the little book which 5227
Rev 13:10 captivity shall g into captivity: 5227
Rev 16:1 G your ways, and pour out the vials 5227
Rev 16:14 g forth unto the kings of the earth 2607
Rev 17:8 pit, and g into perdition: 5227
Rev 20:8 shall g out to deceive the nations 1831

GOAD
Jgs 3:31 six hundred men with an ox g 4451

GOADS
Ecc 12:11 The words of the wise are as g, 1861

GOAT See also GOATSKINS; SCAPEGOAT.
Ge 15:9 and a she g of three years old, 5795
Le 3:12 if his offering be a g, then he shall 5795
Le 4:24 his hand upon the head of the g, 8163
Le 16:9 Aaron shall bring the g upon which. 8163
Le 16:10 But the g, on which the lot fell to be 8163
Le 16:15 Then shall he kill the g of the sin 8163
Le 16:21 hands upon the head of the live g. 8163
Le 16:21 putting them upon the head of the g. 8163
Le 16:22 the g shall bear upon him all their 8163
Le 16:22 shall let go the g in the wilderness. 8163
Nu 15:27 he shall bring a she g of the first. 5795
Nu 28:22 And one g for a sin offering, to. 8163
Dt 14:4 eat: the ox, the sheep, and the g, 5795
Pr 30:31 A greyhound; an he g also; and. 8495
Eze 43:25 every day a g for a sin offering: 8163
Da 8:5 an he g came from the west. 5795
Da 8:5 and the g had a notable horn 6842
Da 8:21 the rough g is the king of Grecia: 6842

GOATS
Ge 27:9 thence two good kids of the g; 5795
Ge 27:16 put the skins of the kids of the g. 5795
Ge 30:33 speckled and spotted among the g, 5795
Ge 30:35 the she g that were speckled and. 5795
Ge 37:31 killed a kid of the g, and dipped 5795
Ex 12:5 out from the sheep, or from the g. 5795
Le 4:28 his offering, a kid of the g, 5795
Le 5:6 a lamb or a kid of the g, for a sin 5795
Le 9:3 Take ye a kid of the g for a sin. 5795
Le 16:5 two kids of the g for a sin offering, 5795
Le 16:8 shall cast lots upon the two g; 8163
Le 23:19 kid of the g for a sin offering, 5795
Nu 7:16 One kid of the g for a sin offering: 5795
Nu 7:17 five rams, five he g, five lambs of 6260
Nu 7:82 One kid of the g for a sin offering: 5795
Nu 7:83 five he g, five lambs of the first 6260
Nu 15:24 one kid of the g for a sin offering 5795
Nu 28:15 one kid of the g for a sin offering 5795
Nu 29:11 One the g for a sin offering; 5795
1Sa 24:2 men upon the rocks of the wild g. 3277
2Ch 29:23 they brought forth the he g for 8163
Ezr 6:17 offering for all Israel, twelve he g, 5796
Ezr 8:35 twelve he g for a sin offering: 6842
Ps 50:13 of bulls, or drink the blood of g? 6260
Ps 104:18 hills are a refuge for the wild g; 3277
Pr 27:26 and the g are the price of the field 6260
SS 4:1 thy hair is as a flock of g, that 5795
Isa 1:11 the blood of bullocks … or of he g 6260
Isa 34:6 and with the blood of lambs and g, 6260
Jer 50:8 as the he g before the flocks. 6260
Jer 51:40 slaughter like rams with he g. 6260
Eze 34:17 between the rams and the he g 6260
Eze 43:22 shall offer a kid of the g without. 5795
Eze 45:23 a kid of the g daily for a sin. 5795
Zec 10:3 the shepherds, and I punished the g: 6260
Mt 25:32 divideth his sheep from the g: 2056
Mt 25:33 right hand, but the g on the left. 2055
Heb 9:12 Neither by the blood of g and 5131
Heb 9:13 For if the blood of bulls and of g, 5131
Heb 10:4 that the blood of bulls and of g. 5131

GOATS'
Ex 26:7 thou shalt make curtains of g hair 5795
Ex 35:6 scarlet, and fine linen, and g hair, 5795
Nu 31:20 all work of g hair, and all things 5795
1Sa 19:13 put a pillow of g hair for his bolster. 5795
1Sa 19:16 with a pillow of g hair for his bolster, 5795
Pr 27:27 thou shalt have g milk enough for 5795

GOATS'-HAIR See GOATS' and HAIR.

GOATSKINS
Heb 11:37 about in sheepskins and g; 122, 1192

GOBLET
SS 7:2 Thy navel is like a round g. 101

GOD (or god) See also GODDESS; GODHEAD.
Ge 1:1 G created the heaven and the 430
Ge 1:2 Spirit of G moved upon the face. 430
Ge 1:3 And G said, Let there be light:. 430

Ge	1:4	And **G** saw the light, that it was	430
Ge	1:4	and **G** divided the light from the	430
Ge	1:5	And **G** called the light Day, and the	430
Ge	1:7	**G** made the firmament, and divided	430
Ge	1:8	**G** called the firmament Heaven.	430
Ge	1:10	And **G** called the dry land Earth;	430
Ge	1:10	and **G** saw that it was good.	430
Ge	1:12	and **G** saw that it was good.	430
Ge	1:16	And **G** made two great lights: the	430
Ge	1:18	and **G** saw that it was good.	430
Ge	1:21	**G** created great whales, and every	430
Ge	1:21	and **G** saw that it was good.	430
Ge	1:25	**G** made the beast of the earth after	430
Ge	1:25	and **G** saw that it was good.	430
Ge	1:26	And **G** said, Let us make man in	430
Ge	1:27	**G** created man in his own image,	430
Ge	1:27	in the image of **G** created he him;	430
Ge	2:2	the seventh day **G** ended his work	430
Ge	2:3	And **G** blessed the seventh day, and	430
Ge	2:7	the Lord **G** formed man of the dust	430
Ge	2:8	Lord **G** planted a garden eastward	430
Ge	2:15	Lord **G** took the man, and put him	430
Ge	2:16	the Lord **G** commanded the man,	430
Ge	2:18	And the Lord **G** said, It is not good	430
Ge	2:21	the Lord **G** caused a deep sleep to	430
Ge	3:1	hath **G** said, Ye shall not eat of every	430
Ge	3:3	**G** hath said, Ye shall not eat of it,	430
Ge	3:5	For **G** doth know that in the day	430
Ge	3:8	they heard the voice of the Lord **G**	430
Ge	3:9	And the Lord **G** called unto Adam,	430
Ge	3:13	the Lord **G** said unto the woman,	430
Ge	3:14	the Lord **G** said unto the serpent,	430
Ge	3:21	did the Lord **G** make coats of skins,	430
Ge	5:1	in the likeness of **G** made he him	430
Ge	5:24	And Enoch walked with **G**: and he	430
Ge	5:24	And he was not; for **G** took him	430
Ge	6:2	the sons of **G** saw the daughters	430
Ge	6:5	And **G** saw that the wickedness of	3068
Ge	6:9	and Noah walked with **G**	430
Ge	6:11	earth also was corrupt before **G**,	430
Ge	8:1	And **G** remembered Noah, and every	430
Ge	9:1	and **G** blessed Noah and his sons,	430
Ge	9:6	in the image of **G** made he man	430
Ge	9:8	**G** spake unto Noah, and to his sons	430
Ge	9:16	between **G** and every living creature	430
Ge	9:27	**G** shall enlarge Japheth, and he	430
Ge	14:18	was the priest of the most high **G**.	410
Ge	16:13	Thou **G** seest me: for she said,	410
Ge	17:1	I am the Almighty **G**; walk before	410
Ge	17:7	to be a **G** unto thee, and to thy seed	430
Ge	17:8	possession; and I will be their **G**.	430
Ge	19:29	when **G** destroyed the cities of the	430
Ge	19:29	that **G** remembered Abraham,	430
Ge	20:11	the fear of **G** is not in this place;	430
Ge	20:13	**G** caused me to wander from my	430
Ge	21:6	**G** hath made me to laugh, so that	430
Ge	21:17	and the angel of **G** called to Hagar	430
Ge	21:17	**G** hath heard the voice of the lad	430
Ge	22:1	**G** did tempt Abraham, and said	430
Ge	22:8	**G** will provide himself a lamb for a	430
Ge	22:12	now I know that thou fearest **G**,	430
Ge	26:24	I am the **G** of Abraham thy father:	430
Ge	27:28	**G** give thee of the dew of heaven,	430
Ge	28:12	the angels of **G** ascending and	430
Ge	28:20	If **G** will be with me, and will keep	430
Ge	30:6	Rachel said, **G** hath judged me, and	430
Ge	30:17	**G** hearkened unto Leah, and she	430
Ge	30:22	**G** remembered Rachel, and **G**	430
Ge	31:11	the angel of **G** spake unto me in a	430
Ge	31:50	**G** is witness betwixt me and thee	430
Ge	32:1	and the angels of **G** met him.	430
Ge	32:30	for I have seen **G** face to face,	430
Ge	33:10	as though I had seen the face of **G**,	430
Ge	35:9	And **G** appeared unto Jacob again	430
Ge	40:8	Do not interpretations belong to **G**?	430
Ge	41:38	a man in whom the Spirit of **G** is?	430
Ge	44:16	**G** hath found out the iniquity of	430
Ge	45:5	for **G** did send me before you to	430
Ge	45:7	**G** sent me before you to preserve	430
Ge	45:8	not you that sent me hither, but **G**:	430
Ge	50:19	for am I in the place of **G**?	430
Ge	50:20	**G** meant it unto good, to bring to	430
Ex	1:17	But the midwives feared **G**, and did	430
Ex	1:20	**G** dealt well with the midwives:	430
Ex	2:24	and **G** remembered his covenant	430
Ex	3:4	**G** called unto him out of the midst	430
Ex	3:6	I am the **G** of thy father,	430
Ex	3:6	the **G** of Abraham, the **G** of Isaac	430
Ex	3:6	and the **G** of Jacob	430
Ex	3:6	for he was afraid to look upon **G**.	430
Ex	3:14	**G** said unto Moses, I Am that I Am:	430
Ex	4:16	thou shalt be to him instead of **G**.	430
Ex	8:10	none like unto the Lord our **G**.	430
Ex	8:19	This is the finger of **G**: and	430
Ex	10:8	Go, serve the Lord your **G**: but who	430
Ex	14:19	the angel of **G**, which went before	430
Ex	16:3	Would to **G** we had died by the hand of	
Ex	18:5	he encamped at the mount of **G**:	430
Ex	18:16	make them know the statutes of **G**,	430
Ex	18:21	able men, such as fear **G**, men of	430
Ex	20:2	I am the Lord thy **G**, which have	430
Ex	20:5	am a jealous **G**, visiting the iniquity	410
Ex	20:7	name of the Lord thy **G** in vain;	430
Ex	20:10	is the sabbath of the Lord thy **G**:	430
Ex	20:19	let not **G** speak with us, lest we die	430
Ex	20:20	**G** is come to prove you, and that	430
Ex	20:21	the thick darkness where **G** was	430
Ex	29:46	know that I am the Lord their **G**,	430
Ex	31:3	have filled him with the spirit of **G**,	430
Ex	31:18	stone, written with the finger of **G**.	430
Ex	32:16	And the tables were the work of **G**,	430
Ex	32:16	the writing was the writing of **G**,	430
Ex	34:14	For thou shalt worship no other **g**	410
Ex	34:14	name is Jealous, is a jealous **G**:	410
Ex	35:31	hath filled him with the spirit of **G**,	430
Le	19:2	for I the Lord your **G** am holy	430
Le	20:7	be ye holy, for I am the Lord your **G**.	430
Le	21:6	not profane the name of their **G**.	430
Le	21:12	profane the sanctuary of his **G**; for	430
Le	24:15	Whosoever curseth his **G** shall	430
Nu	16:22	the **G** of the spirits of all flesh,	430
Nu	22:20	**G** came unto Balaam at night,	430
Nu	22:38	word that **G** putteth in my mouth,	430
Nu	23:8	How shall I curse, whom **G** hath	410
Nu	23:19	**G** is not a man, that he should	410
Nu	24:2	the spirit of **G** came upon him	430
Nu	24:23	who shall live when **G** doeth this!	410
Nu	25:13	because he was zealous for his **G**,	430
Nu	27:16	the **G** of the spirits of all flesh,	430
Dt	3:24	what **G** is there in heaven or in earth,	410
Dt	4:24	the Lord thy **G** is a consuming fire,	430
Dt	4:24	consuming fire, even a jealous **G**.	410

Dt	4:31	(For the Lord thy **G** is a merciful	430
Dt	4:31	(For the Lord … is a merciful **G**;)	410
Dt	4:32	since the day that **G** created man	430
Dt	4:33	Did ever people hear the voice of **G**	430
Dt	4:39	the Lord he is **G** in heaven above,	430
Dt	5:11	the name of the Lord thy **G** in vain:	430
Dt	5:14	is the sabbath of the Lord thy **G**:	430
Dt	5:24	that **G** doth talk with man, and he	430
Dt	5:26	hath heard the voice of the living **G**	430
Dt	6:4	The Lord our **G** is one Lord:	430
Dt	6:5	And thou shalt love the Lord thy **G**	430
Dt	6:15	(For the Lord thy **G** is a jealous	430
Dt	6:15	Lord … is a jealous **G** among you)	410
Dt	6:16	Ye shall not tempt the Lord your **G**,	430
Dt	7:9	that the Lord thy **G**, he is **G**,	430
Dt	9:10	stone written with the finger of **G**;	430
Dt	9:26	O Lord **G**, destroy not thy people	3069
Dt	10:12	what doth the Lord thy **G** require	430
Dt	10:12	of thee, but to fear the Lord thy **G**,	430
Dt	10:12	and to serve the Lord thy **G** with all	430
Dt	10:17	For the Lord your **G**, is **G** of gods,	430
Dt	10:21	He is thy praise, and he is thy **G**,	430
Dt	11:13	to love the Lord your **G**, and to	430
Dt	11:22	to love the Lord your **G**, to walk	430
Dt	11:27	if ye obey the … of the Lord your **G**,	430
Dt	11:28	not obey the … of the Lord your **G**,	430
Dt	12:20	When the Lord thy **G** shall enlarge	430
Dt	13:3	for the Lord your **G** proveth you,	430
Dt	14:21	an holy people unto the Lord thy **G**,	430
Dt	14:23	mayest learn to fear the Lord thy **G**	430
Dt	16:1	the passover unto the Lord thy **G**:	430
Dt	16:10	feast of weeks unto the Lord thy **G**	430
Dt	17:19	may learn to fear the Lord his **G**,	430
Dt	19:9	to love the Lord thy **G**, and to	430
Dt	21:23	he that is hanged is accursed of **G**;)	430
Dt	22:5	abomination unto the Lord thy **G**.	430
Dt	23:5	but the Lord thy **G** turned the curse	430
Dt	23:5	because the Lord thy **G** loved thee.	430
Dt	26:1	land which the Lord thy **G** giveth	430
Dt	26:19	an holy people unto the Lord thy **G**,	430
Dt	27:3	Lord thy **G** giveth thee, a land that	430
Dt	28:58	fearful name, The Lord thy **G**;	430
Dt	28:67	shall say, Would **G** it were even!	
Dt	28:67	shall say, Would **G** it were morning!	
Dt	29:12	covenant with the Lord thy **G**,	430
Dt	29:29	things belong unto the Lord our **G**:	430
Dt	30:6	thy **G** will circumcise thine heart,	430
Dt	30:6	love the Lord thy **G** with all thine	430
Dt	32:4	a **G** of truth and without iniquity,	410
Dt	32:17	sacrificed unto devils, not to **G**;	433
Dt	33:27	The eternal **G** is thy refuge, and	430
Jos	1:9	for the Lord thy **G** is with thee	430
Jos	1:13	Lord your **G** hath given you rest,	430
Jos	2:11	the Lord your **G**, he is **G** in heaven	430
Jos	3:10	know that the living **G** is among	410
Jos	4:24	fear the Lord your **G** for ever	430
Jos	10:42	Lord **G** of Israel fought for Israel	430
Jos	14:8	I wholly followed the Lord my **G**	430
Jos	14:9	wholly followed the Lord my **G**	430
Jos	23:10	for the Lord your **G**, he it is that	430
Jgs	6:10	I am the Lord your **G**; fear not	430
Jgs	6:20	And the angel of **G** said unto him,	430
Jgs	8:34	remembered not the Lord their **G**,	430
Jgs	9:13	which cheereth **G** and man, and go	430
Jgs	9:23	Then **G** sent an evil spirit between	430
Jgs	13:5	a Nazarite unto **G** from the womb:	430
Jgs	13:6	the countenance of an angel of **G**,	430
Jgs	13:22	surely die, because we have seen **G**	430
Jgs	16:17	Nazarite unto **G** from my mother's	430
Jgs	16:23	great sacrifice unto Dagon their **g**,	430
Ru	1:16	my people, and thy **G** my **G**:	430
1Sa	2:2	neither is there any rock like our **G**	430
1Sa	2:3	the Lord is a **G** of knowledge,	410
1Sa	3:17	**G** do so to thee, and more also,	430
1Sa	4:13	his heart trembled for the ark of **G**	430
1Sa	5:1	the Philistines took the ark of **G**,	430
1Sa	5:7	upon us, and upon Dagon our **g**	430
1Sa	9:6	now, there is in this city a man of **G**,	430
1Sa	10:9	**G** gave him another heart: and all	430
1Sa	10:10	and the Spirit of **G** came upon him,	430
1Sa	10:19	ye have this day rejected your **G**,	430
1Sa	11:6	And the Spirit of **G** came upon Saul	430
1Sa	12:23	**G** forbid that I should sin against	
1Sa	16:15	evil spirit from **G** troubleth thee	430
1Sa	16:23	evil spirit from **G** was upon Saul,	430
1Sa	17:26	defy the armies of the living **G**?	430
1Sa	17:46	know that there is a **G** in Israel	430
1Sa	18:10	evil spirit from **G** came upon Saul,	430
2Sa	3:35	So do **G** to me, and more also,	430
2Sa	6:6	put forth his hand to the ark of **G**,	430
2Sa	6:7	**G** smote him there for his error;	430
2Sa	7:18	he said, Who am I, O Lord **G**?	3069
2Sa	7:22	neither is there any **G** beside thee,	430
2Sa	14:14	neither doth **G** respect any person:	430
2Sa	14:20	to the wisdom of an angel of **G**,	430
2Sa	18:33	would **G** I … died for thee, O Absalom,	
2Sa	19:13	**G** do so to me, and more also, if	430
2Sa	19:27	my lord the king is as an angel of **G**:	430
2Sa	22:31	As for **G**, his way is perfect;	410
2Sa	22:32	For who is **G**, save the Lord?	410
2Sa	22:32	and who is a rock, save our **G**?	430
2Sa	23:3	must be just, ruling in the fear of **G**	430
1Ki	2:23	**G** do so to me, and more also, if	430
1Ki	4:29	And **G** gave Solomon wisdom and	430
1Ki	8:23	there is no **G** like thee, in heaven	430
1Ki	8:27	will **G** indeed dwell on the earth?	430
1Ki	8:60	earth may know that the Lord is **G**	430
1Ki	13:31	wherein the man of **G** is buried;	430
1Ki	15:3	not perfect with the Lord his **G**,	430
1Ki	17:24	I know that thou art a man of **G**,	430
1Ki	18:21	If the Lord be **G**, follow him: but	430
1Ki	18:24	and the **G** that answereth by fire	430
1Ki	18:24	answereth by fire, let him be **G**	430
1Ki	22:53	provoked to anger the Lord **G** of	430
2Ki	1:10	If I be a man of **G**, then let the fire	430
2Ki	1:12	If I be a man of **G**, let fire come	430
2Ki	1:12	fire of **G** came down from heaven,	430
2Ki	1:16	not because there is no **G** in Israel	430
2Ki	2:14	Where is the Lord **G** of Elijah?	430
2Ki	4:21	laid him on the bed of the man of **G**	430
2Ki	5:7	Am I **G**, to kill and to make alive	430
2Ki	5:15	now I know that there is no **G** in	430
2Ki	6:6	the man of **G** said, Where fell it?	430
2Ki	6:31	**G** do so and more also to me, if	430
2Ki	19:19	thou art the Lord **G**, even thou only,	430
2Ki	23:21	the passover unto the Lord your **G**,	430
1Ch	5:26	the **G** of Israel stirred up the spirit	430
1Ch	13:3	let us bring again the ark of our **G**	430
1Ch	13:12	David was afraid of **G** that day,	430
1Ch	17:16	Who am I, O Lord **G**, and what is	430
1Ch	17:20	neither is there any **G** beside thee,	430
1Ch	21:17	And David said unto **G**, Is it not I	430

2Ch	2:5	for great is our **G** above all gods	430
2Ch	4:19	vessels that were for the house of **G**	430
2Ch	6:14	**G** of Israel, there is no **G** like thee	430
2Ch	6:42	O Lord **G**, turn not away the face	430
2Ch	13:10	But as for us, the Lord is our **G**,	430
2Ch	14:2	right in the eyes of the Lord his **G**:	430
2Ch	14:11	O Lord, thou art our **G**; let not	430
2Ch	15:3	Israel hath been without the true **G**,	430
2Ch	19:7	is no iniquity with the Lord our **G**,	430
2Ch	20:6	art not thou **G** in heaven?	430
2Ch	20:29	fear of **G** was on all the kingdoms	430
2Ch	20:30	his **G** gave him rest round about	430
2Ch	22:12	was hid in the house of **G** six years:	430
2Ch	29:10	covenant with the Lord **G** of Israel,	430
2Ch	30:5	passover unto the Lord **G** of Israel	430
2Ch	30:9	for the Lord your **G** is gracious and	430
2Ch	30:19	That prepareth his heart to seek **G**,	430
2Ch	32:11	The Lord our **G** shall deliver us	430
2Ch	33:13	knew that the Lord he was **G**	430
2Ch	36:16	they mocked the messengers of **G**,	430
2Ch	36:19	And they burnt the house of **G**,	430
Ezr	1:2	The Lord **G** of heaven hath given	430
Ezr	3:4	freewill offering for the house of **G**	430
Ezr	3:5	them whose spirit **G** hath raised,	430
Ezr	3:2	builded the altar of the **G** of Israel	430
Ezr	4:2	for we seek your **G**, as ye do;	430
Ezr	4:24	ceased the work of the house of **G**	426
Ezr	5:13	a decree to build this house of **G**	426
Ezr	5:14	gold and silver of the house of **G**,	426
Ezr	5:17	build this house of **G** at Jerusalem	426
Ezr	7:9	according to the good hand of his **G**	430
Ezr	8:22	The hand of our **G** is upon all them	430
Ezr	9:6	O my **G**, I am ashamed and blush	430
Ezr	9:6	to lift up my face to thee, my **G**:	430
Ezr	9:9	yet our **G** hath not forsaken us	430
Ne	1:5	the great and terrible **G**, that	410
Ne	2:4	So I prayed to the **G** of heaven	430
Ne	2:20	The **G** of heaven, he will prosper us;	430
Ne	7:2	a faithful man, and feared **G** above	430
Ne	9:3	book of the law of the Lord their **G**	430
Ne	9:31	thou art a gracious and merciful **G**	410
Ne	9:32	terrible **G**, who keepest covenant	410
Ne	13:11	Why is the house of **G** forsaken?	430
Ne	13:14	Remember me, O my **G**, concerning	430
Ne	13:29	Remember them, O my **G**, because	430
Ne	13:31	Remember me, O my **G**, for good	430
Job	1:1	that feared **G**, and eschewed evil	430
Job	1:5	and cursed **G** in their hearts	430
Job	1:6	when the sons of **G** came to present	430
Job	1:8	that feareth **G**, and escheweth evil?	430
Job	1:9	said, Doth Job fear **G** for nought?	430
Job	1:16	The fire of **G** is fallen from heaven	430
Job	1:22	sinned not, nor charged **G** foolishly	430
Job	2:1	a day when the sons of **G** came	430
Job	2:3	upright man, one that feareth **G**,	430
Job	2:9	retain thine integrity? curse **G**,	430
Job	2:10	we receive good at the hand of **G**,	430
Job	4:17	mortal man be more just than **G**?	433
Job	8:3	Doth **G** pervert judgment? or doth	410
Job	8:20	**G** will not cast away a perfect man	410
Job	11:5	But oh that **G** would speak, and	433
Job	11:6	know therefore that **G** exacteth of	433
Job	11:7	Canst thou by searching find out **G**?	433
Job	13:7	Will ye speak wickedly for **G**?	410
Job	16:20	eye poureth out tears unto **G**	433
Job	19:26	yet in my flesh shall I see **G**:	433

Job	21:22	Shall any teach **G** knowledge?	410
Job	22:12	Is not **G** in the height of heaven?	433
Job	25:4	How then can man be justified with **G**?	410
Job	33:12	thee, that **G** is greater than man	433
Job	33:14	For **G** speaketh once, yea twice,	410
Job	34:5	**G** hath taken away my judgment	410
Job	34:12	Yea, surely **G** will not do wickedly,	410
Job	35:10	Where is **G** my maker, who giveth	433
Job	36:26	**G** is great, and we know him not,	410
Job	37:14	consider the wondrous works of **G**	410
Job	37:22	with **G** is terrible majesty	433
Job	38:7	all the sons of **G** shouted for joy?	430
Ps	3:2	There is no help for him in **G**	430
Ps	4:1	O **G** of my righteousness: thou	430
Ps	5:4	art not a **G** that hath pleasure in	410
Ps	7:1	my **G**, in thee do I put my trust;	430
Ps	7:9	the righteous **G** trieth the hearts	430
Ps	10:4	**G** is not in all his thoughts	430
Ps	14:1	said in his heart, There is no **G**	430
Ps	18:30	As for **G**, his way is perfect:	410
Ps	18:31	For who is **G** save the Lord?	433
Ps	18:31	or who is a rock save our **G**?	430
Ps	18:46	the **G** of my salvation be exalted	430
Ps	19:1	heavens declare the glory of **G**;	410
Ps	22:1	My **G**, my **G**, why hast thou forsaken	410
Ps	22:10	art my **G** from my mother's belly	410
Ps	25:2	O my **G**, I trust in thee: let me not	430
Ps	33:12	is the nation whose **G** is the Lord;	430
Ps	36:1	is no fear of **G** before his eyes	430
Ps	37:31	The law of his **G** is in his heart;	430
Ps	42:1	so panteth my soul after thee, O **G**	430
Ps	42:2	My soul thirsteth for **G**	430
Ps	42:2	for the living **G**: when shall	410
Ps	42:3	say unto me, Where is thy **G**?	430
Ps	42:4	I went with them to the house of **G**,	430
Ps	42:5	hope thou in **G**: for I shall yet	430
Ps	42:11	hope thou in **G**: for I shall yet	430
Ps	43:5	hope in **G**: for I shall yet praise	430
Ps	44:21	Shall not **G** search this out?	430
Ps	46:1	**G** is our refuge and strength, a	430
Ps	46:4	shall make glad the city of **G**,	430
Ps	46:5	**G** is in the midst of her; she shall	430
Ps	46:5	not be moved: **G** shall help her,	430
Ps	47:7	**G** is the King of all the earth:	430
Ps	48:14	this **G** is our **G** for ever and ever:	430
Ps	50:3	Our **G** shall come, and shall not	430
Ps	50:7	I am **G**, even thy **G**	430
Ps	51:10	Create in me a clean heart, O **G**;	430
Ps	51:17	sacrifices of **G** are a broken spirit:	430
Ps	51:17	a broken and a contrite heart, O **G**,	430
Ps	53:1	said in his heart, There is no **G**	430
Ps	56:4	In **G** I will praise his word,	430
Ps	56:4	in **G** I have put my trust;	430
Ps	56:9	this I know; for **G** is for me	430
Ps	56:13	I may walk before **G** in the light	430
Ps	57:5	exalted, O **G**, above the heavens;	430
Ps	57:7	My heart is fixed, O **G**, my heart is	430
Ps	60:12	Through **G** we shall do valiantly:	430
Ps	62:1	Truly my soul waiteth upon **G**:	430
Ps	62:5	My soul, wait thou only upon **G**;	430
Ps	62:11	**G** hath spoken once; twice have I	430
Ps	62:11	that power belongeth unto **G**	430
Ps	66:1	Make a joyful noise unto **G**, all ye	430
Ps	66:3	Say unto **G**, How terrible art thou	430
Ps	66:16	Come and hear, all ye that fear **G**,	430
Ps	67:1	**G** be merciful unto us, and bless	430

Ps	67:3	Let the people praise thee, O **G**;	430
Ps	67:6	**G**, even our own **G**, shall bless us	430
Ps	68:2	wicked perish at the presence of **G**.	430
Ps	69:3	eyes fail while I wait for my **G**.	430
Ps	69:32	your heart shall live that seek **G**	430
Ps	71:19	O **G**, who is like unto thee!	430
Ps	72:18	be the Lord **G**, the **G** of Israel,	430
Ps	73:1	Truly **G** is good to Israel,	430
Ps	73:11	they say, How doth **G** know?	410
Ps	73:26	but **G** is the strength of my heart	430
Ps	73:28	is good for me to draw near to **G**:	430
Ps	73:28	have put my trust in the Lord **G**,	3069
Ps	74:8	burned up all the synagogues of **G**	410
Ps	74:12	For **G** is my King of old, working	430
Ps	76:11	Vow, and pay unto the Lord your **G**:	430
Ps	77:9	Hath **G** forgotten to be gracious?	410
Ps	77:13	sanctuary: who is so great a **G** as	410
Ps	77:13	who is so great ... as our **G**?	430
Ps	77:14	Thou art the **G** that doest wonders:	410
Ps	78:7	they might set their hope in **G**,	430
Ps	78:7	and not forget the works of **G**,	410
Ps	78:10	They kept not the covenant of **G**,	430
Ps	78:22	Because they believed not in **G**,	430
Ps	79:10	the heathen say, Where is their **G**?	430
Ps	81:1	make a joyful noise unto the **G** of	430
Ps	81:9	There shall no strange **g** be in thee:	410
Ps	84:2	flesh crieth out for the living **G**	410
Ps	84:10	doorkeeper in the house of my **G**	430
Ps	86:10	wondrous things: thou art **G** alone	430
Ps	87:3	are spoken of thee, O city of **G**	430
Ps	90:2	everlasting to everlasting, thou art **G**.	410
Ps	94:7	neither shall the **G** of Jacob regard it.	430
Ps	95:3	For the Lord is a great **G**, and a	410
Ps	95:7	For he is our **G**; and we are the	430
Ps	99:8	thou wast a **G** that forgavest them	410
Ps	100:3	Know ye that the Lord he is **G**:	430
Ps	104:33	I will sing praise to my **G** while I	430
Ps	107:11	rebelled against the words of **G**,	410
Ps	108:1	O **G**, my heart is fixed; I will sing	430
Ps	108:5	Be thou exalted, O **G**, above the	430
Ps	113:5	Who is like unto the Lord our **G**,	430
Ps	115:2	heathen say, Where is now their **G**?	430
Ps	115:3	But our **G** is in the heavens: he	430
Ps	116:5	yea, our **G** is merciful	430
Ps	119:115	keep the commandments of my **G**	430
Ps	136:26	give thanks unto the **G** of heaven:	410
Ps	139:23	Search me, O **G**, and know my	410
Ps	143:10	for thou art my **G**: thy spirit	430
Ps	146:2	I will sing praises unto my **G** while	430
Ps	146:5	Happy is he that hath the **G** of	410
Ps	146:5	whose hope is in the Lord his **G**:	430
Ps	147:1	good to sing praises unto our **G**;	430
Pr	2:5	and find the knowledge of **G**.	430
Pr	2:17	forgetteth the covenant of her **G**	430
Pr	3:4	understanding in the sight of **G** and	430
Pr	25:2	the glory of **G** to conceal a thing:	430
Pr	30:5	Every word of **G** is pure: he is a	433
Pr	30:9	take the name of my **G** in vain	430
Ecc	1:13	this sore travail hath **G** given to	430
Ecc	2:24	that it was from the hand of **G**	430
Ecc	3:11	find out the work that **G** maketh	430
Ecc	3:14	whatsoever **G** doeth, it shall be for	430
Ecc	3:14	**G** doeth it, that men should fear	430
Ecc	3:15	and **G** requireth that which is past	430
Ecc	3:17	**G** shall judge the righteous and the	430
Ecc	5:1	when thou goest to the house of **G**	430
Ecc	5:2	utter anything before **G**: for **G** is	430
Ecc	5:4	When thou vowest a vow unto **G**,	430
Ecc	5:18	of his life, which **G** giveth him:	430
Ecc	6:2	man to whom **G** hath given riches,	430
Ecc	6:2	yet **G** giveth him not power to eat	430
Ecc	7:13	Consider the work of **G**: for who	430
Ecc	7:26	pleaseth **G** shall escape from her;	430
Ecc	7:29	that **G** hath made man upright;	430
Ecc	8:17	Then I beheld all the work of **G**,	430
Ecc	9:7	for **G** now accepteth thy works	430
Ecc	11:9	**G** will bring thee into judgment	430
Ecc	12:7	spirit shall return unto **G** who gave it	430
Ecc	12:13	matter: Fear **G**, and keep his	430
Ecc	12:14	For **G** shall bring every work into	430
Isa	1:10	give ear unto the law of our **G**,	430
Isa	7:11	Ask thee a sign of the Lord thy **G**;	430
Isa	7:13	but will ye weary my **G** also?	430
Isa	8:10	it shall not stand: for **G** is with us	410
Isa	8:19	not a people seek unto their **G**?	430
Isa	9:6	The mighty **G**, The everlasting	410
Isa	13:19	be as when **G** overthrew Sodom	430
Isa	14:13	my throne above the stars of **G**	410
Isa	21:17	the Lord **G** of Israel hath spoken	430
Isa	25:1	O Lord, thou art my **G**; I will exalt	430
Isa	25:8	the Lord **G** will wipe away tears	3069
Isa	25:9	said in that day, Lo, this is our **G**;	430
Isa	29:23	and shall fear the **G** of Israel	430
Isa	30:18	for the Lord is a **G** of judgment:	430
Isa	35:4	your **G** will come with vengeance,	430
Isa	35:4	even **G** with a recompence;	430
Isa	36:7	We trust in the Lord our **G**: is it	430
Isa	37:16	thou art the **G**, even thou alone,	430
Isa	37:17	hath sent to reproach the living **G**	430
Isa	40:1	comfort ye my people, saith your **G**	430
Isa	40:3	in the desert a highway for our **G**	430
Isa	40:8	but the word of our **G** shall stand	430
Isa	40:9	the cities of Judah, Behold your **G**!	430
Isa	40:18	To whom then will ye liken **G**?	410
Isa	41:10	be not dismayed; for I am thy **G**:	430
Isa	43:3	I am the Lord thy **G**, the Holy One of	430
Isa	43:10	before me there was no **G** formed,	410
Isa	44:6	and beside me there is no **G**.	430
Isa	44:8	Is there a **G** beside me? yea,	433
Isa	44:8	there is no **G**; I know not any.	6697
Isa	44:15	he maketh a **g**, and worshippeth it;	410
Isa	45:14	there is none else, there is no **G**.	430
Isa	45:20	pray unto a **g** that cannot save	410
Isa	45:21	there is no **G** else beside me;	430
Isa	45:22	for I am **G**, and there is none else	410
Isa	46:9	for I am **G**, and there is none else;	410
Isa	46:9	I am **G**, and there is none like me,	430
Isa	52:7	saith unto Zion, Thy **G** reigneth!	430
Isa	52:10	shall see the salvation of our **G**.	430
Isa	53:4	stricken, smitten of **G**, and afflicted	430
Isa	54:5	The **G** of the whole earth shall he	430
Isa	55:7	our **G**, for he will abundantly pardon	430
Isa	57:21	no peace, saith my **G**, to the wicked.	430
Isa	61:1	Spirit of the Lord **G** is upon me;	3069
Isa	61:2	the day of vengeance of our **G**;	430
Isa	64:4	neither hath the eye seen, O **G**,	430
Jer	1:6	Lord **G**! behold, I cannot speak:	3069
Jer	2:19	fear is not in thee, saith the Lord **G**,	3069
Jer	3:23	our **G** is the salvation of Israel.	430
Jer	3:25	sinned against the Lord our **G**,	430
Jer	10:10	But the Lord is the true **G**,	430
Jer	10:10	he is the living **G**, and an	430

Jer	13:16	Give glory to the Lord your **G**,	430
Jer	23:23	Am I a **G** at hand, saith the Lord,	430
Jer	23:23	and not a **G** afar off?	430
Jer	23:36	perverted the words of the living **G**,	430
Jer	24:7	and I will be their **G**: for they shall	430
Jer	26:13	obey the voice of the Lord your **G**;	430
Jer	32:18	the Great, the Mighty **G**, the Lord	410
Jer	32:27	I am the Lord, the **G** of all flesh:	430
Jer	32:38	my people, and I will be their **G**	430
Jer	42:6	obey the voice of the Lord our **G**,	430
Jer	42:6	obey the voice of the Lord our **G**.	430
Jer	42:20	Pray for us unto the Lord our **G**;	430
Jer	50:28	vengeance of the Lord our **G**,	430
Jer	50:40	As **G** overthrew Sodom and.	430
La	3:41	our heart with our hands unto **G**	410
Eze	1:1	opened, and I saw visions of **G**	430
Eze	8:4	glory of the **G** of Israel was there	430
Eze	9:3	glory of the **G** of Israel was gone	430
Eze	11:20	my people, and I will be their **G**.	430
Eze	11:24	in a vision by the Spirit of **G**	430
Eze	13:9	shall know that I am the Lord **G**.	3069
Eze	13:16	there is no peace, saith the Lord **G**	3069
Eze	16:23	woe unto thee! saith the Lord **G**;)	3069
Eze	16:48	saith the Lord **G**, Sodom thy	3069
Eze	17:9	saith the Lord **G**; Shall it prosper?	3069
Eze	20:19	I am the Lord your **G**; walk in my	430
Eze	20:20	know that I am the Lord your **G**.	430
Eze	24:24	shall know that I am the Lord **G**.	3069
Eze	26:14	have spoken it, saith the Lord **G**	3069
Eze	28:2	and thou hast said, I am a **G**,	410
Eze	28:2	I sit in the seat of **G**, in the midst	430
Eze	28:2	thou art a man, and not **G**, though	410
Eze	28:2	set thine heart as the heart of **G**	430
Eze	28:6	set thine heart as the heart of **G**;	430
Eze	28:9	but thou shalt be a man, and no **G**,	410
Eze	28:13	been in Eden the garden of **G**;	430
Eze	28:14	was upon the holy mountain of **G**;	430
Eze	28:16	profane out of the mountain of **G**	430
Eze	28:24	shall know that I am the Lord **G**.	3069
Eze	28:26	know that I am the Lord their **G**.	430
Eze	31:9	were in the garden of **G**, envied him.	430
Eze	33:11	saith the Lord **G**, I have no pleasure.	3069
Eze	34:11	Lord **G**; Behold, I, even I will search.	3069
Eze	34:17	saith the Lord **G**; Behold, I judge	3069
Eze	34:24	And I the Lord will be their **G**,	430
Eze	36:22	the Lord **G**; I do not this for your.	3069
Eze	36:28	my people, and I will be your **G**	430
Eze	37:3	I answered, O Lord **G**, thou knowest.	3069
Eze	37:5	saith the Lord **G** unto these bones;	3069
Eze	37:27	I will be their **G**, and they shall be	430
Eze	44:2	the Lord, the **G** of Israel hath entered	430
Da	1:2	the vessels of the house of **G**	430
Da	1:2	into the treasure house of his **g**.	430
Da	1:17	**G** gave them knowledge and skill	430
Da	2:28	is a **G** in heaven that revealeth.	426
Da	2:47	that your **G** is a **G** of gods	426
Da	3:15	who is that **G** that shall deliver you	426
Da	3:17	**G** whom we serve is able to deliver.	426
Da	3:25	the fourth is like the Son of **G**.	426
Da	3:28	worship any **g**, except their own **G**	426
Da	3:29	is no other **G** that can deliver	426
Da	5:21	knew that the most high **G** ruled	426
Da	5:23	the **G** in whose hand thy breath is	426
Da	5:26	**G** hath numbered thy kingdom,	426
Da	6:7	shall ask a petition of any **G** or	426
Da	6:20	servant of the living **G**, is thy **G**.	426
Da	6:22	My **G** hath sent his angel, and	426
Da	6:26	and fear before the **G** of Daniel:	426
Da	6:26	for he is the living **G**, and stedfast.	426
Da	9:4	O Lord, the great and dreadful **G**,	410
Da	9:9	To the Lord our **G** belong mercies	430
Da	9:14	for the Lord our **G** is righteous	430
Da	11:32	that do know their **G** shall be strong	430
Da	11:36	magnify himself above every **g**	410
Hos	1:9	my people, and I will not be your **G**	
Hos	1:10	Ye are the sons of the living **G**.	410
Hos	4:6	hast forgotten the law of thy **G**,	430
Hos	6:6	the knowledge of **G** more than	430
Hos	7:10	return to the Lord their **G**,	430
Hos	9:1	hast gone a whoring from thy **G**,	430
Hos	11:9	for I am **G**, and not man;	410
Hos	13:4	and thou shalt know no **g** but me:	430
Joel	2:14	offering unto the Lord your **G**?	430
Joel	2:17	the people, Where is their **G**?	430
Joel	2:27	I am the Lord your **G**, and none else:	430
Am	3:7	the Lord **G** will do nothing, but he.	3069
Am	4:2	The Lord **G** hath sworn by his	3069
Am	4:11	as **G** overthrew Sodom and	430
Am	4:12	prepare to meet thy **G**, O Israel.	430
Am	4:13	The Lord, The **G** of hosts, is his name.	430
Am	5:14	the **G** of hosts, shall be with you	430
Am	5:15	Lord **G** of hosts will be gracious	430
Am	5:27	whose name is The **G** of hosts.	430
Am	6:8	Lord **G** hath sworn by himself,	3069
Am	7:2	O Lord **G**, forgive, I beseech thee:	3069
Am	7:5	O Lord **G**, cease, I beseech the:	3069
Jnh	1:6	call upon thy **G**, if so be that **G**	430
Jnh	1:9	I fear the Lord, the **G** of heaven,	430
Jnh	3:5	the people of Nineveh believed **G**,	430
Jnh	3:9	Who can tell if **G** will turn and	430
Jnh	3:10	**G** saw their works, that they	430
Jnh	3:10	**G** repented of the evil, that he	430
Jnh	4:2	I knew that thou art a gracious **G**,	410
Jnh	4:6	the Lord **G** prepared a gourd,	430
Jnh	4:7	But **G** prepared a worm when the	430
Jnh	4:9	**G** said to Jonah, Doest thou well	430
Mic	1:2	Lord **G** be witness against you,	3069
Mic	3:7	for there is no answer of **G**.	430
Mic	6:8	and to walk humbly with thy **G**?	430
Mic	7:10	Where is the Lord thy **G**? mine	430
Mic	7:18	Who is a **G** like unto thee, that	410
Na	1:2	**G** is jealous and the Lord revengeth	410
Hab	3:19	The Lord **G** is my strength, and	136
Zep	3:17	The Lord thy **G** in the midst of thee.	430
Zec	6:15	obey the voice of the Lord your **G**	430
Zec	8:23	we have heard that **G** is with you	430
Zec	9:14	Lord **G** shall blow the trumpet	3069
Mal	2:10	one father? hath not one **G** created us?	410
Mal	2:11	married the daughter of a strange **g**.	410
Mal	2:17	Where is the **G** of judgment?	430
Mal	3:8	Will a man rob **G**? Yet ye have	430
Mal	3:14.	It is vain to serve **G**: and what	430
Mt	1:23	being interpreted is, **G** with us	*2316*
Mt	2:12	being warned of **G** in a dream that	
Mt	2:22	warned of **G** in a dream, he turned	
Mt	3:9	**G** is able of these stones to raise	*2316*
Mt	3:16	he saw the Spirit of **G** descending	*2316*
Mt	4:3	If thou be the Son of **G**, command.	*2316*
Mt	4:4	**proceedeth out of the mouth of G**	*2316*
Mt	4:6	if thou be the Son of **G**, cast thyself	*2316*
Mt	4:7	**shalt not tempt the Lord thy G**	*2316*
Mt	5:8	**pure in heart; for they shall see G.**	*2316*

Mt	5:9	shall be called the children of G.	2316
Mt	6:24	Ye cannot serve G and mammon.	2316
Mt	6:30	G so clothe the grass of the field.	2316
Mt	6:33	seek ye first the kingdom of G,	2316
Mt	8:29	Jesus, thou Son of G? art thou.	2316
Mt	12:28	cast out devils by the Spirit of G,	2316
Mt	12:28	the kingdom of G is come unto	2316
Mt	14:33	Of a truth thou art the Son of G.	2316
Mt	15:3	commandment of G by your tradition.	2316
Mt	15:6	commandment of G of none effect	2316
Mt	15:31	and they glorified the G of Israel	2316
Mt	16:16	art the Christ, the Son of the living G.	2316
Mt	19:6	therefore G hath joined together	2316
Mt	19:17	none good but one, that is, G:.	2316
Mt	19:24	to enter into the kingdom of G.	2316
Mt	19:26	but with G all things are possible.	2316
Mt	21:31	go into the kingdom of G before you.	2316
Mt	21:43	kingdom of G shall be taken from	2316
Mt	22:29	the scriptures, nor the power of G	2316
Mt	22:30	but are as the angels of G in heaven.	2316
Mt	22:32	G is not the G of the dead, but of.	2316
Mt	22:37	Thou shalt love the Lord thy G.	2316
Mt	23:22	sweareth by the throne of G, and	2316
Mt	26:61	to destroy the temple of G, and to	2316
Mt	26:63	I adjure thee by the living G,	2316
Mt	27:40	If thou be the Son of G, come down	2316
Mt	27:43	He trusted in G; let him deliver.	2316
Mt	27:43	for he said, I am the Son of G	2316
Mt	27:46	My G, my G, why hast thou.	2316
Mt	27:54	Truly this was the Son of G	2316
Mk	1:14	the gospel of the kingdom of G,	2316
Mk	1:15	the kingdom of G is at hand:	2316
Mk	2:7	who can forgive sins but G only?	2316
Mk	3:11	saying, Thou art the Son of G	2316
Mk	3:35	the will of G, the same is my brother	2316
Mk	4:11	the mystery of the kingdom of G:	2316
Mk	4:26	So is the kingdom of G, as if	2316
Mk	4:30	shall we liken the kingdom of G?	2316
Mk	5:7	thou Son of the most high G?	2316
Mk	7:9	ye reject the commandment of G.	2316
Mk	7:13	Making the word of G of none	2316
Mk	8:33	not the things that be of G, but	2316
Mk	9:1	seen the kingdom of G come in	2316
Mk	9:47	to enter into the kingdom of G.	2316
Mk	10:6	G made them male and female.	2316
Mk	10:9	therefore G hath joined together,	2316
Mk	10:14	for of such is the kingdom of G	2316
Mk	10:15	shall not receive the kingdom of G	2316
Mk	10:18	is none good but one, that is, G.	2316
Mk	10:23	enter into the kingdom of G!	2316
Mk	10:24	to enter into the kingdom of G!	2316
Mk	10:25	to enter into the kingdom of G.	2316
Mk	10:27	it is impossible, but not with G:	2316
Mk	10:27	for with G all things are possible.	2316
Mk	11:22	saith unto them, Have faith in G.	2316
Mk	12:14	teachest the way of G in truth:	2316
Mk	12:17	to G the things that are God's.	2316
Mk	12:24	scriptures, neither the power of G?	2316
Mk	12:26	how in the bush, G spake unto him	2316
Mk	12:27	He is not the G of the dead,	2316
Mk	12:27	but the G of the living:.	2316
Mk	12:29	The Lord our G is one Lord:.	2316
Mk	12:30	thou shalt love the Lord thy G	2316
Mk	12:32	for there is one G; and there is	2316
Mk	12:34	not far from the kingdom of G.	2316
Mk	14:25	drink it new in the kingdom of G	2316
Mk	15:34	My G, my G, why hast thou.	2316
Mk	15:39	Truly this man was the Son of G.	2316
Mk	15:43	also waited for the kingdom of G	2316
Mk	16:19	and sat on the right hand of G	2316
Lk	1:19	that stand in the presence of G;	2316
Lk	1:26	Gabriel was sent from G unto a	2316
Lk	1:30	for thou hast found favour with G	2316
Lk	1:35	of thee shall be called the Son of G.	2316
Lk	1:37	with G nothing shall be impossible	2316
Lk	1:47	hath rejoiced in G my Saviour.	2316
Lk	1:68	Blessed be the Lord G of Israel;	2316
Lk	1:78	the tender mercy of our G;	2316
Lk	2:13	of the heavenly host praising G.	2316
Lk	2:14	Glory to G in the highest, and on	2316
Lk	2:20	returned, glorifying and praising G.	2316
Lk	2:40	and the grace of G was upon him.	2316
Lk	2:52	and in favour with G and man.	2316
Lk	3:6	all flesh shall see the salvation of G.	2316
Lk	3:8	G is able of these stones to raise	2316
Lk	4:3	If thou be the Son of G, command.	2316
Lk	4:4	alone, but by every word of G.	2316
Lk	4:9	thou be the Son of G, cast thyself	2316
Lk	4:12	shalt not tempt the Lord thy G.	2316
Lk	4:34	who thou art, the Holy One of G	2316
Lk	4:41	Thou art Christ the Son of G.	2316
Lk	5:21	Who can forgive sins, but G alone?.	2316
Lk	5:26	and they glorified G, and were filled	2316
Lk	6:4	How he went into the house of G,	2316
Lk	6:12	continued all night in prayer to G.	2316
Lk	6:20	for yours is the kingdom of G.	2316
Lk	7:16	That G hath visited his people,	2316
Lk	7:28	least in the kingdom of G is greater	2316
Lk	8:10	mysteries of the kingdom of G:	2316
Lk	8:11	The seed is the word of G	2316
Lk	8:21	which hear the word of G, and do	2316
Lk	8:39	how great things G hath done.	2316
Lk	9:2	to preach the kingdom of G, and	2316
Lk	9:27	till they see the kingdom of G.	2316
Lk	9:43	amazed at the mighty power of G.	2316
Lk	9:60	and preach the kingdom of G.	2316
Lk	9:62	back, is fit for the kingdom of G.	2316
Lk	10:9	The kingdom of G is come nigh	2316
Lk	10:11	the kingdom of G is come nigh	2316
Lk	10:27	Thou shalt love the Lord thy G	2316
Lk	11:20	But if I with the finger of G cast.	2316
Lk	11:20	no doubt the kingdom of G is	2316
Lk	11:28	are they that hear the word of G	2316
Lk	11:42	over judgment and the love of G:.	2316
Lk	12:6	one of them is forgotten before G?.	2316
Lk	12:8	confess before the angels of G:	2316
Lk	12:9	be denied before the angels of G	2316
Lk	12:21	and is not rich toward G	2316
Lk	12:24	G feedeth them: how much more.	2316
Lk	12:28	G so clothed the grass, which is	2316
Lk	12:31	rather seek ye the kingdom of G;	2316
Lk	13:13	was made straight, and glorified G.	2316
Lk	13:18	what is the kingdom of G like?	2316
Lk	13:20	shall I liken the kingdom of G?	2316
Lk	13:28	the prophets, in the kingdom of G,	2316
Lk	13:29	sit down in the kingdom of G.	2316
Lk	14:15	eat bread in the kingdom of G	2316
Lk	15:10	in the presence of the angels of G	2316
Lk	16:13	Ye cannot serve G and mammon	2316
Lk	16:15	but G knoweth your hearts; for	2316
Lk	16:15	is abomination in the sight of G.	2316
Lk	16:16	the kingdom of G is preached, and	2316

Lk	17:20	**kingdom of G cometh not with**	*2316*
Lk	17:21	**the kingdom of G is within you.**	*2316*
Lk	18:4	**Though I fear not G, nor regard.**	*2316*
Lk	18:7	**shall not G avenge his own elect.**	*2316*
Lk	18:11	**G, I thank thee, that I am not as**	*2316*
Lk	18:13	**G be merciful to me a sinner.**	*2316*
Lk	18:16	**for of such is the kingdom of G**	*2316*
Lk	18:17	**shall not receive the kingdom of G**	*2316*
Lk	18:19	**None is good, save one, that is, G.**	*2316*
Lk	18:24	**enter into the kingdom of G!**	*2316*
Lk	18:25	**enter into the kingdom of G.**	*2316*
Lk	18:27	**with men are possible with G.**	*2316*
Lk	20:16	heard it, they said, **G** forbid	*3361, 1096*
Lk	20:21	but teachest the way of **G** truly:	*2316*
Lk	20:37	**the Lord the G of Abraham,**	*2316*
Lk	20:37	**G of Isaac, and the G of Jacob.**	*2316*
Lk	20:38	**For he is not a G of the dead,**	*2316*
Lk	21:31	**the kingdom of G is nigh at hand**	*2316*
Lk	22:16	**be fulfilled in the kingdom of G.**	*2316*
Lk	22:18	**the kingdom of G shall come.**	*2316*
Lk	22:69	**the right hand of the power of G.**	*2316*
Lk	22:70	Art thou then the Son of **G**?	*2316*
Lk	23:35	if he be Christ, the chosen of **G**.	*2316*
Lk	23:40	Dost not thou fear **G**, seeing thou	*2316*
Lk	23:51	waited for the kingdom of **G**.	*2316*
Lk	24:53	temple, praising and blessing **G**.	*2316*
Jn	1:1	was with **G**, and the Word was **G**	*2316*
Jn	1:2	same was in the beginning with **G**	*2316*
Jn	1:6	There was a man sent from **G**,	*2316*
Jn	1:12	power to become the sons of **G**,	*2316*
Jn	1:13	nor of the will of man, but of **G**.	*2316*
Jn	1:18	No man hath seen **G** at any time;	*2316*
Jn	1:29	and saith, Behold the Lamb of **G**	*2316*
Jn	1:34	bare record that this is the Son of **G**.	*2316*
Jn	1:36	he saith, Behold the Lamb of **G**!	*2316*
Jn	1:51	**and the angels of G ascending**	*2316*
Jn	3:2	thou art a teacher, come from **G**	*2316*
Jn	3:2	thou doest, except **G** be with him	*2316*
Jn	3:3	**he cannot see the kingdom of G.**	*2316*
Jn	3:5	**enter into the kingdom of G**	*2316*
Jn	3:16	**G so loved the world, that he**	*2316*
Jn	3:17	**G sent not his Son into the world.**	*2316*
Jn	3:18	**of the only begotten Son of G.**	*2316*
Jn	3:21	**that they are wrought in G**	*2316*
Jn	3:33	hath set to his seal that **G** is true	*2316*
Jn	3:34	For he whom **G** hath sent speaketh	*2316*
Jn	3:34	words of **G**: for **G** giveth not the	*2316*
Jn	3:36	the wrath of **G** abideth on him	*2316*
Jn	4:10	**If thou knewest the gift of G,**	*2316*
Jn	4:24	**G is a Spirit: and they that worship**	*2316*
Jn	5:18	said also that **G** was his Father,	*2316*
Jn	5:18	making himself equal with **G**	*2316*
Jn	5:42	**ye, have not the love of G in you.**	*2316*
Jn	5:44	**honour that cometh from G only?**	*2316*
Jn	6:29	**This is the work of G, that ye believe**	*2316*
Jn	6:33	**For the bread of G is he which**	*2316*
Jn	6:45	**And they shall be all taught of G**	*2316*
Jn	6:46	**he which is of G, he hath seen.**	*2316*
Jn	6:69	that Christ, the Son of the living **G**.	*2316*
Jn	7:17	**doctrine, whether it be of G, or**	*2316*
Jn	8:40	**truth which I have heard of G:**	*2316*
Jn	8:41	we have one Father, even **G**	*2316*
Jn	8:42	**G were your Father, ye would love me**	*2316*
Jn	8:42	**proceeded forth, and came from G;**	*2316*
Jn	8:47	**that is of G heareth God's words:**	*2316*
Jn	8:47	**them not, because ye are not of G**	*2316*
Jn	9:16	This man is not of **G**, because he	*2316*
Jn	9:31	we know that **G** heareth not sinners:	*2316*
Jn	9:31	if any man be a worshipper of **G**,	*2318*
Jn	9:33	If this man were not of **G**, he.	*2316*
Jn	9:35	**Dost thou believe on the Son of G?**	*2316*
Jn	10:33	thou, being a man, makest thyself **G**.	*2316*
Jn	10:35	**unto whom the word of G came,**	*2316*
Jn	10:36	**because I said, I am the Son of G?**	*2316*
Jn	11:4	**unto death, but for the glory of G,**	*2316*
Jn	11:4	**the Son of G might be glorified**	*2316*
Jn	11:22	thou wilt ask of **G**, **G** will give it thee.	*2316*
Jn	11:40	**thou shouldest see the glory of G?**	*2316*
Jn	12:43	of men more than the praise of **G**	*2316*
Jn	13:3	was come from **G**, and went to **G**;	*2316*
Jn	13:31	**glorified, and G is glorified in him.**	*2316*
Jn	13:32	**If G be glorified in him, G shall also**	*2316*
Jn	14:1	ye believe in **G**, believe also in me.	*2316*
Jn	16:2	**will think that he doeth G service**	*2316*
Jn	17:3	**might know thee the only true G**	*2316*
Jn	19:7	he made himself the Son of **G**.	*2316*
Jn	20:17	**ascend … to my G, and your G**	*2316*
Jn	20:28	said unto him, My Lord and my **G**.	*2316*
Jn	20:31	Jesus is the Christ, the Son of **G**;	*2316*
Jn	21:19	by what death he should glorify **G**	*2316*
Ac	1:3	pertaining to the kingdom of **G**:	*2316*
Ac	2:11	tongues the wonderful works of **G**	*2316*
Ac	2:23	counsel and foreknowledge of **G**,	*2316*
Ac	2:24	Whom **G** hath raised up, having	*2316*
Ac	2:32	This Jesus hath **G** raised up,	*2316*
Ac	2:36	that **G** hath made that same Jesus,	*2316*
Ac	2:39	as many as the Lord our **G** shall call.	*2316*
Ac	3:15	whom **G** hath raised from the dead;	*2316*
Ac	3:22	prophet shall the Lord your **G** raise up	*2316*
Ac	3:26	**G**, having raised up his Son Jesus,	*2316*
Ac	4:10	whom **G** raised from the dead,	*2316*
Ac	4:19	hearken unto you more than unto **G**,	*2316*
Ac	4:24	thou art **G**, which hast made heaven,	*2316*
Ac	5:4	not lied unto men, but unto **G**.	*2316*
Ac	5:29	ought to obey **G** rather than men.	*2316*
Ac	5:30	**G** of our fathers raised up Jesus,	*2316*
Ac	5:39	if it be of **G**, ye cannot overthrow it;	*2316*
Ac	5:39	ye be found even to fight against **G**.	*2314*
Ac	6:7	And the word of **G** increased; and	*2316*
Ac	7:2	The **G** of glory appeared unto our	*2316*
Ac	7:37	shall the Lord your **G** raise up	*2316*
Ac	7:55	and saw the glory of **G**, and Jesus	*2316*
Ac	7:55	Jesus … on the right hand of **G**,	*2316*
Ac	7:56	Son of man … the right hand of **G**	*2316*
Ac	8:20	hast thought that the gift of **G** may	*2316*
Ac	8:21	heart is not right in the sight of **G**	*2316*
Ac	10:2	one that feared **G** with all his house,	*2316*
Ac	10:3	an angel of **G** coming in to him,	*2316*
Ac	10:15	What **G** hath cleansed, that call not	*2316*
Ac	10:22	a just man, and one that feareth **G**,	*2316*
Ac	10:34	that **G** is no respecter of persons:	*2316*
Ac	10:40	Him **G** raised up the third day,	*2316*
Ac	11:17	what was I, that I could withstand **G**?	*2316*
Ac	12:22	the voice of a **g**, and not of a man	*2316*
Ac	12:23	because he gave not **G** the glory:	*2316*
Ac	13:17	The **G** of the people of Israel.	*2316*
Ac	13:30	But **G** raised him from the dead:	*2316*
Ac	13:37	But he, whom **G** raised again, saw	*2316*
Ac	14:15	from these vanities unto the living **G**,	*2316*
Ac	15:8	And **G**, which knoweth the hearts,	*2316*
Ac	15:10	now therefore why tempt ye **G**	*2316*
Ac	15:18	Known unto **G** are all his works	*2316*

G

1Co	3:17	for the temple of **G** is holy, which	*2316*
1Co	3:19	this world is foolishness with **G**	*2316*
1Co	4:1	stewards of the mysteries of **G**.	*2316*
1Co	4:5	shall every man have praise of **G**.	*2316*
1Co	4:20	the kingdom of **G** is not in word,	*2316*
1Co	5:13	them that are without **G** judgeth	*2316*
1Co	6:10	shall inherit the kingdom of **G**.	*2316*
1Co	6:15	of an harlot? **G** forbid.	*3361, 1096*
1Co	6:20	therefore glorify **G** in your body,	*2316*
1Co	7:40	also that I have the Spirit of **G**.	*2316*
1Co	8:3	But if any man love **G**, the same	*2316*
1Co	8:4	there is none other **G** but one	*2316*
1Co	8:6	there is but one **G**, the Father	*2316*
1Co	10:13	**G** is faithful, who will not suffer	*2316*
1Co	10:20	sacrifice to devils, and not to **G**.	*2316*
1Co	10:31	ye do, do all to the glory of **G**	*2316*
1Co	11:3	and the head of Christ is **G**	*2316*
1Co	11:7	as he is the image and glory of **G**	*2316*
1Co	11:13	woman pray unto **G** uncovered?	*2316*
1Co	11:22	or despise ye the church of **G**, and	*2316*
1Co	12:6	it is the same **G** which worketh	*2316*
1Co	14:2	speaketh not unto men, but unto **G**:	*2316*
1Co	14:18	thank my **G**, I speak with tongues	*2316*
1Co	14:25	report that **G** is in you of a truth.	*2316*
1Co	14:33	**G** is not the author of confusion,	*2316*
1Co	15:9	I persecuted the church of **G**.	*2316*
1Co	15:10	But by the grace of **G** I am what	*2316*
1Co	15:15	are found false witnesses of **G**;	*2316*
1Co	15:15	have testified of **G** that he raised	*2316*
1Co	15:24	delivered up the kingdom to **G**,	*2316*
1Co	15:28	that **G** may be all in all	*2316*
1Co	15:34	some have not the knowledge of **G**.	*2316*
1Co	15:57	But thanks be to **G**, which giveth	*2316*
2Co	1:3	and the **G** of all comfort;	*2316*
2Co	1:9	but in **G** which raiseth the dead:	*2316*
2Co	1:19	For the Son of **G**, Jesus Christ,	*2316*
2Co	1:20	For all the promises of **G** in him	*2316*
2Co	2:14	Now thanks be unto **G**, which	*2316*
2Co	2:17	many, which corrupt the word of **G**:	*2316*
2Co	3:3	with the Spirit of the living **G**;.	*2316*
2Co	3:5	but our sufficiency is of **G**;.	*2316*
2Co	4:4	who is the image of **G**, should	*2316*
2Co	4:6	For **G**, who commanded the light	*2316*
2Co	4:6	of the knowledge of the glory of **G**.	*2316*
2Co	4:7	excellency of the power may be of **G**,	*2316*
2Co	5:18	And all things are of **G**, who hath	*2316*
2Co	5:19	To wit, that **G** was in Christ,	*2316*
2Co	5:21	the righteousness of **G** in him	*2316*
2Co	6:1	receive not the grace of **G** in vain,	*2316*
2Co	6:16	hath the temple of **G** with idols?	*2316*
2Co	6:16	ye are the temple of the living **G**;	*2316*
2Co	6:16	walk in them; and I will be their **G**,	*2316*
2Co	7:1	perfecting holiness in the fear of **G**.	*2316*
2Co	9:7	for **G** loveth a cheerful giver.	*2316*
2Co	9:15	Thanks be unto **G** for his … gift.	*2316*
2Co	10:4	mighty through **G** to the pulling	*2316*
2Co	10:5	itself against the knowledge of **G**,	*2316*
Gal	1:10	For do I now persuade men, or **G**?	*2316*
Gal	2:6	**G** accepteth no man's person:)	*2316*
Gal	2:20	live by the faith of the Son of **G**,	*2316*
Gal	2:21	I do not frustrate the grace of **G**:	*2316*
Gal	3:6	Even as Abraham believed **G**, and	*2316*
Gal	3:20	not a mediator of one, but **G** is one	*2316*
Gal	4:4	**G** sent forth his Son, made of a	*2316*
Gal	4:6	**G** hath sent forth the Spirit of his	*2316*
Gal	4:9	now, after that ye have known **G**,	*2316*
Gal	4:9	or rather are known of **G**,	*2316*
Gal	6:7	**G** is not mocked: for whatsoever	*2316*
Gal	6:14	**G** forbid that I should glory	*3361, 1096*
Eph	2:4	But **G**, who is rich in mercy, for his	*2316*
Eph	2:8	of yourselves: it is the gift of **G**:	*2316*
Eph	3:7	gift of the grace of **G** given unto me.	*2316*
Eph	3:19	be filled with all the fulness of **G**.	*2316*
Eph	4:6	One **G** and Father of all, who is	*2316*
Eph	4:13	of the knowledge of the Son of **G**.	*2316*
Eph	4:30	And grieve not the holy Spirit of **G**,	*2316*
Eph	5:2	sacrifice to **G** for a sweetsmelling	*2316*
Eph	5:6	cometh the wrath of **G** upon the	*2316*
Eph	5:21	one to another in the fear of **G**	*2316*
Eph	6:6	the will of **G** from the heart;	*2316*
Eph	6:11	Put on the whole armour of **G**,	*2316*
Eph	6:13	unto you the whole armour of **G**,	*2316*
Eph	6:17	the Spirit which is the word of **G**:	*2316*
Php	1:3	I thank my **G** upon every	*2316*
Php	1:8	For **G** is my record, how greatly I	*2316*
Php	2:6	Who, being in the form of **G**.	*2316*
Php	2:6	it not robbery to be equal with **G**:	*2316*
Php	2:9	**G** also hath highly exalted him,	*2316*
Php	3:3	which worship **G** in the spirit, and	*2316*
Php	3:14	the prize of the high calling of **G**	*2316*
Php	3:19	whose **G** is their belly, and whose	*2316*
Php	4:7	And the peace of **G**, which passeth	*2316*
Php	4:18	acceptable, well pleasing to **G**.	*2316*
Php	4:19	my **G** shall supply all your need	*2316*
Col	1:6	and knew the grace of **G** in truth:	*2316*
Col	1:15	is the image of the invisible **G**,	*2316*
Col	1:25	dispensation of **G** which is given	*2316*
Col	3:1	sitteth on the right hand of **G**.	*2316*
Col	3:3	your life is hid with Christ in **G**.	*2316*
Col	3:6	wrath of **G** Cometh on the children	*2316*
Col	3:12	as the elect of **G**, holy and beloved,	*2316*
Col	3:15	And let the peace of **G** rule in	*2316*
Col	3:22	in singleness of heart, fearing **G**:	*2316*
1Th	1:4	knowing … your election of **G**	*2316*
1Th	1:9	and how ye turned to **G** from idols	*2316*
1Th	1:9	to serve the living and true **G**;	*2316*
1Th	2:2	to speak unto you the gospel of **G**	*2316*
1Th	2:4	not as pleasing men, but **G**, which	*2316*
1Th	2:5	of covetousness; **G** is witness:	*2316*
1Th	2:8	gospel of **G** only, but also our own	*2316*
1Th	2:12	That ye would walk worthy of **G**.	*2316*
1Th	2:13	but as it is in truth, the word of **G**	*2316*
1Th	4:3	For this is the will of **G**, even	*2316*
1Th	4:5	as the Gentiles which know not **G**:	*2316*
1Th	4:7	For **G** hath not called us unto	*2316*
1Th	4:8	despiseth not man, but **G**, who	*2316*
1Th	4:14	which sleep in Jesus will **G** bring.	*2316*
1Th	5:18	for this is the will of **G** in Christ	*2316*
2Th	2:4	he as **G** sitteth in the temple of **G**	*2316*
2Th	2:11	**G** shall send them strong delusion	*2316*
2Th	2:13	**G** hath from the beginning chosen	*2316*
1Ti	1:11	glorious gospel of the blessed **G**,	*2316*
1Ti	1:17	the only wise **G**, be honour and	*2316*
1Ti	2:5	For there is one **G**, and one	*2316*
1Ti	2:5	one mediator between **G** and men,	*2316*
1Ti	3:15	behave thyself in the house of **G**	*2316*
1Ti	3:15	which is the church of the living **G**,	*2316*
1Ti	4:4	For every creature of **G** is good,	*2316*
1Ti	4:10	because we trust in the living **G**,	*2316*
1Ti	6:1	name of **G** and his doctrine be not	*2316*
1Ti	6:17	in the living **G**, who giveth us richly	*2316*
2Ti	1:6	that thou stir up the gift of **G**,	*2316*

2Ti	1:7	For **G** hath not given us the spirit	*2316*
2Ti	2:9	but the word of **G** is not bound	*2316*
2Ti	2:15	to shew thyself approved unto **G**,	*2316*
2Ti	2:19	the foundation of **G** standeth sure,	*2316*
2Ti	2:25	if **G** peradventure will give them	*2316*
2Ti	3:4	of pleasure more than lovers of **G**;	*5377*
2Ti	3:16	is given by inspiration of **G**,	*2315*
2Ti	3:17	That the man of **G** may be perfect,	*2316*
Tit	1:2	which **G**, that cannot lie, promised	*2316*
Tit	2:5	the word of **G** be not blasphemed	*2316*
Tit	2:10	the doctrine of **G** our Saviour	*2316*
Heb	1:1	**G**, who at sundry times and in	*2316*
Heb	1:6	all the angels of **G** worship him	*2316*
Heb	1:8	Thy throne, O **G**, is for ever and	*2316*
Heb	3:4	but he that built all things is **G**.	*2316*
Heb	3:12	in departing from the living **G**	*2316*
Heb	4:4	**G** did rest the seventh day from	*2316*
Heb	4:9	therefore a rest to the people of **G**	*2316*
Heb	4:12	For the word of **G** is quick, and	*2316*
Heb	6:1	dead works, and of faith toward **G**,	*2316*
Heb	6:3	And this will we do, if **G** permit	*2316*
Heb	6:5	have tasted the good word of **G**,	*2316*
Heb	6:10	For **G** is not unrighteous to forget	*2316*
Heb	6:18	it was impossible for **G** to lie,	*2316*
Heb	7:1	priest of the most high **G**, who	*2316*
Heb	7:3	but made like unto the Son of **G**;	*2316*
Heb	9:14	dead works to serve the living **G**?	*2316*
Heb	10:9	Lo, I come to do thy will, O **G**.	*2316*
Heb	10:29	trodden under foot the Son of **G**,	*2316*
Heb	10:31	fall into the hands of the living **G**	*2316*
Heb	10:36	after ye have done the will of **G**,	*2316*
Heb	11:3	were framed by the word of **G**.	*2316*
Heb	11:4	faith Abel offered unto **G** a more	*2316*
Heb	11:5	**G** had translated him: for before	*2316*
Heb	11:5	this testimony, that he pleased **G**.	*2316*
Heb	11:6	he that cometh to **G** must believe	*2316*
Heb	11:7	Noah, being warned of **G** of things	
Heb	11:10	whose builder and maker is **G**.	*2316*
Heb	11:16	wherefore **G** is not ashamed to be	*2316*
Heb	11:16	ashamed to be called their **G**:	*2316*
Heb	12:2	the right hand of the throne of **G**.	*2316*
Heb	12:7	**G** dealeth with you as with sons;	*2316*
Heb	12:22	and unto the city of the living **G**,	*2316*
Heb	12:23	and to **G** the Judge of all, and to	*2316*
Heb	12:28	serve **G** acceptably with reverence	*2316*
Heb	12:29	for our **G** is a consuming fire	*2316*
Heb	13:4	and adulterers **G** will judge	*2316*
Heb	13:7	spoken unto you the word of **G**:	*2316*
Heb	13:15	sacrifice of praise to **G** continually,	*2316*
Heb	13:16	such sacrifices **G** is well pleased	*2316*
Heb	13:20	Now the **G** of peace, that brought	*2316*
Jas	1:5	let him ask of **G**, that giveth to all	*2316*
Jas	1:13	he is tempted, I am tempted of **G**:	*2316*
Jas	1:13	for **G** cannot be tempted with evil,	*2316*
Jas	1:20	worketh not the righteousness of **G**,	*2316*
Jas	1:27	religion and undefiled before **G**	*2316*
Jas	2:19	Thou believest that there is one **G**;	*2316*
Jas	2:23	Abraham believed **G**, and it was	*2316*
Jas	2:23	and he was called the Friend of **G**,	*2316*
Jas	3:9	Therewith bless we **G**, even the	*2316*
Jas	3:9	are made after the similitude of **G**,	*2316*
Jas	4:4	of the world is enmity with **G**?	*2316*
Jas	4:4	of the world is the enemy of **G**	*2316*
Jas	4:6	**G** resisteth the proud, but giveth	*2316*
Jas	4:7	Submit yourselves therefore to **G**	*2316*
Jas	4:8	Draw nigh to **G**, and he will draw	*2316*
1Pe	1:2	foreknowledge of **G** the Father,	*2316*
1Pe	2:17	Fear **G**. Honour the king	*2316*
1Pe	2:19	if a man for conscience toward **G**	*2316*
1Pe	3:4	is in the sight of **G** of great price	*2316*
1Pe	3:5	holy women also, who trusted in **G**	*2316*
1Pe	3:15	the Lord **G** in your hearts: and	*2316*
1Pe	3:17	it is better, if the will of **G** be so,	*2316*
1Pe	3:21	of a good conscience toward **G**,)	*2316*
1Pe	3:22	and is on the right hand of **G**;	*2316*
1Pe	4:2	lusts of men, but to the will of **G**,	*2316*
1Pe	4:6	live according to **G** in the spirit	*2316*
1Pe	4:11	let him speak as the oracles of **G**;	*2316*
1Pe	4:11	as of the ability which **G** giveth:	*2316*
1Pe	4:16	let him glorify **G** on this behalf	*2316*
1Pe	4:17	must begin at the house of **G**:	*2316*
1Pe	4:17	that obey not the gospel of **G**?	*2316*
1Pe	5:2	Feed the flock of **G** which is among	*2316*
1Pe	5:5	**G** resisteth the proud, and giveth	*2316*
1Pe	5:6	under the mighty hand of **G**,	*2316*
1Pe	5:10	But the **G** of all grace, who hath	*2316*
2Pe	1:17	For he received from **G** the Father	*2316*
2Pe	1:21	holy men of **G** spake as they were	*2316*
2Pe	2:4	For if **G** spared not the angels that	*2316*
2Pe	3:5	that by the word of **G** the heavens	*2316*
2Pe	3:12	unto the coming of the day of **G**,	*2316*
1Jn	1:5	that **G** is light, and in him is no	*2316*
1Jn	2:5	verily is the love of **G** perfected:	*2316*
1Jn	2:14	and the word of **G** abideth in you,	*2316*
1Jn	2:17	doeth the will of **G** abideth for ever	*2316*
1Jn	3:1	should be called the sons of **G**:	*2316*
1Jn	3:2	now are we the sons of **G**, and	*2316*
1Jn	3:9	is born of **G** doth not commit sin;	*2316*
1Jn	3:9	sin, because he is born of **G**.	*2316*
1Jn	3:10	doeth not righteousness is not of **G**,	*2316*
1Jn	3:16	Hereby perceive we the love of **G**,	
1Jn	3:17	how dwelleth the love of **G** in him?	*2316*
1Jn	3:20	**G** is greater than our heart, and	*2316*
1Jn	4:2	Hereby know ye the Spirit of **G**:	*2316*
1Jn	4:2	Christ is come in the flesh is of **G**:	*2316*
1Jn	4:3	is come in the flesh is not of **G**:	*2316*
1Jn	4:4	Ye are of **G**, little children, and	*2316*
1Jn	4:6	We are of **G**: he that knoweth **G**	*2316*
1Jn	4:6	he that is not of **G** heareth not us	*2316*
1Jn	4:7	for love is of **G**; and every one that	*2316*
1Jn	4:7	loveth is born of **G**, and knoweth **G**	*2316*
1Jn	4:8	knoweth not **G**; for **G** is love	*2316*
1Jn	4:9	manifested the love of **G** toward us,	*2316*
1Jn	4:9	**G** sent his only begotten Son into	*2316*
1Jn	4:10	not that we loved **G**, but that he	*2316*
1Jn	4:11	if **G** so loved us, we ought also to	*2316*
1Jn	4:12	No man hath seen **G** at any time	*2316*
1Jn	4:12	**G** dwelleth in us, and his love is	*2316*
1Jn	4:15	that Jesus Christ is the Son of **G**,	*2316*
1Jn	4:15	**G** dwelleth in him, and he in **G**.	*2316*
1Jn	4:16	love that **G** hath to us. **G** is love;	*2316*
1Jn	4:16	dwelleth in **G**, and **G** in him	*2316*
1Jn	4:20	If a man say, I love **G**, and hateth,	*2316*
1Jn	4:20	he love **G** whom he hath not seen?	*2316*
1Jn	4:21	he who loveth **G** love his brother	*2316*
1Jn	5:1	Jesus is the Christ is born of **G**:	*2316*
1Jn	5:2	the children of **G**, when we love **G**,	*2316*
1Jn	5:3	For this is the love of **G**, that	*2316*
1Jn	5:4	is born of **G** overcometh the world:	*2316*
1Jn	5:5	that Jesus is the Son of **G**?	*2316*
1Jn	5:9	men, the witness of **G** is greater:	*2316*
1Jn	5:10	He that believeth on the Son of **G**	*2316*

1Jn	5:10	he that believeth not **G** hath made	*2316*
1Jn	5:10	the record that **G** gave of his Son	*2316*
1Jn	5:11	**G** hath given to us eternal life,	*2316*
1Jn	5:12	hath not the Son of **G** hath not life.	*2316*
1Jn	5:13	on the name of the Son of **G**;	*2316*
1Jn	5:13	believe on the name of the Son of **G**	*2316*
1Jn	5:18	whosoever is born of **G** sinneth	*2316*
1Jn	5:18	but he that is begotten of **G**	*2316*
1Jn	5:19	And we know that we are of **G**, and	*2316*
1Jn	5:20	we know that the Son of **G** is come,	*2316*
1Jn	5:20	This is the true **G**, and eternal life.	*2316*
2Jn	9	the doctrine of Christ, hath not **G**	*2316*
2Jn	10	house, neither bid him **G** speed:	
3Jn	11	He that doeth good is of **G**: but	*2316*
3Jn	11	he that doeth evil hath not seen **G**	*2316*
Jude	4	grace of our **G** into lasciviousness,	*2316*
Jude	4	and denying the only Lord **G**,	*2316*
Jude	21	Keep yourselves in the love of **G**,	*2316*
Jude	25	To the only wise **G** our Saviour,	*2316*
Rev	1:1	Revelation, which **G** gave unto him,	*2316*
Rev	2:7	**in the midst of the paradise of G,**	*2316*
Rev	2:18	**These things saith the Son of G,**	*2316*
Rev	3:1	**that hath the seven Spirits of G,**	*2316*
Rev	3:2	**found thy works perfect before G.**	*2316*
Rev	3:12	**a pillar in the temple of my G,**	*2316*
Rev	3:12	**upon him the name of my G,**	*2316*
Rev	3:14	**beginning of the creation of G;**	*2316*
Rev	4:5	which are the seven Spirits of **G**	*2316*
Rev	5:6	the seven Spirits of **G** sent forth	*2316*
Rev	5:9	and hast redeemed us to **G** by thy	*2316*
Rev	5:10	made us unto our **G** kings and priests	*2316*
Rev	6:9	that were slain for the word of **G**,	*2316*
Rev	7:2	having the seal of the living **G**:	*2316*
Rev	7:10	Salvation to our **G** which sitteth	*2316*
Rev	7:17	**G** shall wipe away all tears from	*2316*
Rev	8:2	seven angels which stood before **G**;	*2316*
Rev	9:4	not the seal of **G** in their foreheads.	*2316*
Rev	9:13	the golden altar which is before **G**,	*2316*
Rev	10:7	mystery of **G** should be finished	*2316*
Rev	11:11	the Spirit of life from **G** entered	*2316*
Rev	11:13	and gave glory to the **G** of heaven	*2316*
Rev	11:16	their faces, and worshipped **G**,	*2316*
Rev	11:17	O Lord **G** Almighty, which art, and	*2316*
Rev	11:19	temple of **G** was opened in heaven,	*2316*
Rev	12:10	kingdom of our **G**, and the power	*2316*
Rev	12:10	accused them before our **G** day	*2316*
Rev	12:17	keep the commandments of **G**	*2316*
Rev	13:6	his mouth in blasphemy against **G**,	*2316*
Rev	14:7	Fear **G**, and give glory to him;	*2316*
Rev	14:10	drink of the wine of the wrath of **G**,	*2316*
Rev	14:12	that keep the commandments of **G**,	*2316*
Rev	14:19	great winepress of the wrath of **G**.	*2316*
Rev	15:1	in them is filled up the wrath of **G**	*2316*
Rev	15:2	sea of glass, having the harps of **G**	*2316*
Rev	15:3	the song of Moses the servant of **G**,	*2316*
Rev	15:3	are thy works, Lord **G** Almighty;	*2316*
Rev	15:7	vials full of the wrath of **G**, who	*2316*
Rev	15:8	smoke from the glory of **G**, and	*2316*
Rev	16:1	out the vials of the wrath of **G**	*2316*
Rev	16:9	and blasphemed the name of **G**,	*2316*
Rev	16:11	And blasphemed the **G** of heaven	*2316*
Rev	16:14	of that great day of **G** Almighty	*2316*
Rev	16:21	men blasphemed **G** because of the	*2316*
Rev	17:17	For **G** hath put in their hearts	*2316*
Rev	17:17	the words of **G** shall be fulfilled	*2316*
Rev	18:5	**G** hath remembered her iniquities	*2316*
Rev	18:8	is the Lord **G** who judgeth her	*2316*
Rev	18:20	for **G** hath avenged you on her	*2316*
Rev	19:1	and power, unto the Lord our **G**:	*2316*
Rev	19:6	the Lord **G** omnipotent reigneth.	*2316*
Rev	19:9	These are the true sayings of **G**	*2316*
Rev	19:10	worship **G**: for the testimony of	*2316*
Rev	19:13	his name is called The Word of **G**.	*2316*
Rev	19:15	fierceness and wrath of Almighty **G**	*2316*
Rev	19:17	unto the supper of the great **G**;	*2316*
Rev	20:9	came down from **G** out of heaven,	*2316*
Rev	20:12	small and great, stand before **G**;	*2316*
Rev	21:2	coming down from **G** out of heaven,	*2316*
Rev	21:3	the tabernacle of **G** is with men,	*2316*
Rev	21:3	and **G** himself shall be with them,	*2316*
Rev	21:4	And **G** shall wipe away all tears	*2316*
Rev	21:22	Lord **G** Almighty and the Lamb	*2316*
Rev	21:23	for the glory of **G** did lighten it,	*2316*
Rev	22:1	the throne of **G** and of the Lamb.	*2316*
Rev	22:3	the throne of **G** and of the Lamb	*2316*
Rev	22:5	for the Lord **G** giveth them light:	*2316*
Rev	22:6	the Lord **G** of the holy prophets	*2316*
Rev	22:9	sayings of this book: worship **G**	*2316*
Rev	22:18	**G** shall add unto him the plagues	*2316*
Rev	22:19	**G** shall take away his part out of	*2316*

GODDESS

1Ki	11:33	Ashtoreth the **g** of the Zidonians,	430
Ac	19:27	the temple of the great **g** Diana	*2299*
Ac	19:37	nor yet blasphemers of your **g**.	*2299*

GODHEAD

Ac	17:29	think that the **G** is like unto gold,	*2304*
Ro	1:20	even his eternal power and **G**;	*2305*
Col	2:9	all the fulness of the **G** bodily.	*2320*

GODLINESS See also UNGODLINESS.

1Ti	2:2	life in all **g** and honesty.	*2150*
1Ti	2:10	becometh women professing **g**)	*2317*
1Ti	3:16	great is the mystery of **g**: God	*2150*
1Ti	4:7	and exercise thyself rather unto **g**	*2150*
1Ti	4:8	but **g** is profitable unto all things,	*2150*
1Ti	6:3	doctrine which is according to **g**;	*2150*
1Ti	6:5	supposing that gain is **g**: from such	*2150*
1Ti	6:6	**g** with contentment is great gain.	*2150*
1Ti	6:11	follow after righteousness, **g**, faith,	*2150*
2Ti	3:5	Having a form of **g**, but denying	*2150*
2Pe	1:3	pertain unto life and **g**, through	*2150*
2Pe	1:6	patience; and to patience **g**;	*2150*
2Pe	1:7	And to **g** brotherly kindness;	*2150*
2Pe	3:11	in all holy conversation and **g**,	*2150*

GODLY See also UNGODLY.

Ps	12:1	Help, Lord; for the **g** man ceaseth;	2623
Ps	32:6	this shall every one that is **g** pray	2623
Mal	2:15	That he might seek a **g** seed.	430
2Co	1:12	simplicity and **g** sincerity, not	*2316*
2Co	7:10	**g** sorrow worketh repentance	*2596, 2316*
2Co	11:2	jealous over you with **g** jealousy:	*2596, 2316*
1Ti	1:4	questions, rather than **g** edifying.	*2316*
2Ti	3:12	all that will live **g** in Christ Jesus	*2153*
Tit	2:12	live soberly, righteously, and **g**.	*2153*
2Pe	2:9	knoweth how to deliver the **g** out	*2152*

GOD'S

Nu	22:22	And **G** anger was kindled because	430
2Ch	20:15	for the battle is not your's, but **G**	430
Ne	10:29	to walk in **G** law which was given	430
Job	33:6	according to thy wish in **G** stead:	410

Job	35:2	My righteousness is more than **G**?	410
Mt	5:34	**by heaven; for it is G throne:**	*2316*
Mt	22:21	**unto God the things that are G.**	*2316*
Lk	18:29	**for the kingdom of G sake,**	*2316*
Jn	8:47	**that is of God heareth G words:**	*2316*
Ro	8:33	thing to the charge of **G** elect?	*2316*
Ro	10:3	being ignorant of **G** righteousness,	*2316*
1Co	3:9	Ye are **G** husbandry, ye are **G** building,	*2316*
1Co	3:23	ye are Christ's; and Christ is **G**.	*2316*
1Co	6:20	body, and in your spirit, which are **G**.	*2316*
1Pe	5:3	as being lords over **G** heritage,	*2316*

GODS

Ge	3:5	ye shall be as **g**, knowing good	430
Ge	31:30	wherefore hast thou stolen my **g**?	430
Ge	35:2	the strange **g** that are among you,	430
Ge	35:4	gave unto Jacob all the strange **g**.	430
Ex	12:12	all the **g** of Egypt I will execute	430
Ex	18:11	the Lord is greater than all **g**:	430
Ex	20:3	shalt have no other **g** before me	430
Ex	23:13	mention of the name of other **g**,	430
Ex	23:24	Thou shalt not bow down to their **g**,	430
Ex	32:23	Make us **g**, which shall go before	430
Ex	34:15	and they go a whoring after their **g**,	430
Ex	34:16	thy sons go a whoring after their **g**,	430
Ex	34:17	Thou shalt make thee no molten **g**.	430
Le	19:4	nor make to yourselves molten **g**:	430
Dt	5:7	Thou shalt have none other **g** before	430
Dt	6:14	the **g** of the people which are round	430
Dt	12:3	down the graven images of their **g**,	430
Dt	12:30	enquire not after their **g**, saying,	430
Dt	12:30	did these nations serve their **g**?	430
Dt	12:31	have burnt in the fire to their **g**.	430
Dt	13:6	Let us go and serve other **g**, which	430
Dt	13:7	the **g** of the people which are round	430
Dt	13:13	Let us go and serve other **g**, which	430
Dt	18:20	shall speak in the name of other **g**,	430
Dt	28:36	shalt thou serve other **g**, wood and	430
Dt	29:26	For they went and served other **g**,	430
Dt	29:26	them, **g** whom they knew not, and	430
Dt	31:16	whoring after the **g** of the strangers	430
Jos	22:22	Lord God of **g**, the Lord God of **g**,	430
Jos	24:16	forsake the Lord, to serve other **g**;	430
Jgs	2:3	their **g** shall be a snare unto you.	430
Jgs	5:8	They chose new **g**; then was war	430
Jgs	10:14	unto the **g** which ye have chosen;	430
Jgs	10:16	And they put away the strange **g**.	430
Jgs	18:24	taken away my **g** which I made,	430
Ru	1:15	unto her people, and unto her **g**:	430
1Sa	4:8	out of the hand of these mighty **G**?	430
1Sa	17:43	Philistine cursed David by his **g**	430
1Sa	28:13	saw **g** ascending out of the earth.	430
1Ki	9:9	and have taken hold upon other **g**,	430
1Ki	11:4	turned away his heart after other **g**:	430
1Ki	18:24	call ye on the name of your **g**,	430
1Ki	19:2	So let the **g** do to me, and more	430
1Ki	20:10	The **g** do so unto me, and more	430
1Ki	20:23	Their **g** are **g** of the hills;	430
2Ki	17:29	every nation made **g** of their own,	430
2Ki	18:33	Hath any of the **g** of the nations	430
2Ki	19:12	Have the **g** of the nations delivered	430
2Ki	19:18	And have cast their **g** into the fire:	430
2Ki	19:18	for they were no **g**, but the work	430
1Ch	16:25	he also is to be feared above all **g**	430
2Ch	2:5	for great is our God above all **g**.	430
2Ch	28:25	to burn incense unto other **g**, and	430
2Ch	34:25	have burned incense unto other **g**,	430
Ezr	1:7	had put them in the house of his **g**;	430
Ps	82:6	I have said, Ye are **g**; and all of you	430
Ps	86:8	Among the **g** there is none like unto	430
Ps	95:3	and a great King above all **g**.	430
Ps	96:4	he is to be feared above all **g**.	430
Ps	97:9	thou art exalted far above all **g**.	430
Isa	37:19	And have cast their **g** into the fire:	430
Jer	2:11	changed their **g**, which are yet no **g**?	430
Jer	7:6	walk after other **g** to your hurt:	430
Jer	7:9	after other **g** whom ye know not;	430
Jet	10:11	**g** that have not made the heavens	426
Jer	16:13	there shall ye serve other **g** day and	430
Jer	16:20	unto himself, and they are no **g**?	430
Jer	35:15	and go not after other **g** to serve	430
Jer	44:5	to burn no incense unto other **g**.	430
Da	2:47	your God is a God of **g**, and a Lord	426
Da	3:12	they serve not thy **g**, nor worship	426
Da	4:9	the spirit of the holy **g** is in thee,	426
Da	5:4	praised the **g** of gold, and of silver,	426
Da	5:11	in whom is the spirit of the holy **g**;	426
Da	11:36	things against the God of **g**, and	410
Hos	3:1	look to other **g**, and love flagons	430
Hos	14:3	work of our hands, Ye are our **g**	430
Na	1:14	out of the house of thy **g** will I	430
Jn	10:34	**in your law, I said, Ye are g?**	*2316*
Jn	10:35	**If he called them g, unto whom**	*2316*
Ac	7:40	Make us **g** to go before us: for as	*2316*
Ac	19:26	that they be no **g**, which are made	*2316*
Gal	4:8	them which by nature are no **g**	*2316*

GOD-WARD

Ex	18:19	Be thou for the people to **G**,	4136, 430
2Co	3:4	have we through Christ to **G**.	*4314, 2316*
1Th	1:8	your faith to **G** is spread	*4314, 2316*

GOEST

Ge	28:15	thee in all places whither thou **g**,	3212
Ge	32:17	Whose art thou? and whither **g**.	3212
Ex	34:12	the land whither thou **g**, lest it be	935
Dt	7:1	land whither thou **g** to possess it,	935
Dt	11:10	land, whither thou **g** in to possess	935
Dt	12:29	before thee, whither thou **g** to	935
Dt	20:1	When thou **g** out to battle against	3318
Dt	21:10	When thou **g** forth to war against	3318
Dt	28:6	blessed shalt thou be when thou **g** out.	3318
Dt	28:19	cursed shalt thou be when thou **g** out.	3318
Dt	30:16	land whither thou **g** to possess it.	935
Dt	32:50	in the mount whither thou **g** up,	5927
Jos	1:7	prosper whithersoever thou **g**.	3212
Jos	1:9	with thee whithersoever thou **g**	3212
Jgs	19:17	old man said, Whither **g** thou?	3212
Ru	1:16	for whither thou **g**, I will go;	3212
1Sa	28:22	strength, when thou **g** on thy way.	3212
Ps	44:9	and **g** not forth with our armies.	3318
Pr	4:12	When thou **g**, thy steps shall not.	3212
Pr	6:22	When thou **g**, it shall lead thee;	1980
Ecc	5:1	when thou **g** to the house of God,	3212
Ecc	9:10	in the grave, whither thou **g**	1980
Zec	2:2	Whither **g** thou? And he said.	1980
Mt	8:19	follow thee whithersoever thou **g**	*565*
Lk	9:57	follow thee whithersoever thou **g**	*565*
Lk	12:58	**When thou g with thine adversary**	*5217*
Jn	13:36	Lord, whither **g** thou? Jesus	*5217*
Jn	14:5	Lord, we know not whither thou **g**.	*5217*
Jn	16:5	**you asketh me, Whither g thou?**	*5217*

GOETH

Book	Ref	Context	No.
Ex	7:15	he **g** out unto the water; and thou	3318
Ex	28:29	when he **g** in unto the holy place,	935
Le	11:27	And whatsoever **g** upon his paws,	1980
Le	11:42	Whatsoever **g** upon the belly, and	1980
Le	11:42	and whatsoever **g** upon all four,	1980
Le	22:3	that **g** unto the holy things,	7126
Nu	5:29	when a wife **g** aside to another	7847
Dt	11:30	where the sun **g** down, in the	3996
Dt	20:4	God is he that **g** with you, to	1980
Dt	24:13	when the sun **g** down, that he may	935
Jgs	5:31	sun when he **g** forth in his might	3318
Jgs	20:31	one **g** up to the house of God,	5927
2Ki	5:18	when my master **g** into the house	935
Job	37:2	the sound that **g** out of his mouth.	3318
Job	41:20	Out of his nostrils **g** smoke, as out	3318
Job	41:21	and a flame **g** out of his mouth	3318
Ps	41:6	when he **g** abroad, he telleth it	3318
Ps	97:3	A fire **g** before him, and burneth	3212
Ps	126:6	He that **g** forth and weepeth,	3212
Pr	6:29	that **g** in to his neighbour's wife;	935
Pr	7:22	He **g** after her straightway,	1980
Pr	7:22	as an ox **g** to the slaughter,	925
Pr	11:10	When it **g** well with the righteous,	
Pr	16:18	Pride **g** before destruction, and an	
Pr	20:19	He that **g** about as a talebearer	1980
Pr	26:20	no wood is, there the fire **g** out:	3518
Pr	31:18	her candle **g** not out by night.	3518
Ecc	3:21	the spirit of man that **g** upward,	5927
Ecc	3:21	of the beast that **g** downward	3381
Ecc	12:5	because man **g** to his long home,	1980
Isa	55:11	So shall my word be that **g** forth	3318
Jer	6:4	the day **g** away, for the shadows	6437
Jer	22:10	weep sore for him that **g** away:	1980
Eze	7:14	but none **g** to the battle: for my	1980
Hos	6:4	as the early dew it **g** away	1980
Zec	5:3	This is the curse that **g** forth.	3318
Mt	8:9	say to this man; Go, and he **g**	*4198*
Mt	13:44	**and for joy thereof g and selleth**	*5217*
Mt	15:11	**that which g into the mouth**	*1525*
Mt	15:17	**g into the belly, and is cast out**	*5562*
Mt	17:21	**this kind g not out but by prayer**	*1607*
Mt	26:24	**The Son of man g as it is written**	*5217*
Mk	14:21	**The Son of man indeed g, as it is**	*5217*
Lk	7:8	I say unto one, Go, and he **g**;	*4198*
Lk	22:22	**the Son of man g, as it was**	*4198*
Jn	3:8	**it cometh, and whither it g:**	*5217*
Jn	7:20	devil: who **g** about to kill thee?	*2212*
Jn	10:4	**he g before them, and the sheep**	*4198*
Jn	12:35	**knoweth not whither he g**	*5217*
1Co	6:6	But brother **g** to law with brother,	
Jas	1:24	beholdeth himself, and **g** his way,	*565*
1Jn	2:11	and knoweth not whither he **g**,	*5217*
Rev	14:4	the Lamb whithersoever he **g**.	*5217*
Rev	17:11	and **g** into perdition.	*5217*
Rev	19:15	his mouth **g** a sharp sword,	*1607*

GOING

Book	Ref	Context	No.
Ge	15:12	And when the sun was **g** down,	935
Ex	17:12	until the **g** down of the sun.	935
Ex	23:4	enemy's ox or his ass **g** astray,	8582
Ex	37:19	branches **g** out of the candlestick	3318
Le	11:20	that creep, **g** upon all four	1980
Dt	16:6	at the **g** down of the sun, at the	935
Jos	6:11	**g** about it once: and they came	5362
Jos	10:27	the time of the **g** down of the sun,	935
Jos	23:14	I am **g** the way of all the earth:	1980
Jgs	19:18	now **g** to the house of the Lord;	1980
1Sa	10:3	meet thee three men **g** up to God	5927
1Sa	29:6	thy **g** out and thy coming in with	3318
2Sa	3:25	know thy **g** out and thy coming in,	4161
2Ch	18:34	the time of the sun **g** down he	935
Ne	3:32	**g** up of the corner unto the sheep	5944
Job	1:7	From **g** to and fro in the earth,	7751
Job	2:2	From **g** to and fro in the earth, and	7751
Ps	19:6	His **g** forth is from the end of	4161
Ps	50:1	the sun unto the **g** down thereof	3996
Ps	104:19	the sun knoweth his **g** down	3996
Ps	113:3	unto the **g** down of the same.	3996
Pr	7:27	**g** down to the chambers of death.	3381
Pr	14:15	prudent man looketh well to his **g**	838
Pr	30:29	go well, yea, four are comely in **g**:	3212
Isa	13:10	shall be darkened in his **g** forth,	3318
Isa	37:28	I know thy abode, and thy **g** out,	3318
Eze	40:37	**g** up to it had eight steps,	4608
Da	6:14	laboured till the **g** down of the sun	4606
Da	9:25	the **g** forth of the commandment	4161
Mal	1:11	unto the **g** down of the same.	3996
Mt	26:46	**Rise, let us be g: behold, he**	*71*
Mk	6:31	there were many coming and **g**,	*5217*
Lk	14:31	**g to make war against another**	*4198*
Ac	9:28	coming in and **g** out at Jerusalem,	*1607*
1Ti	5:24	**g** before to judgment; and some	*4254*
1Pe	2:25	ye were as sheep **g** astray;	*4105*

GOINGS See also OUTGOINGS.

Book	Ref	Context	No.
Nu	33:2	journeys according to their **g** out,	4161
Jos	16:8	the **g** out thereof were at the sea	8444
Ps	40:2	a rock, and established my **g**	838
Pr	5:21	and he pondereth all his **g**	4570
Pr	20:24	Man's **g** are of the Lord; how	4703
Isa	59:8	there is no judgment in their **g**	4570
Mic	5:2	whose **g** forth have been from of	4163

GOLD See also GOLDSMITH.

Book	Ref	Context	No.
Ge	2:12	And the **g** of that land is good:	2091
Ge	13:2	in cattle, in silver, and in **g**.	2091
Ge	24:35	flocks, and herds, and silver, and **g**,	2091
Ge	24:53	jewels of silver, and jewels of **g**,	2091
Ge	41:42	put a **g** chain about his neck;	2091
Ge	44:8	out of thy lord's house silver or **g**?	2091
Ex	3:22	jewels of silver, and jewels of **g**,	2091
Ex	20:23	Shall ye make unto you gods of **g**.	2091
Ex	25:11	make upon it a crown of **g** round.	2091
Ex	25:17	make a mercy seat of pure **g**:	2091
Ex	25:18	cherubims of **g**, of beaten work	2091
Ex	25:31	shalt make a candlestick of pure **g**:	2091
Ex	28:26	And thou shalt make two rings of **g**,	2091
Ex	32:31	and have made them gods of **g**	2091
Ex	39:25	and they made bells of pure **g**, and	2091
Ex	39:30	of the holy crown of pure **g**,	2091
Dt	7:25	shalt not desire the silver or **g** that	2091
Dt	17:17	multiply to himself silver and **g**	2091
2Sa	8:7	And David took the shields of **g**	2091
2Sa	8:11	Silver and **g** that he had dedicated	2091
1Ki	10:14	weight of **g** that came to Solomon	2091
1Ki	10:16	two hundred targets of beaten **g**:	2091
1Ki	10:18	and overlaid it with the best **g**.	2091
1Ki	12:28	made two calves of **g**, and said	2091
1Ki	20:3	Thy silver and thy **g** is mine; thy	2091
2Ki	12:13	vessels of **g**, or vessels of silver,	2091
2Ki	16:8	Ahaz took the silver and **g** that	2091

2Ki 24:13	cut in pieces all the vessels of **g**	2091
1Ch 18:7	And David took the shields of **g**	2091
1Ch 29:5	The **g** for things of **g**, and the silver	2091
2Ch 4:21	made he of **g**, and that perfect **g**;	2091
2Ch 9:14	brought **g** and silver to Solomon	2091
2Ch 9:17	ivory, and overlaid it with pure **g**	2091
2Ch 9:18	with a footstool of **g**, which were	2091
2Ch 9:20	vessels of king Solomon were of **g**,	2091
2Ch 12:9	carried away also the shields of **g**	2091
2Ch 25:24	he took all the **g** and the silver,	2091
Ezr 8:28	the silver and the **g** are a freewill	2091
Est 1:6	the beds were of **g** and silver,	2091
Est 8:15	with a great crown of **g**, and with	2091
Job 28:15	It cannot be gotten for **g**,	5458
Job 31:24	If I have made **g** my hope,	2091
Ps 19:10	More to be desired are they than **g**,	2091
Ps 19:10	yea, than much fine **g**:	6337
Ps 21:3	thou settest a crown of pure **g** on	6337
Ps 119:72	better unto me than thousands of **g**.	2091
Ps 119:127	love thy commandments above **g**;	2091
Ps 119:127	yea, above fine **g**	6337
Pr 3:14	and the gain thereof than fine **g**,	2742
Pr 8:10	knowledge rather than choice **g**	2742
Pr 8:19	My fruit is better than **g**;	2742
Pr 8:19	yea, than fine **g**; and my	6337
Pr 11:22	a jewel of **g** in a swine's snout,	2091
Pr 16:16	better is it to get wisdom than **g**!	2742
Pr 22:1	favour rather than silver and **g**	2091
Pr 25:11	apples of **g** in pictures of silver.	2091
Pr 25:12	As an earring of **g**, and	2091
Pr 25:12	an ornament of fine **g**, so is a	3800
Ecc 2:81	gathered me also silver and **g**,	2091
SS 5:11	His head is as the most fine **g**,	6337
Isa 2:7	land also is full of silver and **g**,	2091
Isa 13:12	a man more precious than fine **g**;	6337
Isa 31:7	idols of silver, and his idols of **g**:	2091
La 4:1	How is the **g** become dim!	2091
La 4:1	how is the most fine **g** changed!	3800
La 4:2	sons of Zion, comparable to fine **g**,	6337
Da 2:32	This image's head was of fine **g**,	1722
Da 2:38	Thou art this head of **g**	1722
Da 3:1	the king made an image of **g**, whose	1722
Da 5:4	and praised the gods of **g**, and of	1722
Da 5:23	praised the gods of silver, and **g**,	1722
Da 5:29	and put a chain of **g** about his neck,	1722
Da 11:8	precious vessels of silver and of **g**;	2091
Da 11:43	have power over the treasures of **g**	2091
Hos 2:8	multiplied her silver and **g**, which	2091
Joel 3:5	ye have taken my silver and my **g**,	2091
Hab 2:19	it is laid over with **g** and silver,	2091
Zep 1:18	Neither their silver nor their **g**.	2091
Hag 2:8	The silver is mine, and the **g**	2091
Zec 13:9	and will try them as **g** is tried:	2091
Mal 3:3	and purge them as **g** and silver,	2091
Mt 10:9	**Provide neither g, nor silver, nor**	*5557*
Mt 23:16	**swear by the g of the temple,**	*5557*
Mt 23:17	**temple that sanctifieth the g?**	*5557*
Ac 3:6	said, Silver and **g** have I none;	*5553*
Ac 17:29	that the Godhead is like unto **g**,	*5557*
Ac 20:33	have coveted no man's silver, or **g**,	*5555*
1Co 3:12	upon this foundation **g**, silver,	*5557*
2Ti 2:20	not only vessels of **g** and of silver,	*5552*
1Pe 1:7	much more precious than of **g**	*5555*
1Pe 1:18	corruptible things, as silver and **g**,	*5553*
1Pe 3:3	the hair, and of wearing of **g**,	*5553*
Rev 3:18	**to buy of me g tried in the fire,**	*5553*
Rev 4:4	had on their heads crowns of **g**	*5552*
Rev 9:7	were as it were crowns like **g**,	*5557*
Rev 9:20	devils, and idols of **g**, and	*5552*
Rev 17:4	decked with **g** and precious	*5557*
Rev 18:12	The merchandise of **g**, and silver,	*5557*
Rev 18:16	decked with **g**, and precious stones,	*5557*
Rev 21:18	and the city was pure **g**, like unto	*5553*
Rev 21:21	the street of the city was pure **g**,	*5553*

GOLDEN

Ge 24:22	the man took a **g** earring of half a	2091
Ex 25:25	thou shalt make a **g** crown to the	2091
Ex 39:38	the **g** altar, and the anointing oil,	2091
Ex 40:26	he put the **g** altar in the tent	2091
Nu 4:11	upon the **g** altar they shall spread	2091
Jgs 8:26	the weight of the **g** earrings that he	2091
2Ch 4:19	the **g** altar also, and the tables	2091
Est 4:11	king shall hold out the **g** sceptre,	2091
Est 5:2	held out to Esther the **g** sceptre.	2091
Est 8:4	out the **g** sceptre toward Esther.	2091
Ecc 12:6	be loosed, or the **g** bowl be broken,	2091
Da 3:10	fall down and worship the **g** image:	1722
Da 3:18	worship the **g** image which thou.	1722
Da 5:2	commanded to bring the **g** and	1722
Heb 9:4	Which had the **g** censer, and the	*5552*
Rev 1:12	turned, I saw seven **g** candlesticks;	5552
Rev 1:13	about the paps with a **g** girdle.	5552
Rev 2:1	**midst of the seven g candlesticks;**	*5552*
Rev 5:8	harps, and **g** vials full of odours,	*5552*
Rev 8:3	having a **g** censer; and there was	*5552*
Rev 8:3	upon the **g** altar which was before	*5552*
Rev 9:13	from the four horns of the **g** altar	*5552*
Rev 14:14	having on his head a **g** crown,	*5552*
Rev 15:6	their breasts girded with **g** girdles	*5552*
Rev 15:7	seven **g** vials full of the wrath of	*5552*
Rev 17:4	having a **g** cup in her hand full	*5552*
Rev 21:15	had a **g** reed to measure the city,	*5552*

GOLDSMITH

Isa 40:19	and the **g** spreadeth it over with	6884
Isa 46:6	and hire a **g**; and he maketh it.	6884

GOLDSMITHS

Ne 3:32	repaired the **g** and the merchants.	6884

GONE See also AGONE.

Ge 27:30	Jacob was yet scarce **g** out from	3318
Ge 44:4	when they were **g** out of the city,	3318
Ex 9:29	As soon as I am **g** out of the city,	3318
Le 17:7	whom they have **g** a whoring.	
Nu 5:20	if thou hast **g** aside to another.	7847
Nu 16:46	is wrath **g** out from the Lord;	3318
Dt 17:3	hath **g** and served other gods,	3212
Dt 23:23	That which is **g** out of thy lips.	4161
Dt 27:4	when ye be **g** over Jordan, that	5674
Dt 32:36	he seeth that their power is **g**.	235
Jos 4:23	before us, until we were **g** over:	5674
Jos 23:16	have **g** and served other gods,	1980
Jgs 4:14	is not the Lord **g** out before thee?	3318
Ru 1:13	hand of the Lord is **g** out against	3318
2Sa 3:22	him away, and he was **g** in peace.	3212
2Sa 3:24	sent him away, and he is quite **g**?	3212
2Sa 17:20	They be **g** over the brook of water	5674
2Ki 1:6	bed on which thou art **g** up,	5927
Job 1:5	the days of their feasting were **g**	5362
Ps 19:4	line is **g** out through all the earth,	3318
Ps 38:4	mine iniquities are **g** over mine	5674

Ps	42:4	I had **g** with the multitude,	5674
Ps	47:5	God is **g** up with a shout, the Lord	5927
Ps	77:8	Is his mercy clean **g** for ever?	656
Ps	89:34	nor alter the thing that is **g** out	4161
Ps	103:16	wind passeth over it, and it is **g**;	369
Ps	109:23	I am **g** like the shadow when it	1980
Ps	119:176	I have **g** astray like a lost sheep;	8582
Ps	124:4	the stream had **g** over our soul:	5674
Pr	7:19	he is **g** a long journey:	1980
Pr	20:14	but when he is **g** his way, then he	235
SS	2:11	is past, the rain is over and **g**;	1980
SS	6:2	beloved is **g** down into his garden,	3381
Isa	38:8	is **g** down in the sun dial of Ahaz,	3381
Isa	45:23	the word is **g** out of my mouth	3318
Isa	51:5	my salvation is **g** forth, and mine	3318
Isa	53:6	All we like sheep have **g** astray;	8582
Isa	57:8	to another than me, and art **g** up;	5927
Jer	2:23	I have not **g** after Baalim? see	1980
Jer	14:2	and the cry of Jerusalem is **g** up	5927
Jer	23:19	a whirlwind of the Lord is **g** forth	3318
La	1:5	her children are **g** into captivity	1980
La	1:18	young men are **g** into captivity.	1980
Eze	9:3	glory of the God of Israel was **g**	5927
Eze	32:24	which are **g** down uncircumcised.	3381
Eze	32:27	**g** down to hell with their weapons	3381
Da	2:5	The thing is **g** from me: if ye will	230
Am	8:5	When will the new moon be **g**,	5674
Jnh	1:5	Jonah was **g** down into the sides	3381
Mt	12:43	**unclean spirit is g out of a man,**	*1831*
Mt	18:12	**and one of them be g astray,**	*4105*
Mt	25:8	**oil; for our lamps are g out**	*4570*
Mk	7:29	**the devil is g out of thy daughter**	*1831*
Lk	8:46	**that virtue is g out of me.**	*1831*
Lk	11:14	when the devil was **g** out, the	*1831*
Lk	11:24	unclean spirit is **g** out of a man	*1831*
Lk	24:28	though he would have **g** further	*4198*
Jn	12:19	behold, the world is **g** after him	*565*
Ac	27:28	when they had **g** a little further,	*1339*
Ro	3:12	They are all **g** out of the way,	*1578*
1Pe	3:22	Who is **g** into heaven, and is on	*4198*
2Pe	2:15	and are **g** astray, following the	*4105*
1Jn	4:1	false prophets are **g** out into the	*1831*
Jude	11	they have **g** in the way of Cain,	*4198*

GOOD See also BEST; BETTER; GOODMAN.

Ge	1:4	God saw the light, that it was **g**:	2896
Ge	1:10	God saw that it was **g**.	2896
Ge	1:12	God saw that it was **g**.	2896
Ge	1:18	God saw that it was **g**.	2896
Ge	1:21	God saw that it was **g**.	2896
Ge	1:25	God saw that it was **g**.	2896
Ge	1:31	made, and, behold, it was very **g**.	2896
Ge	2:9	pleasant to the sight and **g** for food;	2896
Ge	2:9	tree of knowledge of **g** and evil	2896
Ge	2:12	And the gold of that land is **g**:	2896
Ge	2:17	tree of the knowledge of **g** and evil,	2896
Ge	2:18	not **g** that the man should be alone;	2896
Ge	3:5	be as gods, knowing **g** and evil	2896
Ge	3:6	saw that the tree was **g** for food,	2896
Ge	3:22	to know **g** and evil: and now, lest	2896
Ge	19:8	do ye to them as is **g** in your eyes;	2896
Ge	24:50	cannot speak unto thee bad or **g**.	2896
Ge	31:29	not to Jacob either **g** or bad	2896
Ge	32:12	saidst, I will surely do thee **g**,	3190
Ge	41:24	thin ears devoured the seven **g**	2896
Ge	41:26	The seven **g** kine are seven years;	2896
Ge	41:26	and the seven **g** ears are seven	2896
Ge	41:47	was **g** in the eyes of Pharaoh,	3190
Ge	44:4	have ye rewarded evil for **g**?	2896
Ge	45:20	for the **g** of all the land of Egypt	2898
Ge	46:29	and wept on his neck a **g** while	5750
Ge	50:20	God meant it unto **g**, to bring to	2896
Ex	18:17	The thing that thou doest is not **g**	2896
Ex	22:14	he shall surely make it **g**.	7999
Ex	22:15	he shall not make it **g**:	7999
Le	5:4	to do evil, or to do **g**, whatsoever	3190
Le	27:10	nor change it, a **g** for a bad,	2896
Le	27:10	or a bad for a **g**:	2896
Le	27:14	estimate it, whether it be **g** or bad:	2896
Nu	23:19	and shall he not make it **g**?	6965
Dt	1:35	evil generation see that **g** land,	2896
Dt	1:39	no knowledge between **g** and evil,	2896
Dt	4:21	should not go in unto that **g** land,	2896
Dt	4:22	go over, and possess that **g** land	2896
Dt	8:16	to do thee **g** at thy latter end;	3190
Dt	30:15	before thee this day life and **g**,	2896
Dt	31:6	Be strong and of a **g** courage, fear not.	
Jos	1:8	then thou shalt have **g** success.	
Jos	1:18	only be strong, and of a **g** courage;	
Jos	21:45	failed not ought of any **g** thing	2896
Jos	23:13	perish from off this **g** land which	2896
1Sa	1:23	Do what seemeth thee **g**; tarry	2896
1Sa	2:24	for it is no **g** report that I hear:	2896
1Sa	3:18	let him do what seemeth him **g**	2896
1Sa	24:19	the Lord reward thee **g** for that	2896
1Sa	25:21	and he hath requited me evil for **g**.	2896
2Sa	13:22	brother Amnon neither **g** nor bad:	2896
2Sa	14:17	the king to discern **g** and bad:	2896
2Sa	16:12	will requite me **g** for his cursing.	2896
2Sa	19:35	can I discern between **g** and evil?	2896
1Ki	3:9	may discern between **g** and bad:	2896
1Ki	8:36	teach them the **g** way wherein they	2896
1Ki	8:56	one word of all his **g** promise,	2896
1Ki	22:8	not prophesy **g** concerning me,	2896
1Ch	19:13	do that which is **g** in his sight	2896
1Ch	28:20	Be strong, and of **g** courage; and do it:	
2Ch	18:7	for he never prophesied **g** unto me,	2896
2Ch	30:18	The **g** Lord pardon every one	2896
Ezr	3:11	because he is **g**, for his mercy	2896
Ezr	7:9	according to the **g** hand of his God	2896
Ezr	10:4	be of **g** courage, and do it	
Ne	2:8	to the **g** hand of my God upon me.	2896
Ne	5:19	Think upon me, my God, for **g**,	2896
Ne	9:20	Thou gavest also thy **g** spirit to	2896
Ne	13:14	and wipe not out my **g** deeds	2617
Ne	13:31	Remember me, O my God, for **g**	2896
Est	5:4	If it seem **g** unto the king,	2895
Est	9:22	and from mourning into a **g** day:	2896
Job	2:10	we receive **g** at the hand of God,	2896
Job	7:7	mine eye shall no more see **g**.	2896
Job	24:21	and doeth not **g** to the widow.	3190
Job	30:26	I looked for **g**, then evil came	2896
Ps	14:1	works, there is none that doeth **g**	2896
Ps	14:3	filthy: there is none that doeth **g**,	2896
Ps	34:8	taste and see that the Lord is **g**:	2896
Ps	34:10	Lord shall not want any **g** thing	2896
Ps	34:14	Depart from evil, and do **g**; seek	2896
Ps	35:12	They rewarded me evil for **g** to the	2896
Ps	36:4	himself in a way that is not **g**;	2896
Ps	37:3	Trust in the Lord, and do **g**:	2896
Ps	37:23	The steps of a **g** man are ordered	
Ps	37:27	Depart from evil, and do **g**; and	2896

Ps	38:20	They also that render evil for **g**.	2896
Ps	45:1	My heart is inditing a **g** matter:	2896
Ps	52:3	Thou lovest evil more than **g**;	2896
Ps	53:1	iniquity: there is none that doeth **g**	2896
Ps	53:3	filthy: there is none that doeth **g**.	2896
Ps	73:1	Truly God is **g** to Israel,	2896
Ps	84:11	no **g** thing will he withhold from	2896
Ps	100:5	For the Lord is **g**; his mercy is	2896
Ps	103:5	thy mouth with **g** things: so that.	2896
Ps	106:1	for he is **g**: for his mercy endureth	2896
Ps	107:1	for he is **g**: for his mercy endureth	2896
Ps	109:5	have rewarded me evil for **g**,	2896
Ps	111:10	a **g** understanding have all they.	2896
Ps	118:29	for he is **g**; for his mercy endureth	2896
Ps	143:10	thy spirit is **g**; lead me into the	2896
Ps	145:9	The Lord is **g** to all: and his tender.	2896
Pr	2:20	mayest walk in the way of **g** men	2896
Pr	3:27	Withhold not **g** from them to whom	2896
Pr	4:2	For I give you **g** doctrine,	2896
Pr	11:17	merciful man doeth **g** to his own soul.	1580
Pr	11:23	desire of the righteous is only **g**:	2896
Pr	12:2	A **g** man obtaineth favour of the	2896
Pr	12:14	A man shall be satisfied with **g**	2896
Pr	13:22	A **g** man leaveth an inheritance.	2896
Pr	14:19	The evil bow before the **g**; and the	2896
Pr	15:3	beholding the evil and the **g**	2896
Pr	17:13	Whoso rewarded evil for **g**, evil	2896
Pr	17:20	hath a froward heart findeth no **g**:	2896
Pr	17:22	A merry heart doeth **g** like a	3190
Pr	17:26	Also to punish the just is not **g**,	2896
Pr	18:5	It is not **g** to accept the person of	2896
Pr	18:22	findeth a wife findeth a **g** thing,	2896
Pr	20:23	and a false balance is not **g**.	2896
Pr	22:1	**g** name is rather to be chosen than	
Pr	25:25	so is **g** news from a far country.	2896
Pr	25:27	It is not **g** to eat much honey:	2896
Pr	28:10	the upright shall have **g** things	2896
Pr	28:21	To have respect of persons is not **g**:	2896
Pr	31:12	She will do him **g** and not evil.	2896
Ecc	2:26	God giveth to a man that is **g** in.	2896
Ecc	3:12	I know that there is no **g** in them,	2896
Ecc	4:8	and bereave my soul of **g**?	2896
Ecc	6:12	who knoweth what is **g** for man	2896
Ecc	7:1	a **g** name is better than precious	
Ecc	7:11	Wisdom is **g** with an inheritance:	2896
Ecc	7:20	just man upon earth, that doeth **g**,	2896
Ecc	9:18	but one sinner destroyeth much **g**	2896
Ecc	11:6	whether they both shall be alike **g**	2896
Ecc	12:14	whether it be **g**, or whether it be evil.	2896
Isa	5:20	them that call evil **g**, and **g** evil;	2896
Isa	7:16	to refuse the evil, and choose the **g**,	2896
Isa	39:8	**G** is the word of the Lord which.	2896
Isa	40:9	O Zion, that bringest **g** tidings, get	1319
Isa	61:1	preach **g** tidings unto the meek;	1319
Isa	65:2	walketh in a way that was not **g**,	2896
Jer	4:22	to do **g** they have no knowledge	3190
Jer	8:15	looked for peace, but no **g** came;	2896
Jer	10:5	neither also is it in them to do **g**.	3190
Jer	17:6	and shall not see when **g** cometh;	2896
Jer	18:4	seemed **g** to the potter to make it	3474
Jer	18:20	Shall evil be recompensed for **g**?	2896
Jer	21:10	this city for evil, and not for **g**,	2896
Jer	33:11	for the Lord is **g**; for his mercy	2896
Jer	42:6	Whether it be **g**, or whether it be	2896
La	3:25	The Lord is **g** unto them that wait	2896
La	3:26	It is **g** that a man should both hope	2896
La	3:27	It is **g** for a man that he bear the.	2896
Eze	34:14	I will feed them in a **g** pasture,	2896
Da	4:2	I thought it **g** to shew the signs	8232
Hos	8:3	cast off the thing that is **g**.	2896
Am	5:14	Seek **g**, and not evil, that ye may.	2896
Am	5:15	Hate the evil, and love the **g**,	2896
Am	9:4	upon them for evil, and not for **g**.	2896
Mic	3:2	Who hate the **g**, and love the evil;	2896
Mic	6:8	shewed thee, O man, what is **g**;	2896
Mic	7:2	The **g** man is perished out of the	2623
Zep	1:12	heart, The Lord will not do **g**,	3190
Zec	1:13	**g** words and comfortable words	2896
Mal	2:17	Every one that doeth evil is **g** in	2896
Mt	5:13	it is henceforth **g** for nothing	2480
Mt	5:44	do **g** to them that hate you, and	2573
Mt	5:45	sun to rise on the evil and on the **g**,	18
Mt	7:11	to give **g** gifts unto your children,	18
Mt	7:17	Even so every **g** tree bringeth forth	18
Mt	7:17	tree bringeth forth **g** fruit; but a.	2570
Mt	7:18	A **g** tree cannot bring forth evil	18
Mt	9:2	be of **g** cheer; thy sins be forgiven	
Mt	11:26	for so it seemed **g** in thy sight.	2107
Mt	12:34	can ye, being evil, speak **g** things?	18
Mt	12:35	A **g** man out of the **g** treasure of.	18
Mt	13:8	fell into **g** ground, and brought,	2570
Mt	13:38	the **g** seed are the children of the	2570
Mt	14:27	Be of **g** cheer; it is I; be not afraid.	
Mt	17:4	Lord, it is **g** for us to be here:.	2570
Mt	19:10	with his wife, it is not **g** to marry	4851
Mt	19:16	what **g** thing shall I do, that I may	18
Mt	19:17	callest thou me **g**? there is none **g**.	18
Mt	20:15	Is thine eye evil, because I am **g**?	18
Mt	25:23	Well done, **g** and faithful servant;.	18
Mt	26:24	it had been **g** for that man if he	18
Mk	3:4	to do **g** on the sabbath days, or to	15
Mk	4:8	And other fell on **g** ground, and.	2570
Mk	4:20	which are sown on **g** ground;	2570
Mk	6:50	Be of **g** cheer; it is I; be not afraid.	
Mk	9:50	Salt is **g**: but if the salt have lost	2750
Mk	10:18	callest thou me **g**? there is none **g**.	18
Lk	1:3	It seemed **g** to me also, having had	
Lk	2:10	bring you **g** tidings of great joy,	2097
Lk	2:14	earth peace, **g** will toward men	2107
Lk	6:9	on the sabbath days to do **g**, or to	15
Lk	6:27	do **g** to them which hate you,	2573
Lk	6:33	do **g** to them which do **g** to you,	15
Lk	6:35	do **g**, and lend, hoping for nothing	15
Lk	6:38	**g** measure, pressed down, and	2570
Lk	6:43	For a **g** tree bringeth not forth	2570
Lk	6:45	A **g** man out of the **g** treasure of.	18
Lk	8:15	But that on the **g** ground are they	2570
Lk	8:48	Daughter, be of **g** comforteth: thy	
Lk	9:33	it is **g** for us to be here: and let	2570
Lk	10:42	and Mary hath chosen that **g** part,	18
Lk	11:13	know how to give **g** gifts unto your	18
Lk	12:32	your Father's **g** pleasure to give	
Lk	14:34	Salt is **g**: but if the salt have lost	2570
Lk	18:19	Why callest thou me **g**? none is **g**,	18
Lk	23:50	and he was a **g** man, and a just:.	18
Jn	1:46	Can there any **g** thing come out	18
Jn	2:10	but thou hast kept the **g** wine	2570
Jn	10:14	I am the **g** shepherd, and know	2570
Jn	10:33	For a **g** work we stone thee not;	2570
Jn	16:33	but be of **g** cheer; I have overcome	
Ac	9:36	this woman was full of **g** works.	18
Ac	10:38	went about doing **g**, and healing.	2109

Ac 15:38 Paul thought not **g** to take him......... *515*
Ac 18:18 this tarried there yet a **g** while, ... *2425*
Ac 23:1 I have lived in all **g** conscience until...... *18*
Ac 23:11 **Be of g cheer, Paul: for as thou hast**
Ro 3:8 Let us do evil, that **g** may come?......... *18*
Ro 3:12 there is none that doeth **g**, no, not *5544*
Ro 5:7 for a **g** man some would even dare....... *18*
Ro 7:18 in my flesh,) dwelleth no **g** thing:........ *18*
Ro 7:19 For the **g** that I would I do not:.......... *18*
Ro 7:21 a law, that when I would do **g**......... *2570*
Ro 8:28 all things work together for **g** to *18*
Ro 10:15 and bring glad tidings of **g** things! *18*
Ro 12:2 that ye may prove what is that **g**......... *18*
Ro 12:9 is evil; cleave to that which is **g**.......... *18*
Ro 12:21 of evil, but overcome evil with **g**. *18*
Ro 14:16 Let not then your **g** be evil spoken of..... *18*
1Co 5:6 Your glorying is not **g**. Know ye *2570*
1Co 7:1 It is **g** for a man not to touch a *2570*
1Co 15:33 evil communications corrupt **g**........ *5545*
2Co 9:8 may abound to every **g** work: *18*
Gal 6:10 let us do **g** unto all men, especially....... *18*
Eph 2:10 created in Christ Jesus unto **g** *18*
Eph 6:7 With **g** will doing service, as to *2133*
Php 1:6 he which hath begun a **g** work in *18*
Php 2:13 to will and to do of his **g** pleasure.
Php 4:8 whatsoever things are of **g** report; *2163*
Col 1:10 being fruitful in every **g** work,........... *18*
1Th 5:15 but ever follow that which is **g**,.......... *18*
1Th 5:21 things; hold fast that which is **g**........ *2570*
1Ti 1:5 a pure heart, and of a **g** conscience, ... *18*
1Ti 1:8 But we know that the law is **g** *2570*
1Ti 1:19 Holding faith, and a **g** conscience; *18*
1Ti 3:1 of a bishop, he desireth a **g** work....... *2570*
1Ti 3:2 vigilant, sober, of **g** behaviour,
1Ti 4:4 For every creature of God is **g**, ... *2570*
1Ti 4:6 of faith and of **g** doctrine, ... *2570*
1Ti 6:12 Fight the **g** fight of faith, lay hold *2570*
1Ti 6:13 Pilate witnessed a **g** confession;........ *2570*
2Ti 2:3 as a **g** soldier of Jesus Christ.......... *2570*
2Ti 2:21 and prepared unto every **g** work. *18*
2Ti 3:17 throughly furnished unto all **g** works. *18*
2Ti 4:7 I have fought a **g** fight, I have *2570*
Tit 2:7 thyself a pattern of **g** works:.......... *2570*
Tit 2:14 peculiar people, zealous of **g** works..... *2570*
Tit 3:8 be careful to maintain **g** works......... *2570*
Tit 3:8 These things are **g** and profitable *2570*
Heb 5:14 to discern both **g** and evil............ *2570*
Heb 6:5 have tasted the **g** word of God......... *2570*
Heb 9:11 an high priest of **g** things to come,....... *18*
Heb 10:1 a shadow of **g** things to come,........... *18*
Heb 10:24 provoke unto love and to **g** works: *2570*
Heb 11:2 by it the elders obtained a **g** report
Heb 11:39 obtained a **g** report through faith
Heb 13:18 we trust we have a **g** conscience,....... *2570*
Heb 13:21 Make you perfect in every **g** work........ *18*
Jas 1:17 Every **g** gift and every perfect gift *18*
Jas 2:3 Sit thou here in a **g** place
Jas 4:17 him that knoweth to do **g** and doeth ... *2570*
1Pe 3:10 he that will love life, and see **g** days,...... *18*
1Pe 3:11 Let him eschew evil, and do **g**;........... *18*
1Pe 3:13 be followers of that which is **g**? *18*
1Pe 3:21 answer of a **g** conscience toward......... *18*
1Jn 3:17 whoso hath this world's **g**, and *979*
3Jn 11 which is evil, but that which is **g**......... *18*
3Jn 11 He that doeth **g** is of God: *15*

GOODLIER

1Sa 9:2 of Israel a **g** person than he: from...... 2896

GOODLIEST

1Sa 8:16 your **g** young men, and your asses,..... 2896
1Ki 20:3 thy children, even the **g**, are mine...... 2896

GOODLY

Ge 39:6 Joseph was a **g** person,.......... 3303, 8389
Ex 2:2 saw him that he was a **g** child,......... 2896
Nu 24:5 How **g** are thy tents, O Jacob, ... 2896
1Sa 9:2 a choice young man, and a **g**: 2896
2Sa 23:21 he slew an Egyptian, a **g** man;......... 4758
2Ch 36:10 with the **g** vessels of the house 2532
2Ch 36:19 destroyed all the **g** vessels thereof, ... 4261
Ps 80:10 thereof were like the **g** cedars 410
Hos 10:1 of his land they have made **g** images ... 2896
Mt 13:45 **merchant man, seeking g pearls:** *2573*
Lk 21:5 adorned with **g** stones and gifts,....... *2573*
Jas 2:2 in **g** apparel, and there come *2986*

GOODMAN

Pr 7:19 For the **g** is not at home, he is gone *376*
Mt 20:11 **against the g of the house** *3611*
Mt 24:43 **if the g of the house had known**....... *3611*
Lk 12:39 **g of the house had known what** *3611*
Lk 22:11 **shall say unto the g of the house,** *3611*

GOODNESS

Ex 33:19 make all my **g** pass before thee,........ 2898
Ex 34:6 and abundant in **g** and truth, ... 2617
1Ch 17:26 promised this **g** unto thy servant;...... 2896
Ps 16:2 my **g** extendeth not to thee;........... 2896
Ps 23:6 Surely **g** and mercy shall follow me 2896
Ps 27:13 see the **g** of the Lord in the land....... 2898
Ps 33:5 earth is full of the **g** of the Lord........ 2617
Ps 65:4 satisfied with the **g** of thy house, ... 2898
Ps 107:8 would praise the Lord for his **g**, ... 2617
Jer 31:14 people shall be satisfied with my **g**, ... 2898
Hos 6:4 your **g** is as a morning cloud, ... 2617
Ro 2:4 not knowing that the **g** of God *5543*
Ro 11:22 the **g** and severity of God: *5544*
Gal 5:22 longsuffering, gentleness, **g**, faith,........ *19*
Eph 5:9 the fruit of the Spirit is in all **g** *19*

GOODNESS'

Ps 25:7 remember thou me for thy **g** sake, ... 2898

GOODS

Ge 14:16 he brought back all the **g**, and also..... 7399
Ex 22:8 his hand unto his neighbour's **g** 4399
Ex 22:11 his hand unto his neighbour's **g**;....... 4399
Ne 9:25 houses full of all **g**, wells digged,....... 2898
Eze 38:12 which have gotten cattle and **g**,........ 7075
Zep 1:13 their **g** shall become a booty,.......... 2428
Mt 12:29 **and spoil his g, except he first**......... *4632*
Mt 24:47 **make him ruler over all his g**.......... *5224*
Lk 11:21 **his palace, his g are in peace:**.......... *5224*
Lk 12:19 **thou hast much g laid up for many** *18*
Lk 15:12 **me the portion of g that falleth** *3776*
Lk 16:1 **him that he had wasted his g**.......... *5224*
Lk 19:8 Lord, the half of my **g** I give to the..... *5224*
Ac 2:45 And sold their possessions and **g**,...... *5223*
1Co 13:3 though I bestow all my **g** to feed....... *5224*
Rev 3:17 **I am rich, and increased with g,** *4147*

GOPHER

Ge 6:14 Make thee an ark of **g** wood;.......... 1613

GORE

Ex	21:28	If an ox **g** a man or a woman,	5055

GORGEOUS

Lk	23:11	arrayed him in a **g** robe, and sent	*2986*

GORGEOUSLY

Eze	23:12	and rulers clothed most **g**,	4358
Lk	7:25	they which are **g** apparelled,	*1741*

GOSPEL

Mt	4:23	preaching the **g** of the kingdom,	*2098*
Mt	9:35	preaching the **g** of the kingdom,	*2098*
Mt	24:14	this **g** of the kingdom shall be	*2098*
Mt	26:13	wheresoever this **g** shall be preached	*2098*
Mk	1:1	beginning of the **g** of Jesus Christ,	*2098*
Mk	1:15	repent ye, and believe the **g**	*2098*
Mk	13:10	the **g** must first be published	*2098*
Mk	14:9	this **g** shall be preached through	*2098*
Mk	16:15	preach the **g** to every creature	*2098*
Lk	4:18	to preach the **g** to the poor;	*2097*
Lk	20:1	in the temple, and preached the **g**,	*2097*
Ac	20:24	to testify the **g** of the grace of God.	*2098*
Ro	1:9	my spirit in the **g** of his Son,	*2098*
Ro	1:16	For I am not ashamed of the **g**	*2098*
Ro	10:15	them that preach the **g** of peace,	*2097*
Ro	15:19	have fully preached the **g** of Christ.	*2098*
1Co	4:15	have begotten you through the **g**.	*2098*
1Co	9:12	we should hinder the **g** of Christ.	*2098*
1Co	9:16	woe is unto me, if I preach not the **g**!	*2097*
1Co	9:18	that I abuse not my power in the **g**.	*2098*
2Co	4:3	But if our **g** be hid, it is hid to them.	*2098*
2Co	4:4	lest the light of the glorious **g** of	*2098*
2Co	9:13	subjection unto the **g** of Christ,	*2098*
Gal	1:7	and would pervert the **g** of Christ	*2098*
Gal	1:8	preach any other **g** unto you than	*2097*
Gal	1:9	if any man preach any other **g**	*2097*
Gal	2:14	according to the truth of the **g**,	*2098*
Eph	1:13	word of truth ... **g** of your salvation:	*2098*
Eph	6:15	the preparation of the **g** of peace;	*2098*
Eph	6:19	make known the mystery of the **g**,	*2098*
Php	1:17	I am set for the defence of the **g**.	*2098*
Php	1:27	be as it becometh the **g** of Christ:	*2098*
Col	1:23	moved away from the hope of the **g**,	*2098*
1Th	1:5	For our **g** came not unto you	*2098*
1Th	2:4	to be put in trust with the **g**,	*2098*
1Ti	1:11	the glorious **g** of the blessed God,	*2098*
2Ti	1:10	immortality to light through the **g**:	*2098*
Heb	4:2	For unto us was the **g** preached	*2097*
1Pe	4:17	them that obey not the **g** of God?	*2098*
Rev	14:6	having the evelasting **g** to preach	*2098*

GOSPEL'S

Mk	8:35	his life for my sake and the **g**,	*2098*
Mk	10:29	or lands, for my sake, and the **g**,	*2098*
1Co	9:23	And this I do for the **g** sake,	*2098*

GOT See also FORGOT; GAT; GOTTEN.

Ge	39:12	in her hand, and fled, and **g** him out	3318
Ecc	2:7	I **g** me servants and maidens,	7069

GOTTEN See also BEGOTTEN; FORGOTTEN.

Ge	4:1	I have **g** a man from the Lord.	7069
Ge	12:5	souls that they had **g** in Haran;	6213
Ex	14:18	I have **g** me honour upon Pharaoh	7408
Le	6:4	thing which he hath deceitfully **g**,	
Dt	8:17	mine hand hath **g** me this	6213
Job	28:15	It cannot be **g** for gold, neither	5414
Ps	98:1	holy arm, hath **g** him the victory.	
Pr	13:11	Wealth **g** by vanity shall be	
Jer	48:36	riches that he hath **g** are perished	6213
Eze	28:4	thou hast **g** thee riches,	6213
Da	9:15	and hast **g** thee renown, as at this	6213
Rev	15:2	them that had **g** the victory	

GOURD

Jnh	4:6	Jonah was exceeding glad of the **g**.	7021
Jnh	4:9	thou well to be angry for the **g**?	7021
Jnh	4:10	Thou hast had pity on the **g**,	7021

GOVERN

1Ki	21:7	Dost thou now **g** the kingdom of	6213
Job	34:17	Shall even he that hateth right **g**?	2280
Ps	67:4	and **g** the nations upon earth	5148

GOVERNMENT

Isa	9:6	the **g** shall be upon his shoulder:	4951
Isa	9:7	Of the increase of his **g** and peace	4951
Isa	22:21	and I will commit thy **g** into his	4475
2Pe	2:10	despise **g**. Presumptuous are they	2963

GOVERNOR

Ge	42:6	Joseph was the **g** over the land	7989
Ge	45:26	and he is **g** over all the land	4910
2Ch	1:2	to every **g** in all Israel, the chief	5387
Ezr	5:3	them Tatnai, **g** on this side the	6347
Ne	5:14	have not eaten the bread of the **g**	6346
Ps	22:28	he is the **g** among the nations.	4910
Jer	20:1	chief **g** in the house of the Lord,	5057
Mal	1:8	offer it now unto thy **g**; will he be	6346
Mt	2:6	shall come a **G**, that shall rule	*2233*
Mt	27:2	him to Pontius Pilate the **g**.	*2232*
Mt	27:14	that the **g** marvelled greatly	*2232*
Mt	27:15	the **g** was wont to release unto	*2232*
Lk	2:2	when Cyrenius was **g** of Syria.)	*2230*
Jn	2:8	And bear unto the **g** of the feast.	*755*
Ac	7:10	and he made him **g** over Egypt	*2233*
Jas	3:4	helm, whithersoever the **g** listeth	*2116*

GOVERNOR'S

Mt	28:14	And if this come to the **g** ears,	*2232*

GOVERNORS

Jgs	5:9	My heart is toward the **g** of Israel,	2710
1Ch	24:5	the **g** of the sanctuary, and **g** of	8269
Ne	2:9	I came to the **g** beyond the river	6346
Ne	5:15	But the former **g** that had been	6346
Zec	12:5	the **g** of Judah shall say in their heart,	441
Zec	12:6	make the **g** of Judah like an hearth of	441
Mt	10:18	And ye shall be brought before **g**	*2232*
Gal	4:2	But is under tutors and **g** until	*3623*
1Pe	2:14	unto **g**, as unto them that are sent	*2232*

GRACE See also DISGRACE.

Ge	6:8	Noah found **g** in the eyes of	2580
Ge	39:4	And Joseph found **g** in his sight,	2580
Ex	33:16	thy people have found **g** in thy sight?	2580
Ru	2:10	Why have I found **g** in thine eyes,	2580
1Sa	1:18	handmaid find **g** in thy sight	2580
Ezr	9:8	for a little space **g** hath been shewed	8467
Est	2:17	she obtained **g** and favour in his	2580
Ps	84:11	the Lord will give **g** and glory:	2580
Pr	1:9	an ornament of **g** unto thy head,	2580
Pr	3:34	but he giveth **g** unto the lowly.	2580
Pr	22:11	for the **g** of his lips the king shall	2580
Lk	2:40	and the **g** of God was upon him	*5485*

Jn 1:14 of the Father,) full of **g** and truth....... *5485*
Jn 1:16 have all we received, and **g** for **g** *5485*
Jn 1:17 **g** and truth came by Jesus Christ....... *5485*
Ac 4:33 and great **g** was upon them all......... *5485*
Ac 11:23 had seen the **g** of God, was glad,....... *5485*
Ac 13:43 them to continue in the **g** of God. *5485*
Ro 3:24 Being justified freely by his **g**.......... *5485*
Ro 4:4 not reckoned of **g**, but of debt......... *5485*
Ro 4:16 of faith, that it might be by **g**; *5455*
Ro 5:15 the **g** of God, and the gift by **g** *5485*
Ro 5:20 **g** did much more abound:............ *5455*
Ro 6:1 continue in sin, that **g** may abound? ... *5485*
Ro 6:14 are not under the law, but under **g**..... *5485*
Ro 6:15 not under the law, but under **g**? *5485*
Ro 11:6 if by **g**, then is it no more of works:.... *5485*
Ro 11:6 otherwise **g** is no more **g** *5485*
1Co 15:10 by the **g** of God I am what I am:....... *5485*
2Co 6:1 ye receive not the **g** of God in vain. *5485*
2Co 8:7 see that ye abound in this **g** also *5485*
2Co 9:8 God is able to make all **g** abound *5485*
2Co 12:9 **My g is sufficient for thee: for my** *5485*
Gal 2:21 I do not frustrate the **g** of God:......... *5485*
Gal 5:4 by the law; ye are fallen from **g**........ *5485*
Ep 2:5 with Christ, (by **g** ye are saved;) *5485*
Ep 2:7 the exceeding riches of his **g** *5485*
Ep 2:8 by **g** are ye saved through faith;........ *5485*
Ep 3:2 the dispensation of the **g** of God *5485*
Ep 4:29 it may minister **g** unto the hearers *5485*
Col 1:6 and knew the **g** of God in truth:....... *5485*
Col 4:6 your speech be always with **g**.......... *5485*
Tit 3:7 That being justified by his **g**, we *5485*
Heb 2:9 by the **g** of God should taste death..... *5485*
Heb 4:16 come boldly unto the throne of **g**...... *5485*
Heb 4:16 and find **g** to help in time of need...... *5485*
Heb 10:29 done despite unto the Spirit of **g**?...... *5485*
Heb 12:15 lest any man fail of the **g** of God; *5485*
Jas 4:6 But he giveth more **g**. Wherefore *5485*
Jas 4:6 but giveth **g** unto the humble *5485*
1Pe 3:7 heirs together of the **g** of life; *5485*
1Pe 4:10 stewards of the manifold **g** of God..... *5485*
1Pe 5:5 proud, and giveth **g** to the humble..... *5485*
1Pe 5:10 But the God of all **g**, who hath *5485*
1Pe 5:12 true **g** of God wherein ye stand........ *5485*
Rev 1:4 **G** be unto you, and peace, from *5485*
Rev 22:21 The **g** of our Lord Jesus Christ be...... *5485*

GRACIOUS

Ex 33:19 **g** to whom I will be **g**, and will 2603
Ex 34:6 The Lord God, merciful and **G**........ 2587
2Sa 12:22 whether God will be **g** to me, that 2603
Ne 9:17 ready to pardon, **g** and merciful,....... 2587
Ps 77:9 Hath God forgotten to be **g** ?.......... 2589
Ps 103:8 the Lord is merciful and **g**, slow to..... 2587
Ps 111:4 Lord is **g** and full of compassion....... 2587
Ps 112:4 he is **g**, and full of compassion 2587
Ps 116:5 **G** is the Lord, and righteous; yea,...... 2587
Ps 145:8 Lord is **g**, and full of compassion;...... 2587
Ecc 10:12 words of a wise man's mouth are **g**:.... 2580
Joel 2:13 is **g** and merciful, slow to anger, ... 2587
Jnh 4:2 I knew that thou art a **g** God, ... 2587
Lk 4:22 wondered at the **g** words which *5485*
1Pe 2:3 ye have tasted that the Lord is **g** *5543*

GRACIOUSLY

Ge 33:11 God hath dealt **g** with me, and 2603
Hos 14:2 receive us **g**: so will we render......... 2896

GRAFF

Ro 11:23 God is able to **g** them in again *1461*

GRAFFED See also UNGRAFFED.

Ro 11:19 broken off, that I might be **g** in........ *1461*
Ro 11:23 not still in unbelief, shall be **g** in: *1461*
Ro 11:24 and wert **g** contrary to nature......... *1461*

GRAIN

Mt 13:31 **like to a g of mustard seed,** *2848*
Mt 17:20 **faith as a g of mustard seed, ye**........ *2848*
Lk 13:19 **It is like a g of mustard seed,**.......... *2848*
Lk 17:6 **faith as a g of mustard seed, ye**........ *2848*

GRANDMOTHER

2Ti 1:5 which dwelt first in thy **g** Lois, ... *3125*

GRANT

Le 25:24 shall **g** a redemption for the land 5414
1Sa 1:17 God of Israel **g** thee thy petition....... 5414
Est 5:8 it please the king to **g** my petition,..... 5414
Ps 85:7 O Lord, and **g** us thy salvation 5414
Ps 140:8 **G** not, O Lord, the desires of the....... 5414
Mt 20:21 **G** that these my two sons may......... *2036*
Mk 10:37 **G** unto us that we may sit, one *1325*
Rev 3:21 **him that overcometh will I g to sit**..... *1325*

GRANTED

1Ch 4:10 God **g** him that which he requested. 935
2Ch 1:12 and knowledge is **g** unto thee;......... 5414
Ezr 7:6 and the king **g** him all his request, ... 5414
Ne 2:8 And the king **g** me, according to....... 5414
Est 5:6 petition? and it shall be **g** thee: 5414
Est 9:12 petition? and it shall be **g** thee: 5414
Pr 10:24 desire of the righteous shall be **g**....... 5414
Ac 3:14 a murderer to be **g** unto you;.......... *5483*
Ac 11:18 Gentiles **g** repentance unto life *1325*

GRAPE

Le 19:10 neither shalt thou gather every **g**....... 6528
Dt 32:14 drink the pure blood of the **g** 6025
Jer 31:30 every man that eateth the sour **g**, ... 1155

GRAPEGATHERERS

Ob 5 if the **g** came to thee, would they 1219

GRAPES

Ge 49:11 and his clothes in the blood of **g**: 6025
Le 25:5 neither gather the **g** of thy vine........ 6025
Nu 6:3 shall he drink any liquor of **g** 6025
Dt 23:24 thou mayest eat **g** thy fill at thine 6025
Dt 32:32 their **g** are **g** of gall, their clusters 6025
SS 2:15 for our vines have tender **g** 5563
Jer 8:13 there shall be no **g** on the vine,........ 6025
Eze 18:2 The fathers have eaten sour **g**,......... 1154
Hos 9:10 found Israel like **g** in the wilderness; ... 6025
Ob 5 would they not leave some **g**? 6025
Mt 7:16 **Do men gather g of thorns, or** *4718*
Lk 6:44 **of a bramble bush gather they g**....... *4718*
Rev 14:18 **the earth; for her g are fully ripe** *4718*

GRASS

Ge 1:11 Let the earth bring forth **g**, the 1877
Ge 1:12 earth brought forth **g**, and herb 1877
Nu 22:4 ox licketh up the **g** of the field......... 3418
2Sa 23:4 tender **g** springing out of the earth 1877
Ps 37:2 shall soon be cut down like the **g** 2682
Ps 90:5 in the morning they are like **g**......... 2682
Ps 92:7 When the wicked spring as the **g** 6212

Ps	102:4	is smitten, and withered like **g**;	6212
Ps	103:15	As for man, his days are as **g**:	2682
Ps	129:6	as the **g** upon the housetops,	2682
Pr	19:12	his favour is as dew upon the **g**.	6212
Isa	40:6	What shall I cry? All flesh is **g**	2682
Isa	40:7	The **g** withereth, the flower fadeth:	2682
Da	4:25	and they shall make thee to eat **g**	6211
Da	4:33	did eat **g** as oxen, and his body	6211
Da	5:21	they fed him with **g** like oxen	6211
Mt	6:30	**God so clothe the g of the field,**	*5528*
Lk	12:28	If then God so clothe the **g**	*5528*
Jas	1:10	as the flower of the **g** he shall pass	*5528*
1Pe	1:24	For all flesh is as **g**, and all the	*5528*
1Pe	1:24	glory of man as the flower of **g**	*5528*
1Pe	1:24	The **g** withereth, and the flower	*5528*
Rev	9:4	should not hurt the **g** of the earth,	*5528*

GRASSHOPPER

Le	11:22	kind, and the **g** after his kind	2284

GRASSHOPPERS

Nu	13:33	we were in our own sight as **g**	2284
Jgs	6:5	they came as **g** for multitude;	697
Isa	40:22	the inhabitants thereof are as **g**;	2284
Jer	46:23	because they are more than the **g**	697

GRAVE See also ENGRAVE; GRAVECLOTHES; GRAVEN.

Ge	37:35	go down into the **g** unto my son	7585
Ge	42:38	gray hairs with sorrow to the **g**.	7585
Ge	44:31	our father with sorrow to the **g**.	7585
Ex	28:9	and **g** on them the names of	6605
1Ki	2:6	head go down to the **g** in peace	7585
1Ki	13:30	he laid his carcase in his own **g**:	6913
Job	14:13	wouldest hide me in the **g**, that	7585
Job	21:13	in a moment go down to the **g**	7585
Ps	6:5	in the **g** who shall give thee	7585
Ps	49:14	beauty shall consume in the **g**	7585
Ps	49:15	my soul from the power of the **g**:	7585
Ps	88:5	like the slain that lie in the **g**,	6913
Ps	88:11	be declared in the **g**? or thy	6913
Ps	89:48	his soul from the hand of the **g**?	7585
Pr	1:12	swallow them up alive as the **g**;	7585
Ecc	9:10	knowledge, nor wisdom, in the **g**	7585
SS	8:6	death; jealousy is cruel as the **g**:	7585
Isa	14:19	thou art cast out of thy **g** like an	6913
Isa	38:18	the **g** cannot praise thee, death	7585
Jer	20:17	my mother might have been my **g**,	6913
Hos	13:14	O **g**, I will be thy destruction:	7585
Jn	11:17	he had lain in the **g** four days	*3419*
Jn	12:17	he called Lazarus out of his **g**,	*3419*
1Co	15:55	sting? O **g**, where is thy victory?	*86*
1Ti	3:8	Likewise must the deacons be **g**,	*4586*
1Ti	3:11	Even so must their wives be **g**,	*4586*
Tit	2:2	aged men be sober, **g**, temperate,	*4586*

GRAVECLOTHES

Jn	11:44	bound hand and foot with **g**	*2750*

GRAVED See also GRAVEN.

1Ki	7:36	he **g** cherubims, lions, and palm	6605
2Ch	3:7	and **g** cherubims on the walls.	6605

GRAVEL

Pr	20:17	his mouth shall be filled with **g**.	2687
Isa	48:19	offspring of thy bowels like the **g**	4579
La	3:16	broken my teeth with **g** stones	2687

GRAVEN See also GRAVED; ENGRAVEN.

Ex	20:4	not make unto thee any **g** image,	6459
Ex	32:16	of God, **g** upon the tables	2801
Le	26:1	make you no idols nor **g** image,	6459
Dt	5:8	shalt not make thee any **g** image,	6459
Dt	7:25	The **g** images of their gods shall	6456
Dt	27:15	maketh any **g** or molten image	6459
Jgs	17:4	who made thereof a **g** image and	6459
Jgs	18:30	children of Dan set up the **g** image:	6459
2Ch	33:19	up groves and **g** images, before	6456
Job	19:24	they were **g** with an iron pen	2672
Ps	78:58	to jealousy with their **g** images	6456
Ps	97:7	they that serve **g** images, that	6459
Isa	21:9	all the **g** images of her gods	6456
Isa	42:8	neither my praise to **g** images	6456
Isa	42:17	that trust in **g** images, that say	6459
Isa	44:17	maketh a god, even his **g** image:	6459
Isa	49:16	I have **g** thee upon the palms	2710
Jer	8:19	me to anger with their **g** images,	6456
Jer	17:1	**g** upon the table of their heart,	2790
Jer	51:47	the **g** images of Babylon: and her	6456
Hos	11:2	and burned incense to **g** images	6456
Hab	2:18	the maker thereof hath **g** it;	6458
Ac	17:29	stone, **g** by art and man's device	*5480*

GRAVE'S

Ps	141:7	are scattered at the **g** mouth,	7585

GRAVES

Ex	14:11	Because there were no **g** in Egypt,	6913
2Ch	34:4	strowed it upon the **g** of them.	6913
Jer	26:23	cast his dead body into the **g** of	6913
Eze	32:25	her **g** are round about him:	6913
Eze	37:12	I will open your **g**, and cause you	6913
Eze	37:12	you to come up out of your **g**	6913
Eze	39:11	give unto Gog a place there of **g**	6913
Mt	27:52	the **g** were opened; and many	*3419*
Mt	27:53	And came out of the **g** after his	*3419*
Lk	11:44	**for ye are as g which appear not,**	*3419*
Jn	5:28	**that are in the g shall hear his**	*3419*
Rev	11:9	their dead bodies to be put in **g**	*3418*

GRAVING

Ex	32:4	fashioned it with a **g** tool,	2747
Zec	3:9	I will engrave the **g** thereof,	6603

GRAVITY

1Ti	3:4	children in subjection with all **g**;	*4587*
Tit	2:7	uncorruptness, **g**, sincerity,	*4587*

GRAY See also GREY.

Ge	42:38	down my **g** hairs with sorrow	7872
Dt	32:25	also with the man of **g** hairs	7872
Pr	20:29	beauty of old men is the **g** head.	7872

GRAYHEADED See also GREYHEADED.

1Sa	12:2	I am old and **g**; and, behold, my	7867
Ps	71:18	Now also when I am old and **g**,	7872

GREASE

Ps	119:70	Their heart is as fat as **g**;	2459

GREAT

Ge	1:16	And God made two **g** lights; the	1419
Ge	1:21	God created **g** whales, and every	1419
Ge	6:5	that the wickedness of man was **g**	7227
Ge	7:11	fountains of the **g** deep broken up,	7227
Ge	12:2	I will make of thee a **g** nation, and	1419
Ge	12:2	bless thee, and make thy name **g**;	1431

Ge	13:6	for their substance was **g**, so that	7227
Ge	15:1	and thy exceeding **g** reward	7235
Ge	17:20	and I will make him a **g** nation	1419
Ge	18:18	become a **g** and mighty nation,	1419
Ge	18:20	cry of Sodom and Gomorrah is **g**,	7227
Ge	19:11	with blindness, both small and **g**:	1419
Ge	20:9	and on my kingdom a **g** sin?	1419
Ge	21:18	for I will make him a **g** nation	1419
Ge	29:2	**g** stone was upon the well's mouth	1419
Ge	39:9	then can I do this **g** wickedness	1419
Ge	41:29	years of **g** plenty throughout	1419
Ex	3:3	and see this **g** sight, why the bush	1419
Ex	7:4	the land of Egypt by **g** judgments	1419
Ex	11:3	the man Moses was very **g** in the	1419
Ex	11:8	out from Pharaoh in a **g** anger	2750
Ex	12:30	and there was a **g** cry in Egypt;	1419
Ex	18:22	every **g** matter they shall bring	1419
Ex	32:30	Ye have sinned a **g** sin: and now	1419
Ex	32:31	this people have sinned a **g** sin	1419
Le	14:17	his right hand, and upon the **g** toe	
Nu	13:32	we saw in it are men of a **g** stature	
Nu	14:18	of **g** mercy, forgiving iniquity	7227
Dt	1:7	the **g** river, the river Euphrates	1419
Dt	1:17	hear the small as well as the **g**;	1419
Dt	2:21	A people **g**, and many, and tall,	1419
Dt	4:7	For what nation is there so **g**, who	1419
Dt	8:15	that **g** and terrible wilderness	1419
Dt	10:17	a **g** God, a mighty, and a terrible,	1419
Dt	18:16	let me see this **g** fire any more	1419
Jos	6:5	people shall shout with a **g** shout;	1419
Jos	17:15	If thou be a **g** people, then get thee	7227
Jgs	5:15	there were **g** thoughts of heart	1419
Jgs	5:16	there were **g** searchings of heart	1419
Jgs	16:5	see wherein his **g** strength lieth,	1419
Jgs	16:23	to offer a **g** sacrifice unto Dagon	1419
1Sa	4:5	all Israel shouted with a **g** shout	1419
1Sa	4:10	and there was a very **g** slaughter;	1419
1Sa	12:16	stand and see this **g** thing, which	1419
1Sa	12:17	see that your wickedness is **g**,	7227
1Sa	12:24	how **g** things he hath done for you	1431
1Sa	15:22	Hath the Lord as **g** delight in burnt	
2Sa	7:19	house for a **g** while to come	7350
2Sa	12:14	thou hast given **g** occasion to the	5006
2Sa	22:36	thy gentleness hath made me **g**	7235
2Sa	23:12	and the Lord wrought a **g** victory	1419
1Ki	3:9	to judge this thy so **g** a people?	3515
1Ki	8:42	they shall hear of thy **g** name	1419
1Ki	10:2	to Jerusalem with a very **g** train,	3515
1Ki	10:18	king made a **g** throne of ivory,	1419
2Ki	17:21	Lord, and made them sin a **g** sin	1419
2Ki	18:17	with a **g** host against Jerusalem	3515
2Ki	18:28	Hear the word of the **g** king	1419
2Ki	25:9	every **g** man's house burnt he	1419
1Ch	17:17	house for a **g** while to come,	7350
1Ch	21:13	I am in a **g** strait: let me fall	3966
1Ch	21:13	Lord; for very **g** are his mercies:	7227
2Ch	2:5	the house which I build is **g**:	1419
2Ch	2:5	for **g** is our God above all gods	1419
2Ch	9:17	the king made a **g** throne of ivory,	1419
2Ch	25:10	they returned home in **g** anger	2750
2Ch	28:5	a **g** multitude of them captives,	1419
Ezr	5:8	to the house of the **g** God, which	7229
Ezr	5:11	which a **g** king of Israel builded	7229
Ne	1:5	the **g** and terrible God, that keepeth	1419
Ne	4:14	the Lord, which is **g** and terrible,	1419
Ne	6:3	I am doing a **g** work, so that I	1419
Ne	13:27	to do all this **g** evil, to transgress	1419
Est	4:3	was **g** mourning among the Jews,	1419
Est	8:15	with the **g** crown of gold, and with	1419
Est	10:3	**g** among the Jews, and accepted	1419
Job	1:3	a very **g** household; so that this	7227
Job	1:19	a **g** wind from the wilderness,	1419
Job	2:13	saw that his grief was very **g**	1431
Job	5:9	doeth **g** things and unsearchable;	1419
Job	32:9	**G** men are not always wise:	7227
Job	36:26	God is **g**, and we know him not	7689
Ps	19:11	keeping of them there is **g** reward	7227
Ps	21:5	His glory is **g** in thy salvation:	1419
Ps	25:11	pardon mine iniquity; for it is **g**	7227
Ps	47:2	he is a **g** king over all the earth	1419
Ps	48:1	**G** is the Lord, and greatly to be	1419
Ps	57:10	thy mercy is **g** unto the heavens	1419
Ps	77:13	who is so **g** a God as our God?	1419
Ps	92:5	how **g** are thy works! and thy	1431
Ps	95:3	the Lord is a **g** God, and a **g** King	1419
Ps	96:4	the Lord is **g**, and greatly to be	1419
Ps	108:4	thy mercy is **g** above the heavens:	1419
Ps	111:2	The works of the Lord are **g**,	1419
Ps	117:2	merciful kindness is **g** toward us:	1396
Ps	119:165	**G** peace have they which love thy	7227
Ps	126:3	Lord hath done **g** things for us;	1431
Ps	139:17	O God! how **g** is the sum of them!	6105
Ps	145:3	**G** is the Lord, and greatly to be	1419
Ps	145:8	slow to anger, and of **g** mercy	1419
Pr	13:7	himself poor, yet hath **g** riches	7227
Pr	14:29	to wrath is of **g** understanding:	7227
Pr	15:16	Lord than **g** treasure and trouble	7227
Pr	16:8	than **g** revenues without right	7230
Pr	18:9	brother to him that is a **g** waster	1167
Pr	18:16	and bringeth him before **g** men	1419
Pr	19:19	A man of **g** wrath shall suffer	
Pr	22:1	rather to be chosen than **g** riches,	7227
Pr	25:6	stand not in the place of **g** men:	1419
Pr	26:10	The **g** God that formed all things	7227
Pr	28:12	men do rejoice, there is **g** glory:	7227
Ecc	1:16	I am come to **g** estate, and have	1431
Ecc	1:16	heart had **g** experience of wisdom	7235
Ecc	2:21	This also is vanity and a **g** evil	7227
Isa	2:9	and, the **g** man humbleth himself:	
Isa	12:6	for **g** is the Holy One of Israel	1419
Isa	36:4	the **g** king, the king of Assyria	1419
Isa	53:12	divide him a portion with the **g**,	7227
Isa	54:7	with **g** mercies will I gather thee	1419
Jer	10:6	Lord; thou art **g**, and thy name is **g**	1419
Jer	13:9	and the **g** pride of Jerusalem	7227
Jer	26:19	procure **g** evil against our souls,	1419
Jer	30:7	Alas! for that day is **g**, so that	1419
Jer	32:18	the **G**, the Mighty God, the Lord	1419
Jer	32:19	**G** in counsel, and mighty in work:	1419
Jer	44:7	ye this **g** evil against your souls,	1419
La	2:13	thy breach is **g** like the sea: who	1419
La	3:23	every morning: **g** is thy faithfulness	7227
Eze	3:12	behind me a voice of a **g** rushing,	1419
Eze	17:3	eagle with **g** wings, full of	1419
Eze	21:14	it is the sword of the **g** men that	1419
Eze	29:3	**g** dragon that lieth in the midst	1419
Eze	36:23	I will sanctify my **g** name, which	1419
Da	2:6	and rewards and **g** honour:	7390
Da	2:45	the **g** God hath made known to	7229
Da	2:48	the king made Daniel a **g** man	7236
Da	4:30	Is not this **g** Babylon, that I	7227
Da	5:1	the king made a **g** feast to a	7227

Da	7:3	And four **g** beasts came up from	7260
Da	7:7	and it had **g** iron teeth:	7260
Da	7:17	These **g** beasts, which are four,	7260
Da	8:8	the **g** horn was broken;	1419
Da	9:4	the **g** and dreadful God, keeping	1419
Da	9:12	by bringing upon us a **g** evil:	1419
Da	12:1	the **g** prince which standeth for	1419
Joel	2:2	a **g** people and a strong; there	7227
Joel	2:11	of the Lord is **g** and very terrible;	1419
Joel	2:31	the **g** and the terrible day of the	1419
Jnh	1:2	go to Nineveh, that **g** city, and cry	1419
Jnh	1:17	prepared a **g** fish to swallow up	1419
Jnh	3:2	go unto Nineveh, that **g** city, and	1419
Jnh	3:3	**g** city of three days' journey	1419
Zep	1:14	The **g** day of the Lord is near	1419
Zec	7:12	came a **g** wrath from the Lord	1419
Zec	12:11	In that day shall there be a **g**	1431
Mal	1:14	for I am a **g** King, saith the Lord	1419
Mal	4:5	coming of the **g** and dreadful day	1419
Mt	2:18	and **g** mourning, Rachel weeping	*4183*
Mt	4:16	which sat in darkness saw **g** light;	*3173*
Mt	5:12	**for g is your reward in heaven:**	*4183*
Mt	5:19	**shall be called g in the kingdom**	*3173*
Mt	5:35	**for it is the city of the g King**	*3173*
Mt	6:23	**how g is that darkness!**	*4214*
Mt	7:27	**and g was the fall of it**	*3173*
Mt	8:10	**I have not found so g faith, no,**	*5118*
Mt	8:24	arose a **g** tempest in the sea,	*3173*
Mt	8:26	the sea; and there was a **g** calm	*3173*
Mt	13:46	**found one pearl of g price, went**	*4186*
Mt	15:28	**O woman, g is thy faith: be it**	*3173*
Mt	19:22	sorrowful: for he had **g** possessions	*4183*
Mt	20:25	**that are g exercise authority**	*3171*
Mt	20:26	**whosoever will be g among you,**	*3173*
Mt	20:29	a **g** multitude followed him	*4183*
Mt	22:38	**is the first and g commandment**	*3173*
Mt	24:21	**then shall be g tribulation, such**	*3173*
Mt	24:24	**shall shew g signs and wonders;**	*3173*
Mt	24:30	**of heaven with power and g glory**	*4183*
Mt	24:31	**with a g sound of a trumpet, and**	*3173*
Mt	26:47	and with him a **g** multitude with	*4183*
Mt	27:60	he rolled a **g** stone to the door	*3173*
Mt	28:2	there was a **g** earthquake: for the	*3173*
Mt	28:8	with fear and **g** joy; and did run	*5173*
Mk	1:35	rising up a **g** while before day,	*3029*
Mk	3:8	heard what **g** things he did	*3745*
Mk	4:32	**and shooteth out g branches; so**	*3173*
Mk	5:19	**tell them how g things the Lord**	*3745*
Mk	10:48	but he cried the more a **g** deal,	*4183*
Mk	13:2	**Seest thou these g buildings?**	*3173*
Mk	13:26	**in the clouds with g power and glory**	*4183*
Mk	16:4	rolled away: for it was very **g**	*3173*
Lk	1:15	For he shall be **g** in the sight of	*3173*
Lk	1:32	He shall be **g**, and shall be called	*3173*
Lk	1:49	hath done to me **g** things; and	*3167*
Lk	2:5	his espoused wife, being **g** with child	
Lk	2:10	I bring you good tidings of **g** joy,	*3173*
Lk	2:36	she was of a **g** age, and had lived	*4183*
Lk	4:38	was taken with a **g** fever; and	*3173*
Lk	6:17	a **g** multitude of people out of all	*4183*
Lk	6:23	**your reward is g in heaven: for**	*4183*
Lk	6:35	**and your reward shall be g, and**	*4183*
Lk	6:49	**and the ruin of that house was g**	*3173*
Lk	7:9	**I have not found so g faith, no,**	*5118*
Lk	7:16	That a **g** prophet is risen up	*3173*
Lk	8:39	**how g things God hath done**	*3745*
Lk	10:2	**The harvest truly is g, but the**	*4183*
Lk	10:13	**they had a g while ago repented,**	*3819*
Lk	14:16	**A certain man made a g supper,**	*3173*
Lk	14:32	**while the other is yet a g way off,**	*4183*
Lk	15:20	**when he was yet a g way off,**	*3112*
Lk	16:26	**there is a g gulf fixed: so that**	*3173*
Lk	21:11	**g earthquakes shall be in divers**	*3173*
Lk	21:11	**and g signs shall there be**	*3173*
Lk	21:23	**shall be g distress in the land,**	*3173*
Lk	21:27	**cloud with power and g glory**	*4183*
Lk	22:44	as it were **g** drops of blood	
Lk	24:52	returned to Jerusalem with **g** joy:	*3173*
Jn	5:3	a **g** multitude of impotent folk,	*4183*
Jn	7:37	that **g** day of the feast, Jesus	*3173*
Jn	21:11	the net to land full of **g** fishes	*3173*
Ac	2:20	before that **g** and notable day of	*3173*
Ac	4:33	and **g** grace was upon them all	*3173*
Ac	5:5	and **g** fear came on all them that	*3173*
Ac	6:7	and a **g** company of the priests	*4183*
Ac	6:8	**g** wonders and miracles among	*3173*
Ac	9:16	**how g things he must suffer for**	*3745*
Ac	10:11	as it had been a **g** sheet knit at	*3173*
Ac	11:5	as it had been a **g** sheet, let down	*3273*
Ac	11:21	and a **g** number believed, and	*4183*
Ac	16:26	there was a **g** earthquake, so that	*3173*
Ac	19:28	**G** is Diana of the Ephesians	*3173*
Ac	21:40	there was made a **g** silence, he	*4183*
Ac	22:6	shone from heaven a **g** light round	*2425*
Ac	23:14	bound ourselves under a **g** curse	
Ac	24:2	by thee we enjoy **g** quietness,	*4183*
Ac	24:7	with **g** violence took him away	*4183*
Ac	28:29	**g** reasoning among themselves	*4183*
1Co	16:9	a **g** door and effectual is opened	*3173*
2Co	1:10	delivered us from so **g** a death,	*5082*
Eph	2:4	for his **g** love wherewith he loved us,	*4183*
Eph	5:32	This is a **g** mystery: but I speak	*3173*
1Ti	3:16	**g** is the mystery of godliness:	*3173*
1Ti	6:6	godliness with contentment is **g** gain.	*3173*
2Ti	2:20	But in a **g** house there are not	*3173*
Tit	2:13	glorious appearing of the **g** God	*3173*
Heb	2:3	if we neglect so **g** salvation;	*5082*
Heb	4:14	that we have a **g** high priest,	*3173*
Heb	7:4	consider how **g** this man was,	*4080*
Heb	10:32	ye endured a **g** fight of afflictions;	*4183*
Heb	10:35	hath **g** recompence of reward	*3173*
Heb	12:1	with so **g** a cloud of witnesses,	*5118*
Heb	13:20	that **g** shepherd of the sheep,	*3173*
Jas	3:5	little member, and boasteth **g** things	*3166*
Jas	3:5	how **g** a matter a little fire kindleth!	*2245*
1Pe	3:4	is in the sight of God of **g** price	*4185*
2Pe	1:4	exceeding **g** and precious promises:	*3176*
2Pe	3:10	shall pass away with a **g** noise,	
Jude	6	unto the judgment of the **g** day	*3173*
Rev	1:10	and heard behind me a **g** voice,	*3173*
Rev	2:22	**into g tribulation, except they**	*3173*
Rev	6:4	was given unto him a **g** sword	*3173*
Rev	6:12	and, lo, there was a **g** earthquake;	*3173*
Rev	6:17	the **g** day of his wrath is come;	*3173*
Rev	7:9	and, lo, a **g** multitude, which no	*4183*
Rev	7:14	which came out of **g** tribulation,	*3173*
Rev	8:8	as it were a **g** mountain burning	*3173*
Rev	8:10	there fell a **g** star from heaven,	*3173*
Rev	9:2	as the smoke of a **g** furnace; and	*3173*
Rev	11:8	in the street of the **g** city, which	*3173*
Rev	11:11	**g** fear fell upon them which saw	*3173*
Rev	11:12	they heard a **g** voice from heaven	*3173*

Rev	11:13	same hour was there a **g** earthquake,	*3173*
Rev	11:15	there were **g** voices in heaven,	*3173*
Rev	11:17	hast taken to thee thy **g** power,	*3173*
Rev	11:18	that fear thy name, small and **g**;	*3173*
Rev	11:19	and an earthquake, and **g** hail	*3173*
Rev	12:1	a **g** wonder in heaven; a woman	*3173*
Rev	12:3	**g** red dragon, having seven heads	*3173*
Rev	12:9	And the **g** dragon was cast out	*3173*
Rev	12:12	devil … having **g** wrath, because he	*3173*
Rev	12:14	two wings of a **g** eagle, that she	*3173*
Rev	13:2	and his seat, and **g** authority	*3173*
Rev	13:13	he doeth **g** wonders, so that he	*3173*
Rev	13:16	he causeth all, both small and **g**,	*3173*
Rev	14:2	as the voice of a **g** thunder:	*3173*
Rev	14:19	into the **g** winepress of the wrath	*3173*
Rev	15:1	**g** and marvellous, seven angels	*3173*
Rev	15:3	**G** and marvelous are thy works,	*3173*
Rev	16:1	I heard a **g** voice out of the temple	*3173*
Rev	16:9	men were scorched with **g** heat,	*3173*
Rev	16:14	of that **g** day of God Almighty,	*3173*
Rev	16:17	came a **g** voice out of the temple	*3173*
Rev	16:18	there was a **g** earthquake, such as	*3173*
Rev	16:19	the **g** city was divided into three	*3173*
Rev	16:19	**g** Babylon came in remembrance	*3173*
Rev	17:1	judgment of the **g** whore that	*3173*
Rev	17:5	Mystery, Babylon The **G**, The	*3173*
Rev	17:18	is that **g** city, which reigneth over	*3173*
Rev	18:1	from heaven, having **g** power;	*3173*
Rev	18:2	Babylon the **g** is fallen, is fallen,	*3173*
Rev	18:10	Alas, alas that **g** city Babylon, that	*3173*
Rev	18:17	so **g** riches is come to nought	*5118*
Rev	18:18	What city is like unto this **g**	*3173*
Rev	18:21	took up a stone like a **g** millstone,	*3173*
Rev	18:21	shall that **g** city Babylon be thrown	*3173*
Rev	19:1	I heard a **g** voice of much people	*3173*
Rev	19:2	hath judged the **g** whore, which	*3173*
Rev	19:17	unto the supper of the **g** God;	*3173*
Rev	19:18	free and bond, both small and **g**	*3173*
Rev	20:1	and a **g** chain in his hand	*3173*
Rev	20:11	I saw a **g** white throne, and him	*3173*
Rev	20:12	I saw the dead, small and **g**,	*3173*
Rev	21:3	I heard a **g** voice out of heaven	*3173*
Rev	21:10	spirit to a **g** and high mountain,	*3173*
Rev	21:10	and shewed me that **g** city,	*3173*
Rev	21:12	had a wall **g** and high, and had	*3173*

GREATER

Ge	1:16	the **g** light to rule the day, and	1419
Ge	4:13	punishment is **g** than I can bear	1419
Ge	39:9	none **g** in this house than I;	1419
Ge	41:40	in the throne will I be **g** than thou	1431
Ex	18:11	the Lord is **g** than all gods;	1419
Nu	14:12	make of thee a **g** nation and	1419
Dt	1:28	The people is **g** and taller than	1419
Dt	7:1	seven nations **g** and mightier	7227
Dt	9:14	nation mightier and **g** than they	7227
Dt	11:23	ye shall possess **g** nations and	1419
2Sa	13:15	he hated her was **g** than the love	1419
2Sa	13:16	evil in sending me away is **g** than	1419
1Ki	1:47	and make his throne **g** than thy	
Est	9:4	this man Mordecai waxed **g** and	1419
Job	33:12	thee, that God is **g** than man	7235
La	4:6	people is **g** than the punishment	1431
Eze	8:15	shalt see **g** abominations than	1419
Hag	2:9	house shall be **g** than the former,	1419
Mt	11:11	**hath not risen a g than John the**	*3187*
Mt	12:6	**in this place is one g than the temple**	*3187*
Mt	12:41	**behold, a g than Jonas is here**	*1419*
Mt	12:42	**behold, a g than Solomon is here**	*1419*
Mt	23:14	**ye shall receive the g damnation,**	*4055*
Mk	12:40	**these shall receive g damnation**	*4055*
Lk	11:31	**behold, a g than Solomon is here.**	*4119*
Lk	11:32	**behold, a g than Jonas is here.**	*4119*
Lk	12:18	**pull down my barns, and build g;**	*3187*
Lk	20:47	**same shall receive g damnation**	*4055*
Lk	22:27	**For whether is g, he that sitteth**	*3137*
Jn	1:50	**thou shalt see g things than these**	*3137*
Jn	4:12	Art thou **g** than our father Jacob,	*3187*
Jn	5:36	**But I have g witness than that**	*3137*
Jn	10:29	**them me, is g than all; and no man**	*3187*
Jn	13:16	**The servant is not g than his lord;**	*3137*
Jn	13:16	**neither he that is sent g than he**	*3187*
Jn	14:12	**g works than these shall he do;**	*3137*
Jn	14:28	**for my Father is g than I**	*3187*
Jn	15:13	**G love hath no man than this,**	*3137*
Jn	15:20	**The servant is not g than his lord;**	*3137*
Jn	19:11	**me unto thee hath the g sin.**	*3137*
Ac	15:28	to lay upon you no **g** burden than	*4119*
1Co	14:5	for **g** is he that prophesieth than	*3187*
1Co	15:6	the **g** part remain unto this present,	*4119*
Heb	6:13	could swear by no **g**, he sware by	*3187*
Heb	9:11	a **g** and more perfect tabernacle,	*3187*
Heb	11:26	reproach of Christ **g** riches than	*3187*
Jas	3:1	shall receive the **g** condemnation	*3187*
2Pe	2:11	angels, which are **g** in power and	*3187*
1Jn	3:20	God is **g** than our heart, and	*3187*
1Jn	4:4	because **g** is he that is in you, than	*3187*
1Jn	5:9	of men, the witness of God is **g**:	*3187*
3Jn	4	I have no **g** joy than to hear that	*3186*

GREATEST

Job	1:3	was the **g** of all the men of the	1419
Jer	6:13	the least even unto the **g** of them	1419
Jer	31:34	least of them unto the **g** of them,	1419
Jer	42:8	people from the least even to the **g**,	1419
Jnh	3:5	the **g** of them even to the least of	1419
Mt	18:4	**the same is g in the kingdom of**	*3187*
Mt	23:11	**But he that is g among you shall**	*3187*
Mk	9:34	themselves, who should be the **g**.	*3187*
Lk	9:46	which of them should be **g**,	*3187*
Lk	22:26	**but he that is g among you, let**	*3187*
Ac	8:10	gave heed, from the least to the **g**,	*3173*
1Co	13:13	but the **g** of these is charity	*3187*
Heb	8:11	know me, from the least to the **g**	*3173*

GREATLY

Ge	3:16	I will **g** multiply thy sorrow and	
Ge	7:18	were increased **g** upon the earth;	3966
Ge	32:7	Jacob was **g** afraid and distressed:	3966
Ex	19:18	and the whole mount quaked **g**	3966
Nu	11:10	anger of the Lord was kindled **g**;	3966
Nu	14:39	Israel: and the people mourned **g**.	3966
Jos	10:2	they feared **g**, because Gibeon	3966
Jgs	2:15	and they were **g** distressed	3966
Jgs	6:6	And Israel was **g** impoverished	3966
1Sa	11:6	and his anger was kindled **g**	3966
1Sa	12:18	all the people **g** feared the Lord and	3966
1Sa	17:11	they were dismayed, and **g** afraid	3966
1Sa	28:5	afraid, and his heart **g** trembled	3966
1Sa	30:6	And David was **g** distressed; for	3966
2Sa	12:5	anger was **g** kindled against the man	3966
2Sa	24:10	have sinned **g** in that I have done:	3966

1Ch 16:25 great is the lord, and **g** to be praised: . . . 3966
1Ch 21:8 said unto God, I have sinned **g**, ... 3966
2Ch 33:12 humbled himself **g** before the God of. . . 3966
Job 3:25 thing which I **g** feared is come upon
Ps 28:7 therefore my heart **g** rejoiceth; and
Ps 38:6 I am bowed down **g**; I go mourning. . . . 3966
Ps 48:1 Lord, and **g** to be praised in the city. . . . 3966
Ps 62:2 defence; I shall not be **g** moved. 7227
Ps 89:7 God is **g** to be feared in the 7227
Ps 96:4 and **g** to be praised: he is to be feared. . . 3966
Ps 112:1 delighteth **g** in his commandments 3966
Ps 145:3 is the Lord, and **g** to be praised; 3966
Pr 23:24 father of the righteous shall **g** rejoice:
Isa 61:10 I will **g** rejoice in the Lord, my soul
Jer 4:10 thou hast **g** deceived this people
Eze 20:13 and my sabbaths they **g** polluted: 3966
Da 5:9 was king Belshazzar **g** troubled 7690
Da 10:19 O man **g** beloved, fear not:
Ob 2 the heathen: thou art **g** despised 3966
Zec 9:9 Rejoice **g**, O daughter of Zion; 3966
Mt 27:14 that the governor marvelled **g**. 3029
Mt 27:54 feared **g**, saying, Truly this was the *4970*
Mk 12:27 **the living: ye therefore do g err**. *4183*
Jn 3:29 friend of the bridegroom…rejoiceth **g**. . *5479*
Php 1:8 how **g** I long after you all in the *1971*
Php 4:10 I rejoiced in the Lord **g**, that now *3171*
2Ti 1:4 **G** desiring to see thee, being *1971*
2Ti 4:15 he hath **g** withstood our words *3029*
1Pe 1:6 Wherein ye **g** rejoice, though now for
2Jn 4 rejoiced **g** that I found of thy children . . *3029*
3Jn 3 I rejoiced **g**, when the brethren came . . . *3029*

GREATNESS
Ex 15:7 And in the **g** of thine excellency 7230
Ex 15:16 by the **g** of thine arm they shall be 1419
Nu 14:19 according unto the **g** of thy mercy, ... 1433
Dt 3:24 shew thy servant thy **g**, and thy. 1433
Dt 5:24 shewed his glory and his **g**, and we. 1433
Dt 32:3 Lord: ascribe ye **g** unto our God. 1433
1Ch 17:21 thee a name of **g** and terribleness 1420
1Ch 29:11 Thine, O Lord, is the **g**, and. 1420
2Ch 9:6 half of the **g** of thy wisdom was not. . . . 4768
Ne 13:22 according to the **g** of thy mercy 7230
Est 10:2 the **g** of Mordecai, whereunto the. 1420
Ps 66:3 through the **g** of thy power shall. 7230
Ps 145:3 and his **g** is unsearchable 1420
Ps 150:2 according to his excellent **g** 1433
Pr 5:23 and in the **g** of his folly he shall go. 7230
Isa 57:10 wearied in the **g** of thy way;. 7230
Eze 31:18 and in **g** among the trees of Eden? 1433
Da 7:27 **g** of the kingdom under the whole. 7238
Eph 1:19 exceeding **g** of his power to us-ward . . . *3174*

GREAVES
1Sa 17:6 he had **g** of brass upon his legs, ... 4697

GREEDILY
Pr 21:26 He coveteth **g** all the day long: 8378
Eze 22:12 thou hast **g** gained of thy neighbours
Jude 11 ran **g** after the error of Balaam *1632*

GREEDINESS
Eph 4:19 to work all uncleanness with **g**. *4124*

GREEDY
Ps 17:12 as a lion that is **g** of his prey 3700
Pr 1:19 ways of every one that is **g** of gain;. 1214
Pr 15:27 He that is **g** of gain troubleth his 1214
Isa 56:11 **g** dogs which can never have. 5794, 5315
1Ti 3:3 no striker, not **g** of filthy lucre; *866*
1Ti 3:8 to much wine, not **g** of filthy lucre; *146*

GREEN
Ge 1:30 have given every **g** herb for meat:. 3418
Ge 9:3 even as the **g** herb have I given 3418
Ex 10:15 there remained not any **g** thing. 3418
Jgs 16:7 bind me with seven **g** withs that. 3892
1Ki 14:23 high hill, and under every **g** tree 7488
2Ch 28:4 the hills, and under every **g** tree 7488
Job 39:8 he searcheth after every **g** thing. 3387
Ps 23:2 maketh me to lie down in **g** pastures:. . . 1877
Ps 37:2 grass, and wither as the **g** herb 3418
Ps 52:8 am like a **g** olive tree in the house. 7488
Isa 15:6 grass faileth, there is no **g** thing. 3418
Isa 57:5 under every **g** tree, slaying the. 7488
Jer 2:20 under every **g** tree thou wanderest 7488
Jer 3:13 under, every **g** tree, and ye have 7488
Jer 17:8 cometh, but her leaf shall be **g**; 7488
Eze 6:13 under every **g** tree, and under. 7488
Eze 17:24 have dried up the **g** tree, and. 3892
Eze 20:47 shall devour every **g** tree in thee, ... 3892
Lk 23:31 **they do these things in a g tree**, ... *5200*
Rev 8:7 and all **g** grass was burnt up *5515*
Rev 9:4 neither any **g** thing, neither any *5515*

GREET
1Sa 25:5 go to Nabal, and **g** him in 7592, 7965
Ro 16:3 **G** Priscilla and Aquila my. *782*
1Co 16:20 brethren **g** you. **G** ye one another *782*
2Co 13:12 **G** one another with an holy kiss, ... *782*
1Th 5:26 **G** all the brethren with an holy *782*
Tit 3:15 **G** them that love us in the faith. *782*
1Pe 5:14 **G** ye one another with a kiss of. *782*

GREETING
Ac 23:26 excellent governor Felix sendeth **g** *5463*
Jas 1:1 which are scattered abroad, **g** *5463*

GREETINGS
Mt 23:7 **And g in the markets, and to be** *783*
Lk 11:43 **synagogues and g in the markets** *783*
Lk 20:46 **love g in the markets, and the**. *783*

GREW
Ge 2:5 every herb of the field before it **g**:. 6779
Ge 19:25 that which **g** upon the ground 6780
Ge 21:20 God was with the lad; and he **g**, ... 1431
Ge 25:27 And the boys **g**: and Esau was. 1431
Ge 47:27 had possession therein, and **g**,. 6509
Ex 1:12 the more they multiplied and **g** 6555
1Sa 2:21 child Samuel **g** before the Lord. 1431
2Sa 12:3 it **g** up together with him, and 1431
Da 4:11 The tree **g**, and was strong, and 7236
Da 4:20 tree that thou sawest, which **g**. 7236
Mk 4:7 **thorns g up, and choked it, and it** *305*
Mk 5:26 nothing bettered, but rather **g** worse,. . . *2064*
Lk 1:80 And the child **g**, and waxed strong *837*
Lk 2:40 And the child **g**, and waxed strong *837*
Lk 13:19 **it g, and waxed a great tree;**. *837*
Ac 12:24 the word of God **g** and multiplied *837*
Ac 19:20 So mightily **g** the word of God *837*

GREY (so most editions here) See also GRAY.
Pr 20:29 beauty of old men is the **g** head 7872

GREYHEADED (so most editions here)
Ps 71:18 Now also when I am old and **g**, ... 7872

GRIEF
Ge 26:35 Which were a **g** of mind unto Isaac 4786
1Sa 1:16 my complaint and **g** have I spoken. 3708
Job 2:13 they saw that his **g** was very great 3511
Job 6:2 that my **g** were thoroughly weighed, . . . 3708
Ps 6:7 eye is consumed because of **g**; 3708
Ps 31:9 mine eye is consumed with **g**, yea, ... 3708
Ps 31:10 For my life is spent with **g**,. 3015
Pr 17:25 A foolish son is a **g** to his father, ... 3708
Ecc 1:18 For in much wisdom is much **g**: 3708
Isa 53:3 of sorrows, and acquainted with **g**:. 2483
Isa 53:10 bruise him; he hath put him to **g**: 2470
Jer 10:19 Truly this is a **g**, and I must bear it. 2483
Jer 45:3 Lord hath added **g** to my sorrow; 3015
La 3:32 though he cause **g**, yet will he 3013
Jnh 4:6 head, to deliver him from his **g**. 7451
Heb 13:17 do it with joy, and not with **g**: *4727*
1Pe 2:19 conscience toward God endure **g**, ... *3077*

GRIEFS
Isa 53:4 hath borne our **g**, and carried our 2483

GRIEVANCE
Hab 1:3 and cause me to behold **g**? 5999

GRIEVE
1Sa 2:33 thine eyes, and to **g** thine heart: 109
Ps 78:40 wilderness, and **g** him in the desert!. . . . 6087
La 3:33 afflict willingly nor **g** the children of. . . . 3013
Eph 4:30 And **g** not the holy spirit of God, ... *3076*

GRIEVED
Ge 6:6 the earth, and it **g** him at his heart, ... 6087
Ge 45:5 be not **g**, nor angry with yourselves,. . . . 6087
Jgs 10:16 soul was **g** for the misery of Israel 7114
1Sa 1:8 why is thy heart **g**? am not I better 7489
1Sa 15:11 it **g** Samuel; and he cried unto 2734
1Sa 20:34 was **g** for David, because his father. 6087
1Sa 30:6 the soul of all the people was **g**, ... 4784
2Sa 19:2 the king was **g** for his son 6087
Ne 8:11 for the day is holy; neither be ye **g** 6087
Est 4:4 Then was the queen exceedingly **g**;. 2342
Job 4:2 commune with thee, wilt thou be **g**? . . . 3811
Job 30:25 was not my soul **g** for the poor? 5701
Ps 95:10 Forty years long was I **g** with. 6962
Ps 112:10 The wicked shall see it, and be **g**; 3707
Ps 119:158 beheld the transgressors, and was **g**;. . . . 6962
Ps 139:21 am not I **g** with those that rise up 6962
Isa 54:6 thee as a woman forsaken and **g**. 6087
Da 7:15 I Daniel was **g** in my spirit. 3735
Mk 3:5 **g** for the hardness of their hearts *4818*
Mk 10:22 sad at that saying, and went away **g**: *3076*
Jn 21:17 Peter was **g** because he said unto *3076*
Ac 4:2 **g** that they taught the people, ... *1278*
Ac 16:18 Paul, being **g**, turned and said to. *1278*
2Co 2:4 not that ye should be **g**, but that. *3076*
Heb 3:17 But with whom was he **g** forty years?. . . *4360*

GRIEVETH
Ru 1:13 for it **g** me much for your sakes 4843
Pr 26:15 it **g** him to bring it again to his. 3811

GRIEVOUS
Ge 12:10 the famine was **g** in the land 3515
Ge 18:20 and because their sin is very **g**; 3513
Ge 21:11 the thing was very **g** in Abraham's 7489
Ge 21:12 Let it not be **g** in thy sight because 7489
Ge 41:31 following; for it shall be very **g** 3515
Ex 8:24 there came a **g** swarm of flies 3515
Ex 9:3 there shall be a very **g** murrain 3515
Ex 9:18 will cause it to rain a very **g** hail,. 3515
Ex 9:24 fire mingled with the hail, very **g**,. 3515
1Ki 2:8 cursed me with a **g** curse in the 4834
1Ki 12:4 Thy father made our yoke **g** 7185
Ps 31:18 be put to silence; which speak **g** 6277
Pr 15:1 wrath: but **g** words stir up anger. 6089
Pr 15:10 Correction is **g** unto him that 7451
Ecc 2:17 under the sun is **g** unto me: for. 7451
Isa 15:4 out; his life shall be **g** unto him. 3415
Jer 10:19 is me for my hurt! my wound is **g**: 2470
Na 3:19 of thy bruise; thy wound is **g**: 2470
Mt 23:4 **heavy burdens and g to be borne,** *1418*
Lk 11:46 **burdens g to be borne, and ye.** *1418*
Ac 20:29 shall **g** wolves enter in among you, ... *926*
Php 3:1 to me indeed is not **g**, but for *3636*
Heb 12:11 present seemeth to be joyous, but **g**:. . . . *3077*
1Jn 5:3 and his commandments are not **g** *926*
Rev 16:2 a noisome and **g** sore upon the men. . . . *4190*

GRIEVOUSLY
Isa 9:1 afterward did more **g** afflict her 3513
Jer 23:19 fall **g** upon the head of the wicked. 2342
La 1:8 Jerusalem hath **g** sinned; 2399
Eze 14:13 sinneth against me by trespassing **g**,. . . . 4604
Mt 8:6 sick of the palsy, **g** tormented *1171*
Mt 15:22 daughter is **g** vexed with a devil *2560*

GRIND
Jgs 16:21 and he did **g** in the prison house 2912
Job 31:10 Then let my wife **g** unto another, ... 2912
La 5:13 They took the young men to **g** 2911
Mt 21:44 **shall fall, it will g him to powder,** *3039*
Lk 20:18 **shall fall, it will g him to powder** *3039*

GRINDERS
Ecc 12:3 the **g** cease because they are few,. 2912

GRINDING
Mt 24:41 **Two women shall be g at the mill;** *229*
Lk 17:35 **Two women shall be g together;** *229*

GRISLED
Ge 31:10 ringstraked, speckled, and **g**, ... 1261
Ge 31:12 are ringstraked, speckled, and **g**; 1261
Zec 6:3 forth chariot **g** and bay horses 1261

GROAN
Jer 51:52 all her land the wounded shall **g**. 602
Joel 11:18 How do the beasts **g**! the herds 584
Ro 8:23 we ourselves **g** within ourselves. *4727*
2Co 5:2 in this we **g**, earnestly desiring to *4727*
2Co 5:4 we that are in this tabernacle do **g**, ... *4727*

GROANED
Jn 11:33 **g** in the spirit, and was troubled, ... *1690*

GROANETH
Ro 8:22 **g** and travaileth in pain together. *4959*

GROANING
Ex 2:24 heard their **g**, and God remembered . . . 5009
Job 23:2 my stroke is heavier than my **g**,. 585
Ps 6:6 I am weary with my **g**; all the 585
Ps 102:20 To hear the **g** of the prisoner; 603

Jn 11:38 therefore again **g** in himself *1690*
Ac 7:34 I have heard their **g**, and am come *4726*

GROANINGS
Jgs 2:18 because of their **g** by reason of 5009
Eze 30:24 the **g** of a deadly wounded man 5009
Ro 8:26 with **g** which cannot be uttered *4726*

GROPE
Dt 28:29 thou shalt **g** at noonday, as the 4959
Job 5:14 **g** in the noonday as in the night 4959
Job 12:25 They **g** in the dark without light, ... 4959
Isa 59:10 We **g** for the wall like the blind, ... 1659
Isa 59:10 and we **g** as if we had no eyes: 1659

GROPETH
Dt 28:29 as the blind **g** in darkness, and 4959

GROSS
Isa 60:2 earth, and **g** darkness the people: 6205
Jer 13:16 of death, and make it **g** darkness 6205
Mt 13:15 **this people's heart is waxed g,** *3975*
Ac 28:27 the heart of this people is waxed **g**, ... *3975*

GROUND See also AGROUND.
Ge 2:5 there was not a man to till the **g** 127
Ge 2:6 and watered the whole face of the **g** 127
Ge 2:7 formed man of the dust of the **g**, ... 127
Ge 2:9 out of the **g** made the Lord God to 127
Ge 2:19 out of the **g** the Lord God formed 127
Ge 3:17 cursed is the **g** for thy sake; 127
Ge 3:19 eat bread, till thou return unto the **g**; 127
Ge 3:23 to till the **g** from whence he was 127
Ge 4:2 but Cain was a tiller of the **g** 127
Ge 4:10 blood crieth unto me from the **g** 127
Ge 5:29 the **g** which the Lord hath cursed 127
Ge 7:23 which was upon the face of the **g**, ... 127
Ge 8:8 abated from off the face of the **g**; 127
Ge 8:13 behold, the face of the **g** was dry 127
Ge 18:2 and bowed himself toward the **g**, ... 776
Ge 19:1 with his face toward the **g**, ... 776
Ge 33:3 himself to the **g** seven times, ... 776
Ge 38:9 he spilled it on the **g**, lest that he 776
Ge 44:14 and they fell before him on the **g**, ... 776
Ex 3:5 whereon thou standest is holy **g** 127
Ex 4:3 And he said, Cast it on the **g**, ... 776
Ex 14:16 shall go on dry **g** through the
Ex 14:22 midst of the sea upon the dry **g**
Ex 32:20 the fire, and **g** it to powder, ... 2912
Le 20:25 that creepeth on the **g**, which I 127
Nu 16:31 **g** clave asunder that was under 127
Dt 4:18 anything that creepeth on the **g**, ... 127
Dt 9:21 **g** it very small, even until it was 2912
Dt 15:23 shalt pour it upon the **g** as water 776
Jos 3:17 stood firm on dry **g** in the midst
Jos 3:17 Israelites passed over on dry **g**,
Jos 24:32 a parcel of **g** which Jacob bought 7704
Jgs 6:39 and upon all the **g** let there be dew 776
Jgs 13:20 and fell on their faces to the **g** 776
1Sa 3:19 let none of his words fall to the **g** 776
1Sa 14:45 not one hair of his head fall to the **g**; 776
1Sa 28:14 and stooped with his face to the **g**, ... 776
2Sa 2:22 should I smite thee to the **g**? 776
2Sa 14:4 she fell on her face to the **g**, and did 776
2Sa 14:22 Joab fell to the **g** on his face 776
2Sa 18:11 thou not smite him there to the **g**? 776
2Ki 2:8 so that they two went over on dry **g**,
2Ki 2:15 themselves to the **g** before him 776
Ne 10:37 the tithes of our **g** unto the Levites, ... 127
Job 1:20 down upon the **g**, and worshipped, ... 776
Job 2:13 they sat down with him upon the **g** 776
Ps 89:44 cast his throne down to the **g** 776
Ps 105:35 and devoured the fruit of their **g** 127
Ps 143:3 hath smitten my life down to the **g**; 776
Ps 147:6 casteth the wicked down to the **g** 776
Isa 21:9 her gods he hath broken unto the **g** 776
Isa 28:24 and break the clods of his **g**? 127
Isa 29:4 familiar spirit, out of the **g**, and 776
Isa 47:1 sit on the **g**: there is no throne, ... 776
Jer 4:3 Break up your fallow **g**, and sow
La 2:2 hath brought them down to the **g**: 776
La 2:10 sit upon the **g**, and keep silence: 776
Eze 12:12 that he see not the **g** with his eyes 776
Eze 19:13 wilderness, in a dry and thirsty **g** 776
Eze 38:20 every wall shall fall to the **g** 776
Da 8:10 the host and of the stars to the **g**, ... 776
Da 8:12 it cast down the truth to the **g**; 776
Hos 2:18 with the creeping things of the **g**: 127
Hos 10:12 mercy; break up your fallow **g**:
Ob 3 Who shall bring me down to the **g**? 776
Zec 8:12 and the **g** shall give her increase, ... 776
Mt 10:29 **shall not fall on the g without** *1093*
Mt 13:8 **But other fell into good g, and** *1093*
Mt 13:23 **received seed into the good g is** *1093*
Mk 4:5 **some fell on stony g, where it**
Mk 4:8 **other fell on good g, and did** *1093*
Mk 4:26 **man should cast seed into the g;** *1093*
Mk 14:35 fell on the **g**, and prayed that, if it *1093*
Lk 8:8 **other fell on good g, and sprang** *1093*
Lk 8:15 **But that on the good g are they,** *1093*
Lk 12:16 **g of a certain rich man brought** *5561*
Lk 13:7 **down; why cumbereth it the g?** *1093*
Lk 14:18 **I have bought a piece of g, and I,** *68*
Lk 19:44 **shall lay thee even with the g** *1474*
Lk 22:44 of blood falling down to the **g** *1093*
Jn 8:6 with his finger wrote on the **g**, ... *1093*
Jn 8:8 stooped down, and wrote on the **g** *1093*
Jn 9:6 he spat on the **g**, and made day *5476*
Ac 7:33 where thou standest is holy **g** *1093*
Ac 22:7 I fell unto the **g**, and heard *1475*
1Ti 3:15 the pillar and **g** of the truth *1477*

GROUNDED
Eph 3:17 ye, being rooted and **g** in love, ... *2311*
Col 1:23 continue in the faith **g** and settled, ... *2311*

GROVE
Ge 21:33 And Abraham planted a **g** in 815
Dt 16:21 Thou shalt not plant thee a **g** 842
Jgs 6:30 he hath cut down the **g** that was 842
1Ki 15:13 she had made an idol in a **g**; 842
2Ki 17:16 even two calves, and made a **g**, ... 842
2Ki 21:7 set a graven image of the **g** that 842
2Ki 23:4 for Baal, and for the **g**, and for 842
2Ki 23:6 he brought out the **g** from the 842
2Ki 23:15 to powder, and burned the **g** 842

GROVES
Ex 34:13 images, and cut down their **g** 842
Dt 12:3 and burn their **g** with fire; 842
Jgs 3:7 and served Baalim and the **g** 842
1Ki 14:15 because they have made their **g**, ... 842
1Ki 18:19 prophets of the **g** four hundred 842
2Ki 18:4 the images, and cut down the **g**, ... 842
2Ch 19:3 thou hast taken away the **g** 842

2Ch 24:18 fathers, and served **g** and idols: 842
2Ch 31:1 in pieces, and cut down the **g**, 842
2Ch 34:4 the **g**, and the carved images, 842
Isa 17:8 made, either the **g**, or the images 842
Isa 27:9 the **g** and images shall not stand 842
Mic 5:14 I will pluck up thy **g** out of the 842

GROW See also GREW.
Ge 2:9 the Lord God to **g** every tree 6779
Ge 48:16 and let them **g** into a multitude 1711
Nu 6:5 locks of the hair of his head **g** 1431
Jgs 16:22 the hair of his head began to **g** 6779
2Sa 23:5 although he make it not to **g** 6779
2Ki 19:29 such things as **g** of themselves, 5599
Ezr 4:22 why should damage **g** to the hurt 7680
Job 8:11 Can the rush **g** up without mire? 1342
Job 8:11 can the flag **g** without water? 1342
Job 31:40 Let thistles **g** instead of wheat, 3318
Ps 92:12 shall **g** like a cedar in Lebanon 7685
Ps 104:14 causeth the grass to **g** for the 6779
Ps 147:8 who maketh grass to **g** upon the 6779
Ecc 11:5 nor how the bones do **g** in the womb
Isa 11:1 Branch shall **g** out of his roots: 6509
Isa 53:2 For he shall **g** up before him as a 5927
Jer 33:15 Branch of righteousness to **g** up 6779
Eze 44:20 nor suffer their locks to **g** long; 7971
Eze 47:12 on that side, shall **g** all trees for meat 5927
Hos 14:5 he shall **g** as the lily, and cast 6524
Jnh 4:10 neither madest it **g**; which came 1431
Zec 6:12 and he shall **g** up out of his place, 6779
Mal 4:2 forth, and **g** up as calves of the stall 6335
Mt 6:28 **the lilies of the field, how they g;** *837*
Mt 13:30 **both g together until the harvest;** *4886*
Mt 21:19 **no fruit g on thee henceforward** *1096*
Mk 4:27 **the seed should spring and g up,** *3373*
Lk 12:27 **Consider the lilies how they g:** *837*
Eph 4:15 may **g** up into him in all things *837*
1Pe 2:2 of the word, that ye may **g** thereby: *837*
2Pe 3:18 But **g** in grace, and in the knowledge *837*

GROWETH
Ex 10:5 every tree which **g** for you out of 6779
Le 13:39 freckled spot that **g** in the skin; 6524
Le 25:5 That which **g** of it own accord 5599
Le 25:11 reap that which **g** of itself in it, 5599
Dt 29:23 nor any grass **g** therein, like the 5927
Jgs 19:9 the day **g** to an end, lodge here, 2583
Ps 90:5 they are like grass which **g** up. 2498
Ps 90:6 morning it flourisheth, and **g** up; 2498
Ps 129:6 which withereth afore it **g** up: 8025
Isa 37:30 eat this year such as **g** of itself; 5599
Mk 4:32 **when it is sown, it g up, and** *305*
Eph 2:21 **g** unto an holy temple in the Lord; *837*
2Th 1:3 because that your faith **g** exceedingly, *5232*

GROWN
Ge 38:14 she saw that Shelah was **g**, and 1431
Ex 2:11 when Moses was **g**, that he went 1431
Ru 1:13 ye tarry for them till they were **g**? 1431
2Sa 10:5 until your beards be **g**, and then 6779
1Ki 12:10 young men that were **g** up with him 1431
2Ki 4:18 when the child was **g**, it fell on a day 1431
1Ch 19:5 at Jericho until your beards be **g**, 6779
Ezr 9:6 our trespass is **g** up unto the heavens 1431
Ps 144:12 as plants **g** up in their youth; 1431
Pr 24:31 it was all **g** over with thorns, 5927
Jer 50:11 ye are **g** fat as the heifer at grass, 6335

Da 4:22 O king, that are **g** and become strong: 7236
Da 4:22 thy greatness is **g**, and reacheth unto 7236
Da 4:33 till his hairs were **g** like eagles' feathers 7236
Mt 13:32 **but when it is g, it is the greatest** *837*

GROWTH
Am 7:1 lo, it was the latter **g** after the king's 3954

GRUDGE
Le 19:18 bear any **g** against the children 5201
Ps 59:15 and **g** if they be not satisfied. 3885
Jas 5:9 **G** not one against another, *4727*

GRUDGING
1Pe 4:9 hospitality one to another without **g** *1112*

GRUDGINGLY
2Co 9:7 give; not **g**, or of necessity: *1537, 3077*

G

GUARD See also SAFEGUARD.
Ge 39:1 officer of Pharaoh, captain of the **g**, 2876
Ge 40:4 of the **g** charged Joseph with them, 2876
Ge 41:12 servant to the captain of the **g**; 2876
2Sa 23:23 And David set him over his **g** 4928
2Ki 10:25 Jehu said to the **g** and to the captains 7323
2Ki 11:6 third part at the gate behind the **g**: 7323
2Ki 11:11 **g** stood, every man with his weapons 7323
2Ki 11:13 Athaliah heard the noise of the **g** 7323
2Ki 11:19 gate of the **g** to the king's house 7323
2Ki 25:11 the captain of the **g** carry away 2876
2Ki 25:12 the captain of the **g** left of the poor 2876
2Ki 25:15 the captain of the **g** took away 2876
2Ch 12:11 the **g** came and fetched them, 7323
Ne 4:22 in the night they may be a **g** to us, 4929
Jer 39:10 the captain of the **g** left of the poor 2876
Jer 40:1 the captain of the **g** had let him go 2876
Jer 40:2 the captain of the **g** took Jeremiah, 2876
Jer 40:5 captain of the **g** gave him victuals 2876
Jer 52:14 the captain of the **g**, brake down 2876
Jer 52:15 the captain of the **g** carried away 2876
Eze 38:7 thee, and be thou a **g** unto them 4929
Da 2:14 captain of the king's **g**,which was 2877
Ac 28:16 to the captain of the **g**: but Paul was *4759*

GUARD'S
Ge 41:10 captain of the **g** house, both me and 2876

GUEST
Lk 19:7 to be **g** with a man that is a sinner *2647*

GUESTCHAMBER
Mk 14:14 **The Master saith, Where is the g,** *2646*
Lk 22:11 **saith unto thee, Where is the g,** *2646*

GUESTS
1Ki 1:41 all the **g** that were with him heard it 7121
Pr 9:18 her **g** are in the depths of hell. 7121
Zep 1:7 a sacrifice, he hath bid his **g** 7121
Mt 22:10 **the wedding was furnished with g** *345*
Mt 22:11 **when the king came to see the g,** *345*

GUIDE
Job 38:32 canst thou **g** Arcturus with his 5148
Ps 25:9 The meek will he **g** in judgment: 1869
Ps 31:3 thy name's sake lead me, and **g** me. 5095
Ps 32:8 I will **g** thee with mine eye. 3289
Ps 48:14 he will be our **g** even unto death 5090
Ps 55:13 my **g**, and mine acquaintance 441
Ps 73:24 Thou shalt **g** me with thy counsel, 5148

Ps	112:5	will **g** his affairs with discretion	3557
Pr	2:17	forsaketh the **g** of her youth,	441
Pr	6:7	having no **g**, overseer, or ruler,	7101
Pr	11:3	integrity of the upright shall **g** them:	5148
Pr	23:19	be wise, and **g** thine heart in the way	833
Isa	51:18	There is none to **g** her among all	5095
Isa	58:11	And the Lord shall **g** thee	5148
Jer	3:4	Father, thou art the **g** of my youth?	441
Mic	7:5	put ye not confidence in a **g**:	441
Lk	1:79	**g** our feet into the way of peace	*2720*
Jn	16:13	**he will g you into all truth:**	*3594*
Ac	1:16	was **g** to them that took Jesus	*3595*
Ac	8:31	except some man should **g** me?	*3594*
Ro	2:19	thyself art a **g** of the blind, a light	*3595*
1Ti	5:14	**g** the house, give none occasion	*3616*

GUIDED

Ex	15:13	thou hast **g** them in thy strength	5095
2Ch	32:22	all other, and **g** them on every side	5095
Job	31:18	a father, and I have **g** her from my	5148
Ps	78:52	**g** them in the wilderness like a flock.	5090
Ps	78:72	**g** them by the skilfulness of his	5148

GUIDES

Mt	23:16	**Woe unto you, ye blind g, which**	*3595*
Mt	23:24	**Ye blind g, which strain at a gnat**	*3595*

GUILE

Ex	21:14	to slay him with **g**; thou shalt	6195
Ps	32:2	in whose spirit there is no **g**.	7423
Ps	34:13	and thy lips from speaking **g**	4820
Ps	55:11	deceit and **g** depart not from her	4820
Jn	1:47	**Israelite indeed, in whom is no g!**	*1388*
2Co	12:16	being crafty, I caught you with **g**.	*1388*
1Th	2:3	nor of uncleanness, nor in **g**:	*1388*
1Pe	2:1	laying aside all malice, and all **g**	*1388*
1Pe	2:22	neither was **g** found in his mouth:	*1388*
1Pe	3:10	his lips that they speak no **g**:	*1388*
Rev	14:5	in their mouth was found no **g**:	*1388*

GUILT See also GUILTLESS; INNOCENT.

Dt	19:13	Shalt put away the **g** of innocent	
Dt	21:9	put away the **g** of innocent blood	

GUILTINESS See also BLOODGUILTINESS.

Ge	26:10	shouldest have brought **g** upon us	817

GUILTLESS

Ex	26:7	the Lord will not hold him **g**.	5352
Nu	5:31	the man be **g** from iniquity,	5352
Nu	32:22	be **g** before the Lord, and before	5355
Dt	5:11	the Lord will not hold him **g**.	5352
Jos	2:19	upon his head, and we will be **g**:	5355
1Sa	26:9	the Lord's anointed, and be **g**?	5352
2Sa	3:28	I and my kingdom are **g**.	5355
2Sa	14:9	the king and his throne be **g**	5355
1Ki	2:9	hold him not **g**: for thou art	5352
Mt	12:7	**would not have condemned the g**	*335*

GUILTY

Ge	42:21	verily **g** concerning our brother,	816
Ex	34:7	and that will by no means clear the **g**;	
Le	4:13	should not be done, and are **g**;	816
Le	4:22	should not be done, and is **g**;	816
Le	4:27	ought not to be done, and be **g**;	816
Le	5:17	though he wist it not, yet is he **g**,	816
Le	6:4	because he hath sinned, and is **g**, that	816
Nu	5:6	the Lord, and that person be **g**;	816
Nu	14:18	and by no means clearing the **g**	
Nu	35:27	the slayer; he shall not be **g** of blood:	
Nu	35:31	a murderer, which is **g** of death:	7563
Pr	30:10	curse thee, and thou be found **g**	816
Eze	22:4	Thou art become **g** in thy blood	816
Zec	11:5	slay them, and hold themselves not **g**:	816
Mt	23:18	**bye the gift that is upon it, he is g**	*3784*
Mt	26:66	answered and said, He is **g** of death	*1777*
Mk	14:64	condemned him to be **g** of death	*1777*
Ro	3:19	world may become **g** before God	*5257*
1Co	11:27	shall be **g** of the body and blood	*1777*
Jas	2:10	offend in one point, he is **g** of all	*1777*

GULF

Lk	16:26	**us and you there is a great g fixed:**	*5490*

GUSHED

1Ki	18:28	till the blood **g** out upon them	8210
Ps	78:20	smote the rock, that the waters **g** out,	2100
Isa	48:21	the rock also, and the waters **g** out	2100
Ac	1:18	midst, and all his bowels **g** out	*1632*

GUTTER

2Sa	5:8	Whosoever getteth up to the **g**	6794

GUTTERS

Ge	30:38	rods ... before the flocks in the **g**	7298

H

HABITATION

Ex	15:2	and I will prepare him an **h**;	5115
Ex	15:13	in thy strength unto the holy **h**	5116
Dt	26:15	Look down from thy holy **h**,	4583
1Sa	2:29	I have commanded in my **h**;	4583
2Ch	6:2	have built an house of **h** for thee,	2073
Eze	7:15	Israel, whose **h** is in Jerusalem,	4907
Ps	33:14	From the place of his **h** he looketh	3427
Ps	68:5	the widows, is God in his holy **h**	4583
Ps	89:14	judgment … the **h** of thy throne:	4349
Ps	97:2	judgment are the **h** of his throne	4349
Ps	132:5	**h** for the mighty God of Jacob	4908
Pr	3:33	but he blesseth the **h** of the just	5116
Isa	27:10	and the **h** forsaken, and left like	5116
Isa	32:18	people shall dwell in a peaceable **h**,	5116
Isa	35:7	in the **h** of dragons, where each	5116
Isa	63:15	behold from the **h** of thy holiness	2073
Jer	9:6	Thine **h** is in the midst of deceit;	3427
Jer	25:30	utter his voice from his holy **h**;	4583
Jer	33:12	an **h** of shepherds causing their	5116
Jer	50:7	the **h** of justice, even the Lord,	5116
Ob	3	whose **h** is high; that saith in his	3427
Hab	3:11	and moon stood still in their **h**	2073
Zec	2:13	is raised up out of his holy **h**	4583
Ac	17:26	and the bounds of their **h**;	*2733*
Eph	2:22	for an **h** of God through the	*2732*
Jude	6	but left their own **h**, he hath	*3613*
Rev	18:2	and is become the **h** of devils	*2732*

HABITATIONS

Ex	12:20	in all your **h** shall ye eat	4186
Ex	35:3	kindle no fire throughout your **h**	4186
Nu	15:2	the land of your **h**, which I give	4186
Ps	74:20	are full of the **h** of cruelty	4999
Jer	9:10	and for the **h** of the wilderness	4999
Jer	21:13	or who shall enter into our **h**?	4585
Jer	25:37	the peaceable **h** are cut down	4999
La	2:2	swallowed up all the **h** of Jacob,	4999
Am	1:2	**h** of the shepherds shall mourn,	4999
Lk	16:9	**receive you into everlasting h**	*4633*

HAIL

Ex	9:18	to rain a very grievous **h**, such as	1259
Ex	9:24	was **h**, and fire mingled with the **h**,	1259
Ex	9:25	the **h** smote every herb of the field,	1259
Ex	9:26	of Israel were, was there no **h**	1259
Ex	9:34	saw that the rain and the **h** and	1259
Ex	10:12	even all that the **h** hath left	1259
Ps	18:12	thick clouds passed, **h** stones and	1259
Ps	18:13	his voice; **h** stones and coals of	1259
Ps	105:32	He gave them **h** for rain, and	1259
Ps	148:8	Fire, and **h**; snow, and vapours;	1259
Isa	28:17	the **h** shall sweep away the refuge	1259
Mt	26:49	and said, **H**, master; and kissed	*5463*
Mt	27:29	mocked him, saying, **H**, King of the	*5463*
Mt	28:9	Jesus met them, saying, All **h**	*5463*
Mk	15:18	salute him, **H**, King of the Jews!	*5463*
Lk	1:28	**H** thou that art highly favoured,	*5463*
Jn	19:3	And said, **H**, King of the Jews!	*5463*
Rev	8:7	followed **h** and fire mingled with	*5464*
Rev	11:19	and an earthquake, and great **h**	*5464*
Rev	16:21	because of the plague of the **h**;	*5464*

HAILSTONES

Jos	10:11	more which died with **h** than	68, 1259
Isa	30:30	scattering, and tempest, and **h**	68, 1259
Eze	13:13	and great **h** in my fury to	68, 417
Eze	38:22	and great **h**, fire, and brimstone	68, 417

HAIR

Ex	26:7	shalt make curtains of goats' **h** to	
Le	13:3	and when the **h** in the plague is	8181
Le	13:40	whose **h** is fallen off his head, he	4803
Le	14:9	eyebrows, even all his **h** he shall	8181
Nu	6:5	let the locks of the **h** of his head	8181
Nu	6:19	of the Nazarite, after the **h** of his	
Jgs	16:22	the **h** of his head began to grow	8181
Jgs	20:16	could sling stones at an **h** breadth,	8185
1Sa	14:45	there shall not one **h** of his head	8185
2Sa	14:26	he weighed the **h** of his head	8181
Ezr	9:3	plucked off the **h** of my head	8181
Job	4:15	the **h** of my flesh stood up:	8185
Isa	50:6	to them that plucked off the **h**:	
Jer	7:29	Cut off thine **h**, O Jerusalem, and	5145
Eze	5:1	balances to weigh and divide the **h**	
Da	3:27	nor was an **h** of their head singed,	8177
Da	7:9	and the **h** of his head like the pure	8177
Mt	5:36	**canst not make one h white or**	*2359*
Mk	1:6	John was clothed with camel's **h**,	*2359*
Lk	21:18	**But there shall not an h of your**	*2359*
Jn	11:2	and wiped his feet with her **h**,	*2359*
Jn	12:3	wiped his feet with her **h**:	*2359*
Ac	27:34	shall not an **h** fall from the head	*2359*
1Co	11:14	if a man have long **h**, it is a	*2863*
1Co	11:15	But if a woman have long **h**, it is a	*2863*
1Ti	2:9	not with broided **h**, or gold, or	*4117*
1Pe	3:3	of plaiting the **h**, and of wearing	*2359*
Rev	6:12	black as sackcloth of **h**,	*5155*
Rev	9:8	And they had **h** as the **h** of	*2359*

HAIR-BREADTH See HAIR and BREADTH.

HAIRS

Ge	42:38	bring down my gray **h** with sorrow	
Ps	40:12	they are more than the **h** of mine	8185
Ps	69:4	cause are more than the **h** of mine	8185
Isa	46:4	even to hoar **h** will I carry you:	
Da	4:33	his **h** were grown like eagles'	8177
Mt	10:30	**the very h of your head are all**	*2359*
Lk	7:44	**wiped them with the h of her**	*2359*
Lk	12:7	**But even the very h of your head**	*2359*
Rev	1:14	His head and his **h** were white	*2359*

HAIRY

Ge	27:11	Esau my brother is a **h** man, and	8163
2Ki	1:8	answered him, He was an **h**	1167, 8181

HALE

Lk	12:58	**lest he h thee to the judge,**	*2694*

HALF

Ex	24:6	Moses took **h** of the blood, and	2677
Ex	30:13	**h** a shekel after the shekel of the	4276
Le	6:20	**h** of it in the morning, and **h**	4276
Nu	12:12	of whom the flesh is **h** consumed	2677
Nu	31:36	the **h**, which was the portion	4275
Nu	34:14	and **h** the tribe of Manasseh have	2677
Jos	8:33	**h** of them over against mount	2677

Jos	22:7	Now to the one **h** of the tribe of	2677
2Sa	10:4	shaved off the one **h** of their beards,	2677
1Ki	3:25	give **h** to the one, and **h** to the	2677
1Ki	10:7	the **h** was not told me: thy wisdom	2677
1Ki	13:8	If thou wilt give me **h** thine house,	2677
2Ch	9:6	the one **h** of the greatness of thy	2677
Ne	4:21	**h** of them held the spears	2677
Ne	13:24	their children spake **h** in the	2677
Est	7:2	even to the **h** of the kingdom	2677
Ps	55:23	shall not live out **h** their days;	2673
Eze	16:51	Neither hath Samaria committed **h**	2677
Da	12:7	for a time, times, and an **h**; and	2677
Zec	14:2	**h** of the city shall go forth into	2677
Zec	14:4	**h** of the mountain shall remove	2677
Mk	6:23	it thee, unto the **h** of my kingdom.	*2255*
Lk	10:30	**departed, leaving him h dead.**	*2253*
Lk	19:8	the **h** of my goods I give to the	*2255*
Rev	8:1	about the space of **h** an hour	*2256*
Rev	11:9	three days and an **h**, and shall not	*2255*
Rev	11:11	three days and an **h** the Spirit of life.	*2255*
Rev	12:14	a time, and times, and **h** a time,	*2255*

HALL

Mt	27:27	took Jesus into the common **h**,	*4232*
Mk	15:16	into the **h**, called Praetorium	*833*
Jn	18:28	led … unto the **h** of judgment:	*4232*
Jn	18:33	Pilate entered … the judgment **h**	*4232*
Jn	19:9	went again into the judgment **h**,	*4232*

HALLELUJAH See ALLELUIA.

HALLOW

Ex	29:1	to **h** them, to minister unto me	6942
Le	16:19	cleanse it, and **h** it from the	6942
Le	22:2	those things which they **h** unto me:	6942
Le	22:32	I am the Lord which **h** you,	6942
Le	25:10	And ye shall **h** the fiftieth year,	6942
Jer	17:27	to **h** the sabbath day, and not to	6942
Eze	20:20	**h** my sabbaths; and they shall be	6942

HALLOWED

Ex	20:11	blessed the sabbath day and **h** it	6942
Ex	29:21	and he shall be **h**, and his garments,	6942
Le	12:4	she shall touch no **h** thing, nor	6944
Le	19:8	profaned the **h** thing of the Lord:	6944
Le	22:32	I will be **h** among the children	6942
Nu	3:13	I **h** unto me all the firstborn	6942
Dt	26:13	I have brought away the **h** things	6944
1Sa	21:6	the priest gave him **h** bread; for	6944
1Ki	9:3	I have **h** this house, which thou	6942
2Ki	12:18	all the **h** things that Jehoshaphat,	6944
2Ch	7:7	Moreover Solomon **h** the middle	6942
Mt	6:9	**in heaven, H be thy name.**	*37*
Lk	11:2	**in heaven, H be thy name.**	*37*

HALT

1Ki	18:21	How long **h** ye between two	6452
Mt	18:8	**to enter into life h or maimed.**	*5560*
Mk	9:45	**better for thee to enter h into life,**	*5560*
Lk	14:21	**the maimed, and the h, and the**	*5560*

HAMMER

Jgs	5:26	and with the **h** she smote Sisera	
1Ki	6:7	neither **h** nor axe nor any tool of	4717
Jer	23:29	like a **h** that breaketh the rock	6360

HAMMERS

Isa	44:12	and fashioneth it with **h**, and	4717
Jer	10:4	fasten it with nails and with **h**,	4717

HAND

Ge	3:22	now, lest he put forth his **h**, and	3027
Ge	4:11	thy brother's blood from thy **h**;	3027
Ge	9:5	at the **h** of every man's brother	3027
Ge	16:6	Behold, thy maid is in thy **h**;	3027
Ge	16:12	his **h** will be against every man,	3027
Ge	19:16	the men laid hold upon his **h**, and	3027
Ge	22:12	Lay not thine **h** upon the lad,	3027
Ge	24:9	the servant put his **h** under the	3027
Ge	25:26	and his **h** took hold on Esau's heel:	3027
Ge	32:11	of my brother, from the **h** of Esau:	3027
Ge	37:27	and let not our **h** be upon him;	3027
Ge	38:20	his pledge from the woman's **h**	3027
Ge	38:30	had the scarlet thread upon his **h**	3027
Ge	39:6	left all that he had in Joseph's **h**;	3027
Ge	39:12	left his garment in her **h**, and fled,	3027
Ge	39:22	committed to Joseph's **h** all the	3027
Ge	41:42	put it upon Joseph's **h**, and	3027
Ex	3:19	let you go, no, not by a mighty **h**	3027
Ex	4:4	it became a rod in his **h**	3709
Ex	4:6	behold, his **h** was leprous as snow	3027
Ex	6:1	and with a strong **h** shall he drive	3027
Ex	10:21	Stretch out thine **h** toward heaven,	3027
Ex	13:9	for with a strong **h** hath the Lord	3027
Ex	14:26	Stretch out thine **h** over the sea,	3027
Ex	15:6	thy right **h**, O Lord, hath dashed	3225
Ex	17:11	Moses held up his **h**, that Israel	3027
Ex	17:11	and when he let down his **h**,	3027
Ex	19:13	There shall not an **h** touch it,	3027
Ex	21:24	tooth for tooth, **h** for **h**, foot	3027
Ex	29:20	upon the thumb of their right **h**,	3027
Ex	33:22	and will cover thee with my **h**	3709
Ex	33:23	And I will take away mine **h**,	3709
Ex	34:4	took in his **h** the two tables of	3027
Le	1:4	he shall put his **h** upon the head	3027
Le	4:33	lay his **h** upon the … sin	3027
Le	14:17	the rest of the oil that is in his **h**	3709
Nu	11:23	Is the Lord's **h** waxed short?	3027
Nu	20:17	we will not turn to the right **h** nor	3225
Nu	22:31	sword drawn in his **h**: and he	3027
Nu	35:18	if he smite him with an **h** weapon	3027
Nu	35:21	in enmity smite him with his **h**	3027
Nu	35:25	out of the **h** of the revenger of	3027
Dt	3:24	thy mighty **h**: for what God	3027
Dt	4:34	and by a mighty **h**, and by a	3027
Dt	8:17	the might of mine **h** hath gotten	3027
Dt	9:26	out of Egypt with a mighty **h**	3027
Dt	15:7	nor shut thine **h** from thy poor	3027
Dt	16:10	a freewill offering of thine **h**	3027
Dt	17:20	to the right **h**, or to the left: to the	3225
Dt	19:12	into the **h** of the avenger of blood	3027
Dt	19:21	for tooth, **h** for **h**, foot for foot	3027
Dt	30:9	every work of thine **h**, in the	3027
Dt	32:27	Our **h** is high, and the Lord	3027
Dt	32:35	the day of their calamity is at **h**,	7138
Dt	32:39	that can deliver out of my **h**	3027
Jos	6:2	I have given into thine **h** Jericho	3027
Jos	8:26	Joshua drew not his **h** back	3027
Jos	20:9	by the **h** of the avenger of blood,	3027
Jos	21:44	all their enemies into their **h**	3027
Jgs	2:18	out of the **h** of their enemies all	3027
Jgs	3:21	Ehud put forth his left **h**, and took	3027
Jgs	4:9	Sisera into the **h** of a woman	3027
Jgs	5:26	She put her **h** to the nail,	3027
Jgs	6:36	If thou wilt save Israel by mine **h**	3027
Jgs	7:2	Mine own **h** hath saved me	3027

Jgs	7:6	putting their **h** to their mouth	3027
Jgs	7:16	put a trumpet in every man's **h**.	3027
Jgs	15:17	cast away the jawbone out of his **h**.	3027
Jgs	16:18	and brought money in their **h**.	3027
Jgs	16:23	Samson our enemy into our **h**	3027
Jgs	16:29	the one with his right **h**, and of the	3225
Ru	1:13	the **h** of the Lord is gone out.	3027
1Sa	5:7	his **h** is sore upon us, and upon	3027
1Sa	5:11	**h** of God was very heavy there	3027
1Sa	12:3	or of whose **h** have I received any.	3027
1Sa	14:19	unto the priest; Withdraw thine **h**	3027
1Sa	14:26	no man put his **h** to his mouth:	3027
1Sa	17:40	his sling was in his **h**:	3027
1Sa	17:57	the head of the Philistine in his **h**.	3027
1Sa	18:10	there was a javelin in Saul's **h**	3027
1Sa	19:5	he did put his life in his **h**, and	3709
1Sa	19:9	with his javelin in his **h**:	3027
1Sa	22:17	their **h** also is with David, and	3027
1Sa	24:10	I will not put forth mine **h**	3027
1Sa	24:11	see the skirt of thy robe in my **h**:	3027
1Sa	26:23	delivered thee into my **h** to day.	3027
1Sa	27:1	perish one day by the **h** of Saul:	3027
2Sa	2:21	Turn thee aside to thy right **h**	3225
2Sa	4:11	require his blood of your **h**, and.	3027
2Sa	11:14	sent it by the **h** of Uriah.	3027
2Sa	13:10	chamber, that I may eat of thine **h**,	3027
2Sa	14:19	Is not the **h** of Joab with thee	3027
2Sa	16:8	into the **h** of Absalom thy son:	3027
2Sa	18:12	yet would I not put forth mine **h**	3027
2Sa	18:14	And he took three darts in his **h**.	3709
2Sa	20:10	the sword that was in Joab's **h**:	3027
2Sa	21:20	that had on every **h** six fingers,	3027
2Sa	23:10	smote the Philistines until his **h**	3027
2Sa	23:21	the Egyptian had a spear in his **h**;	3027
2Sa	24:14	fall now into the **h** of the Lord;	3027
2Sa	24:16	It is enough: stay now thine **h**.	3027
1Ki	11:12	rend it out of the **h** of thy son.	3027
1Ki	11:31	rend the kingdom out of the **h** of.	3027
1Ki	13:4	And his **h**, which he put forth.	3027
1Ki	13:6	that my **h** may be restored me	3027
1Ki	18:44	out of the sea, like a man's **h**	3709
1Ki	18:46	the **h** of the Lord was on Elijah;	3027
1Ki	22:15	deliver it into the **h** of the king	3027
1Ki	22:34	Turn thine **h**, and carry me out	3027
2Ki	4:29	take my staff in thine **h**, and go.	3027
2Ki	7:17	the lord on whose **h** he leaned	3027
2Ki	8:8	Take a present in thine **h**, and go,	3027
2Ki	13:16	Put thine **h** upon the bow	3027
2Ki	14:5	kingdom was confirmed in his **h**,	3027
2Ki	18:33	out of the **h** of the king of Assyria?	3027
2Ki	18:35	deliver Jerusalem out of mine **h**?	3027
1Ch	4:10	that thine **h** might be with me	3027
1Ch	11:23	the spear out of the Egyptian's **h**	3027
1Ch	12:2	could use both the right **h** and the	3231
1Ch	13:10	because he put his **h** to the ark:	3027
1Ch	20:6	six on each **h**, and six on each foot:	
1Ch	21:13	me fall now into the **h** of the Lord;	3027
1Ch	21:13	but let me not fall into the **h** of man.	3027
1Ch	21:15	It is enough, stay now thine **h**.	3027
1Ch	28:19	in writing by his **h** upon me,	3027
1Ch	29:12	and in thine **h** is power and might;	3027
1Ch	29:12	and in thine **h** it is to make great,	3027
1Ch	29:16	cometh of thine **h**, and is all thine	3027
2Ch	17:5	stablished the kingdom in his **h**;	3027
2Ch	18:18	of heaven standing on his right **h**	3225
2Ch	20:6	and in thine **h** is there not power	3027
2Ch	23:7	man with his weapons in his **h**;	3027
2Ch	32:15	God deliver you out of mine **h**?	3027
Ezr	6:12	that shall put to their **h** to alter.	3028
Ezr	8:18	by the good **h** of our God upon us.	3027
Ezr	8:22	The **h** of our God is upon all	3027
Ne	1:10	great power, and by thy strong **h**	3027
Ne	4:17	and with the other **h** held a weapon	
Est	5:2	golden sceptre that was in his **h**	3027
Est	6:2	who sought to lay **h** on the king.	3027
Job	1:11	put forth thine **h** now, and touch	3027
Job	2:5	put forth thine **h** now, and touch	3027
Job	2:6	Behold, he is in thine **h**; but save	3027
Job	33:7	neither shall my **h** be heavy upon.	405
Job	35:7	or what receiveth he of thine **h**?	3027
Job	37:7	He sealeth up the **h** of every man;	3027
Job	40:4	I will lay mine **h** upon my mouth.	3027
Job	40:14	thine own right **h** can save thee	3225
Ps	10:14	spite, to requite it with thy **h**:	3027
Ps	16:8	he is at my right **h**, I shall not be	3225
Ps	16:11	at thy right **h** there are pleasures.	3225
Ps	20:6	the saving strength of his right **h**	3225
Ps	26:10	and their right **h** is full of bribes.	3225
Ps	31:5	Into thine **h** I commit my spirit:.	3027
Ps	31:15	My times are in thy **h**: deliver me	3027
Ps	32:4	day and night thy **h** was heavy	3027
Ps	39:10	consumed by the blow of thine **h**.	3027
Ps	48:10	thy right **h** is full of righteousness.	3225
Ps	75:8	in the **h** of the Lord there is a cup	3027
Ps	80:17	upon the man of thy right **h**	3225
Ps	89:48	his soul from the **h** of the grave?.	3027
Ps	91:7	ten thousand at thy right **h**; but	3225
Ps	104:28	thou openest thine **h**, they are.	3027
Ps	109:6	let Satan stand at his right **h**	3225
Ps	118:16	right **h** of the Lord doeth valiantly.	3225
Ps	123:2	eyes of a maiden unto the **h** of her.	3027
Ps	127:4	As arrows are in the **h** of a mighty	3027
Ps	137:5	let my right **h** forget her cunning	3225
Ps	139:10	there shall thy **h** lead me, and	3027
Ps	139:10	thy right **h** shall hold me,.	3225
Ps	144:11	right **h** is a right **h** of falsehood	3225
Ps	149:6	a two-edged sword in their **h**;	3027
Pr	1:24	I have stretched out my **h**, and no	3027
Pr	3:27	in the power of thine **h** to do it.	3027
Pr	4:27	Turn not to the right **h** nor to the	3227
Pr	10:4	but the **h** of the diligent maketh	3027
Pr	11:21	Though **h** join in **h**, the wicked	3027
Pr	16:5	though **h** join in **h**, he shall not	3027
Pr	17:16	is there a price in the **h** of a fool	3027
Pr	19:24	A slothful man hideth his **h** in his	3027
Pr	21:1	The king's heart is in the **h** of the	3027
Pr	26:6	a message by the **h** of a fool.	3027
Pr	26:9	into the **h** of a drunkard, so is a	3027
Pr	30:32	lay thine **h** upon thy mouth	3027
Pr	31:20	She stretcheth out her **h** to the	3709
Ecc	5:15	which he may carry away in his **h**.	3027
Ecc	7:18	from this withdraw not thine **h**:	3027
Ecc	9:1	their works, are in the **h** of God:.	3027
Ecc	9:10	Whatsoever thy **h** findeth to do,	3027
Ecc	10:2	wise man's heart is at his right **h**;	3225
Ecc	11:6	evening withhold not thine **h**:.	3027
SS	2:6	His left **h** is under my head,	8040
Isa	1:12	who hath required this at your **h**,	3027
Isa	1:25	I will turn my **h** upon thee,	3027
Isa	5:25	but his **h** is stretched out still	3027
Isa	6:6	having a live coal in his **h**,	3027
Isa	9:17	but his **h** is stretched out still	3027

Isa	10:5	the staff in their **h** is mine	3027
Isa	10:13	the strength of mine **h** I have done	3027
Isa	11:8	put his **h** on the cockatrice's den	3027
Isa	13:6	the day of the Lord is at **h**;	7138
Isa	14:27	and his **h** is stretched out, and who	3027
Isa	19:16	the shaking of the **h** of the Lord	3027
Isa	22:21	commit thy government into his **h**:	3027
Isa	26:11	when thy **h** is lifted up, they will	3027
Isa	28:2	cast down to the earth with the **h**.	3027
Isa	36:6	it will go into his **h**, and pierce	3709
Isa	37:10	into the **h** of the king of Assyria	3027
Isa	38:6	thee and this city out of the **h**	3709
Isa	40:2	received of the Lord's **h** double	3027
Isa	41:10	right **h** of my righteousness	3225
Isa	41:20	the **h** of the Lord hath done this	3027
Isa	43:13	none that can deliver out of my **h**:	3027
Isa	48:13	and my right **h** hath spanned the	3225
Isa	49:22	I will lift up mine **h** to the	3027
Isa	50:2	Is my **h** shortened at all, that it	3027
Isa	51:16	the shadow of mine **h**, that I may	3027
Isa	56:2	keepeth his **h** from doing … evil	3027
Isa	59:1	the Lord's **h** is not shortened,	3027
Isa	62:3	crown of glory in the **h** of the Lord,	3027
Isa	62:8	Lord hath sworn by his right **h**,	3225
Isa	63:12	That led them by the right **h** of	3225
Isa	64:8	we all are the work of thy **h**.	3027
Jer	1:9	the Lord put forth his **h**, and	3027
Jer	12:7	soul into the **h** of her enemies	3709
Jer	18:4	marred in the **h** of the potter:	3027
Jer	18:6	as the clay is in the potter's **h**.	3027
Jer	18:6	so are ye in mine **h**, O house	3027
Jer	20:4	into the **h** of the king of Babylon,	3027
Jer	23:23	Am I a God at **h**, saith the Lord	7138
Jer	25:15	the wine cup of this fury at my **h**	3027
Jer	26:14	I am in your **h**: do with me	3027
Jer	29:21	into the **h** of Nebuchadrezzar king	3027
Jer	34:3	thou shalt not escape out of his **h**.	3027
Jer	34:21	give into the **h** of their enemies	3027
Jer	36:14	Take in thine **h** the roll wherein	3027
Jer	38:16	into the **h** of these men that seek	3027
Jer	38:23	shall be taken by the **h** of the king	3027
Jer	40:4	the chains … were upon thine **h**	3027
Jer	42:11	and to deliver you from his **h**,	3027
Jer	51:7	a golden cup in the Lord's **h**,	3027
La	1:7	her people fell into the **h** of the	3027
La	1:10	The adversary … spread out his **h**	3027
La	5:8	that doth deliver us out of their **h**	3027
Eze	1:3	the **h** of the Lord was there upon	3027
Eze	3:18	blood will I require at thine **h**.	3027
Eze	3:20	blood will I require at thine **h**.	3027
Eze	8:11	every man his censer in his **h**;	3027
Eze	10:2	fill thine **h** with coals of fire	2651
Eze	10:8	the form of a man's **h** under their	3027
Eze	12:23	The days are at **h**, and the effect	7126
Eze	16:46	daughters that dwell at thy left **h**:	8040
Eze	16:49	neither did she strengthen the **h**	3027
Eze	20:34	ye are scattered, with a mighty **h**,	3027
Eze	23:31	will I give her cup into thine **h**	3027
Eze	28:9	in the **h** of him that slayeth thee	3027
Eze	33:6	will I require at the watchman's **h**.	3027
Eze	33:8	his blood will I require at thine **h**.	3027
Eze	34:10	I will require my flock at their **h**,	3027
Eze	37:17	they shall become one in thine **h**	3027
Eze	40:5	and in the man's **h** a measuring	3027
Da	3:17	he will deliver us out of thine **h**	3028
Da	4:35	none can stay his **h**, or say	3028
Da	5:5	came forth fingers of a man's **h**.	3028
Da	5:23	and the God in whose **h** thy breath	3028
Da	8:7	deliver the ram out of his **h**.	3027
Da	8:25	but he shall be broken without **h**	3027
Da	10:10	an **h** touched me, which set me	3027
Da	12:7	and his left **h** unto heaven,	8040
Hos	12:7	the balances of deceit are in his **h**:	3027
Joel	1:15	the day of the Lord is at **h**	7138
Joel	2:1	the day of the Lord … is nigh at **h**;	
Am	7:7	with a plumbline in his **h**.	3027
Am	9:2	into hell, thence shall mine **h** take	3027
Jnh	4:11	between their right … and … left **h**.	8040
Mic	2:1	it is in the power of their **h**	3027
Mic	5:12	cut off witchcrafts out of thine **h**;	3027
Hab	3:4	he had horns coming out of his **h**:	3027
Zep	1:7	the day of the Lord is at **h**:	7138
Zec	3:1	Satan standing at his right **h** to	3225
Zec	13:7	I will turn mine **h** upon the little	3027
Mal	1:13	should I accept this of your **h**?	3027
Mt	3:2	for the kingdom of heaven is at **h**.	*1448*
Mt	4:17	**for the kingdom of heaven is at h.**	*1448*
Mt	5:30	**if thy right h offend thee, cut it**	*5495*
Mt	6:3	**know what thy right h doeth**	
Mt	8:3	Jesus put forth his **h**, and touched	*5495*
Mt	10:7	**The kingdom of heaven is at h**	*1448*
Mt	12:13	to the man, **Stretch forth thine h**	*5495*
Mt	18:8	**if thy h or thy foot offend thee,**	*5495*
Mt	20:23	**to sit on my right h, and on my**	
Mt	22:13	**Bind him h and foot, and take**	*5495*
Mt	22:44	**Sit thou on my right h, till I make**	
Mt	25:33	**shall set the sheep on his right h,**	
Mt	26:18	**The Master saith, My time is at h;**	*1451*
Mt	26:23	**He that dippeth his h with me**	*5495*
Mt	26:45	**behold, the hour is at h, and the.**	*1448*
Mt	26:46	**he is at h that doth betray me.**	*1448*
Mt	26:64	**sitting on the right h of power,**	
Mt	27:29	his head, and a reed in his right **h**:	
Mk	1:15	**the kingdom of God is at h:**	*1448*
Mk	3:5	**Stretch forth thine h.** And he	*5495*
Mk	5:41	took the damsel by the **h**, and said	*5495*
Mk	9:43	**if thy h offend thee, cut it off:**	*5495*
Mk	10:40	**sit on my right h and on my left h**	
Mk	12:36	**Sit thou on my right h, till I make**	
Mk	14:42	**lo, he that betrayeth me is at h**	*1448*
Mk	14:62	**sitting on the right h of power**	
Mk	16:19	and sat on the right **h** of God	
Lk	9:62	**No man, having put his h to the.**	*5495*
Lk	15:22	**put a ring on his h, and shoes**	*5495*
Lk	20:42	**my Lord, Sit thou on my right h,**	
Lk	21:30	**that summer is now nigh at h**	
Lk	21:31	**kingdom of God is nigh at h**	
Lk	22:21	**the h of him that betrayeth me.**	*5495*
Lk	22:69	**sit on the right h of the power of**	
Jn	10:28	**any man pluck them out of my h.**	*5495*
Jn	18:22	struck Jesus with the palm of his **h**,	
Jn	20:27	**reach hither thy h, and thrust**	*5495*
Ac	2:33	being by the right **h** of God exalted,	
Ac	2:34	my Lord, Sit thou on my right **h**,	
Ac	5:31	hath God exalted with his right **h**.	*5495*
Ac	7:55	Jesus standing on the right **h** of God,	
Ac	9:8	they led him by the **h**, and	*5496*
Ac	9:12	**coming in, and putting his h on**	*5495*
Ac	22:11	being led by the **h** of them that	*5496*
Ro	8:34	even at the right **h** of God, who also	
Ro	13:12	night is far spent, the day is at **h**:	*1448*
1Co	12:21	And the eye cannot say unto the **h**	*5495*

Eph 1:20 set him at his own right **h** in the
Php 4:5 unto all men. The Lord is at **h**. *1451*
Col 3:1 Christ sitteth on the right **h** of God,
2Th 2:2 as that the day of Christ is at **h** *1764*
2Ti 4:6 the time of my departure is at **h** *2186*
Heb 1:3 the right **h** of the Majesty on high;
Heb 1:13 Sit on my right **h**, until I make
Heb 8:1 set on the right **h** of the throne
Heb 10:12 sat down on the right **h** of God;
Heb 12:2 is set down at the right **h** of the
1Pe 3:22 is on the right **h** of God; angels, and
1Pe 4:7 the end of all things is at **h**: *1448*
1Pe 5:6 under the mighty **h** of God, that. *5495*
Rev 1:3 therein: for the time is at **h** *1451*
Rev 1:16 he had in his right **h** seven stars:. *5495*
Rev 5:1 I saw in the right **h** of him that sat
Rev 6:5 him had a pair of balances in his **h**. *5495*
Rev 10:2 he had in his **h** a little book. *5495*
Rev 10:10 book out of the angel's **h**, and ate. *5495*
Rev 13:16 to receive a mark in their right **h** *5495*
Rev 14:9 mark in his forehead, or in his **h**, ... *5495*
Rev 14:14 and in his **h** a sharp sickle *5495*
Rev 17:4 having a golden cup in her **h** full of. . . . *5495*
Rev 20:1 pit and a great chain in his **h**. *5495*
Rev 22:10 of this book: for the time is at **h** *1451*

HANDBREADTH See also BREADTH.
2Ch 4:5 And the thickness of it was an **h**. 2947
Ps 39:5 thou hast made my days as an **h**; 2947

HANDFUL
Le 5:12 priest shall take his **h** of it,. 4393, 7062
Le 6:15 shall take of it his **h**, of the flour. 7062
1Ki 17:12 an **h** of meal in a barrel,. 4393, 3709
Ecc 4:6 Better is an **h** with quietness, ... 4393, 3709
Jer 9:22 as the **h** after the harvestman,. 5995

HANDFULS
Ge 41:47 the earth brought forth by **h** 7062
Ru 2:16 let fall also some of the **h** of purpose . . . 6653

HANDKERCHIEFS
Ac 19:12 brought unto the sick **h** or aprons,. *4676*

HANDLE
Ps 115:7 They have hands, but they **h** not: 4184
Jer 2:8 and they that **h** the law knew 8610
Lk 24:39 **h me, and see; for a spirit** *5584*
Col 2:21 **Touch not; taste not; h not;**. *2345*

HANDLETH
Pr 16:20 He that **h** a matter wisely shall 5921

HANDLING
2Co 4:2 **h** the word of God deceitfully *2389*

HANDMAID See also MAID.
Ge 25:12 the Egyptian, Sarah's **h**, bare unto 8198
Ge 35:25 the sons of Bilhah, Rachel's **h**;. 8198
Ge 35:26 And the sons of Zilpah, Leah's **h**; 8198
1Sa 1:11 the affliction of thine **h**, and 519
1Sa 25:28 forgive the trespass of thine **h** 519
1Sa 28:21 thine **h** hath obeyed thy voice, ... 8198
2Sa 14:6 And thy **h** had two sons, and they 8198
1Ki 1:13 O king, swear unto thine **h**,. 519
1Ki 3:20 while thine **h** slept, and laid it. 519
2Ki 4:16 man of God, do not lie unto thine **h** . . . 8198
Pr 30:23 and an **h** that is heir to her 8198
Lk 1:38 Behold the **h** of the Lord; be it *1399*

HANDMAIDEN See also MAIDEN.
Lk 1:48 regarded the low estate of his **h**. *1399*

HANDMAIDS See also MAIDENS; MAIDS.
Ge 33:2 he put the **h** and their children. 8198
2Sa 6:20 in the eyes of the **h** of his servants 519
Joel 2:29 upon the **h** in those days will I 8198

HANDS
Ge 16:9 and submit thyself under her **h**. 3027
Ge 27:22 but the **h** are the **h** of Esau 3027
Ge 37:22 rid him out of their **h**, to deliver. 3027
Ge 39:1 bought him out of the **h** of the. 3027
Ex 17:12 But Moses' **h** were heavy; and 3027
Ex 30:21 they shall wash their **h** and their. 3027
Ex 32:19 he cast the tables out of his **h**,. 3027
Ex 40:31 washed their **h** and their feet. 3027
Le 4:15 lay their **h** upon the head of the 3027
Le 8:18 laid their **h** upon … of the bullock 3027
Le 8:22 laid their **h** upon the … of the ram 3027
Nu 6:19 upon the **h** of the Nazarite, after. 3709
Dt 4:28 the work of men's **h**, wood and. 3027
Dt 17:7 The **h** of the witnesses shall be 3027
Dt 31:29 anger through the work of your **h** 3027
Jgs 7:20 held the lamps in their left **h**, and. 3027
Jgs 19:27 her **h** were upon the threshold 3027
1Sa 5:4 both the palms of his **h** were cut 3027
2Sa 2:7 now let your **h** be strengthened,. 3027
2Sa 4:12 cut off their **h** and their feet,. 3027
2Sa 16:21 the **h** of all that are with thee 3027
2Sa 21:9 he delivered them into the **h** of. 3027
2Sa 22:35 He teacheth my **h** to war; so that 3027
2Ki 4:34 and his **h** upon his **h**: 3709
2Ki 9:35 the feet, and the palms of her **h** 3027
2Ki 13:16 put his **h** upon the king's **h** 3027
2Ki 22:17 the works of their **h**; therefore 3027
2Ch 23:15 they laid **h** on her; and when 3027
Ezr 4:4 weakened the **h** of the people of. 3027
Ezr 6:22 to strengthen their **h** in the 3027
Ezr 10:19 gave their **h** that they would 3027
Ne 2:18 they strengthened their **h** for. 3027
Ne 13:21 ye do so again, I will lay **h** on you. 3027
Job 1:10 hast blessed the work of his **h**, ... 3027
Job 9:30 and make my **h** never so clean;. 3709
Job 34:19 they all are the work of his **h**. 3027
Ps 7:3 if there be iniquity in my **h**;. 3709
Ps 9:16 snared in the work of his own **h**. 3709
Ps 18:24 the cleanness of my **h** in his 3027
Ps 18:34 He teacheth my **h** to war, so that 3027
Ps 22:16 they pierced my **h** and my feet 3027
Ps 24:4 He that hath clean **h**, and a pure. 3709
Ps 44:20 stretched out our **h** to a strange 3709
Ps 47:1 O clap your **h**, all ye people; 3709
Ps 91:12 shall bear thee up in their **h**. 3709
Ps 95:5 his **h** formed the dry land 3027
Ps 102:25 heavens are the work of thy **h** 3027
Ps 115:7 They have **h**, but they handle not: 3027
Ps 144:1 teacheth my **h** to war, and my. 3027
Pr 6:10 a little folding of the **h** to sleep: 3027
Pr 6:17 and **h** that shed innocent blood,. 3027
Pr 12:14 the recompence of a man's **h** shall 3027
Pr 14:1 plucketh it down with her **h** 3027
Pr 17:18 void of understanding striketh **h**,. 3709
Pr 24:33 a little folding of the **h** to sleep: 3027
Pr 30:28 The spider taketh hold with her **h**,. 3027
Pr 31:19 She layeth her **h** to the spindle,. 3027
Pr 31:20 reacheth forth her **h** to the needy. 3027

Ecc 4:5 The fool foldeth his **h** together,........3027
Ecc 4:6 than both the **h** full with travail.......2651
Ecc 10:18 through idleness of the **h** the..........3027
Isa 1:15 your **h** are full of blood..............3027
Isa 2:8 worship the work of their own **h**,......3027
Isa 5:12 consider the operation of his **h**........3027
Isa 35:3 Strengthen ye the weak **h**, and........3027
Isa 45:9 or thy work, He hath no **h**?...........3027
Isa 45:12 I, even my **h**, have stretched out.......3027
Isa 49:16 thee upon the palms of my **h**;.........3709
Isa 59:3 your **h** are defiled with blood, and.....3709
Isa 65:2 I have spread out my **h** all the day.....3027
Jer 6:24 our **h** wax feeble: anguish hath........3027
Jer 25:7 works of your **h** to your own hurt.....3027
Jer 47:3 their children for feebleness of **h**;......3027
La 1:14 hath delivered me into their **h**,........3027
La 2:15 All that pass by clap their **h**...........3709
La 3:41 lift up our heart with our **h**...........3709
La 4:2 the work of the **h** of the potter!.......3027
Eze 1:8 And they had the **h** of a man.........3027
Eze 10:12 and their **h**, and their wings..........3027
Eze 13:22 strengthened the **h** of the wicked,......3027
Eze 21:7 all **h** shall be feeble, and every.........3027
Eze 23:37 blood is in their **h**, and with..........3027
Da 2:45 cut out of the mountain without **h**,....3028
Da 3:15 that shall deliver you out of my **h**?.....3028
Hos 14:3 any more to the work of our **h**,........3027
Mic 7:3 they may do evil with both **h**.........3709
Hag 2:14 so is every work of their **h**;...........3027
Zec 8:13 fear not, but let your **h** be strong......3027
Zec 13:6 are these wounds in thine **h**?..........3027
Mt 4:6 in their **h** they shall bear thee up......*5495*
Mt 15:20 **but to eat with unwashen h**...........*5495*
Mt 17:22 **shall be betrayed into the h of**........*5495*
Mt 18:8 **rather than having two h or two**......*5495*
Mt 26:45 **is betrayed into the h of sinners**.......*5495*
Mt 26:67 smote him with the palms of their **h**,
Mt 27:24 washed his **h** before the multitude,.....*5495*
Mk 9:31 **is delivered into the h of men,**........*5495*
Mk 9:43 **than having two h to go into hell,**.....*5495*
Mk 14:41 **is betrayed into the h of sinners**.......*5495*
Mk 14:58 this temple that is made with **h**,.......*5499*
Mk 14:58 will build another made without **h**......*886*
Mk 14:65 strike him with the palms of their **h**
Mk 16:18 **they shall lay h on the sick, and**.......*5495*
Lk 4:11 And in their **h** they shall bear thee.....*5495*
Lk 4:40 laid his **h** on every one of them,.......*5495*
Lk 9:44 **shall be delivered into the h of**........*5495*
Lk 21:12 **they shall lay their h on you,**..........*5495*
Lk 22:53 **ye stretched forth no h against**........*5495*
Lk 23:46 **into thy h I commend my spirit:**......*5495*
Lk 24:39 **Behold my h and my feet, that it**......*5495*
Jn 7:30 but no man laid **h** on him, because....*5495*
Jn 8:20 and no man laid **h** on him; for........*4084*
Jn 13:3 given all things into his **h**, and........*5495*
Jn 13:9 but also my **h** and my head...........*5495*
Jn 19:3 and they smote him with their **h**......*4475*
Jn 20:27 **thy finger, and behold my h;**..........*5495*
Jn 21:18 **thou shalt stretch forth thy h,**.........*5495*
Ac 2:23 by wicked **h** have crucified and........*5495*
Ac 6:6 prayed, they laid their **h** on them......*5495*
Ac 7:48 not in temples made with **h**;..........*5499*
Ac 8:18 laying on of the apostles' **h**...........*5495*
Ac 17:24 not in temples made with **h**;..........*5499*
Ac 19:6 when Paul had laid his **h** upon........*5495*
Ac 19:11 special miracles by the **h** of Paul:......*5495*
Ac 19:26 no gods, which are made with **h**:......*5495*
2Co 5:1 an house not made with **h**, eternal......*886*
Gal 2:9 the right **h** of fellowship: that.........*1188*
Col 2:11 the circumcision made without **h**,......*886*
1Ti 2:8 lifting up holy **h**, without wrath.......*5495*
1Ti 4:14 with the laying on of the **h** of the......*5495*
1Ti 5:22 Lay **h** suddenly on no man, neither....*5495*
Heb 1:10 heavens are the works of thine **h**:......*5495*
Heb 2:7 set him over the works of thy **h**:.......*5495*
Heb 6:2 of baptisms, and of laying on of **h**,.....*5495*
Heb 9:11 tabernacle, not made with **h**, that......*5499*
Heb 9:24 into the holy places made with **h**,......*5499*
Heb 10:31 to fall into the **h** of the living God.....*5495*
Heb 12:12 lift up the **h** which hang down........*5495*
Jas 4:8 Cleanse your **h**, ye sinners; and........*5495*
1Jn 1:1 and our **h** have handled, of the........*5495*
Rev 7:9 white robes, and palms in their **h**;.....*5495*
Rev 9:20 not of the works of their **h**, that.......*5495*
Rev 20:4 upon their foreheads, or in their **h**;....*5495*

HANDWRITING

Col 2:14 Blotting out the **h** of ordinances.......*5498*

HANDYWORK

Ps 19:1 firmament sheweth his **h**........4639, 3027

HANG

Nu 25:4 and **h** them up before the Lord........3363
Dt 28:66 thy life shall **h** in doubt before........8511
Est 6:4 to **h** Mordecai on the gallows.........8518
Est 7:9 Then the king said, **H** him thereon....8518
La 2:10 the virgins of Jerusalem **h** down.......3381
Mt 22:40 **h all the law and the prophets**.........*2910*
Ac 28:4 venomous beast **h** on his hand........*2910*
Heb 12:12 lift up the hands which **h** down,.......*3935*

HANGED

Ge 40:22 But he **h** the chief baker:.............8518
Dt 21:23 he that is **h** is accursed of God;........8518
Jos 8:29 the king of Ai he **h** on a tree..........8518
2Sa 17:23 and **h** himself, and died, and was......2614
2Sa 18:10 I saw Absalom **h** in an oak............8518
2Sa 21:13 the bones of them that were **h**........3363
Ezr 6:11 let him be **h** thereon; and let his.......4223
Est 5:14 king that Mordecai may be **h**.........8518
Est 7:10 So they **h** Haman on the gallows......8518
Est 9:14 and they **h** Haman's ten sons.........8518
Ps 137:2 We **h** our harps upon the willows......8518
La 5:12 Princes are **h** up by their hand:........8518
Mt 18:6 **that a millstone were h about his**......*2910*
Mt 27:5 departed, and went and **h** himself......*519*
Mk 9:42 **that a millstone were h about his**......*4029*
Lk 17:2 **that a millstone were h about his**......*4029*
Lk 23:39 of the malefactors which were **h**.......*2910*
Ac 5:30 whom ye slew and **h** on a tree.........*2910*
Ac 10:39 whom they slew and **h** on a tree.......*2910*

HANGETH

Job 26:7 and **h** the earth upon nothing.........8518
Gal 3:13 Cursed is every one that **h** on a........*2910*

HAPLY

Lk 14:29 **Lest h, after he hath laid the**..........*3379*
Ac 5:39 lest **h** ye be found even to fight........*3379*
Ac 17:27 if **h** they might feel after him...........*686*

HAPPEN

Pr 12:21 There shall no evil **h** to the just:........579
Mk 10:32 what things should **h** unto him........*4819*

HAPPENED

1Sa 6:9	it was a chance that **h** to us	1961
Jer 44:23	therefore this evil is **h** unto you	7122
Lk 24:14	of all these things which had **h**	*4819*
Ro 11:25	blindness in part is **h** to Israel,	*1096*
1Co 10:11	all these things **h** unto them for	*4819*
1Pe 4:12	as though some strange thing **h**	*4819*

HAPPENETH

Ecc 2:14	that one event **h** to them all.	7136
Ecc 9:11	time and chance **h** to them all.	7136

HAPPY

Dt 33:29	**H** art thou, O Israel: who is like	835
2Ch 9:7	**H** are thy men, and **h** are these	835
Job 5:17	**h** is the man whom God correcteth:	835
Ps 127:5	**H** is the man that hath his quiver	835
Ps 144:15	**h** is that people, whose God is the	835
Ps 146:5	**H** is he that hath the God	835
Pr 3:13	**H** is the man that findeth wisdom	835
Pr 14:21	hath mercy on the poor, **h** is he	835
Pr 16:20	trusteth in the Lord, **h** is he	835
Pr 28:14	**H** is the man that feareth alway:	835
Pr 29:18	he that keepeth the law, **h** is he	835
Jn 13:17	**h are ye if you do them**	*3107*
Jas 5:11	we count them **h** which endure	*3106*
1Pe 3:14	for righteousness's sake, **h** are ye;	*3107*
1Pe 4:14	for the name of Christ, **h** are ye;	*5107*

HARD

Ge 18:14	Is any thing too **h** for the Lord?	6381
Ex 1:14	their lives bitter with **h** bondage	7186
Ex 18:26	**h** causes they brought unto Moses	7186
Dt 1:17	the cause that is too **h** for you	7185
Dt 17:8	If there arise a matter too **h** for	6381
2Ki 2:10	Thou hast asked a **h** thing:	7185
2Ch 9:1	prove Solomon with **h** questions	2420
Ps 63:8	My soul followeth **h** after thee:	1692
Pr 13:15	the way of transgressors is **h**	386
Jer 32:17	and there is nothing too **h** for thee:	6381
Jer 32:27	is there any thing too **h** for me?	6381
Eze 3:6	and of an **h** language, whose words	3515
Jnh 1:13	men rowed **h** to bring it to the land;	
Mt 25:24	**that thou art an h man, reaping**	*4642*
Mk 10:24	**how h is it for them that trust**	*1422*
Jn 6:60	This is an **h** saying; who can	*4642*
Ac 9:5	**h for thee to kick against the**	*4642*
Ac 26:14	it is **h** for thee to kick against	*4642*
Heb 5:11	things to say, and **h** to be uttered,	*1421*
2Pe 3:16	some things **h** to be understood	*1425*

HARDEN

Ex 4:21	but I will **h** his heart, that he	2388
Ex 7:3	I will **h** Pharaoh's heart, and	7185
Ex 14:4	I will **h** Pharaoh's heart, that he	2388
Dt 15:7	thou shalt not **h** thine heart, nor	553
Jos 11:20	was of the Lord to **h** their hearts,	2388
Ps 95:8	**H** not your heart, as in the	7185
Heb 3:8	**H** not your hearts, as in the	*4645*
Heb 3:15	voice, **h** not your hearts, as in the	*4645*
Heb 4:7	his voice, **h** not your hearts	*4645*

HARDENED

Ex 7:14	Pharaoh's heart is **h**, he refuseth	3515
Ex 8:15	he **h** his heart, and hearkened not	3513
Ex 9:7	And the heart of Pharaoh was **h**,	3515
Ex 9:34	sinned yet more, and **h** his heart	3513
Ex 10:1	I have **h** his heart, and the heart	3513
Ex 14:8	the Lord **h** the heart of Pharaoh	2388
Dt 2:30	the Lord thy God **h** his spirit,	7185
1Sa 6:6	and Pharaoh **h** their hearts?	3513
2Ki 17:14	would not hear, but **h** their necks	7185
2Ch 36:13	and **h** his heart from turning	553
Ne 9:17	but **h** their necks, and in their	7185
Ne 9:29	**h** their neck, and would not hear	7185
Job 39:16	She is **h** against her young	7188
Isa 63:17	from thy ways, and **h** our heart	7188
Jer 7:26	but **h** their neck: they did worse	7185
Jer 19:15	they have **h** their necks, that	7185
Da 5:20	up, and his mind **h** in pride	8631
Mk 6:52	loaves: for their heart was **h**.	*4456*
Mk 8:17	**have ye your heart yet h?**	*4456*
Jn 12:40	blinded their eyes, and **h** their	*4456*
Ac 19:9	But when divers were **h**, and	*4645*
Heb 3:13	**h** through the deceitfulness of sin	*4645*

HARDENETH

Pr 21:29	A wicked man **h** his face: but as	5810
Pr 28:14	but he that **h** his heart shall fall	7185
Pr 29:1	being often reproved **h** his neck,	7185
Ro 9:18	mercy, and whom he will he **h**	*4645*

HARDER

Pr 18:19	A brother offended is **h** to be won	
Jer 5:3	made their faces **h** than a rock;	2388

HARDLY

Ge 16:6	And when Sarai dealt **h** with her,	6031
Mt 19:23	**a rich man shall h enter into**	*1423*
Mk 10:23	**How h shall they that have riches**	*1423*
Lk 18:24	**How h shall they that have riches**	*1423*

HARDNESS

Mt 19:8	**because of the h of your hearts**	*4641*
Mk 3:5	grieved for the **h** of their hearts,	*4457*
Mk 10:5	**For the h of your heart he wrote**	*4641*
Mk 16:14	their unbelief and **h** of heart,	*4641*
Ro 2:5	thy **h** and impenitent heart	*4643*
2Ti 2:3	therefore endure **h**, as a good	*2553*

HARLOT

Ge 34:31	with our sister as with an **h**?	2181
Ge 38:15	he thought her to be an **h**;	2181
Ge 38:24	daughter in law hath played the **h**;	2181
Le 21:14	or profane, or an **h**, these shall	2181
Jos 6:17	only Rahab the **h** shall live, she	2181
Jgs 16:1	saw there an **h**, and went	2181
Pr 7:10	a woman with the attire of an **h**,	2181
Isa 1:21	the faithful city become an **h**!	2181
Isa 23:15	years shall Tyre sing as an **h**.	2181
Jer 3:1	played the **h** with many lovers;	2181
Jer 3:8	but went and played the **h** also	2181
Eze 16:15	and playedst the **h** because of thy	2181
Eze 23:44	unto a woman that playeth the **h**:	2181
Hos 2:5	their mother hath played the **h**:	2181
Joel 3:3	have given a boy for an **h**,	2181
Mic 1:7	shall return to the hire of an **h**	2181
Na 3:4	of the well-favoured **h**, the mistress	2181
1Co 6:16	is joined to an **h** is one body?	*4204*
Heb 11:31	By faith the **h** Rahab perished not	*4204*
Jas 2:25	was not Rahab the **h** justified by	*4204*

HARLOTS

1Ki 3:16	two women, that were **h**, unto the	2181
Pr 29:3	he that keepeth company with **h**	2181
Mt 21:31	**and the h go into the kingdom**	*4204*

Mt 21:32	**and the h believed him: and ye,**	*4204*
Lk 15:30	**devoured thy living with h, thou**	*4204*
Rev 17:5	mother of **h** and abominations	*4204*

HARM

Nu 35:23	his enemy, neither sought his **h**:	7451
1Sa 26:21	I will no more do thee **h**,	7489
2Ki 4:41	there was no **h** in the pot	1697, 7451
Ps 105:15	and do my prophets no **h**	7489
Pr 3:30	if he have done thee no **h**.	7451
Jer 39:12	look well to him, and do him no **h**;	7451
Ac 16:28	Do thyself no **h**: for we are all	*2556*
Ac 28:6	saw no **h** come to him, they	*824*
1Pe 3:13	who is he that will **h** you,	*2559*

HARMLESS

Mt 10:16	**wise as serpents, and h as doves**	*185*
Php 2:15	That ye may be blameless and **h**,	*185*
Heb 7:26	who is holy, **h**, undefiled,	*172*

HARNESS

1Ki 22:34	between the joints of the **h**:	8302
Jer 46:4	**H** the horses; and get up, ye	631

HARP

1Sa 16:23	David took an **h**, and played	3658
1Ch 25:3	who prophesied with a **h**, to give	3658
Job 30:31	My **h** also is turned to mourning	3658
Ps 49:4	open my dark saying upon the **h**	3658
Ps 71:22	unto thee will I sing with the **h**,	3658
Ps 92:3	upon the **h** with a solemn sound	3658
Ps 147:7	sing praise upon the **h** unto our	3658
Isa 24:8	endeth, the joy of the **h** ceaseth	3658
1Co 14:7	giving sound, whether pipe or **h**,	*2788*

HARPERS

Rev 14:2	I heard the voice of **h** harping	*2790*

HARPS

1Ki 10:12	**h** also and psalteries for singers:	3658
1Ch 25:1	who should prophesy with **h**, with	3658
Ps 137:2	We hanged our **h** upon the willows	3658
Eze 26:13	sound of thy **h** shall be no more	3658
Rev 5:8	having every one of them **h**,	*2788*
Rev 14:2	of harpers harping with their **h**:	*2788*
Rev 15:2	sea of glass, having the **h** of God	*2788*

HART

Ps 42:1	As the **h** panteth after the water	354
SS 2:9	is like a roe or a young **h**:	354
Isa 35:6	shall the lame man leap as an **h**,	354

HARVEST

Ge 8:22	seedtime and **h**, and cold and	7105
Ex 23:16	the feast of **h**, the firstfruits of	7105
Le 19:9	when ye reap the **h** of your land,	7105
Dt 24:19	When thou cuttest down thine **h**	7105
Jos 3:15	all his banks all the time of **h**,	7105
Ru 2:21	until they have ended all my **h**	7105
1Sa 12:17	Is it not wheat **h** to day?	7105
2Sa 21:9	were put to death in the days of **h**,	7105
2Sa 21:10	from the beginning of **h** until	7105
Pr 6:8	and gathereth her food in the **h**	7105
Pr 10:5	he that sleepeth in **h** is a son	7105
Pr 20:4	therefore shall he beg in **h**, and	7105
Pr 25:13	the cold of snow in the time of **h**,	7105
Pr 26:1	as rain in **h**, so honour is not	7105
Isa 17:11	the **h** shall be a heap in the day of	7105
Isa 18:4	like a cloud of dew in the heat of **h**	7105
Isa 23:3	the **h** of the river, is her revenue;	7105
Jer 5:17	they shall eat up thine **h**, and thy	7105
Jer 8:20	The **h** is past, the summer is	7105
Hos 6:11	he hath set an **h** for thee,	7105
Joel 1:11	the **h** of the field is perished	7105
Joel 3:13	the sickle, for the **h** is ripe:	7105
Mt 9:37	**The h truly is plenteous, but the**	*2325*
Mt 9:38	**Lord of the h, that he will send**	*2326*
Mt 9:38	**send forth labourers into his h**	*2326*
Mt 13:39	**the h is the end of the world;**	*2326*
Mk 4:29	**the sickle, because the h is come**	*2326*
Lk 10:2	**The h truly is great, but the**	*2326*
Jn 4:35	**four months, and then cometh h?**	*2326*
Rev 14:15	the **h** of the earth is ripe	*2326*

HASTE

Ge 19:22	**H** thee, escape thither: for I	4116
Ex 10:16	called for Moses and Aaron in **h**;	4116
Ex 12:11	ye shall eat it in **h**: it is the	2649
Ex 12:33	send them out of the land in **h**;	4416
1Sa 9:12	make **h** now, for he came to day	4116
1Sa 21:8	the king's business required **h**	5169
2Sa 4:4	as she made **h** to flee, that he fell	2648
Ezr 4:23	they went up in **h** to Jerusalem	924
Ps 31:22	For I said in my **h** I am cut off from	2648
Ps 38:22	Make **h** to help me, O Lord	2363
Ps 116:11	I said in my **h**, All men are liars	2648
Ps 119:60	I made **h**, and delayed not to keep	2363
Pr 1:16	evil, and make **h** to shed blood	4116
Pr 28:20	but he that maketh **h** to be rich	213
Isa 28:16	he that believeth shall not make **h**	2363
Isa 59:7	they make **h** to shed innocent	4116
Jer 9:18	make **h**, and take up a wailing	4116
Da 3:24	was astonished, and rose up in **h**,	927
Da 6:19	and went in **h** unto the den of lions	927
Lk 19:5	**Zacchaeus, make h, and come**	*4692*

HASTED

Ex 5:13	the taskmasters **h** them, saying,	213
Jos 10:13	**h** not to go down about a whole	213
1Sa 25:23	when Abigail saw David, she **h**,	4116
Est 6:12	**h** to his house mourning, and	1765
Ps 104:7	voice of thy thunder they **h** away	2648

HASTEN

Isa 5:19	make speed, and **h** his work	2363
Isa 60:22	I the Lord will **h** it in his time	2363
Jer 1:12	I will **h** my word to perform it,	8245

HASTENED

Ge 19:15	then the angels **h** Lot, saying	213
Jer 17:16	I have not **h** from being a pastor	213

HASTETH

Pr 7:23	as a bird **h** to the snare,	4116
Pr 19:2	and he that **h** with his feet sinneth	213
Pr 28:22	He that **h** to be rich hath an evil	926
Hab 1:8	fly as the eagle that **h** to eat	2363
Zep 1:14	is near, it is near, and **h** greatly,	4116

HASTILY

Ge 41:14	brought him **h** out of the dungeon	7323
Jgs 9:54	he called **h** unto the young man	4120
Pr 20:21	inheritance may be gotten **h** at	926
Pr 25:8	Go not forth **h** to strive, lest thou	4118

HASTING

Isa 16:5	judgment, and **h** righteousness	4106
2Pe 3:12	**h** unto the coming of the day of	*4692*

HASTY

Pr	14:29	but he that is **h** of spirit exalteth	7116
Pr	21:5	every one that is **h** only to want	213
Pr	29:20	thou a man that is **h** in his words	213
Ecc	5:2	let not thine heart be **h** to utter	4116
Ecc	7:9	Be not **h** in thy spirit to be	926
Ecc	8:3	Be not **h** to go out of his sight:	926
Da	2:15	Why is the decree so **h** from the	2685
Hab	1:6	that bitter and **h** nation, which	4116

HATE

Ge	26:27	come ye to me, seeing ye **h** me,	8130
Ge	50:15	Joseph will peradventure **h** us,	7852
Ex	20:5	fourth generation of them that **h**	8130
Le	19:17	Thou shalt not **h** thy brother in	8130
Le	26:17	they that **h** you shall reign over	8130
Dt	7:10	repayeth them that **h** him to their	8130
Dt	19:11	But if any man **h** his neighbour,	8130
Dt	22:13	go in unto her, and **h** her	8130
Dt	24:3	And if the latter husband **h** her,	8130
Dt	32:41	and will reward them that **h** me	8130
Jgs	11:7	Did not ye **h** me, and expel me out	8130
Jgs	14:16	Thou dost but **h** me, and lovest me	8130
2Sa	22:41	that I might destroy them that **h**	8130
1Ki	22:8	but I **h** him; for he doth not	8130
2Ch	19:2	and love them that **h** the Lord?	8130
Ps	25:19	they **h** me with cruel hatred	8130
Ps	34:21	and they that **h** the righteous	8130
Ps	38:19	they that **h** me wrongfully are	8130
Ps	69:4	They that **h** me without a cause	8130
Ps	69:14	delivered from them that **h** me,	8130
Ps	86:17	that they which **h** me may see it	8130
Ps	97:10	Ye that love the Lord, **h** evil:	8130
Ps	119:104	therefore I **h** every false way	8130
Ps	119:113	I **h** vain thoughts: but thy law	8130
Ps	119:128	right: and I **h** every false way	8130
Ps	119:163	I **h** and abhor lying: but thy law	8130
Ps	139:21	I **h** them, O Lord, that **h** thee?	8130
Pr	1:22	scorning, and fools **h** knowledge?	8130
Pr	6:16	These six things doth the Lord **h**:	8130
Pr	8:13	The fear of the Lord is to **h** evil:	8130
Pr	8:13	and the froward mouth, do I **h**	8130
Pr	8:36	all they that **h** me love death	8130
Pr	9:8	Reprove not a scorner, lest he **h**	8130
Pr	19:7	the brethren of the poor do **h** him:	8130
Pr	25:17	he be weary of thee, and so **h** thee	8130
Pr	29:10	The bloodthirsty **h** the upright:	8130
Ecc	3:8	A time to love, and a time to **h**;	8130
Isa	61:8	I **h** robbery for burnt offering; and	8130
Jer	44:4	this abominable thing that I **h**.	8130
Da	4:19	the dream be to them that **h** thee,	8131
Am	5:15	**H** the evil, and love the good,	8130
Am	5:21	I **h**, I despise your feast days,	8130
Mic	3:2	Who **h** the good, and love the evil;	8130
Mt	5:43	**shalt love thy neighbour, and h**	*3404*
Mt	5:44	**do good to them that h you**	*3404*
Mt	6:24	**for either he will h the one,**	*3404*
Mt	24:10	**another, and shall h one another.**	*3404*
Lk	6:22	**when men shall h you, and when**	*3404*
Lk	6:27	**enemies, do good to them which h**	*3404*
Lk	14:26	**and h not his father, and mother,**	*3404*
Lk	16:13	**either he will h the one, and love**	*3404*
Jn	7:7	**cannot h you; but me it hateth,**	*3404*
Jn	15:18	**If the world h you, ye know that**	*3404*
Ro	7:15	do I not; but what I **h**, that do I	*3404*
1Jn	3:13	my brethren, if the world **h** you	*3404*
Rev	2:6	**Nicolaitanes, which I also h.**	*3404*
Rev	2:15	**the Nicolaitanes, which thing I h**	*3404*
Rev	17:16	these shall **h** the whore, and shall	*3404*

HATED

Ge	27:41	And Esau **h** Jacob because of the	7852
Ge	29:31	the Lord saw that Leah was **h**,	8130
Ge	37:8	they **h** him yet the more for his	8130
Dt	1:27	Because the Lord **h** us, he hath	8135
Dt	4:42	**h** him not in times past;	8130
Dt	9:28	and because he **h** them, he hath	8135
Dt	19:6	as he **h** him not in time past.	8130
Dt	21:15	firstborn son be her's that was **h**:	8146
Jos	20:5	neighbour unwittingly, and **h** him	8130
2Sa	13:15	Then Amnon **h** her exceedingly; so	8130
2Sa	13:22	for Absalom **h** Amnon, because he	8130
Ps	26:5	I have **h** the congregation of evil	8130
Ps	31:6	I have **h** them that regard lying	8130
Ps	55:12	neither was it he that **h** me that	8130
Ps	106:41	they that **h** them ruled over them	8130
Pr	1:29	For that they **h** knowledge, and	8130
Pr	14:17	a man of wicked devices is **h**	8130
Pr	14:20	The poor is **h** even of his own	8130
Ecc	2:17	Therefore I **h** life; because the	8130
Ecc	2:18	Yea, I **h** all my labour which I had	8130
Isa	66:5	Your brethren that **h** you, that	8130
Eze	16:37	with all them that thou hast **h**;	8130
Mt	10:22	**ye shall be h of all men for my**	*3404*
Mt	24:9	**ye shall be h of all nations**	
Mk	13:13	**ye shall be h of all men for my**	*3404*
Lk	19:14	**But his citizens h him, and sent**	*3404*
Lk	21:17	**And ye shall be h of all men my**	*3404*
Jn	15:18	**ye know that it h me before it**	*3404*
Jn	15:24	**they both seen and h both me**	*3404*
Jn	15:25	**They h me without a cause**	*3404*
Jn	17:14	**the world hath h them, because**	*3404*
Ro	9:13	I loved, but Esau have I **h**.	*3404*
Eph	5:29	no man ever yet **h** his own flesh;	*3404*
Heb	1:9	loved righteousness, and **h** iniquity;	*3404*

HATERS

Ro	1:30	**h** of God, despiteful, proud,	*2319*

HATEST

2Sa	19:6	thine enemies, and **h** thy friends	8130
Ps	5:5	thou **h** all workers of iniquity	8130
Rev	2:6	**thou h the deeds of … Nicolaitanes,**	*3404*

HATETH

Ex	23:5	see the ass of him that **h** thee	8130
Dt	7:10	will not be slack to him that **h** him,	8130
Dt	16:22	image; which the Lord thy God **h**.	8130
Dt	22:16	unto this man to wife, and he **h** her;	8130
Ps	11:5	him that loveth violence his soul **h**.	8130
Pr	12:1	but he that **h** reproof is brutish	8130
Pr	13:5	A righteous man **h** lying: but a	8130
Pr	13:24	He that spareth his rod **h** his son:	8130
Pr	15:10	and he that **h** reproof shall die	8130
Pr	15:27	but he that **h** gifts shall live	8130
Pr	26:28	A lying tongue **h** those that are	8130
Pr	28:16	he that **h** covetousness shall	8130
Pr	29:24	partner with a thief **h** his own soul:	8130
Isa	1:14	your appointed feasts my soul **h**:	8130
Jn	3:20	**h the light, neither cometh to**	*3404*
Jn	7:7	**cannot hate you; but me it h,**	*3404*
Jn	12:25	**he that h his life in this world**	*3404*
Jn	15:19	**world, therefore the world h you**	*3404*

Jn 15:23 **He that h me h my Father also** *3404*
1Jn 2:9 is in the light, and **h** his brother, ... *3404*
1Jn 2:11 But he that **h** his brother is in *3404*
1Jn 3:15 Whosoever **h** his brother, is a *3404*
1Jn 4:20 and **h** his brother, he is a liar: *3404*

HATING

Jude 23 **h** even the garment spotted by the *3404*

HATRED

Nu 35:20 But if he thrust him of **h** 8135
2Sa 13:15 that the **h** wherewith he hated her 8135
Ps 25:19 and they hate me with cruel **h** 8135
Ps 109:5 evil for good, and **h** for my love.. 8135
Ps 139:22 I hate them with perfect **h**: 8135
Pr 10:12 **H** stirreth up strifes: but love.......... 8135
Pr 10:18 He that hideth **h** with lying lips, ... 8135
Pr 15:17 than a stalled ox and **h** therewith.. 8135
Pr 26:26 Whose **h** is covered by deceit, his 8135
Ecc 9:1 no man knoweth either love or **h** 8135
Ecc 9:6 Also their love, and their **h**, and 8135
Eze 35:5 thou hast had a perpetual **h**, and 342
Eze 35:11 which thou hast used out of thy **h** 8135
Hos 9:7 thine iniquity, and the great **h**......... 4895
Hos 9:8 **h** in the house of his God............. 4895

HAUGHTINESS

Isa 2:17 the **h** of men shall be made low:....... 7312
Isa 13:11 will lay low the **h** of the terrible 1346
Jer 48:29 and the **h** of his heart. 7312

HAUGHTY

Ps 131:1 my heart is not **h**, nor mine eyes 1361
Pr 16:18 and an **h** spirit before a fall.. 1363
Pr 18:12 destruction the heart of man is **h**, ... 1361
Pr 21:24 Proud and **h** scorner is his name, ... 3093
Isa 3:16 the daughters of Zion are **h**, ... 1361
Eze 16:50 And they were **h**, and committed 1361
Zep 3:11 shalt no more be **h** because of my 1361

HAVEN

Ps 107:30 them unto their desired **h** 4231

HAVOCK

Ac 8:3 Saul, he made **h** of the church......... *3075*

HAWK

Le 11:16 cuckow, and the **h** after his kind, ... 5322
Job 39:26 Doth the **h** fly by thy wisdom, ... 5322

HAZARDED

Ac 15:26 Men that have **h** their lives for......... *3860*

HEAD

Ge 3:15 it shall bruise thy **h**, and thou 7218
Ge 40:13 shall Pharaoh lift up thine **h**, and...... 7218
Ex 29:6 put the mitre upon his **h**, and put 7218
Ex 29:7 oil, and pour it upon his **h**, and 7218
Ex 29:10 hands upon the **h** of the bullock, ... 7218
Ex 29:17 unto his pieces, and unto his **h** 7218
Ex 29:19 their hands upon the **h** of the ram. 7218
Le 1:15 wring off his **h**, and burn it on the..... 7218
Le 4:29 upon the **h** of the sin offering, ... 7218
Le 13:40 whose hair is fallen off his **h**,.......... 7218
Le 14:18 the **h** of him that is to be cleaned: 7218
Nu 6:5 shall no razor come upon his **h**:........ 7218
Nu 6:7 of his God is upon his **h**.............. 7218
Nu 6:18 the hair of the **h** of his separation, ... 7218
Jos 2:19 his blood shall be upon his **h**, ... 7218
Jos 2:19 his blood shall be on our **h**, ... 7218
Jos 11:10 was the **h** of all those kingdoms 7218
Jgs 5:26 Sisera, she smote off his **h**, ... 7218
Jgs 9:53 of a millstone upon Abimelech's **h**, ... 7218
Jgs 16:17 hath not come a rasor upon mine **h**; ... 7218
1Sa 5:4 and the **h** of Dagon and both the...... 7218
1Sa 17:7 and his spear's **h** weighed six.......... 3852
1Sa 17:54 David took the **h** of the Philistine, ... 7218
2Sa 1:16 Thy blood be upon thy **h**; for 7218
2Sa 3:8 Am I a dog's **h**, which against 7218
2Sa 3:29 Let it rest on the **h** of Joab............ 7218
2Sa 13:19 Tamar put ashes on her **h**, and 7218
2Sa 14:26 he weighed the hair of his **h** at two 7218
2Sa 20:21 his **h** shall be thrown to thee over...... 7218
1Ki 2:6 let not his hoar **h** go down to the grave
1Ki 2:32 return his blood upon his own **h** 7218
1Ki 2:37 blood shall be upon thine own **h** 7218
2Ki 2:23 thou bald **h**; go up, thou bald **h**.
2Ki 6:5 the axe **h** fell into the water: 1270
1Ch 29:11 thou art exalted as **h** above all......... 7218
Ezr 9:3 plucked off the hair of my **h** and 7218
Est 2:17 he set the royal crown upon her **h**,..... 7218
Job 1:20 rent his mantle, and shaved his **h**, ... 7218
Ps 21:3 a crown of pure gold on his **h**......... 7218
Ps 22:7 the lip, they shake the **h**, saying, ... 7218
Ps 23:5 thou anointest my **h** with oil; 7218
Ps 40:12 more than the hairs of mine **h**:........ 7218
Ps 69:4 more than the hairs of mine **h**:........ 7218
Ps 118:22 become the **h** stone of the corner: 7218
Pr 4:9 shall give to thine **h** an ornament...... 7218
Pr 10:6 Blessings are upon the **h** of the........ 7218
Pr 16:31 The hoary **h** is a crown of glory,
Pr 20:29 the beauty of old men is the gray **h**
Pr 25:22 heap coals of fire upon his **h**; 7218
Ecc 2:14 The wise man's eyes are in his **h**; 7218
SS 2:6 His left hand is under my **h**, ... 7218
SS 5:11 His **h** is as the most fine gold, ... 7218
Isa 1:6 the sole of the foot even unto the **h** 7218
Isa 9:15 ancient and honourable, he is the **h**; ... 7218
Isa 51:20 they lie at the **h** of all the streets, ... 7218
Isa 59:17 an helmet of salvation upon his **h**:..... 7218
Jer 23:19 grievously upon the **h** of the wicked ... 7218
La 3:54 Waters flowed over mine **h**; then I 7218
La 5:16 The crown is fallen from our **h**: 7218
Eze 8:3 took me by a lock of mine **h**; 7218
Eze 9:10 recompense their way upon their **h** 7218
Eze 16:12 a beautiful crown upon thine **h** 7218
Eze 16:25 high place at every **h** of the way,....... 7218
Eze 16:43 recompense thy way upon thine **h**,..... 7218
Eze 33:4 his blood shall be upon his own **h** 7218
Da 1:10 me endanger my **h** to the king 7218
Da 2:38 Thou art this **h** of gold. 7217
Da 3:27 nor was an hair of their **h** singed, ... 7217
Da 4:5 the visions of my **h** troubled me....... 7217
Da 7:15 the visions of my **h** troubled me....... 7217
Am 2:7 of the earth on the **h** of the poor, ... 7218
Ob 15 shall return upon thine own **h** 7218
Jnh 2:5 weeds were wrapped about my **h** 7218
Zec 3:5 them set a fair mitre upon his **h** 7218
Mt 5:36 **Neither shalt thou swear by thy h**, ... *2776*
Mt 6:17 **when thou fastest, anoint thine h**, ... *2776*
Mt 8:20 **hath not where to lay his h** *2776*
Mt 10:30 **hairs of your h are all numbered** *2776*
Mt 14:8 Give me here John Baptist's **h** in....... *2776*
Mt 21:42 **is become the h of the corner:** *2776*
Mt 26:7 ointment, and poured it on his **h**,...... *2776*

Mt 27:29 of thorns, they put it upon his **h**, ... *2776*
Mt 27:30 the reed, and smote him on the **h**. *2776*
Mt 27:37 set up over his **h** his accusation........ *2776*
Mk 12:10 **is become the h of the corner:** *2776*
Mk 14:3 the box, and poured it on his **h**........ *2776*
Lk 7:44 **them with the hairs of her h** *2776*
Lk 7:46 **My h with oil thou didst not**.......... *2776*
Lk 9:58 **hath not where to lay his h** *2776*
Lk 12:7 **hairs of your h are all numbered.**...... *2776*
Lk 20:17 **is become the h of the corner?** *2776*
Lk 21:18 **shall not an hair of your h perish.** *2776*
Jn 13:9 but also my hands and my **h** *2776*
Jn 19:2 of thorns, and put it on his **h**, and *2776*
Jn 19:30 and he bowed his **h**, and gave up *2776*
Ac 4:11 is become the **h** of the corner *2776*
Ro 12:20 shalt heap coals of fire on his **h**........ *2776*
1Co 11:3 the **h** of every man is Christ; and *2776*
1Co 11:3 the **h** of the woman is the man; *2776*
1Co 11:3 and the **h** of Christ is God............ *2776*
1Co 11:4 prophesying, having his **h** covered,..... *2776*
1Co 11:5 uncovered dishonoureth her **h**:........ *2776*
1Co 11:7 indeed ought not to cover his **h**,....... *2776*
1Co 12:21 nor again the **h** to the feet, I have...... *2776*
Eph 1:22 gave him to be **h** over all things *2776*
Eph 4:15 which is the **h**, even Christ: *2776*
Eph 5:23 the husband is the **h** of the wife *2776*
Eph 5:23 as Christ is the **h** of the church: *2776*
Col 1:18 he is the **h** of the body, the church: *2776*
Col 2:10 the **h** of all principality and power: *2776*
Col 2:19 And not holding the **H**, from *2776*
1Pe 2:7 same is made the **h** of the corner,...... *2776*
Rev 1:14 His **h** and his hairs were white *2776*
Rev 10:1 and a rainbow was upon his **h**,........ *2776*
Rev 12:1 her **h** a crown of twelve stars: *2776*
Rev 14:14 having on his **h** a golden crown,....... *2776*
Rev 19:12 and on his **h** were many crowns; *2776*

HEADLONG

Ac 1:18 of iniquity; and falling **h**, he burst *4248*

HEADS

Ex 18:25 and made them **h** over the people,..... 7218
Le 10:6 Uncover not your **h**, neither rend...... 7218
Nu 8:12 hands upon the **h** of the bullocks: 7218
Nu 25:4 Take all the **h** of the people 7218
Dt 1:15 and made them **h** over you,........... 7218
Jos 7:6 Israel, and put dust upon their **h** 7218
1Sa 29:4 it not be with the **h** of these men? 7218
1Ki 20:32 and put ropes on their **h**, and came.... 7218
2Ki 10:7 put their **h** in baskets, and sent........ 7218
1Ch 12:19 Saul to the jeopardy of our **h** 7218
Job 2:12 sprinkled dust upon their **h**........... 7218
Ps 24:7 Lift up your **h**, O ye gates; and 7218
Ps 24:9 Lift up your **h**, O ye gates; even........ 7218
Ps 74:13 thou brakest the **h** of the dragons...... 7218
Ps 74:14 Thou brakest the **h** of leviathan 7218
Isa 35:10 and everlasting joy upon their **h**: 7218
La 2:10 have cast up dust upon their **h**;........ 7218
La 2:10 of Jerusalem hang down their **h** 7218
Eze 1:22 upon the **h** of the living creature 7218
Eze 11:21 their way upon their own **h**, saith...... 7218
Eze 22:31 have I recompensed upon their **h**, ... 7218
Eze 23:42 beautiful crowns upon their **h**......... 7218
Eze 27:30 shall cast up dust upon their **h**,........ 7218
Eze 32:27 laid their swords under their **h**,........ 7218
Da 7:6 the beast had also four **h**; and......... 7217
Mic 3:11 The **h** thereof judge for reward, ... 7218

Mt 27:39 by reviled him, wagging their **h**, ... *2776*
Mk 15:29 railed on him, wagging their **h**,........ *2776*
Lk 21:28 **look up, and lift up your h;**........... *2776*
Ac 18:6 Your blood be upon your own **h**; *2776*
Rev 4:4 they had on their **h** crowns of gold *2776*
Rev 9:7 on their **h** were as it were crowns *2776*
Rev 12:3 having seven **h** and ten horns, and..... *2776*
Rev 12:3 and seven crowns upon his **h** *2776*
Rev 13:1 upon his **h** the name of blasphemy *2776*
Rev 17:7 hath the seven **h** and ten horns. *2776*
Rev 17:9 The seven **h** are seven mountains, ... *2776*
Rev 18:19 they cast dust on their **h**, and cried,.... *2776*

HEADY

2Ti 3:4 Traitors, **h**, highminded, lovers *4312*

HEAL

Nu 12:13 **H** her now, O God, I beseech 7495
Dt 32:39 I make alive; I wound, and I **h**: 7495
2Ki 20:5 I will **h** thee: on the third day 7495
2Ch 7:14 their sin, and will **h** their land......... 7495
Ps 6:2 O Lord, **h** me; for my bones are 7495
Ps 41:4 be merciful unto me: **h** my soul;....... 7495
Ecc 3:3 A time to kill, and a time to **h**; 7495
Isa 57:18 I have seen his ways, and will **h**........ 7495
Jer 3:22 and I will **h** your backslidings. 7495
Jer 17:14 **H** me, O Lord, and I shall be.......... 7495
La 2:13 great like the sea: who can **h** thee? 7495
Hos 6:1 he hath torn, and he will **h** us; he...... 7495
Hos 14:4 I will **h** their backsliding, I will........ 7495
Zec 11:16 nor **h** that that is broken,............. 7495
Mt 8:7 unto him, **I will come and h him** *2323*
Mt 10:1 and to **h** all manner of sickness........ *2323*
Mt 10:8 **H the sick, cleanse the lepers,** *2323*
Mt 12:10 lawful to **h** on the sabbath days?....... *2323*
Mk 3:2 he would **h** on the sabbath day; *2323*
Mk 3:15 to have power to **h** sicknesses,......... *2323*
Lk 4:18 **sent me to h the brokenhearted,**....... *2390*
Lk 4:23 **proverb, Physician, h thyself:** *2323*
Lk 6:7 he would **h** on the sabbath day; *2323*
Lk 9:2 kingdom of God, and to **h** the sick..... *2390*
Lk 10:9 **h the sick that are therein, and**........ *2323*
Lk 14:3 **lawful to h on the sabbath day?** *2323*
Jn 4:47 would come down, and **h** his son: *2390*
Jn 12:40 be converted, and I should **h** them..... *2390*

HEALED

Ex 21:19 shall cause him to be thoroughly **h** 7495
Le 14:3 if the plague of leprosy be **h** in 7495
Le 14:48 clean, because the plague is **h** 7495
Dt 28:27 itch, whereof thou canst not be **h**...... 7495
2Ki 2:21 the Lord, I have **h** these waters;........ 7495
2Ki 9:15 king Joram was returned to be **h** 7495
2Ch 30:20 to Hezekiah, and **h** the people......... 7495
Ps 30:2 cried unto thee, and thou hast **h** me.... 7495
Ps 107:20 He sent his word, and **h** them, ... 7495
Isa 6:10 their heart, and convert, and be **h**...... 7495
Isa 53:5 and with his stripes we are **h**.......... 7495
Jer 8:11 For they have **h** the hurt of the........ 7495
Jer 15:18 incurable, which refuseth to be **h**? 7495
Jer 17:14 Heal me, O Lord, and I shall be **h**; 7495
Eze 34:4 have ye **h** that which was sick,......... 7495
Eze 47:8 the sea, the waters shall be **h** 7495
Eze 47:11 marishes thereof shall not be **h**; 7495
Hos 7:1 When I would have **h** Israel, then...... 7495
Mt 8:8 only, and my servant shall be **h**........ *2390*
Mt 8:13 servant was **h** in the selfsame *2390*

Mt	12:15	followed him, and he **h** them all;	*2323*
Mt	14:14	toward them, and he **h** their sick.	*2323*
Mt	15:30	at Jesus' feet; and he **h** them:	*2323*
Mt	21:14	him in the temple; and he **h** them	*2323*
Mk	3:10	For he had **h** many; insomuch	*2323*
Mk	5:29	that she was **h** of that plague	*2390*
Lk	4:40	on every one of them, and **h** them.	*2323*
Lk	6:19	virtue out of him, and **h** them all	*2390*
Lk	7:7	word, and my servant shall be **h**	*2390*
Lk	8:2	women, which had been **h** of evil	*2390*
Lk	9:11	**h** them that had need of healing.	*2390*
Lk	9:42	and **h** the child, and delivered	*2390*
Lk	13:14	Jesus had **h** on the sabbath day,	*2323*
Lk	17:15	when he saw that he was **h**,	*2390*
Lk	22:51	he touched his ear, and **h** him.	*2390*
Ac	3:11	man which was **h** held Peter and	*2390*
Ac	4:14	beholding the man which was **h**	*2323*
Ac	5:16	and they were **h** every one	*2323*
Ac	14:9	perceiving that he had faith to be **h**,	*4982*
Heb	12:13	the way: but let it rather be **h**	*2390*
Jas	5:16	one for another, that ye may be **h**	*2390*
1Pe	2:24	by whose stripes ye were **h**.	*2390*
Rev	13:3	his deadly wound was **h**: and all	*2323*
Rev	13:12	beast, whose deadly wound was **h**	*2323*

H

HEALETH

Ex	15:26	for I am the Lord that **h** thee.	7495
Ps	103:3	iniquities; who **h** all thy diseases;	7495
Ps	147:3	He **h** the broken in heart, and	7495
Isa	30:26	and **h** the stroke of their wound	7495

HEALING

Jer	14:19	us, and there is no **h** for us?	4832
Jer	14:19	and for the time of **h**, and behold.	4832
Jer	30:13	up: thou hast no **h** medicines	8585
Na	3:19	There is no **h** of thy bruise;	3545
Mal	4:2	arise with **h** in his wings;	4832
Mt	4:23	**h** all manner of sickness and all	*2323*
Lk	9:11	healed them that had need of **h**	*2322*
1Co	12:9	gifts of **h** by the same Spirit;	*2386*
1Co	12:30	Have all the gifts of **h**? do all	*2386*
Rev	22:2	were for the **h** of the nations.	*2322*

HEALTH

Ge	43:28	servant our father is in good **h**	7965
Ps	42:11	who is the **h** of my countenance,	3444
Pr	3:8	It shall be **h** to thy navel, and	7500
Pr	4:22	find them, and **h** to all their flesh.	4832
Pr	12:18	but the tongue of the wise is **h**	4832
Pr	16:24	the soul, and **h** to the bones.	4832
Jer	8:15	and for a time of **h**, and behold	4832
Jer	30:17	For I will restore **h** unto thee,	724

HEAP

Ge	31:52	This **h** be witness, and this pillar	1530
Ex	15:8	the floods stood upright as an **h**,	5067
Dt	13:16	and it shall be an **h** for ever;	8510
Jos	3:13	and they shall stand upon an **h**.	5067
Jos	7:26	over him a great **h** of stones	1530
Jos	8:28	Ai, and made it an **h** for ever, even	8510
Job	16:4	I could **h** up words against you,	2266
Job	36:13	hypocrites in heart **h** up wrath:	7760
Ps	33:7	waters of the sea together as an **h**:	5067
Ps	78:13	made the waters to stand as an **h**	5067
Pr	25:22	shall **h** coals of fire upon his head,	2846
Ecc	2:26	gather and to **h** up, that he may	3664
Isa	17:1	city, and it shall be a ruinous **h**	4596
Eze	24:10	**H** on wood, kindle the fire,	7235
Hab	3:15	through the **h** of great waters	2563
Ro	12:20	shalt **h** coals of fire on his head.	*4987*
2Ti	4:3	they **h** to themselves teachers,	*2002*

HEAPED

Zec	9:3	and **h** up silver as the dust, and.	6651
Jas	5:3	Ye have **h** treasures together for	*2343*

HEAPETH

Hab	2:5	nations, and **h** unto him all people:	6908

HEAPS

Jgs	15:16	the jawbone of an ass, **h** upon **h**,	2565
Ne	4:2	stones out of the **h** of the rubbish	6194
Ps	79:1	they have laid Jerusalem on **h**	5856
Isa	37:26	defenced cities into ruinous **h**.	1530
Jer	9:11	I will make Jerusalem **h**, and a	1530
Jer	26:18	Jerusalem shall become **h**, and	5856
Jer	51:37	And Babylon shall become **h**, a.	1530
Mic	3:12	Jerusalem shall become **h**, and	5856

HEAR

Ge	21:6	that all that **h** will laugh with me.	8085
Ge	42:21	besought us, and we would not **h**;	8085
Ex	20:19	Speak thou with us, and we will **h**:	8085
Le	5:1	sin and **h** the voice of swearing,	8085
Nu	30:4	And her father **h** her vow, and	8085
Dt	4:28	which neither see, nor **h**, nor eat,	8085
Dt	4:33	Did ever people **h** the voice of God	8085
Dt	5:27	and **h** all that the Lord our God	8085
Dt	6:4	**H**, O Israel: The Lord our God is	8085
Dt	9:1	**H**, O Israel: Thou art to pass over.	8085
Dt	18:16	Let me not **h** again the voice of.	8085
Dt	29:4	eyes to see, and ears to **h**, unto this	8085
Dt	30:12	that we may **h** it, and do it?	8085
Dt	31:13	may **h**, and learn to fear the.	8085
Jos	3:9	hither, and **h** the words of the Lord	8085
Jos	6:5	when ye **h** the sound of the trumpet,	8085
1Sa	2:24	for it is no good report that I **h**:	8085
1Sa	15:14	the lowing of the oxen which I **h**?	8085
2Sa	15:10	as ye **h** the sound of the trumpet,	8085
1Ki	4:34	people to **h** the wisdom of Solomon,	8085
1Ki	8:39	Then **h** thou in heaven thy	8085
1Ki	10:24	sought to Solomon, to **h** his wisdom,	8085
1Ki	18:26	O Baal, **h** us. But there was no	6030
1Ki	18:37	**H** me, O Lord, **h** me, that this	6030
2Ki	7:6	Syrians to **h** a noise of chariots,	8085
2Ki	18:28	**H** the word of the great king, the	8085
2Ki	19:7	and he shall **h** a rumour, and shall	8085
2Ch	6:23	Then **h** thou from heaven, and	8085
2Ch	7:14	then will I **h** from heaven, and	8085
Ne	4:4	**H**, O our God: for we are despised:	8085
Ne	4:20	ye **h** the sound of the trumpet,	8085
Job	35:13	God will not **h** vanity, neither will	8085
Ps	4:1	mercy upon me, and **h** my prayer.	8085
Ps	13:3	Consider and **h** me, O Lord my	6030
Ps	20:1	**h** thee in the day of trouble;	6030
Ps	20:6	will **h** him from his holy heaven	6030
Ps	34:2	the humble shall **h** thereof, and be	8085
Ps	39:12	**H** my prayer, O Lord, and give	8085
Ps	55:19	God shall **h**, and afflict them, even	8085
Ps	60:5	with thy right hand, and **h** me.	6030
Ps	66:16	Come and **h**, all ye that fear God,	8085
Ps	66:18	in my heart, the Lord will not **h** me:	8085
Ps	85:8	**h** what God the Lord will speak:	8085
Ps	94:9	planted the ear, shall he not **h**?	8085

Ps	95:7	To day if ye will **h** his voice,	8085
Ps	115:6	They have ears, but they **h** not:	8085
Ps	135:17	They have ears, but they **h** not;	238
Ps	143:7	**H** me speedily, O Lord: my	6030
Ps	143:8	Cause me to **h** thy lovingkindness	8085
Pr	1:5	wise man will **h**, and will increase	8085
Pr	1:8	**h** the instruction of thy father,	8085
Pr	4:10	**H**, O my son, and receive my	8085
Pr	8:6	**H**; for I will speak of excellent	8085
Pr	8:33	**H** instruction, and be wise, and	8085
Pr	19:27	Cease, my son, to **h** the instruction	8085
Pr	22:17	ear, and **h** the words of the wise,	8085
Ecc	5:1	be more ready to **h**, than to give	8085
Ecc	7:5	better to **h** the rebuke of the wise,	8085
Ecc	7:5	for a man to **h** the song of fools	8085
Ecc	12:13	us **h** the conclusion of the whole	8085
Isa	1:10	**H** the word of the Lord, ye rulers	8085
Isa	1:15	make many prayers, I will not **h**:	8085
Isa	18:3	when he bloweth a trumpet, **h** ye	8085
Isa	28:14	**h** the word of the Lord, ye scornful	8085
Isa	29:18	And in that day shall the deaf **h** the	8085
Isa	30:9	children that will not **h** the law of	8085
Isa	30:21	ears shall **h** a word behind thee,	8085
Isa	36:13	**H** ye the words of the great king,	8085
Isa	37:7	and he shall **h** a rumour, and	8085
Isa	41:17	I the Lord will **h** them, I the God	6030
Isa	42:18	**H**, ye deaf; and look, ye blind,	8085
Isa	43:9	or let them **h**, and say, It is truth.	8085
Isa	55:3	**h**, and your soul shall live; and I	8085
Isa	59:1	his ear heavy, that it cannot **h**:	8085
Isa	59:2	face from you, that he will not **h**.	8085
Isa	65:12	when I spake, ye did not **h**; but	8085
Isa	66:4	when I spake, they did not **h**: but	8085
Jer	4:21	and **h** the sound of the trumpet?	8085
Jer	5:21	which have ears, and **h** not:	8085
Jer	6:19	**H**, O earth: behold, I will bring	8085
Jer	7:16	to me: for I will not **h** thee.	8085
Jer	9:10	can men **h** the voice of the cattle;	8085
Jer	11:10	which refused to **h** my words,	8085
Jer	11:14	for I will not **h** them in the time	8085
Jer	13:10	people, which refuse to **h** my words,	8085
Jer	13:17	But if ye will not **h** it, my soul shall	8085
Jer	17:23	neck stiff, that they might not **h**,	8085
Jer	20:16	let him **h** the cry in the morning,	8085
Jer	22:5	But if ye will not **h** these words,	8085
Jer	22:21	but thou saidst, I will not **h**	8085
Jer	29:19	but ye would not **h**, saith the Lord.	8085
Jer	31:10	**H** the word of the Lord, O ye	8085
Jer	33:9	which shall **h** all the good that I do	8085
Jer	36:3	Judah will **h** all the evil which I	8085
Jer	36:25	the roll: but he would not **h** them	8085
Jer	38:25	if the princes **h** that I have talked	8085
Jer	42:14	nor **h** the sound of the trumpet,	8085
La	1:18	**h**, I pray you, all people, and	8085
Eze	3:11	whether they will **h**, or whether	8085
Eze	3:27	He that heareth, let him **h**; and he	8085
Eze	8:18	a loud voice, yet will I not **h** them	8085
Eze	12:2	they have ears to **h**, and **h** not:	8085
Eze	13:19	lying to my people that **h** your lies?	8085
Eze	16:35	O harlot, **h** the word of the Lord:	8085
Eze	33:31	and they **h** thy words, but they will	8085
Eze	33:32	for they **h** thy words, but they do	8085
Eze	34:7	ye shepherds, **h** the word of the	8085
Eze	37:4	O ye dry bones, **h** the word of the	8085
Da	3:15	time ye **h** the sound of the cornet,	8086
Da	5:23	which see not, nor **h**, nor know:	8086
Da	9:19	O Lord, **h**; O Lord, forgive; O Lord,	8085
Joel	1:2	**H** this, ye old men, and give ear,	8085
Am	5:1	**H** ye this word which I take up	8085
Am	5:23	I will not **h** the melody of thy viols,	8085
Am	8:4	**H** this, O ye that swallow up the	8085
Mic	1:2	**H**, all ye people; hearken, O earth,	8085
Mic	3:4	the Lord, but he will not **h** them:	6030
Mic	6:2	**H** ye...the Lord's controversy,	8085
Zec	1:4	but they did not **h**, nor hearken	8085
Zec	7:12	lest they should **h** the law, and the	8085
Zec	7:13	as he cried, and they would not **h**;	8085
Zec	7:13	so they cried, and I would not **h**,	8085
Zec	10:6	Lord their God, and will **h** them.	6030
Mal	2:2	If ye will not **h**, and if ye will not	8085
Mt	10:14	not receive you, nor **h** your words,	*191*
Mt	10:27	what ye **h** in the ear, that preach	*191*
Mt	11:15	He that hath ears to **h**, let him **h**	*191*
Mt	12:42	to **h** the wisdom of Solomon; and,	*191*
Mt	13:9	Who hath ears to **h**, let him.	*191*
Mt	13:14	hearing ye shall **h**, and shall not	*191*
Mt	13:16	they see: and your ears, for they **h**	*191*
Mt	13:43	Who hath ears ... let him **h**.	*191*
Mt	17:5	whom I am well pleased; **h** ye him	*191*
Mt	18:15	if he shall **h** thee, thou hast gained.	*191*
Mt	18:17	but if he neglect to **h** the church,	*3878*
Mt	24:6	ye shall **h** of wars and rumours of	*191*
Mk	4:20	such as **h** the word, and receive it,	*191*
Mk	4:23	any man have ears to **h**, let him **h**	*191*
Mk	4:24	Take heed what ye **h**: with what	*191*
Mk	7:16	any man have ears to **h**, let him **h**	*191*
Mk	8:18	see ye not? having ears, **h** ye not?	*191*
Mk	9:7	This is my beloved Son: **h** him	*191*
Mk	12:29	**H**, O Israel; the Lord our God is	*191*
Mk	13:7	ye shall **h** of wars and rumours of	*191*
Lk	6:27	I say unto you which **h**, Love your	*191*
Lk	8:8	He that hath ears to **h**, let him **h**	*191*
Lk	8:18	Take heed therefore how ye **h**: for	*191*
Lk	9:35	This is my beloved Son: **h** him.	*191*
Lk	11:31	to **h** the wisdom of Solomon; and,	*191*
Lk	14:35	He that hath ears to **h**, let him **h**	*191*
Lk	16:2	How is it that I **h** this of thee?	*191*
Lk	16:29	and the prophets; let them **h** them.	*191*
Lk	16:31	they **h** not Moses and the prophets,	*191*
Lk	18:6	said, **H** what the unjust judge saith.	*191*
Lk	21:38	to him in the temple, for to **h** him.	*191*
Jn	5:25	the dead shall **h** the voice of God:	*191*
Jn	5:25	God: and they that **h** shall live.	*191*
Jn	5:28	are in the graves shall **h** his voice,	*191*
Jn	5:30	as I **h**, I judge; and my judgment is	*191*
Jn	6:60	This is an hard saying; who can **h** it?	*191*
Jn	7:51	law judge any man, before it **h** him,	*191*
Jn	8:47	ye therefore **h** them not, because ye	*191*
Jn	9:27	wherefore would ye **h** it again?	*191*
Jn	10:3	and the sheep **h** his voice: and he	*191*
Jn	10:16	and they shall **h** my voice; and they	*191*
Jn	10:27	My sheep **h** my voice, and I know	*191*
Jn	12:47	if any man **h** my words, and believe	*191*
Jn	14:24	the word which ye **h** is not mine,	*191*
Jn	16:13	whatsoever he shall **h**, that shall he	*191*
Ac	2:8	**h** we every man in our own tongue,	*191*
Ac	3:22	shall ye **h** in all things whatsoever.	*191*
Ac	3:23	which will not **h** that prophet,	*191*
Ac	13:7	and desired to **h** the word of God.	*191*
Ac	17:32	We will **h** thee again of this matter.	*191*
Ac	28:26	Hearing ye shall **h**, and shall not	*191*
Ro	10:14	shall they **h** without a preacher?	*191*

Ro	11:8	see, and ears that they should not **h**;	*191*
1Co	11:18	I **h** that there be divisions among	*191*
Gal	4:21	under the law, do ye not **h** the law?	*191*
1Ti	4:16	save thyself, and them that **h** thee.	*191*
Heb	3:7	to day if ye will **h** his voice,	*191*
Heb	3:15	to day if ye will **h** his voice,	*191*
Heb	4:7	said, To day if ye will **h** his voice,	*191*
Jas	1:19	let every man be swift to **h**, slow to	*191*
1Jn	5:15	that he **h** us, whatsoever we ask,	*191*
3Jn	4	no greater joy than to **h** that my	*191*
Rev	1:3	that **h** the words of this prophecy,	*191*
Rev	2:7	that hath an ear, let him **h**	*191*
Rev	2:11	that hath an ear, let him **h**	*191*
Rev	2:17	that hath an ear, let him **h**	*191*
Rev	2:29	that hath an ear, let him **h**	*191*
Rev	3:6	He that hath an ear, let him **h**	*191*
Rev	3:13	He that hath an ear, let him **h**	*191*
Rev	3:20	if any man **h** my voice, and open	*191*
Rev	3:22	He that hath an ear, let him **h**	*191*
Rev	9:20	neither can see, nor **h**, nor walk:	*191*
Rev	13:9	If any man have an ear, let him **h**	*191*

HEARD

Ge	3:8	And they **h** the voice of the Lord	8085
Ge	3:10	I **h** thy voice in the garden, and I	8085
Ge	18:10	Sarah **h** it in the tent door, which	8085
Ge	21:17	And God **h** the voice of the lad;	8085
Ex	2:15	Now when Pharaoh **h** this thing, he	8085
Ex	2:24	And God **h** their groaning, and	8085
Ex	23:13	neither let it be **h** out of thy mouth.	8085
Nu	7:89	then he **h** the voice of one speaking	8085
Nu	11:1	and the Lord **h** it; and his anger	8085
Nu	12:2	also by us? And the Lord **h** it	8085
Nu	14:14	have **h** that thou Lord art among	8085
Dt	4:32	thing is, or hath been **h** like it?	8085
Dt	4:33	of the fire, as thou hast **h**, and live?	8085
Dt	5:26	hath **h** the voice of the living God	8085
Jos	2:11	as soon as we had **h** these things,	8085
1Sa	1:13	lips moved, but her voice was not **h**;	8085
1Sa	2:22	and **h** all that his sons did unto all	8085
2Sa	7:22	to all that we have **h** with our ears.	8085
1Ki	4:34	earth, which had **h** of his wisdom.	8085
1Ki	10:7	exceedeth the fame which I **h**	8085
1Ki	21:27	to pass, when Ahab **h** those words,	8085
2Ki	19:11	hast **h** what the kings of Assyria	8085
2Ki	20:5	**h** thy prayer, I have seen thy tears,	8085
2Ch	15:8	And when Asa **h** these words, and	8085
2Ch	20:29	they had **h** that the Lord fought	8085
2Ch	30:27	and their voice was **h**, and their	8085
2Ch	33:13	and **h** his supplication, and brought	8085
2Ch	34:19	king had **h** the words of the law,	8085
2Ch	34:27	I have even **h** thee also, saith the	8085
Ezr	3:13	shout, and the noise was **h** afar off	8085
Ezr	9:3	And when I **h** this thing, I rent my	8085
Ne	1:4	when I **h** these words, that I sat	8085
Ne	4:7	**h** that the walls of Jerusalem were	8085
Ne	4:15	our enemies **h** that it was known	8085
Ne	6:16	when all our enemies **h** thereof,	8085
Job	2:11	when Job's three friends **h** of all	8085
Job	16:2	I have **h** many such things:	8085
Job	42:5	I have **h** of thee by the hearing of	8085
Ps	3:4	and he **h** me out of his holy hill.	6030
Ps	6:8	hath **h** the voice of my weeping.	8085
Ps	19:3	language, where their voice is not **h**,	8085
Ps	34:4	I sought the Lord, and he **h** me,	6030
Ps	34:6	poor man cried, and the Lord **h**	8085
Ps	48:8	As we have **h**, so have we seen in	8085
Ps	62:11	twice have I **h** this; that power	8085
Ps	76:8	didst cause judgment to be **h** from	8085
Ps	81:5	**h** a language that I understood not	8085
Ps	120:1	cried unto the Lord, and he **h** me.	6030
Pr	21:13	cry himself, but shall not be **h**.	6030
Ecc	9:16	despised, and his words are not **h**.	8085
Ecc	9:17	words of wise men are **h** in quiet	8085
Isa	6:8	Also I **h** the voice of the Lord,	8085
Isa	30:30	cause his glorious voice to be **h**,	8085
Isa	40:28	hast thou not **h**, that the everlasting	8085
Isa	49:8	In an acceptable time have I **h**	6030
Isa	64:4	men have not **h**, nor perceived by	8085
Isa	65:19	voice of weeping shall be no more **h**	8085
Jer	3:21	voice was **h** upon the high places,	8085
Jer	7:13	early and speaking, but ye **h** not;	8085
Jer	8:6	I hearkened and **h**, but they spake	8085
Jer	23:18	hath perceived and **h** his word?	8085
Jer	30:5	We have **h** a voice of trembling,	8085
Jer	35:17	unto them, but they have not **h**;	8085
Jer	38:7	**h** that they had put Jeremiah in	8085
Jer	49:21	noise thereof was **h** in the Red sea	8085
La	1:21	mine enemies have **h** of my trouble;	8085
Eze	1:28	and I **h** a voice of one that spake	8085
Eze	3:12	I **h** behind me a voice of great	8085
Eze	33:5	He **h** the sound of the trumpet,	8085
Da	5:14	have even **h** of thee, that the spirit	8086
Da	8:16	And I **h** a man's voice between the	8085
Da	10:12	thy words were **h**, and I am come	8085
Da	12:8	And I **h**, but I understood not:	8085
Jnh	2:2	and he **h** me; out of the belly of	6030
Mic	5:15	heathen, such as they have not **h**	8085
Na	2:13	thy messengers shall no more be **h**	8085
Hab	3:2	O Lord, I have **h** thy speech, and	8085
Zec	8:23	for we have **h** that God is with you	8085
Mt	2:3	When Herod the king had **h** these	*191*
Mt	2:18	In Rama was there a voice **h**,	*191*
Mt	4:12	Jesus had **h** that John was cast into	*191*
Mt	5:21	Ye have **h** that it was said by	*191*
Mt	5:27	Ye have **h** that it was said by	*191*
Mt	5:33	ye have **h** that it hath been said by	*191*
Mt	5:38	Ye have **h** that it hath been	*191*
Mt	5:43	Ye have **h** that it hath been	*191*
Mt	6:7	be **h** for their much speaking	*1522*
Mt	9:12	But when Jesus **h** that, he said unto	*191*
Mt	11:2	when John had **h** in the prison the	*191*
Mt	13:17	ye hear, and have not **h** them.	*191*
Mt	19:22	when the young man **h** that saying,	*191*
Mt	20:24	when the ten **h** it, they were moved	*191*
Mt	22:7	the king **h** thereof, he was wroth:	*191*
Mt	26:65	now ye have **h** his blasphemy.	*191*
Mk	3:21	when his friends **h** of it, they went	*191*
Mk	4:15	when they have **h**, Satan cometh	*191*
Mk	5:36	As soon as Jesus **h** the word that	*191*
Mk	14:58	We **h** him say, I will destroy this	*191*
Mk	14:64	Ye have **h** the blasphemy: what	*191*
Mk	16:11	when they had **h** that he was alive,	*191*
Lk	1:13	for thy prayer is **h**; and thy wife	*1522*
Lk	1:66	**h** them laid them up in their hearts,	*191*
Lk	2:18	all they that **h** it, wondered at those	*191*
Lk	2:47	all that **h** him were astonished at his	*191*
Lk	4:28	when they **h** these things, were filled	*191*
Lk	7:22	what things ye have seen and **h**;	*191*
Lk	8:15	having **h** the word, keep it, and	*191*
Lk	10:24	ye hear, and have not **h** them.	*191*
Lk	10:39	sat at Jesus' feet, and **h** his word.	*191*

Lk 12:3 in darkness shall be **h** in the light; *191*
Lk 18:23 he **h** this, he was very sorrowful: *191*
Lk 18:26 **h** it said, Who then can be saved? *191*
Lk 20:16 they **h** it, they said, God forbid.. . . . . *191*
Lk 22:71 ourselves have **h** of his own mouth. *191*
Jn 4:42 for we have **h** him ourselves, and *191*
Jn 5:37 Ye have neither **h** his voice at any. *191*
Jn 6:45 Every man therefore that hath **h**, ... *191*
Jn 8:6 the ground, as though he **h** them not. . . . *191*
Jn 8:26 those things which I have **h** of him *191*
Jn 8:40 the truth, which I have **h** of God: *191*
Jn 9:32 Since the world began was it not **h**. *191*
Jn 11:4 Jesus **h** that, he said, This sickness *191*
Jn 11:41 I thank thee that thou hast **h** me. *191*
Jn 12:18 **h** that he had done this miracle. *191*
Jn 12:29 and **h** it, said that it thundered: *191*
Jn 12:34 have **h** out of the law that Christ *191*
Jn 14:28 Ye have **h** how I said unto you, I. *191*
Jn 15:15 things that I have **h** of my Father. *191*
Jn 19:8 When Pilate … **h** that saying, he was. . . . *191*
Ac 1:4 which, saith he, ye have **h** of me. *191*
Ac 2:6 every man **h** them speak in his own. *191*
Ac 4:4 of them which **h** the word believed; *191*
Ac 5:5 fear came on all them that **h** these *191*
Ac 6:11 We have **h** him speak blasphemous *191*
Ac 9:4 he fell to the earth, and **h** a voice *191*
Ac 9:13 I have **h** by many of this man, how *191*
Ac 10:46 they **h** them speak with tongues, ... *191*
Ac 11:7 I **h** a voice saying unto me, Arise, ... *191*
Ac 19:2 We have not so much as **h** whether *191*
Ac 21:20 when they **h** it, they glorified the *191*
Ac 22:7 **h** a voice saying unto me, Saul, Saul, ... *191*
Ac 22:9 **h** not the voice of him that spake to. *191*
Ac 26:14 I **h** a voice speaking unto me, and *191*
Ro 10:14 in him of whom they have not **h**? *191*
Ro 15:21 that have not **h** shall understand. *191*
1Co 2:9 Eye hath not seen, nor ear **h**, ... *191*
2Co 6:2 I have **h** thee in a time accepted, ... *1873*
2Co 12:4 into paradise, and **h** unspeakable *191*
Php 4:9 both learned, and received, and **h**, ... *191*
Col 1:4 Since we **h** of your faith in Christ. *191*
Col 1:9 since the day we **h** it, do not cease *191*
2Ti 2:2 the things that thou hast **h** of me *191*
Heb 2:1 heed to the things which we have **h**, ... *191*
Heb 2:3 confirmed unto us by them that **h** *191*
Heb 5:7 and was **h** in that he feared; *1522*
Heb 12:19 which voice they that **h** intreated *191*
Jas 5:11 Ye have **h** of the patience of Job, ... *191*
2Pe 1:18 voice which came from heaven we **h**, ... *191*
1Jn 1:1 which we have **h**, which we have seen . . . *191*
1Jn 1:3 we have seen and **h** declare we *191*
1Jn 2:18 have **h** that antichrist shall come, ... *191*
1Jn 2:24 which ye have **h** from the beginning *191*
1Jn 4:3 ye have **h** that it should come; *191*
Rev 1:10 **h** behind me a great voice, as of a. *191*
Rev 3:3 how thou hast received and **h**, and. *191*
Rev 4:1 first voice which I **h** was as it were *191*
Rev 5:11 I **h** the voice of many angels round *191*
Rev 6:1 I **h**, as it were, the noise of thunder, ... *191*
Rev 7:4 I **h** the number of them which were. *191*
Rev 8:13 I beheld, and **h** an angel flying *191*
Rev 9:16 and I **h** the number of them *191*
Rev 10:4 I **h** a voice from heaven saying unto. *191*
Rev 12:10 I **h** a loud voice saying in heaven, ... *191*
Rev 14:2 I **h** a voice from heaven, as the voice *191*
Rev 14:13 I **h** a voice from heaven saying unto. *191*
Rev 18:4 I **h** another voice from heaven, ... *191*
Rev 18:22 trumpeters, shall be **h** no more at all *191*
Rev 19:1 I **h** a great voice of much people. *191*
Rev 19:6 I **h**, as it were, the voice of a great. *191*
Rev 21:3 I **h** a great voice out of heaven *191*
Rev 22:8 I John saw these things, and **h** them. *191*

HEARER

Jas 1:23 if any be a **h** of the word, and not. *202*
Jas 1:25 he being not a forgetful **h**, but. *202*

HEARERS

Ro 2:13 For not the **h** of the law are just *202*
Eph 4:29 may minister grace unto the **h** *191*
2Ti 2:14 but to the subverting of the **h** *191*
Jas 1:22 doers of the word, and not **h** only, ... *202*

HEAREST

1Ki 8:30 and when thou **h**, forgive. 8085
Ps 65:2 O thou that **h** prayer, unto thee 8085
Jn 3:8 and thou **h** the sound thereof, but. *191*
Jn 11:42 I knew that thou **h** me always: *191*

HEARETH

Ex 16:8 that the Lord **h** your murmurings 8085
Dt 29:19 when he **h** the words of this curse, ... 8085
1Sa 3:9 Speak, Lord; for thy servant **h**. 8085
1Sa 3:11 of every one that **h** it shall tingle. 8085
2Ki 21:12 that whosoever **h** of it, both his ears . . . 8085
Ps 38:14 I was as a man that **h** not, ... 8085
Ps 69:33 for the Lord **h** the poor, and 8085
Pr 13:1 wise son **h** his father's instruction: 8085
Pr 13:1 but a scorner **h** not rebuke. 8085
Pr 13:8 riches: but the poor **h** not rebuke. 8085
Pr 15:29 he **h** the prayer of the righteous.. 8085
Pr 15:31 The ear that **h** the reproof of life 8085
Pr 18:13 answereth a matter before he **h** it, ... 8085
Pr 25:10 Lest he that **h** it put thee to shame, ... 8085
Isa 41:26 there is none that **h** your words. 8085
Isa 42:20 opening the ears, but he **h** not. 8085
Jer 19:3 whosoever **h**, his ears shall tingle 8085
Eze 3:27 He that **h**, let him hear; and he. 8085
Eze 33:4 Then whosoever **h** the sound of the. . . . 8085
Mt 7:24 whosoever **h** these sayings of mine, ... *191*
Mt 7:26 every one that **h** these sayings of *191*
Mt 13:19 one **h** the word of the kingdom, ... *191*
Mt 13:23 good ground is he that **h** the word, ... *191*
Lk 6:47 cometh to me, and **h** my sayings, ... *191*
Lk 6:49 he that **h**, and doeth not, is like *191*
Lk 10:16 He that **h** you **h** me; and he that. *191*
Jn 5:24 He that **h** my word, and believeth *191*
Jn 8:47 He that is of God **h** God's words: *191*
Jn 9:31 we know that God **h** not sinners: *191*
Jn 9:31 of God, and doeth his will, him he **h** *191*
Jn 18:37 one that is of the truth **h** my voice. *191*
1Jn 4:6 he that knoweth God **h** us; he that. *191*
1Jn 5:14 thing according to his will, he **h** us: *191*
Rev 22:17 And let him that **h** say, Come. *191*
Rev 22:18 that **h** the words of the prophecy of. *191*

HEARING

Dt 31:11 this law before all Israel in their **h**. 241
2Sa 18:12 for in our **h** the king charged thee 241
Job 42:5 heard of thee by the **h** of the ear: 8088
Pr 20:12 The **h** ear, and the seeing eye, ... 8085
Pr 28:9 turneth away his ear from **h** the law, . . . 8085
Ecc 1:8 seeing, nor the ear filled with **h**. 8085
Isa 11:3 reprove after the **h** of his ears: 4926

Isa	21:3	I was bowed down at the **h** of it;	8085
Isa	33:15	stoppeth his ears from **h** of blood,	8085
Eze	9:5	to the others he said in mine **h**,	241
Am	8:11	but of **h** the words of the Lord:	8085
Mt	13:13	**seeing see not; and h they hear not**	*191*
Mt	13:14	**By h ye shall hear, and shall not**	*189*
Mt	13:15	**and their ears are dull of h,**	*191*
Mk	6:2	and many **h** him were astonished,	*191*
Ac	9:7	**h** a voice, but seeing no man.	*191*
Ac	28:26	**H** ye shall hear, and shall not.	*289*
Ac	28:27	and their ears are dull of **h**,	*191*
Ro	10:17	So then faith cometh by **h**,	*189*
Ro	10:17	and **h** by the word of God.	*189*
1Co	12:17	body were an eye, where were the **h**?	*189*
Gal	3:2	of the law, or by the **h** of faith?	*189*
Gal	3:5	of the law, or by the **h** of faith?	*189*
Heb	5:11	to be uttered, seeing ye are dull of **h**.	*189*
2Pe	2:8	them, in seeing and **h**, vexed his	*189*

HEARKEN

Ge	21:12	said unto thee, **h** unto her voice;	8085
Ex	4:1	they will not believe me, nor **h** unto	8085
Ex	11:9	Pharaoh shall not **h** unto you:	8085
Ex	15:26	If thou wilt diligently **h** to the voice	8085
Le	26:21	will not **h** unto me; I will bring	8085
Dt	7:12	if ye **h** to these judgments, and	8085
Dt	13:3	Thou shalt not **h** unto the words	8085
Dt	17:12	not **h** unto the priest that standeth	8085
Dt	26:17	judgments, and to **h** unto his voice:	8085
Dt	28:1	shalt **h** diligently unto the voice of	8085
Dt	28:15	if thou wilt not **h** unto the voice of	8085
Jgs	2:17	would not **h** unto their judges,	8085
Jgs	19:25	But the men would not **h** to him:	8085
1Sa	8:7	**H** unto the voice of the people in all	8085
1Sa	8:9	Now therefore **h** unto their voice:	8085
1Sa	8:22	**H** unto their voice, and make them	8085
1Sa	15:22	better ... to **h** than the fat of rams	7181
1Sa	30:24	For who will **h** unto you in this	8085
1Ki	11:38	thou wilt **h** unto all that I command	8085
2Ki	18:32	and **h** not unto Hezekiah, when he	8085
2Ch	10:16	the king would not **h** unto them,	8085
Ne	13:27	Shall we then **h** unto you to do all	8085
Ps	45:10	**H**, O daughter, and consider, and	8085
Ps	58:5	not **h** to the voice of charmers,	8085
Ps	81:11	But my people would not **h** to my	8085
Pr	23:22	**H** unto thy father that begat thee	8085
Pr	29:12	If a ruler **h** to lies, all his servants	7181
Isa	34:1	**h**, ye people: let the earth hear,	7181
Isa	48:12	**H** unto me, O Jacob and Israel,	8085
Isa	51:1	**H** to me ye that follow after.	8085
Isa	51:7	**H** unto me, ye that know	8085
Jer	6:17	But they said, We will not **h**.	7181
Jer	11:11	cry unto me, I will not **h** unto them	8085
Jer	17:24	to pass, if ye diligently **h** unto me,	8085
Jer	23:16	**H** not unto the words of the	8085
Jer	26:3	If so be they will **h**, and turn every	8085
Jer	27:9	**h** not ye to your prophets, nor to	8085
Jer	27:16	**H** not to the words of your	8085
Jer	27:17	**H** not unto them; serve the king of	8085
Jer	38:15	counsel, wilt thou not **h** unto me?	8085
Jer	44:16	of the Lord, we will not **h** unto thee.	8085
Eze	3:7	the house of Israel will not **h** unto	8085
Mic	1:2	**h**, O earth, and all that therein is:	7181
Zec	7:11	they refused to **h** and pulled away	7181
Mk	7:14	**H unto me every one of you,**	*191*
Ac	4:19	right in the sight of God to **h** unto	*191*

HEARKENED

Ge	3:17	hast **h** unto the voice of thy wife,	8085
Ge	39:10	that he **h** not unto her, to lie by her,	8085
Ex	6:9	they **h** not unto Moses for anguish	8085
Ex	7:13	Pharaoh's heart, that he **h** not	8085
Ex	16:20	they **h** not unto Moses; but some	8085
Dt	9:23	believed him not, nor **h** to his voice	8085
Dt	18:14	**h** unto observers of times, and unto	8085
1Sa	2:25	**h** not unto the voice of their father,	8085
1Ki	12:15	the king **h** not unto the people;	8085
2Ki	22:13	because our fathers have not **h** unto	8085
Ne	9:29	**h** not unto thy commandments, but	8085
Ps	81:13	Oh that my people had **h** unto me,	8085
Isa	48:18	hadst **h** to my commandments!	7181
Jer	7:24	But they **h** not, nor inclined their	8085
Jer	29:19	they have not **h** to my words, saith	8085
Jer	34:17	have not **h** unto me, in proclaiming	8085
Da	9:6	have we **h** unto thy servants the	8085
Mal	3:16	and the Lord **h**, and heard it, and	7181

HEART

Ge	6:5	thoughts of his **h** was only evil	3820
Ge	6:6	earth, and it grieved him at his **h**	3820
Ge	8:21	the imagination of man's **h** is evil.	3820
Ge	20:5	integrity of my **h** and innocency.	3824
Ge	27:41	Esau said in his **h**, The days of	3820
Ex	4:21	I will harden his **h**, that he shall	3820
Ex	7:23	neither did he set his **h** to this also.	3820
Ex	9:14	send all my plagues upon thine **h**.	3820
Ex	14:4	will harden Pharaoh's **h**, that he	3820
Ex	23:9	for ye know the **h** of a stranger	5315
Ex	35:21	every one whose **h** stirred him up	3820
Ex	36:2	every one whose **h** stirred him up	3820
Le	19:17	not hate thy brother in thine **h**:	3824
Nu	15:39	that ye seek not after your own **h**	3824
Dt	4:9	lest they depart from thy **h** all the	3824
Dt	4:29	if thou seek him with all thy **h** and	3824
Dt	6:5	the Lord thy God with all thine **h**,	3824
Dt	10:16	the foreskin of your **h**, and be no	3824
Dt	11:13	serve him with all your **h** and with	3824
Dt	11:16	that your **h** be not deceived, and ye	3824
Dt	11:18	lay up these my words in your **h**.	3824
Dt	13:3	the Lord your God with all your **h**	3824
Dt	15:9	be not a thought in thy wicked **h**	3824
Dt	19:6	the slayer, while his **h** is hot, and	3824
Dt	26:16	keep and do them with all thine **h**	3824
Dt	28:28	blindness, and astonishment of **h**:	3824
Dt	29:19	walk in the imagination of mine **h**,	3820
Dt	30:2	all thine **h**, and with all thy soul;	3824
Dt	30:6	thy God will circumcise thine **h**,	3824
Dt	30:6	Lord thy God with all thine **h**, and	3824
Dt	30:17	if thine **h** turn away, so that thou	3824
Jos	5:1	their **h** melted, neither was there	3824
Jos	14:8	made the **h** of the people melt:	3820
Jos	22:5	to serve him with all your **h** and	3824
Jgs	16:15	thee, when thine **h** is not with me?	3820
Jgs	16:18	for he hath shewed me all his **h**	3820
Jgs	19:5	Comfort thine **h** with a morsel of	3820
1Sa	1:13	Now Hannah, she spake in her **h**:	3820
1Sa	10:9	Samuel, God gave him another **h**:	3820
1Sa	13:14	sought him a man after his own **h**,	3824
1Sa	16:7	but the Lord looketh on the **h**.	3824
1Sa	17:28	the naughtiness of thine **h**; for thou	3824
1Sa	24:5	David's **h** smote him, because he	3820
1Sa	25:37	that his **h** died within him, and he	3820
2Sa	6:16	and she despised him in her **h**	3820

2Sa	17:10	whose **h** is as the **h** of a lion	3820
2Sa	24:10	David's **h** smote him after that he.	3820
1Ki	2:4	all their **h** and with all their soul.	3824
1Ki	3:9	an understanding **h** to judge thy.	3820
1Ki	3:12	wise and an understanding **h**;	3820
1Ki	8:18	it was in thine **h** to build an house	3824
1Ki	8:39	to his ways, whose **h** thou knowest;	3824
1Ki	8:61	Let your **h** therefore be perfect	3824
1Ki	9:3	mine eyes and mine **h** shall be there	3824
1Ki	11:4	wives turned away his **h** after	3824
1Ki	12:33	which he had devised of his own **h**;	3820
1Ki	15:14	Asa's **h** was perfect with the Lord	3824
2Ki	20:3	in truth and with a perfect **h**,	3824
2Ki	22:19	thine **h** was tender, and thou hast.	3824
2Ki	23:25	turned to the Lord with all his **h**,	3824
1Ch	12:33	rank: they were not of double **h**	3820
1Ch	12:38	came with a perfect **h** to Hebron	3820
1Ch	12:38	were of one **h** to make David king	3824
1Ch	17:2	David, Do all that is in thine **h**;.	3824
1Ch	22:19	set your **h** and your soul to seek	3824
1Ch	28:2	I had in mine **h** to build an house	3824
1Ch	29:9	with perfect **h** they offered willingly	3820
1Ch	29:17	thou triest the **h**, and hast pleasure	3824
1Ch	29:18	the thoughts of the **h** of thy people,.	3824
1Ch	29:19	give ... Solomon my son a perfect **h**,	3824
2Ch	6:8	didst well in that it was in thine **h**	3824
2Ch	6:30	his ways, whose **h** thou knowest;	3824
2Ch	9:23	wisdom, that God had put in his **h**	3820
2Ch	12:14	prepared not his **h** to seek the Lord.	3820
2Ch	15:12	all their **h** and with all their soul;	3824
2Ch	16:9	whose **h** is perfect toward him	3824
2Ch	19:3	hast prepared thine **h** to seek God.	3824
2Ch	25:2	the Lord, but not with a perfect **h**	3824
2Ch	29:10	it is in mine **h** to make a covenant	3824
2Ch	30:19	That prepareth his **h** to seek God,	3824
2Ch	32:26	himself for the pride of his **h**.	3820
2Ch	32:31	might know all that was in his **h**.	3824
Ezr	6:22	turned the **h** of the king of Assyria.	3820
Ne	2:2	nothing else but sorrow of **h**.	3820
Job	38:36	given understanding to the **h**?	7907
Ps	4:4	commune with your own **h** upon	3824
Ps	9:1	thee, O Lord, with my whole **h**;	3820
Ps	10:11	said in his **h**, God hath forgotten:.	3820
Ps	12:2	and with a double **h** do they speak.	3820
Ps	14:1	The fool hath said in his **h**, There.	3820
Ps	19:8	Lord are right, rejoicing the **h**:	3820
Ps	19:14	mouth, and the meditation of my **h**.	3820
Ps	24:4	hath clean hands, and a pure **h**;	3824
Ps	34:18	unto them that are of a broken **h**;	3820
Ps	37:31	The law of his God is in his **h**;.	3820
Ps	44:21	he knoweth the secrets of the **h**.	3820
Ps	51:10	Create in me a clean **h**, O God;.	3820
Ps	51:17	a broken and a contrite **h**, O God.	3820
Ps	53:1	The fool hath said in his **h**, There.	3820
Ps	57:7	My **h** is fixed, O God, my **h** is fixed:.	3820
Ps	66:18	I regard iniquity in my **h**, the Lord.	3820
Ps	69:20	Reproach hath broken my **h**; and	3820
Ps	73:26	but God is the strength of my **h**	3824
Ps	84:2	my **h** and my flesh crieth out for	3820
Ps	95:8	Harden not your **h**, as in the	3824
Ps	119:2	that seek him with the whole **h**.	3820
Ps	119:32	when thou shalt enlarge my **h**.	3820
Ps	131:1	my **h** is not haughty, nor mine eyes	3820
Ps	139:23	Search me ... and know my **h**.	3824
Ps	147:3	He healeth the broken in **h**, and	3820
Pr	2:2	apply thine **h** to understanding;	3820
Pr	3:3	them upon the table of thine **h**:	3820
Pr	3:5	Trust in the Lord with all thine **h**;	3820
Pr	4:23	Keep thy **h** with all diligence; for	3820
Pr	6:25	not after her beauty in thine **h**;	3824
Pr	7:3	them upon the table of thine **h**.	3820
Pr	11:29	shall be servant to the wise of **h**	3820
Pr	13:12	Hope deferred maketh the **h** sick:.	3820
Pr	14:13	in laughter the **h** is sorrowful;.	3820
Pr	15:13	A merry **h** maketh a cheerful	3820
Pr	16:9	A man's **h** deviseth his way; but	3820
Pr	17:22	A merry **h** doeth good like a	3820
Pr	19:21	are many devices in a man's **h**;	3820
Pr	22:15	Foolishness is bound in the **h** of a	3820
Pr	23:7	as he thinketh in his **h**, so is he:	5315
Pr	23:17	Let not thine **h** envy sinners:	3820
Pr	23:26	My son, give me thine **h**, and	3820
Pr	24:17	let not thine **h** be glad when he	3820
Pr	25:3	the **h** of kings is unsearchable	3820
Pr	25:20	he that singeth songs to an heavy **h**	3820
Pr	26:25	are seven abominations in his **h**	3820
Pr	28:26	trusteth in his own **h** is a fool:.	3820
Pr	31:11	The **h** of her husband doth safely.	3820
Ecc	1:13	I gave my **h** to seek and search out	3820
Ecc	1:17	And I gave my **h** to know wisdom,.	3820
Ecc	2:10	I withheld not my **h** from any joy;	3820
Ecc	3:11	he hath set the world in their **h**,	3820
Ecc	5:2	and let not thine **h** be hasty to utter	3820
Ecc	7:2	and the living will lay it to his **h**	3820
Ecc	8:11	the **h** of the sons of men is fully set	3820
Ecc	9:3	**h** of the sons of men is full of evil	3820
SS	4:9	Thou hast ravished my **h**, my	3823
Isa	6:10	and understand with their **h**, and.	3824
Isa	13:7	faint, and every man's **h** shall melt:	3824
Isa	14:13	hast said in thine **h**, I will ascend	3824
Isa	29:13	have removed their **h** far from me,.	3820
Isa	38:3	in truth and with a perfect **h**.	3820
Isa	47:8	that sayest in thine **h**, I am, and	3824
Isa	57:1	and no man layeth it to **h**:	3820
Jer	3:17	the imagination of their evil **h**,	3820
Jer	4:4	take away the foreskins of your **h**,	3824
Jer	7:24	in the imagination of their evil **h**,.	3820
Jer	7:31	not, neither came it into my **h**,	3820
Jer	12:11	because no man layeth it to **h**	3820
Jer	13:10	walk in the imagination of their **h**,.	3820
Jer	15:16	me the joy and rejoicing of mine **h**:	3824
Jer	17:1	graven upon the table of their **h**,	3820
Jer	17:9	The **h** is deceitful above all things,	3820
Jer	17:10	I the Lord search the **h**, I try the	3820
Jer	20:9	word was in mine **h** as a burning	3820
Jer	23:16	they speak a vision of their own **h**,.	3820
Jer	24:7	I will give them an **h** to know me	3820
Jer	29:13	shall search for me with all your **h**	3824
Jer	32:39	will give them one **h**, and one way,.	3820
La	2:19	pour out thine **h** like water before	3820
La	5:15	The joy of our **h** is ceased; our	3820
Eze	11:19	and will give them an **h** of flesh:.	3820
Eze	14:3	have set up their idols in their **h**,	3820
Eze	20:16	for their **h** went after their idols	3820
Eze	21:7	every **h** shall melt, and all hands.	3820
Eze	22:14	can thine **h** endure, or can thine.	3820
Eze	27:31	weep for thee with bitterness of **h**	5315
Eze	28:5	thine **h** is lifted up because of thy.	3824
Eze	28:6	set thine **h** as the **h** of God;	3820
Eze	33:31	**h** goeth after their covetousness	3820
Eze	36:26	and I will give you an **h** of flesh	3820
Eze	44:9	No stranger, uncircumcised in **h**,	3820

Da	1:8	Daniel purposed in his **h** that he	3820
Da	2:30	know the thoughts of thy **h**	3825
Da	4:16	let a beast's **h** be given unto him;	3825
Da	8:25	he shall magnify himself in his **h**,	3824
Da	10:12	didst set thine **h** to understand	3820
Da	11:28	and his **h** shall be against the holy	3824
Hos	4:8	they set their **h** on their iniquity	5315
Hos	10:2	Their **h** is divided; now shall they	3820
Joel	2:12	turn ye even to me with all your **h**,	3824
Joel	2:13	And rend your **h**, and not your	3824
Ob	3	pride of thine **h** hath deceived thee	3820
Na	2:10	and the **h** melteth, and the knees	3820
Zep	1:12	say in their **h**, The Lord will not	3824
Zep	2:15	that said in her **h**, I am, and there	3824
Zec	7:10	evil against his brother in your **h**	3824
Mal	2:2	if ye will not lay it to **h**, to give glory	3820
Mal	4:6	he shall turn the **h** of the fathers to	3820
Mt	5:8	**Blessed are the pure in h; for they**	*2588*
Mt	5:28	**adultery with her already in his h**	*2588*
Mt	6:21	**treasure is, there will your h be**	*2588*
Mt	11:29	**for I am meek and lowly in h:**	*2588*
Mt	12:34	**the abundance of the h the mouth.**	*2588*
Mt	12:40	**three nights in the h of the earth**	*2588*
Mt	13:15	**should understand with their h,**	*2588*
Mt	15:8	**lips; but their h is far from me.**	*2588*
Mt	15:19	**out of the h proceed evil thoughts,**	*2588*
Mt	22:37	**the Lord thy God with all thy h,**	*2588*
Mk	7:6	**lips, but their h is far from me.**	*2588*
Mk	7:19	**Because it entereth not into his h,**	*2588*
Mk	11:23	**and shall not doubt in his h, but**	*2588*
Mk	12:30	**the Lord thy God with all thy h,**	*2588*
Lk	2:19	and pondered them in her **h**	*2588*
Lk	2:51	kept all these sayings in her **h**	*2588*
Lk	6:45	**out of the good treasure of his h**	*2588*
Lk	6:45	**out of the evil treasure of his h.**	*2588*
Lk	6:45	**abundance of the h his mouth**	*2588*
Lk	9:47	perceiving the thought of their **h**,	*2588*
Lk	10:27	the Lord thy God with all thy **h**,	*2588*
Lk	12:34	**treasure is, there will your h be**	*2588*
Lk	24:25	**and slow of h to believe all that**	*2588*
Lk	24:32	Did not our **h** burn within us, while	*2588*
Jn	12:40	eyes, nor understand with their **h**;	*2588*
Jn	13:2	having now put into the **h** of Judas	*2588*
Jn	14:1	**Let not your h be troubled: ye**	*2588*
Jn	14:27	**Let not your h be troubled,**	*2588*
Jn	16:6	**you, sorrow hath filled your h**	*2588*
Jn	16:22	**and your h shall rejoice, and your**	*2588*
Ac	2:46	with gladness and singleness of **h**	*2588*
Ac	4:32	were of one **h**, and of one soul:	*2588*
Ac	5:3	why hath Satan filled thine **h** to lie	*2588*
Ac	7:51	and uncircumcised in **h** and ears	*2588*
Ac	7:54	they were cut to the **h**, and they	*2588*
Ac	8:22	the thought of thine **h** may be	*2588*
Ac	8:37	If thou believest with all thine **h**	*2588*
Ac	28:27	For the **h** of this people is waxed	*2588*
Ro	1:21	and their foolish **h** was darkened	*2588*
Ro	2:5	after thy hardness and impenitent **h**.	*2588*
Ro	2:29	and circumcision is that of the **h**	*2588*
Ro	10:6	Say not in thine **h**, Who shall ascend	*2588*
Ro	10:10	For with the **h** man believeth unto	*2588*
1Co	2:9	have entered in to the **h** of man,	*2588*
2Co	3:3	stone, but in fleshy tables of the **h**	*2588*
2Co	3:15	is read, the vail is upon their **h**	*2588*
2Co	5:12	glory in appearance, and not in **h**.	*2588*
2Co	9:7	as he purposeth in his **h**, so let him	*2588*
Eph	4:18	because of the blindness of their **h**:	*2588*
Eph	5:19	making melody in your **h** to the	*2588*
Eph	6:5	in singleness of your **h**, as unto	*2588*
Eph	6:6	doing the will of God from the **h**;	*5590*
Col	3:22	but in singleness of **h**, fearing God:	*2588*
1Ti	1:5	is charity out of a pure **h**, and of a	*2588*
2Ti	2:22	call on the Lord out of a pure **h**	*2588*
Heb	3:12	be in any of you an evil **h** of	*2588*
Heb	4:12	of thoughts and intents of the **h**	*2588*
Heb	10:22	Let us draw near with a true **h** in	*2588*
Heb	13:9	the **h** be established with grace	*2588*
Jas	1:26	his tongue, but deceiveth his own **h**,	*2588*
1Pe	1:22	ye love one another with a pure **h**	*2588*
2Pe	2:14	an **h** they have exercised with	*2588*
1Jn	3:20	God is greater than our **h**, and	*2588*
1Jn	3:21	if our **h** condemn us not, then have	*2588*
Rev	18:7	for she saith in her **h**, I sit a queen,	*2588*

HEARTED

Ex	35:10	And every wise **h** among you shall	3820
Ex	35:22	as many as were willing **h**, and	3820
Ex	35:25	And all the women that were wise **h**	3820

HEARTH

Ps	102:3	my bones are burned as an **h**	4168
Isa	30:14	a sherd to take fire from the **h**, or	3344
Zec	12:6	like an **h** of fire among the wood	3595

HEARTILY

Col	3:23	whatsoever ye do, do it **h**, as to	*1537, 5590*

HEART'S

Ps	10:3	wicked boasteth of his **h** desire,	5315
Ps	21:2	Thou hast given him his **h** desire,	3820
Ro	10:1	my **h** desire and prayer to God	*2588*

HEARTS

Ex	14:17	will harden the **h** of the Egyptians,	3820
Le	26:36	will send a faintness into their **h**.	3824
Le	26:41	uncircumcised **h** be humbled,	3824
Dt	20:3	let not your **h** faint, fear not, and	3824
Jos	2:11	our **h** did melt, neither did there	3824
Jos	7:5	the **h** of the people melted, and	3824
1Sa	6:6	then do ye harden your **h**, as the	3824
2Sa	15:6	Absalom stole the **h** of the men of	3820
1Ki	8:39	thou only, knowest the **h** of all	3824
1Ch	28:9	for the Lord searcheth all **h**, and	3824
Job	1:5	sinned, and cursed God in their **h**	3824
Ps	7:9	the righteous God trieth the **h** and	3826
Ps	28:3	but mischief is in their **h**	3824
Ps	90:12	may apply our **h** unto wisdom	3824
Pr	15:11	then the **h** of the children of men?	3826
Pr	17:3	for gold: but the Lord trieth the **h**	3826
Pr	21:2	eyes: but the Lord pondereth the **h**	3826
Pr	31:6	unto those that be of heavy **h**	5315
Isa	44:18	see; and their **h**, that they cannot	3826
Jer	32:40	but I will put my fear in their **h**	3824
Eze	13:2	that prophesy out of their own **h**	3820
Hos	7:2	they consider not in their **h** that I	3824
Zec	8:17	none of you imagine evil in your **h**	3820
Mt	9:4	**Wherefore think ye evil in your h?**	*2588*
Mt	18:35	**from your h forgive not every one**	*2588*
Mt	19:8	**because of the hardness of your h**	*4641*
Mk	2:8	**reason ye these things in your h?**	*2588*
Mk	3:5	grieved for the hardness of their **h**,	*2588*
Mk	4:15	**word that was sown in their h**	*2588*
Lk	1:17	to turn the **h** of the fathers to the	*2588*
Lk	1:66	laid them up in their **h**, saying,	*2588*
Lk	2:35	the thoughts of many **h** may be	*2588*

Lk	8:12	**away the word out of their h,**	*2588*
Lk	16:15	**but God knoweth your h: for**	*2588*
Lk	21:26	**Men's h failing them for fear, and**	*674*
Lk	21:34	**any time your h be overcharged**	*2588*
Lk	24:38	**why do thoughts arise in your h?**	*2588*
Ac	15:8	And God which knoweth the **h**,	*2589*
Ro	2:15	work of the law written in their **h**,	*2588*
Ro	5:5	love of God is shed abroad in our **h**	*2588*
Ro	8:27	he that searcheth the **h** knoweth	*2588*
Ro	16:18	deceive the **h** of the simple	*2588*
2Co	1:22	the earnest of the Spirit in our **h**.	*2588*
2Co	3:2	written in our **h**, known and read	*2588*
2Co	4:6	hath shined in our **h**, to give the	*2588*
Gal	4:6	the Spirit of his Son into your **h**,	*2588*
Eph	3:17	That Christ may dwell in your **h** by	*2588*
Php	4:7	shall keep your **h** and minds	*2588*
Col	3:15	let the peace of God rule in your **h**,	*2588*
1Th	2:4	men, but God, which trieth our **h**	*2588*
1Th	3:13	he may stablish your **h** unblamable	*2588*
2Th	2:17	Comfort your **h**, and stablish you	*2588*
Heb	3:8	Harden not your **h**, as in the	*2588*
Heb	3:15	voice, harden not your **h**, as in the	*2588*
Heb	4:7	hear his voice, harden not your **h**	*2588*
Heb	8:10	mind, and write them in their **h**:	*2588*
Heb	10:16	I will put my laws into their **h**,	*2588*
Heb	10:22	having our **h** sprinkled from an evil	*2588*
Jas	3:14	envying and strife in your **h**,	*2588*
Jas	4:8	purify your **h**, ye double minded	*2588*
Jas	5:5	ye have nourished your **h**, as in a	*2588*
Jas	5:8	ye also patient; stablish your **h**:	*2588*
1Pe	3:15	sanctify the Lord God in your **h**:	*2588*
2Pe	1:19	and the day star arise in your **h**:	*2588*
1Jn	3:19	and shall assure our **h** before him	*2588*
Rev	2:23	**which searcheth the reins and h:**	*2588*
Rev	17:17	God hath put in their **h** to fulfil	*2588*

HEARTS'

Ps	81:12	them up unto their own **h** lust:	3820

HEAT

Ge	8:22	and cold and **h**, and summer and	2527
Dt	29:24	meaneth the **h** of this great anger?	2750
Dt	32:34	devoured with burning **h**, and	7565
Ps	19:6	nothing hid from the **h** thereof	2535
Ecc	4:11	lie together, then they have **h**:	2552
Isa	18:4	a cloud of dew in the **h** of harvest	2527
Isa	49:10	neither shall the **h** nor sun smite	8273
Jer	17:8	and shall not see when **h** cometh,	2527
Da	3:19	that they should **h** the furnace	228
Mt	20:12	**borne the burden and h of the**	*2742*
Jas	1:11	no sooner risen with a burning **h**,	*2742*
2Pe	3:10	elements shall melt with fervent **h**,	*2741*
Rev	16:9	men were scorched with great **h**,	*2738*

HEATHEN

Le	26:33	I will scatter you among the **h**,	1471
Le	26:45	land of Egypt in the sight of the **h**,	1471
2Ki	17:8	walked in the statutes of the **h**,	1471
2Ki	17:15	went after the **h** that were round	1471
1Ch	16:24	Declare his glory among the **h**;	1471
2Ch	20:6	over all the kingdoms of the **h**?	1471
2Ch	33:2	unto the abominations of the **h**,	1471
2Ch	33:9	to do worse than the **h**, whom the	1471
Ezr	6:21	the filthiness of the **h** of the land,	1471
Ne	6:16	all the **h** that were about us saw	1471
Ps	2:1	Why do the **h** rage, and the people	1471
Ps	2:8	I shall give thee the **h** for thine	1471
Ps	9:19	let the **h** be judged in thy sight	1471
Ps	33:10	the counsel of the **h** to nought:	1471
Ps	44:11	hast scattered us among the **h**.	1471
Ps	44:14	makest us a byword among the **h**,	1471
Ps	46:6	The **h** raged, the kingdoms were	1471
Ps	46:10	I will be exalted among the **h**,	1471
Ps	47:8	God reigneth over the **h**: God	1471
Ps	59:8	shall have all the **h** in derision.	1471
Ps	79:1	**h** are come into thine inheritance;	1471
Ps	79:10	Wherefore should the **h** say, Where	1471
Ps	96:3	Declare his glory among the **h**,	1471
Ps	102:15	So the **h** shall fear the name of	1471
Jer	9:16	scatter them also among the **h**	1471
Jer	10:2	Learn not the way of the **h**, and	1471
Jer	49:15	make thee small among the **h**,	1471
La	1:3	she dwelleth among the **h**, she	1471
Eze	7:24	I will bring the worst of the **h**,	1471
Eze	16:14	renown went forth among the **h**.	1471
Eze	22:4	made thee a reproach unto the **h**,	1471
Eze	22:15	will scatter thee among the **h**,	1471
Eze	36:6	ye have born the shame of the **h**:	1471
Eze	36:23	**h** shall know that I am the Lord	1471
Eze	37:28	**h** shall know that I the Lord do	1471
Eze	39:23	the **h** shall know that the house	1471
Ob	2	made thee small among the **h**:	1471
Ob	15	the Lord is near upon all the **h**:	1471
Mic	5:15	in anger and fury upon the **h**,	1471
Zec	9:10	he shall speak peace unto the **h**:	1471
Zec	14:18	smite the **h** that come not up	1471
Mal	1:11	name shall be great among the **h**,	1471
Mt	6:7	**not vain repetitions, as the h do:**	*1482*
Mt	18:17	**let him be unto thee as an h man**	*1482*
Ac	4:25	Why did the **h** rage, and the	*1484*
Gal	2:9	that we should go unto the **h**, and	*1484*
Gal	3:8	that God would justify the **h**	*1484*

HEAVE

Ex	29:27	the shoulder of the **h** offering,	8641
Nu	15:21	the Lord an **h** offering in your	8641
Nu	18:19	the **h** offerings of the holy things,	8641

HEAVEN

Ge	1:1	the beginning God created the **h**	8064
Ge	1:8	And God called the firmament **H**.	8064
Ge	7:11	and the windows of **h** were opened	8064
Ge	7:23	things, and the fowl of the **h**; and	8064
Ge	8:2	the windows of **h** were stopped, and	8064
Ge	11:4	whose top may reach unto **h**; and	8064
Ge	28:12	and the top of it reached to **h**: and	8064
Ge	28:17	of God, and this is the gate of **h**	8064
Ex	16:4	I will rain bread from **h** for you;	8064
Ex	20:4	likeness of any thing that is in **h**	8064
Ex	20:11	days the Lord made **h** and earth,	8064
Ex	20:22	that I have talked with you from **h**.	8064
Ex	31:17	days the Lord made **h** and earth,	8064
Dt	3:24	what God is there in **h** or in earth,	8064
Dt	4:19	lest thou lift up thine eyes unto **h**,	8064
Dt	4:26	I call **h** and earth to witness against	8064
Dt	4:32	the one side of **h** unto the other,	8064
Dt	4:39	he is God in **h** above, and upon the	8064
Dt	5:8	likeness of any thing that is in **h**	8064
Dt	10:14	the **h** and the **h** of heavens is the	8064
Dt	26:15	from thy holy habitation, from **h**,	8064
Dt	29:20	blot out his name from under **h**	8064
Dt	30:12	say, Who shall go up for us to **h**,	8064
Dt	30:19	I call **h** and earth to record this day	8064
Dt	32:40	For I lift up my hand to **h**, and say,	8064

Jgs	2:11	he is God in **h** above, and in earth	8064
Jgs	10:13	the sun stood still in the midst of **h**,	8064
1Ki	8:23	is no God like thee, in **h** above, or	8064
1Ki	8:27	**h** and **h** of heavens cannot contain	8064
1Ki	8:30	hear thou in **h** thy dwelling place:	8064
1Ki	8:39	hear thou in **h** thy dwelling place,	8064
1Ki	22:19	all the host of **h** standing by him	8064
2Ki	1:10	then let fire come down from **h**	8064
2Ki	2:11	went up by a whirlwind into **h**,	8064
2Ki	17:16	and worshipped all the host of **h**	8064
2Ki	21:5	he built altars for all the host of **h**	8064
1Ch	21:26	he answered him from **h** by fire	8064
1Ch	29:11	all that is in the **h** and in the earth	8064
2Ch	2:6	**h** and **h** of heavens cannot contain	8064
2Ch	6:14	no God like thee in the **h**, nor in the	8064
2Ch	6:18	**h** and the **h** of heavens cannot	8064
2Ch	6:27	hear thou from **h**, and forgive the	8064
2Ch	7:1	the fire came down from **h**, and	8064
Ezr	1:2	The Lord God of **h** hath given me	8064
Ne	2:20	The God of **h**, he will prosper us;	8064
Ne	9:6	thou hast made **h**, the **h** of heavens,	8064
Ne	9:13	and spakest with them from **h**	8064
Ne	9:15	gavest them bread from **h** for their	8064
Job	1:16	The fire of God is fallen from **h**,	8064
Job	38:33	Knowest thou the ordinances of **h**?	8064
Job	41:11	is under the whole **h** is mine	8064
Ps	11:4	temple, the Lord's throne is in **h**:	8064
Ps	14:2	The Lord looked down from **h** upon	8064
Ps	53:2	God looked down from **h** upon the	8064
Ps	73:25	Whom have I in **h** but thee? and	8064
Ps	89:6	who in the **h** can be compared	7834
Ps	89:29	and his throne as the days of **h**	8064
Ps	103:11	as the **h** is high above the earth,	8064
Ps	115:16	The **h**, even the heavens, are the	8064
Ps	119:89	O Lord, thy word is settled in **h**	8064
Ps	121:2	the Lord, which made **h** and earth	8064
Ps	139:8	If I ascend up into **h**, thou art there:	8064
Pr	23:5	they fly away as an eagle toward **h**	8064
Pr	25:3	The **h** for height, and the earth for	8064
Pr	30:4	Who hath ascended up into **h**, or	8064
Ecc	3:1	time to every purpose under the **h**;	8064
Ecc	5:2	God is in **h**, and thou upon earth:	8064
Isa	14:12	How art thou fallen from **h**, O	8064
Isa	14:13	I will ascend into **h**, I will exalt	8064
Isa	34:4	all the host of **h** shall be dissolved,	8064
Isa	40:12	and meted out **h** with the span	8064
Isa	66:1	The **h** is my throne, and the earth	8064
Jer	7:18	to make cakes to the queen of **h**	8064
Jer	23:24	Do not I fill **h** and earth? saith	8064
Jer	44:17	burn incense unto the queen of **h**,	8064
La	2:1	cast down from **h** unto the earth	8064
La	3:50	Lord look down, and behold from **h**	8064
Eze	8:3	up between the earth and the **h**,	8064
Eze	32:7	I will cover the **h** and make the	8064
Eze	32:8	All the bright lights of **h** will I	8064
Da	2:28	there is a God in **h** that revealeth	8065
Da	2:44	shall the God of **h** set up a kingdom,	8065
Da	4:13	and an holy one came down from **h**;	8065
Da	4:31	there fell a voice from **h**, saying,	8065
Da	4:37	and extol and honour the King of **h**,	8065
Da	9:12	under the whole **h** hath not been	8064
Am	9:6	that buildeth his stories in the **h**,	8064
Na	3:16	thy merchants above the stars of **h**:	8064
Mal	3:10	will not open you the windows of **h**,	8064
Mt	3:17	And lo a voice from **h**, saying,	*3772*
Mt	4:17	**for the kingdom of h is at hand**	*3772*
Mt	5:3	theirs is the kingdom of **h**	*3772*
Mt	5:10	theirs is the kingdom of **h**	*3772*
Mt	5:12	for great is your reward in **h**: for	*3772*
Mt	5:16	glorify your Father which is in **h**	*3772*
Mt	5:18	Till **h** and earth pass, one jot or	*3772*
Mt	5:19	the least in the kingdom of **h**:	*3772*
Mt	5:34	Swear not at all; neither by **h**; for	*3772*
Mt	5:48	Father which is in **h** is perfect	*3772*
Mt	6:1	of your Father which is in **h**	*3772*
Mt	6:9	ye: Our Father which art in **h**,	*3772*
Mt	6:10	will be done in earth, as it is in **h**	*3772*
Mt	6:20	up for yourselves treasures in **h**	*3772*
Mt	7:11	Father which is in **h** give good	*3772*
Mt	7:21	will of my Father which is in **h**,	*3772*
Mt	10:7	saying, The kingdom of **h** is at	*3772*
Mt	10:32	before my Father which is in **h**	*3772*
Mt	11:11	that is least in the kingdom of **h**	*3772*
Mt	12:50	will of my Father which is in **h**,	*3772*
Mt	13:11	the mysteries of the kingdom of **h**,	*3772*
Mt	13:24	kingdom of **h** is likened unto a	*3772*
Mt	13:31	kingdom of **h** is like to a grain	*3772*
Mt	13:33	kingdom of **h** is like unto leaven,	*3772*
Mt	13:44	Again, the kingdom of **h** is like	*3772*
Mt	13:45	Again, the kingdom of **h** is like	*3772*
Mt	13:47	kingdom of **h** is like unto a net	*3772*
Mt	16:17	but thy Father which is in **h**	*3772*
Mt	16:19	thee the keys of the kingdom of **h**	*3772*
Mt	16:19	bind on earth shall be bound in **h**:	*3772*
Mt	18:4	is greatest in the kingdom of **h**	*3772*
Mt	18:10	face of my Father which is in **h**	*3772*
Mt	18:14	of your Father which is in **h**	*3772*
Mt	18:18	bind on earth shall be bound in **h**	*3772*
Mt	18:23	the kingdom of **h** is likened unto	*3772*
Mt	19:14	for of such is the kingdom of **h**	*3772*
Mt	19:21	and thou shalt have treasure in **h**	*3772*
Mt	20:1	kingdom of **h** is like unto a man	*3772*
Mt	21:25	whence was it? from **h**, or of men?	*3772*
Mt	22:2	The kingdom of **h** is like unto a	*3772*
Mt	23:9	one is your Father, which is in **h**	*3772*
Mt	24:29	the stars shall fall from **h**, and	*3772*
Mt	24:30	the sign of the Son of man in **h**	*3772*
Mt	24:30	of man coming of the clouds of **h**	*3772*
Mt	24:35	**H** and earth shall pass away, but	*3772*
Mt	24:36	the angels of **h**, but my Father only	*3772*
Mt	25:1	the kingdom of **h** be likened unto	*3772*
Mt	25:14	For the kingdom of **h** is as a man	*3772*
Mt	26:64	and coming in the clouds of **h**	*3772*
Mt	28:18	given unto me in **h** and in earth	*3772*
Mk	1:11	there came a voice from **h**, saying	*3772*
Mk	11:26	your Father which is in **h** forgive	*3772*
Mk	11:30	John, was it from **h**, or of men?	*3772*
Mk	13:25	the stars of **h** shall fall, and the	*3772*
Mk	13:31	**H** and earth shall pass away: but	*3772*
Mk	13:32	no, not the angels which are in **h**	*3772*
Mk	14:62	and coming in the clouds of **h**	*3772*
Mk	16:19	he was received up into **h**, and sat	*3772*
Lk	4:25	the **h** was shut up three years	*3772*
Lk	6:23	your reward is great in **h**: for in	*3772*
Lk	9:54	command fire to come down from **h**,	*3772*
Lk	10:18	Satan as lightning fall from **h**	*3772*
Lk	10:20	your names are written in **h**.	*3772*
Lk	11:2	say, Our Father which art in **h**,	*3772*
Lk	11:2	will be done, as in **h**, so in earth	*3772*
Lk	15:7	joy shall be in **h** over one sinner	*3772*
Lk	15:21	Father, I have sinned against **h**,	*3772*
Lk	16:17	is easier for **h** and earth to pass	*3772*

Lk	17:29	**rained fire and brimstone from h,**	*3772*
Lk	18:13	**lift up so much as his eyes unto h,**	*3772*
Lk	18:22	**and thou shalt have treasure in h:**	*3772*
Lk	19:38	peace in **h**, and glory in the highest	*3772*
Lk	20:4	**baptism of John, was it from h, or**	*3772*
Lk	21:11	**great signs shall there be from h**	*3772*
Lk	21:26	**the powers of h shall be shaken**	*3772*
Lk	21:33	**H and earth shall pass away: but**	*3772*
Lk	24:51	from them, and carried up into **h**.	*3772*
Jn	1:32	descending from **h** like a dove, and	*3772*
Jn	1:51	**Hereafter ye shall see h open, and**	*3772*
Jn	3:13	**no man hath ascended up to h,**	*3772*
Jn	3:13	**but he that came down from h,**	*3772*
Jn	3:13	**the Son of man which is in h**	*3772*
Jn	3:31	he that cometh from **h** is above all	*3772*
Jn	6:32	**giveth you the true bread from h**	*3772*
Jn	6:33	**is he which cometh down from h,**	*3772*
Jn	6:38	**I came down from h, not to do**	*3772*
Jn	6:42	that he saith, I came down from **h**?	*3772*
Jn	6:51	**which came down from h:**	*3772*
Jn	12:28	Then came there a voice from **h**,	*3772*
Ac	1:11	why stand ye gazing up into **h**?	*3772*
Ac	1:11	as ye have seen him go into **h**	*3772*
Ac	2:2	there came a sound from **h** as of a	*3772*
Ac	4:12	none other name under **h** given	*3772*
Ac	7:42	them up to worship the host of **h**;	*3772*
Ac	7:49	**H** is my throne, and earth is my	*3772*
Ac	9:3	round about him a light from **h**:	*3772*
Ac	10:11	And saw **h** opened, and a certain	*3772*
Ac	11:5	let down from **h** by four corners;	*3772*
Ac	11:9	voice answered me again from **h**,	*3772*
Ac	11:10	and all were drawn up again into **h**,	*3772*
Ac	22:6	there shone from **h** a great light	*3772*
Ac	26:13	I saw in the way a light from **h**,	*3771*
Ro	1:18	wrath of God is revealed from **h**	*3772*
Ro	10:6	heart, Who shall ascend into **h**?	*3772*
1Co	15:47	the second man is the Lord from **h**	*3772*
2Co	12:2	one caught up to the third **h**	*3772*
Gal	1:8	we, or an angel from **h**, preach any	*3772*
Eph	6:9	your Master also is in **h**; neither	*3772*
Php	3:20	For our conversation is in **h**; from	*3772*
Col	4:1	knowing ye also have a Master in **h**	*3772*
1Th	1:10	And to wait for his Son from **h**,	*3772*
1Th	4:16	shall descend from **h** with a shout	*3772*
2Th	1:7	Jesus shall be revealed from **h**	*3772*
Heb	9:24	but into **h** itself, now to appear in	*3772*
Heb	10:34	that ye have in **h** a better and an	*3772*
Heb	12:25	from him that speaketh from **h**:	*3772*
Heb	12:26	shake not the earth only, but also **h**	*3772*
Jas	5:12	swear not neither by **h**, neither	*3772*
1Pe	1:4	not away, reserved in **h** for you	*3772*
1Pe	1:12	the Holy Ghost sent down from **h**;	*3772*
1Pe	3:22	Who is gone into **h**, and is on the	*3772*
2Pe	1:18	this voice which came from **h** we	*3772*
1Jn	5:7	are three that bear record in **h**, the	*3772*
Rev	3:12	**down out of h from my God:**	*3772*
Rev	4:1	behold, a door was opened in **h**:	*3772*
Rev	6:13	the stars of **h** fell unto the earth,	*3772*
Rev	6:14	And the **h** departed as a scroll when	*3772*
Rev	8:1	was silence in **h** about the space of	*3772*
Rev	8:10	and there fell a great star from **h**,	*3772*
Rev	9:1	I saw a star fall from **h** unto the	*3772*
Rev	10:4	I heard a voice from **h** saying unto	*3772*
Rev	11:12	they ascended up to **h** in a cloud;	*3772*
Rev	11:15	were great voices in **h**, saying, The	*3772*
Rev	11:19	the temple of God was opened in **h**,	*3772*
Rev	12:4	third part of the stars of **h**, and did	*3772*
Rev	12:7	And there was war in **h**: Michael	*3772*
Rev	13:13	fire come down from **h** on the earth	*3772*
Rev	14:2	I heard a voice from **h**, as the voice	*3772*
Rev	14:7	worship him that made **h**, and	*3772*
Rev	15:1	I saw another sign in **h**, great and	*3772*
Rev	15:5	the tabernacle of the testimony in **h**	*3772*
Rev	16:11	blasphemed the God of **h** because	*3772*
Rev	18:5	For her sins have reached unto **h**,	*3772*
Rev	19:1	a great voice of much people in **h**,	*3321*
Rev	19:11	And I saw **h** opened, and behold a	*3321*
Rev	20:9	fire came down from God out of **h**,	*3772*
Rev	20:11	face the earth and the **h** fled away;	*3772*
Rev	21:1	I saw a new **h** and a new earth:	*3772*
Rev	21:10	holy Jerusalem, descending out of **h**.	*3772*

HEAVENLY

Mt	6:14	**your h Father will also forgive**	*3770*
Mt	6:26	**yet your h Father feedeth them**	*3770*
Mt	6:32	**h Father knoweth that ye have**	*3770*
Mt	18:35	**shall my h Father do also unto**	*2032*
Lk	2:13	a multitude of the **h** host praising	*3770*
Lk	11:13	**your h Father give the Holy**	*1537, 3772*
Jn	3:12	**believe, if I tell you of h things?**	*2032*
Ac	26:19	not disobedient unto the **h** vision:	*3770*
Eph	1:3	spiritual blessings in **h** places in	*2032*
Eph	2:6	together in **h** places in Christ Jesus:	*2032*
Heb	6:4	tasted of the **h** gift, and were made	*2032*
Heb	8:5	example and shadow of **h** things	*2032*
Heb	11:16	a better country, that is, an **h**;	*2032*
Heb	12:22	of the living God, the **h** Jerusalem,	*2032*

HEAVENS

Ge	2:1	the **h** and the earth were finished,	8064
Dt	10:14	and the heaven of **h** is the Lord's	8064
2Sa	22:10	He bowed the **h** also, and came	8064
1Ki	8:27	heaven of **h** cannot contain thee;	8064
1Ch	16:26	are idols: but the Lord made the **h**	8064
2Ch	2:6	heaven of **h** cannot contain him?	8064
2Ch	6:18	heaven of **h** cannot contain thee;	8064
2Ch	6:25	Then hear thou from the **h**, and	8064
Ne	9:6	hast made heaven, the heaven of **h**,	8064
Job	14:12	till the **h** be no more, they shall not	8064
Ps	2:4	He that sitteth in the **h** shall laugh:	8064
Ps	8:3	When I consider thy **h**, the work of	8064
Ps	19:1	The **h** declare the glory of God;	8064
Ps	33:6	word of the Lord were the **h** made;	8064
Ps	50:6	**h** shall declare his righteousness:	8064
Ps	57:5	Be thou exalted, O God, above the **h**;	8064
Ps	68:4	extol him that rideth upon the **h**	6160
Ps	68:33	To him that rideth upon the **h** of **h**,	8064
Ps	89:11	The **h** are thine, the earth also is	8064
Ps	96:5	are idols: but the Lord made the **h**,	8064
Ps	97:6	The **h** declare his righteousness,	8064
Ps	103:19	hath prepared his throne in the **h**;	8064
Ps	104:2	stretchest out the **h** like a curtain:	8064
Ps	108:5	Be thou exalted, O God, above the **h**:	8064
Ps	115:3	our God is in the **h**: he hath done	8064
Ps	115:16	heaven, even the **h**, are the Lord's:	8064
Ps	136:5	To him that by wisdom made the **h**:	8064
Ps	144:5	Bow thy **h**, O Lord, and come down:	8064
Pr	3:19	hath he established the **h**	8064
Pr	8:27	he prepared the **h**, I was there:	8064
Isa	13:13	Therefore I will shake the **h**, and	8064
Isa	34:4	the **h** shall be rolled together as a	8064
Isa	42:5	he that created the **h**, and stretched	8064
Isa	44:24	that stretcheth forth the **h** alone;	8064

Isa	45:12	have stretched out the **h**, and all	8064
Isa	45:18	saith the Lord that created the **h**;	8064
Isa	48:13	my right hand hath spanned the **h**;	8064
Isa	50:3	I clothe the **h** with blackness, and	8064
Isa	51:6	the **h** shall vanish away like smoke,	8064
Isa	51:13	hath stretched forth the **h**, and laid	8064
Isa	55:9	as the **h** are higher than the earth,	8064
Isa	65:17	I create new **h** and a new earth:	8064
Jer	2:12	Be astonished, O ye **h**, at this, and	8064
Jer	4:23	and the **h**, and thy had no light	8064
Jer	4:28	mourn, and the **h** above be black:	8064
Jer	10:11	gods that have not made the **h**	8065
Jer	10:12	hath stretched out the **h** by his	8064
Jer	10:13	is a multitude of waters in the **h**,	8064
La	3:41	with our hands unto God in the **h**	8064
Eze	1:1	that the **h** were opened, and I saw	8064
Joel	2:10	the **h** shall tremble: the sun and	8064
Joel	2:30	I will shew wonders in the **h** and in	8064
Joel	3:16	the **h** and the earth shall shake:	8064
Hag	2:6	I will shake the **h**, and the earth,	8064
Hag	2:21	I will shake the **h** and the earth;	8064
Zec	6:5	These are the four spirits of the **h**,	8064
Zec	12:1	stretcheth forth the **h**, and layeth	8064
Mt	3:16	lo, the **h** were opened unto him,	*3772*
Mt	24:29	**powers of the h shall be shaken:**	*3772*
Mk	1:10	he saw the **h** opened, and the Spirit	*3772*
Lk	12:33	**a treasure in the h that faileth not**	*3772*
Ac	7:56	Behold, I see the **h** opened, and the	*3772*
2Co	5:1	made with hands, eternal in the **h**	*3772*
Eph	4:10	that ascended up far above all **h**,	*3772*
Heb	1:10	the **h** are the works of thine hands	*3772*
Heb	4:14	priest, that is passed into the **h**,	*3772*
Heb	7:26	and made higher than the **h**;	*3772*
Heb	8:1	the throne of the Majesty in the **h**;	*3772*
Heb	9:23	patterns of things in the **h** should	*3772*
2Pe	3:7	But the **h** and the earth, which are	*3772*
2Pe	3:10	the **h** shall pass away with a great	*3772*
2Pe	3:12	**h** being on fire shall be dissolved,	*3772*
2Pe	3:13	look for new **h** and a new earth,	*3772*

HEAVIER

Pr	27:3	a fool's wrath is **h** than them both,	3513

HEAVINESS

Ps	119:28	My soul melteth for **h**: strengthen	8424
Pr	10:1	foolish son is the **h** of his mother	8424
Pr	12:25	**H** in the heart of man maketh it	1674
Pr	14:13	but the end of that mirth is **h**	8424
Isa	61:3	of praise for the spirit of **h**;	3544
Jas	4:9	to mourning, and your joy to **h**	*2725*

HEAVY

Ex	17:12	Moses' hands were **h**; and they	3515
Ex	18:18	for this thing is too **h** for thee;	3515
Nu	11:14	alone, because it is too **h** for me	3515
1Sa	4:18	for he was an old man, and **h**	3513
1Ki	12:10	Thy father made our yoke **h**, but	3513
Ps	32:4	night thy hand was **h** upon me:	3513
Pr	25:20	that singeth songs to an **h** heart	7451
Pr	27:3	stone is **h**, and the sand weighty:	3514
Pr	31:6	unto those that be of **h** hearts	4751
Isa	30:27	and the burden thereof is **h**:	3514
Isa	59:1	neither his ear **h**, that it cannot	3513
Mt	11:28	**all ye that labour and are h laden**	
Mt	23:4	**For they bind h burdens and**	*926*
Mt	26:43	asleep again: for their eyes were **h**.	*916*

HEBREW

Ge	39:14	he hath brought in a **H** unto us	5680
Ge	41:12	with us a young man, an **H**,	5680
Ex	1:15	Egypt spake to the **H** midwives,	5680
Ex	2:11	spied an Egyptian smiting a **H**,	5680
Jn	19:20	written in **H**, and Greek, and Latin.	*1447*
Ac	26:14	saying in the **H** tongue, **Saul, Saul,**	*1446*
Php	3:5	of Benjamin, an **H** of the Hebrews;	*1446*

HEBREWS

Ex	2:13	two men of the **H** strove together	5680
Ex	3:18	God of the **H** hath met with us:	5680
Ex	9:1	saith the Lord God of the **H**,	5680
1Sa	4:6	great shout in the camp of the **H**?	5680
2Co	11:22	Are they **H**? so am I. Are they	*1445*
Php	3:5	of Benjamin, and Hebrew of the **H**;	*1445*

HEDGE

Job	1:10	not thou made an **h** about him,	7753
Pr	15:19	slothful man is as an **h** of thorns	4881
Isa	5:5	I will take away the **h** thereof,	4881
Eze	22:30	them, that should make up the **h**,	1447
Mic	7:4	upright is sharper than a thorn **h**:	4534

HEED

Ex	10:28	take **h** to thyself, see my face no more	8104
Ex	19:12	Take **h** to yourselves, that ye go not	8104
Dt	4:9	Only take **h** to thyself, and keep thy	8104
Dt	4:23	Take **h** unto yourselves, lest ye	8104
Dt	11:16	Take **h** to yourselves, that your	8104
Dt	12:13	Take **h** to thyself that thou offer not	8104
Jos	22:5	But take diligent **h** to do the	8104
1Ki	2:4	If thy children take **h** to their way,	8104
1Ki	8:25	thy children take **h** to their way,	8104
2Ch	19:6	Take **h** what ye do: for ye judge	7200
Ps	39:1	I said, I will take **h** to my ways,	8104
Ps	119:9	by taking **h** thereto according to	8104
Pr	17:4	wicked doer giveth **h** to false lips;	7181
Jer	18:18	us not give **h** to any of his words	7181
Mal	2:15	Therefore take **h** to your spirit, and	8104
Mt	6:1	**Take h that ye do not your alms**	*4337*
Mt	16:6	**Take h and beware of the leaven**	*3708*
Mt	18:10	**Take h that ye despise not one of**	*3708*
Mt	24:4	**Take h that no man deceive you**	*991*
Mk	4:24	**Take h what ye hear: with what**	*991*
Mk	8:15	**Take h, beware of the leaven of**	*3708*
Mk	13:9	**take h to yourselves: for they shall**	*991*
Mk	13:23	**take ye h: behold, I have foretold**	*991*
Mk	13:33	**Take ye h, watch and pray: for ye**	*991*
Lk	8:18	**Take h therefore how ye hear: for**	*991*
Lk	11:35	**Take h therefore that the light**	*4648*
Lk	12:15	**Take h, … beware of covetousness:**	*3708*
Lk	17:3	**Take h to yourselves: If thy**	*4337*
Lk	21:8	**Take h that ye be not deceived;**	*991*
Lk	21:34	**take h to yourselves, lest at any**	*4337*
Ro	11:21	take **h** lest he also spare not thee	*3708*
1Co	3:10	every man take **h** how he buildeth	*991*
1Co	8:9	But take **h** lest by any means this	*991*
1Co	10:12	thinketh he standeth take **h** lest he	*991*
Gal	5:15	take **h** that ye be not consumed one	*991*
1Ti	1:4	give **h** to fables and endless	*4337*
1Ti	4:1	giving **h** to seducing spirits, and	*4337*
1Ti	4:16	Take **h** unto thyself, and unto the	*1907*
Tit	1:14	Not giving **h** to Jewish fables, and	*4337*
Heb	2:1	the more earnest **h** to the things	*4337*
Heb	3:12	Take **h** brethren, lest there be in	*991*
2Pe	1:19	ye do well that ye take **h**, as unto	*4337*

HEEL
Ge 3:15 head, and thou shalt bruise his **h** 6119
Ge 25:26 his hand took hold on Esau's **h**; 6119
Ps 41:9 hath lifted up his **h** against me 6119
Hos 12:3 He took his brother by the **h** in the 6117
Job 13:18 **hath lifted up his h against me** *4418*

HEIFER
Nu 19:2 bring thee a red **h** without spot, ... 6510
Nu 19:5 one shall burn the **h** in his sight; 6510
Jgs 14:18 If ye had not plowed with my **h**, ye 5697
Heb 9:13 the ashes of an **h** sprinkling the *1151*

HEIGHT
1Sa 16:7 or on the **h** of his stature: 1364
1Sa 17:4 whose **h** was six cubits and a span 1363
Job 22:12 Is not God in the **h** of heaven? and 1363
Pr 25:3 The heaven for **h**, and the earth 7312
Jer 49:16 rock, that holdest the **h** of the hill; 4791
Eze 20:40 in the mountain of the **h** of Israel 4791
Da 4:20 whose **h** reached unto the heaven, ... 7314
Ro 8:39 Nor **h**, nor depth, nor any other *5313*
Eph 3:18 and length, and depth, and **h**; *5311*
Rev 21:16 breadth and the **h** of it are equal. *5311*

HEIR
Ge 15:3 one born in my house is mine **h**. 3423
Ge 15:4 this shall not be thine **h**; but he 3423
Mt 21:38 **is the h; come, let us kill him** *2818*
Ro 4:13 he should be the **h** of the world, ... *2818*
Gal 4:1 That the **h**, as long as he is a child, ... *2818*
Gal 4:7 then an **h** of God through Christ *2818*
Gal 4:30 shall not be **h** with the son of the *2816*
Heb 1:2 whom … appointed **h** of all things, ... *2818*
Heb 11:7 and became **h** of the righteousness *2818*

HEIRS
Ro 4:14 if they which are of the law be **h**, ... *2818*
Ro 8:17 And if children, then **h**; **h** of God, ... *2818*
Gal 3:29 and **h** according to the promise *2818*
Tit 3:7 by his grace, we should be made **h** *2818*
Heb 6:17 to shew unto the **h** of promise *2818*
Heb 11:9 **h** with him of the same promise: *4789*
Jas 2:5 rich in faith, and **h** of the kingdom *2818*
1Pe 3:7 **h** together of the grace of life; *4789*

HELD
Ex 17:11 when Moses **h** up his hand, that. 7311
Nu 30:7 and **h** his peace at her in the day 2790
Ne 4:17 with the other hand **h** a weapon. 2388
Est 8:4 the king **h** out the golden sceptre 3447
Ps 32:9 whose mouth must be **h** in with. 1102
Ps 39:2 I **h** my peace, even from good; 2814
Ps 94:18 thy mercy, O Lord, **h** me up 5582
Da 12:7 when he **h** up his right hand and 7311
Mt 26:63 But Jesus **h** his peace. And the. *4623*
Mk 9:34 But they **h** their peace: for by the *4623*
Mk 14:61 But he **h** his peace, and answered *4623*
Lk 20:26 at his answer, and **h** their peace. *4601*

HELL
Dt 32:22 shall burn unto the lowest **h**,. 7585
Job 26:6 **H** is naked before him, and 7585
Ps 9:17 The wicked shall be turned into **h**, ... 7585
Ps 16:10 thou wilt not leave my soul in **h**; 7585
Ps 18:5 The sorrows of **h** compassed me 7585
Ps 55:15 let them go down quick into **h**:. 7585
Ps 86:13 my soul from the lowest **h**. 7585
Ps 116:3 the pains of **h** gat hold upon me: 7585
Ps 139:8 if I make my bed in **h**, behold, ... 7585
Pr 5:5 death; her steps take hold on **h**. 7585
Pr 7:27 Her house is the way to **h**, going. 7585
Pr 9:18 her guests are in the depths of **h**. 7585
Pr 15:11 **H** and destruction are before the 7585
Pr 15:24 he may depart from **h** beneath 7585
Pr 23:14 and shall deliver his soul from **h**. 7585
Pr 27:20 **H** and destruction are never full; 7585
Isa 5:14 Therefore **h** hath enlarged herself, ... 7585
Isa 14:9 **H** from beneath is moved for thee 7585
Isa 14:15 thou shalt be brought down to **h**, ... 7585
Isa 28:15 and with **h** are we at agreement; 7585
Isa 28:18 agreement with **h** shall not stand; 7585
Isa 57:9 didst debase thyself even unto **h**. 7585
Eze 31:16 I cast him down to **h** with them 7585
Eze 31:17 They also went down into **h** with. 7585
Eze 32:21 speak to him out of the midst of **h**. 7585
Eze 32:27 gone down to **h** with their weapons. . . . 7585
Am 9:2 Though they dig into **h**, thence. 7585
Jnh 2:2 out of the belly of **h** cried I, and. 7585
Hab 2:5 who enlargeth his desire as **h**, and 7585
Mt 5:22 **fool, shall be in danger of h fire** *1067*
Mt 5:29 whole **body should be cast into h**. *1067*
Mt 10:28 **destroy both soul and body in h** *1067*
Mt 11:23 **shalt be brought down to h: for if** *86*
Mt 16:18 **and the gates of h shall not prevail** *86*
Mt 18:9 **two eyes to be cast into h fire** *1067*
Mt 23:15 **the child of h than yourselves**. *1067*
Mt 23:33 **can ye escape the damnation of h?**. *1067*
Mk 9:43 **having two hands to go into h** *1067*
Lk 10:15 **heaven, shalt be thrust down to h** *86*
Lk 12:5 **killed hath power to cast into h;**. *1067*
Lk 16:23 **in h he lift up his eyes, being in** *86*
Ac 2:27 thou wilt not leave my soul in **h** *86*
Ac 2:31 that his soul was not left in **h**. *86*
Jas 3:6 nature; and it is set on fire of **h**. *1067*
2Pe 2:4 sinned, but cast them down to **h**. *5020*
Rev 1:18 **have the keys of h and of death** *86*
Rev 6:8 Death, and **H** followed with him *86*
Rev 20:13 death and **h** delivered up the dead *86*
Rev 20:14 death and **h** were cast into the lake. *86*

HELL-FIRE See HELL and FIRE.

HELMET
1Sa 59:17 an **h** of salvation upon his head;. 3553
Eph 6:17 And take the **h** of salvation, and *4030*
1Th 5:8 and for an **h**, the hope of salvation. *4030*

HELP
Ge 2:18 will make him an **h** meet for him. 5828
Ex 23:5 thou shalt surely **h** with him 5800
Dt 22:4 shalt surely **h** him to lift them up 6965
2Ch 14:11 Lord, it is nothing with thee to **h**, ... 5826
2Ch 19:2 Shouldest thou **h** the ungodly, ... 5826
2Ch 25:8 God hath power to **h**, and to cast 5826
2Ch 32:8 with us is the Lord our God to **h** us 5826
Ps 3:2 soul, There is no **h** for him in God. 3444
Ps 12:1 **H**, Lord; for the godly man 3467
Ps 33:20 Lord: he is our **h** and our shield 5828
Ps 46:1 a very present **h** in trouble. 5833
Ps 94:17 Unless the Lord had been my **h**, ... 5833
Ps 108:12 Give us **h** from trouble: for vain 5833
Ps 108:12 trouble: for vain is the **h** of man. 8668
Ps 121:1 hills, from which cometh my **h**. 5828
Ps 121:2 My **h** cometh from the Lord, which 5828

Ecc 4:10 he hath not another to **h** him up 6965
Isa 10:3 to whom will ye flee for **h**? and........ 5833
Isa 31:1 them that go down to Egypt for **h**;..... 5833
Isa 41:13 unto thee, Fear not; I will **h** thee....... 5826
Isa 50:7 the Lord God will **h** me; therefore 5826
Isa 63:5 I looked, and there was none to **h**; 5826
La 1:7 the enemy, and none did **h** her 5826
La 4:17 eyes as yet failed for our vain **h**: 5833
Eze 32:21 midst of hell with them that **h** him:.... 5826
Da 11:45 to his end, and none shall **h** him 5826
Hos 13:9 thyself; but in me is thine **h**........... 5828
Mt 15:25 worshipped him, saying, Lord, **h** me *997*
Mk 9:24 I believe; **h** thou mine unbelief......... *997*
Lk 10:40 bid her therefore that she **h** me........ *4878*
Ac 16:9 over into Macedonia, and **h** us *997*
Heb 4:16 find grace to **h** in time of need *996*

HELPED
1Sa 7:12 Hitherto hath the Lord **h** us 5826
Est 9:3 officers of the king, **h** the Jews;........ 5375
Ps 28:7 heart trusted in him, and I am **h**:...... 5826
Ps 116:6 I was brought low, and he **h** me 3467
Isa 41:6 They **h** every one his neighbour; 5826
Isa 49:8 in a day of salvation have I **h** thee:..... 5826

HELPER
Ps 10:14 thou art the **h** of the fatherless 5826
Ps 54:4 Behold, God is mine **h**: the Lord is..... 5826
Ps 72:12 poor also, and him that hath no **h** 5826
Heb 13:6 Lord is my **h**, and I will not fear *998*

HELPETH
Ro 8:26 the Spirit also **h** our infirmities: *4878*

HELPING
Ps 22:1 why art thou so far from **h** me,........ 3467
2Co 1:11 Ye also **h** together by prayer for us *4943*

HEM
Mt 9:20 touched the **h** of his garment:......... *2899*
Mt 14:36 only touch the **h** of his garment:....... *2899*

HEN
Mt 23:37 **as a h gathereth her chickens** *3733*
Lk 13:34 **as a h doth gather her brood**.......... *3733*

HERB
Ge 1:11 the **h** yielding seed, and the fruit 6212
Ge 1:29 I have given you every **h** bearing 6212
Ge 9:3 even as the green **h** have I given 6212
Dt 32:2 the small rain upon the tender **h**,...... 1877
Ps 37:2 grass, and wither as the green **h** 1877

HERBS
Ex 12:8 and with bitter **h** they shall eat it
Nu 9:11 with unleavened bread and bitter **h**
Pr 15:17 Better is a dinner of **h** where love...... 3419
Mt 13:32 **grown, it is the greatest among h,** *3001*
Mk 4:32 **and becometh greater than all h,** *3001*
Lk 11:42 **mint and rue and all manner of h,**..... *3001*
Ro 14:2 another, who is weak, eateth **h** *3001*
Heb 6:7 and bringeth forth **h** meet for them.... *1008*

HERD
Le 1:3 offering be a burnt sacrifice of the **h**,... 1241
Le 3:1 peace offering, if he offer it of the **h**; ... 1241
2Sa 12:4 of his own flock and of his own **h** 1241
Jnh 3:7 man nor beast, **h** nor flock, taste 1241
Mt 8:32 the whole **h** of swine ran violently *34*

HERDMEN
Ge 13:8 between my **h** and thy **h**; for we be 7462
Ge 26:20 of Gerar did strive with Isaac's **h**,...... 7462

HERDS
Ge 47:1 and their **h**, and all that they have 1241
Ex 34:3 flocks nor **h** feed before that mount.... 1241
Ne 10:36 firstlings of our **h** and of our flocks, ... 1241
Pr 27:23 thy flocks, and look well to thy **h** 5739
Hos 5:6 and with their **h** to seek the Lord; 1241

HERE
Ge 22:1 Abraham: and he said, Behold, **h** I am
Ge 22:11 Abraham: and he said, **H** am I 2009
Ge 27:18 **H** am I; who art thou, my son?........ 2009
Ge 31:11 saying, Jacob: And I said, **H** am I 2009
Ge 37:13 And he said to him, **H** am I........... 2009
Ge 46:2 Jacob, Jacob. And he said, **H** am I...... 2009
Ex 3:4 Moses. And he said, **H** am I........... 2009
1Sa 3:8 **H** am I; for thou didst call me......... 2005
1Sa 3:16 my son. And he answered, **H** am I 2009
1Sa 12:3 behold, **h** I am: witness against me
2Sa 1:7 And I answered, **H** am I.............. 2009
2Sa 15:26 behold, **h** am I, let him do to me as
Isa 6:8 Then said I, **H** am I; send me 2005
Isa 28:13 line; **h** a little, and there a little;........ 8033
Isa 58:9 shalt cry, and he shall say, **H** I am...... 2009
Mt 17:4 Lord, it is good for us to be **h**:......... *5602*
Mk 6:3 and are not his sisters **h** with us?....... *5602*
Lk 11:31 **a greater than Solomon is h** *5602*
Lk 24:6 He is not **h**, but is risen: remember *5602*
Jn 11:32 if thou hadst been **h**, my brother *5602*
Ac 9:10 And he said, Behold, I am **h**, Lord.
Rev 13:10 **H** is the patience and the faith of *5602*
Rev 13:18 **H** is wisdom. Let him that hath *5602*
Rev 14:12 **H** is the patience of the saints:......... *5602*

HEREAFTER
Isa 41:23 Shew the things that are to come **h**,..... 268
Da 2:29 what should come to pass **h** 311, 1836
Da 2:45 what shall come to pass **h** 311, 1836
Mt 26:64 **H shall ye see the Son of man**...... *575, 737*
Lk 22:69 **H shall the Son of man sit on**..... *575, 3568*
Jn 1:51 **H ye shall see heaven open** *737*
Rev 1:19 **the things which shall be h;**...... *3326, 5023*
Rev 4:1 thee things which must be **h**..... *3326, 5023*

HEREBY
Ge 42:33 **H** shall I know that ye are true men; ... 2063
Nu 16:28 And Moses said, **H** ye shall know 2063
1Co 4:4 yet am I not **h** justified: but...... *1722, 5129*
1Jn 3:16 **H** perceive we the love of God,... *1722, 5129*
1Jn 3:24 **h** we know that he abideth in *1722, 5129*
1Jn 4:2 **H** know ye the Spirit of God: *1722, 5129*
1Jn 4:6 **H** know we the spirit of truth, ... *1537, 5124*

HEREIN
Ge 34:22 Only **h** will the men consent unto 2063
2Ch 16:9 **H** thou hast done foolishly:........... 5921
Jn 4:37 **h is that saying true, One** *1722, 5129*
Jn 15:8 **H is my Father glorified, that** *1722, 5129*
1Jn 4:10 **H** is love, not that we loved God.. *1722, 5129*
1Jn 4:17 **H** is our love made perfect *1722, 5129*

HERESIES
1Co 11:19 there must be also **h** among you........ *139*
Gal 5:20 wrath, strife, seditions, **h**, envyings, ... *139*
2Pe 2:1 shall bring in damnable **h**, even *139*

HERETICK
Tit 3:10 A man that is an **h** after the first........ *141*

HERITAGE
Ex 6:8 and I will give it you for an **h** 4181
Ps 61:5 the **h** of those that fear thy name 3425
Ps 111:6 may give them the **h** of the heathen. ... 5159
Ps 119:111 testimonies have I taken as an **h** 5157
Ps 127:3 Lo, children are an **h** of the Lord:...... 5159
Ps 136:22 Even an **h** unto Israel his servant:...... 5159
Isa 54:17 the **h** of the servants of the Lord,...... 5159
Jer 2:7 and made mine **h** an abomination. 5159
Jer 12:7 I have left mine **h**; I have given the..... 5159
Jer 12:8 Mine **h** is unto me as a lion in the 5159
Jer 12:15 every man to his **h**, and every man 5159
Jer 50:11 O ye destroyers of mine **h**, because 5159
Joel 2:17 give not thine **h** to reproach, that...... 5159
Joel 3:2 for my people and for my **h** Israel,..... 5159
Mic 7:18 the remnant of his **h**? he retaineth 5159
1Pe 5:3 as being lords over God's **h**, but *2819*

HEW
Ex 34:1 **H** thee two tables of stone like 6458
Dt 19:5 with his neighbour to **h** wood, and 2404
2Ch 2:2 thousand to **h** in the mountain,....... 2672
Jer 6:6 **H** ye down trees, and cast them 3772
Da 4:14 **H** down the tree, and cut off his....... 1414
Da 4:23 **H** the tree down, and destroy it;....... 1414

HEWED
Dt 10:3 and **h** two tables of stone like unto 6458
1Sa 15:33 And Samuel **h** Agag in pieces,......... 8158
Jer 2:13 and **h** them out cisterns, broken....... 2672
Hos 6:5 have I **h** them by the prophets;........ 2672

HEWERS
Jos 9:23 bondmen, and **h** of wood and 2404
2Ch 2:18 thousand to be **h** in the mountain 2672

HEWN
Ex 20:25 thou shalt not build it of **h** stone:...... 1496
Pr 9:1 she hath **h** out her seven pillars:....... 2672
Isa 9:10 but we will build with **h** stones: 1496
Isa 51:1 unto the rock whence ye are **h** 2672
Mt 7:19 **is h down, and cast into the fire.** *1581*
Lk 23:53 a sepulchre that was **h** in stone, ... *2991*

HID
Ge 3:8 Adam and his wife **h** themselves....... 2244
Ge 3:10 I was naked; and I **h** myself. 2244
Ge 4:14 and from thy face shall I be **h**;......... 5641
Ex 2:2 child, she **h** him three months......... 6845
Ex 2:12 Egyptian, and **h** him in the sand....... 2934
Ex 3:6 And Moses **h** his face; for he was 5641
Le 4:13 and the thing be **h** from the eyes 5956
Le 5:3 defiled withal, and it be **h** from him;... 5956
Nu 5:13 be **h** from the eyes of her husband, ... 5956
Jos 2:6 **h** them with the stalks of flax,......... 2934
Jos 6:25 because she **h** the messengers 2244
Jos 7:21 are **h** in the earth in the midst......... 2934
1Sa 10:22 hath **h** himself among the stuff........ 2244
1Ki 18:13 how I **h** an hundred men of the 2244
2Ki 4:27 and the Lord hath **h** it from me,....... 5956
2Ch 9:2 nothing **h** from Solomon which....... 5956
2Ch 22:12 **h** in the house of God six years: 2244
Job 3:21 for it more than for **h** treasures;....... 4301
Ps 32:5 and mine iniquity have I not **h**........ 3680
Ps 38:9 my groaning is not **h** from thee 5641
Ps 40:10 I have not **h** thy righteousness 3680
Pr 2:4 for her as for **h** treasures;............. 4301
Isa 28:15 falsehood have we **h** ourselves: 5641
Isa 40:27 My way is **h** from the Lord, and my.... 5641
Isa 50:6 I **h** not my face from shame and....... 5641
Isa 53:3 and we **h** as it were our faces from..... 5641
Isa 59:2 your sins have **h** his face from you, ... 5641
Jer 16:17 is their iniquity **h** from mine eyes...... 6845
Jer 33:5 I have **h** my face from this city......... 5641
Jer 36:26 the prophet: but the Lord **h** them...... 5641
Eze 22:26 **h** their eyes from my sabbaths,......... 5956
Eze 39:23 therefore **h** I my face from them, ... 5641
Zep 2:3 it may be ye shall be **h** in the day 5641
Mt 5:14 **that is set on an hill cannot be h** *2928*
Mt 10:26 **and h, that shall not be known**........ *2927*
Mt 11:25 **because thou hast h these things** *613*
Mt 13:44 **is like unto treasure h in a field;**....... *2928*
Mt 25:25 **and h thy talent in the earth:** *2928*
Mk 4:22 **For there is nothing h, which** *2927*
Lk 1:24 and **h** herself five months, saying *4032*
Lk 8:47 saw that she was not **h**, she came *2990*
Lk 9:45 and it was **h** from them, that they...... *3871*
Lk 10:21 **h these things from the wise**........... *613*
Lk 12:2 **neither h, that shall not be known**..... *2927*
Lk 13:21 **and h in three measures of meal,**...... *1470*
Lk 18:34 and this saying was **h** from them,...... *2928*
Lk 19:42 **now they are h from thine eyes** *2928*
Jn 8:59 but Jesus **h** himself, and went out...... *2928*
2Co 4:3 if our gospel be **h**, it is **h** to them *2572*
Eph 3:9 hath been **h** in God, who created *618*
Col 1:26 which hath been **h** from ages and....... *618*
Col 2:3 In whom are **h** all the treasures......... *614*
Col 3:3 your life is **h** with Christ in God. *2928*
Heb 11:23 was **h** three months of his parents,..... *2924*
Rev 6:15 **h** themselves in the dens and in *2928*

HIDDEN
Le 5:2 and if it be **h** from him; he also 5956
Dt 30:11 it is not **h** from thee, neither is 6381
Job 24:1 times are not **h** from the Almighty..... 6845
Ps 51:6 in the **h** part thou shalt make me...... 5640
Pr 28:12 when the wicked rise, a man is **h** 2664
Isa 45:3 and **h** riches of secret places, that...... 4301
1Co 4:5 bring to the light the **h** things of....... *2927*
2Co 4:2 the **h** things of dishonesty, not *2927*
1Pe 3:4 But let it be the **h** man of the heart,.... *2927*
Rev 2:17 **will I give to eat of the h manna,** *2928*

HIDE
Ge 18:17 Shall I **h** from Abraham that thing..... 3680
Ex 2:3 when she could not longer **h** him, ... 6845
Dt 31:17 and I will **h** my face from them 5641
Jos 2:16 **h** yourselves there three days, ... 2247
Jos 7:19 thou hast done; **h** it not from me...... 3582
1Sa 3:17 I pray thee **h** it not from me: God 3582
1Sa 26:1 Doth not David **h** himself in the 5641
Ps 13:1 how long wilt thou **h** thy face 5641
Ps 17:8 **h** me under the shadow of thy 5641
Ps 27:9 **H** not thy face far from me; put 5641
Ps 51:9 **H** thy face from my sins, and blot...... 5641
Ps 64:2 **H** me from the secret counsel of....... 5641
Ps 78:4 not **h** them from their children........ 3582
Ps 89:46 Lord? wilt thou **h** thyself for ever? 5641
Ps 102:2 **H** not thy face from me in the day 5641
Ps 143:7 **h** not thy face from me, lest I be....... 5641
Pr 2:1 **h** my commandments with thee; 6845
Pr 28:28 wicked rise, men **h** themselves:........ 5641

Isa	1:15	will **h** mine eyes from you: yea,	5956
Isa	2:10	and **h** thee in the dust, for fear of	2934
Isa	3:9	their sin as Sodom, they **h** it not	3582
Isa	26:20	**h** thyself as it were for a little	2247
Isa	29:15	that seek deep to **h** their counsel	5641
Jer	23:24	Can any **h** himself in secret places	5641
Jer	36:19	Go, **h** thee, thou and Jeremiah; and	5641
Eze	28:3	no secret that they can **h** from	6004
Eze	39:29	Neither will I **h** face any more	5641
Da	10:7	so that they fled to **h** themselves.	2244
Jas	5:20	and shall **h** a multitude of sins	*2572*
Rev	6:16	**h** us from the face of him that	*2928*

HIDEST

Job	13:24	Wherefore **h** thou thy face, and	5641
Ps	10:1	why **h** thou thyself in times of	5956
Ps	44:24	Wherefore **h** thou thy face, and	5641
Ps	104:29	Thou **h** thy face, they are troubled:	5641
Isa	45:15	thou art a God that **h** thyself, O	5641

HIDETH

Job	42:3	Who is he that **h** counsel without	5956
Ps	10:11	he **h** his face; he will never see it	5641
Ps	139:12	the darkness **h** not from thee;	2821
Pr	10:18	He that **h** hatred with lying lips,	3680
Pr	19:24	man **h** his hand in his bosom,	2934
Pr	22:3	foreseeth the evil, and **h** himself:	5641
Pr	27:16	Whosoever **h** her **h** the wind, and	6845
Pr	28:27	that **h** his eyes shall have many a	5956
Isa	8:17	that **h** his face from the house of	5641

HIDING

Ps	32:7	Thou art my **h** place; thou shalt	5643
Ps	119:114	art my **h** place and my shield:	5643
Hab	3:4	and there was the **h** of his power.	2253

HIGH

Ge	7:19	all the **h** hills, that were under the	1364
Ge	14:18	was the priest of the most **h** God	5945
Le	21:10	And he that is the **h** priest among	1419
Le	26:30	I will destroy your **h** places, and	1116
Nu	20:17	we will go by the king's **h** way,	
Nu	24:16	the knowledge of the most **H**,	5945
Nu	35:25	in it unto the death of the **h** priest,	1419
Nu	35:28	after the death of the **h** priest the	1419
Dt	26:19	to make thee **h** above all nations.	5945
Dt	32:8	When the most **H** divided to the	5945
Dt	32:27	Our hand is **h**, and the Lord hath	7311
2Sa	1:19	Israel is slain upon thy **h** places:	1116
1Ki	3:2	the people sacrificed in **h** places,	1116
1Ki	11:7	Solomon build an **h** place for	1116
1Ki	13:33	the people priests of the **h** places:	1116
1Ki	14:23	For they also built them **h** places,	1364
1Ki	15:14	the **h** places were not removed:	1116
1Ki	22:43	the **h** places were not taken away;	1116
2Ki	12:3	and burnt incense in the **h** places.	1116
2Ki	17:9	they built them **h** places in all their	1116
2Ki	17:11	burnt incense in all the **h** places,	1116
2Ki	18:4	He removed the **h** places, and brake	1116
2Ki	21:3	For he built up again the **h** places	1116
2Ki	23:13	And the **h** places that were before	1116
2Ki	23:20	slew all the priests of the **h** places	1116
1Ch	11:23	man of great stature, five cubits **h**	
2Ch	11:15	priests for the **h** places, and for	1116
2Ch	33:17	did sacrifice still in the **h** places,	1116
Est	5:14	gallows be made of fifty cubits **h**,	1364
Ps	18:27	but wilt bring down **h** looks	7311
Ps	18:33	and setteth me upon my **h** places.	1116
Ps	47:2	the Lord most **h** is terrible; he is	5945
Ps	50:14	pay thy vows unto the most **H**:	5945
Ps	57:2	I will cry unto God most **h**; unto	5945
Ps	62:9	and men of **h** degree are a lie:	376
Ps	68:18	Thou hast ascended on **h**, thou	4791
Ps	71:19	also, O God, is very **h**, who hast	4791
Ps	73:11	is there knowledge in the most **H**?	5945
Ps	78:17	by provoking the most **H** in the	5945
Ps	78:58	to anger with their **h** places, and	1116
Ps	82:6	of you are children of the most **H**	5945
Ps	83:18	art the most **h** over all the earth.	5945
Ps	91:1	in the secret place of the most **H**	5945
Ps	91:14	I will set him on **h**, because he	7682
Ps	97:9	Lord, art **h** above all the earth:	5945
Ps	101:5	hath an **h** look and a proud heart.	1362
Ps	103:11	the heaven is **h** above the earth,	1361
Ps	107:11	the counsel of the most **H**:	5945
Ps	131:1	matters, or in things too **h** for me	6381
Ps	139:6	it is **h**, I cannot attain unto it	7682
Ps	150:5	him upon the **h** sounding cymbals.	8643
Pr	9:14	a seat in the **h** places of the city,	4791
Pr	18:11	as an **h** wall in his own conceit.	7682
Pr	21:4	An **h** look, and a proud heart, and	7312
Pr	24:7	Wisdom is too **h** for a fool: he	7311
Isa	6:1	upon a throne, **h** and lifted up,	7311
Isa	14:14	clouds; I will be like the most **H**	5945
Isa	26:5	down them that dwell on **h**; the	4791
Isa	32:15	spirit be poured upon us from on **h**,	4791
Isa	33:5	is exalted; for he dwelleth on **h**:	4791
Isa	40:9	get thee up into the **h** mountain;	1364
Isa	57:15	the **h** and lofty One that inhabiteth	7311
Isa	57:15	I dwell in the **h** and holy place,	4791
Jer	2:20	when upon every **h** hill and under	1364
La	3:35	before the face of the most **H**,	5945
La	3:38	Out of the mouth of the most **H**	5945
Eze	6:6	and the **h** places shall be desolate;	1116
Eze	16:31	and makest thine **h** place in every	7413
Eze	21:26	is low, and abase him that is **h**.	1364
Eze	31:4	the deep set him up on **h** with her	7311
Eze	34:6	mountains, and upon every **h** hill:	7311
Eze	34:14	the **h** mountains of Israel shall	4791
Eze	36:2	even the ancient **h** places are ours	1116
Eze	40:2	set me upon a very **h** mountain,	1364
Da	3:26	ye servants of the most **h** God,	5943
Da	4:25	most **H** ruleth in the kingdom	5943
Da	4:34	and I blessed the most **H**, and I	5943
Da	5:18	most **h** God gave Nebuchadnezzar	5943
Da	7:22	given to the saints of the most **H**;	5946
Da	7:25	great words against the most **H**;	5943
Hos	7:16	return, but not to the most **H**	5920
Am	4:13	treadeth upon the **h** places of the	1116
Mic	6:6	and bow myself before the **h** God?	4791
Mt	4:8	up into an exceeding **h** mountain,	*5308*
Mt	26:51	struck a servant of the **h** priest's	*749*
Mt	26:65	Then the **h** priest rent his clothes,	*749*
Mk	5:7	Jesus, thou Son of the most **h** God?	*5310*
Mk	14:53	led Jesus away to the **h** priest: and	*749*
Mk	14:66	one of the maids of the **h** priest:	*749*
Lk	1:78	dayspring from on **h** hath visited	*5311*
Lk	4:5	taking him up into an **h** mountain,	*5308*
Lk	22:54	him into the **h** priest's house. And	*749*
Lk	24:49	**be endued with power from on h.**	*5311*
Jn	18:22	Answerest thou the **h** priest so?	*749*
Ac	7:48	most **H** dwelleth not in temples	*5310*
Ac	9:1	And Saul ... went unto the **h** priest,	*749*

Ac 16:17 are the servants of the most **h** God, ... *5310*
Ac 22:5 the **h** priest doth bear me witness, ... *749*
Ac 23:4 said, Revilest thou God's **h** priest? *749*
Ro 12:16 Mind not **h** things, but condescend *5308*
Ro 13:11 it is **h** time to awake out of sleep:
2Co 10:5 and every **h** thing that exalteth *5313*
Eph 4:8 When he ascended up on **h**, he led..... *5311*
Eph 6:12 spiritual wickedness in **h** places......... *2032*
Php 3:14 the prize of the **h** calling of God in *507*
Heb 1:3 the right hand of the Majesty on **h**; *5308*
Heb 2:17 a merciful and faithful **h** priest in....... *749*
Heb 3:1 consider the Apostle and **H** Priest of *749*
Heb 4:14 that we have a great **h** priest, that is *749*
Heb 4:15 we have not an **h** priest which cannot ... *749*
Heb 5:5 not himself to be made an **h** priest; *749*
Heb 5:10 of God an **h** priest after the order of *749*
Heb 6:20 an **h** priest for ever after the order *749*
Heb 7:27 not daily, as those **h** priests, to offer *749*
Heb 9:7 went the **h** priest alone once every *749*
Heb 9:11 an **h** priest of good things to come, ... *749*
Rev 21:10 spirit to a great and **h** mountain, ... *5308*

HIGHER
1Sa 9:2 he was **h** than any of the people. 1364
Ps 61:2 me to the rock that is **h** than I......... 7311
Ecc 5:8 for he that is **h** than the highest 1364
Isa 55:9 the heavens are **h** than the earth, ... 1361
Isa 55:9 so are my ways **h** than your ways,...... 1361
Lk 14:10 **say unto thee, Friend, go up h** *511*
Ro 13:1 soul be subject unto the **h** powers *5241*
Heb 7:26 and made **h** than the heavens;......... *5301*

HIGHEST
Pr 8:26 **h** part of the dust of the world.......... 7218
Pr 9:3 upon the **h** places of the city, ... 4791
Mt 21:9 of the Lord; Hosanna in the **h**......... *5310*
Mk 11:10 of the Lord: Hosanna in the **h**......... *5310*
Lk 1:32 shall be called the Son of the **H**......... *5310*
Lk 1:35 power of the **H** shall overshadow *5310*
Lk 1:76 be called the prophet of the **H**......... *5310*
Lk 2:14 Glory to God in the **h**, and on earth ... *5310*
Lk 6:35 **ye shall be the children of the H**....... *5310*
Lk 14:8 **sit not down in the h room; lest**....... *4411*
Lk 19:38 peace in heaven, and glory in the **h** *5310*
Lk 20:46 **the h seats in the synagogues,**......... *4410*

HIGHLY
Lk 1:28 said, Hail, thou that art **h** favoured,
Lk 16:15 **which is h esteemed among men** *5308*
Ro 12:3 not to think of himself more **h** than ... *5252*
Php 2:9 God also hath **h** exalted him, and...... *5252*
1Th 5:13 to esteem them very **h** in love *1537, 4053*

HIGHMINDED See also MINDED.
Ro 11:20 by faith. Be not **h**, but fear: *5309*
1Ti 6:17 they be not **h**, nor trust in uncertain ... *5309*
2Ti 3:4 heady, **h**, lovers of pleasures more *5187*

HIGHWAY
Jgs 21:19 on the east side of the **h** that goeth 4546
1Sa 6:12 went along the **h**, lowing as they....... 4546
2Sa 20:12 in blood in the midst of the **h**. And 4546
2Sa 20:12 he removed Amasa out of the **h** into ... 4546
2Sa 20:13 When he was removed out of the **h**, ... 4546
Pr 16:17 The **h** of the upright is to depart 4546
Isa 11:16 there shall be an **h** for the remnant 4546
Isa 35:8 And an **h** shall be there, and a way, ... 4547
Isa 40:3 in the desert a **h** for our God.......... 4546

HIGHWAYS
Isa 33:8 The **h** lie waste, the warfaring man 4546
Mt 22:9 **Go ye therefore into the h,** *1327, 3598*
Lk 14:23 **Go out into the h and hedges,** ... *1327, 3598*

HILL
Ex 17:9 I will stand on the top of the **h** with ... 1389
Nu 14:44 presumed to go up unto the **h** top: 2022
Jos 5:3 of Israel at the **h** of the foreskins....... 1389
1Ki 11:7 in the **h** that is before Jerusalem, ... 2022
1Ki 14:23 groves, on every high **h**, and under 1389
2Ki 17:10 groves in every high **h**, and under 1389
Ps 2:6 my king upon my holy **h** of Zion...... 2022
Ps 3:4 and he heard me out of his holy **h** 2022
Ps 24:3 Who shall ascend into the **h** of the..... 2022
Ps 99:9 our God, and worship at his holy **h**;.... 2022
Isa 30:17 mountain, and as an ensign on an **h** ... 1389
Isa 40:4 mountain and **h** shall be made low:.... 1389
Jer 2:20 when upon every high **h** and under.... 1389
Jer 50:6 they have gone from mountain to **h**, ... 1389
Eze 6:13 altars, upon every high **h**, in all the 1389
Mt 5:14 **A city that is set on an h cannot**....... *3735*
Ac 17:22 Paul stood in the midst of Mars' **h**, ... *697*

HILLS
Ge 49:26 utmost bound of the everlasting **h**..... 1389
1Ki 20:23 Their gods are gods of the **h** 2022
1Ki 20:28 The Lord is God of the **h**, but he is 2022
1Ki 22:17 saw all Israel scattered upon the **h**,..... 2022
Ps 18:7 foundations also of the **h** moved 2022
Ps 50:10 and the cattle upon a thousand **h**...... 2042
Ps 97:5 **h** melted like wax at the presence...... 2022
Ps 104:32 he toucheth the **h**, and they smoke..... 2022
Ps 121:1 I will lift up mine eyes unto the **h**, ... 2022
Pr 8:25 before the **h** was I brought forth: 1389
SS 2:8 mountains, skipping upon the **h**....... 1389
Isa 2:2 shall be exalted above the **h**; and 1389
Isa 5:25 the **h** did tremble, and their........... 2022
Isa 40:12 in scales, and the **h** in a balance?....... 1389
Isa 54:10 depart, and the **h** be removed; but 1389
Isa 55:12 the mountains and the **h** shall break ... 1389
Jer 3:23 salvation is hoped for from the **h**, ... 1389
Hos 4:13 and burn incense upon the **h**, under ... 1389
Hos 10:8 Cover us; and to the **h**, Fall on us. 1389
Joel 3:18 and the **h** shall flow with milk, and 1389
Am 9:13 sweet wine, and all the **h** shall melt 1389
Mic 4:1 it shall be exalted above the **h**; and..... 1389
Na 1:5 the **h** melt, and the earth is burned 1389
Lk 23:30 **Fall on us; and to the h, Cover us**...... *1015*

HINDER
Job 9:12 he taketh away, who can **h** him? 7725
Mk 4:38 he was in the **h** part of the ship, ... *4403*
Ac 8:36 what doth **h** me to be baptized? *2967*
1Co 9:12 we should **h** the gospel..... *5100, 1464, 1325*
Gal 5:7 did **h** you that ye should not obey *848*

HINDERED
Ezr 6:8 unto these men, that they be not **h**...... 989
1Th 2:18 once and again; but Satan **h** us.......... *1465*
1Pe 3:7 of life; that your prayers be not **h**...... *1581*

HINGES
Pr 26:14 As the door turneth upon its **h**, so 6735

HIP
Jgs 15:8 he smote them **h** and thigh with a 7785

HIRE

Dt 23:18 shalt not bring the **h** of a whore, ... 868
Dt 24:15 At his day thou shalt give him his **h**.... 7939
Isa 23:18 her **h** shall be holiness to the Lord:...... 868
Mic 3:11 the priests thereof teach for **h**, and..... 4242
Mt 20:1 **to h labourers into his vineyard**....... *3409*
Lk 10:7 **the labourer is worthy of his h**........ *3408*
Jas 5:4 **h** of the labourers who have reaped.... *3408*

HIRED

Ge 30:16 **h** thee with my son's mandrakes....... 7936
Le 19:13 the wages of him that is **h** shall not 7916
Le 22:10 **h** servant, shall not eat of the holy 7916
Le 25:40 as an **h** servant, and as a sojourner, ... 7916
Dt 23:4 **h** against thee Balaam the son of 7936
Dt 24:14 oppress an **h** servant that is poor 7916
1Sa 2:5 full have **h** out themselves for bread; ... 7936
2Ki 7:6 Israel hath **h** against us the kings 7936
Ezr 4:5 And **h** counsellors against them, to 7936
Ne 13:2 but **h** Balaam against them, that he 7936
Mt 20:7 **him, Because no man hath h, us**....... *3409*
Mt 20:9 **were h about the eleventh hour,**....... *3409*
Lk 15:17 **many h servants of my father's**........ *3407*
Lk 15:19 **make me as one of thy h servants**...... *3407*

HIRELING

Mal 3:5 that oppress the **h** in his wages, ... 7916
Jn 10:13 **because he is an h, and careth not** *3411*

HISS

1Ki 9:8 shall be astonished, and shall **h**; 8319
Jer 19:8 shall be astonished and **h** because 8319
La 2:15 they **h** and wag their head at the....... 8319
Zep 2:15 one that passeth by her shall **h**,........ 8319

HOAR

1Ki 2:6 let not his **h** head go down to the...... 7872

HOARY

Le 19:32 shall rise up before the **h** head,........ 7872
Pr 16:31 The **h** head is a crown of glory, if...... 7872

HOLD

Ge 19:16 the men laid **h** upon his hand......... 2388
Ge 25:26 his hand took **h** on Esau's heel;......... 270
Ex 14:14 for you, and ye shall **h** your peace 2790
Ex 20:7 the Lord will not **h** him guiltless
Dt 5:11 the Lord will not **h** him guiltless
Dt 22:28 and lay **h** on her, and lie with her, ... 8610
Jgs 16:29 Samson took **h** of the two middle 3943
Jgs 19:29 knife, and laid **h** on his concubine, ... 2388
2Sa 6:6 to the ark of God, and took **h** of it; 270
2Sa 13:11 he took **h** of her, and said unto her,.... 2388
1Ki 1:50 caught **h** on the horns of the altar 2388
1Ki 2:9 **h** him not guiltless: for thou art
1Ki 2:28 caught **h** on the horns of the altar...... 2388
2Ki 2:3 Yea, I know it; **h** ye your peace 2814
2Ki 2:5 Yea, I know it; **h** ye your peace 2814
Est 4:11 the king shall **h** out the golden 3447
Job 27:6 My righteousness I **h** fast, and......... 2388
Ps 39:12 **h** not thy peace at my tears: for I 2790
Ps 40:12 iniquities have taken **h** upon me, ... 5381
Ps 48:6 Fear took **h** upon them there, and 270
Ps 83:1 **h** not thy peace, and be not still,....... 2790
Ps 109:1 **H** not thy peace, O God of my 2790
Ps 116:3 the pains of hell gat **h** upon me:....... 4672
Ps 119:53 Horror hath taken **h** upon me 270
Pr 2:19 neither take they **h** of the paths 5381
Pr 3:18 life to them that lay **h** upon her:....... 2388
Pr 4:13 Take fast **h** of instruction; let her 2388
Pr 5:5 to death; her steps take **h** on hell....... 8551
Pr 30:28 spider taketh **h** with her hands, ... 8610
Pr 31:19 and her hands **h** the distaff 8551
Ecc 2:3 and to lay **h** on folly, till I might 270
Isa 4:1 seven women shall take **h** of one 2388
Isa 56:6 it, and taketh **h** of my covenant;....... 2388
Isa 62:1 Zion's sake will I not **h** my peace,...... 2814
Isa 62:6 never **h** their peace day nor night: 2814
Jer 2:13 cisterns, that can **h** no water 3557
Jer 4:19 I cannot **h** my peace, because thou..... 2790
Jer 6:24 anguish hath taken **h** of us, and 2388
Jer 8:5 **h** fast deceit, they refuse to return 2388
Am 6:10 Then shall he say, **H** thy tongue:....... 2013
Na 1:7 a strong **h** in the day of trouble;....... 4581
Zep 1:7 **H** thy peace at the presence of the
Zec 11:5 and **h** themselves not guilty; and 816
Mt 6:24 **or else he will h to the one, and** *472*
Mt 14:3 For Herod had laid **h** on John, and *2902*
Mt 20:31 because they should **h** their peace:..... *4623*
Mt 26:48 kiss, that same is he: **h** him fast........ *2902*
Mk 1:25 **H thy peace, and come out of him.** *5392*
Mk 7:8 **ye h the tradition of men, as the.**...... *2902*
Lk 16:13 **or else he will h to the one, and** *472*
Ro 1:18 **h** the truth in unrighteousness;........ *2722*
1Th 5:21 things; **h** fast that which is good *2722*
1Ti 6:12 of faith, lay **h** on eternal life........... *1949*
1Ti 6:19 that they may lay **h** on eternal life...... *1949*
2Ti 1:13 **H** fast the form of sound words *2192*
Heb 4:14 of God, let us **h** fast our profession..... *2902*
Heb 6:18 lay **h** upon the hope set before us: *2902*
Heb 10:23 Let us **h** fast the profession of our *2722*
Rev 2:14 **that h the doctrine of Balaam,** *2902*
Rev 2:15 **h the doctrine of the Nicolaitanes,**..... *2902*
Rev 2:25 **ye have already h fast till I come** *2902*
Rev 20:2 And he laid **h** on the dragon, that...... *2902*

HOLDETH

Pr 11:12 man of understanding **h** his peace. 2790
Pr 17:28 a fool, when he **h** his peace 2790
Rev 2:1 **saith he that h the seven stars in** *2902*

HOLDING

Isa 33:15 his hands from **h** of bribes............ 8551
Php 2:16 **H** forth the word of life; that I......... *1907*
1Ti 1:19 **H** faith, and a good conscience; *2192*
1Ti 3:9 **H** the mystery of the faith in a *2192*
Tit 1:9 **H** fast the faithful word as he *472*
Rev 7:1 **h** the four winds of the earth,......... *2902*

HOLDS

1Sa 23:14 abode in the wilderness in strong **h**, ... 4679
Ps 89:40 hast brought his strong **h** to ruin 4013
Mic 5:11 and throw down all thy strong **h**:...... 4013
2Co 10:4 to the pulling down of strong **h**;....... *3794*

HOLES

Hag 1:6 wages to put it into a bag with **h**....... 5344
Lk 9:58 **Foxes have h, and the birds of**......... *5454*

HOLIER

Isa 65:5 near to me; for I am **h** than thou 6942

HOLIEST

Heb 9:3 which is called the **H** of all: *39*
Heb 9:8 the way into the **h** of all was not......... *39*
Heb 10:19 into the **h** by the blood of Jesus,......... *39*

HOLINESS

Ex 15:11	who is like thee, glorious in **h**,	6944
Ex 28:36	of a signet, **H** to the Lord	6944
Ex 39:30	of a signet, **H** to the Lord	6944
1Ch 16:29	worship the Lord in the beauty of **h**.	6944
Ps 29:2	worship the Lord in the beauty of **h**.	6944
Ps 47:8	sitteth upon the throne of his **h**	6944
Ps 89:35	Once have I sworn by my **h** that I	6944
Ps 96:9	worship the Lord in the beauty of **h**:	6944
Isa 35:8	and it shall be called The way of **h**,	6944
Isa 63:15	behold from the habitation of thy **h**.	6944
Jer 2:3	Israel was **h** unto the Lord, and the	6944
Jer 23:9	and because of the words of his **h**	6944
Am 4:2	The Lord God hath sworn by his **h**	6944
Zec 14:20	of the horses, **H** unto the Lord;	6944
Mal 2:11	Judah hath profaned the **h** of the	6944
Lk 1:75	In **h** and righteousness before him	*3742*
Ro 1:4	power, according to the spirit of **h**	*42*
Ro 6:19	servants to righteousness unto **h**.	*38*
2Co 7:1	perfecting **h** in the fear of God	*42*
Eph 4:24	in righteousness and true **h**	*3742*
1Th 3:13	hearts unblameable in **h** before God	*42*
1Th 4:7	us unto uncleanness, but unto **h**.	*38*
1Ti 2:15	faith ... charity and **h** with sobriety	*38*
Tit 2:3	be in behaviour as becometh **h**,	*2412*
Heb 12:10	that we might be partakers of his **h**	*41*
Heb 12:14	Follow peace with all men, and **h**,	*38*

HOLLOW

Ge 32:25	him, he touched the **h** of his thigh;	3709
Isa 40:12	the waters in the **h** of his hand	8168

HOLY

Ex 3:5	whereon thou standest is **h** ground	6944
Ex 20:8	the sabbath day, to keep it **h**	6942
Ex 26:33	between the **h** place and the most **h**.	6944
Ex 28:29	when he goeth in unto the **h** place,	6944
Ex 28:43	the altar to minister in the **h** place;	6944
Ex 29:37	toucheth the altar shall be **h**	6944
Ex 30:10	it is most **h** unto the Lord	6944
Ex 30:29	whatsoever toucheth them ... be **h**	6942
Ex 40:13	put upon Aaron the **h** garments,	6944
Le 6:16	shall it be eaten in the **h** place;	6918
Le 6:17	it is most **h**, as is the sin offering,	6944
Le 10:10	difference between **h** and unholy,	6944
Le 11:45	ye shall therefore be **h**, for I am **h**.	6918
Le 16:16	make an atonement for the **h** place,	6944
Le 19:2	for I the Lord your God am **h**.	6918
Le 22:10	shall no stranger eat of the **h** thing:	6944
Le 22:32	Neither shall ye profane my **h** name;	6944
Le 27:28	every devoted thing is most **h** unto	6944
Nu 6:8	separation he is **h** unto the Lord	6918
Dt 14:2	for thou art an **h** people unto the	6918
1Sa 2:2	There is none **h** as the Lord: for	6918
1Ch 22:19	the **h** vessels of God, into the house	6944
2Ch 3:10	in the most **h** house he made two	6944
2Ch 35:3	Put the **h** ark in the house which	6944
Ezr 9:2	**h** seed have mingled themselves	6944
Ne 8:10	for this day is **h** unto our Lord:	6918
Ps 2:6	my king upon my **h** hill of Zion.	6944
Ps 11:4	The Lord is in his **h** temple, the	6944
Ps 16:10	thou suffer thine **H** One to see	2623
Ps 51:11	take not thy **h** spirit from me	6944
Ps 99:3	and terrible name; for it is **h**	6918
Pr 9:10	and the knowledge of the **h** is	6918
Isa 1:4	have provoked the **H** One of Israel	6918
Isa 6:3	said, **H**, **h**, **h**, is the Lord of hosts:	6918
Isa 41:20	the **H** One of Israel hath created it	6918
Isa 43:15	I am the Lord, your **H** One, the	6918
Isa 54:5	Redeemer the **H** One of Israel;	6918
Isa 57:15	I dwell in the high and **h** place,	6918
Eze 22:26	between the **h** and profane,	6944
Eze 45:6	the oblation of the **h** portion:	6944
Da 4:9	the spirit of the **h** gods is in thee	6922
Da 9:24	thy people and upon thy **h** city,	6944
Hab 2:20	but the Lord is in his **h** temple:	6944
Mt 1:18	found with child of the **H** Ghost	*40*
Mt 7:6	**not that which is h unto the dogs,**	*40*
Mt 12:31	**the blasphemy against the H Ghost**	
Mt 28:19	**of the Son, and of the H Ghost:**	*40*
Lk 1:35	that **h** thing which shall be born	*40*
Lk 2:23	womb shall be called **h** to the Lord;	*40*
Lk 2:25	and the **H** Ghost was upon him	*40*
Lk 3:16	baptize you with the **H** Ghost	*40*
Lk 3:22	the **H** Ghost descended in a bodily	*40*
Lk 4:1	Jesus being full of the **H** Ghost	*40*
Lk 12:10	**against the H Ghost it shall**	*40*
Jn 14:26	**Comforter, which is the H Ghost,**	*40*
Jn 20:22	them, **Receive ye the H Ghost:**	*40*
Ac 1:5	**be baptized with the H Ghost not**	*40*
Ac 1:8	**that the H Ghost is come upon**	*40*
Ac 2:4	were all filed with the **H** Ghost,	*40*
Ac 2:27	thine **H** One to see corruption	*3741*
Ac 4:27	of a truth against thy **h** child Jesus,	*40*
Ac 7:55	he, being full of the **H** Ghost,	*40*
Ac 8:17	and they received the **H** Ghost	*40*
Ac 11:24	full of the **H** Ghost and of faith:	*40*
Ac 13:35	thine **H** One to see corruption	*3741*
Ac 19:2	Have ye received the **H** Ghost	*40*
Ac 19:2	whether there be any **H** Ghost	*40*
Ro 7:12	law is **h**, and the commandment **h**,	*40*
Ro 12:1	a living sacrifice, **h**, acceptable unto	*40*
1Co 3:17	for the temple of God is **h**, which	*40*
1Co 6:19	is the temple of the **H** Ghost	*40*
Eph 1:13	sealed with that **h** Spirit of promise,	*40*
Eph 4:30	And grieve not the **h** Spirit of God,	*40*
Col 1:22	to present you **h** and unblameable	*40*
1Ti 2:8	lifting up **h** hands, without wrath	*3741*
2Ti 1:14	by the **H** Ghost which dwelleth	*40*
2Ti 3:15	thou hast known the **h** scriptures,	*2413*
Heb 3:7	as the **H** Ghost saith, To day if	*40*
Heb 7:26	who is **h**, harmless, undefiled,	*3741*
Heb 9:8	The **H** Ghost this signifying	*40*
Heb 9:12	he entered in once into the **h** place	*39*
Heb 9:25	entereth into the **h** place every year	*39*
1Pe 1:12	you with the **H** Ghost sent down	*40*
1Pe 1:15	hath called you is **h**, so be ye **h** in all	*40*
1Pe 2:9	a royal priesthood, an **h** nation, a	*40*
2Pe 1:18	we were with him in the **h** mount	*40*
2Pe 1:21	were moved by the **H** Ghost	*40*
1Jn 2:20	ye have an unction from the **H** One	*40*
Jude 20	yourselves in your most **h** faith,	*40*
Rev 3:7	**saith he that is h, he that is true,**	*40*
Rev 4:8	night, saying, **H**, **h**, **h**, Lord God	*40*
Rev 11:2	the **h** city shall they tread under foot	*40*
Rev 14:10	the presence of the **h** angels, and in	*40*
Rev 15:4	for thou only art **h**: for all nations	*3741*
Rev 21:2	John saw the **h** city, new Jerusalem,	*40*
Rev 22:11	and he that is ... let him be **h** still	*37*

HOME

Ge 43:16	Bring these men **h**, and slay, and	1004
Le 18:9	she be born at **h**, or born abroad,	1004

Dt 24:5 but he shall be free at **h** one year 1004
Jgs 11:9 If ye bring me **h** again to fight 7725
Ru 1:21 hath brought me **h** again empty: 7725
1Sa 18:2 go no more **h** to his father's house 7725
1Ki 13:15 Come **h** with me, and eat bread 1004
1Ch 13:12 shall I bring the ark of God **h** to me?
Ps 68:12 that tarried at **h** divided the spoil. 1004
Pr 7:19 For the goodman is not at **h**, he is 1004
Pr 7:20 will come **h** at the day appointed 1004
Ecc 12:5 man goeth to his long **h**, and the 1004
La 1:20 bereaveth, at **h** there is as death. 1004
Hag 1:9 when ye brought it **h**, I did blow 1004
Mk 5:19 **Go h to thy friends, and tell them** *3624*
Lk 9:61 bid them farewell, which are at **h** at
Lk 15:6 **And when he cometh h, he calleth** *3624*
Jn 19:27 that disciple took her unto his own **h** .. *3624*
1Co 11:34 any man hunger, let him eat at **h**, ... *3624*
1Co 14:35 let them ask their husbands at **h** *3624*
2Co 5:6 whilst we are at **h** in the body, we *1736*
1Ti 5:4 learn first to shew piety at **h**, and *2398*
Tit 2:5 be discreet, chaste, keepers at **h**, ... *3626*

HONEST See also **DISHONEST.**
Lk 8:15 **which in an h and good heart** *2570*
Ac 6:3 you seven men of **h** report, full of the
Ro 12:17 things **h** in the sight of all men *2570*
2Co 8:21 Providing for **h** things, not only in *2570*
2Co 13:7 but ye should do that which is **h**, ... *2570*
Php 4:8 are true, whatsoever things are **h**, ... *4586*
1Pe 2:12 conversation **h** among the Gentiles: *2570*

HONESTLY
Ro 13:13 Let us walk **h**, as in the day; not *2156*
1Th 4:12 That ye may walk **h** toward them *2156*
Heb 13:18 in all things willing to live **h** *2573*

HONESTY See also **DISHONESTY.**
1Ti 2:2 quiet ... life in all godliness and **h** *4587*

HONEY
Ex 3:8 a land flowing with milk and **h**; 1706
Ex 16:31 of it was like wafers made with **h** 1706
Le 2:11 burn no leaven, nor any **h**, in any 1706
Le 20:24 land that floweth with milk and **h**: 1706
Nu 14:8 land which floweth with milk and **h** ... 1706
Dt 31:20 that floweth with milk and **h**; and 1706
Dt 32:13 made him to suck **h** out of the rock, ... 1706
Jgs 14:9 had taken the **h** out of the carcase 1706
Jgs 14:18 What is sweeter than **h**? and what 1706
1Sa 14:29 because I tasted a little of this **h** 1706
1Sa 14:43 I did but taste a little **h** with the 1706
2Ki 18:32 a land of oil olive and of **h**, that ye 1706
Ps 19:10 gold: sweeter also than **h** and the 1706
Ps 81:16 and with **h** out of the rock should I 1706
Ps 119:103 yea, sweeter than **h** to my mouth!. 1706
Pr 24:13 son, eat thou **h**, because it is good; 1706
Pr 25:16 Hast thou found **h**? eat so much as 1706
Pr 25:27 It is not good to eat much **h**: so for 1706
SS 4:11 **h** and milk are under thy tongue; 1706
Isa 7:22 for butter and **h** shall every one eat 1706
Jer 32:22 a land flowing with milk and **h**; 1706
Eze 3:3 in my mouth as **h** for sweetness 1706
Mt 3:4 his meat was locusts and wild **h** *3192*
Rev 10:10 it was in my mouth sweet as **h**: *3192*

HONEYCOMB
1Sa 14:27 and dipped it in an **h**, and put ... 3295, 1706
Ps 19:10 also than honey and the **h** 5317, 6688
Pr 5:3 a strange woman drop as an **h** 5317
Pr 16:24 Pleasant words are as an **h**....... 6688, 1706
Pr 24:13 the **h**, which is sweet to thy taste: 5317
Pr 27:7 The full soul loatheth an **h**; but to 5317

HONOUR See also **DISHONOUR**
Ex 14:17 and I will get me **h** upon Pharaoh, ... 3513
Ex 20:12 **H** thy father and thy mother: that 3513
Le 19:15 nor **h** the person of the mighty: 1921
Nu 24:11 Lord hath kept thee back from **h** 3519
Dt 5:16 **H** thy father and thy mother, as 3513
Jgs 13:17 come to pass we may do thee **h**? 3513
1Sa 2:30 them that **h** me I will **h**, and they 3513
2Sa 6:22 of them shall I be had in **h** 3513
1Ki 3:13 hast not asked, both riches, and **h**; 3519
1Ch 29:12 Both riches and **h** come of thee 3519
2Ch 1:12 give thee riches, and wealth, and **h**, ... 3519
2Ch 17:5 he had riches and **h** in abundance 3519
2Ch 32:27 exceeding much riches and **h**: and 3519
2Ch 32:33 inhabitants of Jerusalem did him **h** 3519
Est 1:20 shall give to their husbands **h**, both 3366
Est 6:3 What **h** and dignity hath been done ... 3366
Est 6:6 whom the king delighteth to **h**? 3366
Est 8:16 light, and gladness, and joy, and **h** 3366
Ps 8:5 crowned him with glory and **h** 1926
Ps 21:5 **h** and majesty hast thou laid upon 1935
Ps 26:8 the place where thine **h** dwelleth 3519
Ps 49:12 man being in **h** abideth not: he is 3366
Ps 49:20 that is in **h**, and understandeth not, ... 3366
Ps 66:2 Sing forth the **h** of his name:. 3519
Ps 96:6 **H** and majesty are before him: 1935
Ps 149:9 written: this **h** have all his saints 1926
Pr 3:9 **H** the Lord with thy substance 3513
Pr 4:8 she shall bring thee to **h**, when 3513
Pr 5:9 Lest thou give thine **h** unto others, ... 1935
Pr 8:18 Riches and **h** are with me; yea, ... 3519
Pr 11:16 A gracious woman retaineth **h** 3519
Pr 14:28 multitude of people is the king's **h** 1927
Pr 15:33 wisdom; and before **h** is humility 3519
Pr 18:12 haughty, and before **h** is humility 3519
Pr 20:3 It is an **h** for a man to cease from 3519
Pr 21:21 findeth life, righteousness, and **h** 3519
Pr 22:4 the Lord are riches, and **h**, and life. 3519
Pr 25:2 but the **h** of kings is to search out 3519
Pr 26:1 harvest, so **h** is not seemly for a fool ... 3519
Pr 26:8 so is he that giveth **h** to a fool 3519
Pr 29:23 **h** shall uphold the humble in spirit 3519
Pr 31:25 Strength and **h** are her clothing; 1926
Ecc 6:2 riches, wealth, and **h**, so that he 3519
Ecc 10:1 is in reputation for wisdom and **h** 3519
Isa 29:13 with their lips do **h** me, but have 3513
Isa 58:13 and shall **h** him, not doing thine 3513
Da 2:6 me gifts and rewards and great **h** 3367
Da 4:30 of my power, and for the **h** of my 3367
Da 4:36 mine **h** and brightness returned 1923
Da 4:37 extol and **h** the King of heaven, all 1922
Da 5:18 and majesty, and glory, and **h**: 1923
Da 11:38 his fathers knew not shall he **h** 3513
Mal 1:6 I be a father, where is mine **h**? 3519
Mt 13:57 **A prophet is not without h, save in** *820*
Mt 15:4 **H thy father and mother: and he** *5091*
Mt 15:6 **h not his father or his mother, he.** *5091*
Mt 19:19 **H thy father and thy mother:** *5097*
Mk 6:4 **A prophet is not without h, but in** *820*
Mk 7:10 **H thy father and thy mother;** *5091*
Mk 10:19 **not, H thy father and mother.** *5091*

Lk	18:20	**H, thy father and thy mother.**	*5091*
Jn	4:44	hath no **h** in his own country	*5092*
Jn	5:23	**the Son, even as they h the father.**	*5091*
Jn	5:41	**I receive not h from men**	*1391*
Jn	5:44	**the h that cometh from God only?**	*1391*
Jn	8:49	**but I h my Father, and ye do**	*5091*
Jn	8:54	Jesus answered, If I **h** myself,	*1392*
Jn	12:26	**serve me, him will my Father h**	*5091*
Ro	2:7	for glory and **h** and immortality	*5092*
Ro	9:21	to make one vessel unto **h**, and	*5092*
Ro	12:10	love; in **h** preferring one another;	*5092*
Ro	13:7	fear to whom fear; **h** to whom **h**.	*5092*
1Co	12:23	these we bestow more abundant **h**;	*5092*
Eph	6:2	**H** thy father and mother; which	*5091*
1Th	4:4	his vessel in sanctifiction and **h**;	*5092*
1Ti	1:17	be **h** and glory for ever and ever	*5092*
1Ti	5:3	**H** widows that are widows indeed	*5091*
1Ti	5:17	be counted worthy of double **h**,	*5092*
1Ti	6:1	their own masters worthy of all **h**.	*5092*
2Ti	2:20	some to **h**, and some to dishonour	*5092*
2Ti	2:21	be a vessel unto **h**, sanctified, and	*5092*
Heb	2:9	death, crowned with glory and **h**;	*5092*
Heb	3:3	builded the house hath more **h**	*5092*
Heb	5:4	no man taketh this **h** unto himself,	*5092*
1Pe	1:7	might be found unto praise and **h**	*5092*
1Pe	2:17	**H** all men. Love the brotherhood	*5091*
1Pe	2:17	Fear God. **H** the king	*5091*
1Pe	3:7	giving **h** unto the wife, as unto	*5092*
2Pe	1:17	from God the Father **h** and glory	*5092*
Rev	4:9	beasts give glory and **h** and thanks	*5092*
Rev	4:11	to receive glory and **h** and power:	*5092*
Rev	5:12	and **h**, and glory, and blessing	*5092*
Rev	5:13	Blessing, and **h**, and glory, and	*5092*
Rev	7:12	**h**, and power, and might, be unto	*5092*
Rev	19:1	Salvation, and glory, and **h**, and	*5092*
Rev	19:7	and rejoice, and give **h** to him:	*1391*
Rev	21:24	do bring their glory and **h** into it	*5092*

HONOURABLE

Ge	34:19	was more **h** than all the house of	3513
1Sa	9:6	man of God, and he is an **h** man;	3513
2Sa	23:23	He was more **h** than the thirty	3513
1Ch	11:21	three, he was more **h** than the two;	3513
Ps	111:3	His work is **h** and glorious: and	1935
Isa	3:5	ancient, and ... base against the **h**	3519
Isa	9:15	ancient and **h**, he is the head;	5375, 6440
Isa	23:9	contempt all the **h** of the earth	3513
Isa	42:21	magnify the law, and make it **h**	142
Na	3:10	and they cast lots for her **h** men,	3513
Lk	14:8	**more h man than thou be bidden**	*1784*
1Co	4:10	ye are **h**, but we are despised	*1741*
1Co	12:23	body, which we think to be less **h**,	*820*
Heb	13:4	Marriage is **h** in all, and the bed	*5093*

HONOURED

Ex	14:4	and I will be **h** upon Pharaoh,	3513
Pr	13:18	that regardeth reproof shall be **h**	3513
Pr	27:18	waiteth on his master shall be **h**	3513
Isa	43:23	hast thou **h** me with thy sacrifices	3513
La	1:8	all that **h** her despise her, because	3513
Da	4:34	and **h** him that liveth for ever,	1922
1Co	12:26	one member be **h**, all the members	*1392*

HONOUREST See also **DISHONOUREST.**

1Sa	2:29	and **h** thy sons above me, to make	3513

HONOURETH See also **DISHONOURETH.**

Ps	15:4	but he **h** them that fear the Lord	3513
Pr	12:9	better than he that **h** himself, and	3513
Pr	14:31	that **h** him hath mercy on the poor	3513
Mal	1:6	A son **h** his father, and a servant	3513
Mt	15:8	**mouth, and h me with their lips;**	*5091*
Mk	7:6	**This people h me with their lips,**	*5091*
Jn	5:23	**that h not the Son h not the**	*5091*
Jn	8:54	**it is my Father that h me; of**	*1392*

HOOF

Ex	10:26	shall not an **h** be left behind;	6541
Le	11:3	Whatsoever parteth the **h**, and is	6541
Dt	14:6	And every beast that parteth the **h**.	6541

HOOFS

Ps	69:31	or bullock that hath horns and **h**	6536
Isa	5:28	**h** shall be counted like flint	6541
Jer	47:3	the noise of the stamping of the **h**	6541
Eze	26:11	the **h** of his horses shall he tread	6541
Mic	4:13	iron, and I will make thy **h** brass:	6541

H

HOOKS

Eze	38:4	thee back, and put **h** into thy jaws,	2397
Am	4:2	that he will take you away with **h**,	6793

HOPE

Job	7:6	shuttle, and are spent without **h**	8615
Job	8:13	and the hypocrite's **h** shall perish:	8615
Ps	31:24	heart, all ye that **h** in the Lord	3176
Ps	33:18	upon them that **h** in his mercy;	3176
Ps	38:15	in thee, O Lord, do I **h**: thou wilt	3176
Ps	42:5	disquieted in me? **h** thou in God:	3176
Ps	43:5	disquieted within me? **h** in God:	3176
Ps	71:5	For thou art my **h**, O Lord God:	8615
Ps	78:7	they might set their **h** in God,	3689
Ps	119:116	let me not be ashamed of my **h**	7664
Ps	130:5	doth wait, and in his word do I **h**	3176
Ps	130:7	Let Israel **h** in the Lord: for with	3176
Ps	146:5	whose **h** is in the Lord his God:	7664
Ps	147:11	him, in those that **h** in his mercy	3176
Pr	10:28	The **h** of the righteous shall be	8431
Pr	11:7	and the **h** of unjust men perisheth.	8431
Pr	13:12	**H** deferred maketh the heart sick:	8431
Pr	14:32	the righteous hath **h** in his death.	2620
Pr	19:18	Chasten thy son while there is **h**,	8615
Pr	26:12	is more **h** of a fool than of him	8615
Pr	29:20	is more **h** of a fool than of him	8615
Ecc	9:4	joined to all the living there is **h**:	986
Isa	38:18	into the pit cannot **h** for thy truth	7663
Jer	2:25	but thou saidst, There is no **h**:	2976
Jer	14:8	O the **h** of Israel, the saviour	4723
Jer	17:7	Lord, and whose **h** the Lord is,	4009
Jer	17:17	thou art my **h** in the day of evil	4268
Jer	18:12	And they said, There is no **h**:	2976
Jer	50:7	the Lord, the **h** of their fathers	4723
La	3:24	soul; therefore will I **h** in him	3176
La	3:26	good that a man should both **h**	2342
Eze	37:11	bones are dried, and our **h** is lost:	8615
Joel	3:16	Lord will be the **h** of his people	4268
Zec	9:12	the strong hold, ye prisoners of **h**:	8615
Lk	6:34	**to them of whom ye h to receive**	*1679*
Ac	16:19	that the **h** of their gains was gone	*1680*
Ac	23:6	the **h** and resurrection of the dead	*1680*
Ac	26:6	am judged for the **h** of the promise	*1680*
Ro	4:18	Who against **h** believed in **h**, that	*1680*
Ro	5:2	and rejoice in **h** of the glory of God.	*1680*

Ro 5:4 experience; and experience, **h**: *1680*
Ro 5:5 And **h** maketh not ashamed: *1680*
Ro 8:24 but **h** that is seen is not **h**: *1680*
Ro 8:25 But if we **h** for that we see not, *1679*
Ro 15:4 of the scriptures might have **h**. *1680*
Ro 15:13 the God of **h** fill you with all joy and *1680*
1Co 9:10 he, that ploweth should plow in **h**; *1680*
1Co 13:13 And now abideth faith, **h**, charity *1680*
1Co 15:19 If in this life only we have **h** in *1679*
Gal 5:5 wait for the **h** of righteousness by *1680*
Eph 1:18 know what is the **h** of his calling, *1680*
Eph 2:12 having no **h**, and without God in *1680*
Eph 4:4 are called in one **h** of your calling; *7680*
Col 1:5 the **h** which is laid up for you in *1680*
Col 1:27 Christ in you, the **h** of glory: *1680*
1Th 2:19 For what is our **h**, or joy, or crown *1680*
1Th 4:13 even as others which have no **h**. *1680*
1Th 5:8 for an helmet, the **h** of salvation *1680*
Tit 1:2 In **h** of eternal life, which God *1680*
Tit 2:13 Looking for that blessed **h**, and *1680*
Tit 3:7 according to the **h** of eternal life *1680*
Heb 6:11 full assurance of **h** unto the end: *1680*
Heb 6:18 lay hold upon the **h** set before us: *1680*
Heb 6:19 which **h** we have as an anchor of
1Pe 1:3 begotten us again unto a lively **h**. *1680*
1Pe 1:13 and **h** to the end for the grace that *1679*
1Pe 1:21 your faith and **h** might be in God. *1680*
1Pe 3:15 a reason of the **h** that is in you *1680*
1Jn 3:3 every man that hath this **h** in him *1680*

HOPED

Est 9:1 the enemies of the Jews **h** to have 7663
Ps 119:43 for I have **h** in thy judgments 3176
Ps 119:74 because I have **h** in thy word 3176
Ps 119:166 Lord, I have **h** for thy salvation, 7663
Jer 3:23 Truly in vain is salvation **h** for from
Lk 23:8 he **h** to have seen some miracle *1679*
Ac 24:26 He **h** also that the money should *1679*
Heb 11:1 is the substance of things **h** for *1679*

HOPETH

1Co 13:7 believeth all things, **h** all things *1679*

HOPING

Lk 6:35 **and lend, h for nothing again;** *560*

HORN

Ex 21:29 ox were wont to push with his **h**. 2767
1Sa 2:10 and exalt the **h** of his anointed 7161
1Sa 16:1 fill thine **h** with oil, and go, I will 7161
2Sa 22:3 shield, and the **h** of my salvation, 7161
Ps 75:4 to the wicked, Lift not up the **h**: 7161
Ps 89:24 in my name shall his **h** be exalted 7161
Ps 112:9 his **h** shalt be exalted with honour 7161
Ps 148:14 also exalteth the **h** of his people 7161
La 2:3 his fierce anger all the **h** of Israel: 7161
Da 7:8 in this **h** were eyes like the eyes of 7162
Da 7:21 same **h** made war with the saints, 7162
Da 8:8 strong, the great **h** was broken; 7161
Da 8:21 great **h** that is between his eyes 7161
Mic 4:13 I will make thine **h** iron, and I will 7161
Lk 1:69 hath raised up an **h** of salvation *2768*

HORNS

Ge 22:13 ram caught in a thicket by his **h** 7161
Ex 27:2 And thou shalt make the **h** of it 7161
Ex 29:12 and put it upon the **h** of the altar 7161
Ex 30:10 an atonement upon the **h** of it once 7161
Le 4:7 blood upon the **h** of the altar of 7161
Le 8:15 and put it upon the **h** of the altar 7161
Dt 33:17 his **h** are like the **h** of unicorns: 7161
Jos 6:4 ark seven trumpets of rams' **h**: 3104
1Ki 1:51 caught hold on the **h** of the altar, 7161
1Ki 2:28 caught hold on the **h** of the altar 7161
Ps 22:21 me from the **h** of the unicorns 7161
Ps 69:31 or bullock that hath **h** and hoofs 7160
Ps 75:10 **h** of the righteous shall be exalted 7161
Jer 17:1 and upon the **h** of your altars; 7161
Eze 27:15 for a present **h** of ivory and ebony 7161
Eze 43:15 altar and upward shall be four **h**. 7161
Da 7:7 were before it; and it had ten **h** 7162
Da 7:24 And the ten **h** out of this kingdom 7162
Da 8:7 smote the ram, and brake his two **h** 7161
Da 8:20 sawest having two **h** are the kings 7161
Am 3:14 the **h** of the altar shall be cut off, 7161
Am 6:13 Have we not taken to us **h** by our 7161
Hab 3:4 he had **h** coming out of his hand: 7161
Zec 1:18 eyes, and saw, and behold four **h** 7161
Zec 1:21 to cast out the **h** of the Gentiles, 7161
Rev 5:6 having seven **h** and seven eyes, *2768*
Rev 9:13 from the four **h** of the golden altar *2768*
Rev 12:3 having seven heads and ten **h** *2768*
Rev 13:1 sea, having seven heads and ten **h**, *2768*
Rev 13:1 and upon his **h** ten crowns, and *2768*
Rev 13:11 he had two **h** like a lamb, and he *2768*
Rev 17:3 having seven heads and ten **h** *2768*
Rev 17:7 hath the seven heads and ten **h** *2768*
Rev 17:12 the ten **h** which thou sawest are *2768*
Rev 17:16 the ten **h** which thou sawest upon *2768*

HORRIBLE

Ps 40:2 brought me up also out of an **h** pit, 7588
Jer 3:30 A wonderful and **h** thing is 8186
Jer 18:13 Israel hath done a very **h** thing 8186
Jer 23:14 prophets of Jerusalem an **h** thing: 8186
Hos 6:10 I have seen an **h** thing in the house 8186

HORROR

Ge 15:12 an **h** of great darkness fell upon 367
Ps 55:5 and **h** hath overwhelmed me. 6427
Ps 119:53 **H** hath taken hold upon me 2152
Eze 7:18 **h** shall cover them; and shame 6427

HORSE

Ex 15:1 the **h** and his rider hath he thrown 5483
Ex 15:19 For the **h** of Pharaoh went in with 5483
1Ki 20:25 **h** for **h**, and chariot for chariot: 5483
Est 6:8 the **h** that the king rideth upon, 5483
Ps 32:9 Be ye not as the **h**, or as the mule, 5483
Ps 33:17 An **h** is a vain thing for safety: 5483
Ps 76:6 both the chariot and **h** are cast 5483
Ps 147:10 not in the strength of the **h**: 5483
Pr 21:31 The **h** is prepared against the day 5483
Pr 26:3 A whip for the **h**, a bridle for the 5483
Isa 43:17 bringeth forth the chariot and **h**, 5483
Jer 8:6 as the **h** rusheth into the battle 5483
Jer 51:21 break in pieces the **h** and his rider; 5483
Am 2:15 he that rideth the **h** deliver himself 5483
Zec 1:8 behold a man riding upon a red **h**, 5483
Zec 10:3 them as his goodly **h** in the battle 5483
Zec 12:4 smite every **h** with astonishment, 5483
Rev 6:2 I saw, and behold a white **h**: and *2462*
Rev 6:4 went out another **h** that was red: *2462*
Rev 6:5 I beheld, and lo a black **h**; and he *2462*
Rev 6:8 And I looked, and behold a pale **h**: *2462*

Rev	14:20	winepress, even unto the **h** bridles,	*2462*
Rev	19:11	opened, and behold a white **h**;	*2462*
Rev	19:19	war against him that sat on the **h**,	*2462*
Rev	19:21	sword of him that sat upon the **h**,	*2462*

HORSEBACK

2Ki	9:19	Then he sent out a second on **h**,	5483
Est	6:11	on **h** through the street of the city,	7392

HORSEMEN

Ex	14:9	chariots of Pharaoh, and his **h**,	6571
Ex	14:17	his chariots, and upon his **h**	6571
Ex	14:26	their chariots, and upon their **h**	6571
Ex	14:28	covered the chariots, and the **h**,	6571
1Sa	8:11	for his chariots, and to be his **h**;	6571
2Sa	1:6	**h** followed hard after him	1167, 6571
1Ki	4:26	chariots, and twelve thousand **h**	6571
1Ki	10:26	gathered together chariots and **h**	6571
2Ki	2:12	chariot of Israel, and the **h** thereof	6571
2Ki	13:14	chariot of Israel, and the **h** thereof	6571
Ezr	8:22	a band of soldiers and **h** to help us.	6571
Jer	4:29	for the noise of the **h** and bowmen;	6571
Eze	26:10	shall shake at the noise of the **h**,	6571
Da	11:40	with chariots, and with **h**, and with	6571
Hos	1:7	nor by battle, by horses, nor by **h**	6571
Joel	2:4	and as **h**, so shall they run	6571
Hab	1:8	and their **h** shall come from far;	6571
Ac	23:32	they left the **h** to go with him	*2460*
Rev	9:16	the number of the army of the **h**	*2461*

HORSES

Ge	47:17	them bread in exchange for **h**,	5483
Ex	14:9	all the **h** and chariots of Pharaoh	5483
Ex	14:23	even all Pharaoh's **h**, his chariots	5483
Dt	17:16	he shall not multiply **h** to himself,	5483
Dt	20:1	and seest **h**, and chariots, and a	5483
Jos	11:6	thou shalt hough their **h**, and burn	5483
2Sa	8:4	David houghed all the chariot **h** but	
1Ki	4:26	had forty thousand stalls of **h** for	5483
1Ki	18:5	grass to save the **h** and mules alive,	5483
1Ki	22:4	people as thy people, my **h** as thy **h**	5483
2Ki	2:11	a chariot of fire, and **h** of fire, and	5483
2Ki	3:7	as thy people, and my **h** as thy **h**.	5483
2Ki	5:9	Naaman came with his **h** and with	5483
2Ki	6:17	was full of **h** and chariots of fire	5483
2Ki	7:6	noise of chariots, and a noise of **h**,	5483
2Ki	7:7	left their tents, and their **h**, and	5483
2Ki	7:10	but **h** tied, and asses tied, and the	5483
2Ki	9:33	sprinkled on the wall, and on the **h**	5483
2Ki	11:16	way by the which the **h** came into	5483
2Ki	14:20	And they brought him on **h**: and	5483
Ps	20:7	trust in chariots, and some in **h**:	5483
Ecc	10:7	I have seen servants upon **h**, and	5483
Isa	2:7	their land is also full of **h**, neither	5483
Isa	31:1	stay on **h**, and trust in chariots	5483
Isa	31:3	and their **h** flesh, and not spirit.	5483
Isa	66:20	the Lord out of all nations upon **h**,	5483
Jer	4:13	his **h** are swifter than eagles	5483
Jer	5:8	They were as fed **h** in the morning:	5483
Jer	8:16	The snorting of his **h** was heard	5483
Jer	12:5	how canst thou contend with **h**?	5483
Jer	22:4	riding in chariots and on **h**, he	5483
Jer	47:3	stamping of … hoofs of his strong **h**,	5483
Jer	50:42	they shall ride upon **h**, every one	5483
Eze	17:15	that they might give him **h** and	5483
Eze	23:20	whose issue is like the issue of **h**	5483
Eze	26:10	By reason of the abundance of his **h**	5483
Hos	1:7	by battle, by **h**, nor by horsemen	5483
Joel	2:4	of them is as the appearance of **h**;	5483
Am	6:12	Shall **h** run upon the rock? will one	5483
Na	3:2	of the wheels and of the pransing **h**,	5483
Hab	1:8	Their **h** are also swifter than the	5483
Zec	1:8	and behind him were there red **h**,	5483
Zec	6:2	In the first chariot were red **h**;	5483
Zec	6:2	and in the second chariot black **h**;	5483
Zec	6:3	And in the third chariot white **h**;	5483
Zec	6:3	fourth chariot grisled and bay **h**	5483
Zec	6:6	The black **h** which are therein go	5483
Zec	10:5	riders on **h** shall be confounded	5483
Zec	14:20	there be upon the bells of the **h**,	5483
Rev	9:7	of the locusts were like unto **h**	*2462*
Rev	9:9	the chariots of many **h** running to	*2462*
Rev	9:17	And thus I saw the **h** in the vision,	*2462*
Rev	9:17	heads of the **h** were as the heads	*2462*
Rev	19:14	heaven followed him upon white **h**,	*2462*
Rev	19:18	of mighty men, and the flesh of **h**,	*2462*

HORSES'

Jas	3:3	we put bits in the **h** mouths, that	*2462*

HOSANNA (ho-zan´-nah)

Mt	21:9	**H** to the son of David: Blessed	*5614*
Mt	21:15	and saying, **H** to the son of David;	*5614*
Mk	11:9	**H**; Blessed is he that cometh in	*5614*
Mk	11:10	name of the Lord; **H** in the highest	*5614*
Jn	12:13	**H**: Blessed is the King of Israel	*5614*

HOSPITALITY

Ro	12:13	necessity of saints; given to **h**.	*5381*
1Ti	3:2	given to **h**, apt to teach;	*5382*
Tit	1:8	But a lover of **h**, a lover of good	*5382*
1Pe	4:9	Use **h** one to another without	*5382*

HOST

Ge	2:1	finished, and all the **h** of them	6635
Ge	32:2	them, he said, This is God's **h**:	4264
Ex	14:24	troubled the **h** of the Egyptians,	4264
Ex	15:4	Pharaoh's chariots and his **h** hath	2428
Nu	4:3	all that enter into the **h**, to do the	6635
Nu	31:14	wroth with the officers of the **h**,	2428
Dt	2:14	wasted out from among the **h**,	4264
Dt	4:19	stars, even all the **h** of heaven,	6635
Dt	17:3	moon, or any of the **h** of heaven,	6635
Jos	5:14	captain of the **h** of the Lord am	6635
Jos	5:15	captain of the Lord's **h** said unto	6635
Jgs	4:16	all the **h** of Sisera fell upon the	4264
Jgs	7:13	bread tumbled into the **h** of	4264
Jgs	7:21	the **h** ran, and cried, and fled	4264
Jgs	8:11	smote the **h**: for the **h** was secure	4264
1Sa	14:15	there was trembling in the **h**, in	4264
1Sa	14:19	the noise that was in the **h** of the	4264
1Sa	17:46	the carcases of the **h** of the	4264
1Sa	28:5	Saul saw the **h** of the Philistines	4264
1Sa	28:19	also shall deliver the **h** of Israel	4264
2Sa	24:4	and against the captains of the **h**	2428
1Ki	22:19	And all the **h** of heaven standing	6635
1Ki	22:34	hand, and carry me out of the **h**;	4264
2Ki	3:9	there was no water for the **h**, and	4264
2Ki	5:1	Naaman, captain of the **h** of the	6635
2Ki	6:15	an **h** compassed the city both with	2428
2Ki	7:4	let us fall unto the **h** of the	4264
2Ki	7:6	had made the **h** of the Syrians	4264
2Ki	18:17	Hezekiah with a great **h** against	2426
2Ki	21:5	built altars for all the **h** of heaven	6635

2Ki	23:4	grove, and for all the **h** of heaven:	6635
2Ki	23:5	planets, and to all the **h** of heaven	6635
2Ki	25:1	Babylon came, he, and all his **h**,	2428
1Ch	12:22	was a great **h**, like the **h** of God.	4264
2Ch	16:7	the **h** of the king of Syria escaped.	2428
2Ch	18:18	all the **h** of heaven standing on	6635
2Ch	18:33	thou mayest carry me out of the **h**;	6635
2Ch	24:24	the Lord delivered a very great **h**	2428
2Ch	33:3	worshipped all the **h** of heaven,	6635
2Ch	33:5	built altars for all the **h** of heaven.	6635
Ne	9:6	heaven of heavens, with all their **h**,	6635
Ne	9:6	the **h** of heaven worshippeth thee.	6635
Ps	27:3	Though an **h** should encamp	4264
Ps	33:6	all the **h** of them by the breath of.	6635
Ps	33:16	saved by the multitude of an **h**:	2428
Ps	136:15	overthrew Pharaoh and his **h** in	2428
Isa	13:4	mustereth the **h** of the battle.	6635
Isa	24:21	shall punish the **h** of the high ones	6635
Isa	34:4	**h** of heaven shall be dissolved	6635
Isa	34:4	all their **h** shall fall down, as the	6635
Isa	40:26	bringeth out their **h** by number:	6635
Isa	45:12	and all their **h** have I commanded	6635
Jer	8:2	the moon, and all the **h** of heaven,	6635
Jer	19:13	incense unto all the **h** of heaven,	6635
Jer	33:22	**h** of heaven cannot be numbered,	6635
Jer	51:3	men; destroy ye utterly all her **h**	6635
Eze	1:24	of speech, as the noise of an **h**:	4264
Da	8:10	some of the **h** and of the stars.	6635
Da	8:11	himself even to the prince of the **h**,	6635
Ob	20	captivity of this **h** of the children	2426
Zep	1:5	that worship the **h** of heaven.	6635
Lk	2:13	a multitude of the heavenly **h**	*4756*
Lk	10:35	**pence, and gave them to the h,**	*3830*
Ac	7:42	up to worship the **h** of heaven;	*4756*

HOSTAGES

2Ki	14:14	house and **h**, and returned	1121, 8594

HOSTS

Ex	12:41	the **h** of the Lord went out from.	6635
1Sa	1:3	unto the Lord of **h** in Shiloh	6635
1Sa	1:11	O Lord of **h**, if thou wilt indeed	6635
1Sa	4:4	of the covenant of the Lord of **h**,	6635
1Sa	17:45	thee in the name of the Lord of **h**,	6635
2Sa	5:10	the Lord God of **h** was with him	6635
2Sa	7:26	The Lord of **h** is the God over.	6635
1Ki	2:5	did to the two captains of the **h** of	6635
1Ki	18:15	As the Lord of **h** liveth, before.	6635
1Ki	19:10	jealous for the Lord God of **h**:	6635
1Ch	17:24	The Lord of **h** is the God of Israel,	6635
Ps	24:10	Lord of **h**, he is the King of glory	6635
Ps	46:7	The Lord of **h** is with us; the	6635
Ps	69:6	that wait on thee, O Lord God of **h**,	6635
Ps	80:4	O Lord God of **h**, how long wilt	6635
Ps	80:7	Turn us again, O God of **h**, and	6635
Ps	84:3	O Lord of **h**, my King, and my God	6635
Ps	84:12	O Lord of **h**, blessed is the man	6635
Ps	89:8	O Lord God of **h**, who is a strong.	6635
Ps	103:21	Bless ye the Lord, all ye his **h**; ye	6635
Ps	108:11	thou, O God, go forth with our **h**?	6635
Isa	1:9	Except the Lord of **h** had left unto	6635
Isa	2:12	For the day of the Lord of **h** shall.	6635
Isa	5:7	For the vineyard of the Lord of **h**.	6635
Isa	5:16	But the Lord of **h** shall be exalted.	6635
Isa	5:24	cast away the law of the Lord of **h**,	6635
Isa	6:3	Holy, holy, holy, is the Lord of **h**:	6635
Isa	6:5	have seen the King, the Lord of **h**.	6635
Isa	9:13	neither do they seek the Lord of **h**	6635
Isa	9:19	Through the wrath of the Lord of **h**	6635
Isa	13:4	the Lord of **h** mustereth the host	6635
Isa	14:24	The Lord of **h** hath sworn, saying,	6635
Isa	14:27	For the Lord of **h** hath purposed,	6635
Isa	18:7	place of the name of the Lord of **h**,	6635
Isa	19:17	of the counsel of the Lord of **h**	6635
Isa	19:20	for a witness unto the Lord of **h**	6635
Isa	22:5	perplexity by the Lord God of **h**.	6635
Isa	22:12	that day did the Lord God of **h** call	6635
Isa	23:9	The Lord of **h** hath purposed it, to.	6635
Isa	24:23	Lord of **h** shall reign in mount Zion,	6635
Isa	28:5	Lord of **h** be for a crown of glory.	6635
Isa	28:29	cometh forth from the Lord of **h**,	6635
Isa	29:6	be visited of the Lord of **h** with	6635
Isa	31:4	the Lord of **h** come down to fight	6635
Isa	31:5	the Lord of **h** defend Jerusalem;	6635
Isa	37:16	O Lord of **h**, God of Israel, that	6635
Isa	44:6	and his redeemer the Lord of **h**;	6635
Isa	47:4	the Lord of **h** is his name, the	6635
Isa	48:2	Israel; the Lord of **h** is his name	6635
Isa	51:15	roared: The Lord of **h** is his name	6635
Isa	54:5	husband; the Lord of **h** is his name;	6635
Jer	3:19	goodly heritage of the **h** of nations?	6635
Jer	10:16	The Lord of **h** is his name	6635
Jer	11:17	For the Lord of **h**, that planted	6635
Jer	11:20	Lord of **h**, that judgest righteously,	6635
Jer	15:16	by thy name, O Lord God of **h**	6635
Jer	20:12	Lord of **h**, that triest the righteous,	6635
Jer	23:36	living God, of the Lord of **h** our God	6635
Jer	27:18	make intercession to the Lord of **h**,	6635
Jer	30:8	saith the Lord of **h**, that I will break.	6635
Jer	31:35	The Lord of **h** is his name:	6635
Jer	32:18	the Mighty God, the Lord of **h**, is.	6635
Jer	33:11	Praise the Lord of **h**: for the Lord.	6635
Jer	46:10	is the day of the Lord God of **h**,	6635
Jer	50:25	the work of the Lord God of **h** in.	6635
Jer	50:34	strong; the Lord of **h** is his name:	6635
Jer	51:5	Judah of his God, of the Lord of **h**;	6635
Jer	51:19	the Lord of **h** is his name.	6635
Jer	51:57	King, whose name is the Lord of **h**.	6635
Am	4:13	Lord, the God of **h**, is his name	6635
Am	5:14	the Lord, the God of **h**, shall be	6635
Am	5:15	Lord God of **h** will be gracious	6635
Am	5:27	Lord, whose name is The God of **h**	6635
Am	9:5	Lord God of **h** is he that toucheth	6635
Mic	4:4	of the Lord of **h** hath spoken it.	6635
Na	2:13	against thee, saith the Lord of **h**,	6635
Na	3:5	against thee, saith the Lord of **h**;	6635
Hab	2:13	not of the Lord of **h** that the people.	6635
Zep	2:10	against the people of the Lord of **h**	6635
Hag	1:9	Why? saith the Lord of **h**. Because	6635
Hag	2:4	I am with you, saith the Lord of **h**:	6635
Hag	2:7	with glory, saith the Lord of **h**.	6635
Hag	2:9	I give peace, saith the Lord of **h**	6635
Hag	2:23	In that day, saith the Lord of **h**	6635
Zec	1:6	Like as the Lord of **h** thought to do	6635
Zec	1:12	O Lord of **h**, how long wilt thou not	6635
Zec	2:11	that the Lord of **h** hath sent me unto.	6635
Zec	3:10	In that day, saith the Lord of **h**,	6635
Zec	4:6	by my spirit, saith the Lord of **h**	6635
Zec	7:3	were in the house of the Lord of **h**,	6635
Zec	7:12	a great wrath from the Lord of **h**	6635
Zec	8:3	the mountain of the Lord of **h** the	6635
Zec	8:6	in mine eyes? saith the Lord of **h**	6635
Zec	8:21	and to seek the Lord of **h**: I will	6635

Zec 8:22 shall come to seek the Lord of **h** in 6635
Zec 9:15 The Lord of **h** shall defend them; 6635
Zec 10:3 the Lord of **h** hath visited his flock. 6635
Zec 12:5 strength in the Lord of **h** their God 6635
Zec 14:16 worship the King, the Lord of **h**, ... 6635
Zec 14:21 be holiness unto the Lord of **h** 6635
Mal 1:10 pleasure in you, saith … Lord of **h**. 6635
Mal 1:13 snuffed at it, saith the Lord of **h**; 6635
Mal 1:14 a great King, saith the Lord of **h**, ... 6635
Mal 2:2 unto my name, saith the Lord of **h**, ... 6635
Mal 2:7 is the messenger of the Lord of **h**, ... 6635
Mal 3:1 he shall come, saith the Lord of **h**. 6635
Mal 3:5 fear not me, saith the Lord of **h** 6635
Mal 3:10 now herewith, saith the Lord of **h**, ... 6635
Mal 3:14 mournfully before the Lord of **h**? 6635
Mal 4:1 burn them up, saith the Lord of **h**, ... 6635

HOT

Ex 16:21 when the sun waxed **h**, it melted 2552
Ex 22:24 And my wrath shall wax **h**, and I 2734
Ex 32:10 that my wrath may wax **h** against 2734
Ex 32:19 and Moses' anger waxed **h**, and he 2734
Le 13:24 skin whereof there is a **h** burning, ... 784
Dt 19:6 the slayer, while his heart is **h** 3179
Jos 9:12 This our bread we took **h** for our 2525
Jgs 2:14 the anger of the Lord was **h**. 2734
Jgs 2:20 the anger of the Lord was **h**. 2734
Jgs 3:8 anger of the Lord was **h** against 2734
Jgs 10:7 anger of the Lord was **h** against 2734
Ne 7:3 be opened until the sun be **h**; 2527
Ps 6:1 chasten me in thy **h** displeasure 2534
Ps 38:1 chasten me in thy **h** displeasure 2534
Ps 39:3 My heart was **h** within me, while 2552
Ps 78:48 their flocks to **h** thunderbolts 7565
Pr 6:28 Can one go upon **h** coals, and his feet
Eze 24:11 that the brass of it may be **h**, and 3179
Da 3:22 and the furnace exceeding **h**, the 228
Hos 7:7 They are all **h** as an oven, and 2552
1Ti 4:2 conscience seared with a **h** iron; *2743*
Rev 3:15 that thou art neither cold nor **h**: *2200*
Rev 3:15 I would thou wert cold or **h** *2200*
Rev 3:16 lukewarm, and neither cold nor **h**, ... *2200*

HOTTEST

2Sa 11:15 in the forefront of the **h** battle, ... 2389

HOUR

Da 3:15 be cast the same **h** into the midst 8160
Da 4:19 was astonied for one **h**, and his 8160
Da 4:33 The same **h** was the thing fulfilled 8160
Da 5:5 In the same **h** came forth fingers 8160
Mt 8:13 was healed in the selfsame **h** *5610*
Mt 10:19 that same **h** what ye shall speak *5610*
Mt 20:12 these last have wrought but one **h**, ... *5670*
Mt 24:36 that day and **h** knoweth no man *5610*
Mt 24:42 not what **h** your Lord doth come *5610*
Mt 24:44 such an **h** as ye think not the Son. *5610*
Mt 24:50 and in an **h** that he is not aware *5610*
Mt 25:13 ye know neither the day nor the **h** *5610*
Mt 26:40 ye not watch with me one **h**? *5610*
Mt 26:45 the **h** is at hand, and the Son of *5610*
Mt 27:45 the sixth **h** there was darkness. *5610*
Mt 27:46 about the ninth **h** Jesus cried with *5610*
Mk 13:32 day and that **h** knoweth no man, ... *5610*
Mk 14:35 possible, the **h** might pass from *5610*
Mk 14:37 couldest not thou watch one **h**? *5610*
Mk 14:41 it is enough, the **h** is come; *5610*
Mk 15:25 was the third **h**, and they crucified *5610*
Mk 15:34 the ninth **h** Jesus cried with a loud *5610*
Lk 12:39 known what **h** the thief would *5610*
Lk 12:40 cometh at an **h** when ye think. *5610*
Lk 12:46 at an **h** when he is not aware. *5610*
Lk 22:53 this is your **h**, and the power of *5610*
Lk 22:59 And about the space of one **h** after. *5610*
Lk 23:44 over all the earth until the ninth **h** *5610*
Lk 24:33 rose up the same **h**, and returned *5610*
Jn 2:4 with thee? mine **h** is not yet come *5610*
Jn 4:21 Woman, believe me, the **h** cometh, ... *5610*
Jn 4:23 the **h** cometh, and now is, when *5610*
Jn 4:53 knew that it was at the same **h**, ... *5610*
Jn 5:25 The **h** is coming, and now is, ... *5610*
Jn 5:28 the **h** is coming, in the which all *5610*
Jn 7:30 because his **h** was not yet come. *5610*
Jn 8:20 on him; for his **h** was not yet come *5610*
Jn 12:23 **h** is come, that the Son of man *5610*
Jn 12:27 I say? Father, save me from this **h**. *5610*
Jn 12:27 for this cause came I unto this **h** *5610*
Jn 13:1 when Jesus knew that his **h** was *5610*
Jn 16:21 sorrow, because her **h** is come: *5610*
Jn 16:32 the **h** cometh, yea, is now come *5610*
Jn 17:1 and said, Father, the **h** is come: *5610*
Jn 19:14 the passover, and about the sixth **h**. *5610*
Jn 19:27 from that **h** that disciple took her. *5610*
Ac 2:15 seeing it is but the third **h** of the. *5610*
Ac 3:1 the **h** of prayer, being the ninth **h**. *5610*
Ac 16:33 took them the same **h** of the night, ... *5610*
1Co 4:11 this present **h** we both hunger. *5610*
1Co 15:30 stand we in jeopardy every **h**? *5610*
Rev 3:3 shalt not know what **h** I will come *5610*
Rev 3:10 thee from the **h** of temptation. *5610*
Rev 8:1 about the space of half an **h** *2256*
Rev 9:15 prepared for an **h**, and a day, and *5610*
Rev 11:13 same **h** was there a great *5610*
Rev 14:7 for the **h** of his judgment is come: *5610*
Rev 17:12 power as kings one **h** with the. *5610*
Rev 18:10 for in one **h** is thy judgment come *5610*
Rev 18:17 in one **h** so great riches is come *5610*
Rev 18:19 for in one **h** is she made desolate *5610*

HOURS

Jn 11:9 Are there not twelve **h** in the. *5610*
Ac 5:7 about the space of three **h** after, ... *5610*
Ac 19:34 about the space of two **h** cried out, ... *5610*

HOUSE

Ge 12:17 plagued Pharaoh and his **h** with 1004
Ge 15:3 one born in my **h** is mine heir 1004
Ge 17:13 He that is born in thy **h**, and he 1004
Ge 20:13 me to wander from my father's **h** 1004
Ge 28:17 none other but the **h** of God, and 1004
Ge 28:21 again to my father's **h** in peace; 1004
Ge 28:22 set for a pillar, shall be God's **h**: 1004
Ge 31:41 have I been twenty years in thy **h**; 1004
Ge 34:30 I shall be desroyed, I and my **h** 1004
Ge 38:11 Remain a widow at thy father's **h** 1004
Ge 39:5 he had made him overseer in his **h**, ... 1004
Ge 39:9 is none greater in this **h** than I; 1004
Ge 39:11 that Joseph went into the **h** to do 1004
Ge 41:40 Thou shalt be over my **h**, and 1004
Ge 44:14 his brethren came to Joseph's **h**; 1004
Ge 46:27 all the souls of the **h** of Jacob, ... 1004
Ge 47:14 the money into Pharaoh's **h**. 1004
Ex 12:3 of their fathers, a lamb for an **h**: 1004
Ex 12:22 go out at the door of his **h** until 1004

Ex	12:30	there was not a **h** where there was	1004
Ex	12:46	of the flesh abroad out of the **h**;	1004
Ex	13:3	Egypt, out of the **h** of bondage;	1004
Ex	20:2	Egypt out of the **h** of bondage	1004
Ex	20:17	shalt not covet thy neighbour's **h**,	1004
Le	14:38	and shut up the **h** seven days:	1004
Le	14:52	water, sprinkle the **h** seven times:	1004
Le	16:11	atonement for himself, and for his **h**,	1004
Le	22:13	is returned unto her father's **h**, as	1004
Nu	1:2	families, by the **h** of their fathers,	1004
Nu	2:2	the ensign of their father's **h**:	1004
Nu	4:40	families, by the **h** of … fathers,	1004
Nu	12:7	so, who is faithful in all mine **h**.	1004
Nu	17:8	the rod of Aaron for the **h** of Levi	1004
Nu	20:29	thirty days, even all the **h** of Israel	1004
Nu	22:18	give me his **h** full of silver and gold,	1004
Nu	26:2	throughout their fathers' **h**, all	1004
Nu	30:10	if she vowed in her husband's **h**,	1004
Dt	5:6	of Egypt, from the **h** of bondage.	1004
Dt	5:21	thou covet thy neighbour's **h**, his	1004
Dt	6:7	when thou sittest in thine **h**, and	1004
Dt	6:9	write them upon the posts of thy **h**,	1004
Dt	11:20	upon the door posts of thine **h**,	1004
Dt	20:5	let him go and return to his **h**, lest	1004
Dt	20:6	him also go and return unto his **h**,	1004
Dt	20:7	let him go and return unto his **h**,	1004
Dt	20:8	let him go and return unto his **h**,	1004
Dt	22:8	When thou buildest a new **h**, then	1004
Dt	22:21	to play the whore in her father's **h**:	1004
Dt	24:1	hand, and send her out of his **h**	1004
Dt	24:2	when she is departed out of his **h**,	1004
Dt	24:3	hand, and sendeth her out of his **h**;	1004
Dt	25:9	will not build up his brother's **h**	1004
Jos	2:1	went, and came into an harlot's **h**,	1004
Jos	6:22	Go into the harlot's **h**, and bring	1004
Jos	24:15	as for me and my **h**, we will serve	1004
Jos	24:17	of Egypt, from the **h** of bondage,	1004
Jgs	6:15	I am the least in my father's **h**	1004
Jgs	11:2	shalt not inherit in our father's **h**;	1004
Jgs	11:7	and expel me out of my father's **h**?	1004
Jgs	11:31	cometh forth of the doors of my **h**	1004
Jgs	14:15	we burn thee and thy father's **h**	1004
Jgs	16:21	and he did grind in the prison **h**	1004
Jgs	16:29	pillars upon which the **h** stood,	1004
Jgs	16:30	and the **h** fell upon the lords, and	1004
Jgs	17:5	the man Micah had an **h** of gods,	1004
Jgs	19:26	fell down at the door of the man's **h**	1004
Jgs	20:5	beset the **h** round about upon me	1004
Jgs	20:26	came unto the **h** of God, and wept,	1008
Ru	1:8	Go, return each to her mother's **h**:	1004
Ru	4:11	which two did build the **h** of Israel:	1004
1Sa	2:27	appear unto the **h** of thy father,	1004
1Sa	2:33	the increase of thine **h** shall die in	1004
1Sa	2:35	I will build him a sure **h**; and he	1004
1Sa	3:13	that I will judge his **h** for ever for	1004
1Sa	5:2	brought it into the **h** of Dagon,	1004
1Sa	7:2	all the **h** of Israel lamented after	1004
1Sa	19:9	he sat in his **h** with his javelin in	1004
1Sa	22:22	of all the persons of thy father's **h**	1004
1Sa	25:36	he held a feast in his **h**, like the	1004
2Sa	2:4	David king over the **h** of Judah	1004
2Sa	3:1	the **h** of Saul and the **h** of David:	1004
2Sa	3:29	there not fail from the **h** of Joab	1004
2Sa	4:11	a righteous person in his own **h**	1004
2Sa	6:5	and all the **h** of Israel played	1004
2Sa	6:12	ark of God … **h** of Obed-edom	1004
2Sa	6:21	thy father, and before all his **h**.	1004
2Sa	7:2	I dwell in an **h** of cedar, but the ark	1004
2Sa	7:5	Shalt thou build me an **h** for me	1004
2Sa	7:6	I have not dwelt in any **h** since	1004
2Sa	7:13	He shall build an **h** for my name,	1004
2Sa	7:16	And thine **h** and thy kingdom shall	1004
2Sa	7:18	and what is my **h**, that thou hast	1004
2Sa	7:19	hast spoken also of thy servant's **h**	1004
2Sa	9:1	any that is left of the **h** of Saul	1004
2Sa	11:2	upon the roof of the king's **h**:	1004
2Sa	11:10	Uriah went not down unto his **h**,	1004
2Sa	12:8	I gave thee thy master's **h**, and	1004
2Sa	12:8	and gave thee the **h** of Israel and	1004
2Sa	12:10	shall never depart from thine **h**;	1004
2Sa	12:11	against thee out of thine own **h**,	1004
2Sa	13:7	Go now to thy brother Amnon's **h**,	1004
2Sa	14:24	So Absalom returned to his own **h**.	1004
2Sa	16:8	thee all the blood of the **h** of Saul,	1004
2Sa	16:22	a tent upon the top of the **h**;	1004
2Sa	19:28	my father's **h** were but dead men	1004
2Sa	19:30	again in peace unto his own **h**	1004
2Sa	20:3	whom he had left to keep the **h**	1004
2Sa	21:1	It is for Saul, and for his bloody **h**	1004
2Sa	23:5	Although my **h** be not so with God;	1004
2Sa	24:17	me, and against my father's **h**	1004
1Ki	1:53	said unto him, Go to thine **h**.	1004
1Ki	2:36	Build thee an **h** in Jerusalem,	1004
1Ki	3:2	because there was no **h** built unto	1004
1Ki	3:17	I and this woman dwell in one **h**;	1004
1Ki	5:3	my father could not build an **h**	1004
1Ki	5:5	I purpose to build an **h** unto the	1004
1Ki	6:7	nor any tool of iron heard in the **h**,	1004
1Ki	6:12	this **h** which thou art in building,	1004
1Ki	6:14	built the **h**, and finished it.	1004
1Ki	6:37	the foundation of the **h** of the Lord	1004
1Ki	6:38	was the **h** finished throughout	1004
1Ki	7:1	Solomon was building his own **h**	1004
1Ki	7:2	He built also the **h** of the forest	1004
1Ki	7:8	also an **h** for Pharaoh's daughter,	1004
1Ki	7:51	the treasures of the **h** of the Lord	1004
1Ki	8:10	the cloud filled the **h** of the Lord,	1004
1Ki	8:11	glory of the Lord had filled the **h**	1004
1Ki	8:27	how much less this **h** that I have	1004
1Ki	8:29	eyes may be open toward this **h**	1004
1Ki	8:33	supplication unto thee in this **h**	1004
1Ki	8:43	that this **h**, which I have builded,	1004
1Ki	8:44	toward the **h** that I have built	1004
1Ki	8:48	and the **h** which I have built for	1004
1Ki	8:63	Israel, dedicated the **h** of the Lord	1004
1Ki	9:3	I have hallowed this **h**, which thou	1004
1Ki	9:7	and this **h**, which I have hallowed	1004
1Ki	10:4	wisdom, and the **h** that he had built,	1004
1Ki	10:17	in the **h** of the forest of Lebanon.	1004
1Ki	10:21	of the **h** of the forest of Lebanon	1004
1Ki	12:16	now see to thine own **h**, David.	1004
1Ki	12:19	rebelled against the **h** of David	1004
1Ki	12:21	to fight against the **h** of Israel,	1004
1Ki	12:27	sacrifice in the **h** of the Lord at	1004
1Ki	12:31	he made an **h** of high places, and	1004
1Ki	13:34	became sin unto the **h** of Jeroboam,	1004
1Ki	14:8	kingdom away from the **h** of David,	1004
1Ki	14:14	cut off the **h** of Jeroboam that day:	1004
1Ki	14:26	the treasures of the **h** of the Lord,	1004
1Ki	14:26	and the treasures of the king's **h**:	1004
1Ki	15:18	and the treasures of the king's **h**,	1004
1Ki	15:29	he smote all the **h** of Jeroboam;	1004

1Ki	16:3	make thy **h** like the **h** of Jeroboam	1004
1Ki	16:11	that he slew all the **h** of Baasha:	1004
1Ki	16:18	burnt the king's **h** over him with	1004
1Ki	20:6	they shall search thine **h**, and the	1004
1Ki	20:31	the **h** of Israel are merciful kings:	1004
1Ki	21:22	make thine **h** like the **h** of Jeroboam	1004
1Ki	21:22	and like the **h** of Baasha the son of.	1004
1Ki	22:39	and the ivory **h** which he made,	1004
2Ki	4:2	tell me, what hast thou in the **h**?	1004
2Ki	6:32	But Elisha sat in his **h**, and the	1004
2Ki	8:5	cried to the king for her **h** and for	1004
2Ki	9:8	the whole **h** of Ahab shall perish:	1004
2Ki	10:21	and the **h** of Baal was full from.	1004
2Ki	10:27	and brake down the **h** of Baal,	1004
2Ki	11:3	hid in the **h** of the Lord six years	1004
2Ki	11:15	not be slain in the **h** of the Lord.	1004
2Ki	12:7	repair ye not the breaches of the **h**?	1004
2Ki	14:14	were found in the **h** of the Lord	1004
2Ki	15:25	in the palace of the king's **h**, with	1004
2Ki	16:8	gold that was found in the **h** of.	1004
2Ki	18:15	in the treasures of the king's **h**	1004
2Ki	19:14	went up into the **h** of the Lord,	1004
2Ki	19:37	worshipping in the **h** of Nisroch.	1004
2Ki	20:1	Set thine **h** in order; for thou shalt.	1004
2Ki	20:15	What have they seen in thine **h**?	1004
2Ki	20:17	that all that is in thine **h**, and that	1004
2Ki	21:5	the two courts of the **h** of the Lord.	1004
2Ki	21:18	buried in the garden of his own **h**,	1004
2Ki	21:23	and slew the king in his own **h**	1004
2Ki	22:5	to repair the breaches of the **h**,	1004
2Ki	22:8	found the book of the law in the **h**.	1004
2Ki	23:2	king went up into the **h** of the Lord,	1004
2Ki	23:7	that were by the **h** of the Lord,	1004
2Ki	23:11	entering in of the **h** of the Lord,	1004
2Ki	23:12	the two courts of the **h** of the Lord,	1004
2Ki	24:13	the treasures of the **h** of the Lord,	1004
2Ki	25:9	the **h** of the Lord, and the king's **h**,	1004
1Ch	9:27	lodged round about the **h** of God,	1004
1Ch	10:6	sons, and all his **h** died together	1004
1Ch	10:10	his armour in the **h** of their gods,	1004
1Ch	17:4	Thou shalt not build me an **h** to.	1004
1Ch	17:16	I, O Lord God, and what is mine **h**,	1004
1Ch	21:17	be on me, and on my father's **h**;	1004
1Ch	22:5	the **h** that is to be builded for the	1004
1Ch	22:7	it was in my mind to build an **h**	1004
1Ch	22:14	I have prepared for the **h** of the	1004
1Ch	25:6	for the service of the **h** of God,	1004
1Ch	26:27	to maintain the **h** of the Lord.	1004
1Ch	28:20	for the service of the **h** of the Lord.	1004
1Ch	29:3	my affection to the **h** of my God,	1004
2Ch	2:4	build an **h** to the name of the Lord	1004
2Ch	2:5	And the **h** which I build is great:	1004
2Ch	2:6	But who is able to build him an **h**,	1004
2Ch	5:13	**h** was filled with a cloud, even the **h**	1004
2Ch	5:14	glory of the Lord had filled the **h** of.	1004
2Ch	6:5	the tribes of Israel to build an **h** in,	1004
2Ch	6:18	how much less this **h** which I have.	1004
2Ch	6:24	supplication before thee in this **h**;	1004
2Ch	6:32	if they come and pray in this **h**;	1004
2Ch	7:2	priests could not enter into the **h**	1004
2Ch	7:3	the glory of the Lord upon the **h**,	1004
2Ch	7:5	the people dedicated the **h** of God	1004
2Ch	7:12	place to myself for an **h** of sacrifice.	1004
2Ch	7:16	have I chosen and sanctified this **h**,	1004
2Ch	7:20	and this **h**, which I have sanctified	1004
2Ch	7:21	unto this land, and unto this **h**?	1004
2Ch	8:11	My wife shall not dwell in the **h** of.	1004
2Ch	8:16	So the **h** of the Lord was perfected.	1004
2Ch	9:16	in the **h** of the forest of Lebanon.	1004
2Ch	9:20	of the **h** of the forest of Lebanon	1004
2Ch	10:16	and now, David, see to thine own **h**.	1004
2Ch	10:19	rebelled against the **h** of David	1004
2Ch	12:9	the treasures of the **h** of the Lord,	1004
2Ch	15:18	he brought into the **h** of God the	1004
2Ch	16:2	**h** of the Lord, and of the king's **h**,	1004
2Ch	16:10	seer, and put him in a prison **h**;	1004
2Ch	21:7	would not destroy the **h** of David,	1004
2Ch	21:13	slain thy brethren of thy father's **h**,	1004
2Ch	21:17	that was found in the king's **h**,	1004
2Ch	22:7	anointed to cut off the **h** of Ahab	1004
2Ch	22:9	So the **h** of Ahaziah had no power	1004
2Ch	22:10	all the seed royal of the **h** of Judah	1004
2Ch	22:12	them hid in the **h** of God six years:	1004
2Ch	23:6	none come into the **h** of the Lord,	1004
2Ch	23:7	cometh into the **h**, he shall be put	1004
2Ch	23:14	Slay her not in the **h** of the Lord.	1004
2Ch	24:4	minded to repair the **h** of the Lord.	1004
2Ch	24:7	had broken up the **h** of God; and	1004
2Ch	24:12	to repair the **h** of the Lord,	1004
2Ch	24:12	brass to mend the **h** of the Lord.	1004
2Ch	24:14	burnt offerings in the **h** of the Lord	1004
2Ch	24:18	And they left the **h** of the Lord God.	1004
2Ch	24:27	and the repairing of the **h** of God,	1004
2Ch	25:24	that were found in the **h** of God	1004
2Ch	26:19	before the priests in the **h** of the	1004
2Ch	26:21	was cut off from the **h** of the Lord:	1004
2Ch	28:21	a portion out of the **h** of the Lord,	1004
2Ch	28:24	up the doors of the **h** of the Lord,	1004
2Ch	29:3	the doors of the **h** of the Lord,	1004
2Ch	29:18	We have cleansed all the **h** of the	1004
2Ch	29:35	the service of the **h** of the Lord was	1004
2Ch	30:1	should come to the **h** of the Lord	1004
2Ch	31:21	began in the service of the **h** of God,	1004
2Ch	32:21	he was come into the **h** of his god,	1004
2Ch	33:4	he build altars in the **h** of the Lord,	1004
2Ch	33:5	the two courts of the **h** of the Lord	1004
2Ch	33:7	idol … he had made, in the **h** of God,	1004
2Ch	33:15	the idol out of the **h** of the Lord,	1004
2Ch	33:24	him, and slew him in his own **h**	1004
2Ch	34:8	to repair the **h** of the Lord his God.	1004
2Ch	34:15	book of the law in the **h** of the Lord.	1004
2Ch	34:17	money that was found in the **h** of	1004
2Ch	35:3	Put the holy ark in the **h** which	1004
2Ch	36:14	polluted the **h** of the Lord which	1004
2Ch	36:17	sword in the **h** of their sanctuary,	1004
2Ch	36:18	all the vessels of the **h** of God,	1004
2Ch	36:18	the treasures of the **h** of the Lord,	1004
2Ch	36:19	And they burnt the **h** of God, and	1004
Ezr	1:2	charged me to build him an **h** at	1004
Ezr	1:3	and build the **h** of the Lord God of	1004
Ezr	1:4	freewill offering for the **h** of God	1004
Ezr	1:7	the vessels of the **h** of the Lord,	1004
Ezr	2:68	offered freely for the **h** of God	1004
Ezr	3:11	foundation of the **h** of the Lord was	1004
Ezr	3:12	men, that had seen the first **h**,	1004
Ezr	4:24	ceased the work of the **h** of God.	1005
Ezr	5:2	and began to build the **h** of God	1005
Ezr	5:3	commanded you to build this **h**,	1005
Ezr	5:11	and build the **h** that was builded	1005
Ezr	5:13	a decree to build this **h** of God.	1005
Ezr	5:15	let the **h** of God be builded in his.	1005
Ezr	5:16	laid the foundation of the **h** of God.	1005

Ezr	5:17	to build this **h** of God at Jerusalem,	1005
Ezr	6:3	a decree concerning the **h** of God.	1005
Ezr	6:3	Let the **h** be builded, the place	1005
Ezr	6:7	Let the work of this **h** of God alone;	1005
Ezr	6:11	and let his **h** be made a dunghill.	1005
Ezr	6:12	alter and to destroy this **h** of God.	1005
Ezr	7:16	willingly for the **h** of their God,	1005
Ezr	7:20	be needful for the **h** of thy God,	1005
Ezr	9:9	reviving, to set up the **h** of our God,	1004
Ezr	10:1	himself down before the **h** of God,	1004
Ezr	10:9	sat in the street of the **h** of God,	1004
Ne	1:6	I and my father's **h** have sinned.	1004
Ne	6:10	us meet together in the **h** of God,.	1004
Ne	10:38	of the tithes unto the **h** of our God,	1004
Ne	10:39	will not forsake the **h** of our God.	1004
Ne	13:11	Why is the **h** of God forsaken?	1004
Ne	13:14	I have done for the **h** of my God,	1004
Est	1:22	man should bear rule in his own **h**,	1004
Est	2:9	best place of the **h** of the women.	1004
Est	4:13	thou shalt escape in the king's **h**,	1004
Est	4:14	thy father's **h** shall be destroyed:	1004
Est	5:1	upon his royal throne in the royal **h**,	1004
Est	7:8	the queen also before me in the **h**?	1004
Est	8:1	give the **h** of Haman the Jews'.	1004
Est	8:2	set Mordecai over the **h** of Haman.	1004
Est	8:7	have given Esther the **h** of Haman,	1004
Est	9:4	Mordecai was great in the king's **h**	1004
Job	1:10	hedge about him, and about his **h**,	1004
Job	1:13	wine in their eldest brother's **h**:	1004
Job	1:18	wine in their eldest brother's **h**:	1004
Ps	23:6	dwell in the **h** of the Lord for ever	1004
Ps	27:4	I may dwell in the **h** of the Lord all	1004
Ps	42:4	I went with them to the **h** of God,	1004
Ps	66:13	I will go into thy **h** with burnt	1004
Ps	69:9	the zeal of thine **h** hath eaten me	1004
Ps	84:3	the sparrow hath found an **h**, and	1004
Ps	84:10	a doorkeeper in the **h** of my God,	1004
Ps	93:5	holiness becometh thine **h**, O Lord,	1004
Ps	101:2	walk within my **h** with a perfect	1004
Ps	101:7	deceit shall not dwell within my **h**:	1004
Ps	112:3	Wealth and riches shall be in his **h**:	1004
Ps	122:1	Let us go into the **h** of the Lord.	1004
Ps	127:1	Except the Lord build the **h**, they	1004
Pr	2:18	For her **h** inclineth unto death,	1004
Pr	3:33	curse of the Lord is in the **h**	1004
Pr	5:8	come not nigh the door of her **h**:	1004
Pr	6:31	give all the substance of his **h**	1004
Pr	7:8	he went the way to her **h**, and	1004
Pr	7:27	Her **h** is the way to hell, going	1004
Pr	9:1	Wisdom hath builded her **h**, she	1004
Pr	11:29	He that troubleth his own **h** shall	1004
Pr	12:7	the **h** of the righteous shall stand.	1004
Pr	14:1	wise woman buildeth her **h**: but	1004
Pr	14:11	The **h** of the wicked shall be	1004
Pr	15:6	In the **h** of the righteous is much	1004
Pr	15:25	will destroy the **h** of the proud:	1004
Pr	15:27	greedy of gain troubleth his own **h**;	1004
Pr	17:1	than an **h** full of sacrifices with	1004
Pr	17:13	evil shall not depart from his **h**.	1004
Pr	21:9	a brawling woman in a wide **h**	1004
Pr	21:12	considereth the **h** of the wicked:	1004
Pr	24:3	Through wisdom is an **h** builded;	1004
Pr	24:27	and afterwards build thine **h**.	1004
Pr	25:17	thy foot from thy neighbour's **h**;	1004
Pr	25:24	brawling woman and in a wide **h**	1004
Pr	27:10	neither go into thy brother's **h** in	1004
Ecc	2:7	and had servants born in my **h**;	1004
Ecc	5:1	when thou goest to the **h** of God,	1004
Ecc	7:2	better to go to the **h** of mourning,	1004
Ecc	7:2	than to go to the **h** of feasting:	1004
Ecc	7:4	the wise is in the **h** of mourning;	1004
Ecc	7:4	heart of fools is in the **h** of mirth	1004
Ecc	10:18	of the hands the **h** droppeth	1004
Ecc	12:3	the keepers of the **h** shall tremble,	1004
SS	2:4	brought me to the banqueting **h**,	1004
SS	8:7	all the substance of his **h** for love	1004
Isa	2:2	the mountain of the Lord's **h** shall	1004
Isa	2:5	O **h** of Jacob, come ye, and let us	1004
Isa	5:8	Woe unto them that join **h** to **h**	1004
Isa	6:4	and the **h** was filled with smoke.	1004
Isa	8:17	hideth his face from the **h** of Jacob,	1004
Isa	22:22	the key of the **h** of David will I lay	1004
Isa	22:23	a glorious throne to his father's **h**.	1004
Isa	24:10	every **h** is shut up, that no man	1004
Isa	31:2	arise against the **h** of the evildoers,	1004
Isa	37:14	went up unto the **h** of the Lord,	1004
Isa	37:38	worshipping in the **h** of Nisroch.	1004
Isa	38:1	Set thine **h** in order for thou shalt	1004
Isa	39:4	What have they seen in thy **h**? And	1004
Isa	39:4	All that is in mine **h** have they	1004
Isa	39:6	all that is in thine **h**, and that	1004
Isa	42:7	in darkness out of the prison **h**.	1004
Isa	56:7	mine **h** shall be called an **h** of	1004
Isa	58:1	and the **h** of Jacob their sins.	1004
Isa	64:11	Our holy and our beautiful **h**,	1004
Isa	66:1	where is the **h** that ye build unto	1004
Jer	2:26	so is the **h** of Israel ashamed; they,	1004
Jer	5:11	the **h** of Israel and the **h** of Judah.	1004
Jer	7:2	Stand in the gate of the Lord's **h**,	1004
Jer	7:11	Is this **h**, which is called by my	1004
Jer	9:26	**h** of Israel are uncircumcised in	1004
Jer	11:10	the **h** of Israel and the **h** of Judah.	1004
Jer	11:15	hath my beloved to do in mine **h**,	1004
Jer	11:17	**h** of Israel and of the **h** of Judah,	1004
Jer	12:7	I have forsaken mine **h**, I have left	1004
Jer	16:5	enter not into the **h** of mourning,	1004
Jer	18:2	go down to the potter's **h**, and	1004
Jer	18:6	are ye in mine hand, O **h** of Israel	1004
Jer	20:6	all that dwell in thine **h** shall go	1004
Jer	26:12	to prophesy against this **h** and	1004
Jer	27:18	which are left in the **h** of the Lord,	1004
Jer	28:3	place all the vessels of the Lord's **h**	1004
Jer	31:31	new covenant with the **h** of Israel,	1004
Jer	32:34	set their abominations in the **h**,	1004
Jer	33:17	upon the throne of the **h** of Israel;	1004
Jer	36:6	in the Lord's **h** upon the fasting	1004
Jer	36:8	words of the Lord in the Lord's **h**,	1004
Jer	37:15	in prison in the **h** of Jonathan the	1004
Jer	37:17	king asked him secretly in his **h**,	1004
Jer	38:14	the third entry that is in the **h** of	1004
Jer	38:17	and thou shalt live, and thine **h**:	1004
Jer	39:8	Chaldeans burned the king's **h**	1004
Jer	52:13	the **h** of the Lord, and the king's **h**;	1004
Jer	52:17	sea that was in the **h** of the Lord,	1004
La	2:7	made a noise in the **h** of the Lord,	1004
Eze	2:5	for they are a rebellious **h**, yet	1004
Eze	2:8	rebellious like that rebellious **h**:	1004
Eze	3:5	language, but to the **h** of Israel;	1004
Eze	3:7	the **h** of Israel will not hearken	1004
Eze	3:17	a watchman unto the **h** of Israel:	1004
Eze	4:3	shall be a sign to the **h** of Israel.	1004
Eze	4:6	the iniquity of the **h** of Judah forty	1004

Eze	6:11	abominations of the **h** of Israel!	1004
Eze	8:6	that the **h** of Israel committeth	1004
Eze	8:10	and all the idols of the **h** of Israel,	1004
Eze	8:17	Is it a light thing to the **h** of Judah	1004
Eze	9:7	Defile the **h**, and fill the courts	1004
Eze	10:4	the **h** was filled with the cloud,	1004
Eze	12:2	in the midst of a rebellious **h**,	1004
Eze	12:6	thee for a sign unto the **h** of Israel	1004
Eze	12:24	divination within the **h** of Israel.	1004
Eze	14:4	Every man of the **h** of Israel that	1004
Eze	14:7	every one of the **h** of Israel, or of	1004
Eze	17:2	a parable unto the **h** of Israel;	1004
Eze	18:29	O **h** of Israel, are not my ways.	1004
Eze	18:30	I will judge you, O **h** of Israel,.	1004
Eze	18:31	for why will ye die, O **h** of Israel?	1004
Eze	20:13	the **h** of Israel rebelled against me	1004
Eze	20:31	enquired of by you, O **h** of Israel?	1004
Eze	24:3	a parable unto the rebellious **h**,	1004
Eze	33:7	watchman unto the **h** of Israel;	1004
Eze	33:11	for why will ye die, O **h** of Israel?	1004
Eze	33:20	O ye **h** of Israel, I will judge you	1004
Eze	36:37	be enquired of by the **h** of Israel.	1004
Eze	37:11	bones are the whole **h** of Israel:	1004
Eze	39:23	the **h** of Israel went into captivity	1004
Eze	39:25	mercy upon the whole **h** of Israel,	1004
Eze	39:29	out of my spirit upon the **h** of Israel,	1004
Eze	43:4	glory of the Lord came into the **h**,	1004
Eze	43:5	the glory of the Lord filled the **h**,	1004
Eze	43:10	shew the **h** to the **h** of Israel, that	1004
Eze	43:12	Behold, this is the law of the **h**	1004
Eze	44:4	the Lord filled the **h** of the Lord:	1004
Eze	44:5	mark well the entering in of the **h**,	1004
Eze	44:7	sanctuary, to pollute it, even my **h**,	1004
Eze	45:17	reconciliation for the **h** of Israel.	1004
Eze	48:21	the sanctuary of the **h** shall be in	1004
Da	1:2	part of the vessels of the **h** of God:	1004
Da	1:2	into the treasure **h** of his god.	1004
Da	4:30	built for the **h** of the kingdom	1005
Da	5:3	out of the temple of the **h** of God	1005
Da	5:23	brought the vessels of his **h** before	1005
Da	6:10	was signed, he went into his **h**;	1005
Hos	1:7	have mercy upon the **h** of Judah,	1004
Hos	6:10	horrible thing in the **h** of Israel:	1004
Hos	8:1	an eagle against the **h** of the Lord,	1004
Hos	9:15	I will drive them out of mine **h**,	1004
Hos	11:12	and the **h** of Israel with deceit:	1004
Joel	1:16	gladness from the **h** of our God?	1004
Am	2:8	condemned in the **h** of their god.	1004
Am	5:1	even a lamentation, O **h** of Israel.	1004
Am	5:25	forty years, O **h** of Israel?	1004
Am	6:10	to bring out the bones out of the **h**,	1004
Am	7:10	thee in the midst of the **h** of Israel:	1004
Am	9:8	not utterly destroy the **h** of Jacob,	1004
Ob	18	And the **h** of Jacob shall be a fire,	1004
Mic	1:5	and for the sins of the **h** of Israel,	1004
Mic	3:1	and ye princes of the **h** of Israel;	1004
Mic	7:6	enemies are the men of his own **h**	1004
Hab	2:9	an evil covetousness to his **h**,	1004
Zep	2:7	for the remnant of the **h** of Judah;	1004
Hag	1:2	that the Lord's **h** should be built.	1004
Hag	1:4	cieled houses, and this **h** lie waste?	1004
Hag	1:9	Because of mine **h** that is waste,	1004
Hag	2:3	saw this **h** in her first glory	1004
Hag	2:7	and I will fill this **h** with glory,	1004
Hag	2:9	The glory of this latter **h** shall be	1004
Zec	3:7	then thou shalt also judge my **h**,	1004
Zec	5:4	shall enter into the **h** of the thief,	1004
Zec	5:4	the **h** of him that sweareth falsely	1004
Zec	8:19	to the **h** of Judah joy and gladness,	1004
Zec	9:8	And I will encamp about mine **h**	1004
Zec	10:6	I will strengthen the **h** of Judah,	1004
Zec	10:6	and I will save the **h** of Joseph,	1004
Zec	12:8	and the **h** of David shall be as God,	1004
Zec	12:10	I will pour upon the **h** of David,	1004
Zec	13:1	fountain opened to the **h** of David.	1004
Zec	13:6	wounded in the **h** of my friends.	1004
Mt	7:24	which build his **h** upon a rock:	*3614*
Mt	7:26	which built his **h** upon the sand:	*3614*
Mt	10:6	the lost sheep of the **h** of Israel.	*3624*
Mt	10:13	And if the **h** be worthy, let your	*3614*
Mt	12:4	How he entered into the **h** of God,	*3624*
Mt	12:25	city or **h** divided against itself.	*3614*
Mt	12:29	one enter into a strong man's **h**	*3614*
Mt	15:24	the lost sheep of the **h** of Israel.	*3624*
Mt	20:11	against the goodman of the **h**.	*3617*
Mt	21:13	My **h** shall be called the **h** of.	*3624*
Mt	23:38	your **h** is left unto you desolate	*3624*
Mt	24:17	to take any thing out of his **h**:	*3614*
Mt	24:43	goodman of the **h** had known in	*3617*
Mt	24:43	suffered his **h** to be broken up.	*3614*
Mt	26:18	I will keep the passover at thy **h**	
Mk	3:25	if a **h** be divided against itself,	*3614*
Mk	3:27	can enter into a strong man's **h**,	*3614*
Mk	3:27	man; and then he will spoil his **h**	*3614*
Mk	10:29	There is no man that hath left **h**,	*3614*
Mk	11:17	not written, My **h** shall be called	*3624*
Mk	11:17	of all nations the **h** of prayer?	*3624*
Mk	13:35	when the master of the **h** cometh,	*3614*
Mk	14:14	say ye to the goodman of the **h**,	*3617*
Lk	2:4	was of the **h** and lineage of David:	*3624*
Lk	6:4	How he went into the **h** of God,	*3624*
Lk	6:48	He is like a man which built an **h**.	*3614*
Lk	6:48	beat vehemently upon that **h**,	*3614*
Lk	6:49	built an **h** upon the earth; against.	*3614*
Lk	6:49	and the ruin of that **h** was great.	*3614*
Lk	7:44	I entered into thine **h**, thou gavest	*3614*
Lk	8:39	Return to thine own **h**, and shew	*3624*
Lk	8:49	from the ruler of the synagogue's **h**,	
Lk	10:5	first say, Peace be to this **h**.	*3624*
Lk	10:7	of his hire. Go not from **h** to **h**	*3614*
Lk	11:17	a **h** divided against a **h** falleth.	*3624*
Lk	12:39	the goodman of the **h** had known	*3617*
Lk	12:52	there shall be five in one **h**.	*3624*
Lk	13:35	your **h** is left unto you desolate:	*3624*
Lk	14:21	the master of the **h** being angry	*3617*
Lk	15:8	sweep the **h**, and seek diligently	*3614*
Lk	17:31	housetop, and his stuff in the **h**,	*3614*
Lk	18:14	man went down to his **h** justified.	*3624*
Lk	18:29	no man that hath left **h**, or	*3614*
Lk	19:5	for to day I must abide at thy **h**	*3624*
Lk	19:9	day is salvation come to this **h**,	*3624*
Lk	19:46	written, My **h** is the **h** of prayer:	*3624*
Lk	22:11	say unto the goodman of the **h**,	*3614*
Jn	2:16	Father's **h** an **h** of merchandise	*3624*
Jn	2:17	zeal of thine **h** hath eaten me up.	*3624*
Jn	4:53	himself believed, and his whole **h**.	*3614*
Jn	8:35	abideth not in the **h** for ever:	*3614*
Jn	11:20	him: but Mary sat still in the **h**	*3624*
Jn	14:2	my Father's **h** are many mansions:	*3614*
Ac	2:36	let all the **h** of Israel know	*3624*
Ac	2:46	breaking bread from **h** to **h**,	*3624*
Ac	5:42	in the temple, and in every **h**,	*3624*

Ac	7:47	But Solomon built him an **h**	*3624*
Ac	7:49	what **h** will ye build me? saith	*3624*
Ac	9:11	**enquire in the h of Judas for one**	*3614*
Ac	10:2	one that feared God with all his **h**,	*3624*
Ac	11:13	how he had seen an angel in his **h**,	*3624*
Ac	11:14	thou and all thy **h** shall be saved.	*3624*
Ac	16:31	and thou shalt be saved, and thy **h**	*3624*
Ac	16:34	believing in God with all his **h**	*3832*
Ac	18:7	**h** joined hard to the synagogue.	*3614*
Ac	18:8	believed on the Lord with all his **h**;	*3624*
Ac	19:16	they fled out of the **h** naked and	*3624*
Ac	20:20	you publickly, and from **h** to **h**,	*3624*
Ac	28:30	whole years in his own hired **h**,	
2Co	5:1	we know that if our earthly **h** of	*3614*
2Co	5:1	an **h** not made with hands, eternal	*3614*
2Co	5:2	with our **h** which is from heaven:	*3613*
1Ti	3:4	One that ruleth well his own **h**,	*3624*
1Ti	3:5	know not how to rule his own **h**,	*3624*
1Ti	3:15	to behave thyself in the **h** of God,	*3624*
1Ti	5:8	specially for those of his own **h**.	*3609*
1Ti	5:13	wandering about from **h** to **h**;	*3614*
1Ti	5:14	bear children, guide the **h**, give	*3616*
2Ti	2:20	But in a great **h** there are not only	*3614*
Heb	3:2	also Moses was faithful in all his **h**	*3624*
Heb	3:3	hath more honour than the **h**	*3624*
Heb	3:4	every **h** is builded by some man;	*3624*
Heb	3:5	verily was faithful in all his **h**	*3624*
Heb	3:6	But Christ, as a son over his own **h**;	*3624*
Heb	3:6	whose **h** are we, if we hold fast the	*3624*
Heb	8:8	**h** of Israel and with the **h** of Judah:	*3624*
Heb	8:10	I will make with the **h** of Israel	*3624*
Heb	11:7	an ark to the saving of his **h**;	*3624*
1Pe	2:5	stones, are built up a spiritual **h**,	*3624*
1Pe	4:17	must begin at the **h** of God:	*3624*
2Jn	10	receive him not into your **h**,	*3614*

HOUSEHOLD

Ge	31:37	hast thou found of all thy **h** stuff?	1004
Ge	45:11	lest thou, and thy **h**, and all that	1004
Ge	47:12	and all his father's **h**, with bread,	1004
Ex	12:4	if the **h** be too little for the lamb,	1004
Dt	6:22	upon Pharaoh, and upon all his **h**,	1004
Jos	6:25	harlot alive, and her father's **h**,	1004
Jgs	6:27	because he feared his father's **h**,	1004
1Sa	25:17	our master, and against all his **h**:	1004
2Sa	6:11	blessed Obed-edom, and all his **h**.	1004
2Sa	17:23	put his **h** in order, and hanged	1004
2Ki	7:9	we may go and tell the king's **h**.	1004
Ne	13:8	I cast forth all the **h** stuff of Tobiah	1004
Job	1:3	she asses, and a very great **h**;	5657
Pr	31:21	not afraid of the snow for her **h**:	1004
Pr	31:21	for all her **h** are clothed with scarlet.	1004
Pr	31:27	looketh well to the ways of her **h**,	1004
Mt	10:25	**shall they call them of his h?**	*3615*
Mt	10:36	**foes shall be they of his own h**	*3615*
Mt	24:45	**lord hath made ruler over his h,**	*2322*
Lk	12:42	**lord shall make ruler over his h,**	*2322*
Ac	16:15	when she was baptized, and her **h**,	*3624*
1Co	1:16	baptized also the **h** of Stephanas:	*3624*
Gal	6:10	unto them who are of the **h** of faith.	*3609*
Eph	2:19	with the saints, and of the **h** of God;	*3609*
Php	4:22	chiefly they that are of Caesar's **h**	*3614*

HOUSEHOLDER

Mt	13:52	**is like unto a man that is an h,**	*3617*
Mt	20:1	**is like unto a man that is an h,**	*3617*
Mt	21:33	**was a certain h, which planted a**	*3617*

HOUSEHOLDS

Ge	42:33	food for the famine of your **h**,	1004
Ge	45:18	take your father and your **h**, and	1004
Ge	47:24	your food, and for them of your **h**,	1004
Dt	11:6	swallowed them up, and their **h**,	1004
Jos	7:14	Lord shall take shall come by **h**;	1004

HOUSES

Ex	1:21	feared God, that he made them **h**.	1004
Ex	6:14	be the heads of their fathers' **h**:	1004
Ex	8:21	**h** of the Egyptians shall be full of	1004
Ex	10:6	And they shall fill thy **h**, and the	1004
Ex	12:7	on the upper door post of the **h**,	1004
Ex	12:13	for a token upon the **h** where ye are:	1004
Ex	12:19	be no leaven found in your **h**: for	1004
Ex	12:23	destroyer to come in unto your **h** to	1004
Ex	12:27	over the **h** of the children of Israel	1004
Nu	16:32	swallowed them up, and their **h**,	1004
Nu	32:18	We will not return unto our **h**, until	1004
Dt	6:11	and **h** full of all good things, which	1004
Dt	8:12	and hast built goodly **h**, and dwelt	1004
1Ki	9:10	Solomon had built the two **h**, the	1004
2Ki	17:29	put them in the **h** of the high places	1004
2Ki	23:7	brake down the **h** of the sodomites,	1004
2Ki	25:9	and all the **h** of Jerusalem, and	1004
1Ch	29:4	to overlay the walls of the **h** withal:	1004
Ne	5:3	our lands, vineyards, and **h**, that	1004
Ne	7:4	therein, and the **h** were not builded	1004
Ne	9:25	and possessed **h** full of all goods,	1004
Job	1:4	sons went and feasted in their **h**,	1004
Ps	49:11	that their **h** shall continue for ever,	1004
Ps	83:12	us take to ourselves the **h** of God	4999
Pr	1:13	we shall fill our **h** with spoil:	1004
Pr	30:26	yet make they their **h** in the rocks;	1004
Ecc	2:4	I builded me **h**; I planted me	1004
Isa	3:14	the spoil of the poor is in your **h**	1004
Isa	5:9	a truth many **h** shall be desolate,	1004
Isa	6:11	and the **h** without man, and the	1004
Isa	8:14	of offence to both the **h** of Israel,	1004
Isa	13:16	their **h** shall be spoiled, and their	1004
Isa	13:21	and their **h** shall be full of doleful	1004
Isa	22:10	**h** have ye broken down to fortify	1004
Jer	5:7	by troops in the harlots' **h**	1004
Jer	5:27	birds, so are their **h** full of deceit:	1004
Jer	6:12	their **h** shall be turned unto others,	1004
Jer	29:28	build ye **h**, and dwell in them; and	1004
Jer	32:29	on this city, and burn it with the **h**,	1004
Jer	39:8	and the **h** of the people, with fire,	1004
Jer	43:12	fire in the **h** of the gods of Egypt;	1004
La	5:2	turned to strangers, our **h** to aliens.	1004
Eze	7:24	and they shall possess their **h**:	1004
Eze	11:3	say, It is not near; let us build **h**:	1004
Eze	16:41	they shall burn thine **h** with fire,	1004
Eze	26:12	walls and destroy thy pleasant **h**:	1004
Da	2:5	your **h** shall be made a dunghill.	1005
Da	3:29	their **h** shall be made a dunghill:	1005
Joel	2:9	they shall climb up upon the **h**;	1004
Am	3:15	and the **h** of ivory shall perish, and	1004
Mic	2:9	cast out from their pleasant **h**;	1004
Zep	1:9	fill their master's **h** with violence	1004
Hag	1:4	to dwell in your cieled **h**, and this.	1004
Mt	11:8	**wear soft clothing are in kings' h**	*3624*
Mt	19:29	**that hath forsaken h, or brethren,**	*3614*
Mt	23:14	**ye devour widows' h, and for a**	*3614*
Mk	8:3	**away fasting to their own h, they**	*3624*
Mk	12:40	**Which devour widows h, and**	*3614*

Lk	20:47	**Which devour widows' h, and for**	*3614*
Ac	4:34	possessors of lands or **h** sold them,	*3614*
1Co	11:22	ye not **h** to eat and to drink in?	*3614*
1Ti	3:12	their children and their own **h** well	*3624*
2Ti	3:6	sort are they which creep into **h**,	*3614*
Tit	1:11	who subvert whole **h**, teaching	*3624*

HOUSETOP See also HOUSE and TOP.

Pr	21:9	better to dwell in a corner of the **h**,	1406
Pr	25:24	better to dwell in the corner of the **h**,	1406
Mt	24:17	**Let him which is on the h not**	*1430*
Mk	13:15	**him that is on the h not go down**	*1430*
Lk	17:31	**he which shall be upon the h, and**	*1430*
Ac	10:9	Peter went up upon the **h** to pray	*1430*

HOUSETOPS

Ps	129:6	them be as the grass upon the **h**,	1406
Zep	1:5	the host of heaven upon the **h**;	*1406*
Mt	10:27	**the ear, that preach ye upon the h**	*1430*
Lk	12:3	**shall be proclaimed upon the h**	*1430*

HOWL

Isa	13:6	**H** ye; for the day of the Lord	3213
Isa	15:3	every one shall **h**, weeping	3213
Isa	23:14	**H**, ye ships of Tarshish, for your	3213
Isa	52:5	rule over them make them to **h**,	3213
Isa	65:14	and shall **h** for vexation of spirit	3213
Jer	4:8	you with sackcloth, lament and **h**:	3213
Jer	25:34	**H**, ye shepherds, and cry; and	3213
Jer	47:2	the inhabitants of the land shall **h**	3213
Jer	48:39	They shall **h**, saying, How is it	3213
Jer	51:8	fallen and destroyed: **h** for her:	3213
Eze	21:12	Cry and **h**, son of man: for it	3213
Eze	30:2	Thus saith the Lord God; **H** ye,	3213
Joel	1:5	and **h**, all ye drinkers of wine,	3213
Joel	1:13	**h**, ye ministers of the altar; come	3213
Mic	1:8	I will wail and **h**, I will go stripped	3213
Jas	5:1	weep and **h** for your miseries that	*3649*

HOWLED

Hos	7:14	when they **h** upon their beds:	3213

HOWLING

Dt	32:10	and in the waste **h** wilderness; he	3214
Jer	25:36	an **h** of the principal of the flock,	3213
Zec	11:3	voice of the **h** of the shepherds;	3213

HUMBLE

Ex	10:3	long wilt thou refuse to **h** thyself	6031
Dt	8:2	to **h** thee, and to prove thee,	6031
Dt	8:16	that he might **h** thee, and that he	6031
Jgs	19:24	and **h** ye them, and do with them	6031
2Ch	7:14	If my people, … shall **h** themselves,	3665
2Ch	34:27	thou didst **h** thyself before God,	3665
Ps	9:12	he forgetteth not the cry of the **h**	6041
Ps	10:12	up thine hand: forget not the **h**.	6041
Ps	10:17	hast heard the desire of the **h**:	6041
Ps	34:2	**h** shall hear thereof, and be glad	6041
Ps	69:32	The **h** shall see this, and be glad	6041
Pr	6:3	go, **h** thyself, and make sure thy	7511
Pr	16:19	Better it is to be of an **h** spirit	8213
Pr	29:23	but honour shall uphold the **h** in	8217
Isa	57:15	that is of a contrite and **h** spirit,	8217
Isa	57:15	to revive the spirit of the **h**, and	8217
Jer	13:18	the queen, **H** yourselves, sit down:	8213
Mt	18:4	**h** himself as this little child	*5013*
Mt	23:12	**and he that shall h himself shall**	*5013*
2Co	12:21	my God will **h** me among you,	*5013*
Jas	4:6	but giveth grace unto the **h**	*5011*
Jas	4:10	**H** yourselves in the sight of the	*5013*
1Pe	5:5	proud, and giveth grace to the **h**.	*5011*
1Pe	5:6	**H** yourselves therefore under	*5013*

HUMBLED

Le	26:41	their uncircumcised hearts be **h**,	3665
Dt	8:3	And he **h** thee, and suffered thee	6031
Dt	21:14	her, because thou hast **h** her	6031
Dt	22:24	he hath **h** his neighbour's wife:	6031
Dt	22:29	because he hath **h** her, he may not	6031
2Ki	22:19	and thou hast **h** thyself before	3665
2Ch	12:6	Israel and the king **h** themselves;	3665
2Ch	12:7	Lord saw that they **h** themselves,	3665
2Ch	12:12	And when he **h** himself, the wrath	3665
2Ch	32:26	Hezekiah **h** himself for the pride	3665
2Ch	33:12	and **h** himself greatly before the	3665
2Ch	33:19	graven images, before he was **h**:	3665
2Ch	33:23	And **h** not himself before the Lord,	3665
2Ch	33:23	Manasseh his father had **h** himself;	3665
2Ch	36:12	**h** not himself before Jeremiah	3665
Ps	35:13	I **h** my soul with fasting; and	6031
Isa	2:11	The lofty looks of man shall be **h**,	8213
Isa	5:15	and the mighty man shall be **h**,	8213
Isa	5:15	the eyes of the lofty shall be **h**:	8213
Isa	10:33	down, and the haughty shall be **h**.	8213
Jer	44:10	They are not **h** even unto this	1792
La	3:20	remembrances, and is **h** in me	7743
Eze	22:10	thee have they **h** her that was set	6031
Eze	22:11	another in thee hath **h** his sister,	6031
Da	5:22	Belshazzar, hast not **h** thine heart,	8214
Php	2:8	he **h** himself, and became obedient	*5013*

HUMBLENESS

Col	3:12	kindness, **h** of mind, meekness,	*5012*

HUMBLETH

1Ki	21:29	how Ahab **h** himself before me?	3665
1Ki	21:29	because he **h** himself before me,	3665
Ps	10:10	He croucheth, and **h** himself,	7817
Ps	113:6	Who **h** himself to behold the	8213
Isa	2:9	and the great man **h** himself:	8213
Lk	14:11	**that h himself shall be exalted**	*5013*
Lk	18:14	**that h himself shall be exalted**	*5013*

HUMBLY

2Sa	16:4	I **h** beseech thee that I may find	7812
Mic	6:8	love mercy, and to walk **h** with	6800

HUMILIATION

Ac	8:33	In his **h** his judgment was taken	*5014*

HUMILITY

Pr	15:33	wisdom; and before honour is **h**.	6038
Pr	18:12	haughty, and before honour is **h**.	6038
Pr	22:4	By **h** and the fear of the Lord are	6038
Ac	20:19	Serving the Lord with all **h** of	*5012*
Col	2:18	your reward in a voluntary **h** and	*5012*
Col	2:23	and **h**, and neglecting of the body;	*5012*
1Pe	5:5	clothed with **h**: for God resisteth	*5012*

HUNDRED

Ge	6:3	his days shall be an **h** and twenty	3967
Ge	6:15	of the ark shall be three **h** cubits,	3967
Ge	7:24	upon the earth an **h** and fifty days	3967
Ge	8:3	after the end of the **h** and fifty days	3967
Ge	15:13	shall afflict them four **h** years;	3967
Ge	17:17	unto him that is an **h** years old?	3967
Ge	21:5	Abraham was an **h** years old,	3967

Ge	45:22	gave three **h** pieces of silver,	3967
Ge	47:9	of my pilgrimage are an **h** and	3967
Ex	12:40	was four **h** and thirty years.	3967
Ex	12:41	end of the four **h** and thirty years,	3967
Ex	27:18	the court shall be an **h** cubits,	3967
Le	26:8	five of you shall chase an **h**, and an	3967
Le	26:8	**h** of you shall put ten thousand to	3967
Nu	1:46	numbered were six **h** thousand and	3967
Nu	2:32	their hosts were six **h** thousand.	3967
Nu	3:46	two **h** and threescore and thirteen	3967
Nu	11:21	I am, are six **h** thousand footmen;	3967
Nu	16:35	consumed the two **h** and fifty men	3967
Nu	26:10	fire devoured two **h** and fifty men:	3967
Nu	26:51	children of Israel, six **h** thousand	3967
Jos	24:32	Shechem for an **h** pieces of silver:	3967
Jgs	3:31	slew of the Philistines six **h** men	3967
Jgs	4:3	for he had nine **h** chariots of iron;	3967
Jgs	7:7	By the three **h** men that lapped will	3967
Jgs	7:16	he divided the three **h** men into	3967
Jgs	7:22	And the three **h** blew the trumpets,	3967
Jgs	15:4	went and caught three **h** foxes,	3967
Jgs	16:5	one of us eleven **h** pieces of silver	3967
Jgs	17:2	The eleven **h** shekels of silver that	3967
1Sa	17:7	weighed six **h** shekels of iron:	3967
1Sa	18:25	an **h** foreskins of the Philistines,	3967
1Sa	18:27	slew of the Philistines two **h** men;	3967
2Sa	3:14	I espoused to me for an **h** foreskins	3967
2Sa	14:26	hair of his head at two **h** shekels	3967
2Sa	21:16	weighed three **h** shekels of brass	3967
2Sa	23:8	lift up his spear against eight **h**,	3967
2Sa	23:18	lifted up his spear against three **h**,	3967
2Sa	24:9	Israel eight **h** thousand valiant men	3967
2Sa	24:9	of Judah were five **h** thousand men.	3967
1KI	6:1	in the four **h** and eightieth year	3967
1Ki	7:2	the length thereof was an **h** cubits,	3967
1Ki	10:16	made two **h** targets of beaten gold:	3967
1Ki	10:17	he made three **h** shields of beaten	3967
1Ki	11:3	he had seven **h** wives, princesses	3967
1Ki	11:3	and three **h** concubines: and his	3967
1Ki	18:4	Obadiah took an **h** prophets, and	3967
1Ki	18:19	prophets of Baal four **h** and fifty,	3967
1Ki	20:29	an **h** thousand footmen in one day	3967
1Ki	22:6	the prophets together, about four **h**	3967
1Ch	21:3	Lord make his people an **h** times	3967
1Ch	22:14	Lord an **h** thousand talents of gold,	3967
2Ch	2:2	three thousand and six **h** to oversee	3967
2Ch	7:5	an **h** and twenty thousand sheep:	3967
2Ch	13:17	Israel five **h** thousand chosen men.	3967
2Ch	25:9	the **h** talents which I have given to	3967
2Ch	28:6	an **h** and twenty thousand in one	3967
Ezr	2:69	silver, and one **h** priests' garments	3967
Est	1:1	**h** and seven and twenty provinces:	3967
Pr	17:10	man than an **h** stripes into a fool.	3967
Ecc	6:3	If a man beget an **h** children, and	3967
Ecc	8:12	Though a sinner do evil an **h** times,	3967
Isa	65:20	sinner being an **h** years old shall	3967
Eze	4:9	three **h** and ninety days shalt thou	3967
Da	6:1	kingdom an **h** and twenty princes,	3969
Da	8:14	two thousand and three **h** days;	3967
Da	12:11	a thousand two **h** and ninety days.	3967
Da	12:12	three **h** and five and thirty days.	3967
Am	5:3	out by a thousand shall leave an **h**,	3967
Am	5:3	went forth by an **h** shall leave ten,	3967
Mt	18:12	**if a man have an h sheep, and one**	*1540*
Mt	18:28	**which owed him an h pence;**	*1540*
Mk	4:8	**and some sixty, and some an h**	*1540*
Mk	4:20	**some sixty, and some an h.**	*1540*
Lk	7:41	**the one owed five h pence, and**	*4001*
Lk	15:4	**man of you, having an h sheep,**	*1540*
Lk	16:6	**And he said, An h measures of oil.**	*1540*
Lk	16:7	**he said, An h measures of wheat.**	*1540*
Jn	6:7	Two **h** pennyworth of bread is not	*1250*
Jn	12:5	ointment sold for three **h** pence,	*5145*
Ac	7:6	and entreat them evil four **h** years	*5071*
Ac	13:20	the space of four **h** and fifty years,	*5071*
Ro	4:19	when he was about an **h** years old,	*1541*
1Co	15:6	of above five **h** brethren at once;	*4001*
Gal	3:17	was four **h** and thirty years after,	*5071*
Rev	7:4	an **h** and forty and four thousand	*1540*
Rev	9:16	were two **h** thousand thousand:	*3461*
Rev	11:3	a thousand two **h** and threescore	*1250*
Rev	12:6	a thousand two **h** and threescore	*1250*
Rev	13:18	number is Six **h** threescore and six	*5516*
Rev	14:1	him an **h** forty and four thousand,	*1540*
Rev	14:3	the **h** and forty and four thousand,	*1540*

HUNDREDFOLD

Ge	26:12	in the same year an **h**.	3967, 8180
2Sa	24:3	many soever they be, an **h**,	3967, 6471
Mt	13:8	**some an h, some sixtyfold, some**	*1540*
Mt	13:23	**bringeth forth, some an h, some**	*1540*
Mt	19:29	**shall receive an h, and shall**	*1542*
Mk	10:30	**he shall receive an h now in this**	*1542*
Lk	8:8	**sprang up, and bare fruit an h**	*1542*

HUNDREDS

Ex	18:21	rulers of **h**, rulers of fifties,	3967
2Sa	18:4	all the people came out by **h** and	3967
2Ki	11:10	the captains over **h** did the priest	3967
1Ch	13:1	the captains of thousands and **h**,	3967
Mk	6:40	in ranks, by **h**, and by fifties.	*1540*

HUNGER

Ex	16:3	to kill the whole assembly with **h**	7457
Dt	8:3	thee, and suffered thee to **h**,	7456
Dt	28:48	in **h**, and in thirst, and in	7457
Ne	9:15	bread from heaven for their **h**	7457
Ps	34:10	young lions do lack, and suffer **h**:	7456
Pr	19:15	sleep; and idle soul shall suffer **h**	7456
Isa	49:10	They shall not **h** nor thirst;	7456
Jer	38:9	he is like to die for **h** in the place	7457
Jer	42:14	trumpet, nor have **h** of bread;	7456
La	2:19	young children, that faint for **h**.	7457
La	4:9	than they that be slain with **h**:	7457
Eze	34:29	shall be no more consumed with **h**	7457
Mt	5:6	**Blessed are they which do h and**	*3983*
Lk	6:21	**Blessed are ye that h now: for ye**	*3983*
Lk	6:25	**you that are full! for ye shall h**	*3983*
Lk	15:17	**and to spare, and I perish with h!**	*3042*
Jn	6:35	**that cometh to me shall never h;**	*3983*
Ro	12:20	Therefore if thine enemy **h**, feed	*3983*
1Co	4:11	we both **h**, and thirst, and are	*3983*
1Co	11:34	if any man **h**, let him eat at home	*3983*
2Co	11:27	often, in **h** and thirst, in fastings	*3042*
Rev	6:8	to kill with sword, and with **h**	*3042*
Rev	7:16	They shall **h** no more, neither	*3983*

HUNGERED

Lk	4:2	they were ended, he afterward **h**	*3983*

HUNGRED

Mt	4:2	nights, he was afterward an **h**	*3983*
Mt	12:1	his disciples were an **h**, and began	*3983*
Mt	12:3	**David did, when he was an h,**	*3983*

Mt 25:35 I was an **h**, and ye gave me meat: *3983*
Mt 25:37 when saw we thee an **h**, and fed *3983*
Mt 25:42 For I was an **h**, and ye gave me *3983*
Mt 25:44 Lord, when saw we thee an **h**, or *3983*

HUNGRY

1Sa 2:5 and they that were **h** ceased: 7456
2Sa 17:29 The people is **h**, and weary, and 7456
2Ki 7:12 They know that we be **h**; therefore 7456
Ps 50:12 If I were **h**, I would not tell thee: 7456
Ps 107:9 filleth the **h** soul with goodness 7456
Ps 146:7 which giveth food to the **h**. 7456
Pr 6:30 to satisfy his soul when he is **h**; 7456
Pr 25:21 If thine enemy be **h**, give him bread. 7456
Pr 27:7 to the **h** soul every bitter thing is 7456
Isa 8:21 that when they shall be **h**, they 7456
Isa 29:8 be as when an **h** man dreameth 7456
Isa 32:6 to make empty the soul of the **h**. 7456
Isa 44:12 he is **h**, and his strength faileth: 7456
Isa 58:7 Is it not to deal thy bread to the **h** 7456
Isa 58:10 if thou draw out thy soul to the **h**. 7456
Isa 65:13 servants shall eat, but ye shall be **h**: 7456
Eze 18:16 hath given his bread to the **h**. 7456
Lk 1:53 He hath filled the **h** with good *3983*
Ac 10:10 And he became very **h**, and would *4361*
1Co 11:21 one is **h**, and another is drunken, *3983*
Php 4:12 both to be full and to be **h**, both *3983*

HUNT

Ge 27:5 went to the field to **h** for venison, 6679
1Sa 26:20 **h** a partridge in the mountains 7291
Job 38:39 Wilt thou **h** the prey for the lion? 6679
Ps 140:11 evil shall **h** the violent man to 6679
Pr 6:26 adulteress will **h** for the precious 6679
La 4:18 They **h** our steps, that we cannot 6679
Eze 13:18 Will ye **h** the souls of my people, 6679
Eze 13:20 even the souls that ye **h** to make 6679
Mic 7:2 they **h** every man his brother with 6679

HUNTED

Eze 13:21 be no more in your hand to be **h**; 4686

HUNTER

Ge 10:9 Even as Nimrod the mighty **h** 6718
Ge 25:27 Esau was a cunning **h**, a man of 6718
Pr 6:5 as a roe from the hand of the **h**. 6718

HUNTERS

Jer 16:16 and after will I send for many **h** 6719

HUNTING

Pr 12:27 roasteth not that ... he took in **h** 6718

HURT

Ge 4:23 and a young man to my **h** 2250
Ge 26:29 That thou wilt do us no **h**, as we 7451
Ge 31:7 but God suffered him not to **h** me 7489
Ge 31:29 the power of my hand to do you **h**: 7451
Ex 21:22 strive, and **h** a woman with child 5062
Ex 21:35 if one man's ox **h** another's, that he 5062
Ex 22:10 and it die, or be **h**, or driven away, 7665
Ex 22:14 ought of his neighbour, and it be **h** 7665
Jos 24:20 then he will turn and do you **h**, 7489
2Sa 18:32 rise against thee to do thee **h**. 7451
2Ch 25:19 shouldest thou meddle to thine **h**. 7451
Ezr 4:22 grow to the **h** of the kings? 5142
Est 9:2 hand on such as sought their **h**: 7451
Job 35:8 Thy wickedness may **h** a man as thou
Ps 15:4 He that sweareth to his own **h** 7489
Ps 35:4 to confusion that devise my **h**. 7451
Ps 71:13 and dishonour that seek my **h**. 7451
Ecc 5:13 for the owners thereof to their **h**. 7451
Ecc 8:9 ruleth over another to his own **h** 7451
Isa 11:9 They shall not **h** nor destroy in all 7489
Isa 65:25 They shall not **h** nor destroy in all 7489
Jer 6:14 healed also the **h** of the daughter 7667
Jer 7:6 walk after other gods to your **h**: 7451
Jer 10:19 Woe is me for my **h**! my wound is 7667
Jer 25:6 hands; and I will do you no **h**. 7489
Jer 25:7 works of your hands to your own **h**. 7451
Da 3:25 of the fire, and they have no **h**; 2257
Da 6:22 mouths, that they have not **h** me: 2255
Da 6:23 no manner of **h** was found upon 2257
Mk 16:18 deadly thing, it shall not **h** them; *984*
Lk 10:19 nothing shall by any means **h** you *91*
Ac 18:10 no man shall set on thee to **h** *2559*
Rev 2:11 shall not be **h** of the second death *91*
Rev 7:3 **H** not the earth, neither the sea, *91*
Rev 9:10 power was to **h** men five months *91*
Rev 9:19 had heads, and with them they do **h** *91*
Rev 11:5 any man will **h** them, fire proceedeth *91*

HURTFUL

Ezr 4:15 rebellious city, and **h** unto kings 5142
Ps 144:10 his servant from the **h** sword. 7451
1Ti 6:9 and into many foolish and **h** lusts, *983*

HURTING

1Sa 25:34 hath kept me back from **h** thee 7489

HUSBAND

Ge 3:6 and gave also unto her **h** with her; 376
Ge 3:16 and thy desire shall be to thy **h**, 376
Ge 16:3 gave her to her **h** Abram to be his. 376
Ge 29:32 now therefore my **h** will love me. 376
Ge 29:34 time will my **h** be joined unto me, 376
Ge 30:20 now will my **h** dwell with me, 376
Ex 4:25 Surely a bloody **h** art thou to me 2860
Le 19:20 is a bondmaid, betrothed to an **h** 376
Le 21:3 nigh unto him, which hath had no **h**; 376
Le 21:7 take a woman put away from her **h**: 376
Nu 5:19 with another instead of thy **h**; 376
Nu 5:29 aside to another instead of her **h**, 376
Nu 30:6 had at all an **h**, when she vowed, 376
Nu 30:13 it, or her **h** may make it void 376
Nu 30:14 if her **h** altogether hold his peace 376
Dt 21:13 and be her **h**, and she shall be thy 1167
Dt 22:23 is a virgin be betrothed unto an **h** 376
Dt 24:3 if the latter **h** hate her, and write 376
Dt 24:3 or if the latter **h** die, which took her. 376
Dt 25:11 to deliver her **h** out of the hand of 376
Jgs 13:9 but Manoah her **h** was not with her. 376
Jgs 14:15 Entice thy **h**, that he may declare 376
Jgs 20:4 And the Levite, the **h** of the woman 376
Ru 1:3 Elimelech Naomi's **h** died; and she 376
Ru 1:12 way; for I am too old to have a **h** 376
1Sa 1:8 Then said Elkanah her **h** to her, 376
1Sa 2:19 she came up with her **h** to offer 376
2Sa 11:26 heard that Uriah her **h** was dead. 376
2Sa 14:5 widow woman, and mine **h** is dead 376
2Ki 4:1 Thy servant my **h** is dead; and thou 376
2Ki 4:14 she hath no child, and her **h** is old 376
2Ki 4:26 Is it well with thy **h**? is it well with 376
Pr 12:4 woman is a crown to her **h** 1167
Pr 31:11 The heart of her **h** doth safely trust 1167
Pr 31:23 Her **h** is known in the gates. 1167

Pr	31:28	her **h** also, and he praiseth her	1167
Isa	54:5	For thy Maker is thine **h**; the Lord	1167
Jer	3:20	treacherously departeth from her **h**,	1167
Jer	6:11	the **h** with the wife shall be taken	376
Eze	16:32	taketh strangers instead of her **h**!	376
Eze	44:25	or for sister than hath had no **h**	376
Hos	2:2	is not my wife, neither am I her **h**:	376
Hos	2:7	I will go and return to my first **h**;	376
Joel	1:8	sackcloth for the **h** of her youth	1167
Mt	1:19	Then Joseph her **h**, being a just man,	*435*
Mk	10:12	**a woman shall put away her h,**	*435*
Lk	2:36	had lived with an **h** seven years	*435*
Lk	16:18	**her that is put away from her h**	*435*
Jn	4:16	**Go, call thy h, and come hither**	*435*
Jn	4:18	**whom thou now hast is not thy h**	*435*
Ac	5:9	which have buried thy **h** are at the	*435*
Ro	7:2	woman which hath an **h** is bound	*5220*
Ro	7:3	if her **h** be dead, she is free from	*435*
1Co	7:2	let every woman have her own **h**	*435*
1Co	7:3	Let the **h** render unto the wife due	*435*
1Co	7:3	likewise also the wife unto the **h**	*435*
1Co	7:4	power of her own body, but the **h**:	*435*
1Co	7:4	likewise also the **h** hath not power	*435*
1Co	7:10	Let not the wife depart from her **h**:	*435*
1Co	7:11	and let not the **h** put away his wife	*435*
1Co	7:14	the unbelieving **h** is sanctified by	*435*
1Co	7:16	whether thou shalt save thy **h**? or	*435*
1Co	7:34	world, how she may please her **h**	*435*
2Co	11:2	for I have espoused you to one **h**	*435*
Eph	5:23	For the **h** is the head of the wife	*435*
Eph	5:33	wife see that she reverence her **h**	*435*
1Ti	3:2	the **h** of one wife, vigilant, sober,	*435*
Tit	1:6	the **h** of one wife, having faithful	*435*
Rev	21:2	as a bride adorned for her **h**	*435*

HUSBANDMAN

Ge	9:20	Noah began to be an **h**, and he	376, 127
Zec	13:5	I am no prophet, I am an **h**;	5647
Jn	15:1	**true vine, and my Father is the h**	*1092*
2Ti	2:6	The **h** that laboureth must be first	*1092*
Jas	5:7	the **h** waiteth for the precious fruit	*1092*

HUSBANDMEN

Joel	1:11	Be ye ashamed, O ye **h**; howl, O	406
Mt	21:33	**let it out to h, and went into afar**	*1092*
Mt	21:35	**the h took his servants, and beat**	*1092*
Mt	21:40	**what will he do unto those h?**	*1092*
Mk	12:2	**he sent to the h a servant, that he**	*1092*

HUSBANDRY

1Co	3:9	with God: ye are God's **h**, ye are	*1091*

HUSBAND'S

Dt	25:5	perform the duty of an **h** brother	2992
Dt	25:7	My **h** brother refuseth to raise up	2993
Ru	2:1	kinsman of her **h**, a mighty man	376

HUSBANDS

Est	1:20	wives shall give to their **h** honour	1167
Eze	16:45	lothed their **h** and their children:	582
Jn	4:18	**For thou hast had five h; and he**	*435*
1Co	14:35	let them ask their **h** at home: for it	*435*
Eph	5:22	submit yourselves unto your own **h**	*435*
Eph	5:24	be to their own **h** in every thing	*435*
Eph	5:25	**H**, love your wives, even as Christ	*435*
Col	3:18	submit yourselves unto your own **h**,	*435*
Col	3:19	**H**, love your wives, and be not bitter	*435*
1Ti	3:12	deacons be the **h** of one wife, ruling	*435*
Tit	2:4	love their **h**, to love their children,	*5562*
Tit	2:5	obedient to their own **h**, that the	*435*
1Pe	3:1	wives, in subjection to your own **h**;	*435*
1Pe	3:5	in subjection unto their own **h**:	*435*
1Pe	3:7	Likewise, ye **h**, dwell with them	*435*

HUSKS

Lk	15:16	**filled his belly with the h that**	*2769*

HYMN

Mt	26:30	they had sung an **h**, they went out	*5214*
Mk	14:26	they had sung an **h**, they went out	*5214*

HYMNS

Eph	5:19	in psalms and **h** and spiritual	*5215*
Col	3:16	in psalms and **h** and spiritual	*5215*

HYPOCRISIES

1Pe	2:1	and all guile, and **h**, and envies,	*5272*

HYPOCRISY

Isa	32:6	work iniquity, to practise **h**, and	2612
Mt	23:28	**within ye are full of h and**	*5272*
Mk	12:15	knowing their **h**, said unto them,	*5272*
Lk	12:1	**of the Pharisees, which is h**	*5272*
1Ti	4:2	Speaking lies in **h**; having their	*5272*
Jas	3:17	without partiality, and without **h**	*505*

HYPOCRITE

Job	27:8	For what is the hope of the **h**	2611
Job	34:30	That the **h** reign not, lest	120, 2611
Pr	11:9	An **h** with his mouth destroyeth	2611
Isa	9:17	for every one is a **h** and an	2611
Mt	7:5	**Thou h, first cast out the beam**	*5273*
Lk	6:42	**Thou h, cast out first the beam**	*5273*
Lk	13:15	**Thou h, doth not each one of you**	*5273*

HYPOCRITES

Job	15:34	the congregation of **h** shall be	2611
Isa	33:14	hath surprised the **h**	120, 2611
Mt	6:2	**as the h do in the synagogues**	*5273*
Mt	6:5	**thou shalt not be as the h are: for**	*5273*
Mt	6:16	**when ye fast, be not, as the h, of**	*5273*
Mt	15:7	**Ye h, well did Esaias prophesy of**	*5273*
Mt	16:3	**O ye h, ye can discern the face**	*5273*
Mt	22:18	and said, Why tempt ye me, ye **h**?	*5273*
Mt	23:13	**scribes and Pharisees, h! for ye**	*5273*
Mt	23:14	**scribes and Pharisees, h! for ye**	*5273*
Mt	23:15	**scribes and Pharisees, h!**	*5273*
Mt	23:23	**scribes and Pharisees, h!**	*5273*
Mt	23:25	**scribes and Pharisees, h!**	*5273*
Mt	23:27	**scribes and Pharisees, h!**	*5273*
Mt	23:29	**scribes and Pharisees, h! because**	*5273*
Mt	24:51	**him his portion with the h**	*5273*
Mk	7:6	**Esaias prophesied of you h, as**	*5273*
Lk	11:44	**scribes and Pharisees, h! for ye**	*5273*
Lk	12:56	**Ye h, ye can discern the face**	*5273*

HYPOCRITICAL

Ps	35:16	With **h** mockers in feasts, they	2611
Isa	10:6	will send him against an **h** nation,	2611

HYSSOP

Ex	12:22	ye shall take a bunch of **h**, and dip	231
Le	14:51	the cedar wood, and the **h**, and the	231
Nu	19:18	a clean person shall take **h**, and	231
Ps	51:7	Purge me with **h**, and I shall be	231
Jn	19:29	with vinegar, and put it upon **h**,	*5301*
Heb	9:19	water, and scarlet wool, and **h**, and	*5301*

I

IDLE

Ex	5:8	for they be **i**; therefore they cry,	7504
Pr	19:15	and an **i** soul shall suffer hunger	7423
Mt	12:36	**That every i word that men shall**	*692*
Mt	20:6	**Why stand ye here all the day i?**	*692*
Lk	24:11	words seemed to them as **i** tales,	*3026*
1Ti	5:13	And withal they learn to be **i**,	*692*

IDLENESS

Pr	31:27	and eateth not the bread of **i**	6104
Ecc	10:18	and through **i** of the hands the	8220
Eze	16:49	and abundance of **i** was in her	8252

IDOL

1Ki	15:13	Asa destroyed her **i**, and burnt it	4656
2Ch	15:16	because she had made an **i** in a	4656
2Ch	33:7	image, the **i** which he had made,	5566
2Ch	33:15	the **i** out of the house of the Lord,	5566
Isa	48:5	Mine **i** hath done them, and my	6090
Isa	66:3	incense, as if he blessed an **i**	205
Zec	11:17	Woe to the **i** shepherd that leaveth	457
Ac	7:41	and offered a sacrifice unto the **i**,	*1497*
1Co	8:4	we know that an **i** is nothing in	*1497*

IDOLATER

1Co	5:11	a fornicator, or covetous, or an **i**;	*1496*
Eph	5:5	nor covetous man, who is an **i**	*1496*

IDOLATERS

1Co	5:10	or extortioners, or with **i**;	*1496*
1Co	6:9	neither fornicators, nor **i**, nor	*1496*
1Co	10:7	Neither be **i**, as were some of	*1496*
Rev	21:8	**i**, and all liars, shall have their	*1496*
Rev	22:15	and murderers, and **i**, and	*1496*

IDOLATRIES

1Pe	4:3	banquetings, and abominable **i**:	*1495*

IDOLATROUS

2Ki	23:5	he put down the **i** priests, whom	3649

IDOLATRY

1Sa	15:23	stubbornness is as iniquity and **i**	8655
Ac	17:16	he saw the city wholly given to **i**	2712
1Co	10:14	my dearly beloved, flee from **i**	1495
Gal	5:20	**I**, witchcraft, hatred, variance,	*1495*
Col	3:5	and covetousness, which is **i**:	*1495*

IDOLS

Le	19:4	Turn ye not unto **i**, nor make	457
Le	26:1	Ye shall make you no **i** nor graven	457
Le	26:30	upon the carcases of your **i**,	1544
1Sa	31:9	publish it in the house of their **i**,	6091
1Ch	16:26	all the gods of the people are **i**:	457
2Ch	24:18	and served groves and **i**: and	6091
Ps	97:7	that boast themselves of **i**: worship	457
Ps	106:38	sacrificed unto the **i** of Canaan:	6091
Ps	135:15	The **i** of the heathen are silver and	6091
Isa	2:8	Their land also is full of **i**: they	457
Isa	10:11	so do to Jerusalem and her **i**?	6091
Isa	57:5	Enflaming yourselves with **i** under	410
Jer	50:38	and they are mad upon their **i**	367
Eze	6:6	your **i** may be broken and cease	1544
Eze	8:10	and all the **i** of the house of Israel	1544
Eze	14:4	that setteth up his **i** in his heart	1544
Eze	14:6	turn yourselves from your **i**: and	1544
Eze	16:36	with all the **i** of thy abominations	1544
Eze	20:16	for their heart went after their **i**	1544
Eze	20:39	Go ye, serve ye every one his **i**, and	1544
Eze	22:3	maketh **i** against herself to defile	1544
Eze	23:39	had slain their children to their **i**	1544
Eze	36:25	from all your **i**, will I cleanse you	1544
Hos	8:4	their gold have they made them **i**	6091
Mic	1:7	all the **i** thereof will I lay desolate:	6091
Zec	10:2	For the **i** have spoken vanity	8655
Zec	13:2	cut off the names of the **i** out of	6091
Ro	2:22	thou that abhorrest **i**, dost thou	*1497*
1Co	8:1	as touching things offered to **i**, we	*1494*
1Co	10:28	offered in sacrifice unto **i**, eat not	*1494*
1Co	12:2	carried away unto these dumb **i**	*1497*
2Co	6:16	hath the temple of God with **i**?	*1497*
1Th	1:9	ye turned to God from **i** to serve	*1497*
1Jn	5:21	children, keep yourselves from **i**	*1497*
Rev	2:14	**eat things sacrificed unto i, and**	*1494*
Rev	2:20	**and to eat things sacrificed unto i,**	*1494*
Rev	9:20	**i** of gold, and silver, and brass,	*1497*

IF

Ge	4:7	**i** thou doest not well, sin lieth at	518
Ex	32:32	and **i** not, blot me, I pray thee, out	518
Dt	4:29	**i** thou seek him with all thy heart	3588
Jgs	6:31	**i** he be a god, let him plead for	518
1Ki	18:21	**i** the Lord be God, follow him: but	518
2Ch	7:14	**I** my people, which are called by my	
Job	14:14	**I** a man die, shall he live again?	518
Job	35:7	**I** thou be righteous, what givest	518
Job	38:4	declare, **i** thou hast understanding	
Job	38:18	the earth? declare **i** thou knowest	518
Ps	50:12	**I** I were hungry, I would not tell	518
Ps	66:18	**I** I regard iniquity in my heart, the	518
Ps	130:3	**I** thou, Lord, shouldest mark iniquities	518
Ps	139:8	**I** I ascend up into heaven, thou art	518
Ps	139:8	**i** I make my bed in hell, behold	
Ps	139:9	**I** I take the wings of the morning,	
Ps	139:24	And see **i** there be any wicked way	518
Pr	1:10	**i** sinners entice thee, consent thou	518
Pr	2:4	**I** thou seekest her as silver, and	518
Pr	24:10	**I** thou faint in the day of adversity,	
Pr	25:21	**I** thine enemy be hungry, give	518
Ecc	11:8	But **i** a man live many years, and	518
SS	8:7	**i** a man would give all the substance	518
La	1:12	and see **i** there be any sorrow like	518
Eze	3:19	Yet **i** thou warn the wicked, and	3588
Eze	18:10	**I** he beget a son that is a robber,	
Da	3:17	**I** it be so, our God whom we serve	2006
Da	3:18	But **i** not, be it known unto thee,	2006
Jnh	3:9	Who can tell **i** God will turn and	
Mt	4:3	**I** thou be the Son of God, command	*1487*
Mt	4:6	**I** thou be the Son of God, cast	*1487*
Mt	4:9	**i** thou wilt fall down and worship	*1437*
Mt	5:13	**but i the salt have lost his savour,**	*1437*
Mt	5:29	**And i thy right eye offend thee,**	*1487*
Mt	5:46	**For i ye love them which love you,**	*1437*
Mt	6:14	**For i ye forgive men their trespasses**	*1437*
Mt	6:23	**I therefore the light that is in thee**	*1497*
Mt	6:30	**wherefore, i God so clothed the**	*1487*
Mt	7:11	**I ye then, being evil, know how to**	*1487*
Mt	14:28	Lord, **i** it be thou, bid me come	*1487*
Mt	15:14	**And i the blind lead the blind**	*1487*

I

Mt	16:24	I any man will come after me, let	1487
Mt	17:20	I ye have faith as a grain of	1437
Mt	18:19	That i two of you shall agree on	1437
Mt	22:45	I David then call him Lord, how	1487
Mt	27:40	I thou be the Son of God, come	1487
Mt	27:42	I he be the King of Israel, let	1487
Mk	3:25	And i a house be divided against	1437
Mk	4:23	I any man have ears to hear, let him	
Mk	7:11	I a man shall say to his father or	1437
Mk	8:36	i he shall gain the whole world,	1437
Mk	9:23	I thou canst believe, all things	1487
Mk	9:43	i thy hand offend thee, cut it off:	1437
Mk	9:50	i the salt have lost his saltness,	1437
Mk	11:26	But i ye do not forgive, neither	1487
Lk	4:3	I thou be the Son of God,	1487
Lk	4:7	I thou therefore wilt worship me,	1437
Lk	4:9	I thou be the Son of God, cast	1487
Lk	6:32	For i ye love them which love	1487
Lk	6:33	And i ye do good to them which	1437
Lk	9:25	i he gain the whole world, and lose	
Lk	11:13	I ye then, being evil, know how to	1497
Lk	11:36	I thy whole body therefore be full	1487
Lk	14:26	I any man come to me, and hate	1487
Lk	14:34	but i the salt have lost his savour,	1437
Lk	16:31	I they hear not Moses and the	1497
Lk	17:3	and i he repent, forgive him	1437
Lk	17:6	I ye had faith as a grain of	1487
Lk	22:42	i thou be willing, remove this cup	1487
Lk	23:35	let him save himself, i he be Christ,	1487
Lk	23:37	I thou be the king of the Jews, save	1487
Lk	23:39	I thou be Christ, save thyself and	1487
Jn	4:10	I thou knewest the gift of God	1487
Jn	6:51	i any man eat of this bread, he	1437
Jn	8:24	for i ye believe not that I am he,	1437
Jn	8:42	I God were your Father, ye would	1487
Jn	10:24	I thou be the Christ, tell us	1487
Jn	11:40	i thou wouldest believe, thou	1437
Jn	12:26	i any man serve me, him will my	1437
Jn	13:14	I I then, your Lord and Master,	1487
Jn	14:2	i it were not so, I would have told	1490
Jn	14:15	I ye love me, keep my	1437
Jn	15:7	I ye abide in me, and my words	1437
Jn	16:7	for i I go not away, the Comforter	1437
Jn	18:36	i my kingdom were of this world,	1487
Ac	5:39	But i it be of God, ye cannot	1487
Ro	3:3	For what i some do not believe?	1487
Ro	5:17	For i by one man's offence death	1477
Ro	6:8	Now i we be dead with Christ, we	1477
Ro	7:20	Now i I do that I would not, it is	1487
Ro	8:9	Now i any man have not the Spirit	1487
Ro	8:31	I God be for us, who can be	1487
Ro	10:9	That i thou shalt confess with thy	1437
Ro	11:6	i by grace, then is it no more of works	1487
Ro	12:18	I it be possible, as much as lieth	1487
Ro	12:20	Therefore i thine enemy hunger,	1437
1Co	3:14	I any man's work abide which	1487
1Co	9:16	unto me, i I preach not the gospel!	1437
1Co	14:8	i the trumpet give an uncertain	1437
1Co	15:17	And i Christ be not raised, your	1487
1Co	15:19	I in this life only we have hope in	1487
1Co	16:22	I any man love not the Lord Jesus	1487
2Co	5:14	that i one died for all, then were	1487
2Co	5:17	Therefore i any man be in Christ,	1487
Gal	3:29	And i ye be Christ's, then are ye	1487
Gal	6:1	i a man be overtaken in a fault	1437
Php	2:1	I there be … any consolation in	1487
Php	2:1	i any comfort of love	1487
Php	2:1	i any fellowship of the Spirit,	1487
Php	2:1	i any bowels and mercies	1487
Php	4:8	and i there be any praise, think on	1487
Col	3:1	I ye then be risen with Christ	1487
1Ti	5:8	But i any provide not for his own	1487
2Ti	2:13	I we believe not, yet he abideth	1487
2Ti	2:21	I a man therefore purge himself	1437
2Ti	2:25	i God peradventure will give them	3379
Heb	2:3	i we neglect so great salvation;	
Heb	3:7	To day i ye will hear his voice,	1437
Heb	3:15	To day i ye will hear his voice	1437
Heb	4:7	To day i ye will hear his voice	1437
Jas	1:5	I any of you lack wisdom, let him	1487
Jas	4:15	I the Lord will, we shall live, and	1437
1Pe	4:16	Yet i any man suffer as a Christian,	1487
2Pe	1:8	For i these things be in you, and	
2Pe	1:10	for i ye do these things, ye shall never	
2Pe	2:4	For i God spared not the angels	1487
2Pe	2:20	For i after they have escaped the	1487
1Jn	1:6	I we say that we have fellowship	1437
1Jn	1:8	I we say that we have no sin, we	1437
1Jn	1:9	I we confess our sins, he is	1437
1Jn	1:10	I we say that we have not sinned,	1437
1Jn	2:1	And i any man sin, we have an	1437
1Jn	2:15	I any man love the world, the love	1437
1Jn	3:20	For i our heart condemn us, God	1437
1Jn	3:21	i our heart condemn us not	1437
1Jn	4:11	Beloved, i God so loved us, we	1487
1Jn	5:14	i we ask any thing according to	1437
Rev	3:3	I therefore thou shalt not	1437
Rev	3:20	i any man hear my voice, and	1437
Rev	13:9	I any man have an ear, let him	1487
Rev	14:9	I any man worship the beast and	1487
Rev	22:18	I any man shall add unto these	1437
Rev	22:19	And i any man shall take away	1437

IGNORANCE

Le	4:2	If a soul shall sin through i	7684
Nu	15:29	for him that sinneth through i,	7684
Ac	17:30	the times of this i God winked at;	52
1Pe	1:14	to the former lusts in your i:	52
1Pe	2:15	to silence the i of foolish men:	56

IGNORANT

Isa	56:10	they are all i, they are all	3808, 3045
Isa	63:16	though Abraham be i of us	3808, 3045
Ro	1:13	Now I would not have you i,	50
Ro	11:25	that ye should be i of this mystery	50
1Co	10:1	I would not that ye should be i,	50
1Co	12:1	brethren, I would not have you i	50
2Co	1:8	would not, brethren, have you i of	50
2Co	2:11	of us: for we are not i of his devices	50
1Th	4:13	But I would not have you to be i,	50
Heb	5:2	Who can have compassion on the i	50
2Pe	3:5	For this they willingly are i of	2990
2Pe	3:8	beloved, be not i of this one thing	2990

IGNORANTLY

Nu	15:28	for the soul that sinneth i, when	7683
Dt	19:4	Whoso killeth … neighbour i,	1097, 1847
Ac	17:23	Whom therefore ye i worship, him	50
1Ti	1:13	mercy, because I did it i in unbelief	50

ILL

Ps	106:32	so that it went i with Moses for	3415
Ro	13:10	Love worketh no i to his	2556

ILLUMINATED

Heb	10:32	in which, after ye were **i**, ye	*5461*

IMAGE

Ge	1:26	said, Let us make man in our **i**,	6754
Ge	1:27	God created man in his own **i**,	6754
Ge	9:6	for in the **i** of God made he man,	6754
Ex	20:4	not make unto thee any graven **i**,	6754
1Sa	19:13	Michal took an **i**, and laid it in	8655
Isa	44:10	formed a god, or molten a graven **i**	6459
Jer	10:14	is confounded by the graven **i**	6459
Jer	51:17	is confounded by the graven **i**:	6459
Eze	8:3	was the seat of the **i** of jealousy,	5566
Da	3:1	the king made an **i** of gold, whose	6755
Da	3:18	nor worship the golden **i** which	6755
Hab	2:18	the molten **i**, and a teacher of lies,	6755
Mt	22:20	**Whose is this i and superscription?**	*1504*
Mk	12:16	**Whose is this i and superscription?**	*1504*
Lk	20:24	**Whose i and superscription hath**	*1504*
Ro	1:23	into an **i** made like to corruptible	*1504*
Ro	8:29	conformed to the **i** of his Son, that	*1504*
Ro	11:4	not bowed the knee to the **i** of Baal	
1Co	11:7	as he is, the **i** and glory of God:	*1504*
2Co	4:4	gospel of Christ, who is the **i** of God,	*1504*
Col	1:15	Who is the **i** of the invisible God,	*1504*
Col	3:10	after the **i** of him that created him:	*1504*
Heb	1:3	and the express **i** of his person	*5481*
Rev	13:15	**i** of the beast should both speak,	*1504*
Rev	13:15	not worship the **i** of the beast	*1504*
Rev	19:20	and them that worshipped his **i**	*1504*

IMAGES

Ge	31:19	Rachel had stolen the **i** that were	8655
Le	26:30	cut down your **i**, and cast your	2553
2Sa	5:21	And there they left their **i**, and	6091
1Ki	14:9	made thee other gods, and molten **i**,	
2Ki	17:10	they set them up **i** and groves	4676
2Ki	18:4	brake the **i**, and cut down the	4676
2Ch	34:7	beaten the graven **i** into powder	6456
Ps	78:58	him to jealousy with their graven **i**	6456
Ps	97:7	be all they that serve graven **i**,	
Isa	42:8	neither my praise to graven **i**	
Jer	50:38	for it is the land of graven **i**, and	
Eze	6:6	and your **i** may be cut down, and	2553
Eze	21:21	he consulted with **i**, he looked in	8655
Hos	11:2	and burned incense to graven **i**	
Mic	5:13	Thy graven **i** also will I cut off,	4676

IMAGINATION See also IMAGINATIONS.

Ge	6:5	every **i** of the thoughts of his	3336
Ge	8:21	the **i** of man's heart is evil from	3336
Dt	29:19	I walk in the **i** of mine heart,	8307
Dt	31:21	for I know their **i** which they go	3336
1Ch	29:18	keep this for ever in the **i** of the	3336
Jer	3:17	after the **i** of their evil heart	8307
Jer	7:24	and in the **i** of their evil heart	8307
Jer	9:14	the **i** of their own heart, and after	8307
Jer	11:8	one in the **i** of their evil heart:	8307
Jer	13:10	walk in the **i** of their heart, and	8307
Jer	16:12	one after the **i** of his evil heart	8307
Jer	18:12	every one do the **i** of his evil heart	8307
Jer	23:17	after the **i** of his own heart	8307
Lk	1:51	proud in the **i** of their hearts	*1271*

IMAGINATIONS

1Ch	28:9	all the **i** of the thoughts: if thou	3336
Pr	6:18	An heart that deviseth wicked **i**,	4284
Ro	1:21	became vain in their **i**, and their	*1261*
2Co	10:5	Casting down **i**, and every high	*3053*

IMAGINE

Ps	2:1	and the people **i** a vain thing?	1897
Ps	38:12	and **i** deceits all the day long	1897
Ps	140:2	Which **i** mischiefs in their heart:	2803
Pr	12:20	in the heart of them that **i** evil:	2790
Hos	7:15	yet do they **i** mischief against	2803
Na	1:9	What do ye **i** against the Lord?	2803
Zec	7:10	you **i** evil against his brother	2803
Zec	8:17	none of you **i** evil in your hearts	
Ac	4:25	rage, and the people **i** vain things?	*3191*

IMMANUEL (im-man´-u-el) See also EMMANUEL.

Isa	7:14	a son, and shall call his name **I**	6005
Isa	8:8	fill the breadth of the land, O **I**	6005

IMMEDIATELY

Mt	14:31	And **i** Jesus stretched forth his	*2112*
Mt	20:34	**i** their eyes received sight, and	*2112*
Mt	24:29	**i after the tribulation of those**	*2112*
Mt	26:74	the man. And **i** the cock crew	*2112*
Mk	1:12	**i** the spirit driveth him into the	*2117*
Mk	2:8	**i** when Jesus perceived in his	*2112*
Mk	4:15	**Satan cometh i, and taketh away**	*2112*
Mk	4:16	**word, i receive it with gladness;**	*2112*
Mk	4:17	**word's sake, i they are offended**	*2112*
Mk	5:30	Jesus, **i** knowing in himself that	*2112*
Mk	6:27	**i** the king sent an executioner	*2112*
Lk	6:49	**beat vehemently, and i it fell;**	*2112*
Lk	8:44	and **i** her issue of blood stanched	*3916*
Lk	12:36	**they may open unto him i.**	*2112*
Lk	19:11	kingdom of God should **i** appear	*3916*
Lk	19:40	**peace, the stones would i cry out**	
Lk	22:60	And **i**, while he yet spake, the	*3916*
Jn	13:30	received the sop went **i** out:	*2112*
Jn	18:27	again: and **i** the cock crew	*2112*
Rev	4:2	And **i** I was in the spirit: and	*2112*

IMMORTAL See also MORTAL.

1Ti	1:17	Now unto the King eternal, **i**,	*862*

IMMORTALITY See also MORTALITY.

Ro	2:7	glory and honour and **i**, eternal	*861*
1Co	15:53	and this mortal must put on **i**.	*110*
1Ti	6:16	Who only hath **i**, dwelling in the	*110*
2Ti	1:10	hath brought life and **i** to light	*861*

IMMOVABLE See UNMOVABLE.

IMMUTABILITY

Heb	6:17	The **i** of his counsel, confirmed it	*275*

IMMUTABLE

Heb	6:18	That by two **i** things, in which it	*276*

IMPART

Ro	1:11	**i** unto you some spiritual gift,	*3330*

IMPENITENT

Ro	2:5	But, after thy hardness and **i** heart	*279*

IMPLACABLE

Ro	1:31	without natural affection, **i**,	*786*

IMPORTUNITY

Lk	11:8	**yet because of his i he will rise**	*335*

IMPOSED

Heb	9:10	**i** on them until the time of	*1945*

IMPOSSIBLE
Mt 17:20 and nothing shall be **i** unto you *101*
Mt 19:26 With men this is **i**: but with God *102*
Mk 10:27 With men it is **i**, but not with God: *102*
Lk 1:37 with God nothing shall be **i**. *101*
Lk 17:1 is **i** but that offences will come: *418*
Lk 18:27 things which are **i** with men are *102*
Heb 6:4 For it is **i** for those who were once *102*
Heb 6:18 in which it was **i** for God to lie,. *102*
Heb 11:6 without faith it is **i** to please him:. *102*

IMPOVERISHED
Jgs 6:6 And Israel was greatly **i** because 1809
Isa 40:20 is so **i** that he hath no oblation 5533

IMPRISONED
Ac 22:19 know that I **i** and beat in every *5439*

IMPRISONMENT See also IMPRISONMENTS.
Ezr 7:26 or to confiscation of goods, or to **i** 613
Heb 11:36 yea, moreover of bonds and **i**:. *5438*

IMPRISONMENTS
2Co 6:5 In stripes, in **i**, in tumults, in. *5438*

IMPUDENT
Pr 7:13 kissed him, and with an **i** face. 5810
Eze 2:4 **i** children and stiff hearted 7186, 6440
Eze 3:7 all the house of Israel are **i**. 2389, 4696

IMPUTE
1Sa 22:15 king **i** any thing unto his servant 7760
2Sa 19:19 Let not my lord **i** iniquity unto. 2803
Ro 4:8 to whom the Lord will not **i** sin *3049*

IMPUTED
Le 7:18 it be **i** unto him that offereth it: 2803
Le 17:4 blood shall be **i** unto that man; he 2803
Ro 4:11 might be **i** unto them also:. *3049*
Ro 4:22 therefore it was **i** to him for. *3049*
Ro 4:24 to whom it shall be **i**, if we believe *3049*
Ro 5:13 sin is not **i** when there is no law *1677*
Jas 2:23 and it was **i** unto him for. *3049*

IMPUTETH
Ps 32:2 whom the Lord **i** not iniquity. 2803
Ro 4:6 unto whom God **i** righteousness. *3049*

IMPUTING
Hab 1:11 offend, **i** this his power unto his God
2Co 5:19 not **i** their trespasses unto them;. *3049*

INCENSE See also FRANKINCENSE.
Ex 30:1 make an altar to burn **i** upon:. 7004
Ex 30:8 a perpetual **i** before the Lord. 7004
Ex 30:9 Ye shall offer no strange **i** thereon,. 7004
Le 10:1 put fire therein, and put **i** thereon,. 7004
Le 16:12 and his hands full of sweet **i** beaten 7004
Nu 16:17 man his censer, and put **i** in them,. 7004
Nu 16:47 put on **i**, and made an atonement 7004
1Ki 3:3 he sacrificed and burnt **i** in high. 6999
2Ki 22:17 and have burned **i** unto other gods,. . . . 6999
2Ch 26:18 Uzziah, to burn **i** unto the Lord,. 6999
2Ch 26:19 the Lord, from beside the **i** altar 7004
2Ch 28:3 he burnt **i** in the valley of the son. 6999
2Ch 32:12 one altar, and burn **i** upon it? 6999
2Ch 34:25 and have burned **i** unto other gods,. . . . 6999
Isa 1:13 **i** is an abomination unto me; 7004
Isa 65:7 burned **i** upon the mountains, ... 6999
Isa 66:3 he that burneth **i**, as if he blessed 3828
Jer 1:16 have burned **i** unto other gods,. 6999
Jer 7:9 and burn **i** unto Baal, and walk. 6999
Jer 11:12 the gods unto whom they offer **i** 6999
Jer 18:15 they have burned **i** to vanity, and 6999
Mal 1:11 in every place **i** shall be offered. 6999
Lk 1:11 on the right side of the altar of **i**. *2368*
Rev 8:3 there was given unto him much **i**, ... *2368*
Rev 8:4 the smoke of the **i**, which came. *2368*

INCLINE
1Ki 8:58 That he may **i** our hearts unto him,. . . . 5186
Ps 71:2 escape: **i** thine ear unto me, and 5186
Ps 119:36 **I** my heart unto thy testimonies,. 5186
Ps 141:4 **I** not my heart to any evil thing,. 5186
Pr 2:2 thou **i** thine ear unto wisdom, ... 7181
Isa 55:3 **I** your ear, and come unto me: 5186
Da 9:18 O my God, **i** thine ear, and hear; 5186

INCLINED
Ps 40:1 and he **i** unto me, and heard my. 5186
Ps 119:112 I have **i** mine heart to perform 5186
Pr 5:13 nor **i** mine, ear to them that 5186
Jer 7:24 hearkened not, nor **i** their ear,. 5186
Jer 11:8 they obeyed not, nor **i** their ear, ... 5186
Jer 34:14 not unto me, neither **i** their ear. 5186

INCLOSED
Jgs 20:43 Thus they **i** the Benjamites 3803
Ps 17:10 They are **i** in their own fat: with. 5462
Ps 22:16 assembly of the wicked have **i** me: 5362
SS 4:12 A garden **i** is my sister, my. 5274

INCONTINENCY
1Co 7:5 Satan tempt you not for your **i** *192*

INCONTINENT
2Ti 3:3 false accusers, **i**, fierce, despisers *193*

INCORRUPTIBLE See also UNCORRUPTIBLE.
1Co 9:25 corruptible crown; but we an **i** *862*
1Co 15:52 and the dead shall be raised **i**, ... *862*
1Pe 1:4 To an inheritance **i**, and undefiled,. *862*
1Pe 1:23 corruptible seed, but of **i**,. *862*

INCORRUPTION
1Co 15:42 in corruption; it is raised in **i**. 861
1Co 15:50 neither doth corruption inherit **i** *861*
1Co 15:53 must put on **i**, and this mortal *861*
1Co 15:54 corruptible shall have put on **i**, ... *861*

INCREASE
Ge 47:24 to pass in the **i**, that ye shall give. 8393
Le 25:12 ye shall eat the **i** thereof out of 8393
Le 25:36 Take thou no usury of him, or **i**:. 8635
Le 26:4 the land shall yield her **i**, and the 2981
Le 26:20 your land shall not yield her **i** 2981
Dt 14:22 truly tithe all the **i** of thy seed, ... 8393
Dt 26:12 tithing all the tithes of thine **i** the. 8393
Dt 32:22 consume the earth with her **i**, ... 2981
Ezr 10:10 wives, to **i** the trespass of Israel. 3254
Ne 9:37 yieldeth much **i** unto the kings 8393
Job 8:7 thy latter end should greatly **i** 7685
Pr 1:5 man will hear, and will **i** learning; 3254
Pr 3:9 with the firstfruits of all thine **i**. 8393
Pr 9:9 man, and he will **i** in learning 3254
Pr 14:4 much **i** is by the strength of the ox. 8393
Pr 22:16 oppresseth the poor to **i** his riches,. 7235
Pr 28:28 when they perish, the righteous **i** 7235

Ecc 5:10 he that loveth abundance with **i**:........ 8393
Ecc 5:11 When goods **i**, they are increased 7235
Isa 9:7 Of the **i** of his government and........ 4768
Isa 29:19 The meek also shall **i** their joy.......... 3254
Eze 18:13 upon usury, and hath taken **i**:.......... 8635
Hos 4:10 whoredom, and shall not **i**: 6555
Zec 8:12 and the ground shall give her **i**,........ 2981
Lk 17:5 said unto the Lord, **I** our faith.......... *4369*
Jn 3:30 He must **i**, but I must decrease *837*
1Co 3:6 Apollos watered; but God gave the **i**..... *837*
1Co 3:7 watereth; but God that giveth the **i**...... *837*
2Co 9:10 **i** the fruits of your righteousness;........ *837*
Col 2:19 increaseth with the **i** of God............. *838*
1Th 3:12 the Lord make you to **i** and abound.... *4121*
2Ti 2:16 they will **i** unto more ungodliness *4298*

INCREASED

Ge 7:17 and the waters **i**, and bare up the 7235
Ge 7:18 and were **i** greatly upon the earth; 7235
Ex 1:7 were fruitful, and **i** abundantly,........ 8317
2Ch 18:34 And the battle **i** that day: howbeit 5927
Ezr 9:6 for our iniquities are **i** over our........ 7235
Ps 3:1 Lord, how are they **i** that trouble 7231
Ps 49:16 when the glory of his house is **i**;....... 7235
Pr 9:11 and the years of thy life shall be **i** 3254
Ecc 2:9 So I was great, and **i** more than........ 3254
Ecc 5:11 increase, they are **i** that eat them:...... 7231
Jer 5:6 and their backslidings are **i** 6105
Jer 30:14 iniquity; because thy sins were **i** 6105
Jer 30:15 because thy sins were **i**, I have......... 6105
La 2:5 hath **i** in the daughter of Judah......... 7235
Da 12:4 and fro, and knowledge shall be **i** 7235
Hos 4:7 As they were **i**, so they sinned 7230
Hos 10:1 of his fruit he hath **i** the altars; 7235
Lk 2:52 Jesus **i** in wisdom and stature *4298*
Ac 6:7 And the word of God **i**; and the *837*
Ac 9:22 Saul **i** the more in strength, and *1743*
Ac 16:5 the faith, and **i** in number daily........ *4052*
2Co 10:15 having hope, when your faith is **i**,....... *837*
Rev 3:17 **I am rich, and i with goods, and**....... *4147*

INCREASETH

Pr 11:24 is that scattereth, and yet **i**; 3254
Pr 23:28 **i** the transgressors among men. 3254
Pr 24:5 yea, a man of knowledge **i** strength 553
Pr 28:8 that by usury and unjust gain **i**........ 7235
Pr 29:16 are multiplied, transgression **i**......... 7235
Ecc 1:18 he that **i** knowledge **i** sorrow. 3254
Col 2:19 together, **i** with the increase of God...... *837*

INCREASING

Col 1:10 and **i** in the knowledge of God;......... *837*

INCURABLE

Jer 15:18 my wound **i**, which refuseth to be 605
Jer 30:15 thy sorrow is **i** for the multitude........ 605
Mic 1:9 For her wound is **i**: for it is come 605

INDEBTED

Lk 11:4 **forgive every one that is i to us**........ *3784*

INDEED

Ge 17:19 thy wife shall bear thee a son **i**;.......... 61
Ge 37:8 to him, Shalt thou **i** reign over us?
Nu 12:2 Hath the Lord **i** spoken only by
Jos 7:20 **I** I have sinned against the Lord 546
1Ki 8:27 But will God **i** dwell on the earth? 552
1Ch 4:10 Oh that thou wouldest bless me **i**, and
Isa 6:9 people, Hear ye **i**, but understand not;
Isa 6:9 and see ye **i**, but perceive not.
Mt 26:41 **spirit i is willing, but the flesh**......... *3303*
Mk 10:39 **Ye shall i drink of the cup that** *3303*
Mk 14:21 **The Son of man i goeth, as it is** *3303*
Lk 23:41 And we **i** justly; for we receive the *3303*
Lk 24:34 Saying, The Lord is risen **i**, and........ *3689*
Jn 6:55 **For my flesh is meat i**.................. *230*
Jn 6:55 **and my blood is drink i**............... *230*
Jn 7:26 know **i** that this is the very Christ?...... *230*
Jn 8:31 **word, then are ye my disciples i** *230*
Jn 8:36 **make you free, ye shall be free i** *3689*
1Ti 5:16 relieve them that are widows **i**......... *3689*
1Pe 2:4 disallowed **i** of men, but chosen of..... *3303*

INDIGNATION

2Ki 3:27 there was great **i** against Israel: 7110
Ne 4:1 was wroth, and took great **i**, and....... 3707
Est 5:9 he was full of **i** against Mordecai 2534
Ps 69:24 Pour out thine **i** upon them, and 2195
Isa 34:2 **i** of the Lord is upon all nations, ... 7110
Isa 66:14 and his **i** toward his enemies. 2194
Jer 10:10 shall not be able to abide his **i**......... 2195
La 2:6 hath despised in the **i** of his anger 2195
Eze 21:31 I will pour out mine **i** upon thee,....... 2195
Mic 7:9 I will bear the **i** of the Lord,........... 2197
Na 1:6 Who can stand before his **i**? and....... 2195
Zec 1:12 hast had **i** these threescore and 2194
Mal 1:4 whom the Lord hath **i** for ever 2194
Mk 14:4 some that had **i** within themselves,....... *23*
Ac 5:17 Sadducees,) and were filled with **i**, ... *2205*
Ro 2:8 unrighteousness, **i**, and wrath, ... *2372*
2Co 7:11 yea, what **i**, yea, what fear, yea,........... *24*
Rev 14:10 mixture into the cup of his **i**;.......... *3709*

INDITING

Ps 45:1 My heart is **i** a good matter: I speak 7370

INEXCUSABLE

Ro 2:1 Therefore thou art **i**, O man,........... *379*

INFALLIBLE

Ac 1:3 by many **i** proofs, being seen of them

INFANTS

Job 3:16 been; as **i** which never saw light........ 5768
Hos 13:16 their **i** shall be dashed in pieces, ... 5768
Lk 18:15 they brought unto him also **i**, that *1025*

INFERIOR

Job 12:3 I am not **i** to you: yea, who 5307
Job 13:2 I know also: I am not **i** unto you....... 5307
Da 2:39 arise another kingdom **i** to thee,........ 772

INFIDEL

2Co 6:15 hath he that believeth with an **i**?........ *571*
1Ti 5:8 the faith, and is worse than an **i** *571*

INFINITE

Ps 147:5 power: his understanding is **i** 369, 4557

INFIRMITIES

Mt 8:17 Himself took our **i**, and bare our *769*
Lk 8:2 been healed of evil spirits and **i**......... *769*
Ro 8:26 the Spirit also helpeth our **i**: for *769*
Ro 15:1 to bear the **i** of the weak, and not....... *771*
2Co 12:9 will I rather glory in my **i**, that the...... *769*
2Co 12:10 Therefore I take pleasure in **i**, in *769*
Heb 4:15 touched with the feeling of our **i**;....... *769*

INFIRMITY
Pr 18:14 spirit of a man will sustain his **i**; 4245
Lk 13:12 **thou art loosed from thine i** *769*
Ro 6:19 men because of the **i** of your flesh: *769*
Heb 5:2 himself also is compassed with **i** *769*
Heb 7:28 men high priests which have **i**; *769*

INGATHERING
Ex 23:16 and the feast of **i**, which is in the 614
Ex 34:22 the feast of **i** at the year's end 614

INHABIT
Pr 10:30 the wicked shall not **i** the earth 7931
Isa 65:21 shall build houses, and **i** them; 3427
Isa 65:22 shall not build and another **i**; they 3427
Zep 1:13 also build houses, but not **i** them; 3427

INHABITANT
Isa 6:11 Until the cities be wasted without **i** 3427
Isa 12:6 Cry out and shout, thou **i** of Zion: 3427
Jer 9:11 of Judah desolate, without an **i** 3427
Jer 21:13 I am against thee, O **i** of the valley, ... 3427
Jer 26:9 city shall be desolate without an **i**? 3427
Jer 33:10 without man, and without **i**, and 3427
Jer 44:22 and a curse, without an **i**, as at 3427
Jer 51:29 Babylon a desolation without an **i** 3427

INHABITANTS See also INHABITERS.
Ge 34:30 to stink among the **i** of the land, ... 3427
Ex 15:15 all the **i** of Canaan shall melt away 3427
Ex 34:15 a covenant with the **i** of the land, ... 3427
Le 18:25 the land itself vomiteth out her **i** 3427
Nu 13:32 land that eateth up the **i** thereof; 3427
Nu 14:14 they will tell it to the **i** of this land: 3427
Nu 33:53 ye shall dispossess the **i** of the land,
Nu 33:55 will not drive out the **i** of the land 3427
Jos 2:9 all the **i** of the land faint because 3427
Jos 7:9 all the **i** of the land shall hear of it, ... 3427
Jos 9:24 to destroy all the **i** of the land from 3427
Jgs 1:19 not drive out the **i** of the valley, ... 3427
Jgs 2:2 no league with the **i** of this land; 3427
Ru 4:4 Buy it before the **i**, and before the 3427
2Ki 23:2 and all the **i** of Jerusalem with him, ... 3427
1Ch 22:18 the **i** of the land into mine hand; 3427
2Ch 20:18 and the **i** of Jerusalem fell before 3427
2Ch 21:11 caused the **i** of Jerusalem to commit ... 3427
2Ch 34:28 place, and upon the **i** of the same 3427
Ps 33:8 all the **i** of the world stand in awe 3427
Ps 33:14 looketh upon all the **i** of the earth. 3427
Isa 18:3 All ye **i** of the world, and dwellers 3427
Isa 24:1 scattereth abroad the **i** thereof 3427
Isa 26:9 the **i** of the world will learn 3427
Isa 42:11 let the **i** of the rock sing, let them 3427
Jer 25:29 sword upon all the **i** of the earth, ... 3427
La 4:12 the earth and all the **i** of the world, ... 3427
Eze 12:19 Lord God of the **i** of Jerusalem, ... 3427
Da 4:35 all the **i** of the earth are reputed 1753
Hos 4:1 controversy with the **i** of the land, ... 3427
Joel 2:1 let all the **i** of the land tremble: 3427
Mic 6:12 and the **i** thereof have spoken lies, ... 3427
Zec 8:21 the **i** of one city shall go to another, ... 3427
Zec 11:6 I will no more pity the **i** of the land, ... 3427
Zec 12:10 David, and upon the **i** of Jerusalem, ... 3427
Zec 13:1 of David and to the **i** of Jerusalem 3427
Rev 17:2 the **i** of the earth have been made *2730*

INHABITED
Isa 13:20 It shall never be **i**, neither shall it 3427
Jer 50:13 it shall not be **i**, but it shall be 3427
Eze 29:11 it, neither shall it be **i** forty years 3427
Zec 7:7 when Jerusalem was **i** and in 3427
Zec 12:6 and Jerusalem shall be **i** again in 3427

INHABITERS See also INHABITANTS.
Rev 8:13 woe, woe, to the **i** of the earth *2730*
Rev 12:12 Woe to the **i** of the earth and of *2730*

INHABITEST
Ps 22:30 thou that **i** the praises of Israel 3427

INHABITETH
Isa 57:15 high and lofty One that **i** eternity 7931

INHERIT
Ge 15:7 to give thee this land to **i** it 3423
Ge 28:4 that thou mayest **i** the land 3423
Ex 32:13 seed, and they shall **i** it for ever. 5157
Le 20:24 Ye shall **i** their land, and I will 3423
Dt 1:38 for he shall cause Israel to **i** it 5157
1Sa 2:8 to make them **i** the throne of glory: 5157
Ps 37:11 But the meek shall **i** the earth; 3423
Ps 37:29 The righteous shall **i** the land, ... 3423
Pr 3:35 The wise shall **i** glory: but shame 5157
Pr 11:29 his own house shall **i** the wind: 5157
Pr 14:18 The simple **i** folly: but the prudent 5157
Isa 60:21 they shall **i** the land for ever, the 3423
Isa 65:9 and mine elect shall **i** it, and my 3423
Mt 5:5 **meek: for they shall i the earth** *2816*
Mt 19:29 **and shall i everlasting life** *2816*
Mt 25:34 **i the kingdom prepared for you** *2816*
Mk 10:17 shall I do that I may **i** eternal life? *2816*
Lk 10:25 what shall I do to **i** eternal life? *2816*
Lk 18:18 what shall I do to **i** eternal life? *2816*
Gal 5:21 shall not **i** the kingdom of God. *2816*
Heb 6:12 faith and patience **i** the promises *2816*
Rev 21:7 that overcometh shall **i** all things; *2816*

INHERITANCE
Ge 31:14 yet any portion or **i** for us in our 5159
Ex 34:9 our sin, and take us for thine **i** 5157
Nu 18:23 children of Israel they have no **i** 5159
Nu 26:62 because there was no **i** given 5159
Nu 27:7 an **i** among their father's brethren; 5159
Nu 33:54 divide the land by lot for an **i** 5157
Nu 36:2 to give the land for an **i** by lot to 5159
Nu 36:8 daughter, that possesseth an **i** in 5159
Dt 4:20 to be unto him a people of **i**, as ye 5159
Dt 9:29 they are thy people and thine **i**, ... 5159
Dt 18:2 the Lord is their **i**, as he hath said 5159
Dt 32:8 divided to the nations their **i**, ... 5157
Jgs 2:6 every man unto his **i** to possess 5159
1Sa 26:19 from abiding in the **i** of the Lord, ... 5159
2Sa 21:3 ye may bless the **i** of the Lord? 5159
1Ki 8:51 For they be thy people, and thine **i**, ... 5159
1Ch 28:8 leave it for an **i** for your children 5157
2Ch 10:16 we have none **i** in the son of Jesse: 5159
Ezr 9:12 leave it for an **i** to your children 3423
Job 42:15 gave them **i** among their brethren 5159
Ps 2:8 give thee the heathen for thine **i**, ... 5159
Ps 79:1 the heathen are come into thine **i**; 5159
Ps 106:40 that he abhorred his own **i** 5159
Pr 13:22 A good man leaveth an **i** to his 5157
Ecc 7:11 Wisdom is good with an **i**: and by 5159

Jer	10:16	and Israel is the rod of his **i**: The	5159
Jer	32:8	for the right of **i** is thine, and the	3425
La	5:2	Our **i** is turned to strangers, our	5159
Eze	46:18	shall not take of the people's **i** by	5159
Eze	47:22	they shall have **i** with you among	5159
Mt	21:38	**kill him, and let us seize on his i.**	*2817*
Mk	12:7	**kill him, and the i shall be ours**	*2817*
Lk	20:14	**kill him, that the i may be ours.**	*2817*
Gal	3:18	if the **i** be of the law, it is no more	*2817*
Eph	1:11	In whom also we ... obtained an **i**	2820
Eph	1:14	is the earnest of our **i** until the	*2817*
Eph	1:18	of the glory of his **i** in the saints	*2817*
Eph	5:5	hath any **i** in the kingdom of Christ	*2817*
Col	1:12	be partakers of the **i** of the saints	*2819*
Col	3:24	shall receive the reward of the **i**:	*2817*
Heb	1:4	as he hath by **i** obtained a more	*2820*
Heb	9:15	receive the promise of eternal **i**	2817
Heb	11:8	he should after receive for an **i**,	2817
1Pe	1:4	an **i** incorruptible, and undefiled	*2817*

INHERITED

Jer	16:19	Surely our fathers have **i** lies,	5157
Eze	33:24	and he **i** the land: but we are	3423
Heb	12:17	he would have **i** the blessing	*2876*

INIQUITIES

Le	16:21	all the **i** of the children of Israel	5771
Le	26:39	**i** of their fathers shall they pine	5771
Ezr	9:6	our **i** are increased over our head	5771
Ezr	9:13	punished us less than our **i** deserve,	5771
Ps	51:9	my, sins, and blot out all mine **i**	5771
Ps	64:6	They search out **i** they	5766
Ps	103:3	Who forgiveth all thine **i**; who	5771
Ps	103:10	rewarded us according to our **i**	5771
Ps	130:3	If thou, Lord, shouldest mark **i**,	5771
Pr	5:22	His own **i** shall take the wicked	5771
Isa	53:5	he was bruised for our **i**:	5771
Isa	53:11	many; for he shall bear their **i**	5771
Isa	59:2	But your **i** have separated	5771
Isa	59:12	and as for our **i**, we know them;	5771
Isa	64:6	our **i**, like the wind, have taken	5771
Jer	14:7	though our **i** testify against us,	5771
Jer	33:8	and I will pardon all their **i**,	5771
La	4:13	the **i** of her priests, that have	5771
La	5:7	not; and we have borne their **i**	5771
Eze	36:31	in your own sight for your **i** and	5771
Da	4:27	and thine **i** by shewing mercy to	5758
Da	9:13	that we might turn from our **i**,	5771
Da	9:16	sins, and for the **i** of our fathers,	5771
Am	3:2	I will punish you for all your **i**	5771
Mic	7:19	he will subdue our **i**; and thou	5771
Ac	3:26	away every one of you from his **i**	*4189*
Ro	4:7	are they whose **i** are forgiven,	*458*
Heb	8:12	their **i** will I remember no more.	*458*
Heb	10:17	sins and **i** will I remember no more	*458*
Rev	18:5	and God hath remembered her **i**	*92*

INIQUITY

Ge	15:16	**i** of the Amorites is not yet full	5771
Ge	19:15	be consumed in the **i** of the city	5771
Ex	34:7	visiting the **i** of the fathers upon	5771
Le	5:17	yet is he guilty, and shall bear his **i**	5771
Le	26:41	of the punishment of their **i**:	5771
Nu	18:1	shall bear the **i** of the sanctuary:	5771
Dt	32:4	a God of truth and without **i**,	5766
1Sa	3:14	**i** of Eli's house shall not be purged	5771
1Sa	15:23	stubbornness is as **i** and idolatry	205
2Sa	24:10	take away the **i** of thy servant;	5771
2Ch	19:7	is no **i** with the Lord our God,	5766
Ne	4:5	And cover not their **i**, and let not	5771
Job	4:8	that plow **i**, and sow wickedness,	205
Job	11:6	thee less than thine **i** deserveth.	5771
Ps	25:11	O Lord, pardon mine **i**; for it is	5771
Ps	32:2	whom the Lord imputeth not **i**,	5771
Ps	32:5	thee, and mine **i** have I not hid	5771
Ps	38:18	For I will declare mine **i**: I will	5771
Ps	51:2	Wash me thoroughly from mine **i**,	5771
Ps	51:5	I was shapen in **i**; and in sin	5771
Ps	66:18	If I regard **i** in my heart, the Lord	205
Ps	106:43	and were brought low for their **i**	5771
Pr	10:29	shall be to the workers of **i**	205
Pr	16:6	By mercy and truth **i** is purged:	5771
Pr	19:28	mouth of the wicked devoureth **i**	205
Pr	21:15	shall be to the workers of **i**	205
Pr	22:8	that soweth **i** shall reap vanity:	5766
Ecc	3:16	righteousness, that **i** was there	7562
Isa	1:4	nation, a people laden with **i**	5771
Isa	6:7	thine **i** is taken away, and thy sin	5771
Isa	22:14	Surely this **i** shall not be purged.	5771
Isa	32:6	his heart will work **i**, to practice	205
Isa	40:2	her **i** is pardoned: for she hath	5771
Isa	53:6	hath laid on him the **i** of us all.	5771
Isa	59:4	conceive mischief, and bring forth **i**	205
Isa	59:7	their thoughts are thoughts of **i**;	205
Jer	3:13	Only acknowledge thine **i**, that	5771
Jer	16:17	neither is their **i** hid from mine	5771
La	4:6	punishment of the **i** of the daughter	5771
Eze	3:18	same wicked man shall die in his **i**;	5771
Eze	14:10	bear the punishment of their **i**:	5771
Eze	16:49	this was the **i** of thy sister Sodom,	5771
Eze	18:17	not die for the **i** of his father, he	5771
Eze	18:30	so **i** shall not be your ruin.	5771
Eze	28:15	created, till **i** was found in thee	5766
Eze	33:8	that wicked man shall die in his **i**;	5771
Eze	39:23	went into captivity for their **i**:	5771
Hos	8:13	now will he remember their **i**,	5771
Mic	2:1	Woe to them that devise **i**, and	205
Mic	7:18	like unto thee, that pardoneth **i**,	5771
Hab	1:13	evil, and canst not look on **i**:	5999
Zep	3:5	the midst thereof; he will not do **i**:	5766
Zec	3:4	I have caused thine **i** to pass	5771
Zec	3:9	will remove the **i** of that land in one	5771
Mal	2:6	and **i** was not found in his lips:	5766
Mt	7:23	**depart from me, ye that work i**	*458*
Mt	13:41	**that offend, and them which do i:**	*458*
Mt	23:28	**ye are full of hypocrisy and i.**	*458*
Mt	24:12	**because i shall abound, the love of**	*458*
Lk	13:27	**depart from me, all ye workers of i**	*93*
Ac	1:18	a field with the reward of **i**:	*93*
Ac	8:23	of bitterness, and in the bond of **i**	*93*
Ro	6:19	to uncleanness and to **i** unto **i**;	*458*
1Co	13:6	Rejoiceth not in **i**, but rejoiceth in	*93*
2Th	2:7	mystery of **i** doth already work:	*458*
2Ti	2:19	the name of Christ depart from **i**	*93*
Tit	2:14	might redeem us from all **i**, and	*458*
Heb	1:9	loved righteousness, and hated **i**;	*458*
Jas	3:6	And the tongue is a fire, a world of **i**:	*93*
2Pe	2:16	But was rebuked for his **i**: the	*3892*

INJURIOUS

1Ti	1:13	and a persecutor, and **i**: but I	*5197*

INJUSTICE
Job 16:17 Not for any **i** in mine hands: also 2555

INK
2Co 3:3 written not with **i**, but with the........ *3188*

INN
Ge 43:21 when we came to the **i**, that we........ 4411
Ex 4:24 came to pass by the way in the **i**,....... 4411
Lk 2:7 was no room for them in the **i** *2646*
Lk 10:34 **and brought him to an i, and took**..... *3829*

INNER
1Ki 22:25 shalt go into an **i** chamber to hide 2315
Est 4:11 unto the king into the **i** court,......... 6442
Eze 8:16 he brought me into the **i** court 6442
Eze 10:3 and the cloud filled the **i** court......... 6442
Eze 43:5 and brought me into the **i** court; 6442
Ac 16:24 thrust them into the **i** prison, and *2082*
Eph 3:16 might by his Spirit in the **i** man;....... *2080*

INNERMOST
Pr 18:8 down into the **i** parts of the belly....... 2315
Pr 26:22 down into the **i** parts of the belly....... 2315

INNOCENCY
Ge 20:5 and **i** of my hands have I done 5356
Da 6:22 as before him **i** was found in me; 2136

INNOCENT
Ex 23:7 the **i** and righteous slay thou not:...... 5355
Dt 19:10 That **i** blood be not shed in thy........ 5355
Dt 19:13 the guilt of **i** blood from Israel,........ 5355
Dt 27:25 taketh reward to slay an **i** person....... 5355
1Sa 19:5 then wilt thou sin against **i** blood, ... 5355
2Ki 21:16 Manasseh shed **i** blood very much, ... 5355
2Ki 24:4 he filled Jerusalem with **i** blood;....... 5355
Job 4:7 thee, who ever perished, being **i**? 5355
Job 22:19 and the **i** laugh them to scorn. 5355
Job 33:9 without transgression, I am **i**: 2643
Ps 15:5 nor taketh reward against the **i**........ 5355
Ps 19:13 **i** from the great transgression. 5352
Ps 106:38 And shed **i** blood, even the blood...... 5355
Pr 1:11 let us lurk privily for the **i** without..... 5355
Pr 6:17 and hands that shed **i** blood,.......... 5355
Pr 6:29 toucheth her shall not be **i**............ 5352
Pr 28:20 haste to be rich shall not be **i**.......... 5352
Isa 59:7 they make haste to shed **i** blood:....... 5355
Jer 7:6 and shed not **i** blood in this place, ... 5355
Jer 22:3 neither shed **i** blood in this place,...... 5355
Jer 26:15 ye shall surely bring **i** blood upon 5355
Jnh 1:14 and lay not upon us **i** blood: for....... 5355
Mt 27:4 in that I have betrayed the **i** blood....... *121*
Mt 27:24 I am **i** of the blood of this just.......... *121*

INNUMERABLE
Lk 12:1 an **i** multitude of people;............. *3461*
Heb 11:12 sand which is by the sea shore **i**......... *382*
Heb 12:22 and to an **i** company of angels,........ *3461*

INORDINATE
Eze 23:11 was more corrupt in her **i** love 5691
Col 3:5 uncleanness, **i** affection, evil *3806*

INQUIRE See ENQUIRE.

INQUISITION
Dt 19:18 the judges shall make diligent **i**: 1875
Est 2:23 when **i** was made of the matter, ... 1245

INSCRIPTION
Ac 17:23 altar with this **i**, To The Unknown *1924*

INSOMUCH See also FORASMUCH.
Mt 24:24 **i that, if it were possible, they**......... *5620*
Mk 1:45 **i** that Jesus could no more openly *5620*
Lk 12:1 **i** that they trode one upon another,.... *5620*
2Co 1:8 **i** that we despaired even of life:........ *5620*

INSPIRATION
Job 32:8 the **i** of the Almighty giveth them...... 5397
2Ti 3:16 scripture is given by **i** of God,......... *2315*

INSTANT
Lk 2:38 she coming in that **i** gave thanks....... *5610*
2Ti 4:2 be **i** in season, out of season;.......... *2186*

INSTEAD
Ge 4:25 me another seed **i** of Abel,............ 8478
Ex 4:16 and thou shalt be to him **i** of God.
Nu 3:45 the Levites **i** of all the firstborn........ 8478
Nu 5:29 aside to another **i** of her husband, ... 8478
Nu 10:31 thou mayest be to us **i** of eyes. 8478
1Ki 3:7 made thy servant king **i** of David 8478
Est 2:17 and made her queen **i** of Vashti........ 8478
Isa 3:24 sackcloth; and burning **i** of beauty..... 8478
Eze 16:32 taketh strangers **i** of her husband! 8478

INSTRUCT
Dt 4:36 his voice that he might **i** thee:......... 3256
Ne 9:20 also thy good spirit to **i** them,......... 7919
Job 40:2 contendeth with the Almighty **i** him?... 3250
Ps 32:8 I will **i** thee and teach thee in the 7919
Isa 28:26 his God doth **i** him to discretion,...... 3256
Da 11:33 among the people shall **i** many: 995
1Co 2:16 of the Lord, that he may **i** him?........ *4822*

INSTRUCTED
Dt 32:10 he **i** him, he kept him as the apple of.... 995
2Ch 3:3 Solomon was **i** for the building........ 3245
Pr 21:11 when the wise is **i**, he receiveth 7919
Isa 8:11 and **i** me that I should not walk 3256
Isa 40:14 and who **i** him, and taught him 995
Mt 13:52 **is i unto the kingdom of heaven**....... *3100*
Mt 14:8 being before **i** of her mother,.......... *4264*
Lk 1:4 things, wherein thou hast been **i**....... *2727*
Ac 18:25 man was **i** in the way of the Lord;...... *2727*
Ro 2:18 excellent, being **i** out of the law; *2727*
Php 4:12 all things I am **i** both to be full *3453*

INSTRUCTERS
1Co 4:15 ye have ten thousand **i** in Christ, ... *3807*

INSTRUCTING
2Ti 2:25 In meekness **i** those that oppose *3811*

INSTRUCTION
Ps 50:17 Seeing thou hatest **i**, and easiest 4148
Pr 1:2 To know wisdom and **i**; to............ 4148
Pr 1:7 but fools despise wisdom and **i**........ 4148
Pr 5:12 How have I hated **i**, and my heart...... 4148
Pr 5:23 He shall die without **i**; and in the...... 4148
Pr 6:23 reproofs of **i** are the way of life: 4148
Pr 9:9 Give **i** to a wise man, and he will be
Pr 12:1 Whoso loveth **i** loveth knowledge: 4148
Pr 13:1 A wise son heareth his father's **i**:....... 4148
Pr 13:18 shall be to him that refuseth **i**:......... 4148
Pr 15:32 refuseth **i** despiseth his own soul:...... 4148
Pr 15:33 fear of the Lord is the **i** of wisdom; 4148

Pr 16:22 hath it: but the **i** of fools is folly. 4148
Pr 19:27 to hear the **i** that causeth to err. 4148
Pr 23:12 Apply thine heart unto **i**, and 4148
Pr 24:32 I looked upon it, and received **i** 4148
Jer 17:23 they might not hear, nor receive **i**. 4148
2Ti 3:16 correction, for **i** in righteousness: *3809*

INSTRUCTOR
Ro 2:20 An **i** of the foolish, a teacher of *3810*

INSTRUMENT
Nu 35:16 if he smite him with an **i** of iron, 3627
Eze 33:32 voice, and can play well on an **i**:

INSTRUMENTS
Ge 49:5 **i** of cruelty are in their 3627
Nu 4:12 shall take all the **i** of ministry, 3627
1Sa 8:12 his **i** of war, and **i** of his chariots. 3627
1Sa 18:6 with joy, and with **i** of musick. 7991
1Ch 15:16 to be the singers with **i** of musick, 3627
1Ch 16:42 sound, and with musical **i** of God. 3627
2Ch 29:27 with the **i** ordained by David king 3627
Ne 12:36 with the musical **i** of David the. 3627
Ps 68:25 the players on **i** followed after;
Ecc 2:8 as musical **i**, and that of all sorts.
Da 6:18 neither were **i** of musick brought 1761
Am 6:5 invent to themselves **i** of musick, 3627
Zec 11:15 yet the **i** of a foolish shepherd. 3627
Ro 6:13 as **i** of righteousness unto God. *3696*

INSURRECTION
Ezr 4:19 time hath made **i** against kings, 5376
Mk 15:7 bound with them that had made **i** *4955*
Ac 18:12 the Jews made **i** with one accord. *2722*

INTEGRITY
1Ki 9:4 thy father walked, in **i** of heart, 8537
Job 2:3 and still he holdeth fast his **i**, 8538
Job 2:9 him, Dost thou still retain thine **i**? 8538
Job 27:5 till I die I will not remove mine **i** 8538
Job 31:6 that God may know mine **i** 8538
Ps 26:1 Lord; for I have waked in mine **i**: 8537
Pr 11:3 The **i** of the upright shall guide 8538
Pr 19:1 is the poor that walketh in his **i**, 8537
Pr 20:7 The just man walketh in his **i**: his 8537

INTEND
2Ch 28:13 ye **i** to add more to our sins and to 559
Ac 5:28 and **i** to bring this man's blood *1014*

INTENDED
Ps 21:11 For they **i** evil against thee: they 5186

INTENT
2Sa 17:14 **i** that the Lord might bring evil 5668
2Ki 10:19 to the **i** that he might destroy the 4616
Da 4:17 to the **i** that the living may know 1701
1Co 10:6 to the **i** we should not lust after
Eph 3:10 To the **i** that now unto the *2443*

INTENTS
Heb 4:12 of the thoughts and **i** of the heart. *1771*

INTERCESSION
Isa 53:12 and made **i** for the transgressors. 6293
Jer 7:16 for them, neither make **i** to me: 6293
Ro 8:26 the Spirit itself maketh **i** for us *5241*
Ro 8:34 of God, who also maketh **i** for us. *1793*
Heb 7:25 he ever liveth to make **i** for them *1793*

INTERCESSOR
Isa 59:16 wondered that there was no **i**: 6293

INTERPRET
Ge 41:8 there was none that could **i** them 6622
1Co 12:30 all speak with tongues? do all **i**? *1329*
1Co 14:5 speaketh with tongues, except he **i**, *1329*
1Co 14:27 and that by course; and let one **i**. *1329*

INTERPRETATION
Ge 40:12 This is the **i** of it: The three 6623
Jgs 7:15 of the dream, and the **i** thereof, 7667
Pr 1:6 understand a proverb, and the **i**; 4426
Ecc 8:1 who knoweth the **i** of a thing? 6592
Da 2:45 is certain, and the **i** thereof sure. 6591
Da 4:24 This is the **i**, O king, and this is. 6591
Da 5:26 This is the **i** of the thing: Mene; 6591
1Co 12:10 to another the **i** of tongues: *2058*
1Co 14:26 tongue, hath a revelation, hath an **i** *2058*
2Pe 1:20 the scripture is of any private **i** *1955*

INTERPRETATIONS
Ge 40:8 Do not **i** belong to God? tell me 6623
Da 5:16 that thou canst make **i**, and 6591

INTERPRETED
Ge 41:12 him, and he **i** to us our dreams; 6622
Mt 1:23 which being **i** is, God with us. *3177*
Mk 5:41 **cumi;** which is, being **i**, Damsel. *5177*
Mk 15:22 is, being **i**, The place of a skull. *3177*
Mk 15:34 which is, being **i**, My God, my God, *3177*
Jn 1:38 which is to say, being **i**, Master, *2059*
Jn 1:41 which is, being **i**, the Christ. *5177*
Ac 4:36 being **i**, The son of consolation, *3177*

INTERPRETER
Ge 40:8 a dream, and there is no **i** of it. 6622
Ge 42:23 for he spake unto them by an **i**. 3887
Jn 33:23 an **i**, one among a thousand, to. 3887
1Co 14:28 if there be no **i**, let him keep *1328*

INTREAT
Ex 8:8 **I** the Lord, that he may take 6279
Ex 8:29 **i** the Lord that the swarms of flies 6279
Ex 9:28 **I** the Lord (for it is enough) that 6279
Ru 1:16 Ruth said, **I** me not to leave thee, 6293
1Sa 2:25 the Lord, who shall **i** for him? 6419
1Ki 13:6 **I** now the face of the Lord thy. 2470
Pr 19:6 will **i** the favour of the prince:. 2470
1Co 4:13 Being defamed, we **i**: we are. *3870*
1Ti 5:1 an elder, but **i** him as a father; *3870*

INTREATED See also ENTREATED.
Ge 25:21 Isaac **i** the Lord for his wife, 6279
Ex 8:30 out from Pharaoh, and **i** the Lord 6279
Ex 10:18 out from Pharaoh, and **i** the Lord 6279
Jgs 13:8 Then Manoah **i** the Lord, and said, 6279
2Sa 21:14 after that God was **i** for the land. 6279
2Sa 24:25 So the Lord was **i** for the land, and. 6279
1Ch 5:20 in the battle, and he was **i** of them; 6279
Ezr 8:23 God for this: and he was **i** of us 6279
Lk 15:28 **came his father out, and i him** *3870*
Heb 12:19 **i** that the word should not be *3868*
Jas 3:17 and easy to be **i**, full of mercy and *2138*

INTRUDING
Col 2:18 **i** into those things which he hath *1687*

INVADE
Hab 3:16 he will **i** them with his troops 1464

INVADED
1Sa 23:27 for the Philistines have **i** the land 6584
1Sa 30:1 the Amalekites had **i** the south, ... 6584

INVENTED
2Ch 26:15 engines, **i** by cunning men 2803

INVENTIONS
Ps 99:8 thou tookest vengeance of their **i** 5949
Ps 106:39 went a whoring with their own **i** 4611
Pr 8:12 and find out knowledge of witty **i** 4209
Ecc 7:29 but they have sought out many **i** 2810

INVENTORS
Ro 1:30 **i** of evil things, disobedient to *2182*

INVISIBLE
Ro 1:20 For the **i** things of him from the *517*
Col 1:15 Who is the image of the **i** God *517*
Col 1:16 and that are in earth, visible and **i**, ... 517
1Ti 1:17 unto the King eternal, immortal, **i**, ... 517
Heb 11:27 endured, as seeing him who is **i** 517

INVITED
2Sa 13:23 and Absalom **i** all the king's sons 7121
Est 5:12 am I **i** unto her also with the king, ... 7121

INWARD
Job 19:19 All my **i** friends abhorred me: 5475
Job 38:36 hath put wisdom in the **i** parts? 2910
Ps 5:9 their **i** part is very wickedness; 7130
Ps 49:11 Their **i** thought is, that their 7130
Ps 51:6 thou desirest truth in the **i** parts: 2910
Pr 20:27 all the **i** parts of the belly 2315
Jer 31:33 I will put my law in their **i** parts, ... 7130
Ro 7:22 the law of God after the **i** man: *2080*
2Co 4:16 the **i** man is renewed day by day *2081*
2Co 7:15 his **i** affection is more abundant *4698*

INWARDLY
Ps 62:4 their mouth, but they curse **i**. 7130
Mt 7:15 **but i they are ravening wolves** *2081*
Ro 2:29 he is a Jew, which is one **i**: *1722, 2927*

IRON
Le 26:19 I will make your heaven as **i**, and 1270
Nu 35:16 smite him with an instrument of **i**, ... 1270
Dt 3:11 his bedstead was a bedstead of **i**; 1270
Dt 27:5 thou shalt not lift up any **i** tool 1270
Jos 8:31 which no man hath lift up any **i**, ... 1270
Jos 17:16 of the valley have chariots of **i**, ... 1270
1Sa 17:7 weighed six hundred shekels of **i** 1270
1Ki 6:7 any tool of **i** heard in the house 1270
2Ki 6:6 it in thither; and the **i** did swim 1270
1Ch 22:3 David prepared **i** in abundance 1270
Job 19:24 they were graven with an **i** pen 1270
Job 40:18 brass; his bones are like bars of **i**. 1270
Job 41:27 He esteemeth **i** as straw, and brass 1270
Ps 2:9 shalt break them with a rod of **i**; 1270
Pr 27:17 **I** sharpeneth **i**; so a man 1270
Ecc 10:10 If the **i** be blunt, and he do not 1270
Isa 48:4 thy neck is as an **i** sinew, and thy 1270
Jer 17:1 of Judah is written with a pen of **i**, ... 1270
Jer 28:14 have put a yoke of **i** upon the neck. 1270
Da 2:33 His legs of **i**, his feet part of **i** and 6523
Da 2:40 kingdom shall be strong as **i** 6523
Da 2:43 even as **i** is not mixed with clay. 6523
Da 2:45 it brake in pieces the **i**, the brass 6523
Da 7:7 it had great **i** teeth: it devoured 6523
Ac 12:10 they came unto the **i** gate that *4603*
1Ti 4:2 conscience seared with a hot **i**;
Rev 2:27 **shall rule them with a rod of i** *4603*
Rev 12:5 to rule all nations with a rod of **i** *4603*
Rev 19:15 he shall rule them with a rod of **i** *4603*

ISLAND
Job 22:30 shall deliver the **i** of the innocent 336
Ac 27:16 a certain **i** which is called Clauda *3519*
Ac 28:1 knew that the **i** was called Melita *3520*
Ac 28:7 the chief man of the **i**, whose name *3520*
Ac 28:9 which had diseases in the **i**, came, ... *3520*
Rev 6:14 every mountain and **i** were moved *3520*
Rev 16:20 And every **i** fled away, and the *3520*

ISLANDS
Isa 13:22 the wild beasts of the **i** shall cry in 338
Isa 42:12 and declare his praise in the **i** 339
Isa 42:15 I will make the rivers **i**, and I will 339
Isa 59:18 to the **i** he will repay recompence 339
Jer 50:39 beasts of the **i** shall dwell there, ... 339

ISLE
Isa 23:2 Be still, ye inhabitants of the **i**; 339
Isa 23:6 howl, ye inhabitants of the **i** 339
Ac 13:6 gone through the **i** unto Paphos, ... *3520*
Ac 28:11 which had wintered in the **i**, whose *3520*
Rev 1:9 was in the **i** that is called Patmos, ... *3520*

ISLES
Ge 10:5 were the **i** of the Gentiles divided 339
Est 10:1 the land, and upon the **i** of the sea 339
Ps 72:10 and of the **i** shall bring presents: 339
Ps 97:1 the multitude of **i** be glad thereof. 339
Isa 24:15 God of Israel in the **i** of the sea 339
Isa 40:15 taketh up the **i** as a very little thing 339
Isa 41:5 The **i** saw it, and feared; the ends 339
Isa 42:4 and the **i** shall wait for his law 339
Isa 49:1 Listen, O **i**, unto me; and hearken 339
Isa 51:5 the **i** shall wait upon me, and on 339
Isa 60:9 Surely the **i** shall wait for me, and 339
Isa 66:19 to Tubal, and Javan, to the **i** afar off, ... 339
Jer 2:10 pass over the **i** of Chittim, and see; 339
Jer 25:22 the **i** which are beyond the sea, ... 339
Jer 31:10 declare it in the **i** afar off, and say, ... 339
Eze 26:15 the **i** shake at the sound of thy fall, ... 339
Eze 26:18 the **i** tremble in the day of thy fall; 339
Eze 26:18 the **i** that are in the sea shall be 339
Eze 27:15 many **i** were the merchandise of 339
Eze 39:6 them that dwell carelessly in the **i**. 339
Da 11:18 shall he turn his face unto the **i**. 339
Zep 2:11 place, even all the **i** of the heathen 339

ISRAEL (iz´-ra-el)
Ge 32:28 be called no more Jacob, but **I**. 3478
Ge 34:7 because he had wrought folly in **I** 3478
Ge 35:10 Jacob, but **I** shall be thy name; 3478
Ge 37:3 **I** loved Joseph more than all his 3478
Ge 46:30 **I** said unto Joseph, Now let me die. 3478
Ge 47:27 And **I** dwelt in the land of Egypt 3478
Ge 49:28 these are the twelve tribes of **I**. 3478
Ge 50:2 and the physicians embalmed **I** 3478
Ex 2:23 **I** sighed by reason of bondage. 3478
Ex 4:22 Thus saith the Lord, **I** is my son 3478

Ex	5:1	Thus saith the Lord God of **I**, Let	3478
Ex	10:20	would not let the children of **I** go	3478
Ex	12:40	the sojourning of the children of **I**	3478
Ex	14:5	we have let **I** go from serving us?	3478
Ex	14:8	he pursued after the children of **I**	3478
Ex	14:29	children of **I** walked upon dry land	3478
Ex	14:30	**I** saw the Egyptians dead upon	3478
Ex	16:2	children of **I** murmured against	3478
Ex	17:11	held up his hand, that **I** prevailed:	3478
Ex	18:25	Moses chose able men out of all **I**,	3478
Ex	24:10	And they saw the God of **I**: and	3478
Ex	29:45	will dwell among the children of **I**	3478
Ex	31:16	of **I** shall keep the sabbath	3478
Ex	32:20	made the children of **I** drink of it	3478
Ex	34:35	children of **I** saw the face of Moses,	3478
Le	10:11	that ye may teach the children of **I**	3478
Le	16:21	the iniquities of the children of **I**	3478
Le	16:34	the children of **I** for all their sins	3478
Nu	3:41	firstborn among the children of **I**;	3478
Nu	8:18	the firstborn of the children of **I**	3478
Nu	8:19	atonement for the children of **I**	3478
Nu	9:2	children of **I** also keep the passover	3478
Nu	11:4	the children of **I** also wept again,	3478
Nu	18:14	Every thing devoted in **I** shall be	3478
Nu	20:13	children of **I** strove with the Lord,	3478
Nu	23:7	curse me Jacob, and come, defy **I**	3478
Nu	24:17	a Sceptre shall rise out of **I**, and	3478
Nu	25:13	an atonement for the children of **I**	3478
Nu	32:13	Lord's anger was kindled against **I**,	3478
Dt	6:4	Hear, O **I**: The Lord our God is	3478
Dt	9:1	Hear, O **I**: Thou art to pass over	3478
Dt	10:12	**I**, what doth the Lord thy God	3478
Dt	32:49	the children of **I** for a possession:	3478
Jos	4:7	a memorial unto the children of **I**	3478
Jos	5:3	and circumcised the children of **I**	3478
Jos	7:15	because he hath wrought folly in **I**	3478
Jos	10:42	the Lord God of **I** fought for **I**	3478
Jos	14:10	**I** wandered in the wilderness:	3478
Jos	21:43	the Lord gave unto **I** all the land	3478
Jos	22:24	ye to do with the Lord God of **I**?	3478
Jgs	1:1	the children of **I** asked the Lord,	3478
Jgs	1:28	came to pass, when **I** was strong,	3478
Jgs	2:11	**I** did evil in the sight of the Lord,	3478
Jgs	3:7	**I** did evil in the sight of the Lord,	3478
Jgs	3:12	**I** did evil again in the sight of the	3478
Jgs	4:1	**I** again did evil in the sight of the	3478
Jgs	6:1	**I** did evil in the sight of the Lord:	3478
Jgs	10:6	**I** did evil again in the sight of the	3478
Jgs	11:40	the daughters of **I** went yearly to	3478
Jgs	13:1	**I** did evil again in the sight of the	3478
Jgs	17:6	those days there was no king in **I**,	3478
Jgs	21:25	those days there was no king in **I**	3478
Ru	4:11	which two did build the house of **I**	3478
Ru	4:14	that his name may be famous in **I**	3478
1Sa	1:17	God of **I** grant thee thy petition	3478
1Sa	3:11	Behold, I will do a thing in **I**, at	3478
1Sa	4:22	The glory is departed from **I**:	3478
1Sa	5:11	Send away the ark of the God of **I**,	3478
1Sa	17:10	I defy the armies of **I** this day;	3478
1Sa	17:46	may know that there is a God in **I**	3478
1Sa	26:20	king of **I** is come out to seek a flea,	3478
2Sa	1:19	beauty of **I** is slain upon thy high	3478
2Sa	12:12	I will do this thing before all **I**,	3478
2Sa	13:12	such thing ought to be done in **I**	3478
2Sa	15:6	stole the hearts of the men of **I**	3478
2Sa	23:1	Jacob, and the sweet psalmist of **I**,	3478
1Ki	8:34	forgive the sin of thy people **I**	3478
1Ki	9:7	**I** shall be a proverb and a byword	3478
1Ki	10:9	the Lord loved **I** forever, therefore	3478
1Ki	16:26	his sin wherewith he made **I** to sin,	3478
1Ki	18:17	him, Art thou he that troubleth **I**?	3478
1Ki	18:31	came, saying, **I** shall be thy name:	3478
2Ki	1:6	because there is not a God in **I**	3478
2Ki	5:15	no God in all the earth, but in **I**	3478
2Ki	14:27	he would blot out the name of **I**	3478
2Ki	17:6	and carried **I** away into Assyria,	3478
2Ki	17:20	the Lord rejected all the seed of **I**,	3478
2Ki	19:15	O Lord God of **I**, which dwellest	3478
1Ch	11:1	all **I** gathered themselves to David	3478
1Ch	16:17	to **I** for an everlasting covenant	3478
1Ch	17:21	in the earth is like thy people **I**,	3478
1Ch	17:24	is the God of **I**, even a God to **I**	3478
1Ch	21:1	And Satan stood up against **I**,	3478
1Ch	21:14	fell of **I** seventy thousand men	3478
1Ch	27:23	would increase **I** like to the stars	3478
2Ch	2:4	This is an ordinance for ever to **I**	3478
2Ch	6:14	God of **I**, there is no God like thee	3478
2Ch	6:25	and forgive the sin of my people **I**,	3478
2Ch	9:8	because thy God loved **I**, to	3478
2Ch	15:3	**I** hath been without the true God,	3478
2Ch	18:16	**I** scattered upon the mountains	3478
2Ch	24:5	gather of all **I** money to repair the	3478
2Ch	25:7	for the Lord is not with **I**, to wit,	3478
2Ch	34:21	them that are left in **I** and in Judah,	3478
2Ch	35:18	no passover like to that kept in **I**	3478
Ezr	1:3	the house of the Lord God of **I**,	3478
Ezr	3:11	mercy endureth for ever toward **I**	3478
Ezr	7:10	teach in **I** statutes and judgments	3478
Ne	1:6	confess the sins of the children of **I**,	3478
Ne	8:17	had not the children of **I** done so	3478
Ne	13:26	king of **I** sin by these things?	3478
Ps	22:3	that inhabitest the praises of **I**	3478
Ps	25:22	Redeem **I**, O God, out of all his	3478
Ps	73:1	God is good to **I**, even to such as	3478
Ps	81:11	voice; and **I** would none of me	3478
Ps	105:10	to **I** for an everlasting covenant:	3478
Ps	121:4	that keepeth **I** shall neither slumber	3478
Ps	129:1	from my youth, may **I** now say:	3478
Ps	130:8	And he shall redeem **I** from all	3478
Ps	135:4	and **I** for his peculiar treasure	3478
Isa	1:4	provoked the Holy One of **I** unto	3478
Isa	8:18	for signs and for wonders in **I**	3478
Isa	10:22	people **I** be as the sand of the sea,	3478
Isa	17:7	have respect to the Holy One of **I**	3478
Isa	30:11	cause the Holy One of **I** to cease	3478
Isa	41:20	the Holy One of **I** hath created it	3478
Isa	43:15	One, the Creator of **I**, your King	3478
Isa	45:4	servant's sake, and **I** mine elect,	3478
Isa	49:7	Redeemer of **I**, and his Holy One,	3478
Jer	2:3	**I** was holiness unto the Lord, and	3478
Jer	29:23	they have committed villainy in **I**,	3478
Jer	31:31	new covenant with the house of **I**	3478
Jer	50:17	**I** is a scattered sheep; the lions	3478
Jer	51:19	and **I** is the rod of his inheritance	
Jer	51:49	hath caused the slain of **I** to fall,	3478
La	2:1	unto the earth the beauty of **I**	3478
Eze	4:5	bear the iniquity of the house of **I**	3478
Eze	9:9	The iniquity of the house of **I** and	3478
Eze	11:13	a full end of the remnant of **I**?	3478
Eze	11:17	and I will give you the land of **I**	3478
Eze	14:11	house of **I** may go no more astray	3478
Eze	18:31	for why will ye die, O house of **I**?	3478

Eze 20:5 In the day when I chose **I**, and 3478
Eze 20:13 the house of **I** rebelled against me 3478
Eze 21:2 prophesy against the land of **I**. 3478
Eze 22:18 house of **I** is to me become dross: 3478
Eze 35:5 shed blood of the children of **I** by 3478
Eze 36:17 house of **I** dwelt in their own land 3478
Eze 36:21 which the house of **I** had profaned 3478
Eze 37:11 bones are the whole house of **I** 3478
Eze 39:22 house of **I** shall know that I am 3478
Eze 39:25 mercy upon the whole house of **I**, 3478
Eze 39:29 out my spirit upon the house of **I**, 3478
Eze 43:7 shall the house of **I** no more defile, 3478
Eze 44:15 children of **I** went astray from me, 3478
Eze 45:17 reconciliation for the house of **I** 3478
Da 9:11 all **I** have transgressed thy law, 3478
Da 9:20 my sin and the sin of my people **I** 3478
Hos 1:6 have mercy upon the house of **I**; 3478
Hos 1:10 **I** shall be as the sand of the sea 3478
Hos 3:4 **I** shall abide many days without a 3478
Hos 3:5 shall the children of **I** return, and 3478
Hos 7:1 When I would have healed **I**, then 3478
Hos 7:10 the pride of **I** testifieth to his face: 3478
Hos 8:2 **I** shall cry unto me. My God, we 3478
Hos 8:8 **I** is swallowed up: now shall they 3478
Hos 8:14 **I** hath forgotten his Maker, and 3478
Hos 10:1 **I** is an empty vine, he bringeth 3478
Hos 11:1 When **I** was a child, then I loved 3478
Hos 13:9 O **I**, thou hast destroyed thyself; 3478
Hos 14:1 O **I**, return unto the Lord thy God; 3478
Joel 2:27 know that I am in the midst of **I** 3478
Am 2:6 For three transgressions of **I**, and 3478
Am 4:12 prepare to meet thy God, O **I** 3478
Am 5:2 The virgin of **I** is fallen; she shall 3478
Am 7:9 sanctuaries of **I** shall be laid waste; 3478
Am 7:16 sayest, Prophesy not against **I** 3478
Am 8:2 end is come upon my people of **I**; 3478
Mic 1:5 and for the sins of the house of **I** 3478
Mic 2:12 surely gather the remnant of **I**; 3478
Mic 3:8 his transgression, and to **I** his sin. 3478
Mic 6:2 people, and he will plead with **I** 3478
Zep 3:13 remnant of **I** shall not do iniquity, 3478
Zep 3:15 the king of **I**, even the Lord, is in 3478
Mal 2:11 an abomination is committed in **I** 3478
Mt 2:6 that shall rule my people **I** *2474*
Mt 8:10 **found so great faith, no, not in I.** *2474*
Mt 10:6 **to the lost sheep of the house of I** *2474*
Mt 15:24 **the lost sheep of the house of I.** *2474*
Mt 19:28 **judging the twelve tribes of I** *2474*
Mt 27:42 If he be the King of **I**, let him now *2474*
Mk 12:29 **the commandments is, Hear, O I;** *2474*
Mk 15:32 Let Christ the King of **I** descend *2474*
Lk 1:54 He hath holpen his servant **I**, *2474*
Lk 2:25 waiting for the consolation of **I**. *2474*
Lk 2:32 and the glory of thy people **I**. *2474*
Lk 2:34 fall and rising again of many in **I**; *2474*
Lk 7:9 **found so great faith, no, not in I.** *2474*
Lk 22:30 **judging the twelve tribes of I** *2474*
Lk 24:21 he which should have redeemed **I** *2474*
Jn 1:49 Son of God; thou art the King of **I** *2474*
Jn 3:10 **Art thou a master of I, and** *2474*
Ac 1:6 restore again the kingdom to **I**? *2474*
Ac 2:22 Ye men of **I**, hear these words; *2475*
Ac 3:12 Ye men of **I**, why marvel ye at this? *2475*
Ac 5:35 Ye men of **I**, take heed to *2475*
Ac 13:16 Men of **I**, and ye that fear God, *2475*
Ac 13:23 promise raised unto **I** a Saviour *2474*
Ro 9:6 they are not all **I**, which are of **I** *2474*
Ro 9:27 children of **I** be as the sand of the *2474*
Ro 10:1 desire and prayer to God for **I** is, *2474*
Ro 10:19 But I say, Did not **I** know? *2474*
Ro 11:2 intercession to God against **I**, *2474*
Ro 11:25 blindness in part is happened to **I**, 2474
Ro 11:26 And so all **I** shall be saved: as it is *2474*
1Co 10:18 Behold **I** after the flesh: are not *2474*
Gal 6:16 and mercy, and upon the **I** of God *2474*
Eph 2:12 aliens from the commonwealth of **I**, *2474*
Heb 8:8 a new covenant with the house of **I** *2474*
Heb 11:22 the departing of the children of **I**; *2474*
Rev 7:4 of all the tribes of the children of **I**. *2474*
Rev 21:12 twelve tribes of the children of **I** *2474*

ISRAELITE (iz´-ra-el-ite)
Jn 1:47 **Behold an I indeed, in whom is** *2475*
Ro 11:1 For I also am an **I**, of the seed of *2475*

ISRAELITES (iz´-ra-el-ites)
Jos 3:17 the **I** passed over on dry ground, 3478
Jos 13:6 lot unto the **i** for an inheritance, 3478
Ro 9:4 Who are **I**; to whom pertaineth *2475*
2Co 11:22 Are they **I**? so am **I** Are they *2475*

ISSUE
Le 15:2 When any man hath a running **i** 2100
Isa 39:7 thy sons that shall **i** from thee, 3318
Mt 9:20 with an **i** of blood twelve years, *131*
Mk 5:25 had an **i** of blood twelve years *4511*
Lk 8:43 having an **i** of blood twelve years *4511*

ISSUED
Eze 47:12 waters they **i** out of the sanctuary: 3318
Da 7:10 A fiery stream **i** and came forth 5047
Rev 9:17 out of their mouths **i** fire and *1607*

ISSUES
Pr 4:23 for out of it are the **i** of life 8444

ITCHING
2Ti 4:3 teachers, having **i** ears; *2833*

ITSELF
Ge 1:11 whose seed is in **i**, upon the earth:
Dt 14:21 not eat of any thing that died of **i**
Mt 6:34 **take thought for the things of i.** *1438*
Mt 12:25 **Every kingdom divided against i** *1438*
Mk 3:25 **if a house be divided against i,** *1438*
Lk 11:17 **Every kingdom divided against i is** *1438*
Jn 15:4 **the branch cannot bear fruit of i,** *1438*
Jn 21:25 even the world **i** could not contain *846*
Ro 8:16 Spirit **i** beareth witness with our *846*
Ro 8:26 the Spirit **i** maketh intercession for *846*
Ro 14:14 there is nothing unclean of **i**: but *1438*
1Co 11:14 Doth not even nature **i** teach you, *846*
1Co 13:4 charity vaunteth not **i**, is not puffed
1Co 13:5 Doth not behave **i** unseemly,
2Co 10:5 every high thing that exalteth **i**
Eph 4:16 of the body unto the edifying of **i**. *1438*
Heb 9:24 into heaven **i**, now to appear in the *846*
3Jn 12 of all men, and of the truth **i**. *846*

IVORY
1Ki 10:18 the king made a great throne of **i**, 8127
2Ch 9:17 the king made a great throne of **i**, 8127
Am 3:15 houses of **i** shall perish, and the 8127
Am 6:4 That lie upon beds of **i**, and stretch 8127
Rev 18:12 wood, and all manner vessels of **i** *1661*

J

JAILOR
Ac 16:23 charging the **j** to keep them *1200*

JAVELIN
Nu 25:7 and took a **j** in his hand; 7420
1Sa 18:11 And Saul cast the **j**; for he said, I. 2595
1Sa 19:10 David even to the wall with the **j**; 2595
1Sa 20:33 Saul cast a **j** at him to smite him: 2595

JAW See also JAWBONE; JAWS.
Jgs 15:16 with the **j** of an ass have I slain a 3895
Job 41:2 or bore his **j** through with a thorn? 3895

JAWBONE
Jgs 15:15 he found a new **j** of an ass, and........ 3895

JAWS
Ps 22:15 and my tongue cleaveth to my **j**; 4455
Isa 30:28 be a bridle in the **j** of the people, ... 3895
Eze 38:4 thee back, and put hooks into thy **j**, ... 3895
Hos 11:4 that take off the yoke on their **j**, ... 3895

JEALOUS
Ex 20:5 Lord thy God am a **j** God, visiting 7067
Ex 34:14 Lord, whose name is **J**, is a **j** God:...... 7067
Dt 4:24 is a consuming fire, even a **j** God....... 7067
Dt 5:9 for I the Lord thy God am a **j** God. 7067
Dt 6:15 Lord thy God is a **j** God among you) ... 7067
Jos 24:19 he is an holy God; he is a **j** God; 7072
Joel 2:18 Then will the Lord be **j** for his land,.... 7065
Na 1:2 God is **j**, and the Lord revengeth; 7072
Zec 8:2 I was **j** for Zion with great jealousy, ... 7065
Zec 8:2 and I was **j** for her with great fury...... 7065
2Co 11:2 am **j** over you with godly jealousy: *2206*

JEALOUSIES
Nu 5:29 This is the law of **j**, when a wife 7068

JEALOUSY
Nu 5:14 And the spirit of **j** come upon him, ... 7068
Nu 25:11 not the children of Israel in my **j** 7068
Dt 29:20 his **j** shall smoke against that man, ... 7068
Dt 32:21 They have moved me to **j** with that 7065
1Ki 14:22 provoked him to **J** with their sins 7065
Ps 78:58 moved him to **j** with their graven 7065
Pr 6:3 For **j** is the rage of a man: 7068
SS 8:6 as death; **j** is cruel as the grave: 7068
Isa 42:13 he shall stir up **j** like a man of war: 7068
Eze 8:3 was the seat of the image of **j**, ... 7068
Eze 16:38 I will give thee blood in fury and **j** 7068
Eze 16:42 and my **j** shall depart from thee, ... 7068
Eze 23:25 And I will set my **j** against thee, ... 7068
Eze 38:19 in my **j** and in the fire of my wrath 7068
Zep 1:18 be devoured by the fire of his **j** 7068
Zep 3:8 be devoured with the fire of my **j** 7068
Zec 1:14 jealous ... for Zion with a great **j** 7068
Ro 10:19 I will provoke you to **j** by the
Ro 11:11 Gentiles, for to provoke them to **j**
1Co 10:22 Do we provoke the Lord to **j**? are we
2Co 11:2 am jealous over you with godly **j** *2205*

JEHOVAH (je-ho´-vah) **See also GOD; LORD.**
Ex 6:3 name **J** was I not known to them. 3068
Ps 83:18 thou, whose name alone is **J**, art....... 3068
Isa 12:2 **J** is my strength and my song; 3068
Isa 26:4 the Lord **J** is everlasting strength....... 3068

JEHOVAH-JIREH (je-ho´-vah-ji´-reh)
Ge 22:14 called the name of that place **J** 3070

JEHOVAH-NISSI (je-ho´-vah-nis´-si)
Ex 17:15 altar, and called the name of it **J** 3071

JEHOVAH-SHALOM (je-ho´-vah-sha´-lom)
Jgs 6:24 unto the Lord, and called it **J**. 3073

JEOPARDY
1Ch 11:19 for with the **j** of their lives they brought
Lk 8:23 filled with water, and were in **j** *2793*
1Co 15:30 And why stand we in **j** every hour?..... *2793*

JERUSALEM (je-ru´-sa-lem)
2Sa 14:28 Absalom dwelt two full years in **J**, ... 3389
1Ki 2:36 unto him, Build thee an house in **J**, ... 3389
1Ki 11:42 the time that Solomon reigned in **J** 3389
2Ki 18:35 should deliver **J** out of mine hand? 3389
2Ki 21:4 Lord said, In **J** will I put my name...... 3389
2Ki 21:13 wipe **J** as a man wipeth a dish, ... 3389
2Ki 24:4 for he filled **J** with innocent blood; 3389
2Ki 24:14 he carried away all **J**, and all the 3389
2Ki 25:10 down the walls of **J** round about 3389
1Ch 21:15 And God sent an angel unto **J** to 3389
2Ch 11:16 the Lord God of Israel came to **J** 3389
2Ch 12:7 shall not be poured out upon **J**........ 3389
2Ch 26:15 he made in **J** engines, invented 3389
2Ch 28:24 him altars in every corner of **J** 3389
2Ch 30:26 So there was great joy in **J**: for......... 3389
2Ch 33:13 him again to **J** into his kingdom, ... 3389
2Ch 36:19 and brake down the wall of **J**, ... 3389
2Ch 36:23 me to build him an house in **J**, ... 3389
Ezr 1:4 for the house of God that is in **J** 3389
Ezr 4:8 the scribe wrote a letter against **J** 3390
Ezr 4:24 of the house of God which is at **J** 3390
Ezr 5:14 out of the temple that was in **J** 3390
Ezr 5:17 to build this house of God at **J** 3390
Ezr 7:13 their own freewill to go up to **J**, ... 3390
Ne 1:3 the wall of **J** also is broken down, ... 3389
Ne 2:12 God had put in my heart to do at **J**: 3389
Ne 6:7 prophets to preach of thee at **J** 3389
Ne 12:27 at the dedication of the wall of **J**. 3389
Ps 122:3 **J** is builded as a city that is. 3389
Ps 122:6 Pray for the peace of **J**: they shall 3389
Ps 137:6 if I prefer not **J** above my chief joy..... 3389
Ecc 1:12 Preacher was king over Israel in **J**. 3389
Ecc 1:16 they that have been before me in **J**: 3389
Ecc 2:7 above all that were in **J** before me: 3389
SS 3:5 I charge you, O ye daughters of **J** 3389
SS 5:8 I charge you, O daughters of **J**, ... 3389
SS 8:4 I charge you, O daughters of **J**, ... 3389
Isa 3:8 **J** is ruined, and Judah is fallen: 3389
Isa 36:20 Lord should deliver **J** out of my 3389
Isa 40:2 Speak ye comfortably to **J**, and cry..... 3389
Isa 51:17 Awake, awake, stand up, O **J** 3389
Isa 62:7 till he make **J** a praise in the earth...... 3389
Isa 66:13 and ye shall be comforted in **J**. 3389
Jer 2:2 Go and cry in the ears of **J**, saying, ... 3389
Jer 17:27 it shall devour the palaces of **J**. 3389
Jer 23:15 the prophets of **J** is profaneness 3389
Jer 35:11 Come, and let us go to **J** for fear....... 3389
Jer 38:28 he was there when **J** was taken 3389
Jer 39:8 and brake down the walls of **J**. 3389

Jer	40:1	away captive of **J** and Judah,	3389
Jer	51:50	and let **J** come into your mind	3389
Jer	52:14	brake down all the walls of **J** round	3389
Jer	52:29	he carried away captive from **J**	3389
La	1:8	**J** hath grievously sinned;	3389
Eze	8:3	me in the visions of God to **J**	3389
Eze	14:21	my four sore judgments upon **J**,	3389
Eze	14:22	evil that I have brought upon **J**,	3389
Eze	16:2	cause **J** to know her abominations,	3389
Da	1:1	came Nebuchadnezzar ... unto **J**,	3389
Da	5:2	out of the temple which was in **J**;	3390
Da	6:10	open in his chamber toward **J**	3390
Da	9:12	done as hath been done upon **J**	3389
Da	9:25	to restore and to build **J** unto the	3389
Joel	3:1	again the captivity of Judah and **J**,	3389
Joel	3:17	mountain: then shall **J** be holy	3389
Am	2:5	it shall devour the palaces of **J**	3389
Ob	11	his gates, and cast lots upon **J**	3389
Mic	3:10	with blood, and **J** with iniquity	3389
Zep	1:12	that I will search **J** with candles,	3389
Zec	8:3	**J** shall be called a city of truth;	3389
Zec	9:9	shout, O daughter of **J**: behold,	3389
Zec	12:9	the nations that come against **J**	3389
Zec	12:11	there be a great mourning in **J**,	3389
Zec	14:2	I will gather all nations against **J**	3389
Zec	14:8	living waters shall go out from **J**;	3389
Zec	14:17	earth unto **J** to worship the King	3389
Mal	2:11	is committed in Israel and in **J**;	3389
Mt	2:3	was troubled, and all **J** with him	*2414*
Mt	5:35	**neither by J; for it is the city of**	*2414*
Mt	16:21	how that he must go unto **J**, and	*2414*
Mt	20:18	**Behold, we go up to J; and the**	*2414*
Mt	23:37	**O J, J, thou that killest the**	*2419*
Lk	2:38	that looked for redemption in **J**	*2419*
Lk	2:41	his parents went to **J** every year	*2419*
Lk	2:43	child Jesus tarried behind in **J**;	*2419*
Lk	9:51	stedfastly set his face to go to **J**,	*2419*
Lk	13:33	**be that a prophet perish out of J**	*2419*
Lk	13:34	**O J, J, which killest the prophets,**	*2419*
Lk	18:31	unto them, **Behold, we go up to J,**	*2414*
Lk	21:20	**see J compassed with armies,**	*2419*
Lk	21:24	**and J shall be trodden down of**	*2419*
Lk	23:28	**Daughters of J, weep not for me,**	*2419*
Lk	24:47	**among all nations, beginning at J**	*2419*
Lk	24:49	**tarry ye in the city of J, until ye**	*2419*
Ac	1:8	**be witnesses unto me both in J,**	*2419*
Ac	5:28	ye have filled **J** with your doctrine,	*2419*
Ac	6:7	disciples multiplied in **J** greatly;	*2419*
Ac	9:2	might bring them bound unto **J**	*2419*
Ac	9:13	evil he hath done to thy saints at **J**	*2419*
Ac	20:16	to be at **J** the day of Pentecost	*2414*
Ac	20:22	I go bound in the spirit unto **J**,	*2419*
Ac	21:13	to die at **J** for the name of the Lord	*2419*
Ac	22:18	**and get thee quickly out of J**	*2419*
Ac	23:11	**as thou hast testified of me in J,**	*2419*
Ac	26:4	first among mine own nation at **J**,	*2414*
Ro	15:25	But now I go unto **J** to minister	*2419*
Gal	1:18	I went up to **J** to see Peter,	*2414*
Gal	4:26	But **J** which is above is free, which	*2419*
Heb	12:22	of the living God, the heavenly **J**,	*2419*
Rev	3:12	**city of my God, which is new J,**	*2419*
Rev	21:2	saw the holy city, new **J**, coming	*2419*
Rev	21:10	great city, the holy **J**, descending	*2419*

JESTING

Eph	5:4	nor foolish talking, nor **j**, which	*2160*

JESUS (je´-zus) **See also CHRIST; JESUS'; JOSHUA.**

Mt	1:18	birth of **J** Christ was on this wise:	*2424*
Mt	1:21	son, and thou shalt call his name **J**:	*2424*
Mt	4:17	From that time **J** began to preach,	*2424*
Mt	8:29	do with thee, **J**, thou son of God?	*2424*
Mt	9:4	And **J** knowing their thoughts said,	*2424*
Mt	12:15	But when **J** knew it, he withdrew	*2424*
Mt	12:25	**J** knew their thoughts, and said	*2424*
Mt	17:8	they saw no man, save **J** only	*2424*
Mt	20:34	**J** had compassion on them, and	*2424*
Mt	22:18	But **J** perceived their wickedness,	*2424*
Mt	26:59	sought false witness against **J**,	*2424*
Mt	26:63	**J** held his peace. And the high	*2424*
Mt	27:20	ask Barabbas, and destroy **J**	*2424*
Mt	27:37	This Is **J** The King Of The Jews	*2424*
Mk	1:24	do with thee, thou **J** of Nazareth?	*2424*
Mk	1:41	**J**, moved with compassion, put	*2424*
Mk	2:5	When **J** saw their faith, he said	*2424*
Mk	2:8	when **J** perceived in his spirit	*2424*
Mk	5:30	**J**, immediately knowing in	*2424*
Mk	8:17	And when **J** knew it, he saith unto	*2424*
Mk	10:21	Then **J** beholding him loved him,	*2424*
Mk	14:22	**J** took bread, and blessed, and	*2424*
Mk	15:5	**J** yet answered nothing; so that	*2424*
Mk	15:37	and **J** cried with a loud voice, and	*2424*
Mk	15:43	Pilate, and craved the body of **J**	*2424*
Lk	2:43	the child **J** tarried behind in	*2424*
Lk	2:52	And **J** increased in wisdom and	*2424*
Lk	4:1	And **J** being full of the Holy Ghost	*2424*
Lk	5:22	But when **J** perceived their	*2424*
Lk	9:42	And **J** rebuked the unclean spirit,	*2424*
Lk	10:21	In that hour **J** rejoiced in spirit,	*2424*
Lk	13:14	**J** had healed on the sabbath day,	*2424*
Lk	22:47	and drew near unto **J** to kiss him	*2424*
Lk	22:63	the men that held **J** mocked him,	*2424*
Lk	23:20	willing to release **J**, spake again	*2424*
Lk	23:52	Pilate, and begged the body of **J**	*2424*
Jn	1:17	grace and truth came by **J** Christ	*2424*
Jn	2:11	This beginning of miracles did **J**	*2424*
Jn	4:54	the second miracle that **J** did,	*2424*
Jn	6:19	they see **J** walking on the sea, and	*2424*
Jn	7:50	(he that came to **J** by night, being	*846*
Jn	11:13	Howbeit **J** spake of his death: but	*2424*
Jn	11:35	**J** wept.	*2424*
Jn	11:51	that **J** should die for that nation;	*2424*
Jn	12:16	but when **J** was glorified, then	*2424*
Jn	12:21	him, saying, Sir, we would see **J**	*2424*
Jn	13:1	**J** knew that his hour was come	*2424*
Jn	13:3	**J** knowing that the Father had	*2424*
Jn	17:3	**J Christ, whom thou hast sent**	*2424*
Jn	18:4	**J** therefore, knowing all things	*2424*
Jn	18:15	Simon Peter followed **J**, and so	*2424*
Jn	18:22	struck **J** with the palm of his hand	*2424*
Jn	18:28	Then led they **J** from Caiaphas	*2424*
Jn	18:32	the saying of **J** might be fulfilled,	*2424*
Jn	19:5	came **J** forth, wearing the crown	*2424*
Jn	19:9	But **J** gave him no answer	*2424*
Jn	19:19	**J** of Nazareth the King of the	*2424*
Jn	19:26	When **J** therefore saw his mother,	*2424*
Jn	19:28	**J** knowing that all things were	*2424*
Jn	19:40	Then took they the body of **J**,	*2424*
Jn	20:2	the other disciple, whom **J** loved,	*2424*
Jn	20:19	came **J** and stood in the midst,	*2424*
Jn	20:26	then came **J**, the doors being shut,	*2424*
Jn	20:30	many other signs truly did **J** in	*2424*
Jn	20:31	might believe that **J** is the Christ,	*2424*

Jn	21:7	that disciple whom **J** loved saith	*2424*
Jn	21:20	disciple whom **J** loved following;	*2424*
Jn	21:25	many other things which **J** did	*2424*
Ac	1:11	this same **J**, which is taken up	*2424*
Ac	1:16	was guide to them that took **J**	*2424*
Ac	2:32	This **J** hath God raised up,	*2424*
Ac	3:26	God, having raised up his Son **J**,	*2424*
Ac	7:55	**J** standing on the right hand of	*2424*
Ac	9:5	**I am J whom thou persecutest:**	*2424*
Ac	16:31	Believe on the Lord **J** Christ, and	*2424*
Ac	22:8	said unto me, **I am J of Nazareth,**	*2424*
Ac	26:15	**I am J whom thou persecutest.**	*2424*
Ro	5:15	which is by one man, **J** Christ	*2424*
Ro	8:2	law of the Spirit of life in Christ **J**,	*2424*
Ro	13:14	But put ye on the Lord **J** Christ	*2424*
1Co	2:2	save **J** Christ, and him crucified	*2424*
1Co	6:11	justified in the name of the Lord **J**,	*2424*
2Co	4:10	the body the dying of the Lord **J**,	*2424*
2Co	5:18	hath reconciled us … by **J** Christ	*2424*
2Co	11:4	that cometh preacheth another **J**,	*2424*
2Co	13:5	how that **J** Christ is in you, except	*2424*
Gal	2:16	law, but by the faith of **J** Christ	*2424*
Gal	3:28	for ye are an one in Christ **J**	*2424*
Gal	6:17	my body the marks of the Lord **J**	*2424*
Eph	1:5	adoption of children by **J** Christ	*2424*
Eph	2:6	in heavenly places in Christ **J**:	*2424*
Eph	2:10	created in Christ **J** unto good works,	*2424*
Eph	2:20	**J** Christ himself being the chief	*2424*
Php	1:6	perform it until the day of **J** Christ:	*2424*
Php	2:10	That at the name of **J** every knee	*2424*
Php	2:11	confess that **J** Christ is Lord	*2424*
Php	3:14	the high calling of God in Christ **J**	*2424*
Col	1:28	every man perfect in Christ **J**:	*2424*
Col	3:17	do all in the name of the Lord **J**,	*2424*
1Th	3:13	at the coming of our Lord **J** Christ	*2424*
1Th	4:14	which sleep in **J** will God bring	*2424*
2Th	1:7	the Lord **J** shall be revealed from	*2424*
1Ti	1:15	Christ **J** came into the world to save	*2424*
1Ti	2:5	God and men, the man Christ **J**;	*2424*
1Ti	6:14	appearing of our Lord **J** Christ:	*2424*
2Ti	1:10	appearing of our Saviour **J** Christ	*2424*
2Ti	3:12	all that will live godly in Christ **J**	*2424*
Heb	2:9	see **J**, who was made a little lower	*2424*
Heb	6:20	even **J**, made an high priest for ever	*2424*
Heb	7:22	was **J** made a surety of a better	*2424*
Heb	10:19	into the holiest by the blood of **J**	*2424*
Heb	12:2	Looking unto **J** the author and	*2424*
Heb	12:24	And to **J** the mediator of the new	*2424*
Heb	13:8	**J** Christ the same yesterday, and	*2424*
Jas	2:1	not the faith of our Lord **J** Christ,	*2424*
1Pe	1:2	sprinkling of the blood of **J** Christ:	*2424*
1Pe	1:3	hope by the resurrection of **J** Christ	*2424*
1Pe	1:7	glory at the appearing of **J** Christ:	*2424*
1Pe	2:5	acceptable to God by **J** Christ	*2424*
1Pe	5:10	unto his eternal glory by Christ **J**,	*2424*
1Jn	1:7	blood of **J** Christ his Son cleanseth	*2424*
1Jn	2:1	the Father, **J** Christ the righteous:	*2424*
1Jn	4:2	that **J** Christ is come in the flesh	*2424*
1Jn	4:15	shall confess that **J** is the Son of	*2424*
1Jn	5:5	believeth that **J** is the Son of God?	*2424*
Rev	1:1	The Revelation of **J** Christ, which	*2424*
Rev	1:5	from **J** Christ, who is the faithful	*2424*
Rev	14:12	of God, and the faith of **J**	*2424*
Rev	19:10	the testimony of **J** is the spirit of	*2424*
Rev	22:16	**I J have sent mine angel to testify**	*2424*
Rev	22:20	Amen. Even so, come, Lord **J**	*2424*

JESUS' (je´-zus)

Jn	12:9	they came not for **J** sake only, but	*2424*
Jn	13:23	Now there was leaning on **J** bosom	*2424*
2Co	4:5	ourselves your servants for **J** sake	*2424*

JEW (jew)

Est	3:4	he had told them that he was a **J**	3064
Zec	8:23	hold of the skirt of him that is a **J**,	3064
Jn	4:9	being a **J**, askest drink of me,	*2455*
Jn	18:35	Pilate answered, Am I a **J**? Thine	*2455*
Ro	1:16	the **J** first, and also to the Greek	*2453*
Ro	2:29	he is a **J**, which is one inwardly;	*2453*
Ro	3:1	What advantage then hath the **J**?	*2453*
1Co	9:20	And to the Jews I became as a **J**	*2453*

JEWEL

Pr	11:22	As a **j** of gold in a swine's snout	5141
Pr	20:15	lips of knowledge are a precious **j**	*3627*

JEWELS

Ge	24:53	servant brought forth **j** of silver	3627
Ex	3:22	and **j** of gold, and raiment: and ye	3627
Nu	31:50	of **j** of gold, chains, and bracelets,	3627
2Ch	20:25	precious **j**, which they stripped off	3627
2Ch	32:27	and for all manner of pleasant **j**;	3627
Isa	61:10	bride adorneth herself with her **j**	3627
Mal	3:17	that day when I make up my **j**;	5459

JEWISH (jew´-ish)

Tit	1:14	Not giving heed to **J** fables and	*2451*

JEWS (jews)

Ezr	6:14	the elders of the **J** builded, and	3062
Ne	1:2	concerning the **J** that had escaped,	3064
Ne	4:2	and said, What do these feeble **J**?	3064
Est	3:6	Haman sought to destroy all the **J**	3064
Est	4:3	was great mourning among the **J**,	3064
Est	8:17	the fear of the **J** fell upon them	3064
Est	9:5	the **J** smote all their enemies with	3064
Jer	32:12	**J** that sat in the court of the prison	3064
Da	3:12	certain **J** whom thou hast set	3064
Mt	2:2	is he that is born King of the **J**?	*2453*
Mt	27:11	saying, Art thou the King of the **J**?	*2453*
Mt	27:29	him, saying, Hail, King of the **J**!	*2453*
Mt	27:37	This Is Jesus The King Of The **J**	*2453*
Lk	23:37	If thou be the king of the **J**, save	*2453*
Jn	4:9	the **J** have no dealings with the	*2453*
Jn	4:22	**worship: for salvation is of the J.**	*2453*
Jn	5:16	therefore did the **J** persecute Jesus,	*2453*
Jn	5:18	the **J** sought the more to kill him,	*2453*
Jn	7:1	because the **J** sought to kill him	*2453*
Jn	7:13	openly of him for fear of the **J**	*2453*
Jn	8:31	Jesus to those **J** which believed	*2453*
Jn	9:18	the **J** did not believe concerning	*2453*
Jn	10:31	Then the **J** took up stones again	*2453*
Jn	18:33	him, Art thou the King of the **J**?	*2453*
Jn	18:36	**I should not be delivered to the J**	*2453*
Jn	18:39	release unto you the King of the **J**?	*2453*
Jn	19:21	Write not, The King of the **J**; but	*2453*
Jn	19:31	The **J** therefore, … besought Pilate	*2453*
Jn	19:38	but secretly for fear of the **J**	*2453*
Jn	19:40	as the manner of the **J** is to bury	*2453*
Jn	20:19	were assembled for fear of the **J**,	*2453*
Ac	9:23	the **J** took counsel to kill him:	*2453*
Ac	14:2	the unbelieving **J** stirred up the	*2453*
Ac	17:5	But the **J** which believed not	*2453*
Ac	18:12	the **J** made insurrection with one	*2453*

Ac 19:13 Then certain of the vagabond **J**, *2453*
Ac 24:27 willing to shew the **J** a pleasure, *2453*
Ac 25:8 Neither against the law of the **J**, *2453*
Ro 3:29 Is he the God of the **J** only? *2455*
Ro 9:24 called, not of the **J** only, but also *2453*
1Co 9:20 And unto the **J** I became as a Jew, *2453*
2Co 11:24 Of the **J** five times received I forty *2453*
Rev 2:9 **which say they are J, and are not,** *2453*
Rev 3:9 **which say they are J, and are not,** *2453*

JEWS' (jews)
2Ki 18:28 a loud voice in the **J** language, 3066
2Ch 32:18 with a loud voice in the **J** speech 3066
Gal 1:14 profited in the **J** religion above *2454*

JOIN
Pr 11:21 Though hand **j** in hand, the wicked
Pr 16:5 though hand **j** in hand, he shall not be
Isa 56:6 that **j** themselves to the Lord, to 3867
Da 11:6 they shall **j** themselves together; 2266

JOINED
Ge 29:34 will my husband be **j** unto me, 3867
Ezr 4:12 thereof, and **j** the foundations 2338
Ne 4:6 all the wall was **j** together unto 7194
Est 9:27 such as **j** themselves unto them, 3867
Ecc 9:4 to him that is **j** to all the living 977
Isa 14:1 strangers shall be **j** with them, 3867
Zec 2:11 nations shall be **j** to the Lord 3867
Mt 19:6 **therefore God hath j together,** *4801*
Mk 10:9 **therefore God hath j together,** *4801*
1Co 1:10 that ye be perfectly **j** together *2675*
1Co 6:16 not that he which is **j** to an harlot *2853*
1Co 6:17 he that is **j** unto the Lord is one *2853*
Eph 4:16 the whole body fitly **j** together *4883*
Eph 5:31 shall be **j** unto his wife, and they *4347*

JOINT
Ge 32:25 of Jacob's thigh was out of **j**, 3363
Ps 22:14 and all my bones are out of **j** 6504
Eph 4:16 by that which every **j** supplieth, *860*

JOINT-HEIRS
Ro 8:17 heirs of God, and **j** with Christ; *4789*

JOINTS
1Ki 22:34 between the **j** of the harness: 1694
Heb 4:12 spirit, and of the **j** and marrow *719*

JORDAN (jor´-dan)
Ge 13:11 Lot chose him all the plain of **J**; 3383
Nu 32:5 possession, and bring us not over **J** 3383
Nu 32:21 And will go all of you armed over **J** 3383
Dt 4:21 sware that I should not go over **J**, 3383
Jos 3:13 the waters of **J** shall be cut off 3383
Jos 3:17 on dry ground in the midst of **J**, 3383
Jos 4:8 twelve stones out of the midst of **J**, 3383
Jos 4:22 Israel came over this **J** on dry 3383
Jos 22:10 Manasseh built there an altar by **J** 3383
2Ki 5:10 Go and wash in **J** seven times, 3383
Mk 1:9 and was baptized of John in **J** *2446*

JOT
Mt 5:18 **one j or one tittle shall in no wise** *2503*

JOURNEY
Ge 24:21 had made his **j** prosperous or not 1870
Nu 9:13 man that is clean, and is not in a **j**, 1870
Dt 10:11 Arise, take thy **j** before the people, 4550
1Ki 19:7 because the **j** is too great for thee 1870
Ne 2:6 For how long shall thy **j** be? and 4109
Jnh 3:3 great city of three days' **j** 4109
Mt 10:10 **nor scrip for your j, neither two** *3598*
Mk 6:8 should take nothing for their **j** *3598*
Mk 13:34 **of man is as a man taking a far j,** *590*
Lk 2:44 in the company, went a day's **j**; *3598*
La 9:3 **Take nothing for your j, neither** *3598*
Lk 11:6 **a friend of mine in his j is come** *3598*
Lk 15:13 **and took his j into a far country,** *589*
Jnh 4:6 therefore, being wearied with his **j** *3597*
Ac 1:12 from Jerusalem a sabbath day's **j** *3598*
Ac 22:6 as I made my **j**, and was come *4198*

JOURNEYED
Ge 13:11 and Lot **j** east: and they separated 5265
Nu 9:22 abode in their tents, and **j** not: 5265
Lk 10:33 **But a certain Samaritan, as he j,** *3593*
Ac 9:3 as he **j**, he came near Damascus: *4198*
Ac 9:7 the men which **j** with him stood *4922*

JOURNEYINGS
2Co 11:26 in **j** often, in perils of waters, *3597*

JOURNEYS
Ex 40:38 of Israel, throughout all their **j** 4550
Nu 33:2 goings out according to their **j** 4550

JOY See also ENJOY; JOYFUL.
1Ki 1:40 rejoiced with great **j**, so that the 8057
1Ch 29:9 the king also rejoiced with great **j** 8057
1Ch 29:17 now have I seen with **j** thy people, 8057
2Ch 30:26 there was great **j** in Jerusalem: for 8057
Ezr 3:12 and many shouted aloud for **j**: 8057
Ezr 3:13 discern the noise of the shout of **j** 8057
Ezr 6:16 of this house of God with **j** 2305
Ne 8:10 the **j** of the Lord is your strength 2304
Ne 12:43 that the **j** of Jerusalem was heard 8057
Est 8:16 had light, and gladness, and **j**, 8342
Est 9:22 turned unto them from sorrow to **j**, 8057
Job 29:13 the widow's heart to sing for **j** 7442
Job 38:7 all the sons of God shouted for **j**?
Job 41:22 sorrow is turned into **j** before him
Ps 16:11 in thy presence is fullness of **j**; 8057
Ps 30:5 but **j** cometh in the morning 7440
Ps 43:4 God, unto God my exceeding **j**: 1524
Ps 48:2 the **j** of the whole earth, is mount 4885
Ps 51:8 Make me to hear **j** and gladness; 8342
Ps 51:12 unto me the **j** of thy salvation; 8342
Ps 126:5 that sow in tears shall reap in **j** 7440
Ps 137:6 not Jerusalem above my chief **j** 8057
Pr 12:20 but to the counsellors of peace is **j** 8057
Pr 14:10 doth not intermeddle with his **j** 8057
Pr 15:21 Folly is **j** to him that is destitute of 8057
Pr 15:23 man hath **j** by the answer of his 8057
Pr 17:21 and the father of a fool hath no **j** 8056
Pr 21:15 It is **j** to the just to do judgment: 8057
Pr 23:24 begetteth a wise child shall have **j** 8056
Ecc 2:10 withheld not my heart from any **j**; 8057
Ecc 5:20 answereth him in the **j** of his heart 8057
Isa 24:11 all **j** is darkened, the mirth of the 8057
Isa 35:10 with songs and everlasting **j** upon 8057
Isa 51:11 everlasting **j** shall be upon their 8057
Isa 55:12 For ye shall go out with **j**, and be 8057
Isa 66:5 he shall appear to your **j**, and 8057
Jer 15:16 the **j** and rejoicing of mine heart: 8342
La 2:15 beauty, The **j** of the whole earth? 4885

La	5:15	The **j** of our heart is ceased; our	4885
Eze	24:25	the **j** of their glory, the desire of	4885
Hos	9:1	Rejoice not, O Israel, for **j**, as	1524
Hab	3:18	I will **j** in the God of my salvation.	1523
Zep	3:17	he will rejoice over thee with **j**;	8057
Zep	3:17	he will **j** over thee with singing.	1523
Mt	2:10	rejoiced with exceeding great **j**	*5479*
Mt	25:21	**enter thou into the j of thy**	*5479*
Mt	25:23	**enter thou into the j of thy**	*5479*
Mt	28:8	sepulchre with fear and great **j**;	*5479*
Lk	1:44	the babe leaped in my womb for **j**	*20*
Lk	2:10	bring you good tidings of great **j**,	*5479*
Lk	8:13	**hear, receive the word with j;**	*5479*
Lk	15:7	**j shall be in heaven over one**	*5479*
Lk	15:10	**is j in the presence of the angels**	*5479*
Jn	15:11	**and that your j might be full**	*5479*
Jn	16:20	**your sorrow shall be turned into j**	*5479*
Jn	16:22	**your j no man taketh from you**	*5479*
Jn	16:24	**receive, that your j may be full**	*5479*
Jn	17:13	**have my j fulfilled in themselves**	*5479*
Ac	13:52	the disciples were filled with **j**, and	*5479*
Ac	15:3	caused great **j** unto all the brethren.	*5479*
Ro	5:11	**j** in God through our Lord Jesus	*2744*
Ro	14:17	peace, and **j** in the Holy Ghost.	*5479*
Gal	5:22	fruit of the Spirit is love, **j**, peace,	*5479*
Php	2:2	Fulfil ye my **j**, that ye be	*5479*
Php	4:1	and longed for, my **j** and crown,	*5479*
1Th	1:6	affliction, with **j** of the Holy Ghost:	*5479*
1Th	2:19	what is our hope, or **j**, or crown of	*5479*
2Ti	1:4	tears, that I may be filled with **j**;	*5479*
Heb	12:2	who for the **j** that was set before	*5479*
Jas	1:2	count it all **j** when ye fall into	*5479*
Jas	4:9	mourning, and your **j** to heaviness	*5479*
1Pe	1:8	rejoice with **j** unspeakable and full	*5479*
1Jn	1:4	unto you, that your **j** may be full	*5479*
3Jn	4	I have no greater **j** than to hear	*5479*
Jude	24	of his glory with exceeding **j**	*20*

JOYFUL

Job	3:7	let no **j** voice come therein	7445
Ps	5:11	them also that love thy name be **j**.	5970
Ps	35:9	my soul shall be **j** in the Lord:	1523
Ps	98:4	Make a **j** noise unto the Lord, all	
Ps	113:9	and to be a **j** mother of children	8056
Ecc	7:14	In the day of prosperity be **j**, but	2896
Isa	49:13	Sing, O heavens; and be **j**, O earth;	1523
2Co	7:4	I am exceeding **j** in all our	*5479*

JOYFULLY

Ecc	9:9	Live **j** with the wife whom thou	2416
Lk	19:6	came down, and received him **j**.	*5463*

JOYOUS

Isa	23:7	Is this your **j** city, whose antiquity	5947
Heb	12:11	for the present seemeth to be **j**,	5479

JUBILE (ju´-bi-lee)

Le	25:10	it shall be a **j** unto you; and ye	3104
Le	25:13	In the year of this **j** ye shall return	3104
Le	25:28	hath bought it until the year of **j**	3104
Le	25:40	shall serve thee unto the year of **j**	3104
Le	27:18	if he sanctify his field after the **j**,	3104

JUDAEA (ju-de´-ah)

Mt	2:1	Jesus was born in Bethlehem of **J**	*2449*
Mt	2:5	said unto him, In Bethlehem of **J**	*2449*
Mt	24:16	**be in J flee into the mountains:**	*2449*
Mk	13:14	**that be in J flee to the mountains:**	*2449*
Lk	3:1	Pontius Pilate being governor of **J**	*2449*
Lk	21:21	**are in J flee to the mountains;**	*2449*
Ac	1:8	**and in all J, and in Samaria, and**	*2449*
Ac	26:20	and throughout all the coasts of **J**.	*2449*
Ro	15:31	from them that do not believe in **J**;	*2449*

JUDGE

Ge	16:5	the Lord **j** between me and thee.	8199
Ge	18:25	not the **j** of all the earth do right?	8199
Ex	2:14	thee a prince and a **j** over us?	8199
Ex	18:13	that Moses sat to **j** the people:	8199
Ex	18:22	every small matter they shall **j**:	8199
Le	19:15	shalt thou **j** thy neighbour.	8199
Dt	1:16	**j** righteously between every man	8199
Dt	32:36	For the Lord shall **j** his people,	1777
Jgs	11:27	Lord the **J** be **j** this day between	8199
1Sa	8:5	make us a king to **j** us like all the	8199
1Sa	8:20	that our king may **j** us, and go out	8199
1Sa	24:12	The Lord **j** between me and thee,	8199
2Sa	15:4	Oh that I were made **j** in the land,	8199
1Ki	3:9	for who is able to **j** this thy so great	8199
2Ch	1:11	that thou mayest **j** my people,	8199
Ps	7:8	**j** me, O Lord, according to my	8199
Ps	10:18	**j** the fatherless and the oppressed,	8199
Ps	43:1	**J** me, O God, and plead my cause.	8199
Ps	68:5	a **j** of the widows, is God in his	1781
Ps	75:7	God is the **j**: he putteth down one,	8199
Ps	82:2	How long will ye **j** unjustly, and	8199
Ps	98:9	righteousness shall he **j** the world,	8199
Pr	31:9	Open thy mouth, **j** righteously,	8199
Ecc	3:17	God shall **j** the righteous and the	8199
Isa	1:17	**j** the fatherless, plead for the	8199
Isa	1:23	they **j** not the fatherless, neither	8199
Isa	33:22	the Lord is our **j**, the Lord is our	8199
Jer	5:28	right of the needy do they not **j**	8199
Eze	20:4	Wilt thou **j** them, son of man,	8199
Eze	33:20	I will **j** every one after his ways	8199
Joel	3:12	there will I sit to **j** all the heathen	8199
Mic	4:3	And he shall **j** among many people,	8199
Mic	7:3	and the **j** asketh for a reward;	8199
Mt	5:25	**adversary deliver thee to the j,**	*2923*
Mt	7:1	**J not, that ye be not judged**	*2919*
Lk	6:37	**J not, and ye shall not be judged:**	*2919*
Lk	12:58	**him; lest he hale thee to the j,**	*2923*
Lk	18:6	**said, Hear what the unjust j saith**	*2923*
Lk	19:22	**of thine own mouth will I j thee,**	*2919*
Jn	5:30	**as I hear, I j: and my judgment**	*2919*
Jn	7:24	**J not according to the appearance,**	*2919*
Jn	8:15	**Ye j after the flesh; I j no man.**	*2919*
Jn	12:47	**for I came not to j the world,**	*2919*
Jn	18:31	and **j** him according to your law	*2919*
Ac	4:19	you more than unto God, **j** ye	*2919*
Ac	10:42	to be the **J** of quick and dead	*2923*
Ac	13:46	**j** yourselves unworthy of … life	*2919*
Ac	17:31	will **j** the world in righteousness	*2919*
Ro	2:16	God shall **j** the secrets of men	*2919*
Ro	3:6	then how shall God **j** the world?	*2919*
Ro	14:10	But why dost thou **j** thy brother?	*2919*
1Co	4:5	**j** nothing before the time, until	*2919*
1Co	6:2	that the saints shall **j** the world?	*2919*
1Co	6:3	ye not that we shall **j** angels?	*2919*
2Co	5:14	because we thus **j**, that if one	*2919*
Col	2:16	Let no man therefore **j** you in	*2919*
2Ti	4:1	who shall **j** the quick and the dead	*2919*
2Ti	4:8	which the Lord, the righteous **j**,	*2923*

Heb 10:30	again, The Lord shall **j** his people	*2919*
Heb 12:23	to God the **J** of all, and to the	*2923*
Jas 4:11	art not a doer of the law, but a **j**	*2923*
Jas 5:9	the **j** standeth before the door.	*2923*
1Pe 4:5	ready to **j** the quick and the dead.	*2919*
Rev 19:11	he doth **j** and make war.	*2919*

JUDGED

Ge 30:6	And Rachel said, God hath **j** me,	1777
Ex 18:26	they **j** the people at all seasons:	8199
1Sa 7:15	Samuel **j** Israel all the days of his	8199
2Ki 23:22	days of the judges that **j** Israel,	8199
Eze 36:19	according to their doings I **j** them.	8199
Da 9:12	and against our judges that **j** us,	8199
Mt 7:1	Judge not, that ye be not **j**	*2919*
Mt 7:2	judgment ye judge, ye shall be **J**	*2919*
Lk 6:37	Judge not, and ye shall not be **j**	*2919*
Lk 7:43	said unto him, **Thou hast rightly j**	*2919*
Jn 16:11	**the prince of this world is j**	*2919*
Ac 25:10	seat, where I ought to be **j**: to the	*2919*
Ac 26:6	now I stand and am **j** for the hope	*2919*
Ro 2:12	in the law shall be **j** by the law;	*2919*
Ro 3:7	why yet am I also **j** as a sinner?	*2919*
1Co 2:15	things, yet he himself is **j** of no man.	*350*
1Co 10:29	why is my liberty **j** of another	*2919*
1Co 11:32	when we are **j**, we are chastened	*2919*
Heb 11:11	she **j** him faithful who had.	*2233*
Jas 2:12	as they that shall be **j** by the law	*2919*
Rev 11:18	of the dead, that they should be **j**	*2919*
Rev 20:12	the dead were **j** out of those things.	*2919*
Rev 20:13	they were **j** every man according to	*2919*

JUDGES

Ex 21:6	master shall bring him unto the **j**;	430
Ex 21:22	he shall pay as the **j** determine.	6414
Ex 22:9	whom the **j** shall condemn, he shall	430
Dt 19:18	**j** shall make diligent inquisition:	8199
Dt 25:1	that the **j** may judge them; then	8199
Jgs 2:16	Nevertheless the Lord raised up **j**,	8199
Ru 1:1	pass in the days when the **j** ruled,	8199
1Sa 8:1	that he made his sons **j** over Israel.	8199
2Ki 23:22	the days of the **j** that judged Israel,	8199
1Ch 23:4	six thousand were officers and **j**:	8199
Pr 8:16	nobles, even all the **j** of the earth	8199
Isa 40:23	maketh the **j** of the earth as vanity	8199
Da 9:12	against our **j** that judged us, by	8199
Mt 12:27	**therefore they shall be your j.**	*2923*
Lk 11:19	**therefore shall they be your j.**	*2923*
Ac 13:20	And after that he gave unto them **j**	*2923*
Jas 2:4	and are become **j** of evil thoughts?	*2923*

JUDGEST

Ps 51:4	and be clear when thou **j**	8199
Jer 11:20	O Lord of hosts, that **j** righteously,	8199
Ro 2:1	O man, whosoever thou art that **j**;	*2919*
Ro 14:4	Who art thou that **j** another man's	*2919*
Jas 4:12	who art thou that **j** another?	*2919*

JUDGETH

Job 21:22	seeing he **j** those that are high.	8199
Pr 29:14	The king that faithfully **j** the poor,	8199
Jn 5:22	**the Father j no man, but hath**	*2919*
Jn 12:48	**not my words, hath one that j.**	*2919*
1Co 2:15	But he that is spiritual **j** all things,	*350*
1Co 4:4	but he that **j** me is the Lord.	*350*
1Co 5:13	But them that are without God **j**	*2919*
1Pe 1:17	**j** according to every man's work,	*2919*

JUDGING

Isa 16:5	of David, **j**, and seeking judgment,	8199
Mt 19:28	**j the twelve tribes of Israel.**	*2919*
Lk 22:30	**thrones j the twelve tribes of.**	*2919*

JUDGMENT

Ge 18:19	of the Lord, to do justice and **j**;	4941
Ex 28:15	make the breastplate of **j** with	4941
Le 19:15	shall do no unrighteousness in **j**:	4941
Nu 35:12	stand before the congregation in **j**	4941
Dt 1:17	for the **j** is God's: and the cause	4941
Dt 16:19	Thou shalt not wrest **j**; thou shalt.	4941
Dt 24:17	not pervert the **j** of the stranger,	4941
Dt 32:4	all his ways are **j**: a God of truth	4941
1Sa 8:3	and took bribes, and perverted **j**.	4941
1Ki 3:28	wisdom of God was in him, to do **j**	4941
1Ki 7:7	might judge, even the porch of **j**:	4941
1Ki 20:40	said unto him, So shall thy **j** be;	4941
Ezr 7:26	let **j** be executed speedily upon	1780
Job 8:3	Doth God pervert **j**? or doth the	4941
Job 19:7	I cry aloud, but there is no **j**	4941
Job 34:5	and God hath taken away my **j**	4941
Job 34:12	neither will the Almighty pervert **j**	4941
Job 37:23	he is excellent in power, and in **j**,	4941
Job 40:8	Wilt thou also disannul my **j**? wilt	4941
Ps 1:5	ungodly shall not stand in the **j**,	4941
Ps 9:7	he hath prepared his throne for **j**	4941
Ps 33:5	He loveth righteousness and **j**: the	4941
Ps 89:14	Justice and **j** are the habitation	4941
Ps 106:3	Blessed are they that keep **j**, and	4941
Ps 119:84	when wilt thou execute **j** on them	4941
Ps 149:9	execute upon them the **j** written:	4941
Pr 1:3	wisdom, justice, and **j**, and equity;	4941
Pr 13:23	is that is destroyed for want of **j**	4941
Pr 17:23	the bosom to pervert the ways of **j**.	4941
Pr 18:5	to overthrow the righteous in **j**.	4941
Pr 19:28	An ungodly witness scorneth **j**:	4941
Pr 20:8	that sitteth in the throne of **j**.	1779
Pr 21:3	To do justice and **j** is more acceptable	4941
Pr 21:15	It is joy to the just to do **j**: but.	4941
Pr 24:23	to have respect of persons in **j**.	4941
Pr 28:5	Evil men understand not **j**: but	4941
Pr 29:26	every man's **j** cometh from the	4941
Pr 31:5	pervert the **j** of any of the afflicted.	1779
Ecc 5:8	violent perverting of **j** and justice.	4941
Ecc 8:5	heart discerneth both time and **j**	4941
Ecc 8:6	every purpose there is time and **j**,	4941
Ecc 11:9	things God will bring thee into **j**.	4941
Ecc 12:14	God shall bring every work into **j**,	4941
Isa 3:14	The Lord will enter into **j** with the	4941
Isa 5:7	and he looked for **j**, but behold.	4941
Isa 5:16	Lord of hosts shall be exalted in **j**,	4941
Isa 10:2	To turn aside the needy from **j**,	1779
Isa 28:7	err in vision, they stumble in **j**	6417
Isa 30:18	you: for the Lord is a God of **j**:	4941
Isa 40:27	my **j** is passed over from my God?	4941
Isa 42:1	shall bring forth **j** to the Gentiles	4941
Isa 42:3	he shall bring forth **j** unto truth.	4941
Isa 42:4	till he have set **j** in the earth:	4941
Isa 49:4	yet surely my **j** is with the Lord.	4941
Isa 61:8	I the Lord love **j**, I hate robbery	4941
Jer 4:2	in truth, in **j**, and in righteousness;	4941
Jer 5:1	if there be any that executeth **j**,	4941
Jer 8:7	people know not the **j** of the Lord.	4941
Jer 10:24	O Lord, correct me, but with **j**;	4941
Jer 21:12	Execute **j** in the morning, and.	4941

Jer 23:5	execute **j** and justice in the earth.	4941
Jer 33:15	shall execute **j** and righteousness	4941
Jer 51:47	will do **j** upon the graven images	6485
Eze 18:8	executed true **j** between man and	4941
Da 7:10	the **j** was set, and the books were	1780
Da 7:22	**j** was given to the saints of the most.	1780
Hos 12:6	keep mercy and **j**, and wait on thy	4941
Am 5:15	good, and establish **j** in the gate:	4941
Mic 3:1	Israel; Is it not for you to know **j**?	4941
Hab 1:4	therefore wrong **j** proceedeth.	4941
Zep 3:5	morning doth he bring his **j** to light	4941
Zec 7:9	Execute true **j**, and shew mercy.	4941
Zec 8:16	execute the **j** of truth and peace in	4941
Mal 2:17	them; or. Where is the God of **j**?	4941
Mt 5:21	**kill shall be in danger of the j:**	*2920*
Mt 5:22	**a cause shall be in danger of the j:**	*2920*
Mt 7:2	**with what j ye judge, ye shall be.**	*2917*
Mt 10:15	**and Gomorrha in the day of j,**	*2920*
Mt 11:22	**for Tyre and Sidon at the day of j,**	*2920*
Mt 11:24	**the land of Sodom in the day of j,**	*2920*
Mt 12:18	and he shall shew **j** to the Gentiles	*2920*
Mt 12:36	**account thereof in the day of j**	*2920*
Mt 12:41	**The men of Nineveh shall rise in J**	*2920*
Mt 23:23	**of the law, j, mercy, and faith:**	*2920*
Mk 6:11	**and Gomorrah in the day of j,**	*2920*
Lk 10:14	**for Tyre and Sidon at the j, than.**	*2920*
Lk 11:31	**of the south shall rise up in the j**	*2920*
Lk 11:32	**of Nineve shall rise up in the j**	*2920*
Lk 11:42	**pass over j and the love of God:**	*2920*
Jn 5:22	**hath committed all j unto the Son:**	*2920*
Jn 5:30	**as I hear, I judge: and my j is.**	*2920*
Jn 7:24	**appearance, but judge righteous j**	*2920*
Jn 8:16	**And yet if I judge, my j is true:**	*2920*
Jn 9:39	**For j I am come into this world,**	*2917*
Jn 12:31	**Now is the j of this world: now.**	*2920*
Jn 16:8	**sin, and of righteousness, and of j:**	*2920*
Jn 16:11	**Of j, because the prince of this**	*2920*
Jn 18:28	from Caiaphas unto the hall of **j**:	*4232*
Jn 18:28	went not into the **j** hall, lest they.	*4232*
Jn 19:9	And went again into the **j** hall,	*4232*
Jn 19:13	and sat down in the **j** seat in a.	*968*
Ac 8:33	humiliation his **j** was taken away:	*2920*
Ro 2:2	the **j** of God is according to truth	*2917*
Ro 2:3	that thou shalt escape the **j** of God?	*2917*
Ro 2:5	of the righteous **j** of God;	*1341*
Ro 5:16	the **j** was by one to condemnation,	*2917*
Ro 5:18	by the offence of one **j** came upon all	
Ro 14:10	all stand before the **j** seat of Christ.	*968*
1Co 1:10	the same mind and in the same **j**	*1106*
2Co 5:10	appear before the **j** seat of Christ;	*968*
2Th 1:5	token of the righteous **j** of God,	*2920*
Heb 9:27	once to die, but after this the **j**:	*2920*
Jas 2:6	and draw you before the **j** seats?	*2922*
Jas 2:13	For he shall have **j** without mercy,	*2920*
1Pe 4:17	time is come that **j** must begin	*2917*
2Pe 2:3	**j** now of a long time lingereth	*2917*
2Pe 2:4	darkness, to be reserved unto **j**;	*2920*
2Pe 2:9	reserve the unjust unto the day of **j**	*2920*
2Pe 3:7	against the day of **j** and perdition	*2920*
1Jn 4:17	may have boldness in the day of **j**:	*2920*
Jude 6	unto the **j** of the great day	*2920*
Jude 15	To execute **j** upon all, and to	*2920*
Rev 14:7	him; for the hour of his **j** is come:	*2920*
Rev 17:1	thee the **j** of the great whore	*2917*
Rev 18:10	for in one hour is thy **j** come.	*2920*
Rev 20:4	them, and **j** was given unto them:	*2917*

JUDGMENT-HALL See JUDGMENT and HALL.

JUDGMENTS

Ex 7:4	out of the land of Egypt by great **j**	8201
Le 25:18	shall do my statutes, and keep my **j**,	4941
Le 26:15	statutes, or if your soul abhor my **j**,	4941
Le 26:43	because they despised my **j**, and	4941
Dt 4:14	time to teach you statutes and **j**,	4941
Dt 7:12	if ye hearken to these **j**, and keep,	4941
1Ki 11:33	my statutes and my **j**, as did David.	4941
1Ch 16:14	our God; his **j** are in all the earth.	4941
Ezr 7:10	to teach in Israel statutes and **j**	4941
Ne 1:7	nor the statutes, nor the **j**, which	4941
Ne 9:29	but sinned against thy **j**, (which if a	4941
Ps 10:5	thy **j** are far above out of his sight:	4941
Ps 19:9	the **j** of the Lord are true and	4941
Ps 105:7	our God: his **j** are in all the earth.	4941
Ps 119:30	truth: thy **j** have I laid before me.	4941
Ps 119:52	I remembered thy **j** of old, O Lord;	4941
Ps 119:102	I have not departed from thy **j**	4941
Ps 119:120	of thee; and I am afraid of thy **j**	4941
Ps 119:156	quicken me according to thy **j**.	4941
Pr 19:29	**J** are prepared for scorners, and	8201
Isa 26:9	for when thy **j** are in the earth,	4941
Eze 5:6	for they have refused my **j** and my	4941
Eze 14:21	my four sore **j** upon Jerusalem,	8201
Eze 20:19	walk in my statutes, and keep my **j**,	4941
Eze 20:25	and **j** whereby they should not live;	4941
Eze 36:27	ye shall keep my **j**, and do them	4941
Eze 37:24	also walk in my **j**, and observe my	4941
Hos 6:5	thy **j** are as the light that goeth	4941
Zep 3:15	the Lord hath taken away thy **j**,	4941
Ro 11:33	how unsearchable are his **j**, and	*2917*
1Co 6:4	ye have **j** of things pertaining to	*2922*
Rev 15:4	thee; for thy **j** are made manifest.	*1345*
Rev 16:7	true and righteous are thy **j**	*2920*
Rev 19:2	For true and righteous are his **j**:	*2920*

JUDGMENT-SEAT See JUDGMENT and SEAT.

JURISDICTION

Lk 23:7	that he belonged unto Herod's **j**,	*1849*

JUST See also UNJUST.

Ge 6:9	Noah was a **j** man and perfect in	6662
Le 19:36	**J** balances, **j** weights, a **j** ephah	6664
Dt 25:15	a perfect and **j** measure shalt thou	6664
Dt 32:4	without iniquity, **j** and right is he.	6662
2Sa 23:3	He that ruleth over men must be **j**.	6662
Ne 9:33	thou art **j** in all that is brought	6662
Job 4:17	mortal man be more **j** than God?	6663
Job 9:2	how should man be **j** with God?	6663
Job 33:12	in this thou art not **j**: I will	6663
Ps 37:12	The wicked plotteth against the **j**,	6662
Pr 4:18	path of the **j** is as the shining light,	6662
Pr 9:9	teach a **j** man, and he will increase	6662
Pr 10:6	Blessings are upon the head of the **j**:	6662
Pr 10:7	The memory of the **j** is blessed:	6662
Pr 10:20	tongue of the **j** is as choice silver:	6662
Pr 10:31	The mouth of the **j** bringeth forth	6662
Pr 11:1	but a **j** weight is his delight	8003
Pr 11:9	shall the **j** be delivered	6662
Pr 12:13	But the **j** shall come out of trouble.	6662
Pr 12:21	There shall no evil happen to the **j**:	6662
Pr 13:22	of the sinner is laid up for the **j**.	6662
Pr 16:11	A **j** weight and balance are the	4941
Pr 17:15	and he that condemneth the **j**,	6662

Pr 17:26 Also to punish the **j** is not good,....... 6662
Pr 18:17 is first in his own cause seemeth **j**; 6662
Pr 20:7 The **j** man walketh in his integrity: 6662
Pr 21:15 It is joy to the **j** to do judgment:....... 6662
Pr 24:16 For a **j** man falleth seven times, ... 6662
Pr 29:10 upright: but the **j** seek his soul......... 3477
Pr 29:27 man is an abomination to the **j**: 6662
Ecc 7:15 there is a **j** man that perisheth in 6662
Ecc 7:20 there is not a **j** man upon earth, ... 6662
Ecc 8:14 that there be **j** men, unto whom it 6662
Isa 26:7 the way of the **j** is uprightness: 6662
Isa 29:21 aside the **j** for a thing of nought 6662
Isa 45:21 a **j** God and a Saviour; there is none ... 6662
La 4:13 have shed the blood of the **j** in the 6662
Eze 18:5 if a man be **j**, and do that which is 6662
Eze 18:9 he is **j**, he shall surely live, saith........ 6662
Eze 45:10 Ye shall have **j** balances............... 6664
Am 5:12 they afflict the **j**, they take a bribe, ... 6662
Hab 2:4 but the **j** shall live by his faith.......... 6662
Zep 3:5 The **j** Lord is in the midst thereof; 6662
Mt 1:19 her husband, being a **j** man, and....... *1342*
Mt 5:45 **rain on the j and on the unjust**........ *1342*
Mt 13:49 **the wicked from among the j**,......... *1342*
Mt 27:19 nothing to do with that **j** man: *1342*
Mt 27:24 of the blood of this **j** person:.......... *1342*
Lk 1:17 disobedient to the wisdom of the **j**; *1342*
Lk 14:14 **at the resurrection of the j**............ *1342*
Lk 15:7 **over ninety and nine j persons,** *1342*
Jn 5:20 **I judge: and my judgment is j;** *1342*
Ac 3:14 ye denied the Holy One and the **J**, ... *1342*
Ac 7:52 before of the coming of the **J** One;..... *1342*
Ac 22:14 know his will, and see that **J** One *1342*
Ac 24:15 the dead, both of the **j** and unjust...... *1342*
Ro 1:17 written, The **j** shall live by faith........ *1342*
Ro 2:13 of the law are **j** before God,........... *1342*
Ro 3:8 may come? whose damnation is **j**...... *1738*
Ro 3:26 that he might be **j**, and the justifier *1342*
Ro 7:12 commandment holy, and **j**, and *1342*
Gal 3:11 for, The **j** shall live by faith............ *1342*
Php 4:8 honest, whatsoever things are **j**, ... *1342*
Col 4:1 servants that which is **j** and equal; *1342*
Tit 1:8 a lover of good men, sober, **j**, holy,..... *1342*
Heb 2:2 a **j** recompence of reward: *1738*
Heb 10:38 Now the **j** shall live by faith: but *1342*
Heb 12:23 the spirits of **j** men made perfect,...... *1342*
Jas 5:6 have condemned and killed the **j**;...... *1342*
1Pe 3:18 for sins, the **j** for the unjust, that....... *1342*
2Pe 2:7 And delivered **j** Lot, vexed with........ *1342*
1Jn 1:9 and **j** to forgive us our sins, and to *1342*
Rev 15:3 **j** and true are thy ways, thou King *1342*

JUSTICE See also INJUSTICE.
2Sa 8:15 David executed judgment and **j** 6666
2Sa 15:4 unto me, and I would do him **j**! 6663
Job 8:3 or doth the Almighty pervert **j**? 6664
Job 36:17 judgment and **j** take hold on thee...... 4941
Job 37:23 in judgment, and in plenty of **j**: 6666
Ps 82:3 do **j** to the afflicted and needy......... 6663
Ps 89:14 **J** and judgment are the............... 6664
Pr 1:3 of wisdom, **j**, and judgment, and 6664
Pr 21:3 To do **j** and judgment is more......... 6666
Isa 9:7 it with judgment and with **j** from...... 6666
Isa 58:2 ask of me the ordinances of **j**;......... 6664
Isa 59:4 None calleth for **j**, nor any pleadeth.... 6664
Isa 59:9 us, neither doth **j** overtake us:......... 6666
Jer 22:15 and drink, and do judgment and **j**..... 6666
Jer 23:5 shall execute judgment and **j** in the 6666
Jer 31:23 O habitation of **j**, and mountain 6664

JUSTIFICATION
Ro 4:25 and was raised again for our **j**......... *1347*
Ro 5:16 gift is of many offences unto **j**......... *1345*
Ro 5:18 came upon all men unto **j** of life....... *1347*

JUSTIFIED
Job 13:18 cause; I know that I shall be **j** 6663
Job 25:4 How then can man be **j** with God?..... 6663
Ps 51:4 mightest be **j** when thou speakest...... 6663
Ps 143:2 thy sight shall no man living be **j** 6663
Isa 43:9 their witnesses, that they may be **j** 6663
Isa 43:26 declare thou, that thou mayest be **j** 6663
Isa 45:25 shall all the seed of Israel be **j**,......... 6663
Jer 3:11 backsliding Israel hath **j** herself........ 6663
Mt 11:19 **But wisdom is j of her children** *1344*
Mt 12:37 **For by thy words thou shalt be j,** *1344*
Lk 7:35 **wisdom is j of all her children** *1344*
Lk 18:14 **this man went down to his house j** *1344*
Ac 13:39 could not be **j** by the law of Moses..... *1344*
Ro 2:13 but the doers of the law shall be **j**...... *1344*
Ro 3:4 thou mightest be **j** in thy sayings,...... *1344*
Ro 3:20 shall no flesh be **j** in his sight: *1344*
Ro 3:24 Being **j** freely by his grace through *1344*
Ro 3:28 that a man is **j** by faith without the *1344*
Ro 4:2 For if Abraham were **j** by works,....... *1344*
Ro 5:1 being **j** by faith, we have peace *1344*
Ro 5:9 then, being now **j** by his blood,........ *1344*
Ro 8:30 whom he called, them he also **j**: *1344*
Ro 8:30 whom he **j**, them he also glorified *1344*
1Co 4:4 yet am I not hereby **j**: but he that *1344*
1Co 6:11 **j** in the name of the Lord Jesus, ... *1344*
Gal 2:16 is not **j** by the works of the law *1344*
Gal 2:16 might be **j** by the faith of Christ *1344*
Gal 2:16 works of the law shall no flesh be **j**. *1344*
Gal 2:17 if, while we seek to be **j** by Christ,...... *1344*
Gal 3:11 no man is **j** by the law in the sight *1344*
Gal 3:24 Christ, that we might be **j** by faith *1344*
Gal 5:4 whosoever of you are **j** by the law; *1344*
1Ti 3:16 manifest in the flesh, **j** in the Spirit, ... *1344*
Tit 3:7 being **j** by his grace, we should be...... *1344*
Jas 2:21 not Abraham our father **j** by works,.... *1344*
Jas 2:24 then how that by works a man is **j**,..... *1344*
Jas 2:25 not Rahab the harlot **j** by works,....... *1344*

JUSTIFIETH
Pr 17:15 He that **j** the wicked, and he that 6663
Ro 4:5 on him that **j** the ungodly *1344*
Ro 8:33 of God's elect? It is God that **j**......... *1344*

JUSTIFY See also JUSTIFIED.
Ex 23:7 not: for I will not **j** the wicked......... 6663
Dt 25:1 then they shall **j** the righteous, ... 6663
Job 9:20 If I **j** myself, mine own mouth shall.... 6663
Isa 5:23 Which **j** the wicked for reward,........ 6663
Isa 53:11 shall my righteous servant **j** many;..... 6663
Lk 10:29 he, willing to **j** himself, said unto *1344*
Lk 16:15 **which j yourselves before men,**........ *1344*
Ro 3:30 shall **j** the circumcision by faith,....... *1344*
Gal 3:8 would **j** the heathen through faith,..... *1344*

JUSTLY See also UNJUSTLY.
Mic 6:8 but to do **j**, and love mercy 4941
Lk 23:41 And we indeed **j**; for we receive........ *1346*
1Th 2:10 how holy and **j** and unblameably *1346*

KEEP See also KEEPEST; KEEPETH; KEEPING; KEPT.

Ge	2:15	of Eden to dress it and to **k** it	8104
Ge	3:24	way, to **k** the way of the tree of life.	8104
Ge	6:19	the ark, to **k** them alive with thee;	8104
Ge	17:10	is my covenant, which ye shall **k**,	8104
Ex	12:48	and will **k** the passover to the Lord,	6213
Ex	20:6	love me, and **k** my commandments	8104
Ex	20:8	the sabbath day, to **k** it holy.	6942
Ex	23:7	**K** thee far from a false matter;	7368
Ex	31:13	Verily my sabbaths ye shall **k**:	8104
Nu	1:53	**k** the charge of the tabernacle of.	8104
Dt	4:9	and **k** thy soul diligently, lest thou	8104
Dt	5:12	**K** the sabbath day to sanctify it,	8104
Dt	11:22	For if ye shall diligently **k** all these	8104
Dt	16:1	**k** the passover unto the Lord.	6213
Jos	6:18	**k** yourselves from the accursed	8104
Jgs	2:22	as their fathers did **k** it, or not.	8104
2Sa	20:3	whom he had left to **k** the house	8104
1Ki	8:25	**k** with thy servant David my father	8104
1Ki	20:39	unto me, and said, **K** this man:	8104
2Ki	23:3	to **k** his commandments and his	8104
2Ki	23:21	**K** the passover unto the Lord	6213
1Ch	4:10	that thou wouldest **k** me from evil,	6213
1Ch	29:18	**k** this for ever in the imagination	8104
1Ch	29:19	heart, to **k** thy commandments,	8104
2Ch	13:11	we **k** the charge of the Lord our	8104
2Ch	22:9	no power to **k** still the kingdom	6113
2Ch	30:3	they could not **k** it at that time	6213
2Ch	35:18	kings of Israel **k** such a passover	6213
Ne	1:9	and **k** my commandments, and do.	8104
Ne	13:22	they should come and **k** the gates,	8104
Est	3:8	neither **k** they the king's laws:	6213
Job	14:13	**k** me secret, until thy wrath be	
Ps	17:8	**K** me as the apple of the eye	8104
Ps	19:13	**K** back thy servant also from.	2820
Ps	22:29	and none can **k** alive his own soul	
Ps	39:1	I will **k** my mouth with a bridle,	8104
Ps	78:7	God, but **k** his commandments:	5341
Ps	83:1	**K** not thou silence, O God: hold not	
Ps	103:9	neither will he **k** his anger for	5201
Ps	103:18	to such as **k** his covenant, and to	8104
Ps	119:4	us to **k** thy precepts diligently	8104
Ps	119:69	will **k** thy precepts with my whole	5341
Ps	119:129	therefore doth my soul **k** them	5341
Ps	119:136	eyes, because they **k** not thy law	8104
Ps	127:1	except the Lord **k** the city, the	8104
Pr	2:11	thee, understanding shall **k** thee:	5341
Pr	3:21	**k** sound wisdom and discretion:	5341
Pr	3:26	shall **k** thy foot from being taken	8104
Pr	4:4	**k** my commandments, and live.	8104
Pr	4:13	instruction; let her not go: **k** her;	5341
Pr	4:23	**K** thy heart with all diligence;	5341
Pr	6:20	son, **k** thy father's commandment,	5341
Pr	7:5	**k** thee from the strange woman,	8104
Pr	8:32	blessed are they that **k** my ways	8104
Pr	22:5	he that doth **k** his soul shall be far	8104
Ecc	3:6	time to **k**, and a time to cast away;	8104
Ecc	3:7	time to **k** silence, and a time to speak;	
Ecc	5:1	**K** thy foot when thou goest to the	8104
Ecc	8:2	to **k** the king's commandment	8104
Ecc	12:13	God, and **k** his commandments:	8104
Isa	26:3	Thou wilt **k** him in perfect peace	5341
Isa	42:6	hold thine hand, and will **k** thee.	5341
Isa	62:6	mention of the Lord, **k** not silence,	
Jer	3:12	and I will not **k** anger for ever.	5201
Jer	42:4	I will **k** nothing back from you.	4513
Eze	18:21	**k** all my statutes, and do that which.	8104
Hos	12:6	**k** mercy and judgment, and wait	8104
Na	1:15	O Judah, **k** thy solemn feasts,	2287
Hab	2:20	let all the earth **k** silence before him.	
Zec	14:19	up to **k** the feast of tabernacles	2287
Mal	2:7	priest's lips should **k** knowledge	2287
Mt	19:17	**into life, k the commandments.**	*5083*
Mk	7:9	**that ye may k your own tradition.**	*5083*
Lk	4:10	charge over thee, to **k** thee:	*1314*
Lk	8:15	**having heard the word, k it**	*2722*
Lk	11:28	**hear the word of God, and k it.**	*5442*
Jn	8:51	**If a man k my saying, he shall.**	*5083*
Jn	12:25	**world shall k it unto life eternal**	*5442*
Jn	14:15	**ye love me, k my commandments**	*5083*
Jn	15:10	**If ye k my commandments, ye**	*5083*
Jn	17:11	**Holy Father, k through thine own**	*5083*
Jn	17:15	**shouldest k them from the evil.**	*5083*
Ac	5:3	to **k** back part of the price of the	*3557*
Ac	15:24	be circumcised, and **k** the law:	*5083*
Ac	18:21	I must by all means **k** this feast	*4160*
1Co	5:8	**k** the feast, not with old leaven	*1858*
1Co	5:11	unto you not to **k** company.	*4874*
1Co	9:27	I **k** under my body, and bring it	*5299*
1Co	14:34	women **k** silence in the churches:	*4601*
1Co	15:2	ye **k** in memory what I preached	*2722*
Gal	6:13	who are circumcised **k** the law;	*5442*
Eph	4:3	to **k** the unity of the Spirit in the	*5083*
Php	4:7	shall **k** your hearts and minds	*5452*
2Th	3:3	stablish you, and **k** you from evil	*5442*
1Ti	5:22	other men's sins: **k** thyself pure	*5083*
1Ti	6:14	**k** this commandment without	*5083*
1Ti	6:20	**k** that which is committed to thy	*5442*
2Ti	1:12	**k** that which I have committed	*5442*
Jas	1:27	to **k** himself unspotted from the.	*5083*
Jas	2:10	whosoever shall **k** the whole law.	*5083*
1Jn	2:3	him, if we **k** his commandments.	*5083*
1Jn	3:22	because we **k** his commandments.	*5083*
1Jn	5:3	that we **k** his commandments:	*5083*
1Jn	5:21	children, **k** yourselves from idols	*5442*
Jude	21	**K** yourselves in the love of God	*5083*
Jude	24	that is able to **k** you from falling.	*5442*
Rev	1:3	**k** those things which are written.	*5083*
Rev	3:10	**also will k thee from the hour of**	*5083*
Rev	22:9	which **k** the sayings of this book:	*5083*

KEEPER See also DOORKEEPER.

Ge	4:9	know not: Am I my brother's **k**?	8104
Ge	39:22	the **k** of the prison committed to	8269
Ps	121:5	the Lord is thy **k**: the Lord is thy.	8104
SS	1:6	made me **k** of the vineyards; but	5201
Ac	16:27	the **k** of the prison awaking out	*1200*

KEEPERS

Ecc	12:3	day when the **k** of the house shall.	8104
SS	5:7	**k** of the walls took away any veil.	8104
Eze	44:8	ye have set **k** of my charge in my	8104
Mt	28:4	for fear of him the **k** did shake	*5083*
Ac	12:6	**k** before the door kept the prison	*5441*
Ac	12:19	him not, he examined the **k**, and	*5441*
Tit	2:5	discreet, chaste, **k** at home, good.	*3626*

KEEPETH

Dt 7:9	**k** covenant and mercy with them	8104
Ps 34:20	He **k** all his bones: not one of	8104
Ps 121:4	he that **k** Israel shall neither	8104
Pr 13:3	He that **k** his mouth … his life:	5341
Pr 13:3	He that … his mouth **k** his life:	8104
Pr 16:17	he that **k** his way preserveth his	5341
Pr 19:16	**k** the commandment **k** his own	8104
Pr 21:23	tongue **k** his soul from troubles	8104
Pr 24:12	he that **k** thy soul, doth not he	5341
Pr 28:7	Whoso **k** the law is a wise son: but	5341
Pr 29:3	he that **k** company with harlots	
Pr 29:11	a wise man **k** it in till afterwards	7623
Pr 29:18	he that **k** the law, happy is he	8104
Ecc 8:5	Whoso **k** the commandment shall	8104
Isa 26:2	nation which **k** the truth may enter	8104
Isa 56:2	**k** his hand from doing any evil	8104
Lk 11:21	**a strong man armed k his palace,**	*5442*
Jn 7:19	**and yet none of you k the law?**	*4160*
Jn 14:24	**loveth me not k not my sayings:**	*5083*
1Jn 2:5	whoso **k** his word, in him verily is	*5083*
1Jn 5:18	that is begotten of God **k** himself,	*5083*
Rev 2:26	**and k my works unto the end,**	*5083*
Rev 22:7	blessed is he that **k** the sayings of	*5083*

KEEPING

Ex 34:7	**K** mercy for thousands, forgiving	5341
Dt 8:11	God, in not **k** his commandments,	8104
Ps 19:11	in **k** of them there is great reward	8104
Da 9:4	**k** the covenant and mercy to them	8104
Lk 2:8	**k** watch over their flock by night	*5442*
1Co 7:19	**k** of the commandments of God	*5084*
1Pe 4:19	commit the **k** of their souls to him in	

K

KEPT

Ge 39:9	neither hath he **k** back any thing	2820
Ex 3:1	Moses **k** the flock of Jethro his	7462
Ex 16:33	Lord, to be **k** for your generations	4931
Nu 9:7	wherefore are we **k** back, that we	1639
Nu 24:11	hath **k** thee back from honour	4513
Dt 32:10	he **k** him as the apple of his eye	5341
1Sa 13:13	hast not **k** the commandment of	8104
1Sa 26:16	because ye have not **k** your master,	8104
2Sa 22:22	I have **k** the ways of the Lord, and	8104
1Ki 3:6	hast **k** for him this great kindness	8104
1Ki 11:10	but he **k** not that which the Lord	8104
1Ch 10:13	word of the Lord, which he **k** not,	8104
2Ch 30:21	present at Jerusalem **k** the feast	6213
2Ch 35:18	no passover like to that **k** in Israel	6213
2Ch 36:21	as she lay desolate she **k** sabbath,	7673
Ezr 3:4	**k** also the feast of tabernacles,	6213
Ezr 6:19	of the captivity **k** the passover	6213
Ezr 6:22	**k** the feast of unleavened bread	6213
Ne 1:7	have not **k** the commandments,	8104
Ne 9:34	priests, nor our fathers, **k** thy law,	6213
Est 9:28	days should be remembered and **k**	6213
Job 29:21	waited, and **k** silence at my counsel	
Ps 32:3	When I **k** silence, my bones	2790
Ps 50:21	hast thou done, and I **k** silence;	2790
Ps 119:167	My soul hath **k** thy testimonies;	8104
Ecc 2:10	eyes desired I **k** not from them	680
Ecc 5:13	riches **k** for the owners thereof to	8104
SS 1:6	mine own vineyard have I not **k**	5201
Isa 30:29	night when a holy solemnity is **k**;	6942
Jer 16:11	me, and have not **k** my law;	8104
Eze 44:15	that **k** the charge of my sanctuary	8104
Da 5:19	whom he would he **k** alive; and	
Da 7:28	but I **k** the matter in my heart	5202
Am 1:11	and he **k** his wrath for ever	8104
Mal 3:14	is it that we have **k** his ordinance	8104
Mt 14:6	But when Herod's birthday was **k**,	*71*
Mt 19:20	things have I **k** from my youth	*5442*
Lk 2:19	But Mary **k** all these things, and	*4933*
Lk 2:51	his mother **k** all these sayings in	*1301*
Lk 18:21	these have I **k** from my youth up	*5442*
Jn 2:10	hast **k** the good wine until now	*5083*
Jn 12:7	**of my burying hath she k this.**	*5083*
Jn 15:10	**even as I have k my Father's**	*5083*
Jn 15:20	**if they have k my saying, they**	*5083*
Jn 17:12	**the world, I k them in thy name:**	*5083*
Ac 5:2	**k** back part of the price, his wife	*3557*
Ac 15:12	Then all the multitude **k** silence,	*4601*
Ac 20:20	how I **k** back nothing that was	*5288*
Ac 22:2	them, they **k** the more silence:	*3930*
Ac 22:20	**k** the raiment of them that slew	*5442*
Ro 16:25	**k** secret since the world began,	
Gal 3:23	we were **k** under the law, shut up	*5432*
2Ti 4:7	my course, I have **k** the faith	*5083*
Heb 11:28	Through faith he **k** the passover,	*4160*
Jas 5:4	which is of you **k** back by fraud,	*650*
1Pe 1:5	**k** by the power of God through	*5432*
2Pe 3:7	by the same word are **k** in store,	*2343*
Jude 6	which **k** not their first estate,	*5083*
Rev 3:10	**hast k the word of my patience,**	*5083*

KEY

Isa 22:22	the **k** of the house of David will I	4668
Lk 11:52	**taken away the k of knowledge:**	*2807*
Rev 3:7	**true, he that hath the k of David,**	*2807*
Rev 9:1	given the **k** of the bottomless pit	*2407*
Rev 20:1	having the **k** of the bottomless pit	*2807*

KEYS

Mt 16:19	**the k of the kingdom of heaven:**	*2807*
Rev 1:18	**have the k of hell and of death**	*2807*

KICK

1Sa 2:29	Wherefore **k** ye at my sacrifice	1163
Ac 9:5	**for thee to k against the pricks**	*2979*
Ac 26:14	**for thee to k against the pricks.**	*2979*

KID

Ge 37:31	killed a **k** of the goats, and dipped	8163
Ge 38:20	Judah sent the **k** by the hand	1423
Le 9:3	a **k** of the goats for a sin offering:	8163
Le 23:19	shall sacrifice one **k** of the goats	8163
Dt 14:21	seethe a **k** in his mother's milk	1423
Jgs 14:6	him as he would have rent a **k**,	1423
Jgs 15:1	visited his wife with a **k**;	1423, 5795
Isa 11:6	leopard shall lie down with the **k**;	1423
Lk 15:29	**thou never gavest me a k, that I**	*2056*

KIDS

Ge 27:9	thence two good **k** of the goats;	1423
Le 16:5	two kids of the goats for a sin	8163
1Sa 10:3	Beth-el, one carrying three **k**,	1423
1Ki 20:27	them like two little flocks of **k**;	5795

KILL

Ge 4:15	any finding him should **k** him	5221
Ge 12:12	they will **k** me, but they will save	2026
Ge 26:7	place should **k** me for Rebekah;	2026
Ge 27:24	himself, purposing to **k** thee	2026
Ge 37:21	and said, Let us not **k** him	5221

Ex 1:16 it be a son, then ye shall **k** him:........ 4191
Ex 2:14 intendest thou to **k** me, as thou 2026
Ex 4:24 met him, and sought to **k** him 4191
Ex 12:21 your families, and **k** the passover 7819
Ex 16:3 to **k** this whole assembly with......... 4191
Ex 20:13 Thou shalt not **k**.................... 7523
Ex 22:1 ox, or a sheep, and **k** it, or sell it;....... 2873
Ex 22:24 and I will **k** you with the sword;........ 2026
Le 1:5 shall **k** the bullock before the Lord: 7819
Le 3:8 **k** it before the tabernacle of the 7819
Le 14:25 **k** the lamb of the trespass offering, ... 7819
Le 14:50 he shall **k** the one of the birds in 7819
Le 20:4 seed unto Molech, and **k** him not: 4191
Le 20:16 thou shalt **k** the woman, and the 2026
Nu 14:15 thou shalt **k** all this people as one...... 4191
Nu 31:17 **k** every male among the little ones, ... 2026
Nu 35:27 revenger of blood **k** the slayer; 7523
Dt 4:42 should **k** his neighbour unawares, ... 7523
Dt 5:17 Thou shalt not **k**.................... 7523
Dt 12:21 shalt **k** of thy herd and of thy 2076
Dt 13:9 thou shalt surely **k** him; thine......... 2026
Dt 32:39 I **k**, and I make alive; I would 4191
Jgs 13:23 If the Lord were pleased to **k** us 4191
Jgs 16:2 when it is day, we shall **k** him 2026
1Sa 16:2 if Saul hear it, he will **k** me. And....... 2026
1Sa 17:9 fight with me, and to **k** me, then 5221
1Sa 19:2 Saul my father seeketh to **k** thee: 4191
1Sa 24:10 some bade me **k** thee: but mine 2026
2Sa 14:7 that we may **k** him, for the life of...... 4191
2Sa 14:32 any iniquity in me, let him **k** me 4191
1Ki 11:40 sought therefore to **k** Jeroboam 4191
2Ki 5:7 Am I God, to **k** and make alive........ 4191
2Ch 35:6 So **k** the passover, and sanctify 7819
Est 3:13 to **k**, and to cause to perish, all 2026
Ecc 3:3 A time to **k**, and a time to heal;........ 2026
Mt 5:21 **of old time, Thou shalt not k;**......... *5407*
Mt 10:28 **fear not them which k the body**........ *615*
Mt 17:23 **they shall k him, and the third day** *615*
Mt 24:9 **up to be afflicted, and shall k you:**...... *615*
Mt 26:4 take Jesus by subtilty, and **k** him........ *615*
Mk 3:4 **or to do evil? to save life, or to k?**....... *615*
Mk 9:31 **hands of men, and they shall k**......... *615*
Mk 10:19 **Do not k, Do not steal, Do not**........ *5407*
Mk 10:34 **spit upon him, and shall k him:**......... *615*
Mk 12:7 **let us k him, and the inheritance** *615*
Lk 12:4 **not afraid of them that k the body,** *615*
Lk 13:31 depart thence: for Herod will **k** thee..... *615*
Lk 15:23 **hither the fatted calf, and k it;**......... *2380*
Lk 18:20 **not commit adultery, Do not k**........ *5407*
Lk 20:14 **is the heir: come, let us k him**.......... *615*
Lk 22:2 sought how they might **k** him; *337*
Jn 5:18 the Jews sought the more to **k** him...... *615*
Jn 7:1 because the Jews sought to **k** him....... *615*
Jn 7:19 **the law? Why go ye about to k me?** *615*
Jn 8:22 said the Jews, Will he **k** himself? *615*
Jn 8:37 **ye seek to k me, because my word**....... *615*
Jn 10:10 **not, but for to steal, and to k,** *2380*
Ac 7:28 Wilt thou **k** me, as thou didst the....... *337*
Ac 9:24 the gates day and night to **k** him........ *337*
Ac 10:13 to him, Rise, Peter; **k**, and eat *2380*
Ac 26:21 temple, and went about to **k** me....... *1315*
Ro 13:9 Thou shalt not **k**, Thou shalt not *5407*
Jas 2:11 yet if thou **k**, thou art become a *5407*
Jas 4:2 ye **k**, and desire to have, and *5407*
Rev 2:23 **I will k her children with death;**........ *615*
Rev 6:4 that they should **k** one another: *4969*
Rev 6:8 to **k** with sword, and with hunger, ... *615*
Rev 9:5 given that they should not **k** them,...... *615*
Rev 11:7 shall overcome them, and **k** them....... *615*

KILLED

Ge 37:31 **k** a kid of the goats, and dipped 7819
Le 6:25 place where the burnt offering is **k**..... 7819
1Sa 24:11 skirt of thy robe, and **k** thee not, ... 2026
2Sa 12:9 hast **k** Uriah the Hittite with the....... 5221
1Ki 16:10 in and smote him, and **k** him 4191
2Ki 15:25 **k** him, and reigned in his room 4191
2Ch 29:24 And the priests **k** them, and they 7819
Ezr 6:20 **k** the passover for all the children...... 7819
Ps 44:22 for thy sake are we **k** all the day 2026
La 2:21 anger; thou hast **k**, and not pitied 2873
Mt 16:21 be **k**, and be raised again the third 615
Mt 23:31 **of them which k the prophets**......... *5407*
Mk 14:12 when they **k** the passover, ... *2380*
Lk 11:47 **prophets, and your fathers k them**...... *615*
Lk 12:5 **after he hath k hath power to cast**....... *615*
Lk 15:30 **thou hast k for him the fatted**......... *2380*
Lk 22:7 when the passover must be **k**.......... *2380*
Ac 3:15 And **k** the Prince of life, whom God *615*
Ac 16:27 sword, and would have **k** himself,....... *337*
Ac 23:12 eat nor drink till they had **k** Paul *615*
Ro 8:36 For thy sake we are **k** all the day *2289*
Ro 11:3 Lord, they have **k** thy prophets *615*
2Co 6:9 we live; as chastened, and not **k**; *2289*
1Th 2:15 Who both **k** the Lord Jesus, and *615*
Jas 5:6 have condemned and **k** the just;....... *5407*
Rev 6:11 should be **k** as they were, should........ *615*
Rev 9:20 which were not **k** by these plagues *615*
Rev 13:10 sword must be **k** with the sword. *615*
Rev 13:15 the image of the beast should be **k**...... *615*

KILLEST

Mt 23:37 **Jerusalem, thou that k the prophets,** *615*
Lk 13:34 **Jerusalem, which k the prophets**........ *615*

KILLETH

Le 24:17 he that **k** any man shall surely......... 5221
Le 24:18 that **k** a beast shall make it good; 5221
Nu 35:15 one that **k** any person unawares....... 5221
Nu 35:30 Whoso **k** any person, the murderer 5221
Dt 19:4 Whoso **k** his neighbour ignorantly..... 5221
Jos 20:3 slayer that **k** any person unawares 5221
1Sa 2:6 The Lord **k**, and maketh alive:......... 4191
1Sa 17:26 to the man that **k** this Philistine 5221
Pr 21:25 The desire of the slothful **k** him;....... 4191
Jn 16:2 **whosoever k you will think that he** *615*
2Co 3:6 letter **k**, but the spirit giveth life *615*
Rev 13:10 he that **k** with the sword must be....... *615*

KIN See also **KINSFOLK; KINSMAN; KINSWOMAN.**

Le 18:6 any that is near of **k** to him........... 1320
Le 20:19 for he uncovereth his near **k**:.......... 7607
Le 25:25 if any of his **k** come to redeem it,...... 7138
Ru 2:20 man is near of **k** unto us, one of our
Mk 6:4 **country, and among his own k,** *4773*

KIND See also **MANKIND; WOMANKIND.**

Ge 1:11 tree yielding fruit after his **k**,.......... 4327
Ge 1:12 and herb yielding seed after his **k**, ... 4327
Ge 1:21 forth abundantly, after their **k**, ... 4327
Ge 1:21 every winged fowl after his **k**: 4327
Ge 1:24 the living creature after his **k**, ... 4327
Ge 1:24 beast of the earth after his **k**: and 4327

K

2Ch 10:7 If thou be **k** to this people, and........ 2896
Ne 13:20 merchants and sellers of all **k** of ware
Mt 13:47 **the sea, and gathered of every k:** *1085*
Mt 17:21 **this k goeth not out but by prayer**..... *1085*
Mk 9:29 **This k can come forth by nothing,**..... *1085*
Lk 6:35 **he is k unto the unthankful and**....... *5543*
1Co 13:4 Charity suffereth long, and is **k**; *5541*
1Co 15:39 but there is one **k** of flesh of men,
Eph 4:32 And be ye **k** one to another.......... *5543*
Jas 1:18 a **k** of firstfruits of his creatures *5100*
Jas 3:7 For every **k** of beasts, and of.......... *5449*

KINDLE
Ex 35:3 shall **k** no fire throughout your........ 1197
Pr 26:21 is a contentious man to **k** strife........ 2787
Jer 43:12 **k** a fire in the houses of the gods 3341
Eze 20:47 God; Behold, I will **k** a fire in thee,..... 3341
Mal 1:10 neither do ye **k** fire on mine altar....... 215

KINDLED
Ex 4:14 of the Lord was **k** against Moses, ... 2734
Nu 11:1 heard it; and his anger was **k**; 2734
Nu 11:10 anger of the Lord was **k** greatly;....... 2734
Nu 11:33 wrath of the Lord was **k** against 2734
Nu 22:22 And God's anger was **k** because he..... 2734
Nu 32:13 Lord's anger was **k** against Israel
Dt 7:4 the anger of the Lord be **k** against 2734
Dt 11:17 Lord's wrath be **k** against you......... 2734
Dt 29:27 anger of the Lord was **k** against 2734
Dt 31:17 my anger shall be **k** against them 2734
Dt 32:22 For a fire is **k** in mine anger, and 6919
Jos 7:1 anger of the Lord was **k** against 2734
Jos 23:16 shall the anger of the Lord be **k** 2734
Jgs 14:19 And his anger was **k**, and he went 2734
2Sa 6:7 anger of the Lord was **k** against 2734
2Sa 12:5 And David's anger was greatly **k**....... 2734
2Sa 24:1 anger of the Lord was **k** against 2734
2Ki 22:13 wrath of the Lord that is **k** against..... 3341
2Ki 22:17 my wrath shall be **k** against this 3341
2Ki 23:26 his anger was **k** against Judah,......... 2734
2Ch 25:15 anger of the Lord was **k** against 2734
Job 19:11 hath also **k** his wrath against me....... 2734
Job 42:7 My wrath is **k** against thee, and 2734
Ps 2:12 when his wrath is **k** but a little 1197
Ps 78:21 so a fire was **k** against Jacob, and 5400
Isa 5:25 is the anger of the Lord **k** against...... 2734
Jer 17:4 ye have **k** a fire in mine anger,......... 6919
Jer 44:6 was **k** in the cities of Judah and 1197
La 4:11 hath **k** a fire in Zion, and it hath....... 3341
Eze 20:48 see that I the Lord have **k** it: 1197
Zec 10:3 was **k** against the shepherds........... 2734
Lk 12:49 **what will I, if it be already k?** *381*

KINDLETH
Job 41:21 His breath **k** coals, and a flame........ 3857
Jas 3:5 how great a matter a little fire **k**!........ *381*

KINDLY
Ge 24:49 if ye will deal **k** and truly with 2617
Ru 1:8 Lord deal **k** with you, as ye have....... 2617
1Sa 20:8 shall deal **k** with thy servant;.......... 2617
2Ki 25:28 he spake **k** to him, and set his......... 2896
Ro 12:10 Be **k** affectioned one to another *5387*

KINDNESS See also LOVINGKINDNESS.
Jgs 8:35 shewed they **k** to the house of......... 2617
Ru 2:20 not left off his **k** to the living and...... 2617
Ru 3:10 shewed more **k** in the latter end 2617
2Sa 2:6 will requite you this **k**, because 2896
2Sa 9:1 shew him **k** for Jonathan's sake? 2617
2Sa 10:2 as his father shewed **k** unto me........ 2617
1Ki 3:6 hast kept for him this great **k**,......... 2617
1Ch 19:2 because his father shewed **k** to me 2617
2Ch 24:22 king remembered not the **k** which..... 2617
Ne 9:17 slow to anger, and of great **k**, and...... 2617
Est 2:9 him, and she obtained **k** of him;....... 2617
Ps 117:2 For his merciful **k** is great toward...... 2617
Ps 119:76 thy merciful **k** be for my comfort, ... 2617
Ps 141:5 smite me; it shall be a **k**:............. 2617
Pr 19:22 The desire of a man is his **k**: and 2617
Pr 31:26 and in her tongue is the law of **k** 2617
Isa 54:10 my **k** shall not depart from thee, ... 2617
Joel 2:13 slow to anger, and of great **k**, and...... 2617
Jnh 4:2 slow to anger, and of great **k**, and...... 2617
2Co 6:6 by **k**, by the Holy Ghost, by love....... *5544*
Eph 2:7 in his **k** toward us through Christ...... *5544*
Col 3:12 **k**, humbleness of mind, meekness *5544*
Tit 3:4 after that the **k** and love of God *5544*
2Pe 1:7 to godliness brotherly **k**; and to *5360*

KINDRED
Ge 12:1 of thy country, and from thy **k**,........ 4138
Ge 24:40 take a wife for my son of my **k**,........ 4940
Jos 6:23 and they brought out all her **k**,........ 4940
Ru 3:2 And now is not Boaz of our **k**, ... 4130
Est 2:20 Esther had not yet shewed her **k**....... 4138
Est 8:6 to see the destruction of my **k**?........ 4138
Lk 1:61 thy **k** that is called by this name *4772*
Ac 4:6 were of the **k** of the high priest, ... *1085*
Ac 7:14 all his **k**, threescore and fifteen *4772*
Ac 7:19 same dealt subtilly with our **k**, ... *1085*
Rev 5:9 blood out of every **k**, and tongue,...... *5443*
Rev 14:6 every nation, and **k**, and tongue,....... *5443*

KINDREDS
Ps 22:27 all the **k** of the nations shall 4940
Ac 3:25 all the **k** of the earth be blessed........ *3965*
Rev 1:7 all **k** of the earth shall wail............ *5443*
Rev 7:9 of all nations, and **k**, and people....... *5445*
Rev 11:9 and **k** and tongues and nations........ *5443*
Rev 13:7 power was given him over all **k**, ... *5443*

KINDS
Ge 8:19 upon the earth, after their **k** 4940
Jer 15:3 I will appoint over them four **k**, ... 4940
Eze 47:10 fish shall be according to their **k**, ... 4327
1Co 12:10 another divers **k** of tongues; to *1085*
1Co 14:10 so many **k** of voices in the world,...... *1085*

KINE See also COW.
Ge 41:2 river seven well favoured **k** and........ 6510
Ge 41:3 seven other **k** came up after them 6510
Ge 41:20 the lean and ill favoured **k** did eat 6510
Ge 41:26 The seven good **k** are seven years; 6510

KING
Ge 14:18 **k** of Salem brought forth bread 4428
Ge 14:22 Abram said to the **k** of Sodom,........ 4428
Ge 36:31 reigned any **k** over the children........ 4428
Ge 40:1 butler of the **k** of Egypt and his 4428
Ge 40:1 offended their lord the **k** of Egypt 4428
Ge 41:46 stood before Pharaoh **k** of Egypt 4428
Ex 1:8 there arose up a new **k** over Egypt,..... 4428
Ex 1:18 **k** of Egypt called for the midwives, ... 4428

Ex	2:23	of time that the **k** of Egypt died:	4428
Ex	3:19	the **k** of Egypt will not let you go	4428
Ex	14:8	the heart of Pharaoh **k** of Egypt,	4428
Nu	23:21	the shout of a **k** is among them	4428
Dt	7:8	the hand of Pharaoh **k** of Egypt	4428
Dt	17:14	I will set a **k** over me, like as all	4428
Dt	28:36	**k** which thou shalt set over thee,	4428
Jos	8:29	**k** of Ai he hanged on a tree until	4428
Jos	10:1	**k** of Jerusalem had heard how	4428
Jgs	3:14	of Israel served the **k** of Moab	4428
Jgs	4:2	into the hand of Jabin **k** of Canaan,	4428
Jgs	9:15	If in truth ye anoint me **k** over you,	4428
Jgs	17:6	days there was no **k** in Israel,	4428
Jgs	18:1	days there was no **k** in Israel:	4428
Jgs	19:1	when there was no **k** in Israel	4428
Jgs	21:25	days there was no **k** in Israel:	4428
1Sa	2:10	he shall give strength unto his **k**,	4428
1Sa	8:5	make us a **k** to judge us like all	4428
1Sa	8:11	manner of the **k** that shall reign	4428
1Sa	8:18	your **k** which ye shall have chosen	4428
1Sa	8:19	Nay; but we will have a **k** over us;	4428
1Sa	8:20	that our **k** may judge us, and go	4428
1Sa	8:22	unto their voice, and make them a **k**	4428
1Sa	10:19	unto him, Nay, but set a **k** over us	4428
1Sa	10:24	shouted, and said, God save the **k**.	4428
1Sa	11:15	they made Saul **k** before the Lord	4427
1Sa	12:12	the Lord your God was your **k**	4428
1Sa	12:13	behold the **k** whom ye have chosen,	4428
1Sa	12:17	sight of the Lord, in asking you a **k**	4428
1Sa	12:19	all our sins this evil, to ask us a **k**	4428
1Sa	12:25	be consumed, both ye and your **k**.	4428
1Sa	15:23	also rejected thee from being **k**.	4428
1Sa	17:25	**k** will enrich him with great riches	4428
1Sa	18:18	I should be son in law to the **k**?	4428
1Sa	18:25	The **k** desireth not any dowry,	4428
1Sa	21:11	Is not this David the **k** of the land?	4428
1Sa	23:17	and thou shalt be **k** over Israel,	4427
1Sa	24:20	well that thou shalt surely be **k**,	4428
1Sa	26:14	Who art thou that criest to the **k**?	4428
1Sa	26:15	hast thou not kept thy lord the **k**?	4428
2Sa	2:4	David **k** over the house of Judah	4428
2Sa	3:21	gather all Israel unto my lord the **k**,	4428
2Sa	5:3	they anointed David **k** over Israel	4428
2Sa	14:9	the **k** and his throne be guiltless	4428
2Sa	14:17	so is my lord the **k** to discern good	4428
2Sa	14:22	bowed himself, and thanked the **k**:	4428
2Sa	14:22	**k** hath fulfilled the request of his	4428
2Sa	14:33	and the **k** kissed Absalom	4428
2Sa	16:9	this dead dog curse my lord the **k**?	4428
2Sa	16:16	God save the **k**, God save the **k**	4428
2Sa	19:2	how the **k** was grieved for his son	4428
2Sa	19:27	my lord the **k** is as an angel of God:	4428
2Sa	22:51	is the tower of salvation for his **k**:	4428
1Ki	1:1	Now **k** David was old and stricken	4428
1Ki	1:25	him, and say, God save **k** Adonijah	4428
1Ki	1:34	and say, God save **k** Solomon	4428
1Ki	1:43	David hath made Solomon **k**	4427
1Ki	3:25	the **k** said, Divide the living child	4428
1Ki	5:13	**k** Solomon raised a levy out of all	4428
1Ki	9:26	**k** Solomon made a navy of ships	4428
1Ki	10:10	queen of Sheba gave to **k** Solomon	4428
1Ki	11:1	But **k** Solomon loved many strange	4428
1Ki	12:13	the **k** answered the people roughly,	4428
1Ki	12:15	**k** hearkened not unto the people;	4428
1Ki	12:20	and made him **k** over all Israel:	4427
1Ki	22:32	said, Surely it is the **k** of Israel	4428
1Ki	22:34	smote the **k** of Israel between the	4428
2Ki	6:11	which of us is for the **k** of Israel?	4428
2Ki	6:12	telleth the **k** of Israel the words	4428
2Ki	9:18	Thus saith the **k**, Is it peace?	4428
2Ki	9:19	Thus saith the **k**, Is it peace?	4428
2Ki	17:6	the **k** of Assyria took Samaria, and	4428
2Ki	18:11	**k** of Assyria did carry away Israel,	4428
2Ki	19:36	Sennacherib **k** of Assyria departed	4428
2Ki	20:6	out of the hand of the **k** of Assyria;	4428
2Ki	20:18	in the palace of the **k** of Babylon	4428
2Ki	23:25	unto him was there no **k** before him,	4428
2Ki	24:20	rebelled against the **k** of Babylon	4428
2Ki	25:11	that fell away to the **k** of Babylon	4428
1Ch	5:6	**k** of Assyria carried away captive:	4428
1Ch	20:2	David took the crown of their **k**	4428
1Ch	29:22	made Solomon the son of David **k**	4428
2Ch	9:17	the **k** made a great throne of ivory,	4428
2Ch	16:7	thou hast relied on the **k** of Syria,	4428
2Ch	18:31	that they said, It is the **k** of Israel	4428
2Ch	18:33	smote the **k** of Israel between the	4428
2Ch	24:22	**k** remembered not the kindness	4428
2Ch	25:3	that had killed the **k** his father	4428
2Ch	26:1	sixteen years old, and made him **k**	4427
2Ch	26:13	to help the **k** against the enemy	4428
2Ch	26:21	Uzziah the **k** was a leper unto the	4428
2Ch	27:5	He fought also with the **k** of the	4428
2Ch	28:16	**k** Ahaz send unto the kings of	4428
2Ch	36:22	up the spirit of Cyrus **k** of Persia,	4428
Ezr	1:1	up the spirit of Cyrus **k** of Persia,	4428
Ezr	1:7	the **k** brought forth the vessels	4428
Ezr	4:13	Be it known now unto the **k**, that,	4430
Ezr	4:16	We certify the **k** that, if this city be	4430
Ezr	5:11	which a great **k** of Israel builded	4430
Ezr	5:13	**k** Cyrus made a decree to build	4430
Ezr	5:17	let the **k** send his pleasure to us	4430
Ezr	6:1	Darius the **k** made a decree, and	4430
Ezr	7:12	Artaxerxes, **k** of kings, unto Ezra	4430
Ne	2:5	said unto the **k**. If it please the **k**,	4428
Ne	2:7	said unto the **k**, If it please the **k**,	4428
Ne	2:19	ye do? will ye rebel against the **k**?	4428
Ne	6:7	There is a **k** in Judah: and now	4428
Ne	13:26	**k** of Israel sin by these things?	4428
Est	1:10	the heart of the **k** was merry with	4428
Est	1:12	therefore was the **k** very wroth, and	4428
Est	1:19	let the **k** give her royal estate unto	4428
Est	2:1	the wrath of **k** Ahasuerus was	4428
Est	2:17	the **k** loved Esther above all the	4428
Est	3:1	did **k** Ahasuerus promote Haman	4428
Est	3:10	the **k** took his ring from his hand,	4428
Est	4:11	**k** shall hold out the golden sceptre,	4428
Est	5:2	the **k** held out to Esther the golden	4428
Est	5:8	**k** and Haman come to the banquet	4428
Est	5:12	did let no man come in with the **k**.	4428
Est	5:14	to morrow speak thou unto the **k**.	4428
Est	6:1	On that night could not the **k** sleep,	4428
Est	6:3	**k** said, What honour and dignity	4428
Est	6:6	whom the **k** delighteth to honour?	4428
Est	6:7	whom the **k** delighteth to honour,	4428
Est	6:9	whom the **k** delighteth to honour,	4428
Est	7:6	Haman was afraid before the **k** and	4428
Est	7:8	said the **k**, Will he force the queen	4428
Est	7:9	Then the **k** said, Hang him thereon.	4428
Est	8:2	the **k** took off his ring, which he	4428
Est	8:4	the **k** held out the golden sceptre	4428
Est	8:11	Wherein the **k** granted the Jews	4428
Est	10:3	Jew was next unto **k** Ahasuerus,	4428

Job	29:25	chief, and dwelt as a **k** in the army,.	4428
Job	34:18	fit to say to a **k**, Thou art wicked?.	4428
Job	41:34	a **k** over all the children of pride.	4428
Ps	2:6	Yet have I set my **k** upon my holy.	4428
Ps	10:16	The Lord is **K** for ever and ever:.	4428
Ps	24:8	Who is this **K** of glory? The Lord	4428
Ps	24:10	Who is this **K** of glory? The Lord	4428
Ps	29:10	yea, the Lord sitteth **K** for ever.	4428
Ps	47:7	For God is the **K** of all the earth:	4428
Ps	89:18	and the Holy One of Israel is our **k**	4428
Ps	95:3	God, and a great **K** above all gods.	4428
Pr	1:1	the son of David, **k** of Israel;	4428
Pr	16:10	sentence is in the lips of the **k**:	4428
Pr	16:14	The wrath of a **k** is as messengers.	4428
Pr	20:2	The fear of a **k** is as the roaring of	4428
Pr	20:8	A **k** that sitteth in the throne of	4428
Pr	20:26	A wise **k** scattereth the wicked,	4428
Pr	20:28	Mercy and truth preserve the **k**:	4428
Pr	22:11	of his lips the **k** shall be his friend.	4428
Pr	24:21	son, fear thou the Lord and the **k**:	4428
Pr	25:5	away the wicked from before the **k**.	4428
Pr	25:6	thyself in the presence of the **k**,.	4428
Pr	29:4	The **k** by judgment established	4428
Pr	29:14	**k** that faithfully judgeth the poor,.	4428
Pr	30:27	The locusts have no **k**, yet go they	4428
Pr	30:31	**k** against whom there is no rising.	4428
Ecc	1:12	I the Preacher was **k** over Israel in	4428
Ecc	2:12	man do that cometh after the **k**?.	4428
Ecc	4:13	wise child than an old and foolish **k**,	4428
Ecc	8:4	Where the word of a **k** is, there is	4428
Ecc	9:14	there came a great **k** against it,	4428
Ecc	10:16	thee, O land, when thy **k** is a child,.	4428
Ecc	10:20	Curse not the **k**, no not in thy.	4428
SS	3:9	**K** Solomon made himself a chariot	4428
SS	3:11	behold **k** Solomon with the crown.	4428
Isa	6:1	In the year that **k** Uzziah died I saw	4428
Isa	8:21	and curse their **k** and their God,.	4428
Isa	10:12	the stout heart of the **k** of Assyria,	4428
Isa	32:1	a **k** shall reign in righteousness,	4428
Isa	33:17	eyes shall see the **k** in his beauty:	4428
Isa	33:22	is our lawgiver, the Lord is our **k**;	4428
Isa	36:1	Sennacherib **k** of Assyria came up	4428
Isa	36:2	the **k** of Assyria sent Rabshakeh	4428
Isa	36:4	saith the great **k**, the **k** of Assyria,.	4428
Isa	36:14	Thus saith the **k**, Let not Hezekiah.	4428
Isa	36:18	out of the hand of the **k** of Assyria?	4428
Isa	37:1	when **k** Hezekiah heard it, that he	4428
Isa	37:4	**k** of Assyria his master hath sent	4428
Isa	37:10	into the hand of the **k** of Assyria.	4428
Isa	37:21	against Sennacherib **k** of Assyria:	4428
Isa	43:15	One, the creator of Israel, your **K**.	4428
Jer	4:9	that the heart of the **k** shall perish,.	4428
Jer	10:10	living God, and an everlasting **k**:	4428
Jer	23:5	and a **K** shall reign and prosper,	4428
Jer	24:1	**k** of Babylon had carried away	4428
Jer	25:12	I will punish the **k** of Babylon, and	4428
Jer	26:21	the **k** sought to put him to death:.	4428
Jer	27:9	shall not serve the **k** of Babylon:.	4428
Jer	27:17	serve the **k** of Babylon, and live:	4428
Jer	29:16	**k** that sitteth upon the throne of	4428
Jer	30:9	Lord their God, and David their **k**,.	4428
Jer	36:22	Now the **k** sat in the winterhouse.	4428
Jer	36:27	that the **k** had burned the roll,	4428
Jer	37:17	and the **k** asked him secretly in his.	4428
Jer	38:5	for the **k** is not he that can do any	4428
Jer	38:9	My lord the **k**, these men have done	4428
Jer	38:16	Zedekiah the **k** sware secretly unto.	4428
Jer	39:6	the **k** of Babylon slew all the nobles	4428
Jer	40:11	**k** of Babylon had left a remnant of.	4428
Jer	42:11	Be not afraid of the **k** of Babylon,	4428
Jer	46:17	Pharaoh **k** of Egypt is but a noise;	4428
Jer	48:15	the **K**, whose name is the Lord of.	4428
Jer	49:30	**k** of Babylon hath taken counsel.	4428
Jer	50:17	**k** of Babylon hath broken his bones.	4428
Jer	50:18	I will punish the **k** of Babylon and.	4428
Jer	52:10	the **k** of Babylon slew the sons of.	4428
Jer	52:11	**k** of Babylon bound him in chains,	4428
Jer	52:27	the **k** of Babylon smote them, and	4428
Jer	52:31	the head of Jehoiachin **k** of Judah,	4428
La	2:6	of his anger the **k** and the priest.	4428
La	2:9	her **k** and her princes are among	4428
Eze	24:2	**k** of Babylon set himself against	4428
Eze	37:22	and one **k** shall be **k** to them all:.	4428
Eze	37:24	David my servant shall be **k** over	4428
Da	1:2	Lord gave Jehoiakim **k** of Judah	4428
Da	1:5	**k** appointed them a daily provision	4428
Da	2:2	for to shew the **k** his dreams	4428
Da	2:10	there is no **k**, lord, nor ruler,	4430
Da	2:11	is a rare thing that the **k** requireth,.	4430
Da	2:12	For this cause the **k** was angry and.	4430
Da	2:37	Thou, O **k**, art a **k** of kings: for	4430
Da	2:48	the **k** made Daniel a great man,	4430
Da	3:1	the **k** made an image of gold,	4430
Da	3:18	if not, be it known unto thee, O **k**	4430
Da	4:18	This dream I **k** Nebuchadnezzar.	4430
Da	4:37	extol and honour the **K** of heaven,.	4430
Da	5:1	Belshazzar the **k** made a great	4430
Da	5:5	the **k** saw the part of the hand that	4430
Da	5:12	whom the **k** named Belteshazzar:.	4430
Da	5:17	I will read the writing unto the **k**,.	4430
Da	6:17	the **k** sealed it with his own signet,.	4430
Da	6:22	before thee, O **k**, have I done no.	4430
Da	8:23	the full, a **k** of fierce countenance,	4428
Da	11:3	And a mighty **k** shall stand up, that	4428
Da	11:25	**k** of the south shall be stirred up	4428
Da	11:40	**k** of the north shall come against	4428
Hos	7:3	the **k** glad with their wickedness,	4428
Hos	7:5	In the day of our **k** the princes	4428
Hos	10:3	We have no **k**, because we feared	4428
Hos	13:11	I gave thee a **k** in mine anger, and	4428
Jnh	3:6	word came unto the **k** of Nineveh,.	4428
Mic	4:9	no **k** in thee? is thy counsellor.	4428
Zep	3:15	the **k** of Israel, even the Lord, is in	4428
Zec	9:9	behold, thy **K** Cometh unto thee:	4428
Zec	14:9	Lord shall be **k** over all the earth:	4428
Zec	14:16	to worship the **K**, the Lord of hosts,.	4428
Zec	14:17	unto Jerusalem to worship the **K**	4428
Mal	1:14	I am a great **K**, saith the Lord of.	4428
Mt	2:2	is he that is born **K** of the Jews?	*935*
Mt	5:35	**for it is the city of the great K.**	*935*
Mt	14:9	the **k** was sorry: nevertheless for.	*935*
Mt	21:5	Behold, thy **K** cometh unto thee	*935*
Mt	22:7	**when the k heard thereof, he was**	*935*
Mt	27:11	Art thou the **K** of the Jews?	*935*
Mt	27:29	him, saying, Hail, **K** of the Jews!	*935*
Mt	27:37	This Is Jesus The **K** Of The Jews	*935*
Mt	27:42	If he be the **K** of Israel, let him	*935*
Mk	6:14	And **k** Herod heard of him: (for his	*935*
Mk	6:26	the **k** was exceeding sorry: yet for.	*935*
Mk	15:2	him, Art thou the **K** of the Jews?.	*935*
Mk	15:9	release unto you the **K** of the Jews?	*935*
Mk	15:12	whom ye call the **K** of the Jews?	*935*

Mk	15:18	salute him, Hail, **K** of the Jews?	*935*
Mk	15:26	written over, The **K** Of The Jews.	*935*
Mk	15:32	Let Christ the **K** of Israel descend	*935*
Lk	14:31	**Or what k, going to make war**	*935*
Lk	19:38	Blessed be the **K** that cometh in	*935*
Lk	23:2	that he himself is Christ a **K**	*935*
Lk	23:3	Art thou the **K** of the Jews?	*935*
Lk	23:37	If thou be the **K** of the Jews, save	*935*
Lk	23:38	This Is The **K** Of The Jews	*935*
Jn	6:15	take him by force, to make him a **k**,	*935*
Jn	12:15	thy **K** cometh, sitting on an ass's	*935*
Jn	18:33	him, Art thou the **K** of the Jews?	*935*
Jn	18:37	**Thou sayest that I am a k. To this**	*935*
Jn	18:39	unto you the **K** of the Jews?	*935*
Jn	19:3	said, Hail, **K** of the Jews! and they	*935*
Jn	19:14	unto the Jews, Behold your **K**!	*935*
Jn	19:15	unto them. Shall I crucify your **K**?	*935*
Jn	19:15	answered, We have no **k** but Caesar	*935*
Jn	19:19	Jesus Of Nazareth The **K** Of The	*935*
Jn	19:21	Write not, The **K** of the Jews;	*935*
Jn	19:21	that he said, I am **K** of the Jews	*935*
Ac	13:21	And afterward they desired a **k**:	*935*
Ac	17:7	that there is another **k**, one Jesus	*935*
Ac	26:27	**K** Agrippa, believest thou the	*935*
1Ti	1:17	Now unto the **K** eternal, immortal,	*935*
1Ti	6:15	**K** of kings, and Lord of lords;	*935*
Heb	7:1	Melchisedec, **k** of Salem, priest	*935*
Heb	7:2	**K** of Salem, which is, **K** of peace;	*935*
Heb	11:27	not fearing the wrath of the **k**: for	*935*
1Pe	2:13	whether it be to the **k**, as supreme;	*935*
1Pe	2:17	Fear God. Honour the **k**	*935*
Rev	9:11	they had a **k** over them, which is	*935*
Rev	15:3	are thy ways, thou **K** of saints	*935*
Rev	17:14	is Lord of lords, and **K** of kings:	*935*
Rev	19:16	**K** of Kings, And Lord Of Lords,	*935*

KINGDOM

Ge	20:9	on me and on my **k** a great sin?	4467
Ex	19:6	ye shall be unto me a **k** of priests,	4467
Dt	17:20	he may prolong his days in his **k**	4467
1Sa	13:13	Lord have established thy **k** upon	4467
1Sa	13:14	But now thy **k** shall not continue:	4467
1Sa	15:28	The Lord hath rent the **k** of Israel	4468
1Sa	18:8	can he have more but the **k**?	4410
2Sa	3:28	I and my **k** are guiltless before the	4467
2Sa	7:13	I will stablish the throne of his **k**	4467
2Sa	16:8	the **k** into the hand of Absalom	4410
1Ki	2:15	Thou knowest that the **k** was mine,	4410
1Ki	2:22	ask for him the **k** also; for he is	4410
1Ki	10:20	was not the like made in any **k**	4467
1Ki	11:13	I will not rend away all the **k**; but	4467
1Ki	18:10	God liveth, there is no nation or **k**	4467
1Ch	10:14	turned the **k** unto David the son	4410
1Ch	17:11	sons; and I will establish his **k**	4438
1Ch	28:5	the throne of the **k** of the Lord	4438
1Ch	29:11	thine is the **k**, O Lord, and thou	4467
2Ch	12:1	Rehoboam had established the **k**,	4438
2Ch	13:5	gave the **k** over Israel to David	4467
2Ch	14:5	and the **k** was quiet before him	4467
2Ch	29:21	goats, for a sin offering for the **k**	4467
2Ch	36:20	until the reign of the **k** of Persia:	4438
2Ch	36:22	proclamation throughout all his **k**,	4438
Est	1:4	shewed the riches of his glorious **k**	4438
Est	4:14	art come to the **k** for such a time	4438
Est	5:3	even given thee to the half of the **k**	4438
Est	9:30	twenty and seven provinces of the **k**	4438
Ps	22:28	For the **k** is the Lord's; and he	4410
Ps	45:6	sceptre of thy **k** is a right sceptre	4438
Ps	145:13	Thy **k** is an everlasting **k**, and	4438
Ecc	4:14	is born in his **k** becometh poor	4438
Jer	18:7	concerning a **k**, to pluck up, and	4467
Jer	18:9	concerning a **k**, to build and to	4467
Da	2:37	of heaven hath given thee a **k**,	4437
Da	4:3	his **k** is an everlasting **k**, and his	4437
Da	4:17	most High ruleth in the **k** of men,	4437
Da	4:25	most High ruleth in the **k** of men,	4437
Da	4:32	most High ruleth in the **k** of men,	4437
Da	5:7	shall be the third ruler in the **k**	4437
Da	5:26	Mene; God hath numbered thy **k**,	4437
Da	5:28	Peres; Thy **k** is divided, and given	4437
Da	6:7	All the presidents of the **k**, the	4437
Da	7:18	possess the **k** for ever, even for ever	4437
Da	7:27	High, whose **k** is an everlasting **k**,	4437
Da	8:23	And in the latter time of their **k**,	4438
Mt	4:17	**for the k of heaven is at hand**	*932*
Mt	5:3	**spirit: for theirs is the k of heaven.**	*932*
Mt	5:10	**sake: for theirs is the k of heaven**	*932*
Mt	6:10	**Thy k come. Thy will be done in**	*932*
Mt	6:13	**For thine is the k, and the power,**	*932*
Mt	6:33	**seek ye first the k of God, and his**	*932*
Mt	8:12	**children of the k shall be cast out**	*932*
Mt	12:25	**k divided against itself is brought**	*932*
Mt	13:11	**the mysteries of the k of heaven,**	*932*
Mt	13:24	**k of heaven is likened unto a man.**	*932*
Mt	13:31	**k of heaven is like to a grain of**	*932*
Mt	13:33	**k of heaven is like unto leaven,**	*932*
Mt	13:44	**the k of heaven is like unto**	*932*
Mt	13:45	**k of heaven is like unto a merchant**	*932*
Mt	13:47	**the k of heaven is like unto a net,**	*932*
Mt	16:19	**thee the keys of the k of heaven:**	*932*
Mt	16:28	**the Son of man coming in his k**	*932*
Mt	18:23	**k of heaven likened unto a certain**	*932*
Mt	20:1	**k of heaven is like unto a man that**	*932*
Mt	22:2	**The k of heaven is like unto a**	*932*
Mt	25:1	**k of heaven be likened unto ten**	*932*
Mt	25:14	**k of heaven is as a man travelling**	*932*
Mt	25:34	**inherit the k prepared for you from**	*932*
Mt	26:29	**it new with you in my Father's k**	*932*
Mk	1:15	**fulfilled, and the k of God is at**	*932*
Mk	3:24	**if a k be divided against itself,**	*932*
Mk	4:26	**So is the k of God, as if a man**	*932*
Mk	4:30	**Whereunto shall we liken the k of**	*932*
Mk	13:8	**against nation, and k against k:**	*932*
Mk	14:25	**that I drink it new in the k of God**	*932*
Lk	1:33	of his **k** there shall be no end	*932*
Lk	4:43	**preach the k of God to other cities**	*932*
Lk	6:20	**ye poor: for yours is the k of God**	*932*
Lk	7:28	**he that is least in the k of God is**	*932*
Lk	9:62	**looking back, is fit for the k of**	*932*
Lk	10:11	**the k of God is come nigh unto**	*932*
Lk	11:2	**Thy k come. Thy will be done, as**	*932*
Lk	13:29	**and shall sit down in the k of God.**	*932*
Lk	17:21	**behold, the k of God is within you.**	*932*
Lk	18:25	**rich man to enter into the k**	*932*
Lk	19:11	they thought that the **k** of God	*932*
Lk	22:16	**until it be fulfilled in the k of God**	*932*
Lk	22:18	**vine, until the k of God shall come**	*932*
Lk	22:29	**I appoint unto you a k,**	*932*
Lk	22:30	**eat and drink at my table in my k,**	*932*
Lk	23:42	me when thou comest into thy **k**	*932*
Jn	18:36	**answered, My k is not of this world**	*932*
Jn	18:36	**if my k were of this world, then**	*932*

Jn	18:36	**but now is my k not from hence**	*932*
Ac	1:6	wilt thou this time restore again the **k**	*932*
Ac	14:22	tribulation enter into the **k** of God	*932*
Ac	19:8	things concerning the **k** of God	*932*
Ro	14:17	For the **k** of God is not meat and	*932*
1Co	4:20	the **k** of God is not in word, but in	*932*
1Co	6:9	shall not inherit the **k** of God?	*932*
1Co	15:50	blood cannot inherit the **k** of God;	*932*
Col	1:13	us into the **k** of his dear Son:	*932*
Col	4:11	fellow-workers unto the **k** of God,	*932*
1Th	2:12	called you unto his **k** and glory.	*932*
2Th	1:5	be counted worthy of the **k** of God,	*932*
2Ti	4:1	dead at his appearing and his **k**;	*932*
2Ti	4:18	preserve me unto his heavenly **k**:	*932*
Heb	1:8	righteousness is the sceptre of thy **k**.	*932*
Heb	12:28	we receiving a **k** which cannot be	*932*
2Pe	1:11	into the everlasting **k** of our Lord	*932*
Rev	1:9	in the **k** and patience of Jesus	*932*
Rev	12:10	strength, and the **k** of our God,	*932*
Rev	16:10	his **k** was full of darkness; and	*932*
Rev	17:12	which have received no **k** as yet;	*932*
Rev	17:17	give their **k** unto the beast, until	*932*

KINGDOMS

1Ki	4:21	And Solomon reigned over all **k**.	4467
2Ki	19:15	thou alone, of all the **k** of the earth;	4467
2Ki	19:19	all the **k** of the earth may know	4467
2Ch	20:29	the fear of God was on all the **k**	4467
2Ch	36:23	All the **k** of the earth hath the Lord	4467
Ezr	1:2	given me all the **k** of the earth;	4467
Isa	14:16	earth to tremble, that did shake **k**;	4467
Isa	23:17	commit fornication with all the **k**.	4467
Isa	37:16	alone, of all the **k** of the earth:	4467
Isa	37:20	that all the **k** of the earth may know	4467
Isa	47:5	no more be called, The lady of **k**	4467
Jer	15:4	be removed into all **k** of the earth,	4467
Jer	24:9	be removed into the **k** of the earth.	4467
Jer	29:18	be removed to all the **k** of the earth,	4467
Jer	34:17	removed into all the **k** of the earth.	4467
Da	8:22	four **k** shall stand up out of the	4438
Am	6:2	be they better than these **k**?	4467
Na	3:5	nakedness, and the **k** thy shame	4467
Zep	3:8	nations, that I may assemble the **k**,	4467
Hag	2:22	I will overthrow the throne of **k**,	4467
Hag	2:22	I will destroy the strength of the **k**	4467
Mt	4:8	sheweth him all the **k** of the world,	*932*
Lk	4:5	unto him all the **k** of the world in	*932*
Heb	11:33	Who through faith subdued **k**,	*932*
Rev	11:15	The **k** of this world are become	*932*
Rev	11:15	the **k** of our Lord, and of his Christ;	*932*

KING'S

Ge	39:20	where the **k** prisoners were bound:	4428
Nu	20:17	we will go by the **k** high way, we	4428
Nu	21:22	we will go along by the **k** high way,	4428
1Sa	18:26	David well to be the **k** son in law:	4428
2Sa	11:9	slept at the door of the **k** house	4428
2Sa	11:20	And if so be that the **k** wrath arise,	4428
2Sa	13:30	Absalom hath slain all the **k** sons,	4428
2Sa	13:33	think that all the **k** sons are dead:	4428
2Sa	14:1	the **k** heart was toward Absalom.	4428
2Sa	14:28	Jerusalem, and saw not the **k** face.	4428
2Sa	18:20	because the **k** son is dead.	4428
1Ki	1:28	she came into the **k** presence, and	4428
1Ki	2:19	a seat to be set for the **k** mother;	4428
1Ki	13:6	**k** hand was restored him again,	4428
2Ki	10:6	the **k** sons, being seventy persons,	4428
1Ch	21:6	**k** word was abominable to Joab.	4428
2Ch	23:3	Behold, the **k** son shall reign, as	4428
Ne	1:11	man. For I was the **k** cupbearer.	4428
Est	7:10	Then was the **k** wrath pacified.	4428
Ps	61:6	Thou wilt prolong the **k** life: and	4428
Ps	72:1	thy righteousness unto the **k** son.	4428
Ps	99:4	**k** strength also loveth judgment;	4428
Pr	14:28	multitude of people is the **k** honour	4428
Pr	14:35	**k** favour is toward a wise servant:	4428
Pr	16:15	In the light of the **k** countenance	4428
Pr	19:12	The **k** wrath is as the roaring of a	4428
Pr	21:1	The **k** heart is in the hand of the	4428
Ecc	8:2	thee to keep the **k** commandment,	4428
Jer	39:8	the Chaldeans burned the **k** house,	4428
Da	1:3	and of the **k** seed, and of the	4410
Da	1:8	with the portion of the **k** meat,	4428
Da	1:15	did eat the portion of the **k** meat.	4428
Da	3:28	him, and have changed the **k** word,	4430
Da	4:31	the word was in the **k** mouth,	4430
Da	5:6	the **k** countenance was changed,	4430
Heb	11:23	not afraid of the **k** commandment.	*935*

KINGS

Ge	17:6	thee, and **k** shall come out of thee.	4428
Jos	10:17	the five **k** are found hid in a cave	4428
Jos	10:24	your feet upon the necks of these **k**	4428
1Ki	10:23	king Solomon exceeded all the **k**	4428
1Ki	20:31	house of Israel are merciful **k**:	4428
2Ki	11:19	And he sat on the throne of the **k**.	4428
1Ch	20:1	at the time that **k** go out to battle,	4428
2Ch	9:22	passed all the **k** of the earth in	4428
2Ch	9:23	**k** of the earth sought the presence	4428
2Ch	21:20	but not in the sepulchres of the **k**.	4428
2Ch	28:27	the sepulchres of the **k** of Israel:	4428
2Ch	35:18	the **k** of Israel keep such a passover	4428
Ezr	4:15	and hurtful unto **k** and provinces,	4430
Ezr	4:19	hath made insurrection against **k**,	4430
Ezr	4:22	damage grow to the hurt of the **k**?	4430
Job	3:14	With **k** and counsellors of the earth,	4428
Ps	2:2	**k** of the earth set themselves, and	4428
Ps	76:12	he is terrible to the **k** of the earth.	4428
Ps	89:27	higher than the **k** of the earth.	4428
Ps	102:15	and all the **k** of the earth thy glory.	4428
Ps	110:5	shall strike through **k** in the day of	4428
Ps	136:17	To him which smote great **k**: for	4428
Ps	136:18	And slew famous **k**: for his mercy	4428
Ps	138:4	the **k** of the earth shall praise thee,	4428
Ps	144:10	is he that giveth salvation unto **k**:	4428
Pr	8:15	By me **k** reign, and princes decree	4428
Pr	16:12	It is an abomination to **k** to commit	4428
Pr	16:13	Righteous lips are the delight of **k**;	4428
Pr	22:29	business? he shall stand before **k**;	4428
Pr	25:2	but the honour of **k** is to search out.	4428
Pr	25:3	and the heart of **k** is unsearchable.	4428
Pr	31:3	ways to that which destroyeth **k**	4428
Pr	31:4	it is not for **k** to drink wine; nor for	4428
Ecc	2:8	the peculiar treasure of **k** and of	4428
Isa	7:16	shall be forsaken of both her **k**	4428
Isa	19:11	of the wise, the son of ancient **k**?	4428
Isa	49:7	**K** shall see and arise, princes also	4428
Isa	52:15	**k** shall shut their mouths at him:	4428
Isa	60:3	**k** to the brightness of thy rising	4428
Jer	13:13	the **k** that sit upon David's throne,	4428
Jer	20:5	all the treasures of the **k** of Judah	4428
Jer	22:4	**k** sitting upon the throne of David,	4428

Jer	44:9	the wickedness of the **k** of Judah,	4428
La	4:12	The **k** of the earth, and all the	4428
Eze	28:17	I will lay thee before **k**, that they	4428
Eze	32:10	**k** shall be horribly afraid for thee,	4428
Da	2:21	he removeth **k**, and setteth up **k**:	4430
Da	2:44	in the days of these **k** shall the God	4430
Da	2:47	is a God of gods, and a Lord of **k**,	4430
Da	7:17	beasts, which are four, are four **k**,	4430
Da	9:8	to our **k**, to our princes, and to our	4428
Hos	7:7	all their **k** are fallen: there is	4428
Hos	8:4	They have set up **k**, but not by me:	4428
Hab	1:10	they shall scoff at the **k**, and the	4428
Mt	10:18	**governors and k for my sake,**	*935*
Mk	13:9	**before rulers and k for my sake,**	*335*
Lk	10:24	**prophets and k have desired to see**	*935*
Lk	21:12	**k and rulers for my name's sake**	*935*
Ac	4:26	The **k** of the earth stood up, and	*935*
Ac	9:15	**name before the Gentiles, and k,**	*935*
1Ti	2:2	For **k**, and for all that are in	*935*
1Ti	6:15	the King of **k**, and Lord of lords;	*936*
Heb	7:1	returning from the slaughter of **k**,	*935*
Rev	1:5	the prince of the **k** of the earth.	*935*
Rev	1:6	hath made us **k** and priests unto	*935*
Rev	5:10	us unto our God **k** and priests:	*935*
Rev	10:11	and nations, and tongues, and **k**	*935*
Rev	16:12	the way of the **k** of the east might	*935*
Rev	17:10	there are seven **k**: five are fallen,	*935*
Rev	17:12	horns which thou sawest are ten **k**,	*935*
Rev	17:14	he is Lord of lords, and King of **k**:	*935*
Rev	18:9	the **k** of the earth, who have	*935*
Rev	19:16	King of **K**, And Lord Of Lords	*935*
Rev	19:19	the beast, and the **k** of the earth,	*935*
Rev	21:24	the **k** of the earth do bring their	*935*

KINGS'

Pr	30:28	her hands, and is in **k** palaces	4428
Da	11:27	both these **k** hearts shall be to do	4428
Lk	7:25	**and live delicately, are in k courts,**	*933*

KINSFOLK See also KIN.

Job	19:14	My **k** have failed, and my familiar	7138
Lk	2:44	they sought him among their **k**.	*4773*

KINSFOLKS

1Ki	16:11	neither of his **k**, nor of his	1350
2Ki	10:11	his great men, and his **k**, and his	3045
Lk	21:16	**and brethren, and k, and friends**	*4773*

KINSMAN

Nu	5:8	the man have no **k** to recompence	1350
Ru	3:12	howbeit there is a **k** nearer than I.	1350
Ru	4:1	the **k** of whom Boaz spake came	1350
Ru	4:6	the **k** said, I cannot redeem it for	1350
Jn	18:26	being his **k** whose ear Peter cut	*4773*

KINSMEN

Ru	2:20	of kin unto us, one of our next **k**	1350
Ps	38:11	sore; and my **k** stand afar off.	7138
Lk	14:12	**neither thy k, nor thy rich**	*4773*
Ro	9:3	my **k** according to the flesh:	*4773*

KINSWOMAN

Le	18:12	sister: she is thy father's near **k**	7607
Le	18:13	for she is thy mother's near **k**	7607
Pr	7:4	and call understanding thy **k**:	4129

KINSWOMEN

Le	18:17	for they are her near **k**: it is	7608

KISS

Ps	2:12	**K** the Son, lest he be angry, and	5401
Pr	24:26	shall **k** his lips that giveth a right	5401
SS	1:2	Let him **k** me with the kisses of his	5401
Hos	13:2	the men that sacrifice **k** the calves.	5401
Mt	26:48	Whomsoever I shall **k**, that same	*5368*
Mk	14:44	Whomsoever I shall **k**, that same	*5368*
Lk	7:45	**in hath not ceased to k my feet.**	*2705*
Lk	22:48	**thou the Son of man with a k?**	*5370*
Ro	16:16	Salute one another with an holy **k**	*5370*
1Co	16:20	ye one another with an holy **k**.	*5370*
2Co	13:12	Greet one another with an holy **k**.	*5370*
1Th	5:26	all the brethren with an holy **k**	*5370*
1Pe	5:14	ye one another with a **k** of charity	*5370*

KISSED

Ge	29:11	Jacob **k** Rachel, and lifted up his	5401
Ge	33:4	and fell on his neck, and **k** him:	5401
Ge	48:10	he **k** them, and embraced them	5401
Ge	50:1	and wept upon him, and **k** him	5401
Ex	18:7	law, and did obeisance, and **k** him;	5401
1Sa	10:1	poured it upon his head, and **k** him,	5401
1Sa	20:41	they **k** one another, and wept one	5401
1Ki	19:18	every mouth which hath not **k** him.	5401
Ps	85:10	righteousness and peace have **k**	5401
Pr	7:13	So she caught him, and **k** him, and	5401
Mt	26:49	said, Hail, master; and **k** him.	*2705*
Mk	14:45	saith, Master, master; and **k** him.	*2705*
Lk	7:38	and **k** his feet, and anointed them	*2705*
Lk	15:20	**and fell on his neck, and k him.**	*2705*

K

KISSES

Pr	27:6	the **k** of an enemy are deceitful.	5390
SS	1:2	kiss me with the **k** of his mouth:	5390

KNEAD

Ge	18:6	of fine meal, **k** it, and make cakes	3888
Jer	7:18	and the women **k** their dough, to	3888

KNEADED

2Sa	13:8	she took flour, and **k** it, and made	3888
Hos	7:4	raising after he hath **k** the dough,	3888

KNEE

Ge	41:43	they cried before him, Bow the **k**	
Isa	45:23	That unto me every **k** shall bow,	1290
Mt	27:29	they bowed the **k** before him, and	
Ro	11:4	have not bowed the **k** to the image.	*1119*
Ro	14:11	the Lord, every **k** shall bow to me,	*1119*
Php	2:10	name of Jesus every **k** should bow,	*1119*

KNEEL

Ge	24:11	he made his camels to **k** down	1288
Ps	95:6	let us **k** before the Lord our maker.	1288

KNEELED

2Ch	6:13	**k** down upon his knees before	1288
Da	6:10	he **k** upon his knees three times	1289
Lk	22:41	case, and **k** down, and prayed,	*5087, 1119*
Ac	7:60	he **k** down, and cried with a	*5087, 1119*
Ac	9:40	forth, and **k** down, and prayed;	*5087, 1119*

KNEELING

Mk	1:40	beseeching him, and **k** down to him,	*1120*

KNEES

Dt	28:35	The Lord shall smite thee in the **k**,	1290
Jgs	7:6	down upon their **k** to drink water	1290
Jgs	16:19	made him sleep upon her **k**; and	1290

1Ki 19:18 **k** which have not bowed unto Baal, ... 1290
2Ki 1:13 and fell on his **k** before Elijah, ... 1290
2Ki 4:20 he sat on her **k** till noon, and then 1290
2Ch 6:13 kneeled down upon his **k** before all 1290
Ezr 9:5 I fell upon my **k**, and spread out. 1290
Job 3:12 Why did the **k** prevent me? or why 1290
Ps 109:24 My **k** are weak through fasting; 1290
Isa 35:3 hands, and confirm the feeble **k** 1290
Eze 21:7 and all **k** shall be weak as water: 1290
Da 5:6 and his **k** smote one against 755
Da 6:10 kneeled upon his **k** three times a 1291
Da 10:10 which set me upon my **k** and upon 1290
Na 2:10 and the **k** smite together, and 1290
Mr 15:19 bowing their **k** worshipped him. *1119*
Lk 5:8 he fell down at Jesus' **k**, saying, ... *1119*
Eph 3:14 I bow my **k** unto the Father of our *1119*
Heb 12:12 band down, and the feeble **k**; *1119*

KNEW See also **FOREKNEW; KNOW.**

Ge 3:7 and they **k** that they were naked; 3045
Ge 4:1 Adam **k** Eve his wife; and she 3045
Ge 8:11 Noah **k** that the waters were abated 3045
Ge 9:24 **k** what his younger son had done 3045
Ge 28:16 Lord is in this place; and I **k** it not 3045
Ge 39:6 he **k** not ought he had, save the 3045
Ge 42:8 Joseph **k** his brethren, but they **k** 5234
Ge 42:23 they **k** not that Joseph understood 3045
Ex 1:8 over Egypt, which **k** not Joseph. 3045
Nu 22:34 I **k** not that thou stoodest in the 3045
Nu 24:16 and **k** the knowledge of the most 3045
Dt 9:24 Lord from the day that I **k** you. 3045
Dt 32:17 to gods whom they **k** not, to new 3045
Dt 34:10 whom the Lord **k** face to face, ... 3045
Jgs 2:10 which **k** not the Lord, nor yet the 3045
Jgs 14:4 mother **k** not that it was of the 3045
Jgs 19:25 they **k** her, and abused her all the 3045
Jgs 20:34 they **k** not that evil was near them. 3045
1Sa 2:12 of Belial; they **k** not the Lord. 3045
1Sa 22:22 I **k** it that day, when Doeg the 3045
1Sa 23:9 David **k** that Saul secretly practised 3045
1Sa 26:12 and no man saw it, nor **k** it, neither 3045
2Sa 22:44 which I **k** not shall serve me. 3045
Ne 2:16 the rulers **k** not whither I went, ... 3045
Est 1:13 the wise men, which **k** the times, ... 5234
Job 2:12 and **k** him not, they lifted up their 5234
Job 23:3 I **k** where I might find him! 3045
Job 42:3 wonderful for me, which I **k** not. 3045
Ps 35:11 my charge things that I **k** not 3045
Pr 24:12 Behold, we **k** it not; doth not he 3045
Isa 42:16 blind by a way that they **k** not; 3045
Isa 55:5 nations that **k** not thee shall run 3045
Jer 1:5 formed thee in the belly I **k** thee; 3045
Jer 44:3 serve other gods, whom they **k** not, ... 3045
Da 5:21 he **k** that the most high God ruled 3046
Da 6:10 when Daniel **k** that the writing 3046
Hos 11:3 but they **k** not that I healed them 3045
Jnh 1:10 the men **k** that he fled from the 3045
Jnh 4:2 I **k** that thou art a gracious God, ... 3045
Zec 7:14 all the nations whom they **k** not. 3045
Mt 1:25 **k** her not till she had brought *1097*
Mt 7:23 **profess unto them, I never k you:** *1097*
Mt 12:25 Jesus **k** their thoughts, and said. *1492*
Mt 17:12 **already, and they k him not,** *1912*
Mt 24:39 **k not until the flood came, and,** *1097*
Mt 25:24 **I k thee that thou art an … man,** *1097*
Mt 27:18 For he **k** that for envy they had *1492*
Mk 1:34 to speak, because they **k** him. *1492*
Mk 15:10 he **k** that the chief priests had *1097*
Lk 2:43 Joseph and his mother **k** not of it. *1097*
Lk 6:8 But he **k** their thoughts, and said *1492*
Lk 12:47 **servant, which k his lord's will,** *1097*
La 12:48 **he that k not, and did commit** *1097*
Lk 18:34 neither **k** they the things which. *1097*
Lk 23:7 as soon as he **k** that he belonged *1921*
Lk 24:31 were opened, and they **k** him; *1921*
Jn 1:10 by him, and the world **k** him not. *1097*
Jn 2:24 unto them, because he **k** all men, ... *1097*
Jn 2:25 of man: for he **k** what was in man. *1097*
Jn 4:53 father **k** that it was at the same *1097*
Jn 6:6 he himself **k** what he would do. *1492*
Jn 6:61 When Jesus **k** in himself that his *1492*
Jn 6:64 For Jesus **k** from the beginning *1492*
Jn 11:42 **I k that thou hearest me always:** *1492*
Jn 11:57 that, if any man **k** where he were, ... *1097*
Jn 13:1 Jesus **k** that his hour was come *1492*
Jn 13:11 For he **k** who should betray him; *1492*
Jn 16:19 **k** that they were desirous to ask *1097*
Jn 18:2 which betrayed him, **k** the place: *1492*
Jn 20:9 For as yet they **k** not the scripture, ... *1492*
Jn 20:14 and **k** not that it was Jesus. *1492*
Jn 21:4 disciples **k** not that it was Jesus. *1492*
Ac 7:18 king arose, which **k** not Joseph. *1492*
Ac 13:27 because they **k** him not, nor yet the *50*
Ac 22:29 after he **k** that he was a Roman, ... *1921*
Ro 1:21 when they **k** God, they glorified *1097*
1Co 1:21 the world by wisdom **k** not God, ... *1097*
1Co 2:8 of the princes of this world **k**: *1097*
2Co 5:21 him to be sin for us, who **k** no sin; *1097*
Gal 4:8 when ye **k** not God, ye did service *1492*
Col 1:6 and **k** the grace of God in truth: *1921*
Col 2:1 that ye **k** what great conflict I *1492*
1Jn 3:1 us not, because it **k** him not *1097*
Jude 5 though ye once **k** this, how that *1492*
Rev 19:12 a name written, that no man **k**, ... *1492*

KNEWEST

Lk 19:44 **k not the time of thy visitation** *1097*
Jn 4:10 **If thou k the gift of God, and who** *1492*

KNIFE

Ge 22:10 hand, and took the **k** to slay his son. ... 3979
Pr 23:2 put a **k** to thy throat, if thou be a 7915

KNIT

1Sa 18:1 Jonathan was **k** with the soul of 7194
Col 2:2 being **k** together in love, and unto *4822*

KNIVES

1Ki 18:28 their manner with **k** and lancets, ... 2719
Pr 30:14 swords, and their jaw teeth as **k**, ... 3979

KNOCK

Mt 7:7 **k, and it shall be opened unto** *2925*
Lk 11:9 **k, and it shall be opened unto** *2925*
Rev 3:20 **I stand at the door, and k** *2925*

KNOCKETH

Mt 7:8 **to him that k it shall be opened** *2925*
Lk 11:10 **to him that k it shall be opened** *2925*

KNOW See also **FOREKNOW; KNEW.**

Ge 3:5 God doth **k** that in the day ye eat 3045
Ge 3:22 as one of us, to **k** good and evil: 3045
Ge 4:9 I **k** not: Am I my brother's keeper? 3045

Ge	15:8	shall I **k** that I shall inherit it?	3045
Ge	15:13	**K** of a surety that thy seed shall	3045
Ge	19:5	out unto us, that we may **k** them.	3045
Ge	22:12	for now I **k** that thou fearest God,	3045
Ge	48:19	and said, I **k** it, my son, I **k** it:	3045
Ex	3:7	taskmasters; for I **k** their sorrows;.	3045
Ex	5:2	I **k** not the Lord, neither will I let	3045
Ex	7:5	shall **k** that I am the Lord, when I	3045
Ex	10:2	ye may **k** how that I am the Lord..	3045
Ex	18:11	I **k** that the Lord is greater than all	3045
Ex	31:13	that ye may **k** that I am the Lord	3045
Dt	4:39	**K** therefore this day, and consider	3045
Dt	7:9	**K** therefore that the Lord thy God,	3045
Dt	8:2	to **k** what was in thine heart,	3045
Dt	13:3	to **k** whether ye love the Lord your	3045
Dt	31:29	For I **k** that after my death ye will	3045
Jos	2:9	**k** that the Lord hath given you the	3045
Jos	3:7	may **k** that, as I was with Moses,	3045
Jos	4:24	earth might **k** the hand of the Lord,	3045
Jos	23:14	**k** in all your hearts and in all your	3045
Jgs	3:4	to **k** whether they would hearken	3045
Ru	3:11	**k** that thou art a virtuous woman.	3045
1Sa	3:7	Samuel did not yet **k** the Lord,	3045
1Sa	17:46	may **k** that there is a God in Israel.	3045
1Sa	17:47	**k** … the Lord saveth not with sword	3045
1Sa	24:20	I **k** … that thou shalt surely be king,	3045
1Ki	2:42	**K** for a certain, on the day thou	3045
1Ki	3:7	I **k** not how to go out or come in.	3045
2Ki	5:15	I **k** that there is no God in all the	3045
2Ch	20:12	neither **k** we what to do: but our	3045
2Ch	32:31	might **k** all that was in his heart.	3045
Ezr	4:15	and **k** that this city is a rebellious	3046
Ezr	7:25	teach ye them that **k** them not.	3046
Est	2:11	to **k** how Esther did, and what	3045
Job	9:2	I **k** it is so of a truth: but how	3045
Job	11:6	**K** therefore that God exacteth of	3045
Job	19:25	For I **k** that my redeemer liveth,	3045
Job	21:27	Behold, I **k** your thoughts, and	3045
Job	36:26	God is great, and we **k** him not,	3045
Job	37:15	Dost thou **k** when God disposed	3045
Job	42:2	I **k** that thou canst do every thing,	3045
Ps	20:6	Now **k** I that the Lord saveth his.	3045
Ps	39:4	it is; that I may **k** how frail I am.	3045
Ps	46:10	Be still, and **k** that I am God:	3045
Ps	51:6	thou shalt make me to **k** wisdom	3045
Ps	100:3	**K** ye that the Lord he is God: it.	3045
Ps	135:5	For I **k** that the Lord is great,	3045
Ps	139:23	heart: try me, and **k** my thoughts:	3045
Pr	1:2	To **k** wisdom and instruction; to	3045
Pr	4:19	they **k** not at what they stumble.	3045
Pr	10:32	righteous **k** what is acceptable:	3045
Pr	24:12	keepeth thy soul, doth not he **k** it?	3045
Pr	27:23	diligent to **k** the state of thy flocks,	3045
Pr	30:18	for me, yea, four which I **k** not:.	3045
Ecc	1:17	I gave my heart to **k** wisdom,	3045
Ecc	3:14	I **k** that, whatsoever God doeth, it	3045
Ecc	8:16	I applied mine heart to **k** wisdom,	3045
Ecc	9:5	the dead **k** not any thing, neither	3045
Isa	43:10	that ye may **k** and believe me,	3045
Isa	44:8	yea, there is no God; I **k** not any	3045
Isa	49:26	all flesh shall **k** that I the Lord.	3045
Isa	50:7	I **k** that I shall not be ashamed.	3045
Isa	66:18	I **k** their works and their thoughts:	
Jer	9:3	and they **k** not me, saith the Lord.	3045
Jer	10:23	I **k** that the way of man is not in.	3045
Jer	17:9	desperately wicked: who can **k** it?	3045
Jer	24:7	I will give them an heart to **k** me,	3045
Jer	29:11	For I **k** the thoughts that I think.	3045
Jer	44:29	**k** that my words shall surely stand	3045
Eze	5:13	**k** that I the Lord have spoken it	3045
Eze	7:4	and ye shall **k** that I am the Lord	3045
Eze	11:12	And ye shall **k** that I am the Lord:	3045
Eze	12:15	they shall **k** that I am the Lord.	3045
Eze	16:2	Jerusalem to **k** her abominations,	3045
Eze	20:12	**k** that I am the Lord that sanctify	3045
Eze	20:42	ye shall **k** that I am the Lord,	3045
Eze	39:7	heathen shall **k** that I am the Lord,	3045
Da	2:3	spirit was troubled to **k** the dream	3045
Da	2:30	**k** the thoughts of thy heart.	3046
Da	4:32	until thou **k** that the most High	3046
Da	11:32	the people that do **k** their God shall.	3045
Hos	2:20	and thou shalt **k** the Lord.	3045
Hos	9:7	are come; Israel shall **k** it:.	3045
Hos	13:4	and thou shalt **k** no god but me:	3045
Joel	2:27	ye shall **k** that I am in the midst	3045
Am	5:12	I **k** your manifold transgressions	3045
Jnh	1:7	may **k** for whose cause this evil is	3045
Mic	3:1	Is it not for you to **k** judgment?	3045
Mic	4:12	**k** not the thoughts of the Lord,	3045
Mt	6:3	**left hand k what thy right hand**	*1097*
Mt	7:11	**k how to give good gifts unto your**	*1492*
Mt	7:20	**by their fruits ye shall k them.**	*1921*
Mt	9:6	**k that the Son of man hath power**	*1492*
Mt	13:11	**k the mysteries of the kingdom of**	*1097*
Mt	20:22	and said, **Ye k not what ye ask.**	*1492*
Mt	24:42	**for ye k not what hour your Lord**	*1492*
Mt	25:12	**I say unto you, I k you not**	*1492*
Mt	25:13	**ye k neither the day nor the hour.**	*1492*
Mt	26:70	saying, I **k** not what thou sayest.	*1492*
Mt	26:72	with an oath, I do not **k** the man.	*1492*
Mt	26:74	to swear, saying, I **k** not the man.	*1492*
Mk	2:10	**k that the Son of man hath power**	*1492*
Mk	4:11	**to k the mystery of the kingdom**	*1097*
Mk	10:38	unto them, **Ye k not what ye ask:**	*1492*
Mk	12:24	**because ye k not the scriptures,**	*1492*
Lk	1:34	shall this be, seeing I **k** not a man?	*1097*
Lk	5:24	**k that the Son of man hath power**	*1492*
Lk	8:10	**k the mysteries of the kingdom of**	*1097*
Lk	11:13	**k how to give good gifts unto your**	*1492*
Lk	13:25	**you, I k you not whence ye are:**	*1492*
Lk	21:31	**k ye that the kingdom of God is**	*1097*
Lk	22:57	him, saying, Woman, I **k** him not.	*1492*
Lk	22:60	Man, I **k** not what thou sayest.	*1492*
Lk	23:34	**them; for they k not what they**	*1492*
Lk	24:16	that they should not **k** him.	*1921*
Jn	4:22	**Ye worship ye k not what:**	*1492*
Jn	4:42	**k** that this is indeed the Christ,	*1492*
Jn	5:42	**I k you, that ye have not the love**	*1097*
Jn	7:29	**But I k him: for I am from him,**	*1492*
Jn	8:19	**Ye neither k me, nor my Father:**	*1492*
Jn	8:32	**ye shall k the truth, and the truth**	*1097*
Jn	8:37	**I k that ye are Abraham's seed;**	*1097*
Jn	9:21	means he now seeth, we **k** not;	*1492*
Jn	9:25	one thing I **k**, that, whereas I was	*1492*
Jn	10:4	**follow him: for they k his voice.**	*1492*
Jn	10:14	**good shepherd, and k my sheep,**	*1097*
Jn	10:38	**that ye may k, and believe, that**	*1097*
Jn	12:50	**I k that his commandment is life**	*1492*
Jn	13:7	**now; but thou shalt k hereafter**	*1097*
Jn	13:17	**If ye k these things, happy are ye**	*1492*
Jn	14:4	**And whither I go ye k, and the**	*1492*
Jn	14:5	Lord, we **k** not whither thou goest;	*1492*

Jn 14:31 **world may k that I love the** *1097*
Jn 15:18 **k that it hated me before it hated** *1097*
Jn 17:3 **might k thee the only true God,** *1097*
Jn 20:13 I **k** not where they have laid him. *1492*
Jn 21:24 we **k** that his testimony is true. *1492*
Ac 1:7 **not for you to k the times or the** *1097*
Ac 19:15 and Paul I **k**; but who are ye?. *1987*
Ac 22:14 that thou shouldest **k** his will, and *1097*
Ro 3:19 **k** that what things soever the law *1492*
Ro 7:14 For we **k** that the law is spiritual: *1492*
Ro 7:18 For I **k** that in me (that is, in my. *1492*
Ro 8:22 For we **k** that the whole creation *1492*
Ro 8:28 we **k** that all things work together *1492*
1Co 2:2 not to **k** any thing among you, save *1492*
1Co 3:16 **K** ye not that ye are the temple *1492*
1Co 6:3 **K** ye not … we shall judge angels? *1492*
1Co 6:19 **k** ye not … your body is the temple. . . . *1492*
1Co 9:24 **K** ye not that they which run in a. *1492*
1Co 13:12 now I **k** in part; but then shall I *1097*
1Co 13:12 shall I **k** even as also I am known *1921*
1Co 15:58 ye **k** that your labour is not in vain *1492*
2Co 5:1 we **k** that if our earthly house of. *1492*
2Co 13:5 **K** ye not your own selves, how *1921*
Eph 1:18 **k** what is the hope of his calling *1492*
Eph 3:19 And to **k** the love of Christ, which *1097*
Php 3:10 That I may **k** him, and the power *1097*
Php 4:12 I **k** both how to be abased, and. *1492*
Col 4:6 ye may **k** how ye ought to answer. *1492*
1Th 4:4 should **k** how to possess his vessel *1492*
1Ti 1:8 But we **k** that the law is good, ... *1492*
1Ti 3:5 a man **k** not how to rule his own *1492*
2Ti 1:12 for I **k** whom I have believed. *1492*
2Ti 3:1 This **k** also, that in the last days. *1097*
Heb 8:11 for all shall **k** me, from the least *1492*
Jas 4:4 **k** ye not that the friendship of the *1492*
Jas 4:14 **k** not what shall be on the morrow *1987*
1Jn 2:3 hereby we do **k** that we **k** him. *1097*
1Jn 2:5 hereby **k** we that we are in him. *1097*
1Jn 2:20 the Holy One, and ye **k** all things *1492*
1Jn 3:2 we **k** that, when he shall appear, ... *1492*
1Jn 3:14 We **k** that we have passed from. *1492*
1Jn 4:6 Hereby **k** we the spirit of truth,. *1097*
1Jn 4:13 Hereby **k** we that we dwell in him, ... *1097*
1Jn 5:13 may **k** that ye have eternal life. *1492*
1Jn 5:18 We **k** that whosoever is born of God . . . *1492*
1Jn 5:20 we **k** that the Son of God is come, ... *1492*
3Jn 12 and ye **k** that our record is true. *1492*
Rev 2:2 **I k thy works, and thy labour,** *1492*
Rev 2:9 **I k thy works, and tribulation,** *1492*
Rev 2:13 **I k thy works, and where thou** *1492*
Rev 2:19 **I k thy works, and charity, and** *1492*
Rev 2:23 **k that I am he which searcheth**. *1097*
Rev 3:1 **I k thy works, that thou hast a** *1492*
Rev 3:3 **shalt not k what hour I will come** *1097*
Rev 3:8 **I k thy works; behold, I have set**. *1492*
Rev 3:9 **and to k that I have loved thee** *1097*
Rev 3:15 **I k thy works, that thou art**. *1492*

KNOWEST

Ex 10:7 **k** thou not … Egypt is destroyed? 3045
Jgs 15:11 **K** thou not that the Philistines 3045
2Sa 1:5 How **k** thou that Saul and Jonathan. . . . 3045
1Ki 2:15 Thou **k** that the kingdom was mine, . . . 3045
Job 38:5 the measures thereof, if thou **k**? 3045
Job 38:18 the earth? declare if thou **k** it all 3045
Job 38:33 **K** thou the ordinances of heaven? 3045
Ps 139:2 Thou **k** my downsitting and mine 3045
Ps 139:4 lo, O Lord, thou **k** it altogether 3045
Pr 27:1 thou **k** not what a day may bring 3045
Ecc 11:5 so thou **k** not the works of God 3045
Isa 55:5 shalt call a nation that thou **k** not. 3045
Jer 18:23 thou **k** all their counsel against me. 3045
Mk 10:19 **Thou k the commandments, Do** *1492*
Lk 18:20 **Thou k the commandments, Do** *1492*
Lk 22:34 **shalt thrice deny that thou k me** *1492*
Jn 3:10 **of Israel, and k not these things?** *1097*
Jn 13:7 **him. What I do thou k not now;**. *1492*
Jn 19:10 **k** thou not that I have power to *1492*
Jn 21:15 Lord; thou **k** that I love thee *1492*
Jn 21:16 Lord; thou **k** that I love thee *1492*
Jn 21:17 thou **k** that I love thee *1097*
Ac 1:24 which **k** the hearts of all men,. *2589*
Ac 25:10 no wrong, as thou very well **k**. *1921*
Ro 2:18 **k** his will, and approves! the *1097*
1Co 7:16 For what **k** thou, O wife, whether. *1492*
1Co 7:16 or how **k** thou, O man, whether *1492*
2Ti 1:15 This thou **k**, that all they which *1492*
Rev 3:17 **and k not that thou art wretched?** *1492*

KNOWETH

Dt 2:7 he **k** thy walking through this 3045
Dt 34:6 no man **k** of his sepulchre unto 3045
Est 4:14 who **k** whether thou art come to 3045
Job 23:10 he **k** the way that I take: when he 3045
Job 35:15 yet he **k** it not in great extremity: 3045
Ps 1:6 Lord **k** the way of the righteous:. 3045
Ps 44:21 for he **k** the secrets of the heart. 3045
Ps 90:11 Who **k** the power of thine anger? 3045
Ps 94:11 The Lord **k** the thoughts of man, ... 3045
Ps 103:14 he **k** our frame; he remembereth 3045
Ps 139:14 and that my soul **k** right well 3045
Pr 7:23 and **k** not that it is for his life 3045
Pr 9:13 she is simple, and **k** nothing 3045
Pr 9:18 he **k** not that the dead are there;. 3045
Pr 14:10 The heart **k** his own bitterness;. 3045
Pr 24:22 and who **k** the ruin of them both? 3045
Ecc 2:19 who **k** whether he shall be a wise 3045
Ecc 3:21 Who **k** the spirit of man that 3045
Ecc 6:12 who **k** what is good for man in this 3045
Ecc 7:22 also thine own heart **k** that thou 3045
Ecc 8:1 who **k** the interpretation of a 3045
Ecc 8:7 For he **k** not that which shall be: 3045
Ecc 9:1 no man **k** either love or hatred by 3045
Ecc 9:12 For man also **k** not his time: as the 3045
Jer 9:24 that he understandeth and **k** me, ... 3045
Da 2:22 he **k** what is in the darkness, and 3046
Joel 2:14 Who **k** if he will return and repent 3045
Na 1:7 and he **k** them that trust in him 3045
Zep 3:5 not; but the unjust **k** no shame. 3045
Mt 6:8 **k what things ye have need of,** *1492*
Mt 11:27 **no man k the Son, but the Father;** *1921*
Mt 24:36 **of that day and hour k no man,** *1492*
Mk 13:32 **that day and that hour k no man,** *1492*
Lk 10:22 **and no man k who the Son is,** *1097*
Lk 12:30 **k that ye have need of all these**. *1492*
Lk 16:15 **men; but God k your hearts:**. *1097*
Jn 7:49 who **k** not the law are cursed. *1097*
Jn 10:15 **As the Father k me, even so know** *1097*
Jn 12:35 **darkness k not whither he goeth** *1492*
Jn 14:17 **it seeth him not, neither k him:** *1097*
Jn 15:15 **servant k not what his lord doeth:**. *1492*
Ac 15:8 And God, which **k** the hearts, bare *2589*

Ro 8:27 **k** what is the mind of the Spirit *1492*
1Co 2:11 the things of God **k** no man, but *1492*
1Co 3:20 Lord **k** the thoughts of the wise *1097*
1Co 8:2 man think that he **k** any thing *1492*
1Co 11:31 for evermore, **k** that I lie not *1492*
2Ti 2:19 seal, The Lord **k** them that are his *1097*
Jas 4:17 to him that **k** to do good, and *1492*
2Pe 2:9 Lord **k** how to deliver the godly *1492*
1Jn 2:11 **k** not whither he goeth, because *1492*
1Jn 3:1 the world **k** us not, because it *1097*
1Jn 3:20 than our heart, and **k** all things *1097*
1Jn 4:6 he that **k** God heareth us; he that *1097*
1Jn 4:7 loveth is born of God, and **k** God *2097*
1Jn 4:8 He that loveth not, **k** not God; for *1097*
Rev 12:12 he **k** ... he hath but a short time *1492*

KNOWING

Ge 3:5 shall be as gods, **k** good and evil 3045
Mt 9:4 And Jesus **k** their thoughts said *1492*
Mt 22:29 **Ye do err, not k the scriptures,** *1492*
Mk 5:30 **k** in himself that virtue had gone *1921*
Mk 12:15 **k** their hypocrisy, said unto them *1492*
Lk 11:17 **k** their thoughts, said unto them, *1492*
Jn 13:3 Jesus **k** that the Father had given *1492*
Jn 18:4 **k** all things that should come upon *1492*
Jn 19:28 Jesus **k** that all things were now *1492*
Ro 1:32 Who **k** the judgment of God, that *1921*
Ro 2:4 not **k** that the goodness of God *50*
Ro 5:3 **k** that tribulation worketh *1492*
Ro 6:6 **K** this, that our old man is *1097*
Ro 6:9 **K** that Christ being raised from *1492*
Ro 13:11 **k** the time, that now it is high time *1492*
2Co 5:11 **K** therefore the terror of the Lord, *1492*
Gal 2:16 **K** that a man is not justified by *1492*
Eph 6:9 **k** that your Master ... is in heaven; *1492*
Col 3:24 **K** that of the Lord ye shall receive *1492*
Col 4:1 **k** that ye ... have a Master in heaven *1492*
1Ti 1:9 **K** this, that the law is not made *1492*
1Ti 6:4 **k** nothing, but doting about *1987*
2Ti 2:23 **k** that they do gender strifes *1492*
2Ti 3:14 **k** of whom thou hast learned them; *1492*
Tit 3:11 **K** that he that is such is subverted, *1492*
Phm 21 **k** that thou wilt also do more than *1492*
Heb 10:34 **k** in yourselves that ye have in *1097*
Heb 11:8 went out, not **k** whither he went *1987*
Jas 1:3 **K** this, that the trying of your *1097*
Jas 3:1 **k** that we shall receive the greater *1492*
1Pe 3:9 **k** that ye are thereunto called, *1492*
1Pe 5:9 **k** that the same afflictions are *1492*
2Pe 1:14 **K** that shortly I must put off this *1492*
2Pe 1:20 **K** this first, that no prophecy of *1097*
2Pe 3:3 **K** this first, that there shall come *1097*

KNOWLEDGE See also ACKNOWLEDGE; FORE-KNOWLEDGE.

Ge 2:9 the tree of **k** of good and evil 1847
Ge 2:17 the tree of the **k** of good and evil 1847
Le 4:28 he hath sinned, come to his **k**; 3045
Nu 15:24 without the **k** of the congregation, 5869
Dt 1:39 had no **k** between good and evil 3045
1Sa 2:3 the Lord is a God of **k**, and by 1844
2Ch 1:10 Give me now wisdom and **k**, that 4093
Job 34:35 Job hath spoken without **k**, and 1847
Job 35:16 he multiplieth words without **k** 1847
Job 36:4 that is perfect in **k** is with thee 1844
Job 37:16 of him which is perfect in **k**? 1843
Job 38:2 counsel by words without **k**? 1847
Job 42:3 he that hideth counsel without **k**? 1847
Ps 19:2 and night unto night sheweth **k** 1847
Ps 73:11 and is there **k** in the Most High? 1844
Ps 139:6 Such **k** is too wonderful for me; 1847
Ps 144:3 man, that thou takest **k** of him! 3045
Pr 1:7 the Lord is the beginning of **k**: 1847
Pr 1:22 their scorning, and fools hate **k**? 1847
Pr 1:29 For that they hated **k**, and did not 1847
Pr 2:5 the Lord, and find the **k** of God 1847
Pr 2:10 and **k** is pleasant unto thy soul; 1847
Pr 3:20 By his **k** the depths are broken up, 1847
Pr 8:9 and right to them that find **k** 1847
Pr 8:10 and **k** rather than choice gold 1847
Pr 8:12 and find out **k** of witty inventions 1847
Pr 9:10 the **k** of the holy is understanding 1847
Pr 10:14 Wise men lay up **k**; but the mouth 1847
Pr 11:9 but through **k** shall the just be 1847
Pr 12:1 Whoso loveth instruction loveth **k** 1847
Pr 12:23 A prudent man concealeth **k**: 1847
Pr 13:16 Every prudent man dealeth with **k**: 1847
Pr 14:7 perceivest not in him the lips of **k** 1847
Pr 14:18 the prudent are crowned with **k** 1847
Pr 15:2 tongue of the wise useth **k** aright: 1847
Pr 15:7 The lips of the wise disperse **k**: 1847
Pr 15:14 hath understanding seeketh **k**: 1847
Pr 17:27 He that hath **k** spareth his words: 1847
Pr 19:2 Also, that the soul be without **k**, 1847
Pr 19:25 and he will understand **k** 1847
Pr 20:15 the lips of **k** are a precious jewel 1847
Pr 21:11 wise is instructed, he receiveth **k** 1847
Pr 22:12 The eyes of the Lord preserve **k**, 1847
Pr 24:4 by **k** shall the chambers be filled 1847
Pr 24:5 a man of **k** increaseth strength 1847
Pr 28:2 a man of understanding and **k** 3045
Ecc 1:18 increaseth **k** increaseth sorrow 1847
Ecc 2:21 labour is in wisdom, and in **k** 1847
Ecc 2:26 good in his sight wisdom, and **k** 1847
Ecc 7:12 the excellency of **k** is, that wisdom 1847
Ecc 9:10 there is no work, nor device, nor **k**, 1847
Ecc 12:9 wise, he still taught the people **k**; 1847
Isa 5:13 captivity, because they have no **k**: 1847
Isa 11:2 the spirit of **k** and of the fear of 1847
Isa 11:9 shall be full of the **k** of the Lord, 1844
Isa 28:9 Whom shall he teach **k**? and whom 1844
Isa 33:6 wisdom and **k** shall be the stability 1847
Isa 44:19 there **k** nor understanding to say, 1847
Isa 44:25 and maketh their **k** foolish; 1847
Isa 47:10 thy **k**, it hath perverted thee; 1847
Isa 53:11 by his **k** shall my righteous servant 1847
Jer 3:15 which shall feed you with **k** and 1844
Jer 4:22 but to do good they have no **k** 3045
Jer 10:14 Every man is brutish in his **k**: 1847
Jer 51:17 Every man is brutish by his **k**; 1847
Da 1:4 in all wisdom, and cunning in **k**, 1847
Da 1:17 God gave them **k** and skill in all 4093
Da 2:21 wise, and **k** to them that know 998
Da 5:12 as an excellent spirit, and **k**, and 998
Hos 4:1 nor mercy, nor **k** of God in the land 1847
Hos 4:6 people are destroyed for lack of **k**: 1847
Hos 6:6 **k** of God more than burnt offerings 1847
Hab 2:14 be filled with the **k** of the glory of 3045
Mal 2:7 the priest's lips should keep **k**, 1847
Lk 1:77 give **k** of salvation unto his people *1108*
Lk 11:52 **ye have taken away the key of k** *1108*
Ro 1:28 not like to retain God in their **k**, *1922*

Ro	2:20	hast the form of **k** and of the truth	*1108*
Ro	3:20	for by the law is the **k** of sin.	*1922*
Ro	10:2	zeal of God, but not according to **k**	*1922*
Ro	11:33	both of the wisdom and **k** of God!	*1108*
1Co	8:1	**K** puffeth up, but charity edifieth.	*1108*
1Co	8:11	And through thy **k** shall the weak	*1108*
1Co	12:8	the word of **k** by the same Spirit;	*1108*
1Co	13:2	understand all mysteries, and all **k**;	*1108*
1Co	13:8	whether there be **k**, it shall vanish.	*1108*
1Co	15:34	for some have not the **k** of God:	*56*
2Co	4:6	light of the **k** of the glory of God	*1108*
2Co	10:5	exalteth itself against the **k** of God,	*1108*
Eph	1:17	and revelation in the **k** of him:	*1922*
Eph	3:19	love of Christ, which passeth **k**,	*1108*
Eph	4:13	and of the **k** of the Son of God,	*1922*
Php	3:8	excellency of the **k** of Christ Jesus.	*1108*
Col	1:9	be filled with the **k** of his will in	*1922*
Col	2:3	all the treasures of wisdom and **k**.	*1108*
Col	3:10	is renewed in **k** after the image of	*1922*
1Ti	2:4	and to come unto the **k** of the truth.	*1922*
2Ti	3:7	able to come to the **k** of the truth.	*1922*
Heb	10:26	have received the **k** of the truth.	*1922*
Jas	3:13	and endued with **k** among you?	*1990*
1Pe	3:7	dwell with them according to **k**.	*1108*
2Pe	1:5	your faith virtue; and to virtue **k**;	*1108*
2Pe	1:8	nor unfruitful in the **k** of our Lord.	*1922*

K

KNOWN See also UNKNOWN.

Ge	19:8	daughters which have not **k** man;	3045
Ge	45:1	Joseph made himself **k** unto his	3045
Ex	2:14	and said, Surely this thing is **k**.	3045
Le	4:14	they have sinned against it, is **k**.	3045
Nu	12:6	Lord will make myself **k** unto him	3045
Nu	31:17	kill every woman that hath **k** man	3045
Dt	11:28	other gods, which ye have not **k**	3045
Dt	31:13	children, which have not **k** any	3045
Ru	3:3	make not thyself **k** unto the man	3045
1Ki	18:36	it be **k** this day that thou art God	3045
Ezr	4:12	it **k** unto the king, that the Jews	3046
Est	2:22	And the thing was **k** to Mordecai,	3045
Ps	9:16	The Lord is **k** by the judgment	3045
Ps	18:43	a people whom I have not **k** shall	3045
Ps	78:5	make them **k** to their children:	3045
Ps	98:2	Lord hath made **k** his salvation:	3045
Ps	103:7	He made **k** his ways unto Moses,	3045
Ps	106:8	make his mighty power to be **k**.	3045
Ps	119:152	**k** of old that thou hast founded	3045
Ps	139:1	thou hast searched me, and **k** me	3045
Pr	10:9	that perverteth his ways shall be **k**	3045
Pr	12:16	A fool's wrath is presently **k**: but	3045
Pr	20:11	Even a child is **k** by his doings,	5234
Pr	31:23	Her husband is **k** in the gates,	3045
Ecc	5:3	a fool's voice is **k** by multitude of	
Ecc	6:10	already, and it is **k** that it is man:	3045
Isa	12:5	things: this is **k** in all the earth	3045
Isa	40:21	Have ye not **k**? have ye not heard?	3045
Isa	40:28	Hast thou not **k**? hast thou not	3045
Isa	44:18	They have not **k** nor understood:	3045
Isa	64:2	thy name **k** to thine adversaries,	3045
Jer	4:22	is foolish, they have not **k** me;	3045
Jer	19:4	they nor their fathers have **k**	3045
La	4:8	they are not **k** in the streets:	5234
Eze	20:5	and made myself **k** unto them in	3045
Eze	35:11	I will make myself **k** among them,	3045
Eze	38:23	be **k** in the eyes of many nations	3045
Eze	39:7	So will I make my holy name **k** in	3045
Da	2:9	not make **k** unto me the dream,	3046
Da	2:28	**k** to the king Nebuchadnezzar	3046
Da	2:45	God hath made **k** to the king what	3046
Da	3:18	be it **k** unto thee, O king, that we	3046
Da	4:26	have **k** that the heavens do rule	3046
Da	5:17	make **k** to him the interpretation	3046
Hos	5:4	and they have not **k** the Lord	3045
Am	3:2	You only have I **k** of all the	3045
Zec	14:7	day which shall be **k** to the Lord	3045
Mt	10:26	**and hid, that shall not be k**	*1097*
Mt	12:7	**if ye had k what this meaneth,**	*1097*
Mt	12:33	**for the tree is k by his fruit**	*1097*
Mt	24:43	**had k in what watch the thief**	*1492*
Lk	2:15	the Lord hath made **k** unto us.	*1107*
Lk	6:44	**every tree is k by his own fruit**	*1097*
Lk	7:39	**k** who and what manner of woman	*1097*
Lk	12:39	**had k what hour the thief would**	*1492*
Lk	19:42	**Saying, If thou hadst k, even thou,**	*1097*
Lk	24:35	**k** of them in breaking of bread	*1097*
Jn	8:19	**ye should have k my Father also:**	*1492*
Jn	8:55	**Yet ye have not k him; but I**	*1097*
Jn	10:14	**know my sheep, and am k of.**	*1097*
Jn	14:7	**k me, ye should have k my**	*1097*
Jn	14:9	**yet hast thou not k me, Philip?**	*1097*
Jn	15:15	**Father I have made k unto you.**	*1107*
Jn	16:3	**they have not k the Father, nor.**	*1097*
Jn	17:25	**Father, the world hath not k thee:**	*1097*
Jn	17:25	**but I have k thee, and these.**	*1097*
Jn	18:15	that disciple was **k** unto the high	*1110*
Jn	18:16	which was **k** unto the high priest,	*1110*
Ac	2:28	Thou hast made **k** to me the ways	*1107*
Ac	4:10	Be it **k** unto you all, and to all	*1110*
Ac	7:13	Joseph was made **k** to his brethren;	*319*
Ac	23:28	when I would have **k** the cause	*1097*
Ro	3:17	way of peace have they not **k**:	*1097*
Ro	7:7	I had not **k** sin, but by the law:	*1097*
Ro	7:7	I had not **k** lust, except the law	*1492*
Ro	9:22	wrath, and to make his power **k**,	*1107*
Ro	9:23	that he might make **k** the riches	*1107*
Ro	11:34	who hath **k** the mind of the Lord?	*1097*
Ro	16:26	made **k** to all nations for the	*1107*
1Co	2:8	for had they **k** it, they would not	*1097*
1Co	2:16	who hath **k** the mind of the Lord	*1097*
1Co	8:3	love God, the same is **k** of him	*1097*
1Co	13:12	shall I know even as also I am **k**	*1921*
2Co	3:2	our hearts, **k** and read of all men:	*1097*
Gal	4:9	rather are **k** of God, how turn ye	*1097*
Eph	1:9	made **k** unto us the mystery of his	*1107*
Eph	3:5	not made **k** unto the sons of men.	*1107*
Eph	6:21	shall make **k** to you all things:	*1107*
Php	4:5	moderation be **k** unto all men	*1097*
Php	4:6	requests be made **k** unto God	*1107*
Col	1:27	would make **k** what is the riches	*1107*
2Ti	3:10	thou hast fully **k** my doctrine,	*3877*
2Ti	3:15	thou hast **k** the holy scriptures,	*1492*
Heb	3:10	and they have not **k** my ways.	*1097*
2Pe	1:16	we made **k** unto you the power	*1107*
2Pe	2:21	than, after they have **k** it, to turn	*1921*
1Jn	2:13	because ye have **k** the Father	*1097*
1Jn	2:14	**k** him that is from the beginning	*1097*
1Jn	3:6	hath not seen him, neither **k** him.	*1097*
1Jn	4:16	have **k** and believed the love that	*1097*
2Jn	1	also all they that have **k** the truth;	*1097*
Rev	2:24	**have not k the depths of Satan,**	*1097*

L

LABOUR

Ex	20:9	Six days shalt thou **l**, and do all	5647
Jos	24:13	you a land for which ye did not **l**	3021
Ps	105:44	they inherited the **l** of the people;	5999
Ps	107:12	he brought down their heart with **l**;	5999
Ps	127:1	house, they **l** in vain that build it:	5998
Pr	10:16	**l** of the righteous tendeth to life:	6468
Pr	13:11	that gathereth by **l** shall increase	3027
Pr	14:23	In all **l** there is profit: but the	6089
Pr	23:4	**L** not to be rich: cease from thine	3021
Ecc	1:3	What profit hath a man of all his **l**	5999
Ecc	1:8	All things are full of **l**; man	3023
Ecc	2:18	I hated all my **l** which I had taken	5999
Ecc	3:13	and enjoy the good of all his **l**, it is	5999
Ecc	4:8	yet is there no end of all his **l**;	5999
Ecc	4:9	have a good reward for their **l**	5999
Ecc	5:15	shall take nothing of his **l**, which	5999
Ecc	8:17	though a man **l** to seek it out, yet	5998
Isa	22:4	**l** not to comfort me, because of the	213
Isa	55:2	your **l** for that which satisfieth not?	3018
Jer	3:24	shame hath devoured the **l** of our	3018
La	5:5	we **l**, and have no rest	3021
Mic	4:10	and **l** to bring forth, O daughter	1518
Hab	2:13	the people shall **l** in the very fire,	3021
Mt	11:28	**come unto me, all ye that l and.**	*2872*
Jn	6:27	**L not for ... meat which perisheth,**	*2038*
1Co	15:58	your **l** is not in vain in the Lord	*2873*
2Co	5:9	Wherefore we **l**, that, whether	*5389*
Eph	4:28	rather let him **l**, working with his	*2872*
Col	1:29	Whereunto I also **l**, striving	*2872*
1Th	1:3	your work of faith, and **l** of love	*2873*
1Ti	5:17	who **l** in the word and doctrine	*2872*
Heb	4:11	**l** therefore to enter into that rest	*4704*
Rev	2:2	**I know thy works, and thy l, and**	*2873*

LABOURED

Ne	4:21	So we **l** in the work: and half of	6213
Ecc	5:16	hath he that hath **l** for the wind?	5998
Isa	47:12	thou hast **l** from thy youth;	3021
Jn	4:38	**other men l, and ye are entered**	*2872*
1Co	15:10	I **l** more abundantly than they all	*2872*
Php	2:16	not run in vain, neither **l** in vain	*2872*
Rev	2:3	**and for my name's sake hast l,**	*2872*

LABOURER

Lk	10:7	**for the l is worthy of his hire**	2040
1Ti	5:18	**And, The l is worthy of his reward.**	*2040*

LABOURERS See also FELLOWLABOURERS.

Mt	9:37	**is plenteous, but the l are few;**	*2040*
Mt	9:38	**will send forth l into his harvest**	*2040*
Lk	10:2	**truly is great, but the l are few:**	*2040*
Jas	5:4	the hire of the **l** who have reaped	*2040*

LABOURETH

Pr	16:26	He that **l** ... for himself; for	6001
Pr	16:26	**l** for himself; for his mouth	5998
2Ti	2:6	husbandman that **l** must be first	*2872*

LABOURING

Ecc	5:12	The sleep of a **l** man is sweet,	5647
Ac	20:35	so **l** ye ought to support the weak,	*2872*
Col	4:12	**l** fervently for you in prayers	*75*

LABOURS

Dt	28:33	The fruit of thy land, and all thy **l**,	3018
Isa	58:3	pleasure, and exact all your **l**	6092
Jn	4:38	**and ye are entered into their l.**	*2873*
2Co	11:23	in **l** more abundant, in stripes	*2873*
Rev	14:13	that they may rest from their **l**;	*2873*

LACK

Dt	8:9	thou shalt not **l** any thing in it;	2637
Ps	34:10	The young lions do **l**, and suffer	7326
Pr	28:27	giveth unto the poor shall not **l**:	4270
Hos	4:6	are destroyed for **l** of knowledge:	1097
Mt	19:20	from my youth up: what **l** I yet?	*5302*
Php	2:30	to supply your **l** of service toward	*5303*
Jas	1:5	If any of you **l** wisdom, let him	*3007*

LACKED

Dt	2:7	with thee: thou hast **l** nothing	2637
Ne	9:21	wilderness, so that they **l** nothing;	2637
Lk	22:35	**scrip, and shoes, l ye any thing?**	*5302*
Ac	4:34	was there any among them that **l**:	*1729*
Php	4:10	also careful, but ye **l** opportunity	*170*

LACKEST

Mk	10:21	said unto him, **One thing thou l.**	*5302*
Lk	18:22	unto him, **Yet l thou one thing:**	*3007*

LACKETH

Nu	31:49	and there **l** not one man of us	6485
Pr	6:32	with a woman **l** understanding:	2638
2Pe	1:9	that **l** these things is blind,	*3361, 3918*

LACKING

Jgs	21:3	be to day one tribe **l** in Israel?	6485
1Sa	30:19	And there was nothing **l** to them,	5737
1Co	16:17	that which was **l** on your part they	*5303*
2Co	11:9	that which was **l** to me the brethren	*5303*
1Th	3:10	that which is **l** in your faith?	*5303*

LAD

Ge	22:12	Lay not thy hand upon the **l**,	5288
Jgs	16:26	Samson said unto the **l** that held	5288
1Sa	20:38	Jonathan cried after the **l**, Make	5288
2Ki	4:19	said to a **l**, Carry him to his mother	5288
Jn	6:9	There is a **l** here, which hath five	*3808*

LADDER

Ge	28:12	behold a **l** set up on the earth,	5551

LADE

1Ki	12:11	father did **l** you with a heavy yoke	6006
Lk	11:46	**l men with burdens grievous to**	*5412*

LADEN

Mt	11:28	**all ye that labour and are heavy l,**	*5412*
2Ti	3:6	captive silly women **l** with sins,	*4987*

LADIES

Jgs	5:29	Her wise **l** answered her, yea, she	8282
Est	1:18	**l** of Persia and Media say this day	8282

LAD'S

Ge	44:30	his life is bound up in the **l** life;	5288

LADY

Isa	47:5	be called, The **l** of kingdoms	1404
2Jn	1	unto the elect **l** and her children,	*2959*

LAID

Ge 9:23 **l** it upon both their shoulders, ... 7760
Ge 22:9 **l** him on the altar upon the wood. ... 7760
Ge 30:41 Jacob **l** the rods before the eyes ... 7760
Ex 2:3 she **l** it in the flags by the river's ... 7760
Ex 16:34 Aaron **l** it up before the Testimony, ... 3241
Nu 17:7 Moses **l** up the rods before the ... 3241
Dt 26:6 us, and **l** upon us hard bondage:. ... 5414
Dt 34:9 Moses had **l** his hands upon him:. ... 5564
Jos 10:27 **l** great stones in the cave's mouth, ... 7760
Jgs 16:2 **l** wait for him all night in the gate
1Sa 6:11 **l** the ark of the Lord upon the. ... 7760
1Sa 15:27 **l** hold upon the skirt of his mantel
1Sa 19:13 took an image, and **l** it in the bed ... 7760
1Sa 21:12 David **l** up these words in his heart ... 7760
1Ki 3:20 **l** her dead child in my bosom ... 7901
1Ki 6:37 foundation of the house of the Lord **l**,. . 7901
2Ki 4:21 **l** him on the bed of the man of God ... 7901
2Ki 9:25 the Lord **l** this burden upon him;. ... 5375
Ezr 6:3 foundations thereof be strongly **l**;. ... 5446
Est 9:16 they **l** not their hands on the prey, ... 7971
Job 38:4 when I **l** the foundations of the earth?
Ps 3:5 I **l** me down and slept; I awaked; ... 7901
Ps 35:11 **l** to my charge things that I knew
Ps 79:1 they have **l** Jerusalem on heaps ... 7760
Ps 102:25 thou **l** the foundation of the earth:
Ps 119:30 thy judgments have I **l** before me ... 7737
Pr 13:22 of the sinner is **l** up for the just. ... 6845
Isa 6:7 he **l** it upon my mouth, and said, ... 5060
Isa 23:18 it shall not be treasured nor **l** up; ... 2630
Isa 42:25 him, yet he **l** it not to heart ... 7760
Isa 44:28 temple, Thy foundation shall be **l**
Isa 53:6 Lord hath **l** on him the iniquity ... 6293
Isa 64:11 all our pleasant things are **l** waste
Jer 4:7 and thy cities shall be **l** waste
La 4:19 they **l** wait for us in the wilderness
Eze 6:6 your altars may be **l** waste and made
Eze 33:29 I have **l** the land most desolate ... 5414
Da 6:17 and **l** upon the mouth of the den; ... 7760
Hos 11:4 jaws, and I **l** meat unto them. ... 5186
Ob 13 have **l** hands on their substance ... 7971
Jnh 3:6 and he **l** his robe from him,. ... 5674
Hag 2:15 before a stone was **l** upon a stone ... 7760
Hag 2:18 foundation of the Lord's temple was **l**,
Zec 3:9 behold the stone that I have **l** ... 5414
Zec 4:9 **l** the foundation of this house;
Mt 3:10 axe is **l** unto the root of the trees: ... *2749*
Mt 18:28 **he l hands on him, and took him by**
Mt 26:55 **the temple, and ye l no hold on me**
Mt 26:57 they that had **l** hold on Jesus led him
Mt 27:60 **l** it in his own new tomb, which ... *5087*
Mk 6:17 had sent forth and **l** hold upon John,
Mk 14:46 they **l** their hands on him, and ... *1911*
Mk 15:46 **l** him in a sepulchre which was ... *2698*
Lk 2:7 clothes, and **l** him in a manger;. ... *347*
Lk 6:48 **and l the foundation on a rock:** ... *5087*
Lk 14:19 **he hath l the foundation, and** ... *5087*
Lk 16:20 **Lazarus, which was l at his gate,** ... *906*
Lk 19:22 **taking up that I l not down, and.** ... *5087*
Lk 23:26 on him they **l** the cross, that he. ... *2007*
Lk 23:53 **l** it in a sepulchre that was hewn. ... *5087*
Lk 24:12 the linen clothes **l** by themselves, ... *2749*
Jn 7:30 no man **l** hands on him, because ... *1911*
Jn 11:34 **Where have ye l him?** They said ... *5087*
Jn 11:41 the place where the dead was **l** ... *2749*
Jn 19:42 There **l** they Jesus therefore ... *5087*
Jn 20:2 know not where they have **l** him. ... *5087*
Jn 20:15 tell me where thou hast **l** him, and. ... *5087*
Ac 4:35 **l** them down at the apostles' feet: ... *5087*
Ac 5:2 part, and **l** it at the apostles' feet ... *5087*
Ac 6:6 they **l** their hands on them ... 2007
Ac 7:58 witnesses **l** down their clothes at. ... *659*
Ac 16:23 had **l** many stripes upon them, ... *2007*
Ac 20:3 And when the Jews **l** wait for him, ... *1096*
Ac 25:7 **l** many and grievous complaints ... *5342*
Ac 25:16 the crime **l** against him. ... *1462*
Ro 16:4 for my life **l** down their own necks: ... *5294*
1Co 3:10 I have **l** the foundation, and. ... *5087*
1Co 3:11 can no man lay than that is **l**, ... *5087*
Col 1:5 hope which is **l** up for you in. ... *606*
2Ti 4:8 there is **l** up for me a crown of ... *606*
1Jn 3:16 because he **l** down his life for us: ... *5087*
Rev 20:2 he **l** hold on the dragon, that old

LAIN

Nu 5:19 If no man have **l** with thee, and ... 7901
Jn 11:17 had **l** in the grave four days already
Jn 20:12 where the body of Jesus had **l** ... *2749*

LAKE

Lk 8:23 down a storm of wind on the **l**; ... *3041*
Rev 19:20 both were cast alive into a **l** of fire ... *3041*
Rev 20:14 and hell were cast into the **l** of fire ... *3041*
Rev 21:8 their part in the **l** which burneth ... *3041*

LAMA (la´-mah)

Mt 27:46 saying, **Eli, Eli, l sabachthani?** ... *2982*
Mk 15:34 saying, **Eloi, Eloi, l sabachthani?** ... *2982*

LAMB

Ge 22:7 where is the **l** for a burnt offering? ... 7716
Ge 22:8 God will provide himself a **l** for a. ... 7716
Ex 12:4 the household be too little for the **l**, ... 7716
Ex 12:5 Your **l** shall be without blemish, a. ... 7716
Ex 29:39 the other **l** thou shalt offer at even: ... 3532
Le 3:7 If he offer a **l** for his offering, then ... 3775
Le 12:6 she shall bring a **l** of the first year. ... 3532
Le 22:23 **l** that hath any thing superfluous ... 7716
Nu 6:14 one he **l** of the first year without ... 3532
1Sa 17:34 bear, and took a **l** out of the flock: ... 7716
2Sa 12:4 took the poor man's **l**, and dressed. ... 3535
Isa 11:6 wolf also shall dwell with the **l**, ... 3532
Isa 53:7 is brought as a **l** to the slaughter ... 7716
Jer 11:19 But I was like a **l** or an ox that is. ... 3532
Jn 1:29 and saith, Behold the **L** of God ... *286*
Jn 1:36 he saith, Behold the **L** of God!. ... *286*
Ac 8:32 like a **l** dumb before his shearer, so. ... *286*
1Pe 1:19 of Christ, as of a **l** without blemish ... *286*
Rev 5:6 stood a **L** as it had been slain. ... *721*
Rev 5:8 elders fell down before the **L**,. ... *721*
Rev 5:12 Worthy is the **L** that was slain to. ... *721*
Rev 5:13 the throne, and unto the **L** for ever. ... *721*
Rev 6:1 when the **L** opened one of the seals,. ... *721*
Rev 7:9 and before the **L**, clothed with white ... *721*
Rev 7:17 **L** which is in the midst of the throne ... *721*
Rev 12:11 overcame him by the blood of the **L**, ... *721*
Rev 13:8 written in the book of life of the **L** ... *721*
Rev 14:10 angels, and in the presence of the **L**:. ... *721*
Rev 15:3 of God, and the song of the **L**,. ... *721*
Rev 17:14 and the **L** shall overcome them: ... *721*
Rev 19:7 for the marriage of the **L** is come,. ... *721*
Rev 21:14 of the twelve apostles of the **L**. ... *721*

Rev 21:22 Lord God Almighty and the **L** are....... *721*
Rev 22:3 throne of God and of the **L** shall be..... *721*

LAMB'S

Rev 21:9 shew thee the bride, the **L** wife *721*
Rev 21:27 are written in the **L** book of life *721*

LAMBS

Ge 21:29 What mean these seven ewe **l** which ... 3535
Ex 29:38 two **l** of the first year day by day....... 3532
Nu 28:11 seven **l** of the first year without........ 3532
Nu 29:13 and fourteen **l** of the first year;......... 3532
1Sa 15:9 and the **l**, and all that was good,....... 3733
2Ch 29:22 they killed also the **l**, and they......... 3532
Ezr 6:17 two hundred rams, four hundred **l**;..... 563
Ps 37:20 of the Lord shall be as the fat of **l**: 3733
Ps 114:4 and the little hills like **l**.......... 1121, 6629
Pr 27:26 The **l** are for thy clothing, and......... 3532
Isa 40:11 shall gather the **l** with his arm, ... 2922
Jer 51:40 them down like **l** to the slaughter, ... 3733
Eze 46:11 and to the **l** as he is able to give........ 3532
Lk 10:3 **send you forth as l among wolves** *704*
Jn 21:15 He saith unto him, **Feed my l** *721*

LAME

Dt 15:21 as if it be **l**, or blind, or have any ill 6455
2Sa 4:4 had a son that was **l** of his feet 5223
2Sa 9:3 yet a son, which is **l** on his feet 5223
Job 29:15 the blind, and feet was I to the **l** 6455
Pr 26:7 The legs of the **l** are not equal: so...... 6455
Mal 1:13 was torn, and the **l**, and the sick;....... 6455
Mt 11:5 **l walk, the lepers are cleansed,**........ *5560*
Mt 15:31 the **l** to walk, and the blind to see: *5560*
Lk 7:22 **l walk, the lepers are cleansed**......... *5560*
Lk 14:13 **poor, the maimed, the l, the blind:**..... *5560*
Ac 3:2 man **l** from his mother's womb......... *5560*
Heb 12:13 which is **l** be turned out of the way;.... *5560*

LAMENT

Jgs 11:40 to **l** the daughter of Jephthah the 8567
Jer 16:5 neither go to **l** nor bemoan them: 5594
La 2:8 the rampart and the wall to **l**; 56
Eze 27:32 for thee, and **l** over thee, saying, ... 6969
Joel 1:8 **L** like a virgin girded with 421
Mic 2:4 and **l** with a doleful lamentation, ... 5091
Jn 16:20 **That ye shall weep and l, but the** *2354*
Rev 18:9 shall bewail her, and **l** for her *2875*

LAMENTATION

2Sa 1:17 with this **l** over Saul and over 7015
Jer 31:15 in Ramah, **l**, and bitter weeping;........ 5092
La 2:5 daughter of Judah mourning and **l**...... 592
Eze 19:1 up a **l** for the princes of Israel, ... 7015
Am 5:16 such as are skilful of **l** to wailing....... 5092
Mt 2:18 a voice heard, **l**, and weeping. *2355*

LAMENTED

1Sa 28:3 Israel had **l** him, and buried him 5594
2Sa 1:17 And David **l** with this lamentation..... 6969
2Ch 35:25 And Jeremiah **l** for Josiah and all 6969
Jer 16:4 they shall not be **l**; neither shall 5594
Mt 11:17 **unto you, and ye have not l**........... *2875*

LAMP

Ge 15:17 burning **l** that passed between 3940
2Sa 22:29 For thou art my **l**, O Lord: and the..... 5216
Ps 119:105 Thy word is a **l** unto my feet,.......... 5216
Pr 6:23 For the commandment is a **l**; and...... 5216
Pr 20:20 his **l** shall be put out in obscure 5216
Isa 62:1 the salvation thereof as a **l** that 3940
Rev 8:10 heaven, burning as it were a **l**,.......... *2985*

LAMPS

Ex 30:8 when Aaron lighteth the **l** at even, ... 5216
Ex 40:25 he lighted the **l** before the Lord; 5216
Le 24:2 to cause the **l** to burn continually...... 5216
Jgs 7:16 and **l** within the pitchers 3940
Job 41:19 Out of his mouth go burning **l**, ... 3940
Eze 1:13 fire, and like the appearance of **l**: 3940
Da 10:6 lightning, and his eyes as **l** of fire 3940
Mt 25:1 **ten virgins, which took their l**......... *2985*
Mt 25:7 **virgins arose, and trimmed their l**..... *2985*
Mt 25:8 **of your oil; for our l are gone out**...... *2985*
Rev 4:5 seven **l** of fire burning before the *2985*

LAND

Ge 1:9 place, and let the dry **l** appear:
Ge 1:10 and God called the dry **l** Earth; and
Ge 7:22 of all that was in the dry **l**, died
Ge 12:1 unto a **l** that I will shew thee: 776
Ge 12:7 said, Unto thy seed will I give this **l**:..... 776
Ge 13:12 Abram dwelled in the **l** of Canaan,...... 776
Ge 13:15 For all the **l** which thou seest, to........ 776
Ge 15:18 Unto thy seed have I given this **l**........ 776
Ge 19:28 toward all the **l** of the plain, and........ 776
Ge 21:21 him a wife out of the **l** of Egypt 776
Ge 24:7 Unto thy seed will I give this **l**; 776
Ge 26:3 Sojourn in this **l**, and I will be with 776
Ge 28:4 inherit the **l** wherein thou art a......... 776
Ge 28:15 will bring thee again into this **l**; 127
Ge 31:3 Return unto the **l** of thy fathers 776
Ge 35:12 **l** which I gave Abraham and Isaac,...... 776
Ge 35:22 to pass, when Israel dwelt in the **l**, ... 776
Ge 37:1 Jacob dwelt in the **l** wherein his 776
Ge 41:29 plenty throughout all the **l** of Egypt: 776
Ge 41:30 and the famine shall consume the **l**;..... 776
Ge 41:36 that food shall be for store to the **l**...... 776
Ge 41:43 him ruler over all the **l** of Egypt 776
Ge 41:56 famine waxed sore in the **l** of Egypt..... 776
Ge 42:5 the famine was in the **l** of Canaan....... 776
Ge 42:9 nakedness of the **l** ye are come 776
Ge 43:1 And the famine was sore in the **l** 776
Ge 45:10 thou shalt dwell in the **l** of Goshen,..... 776
Ge 47:6 in the **l** of Goshen let them dwell:....... 776
Ge 47:19 buy us and our **l** for bread, and we...... 127
Ge 47:20 Joseph bought all the **l** of Egypt 127
Ge 47:26 made it a law over the **l** of Egypt 127
Ge 48:4 will give this **l** to thy seed after 776
Ge 50:24 the **l** which he sware to Abraham, ... 776
Ex 1:7 and the **l** was filled with them. 776
Ex 3:8 a **l** flowing with milk and honey; 776
Ex 4:9 shall become blood upon the dry **l**.
Ex 6:1 shall he drive them out of his **l**......... 776
Ex 7:3 and my wonders in the **l** of Egypt....... 776
Ex 8:6 frogs came up, and covered the **l**........ 776
Ex 8:7 up frogs upon the **l** of Egypt........... 776
Ex 8:16 lice throughout all the **l** of Egypt 776
Ex 8:17 all the dust of the **l** became lice......... 776
Ex 8:24 **l** was corrupted by reason of ... flies 776
Ex 9:9 small dust in all the **l** of Egypt,......... 776
Ex 9:23 rained hail upon the **l** of Egypt. 776
Ex 9:26 Only in the **l** of Goshen, where the...... 776
Ex 10:22 thick darkness in all the **l** of Egypt...... 776
Ex 11:5 firstborn in the **l** of Egypt shall die, ... 776

L

Ex	12:29	smote all the firstborn in the **l** of	776
Ex	12:33	send them out of the **l** in haste;	776
Ex	13:5	a **l** flowing with milk and honey	776
Ex	13:15	all the firstborn in the **l** of Egypt,	776
Ex	14:29	Israel walked upon dry **l** in the midst	
Ex	18:3	have been an alien in a strange **l**.	776
Ex	20:12	thy days may be long upon the **l**.	127
Ex	23:19	The first of the firstfruits of thy **l**	127
Le	16:22	iniquities unto a **l** not inhabited:	776
Le	18:25	**l** itself vomiteth out her inhabitants	776
Le	25:4	shall be a sabbath of rest unto the **l**,	776
Le	25:9	trumpet sound throughout all your **l**.	776
Le	25:10	liberty throughout all the **l** unto	776
Le	25:24	shall grant a redemption for the **l**.	776
Le	26:4	and the **l** shall yield her increase	776
Le	26:6	And I will give peace in the **l**, and	776
Le	26:34	Then shall the **l** enjoy her sabbaths,	776
Nu	13:16	which Moses sent to spy out the **l**.	776
Nu	13:28	people be strong that dwell in the **l**	776
Nu	13:32	brought up an evil report of the **l**.	776
Nu	14:30	ye shall not come into the **l**,	776
Nu	18:20	shalt have no inheritance in their **l**.	776
Nu	21:22	Let me pass through thy **l**: we will	776
Nu	22:6	that I may drive them out of the **l**	776
Nu	32:7	of Israel from going over into the **l**.	776
Nu	33:53	I have given you the **l** to possess it	776
Nu	34:18	to divide the **l** by inheritance.	776
Nu	35:28	slayer shall return into the **l** of his	776
Nu	35:33	**l** cannot be cleansed of the blood	776
Dt	1:25	is a good **l** which the Lord our God	776
Dt	1:35	this evil generation see that good **l**.	776
Dt	2:20	also was accounted a **l** of giants:	776
Dt	4:21	I should not go in unto that good **l**,	776
Dt	4:22	go over, and possess that good **l**	776
Dt	5:33	ye may prolong your days in the **l**.	776
Dt	6:1	in the **l** whither ye go to possess it:	776
Dt	8:7	into a good **l**, a **l** of brooks of water,	776
Dt	11:12	A **l** which the Lord thy God careth	776
Dt	15:11	poor shall never cease out of the **l**	776
Dt	19:10	innocent blood be not shed in thy **l**,	776
Dt	24:4	thou shalt not cause the **l** to sin	776
Dt	29:22	when they see the plagues of that **l**,	776
Dt	29:23	the whole **l** thereof is brimstone,	776
Dt	29:24	the Lord done thus unto this **l**?	776
Dt	32:10	He found him in a desert **l**, and in	776
Jos	1:6	thou divide for an inheritance the **l**	776
Jos	1:11	to go in to possess the **l**, which the	776
Jos	4:22	Israel came over this Jordan on dry **l**,	
Jos	5:12	they did eat of the fruit of the **l** of	776
Jos	11:16	So Joshua took all that **l**, the hills,	776
Jos	13:2	This is the **l** that yet remaineth: all	776
Jos	14:4	no part unto the Levites in the **l**	776
Jos	14:15	And the **l** had rest from war	776
Jos	18:10	there Joshua divided the **l** unto the	776
Jos	22:11	altar over against the **l** of Canaan,	776
Jos	22:19	the **l** of your possession be unclean,	776
Jos	24:13	you a **l** for which ye did not labour,	776
Jgs	1:27	Canaanites would dwell in that **l**.	776
Jgs	3:11	And the **l** had rest forty years	776
Jgs	6:5	they entered into the **l** to destroy it	776
Jgs	11:13	Because Israel took away my **l**,	776
Jgs	11:17	me, I pray thee, pass through thy **l**:	776
Jgs	18:2	said unto them, Go, search the **l**	776
Jgs	18:17	five men that went to spy out the **l**.	776
Ru	2:11	mother, and the **l** of thy nativity,	776
Ru	4:3	of Moab, selleth a parcel of **l**	7704
1Sa	13:3	the trumpet throughout all the **l**.	776
1Sa	27:1	escape into the **l** of the Philistines;	776
2Sa	9:7	thee all the **l** of Saul thy father;	7704
2Sa	19:9	he is fled out of the **l** for Absalom	776
2Sa	24:13	be three days' pestilence in thy **l**?	776
1Ki	8:36	give rain upon thy **l**, which thou	776
1Ki	9:11	twenty cities in the **l** of Galilee	776
1Ki	18:6	divided the **l** between them to pass	776
2Ki	3:19	mar every good piece of **l** with stones	
2Ki	8:1	also come upon the **l** seven years	776
2Ki	17:27	them the manner of the God of the **l**,	776
2Ki	21:24	people of the **l** made Josiah his son	776
2Ki	25:22	that remained in the **l** of Judah,	776
2Ki	25:24	dwell in the **l**, and serve the king of	776
1Ch	16:18	Unto thee will I give the **l** of Canaan,	776
1Ch	28:8	that ye may possess this good **l**	776
2Ch	6:38	their soul in the **l** of their captivity,	776
2Ch	7:14	their sin, and will heal their **l**.	776
2Ch	19:3	taken away the groves out of the **l**,	776
2Ch	33:25	people of the **l** made Josiah his son	776
2Ch	34:8	when he had purged the **l**, and the	776
2Ch	36:21	until the **l** had enjoyed her sabbaths:	776
Ezr	10:2	strange wives of the people of the **l**	776
Ne	9:11	the midst of the sea on the dry **l**;	
Est	8:17	of the people of the **l** became Jews;	776
Job	1:1	a man in the **l** of Uz, whose name	776
Job	28:13	is it found in the **l** of the living	776
Ps	27:13	of the Lord in the **l** of the living	776
Ps	63:1	for thee in a dry and thirsty **l**, where	776
Ps	66:6	He turned the sea into dry **l**: they	776
Ps	88:12	righteousness in the **l** of forgetfulness?	776
Ps	106:24	they despised the pleasant **l**, they	776
Ps	106:38	and the **l** was polluted with blood	776
Ps	116:9	before the Lord in the **l** of the living	776
Ps	137:4	sing the Lord's song in a strange **l**?	127
Pr	2:21	For the upright shall dwell in the **l**,	776
Pr	28:19	that tilleth his **l** shall have plenty	127
Pr	31:23	he sitteth among the elders of the **l**	776
Ecc	10:17	Blessed art thou, O **l**, when thy king	776
Isa	2:8	Their **l** also is full of idols; they	776
Isa	6:11	man, and the **l** be utterly desolate	127
Isa	8:8	wings shall fill the breadth of thy **l**	776
Isa	9:2	in the **l** of the shadow of death,	776
Isa	13:14	and flee every one into his own **l**	776
Isa	14:25	I will break the Assyrian in my **l**.	776
Isa	18:7	foot, whose **l** the rivers have spoiled,	776
Isa	19:20	the Lord of hosts in the **l** of Egypt:	776
Isa	24:11	darkened, the mirth of the **l** is gone	776
Isa	26:1	this song be sung in the **l** of Judah;	776
Isa	30:6	into the **l** of trouble and anguish	776
Isa	33:17	shall behold the **l** that is very far off	776
Isa	36:17	a **l** like your own **l**, a **l** of corn and	776
Isa	53:8	was cut off out of the **l** of the living:	776
Isa	57:13	trust in me shall possess the **l**,	776
Isa	62:4	thy **l** any more be termed Desolate:	776
Jer	2:2	wilderness, in a **l** that was not sown	776
Jer	2:7	when ye entered, ye defiled my **l**,	776
Jer	3:1	shall not that **l** be greatly polluted?	776
Jer	4:5	say, Blow ye the trumpet in the **l**.	776
Jer	4:20	the whole **l** is spoiled: suddenly are	776
Jer	5:30	horrible thing is committed in the **l**;	776
Jer	7:7	in the **l** that I gave to your fathers,	776
Jer	7:34	the bride: for the **l** shall be desolate	776
Jer	10:18	sling out the inhabitants of the **l**.	776

Jer 11:5 a **l** flowing with milk and honey, ... 776
Jer 12:12 even to the other end of the **l** 776
Jer 14:8 thou be as a stranger in the **l**, and....... 776
Jer 16:6 and the small shall die in this **l** 776
Jer 16:15 I will bring them again into their **l** 127
Jer 22:12 and shall see this **l** no more............ 776
Jer 22:27 But to the **l** whereunto they desire 776
Jer 24:6 I will bring them again to this **l**: 776
Jer 25:11 this whole **l** shall be a desolation, ... 776
Jer 27:10 you, to remove you far from your **l**: 127
Jer 32:20 signs and wonders in the **l** of Egypt, ... 776
Jer 32:22 a **l** flowing with milk and honey; 776
Jer 37:19 come against you, nor against this **l**? 776
Jer 40:4 behold, all the **l** is before thee:.......... 776
Jer 40:9 dwell in the **l**, and serve the king of 776
Jer 42:13 ye say, We will not dwell in this **l**, ... 776
Jer 44:8 unto other gods in the **l** of Egypt,....... 776
Jer 46:12 shame, and thy cry hath filled the **l**: 776
Jer 47:2 the inhabitants of the **l** shall howl....... 776
Jer 50:18 punish the king of Babylon and his **l**, ... 776
Jer 50:22 A sound of battle is in the **l**, and of 776
Jer 51:5 their **l** was filled with sin against........ 776
Jer 51:29 And the **l** shall tremble and sorrow:..... 776
Jer 51:47 her whole **l** shall be confounded, ... 776
Jer 52:6 was no bread for the people of the **l**..... 776
Eze 7:2 come upon the four corners of the **l** 776
Eze 7:23 for the **l** is full of bloody crimes 776
Eze 9:9 great, and the **l** is full of blood, and 776
Eze 12:22 proverb that ye have in the **l** 127
Eze 17:13 hath also taken the mighty of the **l**...... 776
Eze 18:2 proverb concerning the **l** of Israel, ... 127
Eze 21:2 prophesy against the **l** of Israel 127
Eze 21:30 wast created, in the **l** of thy nativity 776
Eze 22:30 stand in the gap before me for the **l** 776
Eze 23:19 played the harlot in the **l** of Egypt....... 776
Eze 29:19 I will give the **l** of Egypt unto 776
Eze 30:13 I will put a fear in the **l** of Egypt. 776
Eze 32:6 will also water with thy blood the **l** 776
Eze 33:24 the **l** is given us for inheritance. 776
Eze 33:25 blood: and shall ye possess the **l**? 776
Eze 34:25 the evil beasts to cease out of the **l** 776
Eze 36:35 **l** that was desolate is become like 776
Eze 38:9 shalt be like a cloud to cover the **l**....... 776
Eze 38:19 a great shaking in the **l** of Israel;......... 127
Eze 45:1 divide by lot the **l** for inheritance, ... 776
Eze 46:3 the people of the **l** shall worship at...... 776
Eze 48:14 nor alienate the firstfruits of the **l**....... 776
Da 11:16 he shall stand in the glorious **l** 776
Da 11:28 return into his **l** with great riches; 776
Da 11:41 shall enter also into the glorious **l**....... 776
Hos 4:1 nor knowledge of God in the **l** 776
Hos 9:3 shall not dwell in the Lord's **l**;.......... 776
Joel 1:10 The field is wasted, the **l** mourneth;..... 127
Joel 2:3 the **l** is as the garden of Eden........... 776
Joel 2:21 Fear not, O **l**; be glad and rejoice:....... 127
Am 7:2 an end of eating the grass of the **l**....... 776
Jnh 1:13 men rowed hard to bring it to the **l**;.... 3004
Jnh 2:10 it vomited out Jonah upon the dry **l** ... 3004
Mic 5:11 And I will cut off the cities of thy **l**...... 776
Na 3:13 gates of thy **l** shall be set wide open 776
Hab 2:17 and for the violence of the **l**............ 776
Zep 1:3 and I will cut off man from off the **l**, ... 127
Zep 1:18 whole **l** shall be devoured by fire 776
Hag 1:11 I called for a drought upon the **l**, ... 776
Zec 1:21 their horn over the **l** of Judah to........ 776
Zec 9:16 lifted up as an ensign upon his **l**........ 127
Zec 13:2 unclean spirit to pass out of the **l**, ... 776
Mt 2:6 thou Bethlehem in the **l** of Juda,....... *1093*
Mt 10:15 **for the l of Sodom and Gomorrha**..... *1093*
Mt 27:45 there was darkness over all the **l** *1093*
Lk 4:25 **famine was throughout all the l;**....... *1095*
Lk 21:23 **shall be great distress in the l** *1093*
Jn 21:11 drew the net to **l** full of great fishes,.... *1093*
Ac 5:3 back part of the price of the **l**?......... *5564*
Ac 5:8 whether ye sold the **l** for so much?..... *5564*
Ac 7:36 and signs in the **l** of Egypt, and in *1093*
Heb 11:9 he sojourned in the **l** of promise, ... *1093*
Heb 11:29 through the Red sea as by dry **l**:
Jude 5 the people out of the **l** of Egypt *1093*

LANDMARK

Dt 19:14 not remove thy neighbour's **l**,......... 1366
Pr 22:28 Remove not the ancient **l**, which....... 1366
Pr 23:10 Remove not the old **l**; and enter 1366

LANDS

Ge 10:5 of the Gentiles divided in their **l**; 776
Ge 47:18 my lord, but our bodies, and our **l** 127
2Ki 19:11 kings of Assyria have done to all **l**, ... 776
1Ch 14:17 fame of David went out into all **l**;....... 776
2Ch 13:9 manner of the nations of other **l**?....... 776
2Ch 32:13 any ways able to deliver their **l** out 776
Ezr 9:11 the filthiness of the people of the **l**...... 776
Ne 5:3 said, We have mortgaged our **l** 7704
Ps 49:11 call their **l** after their own names 127
Ps 66:1 a joyful noise unto God, all ye **l** 776
Ps 100:1 joyful noise unto the Lord, all ye **l** 776
Isa 36:20 they among all the gods of these **l** 776
Jer 27:6 I given all these **l** into the hand of 776
Eze 20:6 honey, which is the glory of all **l**........ 776
Eze 39:27 them out of their enemies' **l**........... 776
Mt 19:29 **children, or l, for my name's sake,** *68*
Mk 10:29 **wife, or children, or l, for my sake,**....... *68*
Ac 4:34 possessors of **l** or houses sold them ... *5564*

LANGUAGE See also LANGUAGES.

Ge 11:1 And the whole earth was of one **l**...... 8193
Ge 11:9 confound the **l** of all the earth:........ 8193
Ne 13:24 and could not speak in the Jews' **l**,
Ne 13:24 according to the **l** of each people 3956
Est 8:9 and unto every people after their **l**..... 3956
Ps 19:3 There is no speech nor **l**, where 1697
Jer 5:15 nation whose **l** thou knowest not, ... 3956
Eze 3:5 strange speech and of an hard **l** 3956
Da 3:29 That every people, nation, and **l**....... 3961
Zep 3:9 will I turn to the people a pure **l**....... 8193
Ac 2:6 heard them speak in his own **l**, ... *1258*

LANGUAGES

Da 3:7 the people, the nations, and the **l**,...... 3961
Da 5:19 people, nations, and **l**, trembled 3961
Da 7:14 that all people, nations, and **l** 3961
Zec 8:23 hold out of all **l** of the nations,........ 3956

LANGUISH

Isa 19:8 spread nets upon the waters shall **l**...... 535
Isa 24:4 the haughty people of the earth do **l** 535
Jer 14:2 mourneth, and the gates thereof **l**....... 535
Hos 4:3 one that dwelleth therein shall **l** 535

LANGUISHED

La 2:8 wall to lament; they **l** together. 535

LANGUISHETH
Isa 24:4 the world l and fadeth away, the 535
Joel 1:10 the new wine is dried up, the oil l. 535

LAP
Ne 5:13 Also I shook my l, and said, So 2684
Pr 16:33 The lot is cast into the l: but the 2436

LAPPED
Jgs 7:7 By the three hundred men that l. 3952

LAPPETH
Jgs 7:5 water with his tongue, as a dog l, ... 3952

LARGE
Ex 3:8 that land unto a good land and a l 7342
2Sa 22:20 me forth also into a l place 4800
Ne 7:4 the city was l and great: but 7342, 3027
Ps 31:8 thou hast set my feet in a l room 4800
Ps 118:5 me, and set me in a l place 4800
Isa 30:23 shall thy cattle feed in l pastures. 7337
Eze 23:32 of thy sister's cup deep and l 7342
Mt 28:12 gave l money unto the soldiers, ... *2425*
Mk 14:15 **he will shew you a l upper room** *3173*
Rev 21:16 the length is as l as the breadth: *5118*

LARGENESS
1Ki 4:29 exceeding much, and l of heart, ... 7341

LASCIVIOUSNESS
Mk 7:22 **wickedness, deceit, l, an evil eye,** *766*
Gal 5:19 fornication, uncleanness, l *766*
Eph 4:19 have given themselves over unto l. *766*
1Pe 4:3 when we walked in l, lusts, excess *766*
Jude 4 turning the grace of our God into l, ... *766*

LAST
Ge 49:1 shall befall you in the l days 319
Nu 23:10 and let my l end be like his! 319
2Sa 23:1 Now these be the l words of David 314
Ne 8:18 from the first day unto the l day, ... 314
Pr 23:32 At the l it biteth like a serpent, ... 319
Isa 41:4 Lord, the first, and with the l: 314
Jer 12:4 said, He shall not see our l end 319
Da 8:3 other, and the higher came up l 314
Mic 4:1 in the l days it shall come to pass, ... 319
Mt 12:45 **l state of that man is worse than** *2078*
Mt 19:30 **many that are first shall be l** *2078*
Mt 20:16 **l shall be first, and the first l** *2078*
Mt 21:37 **But l of all he sent...his son** *5305*
Mt 27:64 the l error shall be worse than *2078*
Mk 9:35 **be first, the same shall be l of all,** *2078*
Lk 11:26 **l state of that man is worse than** *2078*
Lk 12:59 **till thou hast paid the very l mite.** *2078*
Jn 6:39 **raise it up again at the l day** *2078*
Jn 6:40 raise him up at the l day. *2078*
Jn 7:37 In the l day, that great day of the *2078*
Jn 11:24 in the resurrection at the l day *2078*
Jn 12:48 **same shall judge him in the l day.** *2078*
1Co 4:9 hath set forth us the apostles l, ... *2078*
1Co 15:8 And l of all he was seen of me also, ... *2078*
1Co 15:45 the l Adam was made a quickening *2078*
1Co 15:52 twinkling of an eye, at the l trump: *2078*
2Ti 3:1 in the l days perilous times shall *2078*
Heb 1:2 Hath in the l days spoken unto us *2078*
1Pe 1:5 ready to be revealed in the l time. *2078*
1Pe 1:20 manifest in these l times for you, ... *2078*
1Jn 2:18 Little children, it is the l time: and *2078*
Rev 1:11 **and Omega, the first and the l:** *2078*
Rev 1:17 **Fear not; I am the first and the l,** *2078*
Rev 2:8 **things saith the first and the l,** *2078*
Rev 21:9 vials full of the seven l plagues *2078*
Rev 22:13 **and the end, the first and the l.** *2078*

LATCHET
Isa 5:27 nor the l of their shoes be broken: 8288
Mk 1:7 l of whose shoes I am not worthy *2438*
Jn 1:27 shoe's l I am not worthy to unloose *2438*

LATE
Ps 127:2 you to rise up early, to sit up l 309
Mic 2:8 of l my people is risen up as an 865
Jn 11:8 Jews of l sought to stone thee; *3568*

LATTER
Ex 4:8 will believe the voice of the l sign 314
Dt 4:30 even in the l days, if thou turn to 319
Dt 11:14 the first rain and the l rain, ... 4456
Dt 24:3 if the l husband hate her, and 314
Dt 31:29 evil will befall you in the l days; 319
Ru 3:10 shewed more kindness in the l end 314
Job 19:25 stand at the l day upon the earth: 314
Job 29:23 their mouth wide as for the l rain 4456
Job 42:12 the Lord blessed the l end of Job 319
Pr 16:15 favour is as a cloud of the l rain 4456
Pr 19:20 thou mayest be wise in thy l end 319
Jer 3:3 and there hath been no l rain; 4456
Jer 5:24 rain, both the former and the l 4456
Jer 48:47 the captivity of Moab in the l days, ... 319
Eze 38:8 in the l years thou shalt come into 319
Da 2:28 what shall be in the l days 320
Da 10:14 befall thy people in the l days: 319
Da 11:29 not be as the former, or as the l 314
Hos 6:3 as the l and former rain unto the 4456
Joel 2:23 and the l rain in the first month. 4456
Zec 10:1 rain in the time of the l rain; 4456
1Ti 4:1 l times some shall depart from *5305*
Jas 5:7 he receive the early and l rain *5797*
2Pe 2:20 l end is worse with them than the *2078*

LAUGH
Ge 18:13 Wherefore did Sarah l, saying, ... 6711
Ge 21:6 said, God hath made me to l 6712
Ps 2:4 sitteth in the heavens shall l; 7832
Ps 37:13 The Lord shall l at him: for he 7832
Pr 1:26 I also will l at your calamity; I 7832
Ecc 3:4 A time to weep, and a time to l; 7832
Lk 6:21 **ye that weep now: for ye shall l** *1070*
Lk 6:25 **Woe unto you that l now! for ye** *1070*

LAUGHED
Ge 17:17 Abraham fell upon his face, and l, ... 6711
Ge 18:12 Sarah l within herself, saying, ... 6711
Ge 18:15 Sarah denied, saying, I l not; for 6711
Ne 2:19 heard it, they l us to scorn, and 3932
Mt 9:24 And they l him to scorn *2606*
Mk 5:40 they l him to scorn. But when he *2606*

LAUGHTER
Ps 126:2 Then was our mouth filled with l, ... 7814
Pr 14:13 Even in l the heart is sorrowful; 7814
Ecc 2:2 I said of l, It is mad: and of mirth 7814
Ecc 7:3 Sorrow is better than l: for by the 7814
Ecc 7:6 under a pot, so is the l of the fool: 7814
Ecc 10:19 A feast is made for l, and wine 7814
Jas 4:9 let your l be turned to mourning *1071*

LAUNCH

Lk	5:4	L out into the deep, and let down	1877

LAVER

Ex	30:18	Thou shalt also make a l of brass,	3595
Ex	38:8	made the l of brass, and the foot	3595
Ex	40:30	he set the l between the tent of	3595
Le	8:11	the l and his foot, to sanctify them.	3595

LAVERS

1Ki	7:38	Then made he ten l of brass: one	3595
1Ki	7:40	Hiram made the l, and the shovels,	3595

LAW

Ge	19:14	that mocked unto his sons in l	2859
Ge	47:26	Joseph made it a l over the land	2706
Ex	12:49	One l shall be to him that is	8451
Ex	13:9	the Lord's l may be in thy mouth:	8451
Ex	18:17	Moses' father in l said unto him,	2859
Ex	24:12	give thee tables of stone, and a l,	8451
Le	6:25	This is the l of the sin offering:	8451
Le	7:1	is the l of the trespass offering:	8451
Le	7:11	is the l of the sacrifice of peace	8451
Nu	5:29	This is the l of jealousies, when	8451
Nu	15:29	have one l for him that sinneth	8451
Dt	17:11	to the sentence of the l which they	8451
Dt	17:18	write him a copy of this l in a book	8451
Dt	29:29	we may do all the words of this l	8451
Dt	31:11	shalt read this l before all Israel	8451
Dt	31:26	Take this book of the l, and put it	8451
Jos	1:8	This book of the l shall not depart	8451
Jos	8:32	the stones a copy of the l of Moses,	8451
Jos	24:26	words in the book of the l of God,	8451
Ru	3:6	all that her mother in l bade her.	2545
1Sa	4:19	his daughter in l, Phinehas' wife,	3618
2Ki	22:8	I have found the book of the l in	8451
2Ch	6:16	heed to their way to walk in my l,	8451
2Ch	15:3	a teaching priest, and without l	8451
2Ch	19:10	between l and commandment,	8451
2Ch	34:14	priest found a book of the l of the	8451
Ezr	7:6	a ready scribe in the l of Moses,	8451
Ezr	7:10	his heart to seek the l of the Lord,	8451
Ezr	7:12	a scribe of the l of the God of	1882
Ne	8:3	attentive unto the book of the l	8451
Ne	9:26	cast thy l behind their backs, and	8451
Ne	10:29	into an oath, to walk in God's l	8451
Ne	12:44	the portions of the l for the priests	8451
Est	4:11	is one l of his to put him to death,	1881
Ps	1:2	his delight is in the l of the Lord;	8451
Ps	1:2	in his l doth he meditate day and	8451
Ps	19:7	The l of the Lord is perfect,	8451
Ps	37:31	The l of his God is in his heart;	8451
Ps	119:1	who walk in the l of the Lord	8451
Ps	119:51	yet have I not declined from thy l	8451
Ps	119:72	The l of thy mouth is better unto	8451
Ps	119:77	may live: for thy l is my delight.	8451
Ps	119:97	O how love I thy l! it is my	8451
Ps	119:136	eyes, because they keep not thy l	8451
Ps	119:174	O Lord; and thy l is my delight	8451
Pr	1:8	forsake not the l of thy mother:	8451
Pr	3:1	My son, forget not my l; but let	8451
Pr	6:23	is a lamp; and the l is light;	8451
Pr	7:2	my l as the apple of thine eye	8451
Pr	28:7	Whoso keepeth the l is a wise son:	8451
Pr	29:18	he that keepeth the l, happy is he	8451
Pr	31:26	in her tongue is the l of kindness.	8451
Isa	1:10	give ear unto the l of our God, ye	8451
Isa	8:16	seal the l among my disciples	8451
Isa	30:9	will not hear the l of the Lord:	8451
Isa	42:21	he will magnify the l, and make it	8451
Jer	8:8	and the l of the Lord is with us?	8451
Jer	31:33	will put my l in their inward parts,	8451
La	2:9	the l is no more; her prophets also	8451
Eze	43:12	Behold, this is the l of the house.	8451
Da	6:5	him concerning the l of his God.	1882
Da	6:8	l of the Medes and Persians,	1882
Hos	8:1	and trespassed against my l	8451
Am	2:4	have despised the l of the Lord,	8451
Hab	1:4	Therefore the l is slacked, and	8451
Zep	3:4	they have done violence to the l	8451
Mal	2:7	should seek the l at his mouth:	8451
Mal	2:9	but have been partial in the l	8451
Mt	5:17	that I am come to destroy the l,	3557
Mt	5:18	shall in no wise pass from the l,	3557
Mt	7:12	for this is the l and the prophets.	3551
Mt	10:35	daughter in l against her mother	3565
Mt	12:5	have ye not read in the l, how	3551
Mt	22:40	commandments hang all the l and	3557
Mt	23:23	the weightier matters of the l,	3551
Lk	5:17	and doctors of the l sitting by	3547
Lk	10:26	him. What is written in the l?	3551
Lk	16:16	The l and the prophets were until	3551
Lk	16:17	pass, than one tittle of the l to	3551
Jn	1:17	For the l was given by Moses, but	3551
Jn	7:19	and yet none of you keepeth the l?	3551
Jn	7:23	l of Moses should not be broken;	3551
Jn	8:17	It is also written in your l, that	3551
Jn	12:34	have heard out of the l that Christ	3551
Jn	19:7	a l, and by our l he ought to die	3551
Ac	5:34	named Gamaliel, a doctor of the l,	3547
Ac	7:53	received the l by the disposition	3551
Ac	13:39	not be justified by the l of Moses	3551
Ac	15:24	be circumcised, and keep the l;	3551
Ac	19:38	l is open, and there are deputies:	60
Ac	21:20	and they are all zealous of the l:	3551
Ac	22:12	a devout man according to the l	3551
Ac	23:29	be accused of questions of their l	3551
Ac	28:23	Jesus, both out of the l of Moses,	3551
Ro	2:13	the doers of the l shall be justified	3551
Ro	2:14	do ... the things contained in the l,	3551
Ro	2:14	having not the l, are a l unto	3551
Ro	2:15	of the l written in their hearts,	3551
Ro	2:20	knowledge and of the truth in the l	3551
Ro	2:25	but if thou be a breaker of the l	3551
Ro	2:26	keep the righteousness of the l	3551
Ro	3:20	by the deeds of the l there shall no	3551
Ro	3:20	for by the l is the knowledge of sin.	3551
Ro	3:28	by faith without the deeds of the l	3551
Ro	3:31	God forbid: yea, we establish the l	3551
Ro	4:15	Because the l worketh wrath;	3551
Ro	5:13	until the l sin was in the world:	3551
Ro	6:14	ye are not under the l, but under	3551
Ro	6:15	not under the l, but under grace?	3551
Ro	7:2	is bound by the l to her husband so	3551
Ro	7:4	dead to the l by the body of Christ	3551
Ro	7:7	I had not known sin, but by the l:	3551
Ro	7:7	known lust, except the l had said,	3551
Ro	7:8	For without the l sin was dead	3551
Ro	7:12	Wherefore the l is holy, and the	3551
Ro	7:14	For we know that the l is spiritual:	3551
Ro	7:21	I find then a l, that, when I would	3551
Ro	7:22	I delight in the l of God after the	3551

Ro	7:25	mind I myself serve the **l** of God	*3551*
Ro	8:2	the **l** of the Spirit of life in Christ	*3551*
Ro	8:2	me free from the **l** of sin and death	*3551*
Ro	9:31	not attained to the **l** of righteousness,	*3551*
Ro	10:4	For Christ is the end of the **l** for	*3551*
Ro	13:10	love is the fulfilling of the **l**	*3551*
1Co	6:6	brother goeth to **l** with brother,	*2919*
1Co	7:39	wife is bound by the **l** as long as	*3551*
1Co	15:56	sin; and the strength of sin is the **l**	*3551*
Gal	2:16	not justified by the works of the **l**.	*3551*
Gal	2:16	by the works of the **l** shall no flesh	*3551*
Gal	2:21	for if righteousness come by the **l**.	*3551*
Gal	3:11	no man is justified by the **l** in the	*3551*
Gal	3:13	redeemed us from the curse of the **l**,	*3551*
Gal	3:19	Wherefore then serveth the **l**?	*3551*
Gal	3:21	righteousness … have been by the **l**	*3551*
Gal	3:24	the **l** was our schoolmaster to bring	*3551*
Gal	4:4	of a woman, made under the **l**,	*3551*
Gal	4:5	redeem them that were under the **l**,	*3551*
Gal	5:14	all the **l** is fulfilled in one word,	*3551*
Gal	5:23	against such there is no **l**	*3551*
Gal	6:2	and so fulfil the **l** of Christ.	*3551*
Php	3:5	as touching the **l**, a Pharisee;	*3551*
1Ti	1:8	But we know that the **l** is good,	*3551*
Tit	3:9	and strivings about the **l**;	*3544*
Heb	7:5	take tithes...according to the **l**,	*3551*
Heb	7:16	the **l** of a carnal commandment,	*3551*
Heb	7:19	the **l** made nothing perfect, but the	*3551*
Heb	7:28	For the **l** maketh men high priests	*3551*
Heb	9:22	are by the **l** purged with blood;	*3551*
Heb	10:1	**l** having a shadow of good things	*3551*
Heb	10:28	that despised Moses' **l** died without	*3551*
Jas	1:25	into the perfect **l** of liberty,	*3551*
Jas	2:9	sin, and are convinced of the **l** as	*3551*
Jas	2:10	whosoever shall keep the whole **l**	*3551*
Jas	2:12	shall be judged by the **l** of liberty	*3551*
Jas	4:11	not a doer of the **l**, but a judge	*3551*
1Jn	3:4	sin is the transgression of the **l**	*4160, 458*

LAWFUL See also **UNLAWFUL.**

Ezr	7:24	it shall not be **l** to impose toll,	7990
Eze	18:21	and do that which is **l** and right, he	4941
Mt	12:2	is not **l** to do upon the sabbath day	1832
Mt	12:4	**which was not l for him to eat**	*1832*
Mt	12:12	**l to do well on the sabbath days**	*1832*
Mt	19:3	Is it **l** for a man to put away his	*1832*
Mt	22:17	Is it **l** to give tribute unto Caesar	*1833*
Mt	27:6	**It is not l for to put them into the**	*1833*
Mk	2:26	**is not l to eat but for the priests,**	*1833*
Mk	6:18	It is not **l** … to have thy brother's	*1833*
Mk	10:2	**l** for a man to put away his wife?	*1833*
Lk	6:4	**is not l to eat but for the priests**	*1833*
Lk	6:9	**it l on the sabbath days to do**	*1833*
Lk	14:3	**is it l to heal on the sabbath day?**	*1833*
Jn	5:10	it is not **l** for thee to carry thy bed	*1833*
Ac	19:39	be determined in a **l** assembly.	*1772*
Ac	22:25	**l** for you to scourge...a Roman,	*1832*
1Co	6:12	All things are **l** unto me, but all	*1832*
1Co	10:23	all things are **l** for me, but all	*1832*

LAWFULLY

1Ti	1:8	the law is good, if a man use it **l**;	*3545*
2Ti	2:5	he not crowned, except he strive **l**.	*3545*

LAWGIVER

Ge	49:10	nor a **l** from between his feet,	2710
Ps	60:7	of mine head; Judah is my **l**;	2710
Isa	33:22	the Lord is our **l**, the Lord is our	2710
Jas	4:12	There is one **l**, who is able to save	*3550*

LAWLESS

1Ti	1:9	man, but for the **l** and disobedient,	*459*

LAWS

Ge	26:5	my statutes, and my **l**	8451
Ex	18:16	know the statutes of God, and his **l**	8451
Le	26:46	the statutes and judgments and **l**,	8451
Ne	9:13	them right judgments, and true **l**,	8451
Est	1:19	**l** of the Persians and the Medes,	1881
Ps	105:45	observe his statutes, … keep his **l**	8541
Isa	24:5	they have transgressed the **l**.	8451
Eze	44:5	of the Lord, and all the **l** thereof;	8451
Da	7:25	and think to change times and **l**:	1882
Da	9:10	to walk in his **l**, which he set	8451
Heb	8:10	I will put my **l** into their mind	*3551*

LAWYER See also **LAWYERS.**

Mt	22:35	was a **l**, asked him a question,	*3544*
Lk	10:25	a certain **l** stood up, and tempted	*3544*

LAWYERS

Lk	7:30	and **l** rejected the counsel of God	*3544*
Lk	11:46	he said, **Woe unto you also, ye l!**	*3544*
Lk	11:52	**Woe unto you, l! for ye have**	*3544*
Lk	14:3	spake unto the **l** and Pharisees.	*3544*

LAY

Ge	19:33	went in, and **l** with her father;	7901
Ge	22:12	**L** not thine hand upon the lad,	7971
Ge	37:22	**l** no hand upon him; that he	7971
Ex	7:4	I may **l** my hand upon Egypt,	5414
Ex	16:33	**l** it up before the Lord, to be kept	3241
Le	4:4	shall **l** his hand upon the bullock's	*5564*
Le	16:21	Aaron shall **l** both his hands upon	5564
Nu	12:11	thee, **l** not the sin upon us,	7896
Nu	24:9	He couched, he **l** down as a lion,	7901
Dt	11:18	shall ye **l** up these my words in	7760
Dt	21:8	**l** not innocent blood unto thy	5414
Dt	22:25	man only that **l** with her shall die:	7901
Jos	6:26	he shall **l** the foundation thereof	
Jgs	4:22	Sisera **l** dead, and the nail was	5307
Jgs	14:17	her, because she **l** sore upon him:	
Ru	3:14	she **l** at his feet until the morning:	7901
1Sa	26:5	beheld the place where Saul **l**,	7901
2Sa	11:4	in unto him, and he **l** with her;	7901
2Sa	13:5	**L** thee down on thy bed, and make	7901
2Sa	13:31	his garments, and **l** on the earth;	7901
1Ki	13:31	**l** my bones beside his bones:	3241
1Ki	18:23	other bullock, and **l** it on wood,	7760
1Ki	21:27	fasted, and **l** in sackcloth, and	7901
2Ki	4:29	**l** my staff upon the face of the	7760
Ne	13:21	do so again, I will **l** hands on you.	7971
Job	40:4	I will **l** mine hand upon my mouth.	7760
Ps	4:8	I will both **l** me down in peace,	7901
Pr	1:11	with us, let us **l** wait for blood,	
Pr	1:18	they **l** wait for their own blood;	
Pr	7:1	**l** up my commandments with thee.	6845
Pr	10:14	Wise men **l** up knowledge: but the	6845
Pr	30:32	evil, **l** thine hand upon thy mouth.	
Ecc	7:2	the living will **l** it to his heart.	5414
Isa	28:16	**l** in Zion for a foundation a stone,	
Isa	28:17	Judgment also will I **l** to the line,	7760
Isa	51:16	and **l** the foundations of the earth,	
Jer	6:21	will **l** stumblingblocks before	5414

Eze 3:20 I **l** a stumblingblock before him,....... 5414
Eze 6:5 I will **l** the dead carcases of the........ 5414
Eze 23:8 for in her youth they **l** with her,....... 7901
Eze 42:14 there they shall **l** their garments....... 3241
Jnh 1:14 and **l** not upon us innocent blood:..... 5414
Mic 7:16 **l** their hand upon their mouth,........ 7760
Mt 6:19 **L not up for yourselves treasures**
Mt 8:20 **man hath not where to l his head**...... *2827*
Mt 12:11 **will he not l hold on it, and lift it**
Mt 28:6 see the place where the Lord **l**......... *2749*
Mk 5:23 come and **l** thy hands on her, that..... 2007
Mk 16:18 **they shall l hands on the sick,**......... *2007*
Lk 9:58 **man hath not where to l his head**...... *2827*
Jn 10:15 **and I l down my life for the**........... *5087*
Jn 10:17 **love me, because I l down my life,**..... *5087*
Jn 10:18 **taketh it from me, but I l it down**...... *5087*
Jn 10:18 I have power to **l** it down, and I....... *5087*
Jn 15:13 **man l down his life for his friends.**.... *5087*
Ac 7:60 **l** not this sin to their charge........... *2476*
Ro 8:33 Who shall **l** any thing to the charge.... *1458*
Ro 9:33 I **l** in Sion a stumblingstone and....... *5087*
1Co 3:11 other foundation can no man **l**........ *5087*
1Ti 5:22 **L** hands suddenly on no man,.......... *2007*
1Ti 6:12 of faith, **l** hold on eternal life,......... *1949*
Heb 6:18 to **l** hold upon the hope set before us:
Heb 12:1 let us **l** aside every weight, and the...... *659*
1Jn 3:16 we ought to **l** down our lives for....... *5087*

LAYETH

Pr 2:7 He **l** up sound wisdom for the........ 6845
Pr 26:24 lips, and **l** up deceit within him;....... 7896
Pr 31:19 She **l** her hands to the spindle,........ 7971
Isa 56:2 the son of man that **l** hold on it;
Isa 57:1 and no man **l** it to heart: and......... 7760
Zec 12:1 **l** the foundation of the earth, and
Lk 12:21 **he that l up treasure for himself,**
Lk 15:5 **found it, he l it on his shoulders,**...... *2007*

LAYING

Nu 35:20 or hurl at him by **l** of wait, that
Mr 7:8 **l aside the commandment of God,**...... *863*
Ac 8:18 through **l** on of the apostles' hands.... *1936*
Heb 6:1 not **l** again the foundation of.......... *2598*
Heb 6:2 baptisms, and of **l** on of hands,........ *1936*
1Pe 2:1 **l** aside all malice, and all guile,......... *659*

LEAD

Ex 13:21 of a cloud, to **l** them the way;......... 5148
Ex 15:10 sank as **l** in the mighty waters......... 5777
Dt 4:27 whither the Lord shall **l** you........... 5090
Jgs 5:12 and **l** thy captivity captive, thou
Job 19:24 graven with an iron pen and **l**......... 5777
Ps 5:8 **L** me, O Lord, in thy righteousness.... 5148
Ps 31:3 name's sake **l** me, and guide me........ 5148
Ps 61:2 **l** me to the rock that is higher......... 5148
Ps 139:24 and **l** me in the way everlasting........ 5148
Pr 6:22 When thou goest, it shall **l** thee;....... 5148
Pr 8:20 I **l** in the way of righteousness,........ 1980
Isa 3:12 they which **l** thee cause thee to err,...... 833
Isa 11:6 and a little child shall **l** them.......... 5090
Isa 40:11 gently **l** those that are with young...... 5095
Isa 57:18 I will **l** him also, and restore.......... 5148
Jer 6:29 the **l** is consumed of the fire;.......... 5777
Eze 22:20 silver, and brass, and iron, and **l**....... 5777
Zec 5:8 the weight of **l** upon the mouth....... 5777
Mt 6:13 **And l us not into temptation, but**..... *1533*
Mt 15:14 **if the blind l the blind, both shall**...... *3594*
Lk 6:39 them, **Can the blind l the blind?**....... *3594*
Lk 11:4 **And l us not into temptation; but**..... *1533*
Ac 13:11 seeking some to **l** him by the hand..... *5497*
1Ti 2:2 may **l** a quiet and peaceable life........ *1236*
2Ti 3:6 **l** captive silly women laden with........ *162*
Rev 7:17 shall **l** them unto living fountains...... *3594*

LEADERS

Isa 9:16 the **l** of this people cause them to....... 833
Mt 15:14 **alone: they be blind l of the blind**...... *3595*

LEADETH

Ps 23:2 he **l** me beside the still waters......... 5095
Ps 23:3 he **l** me in the paths of............... 5148
Pr 16:29 **l** into the way that is not good......... 3212
Mt 7:13 **is the way, that l to destruction,**........ *520*
Mt 7:14 **narrow is the way, which l unto**........ *520*
Jn 10:3 **sheep by name, and l them out**........ *1806*
Ro 2:4 of God **l** thee to repentance?............ *71*
Rev 13:10 He that **l** into captivity shall go........ *4863*

LEAF See also LEAVES.

Ge 8:11 lo, in her mouth was an olive **l**........ 5929
Le 26:36 the sound of a shaken **l** shall chase..... 5929
Ps 1:3 his **l** also shall not wither; and......... 5929
Isa 34:4 as the **l** falleth off from the vine,....... 5929
Jer 8:13 on the fig tree, and the **l** shall fade;..... 5929
Jer 17:8 cometh, but her **l** shall be green;....... 5929
Eze 47:12 and the **l** thereof for medicine......... 5929

LEAGUE

Jos 9:7 how shall we make a **l** with you?....... 1285
Jgs 2:2 make no **l** with the inhabitants of...... 1285
1Sa 22:8 made a **l** with the son of Jesse,........ 3772
2Sa 5:3 king David made a **l** with them in..... 1285
1Ki 5:12 and they two made a **l** together........ 1285
Eze 30:5 and the men of the land that is in **l**,.... 1285
Da 11:23 after the **l** made with him he shall..... 2266

LEAN

Ge 41:20 **l** and the ill favoured kine did eat...... 7534
Jgs 16:26 pillars ... that I may **l** upon them....... 8172
2Sa 13:4 the king's son, **l** from day to day?...... 1800
Pro 3:5 **l** not unto thine ... understanding..... 8172
Eze 34:20 fat cattle and between the **l** cattle....... 7330
Mic 3:11 yet will they **l** upon the Lord, and...... *8172*

LEANED

2Sa 1:6 behold Saul **l** upon his spear;......... 8172
Am 5:19 house, and **l** his hand on the wall,..... 5564
Jn 21:20 also **l** on his breast at supper,........... *377*

LEANETH

2Sa 3:29 or that **l** on a staff, or that falleth...... 2388

LEANFLESHED

Ge 41:4 ill favoured and **l** kine did eat.... 1851, 1320
Ge 41:19 poor and very ill favoured and **l**,....... 7534

LEANING

Jn 13:23 there was **l** on Jesus' bosom one........ *345*
Heb 11:21 worshipped, **l** upon the top of his staff.

LEANNESS

Ps 106:15 request but sent **l** into their soul....... 7332
Isa 24:16 I said, My **l**, my **l**, woe unto me!....... 7334

LEAP

Le 11:21 feet, to **l** withal upon the earth;........ 5425
Job 41:19 lamps, and sparks of fire **l** out......... 4422

Ps	68:16	Why **l** ye, ye high hills? this is	7520
Isa	35:6	Then shall the lame man **l** as an	1801
Joel	2:5	the tops of mountains shall they **l**,	7540
Zep	1:9	all those that **l** on the threshold,	1801
Lk	6:23	**ye in that day, and l for joy:**	*4640*

LEAPED

1Ki	18:26	they **l** upon the altar which was	6452
Ps	18:29	by my God have I **l** over a wall.	1801
Lk	1:44	the babe **l** in my womb for joy	*4640*
Ac	19:16	the evil spirit was **l** on them, and	*2177*

LEAPING

2Sa	6:16	David **l** and dancing before the	6339
SS	2:8	he cometh **l** upon the mountains,	1801

LEARN

Dt	4:10	that they may **l** to fear me all the	3925
Dt	5:1	that ye may **l** them, and keep, and	3925
Ps	119:71	that I might **l** thy statutes	3925
Ps	119:73	that I may **l** thy commandments	3925
Pr	22:25	Lest thou **l** his ways, and get a	502
Isa	1:17	**L** to do well; seek judgment,	3925
Isa	2:4	neither shall they **l** war any more.	3925
Isa	29:24	that murmured shall **l** doctrine.	3925
Mic	4:3	neither shall they **l** war any more.	3925
Mt	9:13	go ye and **l** what that meaneth,	*3129*
Mt	11:29	**my yoke upon you, and l of me;**	*3129*
Mt	24:32	**Now l a parable of the fig tree;**	*3129*
1Co	14:35	And if they will **l** any thing, let	*3129*
1Ti	1:20	they may **l** not to blaspheme.	*3311*
1Ti	2:11	Let the woman **l** in silence with	*3129*
1Ti	5:4	them **l** first to shew piety at home,	*3129*
Rev	14:3	no man could **l** that song but the	*3129*

LEARNED See also UNLEARNED.

Ps	106:35	the heathen, and **l** their works	3925
Pr	30:3	I neither **l** wisdom, nor have the	3925
Isa	50:4	given me the tongue of the **l**,	3928
Eze	19:6	young lion, and **l** to catch the prey,	3925
Jn	6:45	**heard, and hath l of the Father,**	*3129*
Jn	7:15	this man letters, having never **l**?	*3129*
Ro	16:17	to the doctrine which ye have **l**;	*3129*
Eph	4:20	But ye have not so **l** Christ;	*3129*
Php	4:9	things, which ye have both **l**, and	*3129*
Php	4:11	for I have **l**, in whatsoever state I am	*3129*
2Ti	3:14	knowing of whom thou hast **l** them;	*3129*

LEARNING

Pr	9:9	just man, and he will increase in **l**	3948
Pr	16:23	his mouth, and addeth **l** to his lips.	3948
Da	1:17	them knowledge and skill in all **l**	5612
Ac	26:24	much **l** doth make thee mad.	*1121*
2Ti	3:7	Ever **l**, and never able to come to	*3129*

LEAST

Ge	32:10	I am not worthy of the **l** of all the	
Jgs	6:15	I am the **l** in my father's house.	6810
Jer	31:34	the **l** of them unto the greatest	6996
Jer	49:20	the **l** of the flock shall draw them	6810
Jnh	3:5	of them even to the **l** of them.	6996
Mt	2:6	the **l** among the princes of Juda:	*1646*
Mt	5:19	**one of these l commandments,**	*1646*
Mt	11:11	**is l in the kingdom of heaven is**	*3398*
Mt	13:32	**Which indeed is the l of all seeds:**	*3395*
Lk	9:48	**for he that is l among you all, the**	*3398*
Lk	16:10	**that is faithful in that which is l**	*1646*
Lk	16:10	**he that is unjust in the l is unjust**	*1646*
1Co	15:9	I am the **l** of the apostles, that am	*1646*
Eph	3:8	who am less than the **l** of all saints,	*1647*

LEAVE

Ge	2:24	man **l** his father and his mother,	5800
Le	23:22	thou shalt **l** them unto the poor,	5800
Ru	1:16	said, Intreat me not to **l** thee, or	5800
1Sa	20:28	asked **l** of me to go to Beth-lehem:	
2Sa	14:7	not **l** to my husband neither name	7604
2Ki	2:2	soul liveth, I will not **l** thee	5800
1Ch	28:8	**l** it for an inheritance for your	5157
Ps	16:10	thou wilt not **l** my soul in hell;	5800
Ps	27:9	**l** me not, neither forsake me, O	5203
Ps	141:8	trust; **l** not my soul destitute	6168
Pr	17:14	therefore **l** off contention, before	5203
Ecc	2:18	**l** it unto the man that shall be	3241
Isa	10:3	and where will ye **l** your glory?	5800
Jer	9:2	that I might **l** my people, and go	5800
Jer	49:11	**L** thy fatherless children, I will	5800
Eze	6:8	Yet will I **l** a remnant, that ye may	3498
Eze	23:29	and shall **l** thee naked and bare:	5800
Eze	39:2	and **l** but the sixth part of thee,	8338
Da	4:15	**l** the stump of his roots in the	7662
Joel	2:14	and **l** a blessing behind him;	7604
Am	5:7	**l** off righteousness in the earth,	3241
Mal	4:1	**l** them neither root nor branch	5800
Mt	5:24	**L there thy gift before the altar,**	*863*
Mt	18:12	**doth he not l the ninety and nine,**	*863*
Mt	19:5	**shall a man l father and mother,**	*2641*
Mk	10:7	**a man l his father and mother,**	*2641*
Mk	12:19	and **l** no children, that his brother	*863*
Lk	11:42	**and not to l the other undone.**	*863*
Lk	19:44	**shall not l in thee one stone upon**	*863*
Jn	14:18	**I will not l you comfortless: I will.**	*863*
Jn	14:27	**Peace I l with you, my peace I give.**	*863*
Jn	16:28	**I l the world, and go to the Father**	*863*
Ac	2:27	thou wilt not **l** my soul in hell.	*1459*
Ac	6:2	that we should **l** the word of God,	*2641*
1Co	7:13	dwell with her, let her not **l** him.	*863*
Eph	5:31	a man **l** his father and mother,	*2641*
Heb	13:5	I will never **l** thee, nor forsake	*447*
Rev	11:2	which is without the temple **l** out,	*1544*

LEAVEN

Ex	12:15	put away **l** out of your houses:	7603
Ex	34:25	the blood of my sacrifice with **l**;	2557
Le	10:12	eat it without **l** beside the altar:	4682
Le	23:17	they shall be baken with **l**; they	2557
Am	4:5	sacrifice of thanksgiving with **l**,	2557
Mt	13:33	**kingdom of heaven is like unto l,**	*2219*
Mt	16:6	**beware of the l of the Pharisees**	*2219*
Mk	8:15	**and of the l of Herod**	*2219*
Lk	13:21	**It is like l, which a woman took**	*2219*
1Co	5:6	little **l** leaveneth the whole lump?	*2219*
1Co	5:7	Purge out therefore the old **l**, that	*2219*
1Co	5:8	neither with the **l** of malice and	*2219*
Gal	5:9	little **l** leaveneth the whole lump	*2219*

LEAVENED See also UNLEAVENED.

Ex	12:15	whosoever eateth **l** bread from	2557
Ex	12:34	took their dough before it was **l**,	2557
Ex	13:7	shall no **l** bread be seen with thee,	2557
Ex	23:18	blood of my sacrifice with **l** bread;	2557
Dt	16:4	shall be no **l** bread seen with thee	7603
Hos	7:4	kneaded the dough, until it be **l**	2557
Mt	13:33	**of meal, till the whole was l**	*2220*

LEAVENETH

1Co 5:6 a little leaven **l** the whole lump? *2220*
Gal 5:9 A little leaven **l** the whole lump. *2220*

LEAVES

Ge 3:7 they sewed fig **l** together, and 5929
Jer 36:23 Jehudi had read three or four **l**,........ 1817
Da 4:12 The **l** thereof were fair, and the........ 6074
Da 4:21 Whose **l** were fair, and the fruit........ 6074
Mt 24:32 **yet tender, and putteth forth l,** *5444*
Mk 11:13 seeing a fig tree afar off having **l**, ... *5444*
Rev 22:2 **l** of the trees were for the healing *5444*

LEAVETH

Pr 13:22 A good man **l** an inheritance to his
Pr 28:3 like a sweeping rain which **l** no food
Zec 11:17 the idol shepherd that **l** the flock!...... 5800
Mt 4:11 Then the devil **l** him, and, behold, ... *863*
Jn 10:12 **coming, and l the sheep, and**........... *863*

LEAVING

Lk 10:30 **and departed, l him half dead.**.......... *863*
Ro 1:27 **l** the natural use of the woman, ... *863*
Heb 6:1 **l** the principles of the doctrine of....... *863*
1Pe 2:21 suffered for us, **l** us an example, ... *5277*

LED

Ge 24:27 **l** me to the house of my master's 5148
Ex 15:13 thy mercy hast **l** forth the people 5148
Dt 8:2 God **l** thee these forty years in the 3212
Dt 29:5 **l** you forty years in the wilderness:..... 3212
2Ki 6:19 seek. But he **l** them to Samaria......... 3212
Ps 68:18 high, thou hast **l** captivity captive:
Ps 78:14 also he **l** them with a cloud,........... 5148
Ps 107:7 he **l** them forth by the right way, ... 1869
Pr 4:11 I have **l** thee in right paths. 1869
Isa 9:16 that are **l** of them are destroyed......... 833
Isa 48:21 he **l** them through the deserts: 3212
Isa 55:12 joy, and be **l** forth with peace:......... 2986
Isa 63:12 **l** them by the right hand of Moses 3212
La 3:2 He hath **l** me, and brought me 5090
Eze 39:28 caused them to be **l** into captivity
Am 2:10 and **l** you forty years through the...... 3212
Mt 4:1 Then was Jesus **l** up of the spirit........ *321*
Mt 26:57 had laid hold on Jesus **l** him away....... *520*
Mt 27:2 had bound him, they **l** him away,....... *520*
Mt 27:31 him, and **l** him away to crucify him. *520*
Lk 21:24 **be l away captive into all nations:**....... *163*
Lk 23:1 of them arose, and **l** him unto Pilate...... *71*
Lk 23:26 as they **l** him away, they laid hold....... *520*
Lk 23:32 **l** with him to be put to death............ *71*
Lk 24:50 he **l** them out as far as to Bethany, ... *1806*
Jn 18:13 And **l** him away to Annas first; for *520*
Jn 18:28 Then **l** they Jesus from Caiaphas......... *71*
Jn 19:16 they took Jesus, and **l** him away *520*
Ac 8:32 was **l** as a sheep to the slaughter;......... *71*
Ro 8:14 many as are **l** by the Spirit of God,....... *71*
Gal 5:18 But if ye be **l** of the Spirit, ye are not *71*
Eph 4:8 up on high, he **l** captivity captive,....... *162*
2Ti 3:6 with sins, **l** away with divers lusts,........ *71*
2Pe 3:17 being **l** away with the error of......... *4879*

LEEKS

Nu 11:5 and the **l**, and the onions, and the 2682

LEFT

Ge 11:8 and they **l** off to build the city. 2308
Ge 18:33 had **l** communing with Abraham: 3615
Ge 24:49 turn to the right hand, or to the **l**...... 8040
Ge 32:24 And Jacob was **l** alone; and there 3498
Ge 39:6 **l** all that he had in Joseph's hand;...... 5800
Ge 39:12 he **l** his garment in her hand, and...... 5800
Ge 48:14 his **l** hand upon Manasseh's head...... 8040
Ex 34:25 passover be **l** until the morning........ 3885
Le 14:26 into the palm of his own **l** hand: 8042
Nu 20:17 to the right hand nor to the **l**,......... 8040
Nu 26:25 there was not **l** a man of them,........ 3498
Dt 2:34 every city, we **l** none to remain: 7604
Dt 17:20 to the right hand, or to the **l**:.......... 8040
Jos 8:17 there was not a man **l** in Ai or......... 7604
Jos 11:14 neither **l** they any to breathe........... 7604
Jos 11:22 There was none of the Anakims **l**...... 3498
Jgs 2:21 of the nations which Joshua **l** 5800
Jgs 3:1 are the nations which the Lord **l**, ... 3241
Jgs 4:16 sword: and there was not a man **l**...... 7604
Jgs 7:20 held the lamps in their **l** hands, ... 8040
Ru 2:11 hast **l** thy father and thy mother,....... 5800
Ru 4:14 hath not **l** thee this day without a...... 7673
1Sa 5:4 the stump of Dagon was **l** to him. 7604
1Sa 17:20 and **l** the sheep with a keeper,......... 5203
1Sa 17:28 whom hast thou **l** those few sheep 5203
2Sa 9:1 any that is **l** of the house of Saul, ... 3498
2Sa 15:16 the king **l** ten women, which were 5800
1Ki 9:20 all the people that were **l** of the........ 3498
1Ki 15:29 he **l** not to Jeroboam any that 7604
1Ki 19:10 and I, even I only, am **l**; and 3498
1Ki 19:18 Yet I have **l** me seven thousand........ 7604
2Ki 10:11 until he **l** him none remaining......... 7604
2Ki 17:16 **l** all the commandments of the........ 5800
2Ki 17:18 none **l** but the tribe of Judah only...... 7604
2Ki 19:4 prayer for the remnant that are **l** 4672
1Ch 12:2 hand and the **l** in hurling stones....... 8041
2Ch 8:8 who were **l** after them in the land, ... 3498
2Ch 18:18 on his right hand and on his **l**......... 8040
2Ch 24:18 they **l** the house of the Lord God 5800
2Ch 28:14 armed men **l** the captives and the...... 5800
2Ch 31:10 enough to eat, and have **l** plenty: 3498
2Ch 32:31 God **l** him, to try him, that he......... 5800
Ne 1:2 which were **l** of the captivity.......... 7604
Ne 1:3 remnant that are **l** of the captivity 7604
Ne 6:1 there was no breach **l** therein;......... 3498
Pr 3:16 in her **l** hand riches and honour....... 8040
Pr 4:27 not to the right hand nor to the **l**: 8040
Pr 29:15 a child **l** to himself bringeth his 7971
Ecc 10:2 hand; but a fool's heart at his **l** 8040
SS 2:6 His **l** hand is under my head, and...... 8040
Isa 1:9 the Lord of hosts had **l** unto us........ 3498
Isa 9:20 and he shall eat on the **l** hand......... 8040
Isa 10:14 as one gathereth eggs that are **l**, ... 5800
Isa 30:17 be **l** as a beacon upon the top of a 3498
Isa 30:21 hand, and when ye turn to the **l**....... 8041
Isa 37:4 prayer for the remnant that is **l**........ 4672
Isa 39:6 to Babylon: nothing shall be **l**......... 3498
Jer 12:7 house, I have **l** mine heritage; 5203
Jer 31:2 people which were **l** of the sword. 8300
Jer 38:27 they **l** off speaking with him; for....... 2790
Jer 40:6 the people that were **l** in the land...... 7604
Jer 40:11 had **l** a remnant of Judah, and 5414
Jer 44:18 **l** off to burn incense to the queen...... 2308
Eze 1:10 the face of an ox on the **l** side;......... 8040
Eze 14:22 therein shall be **l** a remnant that....... 3498
Eze 41:11 place that was **l** was five cubits 3240
Da 2:44 kingdom shall not be **l** to other 7662

Da 10:8 I was **l** alone, and saw this great 7604
Da 10:17 me, neither is there breath **l** in me 7604
Da 12:7 hand and his **l** hand unto heaven, ... 8040
Hos 4:10 **l** off to take heed to the Lord. 5800
Joel 1:4 which the palmerworm hath **l**. 3499
Joel 1:4 that which the locust hath **l** hath 3499
Joel 1:4 that which the cankerworm hath **l** 3499
Zec 13:8 but the third shall be **l** therein. 3498
Mt 4:20 they straightway **l** their nets, and *863*
Mt 6:3 **let not thy l hand know what thy** *710*
Mt 8:15 her hand, and the fever **l** her: *863*
Mt 20:23 **sit on my right hand, and on my l,** *2176*
Mt 24:2 **shall not be l here one stone upon** *863*
Mt 24:40 **shall be taken, and the other l.** *863*
Mt 25:33 **right hand, but the goats on the l.** *2176*
Mt 25:41 **say also unto them on the l hand,** *2176*
Mt 27:38 right hand, and another on the **l**. *2176*
Mk 1:20 and they **l** their father Zebedee in. *863*
Mk 8:8 meat that was **l** seven baskets. *4051*
Mk 10:29 **There is no man that hath l house,** *863*
Mk 10:40 **on my l hand is not mine to give;** *2176*
Mk 12:22 the seven had her, and **l** no seed:. *863*
Mk 13:2 **there shall not be l one stone upon** *863*
Mk 14:52 he **l** the linen cloth, and fled from *2641*
Mk 15:27 right hand, and the other on his **l**. *2176*
Lk 5:28 And he **l** all, rose up, and followed *2641*
Lk 13:35 **your house is l unto you desolate:** *863*
Lk 17:34 **be taken, and the other shall be l** *863*
Lk 18:28 Peter said, Lo, we have **l** all, and *863*
Jn 4:52 at the seventh hour the fever **l** him. *863*
Jn 8:29 **the Father hath not l me alone;** *863*
Ac 2:31 his soul was not **l** in hell, neither *2641*
Heb 2:8 **l** nothing that is not put under him. *863*
Jude 6 estate, but **l** their own habitation, ... *620*
Rev 2:4 **because thou hast l thy first love.** *863*
Rev 10:2 sea, and his **l** foot on the earth, ... *2176*

LEFTHANDED
Jgs 20:16 hundred chosen men **l**; 334, 3027, 3225

LEG
Isa 47:2 make bare the **l**, uncover the 7640

LEGION
Mk 5:9 My name is **L**: for we are many. *3003*
Mk 5:15 with the devil, and had the **l**, ... *3003*
Lk 8:30 **What is thy name? And he said, L:** *3003*

LEGIONS
Mt 26:53 **me more than twelve l of angels?** *3003*

LEGS
Le 1:9 inwards and his **l** shall he wash in 3767
Le 11:21 which have **l** above their feet, to 3767
1Sa 17:6 had greaves of brass upon his **l**, ... 7272
Ps 147:10 not pleasure in the **l** of a man. 7785
Pr 26:7 The **l** of the lame are not equal: so 7785
SS 5:15 His **l** are as pillars of marble, set. 7785
Da 2:33 His **l** of iron, his feet part of iron 8243
Am 3:12 out of the mouth of the lion two **l**,. 3767
Jn 19:33 dead already, they brake not his **l**:. *4628*

LEISURE
Mk 6:31 they had no **l** so much as to eat. *2119*

LEND
Ex 22:25 If thou **l** money to any of my 3867
Dt 15:6 thou shalt **l** unto many nations, ... 5670
Dt 15:8 shalt surely **l** him sufficient for his 5670
Dt 23:20 thou mayest **l** upon usury;. 5391
Dt 24:10 When thou dost **l** thy brother any 5383
Dt 28:44 **l** to thee, and thou shalt not **l** to 3867
Lk 6:34 **sinners also l to sinners, to receive** *1155*
Lk 6:35 **and l, hoping for nothing again;** *1155*
Lk 11:5 **him, Friend, l me three loaves;** *5531*

LENDER
Pr 22:7 the borrower is servant to the **l**. 3867
Isa 24:2 as with the **l**, so with the borrower; 3867

LENDETH
Dt 15:2 Every creditor that **l** ought unto 5383
Ps 112:5 good man sheweth favour, and **l**: 3867
Pr 119:17 pity upon the poor **l** unto the Lord;. . . . 3867

LENGTH
Ge 6:15 **l** of the ark shall be three hundred 753
Ge 13:17 walk through the land in the **l** of it. 753
Ex 25:10 cubits and a half shall be the **l**. 753
Ex 27:18 **l** of the court shall be an hundred 753
Dt 3:11 nine cubits was the **l** thereof, and 753
Jgs 3:16 which had two edges, of a cubit **l**;. 753
1Ki 6:2 the **l** thereof was threescore cubits,. 753
1Ki 7:2 the **l** thereof was an hundred cubits, ... 753
Ps 21:4 even **l** of days for ever and ever. 753
Pr 3:2 For **l** of days, and long life, and. 753
Pr 3:16 **L** of days is in her right hand; and 753
Eze 41:15 he measured the **l** of the building. 753
Eze 42:2 the **l** of an hundred cubits was the 753
Eze 48:9 be of five and twenty thousand in **l**, ... 753
Eze 48:18 the residue in **l** over against the. 753
Ro 1:10 at **l** I might have a prosperous. *4218*
Eph 3:18 what is the breadth, and **l**, and *3372*
Rev 21:16 **l** and the breadth and the height. *3372*

LENGTHEN
1Ki 3:14 did walk, then will I **l** thy days. 748
Isa 54:2 **l** thy cords, and strengthen thy 748

LENGTHENED
Dt 25:15 that thy days may be **l** in the land. 748

LENGTHENING
Da 4:27 if it may be a **l** of thy tranquillity. 754

LENT
Ex 12:36 **l** unto them such things as they 7592
Dt 23:19 of any thing that is **l** upon usury:. 5391
1Sa 1:28 also I have **l** him to the Lord; 7592
1Sa 2:20 for the loan which is **l** to the Lord. 7592

LEOPARD
Isa 11:6 the **l** shall lie down with the kid;. 5246
Jer 5:6 a **l** shall watch over their cities:. 5246
Jer 13:23 change his skin, or the **l** his spots? 5246
Da 7:6 I beheld, and to another, like a **l**,. 5245
Hos 13:7 as a **l** by the way will I observe 5246
Rev 13:2 which I saw was like unto a **l**, ... *3917*

LEOPARDS
Hab 1:8 horses also are swifter than the **l**, ... 5246

LEPER
Le 14:2 this shall be the law of the **l** in. 6879
Le 22:4 soever of the seed of Aaron is a **l** 6879
2Sa 3:29 that hath an issue, or that is a **l**, ... 6879
2Ki 5:1 man in valour, but he was a **l** 6879

2Ki 5:11 over the place, and recover the **l** 6879
2Ki 15:5 was a **l** unto the day of his death, ... 6879
2Ch 26:21 Uzziah the king was a **l** unto the 6879
Mt 8:2 there came a **l** and worshipped *3015*
Mt 26:6 in the house of Simon the **l**, ... *3015*
Mk 1:40 there came a **l**, to him, beseeching *3015*
Mk 14:3 in the house of Simon the **l**, as he *3015*

LEPERS

2Ki 7:8 these **l** came to the uttermost part *6879*
Mt 10:8 **sick, cleanse the l, raise the dead,** *3015*
Mt 11:5 **the l are cleansed, and the deaf** *3015*
Lk 4:27 **And many l were in Israel in the** *3015*
Lk 7:22 **the l are cleansed, the deaf hear,** *3015*
Lk 17:12 there met him ten men that were **l**, ... *3015*

LEPROSY

Le 13:3 skin of his flesh, it is a plague of **l**: 6883
Le 13:15 the raw flesh is unclean: it is a **l**. 6883
Le 13:25 unclean: it is the plague of **l**. 6883
Le 13:51 plague is a fretting **l**; it is unclean 6883
Le 13:59 This is the law of the plague of **l** 6883
Le 14:57 when it is clean: this is the law of **l** 6883
Dt 24:8 Take heed in the plague of **l**, that 6883
2Ki 5:3 for he would recover him of his **l** 6883
2Ki 5:27 The **l** therefore of Naaman shall 6883
2Ch 26:19 the **l** even rose up in his forehead 6883
Mt 8:3 immediately his **l** was cleansed *3014*
Lk 5:12 certain city, behold a man full of **l**: *3014*

LEPROUS

Ex 4:6 behold, his hand was **l** as snow 6879
Le 13:44 He is a **l** man, he is unclean: 6879
Nu 12:10 Miriam became **l**, white as snow: 6879
2Ki 7:3 were four **l** men at the entering in 6879
2Ch 26:20 behold, he was **l** in his forehead, ... 6879

LESS

Ex 16:17 and gathered, some more, some **l** 4591
Ex 30:15 the poor shall not give **l** than half 4591
Nu 22:18 the Lord my God, to do **l** or more 6996
Nu 26:54 thou shalt give the **l** inheritance; 4591
Nu 33:54 ye shall give the **l** inheritance: 4591
1Sa 25:36 she told him nothing, **l** or more 6996
1Ki 8:27 how much **l** this house that I have
2Ch 32:15 how much **l** shall your God deliver
Ezr 9:13 punished us **l** than our iniquities 4295
Job 9:14 How much **l** shall I answer him, and
Job 25:6 How much **l** man, that is a worm?
Pr 17:7 a fool: much **l** do lying lips a prince
Pr 19:10 much **l** for a servant to have rule over
Isa 40:17 are counted to him **l** than nothing, ... 657
Mk 4:31 **l than all the seeds that be in the** *3398*
Mk 15:40 Mary the mother of James the **l** *3398*
1Co 12:23 which we think to be **l** honourable, ... *820*
Eph 3:8 am **l** than the least of all saints, ... *1647*
Heb 7:7 the **l** is blessed of the better *1640*

LESSER

Ge 1:16 and the **l** light to rule the night: 6996
Eze 43:14 and from the **l** settle even to the 6996

LEST

Ge 3:3 neither shall ye touch it, **l** ye die 6435
Ge 4:15 **l** any finding him should kill him 1115
Ge 26:9 Because I said, **L** I die for her 6435
Ge 38:11 **L** peradventure he die also, as his 6435
Ex 1:10 **l** they multiply, and it come to pass, ... 6435
Ex 13:17 **L** peradventure the people repent 6435
Ex 20:19 let not God speak with us, **l** we die 6435
Ex 23:33 **l** they make thee sin against me: 6435
Le 10:7 of the congregation, **l** ye die: 6435
Nu 4:15 not touch any holy thing, **l** they die.
Nu 4:20 the holy things are covered, **l** they die.
Nu 16:34 **L** the earth swallow us up also 6435
Dt 4:9 **l** they depart from thy heart all the 6435
Dt 4:23 **l** ye forget the covenant of the Lord 6435
Dt 6:12 Then beware **l** thou forget the Lord, ... 6435
Dt 6:15 **l** the anger of the Lord thy God be 6435
Dt 19:6 **L** the avenger of the blood pursue 6435
Dt 20:5 **l** he die in the battle; and 6435
Dt 24:15 **l** he cry against thee unto the Lord, ... 3808
Jos 24:27 unto you, **l** ye deny your God 6435
1Sa 13:19 **L** the Hebrews make them swords 6435
2Sa 20:6 **l** he get him fenced cities, and 6435
2Ki 2:16 **l** peradventure the Spirit of the 6435
Ps 2:12 Kiss the Son, **l** he be angry, and 6435
Ps 13:3 eyes, **l** I sleep the sleep of death; 6435
Ps 91:12 **l** thou dash thy foot against a 6435
Ps 140:8 device; **l** they exalt themselves
Pr 5:6 **L** thou shouldest ponder the 6435
Pr 5:10 **L** strangers be filled with thy wealth 6435
Pr 20:13 not sleep, **l** thou come to poverty; 6435
Pr 25:17 **l** he be weary of thee, and so hate 6435
Pr 26:4 folly, **l** thou also be like unto him 6435
Pr 26:5 **l** he be wise in his own conceit 6435
Pr 30:9 **L** I be full, and deny thee, and say, ... 6435
Pr 30:9 or **l** I be poor, and steal, and take 6435
Pr 30:10 **l** he curse thee, and thou be found 6435
Pr 31:5 **L** they drink, and forget the law, ... 6435
Isa 6:10 **l** they see with their eyes, and 6435
Jer 4:4 **l** my fury come forth like fire, and 6435
Jer 6:8 **l** my soul depart from thee; 6435
Hos 2:3 **L** I strip her naked, and set her as 6435
Am 5:6 **l** he break out like fire in the house 6435
Zec 7:12 stone, **l** they should hear the law 6435
Mal 4:6 **l** I come and smite the earth with 6435
Mt 4:6 **l** at any time thou dash thy foot *3379*
Mt 5:25 **l at any time the adversary deliver** *3379*
Mt 7:6 **l they trample them under their** *3379*
Mt 15:32 **fasting, l they faint in the way** *3379*
Mt 25:9 **l there be not enough for us and** *3379*
Mt 27:64 **l** his disciples come by night, and *3379*
Mk 13:5 **Take heed l any man deceive you:** *3361*
Mk 14:38 **l ye enter into temptation** *2443, 3361*
Lk 14:8 **l a more honourable man than** *3379*
Lk 14:12 **l they also bid thee again, and a** *3379*
Lk 18:5 **l by her continual coming she** ... *2443, 3361*
Lk 21:34 **l at any time your hearts be** *3379*
Lk 22:46 **l ye enter into temptation** *2443, 3361*
Jn 12:35 **l darkness come upon you:** *2443, 3361*
Ac 28:27 **l** they should see with their eyes *3379*
Ro 11:21 take heed **l** he also spare not thee *3381*
Ro 11:25 **l** ye should be wise in your *2443, 3361*
1Co 1:17 **l** the cross of Christ should be *2443, 3361*
1Co 9:27 **l**...when I have preached to others *3381*
1Co 10:12 he standeth take heed **l** he fall *3361*
2Co 2:11 **L** Satan should get an *2443, 3361*
2Co 4:4 **l** the light of the glorious ... *1519, 3588, 3361*
Gal 6:1 thyself, **l** thou also be tempted *3361*
Eph 2:9 **l** any man should boast *2443, 3361*
Col 2:8 Beware **l** any man spoil you *3361*
Col 3:21 **l** they be discouraged *2443, 3361*

1Th 3:5 **l** by some means the tempter have *3381*
Heb 3:12 **l** there be in any of you an evil *3379*
Heb 4:11 **l** any man fall after the same *2443, 3361*
Heb 11:28 **l** he that destroyed the *2443, 3361*
Heb 12:3 **l** ye be wearied and faint in *2443, 3361*
Heb 12:15 **l** any man fail of the grace of God;..... *3361*
Jas 5:9 **l** ye be condemned: behold *2443, 3361*
2Pe 3:17 beware **l** ye also, being led *2443, 3361*
Rev 16:15 **l** he walk naked, and they see *2443, 3361*

LET
Ge 1:3 And God said, **L** there be light: and
Ge 1:6 **l** it divide the waters from the waters
Ge 1:14 **l** them be for signs, and for seasons
Ge 1:26 **L** us make man in our image, after
Ge 11:4 Go to, **l** us build us a city and a tower,
Ge 18:30 Oh **l** not the Lord be angry, and I
Ge 19:32 **l** us make our father drink wine,
Ge 32:26 I will not **l** thee go, except thou
Ex 3:19 king of Egypt will not **l** you go,........ 5414
Ex 5:1 **L** my people go, that they may
Ex 8:20 **L** my people go, that they may
Ex 9:13 **L** my people go, that they may
Ex 12:10 shall **l** nothing of it remain until the
Ex 14:5 have **l** Israel go from serving us?
Ex 22:7 the thief be found, **l** him pay double
Le 1:3 **l** him offer a male without blemish:
Dt 13:6 **L** us go and serve other gods,
Dt 24:1 **l** him write her a bill of divorcement,
Jgs 6:31 he be a god, **l** him plead for himself
1Sa 3:18 **l** him do what seemeth him good
1Ki 3:26 **L** it be neither mine nor thine, but
1Ki 18:24 that answereth by fire, **l** him be God
2Ki 1:10 **l** fire come down from heaven
Ezr 6:3 **L** the house be builded, the place
Ezr 6:11 set up, **l** him be hanged thereon;
Ne 2:18 And they said, **L** us rise up and build
Job 3:3 **L** the day perish wherein I was born,
Job 40:2 reproveth God, **l** him answer it
Ps 2:3 **L** us break their bands asunder, and
Ps 5:11 **l** all those that put their trust … rejoice:
Ps 25:2 trust in thee: **l** me not be ashamed,
Ps 25:2 **l** not mine enemies triumph over me
Ps 40:16 **l** such as love thy salvation say
Ps 67:3 **L** the people praise thee, O God;
Ps 67:5 **L** the people praise thee, O God;
Ps 69:28 **L** them be blotted out of the book of
Ps 72:19 **l** the whole earth be filled with his
Ps 95:1 **l** us make a joyful noise to the rock
Ps 95:6 **l** us kneel before the Lord our maker
Ps 99:1 Lord reigneth; **l** the people tremble:
Ps 107:2 **L** the redeemed of the Lord say so,
Ps 119:10 O **l** me not wander from thy
Ps 130:7 **L** Israel hope in the Lord: for with
Ps 137:5 **l** my right hand forget her cunning
Ps 150:6 **L** every thing that hath breath praise
Pr 3:3 **L** not mercy and truth forsake thee:
Pr 4:25 **L** thine eyes look right on, and
Pr 7:18 **l** us take our fill of love until the
Pr 23:17 **L** not thine heart envy sinners: but
Pr 27:2 **L** another man praise thee, and not
Ecc 5:2 earth: therefore **l** thy words be few
Ecc 12:13 **L** us hear the conclusion of the whole
SS 1:2 **L** him kiss me with the kisses of his
Isa 1:18 Come now, and **l** us reason together,
Isa 8:13 and **l** him be your dread
Isa 36:14 king, **L** not Hezekiah deceive you:
Isa 43:9 **l** them bring forth their witnesses,
Isa 50:10 **l** him trust in the name of the Lord,
Isa 55:7 **L** the wicked forsake his way, and
Isa 55:7 **l** him return unto the Lord, and
Jer 9:23 **L** not the wise man glory in his
Jer 9:23 **l** not the rich man glory in his riches:
Jer 14:17 **L** mine eyes run down with tears
Jer 18:18 **l** us devise devices against Jeremiah;
Jer 51:50 **l** Jerusalem come into your mind
La 2:18 **l** tears run down like a river day
La 2:18 **l** not the apple of thine eye cease
La 3:41 **L** us lift up our heart with our hands
Eze 1:24 stood, they **l** down their wings 7503
Eze 3:27 God; He that heareth, **l** him hear;
Da 1:12 **l** them give us pulse to eat, and water
Da 4:16 and **l** seven times pass over him
Hos 4:15 the harlot, yet **l** not Judah offend;
Joel 3:10 spears: **l** the weak say, I am strong
Jnh 1:14 **l** us not perish for this man's life, and
Mic 1:2 **l** the Lord God be witness against
Hab 2:20 **l** all the earth keep silence before
Zec 7:10 **l** none of you imagine evil against his
Mal 2:15 **l** none deal treacherously against the
Mt 5:16 **L** your light so shine before men, that
Mt 5:37 **l** your communication be, Yea,
Mt 5:40 thy coat, **l** him have thy cloke also
Mt 7:4 **L** me pull out the mote out of.......... *863*
Mt 8:22 me; and **l** the dead bury their dead...... *863*
Mt 11:15 He that hath ears to hear, **l** him
Mt 15:4 father or mother, **l** him die the
Mt 16:24 **l** him deny himself, and take up his
Mt 17:4 **l** us make here three tabernacles;
Mt 18:17 **l** him be unto thee as an heathen
Mt 19:6 together, **l** not man put asunder
Mt 19:12 able to receive it, **l** him receive it
Mt 20:27 among you, **l** him be your servant:
Mt 21:38 This is the heir; come, **l** us kill him,
Mt 24:16 **l** them which be in Judaea flee
Mt 26:39 be possible, **l** this cup pass from me:
Mt 27:22 all say unto him, **L** him be crucified
Mt 27:42 **l** him now come down from the cross,
Mk 4:9 He that hath ears to hear, **l** him hear
Mk 4:23 man have ears to hear, **l** him hear
Mk 7:10 father or mother, **l** him die the death:
Mk 7:27 her, **L** the children first be filled:........ *863*
Mk 14:6 And Jesus said, **L** her alone; why *863*
Mk 15:32 **L** Christ the King of Israel descend
Lk 5:4 **l** down your nets for a draught........ *5465*
Lk 6:42 **l** me pull out the mote that is in........ *863*
Lk 9:44 **L** these sayings sink down into your
Lk 15:23 kill it; and **l** us eat, and be merry:
Lk 16:29 and the prophets; **l** them hear them
Lk 22:68 ye will not answer me, nor **l** me go...... *630*
Lk 23:35 **l** him save himself, if he be Christ, the
Jn 8:7 you, **l** him first cast a stone at her
Jn 11:16 **L** us also go, that we may die with
Jn 12:7 **L** her alone: against the day of *863*
Jn 12:26 any man serve me, **l** him follow me;
Jn 14:1 **L** not your heart be troubled: ye
Jn 14:27 **L** not your heart be troubled,
Jn 18:8 ye seek me, **l** these go their way:........ *563*
Jn 19:12 If thou **l** this man go, thou art not *630*
Jn 19:24 **L** us not rend it, but cast lots for it,
Ac 1:20 **L** his habitation be desolate,

Ro	3:4	**l** God be true, but every man a liar;	
Ro	6:12	**L** not sin therefore reign in your	
Ro	12:9	**L** love be without dissimulation	
Ro	13:1	**L** every soul be subject unto the	
Ro	13:12	and **l** us put on the armour of light	
Ro	14:5	**L** every man be fully persuaded in	
1Co	1:31	that glorieth, **l** him glory in the Lord	
1Co	4:1	**L** a man so account of us, as of the	
1Co	7:2	**l** every man have his own wife, and	
1Co	7:2	**l** every woman have her own husband	
1Co	7:9	if they cannot contain, **l** them marry:	
1Co	7:11	**l** not the husband put away his wife	
1Co	7:15	the unbelieving depart, **l** him depart	
1Co	10:24	**L** no man seek his own, but every	
1Co	11:28	But **l** a man examine himself, and	
1Co	11:28	so **l** him eat of that bread, and drink	
1Co	14:40	**L** all things be done decently and in	
2Co	9:7	purposeth in his heart, so **l** him give;	
Gal	5:26	**L** us not be desirous of vain glory,	
Gal	6:9	**l** us not be weary in well doing: for	
Eph	4:26	**l** not the sun go down upon your	
Eph	4:28	**L** him that stole steal no more: but	
Php	2:5	**L** this mind be in you, which was also	
Php	4:5	**L** your moderation be known unto all	
Col	3:15	**l** the peace of God rule in your hearts,	
Col	3:16	**L** the word of Christ dwell in you	
Col	4:6	**L** your speech be alway with grace,	
1Ti	4:12	**L** no man despise thy youth; but be	
1Ti	5:17	**L** the elders that rule well be counted	
Heb	4:14	of God, **l** us hold fast our profession	
Heb	4:16	**L** us therefore come boldly unto the	
Heb	10:22	**L** us draw near with a true heart in	
Heb	12:1	**l** us lay aside every weight, and the	
Heb	12:1	**l** us run with patience the race that is	
Jas	1:4	But **l** patience have her perfect work,	
Jas	1:5	you lack wisdom, **l** him ask of God,	
Jas	5:12	**l** your yea be yea; and your nay, nay;	
Jas	5:14	**l** them pray over him, anointing him	
1Pe	4:11	**l** him seek peace, and ensue it	
1Jn	3:7	Little children, **l** no man deceive you:	
1Jn	3:18	little children, **l** us not love in word,	
1Jn	4:7	**L** us love one another for love is of	
Rev	2:7	**l him hear what the Spirit**	
Rev	13:9	If any man have an ear, **l** him hear	
Rev	19:7	**L** us be glad and rejoice, and give	
Rev	22:11	he which is filthy, **l** him be filthy still:	
Rev	22:11	is righteous, **l** him be righteous still:	
Rev	22:17	**l** him take the water of life freely.	

LETTER

2Sa	11:14	David wrote a **l** to Joab, and sent	5612
2Ki	19:14	And Hezekiah received the **l** of the	5612
Ezr	4:8	a **l** against Jerusalem to Artaxerxes	104
Ezr	7:11	this is the copy of the **l** that the king	5406
Ne	2:8	And a **l** unto Asaph the keeper of	107
Est	9:29	to confirm this second **l** of Purim	107
Jer	29:1	words of the **l** that Jeremiah the	5612
Jer	29:29	the priest read this **l** in the ears of	5612
Ac	23:25	he wrote a **l** after this manner:	*1992*
Ro	2:27	who by the **l** and circumcision	*1121*
Ro	2:29	heart, in the spirit, and not in the **l**;	*1121*
2Co	3:6	not of the **l**, but of the spirit:	*1121*
2Co	3:6	the **l** killeth, but the spirit giveth	*1121*
2Co	7:8	though I made you sorry with a **l**,	*1992*
Gal	6:11	Ye see how large a **l** I have	*1121*
Heb	13:22	I have written a **l** unto you in few	*1989*

LETTERS

1Ki	21:8	So she wrote **l** in Ahab's name	5612
2Ch	30:6	posts went with the **l** from the king	107
2Ch	32:17	He wrote also **l** to rail on the Lord	5612
Ne	6:19	And Tobiah sent **l** to put me in fear	107
Est	9:20	Mordecai...sent **l** unto all the Jews	5612
Est	9:30	And he sent the **l** unto all the Jews,	5612
Lk	23:38	written over him in **l** of Greek	*1121*
Jn	7:15	How knoweth this man **l**, having	*1121*
Ac	9:2	And desired of him **l** to Damascus	*1992*
1Co	16:3	whomsoever … approve by your **l**	*1992*
2Co	3:1	you, or **l** of commendation from you?	
2Co	10:10	For his **l**, say they, are weighty	*1992*

LETTETH

2Ki	10:24	he that **l** him go, his life shall be for	
2Th	2:7	only he who now **l** will let, until	*2722*

LEVITE (le´-vite)

Dt	12:19	forsake not the **L** as long as thou	3881
Dt	14:29	the **L**, (because he hath no part	3881
Dt	18:6	if a **L** come from any of thy gates	3881
Dt	26:12	and hast given it unto the **L**,	3881
Jgs	17:13	seeing I have a **L** to my priest	3881
Jgs	18:3	the voice of the young man the **L**	3881
Jgs	20:4	the **L**, the husband of the woman	3881
Lk	10:31	**likewise a L, when he was at the**	*3019*
Ac	4:36	The son of consolation,) a **L**, and	*3019*

LEVITES (le´-vites)

Ex	6:25	the heads of the fathers of the **L**	3881
Nu	1:50	appoint the **L** over the tabernacle	3881
Nu	3:45	the **L** instead of all the firstborn	3881
Nu	3:45	the **L** shall be mine: I am the Lord	3881
Nu	8:12	to make an atonement for the **L**	3881
Nu	8:19	have given the **L** as a gift to Aaron	3881
Nu	18:24	I have given to the **L** to inherit:	3881
Nu	35:7	cities which ye shall give to the **L**	3881
1Sa	6:15	**L** took down the ark of the Lord,	3881
1Ch	15:2	carry the ark of God but the **L**	3881
2Ch	5:12	Also the **L** which were the singers,	3881
2Ch	24:11	king's office by the hand of the **L**	3881
2Ch	29:34	the **L** were more upright in heart	3881
2Ch	30:17	the **L** had the charge of the killing	3881
Ezr	3:8	appointed the **L**, from twenty years	3881
Ne	8:9	and the **L** that taught the people	3881
Ne	9:38	princes, **L**, and priests, seal unto it	3881
Ne	10:37	tithes of our ground unto the **L**,	3881
Ne	11:18	All the **L** in the holy city were two	3881
Ne	12:47	sanctified holy things unto the **L**;	3881
Ne	13:10	portions of the **L** had not been given	3881
Eze	44:10	**L** that are gone far away from me,	3881
Jn	1:19	when the Jews sent priests and **L**	*3019*

LEVY

Nu	31:28	And **l** a tribute unto the Lord of	7311
1Ki	5:13	king Solomon raised a **l** out of all	4522
1Ki	9:15	the **l** which king Solomon raised;	4522
1Ki	9:21	upon those did Solomon **l** a tribute	5927

LEWD

Eze	16:27	which are ashamed of thy **l** way	2154
Eze	23:44	and unto Aholibah, the **l** women	2154
Ac	17:5	certain **l** fellows of the baser sort	*4190*

LEWDLY

Eze	22:11	hath **l** defiled his daughter in law;	2154

LEWDNESS

Jgs	20:6	committed **l** and folly in Israel	2154
Jer	11:15	she hath wrought **l** with many	4209
Jer	13:27	neighings, the **l** of thy whoredom,	2154
Eze	16:43	shalt not commit this **l** above all	2154
Hos	2:10	And now will I discover her **l** in	5040
Hos	6:9	by consent: for they commit **l**	2154
Ac	18:14	a matter of wrong or wicked **l**,	*4467*

LIAR

Job	24:25	who will make me a **l**, and make my	3576
Pr	17:4	a **l** giveth ear to a naughty tongue	8267
Pr	19:22	a poor man is better than a **l**.	376, 3576
Pr	30:6	thee, and thou be found a **l**.	376, 3576
Jer	15:18	thou be altogether unto me as a **l**,	391
Jn	8:44	**for he is a l, and the father of it**	*5583*
Jn	8:55	**him not, I shall be a l like unto**	*5583*
Ro	3:4	let God be true, but every man a **l**;	*5583*
1Jn	1:10	have not sinned, we make him a **l**,	*5583*
1Jn	2:22	Who is a **l** but he that denieth that	*5583*
1Jn	4:20	and hateth his brother, he is a **l**.	*5583*
1Jn	5:10	not God hath made him a **l**;	*5583*

LIARS

Dt	33:29	enemies shall be found **l** unto thee;	3584
Ps	116:11	I said in my haste, All men are **l**	3576
Isa	44:25	frustrated the tokens of the **l**, and	907
Jer	50:36	A sword is upon the **l**; and they	907
1Ti	1:10	for **l**, for perjured persons, and if	*5583*
Tit	1:12	said, The Cretians are alway **l**	*5583*
Rev	2:2	**are not, and hast found them l**	*5571*
Rev	21:8	sorcerers, and idolaters, and all **l**,	*5571*

LIBERAL

Pr	11:25	The **l** soul shall be made fat: and	1293
Isa	32:8	But the **l** deviseth **l** things; and	5081

LIBERALITY

2Co	8:2	abounded unto the riches of their **l**	*572*

LIBERALLY

Dt	15:14	furnish him **l** out of thy flock	6059
Jas	1:5	ask of God, that giveth to all men **l**,	*574*

LIBERTY

Le	25:10	proclaim **l** throughout all the land	1865
Ps	119:45	And I will walk at **l**: for I seek thy	7342
Isa	61:1	to proclaim **l** to the captives, and	1865
Jer	34:16	he had set at **l** at their pleasure,	2670
Jer	34:17	behold, I proclaim a **l** for you, saith	1865
Eze	46:17	then it shall be his to the year of **l**;	1865
Lk	4:18	**to set at l them that are bruised,**	*859*
Ac	26:32	This man might have been set at **l**,	*630*
1Co	7:39	she is at **l** to be married to whom	*1658*
1Co	8:9	any means this **l** of yours become	*1849*
2Co	3:17	the Spirit of the Lord is, there is **l**	*1657*
Gal	2:4	to spy out our **l** which we have in	*1657*
Gal	5:1	the **l** wherewith Christ hath made	*1657*
Gal	5:13	only use not **l** for an occasion to	*1657*
Jas	1:25	looketh into the perfect law of **l**,	*1657*
1Pe	2:16	and not using your **l** for a cloke of	*1657*
2Pe	2:19	While they promise them **l**, they	*1657*

LICE

Ex	8:17	all the dust of the land became **l**.	3654
Ex	8:18	enchantments to bring forth **l**.	3654
Ps	105:31	of flies, and **l** in all their coasts,	3654

LICENCE

Ac	21:40	when he had given him **l**, Paul	*2010*
Ac	25:16	and have **l** to answer for himself	*5117*

LICK

Nu	22:4	Now shall this company **l** up all	3897
1Ki	21:19	of Naboth shall dogs **l** thy blood.	3952
Ps	72:9	and his enemies shall **l** the dust	3897
Mic	7:17	They shall **l** the dust like a serpent,	3897

LICKED

1Ki	18:38	**l** up the water that was in the	3897
1Ki	21:19	where dogs **l** the blood of Naboth	3952
1Ki	22:38	and the dogs **l** up his blood;	3952
Lk	16:21	**the dogs came and l his sores.**	*621*

LIE

Ge	19:32	we will **l** with him, that we may	7901
Ge	39:7	Joseph; and she said, **L** with me	7901
Ex	21:13	if a man **l** not in wait, but God	6658
Ex	23:11	thou shalt let it rest and **l** still;	5203
Le	18:22	Thou shalt not **l** with mankind,	7901
Le	20:18	if a man shall **l** with a woman	7901
Nu	5:13	And a man **l** with her carnally,	7901
Nu	23:24	not **l** down until he eat of the prey,	7901
Dt	22:25	the man force her, and **l** with her:	7901
Dt	25:2	judge shall cause him to **l** down,	5307
Dt	29:20	written in this book shall **l** upon	7257
Ru	3:13	liveth: **l** down until the morning	7901
1Sa	3:9	Eli said unto Samuel, Go, **l** down:	7901
1Sa	22:8	me, to **l** in wait, as at this day?	
1Ki	1:2	him, and let her **l** in thy bosom	7901
2Ki	4:16	do not **l** unto thine handmaid	3576
Ps	23:2	me to **l** down in green pastures:	7257
Ps	62:9	and men of high degree are a **l**:	3576
Pr	12:6	wicked are to **l** in wait for blood:	
Pr	14:5	A faithful witness will not **l**: but	3576
Ecc	4:11	if two **l** together, then they have	7901
Isa	14:30	the needy shall **l** down in safety:	7257
Isa	44:20	Is there not a **l** in my right hand?	3576
Isa	51:20	they **l** at the head of all the streets,	7901
Isa	63:8	people, children that will not **l**	8266
Jer	27:14	for they prophesy a **l** unto you	8267
Jer	28:15	makest this people to trust in a **l**.	8267
Jer	29:21	prophesy a **l** unto you in my name;	8267
Jer	29:31	and he caused you to trust in a **l**:	8267
La	2:21	young and the old **l** on the ground	7901
Eze	4:4	**L** thou also upon thy left side	7901
Eze	4:6	**l** again on thy right side, and thou	7901
Eze	32:28	Shalt **l** with them that are slain	7901
Eze	34:15	I will cause them to **l** down, saith	7257
Hos	7:6	like an oven, whiles they **l** in wait:	
Joel	1:13	**l** all night in sackcloth, ... ministers	3885
Am	6:4	That **l** upon beds of ivory, and	7901
Mic	2:11	in the spirit and falsehood do **l**,	3576
Hab	2:3	the end it shall speak, and not **l**	3576
Zep	2:15	a place for beasts to **l** down in!	4769
Zep	3:13	for they shall feed and **l** down	7257
Zec	10:2	and the diviners have seen a **l**,	8267
Jn	8:44	**When he speaketh a l, he**	*5579*
Jn	20:6	and seeth the linen clothes **l**,	*2749*
Ac	5:3	hath Satan filled thine heart to **l**	*5574*
Ro	1:25	changed the truth of God into a **l**,	*5579*
Ro	9:1	I say the truth in Christ, I **l** not,	*5574*
Eph	4:14	whereby they **l** in wait to deceive;	*3180*
Col	3:9	**L** not one to another, seeing that	*5574*
2Th	2:11	that they should believe a **l**	*5579*

Tit	1:2	life, which God, that cannot **l**,	*893*
Heb	6:18	it was impossible for God to **l**,	*5574*
Jas	3:14	not, and **l** not against the truth	*5574*
1Jn	1:6	darkness, we **l**, and do not the truth:	*5574*
1Jn	2:21	it, and that no **l** is of the truth	*5579*
1Jn	2:27	and is truth, and is no **l**, and even	*5579*
Rev	3:9	**are Jews, and are not, but do l;**	*5574*
Rev	11:8	dead bodies shall **l** in the street of	
Rev	22:15	whosoever loveth and maketh a **l**	*5579*

LIED

1Ki	13:18	drink water. But he **l** unto him	3584
Ps	78:36	**l** unto him with their tongues	3576
Isa	57:11	or feared, that thou hast **l**, and	3576
Ac	5:4	thou hast not **l** unto men, but unto	*5574*

LIERS

Jos	8:14	were **l** in ambush against him	
Jgs	9:25	men of Shechem set **l** in wait for him	
Jgs	16:12	**l** in wait abiding in the chamber	
Jgs	20:38	the men of Israel and the **l** in wait	

LIES

Jgs	16:13	hast mocked me, and told me **l**	3576
Job	13:4	But ye are forgers of **l**, ye are all	8267
Ps	40:4	proud, nor such as turn aside to **l**	3576
Ps	58:3	soon as they be born, speaking **l**	3576
Ps	63:11	them that speak **l** shall be stopped	8267
Ps	101:7	telleth **l** shall not tarry in my sight	8267
Pr	14:5	lie: but a false witness will utter **l**,	3576
Pr	14:25	but a deceitful witness speaketh **l**	3576
Pr	19:5	he that speaketh **l** shall not escape	3576
Pr	29:12	If a ruler hearken to **l**, all his	1697, 8267
Pr	30:8	far from me vanity and **l**:	3576
Isa	9:15	the prophet that teacheth **l**, he is	8267
Isa	28:17	shall sweep away the refuge of **l**,	3576
Isa	59:4	they trust in vanity, and speak **l**;	7723
Jer	9:3	their tongue like their bow for **l**,	8267
Jer	14:14	prophets prophesy **l** in my name:	8267
Jer	16:19	Surely our fathers have inherited **l**	8267
Jer	23:14	commit adultery, and walk in **l**	8267
Jer	23:25	said, that prophesy **l** in my name	8267
Jer	23:32	cause my people to err by their **l**,	8267
Jer	48:30	be so; his **l** shall not so effect it	907
Eze	13:9	that see vanity, and that divine **l**	3576
Eze	13:19	to my people that hear your **l**?	3576
Eze	22:28	vanity, and divining **l** unto them,	3576
Eze	24:12	She hath wearied herself with **l**,	8383
Da	11:27	they shall speak **l** at one table;	3576
Hos	10:13	ye have eaten the fruit of **l**	3585
Hos	12:1	daily increaseth **l** and desolation;	3576
Am	2:4	and their **l** caused them to err,	3576
Mic	6:12	inhabitants thereof have spoken **l**,	8267
Hab	2:18	molten image, and a teacher of **l**,	8267
Zep	3:13	shall not do iniquity, nor speak **l**;	3576
Zec	13:3	speakest **l** in the name of the Lord:	8267
1Ti	4:2	Speaking **l** in hypocrisy; having	*5573*

LIEST

Ge	28:13	land whereon thou **l**, to thee will	7901
Dt	6:7	when thou **l** down, and when thou	7901
Pr	3:24	When thou **l** down, thou shalt not	7901

LIETH

Ge	4:7	doest not well, sin **l** at the door	7257
Ex	22:19	Whosoever **l** with a beast shall	7901
Le	19:20	whosoever **l** carnally with a woman,	7901
Le	20:13	mankind, as he **l** with a woman,	4904
Le	26:34	her sabbaths, as long as it **l** desolate,	
Dt	27:21	that **l** with any manner of beast	7901
Jgs	16:15	told me wherein thy great strength **l**,	
Ru	3:4	when he **l** down, that thou shalt	7901
Ne	2:17	Jerusalem **l** waste, and the gates	
Job	14:12	So man **l** down, and riseth not;	7901
Ps	10:9	**l** in wait secretly as a lion in his	
Ps	41:8	now that he **l** he shall rise up no	7901
Ps	88:7	Thy wrath **l** hard upon me, and	5564
Pr	23:28	She also **l** in wait as for a prey,	
Pr	23:34	as he that **l** upon the top of a mast	7901
Eze	29:3	great dragon that **l** in the midst	6437
Mic	7:5	from her that **l** in thy bosom	7901
Mt	8:6	my servant **l** at home sick of the	*906*
Mk	5:23	daughter **l** at the point of death:	*2192*
Ro	12:18	as much as **l** in you, live peaceably	
1Jn	5:19	the whole world **l** in wickedness	*2749*
Rev	21:16	And the city **l** foursquare, and the	*2749*

LIFE

Ge	1:20	moving creature that hath **l**,	2416
Ge	1:30	the earth, wherein there is **l**,	2416
Ge	2:7	into his nostrils the breath of **l**;	2416
Ge	2:9	the tree of **l** also in the midst of	2416
Ge	3:14	shalt thou eat all the days of thy **l**	2416
Ge	3:22	take also of the tree of **l**, and eat	2416
Ge	3:24	to keep the way of the tree of **l**	2416
Ge	6:17	flesh, wherein is the breath of **l**,	2416
Ge	7:22	whose nostrils was the breath of **l**,	2416
Ge	9:4	But flesh with the **l** thereof, which	5315
Ge	9:5	brother will I require the **l** of man	5315
Ge	18:14	thee, according to the time of **l**,	2416
Ge	19:17	Escape for thy **l**; look not behind	5315
Ge	32:30	face to face, and my **l** is preserved	5315
Ge	44:30	his **l** is bound up in the lad's **l**;	5315
Ge	45:5	did send me before you to preserve **l**	
Ge	47:9	days of the years of my **l** been	2416
Ex	4:19	men are dead which sought thy **l**	5315
Ex	21:23	then thou shalt give **l** for **l**,	5315
Le	17:11	the **l** of the flesh is in the blood:	5315
Nu	35:31	satisfaction for the **l** of a murderer	5315
Dt	4:9	thy heart all the days of thy **l**	2416
Dt	12:23	mayest not eat the **l** with the flesh	5315
Dt	17:19	read therein all the days of his **l**	2416
Dt	19:21	**l** shall go for **l**, eye for eye, tooth	5315
Dt	24:6	for he taketh a man's **l** to pledge	5315
Dt	30:15	set before thee this day **l** and good,	2416
Dt	30:19	I have set before you **l** and death	2416
Dt	30:20	for he is thy **l**, and the length of	2416
Jos	2:14	Our **l** for yours, if ye utter not	5315
Jos	4:14	feared Moses, all the days of his **l**	2416
Jgs	16:30	than they which he slew in his **l**	2416
Ru	4:15	be unto thee a restorer of thy **l**,	5315
1Sa	1:11	unto the Lord all the days of his **l**,	2416
1Sa	18:18	and what is my **l**, or my father's	2416
1Sa	20:1	thy father, that he seeketh my **l**?	5315
1Sa	28:21	and I have put my **l** in my hand	5315
2Sa	1:9	because my **l** is yet whole in me	5315
1Ki	3:11	hast not asked for thyself long **l**;	3117
1Ki	19:2	if I make not thy **l** as the **l** of one	5315
1Ki	19:4	now, O Lord, take away my **l**; for	5315
1Ki	20:42	therefore thy **l** shall go for his **l**,	5315
2Ki	1:14	my **l** now be precious in thy sight	5315
2Ki	8:5	her son, whom Elisha restored to **l**	2421
2Ch	1:11	neither yet hast asked long **l**; but	3117

Ezr	6:10	and pray for the **l** of the king, and	2417
Ne	6:11	go into the temple to save his **l**?	2425
Est	7:7	stood up to make request for his **l**	5315
Job	2:4	a man hath will he give for his **l**	5315
Job	2:6	he is in thine hand; but save his **l**	5315
Job	10:1	My soul is weary of my **l**; I will	2416
Job	33:4	of the Almighty hath given me **l**	2421
Ps	16:11	Thou wilt shew me the path of **l**	2416
Ps	23:6	shall follow me all the days of my **l**	2416
Ps	27:1	the Lord is the strength of my **l**;	2416
Ps	34:12	What man is he that desireth **l**,	2416
Ps	36:9	For with thee is the fountain of **l**	2416
Ps	63:3	lovingkindness is better than **l**,	2416
Ps	91:16	With long **l** will I satisfy him, and	3117
Ps	103:4	redeemeth thy **l** from destruction;	2416
Pr	1:19	taketh away the **l** of the owners	5315
Pr	2:19	take they hold of the paths of **l**	2416
Pr	3:2	For length of days, and long **l**,	2416
Pr	3:18	She is a tree of **l** to them that lay	2416
Pr	3:22	So shall they be **l** unto thy soul,	2416
Pr	4:13	not go: keep her; for she is thy **l**	2416
Pr	4:22	are **l** unto those that find them,	2416
Pr	4:23	for out of it are the issues of **l**	2416
Pr	6:23	of instruction are the way of **l**	2416
Pr	6:26	will hunt for the precious **l**	5315
Pr	8:35	For whoso findeth me findeth **l**,	2416
Pr	9:11	years of thy **l** shall be increased	2416
Pr	10:16	of the righteous tendeth to **l**	2416
Pr	10:17	He is in the way of **l** that keepeth	2416
Pr	11:30	fruit of the righteous is a tree of **l**;	2416
Pr	12:10	man regardeth the **l** of his beast:	5315
Pr	13:3	keepeth his mouth keepeth his **l**	5315
Pr	13:12	desire cometh, it is a tree of **l**	2416
Pr	13:14	law of the wise is a fountain of **l**	2416
Pr	14:27	fear of the Lord is a fountain of **l**,	2416
Pr	15:4	A wholesome tongue is a tree of **l**	2416
Pr	15:24	The way of **l** is above to the wise	2416
Pr	15:31	ear that heareth the reproof of **l**	2416
Pr	18:21	Death and **l** are in the power of the	2416
Pr	22:4	Lord are riches, and honour, and **l**	2416
Pr	31:12	and not evil all the days of her **l**	2416
Ecc	2:3	the heaven all the days of their **l**	2416
Ecc	3:12	to rejoice, and to do good in his **l**	2416
Ecc	5:18	under the sun all the days of his **l**	2416
Ecc	5:20	much remember the days of his **l**;	2416
Ecc	6:12	days of his vain **l** which he spendeth	2416
Ecc	8:15	him of his labour the days of his **l**,	2416
Ecc	9:9	whom thou lovest all the days of the **l**	2416
Isa	38:12	I have cut off like a weaver my **l**	2416
Isa	38:16	these things is the **l** of my spirit:	2416
Jer	8:3	death shall be chosen rather than **l**	2416
Jer	21:8	I set before you the way of **l**, and	2416
Jer	38:2	he shall have his **l** for a prey, and	5315
Jer	38:16	hand of these men that seek thy **l**	5315
Jer	45:5	thy **l** will I give unto thee for a prey	5315
La	2:19	for the **l** of thy young children,	5315
La	3:53	have cut off my **l** in the dungeon,	2416
Eze	13:22	wicked way, by promising him **l**:	2421
Eze	33:15	robbed, walk in the statutes of **l**,	2416
Da	12:2	awake, some to everlasting **l**	2416
Jnh	1:14	let us not perish for this man's **l**	5315
Jnh	4:3	take, I beseech thee, my **l** from me;	5315
Mal	2:5	My covenant was with him **l**	2416
Mt	2:20	which sought the young child's **l**	*5590*
Mt	6:25	**Take no thought for your l, what**	*5590*
Mt	10:39	**He that findeth his l shall lose it:**	*5690*
Mt	16:25	**will lose his l for my sake shall**	*5590*
Mt	19:16	I do, that I may have eternal **l**?	*2222*
Mt	19:29	**and shall inherit everlasting l**	*2222*
Mt	20:28	**to give his l a ransom for many**	*5590*
Mt	25:46	**but the righteous into l, eternal**	*2222*
Mk	3:4	**or to do evil? to save l, or to kill?**	*5590*
Mk	8:35	**will save his l shall lose it;**	*5590*
Mk	9:43	**for thee to enter into l maimed,**	*2222*
Mk	10:30	**in the world to come eternal l**	*2222*
Mk	10:45	**to give his l a ransom for many**	*5590*
Lk	6:9	**evil? to save l, or to destroy it?**	*5590*
Lk	9:24	**will save his l shall lose it:**	*5590*
Lk	12:22	**Take no thought for your l, what**	*5590*
Lk	17:33	**seek to save his l shall lose it;**	*5590*
Lk	17:33	**shall lose his l shall preserve it**	*5590*
Lk	18:30	**in the world to come l, everlasting**	*2222*
Lk	21:34	**drunkenness, and cares of this l,**	*982*
Jn	1:4	In him was **l**; and the **l** was the	*2222*
Jn	3:15	**not perish, but have eternal l**	*2222*
Jn	3:16	**not perish, but have everlasting l**	*2222*
Jn	3:36	on the Son hath everlasting **l**	*2222*
Jn	4:14	**springing up into everlasting l**	*2222*
Jn	4:36	**gathereth fruit unto l eternal:**	*2222*
Jn	5:24	**that sent me, hath everlasting l**	*2222*
Jn	5:24	**but is passed from death unto l**	*2222*
Jn	5:26	**to the Son to have l in himself:**	*2222*
Jn	5:29	**good, unto the resurrection of l;**	*2222*
Jn	5:40	**come to me, that ye might have l**	*2222*
Jn	6:27	**which endureth unto everlasting l,**	*2222*
Jn	6:35	unto them, **I am the bread of l**	*2222*
Jn	6:47	**believeth on me hath everlasting l**	*2222*
Jn	6:48	**I am that bread of l**	*2222*
Jn	6:53	**his blood, ye have no l in you**	*2222*
Jn	6:54	**drinketh my blood, hath eternal l;**	*2222*
Jn	6:68	thou hast the words of eternal **l**	*2222*
Jn	8:12	**but shall have the light of l**	*2222*
Jn	10:10	**I am come that they might have l,**	*2222*
Jn	10:11	**shepherd giveth his l for the sheep**	*5590*
Jn	10:15	**and I lay down my l for the sheep**	*5590*
Jn	10:28	**I give unto them eternal l; and**	*2222*
Jn	11:25	**I am the resurrection, and the l**	*2222*
Jn	12:25	**He that loveth his l shall lose it;**	*5590*
Jn	13:37	I will lay down my **l** for thy sake	*5590*
Jn	13:38	**thou lay down thy l for my sake?**	*5590*
Jn	14:6	**am the way, the truth, and the l**	*2222*
Jn	15:13	**man lay down his l for his friends**	*5590*
Jn	17:3	**this is l eternal, that they might**	*2222*
Jn	20:31	ye might have **l** through his name	*2222*
Ac	3:15	And killed the Prince of **l**, whom	*2222*
Ac	11:18	Gentiles granted repentance unto **l**	*2222*
Ac	13:46	unworthy of everlasting **l**, lo, we	*2222*
Ac	20:10	not yourselves; for his **l** is in him	*5590*
Ac	20:24	count I my **l** dear unto myself,	*5590*
Ro	2:7	honour and immortality, eternal **l**	*2222*
Ro	5:10	we shall be saved by his **l**	*2222*
Ro	6:4	also should walk in newness of **l**	*2222*
Ro	6:23	but the gift of God is eternal **l**	*2222*
Ro	8:6	to be spiritually minded is **l** and	*2222*
Ro	8:10	Spirit is **l** because of righteousness	*2222*
Ro	8:38	neither death, nor **l**, nor angels	*2222*
Ro	11:3	am left alone, and they seek my **l**	*5590*
1Co	3:22	or **l**, or death, or things present,	*2222*
1Co	14:7	even things without **l** giving sound	*895*
1Co	15:19	If in this **l** only we have hope in	*2222*

2Co	1:8	that we despaired even of **l**;	*2198*
2Co	3:6	killeth, but the spirit giveth **l**	*2227*
2Co	4:10	the **l** also of Jesus might be	*2222*
2Co	4:12	death worketh in us, but **l** in you.	*2222*
Gal	2:20	and the **l** which I now live in the flesh	
Gal	6:8	of the Spirit reap **l** everlasting	*2222*
Eph	4:18	being alienated from the **l** of God.	*2222*
Php	1:20	in my body, whether it be by **l**, or	*2222*
Php	2:16	Holding forth the word of **l**; that	*2222*
Php	4:3	whose names are in the book of **l**	*2222*
Col	3:3	your **l** is hid with Christ in God.	*2222*
Col	3:4	When Christ, who is our **l**, shall	*2222*
1Ti	2:2	lead a quiet and peaceable **l** in all	*979*
1Ti	4:8	promise of the **l** that now is, and	*2222*
1Ti	6:19	that they may lay hold on eternal **l**	*2222*
2Ti	1:1	promise of **l** which is in Christ	*2222*
2Ti	2:4	himself with the affairs of this **l**;	*979*
Tit	3:7	according to the hope of eternal **l**	*2222*
Heb	7:3	beginning of days, nor end of **l**;	*2222*
Heb	11:35	received their dead raised to **l** again:	
Jas	1:12	he shall receive the crown of **l**	*2222*
2Pe	1:3	that pertain unto **l** and godliness,	*2222*
1Jn	1:1	have handled, of the Word of **l**;	*2222*
1Jn	2:16	lust of the eyes, and the pride of **l**,	*979*
1Jn	3:14	we have passed from death unto **l**,	*2222*
1Jn	5:11	God hath given to us eternal **l**	*2222*
1Jn	5:11	and this **l** is in his Son.	*2222*
1Jn	5:12	He that hath the Son hath **l**;	*2222*
1Jn	5:12	hath not the Son of God hath not **l**	*2222*
1Jn	5:20	This is the true God, and eternal **l**	*2222*
Jude	21	Lord Jesus Christ unto eternal **l**	*2222*
Rev	2:7	**will I give to eat of the tree of l,**	*2222*
Rev	2:10	**and I will give thee a crown of l,**	*2222*
Rev	3:5	**out his name out of the book of l,**	*2222*
Rev	8:9	were in the sea, and had **l**, died;	*5590*
Rev	13:8	are not written in the book of **l**	*2222*
Rev	17:8	were not written in the book of **l**	*2222*
Rev	20:12	was opened, which is the book of **l**	*2222*
Rev	20:15	not found written in the book of **l**	*2222*
Rev	21:6	fountain of the water of **l** freely.	*2222*
Rev	21:27	written in the Lamb's book of **l**	*2222*
Rev	22:2	was there the tree of **l**, which bare	*2222*
Rev	22:14	may have right to the tree of **l**	*2222*
Rev	22:19	away his part out of the book of **l**,	*2222*

LIFETIME

2Sa	18:18	Absalom in his **l** had taken and	2416
Lk	16:25	**thou in thy l receivedst thy good**	*2222*
Heb	2:15	all their **l** subject to bondage	*2198*

LIFT

Ge	13:14	**L** up now thine eyes, and look	5375
Ge	21:18	Arise, **l** up the lad, and hold him in	5375
Ex	14:16	**l** thou up thy rod, and stretch out	7311
Nu	6:26	The Lord **l** up his countenance	5375
Dt	4:19	And lest thou **l** up thine eyes unto	5375
Dt	27:5	not **l** up any iron tool upon them.	5130
Dt	32:40	For I **l** up my hand to heaven, and	5375
2Sa	23:8	**l** up his spear against eight hundred,	
Ezr	9:6	and blush to **l** up my face to thee,	7311
Job	38:34	Canst thou **l** up thy voice to the	7311
Ps	24:7	**L** up your heads, O ye gates;	5375
Ps	24:7	be ye **l** up, ye everlasting doors;	5375
Ps	24:9	**L** up your heads, O ye gates; even	5375
Ps	63:4	I will **l** up my hands in thy name.	5375
Ps	86:4	thee, O Lord, do I **l** up my soul.	5375
Ps	93:3	voice; the floods **l** up their waves.	5375
Ps	119:48	My hands also will I **l** up unto thy	5375
Ps	121:1	I will **l** up mine eyes unto the hills,	5375
Ecc	4:10	fall, the one will **l** up his fellow:	6965
Isa	2:4	nation shall not **l** up sword against	5375
Isa	5:26	he will **l** up an ensign to the nations	5375
Isa	13:2	**L** ye up a banner upon the high	5375
Isa	40:9	**l** up thy voice with strength;	7311
Isa	40:26	**L** up your eyes on high, and	5375
Isa	49:22	will **l** up mine hand to the Gentiles,	5375
Isa	58:1	**l** up thy voice like a trumpet, and	7311
Isa	59:19	the Lord shall **l** up a standard	5127
Jer	7:16	neither **l** up cry nor prayer for	5375
La	3:41	Let us **l** up our heart with our hands	5375
Eze	11:22	did the cherubims **l** up their wings,	5375
Eze	17:14	be base, that it might not **l** itself up,	5375
Eze	33:25	**l** up your eyes toward your idols,	5375
Zec	5:5	**L** up now thine eyes, and see what	5375
Mt	12:11	**he not lay hold on it, and l it out?**	*1458*
Lk	16:23	**in hell he l up his eyes, and in**	*1869*
Lk	21:28	**then look up, and l up your heads;**	*1869*
Heb	12:12	**l** up the hands which hang down,	*461*
Jas	4:10	of the Lord, and he shall **l** you up	*5322*

LIFTED

Ge	13:10	Lot **l** up his eyes, and beheld all	5375
Ge	22:13	Abraham **l** up his eyes, and looked,	5375
Ge	37:28	and **l** up Joseph out of the pit,	5927
Ge	39:18	pass, as I **l** up my voice and cried,	7311
Ge	40:20	he **l** up the head of the chief butler	5375
Ex	7:20	**l** up the rod, and smote the waters	7311
Nu	20:11	Moses **l** up his hand, and with his	7311
Nu	24:2	Balaam **l** up his eyes, and he saw	5375
Jos	4:18	soles of the priests' feet were **l** up	5423
Jgs	2:4	people **l** up their voice, and wept.	5375
Ru	1:9	and they **l** up their voice, and wept.	5375
1Sa	6:13	**l** up their eyes, and saw the ark,	5375
1Sa	24:16	And Saul **l** up his voice, and wept.	5375
2Sa	3:32	the king **l** up his voice, and wept at	5375
2Sa	20:21	**l** up his hand against the king,	5375
2Sa	23:18	he **l** up his spear against three	5782
2Ki	19:22	and **l** up thine eyes on high? even	5375
1Ch	14:2	for his kingdom was **l** up on high,	5375
2Ch	17:6	heart was **l** up in the ways of the	1361
Job	2:12	they **l** up their voice, and wept;	5375
Ps	30:1	O Lord; for thou hast **l** me up,	1802
Ps	41:9	hath **l** up his heel against me.	1431
Ps	93:3	the floods have **l** up their voice,	5375
Ps	106:26	he **l** up his hand against them,	5375
Pr	30:13	eyes! and their eyelids are **l** up.	5375
Isa	6:1	upon a throne, high and **l** up, and	5375
Jer	51:9	heaven, and is **l** up even to the skies.	5375
Eze	1:19	when the living creatures were **l** up	5375
Eze	1:21	the wheels were **l** up over against	5375
Eze	3:14	So the spirit **l** me up, and took me	5375
Eze	10:15	And the cherubims were **l** up	7426
Eze	10:16	the cherubims **l** up their wings.	5375
Eze	18:12	and hath **l** up his eyes to the idols,	5375
Eze	18:15	neither hath **l** up his eyes to the	5375
Eze	20:23	I **l** up mine hand unto them also	5375
Eze	28:2	Because thine heart is **l** up, and	1361
Eze	28:5	heart is **l** up because of thy riches:	1361
Eze	28:17	was **l** up because of thy beauty,	1361
Da	4:34	I Nebuchadnezzar **l** up mine eyes	5191
Da	5:20	when his heart was **l** up, and his	7313
Da	11:12	multitude, his heart shall be **l** up;	7311

Hab 2:4 soul which is **l** up is not upright....... 6075
Hab 3:10 voice, and **l** up his hands on high...... 5375
Zec 5:9 **l** up the ephah between the earth...... 5375
Zec 9:16 **l** up as an ensign upon his land........ 5264
Mt 17:8 **l** up their eyes, they saw no man,...... 1869
Lk 6:20 he **l** up his eyes on his disciples,........ *1869*
Jn 3:14 **as Moses l up the serpent in the**....... *5312*
Jn 3:14 **so must the Son of man be l up:**....... *5312*
Jn 8:28 **When ye have l up the Son of**......... *5312*
Jn 12:32 **And I, if I be l up from the earth,**...... *5312*
Jn 12:34 thou, The Son of man must be **l** up?... *5312*
Jn 13:18 **me hath l up his heel against me.**...... *1869*
Jn 17:1 Jesus, and **l** up his eyes to heaven,...... *1869*
Ac 2:14 But Peter, ... **l** up his voice, and *1869*
Ac 4:24 **l** up their voice to God with one........ *142*
Ac 9:41 gave her his hand, and **l** her up, ... *450*
Rev 10:5 the earth **l** up his hand to heaven,....... *142*

LIFTETH

1Sa 2:8 **l** up the beggar from the dunghill,..... 7311
Ps 107:25 which **l** up the waves thereof.......... 7311
Ps 147:6 The Lord **l** up the meek: he........... 5749
Isa 18:3 when he **l** up an ensign on the 5375
Na 3:3 horseman **l** up both the bright 5927

LIFTING

Ne 8:6 Amen, with **l** up their hands:.......... 4607
Job 22:29 thou shalt say, There is **l** up; 1466
Ps 141:2 **l** up of my hands as the evening....... 4864
Pr 30:32 hast done foolishly in **l** up thyself, ... 5375
Isa 9:18 mount up like the **l** up of smoke 1348
Isa 33:3 at the **l** up of thyself the nations....... 7427
1Ti 2:8 pray everywhere, **l** up holy hands, ... *1869*

LIGHT

Ge 1:3 Let there be **l**: and there was **l**.......... 216
Ge 1:4 God saw the **l**, that it was good: 216
Ge 1:4 divided the **l** from the darkness......... 216
Ge 1:5 And God called the **l** Day, and the 216
Ge 1:16 the greater **l** to rule the day,........... 3974
Ge 1:16 and the lesser **l** to rule the night: 3974
Ex 13:21 in a pillar of fire, to give them **l**;........ 216
Ex 25:6 Oil for the **l**, spices for anointing 3974
Nu 8:2 the seven lamps shall give **l** over........ 216
Dt 27:16 be he that setteth **l** by his father 7034
Jgs 9:4 hired vain and **l** persons, which 6348
1Sa 18:23 Seemeth it to you a **l** thing to be....... 7043
1Sa 25:36 less or more, until the morning **l** 216
2Sa 17:12 **l** upon him as the dew falleth on 5117
2Sa 21:17 thou quench not the **l** of Israel........ 5216
1Ki 11:36 a **l** alway before me in Jerusalem....... 5216
2Ki 8:19 him to give him alway a **l**, and to 5216
2Ki 20:10 It is a **l** thing for the shadow to........ 7043
Ne 9:12 **l** in the way wherein they should go..... 216
Est 8:16 The Jews had **l**, and gladness, and....... 219
Job 3:4 neither let the **l** shine upon it.......... 5105
Job 3:20 is **l** given to him that is in misery 216
Job 12:22 out to **l** the shadow of death............ 216
Job 12:25 They grope in the dark without **l** 216
Job 18:5 the **l** of the wicked shall be put out,..... 216
Job 18:6 The **l** shall be dark in his tabernacle, ... 216
Job 18:18 shall be driven from **l** into darkness, ... 216
Job 24:13 of those that rebel against the **l**; 216
Job 24:16 the daytime: they know not the **l** 216
Job 28:11 that is hid bringeth he forth to **l**........ 216
Job 29:24 the **l** of my countenance they cast 216
Job 33:30 enlightened with the **l** of the living...... 216
Job 38:24 By what way is the **l** parted, which...... 216
Ps 4:6 the **l** of thy countenance upon us....... 216
Ps 27:1 The Lord is my **l** and my salvation; 216
Ps 56:13 before God in the **l** of the living? 216
Ps 74:16 hast prepared the **l** and the sun........ 3974
Ps 78:14 and all the night with a **l** of fire......... 216
Ps 90:8 sins in the **l** of thy countenance 3974
Ps 105:39 and fire to give **l** in the night. 216
Ps 119:105 my feet, and a **l** unto my path. 216
Ps 139:11 even the night shall be **l** about me....... 216
Ps 139:12 darkness and the **l** are both alike 219
Pr 6:23 is a lamp; and the law is **l**; and 216
Pr 13:9 The **l** of the righteous rejoiceth: 216
Pr 15:30 **l** of the eyes rejoiceth the heart: 3974
Ecc 2:13 folly, as far as **l** excelleth darkness. 216
Ecc 11:7 Truly the **l** is sweet, and a pleasant 216
Isa 2:5 let us walk in the **l** of the Lord.......... 216
Isa 5:30 the **l** is darkened in the heavens 216
Isa 8:20 is because there is no **l** in them. 7837
Isa 9:2 in darkness have seen a great **l** 216
Isa 9:2 death, upon them hath the **l** shined..... 216
Isa 13:10 moon shall not cause her **l** to shine 216
Isa 30:26 the **l** of the sun shall be sevenfold, ... 216
Isa 42:16 will make darkness **l** before them, ... 216
Isa 45:7 I form the **l**, and create darkness: 216
Isa 49:6 It is a **l** thing that thou shouldest 7043
Isa 50:11 walk in the **l** of your fire, and in 217
Isa 51:4 to rest for a **l** of the people............ 216
Isa 58:10 shall thy **l** rise in obscurity, and thy 216
Isa 60:1 Arise, shine; for thy **l** is come, and 216
Isa 60:19 sun shall be no more thy **l** by day; 216
Isa 60:20 Lord shall be thine everlasting **l** 216
Jer 4:23 and the heavens, and they had no **l** 216
Jer 31:35 which giveth the sun for a **l** by day...... 216
Jer 31:35 and of the stars for a **l** by night, ... 216
Eze 8:17 Is it a **l** thing to the house of Judah 7043
Eze 32:7 and the moon shall not give her **l**....... 216
Da 5:11 of thy father **l** and understanding...... 5094
Da 5:14 and that **l** and understanding and 5094
Hos 6:5 thy judgments are as the **l** that 216
Am 5:18 of the Lord is darkness, and not **l**....... 216
Mic 2:1 when the morning is **l**, they practise 216
Mic 7:8 the Lord shall be a **l** unto me........... 216
Mic 7:9 he will bring me forth to the **l**, and 216
Hab 3:11 at the **l** of thine arrows they went, ... 216
Zep 3:4 prophets are **l** and treacherous 6348
Zep 3:5 doth he bring his judgment to **l** 216
Zec 14:6 the **l** shall not be clear, nor dark:........ 216
Mt 4:16 which sat in darkness saw great **l**;...... *5457*
Mt 4:16 shadow of death **l** is sprung up........ *5457*
Mt 5:14 **Ye are the l of the world. A city**........ *5457*
Mt 5:15 **Neither do men l a candle, and**........ *2545*
Mt 5:16 **Let your l so shine before men,** *5457*
Mt 6:22 **The l of the body is the eye: if**......... *5460*
Mt 6:23 **the l that is in thee be darkness,**....... *5457*
Mt 11:30 yoke is easy, and my burden is **l** *1645*
Mt 17:2 his raiment was white as the **l**......... *5457*
Mt 22:5 **they made l of it, and went their** *272*
Mt 24:29 **and the moon shall not give her l,**..... *5338*
Lk 1:79 give **l** to them that sit in darkness...... *2014*
Lk 2:32 A **l** to lighten the Gentiles, and *5457*
Lk 8:16 **they which enter in may see the l**...... *5457*
Lk 11:36 **shining of a candle doth give thee l**.... *5461*
Lk 12:3 **darkness shall be heard in the l;**....... *5457*
Lk 16:8 **wiser than the children of l**........... *5457*

Jn 1:4 and the life was the l of men 5457
Jn 1:5 And the l shineth in darkness; and..... 5457
Jn 1:7 a witness, to bear witness of the L,..... 5457
Jn 1:8 He was not that L, but was sent 5457
Jn 1:9 That was the true L, which 5457
Jn 3:19 men loved darkness rather than l, ... 5457
Jn 3:20 one that doeth evil hateth the l, ... 5457
Jn 5:35 was a burning and a shining l.......... 3088
Jn 8:12 saying, I am the l of the world: 5457
Jn 8:12 darkness, but shall have the l of life.... 5457
Jn 9:5 the world, I am the l of the world...... 5457
Jn 11:10 because there is no l in him........... 5457
Jn 12:35 Yet a little while is the l with you 5457
Jn 12:36 that ye may be the children of l 5457
Jn 12:46 I am come a l into the world, that 5457
Ac 9:3 round about him a l from heaven:..... 5457
Ac 12:7 him, and a l shined in the prison:...... 5457
Ac 13:47 set thee to be a l of the Gentiles,....... 5457
Ac 22:6 shone from heaven a great l round..... 5457
Ac 22:9 that were with me saw indeed the l,.... 5457
Ac 26:13 I saw in the way a l from heaven....... 5457
Ac 26:18 to turn them from darkness to l, ... 5457
Ro 2:19 a l of them which are in darkness...... 5457
Ro 13:12 and let us put on the armour of l...... 5457
1Co 4:5 will bring to l the hidden things 5461
2Co 4:4 l of the glorious gospel of Christ 5462
2Co 4:6 commanded the l to shine out of 5457
2Co 4:17 our l affliction, which is but for a 1645
2Co 6:14 communion hath l with darkness?..... 5457
2Co 11:14 is transformed into an angel of l....... 5457
Eph 5:8 walk as children of l 5457
Eph 5:14 and Christ shall give thee l............ 2077
Col 1:12 the inheritance of the saints in l 5457
1Th 5:5 Ye are the children of l, and.......... 5457
1Pe 2:9 of darkness into his marvelous l....... 5457
2Pe 1:19 as unto a l that shineth in a dark 3088
1Jn 1:5 declare unto you, that God is l 5457
1Jn 1:7 if we walk in the l, as he is in the l,..... 5457
1Jn 2:8 past, and the true l now shineth 5457
1Jn 2:9 He that saith he is in the l, and 5457
Rev 7:16 neither shall the sun l on them, ... 4098
Rev 18:23 l of a candle shall shine no more 5457
Rev 21:23 and the Lamb is the l thereof.......... 3088
Rev 21:24 saved shall walk in the l of it:.......... 5457
Rev 22:5 no candle, neither l of the sun; 5457
Rev 22:5 for the Lord God giveth them l........ 5467

LIGHTED

Ex 40:25 he l the lamps before the Lord; as...... 5927
Jgs 1:14 a field: and she l from off her ass;...... 6795
Jgs 4:15 that Sisera l down off his chariot,...... 3381
Isa 9:8 Jacob, and it hath l upon Israel........ 5307
Lk 8:16 No man, when he hath l a candle. 681

LIGHTEN

1Sa 6:5 he will l his hand from off you,........ 7043
2Sa 22:29 and the Lord will l my darkness........ 5050
Ezr 9:8 that our God may l our eyes, and....... 215
Ps 13:3 l mine eyes, lest I sleep the sleep........ 215
Jnh 1:5 ship into the sea, to l it of them 7043
Lk 2:32 A light to l the Gentiles, and the........ 602
Rev 21:23 the glory of God did l it, and the 5461

LIGHTENED See also ENLIGHTENED.

Ps 34:5 looked unto him, and were l.......... 5102
Ps 77:18 the lightnings l the world: the.......... 215
Ac 27:18 the next day they l the ship;...... 1546, 4160
Ac 27:38 they l the ship, and cast out the........ 2893
Rev 18:1 the earth was l with his glory.......... 5461

LIGHTER

1Ki 12:10 heavy, but make thou it l unto us; 7043
2Ch 10:10 make thou it somewhat l for us;....... 7043
Ps 62:9 they are altogether l than vanity....... 7043

LIGHTETH

Ex 30:8 when Aaron l the lamps at even,....... 5927
Dt 19:5 and l upon his neighbour, that 4672
Jn 1:9 which l every man that cometh........ 5467

LIGHTING

Mt 3:16 like a dove, and l upon him: 2064

LIGHTLY

Ge 26:10 might l have lien with thy wife,........ 4592
Dt 32:15 and l esteemed the Rock of his 5034
1Sa 2:30 despise me shall be l esteemed......... 7043
1Sa 18:23 I am a poor man, and l esteemed? 7034
Jer 4:24 trembled, and all the hills moved l..... 7043
Mk 9:39 that can l speak evil of me. 5055

LIGHTNESS

Jer 3:9 through the l of her whoredom,....... 6963
Jer 23:32 err by their lies, and by their l; 6350
2Co 1:17 was thus minded, did I use l?.......... 7644

LIGHTNING

Job 37:3 his l unto the ends of the earth. 216
Ps 144:6 Cast forth l, and scatter them:......... 1300
Eze 1:13 and out of the fire went forth l........ 1300
Da 10:6 his face as the appearance of l, ... 1300
Zec 9:14 his arrow shall go forth as the l: 1300
Mt 24:27 For as the l cometh out of the east, ... 796
Mt 28:3 His countenance was like l, and 796
Lk 10:18 I beheld Satan as l fall from............ 796
Lk 17:24 For as the l, that lighteneth out of 796

LIGHTNINGS

Ex 19:16 that there were thunders and l 1300
Job 38:35 Canst thou send l, that they may 1300
Ps 18:14 and he shot out l, and discomfited..... 1300
Ps 77:18 the l lightened the world: the earth 1300
Ps 97:4 His l enlightened the world: the 1300
Ps 135:7 he maketh l for the rain; he........... 1300
Jer 10:13 he maketh l with rain, and bringeth.... 1300
Na 2:4 torches, they shall run like the l 1300
Rev 4:5 out of the throne proceeded l and 796
Rev 8:5 were voices, and thunderings, and l,..... 796
Rev 11:19 and there were l, and voices, and 796
Rev 16:18 were voices, and thunders, and l; 796

LIGHTS

Ge 1:14 Let there be l in the firmament of 3974
Ge 1:16 God made two great l; the greater 3974
1Ki 6:4 he made windows of narrow l......... 8261
Ps 136:7 To him that made great l: for his 216
Eze 32:8 bright l of heaven will I make dark 3974
Lk 12:35 about, and your l burning; 3088
Php 2:15 whom ye shine as l in the world; 5458
Jas 1:17 cometh down from the Father of l..... 5457

LIKE

Ex 8:10 that there is none l unto the Lord
Ex 9:14 there is none l me in all the earth...... 3644
Ex 9:24 none l it in all the land of Egypt....... 3644
Ex 15:11 Who is l unto thee, O Lord, among 3644

Ex	24:17	glory of the Lord was **l** devouring fire	
Ex	34:1	two tables of stone **l** unto the first:	
Nu	23:10	and let my last end be **l** his!	3644
Dt	17:14	a king over me, **l** as all the nations	
Dt	33:26	is none **l** unto the God of Jeshurun	
Dt	34:10	prophet since in Israel **l** unto Moses	
Jos	10:14	no day **l** that before it or after it,	
Jgs	13:6	**l** the countenance of an angel of God,	
1Sa	2:2	neither is there any rock **l** our God.	
1Sa	4:9	Be strong, and quit yourselves **l** men,	
1Sa	8:5	us a king to judge us **l** all the nations	
1Sa	10:24	none **l** him among all the people?	3644
1Sa	17:7	his spear was **l** a weaver's beam;	
1Sa	26:15	and who is **l** to thee in Israel?	3644
2Sa	7:22	Lord God: for there is none **l** thee,	3644
1Ki	3:13	be any among the kings **l** unto thee	3644
1Ki	8:23	of Israel, there is no God **l** thee	3644
1Ki	18:44	cloud out of the sea, **l** a man's hand.	
2Ki	5:14	again **l** unto the flesh of a little child,	
2Ki	9:20	the driving is **l** the driving of Jehu	
2Ki	23:25	And **l** unto him was there no king	3644
2Ki	23:25	after him arose there any **l** him	3644
1Ch	17:20	O Lord, there is none **l** thee	3644
1Ch	27:23	would increase Israel **l** to the stars of	
2Ch	4:5	of it **l** the work of the brim of a cup	
2Ch	6:14	no God **l** thee in the heavens, nor	3644
2Ch	35:18	no passover **l** to that kept in Israel	3644
Ne	13:26	nations was there no king **l** him,	3644
Job	1:8	there is none **l** him in the earth	3644
Job	15:16	man, which drinketh iniquity **l** water?	
Job	38:3	Gird up now thy loins **l** a man;	
Job	40:9	Hast thou an arm **l** God?	
Job	40:9	thou thunder with a voice **l** him?	3644
Job	42:8	thing which is right, **l** my servant Job	
Ps	1:3	And he shall be **l** a tree planted by the	
Ps	2:9	dash them in pieces **l** a potter's vessel	
Ps	22:14	I am poured out **l** water, and all my	
Ps	31:12	out of mind: I am **l** a broken vessel.	
Ps	35:10	who is **l** unto thee, which deliverest	3644
Ps	71:19	O God, who is **l** unto thee!	3644
Ps	78:57	were turned aside **l** a deceitful bow	
Ps	78:69	**l** the earth which he hath established	
Ps	79:3	Their blood have they shed **l** water	
Ps	79:5	ever? shall thy jealousy burn **l** fire?	
Ps	86:8	the gods there is none **l** unto thee, O	
Ps	97:5	hills melted **l** wax at the presence of	
Ps	102:3	For my days are consumed **l** smoke,	
Ps	102:11	days are **l** a shadow that declineth;	
Ps	103:13	**L** as a father pitieth his children, so	
Ps	113:5	Who is **l** unto the Lord our God, who	
Ps	119:176	I have gone astray **l** a lost sheep:	
Ps	126:1	of Zion, we were **l** them that dream.	
Ps	144:4	Man is **l** to vanity: his days are as	1819
Pr	17:22	merry heart doeth good **l** a medicine:	
Pr	18:19	contentions are **l** the bars of a castle	
Pr	23:32	**l** a serpent, and stingeth **l** an adder	
Pr	25:11	A word fitly spoken is **l** apples of gold	
Pr	25:19	in time of trouble is **l** a broken tooth,	
Pr	26:4	lest thou also be **l** unto him	7737
Pr	26:17	is **l** one that taketh a dog by the ears.	
Pr	28:3	is **l** a sweeping rain which leaveth no	
Pr	31:14	She is **l** the merchants' ships; she	
SS	2:9	My beloved is **l** a roe or a young	1819
Isa	1:18	though they be red **l** crimson,	1819
Isa	5:30	against them **l** the roaring of the sea:	
Isa	11:16	**l** as it was to Israel in the day that he	
Isa	14:14	clouds; I will be **l** the most High.	1819
Isa	19:16	day shall Egypt be **l** unto women:	
Isa	24:20	shall reel to and fro **l** a drunkard,	
Isa	26:17	**L** as a woman with child, that	3644
Isa	40:11	He shall feed his flock **l** a shepherd.	
Isa	50:7	therefore have I set my face **l** a flint,	
Isa	51:6	the earth shall wax old **l** a garment,	
Isa	53:6	All we **l** sheep have gone astray;	
Isa	59:10	We grope for the wall **l** the blind,	
Isa	59:19	the enemy shall come in **l** a flood,	
Jer	5:19	**L** as ye have forsaken me, and served	
Jer	10:6	as there is none **l** unto thee, O	3644
Jer	21:12	lest my fury go out **l** fire, and burn	
Jer	23:29	**l** a hammer that breaketh the rock in	
Jer	38:9	he is **l** to die for hunger in the place	
Jer	49:19	appoint over her? for who is **l** me?	3644
La	5:10	Our skin was black **l** an oven because	
Eze	23:18	**l** as my mind was alienated from her	
Eze	36:35	is become **l** the garden of Eden;	
Eze	40:3	was **l** the appearance of brass,	
Da	1:19	was found none **l** Daniel, Hananiah,	
Da	3:25	of the fourth is **l** the Son of God	1821
Da	4:33	and his nails **l** birds' claws	
Da	5:21	they fed him with grass **l** oxen, and	
Da	7:5	beast, a second, **l** to a bear, and it	1821
Da	7:6	and to another, **l** a leopard, which had	
Da	7:8	horn were eyes **l** the eyes of man,	
Da	7:9	his throne was **l** the fiery flame, and	
Da	7:13	one **l** the Son of man came with the	
Da	10:6	his feet **l** in colour to polished brass,	
Da	10:18	me one **l** the appearance of a man	
Hos	4:9	And there shall be, **l** people, **l** priest:	
Hos	6:7	**l** men have transgressed the covenant	
Hos	7:6	made ready their heart **l** an oven,	
Joel	1:8	Lament **l** a virgin girded with	
Joel	2:2	there hath not been ever the **l**	3644
Am	5:6	lest he break out **l** fire in the house of	
Jnh	1:4	that the ship was **l** to be broken	2803
Mic	1:8	I will make a wailing **l** the dragons,	
Mic	4:10	of Zion, **l** a woman in travail:	
Mic	7:18	Who is a God **l** unto thee, that	3644
Na	2:8	Nineveh is of old **l** a pool of water:	
Zec	1:6	**L** as the Lord of hosts thought to do	
Zec	14:5	**l** as ye fled from before the earthquake	
Mal	3:2	**l** a refiner's fire, and **l** a fullers' soap:	
Mt	3:16	Spirit of God descending **l** a dove,	*5616*
Mt	6:29	**was not arrayed l one of these**	*5613*
Mt	13:31	**is l to a grain of mustard seed,**	*3664*
Mt	13:33	**kingdom of heaven is l unto leaven**	*3664*
Mt	13:45	**heaven is l unto a merchant man,**	*3664*
Mt	13:47	**kingdom of heaven is l unto a net,**	*3664*
Mt	13:52	**l unto a man that is an householder**	*3664*
Mt	22:2	**of heaven is l unto a certain king,**	*3666*
Mt	22:39	**And the second is l unto it, Thou.**	*3664*
Mt	23:27	**ye are l unto whited sepulchres,**	*3945*
Mt	28:3	His countenance was **l** lightning,	*5613*
Mk	1:10	and the Spirit **l** a dove descending	*5616*
Mk	4:31	**It is l a grain of mustard seed**	*5613*
Lk	6:49	**l a man that without a foundation**	*3664*
Lk	13:21	**It is l leaven, which a woman**	*3664*
Jn	1:32	descending from heaven **l** a dove	*5616*
Jn	7:46	Never man spake **l** this man	*3779*
Ac	2:3	them cloven tongues **l** as of fire,	*5616*
Ac	8:32	**l** a lamb dumb before his shearer	*5613*

Ac 17:29 that the Godhead is **l** unto gold, ... 3664
Ro 1:23 image made **l** to corruptible man, ... 3667
1Co 16:13 the faith, quit you **l** men, be strong. 407
Php 3:21 fashioned **l** unto his glorious body 4332
Heb 4:15 all points tempted **l** as we are, ... 2596, 3665
Heb 7:3 but made **l** unto the Son of God;. 5:17
Jas 5:17 a man subject to **l** passions as we 3663
1Pe 3:21 **l** figure whereunto even baptism. 499
1Jn 3:2 shall appear, we shall be **l** him; 3664
Rev 1:14 and his hairs were white **l** wool, ... 5616
Rev 2:18 **his eyes l unto a flame of fire** 5613
Rev 2:18 **and his feet are l fine brass;**. 3664
Rev 4:6 was a sea of glass **l** unto crystal: 3664
Rev 4:7 And the first beast was **l** a lion, ... 3664
Rev 4:7 and the second beast **l** a calf, and 3664
Rev 4:7 the fourth beast was **l** a flying eagle 3664
Rev 9:7 were as it were crowns **l** gold, ... 3664
Rev 9:10 they had tails **l** unto scorpions, and 3664
Rev 14:14 cloud one sat **l** unto the Son of man,. . . 3664
Rev 21:18 was pure gold, **l** unto clear glass 3664

LIKEMINDED See also MINDED.
Ro 15:5 to be **l** one toward another . . 3588, 846, 5426
Php 2:2 ye my joy, that ye be **l**. 3588, 846, 5426
Php 2:20 For I have no man **l**, who will 2473

LIKEN
Isa 40:18 To whom then will ye **l** God? or 1819
Isa 40:25 To whom then will ye **l** me, or 1819
Isa 46:5 To whom will ye **l** me, and make 1819
La 2:13 thing shall I **l** to thee, O daughter. 1819
Mk 4:30 **shall we l the kingdom of God?** 3666
Lk 13:20 **shall I l the kingdom of God?** 3666

LIKENESS
Ge 1:26 man in our image, after our **l**: 1823
Ge 5:1 man, in the **l** of God made he him; 1823
Ex 20:4 or any **l** of any thing that is in. 8544
Dt 4:25 graven image, or the **l** of any thing, ... 8544
Ps 17:15 satisfied, when I awake, with thy **l** 8544
Isa 40:18 what **l** will ye compare unto him? 1823
Eze 1:5 came the **l** of four living creatures. 1823
Eze 1:5 they had the **l** of a man 1823
Eze 1:28 of the **l** of the glory of the Lord 1823
Eze 10:10 appearances, they four had one **l** 1823
Ac 14:11 come down to us in the **l** of men. 3666
Ro 6:5 be also in the **l** of his resurrection:
Ro 8:3 his own Son in the **l** of sinful flesh, ... 3667
Php 2:7 and was made in the **l** of men: 3667

LIKEWISE
1Sa 31:5 was dead, he fell **l** upon his sword 1571
Est 4:16 I also and my maidens will fast **l**; 3651
Ps 52:5 God shall **l** destroy thee for ever,. 1571
Ecc 7:22 thou thyself **l** hast cursed others 1571
Eze 46:3 **L** the people of the land shall worship
Mt 17:12 **L shall also the Son of man suffer** 3779
Mt 20:10 **they l received every man a penny**. 2532
Lk 6:31 **do to you, do ye also to them l** 3668
Lk 10:37 Jesus unto him, **Go, and do thou l** 3668
Lk 13:3 **ye repent, ye shall all l perish**. 5615
Lk 17:28 **L also as it was in the days of Lot**. 3668
Lk 22:20 **L** also the cup after supper. 5615
Jn 5:19 **doeth, these also doeth the Son l** 3668
Ro 8:26 **L** the Spirit also helpeth our 5615
1Co 7:3 **l** also the wife unto the husband. 3668
1Co 7:4 **l** also the husband hath not power of. . . 3668
1Ti 3:8 **L** must the deacons be grave, not 5615
Tit 2:3 The aged woman **l** that they be in 5615
Tit 2:6 Young men **l** exhort to be sober 5675
Jas 2:25 **L** also was not Rahab the harlot 3668
1Pe 5:5 **L**, ye younger, submit yourselves. 3668
Jude 8 **L** also these filthy dreamers defile 3668

LILIES
2Ch 4:5 brim of a cup, with flowers of **l**; 7799
SS 2:16 I am his: he feedeth among the **l**. 7799
SS 6:3 is mine: he feedeth among the **l** 7799
Mt 6:28 **Consider the l of the field, how** 2918
La 12:27 **Consider the l how they grow:** 2918

LILY
SS 2:1 of Sharon, and the **l** of the valleys 7799
SS 2:2 As the **l** among thorns, so is my 7799
Hos 14:5 unto Israel: he shall grow as the **l**,. 7799

LIMITED
Ps 78:41 and **l** the Holy One of Israel 8428

LIMITETH
Heb 4:7 he **l** a certain day, saying to David, ... 3724

LINE See also PLUMBLINE.
Jos 2:21 bound the scarlet **l** in the window 8615
2Sa 8:2 and with one full **l** to keep alive. 2256
2Ki 21:13 over Jerusalem the **l** of Samaria, ... 6957
Job 38:5 who hath stretched the **l** upon it?. 6957
Ps 19:4 Their **l** is gone out through all the 6957
Isa 28:10 **l** upon **l**, **l** upon **l**; here a 6957
Isa 34:11 out upon it the **l** of confusion, ... 6957
Isa 44:13 he marketh it out with a **l**; he 8279
Am 7:17 thy land shall be divided by **l**; 2256
2Co 10:16 not to boast in another man's **l**. 2583

LINEAGE
Lk 2:4 was of the house and **l** of David:) 3965

LINEN
Ge 41:42 arrayed him in vestures of fine **l**, ... 8336
Ex 26:1 with ten curtains of fine twined **l**, ... 8336
Ex 26:31 make a vail of...fine twined **l** 8336
Ex 39:27 made coats of fine **l** of woven work 8336
Le 16:4 He shall put on the holy **l** coat, ... 906
1Sa 22:18 persons that did wear a **l** ephod. 906
2Sa 6:14 David was girded with a **l** ephod. 906
Est 8:15 with a garment of fine **l** and purple: 948
Pr 7:16 carved works, with fine **l** of Egypt. 948
Pr 31:24 She maketh fine **l**, and selleth it; 5466
Jer 13:1 Go and get thee a **l** girdle, and 6593
Eze 16:13 thy raiment was of fine **l**, and silk, ... 8336
Eze 44:17 shall be clothed with **l** garments; 6593
Da 10:5 behold a certain man clothed in **l**, ... 906
Mt 27:59 he wrapped it in a clean **l** cloth, ... 4616
Mk 14:52 And he left the **l** cloth, and fled. 4616
Mk 15:46 And he bought fine **l**, and took him. . . . 4616
Lk 16:19 **was clothed in purple and fine l**, ... 1040
Lk 24:12 the **l** clothes laid by themselves. 3608
Jn 19:40 of Jesus, and wound it in **l** clothes 3608
Jn 20:5 looking in, saw the **l** clothes lying; 3608
Jn 20:7 not lying with the **l** clothes, but 3608
Rev 15:6 clothed in pure and white **l**, and. 3043
Rev 18:16 city, that was clothed in fine **l**, ... 1039
Rev 19:8 for the fine **l** is the righteousness 1039
Rev 19:14 clothed in fine **l**, white and clean. 1039

LINES

2Sa 8:2 even with two **l** measured he to 2256
Ps 16:6 The **l** are fallen unto me in pleasant. . . . 2256

LINGERED

Ge 19:16 And while he **l**, the men laid hold 4102
Ge 43:10 For except we had **l**, surely now 4102

LINGERETH

2Pe 2:3 judgment now of a long time **l** not, ... *691*

LINTEL

Ex 12:23 when he seeth the blood upon the **l**, . . . 4947
Am 9:1 he said, Smite the **l** of the door, ... 3730

LION

Ge 49:9 stooped down, he couched as a **l**, ... 738
Nu 23:24 people shall rise up as a great **l**,. 3833
Jgs 14:9 honey out of the carcase of the **l**. 738
Jgs 14:18 and what is stronger than a **l**? 738
1Sa 17:36 slew both the **l** and the bear: 738
2Sa 17:10 whose heart is as the heart of a **l**. 738
1Ki 13:24 **l** met him by the way, and slew him: 738
1Ch 11:22 and slew a **l** in a pit in a snowy day. 738
Ps 7:2 Lest he tear my soul like a **l**,. 738
Ps 10:9 in wait secretly as a **l** in his den: 738
Pr 19:12 king's wrath is as the roaring of a **l**; 3715
Pr 20:2 of a king is as the roaring of a **l**: 3715
Pr 26:13 man saith, There is a **l** in the way; 738
Pr 28:1 but the righteous are bold as a **l** 3715
Pr 28:15 As a roaring **l**, and a ranging bear; 739
Pr 30:30 A **l** which is strongest among 3918
Ecc 9:4 living dog is better than a dead **l**. 738
Isa 5:29 Their roaring shall be like a **l**, ... 3833
Isa 21:8 And he cried, A **l**: My lord, I stand 738
Jer 2:30 your prophets, like a destroying **l** 738
Jer 4:7 The **l** is come up from his thicket. 738
Jer 12:8 Mine heritage is unto me as a **l** in. 738
Jer 49:19 Behold, he shall come up like a **l**. 738
La 3:10 in wait, and as a **l** in secret places.. 738
Eze 1:10 the face of a **l**, on the right side: 738
Eze 10:14 man, and the third the face of a **l** 738
Eze 22:25 like a roaring **l** ravening the prey;. 738
Eze 32:2 art like a young **l** of the nations, ... 3715
Eze 41:19 face of a young **l** toward the palm 3715
Da 7:4 first was like a **l**, and had eagle's 738
Hos 5:14 a young **l** to the house of Judah:. 3715
Joel 1:6 whose teeth are the teeth of a **l**,. 738
Am 3:4 Will a **l** roar in the forest, when he 738
Am 3:12 taketh out of the mouth of the **l**. 738
Mic 5:8 as a young **l** among the flocks of. 3715
Na 2:12 The **l** did tear in pieces enough. 738
2Ti 4:17 delivered out of the mouth of the **l** *3023*
1Pe 5:8 adversary the devil, as a roaring **l**,. *3023*
Rev 4:7 And the first beast was like a **l**, ... *3023*
Rev 5:5 behold, the **L** of the tribe of Juda,. *3023*
Rev 10:3 loud voice, as when a **l** roareth:. *3023*
Rev 13:2 and his mouth as the mouth of a **l**: *3023*

LIONLIKE

2Sa 23:20 acts, he slew two **l** men of Moab: 739

LION'S

Ge 49:9 Judah is a **l** whelp: from the prey, ... 738
Dt 33:22 of Dan he said, Dan is a **l** whelp: 738
Ps 22:21 Save me from the **l** mouth: for 738

LIONS

2Sa 1:23 eagles, they were stronger than **l**. 738
1Ki 7:36 he graved cherubims, **l**, and palm. 738
1Ki 10:19 and two **l** stood beside the stays.. 738
1Ch 12:8 whose faces were like the faces of **l**, ... 738
Ps 34:10 The young **l** do lack, and suffer. 3715
Ps 58:6 out the great teeth of the young **l**, ... 3715
Ps 104:21 The young **l** roar after their prey, ... 3715
Isa 5:29 lion, they shall roar like young **l**:. 3715
Jer 51:38 They shall roar together like **l**:. 3715
Eze 19:2 A lioness: she lay down among **l**, ... 738
Da 6:16 and cast him into the den of **l**. 744
Da 6:19 and went in haste unto the den of **l** 744
Da 6:20 able to deliver thee from the **l**? 744
Da 6:24 they cast them into the den of **l**, ... 744
Na 2:13 the sword shall devour thy young **l**: 3715
Zep 3:3 princes within her are roaring **l**; 738
Zec 11:3 a voice of the roaring of young **l**; 3715
Heb 11:33 promises, stopped the mouths of **l**, ... *3023*
Rev 9:8 their teeth were as the teeth of **l** *3023*
Rev 9:17 the horses were as the heads of **l**; *3023*

LIP

Le 13:45 put a covering upon his upper **l**,. 822
Ps 22:7 they shoot out the **l**, they shake. 8193
Pr 12:19 The **l** of truth shall be established. 8193

LIPS

Ex 6:12 me, who am of uncircumcised **l**? 8193
Le 5:4 pronouncing with his **l** to do evil 8193
Nu 30:8 that which she uttered with her **l**,. 8193
1Sa 1:13 only her **l** moved, but her voice 8193
Job 2:10 In all this did not Job sin with his **l** 8193
Job 15:6 thine own **l** testify against thee 8193
Ps 12:2 with flattering **l** and with a double. 8193
Ps 12:4 our **l** are our own: who is lord over 8193
Ps 16:4 nor take up their names into my **l** 8193
Ps 31:18 Let the lying **l** be put to silence; 8193
Ps 51:15 O Lord, open thou my **l**; and my 8193
Ps 59:7 their mouth: swords are in their **l**: 8193
Ps 59:12 the words of their **l** let them even. 8193
Ps 63:3 than life, my **l** shall praise thee.. 8193
Ps 71:23 My **l** shall greatly rejoice when I 8193
Ps 106:33 he spake unadvisedly with his **l**. 8193
Ps 119:171 My **l** shall utter praise, when thou 8193
Ps 120:2 my soul, O Lord, from lying **l**,. 8193
Ps 140:3 adders' poison is under their **l**. 8193
Ps 141:3 my mouth; keep the door of my **l**. 8193
Pr 4:24 and perverse **l** put far from thee. 8193
Pr 5:3 For the **l** of a strange woman drop. 8193
Pr 7:21 with the flattering of her **l** she. 8193
Pr 10:13 **l** of him that hath understanding 8193
Pr 10:18 He that hideth hatred with lying **l**, ... 8193
Pr 10:19 but he that refraineth his **l** is wise. 8193
Pr 10:21 The **l** of the righteous feed many:. 8193
Pr 12:22 Lying **l** are abomination to the 8193
Pr 13:3 he that openeth wide his **l** shall. 8193
Pr 14:23 talk of the **l** tendeth only to penury.. . . . 8193
Pr 15:7 **l** of the wise disperse knowledge: 8193
Pr 16:13 Righteous **l** are the delight of kings;. . . . 8193
Pr 16:23 mouth, and addeth learning to his **l**. . . . 8193
Pr 16:27 in his **l** there is as a burning fire.. 8193
Pr 17:4 wicked doer giveth heed to false **l**; 8193
Pr 17:28 he that shutteth his **l** is esteemed 8193
Pr 18:6 A fool's **l** enter into contention 8193
Pr 18:7 and his **l** are the snare of his soul.. 8193

Pr	19:1	he that is perverse in his l, and is a	8193
Pr	20:19	with him that flattereth with his l.	8193
Pr	23:16	when thy l speak right things.	8193
Pr	24:2	and their l talk of mischief.	8193
Pr	24:26	Every man shall kiss his l that	8193
Pr	26:23	Burning l and a wicked heart are	8193
Pr	27:2	a stranger, and not thine own l.	8193
Ecc	10:12	but the l of a fool shall swallow up	8193
SS	4:3	Thy l are like a thread of scarlet,	8193
SS	7:9	the l of those that are asleep to	8193
Isa	6:5	because I am a man of unclean l,	8193
Isa	6:7	said, Lo, this hath touched thy l;	8193
Isa	11:4	with the breath of his l shall he	8193
Isa	28:11	with stammering l and another	8193
Isa	29:13	and with their l do honour me,	8193
Isa	57:19	I create the fruit of the l; Peace,	8193
Isa	59:3	your l have spoken lies, your	8193
Jer	17:16	which came out of my l was right	8193
La	3:62	The l of those that rose up against	8193
Eze	24:17	cover not thy l, and eat not the	8222
Eze	24:22	ye shall not cover your l, nor eat	8222
Eze	36:3	are taken up in the l of talkers,	8193
Da	10:16	of the sons of men touched my l:	8193
Mic	3:7	yea, they shall all cover their l;	8222
Mal	2:6	and iniquity was not found in his l:	8193
Mal	2:7	priest's l should keep knowledge,	8193
Mt	15:8	**and honoureth me with their l;**	*5491*
Mk	7:6	**people honoureth me with their l,**	*5491*
Ro	3:13	the poison of asps is under their l.	*5491*
1Co	14:21	men of other tongues and other l.	*5491*
Heb	13:15	the fruit of our l giving thanks to	*5491*
1Pe	3:10	and his l that they speak no guile:	*5491*

LISTETH

Jn	3:8	**the wind bloweth where it l, and**	*2309*
Jas	3:4	whithersoever ... governor l	*3730, 1014*

LITTLE

Ge	19:20	escape thither, (is it not a l one?)	4705
Ge	43:2	them, Go again, buy us a l food	4592
Ge	50:21	will nourish you, and your l ones	2945
Ex	16:18	he that gathered l had no lack;	4591
Nu	14:31	But your l ones, which ye said	2945
Nu	31:17	kill every male among the l ones,	2945
Dt	7:22	nations before thee by l and l:	4592
Jgs	4:19	I pray thee, a l water to drink;	4592
1Sa	14:29	because I tasted a l of this honey	4592
1Sa	15:17	thou wast l in thine own sight	6996
2Sa	12:3	had nothing, save one l ewe lamb,	6996
2Sa	12:8	and if that had been too l, I would	4592
1Ki	3:7	I am but a l child: I know not how	6996
1Ki	17:12	in a barrel, and a l oil in a cruse:	4592
2Ki	5:14	like unto the flesh of a l child, and	6995
Ps	8:5	made him a l lower than the angels,	4592
Ps	137:9	dasheth thy l ones against the	5768
Pr	6:10	Yet a l sleep, a l slumber,	4592
Pr	10:20	the heart of the wicked is l worth.	4592
Pr	16:8	Better is a l with righteousness,	4592
Pr	24:33	Yet a l sleep, a l slumber,	4592
Pr	30:24	four things which are l upon the	6996
Ecc	5:12	sweet, whether he eat l or much:	4592
SS	2:15	Take us the foxes, the l foxes,	6996
Isa	11:6	and a l child shall lead them.	6995
Isa	29:17	Is it not yet a very l while, and	4592
Isa	60:22	A l one shall become a thousand,	6996
Jer	51:33	yet a l while, and the time of her	4592
Eze	16:47	if that were a very l thing, thou	4592
Da	7:8	up among them another l horn,	2192
Hos	1:4	for yet a l while, and I will avenge	4592
Mic	5:2	thou be l among the thousands of	6810
Hag	1:6	have sown much, and bring in l;	4592
Mt	6:30	**more clothe you, O ye of l faith?**	*3640*
Mt	10:42	**to drink unto one of these l ones**	*3398*
Mt	14:31	**O thou of l faith, wherefore didst**	*3640*
Mt	18:3	**and become as l children**	*3813*
Mt	18:4	**humble himself as this l child,**	*3813*
Mt	18:5	**receive one such l child in my**	*3813*
Mt	18:10	**ye despise not one of these l ones;**	*3398*
Mt	19:14	**Jesus said, Suffer l children, and**	*3813*
Mk	9:42	**shall offend one of these l ones.**	*3398*
Mk	10:15	**the kingdom of God as a l child,**	*3813*
Lk	7:47	**l is forgiven, the same loveth l.**	*3641*
Lk	12:32	**Fear not, l flock; for it is your**	*3398*
Lk	18:17	**the kingdom of God as a l child**	*3813*
Lk	19:3	press, because he was l of stature	*3398*
Lk	19:17	**thou hast been faithful in a very l,**	*1646*
Jn	7:33	**Yet a l while am I with you, and**	*3398*
Jn	12:35	**Yet a l while is the light with you**	*3398*
Jn	13:33	**L children, yet a ... while I am**	*5040*
Jn	14:19	**Yet a l while, and the world seeth**	*3397*
Jn	16:16	**A l while, and ye shall not see me:**	*3397*
Jn	16:19	**A l while, and ye shall not see me.**	*3397*
1Co	5:6	not that a l leaven leaveneth the	*3399*
2Co	8:15	that had gathered l had no lack.	*3641*
2Co	11:1	could bear with me a l in my folly:	*3397*
Gal	5:9	A l leaven leaveneth the whole	*3398*
1Ti	4:8	For bodily exercise profiteth l:	*3641*
1Ti	5:23	a l wine for thy stomach's sake	*3641*
Heb	2:7	him a l lower than the angels;	*1024*
Heb	10:37	For yet a l while, and he that shall	*3397*
Jas	3:5	Even so the tongue is a l member,	*3398*
Jas	3:5	great a matter a l fire kindleth!	*3641*
Jas	4:14	vapour, that appeareth for a l time,	*3641*
1Jn	2:1	My l children, these things write	*5040*
1Jn	2:18	L children, it is the last time: and	*3813*
1Jn	3:7	L children, let no man deceive you:	*5040*
1Jn	3:18	My l children, let us not love in	*5040*
1Jn	4:4	Ye are of God, l children, and have	*5040*
1Jn	5:21	L children, keep yourselves from	*5040*
Rev	3:8	**for thou hast a l strength, and**	*3398*
Rev	6:11	they should rest yet for a l season,	*3398*
Rev	10:2	he had in his hand a l book open:	*974*
Rev	10:9	said unto him, Give me the l book.	*974*
Rev	20:3	that he must be loosed a l season	*3398*

LIVE

Ge	3:22	tree of life, and eat, and l for ever	2425
Ge	17:18	unto God, O that Ishmael might l	2421
Ge	42:18	them the third day, This do, and l;	2421
Ge	45:3	I am Joseph; doth my father yet l?	2416
Ex	1:16	if it be a daughter, the she shall l.	2425
Ex	22:18	Thou shalt not suffer a witch to l.	2421
Le	16:21	hands upon the head of the l goat	2416
Nu	21:8	when he looketh upon it, shall l.	2425
Dt	8:3	that man doth not l by bread only,	2421
Dt	19:5	flee unto one of those cities, and l	2425
Dt	32:40	to heaven, and say, I l for ever.	2416
Jos	6:17	only Rahab the harlot shall l, she	2421
2Sa	12:22	to me, that the child may l?	2416
1Ki	1:31	Let my lord king David l for ever	2421
Ne	2:3	the king, Let the king l for ever:	2421
Est	4:11	the golden sceptre, that he may l	2421

Job 14:14 If a man die, shall he **l** again? 2421
Ps 22:26 him: your heart shall **l** for ever 2421
Ps 55:23 men shall not **l** out half their days;
Ps 69:32 your heart shall **l** that seek God......... 2421
Ps 104:33 sing unto the Lord as long as I **l** 2416
Ps 119:17 that I may **l**, and keep thy word......... 2421
Ps 119:175 Let my soul **l**, and it shall praise 2421
Ps 146:2 While I **l** will I praise the Lord:......... 2416
Pr 4:4 keep my commandments, and **l** 2421
Pr 15:27 but he that hateth gifts shall **l** 2421
Ecc 6:6 Yea, though he **l** a thousand years...... 2421
Ecc 9:9 **L** joyfully with the wife whom 2416
Isa 6:6 me, having a **l** coal in his hand,........ 7531
Isa 49:18 As I **l**, saith the Lord, thou shalt 2416
Isa 55:3 hear, and your soul shall **l**; and I....... 2421
Jer 27:12 serve him and his people, and **l**........ 2421
Jer 38:20 unto thee, and thy soul shall **l**......... 2421
La 4:20 said, Under his shadow we shall **l**...... 2421
Eze 3:21 he doth not sin, he shall surely **l**, ... 2421
Eze 13:19 the souls alive that should not **l**,....... 2421
Eze 14:20 as I **l**, saith the Lord God,............. 2416
Eze 18:9 he is just, he shall surely **l**, saith........ 2421
Eze 18:21 he shall surely **l**, he shall not die, ... 2421
Eze 18:32 wherefore turn yourselves, and **l** ye..... 2421
Eze 20:11 man do, he shall even **l** in them;....... 2425
Eze 20:13 do, he shall even **l** in them; 2425
Eze 33:10 in them, how should we then **l**? 2421
Eze 33:11 wicked turn from his way and **l**:....... 2421
Eze 33:13 righteous, that he shall surely **l**;........ 2421
Eze 37:3 Son of man, can these bones **l**?........ 2421
Eze 37:14 put my spirit in you, and ye shall **l**, ... 2421
Eze 47:9 thing shall **l** whither the river 2425
Da 5:10 spake and said, O king, **l** for ever:...... 2414
Hos 6:2 us up, and we shall **l** in his sight. 2421
Am 5:4 Israel, Seek ye me, and ye shall **l**:....... 2421
Jnh 4:3 is better for me to die than to **l**........ 2416
Hab 2:4 but the just shall **l** by his faith. 2421
Zec 1:5 the prophets, do they **l** for ever? 2421
Zec 13:3 say unto him, Thou shalt not **l**;........ 2421
Mt 4:4 **Man shall not l by bread alone,** *2198*
Lk 4:4 **man shall not l by bread alone,** *2198*
Lk 10:28 **right: this do, and thou shalt l.**........ *2198*
Jn 5:25 **of God: and they that hear shall l.**...... *2198*
Jn 6:51 **of this bread, he shall l forever:** *2198*
Jn 6:57 **hath sent me, and I l by the.**.......... *2198*
Jn 11:25 **though he were dead, yet shall he l:**.... *2198*
Jn 14:19 **because I l, ye shall l also**............. *2198*
Ac 17:28 For in him we **l**, and move, and *2198*
Ac 22:22 for it is not fit that he should **l** *2198*
Ac 28:4 yet vengeance suffereth not to **l**........ *2198*
Ro 1:17 written, The just shall **l** by faith........ *2198*
Ro 6:2 dead to sin, **l** any longer therein? *2198*
Ro 8:13 For if ye **l** after the flesh, ye shall....... *2198*
Ro 12:18 in you, **l** peaceably with all men........ *1514*
Ro 14:8 whether we **l**, we **l** unto the Lord;...... *2198*
1Co 9:14 the gospel should **l** of the gospel. *2198*
2Co 5:15 not henceforth **l** unto themselves, ... *2198*
2Co 6:9 as dying, and, behold, we **l**; as *2198*
2Co 13:11 be of one mind, and **l** in peace;........ *1514*
Gal 2:20 with Christ: nevertheless I **l**; *2198*
Gal 2:20 the life which I now **l** in the flesh *2198*
Gal 2:20 I **l** by the faith of the Son of God,...... *2198*
Gal 3:11 for, The just shall **l** by faith *2198*
Gal 5:25 If we **l** in the Spirit, let us also walk *2198*
Eph 6:3 mayest **l** long on the earth. *2071, 3118*
Php 1:21 For to me to **l** is Christ, and to *2198*
Php 1:22 But if I **l** in the flesh, this is the........ *2198*
2Ti 2:11 with him, we shall also **l** with him:..... *4800*
2Ti 3:12 and all that will **l** godly in Christ *2198*
Heb 10:38 Now the just shall **l** by faith: but....... *2198*
Heb 13:18 in all things willing to **l** honestly........ *390*
Jas 4:15 If the Lord will, we shall **l**, and *2198*
1Pe 4:6 **l** according to God in the spirit. *2198*
2Pe 2:18 escaped from them who **l** in error *390*
1Jn 4:9 that we might **l** through him. *2198*
Rev 13:14 the wound by a sword, and did **l**....... *2198*

LIVED

Ge 9:28 And Noah **l** after the flood three....... 2421
Nu 21:9 beheld the serpent of brass, he **l**....... 2425
Dt 5:26 midst of the fire, as we have, and **l**? 2421
1Ki 12:6 Solomon his father while he yet **l**, ... 2416
Eze 37:10 breath came into them, and they **l**,..... 2421
Lk 2:36 and had **l** with an husband seven *2198*
Jas 5:5 have **l** in pleasure on the earth,......... *5171*
Rev 18:7 glorified herself, and **l** deliciously,
Rev 20:4 they **l** and reigned with Christ a *2198*
Rev 20:5 rest of the dead **l** not again until........ *326*

LIVELY

Ex 1:19 for they are **l**, and are delivered........ 2422
Ac 7:38 the **l** oracles to give unto us: *2198*
1Pe 1:3 begotten us again unto a **l** hope *2198*
1Pe 2:5 as **l** stones, are built up a spiritual...... *2198*

LIVER

Ex 29:22 the caul above the **l**, and the two 3516
Le 9:10 caul above the **l** of the sin offering, ... 3516
Pr 7:23 Till a dart strike through his **l**: 3516
La 2:11 my **l** is poured upon the earth,........ 3516

LIVES

Ge 9:5 your blood of your **l** will I require;..... 5315
Ex 1:14 their **l** bitter with hard bondage,....... 2416
Jos 2:13 and deliver our **l** from death 5315
Jos 9:24 were sore afraid of our **l** because 5315
Jgs 5:18 a people that jeoparded their **l** 5315
2Sa 23:17 that went in jeopardy of their **l**? 5315
Pr 1:18 they lurk privily for their own **l** 5315
Jer 19:7 hands of them that seek their **l**........ 5315
La 5:9 our bread with the peril of our **l**....... 5315
Da 7:12 yet their **l** were prolonged for a........ 2417
Lk 9:56 **is not come to destroy men's l,**........ *5590*
1Jn 3:16 to lay down our **l** for the brethren *5590*
Rev 12:11 loved not their **l** unto the death........ *5590*

LIVEST

Dt 12:19 as long as thou **l** upon the earth 3117
Gal 2:14 **l** after the manner of Gentiles, ... *2198*
Rev 3:1 **name that thou l, and art dead**........ *2198*

LIVETH

Ge 9:3 Every moving thing that **l** shall........ 2416
Dt 5:24 God doth talk with man, and he **l** 2425
Jgs 8:19 as the Lord **l**, if ye had saved 2416
1Sa 1:28 as long as he **l** he shall be lent to....... 3117
1Sa 14:45 as the Lord **l**, there shall not one....... 2416
1Sa 20:31 as long as the son of Jesse **l** upon 2425
1Sa 25:34 as the Lord God of Israel **l**, which...... 2416
1Sa 26:10 As the Lord **l**, the Lord shall smite 2416
1Sa 28:10 saying, As the Lord **l**, there shall no 2416
2Sa 11:11 thy soul **l**, I will not do this thing. 2416
1Ki 3:23 This is my son that **l**, and thy son...... 2416

1Ki	17:23	and Elijah said, See, thy son **l**	2416
1Ki	18:10	As the Lord thy God **l**, there is no	2416
2Ki	2:2	the Lord **l**, and as thy soul **l**,	2416
Job	19:25	For I know that my redeemer **l**,	2416
Ps	18:46	The Lord **l**; and blessed be my	2416
Jer	4:2	The Lord **l**, in truth, in judgment,	2416
Jer	12:16	to swear by my name, The Lord **l**;	2416
Jer	16:14	shall no more be said, The Lord **l**,	2416
Jer	23:7	they shall no more say, The Lord **l**,	2416
Eze	47:9	pass, that every thing that **l**, which	2416
Da	4:34	and honoured him that **l** for ever,	2416
Da	12:7	sware by him that **l** for ever that it	2416
Jn	4:50	unto him, **Go thy way; thy son l**	*2198*
Jn	11:26	**whosoever l and believeth in me,**	*2198*
Ro	6:10	but in that he **l**, he **l** unto God	*2198*
Ro	7:2	law to her husband so long as he **l**;	*2198*
Ro	14:7	For none of us **l** to himself, and no	*2198*
1Co	7:39	the law as long as her husband **l**;	*2198*
2Co	13:4	yet he **l** by the power of God. For	*2198*
Gal	2:20	live; yet not I, but Christ **l** in me:	*2198*
1Ti	5:6	**l** in pleasure is dead while she **l**	*2198*
Heb	7:25	he ever **l** to make intercession	*2198*
1Pe	1:23	word of God, which **l** and abideth	*2198*
Rev	1:18	**I am he that l, and was dead;**	*2198*
Rev	4:9	the throne, who **l** for ever and ever,	*2198*
Rev	4:10	him that **l** for ever and ever,	*2198*
Rev	15:7	wrath of God, who **l** for ever and	*2198*

LIVING See also QUICK.

Ge	1:21	and every **l** creature that moveth,	2416
Ge	2:7	of life; and man became a **l** soul	2416
Ge	2:19	Adam called every **l** creature,	2416
Ge	3:20	because she was the mother of all **l**	2416
Ge	6:19	of every **l** thing of all flesh, two of	2416
Ge	7:23	And every **l** substance was destroyed	
Le	11:46	every **l** creature that moveth in the	2416
Nu	16:48	stood between the dead and the **l**;	2416
Dt	5:26	hath heard the voice of the **l** God	2416
Jos	3:10	know that the **l** God is among you,	2416
1Sa	17:26	defy the armies of the **l** God?	2416
2Sa	20:3	of their death, **l** in widowhood.	2424
1Ki	3:25	king said, Divide the **l** child in two,	2416
2Ki	19:4	hath sent to reproach the **l** God;	2416
Job	12:10	hand is the soul of every **l** thing,	2416
Ps	27:13	of the Lord in the land of the **l**	2416
Ps	42:2	thirsteth for God, for the **l** God:	2416
Ps	56:13	walk before God in the light of the **l**?	2416
Ps	69:28	be blotted out of the book of the **l**	2416
Ps	84:2	my flesh crieth out for the **l** God	2416
Ps	116:9	before the Lord in the land of the **l**	2416
Ps	143:2	sight shall no man **l** be justified,	2416
Ecc	7:2	and the **l** will lay it to his heart.	2416
Ecc	9:4	a **l** dog is better than a dead lion	2416
Ecc	9:5	For the **l** know that they shall die:	2416
Isa	38:19	The **l**, the **l**, he shall praise thee,	2416
Isa	53:8	was cut off out of the land of the **l**	2416
Jer	2:13	me the fountain of **l** waters,	2416
Jer	10:10	is the true God, he is the **l** God,	2416
Jer	11:19	cut him off from the land of the **l**,	2416
Jer	23:36	perverted the words of the **l** God,	2416
La	3:39	Wherefore doth a **l** man complain,	2416
Eze	1:5	the likeness of four **l** creatures	2416
Eze	3:13	noise of the wings of the **l** creatures	2416
Eze	10:15	This is the **l** creature that I saw by	2416
Eze	26:20	shall set glory in the land of the **l**;	2416
Da	4:17	**l** may know that the most High	2417
Da	6:26	God of Daniel: for he is the **l** God,	2417
Hos	1:10	them, Ye are the sons of the **l** God	2416
Mt	16:16	the Christ, the Son of the **l** God	*2198*
Mt	22:32	**the God of the dead, but of the l**	*2198*
Mt	26:63	him, I adjure thee by the **l** God,	*2198*
Mk	12:27	**of the dead, but the God of the l:**	*2198*
Lk	8:43	had spent all her **l** upon physicians	*979*
Lk	15:12	**And he divided unto them his l**	*979*
Lk	15:30	**hath devoured thy l with harlots,**	*979*
Lk	20:38	**God of the dead, but of the l.**	*2198*
Lk	21:4	**hath cast in all the l that she had**	*979*
Lk	24:5	seek ye the **l** among the dead?	*2198*
Jn	4:10	**he would have given thee l water**	*2198*
Jn	6:51	**I am the l bread which came**	*2198*
Jn	6:57	**As the l Father hath sent me, and**	*2198*
Jn	7:38	**belly shall flow rivers of l water**	*2198*
Ac	14:15	from these vanities unto the **l** God,	*2198*
Ro	9:26	be called the children of the **l** God	*2198*
Ro	12:1	present your bodies a **l** sacrifice,	*2198*
1Co	15:45	first man Adam was made a **l** soul;	*2198*
2Co	3:3	but with the Spirit of the **l** God;	*2198*
Col	2:20	why, as though **l** in the world, are	*2198*
1Th	1:9	idols to serve the **l** and true God;	*2198*
1Ti	3:15	which is the church of the **l** God,	*2198*
1Ti	4:10	because we trust in the **l** God, who	*2198*
Tit	3:3	pleasures, **l** in malice and envy,	*1236*
Heb	9:14	dead works to serve the **l** God?	*2198*
Heb	10:20	By a new and **l** way, which he hath	*2198*
Heb	12:22	and unto the city of the **l** God,	*2198*
1Pe	2:4	whom coming, as unto a **l** stone,	*2198*
Rev	7:2	east, having the seal of the **l** God:	*2198*
Rev	16:3	and every **l** soul died in the sea.	*2198*

LO

Ge	8:11	**l**, in her mouth was an olive leaf	2009
Ge	15:3	**l**, one born in my house is mine	2009
Ps	40:7	**L**, I come: in the volume of the	2009
Ps	139:4	but, **l**, O Lord, thou knowest it	2005
Isa	6:7	said, **L**, this hath touched thy lips;	2009
Da	3:25	**L**, I see four men loose, walking	1888
Hag	1:9	for much, and, **l**, it came to little;	2009
Zec	2:10	**l**, I come, and I will dwell in the	
Mt	28:20	**l, I am with you alway, even unto**	*2400*
Lk	2:9	**l**, the angel of the Lord came upon	*2400*
Heb	10:7	**L**, I come (in the volume of the	*2400*
Heb	10:9	**L**, I come to do thy will, O God	*2400*

LOATHETH

Nu	21:5	and our soul **l** this light bread.	6973
Pr	27:7	The full soul **l** an honeycomb; but	947

LOATHSOME

Nu	11:20	nostrils, and it be **l** unto you:	2214
Job	7:5	my skin is broken, and become **l**	3988
Ps	38:7	loins are filled with a **l** disease:	7033
Pr	13:5	a wicked man is **l**, and cometh to	887

LOAVES

Le	23:17	two wave **l** of two tenth deals:	3899
Jgs	8:5	**l** of bread unto the people that	3603
1Sa	10:3	another carrying three **l** of bread	3603
1Sa	21:3	give me five **l** of bread in mine hand	
Mt	14:19	took the five **l**, and the two fishes	*740*
Mt	15:36	he took the seven **l** and the fishes,	*740*
Mt	16:9	**remember the five l of the five**	*740*
Mt	16:10	**Neither the seven l of the four**	*740*
Mk	6:52	considered not the miracle of the **l**:	*740*

Jn	6:9	lad here, which hath five barley **l**,	*740*
Jn	6:26	**but because ye did eat of the l, and**	*740*

LOCK

Eze	8:3	and took me by a **l** of mine head;	6734

LOCKS

Nu	6:5	the **l** of the hair of his head grow	6545
Jgs	16:19	to shave off the seven **l** of his head;	4253
Ne	3:15	thereof, the **l** thereof,	4514
Isa	47:2	uncover thy **l**, make bare the leg,	6777
Eze	44:20	nor suffer their **l** to grow long;	6545

LOCUST

Ex	10:19	not one **l** in all the coasts of Egypt,	697
Le	11:22	ye may eat; the **l** after his kind,	697
Dt	28:38	little in; for the **l** shall consume it	697
Dt	28:42	of thy land shall the **l** consume.	6767
Ps	78:46	and their labour unto the **l**,	697
Ps	109:23	I am tossed up and down as the **l**	697
Joel	1:4	that which the **l** hath left hath the	697
Joel	2:25	you the years that the **l** hath eaten,	697

LOCUSTS

Ex	10:4	will I bring the **l** into thy coast:	697
Ex	10:14	before them there were no such **l**	697
2Ch	7:13	command the **l** to devour the land,	2284
Ps	105:34	He spake, and the **l** came, and	697
Pr	30:27	The **l** have no king, yet go they	697
Isa	33:4	as the running to and fro of **l** shall	1357
Na	3:17	Thy crowned are as the **l**, and thy	697
Mt	3:4	his meat was **l** and wild honey	*200*
Rev	9:3	there came out of the smoke **l** upon	*200*
Rev	9:7	shapes of the **l** were like unto horses	*200*

LODGE

Ge	24:23	thy father's house for us to **l** in?	3885
Jos	4:3	place, where ye shall **l** this night	3885
Jgs	19:20	upon me; only **l** not in the street	3885
Ru	1:16	and where thou lodgest, I will **l**:	3885
2Sa	17:16	**L** not this night in the plains of	3885
Ne	13:21	unto them, Why **l** ye about the wall?	3885
Isa	65:4	graves, and **l** in the monuments	3885
Jer	4:14	How long shall thy vain thoughts **l**.	3885
Mt	13:32	**and l in the branches thereof.**	*2681*

LODGED

Jos	2:1	house, named Rahab, and **l** there	7901
Jos	4:8	them unto the place where they **l**,	4411
1Ch	9:27	**l** round about the house of God,	3885
Ne	13:20	sellers of all kind of ware **l** without	3885
Isa	1:21	judgment; rightousness **l** in it;	3885
Lk	13:19	**fowls of the air l in the branches**	*2681*
1Ti	5:10	children, if she have **l** strangers,	*3580*

LODGEST

Ru	1:16	and where thou **l**, I will lodge:	3885

LOFT

1Ki	17:19	carried him up into a **l**, where he	5944
Ac	20:9	and fell down from the third **l**,	*5152*

LOFTINESS

Isa	2:17	the **l** of man shall be bowed down	1365
Jer	48:29	his **l**, and his arrogancy, and his	1363

LOFTY

Ps	131:1	is not haughty, nor mine eyes **l**:	7311
Pr	30:13	generation, O how **l** are their eyes!	7311
Isa	2:11	**l** looks of man shall be humbled,	1365
Isa	5:15	eyes of the **l** shall be humbled:	1364
Isa	26:5	high; the **l** city, he layeth it low;	7682
Isa	57:7	Upon a **l** and high mountain hast	1364
Isa	57:15	**l** One that inhabiteth eternity,	5375

LOINS

Ge	35:11	and kings shall come out of thy **l**;	2504
Ge	37:34	and put sackcloth upon his **l**,	4975
Ex	1:5	souls that came out of the **l** of Jacob	3409
Ex	12:11	with your **l** girded, your shoes on	4975
Dt	33:11	smite through the **l** of them that	4975
2Sa	20:8	with a sword fastened upon his **l**	4975
1Ki	18:46	and he girded up his **l**, and ran	4975
2Ki	4:29	Gird up thy **l**, and take my staff in	4975
Job	38:3	Gird up now thy **l** like a man; for	2504
Ps	38:7	my **l** are filled with a loathsome	3689
Ps	69:23	make their **l** continually to shake	4975
Pr	31:17	She girdeth her **l** with strength,	4975
Isa	11:5	righteousness ... the girdle of his **l**,	4975
Isa	21:3	Therefore are my **l** filled with pain:	4975
Isa	32:11	and gird sackcloth upon your **l**.	2504
Jer	48:37	cuttings, and upon the **l** sackcloth	4975
Eze	21:6	of man, with the breaking of thy **l**;	4975
Eze	44:18	have linen breeches upon their **l**;	4975
Da	5:6	the joints of his **l** were loosed,	2783
Da	10:5	**l** were girded with fine gold of	4975
Na	2:1	watch the way, make thy **l** strong,	4975
Na	2:10	together, and much pain is in all **l**,	4975
Mt	3:4	and a leathern girdle about his **l**;	3751
Mk	1:6	with a girdle of a skin about his **l**;	*3751*
Lk	12:35	**Let your l be girded about, and**	*3751*
Ac	2:30	to him, that of the fruit of his **l**,	*3751*
Eph	6:14	having your **l** girt about with truth	*3751*
Heb	7:5	they come out of the **l** of Abraham:	*3751*
1Pe	1:13	gird up the **l** of your mind, be sober,	*3751*

LONG

Ge	48:15	the God which fed me all my life **l**	5750
Ex	10:3	How **l** wilt thou refuse to humble	4970
Ex	16:28	How **l** refuse ye to keep my	5704
Ex	20:12	days may be **l** upon the land which	748
Ex	27:9	of an hundred cubits **l** for one side:	753
Le	26:34	sabbaths, as **l** as it lieth desolate,	3117
Nu	9:18	as **l** as the cloud abode upon the	3117
Nu	14:11	how **l** will it be ere they believe me,	5704
Dt	1:6	have dwelt **l** enough in this mount:	7227
Dt	14:24	if the way be too **l** for thee, so that	7235
Dt	20:19	thou shalt besiege a city a **l** time,	7227
Jos	6:5	make a **l** blast with the ram's horn,	4900
Jos	18:3	How **l** are ye slack to go to possess	5704
Jos	24:7	dwelt in the wilderness a **l** season	7227
Jgs	5:28	Why is his chariot so **l** in coming?	954
1Sa	1:14	How **l** wilt thou be drunken? put	5704
1Sa	1:28	as **l** as he liveth he shall be lent to	3117
1Ki	3:11	hast not asked for thyself **l** life;	7227
1Ki	18:21	How **l** halt ye between two	5704
2Ch	26:5	as **l** as he sought the Lord, God	3117
Job	3:21	Which **l** for death, but it cometh	2442
Ps	4:2	how **l** will ye love vanity, and seek	
Ps	13:1	How **l** wilt thou forget me, O Lord?	5704
Ps	35:17	Lord, how **l** wilt thou look on?	5704
Ps	38:6	greatly; I go mourning all the day **l**	
Ps	44:22	for thy sake are we killed all the day **l**;	
Ps	72:5	as **l** as the sun and moon endure	5973
Ps	82:2	How **l** will ye judge unjustly, and	5704

Ps	90:13	Return, O Lord, how **l**? and let it	5704
Ps	91:16	With **l** life will I satisfy him, and	753
Ps	95:10	Forty years **l** was I grieved with this	
Pr	3:2	**l** life, and peace, shall they add	753
Pr	6:9	How **l** wilt thou sleep, O sluggard?	5704
Pr	23:30	They that tarry **l** at the wine; they	
Pr	25:15	By **l** forbearing is a prince	753
Ecc	12:5	because man goeth to his **l** home	5769
Isa	6:11	Then said I, Lord, how **l**? And he	5704
Jer	47:6	how **l** will it be ere thou be quiet?	5704
Da	10:1	but the time appointed was **l**:	1419
Hab	1:2	O Lord, how **l** shall I cry, and thou	5704
Zec	1:12	how **l** wilt thou not have mercy on	5704
Mt	9:15	**mourn, as l as the bridegroom is**	*1909*
Mt	17:17	**how l shall I be with you?**	*2193*
Mt	23:14	**for a pretence make l prayer:**	*3117*
Mk	16:5	side, clothed in a **l** white garment;	
Lk	9:41	**how l shall I be with you, and**	*2193*
Lk	18:7	**him, though he bear l with them?**	*3114*
Lk	20:46	**which desire to walk in l robes,**	
Lk	20:47	**and for a shew make l prayers:**	*3117*
Jn	14:9	**Have I been so l time with you**	*5118*
Ro	7:2	law to her husband so **l** as he liveth;	
Ro	8:36	thy sake we are killed all the day **l**;	
1Co	7:39	as **l** as her husband liveth;	*5550*
1Co	11:14	if a man have **l** hair, it is a shame	*2863*
1Co	11:15	But if a woman have **l** hair, it is a	*2863*
1Co	13:4	Charity suffereth **l**, and is kind;	*3114*
Eph	6:3	thou mayest live **l** on the earth	*2118*
2Pe	1:13	as **l** as I am in this tabernacle, to stir	
Rev	6:10	How **l**, O Lord, holy and true,	*2193*

LONGED

2Sa	13:39	David **l** to go forth unto Absalom:	3615
2Sa	23:15	And David **l**, and said, Oh that one	183
Ps	119:40	I have **l** after thy precepts:	8373
Ps	119:174	I have **l** for thy salvation, O Lord;	8373
Php	4:1	brethren dearly beloved and **l** for	*1973*

LONGER

Ex	9:28	let you go, and ye shall stay no **l**	3254
2Ki	6:33	should I wait for the Lord any **l**?	5750
Lk	16:2	**for thou mayest be no l steward**	*2089*
Ac	25:24	that he ought not to live any **l**	*3370*
Ro	6:2	dead to sin, live any **l** therein?	*2089*
Gal	3:25	we are no **l** under a schoolmaster	*2089*
1Ti	5:23	Drink no **l** water, but use a little	*3371*
1Pe	4:2	he no **l** should live the rest of his	*3371*
Rev	10:6	that there should be time no **l**;	*2089*

LONGETH

Dt	12:20	because thy soul **l** to eat flesh;	183
Ps	63:1	my flesh **l** for thee in a dry and	3642
Ps	84:2	My soul **l**, yea, even fainteth for	3700

LONGING

Dt	28:32	fail with **l** for them all the day long:	
Ps	107:9	he satisfieth the **l** soul, and filleth	8264
Ps	119:20	My soul breaketh for the **l** that it	8375

LONGSUFFERING

Ex	34:6	merciful and gracious, **l**, and	750, 639
Nu	14:18	Lord is **l**, and of great mercy,	750, 639
Ps	86:15	**l**, and plenteous in mercy and	750, 639
Jer	15:15	take me not away in thy **l**:	750, 639
Ro	2:4	goodness and forbearance and **l**;	*3115*
2Co	6:6	by **l**, by kindness, by the Holy	*3115*
Gal	5:22	of the Spirit is love, joy, peace, **l**,	*3115*
Eph	4:2	with **l**, forbearing one another in	*3115*
Col	3:12	humbleness of mind, meekness, **l**;	*3115*
1Ti	1:16	Christ might shew forth all **l**,	*3115*
2Ti	3:10	of life, purpose, faith, **l**, charity	*3115*
2Ti	4:2	exhort with all **l** and doctrine	*3115*
1Pe	3:20	the **l** of God waited in the days of	*3115*
2Pe	3:9	but is **l** to us-ward, not willing	*3114*
2Pe	3:15	the **l** of our Lord is salvation;	*3115*

LOOK

Ge	12:11	thou art a fair woman to **l** upon:	4758
Ge	19:17	**l** not behind thee, neither stay thou	5027
Ge	41:33	**l** out a man discreet and wise	7200
Ex	5:21	The Lord **l** upon you, and judge;	7200
Le	13:3	the priest shall **l** on the plague in	7200
Dt	26:15	**L** down from thy holy habitation,	8259
1Sa	16:7	**L** not on his countenance, or on	5027
2Sa	11:2	was very beautiful to **l** upon	4758
1Ki	18:43	Go up now, **l** toward the sea	5027
Ps	22:17	bones: they **l** and stare upon me	5027
Ps	25:18	**L** upon mine affliction and my	7200
Ps	101:5	hath an high **l** and a proud heart	5869
Ps	119:132	**L** … upon me, and be merciful	6437
Pr	6:17	A proud **l**, a lying tongue, and	5869
Pr	21:4	An high **l**, and a proud heart, and	5869
Pr	27:23	flocks, and **l** well to thy herds	7896
Isa	17:7	day shall a man **l** to his Maker,	8159
Isa	22:4	**L** away from me; I will weep	8159
Isa	31:1	they **l** not unto the Holy One of	8159
Isa	42:18	and **l**, ye blind, that ye may see	5027
Isa	45:22	**L** unto me, and be ye saved, all	6437
Isa	59:11	**l** for judgment, but there is none;	6960
Isa	63:15	**L** down from heaven, and behold	5027
Jer	47:3	the fathers shall not **l** back to their	6437
La	3:50	Till the Lord **l** down, and behold	8259
Jnh	2:4	**l** again toward thy holy temple	5027
Mic	4:11	and let our eye **l** upon Zion	2372
Mic	7:7	Therefore I will **l** unto the Lord;	6822
Hab	2:15	thou mayest **l** on their nakedness!	5027
Zec	12:10	**l** upon me whom they have pierced	5027
Mt	11:3	come, or do we **l** for another?	*4328*
Lk	9:38	I beseech thee, **l** upon my son:	*1914*
Jn	4:35	**up your eyes, and l on the fields;**	*2300*
Jn	19:37	shall **l** on him whom they pierced	*3700*
Ac	6:3	**l** ye out among you seven men of	*1980*
2Co	4:18	**l** not at the things which are seen,	*4648*
2Co	10:7	Do ye **l** on things after the outward	*991*
Php	3:20	whence also we **l** for the Saviour	*553*
2Pe	3:13	**l** for new heavens and a new	*4328*
2Jn	8	**L** to yourselves, that we lose not	*991*
Rev	5:3	open the book, neither to **l** thereon	*991*
Rev	5:4	read the book, neither to **l** thereon	*991*

LOOKED

Ge	6:12	And God **l** upon the earth, and,	*7200*
Ge	19:26	But his wife **l** back from behind	5027
Ge	19:28	he **l** toward Sodom and Gomorrah	8259
Ge	39:23	The keeper of the prison **l** not to	7200
Ex	3:2	he **l**, and, behold, the bush burned	7200
Ex	33:8	**l** after Moses, until he was gone	5027
Dt	9:16	And I **l**, and, behold, ye had sinned	7200
Jgs	5:28	of Sisera **l** out at a window,	8259
1Sa	6:19	had **l** into the ark of the Lord,	7200
Est	2:15	sight of all them that **l** upon her	6437
Job	30:26	When I **l** for good, then evil came	6960

Ps	14:2	Lord **l** down from heaven upon	8259
Ps	102:19	he hath **l** down from the height of	8259
Ps	142:4	I **l** on my right hand, and beheld	5027
Pr	24:32	I **l** upon it, and received instruction	7200
Ecc	2:11	Then I **l** on all the works that my	6437
Isa	5:7	and he **l** for judgment, but behold	6960
Isa	22:11	but ye have not **l** unto the maker	5027
Isa	63:5	I **l**, and there was none to help;	5027
Jer	8:15	We **l** for peace, but no good came;	6960
Eze	1:4	And I **l**, and, behold, a whirlwind	7200
Eze	10:9	when I **l**, behold the four wheels by	7200
Da	1:13	let our countenances be **l** upon	7200
Mk	6:41	he **l** up to heaven, and blessed, and	*308*
Mk	8:24	he **l** up, and said, I see men as trees,	*308*
Lk	2:38	to all them that **l** for redemption	*4327*
Lk	10:32	**came and l on him, and passed by**	*1492*
Lk	22:61	Lord turned, and **l** upon Peter	*1689*
Ac	1:10	they **l** stedfastly toward heaven	*816*
Heb	11:10	**l** for a city which hath foundations	*1551*
1Jn	1:1	which we have **l** upon, and our	*2300*
Rev	4:1	After this I **l**, and, behold, a door	*1492*
Rev	6:8	And I **l**, and behold a pale horse:	*1492*
Rev	14:1	I **l**, and, lo, a Lamb stood on the	*1492*

LOOKETH

Nu	21:8	when he **l** upon it, shall live	7200
1Sa	16:7	man **l** on the outward appearance,	7200
1Sa	16:7	but the Lord **l** on the heart	7200
Ps	104:32	He **l** on the earth, and it trembleth:	5027
Pr	31:27	She **l** well to the ways of her	6822
Mt	5:28	**l on a woman to lust after her**	*991*
Mt	24:50	**in a day when he l not for him,**	*4328*
Jas	1:25	**l** into the perfect law of liberty,	*3879*

LOOKING

Mt	14:19	and **l** up to heaven, he blessed, and	*308*
Lk	9:16	**l** up to heaven, he blessed them	*308*
Lk	9:62	**his hand to the plough, and l back,**	*991*
Jn	20:5	And he stooping down, and **l** in, saw	
Tit	2:13	**L** for that blessed hope, and the	*4327*
Heb	12:2	**L** unto Jesus the author and	*872*
Heb	12:15	**L** diligently lest any man fail of	*1983*
Jude	21	**l** for the mercy of our Lord Jesus	*4327*

LOOKS

Ps	18:27	but wilt bring down high **l**	5869
Isa	2:11	lofty **l** of man shall be humbled	5869
Isa	10:12	Assyria, and the glory of his high **l**	5869
Eze	2:6	words, nor be dismayed at their **l**,	6440

LOOSE See also **UNLOOSE.**

Le	14:7	the living bird **l** into the open field	7971
Dt	25:9	and **l** his shoe from off his foot,	2502
Jos	5:15	**L** thy shoe from off thy foot; for	5394
Job	38:31	Pleiades, or **l** the bands of Orion?	6605
Ps	102:20	**l** those that are appointed to death;	6605
Isa	52:2	**l** thyself from the bands of thy neck,	6605
Isa	58:6	to **l** the bands of wickedness, to	6605
Jer	40:4	I **l** thee this day from the chains	6605
Da	3:25	Lo, I see four men **l**, walking in	8271
Mt	16:19	**whatsoever thou shalt l on earth**	*3089*
Mt	18:18	**whatsoever ye shall l on earth**	*3089*
Lk	13:15	**on the sabbath l his ox or his ass**	*3089*
Lk	19:31	**man ask you, Why do ye l him?**	*3089*
Ac	13:25	of his feet I am not worthy to **l**	*3089*
Rev	5:2, 5	and to **l** the seven seals thereof	*3089*

LOOSED

Ex	28:28	the breastplate be not **l** from the	2118
Ecc	12:6	Or ever the silver cord be **l**, or the	7368
Isa	51:14	exile hasteneth that he may be **l**,	6605
Da	5:6	that the joints of his loins were **l**,	8271
Mt	16:19	**loose on earth shall be l in**	*3089*
Mt	18:27	**with compassion, and l him, and**	*630*
Lk	1:64	and his tongue **l**, and he spake, and	
Lk	13:12	**thou art l from thine infirmity**	*630*
Lk	13:16	**l from this bond on the sabbath**	*3089*
Ro	7:2	is **l** from the law of her husband	*2673*
1Co	7:27	Art thou **l** from a wife? seek not	*3080*
Rev	9:15	And the four angels were **l**, which	3089
Rev	20:3	that he must be **l** a little season	3089
Rev	20:7	Satan shall be **l** out of his prison,	3089

LORD

Ge	2:4	that the **L** God made the earth	3068
Ge	2:7	**L** God formed man of the dust	3068
Ge	2:8	And the **L** God planted a garden	3068
Ge	2:16	the **L** God commanded the man,	3068
Ge	2:19	the **L** God formed every beast	3068
Ge	2:21	**L** God caused a deep sleep to fall	3068
Ge	3:21	the **L** God made coats of skins,	3068
Ge	11:9	the **L** did there confound the	3068
Ge	15:6	And he believed in the **L**; and he	3068
Ge	16:7	the angel of the **L** found her by	3068
Ge	18:14	Is any thing too hard for the **L**?	3068
Ge	19:24	**L** rained upon Sodom and upon	3068
Ge	24:7	The **L** God of heaven, which took	3068
Ge	24:50	thing proceedeth from the **L**:	3068
Ge	27:29	be **l** over thy brethren, and let	1376
Ge	28:13	I am the **L** God of Abraham thy	3068
Ge	28:16	Surely the **L** is in this place; and	3068
Ge	45:9	God hath made me **l** of all Egypt:	113
Ex	5:2	Pharaoh said, Who is the **L**, that	3068
Ex	6:7	know that I am the **L** your God	3068
Ex	9:12	**L** hardened the heart of Pharaoh,	3068
Ex	9:21	regarded not the word of the **L**	3068
Ex	9:27	the **L** is righteous, and I and my	3068
Ex	11:10	the **L** hardened Pharaoh's heart,	3068
Ex	12:14	ye shall keep it a feast to the **L**	3068
Ex	12:23	the **L** will pass over the door,	3068
Ex	13:21	**L** went before them by day in a	3068
Ex	14:8	**L** hardened the heart of Pharaoh	3068
Ex	14:14	The **L** shall fight for you, and ye	3068
Ex	14:27	**L** overthrew the Egyptians in the	3068
Ex	14:31	feared the **L**, and believed the **L**,	3068
Ex	15:26	for I am the **L** that healeth thee	3068
Ex	18:11	the **L** is greater than all gods:	3068
Ex	19:18	the **L** descended upon it in fire:	3068
Ex	20:2	I am the **L** thy God, which have	3068
Ex	20:5	the **L** thy God am a jealous God	3068
Ex	20:7	name of the **L** thy God in vain;	3068
Ex	20:7	the **L** will not hold him guiltless	3068
Ex	20:11	the **L** blessed the sabbath day,	3068
Ex	24:16	glory of the **L** abode upon mount	3068
Ex	24:17	glory of the **L** was like devouring	3068
Ex	28:36	of a signet, Holiness To The **L**	3068
Ex	30:10	it is most holy unto the **L**	3068
Ex	31:17	the **L** made heaven and earth,	3068
Ex	32:14	**L** repented of the evil which he	3068
Ex	33:11	**L** spake unto Moses face to face	3068
Ex	34:14	for the **L**, whose name is Jealous	3068
Ex	39:30	of a signet, Holiness To The **L**	3068
Ex	40:35	the glory of the **L** filled the	3068

Ex	40:38	the cloud of the **L** was upon the	3068
Le	1:9	of a sweet savour unto the **L**	3068
Le	6:22	it is a statute for ever unto the **L**;	3068
Le	9:4	to day the **L** will appear unto you	3068
Le	10:19	accepted in the sight of the **L**?	3068
Le	16:8	one lot for the **L**, and the other	3068
Le	18:4	therein: I am the **L** your God	3068
Le	18:5	he shall live in them: I am the **L**	3068
Le	19:12	the name of thy God: I am the **L**	3068
Le	19:32	and fear thy God: I am the **L**	3068
Le	20:8	I am the **L** which sanctify you	3068
Le	23:20	be holy to the **L** for the priest	3068
Le	23:40	rejoice before the **L** your God	3068
Le	24:11	blasphemed the name of the **L**,	
Le	26:46	laws, which the **L** made between	3068
Le	27:21	jubile, shall be holy unto the **L**	3068
Nu	3:4	offered strange fire before the **L**,	3068
Nu	5:21	**L** make thee a curse and an oath	3068
Nu	6:5	separateth himself unto the **L**	3068
Nu	6:24	The **L** bless thee, and keep thee:	3068
Nu	6:25	**L** make his face shine upon thee,	3068
Nu	6:26	**L** lift up his countenance upon	3068
Nu	11:3	fire of the **L** burnt among them	3068
Nu	11:25	And the **L** came down in a cloud	3068
Nu	11:29	the **L** would put his spirit upon	3068
Nu	12:5	**L** came down in the pillar of the	3068
Nu	14:8	If the **L** delight in us, then he	3068
Nu	14:14	that thou **L** art seen face to face,	3068
Nu	14:18	The **L** is longsuffering, and of	3068
Nu	16:30	if the **L** make a new thing, and	3068
Nu	16:35	there came out a fire from the **L**,	3068
Nu	17:13	the tabernacle of the **L** shall die:	3068
Nu	21:6	**L** sent fiery serpents among the	3068
Nu	22:22	angel of the **L** stood in the way	3068
Nu	22:31	**L** opened the eyes of Balaam	3068
Nu	23:5	**L** put a word in Balaam's mouth,	3068
Nu	27:16	Let the **L**, the God of the spirits	3068
Nu	27:21	judgment of Urim before the **L**	3068
Nu	32:20	go armed before the **L** to war,	3068
Nu	32:23	ye have sinned against the **L**	3068
Dt	1:8	land which the **L** sware unto your	3068
Dt	1:36	he hath wholly followed the **L**	3068
Dt	1:45	the **L** would not hearken to your	3068
Dt	2:30	**L** thy God hardened his spirit	3068
Dt	3:22	**L** your God he shall fight for you	3068
Dt	4:24	**L** thy God is a consuming fire,	3068
Dt	4:31	the **L** thy God is a merciful God;)	3068
Dt	4:39	that the **L** he is God in heaven	3068
Dt	5:11	the **L** will not hold him guiltless	3068
Dt	6:4	Israel: The **L** our God is one **L**:	3068
Dt	6:5	love the **L** thy God with all thine	3068
Dt	6:13	Thou shalt fear the **L** thy God	3068
Dt	6:16	shall not tempt the **L** your God,	3068
Dt	9:10	**L** delivered unto me two tables of	3068
Dt	10:12	what doth the **L** thy God require	3068
Dt	10:17	the **L** your God is God of gods,	3068
Dt	11:12	eyes of the **L** thy God are always	3068
Dt	13:3	ye love the **L** your God with all	3068
Dt	14:2	holy people unto the **L** thy God,	3068
Dt	16:1	the passover unto the **L** thy God:	3068
Dt	17:15	whom the **L** thy God shall choose:	3068
Dt	18:7	minister in the name of the **L** his	3068
Dt	18:13	be perfect with the **L** thy God	3068
Dt	20:18	so should ye sin against the **L**	3068
Dt	23:20	**L** thy God may bless thee in all	3068
Dt	23:21	**L** thy God will surely require it	3068
Dt	24:19	**L** thy God may bless thee in all	3068
Dt	26:7	**L** heard our voice, and looked	3068
Dt	26:8	**L** brought us forth out of Egypt	3068
Dt	26:18	**L** hath avouched thee this day to	3068
Dt	27:6	build the altar of the **L** thy God	3068
Dt	28:1	**L** thy God will set thee on high	3068
Dt	28:8	**L** shall command the blessing	3068
Dt	28:10	art called by the name of the **L**;	3068
Dt	28:28	**L** shall smite thee with madness	3068
Dt	28:58	fearful name, The Lord Thy God;	3068
Dt	28:63	**L** rejoiced over you to do you good,	3068
Dt	28:64	**L** shall scatter thee among all	3068
Dt	29:4	**L** hath not given you an heart to	3068
Dt	29:12	covenant with the **L** thy God	3068
Dt	29:20	**L** shall blot out his name from	3068
Dt	29:25	forsaken the covenant of the **L**	3068
Dt	30:3	**L** thy God will turn thy captivity,	3068
Dt	30:6	**L** thy God will circumcise thine	3068
Dt	30:16	this day to love the **L** thy God	3068
Dt	30:20	thou mayest love the **L** thy God	3068
Dt	31:13	learn to fear the **L** your God, as	3068
Dt	34:1	the **L** shewed him all the land of	3068
Dt	34:10	whom the **L** knew face to face	3068
Jos	1:9	for the **L** thy God is with thee	3068
Jos	2:9	the **L** hath given you the land,	3068
Jos	3:17	the ark of the covenant of the **L**	3068
Jos	4:14	that day the **L** magnified Joshua	3068
Jos	4:23	**L** your God dried up the waters	3068
Jos	5:14	as captain of the host of the **L**	3068
Jos	10:14	man: for the **L** fought for Israel	3068
Jos	11:20	of the **L** to harden their hearts,	3068
Jos	14:9	wholly followed the **L** my God	3068
Jos	18:8	cast lots for you before the **L** in	3068
Jos	22:22	The **L** God of gods, the **L** God	3068
Jos	22:29	turn this day from following the **L**,	3068
Jos	22:34	between us that the **L** is God	3068
Jos	23:16	the covenant of the **L** your God	3068
Jos	24:14	Now therefore fear the **L**, and	3068
Jos	24:19	people, Ye cannot serve the **L**:	3068
Jos	24:21	Nay; but we will serve the **L**	3068
Jos	24:24	The **L** our God will we serve	3068
Jgs	2:12	they forsook the **L** God of their	3068
Jgs	2:15	hand of the **L** was against them	3068
Jgs	2:16	the **L** raised up judges, which	3068
Jgs	2:18	then the **L** was with the judge	3068
Jgs	3:7	and forgat the **L** their God, and	3068
Jgs	3:9	**L** raised up a deliverer to the	3068
Jgs	3:10	Spirit of the **L** came upon him,	3068
Jgs	3:15	the **L** raised them up a deliverer	3068
Jgs	4:2	the **L** sold them into the hand of	3068
Jgs	4:9	**L** shall sell Sisera into the hand	3068
Jgs	5:5	mountains melted ... before the **L**,	3068
Jgs	6:8	**L** sent a prophet unto the children	3068
Jgs	6:11	there came an angel of the **L**,	3068
Jgs	6:13	if the **L** be with us, why then is	3068
Jgs	6:22	seen an angel of the **L** face to face	3068
Jgs	6:34	Spirit of the **L** came upon Gideon,	3068
Jgs	7:18	and say, The sword of the **L**, and	3068
Jgs	10:6	evil again in the sight of the **L**,	3068
Jgs	11:10	The **L** be witness between us,	3068
Jgs	11:27	the **L** the Judge be judge this day	3068
Jgs	11:30	Jephthah vowed a vow unto the **L**,	3068
Jgs	13:1	evil again in the sight of the **L**;	3068
Jgs	13:1	**L** delivered them into the hand	3068

Jgs	13:18	the angel of the **L** said unto him	3068
Jgs	13:20	the angel of the **L** ascended in	3068
Jgs	13:25	the Spirit of the **L** began to move	3068
Jgs	14:4	knew not that it was of the **L**,	3068
Jgs	16:20	wist not that the **L** was departed	3068
Ru	1:17	the **L** do so to me, and more also	3068
Ru	4:11	**L** make the woman that is come	3068
Ru	4:14	Blessed be the **L**, which hath not	3068
1Sa	1:10	and prayed unto the **L**, and wept	3068
1Sa	1:27	the **L** hath given me my petition	3068
1Sa	1:28	liveth he shall be lent to the **L**	3068
1Sa	2:2	There is none holy as the **L**;	3068
1Sa	2:6	The **L** killeth, and maketh alive:	3068
1Sa	2:7	The **L** maketh poor, and maketh	3068
1Sa	2:20	**L** give thee seed of this woman	3068
1Sa	3:4	the **L** called Samuel: and he	3068
1Sa	3:6	the **L** called yet again, Samuel	3068
1Sa	3:7	Samuel did not yet know the **L**,	3068
1Sa	3:8	**L** called Samuel again the third	3068
1Sa	3:8	perceived that the **L** had called	3068
1Sa	3:9	that thou shalt say, Speak, **L**;	3068
1Sa	4:3	fetch the ark of the covenant of the **L**	3068
1Sa	5:6	hand of the **L** was heavy upon	3068
1Sa	6:2	shall we do to the ark of the **L**?	3068
1Sa	6:21	brought again the ark of the **L**;	3068
1Sa	7:10	**L** thundered with a great thunder	3068
1Sa	7:17	there he built an altar unto the **L**	3068
1Sa	10:6	Spirit of the **L** will come upon	3068
1Sa	11:7	fear of the **L** fell on the people,	3068
1Sa	11:13	the **L** hath wrought salvation in	3068
1Sa	12:5	The **L** is witness against you	3068
1Sa	12:6	It is the **L** that advanced Moses	3068
1Sa	12:9	when they forgat the **L** their God	3068
1Sa	12:13	the **L** hath set a king over you	3068
1Sa	12:22	**L** will not forsake his people for	3068
1Sa	12:24	Only fear the **L**, and serve him in	3068
1Sa	13:14	**L** hath sought him a man after	3068
1Sa	14:23	So the **L** saved Israel that day:	3068
1Sa	15:1	**L** sent me to anoint thee to be	3068
1Sa	15:22	the **L** as great delight in burnt	3068
1Sa	15:22	as in obeying the voice of the **L**?	3068
1Sa	15:26	**L** hath rejected thee from being	3068
1Sa	15:28	**L** hath rent the kingdom of Israel	3068
1Sa	15:35	**L** repented that he had made Saul king	3068
1Sa	16:7	**L** seeth not as man seeth; for	3068
1Sa	16:7	but the **L** looketh on the heart	3068
1Sa	16:13	Spirit of the **L** came upon David	3068
1Sa	16:14	Spirit of the **L** departed from Saul,	3068
1Sa	17:37	**L** that delivered me out of the paw	3068
1Sa	17:47	the **L** saveth not with sword and	3068
1Sa	18:28	knew that the **L** was with David,	3068
1Sa	20:15	**L** hath cut off … enemies of David	3068
1Sa	24:6	**L** forbid that I should do this	3068
1Sa	24:15	The **L** therefore be judge, and	3068
1Sa	26:12	deep sleep from the **L** was fallen	3068
1Sa	26:19	**L** have stirred thee up against	3068
1Sa	28:6	the **L** answered him not, neither	3068
1Sa	30:6	encouraged himself in the **L** his	3068
2Sa	3:28	guiltless before the **L** for ever	3068
2Sa	6:14	David danced before the **L** with	3068
2Sa	7:19	a small thing in thy sight, O **L** God;	136
2Sa	7:22	thou art great, O **L** God: for	3068
2Sa	12:1	the **L** sent Nathan unto David	3068
2Sa	12:13	I have sinned against the **L**	3068
2Sa	15:7	which I have vowed unto the **L**,	3068
2Sa	19:7	I swear by the **L**, if thou go not	3068
2Sa	22:2	**L** is my rock, and my fortress	3068
2Sa	22:7	my distress I called upon the **L**,	3068
2Sa	22:21	**L** rewarded me according to my	3068
2Sa	22:31	the word of the **L** is tried: he is	3068
2Sa	22:32	For who is God, save the **L**? and	3068
2Sa	24:16	the **L** repented him of the evil	3068
2Sa	24:16	the angel of the **L** was by the	3068
1Ki	2:4	**L** may continue his word which	3068
1Ki	2:32	**L** shall return his blood upon his	3068
1Ki	2:44	**L** shall return thy wickedness	3068
1Ki	3:3	Solomon loved the **L**, walking in	3068
1Ki	5:4	**L** my God hath given me rest on	3068
1Ki	5:12	the **L** gave Solomon wisdom, as	3068
1Ki	7:51	made for the house of the **L**	3068
1Ki	8:11	glory of the **L** had filled the	3068
1Ki	8:61	be perfect with the **L** our God,	3068
1Ki	10:9	the **L** loved Israel for ever,	3068
1Ki	13:26	**L** hath delivered him unto the lion,	3068
1Ki	14:21	the city which the **L** did choose	3068
1Ki	15:4	the **L** his God give him a lamp	3068
1Ki	15:5	was right in the eyes of the **L**,	3068
1Ki	17:14	the day that the **L** sendeth rain	3068
1Ki	17:22	the **L** heard the voice of Elijah;	3068
1Ki	18:1	the word of the **L** came to Elijah	3068
1Ki	18:3	Obadiah feared the **L** greatly:	3068
1Ki	18:12	Spirit of the **L** shall carry thee	3068
1Ki	18:21	if the **L** be God, follow him: but	3068
1Ki	18:37	know that thou art the **L** God,	3068
1Ki	18:38	Then the fire of the **L** fell, and	3068
1Ki	18:39	**L**, he is the God; the **L**, he is the	3068
1Ki	18:46	the hand of the **L** was on Elijah;	3068
1Ki	19:4	now, O **L**, take away my life; for	3068
1Ki	19:11	the **L** passed by, and a great and	3068
1Ki	19:11	but the **L** was not in the wind:	3068
1Ki	19:11	**L** was not in the earthquake:	3068
1Ki	19:12	but the **L** was not in the fire:	3068
1Ki	20:13	thou shalt know that I am the **L**	3068
1Ki	20:28	said, The **L** is God of the hills	3068
1Ki	22:7	there not here a prophet of the **L**	3068
1Ki	22:19	I saw the **L** sitting on his throne,	3068
1Ki	22:24	went the Spirit of the **L** from me	3068
2Ki	2:3	the **L** will take away thy master	3068
2Ki	2:14	Where is the **L** God of Elijah?	3068
2Ki	2:16	Spirit of the **L** hath taken him	3068
2Ki	3:10	**L** hath called these three kings	3068
2Ki	3:11	there not here a prophet of the **L**,	3068
2Ki	4:28	said, Did I desire a son of my **l**?	113
2Ki	6:17	**L** opened the eyes of the young	3068
2Ki	6:20	And the **L** opened their eyes, and	3068
2Ki	7:2	if the **L** would make windows in	3068
2Ki	7:6	**L** had made the host of Syrians	136
2Ki	8:1	the **L** hath called for a famine;	3068
2Ki	8:10	**L** hath shewed me that he shall	3068
2Ki	8:19	**L** would not destroy Judah for	3068
2Ki	9:25	the **L** laid this burden upon him;	3068
2Ki	10:16	me, and see my zeal for the **L**	3068
2Ki	10:31	to walk in the law of the **L** God	3068
2Ki	10:32	the **L** began to cut Israel short:	3068
2Ki	11:3	hid in the house of the **L** six years	3068
2Ki	12:4	brought into the house of the **L**,	3068
2Ki	13:5	(And the **L** gave Israel a saviour	3068
2Ki	14:3	was right in the sight of the **L**,	3068
2Ki	14:26	the **L** saw the affliction of Israel,	3068
2Ki	17:8	heathen, whom the **L** cast out	3068

2Ki 17:20	**L** rejected all the seed of Israel,	3068
2Ki 17:23	**L** removed Israel out of his sight,	3068
2Ki 17:35	the **L** had made a covenant,	3068
2Ki 17:41	So these nations feared the **L**	3068
2Ki 18:6	he clave to the **L**, and departed	3068
2Ki 18:16	the doors of the temple of the **L**,	3068
2Ki 18:22	me, We trust in the **L** our God:	3068
2Ki 18:30	The **L** will surely deliver us, and	3068
2Ki 19:35	that the angel of the **L** went out,	3068
2Ki 20:9	This sign shalt thou have of the **L**,	3068
2Ki 20:19	Good is the word of the **L** which	3068
2Ki 21:10	**L** spake by his servants the prophets	3068
2Ki 21:22	forsook the **L** God of his fathers,	3068
2Ki 22:19	humbled thyself before the **L**	3068
2Ki 23:3	made a covenant before the **L**,	3068
2Ki 22:13	enquire of the **L** for me, and for	3068
2Ki 23:21	Keep the passover unto the **L**	3068
2Ki 23:26	**L** turned not from the fierceness	3068
2Ki 24:4	which the **L** would not pardon.	3068
1Ch 6:15	when the **L** carried away Judah	3068
1Ch 11:9	for the **L** of hosts was with him	3068
1Ch 11:14	and the **L** saved them by a great	3068
1Ch 13:11	**L** had made a breach upon Uzza:	3068
1Ch 15:2	them hath the **L** chosen to carry	3068
1Ch 16:8	Give thanks unto the **L**, call upon	3068
1Ch 16:23	Sing unto the **L**, all the earth;	3068
1Ch 16:25	For great is the **L**, and greatly	3068
1Ch 16:29	Give unto the **L** the glory due	3068
1Ch 16:29	worship the **L** in the beauty of	3068
1Ch 16:31	the nations, The **L** reigneth.	3068
1Ch 17:20	O **L**, there is none like thee,	3068
1Ch 18:6	Thus the **L** preserved David	3068
1Ch 19:13	let the **L** do that which is good in	3068
1Ch 21:3	why then doth my **l** require this	113
1Ch 21:12	three days the sword of the **L**	3068
1Ch 21:16	and saw the angel of the **L** stand	3068
1Ch 21:30	the sword of the angel of the **L**	3068
1Ch 22:1	This is the house of the **L** God,	3068
1Ch 22:12	Only the **L** give thee wisdom and	3068
1Ch 22:19	your soul to seek the **L** your God;	3068
1Ch 23:25	**L** God of Israel hath given rest	3068
1Ch 28:4	**L** God of Israel chose me before	3068
1Ch 28:5	the **L** hath given me many sons,)	3068
1Ch 28:9	the **L** searcheth all hearts, and	3068
1Ch 28:19	**L** made me understand in writing	3068
1Ch 29:18	O **L** God of Abraham, Isaac, and	3068
1Ch 29:20	worshipped the **L**, and the king	3068
1Ch 29:25	And the **L** magnified Solomon	3068
2Ch 1:1	the **L** his God was with him, and	3068
2Ch 2:11	the **L** hath loved his people,	3068
2Ch 3:1	began to build the house of the **L**	3068
2Ch 5:14	glory of the **L** had filled the house	3068
2Ch 6:1	**L** hath said that he would dwell	3068
2Ch 6:41	arise, O **L** God, into thy resting	3068
2Ch 6:42	O **L** God, turn not away the face	3068
2Ch 7:1	glory of the **L** filled the house	3068
2Ch 7:3	glory of the **L** upon the house,	3068
2Ch 7:12	**L** appeared to Solomon by night	3068
2Ch 8:16	the house of the **L** was perfected	3068
2Ch 11:16	set their hearts to seek the **L** God	3068
2Ch 12:6	and they said, the **L** is righteous	3068
2Ch 13:10	as for us, the **L** is our God, and	3068
2Ch 13:20	the **L** struck him, and he died	3068
2Ch 14:2	right in the eyes of the **L** his God:	3068
2Ch 14:6	because the **L** had given him rest	3068
2Ch 14:11	**L**, it is nothing with thee to help	3068
2Ch 14:11	O **L** thou art our God; let not	3068
2Ch 15:2	The **L** is with you, while ye be	3068
2Ch 15:4	trouble did turn unto the **L** God	3068
2Ch 15:12	seek the **L** God of their fathers	3068
2Ch 16:9	the eyes of the **L** run to and fro	3068
2Ch 17:6	lifted up in the ways of the **L**:	3068
2Ch 17:9	had the book of the law of the **L**	3068
2Ch 17:10	the fear of the **L** fell upon all the	3068
2Ch 18:6	there not here a prophet of the **L**	3068
2Ch 18:18	saw the **L** sitting upon his throne	3068
2Ch 18:22	the **L** hath put a lying spirit in	3068
2Ch 19:6	but for the **L**, who is with you in	3068
2Ch 19:7	no iniquity with the **L** our God,	3068
2Ch 20:3	and set himself to seek the **L**,	3068
2Ch 20:14	Spirit of the **L** in the midst of the	3068
2Ch 20:18	before the **L**, worshipping the **L**	3068
2Ch 20:29	heard that the **L** fought against	3068
2Ch 20:37	the **L** hath broken thy works	3068
2Ch 21:16	**L** stirred up against Jehoram	3068
2Ch 21:18	**L** smote him in his bowels with	3068
2Ch 22:7	the **L** had anointed to cut off the	3068
2Ch 22:9	sought the **L** with all his heart	3068
2Ch 24:4	to repair the house of the **L**	3068
2Ch 24:9	bring in to the **L** the collection	3068
2Ch 24:22	The **L** look upon it, and require	3068
2Ch 25:7	for the **L** is not with Israel, to wit,	3068
2Ch 25:9	**L** is able to give thee much more	3068
2Ch 26:18	Uzziah, to burn incense unto the **L**,	3068
2Ch 26:20	because the **L** had smitten him.	3068
2Ch 28:13	offended against the **L** already,	3068
2Ch 28:19	**L** brought Judah low because of	3068
2Ch 28:21	portion out of the house of the **L**,	3068
2Ch 28:24	the doors of the house of the **L**,	3068
2Ch 29:5	sanctify the house of the **L** God	3068
2Ch 29:10	a covenant with the **L** God of	3068
2Ch 29:11	the **L** hath chosen you to stand	3068
2Ch 29:18	cleansed all the house of the **L**,	3068
2Ch 29:35	house of the **L** was set in order	3068
2Ch 30:8	and serve the **L** your God, that	3068
2Ch 30:9	For if ye turn again unto the **L**,	3068
2Ch 30:9	for the **L** your God is gracious	3068
2Ch 30:18	The good **L** pardon every one	3068
2Ch 31:4	encouraged in the law of the **L**	3068
2Ch 31:6	consecrated unto the **L** their God,	3068
2Ch 31:20	and truth before the **L** his God.	3068
2Ch 32:11	The **L** our God shall deliver us	3068
2Ch 32:17	also letters to rail on the **L** God	3068
2Ch 32:21	the **L** sent an angel, which cut off	3068
2Ch 33:13	knew that the **L** he was God	3068
2Ch 33:16	he repaired the altar of the **L**,	3068
2Ch 34:14	found a book of the law of the **L**	3068
2Ch 34:17	was found in the house of the **L**,	3068
2Ch 34:21	Go, enquire of the **L** for me, and	3068
2Ch 35:1	Josiah kept a passover unto the **L**	3068
2Ch 36:15	the **L** God of their fathers sent to	3068
2Ch 36:18	treasures of the house of the **L**,	3068
2Ch 36:22	**L** stirred up the spirit of Cyrus	3068
2Ch 36:23	the **L** God of heaven given me;	3068
2Ch 36:23	The **L** his God be with him, and	3068
Ezr 1:5	build the house of the **L** which is	3068
Ezr 1:7	the vessels of the house of the **L**,	3068
Ezr 6:22	the **L** had made them joyful, and	3068
Ezr 7:6	hand of the **L** his God upon him	3068
En 7:10	heart to seek the law of the **L**,	3068

Ne	4:14	remember the **L**, which is great.	136
Ne	8:6	Ezra blessed the **L**, the great God.	3068
Ne	8:10	the joy of the **L** is your strength.	3068
Ne	9:3	book of the law of the **L** their	3068
Ne	9:6	Thou, even thou, art **L** alone;	3068
Job	1:7	the **L** said unto Satan, Whence	3068
Job	1:9	Satan answered the **L**, and said,	3068
Job	1:12	forth from the presence of the **L**.	3068
Job	1:21	**L** gave, and the **L** hath taken	3068
Job	1:21	blessed be the name of the **L**,	3068
Job	2:4	Satan answered the **L**, and said,	3068
Job	2:6	the **L** said unto Satan, Behold,.	3068
Job	2:7	forth from the presence of the **L**,	3068
Job	42:9	them: the **L** also accepted Job.	3068
Job	42:10	**L** turned the captivity of Job,	3068
Job	42:10	**L** gave Job twice as much as he	3068
Job	42:11	evil that the **L** had brought upon	3068
Job	42:12	**L** blessed the latter end of Job	3068
Ps	1:2	his delight is in the law of the **L**;	3068
Ps	2:2	against the **L**, and against his.	3068
Ps	3:8	Salvation belongeth unto the **L**:	3068
Ps	4:5	and put your trust in the **L**	3068
Ps	8:1	our **L**, how excellent is thy name.	113
Ps	10:3	covetous, whom the **L** abhorreth	3068
Ps	10:16	The **L** is King for ever and ever:	3068
Ps	11:1	In the **L** put I my trust: how say	3068
Ps	11:4	The **L** is in his holy temple, the.	3068
Ps	11:5	The **L** trieth the righteous: but	3068
Ps	11:7	righteous **L** loveth righteousness;	3068
Ps	12:4	lips are our own: who is **l** over us?	113
Ps	12:6	words of the **L** are pure words:	3068
Ps	14:2	The **L** looked down from heaven	3068
Ps	14:7	**L** bringeth back the captivity of	3068
Ps	15:4	honoureth them that fear the **L**	3068
Ps	16:5	The **L** is the portion of mine.	3068
Ps	16:8	have set the **L** always before me:	3068
Ps	18:2	**L** is my rock, and my fortress,	3068
Ps	18:18	calamity: but the **L** was my stay	3068
Ps	18:28	the **L** my God will enlighten my	3068
Ps	18:30	the word of the **L** is tried:	3068
Ps	18:46	The **L** liveth; and blessed be my	3068
Ps	19:7	The law of the **L** is perfect,	3068
Ps	19:7	the testimony of the **L** is sure,	3068
Ps	19:8	The statutes of the **L** are right,	3068
Ps	19:8	commandment of the **L** is pure,	3068
Ps	19:9	The fear of the **L** is clean,.	3068
Ps	19:9	the judgments of the **L** are true.	3068
Ps	20:6	I that the **L** saveth his anointed;	3068
Ps	21:9	**L** shall swallow them up in his	3068
Ps	23:1	The **L** is my shepherd; I shall.	3068
Ps	23:6	in the house of the **L** for ever.	3068
Ps	24:8	The **L** strong and mighty,	3068
Ps	24:8	the **L** mighty in battle.	3068
Ps	24:10	The **L** of hosts, he is the King of	3068
Ps	25:8	Good and upright is the **L**:	3068
Ps	25:15	Mine eyes are ever toward the **L**;.	3068
Ps	27:1	**L** is my light and my salvation;	3068
Ps	27:1	the **L** is the strength of my life;	3068
Ps	27:4	One thing have I desired of the **L**,	3068
Ps	27:4	may dwell in the house of the **L**,.	3068
Ps	27:13	goodness of the **L** in the land of	3068
Ps	28:1	Unto thee will I cry, O **L** my rock;	3068
Ps	28:7	The **L** is my strength and my.	3068
Ps	29:2	worship the **L** in the beauty of	3068
Ps	30:4	Sing unto the **L**, O ye saints of his,	3068
Ps	31:23	for the **L** preserveth the faithful,	3068
Ps	32:2	the **L** imputeth not iniquity,	3068
Ps	33:4	For the word of the **L** is right;	3068
Ps	33:8	Let all the earth fear the **L**: let	3068
Ps	33:18	eye of the **L** is upon them that fear.	3068
Ps	34:1	I will bless the **L** at all times:	3068
Ps	34:3	O magnify the **L** with me, and	3068
Ps	34:8	taste and see that the **L** is good:	3068
Ps	34:15	The eyes of the **L** are upon the	3068
Ps	34:18	**L** is nigh unto them that are of.	3068
Ps	35:9	my soul shall be joyful in the **L**:	3068
Ps	37:3	Trust in the **L**, and do good; so	3068
Ps	37:4	Delight thyself also in the **L**;	3068
Ps	37:5	Commit thy way unto the **L**;	3068
Ps	37:7	Rest in the **L**, and wait patiently	3068
Ps	37:13	the **L** shall laugh at him; for he	136
Ps	37:18	The **L** knoweth the days of the	3068
Ps	37:23	good man are ordered by the **L**:	3068
Ps	37:24	**L** upholdeth him with his hand.	3068
Ps	37:33	**L** will not leave him in his hand,.	3068
Ps	40:1	I waited patiently for the **L**; and	3068
Ps	40:16	continually, The **L** be magnified.	3068
Ps	47:2	For the **L** most high is terrible;	3068
Ps	48:1	Great is the **L**, and greatly to be	3068
Ps	55:22	Cast thy burden upon the **L**, and	3068
Ps	68:11	The **L** gave the word: great was	136
Ps	68:19	Blessed be the **L**, who daily loadeth	136
Ps	69:31	please the **L** better than an ox	3068
Ps	69:33	For the **L** heareth the poor, and	3068
Ps	75:8	in the hand of the **L** there is a cup,	3068
Ps	76:11	and pay unto the **L** your God:.	3068
Ps	77:7	Will the **L** cast off forever? and	136
Ps	78:65	**L** awaked as one out of a sleep,	136
Ps	84:11	the **L** will give grace and glory:	3068
Ps	86:1	Bow down thine ear, O **L**, hear	3068
Ps	89:1	I will sing of the mercies of the **L**	3068
Ps	89:8	O **L** God of hosts, who is a strong	3068
Ps	89:18	For the **L** is our defence; and the	3068
Ps	89:52	Blessed be the **L** for evermore	3068
Ps	90:17	let the beauty of the **L** our God be	3068
Ps	92:5	O **L**, how great are thy works!	3068
Ps	93:1	The **L** reigneth, he is clothed	3068
Ps	93:4	**L** on high is mightier than the	3068
Ps	94:7	they say, The **L** shall not see.	3050
Ps	94:11	**L** knoweth the thoughts of man,	3068
Ps	94:17	Unless the **L** had been my help,	3068
Ps	94:22	But the **L** is my defence; and my.	3068
Ps	95:6	us kneel before the **L** our maker	3068
Ps	96:1	O sing unto the **L** a new song:.	3068
Ps	96:4	For the **L** is great, and greatly to	3068
Ps	98:1	O sing unto the **L** a new song;.	3068
Ps	98:2	**L** hath made known his salvation:	3068
Ps	98:4	Make a joyful noise unto the **L**,.	3068
Ps	99:9	Exalt the **L** our God, and worship	3068
Ps	100:1	Make a joyful noise unto the **L**,.	3068
Ps	100:2	Serve the **L** with gladness: come	3068
Ps	100:3	Know ye that the **L** he is God:.	3068
Ps	103:1	Bless the **L**, O my soul: and all	3068
Ps	103:2	Bless the **L**, O my soul, and forget	3068
Ps	103:8	The **L** is merciful and gracious,.	3068
Ps	103:13	the **L** pitieth them that fear him	3068
Ps	103:17	mercy of the **L** is from everlasting	3068
Ps	103:22	bless the **L**, O my soul.	3068
Ps	104:31	The glory of the **L** shall endure.	3068
Ps	105:4	Seek the **L**, and his strength:	3050

Ps	106:1	O give thanks unto the **L**; for he	3068
Ps	106:25	not unto the voice of the **L**	3068
Ps	107:1	O give thanks unto the **L**, for he	3068
Ps	107:2	Let the redeemed of the **L** say so,	3068
Ps	107:8	praise the **L** for his goodness,	3068
Ps	110:1	said unto my **L**, Sit thou at my	113
Ps	111:1	will praise the **L** with my whole	3068
Ps	111:4	the **L** is gracious and full of	3068
Ps	111:10	The fear of the **L** is the beginning	3068
Ps	112:7	heart is fixed, trusting in the **L**	3068
Ps	114:7	thou earth, at the presence of the **L**,	113
Ps	115:12	The **L** hath been mindful of us:	3068
Ps	115:14	**L** shall increase you more and	3068
Ps	115:17	The dead praise not the **L**,	3050
Ps	116:1	I love the **L**, because he hath	3068
Ps	116:6	The **L** preserveth the simple:	3068
Ps	116:7	the **L** hath dealt bountifully with	3068
Ps	116:14	I will pay my vows unto the **L**	3068
Ps	117:2	truth of the **L** endureth for ever	3068
Ps	118:4	Let them now that fear the **L** say,	3068
Ps	118:6	The **L** is on my side: I will not	3068
Ps	118:8	It is better to trust in the **L** than	3068
Ps	118:14	The **L** is my strength and song,	3050
Ps	118:15	right hand of the **L** doeth valiantly	3068
Ps	118:24	the day which the **L** hath made;	3068
Ps	119:57	Thou art my portion, O **L**: I	3068
Ps	119:166	**L**, I have hoped for thy salvation,	3068
Ps	121:2	My help cometh from the **L**,	3068
Ps	121:7	**L** shall preserve thee from all	3068
Ps	121:8	**L** shall preserve thy going out	3068
Ps	124:1	been the **L** who was on our side,	3068
Ps	124:8	Our help is in the name of the **L**,	3068
Ps	125:1	trust in the **L** shall be as mount	3068
Ps	125:2	**L** is round about his people from	3068
Ps	127:1	Except the **L** build the house,	3068
Ps	127:3	children are an heritage of the **L**:	3068
Ps	130:6	My soul waiteth for the **L** more	136
Ps	132:13	For the **L** hath chosen Zion; he	3068
Ps	134:3	**L** that made heaven and earth	3068
Ps	135:1	Praise ye the **L**. Praise ye the	3050
Ps	136:1	O give thanks unto the **L**; for he	3068
Ps	138:8	The **L** will perfect that which	3068
Ps	139:1	O **L**, thou hast searched me,	3068
Ps	139:4	O **L**, thou knowest it altogether	3068
Ps	140:12	**L** will maintain the cause of the	3068
Ps	144:3	**L**, what is man, that thou takest	3068
Ps	145:3	Great is the **L**, and greatly to be	3068
Ps	145:14	The **L** upholdeth all that fall,	3068
Ps	146:2	While I live will I praise the **L**: I	3068
Ps	146:8	**L** openeth the eyes of the blind:	3068
Ps	146:8	**L** raiseth them that are bowed	3068
Ps	147:1	Praise ye the **L**: for it is good	3050
Ps	147:5	Great is our **L**, and of great power:	113
Ps	147:6	The **L** lifteth up the meek: he	3068
Ps	149:1	Sing unto the **L** a new song,	3068
Ps	150:6	that hath breath praise the **L**	3050
Pr	1:7	fear of the **L** is the beginning of	3068
Pr	2:5	understand the fear of the **L**,	3068
Pr	2:6	For the **L** giveth wisdom: out of	3068
Pr	3:5	Trust in the **L** with all thine	3068
Pr	3:9	Honour the **L** with thy substance.	3068
Pr	3:12	whom the **L** loveth he correcteth;	3068
Pr	3:26	For the **L** shall be thy confidence,	3068
Pr	3:32	froward is abomination to the **L**:	3068
Pr	5:21	man are before the eyes of the **L**,	3068
Pr	6:16	These six things doth the **L** hate:	3068
Pr	8:13	The fear of the **L** is to hate evil:	3068
Pr	8:22	**L** possessed me in the beginning	3068
Pr	8:35	and shall obtain favour of the **L**	3068
Pr	9:10	fear of the **L** is the beginning of	3068
Pr	10:27	fear of the **L** prolongeth days:	3068
Pr	10:29	The way of the **L** is strength to	3068
Pr	11:1	balance is abomination to the **L**:	3068
Pr	11:20	heart are abomination to the **L**:	3068
Pr	12:2	man obtaineth favour of the **L**:	3068
Pr	12:22	lips are abomination to the **L**:	3068
Pr	14:2	his uprightness feareth the **L**:	3068
Pr	14:26	fear of the **L** is strong confidence:	3068
Pr	14:27	fear of the **L** is a fountain of life,	3068
Pr	15:3	eyes of the **L** are in every place,	3068
Pr	15:11	and destruction are before the **L**:	3068
Pr	15:16	little with the fear of the **L** than	3068
Pr	15:29	The **L** is far from the wicked:	3068
Pr	16:1	of the tongue, is from the **L**	3068
Pr	16:2	but the **L** weigheth the spirits	3068
Pr	16:3	Commit thy works unto the **L**,	3068
Pr	16:7	When a man's ways please the **L**,	3068
Pr	16:9	but the **L** directeth his steps	3068
Pr	17:3	gold: but the **L** trieth the hearts	3068
Pr	18:10	name of the **L** is a strong tower:	3068
Pr	19:14	and a prudent wife is from the **L**	3068
Pr	19:17	upon the poor lendeth unto the **L**;	3068
Pr	19:23	The fear of the **L** tendeth to life:	3068
Pr	20:24	Man's goings are of the **L**; how	3068
Pr	20:27	of man is the candle of the **L**,	3068
Pr	21:1	heart is in the hand of the **L**,	3068
Pr	21:31	of battle: but safety is of the **L**	3068
Pr	22:2	the **L** is the maker of them all	3068
Pr	22:12	eyes of the **L** preserve knowledge,	3068
Pr	22:23	For the **L** will plead their cause,	3068
Pr	24:18	Lest the **L** see it, and it displease	3068
Pr	25:22	and the **L** shall reward thee	3068
Pr	29:13	the **L** lighteneth both their eyes	3068
Pr	31:30	a woman that feareth the **L**, she	3068
Isa	1:9	the **L** of hosts had left unto us a	3068
Isa	1:20	mouth of the **L** hath spoken it	3068
Isa	2:3	go up to the mountain of the **L**,	3068
Isa	2:5	let us walk in the light of the **L**	3068
Isa	2:11	**L** alone shall be exalted in that	3068
Isa	2:12	**L** of hosts shall be upon every	3068
Isa	3:13	The **L** standeth up to plead, and	3068
Isa	4:2	branch of the **L** be beautiful and	3068
Isa	5:24	cast away the law of the **L** of	3068
Isa	6:1	also the **L** sitting upon a throne,	136
Isa	6:3	Holy, holy, holy, is the **L** of	3068
Isa	6:5	seen the king, the **L** of hosts	3068
Isa	6:11	Then said I, **L**, how long? And he	136
Isa	6:12	**L** have removed men far away,	3068
Isa	7:14	**L** himself shall give you a sign;	136
Isa	8:13	Sanctify the **L** of hosts himself;	3068
Isa	9:7	zeal of the **L** of hosts will perform	3068
Isa	10:12	**L** hath performed his whole work	136
Isa	11:2	the spirit of the **L** shall rest upon	3068
Isa	11:15	the **L** shall utterly destroy the	3068
Isa	12:2	**L** Jehovah is my strength and	3050
Isa	13:6	for the day of the **L** is at hand;	3068
Isa	13:9	Behold, the day of the **L** Cometh,	3068
Isa	14:5	**L** hath broken the staff of the	3068
Isa	19:1	the **L** rideth upon a swift cloud,	3068
Isa	19:19	shall there be an altar to the **L**	3068

Isa	19:20	for a witness unto the **L** of hosts	3068
Isa	22:17	the **L** will carry thee away with a	3068
Isa	23:9	The **L** of hosts hath purposed it	3068
Isa	23:18	hire shall be holiness to the **L**:	3068
Isa	24:1	the **L** maketh the earth empty,	3068
Isa	24:21	**L** shall punish the host of the	3068
Isa	24:23	**L** of hosts shall reign in mount	3068
Isa	25:1	O **L**, thou art my God; I will exalt	3068
Isa	25:8	**L** God will wipe away tears from	136
Isa	26:4	Trust ye in the **L** forever: for	3068
Isa	26:4	in the **L** Jehovah is everlasting	3050
Isa	26:11	**L**, when thy hand is lifted up, they	3068
Isa	26:12	**L**, thou wilt ordain peace for us:	3068
Isa	26:16	**L**, in trouble have they visited	3068
Isa	26:21	the **L** cometh out of his place to	3068
Isa	27:3	I the **L** do keep it; I will water it	3068
Isa	29:10	**L** hath poured out upon you the	3068
Isa	30:9	will not hear the law of the **L**:	3068
Isa	30:20	**L** give you the bread of adversity,	136
Isa	30:30	**L** shall cause his glorious voice	3068
Isa	31:3	the **L** shall stretch out his hand,	3068
Isa	31:4	the **L** of hosts come down to fight	3068
Isa	31:5	the **L** of hosts defend Jerusalem;	3068
Isa	33:6	the fear of the **L** is his treasure	3068
Isa	33:22	For the **L** is our judge,	3068
Isa	33:22	the **L** is our lawgiver	3068
Isa	33:22	the **L** is our king; he will save us	3068
Isa	34:6	sword of the **L** is filled with blood,	3068
Isa	34:16	Seek ye out of the book of the **L**,	3068
Isa	36:7	to me, We trust in the **L** our God:	3068
Isa	37:14	and spread it before the **L**	3068
Isa	37:17	Incline thine ear, O **L**, and hear;	3068
Isa	37:17	open thine eyes, O **L**, and see:	3068
Isa	37:20	may know that thou art the **L**,	3068
Isa	37:36	the angel of the **L** went forth,	3068
Isa	38:7	be a sign unto thee from the **L**,	3068
Isa	39:8	Good is the word of the **L** which	3068
Isa	40:3	Prepare ye the way of the **L**	3068
Isa	40:5	glory of the **L** shall be revealed	3068
Isa	40:5	mouth of the **L** hath spoken it	3068
Isa	40:7	spirit of the **L** bloweth upon it:	3068
Isa	40:31	that wait upon the **L** shall renew	3068
Isa	41:17	I the **L** will hear them, I the God	3068
Isa	42:6	I the **L** have called thee in	3068
Isa	42:8	I am the **L**: that is my name:	3068
Isa	42:10	Sing unto the **L** a new song, and	3068
Isa	42:13	**L** shall go forth as a mighty man,	3068
Isa	43:15	I am the **L**, your Holy One, the	3068
Isa	44:5	subscribe with his hand unto the **L**,	3068
Isa	44:23	heavens; for the **L** hath done it:	3068
Isa	44:23	for the **L** hath redeemed Jacob,	3068
Isa	45:3	know that I, the **L**, which call	3068
Isa	45:5	I am the **L**, and there is none else,	3068
Isa	45:8	together, I the **L** have created it	3068
Isa	45:18	the **L** that created the heavens;	3068
Isa	45:24	in the **L** have I righteousness and	3068
Isa	47:4	the **L** of hosts is his name, the	3068
Isa	48:14	The **L** hath loved him: he will	3068
Isa	48:16	the **L** God, and his Spirit, hath	136
Isa	49:1	**L** hath called me from the womb;	3068
Isa	49:5	be glorious in the eyes of the **L**,	3068
Isa	49:7	because of the **L** that is faithful,	3068
Isa	49:26	that I the **L** am thy Saviour and	3068
Isa	50:4	**L** God hath given me the tongue	136
Isa	50:5	**L** God hath opened mine ear, and	136
Isa	50:10	trust in the name of the **L**, and	3068
Isa	51:3	desert like the garden of the **L**;	3068
Isa	51:9	put on strength, O arm of the **L**;	3068
Isa	51:17	drunk at the hand of the **L** the cup	3068
Isa	52:10	**L** hath made bare his holy arm	3068
Isa	53:1	is the arm of the **L** revealed?	3068
Isa	53:6	**L** hath laid on him the iniquity	3068
Isa	53:10	it pleased the **L** to bruise him;	3068
Isa	53:10	pleasure of the **L** shall prosper in	3068
Isa	54:13	children shall be taught of the **L**;	3068
Isa	54:17	heritage of the servants of the **L**,	3068
Isa	55:5	thee because of the **L** thy God,	3068
Isa	55:6	Seek ye the **L** while he may be	3068
Isa	56:3	**L** hath utterly separated me from	3068
Isa	56:6	that join themselves to the **L**, to	3068
Isa	56:6	love the name of the **L**, to be his	3068
Isa	58:5	and an acceptable day to the **L**?	3068
Isa	58:11	the **L** shall guide thee continually	3068
Isa	58:14	thou delight thyself in the **L**;	3068
Isa	59:15	the **L** saw it, and it displeased	3068
Isa	59:19	fear the name of the **L** from the	3068
Isa	59:19	the Spirit of the **L** shall lift up a	3068
Isa	60:1	glory of the **L** is risen upon thee	3068
Isa	60:14	shall call thee, The city of the **L**,	3068
Isa	60:16	I the **L** am thy Saviour and thy	3068
Isa	61:1	Spirit of the **L** God is upon me	136
Isa	61:1	the **L** hath anointed me to preach	3068
Isa	61:2	the acceptable year of the **L**, and	3068
Isa	61:6	be named the Priests of the **L**:	3068
Isa	62:2	the mouth of the **L** shall name	3068
Isa	62:8	**L** hath sworn by his right hand,	3068
Isa	63:7	the lovingkindnesses of the **L**,	3068
Isa	66:5	Hear the word of the **L**, ye that	3068
Isa	66:5	sake, said, Let the **L** be glorified:	3068
Isa	66:15	behold, the **L** will come with fire	3068
Isa	66:16	will the **L** plead with all flesh:	3068
Isa	66:16	the slain of the **L** shall be many	3068
Isa	66:20	for an offering unto the **L** out of	3068
Isa	66:20	vessel into the house of the **L**	3068
Jer	1:6	Ah, **L** God! behold, I cannot speak:	136
Jer	2:6	Where is the **L** that brought us	3068
Jer	2:8	priests said not, Where is the **L**?	3068
Jer	2:17	hast forsaken the **L** thy God,	3068
Jer	2:37	**L** hath rejected thy confidences,	3068
Jer	3:16	The ark of the covenant of the **L**:	3068
Jer	3:21	have forgotten the **L** their God	3068
Jer	3:23	in the **L** our God is the salvation	3068
Jer	3:25	we have sinned against the **L** our	3068
Jer	4:4	Circumcise yourselves to the **L**,	3068
Jer	4:8	anger of the **L** is not turned back	3068
Jer	5:2	though they say, The **L** liveth;	3068
Jer	5:12	They have belied the **L**, and said	3068
Jer	5:24	Let us now fear the **L** our God	3068
Jer	7:29	**L** hath rejected and forsaken the	3068
Jer	8:14	**L** our God hath put us to silence,	3068
Jer	8:14	we have sinned against the **L**	3068
Jer	9:24	**L** which exercise lovingkindness	3068
Jer	10:6	there is none like unto thee, O **L**;	3068
Jer	10:10	the **L** is the true God, he is the	3068
Jer	10:16	The **L** of hosts is his name	3068
Jer	11:16	The **L** called thy name, A green	3068
Jer	11:17	For the **L** of hosts, that planted	3068
Jer	12:3	But thou, O **L**, knowest me: thou	3068
Jer	12:12	sword of the **L** shall devour from	3068
Jer	12:16	swear by my name, The **L** liveth:	3068

Eze	29:6	Egypt shall know that I am the **L**,	3068
Eze	30:3	even the day of the **L** is near,	3068
Eze	33:17	say, the way of the **L** is not equal:	136
Eze	33:20	say, The way of the **L** is not equal	136
Eze	33:22	the hand of the **L** was upon me	3068
Eze	33:23	the word of the **L** came unto me	3068
Eze	34:24	And I the **L** will be their God	3068
Eze	35:10	it; whereas the **L** was there:	3068
Eze	36:20	These are the people of the **L**, and	3068
Eze	36:36	I the **L** build the ruined places	3068
Eze	36:36	I the **L** have spoken it, and I will	3068
Eze	37:1	me out in the spirit of the **L**, and	3068
Eze	37:4	bones, hear the word of the **L**	3068
Eze	37:14	know that I the **L** have spoken it,	3068
Eze	37:28	that I the **L** do sanctify Israel	3068
Eze	40:46	come near to the **L** to minister	3068
Eze	41:22	is the table that is before the **L**	3068
Eze	43:4	glory of the **L** came into the house	3068
Eze	43:5	the glory of the **L** filled the house	3068
Eze	44:3	sit in it to eat bread before the **L**;	3068
Eze	44:4	of the **L** filled the house of the **L**:	3068
Eze	44:5	ordinances of the house of the **L**,	3068
Eze	45:1	shall offer an oblation unto the **L**,	3068
Eze	45:4	come near to minister unto the **L**:	3068
Eze	45:23	prepare a burnt offering to the **L**	3068
Eze	46:12	offerings voluntarily unto the **L**,	3068
Eze	46:14	a perpetual ordinance unto the **L**	3068
Eze	48:35	that day shall be, The **L** is there	3068
Da	2:10	there is no king, **l**, nor ruler, that	7229
Da	2:47	a God of gods, and a **L** of kings,	4756
Da	5:23	thyself against the **L** of heaven;	4756
Da	9:3	And I set my face unto the **L** God,	136
Da	9:4	I prayed unto the **L** my God,	3068
Da	9:9	To the **L** our God belong mercies	136
Da	9:10	we obeyed the voice of the **L** our	3068
Da	9:13	not our prayer before the **L** our	3068
Da	9:14	hath the **L** watched upon the evil,	3068
Da	9:14	**L** our God is righteous in all his	3068
Da	9:20	my supplication before the **L** my	3068
Da	12:8	O my **L**, what shall be the end of	113
Hos	1:7	will save them by the **L** their	3068
Hos	3:1	according to the love of the **L**	3068
Hos	3:5	return, and seek the **L** their God	3068
Hos	3:5	shall fear the **L** and his goodness	3068
Hos	4:1	the **L** hath a controversy with	3068
Hos	4:10	left off to take heed to the **L**	3068
Hos	4:16	the **L** will feed them as a lamb	3068
Hos	5:4	and they have not known the **L**	3068
Hos	5:6	with their herds to seek the **L**;	3068
Hos	6:3	if we follow on to know the **L**:	3068
Hos	8:1	eagle against the house of the **L**,	3068
Hos	8:13	but the **L** accepteth them not;	3068
Hos	9:4	not offer wine offerings to the **L**,	3068
Hos	9:4	not come into the house of the **L**	3068
Hos	10:3	because we feared not the **L**;	3068
Hos	10:12	for it is time to seek the **L**, till	3068
Hos	11:10	They shall walk after the **L**: he	3068
Hos	12:2	**L** hath also a controversy with	3068
Hos	12:5	the **L** is his memorial	3068
Hos	12:14	reproach shall his **L** return unto	113
Hos	13:15	the wind of the **L** shall come up	3068
Joel	1:9	cut off from the house of the **L**;	3068
Joel	1:15	for the day of the **L** is at hand,	3068
Joel	2:1	for the day of the **L** cometh, for	3068
Joel	2:11	for the day of the **L** is great and	3068
Joel	2:14	drink offering unto the **L** your	3068
Joel	2:17	the ministers of the **L**, weep	3068
Joel	2:18	the **L** be jealous for his land	3068
Joel	2:21	for the **L** will do great things	3068
Joel	2:23	and rejoice in the **L** your God:	3068
Joel	2:31	the terrible day of the **L** come	3068
Joel	2:32	shall call on the name of the **L**	3068
Joel	2:32	remnant whom the **L** shall call	3068
Joel	3:14	day of the **L** is near in the valley	3068
Joel	3:16	**L** will be the hope of his people,	3068
Am	1:2	the **L** will roar from Zion, and	3068
Am	2:4	have despised the law of the **L**,	3068
Am	3:6	city, and the **L** hath not done it?	3068
Am	3:7	Surely the **L** God will do nothing,	136
Am	4:2	**L** God hath sworn by his holiness	136
Am	5:6	Seek the **L**, and ye shall live;	3068
Am	5:8	of the earth: The **L** is his name:	3068
Am	5:18	you that desire the day of the **L**!	3068
Am	5:18	the day of the **L** is darkness, and	3068
Am	5:20	not the day of the **L** be darkness	3068
Am	6:10	mention of the name of the **L**	3068
Am	7:3	The **L** repented for this: It shall	3068
Am	7:4	the **L** God called to contend by fire,	136
Am	7:7	the **L** stood upon a wall made by a	136
Am	7:15	**L** took me as I followed the flock,	3068
Am	8:7	**L** hath sworn by the excellency	3068
Am	9:1	saw the **L** standing upon the altar:	136
Am	9:5	**L** God of hosts is he that toucheth	136
Ob	15	the day of the **L** is near upon all	3068
Jnh	1:3	from the presence of the **L**	3068
Jnh	1:4	**L** sent out a great wind into the	3068
Jnh	1:16	the men feared the **L** exceedingly,	3068
Jnh	1:16	and offered a sacrifice unto the **L**,	3068
Jnh	1:17	the **L** had prepared a great fish to	3068
Jnh	2:1	Jonah prayed unto the **L** his God	3068
Jnh	2:9	have vowed. Salvation is of the **L**	3068
Jnh	2:10	the **L** spake unto the fish, and it	3068
Jnh	4:6	the **L** God prepared a gourd, and	3068
Mic	1:2	the **L** God be witness against you	136
Mic	2:7	is the spirit of the **L** straitened?	3068
Mic	3:11	yet will they lean upon the **L**,	3068
Mic	4:5	walk in the name of the **L** our God	3068
Mic	4:7	the **L** shall reign over them in	3068
Mic	4:13	consecrate their gain unto the **L**,	3068
Mic	5:7	many people as a dew from the **L**,	3068
Mic	6:6	shall I come before the **L**, and	3068
Mic	6:7	the **L** be pleased with thousands	3068
Mic	6:8	what doth the **L** require of thee,	3068
Mic	7:8	the **L** shall be a light unto me	3068
Na	1:2	The **L** revengeth, and is furious;	3068
Na	1:3	The **L** is slow to anger, and great	3068
Na	1:7	The **L** is good, a strong hold in	3068
Na	2:2	For the **L** hath turned away the	3068
Hab	1:2	O **L**, how long shall I cry, and	3068
Hab	2:20	But the **L** is in his holy temple:	3068
Hab	3:18	Yet I will rejoice in the **L**, I will	3068
Hab	3:19	The **L** God is my strength, and he	3068
Zep	1:7	for the day of the **L** is at hand:	3068
Zep	1:7	the **L** hath prepared a sacrifice,	3068
Zep	1:12	The **L** will not do good, neither	3068
Zep	1:14	The great day of the **L** is near, it	3068
Zep	2:3	Seek ye the **L**, all ye meek of the	3068
Zep	2:7	the **L** their God shall visit them	3068
Zep	2:11	The **L** will be terrible unto them:	3068
Zep	3:17	**L** thy God in the midst of thee is	3068

Hag	1:14	And the **L** stirred up the spirit of	3068
Zec	1:2	**L** hath been sore displeased with	3068
Zec	1:10	are they whom the **L** hath sent	3068
Zec	1:13	**L** answered the angel that talked	3068
Zec	1:20	**L** shewed me four carpenters	3068
Zec	2:12	**L** shall inherit Judah his portion	3068
Zec	3:2	And the **L** said unto Satan,	3068
Zec	3:2	The **L** rebuke thee, O Satan,	3068
Zec	4:5	these be? And I said, No, my **l**	113
Zec	4:9	that the **L** of hosts hath sent me	3068
Zec	6:9	the word of the **L** came unto me	3068
Zec	6:12	shall build the temple of the **L**:	3068
Zec	6:14	memorial in the temple of the **L**	3068
Zec	8:3	the mountain of the **L** of hosts	3068
Zec	8:9	foundation of the house of the **L**	3068
Zec	8:21	go speedily to pray before the **L**, and	3068
Zec	9:14	the **L** shall be seen over them,	3068
Zec	9:14	the **L** God shall blow the trumpet,	136
Zec	9:15	the **L** of hosts shall defend them;	3068
Zec	9:16	**L** their God shall save them in	3068
Zec	10:1	Ask ye of the **L** rain in the time	3068
Zec	10:3	**L** of hosts hath visited his flock	3068
Zec	10:7	their heart shall rejoice in the **L**	3068
Zec	11:13	the potter in the house of the **L**	3068
Zec	14:1	Behold, the day of the **L** cometh	3068
Zec	14:7	which shall be known to the **L**,	3068
Zec	14:9	in that day shall there be one **L**,	3068
Zec	14:17	to worship the King, the **L** of	3068
Zec	14:20	horses, HOLINESS UNTO THE **L**;	3068
Mal	1:7	The table of the **L** is contemptible	3068
Mal	1:12	The table of the **L** is polluted;	3068
Mal	1:14	unto the **L** a corrupt thing:	136
Mal	2:12	The **L** will cut off the man that	3068
Mal	2:13	the altar of the **L** with tears,	3068
Mal	2:14	the **L** hath been witness between	3068
Mal	2:17	wearied the **L** with your words	3068
Mal	2:17	evil is good in the sight of the **L**,	3068
Mal	3:6	For I am the **L**, I change not;	3068
Mal	4:5	great and dreadful day of the **L**:	3068
Mt	1:20	angel of the **L** appeared unto him	*2962*
Mt	1:22	spoken of the **L** by the prophet,	*2962*
Mt	2:13	angel of the **L** appeareth to Joseph	*2962*
Mt	2:19	an angel of the **L** appeareth in a	*2962*
Mt	3:3	Prepare ye the way of the **L**, make	*2962*
Mt	4:7	shalt not tempt the **L** thy God	*2962*
Mt	4:10	Thou shalt worship the **L** thy God,	*2962*
Mt	5:33	perform unto the **L** thine oaths:	*2962*
Mt	7:21	one that saith unto me, **L**, **L**,	*2962*
Mt	7:22	**L**, **L**, have we not prophesied in	*2962*
Mt	9:38	ye therefore the **L** of the harvest,	*2962*
Mt	12:8	man is **L** even of the sabbath day	*2962*
Mt	15:27	Truth, **L**: yet the dogs eat of the	*2962*
Mt	17:4	**L**, it is good for us to be here: if	*2962*
Mt	21:3	say, The **L** hath need of them;	*2962*
Mt	21:9	that cometh in the name of the **L**;	*2962*
Mt	22:37	love the **L** thy God with all thy	*2962*
Mt	22:43	doth David in spirit call him **L**,	*2962*
Mt	22:44	unto my **L**, Sit thou on my right	*2962*
Mt	22:45	If David then call him **L**, how is	*2962*
Mt	23:39	that cometh in the name of the **L**.	*2962*
Mt	24:42	not what hour your **L** doth come	*2962*
Mt	25:11	virgins, saying, **L**, **L**, open to us	*2962*
Mt	25:21	His **l** said unto him, Well done,	*2962*
Mt	25:21	enter thou into the joy of thy **l**	*2962*
Mt	25:23	His **l** said unto him, Well done,	*2962*
Mt	25:23	enter thou into the joy of thy **l**	*2962*
Mt	25:44	**L**, when saw we thee an	*2962*
Mt	26:22	of them to say unto him, **L**, is it I?	*2962*
Mt	28:2	the angel of the **L** descended from	*2962*
Mt	28:6	Come, see the place where the **L** lay	*2962*
Mk	1:3	Prepare ye the way of the **L**, make	*2962*
Mk	2:28	Son of man is **L** also of the	*2962*
Mk	5:19	how great things the **L** hath done	*2962*
Mk	9:24	**L**, I believe; help thou mine	*2962*
Mk	11:3	ye that the **L** hath need of him;	*2962*
Mk	11:9	that cometh in the name of the **L**	*2962*
Mk	12:9	therefore the **l** of the vineyard do?	*2962*
Mk	12:29	Israel; The **L** our God is one **L**:	*2962*
Mk	12:30	love the **L** thy God with all thy	*2962*
Mk	12:36	to my **L**, Sit thou on my right	*2962*
Mk	13:20	the **L** had shortened those days,	*2962*
Lk	1:6	and ordinances of the **L** blameless	*2962*
Lk	1:11	appeared unto him an angel of the **L**	*2962*
Lk	1:15	shall be great in the sight of the **L**	*2962*
Lk	1:16	shall he turn to the **L** their God	*2962*
Lk	1:17	ready a people prepared for the **L**	*2962*
Lk	1:25	Thus hath the **L** dealt with me in	*2962*
Lk	1:28	highly favoured, the **L** is with thee:	*2962*
Lk	1:38	Behold the handmaid of the **L**; be	*2962*
Lk	1:43	mother of my **L** should come to me?	*2962*
Lk	1:46	said, My soul doth magnify the **L**,	*2962*
Lk	1:58	how the **L** had shewed great mercy	*2962*
Lk	1:68	Blessed be the **L** God of Israel: for	*2962*
Lk	2:9	the angel of the **L** came upon them,	*2962*
Lk	2:9	glory of the **L** shone round about	*2962*
Lk	2:11	a Saviour, which is Christ the **L**	*2962*
Lk	2:15	which the **L** hath made known unto	*2962*
Lk	2:22	Jerusalem, to present him to the **L**;	*2962*
Lk	2:29	**L**, now lettest thou thy servant	*1203*
Lk	2:38	gave thanks likewise unto the **L**,	*2962*
Lk	3:4	Prepare ye the way of the **L**, make	*2962*
Lk	4:8	Thou shalt worship the **L** thy God,	*2962*
Lk	4:12	shalt not tempt the **L** thy God	*2962*
Lk	4:18	Spirit of the **L** is upon me	*2962*
Lk	4:19	the acceptable year of the **L**	*2962*
Lk	5:17	power of the **L** was present to heal	*2962*
Lk	6:5	Son of man is **L** also of the	*2962*
Lk	6:46	why call ye me, **L**, **L**, and do not	*2962*
Lk	10:1	the **L** appointed other seventy also,	*2962*
Lk	10:2	ye therefore the **L** of the harvest,	*2962*
Lk	10:21	O Father, **L** of heaven and earth,	*2962*
Lk	10:27	love the **L** thy God with all thy	*2962*
Lk	11:1	**L**, teach us to pray, as John also	*2962*
Lk	16:3	for my **l** taketh away from me the	*2962*
Lk	16:5	How much owest thou unto my **l**?	*2962*
Lk	16:8	**l** commended the unjust steward,	*2962*
Lk	19:31	Because the **L** hath need of him	*2962*
Lk	19:38	that cometh in the name of the **L**	*2962*
Lk	20:37	calleth the **L** the God of Abraham,	*2962*
Lk	20:42	unto my **L**, Sit thou on my right	*2962*
Lk	20:44	David therefore calleth him **L**,	*2962*
Lk	22:61	**L** turned, and looked upon Peter	*2962*
Lk	23:42	**L**, remember me when thou comest	*2962*
Lk	24:3	found not the body of the **L** Jesus	*2962*
Lk	24:34	The **L** is risen indeed, and hath	*2962*
Jn	1:23	Make straight the way of the **L**, as	*2962*
Jn	4:1	the **L** knew how the Pharisees had	*2962*
Jn	6:68	him, **L**, to whom shall we go?	*2962*
Jn	8:11	She said, no man, **L**. And Jesus	*2962*
Jn	12:13	that cometh in the name of the **L**	*2962*

Jn	12:38	**L**, who hath believed our report?	*2962*
Jn	12:38	the arm of the **L** been revealed?	*2962*
Jn	13:13	**Ye call me Master and L: and ye**	*2962*
Jn	13:16	**servant is not greater than his l;**	*2962*
Jn	15:15	**knowest not what his l doeth:**	*2962*
Jn	15:20	**servant is not greater than his l**	*2962*
Jn	20:2	away the **L** out of the sepulchre.	*2962*
Jn	20:13	they have taken away my **L**, and I	*2962*
Jn	20:18	disciples that she had seen the **L**,	*2962*
Jn	20:20	disciples glad, when they saw the **L**	*2962*
Jn	20:25	said unto him, We have seen the **L**	*2962*
Jn	20:28	said unto him, My **L** and my God.	*2962*
Jn	21:7	loved saith unto Peter, It is the **L**.	*2962*
Jn	21:12	thou? knowing that it was the **L**	*2962*
Jn	21:15	**L**; thou knowest that I love	*2962*
Jn	21:16	**L**; thou knowest that I love	*2962*
Jn	21:17	**L**, thou knowest all things; thou	*2962*
Ac	2:21	the name of the **L** shall be saved	*2962*
Ac	2:34	unto my **L**, Sit thou on my right	*2962*
Ac	2:36	have crucified, both **L** and Christ	*2962*
Ac	2:47	**L** added to the church daily such	*2962*
Ac	3:22	prophet shall the **L** your God raise	*2962*
Ac	4:33	of the resurrection of the **L** Jesus:	*2962*
Ac	5:9	to tempt the Spirit of the **L**?	*2962*
Ac	5:14	believers were ... added to the **L**,	*2962*
Ac	5:10	the angel of the **L** by night opened	*2962*
Ac	7:30	angel of the **L** in a flame of fire in	*2962*
Ac	8:24	Pray ye to the **L** for me, that none	*2962*
Ac	8:39	Spirit of the **L** caught away Philip,	*2962*
Ac	9:5	And he said, Who art thou, **L**?	*2962*
Ac	9:5	And the **L** said, **I am Jesus whom**	*2962*
Ac	9:10	said the **L** in a vision, **Ananias**.	*2962*
Ac	9:27	how he had seen the **L** in the way,	*2962*
Ac	9:42	and many believed in the **L**	*2962*
Ac	10:36	by Jesus Christ: (he is **L** of all:)	*2962*
Ac	10:48	be baptized in the name of the **L**	*2962*
Ac	11:17	who believed on the **L** Jesus Christ;	*2962*
Ac	12:7	the angel of the **L** came upon him	*2962*
Ac	12:11	that the **L** hath sent his angel, and	*2962*
Ac	12:23	the angel of the **L** smote him.	*2962*
Ac	13:11	the hand of the **L** is upon thee, and	*2962*
Ac	13:12	astonished at the doctrine of the **L**.	*2962*
Ac	13:49	the word of the **L** was published	*2962*
Ac	14:3	they speaking boldly in the **L**,	*2962*
Ac	15:17	of men might seek after the **L**,	*2962*
Ac	15:26	for the name of our **L** Jesus Christ	*2962*
Ac	16:14	whose heart the **L** opened, that she	*2962*
Ac	16:15	judged me to be faithful to the **L**,	*2962*
Ac	16:31	Believe on the **L** Jesus Christ, and	*2962*
Ac	17:24	that he is **L** of heaven and earth,	*2962*
Ac	18:8	believed on the **L** with all his house;	*2962*
Ac	19:5	baptized in the name of the **L** Jesus	*2962*
Ac	19:17	name of the **L** Jesus was magnified.	*2962*
Ac	20:19	Serving the **L** with all humility of	*2962*
Ac	20:35	remember the words of the **L** Jesus,	*2962*
Ac	21:14	saying, The will of the **L** be done	*2962*
Ac	22:8	And I answered, Who art thou, **L**?	*2962*
Ac	22:10	And I said, What shall I do, **L**?	*2962*
Ac	23:11	night following the **L** stood by him,	*2962*
Ro	4:8	to whom the **L** will not impute sin	*2962*
Ro	6:23	life through Jesus Christ our **L**.	*2962*
Ro	9:29	the **L** of Sabaoth had left us a seed,	*2962*
Ro	10:9	confess with thy mouth the **L** Jesus,	*2962*
Ro	11:34	who hath known the mind of the **L**?	*2962*
Ro	13:14	But put ye on the **L** Jesus Christ,	*2962*
Ro	14:8	whether we live, we live unto the **L**;	*2962*
Ro	14:8	whether we die, we die unto the **L**:	*2962*
Ro	14:9	be **L** both of the dead and living	*2961*
1Co	1:7	the coming of our **L** Jesus Christ:	*2962*
1Co	1:8	in the day of our **L** Jesus Christ.	*2962*
1Co	1:31	that glorieth, let him glory in the **L**	*2962*
1Co	2:8	not have crucified the **L** of glory.	*2962*
1Co	2:16	who hath known the mind of the **L**	*2962*
1Co	3:20	**L** knoweth the thoughts of the wise,	*2962*
1Co	4:5	before the time, until the **L** come,	*2962*
1Co	4:19	come to you shortly, if the **L** will,	*2962*
1Co	5:5	be saved in the day of the **L** Jesus	*2962*
1Co	6:11	justified in the name of the **L** Jesus,	*2962*
1Co	6:14	God hath both raised up the **L**, and	*2962*
1Co	6:17	is joined unto the **L** is one spirit	*2962*
1Co	7:25	that hath obtained mercy of the **L**	*2962*
1Co	7:32	how he may please the **L**:	*2962*
1Co	7:34	careth for the things of the **L**, that	*2962*
1Co	9:14	Even so hath the **L** ordained that	*2962*
1Co	10:21	Ye cannot drink the cup of the **L**,	*2962*
1Co	10:22	Do we provoke the **L** to jealousy?	*2962*
1Co	11:23	I have received of the **L** that which	*2962*
1Co	11:23	That the **L** Jesus the same night	*2962*
1Co	11:27	bread, and drink this cup of the **L**,	*2962*
1Co	11:27	of the body and blood of the **L**,	*2962*
1Co	12:3	no man can say that Jesus is the **L**,	*2962*
1Co	15:47	second man is the **L** from heaven	*2962*
1Co	15:57	victory through our **L** Jesus Christ	*2962*
1Co	15:58	abounding in the work of the **L**	*2962*
1Co	15:58	your labour is not in vain in the **L**	*2962*
2Co	1:14	are ours in the day of the **L** Jesus	*2962*
2Co	3:17	where the Spirit of the **L** is, there	*2962*
2Co	4:10	the body the dying of the **L** Jesus	*2962*
2Co	4:14	he which raised up the **L** Jesus	*2962*
2Co	5:8	body, and to be present with the **L**	*2962*
2Co	8:5	gave their own selves to the **L**, and	*2962*
2Co	10:8	the **L** hath given us for edification,	*2962*
2Co	10:17	glorieth, let him glory in the **L**	*2962*
2Co	12:8	this thing I besought the **L** thrice,	*2962*
2Co	13:10	power which the **L** hath given me.	*2962*
Gal	6:14	in the cross of our **L** Jesus Christ	*2962*
Gal	6:17	my body the marks of the **L** Jesus.	*2962*
Eph	3:11	he purposed in Christ Jesus our **L**:	*2962*
Eph	4:5	One **L**, one faith, one baptism	*2962*
Eph	5:8	but now are ye light in the **L**: walk	*2962*
Eph	5:17	What the will of the **L** is.	*2962*
Eph	5:22	your own husbands, as unto the **L**	*2962*
Eph	6:1	obey your parents in the **L**: for	*2962*
Eph	6:7	good will doing service, as to the **L**,	*2962*
Eph	6:8	the same shall he receive of the **L**,	*2962*
Eph	6:10	my brethren, be strong in the **L**,	*2962*
Php	2:11	confess that Jesus Christ is **L**, to	*2962*
Php	2:29	Receive him therefore in the **L** with	*2962*
Php	3:8	knowledge of Christ Jesus my **L**:	*2962*
Php	4:1	and crown, so stand fast in the **L**,	*2962*
Php	4:2	they be of the same mind in the **L**	*2962*
Php	4:4	Rejoice in the **L** alway: and again	*2962*
Php	4:5	unto all men. The **L** is at hand	*2962*
Php	4:10	But I rejoiced in the **L** greatly, that	*2962*
Col	1:10	That ye might walk worthy of the **L**.	*2962*
Col	3:17	do all in the name of the **L** Jesus.	*2962*
Col	3:23	ye do, do it heartily, as to the **L**	*2962*
Col	3:24	of the **L** ye shall receive the reward	*2962*
Col	3:24	for ye serve the **L** Christ	*2962*
1Th	3:12	**L** make you to increase and abound	*2962*

1Th	4:6	the **L** is the avenger of all such,	*2962*
1Th	4:16	the **L** himself shall descend from	*2962*
1Th	4:17	the clouds, to meet the **L** in the air:	*2962*
1Th	4:17	and so shall we ever be with the **L**	*2962*
1Th	5:2	day of the **L** so cometh as a thief.	*2962*
2Th	1:7	the **L** Jesus shall be revealed from	*2962*
2Th	1:8	the gospel of our **L** Jesus Christ:	*2962*
2Th	2:13	for you, brethren beloved of the **L**,	*2962*
2Th	3:1	the word of the **L** may have free	*2962*
2Th	3:3	**L** is faithful, who shall stablish	*2962*
2Th	3:5	**L** direct your hearts into the love	*2962*
2Th	3:16	**L** of peace himself give you peace	*2962*
1Ti	6:15	the King of kings, and **L** of lords;	*2962*
2Ti	1:18	**L** grant unto him that he may find	*2962*
2Ti	2:7	**L** give thee understanding in all	*2962*
2Ti	2:19	The **L** knoweth them that are his	*2962*
2Ti	2:22	call on the **L** out of a pure heart	*2962*
2Ti	4:8	which the **L**, the righteous judge	*2962*
2Ti	4:14	the **L** reward him according to his	*2962*
2Ti	4:18	**L** shall deliver me from every evil	*2962*
2Ti	4:22	**L** Jesus Christ be with thy spirit	*2962*
Phm	20	let me have joy of thee in the **L**:	*2962*
Heb	2:3	first began to be spoken by the **L**,	*2962*
Heb	8:11	his brother, saying, Know the **L**:	*2962*
Heb	10:30	The **L** shall judge his people	*2962*
Heb	12:6	whom the **L** loveth he chasteneth,	*2962*
Heb	13:6	boldly say, The **L** is my helper,	*2962*
Jas	1:7	shall receive any thing of the **L**	*2962*
Jas	2:1	**L** of glory, with respect of persons.	
Jas	4:10	yourselves in the sight of the **L**,	*2962*
Jas	4:15	that ye ought to say, If the **L** will	*2962*
Jas	5:4	into the ears of the **L** of Sabaoth	*2962*
Jas	5:11	and have seen the end of the **L**;	*2962*
Jas	5:11	that the **L** is very pitiful, and of	*2962*
Jas	5:15	sick, and the **L** shall raise him up;	*2962*
1Pe	1:25	word of the **L** endureth for ever	*2962*
1Pe	2:3	have tasted that the **L** is gracious	*2962*
1Pe	3:12	For the eyes of the **L** are over the	*2962*
1Pe	3:15	sanctify the **L** God in your hearts:	*2962*
2Pe	1:11	kingdom of our **L** and Saviour	*2962*
2Pe	2:1	denying the **L** that brought them	*1203*
2Pe	2:9	The **L** knoweth how to deliver the	*2962*
2Pe	3:8	one day is with the **L** as a thousand	*2962*
2Pe	3:9	The **L** is not slack concerning his	*2962*
2Pe	3:10	day of the **L** will come as a thief	*2962*
2Pe	3:18	knowledge of our **L** and Saviour	*2962*
Jude	4	and denying the only **L** God,	*2962*
Jude	9	but said, The **L** rebuke thee	*2962*
Jude	14	the **L** cometh with ten thousands	*2962*
Rev	4:8	Holy, holy, holy, **L** God Almighty	*2962*
Rev	4:11	Thou art worthy, O **L**, to receive	*2962*
Rev	6:10	How long, O **L**, holy and true, dost	*1203*
Rev	11:8	where also our **L** was crucified	*2962*
Rev	11:15	are become the kingdoms of our **L**,	*2962*
Rev	14:13	are the dead which die in the **L**	*2962*
Rev	15:3	are thy works, **L** God Almighty;	*2962*
Rev	15:4	Who shall not fear thee, O **L**, and	*2962*
Rev	16:5	Thou art righteous, O **L**, which	*2962*
Rev	17:14	for he is **L** of lords, and King of	*2962*
Rev	18:8	strong is the **L** God which judgeth	*2962*
Rev	19:1	and power, unto the **L** our God:	*2962*
Rev	19:6	the **L** God omnipotent reigneth	*2962*
Rev	19:16	King Of Kings, And **L** of Lords	*2962*
Rev	21:22	for the **L** God Almighty and the	*2962*
Rev	22:5	the **L** God giveth them light: and	*2962*
Rev	22:6	the **L** God of the holy prophets	*2962*
Rev	22:20	Amen. Even so, come, **L** Jesus	*2962*
Rev	22:21	grace of our **L** Jesus Christ be with	*2962*

LORD'S

Ge	44:18	speak a word in my **l** ears, and let	113
Ex	9:29	know how that the earth is the **L**	3068
Ex	12:11	it in haste: it is the **L** passover	3068
Ex	13:12	hast: the male shall be the **L**	3068
Ex	32:26	Who is on the **L** side? let him	3068
Nu	11:23	Is the **L** hand waxed short?	3068
Nu	32:10	**L** anger was kindled the same	3068
Dt	15:2	because it is called the **L** release	3068
1Sa	2:8	the pillars of the earth are the **L**,	3068
1Sa	17:47	for the battle is the **L**, and he will	3068
1Sa	22:21	that Saul had slain the **L** priests	3068
1Sa	24:20	lord; for he is the **L** anointed	3068
2Sa	1:16	I have slain the **L** anointed	3068
2Sa	21:7	**L** oath that was between them,	3068
1Ki	18:13	an hundred men of the **L** prophets	3068
2Ki	11:17	that they should be the **L** people;	3068
2Ki	13:17	The arrow of the **L** deliverance	3068
Ps	11:4	the **L** throne is in heaven: his	3068
Ps	22:28	For the kingdom is the **L**: and	3068
Ps	24:1	earth is the **L**, and the fulness	3068
Ps	113:3	the **L** name is to be praised	3068
Ps	116:19	In the courts of the **L** house, in	3068
Ps	118:23	This is the **L** doing; it is	3068
Ps	137:4	How shall we sing the **L** song in	3068
Pr	16:11	just weight and balance are the **L**	3068
Isa	34:8	is the day of the **L** vengeance,	3068
Isa	40:2	received of the **L** hand double	3068
Isa	59:1	the **L** hand is not shortened, that	3068
Jer	13:17	**L** flock is carried away captive	3068
Jer	25:17	took I the cup at the **L** hand,	3068
Jer	26:2	come to worship in the **L** house,	3068
Jer	28:3	all the vessels of the **L** house	3068
Jer	36:6	ears of the people in the **L** house	3068
Jer	51:6	is the time of the **L** vengeance;	3068
La	2:22	day of the **L** anger none escaped	3068
La	3:22	of the **L** mercies that we are not	3068
Eze	10:4	of the brightness of the **L** glory	3068
Da	9:17	that is desolate, for the **L** sake	136
Hos	9:3	shall not dwell in the **L** land;	3068
Joel	1:9	priests, the **L** ministers, mourn	3068
Ob	21	and the kingdom shall be the **L**.	3068
Mic	6:9	The **L** voice crieth unto the city,	3068
Hab	2:16	the cup of the **L** right hand shall	3068
Zep	1:8	pass in the day of the **L** sacrifice,	3068
Zep	1:18	them in the day of the **L** wrath;	3068
Zep	2:3	be hid in the day of the **L** anger	3068
Hag	2:18	the foundation of the **L** temple	3068
Mt	21:42	**this is the L doing, and it is**	*2962*
Mt	25:18	**in the earth, and hid his l money**	*2962*
Lk	2:26	before he had seen the **L** Christ	*2962*
Lk	12:47	**servant, which knew his l will,**	*2962*
Lk	16:5	**called every one of his l debtors**	*2962*
Ro	14:8	live therefore, or die, we are the **L**.	*2962*
1Co	7:22	being a servant, is the **L** freeman:	*2962*
1Co	10:21	cannot be partakers of the **L** table	*2962*
1Co	10:26	the earth is the **L**, and the fullness	*2962*
1Co	11:26	do shew the **L** death till he come	*2962*
1Co	11:29	himself, not discerning the **L** body	*2962*
1Pe	2:13	ordinance of man for the **L** sake:	*2962*
Rev	1:10	I was in the Spirit on the **L** day	*2960*

LORDS

Ge	19:2	he said, Behold now, my **l**, turn in,	113
Jgs	16:5	**l** of the Philistines came up unto	5633
1Sa	5:8	gathered all the **l** of the Philistines	5633
1Sa	29:6	nevertheless the **l** favour thee not	5633
Ps	136:3	O give thanks to the Lord of **l**:	113
Jer	2:31	say my people, We are **l**;	7300
Da	5:1	a great feast to a thousand of his **l**,	7261
Da	5:23	thou, and thy **l**, thy wives, and thy	7261
Da	6:17	and with the signet of his **l**;	7261
1Co	8:5	there be gods many, and **l** many,)	*2962*
1Ti	6:15	the King of kings, and Lord of **l**;	*2961*
1Pe	5:3	as being **l** over God's heritage	*2634*
Rev	19:16	King of Kings, and Lord of **L**.	*2634*

LORDSHIP

Mk	10:42	**Gentiles exercise l over them;**	*2634*
Lk	22:25	**Gentiles exercise l over them;**	*2961*

LOSE

Jgs	18:25	and thou **l** thy life, with the lives	622
Pr	23:8	vomit up, and **l** thy sweet words	7843
Ecc	3:6	A time to get, and a time to **l**; a	6
Mt	10:39	**He that findeth his life shall l it:**	*622*
Mt	16:25	**will l his life for my sake shall**	*622*
Mt	16:26	**whole world, and l his own soul?**	*2210*
Mk	8:35	**will save his life shall l it;**	*622*
Lk	9:25	**gain the whole world, and l**	*622*
Lk	15:4	**hundred sheep, if he l one of them,**	*622*
Lk	17:33	**shall seek to save his life shall l it;**	*622*
Jn	12:25	**He that loveth his life shall l it;**	*622*
2Jn	8	**l** not those things which we have	*622*

LOSS

Ge	31:39	not unto thee; I bare the **l** of it;	2398
Isa	47:8	shall I know the **l** of children:	7921
Ac	27:22	be no **l** of any man's life among	*580*
1Co	3:15	shall be burned, he shall suffer **l**:	*2210*
Php	3:7	me, those I counted **l** for Christ	*2209*

LOST

Ex	22:9	or for any manner of **l** thing, which	9
Nu	6:12	days that were before shall be **l**,	5307
1Sa	9:20	as for thine asses that were **l** three	6
Ps	119:176	I have gone astray like a **l** sheep;	6
Isa	49:21	seeing I have **l** my children, and.,	7908
Jer	50:6	My people hath been **l** sheep: their	6
Eze	19:5	she had waited, and her hope was **l**,	6
Eze	37:11	bones are dried, and our hope is **l**.	6
Mt	5:13	**but if the salt have l his savour,**	*3471*
Mt	10:6	**the l sheep of the house of Israel**	*622*
Mt	18:11	**is come to save that which was l.**	*622*
Mk	9:50	**if the salt have l his saltness,**	*358, 1096*
Lk	15:6	**I found my sheep which was l.**	*622*
Lk	15:9	**I found the piece which I had l.**	*622*
Lk	15:24	**alive again; he was l, and is found**	*622*
Lk	19:10	**seek and to save that which was l.**	*622*
Jn	6:12	**that remain, that nothing be l.**	*622*
Jn	17:12	**and none of them is l, but the son**	*622*
Jn	18:9	which thou gavest me have I **l** none	*622*
2Co	4:3	be hid, it is hid to them that are **l**:	*622*

LOT

Le	16:8	the two goats; one **l** for the Lord	1486
Le	16:8	and the other **l** for the scapegoat	1486
Nu	33:54	be in the place where his **l** falleth;	1486
Nu	36:3	taken from the **l** of our inheritance	1486
Dt	32:9	Jacob is the **l** of his inheritance	2256
Jos	14:2	By **l** was their inheritance, as the	1486
Jos	21:40	Levites, were by their **l** twelve cities	1486
Jgs	1:3	Come up with me into my **l**, that	1486
1Sa	14:41	Lord God of Israel, Give a perfect **l**	
Est	3:7	they cast Pur, that is, the **l**,	1486
Ps	16:5	of my cup: thou maintainest my **l**	1486
Ps	125:3	rest upon the **l** of the righteous;	1486
Pr	16:33	The **l** is cast into the lap; but the	1486
Pr	18:18	The **l** causeth contentions to cease,	1486
Isa	17:14	and the **l** of them that rob us	1486
Isa	34:17	And he hath cast the **l** for them	1486
Isa	57:6	thy portion; they, they are thy **l**:	1486
Eze	24:6	piece by piece; let no **l** fall upon it	1486
Eze	45:1	when ye shall divide by **l** the land for	
Da	12:13	stand in thy **l** at the end of days	1486
Jnh	1:7	cast lots, and the **l** fell upon Jonah	1486
Lk	1:9	his **l** was to burn incense when	*2975*
Ac	1:26	and the **l** fell upon Matthias;	*2819*
Ac	13:19	he divided their land to them by **l**	*2624*

LOTHE

Ex	7:18	Egyptians shall **l** to drink of the	3811
Eze	6:9	shall **l** themselves for the evils	6962
Eze	20:43	**l** yourselves in your own sight for	6962

LOTHED

Jer	14:19	hath thy soul **l** Zion? why hast	1602
Eze	16:45	which **l** their husbands and their	1602
Zec	11:8	my soul **l** them, and their soul	7114

LOTS

Le	16:8	shall cast **l** upon the two goats;	1486
Jos	18:8	here cast **l** for you before the Lord	1486
Jos	18:10	Joshua cast **l** for them in Shiloh	1486
1Sa	14:42	Cast **l** between me and Jonathan my	
1Ch	25:8	they cast **l**, ward against ward, as	1486
Ne	10:34	we cast the **l** among the priests, the	1486
Ne	11:1	the rest of the people also cast **l**, to	1486
Ps	22:18	them, and cast **l** upon my vesture	1486
Ob	11	gates, and cast **l** upon Jerusalem	1486
Jnh	1:7	So they cast **l**, and the lot fell upon	1486
Mt	27:35	parted his garments, casting **l**:	*2819*
Mk	15:24	garments, casting **l** upon them,	*2819*
Lk	23:34	they parted his raiment, and cast **l**	*2819*
Jn	19:24	Let us not rend it, but cast **l** for it,	*2819*
Ac	1:26	they gave forth their **l**; and the lot	*2819*

LOUD

Ge	39:14	me, and I cried with a **l** voice:	1419
Ex	19:16	voice of the trumpet exceeding **l**;	2389
2Sa	15:23	all the country wept with a **l** voice	1419
2Ch	15:14	sware unto the Lord with a **l** voice,	1419
Ezr	10:12	answered and said with a **l** voice,	1419
Est	4:1	cried with a **l** and a bitter cry;	1419
Ps	98:4	make a **l** noise, and rejoice, and sing	
Ps	150:5	Praise him upon the **l** cymbals:	8085
Pr	27:14	blesseth his friend with a **l** voice,	1419
Eze	8:18	they cry in mine ears with a **l** voice,	1419
Mt	27:46	Jesus cried with a **l** voice, saying	*3173*
Mt	27:50	he had cried again with a **l** voice,	*3173*
Mk	15:34	Jesus cried with a **l** voice, saying,	*3173*
Mk	15:37	And Jesus cried with a **l** voice, and	*3173*
Lk	4:33	devil, and cried out with a **l** voice,	*3173*
Lk	17:15	and with a **l** voice glorified God	*3173*
Lk	19:37	and praise God with a **l** voice for	*3173*
Lk	23:46	Jesus had cried with a **l** voice.	*3173*

Jn	11:43	he cried with a **l** voice, **Lazarus,**	*3173*
Ac	7:60	and cried with a **l** voice, Lord, lay	*3173*
Ac	14:10	Said with a **l** voice, Stand upright	*3173*
Ac	26:24	Festus said with a **l** voice, Paul.	*3173*
Rev	5:12	Saying with a **l** voice, Worthy is.	*3173*
Rev	7:2	with a **l** voice to the four angels,	*3173*
Rev	8:13	saying with a **l** voice, Woe, woe,	*3173*
Rev	14:7	Saying with a **l** voice, Fear God	*3173*
Rev	14:15	crying with a **l** voice to him that	*3173*
Rev	19:17	he cried with a **l** voice, saying to all	*3173*

LOVE

Ge	27:4	make me savoury meat, such as I **l**	157
Ge	29:32	therefore my husband will **l** me	157
Ex	21:5	I **l** my master, my wife, and my	157
Le	19:18	but thou shalt **l** thy neighbour as	157
Dt	5:10	unto thousands of them that **l** me	157
Dt	6:5	thou shalt **l** the Lord thy God with	157
Dt	7:9	mercy with them that **l** him and	157
Dt	7:13	he will **l** thee, and bless thee, and	157
Dt	10:12	to walk in all his ways, and to **l** him	157
Dt	10:19	**L** ye therefore the stranger: for ye	157
Dt	11:1	Therefore thou shalt **l** the Lord thy	157
Dt	13:3	whether ye **l** the Lord your God	157
Dt	30:6	to **l** the Lord thy God with all thine	157
Jos	22:5	to **l** the Lord your God, and to walk	157
Jgs	5:31	let them that **l** him be as the sun	157
Jgs	16:15	How canst thou say, I **l** thee, when	157
2Sa	1:26	me: thy **l** to me was wonderful	160
2Sa	1:26	wonderful, passing the **l** of women.	160
2Sa	13:4	Amnon said unto him, I **l** Tamar	157
1Ki	11:2	Solomon clave unto these in **l**	160
2Ch	19:2	and **l** them that hate the Lord?	157
Ne	1:5	and mercy for them that **l** him and	157
Ps	5:11	let them also that **l** thy name be	157
Ps	18:1	I will **l** thee, O Lord, my strength	7355
Ps	40:16	let such as **l** thy salvation say	157
Ps	97:10	Ye that **l** the Lord, hate evil: he	157
Ps	116:1	I **l** the Lord, because he hath heard.	157
Ps	119:97	O how **l** I thy law! it is my	157
Ps	119:119	dross: therefore I **l** thy testimonies	157
Ps	119:132	to do unto those that **l** thy name	157
Ps	119:159	Consider how I **l** thy precepts:	157
Ps	145:20	Lord preserveth all them that **l** him:	157
Pr	1:22	ye simple ones, will ye **l** simplicity?	157
Pr	4:6	**l** her, and she shall keep thee	157
Pr	8:17	I **l** them that **l** me; and those that	157
Pr	8:21	cause those that **l** me to inherit	157
Pr	8:36	soul: all they that hate me **l** death	157
Pr	10:12	up strifes: but **l** covereth all sins	160
Pr	17:9	covereth a transgression seeketh **l**;	160
Pr	18:21	and they that **l** it shall eat the fruit	157
Pr	20:13	**L** not sleep, lest thou come to	157
Pr	27:5	rebuke is better than secret **l**	160
Ecc	3:8	A time to **l**, and a time to hate; a	157
SS	1:2	for thy **l** is better than wine	1730
SS	1:15	Behold, thou art fair, my **l**; behold	7474
SS	2:4	and his banner over me was **l**	160
SS	2:7	up, nor awake my **l**, till he please	160
SS	2:10	Rise up, my **l**, my fair one, and	7474
SS	3:10	midst thereof being paved with **l**,	160
SS	5:8	that, ye tell him, I am sick of **l**	160
SS	8:4	that ye stir not up, nor awake my **l**	160
SS	8:6	for **l** is strong as death; jealousy	160
SS	8:7	Many waters cannot quench **l**,	160
SS	8:7	all the substance of his house for **l**	160
Isa	38:17	but thou hast in **l** to my soul	2836
Isa	56:6	to **l** the name of the Lord, to be	157
Isa	61:8	For I the Lord **l** judgment, I hate	157
Isa	66:10	be glad with her, all ye that **l** her:	157
Jer	31:3	loved thee with an everlasting **l**:	160
Eze	16:8	behold, thy time was the time of **l**;	1730
Eze	23:17	came to her into the bed of **l**, and	1730
Da	1:9	Daniel into favour and tender **l**	
Hos	3:1	**l** a woman, beloved of her friend,	157
Hos	3:1	to other gods, and **l** flagons of wine	157
Hos	11:4	cords of a man, with bands of **l**:	160
Hos	14:4	backsliding, I will **l** them freely:	157
Am	5:15	Hate the evil, and **l** the good, and	157
Mic	3:2	Who hate the good, and **l** the evil;	157
Mic	6:8	but to do justly, and to **l** mercy,	160
Zec	8:19	therefore **l** the truth and peace	157
Mt	5:43	**Thou shalt l thy neighbour, and**	*25*
Mt	5:44	**But I say unto you, L your enemies,**	*25*
Mt	6:5	**for they l to pray standing in the**	*5368*
Mt	19:19	**shalt l thy neighbour as thyself**	*25*
Mt	22:37	**Thou shalt l the Lord thy God with**	*25*
Mt	24:12	**the l of many shall wax cold**	*26*
Mk	12:33	to **l** him with all the heart, and with	*25*
Mk	12:33	and to **l** his neighbour as himself,	*25*
Mk	12:38	**the scribes, which l to go in long**	*2309*
Lk	6:32	**For if ye l them which l you, what**	*25*
Lk	7:42	**which of them will l him most?**	*25*
Lk	10:27	Thou shalt **l** the Lord thy God with	25
Lk	11:42	**pass over judgment and the l of God:**	*26*
Lk	11:42	**for ye l the uppermost seats in the**	*26*
Lk	16:13	**he will hate the one, and l the**	*25*
Lk	20:46	**and l greetings in the markets,**	*5368*
Jn	5:42	**that ye have not the l of God in you.**	*26*
Jn	8:42	**were your Father, ye would l me:**	*25*
Jn	10:17	**Therefore doth my Father l me,**	*25*
Jn	13:34	**unto you, That ye l one another**	*25*
Jn	13:35	**are my disciples, if ye have l one to**	*26*
Jn	14:15	**ye l me, keep my commandments**	*25*
Jn	14:23	**my Father will l him, and we will**	*25*
Jn	14:31	**may know that I l the Father; and**	*25*
Jn	15:9	**I loved you: continue ye in my l,**	*26*
Jn	15:10	**ye shall abide in my l; even as I have**	*26*
Jn	15:12	**That ye l one another, as I have**	*26*
Jn	15:13	**Greater l hath no man than this,**	*26*
Jn	15:19	**world, the world would l his own:**	*5368*
Jn	17:26	**l wherewith thou hast loved me**	*26*
Jn	21:15	thou knowest that I **l** thee	*5368*
Jn	21:16	thou knowest that I **l** thee	*5368*
Jn	21:17	thou knowest that I **l** thee	*5368*
Ro	5:5	because the **l** of God is shed abroad	*26*
Ro	5:8	God commendeth his **l** toward us.	*26*
Ro	8:28	together for good to them that **l** God.	*25*
Ro	8:35	separate us from the **l** of Christ?	*26*
Ro	8:39	able to separate us from the **l** of God,	*26*
Ro	12:9	Let **l** be without dissimulation.	*26*
Ro	12:10	one to another with brotherly **l**;	*5360*
Ro	13:9	Thou shalt **l** thy neighbour as	*25*
Ro	13:10	therefore **l** is the fulfilling of the law.	*26*
1Co	2:9	hath prepared for them that **l** him	*25*
1Co	4:21	come unto you with a rod, or in **l**;	*26*
1Co	8:3	if any man **l** God, the same is known	*25*
1Co	16:22	If any man **l** not the Lord Jesus	*5368*
2Co	2:4	ye might know the **l** which I have	*26*
2Co	5:14	For the **l** of Christ constraineth us;	*26*
2Co	8:8	and to prove the sincerity of your **l**,	*26*

2Co 11:11 because I **l** you not? God knoweth *25*
2Co 13:11 God of **l** and peace shall be with you *26*
2Co 13:14 the **l** of God, and the communion *26*
Gal 5:13 flesh, but by **l** serve one another *26*
Gal 5:22 the fruit of the Spirit is **l**, joy, peace *26*
Eph 1:4 and without blame before him in **l**: *26*
Eph 2:4 great **l** wherewith he loved us *26*
Eph 3:17 ye, being rooted and grounded in **l**. *26*
Eph 3:19 And to know the **l** of Christ, which *26*
Eph 4:15 speaking the truth in **l**, may grow *26*
Eph 4:16 body unto the edifying of itself in **l**, ... *26*
Eph 5:2 And walk in **l**, as Christ also hath *26*
Eph 5:25 Husbands, **l** your wives, even as *25*
Eph 5:28 So ought men to **l** their wives as *25*
Eph 5:33 so **l** his wife even as himself; and *25*
Php 1:9 your **l** may abound yet more and *26*
Php 2:1 in Christ, if any comfort of **l**, if any *26*
Php 2:2 be likeminded, having the same **l**, ... *26*
Col 2:2 comforted, being knit together in **l**. *26*
Col 3:19 Husbands, **l** your wives, and be not *25*
1Th 1:3 your work of faith, and labour of **l**. *25*
1Th 4:9 are taught of God to **l** one another. *25*
1Th 5:8 on the breastplate of faith and **l** *26*
2Th 2:10 they received not the **l** of the truth *26*
2Th 3:5 direct your hearts into the **l** of God, ... *26*
1Ti 1:14 faith and **l** which is in Christ Jesus *26*
1Ti 6:10 **l** of money is the root of all evil: *5365*
1Ti 6:11 faith, **l**, patience, meekness. *26*
2Ti 1:7 and of **l**, and of a sound mind. *26*
2Ti 4:8 all them also that **l** his appearing *25*
Tit 2:4 to be sober, to **l** their husbands *5362*
Tit 3:15 Greet them that **l** us in the faith *5368*
Phm 5:7 great joy and consolation in thy **l** *26*
Heb 6:10 to forget your work and labour of **l**, ... *26*
Heb 10:24 to provoke unto **l** and to good works: *26*
Heb 13:1 Let brotherly **l** continue *5360*
Jas 1:12 hath promised to them that **l** him *25*
Jas 2:8 shalt **l** thy neighbour as thyself, ye do. *25*
1Pe 1:8 Whom having not seen, ye **l**; in. *25*
1Pe 1:22 ye **l** one another with a pure heart *25*
1Pe 2:17 **L** the brotherhood. Fear God. *25*
1Jn 2:5 in him verily is the **l** of God perfected:. . . . *26*
1Jn 2:15 **L** not the world, neither the things *25*
1Jn 3:1 what matter of **l** the Father hath *26*
1Jn 3:11 that we should **l** one another. *25*
1Jn 3:14 unto life, because we **l** the brethren *25*
1Jn 3:16 Hereby perceive we the **l** of God, ... *26*
1Jn 3:18 little children, let us not **l** in word, ... *25*
1Jn 3:23 Son Jesus Christ, and **l** one another, ... *25*
1Jn 4:7 Beloved, let us **l** one another:. *25*
1Jn 4:8 not knoweth not God; for God is **l**. *26*
1Jn 4:10 Herein is **l**, not that we loved God *26*
1Jn 4:11 us, we ought also to **l** one another *25*
1Jn 4:12 If we **l** one another, God dwelleth in *26*
1Jn 4:16 believed the **l** that God hath to us. *26*
1Jn 4:16 hath to us. God is **l** and he that *26*
1Jn 4:16 that dwelleth in **l** dwelleth in God *26*
1Jn 4:17 Herein is our **l** made perfect, that. *26*
1Jn 4:18 There is no fear in **l**; but perfect *26*
1Jn 4:19 We **l** him, because he first loved us. *25*
1Jn 4:20 If a man say, I **l** God, and hateth *25*
1Jn 4:21 who loveth God **l** his brother also. *25*
1Jn 5:2 know that we **l** the children of God, ... *25*
1Jn 5:3 this is the **l** of God, that we keep. *26*
2Jn 1 her children, whom I **l** in the truth; *25*
2Jn 3 the Son of the Father, in truth and **l**. *26*
2Jn 5 beginning, that we **l** one another *25*
2Jn 6 And this is **l**, that we walk after his *26*
3Jn 1 unto ... Gaius, whom I **l** in the truth. *25*
Jude 2 Mercy unto you, and peace, and **l**. *26*
Jude 21 Keep yourselves in the **l** of God, ... *26*
Rev 2:4 **because thou hast left thy first l.** *26*
Rev 3:19 **As many as I l, I rebuke and** *5368*

LOVED

Ge 25:28 And Isaac **l** Esau, because he did. 157
Ge 25:28 his venison: but Rebekah **l** Jacob. 157
Ge 29:18 Jacob **l** Rachel; and said, I will. 157
Ge 29:30 he **l** also Rachel more than Leah, ... 157
Ge 37:3 Now Israel **l** Joseph more than all. 157
Dt 7:8 But because the Lord **l** you, and 160
1Sa 18:1 and Jonathan **l** him as his own soul. 157
1Sa 18:16 But all Israel and Judah **l** David 157
1Sa 20:17 for he ... him as he **l** his own soul.. 160
2Sa 12:24 name Solomon: and the Lord **l** him. 157
1Ki 10:9 because the Lord **l** Israel for ever 160
1Ki 11:1 Solomon **l** many strange women, ... 157
Est 2:17 And the king **l** Esther above all the. 157
Ps 26:8 Lord, I have **l** the habitation of thy. 157
Ps 47:4 the excellency of Jacob whom he **l** 157
Isa 48:14 The Lord hath **l** him: he will do his 157
Jer 14:10 Thus have they **l** to wander, they 157
Jer 31:3 I have **l** thee with an everlasting 157
Hos 11:1 Israel was a child, then I **l** him, and 157
Mal 1:2 I have **l** you, saith the Lord 157
Mal 1:2 saith the Lord: yet I **l** Jacob 157
Mk 10:21 Jesus beholding him **l** him, and said. *25*
Lk 7:47 **many, are forgiven; for she l much:** *25*
Jn 3:16 **For God so l the world, that he.** *25*
Jn 3:19 **men l darkness rather than light,** *25*
Jn 11:36 the Jews, Behold how he **l** him! *5368*
Jn 12:43 they **l** the praise of men more than *25*
Jn 13:23 one of his disciples, whom Jesus **l**. *25*
Jn 13:34 **as I have l you, that ye also love** *25*
Jn 14:21 **loveth me shall be l of my Father,** *25*
Jn 14:28 **If ye l me, ye would rejoice, because** *25*
Jn 15:9 **As the Father hath l me, so have I.** *25*
Jn 15:12 **ye love one another, as I have l you** *25*
Jn 16:27 **because ye have l me, and have.** *5368*
Jn 17:23 **and hast l them, as thou hast l me** *25*
Jn 17:26 **the love wherewith thou hast l me.** *25*
Jn 21:20 the disciple whom Jesus **l** following;. *25*
Ro 8:37 conquerors through him that **l** us. *25*
Ro 9:13 As it is written, Jacob have I **l**, but. *25*
Gal 2:20 faith of the Son of God, who **l** me, ... *25*
Eph 2:4 his great love wherewith he **l** us, ... *25*
Eph 5:25 even as Christ also **l** the church, ... *25*
2Ti 4:10 me, having **l** this present world, ... *25*
Heb 1:9 hast **l** righteousness, and hated *25*
2Pe 2:15 who **l** the wages of unrighteousness; *25*
1Jn 4:10 Herein is love, not that we **l** God, ... *25*
1Jn 4:11 Beloved, if God so **l** us, we ought *25*
1Jn 4:19 We love him, because he first **l** us *25*
Rev 1:5 Unto him that **l** us, and washed us *25*
Rev 3:9 **feet, and to know that I have l thee.** *25*

LOVELY

2Sa 1:23 and Jonathan were **l** and pleasant. 157
SS 5:16 sweet: yea, he is altogether **l**. 4261
Eze 33:32 art unto them as a very **l** song of 5690
Php 4:8 are pure, whatsoever things are **l**, ... *4375*

LOVER

1Ki	5:1	for Hiram was ever a **l** of David	157
Ps	88:18	**L** and friend hast thou put far from	157
Tit	1:8	But a **l** of hospitality, ... of good	*5382*
Tit	1:8	a **l** of good men, sober, just, holy,	*5358*

LOVERS

Ps	38:11	My **l** and my friends stand aloof	157
Jer	3:1	played the harlot with many **l**;	7453
Jer	30:14	All thy **l** have forgotten thee: they	157
La	1:19	I called for my **l**, but they deceived	157
Eze	16:33	but thou givest thy gifts to all thy **l**	157
Eze	23:22	I will raise up thy **l** against thee,	157
Hos	2:5	I will go after my **l**, that give me my	157
Hos	2:10	her lewdness in the sight of her **l**,	157
2Ti	3:2	men shall be **l** of their own selves	*5367*
2Ti	3:4	highminded, **l** of pleasures more	*5369*
2Ti	3:4	of pleasures more than **l** of God;	*5377*

LOVE'S

Phm	9	for **l** sake I rather beseech thee	*26*

LOVES

Pr	7:18	let us solace ourselves with **l**	159
SS	7:12	forth: there will I give thee my **l**	1730

LOVEST

Ge	22:2	thine only son Isaac, whom thou **l**,	157
2Sa	19:6	In that thou **l** thine enemies, and	157
Ps	45:7	Thou **l** righteousness, and hatest	157
Ecc	9:9	joyfully with the wife whom thou **l**	157
Jn	11:3	behold, he whom thou **l** is sick	*5368*
Jn	21:15	**Jonas, l thou me more than these?**	*25*
Jn	21:16	**Simon, son of Jonas, l thou me?**	*25*
Jn	21:17	**Simon, son of Jonas, l thou me?**	*5368*
Jn	21:17	him the third time, **l** thou me?	*5368*

LOVETH

Ge	27:9	meat for thy father, such as he **l**:	157
Dt	10:18	**l** the stranger, in giving him food	157
Ru	4:15	thy daughter in law, which **l** thee	157
Ps	11:5	him that **l** violence his soul hateth.	157
Ps	11:7	the righteous Lord **l** righteousness;	157
Ps	33:5	He **l** righteousness and judgment:	157
Ps	37:28	the Lord **l** judgment, and forsaketh	157
Ps	87:2	The Lord **l** the gates of Zion more	157
Ps	146:8	down: the Lord **l** the righteous:	157
Pr	3:12	for whom the Lord **l** he correcteth;	157
Pr	12:1	Whoso **l** instruction **l** knowledge:	157
Pr	13:24	that **l** him chasteneth him betimes.	157
Pr	15:12	A scorner **l** not one that reproveth	157
Pr	17:17	friend **l** at all times, and a brother	157
Pr	19:8	that getteth wisdom **l** his own soul:	157
Pr	21:17	that **l** pleasure shall be a poor man:	157
Pr	21:17	that **l** wine and oil shall not be rich	157
Pr	29:3	Whoso **l** wisdom rejoiceth his	157
Ecc	5:10	that **l** silver shall not be satisfied	157
SS	3:1	bed I sought him whom my soul **l**:	157
Isa	1:23	every one **l** gifts, and followeth	157
Mt	10:37	**l father or mother more than me**	*5368*
Mt	10:37	**l son or daughter more than me.**	*5368*
Lk	7:47	**little is forgiven, the same l little.**	*25*
Jn	3:35	Father **l** the Son, and hath given	*25*
Jn	5:20	**Father l the Son, and sheweth**	*5368*
Jn	12:25	**He that l his life shall lose it; and**	5368
Jn	14:21	**keepeth them, he it is that l me:**	*25*
Jn	14:21	**l me shall be loved by my Father,**	*25*
Jn	16:27	**the Father himself l you, because**	*5368*
2Co	9:7	necessity: for God **l** a cheerful giver	*25*
Eph	5:28	bodies. He that **l** his wife **l** himself	*25*
Heb	12:6	For whom the Lord **l** he chasteneth	*25*
1Jn	2:10	**l** his brother abideth in the light	*25*
1Jn	4:7	and every one that **l** is born of God,	*25*
1Jn	4:20	**l** not his brother whom he hath seen,	*25*
1Jn	4:21	he who **l** God love his brother also	*25*
1Jn	5:1	and every one that **l** him that begat	*25*
3Jn	9	**l** to have the preeminence among	*5383*
Rev	22:15	and whosoever **l** and maketh a lie	*5368*

LOVING

Pr	5:19	be as the **l** hind and pleasant roe;	158
Pr	22:1	**l** favour rather than silver and	2896
Isa	56:10	sleeping, lying down, **l** to slumber	157

LOVINGKINDNESS

Ps	26:3	For thy **l** is before mine eyes: and	2617
Ps	36:7	How excellent is thy **l**, O God!	2617
Ps	40:11	let thy **l** and thy truth continually	2617
Ps	63:3	Because thy **l** is better than life,	2617
Ps	92:2	To shew forth thy **l** in the morning,	2617
Ps	103:4	crowneth thee with **l** and tender	2617
Ps	138:2	name for thy **l** and for thy truth:	2617
Ps	143:8	me to hear thy **l** in the morning;	2617
Jer	9:24	I am the Lord which exercise **l**	2617
Jer	32:18	Thou shewest **l** unto thousands	2617
Hos	2:19	judgment, and in **l**, and in mercies	2617

LOVINGKINDNESSES

Ps	25:6	thy tender mercies and thy **l**;	2617
Ps	89:49	Lord, where are thy former **l**,	2617
Isa	63:7	I will mention the **l** of the Lord,	2617

L

LOW

Jgs	11:35	thou hast brought me very **l**, and	3766
1Sa	2:7	rich: he bringeth **l**, and lifteth up	8213
2Ch	28:19	the Lord brought Judah **l** because	3665
Job	40:12	that is proud, and bring him **l**:	3665
Ps	49:2	Both **l** and high, rich and poor,	120
Ps	106:43	were brought **l** for their iniquity	4355
Ps	136:23	remembered us in our **l** estate:	8213
Pr	29:23	A man's pride shall bring him **l**:	8213
Ecc	10:6	dignity, and the rich sit in **l** place	8216
Ecc	12:4	the sound of the grinding is **l**, and	8217
Isa	2:12	up; and he shall be brought **l**:	8213
Isa	26:5	high; the lofty city, he layeth it **l**;	8213
Isa	29:4	speech shall be **l** out of the dust,	7817
Isa	40:4	mountain and hill shall be made **l**:	8213
Eze	21:26	exalt him that is **l**, and abase him	8217
Eze	26:20	thee in the **l** parts of the earth,	8482
Lk	1:48	hath regarded the **l** estate of his	*5014*
Lk	1:52	and exalted them of **l** degree	*5011*
Ro	12:16	but condescend to men of **l** estate	*5011*
Jas	1:10	the rich, in that he is made **l**:	*5014*

LOWER

Ne	4:13	set I in the **l** places behind the	8482
Ps	8:5	him a little **l** than the angels,	2637
Ps	63:9	go into the **l** parts of the earth	8482
Eph	4:9	descended first into the **l** parts	*2737*
Heb	2:7	madest him a little **l** than the angels;	*1642*
Heb	2:9	was made a little **l** than the angels	*1642*

LOWEST

Dt	32:22	and shall burn unto the **l** hell	8482
1Ki	13:33	again of the **l** of the people priests	7098

Ps 86:13 delivered my soul from the l hell 8482
Ps 88:6 Thou hast laid me in the l pit, in 8482
Ps 139:15 wrought in the l parts of the 8482
Lk 14:9 **with shame to take the l room** *2078*

LOWING
1Sa 6:12 l as they went, and turned not 1600
1Sa 15:14 the l of the oxen which I hear? 6963

LOWLINESS
Eph 4:2 With all l and meekness, with *5012*
Php 2:3 in l of mind let each esteem other *5012*

LOWLY
Ps 138:6 yet hath he respect unto the l:......... 8217
Pr 3:34 but he giveth grace unto the l 6041
Pr 11:2 shame: but with the l is wisdom....... 6800
Pr 16:19 be of an humble spirit with the l,...... 6041
Zec 9:9 l, and riding upon an ass, and upon.... 6041
Mt 11:29 **me; for I am meek and l in heart:**...... *5011*

LUCRE
1Sa 8:3 but turned aside after l, and took 1215
1Ti 3:3 no striker, not greedy of filthy l; *866*
1Ti 3:8 much wine, not greedy of filthy l;....... *146*
Tit 1:7 no striker, not given to filthy l; *146*
1Pe 5:2 not for filthy l, but of a ready *147*

LUCRE'S
Tit 1:11 they ought not, for filthy l sake *2771*

LUKEWARM
Rev 3:16 **So then because thou art l, and** *5513*

LUMP
Isa 38:21 had said, Let them take a l of figs, ... 1690
Ro 9:21 same l to make one vessel unto........ *5445*
Ro 11:16 firstfruit be holy, the l is also holy: *5445*
1Co 5:6 little leaven leaveneth the whole l? *5445*
Gal 5:9 little leaven leaveneth the whole l *5445*

LUNATICK
Mt 4:24 and those which were l, and those *4583*
Mt 17:15 son: for he is l, and sore vexed: *4583*

LURK
Pr 1:11 let us l privily for the innocent 6845
Pr 1:18 they l privily for their own lives........ 6845

LURKING
1Sa 23:23 take knowledge of all the l places 4224
Ps 10:8 in the l places of the village: 3993
Ps 17:12 a young lion l in secret places.......... 3427

LUST
Ex 15:9 my l shall be satisfied upon them; 5315
Ps 78:18 heart by asking meat for their l......... 5315
Ps 81:12 them up unto their own hearts l: 8307
Pr 6:25 L not after her beauty in thine 2530
Mt 5:28 **looketh on a woman to l after her** *2530*
Ro 1:27 burned in their l one toward.......... *3715*
1Co 10:6 should not l after evil things *1511, 1938*
Gal 5:16 shall not fulfil the l of the flesh. *1939*
1Th 4:5 Not in the l of concupiscence *3806*
Jas 1:14 he is drawn away of his own l, ... *1939*
Jas 1:15 Then when l hath conceived, it........ *1939*
2Pe 1:4 that is in the world through l *1939*
1Jn 2:16 l of the flesh, and the l of the eyes,..... *1939*
1Jn 2:17 passeth away, and the l thereof:........ *1939*

LUSTED
Nu 11:34 there they buried the people that l...... 183
Ps 106:14 But l exceedingly in the wilderness...... 183
1Co 10:6 after evil things, as they also l *1937*
Rev 18:14 the fruits that thy soul l after are....... *1937*

LUSTETH
Dt 12:15 eat ... whatsoever thy soul l after 183
Dt 12:20 flesh, whatsoever thy soul l after. 183
Dt 14:26 for whatsoever thy soul l after, ... 183
Gal 5:17 For the flesh l against the Spirit,....... *1937*
Jas 4:5 that dwelleth in us l to envy?.......... *1971*

LUSTS
Mk 4:19 **the l of other things entering in,**....... *1939*
Jn 8:44 **and the l of your father ye will**........ *1939*
Ro 1:24 through the l of their own hearts, to ... *1939*
Ro 6:12 ye should obey it in the l thereof....... *1939*
Gal 5:24 the flesh with the affections and l...... *1939*
Eph 2:3 in times past in the l of our flesh,...... *1939*
Eph 4:22 corrupt according to the deceitful l;.... *1939*
2Ti 2:22 Flee also youthful l: but follow *1939*
2Ti 3:6 with sins, led away with divers l *1939*
Tit 2:12 denying ungodliness and worldly l..... *1939*
Jas 4:1 your l that war in your members?...... *2237*
Jas 4:3 ye may consume it upon your l........ *2237*
1Pe 1:14 to the former l in your ignorance: *1939*
1Pe 4:3 walked in lasciviousness, l, excess *1939*
2Pe 2:18 allure through the l of the flesh, ... *1939*
2Pe 3:3 scoffers, walking after their own l...... *1939*
Jude 18 walk after their own ungodly l *1939*

LUSTY
Jgs 3:29 men, all l, and all men of valour; 8082

LYING
Ex 23:5 hateth thee l under his burden,........ 7257
Nu 31:17 hath known man by l with him........ 4904
Dt 21:1 l in the field, and it be not known 5307
Jgs 16:9 Now there were men l in wait
1Ki 22:23 Lord hath put a l spirit in the mouth... 8267
Ps 31:18 Let the l lips be put to silence;......... 8267
Ps 59:12 and for cursing and l, which they...... 3585
Ps 119:163 I hate and abhor l: but thy law 8267
Ps 120:2 Deliver my soul, O Lord, from l lips, ... 8267
Ps 139:3 Thou compassest ... my l down....... 7252
Pr 6:17 proud look, a l tongue, and hands 8367
Pr 10:18 He that hideth hatred with l lips, ... 8367
Pr 12:22 L lips are abomination to the Lord: 8367
Pr 21:6 getting of treasures by a l tongue 8267
Isa 32:7 to destroy the poor with l words, ... 8267
Isa 56:10 l down, loving to slumber............. 7901
Jer 7:4 Trust ye not in l words, saying, ... 8267
Jer 29:23 have spoken l words in my name 8267
La 3:10 He was unto me as a bear l in wait
Eze 13:6 have seen vanity and l divination, ... 3577
Da 2:9 prepared l and corrupt words to....... 3538
Hos 4:2 By swearing, and l, and killing, ... 3584
Jnh 2:8 that observe l vanities forsake 7723
Lk 2:12 swaddling clothes, l in a manger. *2749*
Lk 2:16 Joseph, and the babe l in a manger..... *2749*
Jn 13:25 He then l on Jesus' breast saith *1968*
Jn 20:5 looking in, saw the linen clothes l; *2749*
Eph 4:25 Wherefore putting away l, speak....... *5579*
2Th 2:9 all power and signs and l wonders,..... *5579*

M

MAD
1Sa 21:13 feigned himself **m** in their hands, ... 1984
Pr 26:18 a **m** man who casteth firebrands, ... 3856
Ecc 2:2 I said of laughter, It is **m**: and of ... 1984
Ecc 7:7 oppression maketh a wise man **m**; ... 1984
Isa 44:25 liars, and maketh diviners **m**; ... 1984
Jer 25:16 drink, and be moved, and be **m**, ... 1984
Jer 50:38 and they are **m** upon their idols ... 1984
Jer 51:7 wine; therefore the nations are **m** ... 1984
Hos 9:7 is a fool, the spiritual man is **m**, ... 7696
Jn 10:20 said, He hath a devil, and is **m**; ... *3105*
Ac 12:15 they said unto her, Thou art **m**, ... *3105*
Ac 26:24 learning doth make thee **m** ... *1519, 3130*
1Co 14:23 will they not say that ye are **m**? ... *3105*

MADNESS
Dt 28:28 The Lord shall smite thee with **m**, ... 7697
Ecc 1:17 wisdom, and to know **m**, and folly: ... 1947
Ecc 2:12 behold wisdom, and **m**, and folly: ... 1947
Ecc 7:25 of folly, even of foolishness and **m**: ... 1947
Ecc 9:3 **m** is in their heart while they live, ... 1947
Ecc 10:13 end of his talk is mischievous **m** ... 1948
Lk 6:11 And they were filled with **m**; and ... *454*
2Pe 2:16 voice forbad the **m** of the prophet ... *3913*

MAGICIAN
Da 2:10 that asked such things at any **m**, ... 2749

MAGICIANS
Ge 41:8 and called for all the **m** of Egypt, ... 2748
Ex 7:11 now the **m** of Egypt, they also did ... 2748
Ex 8:19 Then the **m** said unto Pharaoh, ... 2748
Ex 9:11 **m** could not stand before Moses ... 2748
Da 1:20 ten times better than all the **m** and ... 2748
Da 2:27 wise men, the astrologers, the **m**, ... 2749
Da 4:9 O Belteshazzar, master of the **m**, ... 2749
Da 5:11 thy father, made master of the **m**, ... 2749

MAGISTRATE
Jgs 18:7 there was no **m** in the land ... 3423, 6114
Lk 12:58 **with thine adversary to the m,** ... *758*

MAGISTRATES
Ezr 7:25 set **m** and judges, which may ... 8200
Lk 12:11 **unto the synagogues, and unto m,** ... *745*
Ac 16:20 brought them to the **m**, saying, ... *4755*
Tit 3:1 to obey **m**, to be ready to every ... *3980*

MAGNIFICENCE
Ac 19:27 and her **m** should be destroyed, ... *3168*

MAGNIFIED
Ge 19:19 and thou hast **m** thy mercy, ... 1431
Jos 4:14 On that day the Lord **m** Joshua ... 1431
2Sa 7:26 And let thy name be **m** for ever, ... 1431
1Ch 29:25 the Lord **m** Solomon exceedingly ... 1431
2Ch 32:23 was **m** in the sight of all nations ... 5375
Ps 40:16 say continually, The Lord be **m** ... 1431
Ps 70:4 say continually, Let God be **m** ... 1431
Ps 138:2 **m** thy word above all thy name ... 1431
Jer 48:42 hath **m** himself against the Lord ... 1431
La 1:9 for the enemy hath **m** himself ... 1431
Zep 2:10 **m** themselves against the people ... 1431
Ac 19:17 the name of the Lord Jesus was **m** ... *3170*
Php 1:20 also Christ shall be **m** in my body, ... *3170*

MAGNIFY
Jos 3:7 begin to **m** thee in the sight of all ... 1431
Ps 34:3 O **m** the Lord with me, and let us ... 1431
Ps 55:12 me that did **m** himself against me; ... 1431
Isa 42:21 he will **m** the law, and make it ... 1431
Eze 38:23 Thus will I **m** myself, and sanctify ... 1431
Da 11:36 and **m** himself above every god, ... 1431
Lk 1:46 said, My soul doth **m** the Lord, ... *3170*

MAID See also HANDMAID.
Ge 16:2 I pray thee, go in unto my **m**; it ... 8198
Ex 2:5 flags, she sent her **m** to fetch it ... 519
Ex 22:16 if a man entice a **m** that is not ... 1330
Dt 22:14 came to her, I found her not a **m**: ... 1331
Est 2:7 and the **m** was fair and beautiful; ... 5291
Job 31:1 why then should I think upon a **m** ... 1330
Pr 30:19 and the way of a man with a **m** ... 5959
Mt 9:24 **the m is not dead, but sleepeth.** ... *2877*
Mt 9:25 **her by the hand and the m arose** ... *2877*
Mt 26:71 into the porch, another **m** saw him,
Mk 14:69 a **m** saw him again, and began to ... *3814*
Lk 8:54 hand, and called, saying, **M, arise** ... *3816*
Lk 22:56 a certain **m** beheld him as he sat ... *3814*

MAIDEN See also HANDMAIDEN.
2Ch 36:17 compassion upon young man or **m**, ... 1330
Est 2:4 let the **m** which pleaseth the king ... 5291
Ps 123:2 eyes of a **m** unto the hand of her ... 8198

MAIDENS See also HANDMAIDENS.
Ex 2:5 her **m** walked along by the river's ... 5291
Ru 2:23 So she kept fast by the **m** of Boaz ... 5291
1Sa 9:11 found young **m** going out to draw ... 5291
Est 4:16 I also and my **m** will fast likewise; ... 5291
Ps 78:63 **m** were not given to marriage ... 1330
Ps 148:12 Both young men, and **m**; old men, ... 1330
Pr 31:15 household, and a portion to her **m** ... 5291
Ecc 2:7 I got me servants and **m**, and had ... 8198
Lk 12:45 to beat the menservants and **m**, ... *3814*

MAIDS See also HANDMAIDS.
Est 2:9 he preferred her and her **m** unto ... 5291
Job 19:15 my **m**, count me for a stranger: ... 519
Eze 9:6 utterly old and young, both **m**, and ... 1330
Mk 14:66 one of the **m** of the high priest: ... *3814*

MAIDSERVANT
Ex 11:5 unto the firstborn of the **m** that is ... 8198
Ex 20:17 his manservant, nor his **m**, nor his ... 519
Dt 15:17 unto thy **m** thou shalt do likewise ... 519
Dt 16:11 thy manservant, and thy **m**, and ... 519
Jer 34:10 manservant, and every one his **m**, ... 8198

MAIDSERVANTS
Ge 30:43 cattle, and **m**, and menservants, ... 8198
2Sa 6:22 of the **m** which thou hast spoken ... 519

MAIL
1Sa 17:5 he was armed with a coat of **m**; ... 7193

MAIMED
Le 22:22 Blind, or broken, or **m**, or having ... 2782
Mt 15:31 dumb to speak, the **m** to be whole, ... *2948*
Mt 18:8 **thee to enter into life halt or m,** ... *2948*
Lk 14:13 **a feast, call the poor, the m, the** ... *376*

MAINTAIN

1Ki	8:59	that he **m** the cause of his servant,	6213
1Ch	26:27	to **m** the house of the Lord	2388
Job	13:15	I will **m** mine own ways before	3198
Ps	140:12	will **m** the cause of the afflicted,	6213
Tit	3:8	might be careful to **m** good works.	*4291*
Tit	3:14	let ours also learn to **m** good works	*4291*

MAINTAINED

Ps	9:4	hast **m** my right and my cause;	6213

MAINTENANCE

Ezr	4:14	have **m** from the king's palace,	4415
Pr	27:27	and for the **m** for thy maidens.	2416

MAJESTY

1Ch	29:11	glory, and the victory, and the **m**:	1935
1Ch	29:25	bestowed upon him such royal **m**.	1935
Job	37:22	the north: with God is terrible **m**	1935
Ps	29:4	the voice of the Lord is full of **m**.	1926
Ps	93:1	reigneth, he is clothed with **m**;	1348
Ps	96:6	Honour and **m** are before him:	1926
Ps	145:12	the glorious **m** of his kingdom	1926
Isa	2:19	Lord, and for the glory of his **m**,	1347
Isa	26:10	will not behold the m of the Lord	1348
Da	4:36	excellent **m** was added unto me	7238
Da	5:19	And for the **m** that he gave him,	7238
Mic	5:4	in the **m** of the name of the Lord	1347
Heb	1:3	the right hand of the **M** on high;	*3172*
Heb	8:1	throne of the **M** in the heavens;	*3172*
2Pe	1:16	but were eyewitnesses of his **m**	*3168*
Jude	25	be glory and **m**, dominion and	*3172*

MAKER

Job	4:17	a man be more pure than his **m**?	6213
Job	35:10	Where is God my **m**, who giveth	6213
Ps	95:6	us kneel before the Lord our **M**,	6213
Pr	14:31	the poor reproacheth his **M**.	6213
Pr	17:5	the poor reproacheth his **M**.	6213
Pr	22:2	the Lord is the **m** of them all.	6213
Isa	17:7	day shall a man look to his **M**	6213
Isa	45:9	him that striveth with his **M**!	3335
Isa	45:11	the Holy One of Israel, and his **M**	3335
Isa	51:13	And forgettest the Lord thy **m**.	6213
Isa	54:5	For thy **M** is thine husband; The.	6213
Jer	33:2	Thus saith the Lord the **m** thereof,	6213
Hos	8:14	For Israel hath forgotten his **M**	6213
Hab	2:18	the **m** of his work trusteth therein	3335
Heb	11:10	whose builder and **m** is God	*1217*

MAKERS See also PEACEMAKERS; TENTMAKERS.

Isa	45:16	together that are **m** of idols	2796

MALE

Ge	1:27	**m** and female created he them	2145
Ge	5:2	**M** and female created he them;	2145
Ge	7:9	into the ark, the **m** and the female,	2145
Ge	17:23	every **m** among the men of	2145
Ex	12:5	blemish, a **m** of the first year:	2145
Le	1:10	shall bring it a **m** without blemish,	2145
Le	27:3	of the **m**, from twenty years old	2145
Nu	3:15	every **m** from a month old and.	2145
Nu	31:17	kill every **m** among the little ones.	2145
Dt	4:16	figure, the likeness of **m** or female,	2145
Jgs	21:11	Ye shall utterly destroy every **m**.	2145
Mal	1:14	which hath in his flock a **m**, and.	2145
Mt	19:4	**made them m and female,**	*730*
Mk	10:6	**God made them m and female.**	*730*
Lk	2:23	Every **m** that openeth the womb.	*730*
Gal	3:28	free, there is neither **m** nor female:	*730*

MALEFACTOR

Jn	18:30	If he were not a **m**, we would not	*2555*

MALEFACTORS

Lk	23:32	**m**, led with him to be put to death,	*2557*
Lk	23:39	one of the **m** which were hanged	*2557*

MALES

Ex	12:48	let all his **m** be circumcised, and.	2145
Ex	23:17	all thy **m** shall appear before the.	2138
Le	6:29	the **m** among the priests shall eat	2145
Nu	3:40	Number all the firstborn of the **m**	2145
Dt	16:16	all thy **m** appear before the Lord	2138

MALICE

1Co	5:8	the leaven of **m** and wickedness;	*2549*
1Co	14:20	howbeit in **m** be ye children, but in	*2549*
Eph	4:31	be put away from you, with all **m**:	*2549*
Col	3:8	anger, wrath, **m**, blasphemy	*2549*
Tit	3:3	living in **m** and envy, hateful, and.	*2549*
1Pe	2:1	laying aside all **m**, and all guile	*2549*

MALICIOUS

3Jn	10	prating against us with **m** words:	*4190*

MALICIOUSNESS

1Pe	2:16	using your liberty for a cloke of **m**	*2549*

MAMMON (mam′-mon)

Mt	6:24	**Ye cannot serve God and m.**	*3126*
Lk	16:9	**of the m of unrighteousness;**	*3126*
Lk	16:11	**faithful in the unrighteous m,**	*3126*
Lk	16:13	**Ye cannot serve God and m.**	*3126*

MAN

Ge	1:26	said, Let us make **m** in our image,	120
Ge	2:5	there was not a **m** to till the ground.	120
Ge	2:7	Lord God formed **m** of the dust of.	120
Ge	2:7	of life; and **m** became a living soul.	120
Ge	2:16	the Lord God commanded the **m**,	120
Ge	2:13	good that the **m** should be alone;	120
Ge	2:22	woman, and brought her unto the **m**.	120
Ge	2:24	shall a **m** leave his father and his.	376
Ge	3:12	the **m** said, The woman whom thou	120
Ge	3:22	**m** is become as one of us, to know.	120
Ge	3:24	So he drove out the **m**; and he	120
Ge	4:23	I have slain a **m** to my wounding	376
Ge	6:3	shall not always strive with **m**,	120
Ge	6:5	that the wickedness of **m** was great,	120
Ge	6:6	repented the Lord … he had made **m**	120
Ge	6:9	Noah was a just **m** and perfect in	376
Ge	9:6	blood, by **m** shall his blood be shed:	120
Ge	9:6	for in the image of God made he **m**.	120
Ge	20:7	therefore restore the **m** his wife;	376
Ge	27:11	is a hairy **m**, and I am a smooth **m**.	376
Ge	39:2	Joseph, and he was a prosperous **m**;	376
Ge	41:33	look out a **m** discreet and wise	376
Ge	41:38	a **m** in whom the Spirit of God is?	376
Ge	44:17	but the **m** in whose hand the cup is	376
Ge	45:1	Cause every **m** to go out from me	376
Ge	49:6	for in their anger they slew a **m**	376
Ex	2:12	when he saw that there was no **m**.	376
Ex	11:3	**m** Moses was very great in the land	376
Ex	21:12	He that smiteth a **m**, so that he die,	376
Ex	21:29	that he hath killed a **m** or a woman;	376
Ex	21:33	And if a **m** shall open a pit, or if.	376

Ex	21:33	a **m** shall dig a pit, and not cover it	376
Ex	22:1	If a **m** shall steal an ox, or a sheep	376
Ex	22:5	If a **m** shall cause a field or	376
Ex	22:7	If a **m** … deliver unto his neighbour	376
Ex	22:10	If a **m** deliver unto his neighbour	376
Ex	22:10	hurt, or driven away, no **m** seeing it:	
Ex	22:16	And if a **m** entice a maid that is not	376
Le	18:5	which if a **m** do, he shall live in	120
Le	19:3	Ye shall fear every **m** his mother,	376
Le	24:21	he that killeth a **m**, he shall be put	120
Le	25:10	return every **m** unto his possession,	376
Nu	8:17	Israel are mine, both **m** and beast:	120
Nu	9:13	season, that **m** shall bear his sin	376
Nu	19:13	dead body of any **m** that is dead,	120
Nu	21:9	if a serpent had bitten any **m**,	376
Nu	27:18	a **m** in whom is the spirit, and lay	376
Dt	4:32	the day that God created **m** upon	120
Dt	5:24	that God doth talk with **m**, and he	120
Dt	8:3	**m** doth not live by bread only, but	120
Dt	8:5	as a **m** chasteneth his son, so the	376
Dt	12:8	every **m** whatsoever is right in his	376
Dt	15:7	If there be among you a poor **m**	
Dt	16:17	Every **m** shall give as he is able	376
Dt	20:7	what **m** is there that hath betrothed	376
Dt	21:18	**m** have a stubborn and rebellious	376
Dt	22:5	a **m** put on a woman's garment:	1397
Dt	22:25	the **m** force her, and lie with her:	376
Jos	3:12	of Israel, out of every tribe a **m**	376
Jos	5:13	stood a **m** over against him with a	376
Jos	23:10	One **m** of you … chase a thousand:	376
Jgs	13:6	saying, A **m** of God came unto me,	376
Jgs	17:6	every **m** did that which was right	376
Jgs	19:24	unto this **m** do not so vile a thing	376
Jgs	21:25	every **m** did that which was right in	376
Ru	2:20	The **m** is near of kin unto us, one of	376
1Sa	2:25	but if a **m** sin against the Lord, who	376
1Sa	13:14	sought him a **m** after his own heart,	376
1Sa	15:29	for he is not a **m**, that he should	120
1Sa	16:7	for the Lord seeth not as **m** seeth;	120
1Sa	16:7	for **m** looketh on the outward	120
1Sa	26:23	The Lord render to every **m** his	376
2Sa	12:7	said to David, Thou art the **m**	376
2Sa	24:14	let me not fall into the hand of **m**	120
1Ki	9:5	not fail thee a **m** upon the throne	376
1Ki	17:24	I know that thou art a **m** of God,	376
2Ki	1:10	If I be a **m** of God, then let fire come	376
2Ki	1:12	I be a **m** of God, let fire come down	376
2Ki	4:27	the **m** of God said, Let her alone;	376
2Ki	6:17	opened the eyes of the young **m**;	
2Ch	6:36	there is no **m** which sinneth not,)	120
2Ch	7:18	shall not fail thee a **m** to be ruler	376
2Ch	19:6	for ye judge not for **m**, but for the	120
2Ch	25:4	every **m** shall die for his own sin	376
Ne	9:29	(which if a **m** do, he shall live in	120
Job	1:1	and that **m** was perfect and upright,	376
Job	2:4	all that a **m** hath will he give for his	376
Job	4:17	Shall mortal **m** be more just than	582
Job	5:7	Yet **m** is born unto trouble, as the	120
Job	7:1	appointed time to **m** upon earth?	582
Job	9:2	how should **m** be just with God?	582
Job	14:1	**M** that is born of a woman is of	120
Job	25:4	then can **m** be justified with God?	582
Job	32:8	But there is a spirit in **m**: and the	582
Job	33:12	thee, that God is greater than **m**	582
Job	34:21	his eyes are upon the ways of **m**,	376
Ps	1:1	Blessed is the **m** that walketh not	376
Ps	8:4	What is **m**, that thou art mindful	582
Ps	22:6	But I am a worm, and no **m**; a	376
Ps	32:2	Blessed is the **m** unto whom the	120
Ps	36:6	Lord, thou preservest **m** and beast	120
Ps	37:16	little that a righteous **m** hath is better	
Ps	37:23	steps of a good **m** are ordered by	1397
Ps	37:37	for the end of that **m** is peace	376
Ps	39:6	every **m** walketh in a vain shew:	376
Ps	40:4	Blessed is that **m** that maketh the	1397
Ps	56:11	I will not be afraid what **m** can do	120
Ps	62:12	to every **m** according to his work	376
Ps	84:5	Blessed is the **m** whose strength is	120
Ps	89:48	What **m** is he that liveth, and shall	1397
Ps	94:11	Lord knoweth the thoughts of **m**,	120
Ps	103:15	As for **m**, his days are as grass:	582
Ps	118:6	not fear: what can **m** do unto me?	120
Ps	127:5	Happy is the **m** that hath his	1397
Ps	142:4	failed me; no **m** cared for my soul	
Pr	1:5	wise **m** will hear, and will increase	
Pr	3:13	Happy is the **m** that findeth wisdom,	120
Pr	3:30	Strive not with a **m** without cause,	120
Pr	5:21	ways of **m** are before the eyes of	376
Pr	6:27	Can a **m** take fire in his bosom,	376
Pr	6:34	For jealousy is the rage of a **m**:	1397
Pr	12:10	A righteous **m** regardeth the life of	
Pr	13:5	A righteous **m** hateth lying: but a	
Pr	13:22	A good **m** leaveth an inheritance to	
Pr	15:20	a foolish **m** despiseth his mother	120
Pr	16:2	ways of a **m** are clean in his own	376
Pr	16:25	way that seemeth right unto a **m**,	376
Pr	19:6	and every **m** is a friend to him that	
Pr	20:6	but a faithful **m** who can find?	376
Pr	21:2	way of a **m** is right in his own	376
Pr	24:12	to every **m** according to his works?	120
Pr	24:16	For a just **m** falleth seven times, and	
Pr	27:20	the eyes of **m** are never satisfied	120
Pr	28:1	The wicked flee when no **m** pursueth:	
Pr	29:11	wise **m** keepeth it in till afterwards	
Pr	29:22	An angry **m** stirreth up strife, and	376
Pr	29:25	fear of **m** bringeth a snare: but	120
Pr	30:19	and the way of a **m** with a maid	1397
Ecc	1:3	What profit hath a **m** of all his	120
Ecc	2:24	There is nothing better for a **m**,	120
Ecc	3:11	no **m** can find out the work that God	120
Ecc	5:12	The sleep of a labouring **m** is sweet,	
Ecc	6:3	If a **m** beget an hundred children,	376
Ecc	6:12	who can tell a **m** what shall be after	120
Ecc	7:20	there is not a just **m** upon earth,	120
Ecc	7:29	that God hath made **m** upright; but	120
Ecc	8:8	is no **m** that hath power over the	120
Ecc	9:12	For **m** also knoweth not his time:	120
Ecc	11:8	But if a **m** live many years, and	120
Ecc	11:9	Rejoice, O young **m**, in thy youth; and	
Ecc	12:5	because **m** goeth to his long home,	120
Ecc	12:13	for this is the whole duty of **m**	120
Isa	17:7	day shall a **m** look to his Maker,	120
Isa	41:28	For I beheld, and there was no **m**;	376
Isa	51:12	be afraid of a **m** that shall die,	582
Isa	52:14	was so marred more than any **m**,	376
Isa	53:3	a **m** of sorrows, and acquainted with	376
Isa	55:7	the unrighteous **m** his thoughts:	376
Isa	57:1	and no **m** layeth it to heart:	376
Jer	3:1	If a **m** put away his wife, and she	376
Jer	10:23	that the way of **m** is not in himself:	120
Jer	10:23	it is not in **m** that walketh to direct	
Jer	12:11	because no **m** layeth it to heart	376

Jer	16:20	Shall a **m** make gods unto himself,	120
Jer	17:7	is the **m** that trusteth in the Lord,	1397
Jer	22:30	the Lord, Write ye this **m** childless,	376
Jer	22:30	for no **m** of his seed shall prosper,	376
Jer	26:3	turn every **m** from his evil way, that	376
Jer	33:17	David shall never want a **m** to sit	376
Jer	36:3	return every **m** from his evil way;	376
Jer	49:18	the Lord, no **m** shall abide there,	376
Jer	49:18	neither shall a son of **m** dwell in it	120
Jer	50:44	who is a chosen **m**, that I may appoint	
Jer	51:45	deliver ye every **m** his soul from	376
La	3:1	am the **m** that hath seen affliction	1397
La	3:26	It is good that a **m** should both hope	
La	3:27	good for a **m** that he bear the yoke	1397
La	3:39	**m** for the punishment of his sins?	1397
Eze	1:5	they had the likeness of a **m**,	120
Eze	2:1	Son of **m**, stand upon thy feet, and	120
Eze	2:3	Son of **m**, I send thee to the children	120
Eze	2:6	son of **m**, be not afraid of them,	120
Eze	3:17	Son of **m**, I have made thee a	120
Eze	3:18	wicked **m** shall die in his iniquity;	
Eze	3:20	When a righteous **m** doth turn from	
Eze	3:21	if thou warn the righteous **m**, that the	
Eze	12:2	Son of **m**, thou dwellest in the midst	120
Eze	12:27	Son of **m**, behold, they of the house	120
Eze	14:13	Son of **m**, when the land sinneth	120
Eze	16:2	Son of **m**, cause Jerusalem to know	120
Eze	18:5	But if a **m** be just, and do that	376
Eze	18:26	a righteous **m** turneth away from his	
Eze	18:27	when the wicked **m** turneth away from	
Eze	20:13	which if a **m** do, he shall even	120
Eze	22:30	I sought for a **m** among them, that	376
Eze	24:16	Son of **m**, behold, I take away from	120
Eze	28:2	yet thou art a **m**, and not God,	120
Eze	28:9	thou shalt be a **m**, and no God, in	120
Eze	29:11	No foot of **m** shall pass through it,	120
Eze	33:7	O Son of **m**, I have set thee a	120
Eze	37:3	Son of **m**, can these bones live?	120
Eze	40:3	there was a **m**, whose appearance	376
Da	2:25	I have found a **m** of the captives	1400
Da	5:11	There is a **m** in thy kingdom, in	1400
Da	7:13	one like the Son of **m** came with the	606
Da	10:18	one like the appearance of a **m**,	120
Da	10:19	O **m** greatly beloved, fear not:	376
Hos	9:7	is a fool, the spiritual **m** is mad	376
Hos	11:9	for I am God, and not **m**; the Holy	376
Jnh	1:5	and cried every **m** unto his god, and	
Mic	2:11	If a **m** walking in the spirit and	376
Mic	6:8	shewed thee, O **m**, what is good:	120
Zec	1:8	a **m** riding upon a red horse, and	376
Zec	6:12	the **m** whose name is The Branch;	376
Zec	8:16	Speak ye every **m** the truth to his	376
Zec	12:1	and formeth the spirit of **m** within	120
Mal	3:8	Will a **m** rob God? Yet ye have	120
Mt	1:19	her husband, being a just **m**, and	
Mt	4:4	**M shall not live by bread alone,**	*444*
Mt	6:24	**No m can serve two masters: for**	*3762*
Mt	8:20	**the Son of m hath not where to**	*444*
Mt	8:27	What manner of **m** is this, that even	
Mt	11:27	**no m knoweth the Son, but the**	*3762*
Mt	12:8	**the Son of m is Lord even of the**	*444*
Mt	12:32	**a word against the Son of m,**	*444*
Mt	12:35	**A good m out of the good treasure**	*444*
Mt	12:40	**so shall the Son of m be three days**	*444*
Mt	15:11	**goeth into the mouth defileth a m;**	*444*
Mt	16:26	**a m give in exchange for his soul?**	*444*
Mt	18:7	**woe to that m by whom the offence**	*444*
Mt	18:11	**For the Son of m is come to save**	*444*
Mt	18:12	**if a m have an hundred sheep, and**	*444*
Mt	19:3	lawful for a **m** to put away his wife	*444*
Mt	19:5	**this cause shall a m leave father**	*444*
Mt	19:6	**together, let not m put asunder**	*444*
Mt	24:4	**Take heed that no m deceive you**	*5100*
Mt	24:27	**also the coming of the Son of m be**	*444*
Mt	26:24	**by whom the Son of m is betrayed!**	*444*
Mt	26:72	with an oath, I do not know the **m**.	*444*
Mk	2:28	**the Son of m is Lord also of the**	*444*
Mk	4:41	What manner of **m** is this, that even	
Mk	7:23	**from within, and defile the m.**	*444*
Mk	8:31	Son of **m** must suffer many things	*444*
Mk	8:36	**For what shall it profit a m, if he**	*444*
Mk	13:32	**day and that hour knoweth no m,**	*3762*
Mk	14:21	**whom the Son of m is betrayed!**	*444*
Mk	15:39	Truly this **m** was the Son of God	*444*
Lk	4:4	**m shall not live by bread alone.**	*444*
Lk	5:8	me; for I am a sinful **m**, O Lord	*435*
Lk	5:20	him, **M, thy sins are forgiven thee**	*444*
Lk	5:24	**Son of m hath power upon earth**	*444*
Lk	6:5	**the Son of m is Lord also of the**	*444*
Lk	6:30	**Give to every m that asketh of thee;**	
Lk	6:45	**good m out of the good treasure**	*444*
Lk	8:25	What manner of **m** is this! for he	
Lk	9:23	**If any m will come after me, let**	
Lk	9:56	**Son of m is not come to destroy**	*444*
Lk	9:58	**Son of m hath not where to lay**	*444*
Lk	9:62	**No m, having put his hand to the**	*3762*
Lk	11:26	**last state of that m is worse than**	*444*
Lk	11:33	**No m, when he hath lighted a**	*3762*
Lk	12:40	**Son of m cometh at an hour when**	*444*
Lk	17:24	**so shall also the Son of m be in**	*444*
Lk	18:8	**when the Son of m cometh, shall**	*444*
Lk	19:10	**the Son of m is come to seek and**	*444*
Lk	19:14	**will not have this m to reign over**	
Lk	19:30	**colt tied, whereon yet never m sat:**	*444*
Lk	21:27	**see the Son of m coming in a cloud**	*444*
Lk	22:22	**that m by whom he is betrayed!**	*444*
Lk	22:48	**betrayest thou the Son of m**	*444*
Lk	22:56	and said, This **m** was also with him.	
Lk	23:4	the people, I find no fault in this **m**	*444*
Lk	23:14	I, … have found no fault in this **m**.	*444*
Jn	1:6	There was a **m** sent from God, whose	*444*
Jn	1:13	nor of the will of **m**, but of God.	*435*
Jn	1:18	No **m** hath seen God at any time;	*3762*
Jn	1:51	**and descending upon the Son of m**	*444*
Jn	3:3	**Except a m be born again, he**	*5100*
Jn	3:5	**Except a m be born of water and**	*5100*
Jn	3:13	**no m hath ascended up to heaven,**	*3762*
Jn	3:13	**the Son of m which is in heaven**	*444*
Jn	4:29	Come, see a **m**, which told me all	*444*
Jn	6:44	**No m can come to me, except the**	*3762*
Jn	6:51	**if any m eat of this bread, he shall**	
Jn	6:53	**ye eat the flesh of the Son of m,**	*444*
Jn	6:62	**if ye shall see the Son of m ascend**	*444*
Jn	6:65	**no m can come unto me, except,**	*3762*
Jn	7:37	**If any m thirst, let him come unto**	
Jn	7:46	answered, Never **m** spake like this	*444*
Jn	8:10	**hath no m condemned thee?**	*3762*
Jn	9:3	**hath this m sinned, nor his parents:**	
Jn	9:4	**cometh, when no m can work.**	*3762*
Jn	10:18	**No m taketh it from me, but I lay**	*3762*
Jn	10:29	**no m is able to pluck them out of**	*3762*
Jn	12:26	**if any m serve me, him will my**	

Jn 13:31 **said, Now is the Son of m glorified,** *444*
Jn 14:6 **no m cometh unto the Father, but** *3762*
Jn 15:13 **Greater love hath no m than this,** *3762*
Jn 16:21 **joy that a m is born into the world** *444*
Jn 18:14 one **m** should die for the people *444*
Jn 18:31 lawful for us to put any **m** to death: *3762*
Ac 2:8 we every **m** in our own tongue, ... *1520*
Ac 6:5 a **m** full of faith and of the Holy *435*
Ac 7:56 Son of **m** standing on the right hand *444*
Ac 8:10 This **m** is the great power of God.
Ac 9:8 eyes were opened, he saw no **m**. *3762*
Ac 10:2 A devout **m**, and one that feared God
Ac 22:26 thou doest: for this **m** is a Roman. *444*
Ac 23:9 saying, We find no evil in this **m**: *444*
Ro 1:23 image made like to corruptible **m**, ... *444*
Ro 2:1 inexcusable, O **m**, whosoever thou *444*
Ro 3:4 let God be true, but every **m** a liar; *444*
Ro 3:28 a **m** is justified by faith without the *444*
Ro 4:8 Blessed is the **m** to whom the Lord *435*
Ro 5:7 for a righteous **m** will one die:
Ro 7:22 the law of God after the inward **m**: *444*
Ro 7:24 O wretched **m** that I am! who shall *444*
Ro 8:9 if any **m** have not the Spirit of Christ,
Ro 12:17 Recompense to no **m** evil for evil *3367*
Ro 13:8 Owe no **m** any thing, but to love *3367*
Ro 14:5 One **m** esteemeth one day above
Ro 14:5 Let every **m** be fully persuaded in
Ro 14:13 that no **m** put a stumblingblock
1Co 2:9 have entered into the heart of **m**, ... *444*
1Co 2:11 For what **m** knoweth the things *444*
1Co 2:11 knoweth the things of a **m**, save *444*
1Co 2:11 the things of God knoweth no **m**, ... *3762*
1Co 2:15 yet he himself is judged of no **m**. *3762*
1Co 3:5 as the Lord gave to every **m**?
1Co 3:8 and every **m** shall receive his own
1Co 3:10 every **m** take heed how he buildeth
1Co 3:12 if any **m** build upon this foundation
1Co 3:18 Let no **m** deceive himself. *3367*
1Co 3:18 any **m** among you seemeth to be wise
1Co 4:1 Let a **m** so account of us, as of the *444*
1Co 4:2 that a **m** be found faithful *5100*
1Co 6:18 Every sin that a **m** doeth is without *444*
1Co 7:1 good for a **m** not to touch a woman. *444*
1Co 8:2 if any **m** think that he knoweth any
1Co 8:3 But if any **m** love God, the same is
1Co 10:24 Let no **m** seek his own, ... *3367*
1Co 11:3 that the head of every **m** is Christ; *435*
1Co 11:3 the head of the woman is the **m**; *435*
1Co 11:7 the woman is the glory of the **m**. *435*
1Co 11:9 woman; but the woman for the **m** *435*
1Co 15:21 For since by **m** came death *444*
1Co 15:21 by **m** came also the resurrection of. *444*
2Co 4:16 the inward **m** is renewed day by day
2Co 5:17 Therefore if any **m** be in Christ, he is
Gal 3:11 no **m** is justified by the law in the *3762*
Gal 6:1 if a **m** be overtaken in a fault, ye *444*
Gal 6:5 every **m** shall bear his own burden *5100*
Gal 6:7 whatsoever a **m** soweth, that shall *444*
Eph 2:9 works, lest any **m** should boast
Eph 4:24 that ye put on the new **m**, which *444*
Eph 5:6 Let no **m** deceive you with vain *3367*
Eph 5:31 cause shall a **m** leave his father *444*
Php 2:4 Look not every **m** on his own
Php 2:8 being found in fashion as a **m**, ... *444*
Col 1:28 we preach, warning every **m**, and *444*
Col 4:6 how ye ought to answer every **m** *1520*
1Th 5:15 none render evil for evil unto any **m**;
1Ti 1:8 is good, if a **m** use it lawfully; *5100*
1Ti 1:9 the law is not made for a righteous **m**,
1Ti 2:12 nor to usurp authority over the **m**, ... *435*
1Ti 6:3 If any **m** teach otherwise, and
1Ti 6:16 the light which no **m** can approach
1Ti 6:16 whom no **m** hath seen, nor can see: *444*
2Ti 2:4 No **m** that warreth entangleth *3762*
2Ti 3:17 That the **m** of God may be perfect, ... *444*
Heb 2:6 What is **m**, that thou art mindful *444*
Heb 2:6 son of **m**, that thou visitest him? *444*
Heb 2:9 God should taste death for every **m**
Heb 12:15 any **m** fail of the grace of God;
Heb 13:6 not fear what **m** shall do unto me. *444*
Jas 1:8 double minded **m** is unstable in *435*
Jas 1:12 Blessed is the **m** that endureth *435*
Jas 1:13 no **m** say when he is tempted, ... *3367*
Jas 1:13 evil, neither tempteth he any **m**: *3762*
Jas 1:19 let every **m** be swift to hear, slow *444*
Jas 1:20 For the wrath of **m** worketh not the. *435*
Jas 2:2 come in also a poor **m** in vile raiment;
Jas 3:8 the tongue can no **m** tame; it is an *444*
Jas 5:16 fervent prayer of a righteous **m**
Jas 5:17 **m** subject to like passions as we *444*
1Pe 2:19 if a **m** for conscience toward God *5100*
1Jn 2:1 if any **m** sin, we have an advocate
1Jn 2:15 If any **m** love the world, the love
1Jn 3:3 And every **m** that hath this hope
1Jn 4:12 No **m** hath seen God at any time *3762*
1Jn 5:16 If any **m** see his brother sin a sin
Rev 1:13 one like unto the Son of **m**, clothed *444*
Rev 3:7 **that openeth, and no m shutteth;** *3762*
Rev 14:14 cloud one sat like unto the Son of **m**, ... *444*
Rev 19:12 a name written, that no **m** knew *3762*
Rev 22:12 **every m according as his work**
Rev 22:18 every **m** that heareth the words *3956*
Rev 22:18 If any **m** shall add unto these
Rev 22:19 if any **m** shall take away from the

MANGER

Lk 2:7 clothes, and laid him in a **m**; *5336*
Lk 2:12 in swaddling clothes, lying in a **m**. *5336*
Lk 2:16 and the babe lying in the **m**. *5336*

MANIFEST

Lk 8:17 **secret, that shall not be made m;** *5318*
Jn 3:21 **that his deeds may be made m,** *5319*
Jn 9:3 **works of God should be made m** *5319*
1Co 3:13 every man's work shall be made **m**: *5318*
Gal 5:19 Now the works of the flesh are **m**, ... *5318*
Eph 5:13 whatsoever doth make **m** is light *5319*
Col 1:26 but now is made **m** to his saints: *5319*
2Th 1:5 a **m** token of the righteous judgement
1Ti 3:16 God was **m** in the flesh, justified *5319*
2Ti 1:10 is now made **m** by the appearing *5319*
Heb 4:13 creature that is not **m** in his sight: *852*
Heb 9:8 holiest of all was not yet made **m**, ... *5319*
1Pe 1:20 was **m** in these last times for you, ... *5319*
1Jn 3:10 In this the children of God are **m** *5318*
Rev 15:4 for thy judgments are made **m** *5319*

MANIFESTATION

Ro 8:19 for the **m** of the sons of God *602*
1Co 12:7 But the **m** of the Spirit is given to *5321*
2Co 4:2 by **m** of the truth commending *5321*

MANIFESTED
Mk 4:22 nothing hid, which shall not be **m**; *5319*
Jn 17:6 I have **m** thy name unto the men...... *5319*
Ro 3:21 of God without the law is **m**, being *5579*
Tit 1:3 But hath in due times **m** his word *5319*
1Jn 1:2 the life was **m**, and we have seen....... *5319*
1Jn 3:5 that he was **m** to take away our........ *5319*
1Jn 3:8 purpose the Son of God was **m**........ *5319*
1Jn 4:9 **m** the love of God toward us.......... *5319*

MANIFOLD See also MANY.
Ps 104:24 O Lord, how **m** are thy works! in 7231
Am 5:12 I know your **m** transgressions......... 7227
Eph 3:10 the church the **m** wisdom of God...... *4182*
1Pe 1:6 through **m** temptations:.............. *4164*
1Pe 4:10 stewards of the **m** grace of God *4164*

MANKIND See also WOMANKIND.
Le 18:22 Thou shalt not lie with **m**, as with 2145
Le 20:13 If a man also lie with **m**, as he......... 2145
1Co 6:9 nor abusers of themselves with **m**,...... *733*
1Ti 1:10 them that defile themselves with **m**,..... *733*
Jas 3:7 and hath been tamed of **m**:....... *5449, 442*

MANNA (man´-nah)
Ex 16:15 they said one to another, It is **m**:....... 4478
Ex 16:33 and put an omer full of **m** therein,..... 4478
Ex 16:35 children of Israel did eat **m** forty 4478
Dt 8:16 fed thee in the wilderness with **m**, ... 4478
Jos 5:12 And the **m** ceased on the morrow 4478
Ps 78:24 rained down **m** upon them to eat, ... 4478
Jn 6:49 Your fathers did eat **m** in the *3131*
Jn 6:58 not as your fathers did eat **m**, and *3131*
Heb 9:4 was the golden pot that had **m**,........ *3131*
Rev 2:17 will I give to eat of the hidden **m** *3131*

MANNER
Ge 18:11 with Sarah after the **m** of women....... 734
Ge 19:31 us after the **m** of all the earth:......... 1870
Le 24:22 Ye shall have one **m** of law, as 4941
Nu 15:16 One law and one **m** shall be for 4941
1Sa 8:11 **m** of the king that shall reign 4941
2Ki 1:7 What **m** of man was he which 4941
2Ki 17:33 after the **m** of the nations whom 4941
Ps 107:18 Their soul abhorreth all **m** of meat;
SS 7:13 our gates are all **m** of pleasant fruits,
Isa 51:6 dwell therein shall die in like **m**:....... 3654
Jer 13:9 After this **m** will I mar the pride....... 3541
Eze 20:30 after the **m** of your fathers?........... 1870
Eze 23:15 after the **m** of the Babylonians of...... 1823
Eze 23:45 them after the **m** of adulteresses, ... 4941
Am 4:10 pestilence after the **m** of Egypt:........ 1870
Mt 5:11 shall say all **m** of evil against you
Mt 6:9 After this **m** therefore pray ye: *3779*
Mt 8:27 What **m** of man is this, that even *4217*
Mk 4:41 What **m** of man is this, that............ *686*
Mk 13:29 So ye in like **m**, when ye shall see...... *5779*
Lk 1:29 what **m** of salutation this should *4217*
Lk 1:66 What **m** of child shall this be!.......... *686*
Lk 6:23 in the like **m** did their fathers
Lk 8:25 What **m** of man is this! for he.......... *686*
Ac 15:1 circumcised after the **m** of Moses, ... *1485*
1Co 11:25 the same **m** also he took the cup....... *5675*
2Co 7:9 ye were made sorry after a godly **m**,
Jas 1:24 forgetteth what **m** of man he was, ... *3697*
1Pe 1:11 what **m** of time the Spirit of *4169*
1Pe 1:15 ye holy in all **m** of conversation;
1Jn 3:1 what **m** of love the Father hath........ *4217*
Rev 21:19 with all **m** of precious stones
Rev 22:2 of life, which bare twelve **m** of fruits,

MANNERS
Le 20:23 not walk in the **m** of the nation,....... 2708
Eze 11:12 done after the **m** of the heathen 4941
1Co 15:33 communications corrupt good **m**...... *2239*
Heb 1:1 and in divers **m** spake in time past..... *4187*

MAN'S See also WOMAN'S.
Ge 8:21 the ground any more for **m** sake; 120
Ge 8:21 the imagination of **m** heart is evil....... 120
Ge 9:6 Whoso sheddeth **m** blood, by man...... 120
Ge 44:1 every **m** money in his sack's mouth 376
Ex 4:11 him, Who hath made **m** mouth? 120
Le 20:10 adultery with another **m** wife,.......... 376
Dt 24:6 for he taketh a **m** life to pledge
Pr 10:15 The rich **m** wealth is his strong city:
Pr 12:14 recompence of a **m** hands shall be 120
Pr 13:8 ransom of a **m** life are his riches: 376
Pr 16:7 When a **m** ways please the Lord, he 376
Pr 16:9 A **m** heart deviseth his way: but 120
Pr 18:11 The rich **m** wealth is his strong city,
Pr 18:16 A **m** gift maketh room for him, and..... 120
Pr 18:20 A **m** belly shall be satisfied with 376
Pr 19:21 are many devices in a **m** heart; 376
Pr 20:24 **M** goings are of the Lord; how 1397
Pr 27:9 so doth the sweetness of a **m** friend
Pr 29:23 A **m** pride shall bring him low: but 120
Pr 29:26 **m** judgment cometh from the Lord..... 376
Ecc 2:14 The wise **m** eyes are in his head; but
Ecc 8:1 a **m** wisdom maketh his face to......... 120
Ecc 8:5 wise **m** heart discerneth both time
Ecc 9:16 the poor **m** wisdom is despised, and
Ecc 10:2 A wise **m** heart is at his right hand;
Ecc 10:12 The words of a wise **m** mouth are
Isa 13:7 faint, and every **m** heart shall melt: 582
Jer 23:36 every **m** word shall be his burden; 376
Jnh 1:14 let us not perish for this **m** life,......... 376
Mic 7:6 a **m** enemies are the men of his own 376
Mt 10:36 a **m** foes shall be they of his own *444*
Mt 12:29 can one enter into a strong **m** house,
Mk 3:27 man can enter into a strong **m** house,
Lk 12:15 for a **m** life consisteth not in the....... *5100*
Lk 16:21 which fell from the rich **m** table:
Jn 18:17 thou also one of this **m** disciples?....... *444*
Ac 5:28 to bring this **m** blood upon us.......... *444*
Ac 7:58 their clothes at a young **m** feet,........ *3494*
Ro 5:17 For if by one **m** offence death reigned
Ro 5:19 by one **m** disobedience many were...... *444*
Ro 14:4 that judgest another **m** servant? *245*
Ro 15:20 build upon another **m** foundation: *245*
1Co 2:4 with enticing words of **m** wisdom,...... *442*
1Co 3:13 fire shall try every **m** work of what
1Co 3:14 If any **m** work abide which he hath
Jas 1:26 his own heart, this **m** religion is vain
1Pe 1:17 according to every **m** work,

MANSERVANT
Job 31:13 If I did despise the cause of my **m**,..... 5650
Jer 34:10 that every one should let his **m**, ... 5650

MANSIONS
Jn 14:2 my Father's house are many **m**........ *3438*

MANSLAYER

Nu	35:6	which ye shall appoint for the **m**,	7523
Nu	35:12	that the **m** die not, until he stand	7523

MANTLE

Jgs	4:18	tent, she covered him with a **m**	8063
1Sa	15:27	hold upon the skirt of his **m**, and	4598
1Sa	28:14	up; and he is covered with a **m**	4598
2Ki	2:8	Elijah took his **m**, and wrapped it	155
2Ki	2:13	He took up also the **m** of Elijah that	155
Job	1:20	Then Job arose, and rent his **m**,	4598
Job	2:12	they rent every one his **m**, and	4598

MANY See also **MANIFOLD.**

Ge	17:4	shalt be a father of **m** nations	1995
Ge	37:3	and he made him a coat of **m** colours	
Ge	37:32	And they sent the coat of **m** colours,	
Ex	19:21	to gaze, and **m** of them perish	7227
Nu	13:18	they be strong or weak, few or **m**;	7227
Dt	1:11	thousand times as **m** more as ye are,	
Dt	7:1	cast out **m** nations before thee, the	7227
Dt	15:6	thou shalt reign over **m** nations,	7227
Jgs	7:2	are with thee are too **m** for me to	7227
1Sa	14:6	the Lord to save by **m** or by few	7227
1Ki	11:1	Solomon loved **m** strange women	7227
Ezr	5:11	was builded these **m** years ago,	7690
Ne	7:2	man, and feared God above **m**	7227
Ps	3:2	**M** there be which say of my soul	7227
Ps	34:19	**M** are the afflictions of the	7227
Ps	93:4	than the noise of **m** waters, yea	7227
Ps	129:2	**M** a time have they afflicted me	7227
Pr	7:26	**m** strong men have been slain by	3605
Pr	14:20	but the rich hath **m** friends	7227
Pr	19:21	are **m** devices in a man's heart;	7227
Pr	31:29	**M** daughters have done virtuously	7227
Ecc	6:3	and live **m** years, so that the	7227
Ecc	11:1	thou shalt find it after **m** days	7230
Ecc	11:8	But if a man live **m** years, and	7235
Ecc	12:9	out, and set in order **m** proverbs	7235
Ecc	12:12	of making **m** books there is no end;	7235
SS	8:7	**M** waters cannot quench love,	7227
Isa	42:20	Seeing **m** things, but thou	7227
Isa	52:14	As **m** were astonied at thee; his	7227
Jer	3:1	played the harlot with **m** lovers;	7227
Jer	16:16	I will send for **m** fishers, saith	7227
Jer	35:7	that ye may live **m** days in the land	7227
Eze	12:27	he seeth is for **m** days to come	7227
Da	8:26	vision; for it shall be for **m** days	7227
Da	11:26	and **m** shall fall down slain	7227
Da	12:2	**m** of them that sleep in the dust	7227
Da	12:3	they that turn **m** to righteousness	7227
Mic	4:2	**m** nations shall come, and say,	7227
Mic	4:11	Now also **m** nations are gathered	7227
Zec	2:11	**m** nations shall be joined to the	7227
Mal	2:6	did turn **m** away from iniquity.	7227
Mal	2:8	caused **m** to stumble at the law;	7227
Mt	7:13	**m there be which go in thereat:**	*4183*
Mt	7:22	**M will say to me in that day,**	*4183*
Mt	10:31	**of more value than m sparrows**	*4183*
Mt	20:28	**to give his life a ransom for m**	*4183*
Mt	22:14	**m are called, but few are chosen**	*4183*
Mt	25:21	**make thee ruler over m things:**	*4183*
Mt	26:28	**shed for m for the remission of**	*4183*
Mk	5:9	My name is Legion: for we are **m**	*4183*
Mk	9:12	**that he must suffer m things, and**	*4183*
Mk	14:24	**testament, which is shed for m**	*4183*
Lk	2:34	and rising again of **m** in Israel;	*4183*
Lk	2:35	the thoughts of **m** hearts may be	*4183*
Lk	7:47	**thee, Her sins, which are m, are**	*4183*
Lk	9:22	**Son of man must suffer m things,**	*4183*
Lk	12:7	**of more value than m sparrows.**	*4183*
Lk	17:25	**first must he suffer m things,**	*4183*
Lk	21:8	**m shall come in my name,**	*4183*
Jn	1:12	But as **m** as received him, to them	*3745*
Jn	2:23	**m** believed in his name, when they	*4183*
Jn	14:2	**Father's house are m mansions:**	*4183*
Jn	17:2	**give eternal life to as m as thou**	
Jn	20:30	**m** other signs truly did Jesus in	*4183*
Jn	21:25	And there are also **m** other things	*4183*
Ac	9:13	I have heard by **m** of this man,	*4183*
Ro	5:15	the offence of one **m** be dead,	*4183*
Ro	8:14	as **m** as are led by the Spirit of God,	*3745*
1Co	1:26	that not **m** wise men after the flesh,	*4183*
2Co	2:4	I wrote unto you with **m** tears;	*4183*
1Ti	6:9	into **m** foolish and hurtful lusts,	*4183*
1Ti	6:10	pierced … through with **m** sorrows	*4183*
Heb	9:28	once offered to bear the sins of **m**;	*4183*
Jas	3:1	My brethren, be not **m** masters,	*4183*
Jas	3:2	For in **m** things we offend all. If	*4183*
1Jn	2:18	even now are there **m** antichrists;	*4183*
Rev	1:15	his voice as the sound of **m** waters.	*4183*
Rev	2:24	as **m** as have not this doctrine, and	*3745*
Rev	3:19	**m as I love, I rebuke and chasten:**	*3745*
Rev	5:11	and I heard the voice of **m** angels	*4183*
Rev	14:2	heaven, as the voice of **m** waters,	*4183*
Rev	19:6	and as the voice of **m** waters, and	*4183*
Rev	19:12	and on his head were **m** crowns;	*4183*

MARANATHA (mar-an-a´-thah)

1Co	16:22	Christ, let him be Anathema **M**.	*3134*

M

MARCH

Ps	68:7	didst **m** through the wilderness;	6805
Hab	1:6	shall **m** through the breadth of	1980
Hab	3:12	Thou didst **m** through the land in	6805

MARCHED

Ex	14:10	the Egyptians **m** after them;	5265

MARINERS

Jnh	1:5	Then the **m** were afraid, and cried	4419

MARK

Ge	4:15	the Lord set a **m** upon Cain, lest	226
Job	21:5	**M** me, and be astonished, and lay	6437
Ps	37:37	**M** the perfect man, and behold	8104
Ps	130:3	thou, Lord, shouldest **m** iniquities,	8104
Eze	9:4	**m** upon the foreheads of the men	8420
Eze	9:6	any man upon whom is the **m**;	8420
Eze	44:5	Son of man, **m** well, and behold	7760
Php	3:14	press toward the **m** for the prize	*4649*
Rev	13:16	to receive a **m** in their right hand,	*5480*
Rev	14:9	and receive his **m** in his forehead,	*5480*
Rev	15:2	over his image, and over his **m**,	*5480*
Rev	16:2	upon the men which had the **m** of	*5480*
Rev	19:20	had received the **m** of the beast,	*5480*
Rev	20:4	had received his **m** upon their	*5480*

MARKED

Jer	2:22	yet thine iniquity is **m** before me,	3799
Lk	14:7	when he **m** how they chose out	*1907*

MARKEST

Job	10:14	If I sin, then thou **m** me, and	8104

MARKET
Mk 7:4 And when they come from the **m**, ... *58*
Ac 17:17 in the **m** daily with them that met *58*

MARKETPLACE
Mt 20:3 **saw others standing idle in the m**, ... *55*
Lk 7:32 **like unto children sitting in the m**,....... *58*

MARKETPLACES
Mk 12:38 **and love salutations in the m**,........... *58*

MARKETS
Mt 23:7 **greetings in the m, and to be called**...... *58*
Lk 20:46 **robes, and love greetings in the m**,....... *58*

MARKS
Le 19:28 dead, nor print any **m** upon you:...... 7085
Gal 6:17 my body the **m** of the Lord Jesus *4742*

MARRED
Isa 52:14 his visage was so **m** more than 4893
Jer 18:4 vessel that he made of clay was **m**...... 7843
Mk 2:22 **spilled, and the bottles will be m**:....... *622*

MARRIAGE
Ex 21:10 her raiment, and her duty of **m**,....... 5772
Ps 78:63 maidens were not given to **m** 1984
Mt 22:30 **neither marry, nor are given in m**,..... *1548*
Mk 12:25 **neither marry, nor are given in m**;..... *1061*
Lk 20:35 **neither marry, nor are given in m**:..... *1548*
Jn 2:1 there was a **m** in Cana of Galilee;...... *1062*
Heb 13:4 **M** is honourable in all, and the........ *1062*
Rev 19:7 for the **m** of the Lamb is come,........ *1062*

MARRIAGES
Ge 34:9 make ye **m** with us, and give your 2859
Dt 7:3 Neither shalt thou make **m** with....... 2859

MARRIED See also UNMARRIED.
Ex 21:3 if he were **m**, then his wife........ 1166, 802
Nu 12:1 he had **m** an Ethiopian woman........ 3947
Dt 22:22 with a woman **m** to an husband....... 1166
Dt 24:1 hath taken a wife, and **m** her, ... 1166
Pr 30:23 odious woman when she is **m**; 1166
Mal 2:11 **m** the daughter of a strange god....... 1166
Mk 6:17 Philip's wife: for he had **m** her *1060*
Mk 10:12 **husband, and be m to another**,........ *1060*
Lk 14:20 **another said, I have m a wife**,......... *1060*
Lk 17:27 **did eat, they drank, they m wives**, ... *1060*
Ro 7:3 though she be **m** to another man...... *1096*
1Co 7:33 he that is **m** careth for the things *1060*
1Co 7:34 she that is **m** careth for the things *1060*
1Co 7:39 liberty to be **m** to whom she will;...... *1060*

MARRIETH
Mt 19:9 **whoso m her which is put away**....... *1060*
Lk 16:18 **whosoever m her that is put away** *1060*

MARROW
Ps 63:5 satisfied as with **m** and fatness;........ 2459
Pr 3:8 to thy navel, and **m** to thy bones....... 8250
Heb 4:12 spirit, and of the joints and **m**, ... *3452*

MARRY
Ge 38:8 thy brother's wife, and **m** her, ... 2992
Mt 5:32 **shall m her that is divorced**........... *1060*
Mt 19:9 **m another, committeth adultery**:...... *1060*
Mt 22:24 his brother shall **m** his wife, and....... *1918*
Mt 22:30 **in the resurrection they neither m**, ... *1060*
Mk 10:11 **put away his wife, and m another**, ... *1060*
Mk 12:25 **they neither m, nor are given in**....... *1060*
1Co 7:9 they cannot contain, let them **m**: *1060*
1Co 7:9 for it is better to **m** than to burn....... *1060*
1Co 7:28 if a virgin **m**, she hath not sinned...... *1060*
1Co 7:36 will, he sinneth not: let them **m** *1060*
1Ti 4:3 Forbidding to **m**, and commanding.... *1060*
1Ti 5:14 that the younger women **m**, bear *1060*

MARRYING
Ne 13:27 our God in **m** strange wives?.......... 3427
Mt 24:38 **m and giving in marriage, until**....... *1060*

MARS' (marz)
Ac 17:22 Paul stood in the midst of **M** hill,....... *697*

MARTYR
Ac 22:20 blood of thy **m** Stephen was shed, ... *3144*
Rev 2:13 **Antipas was my faithful m, who**....... *3144*

MARTYRS
Rev 17:6 with the blood of the **m** of Jesus: *3144*

MARVEL
Ecc 5:8 in a province, **m** not at the matter:..... 8539
Mk 5:20 done for him: and all men did **m** *2296*
Jn 3:7 **M not that I said unto thee, Ye**........ *2296*
Jn 5:20 **works than these, that ye may m** *2296*
Jn 5:28 **M not at this: for the hour is**.......... *2296*
Jn 7:21 **have done one work, and ye all m** *2296*
Ac 3:12 men of Israel, why **m** ye at this? *2296*
2Co 11:14 And no **m**; for Satan himself is *2298*
Gal 1:6 I **m** that ye are so soon removed....... *2296*
1Jn 3:13 **M** not, my brethren, if the world *2296*
Rev 17:7 unto me, Wherefore didst thou **m**?..... *2296*

MARVELLED
Ge 43:33 and the men **m** one at another 8539
Mt 8:10 When Jesus heard it, he **m**, and........ *2296*
Mt 8:27 the men **m**, saying, What manner...... *2296*
Mt 27:14 that the governor **m** greatly............ *2296*
Mk 6:6 he **m** because of their unbelief......... *2296*
Mk 15:5 answered nothing; so that Pilate **m**..... *2296*
Mk 15:44 Pilate **m** if he were already dead:....... *2296*
Lk 2:33 And Joseph and his mother **m** at *2296*
Jn 4:27 **m** that he talked with the woman: *2296*
Jn 7:15 the Jews **m**, saying, How knoweth...... *2296*
Ac 2:7 they were all amazed and **m**, ... *2296*

MARVELLOUS
1Ch 16:12 Remember his **m** works that he 6381
1Ch 16:24 his **m** works among all nations. 6381
Ps 9:1 I will shew forth all thy **m** works 6381
Ps 17:7 Shew thy **m** lovingkindness, O 6395
Ps 78:12 **M** things did he in the sight of 6382
Ps 98:1 for he hath done **m** things: his 6381
Ps 105:5 Remember his **m** works that he 6381
Ps 118:23 Lord's doing; it is **m** in our eyes........ 6381
Ps 139:14 **m** are thy works: and that my soul..... 6381
Isa 29:14 I will proceed to do a **m** work......... 6381
Da 11:36 speak **m** things against the God of..... 6381
Mic 7:15 will I shew unto him **m** things......... 6381
Zec 8:6 should it also be **m** in mine eyes?...... 6381
Mt 21:42 **doing, and it is m in our eyes?** *2298*
Mk 12:11 **doing, and it is m in our eyes?** *2298*
Jn 9:30 Why herein is a **m** thing, that ye....... *2298*
1Pe 2:9 out of darkness into his **m** light:....... *2298*
Rev 15:1 sign in heaven, great and **m**, seven *2298*
Rev 15:3 Great and **m** are thy works, Lord *2298*

MARVELLOUSLY

2Ch	26:15	for he was **m** helped, till he was	6381
Job	37:5	God thundereth **m** with his voice;	6381
Hab	1:5	and regard, and wonder **m**:	8539

MASTER

Ge	24:10	goods of his **m** were in his hand:	113
Ge	24:12	said, O Lord God of my **m** Abraham,	113
Ge	24:35	Lord hath blessed my **m** greatly;	113
Ge	24:54	he said, Send me away unto my **m**	113
Ge	39:8	my **m** wotteth not what is with me	113
Ex	21:4	If his **m** have given him a wife, and	113
Ex	21:6	his **m** shall bore his ear through	113
Dt	23:15	not deliver unto his **m** the servant	113
1Sa	24:6	I should do this thing unto my **m**,	113
1Sa	26:16	ye have not kept your **m**, the Lord's	113
2Sa	2:7	your **m** Saul is dead, and also the	113
1Ki	22:17	the Lord said, These have no **m**:	113
2Ki	2:3	that the Lord will take away thy **m**:	113
2Ki	2:5	that the Lord will take away thy **m**:	113
2Ki	6:5	said, Alas, **m**! for it was borrowed.	113
2Ch	18:16	These have no **m**; let them return.	113
Pr	27:18	he that waiteth on his **m** shall be	113
Pr	30:10	Accuse not a servant unto his **m**,	113
Isa	24:2	as with the servant, so with his **m**;	113
Da	4:9	Belteshazzar, **m** of the magicians,	729
Da	5:11	father, made **m** of the magicians,	729
Mal	1:6	and if I be a **m**, where is my fear?	113
Mt	10:24	**The disciple is not above his m,**	*1320*
Mt	12:38	**M**, we would see a sign from thee.	*1320*
Mt	17:24	said, Doth not your **m** pay tribute?	*1320*
Mt	23:8	**for one is your M, even Christ;**	*2519*
Mt	23:10	**for one is your M, even Christ.**	*2519*
Mt	26:25	answered and said, **M**, is it I?	*4461*
Mt	26:49	and said, Hail, **m**; and kissed him.	*4461*
Mk	4:38	him, **M**, carest thou not that we	*1320*
Mk	13:35	**when the m of the house cometh,**	*2962*
Mk	14:45	saith, **M**, **m**; and kissed him.	*4461*
Lk	5:5	**M**, we have toiled all the night,	*1988*
Lk	6:40	**The disciple is not above his m:**	*1320*
Lk	6:40	**that is perfect shall be as his m.**	*1320*
Lk	8:24	him, saying, **M**, **m**, we perish.	*1988*
Lk	8:49	is dead; trouble not the **M**	*1320*
Lk	13:25	**When once the m of the house is**	*3617*
Lk	14:21	**m of the house being angry said**	*3617*
Jn	1:38	is to say, being interpreted, **M**,)	*1320*
Jn	3:10	**Art thou a m of Israel, and**	*1320*
Jn	11:28	The **M** is come, and calleth for	*1320*
Jn	13:13	**Ye call me M and Lord: and ye**	*1320*
Jn	13:14	**If I then, your Lord and M, have**	*1320*
Jn	20:16	him, Rabboni; which is to say, **M**	*1320*
Ro	14:4	to his own **m** he standeth or	*2962*
Eph	6:9	that your **M** also is in heaven;	*2962*
Col	4:1	that ye also have a **M** in heaven.	*2962*

MASTERBUILDER See also BUILDER.

1Co	3:10	is given unto me, as a wise **m**,	*753*

MASTER'S

Ge	24:27	me to the house of my **m** brethren.	113
Ge	24:36	And Sarah my **m** wife bore a son to	113
Ge	39:7	**m** wife cast her eyes upon Joseph;	113
2Sa	9:10	thy **m** son shall eat bread alway.	113
2Sa	12:8	I gave thee thy **m** house, and thy.	113
2Ki	6:32	the sound of his **m** feet behind him?	113
2Ti	2:21	and meet for the **m** use, and	*1203*

MASTERS See also TASKMASTERS.

Ps	123:2	look unto the hand of their **m**,	113
Pr	25:13	for he refresheth the soul of his **m**	113
Mt	6:24	**No man can serve two m: for**	*2962*
Mt	23:10	**Neither be ye called m: for one is**	*2519*
Lk	16:13	**No servant can serve two m: for**	*2962*
Ac	16:16	which brought her **m** much gain	*2962*
Eph	6:5	obedient to them that are your **m**.	*2962*
Col	3:22	Servants, obey in all things your **m**.	*2962*
Col	4:1	**M**, give unto your servants that.	*2962*
1Ti	6:1	their own **m** worthy of all honour,	*1203*
1Ti	6:2	And they that have believing **m**	*1203*
Tit	2:9	to be obedient unto their own **m**,	*1203*
Jas	3:1	My brethren, be not many **m**,	*1320*
1Pe	2:18	subject to your **m** with all fear;	*1203*

MASTERS'

Mt	15:27	which fall from their **m** table.	*2962*

MASTERIES

2Ti	2:5	And if a man also strive for **m**, yet	

MASTERY

Da	6:24	and the lions had the **m** of them,	6981
1Co	9:25	every man that striveth for the **m**	

MASTS

Eze	27:5	cedars from Lebanon to make **m**	8650

MATE

Isa	34:16	shall fail, none shall want her **m**:	7468

MATRIX

Ex	13:12	the Lord all that openeth the **m**,	7358
Ex	34:19	All that openeth the **m** is mine;	7358
Nu	3:12	the firstborn that openeth the **m**	7358

M

MATTER

Ex	18:22	every great **m** they shall bring	1697
Ex	18:22	but every small **m** they shall judge:	1697
Ex	23:7	Keep thee far from a false **m**; and	1697
Nu	16:49	that died about the **m** of Korah.	1697
Dt	3:26	speak no more unto me of this **m**	1697
Dt	17:8	If there arise a **m** too hard for thee.	1697
Dt	19:15	shall the **m** be established	1697
1Sa	20:39	Jonathan and David knew the **m**	1697
1Ki	8:59	all times, as the **m** shall require:	1697
1Ki	15:5	only in the **m** of Uriah the Hittite	1697
Ezr	5:5	to cease, till the **m** came to Darius:	2941
Ezr	10:4	for this **m** belongeth unto thee:	1697
Ezr	10:14	fierce wrath of our God for this **m**.	1697
Ne	6:13	they might have **m** for an evil report,	
Est	2:23	inquisition was made of the **m**,.	1697
Ps	45:1	My heart is inditing a good **m**:	1697
Ps	64:5	encourage themselves in an evil **m**:	1697
Pr	11:13	a faithful spirit concealeth the **m**	1697
Pr	16:20	He that handleth a **m** wisely shall.	1697
Pr	17:9	he that repeateth a **m** separateth.	1697
Pr	18:13	answereth a **m** before he heareth	1697
Pr	25:2	of kings is to search out a **m**	1697
Ecc	12:13	the conclusion of the whole **m**:	1697
Da	2:23	made known unto us the king's **m**.	4406
Da	3:16	not careful to answer thee in this **m**.	6600
Da	7:28	me: but I kept the **m** in my heart.	4406
Da	9:23	understand the **m**, and consider	1697
Ac	8:21	neither part nor lot in this **m**:	*3056*
Ac	17:32	We will hear thee again of this **m**	
Ac	19:38	him, have a **m** against any man,	*3056*

1Co	6:1	you, having a **m** against another,	*4229*
2Co	7:11	yourselves to be clear in this **m**	*4229*
1Th	4:6	and defraud his brother in any **m**:	*4229*
Jas	3:5	great a **m** a little fire kindleth!	*5208*

MATTERS

Dt	17:8	**m** of controversy within thy gates:	1697
1Sa	16:18	a man of war, and prudent in **m**,	1697
2Sa	19:29	speakest thou any more of thy **m**?	1697
2Ch	19:11	is over you in all **m** of the Lord;	1697
2Ch	19:11	house of Judah, for all the king's **m**:	1697
Ne	11:24	in all **m** concerning the people.	1697
Est	3:4	whether Mordecai's **m** would stand:	1697
Ps	35:20	devise deceitful **m** against them	1697
Ps	131:1	do I exercise myself in great **m**,	1419
Da	1:20	**m** of wisdom and understanding,	1697
Mt	23:23	**omitted the weightier m of the law,**	
1Co	6:2	ye unworthy to judge the smallest **m**?	
1Pe	4:15	or as a busybody in other men's **m**	

MEALTIME

Ru	2:14	her, At **m** come thou hither,	6256, 400

MEAN

Ex	12:26	unto you, What **m** ye by this service?	
Dt	6:20	What **m** the testimonies, and the	
Jos	4:6	saying, What **m** ye by these stones?	
1Ki	18:45	came to pass in the **m** while,	5704, 3541
Pr	22:29	he shall not stand before **m** men	2823
Isa	2:9	the **m** man boweth down, and the	120
Eze	17:12	Know ye not what these things **m**?	
Mk	9:10	rising from the dead should **m**	*2076*
Ac	10:17	vision … he had seen should **m**,	*1498*
Ac	17:20	know … what these things **m**	*2309, 1511*
Ac	21:13	What **m** ye to weep and to break	*4160*
Ac	21:39	in Cilicia, a citizen of no **m** city:	*767*
Ro	2:15	thoughts the **m** while accusing	*3342*

MEANEST

Ge	33:8	What **m** thou by all this drove which	
Eze	37:18	not shew us what thou **m** by these?	
Jnh	1:6	unto him, What **m** thou, O sleeper?	

MEANETH

1Sa	4:6	What **m** the noise of this great shout	
1Sa	15:14	**m** then this bleating of the sheep	
Isa	10:7	Howbeit he **m** not so, neither	1819
Mt	9:13	**go ye and learn what that m,**	*2076*
Mt	12:7	**if ye had known what this m,**	*2076*
Ac	2:12	one to another, What **m** this?	*2309, 1511*

MEANING

Da	8:15	the vision, and sought for the **m**,	998
1Co	14:11	if I know not the **m** of the voice	*1411*

MEANS

Ex	34:7	that will by no **m** clear the guilty;	
Nu	14:18	and by no **m** clearing the guilty,	
Jgs	16:5	by what **m** we may prevail against	
1Ki	20:39	if by any **m** he be missing, then shall	
Ps	49:7	can by any **m** redeem his brother,	
Pr	6:26	For by **m** of a whorish woman a	1157
Jer	5:31	the priests bear rule by their **m**;	3027
Mal	1:9	this hath been by your **m**: will he	3027
Mt	5:26	**Thou shalt by no m come out**	*3361*
Lk	10:19	**nothing shall by any m hurt you**	*3364*
Jn	9:21	But by what **m** he now seeth, we	*4459*
Ac	4:9	by what **m** he is made whole;	
Ac	18:21	I must by all **m** keep this feast	*3843*
1Co	8:9	heed lest by any **m** this liberty of	*4458*
1Co	9:22	that I might by all **m** save some	*3843*
1Co	9:27	lest that by any **m**, when I have	*4458*
2Co	11:3	lest by any **m**, as the serpent	*4458*
Gal	2:2	lest by any **m** I should run, or had	*4458*
Php	3:11	If by any **m** I might attain unto	*4458*
1Th	3:5	lest by some **m** the tempter have	*4458*
2Th	2:3	no man deceive you by any **m**:	*5158*
2Th	3:16	give you peace always by all **m**	*5158*
Heb	9:15	testament, that by **m** of death,	*1096*

MEANT

Ge	50:20	God **m** it unto good, to bring to	2803
Lk	15:26	**and asked what these things m,**	*1493*
Lk	18:36	pass by, he asked what it **m**	*1498*

MEASURE

Dt	25:15	and just **m** shalt thou have: that	374
2Ki	7:1	shall a **m** of fine flour be sold for	5429
Job	11:9	**m** thereof is longer than the earth,	4055
Job	28:25	and he weigheth the waters by **m**.	4060
Ps	39:4	and the **m** of my days, what it is;	4060
Ps	80:5	them tears to drink in great **m**	7991
Isa	5:14	opened her mouth without **m**:	2706
Isa	40:12	the dust of the earth in a **m**, and	7991
Jer	30:11	but I will correct thee in **m**, and	4941
Jer	46:28	end of thee, but correct thee in **m**;	4941
Jer	51:13	and the **m** of thy covetousness	520
Eze	4:16	and they shall drink water by **m**,	4884
Mt	7:2	**and with what m ye mete, it**	*3358*
Mt	23:32	**Fill ye up then the m of your**	*3358*
Mk	4:24	**with what m ye mete, it shall be**	*3358*
Lk	6:38	**good m, pressed down, and.**	*3358*
Lk	6:38	**For with the same m that ye**	*3358*
Jn	3:34	not the Spirit by **m** unto him	*3358*
Ro	12:3	dealt to every man the **m** of faith	*3358*
2Co	1:8	we were pressed out of **m**.	*5236*
2Co	10:13	not boast of things without our **m**,	*280*
2Co	11:23	in stripes above **m**, in prisons	*5234*
2Co	12:7	lest I should be exalted above **m**	
Gal	1:13	beyond **m** I persecuted the church	*5236*
Eph	4:7	to the **m** of the gift of Christ	*3358*
Eph	4:13	the **m** of the stature of the fulness	*3358*
Eph	4:16	working in the **m** of every part,	*3358*
Rev	6:6	A **m** of wheat for a penny, and	*5518*

MEASURED

Isa	40:12	hath **m** the waters in the hollow	4058
Jer	31:37	If heaven above can be **m**, and the	4058
Jer	33:22	neither the sand of the sea **m**:	4058
Eze	40:5	he **m** the breadth of the building	4058
Eze	47:4	Again he **m** a thousand, and	4058
Hos	1:10	which cannot be **m** nor numbered;	4058
Hab	3:6	He stood, and **m** the earth: he	4128
Mt	7:2	**mete, it shall be m to you again**	*488*
Mk	4:24	**ye mete, it shall be m to you:**	*3354*
Lk	6:38	**withal it shall be m to you again**	*488*
Rev	21:16	and he **m** the city with the reed,	*3354*

MEASURES

Ge	18:6	quickly three **m** of fine meal,	5429
2Ki	7:1	and two **m** of barley for a shekel,	5429
Job	38:5	Who hath laid the **m** thereof, if	4461
Pr	20:10	Divers weights, and divers **m**,	374
Eze	40:24	thereof according to these **m**.	4060
Eze	43:13	these are the **m** of the altar after	4060

Eze 48:16 And these shall be the **m** thereof; 4060
Mt 13:33 **took, and hid in three m of meal,** *4568*
Lk 13:21 **took and hid in three m of meal,** *4568*
Rev 6:6 three **m** of barley for a penny; *5518*

MEASURING
Eze 40:5 in the man's hand a **m** reed of six...... 4060
Zec 2:1 a man with a **m** line in his hand....... 4060
2Co 10:12 they **m** themselves by themselves,...... *3354*

MEAT
Ge 1:29 seed; to you it shall be for **m** 402
Ge 9:3 that liveth shall be **m** for you; 402
Ge 27:4 make me savoury **m**, such as I
Ge 27:14 and his mother made savoury **m**,
Ex 29:41 to the **m** offering of the morning,
Le 2:1 when any will offer a **m** offering
Le 2:11 No **m** offering, which ye shall bring
Le 2:13 to be lacking from thy **m** offering:
Le 2:15 thereon: it is a **m** offering
Le 5:13 be the priest's, as a **m** offering
Le 6:14 this is the law of the **m** offering:
Le 10:12 Take the **m** offering that remaineth
Le 11:34 Of all **m** which may be eaten, that 400
Le 14:20 and the **m** offering upon the altar:
Le 22:11 house: they shall eat of his **m** 3899
Nu 4:16 and the daily **m** offering,
Nu 7:13 flour mingled with oil for a **m** offering
Nu 15:24 with his **m** offering, and his drink
Nu 18:9 every **m** offering of theirs, and
Nu 28:24 **m** of the sacrifice made by fire,........ 3899
Nu 29:11 and the **m** offering of it, and their
Nu 29:39 for your **m** offerings, and for your
Dt 2:6 Ye shall buy **m** of them for money,...... 400
Dt 20:20 that they be not trees for **m**, thou...... 3978
Jgs 13:23 and a **m** offering at our hands,
Jgs 14:14 Out of the eater came forth **m**,........ 3978
1Sa 20:27 cometh not the son of Jesse to **m**,...... 3899
1Sa 20:34 did eat no **m** the second day of the 3899
2Sa 3:35 to eat **m** while it was yet day,.......... 3899
2Sa 13:5 Tamar come, and give me **m**, ... 3899
1Ki 19:8 the strength of that **m** forty days 396
2Ki 3:20 when the **m** offering was offered,
Ezr 7:17 their **m** offerings and their drink
Ne 10:33 for the continual **m** offering, and
Job 38:41 God, they wander for lack of **m** 400
Ps 42:3 My tears have been my **m** day......... 3899
Ps 44:11 us like sheep appointed for **m**; 3978
Ps 69:21 They gave me also gall for my **m**;...... 1267
Ps 78:18 heart by asking **m** for their lust......... 400
Ps 78:30 their **m** was yet in their mouths 400
Ps 104:21 prey, and seek their **m** from God 400
Ps 104:27 give them their **m** in due season........ 400
Ps 107:18 soul abhorreth all manner of **m**;........ 400
Ps 111:5 hath given **m** unto them that fear...... 2964
Ps 145:15 givest them their **m** in due season 400
Pr 6:8 Provideth her **m** in the summer,....... 3899
Pr 23:3 dainties: for they are deceitful **m**....... 3899
Pr 30:22 and a fool when he is filled with **m**;.... 3899
Pr 30:25 prepare their **m** in the summer; 3899
Pr 31:15 giveth **m** to her household, and a...... 2964
Isa 57:6 thou hast offered a **m** offering
Jer 16:4 carcases shall be **m** for the fowls....... 3978
Jer 34:20 dead bodies shall be for **m** unto 3978
La 1:11 given their pleasant things for **m** 400
La 1:19 they sought their **m** to relieve 400
Eze 34:8 flock became **m** to every beast of 402
Eze 46:7 he shall prepare a **m** offering, an
Eze 47:12 shall grow all trees for **m**, whose....... 3978
Da 1:5 a daily provision of the king's **m**, ... 6598
Da 1:16 took away the portion of their **m**, ... 6598
Da 4:21 much, and in it was **m** for all; 4203
Joel 1:13 for the **m** offering and the drink
Am 5:22 offerings and your **m** offerings,
Mal 1:12 even his **m**, is contemptible............ 400
Mt 3:4 his **m** was locusts and wild honey...... *5160*
Mt 6:25 **Is not the life more than m, and** *5160*
Mt 9:10 as Jesus sat at **m** in the house,
Mt 10:10 **the workman is worthy of his m** *5160*
Mt 24:45 **to give them m in due season?** *5160*
Mt 25:35 **an hungred, and ye gave me m:** *5315*
Mt 26:7 poured it on his head, as he sat at **m**
Mk 8:8 broken **m** that was left seven baskets
Lk 9:13 go and buy **m** for all this people *1033*
Lk 12:23 **The life is more than m, and the** *5160*
Lk 12:37 **and make them to sit down to m,**
Lk 12:42 **their portion of m in due season?** *4620*
Lk 14:10 **of them that sit at m with thee**
Lk 17:7 **the field, Go and sit down to m?**
Lk 22:27 **serveth? is not he that sitteth at m?**
Lk 24:41 unto them, **Have ye here any m?**....... *1034*
Jn 4:32 **have m to eat that ye know not**........ *1035*
Jn 4:34 **My m is to do the will of him** *1033*
Jn 6:27 **m which endureth unto**.............. *1035*
Jn 6:55 **For my flesh is m indeed,** *1035*
Jn 21:5 them, **Children, have ye any m?** *4371*
Ro 14:15 Destroy not him with thy **m**, for....... *1033*
Ro 14:17 the kingdom of God is not **m** and *1035*
1Co 3:2 fed you with milk, and not with **m**: *1033*
1Co 8:10 sit at **m** in the idol's temple,
1Co 8:13 if **m** make my brother to offend *1033*
1Co 10:3 did all eat the same spiritual **m**; *1033*
Col 2:16 no man therefore judge you in **m**...... *1035*
Heb 5:14 strong **m** belongeth to them that *5160*
Heb 12:16 morsel of **m** sold his birthright........ *1035*

MEAT-OFFERING See MEAT and OFFERING.

MEATS
Pr 23:6 neither desire thou his dainty **m**:
Mk 7:19 **into the draught, purging all m?**....... *1033*
Ac 15:29 abstain from **m** offered to idols,
1Co 6:13 **M** for the belly, and the belly for....... *1033*
1Ti 4:3 commanding to abstain from **m**....... *1033*
Heb 9:10 Which stood only in **m** and drinks, ... *1033*
Heb 13:9 not with **m**, which have not........... *1033*

MEDDLE
Dt 2:5 **M** not with them; for I will not........ 1624
Dt 2:19 them not, nor **m** with them: 1624
2Ki 14:10 why shouldest thou **m** to thy hurt 1624
Pr 20:19 **m** not with him that flattereth 6148
Pr 24:21 **m** not with them that are given to 6148

MEDDLED
Pr 17:14 contention, before it be **m** with........ 1566

MEDDLETH
Pr 26:17 **m** with strife belonging not to 5674

MEDDLING
2Ch 35:21 forbear thee from **m** with God, who
Pr 20:3 strife: but every fool will be **m** 1566

MEDIATOR

Gal 3:19 by angels in the hand of a **m**. *3316*
Gal 3:20 is not a **m** of one, but God is one
1Ti 2:5 and one **m** between God and men, ... *3316*
Heb 8:6 he is the **m** of a better covenant, ... *3316*
Heb 9:15 he is the **m** of the new testament, ... *3316*
Heb 12:24 Jesus the **m** of the new covenant, ... *3316*

MEDICINE

Pr 17:22 merry heart doth good like a **m**: 1456
Eze 47:12 meat, and the leaf thereof for **m** 8644

MEDICINES

Jer 30:13 bound up; thou hast no healing **m**. 7499
Jer 46:11 in vain shalt thou use many **m**; 7499

MEDITATE

Ge 24:63 went out to **m** in the field at the
Jos 1:8 thou shalt **m** therein day and night 1897
Ps 1:2 his law doth he **m** day and night. 1897
Ps 63:6 **m** on thee in the night watches. 1897
Ps 77:12 I will **m** also of all thy work, and 1897
Ps 119:23 thy servant did **m** in thy statutes. 7878
Ps 119:148 that I might **m** in thy word 7878
Ps 143:5 I **m** on all thy works; I muse on 1897
Isa 33:18 Thine heart shall **m** terror. Where 1897
Lk 21:14 **not to m before what ye shall** *4304*
1Ti 4:15 **M** upon these things; give thyself *3191*

MEDITATION

Ps 19:14 the **m** of my heart, be acceptable 1902
Ps 49:3 **m** of my heart … be understanding. . . . 1900
Ps 119:97 I thy law! it is my **m** all the day 7881
Ps 119:99 for thy testimonies are my **m**. 7881

MEEK

Nu 12:3 man Moses was very **m**, above all. 6035
Ps 22:26 The **m** shall eat and be satisfied: 6035
Ps 25:9 The **m** will he guide in judgment: 6035
Ps 37:11 But the **m** shall inherit the earth; 6035
Ps 76:9 to save all the **m** of the earth 6035
Ps 147:6 The Lord lifteth up the **m**: he 6035
Ps 149:4 will beautify the **m** with salvation. 6035
Isa 11:4 with equity for the **m** of the earth: 6035
Isa 29:19 The **m** also shall increase their joy 6035
Isa 61:1 preach good tidings unto the **m**; 6035
Am 2:7 and turn aside the way of the **m**: 6035
Zep 2:3 ye the Lord, all ye **m** of the earth 6035
Mt 5:5 **Blessed are the m: for they shall** *4239*
Mt 11:29 **for I am m and lowly in heart:** *4235*
Mt 21:5 thee, **m**, and sitting upon an ass, ... *4239*
1Pe 3:4 ornament of a **m** and quiet spirit, ... *4239*

MEEKNESS

Zep 2:3 seek righteousness, seek **m**: it 6038
1Co 4:21 or in love, and in the spirit of **m**? *4236*
2Co 10:1 by the **m** and gentleness of Christ, ... *4236*
Gal 5:23 **M**, temperance: against such *4236*
Gal 6:1 such an one in the spirit of **m**; *4236*
Eph 4:2 With all lowliness and **m**, with *4236*
Col 3:12 of mind, **m**, longsuffering; *4236*
1Ti 6:11 godliness, faith, love, patience, **m** *4236*
2Ti 2:25 In **m** instructing those that oppose *4236*
Tit 3:2 gentle, shewing all **m** unto all men *4236*
Jas 1:21 and receive with **m** the engrafted *4240*
Jas 3:13 his works with **m** of wisdom *4240*
1Pe 3:15 that is in you with **m** and fear: *4240*

MEET

Ge 2:20 was not found an help **m** for him. 5828
Ge 33:4 Esau ran to **m** him, and embraced 7125
Ex 8:26 Moses said, It is not **m** so to do; 3559
Ex 23:4 If thou **m** thine enemy's ox or his. 6293
Ex 25:22 there I will **m** with thee, and I. 3259
Ex 29:43 I will **m** with the children of Israel 3259
Ex 30:6 testimony, where I will **m** … thee: 3259
Dt 3:18 Israel, all that are **m** for the war 1121
2Ki 5:21 down from the chariot to **m** him, ... 7125
Ezr 4:14 was not **m** for us to see the king's. 749
Est 2:9 which were **m** to be given her 7200
Pr 17:12 robbed of her whelps **m** a man. 6298
Pr 22:2 The rich and poor **m** together: the. 6298
Pr 29:13 and the deceitful man **m** together: 6298
Isa 14:9 is moved for thee to **m** thee at thy 7125
Jer 26:14 as seemeth good and **m** unto you. 3477
Jer 27:5 unto whom it seemed **m** unto me 3474
Eze 15:4 burned. Is it **m** for any work? 6743
Hos 13:8 I will **m** them as a bear that is. 6298
Am 4:12 prepare to **m** thy God, O Israel. 7125
Mt 3:8 therefore fruits **m** for repentance: *514*
Mt 15:26 **not m to take the children's,** *2570*
Mt 25:1 **forth to m the bridegroom** *529*
Mk 7:27 **not m to take the children's** *2570*
Lk 15:32 **m that we should make merry,** *1163*
Lk 22:10 **a man m you, bearing a pitcher** *4876*
Ac 26:20 and do works **m** for repentance *514*
Ro 1:27 that recompence … which was **m**. *1163*
1Co 15:9 am not **m** to be called an apostle, ... *2425*
Col 1:12 hath made us **m** to be partakers *2427*
1Th 4:17 to **m** the Lord in the air: *529*
2Ti 2:21 and **m** for the master's use, and *2173*
2Pe 1:13 I think it **m**, as long as I am in *1342*

MEETETH

Ge 32:17 When Esau my brother **m** thee. 6298
Nu 35:19 when he **m** him, he shall slay him 6293

MEETING

1Sa 21:1 was afraid at the **m** of David, ... 7125

MELODY

Am 5:23 I will not hear the **m** of thy viols 2172
Eph 5:19 making **m** in your heart to the *5567*

MELT

Jos 2:11 these things, our hearts did **m**, ... 4549
Jos 14:8 made the heart of the people **m**: 4529
2Sa 17:10 heart of a lion, shall utterly **m**: 4549
Ps 58:7 Let them **m** away as waters which 3988
Isa 13:7 and every man's heart shall **m**: 4549
Eze 21:7 every heart shall **m**, and all hands 4549
Eze 22:20 I will leave you there, and **m** you 5413
Am 9:13 wine, and all the hills shall **m**, ... 4127
Na 1:5 the hills **m**, and the earth is burned 4127
2Pe 3:10 elements shall **m** with fervent *3089*
2Pe 3:12 elements shall **m** with fervent *5080*

MELTED See also MOLTEN.

Ex 16:21 when the sun waxed hot, it **m**. 4549
Jos 5:1 that their heart **m**, neither was 4549
Jos 7:5 the hearts of the people **m**, and 4549
Jgs 5:5 The mountains **m** from before 5140
1Sa 14:16 the multitude **m** away, and they 4127
Ps 22:14 is **m** in the midst of my bowels. 4549
Ps 46:6 he uttered his voice, the earth **m**. 4127

Ps	97:5	hills **m** like wax at the presence	4549
Ps	107:26	their soul is **m** because of trouble	4127
Isa	34:3	mountains ... **m** with their blood	4549
Eze	22:22	As silver is **m** in the midst of the	2046

MELTETH

Ps	58:8	As a snail which **m**, let every one	8557
Ps	68:2	as wax **m** before the fire, so let	4549
Ps	119:28	My soul **m** for heaviness:	1811
Ps	147:18	out this word and **m** them: he	4529
Isa	40:19	The workman **m** a graven image	5258
Jer	6:29	the founder **m** in vain: for the	6884
Na	2:10	and the heart **m**, and the knees	4549

MEMBER

Dt	23:1	or hath his privy **m** cut off, shall not	
1Co	12:14	For the body is not one **m**, but	*3196*
1Co	12:26	And whether one **m** suffer, all the	*3196*
Jas	3:5	Even so the tongue is a little **m**,	*3196*

MEMBERS

Ps	139:16	in thy book all my **m** were written,	
Mt	5:29	**one of thy m should perish,**	*3196*
Ro	6:13	Neither yield ye your **m** as	*3196*
Ro	6:19	as ye have yielded your **m** servants	*3196*
Ro	7:23	But I see another law in my **m**,	*3196*
Ro	12:4	all **m** have not the same office:	*3196*
1Co	6:15	your bodies are the **m** of Christ?	*3196*
1Co	6:15	and make them the **m** of a harlot?	*3196*
1Co	12:12	the body is one, and hath many **m**,	*3196*
1Co	12:18	now hath God set the **m** every one	*3196*
1Co	12:27	body of Christ, and **m** in particular	*3196*
Eph	4:25	for we are **m** one of another	*3196*
Eph	5:30	For we are **m** of his body, of his	*3196*
Col	3:5	Mortify therefore your **m** which	*3196*
Jas	3:6	so is the tongue among our **m**, that	*3196*
Jas	4:1	of your lusts that war in your **m**?	*3196*

MEMORIAL

Ex	3:15	is my **m** unto all generations	2143
Ex	12:14	day shall be unto you for a **m**;	2146
Ex	13:9	and for a **m** between thine eyes	2146
Ex	17:14	Write this for a **m** in a book, and	2146
Ex	28:29	for a **m** before the Lord continually	2146
Ex	30:16	it may be a **m** unto the children	2146
Le	23:24	a **m** of blowing of trumpets, an	2146
Nu	5:15	an offering of **m**, bringing iniquity	2146
Nu	16:40	be a **m** unto the children of Israel	2146
Jos	4:7	these stones shall be for a **m** unto	2146
Ne	2:20	nor right, nor **m**, in Jerusalem	2146
Est	9:28	the **m** of them perish from their	2143
Ps	9:6	their **m** is perished with them	2143
Mt	26:13	**hath done, be told for m of**	*3422*
Mk	14:9	**shall be spoken of for a m of**	*3422*
Ac	10:4	thine alms are come up for a **m**	*3422*

MEMORY

Ps	145:7	utter the **m** of thy great goodness	2143
Pr	10:7	The **m** of the just is blessed: but	2143
Ecc	9:5	for the **m** of them is forgotten	2143
Isa	26:14	and made all their **m** to perish	2143
1Co	15:2	if ye keep in **m** what I preached unto	

MEN

Ge	4:26	then began **m** to call upon the name	
Ge	6:2	daughters of **m** that they were fair;	120
Ge	13:13	the **m** of Sodom were wicked and	582
Ge	18:2	and, lo, three **m** stood by him:	582
Ge	19:8	only unto these **m** do nothing; for	582
Ge	26:7	the **m** of the place should kill me	582
Ex	1:18	and have saved the **m** children alive?	
Ex	18:21	the people able **m**, such as fear God,	582
Nu	16:29	die the common death of all **m**,	120
Jgs	14:10	feast; for so used the young **m** to do	
Ru	2:15	Boaz commanded his young **m**,	
1Sa	4:9	quit yourselves like **m**, and fight	582
1Sa	18:5	and Saul set him over the **m** of war,	582
2Sa	2:32	Joab and his **m** went all night, and	582
2Sa	3:34	as a man falleth before wicked **m**,	1121
2Sa	7:14	chasten him with the rod of **m**	582
2Sa	10:12	let us play the **m** for our people,	2388
2Sa	19:42	the **m** of Judah answered the **m** of	376
2Sa	19:43	the **m** of Israel answered the **m** of	376
1Ki	2:32	two **m** more righteous and better	582
1Ki	4:31	For he was wiser than all **m**; than	120
2Ki	6:20	open the eyes of these **m**, that they	
1Ch	11:19	shall I drink the blood of these **m**.	582
1Ch	11:22	he slew two lionlike **m** of Moab:	
2Ch	6:18	God in very deed dwell with **m** on	120
2Ch	6:30	the hearts of the children of **m**:)	120
2Ch	10:13	forsook the counsel of the old **m**	
2Ch	10:14	them after the advice of the young **m**,	
2Ch	26:15	engines, invented by cunning **m**, to be	
Job	1:3	greatest of all the **m** of the east	1121
Job	37:24	**M** do therefore fear him: he	582
Ps	4:2	O ye sons of **m**, how long will ye	376
Ps	9:20	may know themselves to be but **m**	582
Ps	11:4	his eyelids try, the children of **m**.	120
Ps	12:1	fail from among the children of **m**,	120
Ps	12:8	when the vilest **m** are exalted	1121, 120
Ps	18:4	floods of ungodly **m** made me afraid	
Ps	22:6	a reproach of **m**, and despised of	120
Ps	62:9	**m** of low degree are vanity	1121, 120
Ps	62:9	**m** of high degree are a lie: to be	1121, 376
Ps	107:8	Oh that **m** would praise the Lord for	
Ps	107:8	works to the children of **m**!	120
Ps	116:11	I said in my haste, All **m** are liars	120
Pr	4:14	and go not in the way of evil **m**	
Pr	6:30	**M** do not despise a thief, if he steal to	
Pr	7:26	many ... **m** have been slain by her	
Pr	10:14	Wise **m** lay up knowledge: but the	
Pr	11:7	and the hope of unjust **m** perisheth	
Pr	13:20	walketh with wise **m** shall be wise:	
Pr	15:11	the hearts of the children of **m**?	120
Pr	16:6	fear of the Lord **m** depart from evil	
Pr	17:6	children are the crown of old **m**;	
Pr	20:6	Most **m** will proclaim every one	120
Pr	20:29	glory of young **m** is their strength:	
Pr	20:29	the beauty of old **m** is the gray head	
Pr	24:1	not thou envious against evil **m**	582
Pr	24:9	scorner is an abomination to **m**,	120
Pr	24:19	Fret not thyself because of evil **m**,	
Pr	25:27	for **m** to search their own glory is not	
Pr	26:16	seven **m** that can render a reason	
Pr	28:5	Evil **m** understand not judgment:	582
Pr	28:28	wicked rise, **m** hide themselves:	120
Pr	29:8	Scornful **m** bring a city into a	582
Ecc	3:10	God hath given to the sons of **m**,	120
Ecc	3:14	that **m** should fear before him	
Ecc	3:19	that which befalleth the sons of **m**	120
Ecc	6:1	sun, and it is common among **m**:	120
Ecc	7:2	for that is the end of all **m**; and the	120
Ecc	8:11	heart of the sons of **m** is fully set	120
Ecc	8:14	that there be just **m**, unto whom it	

M

Ecc 8:14 again, there be wicked **m**, to whom it
Ecc 9:3 heart of the sons of **m** is full of evil,..... 120
Ecc 9:11 nor yet riches to **m** of understanding,
Ecc 9:11 nor yet favour to **m** of skill; but time
Isa 2:17 haughtiness of **m** shall be made low:.... 582
Isa 29:13 me is taught by the precept of **m**:....... 582
Isa 29:19 the poor among **m** shall rejoice in 120
Isa 31:3 the Egyptians are **m**, and not God;...... 120
Isa 51:7 fear ye not the reproach of **m**,.......... 582
Isa 53:3 He is despised and rejected of **m**;....... 376
Jer 38:9 **m** have done evil in all that they........ 582
Eze 9:4 mark upon the foreheads of the **m**...... 582
Eze 14:14 these three **m**, Noah, Daniel, and 582
Da 3:24 Did not we cast three **m** bound 1400
Da 3:25 Lo, I see four **m** loose, walking in...... 1400
Da 4:25 High ruleth in the kingdom of **m**, ... 606
Da 4:32 High ruleth in the kingdom of **m**, ... 606
Da 5:21 God ruled in the kingdom of **m**, ... 606
Da 6:26 **m** tremble and fear before the God
Joel 2:28 your old **m** shall dream dreams,
Joel 2:28 your young **m** shall see visions:
Jnh 1:16 the **m** feared the Lord exceedingly,...... 582
Mic 7:2 there is none upright among **m**:......... 120
Mic 7:6 enemies are ... **m** of his house 582
Zec 8:10 I set all **m** every one against his......... 120
Mt 2:1 there came wise **m** from the east to
Mt 2:16 saw that he was mocked of the wise **m**,
Mt 4:19 and I will make you fishers of **m** *444*
Mt 5:11 are ye, when **m** shall revile you,
Mt 5:13 and to be trodden under foot of **m** *444*
Mt 5:16 Let your light so shine before **m**, ... *444*
Mt 6:1 ye do not your alms before **m**, ... *444*
Mt 6:15 if ye forgive not **m** their, ... *444*
Mt 6:16 they may appear unto **m** to fast *444*
Mt 7:12 ye would that **m** should do to you, ... *444*
Mt 10:22 be hated of all **m** for my name's
Mt 10:32 shall confess me before **m**, him......... *444*
Mt 12:36 idle word that **m** shall speak, ... *444*
Mt 16:13 Whom do **m** say that I the Son of *444*
Mt 17:22 be betrayed into the hands of **m**:....... *444*
Mt 19:26 With **m** this is impossible; but *444*
Mk 1:17 make you to become fishers of **m**....... *444*
Mk 7:7 doctrines the commandments of **m**..... *444*
Mk 7:21 out of the heart of **m**, proceed evil...... *444*
Mk 10:27 With **m** it is impossible, but not........ *444*
Lk 2:14 on earth peace, good will toward **m**..... *444*
Lk 6:31 ye would that **m** should do to you, ... *444*
Lk 12:8 confess me before **m**, him shall......... *444*
Lk 12:9 he that denieth me before **m** shall *444*
Lk 17:36 Two **m** shall be in the field;
Lk 18:27 impossible with **m** are possible......... *444*
Lk 21:17 be hated of all **m** for my name's
Lk 22:63 the **m** that held Jesus mocked him, ... *435*
Lk 24:7 delivered into the hands of sinful **m**..... *444*
Jn 1:4 and the life was the light of **m**.......... *444*
Jn 1:7 that all **m** through him might believe
Jn 3:19 **m** loved darkness rather than.......... *444*
Jn 5:23 That all **m** should honour the Son,
Jn 5:41 I receive not honour from **m**........... *444*
Jn 12:43 For they loved the praise of **m** more *444*
Ac 1:11 **m** of Galilee, why stand ye gazing....... *455*
Ac 14:11 down to us in the likeness of **m** *444*
Ac 14:15 We also are **m** of like passions with *444*
Ac 15:26 **M** that have hazarded their lives *444*
Ac 17:30 all **m** every where to repent: *444*
Ac 20:26 I am pure from the blood of all **m**

Ro 1:27 **m** with **m** working that which is........ *730*
Ro 2:16 God shall judge the secrets of **m**........ *444*
Ro 5:12 so death passed upon all **m**, for......... *444*
Ro 5:18 the free gift came upon all **m** unto *444*
Ro 12:18 in you, live peaceably with all **m**........ *444*
1Co 1:25 foolishness of God is wiser than **m**, ... *444*
1Co 1:25 weakness of God is stronger than **m**..... *444*
1Co 1:26 that not many wise **m** after the flesh,
1Co 9:22 I am made all things to all **m**, that I
1Co 13:1 the tongues of **m** and of angels, ... *444*
1Co 15:19 we are of all **m** most miserable *444*
1Co 16:13 faith, quit you like **m**, be strong *407*
2Co 3:2 hearts, known and read of all **m**: *444*
Gal 6:10 let us do good unto all **m**, especially
Eph 4:8 captive, and gave gifts unto **m**.......... *444*
Eph 5:28 So ought **m** to love their wives as *455*
Php 2:7 and was made in the likeness of **m**: *444*
Php 4:5 moderation be known unto all **m**....... *444*
Col 2:8 vain deceit, after the tradition of **m** *444*
Col 2:22 commandments and doctrines of **m**?.... *444*
Col 3:23 as to the Lord, and not unto **m**; *444*
1Th 2:13 ye received it not as the word of **m**, ... *444*
1Ti 2:4 Who will have all **m** to be saved *444*
1Ti 2:5 one mediator between God and **m**, ... *444*
1Ti 2:8 I will ... that **m** pray every where, ... *455*
1Ti 4:10 God, who is the Saviour of all **m**,....... *444*
2Ti 2:2 the same commit thou to faithful **m**,.... *444*
2Ti 2:24 be gentle unto all **m**, apt to teach,
2Ti 3:2 For **m** shall be lovers of their own *444*
Tit 2:11 salvation hath appeared to all **m**, ... *444*
Heb 9:17 is of force after **m** are dead;
Heb 9:27 it is appointed unto **m** once to die,...... *444*
Heb 12:14 Follow peace with all **m**, and holiness,
Heb 12:23 the spirits of just **m** made perfect,
Jas 1:5 that giveth to all **m** liberally, and
Jas 3:9 Therewith curse we **m**, which are....... *444*
1Pe 2:15 silence the ignorance of foolish **m**:...... *444*
1Pe 2:17 Honour all **m**, Love the brotherhood
2Pe 1:21 holy **m** of God spake as they were *444*
1Jn 2:13 I write unto you, young **m**............ *3495*
Rev 9:6 in those days shall **m** seek death *444*
Rev 9:7 their faces were as the faces of **m** *444*
Rev 9:15 year, for to slay the third part of **m**...... *444*
Rev 9:18 three was the third part of **m** killed,..... *444*
Rev 9:20 rest of the **m** which were not killed *444*
Rev 21:3 the tabernacle of God is with **m**,........ *444*

MENDING

Mt 4:21 with ... their father, **m** their nets;....... *2675*
Mk 1:19 also were in the ship **m** their nets...... *2675*

MENPLEASERS

Eph 6:6 Not with eyeservice, as **m**; but as *441*
Col 3:22 not with eyeservice, as **m**; but in........ *441*

MEN'S

Dt 4:28 serve gods, the work of **m** hands,....... 120
1Ki 12:13 forsook the old **m** counsel that they
2Ki 19:18 no gods, but the work of **m** hands,...... 120
Isa 37:19 no gods, but the work of **m** hands 120
Mt 23:27 are within full of dead **m** bones
Lk 9:56 is not come to destroy **m** lives,......... *444*
Lk 21:26 **M** hearts failing them for fear, ... *444*
Ac 17:25 Neither is worshiped with **m** hands *444*
1Ti 5:22 neither be partaker of other **m** sins:
1Pe 4:15 or as a busy body in other **m** matters

M

MENSERVANTS

Ex	21:7	she shall not go out as the **m** do	5650
1Sa	8:16	he will take your **m**, and your	5650
Lk	12:45	shall begin to beat the **m** and	*3816*

MENSTEALERS

1Ti	1:10	with mankind, for **m**, for liars	*405*

MENSTRUOUS

Isa	30:22	cast them away as a **m** cloth;	1739
La	1:17	Jerusalem is as a **m** woman	5079
Eze	18:6	hath come near to a **m** woman,	5079

MENTION

Ge	40:14	and make **m** of me unto Pharaoh,	2142
Ex	23:13	make no **m** of the name of other	2142
Jos	23:7	make **m** of the name of their gods,	2142
1Sa	4:18	when he made **m** of the ark of God,	2142
Ps	71:16	will make **m** of thy righteousness	2142
Isa	12:4	make **m** that his name is exalted.	2142
Isa	26:13	by thee only will we make **m** of thy	2142
Isa	48:1	and make **m** of the God of Israel,	2142
Isa	62:6	ye that make **m** of the Lord, keep	2142
Isa	63:7	**m** the lovingkindness of the Lord,	2142
Jer	20:9	I said, I will not make **m** of him,	2142
Jer	23:36	burden of the Lord shall ye **m** no	2142
Am	6:10	make **m** of the name of the Lord.	2142
Ro	1:9	without ceasing I make **m** of you	*3417*
1Th	1:2	always for you all, making **m** of you	*3417*
Heb	11:22	died, made **m** of the departing of	*3421*

MENTIONED

Eze	18:22	they shall not be **m** unto him:	2142
Eze	18:24	that he hath done shall not be **m**:	2142
Eze	33:16	hath committed shall be **m** unto	2142

MERCHANDISE

Dt	21:14	thou shalt not make **m** of her,	6014
Dt	24:7	maketh **m** of him, or selleth him;	6014
Pr	3:14	is better than the **m** of silver,	5505
Pr	31:18	perceiveth that her **m** is good:	5504
Isa	23:18	**m** and her hire shall be holiness	5504
Eze	26:12	riches, and make a prey of thy **m**:	7404
Eze	27:33	multitude of thy riches and of thy **m**	4627
Eze	27:34	thy **m** and all thy company in the	4627
Eze	28:16	By the multitude of thy **m** they	7404
Jn	2:16	**Father's house an house of m**	*1712*
2Pe	2:3	with feigned words make **m** of you:	
Rev	18:11	no man buyeth their **m** any more;	*1117*

MERCHANT

Pr	31:24	delivereth girdles unto the **m**.	5503
Isa	23:11	against the **m** city, to destroy	3667
Eze	27:3	a **m** of the people for many isles,	7402
Hos	12:7	He is a **m**, the balances of deceit	3667
Mt	13:45	**of heaven is like unto a m man,**	*1713*

MERCHANTS

Ne	13:20	**m** and sellers of all kind of ware	7402
Isa	23:8	crowning city, whose **m** are princes,	5503
Eze	27:36	**m** among the people shall hiss at	5503
Na	3:16	multiplied thy **m** above the stars.	7402
Rev	18:3	the **m** of the earth are waxed rich	*1713*
Rev	18:11	the **m** of the earth shall weep and	*1713*
Rev	18:15	The **m** of these things, which were	*1713*
Rev	18:23	**m** were the great men of the earth;	*1713*

MERCHANTS'

Pr	31:14	She is like the **m** ships; she	5503

MERCIES

Ge	32:10	worthy of the least of all the **m**,	2617
1Ch	21:13	the Lord; for very great are his **m**:	7356
Ne	9:19	thou in thy manifold **m** forsookest	7356
Ne	9:27	according to thy manifold **m** thou	7356
Ne	9:28	deliver them according to thy **m**;	7356
Ps	40:11	not thou thy tender **m** from me,	7356
Ps	51:1	multitude of thy tender **m** blot out	7356
Ps	77:9	he in anger shut up his tender **m**?	7356
Ps	89:1	I will sing of the **m** of the Lord	2617
Ps	103:4	lovingkindness and tender **m**;	7356
Ps	106:45	according to the multitude of his **m**	2617
Ps	119:156	Great are thy tender **m**, O Lord:	7356
Ps	145:9	his tender **m** are over all his works.	7356
Pr	12:10	tender **m** of the wicked are cruel.	7356
Isa	54:7	with great **m** will I gather thee	7356
Isa	55:3	you, even the sure **m** of David	2617
Isa	63:7	on them according to his **m**, and	7356
Jer	42:12	I will shew **m** unto you, that ye may	7356
La	3:22	It is of the Lord's **m** that we are	2617
La	3:32	according ... the multitude of his **m**	2617
Da	2:18	they would desire **m** of the God	7359
Da	9:9	To the Lord our God belong **m**.	7356
Da	9:18	righteousnesses, ... for thy great **m**	7356
Hos	2:19	and in lovingkindness, and in **m**	7356
Zec	1:16	I am returned to Jerusalem with **m**:	7356
Ro	12:1	by the **m** of God, that ye present	*3628*
2Co	1:3	the Father of **m**, and the God of all	*3628*
Php	2:1	of the Spirit, if any bowels and **m**,	*3628*
Col	3:12	bowels of **m**, kindness, humbleness	*3628*

MERCIES'

Ne	9:31	Nevertheless for thy great **m** sake	7356
Ps	6:4	soul: oh save me for thy **m** sake	2617
Ps	31:16	servant: save me for thy **m** sake.	2617
Ps	44:26	help, and redeem us for thy **m** sake.	2617

MERCIFUL See also UNMERCIFUL.

Ex	34:6	The Lord God, **m** and gracious,	7349
Dt	4:31	(For the Lord thy God is a **m** God;)	7349
Dt	21:8	Be **m**, O Lord, unto thy people	3722
2Sa	22:26	With the **m** thou wilt shew thyself	2623
1Ki	20:31	the house of Israel are **m** kings:	2617
2Ch	30:9	Lord your God is gracious and **m**.	7349
Ne	9:17	ready to pardon, gracious and **m**,	7349
Ne	9:31	for thou art a gracious and **m** God.	7349
Ps	18:25	with the **m** thou wilt shew thyself.	2623
Ps	41:4	Lord, be **m** unto me: heal my soul;	2603
Ps	56:1	Be **m** unto me, O God: for man	2603
Ps	57:1	Be **m** unto me, O God, be **m** unto	2603
Ps	67:1	God be **m** unto us, and bless us;	2603
Ps	86:3	Be **m** unto me, O Lord: for I cry	2603
Ps	103:8	the Lord is **m** and gracious, slow	7349
Ps	116:5	and righteous; yea, our God is **m**	7355
Ps	117:2	his **m** kindness is great toward	2617
Ps	119:58	be **m** unto me according to thy	2603
Pr	11:17	The **m** man doeth good to his own	2617
Isa	57:1	and **m** men are taken away, none	2617
Jer	3:12	for I am **m**, saith the Lord, and	2623
Joel	2:13	for he is gracious and **m**, slow to	7349
Jnh	4:2	art a gracious God, and **m**, slow to	7349
Mt	5:7	**Blessed are the m: for they shall**	*1655*
Lk	6:36	**m, as your Father also is m**	*3629*
Lk	18:13	**saying, God be m to me a sinner.**	*2433*
Heb	2:17	be a **m** and faithful high priest	*1655*
Heb	8:12	be **m** to their unrighteousness,	*2436*

MERCY

Ge	39:21	with Joseph, and shewed him **m**	2617
Ex	15:13	Thou in thy **m** hast led forth the	2617
Ex	20:6	shewing **m** unto thousands of them	2617
Ex	25:17	shall make a **m** seat of pure gold:	3727
Ex	25:21	put the **m** seat above upon the ark;	3727
Ex	25:22	with thee from above the **m** seat,	3727
Ex	33:19	shew **m** on whom I will shew **m**.	7355
Ex	34:7	Keeping **m** for thousands,	2617
Le	16:2	appear in the cloud upon the **m** seat	3727
Le	16:15	and sprinkle it upon the **m** seat,	3727
Le	16:15	and before the **m** seat:	3727
Nu	7:89	unto him from off the **m** seat that	3727
Nu	14:18	is longsuffering, and of great **m**	2617
Dt	5:10	shewing **m** unto thousands of them	2617
Dt	7:2	with them, nor shew **m** unto them:	2603
Dt	7:9	covenant and **m** with them that	2617
2Sa	22:51	sheweth **m** to his anointed, unto	2617
1Ki	8:23	covenant and **m** with thy servants	2617
1Ch	16:34	good; for his **m** endureth for ever	2617
2Ch	5:13	good; for his **m** endureth for ever:	2617
Ezr	3:11	his **m** endureth for ever toward	2617
Ezr	7:28	hath extended **m** unto me before	2617
Ezr	9:9	hath extended **m** unto us in the	2617
Ne	1:11	and grant him **m** in the sight of	7356
Ne	9:32	who keepest covenant and **m**, let	2617
Ps	6:2	Have **m** upon me, O Lord; for I	2603
Ps	9:13	Have **m** upon me, O Lord; consider	2603
Ps	13:5	But I have trusted in thy **m**; my	2617
Ps	23:6	goodness and **m** shall follow me	2617
Ps	25:7	according to thy **m** remember thou	2617
Ps	25:10	paths of the Lord are **m** and truth	2617
Ps	27:7	have **m** also upon me, and answer	2603
Ps	31:9	Have **m** upon me, O Lord, for I am	2603
Ps	32:10	Lord, **m** shall compass him about	2617
Ps	33:18	upon them that hope in his **m**;	2617
Ps	36:5	Thy **m**, O Lord, is in the heavens;	2617
Ps	37:21	but the righteous sheweth **m**,	2603
Ps	51:1	Have **m** upon me, O God, according	2603
Ps	57:10	thy **m** is great unto the heavens	2617
Ps	59:16	I will sing aloud of thy **m** in the	2617
Ps	62:12	unto thee, O Lord, belongeth **m**:	2617
Ps	77:8	Is his **m** clean gone for ever? doth	2617
Ps	85:7	Shew us thy **m**, O Lord, and grant	2617
Ps	85:10	**M** and truth are met together;	2617
Ps	86:5	plenteous in **m** unto all them that	2617
Ps	86:13	For great is thy **m** toward me: and	2617
Ps	89:2	said, **M** shall be built up for ever:	2617
Ps	90:14	O satisfy us early with thy **m**; that	2617
Ps	94:18	thy **m**, O Lord, held me up	2617
Ps	100:5	is good; his **m** is everlasting;	2617
Ps	101:1	will sing of **m** and judgment: unto	2617
Ps	103:8	slow to anger, and plenteous in **m**	2617
Ps	103:11	great is his **m** toward them that	2617
Ps	103:17	But the **m** of the Lord is from	2617
Ps	106:1	good: for his **m** endureth for ever	2617
Ps	107:1	good: for his **m** endureth for ever	2617
Ps	108:4	thy **m** is great above the heavens:	2617
Ps	109:16	he remembered not to shew **m**	2617
Ps	115:1	for thy **m**, and for thy truth's sake	2617
Ps	118:1	because his **m** endureth for ever	2617
Ps	119:64	The earth, O Lord, is full of thy **m**:	2617
Ps	123:2	God, until that he have **m** upon us	2603
Ps	130:7	for with the Lord there is **m**, and	2617
Ps	136:1	his **m** endureth for ever	2617
Ps	138:8	thy **m**, O Lord, endureth for ever:	2617
Ps	145:8	slow to anger, and of great **m**	2617
Ps	147:11	him, in those that hope in his **m**	2617
Pr	3:3	Let not **m** and truth forsake thee:	2617
Pr	14:21	but he that hath **m** on the poor,	2603
Pr	14:22	**m** and truth shall be to them that	2617
Pr	14:31	honoureth him hath **m** on the	2603
Pr	16:6	**m** and truth iniquity is purged:	2617
Pr	20:28	**M** and truth preserve the king:	2617
Pr	21:21	righteousness and **m** findeth life,	2617
Pr	28:13	and forsaketh them shall have **m**	7355
Isa	27:11	made them will not have **m** on them	7355
Isa	49:13	and will have **m** upon his afflicted	7355
Isa	54:8	kindness will I have **m** on thee	7355
Isa	55:7	and he will have **m** upon him; and	7355
Jer	6:23	they are cruel, and have no **m**;	7355
Jer	13:14	not pity, nor spare, nor have **m**,	7355
Jer	21:7	neither have pity, nor have **m**	7355
Jer	33:11	for his **m** endureth for ever: and	2617
Jer	33:26	to return, and have **m** on them	7355
Jer	50:42	are cruel, and will not shew **m**:	7355
Eze	39:25	and have **m** upon the whole house	7355
Da	9:4	and **m** to them that love him,	2617
Hos	1:7	have **m** upon the house of Judah,	7355
Hos	2:23	upon her that had not obtained **m**;	7355
Hos	4:1	because there is no truth, nor **m**,	2617
Hos	6:6	For I desired **m**, and not sacrifice;	2617
Hos	10:12	in righteousness, reap in **m**; break	2617
Hos	14:3	in thee the fatherless findeth **m**.	7355
Mic	6:8	but to do justly, and to love **m**,	2617
Mic	7:18	ever, because he delighteth in **m**	2617
Hab	3:2	known; in wrath remember **m**	7355
Zec	10:6	for I have **m** upon them: and they	7355
Mt	5:7	**merciful: for they shall obtain m**	*1653*
Mt	9:13	**I will have m, and not sacrifice:**	*1656*
Mt	9:27	Thou son of David, have **m** on us	*1653*
Mt	12:7	**I will have m, and not sacrifice**	*1656*
Mt	23:23	**the law, judgment, m, and faith:**	*1656*
Lk	1:50	his **m** is on them that fear him	*1656*
Lk	1:58	Lord had shewed great **m** upon her;	*1656*
Lk	1:72	To perform the **m** promised to our	*1656*
Lk	1:78	Through the tender **m** of our God;	*1656*
Lk	16:24	**Father Abraham, have m on me,**	*1653*
Lk	18:39	thou son of David, have **m** on me	*1653*
Ro	9:15	have **m** on whom I will have **m**,	*1653*
Ro	9:16	but of God that sheweth **m**	*1653*
Ro	9:18	on whom he will have **m**, and on	
Ro	9:23	of his glory on the vessels of **m**	*1656*
Ro	11:30	yet have now obtained **m** through	*1653*
Ro	11:32	that he might have **m** upon all	*1653*
2Co	4:1	as we have received **m**, we faint not;	*1653*
Eph	2:4	But God, who is rich in **m**, for his	*1656*
1Ti	1:13	but I obtained **m**, because I did it	*1653*
1Ti	1:16	for this cause I obtained **m**, that	*1653*
Tit	3:5	but according to his **m** he saved us,	*1656*
Heb	4:16	that we may obtain **m**, and find	*1656*
Heb	10:28	Moses' law died without **m** under	*3628*
Jas	2:13	he shall have judgment without **m**,	*448*
Jas	2:13	that hath shewed no **m**;	*1656*
Jas	2:13	and **m** rejoiceth against judgment	*1656*
Jas	3:17	full of **m** and good fruits, without	*1656*
Jas	5:11	is very pitiful, and of tender **m**	*3629*
1Pe	1:3	according to his abundant **m** hath	*1656*
1Pe	2:10	but now have obtained **m**	*1653*
Jude	21	looking for the **m** of our Lord	*1656*

MERCYSEAT See also MERCY and SEAT.
Heb 9:5 of glory shadowing the **m**; ... *2435*

MERRY
Ge 43:34 they drank, and were **m** with him. ... 7937
Jgs 16:25 pass, when their hearts were **m**, ... 2896
Jgs 19:22 they were making their hearts **m** ... 3190
Ru 3:7 and drunk, and his heart was **m** ... 3190
1Sa 25:36 Nabal's heart was **m** within him ... 2896
2Sa 13:28 Amnon's heart is **m** with wine, ... 2896
1Ki 21:7 bread, and let thine heart be **m**: ... 3190
2Ch 7:10 their tents, glad and **m** in heart. ... 2896
Pr 15:13 A **m** heart maketh a cheerful. ... 8056
Pr 15:15 but he that is of a **m** heart hath a ... 2896
Pr 17:22 A **m** heart doeth good like a ... 8056
Ecc 8:15 to eat, and to drink, and to be **m**: ... 8055
Ecc 9:7 drink thy wine with a **m** heart; ... 2896
Ecc 10:19 for laughter, and wine maketh **m**:. ... 8055
Lk 12:19 **thine ease, eat, drink, and be m** ... *2165*
Lk 15:23 **kill it; and let us eat, and be m**: ... *2265*
Lk 15:32 **was meet that we should make m**, ... *2165*
Jas 5:13 Is any **m**? let him sing psalms. ... *2114*
Rev 11:10 rejoice over them, and make **m**, ... *2165*

MESS
Ge 43:34 Benjamin's **m** was five times so ... 4864

MESSAGE
Jgs 3:20 I have a **m** from God unto thee. ... 1697
Pr 26:6 He that sendeth a **m** by the hand ... 1697
Lk 19:14 **him, and sent a m after him**, ... *4242*
1Jn 1:5 is the **m** which we have heard of. ... *1860*
1Jn 3:11 is the **m** that ye heard from the ... *31*

MESSENGER
Ge 50:16 And they sent a **m** unto Joseph, ... 6680
1Sa 4:17 the **m** answered and said, Israel ... 1319
2Sa 11:19 And charged the **m**, saying, When ... 4397
2Sa 15:13 there came a **m** to David, saying, ... 5046
1Ki 19:2 Jezebel sent a **m** unto Elijah, ... 4397
2Ki 5:10 Elisha sent a **m** unto him, saying ... 4397
2Ki 6:32 ere the **m** came to him, he said to. ... 4397
2Ki 9:18 The **m** came to them, but he ... 4397
Job 1:14 And there came a **m** unto Job, and. ... 4397
Pr 13:17 A wicked **m** falleth into mischief: ... 4397
Pr 17:11 a cruel **m** shall be sent against. ... 4397
Pr 25:13 is a faithful **m** to them that send. ... 6735
Jer 51:31 and one **m** to meet another, to ... 5046
Mal 2:7 he is the **m** of the Lord of hosts ... 4397
Mal 3:1 I will send my **m**, and he shall. ... 4397
Mt 11:10 **I send my m before thy face** ... *32*
Mk 1:2 I send my **m** before thy face, which ... *32*
Lk 7:27 **I send my m before thy face**, ... *32*
2Co 12:7 the **m** of Satan to buffet me, lest I. ... *32*

MESSENGERS
Ge 32:3 Jacob sent **m** before him to Esau ... 4397
Jos 6:25 she hid the **m**, which Joshua sent ... 4397
1Sa 19:14 when Saul sent **m** to take David ... 4397
1Sa 19:16 when the **m** were come in, behold ... 4397
1Sa 19:20 Spirit of God was upon the **m** of ... 4397
1Sa 19:21 Saul sent **m** again the third time. ... 4397
2Sa 11:4 And David sent **m**, and took her; ... 4397
2Ki 1:3 meet the **m** of the king of Samaria, ... 4397
2Ch 36:16 But they mocked the **m** of God, and ... 4397
Ne 6:3 I sent **m** unto them, saying, I am ... 4397
Pr 16:14 wrath of a king is as **m** of death:. ... 4397
Isa 18:2 saying, Go, ye swift **m**, to a nation ... 4397
Isa 44:26 performeth the counsel of his **m**; ... 4397
Na 2:13 the voice of thy **m** shall no more be ... 4397
Lk 7:24 when the **m** of John were departed ... *32*
Lk 9:52 And sent **m** before his face: and ... *32*
2Co 8:23 they are the **m** of the churches, ... *652*
Jas 2:25 she had received the **m**, and had ... *32*

MET
Ge 32:1 and the angels of God **m** him. ... 6293
Ge 33:8 thou by all this drove which I **m**? ... 6298
Ex 4:24 Lord **m** him, and sought to kill ... 6298
Ex 5:3 of the Hebrews hath **m** with us: ... 7122
Nu 23:16 Lord **m** Balaam, and put a word ... 7136
Dt 23:4 they **m** you not with bread and. ... 6923
1Sa 10:10 a company of prophets **m** him;. ... 7125
2Sa 18:9 Absalom **m** the servants of David. ... 7122
1Ki 13:24 a lion **m** him by the way, and slew ... 4672
1Ki 18:7 in the way, behold, Elijah **m** him: ... 7125
Ne 13:2 **m** not the children of Israel with ... 6923
Ps 85:10 Mercy and truth are **m** together ... 6298
Pr 7:10 **m** him a woman with the attire ... 7125
Am 5:19 flee from a lion, and a bear **m** him; ... 6293
Mt 8:28 **m** him two possessed with devils, ... *5221*
Mt 28:9 Jesus **m** them, saying, **All hail**. ... *528*
Lk 17:12 **m** him ten men that were lepers, ... *528*
Ac 16:16 with a spirit of divination **m** us, ... *528*
Heb 7:1 who **m** Abraham returning from ... *4876*
Heb 7:10 father, when Melchisedec **m** him. ... *4876*

METE
Mt 7:2 **with what measure ye m, it shall** ... *3354*
Mk 4:24 **with what measure ye m, it shall** ... *3354*
Lk 6:38 **with the same measure that ye m**. ... *3354*

METED
Isa 18:7 a nation **m** out and trodden under ... 6978
Isa 40:12 and **m** out heaven with the span, ... 8505

MICE
1Sa 6:4 and five golden **m**, according to the ... 5909

MIDDLE
Jgs 7:19 in the beginning of the **m** watch; ... 8484
Jgs 16:29 took hold of the two **m** pillars ... 8432
2Sa 10:4 cut off their garments in the **m**. ... 2677
2Ch 7:7 hallowed the **m** of the court that ... 8484
Jer 39:3 came in, and sat in the **m** gate, ... 8484
Eze 1:16 were a wheel in the **m** of a wheel ... 8432
Eph 2:14 hath broken down the **m** wall of. ... *3320*

MIDNIGHT
Ex 11:4 About **m** will I go out into ... 2676, 3915
Ex 12:29 **m** the Lord smote all the, ... 2677, 3915
Jgs 16:3 lay till **m**, and arose at **m**, ... 2677, 3915
Ru 3:8 it came to pass at **m**, that the ... 2677, 3915
1Ki 3:20 arose at **m**, and took my ... 8432, 3915
Ps 119:62 At **m** I will rise to give thanks ... 2676, 3915
Mt 25:6 **at m there was a cry made**, ... *3319, 3571*
Mk 13:35 **or at m, or at the cockcrowing**, ... *3317*
Lk 11:5 **and shall go unto him at m, and** ... *3317*
Ac 16:25 at **m** Paul and Silas prayed, and ... *3317*

MIDST
Ge 1:6 firmament in the **m** of the waters, ... 8432
Ge 2:9 tree of life … in the **m** of the garden, .. 8432
Ge 3:3 which is in the **m** of the garden, ... 8432
Ex 3:2 of fire out of the **m** of a bush: ... 8432

Ex	3:4	unto him out of the **m** of the bush,	8432
Ex	11:4	will I go out into the **m** of Egypt:	8432
Ex	14:16	ground through the **m** of the sea.	8432
Ex	14:22	of Israel went into the **m** of the sea	8432
Ex	24:18	Moses went into the **m** of the cloud,	8432
Ex	33:3	I will not go up in the **m** of thee;	7130
Ex	33:5	I will come up into the **m** of thee	7130
Nu	16:47	ran into the **m** of the congregation;	8432
Dt	4:11	with fire unto the **m** of heaven,.	3820
Dt	4:33	speaking out of the **m** of the fire,	8432
Dt	5:22	mount out of the **m** of the fire,.	8432
Dt	5:24	his voice out of the **m** of the fire:	8432
Dt	5:26	speaking out of the **m** of the fire,	8432
Dt	11:3	did in the **m** of Egypt unto Pharaoh	8432
Dt	13:5	the evil away from the **m** of thee.	7130
Dt	18:15	thee a Prophet from the **m** of thee,	7130
Jos	4:9	twelve stones in the **m** of Jordan,	8432
Jos	4:10	the ark stood in the **m** of Jordan,	8432
Jos	4:18	come up out of the **m** of Jordan,	8432
Jos	7:13	accursed thing in the **m** of thee,	7130
Jos	10:13	sun stood still in the **m** of heaven,	2677
Jgs	15:4	put a firebrand in the **m** between	8432
1Sa	18:10	prophesied in the **m** of the house:	8432
2Sa	1:25	mighty fallen in the **m** of the battle!	8432
2Sa	18:14	was yet alive in the **m** of the oak.	3820
2Sa	23:20	slew a lion in the **m** of a pit in time	8432
1Ki	6:27	one another in the **m** of the house	8432
1Ki	20:39	went out into the **m** of the battle;	7130
2Ch	6:13	had set it in the **m** of the court:	8432
2Ch	20:14	Lord in the **m** of the congregation;	8432
Ne	9:11	through the **m** of the sea on dry	8432
Ps	46:2	be carried into the **m** of the sea;	3820
Ps	46:5	God is in the **m** of her; she shall	7130
Ps	55:11	Wickedness is in the **m** thereof:	7130
Ps	74:12	salvation in the **m** of the earth.	7130
Ps	102:24	me not away in the **m** of my days:	2677
Ps	135:9	and wonders in the **m** of thee,	8432
Ps	137:2	upon the willows in the **m** thereof.	8432
Pr	4:21	keep them in the **m** of thine heart.	8432
Pr	5:14	all evil in the **m** of the congregation	8432
Pr	14:33	that which is in the **m** of fools is.	7130
Pr	23:34	he lieth down in the **m** of the sea,	3820
Pr	30:19	way of a ship in the **m** of the sea;	3820
Isa	6:5	I dwell in the **m** of a people of	8432
Isa	6:12	forsaking in the **m** of the land.	7130
Isa	12:6	Holy One of Israel in the **m** of thee	7130
Isa	16:3	night in the **m** of the noonday;.	8432
Isa	19:14	a perverse spirit in the **m** thereof:.	7130
Isa	24:18	cometh up out of the **m** of the pit	8432
Jer	6:1	flee out of the **m** of Jerusalem,	7130
Jer	9:6	habitation is in the **m** of deceit;	8432
Jer	14:9	thou, O Lord, art in the **m** of us,	7130
Jer	29:8	that be in the **m** of you, deceive	7130
Jer	51:6	Flee out of the **m** of Babylon, and	8432
La	4:13	blood of the just in the **m** of her,	7130
Eze	6:7	the slain shall fall in the **m** of you,	8432
Eze	7:9	abominations that are in the **m** of	8432
Eze	9:4	through the **m** of Jerusalem, and	8432
Eze	10:10	wheel had been in the **m** of a wheel.	8432
Eze	12:2	in the **m** of a rebellious house,	8432
Eze	17:16	in the **m** of Babylon he shall die	8432
Eze	21:32	blood shall be in the **m** of the land;	8432
Eze	22:9	**m** of thee they commit lewdness.	8432
Eze	22:21	ye shall be melted in the **m** thereof.	8432
Eze	26:5	of nets in the **m** of the sea:	8432
Eze	26:12	and thy dust in the **m** of the water	8432
Eze	31:18	lie in the **m** of the uncircumcised.	8432
Eze	32:21	speak to him out of the **m** of hell	8432
Eze	36:23	ye have profaned in the **m** of them;	8432
Eze	39:7	in the **m** of my people Israel;.	8432
Eze	46:10	And the prince in the **m** of them,	8432
Eze	48:10	the Lord shall be in the **m** thereof.	8432
Da	3:23	**m** of the burning fiery furnace.	1459
Da	3:25	loose, walking in the **m** of the fire,	1459
Da	9:27	**m** of the week he shall cause the.	2677
Hos	11:9	man; the Holy One in the **m** of thee:	7130
Joel	2:27	know that I am in the **m** of Israel	7130
Am	7:8	plumbline in the **m** of my people	7130
Am	7:10	in the **m** of the house of Israel:	7130
Hab	2:19	is no breath at all in the **m** of it.	7130
Hab	3:2	in the **m** of the years make known;	7130
Zep	3:5	The just Lord is in the **m** thereof;	7130
Zep	3:12	leave in the **m** of thee an afflicted	7130
Zep	3:17	thy God in the **m** of thee is mighty;	7130
Zec	2:10	and I will dwell in the **m** of thee,	8432
Zec	8:8	shall dwell in the **m** of Jerusalem:	8432
Mt	10:16	**as sheep in the m of wolves:**	*3319*
Mt	18:20	**there am I in the m of them.**	*3319*
Mk	9:36	child, and set him in the **m** of them:	*3319*
Lk	2:46	sitting in the **m** of the doctors,	*3319*
Lk	21:21	**are in the m of it depart out;**	*3319*
Lk	23:45	of the temple was rent in the **m**	*3319*
Lk	24:36	Jesus ... stood in the **m** of them,	*3319*
Jn	7:14	the **m** of the feast Jesus went up	*3322*
Jn	8:9	and the woman standing in the **m**	*3319*
Jn	19:18	either side one, and Jesus in the **m**	*3319*
Jn	20:19	came Jesus and stood in the **m**,	*3319*
Jn	20:26	stood in the **m**, and said, **Peace be**	*3319*
Ac	2:22	God did by him in the **m** of you,	*3319*
Ac	17:22	Paul stood in the **m** of Mars' hill,	*3319*
Php	2:15	in the **m** of a crooked and perverse	*3319*
Rev	1:13	in the **m** of the seven candlesticks	*3319*
Rev	2:1	**m of the seven golden**	*3319*
Rev	2:7	**is in the m of the paradise of**	*3319*
Rev	4:6	in the **m** of the throne, and round	*3319*
Rev	5:6	in the **m** of the elders, stood a Lamb	*3319*
Rev	7:17	which is in the **m** of the throne.	*3319*
Rev	22:2	In the **m** of the street of it, and on	*3319*

MIDWIFE

Ge	35:17	labour, that the **m** said unto her,.	3205
Ge	38:28	**m** took and bound upon his hand a	3205
Ex	1:16	When ye do the office of a **m** to the	3205

MIDWIVES

Ex	1:17	the **m** feared God, and did not as	3205
Ex	1:19	delivered ere the **m** come in	3205
Ex	1:20	God dealt well with the **m**: and the	3205
Ex	1:21	to pass because the **m** feared God,	3205

MIGHT

Nu	14:13	broughtest up this people in thy **m**	3581
Dt	6:5	all thy soul, and with all thy **m**	3966
Dt	8:17	the **m** of mine hand hath gotten	6108
Dt	28:32	there shall be no **m** in thine hand.	410
Jgs	5:31	sun when he goeth forth in his **m**.	1369
Jgs	16:30	he bowed himself with all his **m**;	3581
2Sa	6:14	before the Lord with all his **m**;	5797
2Ki	23:25	all his soul, and with all his **m**,	3966
2Ki	24:16	And all the men of **m**, even seven.	2428
1Ch	7:2	men of **m** in their generations;	2428
1Ch	13:8	before God with all their **m**, and	5797
1Ch	29:2	prepared with all my **m** for the	3581

1Ch 29:12 and in thine hand is power and **m**; 1369
2Ch 20:6 hand is there not power and **m**, ... 1369
2Ch 20:12 no **m** against this great company 3581
Est 10:2 the acts of his power and of his **m**,..... 1369
Ps 145:6 speak of the **m** of thy terrible acts:..... 5807
Ecc 9:10 findeth to do, do it with thy **m**;........ 3581
Isa 11:2 the spirit of counsel and **m**, the 1369
Isa 33:13 that are near, acknowledge my **m**...... 1369
Isa 40:26 names by the greatness of his **m**, ... 202
Isa 40:29 have no **m** he increaseth strength. 202
Jer 9:23 let the mighty man glory in his **m**,..... 1369
Jer 10:6 great, and thy name is great in **m**...... 1369
Eze 32:30 terror they are ashamed of their **m**; 1369
Da 2:23 who hast given me wisdom and **m**, ... 1370
Da 4:30 kingdom by the **m** of my power,....... 8632
Mic 3:8 of judgment, and of **m**, to declare 1369
Mic 7:16 and be confounded at all their **m**: 1369
Zec 4:6 Not by **m**, nor by power, but by 2428
Mt 26:9 this ointment **m** have been sold for *1410*
Ac 26:32 man **m** have been set at liberty, if...... *1410*
Eph 1:21 principality, and power, and **m**,........ *1411*
Eph 6:10 Lord, and in the power of his **m**....... *2479*
Col 1:11 Strengthened with all **m**, ... *1411*
2Pe 2:11 which are greater in power and **m**,..... *1411*
Rev 7:12 power, and **m**, be unto our God *2479*
Rev 13:17 that no man **m** buy or sell, save *1410*

MIGHTIER

Ex 1:9 of Israel are more and **m** than we: 6099
Dt 4:38 thee greater and **m** than thou art,...... 6099
Dt 9:14 a nation **m** and greater than they....... 6099
Ps 93:4 Lord on high is **m** than the noise 117
Ecc 6:10 with him that is **m** than he............ 8623
Mt 3:11 that cometh after me is **m** than I,...... *2478*
Mk 1:7 cometh one **m** than I after me, ... *2478*
Lk 3:16 one **m** than I cometh, the lachet of..... *2478*

MIGHTIEST

1Ch 11:19 These things did these three **m**........ 1368

MIGHTILY

Dt 6:3 that ye may increase **m**, as the......... 3966
Jgs 14:6 Spirit of the Lord came **m** upon him,
Jgs 15:14 Spirit of the Lord came **m** upon him,
Jnh 3:8 sackcloth, and cry **m** unto God: 2393
Ac 18:28 For he **m** convinced the Jews, and *2159*
Col 1:29 which worketh in me **m**......... *1722, 1411*
Rev 18:2 cried **m** with a strong voice...... *1722, 2479*

MIGHTY See also **ALMIGHTY.**

Ge 6:4 the same became **m** men which 1368
Ge 10:9 the **m** hunter before the Lord 1368
Ge 18:18 become a great and **m** nation,......... 6099
Ge 49:24 strong by the hands of the **m** God 46
Ex 1:7 and waxed exceeding **m**; and the 6105
Ex 3:19 let you go, no, not by a **m** hand........ 2389
Ex 15:10 they sank as lead in the **m** waters........ 117
Ex 32:11 great power, and with a **m** hand? 2389
Nu 22:6 people; for they are too **m** for me: 6099
Dt 5:15 out thence through a **m** hand, and..... 2389
Dt 6:21 us out of Egypt with a **m** hand: 2389
Dt 7:8 brought you out with a **m** hand,....... 2389
Dt 7:21 among you, a **m** God and terrible...... 1419
Dt 10:17 a great God, a **m**, and a terrible, ... 1368
Dt 11:2 God, his greatness, his **m** hand, ... 2389
Dt 26:8 forth out of Egypt with a **m** hand,..... 2389
Jos 4:24 the hand of the Lord, that it is **m**:...... 2389
Jos 8:3 thirty thousand **m** men of valour, ... 1368
Jgs 6:12 with thee, thou **m** men of valour 1368
1Sa 2:4 bows of the **m** men are broken, ... 1368
2Sa 1:19 high places: how are the **m** fallen!...... 1368
2Sa 1:25 How are the **m** fallen in the midst 1368
2Sa 23:17 things did these three **m** men 1368
1Ki 1:8 **m** men which belonged to David, ... 1368
1Ki 11:28 Jeroboam was a **m** man of valour:..... 1368
2Ki 24:15 the **m** of the land, those carried he...... 193
Ezr 4:20 been **m** kings also over Jerusalem, ... 8624
Ne 9:32 our God, the great, the **m**, and the..... 1368
Ps 45:3 sword upon thy thigh, O most **m**, ... 1368
Ps 74:15 the flood: thou driedst up **m** rivers...... 386
Ps 78:65 **m** man that shouteth by reason of..... 1368
Ps 89:6 who among the sons of the **m** can 410
Ps 106:2 can utter the **m** acts of the Lord? 1369
Ps 106:8 make his **m** power to be known........ 1369
Ps 127:4 arrows are in the hand of a **m** man;.... 1368
Ps 150:2 Praise him for his **m** acts: praise....... 1369
Pr 16:32 to anger is better than the **m**; 1368
Pr 23:11 For their redeemer is **m**; he shall 2389
Ecc 7:19 more than ten **m** men which are 7989
Isa 9:6 Wonderful, Counsellor, The **m** God, ... 1368
Isa 17:12 like the rushing of **m** waters!.......... 3524
Isa 30:29 the Lord, to the **m** One of Israel. 6697
Isa 49:26 thy Redeemer, the **m** One of Jacob....... 46
Isa 60:16 thy Redeemer, the **m** One of Jacob. 46
Jer 20:11 Lord is with me as a **m** terrible one:.... 1368
Jer 32:18 the Great, the **M** God, the Lord........ 1368
Jer 33:3 shew thee great and **m** things,......... 1219
Jer 51:30 The **m** men of Babylon have forborn... 1368
Eze 20:33 with a **m** hand, and with a............ 2389
Da 4:3 and how **m** are his wonders! 8624
Da 11:25 with a very great and **m** army; 6099
Joel 2:7 They shall run like **m** men; they....... 1368
Joel 3:9 Prepare war, wake up the **m** men,...... 1368
Joel 3:11 thy **m** ones to come down, O Lord..... 1368
Am 2:14 neither shall the **m** deliver himself: 1368
Am 2:16 he that is courageous among the **m**.... 1368
Am 5:12 transgressions and your **m** sins: 6099
Am 5:24 and righteousness as a **m** stream......... 386
Ob 9 thy **m** men, O Teman, shall be 1368
Jnh 1:4 there was a **m** temptest in the sea, ... 1419
Na 2:3 shield of his **m** men is made red, ... 1368
Hab 1:12 O **m** God, thou hast established 6697
Zep 3:17 thy God in the midst of thee is **m**; 1368
Mt 11:23 **if the m works, which have been** *1411*
Mt 13:58 he did not many **m** works there *1411*
Mk 6:2 such **m** works are wrought by his...... *1411*
Mk 6:5 he could there do no **m** work, save..... *1411*
Mk 6:14 **m** works do shew forth themselves..... *1411*
Lk 1:49 he that is **m** hath done to me great..... *1415*
Lk 1:52 put down the **m** from their seats, ... *1413*
Lk 10:13 **if the m works had been done in** *1411*
Lk 15:14 **arose a m famine in that land;** *2478*
Lk 24:19 was a prophet **m** in deed and word *1415*
Ro 15:19 Through **m** signs and wonders, ... *1411*
1Co 1:26 not many **m**, not many noble, are...... *1415*
1Co 1:27 confound the things which are **m**; *2478*
2Co 10:4 but **m** through God to the pulling *1415*
Gal 2:8 **m** in me toward the Gentiles:) *1754*
1Pe 5:6 under the **m** hand of God, that he *2900*

MILE

Mt 5:41 **shall compel thee to go a m, go.** *3400*

MILK

Ge 49:12	wine, and his teeth white with **m**	2461
Ex 3:8	a land flowing with **m** and honey;	2461
Ex 23:19	not seethe a kid in his mother's **m**	2461
Pr 30:33	the churning of **m** bringeth forth	2461
Isa 55:1	buy wine and **m** without money	2461
La 4:7	than snow, they were whiter than **m**,	2461
1Co 3:2	I have fed you with **m**, and not	*1051*
1Co 9:7	eateth not of the **m** of the flock?	*1051*
Heb 5:12	become such as have need of **m**,	*1051*
Heb 5:13	every one that useth **m** is unskilful	*1051*
1Pe 2:2	desire the sincere **m** of the word,	*1051*

MILL

Mt 24:41	**shall be grinding at the m; the**	*3459*

MILLSTONE

2Sa 11:21	woman cast a piece of a **m** upon him	7393
Mt 18:6	**a m were hanged about his**	*3458, 3684*
Mk 9:42	**a m were hanged about his**	*3037, 3457*
Lk 17:2	**a m were hanged about his**	*3458, 3684*
Rev 18:21	took up a stone like a great **m**,	*3458*
Rev 18:22	the sound of a **m** shall be heard no	*3458*

MIND

Le 24:12	**m** of the Lord might be shewed	6310
Dt 18:6	come with all the desire of his **m**	5315
1Sa 2:35	is in mine heart and in my **m**:	5315
1Ch 22:7	was in my **m** to build an house	3824
1Ch 28:9	heart and with a willing **m**: for	5315
Ne 4:6	for the people had a **m** to work	3820
Ps 31:12	forgotten as a dead man out of **m**:	3820
Pr 21:27	he bringeth it with a wicked **m**?	
Pr 29:11	A fool uttereth all his **m**: but a	7307
Isa 26:3	peace, whose **m** is stayed on thee:	3336
Jer 19:5	it, neither came it into my **m**:	3820
Jer 32:35	neither came it into **m**, that	3820
Jer 51:50	let Jerusalem come into your **m**	3824
Eze 11:5	the things that come into your **m**,	7307
Da 5:20	up, and his **m** hardened in pride,	7307
Mt 22:37	**all thy soul, and with all thy m**	*1271*
Mk 5:15	and clothed, and in his right **m**:	*4993*
Mk 12:30	**all thy soul, and with all thy m,**	*1271*
Mk 14:72	Peter called to **m** the word that	*363*
Lk 8:35	Jesus, clothed, and in his right **m**:	*4993*
Lk 10:27	thy strength, and with all thy **m**:	*1271*
Lk 12:29	**neither be ye of doubtful m**	
Ac 17:11	the word with all readiness of **m**,	*4288*
Ac 20:19	the Lord with all humility of **m**,	
Ro 1:28	gave them over to a reprobate **m**,	*3563*
Ro 7:23	warring against the law of my **m**,	*3563*
Ro 7:25	then with the **m** I myself serve the	*3563*
Ro 8:7	carnal **m** is enmity against God:	*5427*
Ro 11:34	hath known the **m** of the Lord?	*3563*
Ro 12:2	by the renewing of your **m**, that	*3563*
Ro 12:16	the same **m** one toward another	*5426*
Ro 12:16	**M** not high things, but condescend	*5426*
Ro 14:5	be fully persuaded in his own **m**.	*3563*
Ro 15:6	may with one **m** and one mouth	*3667*
1Co 2:16	who hath known the **m** of the Lord,	*3563*
1Co 2:16	him? But we have the **m** of Christ	*3563*
2Co 8:12	if there be first a willing **m**, it is	*4288*
2Co 13:11	be of one **m**, live in peace; and	*5426*
Eph 2:3	desires of the flesh and of the **m**;	*1271*
Eph 4:23	renewed in the spirit of your **m**;	*3563*
Php 2:3	in lowliness of **m** let each esteem	*5012*
Php 2:5	Let this **m** be in you, which was	*5426*
Col 1:21	enemies in your **m** by wicked	*1271*
Col 2:18	vainly puffed up by his fleshly **m**,	*3563*
Col 3:12	humbleness of **m**, meekness,	
2Ti 1:7	and of love, and of sound **m**,.	*4995*
Tit 1:15	their **m** and conscience is defiled.	*3563*
Tit 3:1	Put them in **m** to be subject to	*5279*
Phm 14	But without thy **m** would I do	*1106*
Heb 8:10	I will put my laws into their **m**,	*1271*
1Pe 1:13	gird up the loins of your **m**, be	*1271*
1Pe 3:8	be ye all of one **m**, having	*3675*
1Pe 4:1	likewise with the same **m**: for	*1777*
1Pe 5:2	for filthy lucre, but of a ready **m**;	*4290*
Rev 17:9	here is the **m** which hath wisdom.	*3563*
Rev 17:13	These have one **m**, and shall give	*1106*

MINDED See also FEEBLEMINDED; HIGHMINDED; LIKEMINDED.

Ezr 7:13	are **m** of their own freewill to go up	
Mt 1:19	was **m** to put her away privily.	*1014*
Ro 8:6	to be carnally **m** is death;	*5427*
Ro 8:6	spiritually **m** is life and peace	*5427*
Php 3:15	if in any thing ye be otherwise **m**,	*5426*
Tit 2:6	likewise exhort to be sober **m**	*4993*
Jas 1:8	A double **m** man is unstable in all	*1374*
Jas 4:8	purify your hearts, ye double **m**	*1374*

MINDFUL See also UNMINDFUL.

1Ch 16:15	Be ye **m** always of his covenant;	2142
Ne 9:17	neither were **m** of thy wonders that	2142
Ps 8:4	is man, that thou art **m** of him?	2142
Ps 111:5	he will ever be **m** of his covenant	2142
Ps 115:12	The Lord hath been **m** of us: he	2142
Isa 17:10	hast not been **m** of the rock of thy	2142
2Ti 1:4	being **m** of thy tears that I may	*3403*
Heb 2:6	is man, that thou art **m** of him?	*3403*
Heb 11:15	they had been **m** of that country	*3421*
2Pe 3:2	That ye may be **m** of the words.	*3403*

MINDS

2Sa 17:9	they be chafed in their **m**, as a	5315
Ac 28:6	changed their **m**, and said that he	
2Co 3:14	But their **m** were blinded: for until	*3540*
2Co 4:4	hath blinded the **m** of them which	*3540*
2Co 11:3	so your **m** should be corrupted	*3540*
Php 4:7	keep your hearts and **m** through	*3540*
1Ti 6:5	disputings of men of corrupt **m**,	*3563*
2Ti 3:8	men of corrupt **m**, reprobate	*3563*
Heb 10:16	and in their **m** will I write them;	*1271*
Heb 12:3	be wearied and faint in your **m**.	*5590*

MINE

Ex 13:2	both of man and of beast: it is **m**	
Le 25:23	be sold for ever: for the land is **m**;	
2Sa 14:30	See, Joab's field is near **m**, and he	3027
Ps 50:11	the wild beasts of the field are **m**	5978
Pr 23:15	my heart shall rejoice, even **m**.	589
SS 2:16	My beloved is **m**, and I am his: he	
Mt 7:24	**heareth these sayings of m,**	*3450*
Mt 20:15	**me to do what I will with m own?**	*1699*
Mt 20:23	**not m to give, but it shall be given**	*1699*
Mk 9:24	I believe; help thou **m** unbelief	*3450*
Lk 2:30	**m** eyes have seen thy salvation	*3450*
Jn 2:4	**thee? m hour is not yet come**	*3450*
Jn 5:30	**I can of m own self do nothing;**	*1683*
Jn 7:16	**My doctrine is not m, but his that**	*1699*
Jn 8:50	**I seek not m own glory: there is**	*3450*
Jn 10:14	**my sheep, and am known of m.**	*1699*

Jn 16:15 **things that the Father hath are m.** *1699*
Jn 17:10 **all m are thine, and thine are m;** *1699*
Ac 13:22 a man after **m** own heart, which....... *3450*
Ac 21:13 ye to weep and to break **m** heart? *3450*
Ac 26:4 at the first among **m** own nation *3450*
Ro 12:19 Vengeance is **m**; I will repay, saith...... *1698*
1Co 4:3 yea, I judge not **m** own self *1683*
Phm 18 thee ought, put that on **m** account; *1699*
Phm 19 Paul have written it with **m** own hand,
Rev 22:16 **sent m angel to testify unto you** *3450*

MINGLE
Isa 5:22 of strength to **m** strong drink:......... 4537
Da 2:43 **m** themselves with the seed of......... 6151

MINGLED
Le 2:4 cakes of fine flour **m** with oil, or....... 1101
Le 19:19 not sow thy field with **m** seed: 3610
Le 19:19 a garment **m** of linen and woollen..... 3610
Ezr 9:2 the holy seed have **m** themselves....... 6148
Ps 102:9 and **m** my drink with weeping 4537
Ps 106:35 were **m** among the heathen, and....... 6148
Pr 9:2 she hath **m** her wine; she hath 4537
Pr 9:5 drink the wine which I have **m**........ 4537
Isa 19:14 The Lord hath **m** a perverse spirit 4537
Mt 27:34 him vinegar to drink **m** with gall:...... *3396*
Mk 15:23 him to drink wine **m** with myrrh:
Lk 13:1 Pilate had **m** with their sacrifices *3396*
Rev 8:7 followed hail and fire **m** with blood.... *3396*
Rev 15:2 it were a sea of glass **m** with fire:....... *3396*

MINISTER
Ex 28:1 may **m** unto me in the priest's office,
Ex 28:43 the altar to **m** in the holy place; 8334
Nu 1:50 and they shall **m** unto it, and shall..... 8334
Nu 16:9 the congregation to **m** unto them?..... 8334
1Sa 2:11 And the child did **m** unto the Lord 8334
1Ki 8:11 the priests could not stand to **m**....... 8334
2Ch 23:6 and they that **m** of the Levites;........ 8334
Ps 9:8 shall **m** judgment to the people in 1777
Isa 60:10 and their kings shall **m** unto thee: 8334
Jer 33:22 and the Levites that **m** unto me 8334
Eze 42:14 lay their garments where they **m**;...... 8334
Eze 45:4 shall come near to **m** unto the Lord: ... 8334
Mt 20:26 **among you, let him be your m;** *1249*
Mt 20:28 **to be ministered unto, but to m** *1247*
Mk 10:43 **among you, shall be your m:**.......... *1249*
Mk 10:45 **to be ministered unto, but to m,** *1247*
Lk 4:20 he gave it again to the **m**, and sat *5257*
Ac 26:16 **to make thee a m and a witness** *5257*
Ro 13:4 is the **m** of God to thee for good *1249*
Ro 15:8 a **m** of the circumcision for the........ *1249*
Ro 15:16 **m** of Jesus Christ to the Gentiles....... *3011*
Gal 2:17 is therefore Christ the **m** of sin? *1249*
Eph 3:7 Whereof I was made a **m**, according ... *1249*
1Ti 1:4 **m** questions, rather than godly........ *3930*
1Ti 4:6 shalt be a good **m** of Jesus Christ *1249*
Heb 8:2 A **m** of the sanctuary, and of the....... *3011*
1Pe 4:11 if any man **m**, let him do it as of....... *1247*

MINISTERED See also **ADMINISTERED.**
1Sa 2:18 Samuel **m** before the Lord, being 8334
1Sa 3:1 the child Samuel **m** unto the Lord 8334
Est 6:3 king's servants that **m** unto him 8334
Jer 52:18 vessels of brass wherewith they **m**, ... 8334
Eze 44:12 they **m** unto them before their idols, ... 8334
Da 7:10 thousand thousands **m** unto him, ... 8120
Mt 4:11 angels came and **m** unto him *1247*
Mt 8:15 and she arose, and **m** unto them....... *1247*
Mt 20:28 **Son of man came not be m unto,**...... *1247*
Mk 1:13 beasts; and the angels **m** unto him *1247*
Mk 10:45 **of man came not to be m unto,** *1247*
2Co 3:3 to be the epistle of Christ **m** by us,..... *1247*
Heb 6:10 **m** to the saints, and do minister *1247*
2Pe 1:11 an entrance shall be **m** unto you....... *2023*

MINISTERETH
2Co 9:10 Now he that **m** seed to the sower *2023*
Gal 3:5 therefore that **m** to you the Spirit...... *2023*

MINISTERING
Ro 12:7 Or ministry, let us wait on our **m**: *1248*
Ro 15:16 the Gentiles, **m** the gospel of God, ... *2418*
Heb 1:14 Are they not all **m** spirits, sent......... *3010*
Heb 10:11 every priest standeth daily **m** and...... *3008*

MINISTERS
1Ki 10:5 attendance of his **m**, and their......... 8334
Ps 103:21 ye **m** of his, that do his pleasure 8334
Ps 104:4 angels spirits; his **m** a flaming fire:..... 8334
Isa 61:6 shall call you the **M** of our God:....... 8334
Joel 1:9 the priests, the Lord's **m**, mourn....... 8334
Joel 1:13 howl, ye **m** of the altar: come, lie 8334
Lk 1:2 eyewitnesses, and **m** of the word; *5257*
1Co 4:1 account of us, as of ... **m** of Christ, ... *5257*
2Co 3:6 hath made us able **m** of the new....... *1249*
2Co 6:4 approving ourselves as ... **m** of God,... *1249*
2Co 11:15 as the **m** of righteousness; whose *1249*
Heb 1:7 spirits, and his **m** a flame of fire *3011*

MINISTRATION
Lk 1:23 days of his **m** were accomplished,...... *3009*
Ac 6:1 were neglected in the daily **m** *1248*
2Co 3:7 But if the **m** of death, written and *1248*
2Co 3:8 **m** of the spirit be rather glorious? *1248*

MINISTRY
Nu 4:12 take all the instruments of **m**,......... 8335
2Ch 7:6 when David praised by their **m**; 3027
Hos 12:10 by the **m** of the prophets 3027
Ac 1:17 and had obtained part of this **m**....... *1248*
Ac 6:4 prayer, and to the **m** of the word *1248*
Ac 20:24 and the **m**, which I have received *1248*
Ro 12:7 Or **m**, let us wait on ... ministering; ... *1248*
1Co 16:15 addicted ... to the **m** of the saints,) *1248*
2Co 4:1 Therefore seeing we have this **m**, ... *1248*
2Co 5:18 given to us the **m** of reconciliation; *1248*
2Co 6:3 thing, that the **m** be not blamed: *1248*
Eph 4:12 for the work of the **m**, for the *1248*
1Ti 1:12 faithful, putting me into the **m**;........ *1248*
2Ti 4:5 evangelist, make full proof of thy **m**.... *1248*
2Ti 4:11 for he is profitable to me for the **m** *1248*
Heb 8:6 he obtained a more excellent **m** *3009*
Heb 9:21 and all the vessels of the **m** *3009*

MIRACLE
Ex 7:9 you, saying, Shew a **m** for you: 4159
Mk 9:39 **which shall do a m in my name,**....... *1411*
Lk 23:8 hoped to have seen some **m** done...... *4592*
Jn 6:14 they had seen the **m** that Jesus did,..... *4592*
Jn 10:41 him, and said, John did no **m**:......... *4592*

MIRACLES
Nu 14:22 and my **m**, which I did in Egypt........ 226
Jgs 6:13 and where be all his **m** which our...... 6381

M

Jn 2:11 beginning of **m** did Jesus in Cana...... *4592*
Jn 2:23 they saw the **m** which he did.......... *4592*
Jn 3:2 can do these **m** that thou doest........ *4592*
Jn 6:26 **me, not because ye saw the m**......... *4592*
Jn 7:31 will he do more **m** than these *4592*
Jn 9:16 man that is a sinner do such **m**?....... *4592*
Jn 11:47 we? for this man doeth many **m**....... *4592*
Jn 12:37 though he had done so many **m**....... *4592*
Ac 2:22 approved of God among you by **m**..... *1411*
Ac 6:8 did great wonders and **m** among *4592*
Ac 8:6 and seeing the **m** which he did *4592*
Ac 15:12 **m** and wonders God had wrought..... *4592*
Ac 19:11 special **m** by the hands of Paul:........ *1411*
1Co 12:10 To another the working of **m**; to....... *1411*
1Co 12:29 all teachers? are all workers of **m**?...... *1411*
Gal 3:5 worketh **m** among you, doeth he it *1411*
Heb 2:4 and wonders, and with divers **m**, ... *1411*
Rev 13:14 those **m** which he had power to do *4592*
Rev 16:14 the spirits of devils, working **m**, ... *4592*
Rev 19:20 the false prophet that wrought **m**...... *4592*

MIRE
Ps 69:14 Deliver me out of the **m**, and let....... 2916
Isa 10:6 down like the **m** of the streets......... 2563
Isa 57:20 whose waters cast up **m** and dirt 7516
Jer 38:6 so Jeremiah sunk in the **m**............ 2916
Mic 7:10 down as the **m** of the streets 2916
Zec 9:3 fine gold as the **m** of the streets 2916
Zec 10:5 enemies in the **m** of the streets in...... 2916
2Pe 2:22 washed to her wallowing in the **m** *1004*

MIRTH
Ge 31:27 have sent thee away with **m**, and....... 8057
Ps 137:3 that wasted us required of us **m**,....... 8057
Pr 14:13 and the end of that **m** is heaviness..... 8057
Ecc 2:1 to now, I will prove thee with **m**, ... 8057
Ecc 2:2 is mad: and of **m**, What doeth it?...... 8057
Ecc 7:4 heart of fools is in the house of **m** 8057
Ecc 8:15 Then I commended **m**, because a...... 8057
Isa 24:11 the **m** of the land is gone............. 4885
Jer 25:10 will take from them the voice of **m**,.... 8342
Eze 21:10 glitter: should we then make **m**?....... 7797
Hos 2:11 will also cause all her **m** to cease, ... 4885

MIRY
Ps 40:2 an horrible pit, out of the **m** clay,...... 3121
Eze 47:11 But the **m** places thereof and the 1207
Da 2:43 sawest iron mixed with **m** clay 2917

MISCARRYING
Hos 9:14 give them a **m** womb and dry......... 7921

MISCHIEF
Ge 42:4 Lest peradventure **m** befall him 611
Ge 44:29 this also from me, and **m** befall him 611
Ex 21:22 from her, and yet no **m** follow:......... 611
Ex 21:23 if any **m** follow, then thou shalt 611
Ex 32:12 For **m** did he bring them out, to....... 7451
1Sa 23:9 secretly practised **m** against him; 7451
2Sa 16:8 thou art taken in thy **m**, because....... 7451
1Ki 20:7 and see how this man seeketh **m**:...... 7451
2Ki 7:9 light, some **m** will come upon us:...... 5771
Ps 7:16 His **m** shall return upon his own 5999
Ps 10:7 under his tongue is **m** and vanity...... 5999
Ps 26:10 In whose hands is **m**, and their........ 2154
Ps 28:3 but **m** is in their hearts............... 7451
Ps 36:4 He deviseth **m** upon his bed; he........ 205
Ps 52:1 Why boastest thou thyself in **m**,....... 7451
Ps 94:20 thee, which frameth **m** by a law?....... 5999
Ps 119:150 draw nigh that follow after **m**:......... 2154
Pr 4:16 not, except they have done **m**;......... 7489
Pr 6:14 he deviseth **m** continually; he......... 7451
Pr 6:18 feet that be swift in running to **m**, ... 7451
Pr 10:23 It is as sport to a fool to do **m**: 2154
Pr 11:27 he that seeketh **m**, it shall come 7451
Pr 12:21 the wicked shall be filled with **m** 7451
Pr 13:17 wicked messenger falleth into **m**:...... 7451
Pr 17:20 a perverse tongue falleth into **m**....... 7451
Pr 24:2 and their lips talk of **m**............... 5999
Pr 24:16 but the wicked shall fall into **m**......... 7451
Pr 28:14 his heart shall fall into **m**............. 7451
Isa 47:11 **m** shall fall upon thee; thou shalt...... 1943
Isa 59:4 they conceive **m**, and bring forth 5999
Eze 7:26 **M** shall come upon **m**, and 1943
Eze 11:2 these are the men that devise **m**,........ 205
Da 11:27 king's hearts shall be to do **m**,......... 4827
Hos 7:15 do they imagine **m** against me 7451
Ac 13:10 O full of all subtilty and all **m**, ... *4468*

MISCHIEFS
Ps 52:2 Thy tongue deviseth **m**; like a......... 1942
Ps 140:2 Which imagine **m** in their hearts;...... 7451

MISCHIEVOUS
Ps 21:11 they imagined a **m** device, which 4209
Ps 38:12 that seek my hurt speak **m** things, ... 1942
Pr 24:8 evil shall be called a **m** person......... 4209
Ecc 10:13 the end of his talk is **m** madness....... 7451
Mic 7:3 man, he uttereth his **m** desire:......... 1942

MISERABLE
Job 16:2 things: **m** comforters are ye all 5999
1Co 15:19 Christ, we are of all men most **m** *1652*
Rev 3:17 **that thou art wretched, and m**,........ *1652*

MISERIES
La 1:7 days of her affliction and of her **m**..... 4788
Jas 5:1 weep and howl for your **m** that........ *5004*

MISERY
Jgs 10:16 was grieved for the **m** of Israel 5999
Pr 31:7 and remember his **m** no more 5999
Ecc 8:6 the **m** of man is great upon him....... 7451
Ro 3:16 and **m** are in their ways:.............. *5004*

MISSED
1Sa 20:18 and thou shalt be **m**, because thy 6485
1Sa 25:21 nothing was **m** of all that pertained.... 6485

MISSING
1Ki 20:39 if by any means he be **m**, then shall.... 6485

MIST
Ge 2:6 there went up a **m** from the earth....... 108
Ac 13:11 fell on him a **m** and a darkness; *887*
2Pe 2:17 the **m** of darkness is reserved for *2217*

MISTRESS
Ge 16:4 her **m** was despised in her eyes........ 1404
Ge 16:9 said unto her, Return to thy **m**,........ 1404
Pr 30:23 handmaid that is heir to her **m**........ 1404
Isa 24:2 as with the maid, so with her **m**;....... 1404
Na 3:4 the **m** of witchcrafts, that selleth....... 1172

MISUSED
2Ch 36:16 and **m** his prophets, until the 8591

MITE

Lk	12:59	**till thou hast paid the very last m**	*3016*

MITES

Mk	12:42	and she threw in two **m**, which	*3016*
Lk	21:2	widow casting in thither two **m**	*3016*

MITRE

Ex	28:39	shalt make the **m** of fine linen, and	4701
Ex	29:6	put the holy crown upon the **m**	4701
Le	8:9	And he put the **m** upon his head;	4701
Zec	3:5	So they set a fair **m** upon his head,	6797

MIXED

Pr	23:30	wine; they that go to seek **m** wine	4469
Isa	1:22	dross, thy wine **m** with water:	4107
Da	2:43	even as iron is not **m** with clay	6151
Hos	7:8	he hath **m** himself among the	1101
Heb	4:2	not being **m** with faith in them	*4786*

MIXTURE

Ps	75:8	the wine is red; it is full of **m**;	4538
Jn	19:39	brought a **m** of myrrh and aloes,	*3395*
Rev	14:10	is poured out without **m** into the	*194*

MOCK

Ge	39:14	in an Hebrew unto us to **m** us;	6711
Ge	39:17	unto us, came in unto me to **m** me:	6711
Pr	1:26	I will **m** when your fear cometh;	3932
Pr	14:9	Fools make a **m** at sin: but among	3887
Jer	38:19	into their hand, and they **m** me	5953
La	1:7	her, and did **m** at her sabbaths	7832
Eze	22:5	be far from thee, shall **m** thee,	7046
Mt	20:19	**deliver him to the Gentiles to m,**	*1702*
Mk	10:34	**they shall m him, and shall**	*1702*
Lk	14:29	**all that behold it begin to m him,**	*1702*

MOCKED

Ge	19:14	one that **m** unto his sons in law	6711
Nu	22:29	the ass, Because thou hast **m** me:	5953
Jgs	16:15	thou hast **m** me these three times	2048
1Ki	18:27	pass at noon, that Elijah **m** them	2048
2Ki	2:23	children out of the city, and **m** him,	7046
2Ch	36:16	But they **m** the messengers of God,	3931
Ne	4:1	great indignation, and **m** the Jews	3932
Mt	2:16	that he was **m** of the wise men	*1702*
Mt	27:29	the knee before him, and **m** him	*1702*
Lk	18:32	**be m, and spitefully entreated**	*1702*
Lk	22:63	and the men that held Jesus **m** him,	*1702*
Lk	23:11	war set him at nought, and **m** him,	*1702*
Lk	23:36	the soldiers also **m** him, coming	*1702*
Ac	17:32	resurrection of the dead, some **m**:	*5512*
Gal	6:7	Be not deceived; God is not **m**: for	*3456*

MOCKER

Pr	20:1	Wine is a **m**, strong drink is	3887

MOCKERS

Job	17:2	Are there not **m** with me? and doth	2049
Ps	35:16	With hypocritical **m** in feasts, they	3934
Jer	15:17	sat not in the assembly of the **m**,	7832
Jude	18	there should be **m** in the last time	*1703*

MOCKETH

Pr	17:5	Whoso **m** the poor reproacheth	3932
Pr	30:17	The eye that **m** at his father, and	3932
Jer	20:7	in derision daily, every one **m** me	3932

MOCKING

Ge	21:9	she had born unto Abraham, **m**	6711
Mk	15:31	Likewise also the chief priests **m**	*1702*
Ac	2:13	Others **m** said, These men are full	*5512*

MOCKINGS

Heb	11:36	trial of cruel **m** and scourgings,	*1701*

MODERATION

Php	4:5	Let your **m** be known unto all	*1933*

MODEST

1Ti	2:9	adorn themselves in **m** apparel,	*2887*

MOISTURE

Ps	32:4	my **m** is turned into the drought of	3955
Lk	8:6	**it withered ... because it lacked m**	*2429*

MOLES

Isa	2:20	worship, to the **m** and to the bats;	2661

MOLTEN

Ex	32:4	after he had made it a **m** calf:	4541
Ex	32:8	they have made them a **m** calf, and	4541
Ex	34:17	Thou shalt make thee no **m** gods.	4541
Le	19:4	nor make to yourselves **m** gods: I	4541
1Ki	7:23	he made a **m** sea, ten cubits from	3332
2Ch	28:2	made also **m** images for Baalim	4541
Isa	42:17	say to the **m** images, Ye are our	4541
Jer	51:17	for his **m** image is falsehood, and	5262
Eze	24:11	the filthiness of it may be **m** in it,	5413
Mic	1:4	mountains shall be **m** under him,	4549
Na	1:14	graven image and the **m** image:	4541
Hab	2:18	the **m** image, and a teacher of lies,	4541

MOMENT

Eze	33:5	up into the midst of thee in a **m**,	7281
Nu	16:21	that I may consume them in a **m**	7281
Nu	16:45	I may consume them as in a **m**	7281
Ps	30:5	For his anger endureth but a **m**;	7281
Pr	12:19	but a lying tongue is but for a **m**	7281
Isa	26:20	thyself as it were for a little **m**,	7281
Isa	54:8	I hid my face from thee for a **m**;	7281
La	4:6	that was overthrown as in a **m**, and	7281
Eze	32:10	shall tremble at every **m**, and they	7281
Lk	4:5	kingdoms of the world in a **m** of	*4743*
1Co	15:52	In a **m**, in the twinkling of an eye,	*823*
2Co	4:17	affliction, which is but for a **m**,	*3901*

MONEY

Ge	17:13	he that is bought with thy **m**, must	3701
Ge	23:9	for as much **m** as it is worth he	3701
Ge	42:25	to restore every man's **m** into his	3701
Ge	43:12	And take double **m** in your hand;	3701
Ge	47:14	Joseph gathered up all the **m** that	3701
Ex	12:44	man's servant that is bought for **m**,	3701
Ex	21:11	shall she go out free without **m**.	3701
Ex	21:34	give **m** unto the owner of them;	3701
Ex	22:17	pay **m** according to the dowry of	3701
Ex	22:25	If thou lend **m** to any of my people	3701
Ex	30:16	thou shalt take the atonement **m**	3701
Le	22:11	priest buy any soul with his **m**,	3701
Nu	3:49	Moses took the redemption **m** of	3701
Dt	23:19	usury of **m**, usury of victuals, usury	3701
2Ki	12:4	All the **m** of the dedicated things	3701
2Ki	12:10	there was much **m** in the chest,	3701
2Ki	23:35	but he taxed the land to give the **m**	3701
2Ch	24:5	of all Israel **m** to repair the house	3701
Ne	5:4	have borrowed **m** for the king's	3701

Est 4:7 the **m** that Haman had promised...... 3701
Ps 15:5 putteth not out his **m** to usury........ 3701
Pr 7:20 hath taken a bag of **m** with him,........ 3701
Ecc 7:12 is a defence, and **m** is a defence:........ 3701
Ecc 10:19 merry: but **m** answereth all things..... 3701
Isa 52:3 ye shall be redeemed without **m**........ 3701
Isa 55:1 milk without **m** and without price..... 3701
Isa 55:2 do ye spend **m** for that which is not.... 3701
Jer 32:25 Buy thee the field for **m**, and take...... 3701
La 5:4 We have drunken our water for **m**; 3701
Mic 3:11 the prophets thereof divine for **m**:...... 3701
Mt 17:27 **thou shalt find a piece of m: that**...... *4715*
Mt 22:19 **Shew me the tribute m.** And they...... *3546*
Mt 25:27 **have put my m to the exchangers,**....... *694*
Mt 28:15 So they took the **m**, and did as they..... *694*
Mk 12:41 the people cast **m** into the treasury:.... *5475*
Mk 14:11 glad, and promised to give him **m** *694*
Lk 9:3 **nor scrip, neither bread, neither m;**..... *694*
Lk 19:15 **to whom he had given the m, that**...... *694*
Jn 2:15 poured out the changers' **m**, and *2772*
Ac 4:37 land, sold it, and brought the **m**,........ *5536*
Ac 7:16 Abraham bought for a sum of **m** of..... *694*
Ac 8:20 Thy **m** perish with thee, because........ *694*
Ac 24:26 hoped also that **m** should have........ *5536*
1Ti 6:10 the love of **m** is the root of all evil:..... *5365*

MONEYCHANGERS
Mt 21:12 and overthrew the tables of the **m**,...... *2855*
Mk 11:15 and overthrew the tables of the **m**,...... *2855*

MONTH
Ex 12:2 This **m** shall be unto you the.......... 2320
Le 23:5 the fourteenth day of the first **m** at 2320
Le 23:6 on the fifteenth day of the same **m**..... 2320
Le 23:24 seventh **m**, in ... first day of the **m**..... 2320
Le 23:27 tenth day of this seventh **m** there...... 2320
Nu 3:15 every male from a **m** old and 2320
1Sa 20:34 no meat the second day of the **m**:....... 2320
1Ki 4:7 each man his **m** in a year made......... 2320
Ezr 3:6 first day of the seventh **m** began....... 2320
Ne 2:1 it came to pass in the **m** Nisan, in...... 2320
Ne 6:15 twenty and fifth day of the **m** Elul
Est 9:19 fourteenth day of the **m** Adar a day.... 2320
Est 9:21 the fourteenth day of the **m** Adar...... 2320
Jer 39:1 the tenth **m**, came Nebuchadrezzar 2320
Jer 39:2 fourth **m**, the ninth day of the **m**,...... 2320
Da 10:4 and twentieth day of the first **m**,....... 2320
Hos 5:7 now shall a **m** devour them with 2320
Joel 2:23 and the latter rain in the first **m**,
Hag 1:1 sixth **m**, in the first day of the **m**,....... 2320
Zec 1:1 In the eighth **m**, in the second year 2320
Lk 1:26 in the sixth **m** the angel Gabriel *3376*
Lk 1:36 this is the sixth **m** with her, who....... *3376*
Rev 9:15 and a day, and a **m**, and a year, for *3376*
Rev 22:2 and yielded her fruit every **m**:......... *3376*

MONTHS
Ex 2:2 child, she hid him three **m**............ 3391
Ex 12:2 be unto you the beginning of **m**: 2320
Nu 28:14 throughout the **m** of the year 2320
Jgs 11:37 let me alone two **m**, that I may go 2320
2Sa 24:13 flee three **m** before thine enemies,..... 2320
1Ki 11:16 (For six **m** did Joab remain there...... 2320
1Ch 21:12 three **m** to be destroyed before thy..... 2320
Job 39:2 Canst thou number the **m** that they.... 3391
Eze 47:12 forth new fruit according to his **m**, ... 2320
Da 4:29 At the end of twelve **m** he walked...... 3393
Am 4:7 were yet three **m** to the harvest: 2320
Lk 1:24 conceived, and hid herself five **m**,...... *3376*
Lk 4:25 **shut up three years and six m,** *3376*
Jn 4:35 **Say not ye, There are yet four m,** *5072*
Gal 4:10 Ye observe days, and **m**, and times,..... *3376*
Heb 11:23 was hid three **m** of his parents,........ *5150*
Jas 5:17 space of three years and six **m**......... *3376*
Rev 9:5 they should be tormented five **m**:...... *3376*
Rev 9:10 power was to hurt men five **m** *3376*
Rev 11:2 tread under foot forty and two **m**...... *3376*
Rev 13:5 him to continue forty and two **m**...... *3376*

MOON
Ge 37:9 sun ... the **m** and the eleven stars...... 3394
Dt 4:19 the sun, and the **m**, and the stars,...... 3394
Dt 17:3 either the sun, or **m**, or any of the 3394
Jos 10:13 sun stood still, and the **m** stayed, ... 3394
1Sa 20:5 Behold, tomorrow is the new **m**, ... 2320
1Sa 20:18 Tomorrow is the new **m**: and thou..... 2320
1Sa 20:24 and when the new **m** was come,....... 2320
Ps 8:3 **m** and the stars, which thou hast 3394
Ps 72:5 as long as the sun and **m** endure,...... 3394
Ps 81:3 Blow up the trumpet in the new **m** 2320
Ps 104:19 He appointed the **m** for seasons: 3394
Ps 136:9 The **m** and stars to rule by night:...... 3394
Ecc 12:2 **m**, or the stars, be not darkened, ... 3394
Isa 13:10 the **m** shall not cause her light to 3394
Isa 30:26 light of the **m** shall be as the light...... 3842
Jer 8:2 before the sun, and the **m**, and all 3394
Jer 31:35 ordinances of the **m** and of the stars ... 3394
Eze 32:7 and the **m** shall not give her light...... 3394
Joel 2:10 the sun and the **m** shall be dark,....... 3394
Joel 2:31 darkness, and the **m** into blood,....... 3394
Joel 3:15 sun and the **m** shall be darkened,...... 3394
Am 8:5 When will the new **m** be gone,........ 2320
Hab 3:11 The sun and **m** stood still in their 3394
Mt 24:29 **and the m shall not give her light,**..... *4582*
Mk 13:24 **and the m shall not give her light,**..... *4582*
Lk 21:25 **be signs in the sun, and in the m,**...... *4582*
Ac 2:20 darkness, and the **m** into blood *4582*
1Co 15:41 sun, and another glory of the **m**....... *4582*
Col 2:16 or of the new **m**, or of the sabbath..... *3561*
Rev 6:12 hair, and the **m** became as blood;...... *4582*
Rev 8:12 and the third part of the **m**, and the.... *4582*
Rev 21:23 need of the sun, neither of the **m**,...... *4582*

MOONS
2Ch 2:4 on the new **m**, and on the solemn 2320
2Ch 31:3 the new **m**, and for the set feasts,...... 2320
Ezr 3:5 both of the new **m**, and all the set 2320
Ne 10:33 of the sabbaths, of the new **m**, for 2320
Isa 1:13 the new **m** and sabbaths, the.......... 2320
Hos 2:11 her feast days, her new **m**, and her..... 2320

MORE See also EVERMORE; FURTHERMORE; MOREOVER.
Ge 3:1 Now the serpent was **m** subtil than
Ex 10:29 I will see thy face again no **m** 5750
Ex 30:15 The rich shall not give **m**, and......... 7235
Le 26:21 bring seven times **m** plagues upon..... 3254
1Sa 24:17 Thou art **m** righteous than I: for thou
2Sa 19:13 God do so to me, and **m** also, if 3254
1Ki 2:23 God do so to me, and **m** also, if 3254
1Ki 19:2 let the gods do to me, and **m** also, ... 3254
1Ki 20:10 gods do so unto me, and **m** also, if..... 3254
2Ki 6:31 God do so and **m** also to me, if the 3254
Ps 19:10 **M** to be desired are they than gold,

Ps 39:13 before I go hence, and be no **m**
Pr 26:12 there is **m** hope of a fool than of him.
Pr 29:20 there is **m** hope of a fool than of him.
SS 1:4 will remember thy love **m** than wine:
Hab 1:13 the man that is **m** righteous than he?
Mt 11:22 **be m tolerable for Tyre and Sidon** *414*
Mt 12:45 **seven other spirits m wicked than**
Lk 12:7 **of m value than many sparrows** *1308*
Lk 15:21 **am no m worthy to be called** *3765*
Jn 8:11 **I condemn thee: go, and sin no m** *2001*
Ac 20:35 **m blessed to give than to receive** *3122*
Ro 1:25 the creature **m** than the Creator,........ *3844*
Ro 7:17 Now then it is no **m** I that do it *2089*
Ro 11:6 otherwise work is no **m** work *2089*
2Ti 3:4 pleasures **m** than lovers of God; *3123*
Heb 1:4 obtained a **m** excellent name than
Heb 10:2 have had no **m** conscience of sins...... *2089*
Heb 10:17 iniquities will I remember no **m**....... *2089*
Heb 10:18 is, there is no **m** offering for sin........ *2089*
Heb 10:26 remaineth no **m** sacrifice for sins,...... *2089*
Rev 21:1 away; and there was no **m** sea. *2089*
Rev 21:4 there shall be no **m** death, neither *2089*

MOREOVER See also **FURTHERMORE.**

Ge 45:15 **M** he kissed all his brethren, and
Ps 19:11 **M** by them is thy servant warned: 1571
Ecc 12:9 **m**, because the preacher was wise 3148
Mt 6:16 **M when ye fast, be not, as the**......... *1161*
Ro 8:30 **M** whom he did predestinate, them *1161*

MORNING

Ge 1:5 evening and the **m** were the first....... 1242
Ge 19:15 And when the **m** arose, then the....... 7837
Ge 29:25 that in the **m**, behold, it was Leah: 1242
Ex 3:6 **M** he said, I am the God 1242
Ex 12:10 nothing of it remain until the **m**; 1242
Ex 14:24 **m** watch the Lord looked unto the..... 1242
Ex 16:20 some of them left of it until the **m**, ... 1242
Ex 16:21 they gathered it every **m**, every........ 1242
Ex 29:39 one lamb thou shalt offer in the **m**; 1242
Ex 30:7 thereon sweet incense every **m**:........ 1242
Ex 34:25 of the passover be left unto the **m**, ... 1242
Le 6:20 perpetual, half of it in the **m**, and...... 1242
Le 7:15 shall not leave any of it until the **m** 1242
Nu 9:15 the appearance of fire, until the **m**..... 1242
Nu 9:21 cloud abode from even unto the **m** 1242
Dt 28:67 shalt say, Would God it were **m**! 1242
Jgs 6:31 be put to death whilst it is yet **m**: 1242
Jgs 19:25 abused her all … night until the **m**:.... 1242
Ru 3:14 And she lay at his feet until the **m**:..... 1242
2Sa 23:4 riseth, even a **m** without clouds;....... 1242
Ne 4:21 the rising of the **m** till the stars........ 7837
Ne 8:3 water gate from the **m** until midday, ... 216
Job 38:7 When the **m** stars sang together,....... 1242
Job 38:12 Hast thou commanded the **m** since 1242
Ps 30:5 a night, but joy cometh in the **m**,...... 1242
Ps 55:17 and **m**, and at noon, will I pray, ... 1242
Ps 59:16 sing aloud of thy mercy in the **m**:...... 1242
Ps 92:2 forth thy lovingkindness in the **m**,..... 1242
Ps 110:3 holiness from the womb of the **m**:..... 4891
Ps 119:147 prevented the dawning of the **m**, and
Ps 130:6 than they that watch for the **m**:........ 1242
Ps 139:9 If I take the wings of the **m**, and....... 7837
Ps 143:8 hear thy lovingkindness in the **m**; 1242
Pr 7:18 us take our fill of love until the **m**:..... 1242
Pr 27:14 rising early in the **m**, it shall be........ 1242
Ecc 10:16 and thy princes eat in the **m**!.......... 1242
Ecc 11:6 In the **m** sow thy seed, and in the...... 1242
Isa 14:12 heaven, O Lucifer, son of the **m**!....... 7837
Isa 17:14 and before the **m** he is not........... 1242
Isa 38:13 I reckoned till **m**, that, as a lion, so..... 1242
Isa 50:4 he wakeneth **m** by **m**, he wakeneth 1242
Isa 58:8 thy light break forth as the **m**,......... 7837
Jer 21:12 Execute judgment in the **m**, and....... 1242
La 3:23 They are new every **m**: great is thy..... 1242
Eze 7:7 The **m** is come unto thee, O thou...... 6843
Eze 46:15 every **m** for a continual … offering..... 1242
Da 6:19 king arose very early in the **m**, ... 5053
Da 8:26 vision of the evening and the **m** 1242
Hos 6:3 going forth is prepared as the **m**; 7837
Hos 10:15 in a **m** shall the king of Israel 7837
Hos 13:3 they shall be as the **m** cloud, and 1242
Joel 2:2 **m** spread upon the mountains:........ 7837
Am 4:13 that maketh the **m** darkness, and 7837
Am 5:8 the shadow of death into the **m**,........ 1242
Mic 2:1 when the **m** is light, they practise...... 1242
Zep 3:5 every **m** doth he bring his judgment ... 1242
Mt 16:3 **in the m, It will be foul weather** *4404*
Mt 27:1 When the **m** was come, all the chief.... *4405*
Mk 1:35 in the **m**, rising up a great while....... *4404*
Mk 16:2 very early in the **m**, the first day
Lk 24:1 very early in the **m**, they came unto
Jn 8:2 early in the **m** he came again into
Jn 21:4 But when the **m** was now come,....... *4405*
Ac 28:23 the prophets, from **m** till evening...... *4404*
Rev 2:28 **And I will give him the m star**......... *4407*
Rev 22:16 **David, and the bright and m star.** *3720*

MORNING-STAR See **MORNING** and **STAR.**

M

MORROW

Ex 8:10 And he said, To **m**. And he said 4279
Ex 8:29 servants, and from his people, to **m**: ... 4279
Ex 9:5 To **m** the Lord shall do this thing...... 4279
Ex 9:18 to **m** about this time I will cause 4279
Ex 10:4 to **m** will I bring the locusts into 4279
Le 23:16 Even unto the **m** after the seventh 4283
Nu 17:8 that on the **m** Moses went into the..... 4283
Jos 5:12 the manna ceased on the **m** after 4283
1Sa 18:10 to pass on the **m**, that the evil......... 4283
1Sa 19:11 to night, to **m** thou shalt be slain....... 4279
1Sa 20:18 to David, To **m** is the new moon:...... 4279
2Ki 6:28 day, and we will eat my son to **m** 4279
2Ki 7:1 To **m** about this time … a measure 4279
Pr 3:28 come again, and to **m** I will give; 4279
Pr 27:1 Boast not thyself of to **m**; for thou..... 4279
Isa 22:13 and drink; for to **m** we shall die........ 4279
Isa 56:12 to **m** shall be as this day, and much 4279
Mt 6:30 **is, and to m is cast into the oven,**....... *839*
Mt 6:34 **for the m shall take thought for** *839*
Lk 12:28 **and to m is cast into the oven;** *839*
Lk 13:33 **and to m, and the day following:** *839*
Ac 25:17 on the **m** I sat on the judgment *1836*
1Co 15:32 us eat and drink; for to **m** we die........ *839*
Jas 4:13 To day or to **m** we will go into such..... *839*
Jas 4:14 ye know not what shall be on the **m**..... *839*

MORSEL

Ge 18:5 And I will fetch a **m** of bread, and 6595
Jgs 19:5 thine heart with a **m** of bread, and..... 6595
1Sa 28:22 let me set a **m** of bread before......... 6595
1Ki 17:11 Bring me, I pray thee, a **m** of bread 6595
Pr 17:1 Better is a dry **m**, and quietness 6595

Pr 23:8 The **m** which thou hast eaten shalt. 6595
Heb 12:16 one **m** of meat sold his birthright. *1035*

MORTAL See also IMMORTAL.

Job 4:17 **m** man be more just than God? 582
Ro 6:12 therefore reign in your **m** body, ... *2349*
Ro 8:11 also quicken your **m** bodies by his *2349*
1Co 15:53 this **m** must put on immortality. *2349*
2Co 4:11 be made manifest in our **m** flesh. *2349*

MORTALITY See also IMMORTALITY.

2Co 5:4 **m** might be swallowed up of life. *2349*

MORTAR

Pr 27:22 thou shouldest bray a fool in a **m**. 4388

MORTER

Ge 11:3 stone, and slime had they for **m** 2563
Ex 1:14 hard bondage, in **m**, and in brick, ... 2563
Na 3:14 go into clay, and tread the **m**, ... 2563

MORTGAGED

Ne 5:3 We have **m** our lands, vineyards, ... 6148

MORTIFY

Ro 8:13 the Spirit do **m** the deeds of the *2289*
Col 3:5 **M** therefore your members which *3499*

MOST

Ge 14:18 was the priest of the **m** high God 5945
Ge 14:22 unto the Lord, the **m** high God, ... 5945
Ex 26:33 the holy place and the **m** holy. 6944
Ex 29:37 and it shall be an altar **m** holy: 6944
Le 6:17 it is **m** holy, as is the sin offering, ... 6944
Le 7:6 eaten in the holy place: it is **m** holy 6944
Le 21:22 both of the **m** holy, and of the holy. 6944
Le 27:28 every devoted thing is **m** holy unto 6944
Nu 4:19 approach unto the **m** holy things: 6944
Nu 24:16 knew the knowledge of the **m** High, . . . 6944
Dt 32:8 When the **m** High divided to the 6944
2Sa 23:19 Was he not **m** honourable of three?
1Ki 6:16 oracle, even for the **m** holy place. 6944
2Ch 3:10 in the **m** holy house he made two 6944
2Ch 5:7 into the **m** holy place, even under 6944
Ezr 2:63 should not eat of the **m** holy things,
Ne 7:65 should not eat of the **m** holy things, . . . 6944
Ps 7:17 to the name of the Lord **m** high. 5945
Ps 21:7 the mercy of the **m** High he shall 5945
Ps 47:2 For the Lord **m** high is terrible; he 5945
Ps 50:14 pay thy vows unto the **m** High:. 5945
Ps 73:11 there knowledge in the **m** High?. 5945
Ps 78:17 by provoking the **m** High in the 5945
Ps 82:6 you are children of the **m** High. 5945
Ps 83:18 art the **m** High over all the earth. 5945
Ps 91:1 in the secret place of the **m** High 5945
Ps 107:11 the counsel of the **m** High: 5945
Pr 20:6 **M** men will proclaim every one 7230
SS 8:6 which hath a **m** vehement flame
Isa 14:14 clouds; I will be like the **m** High. 5945
Jer 50:31 I am against thee, O thou **m** proud,
La 3:38 Out of the mouth of the **m** High 5945
La 4:1 how is the **m** fine gold changed!. 2896
Eze 2:7 forbear: for they are **m** rebellious.
Eze 44:13 holy things, in the **m** holy place:. 6944
Da 3:20 commanded the **m** mighty men 2429
Da 3:26 ye servants of the **m** high God,. 5943
Da 4:25 know that the **m** High ruleth in 5943
Da 4:34 and I blessed the **m** High, and I 5943
Da 5:21 knew that the **m** high God ruled 5943
Da 7:18 saints of the **m** High shall take 5946
Da 7:25 great words against the **m** High,. 5943
Da 7:27 of the saints of the **m** High, whose. 5945
Da 9:24 and to anoint the **m** Holy 6944
Da 11:39 he do in the **m** strong holds with 4581
Hos 7:16 return, but not to the **m** High: 5920
Hos 11:7 they called them to the **m** High,. 5920
Mic 7:4 the **m** upright is sharper than a thorn
Mt 11:20 **m** of his mighty works were done, ... *4118*
Mk 5:7 thou Son of the **m** high God? I *5310*
Lk 7:42 **which of them will love him m?** *4119*
Lk 8:28 Jesus, thou Son of God **m** high? *5310*
Ac 7:48 **m** High dwelleth not in temples *5310*
Ac 16:17 the servants of the **m** high God, ... *5310*
Ac 26:5 that after the **m** straitest sect of our
1Co 15:19 we are of all men **m** miserable
2Co 12:9 **M** gladly therefore will I rather *2236*
Heb 7:1 Salem, priest of the **m** high God, ... *5370*
Jude 20 yourselves on your **m** holy faith,. *40*
Rev 18:12 manner vessels of **m** precious wood,
Rev 21:11 was like unto a stone **m** precious,

MOST-HIGH See MOST and HIGH.

MOST-HOLY See MOST and HOLY.

MOTE

Mt 7:4 **pull out the m out of thine eye;** *2595*
Lk 6:42 **out the m that is in thine eye,** *2595*

MOTH

Isa 51:8 For the **m** shall eat them up like a 6211
Mt 6:20 **where neither m nor rust doth** *4597*
Lk 12:33 **neither m corrupteth.** *4597*

MOTHEATEN

Jas 5:2 and your garments are **m**. *4598*

MOTHER

Ge 2:24 a man leave his father and his **m**, ... 517
Ge 3:20 because she was the **m** of all living. 517
Ge 27:14 and his **m** made savoury meat, such 517
Ge 44:20 he alone is left of his **m**, and his 517
Ex 20:12 Honour thy father and thy **m**: that. 517
Ex 21:15 that smiteth his father, or his **m**,. 517
Ex 21:17 he that curseth his father, or his **m**, ... 517
Le 18:7 father, or the nakedness of thy **m**,. 517
Le 19:3 Ye shall fear every man his **m**, and 517
Le 20:9 that curseth his father or his **m**; 517
Dt 5:16 Honour thy father and thy **m**, as. 517
Jgs 14:4 But his father and his **m** knew not 517
Jgs 14:6 he told not … his **m** what he had done. . 517
Ru 3:6 to all that her **m** in law bade her. 2545
1Sa 15:33 so shall thy **m** be childless among. 517
2Ch 22:3 **m** was his counsellor to do wickedly 517
Ps 27:10 my father and **m** forsake me,. 517
Ps 35:14 as one that mourneth for his **m** 517
Ps 51:5 and in sin did my **m** conceive me. 517
Ps 109:14 not the sin of his **m** be blotted out. 517
Ps 113:9 and to be a joyful **m** of children.. 517
Pr 1:8 and forsake not the law of thy **m**:. 517
Pr 10:1 foolish son is the heaviness of his **m** 517
Pr 15:20 but a foolish man despiseth his **m** 517
Pr 19:26 chaseth away his **m**, is a son that. 517
Pr 20:20 Whoso curseth his father or his **m**, ... 517
Pr 23:22 despise not thy **m** when she is old. 517
Pr 23:25 Thy father and thy **m** shall be glad, ... 517

Pr	28:24	Whoso robbeth his father or his **m**,	517
Pr	29:15	to himself bringeth his **m** to shame..	517
Pr	30:11	father, and doth not bless their **m**.	517
Pr	30:17	despiseth to obey his **m**, the ravens	517
Pr	31:1	prophecy that his **m** taught him.	517
Isa	8:4	to cry, My father, and my **m**, the	517
Isa	66:13	As one whom his **m** comforteth, so	517
Jer	15:10	Woe is me, my **m**, that thou hast	517
Jer	20:14	not the day wherein my **m** bare me	517
Eze	16:44	As is the **m**, so is her daughter	517
Hos	2:2	Plead with your **m**, plead: for she	517
Hos	4:5	the night, and I will destroy thy **m**	517
Mic	7:6	daughter riseth up against her **m**,	517
Mt	1:18	as his **m** Mary was espoused to	*3384*
Mt	2:13	take the young child and his **m**,	*3384*
Mt	2:20	take the young child and his **m**,	*3384*
Mt	10:35	**and the daughter against her m**,	*3384*
Mt	10:37	**loveth father or m more than**	*3384*
Mt	12:48	**Who is my m? and who are my**	*3384*
Mt	12:49	**Behold my m and my brethren!**	*3384*
Mt	13:55	son? is not his **m** called Mary?	*3384*
Mt	14:8	being before instructed of her **m**,	*3384*
Mt	15:4	**saying, Honour thy father and m:**	*3384*
Mt	15:4	**that curseth father or m, let him**	*3384*
Mt	15:6	**honour not his father or his m,**	*3384*
Mt	19:5	**shall a man leave father and m,**	*3384*
Mt	19:19	**Honour thy father and thy m:**	*3384*
Mt	19:29	**father, or m, or wife, or children,**	*3384*
Mk	3:34	**Behold my m and my brethren!**	*3384*
Mk	5:40	father and the **m** of the damsel,	*3384*
Mk	6:24	said unto her **m**, What shall I ask?	*3384*
Mk	7:10	**Honour thy father and thy m;**	*3384*
Mk	7:10	**Whoso curseth father or m, let**	*3384*
Mk	7:11	**man shall say to his father or m,**	*3384*
Mk	7:12	**do ought for his father or his m;**	*3384*
Mk	10:7	**a man leave his father and m,**	*3384*
Mk	10:19	**not, Honour thy father and m**	*3384*
Lk	2:33	Joseph and his **m** marvelled at	*3384*
Lk	2:34	and said unto Mary his **m**, Behold,	*3384*
Lk	2:43	Joseph and his **m** knew not of it	*3384*
Lk	2:48	and his **m** said unto him, Son, why	*3384*
Lk	2:51	his **m** kept all these sayings in her	*3384*
Lk	8:21	**My m and my brethren are these**	*3384*
Lk	12:53	**the m against the daughter, and**	*3384*
Lk	14:26	**hate not his father, and m, and**	*3384*
Lk	18:20	**Honour thy father and thy m**	
Jn	2:3	**m** of Jesus saith unto him, They	*3384*
Jn	2:5	His **m** saith unto the servants,	*3384*
Jn	19:26	he saith unto his **m**, **Woman,**	*3384*
Jn	19:27	he to the disciple, **Behold thy m!**	*3384*
Ac	1:14	and Mary the **m** of Jesus, and with	*3384*
Gal	4:26	is free, which is the **m** of us all	*3384*
Eph	5:31	shall a man leave his father and **m**	*3384*
Eph	6:2	Honour thy father and **m**, which	*3384*
2Ti	1:5	Lois, and thy **m** Eunice; and I	*3384*
Heb	7:3	Without father, without **m**, without	*282*
Rev	17:5	Great, The **M** of Harlots And	*3384*

MOTHER-IN-LAW See MOTHER and LAW.

MOTHER'S

Ge	24:67	was comforted after his **m** death	517
Ge	27:29	let thy **m** sons bow down to thee:	517
Ge	28:2	daughters of Laban thy **m** brother	517
Le	18:13	for she is thy **m** near kinswoman	517
Dt	14:21	shalt not seethe a kid in his **m** milk	517
Jgs	16:17	unto God from my **m** womb: if I	517
1Sa	20:30	the confusion of thy **m** nakedness?	517
Job	1:21	Naked came I out of my **m** womb,	517
Job	3:10	shut not up the doors of my **m** womb,	
Ps	22:9	when I was upon my **m** breasts.	517
Ps	22:10	thou art my God from my **m** belly	517
Ps	69:8	and an alien unto my **m** children	517
Ps	71:6	that took me out of my **m** bowels:	517
Ecc	5:15	As he came forth of his **m** womb,	517
SS	1:6	my **m** children were angry with me;	517
Isa	50:1	is the bill of your **m** divorcement,	517
Mt	19:12	**were so born from their m womb:**	*3384*
Lk	1:15	Ghost, even from his **m** womb,	*3384*
Jn	3:4	the second time into his **m** womb,	*3384*
Ac	3:2	man lame from his **m** womb was	*3384*
Ac	14:8	being a cripple from his **m** womb,	*3384*
Gal	1:15	separated me from my **m** womb,	*3384*

MOTHERS

La	2:12	They say to their **m**, Where is corn	517
La	5:3	fatherless, our **m** are as widows,	517
Mk	10:30	**and sisters, and m, and children,**	*3384*
1Ti	1:9	of fathers and murderers of **m**,	*3389*
1Ti	5:2	The elder women as **m**; the	*3384*

MOTIONS

Ro	7:5	the **m** of sin, which were by the	*3804*

MOUNT

Ge	22:14	in the **m** of the Lord it shall be	2022
Ex	18:5	he encamped at the **m** of God:	2022
Ex	19:11	sight of all the people upon **m** Sinai.	2022
Ex	19:12	whosoever toucheth the **m** shall be	2022
Ex	19:18	**m** Sinai was altogether on a smoke,	2022
Ex	19:18	and the whole **m** quaked greatly.	2022
Ex	19:20	called Moses up to the top of the **m**;	2022
Ex	19:23	people cannot come up to **m** Sinai:	2022
Ex	24:18	Moses was in the **m** forty days and.	2022
Ex	32:19	and brake them beneath the **m**.	2022
Ex	34:29	when he came down from the **m**,	2022
Dt	5:4	with you face to face in the **m** out	2022
Dt	5:22	unto all your assembly in the **m**	2022
Dt	32:50	die in the **m** whither thou goest up,	2022
2Ch	33:15	altars that he had built in the **m** of	2022
Ne	9:13	camest down also upon **m** Sinai,	2022
Job	39:27	the eagle **m** up at thy command,	1361
Ps	48:2	joy of the whole earth, is **m** Zion,	2022
Ps	74:2	**m** Zion, wherein thou hast dwelt	2022
Ps	78:68	Judah, the **m** Zion which he loved	2022
Ps	107:26	They **m** up to the heaven, they go	5927
Ps	125:1	in the Lord shall be as **m** Zion,	2022
Isa	8:18	of hosts, which dwelleth in **m** Zion	2022
Isa	9:18	**m** up like the lifting up of smoke	55
Isa	24:23	Lord of hosts shall reign in **m** Zion,	2022
Isa	27:13	Lord in the holy **m** at Jerusalem	2022
Isa	40:31	shall **m** up with wings as eagles;	5927
Eze	10:16	wings to **m** up from the earth, the	7311
Joel	2:32	in **m** Zion and in Jerusalem shall	2022
Ob	17	upon **m** Zion shall be deliverance,	2022
Mic	4:7	shall reign over them in **m** Zion	2022
Zec	14:4	in that day upon the **m** of Olives	2022
Mt	24:3	as he sat upon the **m** of Olives, the	*3735*
Mk	13:3	And as he sat upon the **m** of Olives	*3735*
Lk	19:29	Bethany, at the **m** called … Olives,	*3735*
Lk	19:37	at the descent of the **m** of Olives,	*3735*
Lk	21:37	he went out, and abode in the **m**	*3735*
Ac	1:12	from the **m** called Olivet, which is	*3735*

Ac	7:38	which spake to him in the **m** Sina,	*3735*
Heb	8:5	the pattern shewed to thee in the **m**.	*3735*
Heb	12:18	unto the **m** that might be touched,	*3735*
2Pe	1:18	we were with him in the holy **m**	*3735*
Rev	14:1	lo, a Lamb stood on the **m** Sion,	*3735*

MOUNTAIN

Ge	14:10	they that remained fled to the **m**	2022
Ge	19:17	escape to the **m**, lest thou be	2022
Ex	3:12	ye shall serve God upon this **m**.	2022
Ex	19:3	Lord called unto him out of the **m**,	2022
Dt	5:23	(for the **m** did burn with fire,) that	2022
Jos	2:16	Get you to the **m**, lest the pursuers.	2022
Jos	14:12	therefore give me this **m**, whereof.	2022
1Sa	17:3	the Philistines stood on a **m** on the	2022
2Ki	6:17	behold, the **m** was full of horses	2022
Ps	11:1	my soul, Flee as a bird to your **m**?	2022
Isa	2:2	the **m** of the Lord's house shall be	2022
Isa	40:4	and every **m** and hill shall be made	2022
Isa	57:13	land, and shall inherit my holy **m**;	2022
Isa	65:11	that forget my holy **m**, that	2022
Jer	31:23	of justice, and **m** of holiness	2022
Eze	17:23	In the **m** of the height of Israel	2022
Eze	20:40	in the **m** of the height of Israel	2022
Eze	28:16	as profane out of the **m** of God:	2022
Eze	40:2	and set me upon a very high **m**,	2022
Da	9:16	thy city Jerusalem, thy holy **m**:	2022
Joel	2:1	and sound an alarm in my holy **m**:	2022
Zep	3:11	be haughty because of my holy **m**	2022
Hag	1:8	Go up to the **m**, and bring wood,	2022
Zec	14:4	half of the **m** shall remove toward	2022
Mt	4:8	up into an exceeding high **m**,	*3735*
Mt	14:23	went up into a **m** apart to pray:	*3735*
Mt	17:20	**ye shall say unto this m, Remove**	*3735*
Mt	21:21	**also if ye shall say unto this m,**	*3735*
Mk	11:23	**whosoever shall say unto this m,**	*3735*
Lk	3:5	every **m** and hill shall be brought	*3735*
Lk	4:5	taking him up into an high **m**,	*3735*
Lk	9:28	and went up into a **m** to pray	*3735*
Jn	4:20	Our fathers worshipped in this **m**;	*3735*
Jn	4:21	**when ye shall neither in this m,**	*3735*
Heb	12:20	if so much as a beast touch the **m**,	*3735*
Rev	6:14	every **m** and island were moved	*3735*
Rev	8:8	as it were a great **m** burning with	*3735*
Rev	21:10	in the spirit to a great and high **m**,	*3735*

MOUNTAINS

Ge	7:20	prevail; and the **m** were covered	2022
Ge	8:4	the month, upon the **m** of Ararat.	2022
Ex	32:12	them out, to slay them in the **m**,	2022
Dt	12:2	their gods, upon the high **m**, and	2022
Dt	32:22	on fire the foundations of the **m**.	2022
Jgs	5:5	**m** melted from before the Lord,	2022
Jgs	9:36	Thou seest the shadow of the **m** as.	2022
Jgs	11:38	bewailed her virginity upon the **m**.	2022
1Ki	19:11	great and strong wind rent the **m**,	2022
Ps	36:6	righteousness is like the great **m**;	2042
Ps	46:2	the **m** be carried into the midst	2022
Ps	90:2	Before the **m** were brought forth,	2022
Ps	125:2	the **m** are round about Jerusalem	2022
Pr	8:25	Before the **m** were settled, before	2022
Isa	13:4	noise of a multitude in the **m**, like	2022
Isa	34:3	the **m** shall be melted with their	2022
Isa	52:7	How beautiful upon the **m** are the	2022
Isa	55:12	the **m** and the hills shall break	2022
Isa	64:3	the **m** flowed down at thy presence	2022
Jer	4:24	I beheld the **m**, and, lo, they	2022
Jer	13:16	your feet stumble upon the dark **m**,	2022
La	4:19	they pursued us upon the **m**, they	2022
Eze	6:13	in all the tops of the **m**, and under	2022
Eze	7:7	not the sounding again of the **m**,	2022
Eze	22:9	and in thee they eat upon the **m**:	2022
Eze	31:12	upon the **m** and in all the valleys	2022
Eze	36:1	prophesy unto the **m** of Israel, and	2022
Eze	36:4	Ye **m** of Israel, hear the word	2022
Eze	38:20	and the **m** shall be thrown down	2022
Eze	39:17	sacrifice upon the **m** of Israel, that	2022
Hos	10:8	they shall say to the **m**, Cover us;	2022
Joel	2:5	noise of chariots on the tops of **m**	2022
Am	4:13	For, lo, he that formeth the **m**, and	2022
Mic	1:4	the **m** shall be molten under him	2022
Na	1:5	The **m** quake at him, and the hills	2022
Na	1:15	Behold upon the **m** the feet of him	2022
Hab	3:6	the everlasting **m** were scattered	2042
Hab	3:10	**m** saw thee, and they trembled:	2022
Mt	18:12	**goeth into the m, and seeketh**	*3735*
Mt	24:16	**be in Judaea flee into the m:**	*3735*
Mk	5:5	night and day, he was in the **m**,	*3735*
Mk	13:14	**that be in Judaea flee to the m:**	*3735*
Lk	21:21	**are in Judaea flee to the m;**	*3735*
Lk	23:30	**begin to say to the m, Fall on**	*3735*
1Co	13:2	faith, so that I could remove **m**,	*3735*
Rev	6:16	said to the **m** and rocks, Fall on us,	*3735*

MOUNTED

Eze	10:19	**m** up from the earth in my sight:	7426

MOURN

Ge	23:2	Abraham came to **m** for Sarah,	5594
1Sa	16:1	How long wilt thou **m** for Saul	56
Ne	8:9	Lord your God; **m** not, nor weep	56
Job	2:11	together to come to **m** with him.	5110
Pr	5:11	And thou **m** at the last, when they	5098
Pr	29:2	wicked beareth rule, the people **m**	584
Ecc	3:4	a time to **m**, and a time to dance;	5594
Isa	3:26	her gates shall lament and **m**; and	56
Isa	61:2	of our God; to comfort all that **m**;	57
Isa	61:3	To appoint unto them that **m** in	57
Isa	66:10	joy with her, all ye that **m** for her	56
Jer	4:28	For this shall the earth **m**, and the	56
Jer	12:4	How long shall the land **m**, and the	56
La	1:4	The ways of Zion do **m**, because.	57
Eze	7:12	the buyer rejoice, nor the seller **m**:	56
Eze	7:27	The king shall **m**, and the prince	56
Eze	24:16	neither shalt thou **m** nor weep	5594
Hos	4:3	Therefore shall the land **m**, and	56
Joel	1:9	the priests, the Lord's ministers, **m**.	56
Am	1:2	habitations of the shepherds shall **m**,	56
Am	9:5	and all that dwell therein shall **m**:	56
Zec	12:10	and they shall **m** for him, as one.	5594
Mt	5:4	**Blessed are they that m: for they**	*3996*
Mt	9:15	**children of the bridechamber m,**	*3996*
Mt	24:30	**shall all the tribes of the earth m,**	*2875*
Lk	6:25	**now! for ye shall m and weep**	*3996*
Jas	4:9	Be afflicted, and **m**, and weep: let	*3996*
Rev	18:11	earth shall weep and **m** over her;	*3996*

MOURNED

Ge	37:34	loins, and **m** for his son many days	56
Nu	14:39	of Israel: and the people **m** greatly	56
1Sa	15:35	nevertheless Samuel **m** for Saul:	56
2Sa	1:12	And they **m**, and wept, and fasted	5594
2Sa	11:26	was dead, she **m** for her husband	5594

2Sa	13:37	And David **m** for his son every day	56
2Sa	14:2	that had a long time **m** for the dead:	56
1Ki	14:18	and all Israel **m** for him, according	5594
Ezr	10:6	he **m** because of the transgression of	56
Ne	1:4	I ... wept, and **m** certain days, and	56
Zec	7:5	When ye fasted and **m** in the	5594
Mt	11:17	**we have m unto you, and ye have**	*2354*
Mk	16:10	with him, as they **m** and wept	*3996*
Lk	7:32	**we have m to you, and ye have**	*2354*
1Co	5:2	and have not rather **m**, that he	*3996*

MOURNERS

Job	29:25	army, as one that comforteth the **m**	57
Hos	9:4	be unto them as the bread of **m**;	205

MOURNETH

2Sa	19:1	king weepeth and **m** for Absalom	56
Ps	35:14	as one that **m** for his mother	57
Ps	88:9	Mine eye **m** by reason of	1669
Isa	24:4	The earth **m** and fadeth away, the	56
Isa	33:9	the earth **m** and languisheth:	56
Zec	12:10	for him, as one **m** for his only son,	5594

MOURNING

Ge	27:41	The days of **m** for my father are at	60
Ge	37:35	down into the grave unto my son **m**	57
Est	4:3	great **m** among the Jews, ... fasting	60
Ps	30:11	turned for me my **m** into dancing:	4553
Ps	38:6	greatly; I go **m** all the day long	6937
Ps	42:9	go I **m** because of the oppression	6937
Ps	43:2	go I **m** because of the oppression	6937
Ecc	7:2	better to go to the house of **m**, than	60
Ecc	7:4	of the wise is in the house of **m**;	60
Isa	51:11	and sorrow and **m** shall flee away	585
Isa	60:20	the days of thy **m** shall be ended	60
Isa	61:3	beauty for ashes, the oil of joy for **m**,	60
Jer	6:26	make thee **m**, as for an only son	60
Jer	16:5	not into the house of **m**, neither	4798
Jer	31:13	I will turn their **m** into joy, and will	60
La	5:15	ceased; our dance is turned into **m**.	60
Eze	2:10	lamentations, and **m**, and woe	1899
Da	10:2	I Daniel was **m** three full weeks	56
Joel	2:12	and with weeping, and with **m**:	4553
Am	8:10	And I will turn your feasts into **m**,	60
Zec	12:11	there be great **m** in Jerusalem,	4553
Mt	2:18	and great **m**, Rachel weeping for	*3602*
2Co	7:7	your **m**, your fervent mind toward	*3602*
Jas	4:9	laughter be turned to **m**, and your	*3997*
Rev	18:8	day, death, and **m**, and famine;	*3997*

MOUTH

Ge	4:11	hath opened her **m** to receive thy	6310
Ge	8:11	in her **m** was an olive leaf pluckt	6310
Ge	29:2	great stone was upon the well's **m**	6310
Ex	4:11	him, Who hath made man's **m**? or	6310
Ex	4:12	and I will be with thy **m**, and teach	6310
Ex	4:15	will be with thy **m**, and with his **m**,	6310
Ex	13:9	the Lord's law may be in thy **m**:	6310
Nu	12:8	With him will I speak **m** to **m**, even	6310
Nu	16:32	earth opened her **m**, and swallowed	6310
Nu	23:16	Balaam, and put a word in his **m**,	6310
Nu	26:10	earth opened her **m**, and swallowed	6310
Nu	35:30	put to death by the **m** of witnesses:	6310
Dt	8:3	of the **m** of the Lord doth man live	6310
Dt	11:6	earth opened her **m**, and swallowed	6310
Dt	17:6	at the **m** of one witness he shall not	6310
Dt	18:18	and will put my words in his **m**;	6310
Dt	19:15	or at the **m** of three witnesses, shall	6310
Dt	23:23	thou hast promised with thy **m**.	6310
Dt	30:14	is very nigh unto thee, in thy **m**,	6310
Jos	1:8	law shall not depart out of thy **m**;	6310
Jos	6:10	any word proceed out of your **m**,	6310
Jos	9:14	not counsel at the **m** of the Lord	6310
Jgs	7:6	putting their hand to their **m**, were	6310
1Sa	2:1	my **m** is enlarged over mine	6310
1Sa	14:27	honeycomb, ... put his hand to his **m**;	6310
2Sa	1:16	thy **m** hath testified against thee	6310
2Sa	14:3	So Joab put the words in her **m**	6310
2Sa	18:25	be alone, there is tidings in his **m**	6310
2Sa	22:9	and fire out of his **m** devoured:	6310
1Ki	13:21	hast disobeyed the **m** of the Lord	6310
1Ki	17:24	word of the Lord in thy **m** is truth	6310
1Ki	19:18	every **m** which hath not kissed him	6310
1Ki	22:22	spirit in the **m** of all his prophets	6310
2Ki	4:34	child, and put his **m** upon his **m**,	6310
2Ch	18:21	spirit in the **m** of all his prophets	6310
2Ch	35:22	words of Necho from the **m** of God,	6310
Est	7:8	word went out of the king's **m**, and	6310
Job	3:1	After this opened Job his **m**, and	6310
Job	35:16	doth Job open his **m** in vain;	6310
Job	40:4	I will lay mine hand upon my **m**	6310
Job	40:23	he can draw up Jordan into his **m**	6310
Job	41:19	Out of his **m** go burning lamps,	6310
Job	41:21	and a flame goeth out of his **m**.	6310
Ps	5:9	there is no faithfulness in their **m**;	6310
Ps	8:2	Out of ... **m** of babes and sucklings.	6310
Ps	17:3	that my **m** shall not transgress	6310
Ps	19:14	Let the words of my **m**, and the	6310
Ps	32:9	whose **m** must be held in with bit	5716
Ps	33:6	of them by the breath of his **m**	6310
Ps	39:9	I was dumb, I opened not my **m**;	6310
Ps	40:3	he hath put a new song in my **m**,	6310
Ps	50:19	Thou givest thy **m** to evil, and thy	6310
Ps	55:21	The words of his **m** were smoother	6310
Ps	62:4	they bless with their **m**, but they	6310
Ps	73:9	set their **m** against the heavens,	6310
Ps	81:10	open thy **m** wide, and I will fill it	6310
Ps	103:5	satisfieth thy **m** with good things;	5716
Ps	119:72	The law of thy **m** is better unto me	6310
Ps	119:103	yea, sweeter than honey to my **m**!	6310
Ps	119:108	the freewill offerings of my **m**, O	6310
Ps	141:3	Set a watch, O Lord, before my **m**;	6310
Pr	2:6	out of his **m** cometh knowledge	6310
Pr	4:24	put away from thee a froward **m**,	6310
Pr	5:3	and her **m** is smoother than oil:	2441
Pr	6:12	man, walketh with a froward **m**	6310
Pr	8:7	For my **m** shall speak truth; and	2441
Pr	8:13	way, and the froward **m**, do I hate	6310
Pr	10:11	The **m** of a righteous man is a well	6310
Pr	10:14	but the **m** of the foolish is near	6310
Pr	11:9	An hypocrite with his **m** destroyeth	6310
Pr	13:3	He that keepeth his **m** keepeth his	6310
Pr	14:3	In the **m** of the foolish is a rod of	6310
Pr	16:23	heart of the wise teacheth his **m**,	6310
Pr	18:4	The words of a man's **m** are as	6310
Pr	18:7	A fool's **m** is his destruction, and	6310
Pr	19:24	much as bring it to his **m** again	6310
Pr	20:17	his **m** shall be filled with gravel	6310
Pr	21:23	Whoso keepeth his **m** and his	6310
Pr	22:14	The **m** of strange women is a deep	6310
Pr	26:7	so is a parable in the **m** of fools	6310
Pr	26:15	him to bring it again to his **m**	6310
Pr	26:28	and a flattering **m** worketh ruin	6310

Pr	27:2	praise thee, and not thine own **m**;	6310
Pr	30:20	she eateth, and wipeth her **m**, and	6310
Pr	31:9	Open thy **m**, judge righteously	6310
Pr	31:26	She openeth her **m** with wisdom;	6310
Ecc	5:2	Be not rash with thy **m**, and let not	6310
Ecc	5:6	Suffer not thy **m** to cause thy flesh	6310
Ecc	6:7	All the labour of man is for his **m**,	6310
Ecc	10:12	The words of a wise man's **m** are	6310
SS	5:16	His **m** is most sweet; yea, he is	2441
Isa	5:14	opened her **m** without measure:	6310
Isa	6:7	he laid it upon my **m**, and said, Lo,	6310
Isa	9:17	and every **m** speaketh folly. For	6310
Isa	11:4	the earth with the rod of his **m**,	6310
Isa	29:13	people draw near me with their **m**,	6310
Isa	34:16	for my **m** it hath commanded, and	6310
Isa	40:5	the **m** of the Lord hath spoken it	6310
Isa	45:23	the word is gone out of my **m** in	6310
Isa	53:7	is dumb, so he openeth not his **m**	6310
Isa	53:9	neither was any deceit in his **m**.	6310
Isa	59:21	shall not depart out of thy **m**, nor	6310
Jer	1:9	forth his hand, and touched my **m**.	6310
Jer	1:9	I have put my words in thy **m**.	6310
Jer	23:16	and not out of the **m** of the Lord	6310
Jer	32:4	and shall speak with him **m** to **m**,	6310
Jer	36:4	wrote from the **m** of Jeremiah all	6310
Jer	44:17	thing goeth forth out of our own **m**,	6310
Jer	44:26	be named in the **m** of any man of	6310
La	2:16	have opened their **m** against thee:	6310
La	3:29	He putteth his **m** in the dust; if so	6310
La	3:38	Out of the **m** of the most High	6310
Eze	3:3	and it was in my **m** as honey for	6310
Eze	3:27	I will open thy **m**, and thou shalt	6310
Eze	16:63	and never open thy **m** any more	6310
Eze	33:7	thou shalt hear the word at my **m**,	6310
Eze	33:31	with their **m** they shew much love,	6310
Eze	35:13	Thus with your **m** ye have boasted	6310
Da	3:26	near to the **m** of the burning fiery	8651
Da	4:31	the word was in the king's **m**,	6433
Da	6:17	and laid upon the **m** of the den;	6433
Da	7:5	and it had three ribs in the **m** of it	6433
Da	7:8	and a **m** speaking great things,	6433
Hos	6:5	slain them by the words of my **m**:	6310
Mic	6:12	tongue is deceitful in their **m**	6310
Mic	7:5	keep the doors of thy **m** from her	6310
Zec	8:9	words by the **m** of the prophets,	6310
Mal	2:6	The law of truth was in his **m**, and	6310
Mt	4:4	**proceedeth out of the m of God**	*4750*
Mt	12:34	**of the heart the m speaketh**	*4750*
Mt	15:8	**nigh unto me with their m,**	*4750*
Mt	15:11	**that which cometh out of the m,**	*4750*
Mt	18:16	**the m of two or three witnesses**	*4750*
Mt	21:16	**of the m of babes and sucklings**	*4750*
Lk	1:70	spake by the **m** of his holy prophets,	*4750*
Lk	6:45	**of the heart his m speaketh**	*4750*
Lk	19:22	**thine own m will I judge thee,**	*4750*
Lk	21:15	**I will give you a m and wisdom,**	*4750*
Jn	19:29	upon hyssop, and put it to his **m**	*4750*
Ac	3:18	by the **m** of all his prophets, that	*4750*
Ac	3:21	by the **m** of all his holy prophets	*4750*
Ac	8:32	shearer, so opened he not his **m**:	*4750*
Ro	3:19	that every **m** may be stopped, and	*4750*
Ro	10:9	confess with thy **m** the Lord Jesus,	*4750*
Ro	10:10	and with the **m** confession is made	*4750*
1Co	9:9	shalt not muzzle the **m** of the ox	
2Co	13:1	In the **m** of two or three witnesses	*4750*
Eph	4:29	proceed out of your **m**, but that	*4750*
Col	3:8	communication out of your **m**	*4750*
2Th	2:8	consume with the spirit of his **m**,	*4750*
2Ti	4:17	delivered out of the **m** of the lion	*4750*
Jas	3:10	of the same **m** proceedeth blessing	*4750*
1Pe	2:22	neither was guile found in his **m**:	*4750*
Jude	16	**m** speaketh great swelling words,	*4750*
Rev	1:16	and out of his **m** went a sharp	*4750*
Rev	2:16	**them with the sword of my m**	*4750*
Rev	3:16	**hot, I will spue thee out of my m**	*4750*
Rev	9:19	For their power is in their **m**, and	*4750*
Rev	10:10	it was in my **m** sweet as honey:	*4750*
Rev	11:5	fire proceedeth out of their **m**, and	*4750*
Rev	12:15	cast out of his **m** water as a flood	*4750*
Rev	12:16	earth opened her **m**, and swallowed	*4750*
Rev	12:16	which the dragon cast out of his **m**	*4750*
Rev	13:2	and his **m** as the **m** of a lion: and	*4750*
Rev	13:6	And he opened his **m** in blasphemy	*4750*
Rev	14:5	And in their **m** was found no guile:	*4750*
Rev	16:13	come out of the **m** of the dragon,	*4750*
Rev	16:13	and out of the **m** of the beast,	*4750*
Rev	16:13	out of the **m** of the false prophet	*4750*
Rev	19:15	out of his **m** goeth a sharp sword	*4750*

MOUTHS

Dt	31:21	out of the **m** of their seed: for I	6310
Ps	22:13	They gaped upon me with their **m**,	6310
Ps	115:5	They have **m**, but they speak not:	6310
Ps	135:16	They have **m**, but they speak not;	6310
La	3:46	our enemies have opened their **m**	6310
Da	6:22	angel, and hath shut the lions' **m**,	6433
Heb	11:33	promises, stopped the **m** of lions,	*4750*
Jas	3:3	we put bits in the horses' **m**, that	*4750*
Rev	9:17	and out of their **m** issued fire and	*4750*

MOVE See also **REMOVE.**

Le	11:10	of all that **m** in the waters, and of	8318
2Ki	23:18	alone; let no man **m** his bones	5128
Mt	23:4	**will not m them with one of their**	*2795*
Ac	17:28	in him we live, and **m**, and have	*2795*
Ac	20:24	none of these things **m** me	*3056, 4160*

MOVED See also **REMOVED.**

Ge	1:2	the Spirit of God **m** upon the face	7363
Ge	7:21	And all flesh died that **m** upon the	7430
Dt	32:21	They have **m** me to jealousy with that	
1Sa	1:13	only her lips **m**, but her voice was	5128
2Sa	18:33	the king was much **m**, and went	7264
Ps	10:6	said in his heart, I shall not be **m**:	4131
Ps	15:5	doeth these things shall never be **m**	4131
Ps	16:8	at my right hand, I shall not be **m**	4131
Ps	30:6	I said, I shall never be **m**	4131
Ps	55:22	never suffer the righteous to be **m**	4131
Ps	78:58	**m** him to jealousy with their graven	
Ps	93:1	is stablished, that it cannot be **m**	4131
Ps	99:1	cherubims; let the earth be **m**	5120
Ps	121:3	He will not suffer thy foot to be **m**:	4132
Pr	12:3	of the righteous shall not be **m**.	4131
Isa	14:9	Hell from beneath is **m** for thee	7264
Isa	19:1	the idols of Egypt shall be **m** at	5128
Isa	24:19	the earth is **m** exceedingly	4132
Isa	41:7	with nails, that it should not be **m**	4131
Mt	9:36	was **m** with compassion on them,	*4697*
Mt	18:27	**servant was m with compassion,**	*4697*
Mt	20:24	were **m** with indignation against	*23*
Mk	1:41	Jesus, **m** with compassion, put	*4697*
Mk	6:34	and was **m** with compassion toward	*4697*
Mk	15:11	But the chief priests **m** the people,	*353*

Col 1:23 and be not **m** away from the hope *3334*
1Th 3:3 no man should be **m** by these *4525*
Heb 11:7 By faith Noah, … **m** with fear *2125*
Heb 12:28 a kingdom which cannot be **m**, *761*
2Pe 1:21 they were **m** by the Holy Ghost *5342*
Rev 6:14 every mountain and island were **m** *2795*

MOVEDST
Job 2:3 thou **m** me against him, to destroy 5496

MOVETH See also REMOVETH.
Ge 1:21 and every living creature that **m**, 7430
Ge 1:28 over every living thing that **m** upon 7430
Le 11:46 living creature that **m** in the waters, 7430
Pr 23:31 the cup, when it **m** itself aright 1980

MOVING
Ge 9:3 Every **m** thing that liveth shall be 7430
Pr 16:30 **m** his lips he bringeth evil to 7169
Jn 5:3 waiting for the **m** of the water *2796*

MUCH
Ge 34:12 Ask me never so **m** dowry 3966, 7235
Ge 50:20 this day, to save **m** people alive 7227
Nu 16:3 Ye take too **m** upon you, seeing 7227
1Ki 12:28 It is too **m** for you to go up to 7227
2Ch 33:6 wrought **m** evil in the sight of the 7235
Ps 19:10 than gold, yea, than **m** fine gold: 7227
Pr 7:21 With … **m** fair speech she caused 7230
Pr 15:6 of the righteous is **m** treasure: 7227
Pr 15:11 how **m** more then the hearts of the 637
Pr 16:16 How **m** better is it to get wisdom than
Pr 25:27 It is not good to eat **m** honey: 7235
Ecc 1:18 in **m** wisdom is **m** grief: and he 7230
Ecc 5:12 sweet, whether he eat little or **m**: 7235
Ecc 7:16 Be not righteous over **m**; neither 7235
Ecc 7:17 Be not over **m** wicked, neither be 7235
Ecc 9:18 but one sinner destroyeth **m** good 7235
Ecc 10:18 By **m** slothfulness the building
Ecc 12:12 and **m** study is a weariness of the 7235
SS 4:10 how **m** better is thy love than wine!
Eze 23:32 had in derision; it containeth **m** 4767
Eze 33:31 their mouth they shew **m** love,
Da 7:28 my cogitations **m** troubled me, and 7690
Hag 1:6 Ye have sown **m**, and bring in 7235
Hag 1:9 Ye looked for **m**, and lo, it came to 7235
Mt 6:7 **be heard for their m speaking** *4180*
Mt 6:26 **Are ye not m better than they?** *3123*
Mt 6:30 **shall he not m more clothe you, O** *4183*
Lk 6:3 **Have ye not read so m as this,** *3761*
Lk 6:34 **to sinners, to receive as m again** *2470*
Lk 7:26 **you, and m more than a prophet** *4055*
Lk 7:47 **are forgiven; for she loved m:** *4183*
Lk 8:4 **m** people were gathered together, *4183*
Lk 11:13 **how m more shall your heavenly,** *4214*
Lk 12:19 **m goods laid up for many years;** *4183*
Lk 12:28 **m more will he clothe you, O ye** *4214*
Lk 12:48 **unto whomsoever m is given, of** *4183*
Lk 16:5 **how m owest thou unto my lord?** *4214*
Lk 16:10 **is least is faithful also in m:** *4183*
Lk 18:13 **not lift up so m as his eyes unto** *3761*
Jn 12:24 **if it die, it bringeth forth m fruit** *4183*
Jn 14:30 **I will not talk m with you: for** *4183*
Jn 15:8 **glorified, that ye bear m fruit;** *4183*
Ac 5:8 whether ye sold the land for so **m**? *5118*
Ac 9:13 how **m** evil he hath done to thy *3745*
Ac 14:22 through **m** tribulation enter into *4183*
Ac 16:16 brought her masters **m** gain by *4183*
Ac 18:10 **for I have m people in this city** *4183*
Ac 19:2 have not so **m** as heard whether *3761*
Ac 26:24 **m** learning doth make thee mad. *4183*
Ro 1:15 So, as **m** as in me is, I am ready *3588*
Ro 5:10 **m** more, being reconciled, we shall *4183*
Ro 5:15 **m** more the grace of God, and the *4183*
Ro 5:20 grace did **m** more abound: *5245*
Ro 9:22 endured with **m** longsuffering the *4183*
Ro 12:18 as **m** as lieth in you, live peaceably *3588*
1Th 1:6 received the word in **m** affliction, *4183*
1Ti 3:8 not given to **m** wine, not greedy of *4183*
2Ti 4:14 the coppersmith did me **m** evil: *4183*
Tit 2:3 false accusers, not given to **m** wine, *4183*
Heb 1:4 made so **m** better than the angels, *5118*
Heb 7:22 By so **m** was Jesus made a surety *5118*
Heb 8:6 by how **m** also he is the mediator *3745*
Heb 9:14 How **m** more shall the blood of *4274*
Heb 10:25 so **m** the more, as ye see the day *5118*
Heb 10:29 how **m** sorer punishment, suppose *4214*
Heb 12:9 we not **m** rather be in subjection *4183*
Heb 12:20 if so **m** as a beast touch the *2579*
Heb 12:25 **m** more shall not we escape, if we *4183*
Jas 5:16 of a righteous man availeth **m**. *4183*
1Pe 1:7 being **m** more precious than of gold *4183*
Rev 5:4 I wept **m**, because no man was *4183*
Rev 18:7 How **m** she hath glorified herself, *3745*
Rev 18:7 so **m** torment and sorrow give her: *5118*
Rev 19:1 I heard a great voice of **m** people *4183*

MULE
2Sa 18:9 And Absalom rode upon a **m**, and 6505
1Ki 1:38 to ride upon king David's **m**, 6506
Ps 32:9 ye not as the horse, or as the **m**, 6505

MULES
1Ki 10:25 armour, and spices, horses, and **m**, 6505
1Ki 18:5 to save the horses and the **m** alive, 6505

MULTIPLIED
Ex 1:12 them, the more they **m** and grew 7235
Ex 11:9 my wonders may be **m** in the land 7235
Dt 11:21 That your days may be **m**, and the 7235
Job 27:14 If his children be **m**, it is for the 7235
Job 35:6 or if thy transgressions be **m**, 7231
Pr 9:11 For by me thy days shall be **m**, 7235
Pr 29:16 When the wicked are **m**, 7235
Isa 59:12 our transgressions are **m** before 7231
Eze 16:51 thou hast **m** thine abominations 7235
Eze 35:13 have **m** your words against me: 6280
Hos 12:10 **m** visions, and used similitudes, 7235
Na 3:16 **m** thy merchants above the stars 7235
Ac 6:1 number of the disciples was **m**, *4129*
Ac 6:7 of the disciples **m** in Jerusalem *4129*
Ac 12:24 But the word of God grew and **m**. *4129*

MULTIPLIETH
Job 9:17 and **m** my wounds without cause 7235
Job 34:37 us, and **m** his words against God 7235
Job 35:16 he **m** words without knowledge 3527

MULTIPLY
Ge 1:22 Be fruitful, and **m**, and fill the 7235
Ge 1:28 Be fruitful, and **m**, and replenish 7235
Ge 8:17 be fruitful, and **m** upon the earth 7235
Ge 9:1 Be fruitful, and **m**, and replenish 7235
Ge 22:17 I will **m** thy seed as the stars of the 7235

Ex	1:10	lest they **m**, and it come to pass,	7235
Ex	7:3	**m** my signs and my wonders in the	7235
Ex	32:13	I will **m** your seed as the stars of	7235
Dt	7:13	thee, and bless thee, and **m** thee:	7235
Dt	17:16	he shall not **m** horses to himself,	7235
Dt	28:63	you to do you good, and to **m** you;	7235
Jer	33:22	so will I **m** the seed of David my	7235
Heb	6:14	and multiplying I will **m** thee	*4129*

MULTIPLYING

Ge	22:17	in **m** I will multiply thy seed as	7235
Heb	6:14	thee, and **m** I will multiply thee	*4129*

MULTITUDE

Ge	16:10	it shall not be numbered for **m**.	7230
Ge	32:12	which cannot be numbered for **m**	7230
Ex	23:2	shalt not follow a **m** to do evil;	7227
Le	25:16	According to the **m** of years thou	7230
Dt	1:10	day as the stars of heaven for **m**	7230
Dt	28:62	were as the stars of heaven for **m**:	7230
Jgs	7:12	as the sand by the sea side for **m**.	7230
1Sa	13:5	sand which is on the sea shore in **m**:	7230
1Sa	14:16	and, behold, the **m** melted away	1995
1Ki	3:8	be numbered nor counted for **m**	7230
1Ki	8:5	not be told nor numbered for **m**	7230
2Ch	1:9	like the dust of the earth in **m**.	7227
2Ch	20:24	wilderness, they looked unto the **m**,	1995
Job	32:7	**m** of years should teach wisdom.	7230
Ps	5:7	thy house in the **m** of thy mercy:	7230
Ps	5:10	in the **m** of their transgressions;	7230
Ps	49:6	in the **m** of their riches;	7230
Ps	94:19	In the **m** of my thoughts within	7230
Ps	106:7	not the **m** of thy mercies; but	7230
Pr	10:19	In the **m** of words there wanteth	7230
Pr	11:14	in the **m** of counsellors there is	7230
Pr	14:28	In the **m** of people is the king's	7230
Pr	15:22	in the **m** of counsellors they are	7230
Pr	20:15	There is gold, and a **m** of rubies:	7230
Pr	24:6	in **m** of counsellors there is safety	7230
Ecc	5:3	a fool's voice is known by **m** of	7230
Ecc	5:7	For in the **m** of dreams and many	7230
Isa	1:11	the **m** of your sacrifices unto me?	7230
Isa	13:4	The noise of a **m** in the mountains,	1995
Isa	29:5	the **m** of the terrible ones shall be	1995
Isa	47:12	and with the **m** of thy sorceries,	7230
Isa	47:13	wearied in the **m** of thy counsels.	7230
Jer	10:13	is a **m** of waters in the heavens,	1995
Jer	51:16	is a **m** of waters in the heavens;	527
Eze	14:4	according to the **m** of his idols;	7230
Eze	28:18	by the **m** of thine iniquities, by	7230
Eze	39:11	shall they bury Gog and all his **m**:	1995
Da	10:6	of his words like the voice of a **m**	1995
Hos	9:7	mad, for the **m** of thine iniquity,	7230
Mt	13:34	things spake Jesus unto the **m** in	*3793*
Mt	14:19	he commanded the **m** to sit down	*3793*
Mt	15:32	**I have compassion on the m,**	*3793*
Mt	15:35	he commanded the **m** to sit down	*3793*
Mt	21:11	And the **m** said, This is Jesus the	*3793*
Mt	26:47	with him a great **m** with swords	*3793*
Mt	27:20	**m** that they should ask Barabbas,	*3793*
Mk	7:33	And he took him aside from the **m**	*3793*
Mk	8:2	**I have compassion on the m,**	*3793*
Mk	14:43	with him a great **m** with swords	*3793*
Lk	2:13	a **m** of the heavenly host praising	*4128*
Lk	5:6	they inclosed a great **m** of fishes:	*4128*
Jn	21:6	able to draw it for the **m** of fishes	*4128*
Ac	15:12	Then all the **m** kept silence, and	*4128*
Heb	11:12	many as the stars of the sky in **m**,	*4128*
Jas	5:20	death, and shall hide a **m** of sins.	*4128*
1Pe	4:8	for charity shall cover the **m** of sins	*4128*
Rev	7:9	a great **m**, which no man could	*3793*
Rev	19:6	as it were the voice of a great **m**,	*3793*

MULTITUDES

Joel	3:14	**M, m** in the valley of decision:	1995
Mt	8:18	Jesus saw great **m** about him,	*3793*
Mt	15:30	great **m** came unto him, having	*3793*
Ac	5:14	more added to the Lord, **m** both of	*3793*
Ac	13:45	when the Jews saw the **m**, they	*3793*
Rev	17:15	are peoples, and **m**, and nations,	*3793*

MURDER

Ps	10:8	places doth he **m** the innocent:	2026
Ps	94:6	stranger, and **m** the fatherless.	7523
Jer	7:9	Will ye steal, **m**, and commit	7523
Hos	6:9	company of priests **m** in the way	7523
Mt	19:18	Jesus said, **Thou shalt do no m,**	*5407*
Mk	15:7	committed **m** in the insurrection	*5408*
Ro	1:29	full of envy, **m**, debate, deceit	*5408*

MURDERER

Nu	35:16	the **m** shall surely be put to death.	7523
Nu	35:21	for he is a **m**: the revenger of blood	7523
Nu	35:30	**m** shall be put to death by the	7523
Nu	35:31	no satisfaction for the life of a **m**,	7523
2Ki	6:32	this son of a **m** hath sent to take	7523
Jn	8:44	**He was a m from the beginning,**	*443*
Ac	3:14	desired a **m** to be granted unto	*5406*
Ac	28:4	No doubt this man is a **m**, whom,	*5406*
1Pe	4:15	let none of you suffer as a **m**, or as	*5406*
1Jn	3:15	hateth his brother is a **m**: and ye	*443*
1Jn	3:15	know that no **m** hath eternal life.	*443*

MURDERERS

2Ki	14:6	children of the **m** he slew not:	5221
Isa	1:21	lodged in it; but now **m**	7523
Jer	4:31	my soul is wearied because of **m**.	2026
Mt	22:7	**armies, and destroyed those m**	*5406*
Ac	7:52	been now the betrayers and **m**:	*5406*
Ac	21:38	four thousand men that were **m**?	*4607*
1Ti	1:9	and **m** of mothers, for manslayers,	*3389*
Rev	21:8	and the abominable, and **m**, and	*5406*
Rev	22:15	and whoremongers, and **m**, and	*5406*

MURDERS

Mt	15:19	**heart proceed evil thoughts, m**	*5408*
Mk	7:21	**adulteries, fornications, m,**	*5408*
Gal	5:21	Envyings, **m**, drunkenness,	*5408*
Rev	9:21	Neither repented they of their **m**,	*5408*

MURMUR

Ex	16:7	are we, that ye **m** against us?	3885
Ex	16:8	which ye **m** against him: and	3885
Nu	14:27	congregation which **m** against me?	3885
Nu	14:36	congregation to **m** against him,	3885
Nu	16:11	is Aaron, that ye **m** against him?	3885
Jn	6:43	them, **M not among yourselves**	*1111*
1Co	10:10	Neither **m** ye, as some of them also	*1111*

MURMURED

Ex	16:2	children of Israel **m** against Moses,	3885
Nu	14:2	children of Israel **m** against Moses	3885
Nu	16:41	children of Israel **m** against Moses	3885
Dt	1:27	And ye **m** in your tents, and said,	7279

Isa	29:24	they that **m** shall learn doctrine	7279
Lk	5:30	Pharisees **m** against his disciples,	*1111*
Lk	15:2	And the Pharisees and scribes **m**,	*1234*
Lk	19:7	And when they saw it, they all **m**,	*1234*
Jn	6:61	himself that his disciples **m** at it,	*1111*
Jn	7:32	that the people **m** such things	*1111*
1Co	10:10	as some of them also **m**, and were	*1111*

MURMURERS

Jude	16	These are **m**, complainers	*1113*

MURMURING

Ac	6:1	there arose a **m** of the Grecians	*1112*

MURMURINGS

Ex	16:12	have heard the **m** of the children of	8519
Nu	14:27	have heard the **m** of the children of	8519
Nu	17:10	quite take away their **m** from me,	8519
Php	2:14	Do all things without **m** and	*1112*

MUSIC See **MUSICK.**

MUSICAL

1Ch	16:42	and with **m** instruments of God.	7892
Ne	12:36	with the **m** instruments of David	7892
Ecc	2:8	as **m** instruments, and that of all	7705

MUSICIANS

Rev	18:22	of harpers, and **m**, and of pipers	*3451*

MUSICK

2Ch	7:6	with instruments of **m** of the Lord,	7892
Ecc	12:4	all the daughters of **m** shall be	7892
La	3:63	their rising up; I am their **m**	4485
La	5:14	gate, the young men from their **m**	5058
Da	3:15	dulcimer, and all lands of **m**,	2170
Da	6:18	neither were instruments of **m**	
Am	6:5	instruments of **m**, like David	7892
Lk	15:25	**house, he heard m and dancing**	*4858*

MUSING

Ps	39:3	while I was **m** the fire burned:	1901

MUST

Ge	17:13	**m** needs be circumcised:	
Le	23:6	days ye **m** eat unleavened bread.	
2Sa	23:3	that ruleth over men **m** be just,	
Isa	28:10	For precept **m** be upon precept,	
Jer	10:19	Truly this is a grief, and I **m** bear it.	
Mt	16:21	that he **m** go unto Jerusalem,	*1163*
Mt	18:7	**it m needs be that offences come;**	*318*
Mt	24:6	**all these things m come to pass,**	*1163*
Mt	26:54	**be fulfilled, that thus it m be?**	*1163*
Mk	8:31	Son of man **m** suffer many things	*1163*
Mk	9:12	**man, that he m suffer many,**	
Mk	13:7	**for such things m needs be; but**	*1163*
Mk	13:10	**the gospel m first be published.**	*1163*
Mk	14:49	**but the scriptures m be fulfilled**	*2443*
Lk	2:49	**that I m be about my Father's.**	*1163*
Lk	4:43	**I m preach the kingdom of God.**	*1163*
Lk	9:22	**Son of man m suffer many things,**	*1163*
Lk	13:33	**Nevertheless I m walk today,**	*1163*
Lk	14:18	**and I m needs go and see it:**	*2192*
Lk	17:25	**first m he suffer many things,**	*1163*
Lk	19:5	**for to day I m abide at thy**	*1163*
Lk	21:9	**these things m first come to pass;**	*1163*
Lk	22:7	when the passover **m** be killed.	*1163*
Lk	22:37	**m yet be accomplished in me,**	*1163*
Lk	24:7	Son of man **m** be delivered into	*1163*
Lk	24:44	**all things m be fulfilled, which**	*1163*
Jn	3:7	**unto thee, Ye m be born again**	*1163*
Jn	3:14	**so m the Son of man be lifted up:**	*1163*
Jn	3:30	He **m** increase, but I … decrease.	*1163*
Jn	4:4	he **m** needs go through Samaria.	
Jn	4:24	**m worship him in spirit and in.**	*1163*
Jn	9:4	**I m work the works of him that**	*1163*
Jn	10:16	**them also I m bring, and they.**	*1163*
Jn	12:34	The Son of man **m** be lifted up?	*1163*
Jn	20:9	he **m** rise again from the dead.	*1163*
Ac	1:16	**m** needs have been fulfilled,	*1163*
Ac	3:21	Whom the heaven **m** receive until	*1163*
Ac	4:12	men, whereby we **m** be saved.	*1163*
Ac	9:16	**he m suffer for my name's sake**	*1163*
Ac	16:30	Sirs, what **m** I do to be saved?	*1163*
Ac	17:3	Christ **m** needs have suffered,	*1163*
Ac	18:21	I **m** by all means keep this feast.	*1163*
Ac	19:21	been there, I **m** also see Rome.	*1163*
Ac	23:11	**so m thou bear witness also at**	*1163*
1Co	15:25	For he **m** reign, till he hath put all	*1163*
1Co	15:53	corruptible **m** put on incorruption,	
2Co	5:10	For we **m** all appear before the	*1163*
1Ti	3:7	Moreover he **m** have a good report	*1163*
1Ti	3:8	Likewise **m** the deacons be grave, not	
1Ti	3:11	Even so **m** their wives be grave, not	
2Ti	2:6	laboureth **m** be first partaker of	*1163*
2Ti	2:24	servant of the Lord **m** not strive;	*1163*
Tit	1:7	For a bishop **m** be blameless, as	*1163*
Heb	13:17	as they that **m** give account, that	
1Pe	4:17	judgment **m** begin at the house of	
Rev	1:1	which **m** shortly come to pass;	*1163*
Rev	4:1	thee things which **m** be hereafter	*1163*
Rev	10:11	Thou **m** prophesy again before	*1163*
Rev	11:5	he **m** in this manner be killed.	*1163*
Rev	13:10	sword **m** be killed with the sword.	*1163*
Rev	17:10	he **m** continue a short space.	*1163*
Rev	20:3	after that he **m** be loosed a little	*1163*
Rev	22:6	things which **m** shortly be done	*1163*

MUSTARD

Mt	13:31	**heaven is like a grain of m seed,**	*4615*
Mt	17:20	**have faith as a grain of m seed,**	*4615*
Mk	4:31	**It is like a grain of m seed,**	*4615*
Lk	13:19	**It is like a grain of m seed,**	*4615*
Lk	17:6	**ye had faith as a grain of m seed,**	*4615*

MUSTARD-SEED See **MUSTARD** and **SEED.**

MUTABILITY See **IMMUTABILITY.**

MUTABLE See **IMMUTABLE.**

MUZZLE

Dt	25:4	not **m** the ox when he treadeth	2629
1Co	9:9	not **m** the mouth of the ox that	*5552*
1Ti	5:18	not **m** the ox that treadeth out	*5392*

MYRRH

Est	2:12	six months with oil of **m**, and six	4753
Ps	45:8	thy garments smell of **m**, and aloes,	4753
Pr	7:17	I have perfumed my bed with **m**,	4753
SS	1:13	A bundle of **m** is my well beloved	4753
Mt	2:11	gold, and frankincense, and **m**	*4666*
Mk	15:23	to drink wine mingled with **m**:	*4669*
Jn	19:39	a mixture of **m** and aloes, about	*4666*

MYRTLE

Zec	1:8	he stood among the **m** trees that	1918

MYSELF

Ge	3:10	because I was naked; and I hid **m**	
Ge	22:16	By **m** have I sworn, saith the Lord,	
1Ki	22:30	I will disguise **m**, and enter into the	
Ne	5:7	Then I consulted with **m**, and I	
Job	9:20	If I justify **m**, mine own mouth shall	
Job	42:6	I abhor **m**, and repent in dust and	
Ps	18:23	and I kept **m** from mine iniquity	
Ps	101:2	behave **m** wisely in a perfect way	
Ecc	2:3	in mine heart to give **m** unto wine,	
Ecc	2:12	I turned **m** to behold wisdom, and	
Isa	43:21	This people have I formed for **m**; they	
Mic	6:6	and bow **m** before the high God?	
Jn	5:31	**If I bear witness of m, my witness**	*1683*
Jn	8:28	**he, and that I do nothing of m;**	*1683*
Jn	10:18	**from me, but I lay it down of m**	*1683*
Jn	14:3	**again, and receive you unto m;**	*1683*
Jn	17:19	**for their sakes I sanctify m, that**	*1683*
Ac	20:24	count I my life dear unto **m**, so	*1683*
Ro	7:25	the mind I **m** serve the law of God;	
Ro	9:3	could wish that **m** were accursed	*846*
Ro	11:4	reserved to **m** seven thousand	*1683*
1Co	4:4	For I know nothing by **m**; yet am	*1683*
1Co	9:27	to others, I **m** should be a castaway	

MYSTERIES

Mt	13:11	**the m of the kingdom of heaven,**	*3466*
Lk	8:10	**the m of the kingdom of God:**	*3466*
1Co	4:1	and stewards of the **m** of God	*3466*
1Co	13:2	and understand all **m**, and all	*3466*
1Co	14:2	in the spirit he speaketh **m**.	*3466*

MYSTERY

Mk	4:11	**the m of the kingdom of God:**	*3466*
Ro	16:25	to the revelation of the **m**, which	*3466*
1Co	2:7	speak the wisdom of God in a **m**	*3466*
1Co	15:51	I shew you a **m**; We shall not all	*3466*
Eph	1:9	known unto us the **m** of his will	*3466*
Eph	3:9	what is the fellowship of the **m**,	*3466*
Eph	5:32	This is a great **m**: but I speak	*3466*
Eph	6:19	make known the **m** of the gospel,	*3466*
Col	1:26	even the **m** which hath been hid	*3466*
Col	1:27	glory of this **m** among the Gentiles;	*3466*
Col	2:2	acknowledgment of the **m** of God,	*3466*
2Th	2:7	**m** of iniquity doth already work:	*3466*
1Ti	3:9	Holding the **m** of the faith in a	*3466*
1Ti	3:16	great is the **m** of godliness:	*3466*
Rev	1:20	**The m of the seven stars which**	*3466*
Rev	10:7	the **m** of God should be finished,	*3466*
Rev	17:5	written, **M**, Babylon The Great,	*3466*

N

NAIL
Jgs 4:21 and smote the **n** into his temples,...... 3489
Ezr 9:8 to give us a **n** in his holy place,........ 3489
Isa 22:23 fasten him as a **n** in a sure place;....... 3489
Zec 10:4 out of him the **n**, out of him the....... 3489

NAILING
Col 2:14 out of the way, **n** it to his cross:........ *4338*

NAILS
Dt 21:12 shave her head, and pare her **n**;........ 6856
Ecc 12:11 as **n** fastened by the masters of........ 4930
Isa 41:7 and he fastened it with **n**, that it....... 4548
Jer 10:4 it with **n** and with hammers, that...... 4548
Da 4:33 and his **n** like birds' claws............. 2953
Da 7:19 were of iron, and his **n** of brass;....... 2953
Jn 20:25 my finger into the print of the **n**,...... *2247*

NAKED
Ge 2:25 they were both **n**, the man and........ 6174
Ge 3:7 knew that they were **n**; and they....... 5903
Ge 3:10 I was afraid, because I was **n**;.......... 5903
Ge 3:11 Who told thee that thou wast **n**?....... 5903
Ex 32:25 Moses saw that the people were **n**,..... 6544
1Sa 19:24 lay down **n** all that day and all........ 6174
2Ch 28:15 all that were **n** among them, and...... 4636
Job 1:21 **N** came I out out of my mother's...... 6174
Job 24:7 the **n** to lodge without clothing,....... 6174
Job 26:6 Hell is **n** before him, and............. 6174
Ecc 5:15 **n** shall he return to go as he came,..... 6174
Isa 20:2 he did so, walking **n** and barefoot,..... 6174
Isa 20:4 young and old, **n** and barefoot,........ 6174
Isa 58:7 when thou seest the **n**, that thou...... 6174
La 4:21 and shalt make thyself **n**............. 6168
Eze 16:22 youth, when thou wast **n** and bare,.... 5903
Eze 16:39 jewels, and leave thee **n** and bare....... 5903
Eze 18:7 hath covered the **n** with a garment;.... 5903
Eze 23:29 and shall leave thee **n** and bare:....... 5903
Hos 2:3 Lest I strip her **n**, and set her as....... 6174
Am 2:16 the mighty shall flee away **n** in........ 6174
Mic 1:8 howl, I will go stripped and **n**:........ 6174
Hab 3:9 Thy bow was made quite **n**........... 5783
Mt 25:36 **N, and ye clothed me: I was sick**....... *1131*
Mt 25:43 **n, and ye clothed me not: sick,**........ *1131*
Mk 14:51 linen cloth cast about his **n** body;...... *1131*
Jn 21:7 coat unto him, (for he was **n**,) and..... *1131*
Ac 19:16 out of that house **n** and wounded...... *1131*
1Co 4:11 hunger, and thirst, and are **n**,......... *1130*
2Co 5:3 clothed we shall not be found **n**........ *1131*
Heb 4:13 all things are **n** and opened unto...... *1131*
Jas 2:15 If a brother or sister be **n**, and......... *1131*
Rev 3:17 **and poor, and blind, and n:**........... *1131*
Rev 16:15 lest he walk **n**, and they see his........ *1131*
Rev 17:16 and shall make her desolate and **n**,..... *1131*

NAKEDNESS
Ge 9:22 Canaan, saw the **n** of his father........ 6172
Ge 9:23 and they saw not their father's **n**....... 6172
Ge 42:9 to see the **n** of the land ye are......... 6172
Ex 28:42 them linen breeches to cover their **n**;... 6172
Le 18:6 of kin to him, to uncover their **n**:...... 6172
Le 18:17 not uncover the **n** of a woman and.... 6172
Le 20:11 uncovered his father's **n**: both of....... 6172
Le 20:17 and see her **n**, and she see his **n**;....... 6172
Dt 28:48 hunger, and in thirst, and in **n**,........ 5903
1Sa 20:30 the confusion of thy mother's **n**?...... 6172
Isa 47:3 Thy **n** shall be uncovered, yea, thy..... 6172
La 1:8 because they have seen her **n**: yea,..... 6172
Eze 16:37 them, that they may see all thy **n**...... 6172
Eze 22:10 they discovered their father's **n**:....... 6172
Eze 23:29 the **n** of thy whoredoms shall be....... 6172
Hos 2:9 and my flax given to cover her **n**....... 6172
Na 3:5 and I will shew the nations thy **n**,...... 4626
Hab 2:15 that thou mayest look on their **n**!...... 4589
Ro 8:35 famine, or **n**, or peril, or sword?....... *1132*
2Co 11:27 in fastings often, in cold and **n**........ *1132*
Rev 3:18 **the shame of thy n do not appear;**..... *1132*

NAME See also **SURNAME.**
Ge 2:19 creature, that was the **n** thereof........ 8034
Ge 3:20 And Adam called his wife's **n** Eve;..... 8034
Ge 5:2 and called their **n** Adam, in the........ 8034
Ge 11:4 and let us make us a **n**, lest we be...... 8034
Ge 11:9 is the **n** of it called Babel; because..... 8034
Ge 12:2 bless thee, and make thy **n** great;...... 8034
Ge 12:8 and called upon the **n** of the Lord...... 8034
Ge 16:13 she called the **n** of the Lord that....... 8034
Ge 17:5 but thy **n** shall be Abraham;.......... 8034
Ge 17:15 Sarai, but Sarah shall her **n** be......... 8034
Ge 21:33 called there on the **n** of the Lord...... 8034
Ge 26:25 called upon the **n** of the Lord, and..... 8034
Ge 32:28 **n** shall be called no more Jacob,....... 8034
Ge 35:10 Jacob, but Israel shall be thy **n**:........ 8034
Ex 3:13 shall say to me, What is his **n**?......... 8034
Ex 3:15 this is my **n** for ever, and this is........ 8034
Ex 5:23 I came to Pharaoh to speak in thy **n**,... 8034
Ex 6:3 by my **n** Jehovah was I not known..... 8034
Ex 9:16 and that my **n** may be declared........ 8034
Ex 20:7 the **n** of the Lord thy God in vain;..... 8034
Ex 20:7 guiltless that taketh his **n** in vain....... 8034
Ex 20:24 in all places where I record my **n** I..... 8034
Ex 23:13 no mention of the **n** of other gods,.... 8034
Ex 28:21 every one with his **n** shall they be...... 8034
Ex 33:17 in my sight, and I know thee by **n**..... 8034
Ex 34:5 and proclaimed the **n** of the Lord...... 8034
Ex 34:14 the Lord, whose **n** is Jealous, is a....... 8034
Le 19:12 ye shall not swear by my **n** falsely...... 8034
Le 22:32 Neither shall ye profane my holy **n**;.... 8034
Nu 17:2 thou every man's **n** upon his rod....... 8034
Nu 27:4 the **n** of our father be done away...... 8034
Dt 5:11 the **n** of the Lord thy God in vain:..... 8034
Dt 6:13 serve him, and shalt swear by his **n**.... 8034
Dt 10:8 and to bless in his **n**, unto this day..... 8034
Dt 12:11 to cause his **n** to dwell there;.......... 8034
Dt 18:5 to minister in the **n** of the Lord,....... 8034
Dt 18:20 presume to speak a word in my **n**,..... 8034
Dt 18:22 speaketh in the **n** of the Lord, if....... 8034
Dt 22:14 bring up an evil **n** upon her, and...... 8034
Dt 28:58 fear this glorious and fearful **n**,........ 8034
Dt 29:20 blot out his **n** from under heaven...... 8034
Jos 7:9 what wilt thou do unto thy great **n**?.... 8034
Jos 23:7 make mention of the **n** of their gods,.. 8034
Jgs 13:18 Why askest thou thus after my **n**,...... 8034
Ru 4:5 to raise up the **n** of the dead upon..... 8034
Ru 4:14 that his **n** may be famous in Israel...... 8034
1Sa 17:45 to thee in the **n** of the Lord of hosts,... 8034
1Sa 24:21 wilt not destroy my **n** out of my....... 8034

2Sa	7:9	like unto the **n** of the great men	8034
2Sa	7:13	He shall build an house for my **n**,	8034
1Ki	1:47	God make the **n** of Solomon better	8034
1Ki	8:20	an house for the **n** of the Lord God	8034
1Ki	8:43	people of the earth may know thy **n**,	8034
1Ki	11:36	have chosen me to put my **n** there	8034
1Ki	18:24	and I will call on the **n** of the Lord:	8034
1Ki	18:25	call on the **n** of your gods, but put	8034
1Ki	21:8	So she wrote letters in Ahab's **n**,	8034
2Ki	23:27	which I said, My **n** shall be there	8034
1Ch	13:6	cherubims, whose **n** is called on it.	8034
1Ch	16:29	the Lord the glory due unto his **n**:	8034
1Ch	17:8	thee a **n** like the **n** of the great men	8034
1Ch	17:21	to make thee a **n** of greatness and	8034
1Ch	22:9	for his **n** shall be Solomon, and I	8034
2Ch	2:4	build an house to the **n** of the Lord	8034
2Ch	6:20	that thou wouldest put thy **n** there;	8034
2Ch	6:26	and confess thy **n**, and turn from	8034
2Ch	26:15	And his **n** spread far abroad; for	8034
2Ch	33:4	Jerusalem shall my **n** be for ever	8034
2Ch	33:18	spake to him in the **n** of the Lord	8034
Ezr	5:1	in the **n** of the God of Israel, even	8036
Ezr	6:12	hath caused his **n** to dwell there	8036
Ne	1:9	I have chosen to set my **n** there.	8034
Ne	1:11	servants, who desire to fear thy **n**:	8034
Ne	9:5	and blessed be thy glorious **n**,	8034
Ps	5:11	them also that love thy **n** be joyful	8034
Ps	8:1	excellent is thy **n** in all the earth!	8034
Ps	29:2	the Lord the glory due unto his **n**;	8034
Ps	33:21	we have trusted in his holy **n**.	8034
Ps	44:20	we have forgotten the **n** of our God,	8034
Ps	54:1	Save me, O God, by thy **n**, and	8034
Ps	68:4	upon the heavens by his **n** Jah.	8034
Ps	69:36	that love his **n** shall dwell therein	8034
Ps	75:1	thy **n** is near thy wondrous works.	8034
Ps	83:18	thou, whose **n** alone is Jehovah,	8034
Ps	86:11	truth: unite my heart to fear thy **n**	8034
Ps	96:8	the Lord the glory due unto his **n**:	8034
Ps	103:1	that is within me, bless his holy **n**.	8034
Ps	113:3	same the Lord's **n** is to be praised.	8034
Ps	115:1	but unto thy **n** give glory, for thy	8034
Ps	124:8	Our help is in the **n** of the Lord,	8034
Ps	135:13	Thy **n**, O Lord, endureth for ever;	8034
Ps	148:13	for his **n** alone is excellent; his.	8034
Pr	10:7	but the **n** of the wicked shall rot.	8034
Pr	18:10	**n** of the Lord is a strong tower:	8034
Pr	22:1	A good **n** is rather to be chosen	8034
Pr	30:4	is his **n**, and what is his son's **n**,	8034
Pr	30:9	and take the **n** of my God in vain.	8034
Ecc	7:1	A good **n** is better than precious	8034
Isa	7:14	son, and shall call his **n** Immanuel	8034
Isa	9:6	his **n** shall be called Wonderful,	8034
Isa	25:1	will exalt thee, I will praise thy **n**;	8034
Isa	30:27	the **n** of the Lord cometh from far,	8034
Isa	42:8	I am the Lord: that is my **n**: and	8034
Isa	48:11	for how should my **n** be polluted? and	
Isa	50:10	let him trust in the **n** of the Lord,	8034
Isa	51:15	roared: The Lord of hosts is his **n**.	8034
Isa	54:5	the Lord of hosts is his **n**; and thy	8034
Isa	56:5	I will give them an everlasting **n**,	8034
Isa	57:15	eternity, whose **n** is Holy; I dwell	8034
Isa	63:16	redeemer; thy **n** is from everlasting	8034
Isa	65:1	nation that was not called by my **n**	8034
Isa	66:22	shall your seed and your **n** remain	8034
Jer	10:16	The Lord of hosts is his **n**	8034
Jer	11:21	Prophesy not in the **n** of the Lord,	8034
Jer	16:21	shall know that my **n** is The Lord.	8034
Jer	20:9	him, nor speak any more in his **n**.	8034
Jer	23:6	his **n** whereby he shall be called,	8034
Jer	23:27	to forget my **n** by their dreams	8034
Jer	27:15	yet they prophesy a lie in my **n**;	8034
Jer	31:35	roar; The Lord of hosts is his **n**:	8034
Jer	32:18	God, The Lord of hosts, is his **n**,	8034
Jer	32:34	the house which is called by my **n**,	8034
Jer	34:16	But ye turned and polluted my **n**,	8034
Jer	50:34	strong; the Lord of hosts is his **n**:	8034
Jer	51:19	the Lord of hosts is his **n**	8034
La	3:55	I called upon thy **n**, O Lord, out of.	8034
Eze	36:23	I will sanctify my great **n**, which	8034
Eze	43:7	my holy **n**, shall the house of Israel	8034
Da	2:20	Blessed be the **n** of God for ever	8036
Joel	2:26	praise the **n** of the Lord your God	8034
Am	4:13	Lord, The God of hosts, is his **n**	8034
Am	5:8	of the earth: The Lord is his **n**:	8034
Am	6:10	make mention of the **n** of the Lord	8034
Mic	4:5	we will walk in the **n** of the Lord	8034
Zec	6:12	the man whose **n** is The Branch;	8034
Zec	13:9	they shall call on my **n**, and I will	8034
Zec	14:9	there be one Lord, and his **n** one	8034
Mal	1:14	and my **n** is dreadful among the	8034
Mal	3:16	Lord, and that thought upon his **n**.	8034
Mal	4:2	But unto you that fear my **n** shall	8034
Mt	1:21	and thou shalt call his **n** Jesus	*3686*
Mt	1:23	they shall call his **n** Emmanuel,	*3686*
Mt	6:9	**art in heaven, Hallowed by thy n**	*3686*
Mt	7:22	**have we not prophesied in thy n**	*3686*
Mt	10:41	**a prophet in the n of a prophet**	*3686*
Mt	12:21	in his **n** shall the Gentiles trust	*3686*
Mt	18:5	**one such little child in my n**	*3686*
Mt	23:39	**that cometh in the n of the Lord.**	*3686*
Mt	24:5	**many shall come in my n, saying,**	*3686*
Mt	28:19	**them in the n of the Father, and**	*3686*
Mk	5:9	My **n** is Legion: for we are many.	*3686*
Mk	6:14	(for his **n** was spread abroad:) and	*3686*
Mk	9:41	**a cup of water to drink in my n,**	*3686*
Mk	11:10	that cometh in the **n** of the Lord:	*3686*
Mk	13:6	**many shall come in my n, saying,**	*3686*
Lk	1:13	son, and thou shalt call his **n** John.	*3686*
Lk	1:27	David; and the virgin's **n** was Mary.	*3686*
Lk	1:31	a son, and shalt call his **n** Jesus.	*3686*
Lk	1:63	and wrote, saying, His **n** is John.	*3686*
Lk	9:48	**this child in my n receiveth me.**	*3686*
Lk	10:17	are subject unto us through thy **n**.	*3686*
Lk	11:2	**art in heaven, Hallowed be thy n**	*3686*
Lk	13:35	**that cometh in the n of the Lord**	*3686*
Lk	21:8	**many shall come in my n, saying,**	*3686*
Lk	24:47	**be preached in his n among all**	*3686*
Jn	1:12	even to them that believe on his **n**:	*3686*
Jn	3:18	**not believed in the n of the only**	*3686*
Jn	5:43	**I am come in my Father's n, and**	*3686*
Jn	10:3	**he calleth his own sheep by n,**	*3686*
Jn	12:28	**Father, glorify thy n.** Then came	*3686*
Jn	14:13	**whatsoever ye shall ask in my n,**	*3686*
Jn	14:14	**If ye shall ask any thing in my n,**	*3686*
Jn	15:16	**shall ask of the Father in my n,**	*3686*
Jn	16:23	**shall ask the Father in my n, he**	*3686*
Jn	16:26	**At that day ye shall ask in my n:**	*3686*
Jn	17:6	**manifested thy n unto the men**	*3686*
Jn	17:11	**keep through thine own n those.**	*3686*
Jn	17:26	**I have declared unto them thy n,**	*3686*
Jn	20:31	ye might have life through his **n**	*3686*
Ac	2:21	shall call on the **n** of the Lord shall.	*3686*

Ac 3:16 his **n** through faith in his **n** hath *3686*
Ac 4:12 there is none other **n** under heaven *3686*
Ac 4:18 at all nor teach in the **n** of Jesus *3686*
Ac 5:41 worthy to suffer shame for his **n** *3686*
Ac 9:15 **to bear my n before the Gentiles,** *3686*
Ac 10:48 to be baptized in the **n** of the Lord *3686*
Ac 19:5 baptized in the **n** of the Lord Jesus *3686*
Ac 19:17 **n** of the Lord Jesus was magnified *3686*
Ac 26:9 things contrary to the **n** of Jesus of *3686*
Ro 2:24 the **n** of God is blasphemed among *3686*
Ro 9:17 and that my **n** might be declared *3686*
Ro 10:13 shall call upon the **n** of the Lord *3686*
1Co 6:11 in the **n** of the Lord Jesus, and by *3686*
Eph 1:21 and every **n** that is named, not *3686*
Php 2:9 him a **n** which is above every **n**: *3686*
Php 2:10 That at the **n** of Jesus every knee *3686*
Col 3:17 do all in the **n** of the Lord Jesus, *3686*
2Ti 2:19 one that nameth the **n** of Christ *3686*
Heb 1:4 a more excellent **n** than they *3686*
Jas 5:10 have spoken in the **n** of the Lord, *3686*
Jas 5:14 him with oil in the **n** of the Lord: *3686*
1Jn 3:23 believe on the **n** of his Son Jesus *3686*
1Jn 5:13 believe on the **n** of the Son of God; *3686*
1Jn 5:13 believe on the **n** of the Son of God *3686*
Rev 2:17 **and in the stone a new n written,** *3686*
Rev 3:5 **not blot out his n out of the book** *3686*
Rev 3:5 **confess his n before my Father,** *3686*
Rev 6:8 his **n** that sat on him was Death, *3686*
Rev 8:11 **n** of the star is called Wormwood: *3686*
Rev 9:11 Greek tongue hath his **n** Apollyon *3686*
Rev 13:1 upon his heads the **n** of blasphemy *3686*
Rev 13:17 the beast, or the number of his **n** *3686*
Rev 14:11 receiveth the mark of his **n**, *3686*
Rev 17:5 upon her forehead was a **n** written, *3686*
Rev 19:12 and he had a **n** written, that no *3686*
Rev 19:13 his **n** is called The Word of God. *3686*
Rev 19:16 and on his thigh a **n** written, King *3686*
Rev 22:4 his **n** shall be in their foreheads *3686*

NAMED See also SURNAMED.

Isa 61:6 be **n** the Priests of the Lord: 7121
Ro 15:20 gospel, not where Christ was **n**, *3687*
1Co 5:1 so much as **n** among the Gentiles, *3687*
Eph 1:21 and every man that is **n**, not only *3687*
Eph 3:15 family in heaven and earth is **n**, *3687*
Eph 5:3 let it not be once **n** among you, *3687*

NAMELY

Ecc 5:13 **n**, riches kept for the owners thereof
Mk 12:31 **And the second is like, n this, Thou**
Ro 13:9 **n**, Thou shalt love thy neighbour *1722*

NAME'S

1Sa 12:22 his people for his great **n** sake: 8034
Ps 23:3 of righteousness for his **n** sake 8034
Ps 25:11 For thy **n** sake, O Lord, pardon 8034
Ps 79:9 away our sins, for thy **n** sake 8034
Ps 143:11 Quicken me, O Lord, for thy **n** sake: 8034
Isa 48:9 For my **n** sake will I defer mine 8034
Jer 14:21 Do not abhor us, for thy **n** sake, 8034
Eze 36:22 but for mine holy **n** sake, which ye 8034
Mt 10:22 **hated of all men for my n sake:** *3686*
Mt 19:29 **children, or lands, for my n sake,** *3686*
Mt 24:9 **of all nations for my n sake.** *3686*
Mk 13:13 **be hated of all men for my n sake:** *3686*
Lk 21:12 **kings and rulers for my n sake.** *3686*
Jn 15:21 **they do unto you for my n sake,** *3686*
Ac 9:16 **he must suffer for my n sake.** *3686*
1Jn 2:12 are forgiven you for his **n** sake, *3686*
Rev 2:3 **and for my n sake hast laboured,** *3686*

NAMES

Ge 2:20 Adam gave **n** to all cattle, and to 8034
Ex 1:1 are the **n** of the children of Israel, 8034
Ex 28:11 with the **n** of the children of Israel: 8034
Nu 1:18 according to the number of the **n**. 8034
Nu 13:16 **n** of the men which Moses sent 8034
2Sa 23:8 These be the **n** of the mighty men 8034
Ps 147:4 he calleth them all by their **n**. 8034
Isa 40:26 he calleth them all by **n** by the 8034
Lk 10:20 **your n are written in heaven** *3686*
Ac 18:15 if it be a question of words and **n**, *3686*
Php 4:3 whose **n** are in the book of life *3686*
Rev 3:4 **hast a few n even in Sardis which** *3686*
Rev 13:8 whose **n** are not written in the *3686*
Rev 17:8 whose **n** were not written in the *3686*
Rev 21:12 are the **n** of the twelve tribes of the
Rev 21:14 them the **n** of the twelve apostles *3686*

NAMETH

2Ti 2:19 one that **n** the name of Christ *3687*

NAPKIN

Jn 20:7 And the **n**, that was about his head, *4676*

NARROW

Nu 22:26 further, and stood in a **n** place, 6862
Pr 23:27 and a strange woman is a **n** pit. 6862
Isa 49:19 even now be too **n** by reason of 3334
Mt 7:14 **is the gate, and n is the way,** *2346*

NATION See also NATIONS.

Ge 12:2 I will make of thee a great **n**, and 1471
Ge 17:20 and I will make him a great **n** 1471
Ge 18:18 become a great and mighty **n**, and 1471
Ge 20:4 wilt thou slay also a righteous **n**? 1471
Ge 21:18 for I will make him a great **n**. 1471
Ge 46:3 I will there make of thee a great **n**: 1471
Ex 19:6 kingdom of priests, and an holy **n** 1471
Dt 4:7 what **n** is there so great, who hath 1471
Dt 28:50 A **n** of fierce countenance, which 1471
2Sa 7:23 what one **n** in the earth is like thy 1471
1Ki 18:10 there is no **n** or kingdom, whither 1471
2Ki 17:29 every **n** made gods of their own, 1471
1Ch 17:21 what one **n** in the earth is like thy 1471
Ps 33:12 Blessed is the **n** whose God is the 1471
Pr 14:34 Righteousness exalteth a **n**: but 1471
Isa 1:4 Ah sinful **n**, a people laden with 1471
Isa 2:4 **n** shall not lift up sword against **n**, 1471
Isa 26:2 that the righteous **n** which keepeth 1471
Isa 55:5 shalt call a **n** that thou knowest 1471
Isa 65:1 **n** that was not called by my name 1471
Jer 2:11 Hath a **n** changed their gods, which 1471
Jer 5:9 my soul be avenged on such a **n** as 1471
Jer 5:15 I will bring a **n** upon you from far, 1471
Jer 5:29 my soul be avenged on such a **n** as 1471
Jer 18:8 If that **n**, against whom I have 1471
Jer 27:8 that **n** will I punish, saith the Lord, 1471
La 4:17 watched for a **n** that could not save 1471
Da 3:29 every people, **n**, and language, 524
Mic 4:3 **n** shall not lift … sword against **n**, 1471
Hag 2:14 So is this people, and so is this **n** 1471
Mal 3:9 have robbed me, even this whole **n** 1471
Mt 21:43 **to a n bringing forth the fruits** *1484*

N

Mt	24:7	**For n shall rise against n, and**	*1484*
Mk	13:8	**For n shall rise against n, and**	*1484*
Lk	21:10	unto then, **N shall rise against n,**	*1484*
Lk	23:2	found this fellow perverting the **n**,	*1484*
Jn	11:50	and that the whole **n** perish not.	*1484*
Jn	11:51	that Jesus should die for that **n**;	*1484*
Jn	18:35	Thine own **n** and the chief priests	*1484*
Ac	2:5	men, out of every **n** under heaven	*1484*
Ac	10:35	in every **n** he that feareth him,	*1484*
Ro	10:19	and by a foolish **n** I will anger you.	*1484*
Php	2:15	of a crooked and perverse **n**,	*1074*
1Pe	2:9	an holy **n**, a peculiar people;	*1484*
Rev	5:9	and tongue, and people, and **n**;	*1484*
Rev	14:6	every **n**, and kindred, and tongue,	*1484*

NATIONS

Ge	10:32	were the **n** divided in the earth	1471
Ge	17:5	father of many **n** have I made thee.	1471
Ge	18:18	the **n** of earth shall be blessed	1471
Ge	22:18	all the **n** of the earth be blessed;	1471
Ge	25:16	twelve princes according to their **n**;	523
Ge	25:23	Two **n** are in thy womb, and two	1471
Ge	26:4	all the **n** of the earth be blessed;	1471
Dt	2:25	the **n** that are under the whole	5971
Dt	4:6	understanding … the sight of the **n**,	5971
Dt	12:30	How did these **n** serve their gods?	1471
Dt	17:14	like as all the **n** that are about me;	1471
Dt	19:1	Lord thy God hath cut off the **n**,	1471
Dt	29:18	to go and serve the gods of these **n**;	1471
Dt	32:8	the Most High divided to the **n** their	1471
Dt	32:43	Rejoice, O ye **n**, with his people:	1471
Jos	23:13	no more drive out any of these **n**	1471
1Sa	8:5	a king to judge us like all the **n**	1471
2Sa	8:11	dedicated of all **n** which he subdued;	1471
1Ki	14:24	to all the abominations of the **n**	1471
2Ki	18:33	of the gods of the **n** delivered at all	1471
1Ch	14:17	brought the fear of him upon all **n**.	1471
1Ch	16:31	and let men say among the **n**, The	1471
2Ch	7:20	and a byword among all **n**.	5971
2Ch	32:13	the gods of the **n** of those lands	1471
Ezr	4:10	the rest of the **n** whom the great.	524
Ne	1:8	scatter you abroad among the **n**:	5971
Ne	13:26	among many **n** was there no king	1471
Ps	9:17	hell, and all the **n** that forget God.	1471
Ps	22:28	he is the governor among the **n**	1471
Ps	66:7	for ever; his eyes behold the **n**:	1471
Ps	67:4	let the **n** be glad and sing for joy:	3816
Ps	72:17	in him: all **n** shall call him blessed	1471
Ps	96:5	all the gods of the **n** are idols:	5971
Ps	113:4	The Lord is high above all **n**, and	1471
Ps	118:10	All **n** compassed me about: but in	1471
Pr	24:24	people curse, **n** shall abhor him:	3816
Isa	2:4	And he shall judge among the **n**,	1471
Isa	13:4	kingdoms of **n** gathered together:	1471
Isa	17:13	The **n** shall rush like the rushing of	3816
Isa	37:12	Have the gods of the **n** delivered.	1471
Isa	40:15	the **n** are as a drop of a bucket,	1471
Isa	40:17	All **n** before him are as nothing;	1471
Isa	55:5	**n** that knew not thee shall run	1471
Isa	64:2	the **n** may tremble at thy presence!.	1471
Jer	1:5	ordained thee a prophet unto the **n**	1471
Jer	1:10	have this day set thee over the **n**	1471
Jer	10:7	would not fear thee, O King of **n**?	1471
Jer	10:10	and the **n** shall not be able to abide	1471
Jer	25:11	and these **n** shall serve the king.	1471
Jer	25:17	and made all the **n** to drink, unto.	1471
Jer	25:31	Lord hath a controversy with the **n**,	1471
Jer	28:11	of Babylon from the neck of all **n**.	1471
Jer	29:14	I will gather you from all the **n**,	1471
Jer	51:7	her wine; therefore the **n** are mad.	1471
La	1:1	that she was great among the **n**,	1471
Eze	5:6	into wickedness more than the **n**,	1471
Eze	5:14	a reproach among the **n** that are.	1471
Eze	31:6	under his shadow dwelt all great **n**.	1471
Da	5:19	him, all people, **n**, and languages	524
Hos	9:17	shall be wanderers among the **n**	1471
Mic	4:2	many **n** shall come, and say, Come,	1471
Na	3:5	I will shew the **n** thy nakedness.	1471
Hab	2:8	thou hast spoiled many **n**, all the	1471
Hag	2:7	and the desire of all **n** shall come:	1471
Zec	2:11	many **n** shall be joined to the Lord.	1471
Zec	8:22	**n** shall come to seek the Lord of.	1471
Zec	12:9	**n** that come against Jerusalem	1471
Zec	14:2	gather all **n** against Jerusalem to.	1471
Mal	3:12	all **n** shall call you blessed: for ye	1471
Mt	24:9	**ye shall be hated of all n for my**	*1484*
Mt	24:14	**world for a witness unto all n;**	*1484*
Mt	25:32	**before him shall be gathered all n:**	*1484*
Mt	28:19	**Go ye therefore, and teach all n,**	*1484*
Mk	11:17	**called of all n the house of prayer?**	*1484*
Mk	13:10	**first be published among all n**	*1484*
Lk	12:30	**do the n of the world seek after:**	*1484*
Lk	21:24	**be led away captive into all n:**	*1484*
Lk	21:25	**and upon the earth distress of n,**	*1484*
Lk	24:47	**preached in his name among all n,**	*1484*
Ac	13:19	when he had destroyed seven **n** in	*1484*
Ac	14:16	all **n** to walk in their own ways	*1484*
Ac	17:26	made of one blood all **n** of men	*1484*
Ro	4:18	become the father of many **n**,	*1484*
Gal	3:8	In thee shall all **n** be blessed	*1484*
Rev	2:26	**him will I give power over the n.**	*1484*
Rev	7:9	no man could number, of all **n**,	*1484*
Rev	11:9	and **n** shall see their dead bodies.	*1484*
Rev	12:5	was to rule all **n** with a rod of iron:	*1484*
Rev	14:8	she made all **n** drink of the wine	*1484*
Rev	15:4	for all **n** shall come and worship.	*1484*
Rev	16:19	parts, and the cities of the **n** fell:	*1484*
Rev	18:3	For all **n** have drunk of the wine.	*1484*
Rev	18:23	thy sorceries were all **n** deceived	*1484*
Rev	19:15	that with it he should smite the **n**:	*1484*
Rev	20:3	he should deceive the **n** no more	*1484*
Rev	21:24	And the **n** of them which are saved	*1484*
Rev	21:26	glory and honour of the **n** into it	*1484*
Rev	22:2	tree were for the healing of the **n**	*1484*

NATIVE

Jer	22:10	no more, nor see his **n** country.	4138

NATURAL

Ro	1:26	women did change the **n** use into.	*5446*
Ro	1:27	leaving the **n** use of the woman,	*5446*
Ro	1:31	without **n** affection, implacable,	
Ro	11:21	spared not the **n** branches,	*2596, 5449*
1Co	2:14	But the **n** man receiveth not the	*5591*
1Co	15:44	It is sown a **n** body; it is raised a	*5591*
2Ti	3:3	Without **n** affection, trucebreakers,	
Jas	1:23	beholding his **n** face in a glass:	*1083*
2Pe	2:12	But these, as **n** brute beasts, made	*5446*

NATURALLY

Php	2:20	who will **n** care for your state	*1103*
Jude	10	what they know **n**, as brute beasts,	*5447*

NATURE

Ro	1:26	use into that which is against **n**:	*5449*
Ro	2:14	do by **n** the things contained in the	*5449*
Ro	2:27	not uncircumcision which is by **n**,	*5449*
Ro	11:24	of the olive tree which is wild by **n**,	*5449*
1Co	11:14	Doth not even **n** itself teach you,	*5449*
Gal	2:15	We who are Jews by **n**, and not	*5449*
Gal	4:8	unto them which by **n** are no gods	*5449*
Eph	2:3	were by **n** the children of wrath,	*5449*
Heb	2:16	he took not on him the **n** of angels;	
Jas	3:6	and setteth on fire the course of **n**;	*1078*
2Pe	1:4	be partakers of the divine **n**,	*5449*

NAUGHT See also NOTHING; NOUGHT.

Pr	20:14	It is **n**, it is **n**, saith the buyer:	7451

NAUGHTINESS

1Sa	17:28	pride, and the **n** of thine heart;	7455
Jas	1:21	all filthiness and superfluity of **n**,	*2549*

NAUGHTY

Pr	6:12	A **n** person, a wicked man	1100
Pr	17:4	a liar giveth ear to a **n** tongue	1942

NAVEL

Pr	3:8	It shall be health to thy **n**, and	8270
SS	7:2	Thy **n** is like a round goblet,	8326

NAVY

1Ki	9:26	King Solomon made a **n** of ships	590
1Ki	10:22	once in three years came the **n** of	590

NAY See also NO.

Ge	18:15	he said, **N**; but thou didst laugh	3808
Ge	19:2	And they said, **N**: but we will	3808
Ge	42:12	**N**, but to see the nakedness of	3808
Jgs	19:23	**N**, my brethren, ... pray you, do	408
1Sa	8:19	**N**; but we will have a king over	3808
1Sa	12:12	**N**; but a king shall reign over us:	3808
2Sa	13:12	**N**, my brother, do not force me;	408
1Ki	2:30	he said, **N**; but I will die here	3808
Mt	5:37	**be, Yea, yea; N, n:**	*3756*
Lk	12:51	**I tell you, N; but rather division:**	*3780*
Lk	13:3	**you, N: but, except ye repent,**	*3780*
Ro	7:7	**N**, I had not known sin, but by the	*235*
Ro	8:37	**N**, in all these things we are more	*235*
2Co	1:17	there should be yea yea, and **n n**?	*3756*
Jas	5:12	your yea be yea; and your **n**, **n**;	*3756*

NEAR See also NEARER; NEXT; NIGH.

Ge	19:20	this city is **n** to flee unto, and it is	7138
Ge	27:21	unto Jacob, Come **n**, I pray thee,	5066
Ex	14:20	the one came not **n** the other all	7126
Ex	20:21	drew **n** unto the thick darkness	5066
Le	18:6	to any that is **n** of kin to him, to	7607
Nu	16:9	to bring you **n** to himself to do	7138
Jos	3:4	come not **n** unto it, that ye may	7126
Ru	2:20	The man is **n** of kin unto us, one	7138
1Sa	17:40	and he drew **n** to the Philistine	5066
Est	5:2	So Esther drew **n**, and touched	7126
Ps	73:28	is good for me to draw **n** to God:	7132
Pr	7:8	through the street **n** her corner;	681
Pr	10:14	of the foolish is **n** destruction	7138
Pr	27:10	for better is a neighbour that is **n**	7138
Isa	26:17	**n** the time of her delivery, is in	7126
La	4:18	our end is **n**, our days are fulfilled;	7126
Eze	7:7	is come, the day of trouble is **n**	7138
Eze	30:3	the day of the Lord is **n**, a cloudy	7138
Am	6:3	the seat of violence to come **n**;	5066
Ob	15	day of the Lord is **n** upon all the	7138
Zep	1:14	great day of the Lord is **n**, it is **n**,	7138
Mt	24:33	**these things, know that it is n,**	*1451*
Mk	13:28	**leaves, ye know that summer is n:**	*1451*
Lk	21:8	**the time draweth n: go ye not**	*1448*
Lk	22:47	drew **n** unto Jesus to kiss him	*1448*
Heb	10:22	Let us draw **n** with a true heart	*4334*

NEARER

Ru	3:12	there is a kinsman **n** than I	7138
Ro	13:11	is our salvation **n** than when we	*1452*

NECESSARY

Job	23:12	his mouth more than my **n** food	2706
1Co	12:22	seem to be more feeble, are **n**	*316*
Tit	3:14	maintain good works for **n** uses,	*316*
Heb	9:23	was therefore **n** that the patterns	*318*

NECESSITY

Lk	23:17	(For of **n** he must release one	*2192, 318*
Ro	12:13	Distributing to the **n** of saints	*5532*
1Co	7:37	stedfast in his heart, having no **n**,	*318*
1Co	9:16	for **n** is laid upon me; yea, woe is	*318*
2Co	9:7	not grudgingly, or of **n**: for God	*318*
Phm	14	not be as it were of **n**, but willingly	*318*
Heb	7:12	there is made of **n** a change also	*318*
Heb	9:16	there must also of **n** be the death	*318*

NECK See also STIFFNECKED.

Ge	33:4	and fell on his **n**, and kissed him:	6677
Ge	41:42	and put a gold chain about his **n**;	6677
Ge	46:29	fell on his **n**, and he wept on his **n**	6677
2Ki	17:14	like to the **n** of their fathers, that	6203
Pr	3:3	bind them about thy **n**; write	1621
Pr	6:21	heart, and tie them about thy **n**	1621
Pr	29:1	often reproved hardeneth his **n**,	6203
Isa	48:4	and thy **n** is an iron sinew, and	6203
Jer	7:26	their ear, but hardened their **n**	6202
Jer	17:23	their ear, but made their **n** stiff,	6202
Jer	27:8	will not put their **n** under the yoke	6677
Jer	27:11	that bring their **n** under the yoke	6677
Jer	28:14	a yoke of iron upon the **n** of all	6677
Da	5:29	chain of gold about his **n**,	6676
Mt	18:6	**were hanged about his n, and**	*5137*
Mk	9:42	**were hanged about his n, and he**	*5137*
Lk	15:20	**and fell on his n, and kissed him**	*5137*
Lk	17:2	**were hanged about his n, and he**	*5137*

NECKS

2Sa	22:41	given me the **n** of mine enemies,	6203
2Ki	17:14	not hear, but hardened their **n**	6203
Ne	3:5	put not their **n** to the work of	6677
Ne	9:16	proudly, and hardened their **n**,	6203
Isa	3:16	walk with stretched forth **n** and	1627
Jer	19:15	they have hardened their **n**, that	6203
Jer	27:12	Bring your **n** under the yoke of	6677
La	5:5	Our **n** are under persecution: we	6677
Eze	21:29	upon the **n** of them that are slain	6677
Mic	2:3	which ye shall not remove your **n**;	6677
Ro	16:4	for my life laid down their own **n**	*5137*

NECROMANCER

Dt	18:11	spirits, or a wizard, or a **n**,	1875, 4191

NEED

Dt	15:8	lend him sufficient for his **n**, in	4270
2Ch	20:17	Ye shall not **n** to fight in this battle	

Mt	3:14	I have **n** to be baptized of thee,	*5532*
Mt	6:8	what things ye have **n** of,	*5532*
Mt	6:32	ye have **n** of all these things	*5535*
Mt	9:12	be whole **n** not a physician,	*2192, 5532*
Mt	21:3	say, The Lord hath **n** of them;	*5532*
Mt	26:25	further **n** have we of witnesses?	*5532*
Mk	2:17	whole have no **n** of the physician,	*5532*
Mk	2:25	what David did, when he had **n**,	*5532*
Mk	11:3	ye that the Lord hath **n** of him;	*5532*
Mk	14:63	**n** we any further witnesses?	*2192, 5532*
Lk	5:31	are whole **n** not a physician;	*2192, 5532*
Lk	12:30	that ye have **n** of these things	*5535*
Lk	15:7	which **n** no repentance	*2192, 5532*
Lk	19:31	Because the Lord hath **n** of him	*5532*
Lk	19:34	they said, The Lord hath **n** of him	*5532*
Lk	22:71	What **n** we any further witness?	*2192, 5532*
Ac	2:45	to all men, as every man had **n**	*5532*
Ac	4:35	every man according as he had **n**	*5552*
1Co	12:21	to the feet, I have no **n** of you	*5532*
Php	4:12	both to abound and to suffer **n**	
Php	4:19	my God shall supply all your **n**	*5532*
Heb	4:16	and find grace to help in time of **n**	*2121*
Heb	10:36	For ye have **n** of patience, that	*5532*
1Pe	1:6	though now for a season, if **n** be	*1163*
1Jn	2:27	**n** not that any man teach you:	*2192, 5532*
1Jn	3:17	and seeth his brother have **n**, and	*5532*
Rev	3:17	goods, and have **n** of nothing;	*5532*
Rev	21:23	And the city had no **n** of the sun	*5532*
Rev	22:5	they **n** no candle, neither light	*2192, 5532*

NEEDED

Jn	2:25	**n** not that any should testify	*2192, 5532*
Ac	17:25	hands, as though he **n** any thing	*4326*

NEEDETH

Jn	13:10	**n** not save to wash his feet,	*2192, 5532*
Eph	4:28	he may have to give to him that **n**.	*5532*
2Ti	2:15	workman that **n** not to be ashamed	*422*

NEEDFUL

Ezr	7:20	be **n** for the house of thy God	2819
Lk	10:42	But one thing is **n**: and Mary	*5532*
Php	1:24	abide in the flesh is more **n** for you	*316*
Jas	2:16	things which are **n** to the body;	*2006*

NEEDLE

Mt	19:24	to go through the eye of a **n**,	*4476*
Mk	10:25	to go through the eye of a **n**,	*4476*

NEEDLE'S

Lk	18:25	a camel to go through a **n** eye	*4476*

NEEDLEWORK

Ex	38:18	for the gate of the court was **n**,	7551
Ps	45:14	unto the king in raiment of **n**	7553

NEEDS

Ge	17:13	money, must **n** be circumcised:	4135
Ge	19:9	and he will **n** be a judge:	8199
Mt	18:7	for it must **n** be that offences	*318*
Mk	13:7	for such things must **n** be; but the	
Lk	14:18	and I must **n** go and see it:	*318*
Jn	4:4	he must **n** go through Samaria	
Ac	1:16	this scripture must **n** have been	
Ac	17:3	that Christ must **n** have suffered,	
Ro	13:5	ye must **n** be subject, not only	*318*
2Co	11:30	If I must **n** glory, I will glory of	

NEEDY

Dt	15:11	to thy poor, and to thy **n**, in thy land	34
Ps	9:18	the **n** shall not alway be forgotten:	34
Ps	40:17	But I am poor and **n**; yet the Lord	34
Ps	72:12	shall deliver the **n** when he crieth;	34
Ps	82:3	do justice to the afflicted and **n**.	7326
Ps	86:1	Lord, hear me: for I am poor and **n**	34
Ps	109:22	For I am poor and **n**, and my heart	34
Pr	31:9	plead the cause of the poor and **n**.	34
Isa	10:2	turn aside the **n** from judgment	1800
Isa	25:4	a strength to the **n** in his distress	34
Jer	5:28	the right of the **n** do they not judge	34
Eze	18:12	Hath oppressed the poor and **n**,	34
Am	4:1	oppress the poor, which crush the **n**,	34

NEESINGS

Job	41:18	By his **n** a light doth shine, and	5846

NEGLECT

Mt	18:17	And if he shall **n** to hear them,	*3878*
Mt	18:17	but if he **n** to hear the church,	*3878*

NEGLECTING

Col	2:23	and humility, and **n** of the body;	*857*

NEGLIGENT

2Ch	29:11	My sons, be not now **n**: for the	7952
2Pe	1:12	I will not be **n** to put you always	*272*

NEIGHBOUR

Ex	3:22	woman shall borrow of her **n**,	7934
Ex	11:2	let every man borrow of his **n**,	7453
Ex	20:16	bear false witness against thy **n**	7453
Ex	22:14	if a man borrow ought of his **n**,	7453
Le	6:2	and lie unto his **n** in that which	5997
Le	19:13	Thou shalt not defraud thy **n**,	7453
Le	19:18	thou shalt love thy **n** as thyself:	7453
Dt	4:42	which should kill his **n** unawares,	7453
Dt	5:20	bear false witness against thy **n**	7453
Dt	19:11	But if any man hate his **n**, and lie	7453
Dt	27:24	be he that smiteth his **n** secretly	7453
Jos	20:5	because he smote his **n** unwittingly,	7453
2Sa	12:11	and give them unto thy **n**, and he	7453
Job	16:21	God, as a man pleadeth for his **n**!	7453
Ps	12:2	speak vanity every one with his **n**	7453
Pr	3:28	Say not unto thy **n**, Go, and come	7453
Pr	3:29	Devise not evil against thy **n**,	7453
Pr	11:9	with his mouth destroyeth his **n**	7453
Pr	11:12	is void of wisdom despiseth his **n**	7453
Pr	12:26	is more excellent than his **n**:	7453
Pr	14:20	poor is hated even of his own **n**	7453
Pr	14:21	He that despiseth his **n** sinneth:	7453
Pr	16:29	A violent man enticeth his **n**, and	7453
Pr	18:17	his **n** cometh and searcheth him	7453
Pr	24:28	Be not a witness against thy **n**	7453
Pr	25:9	Debate thy cause with thy **n**	7453
Pr	25:18	beareth false witness against his **n**	7453
Pr	26:19	So is the man that deceiveth his **n**	7453
Pr	27:10	better is a **n** that is near than a	7934
Pr	29:5	that flattereth his **n** spreadeth a	7453
Ecc	4:4	for this a man is envied of his **n**	7453
Isa	41:6	They helped every one his **n**; and	7453
Jer	9:8	speaketh peaceably to his **n** with	7453
Jer	22:8	they shall say every man to his **n**,	7453
Jer	49:18	Gomorrah and the **n** cities thereof,	7934
Jer	50:40	Gomorrah and the **n** cities thereof,	7934
Zec	8:16	ye every man the truth to his **n**;	7453

Zec 8:17 evil in your hearts against his **n**; 7453
Mt 5:43 **been said, Thou shalt love thy n,** *4139*
Mt 19:19 **Thou shalt love thy n as thyself** *4139*
Mt 22:39 **Thou shalt love thy n as thyself** *4139*
Mk 12:31 **Thou shalt love thy n as thyself** *4139*
Mk 12:33 and to love his **n** as himself, is *4139*
Lk 10:27 all thy mind; and thy **n** as thyself *4139*
Lk 10:29 said unto Jesus, And who is my **n**? *4139*
Lk 10:36 **was n unto him that fell among** *4139*
Ro 13:9 Thou shalt love thy **n** as thyself. *4139*
Ro 13:10 Love worketh no ill to his **n**: *4139*
Ro 15:2 Let every one of us please his **n**, ... *4139*
Gal 5:14 Thou shalt love thy **n** as thyself. *4139*
Eph 4:25 speak every man truth with his **n** *4139*
Heb 8:11 shall not teach every man his **n**, ... *4139*
Jas 2:8 Thou shalt love thy **n** as thyself, ... *4139*

NEIGHBOUR'S
Ex 20:17 Thou shalt not covet thy **n** house 7453
Ex 20:17 his ass, nor anything that is thy **n** 7453
Ex 22:26 If thou at all take thy **n** raiment 7453
Le 18:20 not lie carnally with thy **n** wife, to 5997
Le 20:10 adultery with his **n** wife 7453
Le 25:14 or buyest ought of thy **n** hand, ye 5997
Dt 5:21 his ass, or any thing that is thy **n**. 7453
Dt 19:14 shalt not remove thy **n** landmark, ... 7453
Dt 27:17 he that removeth his **n** landmark 7453
Job 31:9 or if I have laid wait at my **n** door; 7453
Pr 6:29 So he that goeth in to his **n** wife; 7453
Pr 25:17 thy foot from thy **n** house; lest he 7453
Jer 22:13 useth his **n** service without wages, ... 7453
Eze 18:6 neither hath defiled his **n** wife, ... 7453
Eze 22:11 abomination with his **n** wife; and 7453
Eze 33:26 and ye defile every one his **n** wife: 7453
Zec 11:6 the men every one into his **n** hand, ... 7453

NEIGHBOURS
Ru 4:17 the women her **n** gave it a name, ... 7934
2Ki 4:3 vessels abroad of all thy **n**, even 7934
Ps 28:3 which speak peace to their **n**, but 7453
Ps 44:13 makest us a reproach to our **n**, a 7934
Ps 79:4 We are become a reproach to our **n**, . . . 7934
Ps 89:41 him: he is a reproach to his **n** 7934
Jer 49:10 his brethren, and his **n**, and he is 7934
Eze 22:12 thou hast greedily gained of thy **n** 7453
Eze 23:12 doted upon the Assyrians her **n**, ... 7138
Lk 1:58 And her **n** and her cousins heard *4040*
Lk 14:12 **thy kinsmen, nor thy rich n,** *1069*
Lk 15:6 **calleth together his friends and n,** *1069*
Lk 15:9 **she calleth her friends and her n** *1069*

NEIGHBOURS'
Jer 29:23 adultery with their **n** wives, and 7453

NEITHER See also EITHER.
Ge 3:3 not eat of it, **n** shall ye touch it, ... 3808
Ge 9:11 **n** shall there any more be a flood 3808
Ex 20:23 **n** shall ye make unto you gods of 3808
Ex 30:32 **n** shall ye make any other like it, ... 3808
Le 10:6 **n** rend your clothes; lest ye die, and 3808
Le 22:32 **N** shall ye profane my holy name; 3808
Dt 5:18 **N** shalt thou commit adultery. 3808
Dt 5:19 **N** shalt thou steal 3808
Dt 5:20 **N** shalt thou bear false witness 3808
Dt 5:21 **N** shalt thou desire thy neighbour's 3808
Dt 5:21 **n** shalt thou covet thy neighbour's 3808
Dt 13:8 **n** shall thine eye pity him, ... 3808
Dt 22:5 **n** shall a man put on a woman's 3808
Jos 5:1 **n** was there spirit in them any more, . . . 3808
Jos 8:1 Fear not, **n** be thou dismayed: 408
2Sa 7:22 **n** is there any God beside thee, ... 369
2Sa 14:14 **n** doth God respect any person: 3808
Job 9:33 **N** is there any daysman betwixt 3808
Isa 64:4 **n** hath the eye seen, O God, beside. 3808
Mt 5:15 **N do men light a candle, and put** *3761*
Mt 9:17 **N do men put new wine into old** *3761*
Mt 21:27 **N tell I you by what authority I** *3761*
Jn 8:11 **N do I condemn thee: go, and sin.** *3761*
Jn 14:27 **be troubled, n let it be afraid** *3366*
Ac 2:27 **n** wilt thou suffer thine Holy One *3761*
Ac 4:12 **N** is there salvation in any *2532, 3756*
Ro 8:38 **n** death, nor life, nor angels, nor *3777*
1Co 10:9 **N** let us tempt Christ, as some of *3366*
Eph 4:27 **N** give place to the devil. *3383*
Rev 9:21 **N** repented they of their *2532, 3756*
Rev 21:4 **n** shall there be any more pain: for

NEST See also NESTS.
Dt 32:11 As an eagle stirreth up her **n**, ... 7064
Pr 27:8 a bird that wandereth from her **n**, ... 7064
Jer 49:16 make thy **n** as high as the eagle, ... 7064
Ob 4 thou set thy **n** among the stars, ... 7064
Hab 2:9 that he may set his **n** on high, that 7064

NESTS
Mt 8:20 **and the birds of the air have n;** *2682*
Lk 9:58 **holes, and birds of the air have n;** *2682*

NET See also NETWORK.
Ps 9:15 in the **n** which they hid is their 7568
Ps 31:4 me out of the **n** that they have laid. 7568
Ps 35:7 they hid for me their **n** in a pit, ... 7568
Pr 1:17 **n** is spread in the sight of any bird. 7568
Pr 12:12 wicked desireth the **n** of evil men: 4686
Pr 29:5 spreadeth a **n** for his feet, ... 7568
Ecc 9:12 fishes that are taken in an evil **n**, ... 4686
Isa 51:20 the streets, as a wild bull in a **n** 4364
La 1:13 he hath spread a **n** for my feet, he. 7568
Mt 13:47 **kingdom of heaven is like a n,** *4522*
Lk 5:5 at thy word I will let down the **n**. *1350*
Jn 21:6 **Cast the n on the right side of the** *1350*
Jn 21:11 drew the **n** to land full of great fishes, . . . *1350*

NETHER
Eze 31:14 death, to the **n** parts of the earth, ... 8482
Eze 32:24 into the **n** parts of the earth, which 8482

NETS
Ps 141:10 the wicked fall into their own **n** 4365
Ecc 7:26 whose heart is snares and **n**, and 2764
Eze 26:5 be a place for the spreading of **n**. 2764
Eze 47:10 shall be a place to spread forth **n**; 2764
Mt 4:20 they straightway left their **n**, and. *1350*
Mk 1:18 straightway they forsook their **n** *1350*
Lk 5:4 **let down your n for a draught** *1350*

NEVER
Ge 34:12 Ask me **n** so much dowry and gift,
Le 6:13 upon the altar; it shall **n** go out. 3808
Nu 19:2 and upon which **n** came yoke: 3808
Jgs 2:1 **n** break my covenant with 3808, 5769
2Sa 12:10 sword shall **n** depart. 3808, 5704, 5769
2Ch 18:7 he **n** prophesied good unto me, ... 369
Ps 15:5 these things shall **n** be moved. . . . 3808, 5769
Pr 10:30 righteous shall **n** be removed: 5769, 1077

N

Pr	27:20	Hell and destruction are n full;	3808
Pr	27:20	the eyes of man are n satisfied	3808
Pr	30:15	three things that are n satisfied,	3808
Jer	33:17	shall n want a man to sit upon	3808
Da	12:1	such as n was since there was a	3808
Joel	2:27	and my people shall n be	3808, 5769
Mt	7:23	I n knew you: depart from me,	3763
Mk	3:29	hath n forgiveness,	3756, 1519, 3588, 165
Mk	9:43	that n shall be quenched:	3756
Lk	15:29	and yet thou n gavest me a kid,	3763
Lk	19:30	tied, whereon yet n man sat:	3762
Lk	23:53	wherein n man before was laid	3764
Jn	4:14	give ... shall n thirst;	3364, 1519, 3588, 165
Jn	6:35	that cometh to me shall n hunger;	165
Jn	6:35	believeth on me shall n	3364, 4455
Jn	7:46	N man spake like this man,	3763
Jn	8:51	saying ... shall n see	3364, 1519, 3588, 165
Jn	8:52	shall n taste of death	3364, 1519, 3588, 165
Jn	10:28	shall n perish	3364, 1519, 3588, 165
Jn	11:26	in me shall n	3364, 1519, 3588, 165
1Co	13:8	Charity n faileth: but whether	3763
2Ti	3:7	n able to come to the knowledge	3368
Heb	10:11	which can n take away sins:	3763
Heb	13:5	I will n leave thee, nor forsake	3364
2Pe	1:10	these things, ye shall n fall:	3364, 4219

NEW See also RENEW.

Ex	1:8	arose up a n king over Egypt	2319
Nu	16:30	But if the Lord make a n thing,	1278
2Sa	6:3	set the ark of God upon a n cart,	2319
Ps	96:1	O sing unto the Lord a n song:	2319
Ps	98:1	O sing unto the Lord a n song; for	2319
Ps	149:1	Sing unto the Lord a n song, and	2319
Pr	3:10	presses ... burst out with n wine	8492
Ecc	1:9	there is no n thing under the sun.	2319
Isa	42:9	to pass, and n things do I declare:	2319
Isa	42:10	Sing unto the Lord a n song, and	2319
Isa	43:19	Behold, I will do a n thing; now it	2319
Isa	65:17	create n heavens and a n earth:	2319
Isa	66:22	as the n heavens and the n earth,	2319
Jer	31:22	hath created a n thing in the earth,	2319
Jer	31:31	I will make a n covenant with the	2319
La	3:23	They are n every morning: great	2319
Eze	11:19	I will put a n spirit within you;	2319
Eze	18:31	make you a n heart and a n spirit:	2319
Eze	36:26	a n spirit will I put within you:	2319
Eze	46:1	day of the n moon it shall be opened.	2320
Hos	4:11	and n wine take away the heart	8492
Mt	9:16	of n cloth unto an old garment, for	46
Mt	9:17	men put n wine into old bottles:	3501
Mt	9:17	they put ... wine into n bottles,	2537
Mt	26:28	is my blood of the n testament,	2537
Mk	2:21	piece of n cloth on an old garment:	46
Mk	2:22	putteth n wine into old bottles:	3501
Mk	14:25	drink it n in the kingdom of God.	2537
Lk	5:36	piece of a n garment upon an old;	2537
Lk	5:37	putteth n wine into old bottles;	3501
Lk	22:20	This cup is the n testament in my	2537
Jn	13:34	A n commandment I give unto	2537
1Co	11:25	This cup is the n testament in my	2537
2Co	3:6	able ministers of the n testament;	2537
2Co	5:17	be in Christ, he is a n creature:	2537
Eph	4:24	that ye put on the n man, which	2537
Col	3:10	have put on the n man, which is	3501
Heb	8:8	I will make a n covenant with the	2537
Heb	8:13	A n covenant, he hath made the	2537
Heb	9:15	the mediator of the n testament	2537
Heb	10:20	By a n and living way, which he	4372
Heb	12:24	the mediator of the n covenant,	3501
2Pe	3:13	look for n heavens and a n earth,	2537
Rev	2:17	in the stone a n name written,	2537
Rev	3:12	city of my God, ... is n Jerusalem,	2537
Rev	5:9	they sung a n song, saying, Thou	2537
Rev	14:3	And they sung as it were a n song	2537
Rev	21:1	I saw a n heaven and a n earth:	2537
Rev	21:2	I ... saw the holy city, n Jerusalem,	2537
Rev	21:5	said, Behold, I make all things n	2537

NEWBORN See also BORN.

1Pe	2:2	As n babes, desire the sincere	738

NEWNESS

Ro	6:4	we also should walk in n of life	2538
Ro	7:6	that we should serve in n of spirit	2535

NEWS

Pr	25:25	so is good n from a far country	8052

NEXT

Ru	2:20	of kin unto us, one of our n kinsmen	
1Sa	23:17	Israel, I shall be n unto thee;	4932
Jn	1:29	n day John seeth Jesus coming	1887

NIGH See also NEAR.

Ex	14:10	when Pharaoh drew n, the children	7126
Ex	24:2	Lord: but they shall not come n;	5066
Nu	1:51	stranger that Cometh n shall be	7126
Nu	24:17	I shall behold him, but not n: there	7126
Dt	4:7	who hath God so n unto them, as	7126
Ps	32:6	they shall not come n unto him.	5060
Ps	34:18	n unto them that are of a broken	7126
Ps	69:18	Draw n unto my soul, and	7126
Ps	85:9	his salvation is n them that fear	7138
Ps	88:3	my life draweth n unto the grave,	5060
Ps	91:7	but it shall not come n thee	5066
Ps	145:18	n unto all them that call upon him,	7138
Pr	5:8	come not n the door of her house:	7126
Ecc	12:1	nor the years draw n, when thou	5060
Joel	2:1	Lord cometh, for it is n at hand;	7126
Mt	15:8	draweth n unto me with their	1448
Mt	24:32	ye know that summer is n:	1451
Mk	13:29	come to pass, know that it is n,	1451
Lk	10:9	kingdom of God is come n unto	1448
Lk	10:11	kingdom of God is come n unto	1448
Lk	21:28	for your redemption draweth n	1448
Lk	21:30	that summer is now n at hand	1451
Lk	21:31	the kingdom of God is n at hand	1451
Jn	19:20	Jesus was crucified ... n to the city:	1451
Jn	19:42	for the sepulchre was n at hand	1451
Ro	10:8	The word is n thee, even in thy	1451
Eph	2:13	are made n by the blood of Christ	1451
Php	2:30	work of Christ he was n unto death,	1448
Heb	7:19	by the which we draw n unto God	1448
Jas	4:8	Draw n to God, and he will draw n	1448
Jas	5:8	the coming of the Lord draweth n	1448

NIGHT See also MIDNIGHT.

Ge	1:5	and the darkness he called N	3915
Ge	1:14	to divide the day from the n; and	3915
Ge	1:16	the lesser light to rule the n: he	3915
Ge	8:22	and day and n shall not cease	3915
Ge	46:2	God spake ... in the visions of the n,	3915
Ex	13:21	by n in a pillar of fire, to give	3915
Nu	9:16	and the appearance of fire by n.	3915

1Ki 3:5 to Solomon in a dream by **n**: and...... 3915
1Ki 3:19 this woman's child died in the **n**; 3915
1Ki 8:59 unto the Lord our God day and **n**,...... 3915
Ne 9:12 in the **n** by a pillar of fire, to give 3915
Est 6:1 On that **n** could not the king sleep..... 3915
Job 3:7 let that **n** be solitary, let no joyful...... 3915
Ps 1:2 law doth he meditate day and **n** 3915
Ps 6:6 all the **n** make I my bed to swim;...... 3915
Ps 19:2 and **n** unto **n** sheweth knowledge...... 3915
Ps 136:9 The moon and stars to rule by **n**:...... 3915
Ps 139:11 even the **n** shall be light about me 3915
Ps 139:12 thee; but the **n** shineth as the day: 3915
Pr 31:15 She riseth also while it is yet **n**,........ 3915
Pr 31:18 her candle goeth not out by **n**......... 3915
Ecc 2:23 his heart taketh not rest in the **n**....... 3915
Ecc 8:16 neither day nor **n** seeth sleep with 3915
Isa 21:11 Watchman, what of the **n**?............ 3915
Jer 33:20 not be day and **n** in their seasons; 3915
La 2:18 run down like a river day and **n**:....... 3915
Da 2:19 revealed unto Daniel in a **n** vision...... 3916
Da 7:13 I saw in the **n** visions, and, behold,..... 3916
Jnh 4:10 up in a **n**, and perished in a **n**: 3915
Mt 26:31 **be offended because of me this n**...... *3571*
Mt 26:34 **That this n, before the cock**........... *3571*
Mk 4:27 **should sleep, and rise n and day,** *3571*
Mk 14:27 **be offended because of me this n:** *3571*
Lk 2:8 keeping watch over their flock by **n** *3571*
Lk 6:12 continued all **n** in prayer to God....... *1273*
Lk 12:20 **this n thy soul shall be required**....... *3571*
Jn 9:4 **the n cometh, when no man can** *3571*
Ro 13:12 The **n** is far spent, the day is at *3571*
1Co 11:23 same **n** in which he was betrayed *3571*
1Th 5:2 Lord so cometh as a thief in the **n** *3571*
2Pe 3:10 Lord will come as a thief in the **n**; *3571*
Rev 7:15 serve him day and **n** in his temple:..... *3571*
Rev 20:10 be tormented day and **n** for ever....... *3571*
Rev 21:25 day: for there shall be no **n** there *3571*
Rev 22:5 And there shall be no **n** there; and *3571*

NIGHTS

Ge 7:4 the earth forty days and forty **n**;....... 3915
Ex 24:18 the mount forty days and forty **n**...... 3915
Ex 34:28 the Lord forty days and forty **n**; 3915
Dt 9:25 the Lord forty days and forty **n**, ... 3915
Jnh 1:17 of the fish three days and three **n**...... 3915
Mt 4:2 had fasted forty days and forty **n**,...... *3571*
Mt 12:40 **and three n in the whale's belly;**....... *3571*
Mt 12:40 **three n in the heart of the earth.** *3571*

NINE

Ge 5:27 were **n** hundred sixty and **n** years: 8672
Ge 9:29 of Noah were **n** hundred and fifty 8672
Nu 34:13 to give unto the **n** tribes, and to 8672
Jgs 4:13 even **n** hundred chariots of iron; 8672
Mt 18:12 **he not leave the ninety and n, and**..... *1768*
Lk 15:7 **over ninety and n just persons,** *1768*
Lk 17:17 **ten cleansed? but where are the n?**..... *1767*

NINETY

Ge 17:17 Sarah, that is **n** years old, bear?........ 8673
Ge 17:24 Abraham was **n** years old and nine,.... 8673
Mt 18:12 **doth he not leave the n and nine,**...... *1768*
Lk 15:7 **than over n and nine just persons,**..... *1768*

NINTH

Mt 20:5 **out about the sixth and n hour,** *1766*
Mt 27:45 over all the land unto the **n** hour *1766*
Mt 27:46 the **n** hour Jesus cried with a loud *1766*
Mk 15:34 the **n** hour Jesus cried with a loud *1766*
Lk 23:44 over all the earth until the **n** hour...... *1766*

NO **See also NAY; NONE; NOTHING.**

Ex 20:3 have **n** other gods before me. 3808
Ex 34:14 thou shalt worship **n** other god: 3808
Le 13:26 be **n** white hair in the bright spot, ... 369
Le 13:26 it be **n** lower than the other skin, ... 369
Le 13:31 and that there is **n** black hair in it; 369
Le 13:32 and there be in it **n** yellow hair, ... 3808
Le 16:17 shall be **n** man in the tabernacle....... 3808
Le 16:29 do **n** work at all, whether it be one..... 3808
Le 17:7 shall **n** more offer their sacrifices 3808
Le 17:12 **N** soul of you shall eat blood, ... 3808
Le 17:14 eat the blood of **n** manner of flesh: 3808
Le 19:15 Ye shall do **n** unrighteousness......... 3808
Le 19:35 Ye shall do **n** unrighteousness......... 3808
Le 20:14 there be **n** wickedness among you...... 3808
Le 21:3 him, which hath had **n** husband: 3808
Le 21:21 **N** man that hath a blemish of the seed
Le 22:10 **n** stranger eat of the holy thing: 3808
Le 22:13 or divorced, and have **n** child, and 369
Le 22:13 there shall **n** stranger eat thereof....... 3808
Le 22:21 there shall be **n** blemish therein........ 3808
Le 23:3 ye shall do **n** work therein: it is the..... 3808
Le 23:7 ye shall do **n** servile work 3605, 3808
Le 23:8 ye shall do **n** servile work 3605, 3808
Le 23:21 ye shall do **n** servile work 3605, 3808
Le 23:25 Ye shall do **n** servile work 3605, 3808
Le 23:28 do **n** work in that same day: 3808
Le 23:31 Ye shall do **n** manner of work: it....... 3808
Le 23:35 ye shall do **n** servile work 3605, 3808
Le 23:36 ye shall do **n** servile work 3605, 3808
Le 25:36 Take thou **n** usury of him, or 408
Le 26:1 you **n** idols nor graven image,......... 3808
Le 26:37 have **n** power to stand before your..... 3808
Le 27:26 firstling, **n** man shall sanctify it; 3808
Le 27:28 **n** devoted thing, ... shall be sold . 3605, 3808
Nu 1:53 be **n** wrath upon the congregation..... 3808
Nu 3:4 of Sinai, and they had **n** children:...... 3808
Nu 5:8 have **n** kinsmen to recompense the 369
Nu 5:13 and there be **n** witness against her 369
Nu 5:15 he shall pour **n** oil upon it, nor......... 3808
Nu 5:19 If **n** man have lain with thee, and...... 3808
Nu 6:3 shall drink **n** vinegar of wine, or....... 3808
Nu 6:5 shall **n** rasor come upon his head: 3808
Nu 6:6 Lord ... shall come at **n** dead body..... 3808
Nu 8:19 be **n** plague among the children of..... 3808
Nu 8:25 thereof, and shall serve **n** more: 3808
Nu 8:26 the charge, and shall do **n** service. 3808
Nu 14:18 by **n** means clearing the guilty, ... 3808
Nu 16:40 that **n** stranger, which is not of the..... 3808
Nu 18:5 be **n** wrath any more upon the 3808
Nu 18:20 have **n** inheritance in their land 3808
Nu 18:23 of Israel they have **n** inheritance. 3808
Nu 18:24 they shall have **n** inheritance. 3808
Nu 18:32 ye shall bear **n** sin by reason of it,...... 3808
Nu 19:2 without spot, wherein is **n** blemish, ... 369
Nu 19:15 hath **n** covering bound upon it, is 369
Nu 20:2 was **n** water for the congregation:...... 3808
Nu 20:5 it is **n** place of seed, or of figs, or 3808
Nu 21:5 there is **n** bread, neither is there 369
Nu 22:26 where was **n** way to turn either to 369
Nu 23:23 there is **n** enchantment against........ 3808
Nu 26:33 the son of Hepher had **n** sons, but..... 3808

Nu 26:62 was **n** inheritance given them 3808
Nu 27:3 in his own sin, and had **n** sons......... 3808
Nu 27:4 family, because he hath **n** son? 369
Nu 27:8 If a man die, and have **n** son, then 369
Nu 27:9 And if he have **n** daughter, then ye...... 369
Nu 27:10 And if he have **n** brethren, then ye 369
Dt 1:39 **n** knowledge between good and evil,... 3808
1Ki 8:23 Israel, there is **n** God like thee, ... 369
2Ki 5:15 that there is **n** God in all the earth,...... 369
2Ch 6:14 is **n** God like thee in the heaven,........ 369
2Ch 19:7 **n** iniquity with the Lord our God, ... 369
Ps 14:1 said in his heart, There is **n** God. 369
Ps 19:3 There is **n** speech nor language, ... 369
Ps 23:4 I will fear **n** evil: for thou art with 3808
Ps 36:1 is **n** fear of God before his eyes. 369
Ps 53:1 said in his heart, There is **n** God. 369
Ps 53:3 is none that doeth good, **n**, not one
Pr 11:14 Where **n** counsel is, the people fall: 369
Pr 29:18 Where there is **n** vision, the people 369
Ecc 1:9 there is **n** new thing under the sun. 369
Ecc 2:16 there is **n** remembrance of the wise 369
Ecc 3:11 **n** man can find out the work that 1097
Ecc 5:4 for he hath **n** pleasure in fools: 369
Ecc 12:12 making many books there is **n** end; 369
Isa 9:7 and peace there shall be **n** end, ... 369
Isa 40:28 **n** searching of his understanding 369
Isa 43:10 me there was **n** God formed,.......... 3808
Isa 43:11 and beside me there is **n** saviour........ 369
Isa 44:6 last; and beside me there is **n** God....... 369
Isa 44:8 yea, there is **n** God; I know not any...... 369
Isa 45:5 else, there is **n** God besides me:......... 369
Isa 45:14 there is none else, there is **n** God 657
Isa 45:21 and there is **n** God else beside me; 369
Isa 53:2 **n** beauty that we should desire him. ... 3808
Isa 57:21 There is **n** peace, saith my God, to 369
Eze 18:32 I have **n** pleasure in the death of....... 3808
Eze 33:11 I have **n** pleasure in the death of........ 518
Hos 13:4 for there is **n** saviour beside me 369
Mt 6:24 **N man can serve two masters:** *3762*
Mt 6:25 **Take n thought for your life,** *3361*
Mt 11:27 **n man knoweth the Son, but the** *3762*
Lk 9:62 **N man, having put his hand to**......... *3762*
Lk 10:22 **n man knoweth who the Son is,** *3762*
Lk 16:13 **N servant can serve two masters:**...... *3762*
Jn 1:18 **N** man hath seen God at any time;..... *3762*
Jn 6:44 **N man can come to me, except**......... *3762*
Jn 10:18 **N man taketh it from me, but I** *3762*
Jn 10:29 **n man is able to pluck them out**....... *3762*
Jn 14:6 **n man cometh unto the Father,** *3762*
Jn 19:11 **have n power at all against me,**........ *3756*
Ac 10:34 God is **n** respecter of persons:.......... *3756*
Ro 3:10 There is none righteous, **n**, not one:
Ro 3:12 is none that doeth good, **n**, not one
Ro 3:18 There is **n** fear of God before *3756*
Ro 8:1 therefore now **n** condemnation......... *3762*
Ro 13:1 For there is **n** power but of God: *3756*
Gal 2:16 law shall **n** flesh be justified...... *3756, 3956*
1Ti 6:16 whom **n** man hath seen, nor can see:... *3762*
Heb 9:22 shedding of blood is **n** remission *3756*
Jas 1:13 Let **n** man say when he is tempted, ... *3367*
1Jn 4:12 **N** man hath seen God at any.......... *3762*
1Jn 4:18 There is **n** fear in love; but............ *3756*
Rev 5:4 because **n** man was found worthy *3762*
Rev 21:1 away; and there was **n** more sea *3756*
Rev 21:4 and there shall be **n** more death *3756*
Rev 21:23 And the city had **n** need of the sun,.... *3756*

NOBLE

Est 6:9 one of the king's most **n** princes, ... 6579
Jer 2:21 Yet I had planted thee a **n** vine, wholly
1Co 1:26 mighty, not many **n**, are called;........ *2104*

NOBLEMAN

Lk 19:12 **A certain n went into a far** *2104, 444*
Jn 4:46 there was a certain **n**, whose son........ *937*

NOBLES

1Ki 21:8 to the **n** that were in his city 2715
Ne 3:5 but their **n** put not their necks to....... 117
Ne 10:29 clave to their brethren, their **n**, ... 117
Job 29:10 The **n** held their peace, and their 5057
Ps 149:8 and their **n** with fetters of iron;........ 3513
Pr 8:16 By me princes rule, and **n**, even 5081
Ecc 10:17 when thy king is the son of **n**, and 2715
Jer 39:6 Babylon slew all the **n** of Judah........ 2715
Jnh 3:7 the decree of the king and his **n**,....... 1419

NOISE

Ex 20:18 and the **n** of the trumpet, and the 6963
Ex 32:17 There is a **n** of war in the camp 6963
Jgs 5:11 delivered from the **n** of archers........ 6963
1Sa 4:6 meaneth the **n** of this great shout...... 6963
1Sa 4:14 What meaneth the **n** of this tumult? ... 6963
1Ki 1:45 This is the **n** that ye have heard........ 6963
2Ki 7:6 the Syrians to hear a **n** of chariots,..... 6963
2Ch 23:12 when Athaliah heard the **n** of the...... 6963
Ezr 3:13 discern the **n** of the shout of joy....... 6963
Job 36:29 or the **n** of his tabernacle? 8663
Ps 65:7 Which stilleth the **n** of the seas, ... 7588
Ps 93:4 than the **n** of many waters, yea 6963
Ps 98:4 Make a joyful **n** unto the Lord, all
Ps 100:1 Make a joyful **n** unto the Lord, all ye
Isa 13:4 tumultuous **n** of the kingdoms of 6963
Isa 17:12 make a **n** like the **n** of the seas;........ 1993
Isa 24:18 who fleeth from the **n** of the fear 6963
Isa 29:6 and with earthquake, and great **n**, ... 6963
Isa 33:3 At the **n** of the tumult the people...... 6963
Jer 4:19 my heart maketh a **n** in me; I 1993
Jer 4:29 flee for the **n** of the horsemen......... 6963
Jer 25:31 A **n** shall come even to the ends of..... 7588
Jer 47:3 the **n** of the stamping of the hoofs..... 6963
Jer 49:21 at the cry the **n** thereof was heard 6963
La 2:7 a **n** in the house of the Lord 6963
Eze 1:24 like the **n** of great waters, as the 6963
Eze 3:13 the **n** of the wheels over against 6963
Eze 26:10 shake at the **n** of the horsemen........ 6963
Eze 37:7 as I prophesied, there was a **n**,......... 6963
Eze 43:2 voice was like a **n** of many waters: 6963
Joel 2:5 Like the **n** of chariots on the tops of ... 6963
Na 3:2 The **n** of a whip, and the **n** of the...... 6963
Zep 1:10 the **n** of a cry from the fish gate 6963
2Pe 3:10 shall pass away with a great **n**,......... *4500*
Rev 6:1 heard, as it were the **n** of thunder, ... *5456*

NOISED

Jos 6:27 his fame was **n** throughout all the
Mk 2:1 it was **n** that he was in the house *191*
Lk 1:65 all these sayings were **n** abroad *1255*
Ac 2:6 when this was **n** abroad, the *1096, 5408*

NOISOME

Ps 91:3 fowler, and from the **n** pestilence 1942
Eze 14:15 I cause **n** beasts to pass through 7451
Rev 16:2 fell a **n** and grievous sore upon the..... *2556*

NONE

Ge	41:15	and there is **n** that can interpret it:	369
Ge	41:39	there is **n** so discreet and wise as	369
Ex	8:10	is **n** like unto the Lord our God	369
Ex	9:14	there is **n** like me in all the earth	369
Le	26:17	ye shall flee when **n** pursueth you	369
Dt	4:35	God; there is **n** else beside him	369
Dt	5:7	shalt have **n** other gods before me	
1Sa	2:2	There is **n** holy as the Lord: for	369
2Sa	7:22	for there is **n** like thee, neither is	369
1Ki	3:12	there was **n** like thee before thee	3808
1Ki	8:60	is God, and that there is **n** else	369
1Ch	17:20	O Lord, there is **n** like thee	369
2Ch	20:6	that **n** is able to withstand thee?	369
Ps	14:3	is **n** that doeth good, no, not one	369
Ps	22:29	and **n** can keep alive his own soul	3808
Ps	25:3	**n** that wait on thee be ashamed:	3808
Ps	53:3	there is **n** that doeth good, no, not	369
Ps	69:20	some to take pity, but there was **n**;	369
Ps	73:25	is **n** upon earth that I desire	3808
Pr	1:30	They would **n** of my counsel: they	3808
Pr	2:19	**N** that go unto her return again,	3808
Pr	3:31	and choose **n** of his ways	408
Isa	43:13	is **n** that can deliver out of my hand:	369
Isa	45:5	I am the Lord, and there is **n** else,	369
Isa	45:6	I am the Lord, and there is **n** else	369
Isa	45:14	and there is **n** else, there is no God	369
Isa	45:18	I am the Lord; and there is **n** else	369
Isa	45:21	a Saviour; there is **n** beside me	369
Isa	45:22	for I am God, and there is **n** else	369
Isa	46:9	I am God, and there is **n** like me,	657
Isa	47:10	thou hast said, **n** seeth me. Thy	369
Jer	10:6	as there is **n** like unto thee, O Lord	369
Jer	30:7	day is great, so that **n** is like it:	369
La	1:2	lovers she hath **n** to comfort her:	369
La	1:17	and there is **n** to comfort her: the	369
La	1:21	I sigh: there is **n** to comfort me:	369
Da	4:35	**n** can stay his hand, or say unto	3809
Joel	2:27	the Lord your God, and **n** else:	369
Am	5:2	land; there is **n** to raise her up	369
Zep	2:15	I am, and there is **n** beside me:	657
Zec	8:17	let **n** of you imagine evil in your	408
Mt	15:6	**commandment of God of n effect**	*208*
Mt	19:17	**there is n good but one, that is,**	*3762*
Mk	7:13	**Making … word of God of n effect**	*208*
Mk	10:18	**is n good but one, that is, God**	*3762*
Mk	12:31	**is n other commandment greater**	*3756*
Mk	12:32	God; and there is **n** other but he:	*3756*
Mk	14:55	to put him to death; and found **n**.	*3756*
Lk	18:19	**n is good, save one, that is, God**	*3762*
Jn	17:12	**and n of them is lost, but the son**	*3762*
Ac	4:12	is **n** other name under heaven	*3777*
Ro	3:10	there is **n** righteous, no, not one:	*3756*
Ro	3:11	there is **n** that seeketh after God	*3756*
Ro	3:12	there is **n** that doeth good, no, not	*3756*
Ro	4:14	and the promise made of **n** effect:	*2673*
Ro	8:9	the Spirit of Christ, he is **n** of his	*3756*
Ro	9:6	word of God hath taken **n** effect	*1601*
Ro	14:7	For **n** of us liveth to himself, and	*3762*
1Co	8:4	there is **n** other God but one	*3762*
Gal	3:17	make the promise of **n** effect	*208*
1Th	5:15	**n** render evil for evil unto any	*3361, 5100*
1Ti	5:14	give **n** occasion to the adversary	*3362*
1Pe	4:15	let **n** of you suffer as a murderer,	*3387*
Rev	2:10	**Fear n of those things which thou**	*3367*
Rev	2:24	**put upon you n other burden.**	*3367*

NOON See also AFTERNOON.

Ps	55:17	Evening, and morning, and at **n**,	6672
Isa	58:10	and thy darkness be as the **n** day:	6672
Isa	59:10	we stumble at **n** day as in the	6672
Am	8:9	will cause the sun to go down at **n**,	6672

NOONDAY See also NOON and DAY.

Dt	28:29	And thou shalt grope at **n**, as the	6672
Ps	37:6	light, and thy judgment as the **n**	6672
Ps	91:6	the destruction that wasteth at **n**	6672
Isa	16:3	as the night in the midst of the **n**;	6672

NOR

Jos	1:5	I will not fail thee, **n** forsake thee	3808
1Ki	8:57	let him not leave us, **n** forsake us:	408
2Ch	19:7	**n** respect of persons, **n** taking of gifts	
Job	1:22	not, **n** charged God foolishly	3808
Ps	1:1	**n** standeth in the way of sinners	3808
Ps	1:1	**n** sitteth in the seat of the scornful	3808
Ps	19:3	There is no speech **n** language	369
Ps	37:25	forsaken, **n** his seed begging bread	
Ps	103:10	**n** rewarded us according to our	3808
Ps	121:4	Israel shall neither slumber **n** sleep	3808
Pr	21:30	no … **n** understanding **n** counsel	369
Ecc	9:11	swift, **n** the battle to the strong,	3808
SS	2:7	**n** awake my love, till he please	518
SS	3:5	**n** awake my love, till he please	518
SS	8:4	**n** awake my love, until he please	
Isa	53:2	he hath no form **n** comeliness; and	3808
Jer	51:5	been forsaken, **n** Judah of his God,	
Eze	3:18	**n** speakest to warn the wicked	3808
Da	3:18	**n** worship the golden image	3809
Hos	4:1	because there is no truth, **n** mercy,	369
Hos	4:1	**n** knowledge of God in the land	369
Zec	4:6	Not by might, **n** by power, but by	3808
Mt	22:29	**scriptures, n the power of God**	*3366*
Mt	25:13	**day n the hour wherein the Son**	*3761*
Lk	18:4	**I fear not God, n regard man;**	*3756*
Jn	1:13	of blood, **n** of the will of the flesh,	*3761*
Jn	16:3	**have not known the Father, n me**	*3761*
Ro	8:38	**n** things present, **n** things to come,	*3777*
Ro	8:39	**N** height, **n** depth, **n** any other	*3777*
Ro	9:16	willeth, **n** of him that runneth	*3761*
1Co	2:9	hath not seen, **n** ear heard	*2532, 3756*
Gal	3:28	There is neither Jew **n** Greek	*3767*
Col	3:11	there is neither Greek **n** Jew	*2532*
Heb	13:5	never leave thee, **n** forsake	*3761, 3364*
Rev	3:15	**that thou art neither cold n hot:**	*3777*
Rev	14:11	and they have no rest day **n** night,	*2532*
Rev	21:4	death, neither sorrow, **n** crying	*3777*

NORTH

Job	37:22	Fair weather cometh out of the **n**:	6828
Pr	25:23	The **n** wind driveth away rain:	6828
Isa	41:25	I have raised up one from the **n**,	6828
Jer	1:14	Out of the **n** an evil shall break	6828
Jer	4:6	for I will bring evil from the **n**, and	6828
Jer	6:1	for evil appeareth out of the **n**, and	6828
Jer	50:41	a people shall come from the **n**,	6828
Jer	51:48	shall come unto her from the **n**,	6828
Eze	1:4	a whirlwind came out of the **n**,	6828
Eze	26:7	a king of kings, from the **n**, with	6828
Da	11:15	So the king of the **n** shall come	6828
Zec	2:6	and flee from the land of the **n**,	6828
Zec	14:4	half … shall remove toward the **n**,	6828
Lk	13:29	**from the n, and from the south,**	*1005*
Rev	21:13	on the **n** three gates; on the south	*1005*

N

NOSE
Le 21:18 or a lame, or he that hath a flat **n**, ... 2763
2Ki 19:28 I will put my hook in thy **n**, and 639
Job 41:2 Canst thou put an hook into his **n**? 6396
Pr 30:33 the wringing of the **n** bringeth forth 639
Isa 37:29 therefore will I put my hook in thy **n**, . . . 639
Isa 65:5 These are a smoke in my **n**, a fire 639

NOSES
Ps 115:6 **n** have they, but they smell not: 639

NOSTRILS
Ge 2:7 into his **n** the breath of life; and 639
Ge 7:22 in whose **n** was the breath of life, ... 639
Ex 15:8 with the blast of thy **n** thy waters 639
2Sa 22:9 There went up a smoke out of his **n**, ... 639
2Sa 22:16 at the blast of the breath of his **n** 639
Job 4:9 by the breath of his **n** are they. 639
Job 27:3 and the spirit of God is in my **n**; 639
Job 41:20 Out of his **n** goeth smoke, as out 5156
Ps 18:8 went up a smoke out of his **n**, ... 639
Ps 18:15 at the blast of the breath of thy **n** 639

NOTABLE
Ac 2:20 great and **n** day of the Lord come: *2016*
Ac 4:16 indeed a **n** miracle hath been done *1110*

NOTE
Isa 30:8 in a table, and **n** it in a book, ... 2710
2Th 3:14 **n** that man, and have no company *4598*

NOTED
Da 10:21 is **n** in the scripture of truth: 7559

NOTHING See also NAUGHT.
Ge 19:8 only unto these men do **n**; for . . . 3808, 1697
Ge 26:29 have done unto thee **n** but good. 7535
Ex 12:20 Ye shall eat **n** leavened; in all your 3808
Ex 22:3 if he have **n**, then he shall be sold. 369
Nu 6:4 eat **n** that is made of the vine tree, ... 3808
Nu 16:26 and touch **n** of theirs, lest ye 408, 3605
Dt 20:16 save alive **n** that breatheth: 3808, 3605
Dt 28:55 he hath **n** left him in the siege. 3605
Jos 11:15 left **n** undone of all that the 3808, 1697
1Sa 27:1 there is **n** better for me than that 369
2Sa 12:3 But the poor man had **n**, save. 369, 3605
2Sa 24:24 offer ... that which doth cost me **n** 2600
2Ch 14:11 said, Lord, it is **n** with thee to help 369
Ne 2:2 this is **n** else but sorrow of heart. 369
Est 6:10 **n** fail of all that thou hast spoken. 1697
Job 26:7 and hangeth the earth upon **n** 1099
Pr 8:8 is **n** froward or perverse in them. 369
Pr 9:13 is simple, and knoweth **n**. 1077, 4100
Pr 10:2 Treasures of wickedness profit **n**. 3808
Pr 13:4 the sluggard desireth, and hath **n** 369
Pr 13:7 himself rich, yet hath **n**: 3808, 3605
Pr 20:4 shall he beg in harvest and have **n** 369
Pr 22:27 If thou hast **n** to pay, why should 369
Ecc 2:24 There is **n** better for a man, than 369
Isa 40:17 All nations before him are as **n**; 369
Jer 32:17 there is **n** too hard for thee: 3808, 1697
La 1:12 Is it **n** to you, all ye that pass by? 3808
Da 4:35 of the earth are reputed as **n**: 3809
Mt 5:13 **it is thenceforth good for n, but** *3762*
Mt 10:26 **there is n covered, that shall not**. *3762*
Mt 17:20 **n shall be impossible unto you**. *3762*
Mt 23:16 **shall swear by the temple, it is n;** *3762*
Mt 23:18 **shall swear by the altar, it is n;** *3762*
Mt 26:62 said unto him, Answerest thou **n**? *3762*
Mk 4:22 **there is n hid, which shall** *3756, 5100*
Mk 7:15 **There is n from without a man,** *3762*
Mk 14:60 Jesus, saying, Answerest thou **n**? *3762*
Mk 15:4 again, saying, Answerest thou **n**?. . *3756, 3762*
Lk 1:37 **n** shall be impossible *3756, 3956, 4487*
Lk 8:17 **n is secret, that shall not be made** *3756*
Lk 12:2 **there is n covered, that shall not**. *3762*
Lk 23:9 words; but he answered him **n** *3762*
Lk 23:15 **n** worthy of death is done unto him. . . . *3762*
Lk 23:41 but this man hath done **n** amiss. *3762*
Jn 3:27 A man can receive **n**, except it be *3762*
Jn 5:19 **The Son can do n of himself, but** *3762*
Jn 6:39 **hath given me I should lose n,** *3361, 848*
Jn 8:28 **am he, and that I do n of myself;** *3762*
Jn 8:54 **I honour myself, my honour is n** *3762*
Jn 9:33 man were not of God, he could do **n** . . . *3762*
Jn 15:5 **fruit: for without me ye can do n** *3762*
Jn 16:24 **have ye asked n in my name:** *3762*
Jn 21:3 and that night they caught **n**. *3762*
Ac 26:31 This man doeth **n** worthy of death. *3762*
Ro 14:14 that there is **n** unclean of itself: *3762*
1Co 1:19 will bring to **n** the understanding. *114*
1Co 4:5 Therefore judge **n** before the time *3385*
1Co 8:2 he knoweth **n** yet as he ought to. *3762*
1Co 13:2 and have not charity, I am **n** *3762*
2Co 6:10 as having **n**, and yet possessing *3367*
2Co 13:8 we can do **n** against the truth, ... *3756, 5100*
Php 2:3 Let **n** be done through strife or. *3367*
Php 4:6 Be careful for **n**; but in every thing. *3367*
1Ti 6:7 For we brought **n** into this world, ... *3762*
Heb 7:19 For the law made **n** perfect, but the *3762*
Jas 1:6 let him ask in faith, **n** wavering: *3367*
Rev 3:17 **with goods, and have need of n;** *3762*

NOTICE
2Sa 3:36 all the people took **n** of it, and it. 5234

NOTWITHSTANDING
2Ki 17:14 **N** they would not hear, but
Mt 2:22 **n**, being warned of God in a dream,
Mt 11:11 **n he that is least in the kingdom**
Lk 10:20 **N in this rejoice not, that the** *4133*
2Ti 4:17 **N** the Lord stood with me, and
Rev 2:20 **N I have a few things against thee,** *235*

NOUGHT See also NAUGHT; NOTHING.
Ge 29:15 thou therefore serve me for **n**? 2600
Ne 4:15 had brought their counsel to **n** 6565
Job 1:9 said, Doth Job fear God for **n**? 2600
Ps 33:10 the counsel of the heathen to **n**: 6331
Pr 1:25 ye have set at **n** all my counsel, ... 6544
Isa 8:10 together, and it shall come to **n**; 6565
Isa 29:20 the terrible one is brought to **n**, ... 656
Isa 52:5 my people is taken away for **n**? 2600
Mk 9:12 **many things, and be set at n** *1847*
Ac 5:38 work be of men, it will come to **n**: *2647*
Ro 14:10 why dost thou set at **n** thy brother? *1848*
1Co 1:28 not, to bring to **n** things that are: *2673*

NOURISH
Ge 50:21 I will **n** you, and your little ones 3557
Isa 44:14 an ash, and the rain doth **n** it. 1431

NOURISHED
2Sa 12:3 which he had bought and **n** up: 2421
Ac 7:21 him up, and **n** him for her own son *397*

1Ti 4:6 **n** up in the words of faith and of *1789*
Jas 5:5 ye have **n** your hearts, as in a day *5142*
Rev 12:14 her place, where she is **n** for a time, ... *5142*

NOURISHING
Da 1:5 so **n** them three years, that at the 1431

NOVICE
1Ti 3:6 Not a **n**, lest being lifted up with....... *3504*

NOW
Ge 2:23 This is **n** bones of my bones, and...... 6471
Ge 22:2 Take **n** thy son, thine only son......... 4994
Ge 22:12 for **n** I know that thou fearest God, ... 6258
Ex 3:3 I will **n** turn aside, and see this 4994
Dt 4:32 ask **n** of the days that are past, ... 4994
Dt 10:12 **n**, Israel, what doth the Lord thy....... 6258
1Sa 12:13 **N** therefore behold the king whom 6258
1Sa 17:29 David said, What have I **n** done?....... 6258
2Sa 12:23 **n** he is dead, wherefore should 6258
2Sa 24:14 fall **n** into the hand of the Lord;....... 4994
2Sa 24:16 is enough: stay **n** thine hand 6258
2Ki 7:19 **N**, behold, if the Lord should make
1Ch 21:15 is enough, stay **n** thine hand 6258
1Ch 22:19 **N** set your heart and your soul 6258
2Ch 7:16 For **n** have I chosen and sanctified..... 6258
2Ch 9:13 **N** the weight of gold that came to
Ezr 9:8 And **n** for a little space grace hath 6258
Job 1:6 **N** there was a day when the sons of
Job 1:11 But put forth thine hand **n**, and 4994
Job 2:5 But put forth thine hand **n**, and 4994
Job 17:15 And where is **n** my hope? as for 645
Job 19:23 Oh that my words were **n** written! 645
Job 24:25 if it be not so **n**, who will make......... 645
Job 30:9 And **n** am I their song, yea, I am 6258
Ps 20:6 **N** know I that the Lord saveth his 6258
Ps 115:2 say, Where is **n** their God? 4994
Pr 7:12 **N** is she without, **n** in the streets, ... 6471
Ecc 2:16 which **n** is in the days to come 3528
Ecc 12:1 Remember **n** thy Creator in the days
Isa 1:18 Come **n**, and let us reason 4994
Isa 38:3 Remember **n**, O Lord, I beseech 4994
Jer 4:31 Woe is me **n**! for my soul is........... 4994
Jer 45:3 Woe is me **n**! for the Lord hath........ 4994
Da 5:12 **n** let Daniel be called, and he will...... 3705
Da 6:10 **N** when Daniel knew that the 1768
Mal 1:9 **n**, I pray you, beseech God that........ 6258
Mt 1:18 **N** the birth of Jesus Christ was on *1161*
Mt 1:22 **N** all this was done, that it might *1161*
Mt 11:12 **until n the kingdom of heaven** *737*
Mt 26:45 **Sleep on n, and take your rest:** *3063*
Mt 27:43 let him deliver him **n**, if he will........ *3568*
Mk 8:2 **have n been with me three days,** *2236*
Mk 14:41 **Sleep on n, and take your rest: it** *3063*
Lk 6:21 **Blessed are ye that hunger n: for** *3568*
Lk 6:21 **Blessed are ye that weep n: for ye** *3568*
Lk 11:7 **the door is n shut, and my** *2236*
Lk 16:25 **n he is comforted, and thou art** *3568*
Jn 4:23 **the hour cometh, and n is, when** *3568*
Jn 5:25 **The hour is coming, and n is,** *3568*
Jn 9:25 that, whereas I was blind, **n** I see........ *737*
Jn 13:31 **N is the Son of man glorified,** *3568*
Jn 18:36 **n is my kingdom not from hence** *3568*
Jn 21:14 This is **n** the third time that Jesus...... *2236*
Ro 1:13 **N** I would not have you ignorant,...... *1161*
Ro 6:8 **N** if we be dead with Christ, we *1161*
Ro 7:17 **N** then it is no more I that do it,....... *3570*
Ro 7:20 **N** if I do that I would not, it is no...... *1161*
Ro 8:1 therefore **n** no condemnation to....... *3568*
Ro 8:9 **N** if any man have not the Spirit....... *1161*
Ro 13:11 for **n** is our salvation nearer than *3568*
1Co 15:20 **n** is Christ risen from the dead *3570*
Eph 2:2 the spirit that **n** worketh in the........ *3568*
Eph 3:20 **N** unto him that is able to do *1161*
1Ti 1:17 **N** unto the King eternal, immortal, ... *1161*
Heb 10:38 **N** the just shall live by faith: but *1161*
Heb 11:1 **N** faith is the substance of things *1161*
Heb 12:11 **N** no chastening for the present *1161*
1Pe 3:21 even baptism doth also **n** save us *3568*
1Jn 2:28 **n**, little children, abide in him; *3568*
1Jn 3:2 Beloved, **n** are we the sons of God,..... *3568*
Jude 24 **N** unto him that is able to keep........ *1161*

NUMBER
Ge 15:5 stars, if thou be able to **n** them: 5608
Ex 12:4 it according to the **n** of the souls;...... 4373
Nu 3:40 **N** all the firstborn of the males of...... 6485
1Ch 11:11 **n** of the mighty men whom David..... 4557
Job 36:26 can the **n** of his years be searched...... 4557
Ps 90:12 So teach us to **n** our days, that 4487
Ps 147:4 He telleth the **n** of the stars; he........ 4557
Da 9:2 by books the **n** of the years,........... 4557
Jn 6:10 sat down, in **n** about five thousand...... *706*
Ac 4:4 the **n** of the men was about five *706*
Ac 5:36 to whom a **n** of men, about four *706*
Ac 11:21 and a great **n** believed, and turned *706*
Ac 16:5 the faith, and increased in **n** daily....... *706*
Ro 9:27 the **n** of the children of Israel be........ *706*
Rev 7:9 multitude, which no man could **n**,...... *705*
Rev 13:18 his **n** is Six hundred threescore *706*
Rev 20:8 **n** of whom is as the sand of the sea *706*

NUMBERED
Ge 13:16 then shall thy seed also be **n** 4487
Ex 30:14 among them that are **n**, ... 6485
Nu 4:49 they were **n** by the hand of Moses,..... 6485
2Sa 18:1 David **n** the people that were with 6485
Ps 40:5 them, they are more than can be **n**..... 5608
Ecc 1:15 which is wanting cannot be **n** 4487
Jer 33:22 the host of heaven cannot be **n**, ... 5608
Da 5:26 God hath **n** thy kingdom, and......... 4483
Hos 1:10 which cannot be measured nor **n**; 5608
Mt 10:30 **very hairs of your head are all n**........ *705*
Mk 15:28 he was **n** with the transgressors........ *3049*
Lk 12:7 **very hairs of your head are all n**........ *705*

NUMBEREST
Job 14:16 For now thou **n** my steps: dost 5608

NURSE
Ex 2:7 to thee a **n** of the Hebrew women 3243
1Th 2:7 as a **n** cherisheth her children;......... *5162*

NURSED
Ex 2:9 woman took the child, and **n** it........ 5134

NURTURE
Eph 6:4 **n** and admonition of the Lord......... *3809*

O

OAK

Ge 35:4 Jacob hid them under the **o** which 424
Jos 24:26 set it up there under an **o**, that was 427
Jgs 6:11 under an **o** which was in Ophrah, ... 424
2Sa 18:10 I saw Absalom hanged in an **o**.......... 424
2Sa 18:14 was yet alive in the midst of the **o**....... 424
1Ch 10:12 buried their bones under the **o** in....... 424
Isa 1:30 shall be as an **o** whose leaf fadeth, ... 424
Isa 6:13 and as an **o**, whose substance is in 437
Isa 44:14 taketh the cypress and the **o**, which,..... 437
Eze 6:13 and under every thick **o**, the place 424

OAKS

Isa 1:29 be ashamed of the **o** which ye have 352
Isa 2:13 up, and upon all the **o** of Bashan,....... 437
Hos 4:13 hills, under **o** and poplars and elms, ... 437
Am 2:9 and he was strong as the **o**; yet I........ 437
Zec 11:2 howl. O ye **o** of Bashan; for the......... 437

OAR

Eze 27:29 And all that handle the **o**, the 4880

OARS

Isa 33:21 wherein shall go no galley with **o**...... 7885

OATH

Ge 24:8 shalt be clear from this my **o**.......... 7621
Ge 24:41 shalt thou be clear from this my **o**,...... 423
Ge 26:3 I will perform the **o** which I 7621
Ge 26:28 Let there be now an **o** betwixt us,....... 423
Ge 50:25 Joseph took an **o** of the children....... 7650
Ex 22:11 an **o** of the Lord be between them 7621
Le 5:4 a man shall pronounce with an **o**, ... 7621
Nu 5:19 priest shall charge her by an **o**, ... 7650
Nu 5:21 Lord make thee a curse and an **o** 7621
Nu 30:2 swear an **o** to bind his soul with a 7621
Nu 30:10 her soul by a bond with an **o**; 7621
Nu 30:13 every binding **o** to afflict the soul, ... 7621
Dt 7:8 he would keep the **o** which he had..... 7621
Dt 29:14 do I make this covenant and this **o**; 423
Jos 2:17 will be blameless of this thine **o** 7621
Jos 2:20 then we will be quit of thine **o** 7621
Jos 9:20 because of the **o** which we sware 7621
Jgs 21:5 had made a great **o** concerning him.... 7621
1Sa 14:26 mouth: for the people feared the **o**..... 7621
1Sa 14:28 charged the people with an **o**,......... 7650
2Sa 21:7 Lord's **o** that was between them,....... 7621
1Ki 2:43 thou not kept the **o** of the Lord,........ 7621
1Ki 8:31 **o** come before thine altar in this........ 423
1Ki 18:10 he took an **o** of the kingdom and...... 7650
2Ki 11:4 took an **o** of them in the house of 7650
1Ch 16:16 Abraham, and of his **o** unto Isaac; 7621
2Ch 6:22 the **o** come before the altar in this 423
2Ch 15:15 And all Judah rejoiced at the **o**:........ 7621
Ne 5:12 priests, and took an **o** of them,........ 7650
Ne 10:29 entered into a curse, and into an **o**, ... 7621
Ps 105:9 Abraham, and his **o** unto Isaac; 7621
Ecc 8:2 and that in regard of the **o** of God. 7621
Ecc 9:2 sweareth, as he that feareth an **o**....... 7621
Jer 11:5 That I may perform the **o** which I 7621
Eze 16:59 despised the **o** in breaking the.......... 423
Eze 17:16 whose **o** he despised, and whose........ 423
Eze 17:19 surely mine **o** that he hath despised, ... 423
Da 9:11 the **o** that is written in the law of 7621
Zec 8:17 his neighbour; and love no false **o**:..... 7621
Mt 14:7 he promised with an **o** to give her *3727*
Mt 26:72 he denied with an **o**, I do not know *3727*
Lk 1:73 **o** which he sware to our father *3727*
Ac 2:30 God had sworn with an **o** to him, ... *3727*
Ac 23:21 have bound themselves with an **o**, ... *332*
Heb 6:16 an **o** for confirmation is to them....... *5727*
Heb 6:17 his counsel, confirmed it by an **o**:...... *3727*
Heb 7:20 without an **o** he was made priest:...... *3728*
Heb 7:21 but this with an **o** by him that said..... *3728*
Heb 7:28 the word of the **o**, which was since..... *3728*
Jas 5:12 the earth, neither by any other **o**: *3727*

OATHS

Eze 21:23 sight, to them that have sworn **o**....... 7621
Mt 5:33 **perform unto the Lord thine o**........ *3727*

OBEDIENCE See also DISOBEDIENCE.

Ro 1:5 **o** to the faith among all nations,....... *5218*
Ro 5:19 so by the **o** of one shall many be....... *5218*
Ro 6:16 death, or of **o** unto righteousness? *5218*
Ro 16:19 For your **o** is come abroad unto all *5275*
Ro 16:26 to all nations for the **o** of faith:........ *5218*
1Co 14:34 are commanded to be under **o**,........ *5293*
2Co 7:15 he remembereth the **o** of you all, ... *5218*
2Co 10:5 every thought to the **o** of Christ;....... *5218*
2Co 10:6 when your **o** is fulfilled............... *5218*
Phm 21 Having confidence in thy **o** I wrote *5218*
Heb 5:8 yet learned he **o** by the things *5218*
1Pe 1:2 unto **o** and sprinkling of the blood *5218*

OBEDIENT See also DISOBEDIENT.

Ex 24:7 Lord hath said will we do, and be **o** 8085
Nu 27:20 the children of Israel may be **o** 8085
Dt 4:30 and shalt be **o** unto his voice; 8085
Dt 8:20 ye would not be **o** unto the voice 8085
2Sa 22:45 they hear, they shall be **o** unto me...... 8085
Pr 25:12 so is a wise reprover upon an **o** ear 8085
Isa 1:19 If ye be willing and **o**, ye shall eat...... 8085
Isa 42:24 neither were they **o** unto his law. 8085
Ac 6:7 of the priests were **o** to the faith........ *5219*
Ro 15:18 to make the Gentiles **o**, by word *5218*
2Co 2:9 whether ye be **o** in all things........... *5255*
Eph 6:5 **o** to them that are your masters *5219*
Php 2:8 and became **o** unto death, even......... *5255*
Tit 2:5 good, **o** to their own husbands,........ *5293*
Tit 2:9 to be **o** unto their own masters, ... *5293*
1Pe 1:14 As **o** children, not fashioning.......... *5218*

OBEISANCE

Ge 37:7 about, and made **o** to my sheaf. 7812
Ge 37:9 moon and the eleven stars made **o**..... 7812
Ge 43:28 down their heads, and made **o**,........ 7812
Ex 18:7 meet his father in law, and did **o**, ... 7812
2Sa 1:2 that he fell to the earth, and did **o** 7812
2Sa 14:4 her face to the ground, and did **o**...... 7812
2Sa 15:5 man came nigh to him to do him **o**, ... 7812
1Ki 1:16 Bath-sheba bowed, and did **o** unto..... 7812
2Ch 24:17 of Judah, and made **o** to the king...... 7812

OBEY

Ge 27:8 my son, **o** my voice according to....... 8085
Ge 27:13 only **o** my voice, and go fetch me...... 8085
Ge 27:43 my son, **o** my voice; and arise, flee 8085
Ex 5:2 should **o** his voice to let Israel go? 8085

Ex	19:5	if ye will **o** my voice indeed, and	8085
Ex	23:21	Beware of him, and **o** his voice,	8085
Ex	23:22	if thou shalt indeed **o** his voice,	8085
Dt	11:27	if ye **o** the commandments of the	8085
Dt	11:28	if ye will not **o** the commandments	8085
Dt	13:4	commandments, and **o** his voice,	8085
Dt	21:18	will not **o** the voice of his father,	8085
Dt	21:20	rebellious, he will not **o** our voice;	8085
Dt	27:10	**o** the voice of the Lord thy God,	8085
Dt	28:62	wouldest not **o** the voice of the	8085
Dt	30:2	shalt **o** his voice according to all	8085
Dt	30:8	return and **o** the voice of the Lord,	8085
Dt	30:20	and that thou mayest **o** his voice,	8085
Jos	24:24	we serve, and his voice will we **o**.	8085
1Sa	8:19	refused to **o** the voice of Samuel;	8085
1Sa	12:14	serve him, and **o** his voice, and not	8085
1Sa	12:15	ye will not **o** the voice of the Lord,	8085
1Sa	15:19	didst thou not **o** the voice of the	8085
1Sa	15:22	to **o** is better than sacrifice, and to	8085
Ne	9:17	refused to **o**, neither were mindful	8085
Job	36:11	If they **o** and serve him, they shall	8085
Job	36:12	But if they **o** not, they shall perish	8085
Ps	18:44	they hear of me, they shall **o** me:	8085
Pr	30:17	and despiseth to **o** his mother,	3349
Jer	7:23	**O** my voice, and I will be your	8085
Jer	11:4	**O** my voice, and do them according.	8085
Jer	11:7	and protesting, saying, **O** my voice.	8085
Jer	12:17	if they will not **o**, I will utterly.	8085
Jer	18:10	in my sight, that it **o** not my voice,	8085
Jer	26:13	**o** the voice of the Lord your God;	8085
Jer	35:14	but **o** their father's commandment:	8085
Jer	38:20	**O**, I beseech thee, the voice of the	8085
Jer	42:6	when we **o** the voice of the Lord.	8085
Jer	42:13	neither **o** the voice of the Lord your.	8085
Da	7:27	dominions shall serve and **o** him.	8086
Da	9:11	that they might not **o** thy voice;	8085
Zec	6:15	diligently **o** the voice of the Lord	8085
Mt	8:27	even the winds and the sea **o** him!	*5219*
Mk	1:27	unclean spirits, and they do **o** him.	*5219*
Mk	4:41	even the wind and the sea **o** him?	*5219*
Lk	8:25	winds and water, and they **o** him	*5219*
Lk	17:6	**in the sea; and it should o you.**	*5219*
Ac	5:29	ought to **o** God rather than men	*3980*
Ac	5:32	God hath given to them that **o** him.	*3980*
Ac	7:39	our fathers would not **o**,	5255, 1036
Ro	2:8	and do not **o** the truth, but	*544*
Ro	2:8	the truth, but **o** unrighteousness,	*3982*
Ro	6:12	yield yourselves servants to **o**,	*5218*
Ro	6:16	his servants ye are to whom ye **o**;	*5219*
Gal	3:1	that ye should not **o** the truth.	*3982*
Gal	5:7	that ye should not **o** the truth?	*3982*
Eph	6:1	Children, **o** your parents in the	*5219*
Col	3:20	Children, **o** your parents in all.	*5219*
Col	3:22	**o** in all things your masters	*5219*
2Th	1:8	that **o** not the gospel of our Lord	*5219*
2Th	3:14	if any man **o** not our word by this	*5219*
Tit	3:1	to **o** magistrates, to be ready to	*3980*
Heb	5:9	salvation unto all them that **o**	*5219*
Heb	13:17	**O** them that have the rule over	*3982*
Jas	3:3	horses' mouths, that they may **o**	*3982*
1Pe	3:1	if any **o** not the word, they also.	*544*
1Pe	4:17	them that **o** not the gospel of God?	*544*

OBEYED

Ge	22:18	because thou hast **o** my voice	8085
Ge	26:5	Because that Abraham **o** my voice,	8085
Ge	28:7	Jacob **o** his father and his mother,	8085
Jos	5:6	they **o** not the voice of the Lord:	8085
Jos	22:2	**o** my voice in all that I commanded.	8085
Jgs	2:2	but ye have not **o** my voice: why	8085
Jgs	6:10	dwell: but ye have not **o** my voice	8085
1Sa	15:20	Yea, I have **o** the voice of the Lord,	8085
1Sa	15:24	the people, and **o** their voice.	8085
1Sa	28:21	thine handmaid hath **o** thy voice,	8085
1Ki	20:36	hast not **o** the voice of the Lord,	8085
2Ki	18:12	they **o** not the voice of the Lord	8085
1Ch	29:23	prospered; and all Israel **o** him.	8085
2Ch	11:4	they **o** the words of the Lord, and.	8085
Pr	5:13	have not **o** the voice of my teachers,	8085
Jer	3:13	ye have not **o** my voice, saith the	8085
Jer	3:25	have not **o** the voice of the Lord our	8085
Jer	9:13	and have not **o** my voice, neither	8085
Jer	11:8	Yet they **o** not, nor inclined their	8085
Jer	17:23	they **o** not, neither inclined their	8085
Jer	32:23	but they **o** not thy voice, neither	8085
Jer	35:18	**o** the commandment of Jonadab	8085
Jer	40:3	the Lord, and have not **o** his voice,	8085
Jer	42:21	not **o** the voice of the Lord your	8085
Jer	43:4	**o** not the voice of the Lord, to dwell	8085
Jer	43:7	they **o** not the voice of the Lord:	8085
Jer	44:23	have not **o** the voice of the Lord,	8085
Da	9:10	Neither have we **o** the voice of the	8085
Da	9:14	he doeth: for we **o** not his voice	8085
Zep	3:2	She **o** not the voice; she received.	8085
Hag	1:12	**o** the voice of the Lord their God,	8085
Ro	6:17	have **o** from the heart that form	*5219*
Ro	10:16	they have not all **o** the gospel	*5219*
Php	2:12	my beloved, as ye have always **o**,	*5219*
Heb	11:8	By faith Abraham ... **o**;	*5219*
1Pe	3:6	Even as Sara **o** Abraham, calling	*5219*

OBEYETH

Isa	50:10	that **o** the voice of his servant,	8085
Jer	7:28	a nation that **o** not the voice of the	8085
Jer	11:3	Cursed be the man that **o** not the.	8085

OBEYING

Jgs	2:17	**o** the commandments of the Lord;	8085
1Sa	15:22	as in **o** the voice of the Lord?	8085
1Pe	1:22	purified your souls in **o** the truth	*5218*

OBLATION

Le	2:4	thou bring an **o** of a meat offering	7133
Le	2:13	every **o** of thy meat offering shalt	7133
Le	7:14	one out of the whole **o** for an heave.	7133
Le	22:18	that will offer his **o** for all his vows.	7133
Nu	18:9	every **o** of theirs, every meat	7133
Nu	31:50	We have therefore brought an **o**	7133
Isa	19:21	and shall do sacrifice and **o**; yea	4503
Isa	40:20	so impoverished that he hath no **o**.	8641
Isa	66:3	he that offereth an **o**, as if he	4503
Jer	14:12	they offer burnt offering and an **o**,	4503
Eze	44:30	every **o** all, of every sort of	8641
Eze	45:1	ye shall offer an **o** unto the Lord,	8641
Eze	45:16	give this **o** for the prince in Israel.	8641
Eze	48:10	for the priests, shall be this holy **o**;	8641
Da	2:46	should offer an **o** and sweet odours	4541
Da	9:27	the sacrifice and the **o** to cease,	4503

OBLATIONS

Le	7:38	children of Israel to offer their **o**.	7133
2Ch	31:14	to distribute the **o** of the Lord,	8641
Isa	1:13	Bring no more vain **o**; incense is.	4503

Eze 20:40 and the firstfruits of your **o**, 4864
Eze 44:30 of every sort of your **o**, shall be 8641

OBSCURE
Pr 20:20 shall be put out in **o** darkness. 380

OBSCURITY
Isa 29:18 eyes of the blind shall see out of **o**, 652
Isa 58:10 then shall thy light rise in **o**, and 2822
Isa 59:9 we wait for light, but behold **o**; 2822

OBSERVATION
Lk 17:20 **of God cometh not with o:** *3907*

OBSERVE
Ex 12:17 **o** the feast of unleavened bread; 8104
Ex 12:24 shall **o** this thing for an ordinance 8104
Ex 31:16 **o** the sabbath throughout their 6213
Ex 34:11 **O** thou that which I command 8104
Ex 34:22 thou shalt **o** the feast of weeks, 6213
Le 19:26 ye use enchantment, nor **o** times 6049
Le 19:37 shall ye **o** all my statutes, and 8104
Dt 5:32 shall **o** to do therefore as the Lord 8104
Dt 6:3 O Israel, and **O** to do it; that it 8104
Dt 8:1 commandments … shall ye **o** to do, 8104
Dt 12:1 which ye shall **o** to do in the land, 8104
Dt 12:28 **O** and hear all these words which 8104
Dt 12:32 soever I command you, **o** to do it: 8104
Dt 16:1 **O** the mouth of Abib, and keep the 8104
Dt 16:13 shalt **o** the feast of tabernacles 6213
Dt 28:1 to **o** and to do … his commandments 8104
Dt 28:13 thee this day, to **o** and to do them: 8104
Dt 28:58 wilt not **o** to do all the words of 8104
Dt 31:12 **o** to do all the words of this law: 8104
Jos 1:7, 8 thou mayest **o** to do according to 8104
2Ki 17:37 ye shall **o** to do for evermore; 8104
2Ki 21:8 only if they will **o** to do according 8104
2Ch 7:17 and shalt **o** my statutes and my 8104
Ne 1:5 him and **o** his commandments: 8104
Ne 10:29 to **o** and do all the commandments 8104
Ps 107:43 is wise, and will **o** these things, 8104
Ps 119:34 I shall **o** it with my whole heart 8104
Pr 23:26 and let thine eyes **o** my ways. 5341
Jer 8:7 the swallow **o** the time of their 8104
Eze 20:18 neither **o** their judgments, nor 8104
Eze 37:24 and **o** my statutes, and do them 8104
Hos 13:7 as a leopard by the way will I **o** 7789
Jnh 2:8 They that **o** lying vanities forsake 8104
Mt 23:3 **that o and do; but do not ye** *5083*
Mt 28:20 **Teaching them to o all things** *5083*
Ac 16:21 to receive, neither to **o**, being *4160*
Ac 21:25 that they **o** no such thing, save *5083*
Gal 4:10 Ye **o** days, and months, and *3906*
1Ti 5:21 that thou **o** these things without *5442*

OBSERVED
Ge 37:11 him; but his father **o** the saying 8104
Ex 12:42 is that night of the Lord to be **o** of 8107
Nu 15:22 not **o** all these commandments, 6213
Dt 33:9 they have **o** thy word, and kept 8104
2Sa 11:16 to pass, when Joab **o** the city, 8104
2Ki 21:6 through the fire, and **o** times, 6049
2Ch 33:6 also he **o** times, and used 6049
Mk 6:20 just man and a holy, and **o** him; *4933*
Mk 10:20 all these have I **o** from my youth *5442*

OBSERVER See also OBSERVERS.
Dt 18:10 an **o** of times, or an enchanter, 6049

OBSERVERS
Dt 18:14 hearkened unto **o** of times, and 6049

OBSERVETH
Ecc 11:4 He that **o** the wind shall not sow; 8104

OBSTINATE
Dt 2:30 his spirit, and made his heart **o**, 553
Isa 48:4 Because I knew that thou art **o**, 7186

OBTAIN
Pr 8:35 and shall **o** favour of the Lord 6329
Isa 35:10 they shall **o** joy and gladness, and 5381
Isa 51:11 they shall **o** gladness and joy; and 5381
Da 11:21 and **o** the kingdom by flatteries 2388
Mt 5:7 **merciful: for they shall o mercy** *1653*
Lk 20:35 **accounted worthy to o that world,** *5177*
Ro 11:31 mercy they also may **o** mercy *1653*
1Co 9:24 the prize? So run, that ye may **o**, *2638*
1Co 9:25 do it to **o** a corruptible crown; *2983*
1Th 5:9 to **o** salvation by our Lord Jesus *4047*
2Ti 2:10 that they may also **o** the salvation *5177*
Heb 4:16 that we may **o** mercy, and find *2983*
Heb 11:35 might **o** a better resurrection: *5177*
Jas 4:2 and desire to have, and cannot **o**: *2013*

OBTAINED
Est 5:2 that she **o** favour in his sight: 5375
Hos 2:23 upon her that had not **o** mercy; 5375
Ac 22:28 With a great sum **o** I this freedom *2932*
Ro 11:7 Israel hath not **o** that which he *2013*
Ro 11:30 **o** mercy through their unbelief: *1653*
1Co 7:25 one that hath **o** mercy of the Lord *1653*
Eph 1:11 also we have **o** an inheritance, *2820*
1Ti 1:16 Howbeit for this cause I **o** mercy, *1653*
Heb 1:4 by inheritance **o** a more excellent *2816*
Heb 6:15 endured, he **o** the promise. *2013*
Heb 8:6 he **o** a more excellent ministry, *5177*
Heb 9:12 **o** eternal redemption for us. *2147*
Heb 11:2 by it the elders **o** a good report. *3140*
Heb 11:4 **o** witness that he was righteous, *3140*
Heb 11:33 **o** promises, stopped the mouths of *2013*
Heb 11:39 **o** a good report through faith, *3140*
1Pe 2:10 of God: which had not **o** mercy, *1653*
2Pe 1:1 that have **o** like precious faith *2975*

OBTAINETH
Pr 12:2 A good man **o** favour of the Lord: 6329
Pr 18:22 thing, and **o** favour of the Lord. 6329

OCCASION
Ge 43:18 that he may seek **o** against us, and 1556
Jgs 14:4 sought an **o** against the Philistines: 8385
2Sa 12:14 given great **o** to the enemies of the
Eze 18:3 have **o** any more to use this proverb
Da 6:4 sought to find **o** against Daniel 5931
Ro 7:8 taking **o** by the commandment, *874*
Ro 7:11 taking **o** by the commandment, *874*
Ro 14:13 or an **o** to fall in his brother's way *4625*
Gal 5:13 use not liberty for an **o** to the flesh, *874*
1Ti 5:14 give none **o** to the adversary to *874*
1Jn 2:10 is none **o** of stumbling in him. *4625*

OCCASIONED
1Sa 22:22 **o** the death of all the persons *5437*

OCCASIONS
Job 33:10 Behold, he findeth **o** against me, 8569

O

OCCUPATION

Ge 47:3 unto his brethren, What is your o? 4639
Jnh 1:8 What is thine o? and whence. 4399
Ac 18:3 by their o they were tentmakers. 5078
Ac 19:25 together with the workmen of like o, . . . 5078

OCCUPIED

Heb 13:9 them that have been o therein. 4043

OCCUPY

Lk 19:13 and said unto them, O till I come. 4231

ODIOUS

1Ch 19:6 had made themselves o to David, ... 887
Pr 30:23 o woman when she is married; 8130

ODOUR

Jn 12:3 filled with the o of the ointment. 3744
Php 4:18 an o of a sweet smell, a sacrifice 3744

ODOURS

2Ch 16:14 bed which was filled with sweet o. 1314
Jer 34:5 thee, so shall they burn o for thee;
Da 2:46 an oblation and sweet o unto him 5208
Rev 5:8 golden vials full of o, which are. 2368

OFF See also OFFSPRING.

Ge 7:4 from o the face of the earth. 5921
Nu 7:89 unto him from o the mercy seat 5921
Dt 4:26 utterly perish from o the land 5921
Dt 11:17 ye perish … from o the good land 5921
2Sa 11:2 that David arose from o his bed,. 5921
Isa 6:6 with the tongs from o the altar 5921
Zep 1:2 all things from o the land 5921, 6440
Mt 5:30 right hand offend thee, cut it o, ... 1581
Mt 10:14 city, shake o the dust of your feet. 1621
Mt 18:8 thy foot offend thee, cut them o, ... 1581
Mt 26:51 high priest's, and smote o his ear 851
Mt 26:58 Peter followed him afar o unto the. 575
Mt 27:31 they took the robe o from him 1562
Mt 27:55 women were … beholding afar o,. 575
Mk 5:6 when he saw Jesus afar o, he ran. 575
Mk 6:11 shake o the dust under your feet 1621
Mk 9:43 if thy hand offend thee, cut it o: 609
Mk 9:45 if thy foot offend thee, cut it o: 609
Mk 14:47 of the high priest, and cut o his ear, ... 609
Mk 14:54 Peter followed him afar o, even. 575
Mk 15:20 they took o the purple from him, ... 609
Mk 15:40 were also women looking on afar o: 575
Lk 9:5 shake o the very dust from your. 660
Lk 15:20 when he was yet a great way o, ... 568
Lk 16:23 and seeth Abraham afar o, and. 575
Lk 18:13 publican, standing afar o, would
Lk 22:50 high priest, and cut o his right ear 851
Jn 18:10 servant, and cut o his right ear 609
Jn 18:26 his kinsman whose ear Peter cut o,. 609
Ac 13:51 shook o the dust of their feet. 1621
Ro 11:20 of unbelief they were broken o,. 1575
Ro 13:12 let us … cast o the work of darkness,. . . . 659
Eph 4:22 ye put o concerning the former. 659
Col 2:11 putting o the body of the sins of the 554
Col 3:8 But now ye also put o all these: 659
Col 3:9 put o the old man with his deeds;. 554
1Ti 5:12 they have cast o their first faith 114

OFFENCE

Isa 8:14 a rock of o to both the houses of 4383
Hos 5:15 till they acknowledge their o, and. 816
Mt 16:23 Satan: thou art an o unto me:. 4625
Mt 18:7 that man by whom the o cometh! 4625
Ac 24:16 conscience void of o toward God,. 677
Ro 5:15 not as the o, so also is the free. 3900
Ro 5:17 if by one man's o death reigned 3900
Ro 5:20 entered, that the o might abound. 3900
Ro 9:33 a stumblingstone and rock of o: 4625
Ro 14:20 for that man who eateth with o 4348
1Co 10:32 Give none o, neither to the Jews,. 677
2Co 6:3 Giving no o in any thing, that the. 4349
Gal 5:11 then is the o of the cross ceased 4625
Php 1:10 and without o till the day of Christ; 677
1Pe 2:8 of stumbling, and a rock of o, ... 4625

OFFENCES

Ecc 10:4 for yielding pacifieth great o 2399
Mt 18:7 Woe unto the world because of o! 4625
Mt 18:7 for it must needs be that o come 4625
Lk 17:1 impossible but that o will come: 4625
Ro 4:25 Who was delivered for our o, and. 3900
Ro 5:16 the free gift is of many o unto. 3900
Ro 16:17 them which cause divisions and o 4625

OFFEND

Ps 119:165 law: and nothing shall o them. 4383
Jer 50:7 We o not, because they have sinned 816
Hab 1:11 he shall pass over, and o, imputing. 816
Mt 5:29 if thy right eye o thee, pluck it 4624
Mt 5:30 if thy right hand o thee, cut it off, ... 4624
Mt 13:41 of his kingdom all things that o, ... 4625
Mt 17:27 lest we should o them, go thou to 4624
Mt 18:6 shall o one of these little ones. 4624
Mt 18:8 if thy hand or thy foot o thee, cut 4624
Mk 9:42 shall o one of these little ones. 4624
Mk 9:43 And if thy hand o thee, cut it off:. 4624
Mk 9:45 And if thy foot o thee, cut it off:. 4624
Mk 9:47 And if thine eye o thee, pluck it 4624
Lk 17:2 should o one of these little ones. 4624
Jn 6:61 said unto them, Doth this o you? 4624
1Co 8:13 if meat make my brother to o, ... 4624
Jas 2:10 the whole law, yet o in one point 4417
Jas 3:2 For in many things we o all 4417
Jas 3:2 If any man o not in word, the. 4417

OFFENDED

Ge 20:9 what have I o thee, that thou. 2398
2Ch 28:13 have o against the Lord already, ... 819
Pr 18:19 A brother o is harder to be won 6586
Jer 37:18 What have I o against thee, or. 2398
Mt 11:6 whosoever shall not be o in me, ... 4624
Mt 13:21 of the word, by and by he is o. 4624
Mt 13:57 And they were o in him. But Jesus 4624
Mt 24:10 And then shall many be o, and. 4624
Mt 26:31 All ye shall be o because of me 4624
Mt 26:33 Though all men shall be o because. 4624
Mk 4:17 sake, immediately they are o. 4624
Mk 6:3 with us? And they were o at him. 4624
Mk 14:27 All ye shall be o because of me 4624
Lk 7:23 whosoever shall not be o in me 4624
Jn 16:1 unto you, that ye should not be o 4624
Ro 14:21 brother stumbleth, or is o, or 4624
2Co 11:29 weak? who is o, and I burn not? 4624

OFFENDER

Isa 29:21 That make a man an o for a word 2398
Ac 25:11 if I be an o, or have committed. 91

OFFER

Ge	22:2	**o** him there for a burnt offering	5927
Ex	29:36	thou shalt **o** every day a bullock	6213
Ex	30:9	**o** no strange incense thereon,	5927
Le	1:3	shall **o** it of his own voluntary will	7126
Le	3:1	he shall **o** it without blemish before	7126
Le	6:21	shalt thou **o** for a sweet savour	7126
Le	7:12	If he **o** it for a thanksgiving, then	7126
Le	9:7	**o** the offering of the people, and	6213
Le	17:7	**o** their sacrifices unto devils,	2076
Le	19:5	Lord, ye shall **o** it at your own will	2076
Le	22:22	ye shall not **o** these unto the Lord,	7126
Le	23:37	**o** an offering made by fire	7126
Nu	8:11	Aaron shall **o** the Levites before	5130
Nu	18:26	shall **o** up an heave offering of it	7311
Nu	18:28	ye also shall **o** an heave offering	7311
Nu	18:29	ye shall **o** every heave offering of	7311
Nu	28:2	**o** unto me in their due season	7126
Nu	28:3	which ye shall **o** unto the Lord;	7126
Nu	28:4	lamb shalt thou **o** in the morning,	6213
Nu	28:4	other lamb shalt thou **o** at even;	6213
Nu	28:8	other lamb shalt thou **o** at even:	6213
Nu	28:8	thou shalt **o** it, a sacrifice made by	6213
Nu	28:11	ye shall **o** a burnt offering unto	7126
Nu	28:19	ye shall **o** a sacrifice made by fire,	7126
Nu	28:20	tenth deals shall ye **o** for a bullock,	6213
Nu	28:21	A several tenth deal shalt thou **o** for	6213
Nu	28:24	this manner ye shall **o** daily,	6213
Nu	28:31	shall **o** them beside the continual	6213
Nu	29:2	shall **o** a burnt offering for a sweet	6213
Nu	29:8	shall **o** a burnt offering unto the	7126
Nu	29:13	And ye shall **o** a burnt offering, a	7126
Nu	29:17	shall **o** twelve young bullocks, two	
Dt	12:13	thou **o** not thy burnt offerings in	5927
Dt	12:27	thou shalt **o** thy burnt offerings,	6213
Dt	18:3	from them that **o** a sacrifice,	2076
Dt	27:6	**o** burnt offerings thereon unto	5927
Dt	27:7	thou shalt **o** peace offerings, and	2076
Dt	33:19	shall **o** sacrifices of righteousness:	2076
Jos	22:23	**o** thereon burnt offering or meat	5927
Jos	22:23	if to **o** peace offerings thereon, let	6213
Jgs	3:18	made an end to **o** the present	7126
Jgs	6:26	**o** a burnt sacrifice with the wood	5927
Jgs	11:31	I will **o** it up for a burnt offering	5927
Jgs	13:16	if thou wilt **o** a burnt offering,	6213
Jgs	13:16	thou must **o** it unto the Lord	5927
Jgs	16:23	**o** a great sacrifice unto Dagon	2076
1Sa	1:21	went up to **o** unto the Lord the	2076
1Sa	2:19	husband to **o** the yearly sacrifice	2076
1Sa	2:28	to **o** upon mine altar, to burn	5927
2Sa	24:12	the Lord, I **o** thee three things;	5190
1Ki	9:25	did Solomon **o** burnt offerings	5927
1Ch	21:24	nor **o** burnt offerings without	5927
1Ch	29:17	here, to **o** willingly unto thee	
Ezr	6:10	may **o** sacrifices of sweet savours	7127
Job	42:8	and **o** up for yourselves a burnt	5927
Ps	4:5	**O** the sacrifices of righteousness,	2076
Ps	27:6	**o** in his tabernacle sacrifices of	2076
Ps	50:14	**O** unto God thanksgiving; and	2076
Jer	11:12	gods unto whom they **o** incense:	
Eze	20:31	For when ye **o** your gifts, when	5375
Eze	43:18	**o** burnt offerings thereon, and to	5927
Eze	48:20	**o** the holy oblation foursquare,	7311
Hos	9:4	not **o** wine offerings to the Lord,	5258
Am	5:22	Though ye **o** me burnt offerings	5927
Hag	2:14	which they **o** there is unclean	7126
Mal	1:8	if ye **o** the blind for sacrifice, is it	5066
Mal	1:8	**o** it now unto thy governor; will	7126
Mal	3:3	may **o** unto the Lord an offering	5066
Mt	5:24	**and then come and o thy gift**	*4374*
Mt	8:4	**o the gift that Moses commanded,**	*4374*
Lk	11:12	**an egg, will he o him a scorpion?**	*1929*
Heb	7:27	to **o** up sacrifice, first for his own	*399*
Heb	8:3	man have somewhat also to **o**	*4374*
Heb	8:4	that **o** gifts according to the law:	*4374*
Heb	9:25	that he should **o** himself often	*4374*
Heb	13:15	let us **o** the sacrifice of praise to	*399*
1Pe	2:5	to **o** up spiritual sacrifices	*399*
Rev	8:3	**o** it with the prayers of all saints	*1325*

OFFERED

Ge	8:20	**o** burnt offerings on the altar	5927
Ge	22:13	and **o** him up for a burnt offering	5927
Le	7:15	eaten the same day that it is **o**;	7133
Le	10:1	**o** strange fire before the Lord	7126
Nu	3:4	they **o** strange fire before the Lord,	7126
Nu	7:10	**o** for dedicating of the altar in	7126
Nu	16:35	and fifty men that **o** incense	7126
Nu	28:24	**o** beside the continual burnt	6213
Jgs	5:9	**o** themselves willingly among the	
2Sa	6:17	David **o** burnt offerings and peace	5927
1Ki	8:63	And Solomon **o** a sacrifice of peace	2076
2Ki	3:27	**o** him for a burnt offering upon	5927
1Ch	6:49	his sons **o** upon the altar of the	6999
1Ch	29:9	rejoiced, for that they **o** willingly,	
2Ch	1:6	**o** a thousand burnt offerings upon	5927
2Ch	7:5	And king Solomon **o** a sacrifice of	2076
2Ch	29:7	incense nor **o** burnt offerings	5927
Ezr	2:68	**o** freely for the house of God to	
Ezr	6:3	the place where they **o** sacrifices,	1684
Ezr	7:15	freely **o** unto the God of Israel,	5069
Isa	66:3	oblation, as if he **o** swine's blood;	5927
Jer	32:29	they have **o** incense unto Baal,	6999
Am	5:25	Have ye **o** unto me sacrifices and	5066
Jnh	1:16	**o** a sacrifice unto the Lord, and	2076
Ac	7:42	have ye **o** to me slain beasts and	*4374*
Ac	8:18	was given, he **o** them money	*4374*
Ac	15:29	ye abstain from meats **o** to idols,	*1494*
1Co	8:1	as touching things **o** unto idols,	*1494*
1Co	10:28	This is **o** in sacrifice unto idols,	*1494*
2Ti	4:6	For I am now ready to be **o**, and	*4689*
Heb	5:7	when he had **o** up prayers and	*4374*
Heb	7:27	he did once, when he **o** up himself	
Heb	9:14	**o** himself without spot to God,	*4374*
Heb	9:28	once **o** to bear the sins of many;	*4374*
Heb	10:1	they **o** year by year continually	*4374*
Heb	10:12	he had **o** one sacrifice for sins	*4374*
Heb	11:4	By faith Abel **o** unto God a more	*4374*
Heb	11:17	when he was tried, **o** up Isaac:	*4374*
Jas	2:21	when he had **o** Isaac his son upon	*399*

OFFERETH

Le	6:26	The priest that **o** it for sin shall	2398
Le	22:21	**o** a sacrifice of peace offerings unto	7126
Ps	50:23	Whoso **o** praise glorifieth me:	2076
Isa	66:3	he that **o** an oblation, as if he	5927

OFFERING

Ge	4:4	respect unto Abel and to his **o**:	4503
Ge	22:2	and offer him there for a burnt **o**	
Ge	22:7	where is the lamb for a burnt **o**?	
Ge	22:13	a burnt **o** in the stead of his son	
Ex	29:14	without the camp: it is a sin **o**	

Ex	29:25	an **o** made by fire unto the Lord	
Ex	29:42	This shall be a continual burnt **o**	
Ex	30:15	when they give an **o** unto the Lord,	8641
Ex	36:3	they received of Moses all the **o**,	8641
Le	1:3	If his **o** be a burnt sacrifice of the	7133
Le	1:4	upon the head of the burnt **o**;	
Le	1:9	an **o** made by fire, of a sweet	
Le	1:13	an **o** made by fire, of a sweet	
Le	3:8	his hand upon the head of his **o**,	7133
Le	4:21	it is a sin **o** for the congregation	
Le	4:29	hand upon the head of the sin **o**,	
Le	4:34	blood of the sin **o** with his finger,	
Le	6:9	This is the law of the burnt **o**:	
Le	6:14	And this is the law of the meat **o**:	4503
Le	6:25	saying, This is the law of the sin **o**:	
Le	7:1	this is the law of the trespass **o**:	
Le	7:37	This is the law of the burnt **o**,	
Le	8:29	waved it for a wave **o** before the Lord:	
Le	9:15	And he brought the people's **o**,	7133
Le	10:17	have ye not eaten the sin **o** in the	
Le	14:13	so is the trespass **o**: it is most holy:	
Le	16:9	lot fell, and offer him for a sin **o**	
Le	22:12	not eat of an **o** of the holy things	8641
Nu	5:15	thereon; for it is an **o** of jealousy,	4503
Nu	5:15	**o** of memorial, bringing iniquity	4503
Nu	6:21	**o** unto the Lord for his separation,	7133
Nu	16:15	Respect not thou their **o**: I have	4503
Nu	23:15	Balak, Stand here by thy burnt **o**,	
1Sa	2:17	for men abhorred the **o** of the Lord	4503
1Sa	26:19	against me, let him accept an **o**:	4503
2Ch	8:13	**o** according to the commandment	5927
Ezr	1:4	freewill **o** for the house of God	
Ne	10:33	and for the continual meat **o**,	4503
Ps	40:6	and **o** thou didst not desire;	4503
Ps	51:16	thou delightest not in burnt **o**	
Ps	96:8	bring an **o**, and come into his	4503
Isa	61:8	I hate robbery for burnt **o**;	
Isa	66:20	bring an **o** in a clean vessel into	4503
Jer	11:17	me to anger in **o** incense unto Baal	
Eze	20:28	the provocation of their **o**:	7133
Eze	45:15	pastures of Israel; for a meat **o**,	4503
Joel	1:9	drink **o** is cut off from the house	
Mal	1:10	neither will I accept an **o** at your	4503
Mal	1:11	unto my name, and a pure **o**:	4503
Mal	2:13	he regardeth not the **o** any more,	4503
Mal	3:3	the Lord an **o** in righteousness	4503
Lk	23:36	coming to him, and **o** him vinegar,	*4374*
Ro	15:16	the **o** up of the Gentiles might be	*4376*
Eph	5:2	hath given himself for us an **o** and	*4376*
Heb	10:5	Sacrifice and **o** thou wouldest not,	*4376*
Heb	10:8	Sacrifice and **o** and burnt offerings	*4376*
Heb	10:10	through the **o** of the body of Jesus	*4376*
Heb	10:14	by one **o** he hath perfected for ever	*4376*
Heb	10:18	these is, there is no more **o** for sin	*4376*

OFFERINGS

Ex	36:3	brought yet unto him free **o** every	
Le	7:11	the law of the sacrifice of peace **o**,	
Nu	10:10	the trumpets over your burnt **o**,	
Dt	32:38	drank the wine of their drink **o**?	
1Sa	2:29	chiefest of all the **o** of Israel my	4503
1Sa	15:22	Lord as great delight in burnt **o**	
1Ki	3:4	a thousand burnt **o** did Solomon	
2Ch	31:12	brought in the **o** and the tithes	8641
Ezr	3:4	and offered the daily burnt **o** by	
Ne	12:44	for the treasures, for the **o**, for	8641
Job	1:5	offered burnt **o** according to the	
Ps	16:4	their drink **o** of the blood will I not offer,	
Ps	66:13	go into thy house with burnt **o**:	
Pro	7:14	I have peace **o** with me; this day	
Isa	1:11	I am full of the burnt **o** of rams,	
Jer	7:18	pour out drink **o** unto other gods,	5262
Eze	20:40	and there will I require your **o**,	8641
Hos	6:6	of God more than burnt **o**	
Hos	9:4	shall not offer wine **o** to the Lord,	
Am	5:22	meat **o**, I will not accept them:	4503
Am	5:25	**o** in the wilderness forty years,	4503
Mic	6:6	I come before him with burnt **o**,	
Mal	3:8	we robbed thee? In tithes and **o**	8641
Mk	12:33	all whole burnt **o** and sacrifices	*3646*
Lk	21:4	**cast in unto the o of God:**	*1435*
Heb	10:6	In burnt **o** and sacrifices for sin	*3646*
Heb	10:8	and burnt **o** and offering for sin	*3646*

OFFICE

Ge	41:13	me he restored unto mine **o**, and	3653
Ex	28:1	minister unto me in the priest's **o**,	
1Ch	23:28	their **o** was to wait on the sons of	4612
2Ch	24:11	was brought unto the king's **o** by	6486
Ps	109:8	few; and let another take his **o**	6486
Lk	1:9	to the custom of the priest's **o**	*2405*
Ro	12:4	all members have not the same **o**:	*4234*
1Ti	3:1	If a man desire the **o** of a bishop	*1984*
1Ti	3:10	let them use the **o** of a deacon,	*1247*
1Ti	3:13	that have used the **o** of a deacon	*1247*
Heb	7:5	receive the **o** of the priesthood,	*2405*

OFFICER

Ge	37:36	unto Potiphar, an **o** of Pharaoh's,	5631
2Ki	8:6	appointed unto her a certain **o**,	5631
2Ch	24:11	priest's **o** came and emptied the	6496
Mt	5:25	**the judge deliver thee to the o,**	*5257*
Lk	12:58	**and the o cast thee into prison.**	*4233*

OFFICERS

Ge	40:2	was wroth against two of his **o**,	5631
Ge	41:34	let him appoint **o** over the land,	6496
Ex	5:14	And the **o** of the children of Israel,	7860
Dt	16:18	Judges and **o** shalt thou make thee	7860
1Sa	8:15	give to his **o**, and to his servants	5631
1Ki	5:16	the chief of Solomon's **o** which	5324
1Ch	23:4	six thousand were **o** and judges:	7860
Est	9:3	**o** of the king, helped the Jews;	6213
Jn	7:32	chief priests sent **o** to take him	*5257*
Jn	7:46	The **o** answered, Never man spake	*5257*
Jn	18:12	and **o** of the Jews took Jesus, and	*5257*

OFFICES

1Sa	2:36	pray thee, into one of the priest's **o**,	
2Ch	7:6	And the priests waited on their **o**:	4931
Ne	13:14	of my God, and for the **o** thereof.	4929

OFFSPRING

Isa	44:3	and my blessing upon thine **o**:	6631
Isa	61:9	and their **o** among the people:	6631
Ac	17:28	have said, For we are also his **o**	*1085*
Rev	22:16	**I am the root and the o of David,**	*1085*

OFT

Ps	78:40	How **o** did they provoke him in	
Mt	18:21	how **o** shall my brother sin against	*4212*
1Co	11:25	**this do ye, as o as ye drink it, in**	*3740*

OFTEN

Pr	29:1	He, that being **o** reproved hardeneth	
Mal	3:16	they that feared the Lord spake **o** one	
Mt	23:37	**how o would I have gathered thy.**	*4212*
Lk	13:34	**how o would I have gathered thy**	*4212*
1Co	11:26	For as **o** as ye eat this bread, and	*3740*
2Co	11:26	In journeyings **o**, in perils of	*3740*
Php	3:18	walk, of whom I have told you **o**.	*3740*
1Ti	5:23	stomach's sake and thine **o** infirmities	*4437*

OFTENTIMES

Ecc	7:22	For **o** also thine own heart	6471, 7227
Heb	10:11	and offering **o** the same sacrifices,	*4178*

OIL

Ex	30:25	make it an **o** of holy ointment, an	8081
Ex	40:9	thou shalt take the anointing **o**	8081
Le	8:10	Moses took the anointing **o**, and	8081
Le	8:30	Moses look of the anointing **o**, and	8081
Le	14:16	shall dip his right finger in the **o**.	8081
Le	14:17	the rest of the **o** that is in his hand	8081
Le	21:12	the crown of the anointing **o** of his	8081
Nu	11:8	of it as the taste of fresh **o**	8081
Nu	35:25	was anointed with the holy **o**	8081
Dt	8:8	a land of **o** olive, and honey;	8081
1Sa	10:1	Samuel took a vial of **o**, and poured	8081
1Ki	17:14	neither shall the cruse of **o** fail,	8081
2Ki	4:7	Go, sell the **o**, and pay thy debt,	8081
Ps	23:5	thou anointest my head with **o**;	8081
Ps	45:7	anointed thee with ... **o** of gladness	8081
Ps	55:21	his words were softer than **o**, yet	8081
Ps	104:15	**o** to make his face to shine, and	8081
Pr	5:3	and her mouth is smoother than **o**:	8081
Pr	21:17	he that loveth wine and **o** shall not	8081
Pr	21:20	and **o** in the dwelling of the wise;	8081
Isa	61:3	ashes, the **o** of joy for mourning,	8081
Joel	1:10	is dried up, the **o** languisheth	3323
Joel	2:24	shall overflow with wine and **o**	3323
Mic	6:7	with ten thousands of rivers of **o**?	8081
Mt	25:3	**lamps, and took no o with them:**	*1637*
Mt	25:8	**Give us of your o; for our lamps**	*1637*
Lk	7:46	**My head with o thou didst not**	*1637*
Lk	10:34	**wounds, pouring in o and wine,**	*1637*
Heb	1:9	anointed thee with the **o** of gladness	*1637*
Jas	5:14	anointing him with **o** in the name	*1637*

OINTMENT

Ex	30:25	an **o** compound after the art	7545
2Ki	20:13	the spices, and the precious **o**,	8081
Ps	133:2	like the precious **o** upon the head	8081
Pr	27:9	**O** and perfume rejoice the heart:	8081
Ecc	7:1	name is better than precious **o**;	8081
Ecc	10:1	flies cause the **o** of the apothecary	8081
Mt	26:7	alabaster box of very precious **o**	*3464*
Mt	26:12	**hath poured this o on my body,**	*3464*
Mk	14:3	alabaster box of **o** of spikenard	*3464*
Mk	14:4	Why was this waste of the **o** made?	*3464*
Lk	7:37	brought an alabaster box of **o**,	*3464*
Lk	7:46	**hath anointed my feet with o**	*3464*
Jn	11:2	which anointed the Lord with **o**,	*3464*
Jn	12:3	Mary a pound of **o** of spikenard	*3464*
Jn	12:5	Why was not this **o** sold for three	*3464*

OLD See also ELDER; ELDEST.

Ge	17:17	Sarah, that is ninety years **o**, bear?	1323
Ge	17:24	Abraham was ninety years **o** and	1121
Ge	18:13	a surety bear a child, which am **o**?	2204
Ge	19:31	unto the younger. Our father is **o**,	2204
Ge	21:7	have born him a son in his **o** age	2208
Ge	37:2	Joseph, being seventeen years **o**,	1121
Ge	37:3	he was the son of his **o** age:	2208
Ge	44:20	We have a father, an **o** man, and	2205
Ge	47:8	Jacob, How **o** art thou?	3113, 8140, 3117
Ex	30:14	from twenty years **o** and above	1121
Le	27:3	years **o** even unto sixty years **o**,	1121
Nu	1:3	From twenty years **o** and upward	1121
Dt	2:20	giants dwelt therein in **o** time;	6440
Dt	32:7	Remember the days of **o**, consider	5769
2Sa	2:10	Saul's son was forty years **o** when	1121
2Sa	5:4	David was thirty years **o** when he	1121
1Ki	12:8	forsook the counsel of the **o** men	2205
1Ch	27:23	from twenty years **o** and under:	1121
2Ch	10:13	forsook the counsel of the **o** men	2205
Ezr	3:8	from twenty years **o** and upward,	1121
Ne	9:21	their clothes waxed not **o**, and	1086
Ps	32:3	my bones waxed **o** through my	1086
Ps	74:12	For God is my King of **o**, working	6924
Ps	77:11	will remember thy wonders of **o**.	6924
Ps	93:2	Thy throne is established of **o**:	227
Ps	102:25	Of **o** hast thou laid the foundation	6440
Pr	8:22	of his way, before his works of **o**	227
Pr	17:6	children are the crown of **o** men;	2205
Pr	20:29	beauty of **o** men is the gray head	2205
Pr	22:6	when he is **o**, he will not depart	2204
Pr	23:10	Remove not the **o** landmark; and	5769
Pr	23:22	not thy mother when she is **o**	2204
Ecc	4:13	child than an **o** and foolish long	2205
Isa	25:1	thy counsels of **o** are faithfulness	7350
Isa	46:9	Remember the former things of **o**:	5769
Isa	63:9	and carried them all the days of **o**	5769
Isa	63:11	Then he remembered the days of **o**,	5769
Jer	46:26	be inhabited, as in the days of **o**,	6924
La	1:7	that she had in the days of **o**,	6924
La	2:17	had commanded in the days of **o**:	6924
La	2:21	The young and the **o** lie on the	2205
La	3:4	and my skin hath he made **o**;	1086
La	5:21	turned; renew our days as of **o**	6924
Joel	2:28	your **o** men shall dream dreams,	2205
Am	9:11	I will build it as in the days of **o**:	5769
Mic	5:2	goings forth have been from of **o**,	6924
Mt	2:16	from two years **o** and under,	*1332*
Mt	5:21	**that it was said by them of o time,**	*744*
Mt	5:27	**that it was said by them of o time,**	*744*
Mt	5:33	**hath been said by them of o time,**	*744*
Mt	9:16	**of new cloth unto an o garment,**	*3820*
Mt	9:17	**men put new wine into o bottles:**	*3820*
Mt	13:52	**of his treasure things new and o.**	*3820*
Mk	2:21	**of new cloth on an o garment:**	*3820*
Mk	2:22	**putteth new wine into o bottles:**	*3820*
Lk	1:18	for I am an **o** man, and my wife	*4246*
Lk	2:42	And when he was twelve years **o**,	
Lk	5:36	**of a new garment upon an o;**	*3820*
Lk	5:37	**putteth new wine into o bottles;**	*3820*
Lk	5:39	**new: for he saith, The o is better.**	*3820*
Lk	12:33	**yourselves bags which wax not o,**	*3822*
Jn	3:4	can a man be born when he is **o**?	*1088*
Jn	21:18	**when thou shalt be o, thou shalt**	*1095*
Ac	2:17	your **o** men shall dream dreams:	*4245*
Ac	15:21	Moses of **o** time hath in every city	*744*
Ro	6:6	our **o** man is crucified with him	*3820*
1Co	5:7	Purge out therefore the **o** leaven	*3820*
2Co	3:14	in the reading of the **o** testament;	*3820*
2Co	5:17	creature: **o** things are past away;	*744*

Eph	4:22	That ye put off … the **o** man, which	3820
Col	3:9	that ye have put off the **o** man	3820
Heb	1:11	shall wax **o** as doth a garment;	3822
Heb	8:13	covenant, he hath made the first **o**	3822
1Pe	3:5	in the **o** time the holy women also,	4218
2Pe	1:21	came not in **o** time by the will of	4218
2Pe	2:5	spared not the **o** world, but saved	744
2Pe	3:5	word of God the heavens were of **o**,	1597
1Jn	2:7	The **o** commandment is the word	3820
Jude	4	who were before of **o** ordained to	3819
Rev	12:9	that **o** serpent, called the Devil,	744
Rev	20:2	that **o** serpent, which is the devil,	744

OLIVE

Ge	8:11	in her mouth was an **o** leaf pluckt	2132
Dt	8:8	a land of oil **o**, and honey;	2132
Jgs	9:8	they said unto the **o** tree, Reign.	2132
2Ki	18:32	a land of oil **o** and of honey,	2132
Ps	128:3	thy children like **o** plants round	2132
Jer	11:16	called thy name, A green **o** tree,	2132
Ro	11:24	if thou wert cut out of the **o** tree.	65
Rev	11:4	These are the two **o** trees, and the.	1636

OLIVES

Zec	14:4	in that day upon the mount of **O**,	2132
Mt	24:3	And as he sat upon the mount of **O**,	1636
Mt	26:30	they went out into the mount of **O**	1636
Mk	14:26	they went out into the mount of **O**	1636
Lk	19:29	the mount called the mount of **O**,	1636
Lk	21:37	that is called the mount of **O**.	1636
Lk	22:39	as he was wont, to the mount of **O**;	1636
Jn	8:1	Jesus went unto the mount of **O**.	1636

OLIVET See also MOUNT and OLIVES.

Ac	1:12	from the mount called **O**, which	1638

OMEGA (o´-me-gah)

Rev	1:8	**I am Alpha and O, the beginning**	5598
Rev	1:11	**I am Alpha and O, the first and**	5598
Rev	21:6	**I am Alpha and O, the beginning**	5598
Rev	22:13	**I am Alpha and O, the beginning**	5598

OMITTED

Mt	23:23	**o the weightier matters of the law,**	863

OMNIPOTENT

Rev	19:6	for the Lord God **o** reigneth	3841

ONCE

Ge	18:32	and I will speak yet but this **o**:	6471
Ex	10:17	I pray thee, my sin only this **o**,	6471
Le	16:34	of Israel for all their sins **o** a year.	259
Nu	13:30	Let us go up at **o**, and possess it;	
Jos	6:11	compassed the city, going about it **o**:	259
Jgs	16:28	be at **o** avenged of the Philistines	
Job	33:14	For God speaketh **o**, yea twice, yet	259
Job	40:5	**O** have I spoken; but I will not	259
Ps	62:11	God hath spoken **o**; twice have I.	259
Ps	76:7	in thy sight when **o** thou art angry?	227
Ps	89:35	**O** have I sworn by my holiness that	259
Pr	28:18	perverse in his ways shall fall at **o**	259
Jer	16:21	I will this **o** cause them to know,	6471
Hag	2:6	Yet **o**, it is a little while, and I will	259
Lk	13:25	**When o the master of the house is**	
Ro	6:10	that he died, he died unto sin **o**:	2178
1Co	15:6	above five hundred brethren at **o**;	2178
Gal	1:23	the faith which **o** he destroyed.	4218
Eph	5:3	let it not be **o** named among you,	3366
Heb	6:4	for those who were **o** enlightened,	530
Heb	7:27	for this he did **o**, when he offered	2178
Heb	9:7	the high priest alone **o** every year,	530
Heb	9:27	it is appointed unto men **o** to die,	530
Heb	9:28	So Christ was **o** offered to bear the	530
Heb	10:10	the body of Jesus Christ **o** for all.	2178
Heb	12:26	**o** more I shake not the earth only,	530
1Pe	3:18	Christ also hath **o** suffered for sins,	530
1Pe	3:20	when **o** the longsuffering of God	530
Jude	3	faith which was **o** delivered unto the	530

ONE See also NONE.

Ge	2:24	his wife: and they shall be **o** flesh.	259
Ge	3:6	a tree to be desired to make **o** wise,	
Ge	3:22	the man is become as **o** of us, to	259
Ge	11:1	was of **o** language, and of **o** speech.	259
Ge	19:14	But he seemed as **o** that mocked	
Ge	27:38	Hast thou but **o** blessing, my	259
Ex	12:49	**O** law shall be to him that is	259
Nu	9:14	ye shall have **o** ordinance, both for	259
Nu	15:16	**O** law and **o** manner shall be for	259
Nu	16:22	shall **o** man sin, and wilt thou be	259
Dt	2:36	there was not **o** city too strong for us:	
Dt	4:32	from the **o** side of heaven unto the	
Dt	6:4	Israel: The Lord our God is **o** Lord:	259
Dt	19:5	he shall flee unto **o** of those cities,	259
Jos	23:10	**O** man of you shall chase a	259
Jos	23:14	not **o** thing hath failed of all the	259
Jgs	21:6	**o** tribe cut off from Israel this day	259
1Sa	14:45	there shall not **o** hair of his head fall	
2Sa	7:23	what **o** nation in the earth is like	259
1Ki	4:22	Solomon's provision for **o** day was	259
1Ki	8:56	**o** word of all his good promise,	259
1Ki	18:40	of Baal; let not **o** of them escape	376
1Ch	17:21	what **o** nation in the earth is like	259
2Ch	32:12	Ye shall worship before **o** altar,	259
Job	1:1	**o** that feared God, and eschewed evil	
Job	16:21	**o** might plead for a man with God,	
Job	17:10	I cannot find **o** wise man among you	
Ps	16:10	thine Holy **O** to see corruption	
Ps	27:4	**O** thing have I desired of the Lord,	259
Ps	34:20	bones: not **o** of them is broken	259
Ps	53:3	is none that doeth good, no, not **o**	259
Ps	73:20	As a dream when **o** awaketh; so,	
Ps	75:7	he putteth down **o** and setteth up	
Ps	78:41	and limited the Holy **o** of Israel	
Ps	78:65	the Lord awaked as **o** out of sleep,	
Ps	89:18	the Holy **O** of Israel is our king.	
Pr	1:14	among us; let us all have **o** purse:	259
Ecc	1:4	**O** generation passeth away, and	
Ecc	4:9	Two are better than **o**; because	259
Ecc	9:18	but **o** sinner destroyeth much good	259
Isa	1:4	provoked the Holy **O** of Israel	
Isa	40:26	is strong in power; not **o** faileth	376
Isa	53:6	turned every **o** to his own way;	376
Jer	11:8	walked every **o** in the imagination	376
Eze	11:19	And I will give them **o** heart, and	259
Eze	37:22	**o** king shall be king to them all:	259
Eze	37:24	and they all shall have **o** shepherd:	259
Da	7:13	**o** like the Son of man came with the	
Mal	2:10	hath not **o** God created us? why do	259
Mt	5:18	**heaven and earth pass, o jot or**	1520
Mt	6:27	**can add o cubit unto his stature?**	1520
Mt	13:46	**had found o pearl of great price**	1520
Mt	18:6	**shall offend o of these little ones**	1520
Mt	18:9	**thee to enter into life with o eye,**	3442

Mt	19:17	is none good but o, that is, God:	1520
Mt	23:8	o is your Master, even Christ;	1520
Mt	25:24	had received the o talent	1520
Mt	25:40	it unto o of the least of these my	1520
Mt	26:21	you, that o of you shall betray	1520
Mt	26:40	ye not watch with me o hour?	3391
Mk	9:42	shall offend o of these little ones.	1520
Mk	10:8	And they twain shall be o flesh:	3391
Mk	10:18	is none good but o, that is, God	1520
Mk	10:21	O thing thou lackest: go thy	1520
Mk	12:29	The Lord our God is o Lord:	1520
Mk	12:32	there is o God; and there is none	1520
Mk	14:37	couldest thou not watch o hour?	3391
Lk	3:4	voice of o crying in the wilderness,	
Lk	3:16	but o mightier than I cometh, the	
Lk	10:42	But o thing is needful: and Mary	1520
Lk	12:6	not o of them is forgotten before	1520
Lk	12:25	can add to his stature o cubit?	1520
Lk	15:10	God over o sinner that repenteth	1520
Lk	18:22	Yet lackest thou o thing: sell all.	1520
Jn	4:37	O soweth, and another reapeth.	243
Jn	6:40	every o which seeth the Son, and	
Jn	13:21	that o of you shall betray me	1520
Jn	13:34	unto you, That ye love o another;	240
Jn	15:12	That ye love o another, as I have.	240
Jn	17:22	they may be o, even as we are o:	1520
Ac	4:32	were of o heart and of o soul:	3391
Ac	10:22	a just man, and o that feareth God,	
Ac	13:35	thine Holy O to see corruption	
Ro	1:27	in their lust o toward another;	240
Ro	2:29	But he is a Jew, which is o inwardly;	
Ro	3:10	There is none righteous, no, not o:	1520
Ro	3:30	Seeing it is o God, which shall.	1520
Ro	5:7	for a righteous man will o die:	5100
Ro	5:12	as by o man sin entered into the	1520
Ro	5:15	which is by o man, Jesus Christ,	1520
Ro	5:17	by o man's offence death reigned	1520
Ro	5:18	the righteousness of o the free gift	1520
Ro	5:19	by the obedience of o shall many be.	1520
1Co	5:5	To deliver such an o unto Satan	
1Co	8:4	there is none other God but o.	1520
1Co	8:6	o Lord Jesus Christ, by whom are	1520
1Co	10:8	and fell in o day three and twenty	3391
1Co	12:11	that o and the selfsame Spirit,	1520
1Co	15:39	there is o kind of flesh of men,	243
2Co	5:14	that if o died for all, then were all	1520
Gal	5:14	all the law is fulfilled in o word,	1520
Gal	6:2	Bear ye o another's burdens, and	240
Eph	4:6	O God and Father of all, who is	1520
Eph	4:32	forgiving o another, even as God	1438
Eph	5:21	Submitting yourselves o to another	240
Php	3:13	this o thing I do, forgetting those	1520
Col	3:13	forgiving o another, if any man.	1438
1Ti	3:2	husband of o wife, vigilant, sober,	3391
1Ti	3:4	O that ruleth well his own house,	
Jas	2:10	yet offend in o point, he is guilty	1520
Jas	2:19	believest that there is o God; thou	1520
Jas	4:12	There is o lawgiver, who is able to.	1520
Jas	5:16	Confess your faults o to another,	240
1Pe	3:8	Finally, be ye all of o mind, having	3675
2Pe	3:8	that o day is with the Lord as a	3391
2Pe	3:8	and a thousand years as o day.	3391
1Jn	2:13	ye have overcome the wicked o	
1Jn	4:7	Beloved, let us love o another: for.	240
1Jn	4:11	ye ought also to love o another	240
Rev	1:13	midst ... o like unto the Son of man,	
Rev	6:1	the Lamb opened o of the seals,	3391
Rev	14:14	cloud o sat like unto the Son of man,	
Rev	21:21	pearls; every several gate of o pearl.	1520

ONE'S

Ecc	7:1	day of death than the day of o birth.	

ONES

Pr	1:22	How long, ye simple o, will ye love	
Mt	18:6	shall offend one of these little o	
Mk	9:42	shall offend one of these little o that	
Lk	17:2	He should offend one of these little o	

ONLY

Ge	6:5	his heart was o evil continually.	7535
Ge	22:2	now thy son, thine o son Isaac,	3173
Le	21:23	O he shall not go in unto the vail,	389
Dt	8:3	that man doth not live by bread o,	905
Jos	1:18	o be strong and of a good courage	7535
1Ki	18:22	even I o, remain a prophet of the	905
1Ki	19:14	and I, even I o, am left; and	905
Job	1:15	I o am escaped alone	7535
Job	1:16	I o am escaped alone	7535
Job	1:17	I o am escaped alone	7535
Job	1:19	I o am escaped alone	7535
Ps	51:4	Against thee, thee o, have I sinned,	905
Ps	62:2	He o is my rock and my salvation;	389
Ps	62:5	My soul, wait thou o upon God;	389
Pr	11:23	desire of the righteous is o good:	389
Pr	17:11	An evil man seeketh o rebellion:	389
Ex	7:29	this o have I found, that God hath	905
Isa	37:20	thou art the Lord, even thou o	905
Mt	4:10	God, and him o shalt thou serve	3441
Mt	17:8	they saw no man, save Jesus o	3441
Mt	24:36	of heaven, but my Father o	3441
Mk	5:36	Be not afraid, o believe,	3440
Lk	4:8	God, and him o shalt thou serve.	3441
Lk	8:50	Fear not: believe o, and she shall.	3440
Jn	1:14	as of the o begotten of the Father,)	3439
Jn	1:18	the o begotten Son, which is in the	3439
Jn	3:16	he gave his o begotten Son, that	3439
Jn	3:18	name of the o begotten Son of	3439
Jn	5:44	honour that cometh from God o?	3441
Jn	17:3	might know thee the o true God,	3441
Ro	3:29	Is he the God of the Jews o? is he	3440
1Co	15:19	If in this life o we have hope in	3440
Gal	5:13	o use not liberty for an occasion to	3440
1Ti	1:17	the o wise God, be honour and	3441
1Ti	6:15	is the blessed and o Potentate	3441
1Ti	6:16	Who o hath immortality, dwelling	3441
2Ti	4:11	O Luke is with me. Take Mark,	3441
Jas	2:24	man is justified, and not by faith o.	3440
1Jn	4:9	God sent his o begotten Son into	3439
Jude	25	To the o wise God our Saviour, be	3441
Rev	15:4	for thou o art holy: for all nations	3441

ONLY-BEGOTTEN See ONLY and BEGOTTEN.

OPEN

2Ki	6:17	Lord, I pray thee, o his eyes, that	6491
Job	35:16	doth Job o his mouth in vain;	6475
Ps	51:15	O Lord, o thou my lips; and my	6605
Ps	81:10	o thy mouth wide, and I will fill it	
Pr	13:16	but a fool layeth o his folly	6566
Pr	27:5	O rebuke is better than secret	1540
Isa	22:22	so he shall o, and none shall shut;	6605
Isa	42:7	To o the blind eyes, to bring out	6491

Da 9:18 **o** thine eyes, and behold our ... 6491
Mt 25:11 **saying, Lord, Lord, o to us.** ... *455*
Lk 13:25 **door, saying, Lord, Lord, o unto** ... *455*
Jn 1:51 **Hereafter ye shall see heaven o,** ... *455*
Rev 3:8 **I have set before thee an o door,** ... *455*
Rev 3:20 **hear my voice, and o the door.** ... *455*
Rev 5:2 Who is worthy to **o** the book, and to ... *455*
Rev 5:9 the book, and to **o** the seals thereof: ... *455*
Rev 10:2 he had in his hand a little book **o**: ... *455*

OPENED
Ge 3:7 And the eyes of them both were **o**, ... 6491
Ge 7:11 the windows of heaven were **o**, ... 6605
Ge 8:6 that Noah **o** the window of the ark ... 6605
Job 3:1 After this **o** Job his mouth, and ... 6605
Ps 35:21 they **o** their mouth wide against
Ps 39:9 I was dumb, I **o** not my mouth; ... 6605
Mt 7:7 **knock, and it shall be o unto you:** ... *455*
Mt 27:52 graves were **o**; and many bodies ... *455*
Mk 1:10 he saw the heavens **o**, and the ... *4977*
Lk 3:21 and praying, the heaven was **o**, ... *455*
Lk 11:9 **knock, and it shall be o unto you** ... *455*
Lk 24:31 their eyes were **o**, and they knew ... *1272*
Lk 24:32 while he **o** to us the scriptures? ... *1272*
Ac 7:56 Behold, I see the heavens **o**, and ... *455*
1Co 16:9 door and effectual is **o** unto me ... *455*
Heb 4:13 all things are naked and **o** unto ... *5136*
Rev 4:1 behold, a door was **o** in heaven: ... *455*
Rev 9:2 And he **o** the bottomless pit; and ... *455*
Rev 11:19 the temple of God was **o** in heaven, ... *455*
Rev 19:11 And I saw heaven **o**, and behold a ... *455*
Rev 20:12 before God; and the books were **o**: ... *455*
Rev 20:12 another book was **o**, which is the ... *455*

OPENETH
Ex 13:12 unto the Lord all that **o** the matrix, ... 6363
Ps 146:8 The Lord **o** the eyes of the blind: ... 6491
Lk 2:23 Every male that **o** the womb shall ... *1272*
Rev 3:7 **he that o, and no man shutteth;** ... *455*

OPENING
Ac 17:3 **O** and alleging, that Christ must ... *1272*

OPENLY
Mt 6:4 **shall reward thee o** ... *1722, 3588, 5318*
Jn 7:13 no man spake **o** of him for fear of ... *3954*
Jn 11:54 walked no more **o** among the Jews; ... *3954*
Jn 18:20 **I spake o to the world; I ever.** ... *3954*

OPINIONS
1Ki 18:21 How long halt ye between two **o**? ... 5587

OPPORTUNITY
Mt 26:16 time he sought **o** to betray him ... *2120*
Lk 22:6 sought **o** to betray him unto them ... *2120*
Gal 6:10 As we have therefore **o**, let us do ... *2540*

OPPOSE
2Ti 2:25 instructing those that **o** themselves; ... *476*

OPPOSETH
2Th 2:4 Who **o** and exalteth himself above ... *480*

OPPOSITIONS
1Ti 6:20 and **o** of science falsely so called: ... *477*

OPPRESS
Ex 22:21 neither vex a stranger, nor **o** him: ... 3905
Ex 23:9 Also thou shalt not **o** a stranger: ... 3905
Le 25:17 shall not therefore **o** one another; ... 3238
Ps 10:18 man of the earth may no more **o** ... 6206
Pr 22:22 neither **o** the afflicted in the gate: ... 1792
Am 4:1 which **o** the poor, which crush the ... 6231
Zec 7:10 **o** not the widow, nor the fatherless, ... 6231
Mal 3:5 that **o** the hireling in his wages, ... 6231
Jas 2:6 Do not rich men **o** you, and draw ... *2616*

OPPRESSED
1Sa 12:3 whom have I **o**? or of whose hand ... 7533
Ps 10:18 To judge the fatherless and the **o**, ... 1790
Ps 103:6 and judgment for all that are **o** ... 6231
Ps 146:7 executeth judgment for the **o**: ... 6231
Ecc 4:1 the tears of such as were **o**, ... 6231
Isa 1:17 seek judgment, relieve the **o** ... 2541
Isa 53:7 He was **o**, and he was afflicted, ... 5065
Eze 18:12 Hath **o** the poor and needy, hath ... 3238
Eze 22:29 have **o** the stranger wrongfully ... 6231
Ac 10:38 all that were **o** of the devil; ... *2616*

OPPRESSETH
Pr 14:31 He that **o** the poor reproacheth ... 6231
Pr 22:16 He that **o** the poor to increase his ... 6231
Pr 28:3 A poor man that **o** the poor is like ... 6231

OPPRESSION
Ps 12:5 For the **o** of the poor, for the ... 7701
Ps 42:9 because of the **o** of the enemy? ... 3906
Ps 43:2 because of the **o** of the enemy? ... 3906
Ps 62:10 Trust not in **o**, and become not ... 6233
Ps 107:39 brought low through **o**, affliction, ... 6115
Ecc 5:8 If thou seest the **o** of the poor, ... 6233
Ecc 7:7 Surely **o** maketh a wise man mad; ... 6233
Isa 5:7 for judgment, but behold **o**; ... 4939

OPPRESSIONS
Ecc 4:1 the **o** that are done under the sun: ... 6217

OPPRESSOR
Ps 72:4 and shall break in pieces the **o** ... 6231
Pr 3:31 Envy thou not the **o**, and ... 376, 2555
Pr 28:16 understanding is also a great **o**: ... 4642
Isa 51:13 and where is the fury of the **o**? ... 6693

OPPRESSORS
Ps 54:3 and **o** seek after my soul: they ... 6184
Ps 119:121 justice: leave me not to mine **o** ... 6231
Ecc 4:1 side of their **o** there was power; ... 6231

ORACLE
2Sa 16:23 had enquired at the **o** of God: ... 1697
1Ki 6:22 altar that was by the **o** he overlaid ... 1687
2Ch 5:9 seen from the ark before the **o**; ... 1687
Ps 28:2 up my hands toward thy holy **o** ... 1687

ORACLES
Ro 3:2 were committed the **o** of God. ... *3051*
Heb 5:12 the first principles of the **o** of God; ... *3051*
1Pe 4:11 let him speak as the **o** of God; ... *3051*

ORDAIN
1Ch 17:9 Also I will **o** a place for my people ... 7760
Isa 26:12 Lord, thou wilt **o** peace for us: ... 8239
1Ti 1:5 and **o** elders in every city, as I ... *2525*

ORDAINED
2Ki 23:5 had **o** to burn incense in the ... 5414
2Ch 23:18 with singing, as it was **o** by David.
2Ch 29:27 the instruments **o** by David king of

Ps 8:3	and the stars, which thou hast **o**;	3559
Jer 1:5	and I **o** thee a prophet unto the	5414
Mk 3:14	**o** twelve, that they should be with	*4160*
Jn 15:16	**I have chosen you, and o you.**	*5087*
Ac 10:42	was **o** of God to be the Judge of	*3724*
Ac 13:48	as were **o** to eternal life believed.	*5021*
Ro 13:1	the powers that be are **o** of God	*5021*
1Co 9:14	Lord **o** that they which preach	*1299*
Eph 2:10	**o** that we should walk in them.	*4282*
Heb 8:3	every high priest is **o** to offer gifts.	*2525*

ORDAINETH

Ps 7:13	he **o** his arrows against the.	6466

ORDER

Ge 22:9	there, and laid the wood in **o**.	6186
Ex 40:23	And he set the bread in **o** upon it	6186
2Sa 17:23	city, and put his household in **o**	6680
2Ki 20:1	the Lord, Set thine house in **o**;	6680
Job 23:4	I would **o** my cause before him,	6186
Job 37:19	**o** our speech by reason of darkness	6186
Ps 40:5	be reckoned up in **o** unto thee:	6186
Ps 110:4	ever after the **o** of Melchizedek	1700
Ps 119:133	**O** my steps in thy word: and let	3559
Ecc 12:9	out, and set in **o** many proverbs.	8626
Heb 5:10	priest after the **o** of Melchisedec	*5010*
Heb 6:20	ever after the **o** of Melchisedec.	*5010*
Heb 7:11	not be called after the **o** of Aaron?	*5010*
Heb 7:17	ever after the **o** of Melchisedec.	*5010*

ORDERED

Ps 37:23	of a good man are **o** by the Lord:	3559

ORDINANCE

Ex 12:14	keep it a feast by an **o** for ever.	2708
Ex 12:43	This is the **o** of the passover:	2708
Nu 9:14	ye shall have one **o**, both for the	2708
Isa 58:2	forsook not the **o** of their God:	4941
1Pe 2:13	Submit ... to every **o** of man for.	*2937*

ORDINANCES

Le 18:3	neither shall ye walk in their **o**	2708
Nu 9:12	all the **o** of the passover they shall	2708
Job 38:33	Knowest thou the **o** of heaven?	2708
Isa 58:2	they ask of me the **o** of justice;	4941
Jer 33:25	not appointed the **o** of heaven and.	2708
Eze 11:20	and keep mine **o**, and do them:	4941
Col 2:14	Blotting out the handwriting of **o**.	*1378*
Heb 9:1	had also **o** of divine service, and	*1345*

ORION (o-ri´-on)

Job 38:31	Pleiades, or loose the bands of **O**?	3685
Am 5:8	that maketh the seven stars and **O**,	3685

ORNAMENT

Isa 49:18	thee with them all, as with an **o**,	5716
Eze 7:20	As for the beauty of his **o**, he set	5716
1Pe 3:4	the **o** of a meek and quiet spirit,	

OTHER

Ex 20:3	shalt have no **o** gods before me.	312
Ex 23:13	no mention of the name of **o** gods,	312
Dt 4:32	the one side of heaven unto the **o**,	
Dt 11:28	to go after **o** gods, which ye have not	312
Jos 23:16	have gone and served **o** gods, and.	312
Jgs 2:17	they went a whoring after **o** gods,	312
2Sa 13:16	this evil is ... greater than the **o**	312
1Ki 11:4	turned away his heart after **o** gods:	312
1Ki 14:9	hast gone and made thee **o** gods,	312
Ne 4:17	with the **o** hand held a weapon.	259
Ps 85:10	and peace have kissed each **o**	
Jer 7:9	after **o** gods whom ye know not;	312
Jer 35:15	go not after **o** gods to serve them,	312
Da 3:29	is no **o** God that can deliver after	321
Mt 5:39	**cheek, turn to him the o also**	*243*
Mt 6:24	**will hate the one, and love the o;**	*2087*
Mt 12:45	**with himself seven o spirits.**	*2087*
Mt 13:8	**But o fell into good ground, and**	*243*
Mt 23:23	**and not to leave the o undone.**	*2548*
Mt 24:40	**shall be taken, and the o left.**	*1520*
Mk 4:8	**o fell on good ground, and did**	*243*
Mk 12:31	**is none o commandment greater**	*243*
Mk 12:32	God; and there is none **o** but he:	*243*
Lk 6:29	**on the one cheek offer also the o;**	*243*
Lk 8:8	**And o fell on good ground, and**	*2087*
Lk 11:26	**seven o spirits more wicked than**	*2087*
Lk 11:42	**and not to leave the o undone.**	*2548*
Lk 16:13	**will hate the one, and love the o;**	*2087*
Lk 18:11	**thee, that I am not as o men are,**	*3062*
Jn 10:1	**but climbeth up some o way, the**	*237*
Jn 19:18	crucified him, and two **o** with him,	*243*
Jn 20:2	to the **o** disciple, whom Jesus loved,	*243*
Jn 20:30	And many **o** signs truly did Jesus	*243*
Jn 21:25	also many **o** things which Jesus did,	*243*
Ac 4:12	none **o** name under heaven given	*2087*
1Co 3:11	**o** foundation can no man lay than	*243*
1Co 7:5	Defraud ye not one the **o**, except it	*240*
1Co 8:4	that there is none **o** God but one.	*2087*
Gal 1:8	any **o** gospel unto you than that ... we	
Php 2:3	esteem **o** better than themselves.	*240*
1Ti 1:3	that they teach no **o** doctrine	*2085*
Rev 2:24	**will put upon you none o burden.**	*243*
Rev 17:10	one is, and the **o** is not yet come;	*243*

OTHERS

Ps 49:10	perish, and leave their wealth to **o**	312
Pr 5:9	Lest thou give thine honour unto **o**,	312
Mt 27:42	He saved **o**; himself he cannot.	*243*
Mk 15:31	He saved **o**; himself he cannot save.	*243*
Lk 23:35	He saved **o**; let him save himself,	*243*
Jn 18:34	**thyself, or did o tell it thee of me?**	*243*
1Th 4:13	even as **o** which have no hope.	*3062*

OTHERWISE

2Sa 18:13	**O** I should have wrought	176
1Ki 1:21	**O** it shall come to pass, when my	
2Ch 30:18	passover **o** than it was written.	3808
Ps 38:16	lest **o** they should rejoice over me:	
Mt 6:1	**o ye have no reward of your**	*1490*
Lk 5:36	**if o, then both the new maketh a**	*1490*
Ro 11:6	works: **o** grace is no more grace	*1893*
Ro 11:6	grace: **o** work is no more work	*1893*
Ro 11:22	**o** thou also shalt be cut off.	*1893*
2Co 11:16	if **o**, yet as a fool receive me, that	*1490*
Gal 5:10	that ye will be none **o** minded:	*243*
Php 3:15	if in any thing ye be **o** minded,	*2088*
1Ti 5:25	and they that are **o** cannot be hid	*247*
1Ti 6:3	If any man teach **o**, and consent	*2085*
Heb 9:17	**o** it is of no strength at all while	*1893*

OUGHT See also NAUGHT; NOUGHT.

Ge 34:7	which thing **o** not to be done.	
Ru 1:17	if **o** but death part thee and me	
2Sa 13:12	no such thing **o** to be done in Israel:	
Mt 5:23	**thy brother hath o against thee;**	*5100*
Mt 23:23	**these o ye to have done, and not**	*1163*

O

Mk 11:25 forgive, if ye have o against any: 5100
Lk 24:26 O not Christ to have suffered 1163
Ac 5:29 o to obey God rather than men 1163
Ro 12:3 more highly than he o to think; 1163
Ro 15:1 strong o to bear the infirmities of 3784
Col 4:6 how ye o to answer every man 1163
1Th 4:1 how ye o to walk and to please God, 1163
Jas 4:15 For that ye o to say, If the Lord will
2Pe 3:11 what manner of persons o ye to be 1163
1Jn 2:6 o himself also so to walk, even as 3784
1Jn 3:16 we o to lay down our lives for the 3784
1Jn 4:11 us, we o also to love one another 3784

OUGHTEST

1Ti 3:15 know how thou o to behave thyself 1163

OURSELVES

Ac 6:4 will give o continually to prayer,
2Co 4:2 commending o to every man's 1438
2Co 4:5 o your servants for Jesus' sake 1438
Heb 10:25 the assembling of o together 1438
1Jn 1:8 we deceive o, and the truth is not 1438

OUTER See also UTTER.

Mt 8:12 shall be cast out into o darkness: 1857
Mt 22:13 and cast him into o darkness; 1857
Mt 25:30 servant into o darkness: there 1857

OUTLANDISH

Ne 13:26 him did o women cause to sin 5237

OUTRAGEOUS See also RAGE.

Pr 27:4 Wrath is cruel, and anger is o; 7858

OUTRUN See also RUN.

Jn 20:4 the other disciple did o Peter, 4370, 5032

OUTSIDE

Mt 23:25 ye make clean the o of the cup 1855
Lk 11:39 make clean the o of the cup and 1855

OUTSTRETCHED

Jer 27:5 by my great power by my o arm, 5186

OUTWARD

Mt 23:27 which indeed appear beautiful o, 1855
2Co 4:16 though our o man perish, yet the 1854

OUTWARDLY

Mt 23:38 so ye also o appear righteous 1855
Ro 2:28 is not a Jew, which is one o; 1722, 5318

OVEN

La 5:10 skin was black like an o because 8574
Mt 6:30 and to morrow is cast into the o, 2823
Lk 12:28 and to morrow is cast into the o; 2823

OVER See also MOREOVER.

Ge 1:18 to rule o the day and o the night,
Ge 1:26 have dominion o the fish of the sea,
Ge 37:8 Shalt thou indeed reign o us? 5921
Ex 12:13 I see the blood, I will pass o you, 5921
Ex 30:6 mercy seat that is o the testimony, 5921
Dt 3:27 for thou shalt not go o this Jordan 5674
Dt 9:3 God is he that goeth o before thee; 5674
Jos 3:17 Israelites passed o on dry ground, 5674
Jgs 9:8 the olive tree, Reign thou o us 5921
1Sa 8:19 but we will have a king o us; 5921
1Sa 15:17 Lord anointed thee king o Israel? 5921
1Sa 17:50 David prevailed o the Philistine 4480
2Sa 20:21 shall be thrown to thee o the wall 1157
2Sa 23:3 He that ruleth o men must be just,
2Ki 2:8 they two went o on dry ground 5674
1Ch 22:10 of his kingdom o Israel for ever 5921
2Ch 19:11 chief priest is o you in all matters 5921
Ps 8:6 dominion o the works of thy hands;
Ps 47:2 he is a great King o all the earth. 5921
Ps 103:16 For the wind passeth o it, and it 5674
Pr 25:28 that hath no rule o his own spirit is
Ecc 1:12 I the Preacher was king o Israel 5921
Ecc 7:16 Be not righteous o much; neither 7235
Jer 5:22 roar, yet can they not pass o it? 5674
Eze 47:5 a river that could not be passed o 5674
Da 4:16 and let seven times pass o him 5922
Da 4:23 field, till seven times pass o him; 5922
Jnh 2:3 and thy waves passed o me 5674
Zec 14:9 Lord shall be king o all the earth: 5921
Mt 25:21 hast been faithful o a few things, 1909
Mt 25:23 make thee ruler o many things: 1909
Mk 6:7 gave them power o unclean spirits;
Lk 6:38 shaken together, and running o, 5240
Lk 8:26 which is o against Galilee 495
Lk 9:1 power and authority o all devils, 1909
Lk 10:19 and o all the power of the enemy: 1909
Lk 15:7 o one sinner that repenteth, 1909
Ro 1:28 gave them o to a reprobate mind 3860
Ro 6:14 sin shall not have dominion o you:
Ro 9:5 who is o all, God blessed for ever 1909
Ro 9:21 Hath not the potter power o the clay,
1Ti 2:12 nor to usurp authority o the man, but
Heb 13:17 Obey them that have the rule o you,
Jas 5:14 let them pray o him, anointing 1909
Rev 2:26 will I give power o the nations: 1909
Rev 16:9 which hath power o these plagues: 1909
Rev 17:18 reigneth o the kings of the earth. 1909
Rev 18:20 Rejoice o her, thou heaven, and ye 1909

OVERCAME

Rev 3:21 even as I also o, and am set down 3528
Rev 12:11 o him by the blood of the Lamb 3528

OVERCOME

Lk 11:22 shall come upon him, and o him, 3528
Jn 16:33 of good cheer; I have o the world 3528
Ro 12:21 Be not o of evil 3528
Ro 12:21 but o evil with good 3528
1Jn 2:13 because ye have o the wicked one 3528
Rev 17:14 Lamb, and the Lamb shall o them: 3528

OVERCOMETH

1Jn 5:5 Who is he that o the world, but 3528
Rev 2:7 To him that o will I give to eat of 3528
Rev 2:11 He that o shall not be hurt of the 3528
Rev 2:17 To him that o will I give to eat of 3528
Rev 2:26 he that o, and keepeth my works 3528
Rev 3:5 He that o, the same shall be 3528
Rev 3:12 Him that o will I make a pillar in 3528
Rev 3:21 To him that o will I grant to sit 3528
Rev 21:7 He that o shall inherit all things; 3528

OVERFLOW

Dt 11:4 water of the Red sea to o them 6687
Isa 10:22 decreed shall o with righteousness 7857

OVERFLOWING

Isa 28:15 when the o scourge shall pass 7857
Hab 3:10 the o of the water passed by: the 2230

OVERLAID
Ex 37:2 And he **o** it with pure gold within 6823
1Ki 3:19 in the night; because she **o** it.......... 7901
1Ki 6:20 and he **o** it with pure gold; and........ 6823
1Ki 6:21 Solomon **o** the house within with 6823
1Ki 6:28 And he **o** the cherubims with gold..... 6823
1Ki 6:30 floor of the house he **o** with gold, ... 6823
1Ki 10:18 ivory, and **o** it with the best gold....... 6823
Heb 9:4 covenant **o** round about with gold, ... *4028*

OVERLAY
Ex 25:24 thou shalt **o** it with pure gold, and..... 6823
Ex 30:3 shalt **o** it with pure gold, the top....... 6823

OVERMUCH
2Co 2:7 be swallowed up with **o** sorrow........ *4055*

OVERPASS
Jer 5:28 they **o** the deeds of the wicked:........ 5674

OVERPAST
Ps 57:1 until these calamities be **o** 5674
Isa 26:20 until the indignation be **o** 5674

OVERSEER
Ge 39:4 he made him **o** over his house 6485
Pr 6:7 having no guide, **o**, or ruler, ... 7860

OVERSEERS
2Ch 2:18 **o** to set the people a work............ 5329
2Ch 34:17 it into the hand of the **o**, and to 6485
Ac 20:28 the Holy Ghost hath made you **o**,...... *1985*

OVERSHADOW
Lk 1:35 power of the Highest shall **o** thee: *1982*

OVERSHADOWED
Mt 17:5 behold, a bright cloud **o** them: *1982*
Mk 9:7 there was a cloud that **o** them: *1982*
Lk 9:34 there came a cloud, and **o** them:....... *1982*

OVERSIGHT
Ge 43:12 hand; peradventure it was an **o**........ 4870
2Ch 34:10 the **o** of the house of the Lord......... 6485
1Pe 5:2 among you, taking the **o** thereof, ... *1983*

OVERTAKE
Ex 15:9 enemy said, I will pursue, I will **o**, ... 5381
Dt 19:6 while his heart is hot, and **o** him,...... 5381
Dt 28:45 and shall pursue thee, and **o** thee, ... 5381
Jos 2:5 them quickly; for ye shall **o** them 5381
2Sa 15:14 lest he **o** us suddenly, and bring 5381
Jer 42:16 sword, which ye feared, shall **o** you 5381
Hos 2:7 lovers, but she shall not **o** them;....... 5381
Am 9:10 evil shall not **o** nor prevent us......... 5066
1Th 5:4 that day should **o** you as a thief........ *2638*

OVERTAKEN
Gal 6:1 Brethren, if a man be **o** in a fault,...... *4301*

OVERTHREW
Ex 14:27 and the Lord **o** the Egyptians in 5287
Ps 136:15 But **o** Pharaoh and his host in the 5286
Isa 13:19 God **o** Sodom and Gomorrah, ... 4114
Jer 20:16 be as the cities which the Lord **o**, ... 2015
Jer 50:40 As God **o** Sodom and Gomorrah 4114
Am 4:11 as God **o** Sodom and Gomorrah 4114
Mt 21:12 **o** the tables of the moneychangers *2690*
Mk 11:15 **o** the tables of the moneychangers *2690*
Jn 2:15 changers' money, and **o** the tables;...... *390*

OVERTHROW
Dt 12:3 ye shall **o** their altars, and break 5422
2Sa 10:3 and to spy it out, and to **o** it?.......... 2015
1Ch 19:3 and to **o**, and to spy out the land? 2015
Ps 106:26 to **o** them in the wilderness: 5307
Ps 140:11 hunt the violent man to **o** him 4073
Pr 18:5 to **o** the righteous in judgment........ 5186
Jer 49:18 in the **o** of Sodom and Gomorrah 4114
Hag 2:22 I will **o** the chariots, and those 2015
Ac 5:39 if it be of God, ye cannot **o** it;......... *2647*
2Ti 2:18 already; and **o** the faith of some *396*

OVERTHROWETH
Pr 13:6 but wickedness **o** the sinner........... 5557
Pr 21:12 but God **o** the wicked for their 5557
Pr 22:12 **o** the words of the transgressor........ 5557
Pr 29:4 but he that receiveth gifts **o** it 2040

OVERTHROWN
Ex 15:7 hast **o** them that rose up against....... 2040
Pr 11:11 it is **o** by the mouth of the wicked 2040
Pr 12:7 The wicked are **o**, and are not: 2015
Pr 14:11 house of the wicked shall be **o**:........ 8045
La 4:6 that was **o** as in a moment, and 2015
Da 11:41 and many countries shall be **o**:........ 3782
Jnh 3:4 days, and Nineveh shall be **o** 2015
1Co 10:5 for they were **o** in the wilderness *2693*

OVERTOOK
Ex 14:9 and **o** them encamping by the sea,..... 5381
Jgs 20:42 but the battle **o** them; and them....... 1692
Jer 39:5 **o** Zedekiah in the plains of Jericho: 5381
Jer 52:8 **o** Zedekiah in the plains of Jericho; 5381

OVERWHELMED
Ps 61:2 unto thee, when my heart is **o**: 5848
Ps 77:3 and my spirit was **o**. Selah. 5848
Ps 78:53 not: but the sea **o** their enemies 3680
Ps 142:3 When my spirit was **o** within me,...... 5848
Ps 143:4 is my spirit **o** within me; my 5848

OWE
Ro 13:8 **O** no man any thing, but to love....... *3784*

OWED
Mt 18:24 **o him ten thousand talents** *3781*
Mt 18:28 **which o him an hundred pence:**....... *3784*
Lk 7:41 **the one o five hundred pence, and**..... *3784*

OWEST
Mt 18:28 **saying, Pay me that thou o** *3784*
Lk 16:5 **How much o thou unto my lord?**...... *3784*
Phm 19 **o** unto me even thine own self *4359*

OWETH
Phm 18 wronged thee, or **o** thee ought,......... *3784*

OWLS
Job 30:29 and a companion to **o** 1323, 3284
Isa 13:21 and **o** shall dwell there, and...... 1323, 3284
Mic 1:8 and mourning as the **o**.......... 1323, 3284

OWN
Ge 1:27 So God created man in his **o** image,
Ge 5:3 begat a son in his **o** likeness,
Nu 15:39 that ye seek not after your **o** heart
Dt 12:8 man whatsoever is right in his **o** eyes
Dt 24:16 shall be put to death for his **o** sin.
Jgs 17:6 that which was right in his **o** eyes

O

Jgs 21:25 that which was right in his **o** eyes
1Sa 13:14 sought him a man after his **o** heart,
1Sa 18:3 because he loved him as his **o** soul
1Sa 20:17 for he loved him as he loved his **o** soul
1Ki 8:38 every man the plague of his **o** heart,
2Ki 17:29 every nation made gods of their **o**,
2Ch 25:4 but every man shall die for his **o** sin
Job 9:20 mine **o** mouth shall condemn me:
Job 40:14 that thine **o** right hand can save thee
Ps 4:4 commune with your **o** heart upon
Ps 7:16 mischief shall return upon his **o** head,
Ps 15:4 He that sweareth to his **o** hurt, and
Ps 22:29 and none can keep alive his **o** soul.
Ps 36:2 he flattereth himself in his **o** eyes,
Ps 37:15 sword shall enter into their **o** heart,
Ps 41:9 mine **o** familiar friend, in whom I
Ps 67:6 God, even our **o** God, shall bless us
Ps 81:12 gave them up unto their **o** hearts' lust:
Ps 94:23 bring upon them their **o** iniquity,
Pr 3:5 lean not unto thine **o** understanding
Pr 3:7 Be not wise in thine **o** eyes: fear the
Pr 8:36 that sinneth … wrongeth his **o** soul:
Pr 12:15 way of a fool is right in his **o** eyes:
Pr 20:2 to anger sinneth against his **o** soul.
Pr 20:6 proclaim every one his **o** goodness:
Pr 21:2 way of a man is right in his **o** eyes:
Pr 23:4 be rich: cease from thine **o** wisdom
Pr 25:27 to search their **o** glory is not glory
Pr 25:28 he that hath no rule over his **o** spirit
Pr 26:5 lest he be wise in his **o** conceit
Pr 27:2 a stranger, and not thine **o** lips
Pr 28:26 that trusteth in his **o** heart is a fool:
Pr 30:12 that are pure in their **o** eyes, and yet
Ecc 1:16 I communed with mine **o** heart,
Isa 2:8 worship the work of their **o** hands,
Isa 5:21 them that are wise in their **o** eyes,
Jer 1:16 worshipped the works of their **o** hands
Jer 9:14 after the imagination of their **o** heart,
Jer 18:12 but we will walk after our **o** devices,
Jer 23:16 they speak a vision of their **o** heart,
Jer 23:17 after the imagination of his **o** heart,
Jer 31:30 every one shall die for his **o** iniquity:
Eze 13:3 prophets, that follow their **o** spirit,
Eze 14:20 shall but deliver their **o** souls
Eze 16:15 thou didst trust in thine **o** beauty,
Eze 33:4 his blood shall be upon his **o** head
Eze 36:31 shall ye remember your **o** evil ways,
Da 3:28 worship any god, except their **o** God
Mt 7:3 **the beam that is in thine o eye?**
Mt 16:26 **whole world, and lose his o soul?**
Mk 8:36 **whole world, and lose his o soul?**
Mk 15:20 and put his **o** clothes on him, ... *2398*
Lk 6:41 **the beam that is in thine o eye?** *2398*
Jn 1:11 and his **o** received him not
Jn 5:30 **I can of mine o self do nothing:**
Jn 5:43 **another shall come in his o name,** *2398*
Jn 6:38 **not to do mine o will, but the will**
Jn 7:18 **of himself seeketh his o glory:** *2398*
Jn 8:50 **I seek not mine o glory: there is**
Jn 10:3 **he calleth his o sheep by name,** *2398*
Jn 15:19 **world, the world would love his o** *2398*
Ac 2:8 we every man in our **o** tongue, ... *2398*
Ac 5:4 sold, was it not in thine **o** power?
Ac 13:22 a man after mine **o** heart, which
Ro 1:24 through the lusts of their **o** hearts,
Ro 1:24 to dishonour their **o** bodies between
Ro 8:3 God sending his **o** Son in the *1438*
Ro 8:32 that spared not his **o** Son, but *2398*
Ro 11:24 be graffed into their **o** olive tree? *2398*
Ro 11:25 should be wise in your **o** conceits; *1438*
Ro 14:4 to his **o** master he standeth or. *2398*
Ro 14:5 be fully persuaded in his **o** mind. *2398*
1Co 6:18 sinneth against his **o** body *2398*
1Co 7:4 wife hath not power of her **o** body. *2398*
1Co 10:24 Let no man seek his **o**, but every. *1438*
1Co 13:5 seeketh not her **o**, is not easily. *1438*
Eph 5:28 love their wives as their **o** bodies. *1438*
Php 2:12 work out your **o** salvation with fear *1438*
Heb 9:12 but by his **o** blood he entered in *2398*
Jas 1:14 he is drawn away of his **o** lust, and. *2398*
Jas 1:18 Of his **o** will begat he us with the
Jas 1:22 hearers only, deceiving your **o** selves
2Pe 3:3 scoffers, walking after their **o** lusts,. *2398*
2Pe 3:16 scriptures, unto their **o** destruction *2398*
Rev 1:5 us from our sins in his **o** blood, ... *848*

OWNER

Ex 21:29 and his **o** also shall be put to death 1167
Ex 21:34 The **o** of the pit shall make it good, ... 1167
Ex 22:12 shall make restitution unto the **o** 1167

OWNERS

Pr 1:19 taketh away the life of the **o**. 1167

OX

Ex 20:17 nor his **o**, nor his ass, nor any 7794
Ex 21:28 If an **o** gore a man or a woman, ... 7794
Ex 21:29 the **o** shall be stoned, and his 7794
Dt 25:4 shalt not muzzle the **o** when he 7794
Jgs 3:31 hundred men with an **o** goad:. 1241
Ps 69:31 please the Lord better than an **o** 7794
Pr 7:22 as an **o** goeth to the slaughter, or 7794
Pr 14:4 increase is by the strength of the **o** 7794
Pr 15:17 a stalled **o** and hatred therewith 7794
Isa 66:3 He that killeth an **o** is as if he slew 7794
Lk 13:15 **the sabbath loose his o or his ass.**. *1016*
Lk 14:5 **an ass or an o fallen into a pit,** *1016*
1Co 9:9 not muzzled the mouth of the **o** that. . . *1016*
1Ti 5:18 not muzzled the **o** that treadeth out. . . . *1016*

OXEN

1Sa 15:14 the lowing of the **o** which I hear? 1241
2Sa 6:6 took hold of it; for the **o** shook it 1241
1Ch 13:9 hold the ark; for the **o** stumbled. 1241
2Ch 4:15 One sea, and twelve **o** under it. 1241
2Ch 29:33 six hundred **o** and three thousand 1241
Pr 14:4 Where no **o** are, the crib is clean: 5091
Isa 7:25 shall be for the sending forth of **o** 7794
Da 4:33 and did eat grass as **o**, and his. 8450
Da 5:21 they fed him with grass like **o**, and. 8450
Lk 14:19 **I have bought five yoke of o, and** *1016*
Jn 2:14 that sold **o** and sheep and doves *1016*
Jn 2:15 temple, and the sheep, and the **o**; *1016*
1Co 9:9 corn. Doth God take care for **o**? *1016*

P

PAID

Jnh	1:3	so he **p** the fare thereof, and went	5414
Mt	5:26	**thou hast p the uttermost farthing**	*591*
Lk	12:59	**till thou hast p the very last mite.**	*591*

PAIN

Job	14:22	his flesh upon him shall have **p**,	3510
Ps	48:6	and **p**, as of a woman in travail	2427
Jer	15:18	Why is my **p** perpetual, and my	3511
Rev	16:10	they gnawed their tongues for **p**,	*4192*
Rev	21:4	neither shall there be any more **p**:	*4192*

PAINED

Ps	55:4	My heart is sore **p** within me: and	2342
Joel	2:6	face the people shall be much **p**:	2342
Rev	12:2	in birth, and **p** to be delivered	*928*

PAINS

Ps	116:3	the **p** of hell gat hold upon me:	4712
Ac	2:24	up, having loosed the **p** of death:	*5604*

PAIR

Lk	2:24	A **p** of turtledoves, or two young	*2201*
Rev	6:5	had a **p** of balances in his hand	*2218*

PALACE

1Ch	29:1	**p** is not for man, but for the Lord	1002
Ne	2:8	make beams for the gates of the **p**,	1002
Est	7:8	king returned out of the **p** garden	1055
Est	9:6	in Shushan the **p** the Jews slew	1002
SS	8:9	will build upon her a **p** of silver:	2918
Da	1:4	in them to stand in the king's **p**	1964
Da	4:4	house, and flourishing in my **p**:	1965
Lk	11:21	**strong man armed keepeth his p,**	*833*
Jn	18:15	Jesus into the **p** of the high priest	*833*

PALACES

2Ch	36:19	burnt all the **p** thereof with fire,	759
Ps	45:8	and cassia, out of the ivory **p**,	1964
Isa	13:22	and dragons in their pleasant **p**:	1964

PALE

Isa	29:22	neither shall his face now wax **p**	2357
Rev	6:8	I looked, and behold a **p** horse:	*5515*

PALM

Ex	15:27	and threescore and ten **p** trees:	8558
Le	14:15	into the **p** of his own left hand:	3709
Jgs	4:5	under the **p** tree of Deborah	8560
Ps	92:12	shall flourish like the **p** tree:	8558
SS	7:7	This thy stature is like to a **p** tree,	8558
Jn	12:13	Took branches of **p** trees, and	*5404*
Jn	18:22	struck Jesus with the **p** of his	*4475*

PALMS

1Sa	5:4	both the **p** of his hands were cut	3709
Da	10:10	knees and upon the **p** of my hands	3709
Mt	26:67	smote him with … **p** of their hands,	*4474*
Rev	7:9	robes, and **p** in their hands;	*5404*

PALSY

Mt	4:24	lunatick, and those that had the **p**;	*3885*
Mt	9:2	brought to him a man sick of the **p**,	*3885*
Mk	2:5	he said unto the sick of the **p**, **Son,**	3885
Mk	2:9	easier to say to the sick of the **p**.	*3885*
Ac	9:33	eight years, and was sick of the **p**	*3886*

PAN

Le	2:5	be a meat offering baken in a **p**,	4227
1Sa	2:14	he struck it into the **p**, or kettle,	3595
2Sa	13:9	she took a **p**, and poured them	4958

PANGS

Isa	13:8	**p** and sorrows shall take hold of	6735
Isa	26:17	in pain, and crieth out in her **p**;	2256
Jer	50:43	and **p** as of a woman in travail	2427

PANS

Ex	27:3	make his **p** to receive his ashes,	5518
Nu	11:8	baked it in **p**, and made cakes of	6517
2Ch	35:13	in caldrons, and in **p**, and divided	6745

PANTED

Ps	119:131	I opened my mouth, and **p**: for I	7602
Isa	21:4	My heart **p**, tearfulness	8582

PANTETH

Ps	42:1	the hart **p** after the water brooks	6165
Ps	42:1	so **p** my soul after thee, O God	6165

PAPER

Isa	19:7	The **p** reeds by the brooks, by the	6169
2Jn	12	would not write with **p** and ink:	*5489*

PARABLE

Nu	23:18	he took up his **p**, and said, Rise up,	4912
Job	29:1	Moreover Job continued his **p**,	4912
Ps	49:4	I will incline mine ear to a **p**: I will	4912
Pr	26:7	so is a **p** in the mouth of fools	4912
Mt	13:18	**ye therefore the p of the sower**	*3850*
Mt	13:36	Declare unto us the **p** of the tares	*3850*
Mt	21:33	**Hear another p: There was a**	*3850*
Mt	24:32	**Now learn a p of the fig tree;**	*3850*
Mk	13:28	**Now learn a p of the fig tree;**	*3850*
Lk	8:11	**Now the p is this: The seed is the**	*3850*
Lk	21:29	And he spake to them a **p**: **Behold**	*3850*

PARABLES

Eze	20:49	say of me, Doth he not speak **p**?	4912
Mt	13:13	**Therefore speak I to them in p:**	*3850*
Mt	13:35	saying, I will open my mouth in **p**;	*3850*
Mt	22:1	and spake unto them again by **p**,	*3850*
Mk	4:13	**and how then will ye know all p?**	*3850*
Lk	8:10	**to others in p; that seeing they**	*3850*

PARADISE

Lk	23:43	**To day shalt thou be with me in p**	*3857*
2Co	12:4	How that he was caught up into **p**,	*3857*

PARCEL

Ge	33:19	he bought a **p** of a field, where he	2513
Ru	4:3	selleth a **p** of land, which was our	2513
Jn	4:5	the **p** of ground that Jacob gave	*5564*

PARCHED

Le	23:14	eat neither bread, nor **p** corn, nor	7039
Ru	2:14	he reached her **p** corn, and she	7039
Isa	35:7	**p** ground shall become a pool,	8273

PARDON

Ex	23:21	will not **p** your transgressions:	5375
1Sa	15:25	I pray thee, **p** my sin, and turn	5375
Ne	9:17	but thou art a God ready to **p**,	5547
Job	7:21	dost thou not **p** my transgression,	5375

Ps 25:11 O Lord, **p** mine iniquity; for it is 5545
Isa 55:7 our God, for he will abundantly **p** 5545
Jer 5:7 How shall I **p** thee for this? thy........ 5545

PARDONED
Nu 14:20 I have **p** according to thy word:........ 5545
Isa 40:2 that her iniquity is **p**: for she.......... 7521

PARENTS
Mt 10:21 **shall rise up against their p, and**....... *1118*
Lk 2:27 the **p** brought in the child Jesus,....... *1118*
Lk 2:41 his **p** went to Jerusalem every year *1118*
Lk 18:29 **hath left house, or p, or brethren,** *1118*
Jn 9:3 **hath this man sinned, nor his p:**....... *1118*
Jn 9:23 Therefore said his **p**, He is of age;...... *1118*
Ro 1:30 of evil things, disobedient to **p**,........ *1118*
Eph 6:1 Children, obey your **p** in the Lord:..... *1118*
Col 3:20 obey your **p** in all things: for.......... *1118*
Heb 11:23 was hid three months of his **p**, ... *3962*

PARLOUR
Jgs 3:20 and he was sitting in a summer **p**, ... 5944
1Sa 9:22 and brought them into the **p**, and 3957

PART
Ex 29:26 the Lord: and it shall be thy **p**......... 4490
Le 8:29 of consecration it was Moses' **p**;....... 4940
Nu 18:20 I am thy **p** and thine inheritance 2506
Nu 18:26 the Lord, even a tenth **p** of the tithe.... 2506
Dt 10:9 Levi hath no **p** nor inheritance........ 2506
Jos 15:13 a **p** among the children of Judah,....... 2506
Jos 22:25 ye have no **p** in the Lord: so shall...... 2506
Ru 2:3 hap was to light on a **p** of the field..... 2513
Ru 3:13 perform unto thee the **p** of a kinsman,
1Sa 30:24 his **p** be that tarrieth by the stuff:...... 2506
2Sa 20:1 We have no **p** in David, neither........ 2506
Ne 1:9 unto the uttermost **p** of the heaven
Job 32:17 I said, I will answer also my **p**, ... 2506
Ps 22:18 **p** my garments among them.......... 2505
Ps 51:6 hidden **p** thou shalt make me to know
Pr 17:2 shall have **p** of the inheritance 2505
Da 1:2 with **p** of the vessels of the house...... 7117
Da 2:33 his feet **p** of iron and **p** of clay 4481
Da 2:41 **p** of potters' clay, and **p** of iron, ... 4481
Da 5:5 the king saw the **p** of the hand 6447
Lk 10:42 **Mary hath chosen that good p,**........ *3310*
Lk 11:36 **be full of light, having no p dark,**...... *3313*
Lk 11:39 **but your inward p is full of ravening**
Jn 13:8 **thee not, thou hast no p with me.** *3313*
Ac 1:8 **unto the uttermost p of the earth.**
Ac 5:2 And kept back **p** of the price, his wife
Ac 5:2 brought a certain **p**, and laid it at...... *3313*
Ac 5:3 keep back **p** of the price of the land?
Ro 11:25 in **p** is happened to Israel, until........ *3313*
1Co 13:9 know in **p**, and we prophesy in **p**....... *3313*
1Co 13:10 which is in **p** shall be done away....... *3313*
1Co 13:12 now I know in **p**; but then shall I *3313*
Heb 7:2 Abraham gave a tenth **p** of all; *3307*
Rev 20:6 hath **p** in the first resurrection:........ *3313*
Rev 21:8 liars, shall have their **p** in the lake...... *3313*
Rev 22:19 away his **p** out of the book of life, ... *3313*

PARTAKER
Ps 50:18 and hast been **p** with adulterers........ 2506
1Co 9:10 in hope should be **p** of his hope....... *3348*
1Co 10:30 if I by grace be a **p**, why am I evil...... *3348*
2Ti 1:8 be thou **p** of the afflictions of the...... *4777*
2Ti 2:6 must be first **p** of the fruits *3335*
1Pe 5:1 a **p** of the glory that shall be *2844*
2Jn 11 God speed is **p** of his evil deeds........ *2841*

PARTAKERS
Ro 15:27 made **p** of their spiritual things,....... *2841*
1Co 10:17 for we are all **p** of that one bread *3348*
1Co 10:21 ye cannot be **p** of the Lord's table...... *3348*
2Co 1:7 that as ye are **p** of the sufferings *2844*
Eph 3:6 **p** of his promise in Christ by the *4830*
Php 1:7 gospel, ye are all **p** of my grace *4791*
Heb 3:1 **p** of the heavenly calling, consider *3353*
Heb 3:14 For we are made **p** of Christ, if we *3353*
Heb 6:4 were made **p** of the Holy Ghost,....... *3353*
Heb 12:10 we might be **p** of his holiness.......... *3335*
1Pe 4:13 ye are **p** of Christ's sufferings;......... *2841*
2Pe 1:4 might be **p** of the divine nature,....... *2844*
Rev 18:4 that ye be not **p** of her sins, and *4790*

PARTED
Job 38:24 By what way is the light **p**, which 2505
Mt 27:35 and **p** his garments, casting lots:....... *1266*
Mt 27:35 They **p** my garments among them,..... *1266*

PARTIAL
Mal 2:9 but have been **p** in the law, ... 5375, 6440
Jas 2:4 Are ye not then **p** in yourselves, ... *1252*

PARTIALITY
1Ti 5:21 another, doing nothing by **p** *4346*
Jas 3:17 of mercy and good fruits, without **p**,..... *87*

PARTICULAR
1Co 12:27 of Christ, and members in **p**.......... *3313*
Eph 5:33 every one of you in **p** so love..... *3588, 1520*

PARTITION
1Ki 6:21 made a **p** by the chains of gold........ 5674
Eph 2:14 broken down the middle wall of **p**..... *5418*

PARTLY
Da 2:42 shall be **p** strong, and **p** broken........ 7118
1Co 11:18 you; and I **p** believe it........... *3313, 5100*

PARTNER
Pr 29:24 Whoso is **p** with a thief hateth his 2505
2Co 8:23 he is my **p** and fellowhelper........... *2844*

PARTNERS
Lk 5:7 And they beckoned unto their **p**, ... *3353*
Lk 5:10 Zebedee, which were **p** with Simon *2844*

PARTS
Ge 47:24 four **p** shall be your own, for seed 3027
Le 1:8 Aaron's sons, shall lay the **p**, the 5409
Jos 18:5 they shall divide it into seven **p**........ 2506
2Ki 11:7 two **p** of all you that go forth on....... 3027
Ne 11:1 nine **p** to dwell in other cities......... 3027
Job 26:14 these are **p** of his ways: but how 7098
Ps 136:13 which divided the Red sea into **p**:...... 1506
Pr 20:27 searching all the inward **p** of the belly.
Jer 34:18 and passed between the **p** thereof, ... 1335
Jer 34:19 passed between the **p** of the calf; 1335
Mt 12:42 **from the uttermost p of the earth to**
Jn 19:23 his garments, and made four **p**, ... *3313*
Ro 15:23 having no more place in these **p**, ... *2825*
Eph 4:9 first into the lower **p** of the earth? *3313*
Rev 16:19 great city was divided into three **p**,..... *3313*

PASS

Ge	4:8	it came to **p**, when they were in the	
Ge	8:1	made a wind to **p** over the earth,	5674
Ge	18:3	**p** not away, I pray thee, from thy	5674
Ge	31:52	I will not **p** over this heap to thee,	5674
Ge	32:16	**P** over before me, and put a space	5674
Ge	41:32	and God will shortly bring it to **p**.	6213
Ex	1:21	it came to **p**, because the midwives	
Ex	12:12	For I will **p** through the land of	5674
Ex	12:13	I see the blood, I will **p** over you,	6452
Ex	12:23	the Lord will **p** through to smite.	5674
Ex	15:16	till thy people **p** over, O Lord,	5674
Ex	33:19	make all my goodness **p** before	5674
Ex	33:22	come to **p**, while my glory passeth	
Ex	33:22	thee with my hand while I **p** by:	5674
Le	18:21	seed **p** through the fire to Molech,	5674
Nu	21:23	suffer Israel to **p** through his border:	5674
Nu	32:27	But thy servants will **p** over, every	5674
Nu	32:29	will **p** with you over Jordan, every	5674
Dt	2:27	Let me **p** through thy land: I will	5674
Dt	3:18	ye shall **p** over armed before your.	5674
Dt	9:1	Thou art to **p** over Jordan this day,	5674
Dt	18:10	daughter to **p** through the fire,	5674
Jos	1:11	ye shall **p** over this Jordan, to go	5674
Jos	3:13	come to **p**, as soon as the soles of	
Jos	3:14	it came to **p**, when the people	5674
Jos	6:7	**P** on, and compass the city, and	5674
Jos	22:19	then **p** ye over unto the land of	5674
Jgs	11:17	Let me, I pray thee, **p** through thy	5674
Jgs	11:19	Let us **p**, we pray thee, through	5674
Jgs	13:17	when thy sayings come to **p** we may	935
1Sa	9:27	Bid the servant **p** on before us,	5674
1Sa	16:10	made seven of his sons to **p** before	5674
2Sa	17:16	speedily **p** over; lest the king be	5674
2Sa	17:21	and **p** quickly over the water for	5674
1Ki	11:4	came to **p**, when Solomon was old,	
1Ki	18:27	it came to **p** at noon, that Elijah	
1Ki	21:15	it came to **p**, when Jezebel heard	
2Ki	7:18	came to **p** as the man of God had	
2Ki	16:3	made his son to **p** through … fire,	5674
2Ki	17:17	their daughters to **p** through … fire,	5674
2Ki	19:37	came to **p**, as he was worshipping	
1Ch	15:29	And it came to **p**, as the ark of the	
2Ch	13:15	it came to **p**, that God smote	
Ne	2:14	beast that was under me to **p**	5674
Ne	7:1	it came to **p**, when the wall was	
Ne	13:19	came to **p**, that when the gates of	
Job	6:15	the stream of brooks they **p** away;	5674
Job	11:16	remember it as waters that **p** away:	5674
Job	19:8	fenced up my way that I cannot **p**	5674
Ps	37:7	who bringeth wicked devices to **p**	6213
Ps	136:14	made Israel to **p** through the midst	5674
Pr	4:15	Avoid it, **p** not by it, turn from it,	5674
Pr	8:29	should not **p** his commandment:	5674
Pr	16:30	his lips he bringeth evil to **p**	3615
Pr	19:11	glory to **p** over a transgression.	5674
Pr	22:3	but the simple **p** on, … are punished.	5674
Isa	8:8	And he shall **p** through Judah;	2498
Isa	10:12	shall come to **p**, that when the Lord	
Isa	10:20	come to **p** in that day, that the remnant	
Isa	21:1	whirlwinds in the south **p** through;	2498
Isa	28:15	the overflowing scourge shall **p**.	5674
Isa	28:19	morning by morning shall it **p** over,	5674
Isa	31:9	he shall **p** over to his strong hold	5674
Isa	33:21	neither shall gallant ship **p** thereby	5674
Isa	51:10	a way for the ransomed to **p** over?	5674
Jer	5:22	perpetual decree, that it cannot **p** it:	5674
Jer	5:22	they roar, yet can they not **p** over it?	5674
Jer	22:8	many nations shall **p** by this city,	5674
Jer	51:43	neither doth any son of man **p**	5674
La	1:12	Is it nothing to you, all ye that **p** by?	5674
La	2:15	that **p** by clap their hands at thee;	5674
La	3:44	our prayer should not **p** through.	5674
Eze	5:14	thee, in the sight of all that **p** by	5674
Eze	5:17	and blood shall **p** through thee;	5674
Eze	16:21	to cause them to **p** through the fire	5674
Eze	20:37	will cause you to **p** under the rod,	5674
Eze	29:11	No foot of man shall **p** through it,	5964
Eze	29:11	nor foot of beast shall **p** through it,	5964
Eze	37:2	me to **p** by them round about:	5674
Da	4:16	and let seven times **p** over him.	2499
Da	7:14	dominion, which shall not **p** away,	5709
Da	11:10	and overflow, and **p** through:	5674
Da	11:40	and shall overflow and **p** over.	5674
Am	5:17	for I will **p** through thee, saith the	5674
Jnh	4:8	came to **p**, when the sun did arise,	
Zec	9:8	and no oppressor shall **p** through.	5674
Zec	10:11	**p** through the sea with affliction,	5674
Mt	5:18	**Till heaven and earth p, one jot**	*3928*
Mt	5:18	**one tittle shall in no wise p from**	*3928*
Mt	24:34	**This generation shall not p, till all**	*3928*
Mt	24:35	**Heaven and earth shall p away,**	*3928*
Mt	24:35	**but my words shall not p away.**	*3928*
Mt	26:39	**possible, let this cup p from me:**	*3928*
Mk	4:35	**Let us p over unto the other side.**	*1330*
Mk	13:30	**this generation shall not p, till all.**	*3928*
Mk	14:35	the hour might **p** from him.	*3928*
Lk	1:41	it came to **p**, that, when Elisabeth	
Lk	1:59	came to **p**, that on the eighth day	
Lk	2:1	And it came to **p** in those days, that	
Lk	2:15	came to **p**, as the angels were gone	
Lk	2:15	see this thing which is come to **p**,	
Lk	11:14	came to **p**, when the devil was gone	
Lk	11:42	**p over judgment and the love of.**	*3928*
Lk	16:17	**easier for heaven and earth to p,**	*3928*
Lk	21:32	**This generation shall not p away,**	*3928*
Lk	21:33	**Heaven and earth shall p away:**	*3928*
Lk	21:33	**but my words shall not p away.**	*3928*
Jn	13:19	**when it is come to p, ye may believe**	
Jn	15:25	**But this cometh to p, that the word**	
1Co	7:36	if she **p** the flower of her age,	*5230*
Jas	1:10	of the grass he shall **p** away	*3928*
2Pe	3:10	the heavens shall **p** away with a	*3928*
Rev	1:1	things which must shortly come to **p**.	*1096*

PASSAGE

Jos	22:11	at the **p** of the children of Israel.	1552
Isa	10:29	They are gone over the **p**: they	4569

PASSAGES

Jgs	12:6	and slew him at the **p** of Jordan:	4569
1Sa	14:4	between the **p**, by which Jonathan	4569

PASSED

Ge	12:6	And Abram **p** through the land	5674
Ge	32:10	with my staff I **p** over this Jordan;	5674
Nu	33:8	and **p** through the midst of the sea	5674
Nu	33:51	are **p** over Jordan into the land of.	5674
Jos	2:23	**p** over, and came to Joshua the	5674
Jos	3:17	the Israelites **p** over on dry ground,	5674
Jos	3:17	people were **p** clean over Jordan.	5674
Jos	4:11	the ark of the Lord **p** over, and the.	5674
Jos	15:10	and **p** along unto the side of mount.	5674

2Sa 10:17	Israel together, and **p** over Jordan,	5674
2Sa 17:24	And Absalom **p** over Jordan, he	5674
1Ki 19:19	and Elijah **p** by him, and cast his	5674
2Ki 4:31	Gehazi **p** on before them, and laid	5674
Job 4:15	Then a spirit **p** before my face;	2498
Job 9:26	are **p** away as the swift ships:	2498
Ps 18:12	was before him his thick clouds **p**	5674
Ps 90:9	all our days are **p** away in thy	6437
Isa 40:27	judgment is **p** over from my God?	5674
Da 3:27	the smell of fire had **p** on them.	5709
Jnh 2:3	billows and thy waves **p** over me.	5674
Mt 20:30	when they heard that Jesus **p** by	*3899*
Mk 11:20	as they **p** by, they saw the fig tree	*3899*
Mk 15:29	And they that **p** by railed on him,	*3899*
Lk 10:31	**saw him, he p by on the other side.**	*492*
Lk 10:32	**him, and p by on the other side.**	*492*
Jn 5:24	**but is p from death unto life**	*3327*
Ro 5:12	so death **p** upon all men, for that	*1330*
1Co 10:1	cloud, and all **p** through the sea;	*1330*
2Co 5:17	old things are **p** away; behold, all	*3928*
Heb 4:14	priest, that is **p** into the heavens,	*1330*
Heb 11:29	faith they **p** through he Red sea	*1224*
1Jn 3:14	we have **p** from death unto life,	*3327*
Rev 21:1	and the first earth were **p** away;	*3928*
Rev 21:4	for the former things are **p** away	*565*

PASSEST

Dt 30:18	**p** over Jordan to go to possess it.	5674
Isa 43:2	When thou **p** through the waters,	5674

PASSETH

Le 27:32	whatsoever **p** under the rod, the	5674
Jos 3:11	**p** over before you into Jordan.	5674
Job 30:15	my welfare **p** away as a cloud.	5674
Ps 8:8	**p** through the paths of the seas.	5674
Ps 78:39	a wind that **p** away, and cometh	1980
Pr 10:25	As the whirlwind **p**, so is the	5674
Ecc 1:4	One generation **p** away, and	1980
Isa 29:5	shall be as chaff that **p** away:	5674
Zep 2:15	every one that **p** by her shall hiss,	5674
Eph 3:19	love of Christ, which **p** knowledge,	*5235*
Php 4:7	God, which **p** all understanding,	*5242*
1Jn 2:17	the world **p** away, and the lust	*3855*

PASSING

Pr 7:8	**P** through the street near her	5674
Lk 4:30	he **p** through the midst of them	*1330*
Ac 5:15	the shadow of Peter **p** by might	*2064*

PASSION

Ac 1:3	shewed himself alive after his **p**.	*3958*

PASSIONS

Ac 14:15	We also are men of like **p** with you,	*3663*
Jas 5:17	a man subject to like **p** as we are,	*3663*

PASSOVER

Ex 12:11	eat it in haste: it is the Lord's **p**	6453
Ex 12:43	This is the ordinance of the **p**:	6453
Le 23:5	first month at even is the Lord's **p**	6453
Nu 9:10	he shall keep the **p** unto the Lord.	6453
Dt 16:6	thou shalt sacrifice the **p** at even.	6453
2Ki 23:21	Keep the **p** unto the Lord your God,	6453
2Ch 35:1	Josiah kept a **p** unto the Lord in	6453
2Ch 35:17	that were present kept the **p** at that	6453
2Ch 35:18	was no **p** like to that kept in Israel	6453
Ezr 6:19	children of the captivity kept the **p**	6453
Mt 26:2	**two days is the feast of the p,**	*3957*
Mt 26:17	we prepare for thee to eat the **p**?	*3957*
Mt 26:18	**I will keep the p at thy house**	*3957*
Mt 26:19	them; and they made ready the **p**	*3957*
Lk 22:7	bread, when the **p** must be killed.	*3957*
Lk 22:8	**Go and prepare us the p, that we**	*3957*
Lk 22:11	**I shall eat the p with my**	*3957*
Lk 22:15	**I have desired to eat this p with**	*3957*
Jn 2:13	And the Jews' **p** was at hand, and	*3957*
Jn 12:1	Jesus six days before the **p** came to	*3957*
Jn 18:39	release unto you one at the **p**.	*3957*
1Co 5:7	Christ our **p** is sacrificed for us:	*3957*
Heb 11:28	Through faith he kept the **p**, and	*3957*

PAST

Ex 21:29	to push with his horn in time **p**,	8032
Ex 21:36	the ox hath used to push in time **p**,	8032
Dt 4:42	and hated him not in times **p**; and	8032
1Sa 15:32	Surely the bitterness of death is **p**	5493
2Sa 5:2	in time **p**, when Saul was king over	8032
2Sa 11:27	And when the mourning was **p**,	5493
Job 9:10	doeth great things **p** finding out;	369
Job 17:11	My days are **p**, my purposes are	5674
Ps 90:4	are but as yesterday when it is **p**,	5674
SS 2:11	the winter is **p**, the rain is over	5674
Jer 8:20	harvest is **p**, the summer is ended,	5674
Lk 9:36	the voice was **p**, Jesus was found	*1096*
Ac 14:16	in times **p** suffered all nations	*3944*
Ro 3:25	the remission of sins that are **p**,	*4266*
Ro 11:30	in times **p** have not believed God,	
Gal 1:13	heard of my conversation in time **p**	
Eph 2:2	Wherein in time **p** ye walked	
2Ti 2:18	that the resurrection is **p** already;	*1096*
Heb 1:1	spake in time **p** unto the fathers	*3819*
Heb 11:11	of a child when she was **p** age,	*3844*
1Jn 2:8	because the darkness is **p**, and	*3855*
Rev 9:12	One woe is **p**; and, behold, there	*565*
Rev 11:14	The second woe is **p**; and, behold,	*565*

PASTORS

Jer 10:21	**p** are become brutish, and have	7462
Jer 23:1	Woe be unto the **p** that destroy	7462
Eph 4:11	and some, **p** and teachers;	*4166*

PASTURE

Ge 47:4	servants have no **p** for their flocks;	4829
1Ch 4:40	And they found fat **p** and good, and	4829
Ps 100:3	his people, and the sheep of his **p**.	4830
La 1:6	become like harts that find no **p**,	4829
Eze 34:18	you to have eaten up the good **p**,	4829
Jn 10:9	**shall go in and out, and find p**	*3542*

PASTURES

Ps 23:2	maketh me to lie down in green **p**	4999
Ps 65:13	The **p** are clothed with flocks;	3733
Eze 34:18	your feet the residue of your **p**?	4829

PATH

Ge 49:17	an adder in the **p**, that biteth the	734
Nu 22:24	angel of the Lord stood in a **p** of	4934
Ps 16:11	Thou wilt shew me the **p** of life:	734
Ps 27:11	O Lord, and lead me in a plain **p**,	734
Ps 119:105	my feet, and a light unto my **p**	5410
Ps 139:3	Thou compassest my **p** and my	734
Pr 2:9	and equity; yea, every good **p**	4570
Pr 4:14	Enter not into the **p** of the wicked,	734
Pr 4:18	the **p** of the just is as the shining	734
Pr 5:6	shouldest ponder the **p** of life,	734

PATHS

Job 8:13	So are the **p** of all that forget God;	734
Job 33:11	the stocks, he marketh all my **p**.	734
Ps 17:4	me from the **p** of the destroyer	734
Ps 23:3	me in the **p** of righteousness for	4570
Ps 25:4	thy ways, O Lord; teach me thy **p**	734
Ps 25:10	All the **p** of the Lord are mercy	734
Pr 2:13	leave the **p** of uprightness, to walk	734
Pr 2:18	death, and her **p** unto the dead.	4570
Pr 3:6	him, and he shall direct thy **p**	734
Pr 4:11	wisdom; I have led thee in right **p**	4570
Pr 7:25	her ways, go not astray in her **p**	5410
Pr 8:20	in the midst of the **p** of judgment:	5410
La 3:9	stone, he hath made my **p** crooked.	5410
Mt 3:3	of the Lord, make his **p** straight	*5147*
Heb 12:13	made straight **p** for your feet, lest	*5163*

PATIENCE

Mt 18:26	**Lord, have p with me, and I will**	*3114*
Mt 18:29	**Have p with me, and I will pay**	*3114*
Lk 8:15	**it, and bring forth fruit with p**	*5281*
Lk 21:19	**In your p possess ye your souls**	*5281*
Ro 5:3	that tribulation worketh **p**;	*5281*
Ro 5:4	And **p**, experience; and experience,	*5281*
2Co 6:4	the ministers of God, in much **p**, in	*5281*
1Ti 6:11	godliness, faith, love, **p**, meekness.	*5281*
2Ti 3:10	faith, longsuffering, charity, **p**,	*5281*
Tit 2:2	sound in faith, in charity, in **p**,	*5281*
Heb 12:1	let us run with **p** the race that is	*5281*
Jas 1:3	the trying of your faith worketh **p**	*5281*
Jas 1:4	But let **p** have her perfect work,	*5281*
Jas 5:11	Ye have heard of the **p** of Job,	*5281*
2Pe 1:6	temperance **p**; and to **p** godliness;	*5281*
Rev 1:9	the kingdom and **p** of Jesus Christ,	*5281*
Rev 2:2	**works, and thy labour, and thy p,**	*5281*
Rev 2:3	**hast p, and for my name's sake**	*5281*
Rev 2:19	**faith, and thy p, and thy works;**	*5281*

PATIENT

Ecc 7:8	**p** in spirit is better than the proud	750
Ro 12:12	in hope; **p** in tribulation;	*5278*
1Th 5:14	the weak, be **p** toward all men.	*3114*
2Ti 2:24	gentle unto all men, apt to teach, **p**,	*420*
Jas 5:8	Be ye also **p**; stablish your hearts:	*3114*

PATIENTLY

Ps 37:7	in the Lord, and wait **p** for him:	2342
Ps 40:1	I waited **p** for the Lord; and he	6960
1Pe 2:20	ye take it **p**, this as acceptable with	*5278*

PATRIARCH

Ac 2:29	speak unto you of the **p** David,	*3966*
Heb 7:4	the **p** Abraham gave the tenth of.	*3966*

PATRIARCHS

Ac 7:8	and Jacob begat the twelve **p**	*3966*
Ac 7:9	And the **p**, moved with envy, sold.	*3966*

PATTERN

Ex 25:9	after the **p** of the tabernacle, and	8403
Jos 22:28	the **p** of the altar of the Lord,	8403
1Ti 1:16	**p** to them which should hereafter	*5296*
Tit 2:7	shewing thyself a **p** of good works:	*5179*
Heb 8:5	the **p** shewed to thee in the mount.	*5179*

PATTERNS

Heb 9:23	**p** of things in the heavens should	*5262*

PAVED

Ex 24:10	were a **p** work of a sapphire stone,	3840
SS 3:10	midst thereof being **p** with love,	7528

PAVEMENT

2Ki 16:17	it, and put it upon a **p** of stones	4837
Est 1:6	a **p** of red, and blue, and white	7531
Jn 19:13	in a place that is called the **P**,	*3038*

PAVILION

Ps 18:11	his **p** round about him were dark.	5521
Ps 27:5	he shall hide me in his **p**: in the	5520
Ps 31:20	shalt keep him secretly in a **p**	5521

PAVILIONS

2Sa 22:12	he made darkness **p** round about	5521
1Ki 20:12	drinking, he and the kings in the **p**,	5521

PAW

1Sa 17:37	delivered me out of … **p** of the lion,	3027
1Sa 17:37	and out of the **p** of the bear, he will	3027

PAY

Ex 21:19	he shall **p** for the loss of his time,	5414
Ex 22:7	thief be found, let him **p** double	7999
Ex 22:17	**p** money according to the dowry	8254
2Sa 15:7	let me go and **p** my vow, which I	7999
2Ki 4:7	Go, sell the oil, and **p** thy debt,	7999
Ezr 4:13	will they not **p** toll, tribute, and	5415
Est 4:7	that Haman had promised to **p** to	8254
Ps 22:25	**p** my vows before them that fear	7999
Ps 66:13	offerings: I will **p** thee my vows	7999
Pr 19:17	he hath given will he **p** him again.	7999
Ecc 5:4	a vow unto God, defer not to **p** it;	7999
Ecc 5:5	thou shouldest vow and not **p**.	7999
Mt 18:25	**forasmuch as he had not to p, his**	*591*
Mt 18:28	**saying, P me that thou owest**	*591*
Mt 18:30	**prison, till he should p the debt**	*592*
Mt 23:23	**for ye p tithe of mint and anise**	*586*

PAYED

Pr 7:14	me; this day have I **p** my vows.	7999
Heb 7:9	tithes, **p** tithes in Abraham.	*1183*

P

PEACE

Ge 15:15	thou shalt go to thy fathers in **p**;	7965
Ge 24:21	man wondering at her held his **p**,	2790
Ge 34:5	Jacob held his **p** until they were	2790
Ge 43:23	And he said, **P** be to you, fear not:	7965
Ex 4:18	And Jethro said to Moses, Go in **p**	7965
Ex 20:24	offerings, and thy **p** offerings,	8002
Le 10:3	glorified. And Aaron held his **p**.	1826
Le 26:6	I will give **p** in the land, and ye	7965
Nu 6:26	upon thee, and give thee **p**.	7965
Nu 15:8	vow, or **p** offerings unto the Lord:	8002
Nu 30:4	her father shall hold his **p** at her;	2790
Dt 20:10	against it, then proclaim **p** unto it	7965
Dt 20:11	if it make thee answer of **p**, and	7965
Dt 29:19	I shall have **p**, though I walk in	7965
Jos 9:15	Joshua made **p** with them, and	7965
Jos 10:1	Gibeon had made **p** with Israel.	7999
Jgs 6:23	him, **P** be unto thee; fear not:	7965
Jgs 18:19	they said unto him, Hold thy **p**,	2790
Jgs 19:20	the old man said, **P** be with thee;	7965
1Sa 10:8	sacrifice sacrifices of **p** offerings:	8002
1Sa 20:7	is well; thy servant shall have **p**:	7965
1Sa 20:42	Jonathan said to David, Go in **p**	7965
2Sa 10:19	made **p** with Israel, and served	7999

1Ki	2:5	shed the blood of war in **p**, and	7965
1Ki	5:12	**p** between Hiram and Solomon;	7965
1Ch	12:18	son of Jesse: **p**, **p** be unto thee	7965
Ezr	4:17	unto the rest beyond the river, **P**,	8001
Ne	8:11	Hold your **p**, for the day is holy;	2013
Est	4:14	if thou altogether holdest thy **p**.	2790
Job	5:24	that thy tabernacle shall be in **p**;	7965
Job	33:33	hold thy **p**, and I shall teach thee	2790
Ps	4:8	both lay me down in **p**, and sleep:	7965
Ps	34:14	and do good; seek **p**, and pursue it.	7965
Ps	37:37	for the end of that man is **p**,	7965
Ps	39:2	dumb with silence, I held my **p**,	2814
Ps	72:3	mountains ... bring **p** to the people,	7965
Ps	72:7	abundance of **p** so long as the moon	7965
Ps	85:10	righteousness and **p** have kissed	7965
Ps	109:1	Hold not thy **p**, O God of my	2790
Ps	122:6	Pray for the **p** of Jerusalem: they.	7965
Ps	122:7	**P** be within thy walls, and	7965
Pr	3:2	long life, and **p**, shall they add to	7965
Pr	12:20	but to the counsellors of **p** is joy.	7965
Pr	17:28	Even a fool, when he holdeth his **p**,	2790
Ecc	3:8	a time of war, and a time of **p**.	7965
Isa	9:6	Father, The Prince of **P**	7965
Isa	9:7	increase of his government and **p**.	7965
Isa	26:3	wilt keep him in perfect **p**, whose	7965
Isa	45:7	I make **p**, and create evil: I the	7965
Isa	52:7	good tidings, that publisheth **p**;	7965
Isa	53:5	chastisement of our **p** was upon	7965
Isa	54:10	the covenant of my **p** be removed	7965
Isa	55:12	with joy, and be led forth with **p**:	7965
Isa	57:21	There is no **p**, saith my God, to the	7965
Jer	6:14	saying, **P**, **p**; when there is no **p**	7965
Jer	8:11	saying, **P**, **p**; when there is no **p**	7965
Jer	8:15	We looked for **p**, but no good came;	7965
Jer	23:17	Lord hath said. Ye shall have **p**;	7965
Jer	29:11	thoughts of **p**, and not of evil, to	7965
Eze	13:10	saying, **P**; and there was no **p**;	7965
Da	4:1	earth: **P** be multiplied unto you	8001
Da	8:25	and by **p** shall destroy many;	7962
Mic	3:5	bite with their teeth, and cry, **P**;	7965
Na	1:15	good tidings, that publisheth **p**!	7965
Zec	8:16	execute ... judgment of truth and **p**.	7965
Zec	8:19	therefore love the truth and **p**.	7965
Mal	2:6	he walked with me in **p** and equity,	7965
Mt	10:34	**I am come to send p on earth:**	*1515*
Mt	10:34	**I came not to send p, but a sword.**	*1515*
Mt	26:63	But Jesus held his **p**. And the high	*4623*
Mk	1:25	**Hold thy p, and come out of him.**	*5392*
Mk	4:39	and said unto the sea, **P, be still**	*4623*
Mk	5:34	**go in p, and be whole of thy plague**	*1515*
Mk	9:50	**and have p one with another**	*1518*
Lk	2:14	on earth **p**, good will toward men	*1515*
Lk	2:29	lettest thou thy servant depart in **p**,	*1515*
Lk	4:35	**Hold thy p, and come out of him.**	*5392*
Lk	7:50	**faith hath saved thee; go in p**	*1515*
Lk	10:5	**First say, P be to this house**	*1515*
Lk	10:6	**And if the son of p be there, your**	*1515*
Lk	12:51	**that I am come to give p on earth?**	*1515*
Lk	14:32	**and desireth conditions of p**	*1515*
Lk	19:40	**if these should hold their p, the**	*4623*
Lk	19:42	**things which belong unto thy p!**	*1515*
Lk	24:36	saith unto them, **P be unto you**	*1515*
Jn	14:27	**P I leave with you, my p I give**	*1515*
Jn	16:33	**you, that in me ye might have p**	*1515*
Ac	10:36	preaching **p** by Jesus Christ:	*1515*
Ac	11:18	held their **p**, and glorified God,	*2270*
Ac	18:9	**but speak, and hold not thy p:**	*4623*
Ro	2:10	But glory, honour, and **p**, to every	*1515*
Ro	3:17	the way of **p** have they not known:	*1515*
Ro	5:1	we have **p** with God through our	*1515*
Ro	8:6	be spiritually minded is life and **p**	*1515*
Ro	10:15	that preach the gospel of **p**, and	*1515*
Ro	14:17	but righteousness, and **p**, and joy	*1515*
Ro	15:33	Now the God of **p** be with you all	*1515*
Ro	16:20	God of **p** shall bruise Satan under	*1515*
1Co	14:30	sitteth by, let the first hold his **p**,	*4601*
1Co	14:33	the author of confusion, but of **p**,	*1515*
2Co	13:11	comfort, be of one mind, live in **p**;	*1518*
2Co	13:11	of love and **p** shall be with you	*1515*
Gal	5:22	the fruit of the Spirit is love, joy, **p**,	*1515*
Eph	2:14	For he is our **p**, who hath made	*1515*
Eph	4:3	unity of the Spirit in the bond of **p**	*1515*
Eph	6:15	the preparation of the gospel of **p**;	*1515*
Php	4:7	the **p** of God, which passeth all	*1515*
Col	1:20	made **p** through the blood of his	*1517*
Col	3:15	the **p** of God rule in your hearts,	*1515*
1Th	5:23	And the very God of **p** sanctify you	*1515*
2Th	3:16	the Lord of **p** himself give you **p**.	*1515*
2Ti	2:22	righteousness, faith, charity, **p**.	*1515*
Heb	7:2	King of Salem, which is, King of **p**;	*1515*
Heb	11:31	she had received the spies with **p**	*1515*
Jas	3:18	is sown in **p** of them that make **p**.	*1515*
Rev	6:4	thereon to take **p** from the earth,	*1515*

PEACEABLE

Ge	34:21	These men are **p** with us;	8003
1Ti	2:2	we may lead a quiet and **p** life in.	*2272*
Heb	12:11	the **p** fruit of righteousness unto	*1516*
Jas	3:17	first pure, then **p**, gentle, and easy.	*1516*

PEACEABLY

Ge	37:4	and could not speak **p** unto him.	7965
1Sa	16:4	coming, and said, Comest thou **p**?	7965
Ro	12:18	lieth in you, live **p** with all men.	*1518*

PEACEMAKERS See also MAKERS.

Mt	5:9	**Blessed are the p: for they shall**	*1518*

PEARL

Mt	13:46	**he had found one p of great price,**	*3135*
Rev	21:21	every several gate was of one **p**:	*3135*

PEARLS

Mt	7:6	cast ye your **p** before swine,	*3135*
Mt	13:45	**merchant man, seeking goodly p**	*3135*
1Ti	2:9	hair, or gold, or **p**, or costly array;	*3135*
Rev	21:21	the twelve gates were twelve **p**;	*3135*

PECULIAR

Ex	19:5	ye shall be a **p** treasure unto me	5459
Dt	14:2	thee to be a **p** people unto himself,	5459
Ps	135:4	and Israel for his **p** treasure	5459
Tit	2:14	a **p** people, zealous of good works	*4041*
1Pe	2:9	an holy nation, a **p** people;	*1519, 4047*

PELICAN

Le	11:18	and the **p**, and the gier eagle	6893
Ps	102:6	I am like a **p** of the wilderness:	6893

PEN

Job	19:24	they were graven with an iron **p**	5842
Ps	45:1	tongue is the **p** of a ready writer	5842
Jer	17:1	Judah is written with a **p** of iron,	5842
3Jn	13	with ink and **p** write unto thee:	*2563*

PENCE

Mt	18:28	**which owed him an hundred p:**	*1220*
Lk	7:41	**the one owed five hundred p, and**	*1220*
Lk	10:35	**he took out two p, and gave them**	*1220*
Jn	12:5	ointment sold for three hundred **p**,	*1220*

PENNY

Mt	20:2	**with the labourers for a p a day,**	*1220*
Mt	20:10	**likewise received every man a p**	*1220*
Mk	12:15	**bring me a p, that I may see it**	*1220*
Lk	20:24	**Shew me a p. Whose image and**	*1220*
Rev	6:6	A measure of wheat for a **p**, and	*1220*
Rev	6:6	three measures of barley for a **p**;	*1220*

PENNYWORTH

Mk	6:37	and buy two hundred **p** of bread,	*1220*
Jn	6:7	Two hundred **p** of bread is not	*1220*

PENTECOST (pen´-te-cost)

Ac	2:1	the day of **P** was fully come	*4005*
Ac	20:16	to be at Jerusalem the day of **P**	*4005*
1Co	16:8	I will tarry at Ephesus until **P**	*4005*

PEOPLE

Ge	11:6	Lord said, Behold, the **p** is one	5971
Ge	25:17	died; and was gathered unto his **p**	5971
Ge	25:23	the one **p** shall be stronger than	3816
Ge	25:23	be stronger than the other **p**; and	3816
Ge	27:29	Let **p** serve thee, and nations bow	5971
Ge	32:7	divided the **p** that was with him	5971
Ge	41:55	the **p** cried to Pharaoh for bread:	5971
Ge	48:4	will make of thee a multitude of **p**;	5971
Ge	50:20	is this day, to save much **p** alive	5971
Ex	1:20	the **p** multiplied, and waxed very	5971
Ex	3:7	surely seen the affliction of my **p**	5971
Ex	3:12	thou hast brought forth the **p** out	5971
Ex	4:16	be thy spokesman unto the **p**:	5971
Ex	4:21	that he shall not let the **p** go	5971
Ex	5:1	Let my **p** go, that they may hold a	5971
Ex	5:6	same day the taskmasters of the **p**,	5971
Ex	5:7	Ye shall no more give the **p** straw	5971
Ex	5:12	So the **p** were scattered abroad	5971
Ex	7:4	and my **p** the children of Israel,	5971
Ex	7:14	he refuseth to let the **p** go	5971
Ex	7:16	Let my **p** go, that they may serve	5971
Ex	8:8	and I will let the **p** go, that they	5971
Ex	11:2	Speak now in the ears of the **p**, and	5971
Ex	11:3	the Lord gave the **p** favour in the	5971
Ex	13:17	when Pharaoh had let the **p** go,	5971
Ex	13:17	Lest peradventure the **p** repent	5971
Ex	13:22	of fire by night, from before the **p**	5971
Ex	16:30	So the **p** rested on the seventh day	5971
Ex	17:1	was no water for the **p** to drink	5971
Ex	17:3	the **p** thirsted there for water; and	5971
Ex	17:3	the **p** murmured against Moses,	5971
Ex	17:5	Go on before the **p**, and take with	5971
Ex	20:18	all the **p** saw the thunderings, and	5971
Ex	20:20	Moses said unto the **p**, Fear not:	5971
Ex	20:21	the **p** stood afar off, and Moses	5971
Ex	22:28	gods, now curse the ruler of thy **p**	5971
Ex	30:33	shall even be cut off from his **p**,	5971
Le	9:15	which was the sin offering for the **p**,	5971
Le	9:22	lifted up his hand toward the **p**,	5971
Le	9:23	and came out, and blessed the **p**:	5971
Le	10:3	before all the **p** I will be glorified	5971
Nu	11:16	knowest to be the elders of the **p**,	5971
Nu	11:24	seventy men of the elders of the **p**,	5971
Nu	11:29	that all the Lord's **p** were prophets,	5971
Nu	13:30	Caleb stilled the **p** before Moses	5971
Nu	21:5	And the **p** spake against God, and	5971
Nu	21:6	sent fiery serpents among the **p**,	5971
Dt	4:6	is a wise and understanding **p**	5971
Dt	4:10	Gather me the **p** together, and I	5971
Dt	4:33	Did ever **p** hear the voice of God	5971
Dt	6:14	the gods of the **p** which are round	5971
Dt	7:6	thou art an holy **p** unto the Lord	5971
Dt	7:6	to be a special **p** unto himself,	5971
Dt	7:7	were more in number than any **p**;	5971
Dt	7:7	for ye were the fewest of all **p**:	5971
Dt	28:32	shall be given unto another **p**, and	5971
Dt	28:64	shall scatter thee among all **p**,	5971
Jos	3:6	covenant, and went before the **p**	5971
Jos	3:14	the **p** removed from their tents to	5971
Jos	3:14	ark of the covenant before the **p**;	5971
Jos	3:17	**p** were passed clean over Jordan	1471
Jos	4:2	Take you twelve men out of the **p**,	5971
Jos	5:5	**p** that came out were circumcised:	5971
Jos	7:5	the hearts of the **p** melted, and	5971
Jos	7:13	sanctify the **p**, and say, Sanctify	5971
Jos	8:10	and numbered the **p**, and went up,	5971
Jos	8:16	the **p** that were in Ai were called	5971
Jos	24:2	Joshua said unto all the **p**, Thus	5971
Jos	24:16	**p** answered and said, God forbid	5971
Jos	24:22	And Joshua said unto the **p**, Ye are	5971
Jos	24:24	**p** said unto Joshua, The Lord our	5971
Jos	24:25	made a covenant with the **p** that	5971
Jgs	2:7	the **p** served the Lord all the days	5971
Jgs	7:1	the **p** that were with him, rose up	5971
Jgs	7:3	of the **p** twenty and two thousand;	5971
Jgs	7:4	Gideon, The **p** are yet too many;	5971
Jgs	7:6	the rest of the **p** bowed down upon	5971
Jgs	14:16	a riddle unto the children of my **p**,	5971
Jgs	14:17	the riddle to the children of her **p**	5971
Ru	1:6	the Lord had visited his **p** in giving	5971
Ru	1:10	we will return with thee unto thy **p**	5971
Ru	1:16	thy **p** shall be my **p**, and thy God	5971
Ru	4:4	and before the elders of my **p**. If	5971
Ru	4:11	all the **p** that were in the gate, and	5971
1Sa	6:19	he smote of the **p** fifty thousand	5971
1Sa	9:2	he was higher than any of the **p**	5971
1Sa	9:13	for the **p** will not eat until he come,	5971
1Sa	9:17	this same shall reign over my **p**	5971
1Sa	13:4	**p** were called together after Saul	5971
1Sa	13:5	**p** as the sand which is on the sea	5971
1Sa	13:6	the **p** did hide themselves in caves,	5971
1Sa	13:14	him to be captain over his **p**,	5971
1Sa	13:22	found in the hand of any of the **p**	5971
1Sa	15:1	anoint thee to be king over his **p**,	5971
1Sa	15:8	utterly destroyed all the **p** with	5971
1Sa	15:9	Saul and the **p** spared Agag, and	5971
1Sa	15:15	the **p** spared the best of the sheep	5971
1Sa	15:21	the **p** took of the spoil, sheep and	5971
1Sa	15:30	thee, before the elders of my **p**,	5971
1Sa	30:6	for the **p** spake of stoning him	5971
2Sa	1:12	his son, and for the **p** of the Lord,	5971
2Sa	2:28	a trumpet, and all the **p** stood still	5971
2Sa	3:18	I will save my **p** Israel out of the	5971
2Sa	3:34	And all the **p** wept again over him	5971
1Ki	1:39	the **p** said, God save king Solomon	5971
1Ki	3:2	the **p** sacrificed in high places,	5971
1Ki	3:9	understanding heart to judge thy **p**,	5971
1Ki	3:9	able to judge this thy so great a **p**?	5971
1Ki	5:7	David a wise son over this great **p**	5971

1Ki	18:21	Elijah came unto all the **p**, and	5971
1Ki	18:37	that this **p** may know that thou art	5971
2Ki	6:18	Smite this **p**, I pray thee, with	1471
1Ch	11:2	Thou shalt feed my **p** Israel, and	5971
1Ch	11:2	shalt be ruler over my **p** Israel	5971
1Ch	11:13	**p** fled from before the Philistines,	5971
2Ch	1:9	king over a **p** like the dust of the	5971
2Ch	1:10	who can judge this thy **p**, that is so	5971
2Ch	1:11	that thou mayest judge my **p**, over	5971
2Ch	2:11	Because the Lord hath loved his **p**	5971
2Ch	7:14	If my **p**, which are called by my	5971
2Ch	30:3	neither had the **p** gathered	5971
2Ch	30:13	assembled at Jerusalem much **p**	5971
2Ch	31:4	he commanded the **p** that dwelt in	5971
2Ch	31:8	blessed the Lord, and his **p** Israel	5971
2Ch	31:10	for the Lord hath blessed his **p**:	5971
2Ch	32:8	And the **p** rested themselves upon	5971
2Ch	32:13	done unto all the **p** of other lands?	5971
Ezr	1:3	is there among you of all his **p**?	5971
Ezr	3:11	the **p** shouted with a great shout	5971
Ezr	3:13	the **p** could not discern the noise	5971
Ezr	10:13	But the **p** are many, and it is a time	5971
Ne	4:6	for the **p** had a mind to work	5971
Ne	12:38	and the half of the **p** upon the wall,	5971
Ne	13:24	according to the language of each **p**	5971
Est	1:5	the king made a feast unto all the **p**	5971
Est	1:16	the **p** that are in all the provinces	5971
Est	1:22	and to every **p** after their language,	5971
Est	2:10	Esther had not shewed her **p** nor	5971
Est	3:6	had shewed him the **p** of Mordecai:	5971
Est	3:6	Ahasuerus, even the **p** of Mordecai	5971
Est	3:8	among the **p** in all the provinces	5971
Est	3:12	to every **p** after their language;	5971
Est	3:14	province was published unto all **p**,	5971
Est	7:3	petition, and my **p** at my request:	5971
Est	8:6	the evil that shall come unto my **p**?	5971
Est	8:11	all the power of the **p** and province	5971
Est	8:13	province was published unto all **p**	5971
Est	9:2	for the fear of them fell upon all **p**	5971
Job	34:20	the **p** shall be troubled at midnight	5971
Job	34:30	reign not, lest the **p** be ensnared	5971
Job	36:20	when **p** are cut off in their place	5971
Ps	2:1	and the **p** imagine a vain thing?	3816
Ps	3:8	Lord: thy blessing is upon thy **p**	5971
Ps	7:8	The Lord shall judge the **p**	5971
Ps	14:4	who eat up my **p** as they eat bread,	5971
Ps	14:7	back the captivity of his **p**, Jacob	5971
Ps	22:6	of men, and despised of the **p**	5971
Ps	29:11	Lord will give strength unto his **p**;	5971
Ps	29:11	Lord will bless his **p** with peace	5971
Ps	35:18	I will praise thee among much **p**	5971
Ps	44:2	thou didst afflict the **p**, and cast	3816
Ps	45:10	forget also thine own **p**, and thy	5971
Ps	45:17	shall the **p** praise thee for ever and	5971
Ps	47:1	O clap your hands, all ye **p**: shout;	5971
Ps	47:9	even the **p** of the God of Abraham:	5971
Ps	50:4	the earth, that he may judge his **p**	5971
Ps	50:7	Hear, O my **p**, and I will speak;	5971
Ps	53:6	back the captivity of his **p**, Jacob	5971
Ps	59:11	Slay them not, lest my **p** forget:	5971
Ps	67:3	Let the **p** praise thee, O God; let	5971
Ps	68:30	the bulls, with the calves of the **p**,	5971
Ps	68:30	thou the **p** that delight in war	5971
Ps	72:2	judge thy **p** with righteousness	5971
Ps	72:4	He shall judge the poor of the **p**	5971
Ps	74:18	the foolish **p** have blasphemed thy	5971
Ps	77:14	declared thy strength among the **p**	5971
Ps	77:20	Thou leddest thy **p** like a flock by	5971
Ps	78:1	Give ear, O my **p**, to my law:	5971
Ps	78:20	also? can he provide flesh for his **p**?	5971
Ps	78:62	gave his **p** over also unto the sword;	5971
Ps	79:13	we thy **p** and sheep of thy pasture	5971
Ps	80:4	angry against the prayer of thy **p**?	5971
Ps	85:2	hast forgiven the iniquity of thy **p**	5971
Ps	85:8	for he will speak peace unto his **p**	5971
Ps	89:15	the **p** that know the joyful sound:	5971
Ps	100:3	we are his **p**, and the sheep of his	5971
Ps	144:15	Happy is that **p**, that is in such a	5971
Ps	144:15	happy is that **p**, whose God is the	5971
Pr	11:14	Where no counsel is, the **p** fall:	5971
Pr	11:26	corn, the **p** shall curse him: but	3816
Pr	14:28	of **p** is the king's honour: but in	5971
Pr	14:34	but sin is a reproach to any **p**	3816
Pr	24:24	him shall the **p** curse, nations	5971
Pr	28:15	is a wicked ruler over the poor **p**	5971
Pr	29:2	are in authority, the **p** rejoice: but	5971
Pr	29:18	there is no vision, the **p** perish:	5971
Pr	30:25	The ants are a **p** not strong, yet	5971
Ecc	4:16	There is no end of all the **p**, even	5971
Isa	1:3	not know, my **p** doth not consider	5971
Isa	1:4	nation, a **p** laden with iniquity,	5971
Isa	8:19	should not a **p** seek unto their God?	5971
Isa	9:2	The **p** that walked in darkness have	5971
Isa	11:11	to recover the remnant of his **p**	5971
Isa	11:16	highway for the remnant of his **p**,	5971
Isa	12:4	declare his doings among the **p**	5971
Isa	30:19	For the **p** shall dwell in Zion at	5971
Isa	30:26	bindeth up the breach of his **p**, and	5971
Isa	32:13	Upon the land of my **p** shall come	5971
Isa	40:1	comfort ye my **p**, saith your God	5971
Isa	40:7	upon it: surely the **p** is grass	5971
Isa	53:8	for the transgression of my **p** was	5971
Isa	56:3	utterly separated me from his **p**:	5971
Isa	56:7	called an house of prayer for all **p**	5971
Jer	14:11	Pray not for this **p** for their good	5971
Jer	27:13	Why will ye die, thou and thy **p**, by	5971
Jer	31:33	their God, and they shall be my **p**	5971
Jer	32:38	And they shall be my **p**, and I will	5971
Jer	33:24	they have despised my **p**, that they	5971
La	1:7	**p** fell into the hand of the enemy,	5971
La	1:18	hear, I pray you, all **p**, and behold	5971
Eze	17:9	many **p** to pluck it up by the roots	5971
Eze	17:15	might give him horses and much **p**	5971
Eze	33:3	blow the trumpet, and warn the **p**:	5971
Eze	46:3	the **p** of the land shall worship at	5971
Eze	46:18	my **p** be not scattered every man	5971
Eze	46:20	the utter court, to sanctify the **p**	5971
Da	3:4	O **p**, nations, and languages	5972
Da	3:7	all the **p** heard the sound of the	5972
Da	3:29	That every **p**, nation, … language	5972
Da	9:6	fathers, and to all the **p** of the land	5971
Da	9:15	that hast brought thy **p** forth out	5971
Da	9:19	and thy **p** are called by thy name	5971
Da	9:20	my sin and the sin of my **p** Israel,	5971
Da	9:26	the **p** of the prince that shall come	5971
Da	11:14	the robbers of thy **p** shall exalt	5971
Da	11:15	neither his chosen **p**, neither shall	5971
Da	11:32	but the **p** that do know their God	5971
Da	11:33	among the **p** shall instruct many:	5971
Da	12:1	standeth for the children of thy **p**:	5971
Da	12:7	to scatter the power of the holy **p**	5971
Joel	3:3	And they have cast lots for my **p**;	5971

Jnh	1:8	country? and of what **p** art thou?	5971
Jnh	3:5	So the **p** of Nineveh believed God	582
Mic	5:7	of many **p** as a dew from the Lord,	5971
Mic	5:8	in the midst of many **p** as a lion	5971
Mic	6:16	shall bear the reproach of my **p**	5971
Mic	7:14	Feed thy **p** with thy rod, the flock	5971
Zep	2:9	remnant of my **p** shall possess	1471
Zep	2:10	magnified themselves against … **p**	5971
Zec	8:6	the remnant of this **p** in these days,	5971
Zec	8:8	shall be my **p**, and I will be their	5971
Zec	8:11	not be unto the residue of this **p** as	5971
Zec	8:22	many **p** and strong nations shall	5971
Mt	1:21	shall save his **p** from their sins	*2992*
Mt	2:6	Governor, … shall rule my **p** Israel	*2992*
Mt	4:16	The **p** which sat in darkness saw	*2992*
Mt	7:28	**p** were astonished at his doctrine:	*3793*
Mt	15:8	**p draweth nigh unto me with their**	*2992*
Mt	21:26	shall say, Of men; we fear the **p**;	*3793*
Mt	27:15	to release unto the **p** a prisoner,	*3793*
Mk	7:6	**p honoureth me with their lips,**	*2992*
Mk	9:25	Jesus saw that the **p** came running	*3793*
Mk	11:18	**p** was astonished at his doctrine	*3793*
Mk	12:37	the common **p** heard him gladly	*3793*
Mk	12:41	beheld how the **p** cast money into	*3793*
Lk	1:10	multitude of the **p** were praying	*2992*
Lk	1:17	ready a **p** prepared for the Lord	*2992*
Lk	1:21	And the **p** waited for Zacharias	*2992*
Lk	1:77	knowledge of salvation unto his **p**	*2992*
Lk	2:10	great joy, which shall be to all **p**	*2992*
Lk	2:32	and the glory of thy **p** Israel	*2992*
Lk	3:15	And as the **p** were in expectation	*2992*
Lk	8:40	the **p** gladly received him: for	*3793*
Lk	11:14	dumb spake; and the **p** wondered	*3793*
Lk	19:48	the **p** were very attentive to hear	*2992*
Lk	23:27	followed him a great company of **p**	*2992*
Jn	6:22	**p** which stood on the other side	*3793*
Jn	6:24	**p** therefore saw that Jesus was	*3793*
Jn	7:12	said, Nay; but he deceiveth the **p**:	*3793*
Jn	11:42	**because of the p which stand by I.**	*3793*
Jn	11:50	that one man should die for the **p**,	*2992*
Jn	18:14	that one man should die for the **p**	*2992*
Ac	2:47	and having favour with all the **p**	*2992*
Ac	3:9	the **p** saw him walking and praising	*2992*
Ac	4:1	And as they spake unto the **p**, the	*2992*
Ac	4:8	Ye rulers of the **p**, and elders of	*2992*
Ac	4:10	you all, and to all the **p** of Israel,	*2992*
Ac	4:21	punish them, because of the **p**: for	*2992*
Ac	4:25	and the **p** imagine vain things?	*2992*
Ac	5:13	them: but the **p** magnified them	*2992*
Ac	5:26	they feared the **p**, lest they should	*2992*
Ac	5:34	had in reputation among all the **p**	*2992*
Ac	6:8	wonders and miracles among the **p**	*2992*
Ac	6:12	stirred up the **p**, and the elders	*2992*
Ac	8:9	and bewitched the **p** of Samaria,	*1484*
Ac	10:2	which gave much alms to the **p**	*2992*
Ac	11:24	much **p** was added unto the Lord	*3793*
Ac	13:15	any word of exhortation for the **p**	*2992*
Ac	13:17	God of this **p** of Israel chose our	*2992*
Ac	13:24	of repentance to all the **p** of Israel	*2992*
Ac	13:31	who are his witnesses unto the **p**	*2992*
Ac	14:13	have done sacrifice with the **p**	*3793*
Ac	17:5	sought to bring them out to the **p**	*1218*
Ac	17:8	And they troubled the **p** and the	*3793*
Ac	17:13	thither also, and stirred up the **p**	*3793*
Ac	19:33	have made his defence unto the **p**	*1218*
Ac	21:27	stirred up all the **p**, and laid hands	*3793*
Ac	26:17	**Delivering thee from the p, and**	*2992*
Ac	28:27	the heart of this **p** is waxed gross,	*2992*
Ro	10:19	to jealousy by them that are no **p**	*1484*
Ro	11:1	then, Hath God cast away his **p**?	*2992*
1Co	10:7	The **p** sat down to eat and drink	*2992*
1Co	14:21	other lips will I speak unto this **p**;	*2992*
2Co	6:16	their God, and they shall be my **p**	*2992*
Tit	2:14	a peculiar **p**, zealous of good works	*2992*
Heb	4:9	therefore a rest to the **p** of God	*2992*
Heb	5:3	as for the **p**, so also for himself, to	*2992*
Heb	8:10	God, and they shall be to me a **p**:	*2992*
Heb	9:7	himself, and for the errors of the **p**:	*2992*
Heb	10:30	again, The Lord shall judge his **p**	*2992*
Heb	11:25	suffer affliction with the **p** of God	*2992*
Heb	13:12	sanctify the **p** with his own blood	*2992*
Rev	5:9	and tongue, and **p**, and nation:	*2992*
Rev	7:9	and kindreds, and **p**, and tongues,	*2992*
Rev	18:4	Come out of her, my **p**, that ye be	*2992*
Rev	19:1	a great voice of much **p** in heaven,	*3793*

PEOPLE'S

Mt	13:15	**For this p heart is waxed gross,**	*2992*
Heb	7:27	his own sins, and then for the **p**:	*2992*

PEOPLES

Rev	10:11	prophesy again before many **p**	*2992*
Rev	17:15	where the whore sitteth, are **p**, and	*2992*

PERADVENTURE

Ge	18:24	**P** there be fifty righteous within	194
Ge	18:28	**P** there shall lack five of the fifty	194
Ge	18:29	**P** there shall be forty found there.	194
Ge	18:30	**P** there shall thirty be found there.	194
Ge	18:31	**P** there shall be twenty found there.	194
Ge	18:32	**P** ten shall be found there. And	194
Ge	32:20	his face; **p** he will accept of me	194
Ge	43:12	your hand; **p** it was an oversight:	194
Ge	50:15	Joseph will **p** hate us, and will	3863
Nu	22:11	**p** I shall be able to overcome them,	194
Nu	23:3	**p** the Lord will come to meet me:	194
Nu	23:27	**p** it will please God that thou mayest	194
Jos	9:7	**P** ye dwell among us; and how	194
1Ki	18:5	**p** we may find grass to save the	194
1Ki	18:27	**p** he sleepeth, and must be awaked	194
Ro	5:7	yet **p** for a good man some would	*5029*
2Ti	2:25	if God **p** will give them repentance	*3379*

PERCEIVE

Dt	29:4	hath not given you an heart to **p**,	3045
2Ki	4:9	I **p** that this is an holy man of God,	3045
Job	23:8	and backward, but I cannot **p** him:	995
Pr	1:2	to **p** the words of understanding;	
Ecc	3:22	I **p** that there is nothing better	7200
Mt	13:14	**ye shall see, and shall not p:**	*1492*
Mk	4:12	**seeing they may see, and not p;**	*1492*
Mk	7:18	**Do ye not p, that whatsoever**	*3539*
Mk	8:17	**p ye not yet, neither understand?**	*3539*
Lk	8:46	**I p that virtue is gone out of me.**	*1097*
Jn	4:19	Sir, I **p** that thou art a prophet	*2334*
Ac	10:34	I **p** that God is no respecter of	*2638*
2Co	7:8	**p** that the same epistle hath made	*991*

PERCEIVED

Ge	19:33	he **p** not when she lay down,	3045
Jgs	6:22	Gideon **p** that he was an angel	7200
1Sa	3:8	And Eli **p** that the Lord had called	995
1Sa	28:14	And Saul **p** that it was Samuel,	3045

2Sa 12:19	David **p** that the child was dead:	995
1Ch 14:2	David **p** … the Lord had confirmed	3045
Ne 6:12	I **p** that God had not sent him;	5234
Est 4:1	Mordecai **p** all that was done,	3045
Job 38:18	thou **p** the breadth of the earth?	995
Isa 64:4	have not heard, nor **p** by the ear,	238
Jer 23:18	and hath **p** and heard his word?	7200
Mt 16:8	Which when Jesus **p**, he said unto	*1097*
Mk 2:8	when Jesus **p** in his spirit that	*1921*
Lk 5:22	when Jesus **p** their thoughts, he	*1921*
Lk 20:19	**p** that he had spoken this parable	*1097*
Lk 20:23	But he **p** their craftiness, and said	*2657*
Ac 4:13	**p** that they were unlearned and	*2638*
Gal 2:9	**p** the grace that was given unto	*1097*

PERCEIVEST

Pr 14:7	**p** not in him the lips of knowledge	3045
Lk 6:41	**p not the beam that is in thine**	*2657*

PERCEIVETH

Job 33:14	once, yea twice, yet man **p** it not	7789
Pr 31:18	**p** that her merchandise is good:	2938

PERCEIVING

Lk 9:47	Jesus, **p** the thought of their heart	*1492*
Ac 14:9	**p** that he had faith to be healed,	*1492*

PERDITION

Jn 17:12	**of them is lost, but the son of p;**	*684*
2Th 2:3	of sin be revealed, the son of **p**;	*684*
Rev 17:8	of the bottomless pit, and go into **p**:	*684*
Rev 17:11	is of the seven, and goeth into **p**	*684*

PERES See also UPHARSIN.

Lk 9:47	Jesus, **p** the thought of their heart	*1492*

PERFECT

Ge 6:9	Noah was a just man and **p** in his	8549
Dt 18:13	shalt be **p** with the Lord thy God.	8549
Dt 32:4	He is the Rock, his work is **p**:	8549
2Sa 22:31	As for God, his way is **p**; the word	8549
2Sa 22:33	power: and he maketh my way **p**	8549
1Ki 8:61	Let your heart therefore be **p**.	8003
2Ki 20:3	thee in truth and with a **p** heart,	8003
1Ch 28:9	serve him with a **p** heart and with	8003
1Ch 29:9	with **p** heart they offered willingly	8003
1Ch 29:19	unto Solomon my son a **p** heart,	8003
2Ch 16:9	them whose heart is **p** toward him	8003
2Ch 19:9	faithfully, and with a **p** heart.	8003
2Ch 25:2	of the Lord, but not with a **p** heart.	8003
Job 1:1	and that man was **p** and upright,	8535
Job 8:20	God will not cast away a **p** man,	8535
Job 9:22	destroyeth the **p** and the wicked	8535
Job 22:3	that thou makest thy ways **p**?	8552
Job 36:4	he that is **p** in knowledge is with	8549
Ps 18:30	As for God, his way is **p**: the	8549
Ps 19:7	law of the Lord is **p**, converting.	8549
Ps 37:37	Mark the **p** man, and behold the	8535
Ps 64:4	they may shoot in secret at the **p**:	8535
Ps 101:2	behave myself wisely in a **p** way	8549
Ps 101:2	within my house with a **p** heart	8537
Ps 138:8	will **p** that which concerneth me:	1584
Ps 139:22	I hate them with **p** hatred: I.	8503
Pr 2:21	land, and the **p** shall remain in it.	8549
Pr 4:18	more and more unto the **p** day.	3559
Isa 18:5	when the bud is **p**, and the sour	8552
Isa 38:3	thee in truth and with a **p** heart,	8003
Isa 42:19	who is blind as he that is **p**, and	7999
Eze 28:12	full of wisdom, and **p** in beauty.	3632
Mt 5:48	**Be ye therefore p, even as your**	*5046*
Mt 5:48	**Father which is in heaven is p.**	*5046*
Mt 19:21	**If thou wilt be p, go and sell that**	*5046*
Lk 6:40	**that is p shall be as his master.**	*2675*
Jn 17:23	**that they may be made p in one;**	*5048*
Ac 24:22	more **p** knowledge of that way,	*197*
Ro 12:2	and acceptable, and **p**, will of God.	*5046*
1Co 13:10	But when that which is **p** is come,	*5046*
2Co 12:9	**strength is made p in weakness.**	*5048*
2Co 13:11	Be **p**, be of good comfort, be of.	*2675*
Eph 4:13	unto a **p** man, unto the measure	*5046*
Php 3:12	attained, either were already **p**:	*5048*
Col 1:28	every man **p** in Christ Jesus:	*5046*
Col 4:12	that ye may stand **p** and complete	*5046*
2Ti 3:17	That the man of God may be **p**,	*739*
Heb 2:10	the captain of their salvation **p**	*5048*
Heb 9:9	make him that did the service **p**,	*5048*
Heb 9:11	a greater and more **p** tabernacle,	*5046*
Heb 12:23	to the spirits of just men made **p**	*5048*
Heb 13:21	Make you **p** in every good work	*2675*
Jas 1:4	But let patience have her **p** work,	*5046*
Jas 1:17	and every **p** gift is from above,	*5046*
Jas 1:25	looketh into the **p** law of liberty.	*5046*
Jas 3:2	not in word, the same is a **p** man,	*5046*
1Jn 4:17	Herein is our love made **p**, that	*5048*
1Jn 4:18	but **p** love casteth out fear:	*5046*
1Jn 4:18	that feareth is not made **p** in love	*5048*
Rev 3:2	**have not found thy works p**	*4137*

PERFECTED

2Ch 8:16	So the house of the Lord was **p**.	8003
Lk 13:32	**and the third day I shall be p**	*5048*
Heb 10:14	by one offering he hath **p** for ever	*5048*
1Jn 2:5	in him verily is the love of God **p**:	*5048*
1Jn 4:12	in us, and his love is **p** in us.	*5048*

PERFECTING

2Co 7:1	**p** holiness in the fear of God	*2005*
Eph 4:12	For the **p** of the saints, for the	*2677*

PERFECTION

Job 11:7	find out the Almighty unto **p**?	8503
Job 28:3	darkness, and searcheth out all **p**:	8503
La 2:15	The **p** of beauty, The joy of the	3632
Lk 8:14	**this life, and bring no fruit to p**	*5052*
2Co 13:9	this also we wish, even your **p**.	*2676*
Heb 6:1	of Christ, let us go on unto **p**;	*5051*
Heb 7:11	**p** were by the Levitical priesthood,	*5050*

PERFECTLY

Mt 14:36	as touched were made **p** whole.	*1295*
Ac 18:26	unto him the way of God more **p**.	*197*
1Co 1:10	but that ye be **p** joined together	*2675*
1Th 5:2	know **p** that the day of the Lord	*199*

PERFORM

Ge 26:3	I will **p** the oath which I sware	6965
Ex 18:18	art not able to **p** it thyself alone.	6213
Dt 4:13	which he commanded you to **p**,	6213
Dt 9:5	may **p** the word which the Lord	6965
Ru 3:13	**p** unto thee the part of a kinsman,	
1Sa 3:12	day I will **p** against Eli all things	6965
1Ki 6:12	then will I **p** my word with thee,	6965
2Ki 23:3	to **p** the words of this covenant.	6965
2Ch 10:15	that the Lord might **p** his word.	6965
2Ch 34:31	to **p** the words of the covenant	6213

Est 5:8 my petition, and to **p** my request,...... 6213
Ps 119:106 I have sworn, and I will **p** it, ... 6965
Ps 119:112 heart to **p** thy statutes alway,.......... 6213
Isa 19:21 vow a vow unto the Lord, and **p** it...... 7999
Jer 11:5 **p** the oath which I have sworn......... 6965
Jer 28:6 Lord **p** thy words which thou hast 6965
Jer 33:14 will **p** that good thing which I have 6965
Jer 44:25 We will surely **p** our vows that 6213
Eze 12:25 will I say the word, and will **p** it,....... 6213
Mic 7:20 Thou wilt **p** the truth to Jacob,........ 5414
Mt 5:33 **shalt p unto the Lord thine oaths:** *591*
Lk 1:72 **p** the mercy promised to our.......... *4160*
Ro 4:21 promised, he was able also to **p**........ *4160*
Ro 7:18 how to **p** that which is good I find *2716*
Php 1:6 will **p** it until the day of Jesus *2005*

PERFORMED

1Sa 15:11 hath not **p** my commandments........ 6965
1Ki 8:20 And the Lord hath **p** his word......... 6965
Est 1:15 she hath not **p** the commandment..... 6213
Est 5:6 half of the kingdom it shall be **p**....... 6213
Ps 65:1 and unto thee shall the vow be **p** 7999
Isa 10:12 the Lord hath **p** his whole work 1214
Jer 30:24 he have **p** the intents of his heart:...... 6965
Jer 34:18 not **p** the words of the covenant....... 6965
Lk 1:20 day that these things shall be **p**,........ *1096*
Lk 2:39 **p** all things according to the law *5055*
Ro 15:28 When therefore I have **p** this, ... *2005*

PERFORMETH

Job 23:14 **p** the thing that is appointed for....... 7999
Ps 57:2 unto God that **p** all things for me....... 1584
Isa 44:26 **p** the counsel of his messengers;....... 7999

PERFORMING

Nu 15:3 offering, or a sacrifice in **p** a vow,...... 6381
Nu 15:8 or for a sacrifice in **p** a vow,........... 6381

PERFUME

Ex 30:37 for the **p** which thou shalt make....... 7004
Pr 27:9 Ointment and **p** rejoice the heart: 7004

PERFUMED

Pr 7:17 have **p** my bed with myrrh, aloes,...... 5130
SS 3:6 **p** with myrrh and frankincense,....... 6999

PERHAPS

Ac 8:22 if **p** the thought of thine heart may *686*
2Co 2:7 lest **p** such ... should be swallowed *3381*

PERIL

La 5:9 got our bread with the **p** of our lives,
Ro 8:35 or nakedness, or **p**, or sword? *2794*

PERILOUS

2Ti 3:1 the last days **p** times shall come........ *5467*

PERILS

2Co 11:26 in **p** of waters, in **p** of robbers. *2794*
2Co 11:26 in **p** by mine own countrymen *2794*
2Co 11:26 by the heathen, in **p** in the city,........ *2794*
2Co 11:26 in the city, in **p** in the wilderness,...... *2794*
2Co 11:26 in the wilderness, in **p** in the sea, ... *2794*
2Co 11:26 the sea, in **p** among false brethren;..... *2794*

PERISH

Ge 41:36 land **p** not through the famine......... 3772
Ex 21:26 or the eye of his maid, that it **p**; 7843
Le 26:38 And ye shall **p** among the heathen,........ 6
Nu 24:20 latter end shall be that he **p** for ever. 8
Dt 4:26 shall soon utterly **p** from off the land...... 6
Jos 23:13 until ye **p** from off this good land......... 6
Jos 23:16 shall **p** quickly from off the good 6
Jgs 5:31 So let all thine enemies **p**, O Lord: 6
1Sa 27:1 **p** one day by the hand of Saul: 5595
Est 3:13 to kill, and to cause to **p**, all Jews,......... 6
Est 4:16 according to the law: and if I **p**, I **p**........ 6
Est 9:28 nor the memorial of them **p** from 5486
Job 4:9 By the blast of God they **p**, and by 6
Job 4:20 **p** for ever without any regarding it........ 6
Job 8:13 and the hypocrite's hope shall **p**:.......... 6
Job 31:19 have seen any **p** for want of clothing 6
Job 34:15 All flesh shall **p** together, and man 1478
Ps 1:6 but the way of the ungodly shall **p** 6
Ps 2:12 lest he be angry, and ye **p** from the........ 6
Ps 49:20 not, is like the beasts that **p** 1820
Ps 68:2 let the wicked **p** at ... presence of God..... 6
Ps 112:10 the desire of the wicked shall **p** 6
Ps 146:4 in that very day his thoughts **p** 6
Pr 19:9 and he that speaketh lies shall **p** 6
Pr 21:28 A false witness shall **p**: but the man 6
Pr 29:18 there is no vision, the people **p**: 6544
Isa 26:14 and made all their memory to **p**........... 6
Da 2:18 Daniel and his fellows should not **p** 7
Jnh 1:14 let us not **p** for this man's life, and 6
Jnh 3:9 from his fierce anger, that we **p** not?....... 6
Mt 5:29 **one of thy members should p,** *622*
Mt 8:25 him, saying, Lord, save us: we **p** *622*
Mt 18:14 **one of these little ones should p**........ *622*
Mt 26:52 **the sword shall p with the sword.**....... *622*
Lk 5:37 **be spilled, and the bottles shall p** *622*
Lk 13:3 **repent, ye shall all likewise p**.......... *622*
Lk 15:17 **and to spare, and I p with hunger!**...... *622*
Lk 21:18 **shall not an hair of your head p**........ *622*
Jn 3:15 **believeth in him should not p,** *622*
Jn 3:16 **believeth in him should not p,** *622*
Jn 10:28 **and they shall never p, neither** *622*
Ac 8:20 Thy money **p** with thee,..... *1510, 1519, 684*
Ro 2:12 law shall also **p** without law: *622*
1Co 1:18 cross is to them that **p** foolishness;...... *622*
2Co 4:16 but though our outward man **p**,....... *1311*
Heb 1:11 They shall **p**; but thou remainest;....... *622*
2Pe 3:9 not willing that any should **p**, but....... *622*

PERISHED

Jos 22:20 man **p** not alone in his iniquity........ 1478
Ps 9:6 their memorial is **p** with them............ 6
Ps 10:16 the heathen are **p** out of his land 6
Ps 119:92 should then have **p** in mine affliction...... 6
Ecc 9:6 hatred, and their envy, is now **p**;.......... 6
La 3:18 and my hope is **p** from the Lord: 6
Joel 1:11 because the harvest of the field is **p** 6
Mic 7:2 The good man is **p** out of the earth:....... 6
Lk 11:51 **p between the altar and the temple:**..... *622*
1Co 15:18 are fallen asleep in Christ are **p**......... *622*
Heb 11:31 By faith the harlot Rahab **p** not........ *4881*
Jude 11 and **p** in the gainsaying of Core......... *622*

PERISHETH

Pr 11:7 and the hope of unjust men **p**............ 6
Ecc 7:15 just man that **p** in his righteousness, ... 6
Jn 6:27 **Labour not for the meat which p,** *622*
Jas 1:11 and the grace of the fashion of it **p**: *622*
1Pe 1:7 more precious than of gold that **p**,...... *622*

PERMIT
1Co 16:7 a while with you, if the Lord **p** *2010*
Heb 6:3 And this will we do, if God **p**.......... *2010*

PERMITTED
Ac 26:1 Thou art **p** to speak for thyself......... *2010*
1Co 14:34 it is not **p** unto them to speak; *2010*

PERPETUAL
Ex 30:8 a **p** incense before the Lord 8548
Ex 31:16 generations, for a **p** covenant.......... 5769
Ps 9:6 destructions are come to a **p** end:...... 5331
Jer 5:22 bound of the sea by a **p** decree,........ 5769
Jer 8:5 slidden back by a **p** backsliding?....... 5331
Jer 15:18 Why is my pain **p**, and my wound 5331
Jer 18:16 land desolate, and a **p** hissing;......... 5769
Jer 50:5 to the Lord in a **p** covenant that 5769
Jer 51:39 and sleep a **p** sleep, and not wake, ... 5769
Eze 46:14 by a **p** ordinance unto the Lord 5769
Zep 2:9 and saltpits, and a **p** desolation: 5769

PERPETUALLY
1Ki 9:3 mine heart shall be there **p** 3605, 3117
Am 1:11 all pity, and his anger did tear **p**,....... 5703

PERPLEXED
Est 3:15 drink; but the city Shushan was **p**....... 943
Lk 24:4 as they were much **p** thereabout, ... *1280*
2Co 4:8 we are **p**, but not in despair; *639*

PERPLEXITY
Isa 22:5 and of **p** by the Lord God of hosts..... 3998
Lk 21:25 **earth distress of nations, with p;** *640*

PERSECUTE
Job 19:22 Why do ye **p** me as God, and are 7291
Ps 7:1 save me from all them that **p** me,...... 7291
Ps 35:3 the way against them that **p** me:....... 7291
Ps 119:86 they **p** me wrongfully; help thou 7291
La 3:66 **P** and destroy them in anger 7291
Mt 5:11 **men shall revile you, and p you.**....... *1377*
Mt 5:44 **despitefully use you, and p you;**....... *1377*
Lk 11:49 **of them they shall slay and p:**......... *1559*
Lk 21:12 **their hands on you, and p you,**........ *1377*
Jn 5:16 therefore did the Jews **p** Jesus *1377*
Ro 12:14 Bless them which **p** you: bless, and 1377

PERSECUTED
Ps 119:161 have **p** me without a cause: but........ 7291
Isa 14:6 ruled the nations in anger, is **p**,........ 4783
Mt 5:10 **are p for righteousness' sake:** *1377*
Jn 15:20 **If they have p me, they will also** *1377*
1Co 4:12 we bless; being **p**, we suffer it:......... *1377*
1Co 15:9 because I **p** the church of God......... *1377*
2Co 4:9 **P**, but not forsaken; cast down,........ *1377*
Gal 1:13 measure I **p** the church of God, ... *1377*
Rev 12:13 **p** the woman which brought forth..... *1377*

PERSECUTEST
Ac 9:4 him, **Saul, Saul, why p thou me?**....... *1377*
Ac 9:5 said, **I am Jesus whom thou p:** *1377*
Ac 22:7 me, **Saul, Saul, why p thou me?** *1377*
Ac 22:8 **Jesus of Nazareth, whom thou p** *1377*
Ac 26:14 **Saul, Saul, why p thou me? it is** *1377*
Ac 26:15 **he said, I am Jesus whom thou p** *1377*

PERSECUTION
La 5:5 Our necks are under **p**: we........... 7291
Mt 13:21 **or p ariseth because of the word,**...... *1375*
Ac 8:1 was a great **p** against the church *1375*
Ac 11:19 the **p** that arose about Stephen *2347*
Ro 8:35 shall tribulation, or distress, or **p**,...... *1375*
Gal 6:12 suffer **p** for the cross of Christ......... *1377*
2Ti 3:12 godly in Christ Jesus shall suffer **p** *1377*

PERSECUTIONS
Mk 10:30 **and children, and lands, with p;**....... *1375*
2Co 12:10 **p**, in distresses for Christ's sake: *1375*
2Ti 3:11 **P**, afflictions, which came unto me..... *1375*

PERSECUTORS
Ps 119:157 are my **p** and mine enemies; 7291
Ps 142:6 very low: deliver me from my **p**;....... 7291
La 4:19 Our **p** are swifter than the eagles 7291

PERSON
Le 19:15 not respect the **p** of the poor. 6440
Nu 5:6 the Lord, and that **p** be guilty;......... 5315
Nu 31:19 whosoever hath killed any **p**, and 5315
Nu 35:11 which killeth any **p** at unawares 5315
Nu 35:30 Whoso killeth any **p**, the murderer..... 5315
Nu 35:30 shall not testify against any **p** to 5315
Dt 28:50 shall not regard the **p** of the old,....... 6440
1Sa 16:18 prudent in matters, and a comely **p**,..... 376
2Sa 14:14 neither doth God respect any **p**: 5315
Job 32:21 I pray you, accept any man's **p**,........ 6440
Ps 105:37 not one feeble **p** among their tribes.
Pr 6:12 A naughty **p**, a wicked man, ... 120
Pr 28:17 violence to the blood of any **p**......... 5315
Da 11:21 in his estate shall stand up a vile **p**,
Mal 1:8 or accept thy **p**? saith the Lord 6440
Mt 22:16 thou regardest not the **p** of men....... *4383*
Lk 20:21 neither acceptest thou the **p** of any, ... *4383*
2Co 2:10 forgave I it in the **p** of Christ; *4383*
Heb 1:3 and the express image of his **p** *5287*
Heb 12:16 any fornicator, or profane **p**, as Esau,
2Pe 2:5 but saved Noah the eighth **p**, a

PERSONS
Ge 14:21 said unto Abram, Give me the **p**, ... 5315
Nu 31:28 soul of five hundred, both of the **p**, ... 120
Dt 1:17 shall not respect **p** in judgment;....... 6440
Jgs 9:5 being threescore and ten **p**, upon 376
1Sa 22:18 five **p** that did wear a linen ephod....... 376
Ps 82:2 and accept the **p** of the wicked? 6440
Pr 28:21 To have respect of **p** is not good: 6440
Jnh 4:11 are more than sixscore thousand **p**...... 120
Lk 15:7 **than over ninety and nine just p,**
Ac 10:34 that God is no respecter of **p**: *4381*
Ro 2:11 there is no respect of **p** with God *4382*
Col 3:25 done: and there is no respect of **p**...... *4382*
1Pe 1:17 who without respect of **p** judgeth....... *678*
Jude 16 having men's **p** in admiration *4383*

PERSUADE
1Ki 22:20 Who shall **p** Ahab, that he may........ 6601
1Ki 22:21 the Lord, and said, I will **p** him........ 6601
Isa 36:18 Beware lest Hezekiah **p** you, ... 5496
Gal 1:10 For do I now **p** men, or God? or....... *3982*

PERSUADED
2Ch 18:2 and **p** him to go up with him to....... 5496
Pr 25:15 By long forbearing is a prince **p**,....... 6601
Lk 16:31 **neither will they be p, though one**..... *3982*
Ac 26:26 I am **p** that none of these things....... *3982*
Ro 4:21 And being fully **p** that, what he........ *4135*
Ro 8:38 For I am **p**, that neither death, ... *3982*

Ro 14:5 man be fully **p** in his own mind........ *4135*
Ro 14:14 and am **p** by the Lord Jesus, that....... *3982*
2Ti 1:12 and am **p** that he is able to keep *3982*
Heb 6:9 we are **p** better things of you, and...... *3982*
Heb 11:13 were **p** of them, and embraced *3982*

PERSUADEST
Ac 26:28 thou **p** me to be a Christian........... *3982*

PERSUADING
Ac 19:8 and **p** the things concerning the *3982*
Ac 28:23 **p** them concerning Jesus, both out..... *3982*

PERTAIN
Le 7:20 peace offerings, that **p** unto the Lord,
Le 7:21 offerings, which **p** unto the Lord.
Ro 15:17 in those things which **p** to God.
2Pe 1:3 unto us all things that **p** unto life

PERTAINED
Jos 24:33 in a hill that **p** to Phinehas his son,
2Sa 2:15 which **p** to Ish-bosheth the son of
2Sa 9:9 **p** to Saul and to all his house 1961
2Sa 16:4 are all that **p** unto Mephibosheth.
2Ch 12:4 the fenced cities which **p** to Judah,

PERTAINETH
Le 14:32 get that which **p** to his cleansing.
Dt 22:5 wear that which **p** unto a man,......... 3627
Ro 9:4 to whom **p** the adoption, and the
Heb 7:13 are spoken **p** to another tribe,.......... *3348*

PERTAINING
Ac 1:3 things **p** to the kingdom of God: *4012*
Heb 2:17 high priest in things **p** to God,
Heb 9:9 perfect, as **p** to the conscience;

PERVERSE
Nu 22:32 because thy way is **p** before me: 3399
Dt 32:5 are a **p** and crooked generation........ 6141
1Sa 20:30 son of the **p** rebellious woman,........ 5753
Pr 4:24 and **p** lips put far from thee........... 3891
Pr 12:8 is of a **p** heart shall be despised........ 5753
Pr 17:20 a **p** tongue falleth into mischief........ 2015
Pr 19:1 he that is **p** in his lips, and is a fool 6141
Pr 28:18 **p** in his ways shall fall at once......... 6140
Isa 19:14 The Lord hath mingled a **p** spirit 5773
Mt 17:17 **said, O faithless and p generation,**..... *1294*
Php 2:15 midst of a crooked and **p** nation,....... *1294*

PERVERSELY
1Ki 8:47 We have sinned, and have done **p**, ... 5753
Ps 119:78 for they dealt **p** with me without 5791

PERVERSENESS
Nu 23:21 neither hath he seen **p** in Israel: 5999
Pr 15:4 **p** therein is a breach in the spirit....... 5558

PERVERT
Job 8:3 Doth God **p** judgment? 5791
Job 8:3 or doth the Almighty **p** justice?........ 5791
Pr 17:23 bosom to **p** the ways of judgment 5186
Pr 31:5 forget ... law, and **p** the judgment 8138
Ac 13:10 to **p** the right ways of the Lord? *1294*
Gal 1:7 and would **p** the gospel of Christ *3344*

PERVERTED
1Sa 8:3 and took bribes, and **p** judgment 5186
Job 33:27 sinned, and **p** ... which was right, ... 5753
Jer 23:36 **p** the words of the living God, ... 2015

PERVERTETH
Pr 10:9 that **p** his ways shall be known......... 6140
Pr 19:3 foolishness of man **p** his way: 5557
Lk 23:14 unto me, as one that **p** the people; *654*

PESTILENCE
Ex 5:3 he fall upon us with **p**, or with the..... 1698
2Sa 24:13 there be three days' **p** in thy land?...... 1698
2Sa 24:15 So the Lord sent a **p** upon Israel....... 1698
1Ch 21:14 So the Lord sent **p** upon Israel:........ 1698
Ps 91:3 fowler, and from the noisome **p** 1698
Eze 5:17 **p** and blood shall pass through........ 1698
Eze 7:15 famine and **p** shall devour him........ 1698

PESTILENCES
Mt 24:7 **p, and earthquakes, in divers** *3061*
Lk 21:11 **divers places, and famines, and p;** *3061*

PETITION
1Sa 1:17 God of Israel grant thee thy **p**......... 7596
1Ki 2:20 said, I desire one small **p** of thee; 7596
Est 5:6 What is thy **p**? and it shall be.......... 7596
Est 5:7 and said, My **p** and my request is; 7596
Est 5:8 if it please the king to grant my **p**, ... 7596
Est 7:2 What is thy **p**, queen Esther? and 7596
Est 7:3 let my life be given me at my **p**, ... 7596
Est 9:12 now what is thy **p**? and it shall be...... 7596
Da 6:7 shall ask a **p** of any God or man 1159
Da 6:12 that shall ask a **p** of any God or man
Da 6:13 maketh his **p** three times a day......... 1159

PETITIONS
Ps 20:5 banners: the Lord fulfil all thy **p** 4862
1Jn 5:15 have the **p** that we desired of him. *155*

PHARAOH (fa´-ra-o)
Ge 39:1 Potiphar, an officer of **P**, captain 6547
Ge 40:13 days shall **P** lift up thine head, ... 6547
Ge 40:19 three days shall **P** lift up thy head...... 6547
Ge 41:4 favoured and fat kine. So **P** awoke...... 6547
Ge 41:8 and **P** told them his dream; but 6547
Ge 41:9 Then spake the chief butler unto **P**,.... 6547
Ge 41:10 **P** was wroth with his servants, ... 6547
Ge 41:16 shall give **P** an answer of peace. 6547
Ge 41:17 **P** said unto Joseph, In my dream,...... 6547
Ge 41:25 The dream of **P** is one; God hath 6547
Ge 41:32 dream was doubled unto **P** twice; 6547
Ge 41:34 Let **P** do this, and let him appoint 6547
Ge 41:42 **P** took off his ring from his hand, ... 6547
Ge 41:44 And **P** said unto Joseph, I am **P**,....... 6547
Ge 41:45 And **P** called Joseph's name........... 6547
Ge 41:55 the people cried to **P** for bread: 6547
Ge 42:16 by the life of **P** surely ye are spies 6547
Ge 45:8 he hath made me a father to **P**,........ 6547
Ge 46:31 I will go up, and shew **P**, and say 6547
Ge 47:8 **P** said unto Jacob, How old art........ 6547
Ge 47:10 And Jacob blessed **P**, and went 6547
Ge 47:20 bought all the land of Egypt for **P**;..... 6547
Ge 47:22 did eat their portion which **P** gave..... 6547
Ge 47:24 ye shall give the fifth part unto **P**,...... 6547
Ex 1:11 they built for **P** treasure cities, ... 6547
Ex 2:5 daughter of **P** came down to wash..... 6547
Ex 2:15 Moses fled from the face of **P**, and..... 6547
Ex 3:10 I will send thee unto **P**, that thou...... 6547
Ex 4:21 thou do all those wonders before **P**,.... 6547
Ex 4:22 thou shalt say unto **P**, Thus saith 6547
Ex 5:1 and Aaron went in, and told **P**,........ 6547

P

Ex	5:21	to be abhorred in the eyes of **P**,	6547
Ex	5:23	I came to **P** to speak in thy name,	6547
Ex	6:11	Go in, speak unto **P** king of Egypt,	6547
Ex	6:12	how then shall **P** hear me, who am	6547
Ex	7:1	See, I have made thee a god to **P**:	6547
Ex	7:2	thy brother shall speak unto **P**,	6547
Ex	7:4	But **P** shall not hearken unto you,	6547
Ex	7:9	Take thy rod, and cast it before **P**,	6547
Ex	7:10	Aaron cast down his rod before **P**,	6547
Ex	7:20	were in the river, in the sight of **P**,	6547
Ex	8:24	swarm of flies into the house of **P**,	6547
Ex	8:28	**P** said, I will let you go, that ye	6547
Ex	8:29	swarms of flies may depart from **P**,	6547
Ex	8:29	let not **P** deal deceitfully any more	6547
Ex	8:32	**P** hardened his heart at this time	6547
Ex	9:34	when **P** saw that the rain and the	6547
Ex	10:24	**P** called unto Moses, and said, Go	6547
Ex	10:28	**P** said unto him, Get thee from	6547
Ex	11:5	firstborn of **P** that sitteth upon his	6547
Ex	11:9	**P** shall not hearken unto you;	6547
Ex	12:29	the firstborn of **P** that sat on his	6547
Ex	13:17	when **P** had let the people go, that	6547
Ex	14:4	I will be honoured upon **P**, and	6547
Ex	14:5	heart of **P** and of his servants was	6547
Ex	14:8	The Lord hardened the heart of **P**	6547
Ex	14:10	when **P** drew nigh, the children of	6547
Ex	14:28	all the host of **P** that came into the	6547
Ex	18:4	delivered me from the sword of **P**:	6547
Ex	18:8	all that the Lord had done unto **P**	6547
1Sa	6:6	and **P** hardened their hearts?	6547
1Ki	11:19	great favour in the sight of **P**, so	6547
Ne	9:10	signs and wonders upon **P**, and	6547
Ps	135:9	the midst of thee, O Egypt, upon **P**,	6547
Ps	136:15	**P** and his host in the Red sea:	6547
Eze	32:2	lamentation for **P** king of Egypt	6547
Ro	9:17	For the scripture saith unto **P**,	*5328*

PHARAOH'S (fa´-ra-oze)

Ge	12:15	woman was taken into **P** house	6547
Ge	37:36	unto Potiphar, an officer of **P**, and	6547
Ge	40:13	shalt deliver **P** cup into his hand,	6547
Ge	45:16	fame thereof was heard in **P** house,	6547
Ex	2:7	Then said his sister to **P** daughter,	6547
Ex	2:8	And **P** daughter said unto her, Go.	6547
Ex	2:10	she brought him unto **P** daughter,	6547
Ex	7:3	And I will harden **P** heart, and	6547
Ex	8:19	and **P** heart was hardened, and he	6547
Ex	10:20	the Lord hardened **P** heart,	6547
Ex	11:10	the Lord hardened **P** heart, so that	6547
Ex	14:4	I will harden **P** heart, that he shall	6547
Ex	15:4	**P** chariots and ... hosts hath he cast	6547
Jer	37:5	**P** army was come ... out of Egypt:	6547
Eze	30:24	but I will break **P** arms, and he	6547
Ac	7:21	**P** daughter took him up, and	*5328*
Heb	11:24	be called the son of **P** daughter;	*5328*

PHARISEE (far´-i-see)

Mt	23:26	**Thou blind P, cleanse first that**	*5330*
Lk	18:10	**one a P, and the other a publican**	*5330*
Lk	18:11	**The P stood and prayed thus with**	*5350*
Ac	5:34	a **P**, named Gamaliel, a doctor of	*5330*
Php	3:5	as touching the law, a **P**;	*5330*

PHARISEE'S (far´-i-seze)

Lk	7:36	he went into the **P** house, and sat	*5330*
Lk	7:37	Jesus sat at meat in the **P** house,	*5330*

PHARISEES (far´-i-seze)

Mt	5:20	righteousness of the scribes and **P**,	*5330*
Mt	9:14	Why do we and the **P** fast oft, but	*5330*
Mt	15:12	thou that the **P** were offended,	*5330*
Mt	16:6	**beware of the leaven of the P**	*5330*
Mt	23:2	**scribes and the P sit in Moses'**	*5330*
Mt	23:13	**P, hypocrites!**	*5330*
Mk	2:18	disciples of John and of the **P** fast,	*5330*
Mk	8:15	**beware of the leaven of the P,**	*5330*
Lk	5:17	were **P** and doctors of the law	*5330*
Lk	11:39	**do ye P make clean the outside of**	*5330*
Lk	11:42	**woe unto you, P! for ye tithe mint**	*5330*
Lk	12:1	**Beware ye of the leaven of the P,**	*5330*
Jn	3:1	man of the **P**, named Nicodemus,	*5330*
Jn	4:1	Lord knew how the **P** had heard	*5330*
Jn	7:48	rulers or of the **P** believed on him?	*5330*
Jn	8:3	and **P** brought unto him a woman	*5330*
Jn	11:47	gathered the chief priests and ... **P**.	*5330*
Jn	11:57	the **P** had given a commandment	*5330*
Ac	15:5	of the sect of the **P** which believed,	*5330*

PHILISTINE (fil-is´-tin)

1Sa	17:8	am not I a **P**, and ye servants to	6430
1Sa	17:10	**P** said, I defy the armies of Israel	6430
1Sa	17:16	**P** drew near morning and evening,	6430
1Sa	17:26	done to the man that killeth this **P**.	6430
1Sa	17:33	art not able to go against this **P**	6430
1Sa	17:37	me out of the hand of this **P**.	6430
1Sa	17:41	**P** came on and drew near unto	6430
1Sa	17:42	**P** looked about, and saw David,	6430
1Sa	17:43	the **P** said unto David, Am I a dog,	6430
1Sa	17:43	the **P** cursed David by his gods	6430
1Sa	17:44	the **P** said to David, Come to me,	6430
1Sa	17:49	and smote the **P** in his forehead,	6430
1Sa	17:50	prevailed over the **P** with a sling,	6430
1Sa	17:50	and smote the **P**, and slew him:	6430
1Sa	17:51	David ran, and stood upon the **P**	6430
1Sa	17:54	And David took the head of the **P**,	6430
1Sa	17:57	before Saul with the head of the **P**,	6430
1Sa	19:5	life in his hand, and slew the **P**,	6430
1Sa	21:9	The sword of Goliath the **P**, whom	6430
1Sa	22:10	him the sword of Goliath the **P**	6430

PHILISTINES (fil-is´-tinz)

Ge	21:32	returned into the land of the **P**.	6430
Ge	26:14	servants: and the **P** envied him.	6430
Jgs	3:3	Namely, five lords of the **P**, and	6430
Jgs	10:6	the gods of the **P**, and forsook the	6430
Jgs	13:1	into the hand of the **P** forty years	6430
Jgs	13:5	Israel out of the hand of the **P**	6430
Jgs	16:5	lords of the **P** came up unto her,	6430
Jgs	16:8	lords of the **P** brought up to her	6430
Jgs	16:9	The **P** be upon thee, Samson.	6430
Jgs	16:18	lords of the **P** came up unto her	6430
Jgs	16:21	**P** took him, and put out his eyes	6430
Jgs	16:28	may be at once avenged of the **P**.	6430
Jgs	16:30	Samson said, Let me die with the **P**	6430
1Sa	5:1	And the **P** took the ark of God, and	6430
1Sa	5:8	and gathered all the lords of the **P**	6430
1Sa	6:21	**P** have brought again the ark of	6430
1Sa	7:11	pursued the **P**, and smote them	6430
1Sa	7:13	So the **P** were subdued, and they	6430
1Sa	17:2	the battle in array against the **P**	6430
1Sa	17:3	**P** stood on a mountain on the one	6430
1Sa	17:21	the **P** had put the battle in array,	6430
1Sa	17:51	**P** saw their champion was dead	6430

1Sa 17:52 the wounded of the **P** fell down by 6430
1Sa 17:53 returned from chasing after the **P**, ... 6430
1Sa 18:25 David fall by the hand of the **P**. 6430
1Sa 18:27 slew of the **P** two hundred men;. 6430
1Sa 23:2 Shall I go and smite these **P**? 6430
1Sa 23:2 Go, and smite the **P**, and save 6430
1Sa 23:28 David, and went against the **P**: 6430
1Sa 31:2 the **P** followed hard upon Saul and 6430
1Sa 31:2 **P** slew Jonathan, and Abinadab, ... 6430
1Sa 31:8 when the **P** came to strip the slain, ... 6430
1Sa 31:11 that which the **P** had done to Saul: 6430
2Sa 5:17 all the **P** came up to seek David:. 6430
2Ch 26:7 God helped him against the **P**, ... 6430
Zec 9:6 I will cut off the pride of the **P** 6430

PHILISTINES' (fil-is´-tinz)
Ge 21:34 Abraham sojourned in the **P** land 6430
1Sa 14:1 let us go over to the **P** garrison, ... 6430
1Ch 11:16 **P** garrison was then at Beth-lehem. 6430

PHILOSOPHERS
Ac 17:18 Then certain **p** of the Epicureans, ... *5386*

PHILOSOPHY
Col 2:8 spoil you through **p** and … deceit *5385*

PHYSICIAN
Mt 9:12 **They that be whole need not a p,** *2395*
Mk 2:17 **are whole have no need of the p,** *2395*
Lk 4:23 **me this proverb, P, heal thyself:** *2595*
Lk 5:31 **They that are whole need not a p;** *2395*
Col 4:14 Luke, the beloved **p**, and Demas, ... *2395*

PHYSICIANS
Ge 50:2 and the **p** embalmed Israel 7495
Job 13:4 of lies, ye are all **p** of no value 7495
Mk 5:26 suffered many things of many **p**, ... *2595*
Lk 8:43 had spent all her living upon **p**, ... *2395*

PICTURES
Nu 33:52 destroy all their **p**, and destroy 4906
Pr 25:11 is like apples of gold in **p** of silver. 4906

PIECE
Ge 15:10 laid each **p** one against another: 1335
1Sa 2:36 crouch to him for a **p** of silver and 95
1Sa 2:36 that I may eat a **p** of bread. 6595
1Sa 30:12 gave him a **p** of a cake of figs. 6400
1Ch 16:3 of bread, and a good **p** of flesh,. 829
Ne 3:20 earnestly repaired the other **p**,. 4060
Pr 6:26 a man is brought to a **p** of bread: 3603
Pr 28:21 for a **p** of bread that man will 6595
Eze 24:6 bring it out **p** by **p**; let no lot fall. 5409
Mt 9:16 **putteth a p of new cloth unto an** *1915*
Mt 17:27 **mouth, thou shalt find a p of money:**
Lk 5:36 **putteth a p of a new garment** *1915*
Lk 15:9 **have found the p which I had lost.** *1406*
Lk 24:42 gave him a **p** of a broiled fish, ... *3313*

PIECES
Ge 37:28 Ishmeelites for twenty **p** of silver:
Ge 37:33 Joseph is without doubt rent in **p**
Ge 44:28 and I said, Surely he is torn in **p**;
Ge 45:22 he gave three hundred **p** of silver,
Ex 29:17 And thou shalt cut the ram in **p**, ... 5409
Le 2:6 Thou shalt part it in **p**, and pour 6595
Jgs 19:29 with her bones, into twelve **p**, ... 5409
Jgs 20:6 my concubine, and cut her in **p**,
1Sa 15:33 Samuel hewed Agag in **p** before the
1Ki 11:30 on him, and rent it in twelve **p**: 7168
1Ki 11:31 to Jeroboam, Take thee ten **p**: 7168
2Ki 18:4 brake in **p** the brasen serpent that
2Ki 25:13 did the Chaldees break in **p**, and
2Ch 23:17 brake his altars and his images in **p**,
Job 19:2 soul, and brake me in **p** with words?
Ps 68:30 submit himself with **p** of silver: 7518
Ps 74:14 breakest the heads of leviathan in **p**,
Eze 13:19 of barley and for **p** of bread, ... 6595
Eze 24:4 Gather the **p** thereof into it, even 5409
Da 2:34 of iron and clay, and brake them to **p**
Da 2:44 it shall break in **p** and consume all
Da 2:45 and that it break in **p** the iron, the
Da 3:29 and Abed-nego, shall be cut in **p**, ... 1917
Hos 3:2 her to me for fifteen **p** of silver
Zec 11:12 for my price thirty **p** of silver
Zec 11:13 And I took the thirty **p** of silver, and
Mt 26:15 with him for thirty **p** of silver.
Mt 27:3 brought again the thirty **p** of silver
Mt 27:6 the chief priests took the silver **p**,
Mt 27:9 And they took the thirty **p** of silver
Lk 15:8 **woman having ten p of silver,** *1406*
Ac 19:19 found it fifty thousand **p** of silver

PIERCE
Nu 24:8 **p** them through with his arrows 4272
Isa 36:6 it will go into his hand, and **p** it: 5344
Lk 2:35 shall **p** through thy own soul also,) *1330*

PIERCED
Job 30:17 My bones are **p** in me in the night 5365
Ps 22:16 me: they **p** my hands and my feet. 738
Zec 12:10 look upon me whom they have **p**, ... 1856
Jn 19:34 soldiers with a spear **p** his side, ... *3572*
Jn 19:37 shall look on him whom they **p** *1574*
Rev 1:7 him, and they also which **p** him: *1574*

PIERCING
Heb 4:12 **p** even to the dividing asunder of *1338*

PIGEON
Ge 15:9 and a turtledove, and a young **p** 1469
Le 12:6 and a young **p**, or a turtledove 3123

PIGEONS
Le 5:7 two turtledoves, or two young **p**, ... 3123
Le 5:11 two turtledoves, or two young **p**, ... 3123
Lk 2:24 of turtledoves, or two young **p** *4058*

PILATE (pi´-lut)
Mt 27:2 him to Pontius **P** the governor *4091*
Mt 27:22 **P** saith unto them, What shall I do. *4091*
Mt 27:58 went to **P**, and begged the body of *4091*
Mk 15:2 **P** asked him, Art thou the King of *4091*
Lk 13:1 blood **P** had mingled with their *4091*
Lk 23:12 **P** and Herod were made friends *4091*
Jn 18:35 **P** answered, Am I a Jew? Thine *4091*
Jn 18:38 **P** saith unto him, What is truth? *4091*
Jn 19:5 **P** saith unto them, Behold the man!
Jn 19:15 **P** saith unto them, Shall I crucify *4091*
Jn 19:31 besought **P** that their legs might *4091*
Ac 4:27 both Herod, and Pontius **P**, with *4091*
1Ti 6:13 before Pontius **P** witnessed a good *4091*

PILGRIMAGE
Ge 47:9 The days of the years of my **p** are 4033
Ex 6:4 land of Canaan, the land of their **p**, ... 4033
Ps 119:54 my songs in the house of my **p** 4033

P

PILGRIMS
Heb 11:13 strangers and **p** on the earth. *3927*
1Pe 2:11 I beseech you as strangers and **p**, *3927*

PILLAR
Ge 19:26 him, and she became a **p** of salt, 5333
Ge 31:13 where thou anointedst the **p**, and 4676
Ge 31:45 took a stone, and set it up for a **p** 4676
Ge 35:20 And Jacob set a **p** upon her grave: 4676
Ex 13:21 them by day in a **p** of a cloud, to 5982
Ex 13:21 by night in a **p** of fire, to give them 5982
Ex 33:9 the cloudy **p** descended, and stood. 5982
Nu 12:5 Lord came down in the **p** of the 5982
Ne 9:12 them in the day by a cloudy **p**; 5982
Ne 9:12 and in the night by a **p** of fire, 5982
Ps 99:7 spake unto them in the cloudy **p**: 5982

PILLARS
Ex 24:4 **p**, according to the twelve tribes 4676
Jgs 16:25 and they set him between the **p** 5982
Jgs 16:26 Suffer me that I may feel the **p** 5982
Jgs 16:29 took hold of the two middle **p** 5982
Job 26:11 The **p** of heaven tremble and are 5982
Pr 9:1 she hath hewn out her seven **p**: 5982
Joel 2:30 blood, and fire, and **p** of smoke 8490
Gal 2:9 and John, who seemed to be **p**, *4769*
Rev 10:1 the sun, and his feet as **p** of fire: *4769*

PILLOW
1Sa 19:16 a **p** of goats' hair for his bolster. 3523
Mk 4:38 part of the ship, asleep on a **p**: *4344*

PILLOWS
Ge 28:11 that place, and put them for his **p**, 4763
Ge 28:18 the stone that he had put for his **p**, 4763

PILOTS
Eze 27:27 thy mariners, and thy **p**, thy 2259
Eze 27:29 all the **p** of the sea, shall come 2259

PIN
Jgs 16:14 she fastened it with the **p**, and 3489
Jgs 16:14 went away with the **p** of the beam, 3489

PINE
Isa 60:13 unto thee, the fir tree, the **p** tree, 8410
La 4:9 these **p** away, stricken through 2100
Eze 24:23 shall **p** away for your iniquities, 4743

PINNACLE
Mt 4:5 setteth him on a **p** of the temple *4419*
Lk 4:9 and set him on a **p** of the temple *4419*

PIPE
1Sa 10:5 with a tabret, and a **p**, and a harp, 2485
1Co 14:7 giving sound, whether **p** or harp, *836*

PIPED
1Ki 1:40 and the people **p** with pipes, and 2490
Mt 11:17 **We have p unto you, and ye have** *832*
1Co 14:7 it be known what is **p** or harped? *832*

PIPES
Jer 48:36 mine heart shall sound like **p** for 2485
Eze 28:13 of thy tabrets and of thy **p** was 5345
Zec 4:2 seven **p** to the seven lamps which 4166

PIT
Ge 37:24 took him, and cast him into a **p**: 953
Ge 37:24 **p** was empty, there was no water. 953
Ge 37:28 and lifted up Joseph out of the **p**, 953
Ge 37:29 behold, Joseph was not in the **p**; 953
2Sa 23:20 and slew a lion in the midst of a **p** 953
Job 33:18 keepeth back his soul from the **p**, 7845
Job 33:28 his soul from going into the **p**, 7845
Job 33:30 To bring back his soul from the **p**, 7845
Ps 30:3 that I should not go down to the **p**. 953
Ps 55:23 down into the **p** of destruction: 875
Ps 88:4 with them that go down into the **p**: 953
Pr 1:12 as those that go down into the **p**: 953
Pr 22:14 of strange women is a deep **p**: 7745
Pr 26:27 Whoso diggeth a **p** shall fall. 7845
Pr 28:10 shall fall himself into his own **p**: 7816
Ecc 10:8 He that diggeth a **p** shall fall into 1475
Isa 14:15 down to hell, to the sides of the **p**. 953
Eze 26:20 with them that descend into the **p** 953
Mt 12:11 **it fall into a p on the sabbath day,** *999*
Lk 14:5 **an ass or an ox fallen into a p** *5421*
Rev 9:1 given the key of the bottomless **p** *5421*
Rev 9:2 And he opened the bottomless **p**; *5421*
Rev 11:7 ascendeth out of the bottomless **p**,
Rev 20:3 And cast him into the bottomless **p**,

PITCH
Ex 2:3 daubed it with slime and with **p**, 2203
Nu 1:52 of Israel shall **p** their tents 2583
Jos 4:20 of Jordan, did Joshua **p** in Gilgal 6965
Isa 13:20 neither shall the Arabian **p** tent. 167

PITCHED
Ge 12:8 east of Beth-el, and **p** his tent, 5186
Ge 31:25 Jacob had **p** his tent in the mount: 8628
Ex 17:1 **p** in Rephidim: and there was no 2583
Nu 1:51 when the tabernacle is to be **p**, 2583
Nu 33:15 and **p** in the wilderness of Sinai 2583
Jgs 15:9 the Philistines and **p** in Judah, 2583
1Sa 26:3 And Saul **p** in the hill of Hachilah, 2583
2Sa 6:17 tabernacle that David had **p** for it; 5186
2Sa 17:26 Absalom **p** in the land of Gilead 2583
1Ki 20:27 children of Israel **p** before them 2583
1Ki 20:29 they **p** one over against the other, 2583
1Ch 15:1 the ark of God, and **p** it for a tent. 5186
Jer 52:4 Jerusalem, and **p** against it. 2583
Heb 8:2 which the Lord **p**, and not man *4078*

PITCHER
Ge 24:14 Let down thy **p**, I pray thee, that 3537
Ge 24:16 well, and filled her **p**, and came up. 3537
Ge 24:17 thee, drink a little water of thy **p**. 3537
Ge 24:20 and emptied her **p** into the trough, 3537
Ge 24:43 a little water of thy **p** to drink; 3537
Ge 24:46 let down her **p** from her shoulder 3537
Mk 14:13 **you a man bearing a p of water;** *2765*
Lk 22:10 **meet you, bearing a p of water;** *2765*

PITCHERS
Jgs 7:16 every man's hand, with empty **p**, 3537
Jgs 7:16 and lamps within the **p** 3537
Jgs 7:19 and brake the **p** that were in their 3537
Jgs 7:20 brake the **p**, and held the lamps 3537

PITIED
Ps 106:46 He made them also to be **p** of all 7356
La 2:2 of Jacob, and hath not **p**: 2550

PITIETH
Ps 103:13 Like as a father **p** his children 7355
Ps 103:13 so the Lord **p** them that fear him. 7355

PITIFUL
La 4:10 The hands of the **p** women have....... 7362
Jas 5:11 the Lord is very **p**, and of tender....... *4184*

PITS
1Sa 13:6 rocks, and in high places, and in **p**...... 953
Ps 119:85 The proud have digged **p** for me,...... 7882
La 4:20 the Lord, was taken in their **p**,......... 7825

PITY
Dt 7:16 eye shall have no **p** upon them:......... 2347
Job 19:21 Have **p** upon me, have **p** upon me, ... 2603
Pr 19:17 He that hath **p** upon the poor......... 2603
Pr 28:8 it for him that will **p** the poor......... 2603
Isa 63:9 and in his **p** he redeemed them;........ 2551
Eze 36:21 But I had **p** for mine holy name....... 2550
Jnh 4:10 Thou hast had **p** on the gourd,........ 2347
Mt 18:33 **fellowservant, as I had p on thee?**...... *1653*

PLACE
Ge 18:24 spare the **p** for the fifty righteous...... 4725
Ge 18:26 will spare all the **p** for their sakes...... 4725
Ge 20:11 the fear of God is not in this **p**;........ 4725
Ge 22:14 the name of that **p** Jehovah-jireh:...... 4725
Ge 26:7 men of the **p** should kill me for 4725
Ge 28:11 and lay down in that **p** to sleep........ 4725
Ge 28:16 Surely the Lord is in this **p**; and I...... 4725
Ge 38:14 herself, and sat in an open **p**,......... 6607
Ge 50:19 Fear not: for am I in the **p** of God?
Ex 3:5 **p** whereon thou standest is holy....... 4725
Ex 23:20 into the **p** which I have prepared 4725
Ex 33:21 there is a **p** by me, and thou shalt...... 4725
Le 4:33 sin offering in the **p** where they kill.... 4725
Le 14:42 put them in the **p** of those stones; 8478
Dt 11:24 Every **p** whereon the soles of your 4725
Dt 12:5 **p** which the Lord your God shall 4725
Dt 16:6 at the **p** which the Lord thy God....... 4724
Jos 1:3 Every **p** that the sole of your foot...... 4725
Ru 1:7 forth out of the **p** where she was,...... 4725
Ru 4:10 and from the gate of his **p**: ye are...... 4725
1Sa 3:2 Eli was laid down in his **p**, and his..... 4725
1Sa 3:9 Samuel went and lay down in his **p**.... 4725
1Sa 20:25 side, and David's **p** was empty 4725
1Sa 20:37 lad was come to the **p** of the arrow 4725
1Sa 26:5 David beheld the **p** where Saul lay..... 4725
2Sa 6:17 ark of the Lord, and set it in his **p**,..... 4725
2Sa 18:18 called unto this day, Absalom's **p** 3027
1Ki 8:7 two wings over the **p** of the ark,....... 4725
1Ki 8:8 out in the holy **p** before the oracle,
1Ki 8:21 I have set there a **p** for the ark......... 4725
1Ki 8:43 Hear thou in heaven thy dwelling **p**, ... 4349
1Ki 21:19 **p** where dogs licked the blood of...... 4725
2Ki 22:19 what I spake against this **p**, and 4725
1Ch 15:1 and prepared a **p** for the ark of God,... 4725
1Ch 21:22 me the **p** of this threshingfloor, ... 4725
1Ch 28:11 and of the **p** of the mercy seat,........ 1004
2Ch 6:2 and a **p** for thy dwelling for ever....... 4349
Ezr 5:15 house of God be builded in his **p**....... 870
Ezr 6:5 at Jerusalem, every one to his **p**,........ 870
Ezr 6:5 and **p** them in the house of God....... 5182
Ezr 6:7 build this house of God in his **p**........ 870
Ezr 9:8 and to give us a nail in his holy **p**, ... 4725
Ne 2:3 the **p** of my fathers' sepulchres,........ 1004
Job 8:22 the dwelling **p** of the wicked shall
Job 39:28 the crag of the rock, and the strong **p**
Ps 24:3 or who shall stand in his holy **p**? 4725
Ps 26:8 **p** where thine honour dwelleth........ 4725
Ps 32:7 Thou art my hiding **p**; thou shalt
Ps 68:17 them, as in Sinai, in the holy **p**
Ps 76:2 and his dwelling **p** in Zion
Ps 90:1 Lord, thou hast been our dwelling **p**
Ps 91:1 He that dwelleth in the secret **p** of
Ps 119:114 Thou art my hiding **p** and my
Pr 15:3 eyes of the Lord are in every **p**,........ 4725
Pr 25:6 stand not in the **p** of great men:....... 4725
Isa 22:23 fasten him as a nail in a sure **p**;........ 4725
Isa 46:7 carry him, and set him in his **p**, ... 8478
Isa 46:13 and I will **p** salvation in Zion for 5414
Isa 54:2 Enlarge the **p** of thy tent, and let....... 4725
Isa 60:13 beautify the **p** of my sanctuary; 4725
Isa 60:13 make the **p** of my feet glorious........ 4725
Jer 27:22 up, and restore them to this **p**......... 4725
Jer 28:3 will I bring again into this **p** all........ 4725
Eze 3:12 the glory of the Lord from his **p**....... 4725
Eze 39:11 give unto God a **p** there of graves...... 4725
Eze 42:13 trespass offering; for the **p** is holy...... 4725
Eze 43:7 Son of man, the **p** of my throne....... 4725
Eze 43:7 the **p** of the soles of my feet, where 4725
Da 2:35 no **p** was found for them: and the 870
Joel 3:7 I will raise them out of the **p**.......... 4725
Zec 14:10 be lifted up, and inhabited in her **p**,.... 8478
Zec 14:10 gate unto the **p** of the first gate, ... 4725
Mt 12:6 **in this p is one … than the temple.**.... *5602*
Mt 26:36 them unto a **p** called Gethsemane,..... *5564*
Mt 26:52 **Put up again thy sword into his p** *5117*
Mt 27:33 come unto a **p** called Golgotha........ *5117*
Mt 27:33 that is to say, a **p** of a skull, ... *5117*
Mt 28:6 Come see the **p** where the Lord lay..... *5117*
Mk 16:6 behold the **p** where they laid him...... *5117*
Lk 10:32 **a Levite, when he was at the p**......... *5117*
Lk 16:28 **also come into this p of torment**....... *5117*
Jn 8:37 **my word hath no p in you**............ *5562*
Jn 11:41 from the **p** where the dead was laid
Jn 14:2 **you. I go to prepare a p for you** *5117*
Jn 14:3 **if I go and prepare a p for you,**........ *5117*
Jn 19:13 in a **p** that is called the Pavement,...... *5117*
Jn 19:17 his cross went forth into a **p**
Jn 19:20 the **p** where Jesus was crucified........ *5117*
Jn 19:41 the **p** where he was crucified there..... *5117*
Jn 20:7 wrapped together in a **p** by itself....... *5117*
Ac 1:25 fell, that he might go to his own **p**..... *5117*
Ac 7:33 the **p** where thou standest is holy....... *5117*
Ac 27:8 a **p** which is called The fair havens; *5117*
Ro 12:19 but rather give **p** unto wrath: *5117*
2Co 2:14 his knowledge by us in every **p**........ *5117*
Eph 4:27 Neither give **p** to the devil *5117*
1Th 1:8 in every **p** your faith to God-ward..... *5117*
Heb 9:25 high priest entereth into the holy **p**
Heb 12:17 for he found no **p** of repentance, ... *5117*
Jas 2:3 Sit thou here in a good **p**; and
Jas 3:11 at the same **p** sweet water and......... *3692*
2Pe 1:19 a light that shineth in a dark **p**,........ *5117*
Rev 2:5 **thy candlestick out of this p** *5117*

PLACED
Ge 3:24 he **p** at the east of the garden of....... 7931
Job 20:4 old, since man was **p** upon earth,...... 7760
Ps 78:60 the tent which he **p** among men; 7931
Jer 5:22 have **p** the sand for the bound of....... 776

PLACES
Ex 20:24 **p** where I record my name I will....... 4725
Ex 26:29 rings of gold for **p** for the bars:........ 1004

P

Le 26:30 I will destroy your high **p**, and cut
Nu 33:52 and quite pluck down all their high **p**:
Jos 5:8 they abode in their **p** in the camps..... 8478
1Sa 30:31 to all the **p** where David himself....... 4725
2Ki 18:4 He removed the high **p**, and brake the
2Ki 23:5 and in the **p** round about Jerusalem;
2Ki 23:14 filled their **p** with … bones of men 4725
2Ch 8:11 the **p** are holy, whereunto the ark of
2Ch 20:33 the high **p** were not taken away:
2Ch 21:11 he made high **p** in the mountains
2Ch 33:17 people did sacrifice still in the high **p**,
Ne 4:12 From all **p** whence ye shall return...... 4725
Ne 4:13 set I in the lower **p** behind the wall,.... 4725
Ne 12:27 sought the Levites out of all … **p**, ... 4725
Job 21:28 are the dwelling **p** of the wicked? 168
Ps 16:6 lines are fallen unto me in pleasant **p**;
Ps 17:12 were a young lion lurking in secret **p**
Ps 49:11 their dwelling **p** to all generations;
Ps 103:22 works in all **p** of his dominion:........ 4725
Ps 141:6 judges are overthrown in stony **p**, ... 3027
Pr 8:2 She standeth in the top of high **p**
Isa 32:18 sure dwellings, and in quiet resting **p**;
Isa 40:4 made straight, and the rough **p** plain:
Isa 41:18 I will open rivers in high **p**, and
Isa 45:2 and make the crooked **p** straight:
Jer 13:17 my soul shall weep in secret **p** for
Jer 17:26 and from the **p** about Jerusalem....... 5439
Jer 23:24 Can any hide himself in secret **p** that
Eze 38:20 and the steep **p** shall fall, and every
Am 4:6 and want of bread in all your **p**:....... 4725
Mal 1:4 will return and build the desolate **p**;
Mt 13:5 **Some fell upon stony p, where they**
Mt 13:20 **that received the seed into stony p,**
Lk 21:11 **earthquakes shall be in divers p,**....... *5117*
Eph 1:3 blessings in heavenly **p** in Christ:
Eph 2:6 in heavenly **p** in Christ Jesus:
Eph 6:12 spiritual wickedness in high **p**
Heb 9:24 into the holy **p** made with hands,
Rev 6:14 island were moved out of their **p** *5117*

PLAGUE
Ex 11:1 bring one **p** more upon Pharaoh,...... 5061
Le 13:2 of his flesh like the **p** of leprosy;....... 5061
Le 13:3 skin of his flesh, it is a **p** of leprosy: 5061
Le 13:13 pronounce him clean that hath … **p** ... 5061
Nu 11:33 the people with a very great **p**......... 4347
Nu 14:37 died by the **p** before the Lord 4046
Nu 16:47 the **p** was begun among the people:.... 5063
Nu 16:48 the living; and the **p** was stayed........ 4046
Jos 22:17 was a **p** in the congregation of the 5063
2Sa 24:21 **p** may be stayed from the people 4046
2Sa 24:25 and the **p** was stayed from Israel....... 4046
2Ch 21:14 **p** will the Lord smite thy people....... 4046
Ps 91:10 neither shall any **p** come nigh thy...... 5061
Ps 106:30 judgment: and so the **p** was stayed..... 4046
Mk 5:29 that she was healed of that **p**.......... *3148*
Mk 5:34 **in peace, and be whole of thy p** *3148*
Rev 16:21 God because of the **p** of the hail; *4127*
Rev 16:21 the **p** thereof was exceeding great...... *4127*

PLAGUED
Ge 12:17 Lord **p** Pharaoh and his house 5060
Ex 32:35 the Lord **p** the people, because 5062
Jos 24:51 **p** Egypt, according to that which 5062
Ps 73:14 all the day long have I been **p** 5060

PLAGUES
Ge 12:17 plagued Pharaoh … with great **p**...... 5061
Le 26:21 seven times more **p** upon you......... 4347
Hos 13:14 O death, I will be thy **p**; O grave....... 1698
Mk 3:10 to touch him, as many as had **p** *3148*
Rev 9:20 which were not killed by these **p**....... *4127*
Rev 15:1 angels having the seven last **p**;......... *4127*
Rev 15:8 seven **p** of the seven angels were....... *4127*
Rev 22:18 God shall add unto him the **p** that..... *4127*

PLAIN
Ge 13:11 Lot chose him all the **p** of Jordan; 3603
Ge 13:12 Lot dwelled in the cities of the **p**....... 3603
Ge 14:13 for he dwelt in the **p** of Mamre the 436
Ge 19:29 God destroyed the cities of the **p** 3603
Ge 25:27 Jacob was a **p** man, dwelling in........ 8535
Jos 11:16 Goshen, and the valley, and the **p**...... 6160
Jgs 9:6 by the **p** of the pillar that was in........ 436
Ne 12:28 **p** country round about Jerusalem,..... 3603
Ps 27:11 lead me in a **p** path, because of........ 4334
Pr 15:19 way of the righteous is made **p**........ 5549
Isa 28:25 he hath made **p** the face thereof,....... 7737
Isa 40:4 straight, and the rough places **p**:....... 1237
Jer 21:13 of the valley, and rock of the **p** 4334
Zec 14:10 All the land shall be turned as a **p**...... 6160
Mk 7:35 tongue was loosed, and he spake **p**..... *3723*

PLAINLY
Ex 21:5 if the servant shall **p** say, I love 559
Dt 27:8 all the words of this law very **p** 874
Ezr 4:18 sent unto us hath been **p** read......... 6568
Isa 32:4 shall be ready to speak **p** 6703
Jn 10:24 If thou be the Christ, tell us **p**......... *3954*
Jn 11:14 Then said Jesus unto them **p**, ... *3954*
Jn 16:25 I shall shew you **p** of the Father *3954*
Heb 11:14 declare **p** that they seek a country...... *1718*

PLAINS
Ge 18:1 unto him in the **p** of Mamre: 436
Dt 34:1 Moses went up from the **p** of Moab.... 6160
Jos 4:13 unto battle, to the **p** of Jericho 6160
2Ki 25:5 overtook him in the **p** of Jericho:...... 6160
1Ch 27:28 trees that were in the low **p** was 8219

PLAISTER
Le 14:42 morter, and shall **p** the house 2902
Dt 27:2 great stones, and **p** them with......... 7874
Dt 27:2 great stones, and … them with **p**:...... 7875
Isa 38:21 and lay it for a **p** upon the boil, ... 4799
Da 5:5 **p** of the wall of the king's palace: 1528

PLAITING
1Pe 3:3 outward adorning of **p** the hair, ... *1708*

PLANETS
2Ki 23:5 and to the **p**, and to all the hosts....... 4208

PLANT
Ge 2:5 every **p** of the field before it was....... 7880
2Ki 19:29 sow ye, and reap, and **p** vineyards, ... 5193
Job 14:9 and bring forth boughs like a **p** 5194
Ecc 3:2 a time to **p**, and a time to pluck up 5193
Isa 53:2 grow up before him as a tender **p**,
Jer 42:10 I will **p** you, and not pluck you up: 5193
Eze 34:29 raise up for them a **p** of renown, ... 4302
Da 11:45 **p** the tabernacles of his palace......... 5193
Zep 1:13 and they shall **p** vineyards, but 5193
Mt 15:13 **p, which my heavenly Father** *5451*

PLANTED
Ge 2:8 Lord God **p** a garden eastward 5193
Ge 9:20 husbandman, and he **p** a vineyard: 5193
Ps 1:3 shall be like a tree **p** by the rivers 8362
Ps 92:13 that be **p** in the house of the 8362
Ps 94:9 He that **p** the ear, shall he not 5193
Ecc 3:2 a time to pluck up that which is **p**;..... 5193
Jer 2:21 I had **p** thee a noble vine, wholly 5193
Jer 11:17 the Lord of hosts, that **p** thee, hath..... 5193
Jer 17:8 shall be as a tree **p** by the waters, ... 8362
Mt 15:13 **my heavenly Father hath not p,** *5452*
Mt 21:33 **which p a vineyard, and hedged it** *5452*
Mk 12:1 **A certain man p a vineyard, and** *5452*
Lk 13:6 **had a fig tree p in his vineyard;** *5452*
Lk 17:6 **the root, and be thou p in the sea;** *5452*
Lk 17:28 **they sold, they p, they builded:** *5452*
1Co 3:6 I have **p**, Apollos watered; but *5452*

PLANTETH
Pr 31:16 of her hands she **p** a vineyard 5198
Isa 44:14 he **p** an ash, and the rain doth 5198
1Co 9:7 who **p** a vineyard, and eateth not 5452

PLANTING
Isa 60:21 the branch of my **p**, the work of....... 4302
Isa 61:3 the **p** of the Lord, that he might 4302

PLANTS
Ps 128:3 children like olive **p** round about 8363
SS 4:13 **p** are … orchard of pomegranates,..... 7973
Jer 48:32 thy **p** are gone over the sea, they....... 5189

PLATE
Ex 28:36 thou shalt make a **p** of pure gold,...... 6731
Ex 39:30 they made the **p** of the holy crown..... 6731

PLATES
Ex 39:3 they did beat the gold into thin **p**...... 6341
Nu 16:38 let them make them broad **p** for....... 6341
1Ki 7:30 brasen wheels, and **p** of brass:......... 5633
1Ki 7:36 For on the **p** of the ledges thereof, ... 3871

PLATTED
Mt 27:29 they had **p** a crown of thorns *4120*
Mk 15:17 **p** a crown of thorns, and put it........ *4120*
Jn 19:2 the soldiers **p** a crown of thorns *4120*

PLATTER
Mt 23:25 **outside of the cup and of the p,** *3953*
Mt 23:26 **which is within the cup and p,** *3953*
Lk 11:39 **the outside of the cup and the p;** *4094*

PLAY
Ex 32:6 and to drink, and rose up to **p** 6711
1Sa 21:15 to **p** the mad man in my presence?
2Sa 6:21 therefore will I **p** before the Lord 7832
Job 41:5 thou **p** with him as with a bird? 7832
Ps 33:3 **p** skillfully with a loud noise 5059
Hos 3:3 thou shalt not **p** the harlot, and thou
Hos 4:15 **p** the harlot, yet let not Judah offend;
1Co 10:7 eat and drink, and rose up to **p**........ *3815*

PLAYED
Ge 38:24 daughter in law hath **p** the harlot;
1Sa 16:23 an harp, and **p** with his hand:......... 5059
1Sa 18:10 David **p** with his hand, as at other 5059
1Sa 26:21 I have **p** the fool, and have erred
1Ch 13:8 David and all Israel **p** before God...... 7832

PLAYING
1Sa 16:18 Beth-lehemite that is cunning in **p**, ... 5059
1Ch 15:29 saw king David dancing and **p**:........ 7832
Ps 68:25 were the damsels **p** with timbrels
Zec 8:5 boys and girls **p** in the streets 7832

PLEAD
Jgs 6:31 Will ye **p** for Baal? will ye save......... 7378
Job 16:21 one might **p** for a man with God,...... 3198
Ps 35:1 **P** my cause, O Lord, with them 7378
Pr 119:154 **P** my cause, and deliver me: 7378
Pr 22:23 the Lord will **p** their cause, and........ 7378
Isa 1:17 the fatherless, **p** for the widow 7378
Isa 66:16 will the Lord **p** with all flesh:.......... 8199
Eze 20:36 so will I **p** with you, saith the Lord..... 8199

PLEADED
1Sa 25:39 the Lord that hath **p** the cause 7378
La 3:58 thou hast **p** the causes of my soul; 7378

PLEADETH
Isa 51:22 that **p** the cause of his people 7378
Isa 59:4 for justice, nor any **p** for truth:........ 8199

PLEASANT
Ge 2:9 every tree that is **p** to the sight 2530
Ge 3:6 it was **p** to the eyes, and a tree......... 8378
2Sa 1:23 and Jonathan were lovely and **p** 5273
2Ch 32:27 and for all manner of **p** jewels;........ 2532
Ps 106:24 they despised the **p** land, they......... 2532
Ps 133:1 how **p** it is for brethren to dwell 5273
Ps 147:1 praises unto our God; for it is **p**:....... 5273
Pr 2:10 and knowledge is **p** to thy soul;........ 5276
Pr 9:17 and bread eaten in secret is **p** 5276
Pr 16:24 **P** words are as an honeycomb, ... 5278
SS 7:6 How fair and how **p** art thou, O....... 5276
Isa 54:12 and all thy borders of **p** stones 2656
Jer 3:19 and give thee a **p** land, a goodly 2532
Eze 33:32 song of one that hath a **p** voice........ 3303
Da 10:3 I ate no **p** bread, neither came......... 2530
Na 2:9 glory out of all the **p** furniture 2532

PLEASE
Ex 21:8 If she **p** not her master, who 7451, 5869
1Ki 21:6 else, if it **p** thee, I will give thee 2655
1Ch 17:27 **p** thee to bless the house of thy........ 2974
Ne 2:5 If it **p** the king, and if thy servant...... 2895
Est 1:19 it **p** the king, let there go a royal 2895
Est 5:8 it **p** the king to grant my petition, ... 2895
Est 7:3 if it **p** the king, let my life be given 2895
Job 6:9 it would **p** God to destroy me; 2974
Ps 69:31 shall **p** the Lord better than an ox...... 3190
Pr 16:7 When a man's ways **p** the Lord 7521
Jn 8:29 **do always those things that p him.** *701*
Ro 8:8 that are in the flesh cannot **p** God *700*
1Co 7:32 the Lord, how he may **p** the Lord: *700*
2Ti 2:4 he may **p** him who hath chosen him *700*
Heb 11:6 faith it is impossible to **p** him:......... *2100*

PLEASED
Ge 33:10 of God, and thou wast **p** with me...... 7521
Ge 45:16 and it **p** Pharaoh well, and his ... 3190, 5869
Nu 24:1 Balaam saw that it **p** the Lord 2895
Jgs 14:7 and she **p** Samson well.......... 3477, 5869
1Sa 18:20 Saul, and the thing **p** him 3477, 5869
1Sa 18:26 it **p** David well to be the king's ... 3477, 5869
2Sa 17:4 the saying **p** Absalom well....... 3477, 5869
Ne 2:6 So it **p** the king to send me; and I...... 3190

Est 2:4 And the thing **p** the king; 3190, 5869
Est 5:14 And the thing **p** Haman; and he....... 3190
Ps 51:19 shalt thou be **p** with the sacrifices...... 2654
Ps 135:6 Whatsoever the Lord **p**, that did....... 2654
Isa 53:10 Yet it **p** the Lord to bruise him;........ 2654
Mic 6:7 Lord be **p** with thousands of rams..... 7521
Mt 3:17 beloved Son, in whom I am well **p**..... *2106*
Mt 14:6 danced before them, and **p** Herod *700*
Ac 12:3 And because he saw it **p** the Jews,....... *701*
Ro 15:3 For even Christ **p** not himself;.......... *700*
1Co 1:21 it **p** God by the foolishness of......... *2106*
1Co 15:38 giveth it a body as it hath **p** him, ... *2309*
Heb 11:5 had this testimony, that he **p** God...... *2100*
Heb 13:16 with such sacrifices God is well **p**...... *2100*
2Pe 1:17 beloved son, in whom I am well **p** *2106*

PLEASETH

Ge 16:6 hand; do to her as it **p** thee 2896, 5869
Jgs 14:3 for me; for she **p** me well........ 3477, 5869
Est 2:4 the maiden which **p** the king 3190, 5869
Ecc 7:26 whoso **p** God shall escape 2896, 6440

PLEASING

Est 8:5 the king, and I be **p** in his eyes 2896
Col 1:10 walk worthy of the Lord unto all **p**, ... *699*
1Th 2:4 not as **p** men, but God, which trieth *700*
1Jn 3:22 those things that are **p** in his sight *701*

PLEASURE

1Ch 29:17 heart, and hast **p** in uprightness....... 7521
Est 1:8 do according to every man's **p**......... 7522
Job 22:3 Is it any **p** to the Almighty, that........ 2656
Ps 35:27 **p** in the prosperity of his servant 2655
Ps 51:18 Do good in thy good **p** unto Zion:..... 7522
Ps 149:4 the Lord taketh **p** in his people: 7521
Ecc 12:1 thou shalt say, I have no **p** in them; 2656
Isa 48:14 he will do his **p** on Babylon, and 2656
Isa 53:10 **p** of the Lord shall prosper in his...... 2656
Eze 33:11 no **p** in the death of the wicked;....... 2654
Lk 12:32 **your Father's good p to give you** *2106*
2Co 12:10 Therefore I take **p** in infirmities *2106*
Eph 1:5 according to the good **p** of his will, ... *2107*
Php 2:13 both to will and to do of his good **p**.... *2107*
Heb 10:6 sacrifices … thou hast had no **p** *2106*
Rev 4:11 and for thy **p** they are and were *2307*

PLEASURES

Job 36:11 in prosperity, and their years in **p**...... 5273
Ps 16:11 hand there are **p** for evermore......... *5273*
Lk 8:14 **cares and riches and p of this life,** *2237*
2Ti 3:4 lovers of **p** more than lovers of........ *5559*
Heb 11:25 to enjoy the **p** of sin for a season;...... *2237*

PLEDGE

Ge 38:18 he said, What **p** shall I give thee? 6162
Ge 38:20 his **p** from the woman's hand:......... 6162
Dt 24:10 go into his house to fetch his **p**........ 5667
Job 24:3 they take the widow's ox for a **p** 2254
Pr 27:13 a **p** of him for a strange woman 2254

PLENTEOUS

Ge 41:34 of Egypt in the seven **p** years.......... 7647
Dt 28:11 Lord shall make thee **p** in goods, ... 3498
Ps 103:8 slow to anger, and **p** in mercy......... 7227
Ps 130:7 and with him is **p** redemption 7235
Mt 9:37 **The harvest truly is p, but the**......... *4183*

PLENTEOUSNESS

Ge 41:53 the seven years of **p**, that was in 7647
Pr 21:5 of the diligent tend only to **p**;......... 4195

PLENTIFUL

Ps 68:9 Thou, O God, didst send a **p** rain...... 5071
Jer 2:7 I brought you into a **p** country, ... 3759

PLENTIFULLY

Ps 31:23 and **p** rewardeth the proud doer....... 3499
Lk 12:16 **certain rich man brought forth p:** *2164*

PLENTY

Ge 27:28 the earth, and **p** of corn and wine:..... 7230
Ge 41:29 come seven years of great **p**........... 7647
Ge 41:31 **p** shall not be known in the land 7647
Job 22:25 and thou shalt have **p** of silver 8443
Pr 3:10 So shall thy barns be filled with **p**, ... 7647

PLOUGH

Lk 9:62 **man, having put his hand to the p,** *723*

PLOW

Job 4:8 I have seen, they that **p** iniquity 2790
Pr 20:4 sluggard will not **p** by reason of 2790
1Co 9:10 he that ploweth should **p** in hope; 722

PLOWED

Ps 129:3 The plowers **p** upon my back:......... 2790
Jer 26:18 Zion shall be **p** like a field, and........ 2790
Mic 3:12 Zion for your sake be **p** as a field 2790

PLOWING

1Ki 19:19 was **p** with twelve yoke of oxen........ 2790
Pr 21:4 and the **p** of the wicked, is sin......... 5215
Lk 17:7 **having a servant p or feeding** *722*

PLOWSHARES

Isa 2:4 shall beat their swords into **p**, and 855
Joel 3:10 Beat your **p** into swords, and your 855
Mic 4:3 shall beat their swords into **p**, and 855

PLUCK

Nu 33:52 **p** down all their high places:.......... 8045
Dt 23:25 thou mayest **p** the ears with thine...... 6998
Ps 25:15 he shall **p** my feet out of the net 3318
Ecc 3:2 time to **p** up that which is planted;..... 6131
Jer 12:14 and **p** out the house of Judah from 5428
Jer 45:4 which I have planted I will **p** up 5428
Eze 17:9 to **p** it up by the roots thereof......... 5375
Mt 5:29 **right eye offend thee, p it out,**......... *1808*
Mt 12:1 and began to **p** the ears of corn........ *5089*
Jn 10:28 **any man p them out of my hand** *726*
Jn 10:29 **to p them out of my Father's hand** *726*

PLUCKED

Ru 4:7 a man **p** off his shoe, and gave it....... 8025
2Sa 23:21 **p** the spear out of the Egyptian's....... 1497
Ezr 9:3 **p** off the hair of my head and of....... 4803
Job 29:17 and **p** the spoil out of his teeth........ 7993
Da 11:4 for his kingdom shall be **p** up 5428
Am 4:11 a firebrand **p** out of the burning: 5337
Mk 5:4 had been **p** asunder by him, and....... *1288*
Lk 6:1 his disciples **p** the ears of corn, ... *5089*
Lk 17:6 **Be thou p up by the root, and be** *1610*
Jude 12 twice dead, **p** up by the roots;......... *1610*

PLUMBLINE See also LINE.

Am 7:7 made by a **p**, with a **p** in his hand....... 594
Am 7:8 what seest thou? And I said, A **p**........ 594

POINT

Ge	25:32	said, Behold, I am at the **p** to die:	1980
Eze	21:15	have set the **p** of the sword against	19
Jn	4:47	son: for he was at the **p** of death	*3195*
Jas	2:10	yet offend in one **p**, he is guilty of all	

POINTS

Ecc	5:16	in all **p** as he came, so shall he	5980
Heb	4:15	was in all **p** tempted like as we are,	

POISON

Dt	32:24	with the **p** of serpents of the dust	2534
Ps	140:3	adders' **p** is under their lips	2534
Ro	3:13	the **p** of asps is under their lips:	*2447*
Jas	3:8	an unruly evil, full of deadly **p**	*2447*

POLE

Nu	21:9	of brass, and put it upon a **p**,	5251

POLISHED

Isa	49:2	hid me, and made me a **p** shaft;	1305
Da	10:6	his feet like in colour to **p** brass	7044

POLLUTE

Nu	18:32	neither shall ye **p** the holy things	2490
Nu	35:33	So ye shall not **p** the land wherein	2610
Jer	7:30	is called by my name, to **p** it	2930
Eze	39:7	I will not let them **p** my holy name	2490
Eze	44:7	to **p** it, even my house, when ye	2490
Da	11:31	shall **p** the sanctuary of strength,	2490

POLLUTED

Ex	20:25	thy tool upon it, thou hast **p** it	2490
Ezr	2:62	as **p**, put from the priesthood	1351
Ps	106:38	and the land was **p** with blood	2610
Isa	48:11	how should my name be **p**? and I	2490
Jer	34:16	But ye turned and **p** my name,	2490
Eze	16:6	saw thee **p** in thine own blood	947
Eze	20:16	my statutes, but **p** my sabbaths:	2490
Eze	23:30	because thou art **p** with their idols	2930
Am	7:17	and thou shalt die in a **p** land:	2931
Mic	2:10	because it is **p**, it shall destroy	2930
Zep	3:4	her priests have **p** the sanctuary	2490
Mal	1:12	The table of the Lord is **p**; and the	1351
Ac	21:28	temple, and hath **p** this holy place	*2840*

POLLUTIONS

Ac	15:20	that they abstain from **p** of idols	*234*
2Pe	2:20	have escaped the **p** of the world	*3393*

POMEGRANATE

Ex	28:34	bell and a **p**, a golden bell and a **p**,	7416

POMEGRANATES

Ex	28:33	thou shalt make **p** of blue, and of	7416
Ex	39:25	robe, round about between the **p**;	7416
Nu	20:5	or of figs, or of vines, or of **p**;	7416
SS	7:12	grape appear, and the **p** bud forth:	7416

POMP

Isa	5:14	and their multitude, and their **p**,	7588
Isa	14:11	Thy **p** is brought down to the	1347
Ac	25:23	come, and Bernice, with great **p**	*5325*

PONDER

Pr	4:26	**P** the path of thy feet, and let all	6424
Pr	5:6	thou shouldest **p** the path of life	6424

PONDERED

Lk	2:19	things, and **p** them in her heart	4820

PONDERETH

Pr	5:21	the Lord, and he **p** all his goings	6424
Pr	21:2	eyes: but the Lord **p** the hearts	8505
Pr	24:12	not he that **p** the heart consider it?	8505

POOL

2Ki	18:17	by the conduit of the upper **p**,	1295
Ne	3:15	**p** of Siloah by the king's garden	1295
Isa	35:7	parched ground shall become a **p**,	98
Jn	5:7	is troubled, to put me into the **p**:	*2861*
Jn	9:7	him, **Go, wash in the p of Siloam,**	*2861*

POOLS

Ex	7:19	and upon all their **p** of water	4723
Ps	84:6	a well; the rain also filleth the **p**	1293
Isa	42:15	islands, and I will dry up the **p**	98

POOR

Ge	41:19	kine ... **p** and very ill favoured and	1800
Ex	23:3	shalt thou countenance a **p** man	1800
Dt	15:4	there shall be no **p** among you;	34
Dt	15:7	shut thine hand from thy **p** brother:	34
Dt	15:9	eye be evil against thy **p** brother	34
Dt	15:11	**p** shall never cease out of the land:	34
Ru	3:10	not young men, whether **p** or rich	1800
1Sa	2:7	The Lord maketh **p**, and maketh	3423
Est	9:22	one to another, and gifts to the **p**	34
Job	5:15	he saveth the **p** from the sword	34
Job	5:16	So the **p** hath hope, and iniquity	1800
Ps	34:6	This **p** man cried, and the Lord	6041
Ps	37:14	bow, to cast down the **p** and needy,	6041
Ps	69:33	For the Lord heareth the **p**, and	34
Ps	74:21	the **p** and needy praise thy name	6041
Ps	132:15	I will satisfy her **p** with bread	34
Pr	13:8	but the **p** heareth not rebuke	7326
Pr	14:21	he that hath mercy on the **p**	6035, 6041
Pr	14:31	that oppresseth the **p** reproacheth	1800
Pr	19:1	Better is the **p** that walketh in his	7326
Pr	19:17	that hath pity upon the **p** lendeth	1800
Pr	19:22	and a **p** man is better than a liar	7326
Pr	21:17	loveth pleasure shall be a **p** man:	4270
Pr	28:6	Better is the **p** that walketh in his	1800
Pr	28:8	it for him that will pity the **p**	1800
Pr	29:7	considereth the cause of the **p**:	1800
Pr	29:14	king that faithfully judgeth the **p**:	1800
Pr	31:9	plead the cause of the **p** and needy	6041
Pr	31:20	She stretched out her hand to the **p**;	6041
Ecc	4:13	Better is a **p** and a wise child	4542
Ecc	9:16	the **p** man's wisdom is despised	4542
Isa	14:32	**p** of his people shall trust in it	6041
Isa	41:17	the **p** and needy seek water	6041
Eze	18:17	hath taken off his hand from the **p**,	6041
Da	4:27	by shewing mercy to the **p**; if it	6033
Am	5:11	as your treading is upon the **p**, and	1800
Hab	3:14	was as to devour the **p** secretly	6041
Zec	11:7	even you, O **p** of the flock	6041
Zec	11:11	**p** of the flock that waited upon me	6041
Mt	5:3	**Blessed are the p in spirit: for**	*4434*
Mt	19:21	**that thou hast, and give to the p,**	*4434*
Mt	26:9	sold for much, and given to the **p**	*4434*
Mt	26:11	**ye have the p always with you;**	*4434*
Mk	12:43	**this p widow hath cast more in,**	*4434*
Lk	4:18	**me to preach the gospel to the p;**	*4434*
Lk	6:20	**Blessed be ye p: for yours is the**	*4434*
Lk	19:8	half of my goods I give to the **p**;	*4434*
Lk	21:3	**p widow hath cast in more than**	*4434*
1Co	13:3	I bestow all my goods to feed the **p**,	*4434*

P

2Co 8:9 yet for your sakes he became **p**,........ *4433*
Jas 2:3 say to the **p**, Stand thou there, or *4434*
Jas 2:5 not God chosen the **p** of this world *4434*
Rev 13:16 great, rich and **p**, free and bond,....... *4434*

PORCH
1Ki 7:6 he made a **p** of pillars; the length 197
1Ki 7:19 pillars were of lily work in the **p**, ... 197
1Ch 28:11 to Solomon … the pattern of the **p**,..... 197
Eze 8:16 between the **p** and the altar, were 197
Jn 10:23 in the temple in Solomon's **p**.......... 4745
Ac 3:11 in the **p** that is called Solomon's....... 4745

PORTER
1Ch 9:21 was **p** of the door of the tabernacle 7778
Jn 10:3 **To him the p openeth; and the**........ *2377*

PORTERS
Ezr 2:42 children of the **p**: the children of 7778
Ne 12:45 the **p** kept the ward of their God 7778

PORTION
Ge 14:24 and Mamre: let them take their **p**...... 2506
Nu 31:30 thou shalt take one **p** of fifty, of the..... 270
Dt 21:17 a double **p** of all that he hath:......... 6310
Dt 32:9 For the Lord's **p** is his people;......... 2506
1Sa 1:5 unto Hannah he gave a worthy **p**;...... 4490
2Ki 2:9 double **p** of thy spirit be upon me 6310
Job 20:29 the **p** of a wicked man from God...... 2506
Job 31:2 what **p** of God is there from above?.... 2506
Ps 16:5 Lord is the **p** of mine inheritance...... 4490
Ps 73:26 of my heart, and my **p** for ever 2506
Ps 119:57 Thou art my **p**, O Lord: I have 2506
Ps 142:5 and my **p** in the land of the living 2506
Jer 13:25 the **p** of thy measures from me........ 4490
Jer 51:19 The **p** of Jacob is not like them; 2506
La 3:24 The Lord is my **p**, saith my soul;....... 2506
Da 1:8 with the **p** of the king's meat, nor...... 6598
Da 1:13 eat of the **p** of the king's meat: 6598
Da 4:23 let his **p** be with the beasts of the 2508
Mt 24:51 **him his p with the hypocrites:** *3313*
Lk 12:46 **him his p with the unbelievers**........ *3313*
Lk 15:12 **give me the p of goods that falleth**..... *3313*

PORTIONS
Jos 17:5 fell ten **p** to Manasseh, besides 2256
Ne 12:44 **p** of the law for the priests and........ 4521
Ne 12:47 gave the **p** of the singers and the....... 4521
Eze 47:13 Israel: Joseph shall have two **p**......... 2256

POSSESS
Ge 24:60 let thy seed **p** the gate of those 3423
Nu 13:30 Let us go up at once, and **p** it;......... 3423
Dt 1:8 **p** the land which the Lord sware....... 3423
Dt 1:21 go up and **p** it, as the Lord God of..... 3423
Dt 4:26 ye go over Jordan to **p** it; ye shall 3423
Dt 6:1 in the land whither ye go to **p** it:....... 3423
Dt 6:18 mayest go in and **p** the good land...... 3423
Dt 11:8 be strong, and go in and **p** the land,.... 3423
Dt 11:11 the land, whither ye go to **p** it, is a 3423
Dt 11:23 **p** greater nations and mightier 3423
Dt 19:2 Lord thy God giveth thee to **p** it 3423
Job 7:3 I made to **p** months of vanity......... 5157
Job 13:26 to **p** the iniquities of my youth 3423
Isa 57:13 his trust in me shall **p** the land 5157
Isa 61:7 their land they shall **p** the double: 3423
Da 7:18 **p** the kingdom for ever, even for....... 2631
Ob 17 of Jacob shall **p** their possessions 3423
Lk 18:12 **I give tithes of all that I p** *2932*
Lk 21:19 **In your patience p ye your souls**....... *2932*
1Th 4:4 **p** his vessel in sanctification and....... *2932*

POSSESSED
Nu 21:35 them alive: and they **p** his land........ 3423
Jos 22:9 possession, whereof they were **p**, ... 270
Ne 9:24 children went in and **p** the land 3423
Ps 139:13 For thou hast **p** my reins: thou 7069
Pr 8:22 Lord **p** me in the beginning of 7069
Da 7:22 that the saints **p** the kingdom 2631
Mt 4:24 those which were **p** with devils *1139*
Mt 8:16 many that were **p** with devils; *1139*
Mt 9:32 him a dumb man **p** with a devil *1139*
Mt 12:22 one **p** with a devil, blind, and *1139*
Lk 8:36 was **p** of the devils was healed......... *1139*
Ac 16:16 damsel **p** with a spirit of divination *2192*

POSSESSION
Ge 17:8 Canaan, for an everlasting **p**;........... 272
Ge 23:18 Unto Abraham for a **p** in the.......... 4736
Ge 23:20 Abraham for a **p** of a buryingplace 272
Ge 48:4 seed after thee for an everlasting **p**...... 272
Le 25:34 be sold; for it is their perpetual **p** 272
Dt 2:9 not give thee of their land for a **p**; 3425
Jos 1:15 return unto the land of your **p** 3425
1Ki 21:15 **p** of the vineyard of Naboth the....... 3423
Ps 2:8 parts of the earth for thy **p**............. 272
Ps 69:35 may dwell there, and have it in **p** 3423
Eze 36:2 ancient high places are ours in **p**:...... 4181
Eze 36:3 might be a **p** unto the residue of....... 4181
Eze 44:28 them no **p** in Israel: I am their **p**........ 272
Ac 5:1 with Sapphira his wife, sold a **p**, ... *2933*
Ac 7:5 he would give it to him for a **p**,........ *2697*
Eph 1:14 redemption of the purchased **p**, ... *4047*

POSSESSIONS
Ecc 2:7 great **p** of great and small cattle 4735
Mt 19:22 sorrowful: for he had great **p**.......... *2933*
Mk 10:22 grieved: for he had great **p**............ *2933*
Ac 2:45 And sold their **p** and goods, and....... *2933*

POSSESSOR
Ge 14:19 high God, **p** of heaven and earth:...... 7069
Ge 14:22 God, the **p** of heaven and earth........ 7069

POSSESSORS
Zec 11:5 Whose **p** slay them, and hold 7069
Ac 4:34 **p** of lands or houses sold them, ... *2935*

POSSIBLE
Mt 26:39 **it be p, let this cup pass from me:**..... *1415*
Mk 9:23 **things are p to him that believeth**..... *1415*
Mk 10:27 **God: for with God all things are p**..... *1415*
Mk 14:35 if it were **p**, the hour might pass....... *1415*
Mk 14:36 **Father, all things are p unto thee;**...... *1415*
Lk 18:27 **impossible with men are p with**....... *1415*
Ro 12:18 If it be **p**, as much as lieth in you *1415*
Heb 10:4 it is not **p** that the blood of bulls *102*

POST
Ex 12:7 on the upper door **p** of the houses, ... 4947
Jer 51:31 One **p** shall run to meet another, ... 7323
Eze 40:14 the **p** of the court round about the...... 352

POSTERITY
Ge 45:7 to preserve you a **p** in the earth 7611
Ps 49:13 yet their **p** approve their sayings........ 310
Ps 109:13 Let his **p** be cut off; and in the 319

POSTS

Ex	12:23	the lintel, and on the two side **p**,	4201
Dt	6:9	write them upon the **p** of thy house,	4201
Dt	11:20	write them upon the door **p** of	4201
Jgs	16:3	gate of the city, and the two **p**,	4201
2Ch	3:7	beams, the **p**, and … walls thereof,	5592
Est	3:13	the letters were sent by **p** into all	7323
Est	8:10	and sent letters by **p** on horseback,	7323
Est	8:14	So the **p** that rode upon mules and	7323
Am	9:1	the door, that the **p** may shake:	5592

POT

Ex	16:33	Take a **p**, and put an omer full of	6803
2Ki	4:2	thing in the house, save a **p** of oil	610
Job	41:20	as out of a seething **p** or caldron.	1731
Pr	17:3	The fining **p** is for silver, and the	4715
Heb	9:4	was the golden **p** that had manna,	*4713*

POTS

Ps	68:13	Though ye have lien among the **p**,	8240
Mk	7:4	**p**, brasen vessels, and of tables.	*3582*
Mk	7:8	**as the washing of p and cups:**	*3582*

POTSHERD

Job	2:8	he took him a **p** to scrape himself	2789
Ps	22:15	My strength is dried up like a **p**;	2789
Pr	26:23	and a wicked heart are like a **p**	2789

POTTAGE

Ge	25:30	I pray thee, with that same red **p**;	
Ge	25:34	gave Esau bread and **p** of lentiles;	5138

POTTER

Jer	18:4	was marred in the hand of the **p**.	3335
Jer	18:4	as seemed good to the **p** to make it	3335
Jer	18:6	cannot I do with you as this **p**?	3335
Ro	9:21	not the **p** power over the clay,	*2763*
Rev	2:27	**as the vessels of a p shall they be.**	*2764*

POTTER'S

Jer	18:2	Arise, and go down to the **p** house,	3335
Jer	18:3	I went down to the **p** house, and,	3335
Jer	18:6	Behold, as the clay is in the **p** hand,	3335
Da	2:41	part of **p** clay, and part of iron,	6353
Mt	27:7	bought with them the **p** field, to	*2763*
Mt	27:10	And gave them for the **p** field, as	*2763*

POUND

1Ki	10:17	three **p** of gold went to one shield:	4488
Lk	19:16	**thy p hath gained ten pounds**	*3414*
Lk	19:18	**thy p hath gained five pounds**	*3414*
Lk	19:20	**here is thy p, which I have kept**	*3414*
Lk	19:24	**Take from him the p, and give it.**	*3414*
Jn	19:39	aloes, about a hundred **p** weight	*3046*

POUNDS

Lk	19:13	**and delivered them ten p,**	*3414*
Lk	19:16	**thy pound hath gained ten p.**	*3414*
Lk	19:18	**thy pound hath gained five p**	*3414*
Lk	19:24	**and give it to him that hath ten p.**	*3414*
Lk	19:25	**unto him, Lord, he hath ten p.**	*3414*

POUR

Ex	4:9	river, and **p** it upon the dry land:	8210
Ex	29:7	and **p** it upon his head, and anoint	3332
Le	4:7	shall **p** all the blood of the bullock	8210
Le	14:18	he shall **p** upon the head of him	5414
Le	14:26	priest shall **p** of the oil into the	3332
Jgs	6:20	this rock, and **p** out the broth	8210
2Ki	9:3	the box of oil, and **p** it on his head,	3332
Job	36:27	they **p** down rain according to the	2212
Ps	62:8	**p** out your heart before him: God	8210
Ps	79:6	**P** out thy wrath upon the heathen	8210
Pr	1:23	I will **p** out my spirit unto you, I	5042
Isa	44:3	**p** water upon him that is thirsty,	3332
Isa	44:3	I will **p** my spirit upon thy seed,	3332
Joel	2:28	will **p** out my spirit upon all flesh;	8210
Joel	2:29	those days will I **p** out my spirit	8210
Ac	2:17	**p** out of my Spirit upon all flesh:	*1632*
Ac	2:18	**p** out in those days of my Spirit;	*1632*
Rev	16:1	**p** out the vials of the wrath of God	*1632*

POURED

Ge	35:14	and he **p** a drink offering thereon.	5258
Ex	9:33	the rain was not **p** upon the earth.	5413
Le	8:12	And he **p** of the anointing oil upon	3332
Nu	28:7	cause the strong wine to be **p**	5258
Dt	12:27	**p** out upon the altar of the Lord.	8210
1Sa	1:15	**p** out my soul before the Lord,	8210
1Sa	10:1	vial of oil, and **p** it upon his head,	3332
2Ki	3:11	**p** water on the hands of Elijah	3332
Job	3:24	roarings are **p** out like the waters	5413
Job	29:6	the rock **p** me out rivers of oil;	6694
Job	30:16	now my soul is **p** out upon me;	8210
Ps	45:2	grace is **p** into thy lips: therefore.	3332
Isa	26:16	they **p** out a prayer when thy.	6694
Isa	32:15	spirit be **p** upon us from on high	6168
Isa	57:6	hast thou **p** a drink offering, thou	8210
Isa	53:12	hath **p** out his soul unto death:	6168
La	2:4	Zion: he **p** out his fury like fire	8210
Eze	39:29	**p** out my spirit upon the house	8210
Da	9:11	therefore the curse is **p** upon us,	5413
Mt	26:7	ointment, and **p** it on his head	*2708*
Mt	26:12	**hath p this ointment on my body,**	*906*
Ac	10:45	**p** out the gift of the Holy Ghost	*1632*
Rev	16:3	angel **p** out his vial upon the sea;	*1632*
Rev	16:4	**p** out his vial upon the rivers and	*1632*
Rev	16:8	angel **p** out his vial upon the sun;	*1632*
Rev	16:12	**p** out his vial upon the great river.	*1632*
Rev	16:17	angel **p** out his vial into the air;	*1632*

POURETH

Job	16:20	mine eye **p** out tears unto God	1811
Ps	107:40	He **p** contempt upon princes, and	8210
Pr	15:2	mouth of fools **p** out foolishness	5042
Pr	15:28	of the wicked **p** out evil things	5042
Jn	13:5	After that he **p** water into a bason,	*906*

POURTRAYED

Eze	23:14	she saw men **p** upon the wall,	2707

POVERTY

Ge	45:11	and all that thou hast, come to **p**	3423
Pr	20:13	not sleep, lest thou come to **p**;	3423
Pr	23:21	and the glutton shall come to **p**:	3423
Pr	30:8	give me neither **p** nor riches;	7389
Pr	31:7	Let him drink, and forget his **p**,	7389
2Co	8:9	ye through his **p** might be rich	*4432*
Rev	2:9	**thy works, and tribulation, and p,**	*4432*

POWDER

Ex	32:20	it in the fire, and ground it to **p**,	1854
Mt	21:44	**shall fall, it will grind him to p**	*3039*

POWER

Ge	31:6	with all my **p** I have served your	3581
Ge	31:29	the **p** of my hand to do you hurt:	410

Ge	32:28	prince hast **p** with God and with	8280
Ex	9:16	up, for to shew in thee my **p**;	3581
Ex	15:6	O Lord, is become glorious in **p**:	3581
Dt	8:17	My **p** and the might of mine hand	3581
1Sa	9:1	a Benjamite, a mighty man of **p**	2428
1Sa	30:4	until they had no more **p** to weep	3581
2Sa	22:33	God is my strength and **p**: and	2428
1Ch	29:11	and the **p**, and the glory, and the	1369
1Ch	29:12	in thine hand is **p** and might;	3581
2Ch	25:8	God hath **p** to help, and to cast	3581
Ne	1:10	hast redeemed by thy great **p**,	3581
Est	9:1	Jews hoped to have **p** over them	7980
Est	10:2	the acts of his **p** and of his might	8633
Job	1:12	all that he hath is in thy **p**; only	3027
Job	23:6	against me with his great **p**?	3581
Job	26:12	He divideth the sea with his **p**	3581
Job	37:23	he is excellent in **p**, and in	3581
Job	41:12	not conceal his parts, nor his **p**,	1369
Ps	21:13	so will we sing and praise thy **p**	1369
Ps	49:15	my soul from the **p** of the grave:	3027
Ps	59:16	But I will sing of thy **p**; yea, I	5797
Ps	63:2	To see thy **p** and thy glory, so as I	5797
Ps	66:7	He ruleth by his **p** for ever; his	1369
Ps	106:8	make his mighty **p** to be known	1369
Ps	145:11	thy kingdom, and talk of thy **p**;	1369
Ps	147:5	Great is our Lord, and of great **p**:	3581
Ps	150:1	him in the firmament of his **p**	5797
Pr	18:21	and life are in the **p** of the tongue:	3027
Ecc	8:4	the word of a king is, there is **p**:	7983
Ecc	8:8	no man that hath **p** over the spirit	7989
Isa	40:26	might, for that he is strong in **p**;	3581
Isa	40:29	He giveth **p** to the faint; and to	3581
Jer	27:5	my great **p** and by my outstretched	3581
Jer	32:17	by thy great **p** and stretched out	3581
Da	2:37	given thee a kingdom, **p**, and	2632
Da	3:27	upon whose bodies the fire had no **p**,	7981
Da	6:27	Daniel from the **p** of the lions	3028
Da	11:25	shall stir up his **p** and his courage	3581
Hos	12:3	his strength he had **p** with God:	8280
Hos	12:4	Yea, he had **p** over the angel, and	7786
Hos	13:14	ransom … from the **p** of the grave:	3027
Na	1:3	is slow to anger, and great in **p**,	3581
Hab	2:9	be delivered from the **p** of evil!	3709
Zec	4:6	Not by might, nor by **p**, but by my	3581
Mt	6:13	**kingdom, and the p, and the**	*1411*
Mt	9:6	**Son of man hath p on earth to**	*1849*
Mt	22:29	**the scriptures, nor the p of God.**	*1411*
Mt	24:30	**of heaven with p and great glory.**	*1411*
Mt	26:64	sitting on the right hand of **p**,	*1411*
Mt	28:18	All **p** is given unto me in heaven	*1849*
Mk	9:1	**the kingdom of God come with p**	*1411*
Lk	1:17	him in the spirit and **p** of Elias, to	*1411*
Lk	1:35	**p** of the Highest shall overshadow	*1411*
Lk	4:14	returned in the **p** of the Spirit into	*1411*
Lk	5:17	**p** of the Lord was present to heal	*1411*
Lk	5:24	**Son of man hath p upon earth to.**	*1849*
Lk	9:1	**p** and authority over all devils,	*1411*
Lk	9:43	amazed at the mighty **p** of God	*3168*
Lk	10:19	**unto you p to tread on serpents**	*1849*
Lk	12:5	**killed hath p to cast into hell;**	*1849*
Lk	21:27	**of man coming in a cloud with p**	*1411*
Lk	22:53	**your hour, and the p of darkness.**	*1849*
Lk	24:49	**be endued with p from on high.**	*1411*
Jn	1:12	gave he **p** to become the sons of God,	*1849*
Jn	10:18	**I have p to lay it down, and I**	*1849*
Jn	10:18	**and I have p to take it again.**	*1849*
Jn	17:2	**hast given him p over all flesh,**	*1849*
Jn	19:10	not that I have **p** to crucify thee,	*1849*
Jn	19:10	thee, and have **p** to release thee?	*1849*
Jn	19:11	**have no p at all against me,**	*1849*
Ac	1:7	**the Father hath put in his own p**	*1849*
Ac	1:8	**But ye shall receive p, after that**	*1411*
Ac	4:7	By what **p**, or by what name, have	*1411*
Ac	4:33	great **p** gave the apostles witness	*1411*
Ac	5:4	sold, was it not in thine own **p**?	*1849*
Ac	6:8	Stephen, full of faith and **p**, did	*1411*
Ac	8:19	Saying, Give me also this **p**, that	*1849*
Ac	26:18	**and from the p of Satan unto God,**	*1849*
Ro	1:16	it is the **p** of God unto salvation	*1411*
Ro	1:20	even his eternal **p** and Godhead;	*1411*
Ro	9:21	not the potter **p** over the clay,	*1849*
Ro	9:22	wrath, and to make his **p** known,	*1415*
Ro	13:3	thou then not be afraid of the **p**?	*1849*
Ro	15:13	through the **p** of the Holy Ghost	*1411*
Ro	15:19	by the **p** of the Spirit of God; so	*1411*
1Co	1:18	which are saved it is the **p** of God	*1411*
1Co	1:24	Christ the **p** of God, and the	*1411*
1Co	2:4	demonstration of … Spirit and of **p**:	*1411*
1Co	2:5	of men, but in the **p** of God	*1411*
1Co	5:4	with the **p** of our Lord Jesus Christ,	*1411*
1Co	6:12	not be brought under the **p** of any.	*1850*
1Co	7:4	wife hath not **p** of her own body,	*1850*
1Co	7:4	hath not **p** of his own body, but	*1850*
1Co	9:18	I abuse not my **p** in the gospel	*1849*
1Co	15:43	in weakness; it is raised in **p**:	*1411*
2Co	4:7	excellency of the **p** may be of God,	*1411*
2Co	6:7	the word of truth, by the **p** of God,	*1411*
2Co	13:4	yet he liveth by the **p** of God.	*1411*
Eph	1:19	the exceeding greatness of his **p**	*1411*
Eph	1:19	to the working of his mighty **p**,	*2904*
Eph	1:21	all principality, and **p**, and might,	*1849*
Eph	2:2	to the prince of the **p** of the air,	*1849*
Eph	3:20	to the **p** that worketh in us,	*1411*
Eph	6:10	Lord, and in the **p** of his might.	*2904*
Php	3:10	him, and the **p** of his resurrection,	*1411*
Col	1:13	us from the **p** of darkness, and	*1849*
Col	2:10	the head of all principality and **p**:	*1849*
2Th	1:9	Lord, and from the glory of his **p**;	*2479*
2Ti	1:7	of **p**, and of love, and of a sound	*1411*
2Ti	1:8	gospel according to the **p** of God;	*1411*
2Ti	3:5	but denying the **p** thereof: from	*1411*
Heb	1:3	all things by the word of his **p**,	*1411*
1Pe	1:5	kept by the **p** of God through faith	*1411*
2Pe	1:16	you the **p** and coming of our Lord	*1411*
Jude	25	and majesty, dominion and **p**,	*1849*
Rev	2:26	**will I give p over the nations:**	*1849*
Rev	4:11	to receive glory and honour and **p**:	*1411*
Rev	5:12	Lamb that was slain to receive **p**,	*1411*
Rev	5:13	and honour, and glory, and **p**, be	*2904*
Rev	7:12	**p**, and might, be unto our God	*1411*
Rev	9:3	**p**, as the scorpions of the earth have **p**	*1849*
Rev	9:10	**p** was to hurt men five months,	*1849*
Rev	9:19	their **p** is in their mouth, and in	*1849*
Rev	11:3	I will give **p** unto my two witnesses,	
Rev	12:10	our God, and the **p** of his Christ:	*1849*
Rev	13:2	the dragon gave him his **p**, and	*1411*
Rev	13:12	he exerciseth all the **p** of the first	*1849*
Rev	13:14	miracles which he had **p** to do in	*1325*
Rev	13:15	And he had **p** to give life unto the	*1325*
Rev	14:18	the altar, which had **p** over fire;	*1849*
Rev	16:8	**p** was given unto him to scorch men	
Rev	17:12	receive **p** as kings one hour with	*1849*

Rev 19:1	honour, and **p**, unto the Lord our......	*1411*
Rev 20:6	such the second death hath no **p**,......	*1849*

POWERFUL

Ps 29:4	The voice of the Lord is **p**; the.........	3581
2Co 10:10	his letters, ... are weighty and **p**;.......	*2478*
Heb 4:12	the word of God is quick, and **p**, ...	*1756*

POWERS

Mt 24:29	**p of the heavens shall be shaken:**.......	*1411*
Lk 12:11	**unto magistrates, and p, take ye**.......	*1849*
Ro 8:38	angels, nor principalities, nor **p**,.......	*1411*
Ro 13:1	soul be subject unto the higher **p**......	*1849*
Eph 3:10	and **p** in heavenly places might be	*1849*
Eph 6:12	against principalities, against **p**, ...	*1849*
Heb 6:5	and the **p** of the world to come,.......	*1411*

PRACTISE

Ps 141:4	to **p** wicked works with men that......	5953
Mic 2:1	when the morning is light, they **p** it, ...	6213

PRACTISED

1Sa 23:9	Saul secretly **p** mischief against........	2790
Da 8:12	ground; and it **p**, and prospered.	6213

PRAISE

Ge 29:35	she said, Now will I **p** the Lord:	3034
Dt 10:21	He is thy **p**, and he is thy God, ...	8416
Jgs 5:2	**P** ye the Lord for the avenging	1288
1Ch 16:35	thy holy name, and glory in thy **p**......	8416
1Ch 29:13	thee, and **p** thy glorious name.........	1984
2Ch 20:19	stood up to **p** the Lord God of	1984
2Ch 20:21	should **p** the beauty of holiness,........	1984
2Ch 20:21	the army, and to say, **P** the Lord;.......	3034
Ezr 3:10	**p** the Lord, after the ordinance of......	1984
Ne 9:5	exalted above all blessing and **p**	8416
Ne 12:46	songs of **p** and thanksgiving unto......	8416
Ps 7:17	I will **p** the Lord according to his	3034
Ps 9:1	I will **p** thee, O Lord, with my.........	3034
Ps 9:14	I may shew forth all thy **p** in the.......	8416
Ps 21:13	so will we sing and **p** thy power	2167
Ps 22:25	My **p** shall be of thee in the great......	8416
Ps 28:7	and with my song will I **p** him.........	3034
Ps 33:1	for **p** is comely for the upright.........	8416
Ps 34:1	his **p** shall continually be in my	8416
Ps 35:28	and of thy **p** all the day long...........	8416
Ps 42:11	for I shall yet **p** him, who is the........	3034
Ps 43:4	upon the harp will I **p** thee, O God	3034
Ps 43:5	for I shall yet **p** him, who is the........	3034
Ps 51:15	my mouth shall shew forth thy **p**......	8416
Ps 52:9	I will **p** thee for ever, because	3034
Ps 54:6	I will **p** thy name, O Lord; for it is	3034
Ps 56:10	In God will I **p** his word; in the	1984
Ps 63:3	than life, my lips shall **p** thee..........	7623
Ps 66:2	of his name: make his **p** glorious.......	8416
Ps 67:5	Let the people **p** thee, O God; let	3034
Ps 71:6	my **p** shall be continually of thee.......	8416
Ps 89:5	the heavens shall **p** thy wonders,.......	*3034*
Ps 100:4	and into his courts with **p**:............	8416
Ps 102:21	in Zion, and his **p** in Jerusalem;	8416
Ps 107:8	Oh that men would **p**................	3034
Ps 108:1	I will sing and give **p**, even with	2167
Ps 111:1	**p** the Lord with my whole heart, ...	3034
Ps 112:1	**P** ye the Lord. Blessed is the	1984
Ps 113:9	mother of children. **P** ye the Lord	1984
Ps 117:2	endureth for ever. **P** ye the Lord.	1984
Ps 118:21	I will **p** thee: for thou hast heard	3034
Ps 118:28	Thou art my God, and I will **p** thee:....	3034
Ps 119:175	my soul live, and it shall **p** thee;	1984
Ps 135:3	**P** the Lord; for the Lord is good:	1984
Ps 138:1	will **p** thee with my whole heart:	3034
Ps 139:14	I will **p** thee; for I am fearfully	3034
Ps 145:2	I will **p** thy name for ever and.........	1984
Ps 145:21	shall speak the **p** of the Lord:	8416
Ps 146:2	While I live I will **p** the Lord: I will	1984
Ps 147:1	it is pleasant; and **p** is comely	8416
Ps 148:3	**P** ye him, sun and moon:.............	1984
Ps 148:4	**P** him, ye heavens of heavens, and	1984
Ps 148:5	Let them **p** the name of the Lord:......	1984
Ps 150:1	**P** ye the Lord.	1984
Ps 150:1	**P** God in his sanctuary:..............	1984
Ps 150:2	**P** him for his mighty acts;............	1984
Ps 150:2	**p** him according to his excellent.......	1984
Ps 150:3	**p** him with the psaltery and harp.	1984
Ps 150:4	**P** him with the timbrel and dance:.....	1984
Ps 150:4	**p** him with stringed instruments	1984
Ps 150:5	**P** him upon the loud cymbals:.........	1984
Ps 150:5	**p** him upon the high sounding........	1984
Ps 150:6	that hath breath **p** the Lord.	1984
Pr 27:2	Let another man **p** thee, and not	1984
Pr 28:4	that forsake the law **p** the wicked:......	1984
Pr 31:31	her own works **p** her in the gates	1984
Isa 12:4	**P** the Lord, call upon his name, ...	3034
Isa 38:18	For the grave cannot **p** thee, death.....	3034
Isa 60:18	walls Salvation, and thy gates **P**........	8416
Jer 17:14	I shall be saved: for thou art my **p**	8416
Jer 17:26	sacrifices of **p** unto the house of.......	8426
Jer 33:11	**P** the Lord of hosts: for the Lord	3034
Jer 33:11	shall bring the sacrifice of **p** into	8426
Da 4:37	Now I Nebuchadnezzar **p** and extol....	7624
Joel 2:26	**p** the name of the Lord your God,.....	1984
Zep 3:20	and a **p** among all people of the.......	8416
Mt 21:16	**sucklings thou hast perfected p?**........	*136*
Lk 18:43	when they saw it, gave **p** unto God.	*136*
Lk 19:37	rejoice and **p** God with a loud voice.....	*134*
Jn 9:24	said unto him, Give God the **p**: we.....	*1391*
Jn 12:43	For they loved the **p** of men more	*1391*
Ro 2:29	whose **p** is not of men, but of God.	*1868*
Ro 15:11	again, **P** the Lord, all ye Gentiles;	*134*
Eph 1:6	To the **p** of the glory of his grace,......	*1868*
Eph 1:12	to the **p** of his glory, who first.........	*1868*
Php 1:11	Christ, unto the glory and **p** of God....	*1868*
Php 4:8	if there be any **p**, think on these	*1868*
Heb 13:15	let us offer the sacrifice of **p** to God.....	*133*
1Pe 4:11	whom be **p** and dominion for ever.....	*1391*
Rev 19:5	**P** our God, all ye his servants,..........	*134*

PRAISED

Jgs 16:24	people saw him, they **p** their god:......	1984
1Ch 16:25	is the Lord, and greatly to be **p**:........	1984
2Ch 7:3	and worshipped, and **p** the Lord, ...	3034
Ezr 3:11	great shout, when they **p** the Lord,.....	1984
Ne 5:13	said, Amen, and **p** the Lord, ...	1984
Ps 48:1	greatly to be **p** in the city of our	1984
Ps 96:4	Lord is great, and greatly to be **p**:......	1984
Pr 31:30	feareth the Lord, she shall be **p**........	1984
Da 4:34	I **p** and honoured him that liveth......	7624
Lk 1:64	loosed, and he spake, and **p** God.......	*2127*

PRAISES

Ex 15:11	fearful in **p**, doing wonders?	8416
Ps 22:3	that inhabitest the **p** of Israel..........	8416
Ps 47:6	Sing **p** to God, sing **p**:	

P

Ps 78:4 **p** of the Lord, and his strength,........ 8416
Ps 135:3 Lord is good: sing **p** unto his name;
Ps 147:1 it is good to sing **p** unto our God;
Ac 16:25 prayed, and sang **p** unto God:
1Pe 2:9 shew forth the **p** of him who hath *703*

PRAISING
Ezr 3:11 **p** and giving thanks unto the Lord; 1984
Ps 84:4 thy house: they will be still **p** thee...... 1984
Lk 2:13 heavenly host, **p** God, and saying,....... *134*
Lk 2:20 glorifying and **p** God for all the *134*
Lk 24:53 in the temple, **p** and blessing God....... *134*
Ac 3:8 walking, and leaping, and **p** God........ *134*

PRATING
Pr 10:8 but a **p** fool shall fall. 8193
Pr 10:10 sorrow: but a **p** fool shall fall.......... 8193
3Jn 10 **p** against us with malicious *5396*

PRAY
Ge 12:13 Say, I **p** thee, thou art my sister: 4994
Ge 13:9 separate thyself, I **p** thee, from me:..... 4994
Ge 24:2 Put, I **p** thee, thy hand under my 4994
Ge 24:43 Give me, I **p** thee, a little water of...... 4994
Ge 27:19 I **p** thee, sit and eat of my venison,..... 4994
Ge 27:21 Come near, I **p** thee, that I may........ 4994
Ge 37:6 Hear, I **p** you, this dream which I...... 4994
Ge 50:17 Forgive, I **p** thee now, the trespass 577
Ge 50:17 we **p** thee, forgive the trespass of....... 4994
Ex 5:3 let us go, we **p** thee, three days' 4994
Ex 10:17 forgive, I **p** thee, my sin only this 4994
Jos 2:12 I **p** you, swear unto me by the Lord, ... 4994
Jgs 8:5 Give, I **p** you, loaves of bread unto..... 4994
Jgs 16:28 Lord God, remember me, I **p** thee,..... 4994
Jgs 16:28 strengthen me, I **p** thee, only this 4994
Ru 2:7 I **p** you, let me glean and gather 4994
1Sa 7:5 I will **p** for you unto the Lord......... 6419
1Sa 15:25 I **p** thee, pardon my sin, and turn...... 4994
1Sa 15:30 honour me now, I **p** thee, before....... 4994
1Sa 16:22 Let David, I **p** thee, stand before....... 4994
2Sa 13:5 him, I **p** thee, let my sister Tamar 4994
2Sa 13:6 I **p** thee, let Tamar my sister come,..... 4994
2Sa 13:26 I **p** thee, let my brother Amnon go..... 4994
1Ki 2:17 I **p** thee, unto Solomon the king, ... 4994
1Ki 14:2 wife, Arise, I **p** thee, and disguise 4994
1Ki 17:10 Fetch me, I **p** thee, a little water in 4994
1Ki 17:11 Bring me, I **p** thee, a morsel of 4994
1Ki 17:21 I **p** thee, let this child's soul come...... 4994
2Ki 1:13 O man of God, I **p** thee, let my life, ... 4994
2Ki 2:2 unto Elisha, Tarry here, I **p** thee;....... 4994
2Ki 2:16 let them go, we **p** thee, and seek thy.... 4994
2Ch 7:14 humble themselves, and **p**, and seek.... 6419
Ezr 6:10 **p** for the life of the king, and of 6739
Ne 5:11 Restore, I **p** you, to them, even this 4994
Job 21:15 should we have, if we **p** unto him?..... 6293
Job 22:22 Receive, I **p** thee, the law from his 4994
Job 33:26 He shall **p** unto God, and he will 6279
Ps 5:2 and my God: for unto thee will I **p**..... 6419
Ps 55:17 and morning, and at noon will I **p**..... 7878
Ps 119:76 Let, I **p** thee, thy merciful kindness..... 4994
Ps 122:6 **P** for the peace of Jerusalem: they 7592
Mt 5:44 **P for them which despitefully use.**..... *4336*
Mt 6:5 **to p standing in the synagogues** *4336*
Mt 6:6 **P to thy Father which is in secret;** *4336*
Mt 6:7 **ye p, use not vain repetitions,**......... *4336*
Mt 6:9 **After this manner therefore p ye:**...... *4336*
Mt 14:23 up into a mountain apart to **p**:........ *4336*
Mt 26:36 **ye here, while I go and p yonder**....... *4336*
Mt 26:41 **Watch and p, that ye enter not** *4336*
Mt 26:53 **that I cannot now p to my Father,** *3870*
Mk 11:24 **ye desire, when ye p, believe** *4336*
Mk 13:18 **p ye that your flight be not in the** *4336*
Mk 13:33 **watch and p: for ye know not** *4336*
Lk 6:28 **p for them which despitefully use** *4336*
Lk 11:1 unto him, Lord, teach us to **p**,......... *4336*
Lk 11:2 **When ye p, say, Our Father**........... *4336*
Lk 18:1 men ought always to **p**, and not *4336*
Lk 18:10 **went up into the temple to p;** *4336*
Lk 22:46 **p, lest ye enter into temptation.**....... *4336*
Jn 14:16 **I will p the Father, and he shall.**....... *2065*
Jn 17:9 **I p for them: I p not for the.**.......... *2065*
Jn 17:20 **Neither p I for these alone, but.**....... *2065*
Ac 8:24 **P** ye to the Lord for me, that *1189*
Ac 10:9 went up upon the housetop to **p**....... *4336*
Ro 8:26 we should **p** for as we ought:.......... *4336*
1Co 14:13 tongue **p** that he may interpret *4336*
1Co 14:14 if I **p** in an unknown tongue, my *4336*
1Co 14:15 it then? I will **p** with the spirit, ... *4336*
1Co 14:15 will **p** with the understanding also: *4336*
1Th 5:17 **P** without ceasing.................... *4336*
Jas 5:13 among you afflicted? let him **p** *4336*
Jas 5:14 let them **p** over him, anointing *4336*
Jas 5:16 **p** one for another, that ye may *2172*

PRAYED
Ge 20:17 So Abraham **p** unto God: and......... 6419
Nu 11:2 when Moses **p** unto the Lord,......... 6419
1Sa 1:27 For this child I **p**; and the Lord........ 6419
1Sa 2:1 Hannah **p**, and said, My heart......... 6419
2Ki 6:17 Elisha **p**, and said, Lord, I pray 6419
2Ki 19:15 Hezekiah **p** before the Lord, and....... 6419
Ezr 10:1 Now when Ezra had **p**, and when...... 6419
Ne 2:4 So I **p** to the God of heaven........... 6419
Job 42:10 Job, when he **p** for his friends: 6419
Da 6:10 **p**, and gave thanks before his 6739
Jnh 2:1 Jonah **p** unto the Lord his God........ 6419
Mt 26:39 fell on his face, and **p**, saying, ... *4336*
Mt 26:42 away the second time, and **p** *4336*
Mt 26:44 **p** the third time, saying the same *4336*
Mk 1:35 a solitary place, and there **p**.......... *4336*
Mk 14:35 and **p** that, if it were possible, ... *4336*
Lk 18:11 **stood and p thus with himself,**........ *4336*
Lk 22:44 in an agony he **p** more earnestly: *4336*
Ac 4:31 And when they had **p**, the place *1189*
Ac 16:9 man of Macedonia, and **p** him,........ *3870*
Ac 16:25 Paul and Silas **p**, and sang *4336*
Jas 5:17 he **p** earnestly that it might not........ *4336*
Jas 5:18 he **p** again, and the heaven gave *4336*

PRAYER
2Sa 7:27 heart to pray this **p** unto thee 8605
1Ki 9:3 him, I have heard thy **p** and thy 8605
2Ch 30:27 and their **p** came up to his holy 8605
Ne 1:6 hear the **p** of thy servant, which 8605
Ne 11:17 begin the thanksgiving in **p**: and 8605
Job 16:17 mine hands: also my **p** is pure......... 8605
Ps 4:1 mercy upon me, and hear my **p** 8605
Ps 64:1 Hear my voice, O God, in my **p** 7879
Ps 72:15 **p** also shall be made for him.......... 6419
Ps 88:2 Let my **p** come before thee: incline..... 8605
Ps 109:7 and let his **p** become sin.............. 8605
Pr 15:8 the **p** of the upright is his delight. 8605
Pr 28:9 his **p** shall be an abomination. 8605

Isa 37:4 thy **p** for the remnant that is left. 8605
Isa 56:7 house shall be called an house of **p** 8605
Da 9:13 we not our **p** before the Lord our 2470
Mt 17:21 **not out but by p and fasting.** *4335*
Mt 21:13 **shall be called the house of p; but** *4335*
Mt 21:22 **whatsoever ye shall ask in p,** *4335*
Lk 1:13 not, Zacharias: for thy **p** is heard; *1162*
Lk 19:46 **My house is the house of p: but** *4335*
Ac 6:4 will give ourselves continually to **p**, *4335*
Ac 12:5 but **p** was made without ceasing of *4335*
Ro 12:12 continuing instant in **p**; *4335*
1Co 7:5 give yourselves to fasting and **p**; *4335*
Eph 6:18 Praying always with all **p** and *4535*
Php 1:19 to my salvation through your **p**, *1162*
Php 4:6 every thing by **p** and supplication. *4535*
Jas 5:15 the **p** of faith shall save the sick, *2171*
Jas 5:16 fervent **p** of a righteous man *1162*

PRAYERS

Ps 72:20 **p** of David the son of Jesse are 8605
Mk 12:40 **and for a pretence make long p** *4336*
Ac 2:42 **and in breaking of bread, and in p.** *4335*
Ro 1:9 mention of you always in my **p**; *4335*
2Ti 1:3 have remembrance of thee in my **p** *1162*
Phm 4 mention of thee always in my **p**, *4335*
Heb 5:7 he had offered up **p** ... supplications *1162*
Rev 5:8 odours, which are the **p** of saints. *4335*

PRAYEST

Mt 6:5 **when thou p, thou shalt not be as** *4336*
Mt 6:6 **when thou p, enter into thy closet** *4336*

PRAYETH

1Ki 8:28 thy servant **p** before thee to day: 6419
Ac 9:11 **Saul, of Tarsus: for, behold, he p,** *4336*
1Co 11:5 every woman that **p** or prophesieth *4336*

PRAYING

1Sa 1:12 she continued **p** before the Lord, 6419
Da 6:11 and found Daniel **p** and making. 1156
Mk 11:25 **when ye stand p, forgive, if ye** *4336*
Lk 3:21 Jesus also being baptized, and **p**, *4336*
Eph 6:18 **P** always with all prayer and *4336*
Jude 20 holy faith, **p** in the Holy Ghost, *4336*

PREACH

Ne 6:7 prophets to **p** of thee at Jerusalem, 7121
Isa 61:1 anointed me to **p** good tidings 1319
Mt 10:7 **ye go, p, saying, The kingdom of** *2784*
Mt 10:27 **ear, that p ye upon the housetops.** *2784*
Mk 1:4 **p** the baptism of repentance for the *2784*
Mk 1:38 **towns, that I may p there also:** *2784*
Mk 16:15 **and p the gospel to every creature.** *2784*
Lk 4:18 **me to p the gospel to the poor;** *2097*
Lk 4:18 **to p deliverance to the captives,** *2784*
Lk 4:19 **p the acceptable year of the Lord** *2784*
Ac 5:42 not to teach and **p** Jesus Christ. *2097*
Ro 1:15 I am ready to **p** the gospel to you *2097*
Ro 10:15 shall they **p**, except they be sent? *2784*
Ro 10:15 of them that **p** the gospel of peace, *2097*
1Co 1:23 But we **p** Christ crucified, unto the *2784*
2Co 4:5 For we **p** not ourselves, but Christ *2784*
Gal 1:8 **p** any other gospel unto you than *2097*
Php 1:15 Some indeed **p** Christ even of envy *2784*
Php 1:16 The one **p** Christ of contention, *2605*
2Ti 4:2 **P** the word; be instant in season, *2784*

PREACHED

Ps 40:9 have **p** righteousness in the great 1319
Mt 11:5 **poor have the gospel p to them.** *2097*
Mt 24:14 **be p in all the world for a witness** *2784*
Mk 6:12 and **p** that men should repent. *2784*
Mk 14:9 **this gospel shall be p throughout** *2784*
Lk 7:22 **raised, to the poor the gospel is p.** *2097*
Lk 16:16 **time the kingdom of God is p,** *2097*
Lk 24:47 **should be p in his name among** *2784*
Ac 4:2 **p** through Jesus the resurrection *2605*
Ac 8:25 testified and **p** the word of the *2980*
Ac 9:27 how he had **p** boldly at Damascus *3954*
Ac 10:37 after the baptism which John **p**; *2784*
Ac 13:38 **p** unto you the forgiveness of sins: *2605*
Ac 17:18 because he **p** unto them Jesus, *2907*
1Co 15:1 you the gospel which I **p** unto you, *2097*
1Co 15:12 if Christ be **p** that he rose from the *2784*
2Co 11:4 Jesus, whom we have not **p**, *2784*
2Co 11:7 I have **p** to you the gospel of God. *2097*
Php 1:18 pretence, or in truth, Christ is **p**; *2605*
Heb 4:2 but the word **p** did not profit them, *189*
Heb 4:6 and they to whom it was first **p**. *2097*
1Pe 3:19 and **p** unto the spirits in prison; *2784*
1Pe 4:6 for this cause was the gospel **p** *2097*

PREACHER

Ecc 1:1 words of the **P**, the son of David 6953
Ro 10:14 how shall they hear without a **p**? *2784*
2Pe 2:5 eighth person, a **p** of righteousness, *2783*

PREACHETH

Ac 19:13 you by Jesus whom Paul **p**. *2784*
2Co 11:4 if he that cometh **p** another Jesus, *2784*

PREACHING

Jnh 3:2 unto it the **p** that I bid thee. 7150
Mt 4:23 and **p** the gospel of the kingdom, *2784*
Mt 12:41 **they repented at the p of Jonas;** *2782*
Lk 3:3 **p** the baptism of repentance for *2784*
Lk 9:6 **p** the gospel, and healing every *2097*
Ac 8:12 believed Philip **p** the things *2097*
Ro 16:25 gospel, and the **p** of Jesus Christ, *2782*
1Co 1:18 For the **p** of the cross is to them *3056*
1Co 1:21 by the foolishness of **p** to save *2782*
1Co 15:14 be not risen, then is our **p** vain, *2782*

PRECEPT

Isa 28:10 **p** must be upon **p**, **p** upon **p**; 6673
Isa 28:13 unto them **p** upon **p**, **p** upon **p**; 6673
Mk 10:5 **your heart he wrote you this p** *1785*

PRECEPTS

Ne 9:14 and commandedst them **p**, 4687
Ps 119:4 commanded us to keep thy **p** 6490
Ps 119:15 I will meditate in thy **p**, and have 6490
Ps 119:104 thy **p** I get understanding: 6490
Ps 119:168 kept thy **p** and thy testimonies: 6490

PRECIOUS

Ge 24:53 and to her mother **p** things. 4030
1Sa 3:1 of the Lord was **p** in those days; 3368
1Sa 26:21 my soul was **p** in thine eyes this 3365
Job 28:10 and his eyes seeth every **p** thing. 3366
Ps 49:8 the redemption of their soul is **p**, 3365
Ps 116:15 **P** in the sight of the Lord is the 3368
Ps 126:6 and weepeth, bearing **p** seed, 4901
Pr 3:15 She is more **p** than rubies: and all 3368
Pr 12:27 substance of a diligent man is **p** 3368

Isa 28:16 a tried stone, a **p** corner stone, ... 3368
Da 11:8 **p** vessels of silver and of gold;......... 2532
Mt 26:7 alabaster box of very **p** ointment,....... *927*
1Co 3:12 silver, **p** stones, wood, hay,............ *5093*
1Pe 1:7 more **p** than of gold that perisheth,.... *5093*
1Pe 1:19 But with the **p** blood of Christ, as...... *5093*
1Pe 2:6 Sion a chief corner stone, elect, **p**:...... *1784*
2Pe 1:1 that have obtained the **p** faith *2472*
2Pe 1:4 exceeding great and **p** promises *5093*

PREDESTINATE
Ro 8:29 also did **p** to be conformed to the...... *4309*
Ro 8:30 whom he did **p**, them he also *4309*

PREDESTINATED
Eph 1:5 Having **p** us unto the adoption........ *4309*
Eph 1:11 being **p** according to the purpose...... *4309*

PREEMINENCE
Ecc 3:19 a man hath no **p** above a beast:........ 4195
Col 1:18 all things he might have the **p**......... *4409*
3Jn 9 loveth to have the **p** among them, ... *5383*

PREFERRED
Est 2:9 he **p** her and her maids unto the 8138
Da 6:3 this Daniel was **p** above the........... 5330
Jn 1:15 cometh after me is **p** before me:....... *1096*

PREFERRING
Ro 12:10 love; in honour **p** one another;........ *4285*
1Ti 5:21 without **p** one before another,......... *4299*

PREPARATION
Na 2:3 flaming torches in the day of his **p**, ... 3559
Mt 27:62 that followed the day of the **p**,......... *3904*
Jn 19:14 And it was the **p** of the passover,....... *3904*
Eph 6:15 with the **p** of the gospel of peace;...... *2091*

PREPARE
Ex 15:2 God, and I will **p** him an habitation; ... 4633
Jos 22:26 Let us now **p** to build us an altar, ... 6213
1Sa 7:3 **p** your hearts unto the Lord, and 3559
1Ki 18:44 Ahab, **P** thy chariot, and get thee 631
Est 5:8 banquet that I shall **p** for them, ... 6213
Ps 107:36 they may **p** a city for habitation;....... 3559
Pr 30:25 they **p** their meat in the summer;...... 3559
Isa 40:3 **P** ye the way of the Lord, make........ 6437
Jer 51:12 the watchmen, **p** the ambushes: 3559
Eze 4:15 thou shalt **p** thy bread therewith....... 6213
Eze 46:15 Thus shall they **p** the lamb, and 3559
Am 4:12 thee, **p** to meet thy God, O Israel....... 3559
Mt 11:10 **which shall p thy way before thee** *2680*
Mk 1:3 **P** ye the way of the Lord, make........ *2090*
Lk 7:27 **which shall p thy way before thee** *2680*
Jn 14:2 **told you. I go to p a place for you.** *2090*
Jn 14:3 **And if I go and p a place for you,** *2090*

PREPARED
Ge 24:31 I have **p** the house, and room for 6437
Nu 23:4 unto him, I have **p** seven altars,........ 6186
Jos 4:4 he had **p** of the children of Israel,...... 3559
1Ch 15:1 and **p** a place for the ark of God, ... 3559
1Ch 22:14 I have **p** for the house of the Lord 3559
1Ch 22:14 timber also and stone have I **p**;........ 3559
2Ch 8:16 Now all the work of Solomon was **p** ... 3559
2Ch 12:14 he **p** not his heart to seek the Lord..... 3559
2Ch 35:20 this when Josiah had **p** the temple,..... 3559
Ezr 7:10 Ezra had **p** his heart to seek the law.... 3559
Est 5:4 the banquet that I have **p** for him...... 6213
Est 5:12 banquet that she had **p** but myself; 6213
Est 6:4 the gallows that he had **p** for him...... 3559
Est 7:10 the gallows that he had **p** for.......... 3559
Ps 9:7 he hath **p** his throne for judgment..... 3559
Ps 57:6 They have **p** a net for my steps;........ 3559
Ps 74:16 thou hast **p** the light and the sun 3559
Pr 8:27 When he **p** the heavens, I was......... 3559
Pr 19:29 Judgments are **p** for scorners, and 3559
Pr 21:31 The horse is **p** against the day of....... 3559
Jnh 1:17 **p** a great fish to swallow up........... 4487
Jnh 4:6 And the Lord God **p** a gourd, and 4487
Jnh 4:7 God **p** a worm when the morning 4487
Mt 20:23 **for whom it is p of my Father**......... *2090*
Mt 25:34 **inherit the kingdom p for you** *2090*
Mt 25:41 **p for the devil and his angels:**......... *2090*
2Ti 2:21 use, and **p** unto every good work *2090*
Heb 10:5 not, but a body hast thou **p** me: *2675*
Heb 11:7 **p** an ark to the saving of his house; *2680*
Heb 11:16 God: for he hath **p** for them a city *2090*
Rev 9:15 which were **p** for an hour, and a....... *2090*
Rev 21:2 **p** as a bride adorned for her *2090*

PREPAREST
Nu 15:8 thou **p** a bullock for a burnt 6213
Ps 23:5 Thou **p** a table before me in the 6186

PREPARETH
Job 15:35 vanity, and their belly **p** deceit......... 3559
Ps 147:8 who **p** rain for the earth, who......... 3559

PREPARING
Ne 13:7 in **p** him a chamber in the courts...... 6213
1Pe 3:20 while the ark was a **p**, wherein *2680*

PRESBYTERY
1Ti 4:14 laying on of the hands of the **p**........ *4244*

PRESENCE
Ge 3:8 from the **p** of the Lord God........... 6440
Ge 4:16 Cain went out from the **p** of the....... 6440
Ex 10:11 driven out from Pharaoh's **p**.......... 5869
1Sa 18:11 David avoided out of his **p** twice 6440
1Sa 21:15 to play the mad man in my **p**? 5921
2Ki 5:27 his **p** a leper as white as snow 6440
Est 1:10 in the **p** of Ahasuerus the king 6440
Est 8:15 went out from the **p** of the king 6440
Job 2:7 Satan forth from the **p** of the Lord..... 6440
Ps 16:11 of life: in thy **p** is fulness of joy; 6440
Ps 51:11 Cast me not away from thy **p**; and 6440
Ps 100:2 come before his **p** with singing........ 6440
Ps 139:7 whither shall I flee from thy **p**?........ 6440
Pr 14:7 Go from the **p** of a foolish man,........ 5048
Isa 64:1 mountains might flow ... at thy **p** 6440
Eze 38:20 of the earth, shall shake at my **p**,....... 6440
Jnh 1:10 he fled from the **p** of the Lord......... 6440
Lk 13:26 **have eaten and drunk in thy p,** ...:.... *1799*
Lk 14:10 **in the p of them that sit at meat.** *1799*
Lk 15:10 **there is joy in the p of the angels.** *1799*
Ac 3:13 and denied him in the **p** of Pilate, ... *4383*
1Co 1:29 That no flesh should glory in his **p**..... *1799*
1Th 2:19 in the **p** of our Lord Jesus Christ *1715*
Heb 9:24 to appear in the **p** of God for us: *4383*
Jude 24 faultless before the **p** of his glory *2714*
Rev 14:10 angels, and in the **p** of the Lamb:...... *1799*

PRESENT
Ge 32:13 came to his hand a **p** for Esau......... 4503
Ge 33:10 then receive my **p** at my hand: for 4503

Ex 34:2 Sinai, and **p** thyself there to me........ 5324
Dt 31:14 **p** yourselves in the tabernacle of....... 3320
Jgs 3:15 sent a **p** unto Eglon the king of......... 4503
Jgs 6:18 bring forth my **p**, and set it before 4503
2Ki 18:31 an agreement with me by a **p**,......... 1293
Ezr 8:25 all Israel there **p**, had offered: 4672
Est 4:16 all the Jews that are **p** in Shushan...... 4672
Job 1:6 to **p** themselves before the Lord 3320
Job 2:1 to **p** themselves before the Lord 3320
Ps 46:1 strength, a very **p** help in trouble 4672
Eze 27:15 for a **p** horns of ivory and ebony 814
Da 9:18 **p** our supplications before thee........ 5307
Lk 2:22 Jerusalem, to **p** him to the Lord;....... *3936*
Jn 14:25 **unto you, being yet p with you**........ *3306*
Ro 8:38 nor things **p**, nor things to come,...... *1764*
Ro 12:1 ye **p** your bodies a living sacrifice...... *3936*
1Co 3:22 or things **p**, or things to come; *1764*
1Co 5:3 as absent in body, but **p** in spirit....... *3918*
2Co 5:8 body, and to be **p** with the Lord *1736*
2Co 5:9 that, whether **p** or absent, we may *1736*
2Co 11:2 I may **p** you as a chaste virgin to....... *3936*
Eph 5:27 **p** it to himself a glorious church....... *3936*
Col 1:28 may **p** every man perfect in Christ..... *3936*
2Ti 4:10 me, having loved this **p** world......... *3568*
Jude 24 and to **p** your faultless before the *2476*

PRESENTED

Ge 46:29 Goshen, and **p** himself unto him;...... 7200
Le 16:10 be the scapegoat, shall be **p** alive....... 5975
Jgs 6:19 unto him under the oak, and **p** it...... 5066
1Sa 17:16 evening, and **p** himself forty days...... 3320
Ac 9:41 saints and widows, **p** her alive......... *3936*

PRESENTLY

Pr 12:16 A fool's wrath is **p** known: but a....... 3117
Mt 21:19 And **p** the fig tree withered away *3916*

PRESENTS

1Sa 10:27 him, and brought him no **p**........... 4503
1Ki 4:21 brought **p**, and served Solomon 4503

PRESERVE

Ge 19:32 we may **p** seed of our father 2421
Ge 45:5 did send me before you to **p** life....... 4241
Dt 6:24 that he might **p** us alive, as it is........ 2421
Ps 16:1 **P** me, O God: for in thee do I put 8104
Ps 41:2 The Lord will **p** him, and keep 8104
Ps 64:1 **p** my life from fear of the enemy 5341
Ps 121:7 The Lord shall **p** thee from all evil:..... 8104
Ps 121:8 Lord shall **p** thy going out and thy..... 8104
Pr 14:3 the lips of the wise shall **p** them 8104
Pr 22:12 The eyes of the Lord **p** knowledge,..... 5341
Jer 49:11 children, I will **p** them alive; 2421
Lk 17:33 **shall lose his life shall p it** *2225*
2Ti 4:18 **p** me unto his heavenly kingdom:...... *4982*

PRESERVED

Ge 32:30 God face to face, and my life is **p** 5337
Job 10:12 thy visitation hath **p** my spirit......... 8104
Job 29:2 as in the days when God **p** me;........ 8104
Isa 49:6 and to restore the **p** of Israel:.......... 5336
Mt 9:17 **into new bottles, and both are p**....... *4933*
1Th 5:23 be **p** blameless unto the coming *5083*
Jude 1 and **p** in Jesus Christ, and called: *5083*

PRESERVEST

Ne 9:6 is therein, and thou **p** them all;........ 2421
Ps 36:6 O Lord, thou **p** man and beast 3467

PRESERVETH

Job 36:6 He **p** not the life of the wicked:........ 2421
Ps 31:23 for the Lord **p** the faithful, and 5341
Ps 116:6 the Lord **p** the simple: I was 8104
Pr 16:17 he that keepeth his way **p** his soul 8104

PRESIDENTS

Da 6:2 And over these three **p**; of whom 5632
Da 6:3 preferred above the **p** and princes,..... 5632

PRESS

Joel 3:13 for the **p** is full, the fats overflow;...... 1660
Mk 2:4 not come nigh unto him for the **p**,..... *3793*
Mk 5:27 came in the **p** behind, and touched *3793*
Lk 8:45 multitude throng thee and **p** thee, ... *598*
Php 3:14 I **p** toward the mark for the prize *1377*

PRESSED

Ge 40:11 and **p** them into Pharaoh's cup........ 7818
Jgs 16:16 she **p** him daily with her words,....... 6693
Est 8:14 **p** on by the king's commandment 1765
Lk 6:38 **measure, p down, and shaken**......... *4085*
Ac 18:5 Paul was **p** in the spirit, and........... *4912*

PRESSETH

Ps 38:2 in me, and thy hand **p** me sore........ 5181
Lk 16:16 **preached, and every man p into it**...... *971*

PRESUME

Dt 18:20 shall **p** to speak a word in my 2102
Est 7:5 that durst **p** in his heart to do so?...... 4390

PRESUMPTUOUS

Ps 19:13 thy servant also from **p** sins; 2086
2Pe 2:10 **P** are they, selfwilled, they are *5113*

PRESUMPTUOUSLY

Ex 21:14 man come **p** upon his neighbour, ... 2102
Nu 15:30 But the soul that doeth ought **p**,....... 3027
Dt 18:22 the prophet hath spoken it **p**: 2087

PRETENCE

Mt 23:14 **and for a p make long prayer;**......... *4392*
Mk 12:40 **for a p make long prayers: these**....... *4392*

P

PREVAIL

Ge 7:20 cubits upward did the waters **p**; 1396
1Sa 17:9 but if I **p** against him, and kill him..... 3201
Est 6:13 thou shalt not **p** against him, but...... 3201
Ps 65:3 Iniquities **p** against me: as for our 1396
Da 11:7 deal against them, and shall **p**......... 2388
Mt 16:18 **gates of hell shall not p against**........ *2729*

PREVAILED

Ge 7:18 the waters **p**, and were increased....... 1396
Ge 7:24 And the waters **p** upon the earth 1396
Ex 17:11 held up his hand, that Israel **p**......... 1396
1Sa 17:50 So David **p** over the Philistine......... 2388
Jer 20:7 art stronger than I, and hast **p**: 3201
Da 7:21 the saints, and **p** against them; 3202
Ac 19:20 grew the word of God, and **p**.......... *2480*
Rev 5:5 David hath **p** to open the book, ... *3528*

PREVENT

Ps 119:148 Mine eyes **p** the night watches,........ 6923
1Th 4:15 shall not **p** them which are asleep...... *5348*

PREVENTED

2Sa 22:6 about; the snares of death **p** me;....... 6923
Ps 119:147 I **p** the dawning of the morning....... 6923

Isa 21:14	**p** with their bread him that fled	6923
Mt 17:25	come into the house, Jesus **p** him,	*4399*

PREY

Ge 49:9	from the **p**, my son, thou art gone	2964
Nu 14:3	and our children should be a **p**?	957
Jgs 5:30	have they not divided the **p**; to	7998
Jgs 5:30	**p** of divers colours of needlework,	7998
Est 3:13	to take the spoil of them for a **p**	962
Job 9:26	as the eagle that hasteth to the **p**.	400
Ps 104:21	The young lions roar after their **p**,	2964
Pr 23:28	She also lieth in wait as for a **p**,	2863
Eze 22:25	like a roaring lion ravening the **p**;	2964
Eze 22:27	like wolves ravening the **p**, to shed	2964

PRICE

Le 25:16	thou shalt increase the **p** thereof.	4736
Dt 23:18	the **p** of a dog, into the house of	4242
2Sa 24:24	I will surely buy it of thee at a **p**	4242
Job 28:18	the **p** of wisdom is above rubies	4901
Ps 44:12	increase thy wealth by their **p**	4242
Pr 17:16	a **p** in the hand of a fool to get	4242
Pr 27:26	the goats are the **p** of the field	4242
Pr 31:10	for her **p** is far above rubies	4377
Zec 11:12	for my **p** thirty pieces of silver	7939
Mt 13:46	**had found one pearl of great p,**	*4186*
Mt 27:6	because it is the **p** of blood	*5092*
Ac 5:2	kept back part of the **p**, his wife	*5092*
Ac 5:3	keep back part of the **p** of the land?	*5092*
1Co 6:20	For ye are brought with a **p**	*5092*

PRICKED

Ps 73:21	grieved, and I was **p** in my reins	8150
Ac 2:37	they were **p** in their heart, and	*2669*

PRICKS

Nu 33:55	be **p** in your eyes, and thorns	7899
Ac 9:5	**for thee to kick against the p.**	*2759*
Ac 26:14	**for thee to kick against the p.**	*2759*

PRIDE

1Sa 17:28	I know thy **p**, and the	2087
Job 33:17	purpose, and hide **p** from man	1466
Ps 10:4	through the **p** of his countenance,	1363
Ps 31:20	thy presence from the **p** of man:	7407
Ps 73:6	**p** compasseth them about as a	1346
Pr 16:18	**P** goeth before destruction, and	1347
Pr 29:23	man's **p** shall bring him low: but	1346
Isa 28:1	Woe to the crown of **p**, to the	1348
Jer 49:16	thee, and the **p** of thine heart,	2087
Da 4:37	those that walk in **p** he is able	1466
Da 5:20	his mind hardened in **p**, he was	2103
1Ti 3:6	being lifted up with **p** he fall into	*5187*
1Jn 2:16	lust of the eyes, and the **p** of life	*212*

PRIEST

Ge 14:18	was the **p** of the most high God	3548
Ex 2:16	**p** of Midian had seven daughters:	3548
Ex 31:10	holy garments for Aaron the **p**,	3548
Le 1:7	Aaron the **p** shall put fire upon the	3548
Le 4:3	**p** that is anointed do sin according	3548
Le 4:20	the **p** shall make an atonement for	3548
Le 6:12	the **p** shall burn wood on it every	3548
Le 6:26	The **p** that offereth it for sin shall	3548
Le 7:32	ye give unto the **p** for an heave	3548
Le 13:6	the **p** shall pronounce him clean:	3548
Le 14:12	the **p** shall take one he lamb, and	3548
Le 14:15	**p** shall take some of the log of oil,	3548
Le 17:6	And the **p** shall sprinkle the blood	3548
Le 23:11	the sabbath the **p** shall wave it.	3548
Le 23:20	the **p** shall wave them with the	3548
Le 23:20	shall be holy to the Lord for the **p**	3548
Nu 3:32	Eleazar the son of Aaron the **p**	3548
Jos 20:6	until the death of the high **p** that	3548
1Sa 1:9	Now Eli the **p** sat upon a seat by a	3548
1Sa 2:14	the fleshhook brought up the **p** took	3548
1Sa 2:35	And I will raise me up a faithful **p**,	3548
1Sa 14:3	son of Eli, the Lord's **p** in Shiloh,	3548
1Sa 21:9	the **p** said, The sword of Goliath.	3548
Ezr 2:63	till there stood up a **p** with Urim	3548
Ezr 7:11	Artaxerxes gave unto Ezra the **p**,	3548
Ne 7:65	till there stood up a **p** with Urim	3548
Ne 8:2	Ezra the **p** brought the law before	3548
Ne 8:9	and Ezra the **p** the scribe, and the	3548
Ps 110:4	art a **p** for ever after the order of	3548
Isa 28:7	the **p** and the prophet have erred	3548
Jer 29:26	The Lord hath made thee **p** in the	3548
La 2:20	the **p** and the prophet be slain in	3548
Eze 44:13	to do the office of a **p** unto me,	3547
Hos 4:4	are as they that strive with the **p**.	3548
Zec 3:1	he shewed me Joshua the high **p**.	3548
Zec 3:8	Hear now, O Joshua the high **p**,	3548
Mt 8:4	**shew thyself to the p, and offer**	*2409*
Mt 26:65	Then the high **p** rent his clothes,	*749*
Mk 1:44	**shew thyself to the p, and offer**	*2409*
Mk 14:47	smote a servant of the high **p**, and	*749*
Lk 1:5	a certain **p** named Zacharias, of	*2409*
Lk 10:31	**there came down a certain p that.**	*2409*
Jn 11:51	but being high **p** that year, he	*749*
Jn 18:19	The high **p** then asked Jesus of his	*749*
Jn 18:22	Answerest thou the high **p** so?	*749*
Ac 5:17	Then the high **p** rose up, and all	*749*
Ac 5:21	But the high **p** came, and they that	*749*
Ac 14:13	Then the **p** of Jupiter, Which was	*2409*
Ac 23:4	said, Revilest thou God's high **p**?	*749*
Heb 2:17	a merciful and faithful high **p** in	*749*
Heb 3:1	and High **P** of our profession,	*749*
Heb 4:14	then that we have a great high **p**,	*749*
Heb 4:15	For we have not an high **p** which	*749*
Heb 5:6	Thou art a **p** forever after the	*2409*
Heb 5:10	of God an high **p** after the order of	*749*
Heb 7:1	**p** of the most high God, who met	*2409*
Heb 7:3	of God; abideth a **p** continually	*2409*
Heb 7:17	Thou art a **p** for ever after the	*2409*
Heb 8:1	We have such an high **p**, who is set	*749*
Heb 9:7	went the high **p** alone once every	*749*
Heb 9:11	But Christ being come an high **p** of	*749*
Heb 9:25	high **p** entereth into the holy place	*749*
Heb 10:11	**p** standeth daily ministering and	*2409*
Heb 13:11	sanctuary by the high **p** for sin,	*749*

PRIESTHOOD

Ex 40:15	shall surely be an everlasting **p**	3550
Nu 25:13	the covenant of an everlasting **p**;	3550
Jos 18:7	**p** of the Lord is their inheritance:	3550
Ezr 2:62	they, as polluted, put from the **p**.	3550
Ne 13:29	because they have defiled the **p**,	3550
Ne 13:29	and the covenant of the **p**, and of	3550
Heb 7:11	perfection were by the Levitical **p**,	*2420*
Heb 7:14	Moses spake nothing concerning **p**	*2420*
Heb 7:24	ever, hath an unchangeable **p**	*2420*
1Pe 2:5	up a spiritual house, an holy **p**,	*2406*
1Pe 2:9	a chosen generation, a royal **p**,	*2406*

PRIEST'S

Ex	28:1	minister unto me in the **p** office,	3547
Le	7:14	shall be the **p** that sprinkleth the	3548
Jgs	18:20	And the **p** heart was glad, and he	3548
Mal	2:7	the **p** lips should keep knowledge,	3548
Mt	26:51	struck a servant of the high **p**,	*749*
Mt	26:58	him afar off unto the high **p** palace	*749*
Lk	1:8	executed the **p** office before God.	*2407*
Lk	22:54	brought him into the high **p** house	*749*
Jn	18:10	it, and smote the high **p** servant	*749*

PRIESTS

Ge	47:22	the **p** had a portion assigned them.	3548
Ex	19:6	shall be unto me a kingdom of **p**,	3548
Le	1:5	the **p**, Aaron's sons, shall bring	3548
Le	6:29	the males among the **p** shall eat	3548
Nu	3:3	Aaron, the **p** which were anointed	3548
Jos	3:3	and the **p** the Levites bearing it,	3548
Jos	3:8	command the **p** that bear the ark.	3548
Jos	3:13	feet of the **p** that bear the ark of	3548
Jos	3:14	**p** bearing the ark of the covenant.	3548
Jos	4:9	the feet of the **p** which bare the ark	3548
Jos	4:16	Command the **p** that bear the ark	3548
Jos	6:12	the **p** took up the ark of the Lord.	3548
1Sa	22:17	hand to fall upon the **p** of the Lord	3548
1Sa	22:21	that Saul had slain the Lord's **p**.	3548
1Ki	8:3	came, and the **p** took up the ark.	3548
1Ki	8:6	the **p** brought in the ark of the	3548
2Ch	5:7	the **p** brought in the ark of the	3548
2Ch	5:11	**p** that were present were sanctified,	3548
2Ch	5:14	**p** could not stand to minister by.	3548
Ezr	9:1	The people of Israel, and the **p**,	3548
Ezr	9:7	have we, our kings, and our **p**,	3548
Ne	3:22	after him repaired the **p**, the men	3548
Ne	9:38	Levites, and **p**, seal unto it	3548
Ps	132:9	**p** be clothed with righteousness;	3548
Ps	132:16	also clothe her **p** with salvation:	3548
Hos	5:1	Hear ye this, O **p**; and hearken, ye	3548
Hos	6:9	so the company of **p** murder in the	3548
Joel	1:13	yourselves, and lament, ye **p**:	3548
Zep	3:4	her **p** have polluted the sanctuary,	3548
Mt	2:4	gathered all the chief **p** and scribes.	*749*
Mt	12:4	**were with him, but only for the p?**	*2409*
Mt	12:5	**the p in the temple profane the**	*2409*
Mt	20:18	**shall be betrayed unto the chief p**	*749*
Mt	27:20	chief **p** and elders persuaded the.	*749*
Mt	27:41	also the chief **p** mocking him, with	*749*
Mk	2:26	**is not lawful to eat but for the p,**	*2409*
Mk	10:33	**shall be delivered unto the chief p,**	*749*
Mk	14:1	the chief **p** and the scribes sought.	*749*
Mk	14:55	And the chief **p** and all the council.	*749*
Mk	15:3	the chief **p** accused him of many	*749*
Mk	15:11	But the chief **p** moved the people.	*749*
Lk	3:2	and Caiaphas being the high **p**, the	*749*
Lk	6:4	**lawful to eat but for the p alone?**	*2409*
Lk	9:22	**rejected of the elders and chief p**	*749*
Lk	17:14	**Go shew yourselves unto the p.**	*2409*
Ac	4:1	spake unto the people, the **p**, and	*2409*
Ac	6:7	the **p** were obedient to the faith.	*2409*
Heb	7:21	**p** were made without an oath;	*2409*
Heb	7:23	they truly were many **p**, because	*2409*
Heb	7:27	needeth not daily, as those high **p**,	*749*
Heb	7:28	men high **p** which have infirmity;	*749*
Rev	1:6	made us kings and **p** unto god	*2409*
Rev	5:10	us unto our God kings and **p**: and	*2409*
Rev	20:6	they shall be **p** of God and of	*2409*

PRIESTS'

Jos	4:3	place where the **p** feet stood firm	3548
Jos	4:18	the soles of the **p** feet were lifted.	3548

PRINCE

Ge	23:6	thou art a mighty **p** among us:	5387
Ex	2:14	thee a **p** and a judge over us?	8269
Nu	17:6	him a rod apiece, for each **p** one,	5387
Nu	34:23	the **p** of the children of Joseph, for.	5387
Job	21:28	say, Where is the house of the **p**?	5081
Job	31:37	as a **p** would I go near unto him.	5057
Pr	17:7	fool: much less do lying lips a **p**	5081
Pr	19:6	will intreat the favour of the **p**:	5081
Isa	9:6	everlasting Father, ... **P** of Peace.	8269
Eze	34:24	servant David a **p** among them;	5387
Eze	37:25	my servant David shall be their **p**.	5387
Da	1:7	the **p** of the eunuchs gave names:	8269
Da	1:8	requested of the **p** of the eunuchs	8269
Da	1:10	**p** of the eunuchs said unto Daniel,	8269
Da	8:25	stand up against the **P** of princes;	8269
Da	9:25	unto the Messiah the **P** shall be	5057
Da	10:21	these things, but Michael your **p**.	8269
Da	12:1	**p** which standeth for the children.	8269
Mt	12:24	by Beelzebub the **p** of the devils	*758*
Mk	3:22	by the **p** of the devils casteth he out	*758*
Jn	12:31	**shall p of this world be cast out.**	*758*
Jn	14:30	**the p of this world Cometh, hath**	*758*
Jn	16:11	**the p of this world is judged.**	*758*
Ac	3:15	killed the **P** of life, whom God hath	*747*
Ac	5:31	right hand to be a **P** and a Saviour,	*747*
Eph	2:2	to the **p** of the power of the air,	*758*

PRINCE'S

Eze	45:17	the **p** part to give burnt offerings,	5387

PRINCES

Ge	12:15	The **p** also of Pharaoh saw her,	8269
Nu	1:16	**p** of the tribes of their fathers,	5387
Nu	1:44	the **p** of Israel, being twelve men:	5387
Nu	7:3	a wagon for two of the **p**, and for	5387
Nu	7:10	the **p** offered for dedicating of the	5387
Nu	22:35	Balaam went with the **p** of Balak.	8269
Jos	9:15	**p** of the congregation sware unto	5387
Jos	9:19	**p** said unto all the congregation,	5387
Jgs	5:3	O ye kings; give ear, O ye **p**; I	7336
1Sa	29:4	the **p** of the Philistines were wroth.	8269
Ezr	7:28	and before all the kings mighty **p**	8269
Ezr	8:20	David and the **p** had appointed for	8269
Ne	9:38	our **p**, Levites, and priests, seal	8269
Ne	12:31	Then I brought up the **p** of Judah	8269
Est	1:11	the people and the **p** her beauty:	8269
Est	1:14	the seven **p** of Persia and Media	8269
Job	12:19	He leadeth **p** away spoiled, and	3548
Job	12:21	poureth contempt upon **p**, and.	5081
Job	29:9	The **p** refrained talking, and laid.	8269
Ps	68:31	**P** shall come out of Egypt;	2831
Ps	118:9	than to put confidence in **p**.	5081
Ps	119:23	**P** also did sit and speak against.	8269
Ps	146:3	Put not your trust in **p**, nor in the	5081
Pr	8:16	By me **p** rule, and nobles, even	8269
Pr	31:4	wine; nor for **p** strong drink:	7336
Ecc	10:7	**p** walking as servants upon the	8269
Ecc	10:17	and thy **p** eat in due season, for	8269
Isa	10:8	Are not my **p** altogether kings?	8269
Isa	21:5	arise, ye **p**, and anoint the shield.	8269
Jer	1:18	against the **p** thereof, against the	8269
Jer	8:1	the bones of his **p**, and the bones	8269

Jer 17:25 **p** sitting upon the throne of David, ... 8269
Jer 32:32 their kings, their **p**, their priests 8269
Jer 35:4 was by the chamber of the **p**, which.... 8269
Jer 36:21 the **p** which stood beside the king 8269
Jer 38:4 the **p** said unto the king, We 8269
Jer 41:1 the **p** of the king, even ten men 7227
La 5:12 **P** are hanged up by their hand:........ 8269
Eze 17:12 the king thereof, and the **p** thereof, ... 8269
Eze 32:29 is Edom, her kings, and all her **p**, ... 5387
Eze 39:18 the blood of the **p** of the earth,........ 5387
Da 3:2 king sent to gather together the **p**, ... 324
Da 8:25 stand up against the Prince of **p**; 8269
Da 10:13 Michael, one of the chief **p**, came...... 8269
Zep 3:3 **p** within her are roaring lions; 8269
Mt 2:6 not the least among the **p** of Juda; *2232*
Mt 20:25 that the **p** of the Gentiles exercise *758*
1Co 2:6 nor the **p** of this world, that............ *758*
1Co 2:8 none of the **p** of this world knew:....... *758*

PRINCIPAL
Ex 30:23 thou also unto thee **p** spices,.......... 7218
2Ki 25:19 the **p** scribe of the host, which 8269
Pr 4:7 Wisdom is the **p** thing; therefore 7225
Isa 16:8 have broken down the **p** plants........ 8291
Mic 5:5 shepherds, and eight **p** men........... 5257
Ac 25:23 **p** men of the city, ... *3588, 2596, 1851, 5607*

PRINCIPALITIES
Jer 13:18 your **p** shall come down, even......... 4761
Ro 8:38 nor **p**, nor powers, nor things *746*
Eph 6:12 but against **p**, against powers, ... *746*
Col 2:15 And having spoiled **p** and powers, ... *746*
Tit 3:1 mind to be subject to **p** and powers, ... *746*

PRINCIPALITY
Eph 1:21 Far above all **p**, and power, and......... *746*
Col 2:10 is the head of all **p** and power: *746*

PRINCIPLES
Heb 5:12 the first **p** of the oracles of God;....... *4747*
Heb 6:1 leaving the **p** of the doctrine of......... *746*

PRINT
Le 19:28 dead, nor **p** any marks upon you:...... 5414
Jn 20:25 in his hands the **p** of the nails, ... *5179*
Jn 20:25 my finger into the **p** of the nails,....... *5179*

PRINTED
Job 19:23 oh that they were **p** in a book! 2710

PRISON
Ge 39:20 and he was there in the **p**........ 1004, 5470
Ge 39:21 sight of the keeper of the **p** 1004, 5470
Jgs 16:21 and he did grind in the **p** house 631
Jgs 16:25 for Samson out of the **p** house;......... 631
1Ki 22:27 Put this fellow in the **p**, and 1004, 3608
Ne 12:39 and they stood still in the **p** gate....... 4307
Ps 142:7 Bring my soul out of **p**, that I 4525
Ecc 4:14 out of **p** he cometh to reign 1004, 612
Isa 42:7 bring out the prisoners from the **p**..... 4525
Isa 53:8 He was taken from **p** and from........ 6115
Jer 37:21 Jeremiah into the court of the **p** 4307
Jer 39:15 was shut up in the court of the **p** 4307
Mt 4:12 heard that John was cast into **p**........ *3860*
Mt 5:25 officer, and thou be cast into **p**........ *5438*
Mt 14:3 put him in **p** for Herodias' sake........ *5438*
Mt 14:10 sent, and beheaded John in the **p** *5438*
Mt 18:30 went and cast him into **p**, till he....... *5438*
Mt 25:36 I was in **p**, and ye came unto me *5438*
Mt 25:39 when saw we thee sick, or in **p** *5438*
Mt 25:43 sick, and in **p**, and ye visited me....... *5438*
Mt 25:44 or sick, or in **p**, and did not........... *5438*
Lk 3:20 all, that he shut up John in **p**.......... *5438*
Lk 22:33 ready to go with thee, both into **p**, ... *5438*
Jn 3:24 For John was not yet cast into **p** *5438*
Ac 5:19 Lord by night opened the **p** doors *5438*
Ac 16:23 they cast them into **p**, charging........ *5438*
Ac 16:24 thrust them into the inner **p**, and...... *5438*
Ac 16:27 keeper of the **p** awaking out of *1200*
Ac 16:27 and seeing the **p** doors open, he *5438*
Ac 16:36 keeper of the **p** told this saying to...... *1200*
1Pe 3:19 preached unto the spirits in **p**; *5438*
Rev 2:10 devil cast some of you into **p**,......... *5438*
Rev 20:7 Satan shall be loosed out of his **p**,...... *5438*

PRISONER
Ps 102:20 To hear the groaning of the **p**;.......... 615
Mt 27:15 to release unto the people a **p**,......... *1198*
Eph 3:1 Paul, the **p** of Jesus Christ for you *1198*
2Ti 1:8 of our Lord, nor of me his **p**:.......... *1198*

PRISONERS
Ge 39:20 where the king's **p** were bound:......... 615
Ge 39:22 all the **p** that were in the prison;........ 615
Isa 24:22 as **p** are gathered in the pit, and 616
Zec 9:12 to the strong hold, ye **p** of hope:........ 615
Ac 16:25 unto God: and the **p** heard them *1198*
Ac 16:27 supposing that the **p** had been fled..... *1198*

PRISONS
Lk 21:12 up to the synagogues, and into **p**,...... *5438*
2Co 11:23 in **p** more frequent, in deaths oft *5438*

PRIVATE
2Pe 1:20 scripture is of any **p** interpretation..... *2398*

PRIVATELY
Mt 24:3 disciples came unto him **p**....... *2596, 2398*
Mk 13:3 John and Andrew asked him **p**, .. 2596, 2398
Ac 23:19 and went with him aside **p**, and .. 2596, 2398

PRIVILY
1Sa 24:4 cut off the skirt of Saul's robe **p** 3909
Ps 31:4 net that they have laid **p** for me:....... 2934
Ps 142:3 have they **p** laid a snare for me 2934
Mt 1:19 was minded to put her away **p** *2977*
Mt 2:7 when he had **p** called the wise men,.... *2977*

PRIVY
1Ki 2:44 which thine heart is **p** to, that......... 3045
Ac 5:2 price, his wife also being **p** to it, ... *4894*

PRIZE
1Co 9:24 run all, but one receiveth the **p**? *1017*
Php 3:14 mark for the **p** of the high calling...... *1017*

PROCEED
Jos 6:10 any word **p** out of your mouth, ... 3318
Isa 29:14 I will **p** to do a marvellous work....... 3254
Mt 15:18 things which **p** out of the mouth *1607*
Mt 15:19 out of the heart **p** evil thoughts,....... *1831*
Eph 4:29 communication **p** out ... your mouth, . *1607*

PROCEEDED
Nu 30:12 then whatsoever **p** out of her lips...... 4161
Lk 4:22 words which **p** out of his mouth....... *1607*
Jn 8:42 for I **p** forth and came from God; *1831*

Rev 4:5 out of the throne **p** lightnings *1607*
Rev 19:21 which sword **p** out of his mouth: *1607*

PROCEEDETH
Ge 24:50 The thing **p** from the Lord: we 3318
1Sa 24:13 Wickedness **p** from the wicked: 3318
Mt 4:4 **word that p out of the mouth of** *1607*
Jn 15:26 **truth, which p from the Father,** *1607*
Jas 3:10 mouth **p** blessing and cursing *1831*

PROCESS
Ge 4:3 And in **p** of time it came to pass 7093
Ex 2:23 it came to pass in **p** of time, that 7227

PROCLAIM
Ex 33:19 and I will **p** the name of the Lord 7121
Le 25:10 **p** liberty throughout all the land 7121
Jgs 7:3 **p** in the ears of the people, saying, ... 7121
Isa 61:1 to **p** liberty to the captives, and 7121
Isa 61:2 **p** the acceptable year of the Lord, ... 7121
Jer 34:8 Jerusalem, to **p** liberty unto them; 7121
Joel 3:9 **P** ye this among the Gentiles; 7121
Am 4:5 **p** and publish the free offerings: 7121

PROCLAIMED
Ex 34:5 there, and **p** the name of the Lord.. 7121
2Ki 23:16 man of God **p**, who **p** these words. 7121
2Ch 20:3 and **p** a fast throughout all Judah 7121
Ezr 8:21 Then I **p** a fast there, at the river 7121
Jer 36:9 that they **p** a fast before the Lord 7121
Jnh 3:5 and **p** a fast, and put on sackcloth, ... 7121
Jnh 3:7 he caused it to be **p** and published 2199
Lk 12:3 **shall be p upon the housetops** *2784*

PROCLAIMING
Jer 34:15 in **p** liberty every man to his 7121
Jer 34:17 **p** liberty, every one to his brother 7121
Rev 5:2 strong angel **p** with a loud voice, ... *2784*

PROCLAMATION
Ex 32:5 and Aaron made **p**, and said, To 7121
1Ki 22:36 went a **p** throughout the host 7440
2Ch 24:9 they made a **p** through Judah 6963

PROFANE
Le 18:21 shalt thou **p** the name of thy God: 2490
Le 21:12 nor **p** the sanctuary of his God; 2490
Le 22:2 that they **p** not my holy name in 2490
Eze 21:25 thou, **p** wicked prince of Israel 2491
Mt 12:5 **priests in the temple p the sabbath,** *953*
1Ti 4:7 But refuse **p** and old wives' fables *952*
1Ti 6:20 avoiding **p** and vain babblings, and *952*

PROFANED
Le 19:8 hath **p** the hallowed thing of the 2490
Ps 89:39 thou hast **p** his crown by casting 2490
Mal 2:11 hath **p** the holiness of the Lord 2490

PROFESS
Dt 26:3 him, I **p** this day unto the Lord 5046
Mt 7:23 **then will I p unto them, I never** *3570*
Tit 1:16 They **p** that they know God; but *3670*

PROFESSED
2Co 9:13 for your **p** subjection unto the *3671*
1Ti 6:12 hast **p** a good profession before *3670*

PROFESSING
Ro 1:22 **P** themselves to be wise, they *5335*
1Ti 6:21 some **p** have erred concerning the *1861*

PROFESSION
1Ti 6:12 good **p** before many witnesses *3671*
Heb 3:1 Apostle and High Priest of our **p**, ... *3671*
Heb 4:14 Son of God, let us hold fast our **p**, ... *3671*
Heb 10:23 Let us hold fast the **p** of our faith *3671*

PROFIT
Ge 25:32 what **p** shall this birthright do to me?
Ge 37:26 What **p** is it if we slay our brother 1215
Est 3:8 for the king's **p** to suffer them 7737
Job 35:3 and, What **p** shall I have, if I be 3276
Ps 30:9 What **p** is there in my blood, when 1215
Pr 11:4 Riches **p** not in the day of wrath: 3276
Pr 14:23 In all labour there is **p**: but the 4195
Ecc 2:11 and there was no **p** under the sun 3504
Ecc 7:11 is **p** to them that see the sun 3148
Jer 7:8 trust in lying words, that cannot **p** 3276
Mk 8:36 **For what shall it p a man, if he** *5623*
Ro 3:1 what **p** is there of circumcision? *5622*
1Co 7:35 And this I speak for your own **p**; *4851*
1Co 12:7 is given to every man to **p** withal *4851*
Gal 5:2 Christ shall **p** you nothing. *5623*
Heb 4:2 word preached did not **p** them, ... *5623*
Jas 2:14 What doth it **p**, my brethren, ... *3786*

PROFITABLE
Job 22:2 Can a man be **p** unto God, as he 5532
Mt 5:29 **it is p for thee that one of thy** *4851*
1Ti 4:8 godliness is **p** unto all things *5624*
2Ti 3:16 and is **p** for doctrine, for reproof, ... *5624*
2Ti 4:11 for he is **p** to me for the ministry *2173*

PROFITED
Job 33:27 which was right, and it **p** me not; 7737
Mt 16:26 **For what is a man p, if he shall** *5623*
Mk 7:11 **thou mightest be p by me; he** *5623*

PROFITETH
Hab 2:18 What **p** the graven image that the 3276
Jn 6:63 **the flesh p nothing: the words** *5623*
1Co 13:3 have not charity, it **p** me nothing *5623*
1Ti 4:8 For bodily exercise **p** little: *5624, 2076*

PROLONG
Dt 4:26 shall not **p** your days upon it, but 748
Dt 17:20 he may **p** his days in his kingdom, ... 748
Job 6:11 mine end, that I should **p** my life? 748
Ecc 8:13 neither shall he **p** his days, which 748
Isa 53:10 seed, he shall **p** his days, and the 748

PROLONGED
Dt 5:16 that thy days may be **p**, and that 748
Ecc 8:12 his days be **p**, yet surely I know 743
Da 7:12 lives were **p** for a season and 754, 3052

PROLONGETH
Pr 10:27 The fear of the Lord **p** days: but 3254
Ecc 7:15 a wicked man that **p** his life in 748

PROMISE
2Ch 1:9 let thy **p** unto David my father be 1697
Ne 5:12 should do according to this **p** 1697
Ps 77:8 doth his **p** fail for evermore? 562
Ps 105:42 he remembered his holy **p**, and 1697
Lk 24:49 **the p of my Father upon you:** *1860*
Ac 1:4 **but wait for the p of the Father,** *1860*
Ac 2:33 Father, the **p** of the Holy Ghost *1860*
Ac 26:6 for the hope of the **p** made of God *1860*
Ro 4:14 and the **p** made of none effect: *1860*

Ro 4:20 He staggered not at the **p** of God *1860*
Ro 9:9 this is the word of **p**, At this time *1860*
Gal 3:14 the **p** of the Spirit through faith......... *1860*
Gal 3:17 should make the **p** of none effect *1860*
Gal 3:18 but God gave it to Abraham by **p** *1860*
Gal 3:22 that the **p** by faith of Jesus Christ *1860*
Gal 4:28 as Isaac was, are the children of **p** *1860*
Eph 1:13 sealed with that holy Spirit of **p** *1860*
Eph 3:6 partakers of his **p** in Christ by the *1860*
Eph 6:2 is the first commandment with **p**; *1860*
2Ti 1:1 the **p** of life which is in Christ......... *1860*
Heb 6:13 when God made **p** to Abraham, ... *1861*
Heb 6:15 endured, he obtained the **p** *1860*
Heb 9:15 the **p** of eternal inheritance *1860*
Heb 10:36 of God, ye might receive the **p** *1860*
Heb 11:9 faith he sojourned in the land of **p**..... *1860*
Heb 11:39 through faith, received not the **p**....... *1860*
2Pe 3:4 Where is the **p** of his coming?......... *1860*
2Pe 3:9 is not slack concerning his **p** *1860*

PROMISED

Ex 12:25 according as he hath **p**, that ye 1696
Nu 14:40 place which the Lord hath **p** 559
Dt 6:3 Lord God of thy fathers hath **p**........ 1696
Dt 10:9 as the Lord thy God **p** him 1696
Jos 23:15 the Lord your God **p** you; which 1696
1Ki 2:24 hath made me an house, as he **p**, ... 1696
1Ki 5:12 Solomon wisdom, as he **p** him:........ 1696
1Ki 8:20 throne of Israel, as the Lord **p**......... 1696
1Ki 9:5 as I **p** to David thy father, saying, ... 1696
Ne 9:23 which thou hadst **p** to their fathers 559
Est 4:7 money that Haman had **p** to pay 559
Mt 14:7 he **p** with an oath to giver her......... 3670
Ro 1:2 he had **p** afore by his prophets 4279
Tit 1:2 God, that cannot lie, **p** before the...... *1861*
Heb 11:11 judged him faithful who had **p**........ *1861*
Jas 2:5 kingdom which he hath **p** to them..... *1861*

PROMISES

2Co 1:20 For all the **p** of God in him are yea, ... *1860*
Gal 3:21 the law then against the **p** of God?..... *1860*
Heb 6:12 faith and patience inherit the **p**........ *1860*
Heb 7:6 and blessed him that had the **p**........ *1860*
Heb 11:13 faith, not having received the **p**........ *1860*
Heb 11:33 obtained **p**, stopped the mouths of..... *1860*
2Pe 1:4 exceeding great and precious **p**: *1862*

PROMOTE

Nu 22:17 I will **p** thee unto very great........... 3513
Nu 22:37 able indeed to **p** thee to honour? 3513
Est 3:1 did king Ahasuerus **p** Haman 1431
Pr 4:8 Exalt her, and she shall **p** thee: 7311

PROMOTED

Jgs 9:13 go to be **p** over the trees?............. 5128
Est 5:11 wherein the king had **p** him 1431
Da 3:30 Then the king **p** Shadrach,............ 6744

PROMOTION

Ps 75:6 **p** cometh neither from the east........ 7311
Pr 3:35 but shame shall be the **p** of fools 7311

PRONOUNCE

Le 5:4 that a man shall **p** with an oath 981
Le 13:44 priest shall **p** him utterly unclean;
Jgs 12:6 he could not frame to **p** it right 1696

PRONOUNCED

Ne 6:12 he **p** this prophecy against me: 1696
Jer 36:7 Lord hath **p** against this people........ 1696
Jer 36:31 evil that I have **p** against them;........ 1691

PROOF

2Co 8:24 **p** of your love, and of our boasting *1732*
Php 2:22 But ye know the **p** of him, that *1382*
2Ti 4:5 make full **p** of thy ministry *4135*

PROPER

1Co 7:7 every man hath his **p** gift of God,...... *2398*
Heb 11:23 they saw he was a **p** child; *791*

PROPHECIES

1Co 13:8 whether there be **p**, they shall *4394*
1Ti 1:18 the **p** which went before on thee....... *4394*

PROPHECY

Pr 31:1 the **p** that his mother taught him 4853
Da 9:24 to seal up the vision and **p**, and 5030
Mt 13:14 **them is fulfilled the p of Esaias,** *4394*
1Co 12:10 working of miracles; to another **p**; *4394*
1Co 13:2 though I have the gift of **p**, and........ *4394*
2Pe 1:19 have also a more sure word of **p**; *4397*
2Pe 1:20 that no **p** of the scripture is of any..... *4394*
2Pe 1:21 For the **p** came not in old time by *4394*
Rev 22:7 the sayings of the **p** of this book....... *4394*

PROPHESIED

Nu 11:25 spirit rested upon them, they **p**........ 5012
1Sa 10:11 he **p** among the prophets, that the 5012
1Sa 19:20 of Saul, and they also **p** 5012
1Sa 19:24 **p** before Samuel in like manner,....... 5012
Ezr 5:1 **p** unto the Jews that were in 5013
Jer 20:1 that Jeremiah **p** these things 5012
Eze 37:7 So I **p** as I was commanded: 5012
Mt 7:22 **Lord, have we not p in thy name?**...... *4395*
Mt 11:13 **prophets and the law p until John** *4595*
Mk 7:6 **Well hath Esaias p of you** *4395*
Lk 1:67 the Holy Ghost, and **p**, saying......... *4395*
Jn 11:51 he **p** that Jesus should die for that *4395*
Ac 19:6 and they spake with tongues, and **p** *4395*
1Co 14:5 with tongues, but rather that ye **p**: *4395*
Jude 14 Adam, **p** of these, saying, Behold,...... *4395*

PROPHESIETH

Jer 28:9 The prophet which **p** of peace......... 5012
1Co 11:5 or **p** with her head uncovered......... *4395*
1Co 14:3 But he that **p** speaketh unto men *4395*
1Co 14:4 but he that **p** edifieth the church *4395*
1Co 14:5 greater is he that **p** than he that *4395*

PROPHESY

1Sa 10:6 thou shalt **p** with them, and shalt...... 5012
1Ch 25:1 who should **p** with harps, with 5012
Isa 30:10 **P** not unto us right things, speak 2372
Jer 11:21 **P** not in the name of the Lord 5012
Eze 21:2 and **p** against the land of Israel, ... 5012
Eze 21:9 Son of man, **p**, and say, Thus saith..... 5012
Eze 34:2 **p** against the shepherds of Israel, ... 5012
Joel 2:28 sons and your daughters shall **p** 5012
Mt 15:7 **well did Esaias p of you, saying,** *4395*
Mt 26:68 **P** unto us, thou Christ, Who is he *4395*
Mk 14:65 him, and to say unto him, **P**:.......... *4395*
Lk 22:64 **P**, who is it that smote thee? *4395*
Ac 2:18 of my Spirit; and they shall **p**:......... *4395*
1Co 13:9 we know in part, and we **p** in part *4395*

1Co	14:1	gifts, but rather that ye may **p**	*4595*
1Co	14:24	if all **p**, and there come in one that	*4595*
Rev	10:11	Thou must **p** again before many	*4395*
Rev	11:3	shall **p** a thousand two hundred	*4395*

PROPHESYING

1Sa	10:13	when he had made an end of **p**,	5012
1Co	11:4	Every man praying or **p**, having	*4395*
1Co	14:6	or by knowledge, or by **p**, or by	*4394*

PROPHET

Ge	20:7	for he is a **p**, and he shall pray for	5030
Ex	7:1	Aaron thy brother shall be thy **p**	5030
Dt	18:15	thy God will raise up unto thee a **P**	5030
Dt	18:18	I will raise them up a **P** from	5030
Dt	34:10	arose not a **p** since in Israel like	5030
1Sa	3:20	established to be a **p** of the Lord	5030
2Sa	24:11	of the Lord came unto the **p** Gad	5030
1Ki	1:34	Nathan the **p** anoint him there	5030
1Ki	13:11	there dwelt an old **p** in Beth-el;	5030
1Ki	18:22	I only, remain a **p** of the Lord;	5030
1Ki	18:36	Elijah the **p** came near, and said,	5030
1Ki	19:16	thou anoint to be **p** in thy room	5030
1Ki	22:7	Is there not here a **p** of the Lord	5030
2Ki	6:12	but Elisha, the **p** that is in Israel,	5030
2Ki	14:25	Jonah the son of Amittai, the **p**,	5030
2Ki	20:11	Isaiah the **p** cried unto the Lord:	5030
1Ch	17:1	David said to Nathan the **p**, Lo, I	5030
2Ch	36:12	Jeremiah the **p** speaking from the	5030
Ezr	5:1	Haggai the **p**, and Zechariah the	5029
Isa	37:2	unto Isaiah the **p** the son of Amoz.	5030
Isa	39:3	Isaiah the **p** unto king Hezekiah,	5030
Jer	1:5	ordained thee a **p** unto the nations	5030
Jer	28:10	from off the **p** Jeremiah's neck,	5030
Jer	28:17	So Hananiah the **p** died the same	5030
Jer	38:10	take up Jeremiah the **p** out of the	5030
Da	9:2	the Lord came to Jeremiah the **p**,	5030
Hos	12:13	by a **p** the Lord brought Israel out	5030
Am	7:14	I was no **p**, neither was I a	5030
Hab	3:1	A prayer of Habakkuk the **p** upon	5030
Hag	1:1	word of the Lord by Haggai the **p**	5030
Mal	4:5	Behold, I will send you Elijah the **p**	5030
Mt	1:22	was spoken of the Lord by the **p**,	*4396*
Mt	2:17	which was spoken by Jeremy the **p**,	*4396*
Mt	3:3	that was spoken of by the **p** Esaias,	*4396*
Mt	10:41	**a p in the name of a p shall**	*4396*
Mt	11:9	**what went ye out for to see? A p?**	*4396*
Mt	12:39	**to it, but the sign of the p Jonas:**	*4396*
Mt	13:57	**A p is not without honour, save**	*4396*
Mt	14:5	because they counted him as a **p**	*4396*
Mt	21:11	This is Jesus the **p** of Nazareth of	*4396*
Mt	21:26	people; for all hold John as a **p**	*4396*
Mt	24:15	**spoken of by Daniel the p, stand**	*4396*
Mk	6:15	others said, That it is a **p**, or as one	*4396*
Lk	1:76	be called the **p** of the Highest:	*4396*
Lk	4:24	**No p is accepted in his own**	*4396*
Lk	4:27	**Israel in the time of Eliseus the p;**	*4396*
Lk	7:28	**a greater p than John the Baptist:**	*4396*
Lk	13:33	**that a p perish out of Jerusalem,**	*4396*
Lk	24:19	which was a **p** mighty in deed and	*4396*
Jn	1:21	Art thou that **p**? And he answered	*4396*
Jn	1:25	Christ, nor Elias, neither that **p**?	*4396*
Jn	4:19	Sir, I perceive that thou art a **p**	*4396*
Jn	4:44	that a **p** hath no honour in his own	*4396*
Jn	7:40	said, Of a truth this is the **P**	*4396*
Jn	7:52	look: for out of Galilee ariseth no **p**	*4396*
Ac	2:16	which was spoken by the **p** Joel;	*4396*
Ac	3:22	A **p** shall the Lord your God raise	*4396*
Ac	13:20	fifty years, until Samuel the **p**	*4396*
Ac	28:25	the Holy Ghost by Esaias the **p**	*4396*
Rev	20:10	where the beast and the false **p** are,	*5578*

PROPHETESS

Ex	15:20	Miriam the **p**, the sister of Aaron	5031
Jgs	4:4	Deborah, a **p**, the wife of Lapidoth,	5031
Lk	2:36	was one Anna, a **p**, the daughter	*4398*
Rev	2:20	**Jezebel, which calleth herself a p,**	*4398*

PROPHETS

1Sa	10:5	meet a company of **p** coming down	5030
1Sa	10:11	Kish? Is Saul also among the **p**?	5030
1Sa	10:12	proverb, Is Saul also among the **p**?	5030
1Ki	18:4	Jezebel cut off the **p** of the Lord	5030
1Ki	18:4	Obadiah took an hundred **p**, and	5030
1Ki	18:13	an hundred men of the Lord's **p**	5030
1Ki	18:19	**p** of Baal four hundred and fifty,	5030
1Ki	18:22	Baal's **p** are four hundred and fifty	5030
1Ki	18:25	said unto the **p** of Baal, Choose	5030
1Ki	19:1	how he had slain all the **p** with the	5030
2Ki	2:15	And when the sons of the **p** which	5030
2Ki	4:1	of the wives of the sons of the **p**	5030
2Ki	6:1	the sons of the **p** said unto Elisha	5030
Ne	9:26	slew thy **p** which testified against	5030
Ps	105:15	anointed, and do my **p** no harm	5030
Isa	30:10	to the **p**, Prophesy not unto us	2374
Eze	13:3	Woe unto the foolish **p** that follow	5030
Eze	13:4	**p** are like the foxes in the deserts	5030
Am	2:11	And I raised up of your sons for **p**,	5030
Mic	3:5	the **p** that make my people err,	5030
Zec	7:7	Lord hath cried by the former **p**,	5030
Mt	2:23	which was spoken by the **p**,	*4396*
Mt	5:12	**so persecuted they the p which**	*4396*
Mt	5:17	**come to destroy the law, or the p:**	*4396*
Mt	7:15	**Beware of false p, which come to**	*5578*
Mt	16:14	others, Jeremias, or one of the **p**	*4396*
Mt	22:40	**hang all the law and the p**	*4396*
Mt	23:30	**with them in the blood of the p**	*4396*
Mt	23:34	**behold, I send unto you p, and**	*4396*
Mt	24:11	**And many false p shall rise, and**	*5578*
Mt	26:56	**of the p might be fulfilled**	*4396*
Mk	8:23	Elias; and others, One of the **p**	*4396*
Mk	13:22	**false Christs and false p shall rise,**	*5578*
Lk	9:8	one of the old **p** was risen again	*4396*
Lk	10:24	**many p and kings have desired**	*4396*
Lk	11:49	**I will send them p and apostles,**	*4396*
Lk	13:34	**Jerusalem, which killeth the p**	*4396*
Lk	16:16	**law and the p were until John:**	*4396*
Lk	16:29	**him, They have Moses and the p;**	*4396*
Lk	24:25	**believe all that the p have spoken;**	*4396*
Lk	24:44	**in the law of Moses, and in the p,**	*4396*
Jn	6:45	**It is written in the p, And they**	*4396*
Ac	3:21	by the mouth of all his holy **p**	*4396*
Ac	24:14	written in the law and in the **p**	*4396*
Ro	1:2	by his **p** in the holy scriptures,)	*4396*
Ro	11:3	Lord, they have killed thy **p**, and	*4396*
1Co	12:28	apostles, secondarily **p**, thirdly	*4396*
1Co	12:29	are all **p**? are all teachers? are all	*4396*
1Co	14:29	Let the **p** speak two or three, and	*4396*
Eph	4:11	gave some, apostles; and some, **p**	*4396*
Heb	11:32	also, and Samuel, and of the **p**:	*4396*
Rev	18:20	heaven, and ye holy apostles and **p**	*4396*
Rev	18:24	was found the blood of **p**, and of	*4396*

PROPITIATION

Ro	3:25	a **p** through faith in his blood	*2435*
1Jn	2:2	he is the **p** for our sins: and not	*2434*
1Jn	4:10	his Son to be the **p** for our sins	*2434*

PROPORTION

1Ki	7:36	according to the **p** of every one	4626
Ro	12:6	according to the **p** of faith;	*356*

PROSPER

Ge	24:40	angel with thee and **p** thy way;	6743
Jos	1:7	**p** whithersoever thou goest,	7919
1Ki	2:3	mayest **p** in all that thou doest,	7919
Ne	1:11	and **p**, I pray thee, thy servant this	6743
Ne	2:20	The God of heaven, he will **p** us;	6743
Ps	1:3	and whatsoever he doeth shall **p**.	6743
Pr	28:13	covereth his sins shall not **p**.	6743
Isa	53:10	of the Lord shall **p** in his hand	6743
Jer	23:5	a King shall reign and **p**, and	7919
Da	8:25	shall cause craft to **p** in his hand:	6743
3Jn	2	thou mayest **p** and be in health,	*2137*

PROSPERED

Ge	24:56	seeing the Lord hath **p** my way;	6743
Jgs	4:24	hand of the children of Israel **p**,	1980
2Ch	32:30	And Hezekiah **p** in all his works	6743
Job	9:4	himself against him, and hath **p**?	7999
Da	6:28	Daniel **p** in the reign of Darius,	6744
1Co	16:2	him in store, as God hath **p** him,	*2137*

PROSPERETH

Ps	37:7	because of him who **p** in his way,	6743
Pr	17:8	whithersoever it turneth, it **p**.	7919
3Jn	2	be in health, even as thy soul **p**	*2137*

PROSPERITY

Job	36:11	they shall spend their days in **p**,	2896
Ps	35:27	pleasure in the **p** of his servant	7965
Pr	1:32	the **p** of fools shall destroy them.	7962
Ecc	7:14	In the day of **p** be joyful, but in	2896
Zec	1:17	My cities through **p** shall yet be	2896

PROSPEROUS

Ge	39:2	Joseph, and he was a **p** man;	6743
Jos	1:8	then thou shalt make thy way **p**,	6743
Ro	1:10	I might have a **p** journey by the	*2137*

PROTEST

1Sa	8:9	howbeit yet **p** solemnly unto them,	5749
1Co	15:31	I **p** by your rejoicing which I have	*3513*

PROTESTED

1Ki	2:42	by the Lord, and **p** unto thee,	5749
Zec	3:6	angel of the Lord **p** unto Joshua,	5749

PROUD

Job	26:12	he smiteth through the **p**.	7293
Ps	12:3	tongue that speaketh **p** things:	1419
Ps	119:85	The **p** have digged pits for me,	2086
Ps	138:6	but the **p** he knoweth afar off	1364
Pr	6:17	A **p** look, a lying tongue, and	7311
Pr	16:5	Every one that is **p** in heart is an	1362
Pr	21:4	high look, and a **p** heart, and the	7342
Pr	21:24	**P** and haughty scorner is his	2086
Pr	28:25	He that is of a **p** heart stirreth up	7342
Jer	50:32	the most **p** shall stumble and fall	2087
Lk	1:51	the **p** in the imagination of their	*5244*
Ro	1:30	of God, despiteful, **p**, boasters	*5244*
Jas	4:6	God resisteth the **p**, but giveth	*5244*

PROUDLY

1Sa	2:3	Talk no more so exceeding **p**; let	1364
Ne	9:29	yet they dealt **p**, and hearkened	2102
Ps	17:10	with their mouth they speak **p**	1348
Isa	3:5	the child shall behave himself **p**	7292

PROVE

Ex	20:20	Fear not: for God is come to **p** you,	5254
Jgs	2:22	through them I may **p** Israel,	5254
2Ch	9:1	to **p** Solomon with hard questions	5254
Ps	26:2	Examine me, O Lord, and **p** me;	5254
Da	1:12	**P** thy servants, I beseech thee, ten	5254
Lk	14:19	**yoke of oxen, and I go to p them:**	*1381*
Jn	6:6	And this he said to **p** him: for he	*3985*
Ro	12:2	that ye may **p** what is that good	*1381*
1Th	5:21	**P** all things; hold fast that which	*1381*

PROVED

Ge	42:15	Hereby ye shall be **p**: By the life	974
1Sa	17:39	with these; for I have not **p** them	5254
Ecc	7:23	All this have I **p** by wisdom: I	5254
Da	1:14	this matter, and **p** them ten days.	5254
1Ti	3:10	let these also first be **p**; then let	*1381*
Heb	3:9	your fathers tempted me, **p** me,	*1381*

PROVERB

1Sa	10:12	Therefore it became a **p**, Is Saul	4912
1Sa	24:13	As saith the **p** of the ancients,	4912
1Ki	9:7	Israel shall be a **p** and a byword	4912
Pr	1:6	To understand a **p**, and the	4912
Eze	14:8	and will make him a sign and a **p**,	4912
Lk	4:23	**Ye will surely say unto me this p,**	*3850*
Jn	16:29	thou plainly, and speakest no **p**.	*3942*
2Pe	2:22	unto them according to the true **p**,	*3942*

PROVERBS

1Ki	4:32	And he spake three thousand **p**:	4912
Pr	1:1	The **p** of Solomon the son of David,	4912
Ecc	12:9	out, and set in order many **p**.	4912
Jn	16:25	**have I spoken unto you in p:**	*3942*

PROVIDE

Ge	22:8	God will **p** himself a lamb for a	7200
Ex	18:21	**p** out of all the people able men	2372
Mt	10:9	**P neither gold, nor silver, nor**	*2532*
Ro	12:17	**P** things honest in the sight of	*4306*
1Ti	5:8	But if any **p** not for his own, and	*4306*

PROVIDED

Dt	33:21	And he **p** the first part for himself,	7200
1Sa	16:1	have **p** me a king among his sons	7200
2Ch	32:29	he **p** him cities, and possessions	6213
Heb	11:40	God having **p** some better thing	*4265*

PROVIDETH

Job	38:41	Who **p** for the raven his food?	3559
Pr	6:8	**P** her meat in the summer, and	3559

PROVINCE

Ezr	5:8	that we went into the **p** of Judea,	4083
Ne	1:3	The remnant that are left … in the **p**	4082
Est	3:12	governors that were over every **p**,	4082
Da	2:48	ruler over the whole **p** of Babylon,	4083
Da	2:49	over the affairs of the **p** of Babylon:	4083
Ac	25:1	when Festus was come into the **p**,	*1885*

PROVINCES

Est	1:16	in all the **p** of the king Ahasuerus	4082
Est	1:22	he sent letters into all the king's **p**	4082

Est 8:9 hundred twenty and seven **p**, unto..... 4082
Da 3:2 the rulers of the **p**, to come to the 4082

PROVING

Ac 9:22 **p** that this is very Christ.............. *4822*
Eph 5:10 **P** what is acceptable unto the Lord..... *1381*

PROVISION

Ge 42:25 and to give them **p** for the way: 6720
Jos 9:5 of their **p** was dry and mouldy 6718
Jos 9:12 our bread we took hot for our **p**....... 6679
Ps 132:15 I will abundantly bless her **p**: I 6718
Da 1:5 them a daily **p** of the king's meat 1697
Ro 13:14 and make not **p** for the flesh, to *4307*

PROVOCATION

Job 17:2 not mine eye continue in their **p**?...... 4784
Ps 95:8 not your heart, as in the **p**, and........ 4808
Jer 32:31 For this city hath been to me as a **p**.... 5921
Heb 3:15 harden not your hearts, as in the **p**,.... *3894*

PROVOKE

Ex 23:21 and obey his voice, **p** him not; 4843
Nu 14:11 How long will this people **p** me?....... 5006
1Ki 16:26 sin, to **p** the Lord God of Israel to anger
Job 12:6 and they that **p** God are secure; 7264
Ps 78:40 did they **p** him in the wilderness,...... 4784
Jer 32:29 unto other gods, to **p** me to anger
Ro 10:19 saith, I will **p** you to jealousy by *3863*
Ro 11:11 Gentiles, for to **p** them to jealousy...... *3863*
Eph 6:4 **p** not your children to wrath: *3949*
Heb 10:24 to **p** unto love and to good works: *3948*

PROVOKED

Nu 16:30 that these men have **p** the Lord........ 5006
Dt 32:16 **p** him to jealousy with strange 3707
1Sa 1:6 And her adversary also **p** her sore,..... 3707
1Ch 21:1 and **p** David to number Israel. 5496
Ezr 5:12 **p** the God of heaven unto wrath....... 7265
Ps 106:33 Because they **p** his spirit, so that....... 4784
Ps 106:43 but they **p** him with their counsel 4784
Isa 1:4 have **p** the Holy One of Israel 5006
1Co 13:5 is not easily **p**, thinketh no evil;........ *3947*
2Co 9:2 and your zeal hath **p** very many *2042*

PROVOKING

Dt 32:19 because of the **p** of his sons, and 3707
Ps 78:17 by **p** the most High in the 4784
Gal 5:26 **p** one another, envying one *4292*

PRUDENCE

Pr 8:12 I wisdom dwell with **p**, and find....... 6195
Eph 1:8 toward us in all wisdom and **p**;........ *5428*

PRUDENT

1Sa 16:18 a man of war, and **p** in matters, ... 995
Pr 12:16 but a **p** man covereth shame 6175
Pr 12:23 A **p** man concealeth knowledge:....... 6175
Pr 14:8 wisdom of the **p** is to understand...... 6175
Pr 14:18 the **p** are crowned with knowledge..... 6175
Pr 16:21 wise in heart shall be called **p**:.......... 995
Pr 19:14 and a **p** wife is from the Lord 7919
Pr 22:3 A **p** man foreseeth the evil, and 6175
Isa 29:14 the understanding of their **p** men....... 995
Mt 11:25 **these things from the wise and p,**...... *4908*
1Co 1:19 the understanding of the **p** *4908*

PRUNING

Isa 18:5 cut off the sprigs with **p** hooks,........ 4211

PRUNINGHOOKS

Isa 2:4 and their spears into **p**:............... 4211
Joel 3:10 swords, and your **p** into spears:........ 4211
Mic 4:3 and their spears into **p**:............... 4211

PSALM

1Ch 16:7 David delivered first this **p** to thank
Ps 81:2 Take a **P**, and bring hither the......... 2172
Ps 98:5 the harp, and the voice of a **p** 2172
Ac 13:33 it is also written in the second **p**, ... *5568*
1Co 14:26 every one of you hath a **p**, hath a *5568*

PSALMS

Ps 105:2 Sing unto him, sing **p** unto him:....... 2167
Lk 20:42 **himself saith in the book of P,**........ *5568*
Lk 24:44 **and in the p, concerning me** *5568*
Ac 1:20 it is written in the book of **P**, Let *5568*
Eph 5:19 Speaking to yourselves in **p** and *5568*
Col 3:16 admonishing one another in **p** and *5568*

PSALTERIES

2Sa 6:5 even on harps, and on **p**, and on 5035
1Ch 16:5 and Jeiel with **p** and with harps;....... 3627
2Ch 20:28 they came to Jerusalem with **p** and 5035
Ne 12:27 with cymbals, **p**, and with harps....... 5035

PSALTERY

1Sa 10:5 from the high place with a **p**, ... 5035
Ps 57:8 awake, **p** and harp: I myself will 5035
Ps 71:22 also praise thee with the **p**, even 3627
Ps 150:3 praise him with the **p** and harp 5035
Da 3:5 **p**, dulcimer, and all kinds of 6460
Da 3:7 **p**, and all kinds of musick,............ 6460

PUBLICAN

Mt 10:3 Thomas, and Matthew the **p**: *5057*
Lk 5:27 and saw a **p**, named Levi, sitting....... *5057*
Lk 18:10 **one a Pharisee, and the other a p**...... *5057*
Lk 18:11 **adulterers, or even as this p**........... *5057*
Lk 18:13 **And the p, standing afar off,**.......... *5057*

PUBLICANS

Mt 5:46 **ye? do not even the p the same?** *5057*
Mt 9:10 many **p** and sinners came and sat...... *5057*
Mt 11:19 **a friend of p and sinners** *5057*
Mt 21:31 **That the p and the harlots go into**..... *5057*
Lk 3:12 Then came also **p** to be baptized....... *5057*
Lk 7:29 the **p**, justified God, being baptized *5057*
Lk 19:2 which was the chief among the **p** *754*

PUBLICK

Mt 1:19 willing to make her a **p** example, ... *3856*

PUBLISH

Dt 32:3 I will **p** the name of the Lord:......... 7121
1Sa 31:9 to **p** it in the house of their idols 1319
Ps 26:7 That I may **p** with the voice of 8085
Jer 4:5 and **p** in Jerusalem: and say, Blow...... 8085
Jer 31:7 **p** ye, praise ye, and say, O Lord, ... 8085
Mk 1:45 went out, and began to **p** it much, ... *2784*

PUBLISHED

Est 1:20 be **p** throughout all his empire........ 8085
Jnh 3:7 **p** through Nineveh by the decree 559
Mk 13:10 **must first be p among all nations.**..... *2784*
Lk 8:39 and **p** throughout the whole city *2784*
Ac 13:49 And the word of the Lord was **p**....... *1308*

PUBLISHETH
Isa 52:7 good tidings, that **p** peace;............ 8085
Isa 52:7 tidings of good, that **p** salvation; 8085
Na 1:15 good tidings, that **p** peace!............ 8085

PUFFED
1Co 5:2 ye are **p** up, and have not rather *5448*
1Co 13:4 vaunteth not itself, is not **p** up *5448*
Col 2:18 vainly **p** up by his fleshly mind........ *5448*

PUFFETH
1Co 8:1 Knowledge **p** up, but charity.......... *5448*

PULL
Ps 31:4 **P** me out of the net that they 3318
Eze 17:9 shall he not **p** up the roots............ 5423
Lk 6:42 **P out the mote that is in thine** *1544*
Lk 6:42 **to p out the mote that is in thy**........ *1544*
Lk 12:18 **I will p down my barns, and**.......... *2507*

PULLED
Ge 8:9 **p** her in unto him into the ark 4026
Ge 19:10 and **p** Lot into the house to them, ... 935
Am 9:15 no more be **p** up out of their land 5428
Ac 23:10 Paul should have been **p** in pieces...... *1288*

PULLING
2Co 10:4 to the **p** down of strong holds;) *2506*
Jude 23 with fear, **p** them out of the fire;........ *726*

PULPIT
Ne 8:4 the scribe stood upon a **p** of wood, ... 4026

PULSE
Da 1:12 and let them give us **p** to eat, and...... 2235
Da 1:16 should drink; and gave them **p**........ 2235

PUNISH
Le 26:18 I will **p** you seven times more for...... 3256
Pr 17:26 Also to **p** the just is not good, nor 6064
Isa 13:11 I will **p** the world for their evil, and.... 6485
Jer 25:12 that I will **p** the king of Babylon....... 6485
Jer 27:8 that nation will I **p**, saith the Lord,..... 6485
Ac 4:21 how they might **p** them, because *2849*

PUNISHED
Ex 21:21 a day or two, he shall not be **p**:........ 5358
Ex 21:22 he shall be surely **p**, according as 6064
Pr 21:11 When the scorner is **p**, the simple 6064
Pr 22:3 but the simple pass on, and are **p**...... 6064
Jer 44:13 as I have **p** Jerusalem, by the 6485
2Th 1:9 **p** ... everlasting destruction *1349, 5099*
2Pe 2:9 unto the day of judgment to be **p**: *2849*

PUNISHMENT
Ge 4:13 My **p** is greater than I can bear 5771
Le 26:41 accept of the **p** of their iniquity:....... 5771
Pr 19:19 man of great wrath shall suffer **p**:...... 6066
Eze 14:10 shall bear the **p** of their iniquity: 5771
Mt 25:46 shall go away into everlasting **p**........ *2851*
2Co 2:6 Sufficient to such a man is this **p** *2009*
1Pe 2:14 sent by him for the **p** of evildoers...... *1557*

PURCHASE
Ge 49:32 The **p** of the field and of the cave...... 4735
1Ti 3:13 **p** to themselves a good degree, ... *4046*

PURCHASED
Ex 15:16 pass over, which thou hast **p**.......... 7069
Ps 74:2 which thou hast **p** of old; the rod of.... 7069
Ac 1:18 man **p** a field with the reward of....... *2932*
Ac 8:20 gift of God may be **p** with money...... *2932*
Ac 20:28 he hath **p** with his own blood......... *4046*
Eph 1:14 redemption of the **p** possession,....... *4047*

PURE
Ex 25:11 thou shalt overlay it with **p** gold, ... 2889
Le 24:2 bring unto thee **p** oil olive beaten...... 2134
Le 24:6 upon the **p** table before the Lord 2888
2Sa 22:27 the **p** thou wilt shew thyself **p**; 1305
1Ki 5:11 and twenty measures of **p** oil:.......... 3795
Job 4:17 a man be more **p** than his Maker? 2891
Job 16:17 in mine hands: also my prayer is **p**..... 2134
Ps 19:8 commandment of the Lord is **p**,....... 1249
Ps 119:140 Thy word is very **p**: therefore 6884
Pr 20:9 heart clean, I am **p** from my sin? 2891
Pr 21:8 but as for the **p**, his work is right 2134
Pr 30:5 Every word of God is **p**: he is a........ 6884
Mal 1:11 unto my name, and a **p** offering: 2889
Mt 5:8 **Blessed are the p in heart: for**......... *2513*
Ac 20:26 I am **p** from the blood of all men...... *2513*
Php 4:8 are just, whatsoever things are **p**......... *53*
1Ti 3:9 of the faith in a **p** conscience, ... *2513*
2Ti 2:22 call on the Lord out of a **p** heart....... *2513*
Heb 10:22 our bodies washed with **p** water....... *2513*
Jas 3:17 wisdom that is from above is first **p**, ... *53*
1Pe 1:22 love one another with a **p** heart *2513*
Rev 15:6 clothed in **p** and white linen, and...... *2513*

PURENESS
Pr 22:11 He that loveth **p** of heart, for the 2890
2Co 6:6 By **p**, by knowledge, by.................. *54*

PURGE
Ps 51:7 **P** me with hyssop, and I shall be....... 2398
Ps 79:9 deliver us, and **p** away our sins 3722
Da 11:35 to **p**, and to make them white, ... 1305
1Co 5:7 **P** out therefore the old leaven, ... *1571*
2Ti 2:21 If a man therefore **p** himself from *1571*
Heb 9:14 **p** your conscience from dead.......... *2511*

PURGED
Pr 16:6 mercy and truth iniquity is **p**:......... 3722
Isa 6:7 is taken away, and thy sin **p**........... 3722
Isa 27:9 shall the iniquity of Jacob be **p**;........ 3722
Heb 1:3 had by himself **p** our sins........ *4160, 2512*
Heb 9:22 are by the law **p** with blood; *2511*
2Pe 1:9 that he was **p** from his old sins *2512*

PURIFICATION
Nu 19:9 of separation: it is a **p** for sin.......... 2403
Est 2:3 their things for **p** be given them:....... 8562
Est 2:9 speedily gave her her things for **p**, ... 8562
Lk 2:22 And when the days of her **p**.......... *2512*

PURIFIED
Le 8:15 with his finger, and **p** the altar, ... 2398
Ps 12:6 furnace of earth, **p** seven times 2212
Da 12:10 Many shall be **p**, and made 1305
1Pe 1:22 ye have **p** your souls in obeying,......... *48*

PURIFIER
Mal 3:3 sit as a refiner and **p** of silver:......... 2891

PURIFIETH
Nu 19:13 and **p** not himself, defileth the 2398
1Jn 3:3 hath this hope in him **p** himself,......... *48*

PURIFY
- Nu 19:19 the seventh day he shall **p** himself, 2398
- Eze 43:26 shall they purge the altar and **p** it; 2891
- Jn 11:55 the passover, to **p** themselves *48*
- Tit 2:14 **p** unto himself a peculiar people, *2511*
- Jas 4:8 **p** your hearts, ye double minded *48*

PURIFYING
- Le 12:4 the days of her **p** be fulfilled 2892
- Est 2:12 things for the **p** of the women;) 8562
- Ac 15:9 them, **p** their hearts by faith *2511*
- Heb 9:13 sanctifieth to the **p** of the flesh: *2514*

PURIM (pu´-rim)
- Est 9:26 called these days **P** after the 6332
- Est 9:28 these days of **P** should not fail 6332

PURITY
- 1Ti 4:12 charity, in spirit, in faith, in **p** *47*
- 1Ti 5:2 the younger as sisters, with all **p** *47*

PURPLE
- Ex 28:6 ephod of gold, of blue, and of **p**, 713
- Ex 36:37 tabernacle door of blue, and **p**, and 713
- Nu 4:13 and spread a **p** cloth thereon: 713
- Jgs 8:26 **p** raiment that was on the kings of 713
- Est 8:15 a garment of fine linen and **p**: 713
- Pr 31:22 tapestry; her clothing is silk and **p** 713
- Eze 27:16 emeralds, **p**, and broidered work, 713
- Mk 15:17 they clothed him with **p**, and *4209*
- Lk 16:19 **was clothed in p and fine linen,** *4209*
- Jn 19:2 and they put on him a **p** robe *4210*
- Jn 19:5 crown of thorns, and the **p** robe *4210*
- Ac 16:14 Lydia, a setter of **p**, of the city of *4211*
- Rev 17:4 arrayed in **p** and scarlet colour, *4209*

PURPOSE
- Ru 2:16 of the handfuls of **p** for her, and 7997
- 1Ki 5:5 I **p** to build an house unto the 559
- Ezr 4:5 against them, to frustrate their **p**; 6098
- Ne 8:4 which they had made for the **p**; 1697
- Pr 20:18 **p** is established by counsel: and 4284
- Ecc 3:1 to every **p** under the heaven: 2656
- Ecc 3:17 a time there for every **p** and for 2656
- Ac 11:23 with **p** of heart they would cleave *4286*
- Ac 26:16 **have appeared unto thee for this p,**
- Ro 8:28 are the called according to his **p** *4286*
- Ro 9:11 the **p** of God according to election *4286*
- Eph 3:11 the eternal **p** which he purposed *4286*

PURPOSED
- Ps 17:3 I am **p** that my mouth shall not 2161
- Isa 14:27 For the Lord of hosts hath **p**, and 3289
- La 2:8 The Lord hath **p** to destroy the 2803
- Da 1:8 Daniel **p** in his heart that he 7760
- Ac 19:21 Paul **p** in the spirit, when he had *5087*
- Eph 1:9 which he hath **p** in himself: *4388*
- Eph 3:11 which he **p** in Christ Jesus our *4160*

PURPOSES
- Job 17:11 my **p** are broken off, even the 2154
- Isa 19:10 shall be broken in the **p** thereof, 8356

PURSE
- Mk 6:8 no bread, no money in their **p**: *2223*
- Lk 10:4 **Carry neither p, nor scrip, nor** *905*
- Lk 22:35 **I sent you without p, and scrip,** *905*

PURSUE
- Ge 35:5 did not **p** after the sons of Jacob 7291
- Jos 2:5 **p** after them quickly; for ye shall 7291
- 1Sa 30:8 Shall I **p** after this troop? shall I 7291
- 2Sa 17:1 I will arise and **p** after David this 7291
- Job 30:15 they **p** my soul as the land: and 7291
- Ps 34:14 and do good seek peace, and **p** it 7291

PURSUED
- Ex 14:8 he **p** after the children of Israel: 7291
- Ex 14:9 But the Egyptians **p** after them, 7291
- Ex 14:23 And the Egyptians **p**, and went in 7291
- Jos 2:7 the men **p** after them the way to 7291
- Jos 8:16 and they **p** after Joshua, and were 7291
- Jos 24:6 the Egyptians **p** after your fathers 7291
- Jgs 1:6 they **p** after him, and caught him, 7291
- Jgs 7:23 and **p** after the Midianites. 7291
- Jgs 8:12 he **p** after them, and took the two 7291
- Ps 18:37 I have **p** mine enemies, and 7291
- Isa 41:3 He **p** them, and passed safely; 7291

PURSUERS
- Jos 2:16 mountain, lest the **p** meet you; 7291
- Jos 8:20 turned back upon the **p** 7291

PURSUETH
- Pr 11:19 tendeth to life: so he that **p** evil 7291
- Pr 13:21 Evil **p** sinners: but to the 7291
- Pr 28:1 The wicked flee when no man **p** 7291

PURSUING
- Jgs 8:4 were with him, faint, yet **p** them 7291
- 1Sa 23:28 Saul returned from **p** after David, 7291

PUSH
- Ex 21:32 ox shall **p** a manservant or a 5055
- Dt 33:17 **p** the people together to the ends 5055
- Job 30:12 they **p** away my feet, and they 7971
- Ps 44:5 thee will we **p** down our enemies: 5055

PUT
- Ge 2:8 there he **p** the man who he had 7760
- Ge 2:15 **p** him into the garden of Eden to 3240
- Ge 3:15 I will **p** enmity between thee and 7896
- Ge 24:2 **P**, I pray thee, thy hand under 7760
- Ge 35:2 **P** away the strange gods that are 5493
- Ge 39:20 him, and **p** him into the prison, 5414
- Ge 43:22 who **p** our money in our sacks. 7760
- Ge 44:2 **p** my cup, the silver cup, in the 7760
- Ge 50:26 and he was **p** in a coffin in Egypt. 3455
- Ex 3:5 **p** off thy shoes from off thy feet, 5394
- Ex 16:33 and **p** an omer full of manna 5414
- Ex 17:12 took a stone, and **p** it under him, 7760
- Ex 25:16 shalt **p** into the ark the testimony 5414
- Ex 25:21 **p** the mercy seat above upon the 5414
- Ex 33:22 I will **p** thee in a clift of the rock, 7760
- Ex 34:33 with them, he **p** a vail on his face 5414
- Le 8:15 **p** it upon the horns of the altar 5414
- Le 8:23 **p** it upon the tip of Aaron's right 5414
- Le 10:1 his censer, and **p** fire therein, 5414
- Nu 1:51 that cometh nigh shall be **p** to death.
- Nu 6:27 they shall **p** my name upon the 7760
- Nu 11:29 the Lord would **p** his spirit upon 5414
- Nu 21:9 of brass, and **p** it upon a pole, and 7760
- Nu 23:5 Lord **p** a word in Baalam's mouth, 7760
- Dt 10:2 and thou shalt **p** them in the ark 7760
- Dt 10:5 **p** the tables in the ark which I had 7760
- Dt 17:12 shalt **p** away the evil from Israel. 1197

Dt	21:9	**p** away the guilt of innocent blood.	1197
Dt	24:16	fathers shall not be **p** to death for the	
Dt	24:16	children be **p** to death for the fathers:	
Dt	24:16	shall be **p** to death for his own sin.	
Dt	28:48	**p** a yoke of iron upon the neck	5414
Dt	31:26	law, and **p** it in the side of the ark.	7760
Jos	24:14	and **p** away the gods which your	5493
Jgs	5:26	She **p** her hand to the nail, and her	7971
Jgs	6:21	angel of the Lord **p** forth the end	7971
Jgs	7:16	**p** a trumpet in every man's hand,	5414
Jgs	12:3	I **p** my life in my hands, and	7760
Jgs	14:12	I will now **p** forth a riddle unto	2330
Jgs	16:21	took him, and **p** out his eyes, and	5365
1Sa	17:49	And David **p** his hand in his bag,	7971
2Sa	6:6	Uzzah **p** forth his hand to the ark.	7971
2Sa	12:13	Lord also hath **p** away thy sin;	5674
2Sa	12:31	therein, and **p** them under saws	7760
2Ki	13:16	**P** thine hand upon the bow.	7392
2Ki	13:16	Elisha **p** his hands upon the king's	7760
1Ch	21:27	and he **p** up his sword again into	7725
2Ch	33:7	Israel, will I **p** my name for ever:	7760
Ezr	1:7	**p** them in the house of his gods;	5414
Ezr	6:12	shall **p** to their hand to alter and	7972
Ne	2:12	**p** in my heart to do at Jerusalem:	5414
Ne	7:5	And my God **p** into mine heart to	5414
Est	5:1	Esther **p** on her royal apparel,	3847
Est	8:3	to **p** away the mischief of Haman	5674
Job	1:12	himself **p** not forth thine hand.	7971
Job	18:6	his candle shall be **p** out with him.	1846
Ps	4:5	and **p** your trust in the Lord	
Ps	4:7	Thou hast **p** gladness in my heart,	5414
Ps	8:6	hast **p** all things under his feet:	7896
Ps	18:22	not **p** away his statutes from me.	5493
Ps	36:7	**p** their trust under the shadow of thy	
Ps	40:3	hath **p** a new song in my mouth,	5414
Ps	56:8	**p** thou my tears into thy bottle:	5414
Ps	73:28	I have **p** my trust in the Lord God,	7896
Pr	13:9	lamp of the wicked shall be **p** out.	1846
Pr	23:2	And **p** a knife to thy throat, if thou	7760
Isa	1:16	**p** away the evil of your doings	5493
Isa	5:20	**p** darkness for light, and light for	7760
Isa	5:20	that **p** bitter for sweet, and sweet	7760
Isa	63:11	that **p** his holy Spirit within him?	7760
Jer	1:9	Then the Lord **p** forth his hand,	7971
Jer	20:2	and **p** him in the stocks that were	5414
Jer	52:11	he **p** out the eyes of Zedekiah;	5786
Jer	52:11	**p** him in prison till the day of his	5411
Eze	11:19	I will **p** a new spirit within you;	5414
Eze	17:2	Son of man, **p** forth a riddle, and	2330
Da	5:29	and **p** a chain of gold about his neck,	
Joel	3:13	**P** ye in the sickle, for the harvest	7971
Mt	1:19	was minded to **p** her away privily	*630*
Mt	5:15	**candle, and p it under a bushel,**	*5087*
Mt	5:31	**Whosoever shall p away his wife,**	*630*
Mt	6:25	**for your body, what ye shall p on**	*1749*
Mt	9:17	**men p new wine into old bottles:**	*906*
Mt	10:21	**and cause them to be p to death.**	*2289*
Mt	12:18	I will **p** my spirit upon him, and	*5087*
Mt	13:24	parable **p** he forth unto them,	*3908*
Mt	19:3	for a man to **p** away his wife for	*630*
Mt	19:6	**together, let not man p asunder**	*5562*
Mt	25:27	**p my money to the exchangers,**	*906*
Mt	26:52	**P up again thy sword into his**	*654*
Mt	27:28	him, and **p** on him a scarlet robe	*4060*
Mt	27:29	thorns, they **p** it upon his head,	*2007*
Mt	27:31	and **p** his own raiment on him,	*1746*
Mk	1:14	after that John was **p** in prison,	*3860*
Mk	7:33	**p** his fingers into his ears, and he	*906*
Mk	8:25	**p** his hands again upon his eyes,	*2007*
Mk	13:12	**shall cause them to be p to death.**	*2289*
Mk	15:17	thorns, and **p** it about his head,	*4060*
Mk	15:36	full of vinegar, and **p** it on a reed,	*4060*
Lk	9:62	**having p his hand to the plough,**	*1911*
Lk	15:22	**the best robe, and p it on him;**	*1746*
Lk	15:22	**p a ring on his hand, and shoes**	*1325*
Lk	18:33	**scourge him, and p him to death:**	*615*
Jn	5:7	troubled, to **p** me into the pool:	*906*
Jn	9:15	He **p** clay upon mine eyes, and I	*2007*
Jn	13:2	now **p** into the heart of Judas	*906*
Jn	18:11	**P up thy sword into the sheath:**	*906*
Jn	19:19	a title, and **p** it on the cross	*5087*
Jn	20:25	**p** my finger into the print of the	*906*
Ac	1:7	**Father hath p in his own power.**	*5087*
Ac	7:33	**P** off thy shoes from thy feet:	*3089*
Ro	13:14	But **p** ye on the Lord Jesus Christ,	*1746*
Ro	14:13	that no man **p** a stumblingblock.	*5087*
1Co	13:11	a man, I **p** away childish things.	*2673*
1Co	15:25	hath **p** all enemies under his feet	*5087*
1Co	15:53	corruptible must **p** on incorruption	*1746*
1Co	15:53	this mortal must **p** on immortality.	*1746*
Gal	3:27	into Christ have **p** on Christ.	*1746*
Eph	1:22	hath **p** all things under his feet,	*5293*
Eph	4:24	that ye **p** on the new man, which	*1746*
Eph	6:11	**P** on the whole armour of God,	*1746*
Col	3:8	also **p** off all these; anger, wrath,	*659*
1Th	2:4	to be **p** in trust with the gospel,	*4160*
Phm	18	ought, **p** that on mine account;	*1677*
Heb	2:5	**p** in subjection the world to come,	*5293*
Heb	2:8	nothing that is not **p** under him,	*506*
Heb	2:8	not yet all things **p** under him.	*5293*
Heb	6:6	and **p** him to an open shame.	*3856*
Heb	9:26	to **p** away sin by the sacrifice of	*115*
Heb	10:16	I will **p** my laws into their hearts,	*1325*
Jas	3:3	we **p** bits in the horses' mouths,	*906*
2Pe	1:14	I must **p** off this my tabernacle,	*595*
Rev	2:24	**p** upon you none other burden.	*906*
Rev	11:9	their dead bodies to be **p** in graves.	*5087*
Rev	17:17	**p** in their hearts to fulfil his will,	*1325*

PUTTETH

Dt	25:11	and **p** forth her hand, and taketh	7971
Job	28:9	**p** forth his hand upon the rock;	7971
Ps	75:7	he **p** down one, and setteth up	8213
Pr	28:25	he that **p** his trust in the Lord shall be	
Eze	14:4	**p** the stumblingblock of his	7760
Mt	9:16	**P a piece of new cloth unto an old**	*1911*
Mt	24:32	**is yet tender, and p forth leaves,**	*1631*
Mk	2:22	**man p new wine into old bottles:**	*906*
Mk	4:29	**immediately he p in the sickle,**	*649*
Lk	5:37	**man p new wine into old bottles;**	*906*
Lk	11:33	**a candle, p it in a secret place,**	*5087*

PUTTING

Isa	58:9	**p** forth of the finger, and speaking	7971
Ac	9:12	**coming in, and p his hand on him,**	*2007*
Eph	4:25	Wherefore **p** away lying, speak	*659*
Col	2:11	**p** off the body of the sins of the	*555*
1Th	5:8	**p** on the breastplate of faith and	*1746*
2Ti	1:6	in thee by the **p** on of my hands.	*1936*
1Pe	3:21	the **p** away of the filth of the flesh,	*595*
2Pe	1:13	you up by **p** you in remembrance;	*5279*

Q

QUAILS
Ex 16:13 pass, that at even the **q** came up, ... 7958
Nu 11:31 brought **q** from the sea, and let........ 7958
Nu 11:32 next day, and they gathered the **q**...... 7958
Ps 105:40 people asked, and he brought **q**,....... 7958

QUAKE See also EARTHQUAKE.
Joel 2:10 The earth shall **q** before them; 7264
Nu 1:5 The mountains **q** at him, and the...... 7493
Mt 27:51 and the earth did **q**, and the rocks *4579*
Heb 12:21 said, I exceedingly fear and **q**:) *1790*

QUAKED
Ex 19:18 and the whole mount **q** greatly........ 2729
1Sa 14:15 also trembled, and the earth **q**:........ 7264

QUAKING
Eze 12:18 Son of man, eat thy bread with **q**,...... 7494
Da 10:7 but a great **q** fell upon them, so 2731

QUARREL
Le 26:25 avenge the **q** of my covenant: 5359
2Ki 5:7 see how he seeketh a **q** against me 579
Mk 6:19 Herodias had a **q** against him,......... *1758*
Col 3:13 if any man have a **q** against any:....... *3437*

QUARRIES
Jgs 3:19 from the **q** that were by Gilgal,........ 6456
Jgs 3:26 and passed beyond the **q**, and......... 6456

QUARTER
Ge 19:4 all the people from every **q**:........... 7098
Isa 56:11 every one for his gain, from his **q**...... 7098
Mk 1:45 they came to him from every **q**........ *3836*

QUARTERS
Ex 13:7 leaven seen with thee in all thy **q** 1366
Jer 49:36 winds from the four **q** of heaven,....... 7098
Ac 16:3 the Jews which were in those **q**:........ *5117*
Ac 28:7 In the same **q** were possessions........ *5117*
Rev 20:8 are in the four **q** of the earth, ... *1137*

QUATERNIONS
Ac 12:4 delivered him to four **q** of soldiers *5069*

QUEEN
1Ki 10:1 the **q** of Sheba heard of the fame 4436
1Ki 10:10 which the **q** of Sheba gave to king 4436
1Ki 10:13 unto the **q** of Sheba all her desire, ... 4436
1Ki 15:13 even her he removed from being **q**, ... 1377
2Ch 9:1 **q** of Sheba heard of the fame of 4436
2Ch 9:3 **q** of Sheba had seen the wisdom of 4436
2Ch 15:16 he removed her from being **q**,......... 1377
Ne 2:6 me, (the **q** also sitting by him,)........ 7694
Est 1:12 the **q** Vashti refused to come at the..... 4436
Est 1:15 do unto the **q** Vashti according to...... 4436
Est 1:17 deed of the **q** shall come abroad....... 4436
Est 1:18 have heard of the deed of the **q**........ 4436
Est 2:17 and made her **q** instead of Vashti. 4427
Est 2:22 who told it unto Esther the **q**;......... 4436
Est 4:4 was the **q** exceedingly grieved; 4436
Est 5:2 Esther the **q** standing in the court,..... 4436
Est 5:12 the **q** did let no man come in with..... 4436
Est 7:2 What is thy petition, **q** Esther? 4436
Est 7:5 said unto Esther the **q**, Who is he, ... 4436
Est 7:8 Will he force the **q** also before me 4436
Est 8:1 Jews' enemy unto Esther the **q** 4436
Est 9:31 Esther the **q** had enjoined them,....... 4436
Jer 7:18 to make cakes to the **q** of heaven,...... 4446
Jer 44:18 to burn incense to the **q** of heaven, ... 4446
Jer 44:25 to burn incense to the **q** of heaven, ... 4446
Da 5:10 the **q** spake and said, O king, live 4433
Mt 12:42 **The q of the south shall rise up in** *938*
Lk 11:31 **The q of the south shall rise up in** *938*
Rev 18:7 for she saith in her heart, I sit a **q** *938*

QUEENS
SS 6:8 are threescore **q**, and fourscore........ 4436
Isa 49:23 and their **q** thy nursing mothers: 8282

QUENCH See also UNQUENCHABLE.
2Sa 21:17 that thou **q** not the light of Israel. 3518
SS 8:7 Many waters cannot **q** love,........... 3518
Isa 42:3 the smoking flax shall he not **q**: 3518
Jer 4:4 fire, and burn that none can **q** it, ... 3518
Jer 21:12 fire, and burn that none can **q** it, ... 3518
Mt 12:20 and smoking flax shall he not **q**,....... *4570*
Eph 6:16 **q** all the fiery darts of the wicked *4570*
1Th 5:19 **Q** not the Spirit. *4570*

QUENCHED
Nu 11:2 unto the Lord, the fire was **q**.......... 8257
2Ki 22:17 this place, and shall not be **q**.......... 3518
2Ch 34:25 this place, and shall not be **q**.......... 3518
Isa 34:10 It shall not be **q** night nor day;......... 3518
Isa 66:24 die, neither shall their fire be **q**; 3518
Jer 7:20 it shall burn, and shall not be **q** 3518
Jer 17:27 of Jerusalem, and it shall not be **q** 3518
Eze 20:47 the flaming flame shall not be **q** 3518
Eze 20:48 have kindled it: it shall not be **q** 3518
Mk 9:43 **into the fire that never shall be q** *762*
Mk 9:48 **dieth not, and the fire is not q,**........ *4570*
Heb 11:34 **Q** the violence of fire, escaped the *4570*

QUESTION
Mk 8:11 began to **q** with him, seeking of *4802*
Mk 11:29 **I will also ask of you one q, and**....... *3056*
Mk 12:34 man after that durst ask him any **q**:
Ac 18:15 if it be a **q** of words and names, ... *2213*
Ac 19:40 we are in danger to be called in **q**...... *1458*
Ac 23:6 of the dead I am called in **q**........... *2919*
Ac 24:21 I am called in **q** by you this day........ *2919*

QUESTIONED
Mk 1:27 that they **q** among themselves, ... *4802*
Lk 23:9 he **q** with him in many words; *1905*

QUESTIONS
1Ki 10:3 And Solomon told her all her **q** 1697
2Ch 9:1 to prove Solomon with hard **q** at 2420
Mt 22:46 that day forth ask him any more **q**
Ac 23:29 to be accused of **q** of their law. *2213*
Ac 26:3 to be expert in all customs and **q** *2213*
1Ti 1:4 genealogies, which minister **q**,......... *2214*
1Ti 6:4 about **q** and strifes of words,.......... *2214*
2Ti 2:23 But foolish and unlearned **q** avoid, ... *2214*
Tit 3:9 avoid foolish **q**, and genealogies,....... *2214*

QUICK See also ALIVE; LIVING.
Nu 16:30 and they go down **q** into the pit; 2416
Ps 55:15 and let them go down **q** into hell: 2416
Ac 10:42 to be the Judge of **q** and dead.......... *2198*

2Ti 4:1 shall judge the **q** and the dead at....... *2198*
Heb 4:12 the word of God is **q**, and powerful,.... *2198*
1Pe 4:5 ready to judge the **q** and the dead...... *2198*

QUICKEN
Ps 119:25 **q** thou me according to thy word...... 2421
Ps 119:40 **q** me in thy righteousness 2421
Ps 119:88 **Q** me after thy lovingkindness; so...... 2421
Ps 119:156 **q** me according to thy judgments...... 2421
Ps 119:159 **q** me, O Lord, according to thy........ 2421
Ro 8:11 also **q** your mortal bodies by his....... *2227*

QUICKENED
Eph 2:1 you hath he **q**, who were dead
Eph 2:5 hath **q** us together with Christ,........ *4806*
Col 2:13 flesh, hath he **q** together with him,..... *4806*
1Pe 3:18 in the flesh, but **q** by the Spirit:........ *2227*

QUICKENETH
Jn 5:21 **raiseth up the dead, and q them;** *2227*
Jn 5:21 **even so the Son q whom he will.** *2227*
Jn 6:63 **It is the spirit that q; the flesh**......... *2227*
Ro 4:17 even God, who **q** the dead, and........ *2227*
1Ti 6:13 the sight of God, who **q** all things,..... *2227*

QUICKENING
1Co 15:45 last Adam was made a **q** spirit......... *2227*

QUICKLY
Dt 11:17 lest ye perish **q** from off the good...... 4120
Dt 28:20 and until thou perish **q**; because....... 4118
Jos 23:16 ye shall perish **q** from off the good..... 4120
2Sa 17:16 Now therefore send **q**, and tell 4120
Ecc 4:12 a threefold cord in not **q** broken....... 4120
Mt 5:25 **Agree with thine adversary q,**......... *5035*
Mt 28:7 And go **q**, and tell his disciples *5035*
Mt 28:8 departed **q** from the sepulchre *5035*
Mk 16:8 they went out **q**, and fled from the..... *5035*
Jn 13:27 unto him, **That thou doest, do q** *5032*
Rev 2:5 **or else I will come unto thee q,**........ *5035*
Rev 2:16 **or else I will come unto thee q,**........ *5035*
Rev 3:11 **Behold, I come q: hold that fast** *5035*
Rev 22:7 **Behold, I come q:** blessed is he *5035*
Rev 22:12 **I come q; and my reward is with** *5035*
Rev 22:20 saith, **Surely I come q.** Amen.......... *5035*

QUIET
Jgs 18:27 a people that were at **q** and secure:..... 8252
2Ch 20:30 the realm of Jehoshaphat was **q**:....... 8252
Job 3:26 had I rest, neither was I **q**;............ 5117
Pr 1:33 and shall be **q** from fear of evil. 7599
Ecc 9:17 of wise men are heard in **q** more 5183
Isa 7:4 Take heed, and be **q**; fear not,......... 8252
Isa 14:7 whole earth is at rest, and is **q**: 8252
Isa 33:20 shall see Jerusalem a **q** habitation, ... 7600
Jer 30:10 shall be in rest, and be **q**, and 7599
Eze 16:42 be **q**, and will be no more angry. 8252
Ac 19:36 ye ought to be **q**, and to do *2687*
1Th 4:11 that ye study to be **q**, and to do........ *2270*
1Ti 2:2 may lead a **q** and peaceable life........ *2263*
1Pe 3:4 ornament of a meek and **q** spirit,...... *2272*

QUIETETH
Job 37:17 he **q** the earth by the south wind? 8252

QUIETLY
2Sa 3:27 in the gate to speak with him **q**,....... 7987
La 3:26 **q** wait for the salvation of the Lord

QUIETNESS
Jgs 8:28 the country was in **q** forty years 8252
1Ch 22:9 will give peace and **q** unto Israel....... 8253
Job 34:29 When he giveth **q**, who then can 8252
Pr 17:1 is a dry morsel, and **q** therewith, ... 7962
Ecc 4:6 Better is an handful with **q**, than 5183
Isa 30:15 in **q** and in confidence shall be 8252
Isa 32:17 **q** and assurance for ever.............. 8252
2Th 3:12 that with **q** they work, and eat......... *2271*

QUIT
1Sa 4:9 and **q** yourselves like men,............ 1961
1Co 16:13 faith, **q** you like men, be strong......... *407*

QUITE
Nu 17:10 **q** take away their murmurings 3615
2Sa 3:24 hast sent him away, and he is **q** gone?

QUIVER
Job 39:23 The **q** rattleth against him, the 827
Ps 127:5 Happy is the man that hath his **q** 827
Isa 49:2 shaft; in his **q** hath he hid me;.......... 827
Jer 5:16 Their **q** is as an open sepulchre, ... 827
La 3:13 of his **q** to enter into my reins. 827

QUIVERED
Hab 3:16 trembled; my lips **q** at the voice:....... 6750

R

RABBI (rab´-bi)
Mt 23:7 and to be called of men, **R**, **R** *4461*
Mt 23:8 But be not ye called **R**: for one is *4462*
Jn 1:38 They said unto him, **R**, (which is *4461*
Jn 1:49 him, **R**, thou art the Son of God; *4461*
Jn 3:2 **R**, we know … thou art a teacher *4461*
Jn 6:25 **R**, when camest thou hither? *4461*

RACE
Ecc 9:11 the **r** is not to the swift, nor the 4793
1Co 9:24 they which run in a **r** run all, but *4712*
Heb 12:1 patience the **r** that is set before us, ... *73*

RAGE See also **OUTRAGEOUS.**
2Ki 5:12 he turned and went away in a **r**. 2534
2Ki 19:28 Because thy **r** against me and thy 7264
2Ch 28:9 slain them in a **r** that reacheth 2197
Job 40:11 Cast abroad the **r** of thy wrath: 5678
Ps 2:1 Why do the heathen **r**, and the 7283
Pr 6:34 For jealousy is the **r** of a man: 2534
Pr 29:9 whether he **r** or laugh, there is 7264
Isa 37:28 coming in, and thy **r** against me 7264
Da 3:13 Nebuchadnezzar in his **r** and 7266
Hos 7:16 sword for the **r** of their tongue: 2195
Na 2:4 The chariots shall **r** in the streets, ... 1984
Ac 4:25 Why did the heathen **r**, and the *5433*

RAGETH
Pr 14:16 but the fool **r**, and is confident 5674

RAGING
Ps 89:9 Thou rulest the **r** of the sea: 1348
Pr 20:1 is a mocker, strong drink is **r**: 1993
Jnh 1:15 and the sea ceased from her **r** 2197
Lk 8:24 the wind and the **r** of the water. *2830*
Jude 13 **R** waves of the sea, foaming out *66*

RAGS
Pr 23:21 shall clothe a man with **r** 7168
Isa 64:6 righteousnesses are as filthy **r**; 899

RAIL
2Ch 32:17 also letters to **r** on the Lord God. 2778

RAILED
1Sa 25:14 our master; and he **r** on them 5860
Mk 15:29 And they that passed by **r** on him, ... *987*
Lk 23:39 which were hanged **r** on him, ... *987*

RAILING
1Pe 3:9 rendering evil for evil, or **r** for **r**: *3059*
2Pe 2:11 bring not **r** accusation against *989*
Jude 9 bring against him a **r** accusation *988*

RAIMENT
Ge 27:27 and he smelled the smell of his **r**, ... 899
Ge 45:22 of silver, and five changes of **r** 8071
Ex 22:26 take thy neighbour's **r** to pledge, ... 8008
Ex 22:27 only, it is his **r** for his skin: 8071
Dt 8:4 Thy **r** waxed not old upon thee. 8071
Dt 10:18 stranger, in giving him food and **r** 8071
Dt 24:13 that he may sleep in his own **r** 8008
Dt 24:17 nor take a widow's **r** to pledge: 899
Est 4:4 and she sent **r** to clothe Mordecai, ... 899
Isa 14:19 as the **r** of those that are slain 3830
Mt 6:25 than meat, and the body than **r**? *1742*
Mt 6:28 And why take ye thought for **r**? *1742*
Mt 11:8 to see? A man clothed in soft **r**? *2440*
Mt 17:2 his **r** was white as the light. *2440*
Mt 28:3 and his **r** white as snow: *1742*
Mk 9:3 his **r** became shining, exceeding *2440*
Lk 7:25 to see? A man clothed in soft **r**? *2440*
Lk 9:29 his **r** was white and glistering *2441*
Lk 12:23 meat, and the body is more than **r**. *1742*
Lk 23:34 they parted his **r**, and cast lots. *2440*
Jn 19:24 They parted my **r** among them. *2440*
Ac 22:20 kept the **r** of them that slew him. *2440*
1Ti 6:8 And having food and **r** let us be *4629*
Jas 2:2 come in also a poor man in vile **r**; *2066*
Rev 3:5 same shall be clothed in white **r**; *2440*
Rev 3:18 and white **r**, that thou mayest be *2440*
Rev 4:4 elders sitting, clothed in white **r**; *2440*

RAIN
Ge 7:12 the **r** was upon the earth forty 1653
Ex 16:4 will **r** bread from heaven for you; 4305
Le 26:4 I will give you **r** in due season. 1653
Dt 11:11 drinketh water of the **r** of heaven: 4306
Dt 28:24 make the **r** of thy land powder and 4306
Dt 32:2 My doctrine shall drop as the **r**, my 4306
2Sa 23:4 the earth by clear shining after **r**. 4306
1Ki 8:35 is shut up, and there is no **r**. 4306
1Ki 17:1 shall not be dew nor **r** these years, ... 4306
1Ki 18:41 is a sound of abundance of **r**. 1653
2Ch 6:26 is shut up, and there is no **r**. 4306
2Ch 7:13 shut up heaven that there be no **r**, ... 4306
Job 38:26 To cause it to **r** on the earth. 4305
Ps 11:6 Upon the wicked he shall **r** snares, ... 4305
Pr 16:15 favour is as a cloud of the latter **r** 4456
Pr 25:14 is like clouds and wind without **r** 1653
Pr 25:23 The north wind driveth away **r**: so 1653
Pr 26:1 and as **r** in harvest, so honour is. 4306
Pr 28:3 sweeping **r** which leaveth no food 4306
Ecc 11:3 If the clouds be full of **r**, they 1653
Isa 55:10 For as the **r** cometh down, and the. 1653
Jer 5:24 the Lord our God, that giveth **r**. 1653
Jer 14:22 of the Gentiles that can cause **r**? 1653
Hos 10:12 and **r** righteousness upon you. 3384
Am 4:7 it not to **r** upon another city: 4305
Mt 5:45 sendeth **r** on the just and on the. *1026*
Mt 7:25 And the **r** descended, and the *1028*
Jas 5:17 earnestly that it might not **r**: *1026*
Rev 11:6 it **r** not in the days of their. *1026, 5205*

RAINBOW
Rev 4:3 was a **r** round about the throne *2463*
Rev 10:1 a **r** was upon his head, and his *2463*

RAINED
Ge 19:24 **r** upon Sodom and Gomorrah 4305
Ex 9:23 **r** hail upon the land of Egypt 4305
Ps 78:24 **r** down manna upon them to eat, ... 4305
Lk 17:29 **r** fire and brimstone from heaven, ... *1026*
Jas 5:17 **r** not on the earth for the space of *1026*

RAINY
Pr 27:15 **r** day and contentious woman are 5464

RAISE
Dt 18:15 God will **r** up unto thee a Prophet 6965
Dt 25:7 to **r** up unto his brother a name 6965

R

Ru	4:10	**r** up the name of the dead upon	6965
1Sa	2:35	will **r** me up a faithful priest, that	6965
2Sa	12:11	I will **r** up evil against thee out of	6965
2Sa	12:17	him, to **r** him up from the earth:	6965
Ps	41:10	merciful unto me, and **r** me up,	6965
Isa	58:12	thou shalt **r** up the foundation	6965
Jer	23:5	**r** unto David a righteous Branch,	6965
Jer	50:32	fall, and none shall **r** him up:	6965
Eze	23:22	will **r** up thy lovers against thee,	5782
Hos	6:2	in the third day he will **r** us up, and	6965
Am	5:2	land; there is none to **r** her up	6965
Am	9:11	day will I **r** up the tabernacle of	6965
Hab	1:6	lo, I **r** up the Chaldeans, that	6965
Mt	10:8	**cleanse the lepers, r the dead,**	*1453*
Lk	3:8	to **r** up children unto Abraham	*1453*
Lk	20:28	and **r** up seed unto his brother	*1817*
Jn	6:40	**will r him up at the last day.**	*450*
Ac	2:30	**r** up Christ to sit on his throne;	*450*
Ac	26:8	you, that God should **r** the dead?	*1453*
1Co	6:14	will also **r** up us by his own power	*1825*
2Co	4:14	shall **r** up us also by Jesus,	*1453*
Heb	11:19	that God was able to **r** him up	*1453*
Jas	5:15	sick, and the Lord shall **r** him up;	*1453*

RAISED

Ex	9:16	for this cause have I **r** thee up	5975
Jgs	2:16	Nevertheless the Lord **r** up judges,	6965
2Sa	23:1	the man who was **r** up on high,	6965
1Ki	9:15	king Solomon **r**; for to build	5927
Ezr	1:5	all them whose spirit God had **r**,	5782
Isa	14:9	**r** up from their thrones all the	6965
Isa	45:13	I have **r** him up in righteousness	5782
Jer	51:11	the Lord hath **r** up the spirit of	5782
Zec	2:13	is **r** up out of his holy habitation	5782
Mt	11:5	**the deaf hear, the dead are r up,**	*1453*
Mt	16:21	and be **r** again the third day	*1453*
Mt	17:23	**the third day he shall be r again**	*1453*
Lk	7:22	**the deaf hear, the dead are r, to**	*1453*
Lk	9:22	**be slain, and be r the third day**	*1453*
Lk	20:37	**Now that the dead are r, even**	*1453*
Jn	12:17	**r** him from the dead, bare record	*1453*
Ac	2:32	This Jesus hath God **r** up, whereof	*450*
Ac	3:26	God, having **r** up his Son Jesus,	*450*
Ac	5:30	God of our fathers **r** up Jesus,	*1453*
Ac	10:40	Him God **r** up the third day, and	*1453*
Ac	13:23	**r** unto Israel a Saviour, Jesus:	*1453*
Ac	13:30	But God **r** him from the dead:	*1453*
Ac	13:33	in that he hath **r** up Jesus again;	*450*
Ro	4:24	believe on him that **r** up Jesus	*1453*
Ro	4:25	was **r** again for our justification	*1453*
Ro	6:4	as Christ was **r** up from the dead	*1453*
Ro	6:9	Christ being **r** from the dead dieth	*1453*
Ro	7:4	to him who is **r** from the dead,	*1453*
Ro	8:11	him that **r** up Jesus from the dead	*1453*
Ro	10:9	God hath **r** him from the dead	*1453*
1Co	6:14	God hath both **r** up the Lord, and	*1453*
1Co	15:16	dead rise not, then is not Christ **r**:	*1453*
1Co	15:17	Christ be not **r**, your faith is vain;	*1453*
1Co	15:42	corruption, it is **r** in incorruption:	*1453*
1Co	15:43	sown in dishonour, it is **r** in glory:	*1453*
1Co	15:43	sown in weakness; it is **r** in power:	*1453*
1Co	15:44	body; it is **r** a spiritual body	*1453*
1Co	15:52	dead shall be **r** incorruptible, and	*1453*
Eph	1:20	when he **r** him from the dead, and	*1453*
Eph	2:6	hath **r** us up together, and made	*4891*
Col	2:12	who hath **r** him from the dead	*1453*
1Th	1:10	whom he **r** from the dead, even	*1453*
Heb	11:35	received their dead **r** to life again:	*386*
1Pe	1:21	God, that **r** him up from the dead	*1453*

RAISETH

1Sa	2:8	He **r** up the poor out of the dust,	6965
Ps	145:14	**r** up all those that be bowed down	2210
Jn	5:21	**For as the Father r up the dead,**	*1453*
2Co	1:9	but in God which **r** the dead:	*1453*

RAM

Ge	22:13	**r** caught in a thicket by his horns:	352
Ex	29:15	their hands upon the head of the **r**.	352
Ex	29:18	burn the whole **r** upon the altar:	352
Ex	29:19	And thou shalt take the other **r**;	352
Ex	29:32	his sons shall eat the flesh of the **r**	352
Le	5:15	unto the Lord a **r** without blemish	352
Le	8:22	the other **r**, the **r** of consecration:	352
Nu	5:8	the **r** of the atonement, whereby an	352
Nu	23:2	on every altar a bullock and a **r**.	352
Eze	43:23	a **r** out of the flock without blemish.	352
Da	8:7	and there was no power in the **r** to	352

RAMS

Ge	31:38	and the **r** of the flock have I not	352
Le	8:2	for the sin offering, and two **r**,	352
1Sa	15:22	and to hearken than the fat of **r**	352
1Ch	29:21	a thousand bullocks, a thousand **r**,	352
Isa	1:11	am full of the burnt offerings of **r**,	352
Eze	4:2	set battering **r** against it round	3733
Eze	21:22	battering **r** against the gates,	3733
Mic	6:7	be pleased with thousands of **r**,	352

RAMS'

Ex	36:19	for the tent of **r** skins dyed red,	352
Jos	6:13	bearing seven trumpets of **r** horns	3104

RAN See also **RUN.**

Ge	18:2	he **r** to meet them from the tent	7323
Ge	33:4	Esau **r** to meet him, and embraced.	7323
1Sa	17:51	Therefore David **r**, and stood upon	7323
1Ki	18:46	**r** before Ahab to the entrance of	7323
Ps	105:41	**r** in the dry places like a river	1980
Jer	23:21	not sent these prophets, yet they **r**:	7323
Mt	8:32	swine **r** violently down a steep	*3729*
Mk	5:6	afar off, he **r** and worshipped him,	*5143*
Mk	5:13	**r** violently down a steep place	*3729*
Mk	15:36	one **r** and filled a spunge full of	*5143*
Lk	8:33	herd **r** violently down a steep	*3729*
Lk	15:20	**r, and fell on his neck, and kissed**	*5143*
Jn	20:4	So they **r** both together: and the	*5143*
Ac	12:14	the gate for gladness, but **r** in	*1532*
Jude	11	**r** greedily after the error of Balaam	

RANG

1Sa	4:5	shout, so that the earth **r** again	1949
1Ki	1:45	rejoicing, so that the city **r** again	1949

RANGING

Pr	28:15	As a roaring lion, and a **r** bear;	8264

RANK

Ge	41:7	devoured the seven **r** and full ears	1277
1Ch	12:33	thousand, which could keep **r**:	5737

RANKS

Joel	2:7	and they shall not break their **r**:	734

RANSOM
Ex 21:30 the **r** of his life whatsoever is.......... 6306
Ex 30:12 give every man a **r** for his soul 3724
Job 36:18 then a great **r** cannot deliver thee...... 3724
Pr 6:35 He will not regard any **r**; neither....... 3724
Pr 13:8 The **r** of a man's life are his riches:..... 3724
Pr 21:18 The wicked shall be a **r** for the 3724
Isa 43:3 I gave Egypt for thy **r**, Ethiopia........ 3724
Hos 13:14 I will **r** them from the power of 6299
Mt 20:28 **and to give his life a r for many,**....... *3083*
Mk 10:45 **and to give his life a r for many.**....... *3083*
1Ti 2:6 Who gave himself a **r** for all, to be *487*

RARE
Da 2:11 a **r** thing that the king requireth, ... 3358

RASE
Ps 137:7 **R** it, **r** it, even to the foundation....... 6168

RASH
Ecc 5:2 Be not **r** with thy mouth, and let 926

RASHLY
Ac 19:36 to be quiet, and to do nothing **r**....... *4312*

RATE
2Ki 25:30 of the king, a daily **r** for every day,..... 1697
2Ch 8:13 Even after a certain **r** every day........ 1697

RATHER
Job 7:15 strangling, and death **r** than my life,
Job 32:2 he justified himself **r** than God.
Job 36:21 hast thou chosen **r** than affliction.
Ps 52:3 lying **r** than to speak righteousness.
Ps 84:10 I had **r** be a doorkeeper in the.......... 977
Pr 8:10 and knowledge **r** than choice gold 408
Pr 16:16 understanding **r** to be chosen than
Pr 17:12 a man, **r** than a fool in his folly......... 408
Pr 22:1 A good name is **r** to be chosen than
Jer 8:3 And death shall be chosen **r** than life
Mt 10:6 **But go r to the lost sheep of the**....... *3123*
Mt 10:28 **r fear him which is able to**............ *3123*
Mt 18:9 **r than having two eyes to be cast**...... *2228*
Mt 27:24 but that **r** a tumult was made, he *3123*
Mk 5:26 nothing bettered, but **r** grew worse,.... *3123*
Lk 10:20 **but r rejoice, because your names**..... *3123*
Lk 11:41 **r give alms of such things as ye.**....... *4133*
Lk 12:31 **But r seek ye the kingdom of**......... *4133*
Lk 18:14 **to his house justified r than the other:**
Jn 3:19 **men loved darkness r than light,**....... *3123*
Ro 8:34 died, yea **r**, that is risen again *3123*
Ro 12:19 but **r** give place unto wrath: for
1Co 5:2 puffed up, and have not **r** mourned, ... *3123*
1Co 6:7 Why do ye not **r** take wrong? why *3123*
1Co 6:7 **r** suffer yourselves to be defrauded?.... *3123*
1Co 7:21 thou mayest be made free, use it **r** *3123*
1Co 9:12 this power over you, are not we **r**? *3123*
1Co 14:1 gifts, but **r** that ye may prophesy....... *3123*
1Co 14:19 I had **r** speak five words with my *2309*
2Co 2:7 ye ought **r** to forgive him, and......... *3123*
2Co 5:8 **r** to be absent from the body, and...... *3123*
2Co 12:9 will I **r** glory in my infirmities......... *3123*
Gal 4:9 known God, or **r** are known of God,... *3123*
Heb 11:25 Choosing **r** to suffer affliction with *3123*

RAVEN
Ge 8:7 And he sent forth a **r**, which went 6158
Job 38:41 Who provideth for the **r** his food? 6158

RAVENS
1Ki 17:4 the **r** to feed thee there............... 6158
Ps 147:9 food, and to the young **r** which cry 6158
Pr 30:17 the **r** of the valley shall pick it out,..... 6158
Lk 12:24 **Consider the r: for thy neither**........ *2876*

RAVENING
Ps 22:13 mouths, as a **r** and a roaring lion 2963
Eze 22:25 like a roaring lion **r** the prey; they 2963
Eze 22:27 are like wolves **r** the prey, to shed...... 2963
Mt 7:15 **but inwardly they are r wolves.**......... *727*
Lk 11:39 **part is full of r and wickedness.**........ *724*

RAVENOUS
Isa 35:9 there, nor any **r** beast shall go up 6530
Isa 46:11 Calling a **r** bird from the east, the...... 5861
Eze 39:4 give thee unto the **r** birds of every 5861

RAVIN
Ge 49:27 Benjamin shall **r** as a wolf: in the 2963
Na 2:12 with prey, and his dens with **r**......... 2966

RAVISHED
Pr 5:19 be thou **r** always with her love 7686
Isa 13:16 shall be spoiled, and their wives **r**...... 7693
La 5:11 They **r** the women in Zion, and 6031
Zec 14:2 houses rifled, and the women **r**; 7693

RAW
Le 13:15 for the **r** flesh is unclean: it is a........ 2416

RAZOR
Nu 6:5 shall no **r** come upon his head:........ 8593
Jgs 13:5 and no **r** shall come on his head: 4177
Jgs 16:17 hath not come a **r** upon mine head;.... 4177
1Sa 1:11 shall no **r** come upon his head......... 4177
Isa 7:20 Lord shave with a **r** that is hired, ... 8593

REACH
Ge 11:4 tower, whose top may **r** unto heaven;
Le 26:5 vintage shall **r** unto ... sowing time: ... 5381
Isa 30:28 overflowing stream, shall **r** to the...... 2673
Jn 20:27 **R hither thy finger, and behold.**....... *5342*
Jn 20:27 **r hither thy hand, and thrust it.**....... *5342*
2Co 10:13 us, a measure to **r** even unto you *2185*

REACHED
Ge 28:12 and the top of it **r** to heaven: and...... 5060
Jos 19:11 **r** to the river ... before Jokneam; 6293
Da 4:11 the height thereof **r** unto heaven 4291
Da 4:20 whose height **r** unto the heaven,....... 4291
Rev 18:5 For her sins have **r** unto heaven,........ *190*

REACHETH
2Ch 28:9 in a rage that **r** up unto heaven........ 5060
Ps 36:5 thy faithfulness **r** unto the clouds.
Ps 108:4 and thy truth **r** unto the clouds.
Pr 31:20 **r** forth her hands to the needy 7971
Jer 4:10 the sword **r** unto the soul............. 5060
Jer 4:18 because it **r** unto thine heart.......... 5060
Jer 51:9 for her judgment **r** unto heaven,....... 5060
Da 4:22 is grown, and **r** unto heaven 4291

REACHING
2Ch 3:11 **r** to the wing of the other cherub...... 5060
Php 3:13 **r** forth unto those things which *1901*

READ
Ex 24:7 **r** in the audience of the people: 7121
Dt 17:19 **r** therein all the days of his life:........ 7121

Dt	31:11	shalt **r** this law before all Israel	7121
Jos	8:34	he **r** all the words of the law,	7121
2Ki	5:7	the king of Israel had **r** the letter,	7121
2Ki	19:14	hand of the messengers, and **r** it:	7121
2Ki	22:16	which the king of Judah hath **r**:	7121
2Ki	23:2	he **r** in their ears all the words of	7121
Ezr	4:23	Artaxerxes' letter was **r** before	7123
Ne	8:8	they **r** in the book in the law of God	7121
Ne	9:3	**r** in the book of the law of the Lord	7121
Ne	13:1	day they **r** in the book of Moses	7121
Est	6:1	and they were **r** before the king	7121
Isa	29:11	**R** this, I pray thee: and he saith,	7121
Isa	29:12	**R** this, I pray thee: and he saith,	7121
Jer	36:6	shalt **r** them in the ears of all Judah	7121
Jer	36:15	ears. So Baruch **r** it in their ears	7121
Jer	36:21	Jehudi **r** it in the ears of the king	7121
Jer	51:61	see, and shalt **r** all these words;	7121
Da	5:7	Whosoever shall **r** this writing,	7123
Da	5:17	I will **r** the writing unto the king,	7123
Mt	12:3	**Have ye not r what David did,**	*314*
Mt	12:5	**Or have ye not r in the law, how**	*314*
Mt	19:4	**Have ye not r, that he which made**	*314*
Mt	21:16	**have ye never r, Out of the mouth**	*314*
Mt	21:42	**Did ye never r in the scriptures,**	*314*
Mt	22:31	**have ye not r that which was**	*314*
Mk	2:25	**Have ye never r what David did**	*314*
Mk	12:10	**And have ye not r this scripture;**	*314*
Mk	12:26	**ye not r in the book of Moses,**	*314*
Lk	4:16	sabbath day, and stood up for to **r**	*314*
Lk	6:3	**Have ye not r so much as this,**	*314*
Jn	19:20	This title then **r** many of the Jews:	*314*
Ac	8:30	heard him **r** the prophet Esaias	*314*
Ac	13:27	prophets which are **r** every sabbath	*314*
Ac	15:31	when they had **r**, they rejoiced	*314*
2Co	3:2	our hearts, known and **r** of all men:	*314*
2Co	3:15	even unto this day, when Moses is **r**,	*314*
Col	4:16	that it be **r** also in the church of the	*314*
1Th	5:27	be **r** unto all the holy brethren	*314*
Rev	5:4	worthy to open and to **r** the book,	*314*

READEST

Lk	10:26	**is written in the law? how r thou?**	*314*
Ac	8:30	Understandest thou what thou **r**?	*314*

READETH

Hab	2:2	tables, that he may run that **r** it	7121
Mt	24:15	**(whoso r, let him understand:)**	*314*
Mk	13:14	**(let him that r understand,) then**	*314*
Rev	1:3	Blessed is he that **r**, and they that	*314*

READINESS

Ac	17:11	received the word with all **r** of	*4288*
2Co	8:11	that as there was a **r** to will, so	*4288*

READING

Ne	8:8	caused them to understand the **r**	4744
Jer	51:63	hast made an end of **r** this book,	7121
2Co	3:14	away in the **r** of the old testament;	*320*
1Ti	4:13	Till I come, give attendance to **r**,	*320*

READY

Ge	46:29	And Joseph made **r** his chariot	631
Ex	17:4	they be almost **r** to stone me	5750
Ex	19:11	And be **r** against the third day:	3559
Nu	32:17	But we ourselves will go **r** armed	2363
Dt	26:5	Syrian **r** to perish was my father,	
Jgs	6:19	Gideon went in, and made **r** a kid,	
2Sa	15:15	thy servants are **r** to do whatsoever	
1Ki	6:7	was built of stone made **r** before	8003
1Ch	28:2	and had made **r** for the building:	3559
Ezr	7:6	a **r** scribe in the law of Moses	4106
Ne	9:17	but thou art a God **r** to pardon,	
Est	3:14	they should be **r** against that day	6264
Est	8:13	Jews should be **r** against that day	6264
Job	29:13	blessing of him that was **r** to perish	
Ps	11:2	make **r** their arrow upon the string,	3559
Ps	21:12	thou shalt make **r** thine arrows	3559
Ps	45:1	tongue is the pen of a **r** writer	4106
Ps	86:5	Lord, art good, and **r** to forgive;	
Ps	88:15	and **r** to die from my youth up:	
Pr	31:6	drink unto him that is **r** to perish,	4131
Ecc	5:1	be more **r** to hear, than to give	7138
Isa	38:20	The Lord was **r** to save me: therefore	
Isa	51:13	as if he were **r** to destroy? and	3559
Eze	7:14	the trumpet, even to make all **r**;	3559
Da	3:15	if ye be **r** that at what time ye	6263
Hos	7:6	made **r** their heart like an oven	7126
Mt	22:8	**The wedding is r, but they which**	*2092*
Mt	24:44	**Therefore be ye also r: for in**	*2092*
Mt	25:10	**they that were r went in with**	*2092*
Mt	26:19	and they made **r** the passover	*2090*
Mk	14:15	**prepared: there make r for us**	*2090*
Mk	14:16	and they made **r** the passover	*2090*
Mk	14:38	**spirit truly is r, but the flesh**	*4289*
Lk	1:17	**r** a people prepared for the Lord	*2090*
Lk	12:40	**Be ye therefore r also: for the**	*2092*
Lk	22:13	and they made **r** the passover	*2090*
Lk	22:33	Lord, I am **r** to go with thee, both	*2092*
Jn	7:6	**come: but your time is alway r**	*2092*
Ac	10:10	they made **r**, he fell into a trance	*3903*
Ac	23:15	he come near, are **r** to kill him	*2092*
Ro	1:15	am **r** to preach the gospel to you	*4289*
2Co	12:14	third time I am **r** to come to you;	*2093*
2Ti	4:6	For I am now **r** to be offered, and	*4689*
Heb	8:13	waxeth old is **r** to vanish away	*1451*
1Pe	1:5	**r** to be revealed in the last time	*2092*
1Pe	3:15	and be **r** always to give an answer	*2092*
1Pe	4:5	**r** to judge the quick and the dead	*2093*
1Pe	5:2	for filthy lucre, but of a **r** mind;	*4289*
Rev	3:2	**which remain, that are r to die:**	*3195*
Rev	12:4	the woman … **r** to be delivered	*3195*
Rev	19:7	and his wife hath made herself **r**	*2090*

REAP

Le	19:9	shalt not wholly **r** the corners of	
Le	25:11	neither **r** that which groweth of	7114
Ru	2:9	eyes be on the field that they do **r**,	7114
Job	4:8	and sow wickedness, **r** the same	7114
Ps	126:5	that sow in tears shall **r** in joy	7114
Pr	22:8	soweth iniquity shall **r** vanity:	7114
Ecc	11:4	regardeth the clouds shall not **r**	7114
Jer	12:13	sown wheat, but shall **r** thorns:	7114
Hos	8:7	and they shall **r** the whirlwind:	7114
Hos	10:12	in righteousness, **r** in mercy;	7114
Mic	6:15	shalt sow, but thou shalt not **r**;	7114
Mt	6:26	**neither do they r, nor gather**	*2325*
Mt	25:26	**I r where I sowed not, and gather**	*2325*
Lk	12:24	**ravens: for they neither sow nor r**	*2325*
Jn	4:38	**to r that whereon ye bestowed no**	*2325*
1Co	9:11	if we shall **r** your carnal things?	*2325*
2Co	9:6	sparingly shall **r** also sparingly;	*2325*
Gal	6:7	man soweth, that shall he also **r**	*2325*
Gal	6:8	of the Spirit **r** life everlasting	*2325*

Gal 6:9 for in due season we shall **r**, if we...... *2325*
Rev 14:15 Thrust in thy sickle, and **r**: for......... *2325*

REAPED
Hos 10:13 wickedness, ye have **r** iniquity; 7114
Jas 5:4 the cries of them which have **r** *2325*
Rev 14:16 the earth; and the earth was **r** *2325*

REAPER
Am 9:13 the plowman shall overtake the **r**,...... 7114

REAPERS
Ru 2:3 gleaned in the field after the **r**: 7114
Mt 13:30 **I will say to the r, Gather ye** *2327*
Mt 13:39 **world; and the r are the angels** *2327*

REAPEST
Le 23:22 corners of thy field when thou **r**, ... 7114
Lk 19:21 **and r that thou didst not sow**......... *2325*

REAPETH
Jn 4:36 **he that r receiveth wages, and**......... *2325*
Jn 4:37 **true, One soweth, and another r**....... *2325*

REAPING
Mt 25:24 **r where thou hast not sown, and** *2325*
Lk 19:22 **down, and r that I did not sow:** *2325*

REAR
Jn 2:20 wilt thou **r** it up in three days? *1453*

REARED
Ex 40:18 Moses **r** up the tabernacle, and........ 6965
Nu 9:15 day that the tabernacle was **r** up....... 6965
2Ch 33:3 and he **r** up altars for Baalim, and 6965

REASON
Ge 47:13 Canaan fainted by **r** of the famine 6440
Ex 2:23 Israel sighed by **r** of the bondage,...... 4480
Ex 3:7 cry by **r** of their taskmasters;.......... 6440
Dt 5:5 for ye were afraid by **r** of the fire,...... 6440
1Sa 12:7 may **r** with you before the Lord 8199
2Ch 5:14 not stand to minister by **r** of the....... 6440
Job 13:3 and I desire to **r** with God 3198
Job 17:7 Mine eye also is dim by **r** of sorrow
Ps 78:65 man that shouteth by **r** of wine
Ps 90:10 if by **r** of strength they be fourscore
Pr 20:4 will not plow by **r** of the cold;
Pr 26:16 seven men that can render a **r**......... 2940
Ecc 7:25 out wisdom, and the **r** of things, ... 2808
Isa 1:18 Come now, and let us **r** together, ... 3198
Da 4:36 time my **r** returned unto me; 4486
Jnh 2:2 I cried by **r** of mine affliction unto the
Mt 16:8 **why r ye among yourselves,** *1260*
Mk 2:8 **Why r ye these things in your**......... *1260*
Mk 8:17 **Why r ye, because ye have no** *1260*
Lk 5:22 them, **What r ye in your hearts?**....... *1260*
Ac 18:14 **r** would that I should bear with *3056*
2Co 3:10 by **r** of the glory that excelleth......... *1752*
1Pe 3:15 a **r** of the hope that is in you with *3056*
2Pe 2:2 by **r** of whom the way of truth *1223*

REASONABLE See also UNREASONABLE.
Ro 12:1 unto God, which is your **r** service...... *3050*

REASONED
Mt 16:7 they **r** among themselves, saying, ... *1260*
Mt 21:25 they **r** among themselves, saying, ... *1260*
Mk 2:8 that they so **r** among themselves, ... *1260*
Lk 20:14 **they r among themselves, saying,**...... *1260*
Lk 24:15 they communed together and **r**,........ *4802*
Ac 17:2 **r** with them out of the scriptures,...... *1256*
Ac 18:4 **r** in the synagogue every sabbath,...... *1256*
Ac 18:19 synagogue, and **r** with the Jews........ *1256*
Ac 24:25 And as he **r** of righteousness, ... *1256*

REASONING
Mk 12:28 having heard them **r** together *4802*
Lk 9:46 Then there arose a **r** among them, ... *1261*

REASONS
Job 32:11 I gave ear to your **r**, whilst ye.......... 8394
Isa 41:21 bring forth your strong **r**, saith the

REBEL
Nu 14:9 Only **r** not ye against the Lord 4775
Jos 1:18 doth **r** against thy commandment,..... 4784
Jos 22:16 **r** this day against the Lord? 4775
1Sa 12:14 not **r** against the commandment 4784
Ne 6:6 that thou and the Jews think to **r**:...... 4775
Isa 1:20 But if ye refuse and **r**, ye shall be 4784

REBELLED
Nu 20:24 because ye **r** against my word at....... 4784
Dt 9:23 ye **r** against the commandment of 4784
1Ki 12:19 So Israel **r** against the house of........ 6586
2Ki 18:7 he **r** against the king of Assyria........ 4775
2Ch 36:13 **r** against king Nebuchadnezzar, ... 4775
Ne 9:26 disobedient, and **r** against thee, ... 4775
Ps 5:10 for they have **r** against thee,.......... 4784
Ps 107:11 they **r** against the words of God,....... 4784
Isa 1:2 and they have **r** against me 6586
Isa 63:10 they **r**, and vexed his holy Spirit:....... 4784
La 1:18 **r** against his commandment:.......... 4784
La 3:42 We have transgressed and have **r**:...... 4784
Eze 20:8 they **r** against me, and would not..... 4784
Eze 20:13 **r** against me in the wilderness: 4784
Da 9:5 have **r**, even by departing from........ 4775
Da 9:9 though we have **r** against him; 4775

REBELLION
Dt 31:27 I know thy **r**, and thy stiff neck: 4805
1Sa 15:23 For **r** is as the sin of witchcraft,........ 4805
Ezr 4:19 **r** and sedition have been made........ 4776
Pr 17:11 An evil man seeketh only **r**:........... 4805
Jer 28:16 because thou hast taught **r** against..... 5627
Jer 29:32 he hath taught **r** against the Lord...... 5627

REBELLIOUS
Dt 9:7 ye have been **r** against the Lord........ 4784
Dt 9:24 Ye have been **r** against the Lord 4784
Dt 21:18 a man have a stubborn and **r** son...... 4784
1Sa 20:30 son of the perverse **r** woman, do 4780
Ezr 4:15 and know that this city is a **r** city,...... 4779
Ps 66:7 let not the **r** exalt themselves.......... 5637
Ps 78:8 a stubborn and **r** generation; a 4784
Isa 30:1 Woe to the **r** children, saith the........ 5637
Isa 65:2 hands all the day unto a **r** people,...... 5637
Jer 5:23 hath a revolting and a **r** heart;......... 4784
Eze 2:6 looks, though they be a **r** house 4805
Eze 3:27 forbear: for they are a **r** house......... 4805
Eze 12:2 dwellest in the midst of a **r** house, ... 4805
Eze 17:12 Say now to the **r** house, Know ye 4805

REBELS
Nu 17:10 kept for a token against the **r**; 4805
Nu 20:10 Hear now, ye **r**; must we fetch......... 4784
Eze 20:38 purge out from among you the **r** 4775

REBUKE See also UNREBUKABLE.

Le	19:17	in any wise **r** thy neighbour, and	3198
Dt	28:20	upon thee cursing, vexation and **r**,	4045
Ru	2:16	may glean them, and **r** her not	1605
Ps	6:1	O Lord, **r** me not in thine anger,	3198
Ps	18:15	were discovered at thy **r**, O Lord,	1606
Ps	38:1	O Lord, **r** me not in thy wrath:	3198
Pr	9:8	**r** a wise man, and he will love	3198
Pr	13:1	but a scorner heareth not **r**	1606
Pr	13:8	riches: but the poor heareth not **r**.	1606
Pr	27:5	Open **r** is better than secret love	8433
Ecc	7:5	is better to hear the **r** of the wise,	1606
Isa	2:4	and shall **r** many people:	3198
Isa	25:8	**r** of his people shall he take away	2781
Isa	30:17	shall flee at the **r** of one; at the	1606
Isa	50:2	behold, at my **r** I dry up the sea, I	1606
Jer	15:15	for thy sake I have suffered **r**	2781
Mic	4:3	and **r** strong nations afar off;	3198
Zec	3:2	The Lord **r** thee, O Satan; even	1605
Mt	16:22	took him, and began to **r** him,	*2008*
Mk	8:32	took him, and began to **r** him	*2008*
Lk	17:3	**trespass against thee, r him; and**	*2008*
Php	2:15	the sons of God, without **r**, in the	*298*
1Ti	5:1	**R** not an elder, but intreat him as	*1969*
1Ti	5:20	Them that sin **r** before all, that	*1651*
2Ti	4:2	**r**, exhort with all longsuffering	*2008*
Tit	1:13	Wherefore **r** them sharply, that	*1651*
Jude	9	but said, The Lord **r** thee	*2008*
Rev	3:19	**many as I love, I r and chasten:**	*1651*

REBUKED

Ge	37:10	and his father **r** him, and said	1605
Ps	106:9	He **r** the Red sea also, and it was	1605
Mt	8:26	and **r** the winds and the sea; and	*2008*
Mt	17:18	And Jesus **r** the devil; and he	*2008*
Mk	1:25	And Jesus **r** him, saying, **Hold thy**	*2008*
Mk	4:39	he arose, and **r** the wind, and said	*2008*
Mk	8:33	he **r** Peter, saying, **Get thee behind**	*2008*
Lk	4:35	And Jesus **r** him, saying, **Hold thy**	*2008*
Lk	4:39	and **r** the fever; and it left her:	*2008*
Lk	8:24	he arose, and **r** the wind and the	*2008*
Lk	9:42	Jesus **r** the unclean spirit, and	*2008*
Lk	9:55	he turned, and **r** them, and said,	*2008*
Lk	23:40	But the other answering **r** him,	*2008*
Heb	12:5	nor faint when thou art **r** of him:	*1651*
2Pe	2:16	But was **r** for his iniquity: the	*2192, 1649*

REBUKETH

Pr	9:7	he that **r** a wicked man getteth	3198
Pr	28:23	He that **r** a man afterwards shall	3198
Am	5:10	They hate him that **r** in the gate,	3198
Na	1:4	He **r** the sea, and maketh it dry,	1605

REBUKING

2Sa	22:16	discovered, at the **r** of the Lord	1606
Lk	4:41	he **r** them suffered them not to	*2008*

RECALL

La	3:21	This I **r** to my mind, therefore	7725

RECEIVE

Ge	4:11	mouth to **r** thy brother's blood	3947
Dt	9:9	the mount to **r** the tables of stone	3947
2Ki	5:16	before whom I stand, I will **r** none	3947
2Ch	7:7	not able to **r** the burnt offerings,	3557
Job	2:10	of God, and shall we not **r** evil?	6901
Ps	6:9	the Lord will **r** my prayer.	3947
Ps	73:24	and afterward **r** me to glory	3947
Pr	1:3	To **r** the instruction of wisdom	3947
Pr	2:1	My son, if thou wilt **r** my words	3947
Pr	8:10	**R** my instruction, and not silver;	3947
Isa	57:6	Should I **r** comfort in these?	5162
Jer	5:3	they have refused to **r** correction:	3947
Jer	17:23	might not hear, nor **r** instruction	3947
Eze	3:10	speak unto thee **r** in thine heart,	3947
Da	2:6	ye shall **r** of me gifts and rewards	6902
Mal	3:10	shall not be room enough to **r** it	
Mt	10:14	**whosoever shall not r you, nor**	*1209*
Mt	10:41	**shall r a prophet's reward; and**	*2983*
Mt	11:5	**blind r their sight, and the lame**	*308*
Mt	11:14	**if ye will r it, this is Elias, which**	*1209*
Mt	18:5	**whoso shall r one such little child**	*1209*
Mt	19:11	**All men cannot r this saying, save**	*5562*
Mt	21:22	**in prayer, believing, ye shall r**	*2983*
Mt	23:14	**ye shall r the greater damnation**	*2983*
Mk	4:16	**immediately r it with gladness;**	*2983*
Mk	6:11	**whosoever shall not r you, nor**	*1209*
Mk	9:37	**shall r one of such children in**	*1209*
Mk	9:37	**whosoever shall r me, receiveth**	*1209*
Mk	10:15	**shall not r the kingdom of God**	*1209*
Mk	10:51	Lord, that I might **r** my sight	*308*
Mk	11:24	**ye pray, believe that ye r them,**	*2983*
Mk	12:40	**these shall r greater damnation**	*2983*
Lk	6:34	**to them of whom ye hope to r,**	*618*
Lk	8:13	**they hear, r the word with joy;**	*1209*
Lk	9:5	**whosoever will not r you, when**	*1209*
Lk	9:48	**shall r this child in my name**	*1209*
Lk	9:48	**whosoever shall r me receiveth**	*1209*
Lk	10:10	**they r you not, go your ways out**	*1209*
Lk	18:17	**shall not r the kingdom of God as**	*1209*
Lk	18:41	said, Lord, that I may **r** my sight	*308*
Lk	19:12	**to r for himself a kingdom, and**	*2983*
Lk	20:47	**same shall r greater damnation**	*2983*
Lk	23:41	for we **r** the due reward of our	*618*
Jn	3:27	A man can **r** nothing, except it be	*2983*
Jn	5:41	**I r not honour from men**	*2983*
Jn	5:43	**Father's name, and ye r me not:**	*2983*
Jn	14:3	**again, and r you unto myself;**	*3880*
Jn	16:24	**ask, and ye shall r, that your joy**	*2983*
Jn	20:22	unto them, **R ye the Holy Ghost:**	*2983*
Ac	1:8	**But ye shall r power, after that**	*2983*
Ac	2:38	shall **r** the gift of the Holy Ghost	*2983*
Ac	7:59	and saying, Lord Jesus, **r** my spirit	*1209*
Ac	8:15	that they might **r** the Holy Ghost:	*2983*
Ac	9:12	**on him, that he might r his sight**	*308*
Ac	10:43	in him shall **r** remission of sins	*2983*
Ac	20:35	**is more blessed to give than to r**	*2983*
Ac	26:18	**they may r forgiveness of sins**	*2983*
Ro	13:2	shall **r** to themselves damnation	*2983*
Ro	14:1	that is weak in the faith **r** ye,	*4355*
1Co	3:8	man shall **r** his own reward	*2983*
1Co	4:7	hast thou that thou didst not **r**?	*2983*
2Co	5:10	**r** the things done in his body,	*2865*
2Co	6:1	ye **r** not the grace of God in vain	*1209*
2Co	7:2	**R** us; we have wronged no man	*5562*
2Co	11:4	of if ye **r** another spirit, which ye	*2983*
Gal	3:14	might **r** the promise of the Spirit	*2983*
Gal	4:5	we might **r** the adoption of sons	*618*
Col	3:24	**r** the reward of the inheritance:	*618*
Col	3:25	**r** for the wrong which he hath	*2865*
1Ti	5:19	an elder **r** not an accusation, but	*3858*
Phm	17	a partner, **r** him as myself	*4355*
Heb	9:15	might **r** the promise of eternal	*2983*

Heb 10:36 of God, ye might **r** the promise........ *2865*
Jas 1:12 is tried, he shall **r** the crown of life, ... *2983*
Jas 1:21 **r** with meekness the engrafted *1209*
Jas 3:1 shall **r** the greater condemnation *2983*
Jas 4:3 Ye ask, and **r** not, because ye ask....... *2983*
1Pe 5:4 **r** a crown of glory that fadeth not *2865*
2Pe 2:13 **r** the reward of unrighteousness, ... *2865*
1Jn 3:22 whatsoever we ask, we **r** of him, ... *2983*
1Jn 5:9 If we **r** the witness of men, the *2983*
Rev 4:11 to **r** glory and honour and power: *2983*
Rev 5:12 Lamb that was slain to **r** power........ *2983*
Rev 13:16 to **r** a mark in their right hand,........ *1325*
Rev 14:9 **r** his mark in his forehead, or in *2983*
Rev 17:12 but **r** power as kings one hour with *2983*
Rev 18:4 and that ye **r** not of her plagues *2983*

RECEIVED

Nu 23:20 I have **r** commandment to bless:....... 3947
Jos 18:2 had not yet **r** their inheritance 2505
Jgs 13:23 would not have **r** a burnt offering 3947
Ps 68:18 thou hast **r** gifts for men; yea, for 3947
Isa 40:2 hath **r** of the Lord's hand double 3947
Mt 10:8 freely ye have r, freely give, ... *2983*
Mt 20:9 hour, they r every man a penny *2983*
Mt 20:10 that they should have r more; *2983*
Mt 20:34 and immediately their eyes **r** sight,...... *308*
Mt 25:24 which had r the one talent came *2983*
Mt 25:27 have r mine own with usury *2865*
Mk 16:19 he was **r** up into heaven, and sat on *353*
Lk 10:38 Martha **r** him into her house.......... *5264*
Lk 15:27 he hath r him safe and sound *618*
Lk 18:43 And immediately he **r** his sight, ... *308*
Jn 1:11 his own, and his own **r** him not *3880*
Jn 1:12 as many as **r** him, to them gave........ *2983*
Jn 1:16 And of his fulness have all we **r**, ... *2983*
Jn 9:15 asked him how he had **r** his sight *308*
Jn 19:30 Jesus therefore had **r** the vinegar, ... *2983*
Ac 1:9 a cloud **r** him out of their sight........ *5274*
Ac 8:17 them, and they **r** the Holy Ghost,...... *2983*
Ac 10:47 **r** the Holy Ghost as well as we?........ *2983*
Ac 17:11 they **r** the word with all readiness...... *1209*
Ac 19:2 Have ye **r** the Holy Ghost since ye *2983*
Ro 4:11 And he **r** the sign of circumcision,..... *2983*
Ro 5:11 we have now **r** the atonement......... *2983*
Ro 8:15 ye have **r** the Spirit of adoption,....... *2983*
1Co 4:7 glory, as if thou hadst not **r** it? *2983*
1Co 15:3 you first of all that which I also **r**,...... *3880*
2Co 4:1 as we have **r** mercy, we faint not; *1653*
Gal 3:2 **R** ye the Spirit by the works of *2983*
Col 2:6 As ye have therefore **r** Christ Jesus *3880*
1Th 1:6 **r** the word in much affliction *1209*
1Th 2:13 ye **r** it not as the word of men......... *1209*
2Th 2:10 they **r** not the love of the truth,........ *1209*
1Ti 3:16 on in the world, **r** up into glory *353*
Heb 2:2 **r** a just recompense of reward; *2983*
Heb 11:13 not having **r** the promises, but *2983*
Heb 11:35 Women **r** their dead raised to life *2983*
1Pe 1:18 vain conversation **r** by tradition
2Pe 1:17 he **r** from God the Father honour...... *2983*
Rev 2:27 shivers: even as I r of my Father. *2983*
Rev 17:12 which have **r** no kingdom as yet; *2983*
Rev 19:20 that had **r** the mark of the beast *2983*
Rev 20:4 **r** his mark upon their foreheads *2983*

RECEIVEDST

Lk 16:5 in thy lifetime r thy good things, ... *618*

RECEIVETH

Pr 21:11 wise is instructed, he **r** knowledge 3947
Pr 29:4 but he that **r** gifts overthroweth it
Jer 7:28 Lord their God, nor **r** correction:...... 3947
Mt 7:8 For every one that asketh r; and *2983*
Mt 10:40 that r me r him that sent me *1209*
Mk 9:37 little children in my name, r me: *1209*
Lk 9:48 receive me r him that sent me: *1209*
Lk 11:10 every one that asketh r; and he *2983*
Lk 15:2 This man **r** sinners, and eateth *4327*
Jn 13:20 he that r me r him that sent me *2983*
1Co 2:14 the natural man **r** not the things....... *1209*
1Co 9:24 race run all, but one **r** the prize? *2983*
Heb 12:6 scourgeth every son whom he **r** *3858*
Rev 2:17 man knoweth saving he that r it. *2983*
Rev 14:11 whosoever **r** the mark of his name. *2983*

RECEIVING

Ro 1:27 **r** in themselves that recompence........ *618*
1Pe 1:9 **R** the end of your faith, even the....... *2865*

RECKON

Le 27:23 priest shall **r** unto him the worth 2803
Mt 18:24 And when he had begun to r, one *4865*
Ro 6:11 **r** ye also yourselves to be dead......... *3049*
Ro 8:18 For I **r** that the sufferings of this....... *3049*

RECKONED

2Ki 12:15 they **r** not with the men, into 2803
1Ch 9:1 all Israel were **r** by genealogies;........ 3187
Ezr 2:62 those that were **r** by genealogy,........ 3187
Ne 7:5 that they might be **r** by genealogy 3187
Ps 40:5 cannot be **r** up in order unto thee:
Lk 22:37 was r among the transgressors: *3049*
Ro 4:9 say that faith was **r** to Abraham *3049*

RECKONING

2Ki 22:7 there was no **r** made with them 2803

RECOMPENCE

Dt 32:35 me belongeth vengeance, and **r**; 8005
Pr 12:14 the **r** of a man's hands shall be 1576
Isa 35:4 vengeance, even God with a **r**; he...... 1576
Isa 66:6 that rendereth **r** to his enemies........ 1576
La 3:64 Render unto them a **r**, O Lord 1576
Hos 9:7 the days of **r** are come; Israel, ... 7966
Lk 14:12 thee again, and a r be made thee *468*
Ro 1:27 **r** of their error which was meet......... *489*
Heb 2:2 received a just **r** of reward;............ *3405*
Heb 10:35 which hath great **r** of reward.......... *3405*
Heb 11:26 respect unto the **r** of the reward *3405*

RECOMPENCES

Isa 34:8 year of **r** for the controversy of........ 7966
Jer 51:56 for the Lord God of **r** shall surely...... 1578

RECOMPENSE

Ru 2:12 The Lord **r** thy work, and a full........ 7999
Pr 20:22 Say not thou, I will **r** evil; but 7999
Jer 16:18 And first I will **r** their iniquity......... 7999
Jer 50:29 **r** her according to her work; 7999
Eze 7:4 I will **r** thy ways upon thee, and 5414
Eze 11:21 **r** their way upon their own heads...... 5414
Eze 17:19 even it will I **r** upon his own head 5414
Eze 23:49 they shall **r** your lewdness upon 5414
Hos 12:2 to his doings will he **r** him............ 7725
Lk 14:14 they cannot r thee: for thou shalt *467*
Ro 12:17 **R** to no man evil for evil. Provide....... *591*

2Th 1:6 with God to **r** tribulation to them *467*
Heb 10:30 unto me, I will **r**, saith the Lord *467*

RECOMPENSED
2Sa 22:21 of my hands hath he **r** me 7725
Ps 18:24 the Lord **r** me according to my 7725
Pr 11:31 righteous shall be **r** in the earth: 7999
Lk 14:14 **thou shalt be r at the resurrection.** *467*
Ro 11:35 and it shall be **r** unto him again? *467*

RECONCILE
Eph 2:16 **r** both unto God in one body by the *604*
Col 1:20 him to **r** all things unto himself; *604*

RECONCILED
Mt 5:24 **first be r to thy brother, and** *1259*
Ro 5:10 **r** to God by the death of his Son *2644*
1Co 7:11 unmarried, or be **r** to her husband: *2644*
2Co 5:18 of God, who hath **r** us to himself by ... *2644*
2Co 5:20 in Christ's stead, be ye **r** to God *2644*
Col 1:21 wicked works, yet now hath he **r**. *604*

RECONCILIATION
Le 8:15 sanctified it, to make **r** upon it 3722
2Ch 29:24 made **r** with their blood upon the 2398
Eze 45:17 to make **r** for the house of Israel. 3722
Da 9:24 and to make **r** for iniquity, and to 3722
2Co 5:18 hath given to us the ministry of **r**; *2643*
2Co 5:19 committed unto us the word of **r**; *2643*
Heb 2:17 make **r** for the sins of the people *2433*

RECONCILING
Ro 11:15 of them be the **r** of the world, ... *2643*
2Co 5:19 Christ, **r** the world unto himself *2644*

RECORD
Ex 20:24 where I **r** my name I will come 2142
Dt 30:19 heaven and earth to **r** this day 5749
Dt 31:28 heaven and earth to **r** against 5749
Job 16:19 in heaven, and my **r** is on high 7717
Jn 1:34 bare **r** that this is the Son of God *3140*
Jn 8:14 **of myself, yet my r is true: for** *3141*
Jn 12:17 raised him from the dead, bare **r** *3140*
Jn 19:35 And he that saw it bare **r**, and *3140*
Ac 20:26 I take you to **r** this day, that I am *3143*
Ro 10:2 bear them **r** that they have a zeal *3140*
Gal 4:15 for I bear you **r**, that, if it had *3140*
Php 1:8 For God is my **r**, how greatly I *3144*
1Jn 5:7 are three that bear **r** in heaven *3140*
1Jn 5:10 the **r** that God gave of his Son *3141*
3Jn 12 and ye know that our **r** is true *3141*
Rev 1:2 Who bare **r** of the word of God *3140*

RECOVER
2Ki 1:2 whether I shall **r** of this disease 2421
2Ki 8:8 saying, Shall I **r** of this disease? 2421
2Ki 8:10 him, Thou mayest certainly **r**: 2421
Ps 39:13 spare me, that I may **r** strength, ... 1082
Isa 38:16 so wilt thou **r** me, and make me to 2492
Mk 16:18 on the sick, and they shall **r**. *2192, 2573*

RECOVERED
1Sa 30:19 had taken to them: David **r** all 7725
1Sa 30:22 ought of the spoil that we have **r**, ... 5337
Jer 8:22 of the daughter of my people **r**? 5927

RED
Ge 25:25 And the first came out **r**, all over 132
Ge 25:30 thee, with that same **r** pottage; 122
Ex 36:19 for the tent of rams' skins dyed **r**, ... 119
Nu 19:2 bring thee a **r** heifer without spot, ... 122
Pr 23:31 thou upon the wine when it is **r**, ... 119
Isa 1:18 though they be **r** like crimson, ... 119
Zec 1:8 behold a man riding upon a **r** horse, ... 122
Mt 16:2 **be fair weather: for the sky is r** *4449*
Mt 16:3 **day: for the sky is r and lowring** *4449*
Rev 6:4 out another horse that was **r**: *4450*
Rev 12:3 behold a great **r** dragon, having *4450*

RED SEA
Ex 13:18 way the wilderness of the **R** sea: 5488
Ex 15:4 also are drowned in the **R** sea 5488
Dt 2:1 wilderness by the way of the **R** sea, ... 5488
Dt 11:4 the water of the **R** sea to overflow 5488
Jos 2:10 dried up the water of the **R** sea 5488
Ne 9:9 heardest their cry by the **R** sea; 5488
Ps 106:9 He rebuked the **R** sea also, and it 5488
Ps 136:15 Pharaoh and his host in the **R** sea: 5488
Ac 7:36 land of Egypt, and in the **R** sea, ... *2281*
Heb 11:29 passed through the **R** sea as by dry *2281*

REDEEM
Ex 13:13 firstborn of man … shalt thou **r**. 6299
Le 25:29 within a full year may he **r** it 1353
Le 27:13 But if he will at all **r** it, then he 1350
Le 27:20 And if he will not **r** the field, or if 1350
Nu 18:15 firstborn of man shalt thou … **r**. 6299
Ru 4:4 if thou wilt not **r** it, then tell me, ... 1350
Ru 4:6 I cannot **r** it for myself, lest I mar 1350
Ne 5:5 neither is it in our power to **r** them;
Ps 25:22 **R** Israel, O God, out of all his 6299
Ps 44:26 and **r** us for thy mercies' sake 6299
Ps 49:7 can by any means **r** his brother, ... 6299
Ps 72:14 He shall **r** their soul from deceit 1350
Isa 50:2 shortened at all, that it cannot **r**? 6304
Hos 13:14 grave; I will **r** them from death: 1350
Gal 4:5 To **r** them that were under the *1805*
Tit 2:14 he might **r** us from all iniquity *3084*

REDEEMED
Ge 48:16 Angel which **r** me from all evil 1350
Ex 21:8 then shall he let her be **r**: 6299
Le 19:20 not at all **r**, nor freedom given her; 6299
Le 25:30 **r** within the space of a full year, ... 1350
Le 25:54 And if he be not **r** in these years, ... 1350
Le 27:29 None devoted, … shall be **r**; 6299
Dt 13:5 **r** you out of the house of bondage, ... 6299
2Sa 4:9 hath **r** my soul out of all adversity 6299
1Ki 1:29 hath **r** my soul out of all distress 6299
Ne 1:10 thou hast **r** by thy great power 6299
Ps 31:5 hast **r** me, O Lord God of truth 6299
Ps 71:23 and my soul, which thou hast **r** 6299
Ps 107:2 Let the **r** of the Lord say so, whom 1350
Ps 136:24 And hath **r** us from our enemies: 6561
Isa 1:27 Zion shall be **r** with judgment, ... 6299
Isa 43:1 Fear not: for I have **r** thee, I have 1350
Isa 44:22 return unto me; for I have **r** thee 1350
Isa 51:11 the **r** of the Lord shall return, ... 6299
Isa 62:12 The holy people, The **r** of the Lord: 1350
Isa 63:9 his love and in his pity he **r** them; 1350
La 3:58 of my soul; thou hast **r** my life 1350
Hos 7:13 though I have **r** them, yet they 6299
Lk 1:68 for he hath visited and **r** his people *3085*
Lk 24:21 he which should have **r** Israel: *3084*
Gal 3:13 Christ hath **r** us from the curse *1805*
1Pe 1:18 not **r** with corruptible things *3084*

Rev 5:9 and hast **r** us to God by thy blood *59*
Rev 14:4 These were **r** from among men.......... *59*

REDEEMER

Job 19:25 I know that my **r** liveth, and that 1350
Ps 19:14 O Lord, my strength, and my **r**........ 1350
Pr 23:11 For their **r** is mighty; he shall 1350
Isa 44:24 thy **r**, and he that formed thee 1350
Isa 47:4 As for our **r**, the Lord of hosts is his.... 1350
Isa 49:7 the **R** of Israel, and his Holy One, ... 1350
Isa 49:26 Lord am thy Saviour and thy **R**,....... 1350
Isa 54:5 and thy **R** the Holy One of Israel;...... 1350
Isa 63:16 thou, O Lord, art our father, our **r**;..... 1350
Jer 50:34 Their **R** is strong; The Lord of......... 1350

REDEEMETH

Ps 34:22 Lord **r** the soul of his servants: 6299
Ps 103:4 Who **r** thy life from destruction;....... 1350

REDEEMING

Eph 5:16 **R** the time, because the days are *1805*
Col 4:5 them that are without, **r** the time *1805*

REDEMPTION

Le 25:52 give him again the price of his **r**....... 1353
Ps 49:8 (For the **r** of their soul is precious,..... 6306
Ps 130:7 mercy, and with him is plenteous **r** 6304
Jer 32:8 the **r** is thine; buy it for thyself......... 1353
Lk 2:38 that looked for **r** in Jerusalem *3085*
Lk 21:28 **heads; for your r draweth nigh**......... *629*
Ro 3:24 through the **r** that is in Christ Jesus:..... *629*
Eph 1:7 whom we have **r** through his blood,..... *629*
Eph 4:30 ye are sealed unto the day of **r**.......... *629*
Col 1:14 whom we have **r** through his blood *629*
Heb 9:12 having obtained eternal **r** for us *3085*
Heb 9:15 for the **r** of the transgressions that *629*

REDOUND

2Co 4:15 of many **r** to the glory of God......... *4052*

REED

1Ki 14:15 as a **r** is shaken in the water, ... 7070
2Ki 18:21 upon the staff of this bruised **r**, ... 7070
Isa 42:3 A bruised **r** shall he not break, and..... 7070
Eze 40:3 in his hand, and a measuring **r**; 7070
Mt 11:7 **to see? A r shaken with the wind?**...... *2563*
Mt 12:20 A bruised **r** shall he not break, and..... *2563*
Mt 27:29 head, and a **r** in his right hand:........ *2563*
Mt 27:48 it with vinegar, and put it on a **r**, ... *2563*
Mk 15:19 smote him on the head with a **r**,....... *2563*
Mk 15:36 full of vinegar, and put it on a **r**,....... *2563*
Lk 7:24 **to see? A r shaken with the wind?**...... *2563*
Rev 21:15 talked with me had a golden **r** to *2563*

REFINE

Zec 13:9 will **r** them as silver is refined,......... 6884

REFINED

1Ch 28:18 for the altar of incense **r** gold 2212
1Ch 29:4 seven thousand talents of **r** silver,...... 2212
Isa 48:10 I have **r** thee, but not with silver; 6884
Zec 13:9 and will refine them as silver is **r**,...... 6884

REFINER'S

Mal 3:2 for he is like a **r** fire, and like.......... 6884

REFRAIN

Ge 45:1 Joseph could not **r** himself before....... 662
Job 7:11 I will not **r** my mouth; I will 2820
Pr 1:15 them; **r** thy foot from their path: 4513
Ecc 3:5 and a time to **r** from embracing; 7368
Jer 31:16 **R** thy voice from weeping, and 4513
1Pe 3:10 let him **r** his tongue from evil,......... *3973*

REFRAINED

Ps 40:9 I have not **r** my lips, O Lord, thou 3607
Ps 119:101 **r** my feet from every evil way,......... 3601
Isa 42:14 I have been still and **r** myself: 662
Jer 14:10 they have not **r** their feet 2820

REFRAINETH

Pr 10:19 sin: but he that **r** his lips is wise 2820

REFRESHED

Ex 23:12 and the stranger, may be **r**............ 5314
Ex 31:17 seventh day he rested, and was **r**....... 5314
Ro 15:32 of God, and may with you be **r**........ *4875*
1Co 16:18 they have **r** my spirit and yours: *373*
2Ti 1:16 he oft **r** me, and was not ashamed *404*

REFRESHETH

Pr 25:13 for he **r** the soul of his masters 7725

REFRESHING

Ac 3:19 the times of **r** shall come from *403*

REFUGE

Nu 35:6 there shall be six cities for **r**........... 4733
Nu 35:15 These six cities shall be a **r**, both....... 4733
Jos 20:2 Appoint out for you cities of **r**,........ 4733
Jos 20:3 your **r** from the avenger of blood. 4733
2Sa 22:3 my high tower, and my **r**, my 4498
Ps 46:1 God is our **r** and strength, a very 4268
Ps 46:7 us; the God of Jacob is our **r**.......... 4869
Ps 57:1 of thy wings will I make my **r**......... 2620
Ps 59:16 and **r** in the day of my trouble 4498
Ps 62:7 my strength, and my **r**, is in God 4268
Ps 91:2 Lord, He is my **r** and my fortress:...... 4268
Ps 94:22 and my God is the rock of my **r**....... 4268
Ps 142:4 **r** failed me; no man cared for 4498
Ps 142:5 Thou art my **r** and my portion in...... 4268
Pr 14:26 his children shall have a place of **r** 4268
Isa 28:15 for we have made lies our **r**, and....... 4268
Isa 28:17 hail shall sweep away the **r** of lies, ... 4268
Jer 16:19 and my **r** in the day of affliction, ... 4498
Heb 6:18 have fled for **r** to lay hold upon the *2703*

REFUSE

Ex 4:23 if thou **r** to let him go, behold, I........ 3985
Ex 10:3 long wilt thou **r** to humble thyself 3985
Ex 16:28 **r** ye to keep my commandments 3985
Ex 22:17 utterly **r** to give her unto him,......... 3985
Pr 8:33 and be wise, and **r** it not 6544
Pr 21:7 because they **r** to do judgment 3985
Pr 21:25 him; for his hands **r** to labour......... 3985
Isa 1:20 But if ye **r** and rebel, ye shall be 3985
Isa 7:15 that he may know to **r** the evil 3988
Jer 9:6 through deceit they **r** to know me,..... 3985
Jer 13:10 people, which **r** to hear my words 3987
Ac 25:11 worthy of death, I **r** not to die: *3868*
1Ti 4:7 **r** profane and old wives' fables *3868*
1Ti 5:11 But the younger widows **r**: for......... *3868*
Heb 12:25 that ye **r** not him that speaketh........ *3868*

REFUSED

Ge 37:35 but he **r** to be comforted; and he 3985
Ge 39:8 he **r**, and said unto his master's........ 3985
Nu 20:21 Edom **r** to give Israel passage 3985

1Sa 8:19 the people **r** to obey the voice of....... 3985
1Ki 21:15 which he **r** to give thee for money:..... 3985
2Ki 5:16 he urged him to take it; but he **r**....... 3985
Ne 9:17 **r** to obey, neither were mindful of 3985
Ps 77:2 not: my soul **r** to be comforted........ 3985
Ps 78:10 of God, and **r** to walk in his law;....... 3985
Ps 118:22 The stone which the builders **r** is 3988
Pr 1:24 Because I have called, and ye **r**;........ 3985
Jer 5:3 they have **r** to receive correction: 3985
Jer 31:15 **r** to be comforted for her children,..... 3985
Eze 5:6 they have **r** my judgments and 3988
Zec 7:11 But they **r** to hearken, and pulled...... 3985
Ac 7:35 Moses whom they **r**, saying, Who....... *720*
1Ti 4:4 is good, and nothing to be **r**,........... *579*
Heb 11:24 **r** to be called the son of Pharaoh's *720*

REFUSETH
Ex 7:14 hardened, he **r** to let the people go. 3985
Nu 22:13 the Lord **r** to give me leave to go 3985
Dt 25:7 My husband's brother **r** to raise up 3985
Pr 10:17 but he that **r** reproof erreth........... 5800
Pr 15:32 He that **r** instruction despiseth........ 6544
Jer 15:18 incurable, which **r** to be healed?....... 3985

REGARD
Ge 45:20 Also **r** not your stuff;...... 5869, 2347, 5921
Le 19:31 **R** not them that have familiar......... 6437
Dt 28:50 shall not **r** the person of the old, ... 5375
1Sa 4:20 answered not, neither did she **r** it...... 3820
Job 35:13 neither will the Almighty **r** it.......... 7789
Job 36:21 Take heed, **r** not iniquity: for.......... 6437
Ps 28:5 they **r** not the works of the Lord, ... 995
Ps 66:18 If I **r** iniquity in my heart, the......... 7200
Ps 94:7 neither shall the God of Jacob **r** it....... 995
Ps 102:17 will **r** the prayer of the destitute,....... 6437
Pr 6:35 He will not **r** any ransom;....... 5375, 6440
Ecc 8:2 that in **r** of the oath of God...... 5921, 1700
Isa 5:12 they **r** not the work of the Lord,....... 5027
La 4:16 he will no more **r** them: they.......... 5027
Da 11:37 shall he **r** the God of his fathers,........ 995
Mal 1:9 means: will he **r** your persons? 5375
Lk 18:4 **I fear not God, nor r man;**............ *1788*

REGARDED
1Ch 17:17 **r** me according to the estate of a....... 7200
Ps 106:44 Nevertheless he **r** their affliction, ... 7200
Pr 1:24 out my hand, and no man **r**;.......... 7181
Da 3:12 men, O king, have not **r** thee:.... 7761, 2942
Lk 1:48 he hath **r** the low estate of his *1914*
Lk 18:2 **feared not God, neither r man:**........ *1788*
Heb 8:9 and I **r** them not, saith the Lord *272*

REGARDEST
Mt 22:16 for thou **r** not the person of men *991*
Mk 12:14 for thou **r** not the person of men *991*

REGARDETH
Dt 10:17 **r** not persons, nor taketh reward;...... 5375
Job 34:19 nor **r** the rich more than the poor? 5234
Pr 12:10 man **r** the life of his beast:............ 3045
Pr 13:18 that **r** reproof shall be honoured 8104
Pr 15:5 but he that **r** reproof is prudent 8104
Ecc 5:8 that is higher than the highest **r**;....... 8104
Ecc 11:4 that **r** the clouds shall not reap 7200
Da 6:13 of Judah, **r** not thee, O king 7761, 2942
Mal 2:13 he **r** not the offering any more,........ 6437
Ro 14:6 **r** the day, **r** it unto the Lord; *5425*

REGARDING
Job 4:20 perish for ever without any **r** it........ 7760
Php 2:30 nigh unto death, not **r** his life *3851*

REGENERATION
Mt 19:28 **the r when the Son of man shall**....... *3824*
Tit 3:5 he saved us, by the washing of **r**,....... *3824*

REGION
Mt 4:16 sat in the **r** and shadow of death....... *5561*
Ac 13:49 published throughout all the **r** *5561*

REGISTER
Ezr 2:62 sought their **r** among those that....... 3791
Ne 7:64 sought their **r** among those that....... 3791

REHEARSE
Jgs 5:11 shall they **r** the righteous acts of....... 8567

REHEARSED
1Sa 17:31 spake, they **r** them before Saul:........ 5046
Ac 14:27 they **r** all that God had done with....... *312*

REIGN
Ge 37:8 him, Shalt thou indeed **r** over us?...... 4427
Ex 15:18 The Lord shall **r** for ever and ever...... 4427
1Sa 8:7 me, that I should not **r** over them 4427
1Sa 12:12 Nay; but a king shall **r** over us: 4427
2Sa 3:21 **r** over all that thine heart desireth 4427
1Ki 1:30 Solomon thy son shall **r** after me,...... 4427
1Ki 11:37 **r** according to all that thy soul 4427
Job 34:30 That the hypocrite **r** not, lest the 4427
Ps 146:10 The Lord shall **r** for ever, even thy 4427
Pr 8:15 By me kings **r**, and princes decree 4427
Ecc 4:14 For out of prison he cometh to **r**;...... 4427
Isa 24:23 the Lord of hosts shall **r** in mount..... 4427
Isa 32:1 a king shall **r** in righteousness......... 4427
Jer 23:5 and a King shall **r** and prosper 4427
Jer 33:21 have a son to **r** upon his throne;....... 4427
Da 6:28 this Daniel prospered in the **r** of....... 4437
Lk 1:33 **r** over the house of Jacob for ever; *936*
Lk 19:14 **not have this man to r over us** *936*
Lk 19:27 **not that I should r over them,** *936*
Ro 5:17 shall **r** in life by one, Jesus Christ.)...... *936*
Ro 5:21 grace **r** through righteousness unto *936*
Ro 6:12 Let not sin ... **r** in your mortal body *936*
Ro 15:12 shall rise to **r** over the Gentiles;.......... *757*
1Co 4:8 us: and I would to God ye did **r** *936*
1Co 15:25 For he must **r**, till he hath put all *936*
2Ti 2:12 suffer, we shall also **r** with him:........ *4821*
Rev 5:10 and we shall **r** on the earth *936*
Rev 11:15 and he shall **r** for ever and ever......... *936*
Rev 20:6 shall **r** with him a thousand years....... *936*
Rev 22:5 and they shall **r** for ever and ever *936*

REIGNED
1Ki 2:11 that David **r** over Israel were forty 4427
1Ki 4:21 And Solomon **r** over all kingdoms..... 4910
2Ki 15:10 and slew him, and **r** in his stead 4427
2Ki 15:14 and slew him, and **r** in his stead 4427
2Ki 15:25 he killed him, and **r** in his room....... 4427
2Ki 15:30 and slew him, and **r** in his stead 4427
2Ch 9:26 And he **r** over all the kings from....... 4910
Ro 5:14 death **r** from Adam to Moses, even...... *936*
Ro 5:17 one man's offence death **r** by one; *936*
Ro 5:21 as sin hath **r** unto death, even so........ *936*
Rev 11:17 thee thy great power, and hast **r** *936*
Rev 20:4 and **r** with Christ a thousand years...... *936*

REIGNETH

1Sa	12:14	and also the king that **r** over you	4427
1Ch	16:31	among the nations, The Lord **r**	4427
Ps	47:8	God **r** over the heathen: God	4427
Ps	93:1	The Lord **r**, he is clothed with	4427
Ps	96:10	the heathen that the Lord **r**:	4427
Ps	97:1	The Lord **r**; let the earth rejoice;	4427
Ps	99:1	The Lord **r**; let the people	4427
Pr	30:22	For a servant when he **r**; and a	4427
Isa	52:7	that saith unto Zion, Thy God **r**!	4427
Rev	17:18	which **r** over the kings of the	*2192, 932*
Rev	19:6	for the Lord God omnipotent **r**.	*936*

REIGNING

1Sa	16:1	rejected him from **r** over Israel?	4427

REINS

Ps	7:9	God trieth the hearts and **r**	3629
Ps	26:2	prove me; try my **r** and my heart	3629
Jer	11:20	that triest the **r** and the heart	3629
Jer	17:10	Lord search the heart, I try the **r**.	3629
Rev	2:23	**which searcheth the r and hearts:**	*3510*

REJECT

Hos	4:6	I will also **r** thee, and thou shalt	3988
Mk	7:9	**well ye r the commandment of**	*114*
Tit	3:10	first and second admonition **r**;	*3868*

REJECTED

1Sa	8:7	they have **r** me, that I should not	3988
1Sa	15:26	Lord hath **r** thee from being king	3988
1Sa	16:1	**r** him from reigning over Israel?	3988
2Ki	17:20	the Lord **r** all the seed of Israel,	3988
Isa	53:3	He is despised and **r** of men; a	2310
La	5:22	thou hast utterly **r** us; thou art	3988
Mt	21:42	**The stone which the builders r,**	*593*
Mk	8:31	and be **r** of the elders, and of the	*593*
Mk	12:10	**The stone which the builders r is**	*593*
Lk	7:30	and lawyers **r** the counsel of God	*114*
Lk	9:22	**be r of the elders and chief priests.**	*593*
Lk	17:25	**things, and be r of this generation**	*593*
Lk	20:17	**The stone which the builders r,**	*593*
Heb	12:17	inherited the blessing, he was **r**:	*593*

REJECTETH

Jn	12:48	**He that r me, and receiveth not**	*114*

REJOICE

Le	23:40	shall **r** before the Lord your God	8055
Dt	26:11	thou shalt **r** in every good thing	8056
Dt	28:63	Lord will **r** over you to destroy	7797
Dt	30:9	will again **r** over thee for good,	7797
Jgs	16:23	unto Dagon their god, and to **r**:	8057
1Sa	19:5	thou sawest it, and didst **r**;	8055
Ne	12:43	had made them **r** with great joy:	8055
Ps	5:11	that put their trust in thee **r**:	8055
Ps	13:5	my heart shall **r** in thy salvation	1523
Ps	33:1	**R** in the Lord, O ye righteous:	7442
Ps	33:21	For our heart shall **r** in him	8055
Ps	40:16	Let all those that seek thee **r**	7797
Ps	51:8	bones … thou hast broken may **r**	1523
Ps	63:7	the shadow of thy wings will I **r**	7442
Ps	89:16	thy name shall they **r** all the day:	1523
Ps	97:1	Lord reigneth; let the earth **r**;	1523
Ps	118:24	made; we will **r** and be glad in it	1523
Pr	2:14	Who **r** to do evil, and delight	8056
Pr	5:18	and **r** with the wife of thy youth.	8055
Pr	23:24	father of the righteous shall … **r**:	1523
Pr	24:17	**R** not when thine enemy falleth,	8055
Pr	28:12	When righteous men do **r**, there	5970
Ecc	3:22	a man should **r** in his own works;	8055
Ecc	4:16	that come after shall not **r** in him	8055
Ecc	11:8	live many years, and **r** in them all;	8055
Ecc	11:9	**R**, O young man, in thy youth;	8055
Isa	9:3	men **r** when they divide the spoil.	1523
Isa	62:5	bride, so shall thy God **r** over thee	7797
Isa	66:10	**r** for joy with her, all ye that	7797
Jer	31:13	make them **r** from their sorrow	8057
Jer	32:41	I will **r** over them to do them good,	7797
La	2:17	caused thine enemy to **r** over thee,	8055
Eze	7:12	let not the buyer **r**, nor the seller	8055
Hos	9:1	**R** not, O Israel, for joy, as other	8055
Zep	3:14	be glad and **r** with all the heart, O	5937
Zec	9:9	**R** greatly, O daughter of Zion;	1523
Mt	5:12	**R, and be exceeding glad: for**	*5463*
Lk	1:14	and many shall **r** at his birth	*5463*
Lk	6:23	**R ye in that day, and leap for**	*5463*
Lk	10:20	**but rather r, because your names**	*5463*
Lk	15:6	**R with me; for I have found my**	*4796*
Jn	14:28	**If ye loved me, ye would r,**	*5463*
Jn	16:20	**lament, but the world shall r:**	*5463*
Jn	16:22	**again, and your heart shall r**	*5463*
Ro	5:2	and **r** in hope of the glory of God	*2744*
Gal	4:27	**R**, thou barren that bearest not;	*2165*
Php	2:16	that I may **r** in the day of Christ	*2745*
Php	2:17	faith, I joy, and **r** with you all.	*4796*
Php	4:4	**R** in the Lord alway:	*5463*
1Th	5:16	**R** evermore.	*5463*
1Pe	1:8	ye **r** with joy unspeakable and full	*21*
Rev	19:7	Let us be glad and **r**, and give	*21*

REJOICED

Dt	28:63	Lord **r** over you to do you good,	7797
1Sa	6:13	and saw the ark, and **r** to see it	8055
1Ch	29:9	the people **r**, for that they offered	8055
Ne	12:43	offered great sacrifices, and **r**:	8055
Ps	35:15	But in mine adversity they **r**, and	8055
Ps	119:14	**r** in the way of thy testimonies	7797
Ecc	2:10	for my heart **r** in all my labour	8055
Mt	2:10	they **r** with exceeding great joy	*5463*
Lk	1:47	my spirit hath **r** in God my Saviour	*21*
Lk	10:21	In that hour Jesus **r** in spirit	*21*
Jn	8:56	**father Abraham r to see my day:**	*21*
2Jn	4	I **r** greatly that I found of thy	*5463*

REJOICETH

Ps	28:7	therefore my heart greatly **r**;	5937
Pr	11:10	with the righteous, the city **r**:	5970
Pr	13:9	The light of the righteous **r**: but	8055
Pr	15:30	The light of the eyes **r** the heart:	8055
Pr	29:3	Whoso loveth wisdom **r** his father:	8055
Isa	62:5	the bridegroom **r** over the bride,	4885
Eze	35:14	When the whole earth **r**, I will	8055
Mt	18:13	**he r more of that sheep, than of**	*5463*
Jn	3:29	**r** … because of the bridegroom's	*5463*
1Co	13:6	**R** not in iniquity,	*5463*
Jas	2:13	and mercy **r** against judgment.	*2620*

REJOICING

Ps	19:8	of the Lord are right, **r** the heart:	8055
Pr	8:30	his delight, **r** always before him;	7832
Pr	8:31	**R** in the habitable part of his	7832
Isa	65:18	I create Jerusalem a **r**, and her	1525
Jer	15:16	me the joy and **r** of mine heart:	8057
Lk	15:5	**he layeth it on his shoulders, r**	*5463*

Ac 5:41 **r** that they were counted worthy to *5463*
Ro 12:12 **R** in hope; patient in tribulation; *5463*
2Co 1:12 For our **r** is this, the testimony of *2746*
2Co 6:10 As sorrowful, yet always **r**, as *5463*
1Th 2:19 is our hope, or joy, or crown of **r**? *2746*
Jas 4:16 your boastings: all such **r** is evil. *2746*

RELEASE
Dt 15:1 seven years thou shalt make a **r**. 8059
Mt 27:17 will ye that I **r** unto you? Barabbas, ... *630*
Mk 15:11 rather **r** Barabbas unto them *630*
Lk 23:20 Pilate therefore, willing to **r** Jesus, ... *630*
Jn 18:39 **r** unto you one at the passover: *630*

RELEASED
Mt 27:26 Then **r** he Barabbas unto them: *630*
Mk 15:15 the people, **r** Barabbas unto them *630*

RELIEVE
Isa 1:17 seek judgment, **r** the oppressed 833
La 1:16 comforter that should **r** my soul is 7725

RELIGION
Ac 26:5 sect of our **r** I lived a Pharisee. *2356*
Jas 1:26 own heart, this man's **r** is vain *2356*
Jas 1:27 Pure **r** and undefiled before God *2356*

RELIGIOUS
Jas 1:26 any man among you seem to be **r**. *2357*

REMAIN
Ex 12:10 nothing of it **r** until the morning; 3498
Le 19:6 ought **r** until the third day, it shall 3498
Le 25:28 **r** in the hand of him that ... bought ... 1961
Nu 33:55 those which ye let **r** of them shall 3498
Dt 19:20 which **r** shall hear, and fear, and 7604
Dt 21:23 His body shall not **r** all night 3885
Jos 2:11 **r** any more courage in any man, ... 6965
1Ki 18:22 I only, **r** a prophet of the Lord; 3498
Pr 2:21 land, and the perfect shall **r** in it 3498
Pr 21:16 **r** in the congregation of the dead 5117
Jer 8:3 residue ... that **r** of this evil family 7604
Jer 27:21 the vessels that **r** in the house of 3498
Eze 17:21 and they that **r** shall be scattered 7604
Am 6:9 if there **r** ten men in one house 3498
Jn 6:12 **Gather up the fragments that r,** *4052*
Jn 15:11 **that my joy might r in you, and** *3306*
Jn 15:16 **and that your fruit should r** *3306*
Jn 19:31 bodies should not **r** upon the cross *3306*
1Co 7:11 if she depart, let her **r** unmarried, ... *3306*
1Th 4:15 and **r** unto the coming of the Lord *4035*
1Th 4:17 are alive and **r** shall be caught up *4035*
Rev 3:2 **strengthen the things which r,** *3062*

REMAINDER
Ex 29:34 thou shalt burn the **r** with fire; 3498
Le 6:16 the **r** thereof shall Aaron and his 3498
Ps 76:10 the **r** of wrath shalt thou restrain 7611

REMAINED
Ge 7:23 Noah only **r** alive, and they that 7604
Nu 35:28 have **r** in the city of his refuge 3427
Dt 3:11 only Og king of Bashan **r** of the 7604
Jos 10:20 the rest which **r** of them entered 8277
Jos 11:22 in Gath, and in Ashdod, there **r** 7604
Jos 13:12 who **r** of the remnant of the giants: 7604
Jos 18:2 **r** among the children of Israel 3498
Jos 21:20 which **r** of the children of Kohath, ... 3498
Jos 21:26 of the children of Kohath that **r** 3498
Jgs 7:3 and there **r** ten thousand 7604
1Sa 11:11 they which **r** were scattered, so that 7604
1Sa 23:14 **r** in a mountain in the wilderness 3427
1Sa 24:3 his men **r** in the sides of the cave 3427
2Sa 13:20 Tamar **r** desolate in her brother 3427
1Ki 22:46 which **r** in the days of his father 7604
2Ki 10:17 he slew all that **r** unto Ahab in 7604
2Ki 24:14 none **r**, save the poorest sort of 7604
Ecc 2:9 also my wisdom **r** with me 5975
Mt 11:23 **it would have r until this day** *3306*
Mt 14:20 fragments that **r** twelve baskets *4052*
Lk 9:17 that **r** to them twelve baskets *4052*
Ac 5:4 Whiles it **r**, was it not thine own? *3306*

REMAINEST
La 5:19 Thou, O Lord, **r** for ever; thy 3427

REMAINETH
Ge 8:22 While the earth **r**, seedtime and 3117
Ex 12:10 which **r** of it until the morning 3498
Jos 8:29 heap of stones, that **r** unto this day.
1Sa 16:11 There **r** yet the youngest, and 7604
Ezr 1:4 whosoever **r** in any place where 7604
Isa 4:3 he that **r** in Jerusalem, shall be 3498
Jer 38:2 He that **r** in this city shall die by 3427
Eze 6:12 he that **r** and is besieged shall die 7604
Hag 2:5 so my spirit **r** among you: fear ye 5975
Jn 9:41 **say, We see; therefore your sin r** *3306*
2Co 3:11 more that which **r** is glorious *3306*
2Co 3:14 for until this day **r** the same vail *3306*
2Co 9:9 poor: his righteousness **r** for ever *3306*
Heb 4:9 **r** therefore a rest to the people of *620*
Heb 10:26 there **r** no more sacrifice for sins *620*
1Jn 3:9 his seed **r** in him: and he cannot *3306*

REMAINING
Jos 10:40 left none **r**, but utterly destroyed 8300
Ob 18 not be any **r** of the house of Esau; 8300
Jn 1:33 Spirit descending, and **r** on him *3306*

REMEDY
2Ch 36:16 his people, till there was no **r**. 4832
Pr 6:15 shall he be broken without **r** 4832
Pr 29:1 be destroyed, and that without **r**. 4832

REMEMBER
Ge 9:16 I may **r** the everlasting covenant 2142
Ge 40:23 did not the chief butler **r** Joseph, ... 2142
Ex 13:3 **R** this day, in which ye came out 2142
Ex 20:8 **R** the sabbath day, to keep it holy 2142
Le 26:45 will for their sakes **r** the covenant 2142
Dt 5:15 And **r** that thou wast a servant in 2142
Dt 9:7 **R**, and forget not, how thou 2142
2Sa 14:11 let the king **r** the Lord thy God 2142
2Ki 20:3 **r** now how I have walked before 2142
Ne 13:31 **R** me, O my God, for good 2142
Ps 25:7 **R** not the sins of my youth, nor 2142
Ps 63:6 When I **r** thee upon my bed, and 2142
Ps 89:47 **R** how short my time is: wherefore 2142
Ps 137:6 If I do not **r** thee, let my tongue 2142
Pr 31:7 poverty, and **r** his misery no more. 2142
Ecc 5:20 not much **r** the days of his life; 2142
Ecc 11:8 yet let him **r** the days of darkness; 2142
Ecc 12:1 **R** now thy Creator in the days of 2142
Isa 38:3 **R** now, O Lord, I beseech thee, ... 2142
Isa 64:9 O Lord, neither **r** iniquity for ever: 2142
Jer 31:34 and I will **r** their sin no more 2142

La 5:1 R, O Lord, what is come upon us: 2142
Eze 36:31 Then shall ye r your own evil ways, 2142
Hos 7:2 that I r all their wickedness: 2142
Hos 8:13 now will he r their iniquity, and 2142
Mt 16:9 neither r the five loaves of the 3421
Lk 1:72 and to r his holy covenant; 3415
Lk 16:25 Son, r that thou in thy lifetime 3415
Lk 17:32 R Lot's wife 3421
Lk 23:42 r me when thou comest into thy 3415
Jn 16:4 ye may r that I told you of them 3421
Ac 20:31 r, that by the space of three years 3421
2Ti 2:8 R that Jesus Christ of the seed of 3421
Heb 8:12 their iniquities will I r no more 3415
Heb 10:17 sins and iniquities will I r no more 3415
Heb 13:7 R them which have the rule over 3421
Rev 2:5 R therefore from whence thou 3421
Rev 3:3 R therefore how thou hast 3421

REMEMBERED

Ge 42:9 And Joseph r the dreams which he 2142
Ex 2:24 God r his covenant with Abraham 2142
Jgs 8:34 children of Israel r not the Lord 2142
Ps 78:35 they r that God was their rock, 2142
Ps 78:39 For he r that they were but flesh; 2142
Ps 105:42 For he r his holy promise, and 2142
Isa 65:17 and the former shall not be r, nor 2142
Eze 3:20 which he hath done shall not be r; 2142
Eze 21:24 ye have made your iniquity to be r 2142
Eze 33:13 his righteousnesses shall not be r; 2142
Mt 26:75 And Peter r the word of Jesus, 3415
Lk 22:61 And Peter r the word of the Lord, 5279
Rev 18:5 and God hath r her iniquities 3421

REMEMBEREST

Mt 5:23 and there r that thy brother 3415

REMEMBERETH

Ps 103:14 our frame; he r that we are dust 2142
La 1:9 she r not her last end; therefore 2142
Jn 16:21 child, she r no more the anguish, 3421

REMEMBRANCE

Nu 5:15 memorial, bringing iniquity to r 2142
Dt 32:26 I would make the r of them to cease 2143
Ps 6:5 For in death there is no r of thee: 2143
Ps 34:16 to cut off the r of them from the 2143
Ps 83:4 name of Israel may be no more in r 2142
Ecc 1:11 There is no r of former things; 2146
Isa 43:26 Put me in r: let us plead together 2142
Lk 22:19 given for you: this do in r of me 364
Jn 14:26 and bring all things to your r 5279
1Co 11:24 broken for you: this do in r of me 364
1Co 11:25 as oft as ye drink it, in r of me 364
Php 1:3 thank … God upon every r of you, 3417
2Ti 1:5 I call to r the unfeigned faith 5280
2Ti 1:6 I put thee in r that thou stir up 363
Heb 10:3 there is a r again made of sins 364
2Pe 1:12 you always in r of these things, 5179
2Pe 1:15 to have these things always in r 3418
Jude 5 I will therefore put you in r 5179

REMISSION

Mt 26:28 is shed for many for the r of sins 859
Mk 1:4 of repentance for the r of sins 859
Lk 1:77 his people by the r of their sins, 859
Lk 3:3 of repentance for the r of sins; 859
Lk 24:47 and r of sins should be preached 859
Ac 2:38 of Jesus Christ for the r of sins, 859
Ac 10:43 in him shall receive r of sins 859
Ro 3:25 for the r of sins that are past, 3929
Heb 9:22 without shedding of blood is no r 859
Heb 10:18 Now where r of these is, there is no 859

REMIT

Jn 20:23 Whose soever sins ye r, they are 863

REMITTED

Jn 20:23 ye remit, they are r unto them; 863

REMNANT

Le 5:13 the r shall be the priest's, as a meat
Dt 3:11 remained of the r of giants; 3499
1Ki 22:46 the r of the sodomites, which 3499
2Ch 30:6 and he will return to the r of you, 7604
Ezr 9:8 our God, to leave us a r to escape,
Ne 1:3 r that are left of the captivity 7604
Isa 10:20 in that day, that the r of Israel, 7605
Isa 37:32 of Jerusalem shall go forth a r 7611
Jer 44:14 none of the r of Judah, which are 7611
Am 5:15 be gracious unto the r of Joseph 7611
Mic 5:8 the r of Jacob shall be among the 7611
Hab 2:8 all the r of the people shall spoil 3499
Zep 3:13 r of Israel shall not do iniquity, 7611
Hag 1:12 with all the r of the people, obeyed 7611
Zec 8:12 the r of this people to possess all 7611
Mt 22:6 And the r took his servants, and 3062
Ro 9:27 of the sea, a r shall be saved: 2640
Ro 11:5 is a r according to the election of 3005
Rev 11:13 the r were affrighted, and gave 3062
Rev 19:21 the r were slain with the sword of 3062

REMOVE

Dt 19:14 not r thy neighbour's landmark 5253
2Ki 23:27 will r Judah also out of my sight, 5493
Ps 119:29 R from me the way of lying: and 5493
Pr 4:27 nor to the left: r thy foot from evil 5493
Pr 5:8 R thy way far from her, and come 7368
Pr 22:28 R not the ancient landmark 5253
Pr 23:10 R not the old landmark; and 5253
Pr 30:8 R far from me vanity and lies: 7368
Ecc 11:10 r sorrow from thy heart, and put 5493
Isa 13:13 the earth shall r out of her place, 7493
Jer 27:10 you, to r you far from your land; 7368
Eze 45:9 r violence and spoil, and execute 5493
Zec 3:9 I will r the iniquity of that land in 4185
Mt 17:20 to yonder place; and it shall r; 3327
Lk 22:42 be willing, r this cup from me: 3911
1Co 13:2 faith, so that I could r mountains, 3179
Rev 2:5 r thy candlestick out of his 2795

REMOVED

Ge 8:13 Noah r the covering of the ark 5493
Ex 14:19 angel r … and went behind them; 5265
Dt 28:25 be r into all the kingdoms of the 2189
1Sa 6:3 why his hand is not r from you 5493
2Ki 17:23 the Lord r Israel out of his sight, 5493
Ps 46:2 we fear, though the earth be r 4171
Ps 103:12 far hath he r our transgressions 7368
Isa 29:13 but have r their heart far from me, 7368
Isa 54:10 shall depart, and the hills be r; 4131
Jer 29:18 them to be r to all the kingdoms 2189
La 1:8 sinned; therefore she is r 5206
Mic 2:4 how hath he r it from me! 4185
Mt 21:21 Be thou r, and be thou cast into 142

Mk 11:23 Be thou r, and be thou cast into........ *142*
Gal 1:6 I marvel that ye are so soon **r** *3346*

REMOVETH
Dt 27:17 that **r** his neighbour's landmark. 5253
Ecc 10:9 Whoso **r** stones shall be hurt.......... 5265
Da 2:21 he **r** kings, and setteth up kings:....... 5709

REND See also RENT.
Le 21:10 his head, nor **r** his clothes;............ 6533
1Ki 11:11 surely **r** the kingdom from thee 7167
1Ki 11:12 will **r** it out of the hand of thy son..... 7167
1Ki 11:13 I will not **r** away all the kingdom;...... 7167
Ecc 3:7 A time to **r**, and a time to sew; a....... 7167
Isa 64:1 that thou wouldest **r** the heavens,...... 7167
Joel 2:13 And **r** your heart, and not your 7167
Mt 7:6 feet, and turn again and r you *4486*
Jn 19:24 Let us not **r** it, but cast lots for it....... *4977*

RENDER
Dt 32:41 will **r** vengeance to mine enemies, ... 7725
1Sa 26:23 **r** to every man his righteousness 7725
2Ch 6:30 **r** unto every man according unto...... 5415
Ps 38:20 They also that **r** evil for good are 7999
Ps 94:2 earth: **r** a reward to the proud......... 7725
Ps 116:12 What shall I **r** unto the Lord for....... 7725
Pr 24:12 not he **r** to every man according to 7725
Pr 24:29 **r** to the man according to his work 7725
Pr 26:16 seven men that can **r** a reason......... 7725
Jer 51:6 he will **r** unto her a recompence....... 7999
La 3:64 **R** unto them a recompence, O 7725
Hos 14:2 so will we **r** the calves of our lips....... 7999
Mt 22:21 R therefore unto Caesar the *591*
Mk 12:17 R to Caesar the things that are *591*
Lk 20:25 R therefore unto Caesar the *591*
Ro 2:6 will **r** to every man according to his..... *591*
1Co 7:3 Let the husband **r** unto the wife due *591*
1Th 3:9 what thanks can we **r** to God again *467*
1Th 5:15 that none **r** evil for evil unto any *591*

RENEW
1Sa 11:14 Gilgal, and **r** the kingdom there 2318
Ps 51:10 and **r** a right spirit within me.......... 2318
Isa 40:31 the Lord shall **r** their strength; 2498
Isa 41:1 and let the people **r** their strength:..... 2498
La 5:21 be turned; **r** our days as of old......... 2318
Heb 6:6 to **r** them again unto repentance:....... *340*

RENEWED
Ps 103:5 thy youth is **r** like the eagle's........... 2318
2Co 4:16 the inward man is **r** day by day.......... *341*
Eph 4:23 be **r** in the spirit of your mind;......... *365*
Col 3:10 which is **r** in knowledge after the *341*

RENEWEST
Ps 104:30 and thou **r** the face of the earth........ 2318

RENEWING
Ro 12:2 transformed by the **r** of your mind,..... *342*
Tit 3:5 regeneration, ... **r** of the Holy Ghost; ... *342*

RENOUNCED
2Co 4:2 But have **r** the hidden things of......... *550*

RENOWN
Ge 6:4 men which were of old, men of **r**...... 8034
Nu 16:2 in the congregation, men of **r**......... 8034
Da 9:15 hast gotten thee **r**, as at this day;....... 8034

RENOWNED
Eze 26:17 the **r** city, which wast strong in........ 1984

RENT
Ge 37:29 in the pit; and he **r** his clothes......... 7167
Ge 37:34 And Jacob **r** his clothes, and put....... 7167
Nu 14:6 searched the land, **r** their clothes:...... 7167
Jgs 14:6 as he would have **r** a kid, and he....... 8156
1Sa 15:28 The Lord hath **r** the kingdom of....... 7167
1Sa 28:17 Lord hath **r** the kingdom out of 7167
1Ki 14:8 And **r** the kingdom away from the..... 7167
1Ki 19:11 and strong wind **r** the mountains, ... 6561
Job 1:20 Then Job arose, and **r** his mantle,...... 7167
Job 2:12 they **r** every one his mantle, and....... 7167
Mt 26:65 Then the high priest **r** his clothes, ... *1284*
Mt 27:51 veil of the temple was **r** in twain....... *4977*
Mt 27:51 earth did quake, and the rocks **r**; *4977*
Mk 2:21 the old, and the r is made worse. *4978*
Mk 9:26 the spirit cried, and **r** him sore,........ *4682*
Mk 14:63 Then the high priest **r** his clothes, ... *1284*
Mk 15:38 veil of the temple was **r** in twain....... *4977*
Lk 23:45 the veil of the temple was **r** in the...... *4977*

REPAIR
2Ki 12:7 Why **r** ye not the breaches of the 2388
2Ch 34:10 Lord, to **r** and amend the house: 918

REPAIRED
1Ki 18:30 **r** the altar of the Lord that was........ 7495
2Ki 12:14 **r** therewith the house of the Lord...... 2388
2Ch 33:16 he **r** the altar of the Lord, and......... 1129

REPAY
Dt 7:10 him, he will **r** him to his face.......... 7999
Lk 10:35 when I come again, I will r thee......... *591*
Ro 12:19 is mine; I will **r**, saith the Lord.......... *467*
Phm 19 with mine own hand, I will **r** it: *661*

REPAYED
Pr 13:21 to the righteous good shall be **r**........ 7999

REPEATETH
Pr 17:9 he that **r** a matter separateth.......... 8138

REPENT
Ex 32:12 **r** of this evil against thy people. 5162
1Sa 15:29 he is not a man, that he should **r** 5162
Job 42:6 myself, and **r** in dust and ashes........ 5162
Jer 18:8 **r** of the evil that I thought to do....... 5162
Jer 26:3 that I may **r** me of the evil, which...... 5162
Jer 26:13 and the Lord will **r** him of the evil..... 5162
Jer 42:10 I **r** me of the evil that I have done 5162
Eze 14:6 **R**, and turn ... from your idols; 7725
Eze 24:14 will I spare, neither will I **r**;........... 5162
Joel 2:14 knoweth if he will return and **r**, ... 5162
Jnh 3:9 Who can tell if God will turn and **r**,.... 5162
Mt 3:2 **R** ye: for the kingdom of heaven....... *3340*
Mt 4:17 R: for the kingdom of heaven *3340*
Mk 1:15 r ye, and believe the gospel............ *3340*
Lk 13:3, 5 except ye r, ye shall all likewise *3340*
Lk 16:30 them from the dead, they will r *3340*
Lk 17:3 him; and if he r, forgive him. *3340*
Ac 2:38 **R**, and be baptized every one of you ... *3340*
Ac 17:30 all men every where to **r**: *3340*
Ac 26:20 that they should **r** and turn to God,.... *3340*
Heb 7:21 The Lord sware and will not **r**, ... *3338*
Rev 2:5 whence thou art fallen, and r,......... *3340*
Rev 2:16 R; or else I will come unto thee *3340*

Rev 2:22 except they **r** of their deeds........... *3340*
Rev 3:19 be zealous therefore, and **r** *3340*

REPENTANCE

Mt 3:8 Bring forth … fruits meet for **r**: *3341*
Mt 3:11 baptize you with water unto **r**......... *3341*
Mt 9:13 the righteous, but sinners to **r** *3341*
Mk 1:4 and preach the baptism of **r** for the *3341*
Mk 2:17 the righteous, but sinners to **r** *3341*
Lk 3:3 preaching the baptism of **r** for the *3341*
Lk 3:8 Bring forth … fruits worthy of **r**,...... *3341*
Lk 5:32 the righteous, but sinners to **r** *3341*
Lk 15:7 just persons, which need no **r**......... *3341*
Lk 24:47 And that **r** and remission of sins *3341*
Ac 5:31 to give **r** to Israel, and forgiveness...... *3341*
Ac 11:18 to the Gentiles granted **r** unto life...... *3341*
Ac 20:21 **r** toward God, and faith toward *3341*
Ac 26:20 to God, and do works meet for **r** *3341*
Ro 2:4 goodness of God leadeth thee to **r**? *3341*
Ro 11:29 and calling of God are without **r**........ *278*
2Co 7:10 For godly sorrow worketh **r** to *3341*
2Ti 2:25 God peradventure will give them **r**..... *3341*
Heb 6:6 to renew them again unto **r**; *3341*
Heb 12:17 for he found no place of **r**, though..... *3341*
2Pe 3:9 but that all should come to **r**.......... *3341*

REPENTED

Ge 6:6 **r** the Lord that he had made man...... 5162
Ex 32:14 Lord **r** of the evil which he thought.... 5162
Jgs 2:18 for it **r** the Lord because of their....... 5162
Jgs 21:15 the people **r** them for Benjamin, ... 5162
1Sa 15:35 Lord **r** that he had made Saul king..... 5162
2Sa 24:16 the Lord **r** him of the evil, and said 5162
1Ch 21:15 beheld, and he **r** him of the evil,....... 5162
Ps 106:45 **r** according to the multitude of his..... 5162
Jer 26:19 the Lord **r** him of the evil which....... 5162
Am 7:3 Lord **r** for this: It shall not be,......... 5162
Am 7:6 Lord **r** for this: This also shall not 5162
Jnh 3:10 God **r** of the evil, that he had said 5162
Zec 8:14 saith the Lord of hosts, and I **r** not: 5162
Mt 11:21 have **r** long ago in sackcloth *3340*
Mt 12:41 they **r** at the preaching of Jonas;....... *3340*
Mt 21:29 but afterward he **r**, and went.......... *3338*
Mt 27:3 that he was condemned, **r** himself,..... *3338*
Lk 10:13 they had a great while ago **r**,.......... *3340*
Lk 11:32 they **r** at the preaching of Jonas;....... *3340*
2Co 7:10 worketh repentance … not to be **r** of: ... *278*
2Co 12:21 and have not **r** of the uncleanness *3340*
Rev 2:21 of her fornication; and she **r** not........ *340*
Rev 9:20 **r** not of the works of their hands,...... *3340*
Rev 9:21 Neither **r** they of their murders........ *3340*
Rev 16:9 and they **r** not to give him glory. *3340*
Rev 16:11 sores, and **r** not of their deeds. *3340*

REPENTETH

Ge 6:7 it **r** me that I have made them......... 5162
1Sa 15:11 It **r** me that I have set up Saul to....... 5162
Joel 2:13 kindness, and **r** him of the evil......... 5162
Lk 15:7 in heaven over one sinner that **r**, ... *3340*
Lk 15:10 angels … over one sinner that **r**....... *3340*

REPENTING

Jer 15:6 destroy thee; I am weary with **r**........ 5162

REPETITIONS

Mt 6:7 But when ye pray, use not vain **r**,....... *945*

REPLENISH

Ge 1:28 and multiply, and **r** the earth, and 4390
Ge 9:1 and multiply, and **r** the earth.......... 4390

REPLENISHED

Jer 31:25 and I have **r** every sorrowful soul. 4390

REPLIEST

Ro 9:20 who art thou that **r** against God? *470*

REPORT

Ge 37:2 brought unto his father their evil **r**..... 1681
Ex 23:1 Thou shalt not raise a false **r**.......... 8088
Nu 13:32 brought up an evil **r** of the land 1681
Nu 14:37 men that did bring up an evil **r**........ 1681
Ne 6:13 might have matter for an evil **r**, ... 8034
Pr 15:30 a good **r** maketh the bones fat......... 8052
Isa 53:1 Who hath believed our **r**? and to 8052
Jn 12:38 Lord, who hath believed our **r**?......... *189*
Ac 6:3 among you seven men of honest **r** *3140*
Ro 10:16 Lord, who hath believed our **r**?......... *189*
Php 4:8 whatsoever things are of good **r**;....... *2163*
Heb 11:2 it the elders obtained a good **r**......... *3140*

REPORTED

Mt 28:15 commonly **r** among the Jews.......... *1310*
1Co 5:1 **r** commonly that there is fornication.... *191*
1Ti 5:10 Well **r** of for good works; if she have ... *3140*

REPROACH

Ge 30:23 said, God hath taken away my **r** 2781
2Ki 19:16 hath sent him to **r** the living God. 2778
Ps 22:6 a **r** of men, and despised of the........ 2781
Ps 39:8 make me not the **r** of the foolish....... 2781
Ps 69:20 **R** hath broken my heart; and I 2781
Ps 79:4 are become a **r** to our neighbours,..... 2781
Ps 89:41 him: he is a **r** to his neighbours........ 2781
Ps 102:8 Mine enemies **r** me all the day;........ 2778
Ps 119:39 Turn away my **r** which I fear: for 2781
Pr 6:33 his **r** shall not be wiped away.......... 2781
Pr 14:34 but sin is a **r** to any people............ 2617
Pr 19:26 causeth shame, and bringeth **r** 2659
Isa 37:4 hath sent to **r** the living God, and...... 2778
Isa 37:17 hath sent to **r** the living God. 2778
Isa 51:7 fear ye not the **r** of men, neither....... 2781
Isa 54:4 remember the **r** of thy widowhood 2781
Jer 6:10 word of the Lord is unto them a **r**;..... 2781
Jer 23:40 bring an everlasting **r** upon you,....... 2781
Jer 31:19 I did bear the **r** of my youth........... 2781
Jer 44:8 a **r** among all the nations of the 2781
La 5:1 us: consider, and behold our **r**......... 2781
Lk 1:25 to take away my **r** among men......... *3681*
Lk 6:22 and shall **r** you, and cast out.......... *3679*
1Ti 3:7 fall into **r** and … snare of the devil..... *3680*
Heb 11:26 Esteeming the **r** of Christ greater *3680*
Heb 13:13 without the camp, bearing his **r**........ *3680*

REPROACHED

Ps 55:12 it was not an enemy that **r** me;........ 2778
Ps 69:9 reproaches of them that **r** thee are 2778
Isa 37:23 hast thou **r** and blasphemed? 2778
Ro 15:3 reproaches of them that **r** thee *3679*
1Pe 4:14 If ye be **r** for the name of Christ, ... *3679*

REPROACHES

Ps 69:9 the **r** of them that reproached thee..... 2781
Ro 15:3 The **r** of them that reproached thee *3679*
Heb 10:33 both by **r** and afflictions; and *3680*

R

REPROACHETH
Pr 14:31 oppresseth the poor **r** his Maker: 2778
Pr 17:5 mocketh the poor **r** his Maker: 2778
Pr 27:11 that I may answer him that **r** me 2778

REPROBATE
Ro 1:28 God gave them over to a **r** mind, ... *96*
2Ti 3:8 minds, **r** concerning the faith. *96*
Tit 1:16 and unto every good work **r** *96*

REPROBATES
2Co 13:5 Christ is in you, except ye be **r**? *96*

REPROOF
Pr 1:23 Turn you at my **r**: behold, I will 8433
Pr 1:25 counsel, and would none of my **r**. 8433
Pr 1:30 my counsel: they despised all my **r**. 8433
Pr 10:17 but he that refuseth **r** erreth. 8433
Pr 15:5 but he that regardeth **r** is prudent. 8433
Pr 15:10 way: and he that hateth **r** shall die 8433
Pr 15:31 The ear that heareth the **r** of life. 8433
Pr 17:10 A **r** entereth more into a wise 1606
Pr 29:15 The rod and **r** give wisdom: but 8433
2Ti 3:16 for doctrine, for **r**, for correction, ... *1650*

REPROOFS
Pr 6:23 **r** of instruction are the way of life: 8433

REPROVE See also **UNREPROVABLE.**
Ps 50:21 I will **r** thee, and set them in order. 3198
Pr 9:8 **R** not a scorner, lest he hate thee: 3198
Pr 19:25 and **r** one that hath understanding, ... 3198
Pr 30:6 lest he **r** thee, and thou be found a. 3198
Hos 4:4 let no man strive, nor **r** another:. 3198
Jn 16:8 **come, he will r the world of sin.,** *1651*
Eph 5:11 of darkness, but rather **r** them. *1651*
2Ti 4:2 **r**, rebuke, exhort with all *1651*

REPROVED
Pr 29:1 being often **r** hardeneth his neck, ... 8433
Jn 3:20 **light, lest his deeds should be r.** *1651*

REPROVETH
Job 40:2 he that **r** God, let him answer it. 3198
Pr 9:7 He that **r** a scorner getteth to 3256
Pr 15:12 scorner loveth not one that **r** him: 3198
Isa 29:21 a snare for him that **r** in the gate, ... 3198

R

REPUTATION
Php 2:7 But made himself of no **r**, and *2758*
Php 2:29 gladness; and hold such in **r** *1784*

REQUEST
Ne 2:4 me, For what dost thou make **r**? 1245
Est 5:3 queen Esther? and what is thy **r**?. 1246
Est 7:7 Haman stood up to make **r** for his. 1245
Est 9:12 what is thy **r** further? and it shall 1246
Php 1:4 for you all making **r** with joy, ... *1162*

REQUESTED
1Ki 19:4 he **r** for himself that he might die; 7592
Da 2:49 Then Daniel **r** of the king, and he 1156

REQUESTS
Php 4:6 let your **r** be made known unto God.. . . . *155*

REQUIRE
Dt 10:12 doth the Lord thy God **r** of thee, ... 7592
Ezr 7:21 the God of heaven, shall **r** of you,. 7593
Ps 10:13 in his heart, Thou wilt not **r** it. 1875
Eze 3:18 blood will I **r** at thine hand. 1245
Eze 3:20 blood will I **r** at thine hand. 1245
Eze 33:6 blood will I **r** at the watchman's 1875
Eze 33:8 his blood will I **r** at thine hand. 1245
Eze 34:10 I will **r** my flock at their hand, ... 1875
Mic 6:8 and what doth the Lord **r** of thee, ... 1875
1Co 1:22 the Jews **r** a sign, and the Greeks. *154*

REQUIRED
Ge 42:22 behold, also his blood is **r** 1875
Ex 12:36 lent unto them such things as they **r**.
2Ch 8:14 priests, as the duty of every day **r**: 3117
Ezr 3:4 as the duty of every day **r**; 3117
Ps 40:6 and sin offering hast thou not **r** 7592
Ps 137:3 us away captive **r** of us a song; 7592
Pr 30:7 Two things have I **r** of thee; deny 7592
Isa 1:12 who hath **r** this at your hand, to. 1245
Lk 11:51 **It shall be r of this generation.** *1567*
Lk 12:20 **night thy soul shall be r of thee:**. *523*
Lk 12:48 **is given, of him shall be much r** *2212*
Lk 19:23 **have r mine own with usury?** *4238*
Lk 23:24 that it should be as they **r**. *155*
1Co 4:2 Moreover it is **r** in stewards, that *2212*

REQUITE
Ge 50:15 and will certainly **r** us all the evil 7725
Dt 32:6 Do ye thus **r** the Lord, O foolish. 1580
Jer 51:56 God of recompences shall surely **r** 7999
1Ti 5:4 at home, and to **r** their parents: *287, 591*

REQUITED
1Sa 25:21 and he hath **r** me evil for good. 7725

REREWARD
Jos 6:9 and the **r** came after the ark, the. 622
Isa 52:12 the God of Israel will be your **r**. 622
Isa 58:8 the glory of the Lord shall be thy **r**. 622

RESCUE
Ps 35:17 look on? **r** my soul from their. 7725

RESCUED
1Sa 14:45 So the people **r** Jonathan, that he 6299
1Sa 30:18 away: and David **r** his two wives. 5337
Ac 23:27 came I with an army, and **r** him,. *1807*

RESEMBLE
Lk 13:18 **like? and whereunto shall I r it?** *3666*

RESERVE
Jer 3:5 Will he **r** his anger for ever? will. 5201
Jer 50:20 for I will pardon them whom I **r** 7604
2Pe 2:9 to **r** the unjust unto the day of *5083*

RESERVED
Ge 27:36 thou not **r** a blessing for me?. 680
Job 21:30 is **r** to the day of destruction? 2820
Job 38:23 Which I nave **r** against the time of. 2820
Ro 11:4 I have **r** to myself seven thousand. *2641*
1Pe 1:4 not away, **r** in heaven for you, ... *5083*
2Pe 2:4 darkness, to be **r** unto judgment; *5083*
2Pe 3:7 **r** unto fire against the day of. *5083*
Jude 6 hath **r** in everlasting chains under *5083*
Jude 13 to whom is **r** the blackness of *5083*

RESERVETH
Jer 5:24 **r** unto us the appointed weeks of. 8104
Na 1:2 and he **r** wrath for his enemies. 5201

RESIDUE

Ne	11:20	the **r** of Israel, of the priests, and	7605
Isa	28:5	of beauty, unto the **r** of his people,.	7605
Isa	44:17	the **r** thereof he maketh a god,	7611
Jer	27:19	the **r** of the vessels that remain in	3499
Jer	52:15	**r** of the people that remained in	3499
Eze	36:4	derision to the **r** of the heathen	7611
Eze	48:21	And the **r** shall be for the prince,	3498
Mal	2:15	Yet had he the **r** of the spirit	7605
Mk	16:13	they went and told it unto the **r**:	*3062*
Ac	15:17	**r** of the men might seek after the	*2645*

RESIST

Zec	3:1	at his right hand to **r** him	7853
Mt	5:39	**I say unto you, That ye r not evil**	*436*
Lk	21:15	**shall not be able to gainsay nor r**	*436*
Ac	6:10	were not able to **r** the wisdom and	*436*
Ac	7:51	ears, ye do always **r** the Holy Ghost:	*496*
Ro	13:2	and they that **r** shall receive to	*436*
2Ti	3:8	Moses, so do these also **r** the truth:	*436*
Jas	4:7	**R** the devil, and he will flee from	*436*
Jas	5:6	the just; and he doth not **r** you	*498*
1Pe	5:9	Whom **r** stedfast in the faith,	*436*

RESISTED

Ro	9:19	find fault? For who hath **r** his will?	*436*
Heb	12:4	Ye have not yet **r** unto blood,	*478*

RESISTETH

Ro	13:2	**r** the ordinance of God: and they	*436*
Jas	4:6	God **r** the proud, but giveth grace	*498*
1Pe	5:5	God **r** the proud, and giveth grace	*498*

RESOLVED

Lk	16:4	**I am r what to do, that, when I**	*1097*

RESORT

Mk	10:1	and the people **r** unto him again,	*4848*
Jn	18:20	**whither the Jews always r;**	*4905*

RESORTED

Mk	2:13	and all the multitude **r** unto him,	*2064*
Jn	10:41	many **r** unto him, and said, John	*2064*
Jn	18:2	Jesus ofttimes **r** thither with his	*4863*

RESPECT

Ge	4:4	And the Lord had **r** unto Abel	8159
Le	19:15	not **r** the person of the poor,	5375
Nu	16:15	Lord, **R** not thou their offering:	6437
Dt	1:17	shall not **r** persons in judgment;	5234
Dt	16:19	thou shalt not **r** persons, neither	5234
2Sa	14:14	neither doth God **r** any person:	5375
1Ki	8:28	have thou **r** unto the prayer of	6437
2Ki	13:23	had **r** unto them, because of his	6437
2Ch	19:7	Lord our God, nor **r** of persons,	4856
Ps	138:6	yet hath he **r** unto the lowly:	7200
Pr	24:23	have **r** of persons in judgment	5234
Pr	28:21	To have **r** of persons is not good:	5234
Isa	17:7	have **r** to the Holy One of Israel.	7200
Ro	2:11	there is no **r** of persons with God.	*4382*
2Co	3:10	glorious had no glory in this **r**,	*3313*
Eph	6:9	is there **r** of persons with him.	*3382*
Php	4:11	Not that I speak in **r** of want: for	*2596*
Col	2:16	or in **r** of an holy day, or of the	*3313*
Col	3:25	and there is no **r** of persons.	*4382*
Jas	2:1	Lord of glory, with **r** of persons	*4382*
Jas	2:9	But if ye have **r** to persons, ye	*4380*
1Pe	1:17	who without **r** of persons judgeth	*678*

RESPECTER

Ac	10:34	that God is no **r** of persons:	*4381*

RESPECTETH

Job	37:24	**r** not any that are wise of heart.	7200
Ps	40:4	and **r** not the proud, nor such as	6437

RESPITE

Ex	8:15	when Pharaoh saw that there was **r**	7309
1Sa	11:3	Give us seven days **r**, that we	7503

REST

Ge	8:9	dove found no **r** for the sole of her	4494
Ex	16:23	is the **r** of the holy sabbath unto	7677
Ex	23:12	on the seventh day thou shalt **r**.	7673
Ex	31:15	the seventh is the sabbath of **r**,	7677
Le	25:4	be a sabbath of **r** unto the land,	7677
Jos	1:13	Lord your God hath given you **r**,	5117
Jos	22:4	hath given **r** unto your brethren,	5117
Ru	1:9	grant you that ye may find **r**,	4496
2Ki	2:15	spirit of Elijah doth **r** on Elisha.	5117
1Ch	22:18	he not given you **r** on every side?	5117
2Ch	14:7	he hath given us **r** on every side.	5117
Job	3:13	have slept: then had I been at **r**,	5117
Ps	37:7	**R** in the Lord, and wait patiently	1826
Pr	6:35	neither will he **r** content, though thou	
Pr	29:9	he rage or laugh, there is no **r**	5183
Pr	29:17	thy son, and he shall give thee **r**:	5117
Ecc	2:23	his heart taketh not **r** in the night	
Isa	11:2	spirit of the Lord shall **r** upon	5117
Isa	57:20	troubled sea, when it cannot **r**,	8252
Isa	62:1	for Jerusalem's sake I will not **r**,	8252
Isa	63:14	Spirit of the Lord caused him to **r**:	5117
Jer	6:16	and ye shall find **r** for your souls.	4771
La	1:3	the heathen, she findeth no **r**:	4494
La	2:18	day and night: give thyself no **r**;	6314
Da	2:18	the **r** of the wise men of Babylon.	7606
Zep	3:17	he will **r** in his love, he will joy	2790
Zec	1:11	the earth sitteth still, and is at **r**.	8252
Mt	11:28	**heavy laden, and I will give you r**	*373*
Mt	11:29	**ye shall find r unto your souls.**	*372*
Mt	12:43	**seeking r, and finding none.**	*372*
Mt	26:45	**Sleep on now, and take your r:**	*373*
Mk	14:41	**Sleep on now, and take your r:**	*373*
2Co	12:9	power of Christ may **r** upon me.	*1981*
Heb	3:11	They shall not enter into my **r**.)	*2663*
Heb	4:4	God did **r** the seventh day from	*2664*
Heb	4:8	For if Jesus had given them **r**,	*2664*
Heb	4:9	therefore a **r** to the people of God	*4520*
Heb	4:11	labour therefore to enter into that **r**,	*2663*
Rev	4:8	and they **r** not day and night,	*2192, 372*
Rev	6:11	they should **r** yet for a little season,	*373*
Rev	14:11	and they have no **r** day nor night,	*372*
Rev	20:5	the **r** of the dead lived not again	*3062*

RESTED

Ge	2:2	he **r** on the seventh day from all	7673
Ex	20:11	in them is, and **r** the seventh day:	5117
Ex	31:17	and on the seventh day he **r**, and	7673
Nu	11:25	when the spirit **r** upon them, they	5117
Jo	11:23	tribes. And the land **r** from war.	8252
Lk	23:56	and **r** the sabbath day according	*2270*

RESTETH

Pr	14:33	Wisdom **r** in the heart of him that	5117
Ecc	7:9	for anger **r** in the bosom of fools.	5117
1Pe	4:14	spirit of glory and of God **r** upon	*373*

RESTITUTION
Ex 22:6 kindled … fire shall surely make r 7999
Ex 22:12 he shall make r unto the owner 7999
Ac 3:21 until the times of r of all things 605

RESTORE
Ge 20:7 r the man his wife; for he is a 7725
Ge 42:25 r every man's money into his sack,..... 7725
Ex 22:1 he shall r five oxen for an ox, and...... 7999
Ex 22:4 ass, or sheep; he shall r double......... 7999
Nu 35:25 r him to the city of his refuge 7725
2Sa 9:7 will r thee all the land of Saul thy...... 7725
2Ki 8:6 R all that was hers, and all the......... 7725
Ps 51:12 R unto me the joy of thy 7725
Pr 6:31 he be found, he shall r sevenfold;...... 7999
Isa 42:22 for a spoil, and none saith, R.......... 7725
Isa 57:18 r comforts unto him and to his 7999
Da 9:5 to r and to build Jerusalem unto 7725
Joel 2:25 I will r to you the years that the 7999
Mt 17:11 **shall first come, and r all things** 600
Lk 19:8 false accusation, I r him fourfold........ 591
Ac 1:6 r again the kingdom to Israel?.......... 600
Gal 6:1 r such an one in the spirit of.......... 2675

RESTORED
Ge 40:21 And he r the chief butler unto his 7725
1Ki 13:6 the king's hand was r him again, ... 7725
2Ki 8:1 whose son he had r to life,............ 2421
Ezr 6:5 be r, and brought again unto the 8421
Eze 18:7 but hath r to the debtor his pledge, ... 7725
Mk 8:25 and he was r, and saw every man 600
Lk 6:10 his hand was r whole as the other. 600
Heb 13:19 that I may be r to you the sooner 600

RESTORER
Ru 4:15 shall be unto thee a r of thy life, ... 7725

RESTORETH
Ps 23:3 He r my soul: he leadeth me in........ 7725
Mk 9:12 **cometh first, and r all things;** 600

RESTRAIN
Ps 76:10 remainder of wrath shalt thou r....... 2296

RESTRAINED
Ge 8:2 and the rain from heaven was r;....... 3607
Ge 11:6 now nothing will be r from them, ... 1219
1Sa 3:13 vile, and he r them not. 3543

RESTRAINT
1Sa 14:6 there is no r to the Lord to save 4622

RESURRECTION
Mt 22:30 **For in the r they neither marry,** 386
Mt 22:31 **But as touching the r of the dead,** 386
Mt 27:53 came out the graves after his r,........ 1454
Mk 12:18 Sadducees, which say there is no r;...... 386
Lk 14:14 **be recompensed at the r of the** 386
Lk 20:36 **God, being the children of the r** 386
Jn 5:29 **have done good, unto the r of life;** 386
Jn 5:29 **done evil, unto the r of damnation.** 386
Jn 11:24 rise again in the r at the last day......... 386
Jn 11:25 unto her, **I am the r, and the life:** 386
Ac 2:31 this before spake of the r of Christ, ... 386
Ac 4:2 through Jesus the r from the dead....... 386
Ac 17:18 preached unto them Jesus, and … r..... 386
Ac 23:8 Sadducees say that there is no r,........ 386
Ac 24:15 that there shall be a r of the dead,....... 386
Ro 1:4 of holiness, by the r from the dead: 386
Ro 6:5 be also in the likeness of his r:.......... 386
1Co 15:13 But if there be no r of the dead, then.... 386
1Co 15:21 by man came also the r of the dead...... 386
Php 3:10 know him, and the power of his r,...... 386
2Ti 2:18 saying that the r is past already; 386
Heb 6:2 of r of the dead, and of eternal 386
Heb 11:35 that they might obtain a better r: 386
1Pe 1:3 lively hope by the r of Jesus Christ 386
1Pe 3:21 God,) by the r of Jesus Christ:.......... 386
Rev 20:5 were finished. This is the first r......... 386

RETAIN
Job 2:9 Dost thou still r thine integrity? 2388
Pr 11:16 honour, and strong men r riches,...... 8551
Ecc 8:8 over the spirit to r the spirit;.......... 3607
Jn 20:23 **whose soever sins ye r, they are** 2902

RETAINETH
Pr 3:18 and happy is every one that r her. 8551
Pr 11:16 A gracious woman r honour: and 8551
Mic 7:18 he r not his anger for ever,............ 2388

RETIRED
Jgs 20:39 the men of Israel r in the battle,....... 2015
2Sa 20:22 they r from the city, every man........ 6327

RETURN
Ge 3:19 art, and unto dust shalt thou r 7725
Ge 18:14 time appointed I will r unto thee,...... 7725
Ge 31:3 R unto the land of thy fathers, and..... 7725
Le 25:10 r every man unto his possession, ... 7725
Nu 14:3 not better for us to r into Egypt? 7725
Ru 1:16 or to r from following after thee: 7725
1Sa 15:26 unto Saul, I will not r with thee:....... 7725
1Sa 26:21 r, my son David: for I will no 7725
2Sa 12:23 him, but he shall not r to me.......... 7725
1Ki 2:33 blood … r upon the head of Joab,..... 7725
1Ki 8:48 r unto thee with all their heart,........ 7725
1Ki 22:28 If thou r at all in peace, the Lord 7725
2Ki 20:10 shadow r backward ten degrees........ 7725
2Ch 30:6 he will r to the remnant of you, ... 7725
Job 1:21 and naked shall I r thither: the 7725
Ps 6:4 R, O Lord, deliver my soul: oh 7725
Ps 80:14 R, we beseech thee, O God of 7725
Ps 94:15 shall r unto righteousness: and........ 7725
Ps 104:29 they die, and r to their dust. 7725
Ps 116:7 R unto thy rest, O my soul; for 7725
Pr 2:19 None that go unto her r again,........ 7725
Pr 26:27 rolleth a stone, it will r upon him. 7725
Ecc 12:7 the dust r to the earth as it was: 7725
Ecc 12:7 shall r unto God who gave it.......... 7725
SS 6:13 R, r, O Shulamite;................... 7725
Isa 10:21 The remnant shall r, even the 7725
Isa 44:22 r unto me; for I have redeemed 7725
Isa 55:7 and let him r unto the Lord, and 7725
Isa 55:11 it shall not r unto me void, but it 7725
Jer 3:22 R, ye backsliding children, and I....... 7725
Jer 5:3 than a rock; they have refused to r. 7725
Jer 22:10 for he shall r no more, nor see his 7725
Jer 23:14 none doth r from his wickedness:...... 7725
Jer 23:20 The anger of the Lord shall not r 7725
Jer 24:7 r unto me with their whole heart...... 7725
Jer 35:15 R ye now every man from his evil 7725
Eze 18:23 not that he should r from his ways, ... 7725
Da 11:29 At the time appointed he shall r, ... 7725
Hos 2:7 I will go and r to my first husband; 7725
Hos 6:1 Come, and let us r unto the Lord: 7725

Hos 7:16 They **r**, but not to the most High: 7725
Hos 14:1 O Israel, **r** unto the Lord thy God; 7725
Joel 2:14 knoweth if he will **r** and repent, ... 7725
Mal 3:7 **R** unto me, and I will **r** unto you.. 7725
Mt 2:12 that they should not **r** to Herod,........ *844*
Mt 10:13 **worthy, let your peace r to you** *1994*
Mt 12:44 **will r into my house from whence** *1994*
Mt 24:18 **him which is in the field r back** *1994*
Lk 8:39 **R to thine own house, and shew**....... *5290*
Lk 12:36 **when he will r from the wedding;** *360*
Lk 17:31 **field, let him likewise not r back.** *1994*
Lk 19:12 **to receive ... a kingdom, and to r**...... *5290*
Ac 13:34 now no more to **r** to corruption, ... *5290*

RETURNED

Ge 8:3 the waters **r** from off the earth 7725
Ge 8:12 dove; which **r** not again unto him 7725
Ge 37:29 And Reuben **r** unto the pit; and,....... 7725
Ex 14:27 and the sea **r** to his strength when 7725
Nu 13:25 they **r** from searching of the land...... 7725
1Sa 17:15 David went and **r** from Saul to feed.... 7725
2Sa 1:22 and the sword of Saul **r** not empty..... 7725
2Sa 3:16 unto him, Go, return. And he **r**........ 7725
2Sa 3:27 when Abner was **r** to Hebron, Joab 7725
2Sa 6:20 David **r** to bless his household 7725
2Sa 8:13 he **r** from smiting of the Syrians....... 7725
2Sa 10:14 So Joab **r** from the children of 7725
2Sa 11:4 and she **r** unto her house. 7725
2Sa 12:31 all the people **r** unto Jerusalem........ 7725
2Sa 16:8 hath **r** upon thee all the blood of 7725
2Ki 5:15 And he **r** to the man of God, he and ... 7725
2Ch 32:21 he **r** with shame of face to his own..... 7725
Ezr 5:11 thus they **r** us answer, saying, We 8421
Ne 4:15 we **r** all of us to the wall, every one 7725
Ecc 4:1 So I **r**, and considered all the.......... 7725
Ecc 9:11 I **r**, and saw under the sun, that 7725
Isa 38:8 So the sun **r** ten degrees, by which 7725
Jer 14:3 they **r** with their vessels empty:........ 7725
Jer 43:5 that were **r** from all nations, ... 7725
Da 4:34 mine understanding **r** unto me........ 7725
Zec 7:14 that no man passed through nor **r**: 7725
Mk 14:40 when he **r**, he found them asleep *5290*
Lk 2:43 as they **r**, the child Jesus tarried........ *5290*
Lk 4:1 of the Holy Ghost **r** from Jordan,...... *5290*
Lk 4:14 Jesus **r** in the power of the Spirit....... *5290*
Lk 17:18 **found that r to give glory to God,** *5290*
Lk 23:56 And they **r**, and prepared spices *5290*
Lk 24:52 and **r** to Jerusalem with great joy:...... *5290*
1Pe 2:25 but are now **r** unto the Shepherd *1994*

RETURNETH

Pr 26:11 As a dog **r** to his vomit, ... 7725

RETURNING

Ac 8:28 Was **r**, and sitting in his chariot *5290*
Heb 7:1 **r** from the slaughter of the kings *5290*

REVEAL

Da 2:47 seeing thou couldest **r** this secret 1541
Mt 11:27 **to whomsoever the Son will r him.** *601*
Lk 10:22 **he to whom the Son will r him**......... *601*
Gal 1:16 To **r** his Son in me, that I might *601*

REVEALED

Dt 29:29 those things which are **r** belong 1540
1Sa 3:7 word of the Lord yet **r** unto him....... 1540
Isa 40:5 the glory of the Lord shall be **r**, ... 1540
Isa 53:1 to whom is the arm of the Lord **r**?..... 1540
Jer 11:20 for unto thee have I **r** my cause........ 1540
Da 2:19 was the secret **r** unto Daniel in a....... 1541
Da 2:30 is not **r** to me for any wisdom......... 1541
Mt 10:26 **covered, that shall not be r; and** *601*
Mt 11:25 **and hast r them unto babes.**........... *601*
Mt 16:17 **and blood hath not r it unto thee,** *601*
Lk 2:26 **r** unto him by the Holy Ghost, ... *5557*
Lk 2:35 thoughts of many hearts may be **r**....... *601*
Lk 10:21 **and hast r them unto babes:**........... *601*
Lk 12:2 **covered, that shall not be r;**........... *601*
Lk 17:30 **the day when the Son of man is r**....... *601*
Jn 12:38 hath the arm of the Lord been **r**? *601*
Ro 1:17 righteousness of God **r** from faith *601*
Ro 1:18 the wrath of God is **r** from heaven...... *601*
Ro 8:18 the glory which shall be **r** in us......... *601*
1Co 2:10 hath **r** them unto us by his Spirit:....... *601*
1Co 3:13 it, because it shall be **r** by fire;.......... *601*
Gal 3:23 faith which should afterwards be **r**...... *601*
Eph 3:5 as it is now **r** unto his holy apostles *601*
2Th 1:7 when the Lord Jesus shall be **r** from..... *602*
2Th 2:3 and that man of sin be **r**, the son *601*
2Th 2:6 that he might be **r** in his time *601*
2Th 2:8 then shall that Wicked be **r**, whom...... *601*
1Pe 1:5 ready to be **r** in the last time *601*
1Pe 1:12 Unto whom it was **r**, that not unto...... *601*
1Pe 4:13 when his glory shall be **r**, ye may *602*

REVEALER

Da 2:47 and a **r** of secrets, seeing thou......... 1541

REVEALETH

Pr 11:13 A talebearer **r** secrets: but he.......... 1540
Pr 20:19 about as a talebearer **r** secrets:......... 1540
Da 2:22 He **r** the deep and secret things:........ 1541
Da 2:28 is a God in heaven that **r** secrets, ... 1541
Da 2:29 he that **r** secrets maketh known to..... 1541
Am 3:7 he **r** his secret unto his servants 1540

REVELATION

Ro 2:5 and **r** of the righteous judgment of *602*
Ro 16:25 according to the **r** of the mystery *602*
1Co 14:6 I shall speak to you either by **r**, or....... *602*
1Co 14:26 doctrine, hath a tongue, hath a **r**, ... *602*
Gal 1:12 it, but by the **r** of Jesus Christ.. .... *602*
Gal 2:2 And I went up by **r**, and............... *602*
Eph 1:17 unto you the spirit of wisdom and **r** *602*
Eph 3:3 How that by **r** he made known unto *602*
1Pe 1:13 unto you at the **r** of Jesus Christ; *602*
Rev 1:1 The **R** of Jesus Christ, which God....... *602*

REVELATIONS

2Co 12:1 come to visions and **r** of the Lord....... *602*
2Co 12:7 through the abundance of the **r**,........ *602*

REVENGE

Jer 15:15 me, and **r** me of my persecutors; 5358
2Co 10:6 readiness to **r** all disobedience, ... *1556*

REVENGER

Nu 35:19 The **r** of blood himself shall slay....... 1350
Ro 13:4 a **r** to execute wrath upon him *1558*

REVENGERS

2Sa 14:11 suffer the **r** of blood to destroy........ 1350

REVENGETH

Na 1:2 God is jealous, and the Lord **r**; 5358
Na 1:2 the Lord **r**, and is furious; the......... 5358

R

REVENUE
Ezr 4:13 shalt endamage the **r** of the kings....... 674
Pr 8:19 gold; and my **r** than choice silver 8393

REVENUES
Pr 15:6 in the **r** of the wicked is trouble 8393
Pr 16:8 than great **r** without right............ 8393

REVERENCE
Le 19:30 sabbaths, and **r** my sanctuary:......... 3372
Ps 89:7 to be had in **r** of all them that......... 3372
Mt 21:37 son, saying, They will **r** my son........ *1788*
Mk 12:6 them, saying, They will **r** my son....... *1788*
Lk 20:13 they will **r** him when they see.......... *1788*
Eph 5:33 wife see that she **r** her husband........ *5399*
Heb 12:9 us, and we gave them **r**: *1788*
Heb 12:28 acceptably with **r** and godly fear: *127*

REVEREND
Ps 111:9 ever: holy and **r** is his name........... 3372

REVERSE
Nu 23:20 hath blessed; and I cannot **r** it......... 7725

REVILE
Mt 5:11 are ye, when men shall **r** you, ... *3679*

REVILED
Mt 27:39 And they that passed by **r** him,......... *987*
Mk 15:32 were crucified with him **r** him *3679*
1Co 4:12 being **r**, we bless; being................ *3058*
1Pe 2:23 Who, when he was **r**, … not again;..... *3058*
1Pe 2:23 Who when he was … ,**r** not again;...... *486*

REVILEST
Ac 23:4 said, **R** thou God's high priest? *3058*

REVILINGS
Isa 51:7 neither be ye afraid of their **r**.......... 1421

REVIVE
Ps 85:6 Wilt thou not **r** us again: that thy...... 2421
Ps 138:7 midst of trouble, thou wilt **r** me: 2421
Isa 57:15 **r** the heart of the contrite ones........ 2421
Hab 3:2 **r** thy work in the midst of the......... 2421

REVIVED
1Ki 17:22 came into him again, and he **r** 2421
2Ki 13:21 touched the bones of Elisha, he **r**,...... 2421
Ro 7:9 the commandment came, sin **r**, ... *326*
Ro 14:9 Christ both died, and rose, and **r**,....... *326*

REVIVING
Ezr 9:9 to give us a **r**, to set up the house 4241

REVOLTED
Jer 5:23 heart: they are **r** and gone 5493

REVOLTERS
Hos 5:2 the **r** are profound to make a 7846
Hos 9:15 no more: all their princes are **r** 5637

REWARD
Ge 15:1 shield, and thy exceeding great **r**. 7939
Dt 10:17 not persons, nor taketh **r**............. 7810
Dt 27:25 **r** to slay an innocent person:.......... 7810
Dt 32:41 and will **r** them that hate me.......... 7999
2Sa 3:39 the Lord shall **r** the doer of evil........ 7999
Ps 19:11 keeping of them there is great **r** 6118
Ps 58:11 there is a **r** for the righteous:.......... 6529
Ps 127:3 the fruit of the womb is his **r**.......... 7939
Pr 24:14 then there shall be a **r**, and thy 319
Pr 25:22 head, and the Lord shall **r** thee 7999
Ecc 4:9 have a good **r** for their labour......... 7939
Ecc 9:5 neither have they any more a **r**;........ 7939
Isa 40:10 behold, his **r** is with him, and his 7939
Isa 62:11 his **r** is with him, and his work 7939
Mic 7:3 and the judge asketh for a **r**; 7966
Mt 5:12 for great is your **r** in heaven: for....... *3408*
Mt 5:46 which love you, what **r** have ye? *3408*
Mt 6:2 I say unto you, They have their **r** *3408*
Mt 6:6 seeth in secret shall **r** thee openly....... *591*
Mt 6:16 I say unto you, They have their **r** *3408*
Mt 6:18 seeth in secret, shall **r** thee. *591*
Mt 10:41 shall receive a prophet's **r**; and *3408*
Mt 10:42 he shall in no wise lose his **r** *3408*
Mt 16:27 he shall **r** every man according......... *591*
Mk 9:41 unto you, he shall not lose his **r** *3408*
Lk 6:23 behold, your **r** is great in heaven:...... *3408*
Lk 6:35 your **r** shall be great, and ye *3408*
Lk 23:41 we receive the due **r** of our deeds:....... *514*
1Co 3:14 thereupon, he shall receive a **r**......... *3408*
1Co 9:17 do this thing willingly, I have a **r**....... *3408*
Col 2:18 Let no man beguile you of your **r**...... *2603*
Col 3:24 receive the **r** of the inheritance:......... *469*
1Ti 5:18 The labourer is worthy of his **r** *3408*
2Ti 4:14 the Lord **r** him according to his *591*
Heb 2:2 received a just recompence of **r**; *3405*
Heb 10:35 hath a great recompence of **r**. *3405*
Heb 11:26 unto the recompence of the **r**.......... *3405*
2Pe 2:13 receive the **r** of the unrighteousness, ... *3408*
Rev 22:12 my **r** is with me, to give every......... *3408*

REWARDED
Ge 44:4 Wherefore have ye **r** evil for good?..... 7999
2Ch 15:7 weak: for your work shall be **r**......... 7939
Ps 35:12 They **r** me evil for good to the 7999
Ps 103:10 **r** us according to our iniquities........ 1580
Ps 109:5 And they have **r** me evil for good, ... 7760
Pr 13:13 the commandment shall be **r** 7999
Rev 18:6 Reward her even as she **r** you,........... *591*

REWARDER
Heb 11:6 a **r** of them that diligently seek *3406*

REWARDETH
Ps 31:23 and plentifully **r** the proud doer....... 7999
Ps 137:8 **r** thee as thou hast served us 7999
Pr 17:13 Whoso **r** evil for good, evil shall....... 7725
Pr 26:10 formed all things both **r** the fool,...... 7936

REWARDS
Nu 22:7 the **r** of divination in their hand;
Isa 1:23 gifts, and followeth after **r** 8021
Da 2:6 ye shall receive of me gifts and **r**....... 5023
Da 5:17 thyself, and give thy **r** to another;...... 5023
Hos 2:12 These are my **r** that my lovers.......... 866

RIB
Ge 2:22 And the **r**, … made he a woman 6763

RIBS
Ge 2:21 took one of his **r**, and closed up 6763

RICH See also ENRICH.
Ge 13:2 And Abram was very **r** in cattle,........ 3513
Ex 30:15 The **r** shall not give more, and 6223
1Sa 2:7 Lord maketh poor, and maketh **r**: 6238
Ps 49:16 thou afraid when one is made **r** 6238

Pr 10:4 the hand of the diligent maketh **r**...... 6238
Pr 10:22 blessing of the Lord, it maketh **r**, ... 6238
Pr 13:7 There is that maketh himself **r**,........ 6238
Pr 14:20 but the **r** hath many friends........... 6223
Pr 18:23 but the **r** answereth roughly 6223
Pr 22:2 The **r** and poor meet together:........ 6223
Pr 22:7 The **r** ruleth over the poor, and........ 6223
Pr 23:4 Labour not to be **r**: cease from 6238
Pr 28:6 is perverse ... though he be **r** 6223
Pr 28:11 **r** man is wise in his own conceit:...... 6223
Pr 28:20 he that maketh haste to be **r** shall...... 6238
Pr 28:22 hasteth to be **r** hath an evil eye, ... 1952
Ecc 5:12 abundance of the **r** will not suffer 6223
Ecc 10:20 curse not the **r** in thy bedchamber: 6223
Jer 9:23 not the **r** man glory in his riches:...... 6223
Hos 12:8 Ephraim said, Yet I am become **r** 6238
Zec 11:5 Blessed be the Lord; for I am **r** 6238
Mt 19:23 **a r man shall hardly enter into**........ *4145*
Mt 19:24 **than for a r man to enter into the** *4145*
Mt 27:57 there came a **r** man of Arimathaea, ... *4145*
Mk 10:25 **than for a r man to enter into the** *4145*
Lk 1:53 the **r** he hath sent empty away......... *4147*
Lk 6:24 **But woe unto you that are r!**.......... *4145*
Lk 12:21 **himself, and is not r toward God**...... *4147*
Lk 14:12 **kinsmen, nor thy r neighbours;** *4145*
Lk 16:1 **There was a certain r man,** *4145*
Lk 16:19 **There was a certain r man,** *4145*
Lk 16:21 **which fell from the r man's table:**...... *4145*
Lk 18:23 very sorrowful: for he was very **r**....... *4145*
Lk 18:25 **than for a r man to enter into the** *4145*
Ro 10:12 is **r** unto all that call upon him........ *4147*
2Co 8:9 though he was **r**, yet for your *4145*
Eph 2:4 God, who is **r** in mercy, for his *4145*
1Ti 6:9 that will be **r** fall into temptation *4147*
1Ti 6:17 Charge them that are **r** in this......... *4145*
1Ti 6:18 that they be **r** in good works *4147*
Jas 1:10 But the **r**, in that he is made low: *4145*
Jas 2:5 the poor of this world **r** in faith *4145*
Jas 2:6 Do not **r** men oppress you, and *4145*
Rev 2:9 **and poverty, (but thou art r)**.......... *4145*
Rev 3:17 **Because thou sayest, I am r, and**....... *4145*
Rev 3:18 **in the fire, that thou mayest be r;**...... *4147*
Rev 18:3 merchants of the earth ... waxed **r**..... *4147*

RICHER
Da 11:2 fourth shall be far **r** than they all:...... 6238

RICHES
Jos 22:8 Return with much **r** unto your........ 5233
1Sa 17:25 king will enrich him with great **r**,...... 6239
1Ki 3:11 neither hast asked **r** for thyself,........ 6239
1Ki 10:23 exceeded ... kings of the earth for **r**.... 6239
1Ch 29:12 Both **r** and honour come of thee 6239
2Ch 1:12 I will give thee **r**, and wealth, and...... 6239
2Ch 9:22 passed ... the kings of the earth in **r** ... 6239
2Ch 17:5 he had **r** and honour in abundance 6239
2Ch 32:27 Hezekiah had exceeding much **r**....... 6239
Est 1:4 the **r** of his glorious kingdom and 6239
Est 5:11 told them of the glory of his **r**, and 6239
Ps 37:16 better than the **r** of many wicked 1995
Ps 39:6 he heapeth up **r**, and knoweth not who
Ps 49:6 boast ... in the multitude of their **r**;.... 6239
Ps 52:7 trusted in the abundance of his **r**,...... 6239
Ps 62:10 if **r** increase, set not your heart........ 2428
Ps 104:24 them all: the earth is full of thy **r** 7075
Ps 119:14 testimonies, as much as in all **r**........ 1952
Pr 3:16 in her left hand **r** and honour......... 6239
Pr 8:18 yea, durable **r** and righteousness....... 1952
Pr 11:4 **R** profit not in the day of wrath:....... 1952
Pr 11:28 He that trusteth in his **r** shall fall:...... 6239
Pr 13:7 himself poor, yet hath great **r** 1952
Pr 13:8 ransom of a man's life are his **r**........ 6239
Pr 14:24 The crown of the wise is their **r**;....... 6239
Pr 22:1 rather to be chosen than great **r** 6239
Pr 22:16 oppresseth the poor to increase his **r**,
Pr 23:5 **r** certainly make themselves wings:
Pr 27:24 For **r** are not for ever: and doth 2633
Pr 30:8 give me neither poverty nor **r**; 6239
Ecc 4:8 neither is his eye satisfied with **r**: 6239
Ecc 5:13 **r** kept for the owners thereof to 6239
Ecc 6:2 A man to whom God hath given **r**, ... 6239
Ecc 9:11 nor yet **r** to men of understanding, ... 6239
Isa 10:14 found as a nest the **r** of the people: 2428
Isa 45:3 and hidden **r** of secret places, ... 4301
Jer 9:23 not the rich man glory in his **r**:........ 6239
Jer 17:11 he that getteth **r**, and not by right, ... 6239
Eze 28:5 heart is lifted up because of thy **r**:...... 2428
Da 11:28 return into his land with great **r**; 7399
Mt 13:22 **world, and the deceitfulness of r,**...... *4149*
Mk 4:19 **world, and the deceitfulness of r,**...... *4149*
Mk 10:23 **they that have r enter into the** *5536*
Mk 10:24 **that trust in r to enter into the**........ *5536*
Lk 8:14 **are choked with cares and r and**....... *4149*
Lk 16:11 **commit to your trust the true r?**
Lk 18:24 they that have **r** enter into the......... *5536*
Ro 2:4 Or despisest thou the **r** of his *4149*
Ro 9:23 make known the **r** of his glory on *4149*
Ro 11:33 depth of the **r** both of the wisdom..... *4149*
Eph 1:7 according to the **r** of his grace; *4149*
Eph 1:18 **r** of the glory of his inheritance in *4149*
Eph 2:7 shew the exceeding **r** of his grace *4149*
Eph 3:8 the unsearchable **r** of Christ;.......... *4149*
Eph 3:16 according to the **r** of his glory, to *4149*
Php 4:19 to his **r** in glory by Christ Jesus. *4149*
Col 1:27 the **r** of the glory of this mystery *4149*
Col 2:2 unto all **r** of the full assurance of *4149*
1Ti 6:17 nor trust in uncertain **r**, but in the..... *4149*
Heb 11:26 reproach of Christ greater **r**........... *4149*
Jas 5:2 Your **r** are corrupted, and your *4149*
Rev 5:12 was slain to receive power, and **r**, ... *4149*
Rev 18:17 hour so great **r** is come to nought *4149*

RICHLY
Col 3:16 the word of Christ dwell in you **r**...... *4146*
1Ti 6:17 who giveth us **r** all things to enjoy;..... *4146*

RIDDLE
Jgs 14:12 I will now put forth a **r** unto you:...... 2420
Eze 17:2 Son of man, put forth a **r**, and 2420

RIDE See also RODE.
Ge 41:43 he made him to **r** in the second 7392
1Ki 1:33 cause Solomon my son to **r** upon...... 7392
Ps 45:4 And in thy majesty **r** prosperously..... 7392

RIDER
Jer 51:21 break in pieces the horse and his **r**; 7392

RIDERS
Zec 10:5 **r** on horses shall be confounded....... 7392

RIDETH
Dt 33:26 who **r** upon the heaven in thy help, ... 7392
Est 6:8 and the horse that the king **r** upon, ... 7392

Ps	68:33	**r** upon the heavens of heavens,	7392
Isa	19:1	the Lord **r** upon a swift cloud, and	7392

RIDING

Zec	1:8	behold a man **r** upon a red horse,	7392
Zec	9:9	lowly, and **r** upon an ass, and	7392

RIGHT See also UPRIGHT.

Ge	18:25	the Judge of all the earth do **r**?	4941
Ex	15:6	Thy **r** hand, O Lord, is become	3225
Ex	15:26	do that which is **r** in his sight,	3477
Le	8:23	it upon the tip of Aaron's **r** ear,	3233
Le	14:27	shall sprinkle with his **r** finger	3233
Nu	22:26	either to the **r** hand or to the left	3225
Dt	12:8	whatsoever is **r** in his own eyes	3477
Dt	12:25	do that which is **r** in the sight of	3477
Dt	21:17	the **r** of the firstborn is his	4941
Dt	32:4	without iniquity, just and **r** is he	3477
Jgs	17:6	every man did that which was **r**	3477
Jgs	21:25	every man did that which was **r** in	3477
1Sa	12:23	teach you the good and the **r** way:	3477
2Sa	19:43	we have also more **r** in David than ye:	
1Ki	15:5	David did that which was **r** in the	3477
2Ki	10:15	Is thine heart **r**, as my heart is	3477
Ezr	8:21	God, to seek of him a **r** way for us,	3477
Ne	9:13	and gavest them **r** judgments	3477
Ps	9:4	maintained my **r** and my cause;	4941
Ps	16:11	at thy **r** hand there are pleasures	3225
Ps	19:8	The statutes of the Lord are **r**,	3477
Ps	33:4	For the word of the Lord is **r**; and	3477
Ps	45:6	of thy kingdom is a **r** sceptre	4334
Ps	51:10	and renew a **r** spirit within me	3559
Ps	110:1	Sit thou at my **r** hand, until I make	3225
Ps	139:14	and that my soul knoweth **r** well	3966
Pr	4:27	Turn not to the **r** hand nor to the	3225
Pr	12:15	way of a fool is **r** in his own eyes:	3477
Pr	14:12	There is a way which seemeth **r**	3477
Pr	16:25	There is a way that seemeth **r**	3477
Pr	21:2	Every way of a man is **r** in his own	3477
Isa	30:10	Prophesy not unto us **r** things	5229
Isa	41:10	the **r** hand of my righteousness	3225
Jer	32:7	**r** of redemption is thine to buy it	4941
Zec	11:17	his **r** eye shall be utterly darkened	3225
Mt	5:29	**if thy r eye offend thee, pluck it**	*1188*
Mt	5:39	**shall smite thee on thy r cheek,**	*1188*
Mt	6:3	**hand know what thy r hand**	*1188*
Mt	20:23	**but to sit on my r hand, and on**	*1188*
Mt	22:44	**Sit thou on my r hand, till I make**	*1188*
Mt	25:33	**shall set the sheep on his r hand,**	*1188*
Mt	26:64	**sitting on the r hand of power,**	*1188*
Mk	10:37	we may sit, one on thy **r** hand	*1188*
Mk	10:40	**But to sit on my r hand and on**	*1188*
Jn	18:10	servant, and cut off his **r** ear	*1188*
Ac	2:34	my Lord, Sit thou on my **r** hand	*1188*
Ac	7:56	standing on the **r** hand of God	*1188*
Ac	8:21	thy heart is not **r** in the sight of	*2117*
Ro	8:34	who is even at the **r** hand of God,	*1188*
Gal	2:9	gave ... the **r** hands of fellowship;	*1188*
Col	3:1	sitteth on the **r** hand of God	*1188*
Heb	1:3	the **r** hand of the Majesty on high;	*1188*
Heb	1:13	he at any time, Sit on my **r** hand	*1188*
Heb	10:12	sat down on the **r** hand of God;	*1188*
Heb	12:2	at the **r** hand of the throne of God	*1188*
1Pe	3:22	and is on the **r** hand of God;	*1188*
Rev	1:16	he had in his **r** hand seven stars:	*1188*
Rev	1:20	**which thou sawest in my r hand,**	*1188*
Rev	2:1	**the seven stars in his r hand,**	*1188*
Rev	10:2	and he set his **r** foot upon the sea	*1188*
Rev	13:16	to receive a mark in their **r** hand,	*1188*
Rev	22:14	they may have **r** to the tree of life,	*1849*

RIGHTEOUS See also UNRIGHTEOUS.

Ge	18:24	Peradventure there be fifty **r**	6662
Ge	18:25	to slay the **r** with the wicked: and	6662
1Sa	24:17	to David, Thou art more **r** than I:	6662
2Ch	12:6	and they said, The Lord is **r**	6662
Ezr	9:15	O Lord God of Israel, thou art **r**	6662
Ps	1:6	the Lord knoweth the way of the **r**:	6662
Ps	7:9	for the **r** God trieth the hearts and	6662
Ps	37:16	little that a **r** man hath is better	6662
Ps	37:25	yet have I not seen the **r** forsaken,	6662
Ps	107:42	The **r** shall see it, and rejoice:	3477
Ps	145:17	The Lord is **r** in all his ways, and	6662
Pr	10:11	mouth of a **r** man is a well of life:	6662
Pr	12:10	A **r** man regardeth the life of his	6662
Pr	13:5	A **r** man hateth lying: but a	6662
Pr	14:32	but the **r** hath hope in his death	6662
Pr	16:13	**R** lips are the delight of kings;	6664
Ecc	7:16	Be not **r** over much; neither make	6662
Jer	23:5	will raise unto David a **r** Branch,	6662
Da	9:14	Lord our God is **r** in all his works	6662
Am	2:6	because they sold the **r** for silver,	6662
Mt	9:13	**for I am not come to call the r**	*1342*
Mt	13:43	**shall the r shine forth as the sun**	*1342*
Mt	23:35	**blood of r Abel unto the blood of**	*1342*
Mk	2:17	**I came not to call the r, but**	*1342*
Lk	5:32	**I came not to call the r, but**	*1342*
Jn	17:25	**O r Father, the world hath not**	*1342*
Ro	3:10	There is none **r**, no, not one:	*1342*
Ro	5:7	scarcely for a **r** man will one die:	*1342*
2Th	1:5	token of the **r** judgment of God	*1342*
1Ti	1:9	the law is not made for a **r** man	*1342*
2Ti	4:8	which the Lord, the **r** judge, shall	*1342*
Jas	5:16	prayer of a **r** man availeth much	*1342*
1Pe	3:12	the eyes of the Lord are over the **r**,	*1342*
2Pe	2:8	vexed his **r** soul from day to day,	*1342*
Rev	16:7	true and **r** are thy judgments	*1342*
Rev	19:2	For true and **r** are his judgments:	*1342*
Rev	22:11	be filthy still: and he that is **r**,	*1342*
Rev	22:11	let him be **r** still: and he that is	*1344*

RIGHTEOUSLY See also UNRIGHTEOUSLY.

Dt	1:16	judge **r** between every man and	6664
Ps	96:10	he shall judge the people **r**	4339
Pr	31:9	Open thy mouth, judge **r**, and	6664
Jer	11:20	O Lord of hosts, that judges **r**,	6664
Tit	2:12	we should live soberly, **r**, and	*1346*
1Pe	2:23	himself to him that judgeth **r**:	*1346*

RIGHTEOUSNESS See also UNRIGHTEOUSNESS.

Ge	15:6	and he counted it to him for **r**	6666
Job	35:2	saidst, My **r** is more than God's?	6664
Job	36:3	and will ascribe **r** to my Maker	6664
Ps	4:1	me when I call, O God of my **r**:	6664
Ps	9:8	And he shall judge the world in **r**,	6664
Ps	72:1	and thy **r** unto the king's son	6666
Ps	85:10	**r** and peace have kissed each	6664
Ps	97:6	The heavens declare his **r**, and	6664
Ps	98:9	with **r** shall he judge the world,	6664
Ps	103:17	and his **r** unto children's children;	6666
Pr	11:19	As **r** tendeth to life: so he that	6666
Pr	14:34	**R** exalteth a nation: but sin is a	6666
Pr	16:8	Better is a little with **r** than great	6666

Pr 25:5 throne shall be established in **r**........ 6664
Isa 11:4 with **r** shall he judge the poor, ... 6664
Isa 32:1 Behold, a king shall reign in **r**, ... 6664
Jer 23:6 he shall be called, The Lord Our **R**..... 6664
Jer 33:15 Branch of **r** to grow up unto David;.... 6666
Jer 33:16 shall be called, The Lord our **r** 6664
Da 12:3 that turn many to **r** as the stars........ 6663
Hos 10:12 Sow to yourselves in **r**, reap in......... 6666
Mic 7:9 the light, and I shall behold his **r** 6666
Mal 4:2 Sun of **r** arise with healing in his 6666
Mt 5:6 **do hunger and thirst after r:**.......... *1343*
Mt 5:20 **shall exceed the r of the scribes** *1343*
Mt 6:33 **the kingdom of God, and his r;** *1343*
Jn 16:8 **reprove the world of sin, and of r,**..... *1343*
Jn 16:10 **Of r, because I go to my Father,**....... *1343*
Ro 1:17 therein is the **r** of God revealed......... *1343*
Ro 3:25 to declare his **r** for the remission *1343*
Ro 4:3 and it was counted unto him for **r**..... *1343*
Ro 4:6 man, unto whom God imputeth **r**..... *1343*
Ro 4:9 was reckoned to Abraham for **r**........ *1343*
Ro 4:22 it was imputed to him for **r**........... *1343*
Ro 5:18 by the **r** of one the free gift came *1345*
Ro 5:21 so might grace reign through **r**........ *1343*
Ro 8:10 but the Spirit is life because of **r**....... *1343*
Ro 10:4 Christ is the end of the law for **r**....... *1343*
Ro 10:10 the heart man believeth unto **r**;........ *1343*
Gal 3:6 and it was accounted to him for **r**...... *1343*
Eph 4:24 is created in **r** and true holiness *1343*
Eph 6:14 and having on the breastplate of **r** *1343*
Php 3:9 the **r** which is of God by faith:......... *1343*
2Ti 2:22 but follow **r**, faith, charity, peace....... *1343*
2Ti 3:16 for correction, for instruction in **r**:..... *1343*
2Ti 4:8 there is laid up for me a crown of **r**,.... *1343*
Tit 3:5 Not by works of **r** which we have *1343*
Heb 1:9 hast loved **r**, and hated iniquity;....... *1343*
Heb 7:2 being by interpretation King of **r** *1343*
Heb 11:7 heir of the **r** which is by faith *1343*
Jas 3:18 And the fruit of **r** is sown in peace..... *1343*
1Jn 2:29 every one that doeth **r** is born of *1343*
1Jn 3:10 whosoever doeth not **r** is not of God, .. *1343*

RIGHTEOUSNESS'
Mt 5:10 **which are persecuted for r sake:**....... *1343*
1Pe 3:14 But and if ye suffer for **r** sake *1343*

RIGHTEOUSNESSES
Isa 64:6 and all our **r** are as filthy rags;......... 6666

RIGHTLY See also UPRIGHTLY.
Ge 27:36 he said, Is not he **r** named Jacob?...... 3588
Lk 7:43 said unto him, **Thou hast r judged.**.... *3723*
2Ti 2:15 ashamed, **r** dividing the word of truth.

RING
Ge 41:42 Pharaoh took off his **r** from his 2885
Est 8:10 and sealed it with the king's **r**, and..... 2885
Lk 15:22 **put a r on his hand, and shoes on** *1146*
Jas 2:2 assembly a man with a gold **r**,......... *5554*

RINGS See also EARRINGS.
Ex 25:15 staves shall be in the **r** of the ark:....... 2885
Ex 25:26 and put the **r** in the four corners 2885
Eze 1:18 and their **r** were full of eyes round..... 1354

RINSED
Le 15:11 and hath not **r** his hands in water, ... 7857
Le 15:12 vessel of wood shall be **r** in water...... 7857

RIOTING
Ro 13:13 not in **r** and drunkenness, not in *2970*

RIOTOUS
Pr 28:7 is a companion of **r** men shameth 2151
Lk 15:13 **wasted his substance with r living.**...... *811*

RIPE See also FIRSTRIPE; UNRIPE.
Joel 3:13 in the sickle, for the harvest is **r**:....... 1310
Rev 14:15 for the harvest of the earth is **r**........ *3583*

RIPPED
2Ki 15:16 the women ... with child he **r** up...... 1234
Hos 13:16 women with child shall be **r** up 1234
Am 1:13 have **r** up the women with child of..... 1234

RISE See also ARISE; ROSE.
Nu 24:17 a Sceptre shall **r** out of Israel, and...... 6965
Dt 2:24 **R** ye up, take your journey, and 6965
Ne 2:18 they said, Let us **r** up and build........ 6965
Ps 35:11 False witnesses did **r** up; they laid...... 6965
Ps 127:2 It is vain for you to **r** up early, to 6965
SS 2:10 **R** up, my love, my fair one, and 6965
Isa 32:9 **R** up, ye women that are at ease;....... 6965
La 1:14 from whom I am not able to **r** up 6965
Am 8:14 shall fall, and never **r** up again 6965
Mt 5:45 **he maketh his sun to r on the evil** *393*
Mt 12:41 **men of Nineveh shall r in judgment**
Mt 20:19 **and the third day he shall r again.**...... *450*
Mt 24:7 **For nation shall r against nation,**...... *1453*
Mt 24:11 **And many false prophets shall r,** *1453*
Mt 26:46 **R, let us be going: behold, he is at** *1453*
Mt 27:63 After three days I will **r** again *1453*
Mk 3:26 **And if Satan r up against himself,** *450*
Mk 8:31 and after three days **r** again............ *450*
Mk 9:31 **be killed, he shall r the third day.**...... *450*
Mk 10:34 **and the third day he shall r again.**...... *450*
Mk 12:25 **when they shall r from the dead,** *450*
Mk 13:8 **For nation shall r against nation,**...... *1453*
Mk 13:12 **shall r up against their parents,** *1881*
Mk 13:22 **Christs and false prophets shall r,** *1453*
Mk 14:42 **R up, let us go; lo, he that** *1453*
Lk 5:23 **thee; or to say, R up and walk?**........ *1453*
Lk 11:32 **Nineve shall r up in the judgment**...... *450*
Lk 12:54 **ye see a cloud r out of the west.**........ *393*
Lk 18:33 **and the third day he shall r again.**...... *450*
Lk 21:10 **Nation shall r against nation,**......... *1453*
Lk 22:46 **r and pray, lest ye enter into** *450*
Lk 24:7 crucified, and the third day **r** again...... *450*
Lk 24:46 **to r from the dead the third day:** *450*
Jn 11:23 her, **Thy brother shall r again**.......... *450*
Jn 20:9 he must **r** again from the dead *450*
Ac 3:6 name of Jesus ... of Nazareth **r** up..... *1453*
1Co 15:15 up, if so be that the dead **r** not *1453*
1Co 15:16 if the dead **r** not, ... is not Christ...... *1453*
1Co 15:29 the dead, if the dead **r** not at all?....... *1453*
1Co 15:32 advantageth it me, if the dead **r** *1453*
1Th 4:16 the dead in Christ shall **r** first:.......... *450*
Heb 7:11 that another priest should **r** after *450*
Rev 11:1 **R**, and measure the temple of......... *1453*
Rev 13:1 saw a beast **r** up out of the sea.......... *305*

RISEN
Ps 20:8 but we are **r**, and stand upright........ 6965
Ps 86:14 O God, the proud are r up againts me.. 6965
Is 60:1 the glory of the Lord is r upon thee.... 2224
Mt 11:11 **hath not r a greater than John** *1453*

Mt	17:9	**the Son of man be r again from**	*450*
Mt	26:32	**But after I am r again, I will go**	*1453*
Mt	27:64	the people, He is **r** from the dead:	*1453*
Mt	28:6	He is not here: for he is **r**, as he	*1453*
Mk	14:28	**after that I am r, I will go before**	*1453*
Mk	16:6	he is **r**; he is not here: behold the	*1453*
Mk	16:9	Jesus was **r** early the first day of	*450*
Lk	7:16	a great prophet is **r** up among us;	*1453*
Lk	13:25	**the master of the house is r up,**	*1453*
Lk	24:6	He is not here, but is **r**: remember	*1453*
Lk	24:34	The Lord is **r** indeed, and hath	*1453*
Ro	8:34	died, yea rather, that is **r** again,	*1453*
1Co	15:13	of the dead, then is Christ not **r**:	*1453*
1Co	15:14	And if Christ be not **r**, then is our	*1453*
1Co	15:20	But now is Christ **r** from the dead,	*1453*
Col	2:12	**r** with him through the faith of	*4891*
Col	3:1	If ye then be **r** with Christ, seek	*4891*
Jas	1:11	sun is … **r** with a burning heat,	*393*

RISEST

Dt	6:7	liest down, and when thou **r** up	6965
Dt	11:19	liest down, and when thou **r** up	6965

RISETH See also **ARISETH.**

Pr	24:16	falleth seven times, and **r** up again:	6965
Pr	31:15	She **r** also while it is yet night, and	6965
Jer	46:8	Egypt **r** up like a flood, and his	5927
Mic	7:6	daughter **r** up against her mother.	6965
Jn	13:4	He **r** from supper, and laid aside	*1453*

RISING See also **SUNRISING; UPRISING.**

2Ch	36:15	**r** up betimes, and sending;	7925
Ps	113:3	From the **r** of the sun unto the	4217
Pr	27:14	**r** early in the morning, it shall be	7925
Pr	30:31	against whom there is no **r** up.	510
La	3:63	sitting down, and their **r** up;	7012
Mal	1:11	from the **r** of the sun even unto	4217
Mk	1:35	**r** up a great while before day, he	*450*
Mk	9:10	the **r** from the dead should mean	*305*
Mk	16:2	the sepulchre at the **r** of the sun	*393*
Lk	2:34	and **r** again of many in Israel;	*386*

RITES

Nu	9:3	according to all the **r** of it, and	2708

RIVER

Ge	2:10	a **r** went out of Eden to water the	5104
Ge	2:13	the name of the second **r** is Gihon:	5104
Ge	2:14	name of the third **r** is Hiddekel:	5104
Ge	2:14	And the fourth **r** is Euphrates	5104
Ge	41:2	came up out of the **r** seven … kine	2975
Ex	1:22	Every son … ye shall cast into the **r**	2975
Ex	2:5	came down to wash herself at the **r**;	2975
Ex	7:21	And the fish that was in the **r** died;	2975
Ex	8:3	And the **r** shall bring forth frogs	2975
Jos	13:16	city that is in the midst of the **r**,	5158
Ps	36:8	drink of the **r** of thy pleasures.	5158
Ps	46:4	There is a **r**, the streams whereof	5104
Ps	72:8	and from the **r** unto the ends of	5104
Ps	105:41	they ran in the dry places like a **r**	5104
Isa	7:20	namely, by them beyond the **r**,	5104
Isa	48:18	then had thy peace been as a **r**,	5104
Isa	66:12	I will extend peace to her like a **r**,	5104
La	2:18	let tears run down like a **r** day.	5158
Eze	29:3	My **r** is mine own, and I have	2975
Da	12:7	was upon the waters of the **r**,	2975
Zec	9:10	from the **r** even to the ends of the	5104
Mk	1:5	baptized of him in the **r** of Jordan,	*4215*
Rev	9:14	bound in the great **r** Euphrates	*4215*
Rev	16:12	vial upon the great **r** Euphrates;	*4215*
Rev	22:1	shewed me a pure **r** of water of life,	*4215*

RIVERS

Ex	7:19	upon their streams, upon their **r**,	2975
Ex	8:5	over the **r**, and over the ponds,	2975
Le	11:10	scales in the seas, and in the **r**,	5158
Ps	1:3	a tree planted by the **r** of water,	6388
Ps	78:16	caused waters to run down like **r**	5104
Ps	119:136	**R** of waters run down mine	6388
Ps	137:1	By the **r** of Babylon, there we sat	5104
Pr	21:1	hand of the Lord, as the **r** of water:	6388
Ecc	1:7	All the **r** run into the sea; yet the	5158
Isa	32:2	as **r** of water in a dry place	6388
Isa	50:2	the sea, I make the **r** a wilderness:	5103
Jer	31:9	them to walk by the **r** of waters	5158
La	3:48	runneth down with **r** of water	6388
Eze	6:3	hills, to the **r**, and to the valleys;	650
Eze	30:12	And I will make the **r** dry, and sell	2975
Eze	32:6	and the **r** shall be full of thee	650
Eze	32:14	and cause their **r** to run like oil	5104
Eze	35:8	and in all thy **r**, shall they fall that	650
Joel	3:18	**r** of Judah shall flow with waters	650
Mic	6:7	or with ten thousands of **r** of oil?	5158
Hab	3:8	the Lord displeased against the **r**?	5104
Jn	7:38	**belly shall flow r of living water.**	*4215*
Rev	8:10	it fell upon the third part of the **r**,	*4215*
Rev	16:4	poured out his vial upon the **r** and	*4215*

ROAR See also **UPROAR.**

1Ch	16:32	Let the sea **r**, and the fulness	7481
Ps	96:11	let the sea **r**, and the fulness	7481
Ps	98:7	Let the sea **r**, and the fulness	7481
Ps	104:21	The young lions **r** after their prey,	7580
Isa	5:29	lion, they shall **r** like young lions:	7580
Isa	5:29	yea, they shall **r**, and lay hold of	5098
Isa	5:30	that day they shall **r** against them	5098
Jer	25:30	The Lord shall **r** from on high,	7580
Jer	31:35	the sea when the waves thereof **r**;	1993
Jer	50:42	their voice shall **r** like the sea, and	1993
Jer	51:38	They shall **r** together like lions:	7580
Hos	11:10	the Lord: he shall **r** like a lion:	7580
Joel	3:16	The Lord also shall **r** out of Zion,	7580
Am	1:2	he said, The Lord will **r** from Zion,	7580
Am	3:4	Will a lion **r** in the forest, when he	7580

ROARED

Ps	38:8	**r** by reason of the disquietness of	7580
Isa	51:15	divided the sea, whose waves **r**:	1993
Am	3:8	The lion hath **r**, who will not fear?	7580

ROARETH

Job	37:4	After it a voice **r**: he thundereth	7580
Jer	6:23	mercy; their voice **r** like the sea;	1993
Rev	10:3	a loud voice, as when a lion **r**:	*3455*

ROARING

Job	4:10	The **r** of the lion, and the voice of	7581
Ps	22:1	me, and from the words of my **r**?	7581
Ps	22:13	as a ravening and a **r** lion	7580
Ps	32:3	my bones waxed old through my **r**.	7581
Pr	19:12	king's wrath is as the **r** of a lion;	5099
Pr	20:2	fear of a king is as the **r** of a lion:	5099
Pr	28:15	As a **r** lion, and a ranging bear;	5098
Isa	5:30	shall roar … like the **r** of the sea:	5100

Zec 11:3 a voice of the **r** of young lions; 7581
Lk 21:25 the sea and the waves **r**; *2278*
1Pe 5:8 devil, as a **r** lion, walketh about, *5612*

ROARINGS
Job 3:24 **r** are poured out like the waters 7581

ROAST
Ex 12:8 the flesh in that night, **r** with fire, 6748
Ex 12:9 at all with water, but **r** with fire; 6748
1Sa 2:15 Give flesh to **r** for the priest; for 6740

ROASTED
2Ch 35:13 And they **r** the passover with fire 1310
Jer 29:22 whom the king of Babylon **r** in the 7033

ROASTETH
Pr 12:27 slothful man **r** not that which he 2760

ROB
Pr 22:22 **R** not the poor, because he is 1497
Isa 10:2 that they may **r** the fatherless! 962
Mal 3:8 Will a man **r** God? Yet ye have 6906

ROBBED
Ps 119:61 bands of the wicked have **r** me: 5749
Pr 17:12 Let a bear **r** of her whelps meet a 7909
Isa 42:22 But this is a people **r** and spoiled; 962
Eze 33:15 pledge, give again that he had **r**, 1500
Mal 3:8 man rob God? Yet ye have **r** me 6906
Mal 3:9 for ye have **r** me, even this whole 6906
2Co 11:8 I **r** other churches, taking wages *4813*

ROBBER
Eze 18:10 If he beget a son that is a **r**, a 6530
Jn 10:1 **way, the same is a thief and a r** *3027*
Jn 18:40 Barabbas. Now Barabbas was a **r**. *3027*

ROBBERS
Jer 7:11 become a den of **r** in your eyes? 6530
Eze 7:22 for the **r** shall enter into it, and 6530
Jn 10:8 **came before me are thieves and r** *3027*
2Co 11:26 in perils of waters, in perils of **r** *3027*

ROBBERY
Pr 21:7 The **r** of the wicked shall destroy 7701
Isa 61:8 I hate **r** for burnt offering; and 1498
Na 3:1 city! it is all full of lies and **r**; the 6563
Php 2:6 it not **r** to be equal with God: *725*

ROBBETH
Pr 28:24 Whoso **r** his father or his mother, 1497

ROBE See also WARDROBE.
1Sa 18:4 Jonathan stripped himself of the **r** 4598
1Sa 24:4 cut off the skirt of Saul's **r** privily 4598
1Ch 15:27 David was clothed with a **r** of fine 4598
Job 29:14 my judgment was as a **r** and a 4598
Isa 61:10 me with the **r** of righteousness, 4598
Mt 27:28 him, and put on him a scarlet **r**. *5511*
Mt 27:31 they took the **r** off from him, and *5511*
Lk 15:22 **Bring forth the best r, and put it** *4749*
Lk 23:11 and arrayed him in a gorgeous **r**, *2066*
Jn 19:2 and they put on him a purple **r**, *2440*
Jn 19:5 crown of thorns, and the purple **r**, *2440*

ROBES
2Sa 13:18 for with such **r** were the king's 4598
Lk 20:46 which desire to walk in long **r** *4749*
Rev 6:11 white **r** were given unto every one *4749*
Rev 7:9 clothed with white **r**, and palms in *4749*
Rev 7:14 have washed their **r**, and made *4749*

ROCK
Ex 33:22 I will put thee in a clift of a **r**, and 6697
Nu 20:11 with his rod he smote the **r** twice: 5553
Dt 32:4 He is the **R**, his work is perfect: 6697
Dt 32:15 esteemed the **R** of his salvation. 6697
Dt 32:18 Of the **R** that begat thee thou art 6697
Dt 32:30 except their **R** and sold them, and 6697
Dt 32:31 For their **r** is not as our **R**, even 6697
Dt 32:37 gods, their **r** in whom they trusted, 6697
1Sa 2:2 is there any **r** like our God 6697
2Sa 22:2 said, The Lord is my **r**, and my 5553
2Sa 22:32 and who is a **r**, save our God? 6697
2Sa 22:47 Lord liveth; and blessed be my **r**; 6697
2Sa 22:47 the God of the **r** of my salvation. 6697
Ps 18:2 The Lord is my **r**, and my fortress, 5553
Ps 27:5 me; he shall set me up upon a **r** 6697
Ps 42:9 I will say unto God my **r**, Why hast 5553
Ps 61:2 lead me to the **r** that is higher 6697
Ps 62:6 He only is my **r** and my salvation: 6697
Ps 78:20 he smote the **r**, that the waters 6697
Ps 78:35 remembered that God was their **r**, 6697
Ps 92:15 he is my **r**, and there is no 6697
Pr 30:19 the way of a serpent upon a **r**; 6697
Isa 2:10 Enter into the **r**, and hide thee 6697
Isa 8:14 stumbling and for a **r** of offence 6697
Isa 32:2 shadow of a great **r** in a weary land 5553
Jer 23:29 hammer that breaketh the **r** in 5553
Mt 7:24 **which built his house upon a r** *4073*
Mt 16:18 **this r I will build my church;** *4073*
Mt 27:60 which he had hewn out in the **r**: *4073*
Mk 15:46 sepulchre ... was hewn out of a **r**, *4073*
Lk 6:48 **it: for it was founded upon a r** *4073*
Lk 8:6 **And some fell upon a r; and as** *4073*
Ro 9:33 a stumblingstone and **r** of offence: *4073*
1Co 10:4 they drank of that spiritual **R** that *4073*
1Co 10:4 them: and that **R** was Christ *4073*
1Pe 2:8 a **r** of offence, even to them which *4073*

ROCKS
Nu 23:9 from the top of the **r** I see him, 6697
Job 28:10 cutteth out rivers among the **r**; 6697
Ps 104:18 goats; and the **r** for the conies 5553
Pr 30:26 make they their houses in the **r**: 5553
Isa 2:21 To go into the clefts of the **r**, and 6697
Na 1:6 the **r** are thrown down by him 6697
Mt 27:51 earth did quake, and the **r** rent; *4073*
Rev 6:16 And said to the mountains and **r**, *4073*

ROD
Ex 7:9 Take thy **r**, and cast it before 4294
Ex 7:12 Aaron's **r** swallowed up their rods 4294
Ex 14:16 but lift thou up thy **r**, and stretch 4294
Ex 21:20 his servant, or his maid, with a **r**, 7626
Nu 17:2 thou every man's name upon his **r**. 4294
Ps 2:9 shalt break them with a **r** of iron; 7626
Ps 23:4 **r** and thy staff they comfort me 7626
Pr 10:13 a **r** is for the back of him that is 7626
Pr 13:24 that spareth his **r** hateth his son: 7626
Pr 14:3 mouth of ... foolish is a **r** of pride: 2415
Pr 22:8 and the **r** of his anger shall fail 7626
Pr 22:15 **r** of correction shall drive it far 7626
Pr 23:13 for if thou beatest him with the **r**, 7626
Pr 23:14 Thou shalt beat him with the **r**, 7626
Pr 26:3 the ass, and a **r** for the fool's back 7626

Pr 29:15 The **r** and reproof give wisdom: 7626
Isa 11:1 forth a **r** out of the stem of Jesse, ... 2415
Isa 11:4 smite the earth with the **r** of his 7626
Jer 51:19 Israel is the **r** of his inheritance: 7626
La 3:1 seen affliction by the **r** of his wrath 7626
Eze 20:37 cause you to pass under the **r**, ... 7626
1Co 4:21 shall I come unto you with a **r**, or...... *4464*
Heb 9:4 Aaron's **r** that budded, and the *4464*
Rev 2:27 **shall rule them with a r of iron;** *4464*
Rev 11:1 was given me a reed like unto a **r**:...... *4464*
Rev 12:5 to rule all nations with a **r** of iron:..... *4464*
Rev 19:15 he shall rule them with a **r** of iron:..... *4464*

RODE See also **RIDE.**
2Sa 18:9 Absalom **r** upon a mule, and the 7392
2Sa 22:11 he **r** upon a cherub, and did fly: 7392
Ne 2:12 me, save the beast that I **r** upon 7392
Ps 18:10 he **r** upon a cherub, and did fly: 7392

RODS
Ge 30:37 Jacob took him **r** of green poplar 4731
Ex 7:12 Aaron's rod swallowed up their **r** 4294
Nu 17:6 fathers' houses, even twelve **r**: 4294
2Co 11:25 Thrice was I beaten with **r**, once....... *4463*

ROE
Pr 5:19 the loving hind and pleasant **r**; 3280
Pr 6:5 Deliver thyself as a **r** from the......... 6643
SS 2:17 be thou like a **r** or a young hart 6643
SS 8:14 thou like to a **r** or to a young hart 6643

ROES
SS 2:7 by the **r**, and by the hinds of the....... 6643
SS 3:5 by the **r**, and by the hinds of the....... 6643

ROLL
Jos 10:18 **R** great stones upon the mouth of 1556
1Sa 14:33 **r** a great stone unto me this day 1556
Jer 36:6 and read in the **r**, which thou hast 4039
Eze 3:1 eat this **r**, and go speak unto the....... 4040
Zec 5:1 and looked, and behold a flying **r**...... 4040
Zec 5:2 I see a flying **r**; the length thereof...... 4040
Mk 16:3 Who shall **r** us away the stone.......... *617*

ROLLED
Ge 29:10 **r** the stone from the well's mouth, ... 1556
Isa 9:5 noise, and garments **r** in blood; 1556
Isa 34:4 the heavens shall be **r** together as 1556
Mt 27:60 and he **r** a great stone to the door...... *4351*
Mt 28:2 came and **r** back the stone from *617*
Mk 15:46 and **r** a stone unto the door of the *4351*
Mk 16:4 saw that the stone was **r** away:.......... *617*
Lk 24:2 stone **r** away from the sepulchre *617*
Rev 6:14 as a scroll when it is **r** together;........ *1507*

ROMANS (ro´-muns)
Jn 11:48 **R** shall come and take away both *4514*

ROOF
Jgs 16:27 upon the **r** about three thousand 1406
Ps 137:6 cleave to the **r** of my mouth; if I....... 2441
Mk 2:4 uncovered the **r** where he was: *4721*
Lk 7:6 thou shouldest enter under my **r** *4721*

ROOM
1Ki 8:20 I am risen up in the **r** of David my..... 8478
2Ki 15:25 he killed him, and reigned in his **r** 8478
Pr 18:16 A man's gift maketh **r** for him, ... 7337
Mal 3:10 shall not be **r** enough to receive it.
Mk 14:15 **shew you a large upper r furnished.**..... *508*
Lk 2:7 there was no **r** for them in the......... *5117*
Lk 12:17 **no r where to bestow my fruits?.**
Lk 14:10 **sit down in the lowest r; that.**......... *5117*
Lk 22:12 **you a large upper r furnished:**
1Co 14:16 occupieth the **r** of the unlearned *5117*

ROOMS
Ge 16:14 **r** shalt thou make in the ark, and 7064
Mt 23:6 **love the uppermost r at feasts**......... *4411*
Mk 12:39 **and the uppermost r at feasts:** *4411*
Lk 20:46 **synagogues, ... the chief r at feasts;**.... *4411*

ROOT
Pr 12:3 **r** of the righteous shall not be......... 8328
Pr 12:12 **r** of the righteous yieldeth fruit........ 8328
Isa 11:10 that day there shall be a **r** of Jesse, ... 8328
Mt 3:10 ax is laid unto the **r** of the trees: *4491*
Mt 13:6 **and because they had no r, they**....... *4491*
Mt 13:21 **Yet hath he not r in himself, but**....... *4491*
Mk 4:17 **And have no r in themselves, and** *4491*
Lk 3:9 axe is laid unto the **r** of the trees: *4491*
Lk 8:13 **these have no r, which for a while** *4491*
Lk 17:6 **Be thou plucked up by the r, and**...... *1610*
1Ti 6:10 love of money is the **r** of all evil:....... *4491*
Heb 12:15 lest any **r** of bitterness springing....... *4491*
Rev 5:5 the tribe of Juda, the **R** of David....... *4491*
Rev 22:16 **the r and the offspring of David,** *4491*

ROOTED
Pr 2:22 transgressors shall be **r** out of it 5255
Mt 15:13 **hath not planted, shall be r up** *1610*
Eph 3:17 ye, being **r** and grounded in love *4492*
Col 2:7 **R** and built up in him, and *4492*

ROOTS
Isa 11:1 a Branch shall grow out of his **r** 8328
Eze 17:9 shall he not pull up the **r** thereof,...... 8328
Mk 11:20 the fig tree dried up from the **r**........ *4491*
Jude 12 twice dead, plucked up by the **r**; *1610*

ROSE
Ge 4:8 **r** up against Abel his brother, ... 6965
Ex 12:30 And Pharaoh **r** up in the night, he..... 6965
Ex 32:6 eat and to drink, and **r** up to play...... 6965
Ex 33:10 the people **r** up and worshipped, ... 6965
Jgs 6:21 and there **r** up fire out of the rock,..... 5927
1Ki 2:19 And the king **r** up to meet her, and 6965
1Ki 3:21 I **r** in the morning to give my child 6965
Ne 4:14 And I looked, and **r** up, and said 6965
Ps 124:2 our side, when men **r** up against us:.... 6965
SS 2:1 I am the **r** of Sharon, and the lily 2261
Da 8:27 I **r** up, and did the king's business;..... 6965
Jnh 1:3 Jonah **r** up to flee unto Tarshish 6965
Lk 5:28 he left all, **r** up, and followed him. *450*
Lk 16:31 **though one r from the dead.**........... *450*
Lk 24:33 And they **r** up the same hour, and *450*
Ro 14:9 this end Christ both died, and **r** *450*
1Co 10:7 to eat and drink, and **r** up to play....... *450*
1Co 15:4 and that he **r** again the third day....... *1453*
1Co 15:12 preached that he **r** from the dead *1453*
2Co 5:15 which died for them, and **r** again *1453*
1Th 4:14 that Jesus died and **r** again, even........ *450*
Rev 19:3 her smoke **r** up for ever and ever 305

ROT
Nu 5:22 belly to swell, and thy thigh to **r**:....... 5307
Pr 10:7 the name of the wicked shall **r**......... 7537

ROTTENNESS

Pr	12:4	ashamed is as **r** in his bones	7538
Pr	14:30	flesh: but envy the **r** of the bones	7538
Isa	5:24	so their root shall be as **r**, and	4716

ROUGH

Lk	3:5	the **r** ways shall be made smooth;	*5138*

ROUGHLY

Ge	42:30	spake **r** to us, and took us for spies	7186
1Sa	20:10	what if thy father answer thee **r**?	7186
1KI	12:13	the king answered the people **r**	7186
Pr	18:23	but the rich answereth **r**.	5794

ROUND

Ex	29:20	the blood upon the altar **r** about,	5439
Le	8:24	the blood upon the altar **r** about	5439
Le	9:12	sprinkled **r** about upon the altar.	5439
Nu	1:50	encamp **r** about the tabernacle	5439
Nu	1:53	the Levites shall pitch **r** about the	5439
Jos	21:44	the Lord gave them rest **r** about,	5439
1Sa	23:26	compassed David and his men **r** about	
1Ki	3:1	and the wall of Jerusalem **r** about.	5439
1Ki	4:24	had peace on all sides **r** about him	5439
2Ki	25:10	the walls of Jerusalem **r** about.	5439
Ps	22:12	bulls of Bashan have beset me **r**	3803
Ps	34:7	encampeth **r** about them that fear	5439
Ps	125:2	so the Lord is **r** about his people	5439
SS	7:2	navel is like a **r** goblet, which	5469
Isa	42:25	it hath set him on fire **r** about,	5439
Isa	49:18	Lift up thine eyes **r** about, and	5439
Isa	60:4	Lift up thine eyes **r** about, and see:	5439
Jer	52:14	all the walls of Jerusalem **r** about	5439
La	2:3	fire, which devoureth **r** about.	5439
La	2:22	a solemn day my terrors **r** about,	5439
Eze	1:18	full of eyes **r** about them four	5439
Eze	10:12	wheels, were full of eyes **r** about,	5439
Eze	32:26	her graves are **r** about him:	5439
Zec	2:5	be unto her a wall of fire **r** about,	5439
Mt	21:33	**vineyard, and hedged it r about,**	
Mk	3:5	had looked **r** about on them with	*4017*
Lk	2:9	glory of the Lord shone **r** about	*4034*
Lk	19:43	**compass thee r, and keep thee in**	*4033*
Ac	9:3	there shined **r** about him a light	*4015*
Ac	22:6	heaven a great light **r** about me.	*4015*
Heb	9:4	overlaid **r** about with gold,	*3840*
Rev	4:3	was a rainbow **r** about the throne,	*2943*
Rev	7:11	angels stood **r** about the throne,	*2943*

ROUSE

Ge	49:9	an old lion; who shall **r** him up?	6965

ROWED

Jnh	1:13	men **r** hard to bring it to the land;	2864

ROWS

Ex	28:17	of stones, even four **r** of stones:	2905
Le	24:6	And thou shalt set them in two **r**	4634

ROYAL

1Ki	10:13	Solomon gave her of his **r** bounty	4428
2Ki	11:1	arose and destroyed all the seed **r**	4467
1Ch	29:25	such **r** majesty as had not been	4438
2Ch	22:10	the seed **r** of the house of Judah.	4467
Est	1:7	**r** wine in abundance, according	4438
Est	2:17	he set the **r** crown upon her head	4438
Est	5:1	Esther put on her **r** apparel, and	4438
Est	6:8	Let the **r** apparel be brought	4438
Est	8:15	in **r** apparel of blue and white,	4438
Isa	62:3	**r** diadem in the hand of thy God.	4410
Ac	12:21	Herod, arrayed in **r** apparel, sat	*937*
Jas	2:8	If ye fulfil the **r** law according to	*937*
1Pe	2:9	a **r** priesthood, an holy nation, a	*934*

RUBIES

Job	28:18	the price of wisdom is above **r**	6443
Pr	3:15	She is more precious than **r**: and	6443
Pr	8:11	For wisdom is better than **r**; and	6443
Pr	31:10	woman? for her price is far above **r**	6443

RUDDY

1Sa	17:42	for he was but a youth, and **r**, and	132
SS	5:10	My beloved is white and **r**, the	122

RUDIMENTS

Col	2:8	after the **r** of the world, and not	*4747*
Col	2:20	be dead … from the **r** of the world,	*4747*

RUIN

2Ch	28:23	But they were the **r** of him, and	3782
Pr	24:22	who knoweth the **r** of them both?	6365
Pr	26:28	and a flattering mouth worketh **r**.	4072
Eze	18:30	so iniquity shall not be your **r**.	4383

RUINED

Isa	3:8	For Jerusalem is **r**, and Judah is	3782
Eze	36:36	that I the Lord build the **r** places,	2040

RUINOUS

Isa	37:26	waste defenced cities into **r** heaps.	5327

RUINS

Am	9:11	and I will raise up his **r**, and I will	2034
Ac	15:16	I will build again the **r** thereof,	*2679*

RULE See also UNRULY.

Ge	1:16	the greater light to **r** the day,	4475
Ge	3:16	husband, and he shall **r** over thee	4910
Jgs	8:23	you: the Lord shall **r** over you	4910
Est	1:22	should bare **r** in his own house	8323
Est	9:1	Jews had **r** over them that hated	7980
Ps	136:8	The sun to **r** by day: for his	4475
Ps	136:9	The moon and stars to **r** by night:	4475
Pr	8:16	By me princes **r**, and nobles,	8323
Pr	17:2	servant shall have **r** over a son that	4910
Pr	19:10	a servant to have **r** over princes.	4910
Pr	25:28	hath no **r** over his own spirit is	4623
Pr	29:2	but when the wicked beareth **r**	4910
Isa	19:4	a fierce king shall **r** over them,	4910
Isa	63:19	thou never barest **r** over them;	4910
Eze	29:15	shall no more **r** over the nations	7287
Da	4:26	known that the heavens do **r**.	7990
Da	11:3	that shall **r** with great dominion,	4910
Joel	2:17	the heathen should **r** over them:	4910
Zec	6:13	shall sit and **r** upon his throne;	4910
Mt	2:6	that shall **r** my people Israel.	*4165*
Mk	10:42	**accounted to r over the Gentiles**	*757*
1Co	15:24	he shall have put down all **r** and	*746*
Col	3:15	the peace of God **r** in your hearts	*1018*
1Ti	3:5	know not how to **r** his own house,	*4291*
1Ti	5:17	the elders that **r** well be counted	*4291*
Heb	13:7	them which have the **r** over you,	*2233*
Rev	2:27	**shall r them with a rod of iron;**	*4165*
Rev	12:5	**r** all nations with a rod of iron:	*4165*
Rev	19:15	he shall **r** them with a rod of iron:	*4165*

R

RULED
Ru 1:1 in the days when the judges **r**,......... 8199
Ezr 4:20 which have **r** over all countries........ 7990
Isa 14:6 he that **r** the nations in anger, is....... 7287
La 5:8 Servants have **r** over us: there is....... 4910
Eze 34:4 and with cruelty have ye **r** them. 7287
Da 5:21 God **r** in the kingdom of men,........ 7990

RULER
Ge 41:43 he made him **r** over all the land of
2Ch 7:18 fail thee a man to be **r** in Israel........ 4910
Ne 3:9 **r** of the half part of Jerusalem. 8269
Ne 3:12 **r** of the half part of Jerusalem, he...... 8269
Ps 105:21 house, and **r** of all his substance: 4910
Pr 23:1 When thou sittest to eat with a **r** 4910
Pr 28:15 is a wicked **r** over the poor people 4910
Pr 29:12 If a **r** hearken to lies, all his........... 4910
Ecc 10:4 the spirit of the **r** rise up against....... 4910
Ecc 10:5 which proceedeth from the **r**.......... 7989
Da 2:10 there is no king, lord, no **r**, that 7990
Da 2:38 hath made thee **r** over them all. 7981
Da 2:48 him **r** over the whole province of...... 7981
Da 5:7, 16 be the third **r** in the kingdom......... 7981
Da 5:29 be the third **r** in the kingdom......... 7990
Mt 25:21 **make thee r over many things:**........ *2525*
Lk 12:42 **shall make r over his household,** *2535*
Jn 3:1 named Nicodemus, a **r** of the Jews: *758*

RULER'S
Pr 29:26 Many seek the **r** favour; but every 4910

RULERS
Ge 47:6 then make them **r** over my cattle 8269
Ezr 9:2 **r** hath been chief in this trespass....... 5461
Ne 2:16 the **r** knew not whither I went,........ 5461
Ps 2:2 and the **r** take counsel together........ 7336
Jer 33:26 to be **r** over the seed of Abraham...... 4910
Eze 23:12 and **r** clothed most gorgeously........ 5461
Mk 13:9 **before r and kings for my sake,**........ *2232*
Lk 21:12 **kings and r for my name's sake.**....... *2232*
Lk 23:35 the **r** also with them derided him, ... *758*
Lk 24:20 chief priests and our **r** delivered........ *758*
Jn 7:26 Do the **r** know indeed that this is....... *758*
Ro 13:3 **r** are not a terror to good works,........ *758*
Eph 6:12 against the **r** of the darkness of........ *2888*

RULEST
2Ch 20:6 **r** not thou over all the kingdoms 4910
Ps 89:9 Thou **r** the raging of the sea: when 4910

RULETH
2Sa 23:3 He that **r** over men must be just, ... 4910
Ps 59:13 let them know that God **r** in Jacob..... 4910
Ps 66:7 He **r** by his power for ever; his 4910
Ps 103:19 and his kingdom **r** over all............ 4910
Pr 16:32 he that **r** his spirit than he that........ 4910
Pr 22:7 The rich **r** over the poor, and the...... 4910
Ecc 8:9 wherein one man **r** over another 7980
Ecc 9:17 the cry of him that **r** among fools 4910
Da 4:25 that the most High **r** in the........... 7980
Hos 11:12 but Judah yet **r** with God, and is....... 7300
Ro 12:8 he that **r**, with diligence; he that....... 4291
1Ti 3:4 One that **r** well his own house,........ 4291

RULING
2Sa 23:3 must be just, **r** in the fear of God...... 4910
1Ti 3:12 **r** their children and their own......... *4291*

RUMOUR
2Ki 19:7 and he shall hear a **r**, and shall........ 8052
Jer 49:14 I have heard a **r** from the Lord........ 8052
Ob 1 We have heard a **r** from the Lord...... 8052
Lk 7:17 And this **r** of him went forth.......... *3056*

RUMOURS
Mt 24:6 **shall hear of wars and r of wars:**........ *189*
Mk 13:7 **shall hear of wars and r of wars,**........ *189*

RUN See also OUTRUN; RAN.
Jer 18:25 lest angry fellows **r** upon thee......... 6293
1Sa 20:36 **R**, find out now the arrows which 7323
2Ki 4:22 that I may **r** to the man of God,....... 7323
2Ki 5:20 **r** after him, and take somewhat 7323
2Ch 16:9 the eyes of the Lord **r** to and from..... 7751
Ps 19:5 rejoiceth as a strong man to **r** a........ 7323
Ps 119:32 **r** the way of thy commandments...... 7323
Ps 119:136 of waters **r** down mine eyes........... 3381
Pr 1:16 For their feet **r** to evil, and make....... 7323
Ecc 1:7 All the rivers **r** into the sea; yet........ 1980
Isa 40:31 they shall **r**, and not be weary; 7323
Isa 55:5 that knew not thee shall **r** unto thee.... 7323
Isa 59:7 Their feet **r** to evil, and they make..... 7323
Jer 9:18 our eyes may **r** down with tears,....... 3381
Jer 13:17 weep sore, and **r** down with tears, ... 3381
Jer 14:17 Let mine eyes **r** down with tears....... 3381
La 2:18 let tears **r** down like a river day........ 3381
Eze 24:16 neither shall thy tears **r** down........... 935
Am 8:12 shall **r** to and fro to seek the word..... 7751
Zec 4:10 **r** to and fro through the whole........ 7751
1Co 9:24 that they which **r** in a race **r** all........ *5143*
Gal 2:2 means I should **r**, or had **r**, in vain..... *5143*
Php 2:16 that I have not **r** in vain, neither....... *5143*
Heb 12:1 let us **r** with patience the race that..... *5143*

RUNNETH
Ps 23:5 my head with oil; my cup **r** over....... 7310
Ps 147:15 earth: his word **r** very swiftly.......... 7323
Pr 18:10 the righteous **r** into it, and is safe...... 7323
La 1:16 eye, mine eye **r** down with water, ... 3381
La 3:48 Mine eye **r** down with rivers of........ 3381
Mt 9:17 **bottles break, and the wine r out,**...... *1632*
Ro 9:16 him that willeth, nor of him that **r**..... *5143*

RUNNING See also OVERRUNNING.
2Sa 18:26 the watchman saw another man **r**:..... 7323
Pr 5:15 **r** waters out of thine own well 5140
Pr 6:18 feet that be swift in **r** to mischief,...... 7323
Lk 6:38 **and shaken together, and r over,**....... *5240*
Rev 9:9 of many horses **r** to battle. *5143*

RUSHING
Isa 17:12 and to the **r** of nations, that make 7588
Jer 47:3 at the **r** of his chariots, and at the...... 7494
Eze 3:12 behind me a voice of a great **r**......... 7494
Ac 2:2 from heaven as of a **r** mighty wind, ... *5342*

RUST
Mt 6:19 **where moth and r doth corrupt,** *1035*
Mt 6:20 **neither moth nor r doth corrupt,**...... *1035*

S

SABACHTHANI (sa-bak´-tha-ni)

Mt	27:46	loud voice, saying, Eli, Eli, lama **s**?	*4518*
Mk	15:34	voice, saying, Eloi, Eloi, lama **s**?	*4518*

SABAOTH (sab´-a-oth)

Ro	9:29	Except the Lord of **S** had left us a	*4519*
Jas	5:4	into the ears of the Lord of **s**	*4519*

SABBATH

Ex	16:23	rest of the holy **s** unto the Lord:	7676
Ex	20:8	Remember the **s** day, to keep it holy.	7676
Ex	20:10	seventh day is the **s** of the Lord thy	7676
Ex	20:11	the Lord blessed the **s** day, and	7676
Ex	31:14	Ye shall keep the **s** therefore; for it	7676
Le	16:31	It shall be a **s** of rest unto you, and.	7676
Le	23:16	unto the morrow after the seventh **s**	7676
Le	23:24	shall ye have a **s**, a memorial of	7677
Le	23:32	unto even, shall ye celebrate your **s**	7676
Le	25:4	shall be a **s** of rest unto the land,	7676
Le	25:4	a **s** for the Lord: Thou shalt neither	7676
Nu	15:32	gathered sticks upon the **s** day	7676
Nu	28:10	is the burnt offering of every **s**,	7676
Dt	5:12	Keep the **s** day to sanctify it, as the	7676
2Ch	36:21	as she lay desolate she kept **s**	7673
Ne	13:17	that ye do, and profane the **s** day?	7676
Ne	13:22	keep the gates, to sanctify the **s** day	7676
Isa	58:13	and call the **s** a delight, the holy of	7676
Jer	17:24	but hallow the **s** day, to do no work	7676
Eze	46:12	offerings, as he did on the **s** day:	7676
Am	8:5	and the **s**, that we may set forth	7676
Mt	12:2	is not lawful to do upon the **s** day:	*4521*
Mt	12:8	**of man is Lord even of the s day.**	*4521*
Mt	12:10	Is it lawful to heal on the **s** days?	*4521*
Mt	12:11	**if it fall into a pit on the s day,**	*4521*
Mt	12:12	**is lawful to do well on the s days.**	*4521*
Mt	24:20	**the winter, neither on the s day:**	*4521*
Mk	2:27	**The s was made for man, and not**	*4521*
Mk	2:27	**for man, and not man for the s:**	*4521*
Mk	2:28	**Son of man is Lord also of the s.**	*4521*
Mk	3:4	**it lawful to do good on the s days,**	*4521*
Lk	4:31	and taught them on the **s** days	*4521*
Lk	6:1	pass on the second **s** after the first,	*4521*
Lk	6:5	**Son of man is Lord also of the s.**	*4521*
Lk	6:7	whether he would heal on the **s**	*4521*
Lk	6:9	**lawful on the s days to do good,**	*4521*
Lk	13:15	**one of you on the s loose his ox**	*4521*
Lk	14:3	**Is it lawful to heal on the s day?**	*4521*
Lk	14:5	**straightway pull him out on the s**	*4521*
Lk	23:56	and rested the **s** day according to	*4521*
Jn	5:10	It is the **s** day: it is not lawful for	*4521*
Jn	5:18	he not only had broken the **s**, but	*4521*
Jn	7:23	**on the s day receive circumcision,**	*4521*
Jn	7:23	**every whit whole on the s day?**	*4521*
Jn	9:16	because he keepeth not the **s** day	*4521*
Jn	19:31	remain upon the cross on the **s** day,	*4521*
Jn	19:31	(for that **s** day was an high day,)	*4521*
Ac	1:12	from Jerusalem a **s** day's journey	*4521*
Ac	13:27	prophets which are read every **s**	*4521*
Ac	15:21	read in the synagogues every **s** day	*4521*
Ac	17:2	three **s** days reasoned with them	*4521*
Ac	18:4	reasoned in the synagogue every **s**	*4521*
Col	2:16	of the new moon, or of the **s** days:	*4521*

SABBATH-DAY See SABBATH and DAY.

SABBATHS

Ex	31:13	Verily my **s** ye shall keep: for it	7676
Le	19:3	and his father, and keep my **s**:	7676
Le	19:30	Ye shall keep my **s**, and reverence	7676
Le	25:8	thou shalt number seven **s** of years	7676
Le	26:34	shall the land rest, and enjoy her **s**	7676
Le	26:35	because it did not rest in your **s**	7676
2Ch	8:13	on the **s**, and on the new moons.	7676
2Ch	36:21	until the land had enjoyed her **s**:	7676
Isa	1:13	the new moons and **s**, the calling	7676
La	1:7	saw her, and did mock at her **s**	4868
La	2:6	feasts and **s** to be forgotten in	7676
Eze	20:12	Moreover also I gave them my **s**	7676
Eze	20:13	and my **s** they greatly polluted:	7676
Eze	22:26	and have hid their eyes from my **s**	7676
Eze	44:24	and they shall hallow my **s**.	7676
Hos	2:11	her new moons, and her **s**, and all	7676

SACK

Ge	42:35	bundle of money was in his **s**:	8242
Ge	44:12	the cup was found in Benjamin's **s**	572

SACKCLOTH

Ge	37:34	clothes, put **s** upon his loins, and	8242
1Ki	20:31	us, I pray thee, put **s** on our loins,	8242
1Ki	21:27	and fasted, and lay in **s**, and went	8242
2Ki	19:1	clothes, and covered himself with **s**,	8242
2Ki	19:2	elders of the priests, covered with **s**,	8242
Est	4:2	into the king's gate clothed with **s**	8242
Est	4:4	and to take away his **s** from him:	8242
Ps	69:11	I made **s** also my garment; and I.	8242
Isa	20:2	and loose the **s** from off thy loins,	8242
Isa	37:1	and covered himself with **s**, and	8242
Isa	50:3	and I make **s** their covering.	8242
Isa	58:5	to spread **s** and ashes under him?	8242
Jer	4:8	gird you with **s**, lament and howl:	8242
La	2:10	they have girded themselves with **s**.	8242
Joel	1:8	Lament like a virgin girded with **s**	8242
Joel	1:13	come, lie all night in **s**, ye ministers	8242
Jnh	3:5	proclaimed a fast, and put on **s**,	8242
Jnh	3:8	man and beast be covered with **s**,	8242
Mt	11:21	**repented long ago in s and ashes**	*4526*
Lk	10:13	**repented, sitting in s and ashes.**	*4526*
Rev	6:12	the sun became black as **s** of hair,	*4526*
Rev	11:3	and threescore days, clothed in **s**.	*4526*

SACKS

Ge	42:25	Joseph commanded to fill their **s**	3672
Ge	43:18	money that was returned in our **s**	572
Ge	43:23	hath given you treasure in your **s**	572
Ge	44:1	saying, Fill the men's **s** with food,	572

SACRIFICE

Ex	3:18	we may **s** to the Lord our God.	2076
Ex	5:8	Let us go and **s** to our God	2076
Ex	8:26	shall we **s** the abomination of the	2076
Ex	12:27	It is the **s** of the Lord's passover,	2077
Ex	23:18	not offer the blood of my **s** with	2077
Ex	29:28	of the **s** of their peace offerings,	2077
Ex	30:9	incense thereon, nor burnt **s**, nor	
Ex	34:15	call thee, and thou eat of his **s**;	2077
Ex	34:25	the **s** of the feast of the passover be	2077
Le	1:3	offering be a burnt **s**, of the herd,	

S

Le	1:9	to be a burnt **s**, an offering made	
Le	3:1	oblation be a **s** of peace offering,	2077
Le	3:6	offering for a **s** of peace offering.	2077
Le	7:11	law of the **s** of peace offerings,	2077
Le	7:12	offer with the **s** of thanksgiving	2077
Le	7:15	the flesh of the **s** of his peace.	2077
Le	7:16	if the **s** of his offering be a vow,	2077
Le	8:21	a burnt **s** for a sweet savour,	
Nu	6:18	it in the fire which is under the **s**	2077
Nu	7:88	all the oxen for the **s** of the peace	2077
Nu	15:25	**s** made by fire unto the Lord, and	
Dt	16:2	shalt therefore **s** the passover.	2076
Dt	16:6	thou shalt **s** the passover at even,	2076
Dt	17:1	shalt not **s** unto the Lord thy God	2076
Jgs	6:26	offer a burnt **s** with the wood of	
Jgs	16:23	a great **s** unto Dagon their god,	2077
1Sa	1:21	offer unto the Lord the yearly **s**,	2077
1Sa	2:19	her husband to offer the yearly **s**.	2077
1Sa	3:14	shall not be purged with **s** nor	2077
1Sa	9:13	come, because he doth bless the **s**;	2077
1Sa	15:22	to obey is better than **s**, and to	2077
1Sa	16:5	I am come to **s** unto the Lord:	2076
1Sa	20:6	there is a yearly **s** there for all the	2077
1Sa	20:29	our family hath a **s** in the city;	2077
2Sa	24:22	here be oxen for burnt **s**, and	
1Ki	12:27	If this people go up to do **s** in the.	2077
1Ki	18:33	and pour it on the burnt **s**, and	
1Ki	18:38	fell, and consumed the burnt **s**,	
2Ki	10:19	I have a great **s** to do to Baal;.	2077
2Ki	17:35	nor serve them, nor **s** to them:	2076
2Ki	17:36	worship, and to him shall ye do **s**	2076
2Ch	2:6	save only to burn **s** before him?	
2Ch	7:12	place to myself for an house of **s**.	2077
Ezr	9:4	I sat astonied until … evening **s**	4503
Ne	4:2	will they **s**? will they make an	2076
Ps	40:6	**S** and offering thou didst not	2077
Ps	50:5	made a covenant with me by **s**	2077
Ps	51:16	For thou desirest not **s**; else	2077
Ps	141:2	up of my hands as the evening **s**.	4503
Pr	15:8	**s** of the wicked is an abomination	2077
Pr	21:3	more acceptable to the Lord than **s**	2077
Pr	21:27	**s** of the wicked is abomination:	2077
Ecc	5:1	to hear, than to give the **s** of fools:	2077
Jer	33:11	that shall bring the **s** of praise	
Da	8:11	by him the daily **s** was taken away,	
Da	8:12	daily **s** by reason of transgression,	
Da	9:27	**s** and the oblation to cease,	2077
Da	11:31	and shall take away the daily **s**,	
Da	12:11	the daily **s** shall be taken away,	
Hos	4:14	whores, and they **s** with harlots:	2076
Hos	6:6	for I desired mercy, and not **s**;	2077
Hos	13:2	the men that **s** kiss the calves.	2076
Jnh	1:16	and offered a **s** unto the Lord,	2077
Jnh	2:9	will **s** unto thee with the voice of	2076
Zep	1:7	for the Lord hath prepared a **s**,	2077
Mal	1:8	And if ye offer the blind for **s**, is it	2076
Mt	9:13	**I will have mercy, and not s: for**	*2378*
Mt	12:7	**I will have mercy, and not s, ye**	*2378*
Mk	9:49	**every s shall be salted with salt**	*2378*
Lk	2:24	And to offer a **s** according to that	*2378*
Ac	7:41	and offered **s** unto the idol, and	*2378*
Ac	14:18	they had not done **s** unto them.	*2380*
Ro	12:1	ye present your bodies a living **s**,	*2378*
1Co	10:20	they **s** to devils, and not to God:	*2380*
1Co	10:28	This is offered in **s** unto idols, eat	*1494*
Eph	5:2	for us an offering and a **s** to God	*2378*
Php	2:17	the **s** and service of your faith,	*2378*
Php	4:18	**s** acceptable, wellpleasing to God	*2378*
Heb	7:27	to offer up **s**, first for his own sins,	*2378*
Heb	9:26	to put away sin by the **s** of himself.	*2378*
Heb	10:5	**S** and offering thou wouldest not	*2378*
Heb	10:12	after he had offered one **s** for sins.	*2378*
Heb	10:26	remaineth no more **s** for sins,	*2378*
Heb	11:4	God a more excellent **s** than Cain.	*2378*
Heb	13:15	let us offer the **s** of praise to God	*2378*

SACRIFICED

Ex	32:8	it, and have **s** thereunto, and said	2076
Dt	32:17	They **s** unto devils, not to God; to	2076
1Sa	2:15	said to the man that **s**, Give flesh	2076
2Sa	6:13	six paces, he **s** oxen and fatlings.	2076
1Ki	3:3	only he **s** and burnt incense in high	2076
1Ki	11:8	incense and **s** unto their gods.	2076
2Ch	5:6	**s** sheep and oxen, which could not.	2076
2Ch	34:4	graves of them that … **s** unto them.	2076
Ps	106:37	**s** their sons and their daughters	2076
Ps	106:38	they **s** unto the idols of Canaan:	2076
Eze	16:20	thou **s** unto them to be devoured.	2076
Hos	11:2	they **s** unto Baalim, and burned	2076
1Co	5:7	Christ our passover is **s** for us:	*2380*
Rev	2:14	**to eat things s unto idols, and to**	*1494*
Rev	2:20	**and to eat things s unto idols**	*1494*

SACRIFICES

Ex	10:25	give us also **s** and burnt offerings,	2077
Le	7:32	of the **s** of your peace offerings.	2077
Le	10:14	out of the **s** of peace offerings of	2077
Le	17:7	no more offer their **s** unto devils,	2077
Nu	10:10	over the **s** of your peace offerings;	2077
Dt	12:6	and your **s**, and your tithes, and	2077
Dt	12:11	your burnt offerings, and your **s**,	2077
Dt	12:27	the blood of thy **s** shall be poured	2077
Jos	22:27	with our **s**, and with our peace	2077
Jos	22:28	not for burnt offerings, nor for **s**:	2077
1Sa	15:22	delight in burnt offerings and **s**, as	2077
2Ch	7:1	the burnt offerings and the **s**; and	2077
Ezr	6:3	the place where they offered **s**,	1685
Ps	4:5	Offer the **s** of righteousness, and	2077
Ps	27:6	I offer in his tabernacle **s** of joy;	2077
Ps	51:17	The **s** of God are a broken spirit:	2077
Ps	51:19	with the **s** of righteousness, with	2077
Ps	106:28	and ate the **s** of the dead	2077
Pr	17:1	than an house full of **s** with strife.	2077
Isa	1:11	the multitude of your **s** unto me?	2077
Isa	43:23	hast thou honoured me with thy **s**	2077
Isa	43:24	thou filled me with the fat of thy **s**	2077
Isa	56:7	**s** shall be accepted upon mine	2077
Jer	6:20	nor your **s** sweet unto me	2077
Eze	20:28	and they offered there their **s**,	2077
Hos	8:13	flesh for the **s** of mine offerings,	2077
Hos	9:4	their **s** shall be unto them as the	2077
Am	5:25	ye offered unto me **s** and offerings	2077
Mk	12:33	all whole burnt offerings and **s**	*2378*
Lk	13:1	Pilate had mingled with their **s**	*2378*
Ac	7:42	offered to me slain beasts and **s**.	*2378*
1Co	10:18	which eat of the **s** partakers of the	*2378*
Heb	8:3	is ordained to offer gifts and **s**:	*2378*
Heb	9:9	were offered both gifts and **s**, that.	*2378*
Heb	9:23	with better **s** than these.	*2378*
Heb	10:1	can never with those **s** which they	*2378*
Heb	10:3	in those **s** there is a remembrance	
Heb	10:6	In burnt offerings and **s** for sin thou	

Heb 10:11 offering oftentimes the same **s** *2378*
Heb 13:16 with such **s** God is well pleased. *2378*
1Pe 2:5 to offer up spiritual **s**, acceptable *2378*

SACRIFICETH
Ex 22:20 He that **s** unto any god, save unto 2076
Ecc 9:2 him that **s**, and to him that **s** not:...... 2076
Isa 65:3 **s** in gardens, and burneth incense 2076
Isa 66:3 he that **s** a lamb, as if he cut off a 2076
Mal 1:14 **s** unto the Lord a corrupt thing:....... 2076

SACRIFICING
1Ki 8:5 **s** sheep and oxen, that could not....... 2076
1Ki 12:32 **s** unto the calves that he had made: 2076

SACRILEGE
Ro 2:22 idols, dost thou commit **s**?............ *2416*

SAD
Ge 40:6 them, and, behold, they were **s** 2196
1Sa 1:18 and her countenance was no more **s**
1Ki 21:5 Why is thy spirit so **s**, that thou 5620
Ne 2:3 should not my countenance be **s**,...... 7489
Eze 13:22 made the heart of the righteous **s**, ... 3512
Mt 6:16 **hypocrites, of a s countenance:**........ *4659*
Mk 10:22 he was **s** at that saying, and went *4768*
Lk 24:17 **to another, as ye walk, and are s?** *4659*

SADDUCEES (sad´-du-sees)
Mt 16:6 **leaven of the Pharisees and ... S.**...... *4523*
Mt 16:11 **leaven of the Pharisees and ... S?**...... *4523*
Mt 22:34 that he had put the **S** to silence, ... *4523*
Ac 23:6 perceived that the one part were **S**,..... *4523*
Ac 23:8 **S** say that there is no resurrection, ... *4523*

SADNESS
Ecc 7:3 by the **s** of the countenance the 7455

SAFE
2Sa 18:29 Is the young man Absalom **s**? 7965
Ps 119:117 Hold ... me up, and I shall be **s**:....... 3467
Pr 18:10 runneth into it, and is **s** 7682
Pr 29:25 his trust in the Lord shall be **s**......... 7682
Isa 5:29 prey, and shall carry it away **s**,......... 6403
Eze 34:27 and they shall be **s** in their land,........ 983
Lk 15:27 **he hath received him s and sound.**..... *5198*
Php 3:1 is not grievous, but for you it is **s** *809*

SAFELY
Le 26:5 the full, and dwell in your land **s** 983
1Ki 4:25 And Judah and Israel dwelt **s**, every 983
Ps 78:53 he led them on **s**, so that they feared 983
Pr 1:33 hearkeneth unto me shall dwell **s**,....... 983
Pr 3:23 Then shalt thou walk in thy way **s**,...... 983
Pr 31:11 of her husband doth **s** trust in her,
Jer 23:6 be saved, and Israel shall dwell **s**: 983
Jer 32:37 and I will cause them to dwell **s**:........ 983
Jer 33:16 saved, and Jerusalem shall dwell **s**: 983
Eze 28:26 And they shall dwell **s** therein, and...... 983
Eze 34:28 they shall dwell **s**, and none shall 983
Eze 38:8 and they shall dwell **s** all of them........ 983
Eze 38:14 my people of Israel dwelleth **s**, ... 983
Eze 39:26 when they dwelt **s** in their land, ... 983
Hos 2:18 and will make them to lie down **s**....... 983
Zec 14:11 but Jerusalem shall be **s** inhabited 983
Mk 14:44 take him, and lead him away **s** *806*
Ac 16:23 charging the jailor to keep them **s**....... *806*

SAFETY
Le 25:18 and ye shall dwell in the land in **s**....... 983
Dt 12:10 round about, so that ye dwell in **s**; 983
Dt 33:12 beloved of the Lord shall dwell in **s** 983
Dt 33:28 Israel then shall dwell in **s** alone: 983
Job 3:26 I was not in **s**, neither had I rest,....... 7951
Ps 4:8 Lord, only makest me dwell in **s**, ... 983
Ps 33:17 An horse is a vain thing for **s**: 8668
Pr 11:14 multitude of counsellers there is **s** 8668
Pr 21:31 day of battle: but **s** is of the Lord....... 8668
Pr 24:6 multitude of counsellers there is **s** 8668
Isa 14:30 and the needy shall lie down in **s**,....... 983
Ac 5:23 prison ... found we shut with all **s**, ... *803*
1Th 5:3 when they shall say, Peace and **s**;........ *803*

SAIL
Isa 33:23 they could not spread the **s** 5251
Ac 27:17 strake **s**, and so were driven........... *4632*
Ac 27:24 thee all them that **s** with thee *4126*

SAILED
Lk 8:23 But as they **s** he fell asleep: and........ *4126*
Ac 15:39 took Mark, and **s** unto Cyprus;........ *1602*
Ac 18:21 God will. And he **s** from Ephesus *321*
Ac 20:13 before to ship, and **s** unto Assos *321*
Ac 27:7 when we had **s** slowly many days,...... *1020*

SAILING
Ac 27:9 and when **s** was now dangerous *4144*

SAINT
Ps 106:16 and Aaron the **s** of the Lord 6918
Da 8:13 Then I heard one **s** speaking 6918

SAINTS
Dt 33:2 came with ten thousands of **s** 6944
1Sa 2:9 He will keep the feet of his **s**,.......... 2623
2Ch 6:41 and let thy **s** rejoice in goodness....... 2623
Ps 30:4 Sing unto the Lord, O ye **s** of his,...... 2623
Ps 31:23 O love the Lord, all ye his **s**: for........ 2623
Ps 34:9 O fear the Lord, ye his **s**: for 6918
Ps 37:28 and forsaketh not his **s**; they are 2623
Ps 89:7 be feared in the assembly of the **s**...... 6918
Ps 97:10 he preserveth the souls of his **s**;........ 2623
Ps 116:15 of the Lord is the death of his **s**........ 2623
Ps 145:10 Lord; and thy **s** shall bless thee 2623
Ps 149:1 praise in the congregation of **s** 2623
Ps 149:9 this honour have all his **s**. Praise....... 2623
Pr 2:8 and preserveth the way of his **s**........ 2623
Da 7:18 the **s** of the most High shall take 6922
Da 7:21 same horn made war with the **s**,....... 6922
Da 7:22 judgment was given to the **s** of the..... 6922
Da 7:25 wear out the **s** of the most High, ... 6922
Zec 14:5 shall come, and all the **s** with thee 6918
Mt 27:52 bodies of the **s** which slept arose......... *40*
Ac 9:13 much evil he hath done to thy **s** at *40*
Ac 9:41 when he had called the **s** and widows *40*
Ac 26:10 many of the **s** did I shut up in prison..... *40*
Ro 3:27 he maketh intercession for the **s** *40*
Ro 12:13 Distributing to the necessity of **s**; *40*
Ro 15:25 Jerusalem to minister unto the **s**......... *40*
1Co 1:2 in Christ Jesus, called to be **s**, ... *40*
1Co 6:1 the unjust, and not before the **s**? *40*
1Co 6:2 that the **s** shall judge the world? *40*
1Co 16:1 concerning the collection for the **s** *40*
1Co 16:15 addicted ... to the ministry of the **s**,)..... *40*
2Co 8:4 fellowship of ... ministering to the **s** *40*

2Co	9:12	not only supplieth the want of the s.	*40*
Eph	1:18	the glory of his inheritance in the s	*40*
Eph	2:19	fellowcitizens with the s, and of the	*40*
Eph	3:8	who am less than the least of all s.	*40*
Eph	3:18	to comprehend with all s what is the	*40*
Eph	4:12	For the perfecting of the s, for the	*40*
Eph	5:3	named among you, as becometh s;	*40*
Eph	6:18	and supplication for all s;	*40*
Col	1:12	of the inheritance of the s in light:	*40*
Col	1:26	but now is made manifest to his s:	*40*
1Th	3:13	the coming of … Christ with all his s	*40*
2Th	1:10	he shall come to be glorified in his s	*40*
Heb	6:10	in that ye have ministered to the s,	*40*
Jude	3	faith … once delivered unto the s.	*40*
Jude	14	cometh with ten thousands of his s,	*40*
Rev	5:8	odours, which are the prayers of s	*40*
Rev	8:3	offer it with the prayers of all s	*40*
Rev	8:4	came with the prayers of the s,	*40*
Rev	13:7	unto him to make war with the s,	*40*
Rev	13:10	the patience and the faith of the s,	*40*
Rev	16:6	shed the Blood of s and prophets,	*40*
Rev	17:6	drunken with the blood of the s,	*40*
Rev	18:24	the blood of prophets, and of s, and.	*40*
Rev	19:8	fine linen is the righteousness of s	*40*
Rev	20:9	and compassed the camp of the s.	*40*

SAKE

Ge	3:17	cursed is the ground for thy s;	5668
Ge	8:21	the ground any more for man's s;	5668
Ge	12:13	it may be well with me for thy s;	5668
Ge	18:32	I will not destroy it for ten's s	5668
Ge	20:11	they will slay me for my wife's s	1697
Ge	30:27	Lord hath blessed me for thy s	1558
Ex	21:26	let him go free for his eye's s	8478
Ex	21:27	shall let him go free for his tooth's s.	8478
Nu	25:11	zealous for my s among them,	7068
1Sa	12:22	his people for his great name's s:	5668
2Sa	5:12	kingdom for his people Israel's s.	5668
2Sa	9:1	him kindness for Jonathan's s?	5668
2Sa	18:5	gently for my s with the young man	
1Ki	11:12	not do it for David thy father's s:	4616
1Ki	11:13	Jerusalem's s which I have chosen.	4616
1Ki	11:32	one tribe for my servant David's s	4616
1Ki	15:4	for David's s did the Lord his God	4616
2Ki	19:34	this city, to save it, for mine own s	4616
2Ki	20:6	defend this city for mine own s.	4616
Ne	9:31	for thy great mercies' s thou didst	
Job	19:17	for the children's s of my own body	
Ps	23:3	of righteousness for his name's s	4616
Ps	25:7	me for thy goodness s, O Lord	4616
Ps	25:11	For thy name's s, O Lord, pardon	4616
Ps	31:3	for thy name's s lead me, and	4616
Ps	44:26	redeem us for thy mercies' s	4616
Ps	69:7	for thy s I have borne reproach	5921
Ps	79:9	away our sins, for thy name's s	4616
Ps	106:8	he saved them for his name's s	4616
Isa	43:25	thy transgressions for mine own s,	4616
Isa	45:4	For Jacob my servant's s and	4616
Isa	48:11	mine own s, even for mine own s.	4616
Isa	62:1	Zion's s will I not hold my peace,	4616
Isa	66:5	that cast you out for my name's s.	4616
Jer	14:21	Do not abhor us, for thy name's s.	4616
Jer	15:15	for thy s I have suffered rebuke	
Eze	20:9	I wrought for my name's s.	4616
Eze	36:22	but for mine holy name's s, which	
Da	9:17	that is desolate, for the Lord's s.	4616
Da	9:19	not, for thine own s, O my God:	4616
Jnh	1:12	for my s this great tempest is	7945
Mic	3:12	shall Zion for your s be plowed as	1558
Mt	5:10	persecuted for righteousness' s.	*1752*
Mt	5:11	evil against you falsely, for my s	*1752*
Mt	10:18	governors and kings for my s, for.	*1752*
Mt	10:22	hated of all men for my name's s	
Mt	10:39	that loseth his life for my s shall	*1752*
Mt	16:25	will lose his life for my s shall	*1752*
Mt	19:12	for the kingdom of heaven's s	
Mt	19:29	or lands, for my name's s, shall	*1752*
Mt	24:9	of all nations for my name's s	
Mt	24:22	the elect's s those days shall be	
Mk	4:17	persecution ariseth for the word's s,	
Mk	6:26	yet for his oath's s, and for their	
Mk	8:35	shall lose his life for my s and	*1752*
Mk	10:29	lands, for my s, and the gospel's,	*1752*
Mk	13:9	before rulers and kings for my s.	*1752*
Mk	13:13	hated of all men for my name's s	
Mk	13:20	for the elect's s, whom he hath	
Lk	6:22	as evil, for the Son of man's s	*1752*
Lk	9:24	will lose his life for my s, the	*1752*
Lk	18:29	for the kingdom of God's s	*1752*
Lk	21:12	kings and rulers for my name's s	*1752*
Lk	21:17	hated of all men for my name's s	
Jn	12:9	they came not for Jesus' s only	
Jn	13:37	I will lay down my life for thy s	
Jn	13:38	thou lay down thy life for my s?	
Jn	14:11	believe me for the very works' s	
Jn	15:21	they do unto you for my name's s,	
Ac	9:16	he must suffer for my name's s	
Ro	8:36	For thy s we are killed all the day	*1752*
Ro	13:5	wrath, but also for conscience s	
1Co	4:10	We are fools for Christ's s, but ye	
1Co	10:25	no question for conscience s:	
1Co	10:27	no question for conscience s:	
1Co	10:28	eat not for his s that shewed it,	
2Co	4:5	your servants for Jesus' s	
2Co	4:11	delivered unto death for Jesus' s	
2Co	12:10	in distresses for Christ's s: for	
Eph	4:32	for Christ's s hath forgiven you.	*1722*
Php	1:29	him, but also to suffer for his s;	
Col	1:24	Christ in my flesh for his body's s,	
Col	3:6	For which things's s the wrath of	
1Th	5:13	highly in love for their work's s	
1Ti	5:23	a little wine for thy stomach's s	
Tit	1:11	they ought not, for filthy lucre's s	
Phm	9	Yet for love's s I rather beseech	
1Pe	2:13	ordinance of man for the Lord's s:	
1Pe	3:14	if ye suffer for righteousness' s	
1Jn	2:12	are forgiven you for his name's s	
2Jn	2	For the truth's s, which dwelleth	
3Jn	7	for his name's s they went forth,	
Rev	2:3	and for my name's s hast laboured,	

SAKES

Ge	18:26	will spare all the place for their s	5668
Le	26:45	for their s remember the covenant	
Dt	1:37	was angry with me for your s	1558
Dt	3:26	was wroth with me for your s,	6616
Dt	4:21	was angry with me for your s,	1697
Ru	1:13	it grieveth me much for your s that	
1Ch	16:21	he reproved kings for their s	5921
Ps	106:32	it went ill with Moses for their s,	5668
Eze	36:22	I do not this for your s, O house of	6616
Mal	3:11	I will rebuke the devourer for your s	

S

Jn	11:15	**glad for your s that I was not there,**	
Jn	12:30	**not because of me, but for your s**	
Jn	17:19	**And for their s I sanctify myself,**	
Ro	11:28	are beloved for the fathers' **s**	
1Co	9:10	For our **s**, no doubt, this is written	
2Co	8:9	yet for your **s** he became poor,	
2Ti	2:10	endure all things for the elect's **s**	

SALT

Ge	19:26	him, and she became a pillar of **s**	4417
Le	2:13	offering shalt thou season with **s**	4417
Le	2:13	the **s** of the covenant of thy God.	4417
Nu	18:19	it is a covenant of **s** for ever before	4417
Dt	29:23	land thereof is brimstone, and **s**,	4417
Jos	3:16	the sea of the plain, even the **s** sea,	4417
2Ki	2:21	the waters, and cast the **s** in there,	4417
2Ch	13:5	and to his sons by a covenant of **s**?	4417
Job	6:6	is unsavoury be eaten without **s**?	4417
Eze	43:24	priests shall cast **s** upon them,	4417
Mt	5:13	**Ye are the s of the earth: but if**	*217*
Mk	9:49	**sacrifice shall be salted with s**	*251*
Mk	9:50	**S is good: but if the s have lost**	*217*
Mk	9:50	**Have s in yourselves, and have**	*217*
Lk	14:34	**S is good: but if the s have lost**	*217*
Col	4:6	alway with grace, seasoned with **s**,	*217*
Jas	3:12	both yield **s** water and fresh.	*252*

SALTED

Eze	16:4	not **s** at all, nor swaddled at all.	4414
Mt	5:13	**savour, wherewith shall it be s?**	*233*
Mk	9:49	**For every one shall be s with fire,**	*233*
Mk	9:49	**every sacrifice shall be s with salt.**	*233*

SALT-SEA See SALT and SEA.

SALUTATION

Lk	1:29	what manner of **s** this should be.	*783*
Lk	1:44	voice of thy **s** sounded in mine ears,	*785*

SALUTATIONS

Mk	12:38	**and love s in the marketplaces,**	*783*

SALUTE

1Sa	13:10	to meet him, that he might **s** him	1288
1Sa	25:14	of the wilderness to **s** our master;	1288
2Ki	4:29	if thou meet any man, **s** him not;	1288
2Ki	4:29	and if any **s** thee, answer him not	1288
Mt	5:47	**And if ye s your brethren only,**	*782*
Mt	10:12	**when ye come into an house, s it**	*782*
Mk	15:18	began to **s** him, Hail, King of the	*782*
Lk	10:4	**shoes: and s no man by the way.**	*782*

SALVATION

Ge	49:18	I have waited for thy **s**, O Lord.	3444
Ex	14:13	stand still, and see the **s** of the Lord,	3444
Ex	15:2	and song, and he is become my **s**:	3444
Dt	32:15	lightly esteemed the Rock of his **s**.	3444
1Sa	2:1	enemies; because I rejoice in thy **s**	3444
1Sa	11:13	Lord hath wrought **s** in Israel.	8668
1Sa	14:45	wrought this great **s** in Israel?	3444
1Sa	19:5	Lord wrought a great **s** for all	8668
2Sa	22:36	also given me the shield of thy **s**:	3468
2Sa	22:47	be the God of the rock of my **s**	3468
2Sa	23:5	this is all my **s**, and all my desire,	3468
1Ch	16:23	shew forth from day to day his **s**.	3444
2Ch	6:41	thy priests, … be clothed with **s**,	8668
Ps	3:8	**S** belongeth unto the Lord: thy	3444
Ps	13:5	my heart shall rejoice in thy **s**	3444
Ps	14:7	Oh that the **s** of Israel were come	3444
Ps	18:46	and let the God of my **s** be exalted	3468
Ps	24:5	righteousness from … God of his **s**	3468
Ps	27:1	Lord is my light and my **s**; whom	3468
Ps	37:39	**s** of the righteous is of the Lord:	8668
Ps	40:10	declared thy faithfulness and thy **s**:	8668
Ps	51:12	Restore unto me the joy of thy **s**;	3468
Ps	53:6	Oh that the **s** of Israel were come	3444
Ps	62:2	He only is my rock and **s**; he	3444
Ps	68:20	that is our God is the God of **s**;	4190
Ps	69:29	let thy **s**, O God, set me up on high.	3444
Ps	78:22	in God, and trusted not in his **s**:	3444
Ps	85:7	mercy, O Lord, and grant us thy **s**	3468
Ps	85:9	his **s** is nigh them that fear him;	3468
Ps	96:2	shew forth his **s** from day to day.	3444
Ps	98:3	earth have seen the **s** of our God.	3444
Ps	118:21	heard me, and art become my **s**	3444
Ps	119:81	My soul fainteth for thy **s**: but I	8668
Ps	119:123	Mine eyes fail for thy **s**, and for	3444
Ps	119:155	**S** is far from the wicked: for they	3444
Ps	119:174	I have longed for thy **s**, O Lord;	3444
Ps	132:16	also clothe her priests with **s**:	3468
Ps	144:10	It is he that giveth **s** unto kings:	8668
Ps	149:4	he will beautify the meek with **s**	3444
Isa	12:2	my song; he also is become my **s**	3444
Isa	17:10	hast forgotten the God of thy **s**,	3468
Isa	25:9	will be glad and rejoice in his **s**	3444
Isa	33:2	our **s** also in the time of trouble	3444
Isa	45:17	in the Lord with an everlasting **s**:	8668
Isa	46:13	be far off, and my **s** shall not tarry:	8668
Isa	49:6	be my **s** unto the end of the earth.	3444
Isa	51:6	but my **s** shall be for ever, and my	3444
Isa	52:7	tidings of good, that publisheth **s**;	3444
Isa	52:10	earth shall see the **s** of our God	3444
Isa	59:17	and an helmet of **s** upon his head;	3444
Isa	60:18	but thou shalt call thy walls **S**, and	3444
Isa	62:11	of Zion, Behold, thy **s** cometh;	3468
Jer	3:23	Truly in vain is **s** hoped for from the	
Jer	3:23	Lord our God is the **s** of Israel.	8668
La	3:26	quietly wait for the **s** of the Lord.	8668
Jnh	2:9	I have vowed. **S** is of the Lord.	3444
Mic	7:7	I will wait for the God of my **s**:	3468
Hab	3:13	even for **s** with thine anointed;	3468
Hab	3:18	Lord, I will joy in the God of my **s**	3468
Zec	9:9	he is just, and having **s**; lowly,	3467
Lk	1:69	hath raised up an horn of **s** for us	*4991*
Lk	2:30	For mine eyes have seen thy **S**,	*4992*
Lk	3:6	And all flesh shall see the **s** of God	*4992*
Lk	19:9	**This day is s come to this house,**	*4991*
Jn	4:22	**we worship: for s is of the Jews.**	*4991*
Ac	4:12	Neither is there **s** in any other: for	*4991*
Ac	28:28	**s** of God is sent unto the Gentiles,	*4992*
Ro	1:16	power of God unto **s** to every one	*4991*
Ro	10:10	mouth confession is made unto **s**.	*4991*
Ro	11:11	their fall **s** is come unto the Gentiles,	*4991*
Ro	13:11	**s** nearer than when we believed.	*4991*
2Co	6:2	time: behold, now is the day of **s**.)	*4991*
2Co	7:10	sorrow worketh repentance to **s**	*4991*
Eph	6:17	And take the helmet of **s**, and the	*4992*
Php	2:12	work out your own **s** with fear and	*4991*
1Th	5:8	and for an helmet, the hope of **s**.	*4991*
2Th	2:13	you to **s** through sanctification of	*4991*
2Ti	2:10	also obtain the **s** which is in Christ.	*4991*
2Ti	3:15	are able to make thee wise unto **s**	*4991*
Tit	2:11	the grace of God that bringeth **s**	*4992*
Heb	2:3	we escape, if we neglect so great **s**;	*4991*

Heb 2:10 make the captain of their **s** perfect..... 4991
Heb 5:9 author of eternal **s** unto all them 4991
Heb 9:28 the second time without sin unto **s** 4991
1Pe 1:9 your faith, even the **s** of your souls..... 4991
1Pe 1:10 Of which **s** the prophets have 4991
2Pe 3:15 the longsuffering of our Lord is **s**; 4991
Jude 3 to write unto you of the common **s**,.... 4991
Rev 7:10 **S** to our God which sitteth upon 4991
Rev 12:10 Now is come **s**, and strength, and...... 4991
Rev 19:1 saying, Alleluia; **S**, and glory,.......... 4991

SAMARITAN (sa-mar´-i-tun)
Lk 10:33 **But a certain S, as he journeyed,** 4541
Lk 17:16 him thanks: and he was a **S** 4541

SAME
Ge 15:18 **s** day the Lord made a covenant....... 1931
Ge 26:24 Lord appeared unto him the **s** night,... 1931
Le 7:15 be eaten the **s** day that it is offered;
Le 7:16 be eaten the **s** day that he offereth
Le 19:6 be eaten the **s** day ye offer it, and on
Le 22:30 the **s** day it shall be eaten up; ye 1931
Le 23:28 ye shall do no work in that **s** day:...... 6106
1Ch 16:17 confirmed the **s** to Jacob for a law,
Job 4:8 and sow wickedness, reap the **s**
Ps 102:27 But thou art the **s**, and thy years....... 1931
Ps 105:10 confirmed the **s** unto Jacob for a law,
Ps 113:3 the sun unto the going down of the **s**
Pr 28:24 **s** is the companion of a destroyer...... 1931
Ecc 9:15 man remembered that **s** poor man..... 1931
Eze 3:18 the **s** wicked man shall die in his 1931
Eze 23:38 defiled my sanctuary in the **s** day,...... 1931
Eze 24:2 against Jerusalem this **s** day. 6106
Eze 38:18 the **s** time when Gog shall come....... 1931
Da 3:15 be cast the **s** hour into the midst of
Da 4:33 **s** hour was the thing fulfilled upon
Da 4:36 the **s** time my reason returned unto
Da 5:5 **s** hour came forth fingers of a man's
Da 7:21 **s** horn made war with the saints, ... 1797
Da 12:1 was a nation even to that **s** time:....... 1931
Mal 1:11 even unto the going down of the **s**
Mt 5:19 **the s shall be called great in the** 3778
Mt 5:46 **do not even the publicans the s?**........ 546
Mt 10:19 **that s hour what ye shall speak.** 1565
Mt 12:50 **the s is my brother, and sister,** 846
Mt 18:4 **the s is greatest in the kingdom** 3778
Mt 21:42 **s is become the head of the corner.**.... 3778
Mt 24:13 **unto the end, the s shall be saved**...... 3778
Mt 26:23 **in the dish, the s shall betray me** 3778
Mt 26:44 the third time, saying the **s** words....... 846
Mt 26:48 Whomsoever I ... kiss, that **s** is he:...... 846
Mt 27:44 with him, cast the **s** in his teeth......... 846
Mk 3:35 **s is my brother, and my sister,** 3778
Mk 9:35 **to be first, the s shall be last of all,**
Mk 13:13 **unto the end, the s shall be saved**...... 3778
Mk 14:44 Whomsoever I ... kiss, that **s** is he;...... 846
Lk 2:8 were in the **s** country shepherds 846
Lk 6:33 **for sinners also do even the s** 846
Lk 6:38 **s measure that ye mete withal it**........ 846
Lk 7:47 **little is forgiven, the s loveth little**
Lk 9:24 **for my sake, the s shall save it**......... 3778
Lk 9:48 **among you all, the s shall be**.......... 3778
Lk 12:12 **the s hour what ye ought to say** 846
Lk 17:29 **s day that Lot went out of Sodom it**
Lk 20:17 **s is become ... head of the corner?**..... 3778
Lk 20:47 **s ... receive greater damnation.** 3778
Lk 23:40 thou art in the **s** condemnation?........ 846
Lk 23:51 (The **s** had not consented to the....... 3778
Jn 1:2 **s** was in the beginning with God 3778
Jn 1:7 The **s** came for a witness, to bear 3778
Jn 4:53 knew that it was at the **s** hour,......... 1565
Jn 10:1 **way, the s is a thief and a robber** 1565
Jn 12:48 **s shall judge him in the last day.**....... 1565
Jn 15:5 **the s bringeth forth much fruit:**....... 3778
Ac 1:11 this **s** Jesus, which is taken up from 3778
Ac 2:36 that God hath made that **s** Jesus, ... 5126
Ac 2:41 **s** day there were added unto them 1565
Ac 16:18 her. And he came out the **s** hour. 846
Ac 18:3 because he was of the **s** craft, he 3673
Ro 1:32 not only do the **s**, but have pleasure..... 846
Ro 2:1 thou that judgest doest the **s** things...... 846
Ro 9:21 the **s** lump to make one vessel unto 846
Ro 12:4 all members have not the **s** office;....... 846
Ro 12:16 Be of the **s** mind one toward another.... 846
1Co 1:10 the **s** mind and in the **s** judgment....... 846
1Co 7:20 every man abide in the **s** calling 5026
1Co 10:3 did all eat the **s** spiritual meat; 846
1Co 10:4 did all drink the **s** spiritual drink:....... 846
1Co 11:23 **s** night in which he was betrayed 846
1Co 11:25 **s** manner also he took the cup,......... 5615
1Co 12:4 diversities of gifts, but the **s** Spirit....... 846
1Co 12:6 it is the **s** God which worketh all........ 846
1Co 12:8 word of knowledge by the **s** Spirit;...... 846
1Co 12:9 To another faith by the **s** Spirit;......... 846
1Co 12:9 the gifts of healing by the **s** Spirit; 846
1Co 15:39 All flesh is not the **s** flesh: but 846
2Co 3:14 day remaineth the **s** vail untaken 846
2Co 3:18 are changed into the **s** image from...... 846
2Co 4:13 We having the **s** spirit of faith, ... 846
2Co 12:18 walked we not in the **s** spirit? 846
Gal 3:7 the **s** are the children of Abraham 3778
Eph 4:10 is the **s** also that ascended up........... 846
Php 2:2 ye be likeminded, having the **s** love 846
Php 3:16 let us walk by the **s** rule, let us.......... 846
Php 3:16 rule, let us mind the **s** thing............ 846
2Ti 2:2 **s** commit thou to faithful men,........ 5023
Heb 4:11 fall after the **s** example of unbelief....... 846
Heb 10:11 offering oftentimes the **s** sacrifices,...... 846
Heb 11:9 the heirs with him of the **s** promise:
Heb 13:8 Jesus Christ the **s** yesterday, and 846
Jas 3:2 not in word, the **s** is a perfect man, ... 3778
Jas 3:10 Out of the **s** mouth proceedeth......... 846
Jas 3:11 the **s** place sweet water and bitter? 846
1Pe 2:7 **s** is made the head of the corner, ... 3778
1Pe 4:4 with them to the **s** excess of riot, ... 846
Rev 3:5 **the s shall be clothed in white.**......... 3778
Rev 11:13 **s** hour was ... a great earthquake,...... 1565

SANCTIFICATION
1Co 1:30 righteousness, ... **s**, and redemption:..... 38
1Th 4:3 this is the will of God, even your **s**,....... 38
1Th 4:4 possess his vessel in **s** and honour;....... 38
2Th 2:13 to salvation through **s** of the Spirit....... 38
1Pe 1:2 Father, through **s** of the Spirit, unto...... 38

SANCTIFIED
Ge 2:3 blessed the seventh day, and **s** it:....... 6942
Ex 29:43 tabernacle shall be **s** by my glory....... 6942
Le 8:30 and **s** Aaron, and his garments,........ 6942
Le 10:3 I will be **s** in them that come nigh 6942
Le 27:19 if he that **s** the field will in any wise 6942
Nu 8:17 land of Egypt I **s** them for myself. 6942

Dt	32:51	because ye **s** me not in the midst	6942
1Sa	21:5	it were **s** this day in the the vessel	6942
1Ch	15:14	priests and … Levites **s** themselves	6942
2Ch	7:16	have I chosen and **s** this house,	6942
2Ch	30:3	had not **s** themselves sufficiently,	6942
2Ch	30:15	were ashamed, and **s** themselves,	6942
Ne	12:47	they **s** holy things unto the Levites;	6942
Job	1:5	about that Job sent and **s** them, and	6942
Isa	5:16	is holy shall be **s** in righteousness	6942
Jer	1:5	camest … out of the womb I **s** thee,	6942
Eze	20:41	will be **s** in you before the heathen.	6942
Jn	10:36	**whom the Father hath s, and sent**	*37*
Jn	17:19	**also might be s through the truth**	*37*
Ac	26:18	**among them which are s by faith**	*37*
Ro	15:16	being **s** by the Holy Ghost.	*37*
1Co	6:11	but ye are washed, but ye are **s**, but	*37*
1Co	7:14	unbelieving husband is **s** by the wife,	*37*
1Co	7:14	unbelieving wife is **s** by the husband:	*37*
1Ti	4:5	For it is **s** by the word of God and	*37*
2Ti	2:21	**s**, and meet for the master's use, and	*37*
Heb	10:14	perfected for ever them that are **s**	*37*

SANCTIFIETH

Mt	23:17	**gold, or the temple that s the gold?**	*37*
Mt	23:19	**gift, or the altar that s the gift?**	*37*
Heb	2:11	that **s** and they who are sanctified	*37*
Heb	9:13	**s** to the purifying of the flesh:	*37*

SANCTIFY

Ex	13:2	**S** unto me all the firstborn,	6942
Ex	19:10	and **s** them to day and to morrow,	6942
Ex	19:22	let the priests … **s** themselves,	6942
Ex	19:23	bounds about the mount, and **s** it.	6942
Ex	29:37	atonement for the altar, and **s** it;	6942
Ex	29:44	And I will **s** the tabernacle of the	6942
Ex	31:13	that I am the Lord that doth **s** you.	6942
Le	8:12	head, and anointed him, to **s** him.	6942
Le	20:7	**S** yourselves therefore, and be ye.	6942
Le	20:8	them: I am the Lord which **s** you.	6942
Le	27:18	if he **s** his field after the jubile,	6942
Le	27:26	Lord … s firstling, no man shall **s** it;	6942
Nu	11:18	**S** yourselves against to morrow,	6942
Nu	20:12	**s** me in the eyes of the children of	6942
Nu	27:14	**s** me at the water before their eyes:	6942
Dt	5:12	Keep the sabbath day to **s** it, as the	6942
Dt	15:19	shalt **s** unto the Lord thy God:	6942
Jos	3:5	said unto the people, **S** yourselves:	6942
Jos	7:13	**S** yourselves against to morrow:	6942
1Sa	16:5	**s** yourselves, and come with me to	6942
1Ch	15:12	**s** yourselves, both ye and your	6942
2Ch	29:5	and **s** the house of the Lord God of	6942
2Ch	29:34	upright in heart to **s** themselves	6942
Ne	13:22	keep the gates, to **s** the sabbath day	6942
Isa	8:13	**S** the Lord of hosts himself; and	6942
Eze	20:12	that I am the Lord that **s** them	6942
Eze	36:23	And I will **s** my great name, which	6942
Joel	1:14	**S** ye a fast, call a solemn assembly,	6942
Jn	17:17	**S them through thy truth: thy**	*37*
Jn	17:19	**for their sakes I s myself, that they**	*37*
1Th	5:23	the very God of peace **s** you wholly;	*37*
Heb	13:12	he might **s** the people with his own	*37*
1Pe	3:15	But **s** the Lord God in your hearts:	*37*

SANCTUARIES

Le	21:23	that he profane not my **s**: for I	4720
Jer	51:51	strangers are come into the **s** of	4720
Eze	28:18	Thou hast defiled thy **s** by the	4720

SANCTUARY

Ex	25:8	let them make me a **s**; that I may	4720
Ex	30:13	shekel after the shekel of the **s**:	6944
Ex	36:3	the work of the service of the **s**,	6944
Ex	36:6	work for the offering of the **s**	6944
Le	4:6	the Lord, before the vail of the **s**	6944
Le	16:33	make an atonement for the holy **s**,	4720
Le	19:30	my sabbaths, and reverence my **s**:	4720
Le	20:3	to defile my **s**, and to profane my	4720
Le	26:2	my sabbaths, and reverence my **s**:	4720
Nu	8:19	of Israel come nigh unto the **s**.	6944
Nu	18:1	shall bear the iniquity of the **s**:	4720
Nu	18:3	not come nigh the vessels of the **s**	6944
Nu	18:5	ye shall keep the charge of the **s**,	6944
Nu	19:20	hath defiled the **s** of the Lord:	4720
1Ch	22:19	build ye the **s** of the Lord God,	4720
1Ch	28:10	thee to build an house for the **s**:	4720
2Ch	26:18	go out of the **s**; for thou hast	4720
Ps	63:2	so as I have seen thee in the **s**	6944
Ps	73:17	Until I went into the **s** of God;	4720
Ps	77:13	Thy way, O God, is in the **s**: who is.	6944
Ps	96:6	strength and beauty are in his **s**	4720
Ps	102:19	down from the height of his **s**;	6944
Ps	134:2	Lift up your hands in the **s**, and	6944
Isa	8:14	he shall be for a **s**; but for a stone	4720
Isa	60:13	to beautify the place of my **s**;	4720
Isa	63:18	adversaries … trodden down thy **s**	4720
La	1:10	the heathen entered into her **s**,	4720
La	2:7	he hath abhorred his **s**, he hath	4720
La	2:20	prophet be slain in … **s** of the Lord?	4720
La	4:1	stones of the **s** are poured out in	6944
Eze	5:11	because thou hast defiled my **s**	4720
Eze	8:6	that I should go far off from my **s**?	4720
Eze	11:16	yet will I be to them as a little **s** in	4720
Eze	23:38	have defiled my **s** in the same day.	4720
Eze	24:21	Behold, I will profane my **s**, the	4720
Eze	37:26	will set my **s** in the midst of them	4720
Eze	44:7	have brought into my **s** strangers,	
Eze	44:27	inner court, to minister in the **s**,	6944
Eze	48:21	**s** of the house shall be in the midst	4720
Da	8:11	the place of his **s** was cast down.	4720
Da	8:14	days; then shall the **s** be cleansed	6944
Da	9:17	cause thy face to shine upon thy **s**	4720
Da	9:26	shall destroy the city and the **s**;	6944
Da	11:31	shall pollute the **s** of strength, and	4720
Zep	3:4	her priests have polluted the **s**,	6944
Heb	8:2	A minister of the **s**, and of the true.	*39*
Heb	9:1	of divine service, and a worldly **s**	*39*
Heb	13:11	whose blood is brought into the **s**.	*39*

S

SAND

Ge	22:17	**s** which is upon the sea shore;	2344
Ge	32:12	make thy seed as the **s** of the sea,	2344
Ex	2:12	the Egyptian, and hid him in the **s**	2344
Jgs	7:12	the **s** by the sea side for multitude.	2344
1Ki	4:20	many, as the **s** which is by the sea	2344
1Ki	4:29	as the **s** that is on the sea shore.	2344
Job	6:3	be heavier than the **s** of the sea:	2344
Ps	78:27	fowls like as the **s** of the sea:	2344
Ps	139:18	are more in number than the **s**:	2344
Pr	27:3	stone is heavy, and the **s** weighty;	2344
Isa	10:22	people Israel be as the **s** of the sea,	2344
Jer	5:22	have placed the **s** for the bound of	2344
Jer	15:8	to me above the **s** of the seas:	2344
Jer	33:22	neither the **s** of the sea measured:	2344
Hos	1:10	Israel shall be as the **s** of the sea,	2344

Mt	7:26	which built his house upon the **s**:	*285*
Ro	9:27	of Israel be as the **s** of the sea,	*285*
Heb	11:12	as the **s** which is by the sea shore	*285*
Rev	13:1	And I stood upon the **s** of the sea,	*285*
Rev	20:8	the number … is as the **s** of the sea	*285*

SANDALS

Mk	6:9	But be shod with **s**; and not put	*4547*
Ac	12:8	Gird thyself, and bind on thy **s**	*4547*

SANG

Ex	15:1	Then **s** Moses and the children of	7891
Jgs	5:1	Then **s** Deborah and Barak the	7891
1Sa	29:5	Is not this David, of whom they **s**	6030
Ezr	3:11	And they **s** together by course in	6030
Job	38:7	the morning stars **s** together, and	7442
Ac	16:25	prayed, and **s** praises unto God:	*5214*

SANK

Ex	15:5	they **s** into the bottom as a stone	3381
Ex	15:10	**s** as lead in the mighty waters.	6749

SAP

Ps	104:16	The trees of the Lord are full of **s**;	

SAT

Ge	18:1	he **s** in the tent door in the heat	3427
Ge	19:1	and Lot **s** in the gate of Sodom:	3427
Ex	12:29	firstborn of Pharaoh that **s** on his	3427
Ex	18:13	that Moses **s** to judge the people:	3427
Ru	4:1	to the gate, and **s** him down there:	3427
1Sa	4:13	Eli **s** upon a seat by the wayside	3427
1Sa	19:9	as he **s** in his house with his javelin	3427
1Sa	28:23	from the earth, and **s** upon the bed	3427
2Sa	19:8	the king arose, and **s** in the gate.	3427
1Ki	2:12	**s** Solomon upon the throne of David	3427
1Ki	16:11	reign, as soon as he **s** on his throne,	3427
1Ki	19:4	and **s** down under a juniper tree:	3427
2Ki	4:20	mother, he **s** on her knees till noon.	3427
Ezr	9:4	and I **s** astonied until the evening.	3427
Ne	1:4	I **s** down and wept, and mourned	3427
Ne	8:17	booth, and **s** under the booths:	3427
Est	2:21	while Mordecai **s** in the king's gate,	3427
Job	2:8	and he **s** down among the ashes.	3427
Job	2:13	**s** down with him upon the ground	3427
Ps	26:4	I have not **s** with vain persons,	3427
Ps	137:1	rivers of Babylon, there we **s** down,	3427
Jer	15:17	I **s** alone because of thy hand: for	3427
Da	2:49	but Daniel **s** in the gate of the king.	
Jnh	3:6	with sackcloth, and **s** in ashes	3427
Jnh	4:5	and **s** on the east side of the city,	3427
Mt	4:16	The people which **s** in darkness	*2521*
Mt	9:10	sinners came and **s** down with him	*4873*
Mt	26:55	**I s daily with you teaching in the**	*2516*
Mt	26:69	Now Peter **s** without in the palace:	*2521*
Mt	28:2	stone from the door, and **s** upon it.	*2521*
Mk	2:15	sinners **s** also together with Jesus	*4873*
Mk	6:22	Herod and them that **s** with him,	*4873*
Mk	10:46	**s** by the highway side begging.	*2521*
Mk	11:2	**colt tied, whereon never man s**	*2523*
Mk	12:41	Jesus **s** over against the treasury,	*2523*
Mk	16:14	unto the eleven as they **s** at meat.	*345*
Mk	16:19	and **s** on the right hand of God.	*2523*
Lk	7:15	he that was dead **s** up, and began	*339*
Lk	10:39	Mary which also **s** at Jesus' feet,	*3869*
Lk	19:30	**colt tied, whereon never yet man s.**	*2523*
Lk	24:30	as he **s** at meat with them, he took	*2525*
Jn	19:13	**s** down in the judgment seat in a	*2523*
Ac	2:3	of fire, and it **s** upon each of them.	*2523*
Ac	6:15	all that **s** in the council, looking	*2516*
Ac	12:21	**s** upon his throne, and made an	2523
Ac	20:9	And there **s** in a window a certain	*2521*
1Co	10:7	people **s** down to eat and drink,	*2523*
Heb	1:3	**s** down on the right hand of the	*2523*
Heb	10:12	**s** down on the right hand of God;	*2523*
Rev	4:2	heaven, and one **s** on the throne.	*2521*
Rev	4:3	he that **s** was to look upon like a	*2521*
Rev	4:9	thanks to him that **s** on the throne,	*2521*
Rev	6:2	he that **s** on him had a bow; and a	*2521*
Rev	6:4	was given to him that **s** thereon to	*2521*
Rev	6:5	**s** on him had a pair of balances	*2521*
Rev	6:8	his name that **s** on him was Death,	*2522*
Rev	11:16	which **s** before God on their seats,	*2521*
Rev	14:14	one **s** like unto the Son of man,	*2521*
Rev	19:4	God that **s** on the throne, saying,	*2522*
Rev	19:11	that **s** upon him was called Faithful	*2521*
Rev	19:21	sword of him that **s** upon the horse,	*2521*
Rev	20:4	thrones, and they **s** upon them,	*2523*
Rev	20:11	white throne, and him that **s** on	*2522*
Rev	21:5	he that **s** upon the throne said,	*2522*

SATAN (sa´-tun)

1Ch	21:1	**S** stood up against Israel, and	7854
Job	1:6	and **S** came also among them.	7854
Job	1:12	Lord said unto **S**, Behold, all that	7854
Job	1:12	**S** went forth from the presence of	7854
Job	2:1	and **S** came also among them to	7854
Job	2:6	Lord said unto **S**, Behold, he is in	7854
Job	2:7	went **S** forth from the presence of	7854
Ps	109:6	and let **S** stand at his right hand	7854
Zec	3:2	Lord rebuke thee, O **S**; even the	7854
Mt	4:10	unto him, **Get thee hence, S:**	*4567*
Mt	12:26	**if S cast out S, he is divided**	*4567*
Mt	16:23	**Get thee behind me, S: thou art**	*4567*
Mk	1:13	forty days, tempted of **S**; and was	*4567*
Mk	3:23	parables, **How can S cast out S?**	*4567*
Mk	4:15	**S cometh immediately, and**	*4567*
Mk	8:33	saying, **Get thee behind me, S**	*4567*
Lk	4:8	unto him, **Get thee behind me, S**	*4567*
Lk	10:18	**I beheld S as lightning fall from**	*4567*
Lk	13:16	**of Abraham, whom S hath bound,**	*4567*
Lk	22:3	Then entered **S** into Judas	*4567*
Lk	22:31	**S hath desired to have you, that**	*4567*
Jn	13:27	after the sop **S** entered into him	*4567*
Ac	5:3	why hath **S** filled thine heart to lie	*4567*
Ac	26:18	**from the power of S unto God,**	*4567*
Ro	16:20	bruise **S** under your feet shortly	*4567*
1Co	5:5	To deliver such an one unto **S**	*4567*
1Co	7:5	that **S** tempt you not for your	*4567*
2Co	2:11	**S** should get an advantage of us:	*4567*
2Co	11:14	**S** himself is transformed into an	*4567*
2Co	12:7	the messenger of **S** to buffet me,	*4567*
1Th	2:18	and again; but **S** hindered us	*4567*
2Th	2:9	coming is after the working of **S**	*4567*
1Ti	1:20	whom I have delivered unto **S**,	*4567*
1Ti	5:15	are already turned aside after **S**,	*4567*
Rev	2:9	**not, but are the synagogue of S**	*4567*
Rev	2:13	**among you, where S dwelleth**	*4567*
Rev	2:24	**have not known the depths of S,**	*4567*
Rev	3:9	**make them of the synagogue of S,**	*4567*
Rev	12:9	serpent, called the Devil, and **S**,	*4567*
Rev	20:2	serpent, which is the Devil, and **S**,	*4567*
Rev	20:7	**S** shall be loosed out of his prison,	*4567*

SATAN'S (sa´-tuns)

Rev	2:13	**dwellest, even where S seat is:**	*4567*

SATIATED

Jer	31:25	I have **s** the weary soul, and I	7301

SATISFACTION

Nu	35:31	no **s** for the life of a murderer,	3724
Nu	35:32	no **s** for him that is fled to the city	3724

SATISFIED

Ex	15:9	my lust shall be **s** upon them; I	4390
Le	26:26	and ye shall eat, and not be **s**.	7646
Ps	17:15	I shall be **s**, when I awake, with	7646
Ps	22:26	The meek shall eat and be **s**: they	7646
Ps	65:4	we shall be **s** with the goodness of	7646
Ps	81:16	of the rock should I have **s** thee	7649
Ps	105:40	**s** them with the bread of heaven	7649
Pr	12:11	He that tilleth his land shall be **s**.	7646
Pr	12:14	A man shall be **s** with good by the	7646
Pr	18:20	A man's belly shall be **s** with the	7646
Pr	19:23	he that hath it shall abide **s**; he	7649
Pr	20:13	and thou shalt be **s** with bread	7646
Pr	27:20	so the eyes of man are never **s**.	7646
Pr	30:15	are three things that are never **s**,	7646
Ecc	1:8	the eye is not **s** with seeing, nor	7646
Ecc	4:8	neither is his eye **s** with riches;	7646
Ecc	5:10	He that loveth silver shall not be **s**	7646
Isa	53:11	travail of his soul, and shall be **s**	7646
Jer	31:14	and my people shall be **s** with my	7646
Eze	16:29	and yet thou wast not **s** herewith	7646
Joel	2:26	ye shall eat in plenty, and be **s**	7646
Am	4:8	drink water; but they were not **s**.	7646
Mic	6:14	Thou shalt eat, but not be **s**; and	7646
Hab	2:5	and is as death, and cannot be **s**,	7646

SATISFIEST

Ps	145:16	**s** the desire of every living thing	7646

SATISFIETH

Ps	103:5	**s** thy mouth with good things;	7646
Ps	107:9	he **s** the longing soul, and filleth	7646
Isa	55:2	your labour for that which **s** not?	7654

SATISFY

Ps	90:14	O **s** us early with thy mercy; that	7646
Ps	91:16	With long life will I **s** him, and	7646
Ps	132:15	I will **s** her poor with bread	7646
Pr	5:19	let her breasts **s** thee at all times;	7301
Pr	6:30	if he steal to **s** his soul when he	4390
Isa	58:10	hungry, and **s** the afflicted soul;	7646
Isa	58:11	**s** thy soul in drought, and make	7646
Eze	7:19	they shall not **s** their souls,	7646
Mk	8:4	can a man **s** these men with bread	*5526*

SATISFYING

Pr	13:25	righteous eateth to the **s** of his soul:	7648
Col	2:23	in any honour to the **s** of the flesh	*4140*

SAVE

Ge	45:7	**s** your lives by a great deliverance	2421
Ge	50:20	is this day, to **s** much people alive	2421
Ex	1:22	and every daughter ye shall **s** alive	2421
Ex	22:20	any god, **s** unto the Lord only	1115
Nu	14:30	**s** Caleb the son of Jephunneh	3588, 518
Nu	26:65	**s** Caleb the son of Jephunneh	3588, 518
Dt	22:27	cried, and there was none to **s** her	3467
Dt	28:29	evermore, and no man shall **s** thee	3467
Jos	2:13	that ye will **s** alive my father,	2421
Jgs	6:15	Lord, wherewith shall I **s** Israel?	3467
Jgs	6:31	ye plead for Baal? will ye **s** him?	3467
Jgs	6:37	thou wilt **s** Israel by mine hand	3467
1Sa	10:24	shouted, and said, God **s** the king	2421
1Sa	11:3	and then, if there be no man to **s** us,	3467
1Sa	14:6	is no restraint to the Lord to **s** by	3467
1Sa	19:11	If thou **s** not thy life to night	4422
2Sa	12:3	nothing, **s** one little ewe lamb	3588, 518
2Sa	16:16	God **s** the king, God **s** the king	2421
2Sa	22:32	For who is God, **s** the Lord? and	1107
2Sa	22:32	and who is a rock, **s** our God?	1107
2Sa	22:42	looked, but there was none to **s**;	3467
1Ki	1:39	people said, God **s** king Solomon	2421
1Ki	15:5	**s** only in the matter of Uriah the	
2Ki	7:4	if they **s** us alive, we shall live;	2421
2Ki	11:12	hands, and said, God **s** the king	2421
2Ki	19:34	I will defend this city, to **s** it, for	3467
1Ch	16:35	**S** us, O God of our salvation	3467
2Ch	5:10	nothing in the ark **s** the two tables	7535
2Ch	23:11	him, and said, God **s** the king	2421
Ne	6:11	go into the temple to **s** his life?	2425
Job	2:6	he is in thine hand; but **s** his life	8104
Job	40:14	thine own right hand can **s** thee	3467
Ps	6:4	soul: oh **s** me for thy mercies' sake	3467
Ps	18:31	For who is God **s** the Lord?	1107
Ps	18:31	or who is a rock **s** our God?	2108
Ps	18:41	but there was none to **s** them:	3467
Ps	31:16	**s** me for thy mercies' sake	3467
Ps	44:3	neither did their own arm **s** them:	3467
Ps	54:1	**S** me, O God, by thy name, and	3467
Ps	59:2	and **s** me from bloody men	3467
Ps	69:1	**S** me, O God; for the waters are	3467
Ps	69:35	For God will **s** Zion, and will build	3467
Ps	72:4	he shall **s** the children of the needy,	3467
Ps	72:13	and shall **s** the souls of the needy	3467
Ps	76:9	to **s** all the meek of the earth	3467
Ps	86:2	**s** thy servant that trusteth in	3467
Ps	109:31	to **s** him from those that condemn	3467
Ps	119:94	I am thine, **s** me; for I have	3467
Ps	138:7	and thy right hand shall **s** me	3467
Pr	20:22	on the Lord, and he shall **s** thee	3467
Isa	25:9	waited for him, and he will **s** us:	3467
Isa	33:22	the Lord is our king; he will **s** us	3467
Isa	35:4	your God ... will come and **s** you	3467
Isa	38:20	The Lord was ready to **s** me:	3467
Isa	45:20	and pray unto a god that cannot **s**	3467
Isa	47:15	to his quarter; none shall **s** thee	3467
Isa	49:25	with thee, and I will **s** thy children	3467
Isa	59:1	is not shortened, that it cannot **s**;	3467
Isa	63:1	in righteousness, mighty to **s**.	3467
Jer	2:27	they will say, Arise, and **s** us	3467
Jer	11:12	shall not **s** them at all in the time	3467
Jer	14:9	as a mighty man that cannot **s**?	3467
Jer	17:14	**s** me, and I shall be saved: for thou	3467
Jer	31:7	**s** thy people, the remnant of Israel	3467
Jer	46:27	I will **s** thee from afar off, and thy	3467
La	4:17	for a nation that could not **s** us	3467
Eze	3:18	from his wicked way, to **s** his life;	2421
Eze	13:18	will ye **s** the souls alive that come	2421
Eze	18:27	and right, he shall **s** his soul alive	2421
Eze	34:22	Therefore will I **s** my flock, and	3467
Hab	1:2	of violence, and thou wilt not **s**!	3467
Zep	3:17	he will **s**, he will rejoice over thee	3467
Zec	8:13	so will I **s** you, and ye shall be a	3467
Zec	9:16	the Lord their God shall **s** them in	3467
Zec	10:6	I will **s** the house of Joseph, and I	3467

Mt 1:21 shall **s** his people from their sins....... *4982*
Mt 8:25 him, saying, Lord, **s** us: we perish...... *4982*
Mt 11:27 any man the Father, s the Son,........ *1508*
Mt 13:57 honour, s in his own country, and..... *1508*
Mt 14:30 sink, he cried, saying, Lord, **s** me...... *4982*
Mt 16:25 whosoever will s his life shall......... *4982*
Mt 17:8 they saw no man, **s** Jesus only......... *1508*
Mt 18:11 is come to s that which was lost....... *4982*
Mt 19:11 saying, s they to whom it is given....... *235*
Mt 27:40 buildest it in three days, **s** thyself....... *4982*
Mt 27:42 saved others; himself he cannot **s**...... *4982*
Mk 3:4 or to do evil? to s life, or to kill?....... *4982*
Mk 5:37 no man to follow him, **s** Peter, and..... *1508*
Mk 8:35 whosoever will s his life shall......... *4982*
Mk 9:8 saw no man any more, **s** Jesus only...... *235*
Mk 15:30 **S** thyself, and come down from........ *4982*
Mk 15:31 saved others; himself he cannot **s**...... *4982*
Lk 6:9 do evil? to s life, or to destroy it?...... *4982*
Lk 9:24 for my sake, the same shall s it........ *4982*
Lk 9:56 to destroy men's lives, but to s........ *4982*
Lk 17:18 to give glory to God, s this stranger.... *1508*
Lk 17:33 seek to s his life shall lose it;.......... *4982*
Lk 18:19 none is good, s one, that is, God....... *1508*
Lk 19:10 seek and to s that which was lost...... *4982*
Lk 23:35 let him **s** himself, if he be Christ,...... *4982*
Lk 23:37 be the king of the Jews, **s** thyself........ *4982*
Lk 23:39 If thou be Christ, **s** thyself and us...... *4982*
Jn 6:46 s he which is of God, he hath......... *1508*
Jn 12:27 Father, s me from this hour:.......... *4982*
Jn 12:47 the world, but to s the world.......... *4982*
Jn 13:10 needeth not s to wash his feet,........ *2228*
Ac 27:43 the centurion, willing to **s** Paul........ *1295*
1Co 2:2 **s** Jesus Christ, and him crucified....... *1508*
1Co 2:11 **s** the spirit of man which is in him?.... *1508*
1Co 9:22 that I might by all means **s** some...... *4982*
2Co 11:24 received I forty stripes **s** one.......... *3844*
Gal 6:14 **s** in the cross of our Lord Jesus........ *1508*
1Ti 1:15 came into the world to **s** sinners;...... *4982*
Heb 5:7 that was able to **s** him from death,..... *4982*
Heb 7:25 also to **s** them to the uttermost........ *4982*
Jas 1:21 word, which is able to **s** your souls..... *4982*
Jas 2:14 have not works? can faith **s** him?...... *4982*
Jas 4:12 who is able to **s** and to destroy: who... *4982*
Jas 5:15 the prayer of faith shall **s** the sick,...... *4982*
Jas 5:20 his way shall **s** a soul from death,...... *4982*
1Pe 3:21 even baptism doth also now **s** us...... *4982*
Jude 23 others **s** with fear, pulling them........ *4982*
Rev 13:17 or sell, **s** he that had the mark......... *1508*

S

SAVED

Ex 1:17 but **s** the men children alive.......... 2421
Ex 14:30 the Lord **s** Israel that day out of....... 3467
Jos 6:25 Joshua **s** Rahab the harlot alive........ 2421
Jgs 7:2 saying, Mine own hand hath **s** me..... 3467
Jgs 8:19 if ye had **s** them alive I would not..... 2421
1Sa 14:23 So the Lord **s** Israel that day: and...... 3467
2Sa 19:5 which this day have **s** thy life.......... 4422
2Sa 22:4 so shall I be **s** from mine enemies...... 3467
2Ch 32:22 Thus the Lord **s** Hezekiah and the..... 3467
Ps 18:3 so shall I be **s** from mine enemies...... 3467
Ps 34:6 and **s** him out of all his troubles....... 3467
Ps 80:3 face to shine; and we shall be **s**........ 3467
Ps 106:8 he **s** them for his name's sake......... 3467
Ps 107:13 he **s** them out of their distresses....... 3467
Pr 28:18 walketh uprightly shall be **s**: but....... 3467
Isa 45:17 But Israel shall be **s** in the Lord........ 3467
Isa 45:22 Look unto me, and be ye **s**, all the..... 3467
Isa 63:9 the angel of his presence **s** them:...... 3467
Jer 8:20 summer is ended, and we are not **s**.... 3467
Jer 17:14 save me, and I shall be **s**: for thou...... 3467
Jer 23:6 In his days Judah shall be **s**, and....... 3467
Jer 33:16 In those days shall Judah be **s**,......... 3467
Mt 10:22 endureth to the end shall be s......... *4982*
Mt 19:25 amazed, saying, Who then can be **s**?.... *4982*
Mt 24:13 unto the end, the same shall be s...... *4982*
Mt 24:22 there should no flesh be s: but........ *4982*
Mt 27:42 He **s** others; himself he cannot........ *4982*
Mk 16:16 and is baptized shall be s;............ *4982*
Lk 7:50 Thy faith hath s thee; go in........... *4982*
Lk 8:12 lest they should believe and be s...... *4982*
Lk 13:23 him, Lord, are there few that be **s**?..... *4982*
Lk 18:26 heard it said, Who then can be **s**?...... *4982*
Lk 18:42 thy sight: thy faith hath s thee........ *4982*
Lk 23:35 He **s** others; let him save himself,...... *4982*
Jn 3:17 the world through him might be s..... *4982*
Jn 5:34 things I say, that ye might be s........ *4982*
Jn 10:9 if any man enter in, he shall be s,...... *4982*
Ac 2:21 on the name of the Lord shall be **s**..... *4982*
Ac 2:47 church daily such as should be **s**....... *4982*
Ac 4:12 among men, whereby we must be **s**.... *4982*
Ac 11:14 thou and all thy house shall be **s**....... *4982*
Ac 16:30 said, Sirs, what must I do to be **s**?...... *4982*
Ac 16:31 thou shalt be **s**, and thy house......... *4982*
Ac 27:31 abide in the ship, ye cannot be **s**....... *4982*
Ro 5:10 reconciled, we shall be **s** by his life..... *4982*
Ro 8:24 For we are **s** by hope: but hope........ *4982*
Ro 9:27 of the sea, a remnant shall be **s**........ *4982*
Ro 10:1 Israel is, that they might be **s**.......... *4991*
Ro 10:9 from the dead, thou shalt be **s**......... *4982*
Ro 10:13 the name of the Lord shall be **s**........ *4982*
Ro 11:26 And so all Israel shall be **s**: as it........ *4982*
1Co 1:18 unto us which are **s** it is the power..... *4982*
1Co 3:15 but he himself shall be **s**; yet so........ *4982*
1Co 5:5 the spirit may be **s** in the day of....... *4982*
Eph 2:5 with Christ, (by grace ye are **s**;)........ *4982*
Eph 2:8 by grace are ye **s** through faith;........ *4982*
1Th 2:16 the Gentiles that they might be **s**,...... *4982*
2Th 2:10 of the truth, that they might be **s**...... *4982*
1Ti 2:4 Who will have all men to be **s**, and..... *4982*
1Ti 2:15 she shall be **s** in childbearing, if........ *4982*
Tit 3:5 but according to his mercy he **s** us,..... *4982*
1Pe 3:20 is, eight souls were **s** by water......... *1295*
1Pe 4:18 And if the righteous scarcely be **s**,..... *4982*
2Pe 2:5 but **s** Noah the eighth person, a....... *5442*
Jude 5 **s** the people out of the land of........ *4982*
Rev 21:24 which are **s** shall walk in the light...... *4982*

SAVETH

1Sa 14:39 the Lord liveth, which **s** Israel,........ 3467
1Sa 17:47 Lord **s** not with sword and spear:...... 3467
Ps 7:10 God, which **s** the upright in heart..... 3467
Ps 20:6 know I that the Lord **s** his anointed;... 3467
Ps 34:18 **s** such as be of a contrite spirit........ 3467

SAVING

Ps 20:6 the **s** strength of his right hand........ 3468
Ps 28:8 the **s** strength of his anointed......... 3444
Mt 5:32 s for the cause of fornication,......... *3924*
Lk 4:27 cleansed, s Naaman the Syrian......... *1508*
Heb 10:39 that believe to the **s** of the soul........ *4047*
Heb 11:7 an ark to the **s** of his house; by........ *4991*
Rev 2:17 knoweth s he that receiveth it.......... *1508*

SAVIOUR

2Ki	13:5	(And the Lord gave Israel a **s**, so	3467
Ps	106:21	They forgat God their **s**, which had	3467
Isa	19:20	he shall send them a **s**, and a great	3467
Isa	43:3	God, the Holy One of Israel, thy **S**	3467
Isa	43:11	Lord; and beside me there is no **s**	3467
Isa	45:21	a just God and a **S**; there is none	3467
Isa	49:26	know that I the Lord am thy **S** and	3467
Isa	60:16	know that I the Lord am thy **S** and	3467
Hos	13:4	me: for there is no **s** beside me	3467
Lk	1:47	spirit hath rejoiced in God my **S**	*4990*
Lk	2:11	this day in the city of David a **S**	*4990*
Jn	4:42	the Christ, the **S** of the world	*4990*
Ac	5:31	right hand to be a Prince and a **S**	*4990*
Ac	13:23	his promise raised unto Israel a **S**,	*4990*
Eph	5:23	church: and he is the **s** of the body	*4990*
Php	3:20	we look for the **S**, the Lord Jesus	*4990*
1Ti	4:10	God, who is the **S** of all men	*4990*
2Ti	1:10	appearing of our **S** Jesus Christ	*4990*
Tit	2:10	the doctrine of God our **S** in all	*4990*
Tit	2:13	great God and our **S** Jesus Christ	*4990*
Tit	3:4	and love of God our **S** toward man	*4990*
2Pe	1:1	righteousness of God and our **S**	*4990*
2Pe	1:11	kingdom of our Lord and **S** Jesus	*4990*
2Pe	2:20	the knowledge of the Lord and **S**	*4990*
2Pe	3:18	the knowledge of our Lord and **S**	*4990*
1Jn	4:14	Father sent the Son to be the **S** of	*4990*
Jude	25	To the only wise God our **S**, be	*4990*

SAVIOURS

Ne	9:27	mercies thou gavest them **s**, who	3467

SAVOUR

Ge	8:21	And the Lord smelled a sweet **s**;	7381
Ex	29:18	it is a sweet **s**, an offering made by	7381
Ex	29:25	for a sweet **s** before the Lord:	7381
Ex	29:41	for a sweet **s**, an offering made by	7381
Le	2:12	be burnt on the altar for a sweet **s**	7381
Le	8:28	were consecrations for a sweet **s**:	7381
Le	23:13	by fire unto the Lord for a sweet **s**:	7381
Le	23:18	by fire, of sweet **s** unto the Lord	7381
Le	26:31	not smell the **s** of your sweet odours	7381
Nu	15:14	by fire, of a sweet **s** unto the Lord;	7381
Nu	15:24	for a sweet **s** unto the Lord, with	7381
Nu	28:6	in mount Sinai for a sweet **s**,	7381
Nu	28:24	by fire, of a sweet **s** unto the Lord:	7381
Ecc	10:1	apothecary to send … a stinking **s**:	7381
Eze	6:13	did offer sweet **s** to all their idols	7381
Eze	20:41	I will accept you with your sweet **s**	7381
Mt	5:13	**but if the salt have lost his s,**	*3471*
Lk	14:34	**but if the salt have lost his s,**	*3471*
2Co	2:15	are unto God a sweet **s** of Christ,	*2175*
2Co	2:16	we are the **s** of death unto death;	*3744*
2Co	2:16	to the other the **s** of life unto life	*3744*
Eph	5:2	to God for a sweetsmelling **s**	*3744*

SAVOUREST

Mt	16:23	**s not the things that be of God,**	*5426*
Mk	8:33	**s not the things that be of God,**	*5426*

SAVOURS

Ezr	6:10	sweet **s** unto the God of heaven,	5208

SAVOURY

Ge	27:4	make me **s** meat, such as I love,	4303
Ge	27:14	his mother made **s** meat, such as	4303
Ge	27:31	And he also had made **s** meat, and	4303

SAW

Ge	1:4	God **s** the light, that it was good:	7200
Ge	1:31	God **s** every thing that he had made,	7200
Ge	3:6	woman **s** that the tree was good	7200
Ge	6:2	the sons of God **s** the daughters of	7200
Ge	6:5	God **s** that the wickedness of man	7200
Ge	9:22	**s** the nakedness of his father	7200
Ge	21:19	her eyes, and she **s** a well of water:	7200
Ge	29:31	the Lord **s** that Leah was hated	7200
Ge	32:25	he **s** that he prevailed not against	7200
Ge	37:4	**s** that their father loved him more	7200
Ge	39:13	she **s** that he had left his garment	7200
Ge	42:7	And Joseph **s** his brethren, and he	7200
Ex	2:5	when she **s** the ark among the flags,	7200
Ex	3:4	Lord **s** that he turned aside to see	7200
Ex	14:30	and Israel **s** the Egyptians dead	7200
Ex	24:10	And they **s** the God of Israel: and	7200
Ex	32:1	the people **s** that Moses delayed	7200
Ex	32:25	Moses **s** that the people were naked;	7200
Ex	34:35	children of Israel **s** … face of Moses,	7200
Nu	13:33	we **s** the giants, the sons of Anak,	7200
Nu	22:23	And the ass **s** the angel of the Lord	7200
Dt	4:12	of the words, but **s** no similitude;	7200
Jos	7:21	I **s** among the spoils a goodly	7200
Jgs	16:18	when Delilah **s** that he had told all	7200
1Sa	13:11	I **s** that the people were scattered	7200
1Sa	17:42	Philistine looked about, … **s** David	7200
1Sa	17:51	Philistines **s** their champion was	7200
1Sa	18:28	Saul **s** and knew that the Lord was	7200
1Sa	26:12	no man **s** it, or knew it, neither	7200
1Sa	28:12	when the woman **s** Samuel, she	7200
1Sa	28:13	I **s** gods ascending out of the	7200
1Sa	31:5	armourbearer **s** … Saul was dead,	7200
2Sa	6:16	**s** king David leaping and dancing	7200
2Sa	11:2	he **s** a woman washing herself;	7200
2Sa	14:28	and **s** not the king's face	7200
1Ki	18:39	when all the people **s** it, they fell	7200
1Ki	22:17	I **s** all Israel scattered upon the	7200
1Ki	22:19	I **s** the Lord sitting on his throne,	7200
2Ki	6:17	eyes of the young man; and he **s**:	7200
2Ki	6:20	Lord opened their eyes, and they **s**;	7200
1Ch	21:16	and **s** the angel of the Lord stand	7200
2Ch	18:18	**s** the Lord sitting upon his throne	7200
Est	3:5	Haman **s** that Mordecai bowed not	7200
Est	5:9	Haman **s** Mordecai in the king's	7200
Job	2:13	**s** that his grief was very great	7200
Ps	73:3	I **s** the prosperity of the wicked	7200
Pr	24:32	Then I **s**, and considered it well:	2372
Ecc	2:13	I **s** that wisdom excelleth folly, as	7200
Ecc	8:10	And so I **s** the wicked buried, who	7200
Ecc	9:11	I returned, and **s** under the sun	7200
SS	3:3	**S** ye him whom my soul loveth?	7200
Isa	6:1	I **s** also the Lord sitting upon a	7200
Isa	59:16	And he **s** that there was no man	7200
Jer	3:7	her treacherous sister Judah **s** it	7200
La	1:7	adversaries **s** her, and did mock at	7200
Eze	1:28	when I **s** it, I fell upon my face, and	7200
Da	4:5	I **s** a dream which made me afraid	2370
Da	10:7	And I Daniel alone **s** the vision:	7200
Am	9:1	I **s** the Lord standing upon the	7200
Jnh	3:10	And God **s** their works, that they	7200
Hag	2:3	that **s** this house in her first glory?	7200
Mt	2:9	the star, which they **s** in the east,	*1492*
Mt	2:11	**s** the young child with Mary his	*2147*
Mt	2:16	when he **s** that he was mocked of	*1492*
Mt	3:16	he **s** the Spirit of God descending	*1492*

Mt 4:16 which sat in darkness **s** great light; 1492
Mt 9:36 But when he **s** the multitudes, he 1492
Mt 12:22 blind and dumb both spake and **s** 991
Mt 14:26 disciples **s** him walking on the sea 1492
Mt 17:8 they **s** no man, save Jesus only. 1492
Mt 25:38 **When s we thee a stranger, and** 1492
Mt 25:39 **when s we thee sick, or in prison,** 1492
Mt 25:44 **Lord, when s we thee an hungred,** 1492
Mk 1:10 he **s** the heavens opened, and the 1492
Mk 6:49 they **s** him walking upon the sea. 1492
Mk 9:8 **s** no man any more, save Jesus 1492
Mk 16:4 **s** that the stone was rolled away: 2334
Mk 16:5 **s** a young man sitting on the right 1492
Lk 1:12 And when Zacharias **s** him, he was. 1492
Lk 5:8 When Simon Peter **s** it, he fell down 1492
Lk 10:31 **when he s him, he passed by on** 1492
Lk 10:33 **when he s him, he had compassion** 1492
Lk 15:20 **father s him, and had compassion,** 1492
Lk 21:2 **s** also a certain poor widow casting 1492
Jn 1:32 I **s** the Spirit descending from 2300
Jn 1:48 **wast under the fig tree, I s thee** 1492
Jn 8:10 and **s** none but the woman, he said 2300
Jn 8:56 **my day: and he s it, and was glad** 1492
Jn 9:1 **s** a man which was blind from his 1492
Jn 19:26 When Jesus therefore **s** his mother, 1492
Jn 19:33 and **s** that he was dead already 1492
Jn 20:5 in, **s** the linen clothes lying, yet 991
Ac 7:55 and **s** the glory of God, and Jesus 1492
Ac 9:8 eyes were opened, he **s** no man: 991
Ac 13:37 God raised again, **s** no corruption. 1492
Ac 22:9 were with me **s** indeed the light 2300
Ac 26:13 I **s** in the way a light from heaven, 1492
Rev 1:12 I **s** seven golden candlesticks; 1492
Rev 1:17 when I **s** him, I fell at his feet as 1492
Rev 4:4 I **s** four and twenty elders sitting, 1492
Rev 6:2 And I **s**, and behold a white horse: 1492
Rev 6:9 **s** under the altar the souls of them 1492
Rev 9:1 I **s** a star fall from heaven unto the 1492
Rev 10:5 angel which I **s** stand upon the sea 1492
Rev 17:6 I **s** the woman drunken with the. 1492
Rev 18:18 they **s** the smoke of her burning 3708
Rev 19:11 I **s** heaven opened, and behold a 1492
Rev 19:17 I **s** an angel standing in the sun; 1492
Rev 19:19 I **s** the beast, and the kings of the 1492
Rev 20:1 And I **s** an angel come down from 1492
Rev 20:4 **s** thrones, and they sat upon them, 1492
Rev 20:4 and I **s** the souls of them that were
Rev 20:11 I **s** a great white throne, and him 1492
Rev 20:12 And I **s** the dead, small and great 1492
Rev 21:1 I **s** a new heaven and a new earth: 1492
Rev 21:2 And I John **s** the holy city, new 1492
Rev 21:22 I **s** no temple therein: for the Lord 1492
Rev 22:8 I John **s** these things, and heard 991

SAWEST
Ps 50:18 When thou **s** a thief, then thou 7200
Da 2:31 king, **s**, and behold a great image 2370
Da 4:20 The tree that thou **s**, which grew, 2370
Da 8:20 The ram which thou **s** having two 7200
Rev 1:20 **of the seven stars which thou s** 1492
Rev 1:20 **candlesticks which thou s are the** 1492
Rev 17:8 The beast that thou **s** was, and is 1492
Rev 17:12 the ten horns which thou **s** are ten 1492

SAWN
Heb 11:37 were stoned, they were **s** asunder 4249

SAYINGS
Jgs 13:17 that when thy **s** come to pass we. 1697
Ps 78:2 parable: I will utter dark **s** of old: 2420
Pr 1:6 words of the wise, and their dark **s**. 2420
Mt 7:24 **whosoever heareth these s of** 3056
Mt 7:26 **one that heareth these s of mine,** 3056
Lk 2:51 but his mother kept all these **s** in 4487
Lk 6:47 **heareth my s, and doeth them** 3056
Lk 9:44 **Let these s sink down into your ears** 3056
Jn 14:24 **loveth me not keepeth not my s** 3056
Ro 3:4 mightest be justified in thy **s**, 3056
Rev 19:9 me, These are the true **s** of God 3056
Rev 22:6 me, These **s** are faithful and true: 3056
Rev 22:7 that keepeth the **s** of the prophecy 3056
Rev 22:10 Seal not the **s** of the prophecy of. 3056

SCABBARD
Jer 47:6 put up thyself into thy **s**, rest, and 8593

SCALES
Le 11:9 whatsoever hath fins and **s** in the 7193
Dt 14:10 hath not fins and **s** ye may not eat; 7193
Isa 40:12 and weighed the mountains in **s**, 6425
Ac 9:18 fell from his eyes as it had been **s**: 3013

SCALETH
Pr 21:22 wise man **s** the city of the mighty. 5927

SCAPEGOAT
Le 16:8 Lord, and the other lot for the **s** 5799
Le 16:10 him go for a **s** into the wilderness 5799

SCARCELY
Ro 5:7 **s** for a righteous man will one die: 3433
1Pe 4:18 if the righteous **s** be saved, where 3433

SCARCENESS
Dt 8:9 thou shalt eat bread without **s**, 4544

SCARLET
Ge 38:28 bound upon his hand a **s** thread. 8144
Ex 26:1 and blue, and purple, and **s**. 8144, 8438
Ex 26:31 vail of blue, and purple, and **s**, 8144, 8438
Le 14:4 cedar wood, and **s**, and hyssop: 8144, 8438
Jos 2:21 bound the **s** line in the window 8144
2Sa 1:24 over Saul, who clothed you in **s** 8144
Pr 31:21 household are clothed with **s**. 8144
SS 4:3 Thy lips are like a thread of **s**, 8144
Isa 1:18 though your sins be as **s**, they 8144
La 4:5 they that were brought up in **s** 8144
Da 5:16 thou shalt be clothed with **s**, and 711
Da 5:29 they clothed Daniel with **s**, and put 711
Na 2:3 red, the valiant men are in **s**: 8529
Mt 27:28 him, and put on him a **s** robe 2847
Heb 9:19 water, and **s** wool, and hyssop, 2847
Rev 17:3 woman sit upon a **s** coloured beast, 2847
Rev 17:4 arrayed in purple and **s** colour, 2847
Rev 18:16 in fine linen, and purple, and **s**, 2847

SCARLET-COLOURED See SCARLET.

SCATTER
Ge 11:9 did the Lord **s** them abroad upon. 6327
Le 26:33 I will **s** you among the heathen, 2210
Dt 4:27 shall **s** you among the nations, 6327
Dt 28:64 Lord shall **s** thee among all people, 6327
Dt 32:26 said, I would **s** them into corners, 6284
Ne 1:8 **s** you abroad among the nations: 6327
Ps 68:30 **s** thou the people that delight in. 967

Ps 144:6 Cast forth lightning, and **s** them: 6327
Isa 41:16 and the whirlwind shall **s** them: 6327
Jer 9:16 **s** them also among the heathen, 6327
Jer 23:1 that destroy and **s** the sheep of my 6327
Eze 5:10 remnant … will I **s** into all the winds 2219
Eze 5:12 and I will **s** a third part into all the 2219
Eze 6:5 **s** your bones … about your altars 2219
Eze 10:2 coals … and **s** them over the city 2236
Da 11:24 he shall **s** among them the prey, 967
Da 12:7 to **s** the power of the holy people, 5310
Hab 3:14 came out as a whirlwind to **s** me: 6327
Zec 1:21 over the land of Judah to **s** it 2219

SCATTERED
Ge 11:8 So the Lord **s** them abroad from 6327
Nu 10:35 Lord, and let thine enemies be **s**; 6327
2Sa 22:15 he sent out arrows, and **s** them; 6327
1Ki 22:17 I saw all Israel **s** upon the hills, as 6327
2Ch 18:16 all Israel **s** upon the mountains, 6327
Est 3:8 is a certain people **s** abroad and 6340
Ps 18:14 sent out his arrows, and **s** them; 6327
Ps 44:11 and hast **s** us among the heathen 2219
Ps 53:5 God hath **s** the bones of him that 6340
Ps 60:1 hast cast us off, thou hast **s** us 6555
Ps 68:1 God arise, let his enemies be **s**. 6327
Ps 92:9 the workers of iniquity shall be **s** 6504
Ps 141:7 Our bones are **s** at the grave's 6340
Isa 18:2 to a nation **s** and peeled, to a 4900
Jer 3:13 hast **s** thy ways to the strangers 6340
Jer 23:2 Ye have **s** my flock, and driven 6327
Jer 30:11 all nations whither I have **s** thee, 6327
Jer 31:10 He that **s** Israel will gather him, 2219
Jer 50:17 Israel is a **s** sheep; the lions have 6340
Eze 6:8 shall be **s** through the countries 2219
Eze 11:16 have **s** them among the countries 6327
Eze 17:21 shall be **s** toward all winds: 6566
Eze 20:34 of the countries wherein ye are **s** 6327
Eze 28:25 the people among whom they are **s** 6327
Eze 34:6 was **s** upon all the face of the earth, 6327
Eze 34:12 he is among his sheep that are **s** 6566
Eze 36:19 And I **s** them among the heathen, 6327
Joel 3:2 they have **s** among the nations 6327
Hab 3:6 the everlasting mountains were **s**, 6327
Zec 7:14 I **s** them with a whirlwind among
Zec 13:7 and the sheep shall be **s**: and I 6327
Mt 9:36 were **s** abroad, as sheep having no *4496*
Mt 26:31 **of the flock shall be s abroad** *1287*
Mk 14:27 **shepherd, and the sheep shall be s** *1287*
Lk 1:51 **s** the proud in the imagination of *1287*
Jn 11:52 children of God that were **s** abroad *1287*
Jn 16:32 **is now come, that ye shall be s,** *4650*
Ac 8:4 they that were **s** abroad went *1289*
Jas 1:1 twelve tribes which are **s** abroad, *1290*

SCATTERETH
Ps 147:16 he **s** the hoarfrost like ashes 6340
Pr 11:24 There is that **s**, and yet increaseth; 6340
Pr 20:8 **s** away all evil with his eyes 2219
Pr 20:26 A wise king **s** the wicked, and 2219
Isa 24:1 **s** abroad the inhabitants thereof 6327
Mt 12:30 **gathereth not with me s abroad** *4650*
Lk 11:23 **he that gathereth not with me s** *4650*
Jn 10:12 **catcheth them, and s the sheep** *4650*

SCEPTRE
Ge 49:10 **s** shall not depart from Judah, 7626
Nu 24:17 and a **S** shall rise out of Israel, 7626
Est 4:11 king shall hold out the golden **s**, 8275
Est 5:2 held out to Esther the golden **s**, 8275
Est 8:4 out the golden **s** toward Esther 8275
Ps 45:6 the **s** of thy kingdom is a right **s** 7626
Zec 10:11 the **s** of Egypt shall depart away 7626
Heb 1:8 a **s** of righteousness is the **s** of *4464*

SCHISM
1Co 12:25 there should be no **s** in the body; *4978*

SCHOOLMASTER
Gal 3:24 law was our **s** to bring us unto *3807*
Gal 3:25 we are no longer under a **s**. *3807*

SCIENCE
Da 1:4 knowledge, and understanding **s**, 4093
1Ti 6:20 oppositions of **s** falsely so called: *1108*

SCOFFERS
2Pe 3:3 shall come in the last days **s**, *1703*

SCORCH
Rev 16:8 unto him to **s** men with fire *2739*

SCORCHED
Mt 13:6 **the sun was up, they were s;** *2739*
Mk 4:6 **when the sun was up, it was s;** *2739*
Rev 16:9 And men were **s** with great heat *2739*

SCORE See **FOURSCORE; SIXSCORE; THREESCORE.**

SCORN
2Ki 19:21 thee, and laughed thee to **s**;
Ne 2:19 heard it, they laughed us to **s**
Job 16:20 My friends **s** me: but mine eye 3887
Job 22:19 and the innocent laugh them to **s**
Ps 22:7 they that see me laugh me to **s**:
Ps 44:13 a **s** and a derision to them that 3933
Ps 79:4 a **s** and derision to them that are 3933
Eze 23:32 thou shalt be laughed to **s** and
Mt 9:24 **sleepeth.** … they laughed him to **s** *2606*
Mk 5:40 And they laughed him to **s** But *2606*
Lk 8:53 they laughed him to **s**, knowing *2606*

SCORNER
Pr 9:8 Reprove not a **s**, lest he hate thee: 3887
Pr 13:1 but a **s** heareth not rebuke 3887
Pr 14:6 A **s** seeketh wisdom, and findeth 3887
Pr 15:12 a **s** loveth not one that reproveth 3887
Pr 19:25 Smite a **s**, and the simple will 3887
Pr 22:10 Cast out the **s**, and contention 3887
Pr 24:9 the **s** is an abomination to men 3887
Isa 29:20 the **s** is consumed, and all that 3887

SCORNERS
Pr 1:22 the **s** delight in their scorning, 3887
Pr 3:34 Surely he scorneth the **s**: but he 3887
Hos 7:5 he stretched out his hand with **s**. 3945

SCORNETH
Pr 3:34 Surely he **s** the scorners: but he 3887
Pr 19:28 An ungodly witness **s** judgment: 3887

SCORNFUL
Ps 1:1 nor sitteth in the seat of the **s** 3887
Pr 29:8 **S** men bring a city into a snare: 3944

SCORNING
Job 34:7 who drinketh up **s** like water? 3933
Ps 123:4 the **s** of those that are at ease, 3933
Pr 1:22 the scorners delight in their **s**, 3944

SCORPION

Lk	11:12	**ask an egg, will he offer him a s?**	*4651*
Rev	9:5	torment was as the torment of a **s**	*4651*

SCORPIONS

Dt	8:15	were fiery serpents, and **s**, and	6137
1Ki	12:11	but I will chastise you with **s**	6137
Eze	2:6	thee, and thou dost dwell among **s**	6137
Lk	10:19	**power to tread on serpents and s,**	*4651*
Rev	9:3	as the **s** of the earth have power	*4651*
Rev	9:10	And they had tails like unto **s**, and	*4651*

SCOURGE

Isa	28:15	overflowing **s** shall pass through,	7885
Isa	28:18	overflowing **s** shall pass through,	7752
Mt	10:17	**will s you in their synagogues;**	*3164*
Mt	20:19	**to mock, and to s, and to crucify**	*3164*
Mt	23:34	**some of them shall ye s in your**	*3164*
Mk	10:34	**shall s him, and shall spit upon**	*3164*
Lk	18:33	**they shall s him, and put him to**	*3164*
Jn	2:15	he had made a **s** of small cords,	*5416*
Ac	22:25	Is it lawful for you to **s**...a Roman	*3147*

SCOURGED

Mt	27:26	and when he had **s** Jesus, he	*5417*
Mk	15:15	when he had **s** him, to be crucified.	*5417*
Jn	19:1	therefore took Jesus, and **s** him.	*3146*

SCOURGETH

Heb	12:6	**s** every son whom he receiveth.	*3146*

SCOURGING

Ac	22:24	that he should be examined by **s**;	*3148*

SCOURGINGS

Heb	11:36	trial of cruel mockings and **s**	*3148*

SCRAPE

Le	14:41	the dust that they **s** off without	7096
Job	2:8	a potsherd to **s** himself withal;	1623

SCRIBE

2Ki	12:10	the king's **s** and the high priest	5608
Ezr	7:6	a ready **s** in the law of Moses,	5608
Ezr	7:12	**s** of the law of ... God of heaven,	5613
Ezr	7:21	**s** of the law of ... God of heaven,	5613
Ne	8:4	And Ezra the **s** stood upon a pulpit	5608
Ne	8:9	and Ezra the priest the **s**, and the	5608
Isa	33:18	Where is the **s**? where is the	5608
Jer	36:32	roll, and gave it to Baruch the **s**,	5608
Jer	37:15	in the house of Jonathan the **s**: for	5608
Jer	37:20	to the house of Jonathan the **s**, lest	5608
Mt	8:19	And a certain **s** came, and said	*1122*
Mt	13:52	**every s which is instructed unto**	*1122*
Mk	12:32	the **s** said unto him, Well, Master,	*1122*
1Co	1:20	Where is the wise? where is the **s**?	*1122*

SCRIBES

Jer	8:8	he it; the pen of the **s** is in vain	5608
Mt	2:4	chief priests and **s**...he demanded	*1122*
Mt	5:20	**exceed the righteousness of the s**	*1122*
Mt	7:29	having authority, and not as the **s**	*1122*
Mt	17:10	Why then say the **s** that Elias must	*1122*
Mt	20:18	**shall be betrayed...unto the s,**	*1122*
Mt	21:15	when the chief priests and **s** saw	*1122*
Mt	23:2	**s and the Pharisees sit in Moses'**	*1122*
Mt	23:13	**But woe unto you, s and Pharisees,**	*1122*
Mt	23:34	**send...prophets, and wise men, and s**	*1122*
Mt	26:57	**s** and the elders were assembled	*1122*
Mt	27:41	mocking him, with the **s** and elders,	*1122*
Mk	1:22	had authority, and not as the **s**	*1122*
Mk	2:16	the **s** and Pharisees saw him eat	*1122*
Mk	9:16	he asked the **s**, **What question ye**	*1122*
Mk	10:33	**delivered...unto the s**	*1122*
Mk	12:35	**say the s that Christ is the Son of**	*1122*
Mk	12:38	**Beware of the s, which love to**	*1122*
Mk	14:1	chief priests and the **s** sought how	*1122*
Lk	5:21	**s** and ... Pharisees began to reason,	*1122*
Lk	5:30	their **s** and Pharisees murmured	*1122*
Lk	6:7	the **s** and Pharisees watched him	*1122*
Lk	9:22	**be rejected of the...and s,**	*1122*
Lk	11:44	**Woe unto you, s and Pharisees,**	*1122*
Lk	20:46	**Beware of the s, which desire to**	*1122*
Lk	23:10	chief priests and **s**...accused him.	*1122*
Jn	8:3	**s** and Pharisees brought unto him	*1122*
Ac	23:9	**s** that were of the Pharisees' part	*1122*

SCRIP

1Sa	17:40	bag which he had, even in a **s**;	3219
Mk	6:8	no **s**, no bread, no money in their	*4082*
Lk	9:3	**neither staves, nor s, neither**	*4082*
Lk	22:36	**him take it, and likewise his s:**	*4082*

SCRIPTURE

Da	10:21	which is noted in the **s** of truth:	3791
Mk	15:28	the **s** was fulfilled, which saith,	*1124*
Lk	4:21	**This day is this s fulfilled in your**	*1124*
Jn	2:22	they believed the **s**, and the word	*1124*
Jn	10:35	**and the s cannot be broken;**	*1124*
Jn	13:18	**that the s may be fulfilled, He**	*1124*
Jn	17:12	**that the s might be fulfilled.**	*1124*
Jn	19:24	that the **s** might be fulfilled, which	*1124*
Jn	19:28	that the **s** might be fulfilled, saith,	*1124*
Jn	19:36	**s** should be fulfilled, A bone of him	*1124*
Jn	20:9	For as yet they knew not the **s**	*1124*
Ac	1:16	**s** must needs have been fulfilled,	*1124*
Gal	3:8	the **s**, foreseeing that God would	*1124*
Gal	3:22	the **s** hath concluded all under sin	*1124*
2Ti	3:16	All **s** is given by inspiration of God,	*1124*
Jas	2:8	the royal law according to the **s**,	*1124*
Jas	2:23	And the **s** was fulfilled which saith,	*1124*
Jas	4:5	Do ye think that the **s** saith in vain,	*1124*
2Pe	1:20	no prophecy of the **s** is of ... private	*1124*

SCRIPTURES

Mt	21:42	**Did ye never read in the s, The**	*1124*
Mt	22:29	**Ye do err, not knowing the s,**	*1124*
Mt	26:54	**how then shall the s be fulfilled,**	*1124*
Mt	26:56	**s of the prophets might be**	*1124*
Mk	12:24	**err, because ye know not the s**	*1124*
Mk	14:49	**not: but the s must be fulfilled**	*1124*
Lk	24:27	expounded unto them in all the **s**	*1124*
Lk	24:32	and while he opened to us the **s**?	*1124*
Lk	24:45	that they might understand the **s**,	*1124*
Jn	5:39	**Search the s; for in them ye**	*1124*
Ac	17:2	reasoned with them out of the **s**,	*1124*
Ac	17:11	and searched the **s** daily, whether	*1124*
Ac	18:28	shewing by the **s** that Jesus was	*1124*
Ro	1:2	afore by his prophets in the holy **s**,)	*1124*
Ro	15:4	patience and comfort of the **s** might	*1124*
Ro	16:26	by the **s** of the prophets, according	*1124*
1Co	15:3	died for our sins according to the **s**;	*1124*
1Co	15:4	the third day according to the **s**	*1124*
2Ti	3:15	child thou hast known the holy **s**,	*1121*
2Pe	3:16	wrest, as they do also the other **s**,	*1124*

S

SCROLL

Isa	34:4	shall be rolled together as a **s**.	5612
Rev	6:14	And the heaven departed as a **s**	*975*

SEA

Ge	1:26	dominion over the fish of the **s**,	3220
Ge	1:28	dominion over the fish of the **s**,	3220
Ge	9:2	and upon all the fishes of the **s**;	3220
Ge	22:17	sand which is upon the **s** shore;	3220
Ge	32:12	make thy seed as the sand of the **s**,	3220
Ge	49:13	shall dwell at the haven of the **s**;	3220
Ex	13:18	way of the wilderness of the Red **s**	3220
Ex	14:9	overtook them encamping by the **s**,	3220
Ex	14:16	stretch out thine hand over the **s**,	3220
Ex	14:21	**s** to go back by a strong east wind	3220
Ex	14:22	midst of the **s** upon the dry ground:	3220
Ex	14:23	in after them to the midst of the **s**,	3220
Ex	14:27	stretched forth his hand over the **s**,	3220
Ex	14:29	upon dry land in the midst of the **s**;	3220
Ex	14:30	Egyptians dead upon the **s** shore	3220
Ex	15:1	rider hath he thrown into the **s**.	3220
Ex	15:21	rider hath he thrown into the **s**.	3220
Ex	20:11	the **s**, and all that in them is, and	3220
Nu	11:31	and brought quails from the **s**, and	3220
Nu	14:25	wilderness by the way of the Red **s**.	3220
Dt	11:4	the Red **s** to overflow them as they.	3220
Dt	30:13	Who shall go over the **s** for us, and	3220
Jos	2:10	up the water of the Red **s** for you,	3220
Jos	4:23	Lord your God did to the Red **s**,	3220
Jos	11:4	the sand that is upon the **s** shore	3220
Jos	23:4	even unto the great **s** westward.	3220
Jos	24:7	and brought the **s** upon them, and.	3220
Jgs	7:12	sand by the **s** side for multitude.	3220
Jgs	11:16	by the wilderness unto the Red **s**,	3220
2Sa	22:16	the channels of the **s** appeared, the.	3220
1Ki	4:20	as the sand which is by the **s** in	3220
1Ki	4:29	as the sand that is on the **s** shore.	3220
1Ki	7:23	And he made a molten **s**, ten cubits	3220
1Ki	18:44	ariseth a little cloud out of the **s**,	3220
2Ki	16:17	down the **s** from off the brasen.	3220
2Ki	25:13	the brasen **s** that was in the house	3220
1Ch	16:32	Let the **s** roar, and the fulness	3220
2Ch	4:6	**s** was for the priests to wash in.	3220
Ne	9:11	And thou didst divide the **s** before	3220
Job	6:3	be heavier than the sand of the **s**	3220
Job	26:12	He divideth the **s** with his power,	3220
Job	28:14	and the **s** saith, It is not with me.	3220
Job	38:8	Or who shut up the **s** with doors,	3220
Ps	33:7	He gathereth the waters of the **s**	3220
Ps	46:2	be carried into the midst of the **s**;	3220
Ps	66:6	he turned the **s** into dry land: they	3220
Ps	72:8	have dominion also from **s** to **s**,	3220
Ps	77:19	Thy way is in the **s**, and thy path	3220
Ps	78:27	fowls like as the sand of the **s**	3220
Ps	89:9	Thou rulest the raging of the **s**	3220
Ps	95:5	The **s** is his, and he made it: and.	3220
Ps	96:11	let the **s** roar, and the fulness	3220
Ps	98:7	let the **s** roar, and the fulness	3220
Ps	106:9	He rebuked the Red **s** also, and it	3220
Ps	136:15	Pharaoh and his host in the Red **s**	3220
Ps	139:9	in the uttermost parts of the **s**;	3220
Ps	146:6	the **s**, and all that therein is:.	3220
Pr	8:29	When he gave to the **s** his decree,	3220
Pr	23:34	lieth down in the midst of the **s**,	3220
Pr	30:19	way of a ship in the midst of the **s**;	3220
Ecc	1:7	into the **s**; yet the **s** is not full;	3220
Isa	10:22	Israel be as the sand of the **s**,	3220
Isa	11:9	the Lord, as the waters cover the **s**	3220
Isa	21:1	The burden of the desert of the **s**	3220
Isa	23:11	stretched out his hand over the **s**,	3220
Isa	24:15	God of Israel in the isles of the **s**.	3220
Isa	27:1	slay the dragon that is in the **s**.	3220
Isa	43:16	which maketh a way in the **s**, and.	3220
Isa	48:18	righteousness as the waves of the **s**.	3220
Isa	51:10	made the depths of the **s** a way for.	3220
Isa	57:20	the wicked are like the troubled **s**,	3220
Isa	63:11	that brought them up out of the **s**	3220
Jer	5:22	the sand for the bound of the **s**.	3220
Jer	6:23	their voice roareth like the **s**; and	3220
Jer	31:35	which divideth the **s** when the	3220
Jer	33:22	the sand of the **s** measured: so	3220
Jer	50:42	their voice shall roar like the **s**,	3220
Jer	52:17	the brasen **s** that was in the house	3220
La	2:13	for thy breach is great like the **s**.	3220
Eze	26:5	of nets in the midst of the **s**: for	3220
Eze	26:17	which wast strong in the **s**, she and	3220
Da	7:3	great beasts came up from the **s**,	3221
Hos	1:10	Israel shall be as ... sand of the **s**,	3220
Am	5:8	that calleth for the waters of the **s**,	3220
Am	8:12	And they shall wander from **s** to **s**,	3220
Am	9:6	that calleth for the waters of the **s**,	3220
Jnh	1:4	was a mighty tempest in the **s**, so	3220
Jnh	1:9	which hath made the **s** and the dry	3220
Jnh	1:12	up, and cast me forth into the **s**;	3220
Jnh	1:15	and the **s** ceased from her raging	3220
Mic	7:19	their sins into the depths of the **s**	3220
Na	1:4	He rebuketh the **s**, and maketh it	3220
Hab	2:14	the Lord, as the waters cover the **s**	3220
Hab	3:8	was thy wrath against the **s**, that	3220
Hag	2:6	shake the heavens, and the **s**,	3220
Zec	9:4	he will smite her power in the **s**;	3220
Zec	9:10	dominion shall be from **s** even to **s**,	3220
Zec	14:8	half of them toward the former **s**,	3220
Mt	8:26	and rebuked the winds and the **s**;	*2281*
Mt	8:27	even the winds and the **s** obey him!	*2281*
Mt	8:32	down a steep place into the **s**, and	*2281*
Mt	13:47	**a net, that was cast into the s,**	*2281*
Mt	14:25	went unto them, walking on the **s**,	*2281*
Mt	14:26	disciples saw him walking on the **s**,	*2281*
Mt	17:27	**thou to the s, and cast an hook,**	*2281*
Mt	18:6	**drowned in the depth of the s.**	*2281*
Mt	21:21	**and be thou cast into the s**	*2281*
Mt	23:15	**compass s and land to make one**	*2281*
Mk	4:39	and said unto the **s**, **Peace, be still**	*2281*
Mk	4:41	even the wind and the **s** obey him?	*2281*
Mk	5:13	down a steep place into the **s**,	*2281*
Mk	6:48	unto them, walking upon the **s**,	*2281*
Mk	6:49	they saw him walking upon the **s**,	*2281*
Mk	9:42	**neck, and he were cast into the s**	*2281*
Mk	11:23	**and be thou cast into the s;**	*2281*
Lk	17:2	**his neck, and he cast into the s,**	*2281*
Lk	17:6	**root, and be thou planted in the s**	*2281*
Jn	6:19	they see Jesus walking on the **s**,	*2281*
Jn	21:7	and did cast himself into the **s**	*2281*
Ac	4:24	made heaven, and earth, and the **s**,	*2281*
Ac	7:36	in the Red **s**, and in the wilderness	*2281*
Ac	14:15	made heaven, and earth, and the **s**,	*2281*
Ro	9:27	of Israel be as the sand of the **s**,	*2281*
1Co	10:1	cloud, and all passed through the **s**;	*2281*
2Co	11:26	in perils in the **s**, in perils among	*2281*
Heb	11:12	is by the **s** shore innumerable.	*2281*
Heb	11:29	passed through the Red **s** as by dry	*2281*

Jas 1:6 that wavereth is like a wave of the **s** *2281*
Rev 4:6 was a **s** of glass like unto crystal:....... *2281*
Rev 7:3 Hurt not the earth, neither the **s**, ... *2281*
Rev 8:8 with fire was cast into the **s**: and....... *2281*
Rev 8:8 third part of the **s** became blood;....... *2281*
Rev 10:2 and he set his right foot upon the **s**,.... *2281*
Rev 10:5 angel which I saw stand upon the **s** *2281*
Rev 10:6 **s**, and the things which are therein, ... *2281*
Rev 10:8 the angel which standeth upon the **s** ... *2281*
Rev 12:12 inhabiters of the earth and of the **s**! *2281*
Rev 13:1 And I stood upon the sand of the **s**,.... *2281*
Rev 13:1 and saw a beast rise up out of the **s**,.... *2281*
Rev 15:2 were a **s** of glass mingled with fire:..... *2281*
Rev 16:3 poured out his vial upon the **s**; and *2281*
Rev 16:3 and every living soul died in the **s**...... *2281*
Rev 18:19 made rich all that had ships in the **s**.... *2281*
Rev 18:21 millstone, and cast it into the **s**,........ *2281*
Rev 20:8 of whom is as the sand of the **s**........ *2281*
Rev 20:13 **s** gave up the dead which were in it;.... *2281*
Rev 21:1 away; and there was no more **s**........ *2281*

SEAL
1Ki 21:8 name, and sealed them with his **s**, ... 2368
Ne 9:38 Levites, and priests, **s** unto if.......... 2856
Est 8:8 name, and **s** it with the king's ring:..... 2856
SS 8:6 Set me as a **s** upon thine heart,......... 2368
Jer 32:44 subscribe evidences, and **s** them, ... 2856
Da 9:24 to **s** up the vision and prophecy,....... 2856
Da 12:4 shut up the words, and **s** the book, ... 2856
Jn 3:33 hath set to his **s** that God is true. *4972*
Ro 4:11 **s** of the righteousness of the faith...... *4973*
2Ti 2:19 of God standeth sure, having this **s**,.... *4973*
Rev 6:3 when he had opened the second **s**,..... *4973*
Rev 6:5 when he had opened the third **s**,....... *4973*
Rev 6:7 when he had opened the fourth **s**, ... *4973*
Rev 6:9 and when he had opened the fifth **s**, ... *4973*
Rev 6:12 when he had opened the sixth **s**,....... *4973*
Rev 7:2 east, having the **s** of the living God: *4973*
Rev 8:1 when he had opened the seventh **s**, ... *4973*
Rev 9:4 not the **s** of God in their foreheads..... *4973*
Rev 10:4 **S** up those things which the seven *4972*
Rev 20:3 shut him up, and set a **s** upon him, ... *4972*
Rev 22:10 **S** not the sayings of the prophecy...... *4972*

SEALED
Dt 32:34 and **s** up among my treasures? 2856
1Ki 21:8 name, and **s** them with his seal, ... 2856
Est 8:8 name, and **s** with the kings ring,....... 2856
Isa 29:11 and he saith, I cannot; for it is **s** 2856
Jer 32:10 subscribed the evidence, and **s** it, ... 2856
Da 6:17 the king **s** it with his own signet....... 2857
Da 12:9 up and **s** till the time of the end........ 2856
Jn 6:27 **for him hath God the Father s** *4972*
2Co 1:22 Who hath also **s** us, and given the *4972*
Eph 1:13 **s** with that holy Spirit of promise, ... *4972*
Eph 4:30 are **s** unto the day of redemption *4972*
Rev 5:1 the backside, **s** with seven seals........ *2696*
Rev 7:3 we have **s** the servants of our God *4972*
Rev 7:4 there were **s** an hundred and forty..... *4972*

SEALETH
Job 9:7 riseth not; and **s** up the stars. 2856
Job 37:7 He **s** up the hand of every man;....... 2856

SEALING
Mt 27:66 **s** the stone, and setting a watch. *4972*

SEALS
Rev 5:2 book, and to loose the **s** thereof?....... *4973*
Rev 5:9 the book, and to open the **s** thereof:.... *4973*
Rev 6:1 when the Lamb opened one of the **s**,... *4973*

SEARCH
Le 27:33 He shall not **s** whether it be good...... 1239
Nu 13:2 men, that they may **s** the land of 8446
Nu 13:32 through which we have gone to **s**...... 8446
Nu 14:7 which we passed through to **s** it,....... 8446
Nu 14:38 of the men that went to **s** the land,..... 8446
Dt 1:22 and they shall **s** us out the land, ... 2658
Dt 13:14 shalt thou enquire, and make **s**, ... 2713
Jos 2:3 be come to **s** out all the country........ 2658
Jgs 18:2 said unto them, Go, **s** the land:......... 2713
1Sa 23:23 that I will **s** him out throughout....... 2664
1Ki 20:6 and they shall **s** thine house, and 2664
2Ki 10:23 **S**, and look that there be here 2664
Ezr 4:15 **s** may be made in the book of the 1240
Ezr 5:17 be **s** made in the king's treasure 1240
Ezr 6:1 **s** was made in the house of the........ 1240
Ps 44:21 Shall not God **s** this out? for he........ 2713
Ps 64:6 They **s** out iniquities; they............ 2664
Ps 77:6 and my spirit made diligent **s** 2664
Ps 139:23 **S** me ... and know my heart: 2713
Pr 25:2 honour of kings is to **s** out a matter. ... 2713
Pr 25:27 to **s** their own glory is not glory....... 2714
Ecc 1:13 to seek and **s** out by wisdom.......... 8446
Jer 17:10 I the Lord **s** the heart, I try the 2713
Jer 29:13 shall **s** for me with all your heart 1875
La 3:40 Let us **s** and try our ways, and......... 2664
Eze 34:8 did my shepherds **s** for my flock, ... 1875
Eze 39:14 end of seven months shall they **s** 2713
Zep 1:12 I will **s** Jerusalem with candles,........ 2664
Mt 2:8 **s** diligently for the young child;........ *1833*
Jn 5:39 **S the scriptures; for in them ye**........ *2045*
Jn 7:52 **S**, and look: for out of Galilee *2045*

SEARCHED
Ge 31:35 he **s**, but found not the images......... 2664
Nu 13:32 of the land which they had **s** unto 8446
Nu 14:6 were of them that **s** the land, rent...... 8446
Nu 14:34 of the days in which ye **s** the land, ... 8446
Job 36:26 the number of his years be **s** out....... 2714
Ps 139:1 O Lord, thou hast **s** me, and 2713
Ac 17:11 **s** the scriptures daily, whether.......... *350*
1Pe 1:10 have enquired and **s** diligently......... *1830*

SEARCHEST
Pr 2:4 and **s** for her as for hid treasures;...... 2664

SEARCHETH
1Ch 28:9 for the Lord **s** all hearts, and 1875
Pr 18:17 his neighbour cometh and **s** him 2713
Pr 28:11 hath understanding **s** him out......... 2713
Ro 8:27 And he that **s** the hearts knoweth...... *2045*
1Co 2:10 for the Spirit **s** all things, yea, the *2045*
Rev 2:23 **he which s the reins and hearts:**....... *2045*

SEARCHING
Nu 13:25 they returned from **s** of the land....... 8446
Job 11:7 Canst thou by **s** find out God? 2714
Pr 20:27 **s** all the inward parts of the belly....... 2664
Isa 40:28 is no **s** of his understanding 2714
1Pe 1:11 **S** what, or what manner of time....... *2045*

SEARED
1Ti 4:2 conscience **s** with a hot iron;.......... *2743*

SEAS

Ge	1:10	of the waters called he **S**: and	3220
Le	11:9	and scales in the waters, in the **s**,	3220
Le	11:10	have not fins and scales in the **s**,	3220
Ne	9:6	the **s**, and all that is therein, and	3220
Ps	8:8	passeth through the paths of the **s**	3220
Ps	24:2	For he hath founded it upon the **s**,	3220
Ps	65:7	Which stilleth the noise of the **s**,	3220
Ps	69:34	the **s**, and every thing that moveth	3220
Ps	135:6	earth, in the **s**, and all deep places.	3220
Jer	15:8	to me above the sand of the **s**	3220
Eze	27:27	shall fall into the midst of the **s** in	3220
Eze	28:2	seat of God, in the midst of the **S**;	3220
Eze	28:8	that are slain in the midst of the **s**	3220
Da	11:45	of his palace between the **s** in the	3220

SEA-SHORE See SEA and SHORE.

SEASON

Ex	13:10	keep this ordinance in his **s** from	4150
Le	2:13	offering shalt thou **s** with salt;	4414
Le	26:4	I will give you rain in due **s**, and	6256
Nu	9:2	the passover at his appointed **s**	4150
Nu	9:13	of the Lord in his appointed **s**,	4150
Dt	11:14	the rain of your land in his due **s**,	6256
Dt	28:12	the rain unto thy land in his **s**,	6256
2Ki	4:17	bare a son at that **s** that Elisha had	4150
2Ch	15:3	a long **s** Israel hath been without	3117
Ps	1:3	bringeth forth his fruit in his **s**;	6256
Ps	22:2	in the night **s**, and am not silent	
Ps	145:15	givest them their meat in due **s**.	6256
Pr	15:23	a word spoken in due **s**, how good	6256
Ecc	3:1	To every thing there is a **s**, and a	2165
Isa	50:4	know how to speak a word in **s** to	
Jer	33:20	not be day and night in their **s**;	6256
Da	7:12	their lives were prolonged for a **s**	2166
Mk	9:50	**saltness, wherewith will ye s it?**	*741*
Lk	1:20	which shall be fulfilled in their **s**.	*2540*
Lk	4:13	he departed from him for a **s**.	*2540*
Lk	23:8	he was desirous to see him of a long **s**,	
Jn	5:35	**ye were willing for a s to rejoice**	*5610*
Ac	13:11	blind, not seeing the sun for a **s**	*2540*
Ac	24:25	when I have a convenient **s**, I will	*2540*
Gal	6:9	for in due **s** we shall reap, if we	*2540*
2Ti	4:2	Preach the word; be instant in **s**,	*2121*
Heb	11:25	enjoy the pleasures of sin for a **s**;	*4340*
1Pe	1:6	rejoice, though now for a **s**, if	*3641*
Rev	20:3	that he must be loosed a little **s**.	*5550*

SEASONED

Lk	14:34	**his savour, wherewith shall it be s?**	*741*
Col	4:6	be alway with grace, **s** with salt,	*741*

SEASONS

Ge	1:14	let them be for signs, and for **s**,	4150
Ex	18:22	them judge the people at all **s**:	6256
Le	23:4	which ye shall proclaim in their **s**	4150
Ps	104:19	He appointed the moon for **s**:	4150
Da	2:21	he changeth the times and the **s**:	2166
Ac	1:7	**for you to know the times or the s,**	*2540*
1Th	5:1	of the times and the **s**, brethren	*2540*

SEAT See also **MERCYSEAT.**

Ex	25:17	shalt make a mercy **s** of pure gold:	
Ex	25:21	put the mercy **s** above upon the ark;	
Ex	26:34	put the mercy **s** upon the ark of the	
Ex	37:6	he made the mercy **s** of pure gold:	
Le	16:2	within the vail before the mercy **s**,	
Le	16:15	and sprinkle it upon the mercy **s**,	
Nu	7:89	unto him from off the mercy **s** that	
1Sa	4:13	lo, Eli sat upon a **s** by the wayside.	3678
1Sa	4:18	he fell from off the **s** backward by	3678
Ps	1:1	nor sitteth in the **s** of the scornful.	4186
Pr	9:14	on a **s** in the high places of the	3678
Eze	8:3	the **s** of the image of jealousy,	4186
Eze	28:2	I am a God, I sit in the **s** of God,	4186
Mt	27:19	he was set down on the judgment **s**,	*968*
Jn	19:13	and sat down in the judgment **s** in a	*968*
Ac	25:10	Paul, I stand at Caesar's judgment **s**,	*968*
Ro	14:10	before the judgment **s** of Christ.	*968*
2Co	5:10	before the judgment **s** of Christ;	*968*
Rev	2:13	**dwellest, even where Satan's s is:**	*2332*
Rev	13:2	power, and his **s**, and great authority.	*2332*
Rev	16:10	out his vial upon the **s** of the beast;	*2332*

SEATS

Mt	23:6	**and the chief s in the synagogues,**	*4410*
Mk	11:15	and the **s** of them that sold doves;	*2515*
Mk	12:39	**the chief s in the synagogues, and**	*4410*
Lk	11:43	**uppermost s in the synagogues,**	*4410*
Lk	20:46	**the highest s in the synagogues,**	*4410*
Jas	2:6	draw you before the judgment **s**?	
Rev	4:4	upon the **s** I saw four and twenty	*2362*

SECOND

Ge	1:8	and the morning were the **s** day	8145
Ge	22:15	Abraham out of heaven the **s** time,	8145
Ge	41:5	he slept and dreamed the **s** time:	8145
Ex	39:11	the **s** row, an emerald, a sapphire,	8145
Le	5:10	offer the **s** for a burnt offering.	8145
Jos	5:2	circumcise … of Israel the **s** time.	8145
Jos	6:14	**s** day they compassed the city once,	8145
Jos	19:1	And the **s** lot came forth to Simeon,	8145
1Sa	20:34	eat no meat the **s** day of the month:	8145
1Ki	9:2	appeared to Solomon the **s** time,	8145
1Ki	18:34	And he said, Do it the **s** time.	8138
1Ki	19:7	angel … came again the **s** time,	8145
2Ki	9:19	Then he sent out a **s** on horseback,	8145
1Ch	29:22	made Solomon … king the **s** time,	8145
Ezr	4:24	the **s** year of the reign of Darius	8648
Est	7:2	said again unto Esther on the **s** day	8145
Est	9:29	to confirm this **s** letter of Purim	8145
Ecc	4:8	is one alone, and there is not a **s**;	8145
Isa	11:11	shall set his hand again the **s** time	8145
Eze	10:14	the **s** face was the face of a man,	8145
Da	7:5	another beast, a **s**, like to a bear,	8578
Zec	6:2	and in the **s** chariot black horses;	8145
Mt	21:30	**came to the s, and said likewise**	*1208*
Mt	22:39	**s is like unto it, Thou shalt love**	*1208*
Mt	26:42	He went away again the **s** time,	*1208*
Mk	12:31	**the s is like, … Thou shalt love.**	*1208*
Mk	14:72	And the **s** time the cock crew	*1208*
Lk	12:38	**if he shall come in the s watch,**	*1208*
Lk	19:18	**s came, saying, Lord, thy pound**	*1208*
Jn	3:4	the **s** time into his mother's womb,	*1208*
Jn	4:54	again the **s** miracle that Jesus did,	*1208*
Jn	21:16	He saith to him again the **s** time,	*1208*
Ac	7:13	the **s** time Joseph was made known	*1208*
Ac	10:15	spake unto him again the **s** time,	*1208*
Ac	13:33	as it is also written in the **s** psalm,	*1208*
1Co	15:47	the **s** man is the Lord from heaven.	*1208*
2Co	1:15	that ye might have a **s** benefit;	*1208*
Tit	3:10	after the first and **s** admonition	*1208*

Heb 8:7 no place have been sought for the **s** *1208*
Heb 9:7 into the **s** went the high priest......... *1208*
Heb 9:28 he appear the **s** time without sin....... *1208*
Heb 10:9 first, that he may establish the **s** *1208*
Rev 2:11 **shall not be hurt of the s death**........ *1208*
Rev 4:7 a lion, and the **s** beast like a calf,....... *1208*
Rev 6:3 and when he had opened the **s** seal,.... *1208*
Rev 11:14 The **s** woe is past; and, behold, the..... *1208*
Rev 16:3 And the **s** angel poured out his vial *1208*
Rev 20:6 on such the **s** death hath no power, ... *1208*
Rev 20:14 lake of fire. This is the **s** death......... *1208*
Rev 21:8 brimstone: which is the **s** death........ *1208*

SECRET
Ge 49:6 soul, come not thou into their **s**;....... 5475
Dt 29:29 **s** things belong unto the Lord......... 5641
Jgs 13:18 after my name, seeing it is **s**?.......... 6383
Ps 10:8 in the **s** places doth he murder 4565
Ps 18:11 He made darkness his **s** place;......... 5643
Ps 19:12 cleanse thou me from **s** faults.......... 5641
Ps 25:14 The **s** of the Lord is with them 5475
Ps 64:2 Hide me from the **s** counsel of the..... 5475
Ps 64:4 may shoot in **s** at the perfect: 4565
Ps 90:8 thee, our **s** sins in the light of thy...... 5956
Ps 91:1 dwelleth in the **s** place of the most..... 5643
Ps 139:15 from thee, when I was made in **s**,...... 5643
Pr 3:32 but his **s** is with the righteous. 5475
Pr 9:17 and bread eaten in **s** is pleasant......... 5643
Pr 21:14 A gift in **s** pacifieth anger: and a....... 5643
Pr 25:9 and discover not a **s** to another:....... 5475
Pr 27:5 rebuke is better than **s** love............ 5641
Ecc 12:14 judgment, with every **s** thing.......... 5956
Isa 45:3 hidden riches of **s** places, that......... 4565
Isa 45:19 I have not spoken in **s**, in a dark....... 5643
Isa 48:16 I have not spoken in **s** from the 5643
Jer 2:34 I have not found it by **s** search, but
Jer 13:17 weep in **s** places for your pride; 4565
Jer 23:24 Can any hide himself in **s** places....... 4565
La 3:10 in wait, and as a lion in **s** places........ 4565
Eze 7:22 and they shall pollute my **s** place:...... 6845
Eze 28:3 is no **s** that they can hide from 5640
Da 2:19 **s** revealed unto Daniel in a night 7328
Da 2:22 revealeth the deep and **s** things: 5642
Da 2:30 this **s** is not revealed to me for 7328
Da 2:47 seeing thou couldest reveal this **s** 7328
Da 4:9 and no **s** troubleth me, tell me the..... 7328
Am 3:7 revealeth his **s** unto his servants 5475
Mt 6:4 **That thine alms may be in s: and**...... *2927*
Mt 6:6 **pray to thy Father which is in s;**....... *2927*
Mt 6:18 **thy Father, which seeth in s,** *2927*
Mt 13:35 things which have been kept **s**......... *2928*
Mt 24:26 **behold, he is in the s chambers;**....... *5009*
Mk 4:22 **neither was any thing kept s, but** *614*
Lk 8:17 **For nothing is s, that shall not** *2927*
Lk 11:33 **a candle, putteth it in a s place,**........ *2926*
Jn 7:4 no man that doeth any thing is **s**,...... *2927*
Jn 7:10 not openly, but as it were in **s** *2927*
Jn 18:20 **and in s have I said nothing;**.......... *2927*
Ro 16:25 was kept **s** since the world began,...... *4601*
Eph 5:12 which are done of them in **s**.......... *2931*

SECRETLY
Ge 31:27 didst thou flee away **s**, and steal 2244
Dt 13:6 entice thee **s**, saying, Let us go......... 5643
Dt 27:24 he that smiteth his neighbour **s** 5643
Jos 2:1 out of Shittim two men to spy **s**, ... 2791
1Sa 23:9 Saul **s** practised mischief against....... 2790
2Sa 12:12 For thou didst it **s**: but I will do 5643
2Ki 17:9 the children of Israel did **s** those....... 2644
Ps 10:9 He lieth in wait **s** as a lion in his....... 4565
Jer 37:17 king asked him **s** in his house, ... 5643
Jer 38:16 the king sware **s** unto Jeremiah, ... 5643
Hab 3:14 was as to devour the poor **s**........... 4565
Jn 11:28 way, and called Mary her sister **s**, ... *2977*
Jn 19:38 Jesus, but **s** for fear of the Jews,........ *2928*

SECRETS
Ps 44:21 for he knoweth the **s** of the heart 8587
Pr 11:13 A talebearer revealeth **s**: but he........ 5475
Pr 20:19 about as a talebearer revealeth **s** 5475
Da 2:28 a God in heaven that revealeth **s**, ... 7328
Da 2:47 lord of kings, and a revealer of **s**, ... 7328
Ro 2:16 God shall judge the **s** of men.......... *2927*
1Co 14:25 the **s** of his heart made manifest; *2927*

SECT
Ac 24:5 ringleader of the **s** of the Nazarenes; *139*
Ac 26:5 the most straitest **s** of our religion *139*
Ac 28:22 for as concerning this **s** we know *139*

SECURE
Jgs 18:10 ye shall come unto a people **s**, and...... 982
Mt 28:14 will persuade him, and **s** you...... *4160, 275*

SECURELY
Pr 3:29 seeing he dwelleth **s** by thee............ 983
Mic 2:8 pass by **s** as men averse from war 983

SEDITION
Ezr 4:19 rebellion and **s** have been made 849
Lk 23:25 for **s** and murder was cast into *4714*
Ac 24:5 a mover of **s** among all the Jews *4714*

SEDUCE
Mk 13:22 **to s, if it were possible, even the**........ *635*
1Jn 2:26 you, concerning them that **s** you....... *4105*
Rev 2:20 **to teach and to s my servants to**....... *4105*

SEDUCED
2Ki 21:9 Manasseh **s** them to do more evil...... 8582
Eze 13:10 they have **s** my people, saying, ... 2937

SEDUCERS
2Ti 3:13 and **s** shall wax worse and worse,...... *1114*

SEDUCETH
Pr 12:26 the way of the wicked **s** them 8582

SEDUCING
1Ti 4:1 giving heed to **s** spirits, and........... *4108*

SEED
Ge 1:11 the herb yielding **s**, and the fruit....... 2233
Ge 1:12 yielding fruit, whose **s** was in itself, ... 2233
Ge 1:29 given you every herb bearing **s**,........ 2233
Ge 3:15 and between thy **s** and her **s**;.......... 2233
Ge 4:25 appointed me another **s** instead of..... 2233
Ge 7:3 to keep **s** alive upon the face of all 2233
Ge 9:9 with you, and with your **s** after you;.... 2233
Ge 12:7 Unto thy **s** will I give this land:........ 2233
Ge 13:16 I will make thy **s** as the dust of the..... 2233
Ge 15:3 Behold, to me thou hast given no **s** 2233
Ge 15:5 said unto him, So shall thy **s** be........ 2233
Ge 15:18 Unto thy **s** have I given this land,...... 2233
Ge 16:10 I will multiply thy **s** exceedingly,....... 2233
Ge 17:7 between me and thee and thy **s**........ 2233

S

Ge	17:19	covenant, and with his **s** after him	2233
Ge	19:32	may preserve **s** of our father	2233
Ge	21:12	for in Isaac shall thy **s** be called	2233
Ge	22:17	I will multiply thy **s** as the stars of	2233
Ge	22:18	And in thy **s** shall all the nations of	2233
Ge	24:7	Unto thy **s** will I give this land;	2233
Ge	26:4	give unto thy **s** all these countries;	2233
Ge	26:4	and in thy **s** shall all the nations of	2233
Ge	28:4	to thee, and to thy **s** with thee;	2233
Ge	28:14	And thy **s** shall be as the dust of	2233
Ge	32:12	make thy **s** as the sand of the sea	2233
Ge	35:12	to thy **s** after thee will I give the	2233
Ge	38:8	her, and raise up **s** to thy brother	2233
Ge	38:9	that he should give **s** to his brother	2233
Ge	47:23	here is **s** for you, and ye shall sow	2233
Ge	48:4	and will give this land to thy **s** after	2233
Ge	48:19	his **s** shall become a multitude of	2233
Ex	16:31	and it was like coriander **s**, white;	2233
Ex	32:13	I will multiply your **s** as the stars	2233
Ex	33:1	saying, Unto thy **s** will I give it:	2233
Le	18:21	any of thy **s** pass through the fire	2233
Le	19:19	not sow thy field with mingled **s**	
Le	20:3	he hath given of his **s** unto Molech,	2233
Le	21:21	hath a blemish of the **s** of Aaron.	2233
Le	22:4	What man soever of the **s** of Aaron	2233
Le	26:16	and ye shall sow your **s** in vain, for	2233
Nu	11:7	And the manna was as coriander **s**.	2233
Nu	14:24	he went; and his **s** shall possess it	2233
Nu	16:40	which is not of the **s** of Aaron,	2233
Nu	25:13	shall have it, and his **s** after him	2233
Dt	1:8	unto them and to their **s** after them	2233
Dt	4:37	he chose their **s** after them, and	2233
Dt	14:22	truly tithe all the increase of thy **s**.	2233
Dt	28:46	a wonder, and upon thy **s** for ever	2233
Dt	30:6	thine heart, and the heart of thy **s**,	2233
Dt	30:19	that both thou and thy **s** may live:	2233
Dt	34:4	saying, I will give it unto thy **s**.	2233
Ru	4:12	**s** which the Lord shall give thee	2233
1Sa	2:20	The Lord give thee **s** of this woman	2233
1Sa	8:15	he will take the tenth of your **s**	2233
1Sa	20:42	between my **s** and thy **s** for ever	2233
1Sa	24:21	thou wilt not cut off my **s** after me,	2233
2Sa	4:8	king this day of Saul, and of his **s**	2233
2Sa	22:51	David, and to his **s** for evermore.	2233
1Ki	11:39	I will for this afflict the **s** of David,	2233
2Ki	5:27	unto thee, and unto thy **s** for ever	2233
2Ki	11:1	arose and destroyed all the **s** royal	2233
2Ki	17:20	the Lord rejected all the **s** of Israel,	2233
1Ch	17:11	that I will raise up thy **s** after thee,	2233
Ezr	2:59	their father's house, and their **s**.	2233
Ezr	9:2	holy **s** have mingled themselves	2233
Ne	9:2	**s** of Israel separated themselves.	2233
Ne	9:8	to give it, I say, to his **s**, and hast	2233
Est	6:13	if Mordecai be of the **s** of the Jews,	2233
Est	9:28	memorial ... perish from their **s**.	2233
Est	10:3	and speaking peace to all his **s**.	2233
Ps	18:50	David, and to his **s** for evermore.	2233
Ps	21:10	**s** from among the children of men.	2233
Ps	25:13	and his **s** shall inherit the earth.	2233
Ps	37:25	forsaken, nor his **s** begging bread	2233
Ps	37:28	the **s** of the wicked shall be cut off	2233
Ps	69:36	**s** also of his servants shall inherit	2233
Ps	89:4	Thy **s** will I establish for ever, and.	2233
Ps	89:29	His **s** also will I make to endure for	2233
Ps	89:36	His **s** shall endure for ever, and his	2233
Ps	126:6	and weepeth, bearing precious **s**.	2233
Pr	11:21	but the **s** of the righteous shall be.	2233
Ecc	11:6	In the morning sow thy **s**, and in	2233
Isa	1:4	a **s** of evildoers, children that are	2233
Isa	14:20	the **s** of evildoers shall never be	2233
Isa	41:8	the **s** of Abraham my friend	2233
Isa	44:3	I will pour my spirit upon thy **s**	2233
Isa	45:19	I said not unto the **s** of Jacob, Seek.	2233
Isa	45:25	In the Lord shall all the **s** of Israel	2233
Isa	53:10	he shall see his **s**, he shall prolong.	2233
Isa	57:3	**s** of the adulterer and the whore.	2233
Isa	57:4	of transgression, a **s** of falsehood,	2233
Isa	61:9	the **s** which the Lord hath blessed.	2233
Isa	65:23	are the **s** of the blessed of the Lord,	2233
Isa	66:22	your **s** and your name remain	2233
Jer	2:21	thee a noble vine, wholly a right **s**	2233
Jer	22:28	are they cast out, he and his **s**, and	2233
Jer	22:30	for no man of his **s** shall prosper	2233
Jer	30:10	**s** from the land of their captivity;	2233
Jer	31:27	**s** of man, and with the **s** of beast	2233
Jer	31:36	**s** of Israel also shall cease from	2233
Jer	31:37	cast off all the **s** of Israel for all	2233
Jer	33:22	will I multiply the **s** of David my	2233
Jer	33:26	I will not take any of his **s** to be	2233
Jer	33:26	to be rulers over the **s** of Abraham,	2233
Jer	35:7	nor sow **s**, nor plant vineyard,	2233
Jer	36:31	I will punish him and his **s** and his	2233
Jer	46:27	**s** from the land of their captivity;	2233
Eze	17:13	And hath taken of the king's **s**, and	2233
Eze	20:5	unto the **s** of the house of Jacob	2233
Da	2:43	themselves with the **s** of men:	2234
Am	9:13	of grapes him that soweth **s**;	2233
Hag	2:19	Is the **s** yet in the barn? yea, as	2233
Zec	8:12	for the **s** shall be prosperous; the	2233
Mal	2:15	one? That he might seek a godly **s**	2233
Mt	13:20	**received the s into stony places,**	*4687*
Mt	13:22	**that received s among the thorns**	*4687*
Mt	13:23	**received s into the good ground**	*4687*
Mt	13:24	**which sowed good s in his field:**	*4690*
Mt	13:27	**not thou sow good s in thy field?**	*4690*
Mt	13:31	**heaven ... a grain of mustard s,**	
Mt	13:37	the good **s** is the Son of man;	*4690*
Mt	13:38	**the good s are the children of the.**	*4690*
Mt	17:20	**ye have faith as a grain of mustard s,**	
Mk	4:31	**It is like a grain of mustard s,**	*4690*
Mk	12:22	the seven had her, and left no **s**	*4690*
Lk	1:55	to Abraham, and to his **s** for ever	*4690*
Lk	8:5	**A sower went out to sow his s.**	*4703*
Lk	8:11	**is this: The s is the word of God**	*4703*
Lk	13:19	**It is like a grain of mustard s, which.**	
Lk	17:6	**ye had faith as a grain of mustard s**	
Jn	7:42	Christ cometh of the **s** of David,	*4690*
Jn	8:33	We be Abraham's **s**, and were	*4690*
Jn	8:37	**I know that ye are Abraham's s;**	*4690*
Ac	3:25	in thy **s** shall all the kindreds of.	*4690*
Ac	7:6	his **s** should sojourn in a strange	*4690*
Ac	13:23	Of this man's **s** hath God according	*4690*
Ro	1:3	which was made of the **s** of David	*4690*
Ro	4:18	was spoken, So shall thy **s** be	*4690*
Ro	9:8	of the promise are counted for the **s**	*4690*
Ro	9:29	the Lord of Sabaoth had left us a **s**,	*4690*
1Co	15:38	him, and to every **s** his own body	*4690*
2Co	9:10	he that ministereth **s** to the sower	*4690*
2Co	11:22	Are they the **s** of Abraham? so am	*4690*
Gal	3:16	one, And to thy **s**, which is Christ	*4690*
Gal	3:19	till the **s** should come to whom the	*4690*
Gal	3:29	Christ's, then are ye Abraham's **s**.	*4690*

2Ti	2:8	Jesus Christ of the **s** of David was	*4690*
Heb	2:16	he took on him the **s** of Abraham	*4690*
Heb	11:18	That in Isaac shall thy **s** be called:	*4690*
1Pe	1:23	born again, not of corruptible **s**	*4701*
1Jn	3:9	for his **s** remaineth in him: and	*4690*
Rev	12:17	war with the remnant of her **s**	*4690*

SEEDS

Dt	22:9	not sow thy vineyard with divers **s**	
Mt	13:4	**some s fell by the way aide, and the**	
Mt	13:32	**which indeed is the least of all s**	*4690*
Mk	4:31	**is less than all the s that be**	*4690*
Gal	3:16	He saith not, And to **s**, as of many;	*4690*

SEEK

Ge	43:18	that he may **s** occasion against us,	1556
Le	19:31	neither **s** after wizards, to be	1245
Nu	15:39	ye **s** not after your own heart and	8446
Nu	16:10	thee: and **s** ye the priesthood also?	1245
Nu	24:1	times, to **s** for enchantments	7125
Dt	4:29	if thou **s** him with all thy heart	1875
Dt	22:2	with thee until thy brother **s** after it	1875
Dt	23:6	Thou shalt not **s** their peace nor	1875
1Sa	10:2	which thou wentest to **s** are found:	1245
1Sa	16:16	to **s** out a man, who is a cunning	1245
1Sa	23:15	Saul was come out to **s** his life:	1245
1Sa	25:26	they that **s** evil to my lord, be as	1245
1Sa	26:20	king of Israel is come out to **s** a flea,	1245
1Sa	27:1	to **s** me any more in any coast of	1245
1Sa	28:7	**S** me a woman that hath a	1245
1Ki	18:10	my lord hath not sent to **s** thee:	1245
1Ki	19:10	they **s** my life, to take it away	1245
1Ki	19:14	they **s** my life, to take it away	1245
2Ki	2:16	go, we pray thee, and **s** thy master:	1245
2Ki	6:19	bring you to the man whom ye **s**	1245
1Ch	16:11	**S** the Lord and his strength,	1875
1Ch	16:11	strength, **s** his face continually	1245
1Ch	22:19	your soul to **s** the Lord your God;	1875
1Ch	28:9	if thou **s** him, he will be found of	1875
2Ch	7:14	**s** my face, and turn from their	1245
2Ch	11:16	set their hearts to **s** the Lord God	1245
2Ch	12:14	prepared not his heart to **s** the	1875
2Ch	15:2	if ye **s** him, he will be found of you;	1875
2Ch	15:12	into a covenant to **s** the Lord God	1875
2Ch	15:13	whosoever would not **s** the Lord	1875
2Ch	19:3	hast prepared thine heart to **s** God	1875
2Ch	20:3	and set himself to **s** the Lord, and	1875
2Ch	30:19	prepareth his heart to **s** God, the	1875
2Ch	31:21	the commandments, to **s** his God,	1875
2Ch	34:3	began to **s** after the God of David	1875
Ezr	4:2	for we **s** your God, as ye do; and	1875
Ezr	6:21	land, to **s** the Lord God of Israel,	1875
Ezr	7:10	his heart to **s** the law of the Lord	1875
Ezr	8:21	to **s** of him a right way for us, and	1245
Ezr	8:22	upon all them for good that **s** him;	1245
Ezr	9:12	nor **s** their peace or their wealth	1875
Ne	2:10	to **s** the welfare of the children of	1245
Job	5:8	I would **s** unto God, and unto God	1875
Job	7:21	thou shalt **s** me in the morning	7836
Ps	4:2	love vanity, and **s** after leasing?	1245
Ps	9:10	not forsaken them that **s** thee	1875
Ps	10:4	countenance, will not **s** after God:	1875
Ps	14:2	that did understand, and **s** God	1875
Ps	24:6	the generation of them that **s** him	1875
Ps	27:4	of the Lord, that will I **s** after;	1245
Ps	27:8	unto thee, Thy face, Lord, will I **s**	1245
Ps	34:10	that **s** the Lord shall not want	1875
Ps	34:14	do good; **s** peace, and pursue it	1245
Ps	35:4	put to shame that **s** after my soul:	1245
Ps	40:14	that **s** after my soul to destroy it;	1245
Ps	40:16	Let all those that **s** thee rejoice	1245
Ps	63:1	art my God; early will I **s** thee:	7836
Ps	69:6	not those that **s** thee be confounded	1245
Ps	70:4	all those that **s** thee rejoice and be	1245
Ps	71:24	unto shame, that **s** my hurt	1245
Ps	83:16	that they may **s** thy name, O Lord	1245
Ps	104:21	prey, and **s** their meat from God	1245
Ps	105:3	of them rejoice that **s** the Lord	1245
Ps	119:2	that **s** him with the whole heart	1875
Ps	119:45	at liberty: for I **s** thy precepts	1875
Ps	119:155	wicked: for they **s** not thy statutes	1875
Pr	1:28	they shall **s** me early, but they	7836
Pr	7:15	diligently to **s** thy face, and I have	7836
Pr	8:17	those that **s** me early shall find me	7836
Pr	21:6	to and fro of them that **s** death	1245
Pr	23:30	they that go to **s** mixed wine	2713
Pr	23:35	shall I awake? I will **s** it yet again	1245
Pr	28:5	they that **s** the Lord understand	1245
Pr	29:10	the upright: but the just **s** his soul	1245
Pr	29:26	Many **s** the ruler's favour; but	1245
Ecc	1:13	my heart to **s** and search out by	1875
Ecc	7:25	to search, and to **s** out wisdom	1245
Ecc	8:17	though a man labour to **s** it out,	1245
SS	3:2	will **s** him whom my soul loveth:	1245
Isa	1:17	**s** judgment, relieve the oppressed	1875
Isa	8:19	should not a people **s** unto their God?	1875
Isa	9:13	them, neither do they **s** the Lord	1875
Isa	11:10	to it shall the Gentiles **s**: and his	1875
Isa	19:3	and they shall **s** to the idols, and to	1875
Isa	26:9	within me will I **s** thee early:	7836
Isa	31:1	of Israel, neither **s** the Lord!	1875
Isa	34:16	**S** ye out of the book of the Lord	1875
Isa	41:17	When the poor and needy **s** water,	1245
Isa	45:19	the seed of Jacob, **S** ye me in vain:	1245
Isa	51:1	righteousness, ye that **s** the Lord:	1245
Isa	55:6	**S** ye the Lord while he may be	1875
Isa	58:2	Yet they **s** me daily, and delight	1875
Jer	2:33	trimmest thou thy way to **s** love?	1245
Jer	22:25	into the hand of them that **s** thy life,	1245
Jer	29:13	ye shall **s** me, and find me, when	1245
Jer	30:14	forgotten thee; they **s** thee not;	1875
Jer	34:21	the hand of them that **s** their life	1245
Jer	38:16	hand of these men that **s** thy life	1245
Jer	45:5	great things for thyself? **s** them not:	1245
Jer	50:4	shall go, and **s** the Lord their God	1245
La	1:11	All her people sigh, they **s** bread;	1245
Eze	7:25	they shall **s** peace, and there shall	1245
Eze	7:26	shall they **s** a vision of the prophet;	1245
Eze	34:6	none did search or **s** after them	1245
Eze	34:11	search my sheep, and **s** them out,	1239
Eze	34:12	so will I **s** out my sheep, and will	1239
Eze	34:16	I will **s** that which was lost, and	1245
Hos	2:7	she shall **s** them, but shall not	1245
Hos	3:5	**s** the Lord their God, and David	1245
Hos	5:15	affliction they will **s** me early	7836
Hos	7:10	their God, nor **s** him for all this	1245
Hos	10:12	for it is time to **s** the Lord, till he	1875
Am	5:4	Israel, **S** ye me, and ye shall live:	1875
Am	5:6	**S** the Lord, and ye shall live; lest	1875
Am	5:8	**S** him that maketh the seven stars	
Am	5:14	**S** good, and not evil, that ye may	1875
Am	8:12	to and fro to **s** the word of the Lord,	1245

Zep	2:3	**S** ye the Lord, all ye meek of the	1245
Zep	2:3	**s** righteousness, **s** meekness: it	1245
Zec	8:21	Lord, and to **s** the Lord of hosts:	1245
Zec	8:22	shall come to **s** the Lord of hosts	1245
Zec	12:9	I will **s** to destroy all the nations	1245
Mal	2:7	should **s** the law at his mouth:	1245
Mal	2:15	That he might **s** a godly seed	1245
Mal	3:1	and the Lord, whom ye **s**, shall	1245
Mt	2:13	**s** the young child to destroy him	*2212*
Mt	6:32	**all these things do the Gentiles s:)**	*1934*
Mt	6:33	**But s ye first the kingdom of God**	*2212*
Mt	7:7	**s, and ye shall find; knock**	*2212*
Mt	28:5	ye **s** Jesus, which was crucified	*2212*
Mk	1:37	said unto him, All men **s** for thee	*2212*
Mk	3:32	thy brethren without **s** for thee	*2212*
Mk	8:12	**this generation s after a sign?**	*1934*
Mk	16:6	Ye **s** Jesus of Nazareth, which was	*2212*
Lk	11:9	**s, and ye shall find; knock**	*2212*
Lk	11:29	**they s a sign; and there shall no**	*1934*
Lk	12:29	**And s not ye what ye shall eat,**	*2212*
Lk	12:30	**the nations of the world s after:**	*1934*
Lk	12:31	**rather s ye the kingdom of God:**	*2212*
Lk	13:24	**for many, … will s to enter in,**	*2212*
Lk	17:33	**shall s to save his life shall lose it**	*2212*
Lk	19:10	**to s and to save that which was lost**	*2212*
Lk	24:5	**s** ye the living among the dead?	*2212*
Jn	1:38	and saith unto them, **What s ye?**	*2212*
Jn	5:30	**because I s not mine own will,**	*2212*
Jn	5:44	**s not the honour that cometh**	*2212*
Jn	6:26	**Ye s me, not because ye saw**	*2212*
Jn	7:25	not this he, whom they **s** to kill?	*2212*
Jn	7:34	**Ye shall s me, and shall not find me**	*2212*
Jn	8:21	**ye shall s me, and shall die in your**	*2212*
Jn	8:37	**ye s to kill me, because my**	*2212*
Jn	8:40	**But now ye s to kill me, a man**	*2212*
Jn	8:50	**And I s not mine own glory:**	*2212*
Jn	18:4	and said unto them, **Whom s ye?**	*2212*
Jn	18:7	asked he them again, **Whom s ye?**	*2212*
Jn	18:8	**if therefore ye s me, let these**	*2212*
Ac	10:19	him, Behold, three men **s** thee	*2212*
Ac	17:27	That they should **s** the Lord, if haply	*2212*
Ro	11:3	am left alone, and they **s** my life	*2212*
1Co	1:22	and the Greeks **s** after wisdom:	*2212*
1Co	7:27	unto a wife? **s** not to be loosed	*2212*
1Co	7:27	loosed from a wife? **s** not a wife	*2212*
1Co	10:24	Let no man **s** his own, but every	*2212*
1Co	14:12	**s** that ye may excel to the edifying	*2212*
2Co	12:14	for I **s** not yours, but you: for the	*2212*
2Co	13:3	ye **s** a proof of Christ speaking in	*2212*
Gal	1:10	or do I **s** to please men? for if I	*2212*
Gal	2:17	while we **s** to be justified by Christ,	*2212*
Php	2:21	For all **s** their own, not the things	*2212*
Col	3:1	**s** those things which are above,	*2212*
Heb	11:6	of them that diligently **s** him	*1567*
Heb	11:14	plainly that they **s** a country	*1934*
Heb	13:14	city, but we **s** one to come	*1934*
1Pe	3:11	let him **s** peace, and ensue it	*2212*
Rev	9:6	in those days shall men **s** death,	*2212*

SEEKEST

Ge	37:15	asked him, saying, What **s** thou?	1245
Pr	2:4	If thou **s** her as silver, and	1245
Jer	45:5	**s** thou great things for thyself?	1245
Jn	4:27	yet no man said, What **s** thou?	*2212*
Jn	20:15	**why weepest thou? whom s**	*2212*

SEEKETH

1Sa	19:2	Saul my father **s** to kill thee: now	1245
1Sa	22:23	for he that **s** my life **s** thy life:	1245
1Sa	24:9	saying, Behold, David **s** thy hurt?	1245
2Ki	5:7	see how he **s** a quarrel against me	579
Ps	37:32	the righteous, and **s** to slay him	1245
Pr	11:27	**s** good procureth favour: but	7836
Pr	11:27	he that **s** mischief, it shall come	1875
Pr	14:6	A scorner **s** wisdom, and findeth	1245
Pr	15:14	hath understanding **s** knowledge:	1245
Pr	17:9	covereth a transgression **s** love;	1245
Pr	17:11	an evil man **s** only rebellion:	1245
Pr	17:19	exalteth his gate **s** destruction	1245
Pr	18:1	**s** and intermeddleth with all wisdom	1245
Pr	18:15	the ear of the wise **s** knowledge	1245
Ecc	7:28	Which yet my soul **s**, but I find	1245
Jer	5:1	executeth judgment, … **s** the truth;	1245
Jer	38:4	**s** not the welfare of this people,	1875
Eze	34:12	As a shepherd **s** out his flock in	1243
Mt	7:8	**receiveth; and he that s findeth;**	*2212*
Mt	12:39	**evil … generation s after a sign;**	*1934*
Mt	16:4	**wicked … generation s after**	*1934*
Mt	18:12	**and s that which is gone astray?**	*2212*
Lk	11:10	**receiveth; and he that s findeth;**	*2212*
Jn	4:23	**the Father s such to worship**	*2212*
Jn	8:50	**there is one that s and judgeth**	*2212*
Ro	3:11	there is none that **s** after God	*1567*
Ro	11:7	not obtained that which he **s** for;	*1934*
1Co	13:5	itself unseemly, **s** not her own	*2212*

SEEKING

Isa	16:5	judging, and **s** judgment, and	1875
Mt	12:43	**places, s rest, and findeth none**	*2212*
Mt	13:45	**a merchant man, s goodly pearls:**	*2212*
Mk	8:11	him, **s** of him a sign from heaven,	*2212*
Lk	2:45	back again to Jerusalem, **s** him	*2212*
Lk	11:24	**walketh through dry places, s**	*2212*
Lk	13:7	**three years I come s fruit on**	*2212*
Ac	13:8	**s** to turn away the deputy from the	*2212*
Ac	13:11	**s** some to lead him by the hand	*2212*
1Co	10:33	not **s** mine own profit, but the	*2212*
1Pe	5:8	about, **s** whom he may devour:	*2212*

SEEM

Ge	27:12	shall **s** to him as a deceiver;	1961, 5869
Jos	24:15	**s** evil unto you to serve the	1961, 5869
1Sa	24:4	as it shall **s** good unto thee	1961, 5869
1Ki	21:2	if it **s** good to thee, I will give	1961, 5869
Ezr	5:17	if it **s** good to the king, let there be	
Ne	9:32	let not all the trouble **s** little	4591
Est	5:4	If it **s** good unto the king, let the	
Jer	40:4	If it **s** good unto thee to come	5869
1Co	11:16	if any man **s** to be contentious,	*1380*
1Co	12:22	body, which **s** to be more feeble,	*1380*
Heb	4:1	of you should **s** to come short of it	*1380*
Jas	1:26	man among you **s** to be religious,	*1380*

SEEMED

Ge	19:14	he **s** as one that mocked unto	1961, 5869
Ge	29:20	**s** unto him but a few days	1961, 5869
Jer	18:4	as **s** good to the potter to make it	5869
Mt	11:26	**for so it s good in thy sight**	*1096, 2107*
Lk	10:21	**for so it s good in thy sight**	*1096, 2107*
Lk	24:11	words **s** to them as idle tales, and	*5316*
Ac	15:28	For it **s** good to the Holy Ghost,	*1380*

S

SEEMETH
Nu 16:9 **S** it but a small thing unto you,
Jos 9:25 as it **s** good and right unto thee 5869
Jgs 10:15 us whatsoever **s** good unto thee;....... 5869
Jgs 19:24 unto them what **s** good unto you: 5869
1Sa 3:18 let him do what **s** him good 5869
1Sa 11:10 with us all that **s** good unto you 5869
1Sa 18:23 **S** it to you a light thing to be a 5869
2Sa 10:12 Lord do that which **s** him good 5869
2Sa 15:26 him do to me as **s** good unto him 5869
2Sa 18:4 What **s** you best I will do............. 5869
Est 3:11 with them as it **s** good to thee......... 5869
Pr 14:12 a way which **s** right unto a man 6440
Pr 16:25 is a way that **s** right unto a man 6440
Pr 18:17 that is first in his own cause **s** just;
Jer 26:14 do with me as **s** good and meet 5869
Jer 40:4 it **s** good and convenient for thee...... 5869
Jer 40:5 wheresoever it **s** convenient unto 5869
Eze 34:18 **S** it a small thing unto you to have
Lk 8:18 **even that which he s to have** *1380*
Ac 17:18 He **s** to be a setter forth of strange *1380*
1Co 3:18 you **s** to be wise in this world *1380*
Heb 12:11 for the present **s** to be joyous, but...... *1380*

SEEMLY See also **UNSEEMLY.**
Pr 19:10 Delight is not **s** for a fool; much....... 5000
Pr 26:1 so honour is not **s** for a fool 5000

SEER
1Sa 9:9 Prophet was beforetime called a **S.**) 7200
2Ch 16:10 Then Asa was wroth with the **s,** 7200
Am 7:12 O thou **s,** go, flee thee away into....... 2374

SEERS
Isa 29:10 your rulers, the **s** hath he covered...... 2374
Isa 30:10 Which say to the **s,** See not; and 7200
Mic 3:7 Then shall the **s** be ashamed, and...... 2374

SEETHE
Ex 23:19 not **s** a kid in his mother's milk 1310
Ex 29:31 and **s** his flesh in the holy place 1310
Dt 14:21 not **s** a kid in his mother's milk 1310
2Ki 4:38 and **s** pottage for the sons of the....... 1310

SEIZE
Job 3:6 that night, let darkness **s** upon it:....... 3947
Ps 55:15 Let death **s** upon them, and let 3451
Mt 21:38 **and let us s on his inheritance** *2722*

SEIZED
Jer 49:24 to flee, and fear hath **s** on her 2388

SELF
Jn 5:30 **I can of mine own s do nothing:** *1683*
Jn 17:5 **glorify thou me with thine own s.**...... *4572*
1Co 4:3 yea, I judge not mine own **s.**.......... *1683*
Phm 19 owest unto me even thine own **s.**...... *4572*
1Pe 2:24 Who his own **s** bare our sins in his...... *846*

SELFSAME
Ex 12:41 even the **s** day it came to pass, ... 2088, 6106
Ex 12:51 And it came to pass the **s** day,.... 2088, 6106
Mt 8:13 servant was healed in the **s** hour....... *1565*
1Co 12:11 worketh that one and the **s** Spirit *846*
2Co 5:5 wrought us for the **s** thing is...... 846, 5124

SELFWILLED
Tit 1:7 not **s,** not soon angry, not given to...... *829*
2Pe 2:10 Presumptuous are they, **s,** they *829*

SELL
Ge 25:31 said, **S** me this day thy birthright 4376
Ge 37:27 and let us **s** him to the Ishmeelites, ... 4376
Ex 21:35 then they shall **s** the live ox, and....... 4376
Ex 22:1 ox, or a sheep, and kill it, or **s** it;....... 4376
Le 25:29 **s** a dwelling house in a walled city 4376
Dt 14:21 thou mayest **s** it unto an alien: 4376
Jgs 4:9 the Lord shall **s** Sisera into the 4376
1Ki 21:25 did **s** himself to work wickedness...... 4376
2Ki 4:7 Go, **s** the oil, and pay thy debt, and 4376
Ne 10:31 victuals on the sabbath day to **s,**....... 4376
Pr 23:23 Buy the truth, and **s** it not; also........ 4376
Mt 19:21 **go and s that thou hast, and give.**..... *4453*
Mt 25:9 **go ye rather to them that s, and** *4453*
Mk 10:21 **s whatsoever thou hast, and give** *4453*
Lk 12:33 **S that ye have, and give alms;** *4453*
Lk 18:22 **s all that thou hast, and** *4453*
Lk 22:36 **no sword, let him s his garment,** *4453*
Jas 4:13 and buy and **s,** and get gain: *1710*
Rev 13:17 that no man might buy or **s,** save *4453*

SELLER
Isa 24:2 as with the buyer, so with the **s;** 4376
Eze 7:12 buyer rejoice, nor the **s** mourn:........ 4376
Ac 16:14 named Lydia, a **s** of purple 4211

SELLETH
Ex 21:16 that stealeth a man, and **s** him,........ 4376
Dt 24:7 merchandise of him, or **s** him; 4376
Pr 11:26 upon the head of him that **s** it 7666
Pr 31:24 She maketh fine linen, and **s** it;........ 4376
Na 3:4 **s** nations through her whoredoms, ... 4376
Mt 13:44 **goeth and s all that he hath, and** *4453*

SELVES
Ac 20:30 Also of your own **s** shall men arise, ... *846*
2Co 13:5 Know ye not your own **s,** how that..... *1438*
2Ti 3:2 men shall be lovers of their own **s,**..... *5367*
Jas 1:22 hearers only, deceiving your own **s**...... *846*

SEND
Ge 24:40 will **s** his angel with thee, and......... 7971
Ge 38:17 thou give me a pledge, till thou **s** it?.... 7971
Ge 43:8 **S** the lad with me, and we will 7971
Ge 45:5 For God did **s** me before you to 7971
Ex 3:10 I will **s** thee unto Pharaoh, that........ 7971
Ex 9:14 will at this time **s** all my plagues....... 7971
Ex 23:20 I **s** an Angel before thee, to keep....... 7971
Le 26:22 will also **s** wild beasts among you...... 7971
Le 26:25 I will **s** the pestilence among you;...... 7971
Le 26:36 I will **s** a faintness into their 935
Nu 13:2 **S** thou men, that may search the....... 7971
Dt 24:1 hand, and **s** her out of his house....... 7971
Dt 28:20 The Lord shall **s** upon the cursing 7971
Jos 18:4 I will **s** them, and they shall rise,....... 7971
1Sa 5:11 **S** away the ark of the God of Israel, ... 7971
1Sa 6:3 **s** it not empty; but in any wise 7971
1Sa 16:11 said unto Jesse, **S** and fetch him:....... 7971
1Sa 20:21 I will **s** a lad, saying, Go, find out 7971
1Sa 20:31 now **s** and fetch him unto me, for 7971
2Sa 11:6 saying, **S** me Uriah the Hittite......... 7971
2Ki 2:16 valley. And he said, Ye shall not **s** 7971
Ezr 5:17 let the king **s** his pleasure to us 7972
Ne 2:6 So it pleased the king to **s** me;......... 7971
Ps 43:3 O **s** out thy light and thy truth:........ 7971
Ps 57:3 He shall **s** from heaven, and save 7971
Ps 57:3 God shall **s** forth his mercy and his 7971

Ps 118:25	I beseech thee, **s** now prosperity	
Pr 10:26	is the sluggard to them that **s** him	7971
Pr 22:21	of truth to them that **s** unto thee?	7971
Pr 25:13	messenger to them that **s** him:	7971
Ecc 10:1	to **s** forth a stinking savour	5042
Isa 6:8	Whom shall I **s**, and who will go	7971
Isa 6:8	Then said I, Here am I; **s** me	7971
Isa 19:20	and he shall **s** them a saviour, and	7971
Jer 1:7	shalt go to all that I shall **s** thee,	7971
Jer 24:10	I will **s** the sword, the famine, and	7971
Jer 25:15	nations, to whom I **s** thee, to drink	7971
Jer 42:5	the Lord thy God shall **s** thee to us	7971
Jer 43:10	I will **s** and take Nebuchadrezzar	7971
Eze 2:3	I **s** thee to the children of Israel	7971
Eze 7:3	and I will **s** mine anger upon thee,	7971
Eze 14:21	when I **s** my four sore judgments	7971
Am 2:2	But I will **s** a fire upon Moab, and	7971
Am 2:5	But I will **s** a fire upon Judah, and	7971
Am 8:11	that I will **s** a famine in the land	7971
Mal 2:2	I will even **s** a curse upon you, and	7971
Mal 3:1	Behold, I will **s** my messenger,	7971
Mal 4:5	I will **s** you Elijah the prophet	7971
Mt 9:38	**s forth labourers into his harvest.**	*1544*
Mt 10:16	**I s you forth as sheep in the midst**	*649*
Mt 10:34	**I come not to s peace, but a sword.**	*906*
Mt 11:10	**I s my messenger before thy face,**	*649*
Mt 13:41	**Son of man shall s forth his angels,**	*649*
Mt 15:23	**S** her away; for she crieth after us.	*630*
Mt 15:32	**I will not s them away fasting, lest.**	*630*
Mt 21:3	**and straightway he will s them**	*649*
Mt 23:34	**behold, I s unto you prophets, and**	*649*
Mt 24:31	**he shall s his angels with a great**	*649*
Mk 1:2	I **s** my messenger before thy face	*649*
Mk 5:12	**S** us into the swine, that we may	*3992*
Mk 6:7	to **s** them forth by two and two;	*649*
Mk 8:3	**if I s them away fasting to their**	*630*
Mk 13:27	**then shall he s his angels, shall**	*649*
Lk 7:27	**I s my messenger before thy face,**	*649*
Lk 10:2	**s forth labourers into his harvest.**	*1544*
Lk 10:3	**s you forth as lambs among wolves.**	*649*
Lk 11:49	**I will s them prophets and apostles,**	*649*
Lk 12:49	**I am come to s fire on the earth;**	*906*
Lk 16:24	**s Lazarus, that he may dip the tip**	*3992*
Lk 20:13	**I will s my beloved son: it may be**	*3992*
Lk 24:49	**I s the promise of my Father upon**	*649*
Jn 13:20	**whomsoever I s receiveth me;**	*3992*
Jn 14:26	**the Father will s in my name,**	*3992*
Jn 15:26	**I will s unto you from the Father,**	*3992*
Jn 16:7	**if I depart, I will s him unto you.**	*3992*
Jn 17:8	**have believed that thou didst s me.**	*649*
Jn 20:21	**hath sent me, even so s I you**	*3992*
Ac 10:22	angel to **s** for thee into his house	*3343*
Ac 22:21	**I will s thee far hence unto the**	*1821*
Ac 26:17	**Gentiles, unto whom now I s thee,**	*649*
2Th 2:11	God shall **s** them strong delusion	*3992*
Jas 3:11	fountain **s** forth at the same time	*1032*
Rev 1:11	**s it unto the seven churches**	*3992*
Rev 11:10	and shall **s** gifts one to another;	*3992*

SENDEST

Jos 1:16	whithersoever thou **s** us, we will	7971
Ps 104:30	Thou **s** forth thy spirit, they are	7971

SENDETH

Dt 24:3	hand, and **s** her out of his house;	7971
1Ki 17:14	until the day that the Lord **s** rain	5414
Ps 147:15	He **s** forth his commandment upon	7971
Ps 147:18	He **s** out his word, and melteth	7971
Pr 26:6	**s** a message by the hand of a fool	7971
Mt 5:45	**and s rain on the just and on the**	*1026*
Mk 11:1	he **s** forth two of his disciples	*649*
Mk 14:13	And he **s** forth two of his disciples,	*649*
Lk 14:32	**he s an ambassage, and desireth**	*649*

SENDING

2Sa 13:16	this evil in **s** me away is greater	7971
Ps 78:49	by **s** evil angels among them	4917
Jer 7:25	daily rising up early and **s** them:	7971
Jer 25:4	prophets, rising early and **s** them;	7971
Jer 26:5	both rising up early, and **s** them	7971
Jer 29:19	rising up early and **s** them;	7971
Jer 35:15	rising up early and **s** them,	7971
Jer 44:4	prophets, rising early and **s** them,	7971
Ro 8:3	God **s** his own Son in the likeness	*3992*

SENSE

Ne 8:8	of God distinctly, and gave the **s**,	7922

SENSES

Heb 5:14	have their **s** exercised to discern	*145*

SENSUAL

Jas 3:15	above but is earthly, **s**, devilish	*5591*
Jude 19	**s**, having not the Spirit	*5591*

SENT

Ge 3:23	Lord God **s** him forth from … Eden	7971
Ge 8:12	**s** forth the dove; which returned	7971
Ge 19:13	the Lord hath **s** us to destroy it	7971
Ge 19:29	and **s** Lot out of the midst of the	7971
Ge 31:42	thou hadst **s** me away now empty	7971
Ge 37:32	they **s** the coat of many colours	7971
Ge 38:25	she **s** to her father in law, saying	7971
Ge 45:7	God **s** me before you to preserve	7971
Ge 45:8	it was not you that **s** me hither,	7971
Ex 3:14	of Israel, I Am hath **s** me unto you	7971
Nu 14:36	which Moses **s** to search the land	7971
Nu 16:28	shall know that the Lord hath **s** me	7971
Nu 21:6	Lord **s** fiery serpents among the	7971
Dt 24:4	former husband, which **s** her away,	7971
Jos 6:17	she hid the messengers that we **s**	7971
Jos 14:11	I was in the day that Moses **s** me:	7971
Jgs 6:14	the Midianites: have not I **s** thee?	7971
Jgs 7:8	he **s** all the rest of Israel every	7971
Jgs 9:23	Then God **s** an evil spirit between	7971
Jgs 11:38	And he **s** her away for two months:	7971
Jgs 20:6	**s** her throughout all the country	7971
1Sa 3:10	answered, Speak; for thy **s** heareth	5650
1Sa 12:8	then the Lord **s** Moses and Aaron,	7971
1Sa 12:18	Lord **s** thunder and rain that day:	5414
1Sa 15:1	The Lord **s** me to anoint thee to be	7971
1Sa 19:14	Saul **s** messengers to take David	7971
1Sa 20:22	for the Lord hath **s** thee away	7971
2Sa 10:4	to their buttocks, and **s** them away	7971
2Sa 11:1	that David **s** Joab, and his servants	7971
2Sa 11:4	David **s** messengers, and took her;	7971
2Sa 11:5	**s** and told David, and said, I am	7971
2Sa 11:14	and **s** it by the hand of Uriah	7971
2Sa 12:1	the Lord **s** Nathan unto David	7971
2Sa 15:10	Absalom **s** spies throughout all	7971
2Sa 24:13	I shall return to him that **s** me	7971
2Sa 24:15	So the Lord **s** a pestilence upon	5414
1Ki 2:42	king **s** and called for Shimei	7971

1Ki	14:6	I am **s** to thee with heavy tidings	7971
1Ki	20:7	for he **s** unto me for my wives, and	7971
1Ki	21:11	did as Jezebel had **s** unto them	7971
2Ki	1:6	turn again unto the king that **s** you,	7971
2Ki	1:9	the king **s** unto him a captain of	7971
2Ki	1:11	he **s** unto him another captain of	7971
2Ki	1:13	he **s** again a captain of the third	7971
2Ki	5:8	rent his clothes, that he **s** to the king,	7971
2Ki	5:22	My master hath **s** me, saying	7971
2Ki	6:32	how this son of a murderer hath **s**	7971
2Ki	11:4	Jehoiada **s** and fetched the rulers	7971
2Ki	17:26	he hath **s** lions among them, and,	7971
2Ki	18:17	the king of Assyria **s** Tartan and	7971
2Ki	18:27	my master **s** me to thy master, and	7971
2Ki	19:4	hath **s** to reproach the living God;	7971
2Ki	24:2	**s** them against Judah to destroy it	7971
1Ch	19:3	he hath **s** comforters unto thee?	7971
1Ch	19:4	their buttocks, and **s** them away	7971
1Ch	21:14	Lord **s** pestilence upon Israel:	5414
1Ch	21:15	God **s** an angel unto Jerusalem to	7971
2Ch	24:19	he **s** prophets to them, to bring	7971
2Ch	25:15	he **s** unto him a prophet, which	7971
2Ch	34:26	who **s** you to enquire of the Lord	7971
Ezr	4:11	copy of the letter that they **s** unto	7972
Ezr	4:17	**s** the king an answer unto Rehum	7972
Ezr	5:7	They **s** a letter unto him, wherein	7972
Ezr	6:13	that which Darius the king had **s**	7972
Ne	6:3	I **s** messengers unto them, saying	7971
Ne	6:12	I perceived that God had not **s** him;	7971
Est	1:22	For he **s** letters into all the king's	7971
Est	3:13	letters were **s** by posts into all the	7971
Est	4:4	she **s** raiment to clothe Mordecai,	7971
Est	8:10	and **s** letters by posts on horseback,	7971
Est	9:20	and **s** letters unto all the Jews that	7971
Est	9:30	he **s** the letters unto all the Jews,	7971
Ps	18:14	Yea, he **s** out his arrows, and	7971
Ps	18:16	He **s** from above, he took me, he	7971
Ps	105:26	He **s** Moses his servant; and Aaron	7971
Ps	105:28	He **s** darkness, and made it dark;	7971
Ps	106:15	but **s** leanness into their soul	7971
Ps	111:9	He **s** redemption unto his people:	7971
Pr	17:11	messenger shall be **s** against him	7971
Isa	9:8	The Lord **s** a word into Jacob, and	7971
Isa	37:4	hath **s** to reproach the living God,	7971
Isa	37:17	hath **s** to reproach the living God	7971
Isa	42:19	or deaf, as my messenger that I **s**?	7971
Isa	48:16	God, and his Spirit, hath **s** me	7971
Isa	55:11	prosper in the thing whereto I **s** it	7971
Isa	61:1	**s** me to bind up the brokenhearted,	7971
Jer	14:14	I **s** them not, neither have I	7971
Jer	14:15	I **s** them not, yet they say, Sword	7971
Jer	23:21	I have not **s** these prophets, yet	7971
Jer	25:4	hath **s** unto you all his servants the	7971
Jer	26:5	the prophets, whom I **s** unto you,	7971
Jer	26:15	Lord hath **s** me unto you to speak	7971
Jer	27:15	I have not **s** them, saith the Lord,	7971
Jer	28:9	that the Lord hath truly **s** him	7971
Jer	28:15	The Lord hath not **s** thee; but thou	7971
Jer	29:1	the prophet **s** from Jerusalem unto	7971
Jer	29:9	I have not **s** them, saith the Lord	7971
Jer	29:19	I **s** unto them by my servants the	7971
Jer	29:28	therefore he **s** unto us in Babylon,	7971
Jer	29:31	I **s** him not, and he caused you to	7971
Jer	35:15	**s** also unto you all my servants the	7971
Jer	37:7	**s** you unto me to enquire of me;	7971
Jer	37:17	Zedekiah the king **s**, and took him	7971
Jer	38:14	Then Zedekiah the king **s**, and took	7971
Jer	39:14	Even they **s**, and took Jeremiah	7971
Jer	42:20	ye **s** me unto the Lord your God,	7971
Jer	43:2	Lord our God hath not **s** thee to	7971
Jer	44:4	I **s** unto you all my servants the	7971
La	1:13	From above hath he **s** fire into my	7971
Eze	2:9	behold, an hand was **s** unto me;	7971
Eze	3:5	For thou art not **s** to a people of a	7971
Eze	3:6	Surely, had I **s** thee to them, they	7971
Eze	13:6	and the Lord hath not **s** them: and	7971
Da	3:28	the God … who hath **s** his angel,	7972
Da	5:24	the part of the hand **s** from him;	7972
Da	6:22	My God hath **s** his angel, and hath	7972
Da	10:11	upright: for unto thee am I now **s**	7971
Joel	2:25	great army which I **s** among you	7971
Jnh	1:4	the Lord **s** out a great wind into	2904
Mic	6:4	I **s** before thee Moses, Aaron, and	7971
Zec	1:10	the Lord hath **s** to walk to and fro	7971
Zec	2:8	he **s** me unto the nations which	7971
Zec	2:9	that the Lord of hosts hath **s** me	7971
Zec	2:11	Lord of hosts hath **s** me unto thee	7971
Zec	4:9	Lord of hosts hath **s** me unto you	7971
Zec	6:15	Lord of hosts hath **s** me unto you	7971
Zec	7:12	Lord of hosts hath **s** in his spirit	7971
Mt	2:16	**s** forth, and slew all the children	*649*
Mt	10:5	These twelve Jesus **s** forth, and	*649*
Mt	10:40	**receiveth me receiveth him that s me.**	*649*
Mt	15:24	**I am not s but unto the lost sheep**	*649*
Mt	21:37	**last of all he s unto them his son,**	*649*
Mt	22:3	**s forth his servants to call them**	*649*
Mt	22:4	**he s forth other servants, saying,**	*649*
Mt	22:7	**s forth his armies, and destroyed**	*3992*
Mt	23:37	**stonest them which are s unto thee,**	*649*
Mt	27:19	his wife **s** unto him, saying, Have	*649*
Mk	6:27	the king **s** an executioner, and	*649*
Mk	9:37	**receiveth not me, him that s me**	*649*
Mk	12:3	**beat him, and s him away empty**	*649*
Mk	12:4	**s him away shamefully handled**	*649*
Mk	12:6	**he s him also last unto them.**	*649*
Lk	1:26	the angel Gabriel was **s** from God	*649*
Lk	1:53	the rich he hath **s** empty away	*1821*
Lk	4:18	**s me to heal the brokenhearted, to**	*649*
Lk	4:43	**cities also: for therefore am I s**	*649*
Lk	7:20	John Baptist hath **s** us unto thee,	*649*
Lk	9:2	he **s** them to preach the kingdom	*649*
Lk	9:48	**receive me receiveth him that s me:**	*649*
Lk	10:1	**s** them two and two before his face	*649*
Lk	10:16	**me, despiseth him that s me.**	*649*
Lk	13:34	**stonest them that are s unto thee;**	*649*
Lk	15:15	**s him into his fields to feed swine.**	*3992*
Lk	19:14	**and s a message after him, saying,**	*649*
Lk	20:10	**he s a servant to the husbandmen**	*640*
Lk	20:10	**beat him, and s him away empty**	*1821*
Lk	20:11	**And again he s another servant:**	*3992*
Lk	20:11	**shamefully … s him away empty**	*1821*
Lk	20:12	**And again he s a third: and they**	*3992*
Lk	20:20	**s** forth spies, which should feign	*649*
Lk	22:35	**When I s you without purse, and**	*649*
Lk	23:7	he **s** him to Herod, who himself	*375*
Lk	23:11	robe, and **s** him again to Pilate	*375*
Lk	23:15	nor yet Herod: for I **s** you to him;	*375*
Jn	1:6	There was a man **s** from God	*649*
Jn	1:8	was **s** to bear witness of that Light	
Jn	1:19	Jews **s** priests and Levites from	*649*
Jn	1:22	give an answer to them that **s** us	*3992*
Jn	3:17	**God s not his Son into the world to**	*649*

Jn 3:28 Christ, but that I am **s** before him *649*
Jn 4:34 is to do the will of him that **s** me,...... *3992*
Jn 4:38 I **s** you to reap that whereon ye *649*
Jn 5:24 believeth on him that **s** me, hath *3992*
Jn 5:30 will of the Father which hath **s** me..... *3992*
Jn 5:36 of me, that the Father hath **s** me........ *649*
Jn 5:37 Father himself, which hath **s** me, ... *3992*
Jn 5:38 whom he hath **s**, him ye believe not..... *649*
Jn 6:29 ye believe on him whom he hath **s**...... *649*
Jn 6:38 will, but the will of him **s** me.......... *3992*
Jn 6:39 the Father's will which hath **s** me, ... *3992*
Jn 6:40 this is the will of him that **s** me,....... *3992*
Jn 6:44 Father which hath **s** me draw him:..... *3992*
Jn 6:57 As the living Father hath **s** me,......... *649*
Jn 7:16 is not mine, but his that **s** me.......... *3992*
Jn 7:18 that seeketh his glory that **s** him,...... *3992*
Jn 7:28 that **s** me is true, whom ye know not ... *3992*
Jn 7:29 am from him, and he hath **s** me *649*
Jn 7:33 and then I go unto him that **s** me....... *3992*
Jn 8:16 but I and the Father that **s** me *3992*
Jn 8:18 Father that **s** me beareth witness of.... *3992*
Jn 8:26 he that **s** me is true; and I apeak....... *3992*
Jn 8:29 that **s** me is with me: the Father *3992*
Jn 8:42 came I of myself, but he **s** me *649*
Jn 9:4 work the works of him that **s** me,....... *3992*
Jn 10:36 sanctified, and **s** into the world *649*
Jn 11:42 may believe that thou hast **s** me........ *649*
Jn 12:44 not on me, but on him that **s** me *3992*
Jn 12:45 that seeth me seeth him that **s** me...... *3992*
Jn 12:49 the Father which **s** me, he gave........ *3992*
Jn 13:16 is **s** greater than he that **s** him.......... *652*
Jn 13:20 me receiveth him that **s** me. *3992*
Jn 14:24 mine, but the Father's which **s** me *3992*
Jn 15:21 they know not him that **s** me.......... *3992*
Jn 16:5 I go my way to him that **s** me; *3992*
Jn 17:3 Jesus Christ, whom thou hast **s** *649*
Jn 17:18 As thou hast **s** me into the world, ... *649*
Jn 17:18 have I also **s** them into the world. *649*
Jn 17:21 may believe that thou hast **s** me *649*
Jn 17:23 may know that thou hast **s** me,......... *649*
Jn 17:25 have known that thou hast **s** me........ *649*
Jn 18:24 had **s** him bound unto Caiaphas........ *649*
Jn 20:21 Father hath **s** me, even so send I you.... *649*
Ac 12:11 that the Lord hath **s** his angel *1821*
Ac 13:4 being **s** forth by the Holy Ghost *1599*
Ac 24:26 wherefore he **s** for him the oftener,..... *3343*
Ac 28:28 salvation ... is **s** unto the Gentiles *649*
Ro 10:15 shall they preach, except they be **s**?...... *649*
Gal 4:4 God **s** forth his Son, made of a *1821*
Gal 4:6 God hath **s** forth the Spirit of his *1821*
1Th 3:5 I **s** to know your faith, lest by some *375*
Heb 1:14 **s** forth to minister for them who *649*
Jas 2:25 and had **s** them out another way?...... *1524*
1Pe 1:12 Holy Ghost **s** down from heaven;....... *649*
1Jn 4:9 God **s** his only begotten Son into *649*
1Jn 4:10 and **s** his Son to be the propitiation *649*
1Jn 4:14 Father **s** the Son to be the Saviour *649*
Rev 1:1 he **s** and signified it by his angel *649*
Rev 5:6 seven Spirits of God **s** forth into all *649*
Rev 22:6 God of the holy prophets **s** his angel *649*
Rev 22:16 Jesus have **s** mine angel to testify *3992*

SENTENCE

Dt 17:9 shall shew thee the **s** of judgment: 1697
Pr 16:10 divine **s** is in the lips of the king: 7081
Ecc 8:11 **s** against an evil work is not 6599
Lk 23:24 Pilate gave **s** that it should be *1948*
2Co 1:9 we had the **s** of death in ourselves,...... *610*

SEPARATE

Le 22:2 **s** themselves from the holy things...... 5144
Nu 6:2 to **s** themselves unto the Lord: 5144
Nu 6:3 He shall **s** himself from wine and...... 5144
Nu 8:14 thou **s** the Levites from among the...... 914
Nu 16:21 **S** yourselves from among this 914
1Ki 8:53 **s** them from among all the people 914
Ezr 10:11 **s** yourselves from the people of the 914
Eze 42:13 which are before the **s** place, they...... 1508
Mt 25:32 he shall **s** them one from another, ... *873*
Lk 6:22 shall **s** you from their company,........ *873*
Ac 13:2 **S** me Barnabas and Saul for the *873*
Ro 8:35 shall **s** us from the love of Christ?...... *5562*
Ro 8:39 able to **s** us from the love of God....... *5562*
2Co 6:17 them, and be ye **s**, saith the Lord,....... *873*
Heb 7:26 undefiled, **s** from sinners, and......... *5562*
Jude 19 These be they who **s** themselves,........ *592*

SEPARATED

Ge 25:23 two manner of people shall be **s**....... 6504
Le 20:24 have **s** you from other people 914
Le 20:25 I have **s** from you as unclean. 914
Nu 16:9 God of Israel hath **s** you from the....... 914
Dt 10:8 time the Lord **s** the tribe of Levi, ... 914
Dt 32:8 when he **s** the sons of Adam, he 6504
Dt 33:16 him that was **s** from his brethren....... 5139
1Ch 23:13 and Aaron was **s**, that he should 914
2Ch 25:10 Then Amaziah **s** them, to wit, the....... 914
Ezr 9:1 not **s** themselves from the people of..... 914
Ezr 10:8 himself **s** from the congregation of 914
Ne 9:2 seed of Israel **s** themselves from 914
Ne 10:28 all they that had **s** themselves from 914
Ne 13:3 they **s** from Israel all the mixed......... 914
Pr 18:1 a man, having **s** himself, seeketh....... 6504
Pr 19:4 the poor is **s** from his neighbour 6504
Isa 59:2 your iniquities have **s** between you...... 914
Hos 4:14 themselves are **s** with whores 6504
Hos 9:10 **s** themselves unto that shame;......... 5144
Ro 1:1 apostle, **s** unto the gospel of God,....... *873*
Gal 1:15 who **s** me from my mother's womb *873*

SEPARATETH

Nu 6:5 which he **s** himself unto the Lord, ... 5144
Nu 6:6 that he **s** himself unto the Lord........ 5144
Pr 16:28 and a whisperer **s** chief friends 6504
Pr 17:9 repeateth a matter **s** very friends....... 6504
Eze 14:7 which **s** himself from me, and......... 5144

SEPARATING

Zec 7:3 **s** myself, as I have done these so 5144

SEPARATION

Le 12:2 according to the days of the **s** for 5079
Le 12:5 be unclean two weeks, as in her **s**: 5079
Le 15:25 if it run beyond the time of her **s**; 5079
Nu 6:4 All the days of his **s** shall he eat........ 5145
Nu 6:5 vow of his **s** there shall no razor 5145
Nu 6:8 the days of his **s** he is holy unto 5145
Nu 6:12 be lost, because his **s** was defiled. 5145
Nu 6:13 when the days of his **s** are fulfilled:..... 5145
Nu 6:21 he must do after the law of his **s**....... 5145
Nu 19:9 children of Israel for a water of **s**:...... 5079
Nu 31:23 be purified with the water of **s**:........ 5079
Eze 42:20 to make a **s** between the sanctuary...... 914

SEPULCHRE

Dt	34:6	but no man knoweth of his **s**	6900
1Sa	10:2	shalt find two men by Rachel's **s**	6900
1Ki	13:22	not come unto the **s** of thy fathers	6913
1Ki	13:31	**s** wherein the man of God is buried;	6913
2Ki	13:21	cast the man into the **s** of Elisha:	6913
2Ki	23:17	It is the **s** of the man of God	6913
Ps	5:9	their throat is an open **s**; they	6913
Isa	22:16	that heweth him out a **s** on high	6913
Jer	5:16	Their quiver is as an open **s**, they	6913
Mt	27:60	a great stone to the door of the **s**,	*3419*
Mt	27:64	**s** be made sure until the third day	*5028*
Mt	28:8	they departed quickly from the **s**	*3419*
Mk	16:3	the stone from the door of the **s**?	*3419*
Mk	16:5	And entering into the **s**, they saw	*3419*
Mk	16:8	out quickly, and fled from the **s**;	*3419*
Lk	24:2	the stone rolled away from the **s**	*3419*
Lk	24:9	returned from the **s**, and told all	*3419*
Lk	24:12	arose Peter, and ran unto the **s**;	*3419*
Lk	24:22	which were early at the **s**;	*3419*
Lk	24:24	which were with us went to the **s**,	*3419*
Jn	19:41	in the garden a new **s**, wherein	*3419*
Jn	19:42	day; for the **s** was nigh at hand	*3419*
Jn	20:1	when it was yet dark, unto the **s**	*3419*
Jn	20:2	taken away the Lord out of the **s**	*3419*
Jn	20:4	outrun Peter, and came ... to the **s**	*3419*
Jn	20:6	and went into the **s**, and seeth the	*3419*
Jn	20:8	disciple, which came first to the **s**,	*3419*
Jn	20:11	But Mary stood without at the **s**	*3419*
Ac	2:29	his **s** is with us unto this day	*3418*
Ac	13:29	from the tree, and laid him in a **s**	*3419*
Ro	3:13	Their throat is an open **s**; with	*5028*

SEPULCHRES

2Ki	23:16	and took the bones out of the **s**, and	6913
2Ch	21:20	but not in the **s** of the kings	6913
2Ch	24:25	buried him not in the **s** of the kings	6913
2Ch	28:27	him not into the **s** of the kings of	6913
Ne	2:3	the city, the place of my father's **s**	6913
Mt	23:27	**ye are like unto whited s, which**	*5028*
Mt	23:29	**garnish the s of the righteous,**	*3419*
Lk	11:47	**for ye build the s of the prophets,**	*3419*

SERPENT

Ge	3:1	**s** was more subtil than any beast	5175
Ge	3:4	**s** said unto the woman, Ye shall not	5175
Ge	3:13	The **s** beguiled me, and I did eat	5175
Ge	3:14	Lord God said unto the **s**, Because	5175
Ex	4:3	on the ground, and it became a **s**;	5175
Ex	7:9	Pharaoh, and it shall become a **s**	8577
Ex	7:15	the rod which was turned to a **s**	5175
Nu	21:9	Moses made a **s** of brass, and put	5175
Nu	21:9	when he beheld the **s** of brass, he	5175
2Ki	18:4	the brasen **s** that Moses had made:	5175
Ps	58:4	poison is like the poison of a **s**:	5175
Ps	140:3	sharpened their tongues like a **s**;	5175
Pr	23:32	At the last it biteth like a **s**, and	5175
Pr	30:19	the way of a **s** upon a rock; the way	5175
Ecc	10:11	**s** will bite without enchantment;	5175
Isa	14:29	his fruit shall be a fiery flying **s**	8314
Isa	27:1	punish leviathan the piercing **s**	5175
Isa	30:6	lion, the viper and fiery flying **s**,	8314
Jer	46:22	voice thereof shall go like a **s**;	5175
Am	5:19	hand on the wall, and a **s** bit him.	5175
Mic	7:17	They shall lick the dust like a **s**,	5175
Mt	7:10	**ask a fish, will he give him a s?**	*3789*
Lk	11:11	**will he for a fish give him a s?**	*3789*
Jn	3:14	**as Moses lifted up the s in the**	*3789*
2Co	11:3	as the **s** beguiled Eve through his	*3789*
Rev	12:9	old **s**, called the Devil, and Satan,	*3789*
Rev	12:14	half a time, from the face of the **s**	*3789*
Rev	12:15	the **s** cast out of his mouth water	*3789*
Rev	20:2	old **s**, which is the Devil, and Satan,	*3789*

SERPENTS

Ex	7:12	man his rod, and they became **s**:	8577
Nu	21:6	the Lord sent fiery **s** among the	5175
Dt	8:15	wilderness, wherein were fiery **s**,	5175
Mt	10:16	**be ye therefore wise as s, and**	*3789*
Mt	23:33	**Ye s, ye generation of vipers, how**	*3789*
Mk	16:18	**They shall take up s; and if they**	*3789*
Lk	10:19	**power to tread on s and scorpions,**	*3789*
1Co	10:9	tempted, and were destroyed of **s**	*3789*
Rev	9:19	for their tails were like unto **s**	*3789*

SERVANT

Ge	9:25	a **s** of servants shall he be unto	5650
Ge	9:27	Shem; ... Canaan shall be his **s**	5650
Ge	19:19	thy **s** hath found grace in thy sight	5650
Ge	24:61	the **s** took Rebekah, and went his	5650
Ge	26:24	thy seed for my **s** Abraham's sake	5650
Ge	33:20	Behold, thy **s** Jacob is behind us	5650
Ge	39:17	Hebrew **s**, which thou hast brought	5650
Ge	44:17	the cup is found, he shall be my **s**;	5650
Ge	44:32	thy **s** became surety for the lad	5650
Ge	44:33	let thy **s** abide instead of the lad a	5650
Ex	12:45	an hired **s** shall not eat thereof	7916
Ex	14:31	believed the Lord, and his **s** Moses	5650
Ex	21:2	If thou buy an Hebrew **s**, six years	5650
Ex	21:5	If the **s** shall plainly say, I love my	5650
Ex	21:20	if a man smite his **s**, or his maid	5650
Ex	33:11	but his **s** Joshua, the son of Nun,	8334
Le	22:10	hired **s**, shall not eat of the holy	7916
Le	25:50	according to the time of an hired **s**	7916
Nu	11:11	hast thou afflicted thy **s**? and	5650
Nu	11:28	the son of Nun, the **s** of Moses,	8334
Nu	12:7	My **s** Moses is not so, who is	5650
Nu	12:8	to speak against my **s** Moses?	5650
Nu	14:24	But my **s** Caleb, because he had	5650
Dt	3:24	begun to shew thy **s** thy greatness,	5650
Dt	15:17	door, and he shall be thy **s** for ever	5650
Dt	23:15	not deliver unto his master the **s**	5650
Dt	34:5	So Moses the **s** of the Lord died	5650
Jos	1:7	Moses my **s** commanded thee:	5650
Jos	5:14	What saith my lord unto his **s**?	5650
Jos	11:15	the Lord commanded Moses his **s**,	5650
Jos	14:7	Moses the **s** of the Lord sent me	5650
Jos	22:5	Moses the **s** of the Lord charged	5650
Jgs	19:9	he, and his concubine, and his **s**	5288
1Sa	9:27	Saul, Bid the **s** pass on before us	5288
1Sa	17:32	thy **s** will go and fight with this	5650
1Sa	19:4	Let not the king sin against his **s**,	5650
1Sa	20:8	hast brought thy **s** into a covenant	5650
1Sa	22:8	hath stirred up my **s** against me	5650
1Sa	22:15	for thy **s** knew nothing of all this	5650
1Sa	25:39	and hath kept his **s** from evil: for	5650
1Sa	25:41	handmaid be a **s** to wash the feet	5650
1Sa	26:19	the king hear the words of his **s**	5650
2Sa	3:18	By the hand of my **s** David I will	5650
2Sa	7:5	Go and tell my **s** David, Thus saith	5650
2Sa	7:25	thou hast spoken concerning thy **s**	5650
2Sa	7:26	and let the house of thy **s** David be	5650

2Sa	11:24	and thy **s** Uriah the Hittite is dead	5650
2Sa	13:18	Then his **s** brought her out, and	8334
2Sa	14:19	thy **s** Joab, he bade me, and he	5650
2Sa	15:21	or life, even there also will thy **s** be	5650
2Sa	15:34	Absalom, I will be thy **s**, O king;	5650
2Sa	19:20	thy **s** doth know … I have sinned:	5650
2Sa	19:26	My lord, O king, my **s** deceived me:	5650
2Sa	24:10	take away the iniquity of thy **s**;	5650
1Ki	1:19	Solomon thy **s** hath he not called	5650
1Ki	1:51	to day that he will not slay his **s**	5650
1Ki	2:38	the king hath said, so will thy **s** do	5650
1Ki	3:9	Give … thy **s** an understanding	5650
1Ki	8:26	thou spakest unto thy **s** David my	5650
1Ki	8:59	that he maintain the cause of his **s**	5650
1Ki	11:11	from thee, and will give it to thy **s**	5650
1Ki	11:32	one tribe for my **s** David's sake	5650
1Ki	18:12	I thy **s** fear the Lord from my youth	5650
1Ki	20:40	as thy **s** was busy here and there,	5650
2Ki	4:1	saying, Thy **s** my husband is dead;	5650
2Ki	5:18	the Lord pardon thy **s** in this thing	5650
2Ki	8:13	said, But what, is thy **s** a dog,	5650
2Ki	18:12	Moses … **s** of the Lord commanded	5650
2Ki	24:1	Jehoiakim became his **s** three years	5650
1Ch	17:24	house of David thy **s** be established	5650
1Ch	21:8	thee, do away the iniquity of thy **s**;	5650
2Ch	6:21	unto the supplications of thy **s**	5650
Ne	1:6	mayest hear the prayer of thy **s**	5650
Ne	10:29	was given by Moses the **s** of God	5650
Job	1:8	Hast thou considered my **s** Job,	5650
Job	2:3	Hast thou considered my **s** Job,	5650
Job	41:4	wilt thou take him for a **s** for ever?	5650
Job	42:7	that is right, as my **s** Job hath	5650
Job	42:8	and my **s** Job shall pray for you:	5650
Job	42:8	thing which is right, like my **s** Job	5650
Ps	19:11	by them is thy **s** warned: and in	5650
Ps	19:13	thy **s** also from presumptuous sins;	5650
Ps	31:16	Make thy face to shine upon thy **s**	5650
Ps	86:2	save thy **s** that trusteth in thee	5650
Ps	89:3	I have sworn unto David my **s**,	5650
Ps	105:17	even Joseph, who was sold for a **s**	5650
Ps	116:16	O Lord, truly I am thy **s**;	5650
Ps	119:84	How many are the days of thy **s**?	5650
Ps	119:140	very pure: therefore thy **s** loveth it	5650
Ps	119:176	astray like a lost sheep; seek thy **s**;	5650
Ps	143:2	enter not into judgment with thy **s**	5650
Pr	11:29	and the fool shall be **s** to the wise	5650
Pr	12:9	He that is despised, and hath a **s**,	5650
Pr	14:35	king's favour is toward a wise **s**:	5650
Pr	17:2	A wise **s** shall have rule over a son	5650
Pr	19:10	much less for a **s** to have rule over	5650
Pr	22:7	and the borrower is **s** to the lender.	5650
Pr	29:19	A **s** will not be corrected by words:	5650
Pr	29:21	He that delicately bringeth up his **s**	5650
Pr	30:10	Accuse not a **s** unto his master,	5650
Pr	30:22	For a **s** when he reigneth; and a	5650
Ecc	7:21	lest thou hear thy **s** curse thee:	5650
Isa	20:3	Like as my **s** Isaiah hath walked	5650
Isa	24:2	as with the **s**, so with his master;	5650
Isa	41:8	But thou, Israel, art my **s**, Jacob	5650
Isa	42:1	Behold my **s**, whom I uphold; mine	5650
Isa	42:19	Who is blind, but my **s**? or deaf, as	5650
Isa	42:19	perfect, and blind as the Lord's **s**?	5650
Isa	43:10	and my **s** whom I have chosen:	5650
Isa	48:20	Lord hath redeemed his **s** Jacob	5650
Isa	49:3	my **s**, O Israel, in whom I will be	5650
Isa	49:5	me from the womb to be his **s**,	5650
Isa	49:6	thing that thou shouldest be my **s**	5650
Isa	49:7	nation abhorreth, to a **s** of rulers	5650
Isa	52:13	Behold, my **s** shall deal prudently,	5650
Isa	53:11	shall my righteous **s** justify many;	5650
Jer	2:14	Is Israel a **s**? is he a homeborn	5650
Jer	25:9	and … the king of Babylon, my **s**	5650
Jer	30:10	fear thou not, O my **s** Jacob, saith	5650
Jer	33:21	covenant be broken with David my **s**,	5650
Jer	34:16	and caused every man his **s**, and	5650
Jer	43:10	take … the king of Babylon, my **s**	5650
Jer	46:27	But fear not thou, O my **s** Jacob	5650
Jer	46:28	Fear thou not, O Jacob my **s**, saith	5650
Eze	28:24	land … I have given to my **s** Jacob	5650
Eze	34:24	my **s** David a prince among them;	5650
Eze	37:24	David my **s** shall be king over them;	5650
Da	6:20	O Daniel, **s** of the living God, is	5649
Da	9:11	in the law of Moses the **s** of God,	5650
Zec	3:8	I will bring forth my **s** the BRANCH.	5650
Mal	1:6	son … his father, and a **s** his master:	5650
Mal	4:4	Remember ye the law of Moses my **s**,	5650
Mt	8:13	his **s** was sealed in the selfsame	*3816*
Mt	10:24	**master, nor the s above his lord**	*1401*
Mt	12:18	Behold my **s**, whom I have chosen;	*3816*
Mt	18:32	**O thou wicked s, I forgave thee**	*1401*
Mt	20:27	**chief among you, let him be your s**	*1401*
Mt	23:11	**greatest among you shall be your s**	*1249*
Mt	24:45	**Who then is a faithful and wise s,**	*401*
Mt	24:46	**Blessed is that s, whom his lord**	*1401*
Mt	24:48	**if that evil s shall say in his heart,**	*1401*
Mt	24:50	**lord of that s shall come in a day.**	*1401*
Mt	25:21	**done, thou good and faithful s:**	*1401*
Mt	25:23	**Well done, good and faithful s;**	*1401*
Mt	25:26	**Thou wicked and slothful s, thou.**	*1401*
Mt	25:30	**unprofitable s into outer darkness:**	*1401*
Mt	26:51	and struck a **s** of the high priest's	*1401*
Mk	9:35	**shall be last of all, and s of all**	*1249*
Mk	10:44	**be the chiefest, shall be s of all**	*1401*
Lk	2:29	lettest thou thy **s** depart in peace	*1401*
Lk	7:2	a certain centurion's **s**, who was	*1401*
Lk	7:7	a word, and my **s** shall be healed.	*3816*
Lk	7:8	to my **s**, Do this, and he doeth it.	*1401*
Lk	12:43	**Blessed is that s, whom his lord**	*1401*
Lk	12:45	**But and if that s say in his heart,**	*1401*
Lk	12:46	**lord of that s will come in a day**	*1401*
Lk	12:47	**that s, which knew his lord's will,**	*1401*
Lk	14:17	**And sent his s at supper time to**	*1401*
Lk	14:22	**lord said unto his s, Go out into**	*1401*
Lk	16:13	**No s can serve two masters: for**	*3610*
Lk	17:9	**Doth he thank that s because he**	*1401*
Lk	19:17	**said unto him, Well, thou good s**	*1401*
Lk	19:22	**will I judge thee, thou wicked s**	*1401*
Lk	20:10	**he sent a s to the husbandmen,**	*1401*
Lk	20:11	**And again he sent another s: and**	*1401*
Lk	22:50	them smote the **s** of the high priest,	*1401*
Jn	8:34	**committeth sin is the s of sin**	*1401*
Jn	8:35	**the s abideth not in the house for**	*1401*
Jn	12:26	**I am, there shall also my s be:**	*1249*
Jn	13:16	**The s is not greater than his lord;**	*1401*
Jn	15:15	**s knoweth not what his lord doeth:**	*1401*
Jn	15:20	**The s is not greater than his lord.**	*1401*
Jn	18:10	and smote the high priest's **s**, and	1401
Ro	14:4	that judgest another man's **s**?	*3610*
1Co	7:21	Art thou called being a **s**? care	*1401*
1Co	7:22	is called, being free, is Christ's **s**.	*1401*
1Co	9:19	yet have I made myself **s** unto all,	*1402*
Gal	1:10	I should not be the **s** of Christ.	*1401*

Gal	4:1	a child, differeth nothing from a **s**	*1401*
Gal	4:7	Wherefore thou art no more a **s**	*1401*
Php	2:7	and took upon him the form of a **s**	*1401*
Col	4:12	who is one of you, a **s** of Christ,	*1401*
2Ti	2:24	the **s** of the Lord must not strive;	*1401*
Phm	16	Not now as a **s**, but above a **s**,	*1401*
Heb	3:5	faithful in all his house, as a **s**,	*2324*
Rev	1:1	it by his angel unto his **s** John:	*1401*
Rev	15:3	sing the song of Moses the **s** of God,	*1401*

SERVANT'S

2Sa	7:19	hast spoken also of thy **s** house,	5650
1Ch	17:17	hast also spoken of thy **s** house	5650
Isa	45:4	For Jacob my **s** sake, and Israel	5650
Jn	18:10	ear. The **s** name was Malchus	*1401*

SERVANTS

Ge	9:25	a servant of **s** shall he be unto his	5650
Ge	41:10	Pharaoh was wroth with his **s**, and	5650
Ge	42:11	we are true men, thy **s** are no spies	5650
Ge	42:13	Thy **s** are twelve brethren, the sons	5650
Ge	47:3	Thy **s** are shepherds, both we, and	5650
Ge	47:19	and we and our land will be **s** unto	5650
Ge	50:2	commanded his **s** the physicians	5650
Ex	5:15	dealest thou thus with thy **s**?	5650
Ex	5:16	There is no straw given unto thy **s**,	5650
Ex	9:14	upon thine heart, and upon thy **s**	5650
Ex	9:20	made his **s** and his cattle flee into	5650
Ex	9:34	hardened his heart, he and his **s**	5650
Ex	11:3	in the sight of Pharaoh's **s**, and in	5650
Ex	12:30	up in the night, he, and all his **s**,	5650
Ex	14:5	the heart of Pharaoh and of his **s**	5650
Le	25:42	For they are my **s**, which I brought	5650
Nu	32:27	But thy **s** will pass over, every man	5650
Dt	9:27	Remember thy **s**, Abraham, Isaac,	5650
Dt	32:36	and repent himself for his **s**, when	5650
Dt	32:43	he will avenge the blood of his **s**,	5650
Jos	9:24	Because it was certainly told thy **s**	5650
Jgs	6:27	Then Gideon took ten men of his **s**	5650
1Sa	4:9	ye be not **s** unto the Hebrews, as	5647
1Sa	17:8	not I a Philistine, and ye **s** to Saul?	5650
1Sa	17:9	to kill me, then will we be your **s**	5650
1Sa	17:9	kill him, then shall ye be our **s**	5650
1Sa	18:30	more wisely than all the **s** of Saul;	5650
1Sa	22:17	But the **s** of the king would not put	5650
1Sa	24:7	David stayed his **s** with these words	582
1Sa	28:23	But his **s**, together with the woman	5650
2Sa	8:2	so the Moabites became David's **s**	5650
2Sa	8:6	the Syrians became **s** to David,	5650
2Sa	8:14	they of Edom became David's **s**	5650
2Sa	10:4	Hanun took David's **s**, and shaved	5650
2Sa	13:29	**s** of Absalom did unto Amnon as	5288
2Sa	14:30	Absalom's **s** set the field on fire	5650
2Sa	19:5	shamed this day the face of all thy **s**,	5650
2Sa	20:6	take thou thy lord's **s**, and pursue	5650
1Ki	3:15	and made a feast to all his **s**	5650
1Ki	8:23	covenant and mercy with thy **s**	5650
1Ki	8:36	forgive the sin of thy **s**, and of thy	5650
1Ki	10:8	happy are these thy **s**, which stand	5650
1Ki	12:7	then they will be thy **s** for ever	5650
2Ki	1:13	and the life of these fifty thy **s**, be	5650
2Ki	2:16	be with thy **s** fifty strong men;	5650
2Ki	5:13	his **s** came near, and spake unto	5650
2Ki	7:12	in the night, and said unto his **s**,	5650
2Ki	9:7	I may avenge the blood of my **s**	5650
2Ki	10:19	of Baal, all his **s**, and all his priests;	5647
2Ki	10:23	with you none of the **s** of the Lord,	5650
2Ki	12:21	his **s**, smote him, and he died;	5650
2Ki	14:5	slew his **s** which had slain the king	5650
2Ki	17:13	I sent to you by my **s** the prophets.	5650
2Ki	17:23	had said by all his **s** the prophets	5650
2Ki	21:10	Lord spake by his **s** the prophets	5650
2Ki	21:23	the **s** of Amon conspired against	5650
2Ki	24:2	he spake by his **s** the prophets	5650
2Ki	25:24	Fear not to be the **s** of the Chaldees:	5650
1Ch	18:2	the Moabites became David's **s**	5650
1Ch	18:6	and the Syrians became David's **s**	5650
1Ch	18:13	all the Edomites became David's **s**	5650
1Ch	21:3	king, are they not all my lord's **s**?	5650
2Ch	6:14	and shewest mercy unto thy **s**, that	5650
2Ch	6:23	and judge thy **s**, by requiting the	5650
2Ch	6:27	forgive the sin of thy **s**, and of thy	5650
2Ch	8:18	**s** that had knowledge of the sea;	5650
2Ch	10:7	to them, they will be thy **s** for ever	5650
2Ch	12:8	Nevertheless they shall be his **s**;	5650
2Ch	24:25	his own **s** conspired against him	5650
2Ch	25:3	slew his **s** that had killed the king	5650
2Ch	32:16	his **s** spake yet more against the	5650
2Ch	33:24	And his **s** conspired against him	5650
2Ch	36:20	they were **s** to him and his sons	5650
Ezr	5:11	We are the **s** of the God of heaven	5649
Ezr	9:11	commanded by thy **s** the prophets,	5650
Ne	1:6	for the children of Israel thy **s**, and	5650
Ne	1:11	to the prayer of thy **s**, who desire	5650
Ne	2:20	we his **s** will arise and build: but	5650
Ne	5:15	their **s** bare rule over the people:	5288
Ne	9:36	Behold, we are **s** this day, and for	5650
Ne	13:19	some of my **s** set I at the gates	5288
Job	1:15	have slain the **s** with the edge of the	5288
Job	1:16	burned up the sheep, and the **s**, and	5288
Job	1:17	and slain the **s** with the edge of the	5288
Ps	34:22	Lord redeemeth the soul of his **s**:	5650
Ps	79:10	the revenging of the blood of thy **s**	5650
Ps	90:13	let it repent thee concerning thy **s**	5650
Ps	105:25	people, to deal subtilly with his **s**	5650
Ps	113:1	Praise, O ye **s** of the Lord, praise	5650
Ps	123:2	as the eyes of **s** look unto the hand	5650
Ps	134:1	ye the Lord, all ye **s** of the Lord	5650
Ps	135:1	praise him, O ye **s** of the Lord	5650
Ps	135:9	upon Pharaoh, and upon all his **s**	5650
Ps	135:14	repent himself concerning his **s**	5650
Pr	29:12	to lies, all his **s** are wicked	8334
Ecc	10:7	princes walking as **s** upon the earth	5650
Isa	36:9	of the least of my master's **s**	5650
Isa	36:11	Speak, ... unto thy **s** in the Syrian	5650
Isa	37:5	**s** of king Hezekiah came to Isaiah	5650
Isa	54:17	the heritage of the **s** of the Lord	5650
Isa	56:6	the name of the Lord, to be his **s**	5650
Isa	65:9	inherit it, and my **s** shall dwell there	5650
Isa	65:13	**s** shall eat, but ye shall be hungry:	5650
Isa	65:13	my **s** shall drink, but ye shall be	5650
Isa	65:13	my **s** shall rejoice, but ye shall be	5650
Isa	65:14	my **s** shall sing for joy of heart, but	5650
Isa	65:15	and call his **s** by another name:	5650
Isa	66:14	Lord shall be known toward his **s**	5650
Jer	7:25	even sent unto you all my **s** the	5650
Jer	25:4	sent unto you all his **s** the prophets	5650
Jer	26:5	hearken to the words of my **s** the	5650
Jer	29:19	unto them by my **s** the prophets,	5650
Jer	34:11	caused the **s** and the handmaids	5650
Jer	35:15	I have sent also unto you all my **s**	5650
Jer	36:24	nor any of his **s** that heard all these	5650

Jer	36:31	punish him and his seed and his **s**	5650
Jer	37:2	But neither he, nor his **s**, nor the	5650
Jer	44:4	Howbeit I sent unto you all my **s**	5650
La	5:8	**S** have ruled over us: there is none	5650
Eze	38:17	I have spoken in old time by my **s**	5650
Da	1:12	Prove thy **s**, I beseech thee, ten	5650
Da	3:26	ye **s** of the most high God, come	5649
Da	3:28	delivered his **s** that trusted in him,	5649
Da	9:6	have we hearkened unto thy **s** the	5650
Da	9:10	which he set before us by his **s** the	5650
Joel	2:29	And also upon the **s** and upon the	5650
Am	3:7	revealeth his secret unto his **s** the	5650
Zec	1:6	I commanded my **s** the prophets	5650
Mt	21:35	**husbandmen took his s, and beat**	*1401*
Mt	22:10	**s went out into the highways, and**	*1401*
Mt	22:13	**said the king to the s, Bind him**	*1249*
Mt	25:19	**time the lord of those s cometh,**	*1401*
Mt	26:58	and sat with the **s**, to see the end	*5267*
Mk	13:34	**and gave authority to his s, and to**	*1401*
Mk	14:43	he sat with the **s**, and warmed	*5257*
Mk	14:65	Prophesy: and the **s** did strike him	*5257*
Lk	12:37	**Blessed are those s, whom the**	*1401*
Lk	12:38	**find them so, blessed are those s.**	*1401*
Lk	15:17	**many hired s of my father's have**	*3407*
Lk	15:19	**son: make me as one of thy hired s**	*3407*
Lk	15:22	**But the father said to his s, Bring**	*1401*
Lk	17:10	**say, We are unprofitable s: we**	*1401*
Jn	2:5	His mother saith unto the **s**	*1249*
Jn	2:9	the **s** which drew the water knew:)	*1249*
Jn	15:15	**Henceforth I call you not s;**	*1401*
Jn	18:26	One of the **s** of the high priest,	*1401*
Jn	18:36	**this world, then would my s fight,**	*5257*
Ac	16:17	are the **s** of the most high God	*1401*
Ro	6:16	his **s** ye are to whom ye obey;	*1401*
Ro	6:18	ye became the **s** of righteousness	*1402*
Ro	6:19	your members **s** to uncleanness	*1401*
Ro	6:19	your members **s** to righteousness	*1401*
Ro	6:20	when ye were the **s** of sin, ye were	*1401*
Ro	6:22	and become **s** to God, ye have your	*1402*
1Co	7:23	a price; be not ye the **s** of men	*1401*
2Co	4:5	ourselves your **s** for Jesus' sake	*1401*
Eph	6:5	**S**, be obedient to them that are	*1401*
Eph	6:6	but as the **s** of Christ, doing the	*1401*
Col	3:22	**S**, obey in all things your masters	*1401*
Col	4:1	give unto your **s** that which is just	*1401*
1Ti	6:1	as many **s** as are under the yoke	*1401*
Tit	2:9	Exhort **s** to be obedient unto their	*1401*
1Pe	2:16	maliciousness, but as the **s** of God	*1401*
1Pe	2:18	**S**, be subject to your masters	*3610*
2Pe	2:19	they … are the **s** of corruption;	*1401*
Rev	1:1	to shew unto his **s** things which	*1401*
Rev	2:20	**to teach and to seduce my s to**	*1401*
Rev	7:3	till we have sealed the **s** of our God	*1401*
Rev	10:7	hath declared to his **s** the prophets.	*1401*
Rev	11:18	reward unto thy **s** the prophets,	*1401*
Rev	19:2	hath avenged the blood of his **s** at	*1401*
Rev	19:5	Praise our God, all ye his **s**, and ye	*1401*
Rev	22:3	in it; and his **s** shall serve him:	*1401*
Rev	22:6	sent his angel to shew unto his **s**	*1401*

SERVE

Ge	15:13	is not theirs, and shall **s** them;	5647
Ge	15:14	that nation, whom they shall **s**	5647
Ge	25:23	and the elder shall **s** the younger.	5647
Ge	27:29	Let people **s** thee, and nations bow	5647
Ge	29:18	I will **s** thee seven years for Rachel	5647
Ge	29:25	did not I **s** with thee for Rachel?	5647
Ex	3:12	ye shall **s** God upon this mountain.	5647
Ex	4:23	Let my son go, that he may **s** me:	5647
Ex	8:1	people go, that they may **s** me	5647
Ex	8:20	people go, that they may **s** me	5647
Ex	9:1	my people go, that they may **s** me.	5647
Ex	9:13	my people go, that they may **s** me.	5647
Ex	10:3	my people go, that they may **s** me.	5647
Ex	10:24	Moses, and said, Go ye, **s** the Lord;	5647
Ex	12:31	and go, **s** the Lord, as ye have said	5647
Ex	14:12	better for us to **s** the Egyptians,	5647
Ex	20:5	down thyself to them, nor **s** them:	5647
Ex	21:2	servant, six years he shall **s**: and	5647
Ex	21:6	aul; and he shall **s** him for ever	5647
Ex	23:24	down to their gods, nor **s** them	5647
Ex	23:25	And ye shall **s** the Lord your God	5647
Le	25:40	shall **s** thee unto the year of jubile:	5647
Nu	8:25	thereof, and shall **s** no more:	5647
Nu	18:7	and within the vail; and ye shall **s**:	5647
Nu	18:21	for their service which they **s**, even	5647
Dt	4:19	to worship them, and **s** them, for	5647
Dt	4:28	there ye shall **s** gods, the work of	5647
Dt	5:9	thyself unto them, nor **s** them:	5647
Dt	7:4	me, that they may **s** other gods:	5647
Dt	7:16	neither shalt thou **s** their gods;	5647
Dt	8:19	walk after other gods, and **s** them,	5647
Dt	10:12	to **s** the Lord thy God with all thy	5647
Dt	11:13	and to **s** him with all your heart	5647
Dt	12:30	How did these nations **s** their gods?	5647
Dt	13:2	hast not known, and let us **s** them;	5647
Dt	13:4	and ye shall **s** him, and cleave unto	5647
Dt	13:6	Let us go and **s** other gods	5647
Dt	15:12	unto thee, and **s** thee six years;	5647
Dt	20:11	unto thee, and they shall **s** thee	5647
Dt	28:14	to go after other gods to **s** them	5647
Dt	28:36	and there shalt thou **s** other gods	5647
Dt	28:48	shalt thou **s** thine enemies which	5647
Dt	28:64	and there thou shalt **s** other gods	5647
Dt	29:18	and **s** the gods of these nations;	5647
Dt	31:20	turn unto other gods, and **s** them	5647
Jos	22:5	and to **s** him with all your heart	5647
Jos	23:7	neither **s** them, nor bow yourselves	5647
Jos	24:14	and **s** him in sincerity and in truth:	5647
Jos	24:15	choose you this day whom ye will **s**;	5647
Jos	24:15	and my house, we will **s** the Lord	5647
Jos	24:18	therefore will we also **s** the Lord;	5647
Jos	24:19	Ye cannot **s** the Lord: for he is an	5647
Jos	24:21	Nay; but we will **s** the Lord.	5647
Jos	24:22	have chosen you the Lord, to **s** him	5647
Jos	24:24	The Lord our God will we **s**, and	5647
Jgs	2:19	in following other gods to **s** them,	5647
1Sa	7:3	unto the Lord, and **s** him only:	5647
1Sa	10:7	that thou do as occasion **s** thee;	5647
1Sa	12:14	If ye will fear the Lord, and **s** him.	5647
1Sa	12:20	but **s** the Lord with all your heart;	5647
1Sa	12:24	**s** him in truth with all your heart:	5647
1Sa	17:9	shall ye be our servants, and **s** us	5647
1Sa	26:19	the Lord, saying, Go, **s** other gods.	5647
2Sa	22:44	which I knew not shall **s** me	5647
1Ki	12:4	upon us, lighter, … we will **s** thee.	5647
2Ki	10:18	little; but Jehu shall **s** him much.	5647
2Ki	17:35	nor **s** them, nor sacrifice to them:	5647
2Ki	25:24	land, and **s** the king of Babylon;	5647
1Ch	28:9	**s** him with a perfect heart and with	5647
2Ch	7:19	and shall go and **s** other gods, and	5647
2Ch	29:11	to stand before him, to **s** him,	8334

S

2Ch	30:8	and **s** the Lord your God, that the	5647
2Ch	34:33	all that were present in Israel to **s**	5647
Ps	2:11	**S** the Lord with fear, and rejoice	5647
Ps	22:30	A seed shall **s** him; it shall be	5647
Ps	72:11	before him: all nations shall **s** him.	5647
Ps	97:7	be all they that **s** graven images	5647
Ps	100:2	**S** the Lord with gladness: come	5647
Isa	43:24	hast made me to **s** with thy sins	5647
Isa	60:12	that will not **s** thee shall perish;	5647
Jer	5:19	so shall ye **s** strangers in a land	5647
Jer	11:10	went after other gods to **s** them:	5647
Jer	16:13	ye **s** other gods day and night;	5647
Jer	17:4	will cause thee to **s** thine enemies	5647
Jer	25:6	go not after other gods to **s** them	5647
Jer	25:11	**s** the king of Babylon seventy years	5647
Jer	27:7	And all nations shall **s** him, and	5647
Jer	27:9	Ye shall not **s** the king of Babylon:	5647
Jer	27:12	and **s** him and his people, and live.	5647
Jer	27:13	that will not **s** the king of Babylon?	5647
Jer	27:14	Ye shall not **s** the king of Babylon:	5647
Jer	27:17	**s** the king of Babylon, and live:	5647
Jer	30:9	they shall **s** the Lord their God,	5647
Jer	35:15	go not after other gods to **s** them	5647
Jer	40:9	Fear not to **s** the Chaldeans: dwell	5647
Jer	44:3	**s** other gods, whom they knew not	5647
Eze	20:32	countries, to **s** wood and stone	8334
Eze	20:39	Go ye, **s** ye every one his idols,	5647
Eze	20:40	all of them in the land, **s** me:	5647
Da	3:12	they **s** not thy gods, nor worship	6399
Da	3:17	God whom we **s** is able to deliver	6399
Da	3:18	we will not **s** thy gods, nor worship	6399
Da	7:14	and languages, should **s** him:	6399
Da	7:27	dominions shall **s** and obey him	6399
Zep	3:9	Lord, to **s** him with one consent.	5647
Mal	3:14	Ye have said, It is vain to **s** God:	5647
Mt	4:10	**God, and him only shalt thou s**	*3000*
Mt	6:24	**No man can s two masters: for**	*1398*
Mt	6:24	**Ye cannot s God and mammon**	*1398*
Lk	4:8	**God, and him only shalt thou s**	*3000*
Lk	10:40	my sister hath left me to **s** alone?	*1247*
Lk	15:29	**Lo, these many years do I s thee,**	*1398*
Lk	16:13	**No servant can s two masters: for**	*1398*
Lk	16:13	**Ye cannot s God and mammon**	*1398*
Lk	17:8	**sup, and gird thyself, and s me**	*1247*
Lk	22:26	**he that is chief, as he that doth s**	*1247*
Jn	12:26	**If any man s me, let him follow**	*1247*
Jn	12:26	**if any man s me, him will my**	*1247*
Ac	6:2	leave the word of God, and **s** tables	*1247*
Ac	27:23	of God, whose I am, and whom I **s**	*3000*
Ro	1:9	whom I **s** with my spirit in the	*3000*
Ro	6:6	hence forth we should not **s** sin	*1398*
Ro	7:6	we should **s** in newness of spirit	*1398*
Ro	7:25	mind I myself **s** the law of God;	*1398*
Ro	9:12	her, The elder shall **s** the younger	*1398*
Ro	16:18	such **s** not our Lord Jesus Christ,	*1398*
Gal	5:13	flesh, but by love **s** one another	*1398*
Col	3:24	inheritance for ye **s** the Lord Christ	*1398*
1Th	1:9	idols to **s** the living and true God;	*1398*
Heb	9:14	dead works to **s** the living God?	*3000*
Heb	12:28	whereby we may **s** God acceptably	*3000*
Rev	7:15	**s** him day and night in his temple:	*3000*
Rev	22:3	be in it; and his servants shall **s** him:	*3000*

SERVED

Ge	29:20	Jacob **s** seven years for Rachel;	5647
Ge	29:30	**s** with him yet seven other years.	5647
Ge	31:41	I **s** thee fourteen years for thy two	5647
Dt	12:2	ye shall possess **s** their gods,	5647
Dt	17:3	And hath gone and **s** other gods,	5647
Dt	29:26	For they went and **s** other gods,	5647
Jos	23:16	and have gone and **s** other gods,	5647
Jgs	2:7	people **s** the Lord all the days of	5647
Jgs	2:11	sight of the Lord, and **s** Baalim:	5647
Jgs	3:6	to their sons, and **s** their gods	5647
Jgs	10:6	and **s** Baalim, and Ashtaroth, and	5647
Jgs	10:13	forsaken me, and **s** other gods:,	5647
Jgs	10:16	from among them, and **s** the Lord:	5647
1Sa	7:4	and Ashtaroth, and **s** the Lord only	5647
1Sa	12:10	and have **s** Baalim and Ashtaroth:	5647
2Sa	10:19	made peace with Israel, and **s** them	5647
1Ki	4:21	**s** Solomon all the days of his life.	5647
1Ki	9:9	have worshipped them, and **s** them:	5647
1Ki	16:31	went and **s** Baal, and worshipped	5647
2Ki	10:18	unto them, Ahab **s** Baal a little;	5647
2Ki	17:12	For they **s** idols, whereof the Lord	5647
2Ki	17:16	all the host of heaven, and **s** Baal	5647
2Ki	17:33	the Lord, and **s** their own gods,	5647
2Ki	17:41	Lord, and **s** their graven images,	5647
2Ki	18:7	the king of Assyria, and **s** him not	5647
2Ki	21:3	all the host of heaven, and **s** them	5647
2Ki	21:21	and **s** the idols that his father **s**,	5647
2Ch	7:22	worshipped them, and **s** them:	5647
2Ch	24:18	fathers, and **s** groves and idols:	5647
Ne	9:35	have not **s** thee in their kingdom	5647
Ps	106:36	And they **s** their idols: which	5647
Ps	137:8	rewardeth thee as thou hast **s** us.	1580
Jer	5:19	and **s** strange gods in your land, so	5647
Jer	8:2	have loved, and whom they have **s**,	5647
Jer	16:11	after other gods, and have **s** them,	5647
Jer	22:9	worshipped other gods, and **s** them	5647
Jer	34:14	and when he hath **s** thee six years,	5647
Eze	29:20	labour wherewith he **s** against it,	5647
Hos	12:12	Israel **s** for a wife, and for a wife	5647
Lk	2:37	**s** God with fastings and prayers	*3000*
Jn	12:2	made him a supper; and Martha **s**	*1247*
Ac	13:36	after he had **s** his own generation	*5256*
Ro	1:25	and **s** the creature more than the	*3000*

SERVEST

Da	6:16	Thy God whom thou **s** continually,	6399
Da	6:20	thy God, whom thou **s** continually,	6399

SERVETH

Mal	3:17	spareth his own son that **s** him	5647
Mal	3:18	that **s** God and him that **s** him not.	5647
Lk	22:27	**that sitteth at meat, or he that s?**	*1247*
Lk	22:27	**but I am among you as he that s**	*1247*
Ro	14:18	he that in these things **s** Christ is	*1398*
1Co	14:22	but prophesying **s** not for them that	
Gal	3:19	Wherefore then **s** the law? It was	

SERVICE

Ex	12:26	unto you, What mean ye by this **s**?	5656
Ex	13:5	thou shalt keep this **s** in this month.	5656
Ex	30:16	appoint it for the **s** of the tabernacle	5656
Ex	36:5	than enough for the **s** of the work,	5656
Ex	39:40	vessels of the **s** of the tabernacle	5656
Ex	39:41	The cloths of **s** to do	8278
Ex	39:41	to do **s** in the holy place,	8334
Nu	4:4	shall be the **s** of the sons of Kohath	5656
Nu	4:23	all that enter in to perform the **s**.	5656
Nu	7:5	to every man according to his **s**	5656
Nu	8:19	do the **s** of the children of Israel	5656

S

Nu 8:25 cease waiting upon the **s** thereof, ... 5656
Nu 16:9 to do the **s** of the tabernacle of the..... 5656
Nu 18:4 for all the **s** of the tabernacle: 5656
Nu 18:31 reward for your **s** in the tabernacle..... 5656
Jos 22:27 that we might do the **s** of the Lord..... 5656
1Ch 6:31 whom David set over the **s** of song 3027
1Ch 23:26 nor any vessels of it for the **s** thereof.... 5656
1Ch 25:6 harps, for the **s** of the house of God, ... 5656
1Ch 26:30 the Lord, and in the **s** of the king...... 5656
1Ch 28:20 finished all the work for the **s** of the ... 5656
1Ch 29:5 is willing to consecrate his **s** this....... 3027
2Ch 31:2 every man according to his **s**, the 5656
2Ch 31:21 began in the **s** of the house of God,.... 5656
2Ch 35:2 and encouraged them to the **s** of the ... 5656
2Ch 35:16 all the **s** of the Lord was prepared...... 5656
Ezr 6:18 their courses, for the **s** of God, ... 5673
Ezr 7:19 given thee for the **s** of the house....... 6402
Ne 10:32 the third part of a shekel for the **s** 5656
Jer 22:13 useth his neighbour's **s** without 5647
Eze 29:18 caused his army to serve a great **s**...... 5656
Jn 16:2 **will think that he doeth God s** *2999*
Ro 12:1 God, which is your reasonable **s** *2999*
2Co 11:8 taking wages of them, to do you **s**...... *1248*
Gal 4:8 did **s** unto them which by nature *1398*
Eph 6:7 With good will doing **s**, as to the *1398*
Php 2:17 the sacrifice and **s** of your faith, ... *3009*
Php 2:30 to supply your lack of **s** toward me *3009*
1Ti 6:2 but rather do them **s**, because *1398*
Heb 9:1 had also ordinances of divine **s**, ... *2999*
Heb 9:9 not make him that did the **s** perfect.... *3000*
Rev 2:19 **thy works, and charity, and s,** *1248*

SERVING

Ex 14:5 we have let Israel go from **s** us?........ 5647
Lk 10:40 Martha was cumbered about much **s**, .. *1248*
Ac 20:19 **S** the Lord with all humility of *1398*
Ro 12:11 fervent in spirit; **s** the Lord;........... *1398*
Tit 3:3 **s** divers lusts and pleasures, living...... *1398*

SET

Ge 1:17 God **s** them in the firmament of....... 5414
Ge 4:15 And the Lord **s** a mark upon Cain, ... 7760
Ge 9:13 I do **s** my bow in the cloud, and it 5414
Ge 19:16 forth, and **s** him without the city 3240
Ge 21:2 **s** time of which God had spoken 4150
Ge 28:12 behold a ladder **s** up on the earth...... 5324
Ge 41:41 **s** thee over all the land of Egypt........ 5414
Ex 1:11 they did **s** over them taskmasters 7760
Ex 7:23 neither did he **s** his heart to this also ... 7896
Ex 9:5 And the Lord appointed a **s** time 4150
Ex 32:22 people, that they are **s** on mischief.
Ex 40:5 And thou shalt **s** the altar of gold...... 5414
Ex 40:6 thou shalt **s** the altar of the burnt...... 5414
Ex 40:7 And thou shalt **s** the laver between..... 5414
Ex 40:30 he **s** the laver between the tent of...... 7760
Le 17:10 even **s** my face against that soul 5414
Le 20:6 even **s** my face against that soul,....... 5414
Le 26:1 neither shall ye **s** up any image 5414
Nu 21:8 fiery serpent, and **s** it upon a pole:..... 7760
Nu 27:16 **s** a man over the congregation 6485
Dt 1:21 God hath **s** the land before thee:....... 5414
Dt 4:8 law, which I **s** before you this day? 5414
Dt 7:7 Lord did not **s** his love upon you
Dt 17:14 I will **s** a king over me, like as all....... 7760
Dt 17:15 mayest not **s** a stranger over thee,...... 5414
Dt 28:1 God will **s** thee on high above all 5414
Dt 30:15 I have **s** before thee this day life 5414
Dt 30:19 I have **s** before you life and death, ... 5414
Dt 32:46 **S** your hearts unto all the words....... 7760
Jos 4:9 Joshua **s** up twelve stones in the 6965
Jos 8:8 that ye shall **s** the city on fire: 3341
Jos 8:12 **s** them to lie in ambush between 7760
Jgs 7:5 him shalt thou **s** by himself; 3322
Jgs 9:25 men of Shechem **s** liers in wait for..... 7760
Jgs 16:25 they **s** him between the pillars......... 5975
1Sa 2:8 he hath **s** the world upon them........ 7896
1Sa 5:3 and **s** him in his place again 7725
1Sa 10:19 him, Nay, but **s** a king over us......... 7760
1Sa 12:13 the Lord hath **s** a king over you........ 5414
1Sa 13:8 **s** time that Samuel had appointed:..... 4150
1Sa 15:11 that I have **s** up Saul to be king: 4427
2Sa 6:3 **s** the ark of God upon a new cart, ... 7392
2Sa 7:12 I will **s** up thy seed after thee, ... 6965
2Sa 11:15 **S** ye Uriah in the forefront of the 3051
2Sa 20:5 he tarried longer than the **s** time 4150
1Ki 2:15 that all Israel **s** their faces on me....... 7760
1Ki 6:19 to **s** there the ark of the covenant...... 5414
1Ki 8:21 I have **s** there a place for the ark....... 7760
1Ki 15:4 to **s** up his son after him, and to....... 6965
2Ki 4:10 and let us **s** for him there a bed,....... 7760
2Ki 4:38 **S** on the great pot, and seethe......... 8239
2Ki 25:28 **s** his throne above the throne of....... 5414
1Ch 22:19 **s** your heart and your soul to seek 5414
1Ch 29:3 I have **s** my affection to the house of
2Ch 6:10 and am **s** on the throne of Israel, ... 3427
2Ch 7:19 statutes … which I have **s** before you, .. 5414
2Ch 20:3 and **s** himself to seek the Lord,........ 5414
2Ch 20:17 **s** yourselves, stand ye still, and 3320
2Ch 33:7 And he **s** a carved image, the idol...... 7760
2Ch 35:2 he **s** the priests in their charges, ... 5975
Ezr 2:68 house of God to **s** it up in his place:.... 5975
Ezr 4:16 again, and the walls thereof **s** up, ... 3635
Ezr 5:11 king of Israel builded and **s** up......... 3635
Ezr 6:11 being **s** up, let him be hanged 2211
Ezr 9:9 to **s** up the house of our God, and 7311
Ne 1:9 I have chosen to **s** my name there...... 7931
Ne 2:6 to send me; and I **s** him a time......... 5414
Ne 4:9 **s** a watch against them day and........ 5975
Ne 9:37 kings whom thou hast **s** over us 5414
Ne 10:33 the new moons, for the **s** feasts, ... 4150
Ne 13:11 together, … **s** them in their place. 5975
Est 2:17 **s** the royal crown upon her head:...... 7760
Est 8:2 Esther **s** Mordecai over the house...... 7760
Job 14:13 wouldest appoint me a **s** time, ... 2706
Job 19:8 he hath **s** darkness in my paths. 7760
Job 34:14 If he **s** his heart upon man, if he....... 7760
Ps 2:2 kings of the earth **s** themselves,........ 3320
Ps 2:6 Yet have I **s** my king upon my......... 5258
Ps 4:3 the Lord hath **s** apart him that is 6395
Ps 8:1 hast **s** thy glory above the heavens...... 5414
Ps 10:8 are privily **s** against the poor. 6845
Ps 16:8 have **s** the Lord always before me: 7737
Ps 19:4 hath he **s** a tabernacle for the sun, ... 7760
Ps 20:5 of our God we will **s** up our banners:
Ps 27:5 he shall **s** me up upon a rock 7311
Ps 40:2 clay, and **s** my feet upon a rock, ... 6965
Ps 54:3 they have not **s** God before them....... 7760
Ps 62:10 **s** not your heart upon them........... 7896
Ps 69:29 salvation, O God, **s** me up on high
Ps 73:18 didst **s** them in slippery places:........ 7896
Ps 74:4 they **s** up their ensigns for signs........ 7760
Ps 74:17 hast **s** all the borders of the earth:...... 5324

Ps	78:7	they might **s** their hope in God,	7760
Ps	78:8	that **s** not their heart aright, and	3559
Ps	86:14	and have not **s** thee before them.	7760
Ps	90:8	Thou hast **s** our iniquities before	7896
Ps	91:14	Because he hath **s** his love upon me,	
Ps	101:3	I will **s** no wicked thing before	7896
Ps	102:13	to favour her, yea, the **s** time, is come	
Ps	104:9	Thou hast **s** a bound that they	7760
Ps	109:6	**S** thou a wicked man over him:	6485
Ps	122:5	there are **s** thrones of judgment,	3427
Ps	132:11	thy body will I **s** upon thy throne.	7896
Ps	141:2	be **s** forth before thee as incense;	3559
Ps	141:3	**S** a watch, O Lord, before my	7896
Pr	1:25	have **s** at nought all my counsel,	
Pr	8:23	I was **s** up from everlasting, from	5258
Pr	8:27	he **s** a compass upon the face of	2710
Pr	22:28	landmark, … thy fathers have **s**	6213
Pr	23:5	**s** thine eyes upon that which is not?	5774
Ecc	3:11	he hath **s** the world in their heart,	5414
Ecc	7:14	God also hath **s** the one over	6213
Ecc	8:11	of men is fully **s** in them to do evil.	
Ecc	10:6	Folly is **s** in great dignity, and	5414
Ecc	12:9	and **s** in order many proverbs.	
SS	8:6	**S** me as a seal upon thine heart,	7760
Isa	11:11	the Lord shall **s** his hand again the	
Isa	11:12	**s** up an ensign for the nations,	5375
Isa	14:1	and **s** them in their own land: and	3240
Isa	21:6	Go, **s** a watchman, let him declare	5975
Isa	27:11	women come, and **s** them on fire:	
Isa	38:1	**S** thine house in order: for thou	
Isa	49:22	**s** up my standard to the people:	7311
Isa	50:7	have I **s** my face like a flint, and	7760
Isa	62:6	I have **s** watchmen upon thy walls,	6485
Jer	1:10	this day **s** thee over the nations	6485
Jer	5:26	they **s** a trap, they catch men.	5324
Jer	6:17	Also I **s** watchmen over you,	6965
Jer	7:12	where I **s** my name at the first,	7931
Jer	7:30	they have **s** their abominations in	7760
Jer	9:13	my law which I **s** before them,	5414
Jer	11:13	ye **s** up altars to that shameful	7760
Jer	21:8	I **s** before you the way of life, and	5414
Jer	21:10	I have **s** my face against this city	7760
Jer	23:4	I will **s** up shepherds over them	6965
Jer	24:6	**s** mine eyes upon them for good,	7760
Jer	26:4	law, which I have **s** before you,	5414
Jer	32:20	**s** signs and wonders in the land	7760
Jer	32:34	they **s** their abominations in the	7760
Jer	34:16	had **s** at liberty at their pleasure,	7971
Jer	44:10	I **s** before you and before your	5414
La	3:6	He hath **s** me in dark places, as	3427
La	3:12	and **s** me as a mark for the arrow.	5324
Eze	2:2	**s** me upon my feet, that I heard	5975
Eze	3:24	**s** me upon my feet, and speak with	5975
Eze	4:7	shalt **s** thy face toward the siege of	3559
Eze	6:2	**s** thy face toward the mountains	7760
Eze	9:4	**s** a mark upon the foreheads of	8427
Eze	12:6	I have **s** thee for a sign unto the	5414
Eze	13:17	**s** thy face against the daughters	7760
Eze	14:3	have **s** up their idols in their heart	5927
Eze	14:8	will **s** my face against that man,	5414
Eze	15:7	when I **s** my face against them	7760
Eze	18:2	the children's teeth are **s** on edge?	
Eze	21:2	**s** thy face toward Jerusalem, and	7760
Eze	22:10	her that was **s** apart for pollution.	5079
Eze	23:24	**s** against thee buckler and shield	7760
Eze	23:25	I will **s** my jealousy against thee,	5414
Eze	24:3	**S** on a pot, **s** it on, and also pour	8239
Eze	24:8	I have **s** her blood upon the top of	5414
Eze	24:25	that whereupon they **s** their minds,	4853
Eze	25:2	Son of man, **s** thy face against	7760
Eze	26:9	shall **s** engines of war against thy	5414
Eze	26:20	**s** thee in the low parts of the earth	3427
Eze	28:2, 6	**s** thine heart as the heart of God	5414
Eze	28:14	I have **s** thee so: thou wast upon	5414
Eze	32:8	and **s** darkness upon thy land,	5414
Eze	33:7	I have **s** thee a watchman unto the	5414
Eze	34:23	And I will **s** up one shepherd over	6965
Eze	37:1	and **s** me down in the midst of the	5117
Eze	37:26	will **s** my sanctuary in the midst	5414
Eze	38:2	**s** thy face against God, the land of	7760
Eze	39:9	shall **s** on fire and burn the weapons	1197
Eze	39:15	then shall he **s** up a sign by it,	1129
Eze	39:21	**s** my glory among the heathen	5414
Eze	40:2	**s** me upon a very high mountain,	5117
Eze	40:4	**s** thine heart upon all that I shall	7760
Da	2:44	God of heaven **s** up a kingdom,	6966
Da	3:12	whom thou hast **s** over the affairs	4483
Da	3:18	golden image which thou hast **s** up	6966
Da	5:19	and whom he would he **s** up; and	7313
Da	6:3	to **s** him over the whole realm	6966
Da	6:14	**s** his heart on Daniel to deliver	7761
Da	7:10	judgment was **s**, and the books	3488
Da	10:15	I **s** my face toward the ground,	5414
Da	11:17	He shall also **s** his face to enter	7760
Da	12:11	abomination … maketh desolate **s** up	5414
Hos	4:8	**s** their heart on their iniquity,	5375
Hos	8:4	They have **s** up kings, but not by me:	
Am	7:8	**s** a plumbline in the midst of my	7760
Am	9:4	**s** mine eyes upon them for evil,	7760
Na	3:6	and will **s** thee as a gazingstock	7760
Zec	3:5	they **s** a fair mitre upon his head,	7760
Zec	8:10	I **s** all men every one against his	7971
Mal	3:15	that work wickedness are **s** up;	1129
Mt	5:14	**that is s on an hill cannot be hid.**	*2749*
Mt	10:35	**to s a man at variance against**	*1369*
Mt	18:2	and **s** him in the midst of them,	*2476*
Mt	25:33	**s the sheep on his right hand,**	*2476*
Mt	27:37	**s** up over his head his accusation	*2007*
Mk	4:21	**and not to be s on a candlestick?**	*2007*
Mk	9:12	**must suffer … and be s at nought.**	*1847*
Mk	9:36	and **s** him in the midst of them:	*2476*
Mk	12:1	**s an hedge about it, and digged**	*4060*
Lk	2:34	child is **s** for the fall and rising	*2749*
Lk	4:9	**s** him on a pinnacle of the temple,	*2476*
Lk	4:18	**s at liberty them that are bruised,**	*649*
Lk	9:47	took a child, and **s** him by him	*2476*
Lk	9:51	**s** his face to go to Jerusalem	*4741*
Lk	10:8	**such things as are s before you:**	*3908*
Lk	10:34	**and s him on his own beast,**	*1913*
Lk	11:6	**I have nothing to s before him?**	*3908*
Lk	19:35	the colt, and they **s** Jesus thereon	*1913*
Jn	2:10	beginning doth **s** forth good wine;	*5087*
Jn	3:33	hath **s** to his seal that God is true.	*4972*
Jn	8:3	when they had **s** her in the midst,	*2476*
Ac	4:11	the stone which was **s** at nought	*1848*
Ac	6:13	And **s** up false witnesses, which	*2476*
Ac	12:21	upon a **s** day Herod, arrayed in	*5002*
Ac	13:9	the Holy Ghost, **s** his eyes on him,	*816*
Ac	13:47	**s** thee to be a light of the Gentiles	*5087*
Ac	18:10	**no man shall s on thee to hurt thee.**	*2007*
Ac	26:32	man might have been **s** at liberty,	*630*
Ro	3:25	hath **s** forth to be a propitiation	*4388*

Ro	14:10	dost thou **s** at nought thy brother?	*1848*
1Co	4:9	God hath **s** forth us the apostles	*584*
1Co	6:4	**s** them to judge who are least	*2523*
1Co	10:27	whatsoever is **s** before you, eat,	*3908*
Gal	3:1	Christ hath been evidently **s** forth,	*4270*
Eph	1:20	**s** him at his own right hand in	*2523*
Php	1:17	**s** for the defence of the gospel.	*2749*
Col	3:2	**S** your affection on things above,	*5426*
Heb	2:7	**s** him over the works of thy hands:	*2525*
Heb	6:18	hold upon the hope **s** before us:	*4295*
Heb	8:1	who is **s** on the right hand of the	*2523*
Heb	12:1	the race that is **s** before us,	*4295*
Heb	12:2	for the joy that was **s** before him.	*4295*
Heb	12:2	is **s** down at the right hand of the	*2523*
Jas	3:6	nature; and it is **s** on fire of hell.	*5394*
Rev	3:8	**have s before thee an open door,**	*1325*
Rev	3:21	**am s down with my Father in his**	*2523*
Rev	4:2	behold, a throne was **s** in heaven,	*2749*
Rev	10:2	he **s** his right foot upon the sea.	*5087*
Rev	20:3	him up, and **s** a seal upon him,	*4972*

SETTER

Ac	17:18	to be a **s** forth of strange gods:	*2604*

SETTEST

Dt	23:20	in all that thou **s** thine hand to	4916
Dt	28:8	in all that thou **s** thine hand unto;	4916
Dt	28:20	in all that thou **s** thine hand unto.	4916
Ps	21:3	thou **s** a crown of pure gold on.	7896

SETTETH

Dt	24:15	is poor, and **s** his heart upon it:	5375
Dt	27:16	that **s** light by his father or his.	7034
Ps	36:4	**s** himself in a way that is not good.	3320
Ps	75:7	putteth down one, and **s** up another.	7311
Jer	5:26	they lay wait as he that **s** snares;	7918
Eze	14:4	that **s** up his idols in his heart,	5927
Eze	14:7	and **s** up his idols in his heart,	5927
Da	2:21	removeth kings, and **s** up kings:	6966
Da	4:17	and **s** up over it the basest of men.	6966
Mt	4:5	and **s** him on the pinnacle of the	*2476*
Lk	8:16	**s it on a candlestick, that they**	*2007*
Jas	3:6	**s** on fire the course of nature;	*5394*

SETTING

Mt	27:66	sealing the stone, and **s** a watch.	*3326*

SETTLE

1Ch	17:14	I will **s** him in mine house and	5975
Lk	21:14	**S it therefore in your hearts, not**	*5087*
1Pe	5:10	stablish, strengthen, **s** you.	*2311*

SETTLED

1Ki	8:13	a **s** place for thee to abide in for	4349
2Ki	8:11	he **s** his countenance stedfastly,	5975
Ps	119:89	O Lord, thy word is **s** in heaven.	5324
Pr	8:25	Before the mountains were **s**,	2883
Col	1:23	in the faith grounded and **s**, and.	*1476*

SEVEN

Ge	7:4	**s** days, and I will cause it to rain	7651
Ge	21:28	Abraham set **s** ewe lambs of the	7651
Ge	29:20	Jacob served **s** years for Rachel;	7651
Ge	29:30	served with him yet **s** other years.	7651
Ge	33:3	himself to the ground **s** times,	7651
Ge	41:2	of the river **s** well favoured kine	7651
Ge	41:4	eat up the **s** well favoured and fat	7651
Ge	41:7	devoured the **s** rank and full ears.	7651
Ge	41:20	kine did eat up the first **s** fat kine:	7651
Ge	41:22	**s** ears came up in one stalk, full	7651
Ge	41:29	there come **s** years of great plenty.	7651
Ge	41:30	arise after them **s** years of famine;	7651
Ge	41:48	up all the food of the **s** years,	7651
Ge	41:53	the **s** years of plenteousness, that	7651
Ge	41:54	**s** years of dearth began to come,	7651
Ex	12:15	**S** days shall ye eat unleavened	7651
Ex	12:19	**S** days shall there be no leaven	7651
Ex	13:6	**S** days thou shalt eat unleavened	7651
Ex	22:30	**s** days it shall be with his dam; on	7651
Ex	25:37	shalt make the **s** lamps thereof:	7651
Ex	29:35	**s** days shalt thou consecrate them.	7651
Ex	34:18	**S** days thou shalt eat unleavened	7651
Le	4:6	and sprinkle of the blood **s** times	7651
Le	4:17	sprinkle it **s** times before the Lord,	7651
Le	8:11	thereof upon the altar **s** times,	7651
Le	8:35	congregation day and night **s** days,	7651
Le	12:2	then she shall be unclean **s** days;	7651
Le	14:16	of the oil with his fingers **s** times	7651
Le	14:27	is in his left hand **s** times before	7651
Le	14:38	and shut up the house **s** days:	7651
Le	14:51	and sprinkle the house **s** times:	7651
Le	16:14	of the blood with his finger **s** times	7651
Le	23:8	made by fire unto the Lord **s** days:	7651
Le	23:15	**s** sabbaths shall be complete:	7651
Le	23:34	feast of tabernacles for **s** days unto.	7651
Le	23:36	**S** days ye shall offer an offering.	7651
Le	23:42	Ye shall dwell in booths **s** days; all	7651
Le	25:8	shalt number **s** sabbaths of years	7651
Le	26:18	I will punish you **s** times more	7651
Le	26:21	I will bring **s** times more plagues	7651
Le	26:24	and will punish you yet **s** times.	7651
Le	26:28	chastise you **s** times for your sins	7651
Nu	8:2	the **s** lamps shall give light over.	7651
Nu	12:15	was shut out from the camp **s** days:	7651
Nu	23:1	unto Balak, Build me here **s** altars,	7651
Nu	28:11	**s** lambs of the first year without	7651
Nu	28:17	**s** days shall unleavened bread be.	7651
Nu	28:24	offer daily, throughout the **s** days,	7651
Nu	29:12	keep a feast unto the Lord **s** days:	7651
Nu	29:32	on the seventh day **s** bullocks, two	7651
Dt	7:1	**s** nations greater and mightier	7651
Dt	15:1	**s** years thou shalt make a release.	7651
Dt	16:3	**s** days shalt thou eat unleavened	7651
Dt	16:9	**S** weeks shalt thou number unto	7651
Dt	16:13	the feast of tabernacles **s** days,	7651
Dt	28:7	way, and flee before thee **s** ways.	7651
Dt	31:10	At the end of every **s** years, in the	7651
Jos	6:4	**s** priests shall bear before the ark	7651
Jos	6:13	And **s** priests bearing **s** trumpets	7651
Jos	6:15	they compassed the city **s** times	7651
Jgs	14:17	she wept before him the **s** days,	7651
Jgs	16:19	to shave off the **s** locks of his head;	7651
Ru	4:15	which is better to thee than **s** sons,	7651
1Sa	2:5	so that the barren hath born **s**;	7651
1Sa	10:8	**s** days shalt thou tarry, till I come.	7651
1Sa	11:3	Give us **s** days respite, that we	7651
2Sa	10:18	slew the men of **s** hundred chariots	7651
2Sa	24:13	**s** years of famine come unto thee	7651
1Ki	6:38	it. So was he **s** years in building it.	7651
1Ki	8:65	**s** days and **s** days, even fourteen	7651
1Ki	11:3	he had **s** hundred wives, princesses,	7651
1Ki	18:43	And he said, Go again **s** times.	7651
1Ki	19:18	I have left me **s** thousand in Israel,	7651
2Ki	4:35	the child sneezed **s** times, and the.	7651

2Ki 5:10 Go and wash in Jordan **s** times, ... 7651
2Ki 8:1 also come upon the land **s** years 7651
2Ch 7:8 Solomon kept the feast **s** days 7651
2Ch 30:21 feast of unleavened bread **s** days 7651
2Ch 30:23 took counsel to keep other **s** days: 7651
2Ch 35:17 feast of unleavened bread **s** days. 7651
Ezr 6:22 unleavened bread **s** days with joy: 7651
Ne 8:18 they kept the feast **s** days; and on 7651
Job 1:2 there were born unto him **s** sons 7651
Job 2:13 the ground **s** days and **s** nights,. 7651
Job 5:19 in **s** there shall no evil touch thee 7651
Job 42:13 also **s** sons and three daughters. 7658
Ps 119:164 **S** times a day do I praise thee 7651
Pr 6:16 **s** are an abomination unto him: 7651
Pr 9:1 she hath hewn out her **s** pillars: 7651
Pr 24:16 For a just man falleth **s** times, and 7651
Pr 26:16 **s** men that can render a reason 7651
Pr 26:25 are **s** abominations in his heart 7651
Ecc 11:2 Give a portion to **s**, and also to 7651
Isa 4:1 **s** women shall take hold of one man . . . 7651
Isa 30:26 sevenfold, as the light of **s** days, ... 7651
Jer 34:14 end of **s** years let ye go every man 7651
Jer 52:31 **s** and thirtieth year of the captivity 7651
Eze 39:9 shall burn them with fire **s** years: 7651
Eze 39:14 end of **s** months shall they search. 7651
Eze 43:26 **S** days shall they purge the altar 7651
Eze 45:21 the passover, a feast of **s** days; 7651
Eze 45:23 without blemish daily the **s** days; 7651
Da 3:19 the furnace one **s** times more 7655
Da 4:16 and let **s** times pass over him. 7655
Da 4:23 field, till **s** times pass over him; 7655
Da 4:32 and **s** times shall pass over thee, ... 7655
Da 9:25 the Prince shall be **s** weeks, and 7651
Am 5:8 Seek him that maketh the **s** stars 3598
Zec 3:9 upon one stone shall be **s** eyes: 7651
Zec 4:2 top of it, and his **s** lamps thereon, ... 7651
Zec 4:10 hand of Zerubbabel with those **s**; 7651
Mt 12:45 **s other spirits more wicked than** *2033*
Mt 15:36 And he took the **s** loaves and the *2033*
Mt 16:10 **Neither the s loaves of the four**. *2033*
Mt 18:21 and I forgive him? till **s** times?. *2034*
Mt 18:22 **but, Until seventy times s** *2033*
Mt 22:28 whose wife shall she be of the **s**? *2033*
Mk 8:6 and he took the **s** loaves, and gave *2033*
Mk 8:20 **took ye up? And they said, S** *2033*
Mk 12:22 And the **s** had her, and left no seed. *2033*
Mk 16:9 out of whom he had cast **s** devils.. . . . . . *2033*
Lk 2:36 had lived with an husband **s** years *2033*
Lk 8:2 out of whom went **s** devils. *2033*
Lk 11:26 **him s other spirits more wicked**. *2033*
Lk 17:4 **against thee s times in a day,**. *2034*
Lk 17:4 **and s times in a day turn again**. *2034*
Lk 20:33 them is she? for **s** had her to wife *2033*
Ac 6:3 among you **s** men of honest report,. . . . *2033*
Ac 13:19 destroyed **s** nations in the land of. *2033*
Ac 21:27 And when the **s** days were almost. *2033*
Ro 11:4 to myself **s** thousand men, who *2035*
Heb 11:30 were compassed about **s** days *2033*
Rev 1:4 John to the **s** churches which are *2033*
Rev 1:4 and from the **s** Spirits which are *2033*
Rev 1:11 **the s churches which are in Asia;** *2033*
Rev 1:12 I saw **s** golden candlesticks; *2033*
Rev 1:13 in the midst of the **s** candlesticks *2033*
Rev 1:16 he had in his right hand **s** stars: *2033*
Rev 1:20 **The mystery of the s stars which** *2033*
Rev 1:20 **s stars … angels of the s churches:** *2033*
Rev 1:20 **thou sawest are the s churches** *2033*
Rev 2:1 **he that holdeth the s stars in his**. *2033*
Rev 2:1 **midst of the s golden candlesticks;**. *2033*
Rev 3:1 **s Spirits of God, and the s stars;**. *2033*
Rev 4:5 there were **s** lamps of fire burning *2033*
Rev 4:5 which are the **s** Spirits of God. *2033*
Rev 5:1 the backside, sealed with **s** seals. *2033*
Rev 5:5 and to loose the **s** seals thereof. *2033*
Rev 5:6 slain, having **s** horns and **s** eyes, ... *2033*
Rev 5:6 which are the **s** Spirits of God *2033*
Rev 8:2 And I saw the **s** angels which stood *2033*
Rev 8:2 to them were given **s** trumpets. *2033*
Rev 8:6 **s** angels which had the **s** trumpets *2033*
Rev 10:3 **s** thunders uttered their voices. *2033*
Rev 10:4 **s** thunders had uttered their voices, ... *2033*
Rev 10:4 which the **s** thunders uttered, and *2033*
Rev 11:13 were slain of men **s** thousand: and *2033*
Rev 12:3 having **s** heads and ten horns, and *2033*
Rev 12:3 and **s** crowns upon his heads. *2033*
Rev 13:1 having **s** heads and ten horns, and *2033*
Rev 15:1 **s** angels having the **s** last plagues; *2033*
Rev 15:6 **s** angels came out of the temple,. *2033*
Rev 15:6 having the **s** plagues, clothed in *2033*
Rev 15:7 unto the **s** angels **s** golden vials *2033*
Rev 15:8 the **s** plagues of the **s** angels were *2033*
Rev 16:1 saying to the **s** angels, Go your *2033*
Rev 17:1 the **s** angels which had the **s** vials,. *2033*
Rev 17:3 having **s** heads and ten horns *2033*
Rev 17:7 hath the **s** heads and ten horns. *2033*
Rev 17:9 The **s** heads are **s** mountains, on. *2033*
Rev 17:10 there are **s** kings: five are fallen,. *2033*
Rev 17:11 and is of the **s**, and goeth into *2033*
Rev 21:9 came unto me one of the **s** angels. *2033*
Rev 21:9 **s** vials full of the **s** last plagues, ... *2033*

SEVENFOLD

Ge 4:15 vengeance … be taken on him **s**. 7659
Ge 4:24 If Cain shall be avenged **s**, truly 7659
Ge 4:24 truly Lamech seventy and **s**. 7659
Pr 6:31 if he be found, he shall restore **s**; 7659
Isa 30:26 and the light of the sun shall be **s**. 7659

SEVENS

Ge 7:2 beast thou shalt take to thee by **s**, ... 7651
Ge 7:3 Of fowls also of the air by **s**, the 7651

SEVENTEEN

Ge 37:2 Joseph, being **s** years old 7651, 6240
Ge 47:28 in land of Egypt **s** years:. 7651, 6240

SEVENTH

Ge 2:2 **s** day God ended his work which 7637
Ge 2:2 rested on the **s** day from all his 7637
Ge 2:3 And God blessed the **s** day, and 7637
Ex 12:15 from the first day until the **s** day. 7637
Ex 12:16 in the **s** day there shall be an holy. 7637
Ex 13:6 **s** day shall be a feast to the Lord. 7637
Ex 16:29 go out of his place on the **s** day. 7637
Ex 20:10 **s** day is the sabbath of the Lord 7637
Ex 20:11 in them is, and rested the **s** day: 7637
Ex 21:2 and in the **s** he shall go out free 7637
Ex 23:11 **s** year thou shalt let it rest and lie 7637
Ex 23:12 and on the **s** day thou shalt rest: 7637
Ex 24:16 **s** day he called unto Moses out of. 7637
Ex 31:17 on the **s** day he rested, and was. 7637
Ex 35:2 **s** day there shall be to you an holy 7637
Le 13:27 shall look upon him the **s** day: 7637

Le 16:29 in the **s** month, on the tenth day 7637
Le 23:3 the **s** day is the sabbath of rest, a....... 7637
Le 23:8 the **s** day is an holy convocation: 7637
Le 23:24 the **s** month, in the first day of the..... 7637
Le 23:27 on the tenth day of this **s** month 7637
Le 23:39 in the fifteenth day of the **s** month, ... 7637
Le 25:4 **s** year shall be a sabbath of rest........ 7637
Le 25:20 say, What shall we eat the **s** year? 7637
Nu 6:9 on the **s** day shall he shave it. 7637
Nu 19:12 and on the **s** day he shall be clean: 7637
Nu 19:12 the **s** day he shall not be clean. 7637
Nu 19:19 on the third day, and on the **s** day:..... 7637
Nu 28:25 on the **s** day ye shall have an holy...... 7637
Nu 29:1 in the **s** month, on the first day of 7637
Nu 29:7 on the tenth day of this **s** month 7637
Nu 29:12 on the fifteenth day of the **s** month 7637
Dt 5:14 But the **s** day is the sabbath of the 7637
Dt 15:9 The **s** year, the year of release, is 7637
Dt 15:12 **s** year thou shalt let him go free 7637
Jos 6:4 the **s** day ye shall compass the city 7637
Jos 6:16 And it came to pass at the **s** time,...... 7637
Jos 19:40 the **s** lot came out for the tribe of...... 7637
Jgs 14:17 on the **s** day, that he told her, ... 7637
2Sa 12:18 on the **s** day, that the child died........ 7637
1Ki 18:44 And it came to pass at the **s** time,...... 7637
2Ki 11:4 **s** year Jehoiada sent and fetched 7637
2Ch 5:3 feast which was in the **s** month. 7637
Ne 8:14 booths in the feast of the **s** month:..... 7637
Ne 10:31 and that we would leave the **s** year,..... 7637
Zec 7:5 mourned in the fifth and **s** month, ... 7637
Zec 8:19 the fast of the **s**, and the fast of the..... 7637
Jn 4:52 at the **s** hour the fever left him......... *1442*
Heb 4:4 did rest the **s** day from all his works. ... *1442*
Jude 14 And Enoch also, the **s** from Adam,..... *1442*
Rev 8:1 when he had opened the **s** seal,......... *1442*
Rev 10:7 the days of the voice of the **s** angel, ... *1442*
Rev 11:15 And the **s** angel sounded; and......... *1442*
Rev 16:17 And the **s** angel poured out his vial *1442*

SEVENTY
Ge 4:24 truly Lamech **s** and sevenfold.......... 7657
Ex 1:5 of the lions of Jacob were **s** souls:...... 7657
Nu 11:16 unto me **s** men of the elders of Israel, .. 7657
Nu 11:24 **s** men of the elders of the people,...... 7657
Nu 11:25 him, and gave it unto the **s** elders: 7657
Jgs 9:56 father, in slaying his **s** brethren: 7657
2Ki 10:7 the king's sons, and slew **s** persons, ... 7657
Isa 23:15 end of **s** years shall Tyre sing as an 7657
Isa 23:17 to pass after the end of **s** years, ... 7657
Jer 25:11 serve the king of Babylon **s** years,...... 7657
Jer 25:12 when **s** years are accomplished,......... 7657
Jer 29:10 after **s** years be accomplished at 7657
Eze 8:11 before them **s** men of the ancients 7657
Da 9:2 that he would accomplish **s** years 7657
Da 9:24 **S** weeks are determined upon thy...... 7657
Zec 7:5 even those **s** years, did ye at all fast..... 7657
Mt 18:22 **times: but, Until s times seven.** *1441*
Lk 10:1 the Lord appointed other **s** also, ... *1440*
Lk 10:17 And the **s** returned again with joy, ... *1440*

SEVER
Ex 8:22 **s** in that day the land of Goshen, ... 6395
Ex 9:4 shall **s** between the cattle of Israel...... 6395
Eze 39:14 they shall **s** out men of continual 914
Mt 13:49 **s the wicked from among the just,** *873*

SEVERAL
Nu 28:13 a **s** tenth deal of flour mingled with
2Ch 26:21 death, and dwelt in a **s** house,......... 2669
Mt 25:15 **man according to his s ability;** *2398*
Rev 21:21 every **s** gate was of one pearl: *303, 1520*

SEVERALLY
1Co 12:11 dividing to every man **s** as he will...... *2398*

SEVERED
Le 20:26 and have **s** you from other people,...... 914
Dt 4:41 **s** three cities on this side Jordan 914

SEVERITY
Ro 11:22 Behold ... the goodness and **s** of God:... *663*
Ro 11:22 on them which fell, **s**; but toward *663*

SEW
Ecc 3:7 A time to rend, and a time to **s**; 8609

SEWED
Ge 3:7 they **s** fig leaves together, and 8609
Job 16:15 I have **s** sackcloth upon my skin, ... 8609

SEWETH
Mk 2:21 **No man ... s a piece of new cloth.** *1976*

SHADOW
Ge 19:8 came they under the **s** of my roof...... 6738
Jgs 9:15 come and put your trust in my **s**:...... 6738
Jgs 9:36 Thou seest the **s** of the mountains 6738
2Ki 20:11 brought the **s** ten degrees backward, ... 6738
1Ch 29:15 our days on the earth are as a **s**, ... 6738
Job 8:9 our days upon earth are a **s**:).......... 6738
Job 10:21 land of darkness and the **s** of death;.... 6757
Job 10:22 and of the **s** of death, without any 6757
Job 12:22 bringeth out to light the **s** of death..... 6757
Job 16:16 on my eyelids is the **s** of death;........ 6757
Job 24:17 are in the terrors of the **s** of death...... 6757
Job 34:22 is no darkness, nor **s** of death,......... 6757
Job 38:17 seen the doors of the **s** of death?....... 6757
Ps 17:8 hide me under the **s** of thy wings, ... 6738
Ps 23:4 through the valley of the **s** of death,.... 6757
Ps 36:7 trust under the **s** of thy wings. 6738
Ps 57:1 in the **s** of thy wings will I make....... 6738
Ps 63:7 in the **s** of thy wings will I rejoice. 6738
Ps 91:1 abide under the **s** of the Almighty 6738
Ps 102:11 days are like a **s** that declineth; 6738
Ps 107:10 in darkness and in the **s** of death,...... 6757
Ps 107:14 out of darkness and the **s** of death, ... 6757
Ps 109:23 I am gone like the **s** when it........... 6738
Ps 144:4 days are as a **s** that passeth away....... 6738
Ecc 6:12 vain life which he spendeth as a **s**? 6738
Ecc 8:13 prolong his days, which are as a **s**; 6738
SS 2:3 I sat down under his **s** with great 6738
Isa 4:6 tabernacle for a **s** in the daytime....... 6738
Isa 9:2 dwell in the land of the **s** of death,..... 6757
Isa 16:3 make thy **s** as the night in the 6738
Isa 25:4 from the storm, a **s** from the heat, ... 6738
Isa 30:2 and to trust in the **s** of Egypt!......... 6738
Isa 32:2 **s** of a great rock in a weary land. 6738
Isa 38:8 bring again the **s** of the degrees,....... 6738
Isa 49:2 in the **s** of his hand hath he hid me,.... 6738
Isa 51:16 thee in the **s** of mine hand, ... 6738
Jer 2:6 of drought, and of the **s** of death,...... 6757
Jer 13:16 light, he turn it into the **s** of death,..... 6757
La 4:20 Under his **s** we shall live among 6738
Eze 17:23 the **s** of the branches thereof shall 6738

Eze 31:6 under his **s** dwelt all great nations...... 6738
Da 4:12 beasts of the field had **s** under it, ... 2927
Hos 4:13 because the **s** thereof is good; 6738
Hos 14:7 that dwell under his **s** shall return;..... 6738
Am 5:8 the **s** of death into the morning,....... 6757
Mt 4:16 sat in the region and **s** of death........ *4639*
Mk 4:32 **air may lodge under the s of it** *4639*
Lk 1:79 in darkness and in the **s** of death....... *4639*
Ac 5:15 the **s** of Peter passing by might *4639*
Col 2:17 Which are a **s** of things to come;....... *4639*
Heb 8:5 example and **s** of heavenly things, ... *4639*
Heb 10:1 the law having a **s** of good things *4639*
Jas 1:17 variableness, neither **s** of turning........ *644*

SHADOWING
Heb 9:5 of glory **s** the mercyseat;.............. *2683*

SHADOWS
SS 2:17 day break, and the **s** flee away,......... 6752
SS 4:6 the day break, and the **s** flee away, ... 6752

SHAKE
Ne 5:13 So God **s** out every man from his...... 5287
Job 4:14 which made all my bones to **s**......... 6342
Ps 22:7 shoot out the lip, they **s** the head,...... 5128
Isa 2:19 ariseth to **s** terribly the earth. 6206
Isa 2:21 ariseth to **s** terribly the earth. 6206
Isa 11:15 shall he **s** his hand over the river. 5130
Isa 13:2 **s** the hand, that they may go into 5130
Isa 13:13 I will **s** the heavens, and the........... 7264
Isa 14:16 to tremble, that did **s** kingdoms;....... 7493
Isa 24:18 the foundations of the earth do **s** 7493
Isa 52:2 **S** thyself from the dust; arise, and...... 5287
Jer 23:9 all my bones **s**; I am like a 7363
Eze 26:10 thy walls shall **s** at the noise of 7493
Eze 26:15 the isles **s** at the sound of thy fall,...... 7493
Eze 31:16 nations to **s** at the sound of his fall, ... 7493
Eze 38:20 of the earth, shall **s** at my presence, ... 7493
Da 4:14 **s** off his leaves, and scatter his......... 5426
Joel 3:16 the heavens and the earth shall **s**: 7493
Am 9:1 of the door, that the posts may **s**: 7493
Hag 2:6 little while, and I will **s** the heavens,.... 7493
Hag 2:7 I will **s** all nations, and the desire 7493
Hag 2:21 I will **s** the heavens and the earth;...... 7493
Zec 2:9 I will **s** mine hand upon them, and 5130
Mt 10:14 **or city, s off the dust of your feet.** *1621*
Mt 28:4 for fear of him the keepers did **s**, ... *4579*
Mk 6:11 **s off the dust under your feet for.**...... *1621*
Lk 6:48 **that house, and could not s it: for** *4531*
Lk 9:5 **s off the very dust from your feet**....... *660*
Heb 12:26 once more I **s** not the earth only, ... *4579*

SHAKED
Ps 109:25 upon me they **s** their heads 5128

SHAKEN
Le 26:36 the sound of a **s** leaf chase them; 5086
2Ki 19:21 of Jerusalem hath **s** her head at........ 5128
Ps 18:7 of the hills moved and were **s**,......... 1607
Isa 37:22 of Jerusalem hath **s** her head at........ 5128
Na 2:3 the fir trees shall be terribly **s** 7477
Mt 11:7 **to see? A reed s with the wind?**........ *4531*
Mt 24:29 **powers of the heavens shall be s:** *4531*
Mk 13:25 **that are in heaven shall be s** *4531*
Lk 6:38 **measure, pressed down, s together,** *4532*
Lk 7:24 **to see? A reed s with the wind?**........ *4531*
Lk 21:26 **the powers of heaven shall be s.**........ *4531*
Ac 4:31 the place was **s** where they were *4531*
Ac 16:26 foundations of the prison were **s**:...... *4531*
2Th 2:2 That ye be not soon **s** in mind, or...... *4531*
Heb 12:27 which cannot be **s** may remain. *4531*
Rev 6:13 when she is **s** of a mighty wind. *4579*

SHAKETH
Job 9:6 **s** the earth out of her place, and 7264
Ps 29:8 of the Lord **s** the wilderness;.......... 2342
Isa 33:15 **s** his hands from holding of bribes..... 5287

SHAKING
Job 41:29 he laugheth at the **s** of a spear. 7494
Ps 44:14 a **s** of the head among the people...... 4493
Eze 37:7 was a noise, and behold a **s**, and 7494
Eze 38:19 be a great **s** in the land of Israel;....... 7494

SHAME
Ex 32:25 made them naked unto their **s** 8103
Jgs 18:7 that might put them to **s** in any 3637
1Sa 20:34 because his father had done him **s** 3637
2Sa 13:13 whither shall I cause my **s** to go?....... 2781
2Ch 32:21 with **s** of face to his own land. 1322
Ps 4:2 long will ye turn my glory into **s**?...... 3639
Ps 35:4 put to **s** that seek after my soul: 3637
Ps 40:14 and put to **s** that wish me evil. 3637
Ps 44:7 hast put them to **s** that hated us 954
Ps 53:5 thou hast put them to **s**, because 954
Ps 69:7 reproach; **s** hath covered my face 3639
Ps 71:24 for they are brought unto **s**, that....... 2659
Ps 83:16 Fill their faces with **s**; that they 7036
Ps 83:17 let them be put to **s**, and perish:....... 2659
Ps 89:45 thou hast covered him with **s**........... 955
Ps 119:31 O Lord, put me not to **s**. 954
Pr 3:35 **s** shall be the promotion of fools 7036
Pr 9:7 a scorner getteth to himself **s** 7036
Pr 10:5 in harvest is a son that causeth **s**........ 954
Pr 11:2 pride cometh, then cometh **s**: but...... 7036
Pr 12:16 but a prudent man covereth **s**......... 7036
Pr 13:5 is loathsome, and cometh to **s**. 2659
Pr 13:18 Poverty and **s** shall be to him 7036
Pr 14:35 is against him that causeth **s**............ 954
Pr 17:2 have rule over a son that causeth **s**, ... 954
Pr 18:13 heareth it, it is folly and **s** unto him. ... 3639
Pr 19:26 mother, is a son that causeth **s**,......... 954
Pr 25:8 thy neighbour hath put thee to **s**....... 3637
Pr 25:10 he that heareth it put thee to **s**,........ 2616
Pr 29:15 himself bringeth his mother to **s**........ 954
Isa 20:4 uncovered, to the **s** of Egypt.......... 6172
Isa 22:18 shall be the **s** of thy lord's house....... 7036
Isa 30:3 strength of Pharaoh be your **s**, ... 1322
Isa 47:3 yea, thy **s** shall be seen:............... 2781
Isa 50:6 hid not my face from **s** and spitting. ... 3639
Isa 54:4 for thou shalt not be put to **s**: 2659
Jer 3:24 **s** hath devoured the labour of our 1322
Jer 3:25 We lie down in our **s**, and our......... 1322
Jer 13:26 thy face, that thy **s** may appear 7036
Jer 20:18 days should be consumed with **s**?...... 1322
Jer 23:40 a perpetual **s**, which shall not be....... 3640
Jer 46:12 The nations have heard of thy **s**,....... 7036
Jer 51:51 **s** hath covered our faces: for 3639
Eze 16:52 bear thine own **s** for thy sins that 3639
Eze 16:63 mouth any more because of thy **s**, ... 3639
Eze 32:30 and bear their **s** with them that go..... 3639
Eze 34:29 neither bear the **s** of the heathen 3639
Eze 36:7 about you, they shall bear their **s** 3639
Eze 39:26 After that they have borne their **s**, ... 3639

Eze 44:13 but they shall bear their **s**, and 3639
Da 12:2 to **s** and everlasting contempt 2781
Hos 4:7 will I change their glory into **s** 7036
Hos 9:10 separated themselves unto that **s**; 1322
Mic 7:10 **s** shall cover her which said unto 955
Na 3:5 nakedness and the kingdoms thy **s** 7036
Hab 2:10 hast consulted **s** to thy house by 1322
Zep 3:5 but the unjust knoweth no **s** 1322
Zep 3:19 land where they have been put to **s** 1322
Lk 14:9 **begin with s to take the lowest** *152*
Ac 5:41 worthy to suffer **s** for his name *818*
1Co 4:14 I write not these things to **s** you, but *1788*
1Co 11:14 have long hair, it is a **s** unto him? *819*
1Co 11:22 of God, and **s** them who have not? *2617*
1Co 14:35 **s** for women to speak in the church. *149*
1Co 15:34 of God: I speak this to your **s** *1791*
Eph 5:12 a **s** even to speak of those things *149*
Php 3:19 and whose glory is in their **s**, who *152*
Heb 6:6 afresh, and put him to an open **s** *3856*
Heb 12:2 endured the cross, despising the **s** *152*
Jude 13 the sea, foaming out their own **s**; *152*
Rev 3:18 **s of thy nakedness do not appear;** *152*
Rev 16:15 he walk naked, and they see his **s** *808*

SHAMED See also ASHAMED.
2Sa 19:5 hast **s** this day the faces of all thy 3001
Ps 14:6 Ye have **s** the counsel of the poor, ... 954

SHAMEFACEDNESS
1Ti 2:9 modest apparel, with **s** and sobriety; *127*

SHAMEFULLY
Hos 2:5 that conceived them hath done **s**: 3001
Mk 12:4 **and sent him away s handled** *821*
Lk 20:11 **him also, and entreated him s,** *818*
1Th 2:2 and were **s** entreated, as ye know, ... *5195*

SHAMELESSLY
2Sa 6:20 vain fellows **s** uncovereth himself! 1540

SHAMETH
Pr 28:7 of riotous men **s** his father 3637

SHAPE
Lk 3:22 in a bodily **s** like a dove upon him *1491*
Jn 5:37 **voice at any time, nor seen his s** *1491*

SHAPEN
Ps 51:5 I was **s** in iniquity; and in sin did 2342

SHARP
Ex 4:25 Then Zipporah took a **s** stone, ... 6864
Jos 5:2 unto Joshua, Make thee **s** knives, ... 6697
Ps 45:5 Thine arrows are **s** in the heart 8150
Ps 52:2 mischiefs; like a **s** rasor, working 3913
Ps 57:4 and their tongue a **s** sword 2299
Pr 5:4 wormwood, **s** as a twoedged sword 2299
Isa 5:28 Whose arrows are **s**, and all their 8150
Isa 49:2 made my mouth like a **s** sword; 2299
Rev 1:16 mouth went a **s** twoedged sword: *3691*
Rev 2:12 **hath the s sword with two edges;** *3691*
Rev 14:14 crown, and in his hand a **s** sickle *3691*
Rev 14:17 heaven, he also having a **s** sickle *3691*
Rev 14:18 Thrust in thy **s** sickle, and gather *3691*
Rev 19:15 out of his mouth goeth a **s** sword, ... *3691*

SHARPENED
Ps 140:3 They have **s** their tongues like a 8150
Eze 21:9 A sword, a sword is **s**, and also 2300

SHARPENETH
Job 16:9 mine enemy **s** his eyes upon me 3913
Pr 27:17 Iron **s** iron; so a man **s** the 2300

SHARPER
Mic 7:4 the most upright is **s** than a thorn
Heb 4:12 and **s** than any two edged sword, ... *5114*

SHARPLY
Jgs 8:1 And they did chide with him **s** 2394
Tit 1:13 Wherefore rebuke them **s**, that *664*

SHAVE
Le 14:9 even all his hair he shall **s** off: and 1548
Le 21:5 they **s** off the corner of their beard, ... 1548
Nu 6:18 shall **s** the head of his separation 1548
Nu 8:7 let them **s** all their flesh, and 5674, 8593
Dt 21:12 she shall **s** her head, and pare 1548
Jgs 16:19 to **s** off the seven locks of his head; 1548

SHAVED
2Sa 10:4 **s** off the one half of their beards 1548
Job 1:20 **s** his head, and fell down upon 1494

SHAVEN
Jgs 16:17 if I be **s**, then my strength will go 1548
Jgs 16:22 hair … grow again after he was **s** 1548

SHEAF
Ge 37:7 about, and made obeisance to my **s** 485
Le 23:15 brought the **s** of the wave offering; 6016
Dt 24:19 and hast forgot a **s** in the field 6016

SHEARER
Ac 8:32 like a lamb dumb before his **s**, ... *2751*

SHEARERS
Isa 53:7 as a sheep before her **s** is dumb, so 1494

SHEATH
1Sa 17:51 and drew it out of his **s** thereof, ... 8593
1Ch 21:27 put his sword again into the **s** 5084
Eze 21:30 cause it to return into his **s**? I will 8593
Jn 18:11 **Put up thy sword into the s;** *2336*

SHEAVES
Ge 37:7 behold, your **s** stood round about, ... 485
Ru 2:15 Let her glean even among the **s**, ... 6016
Ps 126:6 rejoicing, bringing his **s** with him 485
Mic 4:12 gather them as the **s** into the floor 5995

SHED
Ge 9:6 by man shall his blood be **s**: for 8210
Ge 37:22 **S** no blood, but cast him into 8210
Ex 22:2 die, there shall no blood be **s** for him
Le 17:4 he hath **s** blood; and that man 8210
Nu 35:33 but by the blood of him that **s** it 8210
Dt 19:10 That innocent blood be not **s** in 8210
Dt 21:7 Our hands have not **s** this blood 8210
1Sa 25:33 me this day from coming to **s** blood
1Ki 2:5 and **s** the blood of war in peace 7760
1Ki 2:31 the innocent blood, which Joab **s** 8210
2Ki 21:16 Manasseh **s** innocent blood very 8210
2Ki 24:4 for the innocent blood that he **s** 8210
1Ch 22:8 Thou hast **s** blood abundantly, and 8210
1Ch 28:3 a man of war, and hast **s** blood 8210
Ps 79:3 Their blood have they **s** like water 8210
Ps 79:10 blood of thy servants which is **s** 8210
Ps 106:38 **s** innocent blood, even the blood 8210
Pr 1:16 to evil, and make haste to **s** blood 8210

Pr	6:17	and hands that **s** innocent blood	8210
Isa	59:7	make haste to **s** innocent blood:	8210
Jer	7:6	**s** not innocent blood in this place	8210
Jer	22:3	neither **s** innocent blood in this	8210
Jer	22:17	and for to **s** innocent blood, and	8210
La	4:13	**s** the blood of the just in the midst.	8210
Eze	16:38	wedlock and **s** blood are judged;.	8210
Eze	22:4	in thy blood that thou hast **s**: and.	8210
Eze	22:9	are men that carry tales to **s** blood:	8210
Eze	22:12	have they taken gifts to **s** blood;	8210
Eze	23:45	manner of women that **s** blood;	8210
Eze	33:25	toward your idols, and **s** blood:.	8210
Joel	3:19	**s** innocent blood in their land.	8210
Mt	23:35	**righteous blood s upon the earth,**	*1632*
Mt	26:28	**s for many for the remission of sins.**	*1632*
Mk	14:24	**testament, which is s for many**	*1632*
Lk	11:50	**which was s from the foundation**	*1632*
Lk	22:20	**in my blood, which is s for you**	*1632*
Ac	22:20	blood of thy martyr Stephen was **s**,	*1632*
Ro	3:15	Their feet are swift to **s** blood:.	*1632*
Ro	5:5	the love of God is **s** abroad in our	*1632*
Tit	3:6	**s** on us abundantly through Jesus.	*1632*
Rev	16:6	For they have **s** the blood of saints	*1632*

SHEDDETH

Ge	9:6	Whoso **s** man's blood, by man	8210
Eze	22:3	The city **s** blood in the midst of it,	8210

SHEDDING

Heb	9:22	and without **s** of blood is no	*130*

SHEEP

Ge	4:2	Abel was a keeper of **s**, but Cain	6629
Ge	31:19	And Laban went to shear his **s**	6629
Ex	22:1	oxen for an ox, and four **s** for a	6629
Ex	22:1	for an ox, and four ... for a **s**.	7716
Ex	22:4	whether it be ox, or ass, or **s**; he	7716
Le	22:21	a freewill offering in beeves or **s**,.	6629
Le	27:26	whether it be ox, or **s**: it is the	7716
Nu	18:17	the firstling of a **s**, or the firstling	3775
Nu	27:17	not as **s** which have no shepherd	6629
Nu	31:37	And the Lord's tribute of the **s** was.	6629
Dt	14:4	eat: the ox, the **s**, and the goat,	3775
Dt	17:1	bullock, or **s**, wherein is blemish.	7716
Dt	28:31	**s** shall be given unto thine enemies,	6629
Jgs	6:4	Israel, neither **s**, nor ox, nor ass.	7716
1Sa	8:17	He will take the tenth of your **s**.	6629
1Sa	14:34	every man his **s**, and slay them	7716
1Sa	15:14	meaneth then this bleating of the **s**	6629
1Sa	15:15	the people spared the best of the **s**	6629
1Sa	16:11	and, behold he keepeth the **s**.	6629
1Sa	17:20	left the **s** with a keeper, and took	6629
1Sa	17:28	whom hast thou left those few **s**	6629
1Sa	17:34	Thy servant kept his father's **s**	6629
1Sa	25:16	we were with them keeping the **s**	6629
2Sa	24:17	but these **s**, what have they done?	6629
1Ki	1:9	Adonijah slew **s** and oxen and fat	6629
1Ki	8:63	hundred and twenty thousand **s**.	6629
1Ki	22:17	as **s** that have not a shepherd:	6629
1Ch	21:17	for these **s**, what have they done?	6629
2Ch	7:5	hundred and twenty thousand **s**.	6629
2Ch	18:16	as **s** that have no shepherd: and	6629
2Ch	31:6	brought in the tithe of oxen and **s**,	6629
Ne	3:1	priests, and they builded the **s** gate;	6629
Ne	5:18	daily was one ox and six choice **s**;	6629
Job	1:3	substance ... was seven thousand **s**,	6629
Job	1:16	hath burned up the **s**, and the	6629
Job	42:12	for he had fourteen thousand **s**.	6629
Ps	44:22	are counted as **s** for the slaughter	6629
Ps	78:52	his own people to go forth like **s**,	6629
Ps	79:13	we thy people and **s** of thy pasture	6629
Ps	95:7	his pasture, and the **s** of his hand	6629
Ps	100:3	his people, and the **s** of his pasture.	6629
Ps	119:176	I have gone astray like a lost **s**;	7716
SS	4:2	Thy teeth are like a flock of **s** that	
Isa	13:14	and as a **s** that no man taketh up:.	6629
Isa	53:6	All we like **s** have gone astray; we	6629
Isa	53:7	and as a **s** before her shearers is	7353
Jer	12:3	them out like **s** for the slaughter	6629
Jer	23:1	and scatter the **s** of my pasture!	6629
Jer	50:6	My people hath been lost **s**: their	6629
Jer	50:17	Israel is a scattered **s**; the lions.	7716
Eze	34:6	My **s** wandered through all the	6629
Eze	34:11	even I, will both search my **s**, and	6629
Eze	34:12	so will I seek out my **s**, and will	6629
Hos	12:12	for a wife, and for a wife he kept **s**	
Mic	5:8	a young lion among the flocks of **s**.	6629
Zec	13:7	and the **s** shall be scattered: and I	6629
Mt	9:36	abroad, as **s** having no shepherd	*4263*
Mt	10:6	**rather to the lost s of the house**	*4263*
Mt	10:16	**send you forth as s in the midst**	*4263*
Mt	12:11	**shall have one s, and if it fall**	*4263*
Mt	12:12	**better then is a man better than a s?**	*4263*
Mt	15:24	**but unto the lost s of the house of**	*4263*
Mt	18:12	**if a man have an hundred s, and**	*4263*
Mt	18:13	**he rejoiceth more of that s, than**	
Mt	25:32	**divideth his s from the goats:**	*4263*
Mt	25:33	**shall set the s on his right hand,**	*4263*
Mt	26:31	**s of the flock shall be scattered**	*4263*
Mk	6:34	were as **s** not having a shepherd:.	*4263*
Mk	14:27	**and the s shall be scattered**	*4263*
Lk	15:6	**I have found my s which was lost.**	*4263*
Jn	2:14	that sold oxen and **s** and doves,.	*4263*
Jn	10:2	**the door is the shepherd of the s**	*4263*
Jn	10:3	**and he calleth his own s by name,**	*4263*
Jn	10:7	**unto you, I am the door of the s.**	*4263*
Jn	10:8	**but the s did not hear them.**	*4263*
Jn	10:11	**shepherd giveth his life for the s.**	*4263*
Jn	10:12	**shepherd, whose own the s are not,**	*4263*
Jn	10:13	**hireling, and careth not for the s**	*4263*
Jn	10:14	**know my s, and am known of mine,**	
Jn	10:15	**and I lay down my life for the s**	*4263*
Jn	10:16	**And other s I have, which are not**	*4263*
Jn	10:26	**ye are not of my s, as I said unto**	*4263*
Jn	10:27	**My s hear my voice, and I know**	*4263*
Jn	21:16	He saith unto him, **Feed my s**	*4263*
Jn	21:17	Jesus saith unto him, **Feed my s**	*4263*
Ac	8:32	He was led as a **s** to the slaughter;.	*4263*
Ro	8:36	accounted as **s** for the slaughter	*4263*
Heb	13:20	Jesus, that great shepherd of the **s**,	*4263*
1Pe	2:25	For ye were as **s** going astray; but	*4263*

SHEEPFOLD

Jn	10:1	**not by the door into the s, but**	*833, 4263*

SHEEP'S

Mt	7:15	**which come to you in s clothing,**	*4263*

SHEEPSKINS

Heb	11:37	they wandered about in **s** and	*3374*

SHEET

Ac	10:11	great **s** knit at the four corners,	*3607*
Ac	11:5	as it had been a great **s**, let down	*3607*

SHEKEL (she´-kul)

Ge 24:22	golden earring of half a **s** weight,	1235
Ex 30:13	sanctuary: (a **s** is twenty gerahs:)	8255
Ex 30:15	shall not give less than half a **s**	8255
Ex 38:26	for every man, that is, half a **s**,	8255
Le 5:15	after the **s** of the sanctuary	8255
Le 27:3	silver, after the **s** of the sanctuary	8255
2Ki 7:1	of fine flour be sold for a **s**, and	8255
2Ki 7:18	Two measures of barley for a **s**	8255
Am 8:5	the ephah small, and the **s** great	8255

SHEKELS

Ex 21:32	unto their master thirty **s** of silver,	8255
Ex 38:24	and seven hundred and thirty **s**,	8255
Le 5:15	with thy estimation by **s** of silver	8255
Le 27:3	estimation shall be fifty **s** of silver.	8255
Le 27:5	shall be of the male twenty **s**	8255
Le 27:5	and for the female ten **s**	8255
Nu 3:47	even take five **s** apiece by the poll,	8255
Nu 18:16	estimation, for the money of five **s**,	8255
Dt 22:19	amerce him in an hundred **s** of silver,	
Dt 22:29	the damsel's father fifty **s** of silver	
Jos 7:21	a wedge of gold of fifty **s** weight,	8255
Jgs 17:3	had restored the eleven hundred **s** of	
Jgs 17:10	and I will give thee ten **s** of silver by	
1Sa 17:5	coat was five thousand **s** of brass	8255
1Sa 17:7	weighed six hundred **s** of iron:	8255
2Sa 14:26	hair of his head two hundred **s**	8255
2Sa 18:12	a thousand **s** of silver in mine hand	
2Sa 21:16	weighed three hundred **s** of brass in	
2Sa 24:24	and the oxen for fifty **s** of silver	8255
1Ch 21:25	for the place six hundred **s** of gold	8255
2Ch 3:9	of the nails was fifty **s** of gold	8255
2Ch 9:15	hundred **s** of beaten gold went to one	
2Ch 9:16	hundred **s** of gold went to one shield	
Jer 32:9	money, even seventeen **s** of silver	8255

SHEPHERD

Ge 46:34	every **s** is an abomination	7462, 6629
Nu 27:17	be not as sheep which have no **s**	7462
1Ki 22:17	hills, as sheep that have not a **s**:	7462
2Ch 18:16	as sheep that have no **s**; and the	7462
Ps 23:1	The Lord is my **s**; I shall not want	7462
Ps 80:1	Give ear, O **S** of Israel, thou that	7462
Ecc 12:11	which are given from one **s**	7462
Isa 40:11	He shall feed his flock like a **s**: he	7462
Isa 44:28	That saith of Cyrus, He is my **s**,	7462
Isa 63:11	of the sea with the **s** of the flock?	7462
Jer 31:10	and keep him, as a **s** doth his flock	7462
Jer 49:19	and who is that **s** that will stand	7462
Jer 50:44	and who is that **s** that will stand	7462
Jer 51:23	in pieces … the **s** and his flock:	7462
Eze 34:8	because there was no **s**, neither did	7462
Eze 34:12	As a **s** seeketh out his flock in the	7462
Eze 34:23	And I will set up one **s** over them	7462
Eze 34:23	feed them, and he shall be their **s**	7462
Eze 37:24	and they all shall have one **s**: they	7462
Am 3:12	As the **s** taketh out of the mouth of	7462
Zec 10:2	troubled, because there was no **s**.	7462
Zec 11:15	yet the instruments of a foolish **s**	7462
Zec 11:16	lo, I will raise up a **s** in the land	7462
Zec 11:17	Woe to the idol **s** that leaveth the	7473
Zec 13:7	smite the **s**, and the sheep shall be	7462
Mt 9:36	abroad, as sheep having no **s**	*4166*
Mt 25:32	**a s divideth his sheep from the**	*4166*
Mt 26:31	**I will smite the s, and the sheep**	*4166*
Mk 6:34	they were as sheep not having a **s**:	*4166*
Mk 14:27	**I will smite the s, and the sheep**	*4166*
Jn 10:2	**in by the door is the s of the sheep.**	*4166*
Jn 10:11	**I am the good s: the good s**	*4166*
Jn 10:12	**that is an hireling, and not the s,**	*4166*
Jn 10:14	**I am the good s, and know my**	*4166*
Jn 10:16	**there shall be one fold, and one s**	*4166*
Heb 13:20	Jesus, that great **s** of the sheep,	*4166*
1Pe 2:25	returned unto the **S** and Bishop of	*4166*
1Pe 5:4	And when the chief **S** shall appear	*750*

SHEPHERDS

Ge 47:3	Thy servants are **s**, both we	7462, 6629
Ex 2:17	And the **s** came and drove them	7462
Isa 31:4	when a multitude of **s** is called forth	7462
Isa 56:11	they are **s** that cannot understand:	7462
Jer 23:4	And I will set up **s** over them which	7462
Jer 3:36	A voice of the cry of the **s**, and an	7462
Jer 50:6	their **s** have caused them to go	7462
Eze 34:2	prophesy against the **s** of Israel	7462
Eze 34:2	should not the **s** feed the flocks?	7462
Eze 34:8	but the **s** fed themselves, and fed	7462
Eze 34:10	Behold, I am against the **s**; and I	7462
Mic 5:5	shall we raise against him seven **s**,	7462
Zec 10:3	anger was kindled against the **s**,	7462
Zec 11:5	and their own **s** pity them not	7462
Zec 11:8	Three **s** also I cut off in one month;	7462
Lk 2:8	same country **s** abiding in the field,	*4166*

SHEW

Ge 12:1	unto a land that I will **s** thee:	7200
Ex 9:16	up, for to **s** in thee my power;	7200
Ex 10:1	that I might **s** these my signs	7896
Ex 18:20	shalt **s** them the way wherein	3045
Ex 33:19	will **s** mercy on whom I will **s** mercy	
Nu 16:5	the Lord will **s** who are his, and	3045
Dt 1:33	to **s** you by what way ye should go,	7200
Dt 5:5	to **s** you the word of the Lord:	5046
Dt 13:17	of his anger, and **s** thee mercy,	5414
Jos 2:12	ye will also **s** kindness unto my	6213
Jos 5:6	he would not **s** them the land	7200
Jgs 4:22	will **s** thee the man … thou seekest	7200
Jgs 6:17	**s** me a sign that thou talkest with	6213
1Sa 3:15	Samuel feared to **s** Eli the vision	5046
1Sa 9:27	I may **s** thee the word of God	8085
1Sa 16:3	I will **s** thee what thou shalt do:	3045
1Sa 22:17	he fled, and did not **s** it to me	1540
1Sa 25:8	young men, and they will **s** thee	5046
2Sa 2:6	**s** kindness and truth unto you:	6213
2Sa 9:7	surely **s** thee kindness for Jonathan	6213
2Sa 10:2	I will **s** kindness unto Hanun the	6213
2Sa 22:26	merciful thou wilt **s** thyself merciful	
2Sa 22:27	the pure thou wilt **s** thyself pure;	
2Sa 22:27	froward thou wilt **s** thyself unsavoury	
1Ki 1:52	If he will **s** himself a worthy man	
1Ki 18:1	saying Go, **s** thyself unto Ahab;	7200
2Ki 6:11	**s** me which of us is for the king	5046
2Ki 7:12	**s** you what the Syrians have done	5046
Ezr 2:59	could not **s** their father's house	5046
Ne 7:61	could not **s** their father's house	5046
Est 1:11	to **s** the people … her beauty:	7200
Ps 4:6	that say, Who will **s** us any good?	7200
Ps 9:1	**s** forth all thy marvellous works	5608
Ps 16:11	Thou wilt **s** me the path of life:	3045
Ps 18:26	the pure thou wilt **s** thyself pure;	
Ps 18:26	froward thou wilt **s** thyself froward	

Ps 25:4 S me thy ways, O Lord; teach me 3045
Ps 25:14 and he will s them his covenant 3045
Ps 39:6 every man walketh in a vain s 6754
Ps 51:15 my mouth shall s forth thy praise 5046
Ps 71:15 shall s forth thy righteousness 5608
Ps 85:7 S us thy mercy, O Lord, and 7200
Ps 86:17 S me a token for good; that they 6213
Ps 88:10 Wilt thou s wonders to the dead? 6213
Ps 92:15 To s that the Lord is upright: he 5046
Ps 94:1 vengeance belongeth, s thyself 3313
Ps 96:2 s … his salvation from day to day 1319
Ps 106:2 who can s forth all his praise? 8085
Ps 109:16 he remembered not to s mercy 6213
Pr 18:24 hath friends must s himself friendly:
Isa 3:9 The s of their countenance doth 1971
Isa 27:11 formed them will s them no favour
Isa 41:23 S the things that are to come, ... 5046
Isa 43:9 this, and s us former things? 8085
Isa 43:21 they shall s forth my praise 5608
Isa 47:6 thou didst s them no mercy; 7760
Isa 49:9 are in darkness, S yourselves 1540
Isa 58:1 s my people their transgression, ... 5046
Isa 60:6 s forth the praises of the Lord 1319
Jer 16:10 shalt s this people all these words 5046
Jer 18:17 I will s them the back, and not 7200
Jer 33:3 s thee great and mighty things 5046
Jer 50:42 they are cruel, and will not s mercy:
Eze 22:2 yea, thou shalt s her all her 3045
Eze 33:31 their mouth they s much love, ... 6213
Eze 37:18 thou not s us what thou meanest 5046
Eze 43:10 s the house to the house of Israel 5046
Eze 43:11 s them the form of the house 3045
Da 2:2 for to s the king his dreams 5046
Da 2:4 and we will s the interpretation 2324
Da 2:24 s unto the king the interpretation 2324
Da 4:2 I thought it good to s the signs 2324
Da 5:12 and he will s the interpretation 2324
Da 11:2 And now will I s thee the truth 5046
Joel 2:30 I will s wonders in the heavens 5414
Na 3:5 I will s the nations thy nakedness 7200
Hab 1:3 Why dost thou s me iniquity, and 7200
Zec 1:9 unto me, I will s thee what these be 7200
Zec 7:9 and s mercy and compassions 6213
Mt 8:4 thy way, s thyself to the priest 1166
Mt 11:4 Go and s John again those things 518
Mt 12:18 shall s judgment to the Gentiles 518
Mt 14:2 mighty works do s … themselves 1754
Mt 16:1 would s them a sign from heaven 1925
Mt 24:24 shall s great signs and wonders; 1325
Mk 13:22 and shall s signs and wonders, to 1325
Mk 14:15 he will s you a large upper room 1166
Lk 1:19 and to s thee these glad tidings 2097
Lk 5:14 but go, and s thyself to the priest, ... 1166
Lk 6:47 I will s you to whom he is like: 5263
Lk 8:39 s how great things God hath done. 1334
Lk 17:14 Go s yourselves unto the priests 1925
Lk 20:24 S me a penny. Whose image and 1925
Lk 20:47 and for a s make long prayers: 4392
Jn 5:20 s him greater works than these, ... 1166
Jn 7:4 things, s thyself to the world 5319
Jn 11:57 knew where he was, he should s it, ... 3377
Jn 14:8 s us the Father, and it sufficeth us 1166
Jn 14:9 sayest thou then, S us the Father? 1166
Jn 16:13 and he will s you things to come 312
Jn 16:14 receive of mine, and shall s it unto 312
Jn 16:15 take of mine, and shall s it unto 312
Jn 16:25 I shall s you plainly of the Father 312
Ac 1:24 s whether of these two thou hast 322
Ac 2:19 I will s wonders in heaven above, ... 1325
Ac 7:3 into the land which I shall s thee 1166
Ac 9:16 I will s him how great things 5263
Ac 16:17 s unto us the way of salvation 2605
Ac 24:27 willing to s the Jews a pleasure, ... 2698
Ro 9:22 What if God, willing to s his wrath, ... 1731
1Co 11:26 ye do s the Lord's death till he 2605
1Co 12:31 s I unto you a more excellent way 1166
1Co 15:51 I s you a mystery; We shall not 3004
Eph 2:7 he might s the exceeding riches 1731
1Ti 5:4 learn first to s piety at home, and 2151
2Ti 2:15 Study to s thyself approved unto 3936
Heb 6:17 to s unto the heirs of promise the 1925
Jas 2:18 s me thy faith without thy works 1166
Jas 2:18 I will s thee my faith by my works 1166
Jas 3:13 let him s out of a good conversation . . . 1166
1Jn 1:2 and s unto you that eternal life 518
Rev 1:1 to s unto his servants things which 1166
Rev 4:1 I will s thee things which must be 1166
Rev 17:1 I will s unto thee the judgment of 1166
Rev 21:9 I will s thee the bride, the Lamb's 1166
Rev 22:6 to s unto his servants the things 1166

SHEWBREAD See also BREAD.

Ex 25:30 shalt set upon the table s 3899, 6440
1Sa 21:6 was no bread there but the s, ... 3899, 6440
Mt 12:4 eat the s, which was not 740, 4286
Mk 2:26 eat the s, which is not lawful 740, 4286
Lk 6:4 and did take and eat the s, ... 740, 4286
Heb 9:2 and the table, and the s; 4286, 740

SHEWED

Ge 32:10 which thou hast s unto thy servant; 6213
Ge 39:21 with Joseph, and s him mercy 5186
Ge 41:25 God hath s Pharaoh what he is 5046
Ex 15:25 and the Lord s him a tree, which 3384
Ex 27:8 as it was s thee in the mount, so 7200
Le 13:49 and shall be s unto the priest: 7200
Nu 8:4 pattern … the Lord had s Moses 7200
Jos 2:12 since I have s you kindness, that 6213
Jgs 13:10 and ran, and s her husband, and 5046
2Sa 10:2 as his father s kindness unto me 6213
2Ki 8:10 Lord hath s me that he shall … die 7200
2Ki 8:13 Lord hath s me thou shalt be king 7200
2Ki 11:4 Lord, and s them the king's son 7200
2Ki 20:13 nothing … that Hezekiah s them not . . . 7200
Est 1:4 he s the riches of his glorious 7200
Est 2:20 Esther had not yet s her kindred 5046
Ps 78:11 his wonders that he had s them 7200
Ps 111:6 hath s his people the power of his 5046
Ps 142:2 him; I s before him my trouble 5046
Pr 26:26 wickedness shall be s before the 1540
Isa 40:14 s … him the way of understanding? . . . 3045
Isa 48:5 before it came to pass I s it thee: 8085
Eze 20:11 and s them my judgments, which 3045
Eze 22:26 neither have they s difference 3045
Mic 6:8 He hath s thee, O man, what is 5046
Mt 28:11 and s unto the chief priests all the 518
Lk 1:51 He hath s strength with his arm; 4160
Lk 4:5 s unto him all the kingdoms of the 1166
Lk 10:37 he said, He that s mercy on him 4160
Lk 14:21 came, and s his lord these things 518
Lk 20:37 even Moses s at the bush, when 3377
Lk 24:40 he s them his hands and his feet 1925

Jn	10:32	**good works have I s you from my**	*1166*
Jn	20:20	he **s** unto them his hands and his	*1166*
Jn	21:1	Jesus **s** himself again to the	*5319*
Jn	21:14	third time that Jesus **s** himself to	*5319*
Ac	1:3	To whom also he **s** himself alive	*3936*
Ac	3:18	**s** by ... mouth of all his prophets	*4293*
Ac	7:26	he **s** himself unto them as they	*3700*
Ac	7:36	**s** wonders and signs in the land	*4160*
Ac	7:52	slain them which **s** before of the	*4293*
Ac	10:40	day, and **s** him openly;	*1325, 1717, 1096*
Ac	11:13	he **s** us how he had seen an angel	*518*
Ac	20:35	I have **s** you all things, how that	*5263*
Ac	28:2	people **s** us no little kindness:	*3930*
1Co	10:28	eat not for his sake that **s** it, and	*3377*
Heb	6:10	which ye have **s** toward his name,	*1731*
Heb	8:5	the pattern **s** to thee in the mount	*1166*
Jas	2:13	without mercy, that hath **s** no mercy;	*4160*
Rev	21:10	and **s** me that great city, the holy	*1166*
Rev	22:1	he **s** me a pure river of water of	*1166*
Rev	22:8	the angel which **s** me these things.	*1166*

SHEWEST

Jn	2;18	What sign **s** thou unto us, seeing	*1166*
Jn	6:30	What sign **s** thou then, that we	*4160*

SHEWETH

Ge	41:28	about to do he **s** unto Pharaoh.	7200
Nu	23:3	and whatsoever he **s** me I will tell.	7200
1Sa	22:8	is none that **s** me that my son	1540, 241
2Sa	22:51	and **s** mercy to his anointed, unto	6213
Ps	19:1	the firmament **s** his handywork	5046
Ps	19:2	night unto night **s** knowledge	2331
Ps	112:5	A good man **s** favour, and lendeth:	
Pr	12:17	He that speaketh truth **s** forth	5046
Isa	41:26	there is none that **s**, yea, there is	5046
Mt	4:8	and **s** him all the kingdoms of the	*1166*
Jn	5:20	**s him all things that himself doeth:**	*1166*
Ro	9:16	runneth, but of God that **s** mercy.	*1653*
Ro	12:8	he that **s** mercy, with cheerfulness.	*1653*

SHEWING

Ex	20:6	**s** mercy unto thousands of them	6213
Dt	5:10	**s** mercy unto thousands of them	6213
Ps	78:4	**s** to the generation to come the	5608
Da	5:12	**s** of hard sentences, and dissolving	263
Lk	1:80	till the day of his **s** unto Israel	*323*
Ac	9:39	**s** the coats and garments which	*1925*
Ac	18:28	**s** by the scriptures that Jesus was	*1925*
2Th	2:4	of God, **s** himself that he is God	*584*
Tit	2:7	**s** thyself a pattern of good works:	*3930*
Tit	3:2	gentle, **s** all meekness unto all men.	*1731*

SHIBBOLETH (shib´-bo-leth) See also SIBBOLETH.

Jgs	12:6	said they unto him, Say now **S**:	7641

SHIELD

Ge	15:1	Fear not, Abram: I am thy **s**, and	4043
1Sa	17:7	one bearing a **s** went before him.	6793
1Sa	17:45	and with a spear, and with a **s**	3591
2Sa	22:3	he is my **s**, and the horn of my	4043
2Sa	22:36	given me the **s** of thy salvation:	4043
1Ki	10:17	three pound of gold went to one **s**	4043
2Ki	19:32	nor come before it with **s**, nor cast	4043
Ps	3:3	But thou, O Lord, art a **s** for me;	4043
Ps	18:35	given me the **s** of thy salvation:	4043
Ps	28:7	The Lord is my strength and my **s**;	4043
Ps	33:20	the Lord: he is our help and our **s**	4043
Ps	59:11	bring them down, O Lord our **s**	4043
Ps	84:11	For the Lord God is a sun and **s**	4043
Ps	91:4	his truth shall be thy **s** and	6793
Ps	115:11	he is their help and their **s**	4043
Ps	119:114	art my hiding place and my **s**	4043
Ps	144:2	my **s**, and he in whom I trust;	4043
Pr	30:5	he is a **s** unto them that put their	4043
Na	2:3	**s** of his mighty men is made red,	4043
Eph	6:16	taking the **s** of faith, wherewith	*2375*

SHIELDS

2Sa	8:7	David took the **s** of gold that were	7982
1Ki	10:17	three hundred **s** of beaten gold;	4043
1Ki	14:26	took away all the **s** of gold which	4043
2Ch	12:10	king Rehoboam made **s** of brass	4043
Ps	47:9	the **s** of the earth belong unto God:	4043
Isa	37:33	nor come before it with **s**, nor	4043
Eze	27:11	hanged their **s** upon thy walls	7982

SHINE

Nu	6:25	Lord make his face **s** upon thee,	215
Job	3:4	neither let the light **s** upon it.	3313
Ps	31:16	thy face to **s** upon thy servant:	215
Ps	67:1	and cause his face to **s** upon us	215
Ps	80:1	between the cherubims, **s** forth.	3313
Ps	80:19	cause thy face to **s**; and we	215
Ps	119:135	thy face to **s** upon thy servant;	215
Ecc	8:1	man's wisdom maketh his face to **s**,	215
Isa	13:10	moon shall not cause her light to **s**.	5050
Isa	60:1	Arise, **s**; for thy light is come,	215
Da	9:17	thy face to **s** upon thy sanctuary	215
Da	12:3	they that be wise shall **s** as the	2094
Mt	5:16	**Let your light so s before men,**	*2989*
Mt	13:43	**Then shall the righteous s forth**	*1584*
Mt	17:2	his face did **s** as the sun, and his	*2989*
2Co	4:4	image of God, should **s** unto them	*826*
2Co	4:6	who commanded the light to **s**	*2989*
Php	2:15	among whom ye **s** as lights in	*5316*
Rev	18:23	light of candle shall **s** no more	*5316*
Rev	21:23	neither of the moon, to **s** in it:	*5316*

SHINED

Job	31:26	If I beheld the sun when it **s**, or	1984
Ps	50:2	perfection of beauty, God hath **s**.	3313
Isa	9:2	upon them hath the light **s**	5050
Eze	43:2	and the earth **s** with his glory	215
Ac	9:3	**s** round about him a light from	*4015*
Ac	12:7	him, and a light **s** in the prison:	*2989*
2Co	4:6	of darkness, hath **s** in our hearts,	*2989*

SHINETH

Ps	139:12	but the night **s** as the day: the	215
Pr	4:18	**s** more and more unto the perfect	215
Mt	24:27	**east, and s even unto the west;**	*5316*
Lk	17:24	**s unto the other part under**	*2989*
Jn	1:5	And the light **s** in darkness; and	*5316*
2Pe	1:19	unto a light that **s** in a dark place,	*5316*
1Jn	2:8	is past, and the true light now **s**	*5316*
Rev	1:16	was as the sun **s** in his strength.	*5316*

SHINING

2Sa	23:4	of the earth by clear **s** after rain	5051
Pr	4:18	path of the just is as the **s** light,	5051
Isa	4:5	the **s** of the flaming fire by night:	5051
Joel	2:10	the stars shall withdraw their **s**:	5051
Joel	3:15	the stars shall withdraw their **s**	5051
Hab	3:11	at the **s** of thy glittering spear	5051

Mk 9:3 And his raiment became **s** *4744*
Lk 11:36 **bright s of a candle doth give** *796*
Lk 24:4 men stood by them in **s** garments: *797*
Jn 5:35 **He was a burning and a s light:** *5316*
Ac 26:13 **s** round about me and them *4034*

SHIP
Pr 30:19 way of a **s** in the midst of the sea; 591
Isa 33:21 oars, neither shall gallant **s** pass 6716
Jnh 1:3 he found a **s** going to Tarshish: 591
Jnh 1:5 gone down into the sides of the **s**; 5600
Mt 4:22 they immediately left the **s** and *4143*
Mt 8:24 the **s** was covered with the waves: *4143*
Mk 1:19 were in the **s** mending their nets *4143*
Mk 4:38 he was in the hinder part of the **s**
Lk 5:3 and taught the people out of the **s**, ... *4143*
Jn 21:6 **the net on the right side of the s,** *4143*
Ac 27:22 man's life among you, but of the **s** *4143*
Ac 27:31 Except these abide in the **s**, ye *4143*

SHIPMEN
1Ki 9:27 **s** that had knowledge of the 582, 591
Ac 27:30 the **s** were about to flee out of the *3492*

SHIPS
Ge 49:13 and he shall be for an haven of **s**; 591
Nu 24:24 **s** shall come from the coast of 6716
1Ki 9:26 made a navy of **s** in Ezion-geber
2Ch 9:21 the **s** of Tarshish bringing gold, ... 591
2Ch 20:37 the **s** were broken, that they were 591
Ps 48:7 Thou breakest the **s** of Tarshish 591
Ps 107:23 They that go down to the sea in **s** 591
Pr 31:14 She is like the merchants' **s**; she 591
Isa 23:14 Howl, ye **s** of Tarshish: for your 591
Eze 27:25 The **s** of Tarshish did sing of thee 591
Lk 5:7 they came, and filled both the **s**, ... *4143*
Jas 3:4 Behold also the **s**, which though *4143*
Rev 8:9 third part of the **s** were destroyed *4143*
Rev 18:19 made rich all that had **s** in the sea *4143*

SHIPWRECK
2Co 11:25 thrice I suffered **s**, a night and a *3489*
1Ti 1:19 Concerning faith have made **s**: *3489*

SHIVERS
Rev 2:27 **potter shall they be broken to s:** *4937*

SHOD
Mk 6:9 But be **s** with sandals; and not 5265
Eph 6:15 your feet **s** with the preparation 5265

SHOE
Dt 25:9 and loose his **s** from off his foot, ... 5275
Dt 29:5 **s** is not waxen old upon thy foot 5275
Jos 5:15 Loose thy **s** from off thy foot; for 5275
Ru 4:7 a man plucked off his **s**, and gave 5275
Ps 60:8 over Edom will I cast out my **s**: 5275
Isa 20:2 and put off thy **s** from thy foot 5275

SHOELATCHET
Ge 14:23 from a thread even to a **s** 8288, 5275

SHOE'S
Jn 1:27 **s** latchet I am not worthy to *5266*

SHOES
Ex 3:5 put off thy **s** from off thy feet, ... 5275
Ex 12:11 your **s** on your feet, and your staff 5275
Dt 33:25 Thy **s** shall be iron and brass; 4515
Jos 9:13 our **s** are become old by reason of 5275
Isa 5:27 nor the latchet of their **s** be broken: 5275
Am 2:6 and the poor for a pair of **s**; 5275
Am 8:6 and the needy for a pair of **s**; 5275
Mt 3:11 whose **s** I am not worthy to bear: *5266*
Mt 10:10 **neither two coats, neither s, nor** *5266*
Mk 1:7 the latchet of whose **s** I am not *5266*
Lk 3:16 the latchet of whose **s** I am not *5266*
Lk 10:4 **neither purse, nor scrip, nor s** *5266*
Lk 15:22 **ring on his hand, and s on his feet:** *5266*
Lk 22:35 **without purse, and scrip, and s,** *5266*
Ac 7:33 Put off thy **s** from thy feet: for the *5266*
Ac 13:25 **s** of his feet I am not worthy to *5266*

SHONE
Ex 34:35 that the skin of Moses' face **s**: and 7160
2Ki 3:22 and the sun **s** upon the water, and 2224
Lk 2:9 and the glory of the Lord **s** round *4034*
Ac 22:6 **s** from heaven a great light round *4015*
Rev 8:12 the day **s** not for a third part of it *5316*

SHOOK
2Sa 6:6 took hold of it; for the oxen **s** it 8058
2Sa 22:8 foundations of heaven moved and **s**, . . . 1607
Ne 5:13 Also I **s** my lap, and said, So God 5287
Ps 68:8 The earth **s**, the heavens also 7493
Ps 77:18 world: the earth trembled and **s** 7493
Ac 13:51 **s** off the dust of their feet against *1621*
Ac 18:6 he **s** his raiment, and said unto *1621*
Ac 28:5 he **s** off the beast into the fire, and *660*
Heb 12:26 Whose voice then **s** the earth: but *4531*

SHOOT
1Sa 20:36 find out now the arrows which I **s** 3384
2Sa 11:20 that they would **s** from the wall? 3384
2Ki 13:17 Then Elisha said, **S** And he shot 3384
2Ki 19:32 into this city, nor **s** an arrow there, ... 3384
2Ch 26:15 **s** arrows and great stones withal 3384
Ps 11:2 privily **s** at the upright in heart 3384
Ps 22:7 they **s** out the lip, they shake the 6362
Ps 64:3 bend their bows to **s** their arrows,
Ps 64:4 may **s** in secret at the perfect: 3384
Ps 64:7 God shall **s** at them with an arrow; 3384
Jer 50:14 bow, **s** at her, spare no arrows: 3034

SHORE
Ge 22:17 the sand which is upon the sea **s**; 8193
Ex 14:30 the Egyptians dead upon the sea **s** 8193
Jos 11:4 that is upon the sea **s** in multitude, ... 8193
1Ki 4:29 as the sand that is on the sea **s** 8193
Mt 13:2 whole multitude stood on the **s** *123*
Mt 13:48 **when it was full, they drew to s,** *123*
Jn 21:4 now come, Jesus stood on the **s**: *123*
Ac 21:5 and we kneeled down on the **s**, and *123*
Heb 11:12 as the sand which is by the sea **s** *5491*

SHORT
Nu 11:23 Is the Lord's hand waxed **s**? 7114
2Ki 10:32 days the Lord began to cut Israel **s**:
Ps 89:47 Remember how **s** my time is: 2465
Ro 3:23 and come **s** of the glory of God; *5302*
Ro 9:28 and cut it **s** in righteousness: *4932*
1Co 7:29 this I say, brethren, the time is **s**: *4958*
Heb 4:1 of you should seem to come **s** of it *5302*
Rev 12:12 knoweth that he hath but a **s** time *3641*
Rev 17:10 he must continue a **s** space *3641*

SHORTENED
Ps 89:45 The days of his youth hast thou **s**: 7114
Pr 10:27 the years of the wicked shall be **s** 7114
Isa 50:2 Is my hand **s** at all, that it cannot 7114
Isa 59:1 Behold, the Lord's hand is not **s**,....... 7114
Mt 24:22 **elect's sake those days shall be s** *2856*
Mk 13:20 **that the Lord had s those days,**........ *2856*

SHORTLY
Ge 41:32 and God will **s** bring it to pass 4116
Jer 27:16 **s** be brought again from Babylon: 4120
Eze 7:8 I **s** pour out my fury upon thee 7138
Ro 16:20 bruise Satan under your feet **s**.... *1722, 5034*
2Ti 4:9 thy diligence to come **s** unto me: *5030*
2Pe 1:14 that **s** I must put off this my *5031*
Rev 1:1 which must **s** come to pass;...... *1722, 5034*
Rev 22:6 things which must **s** be done..... *1722, 5034*

SHOT
Ge 49:23 and **s** at him, and hated him:.......... 7232
Ex 19:13 surely be stoned, or **s** through; 3384
1Sa 20:37 the arrow which Jonathan had **s**, ... 3384
2Sa 11:24 And the shooters **s** from off the wall ... 3384
2Ki 13:17 Then Elisha said, Shoot. And he **s**...... 3384
2Ch 35:23 And the archers **s** at king Josiah;....... 3384
Ps 18:14 an he **s** out lightnings, and 7232
Jer 9:8 tongue is as an arrow **s** out; it 7819

SHOULDER
Ge 24:45 forth with her pitcher on her **s**;........ 7926
Ex 29:27 the **s** of the heave offering, which. 7785
Le 7:34 and the heave **s** have I taken of........ 7785
Le 10:15 heave **s** and the wave breast shall 7785
Nu 6:19 take the sodden **s** of the ram, ... 2220
Jos 4:5 man of you a stone upon his **s**,........ 7926
Ne 9:29 withdrew the **s**, and hardened......... 3802
Isa 9:6 government shall be upon his **s**:........ 7926
Isa 10:27 shall be taken away from off thy **s** 7926
Isa 22:22 house of David will I lay upon his **s**; ... 7926
Eze 12:12 bear upon his **s** in the twilight,........ 3802
Eze 29:18 bald, and every **s** was peeled:.......... 3802
Zec 7:11 to hearken, and pulled away the **s**, ... 3802

SHOULDERS
Ge 9:23 and laid it upon both their **s**, and...... 7926
Ex 28:12 stones upon the **s** of the ephod........ 3802
Dt 33:12 and he shall dwell between his **s**....... 3802
Jgs 16:3 put them upon his **s**, and carried 3802
1Sa 9:2 from his **s** and upward he was......... 7926
1Sa 17:6 a target of brass between his **s**......... 3802
1Ch 15:15 bare the ark of God upon their **s** 3802
2Ch 35:3 shall not be a burden upon your **s**:..... 3802
Isa 49:22 shall be carried upon their **s** 3802
Eze 12:6 sight shalt thou bear it upon thy **s** 3802
Mt 23:4 **borne, and lay them on men's s;**....... *5606*
Lk 15:5 **hath found it, he layeth it on his s,**..... *5606*

SHOUT
Ex 32:18 voice of them that **s** for mastery....... 6030
Nu 23:21 the **s** of a king is among them......... 8643
Jos 6:16 Joshua said unto the people, **S**; for..... 7321
1Sa 4:6 noise of this great **s** in the camp....... 8643
Ezr 3:13 not discern the noise of the **s** of joy 8643
Ps 5:11 let them ever **s** for joy, because 7442
Ps 32:11 **s** for joy, all ye that are upright in...... 7442
Ps 35:27 Let them **s** for joy, and be glad,........ 7442
Ps 47:5 God is gone up with a **s**, the Lord...... 8643
Ps 132:9 and let thy saints **s** for joy 7442
Ps 132:16 her saints shall **s** aloud for joy......... 7442
Isa 12:6 Cry out and **s**, thou inhabitant of...... 7442
Isa 44:23 **s**, ye lower parts of the earth:.......... 7321
Jer 25:30 he shall give a **s**, as they that 6030, 1959
Jer 31:7 **s** among the chief of the nations:...... 6670
La 3:8 when I cry and **s**, he shutteth out 7768
Zep 3:14 **s**, O Israel; be glad and rejoice......... 7321
Zec 9:9 Zion; **s**, O daughter of Jerusalem:...... 7321
Ac 12:22 And the people gave a **s**, saying, ... *2019*
1Th 4:16 descend from heaven with a **s**, ... *2752*

SHOUTED
Ex 32:17 the noise of the people as they **s**....... 7452
Le 9:24 when all the people saw, they **s**........ 7442
Jos 6:20 the people **s** with a great shout, ... 7321
Jgs 15:14 Lehi, the Philistines **s** against him: 7321
1Sa 4:5 all Israel **s** with a great shout, so....... 7321
1Sa 10:24 the people **s**, and said, God save the.... 7321
Ezr 3:12 voice; and many **s** aloud for joy:....... 8643

SHOUTETH
Ps 78:65 man that **s** by reason of wine 7442

SHOUTING
2Sa 6:15 up the ark of the Lord with **s** 8643
1Ch 15:28 up the ark ... of the Lord with **s**....... 8643
Pr 11:10 when the wicked perish, there is **s** 7440
Isa 16:10 singing, neither shall there be **s**: 7321
Jer 20:16 morning, and the **s** at noontide;....... 8643
Jer 48:33 their **s** shall be no **s**.................. 1959
Eze 21:22 to lift up the voice with **s**, ... 8643
Am 1:14 thereof, with **s** in the day of battle 8643

SHOW See SHEW.

SHOWER
Eze 34:26 I will cause the **s** to come down in..... 1653
Lk 12:54 **ye say, There cometh a s; and so**....... *3655*

SHOWERS
Dt 32:2 and as the **s** upon the grass:........... 7241
Ps 72:6 grass: as **s** that water the earth......... 7241
Jer 3:3 the **s** have been withholden, and....... 7241
Jer 14:22 rain? or can the heavens give **s**?........ 7241
Eze 34:26 there shall be **s** of blessing 1653
Mic 5:7 the Lord, as the **s** upon the grass....... 7241

SHRINES
Ac 19:24 which made silver **s** for Diana, ... *3485*

SHUN
2Ti 2:16 But **s** profane and vain babblings:...... *4026*

SHUT
Ge 7:16 him: and the Lord **s** him in 5462
Ge 19:10 house to them, and **s** to the door 5462
Ex 14:3 the wilderness hath **s** them in 5462
Le 13:4 priest shall **s** up him that hath the 5462
Le 13:11 unclean, and shall not **s** him up:....... 5462
Le 13:50 **s** up it that hath the plague seven...... 5462
Le 13:54 he shall **s** it up seven days more:....... 5462
Nu 12:15 Miriam was **s** out from the camp...... 5462
Dt 11:17 **s** up the heaven, that there be no 6113
Dt 15:7 nor **s** thine hand from thy poor 7092
Dt 32:30 and the Lord had **s** them up? 5462
Jos 6:1 Jericho was straitly **s** up because....... 5462
1Sa 1:5 but the Lord had **s** up her womb 5462
1Sa 23:7 for he is **s** in, by entering into a........ 5462

2Sa 20:3	**s** up unto the day of their death	6887
1Ki 8:35	When heaven is **s** up, and there is	6113
2Ki 4:33	and **s** the door upon them twain,	5462
2Ki 6:32	**s** the door, and hold him fast at the	5462
2Ch 7:13	I **s** up heaven that there be no rain,	6113
2Ch 28:24	**s** up the doors of the house of the	5462
Ne 7:3	let them **s** the doors, and bar them:	1479
Ne 13:19	that the gates should be **s**, and	5462
Ps 69:15	not the pit **s** her mouth upon me	332
Ps 77:9	in anger **s** up his tender mercies?	7092
Ecc 12:4	the doors shall be **s** in the streets	5462
Isa 6:10	their ears heavy, and **s** their eyes;	8173
Isa 22:22	he shall open, and none shall **s**;	5462
Isa 22:22	and he shall **s**, and none shall open	5462
Isa 24:10	every house is **s** up, that no man	5462
Isa 44:18	for he hath **s** their eyes, that they	2902
Isa 45:1	and the gates shall not be **s**;	5462
Isa 52:15	kings shall **s** their mouths at him:	7092
Isa 66:9	to bring forth, and **s** the womb?	6113
Jer 20:9	a burning fire **s** up in my bones	6113
Eze 46:2	gate shall not be **s** until … evening	5462
Da 6:22	and hath **s** the lions' mouths, that	5463
Da 12:4	But thou, O Daniel, **s** up the words,	5640
Mt 6:6	**and when thou hast s thy door**	*2808*
Mt 23:13	**for ye s up the kingdom of heaven**	*2808*
Mt 25:10	**the marriage: and the door was s**	*2808*
Lk 4:25	**heaven was s up three years and**	*2808*
Lk 11:7	**the door is now s, and my children**	*2808*
Lk 13:25	**is risen up, and hath s to the door,**	*608*
Jn 20:26	then came Jesus, the doors being **s**	*2808*
Ac 5:23	The prison truly found we **s** with	*2808*
Ac 21:30	and forthwith the doors were **s**	*2808*
Ac 26:10	of the saints did I **s** up in prison	*2623*
Gal 3:23	**s** up unto the faith which should	*4788*
Rev 3:8	**open door, and no man can s it:**	*2808*
Rev 11:6	These have power to **s** heaven, that	*2808*
Rev 20:3	the bottomless pit, and **s** him up,	*2808*
Rev 21:25	the gates of it shall not be **s** at all	*2808*

SHUTTETH

Pr 16:30	He **s** his eyes to devise froward	6095
Pr 17:28	that **s** his lips is esteemed a man	331
Isa 33:15	and **s** his eyes from seeing evil;	6105
La 3:8	and shout, he **s** out my prayer	5640
1Jn 3:17	**s** up his bowels of compassion	2808
Rev 3:7	**he that openeth, and no man s;**	*2808*
Rev 3:7	**and s, and no man openeth;**	*2808*

SIBBOLETH (sib´-bo-leth) **See also SHIBBOLETH.**

Jgs 12:6	and he said **S**: for he could not	5451

SICK

1Sa 19:14	to take David, she said, He is **s**	2470
1Sa 30:13	because three days agone I fell **s**	2470
2Sa 12:15	bare unto David, and it was very **s**	605
2Sa 13:5	on thy bed, and make thyself **s**	2470
1Ki 14:5	of thee for her son; for he is **s**	2470
2Ki 13:14	Elisha was fallen **s** of his sickness	2470
2Ki 20:1	days was Hezekiah **s** unto death.	2470
Ne 2:2	sad, seeing thou art not **s**? this	2470
Pr 13:12	Hope deferred maketh the heart **s**	2470
Pr 23:35	shalt thou say, and I was not **s**;	2470
Isa 1:5	the whole head is **s**, and the whole	2483
Isa 38:1	days was Hezekiah **s** unto death.	2470
Jer 14:18	them that are **s** with famine!	8463
Eze 34:4	have ye healed that which was **s**	2470
Da 8:27	fainted, and was **s** certain days;	2470
Hos 7:5	king the princes have made him **s**	2470
Mk 6:13	will I make thee **s** in smiting thee,	2470
Mal 1:8	if ye offer the lame and **s**, is it not	2470
Mal 1:13	was torn, and the lame, and the **s**;	2470
Mt 4:24	brought unto him all **s** people	*2192, 2560*
Mt 8:16	and healed all that were **s**	*2192, 2560*
Mt 9:12	**physician, but they that are s**	*2192, 2560*
Mt 10:8	**Heal the s, cleanse the lepers,**	*770*
Mt 14:14	toward them, and he healed their **s**	*732*
Mt 25:36	**I was s, and ye visited me: I was**	*770*
Mt 25:39	**when saw we thee s, or in prison,**	*772*
Mt 25:43	**s, and in prison, and ye visited me.**	*772*
Mt 25:44	**naked, or s, or in prison, and did**	*772*
Mk 1:30	Simon's wife's mother lay **s** of a	*4445*
Mk 2:9	**easier to say to the s of the palsy,**	*3885*
Mk 2:17	**physician, but they that are s:**	*2192, 2560*
Mk 6:13	anointed with oil many that were **s**	*732*
Mk 6:56	they laid the **s** in the streets, and	*770*
Mk 16:18	**they shall lay hands on the s,**	*732*
Lk 5:31	**physician; but they that are s**	*2192, 2560*
Lk 9:2	kingdom of God, and to heal the **s**	*770*
Jn 11:2	hair, whose brother Lazarus was **s**.)	*770*
Jn 11:3	behold, he whom thou lovest is **s**	*770*
Ac 5:15	they brought forth the **s** into the	*772*
Ac 19:12	brought unto the **s** handkerchiefs	*770*
Php 2:27	indeed he was **s** nigh unto death:	*770*
Jas 5:14	Is any **s** among you? let him call	*770*
Jas 5:15	prayer of faith shall save the **s**,	*2577*

SICKLE

Dt 23:25	not move a **s** unto thy neighbour's	2770
Joel 3:13	Put ye in the **s**, for the harvest is	4038
Mk 4:29	**immediately he putteth in the s**	*1407*
Rev 14:15	cloud, Thrust in thy **s**, and reap:	*1407*
Rev 14:17	heaven, he also having a sharp **s**	*1407*
Rev 14:19	angel thrust in his **s** into the earth,	*1407*

SICKLY

1Co 11:30	many are weak and **s** among you,	*732*

SICKNESS

Dt 7:15	will take away from thee all **s**.	2483
Dt 28:61	Also every **s**, and every plague	2483
1Ki 8:37	plague, whatsoever **s** there be;	4245
2Ch 21:15	bowels fall out by reason of the **s**	2483
Ps 41:3	wilt make all his bed in his **s**	2483
Ecc 5:17	sorrow and wrath with his **s**	2483
Isa 38:9	sick, and was recovered of his **s**.	2483
Mt 4:23	healing all manner of **s** and all	*3554*
Mt 9:35	healing every **s** and every disease	*3554*
Mt 10:1	to heal all manner of **s** and all	*3554*
Jn 11:4	**This s is not unto death, but for**	*769*

SICKNESSES

Dt 29:22	**s** which the Lord hath laid upon	8463
Mt 8:17	our infirmities, and bare our **s**	*3554*
Mk 3:15	to have power to heal **s** and to	*3554*

SIDE

Ge 38:21	harlot, that was openly by the way **s**?	
Ex 12:23	upon the lintel, and on the two **s** posts	
Ex 27:9	an hundred cubits long for one **s**	6285
Ex 32:26	said, Who is on the Lord's **s**? let him	
Le 1:11	shall kill it on the **s** of the altar	3409
Le 1:15	be wrung out at the **s** of the altar:	7023
Le 5:9	sin offering upon the **s** of the altar;	7023
Nu 32:32	inheritance on this **s** Jordan may	5676

Nu	35:14	give three cities on this **s** Jordan,	5676
Dt	4:32	one **s** of heaven unto the other,	7097
Dt	31:26	in the **s** of the ark of the covenant	6654
Jos	1:15	gave you on this **s** Jordan toward	5676
Jos	14:3	half tribe on the other **s** Jordan:	5676
Jos	22:4	gave you on the other **s** Jordan	5676
Jos	24:3	from the other **s** of the flood, and	5676
Jos	24:14	fathers served on the other **s** of	5676
Jgs	7:12	sand by the sea **s** for multitude	8193
Jgs	8:34	of all their enemies on every **s**:	5439
1Sa	4:18	backward by the **s** of the gate,	3027
2Sa	2:16	thrust his sword in his fellow's **s**;	6654
1Ki	5:3	which were about him on every **s**	
1Ki	5:4	hath given me rest on every **s**	5439
1Ch	22:18	he not given you rest on every **s**?	5439
2Ch	14:7	he hath given us rest on every **s**	5439
Ezr	4:16	have no portion on this **s** the river	5675
Ne	4:18	had his sword girded by his **s**,	4975
Job	1:10	about all that he hath on every **s**?	5439
Ps	12:8	The wicked walk on every **s**, when	5439
Ps	31:13	fear was on every **s**: while they	5439
Ps	71:21	and comfort me on every **s**	5437
Ps	91:7	A thousand shall fall at thy **s**, and	6654
Ps	118:6	Lord is on my **s**; I will not fear:	
Ps	124:1	been the Lord who was on our **s**	
Jer	20:10	defaming of many, fear on every **s**	5439
Jer	49:29	cry unto them, Fear is on every **s**	5439
Eze	1:10	the face of a lion, on the right **s**	3225
Eze	4:6	lie again on thy right **s**, and thou	6654
Eze	4:9	days that thou shalt lie upon thy **s**	6654
Eze	10:3	cherubims stood on the right **s** of	3225
Eze	16:33	come unto thee on every **s** for thy	5439
Eze	28:23	by the sword upon her on every **s**;	5439
Eze	37:21	and will gather them on every **s**	5439
Eze	45:7	other **s** of the oblation of the holy	
Da	7:5	and it raised up itself on one **s**,	7859
Mt	13:4	**some seeds fell by the way s, and**	*3844*
Mt	13:19	**which received seed by the way s**	*3844*
Lk	8:5	**he sowed, some fell by the way s.**	*3844*
Lk	8:12	**Those by the way s are they that**	*3844*
Jn	19:34	with a spear pierced his **s**, and	*4125*
Jn	20:20	unto them his hands and his **s**	*4125*
Jn	20:25	and thrust my hand into his **s**, I	*4125*
Jn	20:27	**thy hand, and thrust it into my s**	*4125*
Jn	21:6	**Cast the net on the right s of the**	*3313*
2Co	4:8	We are troubled on every **s**, yet not	
2Co	7:5	but we were troubled on every **s**;	

SIDES

Ex	25:14	into the rings by the **s** of the ark,	6763
Ex	38:7	the rings on the **s** of the altar	6763
Nu	33:55	your eyes, and thorns in your **s**.	6654
Jos	23:13	and scourges in your **s**, and thorns	6654
Jgs	2:3	they shall be as thorns in your **s**	6654
Eze	10:11	went, they went upon their four **s**;	7253
Eze	32:23	graves are set in the **s** of the pit,	3411
Jnh	1:5	gone down into the **s** of the ship;	3411

SIEGE

Dt	20:19	down … to employ them in the **s**.	4692
Dt	28:55	he hath nothing left in the **s**, and	4692
2Ch	32:10	ye abide in the **s** in Jerusalem?	4692
Jer	19:9	eat the flesh of his friend in the **s**	4692
Eze	4:2	And lay **s** against it, and build a	4692
Eze	4:3	and thou shalt lay **s** against it	6696
Eze	4:7	face toward the **s** of Jerusalem.	4692
Eze	5:2	when the days of the **s** are fulfilled:	4692
Mic	5:1	troops: he hath laid **s** against us:	4692
Na	3:14	Draw thee waters for the **s**, fortify	4692
Zec	12:2	shall be in the **s** both against Judah	4692

SIFT

Isa	30:28	to **s** the nations with the sieve of	5130
Am	9:9	I will **s** the house of Israel among	5128
Lk	22:31	**you, that he may s you as wheat:**	*4617*

SIGH

La	1:11	All her people **s**, they seek bread;	584
La	1:21	They have heard that I **s**: there is	584

SIGHED

Ex	2:23	children of Israel **s** by reason of	584
Mk	7:34	And looking up to heaven, he **s**.	*4727*
Mk	8:12	he **s** deeply in his spirit, and saith	*389*

SIGHING

Ps	12:5	of the poor, for the **s** of the needy	603
Isa	35:10	and sorrow and **s** shall flee away	585
Jer	45:3	fainted in my **s**, and I find no rest.	585

SIGHT

Ge	2:9	every tree that is pleasant to the **s**,	4758
Ge	23:4	may bury my dead out of my **s**.	6440
Ge	39:4	And Joseph found grace in his **s**	5869
Ge	39:21	him favour in the **s** of the keeper	5869
Ex	3:3	turn aside, and see this great **s**,	4758
Ex	11:3	in the **s** of Pharaoh's servants, and	5869
Ex	15:26	wilt do that which is right in his **s**	5869
Ex	19:11	down in the **s** of all the people upon	5869
Ex	24:17	the **s** of the glory of the Lord	4758
Ex	33:17	for thou hast found grace in my **s**	5869
Ex	40:38	in the **s** of all the house of Israel.	5869
Le	10:19	been accepted in the **s** of the Lord?	5869
Nu	13:33	were in our own **s** as grasshoppers,	5869
Nu	27:19	and give him a charge in their **s**	5869
Nu	32:5	if we have found grace in thy **s**, let	5869
Nu	32:13	had done evil in the **s** of the Lord.	5869
Dt	4:25	shall do evil in the **s** of the Lord	5869
Dt	6:18	and good in the **s** of the Lord:	5869
Dt	9:18	wickedly in the **s** of the Lord, to	5869
Dt	21:9	which is right in the **s** of the Lord	5869
Dt	31:7	unto him in the **s** of all Israel,	5869
Dt	31:29	ye will do evil in the **s** of the Lord,	5869
Jos	3:7	magnify thee in the **s** of all Israel,	5869
Jgs	10:6	did evil again in the **s** of the Lord.	5869
1Sa	1:18	handmaid find grace in thy **s**.	5869
1Sa	12:17	ye have done in the **s** of the Lord	5869
1Sa	15:17	thou wast little in thine own **s**.	5869
1Sa	16:22	for he hath found favour in my **s**	5869
2Sa	7:19	was yet a small thing in thy **s**,	5869
2Sa	12:9	of the Lord, to do evil in his **s**?	5869
2Sa	12:11	with thy wives in the **s** of this sun.	5869
2Sa	16:4	thee that I may find grace in thy **s**	5869
2Sa	16:22	concubines in the **s** of all Israel.	5869
1Ki	8:25	shall not fail thee a man in my **s**.	6440
1Ki	11:6	did evil in the **s** of the Lord, and	5869
1Ki	14:22	Judah did evil in the **s** of the Lord	5869
1Ki	21:25	wickedness in the **s** of the Lord.	5869
2Ki	1:13	thy servants, be precious in thy **s**	5869
2Ki	3:18	a light thing in the **s** of the Lord:	5869
2Ki	21:6	wickedness in the **s** of the Lord.	5869
2Ki	23:27	remove Judah also out of my **s**	6440
2Ki	24:3	to remove them out of his **s**, for	6440

1Ch 19:13 do that which is good in his **s** 5869
1Ch 28:8 therefore in the **s** of all Israel the 5869
1Ch 29:25 exceedingly in the **s** of all Israel. 5869
2Ch 6:16 shall not fail thee a man in my **s**. 6440
2Ch 7:20 will I cast out of my **s**, and will. 6440
2Ch 33:6 much evil in the **s** of the Lord. 5869
Est 2:15 favour in the **s** of all them that looked . . 5869
Job 15:15 the heavens are not clean in his **s** 5869
Ps 5:5 foolish shall not stand in thy **s** 5869
Ps 9:19 the heathen be judged in thy **s** 6440
Ps 19:14 be acceptable in thy **s**, O Lord, ... 6440
Ps 51:4 sinned and done this evil in thy **s**. 5869
Ps 76:7 who may stand in thy **s** when once 6440
Ps 90:4 For a thousand years in thy **s** are 5869
Ps 101:7 telleth lies shall not tarry in my **s** 5869
Ps 116:15 Precious in the **s** of the Lord is the. 5869
Ps 143:2 in thy **s** shall no man living be 6440
Pr 1:17 net is spread in the **s** of any bird. 5869
Pr 3:4 understanding in the **s** of God and 5869
Pr 4:3 beloved in the **s** of my mother. 6440
Ecc 2:26 man that is good in his **s** wisdom, ... 6440
Ecc 6:9 Better is the **s** of the eyes than. 4758
Ecc 8:3 Be not hasty to go out of his **s**. 6440
Ecc 11:9 heart, and in the **s** of thine eyes: 4758
Isa 5:21 eyes, and prudent in their own **s**! 6440
Isa 11:3 not judge after the **s** of his eyes, ... 4758
Jer 7:30 of Judah have done evil in my **s**, ... 5869
Jer 32:12 in the **s** of Hanameel mine uncle's 5869
Jer 51:24 they have done in Zion in your **s**, ... 5869
Eze 10:19 mounted up from the earth in my **s**. . . . 5869
Eze 20:43 lothe yourselves in your own **s** 6440
Eze 36:31 lothe yourselves in your own **s** 6440
Da 4:20 and the **s** thereof to all the earth; 2379
Mal 2:17 evil is good in the **s** of the Lord, ... 5869
Mt 11:5 **The blind receive their s, and the** *308*
Mt 11:26 **for so it seemed good in thy s** *1715*
Lk 4:18 **and recovering of s to the blind,** *309*
Lk 10:21 **for so it seemed good in thy s** *1715*
Lk 15:21 **against heaven, and in thy s** *1799*
Lk 16:15 **is abomination in the s of God.** *1799*
Lk 18:42 Jesus said unto him, **Receive thy s** *308*
Lk 24:31 him; and he vanished out of their **s**
Jn 9:11 went and washed, and I received **s** *308*
Ac 1:9 cloud received him out of their **s** *3788*
Ac 4:19 Whether it be right in … **s** of God *1799*
Ac 8:21 heart is not right in the **s** of God. *1799*
Ac 9:9 And he was three days without **s**, ... *991*
Ac 9:12 **him, that he might receive his s** *308*
Ro 3:20 shall no flesh be justified in his **s**. *1799*
Ro 12:17 things honest in the **s** of all men. *1799*
2Co 2:17 the **s** of God speak we in Christ *2714*
2Co 4:2 man's conscience in the **s** of God *1799*
2Co 5:7 (For we walk by faith, not by **s**:) *1491*
Gal 3:11 by the law in the **s** of God, it is *3844*
Col 1:22 and unreproveable in his **s**: *2714*
Heb 4:13 that is not manifest in his **s** *1799*
Heb 12:21 And so terrible was the **s**, that *5324*
Heb 13:21 that which is wellpleasing in his **s**, ... *1799*
Jas 4:10 yourselves in the **s** of the Lord, ... *1799*
1Pe 3:4 is in the **s** of God of great price. *1799*
1Jn 3:22 things that are pleasing in his **s** *1799*
Rev 13:13 on the earth in the **s** of men, ... *1799*
Rev 13:14 power to do in the **s** of the beast; *1799*

SIGHTS
Lk 21:11 **fearful s and great signs shall** *5400*

SIGN
Ex 4:8 will believe the voice of the latter **s**. 226
Ex 31:13 for it is a **s** between me and you 226
Ex 31:17 a **s** between me and the children of 226
Dt 11:18 bind them for a **s** upon your hand, ... 226
Dt 13:2 the **s** or the wonder come to pass, ... 226
Jgs 6:17 me a **s** that thou talkest with me. 226
1Sa 2:34 this shall be a **s** unto thee, that 226
2Ki 20:8 What shall be the **s** that the Lord 226
Isa 7:11 Ask thee a **s** of the Lord thy God; 226
Isa 7:14 the Lord himself shall give you a **s**; 226
Isa 20:3 **s** and wonder upon Egypt and upon 226
Eze 12:11 Say, I am your **s**: like as I have 4159
Eze 14:8 will make him a **s** and a proverb, ... 226
Eze 20:12 to be a **s** between me and them, ... 226
Mt 12:39 **generation seeketh after a s** *4592*
Mt 12:39 **there shall no s be given to it** *4592*
Mt 12:39 **but the s of the prophet Jonas:** *4592*
Mt 16:1 would shew them a **s** from heaven. *4592*
Mt 16:4 **generation seeketh after a s** *4592*
Mt 16:4 **and there … no s be given unto it,** *4592*
Mt 16:4 **but the s of the prophet Jonas** *4592*
Mt 24:3 what shall be the **s** of thy coming, ... *4592*
Mt 24:30 **appear the s of the Son of man in** *4592*
Mt 26:48 that betrayed him gave them a **s**, ... *4592*
Mk 13:4 what shall be the **s** when all these *4592*
Lk 2:12 And this shall be a **s** unto you; Ye *4592*
Lk 2:34 and for a **s** which shall be spoken *4592*
Lk 21:7 what **s** will there be when these. *4592*
Jn 2:18 him, What **s** shewest thou unto us, ... *4592*
Jn 6:30 What **s** shewest thou then, that we *4592*
Ro 4:11 he received the **s** of circumcision, ... *4592*
1Co 1:22 For the Jews require a **s**, and the *4592*
1Co 14:22 Wherefore tongues are for a **s**, ... *4592*
Rev 15:1 I saw another **s** in heaven, great *4592*

SIGNED
Da 6:10 Daniel knew that the writing was **s** 7560

SIGNET
Ge 38:18 Thy **s**, and thy bracelets, and thy. 2368
Ex 28:21 names, like the engravings of a **s**; 2368
Ex 28:36 upon it, like the engravings of a **s**, ... 2368
Ex 39:30 the engravings of a **s**, HOLINESS. 2368
Jer 22:24 were the **s** upon my right hand, ... 2368
Da 6:17 the king sealed it with his own **s**, ... 5824
Hag 2:23 Lord, and will make thee as a **s** 2368

SIGNIFICATION
1Co 14:10 and none of them is without **s** *880*

SIGNIFIED
Ac 11:28 **s** by the spirit that there should be *4591*
Rev 1:1 **s** it by his angel unto his servant. *4591*

SIGNIFIETH
Heb 12:27 **s** the removing of those things *1218*

SIGNIFY
Ac 23:15 the council **s** to the chief captain *1718*
Ac 25:27 to **s** the crimes laid against him. *4591*
1Pe 1:11 of Christ which was in them **s**. *1213*

SIGNIFYING
Jn 12:33 said, **s** what death he should die, ... *4591*
Jn 18:32 spake, **s** what death he should die. *4591*
Jn 21:19 **s** by what death he should glorify. *4591*
Heb 9:8 The Holy Ghost this **s**, that the *1213*

S

SIGNS

Ge	1:14	let them be for **s** and for seasons,	226
Ex	4:9	will not believe also these two **s**,	226
Ex	4:17	rod … wherewith thou shalt do **s**	226
Ex	4:30	did the **s** in the sight of the people.	226
Ex	7:3	my **s** and my wonders in the land of	226
Ex	10:1	might shew these my **s** before him:	226
Nu	14:11	for all the **s** which I have shewed	226
Dt	4:34	by **s**, and by wonders, and by war,	226
Dt	6:22	shewed **s** and wonders, great and sore	226
Dt	7:19	and the **s**, and the wonders, and the	226
Dt	34:11	In all the **s** and the wonders, which	226
Jos	24:17	which did those great **s** in our sight,	226
1Sa	10:9	all those **s** came to pass that day.	226
Ne	9:10	**s** and wonders upon Pharaoh and	226
Ps	74:9	We see not our **s**: there is no more	226
Ps	78:43	How he had wrought his **s** in Egypt,	226
Isa	8:18	are for **s** and for wonders in Israel	226
Jer	10:2	be not dismayed at the **s** of heaven;	226
Da	4:2	I thought it good to shew the **s** and	852
Da	4:3	How great are his **s**! and how	852
Da	6:27	and he worketh **s** and wonders in	852
Mt	16:3	**can ye not discern the s of the times?**	*4592*
Mt	24:24	**shall shew great s and wonders;**	*4592*
Mk	13:22	**and shall shew s and wonders, to**	*4592*
Mk	16:17	**And these s shall follow them that**	*4592*
Mk	16:20	and confirming the word with **s**	*4592*
Lk	1:62	they made **s** to his father, how he	*1770*
Lk	21:11	**s shall there be from heaven**	*4592*
Lk	21:25	**And there shall be s in the sun,**	*4592*
Jn	4:48	**Except ye see s and wonders, ye**	*4592*
Jn	20:30	many other **s** truly did Jesus in the	*4592*
Ac	2:19	above, and **s** in the earth beneath;	*4592*
Ac	2:22	by miracles and wonders and **s**,	*4592*
Ac	2:43	wonders and **s** were done by the	*4592*
Ac	4:30	that **s** and wonders may be done by	*4592*
Ac	5:12	were many **s** and wonders wrought	*4592*
Ac	7:36	shewed wonders and **s** in the land	*4592*
Ac	8:13	Simon … beholding miracles and **s**	*4592*
Ac	14:3	granted **s** and wonders to be done	*4592*
Ro	15:19	**s** and wonders, by the power of the	*4592*
2Co	12:12	Truly the **s** of an apostle were	*4592*
2Th	2:9	working of Satan with all power and **s**	*4592*
Heb	2:4	witness, both with **s** and wonders,	*4592*

SILENCE

Jgs	3:19	thee, O king: who said, Keep **s**.	2013
Job	4:16	there was **s**, and I heard a voice,	1827
Job	29:21	waited, and kept **s** at my counsel.	1826
Ps	31:18	Let the lying lips be put to **s**;	481
Ps	32:3	When I kept **s**, my bones waxed	2790
Ps	35:22	keep not **s**: O Lord, be not far	2790
Ps	39:2	I was dumb with **s**, I held my	1747
Ps	50:3	shall come, and shall not keep **s**	2790
Ps	50:21	hast thou done, and I kept **s**;	2790
Ps	83:1	Keep not thou **s**, O God: hold not	1824
Ps	94:17	my soul had almost dwelt in **s**.	1745
Ps	115:17	neither any that go down into **s**	1745
Ecc	3:7	a time to keep **s**, and a time to	2814
Isa	41:1	Keep **s** before me, O islands; and	2790
Isa	62:6	mention of the Lord, keep not **s**	1824
Isa	65:6	will not keep **s**, but will recompense	2814
Jer	8:14	the Lord our God hath put us to **s**	1826
La	2:10	sit upon the ground, and keep **s**	1826
La	3:28	He sitteth alone and keepeth **s**,	1826
Am	5:13	Therefore the prudent shall keep **s**	1826
Am	8:3	shall cast them forth with **s**	2013
Hab	2:20	holy temple: let all the earth keep **s**	2013
Mt	22:34	he had put the Sadducees to **s**	*5392*
Ac	15:12	Then all the multitude kept **s**,	*4601*
1Co	14:28	let him keep **s** in the church; and	*4601*
1Co	14:34	Let your women keep **s** in the	*4601*
1Ti	2:11	Let the woman learn in **s** with all	*2771*
1Ti	2:12	authority over the man, but to be in **s**	*2771*
1Pe	2:15	put to **s** the ignorance of foolish men	*5392*
Rev	8:1	**s** in heaven … half an hour	*4602*

SILENT

1Sa	2:9	the wicked shall be **s** in darkness;	1826
Ps	22:2	in the night season, and am not **s**.	1747
Ps	28:1	O Lord my rock; be not **s** to me:	2790
Ps	28:1	lest, if thou be **s** to me, I become	2790
Ps	30:12	sing praise to thee and not be **s**.	1826
Ps	31:17	and let them be **s** in the grave	1826
Jer	8:14	cities, and let us be **s** there; for	1826
Zec	2:13	Be **s**, O all flesh, before the Lord:	2013

SILK

Pr	31:22	her clothing is **s** and purple	8336
Eze	16:10	linen, and I covered thee with **s**	4897
Rev	18:12	and purple, and **s** and scarlet,	*2596*

SILLY

Job	5:2	man, and envy slayeth the **s** one	6601
2Ti	3:6	lead captive **s** women laden with	*1133*

SILVER

Ge	13:2	was very rich in cattle, in **s**, and	3701
Ge	20:16	thy brother a thousand pieces of **s**	3701
Ge	23:15	worth four hundred shekels of **s**;	3701
Ge	24:53	servant brought forth jewels of **s**	3701
Ge	37:28	sold Joseph … for twenty pieces of **s**	3701
Ge	44:2	the **s** cup, in the sack's mouth of	3701
Ge	45:22	he gave three hundred pieces of **s**,	3701
Ex	3:22	in her house, jewels of **s**, and	3701
Ex	12:35	of the Egyptians jewels of **s**, and	3701
Ex	20:23	shall not make with me gods of **s**,	3701
Ex	21:32	their master thirty shekels of **s**,	3701
Ex	38:27	the hundred talents of **s** were cast	3701
Le	5:15	with thy estimation by shekels of **s**,	3701
Le	27:3	estimation shall be fifty shekels of **s**,	3701
Le	27:6	be of the male five shekels of **s**	3701
Le	27:6	for the female … three shekels of **s**	3701
Nu	7:85	Each charger of **s** weighing an	3701
Nu	10:2	Make thee two trumpets of **s**; of a	3701
Nu	22:18	would give me his house full of **s** and	3701
Dt	7:25	thou shalt not desire the **s** or gold	3701
Dt	8:13	thy **s** and thy gold is multiplied,	3701
Dt	17:17	multiply to himself **s** and gold.	3701
Dt	22:29	damsel's father fifty shekels of **s**,	3701
Jos	6:19	But all the **s**, and gold, and vessels	3701
Jos	7:22	hid in his tent, and the **s** under it.	3701
Jgs	9:4	him threescore and ten pieces of **s**	3701
Jgs	16:5	of us eleven hundred pieces of **s**	3701
Jgs	17:2	mine ears, behold, the **s** is with me;	3701
Jgs	17:3	dedicated the **s** unto the Lord	3701
Jgs	17:4	took two hundred shekels of **s**,	3701
Jgs	17:10	and I will give thee ten shekels of **s**.	3701
2Sa	8:11	**s** and gold that he had dedicated	3701
2Sa	21:4	We will have no **s** nor gold of Saul,	3701
1Ki	10:21	were of pure gold; none were of **s**.	3701
1Ki	10:27	made **s** to be in Jerusalem as stones,	3701
1Ki	15:18	Asa took all the **s** and the gold	3701

1Ki 20:3 Thy **s** and they gold is mine; thy. 3701
1Ki 20:39 or else thou shalt pay a talent of **s**. 3701
2Ki 5:22 give them, I pray thee, a talent of **s**, ... 3701
2Ki 6:25 was sold for fourscore pieces of **s** 3701
2Ki 14:14 And he took all the gold and **s**, and 3701
2Ki 15:19 gave Pul a thousand talents of **s**,. 3701
2Ki 16:8 Ahaz took the **s** and gold that was 3701
2Ki 18:15 Hezekiah gave him all the **s** that 3701
2Ki 23:33 tribute of an hundred talents of **s**, ... 3701
2Ki 23:35 Jehoiakim gave the **s** and the gold 3701
1Ch 19:6 sent a thousand talents of **s** to hire. 3701
1Ch 22:14 a thousand thousand talents of **s**:. 3701
1Ch 29:4 seven thousand talents of refined **s**, ... 3701
2Ch 1:15 made **s** and gold … as plenteous 3701
2Ch 9:14 brought gold and **s** to Solomon. 3701
2Ch 9:27 king made **s** in Jerusalem as stones, ... 3701
2Ch 21:3 father gave them great gifts of **s**,. 3701
2Ch 32:27 he made himself treasuries for **s**, ... 3701
Ezr 6:5 golden and **s** vessels of the house of. . . . 3702
Ezr 8:28 **s** and the gold are a freewill offering . . . 3701
Est 3:9 I will pay ten thousand talents of **s**. 3701
Ps 12:6 as **s** tried in a furnace of earth, ... 3701
Ps 66:10 thou hast tried us, as **s** is tried. 3701
Ps 115:4 Their idols are **s** and gold, the work. . . . 3701
Ps 119:72 me than thousands of gold and **s** 3701
Ps 135:15 idols of the heathen are **s** and gold, ... 3701
Pr 2:4 If thou seekest her as **s**, and. 3701
Pr 8:10 Receive my instruction, and not **s**; 3701
Pr 10:20 tongue of the just is as choice **s**: 3701
Pr 16:16 rather to be chosen than **s**! 3701
Pr 17:3 fining pot is for **s**, and the furnace 3701
Pr 22:1 and loving favour rather than **s** and. . . . 3701
Pr 25:4 Take away the dross from the **s**, ... 3701
Pr 25:11 like apples of gold in pictures of **s** 3701
Pr 26:23 a potsherd covered with **s** dross 3701
Pr 27:21 fining pot for **s**, and the furnace 3701
Ecc 2:8 I gathered me also **s** and gold, and 3701
Ecc 5:10 shall not be satisfied with **s**;. 3701
Ecc 12:6 Or ever the **s** cord be loosed, or the 3701
SS 3:10 He made the pillars thereof of **s**,. 3701
Isa 1:22 Thy **s** is become dross, thy wine 3701
Isa 2:7 Their land also is full of **s** and gold,. . . . 3701
Isa 13:17 Medes … which shall not regard **s**; 3701
Isa 31:7 man shall cast away his idols of **s**,. 3701
Isa 46:6 and weigh **s** in the balance, and 3701
Isa 48:10 I have refined thee, but not with **s**;. 3701
Isa 60:17 and for iron I will bring **s**, and for 3701
Eze 7:19 shall cast their **s** in the streets,. 3701
Eze 7:19 their **s** and their gold shall not be. 3701
Eze 22:18 they are even the dross of **s** 3701
Eze 22:22 As **s** is melted in the midst of the 3701
Eze 28:4 gold and **s** into thy treasures:. 3701
Da 2:32 gold, his breast and his arms of **s**,. 3702
Da 5:2 to bring the golden and **s** vessels. 3702
Da 5:23 thou hast praised the gods of **s**, ... 3702
Hos 2:8 and multiplied her **s** and gold, ... 3701
Hos 3:2 her to me for fifteen pieces of **s**, ... 3701
Hos 13:2 them molten images of their **s**, and 3701
Joel 3:5 ye have taken my **s** and my gold, ... 3701
Am 2:6 they sold the righteous for **s**, and 3701
Am 8:6 That we may buy the poor for **s**,. 3701
Hab 2:19 it is laid over the gold and **s**, and 3701
Zep 1:18 Neither their **s** nor their gold shall 3701
Hag 2:8 The **s** is mine, and the gold is mine,. . . . 3701
Zec 9:3 heaped up **s** as the dust, and fine 3701
Zec 11:12 for my price thirty pieces of **s** 3701

S

Zec 11:13 I took the thirty pieces of **s**, and 3701
Zec 13:9 and will refine them as **s** is refined, ... 3701
Mal 3:3 and purge them as gold and **s**, ... 3701
Mt 10:9 **Provide neither gold, nor s, nor** *696*
Mt 26:15 with him for thirty pieces of **s**. *694*
Mt 27:5 he cast down the pieces of **s** in the *694*
Lk 15:8 **what woman having ten pieces of s**,. . . . *1406*
Ac 3:6 said, **S** and gold have I none; but *694*
Ac 17:29 the Godhead is like unto gold, or **s**, ... *696*
Ac 19:24 which made **s** shrines for Diana,. *693*
Ac 20:33 I have coveted no man's **s**, or gold,. *694*
1Co 3:12 this foundation gold, **s**, precious. *696*
2Ti 2:20 not only vessels of gold and of **s**, ... *693*
Jas 5:3 Your gold and **s** is cankered; and. *696*
1Pe 1:18 corruptible things, as **s** and gold, ... *694*
Rev 9:20 devils, and idols of gold, and **s**, and *693*
Rev 18:12 The merchandise of gold, and **s**,. *696*

SILVERSMITH
Ac 19:24 certain man named Demetrius, a **s**, ... *695*

SIMILITUDE
Nu 12:8 the **s** of the Lord shall he behold:. 8544
Dt 4:12 voice of the words, but saw no **s**; 8544
Dt 4:15 ye saw no manner of **s** on the day 8544
Da 10:16 **s** of the sons of men touched my 1823
Ro 5:14 the **s** of Adam's transgression. *3667*
Heb 7:15 the **s** of Melchisedec there ariseth. *3665*
Jas 8:9 which are made after the **s** of God *3669*

SIMILITUDES
Hos 12:10 multiplied visions, and used **s**, by. 1819

SIMPLE
Ps 19:7 Lord is sure, making wise the **s**. 6612
Ps 116:6 The Lord preserveth the **s**; I was. 6612
Ps 119:130 giveth understanding unto the **s**. 6612
Pr 1:4 To give subtilty to the **s**, to the 6612
Pr 1:22 How long, ye **s** ones, will ye love. 6612
Pr 1:32 turning away of the **s** shall slay them . . . 6612
Pr 8:5 O ye **s**, understand wisdom: and, ... 6612
Pr 9:13 she is **s**, and knoweth nothing. 6615
Pr 14:15 The **s** believeth every word: but 6612
Pr 19:25 a scorner, and the **s** will beware:. 6612
Pr 22:3 the **s** pass on, and are punished. 6612
Eze 45:20 that erreth, and for him that is **s**. 6612
Ro 16:18 deceive the hearts of the **s** *172*

SIMPLICITY
2Sa 15:11 and they went in their **s**, and they 8537
Pr 1:22 ye simple ones, will ye love **s**? 6612
Ro 12:8 that giveth, let him do it with **s**; *572*
2Co 1:12 that in **s** and godly sincerity, not. *572*
2Co 11:3 from the **s** that is in Christ. *572*

SIN
Ge 4:7 doest not well, **s** lieth at the door 2403
Ge 18:20 because their **s** is very grievous; 2403
Ge 20:9 me and on my kingdom a great **s**? 2401
Ge 31:36 what is my **s**, that thou hast so 2403
Ge 39:9 great wickedness, and **s** against God?. . . 2398
Ge 42:22 saying, Do not **s** against the child; 2398
Ge 50:17 forgive … thy brethren, and their **s**;. . . . 2403
Ex 23:33 lest they make thee **s** against me: 2398
Ex 29:14 without the camp: it is a **s** offering. 2403
Ex 29:36 every day a bullock for a **s** offering. 2403
Ex 32:21 brought so great a **s** upon them? 2401
Ex 32:31 this people have sinned a great **s**. 2401

Ex	32:32	if thou wilt forgive their **s** ... if not	2403
Ex	34:7	iniquity and transgression and **s**,	2402
Le	4:2	a soul shall **s** through ignorance	2398
Le	4:3	If the priest that is anointed do **s**	2398
Le	4:13	Israel **s** through ignorance,	7686
Le	4:21	a **s** offering for the congregation.	2403
Le	4:24	before the Lord: it is a **s** offering.	2403
Le	4:28	Or if his **s**, which he hath sinned,	2403
Le	4:32	if he bring a lamb for a **s** offering,	2403
Le	4:34	take of the blood of the **s** offering	2403
Le	4:35	make an atonement for his **s** that	2403
Le	5:1	if a soul **s**, and hear the voice of	2398
Le	5:7	one for a **s** offering, and the other	2403
Le	5:11	thereon: for it is a **s** offering	2403
Le	5:15	**s** through ignorance, in the holy	2398
Le	5:17	And if a soul **s**, and commit any of	2398
Le	6:17	is most holy, as is the **s** offering,	2403
Le	6:25	This is the law of the **s** offering:	2403
Le	6:26	that offereth it for **s** shall eat it:	2398
Le	6:30	no **s** offering, whereof any of the	2403
Le	7:7	As the **s** offering is, so is the	2403
Le	7:37	and of the **s** offering, and of the	2403
Le	10:16	sought the goat of the **s** offering,	2403
Le	10:17	have ye not eaten the **s** offering in	2403
Le	14:13	as the **s** offering is the priest's, so	2403
Le	16:9	fell, and offer him for a **s** offering.	2403
Le	16:15	he kill the goat of the **s** offering,	2403
Le	19:17	and not suffer **s** upon him.	2399
Le	19:22	for his **s** which he hath done:	2403
Le	24:15	curseth his God shall bear his **s**.	2399
Nu	5:6	commit any **s** that men commit,	2403
Nu	5:7	Then they shall confess their **s**	2403
Nu	6:14	without blemish for a **s** offering,	2403
Nu	9:13	season, that man shall bear his **s**.	2399
Nu	12:11	lay not the **s** upon us, wherein	2403
Nu	15:27	if any soul **s** through ignorance,	2398
Nu	15:27	of the first year for a **s** offering	2403
Nu	18:22	lest they bear **s**, and die	2399
Nu	19:9	separation: it is a purification for **s**.	2403
Nu	27:3	but died in his own **s**, and had no	2399
Nu	32:23	be sure your **s** will find you out.	2403
Dt	9:27	to their wickedness, nor to their **s**:	2403
Dt	21:22	man have committed a **s** worthy	2399
Dt	24:4	thou shalt not cause the land to **s**,	2398
Dt	24:16	shall be put to death for his own **s**	2399
1Sa	2:17	the **s** of the young men was very	2403
1Sa	2:25	but if a man **s** against the Lord,	2398
1Sa	12:23	God forbid that I should **s** against	2398
1Sa	14:34	**s** not against the Lord in eating	2398
1Sa	15:23	rebellion is as the **s** of witchcraft,	2403
1Sa	19:5	wilt thou **s** against innocent blood,	2398
1Sa	20:1	what is my **s** before thy father,	2403
2Sa	12:13	Lord also hath put away thy **s**;	2403
1Ki	8:34	forgive the **s** of thy people Israel,	2403
1Ki	8:36	and forgive the **s** of thy servants,	2403
1Ki	8:46	If they **s** against thee, (for there	2398
1Ki	16:2	hast made my people Israel to **s**,	2398
1Ki	17:18	me to call my **s** to remembrance,	5771
2Ki	12:16	**s** money was not brought into the	
2Ki	14:6	shall be put to death for his own **s**	2399
2Ch	6:22	If a man **s** against his neighbour,	2398
2Ch	6:36	if they **s** against thee, (for there	2398
2Ch	7:14	heaven, and will forgive their **s**,	2403
2Ch	24:4	every man shall die for his own **s**	2403
2Ch	29:24	**s** offering should be made for all	2403
Ezr	6:17	and for a **s** offering for all Israel,	2409
Ne	6:13	should be afraid, and do so, and **s**,	2398
Ne	13:26	Did not Solomon king of Israel **s**	2398
Job	2:10	all this did not Job **s** with his lips	2398
Job	34:37	he addeth rebellion unto his **s**,	2403
Job	35:3	I have, if I be cleansed from my **s**?	2403
Ps	4:4	Stand in awe, and **s** not: commune	2398
Ps	32:1	is forgiven, whose **s** is covered.	2403
Ps	32:5	I acknowledged my **s** unto thee,	2403
Ps	39:1	ways, that I **s** not with my tongue:	2398
Ps	40:6	**s** offering hast thou not required.	2401
Ps	51:2	and cleanse me from my **s**	2403
Ps	51:3	and my **s** is ever before me	2403
Ps	51:5	in **s** did my mother conceive me.	2399
Ps	119:11	that I might not **s** against thee	2398
Pr	10:19	of words there wanteth not **s**.	6588
Pr	14:9	Fools make a mock at **s**: but among	817
Pr	14:34	but **s** is a reproach to any people.	2403
Pr	20:9	heart clean, I am pure from my **s**?	2403
Pr	21:4	and the plowing of the wicked, is **s**.	2403
Pr	24:9	The thought of foolishness is **s**	2403
Ecc	5:6	thy mouth to cause thy flesh to **s**	2398
Isa	3:9	they declare their **s** as Sodom,	2403
Isa	6:7	is taken away, and thy **s** purged.	2403
Isa	30:1	spirit, that they may add **s** to **s**;	2403
Isa	53:10	make his soul an offering for **s**	817
Isa	53:12	he bare the **s** of many, and made	2399
Jer	16:18	their iniquity and their **s** double;	2403
Jer	17:1	**s** of Judah is written with a pen of	2403
Jer	31:34	I will remember their **s** no more.	2403
Jer	51:5	was filled with **s** against the Holy	817
La	4:6	the punishment of the **s** of Sodom,	
Eze	3:20	warning, he shall die in his **s**,	2403
Eze	3:21	man, that the righteous **s** not,	2398
Eze	33:14	if he turn from his **s**, and do that	2403
Eze	43:22	without blemish for a **s** offering;	2403
Da	9:20	my **s** and the **s** of my people, Israel	2403
Hos	4:8	They eat up the **s** of my people,	2403
Am	8:14	that swear by the **s** of Samaria,	819
Mic	6:7	of my body for the **s** of my soul?	2403
Zec	13:1	fountain ... for **s** and ... uncleanness	2403
Mt	12:31	**All manner of s and blasphemy**	*266*
Mt	18:21	oft shall my brother **s** against me,	*264*
Jn	1:29	taketh away the **s** of the world.	*266*
Jn	5:14	**s no more, lest a worse thing**	*264*
Jn	8:7	**He that is without s among you.**	*361*
Jn	8:11	**condemn thee: go, and s no more**	*264*
Jn	8:34	**committeth s is the servant of s,**	*266*
Jn	8:46	**Which of you convinceth me of s?**	*266*
Jn	9:2	Master, who did **s**, this man, or his	*264*
Jn	9:41	**We see; therefore your s remaineth**	*266*
Jn	15:22	**now they have no cloke for their s**	*266*
Jn	16:8	**he will reprove the world of s, and**	*266*
Jn	16:9	**s, because they believe not on me**	*266*
Jn	19:11	**delivered me ... hath the greater s**	*266*
Ac	7:60	Lord, lay not this **s** to their charge	*266*
Ro	3:20	for by the law is the knowledge of **s**	*266*
Ro	4:8	whom the Lord will not impute **s**.	*266*
Ro	5:12	by one man **s** entered into the world,	*266*
Ro	5:13	**s** is not imputed when there is no law	*266*
Ro	5:20	But where **s** abounded, grace did	*266*
Ro	6:1	Shall we continue in **s**, that grace	*266*
Ro	6:2	How shall we that are dead to **s**, live.	*266*
Ro	6:7	For he that is dead is freed from **s**.	*266*
Ro	6:10	in that he died, he died unto **s** once:	*266*
Ro	6:12	Let not **s** therefore reign in your	*266*
Ro	6:13	of unrighteousness unto **s**: but yield	*266*

Ro	6:23	For the wages of **s** is death; but the	*266*
Ro	7:7	Is the law **s**? God forbid. Nay,	*266*
Ro	7:7	I had not known **s**, but by the law:	*266*
Ro	7:8	For without the law **s** was dead.	*266*
Ro	7:14	but I am carnal, sold under **s**.	*266*
Ro	7:17	it, but **s** that dwelleth in me.	*266*
Ro	7:20	it, but **s** that dwelleth in me.	*266*
Ro	8:2	me free from the law of **s** and death.	*266*
Ro	8:3	likeness of sinful flesh, and for **s**,	*266*
Ro	14:23	for whatsoever is not of faith is **s**	*266*
1Co	6:18	Every **s** that a man doeth is without	*265*
1Co	15:34	Awake to righteousness, and **s** not;	*264*
1Co	15:56	The sting of death is **s**; and the	*266*
1Co	15:56	and the strength of **s** is the law	*266*
2Co	5:21	him to be **s** for us, who knew no **s**;	*266*
Gal	3:22	hath concluded all under **s**, that	*266*
Eph	4:26	Be ye angry, and **s** not: let not the	*264*
2Th	2:3	that man of **s** be revealed, the son.	*266*
1Ti	5:20	Them that **s** rebuke before all,	*264*
Heb	4:25	made like as we are, yet without **s**.	*266*
Heb	9:28	appear … without **s** unto salvation.	*266*
Heb	10:6	burnt offerings and sacrifices for **s**	*266*
Heb	10:18	is, there is no more offering for **s**	*266*
Heb	10:26	if we **s** wilfully after that we have	*264*
Heb	11:25	than to enjoy the pleasures of **s** for	*266*
Heb	12:1	the **s** which doth so easily beset us,	*266*
Jas	1:15	it bringeth forth **s**: and **s**, when it	*266*
Jas	2:9	have respect of persons, ye commit **s**	*266*
Jas	4:17	and doeth it not, to him it is **s**.	*266*
1Pe	2:22	Who did no **s**, neither was guile	*266*
1Pe	4:1	in the flesh hath ceased from **s**;	*266*
2Pe	2:14	and that cannot cease from **s**;	*266*
1Jn	1:7	Christ his Son cleanseth us from all **s**.	*266*
1Jn	1:8	If we say that we have no **s**, we	*266*
1Jn	2:1	if any man **s**, we have an advocate	*264*
1Jn	3:4	for **s** is the transgression of the law.	*266*
1Jn	3:8	He that committeth **s** is of the devil;	*266*
1Jn	3:9	is born of God doth not commit **s**;	*266*
1Jn	5:16	if any man see his brother **s**	*264*
1Jn	5:16	There is a **s** unto death: I do not	*266*
1Jn	5:17	All unrighteousness is **s**: and there	*266*
1Jn	5:17	and there is a **s** not unto death.	*266*

SINCE

Ge	46:30	let me die, **s** I have seen thy face,	310
Ex	9:24	all the land of Egypt **s** it became a	227
Dt	4:32	**s** the day that God created man	4480
Dt	34:10	a prophet **s** in Israel like unto	5750
2Ch	30:26	**s** the time of Solomon the son of	
Ne	9:32	**s** the time of the kings of Assyria	
Job	20:4	**s** man was placed upon earth,	4480
Isa	64:4	**s** the beginning of the world men	
Jer	15:7	**s** they return not from their ways.	4480
Jer	44:18	**s** we left off to burn incense	4480, 227
Mt	24:21	**not s the beginning of the world**	*575*
Lk	1:70	which have been **s** the world began:	*575*
Lk	7:45	**this woman s the time I came in.**	*575*
Lk	16:16	**s that time the kingdom of God is**	*575*
Lk	24:21	third day **s** these things were done	*575*
Jn	9:32	**S** the world began was it not	*1557*
Ac	19:2	the Holy Ghost **s** ye believed?	
Ro	16:25	was kept secret **s** the world began,	
1Co	15:21	For **s** by man came death, by man	*1894*
Heb	9:26	**s** the foundation of the world:	*575*
Rev	16:18	such as was not **s** men were	*575, 3739*

SINCERE

Php	1:10	ye may be **s** and without offence.	*1506*
1Pe	2:2	desire the **s** milk of the word, that	*97*

SINCERITY

Jos	24:14	and serve him in **s** and in truth:	8549
1Co	5:8	with the unleavened bread of **s** and	*1505*
2Co	1:12	that in simplicity and godly **s**, not	*1505*
2Co	8:8	and to prove the **s** of your love	*1103*
Tit	2:7	shewing uncorruptness, gravity, **s**,	*861*

SINEW

Ge	32:32	Jacob's thigh in the **s** that shrank.	1517

SINEWS

Eze	37:6	and I will lay **s** upon you, and will	1517

SINFUL

Isa	1:4	Ah **s** nation, a people laden with	2398
Am	9:8	Lord God are upon the **s** kingdom,	2401
Mk	8:38	**this adulterous and s generation:**	*268*
Lk	5:8	from me; for I am a **s** man, O Lord.	*268*
Lk	24:7	delivered into the hands of **s** men,	*268*
Ro	7:13	sin … might become exceeding **s**	*268*
Ro	8:3	own Son in the likeness of **s** flesh,	*266*

SING See also SANG; SUNG.

Ex	15:1	I will **s** unto the Lord, for he hath.	7891
Ex	15:21	**S** ye to the Lord, for he hath	7891
Ex	32:18	the noise of them that **s** do I hear.	6031
Jgs	5:3	I, even I, will **s** unto the Lord;	7891
1Sa	21:11	**s** one to another of him in dances,	6030
1Ch	16:23	**S** unto the Lord, all the earth;	7891
2Ch	23:13	and such as taught to **s** praise,	1984
Job	29:13	the widow's heart to **s** for joy	7442
Ps	13:6	I will **s** unto the Lord, because he	7891
Ps	27:6	sacrifice of joy; I will **s**, yea,	7891
Ps	27:6	I will **s** praises unto the Lord.	2167
Ps	33:3	**S** unto him a new song: play	7891
Ps	57:7	heart is fixed: I will **s** and give praise	7891
Ps	59:16	I will **s** aloud of thy mercy in the	7442
Ps	66:2	**S** forth the honour of his name:	2167
Ps	67:4	the nations be glad and **s** for joy:	7442
Ps	68:4	**S** unto God … extol him that rideth	7891
Ps	89:1	I will **s** of the mercies of the Lord.	7891
Ps	98:1	O **s** unto the Lord a new song; for	7891
Ps	101:1	I will **s** of mercy and judgment:	7891
Ps	104:12	which **s** among the branches.	5414, 6963
Ps	104:33	**s** unto the Lord as long as I live:	7891
Ps	137:3	**S** us one of the songs of Zion	7891
Ps	137:4	**s** the Lord's song in a strange	7891
Ps	147:1	is good to **s** praises unto our God;	2167
Ps	149:1	**S** unto the Lord a new song, and	7891
Ps	149:5	let them **s** aloud upon their beds	7442
Pr	29:6	the righteous doth **s** and rejoice	7442
Isa	23:16	make sweet melody, **s** many songs	
Isa	24:14	shall **s** for the majesty of the	7442
Isa	35:6	and the tongue of the dumb **s**:	7442
Isa	42:11	let the inhabitants of the rock **s**	7442
Isa	49:13	**S**, O heavens; and be joyful, O.	7442
Isa	65:14	servants shall **s** for joy of heart	7442
Hos	2:15	she shall **s** there, as in the days	6030
Zec	2:10	**S** and rejoice, O daughter of Zion:	7442
1Co	14:15	will **s** with the understanding also	*5567*
Jas	5:13	Is any merry? let him **s** psalms	*5567*
Rev	15:3	And they **s** the song of Moses the	*103*

SINGED

Da 3:27	nor was an hair of their head **s**,	2761

SINGERS

2Ch 5:13	as the trumpeters and **s** were as one,	7891
2Ch 20:21	he appointed **s** unto the Lord, and	7891
2Ch 23:13	the **s** with instruments of musick,	7891
2Ch 35:15	And the **s** the sons of Asaph were	7891
Ezr 7:24	Levites, **s**, porters, Nethinims	2171
Ne 11:23	certain portion should be for the **s**,	7891
Ps 68:25	The **s** went before, the players on	7891
Ecc 2:8	I gat me men **s** and women **s**, and	7891

SINGETH

Pr 25:20	so is he that **s** songs to an heavy	7891

SINGING

2Sa 19:35	the voice of **s** men and **s** women?	7891
Ps 100:2	come before his presence with **s**	7445
SS 2:12	time of the **s** of birds is come	2158
Isa 16:10	in the vineyards there shall be no **s**	7442
Isa 44:23	break forth into **s**, ye mountains	7440
Isa 49:13	break forth into **s**, O mountains:	7440
Isa 51:11	return, and come with **s** unto Zion;	7440
Zep 3:17	love, he will joy over thee with **s**	7440
Eph 5:19	**s** and making melody in your hearts	103
Col 3:16	**s** with grace in your hearts to the	103

SINGLE

Mt 6:22	**if therefore thine eye be s, thy**	*573*
Lk 11:34	**therefore when thine eye is s, thy**	*573*

SINGLENESS

Ac 2:46	with gladness and **s** of heart,	*858*
Eph 6:5	in **s** of your heart, as unto Christ;	*572*
Col 3:22	but in **s** of heart, fearing God:	*572*

SINK

Ps 69:2	I **s** in deep mire, where there is	2883
Mt 14:30	beginning to **s**, he cried, saying,	*2670*
Lk 5:7	the ships, so that they began to **s**	*1036*
Lk 9:44	**sayings s down into your ears:**	*5087*

SINNED

Ex 9:27	unto them, I have **s** this time:	2398
Ex 9:34	he **s** yet more, and hardened his	2398
Ex 10:16	I have **s** against the Lord your God,	2398
Ex 32:31	Oh, this people have **s** a great sin	2398
Le 4:22	When a ruler hath **s**, and done	2398
Le 4:23	if his sin, wherein he hath **s**, come	2398
Le 5:5	that he shall confess that he hath **s**	2398
Le 6:4	because he hath **s**, and is guilty	2398
Nu 21:7	We have **s**, for we have spoken	2398
Nu 22:34	I have **s**; for I knew not that thou	2398
Nu 32:23	behold, ye have **s** against the Lord:	2398
Dt 9:16	ye had **s** against the Lord your God,	2398
Jos 7:20	Indeed I have **s** against the Lord	2398
Jgs 10:10	saying, we have **s** against thee,	2398
1Sa 7:6	We have **s** against the Lord.	2398
1Sa 12:10	unto the Lord, and said, We have **s**,	2398
1Sa 15:24	Saul said unto Samuel, I have **s**	2398
1Sa 24:11	and I have not **s** against thee;	2398
2Sa 12:13	Nathan, I have **s** against the Lord	2398
2Sa 24:17	Lo, I have **s**, and I have done	2398
1Ki 8:33	because they have **s** against thee,	2398
1Ki 8:35	because they have **s** against thee;	2398
1Ki 8:50	And forgive thy people that have **s**	2398
1Ch 21:8	said unto God, I have **s** greatly,	2398
1Ch 21:17	even I it is that have **s** and done	2398
2Ch 6:39	forgive thy people which have **s**	2398
Ne 1:6	I and my father's house have **s**	2398
Job 1:5	It may be that my sons have **s**,	2398
Job 1:22	In all this Job **s** no, nor charged	2398
Job 8:4	If thy children have **s** against him,	2398
Ps 51:4	Against thee, thee only, have I **s**,	2398
Ps 78:17	and they **s** yet more against him	2398
Ps 78:32	For all this they **s** still, and believed	2398
Ps 106:6	We have **s** with our fathers, we	2398
Isa 42:24	Lord, he against whom we have **s**?	2398
Isa 43:27	Thy first father hath **s**, and thy	2398
Jer 2:35	because thou sayest, I have not **s**.	2398
Jer 3:25	for we have **s** against the Lord our	2398
Jer 14:7	are many; we have **s** against thee	2398
Jer 40:3	because ye have **s** against the Lord,	2398
La 1:8	Jerusalem hath grievously **s**;	2398
La 5:7	Our fathers have **s**, and are not;	2398
Eze 18:24	and in his sin that he hath **s**, in	2398
Da 9:5	We have **s**, and have committed	2398
Hos 4:7	were increased, so they **s** against me:	2398
Hab 2:10	people, and hath **s** against thy soul.	2398
Zep 1:17	they have **s** against the Lord:	2398
Mt 27:4	I have **s** in that I have betrayed	*264*
Lk 15:21	**Father, I have s against heaven,**	*264*
Jn 9:3	**Neither hath this man s, nor his**	*264*
Ro 3:23	For all have **s**, and come short of	*264*
Ro 5:12	upon all men, for that all have **s**	*264*
1Co 7:28	if a virgin marry, she hath not **s**	*264*
Heb 3:17	was it not with them that had **s**,	*264*
2Pe 2:4	God spared not the angels that **s**,	*264*
1Jn 1:10	If we say that we have not **s**, we	*264*

SINNER

Pr 11:31	much more the wicked and the **s**	2398
Pr 13:6	wickedness overthroweth the **s**	2403
Pr 13:22	wealth of the **s** is laid up for the just	2398
Ecc 2:26	but to the **s** he giveth travail, to	2398
Ecc 8:12	Through a **s** do evil an hundred	2398
Ecc 9:18	but one **s** destroyeth much good	2398
Isa 65:20	the **s** being an hundred years old	2398
Lk 7:39	that toucheth him: for she is a **s**,	*268*
Lk 15:7	**heaven over one s that repenteth,**	*268*
Lk 18:13	**saying, God be merciful to me a s**	*268*
Lk 19:7	to be guest with a man that is a **s**	*268*
Jn 9:16	man that is a **s** do much miracles?	*268*
Jn 9:25	Whether he be a **s** or no, I know not:	*268*
Ro 3:7	why yet am I also judged as a **s**?	*268*
Jas 5:20	converteth the **s** from the error of	*268*
1Pe 4:18	shall the ungodly and the **s** appear?	*268*

SINNERS

Ge 13:13	men of Sodom were wicked and **s**	2400
1Sa 15:18	destroy the **s** the Amalekites,	2400
Ps 1:1	nor standeth in the way of **s**, nor	2400
Ps 1:5	nor **s** in the congregation of the	2400
Ps 25:8	therefore will he teach **s** in the way.	2400
Ps 51:13	**s** shall be converted unto thee	2400
Pr 1:10	if **s** entice thee, consent thou not	2400
Pr 13:21	Evil pursueth **s**: but to the	2400
Pr 23:17	Let not thine heart envy **s**: but be	2400
Isa 13:9	and he shall destroy the **s** thereof	2400
Isa 33:14	The **s** in Zion are afraid; tearfulness	2400
Am 9:10	All the **s** of my people shall die by	2400
Mt 9:11	your Master with publicans and **s**?	*268*
Mt 9:13	**the righteous, but s to repentance.**	*268*

Mk 14:41	**is betrayed into the hands of s?**	*268*
Lk 6:32	**for s also love those that love them.**	*268*
Lk 6:34	**s also lend to s, to receive as**	*268*
Lk 13:2	**were s above all the Galilaeans,**	*268*
Jn 9:31	we know that God heareth not **s**:	*268*
Ro 5:8	while we were yet **s**, Christ died for	*268*
Ro 5:19	disobedience many were made **s**,	*268*
1Ti 1:9	for the ungodly and for **s**, for unholy	*268*
1Ti 1:15	Jesus came into the world to save **s**;	*268*
Heb 7:26	undefiled, separate from **s**, and	*268*
Heb 12:3	contradiction of **s** against himself,	*268*
Jas 4:8	Cleanse your hands, ye **s**; and	*268*

SINNEST

Job 35:6	If thou **s**, what doest thou against	*2398*

SINNETH

Nu 15:29	for him that **s** through ignorance,	6213
Dt 19:15	for any sin, in any sin that he **s**	2398
1Ki 8:46	(for there is no man that **s** not,)	2398
Pr 8:36	**s** against me wrongeth his own	2398
Pr 14:21	He that despiseth his neighbour **s**	2398
Pr 19:2	and he that hasteth with his feet **s**	2398
Pr 20:2	whoso provoketh him to anger **s**	2398
Ecc 7:20	earth, that doeth good, and **s** not	2398
Eze 14:13	when the land **s** against me by	2398
Eze 18:4	mine: the soul that **s**, it shall die	2398
1Co 6:18	fornication **s** against his own body	*264*
1Co 7:36	let him do what he will, he **s** not:	*264*
Tit 3:11	he that is such is subverted, and **s**,	*264*
1Jn 3:6	Whosoever abideth in him **s** not:	*264*
1Jn 3:8	for the devil **s** from the beginning	*264*
1Jn 5:18	whosoever is born of God **s** not;	*264*

SINS

Le 16:16	their transgressions in all their **s**	2403
Le 16:21	their transgressions in all their **s**,	2403
Le 16:34	of Israel for all their **s** once a year	2403
Le 26:28	chastise you seven times for your **s**	2403
Nu 16:26	lest ye be consumed in all their **s**	2403
Dt 9:18	because of all your **s** which ye	2403
Jos 24:19	your transgressions nor your **s**	2403
1Sa 12:19	added unto all our **s** this evil	2403
1Ki 15:3	he walked in all the **s** of his father,	2403
2Ch 28:13	ye intend to add more to our **s**	2403
Ne 9:2	and stood and confessed their **s**,	2403
Ne 9:37	hast set over us because of our **s**:	2403
Ps 19:13	servant also from presumptuous **s**;	
Ps 25:7	Remember not the **s** of my youth	2403
Ps 51:9	Hide thy face from my **s**, and blot	2399
Ps 69:5	and my **s** are not hid from thee	819
Ps 103:10	hath not dealt with us after our **s**;	2399
Pr 10:12	up strifes: but love covereth all **s**	6588
Pr 28:13	that covereth his **s** shall not prosper	6588
Isa 1:18	though your **s** be as scarlet, they	2399
Isa 38:17	hast cast all my **s** behind thy back	2399
Isa 40:2	Lord's hand double for all her **s**	2403
Isa 59:12	thee, and our **s** testify against us:	2403
Jer 30:15	because thy **s** were increased, I	2403
La 3:39	a man for the punishment of his **s**?	2399
La 4:13	For the **s** of her prophets, and the	2403
Eze 16:51	Samaria committed half of thy **s**;	2403
Eze 18:14	that seeth all his father's **s** which	2403
Eze 18:21	all his **s** that he hath committed	2403
Eze 23:49	ye shall bear the **s** of your idols:	2399
Da 4:27	break off thy **s** by righteousness	2408
Da 9:24	to make an end of **s**, and to make	2403
Mic 7:19	their **s** into the depths of the sea	2403
Mt 1:21	shall save his people from their **s**	*266*
Mt 9:6	**hath power on earth to forgive s,**	*266*
Mt 26:28	**for many for the remission of s**	*266*
Mk 1:4	of repentance for the remission of **s**	*266*
Mk 2:7	who can forgive **s** but God only?	*266*
Mk 4:12	**and their s should be forgiven them**	*265*
Lk 7:47	**Her s, which are many, are**	*266*
Lk 11:4	**forgive us our s; for we also**	*266*
Lk 24:47	**remission of s should be preached**	*266*
Jn 8:24	**I am he, ye shall die in your s**	*266*
Jn 9:34	Thou wast altogether born in **s**,	*266*
Jn 20:23	**Whose soever s ye remit, they are**	*266*
Ac 2:38	Jesus Christ for the remission of **s**,	*266*
Ac 3:19	that your **s** may be blotted out,	*266*
Ac 10:43	in him shall receive remission of **s**	*266*
Ac 26:18	**they may receive forgiveness of s,**	*266*
Ro 4:7	forgiven, and whose **s** are covered	*266*
Ro 11:27	when I shall take away their **s**	*266*
1Co 15:3	how that Christ died for our **s**	*266*
1Co 15:17	faith is vain; ye are yet in your **s**	*266*
Gal 1:4	who gave himself for our **s**, that he	*266*
Eph 2:1	who were dead in trespasses and **s**;	*266*
Eph 2:5	Even when we were dead in **s**,	*3900*
Col 1:14	his blood, even the forgiveness of **s**	*266*
Col 2:13	And you, being dead in your **s**	*3900*
1Ti 5:22	be partaker of other men's **s**:	*266*
2Ti 3:6	captive silly women laden with **s**,	*266*
Heb 1:3	he had by himself purged our **s**, sat	*266*
Heb 2:17	reconciliation for the **s** of the people	*266*
Heb 7:27	first for his own **s**, and then for the	*266*
Heb 9:28	once offered to bear the **s** of many:	*266*
Heb 10:11	which can never take away **s**:	*266*
Heb 10:12	after he had offered one sacrifice for **s**	*266*
Heb 10:26	remaineth no more sacrifice for **s**	*266*
Jas 5:15	if he have committed **s**, they shall	*266*
Jas 5:20	and shall hide a multitude of **s**	*266*
1Pe 2:24	own self bare our **s** in his own body	*266*
1Pe 2:24	that we, being dead to **s**, should live	*266*
1Pe 3:18	Christ also hath once suffered for **s**	*266*
1Pe 4:8	shall cover the multitude of **s**	*266*
1Jn 1:9	If we confess our **s**, he is faithful and	*266*
1Jn 2:2	And he is the propitiation for our **s**:	*266*
1Jn 4:10	Son to be the propitiation for our **s**	*266*
Rev 1:5	and washed us from our **s** in his own	*266*
Rev 18:4	that ye be not partakers of her **s**,	*266*

SISTER

Ge 12:13	Say, I pray thee, thou art my **s**	269
Ge 12:19	Why saidst thou, She is my **s**? so I	269
Ge 20:2	said of Sarah his wife, She is my **s**	269
Ge 20:5	Said he not unto me, She is my **s**?	269
Ge 26:7	said, She is my **s**: for he feared	269
Ge 26:9	and how saidst thou, She is my **s**?	269
Ge 30:1	no children, Rachel envied her **s**;	269
Ge 34:14	our **s** to one that is uncircumcised;	269
Ge 34:31	deal with our **s** as with an harlot?	269
Ex 2:7	said his **s** to Pharaoh's daughter	269
Ex 15:20	the prophetess, the **s** of Aaron,	269
Le 18:11	begotten of thy father, she is thy **s**	269
Dt 27:22	Cursed be he that lieth with his **s**,	269
Jgs 15:2	is not her younger **s** fairer than she?	269
2Sa 13:6	let Tamar my **s** come, and make me	269
2Sa 13:32	the day that he forced his **s** Tamar	269
2Ch 22:11	(for she was the **s** of Ahaziah,) hid	269
Pr 7:4	Say unto wisdom, Thou art my **s**;	269

SS	4:9	Thou hast ravished my heart, my **s**,	269
Jer	3:8	her treacherous **s** Judah feared not,	269
Eze	16:49	was the iniquity of thy **s** Sodom	269
Eze	23:31	hast walked in the way of thy **s**;	269
Mt	12:50	**the same is my brother, and s, and**	*79*
Lk	10:39	And she had a **s** called Mary, which	*79*
Lk	10:40	not care that my **s** hath left me to	*79*
Jn	11:5	Now Jesus loved Martha, and her **s**,	*79*
Jn	19:25	his mother, and his mother's **s**.	*79*
1Co	7:15	A brother or a **s** is not under	*79*
Jas	2:15	If a brother or **s** be naked, and	*79*

SISTER'S

Le	20:17	he hath uncovered his **s** nakedness;	269
Eze	23:32	shalt drink of thy **s** cup deep and	269

SISTERS

Eze	16:52	Thou also, which hast judged thy **s**.	269
Eze	16:55	thy **s**, Sodom and her daughters	269
Mt	19:29	**forsaken houses, or brethren, or s,**	*79*
Mk	6:3	and are not his **s** here with us?	*79*
Lk	14:26	**and children, and brethren, and s,**	*79*
1Ti	5:2	the younger as **s**, with all purity	*79*

SIT

Nu	32:6	go to war, and shall ye **s** here?	3427
Jgs	5:10	ye that **s** in judgment, and walk by	3427
Ru	3:18	**S** still, my daughter, until thou	3427
1Sa	20:5	fail to **s** with the king at meat:	3427
2Sa	19:8	Behold, the king doth **s** in the gate	3427
1Ki	1:30	he shall **s** upon my throne in my	3427
1Ki	3:6	him a son to **s** on his throne, as it	3427
2Ki	7:3	Why **s** we here until we die?	3427
2Ki	15:12	Thy sons shall **s** on the throne of	3427
Ps	26:5	and will not **s** with the wicked	3427
Ps	107:10	Such as **s** in darkness and in the	3427
Ps	110:1	**S** thou at my right hand, until I	3427
Ps	127:2	you to rise up early, to **s** up late	3427
Ps	132:12	shall also **s** upon thy throne for	3427
Isa	16:5	he shall **s** upon it in truth in the	3427
Isa	47:1	Come down, and **s** in the dust, O	3427
Jer	13:13	kings that **s** upon David's throne	3427
Jer	33:17	want a man to **s** upon the throne of	3427
La	1:1	How doth the city **s** solitary, that	3427
Eze	26:16	they shall **s** upon the ground, and	3427
Eze	28:2	I **s** in the seat of God, in the midst	3427
Da	7:9	the Ancient of days did **s**, whose	3488
Joel	3:12	there will I **s** to judge all the heathen	3427
Mic	7:8	when I **s** in darkness, the Lord	3427
Zec	3:8	and thy fellows that **s** before thee:	3427
Zec	6:13	shall **s** and rule upon his throne;	3427
Mal	3:3	he shall **s** as a refiner and purifier	3427
Mt	8:11	**shall s down with Abraham, and**	*347*
Mt	19:28	**Son of man shall s in the throne**	*2523*
Mt	19:28	**ye also shall s upon twelve thrones**	*2523*
Mt	20:23	**to s on my right hand, and on**	*2523*
Mt	22:44	**S thou on my right hand, till I**	*2521*
Mt	25:31	**then shall he s upon the throne**	*2523*
Mt	26:36	**S ye here, while I go and pray**	*2523*
Lk	1:79	light to them that **s** in darkness	*2521*
Lk	13:29	**s down in the kingdom of God**	*347*
Lk	14:8	**s not down in the highest room;**	*2625*
Lk	20:42	**Lord, S thou on my right hand,**	*2521*
Lk	22:30	**s on thrones judging the twelve**	*2523*
Lk	22:69	**Son of man s on the right hand**	*2521*
Ac	2:30	raise up Christ to **s** on his throne;	*2523*
Ac	2:34	Lord, **S** thou on my right hand,	*2522*
Eph	2:6	made us **s** together in heavenly	*4776*
Heb	1:13	**S** on my right hand, until I make	*2521*
Jas	2:3	him, **S** thou here in a good place;	*2521*
Rev	3:21	**grant to s with me in my throne,**	*2523*
Rev	17:3	a woman **s** upon a scarlet coloured	*2521*
Rev	18:7	I **s** a queen, and am no widow, and	*2521*

SITTEST

Pr	23:1	When thou **s** to eat with a ruler,	3427
Ac	23:3	**s** thou to judge me after the law,	*2521*

SITTETH

Ex	11:5	Pharaoh that **s** upon his throne,	3427
Le	15:26	and whatsoever she **s** upon shall be	3427
1Ki	1:46	Also Solomon **s** on the throne of	3427
Est	6:10	the Jew, that **s** at the king's gate:	3427
Ps	1:1	nor **s** in the seat of the scornful	3427
Ps	2:4	that **s** in the heavens shall laugh:	3427
Ps	29:10	yea, the Lord **s** King for ever	3427
Ps	47:8	**s** upon the throne of his holiness	3427
Ps	99:1	he **s** between the cherubims; let	3427
Pr	9:14	For she **s** at the door of her house,	3427
Pr	20:8	that **s** in the throne of judgment	3427
Pr	31:23	when he **s** among the elders of the	3427
Jer	29:16	that **s** upon the throne of David	3427
La	3:28	He **s** alone and keepeth silence	3427
Zec	1:11	all the earth **s** still, and is at rest	3427
Mt	23:22	**of God, and by him that s thereon.**	*2522*
Lk	14:28	**s not down first, and counteth**	*2523*
Lk	14:31	**s not down first, and consulteth**	*2523*
Lk	22:27	**is not he that s at meat? but I am**	*345*
Col	3:1	Christ **s** on the right hand of God	*2521*
2Th	2:4	he as God **s** in the temple of God,	*2525*
Rev	5:13	unto him that **s** upon the throne,	*2521*
Rev	6:16	face of him that **s** on the throne,	*2521*
Rev	7:10	our God which **s** upon the throne	*2521*
Rev	7:15	he that **s** on the throne shall dwell	*2521*
Rev	17:1	whore that **s** upon many waters:	*2521*
Rev	17:9	mountains, on which the woman **s**	*2521*
Rev	17:15	where the whore **s**, are peoples,	*2521*

SITTING

Jgs	3:20	and he was **s** in a summer parlour,	3427
1Ki	13:14	and found him **s** under an oak:	3427
1Ki	22:19	I saw the Lord **s** on his throne, and	3427
2Ki	4:38	sons of the prophets were **s** before	3427
2Ch	18:18	I saw the Lord **s** upon his throne,	3427
Est	5:13	Mordecai ... **s** at the king's gate	3427
Isa	6:1	saw also the Lord **s** upon a throne,	3427
Jer	22:30	**s** upon the throne of David, and	3427
La	3:63	Behold their **s** down, and their	3427
Mt	9:9	**s** at the receipt of custom:	*2521*
Mt	11:16	**like unto children s in the markets,**	*2521*
Mt	21:5	unto thee, meek, and **s** upon an ass,	*1910*
Mt	26:64	**Son of man s on the right hand**	*2522*
Mt	27:61	Mary, **s** over against the sepulchre	*2521*
Mk	5:15	**s**, and clothed, and in his right mind	*2521*
Mk	14:62	**Son of man s on the right hand**	*2521*
Mk	16:5	a young man **s** on the right side	*2521*
Lk	2:46	**s** in the midst of the doctors, both	*2516*
Lk	8:35	**s** at the feet of Jesus, clothed, and	*2521*
Lk	10:13	**repented, s in sackcloth and ashes.**	*2521*
Jn	2:14	and the changers of money **s**:	*2521*
Jn	12:15	King Cometh, **s** on an ass's colt	*2521*
Jn	20:12	And seeth two angels in white **s**,	*2516*
Ac	8:28	**s** in his chariot read Esaias the	*2521*
Rev	4:4	I saw four and twenty elders **s**,	*2521*

SITUATION
2Ki 2:19 the **s** of this city is pleasant, as. 4186
Ps 48:2 Beautiful for **s**, the joy of the. 5131

SIX
Ge 7:11 the **s** hundredth year of Noah's life, ... 8337
Ge 46:26 the souls were threescore and **s**; 8337
Ex 16:26 **S** days ye shall gather it; but on. 8337
Ex 20:9 **S** days shalt thou labour, and do. 8337
Ex 20:11 **s** days the Lord made heaven and. 8337
Ex 21:2 servant, **s** years he shall serve: 8337
Ex 23:10 **s** years thou shalt sow thy land,. 8337
Ex 24:16 and the cloud covered it **s** days: 8337
Ex 28:10 **S** of their names on one stone, and 8337
Ex 31:17 **s** days the Lord made heaven and. 8337
Le 23:3 **S** days shall work be done: but 8337
Le 25:3 **S** years thou shalt sow thy field, ... 8337
Nu 11:21 are **s** hundred thousand footmen; 8337
Nu 35:6 there shall be **s** cities for refuge. 8337
Nu 35:15 These **s** cities shall be a refuge. 8337
Dt 5:13 **S** days thou shalt labour, and do. 8337
Dt 16:8 **S** days thou shalt eat unleavened 8337
Jos 6:3 once. Thus shalt thou do **s** days 8337
Jgs 3:31 slew of the Philistines **s** hundred 8337
Ru 3:17 **s** measures of barley gave he me; 8337
1Sa 17:4 height was **s** cubits and a span 8337
1Sa 17:7 spear's head weighed **s** hundred 8337
2Sa 6:13 ark of the Lord had gone **s** paces,. 8337
2Sa 21:20 that had on every hand **s** fingers, ... 8337
1Ki 10:14 Solomon in one year was **s** hundred . . . 8337
1Ki 10:19 The throne had **s** steps, and the 8337
2Ki 13:19 shouldest have smitten five or **s** times; . . 8337
2Ch 2:2 and **s** hundred to oversee them. 8337
2Ch 9:15 **s** hundred shekels of beaten gold 8337
2Ch 22:12 hid in the house of God **s** years: 8337
Ne 5:18 was one ox and **s** choice sheep;. 8337
Est 2:12 and **s** months with sweet odours, ... 8337
Job 5:19 He shall deliver thee in **s** troubles: 8337
Pr 6:16 These **s** things doth the Lord hate: 8337
Isa 6:2 seraphims: each one had **s** wings;. 8337
Jer 34:14 when he hath served thee **s** years 8337
Mk 9:2 after **s** days Jesus taketh with him. *1803*
Lk 13:14 **s** days in which men ought to work *1803*
Jn 2:6 were set there **s** waterpots of stone, ... *1803*
Rev 4:8 each of them **s** wings about him; *1803*
Rev 13:18 is **S** hundred threescore and **s** *5516*

SIXTEEN
2Ki 14:21 Azariah, which was **s** years old,. . . 8337, 6240
2Ch 26:3 **S** years old was Uzziah when. 8337, 6240

SIXTH
Ge 1:31 and the morning were the **s** day 8345
Ex 16:29 on the **s** day the bread of two days; 8345
Le 25:21 blessing upon you in the **s** year, ... 8345
Nu 29:29 on the **s** day eight bullocks, two 8345
Jos 19:32 The **s** lot came out to the children 8345
Eze 39:2 and leave but the **s** part of thee. 8338
Mt 20:5 **out about the s and ninth hour,** *1623*
Mt 27:45 the **s** hour there was darkness *1623*
Lk 1:26 the **s** month the angel Gabriel was *1623*
Lk 1:36 this is the **s** month with her, who *1623*
Lk 23:44 it was about the **s** hour, and there. *1623*
Jn 19:14 passover, and about the **s** hour *1623*
Rev 6:12 when he had opened the **s** seal *1623*
Rev 9:13 the **s** angel sounded, and I heard a *1623*
Rev 16:12 And the **s** angel poured out his vial *1623*

SIXTY
Nu 7:88 the lambs of the first year **s**. This 8346
Mt 13:23 **some an hundredfold, some s,** *1835*
Mk 4:8 **some thirty, and some s, and.** *1835*

SIXTYFOLD
Mt 13:8 **some s, some thirtyfold** *1835*

SKIES
2Sa 22:12 waters, and thick clouds of the **s**. 7834
Ps 18:11 waters and thick clouds of the **s** 7834
Isa 45:8 let the **s** pour down righteousness:. 7834
Jer 51:9 and is lifted up even to the **s** 7834

SKILFUL
1Ch 28:21 every willing **s** man, for any. 2451
Eze 21:31 of brutish men, and **s** to destroy. 2796
Da 1:4 favoured, and **s** in all wisdom 7919
Am 5:16 such as are **s** of lamentation to 3045

SKILL
Ecc 9:11 nor yet favour to men of **s**; but. 3045
Da 1:17 and **s** in all learning and wisdom:. 7919
Da 9:22 to give thee **s** and understanding 7919

SKIN
Ex 22:27 only, it is his raiment for his **s**. 5785
Ex 34:30 behold, the **s** of his face shone; 5785
Ex 34:35 that the **s** of Moses' face shone:. 5785
Le 13:51 or in any work that is made of **s**; 5785
Job 2:4 **S** for **s**, yea, all that a man 5785
Job 16:15 have sewed sackcloth upon my **s**, ... 1539
Job 19:20 escaped with the **s** of my teeth 5785
Job 19:26 though after my **s** worms destroy. 5785
Job 30:30 My **s** is black upon me, and my 5785
Ps 102:5 groaning my bones cleave to my **s** 1320
Jer 13:23 Can the Ethiopian change his **s**, ... 5785
La 4:8 their **s** cleaveth to their bones; it. 5785
La 5:10 Our **s** was black like an oven. 5785
Eze 16:10 and shod thee with badgers' **s**, and
Eze 37:6 upon you, and cover you with **s**,. 5785
Mic 3:3 and flay their **s** from off them; and 5785
Mk 1:6 a girdle of a **s** about his loins; *1193*

SKINS See also GOATSKINS; SHEEPSKINS.
Ge 3:21 did the Lord God make coats of **s**, ... 5785
Ge 27:16 she put the **s** of the kids of the 5785
Ex 26:14 for the tent of rams' **s** dyed red, ... 5785
Ex 36:19 and a covering of badgers' **s** above 5785
Le 16:27 they shall burn in the fire their **s**, ... 5785
Nu 4:10 within a covering of badgers' **s**,. 5785
Nu 31:20 all that is made of **s**, and all work. 5785

SKIPPED
Ps 114:4 The mountains **s** like rams, and 7540

SKIRT
Dt 27:20 he uncovereth his father's **s** 3671
Ru 3:9 spread therefore thy **s** over thine. 3671
1Sa 15:27 laid hold upon the **s** of his mantle 3671
1Sa 24:4 cut off the **s** of Saul's robe privily 3671
1Sa 24:11 see the **s** of thy robe in my hand: 3671
Eze 16:8 and I spread my **s** over thee, and 3671
Hag 2:12 holy flesh in the **s** of his garment,. 3671
Zec 8:23 hold of the **s** of him that is a Jew, ... 3671

SKIRTS
Ps 133:2 down to the **s** of his garments; 6310
Jer 2:34 Also in thy **s** is found the blood of. 3671

Jer 13:26 I discover thy **s** upon thy face 7757
La 1:9 Her filthiness is in her **s**; she 7757
Na 3:5 will discover thy **s** upon thy face, ... 7757

SKULL
2Ki 9:35 found no more of her than the **s**, ... 1538
Mk 15:22 being interpreted, The place of a **s** *2898*
Jn 19:17 into a place called the place of a **s**, ... *2898*

SKY
Dt 33:26 help, and in his excellency on the **s**. 7834
Job 37:18 Hast thou with him spread out the **s**,.. 7834
Mt 16:2 **be fair weather: for the s is red** *3772*
Lk 12:56 **ye can discern the face of the s** *3772*
Heb 11:12 **so many as the stars of the s in** *3772*

SLACK
Dt 7:10 not be **s** to him that hateth him, ... 309
Dt 23:21 thy God, thou shalt not **s** to pay it: 309
Jos 18:3 How long are ye **s** to go to possess 7503
2Ki 4:24 **s** not thy riding for me, except I 6113
Pr 10:4 poor that dealeth with a **s** hand: 7423
Zep 3:16 to Zion, Let not thine hands be **s** 7503
2Pe 3:9 The Lord is not **s** concerning his. *1019*

SLACKNESS
2Pe 3:9 promise, as some men count **s**; *1022*

SLAIN
Ge 4:23 I have **s** a man to my wounding, ... 2026
Ge 34:27 sons of Jacob came upon the **s**, ... 2491
Le 14:51 them in the blood of the **s** bird 7819
Le 26:17 shall be **s** before your enemies: 5062
Nu 14:16 hath **s** them in the wilderness 7819
Nu 19:18 a bone, or one **s**, or one dead, or a 2491
Nu 22:33 surely now also I had **s** thee, and 2026
Nu 23:24 and drink the blood of the **s** 2491
Nu 25:14 was **s** with the Midianitish woman, ... 5221
Nu 31:19 and whosoever hath touched any **s** 2491
Dt 21:1 it be not known who hath **s** him: 2491
Dt 32:42 with the blood of the **s** and of the 2491
Jos 11:6 deliver them up all **s** before Israel: 2491
Jgs 9:18 and have **s** his sons, threescore 2026
Jgs 15:16 of an ass have I **s** a thousand men 5221
Jgs 20:4 husband of the woman that was **s** 7523
1Sa 4:11 Hophni and Phinehas, were **s** 4191
1Sa 18:7 Saul hath **s** his thousands, and 5221
1Sa 19:6 As the Lord liveth, he shall not be **s** 4191
1Sa 19:11 to night, to morrow thou shalt be **s** 4191
1Sa 22:21 Saul had **s** the Lord's priests 2026
1Sa 31:8 the Philistines came to strip the **s**. 2491
2Sa 1:16 saying, I have **s** the Lord's anointed 4191
2Sa 1:19 The beauty of Israel is **s** upon thy. 2491
2Sa 4:11 men have **s** a righteous person in 2026
2Sa 12:9 and hast **s** him with the sword of 2026
2Sa 13:30 Absalom hath **s** all the king's sons 5221
2Sa 21:16 sword, thought to have **s** David 5221
1Ki 13:26 which hath torn him, and **s** him, ... 4191
1Ki 16:16 and hath also **s** the king: 5221
1Ki 19:1 how he had **s** all the prophets 2026
1Ki 19:14 **s** thy prophets with the sword; 2026
2Ki 11:15 Let her not be **s** in the house of the 4191
1Ch 11:11 three hundred **s** by him at one time. ... 2491
2Ch 28:9 **s** them in a rage that reacheth unto 2026
Est 7:4 my people, to be destroyed, to be **s**, ... 2026
Est 9:12 The Jews have **s** and destroyed 2026
Job 1:15 **s** the servants with the edge of 5221
Job 1:17 **s** the servants with the edge of 5221
Pr 7:26 many strong men have been **s** by her... 2026
Pr 22:13 without, I shall be **s** in the streets 7523
Isa 66:16 the **s** of the Lord shall be many. 2491
Jer 9:1 the **s** of the daughter of my people! 2491
Jer 14:18 then behold the **s** with the sword! 2491
Jer 25:33 **s** of the Lord shall be at that day. 2491
Jer 33:5 whom I have **s** in mine anger 5221
Jer 51:49 shall fall the **s** of all the earth. 2491
La 2:21 **s** them in the day of thine anger; 2026
La 3:43 thou hast **s**, thou hast not pitied. 2026
La 4:9 that be **s** with the sword are better 2491
Eze 6:4 down your **s** men before your idols 2491
Eze 9:7 house, and fill the courts with the **s** 2491
Eze 11:6 filled the streets thereof with the **s** 2491
Eze 23:39 when they had **s** their children to 7819
Eze 28:8 that are **s** in the midst of the seas 2491
Eze 32:21 lie uncircumcised, **s** by the sword 2491
Eze 32:25 set her a bed in the midst of the **s**. 2491
Eze 32:31 Pharaoh and all his army **s** by the. 2491
Eze 37:9 breathe upon these **s**, that they 2026
Da 2:13 that the wise men should be **s**; 6992
Da 7:11 I beheld even till the beast was **s**. 6992
Da 11:26 and many shall fall down **s** 2491
Na 3:3 and there is a multitude of **s**, and 2491
Lk 9:22 **be s, and be raised the third day** *615*
Ac 2:23 wicked hands have crucified and **s** *337*
Ac 7:42 have ye offered to me **s** beasts and *4968*
Ac 7:52 they have **s** them which shewed *615*
Ac 13:28 desired they Pilate that he should be **s**... *337*
Ac 23:14 eat nothing until we have **s** Paul *615*
Heb 11:37 were **s** with the sword: *1722, 5408, 599*
Rev 2:13 **martyr, who was s among you** *615*
Rev 5:6 stood a Lamb as it had been **s**, ... *4969*
Rev 5:12 Worthy is the Lamb that was **s** to *4969*
Rev 6:9 that were **s** for the word of God, ... *4969*
Rev 11:13 were **s** of men seven thousand: *615*
Rev 13:8 the Lamb **s** from the foundation. *4969*
Rev 18:24 of all that were **s** upon the earth. *4969*
Rev 19:21 remnant were **s** with the sword of *615*

SLANDER
Nu 14:36 by bringing up a **s** upon the land, ... 1681
Ps 31:13 For I have heard the **s** of many: 1681
Pr 10:18 and he that uttereth a **s**, is a fool. 1681

SLAUGHTER
Jgs 11:33 the vineyards, with a very great **s**, ... 4347
Jgs 15:8 them hip and thigh with a great **s**: 4347
1Sa 17:57 David returned from the **s** of the 5221
1Sa 18:6 David was returned from the **s** of. 5221
2Sa 1:1 David was returned from the **s** of. 5221
Ps 44:22 we are counted as sheep for the **s** 2878
Pr 7:22 as an ox goeth to the **s**, or as a. 2875
Isa 14:21 Prepare **s** for his children for the 4293
Isa 53:7 he is brought as a lamb to the **s**, ... 2875
Jer 12:3 pull them out like sheep for the **s**. 2873
Jer 12:3 and prepare them for the day of **s** 2028
Jer 51:40 them down like lambs to the **s**, ... 2873
Eze 9:2 every man a **s** weapon in his hand; 4660
Zec 11:4 my God; Feed the flock of the **s**; 2028
Zec 11:7 And I will feed the flock of **s**, even 2028
Ac 8:32 He was led as a sheep to the **s**; *4967*
Ro 8:36 are accounted as sheep for the **s** *4967*
Heb 7:1 returning from the **s** of the kings, ... *2871*
Jas 5:5 your hearts, as in a day of **s** *4967*

SLAY

Ge 4:14	one that findeth me shall **s** me	2026
Ge 20:11	they will **s** me for my wife's sake	2026
Ge 22:10	and took the knife to **s** his son	7819
Ge 37:20	let us **s** him, and cast him into	2026
Ge 37:26	What profit is it if we **s** our brother,	2026
Ge 42:37	**S** my two sons, if I bring him not	4191
Ex 2:15	this thing, he sought to **s** Moses	2026
Ex 4:23	I will **s** thy son, even thy firstborn	2026
Ex 5:21	put a sword in their hand to **s** us	2026
Ex 23:7	innocent and righteous **s** thou not:	2026
Le 4:33	**s** it for a sin offering in the place	7819
Le 14:13	he shall **s** the lamb in the place	7819
Dt 27:25	reward to **s** an innocent person:	5221
Jos 13:22	children of Israel **s** with the sword	2026
Jgs 8:19	saved them alive, I would not **s** you	2026
Jgs 9:54	Draw thy sword, and **s** me, that	4191
1Sa 5:10	ark ... to us, to **s** us and our people.	4191
1Sa 5:11	that it **s** us not, and our people:	4191
1Sa 15:3	but **s** both man and woman	4191
1Sa 19:5	blood, to **s** David without a cause?	4191
1Sa 20:8	be in me iniquity, **s** me thyself;	4191
1Sa 22:17	Turn, and **s** the priests of the Lord;	4191
1Ki 3:26	the living child, and in no wise **s** it	4191
1Ki 18:9	into the hand of Ahab, to **s** me?	4191
1Ki 18:12	he cannot find thee, he shall **s** me:	2026
1Ki 18:14	Elijah is here: and he shall **s** me	2026
1Ki 19:17	the sword of Jehu shall Elisha **s**	4191
1Ki 20:36	from me, a lion shall **s** thee	5221
2Ch 23:14	**S** her not in the house of the Lord,	4191
Ne 6:10	for they will come to **s** thee;	2026
Ne 6:10	the night will they come to **s** thee	2026
Job 13:15	Though he **s** me, yet will I trust	6991
Ps 37:32	righteous, and seeketh to **s** him	4191
Ps 109:16	might even **s** the broken in heart	4191
Ps 139:19	Surely thou wilt **s** the wicked	6991
Pr 1:32	away of the simple shall **s** them,	2026
Isa 27:1	he shall **s** the dragon that is in the	2026
Isa 65:15	for the Lord God shall **s** thee, and	4191
Jer 15:3	sword to **s**, and the dogs to tear	2026
Jer 40:15	and I will **s** Ishmael the son of	5221
Jer 40:15	wherefore should he **s** thee, that	5221
Eze 9:6	**S** utterly old and young, both	2026
Eze 40:39	to **s** thereon the burnt offering	7819
Da 2:14	was gone forth to **s** the wise men	6992
Am 9:1	**s** the last of them with the sword:	2026
Hab 1:17	spare continually to **s** the nations?	2026
Lk 19:27	**hither, and s them before me**	*2695*
Jn 5:16	Jesus, and sought to **s** him,	*615*
Ac 5:33	heart, and took counsel to **s** them	*337*
Ac 11:7	unto me, Arise, Peter; **s** and eat	*2380*
Rev 9:15	year, for to **s** the third part of men	*615*

SLAYER

Nu 35:11	that the **s** may flee thither, which	7523
Nu 35:24	between the **s** and the revenger	5221
Nu 35:25	congregation shall deliver the **s**	7523
Nu 35:27	the revenger of blood kill the **s**;	7523
Jos 20:3	That the **s** that killeth any person	7523
Jos 20:6	then shall the **s** return, and come	7523
Jos 21:13	a city of refuge for the **s**;	7523
Eze 21:1	to give it into the hand of the **s**	2026

SLAYETH

Ge 4:15	him, Therefore whosoever **s** Cain,	2026
Dt 22:26	against his neighbour, and **s** him,	7523
Job 5:2	man, and envy **s** the silly one	4191
Eze 28:9	before him that **s** thee, I am God?	2026

SLAYING

Jos 8:24	end of **s** all the inhabitants of Ai	2026
Jgs 9:56	father, in **s** his seventy brethren:	2026
Isa 57:5	**s** the children in the valleys	7819

SLEEP

Ge 2:21	a deep **s** to fall upon Adam, and	3462
Ge 15:12	down, a deep **s** fell upon Abram;	8639
Dt 31:16	thou shalt **s** with thy fathers; and	7901
Jgs 16:14	And he awaked out of **s**, and went	8142
Jgs 16:19	she made him **s** upon her knees;	3462
Jgs 16:20	he awoke out of his **s**, and said,	8142
1Sa 26:12	a deep **s** from the Lord was fallen	8639
Est 6:1	that night could not the king **s**,	8142
Job 7:21	for now shall I **s** in the dust; and	7901
Job 14:12	awake, nor be raised out of their **s**	8142
Ps 4:8	both lay me down in peace, and **s**;	3462
Ps 78:65	the Lord awaked as one out of **s**,	3463
Ps 90:5	as with a flood; they are as a **s**	8142
Ps 121:4	Israel shall neither slumber nor **s**	3462
Pr 3:24	down, and thy **s** shall be sweet,	8142
Pr 6:9	How long wilt thou **s**, O sluggard?	7901
Pr 6:9	when wilt thou arise out of thy **s**?	8142
Pr 6:10	Yet a little **s**, a little slumber, **s**	8142
Pr 6:10	a little folding of the hands to **s**	7901
Pr 24:33	Yet a little **s**, a little slumber, **s**	8142
Pr 24:33	a little folding of the hands to **s**	7901
Ecc 5:12	**s** of a labouring man is sweet,	8142
Ecc 5:12	of the rich will not suffer him to **s**	3462
Isa 5:27	none shall slumber nor **s**; neither	3463
Isa 29:10	out upon you the spirit of deep **s**	8639
Jer 31:26	and my **s** was sweet unto me	8142
Da 6:18	him: and his **s** went from him	8139
Da 8:18	I was in a deep **s** on my face	7290
Mt 1:24	Joseph being raised from **s** did as	*5258*
Mt 26:45	**S on now, and take your rest:**	*2518*
Mk 4:27	**And should s, and rise night and**	*2518*
Lk 22:46	**Why s ye? rise and pray, lest ye**	*2518*
Jn 11:11	**that I may awake him out of s**	*1852*
Jn 11:12	Lord, if he **s**, he shall do well	*2837*
Jn 11:13	had spoken of taking of rest in **s**	*5258*
Ac 20:9	being fallen into a deep **s**;	*5258*
Ac 20:9	he sunk down with **s**, and fell	*5258*
Ro 13:11	it is high time to awake out of **s**	*5258*
1Co 11:30	sickly among you, and many **s**	*2837*
1Co 15:51	We shall not all **s**, but we shall all	*2837*
1Th 4:14	so them also which **s** in Jesus	*2837*
1Th 5:7	For they that **s s** in the night;	*2518*
1Th 5:10	for us, that, whether we wake or **s**,	*2518*

SLEEPEST

Ps 44:23	why **s** thou, O Lord? arise, cast	3462
Mk 14:37	saith unto Peter, **Simon, s thou?**	*2518*
Eph 5:14	Awake thou that **s**, and arise from	*2518*

SLEEPETH

1Ki 18:27	peradventure he **s**, and must be	3463
Mt 9:24	**for the maid is not dead, but s**	*2518*
Jn 11:11	unto them, **Our friend Lazarus s**	*2837*

SLEEPING

1Sa 26:7	Saul lay **s** within the trench, and	3463
Mk 13:36	**coming suddenly he find you s**	*2518*
Ac 12:6	Peter was **s** between two soldiers,	*2837*

SLEPT

Ge	2:21	to fall upon Adam, and he **s**: and	3462
Ge	41:5	And he **s** and dreamed the second	3462
2Sa	11:9	Uriah **s** at the door of the king's	7901
1Ki	2:10	David **s** with his fathers, and was	7901
1Ki	19:5	he lay and **s** under a juniper tree,	3462
Ps	3:5	I laid me down and **s**; I awaked;	3462
Ps	76:5	spoiled, they have **s** their sleep:	5123
Mt	13:25	**But while men s, his enemy**	*2518*
Mt	25:5	**tarried, they all slumbered and s**	*2518*
Mt	27:52	bodies of the saints which **s** arose,	*2837*
Mt	28:13	and stole him away while we **s**.	*2837*
1Co	15:20	the firstfruits of them that **s**.	*2837*

SLEW

Ge	4:8	Abel his brother, and **s** him	2026
Ge	4:25	seed instead of Abel, whom Cain **s**.	2026
Ge	38:7	of the Lord; and the Lord **s** him	4191
Ex	2:12	he **s** the Egyptian, and hid him in.	5221
Ex	13:15	the Lord **s** all the firstborn in the	2026
Nu	31:7	Moses; and they **s** all the males	2026
Jos	8:21	again, and **s** the men of Ai.	5221
Jos	10:26	Joshua smote them, and **s** them,	4191
Jgs	3:31	**s** of the Philistines six hundred	5221
Jgs	9:44	were in the fields, and **s** them	5221
Jgs	9:45	**s** the people that was therein,	2026
Jgs	9:54	say not of me, A woman **s** him	2026
Jgs	12:6	**s** him at the passages of Jordan:	7819
Jgs	14:19	**s** thirty men of them, and took	5221
Jgs	15:15	and **s** a thousand men therewith	5221
Jgs	16:24	our country, which **s** many of us	2491
Jgs	16:30	the dead which he **s** at his death	4191
Jgs	16:30	than they which he **s** in his life	4191
1Sa	17:35	beard, and smote him, and **s** him	4191
1Sa	17:36	Thy servant **s** both the lion and	5221
1Sa	17:50	smote the Philistine, and **s** him;	4191
1Sa	17:51	and **s** him, and cut off his head	4191
1Sa	18:27	**s** of the Philistines two hundred	5221
1Sa	19:5	in his hand, and **s** the Philistine,	5221
1Sa	29:5	Saul **s** his thousands, and David	5221
1Sa	31:2	and the Philistines **s** Jonathan	5221
2Sa	1:10	So I stood upon him, and **s** him	4191
2Sa	10:18	David **s** the men of seven hundred	2126
2Sa	18:15	and smote Absalom, and **s** him	4191
2Sa	21:19	**s** the brother of Goliath the Gittite,	5221
2Sa	23:18	three hundred, and **s** them, and	2491
2Sa	23:20	he **s** two lionlike men of Moab:	5221
2Sa	23:20	and **s** a lion in the midst of a pit	5221
1Ki	18:13	I did when Jezebel **s** the prophets	2026
1Ki	18:40	brook Kishon, and **s** them there	7819
1Ki	19:21	took a yoke of oxen, and **s** them,	2076
1Ki	20:36	him, a lion found him, and **s** him.	5221
2Ki	15:10	**s** him, and reigned in his stead	4191
1Ch	11:23	he **s** an Egyptian, a man of great	5221
1Ch	11:23	and **s** him with his own spear	2026
2Ch	24:22	not the kindness ... but **s** his son	2026
2Ch	24:25	and **s** him on his bed, and he died:	2026
Ne	9:26	and **s** thy prophets which testified	2026
Est	9:6	Jews **s** and destroyed five hundred	2026
Est	9:15	**s** three hundred men at Shushan;	2026
Est	9:16	and **s** of their foes seventy and five.	2026
Ps	78:31	**s** the fattest of them, and smote	2026
Ps	105:29	waters into blood, and **s** their fish.	4191
Ps	135:10	great nations, and **s** mighty kings;	2026
Ps	136:18	And **s** famous kings; for his mercy	2026
Jer	20:17	he **s** me not from the womb; or	4191
La	2:4	**s** all that were pleasant to the eye	2026
Da	3:22	the flame of the fire **s** those men	6992
Mt	2:16	**s** all the children ... in Bethlehem,	337
Mt	21:39	**out of the vineyard, and s him**	*615*
Mt	23:35	**s between the temple and ... altar**	*5407*
Ac	5:30	raised up Jesus, whom ye **s** and	*1315*
Ac	10:39	whom they **s** and hanged on a tree:	*337*
Ro	7:11	deceived me, and by it **s** me	*615*
1Jn	3:12	wicked one, and **s** his brother	*4969*
1Jn	3:12	And wherefore **s** he him? Because	*4969*

SLIDE

Ps	26:1	the Lord; therefore I shall not **s**.	4571
Ps	37:31	his heart; none of his steps shall **s**.	4571

SLIME

Ge	11:3	stone, and **s** had they for morter	2564
Ex	2:3	daubed it with **s** and with pitch,	2564

SLING

Jgs	20:16	could **s** stones at an hair breadth,	7049
1Sa	17:40	and his **s** was in his hand: and he	7050
1Sa	17:50	with a **s** and with a stone,	7050
Pr	26:8	As he that bindeth a stone in a **s**.	4773

SLIP

Job	12:5	He that is ready to **s** with his feet	4571
Ps	17:5	thy paths, that my footsteps **s** not	4131
Heb	2:1	at any time we should let them **s**.	*3901*

SLIPPED

1Sa	19:10	he **s** away out of Saul's presence	6362
Ps	73:2	gone; my steps had well nigh **s**	8210

SLIPPERY

Ps	35:6	Let their way be dark and **s**: and	2519
Ps	73:18	thou didst set them in **s** places:	2513

SLIPPETH

Ps	38:16	when my foot **s**, they magnify	4131
Ps	94:18	When I said, My foot **s**; thy mercy,	4131

SLOTHFUL

Pr	12:24	but the **s** shall be under tribute	7423
Pr	15:19	way of the **s** man is as an hedge	6102
Pr	21:25	The desire of the **s** killeth him;	6102
Pr	22:13	The **s** man saith, There is a lion	6102
Pr	26:13	The **s** man saith, There is a lion in	6102
Pr	26:14	hinges, so doth the **s** upon his bed.	6102
Mt	25:26	**Thou wicked and s servant, thou**	*3636*
Ro	12:11	Not **s** in business; fervent in spirit;	*3636*
Heb	6:12	That ye be not **s**, but followers of	*3576*

SLOTHFULNESS

Pr	19:15	**S** casteth into a deep sleep; and	6103
Ecc	10:18	By much **s** the building decayeth;	6103

SLOW

Ps	103:8	**s** to anger, and plenteous in mercy,	750
Ps	145:8	**s** to anger, and of great mercy	750
Pr	15:18	that is **s** to anger appeaseth strife	750
Pr	16:32	He that is **s** to anger is better than	750
Jnh	4:2	**s** to anger, and of great kindness,	750
Na	1:3	The Lord is **s** to anger, and great in	750
Lk	24:25	**O fools, and s of heart to believe**	*1021*
Jas	1:19	to hear, **s** to speak, **s** to wrath;	*1021*

SLUGGARD

Pr	6:6	Go to the ant, thou **s**; consider	6102
Pr	6:9	How long wilt thou sleep, O **s**?	6102

Pr	20:4	The **s** will not plow by reason of	6102
Pr	26:16	The **s** is wiser in his own conceit	6102

SLUMBER

Ps	121:3	he that keepeth thee will not **s**	5123
Ps	121:4	Israel shall neither **s** nor sleep	5123
Pr	6:10	Yet a little sleep, a little **s**, a little	8572
Ro	11:8	hath given them the spirit of **s**,	*2659*

SMALL

Ge	19:11	with blindness, both **s** and great:	6996
Ge	30:15	a **s** matter that thou hast taken	4592
Ex	18:22	every **s** matter they shall judge:	6990
Ex	18:26	**s** matter they judged themselves	6990
Nu	16:9	it but a **s** thing unto you, that	4592
Nu	16:13	**s** thing that thou hast brought us	4592
Dt	1:17	hear the **s** as well as the great;	6996
1Sa	5:9	men of the city, both **s** and great,	6996
2Sa	17:13	be not one **s** stone found there	1571
1Ki	19:12	and after the fire a still **s** voice	1851
2Ki	23:2	all the people, both **s** and great:	6996
1Ch	17:17	this was a **s** thing in thine eyes,	6994
2Ch	15:13	put to death, whether **s** or great	6996
2Ch	24:24	came with a **s** company of men	4705
Est	1:5	both unto great and **s**, seven days,	6996
Job	8:7	Though thy beginning was **s**, yet	4705
Job	15:11	consolations of God **s** with thee?	4592
Job	36:27	he maketh **s** the drops of water:	1639
Ps	115:13	fear the Lord, both **s** and great	6996
Ps	119:141	I am **s** and despised: yet do not	6810
Pr	24:10	day of adversity, thy strength is **s**	6862
Isa	1:9	left unto us a very **s** remnant,	4592
Isa	54:7	For a **s** moment have I forsaken	6996
Isa	60:22	and a **s** one a strong nation:	6810
Mk	8:7	And they had a few **s** fishes: and	*2485*
Jn	2:15	he had made a scourge of **s** cords	*4979*
Jn	6:9	five barley loaves, ... two **s** fishes:	*3795*
Ac	15:2	no **s** dissension and disputation	*3641*
Ac	19:24	no **s** gain unto the craftsman;	*3641*
Jas	3:4	turned about with a very **s** helm,	*1646*
Rev	11:18	that fear thy name, **s** and great;	*3398*
Rev	20:12	And I saw the dead, **s** and great	*3398*

SMALLEST

1Sa	9:21	of the **s** of the tribes of Israel?	6996
1Co	6:2	unworthy to judge the **s** matters?	*1646*

SMELL

Ge	27:27	he smelled the **s** of his raiment,	*7381*
Ge	27:27	**s** of my son is as the **s** of a field	*7381*
Le	26:31	will not **s** the savour of your sweet	7306
SS	2:13	the tender grape give a good **s**	7381
SS	4:10	and the **s** of thine ointments than	7381
SS	7:8	and the **s** of thy nose like apples;	7381
Isa	3:24	instead of sweet **s** there shall be	1314
Da	3:27	nor the **s** of fire had passed on	7382
Php	4:18	an odour of a sweet **s**, a sacrifice	*2175*

SMELLED

Ge	8:21	And the Lord **s** a sweet savour;	7306
Ge	27:27	and he **s** the smell of his raiment,	7306

SMELLING

SS	5:5	my fingers with sweet **s** myrrh,	5674
SS	5:13	lilies, dropping sweet **s** myrrh.	5674
1Co	12:17	were hearing, where were the **s**?	*3750*

SMITE

Ge	8:21	neither will I again **s** any more	5221
Ex	3:20	**s** Egypt with all my wonders which	5221
Ex	7:17	I will **s** with the rod that is in mine	5221
Ex	8:2	I will **s** all thy borders with frogs:	5062
Ex	8:16	and **s** the dust of the land, that it	5221
Ex	9:15	I may **s** thee and thy people with	5221
Ex	12:12	will **s** all the firstborn in the land of	5221
Ex	12:13	you, when I **s** the land of Egypt	5221
Ex	12:23	pass through to **s** the Egyptians;	5062
Ex	12:23	come in unto your houses to **s** you	5062
Ex	17:6	thou shalt **s** the rock, and there	5221
Dt	19:11	and **s** him mortally that he die, and	5221
Dt	20:13	thou shalt **s** every male thereof	5221
Dt	28:22	shall **s** thee with a consumption,	5221
Dt	28:27	**s** thee with the botch of Egypt,	5221
Dt	28:28	Lord shall **s** thee with madness	5221
Dt	28:35	The Lord shall **s** thee in the knees,	5221
Jos	7:3	thousand men go up and **s** Ai;	6221
1Sa	15:3	Now go and **s** Amalek, and utterly	5221
1Sa	17:46	I will **s** thee, and take thine head	5221
1Sa	18:11	I will **s** David even to the wall with	5221
1Sa	19:10	Saul sought to **s** David even to the	5221
1Sa	20:33	Saul cast a javelin at him to **s** him:	5221
1Sa	26:10	Lord liveth, the Lord shall **s** him;	5062
1Ki	14:15	the Lord shall **s** Israel, as a reed	5221
2Ki	9:7	thou shalt **s** the house of Ahab thy	5221
2Ki	9:27	and said, **S** him also in the chariot	5221
Ps	121:6	The sun shall not **s** thee by day	5221
Pr	19:25	**S** a scorner, and the simple will	5221
Isa	10:24	he shall **s** thee with a rod, and	5221
Isa	49:10	shall the heat nor sun **s** them:	5221
Jer	18:18	and let us **s** him with the tongue,	5221
Eze	39:3	And I will **s** thy bow out of thy left	5221
Am	9:1	**S** the lintel of the door, that the	5221
Mic	5:1	**s** the judge of Israel with a rod	5221
Zec	9:4	and he will **s** her power in the sea;	5221
Zec	12:4	**s** every horse of the people with	5221
Zec	13:7	**s** the shepherd, and the sheep shall	5221
Zec	14:18	the Lord will **s** the heathen that	5062
Mt	5:39	**shall s thee on thy right cheek,**	*4474*
Mk	14:27	**I will s the shepherd, and the**	*3960*
Lk	22:49	Lord, shall we **s** with the sword?	*3960*
Ac	23:2	by him to **s** him on the mouth	*5180*
Ac	23:3	God shall **s** thee, thou whited wall:	*5180*
Rev	11:6	to **s** the earth with all plagues,	*3960*

SMITEST

Ex	2:13	Wherefore **s** thou thy fellow?	5221
Jn	18:23	**evil: but if well, why s thou me?**	*1194*

SMITETH

Ex	21:12	He that **s** a man, so that he die,	5221
Ex	21:15	he that **s** his father, or his mother,	5221
Job	26:12	he **s** through the proud	4272
La	3:30	giveth his cheek to him that **s** him:	5221
Eze	7:9	know that I am the Lord that **s**	5221
Lk	6:29	**that s thee on the one cheek**	*5180*

SMITHS

2Ki	24:14	and all the craftsmen and **s**:	4525
Jer	24:1	with the carpenters and **s**, from	4525

SMITING

Ex	2:11	he spied an Egyptian **s** an Hebrew,	5221
1Ki	20:37	him, so that in **s** he wounded him	5221

SMITTEN

Ex	7:25	that the Lord had **s** the river	5221
Nu	22:28	thou hast **s** me thee three times?	5221
Jgs	20:32	They are **s** down before us, as at	5062
Jgs	20:36	of Benjamin saw that they were **s**	5062
Jgs	20:39	Surely they are **s** down before us,	5062
1Sa	4:2	Israel was **s** before the Philistines:	5062
1Sa	4:3	Wherefore hath the Lord **s** us to	5062
1Sa	5:12	died not were **s** with the emerods:	5221
1Sa	13:4	that Saul had **s** a garrison of the	5221
2Ki	2:14	when he also had **s** the waters,	5221
1Ch	18:9	how David had **s** all the host of	5221
2Ch	26:20	out, because the Lord had **s** him	5060
Job	16:10	they have **s** me upon the cheek	5221
Ps	3:7	**s** all mine enemies upon the cheek	5221
Ps	143:3	he hath **s** my life down to the	1792
Isa	53:4	stricken, **s** of God, and afflicted	5221
Hos	9:16	Ephraim is **s**, their root is dried	5221
Ac	23:3	me to be **s** contrary to the law?	*5180*
Rev	8:12	the third part of the sun was **s**	*4141*

SMOKE

Ex	19:18	Sinai was altogether on a **s**,	6225
Ex	19:18	fire: and the **s** thereof ascended	6227
Ex	19:18	ascended as the **s** of a furnace,	6227
Jos	8:20	the **s** of the city ascended up to	6227
Jos	8:21	and that the **s** of the city ascended,	6227
2Sa	22:9	went up a **s** out of his nostrils, and	6227
Job	41:20	Out of his nostrils goeth **s**, as out	6227
Ps	74:1	thine anger **s** against the sheep	6225
Ps	104:32	toucheth the hills, and they **s**	6225
Pr	10:26	to the teeth, and as **s** to the eyes,	6227
SS	3:6	of the wilderness like pillars of **s**	6227
Isa	4:5	assemblies, a cloud and **s** by day,	6227
Isa	51:6	heavens shall vanish away like **s**,	6227
Hos	13:3	and as the **s** out of the chimney	6227
Joel	2:30	blood, and fire, and pillars of **s**	6227
Rev	9:2	and there arose a **s** out of the pit,	*2586*
Rev	9:2	as the **s** of a great furnace; and the	*2586*
Rev	9:2	was darkened by reason of the **s**	*2586*
Rev	9:3	there came out of the **s** locusts	*2586*
Rev	9:18	killed, by the fire, and by the **s**,	*2586*
Rev	15:8	filled with **s** from the glory of God,	*2586*
Rev	19:3	And her **s** rose up for ever and ever	*2586*

SMOKING

Ex	20:18	the trumpet, and the mountain **s**	6226
Isa	42:3	the **s** flax shall he not quench:	3544
Mt	12:20	and **s** flax shall he not quench,	5187

SMOOTH

Ge	27:11	a hairy man, and I am a **s** man:	2509
Ge	27:16	hands, and upon the **s** of his neck:	2513
1Sa	17:40	chose him five **s** stones out of the	2512
Lk	3:5	the rough ways shall be made **s**;	*3006*

SMOTE

Ex	7:20	**s** the waters that were in the river,	5221
Ex	8:17	his rod, and **s** the dust of the earth,	5221
Ex	9:25	the hail **s** throughout the land of	5221
Ex	9:25	the hail **s** every herb of the field,	5221
Ex	12:27	Egypt, when he **s** the Egyptians	5062
Ex	12:29	the Lord **s** all the firstborn in the	5221
Nu	11:33	Lord **s** the people with a very great	5221
Nu	20:11	with his rod he **s** the rock twice:	5221
Nu	22:23	Balaam **s** the ass, to turn her into	5221
Nu	22:25	the wall: and he **s** her again	5221
Nu	24:10	and he **s** his hands together	5606
Dt	4:46	Moses and the children of Israel **s**,	5221
Jos	7:5	men of Ai **s** of them about thirty	5221
Jos	7:5	and **s** them in the going down:	5221
Jos	8:22	they **s** them, so that they let none	5221
Jos	8:24	unto Ai, and **s** it with the edge of	5221
Jos	10:40	Joshua **s** … the country of the hills,	5221
Jos	10:41	**s** them from Kadesh-barnea even	5221
Jos	20:5	he **s** his neighbour unwittingly	5221
Jgs	4:21	and **s** the nail into his temples,	8628
Jgs	5:26	with the hammer she **s** Sisera	1986
Jgs	5:26	she **s** off his head, when she had	4277
Jgs	7:13	unto a tent, and **s** it that it fell,	5221
Jgs	8:11	Gideon went up … and **s** the host:	5221
Jgs	15:8	**s** them hip and thigh with a great	5221
1Sa	5:6	**s** them with emerods, even Ashdod	5221
1Sa	5:9	**s** the men of the city, both small	5221
1Sa	6:19	even he **s** of the people fifty thousand	
1Sa	15:7	And Saul **s** the Amalekites from	5221
1Sa	17:35	I went out after him, and **s** him,	5221
1Sa	17:35	caught him by his beard, and **s** him,	5221
1Sa	17:49	and **s** the Philistine in his forehead,	5221
1Sa	17:50	with a stone, and **s** the Philistine	5221
1Sa	19:10	and he **s** the javelin into the wall:	5221
1Sa	24:5	afterward, that David's heart **s** him,	5221
1Sa	25:38	the Lord **s** Nabal, that he died	5062
2Sa	2:23	spear **s** him under the fifth rib	5221
2Sa	6:7	and God **s** him there for his error;	5221
2Sa	18:15	and **s** Absalom, and slew him	5221
2Sa	24:10	David's heart **s** him after that he	5221
2Ki	2:8	his mantle, … and **s** the waters	5221
2Ki	2:14	the mantle … and **s** the waters	5221
2Ki	6:18	**s** them with blindness according	5221
2Ki	13:18	And he **s** thrice, and stayed	5221
1Ch	13:10	kindled against Uzza, and he **s** him,	5221
2Ch	13:15	God **s** Jeroboam and all Israel	5062
Ne	13:25	**s** certain of them, and plucked off	5221
Est	9:5	the Jews **s** all their enemies with	5221
Job	1:19	**s** the four corners of the house	5060
Job	2:7	**s** Job with sore boils from the	5221
Ps	78:20	he **s** the rock, that the waters	5221
Ps	78:31	**s** down the chosen men of Israel	3766
Ps	78:51	And **s** all the firstborn in Egypt;	5221
Ps	105:36	He **s** also all the firstborn in their	5221
Ps	135:8	Who **s** the firstborn of Egypt, both	5221
Isa	14:29	rod of him that **s** thee is broken:	5221
Isa	41:7	the hammer him that **s** the anvil,	1986
Jer	20:2	Pashur **s** Jeremiah the prophet,	5221
Jer	37:15	wroth with Jeremiah, and **s** him,	5221
Da	2:34	**s** the image upon his feet that were	4223
Da	2:35	the stone that **s** the image became	4223
Da	5:6	his knees **s** one against another.	5368
Da	8:7	and **s** the ram, and brake his two	5221
Jnh	4:7	and it **s** the gourd that it withered	5221
Mt	26:51	the high priest's, and **s** off his ear	*851*
Mt	26:67	others **s** him with the palms of	*4474*
Mt	26:68	thou Christ, Who is he that **s** thee?	*3817*
Mt	27:30	the reed, and **s** him on the head	*5180*
Lk	18:13	**s upon his breast, saying, God be**	*5180*
Lk	22:63	held Jesus mocked him, … **s** him	*1194*
Lk	22:64	Prophesy, who is it that **s** thee?	*3817*
Lk	23:48	**s** their breasts, and returned	*5180*
Ac	7:24	oppressed, and **s** the Egyptian:	*3960*
Ac	12:7	he **s** Peter on the side, and raised	*3960*
Ac	12:23	angel of the Lord **s** him, because	*3960*

SNARE

Ex	10:7	shall this man be a **s** unto us?	4170
Jgs	8:27	thing became a **s** unto Gideon,	4170
1Sa	28:9	then layest thou a **s** for my life	5367
Job	18:8	feet, and he walketh upon a **s**	7639
Job	18:10	**s** is laid for him in the ground	2256
Ps	69:22	Let their table become a **s** before	6341
Ps	91:3	thee from the **s** of the fowler, and	6341
Ps	119:110	The wicked have laid a **s** for me:	6341
Ps	124:7	bird out of the **s** of the fowlers:	6341
Ps	140:5	The proud have hid a **s** for me, and	6341
Pr	7:23	as a bird hasteth to the **s**, and	6341
Pr	18:7	and his lips are the **s** of his soul	4170
Pr	29:8	Scornful men bring a city into a **s**	6315
Ecc	9:12	birds that are caught in the **s**;	6341
Jer	50:24	I have laid a **s** for thee, and thou	3369
Lk	21:35	**as a s shall it come on all them**	*3803*
1Ti	3:7	reproach and the **s** of the devil	*3803*
2Ti	2:26	themselves out of the **s** of the devil,	*3803*

SNARED

Dt	12:30	thou be not **s** by following them.	5367
Ps	9:16	wicked is **s** in the work of his own	5367
Pr	6:2	**s** with the words of thy mouth,	3369
Isa	8:15	be broken, and be **s**, and be taken.	3369
Isa	42:22	they are all of them **s** in holes	6351

SNARES

Job	22:10	Therefore **s** are round about thee,	6341
Ps	11:6	Upon the wicked he shall rain **s**,	6341
Ps	38:12	seek after my life lay **s** for me:	5367
Ps	64:5	they commune of laying **s** privily;	4170
Pr	13:14	life, to depart from the **s** of death	4170
Pr	22:5	Thorns and **s** are in the way of	6341
Ecc	7:26	whose heart is **s** and nets, and	4685

SNEEZED

2Ki	4:35	and the child **s** seven times, and	2237

SNOW

Ex	4:6	behold, his hand was leprous as **s**.	7950
Nu	12:10	became leprous, white as **s**: and	7950
Job	9:30	If I wash myself with **s** water, and	7950
Job	24:19	and heat consume the **s** waters:	7950
Ps	51:7	me, and I shall be whiter than **s**	7950
Ps	147:16	He giveth **s** like wool: he	7950
Ps	148:8	Fire, and hail; **s**, and vapours;	7950
Pr	25:13	As the cold of **s** in the time of	7950
Pr	26:1	As **s** in summer, and as rain in	7950
Pr	31:21	She is not afraid of the **s** for her	7950
Isa	1:18	scarlet, they shall be as white as **s**;	7950
Da	7:9	whose garment was white as **s**.	8517
Mt	28:3	and his raiment white as **s**	*5510*
Mk	9:3	shining, exceeding white as **s**.	*5510*
Rev	1:14	were white like wool, as white as **s**	*5510*

SNUFFDISHES

Ex	37:23	his snuffers, and his **s**, of pure gold	4289
Nu	4:9	lamps, and his tongs, and his **s**	4289

SNUFFED

Jer	14:6	they **s** up the winds like dragons;	7602
Mal	1:13	ye have **s** at it, saith the Lord of.	5301

SNUFFERS

Ex	37:23	made his seven lamps, and his **s**,	4457
2Ki	12:13	of the Lord bowls of silver, **s**	4212

SOBER

2Co	5:13	or whether we be **s**, it is for your.	*4993*
1Ti	3:2	husband of one wife, vigilant, **s**,	*4998*
1Ti	3:11	wives be grave, not slanderers, **s**,	*3524*
Tit	2:2	That the aged men be **s**, grave,	*3524*
Tit	2:4	teach the young women to be **s**.	*4994*
Tit	2:6	likewise exhort to be **s** minded	*4993*
1Pe	1:13	be **s**, and hope to the end for the	*3525*
1Pe	5:8	Be **s**, be vigilant: because your	*3525*

SOBERLY

Ro	12:3	but to think **s**, according as	*1519, 4993*
Tit	2:12	we should live **s**, righteously, and	*4996*

SOBRIETY

1Ti	2:9	with shamefacedness and **s**; not	*4997*
1Ti	2:15	and charity and holiness with **s**.	*4997*

SOCKETS

Ex	26:19	forty **s** of silver under the twenty	134
Ex	26:19	two **s** under one board for his two	134
Ex	38:30	**s** to the door of the tabernacle	134
SS	5:15	of marble, set upon **s** of fine gold:	134

SOD

Ge	25:29	And Jacob **s** pottage: and Esau	2102
2Ch	35:13	other holy offerings **s** they in pots,	1310

SODDEN

Le	6:28	the earthen vessel wherein it is **s**.	1310
La	4:10	women have **s** their own children:	1310

SOEVER

Le	15:9	what saddle **s** he rideth upon that	834
Dt	12:32	What thing **s** I command you,	834
Mk	6:10	**what place s ye enter into an**	*1437*
Jn	20:23	**Whose s sins ye remit, they**	*3745, 302*
Jn	20:23	**whose s sins ye retain, they**	3745, 302
Ro	8:19	that what things **s** the law saith,	*1437*

SOFT

Job	23:16	For God maketh my heart **s**, and	7401
Pr	15:1	A **s** answer turneth away wrath:	7390
Pr	25:15	and a **s** tongue braketh the bone.	7390
Mt	11:8	**A man clothed in s raiment?**	*3120*

SOFTLY

Ge	33:14	I will lead on **s**, according as the	328
Jgs	4:21	and went **s** unto him, and smote	3814
Ru	3:7	came **s** and uncovered his feet,	3909

SOJOURN

Ge	12:19	went down into Egypt to **s** there;	1481
Ru	1:1	went to **s** in the country of Moab.	1481
Ps	120:5	Woe is me, that I **s** in Mesech, that	1481
Isa	23:7	feet shall carry her afar off to **s**	1481
Isa	52:4	aforetime into Egypt to **s** there;	1481
Ac	7:6	should **s** in a strange land;	*1510, 3941*

SOJOURNED

Ge	21:34	And Abraham **s** in the Philistines'	1481
Ge	32:4	I have **s** with Laban, and stayed.	1481
Ps	105:23	and Jacob **s** in the land of Ham.	1481
Heb	11:9	faith he **s** in the land of promise,	*3939*

SOJOURNER

Ge	23:4	I am a stranger and a **s** with you:	8453
Le	25:47	a **s** or stranger wax rich by thee,	1616
Ps	39:12	and a **s**, as all my fathers were.	8453

SOJOURNERS

Le	25:3	ye are strangers and **s** with me	8453
1Ch	29:15	are strangers before thee, and **s**,	8453

SOJOURNETH

Ex	3:22	of her that **s** in her house, jewels.	1481
Ezr	1:4	remaineth in any place where he **s**,	1481

SOJOURNING

Jgs	19:1	a certain Levite **s** on the side of.	1481
1Pe	1:17	the time of your **s** here in fear:	*3940*

SOLD

Ge	25:33	he **s** his birthright unto Jacob	4876
Ge	37:28	and **s** Joseph to the Ishmeelites for	4876
Ge	37:36	Midianites **s** him into Egypt unto.	4876
Ge	45:4	brother, whom ye **s** into Egypt.	4376
Ge	45:5	yourselves, that ye **s** me hither:	4376
Ge	47:20	Egyptians **s** every man his field,	4376
Ge	47:22	wherefore they **s** not their lands	4376
Le	25:25	redeem that which his brother **s**	4465
Le	25:42	they shall not be **s** as bondmen.	4376
Le	25:48	After … he is **s** he may be redeemed	4376
Dt	32:30	except their Rock had **s** them, and	4376
Jgs	2:14	he **s** them into the hands of their	4376
1Ki	21:20	hast **s** thyself to work evil in the	4376
Ne	13:16	**s** on the sabbath unto the children	4376
Est	7:4	For we are **s**, I and my people, to	4376
Est	7:4	if we had been **s** for bondmen and	4376
Ps	105:17	Joseph, who was **s** for a servant:	4376
Isa	50:1	iniquities have ye **s** yourselves,	4376
Isa	52:3	Ye have **s** yourselves for nought;	4376
La	5:4	money; our wood is **s** unto us	935, 4242
Mt	10:29	**not two sparrows s for a farthing**	*4453*
Mt	13:46	**went and s all that he had, and**	*4097*
Mt	21:12	that **s** and bought in the temple,	*4453*
Mt	21:12	the seats of them that **s** doves,	*4453*
Mt	26:9	ointment might have been **s** for	*4097*
Mk	14:5	**s** for more than three hundred	*4097*
Lk	12:6	**five sparrows s for two farthings,**	*4453*
Lk	17:28	**they bought, they s, they planted**	*4453*
Lk	19:45	to cast out them that **s** therein, and	*4453*
Jn	2:14	in the temple those that **s** oxen and	*4453*
Jn	2:16	said unto them that **s** doves, Take	*4453*
Jn	12:5	this ointment **s** for three hundred	*4097*
Ac	2:45	And **s** their possessions and goods,	*4097*
Ac	4:34	of lands or houses **s** them, and	*4458*
Ac	5:1	Sapphira his wife, **s** a possession,	*4453*
Ac	5:4	and after it was **s**, was it not in	*4097*
Ac	5:8	whether ye **s** the land for so much?	*591*
Ac	7:9	with envy, **s** Joseph into Egypt:	*591*
Ro	7:14	but I am carnal, **s** under sin.	*4097*
1Co	10:25	Whatsoever is **s** in the shambles.	*4453*
Heb	12:16	morsel of meat **s** his birthright.	*591*

SOLDIER

Jn	19:23	made four parts, to every **s** a part;	*4757*
2Ti	2:3	as a good **s** of Jesus Christ.	*4757*
2Ti	2:4	who hath chosen him to be a **s**	*4758*

SOLDIERS

1Ch	7:4	fathers, were bands of **s** for war,	6635
Ezr	8:22	to require of the king a band of **s**	2428
Mt	27:27	the **s** of the governor took Jesus	*4757*
Mt	28:12	they gave large money unto the **s**,	*4757*
Mk	15:16	the **s** led him away into the hall,	*4757*
Lk	23:36	the **s** also mocked him, coming to	*4757*
Jn	19:2	the **s** platted a crown of thorns,	*4757*
Jn	19:23	**s**, when they had crucified Jesus	*4757*
Jn	19:24	These things therefore the **s** did	*4757*
Jn	19:32	Then came the **s**, and brake the	*4757*
Jn	19:34	one of the **s** with a spear pierced.	*4757*
Ac	12:4	him to four quaternions of **s** to.	*4757*
Ac	12:6	Peter was sleeping between two **s**,	*4757*
Ac	23:23	Make ready two hundred **s** to go to	*4757*

SOLE

Ge	8:9	no rest for the **s** of her foot,	3709
Jos	1:3	the **s** of your foot shall tread upon,	3709
2Sa	14:25	from the **s** of his foot even to the	3709
2Ki	19:24	with the **s** of my feet have I dried	3709
Job	2:7	the **s** of his foot unto his crown	3709
Isa	1:6	**s** of the foot even unto the head	3709

SOLEMN

Nu	15:3	in your **s** feasts, to make a sweet	4150
Dt	16:8	seventh day shall be a **s** assembly:	6116
Dt	16:15	thou keep a **s** feast unto the Lord	2287
Ne	8:18	the eighth day was a **s** assembly	6116
Ps	81:3	appointed, on our **s** feast day	2282
La	2:22	called as in a **s** day my terrors	4150

SOLEMNITIES

Isa	33:20	Look upon Zion, the city of our **s**	4150
Eze	45:17	in all **s** of the house of Israel:	4150

SOLEMNITY

Dt	31:10	in the **s** of the year of release,	4150
Isa	30:29	the night when a holy **s** is kept;	2282

SOLEMNLY

Ge	43:3	The man did **s** protest unto us,	5749
1Sa	8:9	howbeit yet protest **s** unto them,	5749

SOLES

Dt	11:24	**s** of your feet shall tread shall be.	3709
Jos	4:18	**s** of the priests' feet were lifted	3709
Isa	60:14	down at the **s** of thy feet; and	3709
Mal	4:3	be ashes under the **s** of your feet	3709

SOLITARY

Job	3:7	Lo, let that night be **s**, let no	1565
Job	30:3	For want and famine they were **s**;	1565
Ps	68:6	God setteth the **s** in families: he	3173
Ps	107:4	in the wilderness in a **s** way;	3452
Isa	35:1	**s** place shall be glad for them;	6723
La	1:1	How doth the city sit **s**, that was	910
Mk	1:35	out, and departed into a **s** place,	*2048*

SOME

Ge	19:19	lest **s** evil take me, and I die:	
Ge	27:3	to the field, and take me **s** venison;	
Ge	37:20	slay him, and cast him into **s** pit	259
Ge	37:20	**S** evil beast hath devoured him:	
Le	4:7	the priest shall put **s** of the blood	
Le	4:17	shall dip his finger in **s** of the blood,	
Le	4:18	put **s** of the blood upon the horns	
Nu	31:3	Arm **s** of yourselves unto the war,	582
Jos	8:22	**s** on this side, and **s** on that side:	428
Ru	2:16	let fall also **s** of the handfuls of	
1Sa	8:11	and **s** shall run before his chariots	
1Ki	14:13	in him there is found **s** good thing.	
2Ch	12:7	I will grant them **s** deliverance;	4592
Ne	2:12	night, I and **s** few men with me;	4592
Ps	20:7	**S** trust in chariots, and **s** in	428
Pr	4:16	away, unless they cause **s** to fall.	

Da	11:35	s of them of understanding shall fall,	
Da	12:2	shall awake, s to everlasting life,	428
Da	12:2	s to shame … everlasting contempt.	428
Mt	13:4	s seeds fell by the way side,	3588, 3303
Mt	13:5	S fell … stony places, where	3588, 243
Mt	13:7	s fell among thorns; and the	3588, 243
Mt	13:8	forth fruit, s an hundredfold,	3588, 3303
Mt	13:8	s sixtyfold, s thirtyfold,	3588, 1161
Mt	13:23	forth, s … hundredfold,	3588, 3033
Mt	13:23	hundredfold, s sixty, s thirty	3588, 1161
Mt	16:14	S say … John the Baptist:	3588, 3033
Mt	16:14	s, Elias; and others, Jeremias,	3588, 3033
Mt	23:34	s of them ye shall kill and crucify;	
Mt	23:34	s of them shall ye scourge in your	
Mt	28:17	worshipped him: but s doubted	3588
Mk	7:2	saw s of his disciples eat bread	5100
Mk	9:1	be s of them that stand here,	5100
Mk	12:5	many others; beating s, and	3588, 3303
Mk	12:5	others; beating … and killing s	3588
Mk	14:65	And s began to spit on him, and to	5100
Lk	9:8	And of s, that Elias had appeared;	5100
Lk	9:19	but s say, Elias; and others say,	243
Jn	6:64	are s of you that believe not	5100
Jn	7:12	for s said, He is a good man:	3588, 3303
Jn	7:41	s said, Shall Christ come out of	243
Ac	5:15	by might overshadow s of them	5100
Ac	17:18	s said, What will this babbler say?	5100
Ac	17:18	s, He seemeth to be a setter forth	3588
Ac	17:32	the resurrection … s mocked:	3588, 3303
Ac	27:44	And the rest, s on boards	3588, 3303
Ac	27:44	on boards, and s on broken pieces	1161
Ac	28:24	s believed the things which	3588, 3303
Ac	28:24	were spoken, and s believed not	3588
Ro	1:11	impart unto you s spiritual gift	5200
Ro	1:13	I might have s fruit among you	5100
Ro	5:7	good man s would even dare to die	5100
1Co	4:18	Now s are puffed up, as though I	5100
1Co	9:22	that I might by all means save s	5100
1Co	15:6	present, but s are fallen asleep.	5100
1Co	15:34	s have not the knowledge of God:	5100
Eph	4:11	And he gave s, apostles;	3588, 3303
Eph	4:11	apostles; and s, prophets; and	3588
Eph	4:11	and s, evangelists; and s, pastors	3588
Php	1:15	S indeed preach Christ even of	5100
Php	1:15	and strife; and s also of good will:	5100
1Ti	1:3	s that they teach no other doctrine,	5100
1Ti	5:24	S men's sins are open beforehand,	5100
2Ti	2:20	and of earth; s to honour,	3588, 3303
2Ti	2:20	to honour, and s to dishonour	3588
Heb	10:25	together, as the manner of s is;	5100
Heb	13:2	thereby s have entertained angels	5100
2Pe	3:9	as s men count slackness; but	5100
Jude	22	s have compassion, making	3588, 3303

SOMEBODY

Lk	8:46	Jesus said, S hath touched me:	5100
Ac	5:36	Theudas, boasting himself to be s;	5100

SOMETHING

1Sa	20:26	S hath befallen him, he is not	4745
Jn	13:29	that he should give s to the poor.	5100
Ac	3:5	expecting to receive s of them.	5100
Gal	6:3	a man think himself to be s, when	5100

SOMETIME

Col	1:21	you, that were s alienated and	4218
1Pe	3:20	Which s were disobedient, when.	4218

SOMETIMES

Eph	2:13	ye who s were far off are made	4218
Eph	5:8	For ye were s darkness, but now	4218

SOMEWHAT

2Ch	10:4	ease thou s the grievous servitude	
2Ch	10:9	Ease s the yoke that thy father did	
2Ch	10:10	but make thou it s lighter for us;	
Lk	7:40	Simon, I have s to say unto thee	5100
2Co	10:8	boast s more of our authority	5100
Heb	8:3	that this man have s also to offer	5100
Rev	2:4	Nevertheless I have s against thee,	

SON

Ge	11:31	Terah took Abram his s, and Lot.	1121
Ge	16:15	Hagar bare Abram a s: and Abram	1121
Ge	17:23	And Abraham took Ishmael his s,	1121
Ge	18:10	lo, Sarah thy wife shall have a s	1121
Ge	21:2	bare Abraham a s in his old age	1121
Ge	21:3	Abraham called the name of his s	1121
Ge	21:7	I have born him a s in his old age.	1121
Ge	21:10	for the s of this bondwoman shall	1121
Ge	22:2	And he said, Take now thy s,	1121
Ge	22:2	thine only s Isaac, whom thou	
Ge	22:6	and laid it upon Isaac his s; and	1121
Ge	22:8	My s, God will provide himself a	1121
Ge	22:9	and bound Isaac his s, and laid	1121
Ge	22:10	and took the knife to slay his s	1121
Ge	22:12	seeing thou hast not withheld thy s	1121
Ge	22:16	thing, and hast not withheld thy s,	1121
Ge	24:4	and take a wife unto my s Isaac.	1121
Ge	25:11	that God blessed his s Isaac;	1121
Ge	27:8	therefore, my s, obey my voice	1121
Ge	27:15	raiment of her eldest s Esau,	1121
Ge	27:18	Here am I; who art thou, my s?	1121
Ge	27:21	that I may feel thee, my s, whether	1121
Ge	27:32	I am thy s, thy firstborn Esau.	1121
Ge	27:42	and called Jacob her younger s,	1121
Ge	45:9	Thus saith thy s Joseph, God hath	1121
Ge	45:28	enough; Joseph my s is yet alive:	1121
Ge	48:19	said, I know it, my s, I know it:	1121
Ex	1:16	if it be a s, then ye shall kill him:	1121
Ex	1:22	Every s that is born ye shall cast	1121
Ex	2:2	woman conceived, and bare a s.	1121
Ex	2:10	daughter, and he became her s,	1121
Ex	20:10	not do any work, thou, nor thy s,	1121
Ex	33:11	Joshua, the s of Nun, a young man,	1121
Nu	4:16	Eleazar the s of Aaron the priest	1121
Nu	13:6	Judah, Caleb the s of Jephunneh.	1121
Nu	23:19	s of man, that he should repent:	1121
Nu	27:8	If a man die, and have no s, then	1121
Dt	1:36	Save Caleb the s of Jephunneh; he	1121
Dt	1:38	But Joshua the s of Nun, which	1121
Dt	6:2	thou, and thy s, and thy son's s,	1121
Dt	8:5	as a man chasteneth his s, so the	1121
Dt	21:18	have a stubborn and rebellious s,	1121
Dt	21:20	our s is stubborn and rebellious,	1121
Jgs	6:11	his s Gideon threshed wheat by	1121
Jgs	11:2	thou art the s of strange woman.	1121
Jgs	17:3	the Lord from my hand for my s	1121
Ru	4:13	her conception, and she bare a s.	1121
1Sa	1:20	that she bare a s, and called his	1121
1Sa	3:6	I called not my s; lie down again	1121
1Sa	3:16	Samuel, and said, Samuel, my s	1121
1Sa	7:1	Eleazar his s to keep the ark of	1121
1Sa	9:2	he had a s, whose name was Saul,	1121

1Sa	14:3	the **s** of Eli, the Lord's priest	1121
1Sa	16:18	a **s** of Jesse the Beth-lehemite	1121
1Sa	16:19	Send me David thy **s**, which is	1121
1Sa	17:55	Abner, whose **s** is this youth? And	1121
1Sa	17:56	thou whose **s** the stripling is	1121
1Sa	17:58	Whose **s** art thou, thou young man?	1121
1Sa	17:58	I am the **s** of thy servant Jesse the	1121
1Sa	20:27	cometh not the **s** of Jesse to meat	1121
1Sa	20:30	Thou **s** of the perverse rebellious	1121
1Sa	20:30	thou hast chosen the **s** of Jesse	1121
1Sa	20:31	For a long as the **s** of Jesse liveth	1121
1Sa	24:16	said, Is this thy voice, my **s** David?	1121
1Sa	25:17	for he is such a **s** of Belial, that a	1121
1Sa	26:17	said, Is this thy voice, my **s** David?	1121
1Sa	26:21	I have sinned: return, my **s** David:	1121
2Sa	1:5	Saul and Jonathan his **s** be dead?	1121
2Sa	1:13	I am the **s** of a stranger, an	1121
2Sa	2:8	took Ish-bosheth, the **s** of Saul	1121
2Sa	9:3	Jonathan hath yet a **s**, which is	1121
2Sa	9:6	Mephibosheth, the **s** of Jonathan,	1121
2Sa	9:6	the **s** of Saul, was come unto David,	1121
2Sa	9:9	I have given unto thy master's **s**	1121
2Sa	9:10	master's **s** may have food to eat:	1121
2Sa	9:10	thy master's **s** shall eat bread	1121
2Sa	13:1	Absalom the **s** of David had a fair	1121
2Sa	13:37	David mourned for his **s** every day	1121
2Sa	18:18	said, I have no **s** to keep my name	1121
2Sa	18:33	said, O my **s** Absalom, my **s**, my **s**.	1121
2Sa	18:33	for thee, O Absalom, my **s**, my **s**!	1121
2Sa	19:2	how the king was grieved for his **s**	1121
2Sa	19:4	with a loud voice, O my **s** Absalom,	1121
2Sa	19:4	Absalom, O Absalom, my **s**, my **s**!	1121
2Sa	20:1	we inheritance in the **s** of Jesse:	1121
2Sa	23:1	David the **s** of Jesse said, and the	1121
1Ki	1:12	life, and the life of thy **s** Solomon	1121
1Ki	1:21	I and my **s** Solomon … be counted	1121
1Ki	3:20	and took my **s** from beside me	1121
1Ki	3:21	it was not my **s**, which I did bear	1121
1Ki	3:22	living is my **s**, … the dead is thy **s**.	1121
1Ki	3:22	dead is thy **s**, … the living is my **s**.	1121
1Ki	3:23	my **s** … liveth, and thy **s** is the dead:	1121
1Ki	3:23	thy **s** is dead, and my **s** is … living	1121
1Ki	5:5	Thy **s**, whom I will set upon thy	1121
1Ki	5:7	hath given unto David a wise **s**	1121
1Ki	12:21	to Rehoboam the **s** of Solomon	1121
1Ki	17:12	go in and dress it for me and my **s**,	1121
1Ki	17:17	the **s** of the woman, the mistress of	1121
1Ki	17:18	to remembrance, and to slay my **s**?	1121
1Ki	17:19	he said unto her, Give me thy **s**.	1121
1Ki	17:20	whom I sojourn, by slaying her **s**?	1121
1Ki	17:23	and Elijah said, See, thy **s** liveth.	1121
2Ki	3:27	took his eldest **s** that should have	1121
2Ki	4:6	that she said unto her **s**, Bring me	1121
2Ki	4:16	time of life, thou shalt embrace a **s**.	1121
2Ki	4:17	and bare a **s** at that season that	1121
2Ki	4:28	said, Did I desire a **s** of my lord?	1121
2Ki	4:36	unto him, he said, Take up thy **s**	1121
2Ki	4:37	and took up her **s**, and went out	1121
2Ki	6:32	See ye how this **s** of a murderer	1121
2Ki	8:1	whose **s** he had restored to life,	1121
2Ki	8:5	whose **s** he had restored to life,	1121
2Ki	8:5	and this is her **s**, whom Elisha	1121
2Ki	11:1	Athaliah … saw that her **s** was dead	1121
2Ki	16:3	made his **s** to pass through the fire,	1121
2Ki	16:7	I am thy servant and thy **s**: come	1121
2Ki	16:20	Hezekiah his **s** reigned in his stead	1121
2Ki	21:6	made his **s** pass through the fire,	1121
2Ki	21:7	said to David, and to Solomon his **s**,	1121
2Ki	21:24	made Josiah his **s** king in his stead	1121
1Ch	5:1	the sons of Joseph the **s** of Israel:	1121
1Ch	6:38	the **s** of Levi, the **s** of Israel	1121
1Ch	6:56	gave to Caleb the **s** of Jephunneh	1121
1Ch	7:29	children of Joseph the **s** of Israel.	1121
1Ch	10:14	kingdom unto David the **s** of Jesse	1121
1Ch	20:6	he also was the **s** of the giant	3205
1Ch	22:5	said, Solomon my **s** is younger and	1121
1Ch	22:11	Now, my **s**, the Lord be with thee;	1121
1Ch	26:24	the **s** of Moses, was ruler over	1121
1Ch	28:5	chosen Solomon my **s** to sit upon	1121
1Ch	28:6	Solomon thy **s**, he shall build	1121
1Ch	28:6	for I have chosen him to be my **s**,	1121
1Ch	28:9	Solomon my **s**, know thou the God	1121
1Ch	28:11	gave to Solomon his **s** the pattern	1121
1Ch	29:1	Solomon my **s**, whom alone God	1121
1Ch	29:19	unto Solomon my **s** a perfect heart,	1121
1Ch	29:22	made Solomon the **s** of David king	1121
1Ch	29:26	David the **s** of Jesse reigned over	1121
1Ch	29:28	Solomon his **s** reigned in his stead	1121
2Ch	2:12	given to David the king a wise **s**,	1121
2Ch	21:17	there was never a **s** left him, save	1121
Job	18:19	shall neither have **s** nor nephew	5209
Job	25:6	the **s** of man, which is a worm?	1121
Job	35:8	may profit the **s** of man	1121
Ps	2:7	hath said unto me, Thou art my **S**;	1121
Ps	2:12	Kiss the **S**, lest he be angry, and	1248
Ps	8:4	**s** of man, that thou visitest him?	1121
Ps	72:20	prayers of David the **s** of Jesse are	1121
Ps	86:16	and save the **s** of thine handmaid	1121
Ps	144:3	or the **s** of man, that thou makest	1121
Ps	146:3	nor in the **s** of man, in whom there	1121
Pr	1:1	of Solomon the **s** of David, king	1121
Pr	1:8	My **s**, hear the instruction of thy	1121
Pr	1:10	My **s**, if sinners entice thee,	1121
Pr	1:15	My **s**, walk not thou in the way	1121
Pr	3:1	My **s**, forget not my law; but let	1121
Pr	3:11	My **s**, despise not the chastening	1121
Pr	3:21	My **s**, let not them depart from	1121
Pr	4:20	My **s**, attend to my words; incline	1121
Pr	6:1	My **s**, if thou be surety for thy	1121
Pr	6:3	Do this now, my **s**, and deliver	1121
Pr	10:1	A wise **s** maketh a glad father:	1121
Pr	10:1	but a foolish **s** is the heaviness of	1121
Pr	10:5	gathereth in summer is a wise **s**:	1121
Pr	10:5	harvest is a **s** that causeth shame	1121
Pr	13:1	A wise **s** heareth his father's	1121
Pr	13:24	that spareth his rod hateth his **s**:	1121
Pr	15:20	A wise **s** maketh a glad father: but	1121
Pr	17:2	servant shall have rule over a **s**	1121
Pr	17:25	A foolish **s** is a grief to his father	1121
Pr	19:13	A foolish **s** is the calamity of his	1121
Pr	19:18	Chasten thy **s** while there is hope	1121
Pr	19:26	is a **s** that causeth shame, and	1121
Pr	19:27	Cease, my **s**, to hear the	1121
Pr	23:15	My **s**, if thine heart be wise, my	1121
Pr	24:21	My **s**, fear thou the Lord and the	1121
Pr	27:11	My **s**, be wise, and make my heart	1121
Pr	28:7	Whoso keepeth the law is a wise **s**:	1121
Pr	29:17	Correct thy **s**, and he shall give	1121
Pr	31:2	my **s**? … what, the **s** of my womb?	1248
Pr	31:2	and what, the **s** of my vows?	1248
Ecc	1:1	of the Preacher, the **s** of David	1121
Isa	1:1	The vision of Isaiah the **s** of Amoz,	1121

Isa	7:1	the **s** of Uzziah, the king of Judah,	1121
Isa	7:14	virgin shall conceive, and bare a **s**,	1121
Isa	8:3	and she conceived, and bare a **s**	1121
Isa	9:6	child is born, unto us a **s** is given:	1121
Isa	14:12	O Lucifer, **s** of the morning! how	1121
Isa	19:11	Pharaoh, I am the **s** of the wise,	1121
Isa	49:15	compassion on the **s** of her womb?	1121
Isa	51:12	and of the **s** of man which shall be	1121
Isa	56:2	and the **s** of man that layeth hold	1121
Jer	6:26	thee mourning, as for an only **s**,	3173
Eze	2:1	**S** of man, stand upon thy feet, and	1121
Eze	2:3	**S** of man, I send thee to the	1121
Eze	2:6	**s** of man, be not afraid of them	1121
Eze	2:8	**s** of man, hear what I say unto	1121
Eze	5:1	**s** of man, take thee a sharp knife,	1121
Eze	8:8	**S** of man, dig now in the wall: and	1121
Eze	21:6	Sigh therefore, thou **s** of man, with	1121
Eze	21:14	**s** of man, prophesy, and smite	1121
Eze	36:1	Also, thou **s** of man, prophesy unto	1121
Eze	37:3	me, **S** of man, can these bones live?	1121
Eze	37:11	**S** of man, these bones are the	1121
Eze	37:16	thou **s** of man, take thee one stick	1121
Da	3:25	of the fourth is like the **S** of God	1247
Da	7:13	one like the **S** of man came with	1247
Da	8:17	unto me, Understand, O **s** of man;	1121
Hos	11:1	him and called my **s** out of Egypt	1121
Hos	13:13	he is an unwise **s**; for he should	1121
Zec	12:10	as one mourneth for his only **s**,	
Mal	1:6	A **s** honoureth his father, and a	1121
Mal	3:17	as a man spareth his own **s** that	1121
Mt	1:1	of Jesus Christ, the **s** of David	*5207*
Mt	1:1	of David, the **s** of Abraham	*5207*
Mt	1:20	Joseph, thou **s** of David, fear not to	*5207*
Mt	1:21	she shall bring forth a **s**, and thou	*5207*
Mt	1:23	child, and shall bring forth a **s**,	*5207*
Mt	1:25	had brought forth her firstborn **s**:	*5207*
Mt	2:15	Out of Egypt have I called my **s**	*5207*
Mt	3:17	This is my beloved **S**, in whom I	*5207*
Mt	4:3	If thou be the **S** of God, command	*5207*
Mt	4:6	If thou be the **S** of God, cast	*5207*
Mt	7:9	his **s** ask bread, will he give him	*5207*
Mt	8:20	**S** of man hath not where to lay	*5207*
Mt	9:2	**S**, be of good cheer; thy sins be	*5048*
Mt	9:6	**S** of man hath power on earth to	*5207*
Mt	9:27	Thou **s** of David, have mercy on us	*5207*
Mt	10:23	Israel, till the **S** of man be come	*5207*
Mt	11:19	The **S** of man came eating and	*5207*
Mt	11:27	and no man knoweth the **S**, but	*5207*
Mt	11:27	any man the Father, save the **S**,	*5207*
Mt	11:27	whomsoever the **S** will reveal him.	*5207*
Mt	12:8	**S** of man is Lord … of the sabbath	*5207*
Mt	12:23	and said, Is not this the **s** of David?	*5207*
Mt	12:40	shall the **S** of man be three days	*5207*
Mt	13:41	The **S** of man shall send forth	*5207*
Mt	13:55	Is not this the carpenter's **s**? is not	*5207*
Mt	16:13	men say that I the **S** of man am?	*5207*
Mt	16:16	the Christ, the **S** of the living God	*5207*
Mt	16:27	**S** of man shall come in the glory	*5207*
Mt	16:28	till they see the **S** of man coming	*5207*
Mt	17:5	This is my beloved **S**, in whom I	*5207*
Mt	17:9	until the **S** of man be risen again.	*5207*
Mt	17:12	shall … the **S** of man suffer of	*5207*
Mt	17:22	**S** of man shall be betrayed into	*5207*
Mt	18:11	For the **S** of man is come to save	*5207*
Mt	20:28	**S** man came not to be ministered	*5207*
Mt	20:30	on us, O Lord, thou **s** of David	*5207*
Mt	21:9	saying Hosanna to the **s** of David:	*5207*
Mt	21:28	**S**, go work to day in my vineyard	*5043*
Mt	21:37	last of all he sent unto them his **s**,	*5207*
Mt	21:37	saying, They will reverence my **s**	*5207*
Mt	21:38	when the husbandmen saw the **s**,	*5207*
Mt	22:2	which made a marriage for his **s**,	*5207*
Mt	22:42	think ye of Christ? whose **s** is he?	*5207*
Mt	22:45	call him Lord, how is he his **s**?	*5207*
Mt	24:30	sign of the **S** of man in heaven:	*5207*
Mt	24:30	**S** of man coming in the clouds	*5207*
Mt	25:31	**S** of man shall come in his glory,	*5207*
Mt	26:63	thou be the Christ, the **S** of God	*5207*
Mt	26:64	the **S** of man sitting on the right	*5207*
Mt	27:40	If thou be the **S** of God, come down	*5207*
Mt	27:43	for he said, I am the **S** of God	*5207*
Mt	27:54	Truly this was the **S** of God	*5207*
Mt	28:19	name of the Father, and of the **S**,	*5207*
Mk	1:1	of Jesus Christ, the **S** of God;	*5207*
Mk	2:5	**S**, thy sins be forgiven thee	*5043*
Mk	9:7	This is my beloved **S**: hear him.	*5207*
Mk	10:45	the **S** of man came not to be	*5207*
Mk	10:47	Jesus, thou **s** of David, have mercy	*5207*
Mk	10:48	Thou **s** of David, have mercy on me.	*5207*
Mk	13:32	neither the **S**, but the Father	*5207*
Mk	14:61	the Christ, the **S** of the Blessed?	*5207*
Mk	14:62	**S** of man sitting on the right	*5207*
Mk	15:39	Truly this man was the **S** of God	*5207*
Lk	1:13	wife Elisabeth shall bear thee a **s**,	*5207*
Lk	1:31	bring forth a **s**, and shalt call his	*5207*
Lk	1:32	shall be called the **S** of the Highest;	*5207*
Lk	1:35	thee shall be called the **S** of God,	*5207*
Lk	1:36	also conceived a **s** in her old age:	*5207*
Lk	1:57	and she brought forth a **s**.	*5207*
Lk	2:7	she brought forth her firstborn **s**,	*5207*
Lk	2:48	**S**, why hast thou thus dealt with	*5043*
Lk	3:2	came unto John the **s** of Zacharias	*5207*
Lk	3:22	Thou art my beloved **S**; in thee	*5207*
Lk	3:23	(as was supposed) the **s** of Joseph,	*5207*
Lk	3:38	which was the **s** of Adam,	
Lk	3:38	which was the **s** of God.	
Lk	4:3	If thou be the **S** of God, command	*5207*
Lk	4:22	they said, Is not this Joseph's **s**?	*5207*
Lk	9:56	**S** of man is not come to destroy.	*5207*
Lk	9:58	the **S** of man hath not where to	*5207*
Lk	15:13	younger **s** gathered all together,	*5207*
Lk	15:19	no more worthy to be called thy **s**	*5207*
Lk	15:21	And the **s** said unto him, Father,	*5207*
Lk	15:21	more worthy to be called thy **s**	*5207*
Lk	15:24	For this my **s** was dead, and is	*5207*
Lk	15:25	Now his elder **s** was in the field:	*5207*
Lk	15:30	as soon as this thy **s** was come	*5207*
Lk	15:31	**S**, thou art ever with me, and all	*5043*
Lk	19:10	For the **S** of man is come to seek	*5207*
Lk	20:41	say they that Christ is David's **s**?	*5207*
Lk	20:44	him Lord, how is he then his **s**?	*5207*
Lk	21:27	the **S** of man coming in a cloud	*5207*
Lk	22:70	all, Art thou then the **S** of God?	*5207*
Lk	24:7	**S** of man must be delivered into	*5207*
Jn	1:18	the only begotten **S**, which is in	*5207*
Jn	1:34	record that this is the **S** of God	*5207*
Jn	1:45	Jesus of Nazareth, the **S** of Joseph.	*5207*
Jn	1:51	descending upon the **S** of man	*5207*
\Jn	3:14	so must the **S** of man be lifted up:	*5207*
Jn	3:16	that he gave his only begotten **S**,	*5207*
Jn	3:17	God sent not his **S** into the world	*5207*
Jn	3:18	of the only begotten **S** of God.	*5207*

Jn 3:35 The Father loveth the **S**, and hath...... *5207*
Jn 3:36 He that believeth on the **S** hath........ *5207*
Jn 3:36 and he that believeth not the **S**........ *5207*
Jn 4:50 unto him, Go thy way; thy **s** liveth..... *5207*
Jn 5:19 The **S** can do nothing of himself,...... *5207*
Jn 5:19 these also doeth the **S** likewise *5207*
Jn 5:21 so the **S** quickeneth whom he will *5207*
Jn 5:26 he given to the **S** to have life *5207*
Jn 6:40 that every one which seeth the **S**,...... *5207*
Jn 6:53 ye eat the flesh of the **S** of man, ... *5207*
Jn 6:69 art that Christ, the **S** of the living...... *5207*
Jn 8:28 ye have lifted up the **S** of man, ... *5207*
Jn 8:35 for ever: but the **S** abideth ever........ *5207*
Jn 8:36 **S** therefore shall make you free, ... *5207*
Jn 10:36 I said, I am the **S** of God?............. *5207*
Jn 11:4 the **S** of God might be glorified *5207*
Jn 12:34 The **S** of man must be lifted up?....... *5207*
Jn 12:34 lifted up? who is this **S** of man?........ *5207*
Jn 13:31 Now is the **S** of man glorified, ... *5207*
Jn 14:13 Father may be glorified in the **S**....... *5207*
Jn 17:1 the hour is come; glorify thy **S**,........ *5207*
Jn 17:1 that thy **S** also may glorify thee:....... *5207*
Jn 17:12 is lost, but the **s** of perdition; *5207*
Jn 19:7 he made himself the **S** of God......... *5207*
Jn 19:26 his mother, Woman, behold thy **s**! *5207*
Jn 20:31 Jesus is the Christ, the **S** of God;....... *5207*
Jn 21:15 **s** of Jonas, lovest thou me more than
Jn 21:16 Simon, **s** of Jonas, lovest thou me?
Jn 21:17 Simon, **s** of Jonas, lovest thou me?
Ac 3:13 fathers ... glorified his **S** Jesus; *3816*
Ac 4:36 interpreted, The **s** of consolation,)..... *5207*
Ac 7:56 the **S** of man standing on the right..... *5207*
Ac 8:37 that Jesus Christ is the **S** of God....... *5207*
Ac 9:20 that he is the **S** of God *5207*
Ac 13:33 Thou art my **S**, this day have I......... *5207*
Ro 1:3 has **S** Jesus Christ our Lord *5207*
Ro 1:4 declared to be the **S** of God with *5207*
Ro 8:29 be conformed to the image of his **S**,.... *5207*
Ro 8:32 He that spared not his own **S**, but *5207*
1Co 1:9 of his **S** Jesus Christ our Lord *5207*
Gal 2:20 I live by the faith of the **S** of God,...... *5207*
Gal 4:4 God sent forth his **S**, made of a........ *5207*
Eph 4:13 of the knowledge of the **S** of God, ... *5207*
Col 1:13 into the kingdom of his dear **S**:........ *5207*
1Th 1:10 to wait for his **S** from heaven.......... *5207*
2Th 2:3 be revealed, the **s** of perdition; *5207*
1Ti 1:2 Timothy, my own **s** in the faith: *5043*
Tit 1:4 To Titus, mine own **s** after the......... *5043*
Heb 1:2 last days spoken unto us by his **S**,...... *5207*
Heb 1:5 Thou art my **S**, this day have I......... *5207*
Heb 1:8 unto the **S** he saith, Thy throne........ *5207*
Heb 2:6 the **s** of man, that thou visitest him? ... *5207*
Heb 5:8 Though he were a **S**, yet learned he *5207*
Heb 6:6 they crucify ... the **S** of God afresh *5207*
Heb 12:6 and scourgeth every **s** whom he *5207*
Heb 12:7 **s** is he whom the father chasteneth..... *5207*
Jas 2:21 offered Isaac his **s** upon the altar?...... *5207*
1Jn 1:7 the blood of Jesus Christ his **S**......... *5207*
1Jn 2:24 ye also shall continue in the **S**, ... *5207*
1Jn 4:9 God sent his only begotten **S** into...... *5207*
1Jn 4:10 his **S** to be the propitiation for our..... *5207*
1Jn 4:15 confess that Jesus is the **S** of God,...... *5207*
1Jn 5:12 He that hath the **S** hath life; and....... *5207*
1Jn 5:12 hath not the **S** of God hath not life..... *5207*
2Jn 3 Jesus Christ, the **S** of the Father,....... *5207*
Rev 1:13 one like unto the **S** of man *5207*
Rev 2:18 These things saith the **S** of God,....... *5207*
Rev 14:14 one sat like unto the **S** of man, ... *5207*

SONG

Ex 15:1 of Israel this **s** unto the Lord, ... 7892
Ex 15:2 The Lord is my strength and **s**,......... 2176
Nu 21:17 Israel sang this **s**, Spring up, O 7892
Dt 31:22 Moses therefore wrote this **s** the....... 7892
Jgs 5:12 Deborah: awake, awake, utter a **s** 7892
1Ch 6:31 David set over the service of **s**......... 7892
1Ch 25:6 the hands of their father for **s** in....... 7892
2Ch 29:27 **s** of the Lord began also with the 7892
Job 30:9 And now am I their **s**, yea, I am 5058
Ps 28:7 and with my **s** will I praise him 7892
Ps 33:3 Sing unto him a new **s**; play........... 7892
Ps 40:3 he hath put a new **s** in my mouth,..... 7892
Ps 42:8 in the night his **s** shall be with me 7892
Ps 69:12 and I was the **s** of the drunkards 5058
Ps 69:30 praise the name of God with a **s**....... 7892
Ps 77:6 I call to remembrance my **s** in the 5058
Ps 96:1 O sing unto the Lord a new **s** 7892
Ps 118:14 The Lord is my strength and **s**,......... 2176
Ps 137:4 How shall we sing the Lord's **s** in a..... 7892
Ps 144:9 I will sing a new **s** unto thee, O........ 7892
Ps 149:1 Sing unto the Lord a new **s**, and....... 7892
SS 1:1 The **s** of songs, which is Solomon's 7892
Isa 5:1 will sing to my wellbeloved a **s** 7892
Isa 12:2 Jehovah is my strength and my **s**;...... 2176
Isa 26:1 this **s** be sung in the land of Judah; 7892
Isa 42:10 Sing unto the Lord a new **s**, and....... 7892
Rev 5:9 And they sung a new **s**, saying......... *5603*
Rev 14:3 And they sung as it were a new **s** *5603*
Rev 14:3 no man could learn that **s** but the *5603*
Rev 15:3 And they sing the **s** of Moses the *5603*
Rev 15:3 and the **s** of the Lamb, saying *5603*

SONGS

1Ki 4:32 and his **s** were a thousand and five..... 7892
Ne 12:46 **s** of praise and thanksgiving unto...... 7892
Job 35:10 maker, who giveth **s** in the night; 2158
Ps 32:7 me about with **s** of deliverance........ 7438
Ps 137:3 Sing us one of the **s** of Zion........... 7892
Pr 25:20 he that singeth **s** to an heavy heart..... 7892
SS 1:1 The song of **s**, which is Solomon's...... 7892
Isa 23:16 make sweet melody, sing many **s**,...... 7892
Isa 35:10 to Zion with **s** and everlasting......... 7440
Am 8:10 and all your **s** into lamentation; 7892
Eph 5:19 psalms and hymns and spiritual **s**...... *5603*
Col 3:16 psalms and hymns and spiritual **s**...... *5603*

SON'S

Ge 11:31 Lot the son of Haran his **s** son,........ 1121
Ge 16:15 Abram called his **s** name, which 1121
Ge 27:25 me, and I will eat of my **s** venison,..... 1121
Ge 27:31 arise, and eat of his **s** venison 1121
Ge 37:32 now whether it be thy **s** coat or no..... 1121
Ge 37:33 knew it, and said, It is my **s** coat; 1121
Dt 6:2 thou, and thy son, and thy **s** son, ... 1121
1Ki 11:35 the kingdom out of his **s** hand 1121
Pr 30:4 his name, and what is his **s** name, ... 1121

SONS

Ge 6:2 the **s** of God saw the daughters of 1121
Ge 6:4 the **s** of God came in unto the 1121
Ge 6:10 Noah begat three **s**, Shem, Ham, ... 1121
Ge 7:13 three wives of his **s** with them......... 1121
Ge 8:18 Noah went forth, and his **s**, and his 1121

Ge	27:29	thy mother's **s** bow down to thee:	1121
Ge	29:34	because I have born him three **s**:	1121
Ge	30:20	me, because I have born him six **s**:	1121
Ge	31:1	he heard the word's of Laban's **s**,	1121
Ge	32:22	womenservants, and his eleven **s**,	3206
Ge	35:22	Now the **s** of Jacob were twelve:	1121
Ge	35:23	The **s** of Leah; Reuben, Jacob's	1121
Ge	35:24	And the **s** of Rachel; Joseph and	1121
Ge	35:25	**s** of Bilhah, Rachel's handmaid;	1121
Ge	35:26	the **s** of Zilpah, Leah's handmaid;	1121
Ge	42:1	Jacob said unto his **s**, Why do ye	1121
Ge	42:5	the **s** of Israel came to buy corn	1121
Ge	42:11	We are all one man's **s**; we are	1121
Ge	42:32	twelve brethren, **s** of our father;	1121
Ge	42:37	Slay my two **s**, if I bring him not	1121
Ge	46:5	**s** of Israel carried Jacob their	1121
Ge	48:8	Israel beheld Joseph's **s**, and said	1121
Ge	48:9	They are my **s**, whom God hath	1121
Ge	50:12	his **s** did unto him according as he	1121
Ge	50:13	his **s** carried him into the land of	1121
Ex	4:20	And Moses took his wife and his **s**	1121
Ex	12:24	to thee and to thy **s** for ever	1121
Ex	28:40	Aaron's **s** thou shalt make coats	1121
Ex	29:9	shalt consecrate Aaron and his **s**	1121
Ex	29:20	the tip of the right ear of his **s**,	1121
Le	8:36	So Aaron and his **s** did all things	1121
Le	9:1	that Moses called Aaron and his **s**	1121
Le	10:1	Nadab and Abihu, the **s** of Aaron,	1121
Le	16:1	the death of the two **s** of Aaron	1121
Nu	3:9	the Levites unto Aaron and to his **s**	1121
Nu	3:10	thou shalt appoint Aaron and his **s**	1121
Nu	4:19	Aaron and his **s** shall go in, and	1121
Nu	4:27	appointment of Aaron and his **s**	1121
Nu	18:1	**s** with thee shall bear the iniquity	1121
Nu	18:2	and thy **s** with thee shall minister	1121
Nu	18:8	to thy **s**, by an ordinance for ever	1121
Nu	18:9	most holy for thee and for thy **s**	1121
Nu	27:3	died in his own sin, and had no **s**	1121
Dt	4:9	teach them thy **s**, and thy sons' **s**,	1121
Dt	18:5	of the Lord, him and his **s** for ever	1121
Dt	32:8	when he separated the **s** of Adam,	1121
Dt	32:19	because of the provoking of his **s**,	1121
Jos	15:14	drove thence the three **s** of Anak,	1121
Jgs	1:20	expelled thence … three **s** of Anak	1121
Jgs	8:30	Gideon had threescore and ten **s**	1121
Jgs	10:4	he had thirty **s** that rode on thirty	1121
Jgs	12:14	he had forty **s** and thirty nephews	1121
Jgs	17:5	and consecrated one of his **s**, who	1121
Jgs	17:11	man was unto him as one of his **s**	1121
Ru	1:5	left of her two **s** and her husband	3206
Ru	1:11	there yet any more **s** in my womb,	1121
Ru	1:12	to night, and should also bear **s**;	1121
Ru	4:15	which is better to thee than seven **s**,	1121
1Sa	1:8	am not I better to thee than ten **s**?	1121
1Sa	3:13	because his **s** made themselves vile,	1121
1Sa	8:1	he made his **s** judges over Israel	1121
1Sa	8:3	his **s** walked not in his ways, but	1121
1Sa	8:5	and thy **s** walk not in thy ways:	1121
1Sa	8:11	He will take your **s**, and appoint	1121
1Sa	16:5	And he sanctified Jesse and his **s**	1121
1Sa	16:10	Jesse made seven of his **s** to pass	1121
1Sa	17:12	was Jesse; and he had eight **s**:	1121
1Sa	17:13	eldest **s** of Jesse … followed Saul	1121
1Sa	17:13	names of his three **s** that went to	1121
1Sa	31:2	hard upon Saul and upon his **s**;	1121
1Sa	31:6	So Saul died, and his three **s**, and	1121

1Sa	31:7	and that Saul and his **s** were dead,	1121
1Sa	31:8	found Saul and his three **s** fallen in	1121
1Sa	31:12	body of Saul and the bodies of his **s**	1121
2Sa	5:13	yet **s** and daughters born to David	1121
2Sa	9:11	at my table, as one of the king's **s**	1121
2Sa	13:23	Absalom invited all the king's **s**	1121
2Sa	13:30	Absalom hath slain all the king's **s**	1121
2Sa	13:32	slain … the young men the king's **s**;	1121
2Sa	13:33	think that all the king's **s** are dead:	1121
2Sa	13:35	king, Behold, the king's **s** come:	1121
2Sa	13:36	the king's **s** came, and lifted up	1121
2Sa	21:16	which was of the **s** of the giant	3211
2Sa	21:18	which was of the **s** of the giant,	3211
1Ki	20:35	man of the **s** of the prophets said	1121
2Ki	4:1	wives of the **s** of the prophets unto	1121
2Ki	10:1	Ahab had seventy **s** in Samaria	1121
1Ch	1:28	The **s** of Abraham; Isaac, and	1121
1Ch	1:34	The **s** of Isaac; Esau and Israel	1121
1Ch	3:1	Now these were the **s** of David	1121
1Ch	3:9	beside the **s** of the concubines, and	1121
1Ch	6:49	But Aaron and his **s** offered upon	1121
1Ch	10:2	hard after Saul, and after his **s**;	1121
1Ch	10:2	and Malchi-shua, the **s** of Saul	1121
1Ch	10:6	So Saul died, and his three **s**, and	1121
1Ch	10:7	and that Saul and his **s** were dead	1121
1Ch	10:8	they found Saul and his **s** fallen in	1121
1Ch	10:12	of Saul, and the bodies of his **s**,	1121
1Ch	23:13	holy things, he and his **s** for ever,	1121
1Ch	23:15	The **s** of Moses were, Gershom, and	1121
1Ch	23:22	Eleazar died, and had no **s**, but	1121
1Ch	23:32	the charge of the **s** of Aaron their	1121
1Ch	24:1	are the divisions of the **s** of Aaron	1121
1Ch	24:30	were the **s** of the Levites after the	1121
2Ch	11:14	Jeroboam and his **s** had cast them	1121
2Ch	13:5	to him and to his **s** by a covenant	1121
2Ch	13:8	Lord in the hand of the **s** of David;	1121
2Ch	21:7	a light to him and to his **s** for ever	1121
2Ch	22:11	among the king's **s** that were slain,	1121
2Ch	29:11	My **s**, be not now negligent: for the	1121
Ezr	6:10	the life of the king, and of his **s**	1123
Ezr	7:23	the realm of the king and his **s**?	1123
Ne	3:3	gate did the **s** of Hassenaah build	1121
Ne	4:14	and fight for your brethren, your **s**	1121
Ne	5:5	we bring into bondage our **s** and	1121
Ne	10:36	Also the firstborn of our **s**, and of	1121
Ne	11:22	Of the **s** of Asaph, the singers were	1121
Est	9:10	The ten **s** of Haman the son of	1121
Est	9:12	palace, and the ten **s** of Haman;	1121
Est	9:13	let Haman's ten **s** be hanged upon	1121
Est	9:25	he and his **s** should be hanged on	1121
Job	1:4	his **s** went and feasted in their	1121
Job	1:5	It may be that my **s** have sinned	1121
Job	1:6	when the **s** of God came to present	1121
Job	1:13	when his **s** and his daughters were	1121
Job	2:1	when the **s** of God came to present	1121
Job	38:7	all the **s** of God shouted for joy?	1121
Job	42:13	also seven **s** and three daughters	1121
Job	42:16	saw his **s**, and his sons' **s**, even	1121
Ps	4:2	O ye **s** of men, how long will ye	1121
Ps	57:4	even the **s** of men, whose teeth are	1121
Ps	58:1	judge uprightly, O ye **s** of men?	1121
Ps	89:6	who among the **s** of the mighty can	1121
Ps	106:37	they sacrificed their **s** and their	1121
Ps	144:12	That our **s** may be as plants grown	1121
Ps	145:12	To make known to the **s** of men	1121
Ecc	1:13	hath God given to the **s** of man to	1121

Ecc 8:11 heart of the **s** of men is fully set in 1121
Ecc 9:3 heart of the **s** of men is full of evil 1121
Ecc 9:12 so are the **s** of men snared in an 1121
Isa 56:5 and a name better than of **s** and 1121
Isa 60:4 thy **s** shall come from far, and thy 1121
Isa 60:9 to bring thy **s** from far, their silver 1121
Jer 32:19 upon all the ways of the **s** of men 1121
Jer 35:5 I set before the **s** of the house of 1121
Jer 48:46 for thy **s** are taken captives, and 1121
Jer 49:1 Hath Israel no **s**? hath he no heir? 1121
La 4:2 precious **s** of Zion, comparable to 1121
Hos 1:10 Ye are the **s** of the living God 1121
Joel 3:8 will sell your **s** and your daughters. 1121
Am 2:11 I raised up of your **s** for prophets. 1121
Zec 9:13 and raised up thy **s**, O Zion 1121
Zec 9:13 against thy **s**, O Greece, and made 1121
Mal 3:3 and he shall purify the **s** of Levi. 1121
Mal 3:6 ye **s** of Jacob are not consumed. 1121
Mt 20:21 Grant that these my two **s** may sit, ... *5207*
Mt 21:28 **A certain man had two s; and he** *5043*
Mk 3:17 which is, The **s** of thunder: *5207*
Mk 3:28 **be forgiven unto the s of men** *5207*
Mk 10:35 James and John, the **s** of Zebedee, ... *5207*
Lk 11:19 **whom do your s cast them out?** *5207*
Lk 15:11 he said, **A certain man had two s:** *5207*
Jn 1:12 he power to become the **s** of God *5043*
Ac 19:14 there were seven **s** of one Sceva, ... *5207*
Ro 8:14 Spirit of God, they are the **s** of God. ... *5207*
Ro 8:19 the manifestation of the **s** of God *5207*
Gal 4:5 might receive the adoption of **s**. *5206*
Gal 4:6 because ye are **s**, God hath sent. *5207*
Gal 4:22 Abraham had two **s**, the one by a *5207*
Heb 2:10 in bringing many **s** unto glory, ... *5207*
Heb 11:21 blessed both the **s** of Joseph: and *5207*
Heb 12:7 God dealeth with you as with **s**; *5207*
1Jn 3:1 we should be called the **s** of God: *5043*
1Jn 3:2 Beloved, now are we the **s** of God, ... *5043*

SONS'

Ge 6:18 wife, and thy **s** wives with thee 1121
Ge 7:7 his wife, and his **s** wives with him, ... 1121
Ge 8:16 sons, and thy **s** wives with thee 1121
Ge 8:18 his wife, and his **s** wives with him: 1121
Ge 46:26 besides Jacob's **s** wives, all the 1121
Ex 29:29 of Aaron shall be his **s** after him 1121
Job 42:16 his **s** sons, even four generations. 1121
Eze 46:16 inheritance thereof shall be his **s**; 1121

SOON

Ge 18:33 as **s** as he had left communing 834
Ex 2:18 How is it that ye are come so **s** 4116
Jos 2:7 as **s** as they which pursued after 834
Jos 3:13 as **s** as the soles of the feet of the
Jos 8:19 as **s** as he had stretched out his hand:
Jos 8:29 and as **s** as the sun was down, Joshua
Jgs 8:33 to pass, as **s** as Gideon was dead 834
1Sa 20:41 And as **s** as the lad was gone, David
2Sa 15:10 As **s** as ye hear the sound of the
1Ki 16:11 as **s** as he sat on his throne, that he
Job 32:22 my maker would **s** take me away 4592
Ps 37:2 shall **s** be cut down like the grass, ... 4120
Ps 90:10 for it is **s** cut off, and we fly away 2440
Ps 106:13 They **s** forgat his works; they 4116
Pr 14:17 that is **s** angry dealeth foolishly: 7116
Isa 66:8 **s** as Zion travailed, she brought 1571
Mt 21:20 How **s** is the fig tree withered 3916
Mk 5:36 As **s** as Jesus heard the word that *2112*
Mk 11:2 **and as s as ye be entered into it,** *2112*
Lk 8:6 **s as it was sprung up, it withered**
Lk 15:30 **as s as this thy son was come,** *3753*
Jn 16:21 **but as s as she is delivered of the** *3752*
Gal 1:6 ye are so **s** removed from him *5030*
2Th 2:2 That ye be not **s** shaken in mind *5030*
Tit 1:7 not **s** angry, not given to wine, no *3711*

SOOTHSAYERS

Isa 2:6 and are **s** like the Philistines, and 6049
Da 2:27 the **s**, shew unto the king; 1505

SOP

Jn 13:26 **He it is, to whom I shall give a s,** *5596*
Jn 13:26 when he had dipped the **s**, he gave *5595*
Jn 13:27 after the **s** Satan entered into him. *5596*
Jn 13:30 He then having received the **s** *5596*

SOPE

Jer 2:22 and take thee much **s**, yet thine. 1287
Mal 3:2 refiner's fire, and like fullers' **s**: 1287

SORCERERS

Ex 7:11 called the wise men and the **s** 3784
Da 2:2 and the **s**, and the Chaldeans, for 3784
Rev 22:15 For without are dogs, and **s**, and *5333*

SORCERIES

Ac 8:11 he had bewitched them with **s**. *3095*
Rev 18:23 by thy **s** were all nations deceived. *5331*

SORE

Ge 20:8 ears: and the men were **s** afraid 3966
Ge 34:25 when they were **s**, that two of 3510
Ge 41:56 the famine waxed **s** in the land of 2388
Ge 43:1 And the famine was **s** in the land 3515
Ex 14:10 them; and they were **s** afraid: 3966
Le 13:43 rising of the **s** be white reddish 5061
Dt 6:22 signs and wonders, great and **s** 7451
Dt 28:59 and **s** sicknesses, and of long 7451
Jgs 15:18 And he was **s** athirst, and called 3966
1Sa 1:6 adversary also provoked her **s** 3708
1Sa 1:10 prayed unto the Lord, and wept **s**
1Sa 28:15 Saul answered, I am **s** distressed; 3966
1Sa 31:3 the battle went **s** against Saul 3513
1Sa 31:3 he was **s** wounded of the archers 3966
1Sa 31:4 would not; for he was **s** afraid. 3966
2Ki 20:3 thy sight. And Hezekiah wept **s**. 1419
Ezr 10:1 for the people wept very **s**
Ne 2:2 of heart. Then I was very **s** afraid, ... 7235
Job 2:7 smote Job with **s** boils from the 7451
Ps 6:3 My soul is also **s** vexed: but thou 3966
Ps 38:8 I am feeble and **s** broken: I 5704, 3966
Ps 118:18 The Lord hath chastened me **s**: but
Ecc 1:13 this **s** travail hath God given to 7451
Isa 38:3 sight. And Hezekiah wept **s** 1419
Eze 14:21 I send my four **s** judgments upon 7451
Da 6:14 was **s** displeased with himself, ... 7690
Mt 17:6 on their face, and were **s** afraid *4970*
Mt 17:15 for he is lunatick, and **s** vexed: *2560*
Mt 21:15 of David; they were **s** displeased, ... *23*
Mk 6:51 were **s** amazed in themselves *3029*
Mk 9:6 to say; for they were **s** afraid *1630*
Mk 9:26 the spirit cried, and rent him **s** *4183*
Mk 14:33 began to be **s** amazed, and to be *1568*
Ac 20:37 they all wept **s**, and fell on Paul's *2425*
Rev 16:2 fell a noisome and grievous **s** upon *1668*

SORES

Lk	16:20	**was laid at his gate, full of s.**	*1669*
Lk	16:21	**the dogs came and licked his s**	*1668*

SORROW

Ge	3:16	said, I will greatly multiply thy **s**	6093
Ge	3:16	in **s** shalt thou bring forth	6089
Ge	3:17	in **s** shalt thou eat of it all the	6093
Ge	42:38	my gray hairs with **s** to the grave	3015
Ge	44:29	my gray hairs with **s** to the grave	7451
1Ch	4:9	Because I bare him with **s**	6090
Ne	2:2	this is nothing else but **s** of heart	7455
Est	9:22	turned unto them from **s** to joy	3015
Job	41:22	**s** is turned into joy before him	1670
Ps	38:17	my **s** is continually before me	4341
Ps	90:10	yet is their strength labour and **s**;	205
Pr	10:10	winketh with the eye causeth **s**	6094
Pr	17:21	begetteth a fool doeth it to his **s**	8424
Ecc	1:18	knowledge increaseth **s**.	4341
Ecc	7:3	**S** is better than laughter: for by	3708
Jer	31:13	make them rejoice from their **s**.	3015
Jer	45:3	Lord hath added grief to my **s**;	4341
La	3:65	Give them **s** of heart, thy curse	4044
Lk	22:45	he found them sleeping for **s**.	*3077*
Jn	16:6	**unto you, s hath filled your heart.**	*3077*
Jn	16:20	**your s shall be turned into joy**	*3077*
2Co	7:10	For godly **s** worketh repentance to	*3077*
2Co	7:10	the **s** of the world worketh death	*3077*
1Th	4:13	that ye **s** not even as others which	*3076*
Rev	21:4	neither **s**, nor crying, neither shall	*3997*

SORROWED

2Co	7:9	sorry, but that ye **s** to repentance:	*3076*
2Co	7:11	thing, that ye **s** after a godly sort,	*3076*

SORROWFUL

1Sa	1:15	lord, I am a woman of a **s** spirit:	7186
Pr	14:13	Even in laughter the heart is **s**;	3510
Jer	31:25	I have replenished every **s** soul	1669
Mt	19:22	that saying, he went away **s**: for	*3076*
Mt	26:22	they were exceeding **s**, and began	*3076*
Mt	26:37	and began to be **s** and very heavy	*3076*
Mt	26:38	**My soul is exceeding s, even unto.**	*4036*
Lk	18:23	when he heard this, he was very **s**	*4036*
Lk	18:24	when Jesus saw that he was very **s**,	*4036*
Jn	16:20	**ye shall be s, but your sorrow**	*3076*

SORROWS

Ex	3:7	taskmasters; for I know their **s**;	4341
2Sa	22:6	**s** of hell compassed me about;	2256
Job	21:17	God distributeth **s** in his anger	2256
Ps	18:4	The **s** of death compassed me	2256
Ps	18:5	**s** of hell compassed me about:	2256
Ps	127:2	sit up late, to eat the bread of **s**	6089
Isa	53:3	a man of **s**, and acquainted with	4341
Isa	53:4	our griefs, and carried our **s**	4341
Da	10:16	vision my **s** are turned upon me,	6735
Mt	24:8	**All these are the beginning of s**	*5604*
Mk	13:8	**these are the beginnings of s.**	*5604*

SORRY

Ne	8:10	neither be ye **s**; for the joy of the	6087
Ps	38:18	iniquity: I will be **s** for my sin	1672
Isa	51:19	thee; who shall be **s** for thee?	5110
Mt	14:9	And the king was **s**: nevertheless	*3076*
2Co	7:8	though I made you **s** with a letter,	*3076*
2Co	7:8	the same epistle hath made you **s**,	*3076*

SORT

Ge	6:19	two of every **s** shalt thou bring into	
Ge	6:20	two of every **s** shall come unto thee,	
Ge	7:14	his kind, every bird of every **s**	3671
Ezr	4:8	to Artaxerxes the king in this **s**	3660
Ne	6:4	unto me four times after this **s**;	1697
Da	1:10	children which are of your **s**?	1524
Da	3:29	God that can deliver after this **s**	
1Co	3:13	every man's work of what **s** it is	*3697*
2Ti	3:6	For of this **s** are they which creep into	

SORTS

Ps	78:45	He sent divers **s** of flies among them,	
Ps	105:31	spake, and there came divers **s** of flies,	
Eze	38:4	clothed with all **s** of armour,	4358

SOUGHT

Ge	43:30	and he **s** where to weep: and he	1245
Ex	2:15	this thing, he **s** to slay Moses	1245
Ex	4:19	the men are dead which **s** thy life	1245
Ex	4:24	Lord met him, and **s** to kill him	1245
1Sa	13:14	Lord hath **s** him a man after his	1245
1Sa	23:14	And Saul **s** him every day, but God	1245
2Sa	3:17	Ye **s** for David in times past to be	1245
2Sa	4:8	Saul thine enemy, which **s** thy life;	1245
1Ki	1:2	Let there be **s** for my lord the king	1245
1Ki	1:3	So they **s** for a fair damsel	1245
1Ki	10:24	And all the earth **s** to Solomon	1245
1Ki	11:40	Solomon **s** … to kill Jeroboam.	1245
2Ch	9:23	earth **s** the presence of Solomon,	1245
2Ch	14:7	we have **s** the Lord our God,	1875
2Ch	15:15	and **s** him with their whole desire;	1245
2Ch	17:4	**s** to the Lord God of his father	1875
2Ch	26:5	he **s** God in the days of Zechariah,	1875
2Ch	26:5	as long as he **s** the Lord, God made	1875
Est	2:2	fair young virgins **s** for the king:	1245
Est	3:6	Haman **s** to destroy all the Jews	1245
Est	6:2	**s** to lay hand on … king Ahasuerus	1245
Ps	34:4	I **s** the Lord, and he heard me,	1875
Ps	77:2	day of my trouble I **s** the Lord:	1875
Ps	119:10	my whole heart have I **s** thee:	1875
Ps	119:94	save me; for I have **s** thy precepts.	1875
Ecc	2:3	I **s** in mine heart to give myself	8446
Ecc	12:10	**s** to find out acceptable words:	1245
SS	3:1	bed I **s** him whom my soul loveth:	1245
Isa	62:12	called, **S** out, A city not forsaken.	1875
Jer	10:21	brutish, and have not **s** the Lord:	1875
Eze	22:30	And I **s** for a man among them.	1245
Da	2:13	they **s** Daniel and his fellows to	1158
Da	6:4	**s** to find occasion against Daniel	1158
Da	8:15	the vision, and **s** for the meaning	1245
Zep	1:6	those that have not **s** the Lord.	1245
Mt	2:20	which **s** the young child's life.	*2212*
Mt	21:46	when they **s** to lay hands on him,	*2212*
Mt	26:16	he **s** opportunity to betray him	*2212*
Mt	26:59	**s** false witness against Jesus, to	*2212*
Mk	11:18	and **s** how they might destroy him:	*2212*
Mk	14:1	scribes **s** how they might take him	*2212*
Lk	2:49	unto them, **How is it that ye s me?**	*2212*
Lk	6:19	whole multitude **s** to touch him:	*2212*
Lk	11:16	him, **s** of him a sign from heaven	*2212*
Lk	13:6	**and he came and s fruit thereon,**	*2212*
Lk	19:3	And he **s** to see Jesus who he was;	*2212*
Jn	5:16	persecute Jesus, and **s** to slay him,	*2212*
Jn	5:18	the Jews **s** the more to kill him,	*2212*
Jn	10:39	they **s** again to take him: but he	*2212*

Jn	11:8	the Jews of late **s** to stone thee;	*2212*
Jn	19:12	thenceforth Pilate **s** to release him:	*2212*
Ac	12:19	And when Herod had **s** for him,	*1934*
Ro	9:32	Because they **s** it not by faith, but	*2212*
1Th	2:6	Nor of men **s** we glory, neither of	*2212*
Heb	12:17	though he **s** it carefully with tears	*1567*

SOUL

Ge	2:7	life; and man became a living **s**	5315
Ge	12:13	and my **s** shall live because of thee	5315
Ge	19:20	a little one?) and my **s** shall live	5315
Ge	27:4	my **s** may bless thee before I die	5315
Ge	27:19	venison, that thy **s** may bless me	5315
Ge	34:3	And his **s** clave unto Dinah the	5315
Ex	30:12	give every man a ransom for his **s**	5315
Le	4:2	If a **s** shall sin through ignorance	5315
Le	17:11	maketh an atonement for the **s**	5315
Le	26:15	or if your **s** abhor my judgments,	5315
Le	26:30	idols, and my **s** shall abhor you	5315
Le	26:43	their **s** abhorred my statutes	5315
Nu	15:27	if any **s** sin through ignorance,	5315
Nu	15:28	make an atonement for the **s** that	5315
Nu	30:2	an oath to bind his **s** with a bond;	5315
Nu	30:6	lips, wherewith she bound her **s**;	5315
Nu	30:13	every binding oath to afflict the **s**	5315
Dt	4:9	and keep thy **s** diligently, lest thou	5315
Dt	4:29	with all thy heart and with all thy **s**	5315
Dt	6:5	all thine heart, and with all thy **s**	5315
Jos	22:5	all your heart and with all your **s**	5315
1Sa	1:10	And she was in bitterness of **s**, and	5315
1Sa	1:15	poured out my **s** before the Lord	5315
1Sa	1:26	as thy **s** liveth, my lord, I am the	5315
1Sa	18:1	that the **s** of Jonathan was knit	5315
1Sa	18:1	was knit with the **s** of David	5315
1Sa	18:1	Jonathan loved him as his own **s**	5315
1Sa	18:3	because he loved him as his own **s**	5315
1Sa	25:26	and as thy **s** liveth, seeing the Lord	5315
2Sa	4:9	who hath redeemed my **s** out of all	5315
2Sa	5:8	blind, that are hated of David's **s**	5315
1Ki	17:21	let this child's **s** come into him	5315
1Ki	17:22	the **s** of the child came into him,	5315
2Ki	2:2	Lord liveth, and as thy **s** liveth,	5315
Job	7:11	complain in the bitterness of my **s**	5315
Job	10:1	My **s** is weary of my life; I will	5315
Job	16:4	if your **s** were in my soul's stead, I	5315
Job	27:8	when God taketh away his **s**?	5315
Job	30:16	now my **s** is poured out upon me;	5315
Job	33:18	keepeth back his **s** from the pit	5315
Job	33:28	He will deliver his **s** from going	5315
Job	33:30	To bring back his **s** from the pit	5315
Ps	6:4	Return, O Lord, deliver my **s**: O	5315
Ps	7:2	Lest he tear my **s** like a lion,	5315
Ps	11:1	how say ye to my **s**, Flee as a bird	5315
Ps	16:10	thou wilt not leave my **s** in hell;	5315
Ps	19:7	Lord is perfect, converting the **s**	5315
Ps	23:3	He restoreth my **s**: he leadeth me	5315
Ps	25:1	thee, O Lord, do I lift up my **s**	5315
Ps	33:20	Our **s** waiteth for the Lord: he is	5315
Ps	34:2	My **s** shall make her boast in the	5315
Ps	34:22	The Lord redeemeth the **s** of his	5315
Ps	35:9	my **s** shall be joyful in the Lord:	5315
Ps	40:14	that seek after my **s** to destroy it;	5315
Ps	42:1	so panteth my **s** after thee, O God	5315
Ps	42:2	My **s** thirsteth for God, for the	5315
Ps	42:4	things, I pour out my **s** in me:	5315
Ps	42:5	Why art thou cast down, O my **s**?	5315
Ps	42:6	God, my **s** is cast down within me:	5315
Ps	55:18	He hath delivered my **s** in peace	5315
Ps	62:1	Truly my **s** waiteth upon God:	5315
Ps	63:1	my **s** thirsteth for thee, my flesh	5315
Ps	63:5	My **s** shall be satisfied as with	5315
Ps	63:8	My **s** followeth hard after thee:	5315
Ps	69:18	Draw nigh unto my **s**, and redeem	5315
Ps	86:2	Preserve my **s**; for I am holy: O	5315
Ps	86:4	unto thee, O Lord, do I lift up my **s**	5315
Ps	103:1	Bless the Lord, O my **s**: and all	5315
Ps	103:2	Bless the Lord, O my **s**, and forget	5315
Ps	103:22	dominion: bless the Lord, O my **s**	5315
Ps	104:1	Bless the Lord, O my **s** O Lord	5315
Ps	104:35	Bless thou the Lord, O my **s**	5315
Ps	107:9	For he satisfieth the longing **s**, and	5315
Ps	107:9	filleth the hungry **s** with goodness	5315
Ps	116:8	hast delivered my **s** from death,	5315
Ps	119:109	My **s** is continually in my hand:	5315
Ps	121:7	all evil: he shall preserve thy **s**	5315
Ps	130:5	I wait for the Lord, my **s** doth wait,	5315
Ps	139:14	and that my **s** knoweth right well	5315
Ps	143:6	my **s** thirsteth after thee, as a	5315
Ps	146:1	Lord. Praise the Lord, O my **s**	5315
Pr	2:10	knowledge is pleasant unto thy **s**;	5315
Pr	3:22	So shall they be life unto thy **s**	5315
Pr	11:25	The liberal **s** shall be made fat:	5315
Pr	13:4	The **s** of the sluggard desireth, and	5315
Pr	13:4	**s** of the diligent shall be made fat	5315
Pr	16:17	keepeth his way preserveth his **s**	5315
Pr	18:7	and his lips are the snare of his **s**	5315
Pr	19:8	getteth wisdom loveth his own **s**:	5315
Pr	19:16	commandment keepeth his own **s**;	5315
Pr	20:2	anger sinneth against his own **s**	5315
Pr	21:10	The **s** of the wicked desireth evil:	5315
Pr	23:14	and shalt deliver his **s** from hell	5315
Pr	25:25	As cold waters to a thirsty **s**, so is	5315
Pr	27:7	The full **s** loatheth an honeycomb;	5315
Pr	27:7	to the hungry **s** every bitter thing	5315
Ecc	2:24	he should make his **s** enjoy good	5315
Ecc	4:8	labour, and bereave my **s** of good?	5315
Ecc	7:28	Which yet my **s** seeketh, but I find	5315
SS	1:7	Tell me, O thou whom my **s** loveth,	5315
SS	5:6	gone: my **s** failed when he spake:	5315
Isa	3:9	Woe unto their **s**! for they have	5315
Isa	26:9	With my **s** have I desired thee in	5315
Isa	42:1	elect, in whom my **s** delighteth;	5315
Isa	51:23	which have said to thy **s**, Bow down,	5315
Isa	53:10	thou shalt make his **s** an offering	5315
Isa	53:11	He shall see of the travail of his **s**	5315
Isa	53:12	hath poured out his **s** unto death:	5315
Isa	55:3	me: hear, and your **s** shall live;	5315
Isa	61:10	my **s** shall be joyful in my God;	5315
Jer	32:41	whole heart and with my whole **s**	5315
Jer	50:19	his **s** shall be satisfied upon mount	5315
La	3:24	Lord is my portion, saith my **s**;	5315
Eze	3:19	but thou hast delivered thy **s**	5315
Eze	18:4	the **s** that sinneth, it shall die.	5315
Eze	18:20	The **s** that sinneth, it shall die.	5315
Jnh	2:7	When my **s** fainted within me I	5315
Mt	10:28	**but are not able to kill the s**	*5590*
Mt	10:28	**to destroy both s and body in hell**	*5590*
Mt	12:18	in whom my **s** is well pleased:	*5590*
Mt	16:26	**whole world, and lose his own s?**	*5590*
Mt	16:26	**a man give in exchange for his s**	*5590*
Mt	22:37	**all thy heart, and with all thy s,**	*5590*
Mt	26:38	**My s is exceeding sorrowful, even**	*5590*

Mk	12:30	**all thy heart, and with all thy s,**	*5590*
Lk	1:46	said, My **s** doth magnify the Lord,	*5590*
Lk	10:27	all thy heart, and with all thy **s**	*5590*
Lk	12:19	**say to my s, S, thou hast much**	*5590*
Lk	12:20	**this night thy s shall be required**	*5590*
Jn	12:27	**Now is my s troubled; and what**	*5590*
Ac	2:27	thou wilt not leave my **s** in hell,	*5590*
Ac	2:31	that his **s** was not left in hell,	*5590*
Ac	2:43	And fear came upon every **s**: and	*5590*
Ro	13:1	Let every **s** be subject unto the	*5590*
1Co	15:45	man Adam was made a living **s**;	*5590*
1Th	5:23	your whole spirit and **s** and body	*5590*
Heb	4:12	dividing asunder of **s** and spirit	*5590*
Heb	6:19	we have as an anchor of the **s**	*5590*
Heb	10:38	my **s** shall have no pleasure in	*5590*
Heb	10:39	that believe to the saving of the **s**	*5590*
1Pe	2:11	lusts, which war against the **s**;	*5590*
2Pe	2:8	vexed his righteous **s** from day to	*5590*
Rev	16:3	and every living **s** died in the sea	*5590*
Rev	18:14	fruits that thy **s** lusted after are	*5590*

SOULS

Ge	12:5	and the **s** that they had gotten in	5315
Ge	46:18	bare unto Jacob, even sixteen **s**	5315
Ge	46:26	all the **s** were threescore and six;	5315
Ge	46:27	born him in Egypt, were two **s**	5315
Ex	1:5	the loins of Jacob were seventy **s**.	5315
Ex	30:15	make an atonement for your **s**	5315
Jos	23:14	all your hearts and in all your **s**,	5315
Ps	97:10	preserveth the **s** of his saints; he	5315
Pr	11:30	life; and he that winneth **s** is wise.	5315
Pr	14:25	A true witness delivereth **s**: but a	5315
Jer	6:16	and ye shall find rest for your **s**.	5315
Eze	18:4	Behold, all **s** are mine; as the soul	5315
Mt	11:29	**and ye shall find rest unto your s,**	*5590*
Lk	21:19	**your patience possess ye your s**	*5590*
Ac	2:41	unto them about three thousand **s**	*5590*
Ac	7:14	kindred, threescore and fifteen **s**	*5590*
Ac	27:37	hundred threescore and sixteen **s**	*5590*
Heb	13:17	for they watch for your **s**, as they	*5590*
Jas	1:21	word, which is able to save your **s**.	*5590*
1Pe	1:9	faith, even the salvation of your **s**	*5590*
1Pe	1:22	have purified your **s** in obeying the	*5590*
1Pe	2:25	Shepherd and Bishop of your **s**.	*5590*
1Pe	3:20	is, eight **s** were saved by water	*5590*
Rev	6:9	under the altar the **s** of them that	*5590*
Rev	20:4	the **s** of them that were beheaded	*5590*

S

SOUND

Le	25:9	trumpet of the jubile to **s** on the	5674
Nu	10:7	blow, but ye shall not **s** an alarm	7321
Jos	6:5	when ye hear the **s** of the trumpet,	6963
Jos	6:20	people heard the **s** of the trumpet,	6963
1Ki	18:41	there is a **s** of abundance of rain.	6963
1Ch	16:5	but Asaph made a **s** with cymbals;	8085
Ne	4:20	ye hear the **s** of the trumpet,	6963
Job	39:24	he that it is the **s** of the trumpet	6963
Ps	47:5	the Lord with the **s** of a trumpet.	6963
Ps	119:80	Let my heart be **s** in thy statutes;	8549
Ps	150:3	him with the **s** of the trumpet:	8629
Pr	2:7	He layeth up **s** wisdom for the	8454
Pr	3:21	keep **s** wisdom and discretion:	8454
Pr	14:30	A **s** heart is the life of the flesh:	4832
Jer	25:10	**s** of the millstones, and the light	6963
Da	3:5	ye hear the **s** of the cornet, flute,	7032
Da	3:7	people heard the **s** of the, cornet,	7032
Da	3:10	that shall hear the **s** of the cornet,	7032
Da	3:15	ye hear the **s** of the cornet, flute,	7032
Joel	2:1	**s** an alarm in my holy mountain:	7321
Mt	6:2	**do not s a trumpet before thee,**	*4537*
Mt	24:31	**with a great s of a trumpet,**	*5456*
Lk	15:27	**he hath received him safe and s**	*5198*
Jn	3:8	**thou nearest the s thereof, but**	*5456*
Ac	2:2	there came a **s** from heaven as of	*2279*
1Co	14:7	even things without life giving **s**	*5456*
1Co	14:8	if the trumpet give an uncertain **s**	*5456*
1Ti	1:10	that is contrary to **s** doctrine;	*5198*
2Ti	1:7	and of love, and of a **s** mind	*4995*
2Ti	1:13	Hold fast the form of **s** words,	*5198*
2Ti	4:3	they will not endure **s** doctrine;	*5198*
Tit	1:9	he may be able by **s** doctrine both	*5198*
Tit	1:13	that they may be **s** in the faith;	*5198*
Tit	2:1	things which become **s** doctrine:	*5198*
Tit	2:2	**s** in faith, in charity, in patience.	*5198*
Tit	2:8	**S** speech, that cannot be	*5199*
Rev	1:15	his voice as the **s** of many waters	*5456*
Rev	8:13	the three angels, which are yet to **s**!	*4537*
Rev	9:9	as the **s** of chariots of many horses	*5456*
Rev	18:22	**s** of a millstone shall be heard no	*5456*

SOUNDED

1Sa	20:12	when I have **s** my father about	2713
Lk	1:44	of thy salutation **s** in mine ears,	*1096*
Rev	8:7	The first angel **s**, and there	*4537*
Rev	8:8	the second angel **s**, and as it were	*4537*
Rev	8:10	the third angel **s**, and there fell a	*4537*
Rev	8:12	the fourth angel **s**, and the third	*4537*
Rev	9:1	the fifth angel **s**, and I saw a star	*4537*
Rev	9:13	the sixth angel **s**, and I heard a	*4537*
Rev	11:15	And the seventh angel **s**; and there	*4537*

SOUNDING

Ps	150:5	him upon the high **s** cymbals.	8643
1Co	13:1	I am become as **s** brass, or a	*2278*

SOUNDNESS

Ps	38:3	no **s** in my flesh because of thine	4974
Ps	38:7	and there is no **s** in my flesh.	4974
Ac	3:16	him hath given him this perfect **s**	*3647*

SOUR

Jer	31:29	The fathers have eaten a **s** grape,	1155
Eze	18:2	The fathers have eaten **s** grapes,	1155

SOUTH

Ge	13:1	had, and Lot with him, into the **s**	5045
Ge	13:3	journey from the **s** … to Beth-el,	5045
Ex	26:35	of the tabernacle toward the **s**.	8486
Jos	10:40	country of the hills, and of the **s**.	5045
Jos	18:19	the salt sea at the **s** end of Jordan:	5045
Jos	18:19	of Jordan: this was the **s** coast	5045
1Sa	20:41	arose out of a place toward the **s**,	5045
1Sa	30:14	to Judah, and upon the **s** of Caleb;	5045
Job	37:9	Out of the **s** cometh … whirlwind:	2315
Job	39:26	stretch her wings toward the **s**?	8486
Ps	89:12	north and the **s** thou hast created.	3225
Ps	126:4	O Lord, as the streams in the **s**	5045
Ecc	11:3	and if the tree fall toward the **s**	1864
Isa	21:1	As whirlwinds in the **s** pass	5045
Da	11:5	the king of the **s** shall be strong,	5045
Da	11:9	So the king of the **s** shall come	5045
Da	11:11	the king of the **s** shall be moved	5045
Da	11:14	stand up against the king of the **s**.	5045

Da	11:15	arms of the **s** shall not withstand,.	5045
Da	11:25	courage against the king of the **s**.	5045
Da	11:25	king of the **s** shall be stirred up to	5045
Da	11:29	return, and come toward the **s**;	5045
Da	11:40	shall the king of the **s** push at	5045
Mt	12:42	**queen of the s shall rise up in**	*3558*
Lk	12:55	**when ye see the s wind blow,**	*3558*
Rev	21:13	three gates; on the **s** three gates;	*3558*

SOUTHWARD

Ge	13:14	**s**, and eastward, and westward:	5045
Ex	40:24	the south side of the tabernacle **s**	5045
Nu	3:29	on the side of the tabernacle **s**.	8486
Jos	18:13	side of Luz, which is Beth-el, **s**;	5045
1Ch	26:15	To Obed-edom **s**; and to his sons	5045
Da	8:4	westward, and northward, and **s**;	5045

SOW

Ge	47:23	for you, and ye shall **s** the land	2232
Ex	23:10	six years thou shalt **s** thy land,.	2232
Le	25:3	Six years thou shalt **s** thy field,	2232
Le	25:4	thou shalt neither **s** thy field, nor	2232
Le	25:22	And ye shall **s** the eight year, and	2232
Job	4:8	plow iniquity, and **s** wickedness	2232
Job	31:8	Then let me **s**, and let another eat;	2232
Ps	126:5	that **s**; in tears shall reap in joy	2232
Ecc	11:4	observeth the wind shall not **s**;	2232
Ecc	11:6	In the morning **s** thy seed, and in	2232
Isa	32:20	Blessed are ye that **s** beside all	2232
Jer	31:27	that I will **s** the house of Israel and	2232
Hos	10:12	**S** to yourselves in righteousness,	2232
Mt	6:26	**fowls of the air: for they s not,**	*4687*
Mt	13:3	**Behold, a sower went forth to s;**	*4687*
Mk	4:3	**there went out a sower to s**	*4687*
Lk	8:5	**A sower went out to s his seed:**	*4687*
Lk	12:24	**for they neither s nor reap;**	*4687*
Lk	19:21	**and reapest that thou didst not s**	*4687*
2Pe	2:22	and the **s** that was washed to her	*5300*

SOWED

Jgs	9:45	down the city, and **s** it with salt.	2232
Mt	13:4	**when he s, some seeds fell by.**	*4687*
Mt	13:24	**unto a man which s good seed in**	*4687*
Mt	13:25	**and s tares among the wheat.**	*4687*
Mt	13:31	**a man took, and s in his field:**	*4687*
Mt	13:39	**enemy that s them is the devil;**	*4687*
Mt	25:26	**knewest that I reap where I s not,**	*4687*
Mk	4:4	**he s, some fell by the way side,**	*4687*

SOWER

Isa	55:10	that it may give seed to the **s**,	2232
Mt	13:3	**Behold, a s went forth to sow;**	*4687*
Mt	13:18	**Hear ye … the parable of the s**	*4687*
Mk	4:14	**The s soweth the word**	*4687*
2Co	9:10	he that ministereth seed to the **s**	*4687*

SOWETH

Pr	6:14	mischief continually; he **s** discord	7971
Pr	6:19	that **s** discord among brethren	7971
Pr	11:18	but to him that **s** righteousness.	2232
Pr	16:28	A froward man **s** strife: and a	7971
Pr	22:8	He that **s** iniquity shall reap.	2232
Am	9:13	treader of grapes him that **s** seed;	4900
Mt	13:37	**that s the good seed is the Son**	*4687*
Mk	4:14	**The sower s the word**	*4687*
Jn	4:36	**that both he that s and he that**	*4687*
Jn	4:37	**true, One s, and another reapeth**	*4687*
2Co	9:6	He which **s** sparingly shall reap.	*4687*
2Co	9:6	he which **s** bountifully shall reap	*4687*
Gal	6:7	whatsoever a man **s**, that shall he	*4687*
Gal	6:8	For he that **s** to his flesh shall of	*4687*
Gal	6:8	but he that **s** to the Spirit shall of	*4687*

SOWN

Ex	23:16	which thou hast **s** in the field:	2232
Jgs	6:3	And so it was when Israel had **s**,	2232
Ps	97:11	Light is **s** for the righteous, and	2232
Isa	61:11	things that are **s** in it to spring	2221
Jer	12:13	They have **s** wheat, but shall reap	2232
Eze	36:9	you, and ye shall be tilled and **s**:	2232
Hos	8:7	For they have **s** the wind, and they	2232
Mt	13:19	**that which was s in his heart**	*4687*
Mt	25:24	**reaping where thou hast not s**	*4687*
Mk	4:15	**way side, where the word is s;**	*4687*
Mk	4:15	**word that was s in their hearts**	*4687*
Mk	4:16	**which are s on stony ground**	*4687*
Mk	4:18	**they which are s among thorns;**	*4687*
Mk	4:20	**they which are s on good ground;**	*4687*
Mk	4:31	**when it is s in the earth, is less**	*4687*
Mk	4:32	**when it is s, it groweth up, and**	*4687*
1Co	15:42	It is **s** in corruption; it is raised in	*4687*
1Co	15:43	It is **s** in dishonour; it is raised in	*4687*
1Co	15:43	it is **s** in weakness; it is raised in	*4687*
1Co	15:44	It is **s** a natural body; it is raised	*4687*

SPACE

Ge	29:14	abode with him the **s** of a month.	3117
Ge	32:16	put a **s** betwixt drove and drove	7305
Jos	3:4	shall be a **s** between you and it	7350
Ezr	9:8	a little **s** grace hath been shewed.	7281
Lk	22:59	And about the **s** of one hour after	*1339*
Ac	5:7	it was about the **s** of three hours.	*1292*
Ac	5:34	to put the apostles forth a little **s**;	*1024*
Ac	15:33	after they had tarried there a **s**,	*5550*
Ac	19:34	about the **s** of two hours cried out,	*1909*
Rev	2:21	**And I gave her s to repent of her**	*5550*
Rev	8:1	in heaven about the **s** of half an hour	

SPAN

Ex	28:16	a **s** shall be the length thereof,	2239
Ex	28:16	a **s** shall be the breadth thereof.	2239
1Sa	17:4	whose height was six cubits and a **s**	2239
Isa	40:12	and meted out heaven with the **s**,	2239

SPANNED

Isa	48:13	my right hand hath **s** the heavens:	2946

SPARE

Ge	18:24	also destroy and not **s** the place	5375
Ge	18:26	will **s** all the place for their sakes.	5375
Dt	13:8	eye pity him, neither shalt thou **s**,	2550
Dt	29:20	The Lord will not **s** him, but then	5545
Job	20:13	Though he **s** it, and forsake it not;	2550
Job	30:10	me, and **s** not to spit in my face.	2820
Ps	39:13	O **s** me, that I may recover.	8159
Ps	72:13	He shall **s** the poor and needy,	2347
Pr	6:34	will not **s** in the day of vengeance.	2550
Pr	19:18	let not thy soul **s** for his crying.	5375
Isa	58:1	Cry aloud, **s** not, lift up thy voice	2820
Jer	13:14	I will not pity, nor **s**, nor have	2347
Jer	50:14	bow, shoot at her, **s** no arrows:	2550
Eze	24:14	I will not go back, neither will I **s**,	2347
Joel	2:17	**S** thy people, O Lord, and give not	2347
Jnh	4:11	should not I **s** Nineveh, that great	2347

Mal 3:17 I will **s** them, as a man spareth 2550
Lk 15:17 **have bread enough and to s,** *4052*
1Co 7:28 trouble in the flesh: but I **s** you *5339*

SPARED
1Sa 15:9 But Saul and the people **s** Agag, ... 2550
1Sa 15:15 people **s** the best of the sheep and 2550
2Sa 21:7 But the king **s** Mephibosheth, the. 2550
2Ki 5:20 my master hath **s** Naaman this 2820
Ps 78:50 he **s** not their soul from death, ... 2820
Ro 8:32 He that **s** not his own Son, but *5339*
2Pe 2:4 if God **s** not the angels that sinned, ... *5339*
2Pe 2:5 And **s** not the old world, but saved. *5339*

SPARETH
Pr 13:24 He that **s** his rod hateth his son: 2820
Pr 17:27 that hath knowledge **s** his words: 2820

SPARINGLY
2Co 9:6 which soweth **s** shall reap also **s**; *5340*

SPARK
Job 18:5 the **s** of his fire shall not shine. 7632
Isa 1:31 as tow, and the maker of it as a **s**, ... 5213

SPARKS
Job 5:7 trouble, as the **s** fly upward. 1121, 7565
Job 41:19 lamps, and **s** of fire leap out. 3590

SPARROW
Ps 84:3 Yea, the **s** hath found an house, ... 6833

SPARROWS
Mt 10:29 **Are not two s sold for a farthing?** *4765*
Mt 10:31 **ye are of more value than many s.** *4765*
Lk 12:6 **not five s sold for two farthings,** *4765*
Lk 12:7 **ye are of more value than many s.** *4765*

SPEAK
Ge 18:27 taken upon me to **s** unto the Lord,. 1696
Ge 24:50 we cannot **s** unto thee bad or good 1696
Ge 32:4 Thus shall ye **s** unto my lord Esau; 559
Ge 44:18 thee, **s** a word in my lord's ears, ... 1696
Ge 50:4 **s**, … in the ears of Pharaoh, saying, ... 1696
Ex 4:14 brother? I know that he can **s** well. 1696
Ex 7:2 thy brother shall **s** unto Pharaoh, ... 1696
Ex 7:9 When Pharaoh shall **s** unto you, ... 1696
Ex 20:19 let not God **s** with us, lest we die. 1696
Ex 23:2 neither shalt thou **s** in a cause to 6030
Ex 23:22 obey his voice, and do all that I **s**; 1696
Le 21:1 **S** unto the priests the sons of 559
Le 21:17 **S** unto Aaron, saying, Whosoever 1696
Nu 7:89 Moses was gone … to **s** with him, ... 1696
Nu 12:6 and will **s** unto him in a dream. 1696
Nu 12:8 With him will I **s** mouth to mouth, ... 1696
Nu 12:8 afraid to **s** against my servant 1696
Nu 14:15 have heard the fame of thee will **s**, ... 559
Nu 20:8 **s** ye unto the rock before their eyes; 1696
Nu 23:5 unto Balak, and thus thou shalt **s** 1696
Nu 23:12 to **s** that which the Lord hath put. 1696
Dt 3:26 **s** no more unto me of this matter 1696
Dt 5:27 **s** thou unto us all that the Lord 1696
Dt 5:27 the Lord our God shall **s** unto thee; 1696
Dt 5:31 **s** unto thee all the commandments, ... 1696
Dt 9:4 **S** not thou in thine heart, after 559
Dt 18:20 presume to **s** a word in my name, ... 1696
Dt 18:20 shall **s** in the name of other gods, ... 1696
Dt 26:5 shalt **s** and say before the Lord 6030
Jos 22:24 children might **s** unto our children, ... 559
Jgs 9:2 **S**, I pray you, in the ears of all the 1696
Jgs 19:3 to **s** friendly unto her, and to bring 1696
Jgs 19:30 it, take advice, and **s** your minds. 1696
1Sa 3:9 **S**, Lord; for thy servant heareth. 1696
1Sa 3:10 **S**; for thy servant heareth. 1696
2Sa 7:17 vision, so did Nathan **s** unto David 1696
1Ki 2:17 said, **S**, I pray thee, unto Solomon 559
1Ki 2:18 I will **s** for thee unto the king. 1696
1Ch 17:15 so did Nathan **s** unto David. 1696
2Ch 18:13 what my God saith, that will I **s** 1696
2Ch 18:23 Spirit … from me to **s** unto thee?. 1696
2Ch 32:17 God of Israel, and to **s** against him. 559
Ne 13:24 could not **s** in the Jews' language 1696
Est 5:14 to morrow **s** thou unto the king 559
Est 6:4 to **s** unto the king to hang Mordecai 559
Job 7:11 will **s** in the anguish of my spirit; 1696
Job 10:1 I will **s** in the bitterness of my soul. 1696
Job 11:5 But oh that God would **s**, and open 1696
Job 13:3 Surely I would **s** to the Almighty, ... 1696
Job 13:7 Will ye **s** wickedly for God? and 1696
Job 16:6 Though I **s**, my grief is not 1696
Job 32:20 I will **s**, that I may be refreshed: 1696
Job 36:2 I have yet to **s** on God's behalf. 4405
Job 41:3 will he **s** soft words unto thee? 1696
Job 42:4 Hear, I beseech thee, and I will **s**. 1696
Ps 2:5 shall he **s** unto them in his wrath, ... 1696
Ps 12:2 and with a double heart do they **s** 1696
Ps 17:10 with their mouth they **s** proudly. 1696
Ps 35:28 shall **s** of thy righteousness and 1897
Ps 49:3 My mouth shall **s** of wisdom; and 1696
Ps 69:12 that sit in the gate **s** against me; 7878
Ps 77:4 I am so troubled that I cannot **s** 1696
Ps 85:8 will hear what God the Lord will **s**. 1696
Ps 85:8 he will **s** peace unto his people,. 1696
Ps 119:46 I will **s** of thy testimonies also. 1696
Ps 119:172 My tongue shall **s** of thy word: 6030
Ps 139:20 For they **s** against thee wickedly,. 559
Ps 145:5 I will **s** of the glorious honour of 7878
Ps 145:21 My mouth shall **s** the praise of the. 1696
Pr 8:6 for I will **s** of excellent things; 1696
Pr 8:7 For my mouth shall **s** truth; and. 1897
Pr 23:9 **S** not in the ears of a fool: for he 1696
Ecc 3:7 to keep silence, and a time to **s**;. 1696
SS 7:9 lips of those that are asleep to **s** 1680
Isa 32:4 the stammerers shall be ready to **s** 1696
Isa 32:6 the vile person will **s** villany, and 1696
Isa 45:19 I the Lord **s** righteousness, I 1696
Isa 52:6 that day that I am he that doth **s** 1696
Isa 56:3 hath joined himself to the Lord, **s**, ... 559
Isa 59:4 they trust in vanity, and **s** lies; 1696
Jer 12:6 though they **s** fair words unto thee. 1696
Jer 23:28 word, let him **s** my word faithfully.. 1696
Jer 32:4 shall **s** with him mouth to mouth, ... 1696
Eze 12:25 For I am the Lord: I will **s**, and 1696
Eze 20:49 of me, Doth he not **s** parables? 4911
Da 3:29 which **s** any thing amiss against 560
Da 7:25 he shall **s** great words against 4449
Da 10:19 said, Let my lord **s**; for thou hast 1696
Da 11:36 shall **s** marvellous things against. 1696
Hos 2:14 and **s** comfortably unto her. 1696
Zec 8:16 **S** ye every man the truth to his. 1696
Mt 10:19 **thought how or what ye shall s.** *2980*
Mt 10:19 **that same hour what ye shall s** *2980*
Mt 10:20 **For it is not ye that s, but the** *2980*
Mt 12:34 **can ye, being evil, s good things?** *2980*
Mt 12:36 **every idle word that men shall s,** *2980*

Mt 13:13 **Therefore s I to them in parables:** *2980*
Mt 15:31 when they saw the dumb to **s**, the...... *2980*
Mk 7:37 the deaf to hear, and the dumb to **s** *2980*
Mk 9:39 **that can lightly s evil of me.** *2551*
Mk 16:17 **they shall s with new tongues;** *2980*
Lk 1:19 and am sent to **s** unto thee, and to *2980*
Lk 1:20 shalt be dumb, and not able to **s**, ... *2980*
Lk 1:22 out, he could not **s** unto them: *2980*
Lk 12:10 **s a word against the Son of man,** *2046*
Jn 3:11 **s that we do know, and testify**......... *2980*
Jn 4:26 unto her, **I that s unto thee am he** *2980*
Jn 6:63 **the words that I s unto you, they** *2980*
Jn 7:17 **of God, or whether I s of myself.** *2980*
Jn 12:49 **I should say, and what I should s** *2980*
Jn 12:50 **whatsoever I s therefore, even as** *2980*
Jn 12:50 **the Father said unto me, so I s** *2980*
Jn 13:18 **I s not of you all: I know whom I**...... *3004*
Jn 14:10 **the words that I s unto you**........... *2980*
Jn 14:10 **I s not of myself: but the Father** *2980*
Jn 16:13 **for he shall not s of himself; but**....... *2980*
Jn 16:13 **he shall hear, that shall he s:** *2980*
Jn 16:25 **no more s unto you in proverbs,** *2980*
Jn 17:13 **these things I s in the world,**.......... *2980*
Ac 2:4 they began to **s** with other tongues, ... *2980*
Ac 2:6 heard them **s** in his own language *2980*
Ac 2:11 we do hear them **s** in our tongues *2980*
Ac 4:20 **s** the things which we have seen *2980*
Ac 4:29 all boldness they may **s** thy word *2980*
Ac 10:46 they heard them **s** with tongues,....... *2980*
Ac 11:15 as I began to **s**, the Holy Ghost fell..... *2980*
Ac 18:9 **Be not afraid, but s, and hold** *2980*
Ac 21:37 Who said, Canst thou **s** Greek?........ *2097*
Ro 6:19 I **s** after the manner of men........... *3004*
Ro 11:13 For I **s** to you Gentiles, inasmuch...... *3004*
1Co 2:7 But we **s** the wisdom of God in a *2980*
1Co 3:1 not **s** unto you as unto spiritual,....... *2980*
1Co 6:5 I **s** to your shame. Is it so, that......... *3004*
1Co 7:35 And this I **s** for your own profit;....... *3004*
1Co 12:30 do all **s** with tongues? do all.......... *2980*
1Co 13:1 I **s** with the tongues of men and of..... *2980*
1Co 14:6 except I shall **s** to you either by........ *2980*
1Co 14:9 spoken? for ye shall **s** into the air *2980*
1Co 14:18 I **s** with tongues more than ye all:...... *2980*
1Co 14:19 I had rather **s** five words with my...... *2980*
1Co 14:27 any man **s** in an unknown tongue,..... *2980*
1Co 14:28 let him **s** to himself, and to God....... *2980*
1Co 14:35 is a shame for women to **s** in the *2980*
1Co 15:34 of God: I **s** this to your shame......... *3004*
2Co 2:17 in the sight of God **s** we in Christ. *2980*
2Co 4:13 we also believe, and therefore **s**; *2980*
Eph 4:25 **s** every man truth with his............ *2980*
Eph 5:32 but I **s** concerning Christ and the...... *3004*
Eph 6:20 boldly, as I ought to **s** *2980*
Php 4:11 Not that I **s** in respect of want: *3004*
1Th 2:4 trust with the gospel, even so we **s**;..... *2980*
Tit 2:1 **s** thou the things which become *2980*
Jas 1:19 to hear, slow to **s**, slow to wrath:....... *2980*
Jas 4:11 **S** not evil one of another,............. *2635*
1Pe 3:10 and his lips that they **s** no guile: *2980*
1Pe 4:11 him **s** as the oracles of God;........... *2980*
2Pe 2:18 when they **s** great swelling words *5350*
2Jn 12 **s** face to face, that our joy may be...... *2980*
3Jn 14 thee, and we shall **s** face to face. *2980*
Rev 2:24 **the depths of Satan, as they s;**......... *3004*
Rev 13:15 image of the beast should both **s**,...... *2980*

SPEAKEST

2Ki 6:12 words ... thou **s** in thy bedchamber.... 1696
Job 2:10 Thou **s** as one of the foolish women ... 1696
Ps 50:20 sittest and **s** against thy brother;....... 1696
Jer 40:16 for thou **s** falsely of Ishmael........... 1696
Jer 43:2 unto Jeremiah, Thou **s** falsely:......... 1696
Eze 3:18 nor **s** to warn the wicked from his 1696
Zec 13:3 thou **s** lies in the name of the Lord:.... 1696
Mt 13:10 Why **s** ... unto them in parables? *2980*
Lk 12:41 Lord, **s** thou this parable unto us,...... *3004*
Ac 17:19 new doctrine, whereof thou **s**, is? *2980*

SPEAKETH

Ex 33:11 to face, as a man **s** unto his friend...... 1696
Nu 23:26 All that the Lord **s**, that I must do?..... 1696
Dt 18:22 When a prophet **s** in the name of...... 1696
Job 17:5 He that **s** flattery to his friends,........ 5046
Job 33:14 God **s** once, yea twice, yet man 1696
Ps 12:3 the tongue that **s** proud things:........ 1696
Ps 37:30 mouth of the righteous **s** wisdom,..... 1897
Pr 6:13 he **s** with his feet, he teacheth 4448
Pr 6:19 A false witness that **s** lies, and he 6315
Pr 12:18 **s** like the piercings of a sword: 981
Pr 14:25 but a deceitful witness **s** lies........... 6315
Pr 19:5 he that **s** lies shall not escape.......... 6315
Pr 19:9 and he that **s** lies shall perish.......... 6315
Jer 9:8 as an arrow shot out; it **s** deceit: 1696
Jer 10:1 word which the Lord **s** unto you,...... 1696
Eze 10:5 of the Almighty God when he **s** 1696
Mt 10:20 **of your Father which s in you.** *2980*
Mt 12:32 **whosoever s a word against the** *2036*
Mt 12:32 **whosoever s against the Holy** *2036*
Mt 12:34 **out ... of the heart the mouth s** *2980*
Jn 3:34 God hath sent **s** the words of God: 2980
Jn 7:18 **He that s of himself seeketh his** *2980*
Jn 8:44 **When he s a lie, he s of his own:**....... *2980*
Ro 10:6 which is of faith **s** on this wise,........ *3004*
1Co 14:2 he that **s** in an unknown tongue....... *2980*
1Co 14:2 **s** not unto men, but unto God: for..... *2980*
1Co 14:2 in the spirit he **s** mysteries. *2980*
1Co 14:3 he that prophesieth **s** unto men *2980*
1Co 14:4 **s** in an unknown tongue edifieth *2980*
1Co 14:5 than he that **s** with tongues, ... *2980*
1Ti 4:1 the Spirit **s** expressly, that in the *3004*
Heb 11:4 and by it he being dead yet **s**.......... *2980*
Heb 12:5 which **s** unto you as unto children, ... *1256*
Jas 4:11 He that **s** evil of his brother, and....... *2635*
Jude 16 mouth **s** great swelling words,......... *2980*

S

SPEAKING

Ge 24:45 before I had done **s** in mine heart,..... 1696
Ex 34:33 till Moses had done **s** with them, ... 1696
Dt 4:33 God **s** out of the midst of the fire, ... 1696
Jgs 15:17 when he had made an end of **s**, ... 1696
Ru 1:18 with her, then she left **s** unto her 1696
1Sa 18:1 had made an end of **s** unto Saul, ... 1696
1Sa 24:16 an end of **s** these words unto Saul,..... 1696
Est 10:3 people, and **s** peace to all his seed...... 1696
Job 1:16 While he was yet **s**, there 1696
Job 1:17 While he was yet **s**, there 1696
Job 1:18 While he was yet **s**, there 1696
Job 32:15 answered no more: they left off **s** 4405
Isa 58:9 forth of the finger, and **s** vanity;....... 1696
Jer 26:7 heard Jeremiah **s** these words in 1696
Da 7:8 man, and a mouth **s** great things....... 4449
Da 8:13 Then I heard one saint **s**, and 1696

Da	9:20	And whiles I was **s**, and praying,	1696
Da	9:21	whiles I was **s** in prayer, even the	1696
Mt	6:7	**shall be heard for their much s**	*4180*
Lk	5:4	Now when he had left **s**, he said	*2980*
Ac	7:44	**s** unto Moses, that he should	*2980*
1Co	12:3	that no man **s** by the Spirit of God	*2980*
1Co	14:6	I come unto you **s** with tongues,	*2980*
2Co	13:3	ye seek a proof of Christ **s** in me,	*2980*
Eph	4:15	**s** the truth in love, may grow up	*226*
Eph	5:19	**S** to yourselves in psalms and	*2980*
Rev	13:5	him a mouth **s** great things and	*2980*

SPEAR

Jos	8:18	Stretch out the **s** that is in thy	3591
Jos	8:18	Joshua stretched out the **s** that	3591
Jos	8:26	wherewith he stretched out the **s**,	3591
Jgs	5:8	a shield or **s** seen among forty	7420
1Sa	13:22	neither sword nor **s** found in the	2595
1Sa	17:7	staff of his **s** was like a weaver's	2595
1Sa	17:45	to me with a sword, and with a **s**,	2595
1Sa	17:47	Lord saveth not with sword and **s**	2595
2Sa	1:6	behold, Saul leaned upon his **s**;	2595
2Sa	21:16	**s** weighed three hundred shekels	7013
2Sa	21:19	of whose **s** was like a weaver's	2595
2Sa	23:21	the Egyptian had a **s** in his hand;	2595
2Sa	23:21	the **s** out of the Egyptian's hand,	2595
2Sa	23:21	hand, and slew him with his own **s**	2595
Job	41:29	he laugheth at the shaking of a **s**	3591
Ps	46:9	bow, and cutteth the **s** in sunder;	2595
Jn	19:34	soldiers with a **s** pierced his side,	*3057*

SPEARMEN

Ps	68:30	Rebuke the company of **s**, the	7070
Ac	23:23	**s** two hundred, at the third hour	*1187*

SPEARS

1Sa	13:19	Hebrews make them swords or **s**	2595
Ne	4:21	half of them held the **s** from the	7420
Job	41:7	irons? or his head with fish **s**?	6767
Isa	2:4	and their **s** into pruninghooks:	2595
Joel	3:10	and your pruninghooks into **s**	7420
Mic	4:3	and their **s** into pruninghooks:	2595

SPECIAL

Dt	7:6	to be a **s** people unto himself	5459
Ac	19:11	God wrought **s** miracles	*3756, 3858, 5177*

SPECIALLY

Ac	25:26	and **s** before thee, O king Agrippa,	*3122*
1Ti	4:10	of all men, **s** of those that believe	*3122*
1Ti	5:8	and **s** for those of his own house	*3122*
Phm	16	servant, a brother beloved, **s** to me,	*3122*

SPECKLED

Ge	31:8	said thus, The **s** shall be thy wages;	5348
Ge	31:8	wages; then all the cattle bare **s**	5348
Ge	31:10	were ringstraked, **s**, and grisled	5348
Ge	31:12	are ringstraked, **s**, and grisled:	5348
Jer	12:9	heritage is unto me as a **s** bird	6641
Zec	1:8	there red horses, **s**, and white	8320

SPEECH

Ge	11:1	was of one language, and of one **s**	1697
Ge	11:7	not understand one another's **s**	8193
Ex	4:10	but I am slow of **s**, and of a slow	6310
1Ki	3:10	**s** pleased the Lord, that Solomon	1697
Job	24:25	and make my **s** nothing worth?	4405
Ps	19:2	Day unto day uttereth **s**, and night	562
Ps	19:3	There is no **s** nor language, where	562
Pr	7:21	With her much fair **s** she caused	3948
Pr	17:7	Excellent **s** becometh not a fool:	8193
SS	4:3	of scarlet, and thy **s** is comely:	4057
Jer	31:23	use this **s** in the land of Judah,	1697
Mt	26:73	them; for thy **s** bewrayeth thee	*2981*
Mk	7:32	and had an impediment in his **s**;	*3424*
Jn	8:43	**Why do ye not understand my s?**	*2981*
1Co	2:1	with excellency of **s** or of wisdom,	*3056*
1Co	2:4	my **s** and my preaching was not	*3056*
Col	4:6	Let your **s** be always with grace,	*3056*
Tit	2:8	Sound **s**, that cannot be condemned;	*3056*

SPEECHES

Nu	12:8	apparently, and not in dark **s**;	2420
Job	6:26	and the **s** of one that is desperate	561
Job	33:1	Job, I pray thee, hear my **s**, and	4405
Ro	16:18	fair **s** deceive the hearts of the	*2129*

SPEECHLESS

Mt	22:12	**wedding garment? And he was s**	*5392*
Lk	1:22	unto them, and remained **s**	*2974*

SPEED

1Sa	20:38	the lad, Make **s**, haste, stay not	4120
2Sa	15:14	make **s** to depart, lest he overtake	4116
Ezr	6:12	a decree; let it be done with **s**	629
2Jn	10	house, neither bid him God **s**	*5463*
2Jn	11	For he that biddeth him God **s** is	*5463*

SPEEDILY

Ge	44:11	they **s** took down every man his	4116
1Sa	27:1	I should **s** escape into the land of	4422
Ezr	7:21	shall require of you, it be done **s**,	629
Est	2:9	and he **s** gave her her things for	926
Ps	31:2	thine ear to me; deliver me **s**:	4120
Ps	69:17	for I am in trouble: hear me **s**	4118
Ps	102:2	in the day when I call answer me **s**	4118
Ecc	8:11	an evil work is not executed **s**,	4120
Zec	8:21	us go **s** to pray before the Lord	1980
Lk	18:8	**that he will avenge them s**	*1722, 5034*

SPEND

Dt	32:23	I will **s** mine arrows upon them	3615
Job	36:11	shall **s** their days in prosperity,	3615
Ps	90:9	we **s** our years as a tale that is	3615
2Co	12:15	I will very gladly **s** and be spent	*2259*

SPENDETH

Pr	21:20	wise; but a foolish man **s** it up	1104
Ecc	6:12	vain life which he **s** as a shadow?	6213

SPENT

Ge	21:15	And the water was **s** in the bottle,	3615
Ge	47:18	my lord, how that our money is **s**;	8552
1Sa	9:7	for the bread is **s** in our vessels,	235
Isa	49:4	I have **s** my strength for nought	3615
Mk	5:26	had **s** all that she had, and was	1159
Lk	8:43	which had **s** all her living upon	*4321*
Lk	15:14	**when he had s all, there arose a**	*1159*
Ro	13:12	The night is far **s**, the day is at	*4298*
2Co	12:15	gladly spend and be **s** for you;	*1550*

SPICE

Ex	35:28	**s**, and oil for the light, and for	1314
1Ki	10:15	of the traffick of the **s** merchants	7402
SS	5:1	gathered my myrrh with my **s**;	1313

SPICES

Ge	43:11	**s**, and myrrh, nuts, and almonds:	5219
Ex	25:6	**s** for anointing oil, and for sweet	1314
1Ki	10:2	with camels that bare **s**, and very	1314
SS	5:13	His cheeks are as a bed of **s**, as	1314
Mk	16:1	and Salome, had bought sweet **s**,	*759*
Lk	23:56	and prepared **s** and ointments;	*759*
Lk	24:1	bringing the **s** which they had	*759*
Jn	19:40	wound it in linen clothes with the **s**,	*759*

SPIDER

Pr	30:28	The **s** taketh hold with her hands,	8079

SPIDER'S

Job	8:14	and whose trust shall be a **s** web	5908
Isa	59:5	eggs, and weave the **s** web:	5908

SPIED

Ex	2:11	And he **s** an Egyptian smiting an	7200
Jos	6:22	men that had **s** out the country,	7270

SPIES

Ge	42:9	and said unto them, Ye are **s**;	7270
Ge	42:11	true men, thy servants are no **s**	7270
Ge	42:14	spake unto you, saying, Ye are **s**.	7270
Ge	42:31	We are true men; we are no **s**	7270
Ge	42:34	I know that ye are no **s**, but that	7270
Nu	21:1	Israel came by the way of the **s**;	871
Jos	6:23	young men that were **s** went in	7270
Lk	20:20	watched him, and sent forth **s**,	*1455*
Heb	11:31	when she had received the **s** with	*2685*

SPIKENARD

SS	4:13	pleasant fruits; camphire, with **s**,	5373
Mk	14:3	box of ointment of **s** very	*3487, 4101*
Jn	12:3	Mary a pound of ointment of **s**	*3487, 4101*

SPILLED

Mk	2:22	**the bottles, and the wine is s,**	*1632*
Lk	5:37	**will burst the bottles, and be s**	*1632*

SPIN

Ex	35:25	that were wise hearted did **s**	2901
Mt	6:28	**they toil not, neither do they s**	*3514*
Lk	12:27	**grow: they toil not, they s not;**	*3514*

SPIRIT

Ge	1:2	**S** of God moved upon the face of	7307
Ge	6:3	My **s** shall not always strive with	7307
Ge	41:38	is, a man in whom the **S** of God is?	7307
Ex	31:3	I have filled him with the **s** of God,	7307
Le	20:27	or woman that hath a familiar **s**,	178
Nu	11:17	take of the **s** which is upon thee,	7307
Nu	11:25	took of the **s** that was upon him,	7307
Nu	11:25	when the **s** rested upon them, they	7307
Nu	11:26	and the **s** rested upon them; and	7307
Nu	11:29	Lord would put his **s** upon them!	7307
Nu	27:18	of Nun, a man in whom is the **s**,	7307
Dt	2:30	the Lord thy God hardened his **s**,	7307
Jgs	6:34	**S** of the Lord came upon Gideon	7307
Jgs	13:25	**S** of the Lord began to move him	7307
Jgs	14:6	**S** of the Lord came mightily upon	7307
Jgs	14:19	the **S** of the Lord came upon him.	7307
Jgs	15:14	**S** of the Lord came mightily upon	7307
1Sa	1:15	I am a woman of a sorrowful **s**	7307
1Sa	11:6	And the **S** of God came upon Saul	7307
1Sa	16:13	**S** of the Lord came upon David	7307
1Sa	16:14	**S** of the Lord departed from Saul	7307
1Sa	16:14	evil **s** from the Lord troubled him	7307
1Sa	16:15	an evil **s** from God troubleth thee	7307
1Sa	16:23	the evil **s** from God was upon Saul,	7307
1Sa	16:23	and the evil **s** departed from him	7307
1Sa	19:20	**S** of God was upon the messengers	7307
1Sa	19:23	the **S** of God was upon him also	7307
1Sa	28:8	divine unto me by the familiar **s**,	178
1Ki	18:12	the **S** of the Lord shall carry thee	7307
2Ki	2:9	double portion of thy **s** be upon me	7307
2Ki	2:15	The **s** of Elijah doth rest on Elisha	7307
2Ki	2:16	**S** of the Lord hath taken him up,	7307
2Ch	18:20	Then there came out a **s**, and stood	7307
2Ch	18:21	be a lying **s** in the mouth of all his	7307
2Ch	18:23	Which way went the **S** of the Lord	7307
2Ch	24:20	the **S** of God came upon Zechariah	7307
Ezr	1:1	up the **s** of Cyrus king of Persia,	7307
Ezr	1:5	all them whose **s** God had raised,	7307
Ne	9:20	gavest also thy good **s** to instruct	7307
Job	7:11	I will speak in the anguish of my **s**;	7307
Job	10:12	visitation hath preserved my **s**.	7307
Job	15:13	that turnest thy **s** against God,	7307
Job	27:3	and the **s** of God is in my nostrils;	7307
Job	32:8	But there is a **s** in man: and the	7307
Job	33:4	The **S** of God hath made me, and	7307
Job	34:14	if he gather unto himself his **s** and	7307
Ps	31:5	Into thine hand I commit my **s**:	7307
Ps	32:2	and in whose **s** there is no guile	7307
Ps	34:18	saveth such as be of a contrite **s**	7307
Ps	51:10	and renew a right **s** within me	7307
Ps	51:11	and take not thy holy **s** from me.	7307
Ps	51:12	and uphold me with thy free **s**	7307
Ps	51:17	sacrifices of God are a broken **s**	7307
Ps	78:8	whose **s** was not stedfast with God	7307
Ps	139:7	Whither shall I go from thy **s**? or	7307
Pr	1:23	I will pour out my **s** unto you, I	7307
Pr	11:13	he that is of a faithful **s** concealeth	7307
Pr	15:13	sorrow of the heart the **s** is broken	7307
Pr	16:18	and an haughty **s** before a fall	7307
Pr	16:32	and he that ruleth his **s** than he	7307
Pr	18:14	but a wounded **s** who can bear?	7307
Pr	20:27	The **s** of man is the candle of the	5397
Pr	25:28	that hath no rule over his own **s**	7307
Pr	29:23	shall uphold the humble in **s**.	7307
Ecc	1:14	all is vanity and vexation of **s**	7307
Ecc	3:21	the **s** of man that goeth upward	7307
Ecc	7:8	and the patient in **s** is better	7307
Ecc	7:8	is better than the proud in **s**	7307
Ecc	7:9	Be not hasty in thy **s** to be angry:	7307
Ecc	12:7	and the **s** shall return unto God	7307
Isa	11:2	**s** of the Lord shall rest upon him,	7307
Isa	30:1	with a covering, but not of my **s**,	7307
Isa	40:13	hath directed the **S** of the Lord,	7307
Isa	42:1	I have put my **s** upon him: he shall	7307
Isa	44:3	I will pour my **s** upon thy seed,	7307
Isa	57:15	that is of a contrite and humble **s**,	7307
Isa	61:1	The **S** of the Lord God is upon me;	7307
Isa	63:11	he that put his holy **S** within him?	7307
Isa	65:14	and shall howl for vexation of **s**	7307
Isa	66:2	him that is poor and of a contrite **s**,	7307
Eze	1:12	whither the **s** was to go, they went;	7307
Eze	2:2	**s** entered into me when he spake	7307
Eze	3:12	Then the **s** took me up, and I heard	7307
Eze	11:5	the **S** of the Lord fell upon me	7307
Eze	11:19	and I will put a new **s** within you;	7307
Eze	18:31	make you a new heart and a new **s**.	7307
Eze	36:26	and a new **s** will I put within you:	7307
Eze	36:27	And I will put my **s** within you,	7307

Eze	37:14	And shall put my **s** in you, and ye	7307
Da	2:1	wherewith his **s** was troubled	7307
Da	2:3	**s** was troubled to know the dream	7307
Da	5:12	Forasmuch as an excellent **s**, and	7308
Da	5:14	that the **s** of the gods is in thee	7308
Da	6:3	because an excellent **s** was in him;	7308
Da	7:15	I Daniel was grieved in my **s** in the	7308
Joel	2:28	I will pour out my **s** upon all flesh;	7307
Joel	2:29	in those days will I pour out my **s**,	7307
Mic	2:7	is the **s** of the Lord straitened?	7307
Zec	4:6	might, nor by power, but by my **s**,	7307
Zec	7:12	sent in his **s** by the former prophets	7307
Zec	12:1	formeth the **s** of man within him	7307
Mt	3:16	he saw the **S** of God descending	*4151*
Mt	4:1	led up of the **s** into the wilderness	*4151*
Mt	5:3	**Blessed are the poor in s: for**	*4151*
Mt	10:20	**S of your Father which speaketh**	*4151*
Mt	14:26	were troubled, saying, It is a **s**;	*5326*
Mt	22:43	**doth David in s call him Lord,**	*4151*
Mt	26:41	**the s indeed is willing, but the**	*4151*
Mk	1:23	a man with an unclean **s**; and he	*4151*
Mk	2:8	Jesus perceived in his **s** that they	*4151*
Mk	5:8	**out of the man, thou unclean s.**	*4151*
Mk	8:12	And he sighed deeply in his **s**, and	*4151*
Mk	9:25	**Thou dumb and deaf s, I charge**	*4151*
Mk	14:38	**The s truly is ready, but the flesh**	*4151*
Lk	1:17	him in the **s** and power of Elias,	*4151*
Lk	1:47	And my **s** hath rejoiced in God my	*4151*
Lk	1:80	child grew, and waxed strong in **s**,	*4151*
Lk	2:27	came by the **S** into the temple:	*4151*
Lk	2:40	child grew, and waxed strong in **s**,	*4151*
Lk	4:1	led by the **S** into the wilderness,	*4151*
Lk	4:14	in the power of the **S** into Galilee:	*4151*
Lk	4:18	**The S of the Lord is upon me,**	*4151*
Lk	11:13	**Father give the Holy S to them**	*4151*
Lk	23:46	**into thy hands I commend my s.**	*4151*
Lk	24:37	supposed that they had seen a **s**	*4151*
Lk	24:39	**for a s hath not flesh and bones,**	*4151*
Jn	1:32	I saw the **S** descending from	*4151*
Jn	1:33	thou shalt see the **S** descending,	*4151*
Jn	3:5	**be born of water and of the S,**	*4151*
Jn	3:6	**that which is born of the S is s**	*4151*
Jn	3:8	**is every one that is born of the S**	*4151*
Jn	4:23	**shall worship the Father in s and**	*4151*
Jn	4:24	**God is a S: and they that worship**	*4151*
Jn	4:24	**him must worship him in s and**	*4151*
Jn	14:17	**Even the S of truth; whom the**	*4151*
Jn	15:26	**the S of truth, which proceedeth**	*4151*
Jn	16:13	**when he, the S of truth, is come,**	*4151*
Ac	2:4	as the **S** gave them utterance	*4151*
Ac	2:17	God, I will pour out of my **S** upon	*4151*
Ac	2:18	pour out in those days of my **S**;	*4151*
Ac	5:9	to tempt the **S** of the Lord?	*4151*
Ac	7:59	saying, Lord Jesus, receive my **s**.	*4151*
Ac	8:39	**S** of the Lord caught away Philip	*4151*
Ac	16:7	but the **S** suffered them not	*4151*
Ac	18:5	Paul was pressed in the **s**, and	*4151*
Ro	2:29	in the **s**, and not in the letter;	*4151*
Ro	7:6	we should serve in newness of **s**,	*4151*
Ro	8:1	not after the flesh, but after the **S**	*4151*
Ro	8:2	the law of the **S** of life in Christ	*4151*
Ro	8:4	not after the flesh, but after the **S**	*4151*
Ro	8:5	after the **S** the things of the **S**	*4151*
Ro	8:9	are not in the flesh, but in the **S**,	*4151*
Ro	8:9	be that the **S** of God dwell in you	*4151*
Ro	8:9	any man have not the **S** of Christ,	*4151*
Ro	8:10	**S** is life because of righteousness	*4151*
Ro	8:11	the **S** of him that raised up Jesus	*4151*
Ro	8:11	by his **S** that dwelleth in you	*4151*
Ro	8:14	many as are led by the **S** of God	*4151*
Ro	8:15	have not received the **s** of bondage	*4151*
Ro	8:15	have received the **S** of adoption,	*4151*
Ro	8:16	**S** itself beareth witness with our	*4151*
Ro	8:26	Likewise the **S** also helpeth our	*4151*
Ro	8:26	**S** itself maketh intercession for us	*4151*
Ro	8:27	knoweth what is the mind of the **S**.	*4151*
Ro	11:8	hath given them the **s** of slumber	*4151*
Ro	12:11	fervent in **s**; serving the Lord;	*4151*
1Co	2:10	revealed them unto us by his **S**:	*4151*
1Co	2:10	for the **S** searcheth all things, yea	*4151*
1Co	2:11	knoweth no man, but the **S** of God	*4151*
1Co	2:14	not the things of the **S** of God	*4151*
1Co	7:34	may be holy both in body and in **s**.	*4151*
1Co	12:3	no man speaking by the **S** of God	*4151*
1Co	12:4	diversities of gifts, but the same **S**.	*4151*
1Co	12:7	of the **S** is given to every man to	*4151*
1Co	12:8	one is given by the **S** the word of	*4151*
1Co	12:8	word of knowledge by the same **S**;	*4151*
1Co	12:9	To another faith by the same **S**;	*4151*
1Co	12:9	the gifts of healing by the same **S**;	*4151*
1Co	12:11	that one and the selfsame **S**	*4151*
1Co	12:13	by one **S** are we all baptized into	*4151*
1Co	12:13	been all made to drink into one **S**.	*4151*
2Co	1:22	and given the earnest of the **S** in	*4151*
2Co	3:3	but with the **S** of the living God;	*4151*
2Co	3:6	not of the letter, but of the **s**: for	*4151*
2Co	3:6	letter killeth, but the **s** giveth life	*4151*
2Co	3:17	Now the Lord is that **S**: and where	*4151*
2Co	3:17	where the **S** of the Lord is, there is	*4151*
Gal	3:2	Received ye the **S** by the works of	*4151*
Gal	3:14	might receive the promise of the **S**	*4151*
Gal	4:29	him that was born after the **S**,	*4151*
Gal	5:5	we through the **S** wait for the hope	*4151*
Gal	5:16	Walk in the **S**, and ye shall not	*4151*
Gal	5:17	For the flesh lusteth against the **S**,	*4151*
Gal	5:17	and the **S** against the flesh: and	*4151*
Gal	5:18	But if ye be led of the **S**, ye are not	*4151*
Gal	5:22	fruit of the **S** is love, joy, peace,	*4151*
Gal	5:25	If we live in the **S**, let us also walk	*4151*
Gal	6:1	such an one in the **s** of meekness;	*4151*
Gal	6:8	soweth to the **S** shall of the **S** reap	*4151*
Eph	1:13	sealed with that holy **S** of promise	*4151*
Eph	2:2	the **s** that now worketh in the	*4151*
Eph	2:18	access by one **S** unto the Father	*4151*
Eph	4:3	to keep the unity of the **S** in the	*4151*
Eph	4:4	There is one body, and one **S**,	*4151*
Eph	4:23	be renewed in the **s** of your mind;	*4151*
Eph	4:30	And grieve not the holy **S** of God,	*4151*
Eph	5:9	(For the fruit of the **S** is in all	*4151*
Eph	5:18	excess; but be filled with the **S**;	*4151*
Eph	6:17	the sword of the **S**, which is the	*4151*
Php	2:1	of love, if any fellowship of the **S**,	*4151*
1Th	5:19	Quench not the **S**	*4151*
1Th	5:23	your whole **s** and soul and body be	*4151*
2Th	2:13	through sanctification of the **S**	*4151*
1Ti	4:1	Now the **S** speaketh expressly	*4151*
2Ti	1:7	hath not given us the **s** of fear;	*4151*
Heb	4:12	the dividing asunder of soul and **s**	*4151*
Heb	9:14	who through the eternal **s** offered	*4151*
Jas	2:26	as the body without the **s** is dead,	*4151*
1Pe	1:11	**S** of Christ which was in them did	*4151*
1Pe	4:6	but live according to God in the **s**.	*4151*

1Jn	3:24	by the **S** which he hath given us	*4151*
1Jn	4:1	Beloved, believe not every **s**, but	*4151*
1Jn	4:2	Hereby know ye the **S** of God:	*4151*
1Jn	4:2	Every **s** that confesseth that Jesus	*4151*
1Jn	4:3	every **s** that confesseth not that	*4151*
1Jn	4:3	this is that **s** of antichrist, whereof	
1Jn	4:6	the **s** of truth, and the **s** of error	*4151*
1Jn	5:6	it is the **S** that beareth witness,	*4151*
1Jn	5:6	witness, because the **S** is truth	*4151*
1Jn	5:8	**s**, and the water, and the blood:	*4151*
Rev	1:10	I was in the **S** on the Lord's day,	*4151*
Rev	2:7	**S saith unto the churches;**	*4151*
Rev	4:2	And immediately I was in the **s**:	*4151*
Rev	17:3	So he carried me away in the **s**	*4151*
Rev	19:10	of Jesus is the **s** of prophecy	*4151*
Rev	22:17	the **S** and the bride say, Come	*4151*

SPIRITS

Le	20:6	turneth after such as have familiar **s**,	178
1Sa	28:3	put away those that had familiar **s**,	178
1Sa	28:9	cut off those that have familiar **s**,	178
Ps	104:4	Who maketh his angels **s**; his	7307
Pr	16:2	eyes; but the Lord weigheth the **s**	7307
Zec	6:5	are the four **s** of the heavens	7307
Mt	8:16	he cast out the **s** with his word	*4151*
Mt	10:1	gave them power against unclean **s**,	*4151*
Mt	12:45	**seven other s more wicked than**	*4151*
Mk	3:11	unclean **s**, when they saw him, fell	*4151*
Lk	10:20	**that the s are subject unto you;**	*4151*
Lk	11:26	**seven other s more wicked than**	*4151*
Ac	8:7	unclean **s**, crying with loud voice,	*4151*
Ac	19:12	and the evil **s** went out of them	*4151*
Ac	19:13	call over them which had evil **s**	*4151*
1Co	12:10	to another discerning of **s**; to	*4151*
1Ti	4:1	giving heed to seducing **s**, and	*4151*
Heb	1:7	Who maketh his angels **s**, and his	*4151*
Heb	12:9	in subjection unto the Father of **s**,	*4151*
Heb	12:23	to the **s** of just men made perfect	*4151*
1Pe	3:19	and preached unto the **s** in prison;	*4151*
1Jn	4:1	try the **s** whether they are of God:	*4151*
Rev	1:4	the seven **S** which are before his	*4151*
Rev	3:1	**he that hath the seven S of God,**	*4151*
Rev	4:5	which are the seven **S** of God	*4151*
Rev	5:6	which are the seven **S** of God sent	*4151*

SPIRITUAL

Hos	9:7	is a fool, the **s** man is mad	7307
Ro	1:11	may impart unto you some **s** gift,	*4152*
Ro	7:14	For we know that the law is **s**: but	*4152*
Ro	15:27	made partakers of their **s** things,	*4152*
1Co	2:13	comparing **s** things with **s**	*4152*
1Co	2:15	But he that is **s** judgeth all things,	*4151*
1Co	3:1	not speak unto you as unto **s**,	*4152*
1Co	10:3	And did all eat the same **s** meat;	*4151*
1Co	10:4	And did all drink the same **s** drink:	*4151*
1Co	10:4	drank of that **s** Rock that followed	*4151*
1Co	12:1	Now concerning **s** gifts, brethren, I	*4152*
1Co	14:1	after charity, and desire **s** gifts,	*4151*
1Co	14:12	as ye are zealous of **s** gifts, seek	*4151*
1Co	15:44	natural body; it is raised a **s** body	*4152*
1Co	15:44	natural body, and there is a **s** body	*4152*
1Co	15:46	that was not first which is **s**, but	*4151*
1Co	15:46	and afterward that which is **s**	*4152*
Gal	6:1	ye which are **s**, restore such an one	*4152*
Eph	5:19	in psalms and hymns and **s** songs,	*4152*
Eph	6:12	against **s** wickedness in high	*4152*
1Pe	2:5	stones, are built up a **s** house,	*4152*
1Pe	2:5	priesthood, to offer up **s** sacrifices,	*4152*

SPIRITUALLY

Ro	8:6	but to be **s** minded is life and	*3588, 4151*
1Co	2:14	because they are **s** discerned	*4153*
Rev	11:8	which **s** is called Sodom and Egypt,	*4153*

SPIT

Nu	12:14	her father had but **s** in her face,	3417
Job	30:10	me, and spare not to **s** in my face	7536
Mt	26:67	Then did they **s** in his face, and	*1716*
Mt	27:30	And they **s** upon him, and took the	*1716*
Mk	7:33	and he **s**, and touched his tongue;	*4429*
Mk	8:23	when he had **s** on his eyes, and put	*4429*
Mk	14:65	And some began to **s** on him, and to	*1716*
Mk	15:19	did **s** upon him, and bowing their	*1716*

SPITEFULLY

Mt	22:6	**servants, and entreated them s,**	*5195*
Lk	18:32	**shall be mocked, and s entreated,**	*5195*

SPITTING

Isa	50:6	hid not my face from shame and **s**	7536

SPITTLE

1Sa	21:13	let his **s** fall down upon his beard	7388
Jn	9:6	ground, and made clay of the **s**,	*4427*

SPOIL

Ex	3:22	and ye shall **s** the Egyptians	5337
Ex	15:9	will overtake, I will divide the **s**;	7998
Jos	8:2	only the **s** thereof, and the cattle	7998
Jos	8:27	**s** of that city Israel took for a prey	7998
1Sa	15:19	but didst fly upon the **s**, and didst	7998
1Sa	15:21	But the people took of the **s**, sheep	7998
1Ch	20:2	he brought also exceeding much **s**	7998
2Ch	25:13	thousand of them, and took much **s**	961
2Ch	28:15	with the **s** clothed all that were	7998
Ezr	9:7	to a **s**, and to confusion of face, as	961
Est	3:13	to take the **s** of them for a prey	7998
Job	29:17	and plucked the **s** out of his teeth	2964
Ps	119:162	word, as one that findeth great **s**	7998
Pr	16:19	than to divide the **s** with the proud	7998
Pr	22:23	and **s** the soul of those that spoiled	6906
Pr	24:15	righteous; **s** not his resting place;	7703
Pr	31:11	so that he shall have no need of **s**	7998
SS	2:15	the little foxes, that **s** the vines:	2254
Isa	42:24	Who gave Jacob for a **s**, and	4882
Isa	53:12	divide the **s** with the strong;	7998
Jer	5:6	wolf of the evenings shall **s** them	7703
Jer	47:4	for the Lord will **s** the Philistines	7703
Eze	26:5	it shall become a **s** to the nations	957
Da	11:24	among them the prey, and **s**, and	7998
Da	11:33	by captivity, and by **s**, many days	961
Mt	12:29	**man's house, and s his goods,**	*1283*
Mt	12:29	**man? and then he will s his**	*1283*
Col	2:8	Beware lest any man **s** you	*4812*

SPOILED

Ge	34:27	came upon the slain, and **s** the city,	962
Ge	34:29	**s** even all that was in the house	962
Ex	12:36	And they **s** the Egyptians	5337
Dt	28:29	be only oppressed and **s** evermore,	1497
2Ki	7:16	out, and **s** the tents of the Syrians	962
Job	12:17	He leadeth counselors away **s**,	7758
Job	12:19	He leadeth princes away **s**, and	7758
Pr	22:23	the soul of those that **s** them	6906

Jer	2:14	he a homeborn slave? why is he **s**?	957
Jer	9:19	heard out of Zion, How are we **s**!	7703
Jer	10:20	My tabernacle is **s**, and all my	7703
Zec	11:3	for their glory is **s**: a voice of the	7703
Zec	11:3	lions; for the pride of Jordan is **s**	7703
Col	2:15	having **s** principalities ... powers,	*554*

SPOILER

Isa	16:4	to them from the face of the **s**:	7703
Isa	16:4	the **s** ceaseth, the oppressors are	7701
Jer	6:26	the **s** shall suddenly come upon us	7703
Jer	51:56	Because the **s** is come upon her,	7703

SPOILERS

Jgs	2:14	the hands of **s** that spoiled them,	8154
1Sa	13:17	the **s** came out of the camp of the	7843
2Ki	17:20	them into the hand of **s**, until	8154
Jer	51:53	yet from me shall **s** come unto her,	7703

SPOILETH

Ps	35:10	the needy from him that **s** him?	1497
Na	3:16	the cankerworm **s**, and fleeth away	6584

SPOILING

Ps	35:12	evil for good to the **s** of my soul	7908
Heb	10:34	took joyfully the **s** of your goods,	*724*

SPOILS

Jos	7:21	among the **s** a goodly Babylonish	7998
Lk	11:22	**he trusted, and divideth his s**	*4661*
Heb	7:4	Abraham gave the tenth of the **s**	*205*

SPOKEN

Ge	12:4	as the Lord had **s** unto him;	1696
Ge	21:1	Lord did unto Sarah as he had **s**	1696
Ge	24:51	son's wife, as the Lord hath **s**	1696
Ge	41:28	thing ... I have **s** unto Pharaoh:	1696
Ge	44:2	to the word that Joseph had **s**	1696
Ex	4:30	which the Lord had **s** unto Moses,	1696
Ex	9:35	go; as the Lord had **s** by Moses	1696
Ex	19:8	All that the Lord hath **s** we will do	1696
Ex	32:13	all this land that I have **s** of will I	559
Nu	10:29	the Lord hath **s** good concerning	1696
Nu	21:7	for we have **s** against the Lord	1696
Nu	23:2	And Balak did as Balaam had **s**;	1696
Nu	23:17	unto him, What hath the Lord **s**?	1696
Nu	23:19	or hath he **s**, and shall he not make	1696
Dt	18:22	thing which the Lord hath not **s**,	1696
Dt	18:22	prophet hath **s** it presumptuously	1696
Dt	26:19	the Lord thy God, as he hath **s**	1696
Jos	6:8	when Joshua had **s** unto the people,	559
Jos	21:45	the Lord had **s** unto the house of	1696
Ru	2:13	for thou hast **s** friendly unto thine	1696
1Sa	1:16	and grief have I **s** hitherto	1696
2Sa	3:18	the Lord hath **s** of David, saying,	559
1Ki	13:3	is the sign which the Lord hath **s**;	1696
2Ki	1:17	of the Lord which Elijah had **s**	1696
2Ch	18:22	the Lord hath **s** evil against thee	1696
Ne	2:18	king's words that he had **s** unto me	559
Est	6:10	nothing fail of all ... thou hast **s**	1696
Est	7:9	who had **s** good for the king,	1696
Job	32:4	Elihu had waited till Job had **s**,	1697
Job	34:35	Job hath **s** without knowledge	1696
Job	42:7	Lord had **s** these words unto Job,	1696
Ps	50:1	God, even the Lord, hath **s**, and	1696
Ps	62:11	God hath **s** once; twice have I	1696
Ps	87:3	Glorious things are **s** of thee, O	1696
Pr	15:23	a word **s** in due season, how good	
Pr	25:11	word fitly **s** is like apples of gold	1696
Isa	1:20	for the mouth of the Lord hath **s** it	1696
Isa	21:17	the Lord God of Israel hath **s** it	1696
Isa	40:5	for the mouth of the Lord hath **s** it	1696
Isa	45:19	I have not **s** in secret, in a dark	1696
Isa	58:14	for the mouth of the Lord hath **s** it	1696
Jer	4:28	because I have **s** it, I have purposed	1696
Jer	23:35	and, What hath the Lord **s**?	1696
Jer	30:2	Write ... all the words that I have **s**	1696
Eze	5:13	I the Lord have **s** it in my zeal	1696
Eze	13:7	have ye not **s** a lying divination	1696
Eze	22:14	I the Lord have **s** it, and will do it	1696
Eze	24:14	I the Lord have **s** it: it shall come	1696
Eze	36:5	in the fire of my jealousy have I **s**	1696
Eze	38:19	and in the fire of my wrath have I **s**,	1696
Da	4:31	Nebuchadnezzar, to thee it is **s**;	560
Da	10:11	when he had **s** this word unto me	1696
Mt	1:22	which was **s** of the Lord by the	*4483*
Mt	2:17	which was **s** by Jeremy the prophet,	*4483*
Mt	2:23	which was **s** by the prophets	*4483*
Mt	3:3	that was **s** of by the prophet Esaias,	*4483*
Mt	22:31	**which was s unto you by God,**	*4483*
Mt	24:15	**s of by Daniel the prophet, stand**	*4483*
Mk	12:12	had **s** the parable against them:	*2036*
Mk	14:9	**be s of for a memorial of her**	*2980*
Lk	2:33	those things which were **s** of him	*2980*
Lk	2:34	for a sign which shall be **s** against;	*483*
Lk	24:25	**all that the prophets have s:**	*2980*
Lk	24:40	when he had thus **s**, he shewed	*2036*
Jn	4:50	word that Jesus had **s** unto him,	*2036*
Jn	9:6	When he had thus **s**, he spat on the	*2036*
Jn	12:49	**For I have not s of myself; but**	*2980*
Jn	16:25	**have I s unto you in proverbs:**	*2980*
Jn	18:23	**If I have s evil, bear witness of**	*2980*
Ac	2:16	which was **s** by the prophet Joel;	*2046*
Ac	3:21	God hath **s** by the mouth of all	*2980*
Ac	13:40	you, which is **s** of in the prophets;	*2046*
Ac	13:45	things which were **s** by Paul	*3004*
Ac	23:9	a spirit or an angel hath **s** to him,	*2980*
Ro	1:8	that your faith is **s** of throughout	*2605*
1Co	14:9	how shall it be known what is **s**?	*2980*
Heb	1:2	last days **s** unto us by his Son,	*2980*
Heb	2:2	word **s** by angels was stedfast,	*2980*
Heb	2:3	the first began to be **s** by the Lord,	*2980*
Heb	9:19	when Moses had **s** every precept	*2980*
Jas	5:10	who have **s** in the name of the	*2980*
2Pe	3:2	**s** before by the holy prophets	*4280*
Jude	17	were **s** before of the apostles	*4280*

SPOONS

Nu	7:86	the gold of the **s** was an hundred	3709
2Ch	4:22	and the **s**, and the censers, of pure	3709
2Ch	24:14	**s** and vessels of gold and silver	3709
Jer	52:18	the bowls, and the **s**, and all the	3709

SPORT

Jgs	16:25	Samson, that he may make us **s**	7832
Jgs	16:25	house; and he made them **s**:	6711
Jgs	16:27	that beheld while Samson made **s**	7832
Pr	10:23	It is as **s** to a fool to do mischief:	7814
Pr	26:19	neighbour, and saith, Am ... I in **s**?	7832

SPORTING

Ge	26:8	behold, Isaac was **s** with Rebekah	6711
2Pe	2:13	**s** themselves with their own	*1792*

SPOT

Le	13:4	If the bright **s** be white in the skin	934
Le	13:19	be a white rising, or a bright **s**,	934
Le	13:23	But if the bright **s** stay in his place	934
Nu	19:2	bring thee a red heifer without **s**,	8549
Nu	28:3	lambs of the first year without **s**	8549
Dt	32:5	their **s** is not … of his children:	3971
Job	11:15	thou lift up thy face without **s**;	3971
SS	4:7	fair, my love; there is no **s** in thee	3971
Eph	5:27	not having **s**, or wrinkle, or any	4696
Heb	9:14	offered himself without **s** to God	299
1Pe	1:19	without blemish and without **s**:	784
2Pe	3:14	found of him in peace, without **s**	784

SPOTS

Le	13:39	if the bright **s** in the skin of their	934
Jer	13:23	his skin, or the leopard his **s**?	2272
2Pe	2:13	**S** they are and blemishes,	*4696*
Jude	12	These are **s** in your feasts of	*4694*

SPOTTED

Ge	30:32	all the speckled and **s** cattle, and	2921
Ge	30:39	ringstraked, speckled, and **s**.	2921
Jude	23	even the garment **s** by the flesh	*4695*

SPOUSE

SS	4:8	with me from Lebanon, my **s**	3618
SS	4:11	Thy lips, O my **s**, drop as the	3618

SPOUSES

Hos	4:13	and your **s** shall commit adultery	3618
Hos	4:14	your **s** when they commit adultery;	3618

SPRANG

Mk	4:5	**and immediately it s up, because**	*1816*
Mk	4:8	**yield fruit that s up and increased,**	*305*
Lk	8:7	**and the thorns s up with it, and**	*4855*
Lk	8:8	**fell on good ground, and s up,**	*5453*
Heb	7:14	that our Lord **s** out of Juda; of	*393*
Heb	11:12	Therefore **s** there even of one, and	*1080*

SPREAD

Ge	10:18	of the Canaanites **s** abroad	6327
Ex	37:9	the cherubims **s** out their wings on	6566
Le	13:5	and the plague **s** not in the skin;	6581
Nu	4:11	altar they shall **s** a cloth of blue,	6566
Nu	4:13	altar, and **s** a purple cloth thereon:	6566
Jgs	8:25	And they **s** a garment, and did cast	6566
Ru	3:9	**s** therefore thy skirt over thine	6566
1Sa	30:16	were **s** abroad upon all the earth.	5203
1Ki	8:7	the cherubims **s** forth their two	6566
1Ki	8:22	**s** forth his hands toward heaven:	6566
1Ki	8:38	and **s** forth his hands toward this	6566
1Ki	8:54	with his hands **s** up to heaven	6566
2Ki	8:15	and **s** it on his face, so … he died:	6566
Ezr	9:5	**s** out my hands unto the Lord my	6566
Job	29:19	My root was **s** out by the waters,	6605
Job	37:18	thou with him **s** out the sky	7554
Ps	105:39	He **s** a cloud for a covering; and	6566
Ps	140:5	they have **s** a net by the wayside;	6566
Pr	1:17	Surely in vain the net is **s** in the	2219
Isa	14:11	the worm is **s** under thee, and the	3331
Isa	33:23	mast, they could not **s** the sail:	6566
Isa	58:5	to **s** sackcloth and ashes under	3331
Isa	65:2	I have **s** out my hands all the day	6566
Jer	8:2	they shall **s** them before the sun	7849
La	1:10	The adversary hath **s** out his hand	6566
La	1:13	he hath **s** a net for my feet, he hath	6566
Eze	12:13	My net also will I **s** upon him, and	6566
Zec	1:17	prosperity shall yet be **s** abroad;	6327
Zec	2:6	**s** you abroad as the four winds	6566
Mt	9:31	**s** abroad his fame in all that	*1310*
Mt	21:8	**s** their garments in the way;	*4766*
Mk	1:28	immediately his fame **s** abroad	*1831*
Ac	4:17	it **s** no further among the people,	*1268*
1Th	1:8	faith to God-ward is **s** abroad;	*1831*

SPREADETH

Le	13:8	the scab **s** in the skin, then the	6581
Dt	32:11	As an eagle … **s** abroad her wings	6566
Job	9:8	Which alone **s** out the heavens	5186
Job	36:30	Behold, he **s** his light upon it.	6566
Pr	29:5	his neighbour **s** a net for his feet.	6566
Isa	25:11	that swimmeth **s** forth his hands	6566
Isa	44:24	**s** abroad the earth by myself;	7554
La	1:17	Zion **s** forth her hands, and there	6566

SPREADING

Le	13:57	thing of skin; it is a **s** plague:	6524
Ps	37:35	**s** himself like a green bay tree	6168
Eze	26:5	be a place for the **s** of nets in the	4894

SPRING

Nu	21:17	sang this song, **S** up, O well;	5927
Jgs	19:25	when the day began to **s**, they let	5927
1Sa	9:26	to pass about the **s** of the day	5927
Job	38:27	bud of the tender herb to **s** forth?	6779
Ps	85:11	Truth shall **s** out of the earth; and	6779
Ps	92:7	When the wicked **s** as the grass,	6524
Isa	45:8	let righteousness **s** up together;	6779
Isa	58:11	like a **s** of water, whose waters	4161
Isa	61:11	and praise to **s** forth before all the	6779
Mk	4:27	**and the seed should s and grow up,**	*985*

SPRINGETH

1Ki	4:33	the hyssop that **s** out of the wall:	3318
Hos	10:4	thus judgment **s** up as hemlock	6524

SPRINGING

Ge	26:19	and found there a well of **s** water	2416
Jn	4:14	**of water s up into everlasting life**	*242*
Heb	12:15	lest any root of bitterness **s** up	*5453*

SPRINGS

Dt	4:49	the plain, under the **s** of Pisgah	794
Jos	15:19	land; give me also **s** of water	1543
Jos	15:19	her the upper **s**, and the nether **s**	1543
Ps	104:10	He sendeth the **s** into the valleys,	4599
Isa	49:10	**s** of water shall he guide them	4002
Jer	51:36	up her sea, and make her **s** dry	4726

SPRINKLE

Ex	9:8	let Moses **s** it toward the heaven	2236
Ex	29:16	and **s** it round about the altar	2236
Ex	29:20	**s** the blood upon the altar round	2236
Ex	29:21	**s** it upon Aaron, and upon his	5137
Le	4:6	**s** of the blood seven times before	5137
Le	4:17	**s** it seven times before the Lord	5137
Le	14:7	**s** upon him that is to be cleansed	5137
Le	16:15	and **s** it upon the mercy seat, and	5137
Isa	52:15	So shall he **s** many nations; the	5137

SPRINKLED

Ex	9:10	Moses **s** it up toward heaven;	2236
Ex	24:6	half of the blood he **s** on the altar.	2236
Ex	24:8	the blood, and **s** it on the people,	2236
Le	8:11	he **s** … upon the altar seven times,	5137

Le 8:19 and Moses **s** the blood upon 2236
Le 8:30 **s** it upon Aaron, and upon his 5137
Le 9:12 he **s** round about upon the altar 2236
2Ki 9:33 of her blood was **s** on the wall 5137
Job 2:12 **s** dust upon their heads toward 2236
Heb 9:19 and **s** both the book, and all the *4473*
Heb 9:21 **s** with blood both the tabernacle *4473*
Heb 10:22 hearts **s** from an evil conscience *4473*

SPRINKLING
Heb 11:28 the passover, and the **s** of blood, ... *4378*
Heb 12:24 to the blood of **s**, that speaketh *4473*
1Pe 1:2 and **s** of the blood of Jesus Christ: *4473*

SPRUNG
Ge 41:6 the east wind **s** up after them 6779
Ge 41:23 the east wind, **s** up after them: 6779
Le 13:42 a leprosy **s** up in his bald head 6524
Mt 13:5 **and forthwith they s up, because** *1816*
Mt 13:7 **the thorns s up, and choked them:** *305*
Mt 13:26 **But when the blade was s up, and** *985*

SPUE
Le 20:22 to dwell therein, **s** you not out 6958
Rev 3:16 **I will s thee out of my mouth** *1692*

SPUNGE
Mt 27:48 a **s**, and filled it with vinegar, ... *4699*
Mk 15:36 ran and filled a **s** full of vinegar *4699*
Jn 19:29 and they filled a **s** with vinegar, ... *4699*

SPY See also ESPIED; ESPY.
Nu 13:16 Moses sent to **s** out the land 8446
Nu 13:17 Moses sent them to **s** out the land 8446
Jos 6:25 Joshua sent to **s** out Jericho 7270
2Sa 10:3 to search the city, and to **s** it out, ... 7270
Gal 2:4 came in privily to **s** out our liberty *2684*

STABLE
1Ch 16:30 the world also shall be **s**, that it 3559
Eze 25:5 will make Rabbah a **s** for camels, ... 5116

STABLISH See also ESTABLISH.
2Sa 7:13 I will **s** the throne of his kingdom 3559
Est 9:21 To **s** this among them, that they 6965
Ps 119:38 **S** thy word unto thy servant, who 6965
1Th 3:13 To the end he may **s** your hearts *4741*
2Th 2:17 and **s** you in every good word and *4741*
Jas 5:8 Be ye also patient; **s** your hearts: *4741*
1Pe 5:10 make you perfect, **s**, strengthen, ... *4741*

STABLISHED See also ESTABLISHED.
Ps 148:6 He hath also **s** them for ever and 5975
Col 2:7 and **s** in the faith, as ye have been *950*

STABLISHETH See also ESTABLISHETH.
Hab 2:12 blood, and **s** a city by iniquity! 3559
2Co 1:21 he which **s** us with you in Christ, ... *950*

STAFF See also STAVES.
Ge 38:18 and thy **s** that is in thine hand 4294
Ge 38:25 the signet, and bracelets, and **s** 4294
Ex 12:11 feet, and your **s** in your hand: 4731
Nu 13:23 bare it between two upon a **s**; 4132
Jgs 6:21 put forth the end of the **s** that was 4938
1Sa 17:7 And the **s** of his spear was like a 2671
1Sa 17:40 And he took his **s** in his hand, and 4731
2Sa 23:7 with iron and the **s** of a spear; 6086
2Ki 4:29 lay my **s** upon the face of the child 4938
2Ki 4:31 and laid the **s** upon the face of the 4938
1Ch 20:5 spear **s** was like a weaver's beam. 6086
Ps 23:4 rod and thy **s** they comfort me 4938
Ps 105:16 he brake the whole **s** of bread 4294
Isa 36:6 Lo, thou trustest in the **s** of this 4938
Eze 4:16 I will break the **s** of bread in 4294
Zec 11:10 And I took my **s**, even Beauty 4731
Zec 11:14 Then I cut asunder mine other **s**, ... 4731
Mk 6:8 for their journey, save a **s** only; *4464*
Heb 11:21 leaning upon the top of his **s** *4464*

STAGGER
Job 12:25 them to **s** like a drunken man. 8582
Ps 107:27 fro, and **s** like a drunken man 5128

STAGGERED
Ro 4:20 He **s** not at the promise of God *1252*

STAIN
Job 3:5 and the shadow of death **s** it; 1350
Isa 63:3 and I will **s** all my raiment 1351

STAIRS
2Ki 9:13 it under him on the top of the **s**, ... 4609
Ne 12:37 up by the **s** of the city of David 4609
Ac 21:35 And when he came upon the **s**, so *304*
Ac 21:40 Paul stood on the **s**, and beckoned *304*

STALK
Ge 41:5 ears of corn came up upon one **s**, ... 7070
Ge 41:22 seven ears came up in one **s**, full 7070

STALL
Am 6:4 calves out of the midst of the **s**; 4770
Mal 4:2 and grow up as calves of the **s** 4770
Lk 13:15 **loose his ox or his ass from the s,** *5396*

STAMMERING
Isa 28:11 with **s** lips and another tongue 3934
Isa 33:19 of a **s** tongue, that thou canst not 3932

STAMP
2Sa 22:43 I did **s** them as the mire of the 1854
Eze 6:11 thine hand, and **s** with thy foot, ... 7554

STAMPED
Dt 9:21 and burnt it with fire, and **s** it, ... 3807
2Ki 23:6 **s** it small to powder, and cast the 1854
2Ki 23:15 **s** it small to powder, and burned 1854
2Ch 15:16 Asa cut down her idol, and **s** it, ... 1854
Da 7:7 **s** the residue with the feet of it: 7512
Da 7:19 and **s** the residue with his feet; 7512

STAND
Ge 19:9 And they said, **S** back. And they 5066
Ex 7:15 thou shalt **s** by the river's brink 5324
Ex 8:20 morning, and **s** before Pharaoh; 3320
Ex 14:13 Fear ye not, **s** still, and see the 3320
Ex 33:10 cloudy pillar **s** at the tabernacle 5975
Ex 33:21 me, and thou shalt **s** upon a rock: 5324
Le 26:37 power to **s** before your enemies 8617
Nu 9:8 **S** still, and I will hear what the 5975
Dt 7:24 no man be able to **s** before thee 3320
Dt 9:2 can **s** before the children of Anak! 3320
Dt 10:8 to **s** before the Lord to minister 5975
Dt 11:25 no man be able to **s** before you: 3320
Jos 1:5 not any man be able to **s** before 3320
Jos 3:8 Jordan, ye shall **s** still in Jordan 5975
Jos 10:8 not a man of them **s** before thee 5975

Jos	10:12	Sun, **s** thou still upon Gibeon;	1826
Jos	23:9	man hath been able to **s** before you	5975
1Sa	6:20	Who is able to **s** before this holy	5975
1Sa	12:7	Now therefore **s** still, that I may	3320
1Sa	16:22	Let David, I pray thee, **s** before me;	5975
1Ki	1:2	and let her **s** before the king, and	5975
1Ki	17:1	of Israel liveth, before whom I **s**,	5975
1Ki	18:15	of hosts liveth, before whom I **s**,	5975
2Ki	6:31	if the head of Elisha ... **s** on him	5975
2Ch	20:17	**s** ye still, and see the salvation of	5975
Ne	9:5	**S** up and bless the Lord your God	6965
Est	3:4	Mordecai's matters would **s**:	5975
Est	8:11	and to **s** for their life, to destroy	5975
Job	19:25	he shall **s** at the latter day upon	6965
Ps	1:5	the ungodly shall not **s** in the	6965
Ps	24:3	or who shall **s** in his holy place?	6965
Ps	109:6	and let Satan **s** at his right hand	5975
Ps	109:31	he shall **s** at the right hand of the	5975
Ps	111:8	They **s** fast for ever and ever, and	5564
Ps	130:3	iniquities, O Lord, who shall **s**?	5975
Ps	135:2	Ye that **s** in the house of the Lord	5975
Pr	22:29	business? he shall **s** before kings:	3320
Pr	22:29	he shall not **s** before mean men	3320
Pr	27:4	but who is able to **s** before envy?	5975
Ecc	8:3	of his sight: **s** not in an evil thing;	5975
Isa	11:10	**s** for an ensign of the people;	5975
Isa	21:8	I **s** ... upon the watchtower	5975
Isa	28:18	agreement with hell shall not **s**;	6965
Isa	40:8	word of our God shall **s** for ever	6965
Isa	51:17	awake, **s** up, O Jerusalem, which	6965
Jer	7:2	**S** in the gate of the Lord's house	5975
Jer	26:2	**S** in the court of the Lord's house	5975
Jer	35:19	want a man to **s** before me for ever	5975
Eze	22:30	**s** in the gap before me for the land,	5975
Da	1:4	in them to **s** in the king's palace	5975
Da	1:5	they might **s** before the king	5975
Da	2:44	kingdoms, and it shall **s** for ever	6966
Da	7:4	and made **s** upon the feet as a man,	6966
Da	8:4	that no beasts might **s** before him	5975
Da	8:7	there was no power in the ram to **s**	5975
Da	8:22	four kingdoms shall **s** up out of the	5975
Da	8:23	dark sentences, shall **s** up	5975
Da	8:25	shall also **s** up against the Prince	5975
Da	11:2	there shall **s** up yet three kings in	5975
Da	11:3	And a mighty king shall **s** up, that	5975
Da	11:6	neither shall he **s**, nor his arm:	5975
Da	11:7	branch of her roots shall one **s** up	5975
Da	11:16	and he shall **s** in the glorious land,	5975
Da	11:17	she shall not **s** on his side, neither	5975
Da	12:1	And at that time shall Michael **s** up,	5975
Da	12:13	**s** in thy lot at the end of the days	5975
Mal	3:2	who shall **s** when he appeareth?	5975
Mt	12:25	**divided against itself shall not s**	*2476*
Mt	12:26	**how shall then his kingdom s?**	*2476*
Mt	12:47	mother and thy brethren **s** without	*2476*
Mt	20:6	**Why s ye here all the day idle?**	*2476*
Mk	3:3	had the withered hand, **S forth**	*1453*
Mk	3:26	**and be divided, he cannot s, but**	*2476*
Mk	11:25	**And when ye s praying, forgive,**	*4739*
Lk	6:8	**Rise up, and s forth in the midst**	*2476*
Jn	11:42	**of the people which s by I said it,**	*4026*
Ac	1:11	why **s** ye gazing up into heaven?	*2476*
Ac	8:38	commanded the chariot to **s** still:	*2476*
Ac	10:26	**S** up; I myself also am a man	*450*
Ac	26:16	**But rise, and s upon thy feet: for**	*2476*
Ro	5:2	faith into this grace wherein we **s**,	*2476*
Ro	14:4	up: for God is able to make him **s**.	*2476*
1Co	2:5	should not **s** in the wisdom of men,	*1510*
2Co	1:24	of your joy; for by faith ye **s**.	*2476*
Gal	5:1	**S** fast therefore in the liberty	*4739*
Eph	6:11	may be able to **s** against the wiles	*2476*
Eph	6:13	evil day, and having done all, to **s**	*2476*
Eph	6:14	**S** therefore, having your loins girt	*2476*
Col	4:12	ye may **s** perfect and complete in	*2476*
Jas	2:3	**S** thou there, or sit here under	*2476*
Rev	3:20	**I s at the door, and knock:**	*2476*
Rev	6:17	come; and who shall be able to **s**?	*2476*
Rev	20:12	I saw the dead, ... **s** before God;	*2476*

STANDARD

Nu	1:52	and every man by his own **s**,	1714
Nu	2:2	of Israel shall pitch by his own **s**,	1714
Isa	49:22	and set up my **s** to the people:	5251
Isa	59:19	Spirit of the Lord shall lift up a **s**	5127
Isa	62:10	stones; lift up a **s** for the people	5251
Jer	4:6	Set up the **s** toward Zion: retire,	5251

STANDEST

Ex	3:5	the place whereon thou **s** is holy	5975
Jos	5:15	the place whereon thou **s** is holy	5975
Ac	7:33	for the place where thou **s** is holy	*2476*
Ro	11:20	broken off, and thou **s** by faith	*2476*

STANDETH

Nu	14:14	and that thy cloud **s** over them,	5975
Dt	1:38	son of Nun, which **s** before thee,	5975
Jgs	16:26	pillars whereupon the house **s**,	3559
Est	6:5	Behold, Haman **s** in the court	5975
Est	7:9	gallows ... **s** in the house of Haman	5975
Ps	1:1	nor **s** in the way of sinners, nor	5975
Ps	33:11	The counsel of the Lord **s** for ever,	5975
Pr	8:2	She **s** in the top of high places, by	5324
SS	2:9	he **s** behind our wall, he looketh	5975
Isa	3:13	The Lord **s** up to plead	5324
Isa	59:14	backward, and justice **s** afar off:	5975
Jn	1:26	but there **s** one among you, whom	*2476*
1Co	10:12	let him that thinketh he **s** take	*2476*
2Ti	2:19	the foundation of God **s** sure	*2476*
Heb	10:11	every priest **s** daily ministering	*2476*

STANDING

Le	26:1	neither rear you up a **s** image,	4676
Nu	22:23	angel of the Lord **s** in the way,	5324
Nu	22:31	angel of the Lord **s** in the way,	5324
1Sa	19:20	Samuel **s** as appointed over them	5975
2Ch	18:18	the host of heaven **s** on his right	5975
Est	5:2	Esther the queen **s** in the court,	5975
Ps	114:8	turned the rock into a **s** water	98
Da	8:6	I had seen **s** before the river	5975
Am	9:1	I saw the Lord **s** upon the altar	5324
Zec	3:1	Satan **s** at his right hand to resist	5975
Mt	6:5	**to pray s in the synagogues**	*2476*
Mt	16:28	**There be some s here, which shall**	*2476*
Mt	20:3	**others s idle in the marketplace**	*2476*
Mt	20:6	**went out, and found others s idle,**	*2476*
Mk	13:14	**desolation, ... s where it ought not,**	*2476*
Lk	1:11	**s** on the right side of the altar of	*2476*
Lk	18:13	**publican, s afar off, would not**	*2476*
Jn	19:26	disciple **s** by, whom he loved	*3936*
Jn	20:14	herself back, and saw Jesus **s**,	*2476*
Ac	2:14	Peter, **s** up with the eleven, lifted	*2476*
Ac	4:14	the man which was healed **s** with	*2476*
Ac	7:55	Jesus **s** on the right hand of God	*2476*

Ac	7:56	Son of man **s** on the right hand of	*2476*
Rev	7:1	four angels **s** on the four corners	*2476*
Rev	18:10	**S** afar off for ... fear of her torment,	*2476*
Rev	19:17	And I saw an angel **s** in the sun;	*2476*

STANK

Ex	7:21	and the river **s**, and the Egyptians.	887
Ex	8:14	upon heaps: and the land **s**	887
Ex	16:20	morning, and it bred worms, and **s**:	887

STAR

Nu	24:17	shall come a **S** out of Jacob, and	3556
Mt	2:2	for we have seen his **s** in the east	*792*
Mt	2:7	what time the **s** appeared	*792*
Mt	2:9	the **s**, which they saw in the east,	*792*
Mt	2:10	When they saw the **s**, they rejoiced	*792*
1Co	15:41	differeth from another **s** in glory	*792*
2Pe	1:19	and the day **s** arise in your hearts:	*5459*
Rev	2:28	**And I will give him the morning s**	*792*
Rev	8:10	there fell a great **s** from heaven,.	*792*
Rev	8:11	name of the **s** is called Wormwood:	*792*
Rev	9:1	I saw a **s** fall from heaven unto the	*792*
Rev	22:16	**and the bright and morning s.**	*792*

STARS

Ge	1:16	the night: he made the **s** also	3556
Ge	15:5	now toward heaven, and tell the **s**,	3556
Ge	22:17	thy seed as the **s** of the heaven,	3556
Ge	26:4	seed to multiply as the **s** of heaven,	3556
Ge	37:9	eleven **s** made obeisance to me	3556
Ex	32:13	your seed as the **s** of heaven, and	3556
Dt	1:10	as the **s** of heaven for multitude	3556
Dt	4:19	the sun, and the moon, and the **s**	3556
Dt	28:62	ye were as the **s** of heaven for	3556
Jgs	5:20	the **s** in their courses fought	3556
1Ch	27:23	Israel like to the **s** of the heavens	3556
Ne	4:21	the morning till the **s** appeared.	3556
Job	3:9	Let the **s** of the twilight ... be dark;	3556
Job	25:5	yea, the **s** are not pure in his sight,	3556
Job	38:7	When the morning **s** sang together,	3556
Ps	8:3	the moon and the **s**, which thou	3556
Ps	136:9	The moon and **s** to rule by night:	3556
Ps	147:4	He telleth the number of the **s**;	3556
Isa	14:13	will exalt my throne above the **s**	3556
Jer	31:35	and of the **s** for a light by night.	3556
Da	12:3	as the **s** for ever and ever	3556
Joel	2:10	the **s** shall withdraw their shining:	3556
Joel	3:15	the **s** shall withdraw their shining.	3556
Am	5:8	Seek him that maketh the seven **s**.	3598
Mt	24:29	**and the s shall fall from heaven,**	*792*
Lk	21:25	**and in the moon, and in the s;**	*798*
Heb	11:12	as the **s** of the sky in multitude,	*798*
Jude	13	wandering **s**, to whom is reserved.	*792*
Rev	1:16	he had in his right hand seven **s**:	*792*
Rev	1:20	**The mystery of the seven s which**	*792*
Rev	1:20	**seven s are the angels of the seven**	*792*
Rev	2:1	**he that holdeth the seven s in his**	*792*
Rev	3:1	**Spirits of God, and the seven s;**	*792*
Rev	6:13	the **s** of heaven fell unto the earth,	*792*
Rev	8:12	moon, and the third part of the **s**;	*792*
Rev	12:1	upon her head a crown of twelve **s**:	*792*
Rev	12:4	the third part of the **s** of heaven,.	*792*

STATE See also ESTATE.

Est	1:7	according to the **s** of the king.	3027
Est	2:18	according to the **s** of the king	3027
Ps	39:5	at his best **s** is altogether vanity.	5324
Pr	27:23	to know the **s** of thy flocks, and	6440
Isa	22:19	and from thy **s** shall he pull thee.	4612
Mt	12:45	**the last s of that man is worse than**	
Php	2:19	comfort, when I know your **s**	*3588, 4012*
Php	2:20	will naturally care for your **s**	*3588, 4012*
Php	4:11	in whatsoever **s** I am, therewith to	

STATURE

Nu	13:32	we saw in it are men of a great **s**.	4060
1Sa	16:7	or on the height of his **s**; because	6967
1Ch	20:6	Gath, where was a man of great **s**,	4060
SS	7:7	This thy **s** is like to a palm tree,.	6967
Mt	6:27	**can add one cubit unto his s?**	2244
Lk	2:52	Jesus increased in wisdom and **s**,	*2244*
Lk	19:3	press, because he was little of **s**	*2244*
Eph	4:13	unto the measure of the **s** of the	*2244*

STATUTE

Ex	15:25	there he made for them a **s** and	2706
Ex	27:21	it shall be a **s** for ever unto their	2708
Ex	29:9	shall be theirs for a perpetual **s**:	2708
Ex	30:21	and it shall be a **s** for ever to them,.	2706
Le	23:41	It shall be a **s** for ever in your	2708
Le	24:9	made by fire by a perpetual **s**	2706
Nu	27:11	children of Israel a **s** of judgment,	2708
Nu	35:29	things shall be for a **s** of judgment	2708
Jos	24:25	set them a **s** and an ordinance in	2706
1Sa	30:25	he made it a **s** and an ordinance.	2706
Da	6:7	together to establish a royal **s**,	7010
Da	6:15	no decree nor **s** which the king.	7010

STATUTES

Ge	26:5	my commandments, my **s**, and my	2708
Ex	15:26	commandments, and keep ... his **s**,	2706
Le	10:11	all the **s** which the Lord hath.	2706
Le	18:5	Ye shall therefore keep my **s**, and	2708
Le	26:3	If ye walk in my **s**, and keep my	2708
Le	26:43	because their soul abhorred my **s**	2708
Dt	4:8	that hath **s** and judgments so	2706
Dt	6:1	are the commandments, the **s**, and.	2706
Dt	6:2	all his **s** and his commandments,	2708
Dt	6:20	mean the testimonies, and the **s**,.	2706
Dt	6:24	commanded us to do all these **s**,.	2706
Dt	11:1	and keep his charge, and his **s**,	2708
Dt	17:19	the words of this law and these **s**,	2706
Dt	26:16	hath commanded thee to do these **s**.	2706
2Sa	22:23	as for his **s**, I did not depart from.	2708
1Ki	3:3	walking in the **s** of David his.	2708
1Ki	11:11	not kept my covenant and my **s**,.	2708
2Ki	17:8	And walked in the **s** of the heathen,	2708
2Ki	17:15	And they rejected his **s**, and his.	2706
2Ki	23:3	his testimonies and his **s** with all	2708
2Ch	7:19	if ye turn away, and forsake my **s**	2708
2Ch	33:8	to the whole law and the **s** and	2706
Ezr	7:10	to teach in Israel **s** and judgments	2706
Ne	1:7	kept the commandments, nor the **s**,	2706
Ne	9:13	laws, good **s** and commandments:	2706
Ps	18:22	I did not put away his **s** from me	2708
Ps	19:8	the **s** of the Lord are right,.	6490
Ps	119:8	I will keep thy **s**: O forsake me not.	2706
Ps	119:12	art thou, O Lord: teach me thy **s**.	2706
Ps	119:48	loved; and I will meditate in thy **s**.	2706
Ps	119:54	Thy **s** have been my songs in the	2706
Ps	119:83	smoke; yet do I not forget thy **s**.	2706
Ps	119:112	mine heart to perform thy **s** alway,.	2706
Jer	44:10	nor in my **s**, that I set before you	2708
Jer	44:23	nor in his **s**, nor in his testimonies;	2708

Eze 11:20 That they may walk in my **s**, and 2708
Eze 20:11 And I gave them my **s**, and shewed 2708
Eze 20:16 walked not in my **s**, but polluted 2708
Eze 20:25 gave them ... **s** that were not good, ... 2706
Eze 33:15 walk in the **s** of life, without 2708
Eze 36:27 cause you to walk in my **s**, and ye.... 2706
Mal 4:4 Israel, with the **s** and judgments.... 2706

STAVES

Ex 25:13 thou shalt make **s** of shittim wood, ... 905
Ex 25:13 **s** into the rings by the sides of the ark ... 905
Ex 27:6 and thou shalt make **s** for the altar, ... 905
Ex 27:7 the **s** shall be put into the rings, ... 905
Ex 30:4 for places for the **s** to bear it withal.... 905
Ex 35:12 the ark, and the **s** thereof, with the.... 905
Ex 35:13 The table, and his **s**, and all his 905
Ex 40:20 the ark, and set the **s** on the ark 905
1Sa 17:43 that thou comest to me with **s**?.... 4731
1Ki 8:7 covered the ark and the **s** thereof 905
1Ki 8:8 they drew out the **s**, that the ends.... 905
1Ki 8:8 **s** were seen out in the holy place.... 905
Zec 11:7 I took unto me two **s**; the one I 4731
Mt 10:10 **coats, neither shoes, nor yet s** *4464*
Mt 26:47 great multitude with swords and **s**, ... *3586*
Mt 26:55 **against a thief with swords and s** *3586*
Lk 9:3 **your journey, neither s, nor scrip,** *4464*
Lk 22:52 **against a thief, with swords and s?** *3586*

STAY

Ge 19:17 neither **s** thou in all the plain;.... 5975
Ex 9:28 let you go, and ye shall **s** no longer. 5975
Ru 1:13 would ye **s** for them from having.... 5702
1Sa 15:16 **S**, and I will tell thee what the.... 7503
2Sa 22:19 calamity: but the Lord was my **s**.... 4937
2Sa 24:16 It is enough: **s** now thine hand 7503
Job 38:37 who can **s** the bottles of heaven,.... 7901
Ps 18:18 calamity: but the Lord was my **s**.... 4937
Pr 28:17 flee to the pit; let no man **s** him.... 8551
SS 2:5 **S** me with flagons, comfort me.... 5564
Isa 10:20 shall **s** upon the Lord, the Holy.... 8172
Isa 31:1 **s** on horses, and trust in chariots,.... 8172
Da 4:35 none can **s** his hand, or say unto 4223

STAYED

Ge 32:4 with Laban, and **s** there until now:.... 309
Ex 17:12 Aaron and Hur **s** up his hands,.... 8551
Nu 25:8 plague was **s** from the children of.... 6113
Jos 10:13 the sun stood still, and the moon **s**, ... 5975
2Sa 24:21 plague may be **s** from the people 6113
2Sa 24:25 and the plague was **s** from Israel.... 6113
2Ki 4:6 not a vessel more. And the oil **s**.... 5975
2Ch 18:34 king ... **s** himself up in his chariot.... 5975
Job 38:11 here shall thy proud waves be **s**?.... 7896
Ps 106:30 and so the plague was **s** 6113
Isa 26:3 peace, whose mind is **s** on thee: 5564
Eze 31:15 and the great waters were **s**:.... 3607

STAYS

1Ki 10:19 and two lions stood beside the **s**.... 3027

STEAD

Ge 22:13 burnt offering in the **s** of his son 8478
Ge 30:2 Am I in God's **s**, who hath withheld 8478
Ge 36:37 died, and Saul ... reigned in his **s**.... 8478
Le 6:22 his sons that is anointed in his **s**.... 8478
Le 16:32 the priest's office in his father's **s**, ... 8478
Jos 5:7 whom he raised up in their **s**.... 8478
2Sa 16:8 Saul, in whose **s** thou hast reigned; 8478
1Ki 1:30 shall sit upon my throne in my **s** 8478
1Ki 11:43 Rehoboam his son reigned in his **s**.... 8478
1Ki 14:27 Rehoboam made in their **s** brasen 8478
2Ki 16:20 Hezekiah his son reigned in his **s** 8478
2Ki 21:24 made Josiah his son king in his **s** 8478
2Ki 21:26 Josiah his son reigned in his **s**.... 8478
1Ch 29:28 Solomon his son reigned in his **s** 8478
2Ch 1:8 and hast made me to reign in his **s**.... 8478
2Ch 9:31 Rehoboam his son reigned in his **s**.... 8478
2Ch 28:27 Hezekiah his son reigned in his **s** 8478
2Ch 33:25 made Josiah his son king in his **s** 8478
Job 16:4 if your soul were in my soul's **s**, I 8478
Job 34:24 number, and set others in their **s** 8478
Pr 11:8 and the wicked cometh in his **s**.... 8478
Ecc 4:15 child that shall stand up in his **s** 8478
2Co 5:20 we pray you in Christ's **s**, be ye *5228*
Phm 13 in they **s** he might have ministered.... *5228*

STEAL

Ge 31:27 secretly, and **s** away from me; 1589
Ex 20:15 Thou shalt not **s** 1589
Ex 22:1 If a man shall **s** an ox, or a sheep,.... 1589
Le 19:11 Ye shall not **s**, neither deal falsely 1589
Dt 5:19 Neither shalt thou **s** 1589
Pr 6:30 if he **s** to satisfy his soul when he 1589
Pr 30:9 or lest I be poor, and **s**, and take.... 1589
Mt 6:19 **thieves break through and s** *2813*
Mt 6:20 **do not break through nor s**.... *2813*
Mt 19:18 **Thou shalt not s, Thou shalt not** *2813*
Mt 27:64 come by night, and **s** him away, ... *2813*
Mk 10:19 **Do not kill, Do not s, Do not** *2813*
Lk 18:20 **Do not kill, Do not s, Do not** *2813*
Jn 10:10 **The thief cometh not, but for to s,**.... *2813*
Ro 2:21 a man should not **s**, dost thou **s**? *2813*
Ro 13:9 shalt not kill, Thou shalt not **s**, ... *2813*
Eph 4:28 Let him that stole **s** no more: but *2813*

STEALETH

Ex 21:16 he that **s** a man, and selleth him.... 1589
Job 27:20 tempest **s** him away in the night.... 1589
Zec 5:3 for every one that **s** shall be cut off.... 1589

STEALING

Dt 24:7 If a man be found **s** any of his 1589
Hos 4:2 and lying, and killing, and **s**, and 1589

STEDFAST

Ps 78:8 whose spirit was not **s** with God.... 589
Ps 78:37 neither were they **s** in his covenant.... 589
Da 6:26 is the living God, and **s** for ever, ... 7011
1Co 15:58 my beloved brethren, be ye **s**, ... *1476*
Heb 2:2 if the word spoken by angels were **s**, ... *949*
Heb 3:14 of our confidence **s** unto the end;.... *949*
Heb 6:19 anchor of the soul, both sure and **s**,.... *949*
1Pe 5:9 Whom resist **s** in the faith,.... *4731*

STEDFASTLY

Ru 1:18 she was **s** minded to go with her.... 553
Lk 9:51 **s** set his face to go to Jerusalem, ... *4741*
Ac 1:10 they looked **s** toward heaven as.... *816*
Ac 2:42 they continued **s** in the apostles'.... *4342*
Ac 6:15 looking **s** on him, saw his face as *816*
Ac 7:55 looked up **s** into heaven, and saw *816*
Ac 14:9 Paul speak: who **s** beholding him, ... *816*
2Co 3:7 could not **s** behold the face of.... *816*

STEDFASTNESS
Col 2:5 and the **s** of your faith in Christ *4733*
2Pe 3:17 the wicked, fall from your own **s**. *4740*

STEEL
2Sa 22:35 bow of **s** is broken by mine arms 5154
Job 20:24 and the bow of **s** shall strike him 5154
Ps 18:34 bow of **s** is broken by mine arms 5154

STEEP
Eze 38:20 **s** places shall fall, and every wall 4095
Mt 8:32 ran violently down a **s** place into *2911*

STEM
Isa 11:1 forth a rod out of the **s** of Jesse, ... 1508

STEP
1Sa 20:3 is but a **s** between me and death, ... 6587
Job 31:7 If my **s** hath turned out of the way. 838

STEPS
Ex 20:26 thou go up by **s** unto mine altar, ... 4609
1Ki 10:19 The throne had six **s**, and the top 4609
1Ki 10:20 and on the other upon the six **s**: 4609
Job 14:16 For now thou numberest my **s**:. 6806
Job 31:4 see my ways, and count all my **s**? 6806
Ps 18:36 hast enlarged my **s** under me 6806
Ps 37:23 The **s** of a good man are ordered 4703
Ps 56:6 they mark my **s**, when they wait 6119
Ps 119:133 Order my **s** in thy word: and let 6471
Pr 4:12 thy **s** shall not be straitened; 6806
Pr 5:5 to death; her **s** take hold on hell 6806
Pr 16:9 way: but the Lord directeth his **s**. 6806
La 4:18 They hunt our **s**, that we cannot. 6806
Da 11:43 the Ethiopians shall be at his **s** 4703
Ro 4:12 walk in the **s** of that faith of our *2487*
1Pe 2:21 that ye should follow his **s**:. *2487*

STEWARD
Ge 43:19 to the **s** of Joseph's house, ... 376, 834, 5921
Ge 44:1 commanded the **s** of his house 834, 5921
Ge 44:4 far off, Joseph said unto his **s**, ... 834, 5921
Mt 20:8 **of the vineyard saith unto his s**, ... *2012*
Lk 12:42 **then is that faithful and wise s**, ... *3623*
Lk 16:1 **a certain rich man, which had a s**; *3623*
Lk 16:2 **for thou mayest be no longer s** *3621*
Lk 16:3 **Then the s said within himself**, ... *3622*
Lk 16:8 **the lord commended the unjust s**, ... *3622*
Tit 1:7 must be blameless, as the **s** of God; *3622*

STEWARDS
1Co 4:1 and **s** of the mysteries of God *3623*
1Co 4:2 Moreover it is required in **s**, that a *3623*
1Pe 4:10 **s** of the manifold grace of God *3623*

STEWARDSHIP
Lk 16:2 **give an account of thy s; for thou**. *3622*
Lk 16:3 **lord taketh away from me the s**; *3622*
Lk 16:4 **when I am put out of the s, they** *3622*

STICK
2Ki 6:6 And he cut down a **s**, and cast it 6086
Job 33:21 bones that were not seen **s** out 8205
Job 41:17 they **s** together, that they cannot. 3920
Ps 38:2 For thine arrows **s** fast in me, and 5181
Eze 37:16 thou son of man, take thee one **s**, ... 6086
Eze 37:16 then take another **s**, and write upon . . . 6086

STICKETH
Pr 18:24 is a friend that **s** closer than a 1695

STICKS
Nu 15:32 they found a man that gathered **s**. 6086
Nu 15:33 they that found him gathering **s** 6086
1Ki 17:10 woman was there gathering of **s** 6086
1Ki 17:12 behold, I am gathering two **s**, that 6086
Eze 37:20 the **s** whereon thou writest shall 6086
Ac 28:3 Paul had gathered a bundle of **s**, ... *5434*

STIFF
Dt 31:27 thy rebellion and thy **s** neck: 7186
Ps 75:5 on high: speak not with a **s** neck. 6277
Jer 17:23 but made their neck **s**, that they 7185

STIFFNECKED
Ex 32:9 and, behold, it is a **s** people: 7186, 6203
Ex 33:3 thee; for thou art a **s** people: 7186, 6203
Ex 33:5 Ye are a **s** people: I will come 7186, 6203
Ac 7:51 Ye **s** and uncircumcised in heart *4644*

STILL
Ge 12:9 going on **s** toward the south 5265
Ex 14:13 not stand **s**, and see the salvation of
Ex 15:16 arm they shall be as **s** as a stone;. 1826
Nu 9:8 them, Stand **s**, and I will hear what
Jos 10:12 Sun, stand thou **s** upon Gibeon; 1826
Jos 10:13 And the sun stood **s**, and the moon 1826
Jos 10:13 So the sun stood **s** in the midst of
Ru 3:18 Then said she, Sit **s**, my daughter
2Sa 11:1 But David tarried **s** at Jerusalem
2Sa 14:32 but his hand is stretched out **s** 5750
1Ki 19:12 and after the fire a **s** small voice 1827
2Ki 12:3 the people **s** sacrificed and burnt 5750
2Ch 20:17 stand ye **s**, and see the salvation of
Ne 12:39 they stood **s** in the prison gate
Job 2:3 **s** he holdeth fast his integrity 5750
Job 37:14 stand **s**, and consider the wondrous 5975
Ps 23:2 leadeth me beside the **s** waters 4496
Ps 46:10 Be **s**, and know that I am God: I 7503
Ps 83:1 thy peace, and be not **s**, O God. 8252
Ps 92:14 They shall **s** bring forth fruit in old 5750
Ps 139:18 when I awake, I am **s** with thee. 5750
Isa 5:25 but his hand is stretched out **s** 5750
Hab 3:11 the sun and moon stood **s** in
Mt 20:32 Jesus stood **s**, and called them *2476*
Mk 4:39 said unto the sea, **Peace, be s**, ... *5392*
Lk 7:14 and they that bare him stood **s** *2476*
Jn 11:20 him: but Mary sat **s** in the house
Ac 8:38 commanded the chariot to stand **s**. *2476*
Rev 22:11 is unjust, let him be unjust **s** *2089*
Rev 22:11 which is filthy, let him be filthy **s**. *2089*
Rev 22:11 righteous, let him be righteous **s**. *2089*
Rev 22:11 he that is holy, let him be holy **s** *2089*

STILLED
Nu 13:30 Caleb **s** the people before Moses, ... 2013
Ne 8:11 So the Levites **s** all the people,. 2814

STING
1Co 15:55 O death, where is thy **s**? O grave, ... *2759*
1Co 15:56 The **s** of death is sin; and the. *2759*

STINK
Ex 7:18 shall die, and the river shall **s**; 887
Ps 38:5 My wounds **s** and are corrupt. 887
Isa 34:3 their **s** shall come up out of their 889

STINKETH

Isa 50:2 their fish **s**, because there is no 887
Jn 11:39 him. Lord, by this time he **s**; *3605*

STIR

Nu 24:9 a great lion: who shall **s** him up?. 6965
Job 41:10 is so fierce that dare **s** him up:. 5782
Ps 35:23 **S** up thyself, and awake to my 5782
Pr 15:1 but grievous words **s** up anger 5927
SS 2:7 ye **s** not up, nor awake my love, ... 5782
Isa 13:17 I will **s** up the Medes against them, ... 5782
Da 11:25 And he shall **s** up his power and. 5782
Ac 19:23 there arose no small **s** about that *5017*
2Ti 1:6 that thou **s** up the gift of God *329*

STIRRED

1Sa 22:8 son hath **s** up my servant against 6965
1Ki 21:25 whom Jezebel his wife **s** up 5496
1Ch 5:26 the God of Israel **s** up the spirit 5782
Ezr 1:1 Lord **s** up the spirit of Cyrus king 5782
Ps 39:2 good; and my sorrow was **s**, ... 5916
Da 11:10 But his sons shall be **s** up, and. 1624
Hag 1:14 And the Lord **s** up the spirit of 5782
Ac 17:13 thither also, and **s** up the people. *4531*
Ac 17:16 his spirit was **s** in him, when *3947*

STIRRETH

Dt 32:11 As an eagle **s** up her nest,. 5782
Pr 10:12 Hatred **s** up strifes: but love. 5782
Pr 15:18 a wrathful man **s** up strife: but 1624
Pr 28:25 is of a proud heart **s** up strife;. 1624
Pr 29:22 An angry man **s** up strife, and a 1624
Lk 23:5 He **s** up the people, teaching *383*

STOCK

Job 14:8 the **s** thereof die in the ground;. 1503
Isa 40:24 their **s** shall not take root in the 1503
Ac 13:26 children of the **s** of Abraham, and *1085*
Php 3:5 the eighth day, of the **s** of Israel, ... *1085*

STOCKS

Job 13:27 puttest my feet also in the **s**, and. 5465
Pr 7:22 a fool to the correction of the **s**; 5914
Jer 20:3 forth Jeremiah out of the **s** 4115
Jer 29:26 put him in prison, and in the **s** 6729
Ac 16:24 and made their feet fast in the **s** *3586*

STOLE

Ge 31:20 Jacob **s** away unawares to Laban 1589
2Sa 15:6 Absalom **s** the hearts of the men 1589
2Ki 11:2 **s** him from among the king's sons 1589
2Ch 22:11 **s** him from among the king's sons 1589
Mt 28:13 and **s** him away while we slept *2813*
Eph 4:28 Let him that **s** steal no more; but *2813*

STOLEN

Ge 31:19 Rachel had **s** the images that were 1589
Ge 31:30 wherefore hast thou **s** my gods? 1589
Ge 31:32 knew not that Rachel had **s** them. 1589
Ex 22:7 and it be **s** out of the man's house;. 1589
Ex 22:12 if it be **s** from him, he shall make 1589
Pr 9:17 **S** waters are sweet, and bread 1589

STONE

Ge 2:12 there is bdellium and the onyx **s**. 68
Ge 11:3 And they had brick for **s**, and slime 68
Ge 28:18 the **s** that he had put for his pillows 68
Ge 28:22 this **s**, which I have set for a pillar, ... 68
Ge 31:45 And Jacob took a **s**, and set it up for 68
Ex 4:25 Zipporah took a sharp **s**, and cut 6697
Ex 17:4 they be almost ready to **s** me. 5619
Ex 20:25 if thou wilt make me an altar of **s**, ... 68
Ex 31:18 two tables of testimony, tables of **s**, ... 68
Ex 34:4 took in his hand the two tables of **s** 68
Le 20:27 they shall **s** them with stones: 7275
Le 24:23 the camp, and **s** him with stones. 7275
Le 26:1 neither shall ye set up any image of **s**. 68
Dt 4:13 he wrote them upon two tables of **s** 68
Dt 9:11 Lord gave me the two tables of **s**, ... 68
Dt 28:36 thou serve other gods, wood and **s**. 68
Jos 4:5 take ye up every man of you a **s** 68
Jos 24:27 this **s** shall be a witness unto us;. 68
Jgs 9:18 and ten persons, upon one **s**, and. 68
1Sa 7:12 Then Samuel took a **s**, and set it. 68
1Sa 17:49 and took thence a **s**, and slang it, ... 68
1Sa 17:49 that the **s** sunk into his forehead; 68
1Sa 17:50 Philistine with a sling and with a **s**, ... 68
1Sa 25:37 within him, and he became as a **s**. 68
1Ki 8:9 in the ark save the two tables of **s**, ... 68
Ne 4:3 shall even break down their **s** wall. 68
Ne 9:11 as a **s** into the mighty waters. 68
Job 41:24 His heart is as firm as a **s**; yea, as. 68
Ps 91:12 lest thou dash thy foot against a **s**. 68
Ps 118:22 The **s** which the builders refused 68
Ps 118:22 is become the head **s** of the corner
Pr 17:8 A gift is as a precious **s** in the eyes 68
Pr 24:31 the **s** wall thereof was broken down. 68
Pr 26:8 As he that bindeth a **s** in a sling,. 68
Pr 26:27 and he that rolleth a **s**, it will return. 68
Pr 27:3 A **s** is heavy, and the sand weighty;. 68
Isa 8:14 but for a **s** of stumbling and for a. 68
Isa 28:16 Zion for a foundation a **s**, a tried **s**, ... 68
Isa 28:16 a precious corner **s**, a sure
Isa 37:19 work of men's hands, wood and **s**: 68
Jer 51:26 not take of thee a **s** for a corner, ... 68
Jer 51:26 nor a **s** for foundations; but thou 68
Da 2:34 that a **s** was cut out without hands, ... 69
Da 2:35 the **s** that smote the image became. 69
Da 2:45 the **s** was cut out of the mountain 69
Da 5:4 of brass, of iron, of wood, and of **s**. 69
Da 5:23 of brass, iron, wood, and **s**, which. 69
Da 6:17 And a **s** was brought, and laid upon. 69
Hab 2:19 to the dumb **s**, Arise, it shall teach!. 68
Mt 4:6 thou dash thy foot against a **s** *3037*
Mt 21:42 **The s which the builders rejected,** *3037*
Mt 21:44 **fall on this s shall be broken:**. *3037*
Mt 24:2 **be left here one s upon another,**. *3037*
Mt 27:60 rolled a great **s** to the door of the *3037*
Mt 27:66 sealing the **s**, and setting a watch. *3037*
Mt 28:2 came and rolled back the **s** from. *3037*
Mk 16:3 roll us away the **s** from the door *3037*
Mk 16:4 they saw that the **s** was rolled *3037*
Lk 4:3 command this **s** that it be made *3037*
Lk 11:11 **is a father, will he give him a s?**. *3037*
Lk 19:44 **leave in thee one s upon another;**. *3037*
Lk 23:53 in a sepulchre that was hewn in **s**, ... *2991*
Jn 1:42 which is by interpretation, A **s**. *4074*
Jn 2:6 were set there six waterpots of **s**,. *3035*
Jn 8:7 **you, let him first cast a s at her.** *3037*
Jn 10:31 Jews took … stones again to **s** him. *3034*
Jn 10:32 **which of those works do ye s me?** *3034*
Jn 10:33 For a good work we **s** thee not;. *3034*
Jn 11:39 Jesus said, **Take ye away the s** *3037*
Jn 11:41 they took away the **s** from the. *3037*
Jn 20:1 seeth the **s** taken away from the *3037*

2Co 3:3	not in tables of **s**, but in fleshy	*3035*
Eph 2:20	himself being the chief corner **s**;	
1Pe 2:4	whom coming, as unto a living **s**,	*3037*
1Pe 2:6	I lay in Sion a chief corner **s**, elect,	*3037*
1Pe 2:7	**s** which the builders disallowed,	*3037*
1Pe 2:8	And a **s** of stumbling, and a rock of	*3037*
Rev 2:17	**and will give him a white s,**	*5586*
Rev 2:17	**and in the s a new name written,**	*5595*
Rev 18:21	mighty angel took up a **s** like a	*3037*
Rev 21:11	like a jasper **s**, clear as crystal;	*3037*

STONED

Ex 19:13	but he shall surely be **s**, or shot	5619
Nu 15:36	**s** him with stones, and he died;	7275
Jos 7:25	And all Israel **s** him with stones,	5619
Jos 7:25	after they had **s** them with stones.	7275
1Ki 12:18	and all Israel **s** him with stones	7275
1Ki 21:13	**s** him with stones, that he died	5619
1Ki 21:14	saying, Naboth is **s**, and is dead	5619
1Ki 21:15	Jezebel heard that Naboth was **s**,	5619
Mt 21:35	**and killed another, and s another**	*3036*
Ac 7:58	him out of the city, and **s** him:	*3036*
Ac 7:59	they **s** Stephen, calling upon God,	*3036*
Ac 14:19	having **s** Paul, drew him out of	*3034*
2Co 11:25	once was I **s**, thrice I suffered	*3034*
Heb 11:37	They were **s**, they were sawn	*3034*
Heb 12:20	it shall be **s**, or thrust through	*3036*

STONES

Ge 31:46	said unto his brethren, Gather **s**;	68
Ge 31:46	and they took **s**, and made an heap:	68
Ex 28:12	put the two **s** upon the shoulders of	68
Ex 28:12	for **s** of memorial unto the children	68
Ex 35:9	onyx **s**, and **s** to be set for the ephod,	68
Ex 39:14	the **s** were according to the names	68
Le 20:27	death: they shall stone them with **s**:	68
Nu 15:35	congregation shall stone him with **s**	68
Nu 15:36	and stoned him with **s**, and he died;	68
Dt 27:2	that thou shalt set thee up great **s**,	68
Dt 27:4	that ye shall set up these **s**, which I	68
Dt 27:6	altar of the Lord thy God of whole **s**:	68
Dt 27:8	write upon the **s** all the words of	68
Jos 4:3	the priests' feet stood firm, twelve **s**,	68
Jos 4:6	saying, What mean ye by these **s**?	68
Jos 4:7	these **s** shall be for a memorial unto	68
Jos 4:8	took up twelve **s** out of the midst of	68
Jos 4:9	Joshua set up twelve **s** in the midst	68
Jos 4:20	those twelve **s**, which they took out	68
Jos 4:21	come, saying, What mean these **s**?	68
Jos 7:25	And all Israel stoned him with **s**,	68
Jos 7:25	after they had stoned them with **s**,	68
Jos 7:26	raised over him a great heap of **s**	68
Jos 10:11	Lord cast down great **s** from heaven	68
Jgs 20:16	could sling **s** at an hair breadth,	68
1Sa 17:40	chose him five smooth **s** out of the	68
2Sa 16:6	And he cast **s** at David, and at all	68
2Sa 16:13	and threw **s** at him, and cast dust	68
1Ki 5:17	and they brought great **s**, costly **s**,	68
1Ki 5:17	hewed **s**, to lay the foundation of	68
1Ki 5:18	prepared timber and **s** to build the	68
1Ki 18:31	Elijah took twelve **s**, according to	68
1Ki 18:32	with the **s** he built an altar in the	68
1Ki 18:38	the wood, and the **s**, and the dust,	68
1Ch 12:2	right hand and the left in hurling **s**	68
2Ch 26:15	to shoot arrows and great **s** withal.	68
Ezr 5:8	which is builded with great **s**, and	69
Job 6:12	Is my strength the strength of **s**? or	68
Job 14:19	waters wear the **s**: thou washest	68
Job 41:30	Sharp **s** are under him: he	2789
Ps 137:9	thy little ones against the **s**.	5553
Ps 144:12	our daughters may be as corner **s**,	2106
Ecc 3:5	A time to cast away **s**, and a time to	68
Ecc 3:5	a time to gather **s** together; a time	68
Ecc 10:9	Whoso removeth **s** shall be hurt	68
Isa 34:11	of confusion, and the **s** of emptiness	68
La 3:16	broken my teeth with gravel **s**,	2687
Mt 3:9	able of these **s** to raise up children	*3037*
Mt 4:3	that these **s** be made bread.	*3037*
Mk 5:5	crying, and cutting himself with **s**	*3037*
Mk 12:4	**and at him they cast s, and**	*3036*
Lk 19:40	**the s would immediately cry out**	*3037*
Jn 8:59	Then took they up **s** to cast at him:	*3037*
Jn 10:31	the Jews took up **s** again to stone	*3037*
1Co 3:12	gold, silver, precious **s**, wood, hay,	*3037*
1Pe 2:5	Ye also, as lively **s**, are built up a	*3037*
Rev 18:16	decked with gold, and precious **s**	*3037*
Rev 21:19	with all manner of precious **s**,	*3037*

STONEST

Mt 23:37	**s them which are sent unto thee,**	*3036*
Lk 13:34	**s them that are sent unto thee;**	*3036*

STONING

1Sa 30:6	for the people spake of **s** him,	5619

STONY

Eze 11:19	take the **s** heart out of their flesh,	68
Mt 13:5	**Some fell upon s places, where**	*4075*
Mt 13:20	**received the seed into s places,**	*4075*
Mk 4:5	**And some fell on s ground, where**	*4075*
Mk 4:16	**which are sown on s ground;**	*4075*

STOOD

Ge 18:2	and, lo, three men **s** by him:	5324
Ge 18:22	Abraham **s** yet before the Lord.	5975
Ge 24:30	he **s** by the camels at the well	5975
Ge 28:13	And, behold, the Lord **s** above it	5324
Ge 37:7	my sheaf arose, and also **s** upright;	5324
Ge 37:7	your sheaves **s** round about, and	
Ge 41:46	years old when he **s** before Pharaoh	5975
Ge 43:15	to Egypt, and **s** before Joseph	5975
Ex 2:4	his sister **s** afar off, to wit what	3320
Ex 2:17	but Moses **s** up and helped them,	6965
Ex 5:20	met Moses … who **s** in the way,	5324
Ex 9:10	furnace, and **s** before Pharaoh;	5975
Ex 15:8	the floods **s** upright as an heap,	5324
Ex 20:18	it, they removed, and **s** afar off.	5975
Ex 20:21	And the people **s** afar off, and	5975
Nu 22:22	angel of the Lord **s** in the way	3320
Nu 22:24	angel of the Lord **s** in a path of	5975
Dt 31:15	pillar of the cloud **s** over the door	5975
Jos 3:17	priests … **s** firm on dry ground	5975
Jos 4:3	where the priests' feet **s** firm,	4673
Jos 4:9	bare the ark of the covenant **s**:	4673
Jos 4:10	which bare the ark **s** in the midst	5975
Jos 5:13	these **s** a man over against him with	5975
Jos 10:13	And the sun **s** still, and the moon	1826
Jos 10:13	So the sun **s** still in the midst of	5975
Jos 11:13	cities that **s** still in their strength,	5975
Jgs 16:29	pillars upon which the house **s**,	3559
1Sa 1:26	I am the woman that **s** by thee	5324
1Sa 3:10	the Lord came, and **s**, and called.	3320
1Sa 17:3	the Philistines **s** on a mountain	5975

1Sa	17:3	Israel **s** on a mountain on the other	5975
1Sa	17:8	he **s** and cried unto the armies of	5975
1Sa	17:26	David spake to the men that **s** by	5975
1Sa	17:51	David ... **s** upon the Philistine, and	5975
2Sa	1:10	So I **s** upon him, and slew him,	5975
1Ki	3:15	**s** before the ark of the covenant of	5975
1Ki	3:16	unto the king, and **s** before him.	5975
1Ki	8:22	Solomon **s** before the altar of the	5975
1Ki	8:55	And he **s**, and blessed all the	5975
1Ki	13:1	Jeroboam **s** by the altar to burn	5975
1Ki	22:21	a spirit, and **s** before the Lord,	5975
2Ki	5:9	**s** at the door of the house of Elisha	5975
2Ki	9:17	there **s** a watchman on the tower	5975
2Ki	23:3	all the people **s** to the covenant	5975
1Ch	21:1	And Satan **s** up against Israel,	5975
1Ch	21:15	angel ... **s** by the threshingfloor	5975
2Ch	6:12	he **s** before the altar of the Lord	5975
2Ch	6:13	upon it he **s**, and kneeled down	5975
Ezr	2:63	till there **s** up a priest with Urim	5975
Ne	7:65	till there **s** up a priest with Urim	5975
Ne	8:4	Ezra the scribe **s** upon a pulpit of	5975
Ne	8:5	he opened it, all the people **s** up:	5975
Est	7:7	Haman **s** up to make request for	5975
Est	8:4	Esther arose, and **s** before the king,	5975
Est	9:16	together, and **s** for their lives,	5975
Job	4:15	face; the hair of my flesh **s** up:	5568
Job	29:8	and the aged arose, and **s** up	5975
Ps	104:6	the waters **s** above the mountains	5975
Ps	106:23	not Moses his chosen **s** before him	5975
Isa	6:2	Above it **s** the seraphims: each one	5975
Eze	3:23	the glory of the Lord **s** there, as	5975
Eze	10:6	went in, and **s** beside the wheels	5975
Eze	37:10	lived, and **s** up upon their feet,	5975
Da	1:19	therefore **s** they before the king	5975
Da	2:2	they came and **s** before the king	5975
Da	2:31	was excellent, **s** before thee;	6966
Da	3:3	and they **s** before the image that	6966
Da	7:10	times ten thousand **s** before him:	6966
Da	8:3	there **s** before the river a ram	5975
Da	8:22	whereas four **s** up for it, four	5975
Da	10:11	this word unto me, I **s** trembling	5975
Da	12:5	behold, there **s** other two, the one	5975
Hab	3:6	He **s**, and measured the earth; he	5975
Hab	3:11	The sun and moon **s** still in their	5975
Zec	3:5	And the angel of the Lord **s** by	5975
Mt	2:9	**s** over where the young child was	*2476*
Mt	12:46	mother and his brethren **s** without,	*2476*
Mt	20:32	And Jesus **s** still, and called them,	*2476*
Mt	27:11	And Jesus **s** before the governor:	*2476*
Mk	14:47	of them that **s** by drew a sword,	*3936*
Mk	14:60	the high priest **s** up in the midst,	*450*
Mk	14:70	they that **s** by said again to Peter	*3936*
Mk	15:35	And some of them that **s** by, when	*3936*
Mk	15:39	centurion, which **s** over against	*3936*
Lk	9:32	and the two men that **s** with him.	*4921*
Lk	17:12	that were lepers, which **s** afar off:	*2476*
Lk	19:8	and Zacchaeus **s**, and said unto the	*2476*
Lk	19:24	**And he said unto them that s by,**	*3936*
Lk	24:4	two men **s** by them in shining	*2186*
Lk	24:36	Jesus ... **s** in the midst of them,	*2476*
Jn	7:37	Jesus **s** and cried, saying, **If any**	*2476*
Jn	18:5	which betrayed him, **s** with them	*2476*
Jn	18:16	But Peter **s** at the door without.	*2476*
Jn	18:18	Peter **s** with them, and warmed	*2476*
Jn	18:22	officers which **s** by struck Jesus	*3936*
Jn	18:25	Peter **s** and warmed himself	*2476*
Jn	19:25	**s** by the cross of Jesus his mother,	*2476*
Jn	20:11	Mary **s** without at the sepulchre	*2476*
Jn	20:19	came Jesus and **s** in the midst, and	*2476*
Jn	20:26	**s** in the midst, and said, **Peace be**	*2476*
Jn	21:4	now come, Jesus **s** on the shore:	*2476*
Ac	1:10	men **s** by them in white apparel;	*2936*
Ac	1:15	days Peter **s** up in the midst of the	*450*
Ac	3:8	And he leaping up **s**, and walked	*2476*
Ac	4:26	The kings of the earth **s** up, and	*3936*
Ac	10:30	**s** before me in bright clothing,	*2476*
Ac	13:16	Then Paul **s** up, and beckoning	*450*
Ac	16:9	There **s** a man of Macedonia, and	*2476*
2Ti	4:16	first answer no man **s** with me,	*4836*
2Ti	4:17	Lord **s** with me, and strengthened	*3936*
Rev	5:6	**s** a Lamb as it had been slain,	*2476*
Rev	7:11	angels **s** round about the throne,	*2476*
Rev	8:2	seven angels which **s** before God;	*2476*
Rev	11:1	and the angel **s**, saying, Rise, and	*2476*
Rev	12:4	and the dragon **s** before the woman	*2476*
Rev	13:1	And I **s** upon the sand of the sea,	*2476*
Rev	14:1	lo, a Lamb **s** on the mount Sion.	*2476*

STOODEST

Nu	22:34	I knew not that thou **s** in the way	5324
Dt	4:10	day that thou **s** before the Lord	5975

STOOP

Job	9:13	proud helpers do **s** under him	7817
Pr	12:25	in the heart of man maketh it **s**:	7812
Mk	1:7	I am not worthy to **s** down and	*2955*

STOOPED

Ge	49:9	he **s** down, he couched as a lion,	3766
1Sa	24:8	David **s** with his face to the earth,	6915
2Ch	36:17	old man, or him that **s** for age:	3486
Jn	8:6	But Jesus **s** down, and with his	*2955*
Jn	8:8	again he **s** down, and wrote on the	*2955*
Jn	20:11	she **s** down, and looked into the	*3879*

STOOPING

Lk	24:12	and **s** down, he beheld the linen	*3879*
Jn	20:5	And he **s** down, and looking in, saw	*3879*

STOP

1Ki	18:44	down, that the rain **s** thee not.	6113
Ps	107:42	and all iniquity shall **s** her mouth	7092
2Co	11:10	no man shall **s** me of this boasting	*5420*

STOPPED

Ge	8:2	the windows of heaven were **s**,	5534
2Ki	3:25	and they **s** all the wells of water,	5640
2Ch	32:4	who **s** all the fountains, and the	5640
Ne	4:7	that the breaches began to be **s**,	5640
Ps	63:11	of them that speak lies shall be **s**	5534
Zec	7:11	**s** their ears, that they should not	3513
Ac	7:57	**s** their ears, and ran upon him	*4912*
Ro	3:19	that every mouth may be **s**, and all	*5420*
Heb	11:33	promises, **s** the mouths of lions	*5420*

STOPPETH

Ps	58:4	like the deaf adder that **s** her ear;	331
Pr	21:13	Whoso **s** his ears at the cry of the	331
Isa	33:15	that **s** his ears from hearing of blood,	331

STORE

Ge	41:36	that food shall be for **s** to the land	6487
Dt	28:5	shall be thy basket and thy **s**	4863
1Ki	9:19	the cities of **s** that Solomon had,	4543
2Ch	11:11	**s** of victual, and of oil and wine.	214

S

Ne 5:18 in ten days **s** of all sorts of wine:....... 7235
Isa 39:6 which thy fathers have laid up in **s**...... 686
1Co 16:2 every one of you lay by him in **s**, ... *2343*
1Ti 6:19 Laying up in **s** for themselves a......... *597*
2Pe 3:7 by the same word are kept in **s**,........ *2343*

STOREHOUSE
Mal 3:10 Bring ye all the tithes into the **s**,........ 214
Lk 12:24 **which neither have s nor barn;**........ *5009*

STOREHOUSES
Ge 41:56 And Joseph opened all the **s**, and 834
Dt 28:8 the blessing upon thee in thy **s**,......... 618
Ps 33:7 heap: he layeth up the depth in **s** 214

STORIES
Ge 6:16 second, and third **s** shalt thou make it.
Am 9:6 that buildeth his **s** in the heaven, ... 4609

STORK
Ps 104:17 as for the **s**, the fir trees are her........ 2624
Jer 8:7 the **s** in the heaven knoweth her....... 2624
Zec 5:9 had wings like the wings of a **s**:........ 2624

STORM
Job 21:18 chaff that the **s** carrieth away.......... 5492
Ps 83:15 and make them afraid with thy **s** 5492
Ps 107:29 He maketh the **s** a calm, so that 5591
Isa 25:4 a refuge from the **s**, a shadow from 2230
Na 1:3 in the whirlwind and in the **s**,......... 8183
Mk 4:37 there arose a great **s** of wind, and...... *2978*
Lk 8:23 there came down a **s** of wind on....... *2978*

STORMY
Ps 107:25 raiseth the **s** wind, which lifteth 5591
Ps 148:8 vapours: **s** wind fulfilling his word: 5591

STOUT
Job 4:11 the **s** lion's whelps are scattered
Da 7:20 look was more **s** than his fellows....... 7229

STOUTHEARTED
Ps 76:5 The **s** are spoiled, they have........ 47, 3820
Isa 46:12 Hearken unto me, ye **s**, that........ 47, 3820

STRAIGHT
Ps 5:8 make thy way **s** before my face......... 3474
Pr 4:25 let thine eyelids look **s** before thee...... 3474
Ecc 1:15 is crooked cannot be made **s**.......... 8626
Ecc 7:13 for who can make that **s**, which he..... 8626
Isa 40:3 make **s** in the desert a highway......... 3474
Isa 40:4 the crooked shall be made **s**, and 4334
Isa 42:16 before them, and crooked things **s**..... 4334
Isa 45:2 and make the crooked places **s**:........ 3474
Jer 31:9 by the river of waters in a **s** way........ 3474
Lk 3:4 way of the Lord, make his paths **s**, ... *2117*
Lk 3:5 and the crooked shall be made **s**, ... *2117*
Lk 13:13 and immediately she was made **s**,....... *461*
Jn 1:23 Make **s** the way of the Lord, as *2116*
Ac 9:11 **into the street which is called S**,....... *2117*
Heb 12:13 And make **s** paths for your feet, ... *3717*

STRAIGHTWAY
1Sa 28:20 Saul fell **s** all along on the earth,....... 4116
Mt 3:16 went up **s** out of the water: and,....... *2117*
Mt 4:20 they **s** left their nets, and followed *2112*
Mt 21:2 **s ye shall find an ass tied, and a** *2112*
Mt 21:3 **of them; and s he will send them.** *2112*
Mt 27:48 And **s** one of them ran, and took a..... *2112*
Mk 1:20 And **s** he called them: and they........ *2112*
Mk 5:29 **s** the fountain of her blood was *2112*
Mk 5:42 **s** the damsel arose, and walked; *2112*
Mk 7:35 And **s** his ears were opened, and....... *2112*
Mk 9:20 he saw him, **s** the spirit tare him; *2112*
Mk 9:24 **s** the father of the child cried out,...... *2112*
Lk 5:39 **drunk old wine s desireth new:**........ *2112*
Lk 12:54 **s ye say, There cometh a shower;** *2112*
Lk 14:5 **not s pull him out on the sabbath** *2112*
Jn 13:32 **himself and shall s glorify him**........ *2117*
Ac 5:10 Then fell she down **s** at his feet, ... *3916*
Jas 1:24 **s** forgetteth what manner of man...... *2112*

STRAIN
Mt 23:24 **blind guides, which s at a gnat,**........ *1368*

STRAIT
1Sa 13:6 Israel saw that they were in a **s**,........ 6887
Job 36:16 remove thee out of the **s** into a........ 6862
Mt 7:13 **Enter ye in at the s gate: for wide**...... *4728*
Mt 7:14 **s is the gate, and narrow is the** *4728*
Lk 13:24 **Strive to enter in at the s gate:** *4728*
Php 1:23 For I am in a **s** betwixt two,........... *4912*

STRAITENED
Job 18:7 steps of his strength shall be **s**, ... 3334
Job 37:10 the breadth of the waters is **s**.......... 4164
Pr 4:12 goest, thy steps shall not be **s**; 3334
Lk 12:50 **am I s till it be accomplished!**......... *4912*

STRAITLY
Mk 3:12 And he **s** charged them that they *4183*
Mk 5:43 he charged them **s** that no man *4183*
Ac 5:28 Did not we **s** command you that ye

STRAITNESS
Job 36:16 broad place, where there is no **s**;....... 4164
Jer 19:9 of his friend in the siege and **s**,........ 4689

STRAITS
Job 20:22 of his sufficiency he shall be in **s**....... 3334
La 1:3 over took her between the **s**........... 4712

STRANGE
Ge 35:2 Put away the **s** gods ... among you,.... 5236
Ge 35:4 gave unto Jacob all the **s** gods 5236
Ge 42:7 but made himself **s** unto them,........ 5234
Ex 2:22 I have been a stranger in a **s** land...... 5237
Ex 30:9 Ye shall offer no **s** incense 2114
Le 10:1 and offered **s** fire before the Lord, ... 2114
Jos 24:20 the Lord, and serve **s** gods, then 5236
Jos 24:23 the **s** gods which are among you, ... 5236
Jgs 11:2 thou art the son of a **s** woman.......... 312
1Ki 11:1 Solomon loved many **s** women, ... 5237
2Ch 33:15 he took away the **s** gods, and the 5236
Ezr 10:10 and have taken **s** wives, to increase..... 5237
Ne 13:27 transgress ... in marrying **s** wives?..... 5237
Job 19:17 My breath is **s** to my wife, ... 2114
Job 31:3 a **s** punishment to the workers 5235
Ps 81:9 shalt thou worship any **s** god.......... 5236
Ps 114:1 Jacob from a people of **s** language;..... 3937
Ps 137:4 sing the Lord's song in a **s** land? 5236
Pr 2:16 deliver thee from the **s** woman,........ 2114
Pr 5:3 the lips of a **s** woman drop as an 2114
Pr 6:24 of the tongue of a **s** woman........... 5237
Pr 7:5 keep thee from the **s** woman, ... 2114
Pr 20:16 a pledge of him for a **s** woman 5237
Pr 21:8 way of man is froward and **s**.......... 2114

S

Pr	22:14	mouth of **s** women is a deep pit:	2114
Pr	23:27	and a **s** woman is a narrow pit.	5237
Pr	23:33	thine eyes shall behold **s** women,	2114
Pr	27:13	a pledge of him for a **s** woman.	5237
Isa	28:21	he may do his work, his **s** work;	2114
Isa	28:21	bring to pass his act, his **s** act.	5237
Jer	5:19	and served **s** gods in your land,.	5236
Da	11:39	most strong holds with a **s** god,	5236
Mal	2:11	married the daughter of a **s** god	5236
Lk	5:26	We have seen **s** things to day	*3861*
Ac	7:6	seed should sojourn in a **s** land;	*245*
Heb	11:9	land of promise, as in a **s** country,	*245*
Heb	13:9	about with divers and **s** doctrines.	*3581*
Jude	7	and going after **s** flesh, are set	*2087*

STRANGER

Ge	15:13	be a **s** in a land that is not theirs,	1616
Ge	17:8	the land wherein thou art a **s**,	4033
Ge	23:4	I am a **s** and a sojourner with you:	1616
Ex	2:22	I have been a **s** in a strange land	1616
Ex	20:10	nor thy **s** that is within thy gates:	1616
Le	25:47	sojourner or **s** wax rich by thee,	8453
Le	25:47	and sell himself unto the **s** or	1616
Nu	1:51	**s** that cometh nigh shall be put	2114
Nu	16:40	no **s**, which is not of the seed	376, 2114
Dt	10:18	and loveth the **s**, in giving him food.	1616
Dt	10:19	Love ye therefore the **s**: for ye	1616
Dt	17:15	mayest not set a **s** over thee	376, 5237
Ru	2:10	knowledge of me, seeing I am a **s**?	5237
2Sa	1:13	answered, I am the son of a **s**	376, 1616
Job	19:15	and my maids, count me for a **s**	2114
Ps	39:12	I am a **s** with thee, and a sojourner	1616
Ps	69:8	I am … a **s** unto my brethren,.	2114
Ps	119:19	I am a **s** in the earth: hide not thy	1616
Pr	2:16	from the **s** which flattereth with	5237
Pr	5:10	thy labours be in the house of a **s**,	5237
Pr	5:20	and embrace the bosom of a **s**?	5237
Pr	6:1	hast stricken thy hand with a **s**,.	2114
Pr	7:5	from the **s** which flattereth with	5237
Pr	11:15	that is surety for a **s** shall smart	2114
Pr	14:10	a **s** doth not intermeddle with his.	2114
Pr	20:16	his garment that surety for a **s**.	2114
Pr	27:2	a **s**, and not thine own lips.	5237
Pr	27:13	his garment that is surety for a **s**,	2114
Ecc	6:2	eat thereof, but a **s** eateth it:	376, 5237
Eze	44:9	**s**, uncircumcised in heart,	1121, 5236
Mt	25:35	**I was a s, and ye took me in:**	*3581*
Mt	25:38	**When saw we thee a s, and took**	*3581*
Mt	25:43	**I was a s, and ye took me not in:**	*3581*
Mt	25:44	**or a s, or naked, or sick, or in**	*3581*
Lk	17:18	**to give glory to God, save this s**	*241*
Lk	24:18	Art thou only a **s** in Jerusalem,	*3939*
Jn	10:5	**And a s will they not follow, but.**	*245*

STRANGERS

Ge	31:15	Are we not counted of him **s**? for	5237
Ge	36:7	and the land wherein they were **s**	4033
Ex	6:4	pilgrimage, wherein they were **s**	1481
Ex	22:21	for ye were **s** in the land of Egypt	1616
Ex	23:9	ye were **s** in the land of Egypt.	1616
Le	19:34	for ye were **s** in the land of Egypt:	1616
Le	20:2	of the **s** that sojourn in Israel, that	1616
Dt	31:16	after the gods of the **s** of the land,	5236
2Sa	22:46	**S** shall fade away, and they	1121, 5236
2Ch	2:17	Solomon numbered all the **s**.	582, 1616
Ne	13:30	Thus cleansed I them from all **s**,.	1121, 5236
Ps	18:45	The **s** shall fade away, and be	1121, 5236
Ps	146:9	The Lord preserveth the **s**; he	1616
Pr	5:10	Lest **s** be filled with thy wealth;	2114
Isa	60:10	sons of **s** shall build up thy walls	5236
Jer	3:13	hast scattered thy ways to the **s**	2114
Jer	51:51	**s** are come into the sanctuaries	2114
La	5:2	Our inheritance is turned to **s**, our	2114
Eze	31:12	And **s**, the terrible of the nations,	2114
Joel	3:17	shall no **s** pass through her any	2114
Ob	11	**s** carried away captive his forces,.	2114
Mt	17:25	**of their own children, or of s?**	*245*
Mt	17:26	Peter saith unto him, Of **s**. Jesus	*245*
Mt	27:7	the potter's field, to bury **s** in.	*3581*
Jn	10:5	**for they know not the voice of s**	*245*
Ac	13:17	dwelt as **s** in … land of Egypt	1722, 3940
Eph	2:12	**s** from the covenants of promise	*3581*
Eph	2:19	ye are no more **s** and foreigners,	*3581*
Heb	11:13	confessed that they were **s** and	*3581*
Heb	13:2	Be not forgetful to entertain **s**	*5381*
1Pe	1:1	to the **s** scattered throughout.	*3927*
1Pe	2:11	I beseech you as **s** and pilgrims,	*3941*

STRANGLED

Ac	15:20	fornication, and from things **s**,	*4156*
Ac	15:29	and from blood, and from things **s**,	*4156*
Ac	21:25	and from **s**, and from fornication	*4156*

STRAW

Ge	24:25	We have both **s** and provender	8401
Ge	24:32	**s** and provender for the camels,	8401
Ex	5:7	give the people **s** to make brick,	8401
Ex	5:7	go and gather **s** for themselves	8401
Ex	5:10	Pharaoh, I will not give you **s**	8401
Ex	5:11	get you **s** where ye can find it: yet	8401
Ex	5:12	to gather stubble instead of **s**.	8401
Ex	5:13	daily tasks, as when there was **s**.	8401
Ex	5:16	is no **s** given unto thy servants	8401
Ex	5:18	for there shall no **s** be given you,	8401
Isa	11:7	and the lion shall eat **s** like the ox	8401

STRAWED

Ex	32:20	powder, and **s** it upon the water	2219
Mt	21:8	the trees, and **s** them in the way.	*4766*
Mt	25:24	**gathering where thou hast not s.**	*1287*
Mt	25:26	**and gather where I have not s.**	*1287*

STREAM

Job	6:15	as the **s** of brooks they pass away;	650
Ps	124:4	us, the **s** had gone over our soul:	5158
Isa	66:12	of the Gentiles like a flowing **s**	5158
Da	7:10	A fiery **s** issued and came forth.	5103
Am	5:24	and righteousness as a mighty **s**	5158
Lk	6:48	**the s beat vehemently upon that**	*4215*
Lk	6:49	**against which the s did beat**	*4215*

STREAMS

Ex	8:5	thine hand with thy rod over the **s**,	5104
Ps	46:4	the **s** whereof shall make glad the	6388
Ps	78:16	He brought **s** also out of the rock,	5140
Ps	126:4	O Lord, as the **s** in the south	650
Isa	34:9	the **s** thereof shall be burned into	5158
Isa	35:6	break out, and **s** in the desert.	5158

STREET

Ge	19:2	we will abide in the **s** all night.	7339
Jgs	19:15	he sat him down in a **s** of the city:	7339
Jgs	19:17	wayfaring man in the **s** of the city:	7339
Jgs	19:20	upon me; only lodge not in the **s**	7339

Ezr	10:9	sat in the **s** of the house of God,	7339
Ne	8:1	**s** that was before the water gate;	7339
Est	4:6	to Mordecai unto the **s** of the city,	7339
Est	6:9	horseback through the **s** of the	7339
Est	6:11	horseback through the **s** of the	7339
Job	18:17	shall have no name in the **s**.	2351, 6440
Pr	7:8	through the **s** near her corner;	7784
Isa	51:23	as the **s**, to them that went over	2351
La	2:19	for hunger in the top of every **s**	2351
La	4:1	poured out in the top of every **s**	2351
Da	9:25	the **s** shall be built again, and the	7339
Ac	9:11	**the s which is called Straight,**	*4505*
Rev	11:8	dead bodies shall lie in the **s** of	*4113*
Rev	21:21	the **s** of the city was pure gold, as it	*4113*
Rev	22:2	In the midst of the **s** of it, and on	*4113*

STREETS

Ps	144:13	and ten thousands in our **s**	2351
Pr	1:20	she uttereth her voice in the **s**	7339
Pr	5:16	abroad, and rivers of waters in the **s**.	7339
Pr	22:13	without, I shall be slain in the **s**	7339
Pr	26:13	a lion in the way; a lion is in the **s**	7339
Isa	15:3	In their **s** they shall gird themselves	2351
Isa	15:3	in their **s**, every one shall howl,	7339
Jer	49:26	her young men shall fall in her **s**,	7339
Jer	50:30	shall her young men fall in the **s**,	7339
La	4:8	they are not known in the **s**.	2351
La	4:14	wandered as blind men in the **s**,	2351
Eze	11:6	filled the **s** thereof with the slain.	2351
Eze	28:23	pestilence, and blood into her **s**;	2351
Zec	8:4	and old women dwell in the **s** of.	7339
Zec	8:5	**s** of the city shall be full of boys	7339
Zec	8:5	and girls playing in the **s** thereof.	7339
Mt	6:2	**in the synagogues and in the s,**	*4505*
Mt	6:5	**and in the corners of the s,**	*4113*
Lk	10:10	**go your ways out into the s of.**	*4113*
Lk	13:26	**and thou hast taught in our s**	*4113*
Lk	14:21	**out quickly into the s and lanes**	*4113*

STRENGTH

Ge	4:12	shall not ... yield unto thee her **s**;	3581
Ge	49:24	But his bow abode in **s**, and the	386
Ex	13:3	by **s** of hand the Lord brought you	2392
Ex	14:27	sea returned to his **s** when the	386
Ex	15:2	The Lord is my **s** and song, and	5797
Nu	23:22	hath as it were the **s** of an unicorn.	8443
Jgs	16:5	and see wherein his great **s** lieth,	3581
Jgs	16:6	Tell me, ... wherein thy great **s** lieth,	3581
Jgs	16:9	the fire. So his **s** was not known.	3581
Jgs	16:15	told me wherein thy great **s** lieth.	3581
Jgs	16:17	shaven, then my **s** will go from me,	3581
Jgs	16:19	him, and his **s** went from him.	3581
1Sa	15:29	the **S** of Israel will not lie nor	5331
1Sa	28:20	and there was no **s** in him; for he	3581
1Sa	28:22	and eat, that thou mayest have **s**,	3581
2Sa	22:33	God is my **s** and power: and he.	4581
2Sa	22:40	hast girded me with **s** to battle:	2428
1Ch	16:11	Seek the Lord and his **s**, seek his	5797
1Ch	16:27	**s** an gladness are in his place.	5797
1Ch	16:28	give unto the Lord glory and **s**	5797
2Ch	6:41	place, thou, and the ark of thy **s**	5797
Ne	8:10	for the joy of the Lord is your **s**	4581
Job	6:11	What is my **s**, that I should hope?	3581
Job	6:12	Is my **s** the **s** of stones? or is my	3581
Job	9:19	If I speak of **s**, lo, he is strong:	3581
Job	18:7	steps of his **s** shall be straitened,	202
Job	26:2	savest ... the arm that hath no **s**?	5797
Job	36:5	he is mighty in **s** and wisdom.	3581
Job	37:6	and to the great rain of his **s**	5797
Job	39:19	Hast thou given the horse **s**?	1369
Job	39:21	the valley, and rejoiceth in his **s**	3581
Ps	18:1	I will love thee, O Lord, my **s**,	2391
Ps	18:2	my God, my **s**, in whom I will.	6697
Ps	19:14	O Lord, my **s**, and my redeemer.	6697
Ps	20:6	with ... saving **s** of his right hand.	1369
Ps	21:13	Be ... exalted, Lord, in thine own **s**	5797
Ps	27:1	Lord is the **s** of my life; of whom	4581
Ps	28:7	The Lord is my **s** and my shield;	5797
Ps	28:8	The Lord is their **s**, and he is the.	5797
Ps	29:1	give unto the Lord glory and **s**	5797
Ps	29:11	Lord will give **s** unto his people;	5797
Ps	31:4	privily for me: for thou art my **s**.	4581
Ps	31:10	my **s** faileth because of mine	3581
Ps	37:39	is their **s** in the time of trouble.	4581
Ps	43:2	For thou art the God of my **s**:	4581
Ps	46:1	God is our refuge and **s**, a very	5797
Ps	59:17	Unto thee, O my **s**, will I sing: for.	5797
Ps	62:7	the rock of my **s**, and my refuge,	5797
Ps	71:9	forsake me not when my **s** faileth.	3581
Ps	71:16	I will go in the **s** of the Lord God:	1369
Ps	73:26	but God is the **s** of my heart, and	6697
Ps	74:13	Thou didst divide the sea by thy **s**	5797
Ps	81:1	Sing aloud unto God our **s**: make.	5797
Ps	90:10	by reason of **s** they be fourscore	1369
Ps	93:1	the Lord is clothed with **s**,	5797
Ps	96:6	**s** and beauty are in his sanctuary	5797
Ps	96:7	give unto the Lord glory and **s**	5797
Ps	105:4	Seek the Lord, and his **s**: seek his	5797
Ps	118:14	The Lord is my **s** and song, and is	5797
Ps	132:8	thy rest; thou, and the ark of thy **s**	5797
Ps	140:7	the Lord, the **s** of my salvation,	5797
Pr	8:14	I am understanding; I have **s**.	1369
Pr	10:29	The way of the Lord is **s** to the	4581
Pr	14:4	increase is by the **s** of the ox.	3581
Pr	20:29	glory of young men is their **s**	3581
Pr	24:5	a man of knowledge increaseth **s**	3581
Pr	24:10	day of adversity, thy **s** is small.	3581
Pr	31:3	Give not thy **s** unto women, nor.	2428
Pr	31:17	She girdeth her loins with **s**, and.	5797
Pr	31:25	**S** and honour are her clothing;	5797
Ecc	9:16	said I, Wisdom is better than **s**	1369
Ecc	10:10	edge, then must he put to more **s**	2428
Ecc	10:17	princes eat in due season, for **s**,	1369
Isa	5:22	men of **s** to mingle strong drink:	2428
Isa	12:2	JEHOVAH is my **s** and my song;	5797
Isa	17:10	been mindful of the rock of thy **s**,	4581
Isa	26:4	Lord Jehovah is everlasting **s**:	6697
Isa	33:6	of thy times, and **s** of salvation:	2633
Isa	40:31	the Lord shall renew their **s**;	3581
Isa	45:24	Lord have I righteousness and **s**	5797
Isa	49:4	I have spent my **s** for nought, and	3581
Isa	49:5	Lord, and my God shall be my **s**.	5797
Isa	51:9	awake, put on **s**, O arm of the Lord;	5797
Isa	63:15	where is thy zeal and thy **s**, the	1369
Jer	16:19	O Lord, my **s**, and my fortress.	5797
La	3:18	My **s** and my hope is perished.	5331
Da	2:37	thee a kingdom, power, and **s**,	8632
Da	2:41	shall be in it of the **s** of the iron,	5326
Da	10:8	and there remained no **s** in me:	3581
Da	10:8	corruption, and I retained no **s**.	3581
Da	10:16	upon me, and I have retained no **s**.	3581
Da	10:17	there remained no **s** in me, neither	3581

S

Joel 2:22 tree and the vine do yield their **s** 2428
Mic 5:4 and feed in the **s** of the Lord.......... 5797
Hab 3:19 The Lord God is my **s**, and he will..... 2428
Zec 12:5 shall be my **s** in the Lord of hosts....... 556
Mk 12:30 **all thy mind, and with all thy s**........ *2479*
Mk 12:33 all the soul, and with all the **s**,......... *2479*
Lk 1:51 He hath shewed **s** with his arm; *2904*
Lk 10:27 all thy soul, and with all thy **s**,......... *2479*
Ac 9:22 But Saul increased the more in **s**, ... *1743*
Ro 5:6 For when we were yet without **s**,........ *772*
1Co 15:56 is sin; and the **s** of sin is the law *1411*
2Co 1:8 pressed out of measure, above **s** *1411*
2Co 12:9 **s is made perfect in weakness**......... *1411*
Heb 9:17 of no **s** at all while the testator *2480*
Heb 11:11 Sara ... received **s** to conceive seed, ... *1411*
Rev 1:16 was as the sun shineth in his **s**......... *1411*
Rev 3:8 **thou hast a little s, and hast**........... *1411*
Rev 5:12 and riches, and wisdom, and **s**,........ *2479*
Rev 12:10 Now is come salvation, and **s**, and *1411*
Rev 17:13 their power and **s** unto the beast....... *1849*

STRENGTHEN
Dt 3:28 and encourage him, and **s** him:......... 553
Jgs 16:28 **s** me, I pray thee, only this once,....... 2388
Ezr 6:22 to **s** their hands in the work of the..... 2388
Ne 6:9 therefore, O God, **s** my hands. 2388
Job 16:5 I would **s** you with my mouth, and 553
Ps 27:14 and he shall **s** thine heart: 553
Ps 41:3 Lord will **s** him upon the bed of....... 5582
Ps 68:28 **s**, O God, that which thou hast........ 5810
Ps 119:28 **s** ... me according unto thy word...... 6965
Isa 35:3 **S** ye the weak hands, and confirm 2388
Isa 41:10 I will **s** thee; yea, I will help thee; 553
Da 11:1 I, stood to confirm and to **s** him....... 4581
Zec 10:6 And I will **s** the house of Judah, ... 1396
Zec 10:12 And I will **s** them in the Lord;......... 1396
Lk 22:32 **art converted, s thy brethren**.......... *4741*
1Pe 5:10 perfect, stablish, **s**, settle you *4599*
Rev 3:2 **and s the things which remain,**........ *4741*

STRENGTHENED
Ge 48:2 Israel **s** himself, and sat upon 2388
Jgs 3:12 Lord **s** Eglon the king of Moab........ 2388
Jgs 7:11 shall thine hands be **s** to go down 2388
2Ch 1:1 Solomon ... was **s** in his kingdom,..... 2388
2Ch 24:13 house of God in his state, and **s** it....... 553
Ezr 7:28 I was **s** as the hand of the Lord my..... 2388
Ne 2:18 **s** their hands for this good work....... 2388
Job 4:3 and thou hast **s** the weak hands 2388
Job 4:4 and thou hast **s** the feeble knees 553
Ps 147:13 he hath **s** the bars of thy gates; 2388
Pr 8:28 he **s** the fountains of the deep: 5810
Da 10:18 appearance of a man, and he **s** me, ... 2388
Da 10:19 he had spoken unto me, I was **s** 2388
Da 10:19 my lord speak; for thou hast **s** me 2388
Ac 9:19 he had received meat, he was **s** *1765*
Eph 3:16 to be **s** with might by his Spirit........ *2901*
Col 1:11 **S** with all might, according to his *1412*
2Ti 4:17 Lord stood with me, and **s** me; *1743*

STRENGTHENETH
Job 15:25 **s** himself against the Almighty 1396
Ps 104:15 and bread which **s** man's heart......... 5582
Ecc 7:19 Wisdom **s** the wise more than ten 5810
Php 4:13 things through Christ which **s** me...... *1743*

STRENGTHENING
Lk 22:43 an angel from heaven, **s** him........... *1765*
Ac 18:23 in order, **s** all the disciples............. *1991*

STRETCH
Ex 3:20 **s** out my hand, and smite Egypt....... 7971
Ex 7:5 I **s** forth mine hand upon Egypt, ... 5186
Ex 7:19 **s** out thine hand upon the waters...... 5186
Ex 8:5 **S** forth thine hand with thy rod 5186
Ex 8:16 **S** out thy rod, and smite the dust 5186
Ex 10:12 **S** out thine hand over ... Egypt 5186
Ex 14:16 and **s** out thine hand over the sea, ... 5186
Ex 14:26 **S** out thine hand over the sea, that..... 5186
Ex 25:20 cherubims ... **s** forth their wings 6566
Jos 8:18 **S** out the spear that is in thy 5186
1Sa 26:9 **s** forth his hand against the Lord's..... 7971
1Sa 26:11 **s** ... mine hand against the Lord's 7971
1Sa 26:23 **s** ... mine hand against the Lord's 7971
Job 30:24 not **s** out his hand to the grave,........ 7971
Ps 143:6 I **s** forth my hands unto thee: 6566
Isa 34:11 **s** out upon it the line of confusion, ... 5186
Mt 12:13 he to the man, **S forth thine hand**...... *1614*
Jn 21:18 **old, thou shalt s forth thy hands,**...... *1614*
2Co 10:14 we **s** not ourselves beyond our *5239*

STRETCHED
Ge 22:10 And Abraham **s** forth his hand, ... 7971
Ge 48:14 And Israel **s** out his right hand, ... 7971
Ex 6:6 will redeem you with a **s** out arm, ... 5186
Ex 8:6 Aaron **s** ... his hand over the waters ... 5186
Ex 8:17 Aaron **s** out his hand with his rod,..... 5186
Ex 9:23 Moses **s** ... his rod toward heaven:..... 5186
Ex 10:13 Moses **s** forth his rod over ... Egypt, ... 5186
Ex 10:22 Moses **s** ... his hand toward heaven; ... 5186
Ex 14:21 Moses **s** out his hand over the sea; 5186
Ex 14:27 Moses **s** forth his hand over the sea,.... 5186
Jos 8:18 Joshua **s** out the spear that he had 5186
Jos 8:19 as soon as he had **s** out his hand: 5186
Jos 8:26 back, wherewith he **s** out the spear, ... 5186
2Sa 24:16 when the angel **s** out his hand......... 7971
1Ki 6:27 **s** ... the wings of the cherubims, ... 6566
1Ki 17:21 he **s** himself upon the child three...... 4058
2Ki 4:34 and he **s** himself upon the child:....... 1457
2Ki 4:35 went up, and **s** himself upon him: 1457
Ps 136:6 To him that **s** out the earth above...... 7554
Ps 136:12 strong hand, and ... a **s** out arm: 5186
Pr 1:24 I have **s** out my hand, and no man..... 5186
Isa 42:5 the heavens, and **s** them out;.......... 5186
Isa 45:12 my hands, have **s** out the heavens, ... 5186
Jer 51:15 and hath **s** out the heaven by his 5186
Eze 1:11 and their wings were **s** upward; 6504
Eze 1:22 **s** forth over their heads above. 5186
Zec 1:16 shall be **s** forth upon Jerusalem........ 5186
Mt 12:13 he **s** it forth; and it was restored *1614*
Mt 12:49 And he **s** forth his hand toward his *1614*
Mt 14:31 Jesus **s** forth his hand, and caught *1614*
Mt 26:51 **s** out his hand, and drew his sword,.... *1614*
Lk 22:53 **ye s forth no hands against me:** *1614*
Ac 12:1 Herod the king **s** forth his hands *1911*
Ro 10:21 I have **s** forth my hands unto a *1600*

STRETCHEST
Ps 104:2 **s** out the heavens like a curtain: 5186

STRETCHETH
Job 15:25 he **s** out his hand against God, ... 5186
Pr 31:20 She **s** out her hand to the poor; 6566

S

Isa 40:22 **s** out the heavens as a curtain, . . . 5186
Isa 44:13 The carpenter **s** out his rule; he . . . 5186

STRETCHING
Isa 8:8 the **s** out of his wings shall fill the . . . 4298
Ac 4:30 By **s** forth thine hand to heal; and . . . *1614*

STRICKEN
Ge 18:11 Sarah were old and well **s** in age; . . . 935
Ge 24:1 Abraham was old, and well **s** in age: . . . 935
Jos 13:1 Now Joshua was old and **s** in years; . . . 935
Jos 23:2 unto them, I am old and **s** in age: . . . 935
Jgs 5:26 and **s** through his temples. . . . 2498
1Ki 1:1 king David was old and **s** in years; . . . 935
Pr 6:1 hast **s** thy hand with a stranger, . . . 8628
Isa 53:4 yet we did esteem him **s**, smitten . . . 5060
Isa 53:8 transgression of my people was he **s** . . . 5061
Jer 5:3 thou hast **s** them, but they have . . . 5221
Lk 1:7 both were now well **s** in years. . . . *4260*
Lk 1:18 man, and my wife well **s** in years. . . . *4260*

STRIFE
Ge 13:7 was a **s** between the herdmen of . . . 7379
Ge 13:8 said unto Lot, Let there be no **s**, . . . 4808
Jgs 12:2 I and my people were at great **s**. . . . 7379
Ps 55:9 have seen violence and **s** in the city . . . 7379
Pr 15:18 A wrathful man stirreth up **s**. . . . 4066
Pr 15:18 that is slow to anger appeaseth **s**. . . . 7379
Pr 16:28 A froward man soweth **s**: and a. . . . 4066
Pr 17:1 an house full of sacrifices with **s** . . . 7379
Pr 17:14 The beginning of **s** is as when one . . . 4066
Pr 17:19 loveth transgression that loveth **s** . . . 4683
Pr 20:3 honour for a man to cease from **s**. . . . 7379
Pr 22:10 yea, **s** and reproach shall cease . . . 1779
Pr 26:17 meddleth with **s** belonging not . . . 7379
Pr 26:20 is no talebearer, the **s** ceaseth. . . . 4066
Pr 26:21 is a contentious man to kindle **s** . . . 7379
Pr 28:25 is of a proud heart stirreth up **s** . . . 4066
Pr 29:22 An angry man stirreth up **s**, and a . . . 4066
Pr 30:33 forcing of wrath bringeth forth **s** . . . 7379
Jer 15:10 a man of **s** and a man of contention . . . 7379
Ro 13:13 wantonness, not in **s** and envying. . . . *2054*
1Co 3:3 you envying and **s**, and divisions, . . . *2054*
Gal 5:20 emulations, wrath, **s**, seditions, . . . *2052*
Php 1:15 preach Christ even of envy and **s**: . . . *2054*
Php 2:3 Let nothing be done through **s** or. . . . *2052*
1Ti 6:4 whereof cometh envy, **s**, railings, . . . *2054*
Heb 6:16 oath … is to them an end of all **s** . . . *485*
Jas 3:14 envying and **s** in your hearts, . . . *2052*
Jas 3:16 For where envying and **s** is, there . . . *2052*

STRIFES
Pr 10:12 Hatred stirreth up **s**: but love . . . 4090
2Ti 2:23 knowing that they do gender **s** . . . *3163*

STRIKE
Ex 12:7 and **s** it on the two side posts . . . 5414
Ex 12:22 **s** the lintel and the two side posts. . . . 5060
Job 17:3 is he that will **s** hands with me? . . . 8628
Ps 110:5 The Lord … shall **s** through kings . . . 4272
Pr 7:23 Till a dart **s** through his liver; as . . . 6398
Pr 17:26 good, nor to **s** princes for equity. . . . 5221
Pr 22:26 Be not … one of them that **s** hands, . . . 8628
Mk 14:65 did **s** him with the palms of their . . . *906*

STRIKER
1Ti 3:3 Not given to wine, no **s**, not greedy . . . *4131*
Tit 1:7 not given to wine, no **s**, not given to . . . *4131*

STRIKETH
Pr 17:18 void of understanding **s** hands, . . . 8628
Rev 9:5 a scorpion, when he **s** a man. . . . *3817*

STRING
Ps 11:2 ready their arrow upon the **s**. . . . 3499
Mk 7:35 the **s** of his tongue was loosed, . . . *1199*

STRINGED
Ps 150:4 praise him with **s** instruments. . . . 4482
Isa 38:20 my songs to the **s** instrument . . . 5058
Hab 3:19 chief singer on my **s** instruments . . . 5058

STRINGS
Ps 21:12 arrows upon thy **s** against the . . . 4340
Ps 33:2 and an instrument of ten **s**

STRIP
Nu 20:26 **s** Aaron of his garments, and put . . . 6584
1Sa 31:8 the Philistines came to **s** the slain . . . 6584
Eze 16:39 shall **s** thee also of thy clothes, . . . 6584
Hos 2:3 Lest I **s** her naked, and set her as. . . . 6584

STRIPE
Ex 21:25 wound for wound, **s** for **s**. . . . 2250

STRIPES
Dt 25:3 Forty **s** he may give him, and . . . 5221
Dt 25:3 him above these with many **s**, . . . 4347
Pr 17:10 than an hundred **s** into a fool. . . . 5221
Pr 19:29 and **s** for the back of fools. . . . 4112
Isa 53:5 and with his **s** we are healed. . . . 2250
Lk 12:47 **will, shall be beaten with many s**
Lk 12:48 **commit things worthy of s, shall** . . . *4127*
Lk 12:48 **shall be beaten with few s. For** . . . *4127*
Ac 16:23 they had laid many **s** upon them, . . . *4127*
Ac 16:33 of the night, and washed their **s**; . . . *4127*
2Co 6:5 In **s**, in imprisonments, in tumults, . . . *4127*
2Co 11:23 in **s** above measure, in prisons. . . . *4127*
2Co 11:24 times received I forty **s** save one.
1Pe 2:24 by whose **s** ye were healed . . . *3468*

STRIPPED
Nu 20:28 Moses **s** Aaron of his garments, . . . 6584
1Sa 18:4 Jonathan **s** himself of the robe . . . 6584
1Sa 19:24 And he **s** off his clothes also, and . . . 6584
1Sa 31:9 off his head, and **s** off his armour, . . . 6584
2Ch 20:25 which they **s** off for themselves, . . . 5337
Job 19:9 He hath **s** me of my glory, and . . . 6584
Job 22:6 and **s** the naked of their clothing. . . . 6584
Mt 27:28 And they **s** him, and put on him a . . . *1562*
Lk 10:30 **which s him of his raiment, and.** . . . *1562*

STRIPT
Ge 37:23 they **s** Joseph out of his coat, his. . . . 6584

STRIVE
Ge 6:3 My spirit shall not … **s** with man, . . . 1777
Ge 26:20 did **s** with Isaac's herdmen, . . . 7378
Ex 21:18 if men **s** together, and one smite. . . . 7378
Ex 21:22 If men **s**, and hurt a woman with . . . 5327
Jgs 11:25 did he ever **s** against Israel, or did . . . 7378
Job 33:13 Why dost thou **s** against him? for . . . 7378
Ps 35:1 Lord, with them that **s** with me: . . . 3401
Pr 3:30 **S** not with a man without cause, . . . 7378
Pr 25:8 Go not forth hastily to **s**, lest thou . . . 7378
Isa 45:9 the potsherd **s** with the potsherds
Hos 4:4 are as they that **s** with the priest. . . . 7378
Mt 12:19 He shall not **s**, nor cry; neither . . . *2051*

Lk 13:24 **S to enter in at the strait gate:**........... *75*
2Ti 2:5 if a man also **s** for masteries, yet........ *118*
2Ti 2:5 not crowned, except he **s** lawfully........ *118*
2Ti 2:14 **s** not about words to no profit,........ *3054*
2Ti 2:24 servant of the Lord must not **s**;........ *3164*

STRIVED

Ro 15:20 so have I **s** to preach the gospel,........ *5389*

STRIVETH

Isa 45:9 unto him that **s** with his Maker!........ 7378
1Co 9:25 every man that **s** for the mastery......... *75*

STRIVING

Php 1:27 one mind **s** together for the faith...... *4866*
Col 1:29 **s** according to his working, which........ *75*
Heb 12:4 resisted unto blood, **s** against sin....... *464*

STRIVINGS

Ps 18:43 delivered me from the **s** of the........ 7379
Tit 3:9 contentions, and **s** about the law;...... *3163*

STROKE

Dt 19:5 his hand fetcheth a **s** with the axe
Dt 21:5 controversy and every **s** be tried:...... 5061
Est 9:5 enemies with the **s** of the sword,........ 4347
Job 23:2 **s** is heavier than my groaning......... 3027
Ps 39:10 Remove thy **s** away from me: I........ 5061
Isa 30:26 and healeth the **s** of their wound...... 4273
Eze 24:16 the desire of thine eyes with a **s**:........ 4046

STRONG

Ge 49:24 were made **s** by the hands of the....... 6339
Ex 6:1 a **s** hand shall he let them go,......... 2389
Ex 6:1 a **s** hand shall he drive them out....... 2389
Ex 10:19 Lord turned a mighty **s** west wind,..... 2389
Ex 13:9 for with a **s** hand hath the Lord....... 2389
Ex 14:21 sea to go back by a **s** east wind........ 5794
Le 10:9 Do not drink wine nor **s** drink, thou,
Nu 6:3 himself from wine and **s** drink, and
Nu 13:18 whether they be **s** or weak, few........ 2389
Nu 13:28 people be **s** that dwell in the land,..... 5794
Dt 2:36 was not one city too **s** for us:.......... 7682
Dt 11:8 that ye may be **s**, and go in and........ 2388
Dt 31:6 Be **s** and of a good courage, fear....... 2388
Dt 31:7 Be **s** and of a good courage, for........ 2388
Dt 31:23 Be **s** and of a good courage, for........ 2388
Jos 1:6 Be **s** and of a good courage: for........ 2388
Jos 1:7 be thou **s** and very courageous,........ 2388
Jos 1:9 Be **s** and of a good courage; be........ 2388
Jos 1:18 only be **s** and of a good courage....... 2388
Jos 10:25 be **s** and of good courage: for.......... 2388
Jos 14:11 As yet I am as **s** this day as I was....... 2389
Jos 23:9 before you great nations and **s**:........ 6099
Jgs 1:28 came to pass, when Israel was **s**,........ 2388
Jgs 13:4 and drink not wine nor **s** drink, and
Jgs 13:7 and now drink no wine nor **s** drink,
Jgs 13:14 neither let her drink wine or **s** drink,
Jgs 14:14 out of the **s** came forth sweetness...... 5794
1Sa 1:15 have drunk neither wine nor **s** drink,
1Sa 4:9 Be **s**, and quit yourselves like.......... 2388
1Sa 14:52 when Saul saw any **s** man, or any...... 1368
1Sa 23:19 not David hide ... with us in **s** holds... 4679
1Sa 23:29 and dwelt in **s** holds at En-gedi........ 4679
2Sa 5:7 David took the **s** hold of Zion:........ 4686
2Sa 10:11 If the Syrians be too **s** for me......... 2388
2Sa 10:11 if the children of Ammon be too **s**..... 2388
1Ki 8:42 great name, and of thy **s** hand,........ 2389
1Ki 19:11 and **s** wind rent the mountains,....... 2389
2Ki 2:16 be with thy servants fifty **s** men;....... 2428
1Ch 22:13 be **s**, and of good courage; dread...... 2388
1Ch 28:20 his son, be **s** and of good courage,..... 2388
2Ch 26:16 But when he was **s**, his heart was...... 2394
2Ch 32:7 Be **s** and courageous, be not.......... 2388
Ezr 9:12 that ye may be **s**, and eat the good..... 2388
Ne 1:10 great power, and by thy **s** hand......... 2389
Job 8:2 of thy mouth be like a **s** wind?........ 3524
Job 9:19 If I speak of strength, lo, he is **s**:........ 533
Job 37:18 spread out the sky, which is **s**,......... 2389
Job 39:28 crag of the rock, and the **s** place........ 4686
Job 40:18 His bones are as **s** pieces of brass;....... 650
Ps 18:17 delivered me from my **s** enemy,....... 5794
Ps 19:5 and rejoiceth as a **s** man to run a...... 1368
Ps 22:12 **s** bulls of Bashan have beset me......... 47
Ps 24:8 The Lord **s** and mighty, the Lord...... 5808
Ps 30:7 made my mountain to stand **s**........ 5797
Ps 31:2 be thou my **s** rock, for an house....... 4581
Ps 71:3 Be thou my **s** habitation,............. 6697
Ps 89:8 who is a **s** Lord like unto thee?........ 2626
Ps 89:10 thine enemies with thy **s** arm.......... 5797
Ps 89:13 **s** is thy hand, and high is thy.......... 5810
Pr 7:26 many **s** men have been slain by........ 6099
Pr 10:15 rich man's wealth is his **s** city:......... 5797
Pr 11:16 honour: and **s** men retain riches....... 6184
Pr 14:26 fear of the Lord is **s** confidence:....... 5797
Pr 18:10 The name of the Lord is a **s** tower:..... 5797
Pr 18:11 The rich man's wealth is his **s** city,..... 5797
Pr 18:19 is harder to be won than a **s** city:...... 5797
Pr 20:1 Wine is a mocker, **s** drink is raging:
Pr 21:14 a reward in the bosom **s** wrath......... 5794
Pr 24:5 A wise man is **s**; yea, a man of......... 5797
Pr 30:25 The ants are a people not **s**, yet........ 5794
Pr 31:4 to drink wine; nor for princes **s** drink:
Pr 31:6 Give **s** drink unto him that is ready to
Ecc 9:11 nor the battle to the **s**, neither yet...... 1368
Ecc 12:3 the **s** men shall bow themselves,....... 2428
SS 8:6 for love is **s** as death; jealousy is....... 5794
Isa 5:22 men of strength to mingle **s** drink:
Isa 25:3 shall the **s** people glorify thee,......... 5794
Isa 26:1 We have a **s** city; salvation will........ 5797
Isa 28:2 the Lord hath a mighty and **s** one,...... 533
Isa 35:4 of a fearful heart, be **s**, fear not:....... 2388
Isa 40:10 Lord God will come with **s** hand,....... 2389
Isa 40:26 might, for that he is **s** in power:........ 533
Isa 41:21 bring forth your **s** reasons, saith....... 6110
Isa 53:12 shall divide the spoil with the **s**;....... 6099
Isa 56:12 we will fill ourselves with **s** drink;
Isa 60:22 and a small one a **s** nation:........... 6099
Jer 48:14 mighty and **s** men for the war?........ 2428
Jer 49:19 against the habitation of the **s**.......... 386
Jer 50:34 Their Redeemer is **s**; the Lord of....... 2389
La 2:2 **s** holds of the daughter of Judah;...... 4013
Eze 3:14 hand of the Lord was **s** upon me....... 2388
Da 2:40 fourth kingdom shall be **s** as iron:..... 8624
Da 2:42 the kingdom shall be partly **s**, and..... 8624
Da 4:11 The tree grew, and was **s**, and the...... 8631
Da 4:20 The tree ... which grew, and was **s**,.... 8631
Da 4:22 king, that art grown and become **s**..... 8631
Da 7:7 and terrible, and **s** exceedingly;........ 8624
Da 8:8 when he was **s**, the great horn......... 6105
Da 10:19 be unto thee, be **s**, yea, be **s**........... 2388
Da 11:5 the king of the south shall be **s**,....... 2388
Da 11:5 and he shall be **s** above him, and...... 2388
Da 11:23 become **s** with a small people......... 6105

Da 11:24	his devices against the **s** holds,	4013
Da 11:32	that do know their God shall be **s**,	2388
Da 11:39	shall he do in the most **s** holds	4581
Joel 2:11	for he is **s** that executeth his word:	6099
Joel 3:10	spears: let the weak say, I am **s**	1368
Mic 4:8	**s** hold of the daughter of Zion,	6076
Na 1:7	a **s** hold in the day of trouble;	4581
Zec 8:9	Let your hands be **s**, ye that hear	2388
Zec 8:13	fear not, but let your hands be **s**	2388
Zec 8:22	**s** nations shall come to seek the	6099
Mt 12:29	**one enter into a s man's house,**	*2478*
Mt 12:29	**except he first bind the s man?**	*2478*
Lk 1:15	drink neither wine nor **s** drink;	*4608*
Lk 1:80	child grew, and waxed **s** in spirit,	*2901*
Lk 2:40	child grew, and waxed **s** in spirit,	*2901*
Lk 11:21	**s man armed keepeth his palace,**	*2478*
Ac 3:16	his name hath made this man **s**,	*4732*
Ro 4:20	was **s** in faith, giving glory to God;	*1743*
Ro 15:1	We then that are **s** ought to bear the	*1415*
1Co 4:10	we are weak, but ye are **s**;	*2478*
1Co 16:13	the faith, quit you like men, be **s**	*2901*
2Co 10:4	to the pulling down of **s** holds;)	*3794*
2Co 12:10	for when I am weak, then am I **s**	*1415*
2Co 13:9	when we are weak, and ye are **s**	*1415*
Eph 6:10	my brethren, be **s** in the Lord	*1743*
2Th 2:11	God shall send them **s** delusion,	*1753*
2Ti 2:1	my son, be **s** in the grace that is	*1743*
Heb 5:7	with **s** crying and tears unto him	*2478*
Heb 5:12	need of milk, and not of **s** meat	*4731*
Heb 5:14	But **s** meat belongeth to them that	*4731*
Heb 6:18	we might have a **s** consolation,	*2478*
Heb 11:34	out of weakness were made **s**,	*1743*
1Jn 2:14	young men, because ye are **s**, and	*2478*
Rev 5:2	I saw a **s** angel proclaiming with	*2478*
Rev 18:2	he cried mightily with a **s** voice	*3173*
Rev 18:8	**s** is the Lord God who judgeth	*2478*

STRONGER

Ge 30:41	the **s** cattle did conceive,	7194
Ge 30:42	were Laban's, and the **s** Jacob's	7194
Nu 13:31	people; for they are **s** than we.	2389
Jgs 14:18	honey? and what is **s** than a lion?	5794
2Sa 1:23	eagles, they were **s** than lions.	1396
2Sa 3:1	but David waxed **s** ... and the	2390
2Sa 13:14	but, being **s** than she, forced her,	2388
1Ki 20:23	therefore they were **s** than we;	2388
Job 17:9	that hath clean hands shall be **s**	555
Ps 105:24	made them **s** than their enemies	6105
Ps 142:6	prosecutors; for they are **s** than I	553
Lk 11:22	**when a s than he shall come**	*2478*
1Co 1:25	the weakness of God is **s** than men	*2478*
1Co 10:22	to jealousy? are we **s** than he?	*2478*

STRONGEST

Pr 30:30	A lion is **s** among beasts,	1368

STRONG-HOLD See STRONG and HOLD.

STROVE

Ge 26:20	Esek; because they **s** with him.	6229
Ge 26:21	another well, and **s** for that also:	7378
Ge 26:22	another well; ... for that they **s** not:	7378
Ex 2:13	men of the Hebrews **s** together:	5327
Nu 20:13	children of Israel **s** with the Lord,	7378
Nu 26:9	who **s** against Moses and against	5327
Nu 26:9	when they **s** against the Lord:	5327
2Sa 14:6	they two **s** together in the field,	5327

STRUCK

2Sa 12:15	the Lord **s** the child that Uriah's	5062
2Ch 13:20	and the Lord **s** him, and he died.	5062
Mt 26:51	**s** a servant of the high priest's,	*3960*
Lk 22:64	him, they **s** him on the face,	*5180*
Jn 18:22	**s** Jesus with the palm of his	*1325, 4475*

STRUGGLED

Ge 25:22	children **s** together within her;	7533

STUBBLE

Ex 5:12	to gather **s** instead of straw.	7179
Job 21:18	They are as **s** before the wind.	8401
Ps 83:13	wheel; as the **s** before the wind.	7179
Joel 2:5	flame of fire that devoureth the **s**,	7179
Mal 4:1	all that do wickedly, shall be **s**	7179
1Co 3:12	precious stones, wood, hay, **s**;	*2562*

STUBBORN

Dt 21:18	man have a **s** and rebellious son,	5637
Dt 21:20	This our son is **s** and rebellious,	5637
Jgs 2:19	doings, nor from their **s** way.	7186
Ps 78:8	a **s** and rebellious generation;	5637
Pr 7:11	(She is loud and **s**; her feet abide	5637

STUBBORNNESS

Dt 9:27	look not unto the **s** of this people,	7190
1Sa 15:23	and **s** is an iniquity and idolatry	6484

STUCK

1Sa 26:7	his spear **s** in the ground at his	4600
Ps 119:31	I have **s** unto thy testimonies:	1692

STUDIETH

Pr 15:28	of the righteous **s** to answer:	1897
Pr 24:2	For their heart **s** destruction, and	1897

STUDY

Ecc 12:12	much **s** is a weariness of the flesh.	3854
1Th 4:11	that ye **s** to be quiet, and to do	*5389*
2Ti 2:15	**S** to shew thyself approved unto	*4704*

STUFF

Ge 31:37	thou hast searched all my **s**,	3627
Ge 31:37	thou found of all thy household **s**?	3627
Ge 45:20	Also regard not your **s**; for the	3627
Ex 22:7	his neighbour money or **s** to keep,	3627
Jos 7:11	put it even among their own **s**	3627
1Sa 10:22	he hath hid himself among the **s**	3627
1Sa 30:24	his part be that tarrieth by the **s**	3627
Ne 13:8	forth all the household **s** of Tobiah	3627
Lk 17:31	**housetop, and his s in the house,**	*4632*

STUMBLE

Pr 3:23	safely, and thy foot shall not **s**	5062
Pr 4:12	thou runnest, thou shalt not **s**	3782
Pr 4:19	they know not at what they **s**	3782
Isa 5:27	shall be weary nor **s** among them;	3782
Isa 28:7	err in vision, they **s** in judgment	6328
Isa 59:10	we **s** at noon day as in the night;	3782
Jer 18:15	caused them to **s** in their ways	3782
Jer 20:11	therefore my persecutors shall **s**,	3782
Da 11:19	shall **s** and fall, and not be found	3782
Mal 2:8	have caused many to **s** at the law;	3782
1Pe 2:8	even to them which **s** at the word,	*4350*

STUMBLED

1Ch 13:9	to hold the ark; for the oxen **s**	8058
Jer 46:12	man hath **s** against the mighty	3782

S

Ro	9:32	they **s** at that stumblingstone;	*4350*
Ro	11:11	Have they **s** that they should fall?	*4417*

STUMBLETH

Pr	24:17	thine heart be glad when he **s**	3782
Jn	11:9	**man walk in the day, he s not,**	*4350*
Jn	11:10	**if a man walk in the night, he s,**	*4350*
Ro	14:21	any thing whereby thy brother **s**,	*4350*

STUMBLING

Isa	8:14	for a stone of **s** and for a rock of.	5063
Isa	57:14	take up the **s** block out of the way	4383
1Pe	2:8	And a stone of **s**, and a rock of	*4348*
1Jn	2:10	there is none occasion of **s** in him	*4625*

STUMBLINGBLOCK

Le	19:14	deaf, nor put a **s** before the blind,	4383
Eze	3:20	iniquity, and I lay a **s** before him,	4383
Eze	7:19	because it is the **s** of their iniquity	4383
Eze	14:3	put the **s** of their iniquity before	4383
Ro	14:13	no man put a **s** or an occasion to	*4348*
1Co	1:23	unto the Jews a **s**, and unto the	*4625*
1Co	8:9	become a **s** to them that are weak	*4348*
Rev	2:14	**to cast a s before the children of**	*4625*

STUMBLINGBLOCKS

Jer	6:21	I will lay **s** before this people	4383
Zep	1:3	sea, and the **s** with the wicked;	4384

STUMBLINGSTONE

Ro	9:32	For they stumbled at that **s**;	*3037, 4348*
Ro	9:33	I lay in Sion a **s** and rock of	*3037, 4348*

SUBDUE

Ge	1:28	and replenish the earth, and **s** it	3533
Ps	47:3	He shall **s** the people under us,	1696
Da	7:24	first, and he shall **s** three kings	8214
Mic	7:19	he will **s** our iniquities; and thou	3533
Zec	9:15	devour, and **s** with sling stones;	3533
Php	3:21	to **s** all things unto himself	*5293*

SUBDUED

Nu	32:22	the land be **s** before the Lord:	3533
Nu	32:29	and the land shall be **s** before you;	3533
Jos	18:1	And the land was **s** before them.	3533
Jgs	4:23	So God **s** on that day Jabin the	3665
1Sa	7:13	So the Philistines were **s**, and they	3665
2Sa	8:1	smote the Philistines, and **s** them:	3665
1Ch	20:4	of the giant: and they were **s**	3665
Ps	18:39	thou hast **s** under me those that	3766
1Co	15:28	all things shall be **s** unto him,	*5293*
Heb	11:33	Who through faith **s** kingdoms,	*2610*

SUBDUETH

Ps	18:47	me, and **s** the people under me	1696
Ps	144:2	trust; who **s** my people under me.	7286
Da	2:40	in pieces and **s** all things: and as	2827

SUBJECT

Lk	2:51	Nazareth, and was **s** unto them:	*5293*
Lk	10:17	devils are **s** unto us through thy	*5293*
Lk	10:20	**that the spirits are s unto you;**	*5293*
Ro	8:7	for it is not **s** to the law of God,	*5293*
Ro	8:20	the creature was made **s** to vanity,	*5293*
Ro	13:1	every soul be **s** unto the higher	*5293*
Ro	13:5	Wherefore ye must needs be **s**, not	*5293*
1Co	14:32	the prophets are **s** to the prophets.	*5293*
1Co	15:28	the Son also himself be **s** unto him	*5293*
Eph	5:24	as the church is **s** unto Christ,	*5293*
Col	2:20	the world, are ye **s** to ordinances,	*1379*
Tit	3:1	in mind to be **s** to principalities	*5293*
Heb	2:15	all their lifetime **s** to bondage	*1777*
Jas	5:17	Elias … a man **s** to like passions	*3663*
1Pe	2:18	Servants, be **s** to your masters	*5293*
1Pe	3:22	powers being made **s** unto him.	*5293*
1Pe	5:5	all of you be **s** one to another, and	*5293*

SUBJECTION

Ps	106:42	brought into **s** under their hand	3665
1Co	9:27	my body, and bring it into **s**	*1396*
1Ti	2:11	woman learn in silence with all **s**	*5292*
1Ti	3:4	his children in **s** with all gravity;	*5292*
Heb	2:5	not put in **s** the world to come,	*5293*
Heb	2:8	Thou hast put all things in **s** under	*5293*
Heb	2:8	in that he put all in **s** under him,	*5293*
Heb	12:9	rather be in **s** unto the Father of	*5293*
1Pe	3:1	be in **s** to our own husbands;	*5293*
1Pe	3:5	in **s** unto their own husbands:	*5293*

SUBMIT

Ge	16:9	and **s** thyself under her hands.	6031
Ps	18:44	strangers shall **s** themselves unto	3584
Ps	68:30	**s** himself with pieces of silver:	7511
Eph	5:22	Wives, **s** yourselves unto your own	*5293*
Col	3:18	Wives, **s** yourselves unto your own	*5293*
Heb	13:17	rule over you, and **s** yourselves:	*5226*
Jas	4:7	**S** yourselves therefore to God.	*5293*
1Pe	2:13	**S** yourselves to every ordinance	*5293*
1Pe	5:5	**s** yourselves unto the elder	*5293*

SUBMITTED

1Ch	29:24	**s** themselves unto Solomon	5414, 3027
Ro	10:3	have not **s** themselves unto the	*5293*

SUBMITTING

Eph	5:21	**S** yourselves one to another in	*5293*

SUBSCRIBE

Isa	44:5	**s** with his hand unto the Lord,	3789
Jer	32:44	and **s** evidences, and seal them,	3789

SUBSCRIBED

Jer	32:10	I **s** the evidence, and sealed it,	3789
Jer	32:12	witnesses that **s** the book of the	3789

SUBSTANCE

Ge	7:4	living **s** that I have made will I	3351
Ge	7:23	And every living **s** was destroyed	3351
Dt	33:11	Bless, Lord, his **s**, and accept the	3428
2Ch	32:29	God had given him **s** very much.	7399
Ezr	8:21	for our little ones, and for all our **s**.	7399
Ezr	10:8	elders, all his **s** should be forfeited,	7399
Job	1:3	His **s** also was seven thousand	4735
Job	1:10	and his **s** is increased in the land.	4735
Ps	139:15	My **s** was not hid from thee,	6108
Ps	139:16	Thine eyes did see my **s**, yet	1564
Pr	3:9	Honour the Lord with thy **s**, and	1952
Pr	6:31	he shall give all the **s** of his house.	1952
Pr	10:3	casteth away the **s** of the wicked.	1942
Pr	12:27	the **s** of a diligent man is precious	1952
SS	8:7	give all the **s** of his house for love,	1952
Isa	6:13	the holy seed shall be the **s** thereof.	4678
Ob	13	laid hands on their **s** in the day of	2428
Mic	4:13	their **s** unto the Lord of the whole	2428
Lk	15:13	**wasted his s with riotous living**	*3776*
Heb	10:34	a better and an enduring **s**.	*5223*
Heb	11:1	faith is the **s** of things hoped for,	*5287*

SUBTIL
Ge 3:1 the serpent was more **s** than any....... 6175
Pr 7:10 attire of an harlot, and **s** of heart....... 5341

SUBTILLY
Ps 105:25 to deal **s** with his servants............. 5230
Ac 7:19 The same dealt **s** with our kindred, ... 2686

SUBTILTY
Ge 27:35 The brother came with **s**, and......... 4820
Pr 1:4 To give **s** to the simple, to the 6195
Mt 26:4 that they might take Jesus by **s**,......... *1388*
Ac 13:10 O full of all **s** and all mischief,......... *1388*
2Co 11:3 beguiled Eve through his **s**............ *3834*

SUBURBS
Le 25:34 field of the **s** of their cities may........ 4054
Jos 21:2 with the **s** thereof for our cattle........ 4054
Jos 21:3 the Lord, these cities and their **s**, ... 4054
Jos 21:8 Levites these cities with their **s**,........ 4054
Jos 21:11 with the **s** thereof round about it. 4054
Jos 21:27 gave Golan in Bashan with her **s**,...... 4054
1Ch 5:16 towns, and in all the **s** of Sharon,...... 4054
1Ch 6:57 Hebron, ... and Libnah with her **s**, ... 4054
2Ch 11:14 left their **s** and their possession, ... 4054
2Ch 31:19 in the fields of the **s** of their cities,..... 4054
Eze 27:28 The **s** shall shake at the sound of 4054

SUBVERT
La 3:36 to **s** a man in his cause, the Lord 5791
Tit 1:11 who **s** whole houses, teaching *396*

SUBVERTING
Ac 15:24 you with words, **s** your souls, ... *384*
2Ti 2:14 profit, but to the **s** of the hearers....... *2692*

SUCCEEDED
Dt 2:12 but the children of Esau **s** them,....... 3423
Dt 2:21 they **s** them, and dwelt in their 3423

SUCCESS
Jos 1:8 and then thou shalt have good **s**....... 7919

SUCCOUR
2Sa 18:3 that thou **s** us out of the city.......... 5826
Heb 2:18 is able to **s** them that are tempted....... *997*

SUCCOURED
2Co 6:2 the day of salvation have I **s** thee:....... *997*

SUCH
Ge 4:20 was the father of **s** as dwell in tents,
Ge 27:4 make me savoury meat, **s** as I love,
Ge 27:9 meat for thy father, **s** as he loveth:
Ge 27:14 savoury meat, **s** as his father loved.
Ge 27:46 the daughters of Heth, **s** as these
Ge 41:19 **s** as I never saw in all the land of 2007
Ge 41:38 Can we find **s** a one as this is, a
Ex 9:18 hail, **s** as hath not been in Egypt........ 834
Ex 9:24 hail, ... **s** as there was none like it in 834
Ex 10:14 there were no **s** locusts as they,........ 3651
Ex 10:14 neither after them shall be **s**
Ex 11:6 cry ... **s** as there was none like it,....... 834
Ex 12:36 they lent unto them **s** things as they
Ex 18:21 **s** as fear God, men of truth, hating
Dt 25:16 For all that do **s** things, and all 428
Jgs 3:2 **s** as before knew nothing thereof;
Jgs 13:23 have told us **s** things as these
Jgs 18:23 that thou comest with **s** a company?
Jgs 19:30 was no **s** deed done nor seen from..... 2063
Ru 4:1 Ho, **s** a one! turn aside, sit down....... 6423
2Sa 9:8 look upon **s** a dead dog as I am?
2Sa 12:8 given unto thee **s** and **s** things......... 2007
2Sa 13:12 no **s** thing ought to be done in 3651
2Sa 19:36 recompense ... with **s** a reward?....... 2063
2Ki 23:22 there was not holden **s** a passover...... 2088
1Ch 29:25 bestowed upon him **s** royal majesty
2Ch 1:12 **s** as none of the kings have had......... 834
2Ch 9:9 **s** spice as the queen of Sheba gave 1932
2Ch 9:11 there were none **s** seen before in....... 1992
2Ch 11:16 **s** as set their hearts to seek the Lord
2Ch 35:18 keep **s** a passover as Josiah kept,
Ezr 7:12 perfect peace, and at **s** a time.......... 3706
Ezr 7:25 all **s** as know the laws of thy God;
Ne 6:11 I said. Should **s** a man as I flee?........ 3644
Est 4:11 **s** to whom the king shall hold out 834
Est 4:14 the kingdom for **s** a time as this?
Job 12:3 knoweth not **s** things as these? 3644
Job 18:21 **s** are the dwellings of the wicked 428
Ps 34:18 saveth **s** as be of a contrite spirit
Ps 37:22 **s** as be blessed of him shall inherit
Ps 40:16 let **s** as love thy salvation say
Ps 70:4 let **s** as love thy salvation say
Ps 139:6 **S** knowledge is too wonderful for me;
Pr 30:20 **S** is the way of an adulterous.......... 3651
Isa 58:5 Is it **s** a fast that I have chosen?........ 2088
Jer 2:10 and see if there be **s** a thing........... 2063
Jer 9:9 soul be avenged on **s** a nation as........ 834
Jer 15:2 Lord; **S** as are for death, to death;
Jer 43:11 and **s** as are for captivity to captivity;
Da 1:4 **s** as had ability in them to stand in
Da 2:10 asked **s** things at any magician 1836
Da 12:1 trouble, **s** as never was since there 834
Mt 18:5 **shall receive one s little child in** *5108*
Mt 19:14 **for of s is the kingdom of heaven**...... *5108*
Mt 24:21 **s as was not since the beginning**....... *3634*
Mt 24:44 **s an hour as ye think not the Son**
Mt 26:18 **Go into the city to s a man, and**....... *1170*
Mk 4:18 **thorns; s as hear the word**............ *3778*
Mk 4:20 **s as hear the word, and receive**........ *3748*
Mk 9:37 **receive one of s children in my**........ *5108*
Mk 10:14 **for of s is the kingdom of God**........ *5108*
Mk 13:7 **for s things must needs be; but**
Lk 10:8 **eat s things as are set before you:**
Lk 11:41 **give alms of s things as ye have;**
Lk 13:2 **because they suffered s things?**........ *5108*
Lk 18:16 **for of s is the kingdom of God**........ *5108*
Jn 4:23 **Father seeketh s to worship him.**...... *5108*
Ac 2:47 church daily **s** as should be saved
Ac 3:6 I none; but **s** as I have give I thee:
Ac 16:24 Who, having received **s** a charge, ... *5108*
Ro 1:32 **s** things are worthy of death,.......... *5108*
Ro 2:3 judgest them which do **s** things........ *5108*
1Co 5:5 To deliver **s** an one unto Satan for *5108*
1Co 10:13 taken you but **s** as is common to man:
2Co 3:12 Seeing then that we have **s** hope *5108*
2Co 12:2 **s** an one caught up to the third........ *5108*
2Co 12:3 And I knew **s** a man, (whether in *5108*
2Co 12:5 Of **s** an one will I glory: yet of......... *5108*
Gal 5:23 against **s** there is no law *5108*
Gal 6:1 restore **s** an one in the spirit of *5108*
2Ti 3:5 power thereof: from **s** turn away....... *5128*
Heb 5:12 are become **s** as have need of milk
Heb 7:26 **s** an high priest became us, who *5108*
Heb 8:1 We have **s** an high priest, who is *5108*

Heb 11:14	For they that say **s** things declare	*5108*
Heb 12:3	him that endured **s** contradiction	*5108*
Heb 13:5	content with **s** things as ye have;	*3588*
Heb 13:16	with **s** sacrifices God is well pleased	*5108*
Jas 4:13	to morrow we will go into **s** a city,	*3592*
Jas 4:16	boastings: all **s** rejoicing is evil	*5108*
2Pe 1:17	there came **s** a voice to him from	*5107*
2Pe 3:14	seeing that ye look for **s** things	*5023*
Rev 16:18	**s** as was not since men were upon	*3634*
Rev 20:6	on **s** the second death hath no	*5130*

SUCK

Dt 32:13	him to **s** honey out of the rock	3243
Dt 33:19	**s** of the abundance of the seas	3243
1Sa 1:23	gave her son **s** until she weaned	3243
Job 20:16	He shall **s** the poison of asps:	3243
Job 39:30	Her young ones also **s** up blood:	5966
Isa 60:16	also **s** the milk of the Gentiles,	3243
Eze 23:34	shalt even drink it and **s** it out,	4680
Joel 2:16	and those that **s** the breasts:	3243
Mk 24:19	**and to them that give s in those**	*2337*
Lk 23:29	**and the paps which never gave s.**	*2337*

SUCKING

Nu 11:12	nursing father beareth the **s** child,	3243
1Sa 7:9	Samuel took a **s** lamb, and offered	2461
Isa 49:15	Can a woman forget her **s** child	5764
La 4:4	The tongue of the **s** child cleaveth	3243

SUCKLINGS

Ps 8:2	Out of the mouth of babes and **s**	3243
Mt 21:16	**Out of the mouth of babes and s**	*2337*

SUDDEN

Job 22:10	thee, and **s** fear troubleth thee;	6597
Pr 3:25	Be not afraid of **s** fear, neither of	6597
1Th 5:3	**then s destruction cometh upon**	*160*

SUDDENLY

Nu 12:4	And the Lord spake **s** unto Moses,	6597
Nu 35:22	if he thrust him **s** without enmity,	6621
2Sa 15:14	lest he overtake us **s**, and bring	4116
Ps 64:4	**s** do they shoot at him, and fear	6597
Ps 64:7	arrow; **s** shall they be wounded	6597
Pr 24:22	For their calamity shall rise **s**;	6597
Pr 29:1	shall **s** be destroyed, and that	6621
Ecc 9:12	time, when it falleth **s** upon them	6597
Isa 47:11	desolation shall come upon thee **s**	6597
Jer 15:8	I have caused him to fall upon it **s**	6597
Jer 51:8	Babylon is **s** fallen and destroyed:	6597
Mal 3:1	seek, shall **s** come to his temple	6597
Mk 9:8	**s**, when they had looked round	*1819*
Mk 13:36	**coming s he find you sleeping**	*1810*
Lk 2:13	And **s** there was with the angel a	*1810*
Ac 2:2	**s** there came a sound from heaven	*869*
Ac 16:26	**s** there was a great earthquake,	*869*
Ac 22:6	**s** there shone from heaven a great	*1810*
1Ti 5:22	Lay hands **s** on no man, neither	*5030*

SUE

Mt 5:40	**if any man will s thee at the law,**	*2919*

SUFFER

Ex 22:18	Thou shalt not **s** a witch to live	
Nu 21:23	Sihon would not **s** Israel to pass	5414
Jgs 15:1	father would not **s** him to go in	5414
Jgs 16:26	**S** me that I may feel the pillars	3240
Est 3:8	not for the king's profit to **s** them	3240
Job 21:3	**S** me that I may speak; and after	5375
Ps 16:10	wilt thou **s** thine Holy One to see	5414
Ps 34:10	young lions do lack, and **s** hunger:	
Ps 55:22	he shall never **s** the righteous to	5414
Ps 121:3	will not **s** thy foot to be moved:	5414
Pr 10:3	will not **s** the … righteous to famish:	
Pr 19:15	sleep; and an idle soul shall **s** hunger	
Pr 19:19	great wrath shall **s** punishment:	5375
Ecc 5:6	**S** not thy mouth to cause thy flesh	5414
Ecc 5:12	the rich will not **s** him to sleep	3240
Mt 3:15	said unto him, **S** it to be so now:	*863*
Mt 8:21	**s** me first to go and bury my	*2010*
Mt 8:31	**s** us to go away into the herd of	*2010*
Mt 17:12	**also the Son of man s of them**	*3958*
Mt 17:17	**with you? how long shall I s you?**	*430*
Mt 19:14	**S little children, and forbid them**	*863*
Mk 8:31	Son of man must **s** many things	*3958*
Mk 9:12	**man, that he must s many things,**	*3958*
Mk 10:14	**S the little children to come unto**	*863*
Lk 9:22	**Son of man must s many things,**	*3958*
Lk 9:41	**shall I be with you, and s you?**	*430*
Lk 18:16	**S little children to come unto me,**	*863*
Lk 22:15	**this passover with you before I s**	*3958*
Lk 24:46	**and thus it behoved Christ to s,**	*3958*
Ac 2:27	wilt thou **s** thine Holy One to see	*1325*
Ac 3:18	prophets, that Christ should **s**	*3958*
Ac 5:41	counted worthy to **s** shame for his	*818*
Ac 9:16	**him how great things he must s**	*3958*
Ac 13:35	shalt not **s** thine Holy One to see	*1325*
Ac 26:23	That Christ should **s**, and that he	*3805*
Ro 8:17	If so be that we **s** with him, that	*4841*
1Co 3:15	shall be burned, he shall **s** loss:	*2210*
1Co 10:13	will not **s** you to be tempted above	*1439*
1Co 12:26	whether one member **s**, all the	*3958*
1Co 12:26	all the members **s** with it; or one	*4841*
Gal 6:12	should **s** persecution for the cross	*1377*
Php 1:29	on him, but also to **s** for his sake;	*3958*
Php 4:12	both to abound and to **s** need	*5302*
1Ti 2:12	I **s** not a woman to teach, nor to	*2010*
2Ti 2:9	Wherein I **s** trouble, as an evil doer,	*2553*
2Ti 2:12	If we **s**, we shall also reign with	*5278*
2Ti 3:12	Christ Jesus shall **s** persecution	*1377*
Heb 11:25	Choosing rather to **s** affliction	*4778*
1Pe 3:14	if ye **s** for righteousness' sake	*3958*
1Pe 3:17	that ye **s** for well doing, than for	*3958*
1Pe 4:15	let none of you **s** as a murderer, or	*3958*
1Pe 4:16	if any man **s** as a Christian, let him	
1Pe 4:19	let them that **s** according to the	*3958*
Rev 2:10	**those things which thou shalt s**	*3958*

SUFFERED

Ge 20:6	**s** I thee not to touch her	5414
Dt 18:14	thy God hath not **s** thee so to do	5414
2Sa 21:10	and **s** neither the birds of the air	5414
Job 31:30	Neither have I **s** my mouth to sin	5414
Ps 105:14	He **s** no man to do them wrong:	3240
Jer 15:15	that for thy sake I have **s** rebuke	5375
Mt 19:8	**s you to put away your wives:**	*2010*
Mt 24:43	**have s his house to be broken up**	*1439*
Mt 27:19	for I have **s** many things this day	*3958*
Mk 5:26	**s** many things of many physicians,	*3958*
Mk 10:4	**s** to write a bill of divorcement	*2010*
Lk 8:51	he **s** no man to go in, save Peter,	*863*
Lk 24:26	**not Christ to have s these things,**	*3958*
Ac 16:7	but the Spirit **s** them not	*1439*
Ac 17:3	that Christ must needs have **s**,	*3958*

2Co 7:12 nor for his cause that **s** wrong, but
2Co 11:25 was I stoned, thrice I **s** shipwreck,
Php 3:8 I have **s** the loss of all things, *2210*
Heb 2:18 he himself hath **s** being tempted *3958*
Heb 5:8 he obedience by the things … he **s**; *3958*
Heb 9:26 For then must he often have **s** *3958*
Heb 13:12 his own blood, **s** without the gate *3958*
1Pe 2:21 because Christ also **s** for us, *3958*
1Pe 2:23 when he **s**, he threatened not; but *3958*
1Pe 3:18 Christ also hath once **s** for sins, *3958*
1Pe 4:1 as Christ hath **s** for us in the flesh *3958*
1Pe 4:1 for he that hath **s** in the flesh hath *3958*

SUFFERETH
Ps 66:9 and **s** not our feet to be moved 5414
Mt 11:12 **kingdom of heaven s violence,** *971*
1Co 13:4 Charity **s** long, and is kind; *3114*

SUFFERING
Jas 5:10 for an example of **s** affliction, *2552*
Jude 7 **s** the vengeance of eternal fire *5254*

SUFFERINGS
2Co 1:5 as the **s** of Christ abound in us, *3804*
2Co 1:7 that as ye are partakers of the **s** *3804*
Php 3:10 and the fellowship of his **s** *3804*
1Pe 4:13 as ye are partakers of Christ's **s**; *3804*
1Pe 5:1 and a witness of the **s** of Christ *3804*

SUFFICE
Dt 3:26 Lord said unto me, Let it **s** thee; 7227
1Pe 4:3 the time past of our life may **s** us *713*

SUFFICETH
Jn 14:8 shew us the Father, and it **s** us *714*

SUFFICIENCY
Job 20:22 In the fullness of his **s** he shall be 5607
2Co 3:5 of ourselves; but our **s** is of God; *2426*
2Co 9:8 always having all **s** in all things, *841*

SUFFICIENT
Pr 25:16 eat so much as is **s** for thee, lest 1767
Mt 6:34 **S unto the day is the evil thereof** *713*
Lk 14:28 **cost, whether he have s to finish it?**
Jn 6:7 pennyworth of bread is not **s** for *714*
2Co 2:6 **S** to such … is this punishment *2425*
2Co 3:5 Not that we are **s** of ourselves to *2425*
2Co 12:9 unto me, **My grace is s for thee** *714*

SUIT
Jgs 17:10 a **s** of apparel, and thy victuals 6187
Job 11:19 many shall make **s** unto thee 2470

SUM
Ex 21:30 be laid on him a **s** of money 3724
Ex 38:21 This is the **s** of the tabernacle, 6485
Nu 1:2 Take ye the **s** of the congregation 7218
2Sa 24:9 the **s** of the number of the people 4557
Est 4:7 the **s** of the money that Haman 6575
Ps 139:17 God! how great is the **s** of them! 7218
Da 7:1 and told the **s** of the matters 7217
Ac 7:16 Abraham bought for a **s** of money *5092*
Ac 22:28 a great **s** obtained I this freedom *2774*

SUMMER
Ge 8:22 cold and heat, and **s** and winter, 7019
Jgs 3:20 and he was sitting in a **s** parlour, 4747
Jgs 3:24 covereth his feet in his **s** chamber 4747
Ps 74:17 thou hast made **s** and winter 7019
Pr 6:8 Provideth her meat in the **s**, and 7019
Pr 10:5 that gathereth in **s** is a wise son: 7019
Pr 26:1 As snow in **s**, and as rain in 7019
Jer 8:20 The harvest is past, the **s** is ended, 7019
Mt 24:32 **leaves, ye know that s is nigh:** *2330*
Lk 21:30 **that s is now nigh at hand** *2330*

SUN
Ge 15:12 And when the **s** was going down, 8121
Ge 15:17 when the **s** went down, and it was 8121
Ge 37:9 the **s** and the moon and the eleven 8121
Ex 16:21 when the **s** waxed hot, it melted 8121
Ex 17:12 until the going down of the **s** 8121
Nu 25:4 up before the Lord against the **s**, 8121
Jos 1:4 sea toward the going down of the **s**, 8121
Jos 10:12 **S**, stand thou still upon Gibeon; 8121
Jos 10:13 And the **s** stood still, and the moon 8121
Jos 10:13 **s** stood still in the midst of heaven, 8121
Jos 10:27 the time of the going down of the **s**, 8121
Jgs 5:31 as the **s** when he goeth forth in his 8121
1Sa 11:9 by that time the **s** be hot, ye shall 8121
2Sa 12:12 before all Israel, and before the **s** 8121
Ne 7:3 he opened until the **s** be hot; 8121
Job 9:7 Which commandeth the **s**, and it 2775
Job 31:26 If I beheld the **s** when it shined, 216
Ps 19:4 hath he set a tabernacle for the **s**, 8121
Ps 72:5 as long as the **s** and moon endure, 8121
Ps 74:16 hast prepared the light and the **s** 8121
Ps 84:11 For the Lord God is a **s** and shield: 8121
Ps 113:3 From the rising of the **s** unto the 8121
Ps 121:6 The **s** shall not smite thee by day, 8121
Ps 136:8 The **s** to rule by day: for his mercy 8121
Ps 148:3 Praise ye him, **s** and moon: praise 8121
Ecc 1:5 the **s** also ariseth, and the **s** goeth 8121
Ecc 1:9 there is no new thing under the **s** 8121
Ecc 1:14 works that are done under the **s**; 8121
Ecc 2:11 and there was no profit under the **s** 8121
Ecc 3:16 under the **s** the place of judgment, 8121
Ecc 4:1 the oppressions … done under the **s** 8121
Ecc 4:3 evil work that is done under the **s** 8121
Ecc 4:7 and I saw vanity under the **s** 8121
Ecc 6:12 what shall be after him under the **s**? 8121
Ecc 8:15 which God giveth him under the **s** 8121
Ecc 11:7 it is for the eyes to behold the **s**: 8121
Ecc 12:2 While the **s**, or the light, or the 8121
SS 1:6 because the **s** hath looked upon me: 8121
SS 6:10 fair as the moon, clear as the **s** 2535
Isa 30:26 moon shall be as the light of the **s** 2535
Isa 30:26 light of the **s** shall be sevenfold 8121
Isa 38:8 is gone down in the **s** dial of Ahaz, 8121
Isa 38:8 So the **s** returned ten degrees, by 8121
Isa 59:19 his glory from the rising of the **s** 8121
Isa 60:19 The **s** shall be no more thy light by 8121
Isa 60:20 Thy **s** shall no more go down; 8121
Jer 15:9 her **s** is gone down while it was yet 8121
Jer 31:35 giveth the **s** for a light by day, 8121
Da 6:14 laboured till … going down of the **s** 8122
Joel 2:10 the **s** and the moon shall be dark, 8121
Joel 2:31 **s** shall be turned into darkness, 8121
Joel 3:15 **s** and the moon shall be darkened, 8121
Am 8:9 cause the **s** to go down at noon, 8121
Jnh 4:8 came to pass, when the **s** did rise, 8121
Jnh 4:8 the **s** beat upon the head of Jonah, 8121
Mal 1:11 from the rising of the **s** even unto 8121
Mal 4:2 the **S** of righteousness arise with 8121

Mt 5:45	he maketh his **s** to rise on the	*2246*
Mt 13:6	**And when the s was up, they were**	*2246*
Mt 13:43	**the righteous shine forth as the s**	*2246*
Mt 17:2	his face did shine as the **s**, and his	*2246*
Mt 24:29	**days shall the s be darkened,**	*2246*
Mk 1:3	when the **s** did set, they brought	*2246*
Mk 16:2	the sepulchre at the rising of the **s**	*2246*
Lk 21:25	**And there shall be signs in the s,**	*2246*
Lk 23:45	And the **s** was darkened, and the	*2246*
Ac 2:20	**s** shall be turned into darkness	*2246*
Ac 13:11	blind, not seeing the **s** for a season.	*2246*
Ac 27:20	when neither **s** nor stars in many	*2246*
1Co 15:41	There is one glory of the **s**, and	*2246*
Eph 4:26	not the **s** go down upon your wrath:	*2246*
Jas 1:11	For the **s** is no sooner risen with a	*2246*
Rev 1:16	as the **s** shineth in his strength	*2246*
Rev 6:12	the **s** became black as sackcloth of	*2246*
Rev 7:16	neither shall the **s** light on them	*2246*
Rev 8:12	the third part of the **s** was smitten,	*2246*
Rev 9:2	the **s** and the air were darkened by	*2246*
Rev 10:1	and his face was as it were the **s**,	*2246*
Rev 12:1	a woman clothed with the **s**, and	*2246*
Rev 16:8	poured out his vial upon the **s**;	*2246*
Rev 19:17	I saw an angel standing in the **s**;	*2246*
Rev 21:23	And the city had no need of the **s**.	*2246*
Rev 22:5	no candle, neither light of the **s**;	*2246*

SUNDRY

Heb 1:1	at **s** times and in divers manners	*4181*

SUNG

Isa 26:1	In that day shall this song be **s** in	7891
Mt 26:30	when they had **s** an hymn, they	*5214*
Mk 14:26	when they had **s** an hymn, they	*5214*
Rev 5:9	they **s** a new song, saying, Thou	*103*
Rev 14:3	**s** as it were a new song before the	*103*

SUNK

1Sa 17:49	the stone **s** into his forehead;	2883
2Ki 9:24	and he **s** down in his chariot	3766
Jer 38:6	mire: so Jeremiah **s** in the mire	2883
Jer 38:22	thy feet are **s** in the mire, and they	2883
Ac 20:9	preaching, he **s** down with sleep	*2702*

SUNRISING See also RISING.

Dt 4:41	side Jordan toward the **s**;	4217, 8121
Jos 1:15	this side Jordan toward the **s**.	4217, 8121
Jos 19:34	upon Jordan toward the **s**	4217, 8121

SUP

Lk 17:8	**Make ready wherewith I may s,**	*1172*
Rev 3:20	**in to him, and will s with him,**	*1172*

SUPERFLUOUS

Le 21:18	hath a flat nose, or any thing **s**,	8311
2Co 9:1	it is **s** for me to write to you:	*4053*

SUPERSCRIPTION

Mt 22:20	them, **Whose is this image and s?**	*1923*
Mk 12:16	them, **Whose is this image and s?**	*1923*
Mk 15:26	the **s** of his accusation was written	*1923*
Lk 20:24	**Whose image and s hath it?** They	*1923*
Lk 23:38	And a **s** also was written over him	*1923*

SUPERSTITIOUS

Ac 17:22	that in all things ye are too **s**	*1174*

SUPPED

1Co 11:25	he took the cup, when he had **s**,	*1172*

SUPPER

Mk 6:21	birthday made a **s** to his lords,	*1173*
Lk 14:12	**thou makest a dinner or a s,**	*1173*
Lk 14:16	**A certain man made a great s,**	*1173*
Lk 14:17	**sent his servant at s time to say**	*1173*
Lk 14:24	**were bidden shall taste of my s.**	*1173*
Lk 22:20	Likewise also the cup after **s**,	*1172*
Jn 13:4	He riseth from **s**, and laid aside	*1173*
Jn 21:20	also leaned on his breast at **s**, and	*1173*
1Co 11:20	this is not to eat the Lord's **s**	*1173*
1Co 11:21	one taketh before other his own **s**.	*1173*
Rev 19:9	unto the marriage **s** of the Lamb	*1173*
Rev 19:17	unto the **s** of the great God;	*1173*

SUPPLANT

Jer 9:4	for every brother will utterly **s**,	6117

SUPPLANTED

Ge 27:36	for he hath **s** me these two times:	6117

SUPPLICATION

1Sa 13:12	I have not made **s** unto the Lord:	2470
1Ki 8:33	make **s** unto thee in this house:	2603
1Ki 8:45	and make **s** unto thee in the land	2603
1Ki 8:52	and unto the **s** of thy people Israel,	8467
1Ki 8:54	all this prayer and **s** unto the Lord	8467
1Ki 9:3	I have heard thy prayer and thy **s**	8467
Est 4:8	the king, to make **s** unto him	2603
Job 8:5	and make thy **s** to the Almighty;	2603
Ps 6:9	The Lord hath heard my **s**; the	8467
Ps 30:8	and unto the Lord I made **s**.	2603
Ps 119:170	Let my **s** come before thee:	8467
Ps 142:1	unto the Lord did I make my **s**	2603
Jer 36:7	present their **s** before the Lord	8467
Da 6:11	and making **s** before his God	2604
Da 9:20	presenting my **s** before the Lord	8467
Ac 1:14	with one accord in prayer and **s**	*1162*
Eph 6:18	with all prayer and **s** in the Spirit,	*1162*
Php 4:6	by prayer and **s** with thanksgiving	*1162*

SUPPLICATIONS

2Ch 6:21	unto the **s** of thy servant, and	8469
Job 41:3	Will he make many **s** unto thee?	8469
Ps 28:2	Hear the voice of my **s**, when I cry	8469
Ps 28:6	he hath heard the voice of my **s**	8469
Ps 140:6	hear the voice of my **s**, O Lord	8469
Ps 143:1	prayer, O Lord, give ear to my **s**	8469
Da 9:3	Lord God, to seek by prayer and **s**	8469
Da 9:17	prayer of thy servant, and his **s**	8469
Da 9:18	for we do not present our **s** before	8469
Zec 12:10	the spirit of grace and of **s**: and	8469
1Ti 2:1	that, first of all, **s**, prayers	*1162*
1Ti 5:5	continueth in **s** and prayers night	*1162*
Heb 5:7	he had offered up prayers and **s**	*2428*

SUPPLIED

1Co 16:17	lacking on your part they have **s**	*378*
2Co 11:9	which came from Macedonia **s**	*4322*

SUPPLIETH

2Co 9:12	not only **s** the want of the saints,	*4322*
Eph 4:16	by that which every joint **s**,	*2024*

SUPPLY

Php 1:19	the **s** of the Spirit of Jesus Christ,	*2024*
Php 2:30	to **s** your lack of service toward	*378*
Php 4:19	But my God shall **s** all your need	*4137*

SUPPORT

Ac	20:35	labouring ye ought to **s** the weak,	*482*
1Th	5:14	**s** the weak, be patient toward all	*472*

SUPPOSE

2Sa	13:32	not my lord **s** that they have slain	559
Lk	7:43	I **s** that he, to whom he forgave	*5274*
Lk	12:51	**S ye that I am come to give**	*1380*
Jn	21:25	I **s** that even the world itself	*3633*
Ac	2:15	these are not drunken, as ye **s**,	*5274*
1Co	7:26	I **s** therefore that this is good for	*3543*
1Pe	5:12	a faithful brother … as I **s**	*3049*

SUPPOSED

Mt	20:10	**s that they should have received**	*3543*
Mk	6:49	sea, they **s** it had been a spirit,	*1380*
Lk	24:37	and **s** that they had seen a spirit	*1380*
Php	2:25	I **s** it necessary to send to you	*2233*

SUPPOSING

Lk	2:44	they, **s** him … in the company,	*3543*
Jn	20:15	She, **s** him to be the gardener	*1380*
Ac	14:19	out of the city, **s** he had been dead,	*3543*
Ac	16:27	**s** that the prisoners had been fled	*3543*
Php	1:16	**s** to add affliction to my bonds:	*3633*
1Ti	6:5	truth, **s** that gain is godliness:	*3543*

SURE

Ge	23:20	were made **s** unto Abraham for a	6965
Ex	3:19	I am **s** … the king of Egypt will not	3045
Nu	32:23	and be **s** your sin will find you out	3045
1Sa	2:35	and I will build him a **s** house;	539
1Sa	25:28	certainly make my lord a **s** house;	539
1Ki	11:38	and build thee a **s** house, as I built	539
Ne	9:38	we make a **s** covenant, and write	548
Job	24:22	riseth up, and no man is **s** of life	539
Ps	19:7	the testimony of the Lord is **s**,	539
Ps	93:5	Thy testimonies are very **s**	539
Ps	111:7	all his commandments are **s**	539
Pr	6:3	thyself, and make **s** thy friend	7292
Pr	11:15	and he that hateth suretiship is **s**	982
Pr	11:18	righteousness shall be a **s** reward	571
Isa	28:16	corner stone, a **s** foundation:	3245
Isa	55:3	you, even the **s** mercies of David	539
Da	2:45	and the interpretation thereof **s**	546
Da	4:26	thy kingdom shall be **s** unto thee,	7011
Mt	27:64	sepulchre be made **s** until the third	*805*
Mt	27:65	your way, make it as **s** as ye can	*805*
Mt	27:66	went, and made the sepulchre **s**	*805*
Lk	10:11	**be ye s of this, that the kingdom**	*1097*
Jn	6:69	are **s** that thou art that Christ	*1097*
Ac	13:34	give you the **s** mercies of David	*4103*
2Ti	2:19	the foundation of God standeth **s**,	*4731*
Heb	6:19	of the soul, both **s** and stedfast,	*804*
2Pe	1:10	make your calling and election **s**	*949*
2Pe	1:19	also a more **s** word of prophecy;	*949*

SURELY

Ge	2:17	thou eatest thereof thou shalt **s** die	
Ge	3:4	unto the woman, Ye shall not **s** die:	
Ge	9:5	**s** your blood … will I require;	389
Ge	18:18	Abraham shall **s** become a great and	
Ge	20:11	**S** the fear of God is not in this	7535
Ge	28:16	said, **S** the Lord is in this place;	403
Ge	28:22	me I will **s** give the tenth unto thee	
Ge	29:14	**S** thou art my bone and my flesh	389
Ge	29:32	**S** the Lord hath looked upon my	3588
Ge	42:16	by the life of Pharaoh **s** ye are spies	
Ge	44:28	**S** he is torn in pieces; and I saw	389
Ge	46:4	and I will also **s** bring thee up again:	
Ge	50:24	God will **s** visit you, and bring you	
Ge	50:25	God will **s** visit you, and ye shall	
Ex	2:14	and said, **S** this thing is known	403
Ex	4:25	**S** a bloody husband art thou to	3588
Ex	13:19	of Israel, saying, God will **s** visit you;	
Ex	18:18	Thou wilt **s** wear away, both thou,	
Ex	19:13	touch it, but he shall **s** be stoned,	3588
Le	20:2	Molech; he shall **s** be put to death:	
Le	20:9	or his mother shall be **s** put to death:	
Le	20:10	the adulteress shall **s** be put to death.	
Le	20:13	they shall **s** be put to death; their	
Le	20:15	a beast, he shall **s** be put to death:	
Le	20:16	beast: they shall **s** be put to death;	
Le	20:27	a wizard, shall **s** be put to death:	
Le	24:16	the Lord, he shall **s** be put to death,	
Le	24:17	any man shall **s** be put to death.	
Nu	13:27	and **s** it floweth with milk and honey;	
Nu	14:23	**S** they shall not see the land	518
Nu	14:35	I will **s** do it unto all this evil	518
Nu	26:65	They shall **s** die in the wilderness	
Nu	35:21	smote him shall **s** be put to death;	
Nu	35:31	death: but he shall be **s** put to death	
Dt	23:21	thy God will **s** require it of thee;	
Dt	31:18	And I will **s** hide my face in that day	
Jos	14:9	**S** the land whereon thy feet have	518
Jgs	6:16	**S** I will be with thee, and thou	3588
Ru	1:10	**S** we will return with thee unto	3588
1Sa	14:39	Jonathan my son, he shall **s** die	3588
1Sa	14:44	for thou shalt **s** die, Jonathan	
1Sa	16:6	**S** the Lord's anointed is before him	389
1Sa	20:31	him unto me, for he shall **s** die	
1Sa	29:6	**S**, as the Lord liveth, thou hast been	
2Sa	9:7	**s** shew the kindness for Jonathan	3588
2Sa	12:5	hath done this thing shall **s** die:	
2Sa	12:14	that is born unto thee shall **s** die	
1Ki	8:13	I have **s** built thee an house to	403
1Ki	11:2	for **s** they will turn away your heart	403
1Ki	11:11	I will **s** rend the kingdom from thee	
2Ki	18:30	The Lord will **s** deliver us, and this	
Job	13:3	**S** I would speak to the Almighty	199
Job	20:20	**S** he shall not feel quietness in	3588
Job	33:8	**S** … hast spoken in mine hearing	389
Job	34:12	Yea, **s** God will not do wickedly	551
Ps	23:6	**S** goodness and mercy shall	389
Ps	39:6	**S** every man walketh in a vain	389
Ps	39:11	like a moth: **s** every man is vanity	389
Ps	76:10	**S** the wrath of man shall praise	3588
Ps	85:9	**S** his salvation is nigh them that	389
Ps	112:6	**S** he shall not be moved for ever:	3588
Ps	139:11	**S** the darkness shall cover me:	389
Ps	139:19	**S** thou wilt slay the wicked, O God:	518
Pr	1:17	**S** in vain the net is spread in the	3588
Pr	10:9	that walketh uprightly walketh **s**	983
Pr	22:16	to the rich, shall **s** come to want	389
Pr	30:33	**S** the churning of milk bringeth	3588
Ecc	4:16	**S** this also is vanity and vexation	3588
Ecc	7:7	**S** oppression maketh a wise man	3588
Ecc	10:11	**S** the serpent will bite without	518
Isa	36:15	saying, The Lord will **s** deliver us:	
Isa	40:7	upon it: **s** the people is grass	403
Isa	45:14	**S** God is in thee; and there is none	389
Isa	45:24	**S**, shall one say, in the Lord have I	389
Isa	53:4	**S** he hath borne our griefs, and	403

Jer 8:13 I will **s** consume them, saith the
Jer 24:8 **s** thus saith the Lord, So will I give..... 3588
Jer 44:25 We will **s** perform our vows that we
Jer 44:25 ye will **s** accomplish your vows, and
Jer 44:25 your vows, and **s** perform your vows
Jer 49:20 **s** he ... make their habitations 518, 3808
Jer 51:56 God of recompences shall **s** requite
Eze 36:5 **S** in the fire of my jealousy 518, 3808
Mt 26:73 **S** thou also art one of them: *230*
Mk 14:70 to Peter, **S** thou art one of them:......... *230*
Lk 1:1 things which are most **s** believed *4135*
Jn 17:8 **known s that I came out from** *230*
Heb 6:14 **S** blessing I will bless thee, and *2229*
Rev 22:20 things saith, **S I come quickly** *3483*

SURETY
Ge 15:13 Know of a **s** that thy seed shall be...... 3045
Ge 18:13 Shall I of a **s** bear a child, which 552
Ge 26:9 said, Behold, of a **s** she is thy wife: 389
Ge 44:32 servant became **s** for the lad unto...... 6148
Job 17:3 down now, put me in a **s** with thee;.... 6148
Ps 119:122 Be **s** for thy servant for good: let....... 6148
Pr 6:1 My son, if thou be **s** for thy friend,..... 6148
Pr 11:15 He that is **s** for a stranger shall 6148
Pr 17:18 becometh **s** in the presence of his...... 6161
Pr 20:16 garment that is **s** for a stranger: 6148
Pr 27:13 garment that is **s** for a stranger 6148
Ac 12:11 Now I know of a **s**, that the Lord *230*
Heb 7:22 made a **s** of a better testament......... *1450*

SURNAME
Isa 44:5 **s** himself by the name of Israel 3655
Mt 10:3 whose **s** was Thaddaeus;.............. *1941*
Ac 10:5 for one Simon, whose **s** is Peter........ *1941*
Ac 12:12 of John, whose **s** was Mark *1941*

SURNAMED
Mk 3:16 And Simon he **s** Peter; *2007, 3686*
Mk 3:17 he **s** them Boanerges, which *2007, 3686*
Lk 22:3 Satan into Judah **s** Iscariot............ *1941*
Ac 4:36 by the apostles was **s** Barnabas *1941*
Ac 15:22 Judas **s** Barsabas, and Silas, chief....... *1941*

SUSTAIN
1Ki 17:9 a widow woman there to **s** thee 3557
Ne 9:21 Yea, forty years didst thou **s** them...... 3557
Ps 55:22 upon the Lord, and he shall **s** thee:..... 3557
Pr 18:14 spirit of a man will **s** his infirmity;..... 3557

SUSTAINED
Ps 3:4 I awaked; for the Lord **s** me........... 5564
Isa 59:16 and his righteousness, it **s** him 5564

SUSTENANCE
Jgs 6:4 left no **s** for Israel, neither sheep, ... 4241
Ac 7:11 and our fathers found no **s** *5527*

SWADDLING
Lk 2:7 and wrapped him in **s** clothes......... *4683*
Lk 2:12 find the babe wrapped in **s** clothes, ... *4683*

SWALLOW
Nu 16:30 open her mouth, and **s** them up....... 1104
Nu 16:34 said, Lest the earth **s** us up also........ 1104
Job 7:19 me alone till I **s** down my spittle?...... 1104
Ps 21:9 Lord shall **s** them up in his wrath...... 1104
Ps 56:1 O God: for man would **s** me up;....... 7602
Ps 56:2 Mine enemies would daily **s** me up:.... 7602
Ps 57:3 reproach of him that would **s** me...... 7602
Ps 69:15 neither let the deep **s** me up, and 1104
Pr 1:12 us **s** them up alive as the grave;........ 1104
Ecc 10:12 the lips of a fool will **s** up himself...... 1104
Isa 25:8 He will **s** up death in victory; and 1104
Am 8:4 this, O ye that **s** up the needy,......... 7602
Jnh 1:17 a great fish to **s** up Jonah. 1104
Mt 23:24 **strain at a gnat, and s a camel.** *2666*

SWALLOWED
Ex 7:12 but Aaron's rod **s** up their rods........ 1104
Ex 15:12 thy right hand, the earth **s** them....... 1104
Nu 26:10 and **s** them up together with Korah, ... 1104
Job 6:3 sea: therefore my words are **s** up....... 3886
Ps 35:25 them not say, We have **s** him up 1104
Ps 106:17 The earth opened and **s** up Dathan,.... 1104
Ps 124:3 Then they had **s** us up quick, when 1104
Jer 51:34 he hath **s** me up like a dragon, he...... 1104
1Co 15:54 written, Death is **s** up in victory *2666*
2Co 2:7 be **s** up with overmuch sorrow *2666*
2Co 5:4 that mortality might be **s** up of life *2666*
Rev 12:16 **s** up the flood which the dragon....... *2666*

SWARE
Ge 24:7 me, and that **s** unto me, saying........ 7650
Ge 24:9 **s** to him concerning that matter....... 7650
Ge 26:3 oath which I **s** unto Abraham thy...... 7650
Ge 31:53 Jacob **s** by the fear of his father........ 7650
Ge 50:24 the land which he **s** to Abraham....... 7650
Ex 33:1 the land which I **s** unto Abraham, ... 7650
Nu 32:11 the land which I **s** unto Abraham, ... 7650
Dt 1:8 which the Lord **s** unto your fathers..... 7650
Dt 8:18 his covenant which he **s** unto thy 7650
Jos 1:6 which I **s** unto their fathers to give..... 7650
Jos 5:6 the Lord **s** that he would not shew..... 7650
1Sa 19:6 and Saul **s**, As the Lord liveth, he 7650
1Sa 20:3 And David **s** moreover, and said, ... 7650
1Ki 2:23 Then King Solomon **s** by the Lord..... 7650
Ezr 10:5 according to this word. And they **s**..... 7650
Ps 95:11 Unto whom I **s** in my wrath that 7650
Ps 132:2 he **s** unto the Lord, and vowed 7650
Da 12:7 and **s** by him that liveth for ever....... 7650
Lk 1:73 The oath which he **s** to our father *3660*
Heb 3:11 So I **s** in my wrath, They shall not *3660*
Heb 3:18 to whom **s** he that they should not..... *3660*
Heb 6:13 by no greater, he **s** by himself,......... *3660*
Heb 7:21 The Lord **s** and will not repent,........ *3660*
Rev 10:6 **s** by him that liveth for ever and....... *3660*

SWAREST
Ex 32:13 to whom thou **s** by thine own self,..... 7650
Nu 11:12 the land which thou **s** unto their 7650
Dt 26:15 as thou **s** unto our fathers, a land...... 7650
Ps 89:49 thou **s** unto David in thy truth? 7650

SWARM
Ex 8:24 there came a grievous **s** of flies 6157
Jgs 14:8 was a **s** of bees and honey in the....... 5712

SWARMS
Ex 8:21 I will send **s** of flies upon thee, ... 6157
Ex 8:21 Egyptians shall be full of **s** of flies...... 6157
Ex 8:31 and he removed the **s** of flies from..... 6157

SWEAR
Ge 21:23 therefore **s** unto me here by God 7650
Ge 21:24 And Abraham said, I will **s** 7650
Ge 24:3 I will make thee **s** by the Lord, the 7650
Ge 25:33 And Jacob said, **S** to me this day; 7650

Ge	50:5	My father made me **s**, saying, Lo, I	7650
Ex	6:8	I did **s** to give it to Abraham	5375
Le	5:4	Or if a soul **s**, pronouncing with	7650
Le	19:12	ye shall not **s** by my name falsely,	7650
Dt	6:13	him, and shalt **s** by his name	7650
Jos	2:12	unto me by the Lord, since I	7650
Jos	2:17	oath which thou hast made us **s**	7650
1Sa	20:17	Jonathan caused David to **s** again,	7650
2Sa	19:7	for I **s** by the Lord, if thou go not	7650
1Ki	1:51	Let king Solomon **s** unto me to	7650
Ezr	10:5	to **s** that they should do according	7650
Ne	13:25	and made them **s** by God, saying	7650
Isa	3:7	In that day shall he **s**, saying, I	5375
Isa	19:18	and **s** to the Lord of hosts; one	7650
Isa	45:23	shall bow, every tongue shall **s**	7650
Isa	48:1	which **s** by the name of the Lord,	7650
Isa	65:16	earth shall **s** by the God of truth;	7650
Jer	4:2	And thou shalt **s**, The Lord liveth	7650
Jer	5:2	Lord liveth; surely they **s** falsely	7650
Jer	7:9	commit adultery, and **s** falsely	7650
Jer	12:16	to **s** by my name, The Lord liveth;	7650
Jer	22:5	I **s** by myself, saith the Lord, that	7650
Jer	32:22	thou didst **s** to their fathers to give	7650
Am	8:14	they that **s** by the sin of Samaria,	7650
Zep	1:5	worship and that **s** by the Lord,	7650
Mt	5:34	**S not at all; neither by heaven;**	*3660*
Mt	5:36	**Neither shalt thou s by thy head,**	*3660*
Mt	23:16	**Whosoever shall s by the temple,**	*3660*
Mt	23:16	**shall s by the gold of the temple,**	*3660*
Mt	23:18	**Whosoever shall s by the altar, it**	*3660*
Mt	23:20	**therefore shall s by the altar,**	*3660*
Mt	23:21	**And whoso shall s by the temple,**	*3660*
Mt	23:22	**And he that shall s by heaven,**	*3660*
Mt	26:74	Then began he to curse and to **s**,	*3660*
Heb	6:13	because he could **s** by no greater,	*3660*
Heb	6:16	For men verily **s** by the greater:	*3660*
Jas	5:12	all things, my brethren, **s** not,	*3660*

SWEARETH

Ps	15:4	He that **s** to his own hurt, and	7650
Ps	63:11	one that **s** by him shall glory:	7650
Isa	65:16	he that **s** in the earth shall swear	7650
Zec	5:4	of him that **s** falsely by my name:	7650
Mt	23:18	**whosoever s by the gift that is.**	*3660*
Mt	23:20	**s by it, and by all things thereon.**	*3660*
Mt	23:21	**s by it, and by him that dwelleth**	*3660*
Mt	23:22	**heaven, s by the throne of God,**	*3660*

SWEARING

Jer	23:10	because of **s** the land mourneth;	423
Hos	10:4	**s** falsely in making a covenant:	422

SWEAT

Ge	3:19	In the **s** of thy face shalt thou eat	2188
Lk	22:44	his **s** was as it were great drops of	*2402*

SWEEP

Isa	28:17	hail shall **s** away the refuge of lies	3261
Lk	15:8	**light a candle, and s the house,**	*4563*

SWEEPING

Pr	28:3	is like a **s** rain that leaveth no	5502

SWEET

Ge	8:21	And the Lord smelled a **s** savour;	5207
Ex	15:25	waters, the waters were made **s**:	4985
Ex	29:25	for a **s** savour before the Lord:	5207
Ex	30:7	burn thereon **s** incense every	5561
Ex	30:23	and of **s** cinnamon half so much,	1314
Ex	31:11	and **s** incense for the holy place:	5561
Ex	40:27	And he burnt **s** incense thereon; as	5561
Le	2:2	by fire, of a **s** savour unto the Lord:	5207
Nu	28:6	in mount Sinai for a **s** savour,	5207
Nu	28:8	by fire, of a **s** savour unto the Lord	5207
2Sa	23:1	and the **s** psalmist of Israel, said	5273
2Ch	13:11	burnt sacrifices and **s** incense:	5561
Ezr	6:10	**s** savours unto the God of heaven,	5208
Ps	55:14	We took **s** counsel together, and	4985
Ps	104:34	My mediation of him shall be **s**	6148
Ps	119:103	How **s** are thy words unto my	4452
Ps	141:6	hear my words; for they are **s**	5276
Pr	3:24	lie down, and thy sleep shall be **s**	6148
Pr	9:17	Stolen waters are **s**, and bread	4985
Pr	13:19	desire accomplished is **s** to the	6148
Pr	16:24	as an honeycomb, **s** to the soul	4966
Pr	20:17	Bread of deceit is **s** to a man; but	6149
Pr	23:8	vomit up, and lose thy **s** words	5273
Pr	27:7	hungry soul every bitter thing is **s**	4966
Ecc	5:12	The sleep of a labouring man is **s**	4966
Ecc	11:7	Truly the light is **s**, and a pleasant	4966
SS	2:14	**s** is thy voice, and thy countenance	6149
SS	5:16	His mouth is most **s**: yea, he is	4477
Isa	5:20	put bitter for **s**, and **s** for bitter!	4966
Isa	23:16	make **s** melody, sing many songs,	3190
Jer	31:26	and my sleep was **s** unto me	6148
Da	2:46	an oblation and **s** odours unto him	5208
Mk	16:1	and Salome, had bought **s** spices	
2Co	2:15	are unto God a **s** savour of Christ	*2175*
Php	4:18	an odour of a **s** smell, a sacrifice	*2175*
Jas	3:11	same place **s** water and bitter?	*1099*
Rev	10:9	it shall be in thy mouth **s** as honey	*1099*
Rev	10:10	and it was in my mouth **s** as honey:	*1099*

SWEETER

Jgs	14:18	What is **s** than honey? and what	4966
Ps	19:10	**s** ... than honey and the honeycomb	4966

SWEETNESS

Jgs	14:14	and out of the strong came forth **s**	4966
Pr	16:21	**s** of the lips increaseth learning	4986
Pr	27:9	so doth the **s** of a man's friend by	4986
Eze	3:3	was in my mouth as honey for **s**	4966

SWEETSMELLING See also SWEET and SMELLING.

Eph	5:2	a sacrifice to God for a **s** savour	*2175*

SWELL

Nu	5:22	to make thy belly to **s**, and thy	6638
Dt	8:4	neither did thy foot **s**, these forty	1216

SWELLING

Ps	46:3	the mountains shake with the **s**	1346
2Pe	2:18	speak great **s** words of vanity	*5246*
Jude	16	mouth speaketh great **s** words,	*5246*

SWEPT

Jer	46:15	Why are thy valiant men **s** away?	5502
Mt	12:44	**findeth it empty, s, and garnished,**	*4563*
Lk	11:25	**he findeth it s and garnished**	*4563*

SWIFT

1Ch	12:8	were as **s** as the roes upon the	4116
Pr	6:18	feet ... be **s** in running to mischief,	4116
Ecc	9:11	that the race is not to the **s**, nor	7031
Isa	19:1	the Lord rideth upon a **s** cloud,	7031
Am	2:15	and he that is **s** of foot shall not	7031

Mal	3:5	I will be a **s** witness against the	4116
Ro	3:15	Their feet are **s** to shed blood:	*3691*
Jas	1:19	let every man be **s** to hear, slow	*5036*
2Pe	2:1	upon themselves **s** destruction	*5031*

SWIFTER

2Sa	1:23	they were **s** than eagles, they	7043
Job	7:6	My days are **s** than a weaver's	7043
Jer	4:13	his horses are **s** than eagles	7043

SWIFTLY

Ps	147:15	earth: his word runneth very **s**	4120
Da	9:21	begin caused to fly **s**, touched me	3288

SWIM

2Ki	6:6	it in thither; and the iron did **s**	6687
Ps	6:6	all the night make I my bed to **s**;	7811
Ac	27:42	lest any of them should **s** out	*1579*
Ac	27:43	they which could **s** should cast	*2860*

SWINE

Dt	14:8	the **s**, because it divideth the hoof,	2386
Mt	7:6	**neither cast ye ... pearls before s,**	*5519*
Mt	8:30	them an herd of my **s** feeding	*5519*
Mt	8:31	us to go away into the heard of **s**	*5529*
Mt	8:32	out, they went into the herd of **s**.	*5519*
Mt	8:32	whole herd of **s** ran violently down	*5519*
Mk	5:11	a great heard of **s** feeding	*5519*
Mk	5:12	Send us into the **s**, that we may	*5529*
Mk	5:13	went out, and entered into the **s**	*5519*
Mk	5:14	they that fed the **s** fled, and told	*5519*
Mk	5:16	the devil, and also concerning the **s**	*5519*
Lk	15:15	**sent him into his fields to feed s.**	*5529*
Lk	15:16	**with the husks that the s did eat:**	*5529*

SWINE'S

Pr	11:22	As a jewel of gold in a **s** snout, so	2386
Isa	66:3	oblation, as if he offered **s** blood;	2386

SWORD

Ge	3:24	a flaming **s** which turned every	2719
Ge	27:40	And by thy **s** shalt thou live, and	2719
Ge	34:25	brethren, took each man his **s**,	2719
Ex	5:3	us with pestilence, or with the **s**	2719
Ex	18:4	delivered me from the **s** of Pharaoh:	2719
Ex	32:27	Put every man his **s** by his side	2719
Nu	20:18	I come out against thee with the **s**	2719
Nu	22:31	way, and his **s** drawn in his hand:	2719
Dt	32:25	The **s** without, and terror within,	2719
Dt	32:41	If I whet my glittering **s**, and mine	2719
Jos	5:13	him with his **s** drawn in his hand:	2719
Jos	24:12	not with thy **s**, nor with thy bow	2719
Jgs	4:16	Sisera fell upon the edge of the **s**;	2719
Jgs	7:20	The **s** of the Lord, and of Gideon	2719
Jgs	7:22	every man's **s** against his fellow,	2719
1Sa	13:22	was neither **s** nor spear found in	2719
1Sa	17:39	girded his **s** upon his armour,	2719
1Sa	17:45	Thou comest to me with a **s**, and	2719
1Sa	17:47	that the Lord saveth not with **s** and	2719
1Sa	17:51	upon the Philistine, and took his **s**,	2719
1Sa	22:10	and gave him the **s** of Goliath the	2719
1Sa	31:4	Draw thy **s**, and thrust me through	2719
1Sa	31:4	Saul took a **s**, and fell upon it	2719
2Sa	12:9	killed Uriah the Hittite with the **s**,	2719
2Sa	12:10	the **s** shall never depart from thine	2719
1Ki	2:8	not put thee to death with the **s**	2719
1Ki	3:24	And the king said, Bring me a **s**	2719
1Ki	19:10	slain thy prophets with the **s**;	2719
1Ki	19:14	slain thy prophets with the **s**;	2719
1Ch	21:30	afraid because of the **s** of the angel.	2719
Ezr	9:7	to the **s**, to captivity, and to a spoil,	2719
Ne	4:18	every one had his **s** girded by his	2719
Est	9:5	enemies with the stroke of the **s**,	2719
Job	1:15	servants with the edge of the **s**;	2719
Job	1:17	servants with the edge of the **s**;	2719
Job	33:18	his life from perishing by the **s**	7973
Ps	22:20	Deliver my soul from the **s**; my	2719
Ps	45:3	Gird thy **s** upon thy thigh, O most	2719
Ps	57:4	arrows, and their tongue a sharp **s**,	2719
Ps	149:6	and a twoedged **s** in their hand;	2719
Pr	5:4	wormwood, sharp as a twoedged **s**.	2719
Pr	12:18	speaketh like the piercings of a **s**.	2719
SS	3:8	every man ... his **s** upon his thigh	2719
Isa	2:4	shall not lift up **s** against nation,	2719
Isa	27:1	great and strong **s** shall punish	2719
Isa	34:6	**s** of the Lord is filled with blood,	2719
Isa	66:16	by his **s** will the Lord plead with	2719
Jer	4:10	the **s** reacheth unto the soul	2719
Jer	5:12	neither shall we see **s** nor famine:	2719
Jer	11:22	the young men shall die by the **s**;	2719
Jer	12:12	for the **s** of the Lord shall devour	2719
Jer	14:12	but I will consume them by the **s**,	2719
Jer	15:2	such as are for the **s**, to the **s**;	2719
Jer	15:3	the **s** to slay, and the dogs to tear	2719
Jer	27:13	die, thou and thy people, by the **s**,	2719
Jer	43:11	and such as are for the **s** to the **s**.	2719
Jer	44:28	a small number that escape the **s**	2719
Jer	47:6	O thou **s** of the Lord, how long will	2719
Jer	50:36	A **s** is upon the liars; and they	2719
Jer	50:37	a **s** is upon her treasures; and they	2719
La	2:21	my young men are fallen by the **s**;	2719
La	4:9	that be slain with the **s** are better	2719
Eze	5:12	and a third part shall fall by the **s**	2719
Eze	6:3	I, even I, will bring a **s** upon you,	2719
Eze	6:8	escape the **s** among the nations,	2719
Eze	11:8	bring a **s** upon you, saith the Lord	2719
Eze	14:17	and say, **S**, go through the land;	2719
Eze	21:9	Say, A **s**, a **s** is sharpened, and	2719
Eze	21:28	say thou, The **s**, the **s** is drawn:	2719
Eze	32:10	I shall brandish my **s** before them:	2719
Eze	32:11	**s** of the king of Babylon shall come	2719
Eze	33:4	if the **s** come, and take him away,	2719
Eze	33:6	if the watchman see the **s** come,	2719
Eze	33:6	if the **s** come, and take any person	2719
Eze	38:21	And I will call for a **s** against him	2719
Eze	38:21	every man's **s** shall be against his	2719
Eze	39:23	enemies: so fell they all by the **s**	2719
Da	11:33	yet they shall fall by the **s**, and by	2719
Hos	1:7	not save them by bow, nor by **s**,	2719
Hos	2:18	and I will break the bow and the **s**	2719
Joel	2:8	and when they fall upon the **s**,	7973
Am	1:11	did pursue his brother with the **s**,	2719
Am	9:10	sinners of my people ... die by the **s**,	2719
Mic	4:3	shall not lift up a **s** against nation,	2719
Na	2:13	the **s** shall devour thy young lions:	2719
Hag	2:22	every one by the **s** of his brother.	2719
Zec	9:13	made thee as the **s** of a mighty man.	2719
Zec	13:7	Awake, O **s**, against my shepherd	2719
Mt	10:34	**I came not to send peace, but a s**	*3162*
Mt	26:52	**Put up again thy s into his.**	*3162*
Mt	26:52	**for all they that take the s**	*3162*
Mt	26:52	**shall perish with the s**	*3162*
Lk	2:35	a **s** ... pierce through thy own soul.	*4501*
Lk	21:24	**shall fall by the edge of the s,**	*3162*

S

Lk	22:36	**he that hath no s, let him sell**	*3162*
Lk	22:49	Lord, shall we smite with the **s**?	*3162*
Jn	18:10	Simon Peter having a **s** drew it,	*3162*
Jn	18:11	Peter, **Put up thy s into the**	*3162*
Ac	12:2	And he killed James … with the **s**.	*3162*
Ac	16:27	doors open, he drew out his **s**, and	*3162*
Ro	8:35	or nakedness, or peril, or **s**?	*3162*
Ro	13:4	for he beareth not the **s** in vain:	*3162*
Eph	6:17	**s** of the Spirit, which is the word	*3162*
Heb	4:12	and sharper than any twoedged **s**	*3162*
Heb	11:34	escaped the edge of the **s**, out of	*3162*
Heb	11:37	tempted, were slain with the **s**	*3162*
Rev	1:16	mouth went a sharp twoedged **s**:	*4501*
Rev	2:12	**hath the sharp s with two edges;**	*4501*
Rev	2:16	**them with the s of my mouth.**	*4501*
Rev	6:4	was given unto him a great **s**	*3162*
Rev	6:8	to kill with **s**, and with hunger,	*4501*
Rev	13:10	he that killeth with the **s**.	*3162*
Rev	13:14	beast, which had the wound by a **s**,	*3162*
Rev	19:15	out of his mouth goeth a sharp **s**	*4501*
Rev	19:21	the remnant were slain with the **s**.	*4501*
Rev	19:21	which **s** proceeded out of his mouth:	

SWORDS

1Sa	13:19	Lest the Hebrews make them **s**	2719
Ps	59:7	their mouths: **s** are in their lips:	2719
Pr	30:14	a generation, whose teeth are as **s**,	2719
Isa	2:4	shall beat their **s** into plowshares,	2719
Eze	28:7	draw their **s** against the beauty of	2719
Eze	32:12	By the **s** of the mighty will I cause	2719
Eze	32:27	have laid their **s** under their heads	2719
Joel	3:10	Beat your plowshares into **s**, and	2719
Mic	4:3	shall beat their **s** into plowshares,	2719
Mt	26:47	with him a great multitude with **s**	*3162*
Mt	26:55	**out as against a thief with s.**	*3162*
Mk	14:43	with him a great multitude with **s**	*3162*
Mk	14:48	**out, as against a thief, with s**	*3162*
Lk	22:38	said, Lord, behold, here are two **s**	*3162*
Lk	22:52	out, as against a thief, with **s**	*3162*

SWORN

Ge	22:16	By myself have I **s** saith the Lord	7650
Ex	17:16	Lord hath **s** that the	3027, 5920, 3676
Le	6:5	about which he hath **s** falsely;	7650
Dt	7:8	keep the oath which he hath **s**.	7650
Dt	29:13	and as he hath **s** unto thy fathers,	7650
Dt	31:7	Lord hath **s** unto their fathers to	7650
Jos	9:19	We have **s** unto them by the Lord	7650
Jgs	21:7	seeing we have **s** by the Lord that	7650
Jgs	21:18	for the children of Israel have **s**	7650
1Sa	3:14	I have **s** unto the house of Eli,	7650
2Sa	3:9	as the Lord hath **s** to David, even	7650
2Ch	15:15	for they had **s** with all their heart,	7650
Ps	24:4	unto vanity, nor **s** deceitfully	7650
Ps	89:3	I have **s** unto David my servant	7650
Ps	89:35	Once have I **s** by my holiness that	7650
Ps	110:4	Lord hath **s**, and will not repent,	7650
Ps	119:106	I have **s**, and I will perform it,	7650
Ps	132:11	Lord hath **s** in truth unto David;	7650
Isa	14:24	The Lord of hosts hath **s**, saying	7650
Isa	45:23	I have **s** by myself, the word is	7650
Isa	54:9	I have **s** that the waters of Noah	7650
Isa	62:8	Lord hath **s** by his right hand, and	7650
Jer	5:7	and **s** by them that are no gods:	7650
Jer	11:5	the oath which I have **s** unto your	7650
Jer	44:26	I have **s** by my great name, saith	7650
Eze	21:23	sight, to them that have **s** oaths:	7650
Am	4:2	Lord God hath **s** by his holiness	7650
Am	6:8	The Lord God hath **s** by himself,	7650
Am	8:7	hath **s** by the excellency of Jacob,	7650
Mic	7:20	which thou has **s** unto our fathers	7650
Ac	2:30	God had **s** with an oath to him,	3660
Ac	7:17	which God had **s** to Abraham, the	3660
Heb	4:3	As I have **s** in my wrath, if they	3660

SYCOMORE

2Ch	1:15	cedar trees made he as the **s** trees	3256
2Ch	9:27	cedar trees made he as the **s** trees	3256
Lk	19:4	climbed up into a **s** tree to see	*4809*

SYNAGOGUE

Mt	13:54	country, he taught them in their **s**	*4864*
Mk	1:21	sabbath day he entered into the **s**,	*4864*
Mk	1:23	in their **s** a man with an unclean	*4864*
Mk	5:36	unto the ruler of the **s**, **Be not**	*752*
Mk	5:38	to the house of the ruler of the **s**,	*752*
Mk	6:2	come, he began to teach in the **s**	*4864*
Lk	4:20	eyes of all them that were in the **s**	*4864*
Lk	7:5	nation, and he hath built us a **s**	*4864*
Lk	8:41	and he was a ruler of the **s**: and	*4864*
Lk	13:14	the ruler of the **s** answered with	*752*
Jn	9:22	he should be put out of the **s**	*656*
Jn	12:42	lest they should be put out of the **s**	*656*
Jn	18:20	**I ever taught in the s, and in the**	*4864*
Ac	6:9	is called the **s** of the Libertines,	*4864*
Ac	13:14	and went into the **s** on the sabbath	*4864*
Ac	13:42	the Jews were gone out of the **s**,	*4864*
Ac	17:17	disputed he in the **s** with the Jews,	*4864*
Ac	18:4	reasoned in the **s** every sabbath,	*4864*
Ac	18:7	whose house joined hard to the **s**	*4864*
Ac	18:26	he began to speak boldly in the **s**	*4864*
Ac	22:19	beat in every **s** them that believed	*4864*
Ac	26:11	I punished them oft in every **s**,	*4864*
Rev	2:9	**are not, but are the s of Satan**	*4864*
Rev	3:9	**make them of the s of Satan,**	*4864*

SYNAGOGUES

Ps	74:8	have burned up all the **s** of God	4150
Mt	4:23	teaching in their **s**, and preaching	4864
Mt	6:2	**as the hypocrites do in the s and**	*4864*
Mt	6:5	**love to pray standing in the s**	*4864*
Mt	10:17	**they will scourge you in their s;**	*4864*
Mt	23:6	**and the chief seats in the s,**	*4864*
Mt	23:34	**them shall ye scourge in your s,**	*4864*
Mk	12:39	**And the chief seats in the s, and**	*4864*
Mk	13:9	**and in the s ye shall be beaten:**	*4864*
Lk	11:43	**the uppermost seats in the s,**	*4864*
Lk	12:11	**when they bring you unto the s,**	*4864*
Lk	13:10	he was teaching in one of the **s**	*4864*
Lk	20:46	**and the highest seats in the s,**	*4864*
Lk	21:12	**delivering you up to the s, and**	*4864*
Jn	16:2	**They shall put you out of the s**	*655*
Ac	9:20	he preached Christ in the **s**, that	*4864*
Ac	13:5	preached the word of God in the **s**	*4864*
Ac	15:21	being read in the **s** every sabbath	*4864*

S

T

TABERNACLE

Ex	25:9	thee, after the pattern of the **t**,	4908
Ex	28:43	come in unto … **t** of … congregation,	168
Ex	30:18	between the **t** of the congregation	168
Ex	30:20	go into the **t** of the congregation,	168
Ex	33:7	called it the **T** of the congregation	168
Ex	33:10	cloudy pillar stand at the **t** door:	168
Ex	36:37	made an hanging for the **t** door	168
Ex	40:34	the glory of the Lord filled the **t**	4908
Ex	40:36	cloud was taken up from over the **t**,	4908
Ex	40:38	cloud of the Lord was upon the **t**	4908
Le	1:3	door of the **t** of the congregation	168
Le	3:13	before the **t** of the congregation:	168
Le	4:4	door of the **t** of the congregation	168
Le	4:7	is in the **t** of the congregation;	168
Le	4:16	blood to the **t** of the congregation:	168
Le	6:16	court of the **t** of the congregation.	168
Le	6:26	court of the **t** of the congregation.	168
Le	6:30	into the **t** of the congregation	168
Le	8:3	door of the **t** of the congregation	168
Le	8:10	anointed the **t** and all … therein.	4908
Le	8:33	not go out of the door of the **t**	168
Le	15:31	defile my **t** that is among them	4908
Le	16:17	no man in the **t** of the congregation	168
Nu	1:50	shall bear the **t**, and all the vessels.	4908
Nu	3:38	before the **t** toward the east, even	4908
Nu	9:22	that the cloud tarried upon the **t**,	4908
Nu	12:5	and stood in the door of the **t**, and.	168
Nu	17:7	before the Lord in the **t** of witness	168
Nu	19:13	himself, defileth the **t** of the Lord;	4908
Jos	22:19	wherein the Lord's **t** dwelleth,	4908
1Ki	2:28	Joab fled unto the **t** of the Lord	168
1Ch	23:26	they shall no more carry the **t**, nor	4908
Ps	15:1	Lord, who shall abide in thy **t**?	168
Ps	19:4	In them hath he set a **t** for the sun,	168
Ps	27:6	will I offer in his **t** sacrifices of joy;	168
Ps	61:4	I will abide in thy **t** for ever: I will	168
Pr	14:11	the **t** of the upright shall flourish	168
La	2:6	he hath violently taken away his **t**,	7900
2Co	5:4	For we that are in this **t** do groan,	*4636*
Heb	9:3	**t** which is called the Holiest of all;	*4633*
Heb	9:11	by a greater and more perfect **t**,	*4633*
2Pe	1:13	as long as I am in this **t**, to stir	*4638*
2Pe	1:14	shortly I must put off this my **t**,	*4638*
Rev	21:3	the **t** of God is with men, and he	*4633*

TABERNACLES

Dt	16:13	observe the feast of **t** seven days	5521
Dt	31:10	the year of release, in the feast of **t**,	5521
2Ch	8:13	feast of weeks, and in the feast of **t**.	5521
Ps	46:4	place of the **t** of the most High	4908
Ps	84:1	How amiable are thy **t**, O Lord of.	4908
Ps	118:15	is in the **t** of the righteous:	168
Zec	14:16	of hosts, and to keep the feast of **t**	5521
Mt	17:4	let us make here three **t**; one for	*4633*
Mk	9:5	let us make three **t**; one for thee,	*4633*
Lk	9:33	let us make three **t**; one for thee	*4633*
Jn	7:2	the Jews' feast of **t** was at hand	*4634*
Heb	11:9	dwelling in **t** with Isaac … Jacob.	*4633*

TABLE

Ex	25:30	thou shalt set upon the **t** shewbread	7979
Ex	26:35	thou shalt set the **t** without the vail,	7979
Le	24:6	upon the pure **t** before the Lord	7979
Nu	3:31	charge shall be the ark, and the **t**,	7979
Nu	4:7	upon the **t** of shewbread they shall.	7979
1Sa	20:34	Jonathan arose from the **t** in fierce	7979
2Sa	9:10	son shall eat bread alway at my **t**.	7979
1Ki	7:48	the altar of gold, and the **t** of gold	7979
Ps	23:5	Thou preparest a **t** before me in the.	7979
Pr	3:3	them upon the **t** of thine heart:	3871
Pr	7:3	write them upon the **t** of thine heart	3871
Pr	9:2	she hath also furnished her **t**.	7979
Isa	30:8	Now go, write it before them in a **t**,	3871
Jer	17:1	graven upon the **t** of their heart,	3871
Eze	41:2	This is the **t** that is before the Lord.	7979
Mal	1:12	say, The **t** of the Lord is polluted;	7979
Mt	15:27	which fall from their masters' **t**,	*5132*
Mk	7:28	yet the dogs under the **t** eat of the	*5132*
Lk	1:63	And he asked for a writing **t**, and	*4093*
Lk	16:21	**fell from the rich man's t**	*5132*
1Co	10:21	cannot be partakers of the Lord's **t**,	*5132*
Heb	9:2	and the **t**, and the shewbread;	*5132*

TABLES

Ex	31:18	two **t** of testimony, **t** of stone,	3871
Ex	32:16	And the **t** were the work of God,	3871
Ex	32:19	and he cast the **t** out of his hands,	3871
Ex	34:4	two **t** of stone like unto the first;	3871
Dt	9:9	**t** of the covenant which the Lord	3871
Dt	10:5	and put the **t** in the ark which I had	3871
1Ki	8:9	in the ark save the two **t** of stone,	3871
1Ch	28:16	gave gold for the **t** of shew bread,	7979
2Ch	4:19	**t** whereon the shewbread was set;	7979
Eze	40:42	four **t** were of hewn stone for the	7979
Hab	2:2	vision, and make it plain upon **t**,	3871
Mt	21:12	the **t** of the moneychangers, and.	*5132*
Mk	11:15	the **t** of the moneychangers,	*5132*
Jn	2:15	money, and overthrew the **t**;	*5132*
Ac	6:2	leave the word of God, and serve **t**	*5132*
2Co	3:3	living God; not in **t** of stone	*4109*
2Co	3:3	but in fleshy **t** of the heart	*4109*
Heb	9:4	budded, and the **t** of the covenant;	*4109*

TAIL

Ex	4:4	thine hand, and take it by the **t**	2180
Dt	28:13	thee the head, and not the **t**;	2180
Dt	28:44	the head, and thou shalt be the **t**.	2180
Isa	9:15	that teacheth lies, he is the **t**.	2180
Rev	12:4	his **t** drew the third part of the	*3769*

TAILS

Rev	9:10	they had **t** like unto scorpions,	*3769*
Rev	9:19	is in their mouth, and in their **t**.	*3769*

TAKE

Ge	22:2	**T** now thy son, thine only son.	3947
Ex	7:9	**T** thy rod, and cast it before.	3947
Ex	20:7	shalt not **t** the name of the Lord.	5375
Nu	3:45	**T** the Levites instead of all the.	3947
Nu	16:3	Ye **t** too much upon you, seeing all	
Nu	35:31	**t** no satisfaction for the life of a	3947
Nu	35:32	**t** no satisfaction for him that is fled	3947
1Ki	19:4	now, O Lord, **t** away my life; for	3947
2Ki	2:1	when the Lord would **t** up Elijah	5927
Job	23:10	But he knoweth the way that I **t**	5978
Ps	2:2	and the rulers **t** counsel together,	
Ps	51:11	and **t** not thy holy spirit from me.	3947

Ps 69:20 I looked for some to **t** pity, but there
Pr 4:13 **T** fast hold of instruction; let her 2388
Pr 5:5 to death; her steps **t** hold on hell 8551
Pr 6:25 let her **t** thee with her eyelids 3947
Pr 6:27 Can a man **t** fire in his bosom, and 2846
Pr 7:18 let us **t** our fill of love until the
Pr 30:9 and **t** the name of my God in vain 8610
Ecc 5:15 and shall **t** nothing of his labour, ... 5375
SS 2:15 **T** us the foxes, the little foxes........... 270
Eze 11:19 **t** the stony heart out of their flesh 5493
Eze 36:26 I will **t** away the stony heart out 5493
Da 7:18 most High shall **t** the kingdom, ... 6902
Da 7:26 they shall **t** away his dominion,........ 5709
Da 11:31 shall **t** away the daily sacrifice,......... 5493
Hos 4:11 and new wine **t** away the heart 3947
Jnh 4:3 O Lord, **t**, I beseech thee, my life....... 3947
Mt 1:20 fear not to **t** unto thee Mary thy....... *3880*
Mt 6:25 **T no thought for your life, what**
Mt 9:6 **t up thy bed, and go unto thine** *142*
Mt 11:29 **T my yoke upon you, and learn of**...... *142*
Mt 15:26 **not meet to t the children's bread,** *2983*
Mt 16:24 **and t up his cross, and follow me**....... *142*
Mt 24:4 **T heed that no man deceive you**
Mt 25:28 **T therefore the talent from him,**........ *142*
Mt 26:26 **and said, T, eat; this is my body** *2983*
Mk 8:34 **deny himself, and t up his cross,**........ *142*
Mk 13:5 **T heed lest any man deceive you:**
Mk 14:22 and said, **T, eat: this is my body** *2983*
Mk 14:36 **unto thee; t away this cup from me:** ... *3911*
Lk 9:3 **them, T nothing for your journey,**...... *142*
Lk 9:23 **himself, and t up his cross daily,**........ *142*
Lk 12:22 **T no thought for your life, what**
Lk 19:24 **T from him the pound, and give it**...... *142*
Lk 21:8 **T heed that ye be not deceived:**
Jn 5:8 him, **Rise, t up thy bed, and walk.** *142*
Jn 10:17 **my life, that I might t it again,** *2983*
Ac 1:20 and his bishoprick let another **t** *2983*
Ac 20:26 I **t** you to record this day, that
1Co 3:10 let every man **t** heed how he buildeth
1Co 11:24 **T, eat: this is my body, which is** *2983*
Eph 6:13 **t** unto you the whole armour of........ *353*
Col 4:17 **T** heed to the ministry which thou
Heb 10:11 which can never **t** away sins: *4014*
Rev 3:11 **hast, that no man t thy crown**......... *2983*
Rev 5:9 Thou art worthy to **t** the book, and *2983*
Rev 22:17 let him **t** the water of life freely........ *2902*
Rev 22:19 if any man shall **t** away from the........ *851*

TAKEN

Ge 2:23 because she was **t** out of Man 3947
Ex 40:36 the cloud was **t** up from over the 5927
Nu 9:22 when it was **t** up, they journeyed 5927
1Sa 4:11 the ark of God was **t**; and the two 3947
2Sa 12:10 hast **t** the wife of Uriah the Hittite 3947
2Ki 2:16 Spirit of the Lord hath **t** him up....... 5375
Job 1:21 gave, and the Lord hath **t** away; 3947
Ps 59:12 let them even be **t** in their pride:....... 3920
Pr 3:26 shall keep thy foot from being **t** 3921
Pr 4:16 and their sleep is **t** away, unless........ 1497
Pr 6:2 **t** with the words of thy mouth 3920
Jer 16:5 **t** away my peace from this people....... 622
Da 5:3 the golden vessels that were **t** out 5312
Da 6:23 So Daniel was **t** up out of the den,..... 5267
Da 8:11 the daily sacrifice was **t** away.......... 7311
Da 12:11 the daily sacrifice shall be **t** away, ... 5493
Mt 13:12 **from him shall be t away even** *142*
Mt 24:40 **one shall be t, and the other** *3880*
Lk 8:18 **from him shall be t even that** *142*
Lk 9:17 there was **t** up of fragments that........ *142*
Lk 17:36 **one shall be t, and the other left**....... *3880*
Lk 19:26 **he hath shall be t away from him**....... *142*
Jn 8:3 unto him a woman **t** in adultery; *2638*
Jn 20:13 they have **t** away my Lord, and I *142*
Ac 1:11 Jesus, which is **t** up from you into *353*
Ac 1:22 same day that he was **t** up from us, ... *353*
1Co 10:13 There hath no temptation **t** you *2983*
2Th 2:7 let, until he be **t** out of the way *1096*
Rev 11:17 thou hast **t** to thee thy great power, ... *2983*

TAKETH

Ex 20:7 guiltless that **t** his name in vain 5375
Dt 5:11 guiltless that **t** his name in vain 5375
Dt 27:25 that **t** reward to slay an innocent 3947
Ps 144:3 is man, that thou **t** knowledge of him!
Pr 16:32 his spirit than he that **t** a city.......... 3920
Pr 17:23 man **t** a gift out of the bosom......... 3947
Pr 26:17 like one that **t** a dog by the ears 2388
Pr 30:28 The spider **t** hold with her hands, ... 8610
Mt 4:5 devil **t** him up into the holy city,....... *3880*
Mt 4:8 devil **t** him up into an exceeding....... *3880*
Mt 10:38 **And he that t not his cross, and** *2983*
Mt 12:45 **t with himself seven other spirits**...... *3880*
Lk 11:26 **and t to him seven other spirits** *3880*
Jn 10:18 **No man t it from me, but I lay it** *142*
1Co 3:19 **t** the wise in their own craftiness *1405*
Heb 5:4 no man **t** this honour unto himself,.... *2983*
Heb 10:9 He **t** away the first, that he may......... *337*

TAKING

2Ch 19:7 respect of persons, nor **t** of gifts 4727
Ps 119:9 by **t** heed thereto according to thy
Mt 6:27 **Which of you by t thought can**
Ro 7:11 For sin, **t** occasion by the *2983*
Eph 6:16 Above all, **t** the shield of faith *353*

TALE

Ex 5:18 yet shall ye deliver the **t** of bricks 8506
Ps 90:9 spend our years as a **t** that is told 1899

TALEBEARER

Le 19:16 down as a **t** among thy people:........ 7400
Pr 11:13 A **t** revealeth secrets: but he...... 1980, 7400
Pr 18:8 The words of a **t** are as wounds,....... 5372
Pr 20:19 about as a **t** revealeth secrets:.......... 7400
Pr 26:20 there is no **t**, the strife ceaseth......... 5372
Pr 26:22 The words of a **t** are as wounds 5372

TALENT

Ex 37:24 Of a **t** of pure gold made he it, and 3603
2Sa 12:30 a **t** of gold with the precious stones:.... 3603
Mt 25:24 **he which had received the one t**....... *5007*
Mt 25:28 **Take therefore the t from him,** *5007*
Rev 16:21 stone about the weight of a **t**.......... *5006*

TALENTS

1Ki 10:10 an hundred and twenty **t** of gold,...... 3603
1Ch 22:14 an hundred thousand **t** of gold........ 3603
1Ch 22:14 a thousand thousand **t** of silver; 3603
Mt 18:24 **which owed him ten thousand t**....... *5007*
Mt 25:15 **unto one he gave five t, and to** *5007*

TALES

Eze 22:9 men that carry **t** to shed blood: 7400
Lk 24:11 words seemed to them as idle **t**, ... *3026*

T

TALITHA (tal´-ith-ah)
Mk 5:41 hand, and said unto her, **T cumi;** *5008*

TALK
Nu 11:17 come down and **t** with thee there: 1696
Dt 5:24 this day that God doth **t** with man..... 1696
Dt 6:7 **t** of them when thou sittest in thine.... 1696
1Sa 2:3 **T** no more so exceeding proudly;...... 1696
Pr 6:22 thou awakest, it shall **t** with thee....... 7878
Pr 14:23 but the **t** of the lips tendeth only 1697
Pr 24:2 and their lips **t** of mischief............ 1696
Ecc 10:13 the end of his **t** is mischievous 6310
Jn 14:30 **Hereafter I will not t much with**....... *2980*

TALKED
Ex 20:22 that I have **t** with you from heaven..... 1696
Ex 34:29 his face shone while he **t** with him..... 1696
Dt 5:4 The Lord **t** with you face to face....... 1696
Zec 1:9 And the angel that **t** with me said...... 1696
Zec 4:1 angel that **t** with me came again....... 1696
Lk 24:32 while he **t** with us by the way, ... *2980*

TALKEST
Jn 4:27 thou? or, Why **t** thou with her?........ *2980*

TALKETH
Jn 9:37 **him, and it is he that t with thee**....... *2980*

TALKING
1Ki 18:27 either he is **t**, or he is pursuing 7879
Mt 17:3 them Moses and Elias **t** with him...... *4814*
Mk 9:4 Moses: and they were **t** with Jesus...... *4814*
Eph 5:4 nor foolish **t**, nor jesting.............. *3473*

TALL
Dt 2:21 A people great, and many, and **t**....... 7311
Dt 9:2 A people great and **t**, the children...... 7311

TALLER
Dt 1:28 people is greater and **t** than we; 7311

TAME
Mk 5:4 neither could any man **t** him.......... *1150*
Jas 3:8 But the tongue can no man **t**; it is *1150*

TAMED
Jas 3:7 and hath been **t** of mankind:.......... *1150*

TANGLE See **ENTANGLE.**

TAPESTRY
Pr 7:16 decked my bed with coverings of **t**,
Pr 31:22 She maketh herself coverings of **t**;

TARE
2Sa 13:31 king arose, and **t** his garments,........ 7167
Mk 9:20 him, straightway the spirit **t** him;...... *4682*
Lk 9:42 devil threw him down, and **t** him. *4952*

TARES
Mt 13:25 **and sowed t among the wheat,**........ *2215*
Mt 13:29 **Nay; lest while ye gather up the t,** *2215*
Mt 13:38 **t are the children of the wicked** *2215*
Mt 13:40 **t are gathered and burned in the** *2215*

TARGETS
1Ki 10:16 two hundred **t** of beaten gold:......... 6793

TARRIED
Nu 9:22 the cloud **t** upon the tabernacle,........ 748
1Sa 13:8 he **t** seven days, according to the....... 3176
2Sa 11:1 But David **t** still at Jerusalem.......... 3427
1Ch 20:1 Rabbah. But David **t** at Jerusalem...... 3427
Mt 25:5 **While the bridegroom, t they all** *5549*
Lk 1:21 that he **t** so long in the temple......... *5549*
Lk 2:43 child Jesus **t** behind in Jerusalem;...... *5278*

TARRIETH
1Sa 30:24 his part be that **t** by the stuff; 3427
Mic 5:7 upon the grass, that **t** not for man,..... 6960

TARRY
Ge 27:44 And **t** with him a few days, until....... 3427
Ex 12:39 out of Egypt, and could not **t**,......... 4102
Le 14:8 **t** abroad out of his tent seven days..... 3427
Jgs 19:10 But the man would not **t** that night, ... 3885
Ru 3:13 **T** this night, and it shall be in the...... 3885
2Ki 2:2 unto Elisha, **T** here, I pray thee; 3427
2Ki 2:4 him, Elisha, **t** here, I pray thee; 3427
2Ki 2:6 unto him, **T**, I pray thee, here;......... 3427
1Ch 19:5 **T** at Jericho until your beards be 3427
Pr 23:30 They that **t** long at the wine; they....... 309
Isa 46:13 off, and my salvation shall not **t** 309
Hab 2:3 not lie: though it **t**, wait for it;......... 4102
Hab 2:3 it will surely come, it will not **t** 309
Mt 26:38 **t ye here, and watch with me**.......... *3306*
Mk 14:34 **unto death: t ye here, and watch**....... *3306*
Lk 24:49 **but t ye in the city of Jerusalem,**....... *2523*
Jn 21:22 **If I will that he t till I come,** *3306*
Jn 21:23 but, If I will that he **t** till
Heb 10:37 come will come, and will not **t** *5549*

TASK
Ex 5:19 from your bricks of your daily **t** 1697

TASKMASTERS See also **MASTERS.**
Ex 1:11 they did set over them **t**......... 8269, 4522
Ex 3:7 their cry by reason of their **t**;.......... 5065

TASKS
Ex 5:13 Fulfill your works, your daily **t**,........ 1697

TASTE
1Sa 14:43 I did but **t** a little honey with the 2938
Job 6:6 there any **t** in the white of an egg? 2940
Ps 34:8 O **t** and see that the Lord is good: 2938
Pr 24:13 honeycomb, which is sweet to thy **t** 2441
SS 2:3 and his fruit was sweet to my **t** 2441
Mt 16:28 **here, which shall not t of death,**....... *1089*
Mk 9:1 **here, which shall not t of death,**....... *1089*
Lk 9:27 **here, which shall not t of death,**....... *1089*
Lk 14:24 **were bidden shall t of my supper**...... *1089*
Jn 8:52 saying, he shall never **t** of death *1089*
Col 2:21 (Touch not; **t** not; handle not;......... *1089*
Heb 2:9 should **t** death for every man *1089*

TASTED
Da 5:2 Belshazzar, whiles he **t** the wine,....... 2942
Mt 27:34 had **t** thereof, he would not drink...... *1089*
Jn 2:9 **t** of the water that was made wine,..... *1089*
Heb 6:4 and have **t** of the heavenly gift, and *1089*
Heb 6:5 And have **t** the good word of God,..... *1089*
1Pe 2:3 ye have **t** that the Lord is gracious *1089*

TATTLERS
1Ti 5:13 idle, but **t** also and busybodies,........ *5397*

TAUGHT
Dt 4:5 Behold, I have **t** you statutes and 3925
2Ki 17:28 **t** them how they should fear the....... 3384

2Ch 6:27 thou hast **t** them the good way,........ 3384
2Ch 30:22 **t** the good knowledge of the Lord:..... 7919
Ps 71:17 thou hast **t** me from my youth:........ 3925
Pr 4:4 He **t** me also, and said unto me,........ 3384
Pr 4:11 I have **t** thee in the way of wisdom;.... 3384
Pr 31:1 prophecy that his mother **t** him....... 3256
Ecc 12:9 he still **t** the people knowledge;........ 3925
Isa 40:13 being his counsellor hath **t** him?....... 3045
Isa 40:14 and **t** him knowledge, and shewed..... 3925
Jer 9:5 have **t** their tongue to speak lies,....... 3925
Mt 7:29 he **t** them as one having......... *2258, 1321*
Mt 13:54 he **t** them in their synagogue.......... *1321*
Mk 1:22 for he **t** them as one that had.... *2258, 1321*
Mk 4:2 **t** them many things by parables,.. *2258, 1321*
Lk 5:3 and **t** the people out of the ship....... *1321*
Lk 19:47 And he **t** daily in the temple..... *2258, 1321*
Jn 6:45 **And they shall be all t of God**......... *1318*
Jn 7:28 cried Jesus in the temple as he **t**,....... *1321*
Jn 8:28 **as my Father hath t me, I speak**....... *1321*
Jn 18:20 **I ever t in the synagogue, and in**....... *1321*
Ac 18:25 **t** diligently the things of the Lord,..... *1321*
Gal 6:6 Let him that is **t** in the word.......... *2727*
Eph 4:21 heard him, and ... been **t** by him,...... *1321*
Col 2:7 in the faith, as ye have been **t**.......... *1321*
1Th 4:9 are **t** of God to love one anther........ *2312*
2Th 2:15 traditions which ye have been **t**........ *1321*
Tit 1:9 faithful word as he hath been **t**........ *1322*
1Jn 2:27 no lie, and even as it hath **t** you........ *1321*
Rev 2:14 **t Balac to cast a stumblingblock**....... *1321*

TAUNT
Jer 24:9 and a proverb, a **t** and a curse,........ 8148
Eze 5:15 So it shall be a reproach and a **t**,....... 1422

TAUNTING
Hab 2:6 and a **t** proverb against him, and...... 4426

TAXATION
2Ki 23:35 of every one according to his **t**, to...... 6187

TAXED
2Ki 23:35 he **t** the land to give the money........ 6186
Lk 2:1 that all the world should be **t**........... *582*
Lk 2:5 be **t** with Mary his espoused wife,....... *582*

TEACH
Ex 4:12 and **t** thee what thou shalt say......... 3384
Ex 4:15 and will **t** you what ye shall do........ 3384
Ex 24:12 written; that thou mayest **t** them...... 3384
Le 14:57 **t** when it is unclean, and when it is.... 3384
Dt 5:31 judgments, which thou shalt **t** them,... 3925
Dt 6:7 shalt **t** them diligently unto thy........ 8150
Dt 17:11 of the law which they shall **t** thee,...... 3384
Jgs 13:8 and **t** us what we shall do unto the..... 3384
1Sa 12:23 I will **t** you the good and the right..... 3384
Job 6:24 **T** me, and I will hold my tongue:...... 3384
Job 37:19 **T** us what we shall say unto him;...... 3045
Ps 25:4 thy ways, O Lord; **t** me thy paths...... 3925
Ps 25:8 will he **t** sinners in the way........... 3384
Ps 32:8 I will instruct thee and **t** thee in the.... 3384
Ps 34:11 I will **t** you the fear of the Lord........ 3925
Ps 51:13 will I **t** transgressors thy ways;......... 3925
Ps 90:12 **t** us to number our days, that we...... 3045
Ps 119:64 of thy mercy: **t** me thy statutes........ 3925
Ps 119:108 O Lord, and **t** me thy judgments...... 3925
Ps 143:10 **T** me to do thy will; for thou art....... 3925
Pr 9:9 **t** a just man, and he will increase...... 3045

Jer 31:34 **t** no more every man his neighbour,... 3925
Eze 44:23 shall **t** my people the difference....... 3384
Da 1:4 whom they might **t** the learning....... 3925
Mic 3:11 and the priests thereof **t** for hire,...... 3384
Mt 5:19 **whosoever shall do and t them,**....... *1321*
Mt 28:19 **Go ye therefore, and t all nations,**..... *3100*
Mk 8:31 he began to **t** them, that the Son of.... *1321*
Lk 11:1 said unto him, Lord, **t** us to pray,...... *1321*
Lk 12:12 **Holy Ghost shall t you in the**......... *1321*
Jn 9:34 born in sins, and dost thou **t** us?....... *1321*
Jn 14:26 **he shall t you all things, and**.......... *1321*
Ac 1:1 that Jesus began both to do and **t**,..... *1321*
Ac 4:18 at all nor **t** in the name of Jesus....... *1321*
1Co 11:14 Doth not even nature itself **t** you,...... *1321*
1Ti 1:3 some that they **t** no other doctrine,.... *2085*
1Ti 2:12 But I suffer not a woman to **t**, nor..... *1321*
1Ti 3:2 given to hospitality, apt to **t**;.......... *1317*
1Ti 4:11 These things command and **t**......... *1321*
1Ti 6:3 If any man **t** otherwise, and........... *2085*
2Ti 2:2 who shall be able to **t** others also...... *1321*
2Ti 2:24 but be gentle unto all men, apt to **t**,.... *1317*
Tit 2:4 **t** the young women to be sober,....... *4994*
Heb 5:12 ye have need that one **t** you again...... *1321*
Heb 8:11 not **t** every man his neighbour,........ *1321*
1Jn 2:27 ye need not that any man **t** you:....... *1321*
Rev 2:20 **to t and to seduce my servants to**...... *1321*

TEACHER
Hab 2:18 the molten image, and a **t** of lies,...... 3384
Jn 3:2 that thou art a **t** come from God:...... *1320*
Ro 2:20 a **t** of babes, which hast the form...... *1320*
1Ti 2:7 a **t** of the Gentiles in faith and......... *1320*

TEACHERS
Ps 119:99 understanding than all my **t**.......... 3925
Pr 5:13 have not obeyed the voice of my **t**..... 3384
Isa 30:20 not thy **t** be removed into a corner..... 3384
1Co 12:29 are all prophets? are all **t**? are all....... *1320*
1Ti 1:7 Desiring to be **t** of the law;........... *3547*
2Ti 4:3 shall they heap to themselves **t**........ *1320*
Tit 2:3 to much wine, **t** of good things;....... *2567*
Heb 5:12 when for the time ye ought to be **t**..... *1320*
2Pe 2:1 there shall be false **t** among you,....... *5572*

TEACHEST
Mt 22:16 true, and **t** the way of God in truth,.... *1321*
Mk 12:14 men, but **t** the way of God in truth:.... *1321*
Lk 20:21 of any, but **t** the way of God truly:..... *1321*
Ac 21:21 that thou **t** all the Jews which are...... *1321*
Ro 2:21 **t** thou not thyself? thou that.......... *1321*

TEACHETH
2Sa 22:35 He **t** my hands to war; so that a....... 3925
Job 36:22 by his power: who **t** like him?......... 3384
Ps 94:10 he that **t** man knowledge, shall not.... 3925
Pr 6:13 his feet, he **t** with his fingers;.......... 3384
Pr 16:23 The heart of the wise **t** his mouth..... 7919
Isa 9:15 prophet that **t** lies, he is the tail........ 3384
Isa 48:17 thy God which **t** thee to profit,........ 3925
1Co 2:13 but which the Holy Ghost **t**........... *1318*
Gal 6:6 unto him that **t** in all good things...... *2727*
1Jn 2:27 as the same anointing **t** you of all...... *1321*

TEACHING
2Ch 15:3 without a **t** priest, and without........ 3384
Jer 32:33 them, rising up early and **t** them,...... 3925
Mt 15:9 **t for doctrines the commandments**.... *1321*

T

Mt 26:55 **sat daily with you t in the temple,** *1321*
Mt 28:20 **T them to observe all things** *1321*
Mk 7:7 **t for doctrines the commandments** *1321*
Mk 14:49 **daily with you in the temple t.** *1321*
Lk 23:5 the people, **t** throughout all Jewry, ... *1321*
Col 1:28 and **t** every man in all wisdom;........ *1321*
Col 3:16 **t** and admonishing one another *1321*
Tit 1:11 **t** things which they ought not, for *1321*
Tit 2:12 **T** us that, denying ungodliness *3811*

TEAR
Ps 7:2 Lest he **t** my soul like a lion, ... 2963
Ps 50:22 lest I **t** you in pieces, and there be...... 2963
Jer 15:3 sword to slay, and the dogs to **t**, ... 5498
Eze 13:20 and I will **t** them from your arms, ... 7167
Na 2:12 The lion did **t** in pieces enough for 2963

TEARETH
Mic 5:8 and **t** in pieces, and none can deliver.... 2963
Mk 9:18 he taketh him, he **t** him: and he *4486*

TEARS
2Ki 20:5 thy prayer, I have seen thy **t**........... 1832
Ps 39:12 my cry; hold not thy peace at my **t**..... 1832
Ps 56:8 put thou my **t** into thy bottle: are...... 1832
Ps 126:5 They that sow in **t** shall reap in joy. 1832
Ecc 4:1 the **t** of such as were oppressed........ 1832
Isa 25:8 Lord God will wipe away **t** from off.... 1832
Jer 9:1 and mine eyes a fountain of **t**, that..... 1832
Jer 13:17 weep sore, and run down with **t**, ... 1832
La 1:2 night, and her **t** are on her cheeks:..... 1832
La 2:18 let **t** run down like a river day and 1832
Eze 24:16 weep, neither shall thy **t** run down..... 1832
Mal 2:13 covering … altar of the Lord with **t**, ... 1832
Mk 9:24 and said with **t**, Lord, I believe;........ *1144*
Lk 7:44 **she hath washed my feet with t,** *1144*
Ac 20:19 humility of mind, and with many **t** *1144*
Ac 20:31 every one night and day with **t** *1144*
2Co 2:4 I wrote unto you with many **t**; not..... *1144*
2Ti 1:4 to see thee, being mindful of thy **t** *1144*
Rev 7:17 and God shall wipe away all **t** from *1144*
Rev 21:4 and God shall wipe away all **t** from *1144*

TEETH
Nu 11:33 the flesh was yet between their **t**, ... 8127
Dt 32:24 also send the **t** of beasts upon them, ... 8127
Ps 3:7 hast broken the **t** of the ungodly....... 8127
Ps 58:6 Break their **t**, O God, in their 8127
Pr 10:26 As vinegar to the **t**, and as smoke...... 8127
Pr 30:14 generation, whose **t** are as swords, ... 8127
Jer 31:29 the children's **t** are set on edge 8127
Eze 18:2 the children's **t** are set on edge?........ 8127
Joel 1:6 whose **t** are the **t** of a lion, and 8127
Mt 8:12 **be weeping and gnashing of t**......... *3599*
Mt 13:42 **be wailing and gnashing of t**.......... *3599*
Mt 13:50 **be wailing and gnashing of t**.......... *3599*
Mt 22:13 **be weeping and gnashing of t**......... *3599*
Mt 24:51 **be weeping and gnashing of t**......... *3599*
Mt 25:30 **be weeping and gnashing of t**......... *3599*
Rev 9:8 were as the **t** of lions

TEKEL (te´-kel)
Da 5:25 Mene, Mene, **T**, Upharsin............. 8625
Da 5:27 **T**; Thou art weighed in the 8625

TELL
Ge 15:5 toward heaven, and **t** the stars, ... 5608
Ge 32:29 said, **T** me, I pray thee, thy name 5046
Ex 9:1 Go in unto Pharaoh, and **t** him,....... 1696
1Ki 18:8 **t** thy lord, Behold, Elijah is here......... 559
Job 1:15 escaped alone to **t** thee. 5046
Job 1:16 escaped alone to **t** thee. 5046
Job 1:17 escaped alone to **t** thee. 5046
Job 1:19 escaped alone to **t** thee. 5046
Ps 22:17 I may **t** all my bones: they look........ 5608
Pr 30:4 is his son's name, if thou canst **t**? 3045
Ecc 6:12 for who can **t** a man what shall be 5046
Ecc 8:7 for who can **t** him when it shall be? 5046
Ecc 10:14 shall be after him, who can **t** him? 5046
Da 2:36 and we will **t** the interpretation......... 560
Jnh 1:8 **T** us, … for whose cause this.......... 5046
Mt 8:4 saith unto him, **See thou t no man;** *2036*
Mt 10:27 **What I t you in darkness, that** *3004*
Mt 17:9 **T the vision to no man, until the** *2036*
Mt 21:27 **Neither t I you by what authority** *3004*
Mk 13:4 **T** us, when shall these things be?....... *2036*
Lk 13:32 **Go ye, and t that fox, Behold, I**........ *2036*
Lk 17:34 **I t you, in that night there shall** *3004*
Gal 4:16 enemy, because I **t** you the truth? *226*

TELLETH
Ps 101:7 he that **t** lies shall not tarry in my...... 1696
Ps 147:4 He **t** the number of the stars; he....... 4487

TEMPERANCE
Gal 5:23 Meekness, **t**: against such there is *1466*
2Pe 1:6 and to **t** patience; and to patience...... *1466*

TEMPERATE
1Co 9:25 for the mastery is **t** in all things 1467
Tit 1:8 of good men, sober, just, holy, **t**;....... *1468*
Tit 2:2 the aged men be sober, grave, **t**, ... *4998*

TEMPERED
1Co 12:24 but God hath **t** the body together, ... *4786*

TEMPEST
Ps 11:6 and brimstone, and an horrible **t** 7307
Isa 54:11 O thou afflicted, tossed with **t**, and..... 5590
Am 1:14 a **t** in the day of the whirlwind:........ 5591
Jnh 1:12 my sake this great **t** is upon you 5591
Mt 8:24 there arose a great **t** in the sea *4578*
Ac 27:18 being exceedingly tossed with a **t** *5492*
Heb 12:18 blackness, and darkness, and **t**, ... *2366*
2Pe 2:17 clouds that are carried with a **t**;........ *2978*

TEMPESTUOUS
Jnh 1:11 for the sea wrought, and was **t** 5490
Ac 27:14 there arose against it a **t** wind,......... *5189*

TEMPLE
1Sa 3:3 lamp … went out in the **t** of the Lord, . 1964
2Ki 11:10 that were in the **t** of the Lord.......... 1004
1Ch 10:10 fastened his head in … **t** of Dagon..... 1004
2Ch 26:16 went into the **t** of the Lord to burn 1964
2Ch 36:7 and put them in his **t** at Babylon 1964
Ezr 5:15 them into the **t** that is in Jerusalem,.... 1965
Ne 6:11 go into the **t** to save his life?.......... 1964
Ps 5:7 will I worship toward thy holy **t** 1964
Ps 11:4 The Lord is in his holy **t**, the Lord's 1964
Ps 68:29 Because of thy **t** at Jerusalem shall 1964
Ps 79:1 thy holy **t** have they denied; they 1964
Ps 138:2 I will worship toward thy holy **t**,....... 1964
Isa 6:1 lifted up, and his train filled the **t**...... 1964
Isa 66:6 a voice from the **t**, a voice of the....... 1964
Jer 51:11 the Lord, the vengeance of his **t**,....... 1964

Eze	41:1	Afterward he brought me to the **t**.	1964
Da	5:3	out of the **t** of the house of God.	1965
Am	8:3	songs of the **t** shall be howlings	1964
Hab	2:20	But the Lord is in his holy **t**: let all	1964
Zec	6:12	he shall build the **t** of the Lord:	1964
Mal	3:1	seek, shall suddenly come to his **t**,	1964
Mt	4:5	setteth him on a pinnacle of the **t**.	2411
Mt	12:5	priests in the **t** profane ... sabbath,	2411
Mt	12:6	place is one greater than the **t**.	2411
Mt	21:12	them that sold and bought in the **t**.	2411
Mt	23:16	Whosoever shall swear by the **t**,	3485
Mt	23:35	slew between the **t** and the altar	3485
Mt	26:55	daily with you teaching in the **t**,	2411
Mt	26:61	I am able to destroy the **t** of God,	3485
Mt	27:51	the veil of the **t** was rent in twain	3485
Mk	11:15	them that sold and bought in the **t**.	2411
Mk	14:49	daily with you in the **t** teaching,	2411
Mk	15:29	Ah, thou that destroyest the **t**,	3485
Mk	15:38	the veil of the **t** was rent in twain	3485
Lk	2:27	he came by the Spirit into the **t**.	2411
Lk	2:46	three days they found him in the **t**	2411
Lk	4:9	and set him on a pinnacle of the **t**	2411
Lk	11:51	between the altar and the **t**	3624
Lk	19:47	And he taught daily in the **t**. But	2411
Lk	22:53	I was daily with you in the **t**,	2411
Lk	23:45	veil of the **t** was rent in the midst	3485
Jn	2:15	he drove them all out of the **t**,	2411
Jn	2:19	Destroy this **t**, and in three days	3485
Jn	2:21	But he spake of the **t** of his body	3485
Jn	10:23	Jesus walked in the **t** in Solomon's	2411
Jn	18:20	in the synagogue, and in the **t**,	2411
Ac	3:10	alms at the Beautiful gate of the **t**	2411
Ac	5:20	and speak in the **t** to the people	2411
Ac	19:27	the **t** of the great goddess Diana	2411
1Co	3:16	ye not that ye are the **t** of God,	3485
1Co	3:17	destroy; for the **t** of God is holy,	3485
1Co	6:19	body is the **t** of the Holy Ghost	3485
2Co	6:16	hath the **t** of God with idols?	3485
2Co	6:16	for ye are the **t** of the living God;	3485
2Th	2:4	he as God sitteth in the **t** of God,	3485
Rev	3:12	make a pillar in the **t** of my God,	3485
Rev	7:15	serve him day and night in his **t**	3485
Rev	11:19	the **t** of God was opened in heaven,	3485
Rev	11:19	was seen in his **t** the ark of his	3485
Rev	15:5	**t** of the tabernacle of the testimony	3485
Rev	15:8	And the **t** was filled with smoke	3485
Rev	15:8	no man was able to enter into the **t**,	3485
Rev	21:22	I saw no **t** therein: for the Lord	3485
Rev	21:22	and the Lamb are the **t** of it	3485

TEMPLES

Jgs	4:21	and smote the nail into his **t**, and	7541
Hos	8:14	his Maker, and buildeth **t**;	1964
Joel	3:5	have carried into your **t** my goodly	1964
Ac	7:48	dwelleth not in **t** made with	3485
Ac	17:24	dwelleth not in **t** made with hands;	3485

TEMPORAL

2Co	4:18	the things which are seen are **t**;	4340

TEMPT

Ge	22:1	things, that God did **t** Abraham	5254
Ex	17:2	me? wherefore do ye **t** the Lord?	5254
Dt	6:16	Ye shall not **t** the Lord your God,	5254
Mt	4:7	shalt not **t** the Lord thy God	1598
Mt	22:18	said, Why **t** ye me, ye hypocrites?	3985
Mk	12:15	said unto them, Why **t** ye me?	3985
Lk	4:12	shalt not **t** the Lord thy God.	1598
Lk	20:23	and said unto them, Why **t** ye me?	3985
Ac	5:9	to **t** the Spirit of the Lord?	3985
1Co	7:5	**t** you not for your incontinency	3985
1Co	10:9	Neither let us **t** Christ, as some of	1598

TEMPTATION

Ps	95:8	in the day of **t** in the wilderness:	4531
Mt	6:13	lead us not into **t**, but deliver	3986
Mt	26:41	and pray, that ye enter not into **t**	3986
Mk	14:38	ye and pray, lest ye enter into **t**.	3986
Lk	8:13	believe, and in time of **t** fall away	3986
Lk	11:4	lead us not into **t**; but deliver	3986
Lk	22:40	Pray that ye enter not into **t**	3986
Lk	22:46	rise and pray, lest ye enter into **t**.	3986
1Co	10:13	There hath no **t** taken you but such	3986
1Co	10:13	with the **t** ... make a way to escape,	3986
1Ti	6:9	will be rich fall into **t** and a snare,	3986
Heb	3:8	in the day of **t** in the wilderness:	3986
Jas	1:12	is the man that endureth **t**	3986
Rev	3:10	will keep thee from the hour of **t**,	3986

TEMPTATIONS

Dt	4:34	by **t**, by signs, and by wonders,	4531
Dt	7:19	The great **t** which thine eyes saw,	4531
Lk	22:28	have continued with me in my **t**.	3986
Jas	1:2	all joy when ye fall into divers **t**;	3986
1Pe	1:6	in heaviness through manifold **t**:	3986
2Pe	2:9	how to deliver the godly out of **t**,	3986

TEMPTED

Ex	17:7	because they **t** the Lord, saying,	5254
Nu	14:22	and have **t** me now these ten times,	5254
Ps	78:18	they **t** God in their heart by asking.	5254
Ps	78:41	they turned back and **t** God, and	5254
Ps	95:9	When your fathers **t** me, proved me,	5254
Ps	106:14	wilderness, and **t** God in the desert	5254
Mt	4:1	wilderness to be **t** of the devil	3985
Mk	1:13	wilderness forty days, **t** of Satan;	3985
Lk	4:2	Being forty days **t** of the devil	3985
1Co	10:9	as some of them also **t**, and were	3985
1Co	10:13	not suffer you to be **t** above that ye	3985
Gal	6:1	thyself, lest thou also be **t**.	3985
1Th	3:5	means the tempter have **t** you	3985
Heb	2:18	is able to succour them that are **t**	3985
Heb	4:15	was in all points **t** like as we are	3985
Jas	1:13	say when he is **t**, I am **t** of God:	3985
Jas	1:13	for God cannot be **t** with evil,	551
Jas	1:14	every man is **t**, when he is drawn	3985

TEMPTETH

Jas	1:13	with evil, neither **t** he any man:	3985

TEMPTING

Mk	10:2	a man to put away his wife? **t** him.	3985
Lk	11:16	others, **t** him, sought of him a sign.	3985
Jn	8:6	This they said, **t** him, that they	3985

TEN

Ge	31:41	hast changed my wages **t** times.	6235
Ex	34:28	the covenant, the **t** commandments,	6235
Le	26:8	you shall put **t** thousand to flight:	7233
Nu	14:22	have tempted me now these **t** times	6235
Dt	4:13	perform, even **t** commandments:	6235
Dt	10:4	the **t** commandments, which the	6235
Dt	32:30	and two put **t** thousand to flight,	7233
Dt	33:2	he came with **t** thousands of saints:	7233
Jgs	20:10	and a thousand out of **t** thousand,	7233

1Sa	1:8	am not I better to thee than **t** sons?	6235
1Sa	18:7	and David his **t** thousands.	7233
1Sa	21:11	and David his **t** thousands?	7233
1Sa	29:5	and David his **t** thousands?	7233
2Ki	20:9	the shadow go forward **t** degrees,	6235
2Ki	20:10	shadow return backward **t** degrees.	6235
Ne	4:12	they said unto us **t** times, From all	6235
Ps	3:6	be afraid of **t** thousands of people,	7233
Ps	90:10	our years are threescore years and **t**;	
Ps	91:7	and **t** thousand at thy right hand;	7233
Ps	144:9	instrument of **t** strings will I sing	6218
Ecc	7:19	the wise more than **t** mighty men	6235
SS	5:10	the chiefest among **t** thousand	7233
Isa	38:8	dial of Ahaz, **t** degrees backward.	6235
Da	1:15	end of **t** days their countenances	6235
Da	1:20	he found them **t** times better than	6235
Da	7:10	**t** thousand times **t** thousand	7240
Da	7:20	the **t** horns that were in his head	6236
Mic	6:7	with **t** thousands of rivers of oil?	7233
Mt	18:24	**owed him t thousand talents.**	*3463*
Mt	25:1	**heaven be likened unto t virgins**	*1176*
Mt	25:28	**it unto him which hath t talents.**	*1176*
Lk	15:8	**woman having t pieces of silver,**	*1176*
Lk	19:24	**give it to him that hath t pounds.**	*1176*
1Co	14:19	**t** thousand words in an unknown.	*3463*
Jude	14	with **t** thousands of his saints	*3461*
Rev	2:10	**ye shall have tribulation t days:**	*1176*
Rev	5:11	was **t** thousand times **t** thousand,	*3461*
Rev	13:1	having seven heads and **t** horns,	*1176*
Rev	17:16	the **t** horns which thou sawest.	*1176*

TENDER

Ge	29:17	Leah was **t** eyed; but Rachel was	7390
Dt	28:56	The **t** and delicate woman among	7390
2Ki	22:19	Because thine heart was **t**, and	7401
Ps	25:6	Remember, O Lord, thy **t** mercies	
Ps	40:11	Withhold not thou thy **t** mercies from	
Ps	51:1	unto the multitude of thy **t** mercies	
Ps	77:9	he in anger shut up his **t** mercies?	
Ps	119:156	Great are thy **t** mercies, O Lord:	
Ps	145:9	his **t** mercies are over all his works	
Pr	4:3	**t** and only beloved in the sight of	7390
Pr	12:10	the **t** mercies of the wicked are cruel	
Isa	53:2	grow up before him as a **t** plant,	3126
Da	1:9	Daniel into favor and **t** love	
Mt	24:32	**When his branch is yet t, and**	*527*
Mk	13:28	**When her branch is yet t, and.**	*527*
Lk	1:78	Through the **t** mercy of our God;	*4698*
Jas	5:11	is very pitiful, and of **t** mercy.	*3629*

TENDERHEARTED

2Ch	13:7	Rehoboam was young and **t**,	7390, 3824
Eph	4:32	**t**, forgiving one another, even as	*2155*

TENDETH

Pr	10:16	The labour of the righteous **t** to life:	
Pr	11:19	As righteousness **t** to life: so he that	
Pr	11:24	more than is meet, but it **t** to poverty	
Pr	14:23	the talk of the lips **t** only to penury	
Pr	19:23	The fear of the Lord **t** to life: and he	

TENOR

Ge	43:7	according to the **t** of these words:	6310
Ex	34:27	for after the **t** of these words I have	6310

TEN'S

Ge	18:32	I will not destroy it for **t** sake.	6235

TENT

Ge	9:21	and he was uncovered within his **t**	168
Ge	13:12	and pitched his **t** toward Sodom.	167
Ge	18:10	And Sarah heard it in the **t** door.	168
Ge	31:34	And Laban searched all the **t**, but	168
Ex	33:8	and stood every man at his **t** door,	168
Ex	39:32	the **t** of the congregation finished:	168
Ex	40:26	altar in the **t** of the congregation	168
Le	14:8	tarry abroad out of his **t** seven days	168
Nu	9:15	namely, the **t** of the testimony:	168
Nu	11:10	every man in the door of his **t**.	168
Nu	19:14	is the law, when a man dieth in a **t**	168
Jos	7:22	it was hid in his **t**, and the silver	168
Jgs	4:17	Sisera fled away on his feet to the **t**.	168
Jgs	4:21	Heber's wife took a nail of the **t**	168
Jgs	7:8	rest of Israel every man unto his **t**	168
1Sa	4:10	and they fled every man into his **t**:	168
2Sa	16:22	So they spread Absalom a **t** upon	168
1Ch	15:1	ark of God, and pitched for it a **t**	168
Ps	78:60	the **t** which he placed among men;	168
Isa	38:12	from me as a shepherd's **t**	168
Isa	54:2	Enlarge the place of thy **t**, and let	168
Jer	37:10	they rise up every man in his **t**,	168

TENTH

Ge	28:22	I will surely give the **t** unto thee	6237
Ex	12:3	In the **t** day of this month they	6218
Ex	16:36	an omer is the **t** part of an ephah	6224
Le	5:11	**t** part of an ephah of fine flour	6224
Le	23:27	Also on the **t** day of this seventh	6218
Le	27:32	the **t** shall be holy unto the Lord.	6224
Nu	18:21	children of Levi … the **t** in Israel	4643
Nu	29:7	on the **t** day of this seventh month.	6218
Dt	23:2	even to his **t** generation shall he	6224
Dt	23:3	even to their **t** generation shall	6224
Jos	4:19	on the **t** day of the first month,	6218
1Sa	8:15	he will take the **t** of your seed	6237
Jer	39:1	**t** month, came Nebuchadrezzar	6224
Jn	1:39	day: for it was about the **t** hour.	*1882*
Heb	7:2	also Abraham gave a **t** part of all;	*1181*
Heb	7:4	Abraham gave the **t** of the spoils.	*1181*
Rev	11:13	and the **t** part of the city fell, and	*1182*

TENTMAKERS See also MAKERS.

Ac	18:3	by their occupation they were **t**.	*4635*

TENTS

Ge	4:20	the father of such as dwell in **t**	168
Ge	25:27	was a plain man, dwelling in **t**.	168
Nu	9:23	of the Lord they rested in the **t**	
Nu	16:26	from the **t** of these wicked men	168
Nu	16:27	out, and stood in the door of their **t**.	168
Nu	24:2	saw Israel abiding in his **t** according	
Nu	24:5	How goodly are thy **t**, O Jacob,	168
Dt	1:27	And ye murmured in your **t**, and	168
Jos	3:14	the people removed from their **t**.	168
Jos	22:6	away: and they went unto their **t**	168
Jos	22:8	with much riches unto your **t**, and	168
Jgs	8:11	by the way of them that dwelt in **t**	168
1Ki	8:66	went unto their **t** joyful and glad	168
1Ki	12:16	to your **t**, O Israel: now see to thine	168
2Ki	7:16	and spoiled the **t** of the Syrians.	4264
1Ch	4:41	smote their **t**, and the habitations	168
2Ch	10:16	So all Israel went to their **t**.	168
2Ch	31:2	in the gates of the **t** of the Lord.	4264
Ezr	8:15	there abode we in **t** three days:	2583
Ps	84:10	than to dwell in the **t** of wickedness.	168

Ps 106:25 But murmured in their **t**, and 168
Jer 4:20 suddenly are my **t** spoiled, and my 168
Jer 30:18 again the captivity of Jacob's **t**. 168
Jer 35:7 but all your days ye shall dwell in **t**; 168
Zec 12:7 also shall save the **t** of Judah first 168

TERAPHIM (ter′-af-im)
Jgs 17:5 and made an ephod, and **t**, and 8655
Jgs 18:18 carved image, the ephod, and the **t**, ... 8655
Hos 3:4 without an ephod, and without **t**:...... 8655

TERMED
Isa 62:4 Thou shalt no more be **t** Forsaken;...... 559
Isa 62:4 thy land any more be **t** Desolate: 559

TERRESTRIAL
1Co 15:40 also celestial bodies, and bodies **t** *1919*
1Co 15:40 and the glory of the **t** is another *1919*

TERRIBLE
Ex 34:10 for it is a **t** thing that I will do......... 3372
Dt 7:21 is among you, a mighty God and **t**..... 3372
Dt 8:15 through ... great and **t** wilderness,..... 3372
Dt 10:17 a great God, a mighty, and a **t**, ... 3372
Dt 10:21 for thee these great and **t** things,....... 3372
Jgs 13:6 of an angel of God, very **t** 3372
2Sa 7:23 to do for you great things and **t**,....... 3372
Ne 1:5 of heaven, the great and **t** God,........ 3372
Ne 4:14 the Lord, which is great and **t**,......... 3372
Ne 9:32 great, the mighty, and the **t** God, ... 3372
Job 37:22 the north: with God is **t** majesty....... 3372
Ps 47:2 For the Lord most high is **t**; he is 3372
Ps 65:5 By **t** things in righteousness wilt....... 3372
Ps 66:3 God, How **t** art thou in thy works!..... 3372
Ps 68:35 O God, thou art **t** out of thy holy...... 3372
Ps 99:3 them praise thy great and **t** name; 3372
Ps 145:6 speak of the might of thy **t** acts: 3372
Isa 13:11 lay low the haughtiness of the **t**. 6184
Isa 25:4 the blast of the **t** ones is as a storm..... 6184
Isa 25:5 the branch of the **t** ones shall be....... 6184
Isa 29:20 For the **t** one is brought to nought, ... 6184
Isa 64:3 When thou didst **t** things which we 3372
La 5:10 an oven because of the **t** famine 2152
Eze 1:22 was as the colour of the **t** crystal, ... 3372
Eze 31:12 the **t** of the nations, have cut him...... 6184
Da 7:7 a fourth beast, dreadful and **t**,.......... 574
Joel 2:11 day of the Lord is great and very **t**;..... 3372
Joel 2:31 the great and the **t** day of the Lord..... 3372
Zep 2:11 The Lord will be **t** unto them:......... 3372
Heb 12:21 so **t** was the sight, that Moses *5398*

TERRIBLENESS
Dt 26:8 and with great **t**, and with signs,....... 4172
1Ch 17:21 thee a name of greatness and **t**,........ 3372
Jer 49:16 Thy **t** hath deceived thee, and the...... 8606

TERRIBLY
Isa 2:19 he ariseth to shake **t** the earth. 6206
Isa 2:21 he ariseth to shake **t** the earth. 6206

TERRIFIED
Dt 20:3 neither be ye **t** because of them;....... 6206
Lk 21:9 **of wars and commotions, be not t** *4422*
Lk 24:37 But they were **t** and affrighted, ... *4422*
Php 1:28 in nothing **t** by your adversaries:....... *4426*

TERROR
Le 26:16 I will even appoint over you **t** 928
Dt 32:25 The sword without, and **t** within,....... 367
Dt 34:12 the great **t** which Moses shewed 4172
Jos 2:9 and that your **t** is fallen upon us, ... 367
Ps 91:5 not be afraid for the **t** by night;........ 6343
Isa 33:18 Thine heart shall meditate **t**. 367
Isa 54:14 and from **t**; for it shall not come....... 4288
Jer 20:4 I will make thee a **t** to thyself, ... 4032
Jer 32:21 strong hand, ... and with great **t**: 4172
Eze 26:21 I will make thee a **t**, and thou 1091
Eze 32:24 which caused their **t** in the land of..... 2851
Eze 32:25 their **t** was caused in the land of....... 2851
Eze 32:27 the **t** of the mighty in the land of...... 2851
Eze 32:32 I have caused my **t** in the land of 2851
Ro 13:3 rulers are not a **t** to good works *5401*
2Co 5:11 Knowing ... the **t** of the Lord, we...... *5401*
1Pe 3:14 be not afraid of their **t**, neither be...... *5401*

TERRORS
Dt 4:34 stretched out arm, and by great **t**,...... 4172
Ps 55:4 the **t** of death are fallen upon me 367
Ps 73:19 they are utterly consumed with **t** 1091
Ps 88:15 while I suffer thy **t** I am distracted 367
Jer 15:8 it suddenly, and **t** upon the city......... 928
La 2:22 a solemn day my **t** round about,....... 4032
Eze 21:12 **t** by reason of the sword shall be....... 4048

TESTAMENT
Mt 26:28 **For this is my blood of the new t**,...... *1242*
Mk 14:24 **This is my blood of the new t**, ... *1242*
Lk 22:20 **This cup is the new t in my blood**,..... *1242*
1Co 11:25 **This cup is the new t in my blood**:..... *1242*
2Co 3:14 away in the reading of the old **t**; *1242*
Heb 7:22 Jesus made a surety of a better **t** *1242*
Heb 9:15 he is the mediator of the new **t**, ... *1242*
Heb 9:16 For where a **t** is, there must also of..... *1242*
Heb 9:18 Whereupon neither the first **t** was
Heb 9:20 This is the blood of the **t** which *1242*
Rev 11:19 seen in his temple the ark of his **t**...... *1242*

TESTATOR
Heb 9:16 necessity be the death of the **t**......... *1303*
Heb 9:17 strength at all while the **t** liveth, ... *1303*

TESTIFIED
Dt 19:18 hath **t** falsely against his brother; 6030
Ru 1:21 seeing the Lord hath **t** against me, ... 6030
Ne 9:26 slew thy prophets which **t** against...... 5749
Ne 13:15 and I **t** against them in the day........ 5749
Jn 4:44 For Jesus himself **t**, that a prophet *3140*
Jn 13:21 he was troubled in spirit, and **t**, ... *3140*
Ac 23:11 **thou hast t of me in Jerusalem** *1263*
1Co 15:15 we have **t** of God that he raised........ *3140*
Heb 2:6 But one in a certain place **t**,........... *1263*
1Pe 1:11 it **t** beforehand the sufferings of *4303*
1Jn 5:9 God which he hath **t** of his Son *3140*
3Jn 3 and **t** of the truth that is in thee,....... *3140*

TESTIFIETH
Hos 7:10 the pride of Israel **t** to his face: 6030
Jn 21:24 disciple which **t** of these things........ *3140*
Heb 7:17 For he **t**, Thou art a priest for ever *3140*
Rev 22:20 He which **t** these things saith, ... *3140*

TESTIFY
Nu 35:30 one witness shall not **t** against......... 6030
Dt 8:19 I **t** against you this day that ye......... 5749
Ps 50:7 Israel, and I will **t** against thee: 5749
Isa 59:12 thee, and our sins **t** against us: 6030
Jer 14:7 though our iniquities **t** against us, ... 6030

Hos 5:5 pride of Israel doth **t** to his face: 6030
Mic 6:3 I wearied thee? **t** against me. 6030
Lk 16:28 **that he may t unto them, lest** *1263*
Jn 3:11 **know, and t that we have seen;** *3140*
Jn 5:39 **and they are they which t of me** *3140*
Jn 7:7 **me it hateth, because I t of it,** *3140*
Jn 15:26 **the Father, he shall t of me** *3140*
Gal 5:3 For I **t** again to every man that is *3143*
Eph 4:17 **t** in the Lord, that ye henceforth *3143*
1Jn 4:14 and do **t** that the Father sent the *3140*
Rev 22:16 **sent mine angel to t unto you** *3140*
Rev 22:18 I **t** unto every man that heareth *4828*

TESTIFYING
Ac 20:21 **T** both to the Jews, and also to *1263*
Heb 11:4 was righteous, God **t** of his gifts: *3140*
1Pe 5:12 and **t** that this is the true grace *1957*

TESTIMONIES
Dt 4:45 These are the **t**, and the statutes, 5713
Dt 6:17 his **t**, and his statutes, which he 5713
Dt 6:20 What mean the **t**, and the statutes, 5713
2Ki 17:15 his **t** which he testified against 5715
2Ki 23:3 keep his commandments and his **t**. 5715
Ne 9:34 thy commandments and thy **t**. 5715
Ps 25:10 as keep his covenant and his **t**, 5713
Ps 78:56 high God, and kept not his **t**, 5713
Ps 93:5 Thy **t** are very sure: holiness 5713
Ps 119:2 Blessed are they that keep his **t**, 5713
Ps 119:14 have rejoiced in the way of thy **t**, 5715
Ps 119:111 Thy **t** have I taken as an heritage. 5715
Ps 119:119 dross: therefore I love thy **t** 571
Ps 119:167 My soul hath kept thy **t**; and I 5713
Jer 44:23 nor in his statutes, nor in his **t**; 5715

TESTIMONY
Ex 16:34 so Aaron laid it up before the **T**, 5715
Ex 25:21 in the ark thou shalt put the **t** 5715
Ex 25:22 which are upon the ark of the **t**, 5715
Ex 26:33 within the vail the ark of the **t**. 5715
Ex 27:21 the vail, which is before the **t**, 5715
Ex 30:36 of it before the **t** in the tabernacle 5715
Ex 31:18 two tables of **t**, tables of stone, 5715
Ex 34:29 the two tables of **t** in Moses' hand 5715
Le 16:13 the mercy seat that is upon the **t**, 5715
Nu 1:50 Levites over the tabernacle of **t**, 5715
Nu 1:53 round about the tabernacle of **t**, 5715
Nu 7:89 seat that was upon the ark of **t**, 5715
2Ki 11:12 upon him, and gave him the **t**. 5715
2Ch 23:11 him the crown, and gave him the **t**, 5715
Ps 19:7 the **t** of the Lord is sure, making 5715
Isa 8:20 To the law and to the **t**: if they 8584
Mt 10:18 **a t against them and the Gentiles.** *3142*
Mk 6:11 **your feet for a t against them** *3142*
Mk 13:9 **for my sake, for a t against them** *3142*
Lk 9:5 **your feet for a t against them** *3142*
Jn 3:33 He that hath received his **t** hath *3141*
Jn 5:34 **But I receive not t from man:** *3141*
Jn 8:17 **that the t of two men is true** *3141*
Jn 21:24 and we know that his **t** is true *3141*
2Co 1:12 is this, the **t** of our conscience *3142*
2Ti 1:8 ashamed of the **t** of our Lord, *3142*
Heb 11:5 had this **t**, that he pleased God *3140*
Rev 1:2 God, and of the **t** of Jesus Christ. *3141*
Rev 12:11 Lamb, and by the word of their **t**; *3141*
Rev 19:10 **t** of Jesus is the spirit of prophecy. *3141*

TETRARCH
Mt 14:1 Herod the **t** heard of the fame of *5076*
Lk 3:1 and Herod being **t** of Galilee, and. *5075*
Lk 3:19 Herod the **t**, being reproved by *5076*

THANK
1Ch 16:4 to **t** and praise the Lord God of 3034
Da 2:23 I **t** thee, and praise thee, O thou 3029
Mt 11:25 **and said, I t thee, O Father, Lord** *1843*
Lk 6:32 **which love you, what t have ye?** *5485*
Lk 18:11 **God, I t thee, that I am not as** *2168*
Jn 11:41 **I t thee that thou hast heard me** *2168*
Php 1:3 **t** my God upon every remembrance *2168*
1Th 2:13 this cause also **t** we God without *2168*
2Ti 1:3 I **t** God, whom I serve from my *2192, 5485*

THANKFUL See also UNTHANKFUL.
Ps 100:4 be **t** unto him, and bless his name 3034
Ro 1:21 him not as God, neither were **t**; *2168*

THANKS
1Ch 16:8 Give **t** unto the Lord, call upon his 3034
1Ch 16:34 O give **t** unto the Lord; for he is 3034
Ps 6:5 in the grave who shall give thee **t**? 3034
Ps 30:4 give **t** at the remembrance of his 3034
Ps 35:18 thee **t** in the great congregation: 3034
Ps 79:13 we thy people … give thee **t** for ever 3034
Ps 119:62 At midnight I will rise to give **t**. 3034
Ps 136:2 O give **t** unto the God of gods: for 3034
Ps 136:26 O give **t** unto the God of heaven: 3034
Da 6:10 prayed, and gave **t** before his God. 3029
Mt 26:27 And he took the cup, and gave **t** *2168*
Mk 8:6 took the seven loaves, and gave **t**. *2168*
Lk 22:17 And he took the cup, and gave **t** *2168*
Lk 22:19 And he took bread, and gave **t**. *2168*
Ro 14:6 he eateth not, and giveth God **t**. *2168*
1Co 11:24 when he had given **t**, he brake it *2168*
1Co 15:57 But **t** be to God, which giveth us. *5485*
2Co 2:14 Now **t** be unto God, which always *5485*
2Co 9:15 **T** be unto God for his unspeakable *5485*
Eph 1:16 Cease not to give **t** for you *2168*
Eph 5:20 Giving **t** always for all things *2168*
Col 3:17 giving **t** to God and the Father by *2168*
1Th 1:2 We give **t** to God always for you *2168*
1Th 5:18 In every thing give **t**: for this is *2168*
1Ti 2:1 and giving of **t**, be made for all men *2169*
Rev 4:9 **t** to him that sat on the throne, *2169*

THANKSGIVING
Le 22:29 offer a sacrifice of **t** unto the Lord 8426
Ps 50:14 Offer unto God **t**; and pay thy vows 8426
Ps 100:4 Enter into his gates with **t**, and 8426
Ps 116:17 I will offer to thee the sacrifice of **t**, 8426
Am 4:5 offer a sacrifice of **t** with leaven, 8426
Jnh 2:9 unto thee with the voice of **t**; 8426
Php 4:6 by prayer and supplication with **t**. *2169*
Col 4:2 and watch in the same with **t**; *2169*
1Ti 4:3 to be received with **t** of them which *2169*
Rev 7:12 and wisdom, and **t**, and honour, *2169*

THANKWORTHY
1Pe 2:19 this is **t**, if a man for conscience *5485*

THEATRE
Ac 19:29 rushed with one accord into the **t**. *2302*

THEFT
Ex 22:3 then he shall be sold for his **t**. 1591

THEFTS
- Mt 15:19 fornications, **t**, false witness, ... 2829
- Mk 7:22 **T**, covetousness, wickedness, ... 2829

THEIRS
- Mt 5:3 for **t** is the kingdom of heaven 846
- Mt 5:10 for **t** is the kingdom of heaven 846

THEREFORE
- Ge 2:24 **T** shall a man leave … father. 5921, 3651
- Ge 18:12 **T** Sarah laughed within herself
- Ge 29:32 now **t** my husband will love me 3588
- Le 11:45 God: ye shall **t** be holy, for I am holy
- Dt 7:9 Know **t** that the Lord thy God, he is
- Dt 10:19 Love ye **t** the stranger: for ye were
- Dt 30:19 **t** choose life, that both thou and thy
- Jgs 3:8 **T** the anger of the Lord was hot
- Job 11:6 Know **t** that God exacteth of thee less
- Job 37:24 Men do **t** fear him: he respecteth 3651
- Ps 46:2 **T** will not we fear, though the.... 5921, 3651
- Ecc 5:2 earth: **t** let thy words be few 5921, 3651
- Ecc 8:11 **t** the heart of the sons of men.... 5921, 3651
- Isa 5:13 **T** my people are gone into............ 3651
- Isa 53:12 **T** will I divide him a portion with 3651
- La 3:24 my soul; **t** will I hope in him..... 5921, 3651
- Hos 4:7 **t** will I change their glory into shame
- Am 5:27 **T** will I cause you to go into captivity
- Jnh 4:2 **T** I fled … unto Tarshish: 5921, 3651
- Mic 7:7 **T** I will look unto the Lord; I will
- Hab 1:4 **T** the law is slacked, and 5921, 3651
- Mt 3:8 Bring forth **t** fruits meet for 3767
- Mt 5:48 ye **t** perfect, even as your Father 3767
- Mt 6:2 **T** when thou doest thine alms, do 3767
- Mt 6:22 if **t** thine eye be single, thy whole 3767
- Mt 6:34 Take **t** no thought for the morrow 3767
- Mt 9:38 Pray ye **t** the Lord of the harvest, ... 3767
- Mt 24:42 Watch **t**: for ye know not what 3767
- Mt 25:13 Watch **t**, for ye know neither the 3767
- Mt 28:19 Go ye **t**, and teach all nations 3767
- Mk 2:28 **T** the Son of man is Lord also of 5620
- Mk 13:35 Watch ye **t**: for ye know not when 3767
- Lk 6:36 Be ye **t** merciful, as your Father 3767
- Lk 12:7 Fear not **t**: ye are of more value 3767
- Lk 20:25 Render **t** unto Caesar the things....... 5106
- Lk 20:44 David **t** calleth him Lord, how is he
- Lk 21:36 Watch ye **t**, and pray always,.......... 3767
- Jn 8:36 If the Son **t** shall make you free, ... 3767
- Jn 11:33 When Jesus **t** saw her weeping......... 3767
- Jn 21:7 **T** that disciple whom Jesus loved 3767
- Ro 2:1 **T** thou art inexcusable, O man 1352
- Ro 5:1 **T** being justified by faith, we 3767
- Ro 6:12 Let not sin **t** reign in your mortal...... 3767
- Ro 8:1 There is **t** now no condemnation 686
- Ro 12:20 **T** if thine enemy hunger, feed 3767
- 1Co 4:5 **T** judge nothing before the time 5620
- 1Co 9:26 I **t** so run, not as uncertainly; so 5106
- 2Co 5:11 Knowing **t** the terror of the Lord 3767
- 2Co 5:17 **T** if any man be in Christ, he is a 5620
- 2Co 7:1 Having **t** these promises, dearly 3767
- Gal 5:1 Stand fast **t** in the liberty 3767
- Col 3:5 Mortify **t** your members which are..... 3767
- 2Ti 2:3 Thou **t** endure hardness, as a good..... 3767
- 2Ti 2:10 **T** I endure all things for the elect's
- 2Ti 2:21 If a man **t** purge himself from these.... 3767
- Heb 10:35 Cast not away **t** your confidence 3767
- Jas 4:7 Submit yourselves **t** to God 3767
- Jas 4:17 **T** to him that knoweth to do good..... 3767
- Jas 5:7 Be patient **t**, brethren, unto the........ 3767
- 1Pe 5:6 Humble yourselves **t** under the 3767
- Rev 2:5 Remember **t** from whence thou 3767
- Rev 3:3 Remember **t** how thou hast........... 3767
- Rev 3:19 chasten: be zealous **t**, and repent 3767

THEREFROM
- 2Ki 3:3 made Israel to sin; he departed not **t**
- 2Ki 13:2 made Israel to sin; he departed not **t**

THICK
- Ex 10:22 there was a **t** darkness in all the 653
- Ex 19:9 Lo, I come unto thee in a **t** cloud,...... 5645
- Ex 19:16 and a **t** cloud upon the mount,........ 3515
- Ex 20:21 Moses drew near unto the **t** darkness
- Dt 4:11 darkness, clouds, and **t** darkness
- Dt 5:22 the cloud, and of the **t** darkness
- 2Sa 22:12 waters, and **t** clouds of the skies
- 2Ch 6:1 he would dwell in the **t** darkness
- Ps 18:11 dark waters and **t** clouds of the
- Ps 74:5 lifted up axes upon the **t** trees......... 5441
- Isa 44:22 blotted out, as a **t** cloud, thy
- Eze 8:11 and a **t** cloud of incense went up 6282
- Joel 2:2 day of clouds and of **t** darkness
- Zep 1:15 a day of clouds and **t** darkness,

THICKET
- Ge 22:13 a ram caught in a **t** by his horns: 5442

THICKETS
- 1Sa 13:6 hide themselves in caves, and in **t**, ... 2337
- Jer 4:29 they shall go into the **t**, and climb 5645

THICKNESS
- 2Ch 4:5 the **t** of it was an handbreadth 5672
- Eze 41:9 The **t** of the wall, which was for 7341

THIEF
- Ex 22:2 If a **t** be found breaking up, and....... 1590
- Ex 22:7 if a **t** be found, let him pay double..... 1590
- Dt 24:7 selleth him; then that **t** shall die;....... 1590
- Pr 6:30 Men do not despise a **t**, if he steal...... 1590
- Pr 29:24 Whoso is partner with a **t** hateth 1590
- Jer 2:26 As the **t** is ashamed when he is 1590
- Mt 24:43 in what watch the **t** would come, ... 2812
- Mt 26:55 Are ye come out as against a **t**......... 3027
- Mk 14:48 Are ye come out, as against a **t**,........ 3027
- Lk 12:33 where no **t** approacheth, neither 2812
- Lk 12:39 what hour the **t** would come, ... 2822
- Jn 10:1 way, the same is a **t** and a robber....... 2812
- Jn 10:10 The **t** cometh not, but for to steal, ... 2812
- Jn 12:6 but because he was a **t**, and had the 2812
- 1Th 5:2 Lord so cometh as a **t** in the night...... 2812
- 1Th 5:4 day should overtake you as a **t**......... 2812
- 1Pe 4:15 you suffer as a murderer, or as a **t**...... 2812
- 2Pe 3:10 Lord will come as a **t** in the night; 2812
- Rev 3:3 watch, I will come on thee as a **t**, ... 2812
- Rev 16:15 Behold, I come as a **t**. Blessed is 2812

THIEVES
- Isa 1:23 rebellious, and companions of **t**....... 1590
- Jer 49:9 if **t** by night, they will destroy till 1590
- Ob 5 If **t** came to thee, if robbers by 1590
- Mt 6:19 where **t** break through and steal: 2812
- Mt 21:13 but ye have made it a den of **t**......... 3027
- Mt 27:38 there two **t** crucified with him; 3027
- Mk 11:17 but ye have made it a den of **t**......... 3027

Mk 15:27 And with him they crucify two t; *3027*
Lk 10:30 to Jericho, and fell among t........... *3027*
Lk 19:46 but ye have made it a den of t......... *3027*
Jn 10:8 that ever came before me are t *2812*
1Co 6:10 Nor t, nor covetous, nor drunkards,.... *2812*

THIGH
Ge 24:9 his hand under the t of Abraham...... 3409
Ge 32:25 hollow of Jacob's t was out of joint,.... 3409
Ge 47:29 I pray thee, thy hand under my t,...... 3409
Nu 5:22 thy belly to swell, and thy t to rot: 3409
Jgs 3:21 took the dagger from his right t 3409
Jer 31:19 instructed, I smote upon my t......... 3409
Eze 24:4 good piece, the t, and the shoulder; 3409
Rev 19:16 and on his t a name written, ... *3382*

THIN
Ge 41:7 And the seven t ears devoured the 1851
Ge 41:27 the seven t and ill favoured kine....... 7534
Ex 39:3 they did beat the gold into t plates,

THINK
Ge 40:14 t on me when it shall be well.......... 2142
2Sa 13:33 t that all the king's sons are dead:....... 559
Ne 5:19 T upon me, my God, for good,......... 2142
Est 4:13 T not with thyself that thou shalt...... 1819
Job 31:1 why then should I t upon a maid? 995
Ecc 8:17 though a wise man t to know it 559
Jer 29:11 the thoughts that I t toward you....... 2803
Eze 38:10 and thou shalt t an evil thought: 2803
Da 7:25 and t to change times and laws: 5452
Mt 5:17 T not that I am come to destroy....... *3543*
Mt 6:7 they t that they shall be heard for *1380*
Mt 9:4 Wherefore t ye evil in your hearts? *1760*
Mt 10:34 T not that I am come to send *3543*
Mt 24:44 such an hour as ye t not the Son *1380*
Lk 12:40 cometh at an hour when ye t not. *1380*
Jn 5:39 in them ye t ye have eternal life:....... *1380*
Jn 16:2 will t that he doeth God service *1380*
Ac 17:29 not to t that the Godhead is like *3543*
Ro 12:3 not to t of himself more highly........ *5252*
1Co 7:36 any man t that he behaveth himself.... *3543*
1Co 8:2 if any man t that he knoweth any...... *1380*
1Co 12:23 which we t to be less honourable *1380*
2Co 11:16 say again, Let no man t me a fool; *1380*
Gal 6:3 if a man t himself to be something..... *1380*
Eph 3:20 abundantly above all that we ask or t ... *3539*
Php 4:8 be any praise, t on these things *3049*
Jas 1:7 that man t that he shall receive *3633*

THINKEST
2Sa 10:3 T thou that David doth honour 5869
Job 35:2 T thou this to be right, that thou 2803
Mt 17:25 him, saying, What t thou, Simon? *1380*
Mt 26:53 T thou that I cannot now pray to...... *1380*
Lk 10:36 Which now of these three, t thou, ... *1380*
Ro 2:3 And t thou this, O man, that judgest ... *3049*

THINKETH
Pr 23:7 For as he t in his heart, so is he: 8176
1Co 10:12 let him that t he standeth take......... *1380*
1Co 13:5 is not easily provoked, t no evil; *3049*

THIRD
Ge 1:13 and the morning were the t day 7992
Ge 22:4 t day Abraham lifted up his eyes....... 7992
Ge 34:25 came to pass on the t day, when 7992
Ge 42:18 Joseph said unto them the t day 7992
Ex 19:15 Be ready against the t day: come....... 7969
Ex 20:5 unto the t and fourth generation 8029
Le 19:6 if ought remain until the t day, it 7992
Nu 14:18 unto the t and fourth generation 8029
Nu 19:12 if he purify not himself the t day 7992
Dt 5:9 unto the t and fourth generation 8029
Dt 26:12 tithes of thine increase the t year 7992
1Sa 19:21 sent messengers again the t time....... 7992
1Ki 12:12 saying, Come to me again the t day 7992
1Ki 18:1 Lord came to Elijah in the t year....... 7992
1Ki 18:34 And he said, Do it the t time.......... 8027
2Ki 11:5 A t part of you that enter in on the 7992
2Ki 19:29 in the t year sow ye, and reap, and 7992
2Ki 20:8 the house of the Lord the t day? 7992
2Ch 23:5 t part shall be at the king's house;...... 7992
Ne 10:32 t part of a shekel for the service 7992
Est 5:1 Now it came to pass on the t day 7992
Eze 5:2 Thou shalt burn with fire a t part...... 7992
Eze 5:12 A t part of thee shall die with the...... 7992
Eze 5:12 I will scatter a t part into all the 7992
Eze 10:14 and the t the face of a lion, and the 7992
Da 5:29 be he t ruler in the kingdom 8531
Hos 6:2 t day he will raise us up, and we 7992
Mt 17:23 and the t day he shall be raised........ *5154*
Mt 20:3 And he went out about the t hour,..... *5154*
Mt 20:19 and the t day he shall rise again *5154*
Mt 27:64 be made sure until the t day, ... *5154*
Mk 9:31 is killed, he shall rise the t day *5154*
Mk 10:34 and the t day he shall rise again *5154*
Mk 15:25 And it was the t hour, and they........ *5154*
Lk 9:22 be slain, and be raised the t day *5154*
Lk 12:38 watch, or come in the t watch, ... *5154*
Lk 13:32 and the t day I shall be perfected....... *5154*
Lk 18:33 and the t day he shall rise again........ *5154*
Lk 24:7 crucified, and the t day rise again *5154*
Lk 24:21 to day is the t day since these.......... *5154*
Lk 24:46 to rise from the dead the t day:........ *5154*
Jn 21:14 t time that Jesus shewed himself....... *5154*
Jn 21:17 said unto him the t time, Lovest thou... *5154*
Ac 10:40 Him God raised up the t day, and...... *5154*
1Co 15:4 he rose again the t day according *5154*
2Co 12:2 an one caught up to the t heaven *5154*
2Co 12:14 t time I am ready to come to you;...... *5154*
Rev 4:7 and the t beast had a face as a man, ... *5154*
Rev 6:5 when he had opened the t seal,......... *5154*
Rev 6:5 I heard the t beast say, Come and *5154*
Rev 8:8 the t part of the sea became blood;..... *5154*
Rev 8:10 And the t angel sounded, and there *5154*
Rev 8:12 the t part of the sun was smitten *5154*
Rev 9:18 three was the t part of men killed...... *5154*
Rev 11:14 behold, the t woe cometh quickly...... *5154*
Rev 12:4 tail drew the t part of the stars of *5154*
Rev 16:4 t angel poured out his vial upon....... *5154*

THIRST
Ex 17:3 our children and our cattle with t?..... 6772
Dt 29:19 heart, to add drunkenness to t 6771
Ne 9:15 for them out of the rock for their t..... 6772
Ps 69:21 in my t they gave me vinegar to 6772
Isa 41:17 and their tongue faileth for t.......... 6772
La 4:4 to the roof of his mouth for t 6772
Hos 2:3 like a dry land, and slay her with t 6772
Am 8:13 virgins and young men faint for t...... 6772
Mt 5:6 hunger and t after righteousness:...... *1372*
Jn 4:13 drinketh ... this water shall t again:.... *1372*
Jn 6:35 that believeth on me shall never t...... *1372*

Jn 7:37 If any man t, let him come unto....... 1372
Jn 19:28 scripture might be fulfilled, saith, I t ... 1372
Ro 12:20 feed him; if he t, give him drink:....... 1372
1Co 4:11 both hunger, and t, and are naked 1372
Rev 7:16 no more, neither t any more;.......... 1372

THIRSTED
Ex 17:3 t there for water; and the people....... 6770
Isa 48:21 they t not when he led them through... 6770

THIRSTETH
Ps 42:2 My soul t for God, for the living....... 6770
Ps 63:1 my soul t for thee, my flesh longeth.... 6770
Ps 143:6 my soul t after thee, as a thirsty
Isa 55:1 Ho, every one that t, come ye to....... 6771

THIRSTY
Jgs 4:19 a little water to drink; for I am t....... 6770
Ps 63:1 longeth for thee in a dry and t land,
Pr 25:21 and if he be t, give him water to....... 6771
Pr 25:25 As cold waters to a t soul, so is good
Isa 21:14 brought water to him that was t....... 6771
Isa 29:8 or as when a t man dreameth, and, ... 6771
Isa 44:3 pour water upon him that is t......... 6771
Isa 65:13 shall drink, but ye shall be t........... 6770
Mt 25:35 I was t, and ye gave me drink:......... 1372
Mt 25:42 I was t, and ye gave me no drink:...... 1372

THIRTEEN
1Ki 7:1 building his own house t years, .. 7969, 6240

THIRTIETH
2Ki 25:27 seven and t year of the captivity of..... 7970

THIRTY
Ge 6:15 cubits, and the height of it t cubits..... 7970
Ge 41:46 And Joseph was t years old when 7970
Ex 12:41 end of the four hundred and t years,... 7970
Nu 4:23 t years old and upward............... 7970
Jgs 14:19 slew t men of them, and took their 7970
2Sa 5:4 David was t years old when he 7970
1Ch 23:3 the age of t years and upward: 7970
Est 4:11 come in unto the king these t days..... 7970
Da 6:7 of any God or man for t days 8533
Zec 11:12 for my price t pieces of silver.......... 7970
Mt 13:23 hundredfold, some sixty, some t....... 5144
Mt 26:15 with him for t pieces of silver 5144
Mt 27:3 brought again the t pieces of silver..... 5144
Mt 27:9 they took the t pieces of silver, the 5144
Lk 3:23 began to be about t years of age,....... 5144
Gal 3:17 four hundred and t years after, ... 5144

THISTLE
Hos 10:8 t shall come up on their altars; 1863

THISTLES
Ge 3:18 and t shall it bring forth to thee;....... 1863
Mt 7:16 grapes of thorns, or figs of t? 5146

THORN
Pr 26:9 As a t goeth up into the hand of a 2336
Mic 7:4 upright is sharper than a t hedge:...... 4534
2Co 12:7 was given to me a t in the flesh, ... 4647

THORNS
Ge 3:18 T also and thistles shall it bring 6975
Jos 23:13 in your sides, and t in your eyes 6796
Jgs 2:3 but they shall be as t in your sides,
Ps 58:9 Before your pots can feel the t, he....... 329
Ps 118:12 they are quenched as the fire of t 6975
Pr 15:19 slothful man is as an hedge of t 2312
Pr 22:5 T and snares are in the way of......... 6791
Pr 24:31 all grown over with t, and nettles 7063
Ecc 7:6 as the crackling of t under a pot, ... 5518
SS 2:2 As the lily among t, so is my love 2336
Isa 7:24 the land shall become briers and t 7898
Mt 7:16 Do men gather grapes of t, or figs 173
Mt 13:7 And some fell among t; 173
Mt 27:29 when they had platted a crown of t,..... 173
Mk 4:7 and the t grew up, and choked it,....... 173
Mk 15:17 platted a crown of t, and put it 174
Lk 8:14 that which fell among t are they, ... 173
Jn 19:5 Jesus forth, wearing the crown of t...... 174
Heb 6:8 that which beareth t and briers is 173

THOROUGHLY See also THROUGHLY.
Ex 21:19 and shall cause him to be t healed...... 7495
2Ki 11:18 his images brake they in pieces t, ... 3190

THOUGHT
Ge 20:11 I t, Surely the fear of God is not 559
Ge 38:15 saw her, he t her to be an harlot;....... 2803
Ge 50:20 as for you, ye t evil against me;........ 2803
Ex 32:14 the evil which he t to do unto his...... 1696
Dt 15:9 there be not a t in thy wicked heart 1697
Dt 19:19 had t to have done unto his brother.... 2161
1Sa 1:13 Eli t she had been drunken............ 2803
1Sa 18:25 Saul t to make David fall by the 2803
2Sa 4:10 t that I would have given ... reward
2Ki 5:11 I t, He will surely come out to me,...... 559
Ne 6:2 But they t to do me mischief.......... 2803
Est 6:6 Haman t in his heart, To whom would... 559
Job 42:2 no t can be withholden from.......... 4209
Ps 64:6 the inward t of every one of them,
Ps 139:2 thou understandest my t afar off....... 7454
Pr 24:9 The t of foolishness is sin: and 2154
Pr 30:32 or if thou hast t evil, lay thine......... 2161
Ecc 10:20 Curse not the king, no not in thy t; 4093
Isa 14:24 Surely as I have t, so shall it come...... 1819
Jer 18:8 the evil that I t to do unto them. 2803
Da 6:3 king t to set him over the whole....... 6246
Am 4:13 declareth unto man what is his t,...... 7807
Mal 3:16 the Lord, and that t upon his name 2803
Mt 1:20 But while he t on these things, ... 1760
Mt 6:25 Take no t for your life, what ye........ 3309
Mt 6:27 you by taking t can add one 3309
Mt 6:34 Take ... no t for the morrow: 3309
Mt 6:34 morrow shall take t for the things 3309
Mt 10:19 take no t how or what ye shall 3309
Mk 13:11 take no t beforehand what ye 4305
Mk 14:72 And when he t thereon, he wept....... 1911
Lk 7:7 neither t I myself worthy to come
Lk 9:47 perceiving the t of their heart,......... 1261
Lk 12:17 And he t within himself, saying,....... 1260
Lk 12:22 Take no t for your life, what ye........ 3309
Lk 19:11 they t that the kingdom of God 1380
Jn 11:13 they t that he had spoken of taking 1380
Jn 13:29 some of them t because Judas had 1380
Ac 8:20 thou hast t that the gift of God........ 3543
Ac 8:22 t of thine heart may be forgiven 1963
1Co 13:11 as a child, I t as a child;............... 3049
2Co 10:5 every t to the obedience of Christ; 3540
Php 2:6 t it not robbery to be equal with....... 2233
Heb 10:29 shall he be t worthy, who hath

THOUGHTS

Ge	6:5	the **t** of his heart was only evil	4284
1Ch	28:9	all the imaginations of the **t**.	4284
1Ch	29:18	of the **t** of the heart of thy people,	4284
Ps	10:4	after God: God is not in all his **t**	4209
Ps	40:5	and thy **t** which are to usward:	4284
Ps	56:5	all their **t** are against me for evil.	4284
Ps	92:5	thy works! and thy **t** are very deep.	4284
Ps	94:11	The Lord knoweth the **t** of man,	4284
Ps	94:19	In the multitude of my **t** within	8312
Ps	119:113	I hate vain **t**: but thy law do I	5588
Ps	139:23	heart: try me, and know my **t**	8312
Ps	146:4	in that very day his **t** perish.	6250
Pr	12:5	The **t** of the righteous are right:	4284
Pr	15:26	**t** of the wicked are an abomination	4284
Pr	21:5	the **t** of the diligent tend only to	4284
Isa	55:7	and the unrighteous man his **t**	4284
Isa	55:8	For my **t** are not your **t**, neither	4284
Isa	55:9	your ways, and my **t** than your **t**	4284
Isa	59:7	blood: their **t** are **t** of iniquity;	4284
Jer	29:11	**t** of peace, and not of evil, to	4284
Da	2:30	mightest know the **t** of thy heart	7476
Da	4:19	one hour, and his **t** troubled him.	7476
Da	5:10	let not thy **t** trouble thee, nor	7476
Mic	4:12	they know not the **t** of the Lord,	4284
Mt	9:4	And Jesus knowing their **t** said,	*1761*
Mt	12:25	Jesus knew their **t**, and said unto	*1761*
Mt	15:19	**out of the heart proceed evil t,**	*1261*
Mk	7:21	**the heart of men, proceed evil t,**	*1261*
Lk	2:35	**t** of many hearts may be revealed	*1261*
Lk	5:22	But when Jesus perceived their **t**,	*1261*
Lk	6:8	he knew their **t**, and said to the	*1261*
Lk	11:17	knowing their **t**, said unto them,	*1270*
Lk	24:38	**and why do t arise in your**	*1261*
1Co	3:20	Lord knoweth the **t** of the wise,	*1261*
Heb	4:12	a discerner of the **t** and intents of	*1761*
Jas	2:4	and are become judges of evil **t**?	*1261*

THOUSAND

Le	26:8	of you shall put ten **t** to flight:	7233
Nu	31:4	Of every tribe a **t**, throughout all	505
Dt	1:11	make you a **t** times so many more	505
Dt	7:9	commandments to a **t** generations;	505
Dt	32:30	How should one chase a **t**, and two	505
Dt	32:30	and two put ten **t** to flight, except	505
Jos	23:10	One man of you shall chase a **t**: for	505
2Sa	18:3	but now thou art worth ten **t** of us:	505
1Ki	4:26	Solomon had forty **t** stalls of horses	505
1Ki	4:26	chariots, and twelve **t** horsemen.	505
1Ki	4:32	And he spake three **t** proverbs:	505
1Ki	4:32	and his songs were a **t** and five	505
1Ki	19:18	Yet I have left me seven **t** in Israel,	505
1Ch	16:15	he commanded to a **t** generations;	505
1Ch	27:1	course were twenty and four **t**.	505
2Ch	1:6	offered a **t** burnt offerings	7239, 505
Job	9:3	he cannot answer him one of a **t**	505
Job	33:23	one among a **t**, to shew unto man	505
Ps	50:10	mine, and the cattle upon a **t** hills.	505
Ps	84:10	a day in thy courts is better than a **t**.	505
Ps	90:4	For a **t** years in thy sight are but as	505
Ps	91:7	A **t** shall fall at thy side, and ten	505
Ps	91:7	and ten **t** at thy right hand; but it	7233
Ps	105:8	he commanded to a **t** generations	505
Ecc	6:6	though he live a **t** years twice told,	505
Ecc	7:28	one man among a **t** have I found;	505
Isa	60:22	A little one shall become a **t**, and a	505
Da	7:10	ten **t** times ten **t** stood before him:	7240
Da	8:14	Unto two **t** and three hundred days;	505
Da	12:11	be a **t** two hundred and ninety days	505
Am	5:3	city that went out by a **t** shall leave	505
Jnh	4:11	sixscore **t** persons that cannot	7239
Mt	14:21	had eaten were about five **t** men,	*4000*
Mt	15:38	they that did eat were four **t** men,	*5070*
Mt	16:9	**the five loaves of the five t,**	*4000*
Mt	16:10	**the seven loaves of the four t,**	*5070*
Mt	18:24	**which owed him ten t talents.**	*3463*
Mk	8:19	**brake the five loaves among five t,**	*4000*
Mk	8:20	**And when the seven among four t,**	*5070*
Lk	14:31	**against him with twenty t?**	*5505*
Ac	2:41	unto them about three **t** souls	*5153*
Ac	4:4	of the men was about five **t**	*5505*
Ro	11:4	reserved to myself seven **t** men,	*2035*
1Co	4:15	ye have ten **t** instructors in Christ,	*3563*
1Co	14:19	ten **t** words in an unknown tongue	*3463*
2Pe	3:8	day is with the Lord as a **t** years,	*5507*
2Pe	3:8	years, and a **t** years as one day.	*5507*
Rev	5:11	of them was ten **t** times ten **t**,	*3461*
Rev	7:4	forty and four **t** of all the tribes.	*5507*
Rev	9:16	horsemen were two hundred **t t**	*3461*
Rev	20:2	Satan, and bound him a **t** years,	*5507*
Rev	20:3	till the **t** years should be fulfilled:	*5507*
Rev	20:4	and reigned with Christ a **t** years.	*5507*
Rev	20:5	until the **t** years were finished.	*5507*
Rev	20:6	and shall reign with him a **t** years	*5507*
Rev	20:7	when the **t** years are expired, Satan	*5507*

THOUSANDS

Ge	24:60	be thou the mother of **t** of millions,	505
Ex	20:6	shewing mercy unto **t** of them that	505
Ex	34:7	Keeping mercy for **t**, forgiving.	505
Dt	5:10	shewing mercy unto **t** of them that	505
1Sa	18:7	and David his ten **t**	505
1Sa	18:8	to me they have ascribed but **t**	505
1Sa	21:11	David his ten **t**?	7233
Ps	3:6	not be afraid of ten **t** of people,	7233
Ps	119:72	unto me than **t** of gold and silver.	505
Jer	32:18	shewest lovingkindness unto **t**,	505
Da	7:10	thousand **t** ministered unto him,	506
Da	11:12	he shall cast down many ten **t**.	7239
Mic	5:2	thou be little among the **t** of Judah,	505
Mic	6:7	or with ten **t** of rivers of oil? shall	7233
Ac	21:20	**t** of Jews there are which believe;	*3461*
Jude	14	cometh with ten **t** of his saints,	*3461*
Rev	5:11	times ten thousand, and **t** of **t**;	*5505*

THREAD

Ge	14:23	take from a **t** even to a shoelatchet,	2339
Ge	38:28	bound upon his hand a scarlet **t**,	
Jos	2:18	shalt bind this line of scarlet **t**,	2339

THREATENED

Ac	4:21	So when they had further **t** them	*4324*
1Pe	2:23	again; when he suffered, he **t** not;	*546*

THREATENINGS

Ac	4:29	And now, Lord, behold their **t**: and	*547*
Ac	9:1	And Saul, yet breathing out **t** and	*547*

THREE

Ge	18:2	and, lo, **t** men stood by him:	7969
Ge	40:12	The **t** branches are **t** days:	7969
Ge	40:18	thereof: the **t** baskets are **t** days:	7969
Ex	2:2	goodly child, she hid him **t** months	7969

Ex 3:18 **t** days' journey into the wilderness, ... 7969
Ex 10:22 in all the land of Egypt **t** days:......... 7969
Ex 23:17 **T** times in the year all thy males 7969
Ex 25:33 **T** bowls made like unto almonds,...... 7969
Le 19:23 **t** years shall it be as uncircumcised..... 7969
Nu 10:33 mount of the Lord **t** days' journey: 7969
Nu 12:4 Come out ye **t** unto the tabernacle..... 7969
Nu 22:28 hast smitten me these **t** times?......... 7969
Dt 16:16 **T** times in a year shall all thy.......... 7969
Dt 17:6 of two witnesses, or **t** witnesses, ... 7969
Dt 19:15 or at the mouth of **t** witnesses, ... 7969
Jos 2:16 and hide yourselves there **t** days,....... 7969
Jgs 14:14 not in **t** days expound the riddle....... 7969
Jgs 16:15 hast mocked me these **t** times, ... 7969
1Sa 10:3 meet thee **t** men going up to God...... 7969
1Sa 20:20 I will shoot **t** arrows on the side 7969
2Sa 23:17 things did these **t** mighty men......... 7969
2Sa 24:12 the Lord, I offer thee **t** things;......... 7969
2Sa 24:13 that there be **t** days' pestilence in 7969
1Ki 4:32 And he spake **t** thousand proverbs: 7969
1Ki 9:25 **t** times in a year did Solomon offer 7969
1Ki 10:17 **t** hundred shields of beaten gold;...... 7969
1Ki 10:22 once in **t** years came the navy of....... 7969
1Ki 11:3 and **t** hundred concubines: and 7969
1Ki 17:21 himself upon the child **t** times,........ 7969
1Ch 11:21 Of the **t**, he was more honourable 7969
1Ch 21:12 Either **t** years' famine;................ 7969
1Ch 21:12 or **t** months to be destroyed before 7969
1Ch 21:12 else **t** days the sword of the Lord,...... 7969
Job 2:11 Job's **t** friends heard of all this evil 7969
Job 32:1 these **t** men ceased to answer Job,...... 7969
Pr 30:15 **t** things that are never satisfied,........ 7969
Pr 30:18 **t** things which are too wonderful 7969
Pr 30:21 For **t** things the earth is disquieted, ... 7969
Pr 30:29 There be **t** things which go well,....... 7969
Isa 20:3 walked naked and barefoot **t** years 7969
Eze 14:14 Though these **t** men, Noah, Daniel, ... 7969
Da 3:24 Did not we cast **t** men bound into 8532
Da 6:13 maketh his petition **t** times a day,...... 8532
Am 2:4 For **t** transgressions of Judah, and 7969
Am 2:6 For **t** transgressions of Israel, and...... 7969
Jnh 1:17 belly of the fish **t** days and nights...... 7969
Jnh 3:3 great city of **t** days' journey............ 7969
Mt 12:40 **as Jonas was t days and t nights** *5140*
Mt 15:32 **continue with me now t days,**......... *5140*
Mt 17:4 let us make here **t** tabernacles;......... *5140*
Mt 18:16 **the mouth of two or t witnesses**....... *5140*
Mt 18:20 **two or t are gathered together in** *5140*
Mt 26:61 of God, and to build it in **t** days........ *5140*
Mt 27:40 and buildest it in **t** days, save.......... *5140*
Mt 27:63 alive, After **t** days I will rise again....... *5140*
Mk 8:2 **have now been with me t days,**........ *5140*
Mk 8:31 killed, and after **t** days rise again....... *5140*
Mk 9:5 and let us make **t** tabernacles; one *5140*
Mk 14:58 within **t** days I will build another *5240*
Mk 15:29 temple, and buildest it in **t** days,....... *5140*
Lk 1:56 abode with her about **t** months,....... *5140*
Lk 4:25 **shut up t years and six months,** *5140*
Lk 9:33 and let us make **t** tabernacles; one *5140*
Lk 10:36 **Which now of these t, thinkest**........ *5140*
Lk 11:5 **him, Friend, lend me t loaves;**......... *5140*
Lk 12:52 **t against two, and two against t.**....... *5140*
Lk 13:21 **and hid in t measures of meal,**........ *5140*
Jn 2:19 **and in t days I will raise it up** *5140*
Jn 2:20 and wilt thou rear it up in **t** days?...... *5140*
Ac 2:41 them about **t** thousand souls. *5153*
Ac 5:7 about the space of **t** hours after, ... *5140*
Ac 28:15 as Appii forum, and The **t** taverns:..... *5140*
1Co 13:13 faith, hope, charity, these **t**; *5140*
1Co 14:27 let it be by two, or at the most by **t**, ... *5140*
2Co 13:1 mouth of two or **t** witnesses shall...... *5140*
1Ti 5:19 but before two or **t** witnesses.......... *5140*
Heb 10:28 mercy under two or **t** witnesses: *5140*
Heb 11:23 was hid **t** months of his parents,....... *5150*
1Jn 5:7 are **t** that bear record in heaven, ... *5140*
1Jn 5:8 are **t** that bear witness in earth,........ *5140*
1Jn 5:8 blood: and these **t** agree in one........ *5140*
Rev 6:6 **t** measures of barley for a penny; *5140*
Rev 11:9 dead bodies **t** days and an half,........ *5140*
Rev 11:11 after **t** days and an half the Spirit *5140*

THREEFOLD

Ecc 4:12 a **t** cord is not quickly broken 8027

THREESCORE

Ge 46:26 all the souls were **t** and six; 8346
2Ch 36:21 sabbath, to fulfil **t** and ten years 7657
Ps 90:10 of our years are **t** years and ten; 7657
Isa 7:8 and within **t** and five years shall 7657
Da 9:26 And after **t** and two weeks shall 8346
Zec 1:12 indignation these **t** and ten years? 7657
Rev 13:18 number is Six hundred **t** and six. *5516*

THRESH

Isa 41:15 thou shalt **t** the mountains, and 1758
Jer 51:33 threshingfloor, it is time to **t** her: 1869
Hab 3:12 thou didst **t** the heathen in anger 1758

THRESHED

Jgs 6:11 Gideon **t** wheat by the winepress,...... 2251

THRESHETH

1Co 9:10 he that **t** in hope should be partaker *248*

THRESHING

Le 26:5 And your **t** shall reach unto the 1786
2Ki 13:7 had made them like the dust by **t**...... 1758
1Ch 21:20 Now Ornan was **t** wheat 1758
Isa 41:15 a new sharp **t** instrument having 4173
Am 1:3 Gilead with **t** instruments of iron: 2742

THRESHINGFLOOR

Nu 18:30 Levites as the increase of the **t**, ... 1637
2Sa 24:24 David bought the **t** and the oxen 1637
1Ch 21:15 angel of the Lord stood by the **t** 1637
2Ch 3:1 had prepared in the **t** of Ornan........ 1637
Jer 51:33 The daughter of Babylon is like a **t**, ... 1637

THRESHINGFLOORS

Da 2:35 like the chaff of the summer **t**; 147

THRESHOLD

Jgs 19:27 and her hands were upon the **t**........ 5592
1Sa 5:4 his hands were cut off upon the **t**; 4670
1Sa 5:5 tread on the **t** of Dagon in Ashdod..... 4670
1Ki 14:17 she came to the **t** of the door, ... 5592
Eze 10:4 and stood over the **t** of the house; 4670
Eze 46:2 shall worship at the **t** of the gate: 4670
Zep 1:9 punish all those that leap on the **t**,..... 4670

THRESHOLDS

Eze 43:8 setting of their threshold by my **t**, ... 5592

THREW

2Sa 16:13 **t** stones at him, and cast dust.......... 5619
2Ki 9:33 her down. So they **t** her down: 8058

Mk	12:42	widow, and she **t** in two mites,	*906*
Lk	9:42	devil **t** him down, and tare him.	*4952*
Ac	22:23	clothes, and **t** dust into the air,	*906*

THRICE

Ex	34:23	**T** in the year shall all your	7969, 6471
2Ki	13:18	And he smote **t**, and stayed.	7969, 6471
Mt	26:34	**crow, thou shalt deny me t**	*5151*
Mt	26:75	thou shalt deny me **t**	
Mk	14:30	**twice, thou shalt deny me t**	*5151*
Lk	22:34	**shalt t deny that thou knowest**	*5151*
Lk	22:61	**cock crow, thou shalt deny me t**	*5151*
Jn	13:38	**crow, till thou hast denied me t**	*5151*
2Co	12:8	this thing I besought the Lord **t**,	*5151*

THROAT

Ps	5:9	their **t** is an open sepulchre; they	1627
Pr	23:2	And put a knife to thy **t**, if thou	3930
Mt	18:28	**and took him by the t, saying,**	*4155*
Ro	3:13	Their **t** is an open sepulchre;	*2995*

THRONE

Ge	41:40	only in the **t** will I be greater	3678
Ex	12:29	of Pharaoh that sat on his **t**.	3678
Dt	17:18	sitteth upon the **t** of his kingdom,	3678
1Sa	2:8	make them inherit the **t** of glory:	3678
2Sa	3:10	to set up the **t** of David over Israel	3678
2Sa	7:16	thy **t** shall be established for ever	3678
2Sa	14:9	the king and his **t** be guiltless.	3678
1Ki	1:30	he shall sit upon my **t** in my stead;	3678
1Ki	1:46	Solomon sitteth on the **t** of the	3678
1Ki	1:47	and make his **t** greater than thy **t**	3678
1Ki	7:7	he made a porch for the **t** where he	3678
1Ki	9:5	thee a man upon the **t** of Israel.	3678
1Ki	10:18	the king made a great **t** of ivory	3678
1Ki	22:19	I saw the Lord sitting on his **t**,	3678
2Ki	25:28	set his **t** above the **t** of the kings	3678
1Ch	17:14	and his **t** shall be established for	3678
1Ch	29:23	Solomon sat on the **t** of the Lord	3678
2Ch	18:18	I saw the Lord sitting upon his **t**,	3678
Est	5:1	king sat upon his royal **t** in the	3678
Ps	11:4	temple, the Lord's **t** is in heaven:	3678
Ps	45:6	Thy **t**, O God, is for ever and ever:	3678
Ps	89:14	are the habitation of thy **t**	3678
Ps	89:36	and his **t** as the sun before me.	3678
Ps	89:44	and cast his **t** down to the ground.	3678
Ps	93:2	Thy **t** is established of old: thou art	3678
Ps	94:20	the **t** of iniquity have fellowship	3678
Ps	97:2	are the habitation of his **t**.	3678
Ps	103:19	hath prepared his **t** in the heavens;	3678
Pr	16:12	**t** is established by righteousness.	3678
Pr	20:8	A king that sitteth in the **t** of	3678
Pr	20:28	and his **t** is upholden by mercy.	3678
Pr	25:5	his **t** shall be established in	3678
Pr	29:14	his **t** shall be established for ever.	3678
Isa	6:1	saw also the Lord sitting upon a **t**,	3678
Isa	9:7	upon the **t** of David, and upon his	3678
Isa	14:13	exalt my **t** above the stars of God:	3678
Isa	66:1	The heaven is my **t**, and the earth	3678
Jer	14:21	do not disgrace the **t** of thy glory:	3678
Jer	36:30	none to sit upon the **t** of David:	3678
La	5:19	**t** from generation to generation	3678
Eze	1:26	upon the likeness of the **t** was the	3678
Eze	10:1	appearance of the likeness of a **t**	3678
Eze	43:7	the place of my **t**, and the place of	3678
Da	5:20	he was deposed from his kingly **t**,	3764
Da	7:9	his **t** was like the fiery flame, and	3764
Jnh	3:6	Nineveh, and he arose from his **t**,	3678
Zec	6:13	he shall be a priest upon his **t**	3678
Mt	5:34	**by heaven; for it is God's t**	*2362*
Mt	19:28	**man shall sit in the t of his glory,**	*2362*
Mt	23:22	**heaven, sweareth by the t of God,**	*2362*
Mt	25:31	**he sit upon the t of his glory:**	*2362*
Lk	1:32	unto him the **t** of his father David:	*2362*
Ac	2:30	raise up Christ to sit on his **t**:	*2362*
Ac	7:49	Heaven is my **t**, and earth is my	*2362*
Heb	1:8	Thy **t**, O God, is for ever and ever:	*2362*
Heb	4:16	come boldly unto the **t** of grace,	*2362*
Heb	8:1	right hand of the **t** of the Majesty	*2362*
Heb	12:2	at the right hand of the **t** of God	*2362*
Rev	3:21	**I grant to sit with me in my t,**	*2362*
Rev	3:21	**set down with my Father in his t**	*2362*
Rev	4:2	and, behold, a **t** was set in heaven,	*2362*
Rev	4:3	was a rainbow round about the **t**,	*2362*
Rev	4:5	out of the **t** proceeded lightnings	*2362*
Rev	4:6	before the **t** there was a sea of	*2362*
Rev	4:10	and cast their crowns before the **t**,	*2362*
Rev	7:11	and fell before the **t** on their faces,	*2362*
Rev	7:17	Lamb which is in the midst of the **t**	*2362*
Rev	20:11	I saw a great white **t**, and him that	*2362*
Rev	21:5	he that sat upon the **t** said, Behold,	*2362*
Rev	22:1	proceeding out of the **t** of God and	*2362*
Rev	22:3	the **t** of God and of the Lamb shall	*2362*

THRONES

Ps	122:5	For there are set **t** of judgment,	3678
Da	7:9	I beheld till the **t** were cast down,	3764
Mt	19:28	**ye also shall sit upon twelve t,**	*2362*
Lk	22:30	**sit on t judging the twelve tribes**	*2362*
Col	1:16	whether they be **t**, or dominions,	*2362*

THROUGHLY See also **THOROUGHLY.**

Ps	51:2	Wash me **t** from mine iniquity,	7235
Jer	7:5	if ye **t** execute judgment between	
Mt	3:12	he will **t** purge his floor, and gather	*1245*
Lk	3:17	he will **t** purge his floor, and will	*1245*
2Ti	3:17	**t** furnished unto all good works	*1822*

THROW

Jgs	2:2	ye shall **t** down their altars:	5422
Jgs	6:25	**t** down the altar of Baal that thy	2040
2Ki	9:33	And he said, **T** her down. So	8058
Jer	1:10	and to destroy, and to **t** down	2040
Jer	31:28	to **t** down, and to destroy, and to	2040

THROWN

Ex	15:1	rider hath he **t** into the sea.	7411
2Sa	20:21	his head shall be **t** to thee over	7993
1Ki	19:14	covenant, **t** down thine altars,	2040
Jer	50:15	are fallen, her walls are **t** down:	2040
La	2:2	he hath **t** down in his wrath the	2040
La	2:17	hath **t** down, and hath not pitied:	2040
Eze	38:20	the mountains shall be **t** down	2040
Na	1:6	and the rocks are **t** down by him	5422
Mt	24:2	**another, that shall not be t down.**	*2647*
Lk	4:35	the devil had **t** him in the midst,	*4496*
Rev	18:21	that great city Babylon be **t** down,	*906*

THRUST

Ex	11:1	he shall surely **t** you out hence	1644
Ex	12:39	because they were **t** out of Egypt,	1644
Nu	25:8	tent, and **t** both of them through,	1856
Nu	35:20	But if he **t** him of hatred, or hurl	1920
Nu	35:22	**t** him suddenly without enmity,	1920

Dt 15:17 **t** it through his ear unto the door, ... 5414
1Sa 11:2 I may **t** out all your right eyes, ... 5365
2Sa 18:14 and **t** them through the heart of. 8628
1Ch 10:4 and **t** me through therewith; 1856
Lk 10:15 **heaven, shall be t down to hell** *2601*
Jn 20:25 nails, and **t** my hand into his side *906*
Jn 20:27 **thy hand, and t it into my side:** *906*
Heb 12:20 stoned, or **t** through with a dart: *2700*
Rev 14:19 the angel **t** in his sickle into the. *906*

THRUSTETH
Job 32:13 God **t** him down, not man. 5086

THUMB
Ex 29:20 and upon the **t** of their right hand, ... 931
Le 8:23 and upon the **t** of his right hand, ... 931
Le 14:25 the **t** of his right hand, ... 931

THUMBS
Jgs 1:7 **t** and their great toes cut off 931, 3027

THUMMIM (thum´-mim)
Ex 28:30 of judgment the Urim and the **T**; 8550
Dt 33:8 Let thy **T** and thy Urim be with 8550
Ezr 2:63 a priest with Urim and with **T** 8550
Ne 7:65 up a priest with Urim and **T** 8550

THUNDER
Ex 9:23 the Lord sent **t** and hail, and the. 6963
Ex 9:29 and the **t** shall cease, neither shall. 6963
1Sa 7:10 the Lord thundered with a great **t**. 6963
1Sa 12:18 the Lord sent **t** and rain that day: 6963
Job 40:9 thou **t** with a voice like him? 7481
Ps 77:18 voice of thy **t** was in the heaven: 7482
Ps 81:7 thee in the secret place of **t** 7482
Ps 104:7 voice of thy **t** they hasted away 7482
Mk 3:17 Boanerges, ... The sons of **t**. *1027*
Rev 6:1 I heard, as it were the noise of **t**, ... *1027*

THUNDERED
2Sa 22:14 The Lord **t** from heaven, and. 7481
Ps 18:13 The Lord also **t** in the heavens, ... 7481

THUNDERETH
Ps 29:3 the God of glory **t**: the Lord is. 7481

THUNDERINGS
Ex 9:28 be no more mighty **t** and hail; 6963
Ex 20:18 and all the people saw the **t**, and. 6963
Rev 4:5 lightnings and **t** and voices: *1027*
Rev 8:5 and there were voices, and **t**, and *1027*
Rev 11:19 were lightnings, and voices, and **t**, ... *1027*
Rev 19:6 and as the voice of mighty **t**. *1027*

THUNDERS
Ex 9:33 **t** and hail ceased, and the rain. 6963
Ex 19:16 that there were **t** and lightnings, ... 6963
Rev 10:4 things which the seven **t** uttered, ... *1027*
Rev 16:18 were voices, and **t**, and lightnings; *1027*

TIDINGS
Ex 33:4 when the people heard these evil **t**, ... 1697
1Sa 4:19 heard the **t** that the ark of God 8052
2Sa 4:4 five years old when the **t** came 8052
2Sa 4:10 thinking to have brought good **t**, ... 1319
2Sa 18:20 but this day thou shalt bear no **t**, ... 1319
Ps 112:7 He shall not be afraid of evil **t**. 8052
Isa 40:9 O Zion, that bringest good **t**, get. 1319
Isa 41:27 one that bringeth good **t** 1319
Isa 52:7 feet of him that bringeth good **t**, ... 1319
Isa 61:1 to preach good **t** unto the meek; 1319
Jer 20:15 man who brought **t** to my father 1319
Jer 37:5 Jerusalem heard **t** of them, ... 8088
Na 1:15 feet of him that bringeth good **t**, ... 1319
Lk 2:10 I bring you good **t** of great joy *2097*
Ac 13:32 And we declare unto you glad **t**, ... *2097*
Ro 10:15 and bring glad **t** of good things! *2097*
1Th 3:6 and brought us good **t** of your faith. . . . *2097*

TIE
Pr 6:21 and **t** them about thy neck. 6029

TIED
Mt 21:2 **straightway ye shall find an ass t**, ... *1210*
Mk 11:2 **ye shall find a colt t, whereon** *1210*
Lk 19:30 **your entering ye shall find a colt t**, ... *1210*

TILE
Eze 4:1 son of man, take thee a **t**, and lay it 3843

TILLAGE
Pr 13:23 Much food is in the **t** of the poor: 5215

TILLED
Eze 36:34 And the desolate land shall be **t**, ... 5647

TILLER
Ge 4:2 but Cain was a **t** of the ground 5647

TILLEST
Ge 4:12 When thou **t** the ground, it shall 5647

TILLETH
Pr 12:11 He that **t** his land shall be 5647
Pr 28:19 He that **t** his land shall have plenty 5647

TIMBER
Ex 31:5 and in carving of **t**, to work in all. 6086
1Ki 5:18 prepared **t** and stones to build the 6086
1Ch 22:14 **t** also and stone have I prepared; 6086
Ezr 5:8 stones, and **t** is laid in the walls, ... 636
Ezr 6:4 of great stones, and a row of new **t**: 636
Ezr 6:11 let **t** be pulled down from his house, ... 636
Hab 2:11 beam out of the **t** shall answer it. 6086

TIMBREL
Ps 81:2 a psalm, and bring hither the **t** 8596
Ps 150:4 Praise him with the **t** and dance 8596

TIMBRELS
Ex 15:20 women went out after her with **t** 8596
Jgs 11:34 came out to meet him with **t** and. 8596
1Ch 13:8 and with psalteries, and with **t** 8596

TIME
Ge 4:3 And in process of **t** it came to pass, ... 3117
Ge 18:10 thee according to the **t** of life; 6256
Ge 18:14 At the **t** appointed I will return
Ge 22:15 out of heaven the second **t**, ... 6256
Ge 24:11 the **t** that women go out to draw 6256
Ex 8:32 hardened his heart at this **t** also, ... 6471
Ex 9:27 unto them, I have sinned this **t**: 6471
Ex 13:14 thy son asketh thee in **t** to come, ... 4279
Nu 20:15 we have dwelt in Egypt a long **t** 3117
Dt 6:20 thy son asketh thee in **t** to come, ... 4279
Dt 19:4 whom he hated not in **t** past; 8543, 8032
Dt 32:35 their foot shall slide in due **t**: for. 6256
Jos 4:6 ask their fathers in **t** to come. 4279
Jos 6:16 it came to pass at the seventh **t** 6471

Jgs 10:14	you in the **t** of your tribulation	6256
2Sa 11:1	at the **t** when kings go forth to	6256
2Sa 24:15	morning even to the **t** appointed:	6256
1Ki 19:2	them by to morrow about this **t**	6256
2Ki 4:16	according to the **t** of life, thou	6256
2Ki 5:26	Is it a **t** to receive money, and to	6256
1Ch 11:11	hundred slain by him at one **t**.	6471
1Ch 20:1	the **t** that kings go out to battle,	6256
Ezr 4:19	city of old **t** hath made insurrection	3118
Est 4:14	to the kingdom for such a **t** as this?	6256
Job 22:16	Which were cut down out of **t**,	6256
Ps 32:6	pray unto thee in a **t** when thou	6256
Ps 56:3	What **t** I am afraid, I will trust in	3117
Ps 69:13	thee, O Lord, in an acceptable **t**	6256
Ps 71:9	Cast me not off in the **t** of old age:	6256
Pr 25:13	cold of snow in the **t** of harvest.	3117
Pr 25:19	an unfaithful man in **t** of trouble	3117
Pr 31:25	and she shall rejoice in **t** to come	3117
Ecc 3:1	a **t** to every purpose under the	6256
Ecc 3:2	A **t** to be born, and a **t** to die;	6256
Ecc 3:3	A **t** to kill, and a **t** to heal;	6256
Ecc 3:4	A **t** to weep, and a **t** to laugh;	6256
Ecc 3:5	A **t** to cast away stones, and a	6256
Ecc 3:6	a **t** to keep, and a **t** to cast away;	6256
Ecc 3:7	a **t** to keep silence, and a **t** to speak;	6256
Ecc 3:8	a **t** of war, and a **t** of peace.	6256
Ecc 3:11	every thing beautiful in his **t**:	6256
Ecc 7:17	shouldest thou die before thy **t**?	6256
Ecc 8:6	to every purpose there is **t** and	6256
Ecc 9:11	**t** and chance happeneth to them all.	6256
Ecc 9:12	For man also knoweth not his **t**:	6256
Isa 49:8	an acceptable **t** have I heard thee	6256
Jer 8:12	**t** of their visitation they shall be	6256
Jer 10:15	**t** of their visitation they shall.	6256
Jer 18:23	with them in the **t** of thine anger	6256
Jer 33:15	at that **t**, will I cause the Branch	6256
Jer 50:16	the sickle in the **t** of harvest:	6256
Jer 50:27	day is come, the **t** of their visitation	6256
La 5:20	ever, and forsake us so long **t**?	3117
Eze 7:7	the **t** is come, the day of trouble	6256
Eze 16:8	behold, thy **t** was the **t** of love;	6256
Eze 30:3	it shall be the **t** of the heathen.	6256
Eze 35:5	sword in the **t** of their calamity.	6256
Da 3:5	at what **t** ye hear the sound of.	5732
Da 4:36	At the same **t** my reason returned	2166
Da 7:25	and times and the dividing of **t**.	5732
Da 12:1	and there shall be a **t** of trouble	6256
Hos 10:12	for it is **t** to seek the Lord, till he	6256
Zec 10:1	rain in the **t** of the latter rain;	6256
Mt 2:7	of them diligently what **t** the star	*5550*
Mt 4:6	lest at any **t** thou dash thy foot	*3379*
Mt 4:17	From that **t** Jesus began to preach,	*5119*
Mt 13:15	**lest at any t they should see.**	*3379*
Mt 24:21	**beginning of the world to this t,**	*2540*
Mt 26:18	**Master saith, My t is at hand;**	*2540*
Mk 4:12	**lest at any t they … be converted,**	*3379*
Mk 4:17	**and so endure but for a t.**	*4340*
Mk 13:19	**which God created unto this t,**	*3568*
Mk 13:33	**for ye know not when the t is**	*2540*
Lk 4:11	lest at any **t** thou dash thy foot	*3379*
Lk 8:13	**and in t of temptation fall away**	*2540*
Lk 16:16	**t the kingdom of God is preached,**	*5119*
Lk 19:44	**knewest not the t of thy visitation**	*2540*
Lk 20:9	**into a far country for a long t.**	*5550*
Lk 21:8	**Christ; and the t draweth near:**	*2540*
Lk 21:34	**at any t … hearts be overcharged.**	*3379*
Jn 1:18	No man hath seen God at any **t**;	*4455*
Jn 3:4	second **t** into his mother's womb	*1208*
Jn 7:6	unto them, **My t is not yet come:**	*2540*
Jn 7:8	**feast; for my t is not yet full.**	*2540*
Jn 14:9	**Have I been so long t with you,**	*5550*
Jn 16:25	**the t cometh, when I shall no**	*5610*
Jn 21:17	He saith unto him the third **t**, **Simon,**	
Ac 1:6	at this **t** restore again the kingdom	*5550*
Ro 5:6	in due **t** Christ died for … ungodly	*2540*
Ro 8:18	sufferings of this present **t** are not	*2540*
Ro 13:11	it is high **t** to awake out of sleep:	*5610*
1Co 4:5	judge nothing before the **t**, until	*2540*
1Co 7:5	except it be with consent for a **t**,	*2540*
1Co 7:29	this I say, brethren, the **t** is short:	*2540*
1Co 15:8	me also, as of one born out of due **t**	
2Co 6:2	now is the accepted **t**; behold, now	*2540*
2Co 13:1	This is the third **t** I am coming to you	
Gal 1:13	heard of my conversation in **t** past	*4218*
Gal 4:4	the fulness of the **t** was come,	*5550*
Eph 2:2	in **t** past ye walked according to	*4218*
Eph 2:12	at that **t** ye were without Christ.	*2540*
Eph 5:16	Redeeming the **t**, because the days	*2540*
Col 3:7	In the which ye also walked some **t**,	*4218*
Col 4:5	that are without, redeeming the **t**	*2540*
2Th 2:6	that he might be revealed in his **t**	*2540*
1Ti 2:6	for all, to be testified in due **t**.	*2540*
2Ti 4:6	the **t** of my departure is at hand	*2540*
Heb 1:1	spake in **t** past unto the fathers	*3819*
Heb 1:5	of the angels said he at any **t**,	*4218*
Heb 1:13	of the angels said he at any **t**,	*4218*
Heb 4:7	David, To day, after so long a **t**;	*5550*
Heb 4:16	and find grace to help in **t** of need	*2121*
Heb 9:28	shall he appear the second **t** without	
Heb 11:32	**t** would fail me to tell of Gibeon.	*5550*
1Pe 1:5	ready to be revealed in the last **t**	*2540*
1Pe 1:11	or what manner of **t** the Spirit of	*2540*
1Pe 4:17	the **t** is come that judgment must.	*2540*
1Pe 5:6	that he may exalt you in due **t**.	*2540*
2Pe 1:21	prophecy came not in old **t** by the	*4218*
1Jn 2:18	Little children, it is the last **t**	*5610*
1Jn 4:12	No man hath seen God at any **t**	*4455*
Rev 1:3	therein: for the **t** is at hand	*2540*
Rev 10:6	that there should be **t** no longer:	*5550*
Rev 12:14	times, and half a **t**, from the face of	*2540*
Rev 14:15	for the **t** is come for thee to reap;	*5610*
Rev 22:10	of this book: for the **t** is at hand	*2540*

TIMES

Ge 31:7	me, and changed my wages ten **t**;	4489
Ex 23:17	Three **t** in the year all thy males	6471
Le 4:6	and sprinkle of the blood seven **t**	6471
Le 14:51	and sprinkle the house seven **t**	6471
Le 19:26	ye use enchantment, nor observe **t**	
Le 25:8	unto thee, seven **t** seven years;	6471
Le 26:21	bring seven **t** more plagues upon	
Le 26:28	chastise you seven **t** for your sins	
Nu 14:22	have tempted me now these ten **t**,	
Nu 22:28	thou hast smitten me these three **t**?	
Dt 1:11	you a thousand **t** so many more	6471
Jos 6:15	they compassed the city seven **t**	6471
Jgs 16:15	hast mocked me these three **t**,	6471
1Ki 17:21	himself upon the child three **t**,	6471
2Ki 5:10	Go and wash in Jordan seven **t**,	6471
2Ki 13:19	shouldest have smitten five or six **t**;	6471
2Ki 21:6	the fire, and observed **t**, and used	
Est 1:13	to the wise men, which knew the **t**,	6256

T

Ps 10:1 hidest thou thyself in **t** of trouble? 6256
Ps 12:6 in a furnace of earth, purified seven **t**
Ps 31:15 My **t** are in thy hand: deliver me. 6256
Ps 34:1 I will bless the Lord at all **t**: his 6256
Ps 62:8 Trust in him at all **t**; ye people. 6256
Pr 5:19 her breasts satisfy thee at all **t**;. 6256
Pr 17:17 A friend loveth at all **t**, and a. 6256
Pr 24:16 For a just man falleth seven **t**, and
Ecc 8:12 a sinner do evil an hundred **t**,
Isa 14:31 shall be alone in his appointed **t**. 4151
Da 1:20 he found them ten **t** better than all
Da 3:19 heat the furnace one seven **t** more
Da 4:16 and let seven **t** pass over him. 5732
Da 6:10 upon his knees three **t** a day, ... 2166
Da 7:10 ten thousand **t** ten thousand stood
Da 7:25 a time and **t** and the dividing of 5732
Da 12:7 shall be for a time, **t**, and an half; 4150
Mt 16:3 **ye not discern ... signs of the t?** *2540*
Mt 18:22 **but, Until seventy t seven** *1441*
Lk 17:4 **seven t in a day turn again to thee,** *2034*
Lk 21:24 **the t of the Gentiles be fulfilled** *2540*
Ac 1:7 **you to know the t of the seasons,** *5550*
Ac 3:21 until the **t** of restitution of all *5550*
Ro 11:30 in **t** past have not believed God. *4218*
2Co 11:24 five **t** received I forty stripes save *3999*
Gal 4:10 observe days, and months, and **t**, ... *2540*
Eph 1:10 the dispensation of the fulness of **t**. *2540*
1Th 5:1 of the **t** and the seasons, brethren. *5550*
1Ti 4:1 latter **t** some shall depart from *5550*
2Ti 3:1 the last days perilous **t** shall come. *5550*
Heb 1:1 who at sundry **t** and in divers
Rev 5:11 was ten thousand **t** ten thousand
Rev 12:14 for a time, and **t**, and half a time. *2540*

TINGLE
1Sa 3:11 of every one that heareth it shall **t** 6750
Jer 19:3 whosoever heareth, his ears shall **t** 6750

TINKLING
1Co 13:1 as sounding brass, or a **t** cymbal *214*

TIP
Ex 29:20 the **t** of the right ear of Aaron, ... 8571
Le 8:24 blood upon the **t** of their right ear, ... 8571
Lk 16:24 **dip the t of his finger in water,** *206*

TITHE
Le 27:30 all the **t** of the land, whether of. 4643
Nu 18:26 Lord, even a tenth part of the **t**. 4643
Dt 14:23 **t** of thy corn, of thy wine, and of 4643
Dt 14:28 forth all the **t** of thine increase 4643
2Ch 31:6 the **t** of holy things which were. 4643
Ne 10:38 the Levites shall bring up the **t** of 4643
Mt 23:23 **for ye pay t of mint and anise** *586*
Lk 11:42 **ye t mint and rue and all manner**. *586*

TITHES
Ge 14:20 hand. And he gave him **t** of all. 4643
Le 27:31 will at all redeem ought of his **t**, ... 4643
Nu 18:28 offering unto the Lord of all your **t**, ... 4643
Dt 26:12 the **t** of thine increase the third. 4643
2Ch 31:12 brought in the offerings and the **t** 4643
Ne 12:44 for the firstfruits, and for the **t** 4643
Am 4:4 and your **t** after three years:. 4643
Mal 3:8 robbed thee? In **t** and offerings 4643
Lk 18:12 **I give t of all that I possess** *586*
Heb 7:9 receiveth **t**, payed **t** in Abraham. *1183*

TITHING
Dt 26:12 third year, which is the year of **t**,. 4643

TITLE
Jn 19:19 And Pilate wrote a **t**, and put it. *5102*

TITTLE
Mt 5:18 **one t shall in no wise pass from** *2762*
Lk 16:17 **pass, than one t of the law to fail**. *2762*

TO-DAY See DAY.

TOE
Le 8:23 upon the great **t** of his right foot. 931
Le 14:25 upon the great **t** of his right foot: 931
Le 14:28 upon the great **t** of his right foot, ... 931

TOES
Le 8:24 the great **t** of their right feet: 931
2Sa 21:20 fingers, and on every foot six **t**, ... 676
Da 2:41 whereas thou sawest the feet and **t**, ... 677

TOGETHER
Ge 1:10 gathering **t** of the waters called he 8425
Ge 3:7 and they sewed fig leaves **t**, and. 8425
Ge 25:22 children struggled **t** within her;
Ex 2:13 two men of the Hebrews strove **t**:
Ex 15:8 the waters were gathered **t**,
Nu 26:10 and swallowed them up **t** with Korah,
Dt 25:5 If brethren dwell **t**, and one of 3162
1Sa 11:11 so that two of them were not left **t**. 3162
2Sa 14:6 and they two strove **t** in the field,
Ne 6:10 Let us meet **t** in the house of God,
Ps 2:2 and the rulers take counsel **t**,. 3162
Ps 33:7 He gathereth the waters of the sea **t**
Ps 34:3 me, and let us exalt his name **t** 3162
Ps 49:2 Both low and high, rich and poor, **t**. . . . 3162
Ps 85:10 Mercy and truth are met **t**
Pr 22:2 The rich and poor meet **t**: the Lord is
Pr 29:13 poor and the deceitful man meet **t**
Ecc 3:5 and a time to gather stones **t**;
Ecc 4:5 fool foldeth his hands **t**, and eateth his
Ecc 4:11 if two lie **t**, then they have heat:
Isa 1:18 Come now, and let us reason **t**, saith
Isa 45:8 let righteousness spring up **t**; I 3162
Isa 45:16 go to confusion **t** that are makers. 3162
Isa 52:9 Break forth into joy, sing **t**, ye
Isa 65:25 the wolf and the lamb shall feed **t**. 259
La 2:8 to lament; they languished **t** 3162
Eze 37:7 bones came **t**, bone to his bone
Am 3:3 Can two walk **t**, except they be 3162
Zec 12:3 people of the earth be gathered **t**
Mt 1:18 before they came **t**, she was found *4905*
Mt 19:6 **What therefore God hath joined t,**. *4801*
Mt 24:31 **gather t his elect from the four**. *1996*
Mt 27:62 and Pharisees came **t** unto Pilate, ... *4863*
Mk 2:15 and sinners sat also **t** with Jesus *4873*
Mk 10:9 **therefore God hath joined t,** *4801*
Mk 13:27 **gather t his elect from the four**. *1996*
Mk 14:59 neither so did their witness agree **t**
Lk 6:38 **pressed down, and shaken t**
Lk 12:1 were gathered **t** an innumerable *1996*
Lk 15:13 **the younger son gathered all t,** *4863*
Lk 17:35 **women ... be grinding t;**. . . . *1909, 3588, 846*
Lk 24:33 and found the eleven gathered **t** *4867*
Jn 11:52 gather **t** in one the children of God *4863*
Jn 20:4 So they ran both **t**: and the *3674*
Jn 20:7 but wrapped **t** in a place by itself. *1794*

T

Ac	15:6	And the apostles and elders came **t**	*4863*
Ro	6:5	planted **t** in the likeness of his	*4854*
Ro	8:17	that we may be also glorified **t**.	*4888*
Ro	8:22	groaneth and travaileth in pain **t**	*4944*
Ro	8:28	that all things work **t** for good.	*4903*
Ro	15:30	strive **t** with me in your prayers	*4865*
1Co	3:9	For we are labourers **t** with God:	*4904*
1Co	11:17	that ye come **t** not for the better	*4905*
2Co	6:14	Be ye not unequally yoked **t** with	*2086*
Eph	2:5	hath quickened us **t** with Christ,	*4806*
Eph	2:6	made us sit **t** in heavenly places.	*4776*
Eph	2:21	all the building fitly framed **t**.	*4883*
Eph	4:16	the whole body fitly joined **t** and	*4883*
Php	1:27	one mind striving **t** for the faith	*4866*
Col	2:2	be comforted, being knit **t** in love,	*4822*
Col	2:13	hath he quickened **t** with him,	*4806*
1Th	4:17	remain shall be caught up **t** with	*260*
1Th	5:10	sleep, we should live **t** with him	*260*
1Th	5:11	Wherefore comfort yourselves **t**	*240*
Heb	10:25	the assembling of ourselves **t**,	*1997*
Jas	5:3	Ye have heaped treasure **t** for the	
1Pe	3:7	being heirs **t** of the grace of life;	*4789*
Rev	16:16	he gathered them **t** into a place	*4863*
Rev	19:17	Come and gather yourselves **t** unto	*4863*
Rev	19:19	armies, gathered **t** to make war	*4863*
Rev	20:8	Magog, to gather them **t** to battle:	*4863*

TOIL

Ge	5:29	our work and **t** of our hands.	6093
Ge	41:51	hath made me forget all my **t**	5999
Mt	6:28	**they t not, neither do they spin:**	*2872*
Lk	12:27	**grow: they t not, they spin not;**	*2872*

TOILED

Lk	5:5	Master, we have **t** all the night,	*2872*

TOKEN

Ge	9:12	This is the **t** of the covenant which	226
Ge	9:13	**t** of a covenant between me and	226
Ge	17:11	**t** of the covenant betwixt me and	226
Ex	3:12	this shall be a **t** unto thee, that I	226
Ex	12:13	the blood shall be to you for a **t**	226
Ex	13:16	shall be for a **t** upon thine hand,	226
Nu	17:10	be kept for a **t** against the rebels;	226
Jos	2:12	father's house, and give me a true **t**	226
Ps	86:17	Shew me a **t** for good; that they	226
Mk	14:44	betrayed him had given them a **t**,	*4958*
Php	1:28	to them an evident **t** of perdition,	*1732*
2Th	1:5	a manifest **t** of the righteous	*1730*
2Th	3:17	which is the **t** in every epistle:	*4592*

TOKENS

Dt	22:15	forth the **t** of the damsel's virginity	
Ps	65:8	uttermost parts are afraid at thy **t**.	226
Ps	135:9	sent **t** and wonders into the midst	226
Isa	44:25	That frustrateth the **t** of the liars,	226

TOLERABLE

Mt	10:15	**It shall be more t for the land of.**	*414*
Mt	11:22	**It shall be more t for Tyre and**	*414*
Mt	11:24	**it shall be more t for the land of.**	*414*
Mk	6:11	**It shall be more t for Sodom and**	*414*
Lk	10:12	**it shall be more t in that day for**	*414*
Lk	10:14	**it shall be more t for Tyre and**	*414*

TOLL

Ezr	4:13	then will they not pay **t**, tribute	4061
Ezr	7:24	it shall not be lawful to impose **t**,	4061

TOMB

Mt	27:60	laid it in his own new **t**, which he	*3419*
Mk	6:29	up his corpse, and laid it in a **t**	*3419*

TOMBS

Mt	8:28	with devils, coming out of the **t**,	*3419*
Mt	23:29	**ye build the t of the prophets,**	*5028*
Mk	5:2	there met him out of the **t** a man	*3419*
Lk	8:27	abode in any house, but in the **t**	*3418*

TO-MORROW See MORROW.

TONGS

Nu	4:9	and his **t**, and his snuffdishes,	4457
2Ch	4:21	lamps, and the **t**, made he of gold.	4457
Isa	6:6	which he had taken with the **t**.	4457
Isa	44:12	The smith with the **t** both worketh	4621

TONGUE

Ge	10:5	every one after his **t**, after their	3956
Ex	4:10	slow of speech, and of a slow **t**	3956
Ex	11:7	Israel shall not a dog move his **t**,	3956
Dt	23:49	whose **t** thou shalt not understand:	3956
Jos	10:21	none moved his **t** against any of	3956
Jgs	7:5	lappeth of the water with his **t**	3956
2Sa	23:2	by me, and his word was in my **t**	3956
Ezr	4:7	letter was written in the Syrian **t**.	762
Job	6:24	Teach me, and I will hold my **t**	2790
Ps	5:9	sepulchre; they flatter with their **t**.	3956
Ps	10:7	under his **t** is mischief and vanity.	3956
Ps	12:3	the **t** that speaketh proud things:	3956
Ps	15:3	He that backbiteth not with his **t**,	3956
Ps	34:13	Keep thy **t** from evil, and thy lips	3956
Ps	39:1	my ways, that I sin not with my **t**	3956
Ps	45:1	my **t** is the pen of a ready writer.	3956
Ps	50:19	to evil, and thy **t** frameth deceit	3956
Ps	51:14	my **t** shall sing aloud of thy	3956
Ps	52:2	Thy **t** deviseth mischiefs; like a	3956
Ps	57:4	arrows, and their **t** a sharp sword	3956
Ps	64:3	Who whet their **t** like a sword, and.	3956
Ps	68:23	and the **t** of thy dogs in the same	3956
Ps	71:24	My **t** also shall talk of thy.	3956
Ps	73:9	their **t** walketh through the earth.	3956
Ps	109:2	spoken against me with a lying **t**.	3956
Ps	119:172	My **t** shall speak of thy word: for	3956
Ps	120:2	lying lips, and from a deceitful **t**.	3956
Ps	139:4	For there is not a word in my **t**,	3956
Pr	6:17	A proud look, a lying **t**, and hands	3956
Pr	6:24	of the **t** of a strange woman.	3956
Pr	10:20	**t** of the just is as choice silver:	3956
Pr	10:31	but the froward **t** shall be cut out	3956
Pr	12:18	but the **t** of the wise is health.	3956
Pr	12:19	but a lying **t** is but for a moment	3956
Pr	15:2	The **t** of the wise useth knowledge	3956
Pr	15:4	A wholesome **t** is a tree of life: but	3956
Pr	16:1	answer of the **t**, is from the Lord.	3956
Pr	17:4	a liar giveth ear to a naughty **t**.	3956
Pr	17:20	a perverse **t** falleth into mischief.	3956
Pr	18:21	and life are in the power of the **t**:	3956
Pr	21:6	lying **t** is a vanity tossed to and fro	3956
Pr	21:23	keepeth his mouth and his **t**	3956
Pr	25:15	and a soft **t** breaketh the bone.	3956
Pr	25:23	angry countenance a backbiting **t**.	3956
Pr	26:28	A lying **t** hateth those that are	3956
Pr	28:23	than he that flattereth with the **t**.	3956
Pr	31:26	and in her **t** is the law of kindness	3956
SS	4:11	honey and milk are under thy **t**;	3956

Isa 30:27 and his **t** as a devouring fire: 3956
Isa 33:19 of a stammering **t**, that thou canst 3956
Isa 35:6 hart, and the **t** of the dumb sing: 3956
Isa 45:23 knee shall bow, every **t** shall swear 3956
Jer 9:5 have taught their **t** to speak lies 3956
Jer 9:8 Their **t** is as an arrow shot out; it 3956
La 4:4 **t** of the sucking child cleaveth to 3956
Mic 6:12 their **t** is deceitful in their mouth. 3956
Hab 1:13 holdest thy **t** when the wicked 2790
Mk 7:33 and he spit, and touched his **t**; *1100*
Lk 1:64 and his **t** loosed, and he spake, and *1100*
Lk 16:24 **finger in water, and cool my t** *1100*
Ac 2:8 hear we every man in our own **t** *1258*
Ac 26:14 and saying in the Hebrew **t, Saul,** *1258*
Ro 14:11 and every **t** shall confess to God *1100*
1Co 14:2 he that speaketh in an unknown **t** *1100*
1Co 14:14 For if I pray in an unknown **t**, my *1100*
1Co 14:19 thousand words in an unknown **t** *1100*
Php 2:11 every **t** should confess that Jesus *1100*
Jas 1:26 be religious, and bridleth not his **t**, *1100*
Jas 3:5 Even so the **t** is a little member, *1100*
Jas 3:6 the **t** is a fire, a world of iniquity: *1100*
Jas 3:8 But the **t** can no man tame; it is *1100*
1Jn 3:18 let us not love in word, neither in **t**; *1100*
Rev 5:9 out of every kindred, and **t**, and *1100*
Rev 14:6 every nation, and kindred, and **t**, *1100*

TONGUES

Ge 10:20 their families, after their **t**, 3956
Ps 55:9 Destroy, O Lord, and divide their **t** 3956
Ps 140:3 sharpened their **t** like a serpent: 3956
Isa 66:18 that I will gather all nations and **t**; 3956
Jer 9:3 they bend their **t** like their bow for 3956
Jer 23:31 that use their **t**, and say, He saith 3956
Mk 16:17 **they shall speak with new t;** *1100*
Ac 2:3 there appeared unto them cloven **t** *1100*
Ac 2:11 we do hear them speak in our **t** the *1100*
Ac 10:46 For they heard them speak with **t** *1100*
Ac 19:6 they spake with **t**, and prophesied *1100*
Ro 3:13 with their **t** they have used deceit; *1100*
1Co 12:10 spirits; to another divers kinds of **t**; *1100*
1Co 13:1 Though I speak with the **t** of men *1100*
1Co 13:8 fail; whether there be **t**, they shall *1100*
1Co 14:5 I would that ye all spake with **t** *1100*
1Co 14:6 if I come unto you speaking with **t** *1100*
1Co 14:22 Wherefore **t** are for a sign, not to *1100*
1Co 14:39 and forbid not to speak with **t** *1100*
Rev 7:9 kindreds, and people, and **t**, stood *1100*
Rev 16:10 and they gnawed their **t** for pain, *1100*
Rev 17:15 and multitudes, and nations, and **t** *1100*

TOOK

Ge 2:21 and he **t** one of his ribs, and 3947
Ge 3:6 she **t** of the fruit thereof, and did 3947
Ge 5:24 and he was not; for God **t** him 3947
Ge 14:11 And they **t** all the goods of Sodom 3947
Ge 22:10 and **t** the knife to slay his son 3947
Ge 27:36 he **t** away my birthright; and, 3947
Ge 37:31 they **t** Joseph's coat, and killed a 3947
Ex 34:4 and **t** in his hand the two tables of 3947
Le 8:23 Moses **t** of the blood of it, and put 3947
Dt 1:23 and I **t** twelve men of you, one of 3947
Dt 9:17 I **t** the two tables, and cast them 8610
Dt 9:21 I **t** your sin, the calf which ye had 3947
Jgs 4:21 Jael Heber's wife **t** a nail of the 3947
Jgs 16:21 the Philistines **t** him, and put out 270
Jgs 16:29 Samson **t** hold of the two middle
1Sa 5:1 the Philistines **t** the ark of God 3947
1Sa 17:54 David **t** the head of the Philistine, 3947
2Sa 13:10 Tamar **t** the cakes which she had 3947
1Ki 14:26 he **t** away all the shields of gold 3947
2Ki 2:13 He **t** up also the mantle of Elijah 7311
2Ki 23:16 **t** the bones out of the sepulchres, 3947
1Ch 10:4 So Saul **t** a sword, and fell upon it 3947
2Ch 34:33 Josiah **t** away all the abominations
Ezr 6:5 Nebuchadnezzar **t** forth out of the 5312
Job 1:15 fell upon them, and **t** them away; 3947
Ps 22:9 art he that **t** me out of the womb 1518
Ps 55:14 We **t** sweet counsel together, and
Pr 12:27 not that which he **t** in hunting:
Ecc 2:20 to despair of all the labour which I **t**
Isa 8:2 I **t** unto me faithful witnesses to
Jer 32:11 I **t** the evidence of the purchase, 3947
La 5:13 They **t** the young men to grind, 5375
Eze 3:12 Then the spirit **t** me up, and I 5375
Eze 3:14 spirit lifted me up, and **t** me away, 3947
Eze 8:3 and **t** me by a lock of mine head; 3947
Eze 11:24 Afterwards the spirit **t** me up, 5375
Eze 43:5 So the spirit **t** me up, and brought 5375
Zec 11:13 And I **t** the thirty pieces of silver, 3947
Mt 1:24 him, and **t** unto him his wife: *3880*
Mt 8:17 saying, Himself **t** our infirmities, *2983*
Mt 9:25 he went in, and **t** her by the hand, *2902*
Mt 14:12 disciples came, and **t** up the body, *142*
Mt 14:19 and **t** the five loaves, and the two *2983*
Mt 14:20 they **t** up of the fragments that *142*
Mt 16:10 **and how many baskets ye t** *2983*
Mt 18:28 **and t him by the throat, saying,** *2902*
Mt 22:15 **t** counsel how they might entangle *2983*
Mt 24:39 **flood came, and t them all away;** *142*
Mt 25:1 **ten virgins, which t their lamps,** *2983*
Mt 25:35 **I was a stranger, and ye t me** *4863*
Mt 25:43 **a stranger, and ye t me not in:** *4863*
Mt 26:26 Jesus **t** bread, and blessed it, and *2983*
Mt 26:27 And he **t** the cup, and gave thanks, *2983*
Mt 26:50 laid hands on Jesus, and **t** him *2902*
Mt 27:6 chief priests **t** the silver pieces, *2983*
Mt 27:9 they **t** the thirty pieces of silver, *2983*
Mt 27:27 **t** Jesus into the common hall *3880*
Mt 27:30 **t** the reed, and smote him on the *2983*
Mt 27:31 they **t** the robe off from him, and *1562*
Mt 27:48 and **t** a spunge, and filled it with *2983*
Mt 28:15 So they **t** the money, and did as *2983*
Mk 6:43 they **t** up twelve baskets full of the *142*
Mk 8:20 **baskets full of fragments t ye** *142*
Mk 8:32 Peter **t** him, and began to rebuke *4355*
Mk 9:36 he **t** a child, and set him in the *2983*
Mk 10:16 he **t** them up in his arms, put his *1723*
Mk 12:8 **they t him, and killed him, and** *2983*
Mk 14:23 he **t** the cup, and when he had *2983*
Mk 14:46 their hands on him, and **t** him *2902*
Mk 14:49 **temple teaching, and ye t me** *2902*
Mk 15:20 they **t** off the purple from him, *1562*
Mk 15:46 **t** him down, and wrapped him in *2507*
Lk 9:16 Then he **t** the five loaves and the *2983*
Lk 9:28 he **t** Peter and John and James, *3880*
Lk 10:34 **him to an inn, and t care of him** *1959*
Lk 15:13 **t his journey into a far country,** *589*
Lk 22:17 he **t** the cup, and gave thanks, *1209*
Lk 22:19 And he **t** bread, and gave thanks, *2983*
Lk 24:30 he **t** bread, and blessed it, and *2983*
Lk 24:43 he **t** it, and did eat before them *2983*

Jn 8:59 **t** they up stones to cast at him: *142*
Jn 10:31 the Jews **t** up stones again to stone *941*
Jn 12:3 Then **t** Mary a pound of ointment *2983*
Jn 12:13 **T** branches of palm trees, and *2983*
Jn 13:4 and **t** a towel, and girded himself....... *2983*
Jn 19:1 Pilate therefore **t** Jesus, and *2983*
Jn 19:23 **t** his garments, and made four *2983*
Jn 19:27 disciple **t** her unto his own home *2983*
Jn 19:40 Then **t** they the body of Jesus,......... *2983*
Ac 1:16 was guide to them that **t** Jesus. *4815*
Ac 9:23 the Jews **t** counsel to kill him: *4823*
Ac 27:35 **t** bread, and gave thanks to God *2983*
1Co 11:23 in which he was betrayed **t** bread:...... *2983*
1Co 11:25 the same manner also he **t** the cup
Php 2:7 **t** upon him the form of a servant, ... *2983*
Col 2:14 and **t** it out of the way, nailing.......... *142*
Heb 2:16 he **t** on him the seed of Abraham. *1949*
Heb 9:19 he **t** the blood of calves and of *2983*
Rev 5:7 **t** the book out of the right hand *4327*
Rev 8:5 the angel **t** the censer, and filled it...... *4327*
Rev 10:10 I **t** the little book out of the........... *4327*
Rev 18:21 a mighty angel **t** up a stone like a *142*

TOOL
Ex 20:25 if thou lift up thy **t** upon it, thou 2719
Ex 32:4 and fashioned it with a graving **t**,
Dt 27:5 shalt not lift up any iron **t** upon them.
1Ki 6:7 any **t** of iron heard in the house,....... 3627

TOOTH
Ex 21:24 Eye for eye, **t** for **t**, hand for........... 8127
Le 24:20 for breach, eye for eye, **t** for **t**.......... 8127
Dt 19:21 **t** for **t**, hand for hand, foot for foot 8127
Pr 25:19 time of trouble is like a broken **t**....... 8127
Mt 5:38 **eye for an eye, and a t for a t**.......... *3599*

TOP
Ge 11:4 whose **t** may reach unto heaven;....... 7218
Ge 28:12 and the **t** of it reached to heaven:...... 7218
Ex 24:17 like ... fire on the **t** of the mount 7218
Nu 14:40 up into the **t** of the mountain, ... 7218
Dt 3:27 Get thee up into the **t** of Pisgah,....... 7218
Jgs 6:26 an altar ... upon the **t** of this rock,..... 7218
1Sa 9:25 with Saul upon the **t** of the house 1406
1Ki 18:42 Elijah went up to the **t** of Carmel; 7218
2Ch 25:12 cast ... down from the **t** of the rock, ... 7218
Est 5:2 and touched the **t** of the sceptre 7218
Pr 8:2 standeth in the **t** of high places, ... 7218
Pr 23:34 he that lieth upon the **t** of a mast. 7218
Isa 30:17 a beacon upon the **t** of a mountain,.... 7218
Isa 42:11 shout from the **t** of the mountains. 7218
La 2:19 for hunger in the **t** of every street...... 7218
La 4:1 poured out in the **t** of every street...... 7218
Eze 24:8 set her blood upon the **t** of a rock 6706
Am 9:3 hide themselves in the **t** of Carmel, ... 7218
Mic 4:1 in the **t** of the mountains, ... 7218
Na 3:10 in pieces at the **t** of all the streets:...... 7218
Mt 27:51 in twain from the **t** to the bottom; *509*
Mk 15:38 in twain from the **t** to the bottom. *509*
Jn 19:23 seam, woven from the **t** throughout..... *509*
Heb 11:21 leaning upon the **t** of his staff *206*

TOPS
Isa 2:21 into the **t** of the ragged rocks,......... 5585
Isa 15:3 on the **t** of their houses, and in........ 1406
Eze 6:13 in all the **t** of the mountains, and...... 7218
Joel 2:5 chariots on the **t** of mountains shall ... 7218

TORCH
Zec 12:6 and like a **t** of fire in a sheaf; 3940

TORCHES
Na 2:4 they shall seem like **t**, they shall 3940
Jn 18:3 with lanterns and **t** and weapons....... *2985*

TORMENT
Mt 8:29 art thou come hither to **t** us before...... *928*
Mk 5:7 thee by God, that thou **t** me not *928*
Lk 8:28 high? I beseech thee, **t** me not *928*
Lk 16:28 **they also come into this place of t** *931*
1Jn 4:18 out fear, because fear hath **t**........... *2851*
Rev 9:5 their **t** was as the **t** of a scorpion, ... *929*
Rev 14:11 the smoke of their **t** ascendeth up....... *929*
Rev 18:7 so much **t** and sorrow give her:......... *929*
Rev 18:10 Standing afar off for ... fear of her **t**, ... *929*
Rev 18:15 stand afar off for the fear of her **t**, ... *929*

TORMENTED
Lk 16:24 **tongue; for I am t in this flame**........ *3600*
Lk 16:25 **he is comforted, and thou art t**........ *3600*
Heb 11:37 being destitute, afflicted, **t**;............ *2558*
Rev 9:5 that they should be **t** five months: *928*
Rev 11:10 these two prophets **t** them that *928*
Rev 14:10 he shall be **t** with fire and brimstone *928*
Rev 20:10 shall be **t** day and night for ever *928*

TORMENTORS
Mt 18:34 **wroth, and delivered him to the t**....... *930*

TORMENTS
Mt 4:24 taken with divers diseases and **t**,........ *931*
Lk 16:23 **hell he lift up his eyes, being in t**,....... *931*

TORN
Ge 31:39 That which was **t** of beasts I 2966
Ge 44:28 Surely he is **t** in pieces; and I.......... 2963
Ex 22:13 not make good that which was **t**....... 2966
Ex 22:31 ye eat any flesh that is **t** of beasts 2966
Le 7:24 fat of that which is **t** with beasts, ... 2966
Le 17:15 or that which was **t** with beasts, ... 2966
Le 22:8 dieth of itself, or is **t** with beasts, ... 2966
1Ki 13:26 unto the lion, which hath **t** him,....... 7665
1Ki 13:28 eaten the carcase, nor **t** the ass 7665
Isa 5:25 carcases were **t** in the midst of 5478
Jer 5:6 out thence shall be **t** in pieces:......... 2963
Eze 4:14 dieth of itself, or is **t** in pieces;......... 2966
Eze 44:31 any thing that is dead of itself, or **t**, ... 2966
Hos 6:1 for he hath **t**, and he will heal us; 2963
Mal 1:13 and ye brought that which was **t**, ... 1497

TORTURED
Heb 11:35 and others were **t**, not accepting *5178*

TOSS
Isa 22:18 violently turn and **t** thee like a 6802
Jer 5:22 the waves thereof **t** themselves,........ 1607

TOSSED
Pr 21:6 a vanity **t** to and fro of them that...... 5086
Isa 54:11 O thou afflicted, **t** with tempest, and
Mt 14:24 the midst of the sea, **t** with waves: *928*
Ac 27:18 exceedingly **t** with a tempest,.......... *5492*
Eph 4:14 **t** to and fro, and carried about *2831*
Jas 1:6 sea driven with the wind and **t** *4494*

TOSSINGS
Job 7:4 I am full of **t** to and fro unto the 5076

TOUCH

Ge	3:3	it, neither shall ye **t** it, lest ye die	5060
Ex	19:12	the mount, or **t** the border of it:	5060
Le	5:2	Or if a soul **t** any unclean thing,	5060
Le	6:27	**t** the flesh thereof shall be holy:	5060
Le	7:21	soul that shall **t** any unclean thing	5060
Le	11:8	and their carcase ye shall not **t**;	5060
Nu	4:15	but they shall not **t** any holy thing,	5060
Nu	16:26	**t** nothing of theirs, lest ye be	5060
Jos	9:19	now therefore we may not **t** them.	5060
Ru	2:9	men that they shall not **t** thee?	5060
2Sa	14:10	and he shall not **t** thee any more.	5060
2Sa	18:12	that none **t** the young man Absalom.	
Job	1:11	and **t** all that he hath, and he will	5060
Job	2:5	and **t** his bone and his flesh, and he	5060
Ps	105:15	**T** not mine anointed, and do my	5060
Isa	52:11	from thence, **t** no unclean thing;	5060
La	4:14	men could not **t** their garments.	5060
La	4:15	it is unclean; depart, depart **t** not:	5060
Hag	2:12	and with his skirt do **t** bread, or	5060
Hag	2:13	by a dead body **t** any of these,	5060
Mt	9:21	If I may but **t** his garment, I shall	*680*
Mt	14:36	might only **t** the hem of his garment:	*680*
Mk	3:10	they pressed upon him for to **t** him,	*680*
Mk	5:28	If I may **t** but his clothes, I shall be	*680*
Mk	6:56	**t** if it were but the border of his	*680*
Mk	8:22	him, and besought him to **t** him.	*680*
Mk	10:13	to him, that he should **t** them:	*680*
Lk	6:19	whole multitude sought to **t** him:	*680*
Lk	11:46	**t not the burdens with one of**	*4379*
Lk	18:15	also infants, that he would **t** them:	*680*
Jn	20:17	Jesus saith unto her, **T me not;**	*680*
1Co	7:1	is good for a man not to **t** a woman.	*680*
2Co	6:17	**t** not the unclean thing: and I will	*680*
Col	2:21	(**T** not; taste not; handle not;	*680*
Heb	11:28	destroyed the firstborn shall **t**	*2345*
Heb	12:20	And if so much as a beast **t** the	*2345*

TOUCHED

Ge	26:29	us no hurt, as we have not **t** thee,	5060
Ge	32:25	him, he **t** the hollow of his thigh;	5060
Ge	32:32	he **t** the hollow of Jacob's thigh	5060
Nu	19:18	and upon him that **t** a bone, or one	5060
Nu	31:19	and whosoever hath **t** any slain,	5060
Jgs	6:21	**t** the flesh and … unleavened cakes;	5060
1Sa	10:26	of men, whose hearts God had **t**.	5060
1Ki	6:27	the wing of the one **t** the one wall,	5060
1Ki	6:27	their wings **t** one another in the	5060
1Ki	19:5	then an angel **t** him, and said unto	5060
1Ki	19:7	and **t** him, and said, Arise and eat;	5060
2Ki	13:21	let down, and **t** the bones of Elisha,	5060
Est	5:2	near, and **t** the top of the sceptre.	5060
Isa	6:7	and said, Lo, this hath **t** thy lips;	5060
Jer	1:9	forth his hand, and **t** my mouth	5060
Eze	3:13	creatures that **t** one another,	5401
Da	8:18	but he **t** me, and set me upright.	5060
Da	9:21	**t** me about the time of the evening	5060
Da	10:10	an hand **t** me, which set me upon	5060
Da	10:16	of the sons of men **t** my lips:	5060
Da	10:18	**t** me one like the appearance of a	5060
Mt	8:3	put forth his hand, and **t** him,	*680*
Mt	8:15	he **t** her hand, and the fever left her:	*680*
Mt	9:20	and **t** the hem of his garment:	*680*
Mt	9:29	Then **t** he their eyes, saying,	*680*
Mt	14:36	many as **t** were made perfectly	*680*
Mt	17:7	Jesus came and **t** them, and said,	*680*
Mt	20:34	on them, and **t** their eyes:	*680*
Mk	1:41	put forth his hand, and **t** him, and	*680*
Mk	5:27	the press behind, and **t** his garment.	*680*
Mk	5:30	press, and said, **Who t my clothes?**	*680*
Mk	6:56	as many as **t** him were made whole	*680*
Mk	7:33	ears, and he spit, and **t** his tongue;	*680*
Lk	5:13	he put forth his hand, and **t** him,	*680*
Lk	7:14	And he came and **t** the bier: and	*680*
Lk	8:44	and **t** the border of his garment:	*680*
Lk	8:45	And Jesus said, **Who t me?** When	*680*
Lk	8:46	Jesus said, **Somebody hath t me:**	*680*
Lk	22:51	And he **t** his ear, and healed him.	*680*
Heb	4:15	**t** with … feeling of our infirmities;	*4834*
Heb	12:18	unto the mount that might be **t**,	*5584*

TOUCHETH

Ge	26:11	He that **t** this man or his wife	5060
Ex	19:12	whosoever **t** the mount shall be	5060
Ex	29:37	whatsoever **t** the altar shall be holy.	5060
Ex	30:29	whatsoever **t** them shall be holy	5060
Le	7:19	the flesh that **t** any unclean thing	5060
Le	11:26	one that **t** them shall be unclean.	5060
Le	15:10	whosoever **t** any thing that was	5060
Le	15:22	whosoever **t** any thing that she	5060
Le	22:4	whoso **t** any thing that is unclean	5060
Nu	19:11	He that **t** the dead body of any man.	5060
Ps	104:32	he **t** the hills, and they smoke.	5060
Pr	6:29	**t** her shall not be innocent.	5060
Hos	4:2	they break out, and blood **t** blood.	5060
Am	9:5	God of hosts is he that **t** the land,	5060
Zec	2:8	he that **t** you **t** the apple of his eye.	5060
Lk	7:39	manner of woman this is … **t** him:	*680*
1Jn	5:18	and that wicked one **t** him not.	*680*

TOUCHING

Le	5:13	an atonement for him as **t** his sin	5921
Job	37:23	**T** the Almighty, we cannot find him	
Jer	1:16	them **t** all their wickedness	5921
Eze	7:13	the vision is **t** the whole multitude	413
Mt	18:19	**shall agree on earth as t any**	*4012*
Mt	22:31	**as t the resurrection of the dead,**	*4012*
Mk	12:26	**And as t the dead, that they.**	*4012*
Lk	23:14	no fault in this man **t** those things	
Ac	21:25	As **t** the Gentiles which believe	*4012*
Ac	24:21	**T** the resurrection of the dead I	*4012*
Ac	26:2	**t** … the things whereof I am accused	*4012*
Ro	11:28	but as **t** the election, they are	*2596*
1Co	8:1	as **t** things offered unto idols,	*4012*
Php	3:5	Hebrews; as **t** the law, a Pharisee;	*2596*
Php	3:6	**t** the righteousness which is in the	*2596*
1Th	4:9	**t** brotherly love ye need not that	*4012*
2Th	3:4	have confidence in the Lord **t** you,	*1909*

TOWARD

Ge	13:12	and pitched his tent **t** Sodom	5704
Ge	15:5	Look now **t** heaven, and tell the stars	
Ge	18:22	faces from thence, and went **t** Sodom:	
Ex	9:10	and Moses sprinkled it up **t** heaven;	
Ex	9:22	Stretch forth thine hand **t** heaven	5921
Ex	10:21	Stretch out thine hand **t** heaven,	5921
Dt	28:54	his eye shall be evil **t** his brother,	
Dt	28:54	and **t** the wife of his bosom,	
Dt	28:56	be evil **t** the husband of her bosom,	
Dt	28:56	and **t** her son, and **t** her daughter,	
Dt	28:57	**t** her children which she shall bear:	
Jgs	13:20	went up **t** heaven from off the altar,	
1Sa	17:48	David hasted, and ran **t** the army	

2Sa 14:1 the king's heart was **t** Absalom 5921
2Ch 6:26 if they pray **t** this place, and confess 413
2Ch 16:9 them whose heart is perfect **t** him 413
Ezr 3:11 mercy endureth for ever **t** Israel 5921
Est 8:4 held out the golden sceptre **t** Esther
Ps 5:7 will I worship **t** thy holy temple 413
Ps 25:15 Mine eyes are ever **t** the Lord; for 413
Ps 85:4 cause thine anger **t** us to cease 5973
Ps 86:13 For great is thy mercy **t** me: and 5921
Ps 103:11 is his mercy **t** them that fear him 5921
Ps 116:12 the Lord for all his benefits **t** me? 5921
Ps 138:2 I will worship **t** thy holy temple, 413
Pr 14:35 The king's favour is **t** a wise servant:
Pr 23:5 they fly away as an eagle **t** heaven
SS 7:10 my beloved's, and his desire is **t** me 5921
Jer 29:11 the thoughts that I think **t** you, 5921
Eze 8:16 backs **t** the temple of the Lord, 413
Eze 48:28 and to the river **t** the great sea 5921
Da 8:8 ones **t** the four winds of heaven.
Mt 14:14 moved with compassion **t** them, *1909*
Lk 2:14 on earth peace, good will **t** men *1722*
Lk 12:21 **himself, and is not rich t God** *1519*
Lk 24:29 for it is **t** evening, and the day is *4314*
Ac 1:10 looked stedfastly **t** heaven as he *1519*
Ac 20:21 to the Greeks, repentance **t** God, *1519*
Ac 22:3 and was zealous **t** God, as ye all are
Ac 24:16 conscience void of offence **t** God, *4314*
Ro 1:27 burned in their lust one **t** another; *1519*
Ro 5:8 God commendeth his love **t** us, *1529*
Ro 15:5 be likeminded one **t** another *1722*
1Co 7:36 himself uncomely **t** his virgin, *1909*
2Co 2:8 would confirm your love **t** him *1519*
Eph 1:8 hath abounded **t** us in all wisdom *1519*
Php 3:14 I press **t** the mark for the prize *2596*
Col 4:5 Walk in wisdom **t** them that are *4314*
1Th 3:12 abound in love one **t** another, *1519*
1Th 4:12 ye may walk honestly **t** them that *4314*
Heb 6:1 dead works, and of faith **t** God, *1909*
1Pe 3:21 of a good conscience **t** God,) *1519*
1Jn 3:21 then have we confidence **t** God *4314*
1Jn 4:9 manifested the love of God **t** us, *2722*

TOWEL
Jn 13:4 and took a **t**, and girded himself. *3012*

TOWER See also WATCHTOWER.
Ge 11:4 to, let us build us a city and a **t**, 4026
2Sa 22:3 my high **t**, and my refuge, my 4869
2Sa 22:51 He is the **t** of salvation for his 1431
2Ki 9:17 there stood a watchman on the **t** 4026
Ps 18:2 of my salvation, and my high **t** 4869
Ps 144:2 my high **t**, and my deliverer; 4869
Pr 18:10 name of the Lord is a strong **t**: 4026
SS 4:4 Thy neck is like the **t** of David 4026
Isa 2:15 And upon every high **t**, and upon 4026
Isa 5:2 and built a **t** in the midst of it, 4026
Jer 6:27 I have set thee for a **t** and a 969
Hab 2:1 my watch, and set me upon the **t**, 4692
Mt 21:33 **a winepress in it, and built a t,** *4444*
Lk 13:4 **upon whom the t in Siloam fell,** *4444*
Lk 14:28 **of you, intending to build a t,** *4444*

TOWERS
2Ch 26:9 Uzziah built **t** in Jerusalem at the 4026
2Ch 26:10 Also he built **t** in the desert, and 4026
2Ch 27:4 the forests he built castles and **t** 4026
Ps 48:12 about her: tell the **t** thereof 4026
Isa 33:18 where is he that counted the **t**? 4026
Eze 26:4 of Tyrus, and break down her **t** 4026
Zep 1:16 cities, and against the high **t** 6438
Zep 3:6 the nations: their **t** are desolate; 6438

TOWN
Jos 2:15 for her house was upon the **t** wall 7023
1Sa 16:4 the elders of the **t** trembled at his 7023
1Sa 23:7 by entering into a **t** that hath gates 5892
Hab 2:12 him that buildeth a **t** with blood, 5892
Mt 10:11 **city or t ye shall enter,** *2968*
Mk 8:26 saying, **Neither go into the t, nor** *2968*
Lk 5:17 were come out of every **t** of Galilee, *2968*
Jn 7:42 out of the **t** of Bethlehem, where *2968*
Jn 11:30 Jesus was not yet come into the **t**, *2968*

TOWNS
Dt 3:5 beside unwalled **t** a great many 5892
Est 9:19 that dwelt in the unwalled **t** 5892
Jer 19:15 upon this city and upon all her **t** 5892
Mk 1:38 **Let us go into the next t, that I** *2969*

TRADE
Ge 34:21 dwell in the land, and **t** therein; 5503
Ge 46:34 Thy servants' **t** hath been about 582
Rev 18:17 sailors, and as many as **t** by sea, *2038*

TRADED
Eze 27:13 they **t** the persons of men and 5414
Mt 25:16 **talents went and t with the same** *2038*

TRADING
Lk 19:15 **much every man had gained by t** *1281*

TRADITION
Mt 15:2 transgress the **t** of the elders? *3862*
Mt 15:3 **commandment of God by your t?** *3862*
Mt 15:6 **of God of none effect by your t** *3862*
Mk 7:8 **ye hold the t of men, as the** *3862*
Mk 7:13 **God of none effect through your t,** *3862*
Col 2:8 vain deceit, after the **t** of men, *3862*
2Th 3:6 not after the **t** which he received *3862*
1Pe 1:18 received by **t** from your fathers;

TRADITIONS
Gal 1:14 zealous of the **t** of my fathers *3862*
2Th 2:15 hold the **t** … ye have been taught, *3862*

TRAFFICK
Ge 42:34 brother, and ye shall **t** in the land 5503
1Ki 10:15 of the **t** of the spice merchants, 4536
Eze 28:5 by thy **t** hast thou increased thy 7404
Eze 28:18 iniquities, by the iniquity of thy **t**; 7404

TRAFFICKERS
Isa 23:8 **t** are the honourable of the earth? 3669

TRAIN
1Ki 10:2 to Jerusalem with a very great **t**, 2428
Pr 22:6 **T** up a child in the way he should 2596
Isa 6:1 up, and his **t** filled the temple 7757

TRAITOR
Lk 6:16 Iscariot, which was also the **t** *4273*

TRAITORS
2Ti 3:4 **T**, heady, highminded, lovers of *4273*

TRAMPLE
Isa 63:3 anger, and **t** them in my fury; 7429
Mt 7:6 **they t them under their feet,** *2662*

TRANCE

Nu	24:16	into a **t**, but having his eyes open:	
Ac	10:10	they made ready, he fell into a **t**,	*1611*
Ac	11:5	and in a **t** I saw a vision, A certain	*1611*
Ac	22:17	prayed in the temple, I was in a **t**;	*1611*

TRANQUILLITY

Da	4:27	it may be a lengthening of thy **t**	7963

TRANSFIGURED

Mt	17:2	And was **t** before them: and his	*3339*
Mk	9:2	and he was **t** before them	*3339*

TRANSFORMED

Ro	12:2	ye **t** by the renewing of your mind,	*3339*
2Co	11:14	Satan himself is **t** into an angel	*3345*
2Co	11:15	**t** as ... ministers of righteousness;	*3345*

TRANSGRESS

Nu	14:41	do ye **t** the commandment of the	5674
1Sa	2:24	ye make the Lord's people to **t**	5674
2Ch	24:20	Why **t** ye the commandments of	5674
Ne	13:27	to **t** against our God in marrying	4603
Ps	17:3	that my mouth shall not **t**	5674
Ps	25:3	ashamed which **t** without cause	898
Pr	28:21	a piece of bread that man will **t**	6586
Jer	2:20	and thou saidst, I will not **t**;	5647
Mt	15:2	thy disciples **t** the tradition of the	*3845*
Mt	15:3	**do ye also t the commandment**	*3845*
Ro	2:27	and circumcision dost **t** the law?	*3848*

TRANSGRESSED

Dt	26:13	I have not **t** thy commandments,	5674
Jos	7:11	and they have also **t** my covenant	5674
Jos	7:15	because he hath **t** the covenant of	5674
Jos	23:16	When ye have **t** the covenant of the	5674
1Sa	14:33	Ye have **t**: roll a great stone unto me	898
1Sa	15:24	for I have **t** the commandment of	5674
1Ki	8:50	wherein they have **t** against thee,	6586
1Ch	5:25	**t** against the God of their fathers,	4603
2Ch	26:16	for he **t** against the Lord his God,	4603
2Ch	36:14	people, **t** very much after all the	4603
Ezr	10:10	Ye have **t**, and have taken strange	4603
Isa	66:24	the men that have **t** against me:	6586
Jer	2:8	the pastors also **t** against me, and	6586
Jer	3:13	that thou hast **t** against the Lord	6586
Jer	33:8	pardon ... whereby they have **t** against me	6586
Jer	34:18	the men that have **t** my covenant,	5674
La	3:42	We have **t** and have rebelled:	6586
Da	9:11	Yea, all Israel have **t** thy law,	5674
Hos	7:13	because they have **t** against me:	6586
Lk	15:29	**neither t I at any time thy**	*3928*

TRANSGRESSETH

Pr	16:10	his mouth **t** not in judgment	4603
Hab	2:5	Yea also, because he **t** by wine,	898
1Jn	3:4	Whosoever committeth sin **t**	*458, 4160*
2Jn	9	Whosoever **t**, and abideth not in	*3845*

TRANSGRESSING

Dt	17:2	Lord thy God, in **t** his covenant,	5674
Isa	59:13	In **t** and lying against the Lord,	6586

TRANSGRESSION

Ex	34:7	forgiving iniquity and **t** and sin,	6588
Nu	14:18	forgiving iniquity and **t**, and by no	6588
1Sa	24:11	is neither evil nor **t** in mine hand,	6588
1Ch	9:1	carried away to Babylon for their **t**	4604
1Ch	10:13	So Saul died for his **t** which he	4604
2Ch	29:19	in his reign did cast away in his **t**,	4604
Ezr	9:4	the **t** of those that had been	4604
Ezr	10:6	he mourned because of the **t** of	4604
Job	7:21	why dost thou not pardon my **t**,	6588
Ps	32:1	Blessed is he whose **t** is forgiven,	6588
Ps	36:1	The **t** of the wicked saith within	6588
Pr	12:13	The wicked is snared by the **t** of	6588
Pr	17:9	He that covereth a **t** seeketh love:	6588
Pr	17:19	He loveth **t** that loveth strife: and	6588
Pr	19:11	and it is his glory to pass over a **t**	6588
Pr	28:2	For the **t** of a land many are the	6588
Pr	28:24	his mother, and saith, It is no **t**:	6588
Pr	29:6	**t** of an evil man there is a snare:	6588
Pr	29:16	are multiplied, **t** increaseth:	6588
Pr	29:22	and a furious man aboundeth in **t**	6588
Isa	53:8	for the **t** of my people was he	6588
Isa	58:1	and shew my people their **t**, and	6588
Eze	33:12	not deliver him in the day of his **t**	6588
Da	8:12	the daily sacrifice by reason of **t**,	6588
Da	8:13	sacrifice, and the **t** of desolation,	6588
Da	9:24	to finish the **t**, and to make an end	6588
Mic	1:5	For the **t** of Jacob is all this, and	6588
Mic	3:8	to declare unto Jacob his **t**, and to	6588
Mic	6:7	shall I give my firstborn for my **t**,	6588
Mic	7:18	passeth by the **t** of the remnant of	6588
Ac	1:25	from which Judas by **t** fell, that	*3845*
Ro	4:15	for where no law is, there is no **t**	*3847*
Ro	5:14	after the similitude of Adam's **t**,	*3847*
1Ti	2:14	woman being deceived was in the **t**	*3847*
Heb	2:2	every **t** and disobedience received	*3847*
1Jn	3:4	the law: for sin is the **t** of the law	*458*

TRANSGRESSIONS

Ex	23:21	not; for he will not pardon your **t**	6588
Le	16:16	because of their **t** in all their sins:	6588
Le	16:21	and all their **t** in all their sins,	6588
Jos	24:19	not forgive your **t** nor your sins	6588
Job	31:33	If I covered my **t** as Adam, by	6588
Job	35:6	if thy **t** be multiplied, what doest	6588
Ps	25:7	not the sins of my youth, nor my **t**	6588
Ps	32:5	I will confess my **t** unto the Lord;	6588
Ps	51:1	thy tender mercies blot out my **t**	6588
Ps	51:3	For I acknowledge my **t**: and my	6588
Ps	65:3	as for our **t**, thou shalt purge them	6588
Ps	103:12	hath he removed our **t** from us	6588
Isa	43:25	blotteth out thy **t** for mine own	6588
Isa	44:22	blotted out, as a thick cloud, thy **t**,	6588
Isa	50:1	your **t** is your mother put away	6588
Isa	53:5	But he was wounded for our **t**, he	6588
Isa	59:12	for our **t** are with us; and as for	6588
Jer	5:6	because their **t** are many, and their	6588
La	1:5	her for the multitude of her **t**	6588
Eze	18:22	All his **t** that he hath committed,	6588
Eze	18:28	away from all his **t** that he hath	6588
Eze	18:30	turn yourselves from all your **t**;	6588
Eze	18:31	Cast away from you all your **t**,	6588
Eze	21:24	in that your **t** are discovered, so	6588
Eze	39:24	according to their **t** have I done	6588
Am	1:3	For three **t** of Damascus, and for	6588
Am	2:4	For three **t** of Judah, and for four,	6588
Am	2:6	For three **t** of Israel, and for four,	6588
Am	5:12	your manifold **t** and your mighty	6588
Mic	1:13	the **t** of Israel were found in thee	6588
Gal	3:19	It was added because of **t**, till the	*3847*
Heb	9:15	the **t** that were under the first	*3847*

TRANSGRESSOR
Pr 21:18 and the **t** for the upright 898
Pr 22:12 overthroweth the words of the **t** 898
Isa 48:8 wast called a **t** from the womb 6586
Gal 2:18 I destroyed, I make myself a **t** *3848*
Jas 2:11 kill, thou art become a **t** of the law..... *3848*

TRANSGRESSORS
Ps 51:13 Then will I teach **t** thy ways; and 6586
Ps 119:158 I beheld the **t**, and was grieved;......... 898
Pr 2:22 and the **t** shall be rooted out of it. 898
Pr 13:2 the soul of the **t** shall eat violence....... 898
Pr 23:28 and increaseth the **t** among men......... 898
Pr 26:10 the fool, and rewardeth **t** 5674
Isa 1:28 the destruction of the **t** and of the 6586
Isa 46:8 men; bring it again to mind, O ye **t** 6586
Isa 53:12 and he was numbered with the **t**;...... 6586
Da 8:23 when the **t** are come to the full, ... 6586
Hos 14:9 them: but the **t** shall fall therein......... 6586
Mk 15:28 And he was numbered with the **t** *459*
Lk 22:37 **he was reckoned among the t:**.......... *459*
Jas 2:9 and are convinced of the law as **t** *3848*

TRANSLATED
Col 1:13 hath **t** us into the kingdom of his...... *3179*
Heb 11:5 By faith Enoch was **t** that he *3346*

TRANSLATION
Heb 11:5 for before his **t** he had this............ *3331*

TRANSPARENT
Rev 21:21 was pure gold, as it were **t** glass........ *1307*

TRAP
Jer 5:26 they set a **t**, they catch men............ 4889
Ro 11:9 table he made a snare, and a **t**, ... *2339*

TRAVAIL
Ge 38:27 came to pass in the time of her **t**, ... 3205
Ex 18:8 all the **t** that had come upon them..... 8513
Ps 48:6 and pain, as of a woman in **t**.......... 3205
Ecc 1:13 this sore **t** hath God given to the....... 6045
Ecc 2:26 to the sinner he giveth **t**, to gather 6045
Ecc 4:4 I considered all **t**, and every right 5999
Ecc 4:6 hands full with **t** and vexation of 5999
Ecc 5:14 But those riches perish by evil **t** 6045
Isa 53:11 He shall see of the **t** of his soul 5999
Isa 54:1 thou that didst not **t** with child: 2342
Jer 4:31 heard a voice as of a woman in **t**, ... 2470
Jer 6:24 us, and pain, as of a woman in **t** 3205
Jer 13:21 sorrows take thee, as a woman in **t**? 3205
Jer 22:23 thee, the pain as of a woman in **t**!...... 3205
Jer 30:6 whether a man doth **t** with child?...... 3205
Jer 50:43 him, and pangs as of a woman in **t**..... 3205
Mic 4:9 have taken thee as a woman in **t**....... 3205
Jn 16:21 **A woman ... in t hath sorrow,** *5088*
Gal 4:19 I **t** in birth again until Christ be *5605*
1Th 5:3 as **t** upon a woman with child; *5604*
2Th 3:8 wrought with labour and **t** night *3449*

TRAVAILED
Ge 38:28 it came to pass, when she **t**, that 3205
1Sa 4:19 dead, she bowed herself and **t**; 3205
Isa 66:7 Before she **t**, she brought forth;......... 2342

TRAVAILEST
Gal 4:27 forth and cry, thou that **t** not: *5605*

TRAVAILETH
Job 15:20 wicked man **t** with pain all his 2342
Ps 7:14 he **t** with iniquity, and hath........... 2254
Isa 13:8 be in pain as a woman that **t**.......... 3205
Isa 21:3 as the pangs of a woman that **t**........ 3205
Jer 31:8 and her that **t** with child together:..... 3205
Mic 5:3 she which **t** hath brought forth: 3205
Ro 8:22 whole creation groaneth and **t** *4944*

TRAVAILING
Isa 42:14 now will I cry like a **t** woman; I 3205
Hos 13:13 The sorrows of a **t** woman shall 3205
Rev 12:2 being with child cried, **t** in birth....... *5605*

TRAVELLER
2Sa 12:4 there came a **t** unto the rich man, ... 1982
Job 31:32 but I opened my doors to the **t**......... 734

TRAVELLETH
Pr 6:11 thy poverty come as one that **t**,........ 1980
Pr 24:34 thy poverty come as one that **t**;........ 1980

TRAVELLING
Isa 63:1 **t** in the greatness of his strength? 6808
Mt 25:14 **is as a man t into a far country,** *589*

TREACHEROUS
Jer 3:8 yet her **t** sister Judah feared not......... 898
Jer 9:2 adulterers, an assembly of **t** men........ 898
Zep 3:4 prophets are light and **t** persons:........ 900

TREACHEROUSLY
Isa 21:2 the treacherous dealer dealeth **t**,........ 898
Isa 33:1 and they dealt not **t** with thee! 898
Isa 48:8 that thou wouldest deal very **t**.......... 898
Jer 3:20 as a wife **t** departeth from her.......... 898
Jer 12:1 are all they happy that deal very **t**? 898
La 1:2 her friends have dealt **t** with her........ 898
Hos 5:7 have dealt **t** against the Lord:........... 898
Hab 1:13 lookest thou upon them that deal **t**,..... 898
Mal 2:10 we deal **t** every man against his......... 898
Mal 2:15 deal **t** against the wife of his youth...... 898
Mal 2:16 to your spirit, that ye deal not **t**......... 898

TREAD
Dt 11:24 the soles of your feet shall **t** shall 1869
Dt 33:29 thou shalt **t** upon their high places..... 1869
Jos 1:3 the sole of your feet shall **t** upon,...... 1869
Ps 7:5 let him **t** down my life upon the....... 7429
Ps 60:12 it is that shall **t** down our enemies 947
Ps 91:13 shalt **t** upon the lion and adder:....... 1869
Ps 108:13 it is that shall **t** down our enemies 947
Isa 1:12 this at your hand, to **t** my courts?...... 7429
Isa 10:6 **t** them down like the mire of 7760, 4823
Isa 16:10 treaders shall **t** out no wine in......... 1869
Isa 26:6 The foot shall **t** it down, even the...... 7429
Isa 63:3 for I will **t** them in mine anger 1869
Jer 25:30 shout, as they that **t** the grapes,........ 1869
Eze 26:11 shall he **t** down all thy streets: 7429
Eze 34:18 ye must **t** down with your feet the 7429
Da 7:23 shall **t** it down, and break it in 1759
Mic 1:3 **t** upon the high places of the.......... 1869
Mic 5:5 and when he shall **t** in our palaces 1869
Mic 6:15 thou shalt **t** the olives, but thou 1869
Zec 10:5 which **t** down their enemies in the...... 947
Mal 4:3 And ye shall **t** down the wicked;....... 6072
Lk 10:19 **you power to t on serpents and** *3961*
Rev 11:2 holy city shall they **t** under foot *3961*

TREADER
Am 9:13 the **t** of grapes him that soweth 1869

TREADERS
Isa 16:10 the **t** shall tread out no wine in........ 1869

TREADETH
Dt 25:4 the ox when he **t** out the corn......... 1758
Job 9:8 and **t** upon the waves of the sea 1869
Isa 41:25 morter, and as the potter **t** clay........ 7429
Isa 63:2 like him that **t** in the winefat?......... 1869
Am 4:13 **t** upon the high places of the earth..... 1869
Mic 5:8 **t** down, and teareth in pieces,......... 7429
1Co 9:9 of the ox that **t** out the corn *248*
1Ti 5:18 muzzle the ox that **t** out the corn *248*
Rev 19:15 and he **t** the winepress of the.......... *3961*

TREADING
Ne 13:15 **t** wine presses on the sabbath,......... 1869
Isa 22:5 is a day of trouble, and of **t** down, ... 4001
Am 5:11 as your **t** is upon the poor,............ 1318

TREASON
2Ki 11:14 rent her clothes, and cried, **T, T** 7195
2Ch 23:13 rent their clothes, and said, **T, T** 7195

TREASURE
Ge 43:23 hath given you **t** in your sacks: 4301
Ex 1:11 they built for Pharaoh **t** cities,......... 4543
Ex 19:5 then ye shall be a peculiar **t** unto me
Dt 28:12 shall open unto thee his good **t**, ... 214
1Ch 29:8 to the **t** of the house of the Lord, ... 214
Ezr 2:69 their ability unto the **t** of the work...... 214
Ezr 5:17 be search made in the king's **t**......... 1596
Ezr 7:20 it out of the king's **t** house........... 1596
Ne 7:70 gave to the **t** a thousand drams of....... 214
Ne 10:38 to the chambers, into the **t** house....... 214
Ps 17:14 whose belly thou fillest with thy hid **t**
Ps 135:4 himself, and Israel for his peculiar **t**
Pr 15:6 house of the righteous is much **t** 2633
Pr 15:16 Lord than great **t** and trouble 214
Pr 21:20 There is **t** to be desired and oil in 214
Ecc 2:8 the peculiar **t** of kings and of the
Isa 33:6 the fear of the Lord is his **t**............. 214
Eze 22:25 they have taken the **t** and............. 2633
Da 1:2 vessels into the **t** house of his god....... 214
Hos 13:15 spoil the **t** of all pleasant vessels 214
Mt 6:21 **where your t is, there will your**........ *2344*
Mt 12:35 **good t of the heart bringeth** *2344*
Mt 13:44 **heaven is like unto t hid in a**.......... *2344*
Mt 13:52 **out of his t things new and old**......... *2344*
Mt 19:21 **and thou shalt have t in heaven:**....... *2344*
Mk 10:21 **and thou shalt have t in heaven:**....... *2344*
Lk 6:45 **evil t of his heart bringeth forth**....... *2344*
Lk 12:21 **he that layeth up t for himself,**........ *2343*
Lk 12:33 **t in the heavens that faileth not,**....... *2344*
Lk 12:34 **where your t is, there will your**........ *2344*
Lk 18:22 **and thou shalt have t in heaven:**....... *2344*
Ac 8:27 who had the charge of all her **t**,........ *1047*
2Co 4:7 we have this **t** in earthen vessels,....... *2344*
Jas 5:3 heaped **t** together for the last.......... *2343*

TREASURED
Isa 23:18 it shall not be **t** nor laid up; for......... 686

TREASURERS
Ezr 7:21 the **t** which are beyond the river, ... 1490
Da 3:2 judges, the **t**, the counsellers,.......... 1411

TREASURES
Dt 32:34 me, and sealed up among my **t**? 214
Dt 33:19 the seas, and of **t** hid in the sand 8226
1Ki 7:51 he put among the **t** of the house of 214
1Ki 14:26 he took away the **t** of the house of...... 214
1Ki 14:26 Lord, and the **t** of the king's house; 214
1Ki 15:18 left in the **t** of the house of the 214
2Ki 12:18 in the **t** of the house of the Lord, ... 214
2Ki 14:14 and in the **t** in the king's house......... 214
2Ki 16:8 and in the **t** in the king's house, ... 214
2Ki 18:15 and in the **t** of the king's house......... 214
2Ki 20:15 among my **t** that I have not shewed..... 214
2Ki 24:13 all the **t** of the house of the Lord,....... 214
2Ch 8:15 any matter, or concerning the **t**......... 214
2Ch 12:9 took away the **t** of the house of the 214
2Ch 16:2 gold out of the **t** of the house of the..... 214
2Ch 36:18 and the **t** of the king, and of his 214
Ezr 6:1 the **t** were laid up in Babylon 1596
Job 3:21 and dig for it more than for hid **t**; 4301
Pr 2:4 and searchest for her as for hid **t**; 4301
Pr 8:21 substance, and I will fill their **t** 214
Pr 10:2 **T** of wickedness profit nothing: but..... 214
Pr 21:6 The getting of **t** by a lying tongue....... 214
Isa 2:7 neither is there any end of their **t**;....... 214
Isa 10:13 people, and have robbed their **t** 6259
Isa 39:2 and all that was found in his **t**: 214
Isa 45:3 I will give thee the **t** of darkness 214
Jer 10:13 bringeth forth the wind out of his **t**..... 214
Jer 15:13 Thy substance and thy **t** will I give...... 214
Jer 20:5 and all the **t** of the kings of Judah....... 214
Jer 41:8 we have **t** in the field, of wheat,........ 4301
Jer 48:7 trusted in thy works and in thy **t**, ... 214
Jer 49:4 that trusted in her **t**, saying, Who 214
Jer 50:37 a sword is upon her **t**; and they......... 214
Jer 51:13 abundant in **t**, thine end is come,....... 214
Jer 51:16 bringeth forth the wind out of his **t**..... 214
Eze 28:4 gotten gold and silver into thy **t** 214
Da 11:43 have power over the **t** of gold and 4362
Mic 6:10 Are there yet the **t** of wickedness 214
Mt 2:11 and when they had opened their **t** *2344*
Mt 6:19 **not up for yourselves t upon earth,**.... *2344*
Mt 6:20 **up for yourselves t in heaven** *2344*
Col 2:3 whom are hid all the **t** of wisdom...... *2344*
Heb 11:26 greater riches than the **t** in Egypt:...... *2344*

TREASURIES
1Ch 28:12 of the **t** of the dedicated things: 214
2Ch 32:27 and he made himself **t** for silver,........ 214
Est 3:9 to bring it into the king's **t**............ 1595
Est 4:7 had promised to pay to the king's **t** 1595
Ps 135:7 he bringeth the wind out of his **t** 214

TREASURY
Jos 6:24 into the **t** of the house of the Lord...... 214
Mt 27:6 lawful for to put them into the **t**....... *2878*
Mk 12:43 **all they which have cast into the t** *1049*
Lk 21:1 men casting their gifts into the **t**....... *1049*
Jn 8:20 These words spake Jesus in the **t**, ... *1049*

TREATISE
Ac 1:1 The former **t** have I made, O.......... *3056*

TREE
Ge 1:11 the fruit **t** yielding fruit after his....... 6086
Ge 1:29 face of all the earth, and every **t**,....... 6086
Ge 2:9 grow every **t** that is pleasant to the..... 6086
Ge 2:9 the **t** of life also in the midst of the 6086

Ge	2:9	**t** of knowledge of good and evil	6086
Ge	2:16	every **t** of the garden thou mayest	6086
Ge	2:17	of the **t** of the knowledge of good	6086
Ge	3:1	Ye shall not eat of every **t** of the	6086
Ge	3:6	woman saw that the **t** was good	6086
Ge	3:6	a **t** to be desired to make one wise,	6086
Ge	3:11	Hast thou eaten of the **t**, whereof I	6086
Ge	3:12	she gave me of the **t**, and I did eat	6086
Ge	3:22	lest he … take also of the **t** of life,	6086
Ge	40:19	thee, and shall hang thee on a **t**;	6086
Ex	9:25	field, and brake every **t** of the field	6086
Ex	10:5	shall eat every **t** which groweth for	6086
Ex	15:25	the Lord shewed him a **t**, which	6086
Le	27:30	of the fruit of the **t**, is the Lord's:	6086
Nu	6:4	eat nothing … made of the vine **t**,	
Dt	12:2	the hills, and under every green **t**:	6086
Dt	20:19	(for the **t** of the field is man's life)	6086
Dt	21:23	not remain all night upon the **t**	6086
Jgs	9:8	they said unto the olive **t**, Reign thou	
Jgs	9:10	And the trees said to the fig **t**,	6086
1Ki	4:33	the cedar **t** that is in Lebanon	6086
1Ki	6:23	he made two cherubims of olive **t**	6086
1Ki	6:32	The two doors also were of olive **t**;	6086
2Ki	3:19	and shall fell every good **t**, and	6086
2Ki	16:4	hills, and under every green **t**	6086
2Ki	17:10	hills, and under every green **t**	6086
Est	2:23	they were both hanged on a **t**:	6086
Ps	1:3	be like a **t** planted by the rivers	6086
Pr	3:18	She is a **t** of life to them that lay	6086
Pr	11:30	fruit of the righteous is a **t** of life;	6086
Pr	13:12	the desire cometh, it is a **t** of life	6086
Pr	15:4	A wholesome tongue is a **t** of life:	6086
Pr	27:18	Whoso keepeth the fig **t** shall eat	
Ecc	11:3	the place where the **t** falleth, there	6086
Isa	40:20	chooseth a **t** that will not rot;	6086
Isa	56:3	eunuch say, Behold, I am a dry **t**.	6086
Isa	57:5	with idols under every green **t**.	6086
Isa	65:22	as the days of a **t** are the days of	6086
Jer	1:11	I said, I see a rod of an almond **t**	
Jer	2:20	and under every green **t** thou	6086
Jer	3:13	the strangers under every green **t**,	6086
Jer	10:3	one cutteth a **t** out of the forest,	6086
Jer	11:19	Let us destroy the **t** with the fruit	6086
Jer	17:8	be as a **t** planted by the waters,	6086
Eze	6:13	under every green **t**, and under	6086
Eze	15:6	As the vine **t** among the trees of	6086
Eze	17:24	have exalted the low **t**, have	6086
Eze	21:10	the rod of my son, as every **t**	6086
Eze	31:8	nor any **t** in the garden of God was	6086
Eze	34:27	**t** of the field shall yield her fruit,	6086
Da	4:10	a **t** in the midst of the earth	363
Da	4:14	Hew down the **t**, and cut off his	363
Da	4:20	The **t** that thou sawest, which grew,	363
Da	4:26	leave the stump of the **t** roots;	363
Hos	14:6	and his beauty shall be as the olive **t**,	
Joel	1:12	dried up, and the fig **t** languisheth;	
Mt	3:10	every **t** which bringeth not forth	*1186*
Mt	7:17	**good t bringeth forth good fruit:**	*1186*
Mt	7:18	**good t cannot bring forth evil**	*1186*
Mt	7:19	**every t that bringeth not forth**	*1186*
Mt	12:33	**for the t is known by his fruit.**	*1186*
Mt	21:19	when he saw a fig **t** in the way, he	*4808*
Mt	21:21	**do this which is done to the fig t,**	*4808*
Mt	24:32	**Now learn a parable of the fig t;**	*4808*
Mk	11:21	fig **t** … thou cursedst is withered	*4808*
Mk	13:28	**Now learn a parable of the fig t;**	*4808*
Lk	3:9	every **t** therefore which bringeth	*1186*
Lk	6:44	**every t is known by his own fruit.**	*1186*
Lk	13:6	**certain man had a fig t planted**	*4808*
Lk	13:19	**it grew, and waxed a great t;**	*1186*
Lk	17:6	**ye might say unto this sycamine t**	
Lk	19:4	climbed up into a sycomore **t** to	*4809*
Lk	23:31	**they do these things in a green t,**	*3586*
Jn	1:50	**thee, I saw thee under the fig t,**	*4808*
Ac	5:30	whom ye slew and hanged on a **t**	*3586*
Ac	10:39	whom they slew and hanged on a **t**:	*3586*
Ro	11:24	be graffed into their own olive **t**?	
Gal	3:13	is every one that hangeth on a **t**:	*3586*
Jas	3:12	Can the fig **t**, my brethren, bear	*4808*
1Pe	2:24	our sins in his own body on the **t**,	*3586*
Rev	2:7	**will I give to eat of the t of life,**	*3586*
Rev	6:13	a fig **t** casteth her untimely figs,	*4808*
Rev	7:1	nor on the sea, nor on any **t**.	*1186*
Rev	9:4	any green thing, neither any **t**;	*1186*
Rev	22:2	the river, was there the **t** of life	*3586*
Rev	22:2	leaves of the **t** were for the healing	*3586*
Rev	22:14	may have right to the **t** of life, and	*3586*

TREES

Ge	3:2	We may eat of the fruit of the **t**.	6086
Ge	3:8	God amongst the **t** of the garden	6086
Ex	10:15	not any green thing in the **t**,	6086
Le	19:23	planted all manner of **t** for food,	6086
Le	23:40	first day the boughs of goodly **t**,	6086
Le	26:4	**t** of the field shall yield their fruit	6086
Le	26:20	neither shall the **t** of the land yield	6086
Dt	6:11	olive **t**, which thou plantedst not	
Dt	16:21	plant thee a grove of any **t** near	6086
Dt	20:19	thou shalt not destroy the **t**	6086
Dt	20:20	they be not **t** for meat, thou shalt	6086
Dt	28:40	shall have olive **t** throughout all thy	
Jos	10:26	them, and hanged them on five **t**:	6086
Jgs	3:13	and possessed the city of palm **t**	
Jgs	9:9	and go to be promoted over the **t**?	6086
Jgs	9:10	And the **t** said to the fig tree, Come	6086
Jgs	9:15	And the bramble said unto the **t**,	6086
1Ki	5:10	Hiram gave Solomon cedar **t**.	6086
1Ki	5:10	fir **t** according to all his desire	6086
1Ki	7:36	cherubims, lions, and palm **t**	
2Ki	3:25	water, and felled all the good **t**:	6086
1Ch	16:33	Then shall the **t** of the wood sing	6086
Ezr	3:7	to bring cedar **t** from Lebanon to	6086
Ne	9:25	and fruit **t** in abundance:	6086
Ne	10:35	the firstfruits of all fruit of all **t**,	6086
Ps	74:5	lifted up axes upon the thick **t**.	6086
Ps	96:12	shall all the **t** of the wood rejoice	6086
Ps	104:16	The **t** of the Lord are full of sap;	6086
Ecc	2:5	I planted **t** in them of all kind of	6086
SS	2:3	apple tree among the **t** of the wood,	6086
Isa	7:2	as the **t** of the wood are moved	6086
Isa	44:14	himself among the **t** of the forest:	6086
Isa	55:12	all the **t** of the field shall clap their	6086
Isa	61:3	might be called **t** of righteousness;	352
Jer	6:6	Hew ye down **t**, and cast a mount	6097
Jer	7:20	upon the **t** of the field, and upon	6086
Jer	17:2	their groves by the green **t** upon	6086
Eze	15:2	a branch which is among the **t** of	6086
Eze	15:6	vine tree among the **t** of the forest,	6086
Eze	17:24	**t** of the field shall know that I the	6086
Eze	20:28	every high hill, and all the thick **t**,	6086
Eze	31:5	above all the **t** of the field,	6086
Eze	31:14	that none of all the **t** by the waters	6086

T

Eze	31:15	all the **t** of the field fainted for	6086
Eze	31:18	in greatness among the **t** of Eden?	6086
Eze	47:12	shall grow all **t** for meat, whose	6086
Joel	1:12	even all the **t** of the field, are	6086
Joel	1:19	hath burned all the **t** of the field	6086
Na	2:3	the fir **t** shall be terribly shaken	
Zec	1:8	he stood among the myrtle **t** that	
Zec	4:11	What are these two olive **t** upon the	
Mt	3:10	axe is laid unto the root of the **t**	*1186*
Mt	21:8	cut down branches from the **t**, and	*1186*
Mk	8:24	and said, I see men as **t** walking	*1186*
Lk	3:9	axe is laid unto the root of the **t**	*1186*
Lk	21:29	**Behold the fig tree, and all the t;**	*1186*
Jn	12:13	Took branches of palm **t**, and	
Jude	12	**t** whose fruit withereth, without	*1186*
Rev	7:3	earth, neither the sea, nor the **t**,	*1186*
Rev	8:7	the third part of **t** was burnt up,	*1186*
Rev	11:4	These are the two olive **t**, and the two	

TREMBLE

Dt	2:25	and shall **t**, and be in anguish	7264
Dt	20:3	faint, fear not, and do not **t**,	2648
Ezr	10:3	those that **t** at the commandment	2730
Ps	60:2	Thou hast made the earth to **t**;	7493
Ps	99:1	Lord reigneth; let the people **t**.	7264
Ps	114:7	**T**, thou earth, at the presence of	2342
Ecc	12:3	the keepers of the house shall **t**.	2111
Isa	5:25	the hills did **t**, and their carcases	7264
Isa	14:16	the man that made the earth to **t**,	7264
Isa	32:11	**T**, ye women that are at ease; be	2729
Isa	64:2	nations may **t** at thy presence!	7264
Isa	66:5	of the Lord, ye that **t** at his word;	2730
Jer	5:22	will ye not **t** at my presence	2342
Jer	10:10	at his wrath the earth shall **t**,	7493
Jer	33:9	they shall fear and **t** for all the	7264
Jer	51:29	the land shall **t** and sorrow: for	7493
Eze	26:16	shall **t** at every moment, and be	2729
Eze	32:10	they shall **t** at every moment	2729
Da	6:26	men **t** and fear before the God of	2112
Hos	11:11	shall **t** as a bird out of Egypt, and	2729
Joel	2:1	all the inhabitants of the land **t**.	7264
Joel	2:10	before them; the heavens shall **t**	7493
Am	8:8	Shall not the land **t** for this, and	7264
Jas	2:19	the devils also believe, and **t**.	*5425*

TREMBLED

Ge	27:33	And Isaac **t** very exceedingly,	2729
Ex	19:16	the people that was in the camp **t**.	2729
Jgs	5:4	earth **t**, and the heavens dropped,	7493
1Sa	4:13	his heart **t** for the ark of God	2730
1Sa	14:15	and the spoilers, they also **t**,	2729
1Sa	16:4	elders of the town **t** at his coming	2729
1Sa	28:5	was afraid, and his heart greatly **t**	2729
2Sa	22:8	Then the earth shook and **t**; the	7493
Ezr	9:4	every one that **t** at the words of	2730
Ps	18:7	Then the earth shook and **t**; the	7493
Ps	77:18	the world: the earth **t** and shook	7264
Ps	97:4	the world: the earth saw, and **t**	2342
Jer	4:24	the mountains, and, lo, they **t**,	7493
Jer	8:16	the whole land **t** at the sound of	7493
Da	5:19	**t** and feared before him:	2112
Hab	3:10	mountains saw thee, and they **t**.	2342
Hab	3:16	I **t** in myself, that I might rest in	7264
Mk	16:8	for they **t** and were amazed	*2192, 5156*
Ac	7:32	Then Moses **t** and durst not	*1790, 1096*
Ac	24:25	Felix **t**, and answered, Go thy	*1719, 1096*

TREMBLETH

Job	37:1	At this also my heart **t**, and is	2729
Ps	104:32	He looketh on the earth, and it **t**	7460
Ps	119:120	My flesh **t** for fear of thee; and	5568
Isa	66:2	contrite spirit, and **t** at my word	2730

TREMBLING

Dt	28:65	shall give thee there a **t** heart,	7268
1Sa	13:7	and all the people followed him **t**.	2729
1Sa	14:15	quaked: so it was a very great **t**	2731
Ezr	10:9	**t** because of this matter, and for	7460
Job	4:14	Fear came upon me, and **t**, which	7460
Ps	2:11	Lord with fear, and rejoice with **t**	7460
Ps	55:5	Fearfulness and **t** are come upon	7460
Isa	51:17	drunken the dregs of the cup of **t**,	8653
Isa	51:22	out of thine hand the cup of **t**,	8653
Jer	30:5	We have heard a voice of **t**, of	2731
Eze	12:18	drink thy water with **t** and with	7269
Eze	26:16	shall clothe themselves with **t**;	2731
Da	10:11	this word unto me, I stood **t**	7460
Zec	12:2	I will make Jerusalem a cup of **t**	7478
Mk	5:33	But the woman fearing and **t**,	*5141*
Lk	8:47	she came **t** and falling down	*5141*
Ac	9:6	he **t** and astonished said, Lord	*5141*
Ac	16:29	and sprang in, and came **t**,	*1096, 1790*
1Co	2:3	and in fear, and in much **t**	*5156*
2Co	7:15	with fear and **t** ye received him	*5156*
Eph	6:5	with fear and **t**, in singleness of	*5156*
Php	2:12	your own salvation with fear and **t**.	*5156*

TRENCH

1Sa	26:5	Saul lay in the **t**, and the people	4570
2Sa	20:15	the city, and it stood in the **t**	2426
1Ki	18:32	and he made a **t** about the altar,	8585
Lk	19:43	**enemies shall cast a t about thee**	*5482*

TRESPASS

Ge	31:36	What is my **t**? what is my sin, that	6588
Ge	50:17	the **t** of thy brethren, and their	6588
Ex	22:9	For all manner of **t**, whether it be	6588
Le	5:6	he shall bring his **t** offering unto	817
Le	5:15	If a soul commit a **t**, and sin	4604
Le	6:2	and commit a **t** against the Lord,	4604
Le	7:1	this is the law of the **t** offering:	817
Le	14:12	lamb, and offer him for a **t** offering	817
Le	14:14	some of the blood of the **t** offering	817
Le	14:21	take one lamb for a **t** offering to be	817
Le	22:16	them to bear the iniquity of **t**,	819
Le	26:40	with their **t** which they trespassed	4604
Nu	5:7	shall recompense his **t** with the	817
Nu	5:27	have done **t** against her husband,	4604
Nu	18:9	every **t** offering of theirs, which	817
Nu	31:16	to commit **t** against the Lord in	4604
Jos	7:1	children of Israel committed a **t** in	4604
Jos	22:20	Achan the son of Zerah commit a **t**	4604
1Sa	6:4	What shall be the **t** offering which	817
1Sa	25:28	forgive the **t** of thine handmaid:	6588
1Ki	8:31	any man **t** against his neighbour,	2398
2Ki	12:16	**t** money and sin money was not	817
1Ch	21:3	will he be a cause of **t** to Israel?	819
2Ch	19:10	warn them that they **t** not against	816
2Ch	24:18	and Jerusalem for this their **t**.	819
2Ch	28:13	add more to our sins and to our **t**	819
2Ch	33:19	all his sins, and his **t** and the	4604
Ezr	9:6	**t** is grown up unto the heavens	819
Ezr	9:13	our evil deeds, and for our great **t**,	819
Ezr	10:10	wives, to increase the **t** of Israel	819

Eze 15:8	because they have committed a **t**,	4604
Eze 17:20	will plead with him there for his **t**	4604
Eze 20:27	have committed a **t** against me,	4604
Eze 46:20	the priests shall boil the **t** offering	817
Da 9:7	their **t** that they have trespassed	4604
Mt 18:15	**if thy brother shall t against thee,**	*264*
Lk 17:4	**if he t against thee seven times in**	*264*

TRESPASSED

Le 5:19	certainly **t** against the Lord	816
Le 26:40	trespass which they **t** against me,	4604
Nu 5:7	unto him against whom he hath **t**	816
Dt 32:51	Because ye **t** against me among	4603
2Ch 26:18	the sanctuary; for thou hast **t**;	4603
2Ch 29:6	For our fathers have **t**, and done	4603
2Ch 30:7	**t** against the Lord God of their	4603
Ezr 10:2	We have **t** against our God, and	4603
Eze 39:26	whereby they have **t** against me,	4603
Da 9:7	that they have **t** against thee	4603
Hos 8:1	my covenant, and **t** against my law	

TRESPASSES

Ezr 9:15	we are before thee in our **t**: for	819
Ps 68:21	as one as goeth on still in his **t**	817
Mt 6:14	**For if ye forgive men their t**	*3900*
Mt 6:15	**But if ye forgive not men their t,**	*3900*
Mt 18:35	**not every one his brother their t**	*3900*
Mk 11:25	**heaven may forgive you your t**	*3900*
2Co 5:19	not imputing their **t** unto them;	*3900*
Eph 2:1	who were dead in **t** and sin;	*3900*
Col 2:13	him, having forgiven you all **t**;	*3900*

TRIAL

Job 9:23	laugh at the **t** of the innocent	4531
Eze 21:13	Because it is a **t**, and what if the	974
2Co 8:2	How that in a great **t** of affliction	*1382*
Heb 11:36	others had **t** of cruel mockings	*3984*
1Pe 1:7	That the **t** of your faith, being	*1383*
1Pe 4:12	the fiery **t** which is to try you,	

TRIBE

Nu 1:4	there shall be a man of every **t**;	4294
Nu 1:49	shalt not number the **t** of Levi,	4294
Nu 13:2	of every **t** of their fathers shall ye	4294
Nu 31:6	to the war, a thousand of every **t**,	4294
Nu 34:18	shall take one prince of every **t**,	4294
Nu 34:19	Of the **t** of Judah, Caleb the son of	4294
Nu 36:6	**t** of their father shall they marry	4294
Nu 36:7	of Israel remove from **t** to **t**	4294
Dt 10:8	the Lord separated the **t** of Levi,	7626
Dt 18:1	all the **t** of Levi, shall have no part	7626
Jos 4:4	of Israel, out of every **t** a man:	7626
Jos 13:14	unto the **t** of Levi he gave none	7626
Jos 13:33	unto the **t** of Levi Moses gave not	7626
Jos 18:4	among you three men for each **t**	7626
Jgs 18:1	the **t** of the Danites sought them	7626
Jgs 18:30	sons were priests to the **t** of Dan	7626
Jgs 20:12	men through all the **t** of Benjamin,	7626
Jgs 21:17	a **t** be not destroyed out of Israel	7626
1Sa 9:21	the families of the **t** of Benjamin?	7626
1Ki 11:13	but will give one **t** to thy son	7626
1Ki 12:20	of David, but the **t** of Judah only	7626
2Ki 17:18	none left but the **t** of Judah only	7626
Ps 78:68	But chose the **t** of Judah, the	7626
Eze 47:23	in what **t** the stranger sojourneth	7626
Php 3:5	of Israel, of the **t** of Benjamin	*5443*
Heb 7:13	spoken pertaineth to another **t**	*5443*
Heb 7:14	of which **t** Moses spake nothing	*5443*
Rev 5:5	the Lion of the **t** of Juda, the Root	*5443*
Rev 7:5	Of the **t** of Juda were sealed twelve	*5443*

TRIBES

Ge 49:28	All these are the twelve **t** of Israel:	7626
Ex 24:4	according to the twelve **t** of Israel	7626
Ex 28:21	they be according to the twelve **t**	7626
Ex 39:14	name, according to the twelve **t**	7626
Nu 24:2	in his tents according to their **t**;	7626
Nu 36:3	to any of the sons of the other **t**	7626
Nu 36:9	every one of the **t** of the children	4294
Dt 1:15	So I took the chief of your **t**, wise	7626
Dt 12:14	Lord shall choose in one of thy **t**	7626
Dt 18:5	hath chosen him out of all thy **t**	7626
Dt 29:21	unto evil out of all the **t** of Israel	7626
Jos 14:4	the children of Joseph were two **t** of	4294
Jgs 18:1	not fallen unto them among the **t**	7626
Jgs 21:8	What one is there of the **t** of Israel	7626
Jgs 21:15	made a breach in the **t** of Israel	7626
1Sa 2:28	choose him out of all the **t** of Israel	7626
1Sa 9:21	of the smallest of the **t** of Israel?	7626
2Sa 5:1	came all the **t** of Israel to David	7626
2Sa 19:9	strife throughout all the **t** of Israel	7626
1Ki 11:31	and will give ten **t** to thee:	7626
1Ch 28:1	princes of Israel, … princes of the **t**	7626
Ezr 6:17	to the number of the **t** of Israel,	7625
Ps 78:55	**t** of Israel to dwell in their tents	7626
Ps 105:37	one feeble person among their **t**	7626
Eze 48:29	divide by lot unto the **t** of Israel	7626
Mt 19:28	**judging the twelve t of Israel**	*5443*
Mt 24:30	**all the t of the earth mourn,**	*5443*
Lk 22:30	**judging the twelve t of Israel**	*5443*
Ac 26:7	Unto which promise our twelve **t**,	*1429*
Jas 1:1	the twelve **t** which are scattered	*5443*
Rev 7:4	all the **t** of the children of Israel	*5443*
Rev 21:12	are the names of the twelve **t** of	*5443*

TRIBULATION

Dt 4:30	When thou art in **t**, and all these	6862
Jgs 10:14	deliver you in the time of your **t**	6869
1Sa 26:24	and let him deliver me out of all **t**	6869
Mt 13:21	**for when t or persecution ariseth**	*2347*
Mt 24:21	**For then shall be great t, such**	*2347*
Mt 24:29	**after the t of those days shall**	*2347*
Mk 13:24	**that t, the sun … be darkened,**	*2347*
Jn 16:33	**In the world ye shall have t: but**	*2347*
Ac 14:22	through much **t** enter into the	*2347*
Ro 2:9	**T** and anguish upon every soul of	*2347*
Ro 5:3	knowing that **t** worketh patience;	*2347*
Ro 8:35	shall **t**, or distress, or persecution	*2347*
Ro 12:12	Rejoicing in hope; patient in **t**;	*2347*
2Co 1:4	Who comforteth us in all our **t**,	*2347*
2Co 7:4	I am exceeding joyful in all our **t**	*2347*
1Th 3:4	before that we should suffer **t**;	*2346*
2Th 1:6	**t** to them that trouble you;	*2347*
Rev 1:9	your brother, and companion in **t**,	*2347*
Rev 2:9	**thy works, and t, and poverty,**	*2347*
Rev 2:10	**and ye shall have t ten days:**	*2347*
Rev 2:22	**adultery with her into great t,**	*2347*
Rev 7:14	they which came out of great **t**,	*2347*

TRIBULATIONS

1Sa 10:19	of all your adversities and your **t**;	6869
Ro 5:3	only so, but we glory in **t** also;	*2347*
Eph 3:13	that ye faint not at my **t** for you,	*2347*
2Th 1:4	persecutions and **t** that ye endure	*2347*

T

TRIBUTARIES
Dt 20:11 found therein shall be t unto thee, ... 4522
Jgs 1:35 prevailed, so that they became t 4522

TRIBUTARY
La 1:1 provinces, how is she become t! 4522

TRIBUTE
Ge 49:15 and became a servant unto t. 4522
Nu 31:28 levy a t unto the Lord of the men. 4371
Dt 16:10 a t of a freewill offering of thine 4530
Jos 16:10 unto this day, and serve under t 4522
Jos 17:13 that they put the Canaanites to t; 4522
Jgs 1:28 that they put the Canaanites to t 4522
1Ki 9:21 Solomon levy a t of bondservice. 4522
2Ki 23:33 put the land to a t of an hundred 6066
2Ch 8:8 make to pay t until this day. 4522
Ezr 4:20 t, and custom, was paid unto them 1093
Ezr 6:8 even of the t beyond the river,. 4061
Ezr 7:24 lawful to impose toll, t, or custom 1093
Ne 5:4 borrowed money for the king's t. 4060
Pr 12:24 but the slothful shall be under t 4522
Mt 17:24 said, Doth not your master pay t?. *1323*
Mt 17:25 **of the earth take custom or t?** *2778*
Mt 22:19 **Shew me the t money.** And they. *2778*
Mk 12:14 Is it lawful to give t to Caesar, or. *2778*
Lk 20:22 lawful for us to give t unto Caesar, ... *5422*
Lk 23:2 and forbidding to give t to Caesar, ... *5411*
Ro 13:6 For for this cause pay ye t also: *5411*
Ro 13:7 t to whom t is due; custom to *5411*

TRIED
2Sa 22:31 perfect; the word of the Lord is t 6884
Job 23:10 when he hath t me, I shall come 974
Job 34:36 is that Job may be t unto the end,. 974
Ps 12:6 as silver t in a furnace of earth,. 6884
Ps 18:30 perfect: the word of the Lord is t 6884
Ps 66:10 thou hast t us, as silver is t. 6884
Ps 105:19 came: the word of the Lord t him. 6884
Isa 28:16 a stone, and a t stone, a precious. 976
Jer 12:3 me, and t mine heart toward thee: 974
Da 12:10 purified, and made white, and t;. 6884
Zec 13:9 and will try them as gold is t. 974
Heb 11:17 when he was t, offered up Isaac: *3985*
Jas 1:12 for when he is t, he shall receive *1384*
1Pe 1:7 though it be t with fire, might be *1381*
Rev 2:2 **thou hast t them which say they**. *3985*
Rev 2:10 **you into prison, that ye may be t;**. *3985*
Rev 3:18 **to buy of me gold t in the fire,** *4448*

TRIEST
1Ch 29:17 my God, that thou t the heart, and. 974
Jer 11:20 that t the reins and the heart, ... 974
Jer 20:12 that t the righteous, and seest the 974

TRIETH
Job 34:3 For the ear t words, as the mouth. 974
Ps 7:9 for the righteous God t the hearts 974
Ps 11:5 The Lord t the righteous: but the 974
Pr 17:3 for gold: but the Lord t the hearts 974
1Th 2:4 but God, which t our hearts *1381*

TRIMMED
Mt 25:7 **virgins arose, and t their lamps.** *2885*

TRIUMPH
Ps 25:2 let not mine enemies t over me. 5970
Ps 47:1 unto God with the voice of t. 7440
Ps 92:4 I will t in the works of thy hands 7442
Ps 94:3 how long shall the wicked t? 5937
2Co 2:14 always causeth us to t in Christ, ... *2358*

TRIUMPHED
Ex 15:1 the Lord, for he hath t gloriously:. 1342

TRODDEN
Dt 1:36 give the land that he hath t upon 1869
Jos 14:9 land whereon thy feet have t shall. 1869
Ps 119:118 hast t down all them that err. 5541
Isa 14:19 the pit; as a carcase t under feet 947
Isa 18:2 a nation meted out and t down, ... 4001
Isa 25:10 straw is t down for the dunghill 1758
Isa 28:18 then ye shall be t down by it 4823
Isa 63:3 I have t the winepress alone; and 1869
Isa 63:18 our adversaries have t down thy 947
Jer 12:10 they have t my portion underfoot, ... 947
La 1:15 the Lord hath t the virgin, the. 1869
Da 8:13 and the host to be t under foot? 4823
Mic 7:10 shall she be t down as the mire of. 4823
Mt 5:13 **and to be t under foot of men.** *2662*
Lk 8:5 **it was t down, and the fowls of** *2662*
Lk 21:24 **Jerusalem shall be t down of the** *3961*
Heb 10:29 who hath t under foot the Son of. *2662*
Rev 14:20 winepress was t without the city, ... *3961*

TRODE
2Ki 7:17 people t upon him in the gate, ... 7429
2Ki 9:33 horses: and he t her under foot. 7429
2Ki 14:9 in Lebanon, and t down the thistle. 7429
Lk 12:1 that they t one upon another, ... *2662*

TROOP
1Sa 30:8 Shall I pursue after this t? shall I. 1416
Ps 18:29 by thee I have run through a t; 1416
Isa 65:11 that prepare a table for that t. 1409
Jer 18:22 bring a t suddenly upon them: 1416
Hos 7:1 the t of robbers spoileth without 1416
Am 9:6 and hath founded his t in the earth;. 92

TROOPS
Jer 5:7 assembled themselves by t in the
Hos 6:9 as t of robbers wait for a man, ... 1416
Hab 3:16 he will invade them with his t

TROUBLE
Jos 6:18 camp of Israel a curse, and t it 5916
Jos 7:25 us? the Lord shall t thee this day. 5916
Jgs 11:35 thou art one of them that t me: 5916
2Ki 19:3 This day is a day of t, and of 6869
1Ch 22:14 in my t I have prepared for the. 6040
2Ch 15:4 they in their t did turn unto the 6862
2Ch 29:8 and he hath delivered them to t 2189
2Ch 32:18 to affright them, and to t them; 926
Ne 9:27 and in the time of their t, when 6869
Ne 9:32 let not all the t seem little before. 8513
Job 3:26 neither was I quiet; yet t came. 7267
Job 5:7 Yet man is born unto t, as the 5999
Job 14:1 is of few days, and full of t. 7267
Job 27:9 his cry when t cometh upon him? 6869
Job 30:25 weep for him that was in t? 7186, 3117
Job 34:29 quietness, who then can make t?. 7561
Job 38:23 reserved against the time of t 6862
Ps 9:9 oppressed, a refuge in times of t 6869
Ps 10:1 hidest thou thyself in times of t?. 6869
Ps 22:11 Be not far from me; for t is near; 6869
Ps 27:5 in the time of t he shall hide me. 7451

Ps 31:9 upon me, O Lord, for I am in **t**: 6887
Ps 37:39 is their strength in the time of **t** 6869
Ps 46:1 strength, a very present help in **t**. 6869
Ps 50:15 And call upon me in the day of **t**: 6869
Ps 59:16 and refuge in the day of my **t** 6862
Ps 60:11 Give us help from **t**: for vain is 6862
Ps 73:5 They are not in **t** as other men; 5999
Ps 77:2 day of my **t** I sought the Lord: 6869
Ps 78:33 in vanity, and their years in **t**. 928
Ps 81:7 Thou calledst in **t**, and I delivered 6869
Ps 91:15 I will be with him in **t**; I will deliver 6869
Ps 107:6 cried unto the Lord in their **t** 6862
Ps 107:26 their soul is melted because of **t** 7451
Ps 108:12 Give us help from **t**: for vain is the 6862
Ps 116:3 upon me: I found **t** and sorrow 6869
Ps 119:143 **T** and anguish have taken hold 6862
Ps 138:7 Though I walk in the midst of **t**, 6869
Pr 11:8 The righteous is delivered out of **t** 6869
Pr 12:13 but the just shall come out of **t**. 6869
Pr 15:6 in the revenues of the wicked is **t** 5916
Pr 15:16 great treasure and **t** therewith. 4103
Pr 25:19 in an unfaithful man in time of **t** 6869
Isa 22:5 For it is a day of **t**, and of 4103
Isa 30:6 Into the land of **t** and anguish. 6869
Isa 33:2 our salvation also in the time of **t**. 6869
Isa 37:3 This day is a day of **t**, and of 6869
Isa 46:7 answer, nor save him out of his **t** 6869
Jer 2:27 in the time of their **t** they will say 7451
Jer 8:15 a time of health, and behold **t**! 1205
Jer 11:12 them at all in the time of their **t** 7451
Jer 14:19 the time of healing, and behold **t**! 1205
Jer 30:7 it is even the time of Jacob's **t**; 6869
La 1:21 mine enemies have heard of my **t**; 7451
Eze 7:7 is come, the day of **t** is near, 4103
Eze 32:13 neither shall the foot of man **t** them 4103
Da 5:10 let not thy thoughts **t** thee, nor let 927
Da 11:44 and out of the north shall **t** him: 926
Da 12:1 and there shall be a time of **t**. 6869
Na 1:7 good, a strong hold in the day of **t**; 6869
Hab 3:16 that I might rest in the day of **t**: 6869
Mk 14:6 **Let her alone; why t ye her?** *2873, 3930*
Lk 7:6 unto him, Lord, **t** not thyself: *4660*
Lk 8:49 is dead; **t** not the Master *4660*
Lk 11:7 **shall answer and say, T me not:** *2873*
1Co 7:28 such shall have **t** in the flesh: *2347*
2Co 1:4 comfort them which are in any **t**, *2347*
Gal 1:7 but there be some that **t** you, and *5015*
Gal 6:17 henceforth let no man **t** me: *2873, 3930*
2Ti 2:9 Wherein I suffer **t** as an evil doer, *2553*
Heb 12:15 of bitterness springing up **t** you, *1776*

TROUBLED

Ge 34:30 Ye have **t** me to make me to stink 5916
Ge 41:8 the morning that his spirit was **t**; 6470
Ge 45:3 for they were **t** at his presence 926
Jos 7:25 Joshua said, Why hast thou **t** us? 5916
1Sa 16:14 evil spirit from the Lord **t** him 1204
1Sa 28:21 Saul, and saw that he was sore **t**, 926
1Ki 18:18 he answered, I have not **t** Israel; 5916
2Ki 6:11 king of Syria was sore **t** for this 5590
Ezr 4:4 Judah, and **t** them in building, 1089
Job 4:5 it toucheth thee, and thou art **t**. 926
Ps 30:7 didst hide thy face, and I was **t** 926
Ps 38:6 I am **t**; I am bowed down greatly; 5753
Ps 77:3 I remembered God, and was **t**: 1993
Ps 77:4 I am so **t** that I cannot speak 6470
Ps 77:16 afraid: the depths also were **t**. 7264
Ps 83:17 Let them be confounded and **t** for 926
Ps 90:7 anger, and by thy wrath are we **t**. 926
Ps 104:29 Thou hidest thy face, they are **t**: 926
Pr 25:26 the wicked is as a **t** fountain 7515
Isa 57:20 But the wicked are like the **t** sea, 1644
Eze 7:27 of the people of the land shall be **t**: 926
Eze 27:35 afraid, they shall be **t** in their 7481
Da 2:3 my spirit was **t** to know the dream 6470
Da 4:5 and the visions of my head **t** me 927
Da 4:19 one hour, and his thoughts **t** him 927
Da 5:9 Then was king Belshazzar greatly **t**, 927
Da 7:15 and the visions of my head **t** me 927
Zec 10:2 they were **t**, because there was no 6031
Mt 2:3 had heard these things, he was **t**, *5015*
Mt 14:26 they were **t**, saying, It is a spirit; *5015*
Mt 24:6 **see that ye be not t: for all these** *2360*
Mk 6:50 For they all saw him, and were **t** *5015*
Mk 13:7 **and rumours of wars, be ye not t:** *2360*
Lk 1:29 she was **t** at his saying, and cast *1298*
Lk 10:41 **careful and t about many things:** *5182*
Lk 24:38 **Why are ye t? and why do** *5015*
Jn 5:4 into the pool, and **t** the water: *5025*
Jn 11:33 groaned in the spirit, ... was **t**, *5015, 1438*
Jn 12:27 **Now is my soul t; and what shall** *5025*
Jn 13:21 he was **t** in spirit, and testified, *5015*
Jn 14:1 **Let not your heart be t: ye believe** *5025*
Jn 14:27 **Let not your heart be t, neither.** *5015*
Ac 15:24 out from us have **t** you with words, *5015*
2Co 4:8 We are **t** on every side, yet not *2346*
2Th 1:7 And to you who are **t** rest with us, *2346*
2Th 2:2 or be **t**, neither by spirit, nor by *2360*
1Pe 3:14 afraid of their terror, neither be **t**; *5015*

TROUBLER

1Ch 2:7 Achar, the **t** of Israel, who 5916

TROUBLES

Dt 31:17 evils and **t** shall befall them; 6869
Job 5:19 He shall deliver thee in six **t**: yea, 6869
Ps 25:22 Israel, O God, out of all his **t**. 6869
Ps 34:6 him, and saved him out of all his **t**. 6869
Ps 34:17 delivereth them out of all their **t**. 6869
Ps 88:3 For my soul is full of **t**: and my 7451
Pr 21:23 tongue keepeth his soul from **t** 6869
Isa 65:16 because the former **t** are forgotten, 6869
Mk 13:8 **and there shall be famines and t.** *5016*

TROUBLEST

Mk 5:35 dead: why **t** thou the Master any *4660*

TROUBLETH

1Sa 16:15 an evil spirit from God **t** thee 1204
1Ki 18:17 him, Art thou he that **t** Israel? 5916
Job 23:16 heart soft, and the Almighty **t** me: 926
Pr 11:17 he that is cruel **t** his own flesh 5916
Pr 11:29 that **t** his own house shall inherit 5916
Pr 15:27 is greedy of gain **t** his own house; 5916
Da 4:9 is in thee, and no secret **t** thee 598
Lk 18:5 **Yet because this widow t me,** *3930, 2873*
Gal 5:10 but he that **t** you shall bear his *5015*

TROUBLING

Job 3:17 There the wicked cease from **t**; 7267
Jn 5:4 the **t** of the water stepped in was *5015*

TRUCEBREAKERS

2Ti 3:3 Without natural affection, **t**, false *786*

TRUE

Ge 42:11	we are **t** men, thy servants are no	3651
2Sa 7:28	art that God, and thy words be **t**,	571
1Ki 22:16	tell me nothing but that which is **t**	571
2Ch 15:3	Israel hath been without the **t** God.	571
Ps 19:9	the judgments of the Lord are **t**	571
Ps 119:160	Thy word is **t** from the beginning:	571
Pr 14:25	A **t** witness delivereth souls: but a	571
Jer 10:10	But the Lord is the **t** God, he is the	571
Da 3:14	Is it **t**, O Shadrach, Meshach, and	6656
Da 6:12	The thing is **t**, according to the	3330
Da 8:26	the morning which was told is **t**:	571
Da 10:1	and the thing was **t**, but the time	571
Zec 7:9	Execute **t** judgment, and shew	571
Mt 22:16	Master, we know that thou art **t**,	*227*
Lk 16:11	**commit to your trust the t riches?**	*228*
Jn 1:9	That was the **t** Light, which lighteth	*228*
Jn 4:23	**when the t worshippers shall**	*228*
Jn 4:37	**herein is that saying t, One soweth,**	*228*
Jn 5:31	**of myself, my witness is not t**	*227*
Jn 6:32	**my Father giveth you the t bread**	*228*
Jn 7:28	**but he that sent me is t, whom ye**	*228*
Jn 8:14	**of myself, yet my record is t**	*227*
Jn 8:16	**yet if I judge, my judgment is t**	*227*
Jn 8:17	**that the testimony of two men is t**	*227*
Jn 15:1	**I am the t vine, and my Father is**	*228*
Jn 17:3	**might know thee the only t God.**	*228*
Jn 19:35	it bare record, and his record is **t**:	*228*
Ro 3:4	let God be **t**, but every man a liar;	*227*
Eph 4:24	righteousness and **t** holiness	*3588, 225*
Php 4:8	brethren, whatsoever things are **t**,	*227*
1Th 1:9	idols to serve the living and **t** God;	*228*
1Ti 3:1	This is a **t** saying, If a man desire	*4103*
Heb 8:2	sanctuary, and of the **t** tabernacle,	*228*
Heb 9:24	which are the figures of the **t**;	*228*
Heb 10:22	Let us draw near with a **t** heart in	*228*
2Pe 2:22	them according to the **t** proverb,	*227*
1Jn 2:8	past, and the **t** light now shineth	*228*
1Jn 5:20	This is the **t** God, and eternal life	*228*
3Jn 12	and ye know that our record is **t**	*227*
Rev 3:7	**saith he that is holy, he that is t,**	*228*
Rev 3:14	**the faithful and t witness, the**	*228*
Rev 15:3	just and **t** are thy ways, thou King	*228*
Rev 16:7	**t** and righteous are thy judgments	*228*
Rev 19:2	**t** and righteous are his judgments:	*228*
Rev 19:11	him was called Faithful and **T**,	*228*
Rev 21:5	for these words are **t** and faithful	*228*
Rev 22:6	These sayings are faithful and **t**:	*228*

TRULY

Nu 14:21	But as **t** as I live, all the earth	199
Jos 2:14	will deal kindly and **t** with thee	571
1Sa 20:3	but **t** as the Lord liveth, and as thy	199
Ps 62:1	**T** my soul waiteth upon God:	389
Ps 73:1	**T** God is good to Israel, even to	389
Ps 116:16	O Lord, **t** I am thy servant; I am	577
Pr 12:22	they that deal **t** are his delight	530
Ecc 11:7	**T** the light is sweet, and a pleasant	
Jer 3:23	**t** in the Lord … is the salvation of	403
Jer 28:9	that the Lord hath **t** sent him	571
Eze 18:9	hath kept my judgments, to deal **t**;	571
Mic 3:8	**t** I am full of power by the spirit	199
Mt 17:11	**Elias t shall first come, and**	*3303*
Mt 27:54	saying, **T** this was the Son of God.	*230*
Mk 14:38	**spirit t is ready, but the flesh**	*3303*
Lk 10:2	**The harvest t is great, but the**	*3303*
Lk 11:48	**T ye bear witness that ye allow**	*686*
Lk 22:22	**t the Son of man goeth, as it**	*3303*
Jn 4:18	**thy husband: in that saidst thou t**	*227*
Jn 20:30	many other signs **t** did Jesus	*3303*
Ac 1:5	**For John t baptized with water;**	*3303*
2Co 12:12	**T** the signs of an apostle were	*3303*
1Jn 1:3	**t** our fellowship is with … Father	*1161*

TRUMP

1Co 15:52	twinkling of an eye, at the last **t**:	*4536*
1Th 4:16	archangel, and with the **t** of God:	*4536*

TRUMPET

Ex 19:13	when the **t** soundeth long, they	3104
Ex 20:18	lightnings, and the noise of the **t**,	7782
Le 25:9	make the **t** sound throughout all	7782
Nu 10:4	And if they blow but with one **t**, then	
Jgs 7:16	he put a **t** in every man's hand,	7782
1Sa 13:3	Saul blew the **t** throughout all the	7782
2Sa 6:15	and with the sound of the **t**	7782
2Sa 20:22	he blew a **t**, and they retired from	7782
1Ki 1:34	blow ye with the **t**, and say, God	7782
1Ki 1:41	when Joab heard the sound of the **t**,	7782
Ps 150:3	Praise him with the sound of the **t**:	7782
Isa 27:13	that the great **t** shall be blown	7782
Isa 58:1	spare not, lift up thy voice like a **t**	7782
Jer 4:19	heard, O my soul, the sound of the **t**,	7782
Jer 6:17	Hearken to the sound of the **t**	7782
Eze 7:14	They have blown the **t**, even to	8628
Eze 33:6	if the watchman … blow not the **t**,	7782
Hos 8:1	Set the **t** to thy mouth. He shall	7782
Joel 2:1	Blow ye the **t** in Zion, and sound	7782
Joel 2:15	Blow the **t** in Zion, sanctify a fast,	7782
Am 3:6	Shall a **t** be blown in the city, and	7782
Zec 9:14	and the Lord God shall blow the **t**,	7782
Mt 6:2	**alms, do not sound a t before**	*4537*
Mt 24:31	**angels with a great sound of a t,**	*4536*
1Co 14:8	if the **t** give an uncertain sound,	*4536*
1Co 15:52	for the **t** shall sound, and the dead	
Heb 12:19	And the sound of a **t**, and the voice	*4536*
Rev 1:10	behind me a great voice, as of a **t**,	*4536*
Rev 4:1	as it were of a **t** talking with me;	*4536*
Rev 8:13	voices of the **t** of the three angels	*4536*
Rev 9:14	to the sixth angel which had the **t**,	*4536*

TRUMPETS

Le 23:24	a sabbath a memorial of blowing of **t**,	
Nu 10:2	Make thee two **t** of silver; of a	2689
Nu 10:8	the priests, shall blow with the **t**;	2689
Nu 10:9	ye shall blow an alarm with the **t**;	2689
Nu 10:10	blow with the **t** over your burnt	2689
Jos 6:4	shall bear before the ark seven **t**	7782
Jos 6:20	when the priests blew with the **t**	7782
Jgs 7:22	And the three hundred blew the **t**,	7782
1Ch 15:24	did blow with the **t** before the ark	2689
2Ch 5:12	twenty priests sounding with **t**:)	2689
Ezr 3:10	the priests in their apparel with **t**	2689
Ne 12:35	certain of the priests' sons with **t**;	2689
Rev 8:2	and to them were given seven **t**	4536

TRUST

Jgs 9:15	and put your **t** in my shadow:	2620
Ru 2:12	whose wings thou art come to **t**	2620
2Sa 22:3	God of my rock; in him will I **t**	2620
2Sa 22:31	a buckler to all them that **t** in him	2620
2Ki 18:22	me, We **t** in the Lord our God:	982
2Ch 32:10	Whereon do ye **t** that ye abide in	982

Job 13:15 he slay me, yet will I **t** in him: 3176
Job 35:14 him; therefore **t** thou in him 2342
Ps 2:12 all they that put their **t** in him 2620
Ps 4:5 and put your **t** to the Lord 982
Ps 11:1 In the Lord put I my **t**: how say 2620
Ps 20:7 Some **t** in chariots, and some in
Ps 25:2 O my God, I **t** in thee: let me 982
Ps 31:1 In thee, O Lord, do I put my **t**; let 2620
Ps 36:7 children of men put their **t** under 2620
Ps 37:3 **T** in the Lord, and do good; so 982
Ps 37:40 save them, because they **t** in him 2620
Ps 40:4 man that maketh the Lord his **t**, 4009
Ps 44:6 For I will not **t** in my bow, neither 982
Ps 49:6 They that **t** in their wealth, and 982
Ps 52:8 I **t** in the mercy of God for ever and 982
Ps 56:3 time I am afraid, I will **t** in thee 982
Ps 56:11 In God have I put my **t**: I will not 982
Ps 62:8 **T** in him at all times; ye people, 982
Ps 71:1 In thee, O Lord, do I put my **t**: let 2620
Ps 71:5 thou art my **t** from my youth 4009
Ps 91:2 fortress: my God; in him will I **t** 982
Ps 91:4 and under his wings shalt thou **t**: 2620
Ps 115:11 Ye that fear the Lord, **t** in the Lord: 982
Ps 118:8 It is better to **t** in the Lord than 2620
Ps 125:1 They that **t** in the Lord shall be as 982
Ps 144:2 my shield, and he in whom I **t**; 2620
Pr 3:5 **T** in the Lord with all thine heart; 982
Pr 22:19 That thy **t** may be in the Lord, I 4009
Pr 30:5 unto them that put their **t** in him. 2620
Pr 31:11 her husband doth safely **t** in her 982
Isa 12:2 I will **t**, and not be afraid: for 982
Isa 26:4 **T** ye to the Lord for ever: for in 982
Isa 36:7 to me, We **t** in the Lord our God: 982
Isa 42:17 ashamed, that **t** in graven images 982
Isa 50:10 let him **t** in the name of the Lord 982
Isa 57:13 he that putteth his **t** in me shall 2620
Isa 59:4 they **t** in vanity, and speak lies; 982
Jer 7:8 ye **t** in lying words, that cannot 982
Jer 7:14 whereto ye **t**, and unto the place 982
Jer 28:15 thou makest this people to **t** in a lie 982
Jer 49:11 alive; and let thy widows **t** in me 982
Eze 16:15 thou didst **t** in thine own beauty, 982
Eze 33:13 if he **t** to his own righteousness, 982
Hos 10:13 because thou didst **t** in thy way, 982
Mic 7:5 **T** ye not in a friend, put ye not 539
Na 1:7 he knoweth them that **t** in him 2620
Mt 12:21 in his name shall the Gentiles **t** *1679*
Mk 10:24 **for them that t in riches to enter** *3982*
Lk 16:11 **commit your t the true riches?** *4100*
Jn 5:45 **you, even Moses, in whom ye t** *1679*
Ro 15:12 to him shall the Gentiles **t** *1679*
2Co 1:9 that we should not **t** in ourselves, *3982*
2Co 1:10 in whom we **t** that he will yet *1679*
2Co 3:4 such **t** have we through Christ to *4006*
Php 3:4 he might **t** in the flesh, I more: *3982*
1Th 2:4 to be put in **t** with the gospel *4100*
1Ti 1:11 which was committed to my **t** *4100*
1Ti 4:10 because we **t** in the living God, *1679*
1Ti 6:17 nor **t** in uncertain riches, but in *1679*
Phm 22 for I **t** that through your prayers *1679*
Heb 2:13 again, I will put my **t** in him *3982*
Heb 13:18 we **t** we have a good conscience *3982*

TRUSTED

Dt 32:37 gods, their rock in whom they **t** 2620
2Ki 18:5 He **t** in the Lord God of Israel; so 982
Ps 13:5 But I have **t** in thy mercy; my 982
Ps 22:4 Our fathers **t** in thee: they **t**, and 982
Ps 22:8 He **t** on the Lord that he would 1556
Ps 26:1 I have **t** also in the Lord; therefore 982
Ps 31:14 But I **t** in thee, O Lord: I said, 982
Ps 41:9 own familiar friend, in whom I **t**, 982
Ps 52:7 but **t** to the abundance of his riches 982
Isa 47:10 For thou hast **t** to thy wickedness: 982
Jer 13:25 forgotten me, and **t** to falsehood 982
Jer 49:4 that **t** to her treasures, saying, 982
Da 3:28 his servants that **t** in him, and 7365
Mt 27:43 He **t** in God; let him deliver him *3982*
Lk 11:22 **him all his armour wherein he t,** *3982*
Lk 18:9 unto certain which **t** in themselves *3982*
Lk 24:21 we **t** that it had been he which *1679*
Eph 1:12 of his glory, who first **t** in Christ *4276*
1Pe 3:5 holy women also, who **t** in God *1679*

TRUSTEDST

Dt 28:52 walls come down, wherein thou **t**, 982
Jer 5:17 thy fenced cities, whereto thou **t**, 982
Jer 12:5 the land of peace, whereto thou **t**, 982

TRUSTEST

2Ki 19:10 God in whom thou **t** deceive thee, 982
Isa 36:6 thou **t** in the staff of this broken 982

TRUSTETH

Ps 32:10 but he that **t** in the Lord, mercy 982
Ps 34:8 blessed is the man that **t** in him 2620
Ps 57:1 for my soul **t** in thee: yea, in the 2620
Ps 84:12 blessed is the man that **t** in thee 982
Ps 115:8 so is every one that **t** in them 982
Ps 135:18 so is every one that **t** in them 982
Pr 11:28 He that **t** in his riches shall fall: 982
Pr 16:20 whoso **t** in the Lord, happy is he 982
Pr 28:26 He that **t** in his own heart is a fool: 982
Jer 17:5 Cursed be the man that **t** in man 982
Jer 17:7 Blessed is the man that **t** in ... Lord 982
Hab 2:18 the maker of his work **t** thereto 982
1Ti 5:5 indeed, and desolate, **t** in God *1679*

TRUTH

Ex 18:21 such as fear God, men of **t**, hating 571
Ex 34:6 and abundant in goodness and **t**, 571
Dt 13:14 and, behold, if it be **t**, and the thing 571
Dt 32:4 a God of **t** and without iniquity 530
Jos 24:14 serve him in sincerity and in **t**: 571
1Sa 12:24 serve him in **t** with all your heart: 571
1Ki 2:4 walk before me in **t** with all their 571
1Ki 17:24 word of the Lord in thy mouth is **t** 571
2Ki 20:3 how I have walked before thee in **t** 571
2Ch 18:15 that thou say nothing but the **t** 571
Ps 25:5 Lead me in thy **t**, and teach me: 571
Ps 25:10 paths of the Lord are mercy and **t** 571
Ps 30:9 praise thee? shall it declare thy **t**? 571
Ps 31:5 hast redeemed me, O Lord God of **t** 571
Ps 33:4 and all his works are done in **t** 530
Ps 43:3 O send out thy light and thy **t**: let 571
Ps 51:6 thou desirest **t** in the inward parts: 571
Ps 57:3 send forth his mercy and his **t** 571
Ps 69:13 hear me, in the **t** of thy salvation 571
Ps 85:10 Mercy and **t** are met together; 571
Ps 85:11 **T** shall spring out of the earth; 571
Ps 86:11 way, O Lord; I will walk in thy **t**: 571
Ps 86:15 and plenteous in mercy and **t** 571
Ps 100:5 his **t** endureth to all generations 530

Ps 108:4 and thy **t** reacheth unto the clouds...... 571
Ps 117:2 the **t** of the Lord endureth for ever...... 571
Ps 119:43 take not the word of **t** utterly out....... 571
Ps 119:142 righteousness, and thy law is the **t**...... 571
Ps 145:18 him, to all that call upon him in **t**....... 571
Pr 3:3 Let not mercy and **t** forsake thee:....... 571
Pr 12:17 He that speaketh **t** sheweth forth....... 530
Pr 14:22 **t** shall be to them that devise good...... 571
Pr 16:6 By mercy and **t** iniquity is purged:...... 571
Pr 23:23 Buy the **t**, and sell it not; also.......... 571
Ecc 12:10 was upright, even words of **t**........... 571
Isa 16:5 sit upon it in **t** in the tabernacle........ 571
Isa 25:1 of old are faithfulness and **t**............ 544
Isa 26:2 which keepeth the **t** may enter in....... 529
Isa 38:3 walked before thee in **t** and with a...... 571
Isa 42:3 shall bring forth judgment unto **t**....... 571
Isa 43:9 or let them hear, and say, It is **t**......... 571
Isa 48:1 but not in **t**, nor in righteousness....... 571
Isa 59:4 for justice, nor any pleadeth for **t**:....... 530
Isa 59:14 for **t** is fallen in the street, and.......... 571
Jer 4:2 The Lord liveth, in **t**, in judgment...... 571
Jer 5:1 judgment, that seeketh the **t**;........... 530
Jer 7:23 **t** is perished, and is cut off from........ 530
Jer 9:3 not valiant for the **t** upon the earth;..... 530
Da 2:47 Of a **t** it is, that your God is a God..... 7187
Da 4:37 whose works are **t**, and his ways....... 7187
Da 7:19 know the **t** of the fourth beast......... 3321
Da 9:13 iniquities, and understand thy **t**........ 571
Hos 4:1 because there is no **t**, nor mercy,........ 571
Zec 8:3 Jerusalem shall be called a city of **t**;..... 571
Zec 8:8 God, in **t** and in righteousness......... 571
Zec 8:16 execute the judgment of **t** and.......... 571
Mal 2:6 The law of **t** was in his mouth, and..... 571
Mt 14:33 Of a **t** thou art the Son of God......... *230*
Mt 15:27 she said, **T**, Lord: yet the dogs......... *3483*
Mk 5:33 before him, and told him all the **t**....... *225*
Lk 4:25 **I tell you of a t, many widows**.......... *225*
Lk 9:27 **But I tell you of a t, there be**........... *230*
Lk 12:44 **a t I say unto you, that he will**.......... *230*
Lk 21:3 **Of a t I say unto you, that this**......... *230*
Lk 22:59 Of a **t** this fellow also was with......... *225*
Jn 1:14 of the Father,) full of grace and **t**....... *225*
Jn 1:17 grace and **t** came by Jesus Christ........ *225*
Jn 3:21 **that doeth t cometh to the light,**........ *225*
Jn 4:24 **worship him in spirit and in t**.......... *225*
Jn 5:33 **and he bare witness unto the t**......... *225*
Jn 8:32 **And ye shall know the t, and the**....... *225*
Jn 8:32 **and the t shall make you free**.......... *225*
Jn 8:40 **a man that hath told you the t,**......... *225*
Jn 8:44 **because there is no t in him**........... *225*
Jn 14:6 **I am the way, the t and the life:**......... *225*
Jn 14:17 **Even the Spirit of t; whom the**......... *225*
Jn 15:26 **the Father, even the Spirit of t,**......... *225*
Jn 16:7 **Nevertheless I tell you the t; It is**....... *225*
Jn 16:13 **he will guide you into all t: for he**....... *225*
Jn 17:17 **Sanctify them through thy t**........... *225*
Jn 17:17 **thy word is t**......................... *225*
Jn 18:37 **Every one that is of the t heareth**....... *225*
Jn 18:38 Pilate saith unto him, What is **t**?........ *225*
Ac 4:27 of a **t** against thy holy child Jesus....... *225*
Ac 10:3 Of a **t** I perceive that God is no......... *225*
Ro 1:18 who hold the **t** in unrighteousness;..... *225*
Ro 1:25 Who changed the **t** of God into a lie,.... *225*
Ro 2:2 judgment of God is according to **t**...... *225*
Ro 2:20 knowledge and of the **t** in the law....... *225*
Ro 3:7 if the **t** of God hath more abounded.... *225*
Ro 9:1 I say the **t** in Christ, I lie not, my........ *225*
1Co 5:8 unleavened bread of sincerity and **t**..... *225*
1Co 13:6 in iniquity, but rejoiceth in the **t**;....... *225*
2Co 6:7 By the word of **t**, by the power of....... *225*
2Co 11:10 As the **t** of Christ is in me, no man...... *225*
2Co 13:8 nothing against the **t**, but for the **t**...... *225*
Gal 3:1 you, that ye should not obey the **t**,...... *225*
Gal 4:16 enemy, because I tell you the **t**?......... *226*
Gal 5:7 you that ye should not obey the **t**?...... *225*
Eph 4:15 speaking the **t** in love, may grow........ *226*
Eph 4:25 speak every man **t** with his............ *226*
Eph 6:14 having your loins girt about with **t**,..... *226*
Col 1:6 and knew the grace of God in **t**:........ *226*
1Th 2:13 but as it is in **t**, the word of God........ *230*
2Th 2:10 they received not the love of the **t**....... *225*
2Th 2:12 be damned who believed not the **t**,..... *225*
2Th 2:13 of the Spirit and belief of the **t**......... *225*
1Ti 2:4 come unto the knowledge of the **t**...... *225*
1Ti 3:15 God, the pillar and ground of the **t**..... *225*
1Ti 6:5 corrupt minds, ... destitute of the **t**..... *225*
2Ti 2:15 rightly dividing the word of **t**.......... *225*
2Ti 2:18 Who concerning the **t** have erred,....... *225*
2Ti 2:25 to the acknowledging of the **t**;.......... *225*
2Ti 3:7 to come to the knowledge of the **t**...... *225*
Jas 1:18 will begat he us with the word of **t**...... *225*
Jas 3:14 glory not, and lie not against the **t**...... *225*
1Pe 1:22 purified your souls in obeying the **t**..... *225*
2Pe 2:2 the way of **t** shall be evil spoken of...... *225*
1Jn 1:8 ourselves, and the **t** is not in us......... *225*
1Jn 2:4 is a liar, and the **t** is not in him......... *225*
1Jn 2:21 know it, and that no lie is of the **t**,...... *225*
1Jn 3:18 in tongue; but in deed and in **t**,......... *225*
1Jn 4:6 Hereby know we the spirit of **t**, and..... *225*
1Jn 5:6 witness, because the Spirit is **t**.......... *225*
2Jn 4 I found of thy children walking in **t**..... *225*
3Jn 4 to hear that my children walk in **t**....... *225*

TRY See also TRIED; TRIEST.

2Ch 32:31 God left him, to **t** him, that he........ 5254
Ps 11:4 his eyelids **t** the children of men........ 974
Ps 139:23 **t** me, and know my thoughts:.......... 974
Jer 6:27 thou mayest know and **t** their way...... 974
Jer 17:10 Lord search the heart, I **t** the reins,...... 974
La 3:40 Let us search and **t** our ways,.......... 2713
Da 11:35 fall, to **t** them, and to purge, and...... 6684
Zec 13:9 and will **t** them as gold is tried:......... 974
1Co 3:13 the fire shall **t** every man's work....... *1381*
1Pe 4:12 fiery trial which is to **t** you....... *4314, 3986*
1Jn 4:1 **t** the spirits whether they are of........ *1381*
Rev 3:10 **t them that dwell upon the earth.**..... *3985*

TRYING

Jas 1:3 **t** of your faith worketh patience....... *1383*

TUMULT

1Sa 4:14 What meaneth the noise of this **t**?..... 1995
2Ki 19:28 against me and thy **t** is come up....... 7600
Ps 65:7 waves, and the **t** of the people......... 1995
Isa 33:3 the noise of the **t** the people fled;...... 1995
Zec 14:13 a great **t** from the Lord shall be........ 4103
Mt 27:24 but that rather a **t** was made, he....... *2351*
Mk 5:38 and seeth the **t**, and them that......... *2351*

TUMULTUOUS

Isa 13:4 a **t** noise of the kingdoms of.......... 7588

T

TURN

Ge	19:2	my lords, **t** in, I pray you, into	5493
Ex	3:3	I will now **t** aside, and see this	5493
Le	19:4	**T** ye not unto idols, nor make to	6437
Nu	14:25	To morrow **t** you, and get you	6437
Nu	22:26	was no way to **t** either to the right	5186
Dt	4:30	if thou **t** to the Lord thy God	7725
Dt	5:32	ye shall not **t** aside to the right	5493
Dt	11:16	ye **t** aside, and serve other gods,	5493
Dt	13:5	spoken to **t** you away from the	5627
Dt	13:17	Lord may **t** from the fierceness of	7725
Dt	17:17	himself, that his heart **t** not away:	5493
Dt	17:20	and that he **t** not aside from the	5493
Dt	30:3	Lord thy God will **t** thy captivity,	7725
Dt	30:10	**t** unto the Lord thy God with all	7725
Dt	30:17	But if thine heart **t** away, as that	6437
Dt	31:20	then will they **t** unto other gods	6437
Jos	1:7	**t** not from it to the right hand or to	5493
Jos	22:16	**t** away this day from following	7725
Jos	24:20	then he will **t** and do you hurt	7725
Jgs	4:18	**T** in, my lord, **t** in to me; fear	5493
1Sa	12:20	**t** not aside from following the Lord,	5493
1Sa	22:17	**T**, and slay the priests of the	5437
2Sa	2:23	Howbeit he refused to **t** aside:	5493
1Ki	8:35	thy name, and **t** from their sin	7725
1Ki	9:6	shall at all **t** from following me,	7725
1Ki	11:2	they will **t** away your heart after	5186
1Ki	13:17	nor **t** again to go by the way that	7725
2Ki	1:6	Go, **t** again unto the king that	7725
2Ki	9:18	with peace? **t** thee behind me	5437
2Ki	17:13	**T** ye from your evil ways, and	7725
2Ch	6:37	**t** and pray unto thee in the land of	7725
2Ch	15:4	they in their trouble did **t** unto the	7725
2Ch	29:10	that his fierce wrath may **t** away	7725
2Ch	30:6	**t** again unto the Lord God of	7725
2Ch	35:22	Josiah would not **t** his face from	5437
Ne	1:9	But if ye **t** unto me, and keep my	7725
Ne	9:26	against them to **t** them to thee,	7725
Ps	4:2	long will ye **t** my glory into shame?	
Ps	7:12	If he **t** not, he will whet his	7725
Ps	22:27	remember and **t** unto the Lord:	7725
Ps	40:4	proud, nor such as **t** aside to lies	7750
Ps	56:9	then shall mine enemies **t** back:	7725
Ps	80:19	**T** us again, O Lord God of hosts	7725
Ps	85:4	**T** us, O God of our salvation, and	7725
Ps	85:8	but let them not **t** again to folly	7725
Ps	101:3	hate … work of them that **t** aside;	7750
Ps	119:37	**T** away mine eyes from	5674
Ps	126:4	**T** again our captivity, O Lord, as	7725
Pr	1:23	**T** you at my reproof: behold, I	7725
Pr	4:15	by it, **t** from it, and pass away	7847
Pr	4:27	**T** not to the right hand nor to	5186
Pr	9:4	is simple, let him **t** in hither:	5493
Pr	25:10	and thine infamy **t** not away,	7725
Pr	29:8	but wise men **t** away wrath	7725
Ecc	3:20	the dust, and all **t** to dust again	7725
SS	2:17	**t**, my beloved, and be thou like a	5437
Isa	10:2	**t** aside the needy from judgment	5186
Isa	13:14	every man **t** to his own people	6437
Isa	19:6	they shall **t** the rivers far away;	2186
Isa	29:21	and **t** aside the just for a thing of	5186
Isa	30:21	ye in it, when ye **t** to the right hand	
Isa	31:6	**T** ye unto him from whom the	7725
Isa	58:13	**t** away thy foot from the sabbath	7725
Jer	2:35	surely his anger shall **t** from me	7725
Jer	3:7	**T** thou unto me. But she	7725
Jer	13:16	he **t** it into the shadow of death	7760
Jer	18:8	**t** from their evil, I will repent of	7725
Jer	26:3	and **t** every man from his evil way	7725
Jer	29:14	and I will **t** away your captivity	7725
Jer	31:13	I will **t** their mourning into joy	2015
Jer	31:18	**t** thou me, and I shall be turned;	7725
La	2:14	iniquity, to **t** away thy captivity;	7725
La	3:35	To **t** aside the right of a man	5186
La	3:40	ways, and **t** again to the Lord	7725
La	5:21	**T** thou us unto thee, O Lord, and	7725
Eze	3:19	he **t** not from his wickedness, nor	7725
Eze	3:20	righteous man doth **t** from his	7725
Eze	8:6	**t** thee yet again, and thou shalt	7725
Eze	14:6	and **t** yourselves from your idols;	7725
Eze	18:21	the wicked will **t** from all his sins	7725
Eze	18:30	Repent, and **t** yourselves from	7725
Eze	33:9	if he do not **t** from his way, he	7725
Eze	33:11	but that the wicked **t** from his way	7725
Eze	33:11	**t** ye, **t** ye from your evil ways; for	7725
Eze	38:4	I will **t** thee back, and put hooks	7725
Da	9:13	we might **t** from our iniquities	7725
Da	12:3	they that **t** many to righteousness, as	
Hos	5:4	their doings to **t** unto their God:	7725
Hos	12:6	Therefore **t** thou to thy God: keep	7725
Joel	2:12	**t** ye even to me with all your heart,	7725
Am	2:4	I will not **t** away the punishment	7725
Am	2:6	I will not **t** away the punishment	7725
Am	2:7	and **t** aside the way of the meek:	5186
Am	8:10	will **t** your feasts into mourning	2015
Jnh	3:8	can tell if God will **t** and repent,	7725
Mic	7:19	He will **t** again, he will have	7725
Zep	2:7	them, and **t** away their captivity	7725
Zep	3:20	when I **t** back your captivity	7725
Zec	1:3	**T** ye unto me, saith the Lord of	7725
Zec	13:7	**t** mine hand upon the little ones	7725
Mal	2:6	did **t** many away from iniquity	7725
Mal	3:5	that **t** aside the stranger from his	5186
Mal	4:6	**t** the heart of the fathers to the	7725
Mt	5:39	**cheek, t to him the other also**	*4762*
Mt	5:42	**borrow of thee t not thou away**	*654*
Mt	7:6	**feet, and t again and rend you**	*4762*
Mk	13:16	**is in the field not t back again**	*1994*
Lk	1:17	to **t** the hearts of the fathers to the	*1994*
Lk	17:4	**and seven times in a day t again**	*1994*
Lk	21:13	**it shall t to you for a testimony**	*576*
Ac	13:46	life, lo, we **t** to the Gentiles	*4762*
Ac	26:18	**to t them from darkness to light,**	*1994*
Ac	26:20	they should repent and **t** to God,	*1994*
2Co	3:16	when it shall **t** to the Lord,	*1994*
Gal	4:9	how **t** ye again to the weak and	*1994*
2Ti	3:5	power thereof: from such **t** away	*665*
2Ti	4:4	they shall **t** away their ears from	*654*
Tit	1:14	of men, that **t** from the truth	*654*
Heb	12:25	we **t** away from him that speaketh	*654*
Jas	3:3	and we **t** about their whole body	*3329*
2Pe	2:21	to **t** from the holy commandment	*1994*
Rev	11:6	over waters to **t** them to blood	*4762*

TURNED

Ge	3:24	flaming sword which **t** every way,	2015
Ge	18:22	men **t** their faces from thence	6437
Ex	3:4	Lord saw that he **t** aside to see	5493
Ex	7:15	the rod which was **t** to a serpent	2015
Ex	7:17	river, and they shall be **t** to blood	2015
Le	13:3	the hair in the plague is **t** white	2015
Nu	22:23	the ass **t** aside out of the way	5186

T

Nu 22:33 and the ass saw me, and **t** from me 5186
Nu 25:4 anger of the Lord may be **t** away....... 7725
Dt 9:15 **t** and came down from the mount..... 6437
Dt 9:16 **t** aside quickly out of the way 5493
Dt 31:18 that they are **t** unto other gods 6437
Jos 8:21 **t** again, and slew the men of Ai. 7725
Jgs 2:17 they **t** quickly out of the way.......... 5493
Jgs 14:8 he **t** aside to see the carcase of......... 5493
Jgs 20:41 when the men of Israel **t** again 2015
Jgs 20:47 six hundred men **t** and fled to the 6437
1Sa 8:3 but **t** aside after lucre, and took 5186
1Sa 15:11 he is **t** back from following me 7725
2Sa 1:22 the bow of Jonathan **t** not back, ... 7734
2Sa 19:2 victory that day was **t** into mourning
1Ki 2:15 howbeit the kingdom is **t** about,....... 5437
1Ki 11:4 wives **t** away his heart after other 5186
1Ki 21:4 upon his bed, and **t** away his face 5437
1Ki 22:33 they **t** back from pursuing him........ 7725
2Ki 1:5 them, Why are ye now **t** back?......... 7725
2Ki 5:12 So he **t** and went away in a rage 6437
2Ki 20:2 Then he **t** his face to the wall, and 5437
2Ki 23:16 as Josiah **t** himself, he spied the........ 6437
2Ki 23:25 that **t** to the Lord with all his.......... 7725
2Ki 23:34 **t** his name to Jehoiakim, and took 5437
2Ki 24:1 he **t** and rebelled against him.......... 7725
1Ch 21:20 Ornan **t** back, and saw the angel; 7725
Ezr 6:22 **t** the heart of the king of Assyria 5437
Ne 13:2 God **t** the curse into a blessing 2015
Job 30:31 My harp also is **t** to mourning, and
Job 37:12 is **t** round about by his counsels: 2015
Job 41:22 sorrow is **t** into joy before him 1750
Job 42:10 the Lord **t** the captivity of Job......... 7725
Ps 9:17 The wicked shall be **t** into hell......... 7725
Ps 30:11 hast **t** for me my mourning into....... 2015
Ps 66:6 He **t** the sea into dry land: they........ 2015
Ps 66:20 which hath not **t** away my prayer 5493
Ps 70:2 let them be **t** backward, and put....... 5472
Ps 78:38 many a time **t** he his anger away....... 7725
Ps 78:41 Yea, they **t** back and tempted God,..... 7725
Ps 78:57 were **t** aside like a deceitful bow 2015
Ps 105:25 He **t** their heart to hate his people,..... 2015
Ps 105:29 He **t** their waters into blood, and 2015
Ps 114:8 **t** the rock into a standing water 2015
Ps 126:1 the Lord **t** again the captivity of 7725
Ecc 2:12 **t** myself to behold wisdom, and 6437
Isa 5:25 all this his anger is not **t** away,......... 7725
Isa 21:4 my pleasure hath he **t** into fear 7760
Isa 53:6 have **t** every one to his own way; 6437
Isa 59:14 judgment is **t** away backward,......... 5253
Isa 63:10 he was **t** to be their enemy, ... 2015
Jer 2:27 they have **t** their back unto me,........ 6437
Jer 3:10 sister Judah hath not **t** unto me 7725
Jer 5:25 Your iniquities have **t** away these 5186
Jer 11:10 They are **t** back to the iniquities of..... 7725
Jer 23:22 have **t** them from their evil way 7725
Jer 31:19 after that I was **t**, I repented; 7725
Jer 32:33 they have **t** unto me the back, and 6437
Jer 34:15 ye were now **t**, and had done right..... 7725
Jer 34:16 But ye **t** and polluted my name........ 7725
Jer 46:21 they also are **t** back, and are fled....... 6437
Jer 50:6 **t** them away on the mountains: 7725
La 1:20 mine heart is **t** within me; for I........ 2015
La 5:2 Our inheritance is **t** to strangers, ... 2015
La 5:15 our dance is **t** into mourning 2015
La 5:21 thee, O Lord, and we shall be **t**;........ 7725
Eze 1:9 they **t** not when they went; 5437
Eze 1:12 and they **t** not when they went........ 5437
Da 9:16 anger and thy fury be **t** away.......... 7725
Hos 14:4 mine anger is **t** away from him........ 7725
Joel 2:31 The sun shall be **t** into darkness 2015
Jnh 3:10 that they **t** from their evil way; 7725
Na 2:2 **t** away the excellency of Jacob......... 7725
Hab 2:16 Lord's right hand shall be **t** unto....... 5437
Zep 1:6 that are **t** back from the Lord;......... 5472
Mt 16:23 But he **t**, and said unto Peter, Get...... *4772*
Lk 2:45 they **t** back again to Jerusalem......... *5290*
Lk 9:55 But he **t**, and rebuked them, and....... *4762*
Lk 22:61 Lord **t**, and looked upon Peter *4762*
Jn 16:20 **your sorrow shall be t into joy** *1096*
Jn 20:14 she **t** herself back, and saw Jesus *4762*
Ac 2:20 The sun shall be **t** into darkness *4762*
Ac 11:21 believed, and **t** unto the Lord *1994*
Ac 16:18 grieved, **t** and said to the spirit,........ *1994*
Ac 17:6 that have **t** the world upside down *387*
1Th 1:9 and how ye **t** to God from idols to *1994*
1Ti 5:15 are already **t** aside after Satan *1824*
2Ti 4:4 truth, and shall be **t** unto fables......... *654*
Heb 11:34 **t** to flight the armies of the aliens *2827*
Jas 3:4 **t** about with a very small helm *3329*
Jas 4:9 let … laughter be **t** to mourning....... *3344*
2Pe 2:22 dog is **t** to his own vomit again; *1994*
Rev 1:12 I **t** to see the voice that spake with *1994*
Rev 1:12 And being **t**, I saw seven golden *1994*

TURNETH
Le 20:6 the soul that **t** after such as have....... 6437
Ps 107:35 He **t** the wilderness into a standing 7760
Ps 146:9 the way of the wicked he **t** upside...... 5791
Pr 15:1 A soft answer **t** away wrath: but 7725
Pr 17:8 whithersoever it **t**, it prospereth 6437
Pr 21:1 he **t** it whithersoever he will 5186
Pr 26:14 As the door **t** upon his hinges, so 5437
Pr 28:9 that **t** away his ear from hearing....... 5493
Pr 30:30 beasts, and **t** not away for any: 7725
Isa 44:25 that **t** wise men backward, and 7725
Jer 14:8 as a wayfaring man that **t** aside........ 5186
La 3:3 **t** his hand against me all the day....... 7725
Eze 18:24 **t** away from his righteousness,
Eze 33:12 day that he **t** from his wickedness; 7725
Am 5:8 and **t** the shadow of death into........ 2015

TURNING
2Ki 21:13 wiping it, and **t** it upside down. 2015
2Ch 36:13 heart from **t** unto the Lord God....... 7257
Pr 1:32 the **t** away of the simple shall slay...... 4878
Isa 29:16 your **t** of things upside down 2017
Jn 21:20 Peter, **t** about, seeth the disciple *1994*
Ac 3:26 in **t** away every one of you from *654*
Jas 1:17 variableness, neither shadow of **t** *5157*
2Pe 2:6 **t** the cities of Sodom … into ashes..... *5077*

TURTLEDOVE
Ps 74:19 O deliver not the soul of thy **t** unto 8449

TURTLEDOVES
Le 1:14 he shall bring his offering of **t**, ... 8449
Le 5:7 two **t**, or two young pigeons, unto 8449
Le 5:11 But if he be not able to bring two **t**,.... 8449
Lk 2:24 A pair of **t**, or two young pigeons...... *5167*

TURTLES
Le 12:8 lamb, then she shall bring two **t** 8449
Le 15:29 day she shall take unto her two **t**....... 8449

TWAIN

Isa	6:2	wings; with **t** he covered his face	8147
Jer	34:18	when they cut the calf in **t**, and	8147
Mt	5:41	**thee to go a mile, go with him t**	*1417*
Mt	19:5	**and they t shall be one flesh?**	*1417*
Mt	21:31	**Whether of them t did the will of**	*1417*
Mt	27:51	the veil of the temple was rent in **t**	*1417*
Mk	10:8	**And they t shall be one flesh: so**	*1417*
Mk	15:38	the veil of the temple was rent in **t**	*1417*
Eph	2:15	make in himself of **t** one new man,	*1417*

TWELFTH

1Ki	19:19	before him, and he with the **t**	8147, 6240
2Ch	34:3	and in the **t** year he began to	8147, 6240
Eze	33:21	it came to pass in the **t** year of	8147, 6240
Rev	21:20	a jacinth; the **t**, an amethyst	*1428*

TWELVE

Ge	17:20	**t** princes shall he beget, and I	8147, 6240
Ge	25:16	**t** princes according to their	8147, 6240
Ge	35:22	Now the sons of Jacob were **t**	8147, 6240
Ge	49:28	these are the **t** tribes of Israel:	8147, 6240
Nu	7:87	were **t** bullocks, the rams **t**,	8147, 6240
Nu	17:2	house of their fathers **t** rods:	8147, 6240
Jos	3:12	take you **t** men out of the	8147, 6240
Jos	4:9	Joshua set up **t** stones in the	8147, 6240
Jgs	19:29	with her bones, into **t** pieces,	8147, 6240
1Ki	4:7	had **t** officers over all Israel,	8147, 6240
1Ki	11:30	on him, and rent it in **t** pieces:	8147, 6240
1Ki	18:31	And Elijah took **t** stones,	8147, 6240
Est	2:12	that she had been **t** months	8147, 6240
Jer	52:20	and **t** brasen bulls that were	8147, 6240
Da	4:29	end of **t** months he walked in	8648, 6236
Mt	9:20	with an issue of blood **t** years,	*1427*
Mt	10:1	called unto him his **t** disciples	*1427*
Mt	10:2	the names of the **t** apostles are	*1427*
Mt	14:20	that remained **t** baskets full	*1427*
Mt	19:28	**ye also shall sit upon t thrones,**	*1427*
Mt	19:28	**judging the t tribes of Israel.**	*1427*
Mt	26:14	Then one of the **t**, called Judas	*1427*
Mt	26:47	lo, Judas, one of the **t**, came, and	*1427*
Mt	26:53	**me more than t legions of angels?**	*1427*
Mk	5:25	had an issue of blood **t** years,	*1427*
Mk	6:43	they took up **t** baskets full of the	*1427*
Mk	14:10	Judas Iscariot, one of the **t**, went	*1427*
Mk	14:20	**It is one of the t, that dippeth**	*1427*
Mk	14:43	spake, cometh Judas, one of the **t**,	*1427*
Lk	2:42	when he was **t** years old, they	*1427*
Lk	6:13	of them he chose **t**, whom also he	*1427*
Lk	9:17	that remained to them **t** baskets	*1427*
Lk	22:30	**judging the t tribes of Israel.**	*1427*
Jn	6:13	filled **t** baskets with the fragments	*1427*
Jn	6:70	**Have not I chosen you t, and one**	*1427*
Jn	11:9	**Are there not t hours in the day?**	*1427*
Ac	7:8	and Jacob begat the **t** patriarchs	*1427*
Ac	26:7	Unto which promise our **t** tribes,	*1429*
1Co	15:5	seen of Cephas, then of the **t**:	*1427*
Jas	1:1	to the **t** tribes which are scattered	*1427*
Rev	7:5	of Juda were sealed **t** thousand	*1427*
Rev	12:1	upon her head a crown of **t** stars:	*1427*
Rev	21:21	the **t** gates were **t** pearls; every	*1427*
Rev	22:2	life, which bare **t** manner of fruits,	*1427*

TWENTY

Ge	31:41	have I been **t** years in thy house; I	6242
Ex	30:14	from **t** years old and above, shall	6242
Le	27:3	male from **t** years old even unto	6242
Le	27:5	years old even unto **t** years old,	6242
Nu	1:3	From **t** years old and upward, all	6242
Nu	7:88	were **t** and four bullocks, the	6242
Nu	8:24	**t** and five years old and upward	6242
Nu	11:19	days, neither ten days, nor **t** days;	6242
Nu	14:29	from **t** years old and upward,	6242
Nu	26:2	from **t** years old and upward,	6242
Nu	32:11	from **t** years old and upward,	6242
1Sa	7:2	time was long; for it was **t** years:	6242
1Ki	9:11	king Solomon gave Hiram **t** cities	6242
1Ch	20:6	fingers and toes were four and **t**,	6242
1Ch	23:24	from the age of **t** years and upward	6242
1Ch	23:27	were numbered from **t** years old	6242
1Ch	27:1	course were **t** and four thousand	6242
2Ch	3:4	the breadth of the house, **t** cubits,	6242
2Ch	3:11	the cherubims were **t** cubits long:	6242
Eze	40:21	the breadth five and **t** cubits	6242
Da	6:1	an hundred and **t** princes	6243
Da	10:13	withstood me one and **t** days:	6242
Zec	5:2	the length thereof is **t** cubits, and	6242
Lk	14:31	**against him with t thousand?**	*1501*
Ac	27:28	sounded, and found it **t** fathoms:	*1501*
Rev	4:4	the throne were four and **t** seats:	*1501*
Rev	4:4	I saw four and **t** elders sitting,	*1501*
Rev	5:8	the four and **t** elders fell down	*1501*
Rev	11:16	four and **t** elders, which sat before	*1501*
Rev	19:4	the four and **t** elders and the four	*1501*

TWENTY'S

Ge	18:31	I will not destroy it for **t** sake	6242

TWICE

Ge	41:32	was doubled unto Pharaoh **t**;	6471
Ex	16:5	**t** as much as they gather daily	4932
Nu	20:11	with his rod he smote the rock **t**	6471
1Ki	11:9	which had appeared unto him **t**	6471
2Ki	6:10	saved himself … not once nor **t**	8147
Job	40:5	Once have I spoken; … yea, **t**; but I	8147
Job	42:10	gave Job **t** as much as he had	4932
Ecc	6:6	he live a thousand years **t** told,	6471
Mk	14:30	**before the cock crow t, thou shalt**	*1364*
Mk	14:72	Before the cock crow **t**, thou shalt	*1364*
Lk	18:12	**I fast t in the week, I give tithes**	*1364*

TWILIGHT

1Sa	30:17	David smote them from the **t**	5399
2Ki	7:7	they arose and fled in the **t**, and	5399
Eze	12:7	I brought it forth in the **t**, and I	5939

TWINKLING

1Co	15:52	In a moment, in the **t** of an eye,	*4493*

TWINS

Ge	25:24	behold, there were **t** in her womb	8380
Ge	38:27	that, behold, **t** were in her womb	8380

T

TWO

Ge	1:16	And God made **t** great lights;	8147
Ge	6:19	**t** of every sort shalt thou bring	8147
Ge	7:15	into the ark, **t** and **t** of all flesh,	8147
Ge	19:1	And there came **t** angels to Sodom	8147
Ge	19:30	in a cave, he and his **t** daughters	8147
Ge	25:23	her, **T** nations are in thy womb,	8147
Ge	27:36	hath supplanted me these **t** times:	6471
Ge	41:50	And unto Joseph were born **t** sons	8147
Ex	2:13	**t** men of the Hebrews strove	8147
Ex	12:22	and the **t** side posts with the blood	8147
Ex	25:18	shalt make **t** cherubims of gold,	8147

Ex	28:9	And thou shalt take t onyx stones,	8147
Ex	28:14	t chains of pure gold at the ends;	8147
Ex	29:38	t lambs of the first year day by day	8147
Ex	31:18	t tables of testimony, tables of	8147
Ex	34:1	Hew thee t tables of stone like	8147
Ex	37:7	And he made t cherubims of gold	8147
Ex	37:7	on the t ends of the mercy seat;	8147
Le	16:1	after the death of the t sons of	8147
Nu	10:2	Make thee t trumpets of silver; of	8147
Nu	28:3	t lambs of the first year without	8147
Nu	28:11	t young bullocks, and one ram,	8147
Nu	31:27	And divide the prey into t parts;	2673
Nu	34:15	The t tribes and the half tribe have	8147
Dt	3:21	God hath done unto these t kings:	8147
Dt	4:13	wrote them upon t tables of stone.	8147
Dt	5:22	he wrote them in t tables of stone,	8147
Dt	9:10	delivered unto me t tables of stone.	8147
Dt	10:3	hewed t tables of stone like unto	8147
Dt	17:6	At the mouth of t witnesses, or	8147
Dt	19:15	at the mouth of t witnesses, or at	8147
Dt	21:15	If a man have t wives, one beloved,	8147
Dt	32:30	and t put ten thousand to flight,	8147
Jos	6:22	the t men that had spied out the	8147
Jos	14:4	children of Joseph were t tribes,	8147
Jgs	3:16	him a dagger which had t edges	8147
Jgs	11:37	let me alone t months, that I may	8147
Jgs	15:4	put a firebrand … between t tails.	8147
Jgs	16:28	of the Philistines for my t eyes,	8147
Jgs	16:29	Samson took hold of the t middle	8147
1Sa	2:34	that shall come upon thy t sons	8147
1Sa	4:17	and thy t sons also, Hophni and	8147
1Sa	11:11	t of them were not left together	8147
1Sa	23:18	they t made a covenant before	8147
1Sa	30:18	and David rescued his t wives	8147
2Sa	14:28	dwelt t full years in Jerusalem,	
2Sa	23:20	he slew t lionlike men of Moab:	8147
1Ki	2:32	fell upon t men more righteous	8147
1Ki	3:25	said, Divide the living child in t,	8147
1Ki	8:9	the ark save the t tables of stone,	8147
1Ki	10:16	king Solomon made t hundred targets	
2Ki	4:1	come to take unto him my t sons	8147
2Ch	5:10	nothing in the ark save the t tables	8147
Ezr	10:13	is this a work of one day or t:	8147
Est	9:27	keep these t days according to	8147
Job	42:7	thee and against thy t friends:	8147
Pr	30:7	T things have I required of thee;	8147
Pr	30:15	The horseleach hath t daughters,	8147
Ecc	4:9	T are better than one; because	8147
Ecc	4:11	Again, if t lie together, then they	8147
Isa	22:11	also a ditch between the t walls for	
Jer	2:13	my people have committed t evils;	8147
Jer	28:3	Within t full years will I bring again	
Eze	37:22	they shall be no more t nations:	8147
Eze	47:13	Israel: Joseph shall have t portions	
Da	8:7	the ram, and brake his t horns:	8147
Da	9:25	and threescore and t weeks:	8147
Da	12:5	there stood other t, the one on this	8147
Da	12:11	thousand t hundred and ninety days.	
Hos	6:2	After t days will he revive us: in the	
Am	1:1	Israel, t years before the earthquake	
Am	3:3	Can t walk together, except they	8147
Zec	4:3	t olive trees by it, one upon the	8147
Zec	4:12	through the t golden pipes empty	8147
Zec	6:1	out from between t mountains;	8147
Mt	2:16	from t years old and under,	*1332*
Mt	6:24	**No man can serve t masters: for**	*1417*
Mt	8:28	met him t possessed with devils,	*1417*
Mt	10:29	**t sparrows sold for a farthing?**	*1417*
Mt	14:17	here but five loaves, and t fishes	*1417*
Mt	18:9	**having t eyes to be cast into hell**	*1417*
Mt	18:16	**mouth of t or three witnesses**	*1417*
Mt	18:19	**if t of you shall agree on earth as**	*1417*
Mt	18:20	**For where t or three are gathered**	*1417*
Mt	20:21	Grant that … my t sons may sit,	*1417*
Mt	21:28	**A certain man had t sons: and he**	*1417*
Mt	22:40	**On these t commandments hang**	*1417*
Mt	24:40	**Then shall t be in the field; the**	*1417*
Mt	24:41	**T women shall be grinding at the**	*1417*
Mt	25:22	**thou deliveredst unto me t talents:**	*1417*
Mt	26:60	At the last came t false witnesses,	*1417*
Mt	27:38	there t thieves crucified with him,	*1417*
Mk	6:41	t fishes divided he among them all	*1417*
Mk	9:43	**having t hands to go into hell,**	*1417*
Mk	12:42	widow, and she threw in t mites,	*1417*
Mk	15:27	with him they crucify t thieves;	*1417*
Mk	16:12	in another form unto t of them,	*1417*
Lk	2:24	turtledoves, or t young pigeons	*1417*
Lk	7:41	**creditor which had t debtors:**	*1417*
Lk	9:16	took the five loaves and the t fishes,	*1417*
Lk	9:30	there talked with him t men,	*1417*
Lk	12:6	**five sparrows sold for t farthings,**	*1417*
Lk	15:11	he said, **A certain man had t sons:**	*1417*
Lk	16:13	**No servant can serve t masters:**	*1417*
Lk	17:35	**T women shall be grinding**	*1417*
Lk	18:10	**T men went up into the temple to**	*1417*
Lk	21:2	widow casting in thither t mites	*1417*
Lk	24:4	t men stood by them in shining	*1417*
Jn	6:7	T hundred pennyworth of bread	*2250*
Jn	6:9	barley loaves, and t small fishes:	*1417*
Jn	8:17	**that the testimony of t men is**	*1417*
Jn	19:18	crucified him, and t other with him,	*1417*
Jn	20:12	And seeth t angels in white sitting,	*1417*
Ac	1:10	t men stood by them in white	*1417*
Ac	12:6	was sleeping between t soldiers,	*1417*
2Co	13:1	the mouth of t or three witnesses	*1417*
Gal	4:22	Abraham had t sons, the one by a	*1417*
Gal	4:24	for these are the t covenants; the	*1417*
Eph	5:31	wife, and they t shall be one flesh.	*1417*
Php	1:23	For I am in a strait betwixt t,	*1417*
1Ti	5:19	but before t or three witnesses	*1417*
Heb	6:18	That by t immutable things, in	*1417*
Heb	10:28	mercy under t or three witnesses:	*1417*
Rev	2:12	**the sharp sword with t edges;**	*1366*
Rev	9:12	there come t woes more hereafter.	*1417*
Rev	9:16	t hundred thousand thousand:	*1417*
Rev	11:3	give power unto my t witnesses,	*1417*
Rev	11:4	the t candlesticks standing before	*1417*
Rev	12:14	given t wings of a great eagle,	*1417*
Rev	13:5	to continue forty and t months.	*1417*
Rev	13:11	and he had t horns like a lamb,	*1417*

TWOEDGED

Ps	149:6	and a t sword in their hand;	6374
Pr	5:4	wormwood, sharp as a t sword	6310
Heb	4:12	and sharper than any t sword,	*1366*
Rev	1:16	of his mouth went a sharp t sword:	*1366*

TWOFOLD

Mt	23:15	**make him t more the child of hell**	*1366*

TWO-HUNDRED See TWO and HUNDRED.

TWO-THOUSAND See TWO and THOUSAND.

U

UNACCUSTOMED See also ACCUSTOMED.
Jer 31:18 as a bullock **u** to the yoke: 3808, 3925

UNADVISEDLY
Ps 106:33 so that he spake **u** with his lips 981

UNAWARES
Ge 31:20 Jacob stole away **u** to Laban 3820, 3824
Nu 35:15 that killeth any person **u** may flee. 7684
Jos 20:9 killeth any person at **u** might flee 7684
Ps 35:8 destruction come upon him at **u**; 3045
Lk 21:34 **and so that day come upon you u** *160*
Gal 2:4 of false brethren **u** brought in *3920*
Heb 13:2 some have entertained angels **u**. *2990*
Jude 4 there are certain men crept in **u**, ... *3921*

UNBELIEF See also BELIEF.
Mt 13:58 works there because of their **u**. *570*
Mt 17:20 said unto them, **Because of your u**. *570*
Mk 6:6 he marvelled because of their **u** *570*
Mk 9:24 Lord, I believe; help thou mine **u** *570*
Mk 16:14 upbraided them with their **u** and *570*
Ro 3:3 shall their **u** make the faith of God. *570*
Ro 4:20 at the promise of God through **u**; *570*
Ro 11:20 because of **u** they were broken off, ... *570*
Ro 11:32 God hath concluded them all in **u**, ... *543*
1Ti 1:13 because I did it ignorantly in **u** *570*
Heb 3:12 be in any of you an evil heart of **u** *570*
Heb 3:19 they could not enter in because of **u** *570*
Heb 4:6 entered not in because of **u**: *543*
Heb 4:11 fall after the same example of **u** *543*

UNBELIEVERS See also BELIEVERS.
Lk 12:46 **him his portion with the u** *571*
1Co 6:6 with brother, and that before the **u**. *571*
1Co 14:23 in those that are unlearned, or **u**. *571*
2Co 6:14 unequally yoked together with **u**. *571*

UNBELIEVING See also BELIEVING.
Ac 14:2 the **u** Jews stirred up the Gentiles, ... *544*
1Co 7:14 the **u** husband is sanctified by the. *571*
1Co 7:14 **u** wife is sanctified by the husband: *571*
1Co 7:15 But if the **u** depart, let him depart *572*
Tit 1:15 are denied and **u** is nothing pure; *571*
Rev 21:8 But the fearful, and **u**, and the. *571*

UNBLAMEABLE See also BLAME.
Col 1:22 to present you holy and **u** and. *299*
1Th 3:13 stablish your hearts **u** in holiness *299*

UNBLAMEABLY
1Th 2:10 justly and **u** we behaved ourselves *274*

UNCERTAIN
1Co 14:8 For if the trumpet gave an **u** sound *82*
1Ti 6:17 nor trust in **u** riches, but in the. *83*

UNCERTAINLY
1Co 9:26 I therefore so run, not as **u**; so fight *82*

UNCHANGEABLE
Heb 7:24 ever, hath an **u** priesthood *532*

UNCIRCUMCISED
Ge 17:14 And the **u** man child whose flesh 6189
Ge 34:14 give our sister to one that is **u**; 6190
Ex 6:30 I am of **u** lips, and how shall. 6189
Ex 12:48 for no **u** person shall eat thereof. 6189
Le 26:41 if then their **u** hearts be humbled, ... 6189
Jos 5:7 for they were **u**, because. 6189
1Sa 17:26 who is this **u** Philistine, that he. 6189
1Ch 10:4 lest these **u** come and abuse me 6189
Jer 6:10 ear is **u**, and they cannot hearken: 6189
Jer 9:26 house of Israel are **u** in the heart 6189
Eze 32:24 are gone down **u** into the nether 6189
Eze 32:30 and they lie **u** with them that be. 6189
Eze 44:9 stranger, **u** in heart, nor **u** in flesh, ... 6189
Ac 7:51 Ye stiffnecked and **u** in heart and *564*
Ac 11:3 Thou wentest in to men **u** *203, 2192*
Ro 4:11 which he had yet being **u**. . . . *1722, 3588, 203*
Ro 4:12 which he had being yet **u**. . . . *1722, 3588, 203*
1Co 7:18 let him not become **u** *1986*

UNCIRCUMCISION
Ro 2:26 if the **u** keep the righteousness *203*
Ro 2:27 And shall not **u** which is by nature, ... *203*
Ro 3:30 by faith, and **u** through faith. *203*
1Co 7:19 is nothing, and **u** is nothing, ... *203*
Gal 2:7 gospel of the **u** was committed unto *203*
Gal 5:6 availeth any thing, nor **u**; but faith *203*
Gal 6:15 availeth any thing, nor **u**, but a *203*

UNCLEAN
Le 7:21 soul that shall touch any **u** thing. 2932
Le 11:26 cheweth the cud, are **u** unto you: 2931
Le 11:27 on all four, those are **u** unto you: 2931
Le 11:47 a difference between the **u** and 2931
Le 12:2 then she shall be **u** seven days; 2930
Le 12:5 then she shall be **u** two weeks,. 2930
Le 13:3 on him, and pronounce him **u** 2930
Le 13:45 upper lip, and shall cry, **U**, **u** 2931
Le 14:57 To teach when it is **u**, and when 2931
Le 15:16 be **u** until the even. 2930
Le 15:24 him, he shall be **u** seven days; 2930
Le 20:21 brother's wife, it is an **u** thing: 5079
Nu 6:7 not make himself **u** for his father,. 2930
Nu 19:19 shall sprinkle upon the **u** on the. 2931
Dt 12:15 **u** and the clean may eat thereof, ... 2931
Dt 14:7 therefore they are **u** unto you.. 2931
Dt 14:8 not the cud, it is **u** unto you: 2931
Dt 14:10 ye may not eat; it is **u** unto you. 2931
Dt 14:19 creeping thing that flieth is **u** unto 2931
Jgs 13:14 strong drink, nor eat any **u** thing: 2932
Ecc 9:2 and to the clean, and to the **u**; 2931
Isa 6:5 because I am a man of **u** lips, and 2931
Isa 6:5 in the midst of a people of **u** lips: 2931
Eze 22:26 between the **u** and the clean, ... 2931
Zec 13:2 **u** spirit to pass out of the land 2932
Mt 10:1 gave them power against **u** spirits, ... *169*
Mt 12:43 **the u spirit is gone out of a man,** *169*
Mk 1:27 commandeth he even the **u** spirits, ... *169*
Mk 3:30 they said, He hath an **u** spirit, ... *169*
Mk 5:2 of the tombs a man with an **u** spirit, ... *169*
Mk 5:8 **out of the man, thou u spirit.** *169*
Mk 6:7 gave them power over **u** spirits;. *169*
Mk 7:25 young daughter had an **u** spirit, ... *169*
Lk 4:36 power he commandeth the **u** spirits, ... *169*
Lk 6:18 that were vexed with **u** spirits: *169*
Lk 8:29 commanded the **u** spirit to come *169*
Lk 9:42 Jesus rebuked the **u** spirit, and *169*
Lk 11:24 **the u spirit is gone out of a man,** *169*

Ac 5:16 which were vexed with **u** spirits:........ *169*
Ac 8:7 For **u** spirits, crying with loud voice, ... *169*
Ac 10:14 any thing that is common or **u** *169*
Ac 10:28 not call any man common or **u**......... *169*
Ac 11:8 nothing common or **u** hath at any...... *169*
Ro 14:14 that there is nothing **u** of itself:........ *2839*
1Co 7:14 else were your children **u**; but *169*
2Co 6:17 Lord, and touch not the **u** thing;......... *169*
Eph 5:5 nor **u** person, nor covetous man, ... *169*
Heb 9:13 of an heifer sprinkling the **u**,.......... *2840*
Rev 16:13 I saw three **u** spirits like frogs *169*
Rev 18:2 a cage of every **u** and hateful bird. *169*

UNCLEANNESS
Le 5:3 Or if he touch the **u** of man 2932
Le 7:20 the Lord, having his **u** upon him,...... 2932
Le 15:31 they die not in their **u**, when they...... 2932
Le 22:3 having his **u** upon him, that soul 2932
Nu 5:19 if thou hast not gone aside to **u** 2932
Dt 24:1 he hath found some **u** in her: 6172
Zec 13:1 of Jerusalem for sin and **u** 5079
Mt 23:27 of dead men's bones, and of all u....... *167*
Ro 1:24 God also gave them up to **u** through *167*
Ro 6:19 yielded your members servants to **u**..... *167*
2Co 12:21 and have not repented of the **u** and *167*
Gal 5:19 are these; Adultery, fornication, **u**, ... *167*
Eph 4:19 to work all **u** with greediness........... *167*
Eph 5:3 But fornication, and all **u**, or.......... *167*
Col 3:5 upon the earth; fornication, **u**, ... *167*
1Th 2:3 not of deceit, nor of **u**, nor in guile:..... *167*
1Th 4:7 For God hath not called us unto **u**, ... *167*
2Pe 2:10 after the flesh in the lust of **u**, ... *3394*

UNCLOTHED
2Co 5:4 not for that we would be **u**, but *1562*

UNCOMELY
1Co 7:36 behaveth himself **u** toward a virgin,..... *807*
1Co 12:23 our **u** parts have more abundant *809*

UNCONDEMNED
Ac 16:37 They have beaten us openly **u**, ... *178*
Ac 22:25 a man that is a Roman, and **u**? *178*

UNCORRUPTIBLE See also INCORRUPTIBLE.
Ro 1:23 changed the glory of the **u** God *862*

UNCORRUPTNESS
Tit 2:7 in doctrine shewing **u**, gravity, ... *90*

UNCOVER
Le 10:6 **U** not your heads, neither rend........ 6544
Le 18:6 kin to him, to **u** their nakedness: 1540
Le 21:10 shall not **u** his head, nor rend his...... 6544
Nu 5:18 Lord, and **u** the woman's head,........ 6544
Ru 3:4 and **u** his feet, and lay thee down; 1540
Isa 47:2 make bare the leg, **u** the thigh, ... 1540
Zep 2:14 for he shall **u** the cedar work.......... 6168

UNCOVERED
Ge 9:21 and he was **u** within his tent 1540
Le 20:18 and she hath **u** the fountain of her..... 1540
Ru 3:7 and **u** his feet, and laid her down. 1540
2Sa 6:20 who **u** himself to day in the eyes of 1540
Isa 20:4 foot, even with their buttocks **u**,........ 2834
Isa 47:3 Thy nakedness shall be **u**, yea,......... 1540
Jer 49:10 bare, I have **u** his secret places, ... 1540
1Co 11:5 or prophesieth with her head **u**......... *177*
1Co 11:13 that a woman pray unto God **u**?........ *177*

UNCOVERETH
Dt 27:20 because he **u** his father's skirt:......... 1540
2Sa 6:20 fellows shamelessly **u** himself!......... 1540

UNCTION
1Jn 2:20 ye have an **u** from the Holy One, ... *5545*

UNDEFILED
Ps 119:1 Blessed are the **u** in the way........... 8549
SS 5:2 sister, my love, my dove, my **u**......... 8535
Heb 7:26 who is holy, harmless, **u**, separate....... *283*
Heb 13:4 is honourable in all, and the bed **u**...... *283*
Jas 1:27 Pure religion and **u** before God......... *283*
1Pe 1:4 an inheritance incorruptible, and **u**,..... *283*

UNDER
Ge 1:9 waters **u** the heaven be gathered....... 8478
Ge 6:17 the breath of life, from **u** heaven; 8478
Ge 24:9 servant put his hand **u** the thigh of 8478
Ex 20:4 or that is in the water **u** the earth: 8478
Dt 2:25 that are **u** the whole heaven, ... 8478
Dt 4:11 near and stood **u** the mountain;....... 8478
Dt 9:14 out their name from **u** heaven:........ 8478
Dt 12:2 the hills, and **u** every green tree:....... 8478
Dt 29:20 blot out his name from **u** heaven....... 8478
Jgs 9:29 to God this people were **u** my hand!
Ru 2:12 **u** whose wings thou art come to....... 8478
2Sa 22:37 Thou hast enlarged my steps **u** me; 8478
1Ki 14:23 high hill, and **u** every green tree 8478
1Ki 18:25 of your gods, but put no fire **u**
2Ki 14:27 the name of Israel from **u** heaven: 8478
2Ki 16:17 off the brasen oxen that were **u** it, ... 8478
2Ki 17:7 from **u** the hand of Pharaoh king...... 8478
1Ch 17:1 the ark ... remaineth **u** curtains 8478
2Ch 28:4 the hills, and **u** every green tree 8478
Job 41:11 whatsoever is **u** the whole heaven is.... 8478
Ps 8:6 thou hast put all things **u** his feet: 8478
Ps 10:7 **u** his tongue is mischief and 8478
Ps 17:8 hide me **u** the shadow of thy wings,
Ps 36:7 their trust **u** the shadow of thy wings
Ps 91:1 shall abide **u** the shadow of the
Ps 91:4 and **u** his wings shalt thou trust:....... 8478
Ecc 1:9 there is no new thing **u** the sun........ 8478
Ecc 2:11 and there was no profit **u** the sun...... 8478
Ecc 2:19 shewed myself wise **u** the sun.......... 8478
Ecc 3:1 time to every purpose **u** the heaven; ... 3478
Ecc 3:16 **u** the sun the place of judgment, ... 8478
Ecc 5:13 evil which I have seen **u** the sun, ... 8478
Ecc 6:1 evil which I have seen **u** the sun, ... 8478
Ecc 6:12 what shall be after him **u** the sun? 8478
Ecc 7:6 the crackling of thorns **u** the pot,...... 8478
Ecc 8:9 every work that is done **u** the sun: 8478
Ecc 8:17 the work that is done **u** the sun:....... 8478
Ecc 9:3 all things that are done **u** the sun, ... 8478
Ecc 9:6 any thing that is done **u** the sun. 8478
Ecc 9:11 and saw **u** the sun, that the race is 8478
Ecc 10:5 evil which I have seen **u** the sun, ... 8478
SS 2:6 His left hand is **u** my head, and 8478
SS 4:11 honey and milk are **u** thy tongue;...... 8478
SS 8:3 His left hand should be **u** my head, ... 8478
Isa 28:15 **u** falsehood have we hid ourselves:
Jer 3:6 and **u** every green tree, and....... 413, 8478
Jer 10:11 earth, and from **u** these heavens 8460
La 3:66 them in anger from **u** the heavens 8478
Eze 6:13 **u** every thick oak, the place where 8478
Eze 10:21 hands of a man was **u** their wings...... 8478
Eze 31:17 that dwelt **u** his shadow in the midst

Da	7:27	the kingdom **u** the whole heaven,	8460
Da	9:12	for **u** the whole heaven hath not	8478
Jnh	4:5	booth, and sat **u** it in the shadow,	8478
Mt	5:13	**and to be trodden u foot of men**	*2662*
Mt	5:15	**a candle, and put it u a bushel,**	*5259*
Mt	8:9	For I am a man **u** authority,	*5259*
Mt	23:37	**her chickens u her wings, and**	*5259*
Mk	7:28	yet the dogs **u** the table eat of the	*5270*
Lk	11:33	**neither u a bushel, but on a**	*5259*
Lk	13:34	**gather her brood u her wings,**	*5259*
Lk	17:24	**out of the one part u heaven,**	*5259*
Jn	1:48	**when thou wast u the fig tree, I**	*5259*
Ac	2:5	out of every nation **u** heaven	*5259*
Ac	4:12	none other name **u** heaven given	*5259*
Ac	23:12	and bound themselves **u** a curse,	*332*
Ro	3:9	Gentiles, that they are all **u** sin;	*5259*
Ro	3:19	saith to them who are **u** the law:	*1722*
Ro	6:15	we are not **u** the law, but **u** grace?	*5259*
Ro	7:14	but I am carnal, sold **u** sin.	*5259*
Ro	16:20	bruise Satan **u** your feet shortly	*5259*
1Co	9:20	that are **u** the law, as **u** the law,	*5259*
1Co	9:27	I keep **u** my body, and bring it	*5299*
1Co	15:25	hath put all enemies **u** his feet	*5259*
1Co	15:27	hath put all enemies **u** his feet	*5259*
Gal	3:22	hath concluded all **u** sin, that	*5259*
Gal	4:4	made of a woman, made **u** the law,	*5259*
Eph	1:22	And hath put all things **u** his feet,	*5259*
Heb	2:8	all things in subjection **u** his feet	*5270*
Heb	10:29	trodden **u** foot the Son of God,	*2662*
1Pe	5:6	**u** the mighty hand of God,	*5259*
Jude	6	in everlasting chains **u** darkness	*5259*
Rev	6:9	I saw **u** the altar the souls of them	*5270*
Rev	11:2	shall they tread **u** foot forty and two	
Rev	12:1	the sun, and the moon **u** her feet,	*5270*

UNDERNEATH

Dt	33:27	**u** are the everlasting arms:	8478

UNDERSTAND

Ge	11:7	may not **u** one another's speech	8085
Ge	41:15	canst **u** a dream to interpret it:	8085
1Ch	28:19	Lord made me **u** in writing by his	7919
Ne	8:7	caused the people to **u** the law:	995
Job	6:24	me to **u** wherein I have erred	995
Ps	19:12	Who can **u** his errors? cleanse	995
Ps	82:5	They knew not, neither will they **u**;	995
Ps	92:6	not; neither doth a fool **u** this.	995
Ps	107:43	**u** the lovingkindness of the Lord	995
Ps	119:100	I **u** more than the ancients, because	995
Pr	1:6	To **u** a proverb, and the	995
Pr	2:5	shalt thou **u** the fear of the Lord,	995
Pr	2:9	Then shalt thou **u** righteousness,	995
Pr	8:5	O ye simple, **u** wisdom: and, ye	995
Pr	14:8	of the prudent is to **u** his way:	995
Pr	19:25	and he will **u** knowledge	995
Pr	20:24	how can a man then **u** his own way?	995
Pr	28:5	they that seek the Lord **u** all things	995
Pr	29:19	for though he **u** he will not answer	995
Isa	6:10	and **u** with the heart, and convert,	995
Isa	43:10	believe me, and **u** that I am he:	995
Isa	44:18	their hearts, that they cannot **u**	7919
Isa	56:11	they are shepherds that cannot **u**	995
Da	9:13	our iniquities, and **u** thy truth	7919
Da	9:25	Know therefore and **u**, that from	7919
Da	10:12	that thou didst set thine heart to **u**,	995
Da	12:10	and none of the wicked shall **u**;	995
Hos	4:14	people that doth not **u** shall fall	995
Mic	4:12	Lord, neither **u** they his counsel:	995
Mt	13:13	**they hear not, neither do they u.**	*4920*
Mt	15:10	and said unto them, Hear, and **u**:	*4920*
Mt	15:17	**Do not ye yet u, that whatsoever**	*3539*
Mt	16:9	**ye not yet u, neither remember**	*3539*
Mt	16:11	**How is it that ye do not u that I**	*3539*
Mt	24:15	**place (whoso readeth, let him u:)**	*3539*
Mk	4:12	**hearing they may hear, and not u**	*4920*
Mk	7:14	**unto me every one of you, and u:**	*4920*
Mk	8:17	**perceive ye not yet, neither u?**	*4920*
Mk	8:21	**them, How is it that ye do not u?**	*4920*
Mk	13:14	**(let him that readeth u,) then let**	*3539*
Lk	8:10	**and hearing they might not u**	*4920*
Lk	24:45	that they might **u** the scriptures	*4920*
Jn	8:43	**Why do ye not u my speech?**	*1097*
Jn	12:40	nor **u** with their heart, and be	*3539*
Ac	28:26	ye shall hear, and shall not **u**	*4920*
Ro	15:21	they that have not heard shall **u**	*4920*
1Co	12:3	Wherefore I give you to **u**, that no	*1107*
1Co	13:2	of prophecy, and **u** all mysteries,	*1492*
Eph	3:4	**u** my knowledge in mystery of	*3539*
Php	1:12	I would ye should **u**, brethren,	*1097*
Heb	11:3	Through faith we **u** that the	*3539*
2Pe	2:12	speak evil of things that they **u** not;	*50*

UNDERSTANDEST

Job	15:9	what **u** thou, which is not in us?	995
Ps	139:2	thou **u** my thought afar off	995
Ac	8:30	said, **U** thou what thou readest?	*1097*

UNDERSTANDETH

1Ch	28:9	and **u** all the imaginations of the	995
Ps	49:20	Man that is in honour, and **u** not,	995
Pr	8:9	They are all plain to him that **u**,	995
Pr	14:6	knowledge is easy unto him that **u**,	995
Jer	9:24	that he **u** and knoweth me, that I	7919
Mt	13:19	**word of the kingdom, and u it**	*4920*
Mt	13:23	**he that heareth the word, and u**	*4920*
Ro	3:11	There is none that **u**, there is none	*4920*
1Co	14:2	for no man **u** him; howbeit in the	*191*
1Co	14:16	seeing he **u** not what thou sayest?	*1492*

UNDERSTANDING

Ex	31:3	of God, in wisdom, and in **u**,	8394
Ex	35:31	spirit of God, in wisdom, in **u**,	8394
Dt	1:13	Take you wise men, and **u**, and	995
1Ki	3:9	Give … thy servant an **u** heart	8085
1Ki	3:12	given thee a wise and an **u** heart;	995
1Ki	4:29	God gave Solomon wisdom and **u**	8394
1Ch	12:32	were men that had **u** of the times,	998
2Ch	26:5	who had **u** in the visions of God:	995
Ezr	8:18	us they brought us a man of **u**,	7922
Ne	8:2	and all that could hear with **u**,	995
Ne	10:28	having knowledge, and having **u**;	995
Job	12:3	But I have **u** as well as you; I am	3824
Job	17:4	thou hast hid their heart from **u**:	7922
Job	34:10	hearken unto me, ye men of **u**:	3824
Job	38:4	the earth? declare, if thou hast **u**.	998
Job	38:36	or who hath given **u** to the heart?	998
Ps	111:10	a good **u** have all they that do his	7922
Ps	119:99	more **u** than all my teachers:	7919
Ps	119:104	Through thy precepts I get **u**:	995
Ps	147:5	of great power: his **u** is infinite	8394
Pr	1:5	a man of **u** shall attain unto wise	995
Pr	2:2	and apply thine heart to **u**;	8394
Pr	2:6	mouth cometh knowledge and **u**	8394

Pr 3:5 and lean not unto thine own **u** ... 998
Pr 3:19 earth; by **u** hath he established the ... 8394
Pr 4:7 and with all thy getting get **u**. ... 998
Pr 6:32 adultery with a woman lacketh **u**: ... 3820
Pr 7:7 youths, a young man void of **u** ... 3820
Pr 9:10 and the knowledge of the holy is **u**. ... 998
Pr 10:13 the back of him that is void of **u**. ... 3820
Pr 11:12 but a man of **u** holdeth his peace ... 8394
Pr 12:11 vain persons is void of **u**. ... 3820
Pr 14:29 is slow to wrath is of great **u**:. ... 8394
Pr 16:16 **u** rather to be chosen than silver! ... 998
Pr 18:2 A fool hath no delight in **u**, but ... 8394
Pr 21:30 no wisdom nor **u** nor counsel. ... 8394
Pr 24:30 vineyard of the man void of **u**; ... 3820
Pr 28:11 the poor that hath **u** searcheth him ... 995
Pr 28:16 The prince that wanteth **u** is also ... 8394
Ecc 9:11 nor yet riches to men of **u**, nor yet ... 995
Isa 11:2 spirit of wisdom and **u**, the spirit ... 998
Isa 29:16 him that framed it, He had no **u**? ... 995
Isa 40:28 there is no searching of his **u**. ... 8394
Jer 5:21 O foolish people, and without **u**; ... 3820
Jer 51:15 stretched out the heaven by his **u** ... 8394
Da 1:4 in knowledge, and **u** science, ... 995
Da 1:17 Daniel had **u** in all visions and ... 995
Da 1:20 in all matters of wisdom and **u**, ... 998
Da 4:34 mine **u** returned unto me, and I ... 4486
Da 9:22 come forth to give thee skill and **u** ... 998
Da 10:1 the thing, and had **u** of the vision. ... 998
Hos 13:2 idols according to their own **u**, ... 8394
Mt 15:16 said, **Are ye also yet without u?** ... *801*
Mk 7:18 them, **Are ye so without u also?** ... *801*
Mk 12:33 all the heart, and with all the **u**, ... *4907*
Lk 1:3 having had perfect **u** of all things ... *3877*
Lk 2:47 him were astonished at his **u** ... *4907*
Lk 24:45 Then opened he their **u**, that they ... *3563*
1Co 1:19 to nothing the **u** of the prudent ... *4907*
1Co 14:14 prayeth, but my **u** is unfruitful. ... *3563*
1Co 14:15 and I will pray with the **u** also: ... *3563*
1Co 14:19 rather speak five words with my **u**, ... *3563*
1Co 14:20 be ye children, but in **u** be men. ... *5424*
Eph 1:18 eyes of your **u** being enlightened; ... *1271*
Eph 5:17 **u** what the will of the Lord is. ... *4920*
Php 4:7 peace of God, which passeth all **u**, ... *3563*
1Ti 1:7 **u** neither what they say, nor. ... *4920*
2Ti 2:7 Lord give thee **u** in all things. ... *4907*
1Jn 5:20 is come, and hath given us an **u**, ... *1271*
Rev 13:18 him that hath **u** count the number. ... *3563*

UNDERSTOOD
Ge 43:23 knew not that Joseph **u** them; ... 8085
1Sa 4:6 they **u** that the ark of the Lord ... 3045
Job 42:3 have I uttered that I **u** not; ... 995
Isa 40:21 ye not **u** from the foundations of ... 995
Da 8:27 at the vision, but none **u** it. ... 995
Da 9:2 I Daniel **u** by books the number of ... 995
Mt 13:51 **them, Have ye u all these things?** ... *4920*
Mk 9:32 But they **u** not that saying, and ... *50*
Lk 2:50 **u** not the saying which he spake ... *4920*
Lk 9:45 they **u** not this saying, and it was ... *50*
Lk 18:34 And they **u** none of these things: ... *4920*
Jn 12:16 These things **u** not his disciples at ... *1097*
Ro 1:20 **u** by the things that are made, ... *3539*
1Co 13:11 I **u** as a child, I thought as a child: ... *5426*
2Pe 3:16 are some things hard to be **u**, ... *1425*

UNDERTAKE
Isa 38:14 Lord, I am oppressed; **u** for me. ... 6148

UNDERTOOK
Est 9:23 Jews **u** to do as they had begun, ... 6901

UNDO
Isa 58:6 to **u** the heavy burdens, and to let ... 5425
Zep 3:19 that time I will **u** all that afflict ... 6213

UNDONE
Jos 11:15 he left nothing **u** of all that the ... 5493
Isa 6:5 Woe is me! for I am **u**; because ... 1820
Mt 23:23 **done, and not to leave the other u**
Lk 11:42 **done, and not to leave the other u**

UNEQUAL See also EQUAL.
Eze 18:25 are not your ways **u**? ... 3808, 8505

UNEQUALLY
2Co 6:14 not **u** yoked together with ... *2086*

UNFAITHFUL See also FAITHFUL.
Pr 25:19 Confidence in an **u** man in time of ... 898

UNFAITHFULLY See also FAITHFULLY.
Ps 78:57 and dealt **u** like their fathers: ... 898

UNFEIGNED
2Co 6:6 by the Holy Ghost, by love **u**, ... *505*
1Ti 1:5 of a good conscience, and of faith **u**. ... *505*
2Ti 1:5 the **u** faith that is in thee, which ... *505*
1Pe 1:22 Spirit unto **u** love of the brethren, ... *505*

UNFRUITFUL
Mt 13:22 **the word, and he becometh u** ... *175*
Mk 4:19 **choke the word, and it becometh u** ... *175*
1Co 14:14 but my understanding is **u**. ... *175*
Eph 5:11 with the **u** works of darkness, ... *175*
Tit 3:14 necessary uses, that they be not **u**. ... *175*
2Pe 1:8 nor **u** in the knowledge of our Lord. ... *175*

UNGODLINESS
Ro 1:18 revealed from heaven against all **u** ... *763*
Ro 11:26 and shall turn away **u** from Jacob: ... *763*
2Ti 2:16 for they will increase unto more **u** ... *763*
Tit 2:12 denying **u** and worldly lusts, we ... *763*

UNGODLY
2Sa 22:5 floods of **u** men made me afraid; ... 1100
2Ch 19:2 Shouldest thou help the **u**, and ... 7563
Job 34:18 wicked? and to princes, Ye are **u**? ... 7563
Ps 1:1 walketh not in the counsel of the **u**, ... 7563
Pr 19:28 An **u** witness scorneth judgment: ... 1100
Ro 4:5 on him that justifieth the **u**, his. ... *765*
Ro 5:6 in due time Christ died for the **u** ... *765*
1Ti 1:9 for the **u** and for sinners, for ... *765*
1Pe 4:18 where shall the **u** and the sinner ... *765*
2Pe 2:6 unto those that after should live **u**; ... *764*
Jude 4 **u** men, turning the grace of our God ... *765*
Jude 15 to convince all that are **u** among. ... *763*
Jude 18 walk after their own **u** lusts. ... *763*

UNHOLY
Le 10:10 difference between holy and **u**, ... 2455
1Ti 1:9 for **u** and profane, for murderers of ... *462*
2Ti 3:2 to parents, unthankful, **u**, ... *462*
Heb 10:29 he was sanctified, an **u** thing, ... *2839*

UNICORN
Nu 23:22 as it were the strength of an **u** ... 7214

Nu 24:8 as it were the strength of an **u** 7214
Job 39:10 Canst thou bind the **u** with his 7214

UNICORNS
Dt 33:17 his horns are like the horns of **u** 7214

UNITE
Ps 86:11 **u** my heart to fear thy name. 3161

UNITY
Ps 133:1 brethren to dwell together in **u**! 3162
Eph 4:3 to keep the **u** of the Spirit in the *1775*
Eph 4:13 we all come in the **u** of the faith,. *1775*

UNJUST
Pr 29:27 An **u** man is an abomination to 5766
Zep 3:5 not; but the **u** knoweth no shame. 5767
Mt 5:45 **rain on the just and on the u**. *94*
Lk 16:10 **is u in the least is u also in much** *94*
Lk 18:6 **said, Hear what the u judge saith** *93*
Lk 18:11 **as other men are, extortioners, u**,. *94*
Ac 24:15 of the dead, both of the just and **u** *94*
1Co 6:1 go to law before the **u**, and not *94*
1Pe 3:18 suffered for sins, the just for the **u**, ... *94*
2Pe 2:9 to reserve the **u** unto the day of. *94*
Rev 22:11 He that is **u**, let him be **u** still:. 91

UNJUSTLY
Ps 82:2 How long will ye judge **u**, and. 5766
Isa 26:10 of uprightness will he deal **u** 5765

UNKNOWN
Ac 17:23 this inscription, To The **U** God. *57*
1Co 14:2 he that speaketh in an **u** tongue

UNLAWFUL See also LAWFUL.
Ac 10:28 an **u** thing for a man that is a Jew. *111*
2Pe 2:8 day to day with their **u** deeds:) *459*

UNLEARNED See also LEARNED.
Ac 4:13 that they were **u** and ignorant men, ... *62*
1Co 14:16 the **u** say Amen at thy giving of. *2399*
2Ti 2:23 foolish and **u** questions avoid,. *521*
2Pe 3:16 that are **u** and unstable wrest, ... *261*

UNLEAVENED See also LEAVENED.
Ge 19:3 did bake **u** bread, and they did 4682
Ex 12:15 Seven days shall ye eat **u** bread;. 4682
Ex 12:17 shall observe the feast of **u** bread;. 4682
Le 2:4 **u** cakes of fine flour mingled with 4682
Nu 9:11 eat it with **u** bread and bitter. 4682
Jgs 6:21 touched the flesh and the **u** cakes; 4682
Ezr 6:22 the feast of **u** bread seven days 4682
Mt 26:17 first day of the feast of **u** bread *106*
Mk 14:1 of the passover, and of **u** bread: *106*
Mk 14:12 the first day of **u** bread, when they *106*
Lk 22:1 Now the feast of **u** bread drew nigh, ... *106*
1Co 5:8 the **u** bread of sincerity and truth. *106*

UNLESS
Ps 27:13 **u** I had believed to see the 3884
Ps 94:17 **U** the Lord had been my help, my 3884
Ps 119:92 **U** thy law had been my delights, I. 3884
Pr 4:16 **u** they cause some to fall. 518, 3808
1Co 15:2 **u** ye have believed in vain. *1622, 1508*

UNLOOSE See also LOOSE.
Mk 1:7 not worthy to stoop down and **u** *3089*
Lk 3:16 whose shoes I am not worthy to **u** *3089*
Jn 1:27 shoe's latchet I am not worthy to **u** *3089*

UNMARRIED See also MARRIED.
1Co 7:11 and if she depart, let her remain **u**,. *22*
1Co 7:32 He that is **u** careth for the things *22*
1Co 7:34 The **u** woman careth for the things *22*

UNMERCIFUL See also MERCIFUL.
Ro 1:31 natural affection, implacable, **u**. *415*

UNMINDFUL See also MINDFUL.
Dt 32:18 Rock that begat thee thou art **u**, ... 7876

UNMOVEABLE
1Co 15:58 brethren, be ye stedfast, **u**, ... *277*

UNPERFECT
Ps 139:16 did see my substance, yet being **u**;

UNPREPARED
2Co 9:4 come with me, and find you **u**, ... *552*

UNPROFITABLE
Mt 25:30 **cast ye the u servant into outer**. *888*
Lk 17:10 **you, say, We are u servants:**. *888*
Ro 3:12 way, they are together become **u**; *889*
Tit 3:9 the law; for they are **u** and vain. *512*
Phm 11 Which in time past was to thee **u**,. *890*
Heb 13:17 with grief: for that is **u** for you. *255*

UNPROFITABLENESS
Heb 7:18 for the weakness and **u** thereof. *512*

UNPUNISHED
Pr 11:21 hand, the wicked shall not be **u**: 5352
Pr 16:5 join in hand, he shall not be **u** 5352
Pr 17:5 is glad at calamities shall not be **u**. 5352
Pr 19:5 A false witness shall not be **u**, ... 5352
Pr 19:9 A false witness shall not be **u**, ... 5352
Jer 25:29 Ye shall not be **u**; for I will call for 5352
Jer 46:28 yet will I not leave thee wholly **u**. 5352

UNQUENCHABLE
Mt 3:12 will burn up the chaff with **u** fire *762*
Lk 3:17 the chaff he will burn with fire **u** *762*

UNREASONABLE See also REASONABLE.
Ac 25:27 seemeth to me **u** to send a prisoner, ...249
2Th 3:2 delivered from **u** and wicked men:. *824*

UNREBUKEABLE See also REBUKE.
1Ti 6:14 commandment without spot, **u**, ... *423*

UNREPROVEABLE See also REPROVE.
Col 1:22 unblameable and **u** in his sight: *410*

UNRIGHTEOUS See also RIGHTEOUS.
Ex 23:1 the wicked to be an **u** witness, ... 2555
Isa 10:1 unto them that decree **u** decrees, ... 205
Isa 55:7 way, and the **u** man his thoughts:. 205
Lk 16:11 **not been faithful in the u mammon**. *94*
Ro 3:5 Is God **u** who taketh vengeance?. *94*
1Co 6:9 **u** shall not inherit the kingdom of *94*
Heb 6:10 God is not **u** to forget your work *94*

UNRIGHTEOUSLY See also RIGHTEOUSLY.
Dt 25:16 all that do **u**, are an abomination 5766

UNRIGHTEOUSNESS See also UNRIGHTEOUSNESS.
Le 19:15 Ye shall do no **u** in judgment:. 5766
Ps 92:15 my rock, and there is no **u** in him, ... 5766
Jer 22:13 that buildeth his house by **u**,. 3808, 6664
Lk 16:9 **friends of the mammon of u**; *93*
Jn 7:18 **same is true, and no u is in him.** *93*

Ro	1:18	of men, who hold the truth in **u**;	*93*
Ro	2:8	but obey **u**, indignation and wrath,	*93*
Ro	3:5	if our **u** commend the righteousness	*93*
Ro	6:13	as instruments of **u** unto sin:	*93*
Ro	9:14	we say then? Is there **u** with God?	*93*
2Co	6:14	hath righteousness with **u**?	*458*
2Th	2:10	deceivableness of **u** in them that	*93*
2Th	2:12	not the truth, but had pleasure in **u**,	*93*
Heb	8:12	**For I will be merciful to their u,**	*93*
2Pe	2:15	Bosor, who loved the wages of **u**;	*93*
1Jn	1:9	sins, and to cleanse us from all **u**.	*93*
1Jn	5:17	All **u** is sin: and there is a sin not	*93*

UNRULY See also **RULE.**

1Th	5:14	brethren, warn them that are **u**,	*813*
Tit	1:6	children not accused of riot or **u**	*506*
Tit	1:10	there are many **u** and vain talkers	*506*
Jas	3:8	it is an **u** evil, full of deadly poison.	*183*

UNSEARCHABLE

Job	5:9	doeth great things and **u**;	369, 2714
Ps	145:3	praised; and his greatness is **u**.	369, 2714
Pr	25:3	and the heart of kings is **u**.	369, 2714
Ro	11:33	how **u** are his judgments, and his	*419*
Eph	3:8	Gentiles the **u** riches of Christ;	*421*

UNSEEMLY See also **SEEMLY.**

Ro	1:27	with men working that which is **u**,	*808*
1Co	13:5	Doth not behave itself **u**, seeketh not	

UNSPEAKABLE

2Co	9:15	Thanks be unto God for his **u** gift	*411*
2Co	12:4	into paradise, and heard **u** words,	*731*
1Pe	1:8	with joy **u** and full of glory:	*412*

UNSPOTTED

Jas	1:27	to keep himself **u** from the world	*784*

UNSTABLE

Jas	1:8	A double minded man is **u** in all	*182*
2Pe	2:14	cease from sin; beguiling **u** souls:	*793*
2Pe	3:16	that are unlearned and **u** wrest,	*793*

UNSTOPPED

Isa	35:5	and the ears of the deaf shall be **u**	6605

UNTHANKFUL See also **THANKFUL.**

Lk	6:35	**is kind unto the u and to the evil.**	*884*
2Ti	3:2	disobedient to parents, **u**, unholy	*884*

UNTIL

Ge	8:7	**u** the waters were dried up from	5704
Ge	26:13	and grew **u** he became very great:	5704
Ge	27:45	**U** thy brother's anger turn	5704
Ge	29:8	**u** all the flocks be gathered	5704
Ge	32:24	with him **u** the breaking of the day	5704
Ex	12:10	nothing of it remain **u** … morning;	5704
Ex	16:20	but some … left of it u the morning	5704
Ex	17:12	**u** the going down of the sun	5704
Nu	11:20	**u** it come out at your nostrils, and	5704
Nu	35:28	**u** the death of the high priest:	5704
Dt	2:14	**u** all the generation of the men of	5704
Dt	9:21	even **u** it was as small as dust:	5704
Jos	1:15	**U** the Lord have given your brethren	5704
Jos	7:13	**u** ye take away the accursed thing	5704
Jos	20:6	**u** the death of the high priest that	5704
Jos	23:13	**u** ye perish from off this good land	5704
Ru	2:17	she gleaned in the field **u** even,	5704
Ru	3:14	she lay at his feet **u** the morning:	5704
1Sa	15:35	to see Saul **u** the day of his death:	5704
1Sa	30:4	**u** they had no more power to	5704, 834
2Sa	23:10	**u** his hand was weary	5704, 3588
1Ki	10:7	**u** I came, and mine eyes had seen.	5704
2Ki	7:3	another, Why sit we here **u** we die?	5704
2Ki	8:11	stedfastly, **u** he was ashamed:	5704
2Ki	17:20	**u** he had cast them out of his	5704
2Ch	36:21	**u** the land had enjoyed her sabbaths	5704
Ezr	4:5	even **u** the reign of Darius king of	5704
Job	26:10	**u** the day and night come to an	5704
Ps	73:17	**U** I went into the sanctuary of God;	5704
Ps	105:19	**U** the time that his word came:	5704
Ps	110:1	**u** I make thine enemies thy footstool	5704
Ps	123:2	**u** that he have mercy upon us	5704
Pr	7:18	take our fill of love **u** the morning:	5704
SS	2:17	**U** the day break, and the shadows	5704
SS	4:6	**U** the day break, and the shadows	5704
Isa	32:15	**U** the spirit be poured upon us	5704
Jer	30:24	**u** he hath performed the intents of	5704
Jer	52:34	a portion **u** the day of his death,	5704
Eze	21:27	more, **u** he come whose right it is;	5704
Da	7:22	**U** the Ancient of days came, and	5704
Da	7:25	**u** a time … times and the dividing.	5704
Mic	5:3	**u** the time … she which travaileth	5704
Mic	7:9	**u** he plead my cause, and execute	5704
Mt	2:15	was there **u** the death of Herod:	*2193*
Mt	11:12	**days of John the Baptist u now.**	*2193*
Mt	17:9	**u the Son of man be risen again**	*2193*
Mt	18:22	**times: but, U seventy times seven.**	*2193*
Mt	24:38	**u the day that Noe entered into**	*891*
Mt	26:29	**u that day when I drink it new**	*2193*
Mt	27:64	be made sure **u** the third day,	*2193*
Mt	28:15	among the Jews **u** this day	*3360*
Mk	14:25	**u that day that I drink it new**	*2193*
Mk	15:33	the whole land **u** the ninth hour	*2193*
Lk	13:35	**u the time … when ye shall say,**	*2193*
Lk	15:4	**that which is lost, u he find it?**	*2193*
Lk	17:27	**u the day that Noe entered into**	*891*
Lk	21:24	**u the times of the Gentiles be**	*891*
Lk	22:16	**u it be fulfilled in the kingdom of**	*2193*
Lk	22:18	**u the kingdom of God shall come.**	*2193*
Lk	23:44	over all the earth **u** the ninth hour	*2193*
Lk	24:49	**u ye be endued with power from**	*2193*
Jn	2:10	hast kept the good wine **u** now.	*2193*
Ac	1:2	**U** the day in which he was taken	*891*
Ac	2:35	**U** I make thy foes thy footstool	*2193*
Ac	3:21	**u** the times of restitution of all	*891*
Ro	5:13	(For **u** the law sin was in the world:	*891*
Ro	8:22	travaileth in pain together **u** now	*891*
Ro	11:25	**u** the fullness of the Gentiles	*891*
1Co	4:5	**u** the Lord come, who both will	*2193*
Gal	4:2	**u** the time appointed of the father	*891*
Gal	4:19	again **u** Christ be formed in you,	*891*
Eph	1:14	**u** … redemption of the purchased	*1519*
Php	1:6	it **u** the day of Jesus Christ:	*891*
2Th	2:7	let, **u** he be taken out of the way	*2193*
1Ti	6:14	**u** the appearing of our Lord	*3360*
Heb	1:13	**u** I make thine enemies thy	*2193*
Heb	9:10	them **u** the time of reformation	*3360*
Jas	5:7	**u** he receive the early and latter	*2193*
2Pe	1:19	**u** the day dawn, and the day star	*2193*
1Jn	2:9	brother, is in darkness even **u** now	*2193*
Rev	6:11	**u** their fellowservants also and	*2193*
Rev	17:17	**u** the words of God … be fulfilled	*891*
Rev	20:5	**u** … thousand years were finished	*2193*

UNTIMELY

Job	3:16	a hidden **u** birth I had not been;	5309
Ecc	6:3	that an **u** birth is better than he	5309

UNWASHEN

Mt	15:20	**to eat with u hands defileth not a.**	*449*
Mk	7:5	elders, but eat bread with **u** hands?	*449*

UNWISE

Dt	32:6	O foolish people and **u**?	3808, 2450
Ro	1:14	both to the wise, and to the **u**	*453*
Eph	5:17	Wherefore be ye not **u**, but	*878*

UNWITTINGLY

Le	22:14	if a man eat of the holy thing **u**,	7684
Jos	20:5	he smote his neighbour **u**,	1097, 1847

UNWORTHILY

1Co	11:29	For he that eateth and drinketh **u**,	*371*

UNWORTHY

Ac	13:46	**u** of everlasting life	*3756, 514*
1Co	6:2	**u** to judge the smallest matters?	*370*

UPBRAIDED

Mk	16:14	and **u** them with their unbelief	*3679*

UPBRAIDETH

Jas	1:5	to all men liberally, and **u** not;	*3679*

UPHARSIN (u-far´-sin) **See also PERES.**

Da	5:25	written, Mene, Mene, Tekel, **U**.	6537

UPHELD

Isa	63:5	unto me; and my fury, it **u** me	5564

UPHOLD

Ps	51:12	and **u** me with thy free spirit	5564
Pr	29:23	but honour shall **u** the humble in	8551
Isa	41:10	I will **u** thee with the right hand of	8551
Isa	42:1	Behold my servant, whom I **u**;	8551

UPHOLDETH

Ps	37:17	but the Lord **u** the righteous	5564
Ps	63:8	after thee: thy right hand **u** me	8551
Ps	145:14	Lord **u** all that fall, and raiseth	5564

UPHOLDING

Heb	1:3	**u** all things by the word of his	*5342*

UPPER

Ex	12:7	on the **u** door post of the houses,	4947
1Ch	28:11	and of the **u** chambers thereof,	5944
2Ch	3:9	he overlaid the **u** chambers with	5944
Mk	14:15	**shew you a large u room furnished.**	*508*
Lk	22:12	**shew you a large u room furnished:**	*508*

UPPERMOST

Ge	40:17	**u** basket there was of all manner	5945
Mt	23:6	**love the u rooms at feasts, and**	*4411*
Mk	12:39	**and the u rooms at feasts:**	*4411*
Lk	11:43	**love the u seats in ... synagogues,**	*4410*

UPRIGHT See also RIGHT.

Ge	37:7	lo, my sheaf arose, and also stood **u**;	
1Sa	29:6	thou hast been **u**, and thy going	3477
Job	1:1	and that man was perfect and **u**,	3477
Job	1:8	a perfect and an **u** man, one that	3477
Job	2:3	a perfect and an **u** man, one that	3477
Ps	7:10	God, which saveth the **u** in heart	3477
Ps	11:2	may privily shoot at the **u** in heart	3477
Ps	25:8	Good and **u** is the Lord: therefore	3477
Ps	32:11	for joy, all ye that are **u** in heart	3477
Pr	10:29	of the Lord is strength to the **u**:	8537
Pr	11:3	The integrity of the **u** shall guide	3477
Pr	11:6	righteousness of the **u** shall deliver	3477
Pr	11:20	are **u** in their way are his delight	8549
Pr	15:8	the prayer of the **u** is his delight.	3477
Pr	16:17	The highway of the **u** is to depart	3477
Pr	28:10	the **u** shall have good things in	8549
Pr	29:10	The bloodthirsty hate the **u**: but	8535
Pr	29:27	is **u** in the way is abomination to	3477
Ecc	7:29	found, that God had made man **u**;	3477
Ecc	12:10	that which was written was **u**,	3476
Da	8:18	but he touched me, and set me **u**	5977
Mic	7:2	and there is none **u** among men:	3477
Hab	2:4	which is lifted up is not **u** in him:	3474

UPRIGHTLY See also RIGHTLY.

Ps	58:1	do ye judge **u**, O ye sons of men?	4339
Ps	84:11	withhold from them that walk **u**.	8549
Pr	10:9	He that walketh **u** walketh surely:	8537
Pr	15:21	man of understanding walketh **u**	3474
Isa	33:15	righteously, and speaketh **u**;	4339
Am	5:10	they abhor him that speaketh **u**	8549
Gal	2:14	they walked not **u** according to	*3716*

UPRIGHTNESS

Dt	9:5	or for the **u** of thine heart, dost	3476
1Ki	9:4	in integrity of heart, and in **u**	3476
1Ch	29:17	**u** of mine heart I have willingly	4339
Job	33:23	thousand, to shew unto man his **u**	3476
Ps	9:8	judgment to the people in **u**	4339
Ps	143:10	good; lead me into the land of **u**.	4334
Pr	2:13	Who leave the paths of **u**, to walk	3476
Pr	14:2	He that walketh in his **u** feareth	3476
Pr	28:6	is the poor that walketh in his **u**,	8537
Isa	26:7	The way of the just is **u**: thou,	4339
Isa	57:2	beds, each one walking in his **u**.	5228

UPRISING See also RISING.

Ps	139:2	my downsitting and mine **u**	6965

UPROAR See also ROAR.

Mt	26:5	there be an **u** among the people	*2351*
Ac	17:5	and set all the city on an **u**.	*2350*
Ac	20:1	And after the **u** was ceased, Paul	*2351*
Ac	21:31	that all Jerusalem was in an **u**	*4797*

UPSIDE

Ps	146:9	way of the wicked he turneth **u** down	
Ac	17:6	that have turned the world **u** down	*389*

UPWARD

Nu	1:3	From twenty years old and **u**, all	4605
Nu	3:15	every male from a month old and **u**	4605
Nu	4:3	From thirty years old and **u**.	4605
Nu	32:11	from twenty years old and **u**,	4605
1Sa	9:2	from his shoulders and **u** he was	4605
1Sa	10:23	people from his shoulders and **u**	4605
Job	5:7	unto trouble, as the sparks fly **u**	1361
Ecc	3:21	the spirit of man that goeth **u**,	4605
Hag	2:15	you, consider from this day and **u**,	4605

URGE

Lk	11:53	the Pharisees began to **u** him	*1758*

URGED

Ge	33:11	and he **u** him, and he took it.	6484
Jgs	16:16	daily with her words, and **u** him,	509

Jgs 19:7 depart, his father in law **u** him:........ 6484
2Ki 2:17 they **u** him till he was ashamed, ... 6484
2Ki 5:16 And he **u** him to take it; but he........ 6484

URGENT
Da 3:22 the king's commandment was **u**, ... 2685

USE See also ABUSE.
Le 19:26 neither shall ye **u** enchantment, ... 5172
Nu 15:39 after which ye **u** to go a whoring:
2Sa 1:18 children of Judah the **u** of the bow:
Jer 23:31 that **u** their tongues, and say, He....... 3947
Jer 46:11 in vain shalt thou **u** many medicines;
Eze 21:21 of the two ways, to **u** divination:....... 7080
Mt 5:44 **them which despitefully u you,** *1908*
Mt 6:7 **ye pray, u not vain repetitions,**
Lk 6:28 **them which despitefully u you,** *1908*
Ac 14:5 to **u** them despitefully, and to *5195*
Ro 1:27 leaving ... natural **u** of the woman, ... *5540*
1Co 7:31 they that **u** this world, as not.......... *5530*
Gal 5:13 **u** not liberty for an occasion to the
1Ti 1:8 is good, if a man **u** it lawfully;......... *5530*
1Ti 3:10 then let them **u** the office of a deacon
1Ti 5:23 **u** a little wine for thy stomach's........ *5530*
2Ti 2:21 and meet for the master's **u**
Heb 5:14 those who by reason of **u** have *1838*
1Pe 4:9 **U** hospitality one to another *5382*

USED See also ABUSED; MISUSED.
2Ki 17:17 **u** divination and enchantments
Eze 22:29 people of the land have **u** oppression,
Mk 2:18 and of the Pharisees **u** to fast: *1510*
Ac 19:19 of them also which **u** curious arts *4238*
1Co 9:12 we have not **u** this power; *5530*
1Th 2:5 time **u** we flattering words....... *1096, 1722*
1Ti 3:13 that have **u** the office of a deacon...... *1247*
Heb 10:33 companions of them that were so **u**. *390*

USETH
Dt 18:10 or that **u** divination, or an observer
Pr 15:2 of the wise **u** knowledge aright:
Pr 18:23 The poor **u** intreaties; but the......... 1696
Heb 5:13 For one that **u** milk is unskillful *3348*

USURER
Ex 22:25 thou shalt not be to him as an **u**, ... 5383

USURP
1Ti 2:12 nor to **u** authority over the man, ... *831*

USURY
Le 25:36 Take thou no **u** of him, or increase: 5392
Dt 23:19 not lend upon **u** to thy brother; 5391
Dt 23:20 a stranger thou mayest lend upon **u**; ... 5391
Ne 5:10 I pray you, let us leave off this **u** 5383
Pr 28:8 He that by **u** and unjust gain.......... 5392
Mt 25:27 **have received mine own with u** *5110*
Lk 19:23 **have required mine own with u?** *5110*

US-WARD
Ps 40:5 and thy thoughts which are to **u**........ 413
Eph 1:19 his power to **u** who believed,..... *1519, 2248*
2Pe 3:9 but is longsuffering to **u**, not..... *1519, 2248*

UTTER See also OUTER.
Le 5:1 if he do not **u** it, then he shall......... 5046
Jos 2:14 yours, if ye **u** not this our business..... 5046
Ps 119:171 My lips shall **u** praise, when........... 5042
Pr 14:5 but a false witness will **u** lies 6315
Pr 23:33 heart shall **u** perverse things 1696
Ecc 1:8 are full of labour; man cannot **u** it: 1696
Ecc 5:2 hasty to **u** any thing before God: 3318
Isa 32:6 and to **u** error against the Lord, ... 1696
Jer 25:30 **u** his voice from his holy 5414
Joel 3:16 and **u** his voice from Jerusalem; 5414
Am 1:2 and **u** his voice from Jerusalem; 5414
Na 1:9 he will make an **u** end: affliction....... 3617
2Co 12:4 it is not lawful for a man to **u** *2980*

UTTERANCE
Ac 2:4 tongues, as the Spirit gave them **u** *669*
Eph 6:19 that **u** may be given unto me, that *5056*
Col 4:3 would open unto us a door of **u**....... *3056*

UTTERED
Nu 30:6 vowed, or **u** ought out of her lips, ... 4008
2Sa 22:14 and the most High **u** his voice 5414
Job 42:3 have I **u** that I understood not;........ 5046
Ps 46:6 he **u** his voice, the earth melted 5414
Ro 8:26 with groanings which cannot be **u** *215*
Heb 5:11 things to say, and hard to be **u**, ... *3004*
Rev 10:4 which the seven thunders **u**, ... *2980*

UTTERETH
Ps 19:2 Day unto day **u** speech, and night 5042
Pr 1:20 she **u** her voice in the streets:.......... 5414
Pr 10:18 and he that **u** a slander, is a fool 3318
Pr 29:11 A fool **u** all his mind: but a wise....... 3318
Jer 10:13 When he **u** his voice, there is a 5414
Jer 51:16 When he **u** his voice, there is a 5414
Mic 7:3 he **u** his mischievous desire: 1696

UTTERING
Isa 59:13 conceiving and **u** from the heart....... 1897

UTTERLY
Le 26:44 I abhor them, to destroy them **u**....... 3615
Nu 15:31 that soul shall be **u** cut off;
Nu 30:12 husband hath **u** made them void
2Sa 17:10 is as the heart of a lion, shall **u** melt:
Ps 19:8 thy statutes: O forsake me not **u**....... 3966
Ps 119:43 word of truth **u** out of my mouth;..... 3966
Isa 2:18 And the idols he shall **u** abolish 3632
Jer 14:19 Hast thou **u** rejected Judah? hath
Jer 51:58 walls of Babylon shall be **u** broken
Mic 2:4 and say, We be **u** spoiled:............. 7703
Na 1:15 through thee; he is **u** cut off 3605
1Co 6:7 there is **u** a fault among you *3654*
2Pe 2:12 and shall **u** perish in their own........ *2704*

UTTERMOST
Ne 1:9 out unto the **u** part of the heaven...... 7097
Ps 2:8 and the **u** parts of the earth for thy 657
Ps 65:8 that dwell in the **u** parts are afraid 7098
Ps 139:9 dwell in the **u** parts of the sea;.......... 319
Mt 5:26 **till thou hast paid the u farthing**....... *2078*
Mt 12:42 **from the u parts of the earth** *4009*
Mk 13:27 **from the u part of the earth** *206*
Ac 1:8 **unto the u part of the earth**........... *2078*
Ac 24:22 I will know the **u** of your matter....... *1231*
1Th 2:16 wrath is come upon them to the **u**..... *5056*
Heb 7:25 able also to save them to the **u** *3838*

V

VAGABOND
Ge 4:14 a fugitive and a **v** in the earth; 5110
Ac 19:13 Then certain of the **v** Jews, *4022*

VAIL See also VEIL.
Ge 38:19 laid by her **v** from her, and put on 6809
Ex 26:33 **v** shall divide unto you between 6532
Ex 34:35 Moses put the **v** upon his face 4533
Ex 40:3 and cover the ark with the **v** 6532
Le 4:17 before the Lord, even before the **v** 6532
Le 16:2 holy place within the **v** before the 6532
Isa 25:7 **v** that is spread over all nations 4541
2Co 3:13 which put a **v** over his face, that *2571*
2Co 3:14 which **v** is done away in Christ
2Co 3:15 read, the **v** is upon their heart *2571*
2Co 3:16 Lord, the **v** shall be taken away *2571*

VAIN
Ex 20:7 name of the Lord thy God in **v**; 7723
Ex 20:7 guiltless that taketh his name in **v**. 7723
Le 26:20 your strength shall be spent in **v**: 7385
Dt 5:11 name of the Lord thy God in **v**: 7723
Jgs 9:4 Abimelech hired **v** and light 7386
1Sa 12:21 then should ye go after **v** things 8414
2Sa 6:20 one of the **v** fellows shamelessly 7386
2Ki 17:15 became **v**, and went after the 1891
Job 21:34 How then comfort ye me in **v** 1892
Job 35:16 doth Job open his mouth in **v**: 1892
Job 41:9 the hope of him is in **v**: shall not 3576
Ps 2:1 and the people imagine a **v** thing? 7385
Ps 26:4 I have not sat with **v** persons 7723
Ps 39:6 every man walketh in a **v** shew:
Ps 60:11 trouble: for **v** is the help of man 7723
Ps 119:113 I hate **v** thoughts: but thy law do I
Ps 127:1 they labour in **v** that build it: 7723
Ps 127:1 the watchman waketh but in **v** 7723
Ps 127:2 It is **v** for you to rise up early, to 7723
Pr 1:17 Surely in **v** the net is spread in 2600
Pr 12:11 he that followeth **v** persons is 7386
Pr 28:19 he that followeth after **v** persons 7386
Pr 30:9 and take the name of my God in **v**.
Pr 31:30 is deceitful, and beauty is **v**: but 1892
Ecc 6:12 all the days of his **v** life which he 1892
Isa 1:13 Bring no more **v** oblations; 7723
Isa 45:18 he created it not in **v**, he formed 8414
Isa 45:19 Seek ye me in **v**: I the Lord speak 8414
Isa 49:4 Then I said, I have laboured in **v** 7385
Jer 3:23 Truly in **v** is salvation hoped for 8267
Jer 4:14 thy **v** thoughts lodge within thee? 205
Jer 10:3 customs of the people are in **v**: 1892
La 2:14 have seen **v** and foolish things 7723
La 4:17 eyes as yet failed for our **v** help: 1892
Eze 6:10 said in **v** that I would do this evil 2600
Eze 13:7 Have ye not seen a **v** vision, and 7723
Zec 10:2 false dreams; they comfort in **v**: 1892
Mal 3:14 have said, It is **v** to serve God: 7723
Mt 6:7 **when ye pray, use not v repetitions,**
Mt 15:9 **But in v they do worship me,** *3155*
Mk 7:7 **Howbeit in v do they worship me,** *3155*
Ac 4:25 and the people imagine **v** things? *2756*
Ro 1:21 became **v** in their imaginations *3154*
1Co 3:20 of the wise, that they are **v** *3152*
1Co 15:2 you, unless ye have believed in **v** *1500*
1Co 15:14 risen, then is our preaching **v**, *2756*
1Co 15:17 be not raised, your faith is **v**; *3152*
1Co 15:58 your labour is not in **v** in the Lord *2756*
2Co 6:1 receive not the grace of God in **v** *2756*
Gal 2:21 the law, then Christ is dead in **v** *1432*
Gal 3:4 many things in **v**? if it be yet in **v** *1500*
Gal 5:26 Let us not be desirous of **v** glory *2755*
Eph 5:6 man deceive you with **v** words: *2756*
Php 2:16 not run in **v**, neither laboured in **v** *2756*
Col 2:8 through philosophy and **v** deceit *2756*
1Ti 1:6 have turned aside unto **v** jangling; *3150*
1Ti 6:20 avoiding profane and **v** babblings *2757*
2Ti 2:16 shun profane and **v** babblings: for *2757*
Tit 1:10 unruly and **v** talkers and deceivers *3151*
Tit 3:9 for they are unprofitable and **v** *3152*
Jas 1:26 own heart, this man's religion is **v**. *3152*
Jas 2:20 O **v** man, that faith without works *2756*
Jas 4:5 think that the scripture saith in **v** *2761*
1Pe 1:18 your **v** conversation received by *3152*

VAINGLORY See also VAIN and GLORY.
Php 2:3 be done through strife or **v**: *2754*

VAINLY
Col 2:18 **v** puffed up by his fleshly mind *1500*

VALIANT
1Sa 14:52 any strong man, or any **v** man 2428
1Sa 16:18 a mighty **v** man, and a man of war 2428
1Sa 18:17 only be thou **v** for me, and 1121, 2428
2Sa 11:16 where he knew that **v** men were 2428
1Ch 10:12 They arose, all the **v** men, and 2428
2Ch 28:6 day, which were all **v** men; 2428
Jer 9:3 they are not **v** for the truth upon 1396
Heb 11:34 waxed **v** in fight, turned to flight *2478*

VALIANTLY
Nu 24:18 enemies; and Israel shall do **v** 2428
1Ch 19:13 and let us behave ourselves **v**. 2388
Ps 60:12 Through God we shall do **v**: for 2428
Ps 108:13 Through God we shall do **v**: for he 2428

VALLEY
Dt 34:6 he buried him in a **v** in the land of 1516
Jos 15:8 of the **v** of the giants northward: 6010
Jos 18:16 the **v** of the giants on the north, 6010
Jgs 1:19 drive out the inhabitants of the **v** 6010
Jgs 16:4 loved a woman in the **v** of Sorek, 5158
2Ki 3:17 yet that **v** shall be filled with water, 5158
1Ch 10:7 men of Israel that were in the **v** 6010
Ps 23:4 through the **v** of the shadow of 1516
Pr 30:17 ravens of the **v** shall pick it out 5158
Isa 22:5 God of hosts in the **v** of vision 1516
Isa 40:4 Every **v** shall be exalted, and 1516
Jer 31:40 the whole **v** of the dead bodies, and 6010
Eze 37:1 midst of the **v** which was full of 1237
Joel 3:14 multitudes in the **v** of decision: 6010
Zec 12:11 in the **v** of Megiddon 1237
Zec 14:4 and there shall be a very great **v**; 1516
Lk 3:5 Every **v** shall be filled, and every *5327*

VALLEYS
Nu 24:6 As the **v** are they spread forth, as 5158
Dt 11:11 possess it, is a land of hills and **v**. 1237
Jos 9:1 Jordan, in the hills, and in the **v**, 8219
Jos 12:8 In the mountains, and in the **v**, 8219

V

1Ki 20:28 hills, but he is not God of the **v**, ... 6010
Job 39:10 or will he narrow the **v** after thee? 6010
SS 2:1 of Sharon, and the lily of the **v** 6010
Isa 22:7 choicest **v** shall be full of chariots, ... 6010
Jer 49:4 Wherefore gloriest thou in the **v**. 6010
Eze 31:12 in all the **v** his branches are fallen, ... 1516
Eze 36:6 hills, to the rivers, and to the **v**, ... 1516
Mic 1:4 the **v** shall be cleft, as wax before 6010

VALOUR
Jgs 6:12 with thee, thou mighty man of **v** 2428
Jgs 11:1 Jephthah … was a mighty man of **v**, . . . 2428
1Ki 11:28 Jeroboam was a mighty man of **v**: 2428
2Ki 5:1 he was also a mighty man in **v**, but 2428
2Ki 24:14 and all the mighty men of **v** 2428
1Ch 5:24 mighty men of **v**, famous men, and 2428
1Ch 12:21 for they were all mighty men of **v**, ... 2428
1Ch 26:32 his brethren, men of **v**, were two 2428
2Ch 32:21 cut off all all the mighty men of **v**, ... 2428

VALUE
Le 27:8 that vowed shall the priest **v** him 6186
Le 27:12 And the priest shall **v** it, whether 6186
Job 13:4 lies, ye are all physicians of no **v** 457
Mt 10:31 **of more v than many sparrows** *1308*
Lk 12:7 **of more v than many sparrows** *1308*

VALUED
Job 28:19 neither shall it be **v** with pure gold. 5541
Mt 27:9 the price of him that was **v** *5091*

VANISH
Isa 51:6 heavens shall **v** away like smoke, ... 4414
1Co 13:8 be knowledge, it shall **v** away. *2673*
Heb 8:13 waxeth old is ready to **v** away *854*

VANISHED
Jer 49:7 the prudent? is their wisdom **v**? 5628
Lk 24:31 and he **v** out of their sight *1096, 855*

VANISHETH
Job 7:9 As the cloud is consumed and **v** 3212
Jas 4:14 for a little time, and then **v** away. *853*

VANITIES
Dt 32:21 me to anger with their **v**. 1892
1Ki 16:13 of Israel to anger with their **v** 1892
Ecc 1:2 Vanity of **v**, saith the Preacher, ... 1892
Ecc 1:2 Preacher, vanity of **v**; all is vanity 1892
Ecc 5:7 words there are also divers **v** 1892
Ecc 12:8 Vanity of **v**, saith the preacher; all. 1892
Jer 8:19 images, and with strange **v**? 1892
Jnh 2:8 that observe lying **v** forsake their 1892
Ac 14:15 from these **v** unto the living God, ... *3152*

VANITY
2Ki 17:15 they followed **v**, and became vain, ... 1892
Job 7:16 let me alone; for my days are **v** 1892
Job 31:5 If I have walked with **v**, or if my 7723
Job 35:13 Surely God will not hear **v**, neither. 7723
Ps 4:2 how long will ye love **v**, and seek 7385
Ps 10:7 under his tongue is mischief and **v**. 205
Ps 12:2 They speak **v** every one with his 7723
Ps 24:4 hath not lifted up his soul unto **v**, ... 7723
Ps 39:5 at his best state is altogether **v**. 1892
Ps 62:9 Surely men of low degree are **v**, ... 1892
Ps 78:33 their days did he consume in **v** 1892
Ps 94:11 thoughts of man, that they are **v**. 1892
Ps 119:37 mine eyes from beholding **v**; 7723
Ps 144:4 Man is like to **v**: his days are as 1892
Ps 144:11 children, whose mouth speaketh **v** 7723
Pr 13:11 Wealth gotten by **v** shall be 1892
Pr 21:6 treasures by a lying tongue is a **v**. 1892
Pr 22:8 that soweth iniquity shall reap **v** 205
Pr 30:8 Remove far from me **v** and lies: 7723
Ecc 1:2 **V** of vanities, saith the Preacher, ... 1892
Ecc 1:14 all is **v** and vexation of spirit 1892
Ecc 2:1 and, behold, this also is **v**. 1892
Ecc 2:11 all was **v** and vexation of spirit, ... 1892
Ecc 2:15 in my heart, that this also is **v** 1892
Ecc 2:21 This also is **v** and a great evil. 1892
Ecc 2:26 also is **v** and vexation of spirit. 1892
Ecc 3:19 above a beast: for all is **v**. 1892
Ecc 4:4 is also **v** and vexation of spirit. 1892
Ecc 4:8 this is also **v**, yea, it is a sore. 1892
Ecc 5:10 with increase: this is also **v**. 1892
Ecc 6:2 this is **v**, and it is an evil disease 1892
Ecc 6:4 for he cometh in with **v**, and. 1892
Ecc 6:11 be many things that increase **v** 1892
Ecc 7:6 laughter of the fool: this is also **v** 1892
Ecc 7:15 have I seen in the days of my **v**: 1892
Ecc 8:10 they had so done: this is also **v** 1892
Ecc 9:9 all the days of the life of thy **v** 1892
Ecc 11:8 be many. All that cometh is **v** 1892
Ecc 11:10 for childhood and youth are **v**. 1892
Ecc 12:8 **V** of vanities, saith the preacher; 1892
Isa 5:18 draw iniquity with cords of **v** 7723
Isa 40:17 to him less than nothing, and **v** 8414
Isa 41:29 they are all **v**; their works are. 205
Isa 59:4 they trust in **v**, and speak lies; 8414
Jer 2:5 from me, and have walked after **v**. 1892
Eze 13:6 They have seen **v** and lying 7723
Eze 21:29 Whiles they see **v** unto thee, ... 7723
Zec 10:2 For the idols have spoken **v**, and. 205
Ro 8:20 creature was made subject to **v** *3153*
Eph 4:17 walk, in the **v** of their mind, ... *3153*
2Pe 2:18 speak great swelling words of **v**. *3153*

VAPOUR
Job 36:27 rain according to the **v** thereof: 108
Ac 2:19 blood, and fire, and **v** of smoke: *822*
Jas 4:14 a **v**, that appeareth for a little time *822*

VAPOURS
Ps 135:7 He causeth the **v** to ascend from. 5387
Jer 10:13 he causeth the **v** to ascend from 5387
Jer 51:16 he causeth the **v** to ascend from 5387

VARIABLENESS
Jas 1:17 with whom is no **v**, neither *3883*

VARIANCE
Mt 10:35 **a man at v against his father,** *1369*
Gal 5:20 **v**, emulations, wrath, strife, ... *2054*

VAUNTETH
1Co 13:4 charity **v** not itself, is not puffed *4068*

VEHEMENT
Jnh 4:8 that God prepared a **v** east wind; 2759
2Co 7:11 yea, what fear, yea, what **v** desire *1972*

VEHEMENTLY
Mk 14:31 But he spake the more **v**, If I *1722, 4053*
Lk 6:48 **stream beat v upon that house,** *4366*
Lk 11:53 Pharisees began to urge him **v**, ... *1171*
Lk 23:10 scribes stood and **v** accused him. *2159*

VEIL See also VAIL.

SS	5:7	the keepers ... took away my **v**	7289
Mt	27:51	**v** of the temple was rent in twain	*2665*
Mk	15:38	**v** of the temple was rent in twain	*2665*
Lk	23:45	**v** of the temple was rent in twain	*2665*
Heb	6:19	entereth into that within the **v**;	*2665*
Heb	9:3	after the second **v**, the tabernacle	*2665*
Heb	10:20	consecrated for us, through the **v**	*2665*

VENGEANCE

Ge	4:15	**v** shall be taken on him sevenfold	5358
Dt	32:41	I will render **v** to mine enemies	5359
Ps	94:1	O God, to whom **v** belongeth, shew	5360
Pr	6:34	he will not spare in the day of **v**	5359
Isa	34:8	For it is the day of the Lord's **v**,	5359
Isa	47:3	I will take **v**, and I will not meet	5359
Isa	61:2	Lord, and the day of **v** of our God;	5359
Jer	11:20	heart, let me see thy **v** on them:	5360
Jer	20:12	heart, let me see thy **v** on them:	5360
Jer	50:28	Lord our God, the **v** of his temple	5360
La	3:60	Thou hast seen all their **v** and all	5360
Eze	25:15	taken **v** with a despiteful heart,	5359
Mic	5:15	execute **v** in anger and fury upon	5359
Na	1:2	will take **v** on his adversaries,	5358
Lk	21:22	**For these be the days of v, that**	*1557*
Ro	3:5	Is God unrighteous who taketh **v**?	*3709*
Ro	12:19	**V** is mine; I will repay, saith the	*1557*
2Th	1:8	In flaming fire taking **v** on them	*1557*
Heb	10:30	**V** belongeth unto me, I will.	*1557*
Jude	7	suffering the **v** of eternal fire	*1349*

VENISON

Ge	25:28	Esau, because he did eat of his **v**:	6718
Ge	27:25	to me, and I will eat of my son's **v**	6718

VERIFIED

Ge	42:20	so shall your words be **v**, and ye	539
1Ki	8:26	let thy word, I pray thee, be **v**,	539
2Ch	6:17	God of Israel, let thy word be **v**,	539

VERILY

Ge	42:21	We are **v** guilty concerning our	61
Ex	31:13	**V** my sabbaths ye shall keep: for	389
1Ki	1:43	**V** our lord king David hath made	61
Ps	39:5	**v** every man at his best state is	389
Mt	5:18	**For v I say unto you, Till heaven**	*281*
Mt	5:26	**V I say unto thee, Thou shalt by**	*281*
Mt	6:2	**V I say unto you, They have**	*281*
Mt	6:5	**V I say unto you, They have**	*281*
Mt	6:16	**V I say unto you, They have**	*281*
Mt	8:10	**V I say unto you, I have not found**	*281*
Mt	10:15	**V I say unto you, It shall be more**	*281*
Mt	10:23	**for v I say unto you, Ye shall not**	*281*
Mt	10:42	**v I say unto you, he shall in no**	*281*
Mt	11:11	**V I say unto you, Among them**	*281*
Mt	13:17	**For v I say unto you, That many**	*281*
Mt	16:28	**V I say unto you, There be some**	*281*
Mt	17:20	**for v I say unto you, If ye have**	*281*
Mt	18:3	**V I say unto you, Except ye be**	*281*
Mt	18:13	**v I say unto you, he rejoiceth**	*281*
Mt	18:18	**V I say unto you, Whatsoever ye**	*281*
Mt	19:23	**V I say unto you, That a rich man.**	*281*
Mt	19:28	**V I say unto you, That ye which**	*281*
Mt	21:21	**V I say unto you, If ye have faith,**	*281*
Mt	21:31	**V I say unto you, That the**	*281*
Mt	23:36	**V I say unto you, All these things.**	*281*
Mt	24:2	**v I say unto you, There shall not**	*281*
Mt	24:34	**V I say unto you, This generation**	*281*
Mt	24:47	**V I say unto you, That he shall**	*281*
Mt	25:12	**V I say unto you, I know you not**	*281*
Mt	25:40	**V I say unto you, Inasmuch as**	*281*
Mt	25:45	**V I say unto you, Inasmuch as**	*281*
Mt	26:13	**V I say unto you, Wheresoever**	*281*
Mt	26:21	**V I say unto you, that one of you**	*281*
Mt	26:34	**V I say unto thee, That this night,**	*281*
Mk	3:28	**V I say unto you, All sins shall be**	*281*
Mk	6:11	**V I say unto you, It shall be more**	*281*
Mk	8:12	**v I say unto you, There shall no**	*281*
Mk	9:1	**V I say unto you, That there be**	*281*
Mk	9:12	**Elias v cometh first, and restoreth**	*3303*
Mk	9:41	**v I say unto you, he shall not lose**	*281*
Mk	10:15	**V I say unto you, Whosoever shall**	*281*
Mk	10:29	**V I say unto you, There is no man**	*281*
Mk	11:23	**v I say unto you, That whosoever**	*281*
Mk	12:43	**V I say unto you, That this poor**	*281*
Mk	13:30	**V I say unto you, that this**	*281*
Mk	14:9	**V I say unto you, Wheresoever**	*281*
Mk	14:18	**V I say unto you, One of you**	*281*
Mk	14:25	**V I say unto you, I will drink no**	*281*
Mk	14:30	**V I say unto thee, That this day,**	*281*
Lk	4:24	**V I say unto you, No prophet is**	*281*
Lk	11:51	**v I say unto you, It shall be**	*3483*
Lk	12:37	**v I say unto you, that he shall**	*281*
Lk	13:35	**and v I say unto you, Ye shall not**	*281*
Lk	18:17	**V I say unto you, Whosoever shall**	*281*
Lk	18:29	**V I say unto you, There is no man**	*281*
Lk	21:32	**V I say unto you, This generation**	*281*
Lk	23:43	**V I say unto thee, To day shalt**	*281*
Jn	1:51	**V, v, I say unto you, Hereafter ye**	*281*
Jn	3:3	**V, v, I say unto thee, Except a**	*281*
Jn	3:5	**V, v, I say unto thee, Except a**	*281*
Jn	3:11	**V, v, I say unto thee, We speak**	*281*
Jn	5:19	**V, v, I say unto you, The Son can**	*281*
Jn	5:24	**V, v, I say unto you, He that**	*281*
Jn	5:25	**V, v, I say unto you, The hour is**	*281*
Jn	6:26	**V, v, I say unto you, Ye seek me,**	*281*
Jn	6:32	**V, v, I say unto you, Moses gave**	*281*
Jn	6:47	**V, v, I say unto you, He that**	*281*
Jn	6:53	**V, v, I say unto you, Except ye**	*281*
Jn	8:34	**V, v, I say unto you, Whosoever**	*281*
Jn	8:51	**V, v, I say unto you, If a man**	*281*
Jn	8:58	**V, v, I say unto you, Before**	*281*
Jn	10:1	**V, v, I say unto you, He that**	*281*
Jn	10:7	**V, v, I say unto you, I am the**	*281*
Jn	12:24	**V, v, I say unto you, Except a**	*281*
Jn	13:16	**V, v, I say unto you, The servant**	*281*
Jn	13:20	**V, v, I say unto you, He that**	*281*
Jn	13:21	**V, v, I say unto you, that one of**	*281*
Jn	13:38	**V, v, I say unto thee, The cock**	*281*
Jn	14:12	**V, v, I say unto you, He that**	*281*
Jn	16:20	**V, v, I say unto you, That ye**	*281*
Jn	16:23	**V, v, I say unto you, Whatsoever**	*281*
Jn	21:18	**V, v, I say unto thee, When thou**	*281*
Ro	10:18	Yes **v**, their sound went into all	*3304*
Heb	2:16	**v** he took not on him the nature of	*1222*
Heb	3:5	Moses **v** was faithful in all his	*3303*
1Jn	2:5	him **v** is the love of God perfected:	*230*

VERY

Ge	1:31	made, and, behold, it was **v** good	3966
Ge	24:16	the damsel was **v** fair to look upon,	3966
Ex	11:3	Moses was **v** great in the land of	3966
Nu	12:3	the man Moses was **v** meek, above	3966

Nu 16:15 Moses was **v** wroth, and said unto 3966
Dt 30:14 But the word is **v** nigh unto thee,...... 3966
Jos 1:7 be thou strong and **v** courageous,...... 3966
Jos 23:6 Be ye therefore **v** courageous to 3966
Jgs 13:6 of an angel of God, **v** terrible:......... 3966
Ru 1:20 hath dealt **v** bitterly with me.......... 3966
2Sa 11:2 the woman was **v** beautiful to look..... 3966
1Ki 10:2 and **v** much gold, and precious........ 3966
2Ki 17:18 the Lord was **v** angry with Israel....... 3966
2Ki 21:16 shed innocent blood **v** much,......... 3966
1Ch 21:13 Lord; for **v** great are his mercies:....... 3966
2Ch 6:18 God in **v** deed dwell with men on 552
2Ch 14:13 they carried away **v** much spoil........ 3966
Est 1:12 therefore was the king **v** wroth,........ 3966
Ps 46:1 a **v** present help in trouble............ 3966
Ps 71:19 righteousness ... O God, is **v** high,..... 5704
Ps 79:8 us: for we are brought **v** low 3966
Ps 89:2 shalt thou establish in the **v** heavens
Ps 92:5 and thy thoughts are **v** deep 3966
Ps 104:1 O Lord my God, thou art **v** great;...... 3966
Ps 146:4 in that **v** day his thoughts perish
Pr 17:9 a matter separateth **v** friends
Pr 27:15 continual dropping in a **v** rainy 5464
Isa 10:25 For yet a **v** little while, and the 4213
Isa 29:17 Is it not yet a **v** little while, and........ 4213
Jer 18:13 Israel hath done a **v** horrible thing..... 3966
La 5:22 thou art **v** wroth against us...... 5704, 3966
Joel 2:11 Lord is great and **v** terrible;........... 3960
Mt 10:30 **But the v hairs of your head are**....... *2532*
Mt 15:28 made whole from that **v** hour......... *1565*
Mt 18:31 **was done, they were v sorry** *4970*
Mt 21:8 a **v** great multitude spread their *4118*
Mt 24:24 **they shall deceive the v elect**.......... *2532*
Mt 26:7 box of **v** precious ointment,............ *927*
Mk 8:1 the multitude being **v** great, and....... *3827*
Mk 14:3 ointment of spikenard **v** precious; *4185*
Mk 14:33 be sore amazed, and to be **v** heavy;....... *85*
Mk 16:2 **v** early in the morning the first day *3029*
Mk 16:4 rolled away: for it was **v** great *4970*
Lk 9:5 **shake off the v dust from your** *2532*
Lk 9:5 **Even the v dust of your city, which**
Lk 12:7 **But even the v hairs of your head**...... *2532*
Lk 12:59 **till thou hast paid the v last mite.**
Lk 19:17 **hast been faithful in a v little,**......... *1646*
Lk 24:1 **v** early in the morning, they came
Jn 7:26 indeed that this is the **v** Christ?......... *230*
Jn 14:11 **else believe me for the v works' sake.**
Ac 9:22 proving that this is **v** Christ............ *846*
Ac 25:10 no wrong, as thou **v** well knowest...... *2566*
2Co 12:15 I will **v** gladly spend and be spent...... *2236*
Php 1:6 Being confident of this **v** thing, that..... *846*
1Th 5:23 the **v** God of peace sanctify you *846*

VESSEL

Nu 19:15 And every open **v**, which hath no...... 3627
Dt 23:24 but thou shalt not put any in thy **v**..... 3627
Ps 2:9 them in pieces like a potter's **v**......... 3627
Ps 31:12 out of mind: I am like a broken **v**...... 3627
Pr 25:4 shall come forth a **v** for the finer....... 3627
Isa 30:14 it as the breaking of the potters' **v**...... 5035
Jer 18:4 so he made it again another **v**, as 3627
Jer 19:11 as one breaketh a potter's **v**, that....... 3627
Jer 22:28 is he a **v** wherein is no pleasure?....... 3627
Jer 25:34 and ye shall fall like a pleasant **v**....... 3627
Jer 32:14 and put them in an earthen **v**, that..... 3627
Hos 8:8 as a **v** wherein is no pleasure.......... 3627
Mk 11:16 carry any **v** through the temple........ *4632*
Lk 8:16 **a candle, covereth it with a v**.......... *4632*
Ac 9:15 **he is a chosen v unto me, to bear**...... *4632*
Ac 10:11 a certain **v** descending unto him....... *4632*
Ac 11:5 saw a vision, A certain **v** descend,...... *4632*
Ro 9:21 lump to make one **v** unto honour *4632*
1Th 4:4 to possess his **v** in sanctification *4632*
2Ti 2:21 he shall be a **v** unto honour, ... *4632*
1Pe 3:7 unto the wife, as unto the weaker **v**,.... *4632*

VESSELS

Ex 27:19 All the **v** of the tabernacle in all 3627
Ex 37:24 pure gold made he it, and all the **v**..... 3627
Ex 40:10 all his **v**, and sanctify the altar: 3627
Le 8:11 anointed the altar and all his **v** 3627
Nu 7:1 the altar and all the **v** thereof,......... 3627
Nu 7:85 the silver **v** weighed two thousand 3627
1Sa 21:5 the **v** of the young men are holy....... 3627
1Ki 7:47 Solomon left all the **v** unweighed...... 3627
1Ki 10:21 Solomon's drinking **v** were of gold, ... 3627
2Ki 4:3 even empty **v**; borrow not a few....... 3627
2Ki 4:6 to pass, when the **v** were full,.......... 3627
2Ki 24:13 cut in pieces all the **v** of gold.......... 3627
2Ch 28:24 together the **v** of the house of God, ... 3627
2Ch 29:19 Moreover all the **v**, which king 3627
Ezr 1:11 All the **v** of gold and of silver were..... 3627
Ezr 5:14 the **v** also of gold and silver of the 3984
Ezr 8:28 **v** are holy also; and the silver.......... 3627
Ne 10:39 where are the **v** of the sanctuary....... 3627
Isa 52:11 clean, that bear the **v** of the Lord 3627
Isa 65:4 abominable things is in their **v**;........ 3627
Jer 14:3 they returned with their **v** empty; 3627
Jer 28:3 bring again into this place all the **v**..... 3627
Jer 52:20 the brass of all these **v** was without 3627
Da 1:2 he brought the **v** into the treasure 3627
Da 5:2 to bring the golden and silver **v**........ 3984
Da 5:23 have brought the **v** of his house 3984
Mt 13:48 **gathered the good into v, but cast** *30*
Mt 25:4 **wise took oil in their v with their**........ *30*
Ro 9:22 **v** of wrath fitted to destruction: *4632*
Ro 9:23 of his glory on the **v** of mercy......... *4632*
2Co 4:7 have this treasure in earthen **v**......... *4632*
2Ti 2:20 are not only **v** of gold and of silver, ... *4632*
Heb 9:21 and all the **v** of the ministry *4632*
Rev 2:27 **as the v of a potter shall they be**....... *4632*

VESTURE

Ps 22:18 them, and cast lots upon my **v** 3830
Ps 102:26 as a **v** shalt thou change them, ... 3830
Mt 27:35 and upon my **v** did they cast lots *2441*
Jn 19:24 and for my **v** they did cast lots *2441*
Heb 1:12 as a **v** shalt thou fold them up......... *4018*
Rev 19:13 clothed with a **v** dipped in blood:...... *2440*
Rev 19:16 on his **v** and on his thigh a name *2440*

VESTURES

Ge 41:42 arrayed him in **v** of fine linen 899

VEX

Ex 22:21 thou shalt neither **v** a stranger, ... 3238
Le 18:18 take a wife to her sister, to **v** her 6887
Le 19:33 in your land, ye shall not **v** him........ 3238
2Sa 12:18 how will he then **v** himself,...... 6213, 7451
Job 19:2 How long will ye **v** my soul, and....... 3013
Ps 2:5 and **v** them in his sore displeasure 926
Isa 7:6 us go up against Judah, and **v** it 6973
Ac 12:1 hands to **v** certain of the church. *2559*

VEXATION

Dt	28:20	shall send upon thee cursing, **v**	4103
Ecc	1:14	all is vanity and **v** of spirit.	7469
Ecc	2:17	for all is vanity and **v** of spirit.	7469
Ecc	4:6	full with travail and **v** of spirit.	7469
Ecc	6:9	this is also vanity and **v** of spirit.	7469
Isa	28:19	shall be a **v** only to understand	2113
Isa	65:14	and shall howl for **v** of spirit	7667

VEXATIONS

2Ch	15:5	but great **v** were upon all the	4103

VEXED

Nu	20:15	Egyptians **v** us, and our fathers:	7489
Jgs	2:18	that oppressed them and **v** them.	1766
Jgs	16:16	so that his soul was **v** unto death:	7114
1Sa	14:47	he turned himself, he **v** them.	7561
2Sa	13:2	Amnon was so **v**, that he fell sick	3334
2Ki	4:27	for her soul is **v** within her:	4843
Ne	9:27	of their enemies, who **v** them:	6887
Job	27:2	Almighty, who hath **v** my soul;	4843
Isa	63:10	rebelled, and **v** his holy Spirit:	6087
Eze	22:7	in thee have they **v** the fatherless	3238
Eze	22:29	and have **v** the poor and needy:	3238
Mt	15:22	is grievously **v** with a devil.	*1139*
Mt	17:15	for he is lunatick, and sore **v**:	*3958*
Lk	6:18	that were **v** with unclean spirits:	*3791*
Ac	5:16	which were **v** with unclean spirits:	*3791*
2Pe	2:8	**v** his righteous soul from day to	*928*

VIAL

Rev	16:2	poured out his **v** upon the earth;	*5357*
Rev	16:3	poured out his **v** upon the sea;	*5357*
Rev	16:4	poured out his **v** upon the rivers.	*5357*
Rev	16:8	poured out his **v** upon the sun;	*5357*
Rev	16:10	poured out his **v** upon the seat	*5357*
Rev	16:12	out his **v** upon the great river	*5357*
Rev	16:17	poured out his **v** into the air;	*5357*

VIALS

Rev	5:8	and golden **v** full of odours, which	*5357*
Rev	15:7	seven golden **v** full of the wrath of	*5357*
Rev	16:1	pour out the **v** of the wrath of God	*5357*
Rev	17:1	angels which had the seven **v**.	*5357*
Rev	21:9	the seven **v** full of the seven last	*5357*

VICTORY

1Ch	29:11	and the glory, and the **v**, and the.	5331
Isa	25:8	He will swallow up death in **v**;	5331
Mt	12:20	he send forth judgment unto **v**.	*3534*
1Co	15:54	Death is swallowed up in **v**	*3534*
1Co	15:55	thy sting? O grave, where is thy **v**?	*3534*
1Jn	5:4	the **v** that overcometh the world.	*3529*
Rev	15:2	had gotten the **v** over the beast	*3528*

VICTUAL

1Ki	4:27	those officers provided **v** for king	3557
2Ch	11:23	he gave them **v** in abundance	4202

VICTUALS

Le	25:37	nor lend him thy **v** for increase.	400
Jos	1:11	people, saying, Prepare you **v**;	6720
Jgs	7:8	the people took **v** in their hand.	6720
1Sa	22:10	and gave him **v**, and gave him.	6720
1Ki	4:7	provided **v** for the king and his.	3557
Ne	10:31	ware or any **v** on the sabbath day	7668
Jer	44:17	for then had we plenty of **v**, and.	3899

VIEW

Jos	2:1	Go **v** the land, even Jericho	7200
Jos	7:2	saying, Go up and **v** the country.	7270

VIEWED

Ezr	8:15	and I **v** the people, and the priests,	995
Ne	2:13	and **v** the walls of Jerusalem	7663

VIGILANT

1Ti	3:2	husband of one wife, **v**, sober, of.	*3524*
1Pe	5:8	Be sober, be **v**; because your	*1127*

VILE

Dt	25:3	thy brother should seem **v** unto	7034
Jgs	19:24	this man do not so **v** a thing	5039
1Sa	3:13	his sons made themselves **v**, and.	7043
Job	40:4	I am **v**; what shall I answer thee?	7043
Isa	32:6	the **v** person will speak villany	5036
Jer	15:19	forth the precious from the **v**,	2151
La	1:11	and consider; for I am become **v**	2151
Na	1:14	make thy grave; for thou art **v**.	7043
Na	3:6	filth upon thee, and make thee **v**	5034
Ro	1:26	gave them up unto **v** affections:	*819*
Php	3:21	Who shall change our **v** body	*5014*
Jas	2:2	also a poor man in **v** raiment:	*4508*

VILEST

Ps	12:8	when the **v** men are exalted	2149

VILLAGE

Mt	21:2	**Go into the v over against you,**	*2968*
Mk	11:2	**Go your way into the v over**	*2968*
Lk	8:1	went throughout every city and **v**,	*2968*
Lk	19:30	**Go ye into the v over against you;**	*2968*
Lk	24:13	same day to a **v** called Emmaus,	*2968*
Lk	24:28	And they drew nigh unto the **v**	*2968*

VILLAGES

Le	25:31	houses of the **v** which have no wall	2691
Jgs	5:7	The inhabitants of the **v** ceased.	6520
1Sa	6:18	of fenced cities, and of country **v**	3724
Est	9:19	Therefore the Jews of the **v**, that	6521
Ps	10:8	in the lurking places of the **v**:	2691
Eze	38:11	go up to the land of unwalled **v**;	6519
Mt	9:35	went about all the cities and **v**.	*2968*
Mt	14:15	that they may go into the **v**, and	*2968*
Mk	6:6	and he went round about the **v**,	*2968*
Mk	6:36	and into the **v**, and buy themselves.	*2968*
Mk	6:56	he entered, into the **v**, or cities, or.	*2968*
Lk	13:22	he went through the cities and **v**,	*2968*
Ac	8:25	preached the gospel in many **v**	*2968*

VILLANY

Isa	32:6	For the vile person will speak **v**,	5039
Jer	29:23	they have committed **v** in Israel	5039

VINE See also VINEDRESSERS; VINEYARD.

Ge	40:9	dream, behold, a **v** was before me;	1612
Le	25:5	the grapes of thy **v** undressed:	5139
Nu	6:4	eat nothing … made of the **v** tree.	3196
Dt	32:32	For their **v** is of the **v** of Sodom,	1612
Jgs	9:12	Then said the trees unto the **v**.	1612
Jgs	13:14	of any thing that cometh of the **v**.	1612
1Ki	4:25	every man under his **v** and under.	1612
2Ki	18:31	eat ye every man of his own **v**, and.	1612
Ps	80:14	and behold, and visit this **v**;	1612
Ps	128:3	Thy wife shall be as a fruitful **v** by	1612
Isa	5:2	and planted it with the choicest **v**,	8321
Isa	24:7	wine mourneth, the **v** languisheth,	1612

Isa 32:12 pleasant fields, for the fruitful v 1612
Jer 2:21 Yet I had planted thee a noble v, ... 8321
Jer 2:21 degenerate plant of a strange v 1612
Jer 6:9 glean the remnant of Israel as a v: 1612
Jer 8:13 there shall be no grapes on the v 1612
Eze 15:2 What is the v tree more than any 1612
Eze 15:6 As the v tree among the trees of 1612
Eze 19:10 Thy mother is like a v in thy blood, ... 1612
Hos 10:1 Israel is an empty v, he bringeth 1612
Joel 1:7 He hath laid my v waste, and 1612
Mic 4:4 sit every man under his v and 1612
Zec 3:10 man his neighbour under the v 1612
Mt 26:29 **henceforth of this fruit of the v,** *288*
Mk 14:25 **drink no more of the fruit of the v,** *288*
Lk 22:18 **not drink of the fruit of the v** *288*
Jn 15:1 **I am the true v, and my Father is.** *288*
Jn 15:5 **I am the v, ye are the branches:** *288*
Jas 3:12 bear olive berries? either a v, figs? *288*
Rev 14:18 gather the clusters of the v of *288*

VINEDRESSERS See also VINE and DRESSER.
2Ki 25:12 the land to be v and husbandmen 3755
Jer 52:16 the land for v and for husbandmen 3755
Joel 1:11 howl, O ye v, for the wheat and for 3755

VINEGAR
Nu 6:3 no v of wine, or v of strong drink, ... 2558
Ps 69:21 my thirst they gave me v to drink 2558
Pr 10:26 As v to the teeth, and as smoke to 2558
Pr 25:20 and as v upon nitre, so is he that 2558
Mt 27:34 v to drink mingled with gall: *3690*
Mt 27:48 took a spunge, and filled it with v *3690*
Mk 15:36 ran and filled a spunge full of v, ... *3690*
Lk 23:36 coming to him, and offering him v *3690*
Jn 19:29 and they filled a spunge with v *3690*
Jn 19:30 when Jesus … had received the v *3690*

VINES
Nu 20:5 place of seed, or of figs, or of v, ... 1612
Ps 78:47 He destroyed their v with hail 1612
Ps 105:33 He smote their v also and their fig 1612
SS 2:15 the little foxes, that spoil the v: 3754
Jer 5:17 they shall eat up thy v and thy fig 1612
Hos 2:12 destroy her v and her fig trees 1612

VINEYARD
Ge 9:20 husbandman, and he planted a v: 3754
Ex 22:5 of the best of his own v, shall he 3754
Le 19:10 And thou shalt not glean thy v, ... 3754
Dt 20:6 man is he that hath planted a v 3754
Dt 23:24 thou comest into thy neighbour's v 3754
Dt 28:30 thou shalt plant a v, and shalt not 3754
1Ki 21:1 that Naboth the Jezreelite had a v, ... 3754
1Ki 21:2 Give me thy v, that I may have it 3754
1Ki 21:7 I will give thee the v of Naboth 3754
Pr 24:30 and by the v of the man void of 3754
Pr 31:16 fruit of her hands she planteth a v 3754
SS 1:6 but mine own v have I not kept 3754
SS 8:12 My v, which is mine, is before me: 3754
Jer 12:10 Many pastors have destroyed my v 3754
Mt 20:1 **to hire labourers into his v** *290*
Mt 20:8 **the lord of the v saith unto his** *290*
Mt 21:28 **said, Son, go work to day in my v.** *290*
Mt 21:33 **householder, which planted a v,** *290*
Mt 21:39 **cast him out of the v, and slew** *290*
Mt 21:40 **the lord therefore of the v cometh,** *290*
Mt 21:41 and will let out his v unto other *290*
Mk 12:1 **A certain man planted a v, and set** *290*
Mk 12:8 **him, and cast him out of the v** *290*
Mk 12:9 **shall therefore the lord of the v do?** *290*
Lk 13:6 **man had a fig tree planted in his v;** *290*
Lk 20:9 **A certain man planted a v, and let** *290*
Lk 20:15 **So they cast him out of the v, and** *290*
1Co 9:7 who planteth a v, and eateth not of *290*

VINEYARDS
Nu 16:14 us inheritance of fields and v: 3754
Nu 22:24 the Lord stood in a path of the v, ... 3754
Dt 28:39 Thou shalt plant v, and dress 3754
Jgs 9:27 and gathered their v, and trode the 3754
Jgs 21:20 saying, Go and lie in wait in the v; 3754
1Sa 8:14 will take your fields, and your v 3754
1Sa 22:7 give every one of you fields and v, ... 3754
2Ki 19:29 year sow ye, and reap, and plant v, ... 3754
Ne 5:3 We have mortgaged our lands, v, ... 3754
Ne 5:5 other men have our lands and v 3754
Ps 107:37 And sow the fields, and plant v 3754
Ecc 2:4 me houses; I planted me v: 3754
SS 1:6 they made me the keeper of the v; 3754
SS 7:12 Let us get up early to the v; let us 3754
Isa 16:10 in the v there shall be no singing 3754
Eze 28:26 shall build houses, and plant v; 3754
Hos 2:15 I will give her her v from thence 3754
Am 4:9 when your gardens and your v and 3754
Am 5:11 ye have planted pleasant v, but ye 3754
Am 5:17 And in all v shall be wailing: for I 3754
Am 9:14 and they shall plant v, and drink 3754
Zep 1:13 they shall plant v, but not drink 3754

VINTAGE
Isa 16:10 I have made their v shouting to cease
Isa 24:13 grapes when the v is done 1210
Isa 32:10 for the v shall fail, the gathering 1210
Zec 11:2 the forest of the v is come down 1208

VIOL
Isa 5:12 And the harp, and the v, the 5035
Am 6:5 That chant to the sound of the v, ... 5035

VIOLATED
Eze 22:26 Her priests have v my law, and 2554

VIOLENCE
Ge 6:11 and the earth was filled with v 2555
Le 6:2 or in a thing taken away by v, or 1498
2Sa 22:3 saviour; thou savest me from v 2555
Ps 11:5 him that loveth v his soul hateth 2555
Ps 72:14 their soul from deceit and v: 2555
Ps 73:6 v covereth them as a garment 2555
Pr 4:17 and drink the wine of v 2555
Pr 10:6 but v covereth the mouth of the 2555
Pr 10:11 but v covereth the mouth of the 2555
Pr 13:2 of the transgressors shall eat v 2555
Pr 28:17 A man that doeth v to the blood 6231
Isa 53:9 because he had done no v 2555
Isa 59:6 and the act of v is in their hands 2555
Isa 60:18 V shall no more be heard in thy 2555
Jer 20:8 I cried out, I cried v and spoil; 2555
Jer 22:3 no wrong, do no v to the stranger, ... 2554
Jer 51:35 The v done to me and to my flesh 2555
Eze 7:23 crimes, and the city is full of v 2555
Eze 8:17 they have filled the land with v, ... 2555
Eze 18:16 neither hath spoiled by v, but 1500
Eze 18:18 spoiled his brother by v, and did 1499
Eze 28:16 filled the midst of thee with v 2555

Joel 3:19	**v** against the children of Judah,	2555
Am 3:10	who store up **v** and robbery in	2555
Am 6:3	cause the seat of **v** to come near;	2555
Jnh 3:8	from the **v** that is in their hands	2555
Mic 2:2	covet fields, and take them by **v**;	1497
Hab 1:2	even cry out unto thee of **v**, and	2555
Hab 1:9	They shall come all for **v**: their	2555
Hab 2:8	for the **v** of the land, of the city	2555
Hab 2:17	for the **v** of the land, of the city	2555
Zep 3:4	they have done **v** to the law	2554
Mal 2:16	one covereth **v** with his garment	2555
Mt 11:12	**kingdom of heaven suffereth v,**	*971*
Lk 3:14	Do **v** to no man, neither accuse	*1286*
Ac 5:26	and brought them without **v**:	*970*
Ac 21:35	the soldiers for the **v** of the people	*970*
Ac 24:7	with great **v** took him away out of	*970*
Ac 27:41	broken with the **v** of the waves	*970*
Heb 11:34	Quenched the **v** of fire, escaped	*1411*
Rev 18:21	**v** shall that great city Babylon be	*3731*

VIOLENT

2Sa 22:49	delivered me from the **v** man	2555
Ps 18:48	hast delivered me from the **v** man	2555
Ps 140:1, 4	preserve me from the **v** man;	2555
Ps 140:11	evil shall hunt the **v** man to	2555
Pr 16:29	A **v** man enticeth his neighbor, and	2555
Ecc 5:8	**v** perverting of judgment and	1499
Mt 11:12	**and the v take it by force.**	*973*

VIOLENTLY

Le 6:4	restore that which he took **v**	1500
La 2:6	**v** taken away his tabernacle	2554
Mt 8:32	of swine ran **v** down a steep place	
Mk 5:13	the herd ran **v** down a steep place	
Lk 8:33	the herd ran **v** down a steep place	

VIPER

Isa 30:6	the **v** and fiery flying serpent	660
Isa 59:5	is crushed breaketh out into a **v**	660
Ac 28:3	there came a **v** out of the heat	*2191*

VIPERS

Mt 3:7	O generation of **v**, who hath	*2191*
Mt 12:34	**O generation of v, how can ye,**	*2191*
Mt 23:33	**ye generation of v, how can ye**	*2191*
Lk 3:7	O generation of **v**, who hath	*2191*

VIRGIN

Ge 24:16	was very fair to look upon, a **v**	1330
Le 21:14	he shall take a **v** of his own people	1330
Dt 22:19	an evil name upon a **v** of Israel:	1330
Dt 22:28	If a man find a damsel that is a **v**	1330
Dt 32:25	both the young man and the **v**, the	1330
2Sa 13:2	for she was a **v**; and Amnon	1330
1Ki 1:2	for my lord the king a young **v**:	1330
2Ki 19:21	The **v** the daughter of Zion hath	1330
Isa 7:14	Behold, a **v** shall conceive, and	5959
Isa 37:22	The **v**, the daughter of Zion, hath	1330
Isa 47:1	O **v** daughter of Babylon, sit on	1330
Isa 62:5	For as a young man marrieth a **v**	1330
Jer 14:17	**v** daughter of my people is broken	1330
Jer 18:13	the **v** of Israel hath done a very	1330
Jer 31:4	thou shalt be built, O **v** of Israel:	1330
Jer 31:21	O **v** of Israel, turn again to these	1330
La 2:13	thee, O **v** daughter of Zion?	1330
Joel 1:8	Lament like a **v** girded with	1330
Am 5:2	The **v** of Israel is fallen; she shall	1330
Mt 1:23	Behold, a **v** shall be with child	*3933*
Lk 1:27	To a **v** espoused to a man whose	*3933*
1Co 7:28	if a **v** marry, she hath not sinned	*3933*
1Co 7:34	also between a wife and a **v**	*3933*
1Co 7:36	himself uncomely toward his **v**	*3933*
1Co 7:37	his heart that he will keep his **v**	*3933*
2Co 11:2	you as a chaste **v** to Christ	*3933*

VIRGINITY

Le 21:13	he shall take a wife in her **v**	1331
Dt 22:15	forth the tokens of the damsel's **v**	1331
Jgs 11:37	bewail my **v**, I and my fellows	1331
Lk 2:36	husband seven years from her **v**;	*3932*

VIRGIN'S

Lk 1:27	and the **v** name was Mary	*3933*

VIRGINS

Ex 22:17	according to the dowry of **v**.	1330
Jgs 21:12	four hundred young **v**, that had	1330
2Sa 13:18	the king's daughters that were **v**	1330
Est 2:2	Let there be fair young **v** sought	1330
Est 2:17	in his sight more than all the **v**:	1330
SS 1:3	therefore do the **v** love thee	5959
SS 6:8	and **v** without number	5959
La 1:4	priests sigh, her **v** are afflicted	1330
La 2:10	the **v** of Jerusalem hang down	1330
Am 8:13	the fair **v** and young men faint for	1330
Mt 25:1	**of heaven be likened unto ten v,**	*3933*
Mt 25:7	**all those v arose, and trimmed**	*3933*
Mt 25:11	**Afterward came also the other v,**	*3933*
Ac 21:9	same man had four daughters, **v**,	*3933*
1Co 7:25	Now concerning **v** I have no	*3933*
Rev 14:4	defiled with women; for they are **v**	*3933*

VIRTUE

Mk 5:30	that **v** had gone out of him	*1411*
Lk 6:19	for there went **v** out of him, and	*1411*
Lk 8:46	**that v has gone out of me**	*1411*
Php 4:8	there be any **v**, and if there be any	*703*
2Pe 1:3	that hath called us to glory and **v**:	*703*
2Pe 1:5	diligence, add to your faith **v**;	*703*

VIRTUOUS

Ru 3:11	know that thou art a **v** woman.	2428
Pr 12:4	A **v** woman is a crown to her	2428
Pr 31:10	Who can find a **v** woman? for her	2428

VISAGE

Isa 52:14	his **v** was so marred more than	4758
La 4:8	Their **v** is blacker than a coal;	8389
Da 3:19	the form of his **v** was changed	600

VISIBLE See also **INVISIBLE.**

Col 1:16	that are in earth, **v** and invisible	*3707*

VISION

Ge 15:1	Lord came unto Abram in a **v**,	4236
Nu 12:6	myself known unto him in a **v**	4758
Nu 24:4	saw the **v** of the Almighty,	4236
Nu 24:16	saw the **v** of the Almighty,	4236
1Sa 3:1	in those days; there was no open **v**	2377
1Sa 3:15	Samuel feared to shew Eli the **v**	4758
Job 20:8	chased away as a **v** of the night	2384
Pr 29:18	Where there is no **v**, the people	2377
Isa 21:2	grievous **v** is declared unto me;	2380
Isa 22:1	The burden of the valley of **v**	2384
Isa 22:5	God of hosts in the valley of **v**	2384
Isa 28:7	they err in **v**, they stumble in	7203
Isa 29:7	shall be as a dream of a night **v**	2377

Isa	29:11	the **v** of all is become unto you as	2380
Jer	14:14	they prophesy unto you a false **v**.	2377
Jer	23:16	they speak a **v** of their own heart,	2377
Eze	7:26	shall they seek a **v** of the prophet;	2377
Eze	11:24	brought me in a **v** by the Spirit of	4758
Eze	12:22	are prolonged, and every **v** faileth?	2377
Eze	12:23	at hand, and the effect of every **v**	2377
Eze	12:24	be no more any vain **v** nor flattering	2377
Eze	12:27	The **v** that he seeth is for many days	2377
Eze	13:7	Have ye not seen a vain **v**, and	4236
Da	2:19	revealed unto Daniel in a night **v**	2376
Da	7:2	and said, I saw in my **v** by night,	2376
Da	8:13	long shall be the **v** concerning the	2377
Da	8:17	the time of the end shall be the **v**	4758
Da	8:26	wherefore shut thou up the **v**; for	2377
Da	9:21	whom I had seen in the **v** at the	2377
Da	9:23	the matter, and consider the **v**.	2377
Da	9:24	and to seal up the **v** and prophecy,	2377
Da	10:1	and had understanding of the **v**	4758
Da	10:7	And I Daniel alone saw the **v**: for	4759
Da	10:14	for yet the **v** is for many days	2377
Mic	3:6	you, that ye shall not have a **v**;	2377
Hab	2:3	the **v** is yet for an appointed time	2377
Zec	13:4	be ashamed every one of his **v**	2384
Mt	17:9	**Tell the v to no man, until the.**	*3705*
Lk	1:22	he had seen a **v** in the temple:	*3701*
Lk	24:23	they had also seen a **v** of angels,	*3701*
Ac	9:12	**seen in a v a man named Ananias**	*3705*
Ac	10:19	While Peter thought on the **v**, the	*3705*
Ac	11:5	and in a trance I saw a **v**, a certain	*3705*
Ac	12:9	angel; but thought he saw a **v**	*3705*
Ac	16:9	a **v** appeared to Paul in the night;	*3705*
Ac	18:9	Lord to Paul in the night by a **v**.	*3705*
Ac	26:19	disobedient unto the heavenly **v**:	*3705*
Rev	9:17	I saw the horses in the **v**, and.	*3076*

VISIONS

Ge	46:2	unto Israel in the **v** of the night	4759
2Ch	26:5	understanding in the **v** of God:	7200
Job	4:13	thoughts from the **v** of the night	2384
Job	7:14	and terrifiest me through **v**:	2384
Eze	1:1	were opened, and I saw **v** of God	4759
Eze	8:3	brought me in the **v** of God to	4759
Eze	13:16	which see **v** of peace for her, and	2377
Eze	40:2	In the **v** of God brought he me	4759
Eze	43:3	and the **v** were like the vision	4759
Da	1:17	understanding in all **v** and	2377
Da	2:28	**v** of thy head upon thy bed, are	2376
Da	4:5	and the **v** of my head trouble me	2376
Da	4:9	tell me the **v** of my dream that I	2376
Da	4:10	Thus were the **v** of mine head in	2376
Da	4:13	I saw in the **v** of my head upon my	2376
Da	7:1	and **v** of his head upon his bed:	2376
Da	7:13	I saw in the night **v**, and, behold	2376
Da	7:15	and the **v** of my head troubled me	2376
Hos	12:10	I have multiplied **v**, and used	2377
Joel	2:28	your young men shall see **v**:	2384
Ac	2:17	and your young men shall see **v**	*3706*
2Co	12:1	I will come to **v** and revelations	*3701*

VISIT

Ge	50:24	God will surely **v** you, and bring	6485
Ex	32:34	the day when I **v** I will **v** their sin	6485
Ps	59:5	Israel, awake to **v** all the heathen:	6485
Ps	89:32	Then will I **v** their transgression	6485
Ps	106:4	people: O **v** me with thy salvation;	6485
Jer	3:16	it; neither shall they **v** it;	6485
Jer	5:9	Shall I not **v** for these things?	6485
Jer	5:29	Shall I not **v** for these things?	6485
Jer	9:9	Shall I not **v** them for these things?	6485
Jer	14:10	their iniquity, and **v** their sins	6485
Jer	15:15	and **v** me, and revenge me of my	6485
Jer	23:2	**v** upon you the evil of your doings,	6485
Jer	27:22	they be until the day that I **v** them,	6485
Jer	29:10	accomplished at Babylon I will **v** you,	6485
Jer	50:31	is come, the time that I will **v** thee	6485
La	4:22	he will **v** thine iniquity, O daughter	6485
Hos	8:13	their iniquity, and **v** their sins:	6485
Hos	9:9	their iniquity, he will **v** their sins	6485
Am	3:14	shall **v** the transgressions of Israel	6485
Am	3:14	I will also **v** the altars of Beth-el:	6485
Zep	2:7	the Lord their God shall **v** them	6485
Ac	15:14	God at the first did **v** the Gentiles	*1980*
Jas	1:27	To **v** the fatherless and widows in	*1980*

VISITATION

Nu	16:29	visited after the **v** of all men;	6486
Job	10:12	thy **v** hath preserved my spirit.	6486
Isa	10:3	And what will ye do in the day of **v**,	6486
Jer	8:12	the time of their **v** they shall be	6486
Jer	10:15	time of their **v** they shall perish.	6486
Jer	51:18	time of their **v** they shall perish	6486
Hos	9:7	The days of **v** are come, the days.	6486
Mic	7:4	of thy watchmen and thy **v** cometh;	6486
Lk	19:44	**knewest not the time of thy v**	*1984*
1Pe	2:12	behold, glorify God in the day of **v**.	*1984*

VISITED

Ge	21:1	the Lord **v** Sarah as he had said,	6485
Ex	4:31	Lord had **v** the children of Israel,	6485
Nu	16:29	if they be **v** after the visitation of	6485
1Sa	2:21	And the Lord **v** Hannah, so that she	6485
Ps	17:3	thou hast **v** me in the night; thou	6485
Pr	19:23	he shall not be **v** with evil	6485
Isa	24:22	after many days shall they be **v**	6485
Isa	26:14	hast thou **v** and destroyed them,	6485
Isa	26:16	Lord, in trouble have they **v** thee,	6485
Isa	29:6-	Thou shalt be **v** of the Lord of	6485
Jer	23:2	them away, and have not **v** them:	6485
Eze	38:8	After many days thou shalt be **v**	6485
Zec	10:3	the Lord of hosts hath **v** his flock	6485
Mt	25:36	**I was sick, and ye v me: I was in**	*1980*
Mt	25:43	**and in prison, and ye v me not**	*1980*
Lk	1:68	hath **v** and redeemed his people,	*1980*
Lk	1:78	dayspring from on high hath **v** us,	*1980*
Lk	7:16	and, That God hath **v** his people.	*1980*

VISITEST

Ps	8:4	the son of man, that thou **v** him?	6485
Heb	2:6	the son of man, that thou **v** him?	*1980*

VISITING

Ex	20:5	**v** the iniquity of the fathers upon	6485
Ex	34:7	**v** the iniquity of the fathers upon	6485
Nu	14:18	**v** the iniquity of the fathers upon	6485
Dt	5:9	**v** the iniquity of the fathers upon	6485

VOCATION See also **CONVOCATION.**

Eph	4:1	walk worthy of the **v** wherewith	*2821*

VOICE

Ge	3:10	I heard thy **v** in the garden, and	6963
Ge	3:17	hearkened unto the **v** of thy wife,	6963
Ge	4:10	**v** of thy brother's blood crieth unto	6963
Ge	21:17	And God heard the **v** of the lad;	6963

Ge	26:5	that Abraham obeyed my **v**, and.......	6963
Ge	27:13	only obey my **v**, and go fetch me	6963
Ge	27:22	The **v** is Jacob's **v**, but the hands.......	6963
Ge	27:38	And Esau lifted up his **v**, and wept.	6963
Ge	39:14	with me, and I cried with a loud **v**.....	6963
Ex	5:2	should obey his **v** to let Israel go?......	6963
Ex	15:26	hearken to the **v** of the Lord thy.......	6963
Ex	18:24	to the **v** of his father in law, and did....	6963
Ex	19:5	if ye will obey my **v** indeed, and	6963
Ex	19:19	and God answered him by a **v**.........	6963
Ex	23:21	Beware of him, and obey his **v**,........	6963
Ex	24:3	all the people answered with one **v**,....	6963
Le	5:1	hear the **v** of swearing, and is a........	6963
Nu	7:89	he heard the **v** of one speaking	6963
Nu	20:16	he heard our **v**, and sent an angel, ...	6963
Nu	21:3	Lord hearkened to the **v** of Israel,......	6963
Dt	1:34	Lord heard the **v** of your words,.......	6963
Dt	4:12	no similitude; only ye heard a **v**	6963
Dt	4:33	**v** of God speaking out of the midst	6963
Dt	5:24	we have heard his **v** out of the.........	6963
Dt	5:25	if we hear the **v** of the Lord our	6963
Dt	18:16	not hear again the **v** of the Lord.......	6963
Dt	21:18	will not obey the **v** of his father,.......	6963
Dt	21:18	or the **v** of his mother, and that,.......	6963
Dt	30:20	that thou mayest obey his **v**, and	6963
Jos	24:24	we serve, and his **v** will we obey,.......	6963
Jgs	2:4	that the people lifted up their **v**........	6963
Ru	1:9	they lifted up their **v** and wept	6963
1Sa	8:19	refused to obey the **v** of Samuel;.......	6963
1Sa	8:22	Hearken unto their **v**, and make.......	6963
1Sa	19:6	hearkened unto the **v** of Jonathan:.....	6963
1Sa	26:17	Is this thy **v**, my son David? And.......	6963
1Sa	28:12	saw Samuel, she cried with a loud **v**: ...	6963
1Sa	30:4	with him lifted up their **v** and wept,....	6963
2Sa	19:4	king cried with a loud **v**, O my son	6963
1Ki	17:22	the Lord heard the **v** of Elijah; and.....	6963
1Ki	18:26	But there was no **v**, nor any that.......	6963
1Ki	19:12	and after the fire a still small **v**	6963
1Ki	20:36	hast not obeyed the **v** of the Lord, ...	6963
Ezr	3:12	their eyes, wept with a loud **v**;.........	6963
Job	2:12	they lifted up their **v**, and wept;	6963
Job	37:5	thundereth marvellously with his **v**;....	6963
Job	38:34	canst thou lift up thy **v** to the clouds ...	6963
Job	40:9	thou thunder with a **v** like him?.......	6963
Ps	6:8	hath heard the **v** of my weeping	6963
Ps	18:6	he heard my **v** out of his temple, ...	6963
Ps	19:3	language, where their **v** is not heard. ...	6963
Ps	29:3	**v** of the Lord is upon the waters:	6963
Ps	29:4	The **v** of the Lord is powerful; the	6963
Ps	46:6	he uttered his **v**, the earth melted......	6963
Ps	64:1	Hear my **v**, O God, in my prayer:......	6963
Ps	74:23	Forget not the **v** of thine enemies:	6963
Ps	95:7	hand. To day if ye will hear his **v**.......	6963
Ps	102:5	By reason of the **v** of my groaning.....	6963
Pr	1:20	she uttereth her **v** in the streets:	6963
Pr	2:3	liftest up thy **v** for understanding;	6963
Pr	5:13	not obeyed the **v** of my teachers, ...	6963
Pr	27:14	blesseth his friend with a loud **v**.......	6963
Ecc	5:3	a fool's **v** is known by multitude of	6963
Ecc	5:6	should God be angry at thy **v**	6963
Ecc	10:20	a bird of the air shall carry the **v**.......	6963
SS	2:8	The **v** of my beloved! behold, he.......	6963
Isa	6:4	moved at the **v** of him that cried,......	6963
Isa	6:8	Also I heard the **v** of the Lord, ...	6963
Isa	29:4	thy **v** shall be, as of one that hath a	6963
Isa	30:30	cause his glorious **v** to be heard,.......	6963
Isa	40:3	The **v** of him that crieth in the	6963
Isa	40:9	tidings, lift up thy **v** with strength;.....	6963
Isa	48:20	with a **v** of singing declare ye, tell......	6963
Isa	65:19	the **v** of weeping shall be no more	6963
Jer	3:21	A **v** was heard upon the high..........	6963
Jer	4:31	the **v** of the daughter of Zion, that.....	6963
Jer	7:23	Obey my **v**, and I will be your God,....	6963
Jer	7:28	that obeyeth not the **v** of the Lord	6963
Jer	10:13	When he uttereth his **v**, there is a......	6963
Jer	18:10	that it obey not my **v**, then I will	6963
Jer	25:30	high, and utter his **v** from his holy.....	6963
Jer	31:16	Refrain thy **v** from weeping, and.......	6963
Jer	32:23	but they obeyed not thy **v**, neither	6963
Jer	50:28	**v** of them that flee and escape out	6963
Jer	51:16	When he uttereth his **v**, there is a......	6963
La	3:56	Thou hast heard my **v**: hide not	6963
Eze	1:28	and I heard a **v** of one that spake	6963
Eze	3:12	behind me a **v** of a great rushing,......	6963
Eze	8:18	they cry in mine ears with a loud **v**	6963
Eze	10:5	as the **v** of the Almighty God when	6963
Eze	33:32	song of one that hath a pleasant **v**	6963
Eze	43:2	and his **v** was like a noise of many	6963
Da	4:31	there fell a **v** from heaven, saying,......	7032
Da	6:20	he cried with a lamentable **v** unto	7032
Da	10:6	like the **v** of a multitude.	6963
Joel	3:16	and utter his **v** from Jerusalem;........	6963
Am	1:2	and utter his **v** from Jerusalem;........	6963
Jnh	2:9	thee with the **v** of thanksgiving;	6963
Mic	6:9	The Lord's **v** crieth unto the city, ...	6963
Hab	3:16	my lips quivered at the **v**	6963
Zep	1:14	even the **v** of the day of the Lord:......	6963
Zep	3:2	She obeyed not the **v**; she received	6963
Zec	11:3	**v** of the howling of the shepherds;.....	6963
Mt	3:3	**v** of one crying in the wilderness	*5456*
Mt	3:17	And lo a **v** from heaven, saying........	*5456*
Mt	17:5	and behold a **v** out of the cloud,.......	*5456*
Mt	27:46	Jesus cried with a loud **v**, saying,.......	*5456*
Mt	27:50	he had cried again with a loud **v**, ...	*5456*
Mk	1:3	**v** of one crying in the wilderness,......	*5456*
Mk	1:11	And there came a **v** from heaven,......	*5456*
Mk	9:7	a **v** came out of the cloud, saying,......	*5456*
Mk	15:34	hour Jesus cried with a loud **v**........	*5456*
Mk	15:37	Jesus cried with a loud **v**, and gave.....	*5456*
Lk	1:44	**v** of thy salutation sounded in mine....	*5456*
Lk	3:4	**v** of one crying in the wilderness	*5456*
Lk	3:22	a **v** came from heaven, which said,.....	*5456*
Lk	9:35	there came a **v** out of the cloud........	*5456*
Lk	9:36	when the **v** was past, Jesus was	*5456*
Lk	23:46	when Jesus had cried with a loud **v**	*5456*
Jn	1:23	**v** of one crying in the wilderness,......	*5456*
Jn	5:25	**shall hear the v of the Son of God.**.....	*5456*
Jn	5:28	**are in the graves shall hear his v,**	*5456*
Jn	5:37	**Ye have neither heard his v at**	*5456*
Jn	10:3	**openeth; and the sheep hear his v:**.....	*5456*
Jn	10:4	**follow him: for they know his v**	*5456*
Jn	10:5	**they know not the v of strangers**	*5456*
Jn	10:16	**and they shall hear my v; and**........	*5456*
Jn	10:27	**My sheep hear my v, and I know**	*5456*
Jn	11:43	**he cried with a loud v, Lazarus,**	*5456*
Jn	12:28	Then came there a **v** from heaven......	*5456*
Jn	12:30	**This v came not because of me,**	*5456*
Jn	18:37	**that is of the truth heareth my v**	*5456*
Ac	7:31	the **v** of the Lord came unto him,......	*5456*
Ac	9:4	and heard a **v** saying unto him,........	*5456*
Ac	9:7	hearing a **v**, but seeing no man.	*5456*
Ac	10:13	there came a **v** to him, Rise, Peter;	*5456*

Ac 11:9 But the **v** answered me again from *5456*
Ac 12:22 is the **v** of a god, and not of a man *5456*
Ac 22:7 heard a **v** saying unto me, Saul *5456*
Ac 22:9 heard not the **v** of him that spake *5456*
Ac 26:14 I heard a **v** speaking unto me, and *5456*
1Co 14:11 if I know not the meaning of the **v** *5456*
1Th 4:16 with the **v** of the archangel, and *5456*
Heb 3:7 saith, To day if ye will hear his **v**, ... *5456*
Heb 3:15 said, To day if ye will hear his **v**, ... *5456*
Heb 4:7 said, To day if ye will hear his **v**, ... *5456*
Heb 12:26 Whose **v** then shook the earth: *5456*
2Pe 1:17 came such a **v** to him from the *5456*
2Pe 1:18 this **v** which came from heaven we *5456*
2Pe 2:16 dumb ass speaking with man's **v** *5456*
Rev 1:15 his **v** as the sound of many waters *5456*
Rev 3:20 **if any man hear my v, and open** *5456*
Rev 5:11 I heard the **v** of many angels round *5456*
Rev 6:7 I heard the **v** of the fourth beast *5456*
Rev 10:7 days of the **v** of the seventh angel, ... *5456*
Rev 14:2 as the **v** of many waters, and *5456*
Rev 14:7 Saying with a loud **v**, Fear God, ... *5456*
Rev 19:1 I heard a great **v** of much people *5456*
Rev 19:6 as the **v** of mighty thunderings *5456*
Rev 21:3 a great **v** out of heaven saying, ... *5456*

VOICES

Lk 23:23 And they were instant with loud **v**,. *5456*
Ac 13:27 nor yet the **v** of the prophets which *5456*
1Co 14:10 so many kinds of **v** in the world,. *5456*
Rev 4:5 lightnings and thunderings and **v** *5456*
Rev 8:5 and there were **v**, and thunderings, ... *5456*
Rev 10:3 seven thunders uttered their **v** *5456*
Rev 11:15 and there were great **v** in heaven *5456*
Rev 11:19 lightnings, and **v**, and thunderings *5456*

VOID

Ge 1:2 the earth was without form, and **v**; 922
Nu 30:13 or her husband may make it **v** 6565
Dt 32:28 For they are a nation **v** of counsel 6
Pr 7:7 a young man **v** of understanding,. 2638
Pr 10:13 of him that is **v** of understanding. 2638
Pr 11:12 He that is **v** of wisdom despiseth 2638
Pr 12:11 vain persons is **v** of understanding 2638
Pr 17:18 a man **v** of understanding striketh 2638
Pr 24:30 of the man **v** of understanding; 2638
Isa 55:11 it shall not return unto me **v**, but 7387
Jer 4:23 and, lo, it was without form, and **v**; 922
Jer 19:7 make **v** the counsel of Judah and 1238
Ac 24:16 conscience **v** of offence toward God *677*
Ro 3:31 make **v** the law through faith? *2673*
Ro 4:14 faith is made **v**, and the promise *2758*
1Co 9:15 man should make my glorying **v** *2758*

VOLUME

Ps 40:7 in the **v** of the book it is written 4039
Heb 10:7 (in the **v** of the book it is written *2777*

VOLUNTARY

Le 1:3 offer it of his own **v** will at the 7522
Le 7:16 offering be a vow, or a **v** offering, ... 5071
Eze 46:12 shalt prepare a **v** burnt offering 5071
Col 2:18 you of your reward in a **v** humility 2309

VOMIT

Job 20:15 and he shall **v** them up again: 6958
Pr 23:8 thou hast eaten shalt thou **v** up, ... 6958
Pr 25:16 thou be filled therewith, and **v** it 6958
Pr 26:11 a dog returneth to his **v**, so a fool 6892
Isa 19:14 drunken man staggereth in his **v** 6892
2Pe 2:22 dog is turned to his own **v** again; *1829*

VOMITED

Jnh 2:10 it **v** out Jonah upon the dry land 6958

VOMITETH

Le 18:25 land itself **v** out her inhabitants 6958

VOW

Ge 28:20 Jacob vowed a **v**, saying, If God 5088
Le 22:21 unto the Lord to accomplish his **v**, ... 5088
Nu 6:2 shall separate themselves to **v** a 5087
Nu 6:2 **v** of a Nazarite, to separate 5088
Nu 15:3 a sacrifice in performing a **v**, or 5088
Nu 21:2 Israel vowed a **v** unto the Lord,. 5088
Nu 30:2 If a man **v** ... unto the Lord 5087
Nu 30:3 a woman also **v** ... unto the Lord, ... 5087
Nu 30:4 her father hear her **v**, and her bond 5088
Nu 30:9 But every **v** of a widow, and of her 5088
Dt 23:18 of the Lord thy God for any **v**: 5088
Dt 23:22 But if thou shalt forbear to **v**, it 5088
Jgs 11:39 according to his **v** which he had 5088
1Sa 1:21 Lord the yearly sacrifice, and his **v**, ... 5088
2Sa 15:7 pray thee, let me go and pay my **v**, ... 5088
Ecc 5:4 When thou vowest a **v** unto God, ... 5088
Ac 18:18 head in Cenchrea: for he had a **v** *2171*
Ac 21:23 four men which have a **v** on them; *2171*

VOWED

Ge 28:20 And Jacob **v** a vow, saying, If God 5087
Le 27:8 according to his ability that **v** shall 5087
Nu 6:21 law of the Nazarite who hath **v**, and 5087
Nu 30:6 at all an husband, when she **v**,. 5088
Jgs 11:30 Jephthah **v** a vow unto the Lord,. 5087
1Sa 1:11 And she **v** a vow, and said, O Lord, ... 5087
Ecc 5:4 pay that which thou hast **v** 5087
Jer 44:25 perform our vows that we have **v**, ... 5087
Jnh 2:9 I will pay that that I have **v** 5087

VOWEST

Dt 12:17 nor any of thy vows which thou **v** 5087
Ecc 5:4 When thou **v** a vow unto God, defer ... 5087

VOWS

Le 23:38 beside all your **v**, and beside all 5088
Nu 29:39 beside your **v**, and your freewill 5088
Nu 30:4 then all her **v** shall stand, and 5088
Nu 30:11 then all her **v** shall stand, and 5088
Dt 12:6 your **v**, and your freewill offerings,. 5088
Dt 12:17 nor any of thy **v** which thou 5088
Ps 50:14 and pay thy **v** unto the most High: 5088
Ps 56:12 Thy **v** are upon me, O God: I will 5088
Ps 61:8 that I may daily perform my **v** 5088
Ps 66:13 offerings: I will pay thee my **v** 5088
Ps 116:14 I will pay my **v** unto the Lord 5088
Ps 116:18 I will pay my **v** unto the Lord 5088
Pr 7:14 me; this day have I payed my **v** 5088
Pr 20:25 holy, and after **v** to make enquiry 5088
Pr 31:2 womb? and what, the son of my **v**? 5088
Jer 44:25 will surely perform our **v** that we 5088
Jnh 1:16 sacrifice unto the Lord, and made **v** 5088
Na 1:15 thy solemn feasts, perform thy **v**: 5088

VULTURE'S

Job 28:7 which the **v** eye hath not seen: 344

VULTURES

Isa 34:15 the **v** also be gathered, every 1772

W

WAFER
Ex 29:23 one cake of oiled bread, and one **w** 7550
Le 8:26 a cake of oiled bread, and one **w**, ... 7550
Nu 6:19 and one unleavened **w**, shall 7550

WAFERS
Ex 16:31 of it was like **w** made with honey 6838
Ex 29:2 **w** unleavened anointed with oil:....... 7550
Le 7:12 unleavened **w** anointed with oil,....... 7550
Nu 6:15 **w** of unleavened bread anointed....... 7550

WAG
Jer 18:16 be astonished, and **w** his head......... 5110
La 2:15 **w** their head at the daughter of........ 5128
Zep 2:15 her shall hiss, and **w** his hand.......... 5128

WAGES
Ge 29:15 tell me what shall thy **w** be?........... 4909
Ge 30:28 Appoint me thy **w**, and I will give...... 7939
Ge 31:7 and changed my **w** ten times; 4909
Ge 31:8 The speckled shall be thy **w**: 7939
Ge 31:41 hast changed my **w** ten times.......... 4909
Ex 2:9 me, and I will give thee thy **w** 7939
Le 19:13 **w** of him that is hired shall not........ 6468
Jer 22:13 neighbour's service without **w**,........ 2600
Eze 29:19 and it shall be the **w** for his army 7939
Hag 1:6 earneth **w** to put it into a bag 7936
Mal 3:5 that oppress the hireling in his **w**,...... 7939
Lk 3:14 and be content with your **w**........... *3800*
Jn 4:36 **And he that reapeth receiveth w,** *3408*
Ro 6:23 For the **w** of sin is death; but the *3800*
2Co 11:8 other churches, taking **w** of them *3800*
2Pe 2:15 loved the **w** of unrighteousness: *3408*

WAGGING
Mt 27:39 by reviled him, **w** their heads *2795*
Mk 15:29 by railed on him, **w** their heads........ *2795*

WAIL
Eze 32:18 **w** for the multitude of Egypt, ... 5091
Mic 1:8 Therefore I will **w** and howl, I.......... 5594
Rev 1:7 kindreds of the earth shall **w**.......... *2875*

WAILED
Mk 5:38 and them that wept and **w** greatly *214*

WAILING
Est 4:3 and fasting, and weeping, and **w**; 4553
Jer 9:19 a voice of **w** is heard out of Zion,...... 5092
Jer 9:20 and teach your daughters **w**,.......... 5092
Eze 7:11 neither shall there be **w** for them 5089
Eze 27:31 bitterness of heart and bitter **w**........ 4553
Am 5:16 **W** shall be in all streets; and 4553
Mic 1:8 I will make a **w** like the dragons 4553
Mt 13:42 **be w and gnashing of teeth.** *2805*
Mt 13:50 **be w and gnashing of teeth.** *2805*
Rev 18:15 of her torment, weeping and **w**, ... *3996*
Rev 18:19 cried, weeping and **w**, saying.......... *3996*

WAIT
Ex 21:13 if a man lie not in **w**, but 6658
Nu 3:10 shall **w** on their priest's office:......... 8104
Nu 35:20 or hurl at him by laying of **w** 6660
Dt 19:11 and lie in **w** for him, and rise up........ 693
Jos 8:4 ye shall lie in **w** against the city, ... 693
Jgs 9:25 set liers in **w** for him in the top of 693
Jgs 16:2 laid **w** for him all night in the gate...... 693
Jgs 16:9 Now there were men lying in **w**,......... 693
Jgs 16:12 there were liers in **w** abiding in......... 693
Jgs 20:38 men of Israel and the liers in **w**, ... 693
Jgs 21:20 go and lie in **w** in the vineyards;........ 693
1Sa 22:13 should rise against me, to lie in **w**....... 693
2Ki 6:33 should I **w** for the Lord any longer?.... 3176
1Ch 23:28 was to **w** on the sons of Aaron 3027
2Ch 13:10 the Levites **w** upon their business:
Ps 10:9 he lieth in **w** to catch the poor: he 693
Ps 25:3 none that **w** on thee be ashamed:...... 6960
Ps 25:5 on thee do I **w** all the day............. 6960
Ps 25:21 preserve me; for I **w** on thee........... 6960
Ps 27:14 thine heart: **w**, I say, on the Lord 6960
Ps 37:7 Lord, and **w** patiently for him: 2342
Ps 37:9 but those that **w** upon the Lord,....... 6960
Ps 37:34 **w** on the Lord, and keep his way, ... 6960
Ps 39:7 And now, Lord, what **w** I for? 6960
Ps 52:9 and I will **w** on thy name; for it is...... 6960
Ps 59:3 For, lo, they lie in **w** for my soul......... 693
Ps 62:5 My soul, **w** thou only upon God; 1826
Ps 69:3 eyes fail while I **w** for my God......... 3176
Ps 69:6 Let not them that **w** on thee,.......... 6960
Ps 71:10 and they that lay **w** for my soul........ 8104
Ps 123:2 so our eyes **w** upon the Lord our
Ps 145:15 The eyes of all **w** upon thee; and 7663
Pr 1:11 let us lay **w** for blood, let us lurk........ 693
Pr 1:18 And they lay **w** for their own blood; 693
Pr 7:12 and lieth in **w** at every corner.) 693
Pr 12:6 the wicked are to lie in **w** for blood:..... 693
Pr 20:22 **w** on the Lord, and he shall save....... 6960
Pr 23:28 She also lieth in **w** as for a prey, ... 693
Pr 24:15 Lay not **w**, O wicked man, against 693
Isa 8:17 and I will **w** upon the Lord, that....... 2442
Isa 30:18 blessed are all they that **w** for him...... 2442
Isa 40:31 they that **w** upon the Lord shall 6960
Isa 49:23 not be ashamed that **w** for me 6960
Isa 59:9 **w** for light, but behold obscurity;...... 6960
Jer 9:8 but in heart he layeth his **w**. 696
Jer 14:22 therefore we will **w** upon thee: for 6960
La 3:10 was unto me as a bear lying in **w** 693
La 3:25 Lord is good unto them that **w**........ 6960
La 3:26 quietly **w** for the salvation of the 1748
Hos 6:9 as troops of robbers **w** for a man,...... 2442
Hos 12:6 and **w** on thy God continually......... 6960
Mic 7:2 they all lie in **w** for blood; they 693
Mic 7:7 **w** for the God of my salvation: 3176
Hab 2:3 though it tarry, **w** for it; because....... 2442
Zep 3:8 Therefore **w** ye upon me, saith the..... 2442
Mk 3:9 a small ship should **w** on him *4342*
Lk 11:54 Laying **w** for him, and seeking to *1748*
Lk 12:36 **like unto men that w for their lord,** *4327*
Ac 1:4 **w for the promise of the Father,** *4037*
Ac 20:3 the Jews laid **w** for him.......... *1096, 1917*
Ac 20:19 by the lying in **w** of the Jews:.......... *1917*
Ac 23:21 for there lie in **w** for him of them...... *1748*
Ac 23:30 the Jews laid **w** for the man, ... *1917*
Ac 25:3 laying **w** in the way to kill *4160, 1747*
Ro 8:25 then do we with patience **w** for it....... *553*
1Co 9:13 they which **w** at the altar are *4332*
Gal 5:5 **w** for the hope of righteousness by...... *553*
Eph 4:14 whereby they lie in **w** to deceive;....... *3180*
1Th 1:10 And to **w** for his Son from heaven,...... *362*

WAITED

Ge	49:18	I have **w** for thy salvation, O Lord.	6960
1Ki	20:38	and **w** for the king by the way,	5975
1Ch	6:32	and then they **w** on their office	5975
2Ch	7:6	the priests **w** on their offices: the	5975
2Ch	17:19	These **w** on the king, beside those	8334
Ne	12:44	priests and for the Levites that **w**	5975
Job	29:21	Unto me men gave ear, and **w**,	3176
Job	30:26	when I **w** for light, there came	3176
Job	32:11	Behold, I **w** for your words; I	3176
Ps	40:1	I **w** patiently for the Lord; and he	6960
Ps	106:13	they **w** not for his counsel:	2442
Ps	119:95	wicked have **w** for me to destroy	6960
Isa	25:9	we have **w** for him, and he will	6960
Isa	33:2	we have **w** for thee: be thou their	6960
Eze	19:5	when she saw that she had **w**,	3176
Zec	11:11	poor of the flock that **w** upon me	8104
Mk	15:43	also **w** for the kingdom of God,	*4327*
Lk	23:51	himself **w** for the kingdom of God.	*4327*
1Pe	3:20	of God **w** in the days of Noah,	*1551*

WAITETH

Job	24:15	the adulterer **w** for the twilight	8104
Ps	33:20	Our soul **w** for the Lord: he is	2442
Ps	62:1	Truly my soul **w** upon God: from	1747
Ps	65:1	Praise **w** for thee, O God, in Sion:	1747
Ps	130:6	My soul **w** for the Lord more than	
Pr	27:18	he that **w** on his master shall be	8104
Isa	64:4	prepared for him that **w** for him.	2442
Da	12:12	Blessed is he that **w**, and cometh to	2442
Mic	5:7	man, nor **w** for the sons of men.	3176
Ro	8:19	**w** for the manifestation of the	*553*
Jas	5:7	husbandman **w** for the precious	*1551*

WAITING

Nu	8:25	they shall cease **w** upon the	6635
Pr	8:34	**w** at the posts of my doors.	8104
Lk	2:25	**w** for the consolation of Israel:	*4327*
Lk	8:40	him: for they were all **w** for him	*4328*
Jn	5:3	**w** for the moving of the water	*1551*
Ro	8:23	**w** for the adoption, to wit, the	*553*
1Co	1:7	**w** for the coming of our Lord Jesus	*553*
2Th	3:5	and into the patient **w** for Christ.	

WAKE

Joel	3:9	**w** up the mighty men, let all the	5782
1Th	5:10	whether we **w** or sleep, we should	*1127*

WAKENED

Joel	3:12	Let the heathen be **w**, and come	5782
Zec	4:1	a man that is **w** out of his sleep,	5782

WAKETH

Ps	127:1	the watchman **w** but in vain	8245

WALK

Ge	13:17	Arise, **w** through the land in the	1980
Ge	17:1	**w** before me, and be thou perfect.	1980
Ge	24:40	The Lord, before whom I **w**, will	1980
Ex	16:4	whether they will **w** in my law, or	3212
Ex	18:20	the way wherein they must **w**	3212
Ex	21:19	and **w** abroad upon his staff,	1980
Le	18:4	mine ordinances, to **w** therein:	3212
Le	20:23	ye shall not **w** in the manners of	3212
Le	26:12	I will **w** among you, and will be	1980
Le	26:21	ye **w** contrary unto me, and will	3212
Le	26:28	**w** contrary unto you also in fury	1980
Dt	8:6	to **w** in his ways, and to fear him	3212
Dt	8:19	**w** after other gods, and serve	1980
Dt	10:12	to **w** in all his ways, and to love	3212
Dt	13:5	thy God commanded thee to **w** in	3212
Dt	26:17	be thy God, and to **w** in his ways,	3212
Dt	29:19	I **w** in the imagination of mine	3212
Dt	30:16	Lord thy God, to **w** in his ways,	3212
Jos	18:8	Go and **w** through the land, and	1980
Jos	22:5	God, and to **w** in all his ways	3212
Jgs	2:22	the way of the Lord to **w** therein,	3212
1Sa	2:30	should **w** before me for ever:	1980
1Sa	8:5	and thy sons **w** not in thy ways:	1980
1Ki	2:4	to **w** before me in truth with all	3212
1Ki	6:12	if thou wilt **w** in my statutes,	3212
1Ki	8:25	**w** before me as thou hast walked	3212
1Ki	8:36	good way wherein they should **w**	3212
1Ki	8:61	Lord our God, to **w** in his statutes,	3212
1Ki	9:4	if thou wilt **w** before me, as David	3212
1Ki	16:31	a light thing for him to **w** in the	3212
2Ki	23:3	the Lord, to **w** after the Lord,	3212
2Ch	6:14	that **w** before thee with all their	1980
2Ch	6:27	good way, wherein they should **w**:	3212
2Ch	7:17	for thee, if thou wilt **w** before me,	3212
Ne	5:9	ye not to **w** in the fear of our God	3212
Ne	10:29	into an oath, to **w** in God's law	3212
Ps	12:8	The wicked **w** on every side,	1980
Ps	23:4	though I **w** through the valley	3212
Ps	56:13	I may **w** before God in the light	1980
Ps	78:10	God, and refused to **w** in his law;	3212
Ps	82:5	they **w** on in darkness:	1980
Ps	86:11	O Lord; I will **w** in thy truth:	1980
Ps	89:15	they shall **w**, O Lord, in the light	1980
Ps	115:7	feet have they, but they **w** not:	1980
Ps	116:9	I will **w** before the Lord in the	1980
Ps	119:1	who **w** in the law of the Lord	1980
Ps	119:45	I will **w** at liberty: for I seek thy	1980
Ps	138:7	I **w** in the midst of trouble, thou	3212
Ps	143:8	know the way wherein I should **w**;	3212
Pr	1:15	**w** not thou in the way with them;	3212
Pr	2:7	buckler to them that **w** uprightly	1980
Pr	2:13	to **w** in the ways of darkness;	3212
Pr	2:20	thou mayest **w** in the way of good	3212
Pr	3:23	shalt thou **w** in thy way safely,	3212
Ecc	4:15	the living which **w** under the sun,	1980
Ecc	6:8	knoweth to **w** before the living?	1980
Ecc	11:9	and **w** in the ways of thine heart,	1980
Isa	2:3	ways, and we will **w** in his paths:	3212
Isa	2:5	let us **w** in the light of the Lord.	3212
Isa	8:11	not **w** in the way of this people,	3212
Isa	30:21	This is the way, **w** ye in it, when	3212
Isa	35:9	but the redeemed shall **w** there:	1980
Isa	40:31	and they shall **w**, and not faint.	3212
Isa	42:5	and spirit to them that **w** therein:	1980
Isa	42:24	for they would not **w** in his ways,	1980
Isa	50:11	**w** in the light of your fire, and in	3212
Isa	59:9	brightness, but we **w** in darkness	1980
Jer	3:17	neither shall they **w** any more	3212
Jer	6:16	is the good way, and **w** therein,	3212
Jer	6:16	they said, We will not **w** therein.	3212
Jer	7:6	**w** after other gods to your hurt:	3212
Jer	7:9	**w** after other gods whom ye know	1980
Jer	7:23	**w** ye in all the ways that I have	1980
Jer	13:10	and **w** after others gods, to serve	1980
Jer	16:12	**w** every one after the imagination	1980
Jer	18:12	we will **w** after our own devices,	1980
Jer	18:15	to **w** in paths, in a way not cast	1980
Jer	23:14	commit adultery, and **w** in lies:	1980

Jer	26:4	not hearken to me, to **w** in my law,	1980
Jer	31:9	cause them to **w** by the rivers of	1980
Jer	42:3	us the way wherein we may **w**,	1980
La	5:18	is desolate, the foxes **w** upon it.	1980
Eze	20:18	**W** ye not in the statutes of your	3212
Eze	33:15	**w** in the statutes of life, without	1980
Eze	36:12	I will cause men to **w** upon you,	3212
Eze	36:27	cause you to **w** in my statutes,	3212
Eze	37:24	they shall also **w** in my judgments,	3212
Da	4:37	those that **w** in pride he is able to	1981
Da	9:10	to **w** in his laws, which he set	3212
Hos	11:10	They shall **w** after the Lord: he	3212
Hos	14:9	right, and the just shall **w** in them:	3212
Joel	2:8	they shall **w** every one in his path:	3212
Am	3:3	Can two **w** together, except they	3212
Mic	4:2	ways, and we will **w** in his paths:	3212
Mic	4:5	will **w** every one in the name of his	3212
Mic	6:8	and to **w** humbly with thy God?	3212
Hab	3:15	didst **w** through the sea with	1869
Hab	3:19	me to **w** upon mine high places	1869
Zep	1:17	that they shall **w** like blind men,	1980
Zec	1:10	to **w** to and fro through the earth.	1980
Zec	3:7	to **w** among these that stand by	4108
Zec	6:7	**w** to and fro through the earth.	1980
Zec	10:12	shall **w** up and down in his name.	1980
Mt	9:5	**thee; or to say, Arise, and w?**	*4043*
Mt	11:5	**and the lame w, the lepers are**	*4043*
Mt	15:31	the lame to **w**, and the blind to see:	*4043*
Mk	7:5	Why **w** not thy disciples according	*4043*
Lk	5:23	**thee; or to say, Rise up and w?**	*4043*
Lk	7:22	**that the blind see, the lame w,**	*4043*
Lk	11:44	**the men that w over them are not**	*4043*
Lk	20:46	**which desire to w in long robes,**	*4043*
Lk	24:17	**ye have one to another, as ye w,**	*4043*
Jn	5:8	him, **Rise, take up thy bed, and w.**	*4043*
Jn	7:1	for he would not **w** in Jewry,	*4043*
Jn	8:12	**me shall not w in darkness,**	*4043*
Jn	11:9	**If any man w in the day, he**	*4043*
Jn	11:10	**But if a man w in the night, he**	*4043*
Jn	12:35	**W while ye have the light, lest**	*4043*
Ac	3:6	Christ of Nazareth rise up and **w**	*4043*
Ac	3:12	we had made this man to **w**?	*4043*
Ac	21:21	neither to **w** after the customs	*4043*
Ro	4:12	also **w** in the steps of that faith	*4748*
Ro	6:4	should **w** in newness of life	*4043*
Ro	8:1	who **w** not after the flesh, but	*4043*
Ro	8:4	who **w** not after the flesh, but	*4043*
Ro	13:13	Let us **w** honestly, as in the day;	*4043*
1Co	3:3	are ye not carnal, and **w** as men?	*4043*
1Co	7:17	called every one, so let him **w**	*4043*
2Co	5:7	(For we **w** by faith, not by sight:)	*4043*
2Co	6:16	dwell in them, and **w** in them;	*1704*
2Co	10:3	For though we **w** in the flesh, we	*4043*
Gal	5:16	**W** in the Spirit, and ye shall not	*4043*
Gal	5:25	Spirit, let us also **w** in the Spirit	*4748*
Gal	6:16	many as **w** according to this rule,	*4748*
Eph	2:10	that we should **w** in them	*4043*
Eph	4:1	that ye **w** worthy of the vocation	*4043*
Eph	4:17	**w** not as other Gentiles **w**	*4043*
Eph	5:2	**w** in love, as Christ also hath loved.	*4043*
Eph	5:8	in the Lord; **w** as children of light:	*4043*
Eph	5:15	See then that ye **w** circumspectly,	*4043*
Php	3:16	let us **w** by the same rule, let us	*4748*
Php	3:17	mark them which **w** so as ye have.	*4043*
Col	1:10	That ye might **w** worthy of the	*4043*
Col	2:6	Jesus the Lord, so **w** ye in him:	*4043*
Col	4:5	**W** in wisdom toward them that	*4043*
1Th	2:12	That ye would **w** worthy of God	*4043*
1Th	4:1	ye ought to **w** and to please God,	*4043*
1Th	4:12	**w** honestly toward them that are	*4043*
2Th	3:11	which **w** among you disorderly,	*4043*
2Pe	2:10	them that **w** after the flesh in the	*4198*
1Jn	1:6	with him, and **w** in darkness,	*4043*
1Jn	1:7	But if we **w** in the light, as he is in	*4043*
1Jn	2:6	in him ought himself also so to **w**	*4043*
2Jn	6	we **w** after his commandments	*4043*
3Jn	4	hear that my children **w** in truth.	*4043*
Jude	18	**w** after their own ungodly lusts.	*4198*
Rev	3:4	**they shall w with me in white:**	*4043*
Rev	9:20	neither can see, nor hear, nor **w**:	*4043*
Rev	16:15	lest he **w** naked, and they see his	*4043*
Rev	21:24	are saved shall **w** in the light of it:	*4043*

WALKED

Ge	5:24	Enoch **w** with God: and he was	1980
Ge	6:9	generations, and Noah **w** with God.	1980
Ex	2:5	her maidens **w** along by the river's	1980
Ex	14:29	children of Israel **w** upon dry land	1980
Le	26:40	they have **w** contrary unto me;	1980
Le	26:41	I also have **w** contrary unto them,	3212
Jos	5:6	**w** forty years in the wilderness	1980
Jgs	2:17	the way which their fathers **w** in,	1980
1Sa	8:3	And his sons **w** not in his ways,	1980
1Sa	12:2	I have **w** before you from my	1980
2Sa	11:2	and **w** upon the roof of the king's	1980
1Ki	3:6	as he **w** before thee in truth, and	1980
1Ki	9:4	as David thy father **w**, in integrity	1980
1Ki	11:33	have not **w** in my ways, to do that	1980
1Ki	15:3	and he **w** in all the sins of his	3212
1Ki	22:52	and **w** in the way of his father, and	3212
2Ki	4:35	and **w** in the house to and fro;	3212
2Ki	13:6	made Israel sin, but **w** therein:	1980
2Ki	16:3	But he **w** in the way of the kings	3212
2Ki	17:19	**w** in the statutes of Israel which	3212
2Ki	20:3	**w** before thee in truth and with a	1980
2Ki	21:21	in all the way that his father **w** in,	1980
2Ki	22:2	and **w** in all the way of David his	3212
2Ch	11:17	they **w** in the way of David and	1980
2Ch	17:3	he **w** in the first ways of his father	1980
2Ch	22:5	He **w** also after their counsel, and	1980
2Ch	34:2	**w** in the ways of David his father,	3212
Est	2:11	Mordecai **w** every day before the	1980
Job	31:5	If I have **w** with vanity, or if my	1980
Job	38:16	thou **w** in the search of the depth?	1980
Ps	26:3	eyes: and I have **w** in thy truth.	1980
Ps	81:12	they **w** in their own counsels.	3212
Isa	9:2	people that **w** in darkness have	1980
Isa	20:3	my servant Isaiah hath **w** naked	1980
Isa	38:3	how I have **w** before thee in truth.	1980
Jer	2:5	and have **w** after vanity, and are	3212
Jer	7:24	but **w** in the counsels and in the	3212
Jer	9:13	obeyed my voice, neither **w** therein;	1980
Jer	11:8	**w** every one in the imagination of	3212
Jer	16:11	have **w** after others gods, and have	3212
Jer	44:10	have they feared, nor **w** in my law,	1980
Eze	11:12	for ye have not **w** in my statutes,	1980
Eze	18:17	judgments, hath **w** in my statutes;	1980
Eze	20:13	they **w** not in my statutes, and	1980
Eze	20:21	they **w** not in my statutes, neither	1980
Eze	23:31	hast **w** in the way of thy sister;	1980
Eze	28:14	hast **w** up and down in the midst	1980
Da	4:29	**w** in the palace of the kingdom	1981

Na	2:11	even the old lion, **w**, and the lion's	1980
Zec	1:11	We have **w** to and fro through the	1980
Mal	2:6	he **w** with me in peace and equity	1980
Mal	3:14	**w** mournfully before the Lord	1980
Mt	14:29	he **w** on the water, to go to Jesus	*4043*
Mk	16:12	form unto two of them, as they **w**,	*4043*
Jn	1:36	looking upon Jesus as he **w**, he	*4043*
Jn	5:9	whole, and took up his bed, and **w**	*4043*
Jn	10:23	Jesus **w** in the temple in Solomon's	*4043*
Jn	11:54	**w** no more openly among the	*4043*
Ac	3:8	he leaping up stood, and **w**, and	*4043*
Ac	14:8	mother's womb, who never had **w**	*4043*
2Co	10:2	as if we **w** according to the flesh.	*4043*
2Co	12:18	you? **w** we not in the same spirit?	*4043*
Gal	2:14	they **w** not uprightly according to	*3716*
Eph	2:2	in time past ye **w** according to the	*4043*
Col	3:7	In the which ye also **w** some time	*4043*
1Pe	4:3	when we **w** in lasciviousness, lusts,	*4198*
1Jn	2:6	also so to walk, even as he **w**	*4043*

WALKEST

Dt	6:7	and when thou **w** by the way,	3212
Isa	43:2	when thou **w** through the fire,	3212

WALKETH

Ge	24:65	man is this that **w** in the field to	1980
Dt	23:14	Lord thy God **w** in the midst of	1980
1Sa	12:2	behold, the king **w** before you:	1980
Job	22:14	and he **w** in the circuit of heaven	1980
Ps	1:1	that **w** not in the counsel of the	1980
Ps	15:2	He that **w** uprightly, and worketh	1980
Ps	73:9	and their tongue **w** through the	1980
Ps	101:6	he that **w** in perfect way, he shall	1980
Ps	104:3	who **w** upon the wings of the wind:	1980
Ps	128:1	the Lord; that **w** in his ways	1980
Pr	10:9	He that **w** uprightly walketh surely:	1980
Pr	13:20	He that **w** with wise men shall be	1980
Pr	14:2	He that **w** in his uprightness	1980
Pr	15:21	of understanding **w** uprightly	1980
Pr	19:1	the poor that **w** in his integrity,	1980
Pr	20:7	The just man **w** in his integrity:	1980
Pr	28:6	poor that **w** in his uprightness,	1980
Pr	28:18	Whoso **w** uprightly shall be saved:	1980
Pr	28:26	but whoso **w** wisely, he shall be	1980
Ecc	2:14	but the fool **w** in darkness: and I	1980
Ecc	10:3	when he that is a fool **w** by the way,	1980
Isa	33:15	He that **w** righteously, and	1980
Isa	50:10	that **w** in darkness, and hath no	1980
Isa	65:2	**w** in a way that was not good,	1980
Jer	23:17	one that **w** after the imagination	1980
Eze	11:21	whose heart **w** after the heart of	1980
Mic	2:7	do good to him that **w** uprightly?	1980
Mt	12:43	**he w through dry places, seeking**	*1330*
Jn	12:35	**he that w in darkness knoweth**	*4043*
2Th	3:6	every brother that **w** disorderly,	*4043*
1Pe	5:8	**w** about, seeking whom he may	*4043*
1Jn	2:11	**w** in darkness, and knoweth not	*4043*
Rev	2:1	**who w in the midst of the seven**	*4043*

WALKING

Ge	3:8	of the Lord God **w** in the garden	1980
1Ki	3:3	**w** in the statutes of David his	3212
Job	1:7	and from **w** up and down in it	1980
Job	2:2	and from **w** up and down in it	1980
Job	31:26	or the moon **w** in brightness:	1980
Ecc	10:7	and princes **w** as servants upon the	1980
Isa	20:2	he did so, **w** naked and barefoot	1980
Isa	57:2	each one **w** in his uprightness.	1980
Da	3:25	loose, **w** in the midst of the fire	1981
Mic	2:11	man **w** in the spirit and falsehood	1980
Mt	14:25	went unto them, **w** on the sea	*4043*
Mt	14:26	the disciples saw him **w** on the sea,	*4043*
Mk	6:49	when they saw him **w** upon the sea,	*4043*
Mk	8:24	up, and said, I see men as trees, **w**.	*4043*
Mk	11:27	and as he was **w** in the temple,	*4043*
Lk	1:6	**w** in all the commandments and	*4198*
Jn	6:19	they see Jesus **w** on the sea, and	*4043*
Ac	3:8	into the temple, **w**, and leaping,	*4043*
Ac	9:31	**w** in the fear of the Lord, and in	*4198*
2Co	4:2	not **w** in craftiness, nor handling	*4043*
2Pe	3:3	scoffers, **w** after their own lusts,	*4198*
2Jn	4	found of thy children **w** in truth,	*4043*
Jude	16	**w** after their own lusts;	*4198*

WALL

Ge	49:6	selfwill they digged down a **w**	7794
Ge	49:22	whose branches run over the **w**:	7791
Ex	14:22	waters were a **w** unto them	2346
Nu	22:25	Balaam's foot against the **w**:	7023
Jos	2:15	her house was upon the town **w**,	2346
Jos	6:20	shout, that the **w** fell down flat	2346
1Sa	18:11	I will smite David even to the **w**	7023
1Sa	19:10	to smite David even to the **w** with	7023
2Sa	11:20	that they would shoot from the **w**?	2346
2Sa	11:21	a millstone upon him from the **w**,	2346
2Sa	11:24	shooters shot from off the **w** upon	2346
2Sa	20:21	shall be thrown to thee over the **w**	2346
1Ki	3:1	the **w** of Jerusalem round about	2346
1Ki	6:27	other cherub touched the other **w**;	7023
1Ki	20:30	**w** fell upon twenty and seven	2346
1Ki	21:23	eat Jezebel by the **w** of Jezreel	2426
2Ki	3:27	for a burnt offering upon the **w**	2346
2Ki	9:33	her blood was sprinkled on the **w**,	7023
2Ki	14:13	brake down the **w** of Jerusalem.	2346
2Ki	18:26	of the people that are on the **w**,	2346
2Ch	32:5	built up all the **w** that was broken,	2346
2Ch	32:18	of Jerusalem that were on the **w**	2346
2Ch	33:14	built a **w** without the city of David	2346
2Ch	36:19	brake down the **w** of Jerusalem.	2346
Ne	1:3	**w** of Jerusalem also is broken	2346
Ne	2:15	by the brook, and viewed the **w**,	2346
Ne	2:17	let us build up the **w** of Jerusalem,	2346
Ne	4:1	heard that we builded the **w**,	2346
Ne	4:6	So built we the **w**; and all the	2346
Ne	4:10	that we are not able to build the **w**	2346
Ne	6:6	which cause thou buildest the **w**,	2346
Ne	6:15	**w** was finished in the twenty and	2346
Ne	12:27	dedication of the **w** of Jerusalem	2346
Ne	13:21	them, Why lodge ye about the **w**?	2346
Ps	18:29	by my God have I leaped over a **w**	7791
Pr	18:11	as an high **w** in his own conceit	2346
Pr	24:31	the stone **w** thereof was broken	1444
Isa	59:10	We grope for the **w** like the blind	7023
Jer	51:44	yea, the **w** of Babylon shall fall	2346
La	2:8	to destroy the **w** of the daughter	2346
Eze	8:8	me, Son of man, dig now in the **w**	7023
Eze	13:12	when the **w** was fallen, shall it not	7023
Eze	13:15	accomplish my wrath upon the **w**,	7023
Eze	38:20	every **w** shall fall to the ground	2346
Eze	41:5	he measured the **w** of the house,	7023
Da	9:25	shall be built again, and the **w**,	2742
Hos	2:6	and make a **w**, that she shall not	1447
Joel	2:7	climb the **w** like men of war;	2346

Am 7:7 upon a **w** made by a plumbline, ... 2346
Hab 2:11 the stone shall cry out of the **w**, ... 7023
Zec 2:5 will be unto her a **w** of fire round. 2346
Ac 9:25 let down by the **w** in a basket. *5038*
Ac 23:3 shall smite thee, thou whited **w**: *5109*
Eph 2:14 broken down the middle **w** of
Rev 21:12 And had a **w** great and high, and *5038*
Rev 21:14 the **w** of the city had twelve *5038*
Rev 21:17 And he measured the **w** thereof, ... *5038*
Rev 21:19 foundations of the **w** of the city *5038*

WALLED See also UNWALLED.

Le 25:29 sell a dwelling house in a **w** city, ... 2346
Dt 1:28 are great and **w** up to heaven; 1219

WALLOW

Jer 6:26 sackcloth, and **w** thyself in ashes: 6428
Jer 25:34 **w** yourselves in the ashes, ye 6428
Eze 27:30 shall **w** themselves in the ashes: 6428

WALLOWING

2Pe 2:22 was washed to her **w** in the mire. *2946*

WALLS

Le 14:39 plague be spread in the **w** of the 7023
Dt 28:52 thy high and fenced **w** come down, ... 2346
1Ki 6:5 against the **w** of the house round 7023
1Ki 6:29 he carved all the **w** of the house 7023
2Ki 25:10 brake down the **w** of Jerusalem. 2346
2Ch 3:7 and graved cherubims on the **w** 7023
2Ch 14:7 make about them **w**, and towers 2346
Ezr 4:13 be builded, and the **w** set up again, ... 7791
Ezr 5:8 and timber is laid in the **w**, and 3797
Ne 2:13 and viewed the **w** of Jerusalem, ... 2346
Ne 4:7 the **w** of Jerusalem were made up, ... 2346
Ps 51:18 build thou the **w** of Jerusalem. 2346
Ps 122:7 Peace be within thy **w**, and 2426
Pr 25:28 is broken down, and without **w** 2346
SS 5:7 keepers of the **w** took away my veil 2346
Isa 22:5 breaking down the **w**, and of. 7023
Isa 56:5 within my **w** a place and a name 2346
Isa 60:10 of strangers shall build up thy **w**, ... 2346
Isa 60:18 thou shalt call thy **w** Salvation, ... 2346
Isa 62:6 I have set watchmen upon thy **w**, ... 2346
Jer 1:15 all the **w** thereof round about, ... 2346
Jer 5:10 Go ye up upon her **w**, and destroy; 8284
Jer 21:4 which besiege you without the **w**,. 2346
Jer 39:4 by the gate betwixt the two **w**:. 2346
Jer 39:8 brake down the **w** of Jerusalem. 2346
Jer 50:15 are fallen, her **w** are thrown down:. 2346
Jer 51:58 broad **w** of Babylon shall be utterly 2346
Jer 52:7 way of the gate between the two **w**, ... 2346
Jer 52:14 brake down all the **w** of Jerusalem 2346
La 2:7 of the enemy the **w** of her palaces; 2346
Eze 26:4 they shall destroy the **w** of Tyrus, ... 2346
Eze 26:10 thy **w** shall shake at the noise of 2346
Eze 38:11 all of them dwelling without **w**, ... 2346
Eze 41:22 and the **w** thereof, were of wood: 7023
Mic 7:11 the day that thy **w** are to be built, ... 1447
Zec 2:4 inhabited as towns without **w**
Heb 11:30 By faith the **w** of Jericho fell *5038*

WANDER

Nu 32:13 he made them **w** in the wilderness 5128
Dt 27:18 he that maketh the blind to **w** out 7686
Ps 55:7 then would I **w** far off, and remain. 5074
Ps 107:40 them to **w** in the wilderness, ... 8582
Ps 119:10 not **w** from thy commandments. 7686
Jer 14:10 Thus have they loved to **w**, they 5128
Jer 48:12 that shall cause him to **w**, and. 6808
Am 8:12 And they shall **w** from sea to sea, ... 5128

WANDERED

Jos 14:10 of Israel **w** in the wilderness:. 1980
Ps 107:4 They **w** in the wilderness in a 8582
La 4:14 They have **w** as blind men in the 5128
Eze 34:6 My sheep **w** through all the. 7686
Heb 11:37 they **w** about in sheepskins and *4022*
Heb 11:38 they **w** in deserts, and in. *4105*

WANDERETH

Pr 21:16 The man that **w** out of the way of 8582
Pr 27:8 so is a man that **w** from his place. 5074
Isa 16:3 outcasts; bewray not him that **w**. 5074
Jer 49:5 none shall gather up him that **w**. 5074

WANDERING

Ge 37:15 behold, he was **w** in the field: 8582
Pr 26:2 As the bird by **w**, as the swallow 5110
Ecc 6:9 the eyes than the **w** of the desire: 1981
Isa 16:2 as a **w** bird cast out of the nest,. 5074
1Ti 5:13 **w** about from house to house;. *4022*
Jude 13 **w** stars, to whom is reserved the *4107*

WANT

Dt 28:57 shall eat them for **w** of all things. 2640
Jgs 18:10 a place where there is no **w** of. 4270
Jgs 19:19 there is no **w** of any thing 4270
Ps 23:1 is my shepherd; I shall not **w**. 2637
Ps 34:9 is no **w** to them that fear him.. 4270
Ps 34:10 Lord shall not **w** any good thing. 2637
Pr 10:21 but fools die for **w** of wisdom. 2638
Pr 13:23 is destroyed for **w** of judgment. 3808
Pr 13:25 the belly of the wicked shall **w** 2637
Pr 14:28 but in the **w** of people is the 657
Pr 21:5 every one that is hasty only to **w**. 4270
Pr 22:16 to the rich, shall surely come to **w** 4270
Pr 24:34 and thy **w** as an armed man. 4270
Isa 34:16 shall fail, none shall **w** her mate:. 6485
Jer 33:17 never **w** a man to sit upon the 3772
La 4:9 for **w** of the fruits of the field.
Mk 12:44 **she of her w did cast in all that**. *5304*
Lk 15:14 **land; and he began to be in w**. *5302*
2Co 8:14 also may be a supply for your **w** *5303*
2Co 9:12 only supplieth the **w** of the saints, ... *5303*
Php 4:11 Not that I speak in respect of **w** *5304*

WANTED

Jer 44:18 we have **w** all things, and have 2637
Jn 2:3 when they **w** wine, the mother of. *5302*
2Co 11:9 I was present with you, and **w**, I *5502*

WANTETH

Pr 9:4 for him that **w** understanding, ... 2638
Pr 10:19 multitude of words there **w** not sin:. . . . 2308
Pr 28:16 The prince that **w** understanding 2638
Ecc 6:2 so that he **w** nothing for his soul 2638

WANTING

2Ki 10:19 whosoever shall be **w**, he shall not 6485
Pr 19:7 with words, yet they are **w** to him. 3808
Ecc 1:15 which is **w** cannot be numbered. 2642
Da 5:27 in the balances, and art found **w**. 2627
Tit 1:5 set in order the things that are **w**, ... *3007*
Tit 3:13 that nothing be **w** unto them. *3007*
Jas 1:4 be perfect and entire, **w** nothing. *3007*

WANTON

1Ti	5:11	begun to wax **w** against Christ,	*2691*
Jas	5:5	pleasure on the earth, and been **w**;	*4684*

WANTONNESS

Ro	13:13	not in chambering and **w**, not in	*766*
2Pe	2:18	through much **w**, those that were	*766*

WANTS

Jgs	19:20	let all thy **w** lie upon me; only	4270
Php	2:25	and he that ministered to my **w**	*5532*

WAR

Ex	13:17	the people repent when they see **w**,	4421
Ex	15:3	The Lord is a man of **w**: the Lord	4421
Ex	17:16	the Lord will have **w** with Amalek	4421
Ex	32:17	There is a noise of **w** in the camp.	4421
Nu	1:45	were able to go forth to **w** in Israel;	6635
Nu	10:9	if ye go to **w** in your land against	4421
Nu	31:6	And Moses sent them to the **w**, a	6635
Nu	32:6	Shall your brethren go to **w**, and	4421
Nu	32:27	over, every man armed for **w**,	6635
Dt	2:16	all the men of **w** were consumed	4421
Dt	3:18	all that are meet for the **w**.	2428
Dt	4:34	signs, and by wonders, and by **w**,	4421
Dt	21:10	When thou goest forth to **w**	4421
Dt	24:5	new wife, he shall not go out to **w**,	6635
Jos	6:3	compass the city, all ye men of **w**,.	4421
Jos	11:18	Joshua made **w** a long time with.	4421
Jos	11:23	And the land rested from **w**.	4421
Jos	14:11	even so is my strength now, for **w**,	4421
Jos	14:15	And the land had rest from **w**	4421
Jgs	3:2	might know, to teach them **w**,	4421
Jgs	5:8	new gods; then was **w** in the gates:	3901
Jgs	11:27	doest me wrong to **w** against me:	3898
Jgs	18:16	appointed with their weapons of **w**	4421
Jgs	20:17	sword: all these were men of **w**	4421
Jgs	21:22	not to each man his wife in the **w**:	4421
1Sa	16:18	and a man of **w**, and prudent in	4421
1Sa	17:33	and he a man of **w** from his youth.	4421
1Sa	18:5	Saul set him over the men of **w**,	4421
1Sa	19:8	there was **w** again: and David	4421
2Sa	1:27	and the weapons of **w** perished!	4421
2Sa	3:1	long **w** between the house of Saul	4421
2Sa	11:19	end of telling the matters of the **w**	4421
2Sa	17:8	thy father is a man of **w**, and will	4421
2Sa	22:35	He teacheth my hands to **w**; so	4421
1Ki	2:5	and shed the blood of **w** in peace,	4421
1Ki	9:22	but they were men of **w**, and his	4421
1Ki	20:18	or whether they be come out for **w**,	4421
1Ki	22:1	continued three years without **w**	4421
2Ki	18:20	counsel and strength for the **w**	4421
2Ki	24:16	that were strong and apt for **w**,	4421
2Ki	25:4	men of **w** fled by night by the way	4421
1Ch	5:22	slain, because the **w** was of God.	4421
1Ch	7:11	fit to go out for **w** and battle.	6635
1Ch	12:8	and men of **w** fit for the battle,	6635
1Ch	12:38	All these men of **w**, that could	4421
1Ch	20:5	And there was **w** again with the	4421
1Ch	20:6	yet again there was **w** at Gath,	4421
1Ch	28:3	thou hast been a man of **w**, and	4421
2Ch	6:34	If thy people go out to **w** against	4421
2Ch	14:6	and he had no **w** in those years;	4421
2Ch	15:19	And there was no more **w** unto the	4421
2Ch	17:10	made no **w** against Jehoshaphat.	3898
2Ch	17:18	ready prepared for the **w**	6635
2Ch	18:3	and we will be with thee in the **w**	4421
2Ch	26:11	men, that went out to **w** by bands,	6635
2Ch	33:14	and put captains of **w** in all the	2428
Job	38:23	against the day of battle and **w**?	4421
Ps	18:34	He teacheth my hands to **w**, so	4421
Ps	27:3	though **w** should rise against me,	4421
Ps	68:30	thou the people that delight in **w**	7128
Ps	120:7	but when I speak, they are for **w**.	4421
Ps	144:1	teacheth my hands to **w**,	4421, 7128
Pr	20:18	and with good advice make **w**.	4421
Pr	24:6	counsel thou shalt make thy **w**:	4421
Ecc	3:8	a time of **w**, and a time of peace	4421
Ecc	9:18	is better than weapons of **w**: but	7128
Isa	2:4	neither shall they learn **w** any	4421
Isa	3:2	mighty man, and the man of **w**,	4421
Isa	7:1	toward Jerusalem to **w** against it,	4421
Isa	21:15	and from the grievousness of **w**	4421
Isa	36:5	I have counsel and strength for **w**:	4421
Isa	41:12	they that **w** against thee shall be	4421
Isa	42:13	stir up jealousy like a man of **w**:	4421
Jer	4:19	of the trumpet, the alarm of **w**	4421
Jer	6:4	Prepare ye **w** against her; arise,	4421
Jer	21:4	I will turn back the weapons of **w**	4421
Jer	28:8	of **w**, and of evil, and of pestilence.	4421
Jer	38:4	the hands of the men of **w** that	4421
Jer	39:4	saw them, and all the men of **w**,	4421
Jer	42:14	Egypt, where we shall see no **w**,	4421
Jer	48:14	mighty and strong men for the **w**?	4421
Jer	49:2	cause an alarm of **w** to be heard in.	4421
Jer	50:30	all her men of **w** shall be cut off in.	4421
Jer	52:7	all the men of **w** fled, and went	4421
Eze	26:9	engines of **w** against thy walls,	6904
Eze	32:27	to hell with their weapons of **w**:	4421
Da	7:21	horn made **w** with the saints,	7129
Da	9:26	unto the end of the **w** desolations	4421
Joel	2:7	shall climb the wall like men of **w**;	4421
Joel	3:9	Prepare **w**, wake up the mighty	4421
Mic	4:3	neither shall they learn **w** any	4421
Lk	14:31	**to make w against another king,**	*4171*
Lk	23:11	Herod with his men of **w** set him	*4753*
2Co	10:3	flesh, we do not **w** after the flesh:	*4754*
1Ti	1:18	them mightest **w** a good warfare;	*4754*
Jas	4:1	lusts that **w** in your members?.	*4754*
Jas	4:2	ye fight and **w**, yet ye have not,	*4170*
1Pe	2:11	lusts, which **w** against the soul;	*4754*
Rev	11:7	pit shall make **w** against them,	*4171*
Rev	12:7	there was **w** in heaven: Michael.	*4171*
Rev	12:17	went to make **w** with the remnant	*4171*
Rev	13:4	who is able to make **w** with him?	*4170*
Rev	13:7	him to make **w** with the saints,	*4171*
Rev	17:14	These … make **w** with the Lamb,	*4170*
Rev	19:11	he doth judge and make **w**.	*4170*
Rev	19:19	to make **w** against him that sat	*4171*

WARD

Ge	42:17	he put them altogether into **w**.	4929
Nu	15:34	they put him in **w**, because it was.	4929
2Sa	20:3	put them in **w**, and fed them,	4931
Ne	12:24	the man of God, **w** over against **w**	4929
Isa	21:8	I am set in my **w** whole nights:	4931
Eze	19:9	they put him in **w** in chains,	5474

WARE

Ne	10:31	the people of the land bring **w** or	4728
Ne	13:16	brought fish, and all manner of **w**,	4377
Ne	13:20	sellers of all kind of **w** lodged	4465
Lk	8:27	devils long time, and **w** no clothes,	*1737*
2Ti	4:15	Of whom be thou **w** also; for he	*5442*

WARES

Eze 27:33	thy **w** went forth out of the seas,	5801
Jnh 1:5	forth the **w** that were in the ship	3627

WARFARE

1Sa 40:2	her, that her **w** is accomplished,	6635
1Co 9:7	who goeth a **w** any time at his	*4754*
2Co 10:4	weapons of our **w** are not carnal,	*4752*
1Ti 1:18	by them mightest war a good **w**;	*4752*

WARM See also LUKEWARM

2Ki 4:34	the flesh of the child waxed **w**	2552
Ecc 4:11	but how can one be **w** alone?	3179
Isa 47:14	there shall not be a coal to **w** at,	2552
Hag 1:6	clothe you, but there is none **w**;	2527

WARMED

Mk 14:54	and **w** himself at the fire	*2328*
Jn 18:25	Simon Peter stood and **w** himself.	*2328*
Jas 2:16	Depart in peace, be ye **w** and filled;	*2328*

WARMING

Mk 14:67	when she saw Peter **w** himself,	*2328*

WARN

2Ch 19:10	**w** them that they trespass not	2094
Eze 3:18	nor speakest to **w** the wicked	2094
Eze 3:21	if thou **w** the righteous man, that	2094
Eze 33:3	the trumpet, and **w** the people;	2094
Eze 33:7	my mouth, and **w** them from me.	2094
Eze 33:8	dost not speak to **w** the wicked	2094
Ac 20:31	I ceased not to **w** every one night	*3560*
1Co 4:14	but as my beloved sons I **w** you	*3560*
1Th 5:14	**w** them that are unruly, comfort	*3560*

WARNED

2Ki 6:10	man of God told him and **w** him of,	2094
Ps 19:11	by them is thy servant **w**: and in	2094
Eze 3:21	shall surely live, because he is **w**;	2094
Eze 33:6	trumpet, and the people be not **w**;	2094
Mt 2:12	being **w** of God in a dream that	*5537*
Mt 3:7	**w** you to flee from the wrath to	*5263*
Lk 3:7	**w** you to flee from the wrath to	*5263*
Ac 10:22	**w** from God by an holy angel to	*5537*
Heb 11:7	being **w** of God of things not seen	*5537*

WARNING

Jer 6:10	whom shall I speak, and give **w**,	5749
Eze 3:17	mouth, and give them **w** from me	2094
Eze 3:20	because thou hast not given him **w**	2094
Eze 33:5	of the trumpet, and took not **w**;	2094
Eze 33:5	taketh **w** shall deliver his soul	2094
Col 1:28	**w** every man, and teaching every	*3560*

WARRED

1Ki 20:1	Samaria, and **w** against it	3898
2Ki 6:8	the king of Syria **w** against Israel,	3898
2Ki 14:28	how he **w**, and how he recovered	3898
2Ch 26:6	and **w** against the Philistines,	3898

WARRETH

2Ti 2:4	No man that **w** entangleth himself	*4754*

WARRING

Ro 7:23	**w** against the law of my mind,	*497*

WARRIOR

Isa 9:5	battle of the **w** is with confused	5431

WARS

Jgs 3:1	had not known all the **w** of Canaan;	4421
1Ki 5:3	the **w** which were about him on	4421
1Ch 22:8	abundantly, and hast made great **w**	4421
2Ch 12:15	there were **w** between Rehoboam	4421
2Ch 16:9	henceforth thou shalt have **w**	4421
Ps 46:9	maketh **w** to cease unto the end of	4421
Mt 24:6	**hear of w and rumours of w:**	*4171*
Lk 21:9	**shall hear of w and commotions,**	*4171*
Jas 4:1	whence come **w** and fightings	*4171*

WASH

Ge 18:4	**w** your feet, and rest yourselves	7364
Ge 19:2	tarry all night, and **w** your feet,	7364
Ex 2:5	daughter of Pharaoh ... down to **w**	7364
Ex 29:4	and shalt **w** them with water.	7364
Ex 30:20	**w** with water, that they die not	7364
Le 6:27	thou shalt **w** that whereon it was	3526
Le 14:9	also he shall **w** his flesh in water,	7364
Le 15:5	toucheth ... bed shall **w** his clothes,	3526
Le 16:24	**w** his flesh with water in the holy	7364
Le 16:26	the scapegoat shall **w** his clothes,	3526
Le 17:16	if he **w** them not, nor bathe his	3526
Le 22:6	unless he **w** his flesh with water	7364
Nu 19:7	Then the priest shall **w** his clothes,	3526
Nu 19:19	purify himself, and **w** his clothes,	3526
Nu 31:34	**w** your clothes on the seventh day,	3526
Dt 23:11	on, he shall **w** himself with water:	7364
Ru 3:3	**W** thyself therefore, and anoint	7364
2Ki 5:10	Go and **w** in Jordan seven times,	7364
2Ki 5:13	he saith to thee, **W**, and be clean?	7364
2Ch 4:6	the sea was for the priests to **w** in.	7364
Job 9:30	If I **w** myself with snow water, and	7364
Ps 26:6	I will **w** mine hands in innocency:	7364
Ps 51:2	**W** me throughly from mine	3526
Ps 51:7	**w** me, and I shall be whiter than	3526
Ps 58:10	**w** his feet in the blood of the	7364
Isa 1:16	**W** you, make you clean; put away	7364
Jer 4:14	**w** thine heart from wickedness,	3526
Mt 6:17	**anoint thine head, and w thy**	*3538*
Mt 15:2	**w** not their hands when they eat	*3538*
Mk 7:4	except they **w**, they eat not	*907*
Lk 7:38	began to **w** his feet with tears,	*1026*
Jn 9:7	him, **Go, w in the pool of Siloam,**	*3538*
Jn 9:11	Go to the pool of Siloam, and **w**.	*3538*
Jn 13:5	and began to **w** the disciples' feet,	*3538*
Jn 13:6	him, Lord, dost thou **w** my feet?	*3538*
Jn 13:8	**If I w thee not, thou hast no part**	*3538*
Jn 13:10	**needeth not save to w his feet,**	*3538*
Jn 13:14	**ought to w one another's feet.**	*3538*
Ac 22:16	be baptized, and **w** away thy sins,	*628*

WASHED

Ge 43:24	water, and they **w** their feet;	7364
Ge 43:31	And he **w** his face, and went out,	7364
Ge 49:11	he **w** his garments in wine, and	3526
Ex 40:31	Aaron and his sons **w** their hands	7364
Ex 40:32	came near unto the altar, they **w**;	7364
Le 13:55	the plague, after that it is **w**:	3526
Le 15:17	shall be **w** with water, and be	3526
Nu 8:21	purified, and they **w** their clothes;	3526
Jgs 19:21	they **w** their feet, and did eat and	7364
2Sa 12:20	David arose from the earth, and **w**,	7364
2Sa 19:24	his beard, nor **w** his clothes,	3526
1Ki 22:38	his blood; and they **w** his armour;	7364
Ps 73:13	and **w** my hands in innocency.	7364
Pr 30:12	yet is not **w** from their filthiness	7364

SS 5:12 rivers of waters, **w** with milk, and...... 7364
Isa 4:4 Lord shall have **w** away the filth 7364
Eze 16:9 I throughly **w** away thy blood 7857
Mt 27:24 **w** his hands before the multitude, ... *633*
Lk 7:44 **she hath w my feet with tears,**......... *1026*
Lk 11:38 he had not first **w** before dinner *907*
Jn 9:7 and **w**, and came seeing............... *3538*
Jn 9:11 I went and **w**, and I received sight...... *3538*
Jn 9:15 mine eyes, and I **w**, and do see......... *3538*
Jn 13:10 **He that is w needeth not save to**....... *3068*
Jn 13:12 So after he had **w** their feet, and *3538*
Jn 13:14 **and Master, have w your feet;** *3538*
Ac 16:33 of the night, and **w** their stripes;....... *3068*
1Co 6:11 but ye are **w**, but ye are sanctified, ... *628*
1Ti 5:10 if she have **w** the saints' feet, if......... *3538*
Heb 10:22 and our bodies **w** with pure water...... *3068*
2Pe 2:22 sow that was **w** to her wallowing *3068*
Rev 1:5 **w** us from our sins in his own......... *3068*
Rev 7:14 and have **w** their robes and made...... *4150*

WASHING

2Sa 11:2 roof he saw a woman **w** herself; 7364
Mk 7:8 **of men, as the w of pots and cups:**...... *909*
Lk 5:2 of them, and were **w** their nets.......... *637*
Eph 5:26 cleanse it with the **w** of water by....... *3067*
Tit 3:5 by the **w** of regeneration, and *3067*

WASHINGS

Heb 9:10 in meats and drinks, and divers **w**,...... *909*

WASTE

Le 26:31 And I will make your cities **w**, ...2723
Dt 32:10 and in the **w** howling wilderness;...... 8414
1Ki 17:14 The barrel of meal shall not **w**,......... 3615
2Ki 19:25 to lay **w** fenced cities into ruinous 7582
Ne 2:17 how Jerusalem lieth **w**, and the........ 2720
Ps 79:7 and laid **w** his dwelling place.......... 8074
Ps 80:13 boar out of the wood doth **w** it, ... 3765
Isa 5:6 I will lay it **w**: it shall not be........... 1326
Isa 23:14 for your strength is laid **w** 7703
Isa 34:10 to generation it shall lie **w**;............ 2717
Isa 51:3 he will comfort all her **w** places;....... 2723
Isa 52:9 ye **w** places of Jerusalem:............. 2723
Isa 61:4 they shall repair the **w** cities, the....... 2721
Isa 64:11 our pleasant things are laid **w**......... 2723
Jer 2:15 yelled, and they made his land **w**:...... 8047
Jer 4:7 and thy cities shall be laid **w**,.......... 5327
Jer 27:17 should this city be laid **w**? 2723
Eze 5:14 Moreover I will make thee **w**, ... 2723
Eze 12:20 are inhabited shall be laid **w**,.......... 2717
Eze 19:7 palaces, and he laid **w** their cities;...... 2717
Eze 35:4 I will lay thy cities **w**, and thou 2723
Joel 1:7 He hath laid my vine **w**, and 8047
Am 7:9 of Israel shall be laid **w**; 2717
Na 2:10 She is empty, and void, and **w**: 1110
Zep 3:6 I made their street **w**, that none 2717
Hag 1:4 houses, and this house lie **w**?.......... 2720
Hag 1:9 Because of mine house that is **w**, ... 2720
Mt 26:8 To what purpose is this **w**?............ *684*
Mk 14:4 Why was this **w** of the ointment........ *684*

WASTED

Dt 2:14 until all the men of war were **w** 8552
1Ki 17:16 And the barrel of meal **w** not,......... 3615
Ps 137:3 they that **w** us required of us.......... 8437
Isa 19:5 the river shall be **w** and dried up 2717
Isa 60:12 those nations shall be utterly **w**........ 2717
Joel 1:10 The field is **w**, the land mourneth;..... 7703
Lk 15:13 **there w his substance with riotous**..... *1287*
Lk 16:1 **unto him that he had w his goods**...... *1287*
Gal 1:13 the church of God, and **w** it: *4199*

WASTER

Pr 18:9 brother to him that is a great **w** 7843
Isa 54:16 I have created the **w** to destroy 7843

WASTETH

Job 14:10 But man dieth, and **w** away: 2522
Ps 91:6 destruction that **w** at noonday 7736
Pr 19:26 He that **w** his father, and 7703

WATCH See also **WATCHMAN; WATCHTOWER.**

Ge 31:49 the Lord **w** between me and thee,...... 6822
Jgs 7:19 they had but newly set the **w**.......... 8104
2Sa 13:34 the young man that kept the **w**........ 6822
2Ki 11:5 keepers of the **w** of the king's 4931
2Ch 20:24 Judah came toward the **w** tower 4707
Ne 4:9 set a **w** against them day and.......... 4929
Ne 7:3 of Jerusalem, every one in his **w**, ... 4929
Ps 90:4 it is past, and as a **w** in the night........ 821
Ps 130:6 than they that **w** for the morning: 8104
Ps 141:3 Set a **w**, O Lord, before my mouth; 8108
Isa 29:20 all that **w** for iniquity are cut off: 8245
Jer 5:6 a leopard shall **w** over their cities:...... 8245
Jer 31:28 so will I **w** over them, to build, and 8245
Jer 44:27 I will **w** over them for evil, and not 8245
Mt 14:25 fourth **w** of the night Jesus went....... 5438
Mt 24:42 **W therefore: for ye know not** *1127*
Mt 24:43 **in what w the thief would come,** *5438*
Mt 26:40 **could ye not w with me one hour?**..... *1127*
Mt 26:41 **W and pray, that ye enter not**......... *1127*
Mt 27:66 sealing the stone, and setting a **w** *2892*
Mk 13:33 **Take ye heed, w and pray: for ye**......... *69*
Mk 13:35 **W ye therefore: for ye know not**....... *1127*
Mk 14:37 **couldest not thou w one hour?**........ *1127*
Mk 14:38 **W ye and pray, lest ye enter into** *1127*
Lk 2:8 keeping **w** over their flock by.......... *5438*
Lk 12:38 **if he shall come in the second w,** *5438*
Lk 21:36 **W ye therefore, and pray always,** *69*
1Co 16:13 **W** ye, stand fast in the faith, quit *1127*
Col 4:2 **w** in the same with thanksgiving;...... *1127*
1Th 5:6 others; but let us **w** and be sober....... *1127*
2Ti 4:5 But **w** thou in all things, endure *3525*
Heb 13:17 they **w** for your souls, as they that *69*
1Pe 4:7 sober, and **w** unto prayer.............. *3525*
Rev 3:3 **If therefore thou shalt not w, I**........ *1127*

WATCHED

La 4:17 **w** for a nation that could not save 6822
Da 9:14 hath the Lord **w** upon the evil, ... 8245
Mt 24:43 **he would have w, and would not** *1127*
Lk 6:7 the scribes and Pharisees **w** him, ... *3906*
Lk 12:39 **he would have w, and not have**........ *1127*
Lk 14:1 the sabbath day, that they **w** him....... *3906*
Lk 20:20 they **w** him, and sent forth spies, ... *3906*
Ac 9:24 they **w** the gates day and night to *3906*

WATCHERS

Jer 4:16 that **w** come from a far country 5341
Da 4:17 matter is by the decree of the **w**,....... 5894

WATCHES

Ps 63:6 meditate on thee in the night **w** 821
Ps 119:148 Mine eyes prevent the night **w**,......... 821
La 2:19 beginning of the **w** pour out thine...... 821

WATCHETH
Ps 37:32 The wicked **w** the righteous, and 6822
Rev 16:15 Blessed is he that **w**, and keepeth *1127*

WATCHFUL
Rev 3:2 **Be w, and strengthen the things** *1127*

WATCHING
1Sa 4:13 sat upon a seat by the wayside **w** 6822
Pr 8:34 heareth me, **w** daily at my gates, ... 8245
La 4:17 in our **w** we have watched for a 6822
Mt 27:54 they that were with him, **w** Jesus, ... *5083*
Lk 12:37 **lord when he cometh shall find w:** *1127*
Eph 6:18 and **w** thereunto with all *69*

WATCHINGS
2Co 6:5 in tumults, in labours, in **w**, in *70*
2Co 11:27 painfulness, in **w** often, in hunger........ *70*

WATCHMAN
2Sa 18:26 the **w** saw another man running: 6822
2Ki 9:17 there stood a **w** on the tower in 6822
Ps 127:1 city, the **w** waketh but in vain.. 8104
Isa 21:11 **W**, what of the night? 8104
Eze 3:17 thee a **w** unto the house of Israel: 6822
Eze 33:7 thee a **w** unto the house of Israel; 6822
Hos 9:8 **w** of Ephraim was with my God: 6822

WATCHMAN'S
Eze 33:6 blood will I require at the **w** hand 6822

WATCHMEN
SS 5:7 The **w** that went about the city 8104
Isa 52:8 Thy **w** shall lift up the voice; 6822
Isa 56:10 His **w** are blind: they are all 6822
Isa 62:6 I have set **w** upon thy walls, O 8104
Jer 6:17 I set **w** over you, saying, Hearken 6822
Jer 31:6 the **w** upon the mount Ephraim 5341
Mic 7:4 the day of thy **w** and thy visitation; 6822

WATCHTOWER See also WATCH and TOWER.
Isa 21:5 the table, watch in the **w**, eat, ... 6844
Isa 21:8 I stand continually upon the **w** in 4707

WATER
Ge 18:4 Let a little **w**, I pray you, be 4325
Ge 21:19 her eyes, and she saw a well of **w**, ... 4325
Ge 24:11 time that women go out to draw **w**
Ge 24:19 I will draw **w** for thy camels also,
Ge 26:20 herdmen, saying, The **w** is ours: 4325
Ge 29:8 mouth; then we **w** the sheep.. 8248
Ge 37:24 was empty, there was no **w** in it 4325
Ge 49:4 Unstable as **w**, thou shalt not excel; 4325
Ex 2:10 Because I drew him out of the **w** 4325
Ex 2:19 and also drew **w** enough for us,
Ex 7:21 not drink of the **w** of the river; 4325
Ex 17:2 said, Give us **w** that we may drink...... 4325
Ex 17:6 there shall come **w** out of it, that 4325
Ex 20:4 that is in the **w** under the earth: 4325
Ex 30:20 they shall wash with **w**, that they 4325
Ex 34:28 did neither eat bread, nor drink **w** 4325
Le 11:32 work is done, it must be put into **w**, ... 4325
Le 14:51 in the running **w**, and sprinkle the..... 4325
Le 15:13 and bathe his flesh in running **w**, ... 4325
Nu 5:17 And the priest shall take holy **w** in 4325
Nu 5:24 the woman to drink the bitter **w**. 4325
Nu 8:7 Sprinkle **w** of purifying upon 4325
Nu 19:9 of Israel for a **w** of separation: 4325
Nu 19:18 take hyssop, and dip it in the **w**, ... 4325
Nu 20:11 and the **w** came out abundantly, ... 4325
Nu 21:5 is no bread, neither is there any **w**; 4325
Nu 21:16 together, and I will give them **w** 4325
Nu 33:14 was no **w** for the people to drink....... 4325
Dt 8:7 good land, a land of brooks and **w**, ... 4325
Dt 8:15 forth **w** out of the rock of flint; 4325
Dt 9:9 neither did eat bread nor drink **w**: 4325
Dt 9:18 did neither eat bread, nor drink **w**,..... 4325
Dt 11:4 he made the **w** of the Red sea to 4325
Dt 12:24 pour it upon the earth as **w**. 4325
Dt 15:23 shalt pour it upon the ground as **w**. 4325
Jos 2:10 dried up the **w** of the Red sea for 4325
Jos 7:5 people melted, and became as **w**. 4325
Jgs 4:19 Give me, ... a little **w** to drink; 4325
Jgs 7:5 Every one that lappeth of the **w** 4325
1Sa 26:12 the cruse of **w** from Saul's bolster; 4325
1Sa 30:12 eaten no bread, nor drunk any **w**, ... 4325
2Sa 14:14 and are as **w** spilt on the ground, ... 4325
1Ki 13:22 hast eaten bread and drunk **w** in 4325
1Ki 18:33 Fill four barrels with **w**, and pour...... 4325
1Ki 18:38 up the **w** that was in the trench. 4325
1Ki 19:6 coals, and a cruse of **w** at his head..... 4325
2Ki 6:5 beam, the axe head fell into the **w** 4325
1Ch 11:17 of the **w** of the well of Beth-lehem, ... 4325
2Ch 32:4 Assyria come, and find much **w**? 4325
Ezr 10:6 he did eat no bread, nor drink **w** 4325
Ne 9:15 forth **w** for them out of the rock 4325
Ne 13:2 of Israel with bread and with **w**, ... 4325
Job 8:11 can the flag grow without **w**? 4325
Job 15:16 which drinketh iniquity like **w**? 4325
Ps 1:3 a tree planted by the rivers of **w**, ... 4325
Ps 6:6 I **w** my couch with my tears 4529
Ps 22:14 I am poured out like **w**, and all 4325
Ps 42:1 hart panteth after the **w** brooks, ... 4325
Ps 79:3 Their blood have they shed like **w** 4325
Ps 114:8 turned the rock into a standing **w**, ... 4325
Pr 8:24 no fountains abounding with **w** 4325
Pr 17:14 is as when one letteth out **w** 4325
Pr 20:5 the heart of man is like deep **w**; 4325
Pr 21:1 of the Lord, as the rivers of **w**:. 4325
Pr 25:21 he be thirsty, give him **w** to drink: 4325
Pr 27:19 As in **w** face answereth to face, so...... 4325
Pr 30:16 the earth that is not filled with **w**;...... 4325
Isa 1:22 dross, thy wine mixed with **w** 4325
Isa 1:30 and as a garden that hath no **w**, ... 4325
Isa 12:3 draw **w** out of the wells of salvation.... 4325
Isa 16:9 I will **w** thee with my tears, O 7301
Isa 27:3 I will **w** it every moment: lest 8248
Isa 30:20 adversity, and the **w** of affliction, ... 4325
Isa 32:2 as rivers of **w** in a dry place, as 4325
Isa 41:17 When the poor and needy seek **w**, ... 4325
Isa 63:12 dividing the **w** before them, to 4325
Jer 2:13 broken cisterns, that can hold no **w** 4325
Jer 8:14 and given us **w** of gall to drink, ... 4325
Jer 23:15 and make them drink the **w** of gall: 4325
Jer 38:6 in the dungeon there was no **w**, ... 4325
La 1:16 mine eye runneth down with **w**, ... 4325
La 2:19 pour out thine heart like **w** before 4325
La 3:48 eye runneth down with rivers of **w** 4325
La 5:4 We have drunken our **w** for money; ... 4325
Eze 4:17 That they may want bread and **w**, ... 4325
Eze 7:17 and all knees shall be weak as **w** 4325
Eze 12:19 drink their **w** with astonishment, ... 4325
Eze 21:7 and all knees shall be weak as **w** 4325
Eze 32:6 also **w** with thy blood the land 8248
Eze 36:25 will I sprinkle clean **w** upon you, ... 4325

Da 1:12 us pulse to eat, and **w** to drink. 4325
Hos 2:5 that give me my bread and my **w**,. 4325
Hos 5:10 my wrath upon them that like **w** 4325
Hos 10:7 is cut off as the foam upon the **w**. 4325
Am 8:11 famine of bread, not a thirst for **w**, ... 4325
Jnh 3:7 let them not feed, nor drink **w**:. 4325
Zec 9:11 out of the pit wherein is no **w**. 4325
Mt 3:11 I indeed baptize you with **w** unto. *5204*
Mt 3:16 went up straightway out of the **w**: *5204*
Mt 10:42 **these little ones a cup of cold w**
Mt 14:29 he walked on the **w**, to go to Jesus. *5204*
Mt 27:24 he took **w**, and washed his hands *5204*
Mk 1:8 I indeed have baptized you with **w**: *5204*
Mk 1:10 coming up out of the **w**, he saw *5204*
Mk 9:41 **cup of w to drink in my name,**. *5204*
Mk 14:13 **you a man bearing a pitcher of w:** *5204*
Lk 3:16 all, I indeed baptize you with **w**; *5204*
Lk 7:44 **thou gavest me no w for my feet:**. *5204*
Lk 8:25 commandeth even the winds and **w**, . . . *5204*
Lk 16:24 **dip the tip of his finger in w,**. *5204*
Lk 22:10 **meet you, bearing a pitcher of w;** *5204*
Jn 1:26 them, saying, I baptize with **w**: *5204*
Jn 1:33 he that sent me to baptize with **w**, ... *5204*
Jn 2:7 them, **Fill the waterpots with w,**. *5204*
Jn 2:9 tasted the **w** that was made wine, ... *5204*
Jn 3:5 **Except a man be born of w and of**. *5204*
Jn 4:10 **he would have given thee living w.**. *5204*
Jn 4:14 **in him a well of w springing up** *5204*
Jn 4:15 Sir, give me this **w**, that I thirst *5204*
Jn 5:4 into the pool, and troubled the **w**. *5204*
Jn 7:38 **belly shall flow rivers of living w.**. *5204*
Jn 19:34 came there out blood and **w** *5204*
Ac 1:5 **For John truly baptized with w;**. *5204*
Ac 8:36 See, here is **w**; what doth hinder *5204*
Ac 10:47 Can any man forbid **w**, that these. *5204*
Ac 11:16 said, **John indeed baptized with w;** *5204*
Eph 5:26 the washing of **w** by the word, ... *5204*
1Ti 5:23 Drink no longer **w**, but use a little *5202*
Heb 10:22 our bodies washed with pure **w** *5204*
Jas 3:11 at the same place sweet **w** and bitter?
Jas 3:12 both yield salt **w** and fresh. *5204*
1Pe 3:20 eight souls were saved by **w**. *5204*
2Pe 2:17 These are wells without **w**, clouds. *504*
2Pe 3:5 standing out of the **w** and in the **w**: *5204*
2Pe 3:6 being overflowed with **w**, perished: *5204*
1Jn 5:6 not by **w** only, but by **w** and blood. *5204*
Jude 12 clouds they are without **w**, carried *504*
Rev 12:15 out of his mouth **w** as a flood *5204*
Rev 16:12 and the **w** thereof was dried up, ... *5204*
Rev 21:6 the fountain of the **w** of life freely. *5204*
Rev 22:1 shewed me a pure river of **w** of life, ... *5204*
Rev 22:17 will, let him take the **w** of life freely *5204*

WATERED

Ge 2:6 **w** the whole face of the ground. 8248
Ge 29:10 **w** the flock of Laban his mother's. 8248
Ex 2:17 helped them, and **w** their flock 8248
Pr 11:25 watereth shall be **w** also himself. 3384
Isa 58:11 and thou shalt be like a **w** garden, ... 7302
Jer 31:12 their soul shall be as a **w** garden; 7302
1Co 3:6 I have planted, Apollos **w**; but. *4222*

WATERETH

Ps 104:13 He **w** the hills from his chambers: 8248
Isa 55:10 **w** the earth, and maketh it bring 7301
1Co 3:7 any thing, neither he that **w**; *4222*
1Co 3:8 planteth and he that **w** are one:. *4222*

WATERING

Job 37:11 by **w** he wearieth the thick cloud:. 7377
Lk 13:15 **stall, and lead him away to w?**. *4222*

WATERS

Ge 1:2 moved upon the face of the **w**. 4325
Ge 1:6 firmament in the midst of the **w**, ... 4325
Ge 1:6 and let it divide the **w** from the **w** 4325
Ge 1:9 Let the **w** under the heaven be 4325
Ge 1:10 together of the **w** called he Seas:. 4325
Ge 1:20 Let the **w** bring forth abundantly 4325
Ge 6:17 bring a flood of **w** upon the earth, ... 4325
Ge 7:18 ark went upon the face of the **w**. 4325
Ge 7:20 cubits upward did the **w** prevail;. 4325
Ge 8:11 Noah knew that the **w** were abated 4325
Ge 9:15 the **w** shall no more become a flood . . . 4325
Ex 7:19 thine hand upon the **w** of Egypt, ... 4325
Ex 8:6 out his hand over the **w** of Egypt;. 4325
Ex 14:21 dry land, and the **w** were divided 4325
Ex 14:28 the **w** returned, and covered the. 4325
Ex 15:10 they sank as lead in the mighty **w**. 4325
Ex 15:23 could not drink of the **w** of Marah, ... 4325
Ex 15:25 the **w** were made sweet: 4325
Le 11:12 hath no fins nor scales in the **w** 4325
Le 11:46 living creature … moveth in the **w**, ... 4325
Dt 5:8 that is in the **w** beneath the earth: 4325
Dt 14:9 shall eat of all that are in the **w**. 4325
Jos 4:7 the **w** of Jordan were cut off before 4325
Jos 4:18 the **w** of Jordan returned unto 4325
Jos 5:1 Lord had dried up the **w** of Jordan. 4325
2Sa 22:17 he drew me out of many **w**;. 4325
2Ki 2:8 smote the **w**, and they were divided. . . . 4325
2Ki 2:14 when he also had smitten the **w**,. 4325
2Ki 2:21 the Lord, I have healed these **w**; 4325
2Ki 5:12 better than all the **w** of Israel?. 4325
2Ch 32:3 men to stop the **w** of the fountains 4325
Ps 18:16 me, he drew me out of many **w** 4325
Ps 23:2 he leadeth me beside the still **w**. 4325
Ps 29:3 voice of the Lord is upon the **w**:. 4325
Ps 33:7 He gathereth the **w** of the sea 4325
Ps 69:1 the **w** are come in unto my soul 4325
Ps 77:19 sea, and thy path in the great **w** 4325
Ps 78:13 he made the **w** to stand as an heap. 4325
Ps 78:20 the rock, that the **w** gushed out, ... 4325
Ps 105:29 He turned their **w** into blood, and 4325
Ps 105:41 the rock, and the **w** gushed out; 4325
Ps 106:11 And the **w** covered their enemies:. 4325
Ps 106:32 angered him also at the **w** of strife, ... 4325
Ps 119:136 Rivers of **w** run down mine eyes, ... 4325
Ps 124:5 proud **w** had gone over our soul. 4325
Ps 136:6 stretched … the earth above the **w**: 4325
Pr 5:15 Drink **w** out of thine own cistern, ... 4325
Pr 8:29 that the **w** should not pass his. 4325
Pr 9:17 Stolen **w** are sweet, and bread 4325
Pr 18:4 of a man's mouth are as deep **w**,. 4325
Pr 25:25 As cold **w** to a thirsty soul, so is 4325
Pr 30:4 hath bound the **w** in a garment?. 4325
Ecc 11:1 Cast thy bread upon the **w**: for 4325
SS 8:7 Many **w** cannot quench love, ... 4325
Isa 11:9 the Lord, as the **w** cover the sea. 4325
Isa 17:12 like the rushing of mighty **w**! 4325
Isa 19:5 And the **w** shall fail from the sea, ... 4325
Isa 19:8 they that spread nets upon the **w** 4325
Isa 28:2 a flood of mighty **w** overflowing, ... 4325
Isa 28:17 **w** shall overflow the hiding place 4325
Isa 40:12 measured the **w** in the hollow of 4325

Isa 43:2 When thou passest through the **w**, 4325
Isa 43:16 sea, and a path in the mighty **w**; 4325
Isa 48:21 caused the **w** to flow out of the rock 4325
Isa 54:9 this is as the **w** of Noah unto me: 4325
Isa 55:1 that thirsteth, come ye to the **w**. 4325
Isa 64:2 the fire causeth the **w** to boil 4325
Jer 2:13 forsaken … the fountain of living **w** 4325
Jer 9:1 Oh that my head were **w**, and mine 4325
Jer 9:18 and our eyelids gush out with **w**. 4325
Jer 10:13 is a multitude of **w** in the heavens, 4325
Jer 17:8 shall be as a tree planted by the **w** 4325
Jer 17:13 the Lord, the fountain of living **w**, 4325
Jer 51:13 O thou that dwellest upon many **w** 4325
Jer 51:16 is a multitude of **w** in the heavens; 4325
Eze 1:24 wings, like the noise of great **w**, 4325
Eze 26:19 thee, and great **w** shall cover thee; 4325
Eze 43:2 voice was like a noise of many **w** 4325
Da 12:7 was upon the **w** of the river, 4325
Joel 3:18 rivers of Judah shall flow with **w**, 4325
Am 5:24 But let judgment run down as **w**, 4325
Am 9:6 he that calleth for the **w** of the sea, 4325
Jnh 2:5 The **w** compassed me about, even 4325
Mic 1:4 as the **w** that are poured down a 4325
Hab 2:14 of the Lord, as the **w** cover the sea 4325
Zec 14:8 **w** shall go out from Jerusalem; 4325
Mt 8:32 the sea, and perished in the **w** *5204*
Mk 9:22 him into the fire, and into the **w** *5204*
2Co 11:26 in perils of **w**, in perils of robbers *4215*
Rev 1:15 his voice as the sound of many **w** *5204*
Rev 7:17 them unto living fountains of **w** *5204*
Rev 8:11 and many men died of the **w**, *5204*
Rev 11:6 have power over **w** to turn them to *5204*
Rev 14:2 heaven, as the voice of many **w** *5204*
Rev 14:7 the sea, and the fountains of **w** *5204*
Rev 16:5 I heard the angel of the **w** say, *5204*
Rev 17:1 whore that sitteth upon many **w** *5204*
Rev 19:6 and as the voice of many **w**, *5204*

WAVE

Le 7:30 for a **w** offering before the Lord. 8573
Le 9:21 for a **w** offering before the Lord; 8573
Le 10:15 for a **w** offering before the Lord; 8573
Nu 5:25 **w** the offering before the Lord 5130
Nu 18:11 the **w** offerings of the children of 8573
Jas 1:6 is like a **w** of the sea driven with *2830*

WAVE-OFFERING See WAVE and OFFERING.

WAVERETH

Jas 1:6 he that **w** is like a wave of the sea *1252*

WAVERING

Heb 10:23 profession of our faith without **w**; *186*
Jas 1:6 let him ask in faith, nothing **w** *1252*

WAVES

2Sa 22:5 the **w** of death compassed me, 4867
Ps 42:7 all thy **w** and thy billows are gone. 4867
Ps 65:7 of the seas, the noise of their **w**, 1530
Ps 88:7 hast afflicted me with all thy **w** 4867
Ps 93:4 yea, than the mighty **w** of the sea 4867
Ps 107:29 so that the **w** thereof are still 1530
Isa 48:18 righteousness as the **w** of the sea: 1530
Isa 51:15 divided the sea, whose **w** roared: 1530
Jer 5:22 the **w** thereof toss themselves, yet 1530
Jer 31:35 the sea when the **w** thereof roar; 1530
Jer 51:55 her **w** do roar like great waters 1530
Jnh 2:3 billows and thy **w** passed over me. 1530
Zec 10:11 and shall smite the **w** in the sea. 1530
Mt 8:24 the ship was covered with the **w** *2949*
Mt 14:24 midst of the sea, tossed with **w** *2949*
Mk 4:37 the **w** beat into the ship, so that it. *2949*
Lk 21:25 **the sea and the w roaring;** *4535*
Jude 13 Raging **w** of the sea, foaming out *2949*

WAX

Ex 22:24 And my wrath shall **w** hot, and I
Ex 32:10 that my wrath may **w** hot against
1Sa 3:2 his eyes began to **w** dim, that he
Ps 22:14 my heart is like **w**; it is melted in 1749
Ps 68:2 as **w** melteth before the fire, so let 1749
Ps 97:5 The hills melted like **w** at the 1749
Isa 50:9 they all shall **w** old as a garment;
Isa 51:6 earth shall **w** old like a garment,
Jer 6:24 our hands **w** feeble: anguish hath
Mic 1:4 shall be cleft, as **w** before the fire, 1749
Mt 24:12 **the love of many shall w cold.** *5594*
Lk 12:33 **yourselves bags which w not old,** *3822*
1Ti 5:11 to **w** wanton against Christ, *2691*
2Ti 3:13 and seducers shall **w** worse and *4298*
Heb 1:11 all shall **w** old as doth a garment; *3822*

WAXED

Ge 41:56 the famine **w** sore in the land of
Ex 16:21 when the sun **w** hot, it melted
Ex 32:19 Moses' anger **w** hot, and he cast
Dt 8:4 Thy raiment **w** not old upon thee
2Sa 3:1 the house of Saul **w** weaker and 1980
Ne 9:21 their clothes **w** not old, and their
Ps 32:3 bones **w** old through my roaring
Da 8:9 horn, which **w** exceeding great
Mt 13:15 **For this people's heart is w gross,** *3975*
Lk 2:40 child grew, and **w** strong in spirit. *2901*
Ac 28:27 the heart of this people is **w** gross, *3975*
Heb 11:34 made strong, **w** valiant in fight, *1096*
Rev 18:3 merchants of the earth are **w** rich *4147*

WAXEN

Ge 19:13 the cry of them is **w** great before
Le 25:25 If thy brother be **w** poor, and
Dt 29:5 clothes are not **w** old upon you
Dt 29:5 thy shoe is not **w** old upon thy foot

WAXETH

Ps 6:7 it **w** old because of all mine enemies
Heb 8:13 and **w** old is ready to vanish away. *1095*

WAY

Ge 3:24 to keep the **w** of the tree of life.
Ge 18:19 they shall keep the **w** of the Lord, 1870
Ge 18:33 And the Lord went his **w**, as soon 3212
Ge 38:16 And he turned unto her by the **w**, 1870
Ex 4:24 came to pass by the **w** in the inn. 1870
Ex 13:18 **w** of the wilderness of the Red sea: 1870
Ex 13:21 of a cloud, to lead them the **w**; 1870
Ex 18:20 the **w** wherein they must walk, 1870
Ex 23:20 before thee to keep thee in the **w**, 1870
Ex 33:3 lest I consume thee in the **w** 1870
Nu 20:17 we will go by the king's high **w** 1870
Nu 21:1 Israel came by the **w** of the spies; 1870
Nu 22:23 the ass turned aside out of the **w**, 1870
Nu 22:31 angel of the Lord standing in the **w**, 1870
Nu 22:32 because thy **w** is perverse before, 1870
Dt 1:33 Who went in the **w** before you, to 1870
Dt 2:1 wilderness by the **w** of the Red sea, 1870
Dt 6:7 when thou walkest by the **w**, and 1870

Dt	8:2	**w** which the Lord thy God led thee	1870
Dt	11:19	when thou walkest by the **w**, when	1870
Dt	14:24	And if the **w** be long for thee, so	1870
Dt	19:6	because the **w** is long, and slay him	1870
Dt	23:4	bread and with water in the **w**	1870
Dt	24:9	God did unto Miriam by the **w**.	1870
Dt	25:18	How he met thee by the **w**, and	1870
Dt	27:18	the blind to wander out of the **w**	1870
Jos	1:8	thou shalt make thy **w** prosperous	1870
Jos	5:4	died in the wilderness by the **w**,	1870
Jos	5:7	had not circumcised them by the **w**	1870
Jos	23:14	I am going the **w** of all the earth:	1870
Jgs	2:17	**w** which their fathers walked in	1870
Jgs	5:10	in judgment, and walk by the **w**	1870
1Sa	9:6	shew us our **w** that we should go	1870
1Sa	12:23	teach you the good and the right **w**	1870
1Sa	15:2	how he laid wait for him in the **w**,	1870
2Sa	13:30	to pass, while they were in the **w**.	1870
2Sa	22:31	As for God, his **w** is perfect;	1870
2Sa	22:33	and he maketh my **w** perfect	1870
1Ki	2:2	I go the **w** of all the earth: be thou	1870
1Ki	2:4	If thy children take heed to their **w**,	1870
1Ki	8:36	good **w** wherein they should walk,	1870
1Ki	13:9	by the same **w** that thou camest	1870
1Ki	13:24	a lion met him by the **w**, and slew	1870
1Ki	22:24	Which **w** went the Spirit of the Lord	2088
2Ki	4:29	take my staff ... and go thy **w**:	
2Ki	5:19	So he departed from him a little **w**	776
2Ki	6:19	This is not the **w**, neither is this	1870
2Ki	9:27	fled by the **w** of the garden house	1870
2Ki	21:22	walked not in the **w** of the Lord	1870
2Ki	22:2	and walked in all the **w** of David	1870
2Ch	6:27	thou hast taught them the good **w**,	1870
2Ch	18:23	Which **w** went the Spirit of the Lord	1870
Ezr	8:21	to seek of him a right **w** for us,	1870
Ezr	8:31	and of such as lay in wait by the **w**	1870
Ne	9:19	them by day, to lead them in the **w**;	1870
Ne	9:19	and the **w** wherein they should go	1870
Job	38:19	is the **w** where light dwelleth?	1870
Job	38:24	By what **w** is the light parted,	1870
Ps	1:1	nor standeth in the **w** of sinners,	1870
Ps	1:6	knoweth the **w** of the righteous:	1870
Ps	1:6	the **w** of the ungodly shall perish	1870
Ps	2:12	angry, and ye perish from the **w**,	1870
Ps	18:30	As for God, his **w** is perfect:	1870
Ps	25:8	will he teach sinners in the **w**	1870
Ps	25:9	and the meek will he teach his **w**	1870
Ps	25:12	teach in the **w** that he shall choose	1870
Ps	27:11	Teach me thy **w**, O Lord, and lead	1870
Ps	32:8	thee in the **w** which thou shalt go:	1870
Ps	37:5	Commit thy **w** unto the Lord:	1870
Ps	37:34	Wait on the Lord, and keep his **w**	1870
Ps	49:13	This their **w** is their folly: yet	1870
Ps	67:2	thy **w** may be known upon earth,	1870
Ps	101:2	behave myself wisely in a perfect **w**	1870
Ps	101:6	he that walketh in a perfect **w**, he	1870
Ps	107:40	the wilderness, where there is no **w**	1870
Ps	119:1	Blessed are the undefiled in the **w**,	1870
Ps	119:9	shall a young man cleanse his **w**?	734
Ps	119:29	Remove from me the **w** of lying:	1870
Ps	119:33	Teach me, ... the **w** of thy statutes;	1870
Ps	119:104	therefore I hate every false **w**	734
Ps	139:24	if there be any wicked **w** in me,	1870
Ps	139:24	and lead me in the **w** everlasting.	1870
Pr	1:15	walk not thou in the **w** with them;	1870
Pr	2:8	and preserveth the **w** of his saints.	1870
Pr	2:12	deliver thee from the **w** of the evil	1870
Pr	2:20	mayest walk in the **w** of good men,	1870
Pr	3:23	shalt thou walk in thy **w** safely	1870
Pr	4:11	taught thee in the **w** of wisdom;	1870
Pr	4:14	go not in the **w** of evil men	1870
Pr	4:19	**w** of the wicked is as darkness:	1870
Pr	5:8	Remove thy **w** far from her, and	1870
Pr	6:23	of instruction are the **w** of life:	1870
Pr	7:8	and he went the **w** to her house,	1870
Pr	7:27	Her house is the **w** to hell, going	1870
Pr	8:13	the evil **w**, and the froward mouth,	1870
Pr	8:20	I lead in the **w** of righteousness, in	734
Pr	9:6	and go in the **w** of understanding	1870
Pr	10:17	He is in the **w** of life that keepeth	734
Pr	10:29	The **w** of the Lord is strength to	1870
Pr	11:5	of the perfect shall direct his **w**	1870
Pr	11:20	upright in their **w** are his delight	1870
Pr	12:15	The **w** of a fool is right in his own	1870
Pr	12:26	the **w** of the wicked seduceth them	1870
Pr	12:28	In the **w** of righteousness is life;	734
Pr	13:6	him that is upright in the **w**	1870
Pr	13:15	but the **w** of transgressors is hard	1870
Pr	14:8	the prudent is to understand his **w**:	1870
Pr	14:12	a **w** which seemeth right unto a	1870
Pr	15:9	**w** of the wicked is an abomination	1870
Pr	15:19	The **w** of the slothful man is	1870
Pr	15:19	the **w** of the righteous man is made	734
Pr	16:9	A man's heart deviseth his **w**: but	1870
Pr	16:17	keepeth his **w** preserveth his soul	1870
Pr	16:25	**w** that seemeth right unto a man	1870
Pr	16:29	him into the **w** that is not good	1870
Pr	16:31	be found in the **w** of righteousness	1870
Pr	19:3	foolishness of man perverteth his **w**	1870
Pr	20:14	but when he is gone his **w**, then he	
Pr	21:1	Every **w** of a man is right in his	1870
Pr	21:8	**w** of man is froward and strange:	1870
Pr	21:29	for the upright, he directeth his **w**	1870
Pr	22:5	snares are in the **w** of the froward:	1870
Pr	22:6	Train up a child in the **w** he should	1870
Pr	23:19	and guide thine heart in the **w**	1870
Pr	26:13	man saith, There is a lion in the **w**;	1870
Pr	28:10	righteous to go astray in an evil **w**,	1870
Pr	29:27	and he that is upright in the **w** is	1870
Pr	30:19	The **w** of an eagle in the air; the	1870
Pr	30:19	**w** of a serpent upon a rock; the	1870
Pr	30:19	**w** of a ship in the midst of the sea;	1870
Pr	30:19	and the **w** of a man with a maid.	1870
Pr	30:20	Such is the **w** of an adulterous	1870
Ecc	11:5	not what is the **w** of the spirit,	1870
Isa	26:7	The **w** of the just is uprightness:	734
Isa	30:21	This is the **w**, walk ye in it	1870
Isa	35:8	shall be called The **w** of holiness;	1870
Isa	40:3	Prepare ye the **w** of the Lord,	1870
Isa	40:14	to him the **w** of understanding?	1870
Isa	40:27	My **w** is hid from the Lord, and my	1870
Isa	43:16	which maketh a **w** in the sea, and	1870
Isa	48:15	he shall make his **w** prosperous	1870
Isa	48:17	by the **w** that thou shouldest go	1870
Isa	51:10	a **w** for the ransomed to pass over?	1870
Isa	53:6	turned every one to his own **w**;	1870
Isa	55:7	Let the wicked forsake his **w**, and	1870
Isa	56:11	they all look to their own **w**, every	1870
Isa	59:8	The **w** of peace they knew not; and	1870
Isa	62:10	prepare ye the **w** of the people;	1870
Isa	65:2	walketh in a **w** that was not good,	1870
Jer	2:17	God, when he led thee by the **w**?	1870

Jer	5:4	they know not the **w** of the Lord,	1870
Jer	10:2	Learn not the **w** of the heathen.	1870
Jer	18:11	ye now every one from his evil **w**,	1870
Jer	21:8	the **w** of life, and the **w** of death	1870
Jer	23:22	have turned them from their evil **w**,	1870
Jer	26:3	turn every man from his evil **w**,	1870
Jer	32:39	give them one heart, and one **w**,	1870
Jer	35:15	ye now every man from his evil **w**,	1870
Jer	42:3	God may shew us the **w** wherein	1870
Eze	3:19	nor from his wicked **w**, he shall die	1870
Eze	18:25	say, The **w** of the Lord is not equal.	1870
Eze	18:25	Is not my **w** equal? are not your	1870
Eze	21:21	stood at the parting of the **w**,	1870
Eze	33:8	to warn the wicked from his **w**	1870
Eze	33:9	if he do not turn from his **w**, he	1870
Eze	33:17	The **w** of the Lord is not equal:	1870
Eze	33:17	as for them, their **w** is not equal	1870
Da	12:13	go thou thy **w** till the end be: for thou	
Hos	2:6	I will hedge up thy **w** with thorns,	1870
Hos	10:13	because thou didst trust in thy **w**	1870
Jnh	3:8	turn every one from his evil **w**	1870
Jnh	3:10	that they turned from their evil **w**;	1870
Na	1:3	Lord hath his **w** in the whirlwind	1870
Zec	10:2	they went their **w** as a flock, they	
Mal	2:8	But ye are departed out of the **w**;	1870
Mal	3:1	he shall prepare the **w** before me:	1870
Mt	2:12	into their own country another **w**	*3598*
Mt	3:3	Prepare ye the **w** of the Lord	*3598*
Mt	5:24	**gift before the altar, and go thy w;**	
Mt	5:25	**whiles thou art in the w with him;**	*3598*
Mt	7:13	**broad is the w, that leadeth to**	*3598*
Mt	7:14	**narrow is the w, which leadeth**	*3598*
Mt	8:4	**but go thy w, shew thyself to the**	
Mt	8:13	said unto the centurion, **Go thy w;**	
Mt	10:5	**Go not into the w of the Gentiles,**	*3598*
Mt	11:10	**shall prepare thy w before thee.**	*3598*
Mt	13:4	**some seeds fell by the w side.**	*3598*
Mt	13:19	**which received seed by the w side.**	*3598*
Mt	15:32	**fasting, lest they faint in the w.**	*3598*
Mt	20:14	**Take that thine is, and go thy w:**	
Mt	20:30	blind men sitting by the **w** side	*3598*
Mt	21:8	spread their garments in the **w**;	*3598*
Mt	22:16	and teachest the **w** of God in truth,	*3598*
Mt	22:22	and left him, and went their **w**	
Mt	27:65	go your **w**, make it as sure as ye can.	
Mk	1:3	Prepare ye the **w** of the Lord,	*3598*
Mk	4:4	**he sowed, some fell by the w side,**	*3598*
Mk	8:3	**houses, they will faint by the w:**	*3598*
Mk	11:4	they went their **w**, and found the colt	
Mk	11:8	spread their garments in the **w**	*3598*
Mk	12:12	and they left him, and went their **w**	
Mk	12:14	teachest the **w** of God in truth:	*3598*
Mk	16:7	But go your **w**, tell his disciples and	
Lk	5:19	find by what **w** they might bring him	
Lk	7:22	**your w, and tell John what things**	
Lk	7:27	**shall prepare thy w before thee.**	*3598*
Lk	8:12	**by the w side are they that hear;**	*3598*
Lk	10:4	**and salute no man by the w.**	*3598*
Lk	10:31	**down a certain priest that w:**	*3598*
Lk	12:58	**thou art in the w, give diligence**	*3598*
Lk	14:32	**the other is yet a great w off,**	*4206*
Lk	15:20	**when he was yet a great w off,**	*3112*
Lk	17:19	**Arise, go thy w: thy faith hath**	
Lk	18:35	blind man sat by the **w** side	*3598*
Lk	19:4	to see him: for he was to pass that **w**	
Lk	20:21	but teachest the **w** of God truly:	*3598*
Lk	24:32	while he talked with us by the **w**,	*3598*
Lk	24:35	what things were done in the **w**,	*3598*
Jn	1:23	Make straight the **w** of the Lord,	*3598*
Jn	4:50	unto him, **Go thy w; thy son liveth.**	
Jn	8:21	**I go my w, and ye shall seek me,**	
Jn	14:5	and how can we know the **w**?	*3598*
Jn	14:6	**I am the w, the truth, and the**	*3598*
Jn	16:5	**I go my w to him that sent me;**	
Jn	18:8	**ye seek me, let these go their w:**	
Ac	9:2	that if he found any of this **w**,	*3598*
Ac	9:15	**Go thy w: for he is a chosen**	
Ac	9:27	how he had seen the Lord in the **w**,	*3598*
Ac	18:26	him the **w** of God more perfectly	*3598*
Ac	19:23	arose no small stir about that **w**	*3598*
Ac	22:4	persecuted this **w** unto the death,	*3598*
Ac	24:14	after the **w** which they call heresy	*3598*
Ac	24:22	more perfect knowledge of that **w**	*3598*
Ro	3:2	Much every **w**: chiefly, because	*5158*
Ro	3:17	**w** of peace have they not known:	*3598*
1Co	10:13	temptation ... make a **w** to escape	*1545*
1Co	12:31	I unto you a more excellent **w**.	*3598*
Col	2:14	took it out of the **w**, nailing it to	*3319*
1Th	3:11	Christ, direct our **w** unto you	*3598*
2Th	2:7	until he be taken out of the **w**	*3319*
Heb	5:2	on them that are out of the **w**;	*4105*
Heb	9:8	the **w** into the holiest of all was	*3598*
Heb	10:20	By a new and living **w**, which he	*3598*
Heb	12:13	is lame be turned out of the **w**;	*1624*
Jas	1:24	beholdeth himself, and goeth his **w**,	*1624*
Jas	2:25	had sent them out another **w**?	*3598*
Jas	5:20	the sinner from the error of his **w**	*3598*
2Pe	2:2	**w** of truth shall be evil spoken of	*3598*
2Pe	2:15	Which have forsaken the right **w**,	*3598*
2Pe	2:21	known the **w** of righteousness,	*3598*
Rev	16:12	the **w** of the kings of the east.	*3598*

WAYFARING

Jgs	19:17	he saw a **w** man in the street of	732
2Sa	12:4	the **w** man that was come unto him;	732
Isa	33:8	lie waste, the **w** man ceaseth:	5674, 734
Jer	9:2	a lodging place of **w** men;	732
Jer	14:8	as a **w** man that turneth aside to	732

WAYS

Le	26:22	your high **w** shall be desolate	1870
Nu	30:15	if he shall any **w** make them void	
Dt	10:12	to walk in all his **w**, and to love	1870
Dt	11:22	to walk in all his **w**, and to cleave	1870
Dt	26:17	to walk in his **w**, and to keep his	1870
Dt	28:25	and flee seven **w** before them:	1870
Dt	28:29	thou shalt not prosper in thy **w**	1870
Dt	32:4	for all his **w** are judgment:	1870
Jos	22:5	to walk in all his **w**, and to keep	1870
1Sa	8:3	And his sons walked not in his **w**,	1870
1Sa	18:14	behaved ... wisely in all his **w**;	1870
2Sa	22:22	For I have kept the **w** of the Lord,	1870
1Ki	2:3	God, to walk in his **w**, to keep his	1870
1Ki	3:14	And if thou wilt walk in my **w**, to	1870
1Ki	8:58	to walk in all his **w**, and to keep	1870
1Ki	11:33	and have not walked in my **w**, to do	1870
1Ki	11:38	and wilt walk in my **w**, and do that	1870
2Ki	17:13	Turn ye from your evil **w**, and	1870
2Ch	6:30	every man according unto all his **w**,	1870
2Ch	7:14	and turn from their wicked **w**;	1870
2Ch	17:3	in the first **w** of his father David	1870
2Ch	27:6	prepared his **w** before the Lord	1870
2Ch	28:2	in the **w** of the kings of Israel	1870

2Ch	32:13	any **w** able to deliver their lands	
2Ch	34:2	and walked in the **w** of David his	1870
Job	13:15	maintain mine own **w** before him	1870
Job	31:4	Doth not he see my **w**, and count	1870
Job	34:21	his eyes are upon the **w** of man,	1870
Job	40:19	He is the chief of the **w** of God:	1870
Ps	10:5	His **w** are always grievous;	1870
Ps	18:21	For I have kept the **w** of the Lord,	1870
Ps	25:4	Shew me thy **w**, O Lord; teach me	1870
Ps	51:13	will I teach transgressors thy **w**;	1870
Ps	81:13	and Israel had walked in my **w**!	1870
Ps	91:11	thee, to keep thee in all thy **w**	1870
Ps	95:10	and they have not known my **w**	1870
Ps	103:7	He made known his **w** unto Moses,	1870
Ps	119:168	for all my **w** are before thee	1870
Ps	128:1	the Lord; that walketh in his **w**	1870
Ps	139:3	and art acquainted with all my **w**	1870
Ps	145:17	The Lord is righteous in all his **w**	1870
Pr	1:19	are the **w** of every one that is greedy	734
Pr	2:13	to walk in the **w** of darkness;	1870
Pr	2:15	Whose **w** are crooked, and they	734
Pr	3:6	In all thy **w** acknowledge him	1870
Pr	3:17	Her **w** are **w** of pleasantness, and	1870
Pr	4:26	and let all thy **w** be established	1870
Pr	5:6	path of life, her **w** are moveable	4570
Pr	5:21	the **w** of man are before the eyes	1870
Pr	6:6	consider her **w**, and be wise:	1870
Pr	7:25	not thine heart decline to her **w**	1870
Pr	8:32	blessed are they that keep my **w**	1870
Pr	10:9	he that perverteth his **w** shall be	1870
Pr	14:2	but he that is perverse in his **w**	1870
Pr	14:12	the end thereof are the **w** of death	1870
Pr	14:14	shall be filled with his own **w**:	1870
Pr	16:2	All the **w** of a man are clean in his	1870
Pr	16:7	When a man's **w** please the Lord	1870
Pr	16:25	the end thereof are the **w** of death	1870
Pr	17:23	to pervert the **w** of judgment	734
Pr	19:16	he that despiseth his **w** shall die	1870
Pr	22:25	Lest thou learn his **w**, and get a	734
Pr	23:26	and let thine eyes observe my **w**	1870
Pr	28:6	than he that is perverse in his **w**	1870
Pr	28:18	that is perverse in his **w** shall fall	1870
Pr	31:3	nor thy **w** to that which destroyeth	1870
Pr	31:27	well to the **w** of her household	1979
Ecc	11:9	and walk in the **w** of thine heart	1870
Isa	2:3	and he will teach us of his **w**, and	1870
Isa	42:24	for they would not walk in his **w**	1870
Isa	45:13	and I will direct all his **w**	1870
Isa	55:8	neither are your **w** my **w**, saith	1870
Isa	55:9	so are my **w** higher than your **w**	1870
Isa	58:2	daily, and delight to know my **w**	1870
Isa	58:13	not doing thine own **w**, nor finding	1870
Isa	63:17	thou made us to err from thy **w**	1870
Isa	66:3	they have chosen their own **w**, and	1870
Jer	6:16	Stand ye in the **w**, and see, and ask	1870
Jer	7:3	Amend your **w** and your doings,	1870
Jer	7:23	walk ye in all the **w** that I have	1870
Jer	12:16	diligently learn the **w** of my people,	1870
Jer	15:7	since they return not from their **w**	1870
Jer	17:10	give every man according to his **w**	1870
Jer	18:15	caused them to stumble in their **w**	1870
Jer	23:12	as slippery **w** in the darkness:	
Jer	26:13	amend your **w** and your doings	1870
La	3:40	Let us search and try our **w**, and	1870
Eze	7:9	recompense thee according to thy **w**	1870
Eze	14:23	ye see their **w** and their doings:	1870
Eze	16:47	more than they in all thy **w**	1870
Eze	16:61	Then thou shalt remember thy **w**	1870
Eze	18:30	every one according to his **w**	1870
Eze	20:43	there shall ye remember your **w**	1870
Eze	20:44	not according to your wicked **w**	1870
Eze	21:21	at the head of the two **w**, to use	1870
Eze	28:15	Thou wast perfect in thy **w** from	1870
Eze	33:11	turn ye, turn ye from your evil **w**;	1870
Eze	36:31	ye remember your own evil **w**,	1870
Da	4:37	are truth, and his **w** judgment:	735
Da	5:23	whose are all thy **w**, hast thou not	735
Hos	4:9	I will punish them for their **w**,	1870
Hos	14:9	for the **w** of the Lord are right, and	1870
Mic	4:2	he will teach us of his **w**, and we	1870
Hab	3:6	did bow: his **w** are everlasting	1979
Hag	1:5	Lord of hosts; Consider your **w**	1870
Hag	1:7	Lord of hosts; Consider your **w**	1870
Zec	1:4	Turn ye now from your evil **w**	1870
Zec	3:7	If thou wilt walk in my **w**, and if	1870
Mal	2:9	as ye have not kept my **w**, but	1870
Mt	22:5	**made light of it, and went their w,**	
Mk	11:4	in a place where two **w** met;	*296*
Lk	3:5	the rough **w** shall be made smooth:	*3598*
Lk	10:3	**Go your w: behold, I send you forth**	
Ac	2:28	made known to me the **w** of life;	*3598*
Ac	13:10	not cease to pervert the right **w** of	*3598*
Ac	14:16	all nations to walk in their own **w**	*3598*
Ro	3:16	and misery are in their **w**:	*3598*
Ro	11:33	and his **w** past finding out!	*3598*
Heb	3:10	and they have not known my **w**	*3598*
Jas	1:8	man is unstable in all his **w**	*3598*
Jas	1:11	the rich man fade away in his **w**	*4197*
2Pe	2:2	shall follow their pernicious **w**;	*684*
Rev	15:3	just and true are thy **w**, thou King	*3598*
Rev	16:1	Go your **w**, and pour out the vials of	

WEAK

Nu	13:18	whether they be strong or **w**,	7504
Jgs	16:17	I shall become **w**, and be like any	2470
2Ch	15:7	and let not your hands be **w**:	7503
Job	4:3	hast strengthened the **w** hands	7504
Ps	6:2	upon me, O Lord; for I am **w**:	536
Ps	109:24	My knees are **w** through fasting;	3782
Isa	14:10	Art thou also become **w** as we?	2470
Eze	7:17	all knees shall be **w** as water	3212
Eze	16:30	How **w** is thine heart, saith the	535
Joel	3:10	let the **w** say, I am strong	2523
Mt	26:41	**is willing, but the flesh is w.**	*772*
Mk	14:38	**truly is ready, but the flesh is w.**	*772*
Ac	20:35	ye ought to support the **w**,	*770*
Ro	4:19	being not **w** in faith, he considered	*770*
Ro	14:1	Him that is **w** in the faith receive	*770*
Ro	14:2	another, who is **w**, eateth herbs	*770*
Ro	15:1	to bear the infirmities of the **w**	*102*
1Co	1:27	chosen the **w** things of the world	*772*
1Co	4:10	we are **w**, but ye are strong;	*772*
1Co	8:7	their conscience being **w** is defiled	*772*
1Co	8:9	stumblingblock to them that are **w**	*770*
1Co	8:11	shall the **w** brother perish,	*770*
1Co	8:12	and wound their **w** conscience	*770*
1Co	9:22	To the **w** became I as **w**,	*770*
1Co	9:22	that I might gain the **w**: I am	*770*
1Co	11:30	many are **w** and sickly among you	*770*
2Co	10:10	but his bodily presence is **w**, and	*770*
2Co	11:29	Who is **w**, and I am not **w**? who is	*770*
2Co	12:10	for when I am **w**, then am I strong	*770*

W

2Co 13:4 For we also are **w** in him, but we *770*
2Co 13:9 when we are **w**, and ye are strong: *770*
1Th 5:14 support the **w**, be patient toward *772*

WEAKEN
Isa 14:12 Lucifer…which didst **w** the nations! ... 2522

WEAKENED
Ezr 4:4 **w** the hands of ... people of Judah, ... 7503
Ne 6:9 hands shall be **w** from the work 7503

WEAKER
2Sa 3:1 house of Saul waxed **w** and **w**......... 1800
1Pe 3:7 the wife, as unto the **w** vessel, ... *772*

WEAKNESS
1Co 1:25 **w** of God is stronger than men......... *772*
1Co 2:3 I was with you in **w**, and in fear,........ *769*
1Co 15:43 it is sown in **w**; it is raised in power:..... *769*
2Co 12:9 **my strength is made perfect in w.** *769*
2Co 13:4 though he was crucified through **w** *769*
Heb 7:18 for the **w** and unprofitableness *772*
Heb 11:34 out of **w** were made strong,............ *769*

WEALTH
Dt 8:17 mine hand hath gotten me this **w**...... 2428
2Ch 1:11 not asked riches, **w**, or honour 5233
2Ch 1:12 I will give thee riches, and **w**, and...... 5233
Est 10:3 seeking the **w** of his people, and....... 2896
Job 21:13 They spend their days in **w**, and in..... 2896
Job 31:25 rejoiced because my **w** was great,...... 2428
Ps 49:6 They that trust in their **w**, and 2428
Ps 49:10 perish, and leave their **w** to others 2428
Pr 5:10 strangers be filled with thy **w**;......... 3581
Pr 10:15 rich man's **w** is his strong city: 1952
Pr 13:11 **W** gotten by vanity shall be........... 1952
Pr 13:22 the **w** of the sinner is laid up for....... 2428
Pr 18:11 rich man's **w** is his strong city......... 1952
Pr 19:4 **W** maketh many friends; but the 1952
Ecc 5:19 God hath given riches and **w**.......... 5233
Ecc 6:2 to whom God hath given riches, **w**..... 5233
Zec 14:14 **w** of all the heathen round about...... 2428
Ac 19:25 that by this craft we have our **w** *2142*
1Co 10:24 his own, but every one another's **w**

WEANED
Ge 21:8 the same day that Isaac was **w**......... 1580
1Sa 1:22 will not go up until the child be **w**, ... 1580
Ps 131:2 my soul is even as a **w** child........... 1580
Isa 11:8 **w** child shall put his hand on the 1580
Isa 28:9 them that are **w** from the milk,......... 1580

WEAPON
Nu 35:18 smite him with an hand **w** of 3627
Ne 4:17 and with the other hand held a **w**...... 7973
Isa 54:17 No **w** that is formed against thee 3627
Eze 9:1 with his destroying **w** in his hand...... 3627

WEAPONS
Dt 1:41 girded on every man his **w** of war,..... 3627
2Sa 1:27 fallen, and the **w** of war perished!...... 3627
2Ch 23:7 every man with his **w** in his hand; 3627
Ecc 9:18 Wisdom is better than **w** of war:....... 3627
Jer 21:4 I will turn back the **w** of war that...... 3627
Eze 32:27 down to hell with their **w** of war:...... 3627
Eze 39:9 shall set on fire and burn the **w** 5402
Jn 18:3 with lanterns and torches and **w**....... *3696*
2Co 10:4 **w** of our warfare are not carnal, ... *3696*

WEAR
Ex 18:18 Thou wilt surely **w** away, both......... 5034
Dt 22:5 woman shall not **w** that which 1961
Dt 22:11 not **w** a garment of divers sorts, ... 3847
Da 7:25 **w** out the saints of the most High,..... 1080
Zec 13:4 **w** a rough garment to deceive: 3847
Mt 11:8 **they that w soft clothing are in**........ *5409*
Lk 9:12 when the day began to **w** away,........ *2827*

WEARIED
Ge 19:11 **w** themselves to find the door. 3811
Isa 43:24 hast **w** me with thine iniquities........ 3021
Jer 4:31 soul is **w** because of murderers........ 5888
Eze 24:12 She hath **w** herself with lies, and....... 3811
Mic 6:3 wherein have I **w** thee? testify 3811
Mal 2:17 **w** the Lord with your words 3021
Mal 2:17 ye say, Wherein have we **w** him? 3021
Heb 12:3 ye be **w** and faint in your minds *2577*

WEARINESS
Ecc 12:12 much study is a **w** of the flesh......... 3024
Mal 1:13 said also, Behold, what a **w** is it! 4972

WEARY
Ge 27:46 I am **w** of my life because of the....... 6973
2Sa 17:2 upon him while he is **w** and weak 3023
2Sa 23:10 Philistines until his hand was **w** 3021
Job 3:17 and there the **w** be at rest............. 3019
Job 10:1 My soul is **w** of my life; I will 5354
Ps 6:6 I am **w** with my groaning; all the 3021
Ps 69:3 I am **w** of my crying: my throat 3021
Pr 3:11 neither be **w** of his correction: 6973
Isa 5:27 None shall be **w** nor stumble.......... 5889
Isa 7:13 but will ye **w** my God also? 3811
Isa 28:12 ye may cause the **w** to rest; 5889
Isa 32:2 shadow of a great rock in a **w** land..... 5889
Isa 40:28 fainteth not, neither is **w**?............ 3021
Isa 40:31 they shall run, and not be **w**; and 3021
Isa 50:4 word in season to him that is **w** 3287
Jer 9:5 **w** themselves to commit iniquity 3811
Jer 15:6 thee, I am **w** with repenting........... 3811
Hab 2:13 the people shall **w** themselves for 3286
Lk 18:5 **her continual coming she w me.**....... *5299*
Gal 6:9 And let us not be **w** in well doing: *1573*
2Th 3:13 brethren, be not **w** in well doing. *1573*

WEATHER
Pr 25:20 taketh away a garment in cold **w**,...... 3117
Mt 16:2 **evening, ye say, It will be fair w:** *2105*
Mt 16:3 **morning, It will be foul w to day:**...... *5494*

WEAVER'S
1Ch 11:23 hand was a spear like a **w** beam;........ 707
1Ch 20:5 spear staff was like a **w** beam. 707
Job 7:6 days are swifter than a **w** shuttle,

WEDDING
Mt 22:8 **The w is ready, but they which**........ *1062*
Mt 22:10 **the w was furnished with guests.** *1062*
Mt 22:12 **in hither not having a w garment?**..... *1062*
Lk 14:8 **art bidden of any man to a w,**......... *1062*

WEDLOCK
Eze 16:38 as women that break **w** and shed 5003

WEEK
Ge 29:28 Jacob did so, and fulfilled her **w** 7620
Da 9:27 the covenant with many for one **w**..... 7620
Mk 16:9 risen early the first day of the **w**,....... *4521*

Lk 18:12 **I fast twice in the w, I give tithes** *4521*
Jn 20:1 the first day of the **w** cometh Mary *4521*
Jn 20:19 being the first day of the **w**, when...... *4521*
Ac 20:7 And upon the first day of the **w** *4521*
1Co 16:2 Upon the first day of the **w** let every ... *4521*

WEEKS
Ex 34:22 thou shalt observe the feast of **w**, ... 7620
Dt 16:10 keep the feast of **w** unto the Lord...... 7620
Da 9:24 Seventy **w** are determined upon 7620
Da 9:25 Unto...the Prince shall be seven **w**,..... 7620
Da 9:25 and threescore and two **w**: the 7620
Da 9:26 threescore and two **w** shall Messiah 7620
Da 10:2 Daniel was mourning three full **w** 7620

WEEP See also CRY.
Ge 43:30 and he sought where to **w**; and he 1058
Nu 11:13 for they **w** unto me, saying, Give 1058
1Sa 30:4 until they had no more power to **w** 1058
2Sa 1:24 daughters of Israel, **w** over Saul, ... 1058
2Sa 12:21 thou didst fast and **w** for the child 1058
2Ch 34:27 rend thy clothes, and **w** before me;..... 1058
Ne 8:9 Lord your God; mourn not, nor **w**..... 1058
Job 30:25 Did not I **w** for him that was in 1058
Ecc 3:4 A time to **w**, and a time to laugh;...... 1058
Isa 22:4 I will **w** bitterly, labour not to 1065
Isa 30:19 thou shalt **w** no more: he will be 1058
Jer 9:1 that I might **w** day and night for 1058
Jer 13:17 my soul shall **w** in secret places for..... 1058
Jer 22:10 **W** ye not for the dead, neither 1058
Jer 22:10 **w** sore for him that goeth away: 1058
La 1:16 For these things I **w**; mine eye......... 1058
Joel 1:5 Awake, ye drunkards, and **w**; and 1058
Joel 2:17 **w** between the porch and the altar,
Zec 7:3 Should I **w** in the fifth month, ... 1058
Mk 5:39 **Why make ye this ado, and w?** *2799*
Lk 6:21 **Blessed are ye that w now: for ye** *2799*
Lk 6:25 **laugh...for ye shall mourn and w.** *2799*
Lk 7:13 on her, and said unto her, **W not.** *2799*
Lk 8:52 he said, **W not; she is not dead,** *2799*
Lk 23:28 **Daughters of Jerusalem, w not for** *2799*
Lk 23:28 **but w for yourselves, and for your** *2799*
Jn 16:20 **you, That ye shall w and lament,** *2799*
Ac 21:13 ye to **w** and to break mine heart? *2799*
Ro 12:15 rejoice, and **w** with them that **w** *2799*
1Co 7:30 they that **w**, as though they wept *2799*
Jas 4:9 Be afflicted, and mourn, and **w**: *2799*
Jas 5:1 **w** and howl for your miseries that *2799*
Rev 5:5 **W** not: behold, the Lion of the tribe.... *2799*
Rev 18:11 merchants of the earth shall **w** *2799*

WEEPEST
1Sa 1:8 to her, Hannah, why **w** thou? 1058
Jn 20:13 Woman, why **w** thou?
Jn 20:15 unto her, **Woman, why w thou?** *2799*

WEEPING
Nu 25:6 were **w** before the door of the......... 1058
Dt 34:8 days of **w** and mourning for Moses 1065
2Sa 15:30 they went up, **w** as they went up. 1058
Ezr 3:13 the noise of the **w** of the people:....... 1065
Ezr 10:1 **w** and casting himself down 1058
Est 4:3 and fasting, and **w**, and wailing; 1065
Job 16:16 My face is foul with **w**, and on my 1065
Ps 6:8 Lord hath heard the voice of my **w**..... 1065
Ps 30:5 **w** may endure for a night, but joy 1065
Isa 15:3 one shall howl, **w** abundantly 1065
Isa 22:12 did the Lord God of hosts call to **w**,.... 1065
Isa 65:19 voice of **w** shall be no more heard 1065
Jer 9:10 will I take up a **w** and wailing......... 1065
Jer 31:15 Rahel **w** for her children refused....... 1058
Joel 2:12 fasting, and with **w**, and with 1065
Mal 2:13 with tears, with **w**, and with crying 1065
Mt 2:18 Rachel **w** for her children, and *2799*
Mt 8:12 **shall be w and gnashing of teeth.** *2805*
Lk 7:38 stood at his feet behind him **w** *2799*
Lk 13:28 **shall be w and gnashing of teeth,** *2805*
Jn 11:33 When Jesus therefore saw her **w**,....... *2799*
Jn 20:11 stood without at the sepulchre **w**:...... *2799*
Ac 9:39 and all the widows stood by him **w** *2799*
Php 3:18 often, and now tell you even **w**,........ *2799*
Rev 18:19 **w** and wailing, saying, Alas, alas *2799*

WEIGH
Ps 58:2 ye **w** the violence of your hands 6424
Isa 26:7 dost **w** the path of the just............ 6424
Isa 46:6 **w** silver in the balance, and hire 8254

WEIGHED
1Sa 2:3 and by him actions are **w**............. 8505
1Sa 17:7 spear's head **w** six hundred shekels of
2Sa 14:26 he **w** the hair of his head at two 8254
2Sa 21:16 spear **w** three hundred shekels
Job 6:2 that my grief were throughly **w**, ... 8254
Job 31:6 Let me be **w** in an even balance 8254
Isa 40:12 and **w** the mountains in scales,........ 8254
Jer 32:10 **w** him the money in the balances...... 8254
Da 5:27 Thou art **w** in the balances, and 8625
Zec 11:12 they **w** for my price thirty pieces 8254

WEIGHETH
Pr 16:2 eyes; but the Lord **w** the spirits........ 8505

WEIGHT
Ex 30:34 of each shall there be a like **w**:
Le 26:26 deliver you your bread again by **w**:..... 4948
Dt 25:15 shalt have a perfect and just **w**, a......... 68
Jos 7:21 wedge of gold of fifty shekels **w** 4948
Jgs 8:26 **w** of the golden earrings that he....... 4948
2Sa 12:30 the **w** thereof was a talent of gold...... 4948
1Ki 10:14 Now the **w** of gold that came to 4948
2Ki 25:16 of all these vessels was without **w**...... 4948
1Ch 22:3 brass in abundance without **w**;........ 4948
1Ch 28:14 of gold by **w** for things of gold, for..... 4948
2Ch 4:18 for the **w** of the brass could not be..... 4948
2Ch 9:13 Now the **w** of gold that came to 4948
Job 28:25 To make the **w** for the winds; and 4948
Pr 11:1 Lord: but a just **w** is his delight.......... 68
Pr 16:11 A just **w** and balance are the 6425
Eze 4:16 and they shall eat bread by **w** 4948
Jn 19:39 aloes, about an hundred pound **w**
2Co 4:17 exceeding and eternal **w** of glory:....... *922*
Heb 12:1 let us lay aside every **w**, and the *3591*
Rev 16:21 every stone about the **w** of a talent: *5006*

WEIGHTIER
Mt 23:23 **omitted the w matters of the law,** *926*

WEIGHTS
Le 19:36 Just balances, just **w**, a just.............. 68
Dt 25:13 shalt not have in thy bag divers **w**, ... 68
Pr 16:11 all the **w** of the bag are his work......... 68
Pr 20:10 Divers **w**, and divers measures, ... 68
Pr 20:23 Divers **w** are an abomination unto....... 68
Mic 6:11 and with the bag of deceitful **w**?......... 68

WEIGHTY

Pr	27:3	A stone is heavy, and the sand **w**;	5192
2Co	10:10	his letters, say they, are **w** and	*926*

WELFARE

Ne	2:10	the **w** of the children of Israel	2896
Jer	38:4	seeketh not the **w** of this people	7965

WELL See also WELLBELOVED; WELLPLEASING.

Ge	4:7	If thou doest **w**, shalt thou not be	3190
Ge	26:25	there Isaac's servants digged a **w**	875
Ge	29:17	was beautiful and **w** favoured	3303
Ge	40:14	think on me when it shall be **w**	3190
Dt	4:40	that it may go **w** with thee, and	3190
Dt	5:16	that it may go **w** with thee, in the	3190
Dt	5:29	that it might be **w** with them, and	3190
Dt	6:3	that it may be **w** with thee, and	3190
Dt	6:18	that it may be **w** with thee, and	3190
Dt	12:28	that it may go **w** with thee,	3190
Dt	19:13	Israel, that it may go **w** with thee	2895
Ru	3:1	thee, that it may be **w** with thee?	3190
2Sa	18:28	and said unto the king, All is **w**	7965
2Sa	23:15	the water of the **w** of Beth-lehem,	953
2Ki	4:26	is it **w** with the child?	7965
2Ki	7:9	said one to another, We do not **w**:	3651
Job	12:3	I have understanding as **w** as you;	71
Ps	48:13	Mark ye **w** her bulwarks	
Ps	128:2	be, and it shall be **w** with thee	2896
Ps	139:14	and that my soul knoweth right **w**	
Pr	5:15	running waters out of thine own **w**	875
Pr	10:11	of a righteous man is a **w** of life:	4726
Pr	30:29	There be three things which go **w**	3190
Pr	31:27	She looketh **w** to the ways of her	6822
Ecc	8:12	be **w** with them that fear God	2896
Ecc	8:13	it shall not be **w** with the wicked	2896
Jer	15:11	to entreat thee **w** in the time of evil	
Da	1:4	was no blemish, but **w** favoured	2896
Jnh	4:4	Doest thou **w** to be angry?	3190
Jnh	4:9	he said, I do **w** to be angry, even	3190
Mt	3:17	Son, in whom I am **w** pleased	*2106*
Mt	12:12	**is lawful to do w on the sabbath**	*2573*
Mt	12:18	in whom my soul is **w** pleased:	*2106*
Mt	17:5	Son, in whom I am **w** pleased;	*2106*
Mt	25:23	**him, W done, good and faithful**	*2095*
Mk	1:11	Son, in whom I am **w** pleased	*2106*
Mk	7:37	He hath done all things **w**	*2573*
Lk	3:22	Son; in thee I am **w** pleased	*2106*
Lk	6:26	**all men shall speak w of you!**	*2573*
Jn	4:11	to draw with, and the **w** is deep:	*5421*
Jn	4:14	**a w of water springing up into**	*4077*
Jn	13:13	**Master and Lord: and ye say w;**	*2573*
Ro	2:7	by patient continuance in **w** doing	*18*
1Co	7:37	he will keep his virgin, doeth **w**	*2573*
1Co	10:5	of them God was not **w** pleased:	*2106*
2Co	6:9	As unknown, and yet **w** known;	*1921*
Gal	5:7	Ye did run **w**; who did hinder you	*2573*
Gal	6:9	let us not be weary in **w** doing:	*2570*
Eph	6:3	That it may be **w** with thee, and	*2095*
Col	3:20	this is **w** pleasing unto the Lord	*2101*
2Th	3:13	be not weary in **w** doing	*2569*
1Ti	3:4	One that ruleth **w** his own house,	*2573*
1Ti	3:13	used the office of a deacon **w**	*2573*
1Ti	5:17	the elders that rule **w** be counted	*2573*
Heb	13:16	such sacrifices God is **w** pleased	*2100*
1Pe	2:15	that with **w** doing ye may put to	*15*
1Pe	2:20	when ye do **w**, and suffer for it, ye	*15*
2Pe	1:17	Son, in whom I am **w** pleased	*2106*

WELLBELOVED See also BELOVED.

SS	1:13	A bundle of myrrh is my **w** unto	1730
Isa	5:1	Now will I sing to my **w** a song of	3039
Mk	12:6	**yet therefore one son, his w, he**	*27*

WELLPLEASING See also WELL and PLEASING.

Php	4:18	a sacrifice acceptable, **w** to God	*2101*
Heb	13:21	you that which is **w** in his sight	*2101*

WELLS

Ge	26:18	Isaac digged again the **w** of water	875
Ex	15:27	where were twelve **w** of water	5869
2Ki	3:25	they stopped all the **w** of water	4599
Isa	12:3	water out of the **w** of salvation	4599
2Pe	2:17	These are **w** without water,	*4077*

WELLSPRING

Pr	16:22	Understanding is a **w** of life unto	4726
Pr	18:4	and the **w** of wisdom as a flowing	4726

WEPT

Ge	27:38	Esau lifted up his voice, and **w**	1058
Ge	42:24	himself about from them, and **w**;	1058
Ge	43:30	into his chamber, and **w** there.	1058
Ge	45:2	And he **w** aloud:	5414, 853, 6963, 1065
Ge	46:29	and **w** on his neck a good while.	1058
Ge	50:17	Joseph **w** when they spake unto	1058
Ex	2:6	child: and, behold, the babe **w**	1058
Nu	11:18	ye have **w** in the ears of the Lord,	1058
Nu	14:1	cried; and the people **w** that night	1058
Dt	1:45	returned and **w** before the Lord;	1058
Jgs	20:23	and **w** before the Lord until even,	1058
Jgs	21:2	lifted up their voices, and **w** sore;	1058
1Sa	1:7	therefore she **w**, and did not eat	1058
2Sa	12:22	child was yet alive, I fasted and **w**	1058
2Sa	15:30	mount Olivet, and **w** as he went up,	1058
2Sa	18:33	the chamber over the gate, and **w**	1058
2Ki	13:14	and **w** over his face, and said, O my	1058
2Ki	22:19	rent thy clothes, and **w** before me;	1058
Ezr	3:12	their eyes, **w** with a loud voice;	1058
Ne	1:4	words, that I sat down and **w**,	1058
Job	2:12	they lifted up their voice, and **w**;	1058
Ps	69:10	When I **w**, and chastened my soul	1058
Ps	137:1	we **w**, when we remembered Zion	1058
Is	38:3	thy sight. And Hezekiah wept sore.	1058
Hos	12:4	he **w** and made supplication unto	1058
Mt	26:75	and he went out, and **w** bitterly	*2799*
Mk	14:72	when he thought thereon, he **w**	*2799*
Lk	7:32	**to you, and ye have not w.**	*2799*
Lk	8:52	all **w**, and bewailed her: but he	*2799*
Lk	19:41	he beheld the city, and **w** over it,	*2799*
Lk	22:62	Peter went out, and **w** bitterly	*2799*
Jn	11:35	Jesus **w**.	*1145*
Jn	20:11	and as she **w**, she stooped down	*2799*
1Co	7:30	that weep, as though they **w** not;	*2799*
Rev	5:4	And I **w** much, because no man	*2799*

WEST

Nu	34:6	this shall be your **w** border.	3220
Jos	15:12	the **w** border was to the great sea,	3220
1Ki	7:25	and three looking toward the **w**	3220
Ps	75:6	from the east, nor from the **w**	4628
Ps	103:12	As far as the east is from the **w**,	4628
Ps	107:3	from the east, and from the **w**	4628
Isa	59:19	the name of the Lord from the **w**	4628
Eze	47:20	**w** side also shall be the great sea	3220
Mt	8:11	**shall come from the east and w,**	*1424*
Mt	24:27	**and shineth even unto the w;**	*1424*

Lk 12:54 **ye see a cloud rise out of the w,** *1424*
Lk 13:29 **from the east, and from the w,** *1424*
Rev 21:13 gates; and on the **w** three gates *1424*

WESTWARD
Nu 3:23 pitch behind the tabernacle **w**......... 3220
Jos 22:7 brethren on this side Jordan **w**.. 3220
Jos 23:4 even unto the great sea **w** 3996, 8121

WET
Da 4:15 be **w** with the dew of heaven, ... 6647
Da 4:33 and his body was **w** with the dew...... 6647
Da 5:21 and his body was **w** with the dew...... 6647

WHALE
Job 7:12 Am I a sea, or a **w**, that thou.......... 8577
Eze 32:2 and thou art as a **w** in the seas:........ 8565

WHALE'S
Mt 12:40 **and three nights in the w belly;** *2785*

WHALES
Ge 1:21 And God created great **w**, and......... 8577

WHAT
Ge 2:19 to see **w** he would call them:.......... 4100
Ge 3:13 **W** is this that thou hast done?......... 4100
Ge 9:24 **w** his younger son had done 853, 834
Ge 32:27 he said unto him, **W** is thy name? 4100
Ex 3:13 shall say to me, **W** is his name?........ 4100
Le 25:20 **W** shall we eat the seventh year?....... 4100
Nu 23:17 him, **W** hath the Lord spoken? 4100
Dt 3:24 for **w** God is there in heaven or 4310
Dt 4:7 For **w** nation is there so great,......... 4310
Dt 8:2 to know **w** was in thine heart 853, 834
Dt 10:12 **w** doth the Lord thy God require 4100
Jos 4:21 saying, **W** mean these stones? 4100
Jos 7:19 tell me now **w** thou hast done; 4100
Jgs 13:17 **W** is thy name, that when thy 4310
Jgs 14:18 down, **W** is sweeter than honey?....... 4100
Ru 4:5 **W** day thou buyest the field
1Sa 3:18 let him do **w** seemeth him good.
1Sa 13:11 Samuel said, **W** hast thou done?....... 4100
1Sa 15:14 **W** meaneth then this bleating of 4100
1Sa 17:29 David said, **W** have I now done?....... 4100
1Sa 18:18 and **w** is my life, or my father's........ 4310
2Sa 3:24 king, and said, **W** hast thou done? 4100
2Sa 7:23 **w** one nation in the earth is like 4310
1Ki 3:5 God said, Ask **w** I shall give thee. 4100
1Ki 12:16 **W** portion have we in David? 4100
1Ki 17:18 **W** have I to do with thee, O thou...... 4100
1Ki 19:13 **W** dost thou here, Elijah?............ 4100
2Ki 2:9 Elisha, Ask **w** I shall do for thee 4100
2Ki 3:13 Israel, **W** have I to do with thee?....... 4100
2Ki 20:8 **W** shall be the sign that the Lord 4100
2Ki 20:15 **W** have they seen in thine house?...... 4100
2Ki 23:17 **W** title is that that I see?............. 4100
1Ch 17:21 **w** one nation in the earth is like 4310
1Ch 21:17 as for these sheep, **w** have they done?
1Ch 29:14 who am I, and **w** is my people,........ 4310
2Ch 1:7 him, Ask **w** I shall give thee 4100
2Ch 10:16 **W** portion have we in David? 4100
2Ch 19:6 the judges, Take heed **w** ye do: 4100
Ne 4:2 **W** do these feeble Jews? will they 4100
Ne 13:17 **W** evil thing is this that ye do,......... 4100
Est 6:6 **W** shall be done unto the man 4100
Job 7:17 **W** is man, that thou shouldest 4100
Job 9:12 will say unto him, **W** doest thou?...... 4100
Job 15:14 **W** is man, that he should be 4100
Job 34:7 **W** man is like Job, who drinketh 4310
Job 35:6 **W** doest thou against him? or if 4100
Job 35:7 be righteous, **w** givest thou him? 4100
Job 35:7 or **w** receiveth he of thine hand?....... 4100
Job 38:24 By **w** way is the light parted 335, 2088
Job 40:4 I am vile; **w** shall I answer thee? 4100
Ps 8:4 **W** is man, that thou art mindful........ 4100
Ps 11:3 destroyed, **w** can the righteous do?..... 4100
Ps 25:12 **W** man is he that feareth the.......... 4310
Ps 34:12 **W** man is he that desireth life 4310
Ps 56:3 **W** time I am afraid, I will trust in
Ps 89:48 **W** man is he that liveth, and 4310
Ps 116:12 **W** shall I render unto the Lord........ 4100
Ps 118:6 not fear: **w** can man do unto me?...... 4100
Ps 144:3 Lord, **w** is man, that thou takest 4100
Pr 4:19 they know not at **w** they stumble 4100
Pr 10:32 the righteous know **w** is acceptable:
Pr 27:1 knowest not **w** a day may bring 4100
Pr 30:4 **w** is his name, and **w** is his son's....... 4100
Ecc 1:3 **W** profit hath a man of all his......... 4100
Ecc 6:8 **w** hath the wise more than the fool? ... 4100
Ecc 6:8 than the fool? **w** hath the poor,........ 4100
Ecc 8:4 may say unto him, **W** doest thou? 4100
Ecc 11:5 not **w** is the way of the spirit, ... 4100
Isa 21:11 night? Watchman, **w** of the night? 4100
Isa 40:6 **W** shall I cry? All flesh is grass, ... 4100
Isa 40:18 **w** likeness will ye compare unto 4100
Isa 45:9 fashioneth it, **W** makest thou?......... 4100
Jer 5:31 **w** will ye do in the end thereof? 4100
Jer 8:6 saying, **W** have I done?............... 4100
Jer 13:21 **W** wilt thou say when he shall 4100
Jer 16:10 **w** is our iniquity: or **w** is our sin....... 4100
Da 2:22 he knoweth **w** is in the darkness, ... 4101
Da 2:28 **w** shall be in the latter days........... 4101
Da 3:5 **w** time ye hear the sound of the 1768
Da 4:35 or say unto him, **W** doest thou? 4101
Da 8:19 know **w** shall be in the last end..... 853, 834
Da 12:8 **w** shall be the end of these things?..... 4100
Am 4:13 declareth unto man **w** is his thought,... 4100
Jnh 1:6 him, **W** meanest thou, O sleeper?...... 4100
Mic 6:8 **w** doth the Lord require of thee,....... 4100
Zec 13:6 **W** are these wounds in thine hands? ... 4100
Mal 1:13 also, Behold, **w** a weariness is it!
Mt 2:7 diligently **w** time … star appeared *3588*
Mt 6:31 **saying, W shall we eat? or** *5101*
Mt 8:27 saying, **W** manner of man is this,...... *4217*
Mt 8:29 **W** have we to do with thee, Jesus,...... *5101*
Mt 10:27 **W I tell you in darkness, that** *3739*
Mt 16:26 **w shall a man give in exchange**........ *5101*
Mt 19:6 **W therefore God hath joined** *3739*
Mt 22:42 **W think ye of Christ? whose son** *5101*
Mt 24:3 **w** shall be the sign of thy coming, ... *5101*
Mt 27:22 **W** shall I do then with Jesus *5101*
Mk 4:41 **W** manner of man is this, that *5101, 686*
Mk 5:9 he asked him, **W is thy name?**......... *5101*
Mk 8:36 **For w shall it profit a man, if** *5101*
Lk 1:66 **W** manner of child shall this...... *5101, 686*
Lk 4:36 saying, **W** a word is this! for with *5101*
Lk 8:25 **W** manner of man is this! *5101, 686*
Lk 8:30 asked him, saying, **W is thy name?**..... *5101*
Lk 10:26 **W is written in the law? how**.......... *5101*
Lk 12:22 **for your life, w ye shall eat;** *5101*
Lk 12:22 **for the body, w ye shall put on..** *5101*
Lk 12:39 **w hour the thief would come,**......... *4169*
Lk 13:18 **w is the kingdom of God like?** *5101*

WHATSOEVER

WHEAT

Jer 23:28	what is the chaff to the **w**? saith	1250
Joel 2:24	the floors shall be full of **w**, and	1250
Am 8:5	sabbath, that we may set forth **w**,	1250
Mt 13:25	**and sowed tares among the w,**	*4621*
Mt 13:30	**but gather the w into my barn.**	*4621*
Lk 16:7	**said, An hundred measures of w.**	*4621*
Lk 22:31	**you, that he may sift you as w:**	*4621*
Jn 12:24	**a corn of w fall into the ground**	*4621*
Rev 6:6	A measure of **w** for a penny, and	*4621*

WHEEL

1Ki 7:33	was like the work of a chariot **w**:	212
Ps 83:13	God, make them like a **w**; as the	1534
Pr 20:26	and bringeth the **w** over them.	212
Ecc 12:6	or the **w** broken at the cistern	1534
Isa 28:27	neither is a cart **w** turned about	212
Eze 1:16	it were a **w** in the middle of a **w**	212
Eze 10:10	a **w** had been in the midst of a **w**	212

WHEELS

Ex 14:25	took off their chariot **w**, that they	212
1Sa 5:28	and their **w** like a whirlwind:	1534
Jer 18:3	he wrought a work on the **w**	70
Eze 1:19	creatures went, the **w** went by them:	212
Eze 1:20	of the living creature was in the **w**	212
Eze 3:13	noise of the **w** over against them,	212
Eze 10:6	Take fire from between the **w**,	1534
Eze 10:9	the four **w** by the cherubims,	212
Eze 10:12	the **w** were full of eyes round about,	212
Eze 11:22	wings, and the **w** beside them; and	212
Eze 23:24	with chariots, wagons, and **w**,	1534
Eze 26:10	of the horsemen, and of the **w**,	1534
Da 7:9	flame, and his **w** as burning fire.	1535

WHELP

Ge 49:9	Judah is a lion's **w**; from the	1482
Dt 33:22	Dan is a lion's **w**: he shall leap	1482
Na 2:11	the lion's **w**, and none made them	1482

WHELPS

2Sa 17:8	as a bear robbed of her **w** in the field:	
Pr 17:12	Let a bear robbed of her **w** meet a	
Jer 51:38	lions: they shall yell as lions' **w**	1484
Eze 19:2	she nourished her **w** among	1482
Hos 13:8	as a bear that is bereaved of her **w**,	
Na 2:12	tear in pieces enough for his **w**,	1484

WHERE

Ge 3:9	and said unto him, **W** art thou?	335
Ge 4:9	unto Cain, **W** is Abel thy brother?	335
Ge 18:9	unto him, **W** is Sarah thy wife?	346
Ge 22:7	**w** is the lamb for a burnt offering?	346
Ex 20:21	the thick darkness **w** God was.	834, 8033
Ex 20:24	**w** I record my name I will come	834
Ex 30:6	**w** I will meet with thee	834, 8033
Ex 30:36	**w** I will meet with thee: it	834, 8033
Nu 9:17	in the place **w** the cloud abode,	834
Ru 1:16	and **w** thou lodgest, I will lodge:	834
Ru 1:17	**W** thou diest, will I die, and there.	834
2Ki 2:14	said, **W** is the Lord God of Elijah?	346
2Ch 3:1	**w** the Lord appeared unto David	834
Job 23:3	Oh that I knew **w** I might find him!	
Job 23:9	**w** he doth work, but I cannot behold	
Job 35:10	**W** is God my maker, who giveth	335
Job 38:4	**W** wast thou when I laid the	375
Job 38:19	**W** is the way **w** light dwelleth?	335
Ps 42:3	say unto me, **W** is thy God?	346
Ps 42:10	say daily unto me, **W** is thy God?	346
Ps 53:5	there in great fear, **w** no fear was:	
Ps 63:1	a dry and thirsty land, **w** no water is;	
Ps 79:10	**W** is their God? let him be known	346
Ps 115:2	heathen say, **W** is now their God?	346
Pr 11:14	**W** no counsel is, the people fall: but	
Pr 14:4	**W** no oxen are, the crib is clean: but	
Pr 15:17	is a dinner of herbs **w** love is	8033
Pr 26:20	**W** no wood is, the fire goeth out:	657
Pr 26:20	**w** there is no talebearer, the strife	
Pr 29:18	**W** there is no vision the people	
Ecc 8:4	**W** the word of a king is, there is	834
Ecc 11:3	place **w** the tree falleth, there it shall	
Isa 33:18	**W** is the scribe? **w** is the receiver?	346
Isa 63:11	**W** is he that brought them up out	346
Isa 63:11	**w** is he that put his holy Spirit	346
Isa 66:1	and **w** is the place of my rest?	335
Jer 2:6	**W** is the Lord that brought us up	346
Jer 2:8	priests said not, **W** is the Lord?	346
Jer 6:16	paths, **w** is the good way, and walk	335
Jer 7:12	**w** I set my name at the first	834, 8033
Jer 17:15	**W** is the word of the Lord? let it	346
Jer 35:7	in the land **w** ye be strangers	834, 8033
Jer 37:19	**W** are now your prophets which	346
La 2:12	mothers, **W** is corn and wine?	346
Eze 11:17	**w** ye have been scattered, and I	834
Eze 21:30	in the place **w** thou wast created	834
Da 8:17	So he came near **w** I stood: and when	
Joel 2:17	among the people, **W** is their God?	346
Mic 7:10	unto me, **W** is the Lord thy God?	346
Mal 1:6	and if I be a master, **w** is my fear?	346
Mal 2:17	or, **W** is the God of judgment?	346
Mt 2:2	**W** is he that is born King of the	*4226*
Mt 2:4	of them **w** Christ should be born.	*4226*
Mt 2:9	stood over **w** the young child was	*3757*
Mt 6:19	**w moth and rust doth corrupt,**	*3699*
Mt 6:19	**w thieves break through and steal:**	*3699*
Mt 6:21	**w your treasure is, there will**	*3699*
Mt 18:20	**For w two or three are gathered**	*3757*
Mt 25:24	**reaping w thou hast not sown,**	*3699*
Mt 28:6	Come, see the place **w** the Lord lay.	*3699*
Mk 9:44	**W their worm dieth not, and**	*3699*
Mk 9:46	**W their worm dieth not, and**	*3699*
Mk 9:48	**W their worm dieth not, and**	*3699*
Mk 16:6	behold the place **w** they laid him.	*3699*
Lk 8:25	said unto them, **W is your faith?**	*4226*
Lk 9:58	**man hath not w to lay his head.**	*4226*
Lk 12:33	**w no thief approacheth, neither**	*3699*
Lk 12:34	**w your treasure is, there will**	*3699*
Jn 3:8	**The wind bloweth w it listeth,**	*3699*
Jn 7:11	at the feast, and said, **W** is he?	*4226*
Jn 7:34	**w I am, thither ye cannot come.**	*3699*
Jn 8:19	said unto him, **W** is thy Father?	*4226*
Jn 11:34	And said, **W have ye laid him?**	*4226*
Jn 12:26	**and w I am, there shall also my**	*3699*
Jn 14:3	**that w I am, there ye may be.**	*3699*
Jn 17:24	**given me be with me w I am:**	*3699*
Jn 19:18	**W** they crucified him, and two	*3699*
Jn 20:2	we know not **w** they have laid	*4226*
Jn 20:13	I know not **w** they have laid him	*4226*
Ac 7:33	**w** thou standest is holy.	*1722, 3739*
Ac 17:30	all men every **w** to repent:	*3837*
Ro 3:27	**W** is boasting then? It is	*4226*
Ro 4:15	for **w** no law is, there is no	*3757*
Ro 5:20	But **w** sin abounded, grace did	*3757*
Ro 9:26	place **w** it was said unto them	*3757*
1Co 1:20	**w** is the disputer of this world?	*4226*

1Co 12:19	one member, **w** were the body?	*4226*
1Co 15:55	O death, **w** is thy sting? O grave	*4226*
1Co 15:55	sting? O grave, **w** is thy victory?	*4226*
2Co 3:17	and **w** the Spirit of the Lord is	*3757*
Col 3:1	**w** Christ sitteth on the right	*3757*
Heb 10:18	**w** remission of these is, there is	*3699*
Jas 3:16	**w** envying and strife is, there is	*3699*
2Pe 3:4	**W** is the promise of his coming?	*4226*
Rev 2:13	**among you, w Satan dwelleth.**	*3699*
Rev 11:8	**w** also our Lord was crucified	*3699*
Rev 12:14	**w** she is nourished for a time, and	*3699*
Rev 17:15	**w** the whore sitteth, are peoples	*3757*
Rev 20:10	**w** the beast and the false prophet	*3699*

WHEREBY

Jer 33:8	**w** they have sinned against me;	834
Lk 1:18	**W** shall I know this? for I	*2596, 5101*
Lk 1:78	**w** the dayspring from on high	*1722, 3739*
Ac 4:12	men, **w** we must be saved	*1722, 3739*
Ro 8:15	**w** we cry, Abba, Father	*1722, 3739*
Ro 14:21	thing **w** thy brother stumbleth,	*1722, 3739*
Eph 4:30	**w** ye are sealed unto the day	*1722, 3739*
Php 3:21	**w** he is able even to subdue all	*3588*
Heb 12:28	grace, **w** we may serve God	*1223, 3739*
1Jn 2:18	**w** we know that it is the last time	*3606*

WHET

Dt 32:41	If I **w** my glittering sword, and	8150
Ps 7:12	he turn not, he will **w** his sword;	3913
Ps 64:3	Who **w** their tongue like a sword,	8150
Ecc 10:10	blunt, and he do not **w** the edge,	7043

WHIP

Pr 26:3	A **w** for the horse, a bridle for the	7752
Na 3:2	The noise of a **w**, and the noise of	7752

WHIPS

1Ki 12:11	father hath chastised you with **w**,	7752
2Ch 10:14	my father chastised you with **w**,	7752

WHIRLWIND

2Ki 2:11	Elijah went up by a **w** into heaven	5591
Job 38:1	Lord answered Job out of the **w**,	5591
Job 40:6	the Lord unto Job out of the **w**,	5591
Ps 58:9	shall take them away as with a **w**,	8175
Pr 1:27	your destruction cometh as a **w**;	5492
Pr 10:25	As the **w** passeth, so is the wicked	5492
Jer 4:13	and his chariots shall be as a **w**	5492
Jer 23:19	a **w** of the Lord is gone forth in	5591
Jer 30:23	**w** of the Lord goeth forth with fury,	5591
Eze 1:4	a **w** came out of the north, a	7307, 5591
Hos 8:7	wind, and they shall reap the **w**:	5492
Am 1:14	a tempest in the day of the **w**	5492
Na 1:3	the Lord hath his way in the **w**	5492
Hab 3:14	came out as a **w** to scatter me:	5590
Zec 7:14	But I scattered them with a **w**	5590

WHISPER

Ps 41:7	All that hate me **w** together	3907
Isa 29:4	thy speech shall **w** out of the dust	6850

WHISPERED

2Sa 12:19	David saw that his servants **w**,	3907

WHISPERER

Pr 16:28	and a **w** separateth chief friends	5372

WHISPERERS

Ro 1:29	debate, deceit, malignity; **w**,	*5588*

WHITE

Ge 40:16	had three **w** baskets on my head:	2751
Le 13:4	If the bright spot be **w** in the skin	3836
Nu 12:10	Miriam became leprous, **w** as snow:	
Jgs 5:10	Speak, ye that ride on **w** asses	6715
2Ch 5:12	brethren, being arrayed in **w** linen	
Est 8:15	king in royal apparel of blue and **w**,	2353
Ecc 9:8	Let thy garments be always **w**;	3836
Isa 1:18	scarlet, they shall be as **w** as snow;	3835
Da 7:9	whose garment was **w** as snow, and	
Da 12:10	shall be purified, and made **w**, and	3835
Joel 1:7	the branches thereof are made **w**	3835
Zec 1:8	there red horses, speckled, and **w**	3836
Zec 6:3	And in the third chariot **w** horses;	3836
Mt 5:36	**not make one hair w or black.**	*3022*
Mt 17:2	his raiment was **w** as the light	*3022*
Mt 28:3	and his raiment **w** as snow:	*3022*
Mk 9:3	shining, exceeding **w** as snow;	*3022*
Mk 16:5	side, clothed in a long **w** garment;	*3022*
Lk 9:29	his raiment was **w** and glistering.	*3022*
Jn 4:35	**for they are w already to harvest.**	*3022*
Jn 20:12	And seeth two angels in **w** sitting	*3022*
Ac 1:10	two men stood by them in **w**.	*3022*
Rev 1:14	His head and his hairs were **w** like	*3022*
Rev 1:14	as **w** as snow; and his eyes were as	*3022*
Rev 2:17	**will give him a w stone, and in**	*3022*
Rev 3:5	**shall be clothed in w raiment;**	*3022*
Rev 4:4	sitting, clothed in **w** raiment; and	*3022*
Rev 6:2	And I saw, and behold a **w** horse:	*3022*
Rev 6:11	**w** robes were given unto every one	*3022*
Rev 7:13	which are arrayed in **w** robes?	*3022*
Rev 7:14	make them **w** in the blood of the	*3021*
Rev 14:14	I looked, and behold a **w** cloud,	*3022*
Rev 15:6	clothed in pure and **w** linen.	*2986*
Rev 19:8	arrayed in fine linen, clean and **w**:	*2986*
Rev 19:11	opened and behold a **w** horse;	*3022*
Rev 19:14	followed him upon **w** horses	*3022*
Rev 19:14	clothed in fine linen, **w** and clean	*3022*
Rev 20:11	I saw a great **w** throne, and him	*3022*

WHITED

Mt 23:27	**for ye are like unto w sepulchres,**	*2867*
Ac 23:3	God shall smite thee, thou **w** wall:	*2867*

WHITER

Ps 51:7	me, and I shall be **w** than snow	3835
La 4:7	snow, they were **w** than milk,	6705

WHO

Ge 3:11	**W** told thee that thou wast naked?	4310
Ge 27:18	Here am I; **w** art thou, my son?	4310
Ge 27:33	Isaac trembled … and said, **W**?	4310
Ex 3:11	And Moses said unto God, **W** am I,	4310
Ex 4:11	him, **w** hath made man's mouth?	4310
Ex 5:2	Pharaoh said, **W** is the Lord, that	4310
Ex 15:11	**W** is like unto thee, O Lord	4310
Ex 15:11	**w** is like thee, glorious in holiness,	4310
Ex 32:26	said, **W** is on the Lord's side?	4310
Nu 16:5	the Lord will shew **w** are his	853, 834
Nu 23:10	**W** can count the dust of Jacob,	4310
Dt 4:7	**w** hath God so nigh unto them,	834
Dt 30:12	**W** shall go up for us to heaven	4310
Dt 33:29	**w** is like unto thee, O people	4310
Jgs 6:29	another, **W** hath done this thing?	4310
Jgs 15:6	said, **W** hath done this?	4310
1Sa 4:8	**w** shall deliver us out of the hand	4310
1Sa 6:20	**W** is able to stand before this holy	4310

1Sa	18:18	David said unto Saul, **W** am I?	4310
1Sa	25:10	**W** is David? and **w** is the son of	4310
2Sa	7:18	**W** am I, O Lord God? and what is	4310
2Sa	12:22	**W** can tell whether God will be	4310
2Sa	22:4	the Lord, **w** is worthy to be praised:	
2Sa	22:32	For **w** is God, save the Lord?	4310
2Sa	22:32	and **w** is a rock, save our God?	
1Ki	3:9	**w** is able to judge this thy so great	4310
1Ch	17:16	**W** am I, O Lord God, and what is	4310
1Ch	29:14	**w** am I, and what is my people,	4310
2Ch	1:10	for **w** can judge this thy people	4310
2Ch	2:6	**w** is able to build him an house	4310
Ezr	5:9	**W** commanded you to build this	4479
Ne	9:7	the God, **w** didst choose Abram	834
Ne	9:32	God, **w** keepest covenant and mercy	
Ne	13:26	like him, **w** was beloved of his God	
Est	4:14	**w** knoweth whether thou art	4310
Est	6:4	the king said, **W** is in the court?	4310
Est	7:5	**W** is he, and where is he, that	4310
Job	13:19	**W** is he that will plead with me?	4310
Job	35:10	maker, **w** giveth songs in the night;	
Job	38:2	**W** is this that darkeneth counsel	4310
Job	38:37	**W** can number the clouds in	4310
Job	41:10	**w** then is able to stand before me?	4310
Job	41:11	**W** hath prevented me, that I	4310
Ps	12:4	are our own: **w** is lord over us?	4310
Ps	14:4	**w** eat up my people as they eat	
Ps	15:1	**w** shall abide in thy tabernacle?	4310
Ps	18:31	For **w** is God save the Lord?	4310
Ps	18:31	or **w** is a rock save our God?	4310
Ps	19:12	**W** can understand his errors?	4310
Ps	24:3	**w** shall stand in his holy place?	4310
Ps	24:8	**W** is this King of glory? The	4310
Ps	24:10	**W** is this King of glory? The	4310
Ps	35:10	say, Lord, **w** is like unto thee	4310
Ps	53:4	**w** eat up my people as they eat	
Ps	59:7	lips: for **w**, say they, doth hear?	4310
Ps	64:5	they say, **W** shall see them?	4310
Ps	68:19	**w** daily loadeth us with benefits,	
Ps	71:19	O God, **w** is like unto thee!	4310
Ps	77:13	**w** is so great a God as our God?	4310
Ps	89:6	**w** in the heaven can be compared	4310
Ps	89:8	**w** is a strong Lord like unto thee?	4310
Ps	90:11	**W** knoweth the power of thine	4310
Ps	103:3	**W** forgiveth all thine iniquities;	
Ps	103:3	iniquities; **w** healeth all thy diseases	
Ps	103:4	**W** redeemeth thy life from	
Ps	103:4	**w** crowneth thee with lovingkindness	
Ps	103:5	**W** satisfieth thy mouth with good	
Ps	104:2	**w** stretchest out the heavens like a	
Ps	104:3	**w** maketh the clouds his chariot:	
Ps	104:4	**W** maketh his angels spirits; his	
Ps	104:5	**W** laid the foundations of the earth,	
Ps	106:2	**W** can utter the mighty acts of	4310
Ps	113:5	**W** is like unto the Lord our God,	4310
Ps	119:1	way, **w** walk in the law of the Lord.	
Ps	124:1	been the Lord **w** was on our side,	
Ps	124:8	the Lord, **w** made heaven and earth.	
Ps	130:3	iniquities, O Lord, **w** shall stand?	4310
Ps	135:8	**W** smote the firstborn of Egypt, both	
Ps	135:10	**W** smote great nations, and slew	
Ps	136:25	**W** giveth food to all flesh: for his	
Ps	147:8	**W** covereth the heaven with clouds,	
Pr	2:13	**W** leave the paths of uprightness, to	
Pr	2:14	**W** rejoice to do evil, and delight in	
Pr	20:6	but a faithful man **w** can find?	4310
Pr	20:9	**W** can say, I have made my heart	4310
Pr	20:25	man **w** devoureth that which is holy	
Pr	21:24	his name **w** dealeth in proud wrath.	
Pr	23:29	**W** hath woe? **w** hath sorrow?	4310
Pr	23:29	**w** hath contentions? **w** hath	4310
Pr	23:29	**w** hath wounds without cause?	4310
Pr	23:29	**w** hath redness of eyes?	4310
Pr	24:22	**w** knoweth the ruin of them both?	4310
Pr	27:4	**w** is able to stand before envy?	4310
Pr	30:4	**W** hath ascended up into heaven,	4310
Pr	30:4	**w** hath gathered the wind in his	4310
Pr	30:4	**w** hath bound the waters in a	4310
Pr	30:4	**w** hath established all the ends of	4310
Pr	30:9	thee, and say, **W** is the Lord?	4310
Pr	31:10	**W** can find a virtuous woman?	4310
Ecc	2:19	And **w** knoweth whether he shall	4310
Ecc	3:21	**W** knoweth the spirit of man that	4310
Ecc	6:12	**w** knoweth what is good for man	4310
Ecc	6:12	for **w** can tell a man what shall be	4310
Ecc	8:4	**w** may say unto him, What doest	4310
Ecc	11:5	the works of God **w** maketh all	834
Ecc	12:7	shall return unto God **w** gave it	834
Isa	1:12	**w** hath required this at your	4310
Isa	6:8	shall I send, and **w** will go for us?	4310
Isa	14:27	out, and **w** shall turn it back?	4310
Isa	29:15	**W** seeth us? and **w** knoweth us?	4310
Isa	40:12	**W** hath measured the waters in	4310
Isa	40:13	**W** hath directed the Spirit of the	4310
Isa	40:14	**w** instructed him, and taught him in	
Isa	50:10	**W** is among you that feareth the	4310
Isa	53:1	**W** hath believed our report? and	4310
Jer	9:12	**w** is he to whom the mouth of the	
Jer	10:7	**W** should not fear thee, O king	4310
La	3:37	**W** is he that saith, and it cometh	4310
Da	2:23	**w** hast given me wisdom and	1768
Da	3:15	**w** is that God that shall deliver	4479
Da	3:23	**w** hath sent his angel, and	1768
Da	6:27	**w** hath delivered Daniel from the	1768
Hos	14:9	**W** is wise, and he shall	4310
Joel	2:11	very terrible; and **w** can abide it?	4310
Joel	2:14	**W** knoweth if he will return and	4310
Am	3:8	hath spoken, **w** can but prophesy?	4310
Jnh	3:9	**W** can tell if God will turn and	4310
Mic	3:2	**W** hate the good, and love the evil;	
Mic	7:18	**W** is a God like unto thee, that	4310
Na	1:6	**w** can abide in the fierceness of his	4310
Hag	2:3	**W** is left among you that saw	4310
Zec	4:10	**w** hath despised the day of small	4310
Mal	3:2	**w** shall stand when he appeareth?	4310
Mt	3:7	**w** hath warned you to flee from	*5101*
Mt	12:48	said unto him … **W is my mother?**	*5101*
Mt	13:9	**W hath ears to hear, let him**	*3588*
Mt	13:43	**W hath ears to hear, let him**	*3588*
Mt	13:46	**W, when he had found one pearl**	*3739*
Mt	18:1	**W** is the greatest in the kingdom	*5101*
Mt	19:25	saying, **W** then can be saved?	*5101*
Mt	21:10	city was moved, saying, **W** is this?	*5101*
Mt	24:45	**W then is a faithful and wise**	*5101*
Mt	26:68	Christ, **W** is he that smote thee?	*5101*
Mk	1:24	I know thee **w** thou art, the Holy	*5101*
Mk	2:7	**w** can forgive sins but God only?	*5101*
Mk	3:33	**W is my mother, or my brethren?**	*5101*
Mk	5:30	and said, **W touched my clothes?**	*5101*
Mk	16:3	**W** shall roll us away the stone	*5101*
Lk	3:7	**w** hath warned you to flee from	*5101*
Lk	5:21	**W** can forgive sins, but God alone?	*5101*

Lk	7:39	**w** and what manner of woman	*5101*
Lk	7:49	**W** is this that forgiveth sins also?	*5101*
Lk	8:45	And Jesus said, **W touched me?**	*5101*
Lk	10:22	**no man knoweth w the Son is,**	*5101*
Lk	10:29	Jesus, And **w** is my neighbour?	*5101*
Lk	12:14	**w made me a judge or a divider**	*5101*
Lk	18:26	it said, **W** then can be saved?	*5101*
Lk	19:3	he sought to see Jesus **w** he was;	*5101*
Lk	22:64	Prophesy, **w** is it that smote thee?	*5101*
Jn	1:19	to ask him, **W** art thou?	*5101*
Jn	1:22	said they unto them, **W** art thou?	*5101*
Jn	1:27	**w** coming after me is preferred	*3588*
Jn	4:10	**and w it is that saith to thee,**	*5101*
Jn	6:64	**w** they were that believed not,	*5101*
Jn	6:64	and **w** should betray him.	*5101*
Jn	8:25	said they unto him, **W** art thou?	*5101*
Jn	9:2	**w** did sin, this man, or his parents,	*5101*
Jn	9:21	**w** hath opened his eyes, we know	*5101*
Jn	9:36	**W** is he, Lord, that I might	*5101*
Jn	12:34	be lifted up? **w** is this Son of man?	*5101*
Jn	12:38	Lord, **w** hath believed our report?	*5101*
Jn	13:11	he knew **w** should betray him:	*3588*
Jn	13:25	saith unto him, Lord, **w** is it?	*5101*
Jn	21:12	durst ask him, **W** art thou?	*5101*
Ac	7:35	**W** made thee a ruler and a judge?	*5101*
Ac	9:5	And he said, **W** art thou, Lord?	*5101*
Ac	19:15	and Paul I know; but **w** are ye?	*5101*
Ac	22:8	I answered, **W** art thou, Lord?	*5101*
Ac	26:15	And I said, **W** art thou, Lord?	*5101*
Ro	1:18	**w** hold … truth in unrighteousness;	*3588*
Ro	1:25	**W** changed the truth of God into	*3748*
Ro	1:25	the Creator, **w** is blessed for ever	*3739*
Ro	1:32	**W** knowing the judgment of God,	*3748*
Ro	2:6	**W** will render to every man	*3739*
Ro	3:5	unrighteous **w** taketh vengeance?	*3588*
Ro	4:18	**W** against hope believed in hope	*3739*
Ro	4:25	**W** was delivered for our offences	*3739*
Ro	7:24	**w** shall deliver me from the body	*5101*
Ro	8:1	**w** walk not after the flesh, but after	
Ro	8:28	**w** are the called according to his	
Ro	8:31	be for us, **w** can be against us?	*5101*
Ro	8:33	**W** shall lay any thing to the	*5101*
Ro	8:34	**W** is he that condemneth? It is	*5101*
Ro	8:34	**w** also maketh intercession for us.	*3739*
Ro	8:35	**W** shall separate us from the	*5101*
Ro	9:5	**w** is over all, God blessed for ever	*3588*
Ro	9:19	For **w** hath resisted his will?	*5101*
Ro	10:6	**W** shall ascend into heaven?	*5101*
Ro	10:7	Or, **W** shall descend into the deep?	*5101*
Ro	11:34	**w** hath known the mind of the	*5101*
Ro	11:34	or **w** hath been his counsellor?	*5101*
Ro	14:4	**W** art thou that judgest another	*5101*
1Co	1:30	**w** of God is made unto us wisdom,	*3739*
1Co	2:16	**w** hath known the mind of the	*5101*
1Co	10:13	**w** will not suffer you to be	*3739*
2Co	1:4	**W** comforteth us in all our	*3588*
2Co	2:16	**w** is sufficient for these things?	*5101*
2Co	4:4	Christ, **w** is the image of God,	*3739*
2Co	5:21	him to be sin for us, **w** knew no sin;	
2Co	11:29	**W** is weak, and I am not weak?	*5201*
Gal	1:4	**W** gave himself for our sins, that	*3588*
Gal	2:20	**w** loved me, and gave himself for	*3588*
Gal	3:1	Galatians, **w** hath bewitched you	*5101*
Eph	1:11	purpose of him **w** worketh all things	
Eph	2:4	But God, **w** is rich in mercy, for his	
Eph	4:19	**W** being past feeling have given	*3748*
Php	2:6	**W**, being in the form of God	
Php	3:21	**W** shall change our vile body	
Col	1:15	**W** is the image of the invisible	*3739*
Col	1:18	**w** is the beginning, the firstborn	*3739*
Col	2:12	**w** hath raised him from the dead	*3588*
Col	3:4	When Christ, **w** is our life, shall	
1Th	2:12	of God, **w** hath called you unto his	*3588*
1Th	5:8	But let us, **w** are of the day, be sober	
1Th	5:10	**W** died for us, that, whether we	*3588*
1Th	5:24	that calleth you, **w** also will do it.	*3739*
1Ti	2:4	**W** will have all men to be saved	*3739*
1Ti	2:6	**W** gave himself a ransom for all,	*3588*
1Ti	5:17	**w** labour in the word and doctrine	
1Ti	6:15	**w** is the … only Potentate	*3588*
1Ti	6:16	**W** only hath immortality	*3588*
1Ti	6:17	**w** giveth us richly all things to	*3588*
2Ti	2:2	**w** shall be able to teach others	*3748*
2Ti	2:4	**w** hath chosen him to be a soldier	
2Ti	2:18	**W** concerning the truth have	*3748*
2Ti	2:26	**w** are taken captive by him at his	
2Ti	4:1	**w** shall judge the quick and the	*3588*
Tit	1:11	**w** subvert whole houses, teaching	*3748*
Heb	1:1	God **w** at sundry times and in divers	
Heb	1:3	**W** being the brightness of his glory	
Heb	2:9	**w** was made a little lower than	*3588*
Heb	6:18	**w** have fled for refuge to lay hold	*3588*
Heb	7:28	Son, **w** is consecrated for evermore	
Heb	8:1	**w** is set on the right hand of the	*3739*
Heb	11:11	judge him faithful **w** had promised	
Heb	11:33	**W** through faith subdued	*3739*
Heb	12:2	**w** for the joy that was set before	*3739*
Heb	12:16	**w** for one morsel of meat sold his	*3739*
Jas	3:13	**W** is a wise man and endued	*5101*
Jas	4:12	destroy: **w** art thou that judgest	*5101*
1Pe	1:17	**w** without respect of persons	*3588*
1Pe	2:9	**w** hath called you out of darkness	
1Pe	2:22	**W** did no sin, neither was guile	*3739*
1Pe	2:23	**W** when he was reviled, reviled not	*3739*
1Pe	2:24	**W** his own self bare our sins in	*3739*
1Pe	4:5	**W** shall give account to him that	*3739*
1Jn	2:22	**W** is a liar but he that denieth	*5101*
1Jn	4:21	he **w** loveth God love his brother	
3Jn	9	**w** loveth to have the preeminence	*3588*
Rev	1:5	Christ, **w** is the faithful witness,	
Rev	2:18	**w hath his eyes like unto a flame.**	*3588*
Rev	4:9	throne, **w** liveth for ever and ever,	*3588*
Rev	5:2	**W** is worthy to open the book	*5101*
Rev	6:17	and **w** shall be able to stand?	*5101*
Rev	10:6	**w** created heaven, and the things	
Rev	15:4	**W** shall not fear thee, O Lord	*5101*
Rev	15:7	God **w** liveth for ever and ever	*3588*

WHOLE

Ge	2:6	and watered the **w** face of the	854, 3605
Ge	7:19	that were under the **w** heaven,	3605
Ge	8:9	were on the face of the **w** earth:	3605
Ge	11:1	the **w** earth was of one language	3605
Nu	10:2	of a **w** piece shalt thou make them	4749
Jos	10:13	not to go down about a **w** day	8549
2Ch	16:9	run to and fro through the **w** earth,	3605
Job	41:11	is under the **w** heaven is mine	3605
Ps	9:1	thee, O Lord, with my **w** heart;	3605
Ps	48:2	joy of the **w** earth, is mount Zion	3605
Ps	72:19	**w** earth be filled with his glory;	854, 3605
Ps	111:1	praise the Lord with my **w** heart	3605
Ps	119:2	that seek him with the **w** heart	3605

Ps 119:10 my **w** heart have I sought thee: 3605
Ps 138:1 I will praise thee with my **w** heart: 3605
Pr 26:26 be shewed before the **w** congregation
Ecc 12:13 for this is the **w** duty of man 3605
Isa 6:3 the **w** earth is full of his glory 3605
Isa 54:5 God of the **w** earth shall he be 3605
Jer 19:11 that cannot be made **w** again: 7495
Jer 24:7 unto me with their **w** heart 3605
Jer 32:41 my **w** heart and with my **w** soul 3605
La 2:15 of beauty, the joy of the **w** earth? 3605
Da 9:12 for under the **w** heaven hath not 3605
Zec 4:10 to and fro through the **w** earth. 3605
Mt 5:29 thy **w** body should be cast *3650*
Mt 6:22 thy **w** body shall be full of light. *3650*
Mt 6:23 **w** body shall be full of darkness. *3650*
Mt 9:12 that be **w** need not a physician, *2480*
Mt 9:22 thy faith hath made thee **w**. *4982*
Mt 16:26 if he shall gain the **w** world, and *3650*
Mt 26:13 be preached in the **w** world, *3650*
Mk 2:17 They that are **w** have no need of *2480*
Mk 5:34 thy faith hath made thee **w**; *4982*
Mk 8:36 if he shall gain the **w** world, and *3650*
Mk 10:52 thy faith hath made thee **w**. *4982*
Mk 15:33 was darkness over the **w** land until *3650*
Lk 5:31 that are **w** need not a physician; *5198*
Lk 9:25 if he gain the **w** world, and lose *3650*
Lk 11:34 thy **w** body also is full of light; *3650*
Jn 5:6 unto him, Wilt thou be made **w**? *5199*
Ro 8:22 that the **w** creation groaneth *3956*
1Co 5:6 little leaven leaveneth the **w** lump? *3650*
1Co 12:17 If the **w** body were an eye, *3650*
Gal 5:9 little leaven leaveneth the **w** lump *3650*
Eph 4:16 the **w** body fitly joined together *3958*
Eph 6:11 Put on the **w** armour of God, that ye
Eph 6:13 take unto you the **w** armour of God,
1Th 5:23 your **w** spirit and soul and body *3648*
Jas 2:10 whosoever shall keep the **w** law, *3650*
Jas 3:2 able also to bridle the **w** body *3650*
1Jn 2:2 also for the sins of the **w** world *3650*
1Jn 5:19 the **w** world lieth in wickedness *3650*
Rev 12:9 which deceiveth the **w** world: *3650*

WHOLESOME
Pr 15:4 A **w** tongue is a tree of life: but 4832
1Ti 6:3 and consent not to **w** words, even *5198*

WHOLLY
Le 6:23 offering ... shall be **w** burnt 3632
Nu 8:16 For they are **w** given unto me from
Job 21:23 full strength, being **w** at ease and 3605
Jer 2:21 thee a noble vine, **w** a right seed: 3605
Jer 46:28 I not leave thee **w** unpunished 5352
Am 8:8 and it shall rise up **w** as a flood; 3605
1Th 5:23 very God of peace sanctify you **w**; *3651*
1Ti 4:15 give thyself **w** to them; that *1510, 1722*

WHORE
Le 19:29 daughter, to cause her to be a **w**; 2181
Le 21:7 shall not take a wife that is a **w**, 2181
Le 21:9 profane herself by playing the **w**, 2181
Dt 23:17 no **w** of the daughters of Israel, 6948
Dt 23:18 shalt not bring the hire of a **w**, 2181
Pr 23:27 For a **w** is a deep ditch; and a 2181
Eze 16:28 hast played the **w** also with the 2181
Rev 17:1 judgment of the great **w** that *4204*
Rev 19:2 for he hath judged the great **w**, *4204*

WHOREDOM
Ge 38:24 behold, she is with child by **w** 2183
Le 19:29 lest the land fall to **w**, and the 2181
Nu 25:1 people began to commit **w** with 2181
Jer 13:27 the lewdness of thy **w**, and thine 2184
Eze 16:17 and didst commit **w** with them 2181
Eze 16:33 unto thee on every side for thy **w** 8457
Eze 23:8 and poured their **w** upon her 8457
Eze 43:7 they, nor their kings, by their **w** 2184
Hos 1:2 land hath committed great **w** 2181
Hos 4:10 they shall commit **w**, and shall not 2181
Hos 4:14 daughters when they commit **w** 2181

WHOREDOMS
2Ki 9:22 as the **w** of thy mother Jezebel 2183
Jer 3:2 hast polluted the land with thy **w** 2184
Eze 16:20 Is this of thy **w** a small matter, 8457
Eze 16:36 discovered through thy **w** with 8457
Eze 23:8 left she her **w** brought from Egypt: 8457
Eze 23:11 more than her sister in her **w** 2183
Hos 1:2 a wife of **w** and children of **w**: 2183
Hos 2:4 for they be the children of **w** 2183
Hos 5:4 spirit of **w** is in the midst of them, 2183
Na 3:4 the **w** of the wellfavoured harlot 2183

WHOREMONGER
Eph 5:5 we know, that no **w**, nor unclean *4205*

WHOREMONGERS
1Ti 1:10 For **w**, for them that defile *4205*
Heb 13:4 **w** and adulterers God will judge *4205*
Rev 21:8 and **w**, and sorcerers, and *4205*
Rev 22:15 are dogs, and sorcerers, and **w**, *4205*

WHORES
Eze 16:33 They give gifts to all **w**: but thou 2181
Hos 4:14 themselves are separated with **w**, 2181

WHORING
Ex 34:15 and they go a **w** after their gods, 2181
Le 17:7 after whom they have gone a **w** 2181
Le 20:5 off, and all that go a **w** after him, 2181
Le 20:6 wizards, to go a **w** after them, I 2181
Dt 31:16 and go a **w** after the gods of the 2181
Jgs 2:17 but they went a **w** after other gods, 2181
Jgs 8:27 all Israel went thither a **w** after it: 2181
Ps 73:27 all them that go a **w** from thee 2181
Ps 106:39 went a **w** with their own inventions. 2181
Eze 6:9 which go a **w** after their idols: 2181
Eze 23:30 hast gone a **w** after the heathen, 2181
Hos 9:1 thou hast gone a **w** from thy God, 2181

WHORISH
Pr 6:26 by means of a **w** woman a man is 2181
Eze 6:9 I am broken with their **w** heart 2181
Eze 16:30 work of an imperious **w** woman; 2181

WHOSO
Ge 9:6 **W** sheddeth man's blood, by man
Nu 35:30 **W** killeth any person, the 3605
Dt 19:4 **W** killeth ... neighbour ignorantly 834
Ps 50:23 **W** offereth praise glorifieth me: and
Ps 101:5 **W** privily slandereth his neighbour,
Pr 6:32 But **w** committeth adultery with a
Pr 8:35 For **w** findeth me findeth life, and
Pr 9:16 **W** is simple, let him turn in 4310
Pr 16:20 **w** trusteth in the Lord, happy is he
Pr 17:5 **W** mocketh the poor reproacheth his

Pr	17:13	**W** rewardeth evil for good, evil shall	
Pr	18:22	**W** findeth a wife findeth a good thing	
Pr	20:20	**W** curseth his father or his mother,	
Pr	21:13	**W** stoppeth his ears at the cry of the	
Pr	28:10	**W** causeth the righteous to go	
Pr	28:24	**W** robbeth his father or his mother,	
Pr	29:25	but **w** putteth his trust in the Lord	
Da	3:11	**w** falleth not … worshippeth,	4479, 1768
Mt	18:6	**w shall offend one of these**	*3739, 302*
Mt	19:9	**w marrieth her which is put**	*3588*
Mk	7:10	**W curseth father or mother, let**	*3588*
Jn	6:54	**W eateth my flesh, and drinketh**	*3588*
Jas	1:25	**w** looketh into the perfect law of	*3588*
1Jn	2:5	**w** keepeth his word, in him	*3739, 302*

WHOSOEVER

Ge	4:15	**W** slayeth Cain, vengeance shall	3605
Ex	19:12	**w** toucheth the mount shall be	3605
Ex	22:19	**w** lieth with a beast shall surely	3605
Ex	31:15	**w** doeth any work in the sabbath	3605
Ex	35:5	**w** is of a willing heart, let him	3605
Le	19:20	**w** lieth carnally with a woman	376, 834
Le	24:15	**W** curseth his God shall bear	376, 834
Nu	31:19	**w** hath killed any person, and	3605
Jos	20:9	**w** killeth any person at unawares	3605
2Ki	21:12	**w** heareth of it, both his ears shall	3605
2Ch	15:13	**w** would not seek the Lord God	3605
Ezr	6:11	that **w** shall alter this word	3605
Ezr	7:26	**w** will not do the law of thy God,	3605
Pr	6:29	**w** toucheth her shall not be	3605
Pr	20:1	**w** is deceived thereby is not wise	3605
Pr	27:16	**W** hideth her hideth the wind, and	
Da	6:7	**w** shall ask a petition of any God	3605
Joel	2:32	**w** shall call on the name of the	834
Mt	5:19	**W therefore shall break one**	*3739, 1437*
Mt	5:21	**w shall kill shall be in**	*3739, 302*
Mt	5:22	**w is angry with his brother**	*3956, 3588*
Mt	5:28	**w looketh on a woman to**	*3956, 3588*
Mt	5:31	**W shall put away his wife,**	*3739, 302*
Mt	5:32	**w shall marry her that is**	*3739, 1437*
Mt	5:39	**w shall smite thee on thy right**	*3748*
Mt	12:32	**w speaketh against the Holy**	*3739, 302*
Mt	12:50	**w shall do the will of my**	*3748, 302*
Mt	13:12	**For w hath, to him shall be**	*3748*
Mt	13:12	**w hath not, from him shall be**	*3748*
Mt	15:5	**W shall say to his father or**	*3739, 302*
Mt	16:25	**w will save his life shall lose**	*3739, 302*
Mt	19:9	**W shall put away his wife,**	*3739, 302*
Mt	20:27	**w will be chief among you,**	*3739, 1437*
Mt	23:12	**w shall exalt himself shall be**	*3748*
Mt	23:16	**W shall swear by the temple,**	*3739, 302*
Mt	23:18	**W shall swear by the altar,**	*3739, 1437*
Mk	8:34	**W will come after me, let him**	*3748*
Mk	8:35	**w shall lose his life for my**	*3736, 302*
Mk	9:41	**w shall give you a cup of**	*3739, 302*
Mk	10:11	**W shall put away his wife,**	*3739, 1437*
Lk	8:18	**w hath, to him shall be**	*3739, 302*
Lk	8:18	**w hath not, from him shall be**	*3739, 302*
Lk	9:24	**For w will save his life shall**	*3739, 302*
Lk	9:24	**w will lose his life for my**	*3739, 302*
Lk	9:26	**w shall be ashamed of me**	*3739, 302*
Lk	9:48	**W shall receive this child**	*3739, 1437*
Lk	14:27	**w doth not bear his cross, and**	*3748*
Lk	16:18	**W putteth away his wife,**	*3956, 3588*
Lk	16:18	**w marrieth her that is put**	*3956, 3588*
Lk	17:33	**W shall seek to save his life**	*3739, 1437*
Lk	17:33	**w shall lose his life shall**	*3739, 1437*
Jn	3:15	**w believeth in him should**	*3956, 3588*
Jn	3:16	**w believeth in him should**	*3956, 3588*
Jn	4:14	**But w drinketh of the water**	*3739, 302*
Jn	8:34	**W committeth sin is the**	*3956, 3588*
Jn	11:26	**w liveth and believeth in me**	*3956, 3588*
Jn	12:46	**w believeth on me should**	*3956, 3588*
Jn	16:2	**w killeth you will think that**	*3956, 3588*
Ac	2:21	**w** shall call on the name of the	*3956, 3739*
Ac	10:43	**w** believeth in him shall	*3956, 3588*
Ac	13:26	**w** among you feareth God, to you	*3588*
Ro	2:1	man, **w** thou art that judgest:	*3956, 3588*
Ro	9:33	**w** believeth on him shall not	*3956, 3588*
Ro	10:11	**W** believeth on him shall not	*3956, 3588*
1Co	11:27	**w** shall eat this bread, and	*3739, 302*
Jas	2:10	**w** shall keep the whole law, and	*3748*
1Jn	2:23	**W** denieth the Son, the same	*3956, 3588*
1Jn	3:4	**W** committeth sin	*3956, 3588*
1Jn	3:6	**W** abideth in him sinneth not:	*3956, 3588*
1Jn	3:6	**w** sinneth hath not seen him	*3956, 3588*
1Jn	3:9	**W** is born of God doth not	*3956, 3588*
1Jn	3:15	**W** hateth his brother is a	*3956, 3588*
1Jn	4:15	**W** shall confess that Jesus is	*3739, 302*
1Jn	5:1	**W** believeth that Jesus is	*3956, 3588*
1Jn	5:18	**w** is born of God sinneth not;	*3956, 3588*
Rev	14:11	**w** receiveth the mark of his name	*1536*
Rev	20:15	**w** was not found written in the	*1536*
Rev	22:15	**w** loveth and maketh a lie	*3956, 3588*
Rev	22:17	**w** will, let him take the water of	*3588*

WICKED

Ge	13:13	the men of Sodom were **w** and	7451
Ex	9:27	and I and my people are **w**	7563
Ex	23:7	not: for I will not justify the **w**	7563
Le	20:17	it is a **w** thing; and they shall	2617
Dt	15:9	be not a thought in thy **w** heart,	1100
Dt	23:9	keep thee from every **w** thing	7451
Dt	25:1	righteous, and condemn the **w**	7563
1Sa	2:9	the **w** shall be silent in darkness;	7563
2Sa	3:34	as a man falleth before **w** men,	5766
1Ki	8:32	thy servants, condemning the **w**,	7563
2Ki	17:11	wrought **w** things to provoke	7451
2Ch	7:14	face, and turn from their **w** ways;	7451
Ne	9:35	turned they from their **w** works.	7451
Job	3:17	There the **w** cease from troubling:	7563
Job	10:15	If I be **w**, woe unto me; and if I be	7561
Job	21:30	the **w** is reserved to the day of	7451
Job	34:36	because of his answers for **w** men.	205
Ps	7:11	God is angry with the **w** every day	
Ps	9:17	**w** shall be turned into hell, and	7563
Ps	10:3	**w** boasteth of his heart's desire,	7563
Ps	10:4	The **w**, through the pride of his	7563
Ps	10:13	doth the **w** contemn God?	7563
Ps	12:8	The **w** walk on every side, when	7563
Ps	17:13	deliver my soul from the **w**, which	7563
Ps	26:5	doers; and will not sit with the **w**	7563
Ps	31:17	let the **w** be ashamed, and let	7563
Ps	32:10	Many sorrows shall be to the **w**:	7563
Ps	37:10	while, and the **w** shall not be:	7563
Ps	37:12	the **w** plotteth against the just,	7563
Ps	37:16	better than the riches of many **w**	7563
Ps	37:21	the **w** borroweth, and payeth not	7563
Ps	37:35	I have seen the **w** in great power,	7563
Ps	50:16	But unto the **w** God saith, What	7563
Ps	58:3	**w** are estranged from the womb:	7563
Ps	58:10	wash his feet in the blood of the **w**.	7563

Ps	64:2	from the secret counsel of the **w**;	7489
Ps	68:2	**w** perish at the presence of God.	7563
Ps	73:3	I saw the prosperity of the **w**.	7563
Ps	82:2	and accept the persons of the **w**?	7563
Ps	91:8	and see the reward of the **w**.	7563
Ps	94:3	how long shall the **w** triumph?	7563
Ps	101:3	set no **w** thing before mine eyes:	1100
Ps	101:4	me: I will not know a **w** person.	7451
Ps	112:10	The **w** shall see it, and be grieved;	7563
Ps	112:10	the desire of the **w** shall perish.	7563
Ps	119:119	puttest away all the **w** of the earth	7563
Ps	119:155	Salvation is far from the **w**: for	7563
Ps	139:19	Surely thou wilt slay the **w**, O God:	7563
Ps	139:24	see if there be any **w** way in me.	6090
Ps	141:10	Let the **w** fall into their own nets,	7563
Ps	146:9	the way of the **w** he turneth upside	7563
Ps	147:6	casteth the **w** down to the ground.	7563
Pr	2:22	**w** shall be cut off from the earth,	7563
Pr	3:33	of the Lord is in the house of the **w**:	7563
Pr	4:14	Enter not into the path of the **w**,	7563
Pr	4:19	The way of the **w** is as darkness:	7563
Pr	6:18	heart that deviseth **w** imaginations,	205
Pr	10:3	casteth away the substance of the **w**	7563
Pr	10:6	covereth the mouth of the **w**.	7563
Pr	10:11	violence covereth … mouth of the **w**	7563
Pr	10:20	the heart of the **w** is little worth.	7563
Pr	10:25	passeth, so is the **w** no more:	7563
Pr	10:27	years of the **w** shall be shortened	7563
Pr	10:28	expectation of the **w** shall perish.	7563
Pr	10:30	the **w** shall not inhabit the earth.	7563
Pr	11:5	**w** shall fall by his own wickedness.	7563
Pr	11:7	When a **w** man dieth, his	7563
Pr	11:10	when the **w** perish, there is shouting.	7563
Pr	11:11	overthrown by the mouth of the **w**	7563
Pr	11:18	The **w** worketh a deceitful work:	7563
Pr	11:21	the **w** shall not be unpunished:	7451
Pr	11:23	the expectation of the **w** is wrath.	7563
Pr	11:31	much more the **w** and the sinner	7563
Pr	12:5	the counsels of the **w** are deceit.	7563
Pr	12:6	words of the **w** are to lie in wait	7563
Pr	12:7	**w** are overthrown, and are not:	7563
Pr	12:10	tender mercies of the **w** are cruel.	7563
Pr	12:12	The **w** desireth the net of evil men:	7563
Pr	12:13	**w** is snared by the transgression	7451
Pr	12:21	**w** shall be filled with mischief.	7563
Pr	12:26	the way of the **w** seduceth them.	7563
Pr	13:5	a **w** man is loathsome, and cometh	7563
Pr	13:9	the lamp of the **w** shall be put out.	7563
Pr	13:17	**w** messenger falleth into mischief:	7563
Pr	14:11	The house of the **w** shall be	7563
Pr	14:17	and a man of **w** devices is hated.	4209
Pr	14:32	The **w** is driven away in his	7563
Pr	15:6	in the revenues of the **w** is trouble	7563
Pr	15:8	sacrifice of the **w** is an abomination.	7563
Pr	15:26	The thoughts of the **w** are an	7451
Pr	15:28	mouth of the **w** poureth out evil	7563
Pr	15:29	The Lord is far from the **w**: but he	7563
Pr	16:4	yea, even the **w** for the day of evil.	7563
Pr	17:4	A **w** doer giveth heed to false lips;	7489
Pr	17:15	He that justifieth the **w**, and he	7563
Pr	17:23	A **w** man taketh a gift out of the	7563
Pr	18:5	good to accept the person of the **w**,	7563
Pr	19:28	mouth of the **w** devoureth iniquity	7563
Pr	20:26	A wise king scattereth the **w**, and	7563
Pr	21:7	The robbery of the **w** shall destroy	7563
Pr	21:10	the soul of the **w** desireth evil:	7563
Pr	21:12	considered the house of the **w**:	7563
Pr	21:12	God overthroweth the **w** for their.	7563
Pr	21:18	The **w** shall be a ransom for the	7563
Pr	21:27	sacrifice of the **w** is abomination:	7563
Pr	21:27	he bringeth it with a **w** mind?	2154
Pr	21:29	A **w** man hardeneth his face: but	7563
Pr	24:15	Lay not wait, O **w** man, against the	7563
Pr	24:16	but the **w** shall fall into mischief.	7563
Pr	24:20	candle of the **w** shall be put out.	7563
Pr	24:24	He that saith unto the **w**, Thou art.	7563
Pr	25:26	man falling down before the **w**.	7563
Pr	26:23	Burning lips and a **w** heart are	7451
Pr	28:1	**w** flee when no man pursueth:	7563
Pr	28:4	that forsake the law praise the **w**:	7563
Pr	28:12	when the **w** rise, a man is hidden.	7563
Pr	28:15	is a **w** ruler over the poor people.	7563
Pr	28:28	the **w** rise, men hide themselves:	7563
Pr	29:2	but when the **w** beareth rule, the	7563
Pr	29:7	the **w** regardeth not to know it.	7563
Pr	29:12	to lies, all his servants are **w**.	7563
Pr	29:16	When the **w** are multiplied,	7563
Pr	29:27	the way is abomination to the **w**.	7563
Ecc	3:17	judge the righteous and the **w**:	7563
Ecc	7:15	a **w** man that prolongeth his life.	7563
Ecc	7:17	Be not over much **w**, neither be	7561
Ecc	8:13	it shall not be well with the **w**,	7563
Ecc	9:2	to the righteous, and to the **w**;	7563
Isa	3:11	Woe unto the **w**! it shall be ill	7563
Isa	5:23	Which justify the **w** for reward,	7563
Isa	11:4	of his lips shall he slay the **w**.	7563
Isa	13:11	evil and the **w** for their iniquity;	7563
Isa	26:10	Let favour be shewed to the **w**, yet	7563
Isa	48:22	peace, saith the Lord, unto the **w**	7563
Isa	53:9	And he made his grave with the **w**,	7563
Isa	55:7	Let the **w** forsake his way, and the	7563
Isa	57:20	the **w** are like the troubled sea,	7563
Isa	57:21	no peace, saith my God, to the **w**	7563
Jer	5:28	they overpass the deeds of the **w**.	7451
Jer	6:29	for the **w** are not plucked away.	7451
Jer	12:1	doth the way of the **w** prosper?	7563
Jer	15:21	thee out of the hand of the **w**,	7451
Jer	17:9	above all things, and desperately **w**.	605
Jer	25:31	give them that are **w** to the sword,	7563
Eze	3:18	to warn the **w** from his **w** way,	7563
Eze	3:18	**w** man shall die in his iniquity;	7563
Eze	3:19	if thou warn the **w**, and he turn	7563
Eze	18:21	if the **w** will turn from all his sins.	7563
Eze	18:23	pleasure … that the **w** should die?	7563
Eze	18:27	**w** man turneth away from his	7563
Eze	21:25	thou, profane **w** prince of Israel,	7563
Eze	21:29	of the **w**, whose day is come, when.	7563
Eze	33:8	speak to warn the **w** from his way,	7563
Eze	33:8	**w** man shall die in his iniquity;	7563
Eze	33:9	warn the **w** of his way to turn from	7563
Eze	33:11	the **w** turn from his way and live:	7563
Eze	33:19	if the **w** turn from his wickedness,	7563
Da	12:10	none of the **w** shall understand;	7563
Mic	6:11	them pure with the **w** balances,	7562
Hab	1:13	when the **w** devoureth the man	7563
Hab	3:13	the head out of the house of the **w**,	7563
Mal	4:3	And ye shall tread down the **w**;	7563
Mt	12:45	**other spirits more w than**	*4191*
Mt	12:45	**be also unto this w generation.**	*4190*
Mt	13:19	**then cometh the w one, and**	*4190*
Mt	13:38	**are the children of the w one;**	*4190*
Mt	13:49	**sever the w from among the just,**	*4190*

Mt	16:4	**A w and adulterous generation**	*4190*
Mt	18:32	**O thou w servant, I forgave thee**	*4190*
Mt	25:26	**Thou w and slothful servant,**	*4190*
Lk	11:26	**other spirits more w than**	*4191*
Lk	19:22	**I judge thee, thou w servant.**	*4190*
Ac	2:23	**w** hands have crucified and slain:	*459*
1Co	5:13	among yourselves that **w** person.	*4190*
Eph	6:16	quench all the fiery darts of the **w**	*4190*
Col	1:21	enemies in your mind by **w** works,	*4190*
2Th	2:8	then shall that **W** be revealed,	*459*
2Th	3:2	from unreasonable and **w** men:	*4190*
2Pe	2:7	with the filthy conversation of the **w**	*113*
2Pe	3:17	led away with the error of the **w**,	*113*
1Jn	2:13	ye have overcome the **w** one.	*4190*
1Jn	2:14	and ye have overcome the **w** one.	*4190*
1Jn	3:12	as Cain, who was of that **w** one,	*4190*
1Jn	5:18	and that **w** one toucheth him not.	*4190*

WICKEDLY

Ge	19:7	I pray you, brethren, do not so **w**.	7489
Dt	9:18	doing **w** in the sight of the Lord,	7451
Jgs	19:23	nay, I pray you, do not so **w**;	7489
2Sa	24:17	I have done **w**: but these sheep,	5753
2Ch	20:35	king of Israel, who did very **w**.	7561
2Ch	22:3	mother was his counsellor to do **w**.	7561
Job	34:12	Yea, surely God will not do **w**,	7561
Ps	106:6	iniquity, we have done **w**	7561
Ps	139:20	For they speak against thee **w**,	4209
Da	9:5	have done **w**, and have rebelled,	7561
Da	9:15	we have sinned, we have done **w**.	7561
Da	11:32	such as do **w** against the covenant	7561
Mal	4:1	all that do **w**, shall be stubble:	7564

WICKEDNESS

Ge	6:5	saw that the **w** of man was great.	7451
Ge	39:9	how then can I do this great **w**, and	7451
Le	18:17	are her near kinswomen: it is **w**	2154
Le	19:29	and the land become full of **w**.	2154
Dt	9:5	but for the **w** of these nations	7564
Dt	9:27	nor to their **w**, nor to their sin:	7562
Dt	17:2	wrought **w** in the sight of the Lord	7451
Dt	28:20	because of the **w** of thy doings,	7455
Jgs	20:12	What **w** is this that is done among	7451
1Sa	12:17	and see that your **w** is great.	7451
1Sa	12:20	Fear not: ye have done all this **w**.	7451
1Sa	24:13	**W** proceedeth from the wicked:	7562
1Sa	25:39	hath returned the **w** of Nabel	7451
2Sa	3:39	the doer of evil according to his **w**.	7451
2Sa	7:10	children of **w** afflict them any	5766
1Ki	1:52	but if **w** shall be found in him,	7451
1Ki	2:44	**w** which thine heart is privy to,	7451
1Ki	2:44	return thy **w** upon thine own head;	7451
1Ki	8:47	perversely, we ... committed **w**;	7561
2Ki	21:6	wrought much **w** in the sight of	7451
1Ch	17:9	the children of **w** waste them	5766
Job	4:8	that plow iniquity, and sow **w**,	5999
Job	22:5	Is not thy **w** great? and thine	7451
Job	35:8	Thy **w** may hurt a man as thou art;	7562
Ps	5:4	not a God that hath pleasure in **w**	7562
Ps	10:15	seek out his **w** till thou find none.	7562
Ps	45:7	righteousness, and hatest **w**	7562
Ps	52:7	strengthened himself in his **w**	1942
Ps	58:2	Yea, in heart ye work **w**; ye.	5766
Ps	84:10	than to dwell in the tents of **w**.	7562
Ps	94:23	shall cut them off in their own **w**	7451
Pr	4:17	For they eat the bread of **w**, and	7562
Pr	10:2	Treasurers of **w** profit nothing:	7562
Pr	11:5	wicked shall fall by his own **w**.	7564
Pr	12:3	shall not be established by **w**.	7562
Pr	13:6	but **w** overthroweth the sinner	7564
Pr	14:32	wicked is driven away in his **w**	7451
Pr	16:12	abomination ... kings to commit **w**.	7562
Pr	21:12	the wicked for their **w**	7451
Pr	30:20	and saith, I have done no **w**.	205
Ecc	3:16	of judgment, that **w** was there;	7562
Ecc	7:15	that prolongeth his life in his **w**	7451
Ecc	7:25	and to know the **w** of folly, even	7562
Ecc	8:8	neither shall **w** deliver those that	7562
Isa	9:18	For **w** burneth as the fire: it shall	7564
Isa	47:10	For thou hast trusted in thy **w**.	7451
Isa	58:6	to loose the bands of **w**, to undo	7562
Jer	2:19	Thine own **w** shall correct thee,	7451
Jer	4:14	wash thine heart from **w**, that	7451
Jer	6:7	waters, so she casteth out her **w**	7451
Jer	7:12	to it for the **w** of my people Israel	7451
Jer	8:6	no man repented him of his **w**,	7451
Jer	12:4	the **w** of them that dwell therein?	7451
Jer	14:16	I will pour their **w** upon them.	7451
Jer	14:20	We acknowledge, O Lord, our **w**,	7562
Jer	22:22	and confounded for all thy **w**	7451
Jer	23:11	in my house have I found their **w**,	7451
Jer	23:14	that none doth return from his **w**.	7451
Jer	44:9	of their wives, and your own **w**,	7451
Jer	44:9	and the **w** of your wives, which.	7451
La	1:22	Let all their **w** come before thee;	7451
Eze	3:19	and he turn not from his **w**, nor	7562
Eze	16:57	Before thy **w** was discovered, as at	7451
Eze	18:27	wicked ... turneth away from his **w**	7564
Eze	31:11	I have driven him out for his **w**.	7562
Eze	33:19	But if the wicked turn from his **w**,	7564
Hos	7:2	hearts that I remember all their **w**:	7451
Hos	7:3	make the king glad with their **w**,	7451
Hos	9:15	for the **w** of their doings I will	7455
Hos	10:13	Ye have plowed **w**, ye have reaped.	7562
Jnh	1:2	for their **w** is come up before me.	7451
Mic	6:10	treasures of **w** in the house of the.	7562
Mt	22:18	but Jesus perceived their **w**, and	*4189*
Mk	7:22	**Thefts, covetousness, w, deceit,**	*4189*
Lk	11:39	**part is full of ravening and w.**	*4189*
Ac	8:22	Repent therefore of this thy **w**,	*2549*
Ac	25:5	man, if there be any **w** in him	*5129, 824*
Ro	1:29	**w**, covetousness, maliciousness;	*4189*
1Co	5:8	with the leaven of malice and **w**;	*4189*
Eph	6:12	against spiritual **w** in high places,	*4189*
1Jn	5:19	and the whole world lieth in **w**	*4190*

WIDE

Dt	15:8	open thine hand **w** unto him,	6605
Ps	81:10	open thy mouth **w**, and I will fill	7337
Ps	104:25	So is this great and **w** sea,	7342, 3027
Pr	13:3	he that openeth **w** his lips shall have	
Pr	25:24	brawling woman and in a **w** house.	2267
Mt	7:13	**for w is the gate, and broad is**	*4116*

WIDOW

Ge	38:11	Remain a **w** at thy father's house,	490
Ex	22:22	Ye shall not afflict any **w**, or	490
Le	22:13	But if the priest's daughter be a **w**,	490
Nu	30:9	But every vow of a **w**, and of her	490
Dt	10:18	judgment of the fatherless and **w**,	490
Dt	14:29	and the fatherless, and the **w**,	490
Dt	16:11	and the fatherless, and the **w**,	490
Dt	24:19	for the fatherless, and for the **w**:	490
Dt	26:13	to the fatherless, and to the **w**,	490

Dt	27:19	of the stranger, fatherless, and **w**.	490
1Ki	17:9	commanded a **w** woman there to	490
Ps	94:6	They slay the **w** and the stranger,	490
Ps	109:9	be fatherless, and his wife a **w**	490
Ps	146:9	he relieveth the fatherless and **w**:	490
Pr	15:25	will establish the border of the **w**	490
Isa	1:17	the fatherless, plead for the **w**	490
Isa	1:23	the cause of the **w** come unto them.	490
Isa	47:8	I shall not sit as a **w**, neither shall I	490
Jer	7:6	stranger, the fatherless, and the **w**,	490
Jer	22:3	stranger, the fatherless, nor the **w**,	490
La	1:1	how is she become as a **w**! she that	490
Eze	22:7	they vexed the fatherless and the **w**	490
Eze	44:22	shall they take for their wives a **w**,	490
Zec	7:10	And oppress not the **w**, nor the	490
Mal	3:5	the hireling in his wages, the **w**,	490
Mk	12:43	**That this poor w hath cast more**	*5503*
Lk	2:37	a **w** of about fourscore and four	*5503*
Lk	4:26	**unto a woman that was a w.**	*5503*
Lk	18:5	**Yet because this w troubleth**	*5503*
Lk	21:2	**w** casting in thither two mites.	*5503*
1Ti	5:5	that is a **w** indeed, and desolate,	*5503*
Rev	18:7	I sit a queen, and am no **w**, and	*5503*

WIDOWHOOD

Ge	38:19	and put on the garments of her **w**	491
2Sa	20:3	the day of their death, living in **w**	491
Isa	47:9	day, the loss of children, and **w**:	489
Isa	54:4	remember the reproach of thy **w**	491

WIDOW'S

Ge	38:14	And she put her **w** garments off	491
Job	24:3	they take the **w** ox for a pledge.	490
Job	29:13	I caused the **w** heart to sing for joy.	490

WIDOWS

Ex	22:24	and your wives shall be **w**, and	490
Ps	68:5	the fatherless, and a judge of the **w**,	490
Isa	9:17	mercy on their fatherless and **w**	490
Isa	10:2	people, that **w** may be their prey,	490
Jer	15:8	Their **w** are increased to me above	490
Jer	18:21	bereaved of their children, and be **w**;	490
Jer	49:11	alive; and let thy **w** trust in me.	490
La	5:3	fatherless, our mothers are as **w**	490
Eze	22:25	made her many **w** in the midst	490
Lk	4:25	**many w were in Israel in the**	*5503*
Ac	6:1	their **w** were neglected in the daily	*5503*
Ac	9:39	all the **w** stood by him weeping,	*5503*
1Co	7:8	therefore to the unmarried and **w**,	*5503*
1Ti	5:3	Honour **w** that are **w** indeed.	*5503*
1Ti	5:11	But the younger **w** refuse: for	*5503*
1Ti	5:16	relieve them that are **w** indeed.	*5503*
Jas	1:27	fatherless and **w** in their affliction,	*5503*

WIDOWS'

Mt	23:14	**for ye devour w houses, and for**	*5503*
Mk	12:40	**Which devour w houses, and for**	*5503*
Lk	20:47	**Which devour w houses, and for**	*5503*

WIFE See also WIVES.

Ge	2:24	and shall cleave unto his **w**	802
Ge	2:25	both naked, the man and his **w**,	802
Ge	3:8	Adam and his **w** hid themselves	802
Ge	3:17	hearkened unto the voice of thy **w**,	802
Ge	4:1	Adam knew Eve his **w**; and she	802
Ge	4:17	Cain knew his **w**; and she conceived,	802
Ge	7:13	the sons of Noah, and Noah's **w**, and	802
Ge	12:18	thou not tell me that she was thy **w**?	802
Ge	12:20	and they sent him away, and his **w**,	802
Ge	16:1	Abram's **w** bare him no children:	802
Ge	16:3	Abram's **w** took Hagar her maid	802
Ge	17:19	Sarah thy **w** shall bare thee a son	802
Ge	18:9	unto him, where is Sarah thy **w**?	802
Ge	18:10	lo, Sarah thy **w** shall have a son.	802
Ge	19:15	take thy **w**, and thy two daughters,	802
Ge	19:26	his **w** looked back from behind him,	802
Ge	20:14	and restored him Sarah his **w**.	802
Ge	24:67	Rebekah, and she became his **w**;	802
Ge	25:1	Then again Abraham took a **w**,	802
Ge	26:7	for he feared to say, She is my **w**;	802
Ge	26:8	was sporting with Rebekah his **w**.	802
Ge	27:46	if Jacob take a **w** of the daughters	802
Ge	29:21	Give me my **w**, for my days are	802
Ge	29:28	gave him Rachel his daughter to **w**	802
Ge	30:4	gave him Bilhah her handmaid to **w**	802
Ge	30:9	her maid, and gave her Jacob to **w**	802
Ge	34:4	saying, Get me this damsel to **w**	802
Ge	34:12	me: but give me the damsel to **w**	802
Ge	38:8	Go in unto thy brother's **w**, and	802
Ge	38:14	she was not given unto him to **w**	802
Ge	39:7	his master's **w** cast her eyes upon	802
Ge	39:19	his master heard the words of his **w**,	802
Ex	18:5	with his sons and his **w** unto Moses	802
Ex	20:17	shalt not covet thy neighbour's **w**,	802
Ex	21:3	then his **w** shall go out with him.	802
Ex	21:4	If his master have given him a **w**,	802
Le	18:8	father's **w** shalt thou not uncover:	802
Le	18:15	she is thy son's **w**; thou shalt not	802
Le	18:16	the nakedness of thy brother's **w**.	802
Le	18:20	lie carnally with thy neighbour's **w**,	802
Le	20:10	adultery with another man's **w**,	802
Le	20:11	man that lieth with his father's **w**	802
Le	20:14	if a man take a **w** and her mother,	802
Le	21:7	shall not take a **w** that is a whore,	802
Le	21:14	take a virgin of his own people to **w**	802
Nu	5:14	and he be jealous of his **w**, and	802
Nu	30:16	between a man and his **w**, between	802
Dt	5:21	shalt thou desire thy neighbour's **w**,	802
Dt	13:6	or the **w** of thy bosom, or thy friend,	802
Dt	20:7	is there that hath betrothed a **w**,	802
Dt	21:11	thou wouldest have her to thy **w**;	802
Dt	22:16	my daughter unto this man to **w**,	802
Dt	22:19	and she shall be his **w**; he may not	802
Dt	22:24	he hath humbled his neighbour's **w**	802
Dt	24:2	she may go and be another man's **w**,	
Dt	24:4	may not take her again to be his **w**,	802
Dt	25:5	the **w** of the dead shall not marry	802
Dt	25:7	his brother's **w** go up to the gate	2994
Dt	25:11	and the **w** of the one draweth near	802
Dt	27:20	he that lieth with his father's **w**;	802
Dt	28:30	Thou shalt betroth a **w**, and another	802
Jgs	13:23	But his **w** said unto him, If the Lord	802
Jgs	14:2	now therefore get her for me to **w**	802
Jgs	14:20	But Samson's **w** was given to his	802
Jgs	21:18	be he that giveth a **w** to Benjamin	802
Ru	4:13	Boaz took Ruth, and she was his **w**.	802
1Sa	18:27	gave him Michal his daughter to **w**	802
1Sa	19:11	and Michal David's **w** told him,	802
2Sa	3:14	Deliver me my **w** Michal, which I	802
2Sa	11:3	of Eliam, the **w** of Uriah the Hittite?	802
2Sa	11:11	and to drink, and to lie with my **w**?	802
2Sa	11:26	when the **w** of Uriah heard that	802
2Sa	12:10	me, and hast taken the **w** of Uriah	802
1Ki	11:19	him to **w** the sister of his own **w**,	802

1Ki 14:2 not known to be the **w** of Jeroboam; 802
2Ch 8:11 My **w** shall not dwell in the house 802
2Ch 21:6 he had the daughter of Ahab to **w** 802
2Ch 25:18 Give thy daughter to my son to **w**. 802
Job 2:9 Then said his **w** unto him, Dost 802
Job 19:17 My breath is strange to my **w**, 802
Ps 128:3 thy **w** shall be as a fruitful vine by 802
Pr 5:18 and rejoice with the **w** of thy youth. 802
Pr 6:29 that goeth in to his neighbour's **w**; 802
Pr 18:22 Whoso findeth a **w** findeth a good 802
Pr 19:13 contentions of a **w** are a continual 802
Pr 19:14 and a prudent **w** is from the Lord. 802
Ecc 9:9 Live joyfully with the **w** whom thou 802
Isa 54:1 the children of the married **w**, 802
Isa 54:6 and a **w** of youth, when thou wast 802
Jer 3:1 If a man put away his **w**, and she 802
Jer 5:8 one neighed after his neighbour's **w**. 802
Jer 16:2 Thou shalt not take thee a **w**, 802
Eze 16:32 as a **w** that committeth adultery, 802
Eze 18:15 hath not defiled his neighbour's **w**, 802
Eze 24:18 at even my **w** died; and I did in the 802
Eze 33:26 defile every one his neighbour's **w** 802
Hos 1:2 take unto thee a **w** of whoredoms 802
Hos 2:2 she is not my **w**, neither am I her 802
Hos 12:12 and for a **w** he kept sheep. 802
Am 7:17 Thy **w** shall be an harlot in the city, 802
Mal 2:14 and the **w** of thy covenant. 802
Mt 1:6 of her that had been the **w** of Urias;
Mt 1:20 not to take unto thee Mary thy **w** *2235*
Mt 5:31 **Whosoever shall put away his w,** *1135*
Mt 5:32 **whosoever shall put away his w,** *1135*
Mt 14:3 sake, his brother Philip's **w**, *1135*
Mt 18:25 **to be sold, and his w, and** *2235*
Mt 19:3 lawful for a man to put away his **w**. *1135*
Mt 19:5 **and shall cleave to his w:** *1135*
Mt 19:9 **Whosoever shall put away his w,** *1135*
Mt 19:29 **or father, or mother, or w, or** *1135*
Mt 22:28 whose **w** shall she be of the seven? *1135*
Mt 27:19 seat, his **w** sent unto him, saying, *1135*
Mk 6:18 for thee to have thy brother's **w**. *1135*
Mk 10:2 for a man to put away his **w**? *1135*
Mk 10:7 **and mother, and cleave to his w;** *1135*
Mk 10:11 **Whosoever shall put away his w,** *1135*
Mk 10:29 **or father, or mother, or w, or** *1135*
Lk 1:13 **w** Elisabeth shall bear thee a son, *1135*
Lk 1:18 and my **w** well stricken in years *1135*
Lk 2:5 taxed with Mary his espoused **w**, *1135*
Lk 3:19 Herodias his brother Philip's **w**, *1135*
Lk 14:20 **I have married a w, and** *1135*
Lk 14:26 **his father, and mother, and w,** *1135*
Lk 16:18 **Whosoever putteth away his w,** *1135*
Lk 17:32 **Remember Lot's w.** *1135*
Lk 18:29 **or parents, or brethren, or w,** *1135*
Ac 5:2 price, his **w** also being privy to it, *1135*
Ac 5:7 his **w**, not knowing what was done, *1135*
1Co 5:1 one should have his father's **w**. *1135*
1Co 7:2 let every man have his own **w**, and *1135*
1Co 7:3 husband render unto the **w** due *1135*
1Co 7:3 also the **w** unto the husband. *1135*
1Co 7:4 **w** hath not power of her own body, *1135*
1Co 7:4 power of his own body, but the **w** *1135*
1Co 7:11 not the husband put away his **w** *1135*
1Co 7:14 husband is sanctified by the **w**, *1135*
1Co 7:14 **w** is sanctified by the husband: *1135*
1Co 7:27 Art thou bound unto a **w**? seek not *1135*
1Co 7:27 loosed from a **w**? seek not a **w**. *1135*
1Co 7:33 world, how he may please his **w** *1135*
1Co 7:39 The **w** is bound by the law as long *1135*
1Co 9:5 power to lead about a sister, a **w**, *1135*
Eph 5:23 the husband is the head of the **w**, *1135*
Eph 5:28 that loveth his **w** loveth himself. *1135*
Eph 5:31 and shall be joined unto his **w**, *1135*
Eph 5:33 so love his **w** even as himself; and *1135*
Eph 5:33 the **w** see that she reverence her *1135*
1Ti 3:2 the husband of one **w**, vigilant, *1135*
1Ti 3:12 deacons be the husbands of one **w**, *1135*
1Ti 5:9 having been the **w** of one man, *1135*
Tit 1:6 the husband of one **w**, having *1135*
1Pe 3:7 giving honour unto the **w**, as unto *1134*
Rev 19:7 his **w** hath made herself ready. *1135*
Rev 21:9 shew thee the bride, the Lamb's **w**. *1135*

WIFE'S

Ge 3:20 And Adam called his **w** name Eve; 802
Ge 20:11 they will slay me for my **w** sake. 802
Mk 1:30 Simon's **w** mother lay sick of a *3994*

WILD

Ge 16:12 And he will be a **w** man; his hand 6501
Le 26:22 also send **w** beasts among you, 7704
Job 6:5 **w** ass bray when he hath grass? 6501
Ps 50:11 the **w** beasts of the field are mine. 2123
Ps 104:18 hills are a refuge for the **w** goats; 3277
Isa 51:20 the streets, as a **w** bull in a net: 8377
Jer 2:24 A **w** ass used to the wilderness, 6501
Jer 14:6 **w** asses did stand in the high 6501
Da 5:21 dwelling was with the **w** asses: 6167
Hos 13:8 the **w** beast shall tear them. 7704
Mt 3:4 his meat was locusts and **w** honey. *66*
Mk 1:13 and was with the **w** beasts; *2342*
Ac 11:6 **w** beasts, and creeping things, and *2342*
Ro 11:17 being a **w** olive tree, wert graffed *65*
Ro 11:24 the olive tree which is **w** by nature, *65*

WILDERNESS

Ge 21:20 and he grew, and dwelt in the **w**, 4057
Ex 3:18 three days' journey into the **w**, that 4057
Ex 4:27 Go into the **w** to meet Moses. 4057
Ex 5:1 may hold a feast unto me in the **w** 4057
Ex 7:16 that they may serve me in the **w**. 4057
Ex 13:18 the way of the **w** of the Red sea: 4057
Ex 14:3 taken us away to die in the **w**? 4057
Ex 15:22 and they went three days in the **w**, 4057
Ex 16:14 upon the face of the **w** there lay a 4057
Le 16:10 him go for a scapegoat into the **w** 4057
Nu 10:31 how we are to encamp in the **w**, 4057
Nu 14:2 would God we had died in this **w**! 4057
Nu 14:29 Your carcases shall fall in this **w**; 4057
Nu 14:33 shall wander in the **w** forty years, 4057
Nu 21:5 us up out of Egypt to die in the **w**? 4057
Nu 24:1 but he set his face toward the **w**. 4057
Nu 26:65 They shall surely die in the **w**. 4057
Nu 27:3 Our father died in the **w**, and he. 4057
Dt 2:7 thy walking through this great **w** 4057
Dt 8:2 thee these forty years in the **w**, 4057
Dt 8:15 through that great and terrible **w**, 4057
Dt 8:16 who fed thee in the **w** with manna, 4057
Dt 9:28 them out to slay them in the **w**. 4057
Dt 29:5 have led you forty years in the **w** 4057
Jos 5:6 Israel walked forty years in the **w**, 4057
Jos 14:10 of Israel wandered in the **w**: 4057
1Sa 4:8 with all the plagues in the **w**. 4057
1Ki 19:4 went a day's journey into the **w**, 4057

Ne 9:21 didst thou sustain them in the **w**, 4057
Job 1:19 came a great wind from the **w**, 4057
Ps 29:8 voice of the Lord shaketh the **w** 4057
Ps 68:7 thou didst march through the **w**; 3452
Ps 72:9 They that dwell in the **w** shall 6728
Ps 78:19 Can God furnish a table in the **w**? 4057
Ps 78:40 oft did they provoke him in the **w**, 4057
Ps 78:52 guided them in the **w** like a flock. 4057
Ps 95:8 in the day of temptation in the **w**: 4057
Ps 106:14 But lusted exceedingly in the **w**, 4057
Ps 106:26 them, to overthrow them in the **w**:. 4057
Ps 107:40 causeth them to wander in the **w**,. 8414
Ps 136:16 led his people through the **w**. 4057
Pr 21:19 It is better to dwell in the **w**, than 4057
Isa 14:17 that made the world a **w**, and 4057
Isa 27:10 forsaken, and left like a **w**: 4057
Isa 41:18 I will make the **w** a pool of water, 4057
Isa 43:19 I will even make a way in the **w**, 4057
Isa 51:3 and he will make her **w** like Eden, 4057
Isa 64:10 Zion is a **w**, Jerusalem a 4057
Jer 2:2 thou wentest after me in the **w**,. 4057
Jer 2:31 Have I been a **w** unto Israel? 4057
Jer 9:2 that I had in the **w** a lodging place 4057
Jer 9:12 and is burned up like a **w**, 4057
Jer 22:6 yet surely I will make thee a **w**, 4057
Jer 31:2 of the sword found grace in the **w**;. 4057
La 4:19 they laid wait for us in the **w**. 4057
Eze 20:13 rebelled against me in the **w**:. 4057
Eze 20:35 bring you into the **w** of the people, 4057
Hos 13:5 I did know thee in the **w**, in the land 4057
Am 2:10 led you forty years through the **w**, 4057
Am 5:25 and offerings in the **w** forty years, 4057
Mt 3:3 the voice of one crying in the **w** *2048*
Mt 4:1 Jesus led up of the spirit into the **w** *2048*
Mt 11:7 **went ye out into the w to see?** *2048*
Mk 1:3 the voice of one crying in the **w**, *2048*
Mk 1:4 John did baptize in the **w**, and *2048*
Mk 1:12 the spirit driveth him into the **w**. *2048*
Mk 1:13 he was there in the **w** forty days,. *2048*
Lk 3:4 The voice of one crying in the **w**, *2048*
Lk 4:1 was led by the Spirit into the **w**, *2048*
Lk 5:16 he withdrew himself into the **w**, *2048*
Lk 7:24 **went ye out into the w for to see?** *2048*
Lk 8:29 was driven of the devil into the **w**.) *2048*
Lk 15:4 **leave the ninety and nine in the w,** *2048*
Jn 1:23 the voice of one crying in the **w**,. *2048*
Jn 3:14 **lifted up the serpent in the w,** *2048*
Jn 6:49 **fathers did eat manna in the w,** *2048*
Ac 7:30 in the **w** of mount Sina an angel. *2048*
Ac 7:44 the tabernacle of witness in the **w**, *2048*
1Co 10:5 for they were overthrown in the **w**. *2048*
2Co 11:26 in the city, in perils in the **w** *2048*
Heb 3:8 in the day of temptation in the **w**. *2048*
Heb 3:17 whose carcases fell in the **w**? *2048*
Rev 12:6 And the woman fled into the **w**, *2048*
Rev 17:3 me away in the spirit into the **w**:. *2048*

WILES

Nu 25:18 For they vex you with their **w**, 5231
Eph 6:11 stand against the **w** of the devil. *3180*

WILFULLY

Heb 10:26 For if we sin **w** after that we have *1596*

WILL See also FREEWILL.

Le 1:3 offer it of his own voluntary **w** 7522
Le 22:19 at your own **w** a male without 7522
Le 22:29 the Lord, offer it at your own **w** 7522
Dt 21:14 shalt let her go whither she **w**;. 5315
Dt 25:7 **w** not perform the duty of my 14
Dt 33:16 for the good **w** of him that dwell in 7522
Ezr 7:18 that do after the **w** of your God 7470
Ps 27:12 over unto the **w** of mine enemies: 5315
Ps 40:8 I delight to do thy **w**, O my God: 7522
Ps 41:2 him unto the **w** of his enemies 5315
Ps 143:10 Teach me to do thy **w**; for thou. 7522
Pr 21:1 he turneth it whithersoever he **w** 2654
Ecc 4:13 who **w** no more be admonished 3045
Isa 30:9 children that **w** not hear the law of. 14
Eze 3:7 house of Israel **w** not hearken unto 14
Eze 3:7 for they **w** not hearken unto me: 14
Eze 16:27 delivered thee unto the **w** of them 5314
Da 4:17 and giveth it to whomsoever he **w**, 6634
Da 4:25 giveth it to whomsoever he **w** 6634
Da 4:32 giveth it to whomsoever he **w** 6634
Da 4:35 to his **w** in the army of heaven,. 6634
Da 8:4 but he did according to his **w**, and 7522
Da 11:3 and do according to his **w** 7522
Da 11:36 king shall do according to his **w**;. 7522
Hos 13:10 I **w** be thy king: where is any 165
Hos 13:14 O death, I **w** be thy plagues; 165
Hos 13:14 O grave, I **w** be thy destruction: 165
Mt 5:40 **if any man w sue thee at the law,** *2309*
Mt 6:10 **Thy w be done in earth, as it is** *2307*
Mt 7:21 **he that doeth the w of my Father** *2307*
Mt 8:3 him, saying, **I w; be thou clean.** *2309*
Mt 9:13 **I w have mercy, and not sacrifice:** *2309*
Mt 11:14 **And if ye w receive it, this is** *2309*
Mt 11:27 **whomsoever the Son w reveal him.** *1014*
Mt 12:7 **I w have mercy, and not sacrifice,** *2309*
Mt 12:50 **do the w of my Father which is** *2307*
Mt 15:32 **I w not send them away fasting,** *2309*
Mt 16:24 **If any man w come after me, let** *2309*
Mt 16:25 **w save his life shall lose it:** *2309*
Mt 18:14 **so it is not the w of your Father** *2307*
Mt 20:15 **to do what I w with mine own?** *2309*
Mt 20:26 **whosoever w be great among you,** *2309*
Mt 20:27 **whosoever w be chief among you,** *2309*
Mt 20:32 **What w ye that I shall do unto** *2309*
Mt 21:29 **He answered and said, I w not:** *2309*
Mt 21:31 **twain did the w of his father?** *2307*
Mt 23:4 **themselves w not move them** *2309*
Mt 26:15 unto them, What **w** ye give me,. *2309*
Mt 26:39 **nevertheless not as I w, but as** *2309*
Mt 26:42 **except I drink it, thy w be done.** *2307*
Mt 27:17 Whom **w** ye that I release unto *2309*
Mt 27:21 of the twain **w** ye that I release *2309*
Mt 27:43 deliver him … if he **w** have him;. *2309*
Mk 1:41 saith unto him, **I w; be thou clean.** *2309*
Mk 3:35 **whosoever shall do the w of God,** *2307*
Mk 8:34 **Whosoever w come after me, let.** *2309*
Mk 8:35 **whosoever w save his life shall** *2309*
Mk 10:43 **whosoever w be great among you,** *2309*
Mk 10:44 **whosoever of you w be … chiefest.** *2309*
Mk 14:7 **whensoever ye w ye may do them** *2309*
Mk 14:36 **nevertheless not what I w, but** *2309*
Mk 15:9 **W** ye that I release unto you the *2309*
Mk 15:12 What **w** ye then that I shall do *2309*
Lk 4:6 and to whomsoever I **w** I give it. *2309*
Lk 5:13 him, saying, **I w: be thou clean.** *2309*
Lk 9:23 **If any man w come after me, let** *2309*
Lk 9:24 **whosoever w save his life shall** *2309*
Lk 10:22 **he to whom the Son w reveal him.** *1014*

Lk	11:2	**Thy w be done, as in heaven, so**	*2307*
Lk	12:47	**knew his lord's w, and prepared**	*2307*
Lk	12:47	**neither did according to his w,**	*2307*
Lk	12:49	**w I, if it, be already kindled?**	*2309*
Lk	13:31	hence: for Herod **w** kill thee.	*2309*
Lk	19:14	**We w not have this man to reign**	*2309*
Lk	22:42	**nevertheless not my w, but thine,**	*2307*
Lk	23:25	but he delivered Jesus to their **w**	*2307*
Jn	1:13	**w** of the flesh, nor of the **w** of man,	*2307*
Jn	4:34	**is to do the w of him that sent me,**	*2307*
Jn	5:21	**the Son quickeneth whom he w.**	*2309*
Jn	5:30	**because I seek not mine own w,**	*2307*
Jn	5:30	**w of the Father which ... sent me.**	*2307*
Jn	5:40	**And ye w not come to me, that ye**	*2309*
Jn	6:38	**but the w of him that sent me.**	*2307*
Jn	6:39	**Father's w which hath sent me.**	*2307*
Jn	6:40	**this is the w of him that sent me,**	*2307*
Jn	6:67	the twelve, **W ye also go away?**	*2309*
Jn	7:17	**If any man ... do his w, he shall**	*2307*
Jn	7:35	Whither **w** he go, that we shall not	*3195*
Jn	7:35	**w** he go unto the dispersed among	*3195*
Jn	8:44	**the lusts of your father ye w do.**	*2309*
Jn	9:27	**w** ye also be his disciples?	*2309*
Jn	15:7	**ye shall ask what ye w, and it**	*2309*
Jn	17:24	**Father, I w that they also, whom**	*2309*
Jn	18:39	**w** ye therefore that I release unto	*1014*
Jn	21:22	**If I w that he tarry till I come,**	*2309*
Ac	13:22	heart, which shall fulfil all my **w**	*2307*
Ac	17:18	said, What **w** this babbler say?	*2309*
Ac	17:31	which he **w** judge the world in	*3195*
Ac	18:21	again unto you, if God **w**	*2309*
Ac	21:14	The **w** of the Lord be done	*2307*
Ac	22:14	that thou shouldest know his **w**,	*2307*
Ro	1:10	by the **w** of God to come unto you.	*2307*
Ro	2:18	knowest his **w**, and approvest the	*2307*
Ro	7:18	for to **w** is present with me; but	*2309*
Ro	9:18	mercy on whom he **w** have mercy,	*2309*
Ro	9:18	and whom he **w** he hardeneth.	*2309*
Ro	9:19	For who hath resisted his **w**?	*1013*
Ro	12:2	acceptable, and perfect, **w** of God.	*2307*
Ro	15:32	you with joy by the **w** of God,	*2307*
1Co	1:1	Jesus Christ through the **w** of God,	*2307*
1Co	4:19	if the Lord **w**,	*2309*
1Co	7:36	let him do what he **w**, he sinneth	*2309*
1Co	7:37	but hath power over his own **w**,	*2307*
1Co	7:39	to be married to whom she **w**;	*2309*
1Co	9:17	but if against my **w**, a dispensation.	*210*
1Co	14:35	And if they **w** learn any thing,	*2309*
2Co	1:1	of Jesus Christ by the **w** of God,	*2307*
2Co	8:5	and unto us by the **w** of God.	*2307*
2Co	8:11	as there was a readiness to **w**	*2309*
Gal	1:4	according to the **w** of God and our	*2307*
Eph	1:5	to the good pleasure of his **w**,	*2307*
Eph	1:9	unto us the mystery of his **w**,	*2307*
Eph	5:17	but ... what the **w** of the Lord is.	*2307*
Eph	6:6	doing the **w** of God from the heart;	*2307*
Eph	6:7	With good **w** doing service, as	*2133*
Php	1:15	strife; and some also of good **w**.	*2107*
Php	2:13	both to **w** and to do of his good	*2309*
Col	1:9	filled with the knowledge of his **w**	*2307*
Col	2:23	a shew of wisdom in **w** worship,	*1479*
Col	4:12	and complete in all the **w** of God	*2307*
1Th	4:3	**w** of God, even your sanctification	*2307*
1Th	5:18	for this is the **w** of God in Christ	*2307*
1Ti	2:4	Who **w** have all men to be saved,	*2309*
1Ti	2:8	I **w** therefore that men pray	*1014*
1Ti	5:11	against Christ, they **w** marry;	*2309*
1Ti	5:14	I **w** therefore that the younger	*1014*
1Ti	6:9	that **w** be rich fall into temptation	*1014*
2Ti	1:1	of Jesus Christ by the **w** of God,	*2307*
2Ti	2:26	are taken captive by him at his **w**	*2307*
2Ti	3:12	and all that **w** live godly in Christ	*2309*
Tit	3:8	these things I **w** that thou affirm	*1014*
Heb	2:4	Ghost, according to his own **w**?	*2308*
Heb	10:7	written of me,) to do thy **w**, O God.	*2307*
Heb	10:9	he, Lo, I come to do thy **w**, O God	*2307*
Heb	10:10	By the which **w** we are sanctified	*2307*
Heb	10:36	after ye have done the **w** of God,	*2307*
Heb	13:21	in every good work to do his **w**,	*2307*
Jas	4:4	therefore **w** be a friend of the	*1014*
Jas	4:15	If the Lord **w**, we shall live, and	*2309*
1Pe	2:15	For so is the **w** of God, that with	*2307*
1Pe	3:10	For he that **w** love life, and see	*2309*
1Pe	3:17	it is better, if the **w** of God be so	*2307*
1Pe	4:2	lusts of men, but to the **w** of God	*2307*
1Pe	4:3	wrought the **w** of the Gentiles,	*2307*
1Pe	4:19	suffer according to the **w** of God	*2307*
2Pe	1:21	not in old time by the **w** of man:	*2307*
1Jn	2:17	he that doeth the **w** of God abideth	*2307*
Jude	5	I **w** ... put you in remembrance	*1014*
Rev	3:16	**I w spue thee out of my mouth.**	*3195*
Rev	11:5	And if any man **w** hurt them,	*2309*
Rev	11:5	and if any man **w** hurt them, he	*2309*
Rev	17:17	put in their hearts to fulfil his **w**	*1106*
Rev	22:17	whosoever **w**, let him take the	*2309*

WILLETH

Ro	9:16	So then it is not of him that **w**,	*2309*

WILLING

Ex	35:5	whosoever is of a **w** heart, let him	5081
Ex	35:21	one whom his spirit made **w**,	5068
Ex	35:29	whose heart made them **w** to	5068
1Ch	28:9	perfect heart and with a **w** mind:	2655
1Ch	28:21	workmanship every **w** skilful.	5081
1Ch	29:5	who then is **w** to consecrate his	5068
Ps	110:3	Thy people shall be **w** in the day.	5071
Isa	1:19	If ye be **w** and obedient, ye shall eat	14
Mt	1:19	not **w** to make her a publick example,	*2309*
Mt	26:41	**the spirit indeed is w, but the**	*4289*
Mk	15:15	Pilate, **w** to content the people,	*1014*
Lk	10:29	But he, **w** to justify himself, said	*2309*
Lk	22:42	**Father, if thou be w, remove this**	*1014*
Lk	23:20	Pilate ... **w** to release Jesus, spake	*2309*
Jn	5:35	**ye were w for a season to rejoice.**	*2309*
Ac	24:27	**w** to shew the Jews a pleasure,	*2309*
Ac	25:9	**w** to do the Jews a pleasure,	*2309*
Ac	27:43	But the centurion, **w** to save Paul,	*1014*
Ro	9:22	if God, **w** to show his wrath, and	*2309*
2Co	5:8	**w** rather to be absent from the	*2106*
2Co	8:3	power they were **w** of themselves;	*830*
2Co	8:12	For if there be first a **w** mind,	*4288*
1Th	2:8	were **w** to have imparted unto you,	*2106*
1Ti	6:18	to distribute, **w** to communicate;	*2843*
Heb	6:17	**w** more abundantly to shew unto	*1014*
Heb	13:18	in all things **w** to live honestly	*2309*
2Pe	3:9	not **w** that any should perish,	*1014*

WILLINGLY

Ex	25:2	every man that giveth it **w** with	5068
Jgs	5:9	that offered themselves **w** among	5068
Jgs	8:25	answered, We will **w** give them	5414
1Ch	29:9	with perfect heart they offered **w**	5068

1Ch 29:17	I have **w** offered all these things:	5068
1Ch 29:17	present here, to offer **w** unto thee.	5068
2Ch 35:8	princes gave **w** unto the people	5071
Ezr 3:5	that **w** offered a freewill offering	5068
Ezr 7:16	offering **w** for the house of their God	5068
Ne 11:2	that **w** offered themselves to dwell at	
Pr 31:13	and worketh **w** with her hands	2656
La 3:33	For he doth not afflict **w**, not	3820
Hos 5:11	because he **w** walked after the	2974
Jn 6:21	they **w** received him into the ship:	*2309*
Ro 8:20	subject to vanity, not **w**, but	*1635*
1Co 9:17	For if I do this thing **w**, I	*1635*
Phm 14	it were of necessity, but **w**	*2596, 1595*
2Pe 3:5	For this they **w** are ignorant of,	*2309*

WILLOWS

Ps 137:2	We hanged our harps upon the **w**	6155
Isa 15:7	carry away to the brook of the **w**	6155
Isa 44:4	grass, as **w** by the water courses	6155

WIN

2Ch 32:1	thought to **w** them for himself	1234
Php 3:8	but dung, that I may **w** Christ	*2770*

WIND

Ge 8:1	God made a **w** to pass over the	7307
Ge 41:27	empty ears blasted with the east **w**	
Ex 10:13	the east **w** brought the locusts	7307
Ex 14:21	sea to go back by a strong east **w**	7307
Ex 15:10	Thou didst blow with thy **w**, the	7307
Nu 11:31	went forth a **w** from the Lord, and	7307
1Ki 19:11	but the Lord was not in the **w**:	7307
2Ki 3:17	Ye shall not see **w**, neither shall	7307
Job 1:19	a great **w** from the wilderness	7307
Job 38:24	scattereth the east **w** upon the earth?	
Ps 1:4	chaff which the **w** driveth away	7307
Ps 18:10	he did fly upon the wings of the **w**	7307
Ps 18:42	small as the dust before the **w**	7307
Ps 35:5	Let them be as chaff before the **w**	7307
Ps 83:13	wheel; as the stubble before the **w**	7307
Ps 103:16	For the **w** passeth over it, and it is	7307
Ps 104:3	walketh upon the wings of the **w**	7307
Ps 147:18	he causeth his **w** to blow, and the	7307
Ps 148:8	stormy **w** fulfilling his word:	7307
Pr 11:29	his own house shall inherit the **w**:	7307
Pr 25:14	like clouds and **w** without rain.	7307
Pr 27:16	hideth her hideth the **w**, and	7307
Pr 30:4	hath gathered the **w** in his fists?	7307
Ecc 5:16	he that hath laboured for the **w**?	7307
Ecc 11:4	observeth the **w** shall not sow;	7307
Isa 7:2	of the wood are moved with the **w**	7307
Isa 11:15	with his mighty **w** shall he shake	7307
Isa 17:13	of the mountains before the **w**	7307
Isa 26:18	have as it were brought forth **w**;	7307
Isa 32:2	be as an hiding place from the **w**	7307
Isa 41:16	and the **w** shall carry them away	7307
Isa 41:29	molten images are **w** and confusion	7307
Isa 57:13	the **w** shall carry them all away;	7307
Jer 5:13	And the prophets shall become **w**,	7307
Jer 10:13	forth the **w** out of his treasures.	7307
Jer 13:24	away by the **w** of the wilderness	7307
Jer 18:17	will scatter them as with an east **w**	7307
Jer 22:22	The **w** shall eat up all thy pastors	7307
Jer 51:1	up against me, a destroying **w**;	7307
Jer 51:16	forth the **w** out of his treasures	7307
Eze 5:2	part thou shalt scatter in the **w**;	7307
Eze 12:14	scatter toward every **w** all that are	7307
Eze 17:10	when the east **w** toucheth it?	7307
Eze 37:9	he unto me, Prophesy unto the **w**.	7307
Da 2:35	and the **w** carried them away, that	7308
Hos 4:19	The **w** hath bound her up in her	7307
Hos 8:7	they have sown the **w**, and they	7307
Am 4:13	mountains, and createth the **w**,	7307
Jnh 1:4	sent out a great **w** into the sea	7307
Zec 5:9	and the **w** was in their wings;	7307
Mt 11:7	**to see? A reed shaken with the w?**	*417*
Mt 14:24	with waves: for the **w** was contrary.	*417*
Mt 14:30	But when he saw the **w** boisterous,	*417*
Mt 14:32	come into the ship, the **w** ceased	*417*
Mk 4:39	And he arose, and rebuked the **w**,	*417*
Mk 4:41	even the **w** and the sea obey him?	*417*
Mk 6:51	into the ship; and the **w** ceased:	*417*
Lk 7:24	**to see? A reed shaken with the w?**	*417*
Lk 12:55	**And when ye see the south w blow,**	
Jn 3:8	**The w bloweth where it listeth,**	*4151*
Jn 6:18	by reason of the great **w** that blew	*417*
Ac 2:2	heaven as of a rushing mighty **w**,	*4157*
Ac 27:15	and could not bear up into the **w**,	*417*
Eph 4:14	about with every **w** of doctrine	*417*
Jas 1:6	wave of the sea driven with the **w**	*416*
Rev 6:13	when she is shaken of a mighty **w**	*417*
Rev 7:1	the **w** should not blow on the earth,	*417*

WINDOW

Ge 6:16	A **w** shalt thou make to the ark,	6672
Ge 8:6	Noah opened the **w** of the ark	2474
Ge 26:8	the Philistines looked out at a **w**	2474
Jos 2:21	she bound the scarlet line in the **w**	2474
1Sa 19:12	let David down through a **w**	2474
2Ki 9:30	her head, and looked out at a **w**	2474
2Ki 13:17	And he said, Open the **w** eastward	2474
1Ch 15:29	looking out at a **w** saw king David	2474
Ac 20:9	sat in a **w** a certain young man	*2376*
2Co 11:33	through a **w** in a basket was I let	*2376*

WINDOWS

Ge 7:11	and the **w** of heaven were opened	699
Ge 8:2	and the **w** of heaven were stopped,	699
2Ki 7:2	Lord would make **w** in heaven,	699
2Ki 7:19	Lord should make **w** in heaven,	699
Isa 24:18	for the **w** from on high are opened,	699
Isa 60:8	and as the doves to their **w**?	699
Eze 40:16	narrow **w** to the little chambers,	2474
Da 6:10	his **w** being open in his chamber	3551
Joel 2:9	shall enter in at the **w** like a thief	2474
Zep 2:14	their voice shall sing in the **w**;	2474
Mal 3:10	will not open you the **w** of heaven	699

WINDS

Job 28:25	To make the weight for the **w**;	7307
Jer 49:32	I will scatter into all **w** them that	7307
Jer 49:36	scatter them toward all those **w**;	7307
Eze 5:12	scatter a third part into all the **w**	7307
Eze 17:21	shall be scattered toward all **w**	7307
Eze 37:9	Come from the four **w**, O breath	7307
Da 7:2	the four **w** of the heaven strove	7308
Da 8:8	ones toward the four **w** of heaven	7307
Da 11:4	toward the four **w** of heaven;	7307
Zec 2:6	as the four **w** of the heaven,	7307
Mt 7:25	**the floods came, and the w**	*417*
Mt 7:27	**the floods came, and the w**	*417*
Mt 8:26	and rebuked the **w** and the sea;	*417*
Mt 8:27	even the **w** and the sea obey him!	*417*
Mt 24:31	**together his elect from the four w,**	*417*

Mk	13:27	**together his elect from the four w,**	*417*
Jas	3:4	are driven of fierce **w**, yet are they	*417*
Jude	12	without water, carried about of **w**;	*417*
Rev	7:1	holding the four **w** of the earth,	*417*

WINE

Ge	9:24	Noah awoke from his **w**, and knew	3196
Ge	14:18	of Salem brought forth bread and **w**	3196
Ge	19:32	let us make our father drink **w**	3196
Ge	19:34	make him drink **w** this night also;	3196
Ge	27:25	he brought him **w**, and he drank	3196
Ge	27:28	earth, and plenty of corn, and **w**.	8492
Ge	49:11	he washed his garments in **w**.	3196
Ge	49:12	His eyes shall be red with **w**,	3196
Le	10:9	Do not drink **w** nor strong drink	3196
Nu	6:3	He shall separate himself from **w**	3196
Nu	6:20	that the Nazarite may drink **w**	3196
Nu	15:5	the fourth part of an hin of **w**.	3196
Nu	15:7	offer the third part of an hin of **w**	3196
Nu	18:12	all the best of the **w**, and of the	8492
Dt	7:13	of thy land, thy corn, and thy **w**,	8492
Dt	12:17	the tithe of thy corn, or of thy **w**,	8492
Dt	14:26	for sheep, or for **w**, or for strong	3196
Dt	28:39	but shalt neither drink of the **w**	3196
Dt	29:6	neither have ye drunk **w** or strong	3196
Dt	32:33	Their **w** is the poison of dragons,	3196
Jgs	9:13	Should I leave my **w**, which	8492
Jgs	13:7	now drink no **w** nor strong drink,	3196
Jgs	19:19	there is bread and **w** also for me,	3196
1Sa	1:14	put away thy **w** from thee	3196
1Sa	1:15	drunk neither **w** nor strong drink,	3196
1Sa	25:37	when the **w** was gone out of Nabal,	3196
2Sa	16:2	and the **w**, that such as be faint	3196
2Ki	18:32	own land, a land of corn and **w**	8492
2Ch	2:10	and twenty thousand baths of **w**.	3196
Ne	2:1	and I took up the **w**, and gave it	3196
Ne	5:15	had taken of them bread and **w**	3196
Ne	13:15	treading **w** presses on the sabbath	1660
Est	5:6	unto Esther at the banquet of **w**.	3196
Est	7:7	arising from the banquet of **w** in	3196
Est	7:8	into the place of the banquet of **w**;	3196
Job	1:13	and drinking **w** in their eldest	3196
Job	1:18	and drinking **w** in their eldest	3196
Ps	60:3	to drink the **w** of astonishment.	3196
Ps	75:8	there is a cup, and the **w** is red;	3196
Ps	78:65	man that shouteth by reason of **w**	3196
Ps	104:15	**w** that maketh glad the heart of	3196
Pr	3:10	shall burst out with new **w**	8492
Pr	4:17	and drink the **w** of violence.	3196
Pr	9:2	beasts; she hath mingled her **w**;	3196
Pr	9:5	and drink of the **w** which I have	3196
Pr	20:1	**W** is a mocker, strong drink is.	3196
Pr	21:17	he that loveth **w** and oil shall not	3196
Pr	23:30	They that tarry long at the **w**;	3196
Pr	23:30	they that go to seek mixed **w**.	4469
Pr	31:4	it is not for kings to drink **w**;	3196
Pr	31:6	and **w** unto those that be of heavy	3196
Ecc	2:3	mine heart to give myself unto **w**	3196
Ecc	9:7	drink thy **w** with a merry heart;	3196
Ecc	10:19	for laughter, and **w** maketh merry:	3196
SS	1:2	for thy love is better than **w**.	3196
SS	1:4	remember thy love more than **w**.	3196
SS	4:10	much better is thy love than **w**!	3196
Isa	5:11	until night, till **w** inflame them!	3196
Isa	5:22	them that are mighty to drink **w**	3196
Isa	16:10	tread out no **w** in their presses;	3196
Isa	22:13	eating flesh, and drinking **w**	3196
Isa	24:9	shall not drink **w** with a song;	3196
Isa	24:11	is a crying for **w** in the streets;	3196
Isa	28:7	they also have erred through **w**,	3196
Isa	49:26	their own blood, as with sweet **w**	6071
Isa	51:21	and drunken, but not with **w**	3196
Isa	55:1	buy **w** and milk without money	3196
Isa	62:8	the stranger shall not drink thy **w**.	8492
Jer	13:12	bottle shall be filled with **w**	3196
Jer	13:12	every bottle shall be filled with **w**?	3196
Jer	23:9	like a man whom **w** hath overcome,	3196
Jer	25:15	Take the **w** cup of this fury at my	3196
Jer	35:6	Ye shall drink no **w**, neither ye	3196
Jer	35:14	commanded his sons not to drink **w**	3196
Jer	48:33	**w** to fail from the winepresses:	3196
Jer	51:7	the nations have drunken of her **w**;	3196
La	2:12	mothers, Where is corn and **w**?	3196
Eze	44:21	Neither shall any priest drink **w**	3196
Da	1:8	nor with the **w** which he drank:	3196
Da	5:2	Belshazzar, whiles he tasted the **w**,	2562
Da	5:4	They drank **w**, and praised the	2562
Da	5:23	concubines, have drunk **w** in them;	2562
Da	10:3	came flesh nor **w** in my mouth,	3196
Hos	2:8	know that I gave her corn, and **w**	8492
Hos	3:1	other gods, and love flagons of **w**,	6025
Hos	4:11	Whoredom and **w** and new	3196
Hos	4:11	and new **w** take away the heart	8492
Hos	7:5	made him sick with bottles of **w**;	3196
Hos	9:2	and the new **w** shall fail in her	8492
Hos	9:4	They shall not offer **w** offerings	8492
Joel	1:10	the new **w** is dried up, the oil	8492
Joel	3:18	shall drop down new **w**,	6071
Am	2:8	drink the **w** of the condemned in	3196
Am	2:12	ye gave the Nazarites **w** to drink;	3196
Am	5:11	but ye shall not drink **w** of them.	3196
Am	6:6	That drink **w** in bowls, and anoint	3196
Am	9:13	the mountains shall drop sweet **w**,	6071
Am	9:14	plant vineyards, and drink the **w**	3196
Mic	6:15	anoint thee with oil; and sweet **w**	8492
Mic	6:15	but shalt not drink **w**.	3196
Hab	2:5	because he transgresseth by **w**,	3196
Zep	1:13	but not drink the **w** thereof.	3196
Hag	1:11	upon the new **w**, and upon the oil	8492
Zec	9:15	and make a noise as through **w**;	3196
Zec	9:17	cheerful, and new **w** the maids	8492
Zec	10:7	heart shall rejoice as through **w**	3196
Mt	9:17	**men put new w into old bottles:**	*3631*
Mt	9:17	**and the w runneth out, and the**	*3631*
Mt	9:17	**they put new w into new bottles,**	*3631*
Mk	2:22	**the new w doth burst the bottles,**	*3631*
Mk	15:23	to drink **w** mingled with myrrh:	*3631*
Lk	1:15	drink neither **w** nor strong drink;	*3631*
Lk	5:37	**putteth new w into old bottles;**	*3631*
Lk	5:38	**But new w must be put into new**	*3631*
Lk	5:39	**also having drunk old w straightway**	
Lk	7:33	**eating bread nor drinking w;**	*3631*
Lk	10:34	**his wounds, pouring in oil and w,**	*3631*
Jn	2:3	saith unto him, They have no **w**	*3631*
Jn	2:9	tasted the water that was made **w**	*3631*
Jn	2:10	hast kept the good **w** until now.	*3631*
Jn	4:46	where he made the water **w**.	*3631*
Ac	2:13	said, These men are full of new **w**.	*1098*
Ro	14:21	to eat flesh, nor to drink **w**.	*3631*
Eph	5:18	And be not drunk with **w**, wherein	*3631*
1Ti	3:3	Not given to **w**, no striker, not	*3943*
1Ti	3:8	not given to much **w**, not greedy	*3631*

1Ti 5:23 use a little **w** for thy stomach's. *3631*
Tit 1:7 not given to **w**, no striker, not *3943*
1Pe 4:3 lusts, excess of **w**, revellings *3632*
Rev 6:6 thou hurt not the oil and the **w** *3631*
Rev 14:8 drink of the **w** of the wrath of her *3631*
Rev 14:10 drink of the **w** of the wrath of God,. . . . *3631*
Rev 16:19 the cup of the **w** of the fierceness *3631*
Rev 17:2 drunk with the **w** of her fornication . . . *3631*
Rev 18:3 have drunk of the **w** of the wrath *3631*
Rev 18:13 and **w**, and oil, and fine flour, and *3631*

WINEPRESS
Nu 18:30 and as the increase of the **w**. 3342
Jgs 6:11 Gideon threshed wheat by the **w** 1660
2Ki 6:27 of the barnfloor, or out of the **w**? 3342
Isa 5:2 of it, and also made a **w** therein:. 3342
Isa 63:3 I have trodden the **w** alone; and 6333
La 1:15 the daughter of Judah, as in a **w**.. 1660
Mt 21:33 **and digged a w in it, and built a** *3025*
Rev 14:19 great **w** of the wrath of God *3025*
Rev 14:20 **w** was trodden without the city. *3025*
Rev 14:20 and blood came out of the **w**, even. *3025*
Rev 19:15 treadeth the **w** of the fierceness . . . *3025, 3631*

WINEPRESSES
Job 24:11 tread their **w**, and suffer thirst. 3342
Jer 48:33 caused wine to fail from the **w** 3342

WING
1Ki 6:24 uttermost part of the one **w** unto 3671
1Ki 6:27 **w** of the one touched the one wall, ... 3671
2Ch 3:11 one **w** of the one cherub was five 3671
2Ch 3:12 joining to … **w** of the other cherub 3671
Isa 10:14 there was none that moved the **w**. 3671
Eze 17:23 it shall dwell all fowl of every **w**;. 3671

WINGED
Ge 1:21 and every **w** fowl after his kind: 3671
Dt 4:17 likeness of any **w** fowl that flieth in 3671

WINGS
Ex 19:4 and how I bare you on eagles' **w**. 3671
Ex 25:20 the mercy seat with their **w** 3671
Ex 37:9 the cherubims spread out their **w**. 3671
Dt 32:11 them, beareth them on her **w** 84
Ru 2:12 under whose **w** thou art come to 3671
2Sa 22:11 was seen upon the **w** of the wind 3671
1Ki 6:27 their **w** touched one another in the 3671
1Ki 8:6 even under the **w** of the cherubims 3671
1Ch 28:18 cherubims, that spread out their **w**,
2Ch 3:11 **w** of the cherubims were twenty. 3671
2Ch 3:13 The **w** of these cherubims spread 3671
2Ch 5:7 even under the **w** of the cherubims;. . . . 3671
Ps 17:8 hide me under the shadow of thy **w**, . . . 3671
Ps 18:10 he did fly upon the **w** of the wind. 3671
Ps 36:7 trust under the shadow of thy **w**. 3671
Ps 55:6 said, Oh that I had **w** like a dove! 83
Ps 57:1 in the shadow of thy **w** will I. 3671
Ps 63:7 the shadow of thy **w** will I rejoice 3671
Ps 91:4 and under his **w** shalt thou trust: 3671
Ps 104:3 walketh upon the **w** of the wind: 3671
Ps 139:9 If I take the **w** of the morning, and 3671
Ecc 10:20 which hath **w** shall tell the matter. 3671
Isa 6:2 the seraphims: each one had six **w**; 3671
Isa 8:8 the stretching out of his **w** shall 3671
Isa 40:31 shall mount up with **w** as eagles; 83
Eze 1:6 faces, and every one had four **w** 3671
Eze 1:8 the hands of a man under their **w** 3671
Eze 1:24 I heard the noise of their **w**, like 3671
Eze 3:13 of the **w** of the living creatures 3671
Eze 10:5 the sound of the cherubims' **w** was 3671
Eze 10:12 and their hands, and their **w**, and. 3671
Eze 10:19 the cherubims lifted up their **w**, ... 3671
Eze 11:22 did the cherubims lift up their **w**,. 3671
Eze 17:3 A great eagle with great **w**,. 3671
Eze 17:7 another great eagle with great **w**. 3671
Da 7:4 was like a lion, and had eagle's **w** 1611
Da 7:4 till the **w** thereof were plucked,. 1611
Hos 4:19 wind hath bound her up in her **w**,. 3671
Zec 5:9 and the wind was in their **w**; for. 3671
Mal 4:2 arise with healing in his **w**; 3671
Mt 23:37 **her chickens under her w**, ... *4420*
Lk 13:34 **gather her brood under her w**, ... *4420*
Rev 4:8 four beasts had each of them six **w**. *4420*
Rev 9:9 sound of their **w** was as the sound *4420*
Rev 12:14 given two **w** of a great eagle, ... *4420*

WINK
Job 15:12 away? and what do thy eyes **w** at. 7335
Ps 35:19 them **w** with the eye that hate me. 7169

WINKED
Ac 17:30 times of this ignorance God **w** at;. *5237*

WINKETH
Pr 6:13 He **w** with his eyes, he speaketh 7169
Pr 10:10 He that **w** with the eye causeth. 7169

WINNETH
Pr 11:30 life; and he that **w** souls is wise. 3947

WINTER
Ge 8:22 cold and heat, and summer and **w**, ... 2779
Ps 74:17 thou hast made summer and **w** 2779
SS 2:11 the **w** is past, the rain is over and 5638
Isa 18:6 the beasts … shall **w** upon them. 2778
Am 3:15 I will smite the **w** house with the 2779
Zec 14:8 in summer and in **w** shall it be 2778
Mt 24:20 **your flight may not be in the w**,. *5494*
Mk 13:18 **your flight may not be in the w**. *5494*
Jn 10:22 of the dedication, and it was in **w**. *5494*
Ac 27:12 haven was not commodious to **w** in, . . . *3915*
2Ti 4:21 thy diligence to come before **w** *5494*
Tit 3:12 for I have determined there to **w**. *3914*

WINTERHOUSE See also WINTER and HOUSE.
Jer 36:22 the king sat in the **w** in the ninth 2779

WIPE
2Ki 21:13 and I will **w** Jerusalem as a man 4229
Ne 13:14 **w** not out my good deeds that I 4229
Isa 25:8 Lord God will **w** away tears from 4229
Lk 7:38 did **w** them with the hairs of her *1591*
Lk 10:11 **on us, we do w off against you:**. *631*
Jn 13:5 and to **w** them with the towel *1591*
Rev 7:17 God shall **w** away all tears from *1813*
Rev 21:4 God shall **w** away all tears from *1813*

WIPED
Pr 6:33 his reproach shall not be **w** away 4229
Lk 7:44 **w them with the hairs of her**. *1591*
Jn 11:2 and **w** his feet with her hair, ... *1591*
Jn 12:3 and **w** his feet with her hair: *1591*

WIPETH
2Ki 21:13 Jerusalem as a man **w** a dish,. 4229
Pr 30:20 she eateth, and **w** her mouth, and. 4229

WISDOM

Ex	28:3	I have filled with the spirit of **w**,	2451
Ex	31:3	with the spirit of God, in **w**,	2451
Ex	35:35	hath he filled with **w** of heart,	2451
Ex	36:2	in whose heart the Lord had put **w**,	2451
Dt	4:6	is your **w** and your understanding	2451
2Sa	14:20	according to the **w** of an angel of	2451
2Sa	20:22	went unto all the people in her **w**	2451
1Ki	2:6	Do therefore according to thy **w**,	2451
1Ki	3:28	saw that the **w** of God was in him,	2451
1Ki	4:29	And God gave Solomon **w** and	2451
1Ki	4:30	Solomon's **w** excelled the **w** of all	2451
1Ki	4:34	people to hear the **w** of Solomon,	2451
1Ki	5:12	And the Lord gave Solomon **w**,	2451
1Ki	10:4	Sheba had seen all Solomon's **w**,	2451
1Ki	10:8	before thee, and that hear thy **w**	2451
1Ki	10:23	of the earth for riches and for **w**.	2451
1Ki	10:24	sought to Solomon, to hear his **w**,	2451
1Ch	22:12	Only the Lord give thee **w** and	7922
2Ch	9:6	greatness of thy **w** was not told	2451
Ezr	7:25	thou, Ezra, after the **w** of thy God,	2452
Job	12:2	people, and **w** shall die with you.	2451
Job	12:12	With the ancient is **w**; and in	2451
Job	28:28	the fear of the Lord, that is **w**;	2451
Job	34:35	and his words were without **w**	7919
Job	36:5	he is mighty in strength and **w**	3820
Job	38:36	hath put **w** in the inward parts?	2451
Job	39:26	Doth the hawk fly by thy **w**, and	998
Ps	51:6	thou shalt make me to know **w**.	2451
Ps	90:12	we may apply our hearts unto **w**.	2451
Ps	104:24	in **w** hast thou made them all:	2451
Ps	111:10	the Lord is the beginning of **w**	2451
Ps	136:5	him that by **w** made the heavens:	8394
Pr	1:2	To know **w** and instruction:	2451
Pr	1:3	To receive the instruction of **w**,	7919
Pr	1:7	fools despise **w** and instruction.	2451
Pr	1:20	**W** crieth without; she uttereth	2454
Pr	2:2	thou incline thine ear unto **w**,	2451
Pr	2:6	For the Lord giveth **w**: out of his	2451
Pr	2:10	When **w** entereth into thine heart,	2451
Pr	3:13	Happy is the man that findeth **w**,	2451
Pr	3:19	Lord by **w** hath founded the earth;	2451
Pr	4:5	Get **w**, get understanding: forget	2451
Pr	4:7	**W** is the principal thing;	2451
Pr	5:1	My son, attend unto my **w**, and	2451
Pr	7:4	Say unto **w**, Thou art my sister;	2451
Pr	8:5	O ye simple, understand **w**: and,	6195
Pr	8:11	For **w** is better than rubies; and	2451
Pr	9:10	of the Lord is the beginning of **w**:	2451
Pr	10:13	hath understanding **w** is found:	2451
Pr	10:21	but fools die for want of **w**	3820
Pr	10:23	man of understanding hath **w**.	2451
Pr	10:31	mouth of the just bringeth forth **w**	2451
Pr	11:2	shame: but with the lowly is **w**	2451
Pr	11:12	He that is void of **w** despiseth his	3820
Pr	12:8	commended according to his **w**	7922
Pr	13:10	but with the well advised is **w**.	2451
Pr	14:6	A scorner seeketh **w**, and findeth	2451
Pr	14:8	**w** of the prudent is to understand	2451
Pr	14:33	**W** resteth in the heart of him that	2451
Pr	15:33	the Lord is the instruction of **w**;	2451
Pr	16:16	better is it to get **w** than gold!	2451
Pr	17:16	price in the hand of a fool to get **w**,	2451
Pr	17:24	**W** is before him that hath	2451
Pr	18:1	and intermeddleth with all **w**.	8454
Pr	19:8	getteth **w** loveth his own soul:	3820
Pr	21:30	There is no **w** nor understanding	2451
Pr	23:4	be rich: cease from thine own **w**	998
Pr	23:9	will despise the **w** of thy words.	7922
Pr	24:3	Through **w** is an house builded;	2451
Pr	24:7	**W** is too high for a fool: he	2454
Pr	24:14	knowledge of **w** be unto thy soul:	2451
Pr	29:3	Whoso loveth **w** rejoiceth his	2451
Pr	29:15	The rod and reproof give **w**: but	2451
Pr	30:3	I neither learned **w**, nor have the	2451
Pr	31:26	She openeth her mouth with **w**;	2451
Ecc	1:16	have gotten more **w** than all they	2451
Ecc	1:17	And I gave my heart to know **w**,	2451
Ecc	1:18	For in much **w** is much grief:	2451
Ecc	2:13	Then I saw that **w** excelleth folly,	2451
Ecc	7:11	**W** is good with an inheritance:	2451
Ecc	7:12	For **w** is a defence, and money is a	2451
Ecc	7:12	**w** giveth life to them that have it.	2451
Ecc	7:19	**W** strengtheneth the wise more	2451
Ecc	7:25	to seek out **w**, and the reason of	2451
Ecc	8:1	a man's **w** maketh his face to	2451
Ecc	8:16	I applied mine heart to know **w**,	2451
Ecc	9:10	nor knowledge, nor **w**, in the grave.	2451
Ecc	9:16	said I, **W** is better than strength:	2451
Ecc	9:16	the poor man's **w** is despised,	2451
Ecc	9:18	**W** is better than weapons of war:	2451
Ecc	10:1	in reputation for **w** and honour	2451
Ecc	10:3	his **w** faileth him, and he saith	3820
Ecc	10:10	but **w** is profitable to direct.	2451
Isa	11:2	the spirit of **w** and understanding,	2451
Isa	29:14	**w** of their wise men shall perish,	2451
Isa	33:6	**w** and knowledge shall be the	2451
Isa	47:10	Thy **w** and thy knowledge, it hath	2451
Jer	9:23	not the wise man glory in his **w**,	2451
Jer	10:12	hath established the world by his **w**,	2451
Jer	51:15	hath established the world by his **w**,	2451
Eze	28:7	swords against the beauty of thy **w**,	2451
Eze	28:17	thou hast corrupted thy **w** by	2451
Da	1:17	and skill in all learning and **w**.	2451
Da	2:20	ever: for **w** and might are his:	2452
Da	2:21	he giveth **w** unto the wise, and	2452
Da	2:30	is not revealed to me for any **w**	2452
Da	5:14	and excellent **w** is found in thee.	2452
Mic	6:9	the man of **w** shall see thy name:	8454
Mt	11:19	**But w is justified of her children.**	*4678*
Mt	12:42	**earth to hear the w of Solomon;**	*4678*
Mk	6:2	**w** is this which is given unto him,	*4678*
Lk	1:17	disobedient to the **w** of the just;	*5428*
Lk	2:40	strong in spirit, filled with **w**	*4678*
Lk	2:52	Jesus increased in **w** and stature,	*4678*
Lk	7:35	**w is justified of all her children.**	*4678*
Lk	11:31	earth to hear the **w** of Solomon;	*4678*
Ac	6:3	full of the Holy Ghost and **w**,	*4678*
Ac	6:10	they were not able to resist the **w**	*4678*
Ac	7:22	in all the **w** of the Egyptians,	*4678*
Ro	11:33	depth of the riches both of the **w**	*4678*
1Co	1:17	not with **w** of words, lest the cross	*4678*
1Co	1:19	I will destroy the **w** of the wise,	*4678*
1Co	1:20	made foolish the **w** of this world?	*4678*
1Co	1:21	the world by **w** knew not God,	*4678*
1Co	1:22	sign, and the Greeks seek after **w**	*4678*
1Co	1:24	the power of God, and the **w** of God.	*4678*
1Co	1:30	who of God is made unto us **w**,	*4678*
1Co	2:4	with enticing words of man's **w**,	*4678*
1Co	2:7	we speak the **w** of God in a	*4678*
1Co	2:13	words which man's **w** teacheth,	*4678*
1Co	3:19	**w** of this world is foolishness with	*4678*

1Co 12:8 given by the Spirit the word of **w**; *4678*
2Co 1:12 not with fleshly **w**, but by the grace *4678*
Eph 1:8 hath abounded toward us in all **w** *4678*
Eph 1:17 you the spirit of **w** and revelation *4678*
Eph 3:10 the church the manifold **w** of God, ... *4678*
Col 1:9 the knowledge of his will in all **w** *4678*
Col 1:28 and teaching every man in all **w**; *4678*
Col 2:3 whom are hid all the treasures of **w** *4678*
Col 2:23 indeed a shew of **w** in will worship, ... *4678*
Col 3:16 Christ dwell in you richly in all **w**; *4678*
Col 4:5 Walk in **w** toward them that are *4678*
Jas 1:5 If any of you lack **w**, let him ask *4678*
Jas 3:13 his works with meekness of **w** *4678*
Jas 3:15 This **w** descendeth not from above, ... *4678*
Jas 3:17 But the **w** that is from above is *4678*
Rev 5:12 and **w**, and strength, and honour, ... *4678*
Rev 7:12 Blessing, and glory, and **w**, and *4678*
Rev 13:18 Here is **w**. Let him that hath *4678*
Rev 17:9 here is the mind which hath **w** *4678*

WISE
Ge 3:6 tree to be desired to make one **w**, ... 7919
Ge 41:33 look out a man discreet and **w**, ... 2450
Ge 41:39 so discreet and **w** as thou art: 2450
Ex 23:8 the gift blindeth the **w**, and 6493
Ex 28:3 speak unto all that are **w** hearted, ... 2450
Ex 35:25 the women that were **w** hearted 2450
Le 7:24 use: but ye shall in no **w** eat of it.
Le 27:19 the field will in any **w** redeem it.
Dt 4:6 is a **w** and understanding people 2450
Dt 16:19 a gift doth blind the eyes of the **w**, ... 2450
Dt 17:15 shalt in any **w** set him king over
Dt 21:23 shalt in any **w** bury him that day;
Jos 6:18 in any **w** keep yourselves from the
Jos 23:12 if ye do in any **w** go back, and cleave
1Sa 6:3 any **w** return him a trespass offering:
2Sa 14:20 and my lord is **w**, according to the 2450
1Ki 2:9 for thou art a **w** man, and knowest 2450
1Ki 3:12 a **w** and an understanding heart; 2450
1Ki 5:7 hath given unto David a **w** son 2450
Est 6:13 Then said his **w** men and Zeresh 2450
Job 5:13 He taketh the **w** in their own 2450
Job 32:9 Great men are not always **w** 2449
Job 37:24 not any that are **w** of heart 2450
Ps 19:7 is sure, making **w** the simple 2449
Ps 36:3 he hath left off to be **w**, and to do 7919
Ps 37:8 fret not thyself in any **w** to do evil.
Ps 49:10 For he seeth that **w** men die, ... 2450
Ps 107:43 Whoso is **w**, and will observe 2450
Pr 1:5 **w** man will hear, and will increase 2450
Pr 3:7 Be not **w** in thine own eyes: fear 2450
Pr 3:35 The **w** shall inherit glory: but 2450
Pr 6:6 consider her ways, and be **w**: 2449
Pr 8:33 Hear instruction, and be **w**, and 2449
Pr 9:8 rebuke a **w** man, and he will love 2450
Pr 9:9 Give instruction to a **w** man, and 2450
Pr 10:1 A **w** son maketh a glad father: 2450
Pr 10:5 gathereth in summer is a **w** son: 7919
Pr 10:14 **W** men lay up knowledge: but 2450
Pr 10:19 he that refraineth his lips is **w**. 7919
Pr 11:30 and he that winneth souls is **w**. 2450
Pr 12:15 hearkeneth unto counsel is **w**. 2450
Pr 12:18 but the tongue of the **w** is health 2450
Pr 13:1 A **w** son heareth his father's 2450
Pr 13:14 law of the **w** is a fountain of life, ... 2450
Pr 13:20 He that walketh with **w** men shall 2450
Pr 14:1 Every **w** woman buildeth her 2454
Pr 14:3 the lips of the **w** shall preserve 2450
Pr 14:16 A **w** man feareth, and departeth 2450
Pr 14:24 The crown of the **w** is their riches: 2450
Pr 14:35 favour is toward a **w** servant: 7919
Pr 15:2 the **w** useth knowledge aright: 2450
Pr 15:7 lips of the **w** disperse knowledge: 2450
Pr 15:20 A **w** son maketh a glad father: but 2450
Pr 16:14 death: but a **w** man will pacify it. 2450
Pr 16:21 **w** in heart shall be called prudent: 2450
Pr 16:23 heart of the **w** teacheth his mouth, ... 2450
Pr 17:2 A **w** servant shall have rule over 7919
Pr 17:10 A reproof entereth more into a **w**. 995
Pr 17:28 holdeth his peace, is counted **w**. 2450
Pr 18:15 the ear of the **w** seeketh knowledge. 2450
Pr 19:20 that thou mayest be **w** in thy 2449
Pr 20:1 is deceived thereby is not **w** 2449
Pr 20:26 A **w** king scattereth the wicked, ... 2450
Pr 21:11 punished, the simple is made **w**: 2449
Pr 21:22 A **w** man scaleth the city of the 2450
Pr 23:15 My son, if thine heart be **w**, my 2449
Pr 24:5 A **w** man is strong; yea, a man of 2450
Pr 24:23 These things also belong to the **w**. 2450
Pr 25:12 a **w** reprover upon an obedient ear. 2450
Pr 26:5 lest he be **w** in his own conceit. 2450
Pr 26:12 thou a man **w** in his own conceit? 2450
Pr 27:11 be **w**, and make my heart glad, ... 2449
Pr 28:7 Whoso keepeth the law is a **w** son: 995
Pr 28:11 rich man is **w** in his own conceit; 2450
Pr 29:8 snare: but **w** men turn away wrath. 2450
Pr 29:9 a **w** man contendeth with a foolish 2450
Pr 30:24 earth, but they are exceeding **w**. 2450
Ecc 2:15 me; and why was I then more **w**? 2449
Ecc 2:16 no remembrance of the **w** more 2450
Ecc 2:16 how dieth the **w** man? as the fool. 2450
Ecc 2:19 he shall be a **w** man or a fool? 2450
Ecc 4:13 Better is a poor and a **w** child, ... 2450
Ecc 7:4 heart of the **w** is in the house of 2450
Ecc 7:5 better to hear the rebuke of the **w**, ... 2450
Ecc 7:7 oppression maketh a **w** man mad; 2450
Ecc 7:19 Wisdom strengthened the **w** 2450
Ecc 7:23 I said, I will be **w**; but it was far 2449
Ecc 8:1 Who is as the **w** man? and who 2450
Ecc 8:5 a **w** man's heart discerneth both 2450
Ecc 8:17 though a **w** man think to know it, ... 2450
Ecc 9:17 The words of **w** men are heard in 2450
Ecc 12:9 because the preacher was **w**, he 2450
Isa 5:21 unto them that are **w** in their own 2450
Isa 19:12 are they? where are thy **w** men? 2450
Isa 29:14 the wisdom of their **w** men shall 2450
Isa 44:25 that turneth **w** men backward, ... 2450
Jer 4:22 they are **w** to do evil, but to do 2450
Jer 8:8 We are **w**, and the law of the Lord 2450
Jer 9:23 the **w** man glory in his wisdom, ... 2450
Jer 10:7 among all the **w** men of the nations. ... 2450
Jer 18:18 nor counsel from the **w**, nor the 2450
Da 2:24 Destroy not the **w** men of Babylon: 2445
Da 2:27 hath demanded cannot the **w** men, ... 2445
Da 4:18 **w** men of my kingdom are not able 2445
Da 5:7 and said to the **w** men of Babylon, ... 2445
Da 12:3 And they that be **w** shall shine 7919
Da 12:10 but the **w** shall understand 7919
Mt 1:18 of Jesus Christ was on this **w**. *3779*
Mt 2:1 there came **w** men from the east *3097*
Mt 2:7 he had privily called the **w** men, ... *3097*
Mt 2:16 that he was mocked of the **w** men *3097*

Mt 5:18 **one tittle shall in no w pass from**
Mt 7:24 **I will liken him unto a w man,** *5429*
Mt 10:16 **be ye therefore w as serpents,** *5429*
Mt 10:42 **he shall in no w lose his reward.**
Mt 11:25 **hast hid these things from the w** *4680*
Mt 23:34 **unto you prophets, and w men,** *4680*
Mt 24:45 **then is a faithful and w servant,** *5429*
Mt 25:4 **But the w took oil in their vessels.** *5429*
Lk 10:21 **hast hid these things from the w** *4680*
Lk 12:42 **is that faithful and w steward,.** *5429*
Jn 6:37 **cometh to me I will in no w cast out.**
Jn 21:1 and on this **w** shewed he himself....... *3779*
Ro 1:22 Professing themselves to be **w**, ... *4680*
Ro 11:25 should be **w** in your own conceits;..... *5429*
Ro 12:16 Be not **w** in your own conceits *5429*
Ro 16:19 you **w** unto that which is good,........ *4680*
Ro 16:27 To God only **w**, be glory through *4680*
1Co 1:19 I will destroy the wisdom of the **w**, ... *4680*
1Co 1:20 Where is the **w**? where is the scribe *4680*
1Co 1:26 not many **w** men after the flesh, ... *4680*
1Co 1:27 of the world to confound the **w**;....... *4680*
1Co 3:10 as a **w** masterbuilder, I have laid *4680*
1Co 3:18 become a fool, that he may be **w**....... *4680*
1Co 3:19 He taketh the **w** in their own.......... *4680*
1Co 3:20 knoweth the thoughts of the **w**, ... *4680*
1Co 4:10 sake, but ye are **w** in Christ;........... *5429*
1Co 6:5 there is not a **w** man among you?...... *4680*
1Co 10:15 I speak as to **w** men; judge ye *5429*
Eph 5:15 not as fools, but as **w**,............... *4680*
1Ti 1:17 the only **w** God, be honour and *4680*
2Ti 3:15 to make thee **w** unto salvation......... *4679*
Jas 3:13 Who is a **w** man and endued with *4680*
Jude 25 To the only **w** God our Saviour, ... *4680*
Rev 21:27 there shall in no **w** enter into it any

WISELY

1Sa 18:30 David behaved himself more **w** 7919
2Ch 11:23 And he dealt **w**, and dispersed of 995
Ps 58:5 charmers, charming never so **w** 2449
Ps 101:2 behave myself **w** in a perfect way 7919
Pr 21:12 The righteous man **w** considereth 7919
Pr 28:26 but whoso walketh **w**, he shall be 2451
Ecc 7:10 for thou dost not enquire **w** 2451
Lk 16:8 **steward, because he had done w.** *5430*

WISE-MEN See WISE and MEN.

WISER

1Ki 4:31 For he was **w** than all men; than....... 2449
Ps 119:98 commandments hast made me **w**...... 2449
Pr 9:9 a wise man, and he will be yet **w**....... 2449
Pr 26:16 sluggard is **w** in his own conceit....... 2450
Lk 16:8 **w than the children of light.** *5429*
1Co 1:25 foolishness of God is **w** than men; *4680*

WISH

Ps 40:14 and put to shame that **w** me evil....... 2655
Ps 73:7 have more than heart could **w** 4906
Ro 9:3 could **w** that myself were accursed..... *2172*
3Jn 2 I **w** above all things that thou *2172*

WISHED

Jnh 4:8 and **w** in himself to die, and said,...... 7592
Ac 27:29 of the stern, and **w** for the day *2172*

WITCH

Ex 22:18 Thou shalt not suffer a **w** to live. 3784
Dt 18:10 of times, or an enchanter, or a **w**,...... 3784

WITCHCRAFT

1Sa 15:23 For rebellion is as the sin of **w**,........ 7081
2Ch 33:6 used enchantments, and used **w**, ... 3784
Gal 5:20 Idolatry, **w**, hatred, variance,.......... *5331*

WITCHCRAFTS

2Ki 9:22 Jezebel and her **w** are so many?........ 3785
Mic 5:12 will cut off **w** out of thine hand;....... 3785
Na 3:4 the mistress of **w**, that selleth 3785
Na 3:4 and families through her **w**. 3785

WITHDRAW

1Sa 14:19 unto the priest, **W** thine hand. 622
Pr 25:17 **W** thy foot from thy neighbour's 3365
Isa 60:20 neither shall thy moon **w** itself:......... 622
Joel 2:10 and the stars shall **w** their shining:...... 622
Joel 3:15 and the stars shall **w** their shining....... 622
2Th 3:6 **w** yourselves from every brother....... *4724*
1Ti 6:5 godliness: from such **w** thyself.......... *868*

WITHDRAWN

La 2:8 not **w** his hand from destroying:....... 7725
Eze 18:8 hath **w** his hand from iniquity,........ 7725
Hos 5:6 he hath **w** himself from them.......... 2502

WITHDREW

Ne 9:29 and **w** the shoulder, and......... 5414, 5437
Eze 20:22 Nevertheless I **w** mine hand,.......... 7725
Lk 5:16 he **w** himself into the wilderness, ... *5298*
Gal 2:12 he **w** and separated himself,........... *5288*

WITHER

Ps 1:3 his leaf also shall not **w**; and 5034
Ps 37:2 grass, and **w** as the green herb......... 5034
Isa 19:6 up: the reeds and flags shall **w**......... 7060
Isa 40:24 blow upon them, and they shall **w**,..... 3001
Jer 12:4 and the herbs of every field **w**, ... 3001
Eze 17:9 cut off the fruit thereof, that it **w**?...... 3001
Eze 17:10 shall it not utterly **w**, when the 3001
Am 1:2 and the top of Carmel shall **w**......... 3001

WITHERED

Ge 41:23 seven ears, **w**, thin, and blasted 6798
Ps 102:4 heart is smitten, and **w** like grass;...... 3001
Ps 102:11 and I am **w** like grass................. 3001
La 4:8 it is **w**, it is become like a stick......... 3001
Eze 19:12 strong rods were broken and **w**; 3001
Joel 1:12 joy is **w** away from the sons of men. ... 3001
Jnh 4:7 and it smote the gourd that it **w**....... 3001
Mt 13:6 **they had no root, they w away.**......... *3583*
Mt 21:20 How soon is the fig tree **w** away!....... *3583*
Mk 4:6 **because it had no root, it w away..** *3583*
Mk 11:21 which thou cursedst is **w** away......... *3583*
Lk 6:6 a man whose right hand was **w**. *3584*
Lk 8:6 **it w … because it lacked moisture.** *3583*
Jn 15:6 **cast forth as a branch, and is w;** *3583*

WITHERETH

Ps 90:6 the evening it is cut down, and **w**...... 3001
Ps 129:6 which **w** afore it groweth up:.......... 3001
Isa 40:8 The grass **w**, the flower fadeth; 3001
Jas 1:11 burning heat, but it **w** the grass, ... *3583*
1Pe 1:24 The grass **w**, and the flower *3583*

W

WITHHELD

Ge 20:6 I also **w** thee from sinning............ 2820
Ge 22:16 hast not **w** thy son, thine only son:..... 2820
Job 31:16 If I have **w** the poor from their........ 4513
Ecc 2:10 I **w** not my heart from any joy;........ 4513

WITHHOLD

2Sa	13:13	for he will not **w** me from thee.	4513
Ps	40:11	**W** not thou thy tender mercies	3607
Ps	84:11	good thing will he **w** from them	4513
Pr	3:27	**W** not good from them to whom it	4513
Pr	23:13	**W** not correction from a child:	4513
Ecc	11:6	in the evening **w** not thine hand:	3240
Jer	2:25	**W** thy foot from being unshod,	4513

WITHIN

Ge	6:14	pitch it **w** and without with pitch.	1004
Ge	9:21	and he was uncovered **w** his tent.	8432
Ge	18:12	Sarah laughed **w** herself, saying,	7130
Ge	18:24	be fifty righteous **w** the city:	8432
Ge	40:19	Yet **w** three days shall Pharaoh	
Ex	20:10	nor thy stranger that is **w** thy gates:	
Ex	37:2	it with pure gold **w** and without,	1004
Le	10:18	not brought in **w** the holy place:	6441
Le	16:15	and bring his blood **w** the vail,	1004
Dt	23:10	he shall not come **w** the camp:	8432
Dt	32:25	The sword without, and terror **w**,	2315
Jos	1:11	**w** three days ye shall pass over	5750
Jgs	7:16	and lamps **w** the pitchers.	8432
1Sa	25:37	that his heart died **w** him, and	7130
2Sa	7:2	ark of God dwelleth **w** curtains.	8432
1Ki	6:21	the house **w** with pure gold:	6441
1Ki	6:27	cherubims **w** the inner house:	8432
Job	32:18	the spirit **w** me constraineth me.	990
Ps	39:3	My heart was hot **w** me, while I	7130
Ps	40:8	God: yea, thy law is **w** my heart.	8432
Ps	42:6	God, my soul is cast down **w** me:	5921
Ps	51:10	and renew a right spirit **w** me.	7130
Ps	94:19	multitude of my thoughts **w** me	7130
Ps	103:1	all that is **w** me, bless his holy	7130
Ps	142:3	my spirit was overwhelmed **w** me,	5921
Pr	26:24	lips, and layeth up deceit **w** him;	7130
Isa	26:9	my spirit **w** me will I seek thee	7130
Isa	63:11	he that put his holy Spirit **w** him?	7130
Jer	23:9	Mine heart **w** me is broken because	7130
La	1:20	mine heart is turned **w** me; for I.	7130
Eze	2:10	it was written **w** and without:	6440
Eze	11:19	and I will put a new spirit **w** you;	7130
Eze	36:27	And I will put my spirit **w** you,	7130
Da	6:12	of any God or man **w** thirty days,	5705
Zec	12:1	formeth the spirit of man **w** him.	7130
Mt	23:26	**first that which is w the cup and**	*1787*
Mt	23:27	**are w full of dead men's bones,**	*2081*
Mt	23:28	**but w ye are full of hypocrisy**	*2081*
Mk	7:23	**All these evil things come from w,**	*2081*
Mk	14:58	**w** three days I will build another	*1223*
Lk	17:21	**the kingdom of God is w you.**	*1787*
Lk	24:32	Did not our heart burn **w** us, while	*1722*
Ro	8:23	we ourselves groan **w** ourselves,	*1722*
Heb	6:19	entereth into that **w** the vail;	*2082*
Rev	4:8	and they were full of eyes **w**.	*2081*
Rev	5:1	on the throne a book written **w**	*2081*

WITHOUT

Ge	1:2	earth was **w** form, and void;	8414
Ge	6:14	pitch it within and **w** with pitch.	2351
Ex	12:5	Your lamb shall be **w** blemish,	8549
Ex	25:11	and **w** shalt thou overlay it,	2351
Ex	29:14	thou burn with fire **w** the camp:	2351
Le	1:3	let him offer a male **w** blemish:	8549
Le	5:15	a ram **w** blemish out of the flocks,	8549
Le	8:17	he burnt with fire **w** the camp;	2351
Le	10:12	eat it **w** leaven beside the altar:	4682
Le	23:18	seven lambs **w** blemish of the first	8549
Le	24:3	**W** the vail of the testimony, in	2351
Nu	6:14	and one ram **w** blemish for peace.	8549
Nu	15:35	him with stones **w** the camp	2351
Nu	20:19	**w** doing any thing else, go through	369
Nu	31:19	ye abide **w** the camp seven days:	2351
Nu	35:22	thrust him suddenly **w** enmity,	3808
Nu	35:22	him any thing **w** laying of wait,	3808
Dt	32:4	a God of truth and **w** iniquity,	369
Jgs	2:23	**w** driving them out hastily;	1115
Ru	4:14	not left thee this day **w** a kinsman,	
1Sa	19:5	blood, to stay David **w** a cause?	2600
2Sa	23:4	riseth, even a morning **w** clouds;	3808
2Ki	18:25	come up **w** the Lord against	1107
2Ch	12:3	people were **w** number that came.	369
2Ch	15:3	Israel hath been **w** the true God,	3808
2Ch	21:20	and departed **w** being desired.	3808
Job	2:3	him, to destroy him **w** cause	2600
Job	34:24	in pieces mighty men **w** number,	3808
Job	34:35	and his words were **w** wisdom.	3808
Job	38:2	counsel by words **w** knowledge?	1097
Job	42:3	that hideth counsel **w** knowledge?	1097
Ps	7:4	him that **w** cause is mine enemy:)	7387
Ps	35:19	the eye that hate me **w** a cause	2600
Ps	119:161	have persecuted me **w** a cause:	2600
Pr	1:20	Wisdom crieth **w**; she uttereth	2351
Pr	3:30	Strive not with a man **w** cause,	2600
Pr	6:15	shall he be broken **w** remedy.	369
Pr	16:8	than great revenues **w** right.	3808
Pr	19:2	that the soul be **w** knowledge,	3808
Pr	22:13	There is a lion **w**, I shall be slain	2351
Pr	23:29	who hath wounds **w** cause?	2600
Pr	24:28	against thy neighbour **w** cause;	2600
Pr	29:1	be destroyed, and that **w** remedy.	369
Isa	6:11	the cities be wasted **w** inhabitant,	369
Isa	10:4	**W** me they shall bow down under	1115
Isa	36:10	now come up **w** the Lord against	1107
Isa	45:17	confounded world **w** end	5769, 5703
Isa	52:3	ye shall be redeemed **w** money	3808
Isa	55:1	and milk **w** money and **w** price.	3808
Jer	2:32	have forgotten me days **w** number.	369
Jer	4:23	the earth, and, lo, it was **w** form,	8414
Jer	15:13	will I give to the spoil **w** price,	3808
Jer	22:13	his neighbour's service **w** wages,	2600
Jer	33:12	desolate **w** man and **w** beast,	369, 5704
La	1:6	**w** strength before the pursuer.	3808
La	3:49	ceaseth not, **w** any intermission,	369
La	3:52	me sore, like a bird, **w** cause.	2600
Eze	17:9	**w** great power or many people to	3808
Eze	46:13	a lamb of the first year **w** blemish:	8549
Da	2:34	a stone was cut out **w** hands,	1768, 3809
Hos	3:4	days **w** a king, and **w** a prince,	369
Mt	5:22	**angry with his brother w a cause**	*1500*
Mt	10:29	**fall on the ground w your Father.**	*427*
Mt	13:34	**w** a parable spake he not unto.	*5565*
Mt	13:57	**A prophet is not w honour, save.**	*820*
Mt	15:16	**Are ye also yet w understanding?**	*801*
Mk	4:11	**unto them that are w, all these**	*1854*
Mk	6:4	**A prophet is not w honour, but**	*820*
Mk	7:15	**There is nothing from w a man,**	*1855*
Mk	7:18	**Are ye so w understanding also?**	*801*
Mk	14:58	will build another made **w** hands.	*886*
Jn	8:7	**He that is w sin among you, let**	*361*
Jn	15:5	**for w me ye can do nothing.**	*5565*
Jn	15:25	**law, They hated me w a cause.**	*1432*
Ac	9:9	And he was three days **w** sight,	*3361*

Ac	12:5	prayer was made **w** ceasing of	*1618*
Ac	14:17	he left not himself **w** witness,	*267*
Ro	1:20	so that they are **w** excuse:	*379*
Ro	1:31	**w** natural affection, implacable,	*794*
Ro	3:3	make the faith of God **w** effect?	*2673*
Ro	10:14	how shall they hear **w** a preacher?	*5565*
Ro	11:29	calling of god are **w** repentance.	*278*
Ro	12:9	Let love be **w** dissimulation.	*505*
1Co	5:13	But them that are **w** God judgeth.	*1854*
1Co	9:21	To them that are **w** law, as **w** law.	*455*
1Co	14:10	none of them is **w** signification.	*880*
2Co	10:13	boast of things **w** our measure,	*280*
Eph	2:12	no hope, and **w** God in the world:	*112*
Eph	3:21	throughout all ages, world **w** end.	
Eph	5:27	it should be holy and **w** blemish.	*299*
Php	1:10	**w** offence till the day of Christ;	*677*
Php	2:14	Do all things **w** murmurings	*5565*
Col	2:11	the circumcision made **w** hands,	*886*
Col	4:5	wisdom toward them that are **w**,	*1854*
1Th	5:17	Pray **w** ceasing.	*89*
1Ti	3:16	**w** controversy great is the mystery	*3672*
Phm	14	**w** thy mind would I do nothing;	*5565*
Heb	4:15	tempted like as we are, yet **w** sin.	*5565*
Heb	9:7	not **w** blood, which he offered for	*5565*
Heb	9:14	offered himself **w** spot to God,	*299*
Heb	9:22	and **w** shedding of blood is no	*5565*
Heb	11:6	**w** faith it is impossible to please	*5565*
Heb	12:14	**w** which no man shall see the	*5565*
Heb	13:5	conversation be **w** covetousness;	*866*
Heb	13:12	own blood, suffered **w** the gate	*1854*
Jas	2:18	shew me thy faith **w** thy works	*5565*
Jas	2:20	man, that faith **w** works is dead?	*5565*
Jas	2:26	as the body **w** the spirit is dead,	*5565*
Jas	2:26	so faith **w** works is dead also.	*5565*
Jas	3:17	**w** partiality, and without hypocrisy.	*87*
Jas	3:17	without partiality, and **w** hypocrisy.	*505*
1Pe	1:19	lamb **w** blemish and without spot:	*299*
1Pe	1:19	lamb without blemish and **w** spot:	*784*

WITHSTAND

Nu	22:32	I went out to **w** thee, because thy	7854
2Ch	13:7	and could not **w** them.	2388
2Ch	13:8	to **w** the kingdom of the Lord.	2388
2Ch	20:6	so that none is able to **w** thee?	3320
Est	9:2	and no man could **w** them; for	5975
Ecc	4:12	against him, two shall **w** him;	5975
Ac	11:17	what was I, that I could **w** God?	*2967*
Eph	6:13	ye may be able to **w** in the evil day,	*436*

WITHSTOOD

2Ch	26:18	And they **w** Uzziah the king, and	5975
Da	10:13	of the kingdom of Persia **w** me.	5975
Gal	2:11	I **w** him to the face, because he was	*436*
2Ti	3:8	as Jannes and Jambres **w** Moses,	*436*
2Ti	4:15	for he hath greatly **w** our words.	*436*

WITNESS See also EYEWITNESS.

Ge	31:50	see, God is **w** betwixt me and thee.	5707
Ge	31:52	and this pillar be **w**, that I will	5711
Ex	20:16	shalt not bear false **w** against thy	5707
Ex	22:13	then let him bring it for **w**, and he	5707
Le	5:1	the voice of swearing, and is a **w**,	5707
Nu	5:13	and there be no **w** against her,	5707
Nu	17:7	the Lord in the tabernacle of **w**.	5715
Nu	18:2	before the tabernacle of **w**	5715
Dt	4:26	I call heaven and earth to **w**.	5749
Dt	5:20	shalt thou bear false **w** against.	5707
Dt	17:6	at the mouth of one **w** he shall not	5707
Dt	19:15	One **w** shall not rise up against a	5707
Dt	19:18	if the **w** be a false **w**, and hath	5707
Dt	31:26	may be there for a **w** against thee.	5707
Jos	22:27	But that it may be a **w** between us,	5707
Jos	22:34	be a **w** between us that the Lord is	5707
Jos	24:27	this stone shall be a **w** unto us;	5713
1Sa	12:3	**w** against me before the Lord,	6030
1Sa	12:5	And they answered, He is **w**.	5707
1Ki	21:10	to bare **w** against him, saying,	5749
Job	16:19	my **w** is in heaven, and my record	5707
Ps	89:37	and as a faithful **w** in heaven.	5707
Pr	6:19	A false **w** that speaketh lies, and	5707
Pr	14:5	A faithful **w** will not lie: but a false	5707
Pr	14:5	lie: but a false **w** will utter lies.	5707
Pr	14:25	A true **w** delivereth souls: but a	5707
Pr	14:25	but a deceitful **w** speaketh lies.	
Pr	19:5	A false **w** shall not be	5707
Pr	19:28	An ungodly **w** scorneth judgment:	5707
Pr	21:28	A false **w** shall perish: but the	5707
Pr	24:28	Be not a **w** against thy neighbour	5707
Pr	25:18	that beareth false **w** against his	5707
Isa	3:9	countenance doth **w** against them;	5707
Isa	19:20	it shall be for a sign and for a **w**	5707
Jer	29:23	I know, and am a **w**, saith the Lord.	5707
Jer	42:5	The Lord be a true and faithful **w**.	5707
La	2:13	thing shall I take to **w** for thee?	5749
Mic	1:2	the Lord God be **w** against you,	5707
Mal	2:14	the Lord hath been **w** between	5749
Mt	15:19	**thefts, false w, blasphemies:**	*5577*
Mt	19:18	**steal, Thou shalt not bare false w,**	*5576*
Mt	24:14	**preached in all the world for a w**	*3142*
Mt	26:59	sought false **w** against Jesus,	*5577*
Mt	27:13	many things they **w** against thee?	*2649*
Mk	10:19	**Do not bear false w, Defraud not,**	*5576*
Mk	14:56	many bare false **w** against him,	*5576*
Mk	14:56	but their **w** agreed not together.	*3141*
Mk	14:59	neither so did their **w** agree	*3141*
Mk	15:4	many things they **w** against thee.	*2649*
Lk	18:20	**Do not bear false w, Honour thy**	*5576*
Jn	1:7	to bear **w** of the Light, that all	*3140*
Jn	1:8	was sent to bear **w** of that Light	*3140*
Jn	1:15	John bare **w** of him, and cried,	*3140*
Jn	3:11	**seen; and ye receive not our w.**	*3141*
Jn	5:31	**If I bear w of myself,**	*3140*
Jn	5:31	**my w is not true.**	*3141*
Jn	5:32	**is another that beareth w of me;.**	*3140*
Jn	5:36	**have greater w than that of John:**	*3141*
Jn	5:36	**works that I do, bear w of me,**	*3140*
Jn	8:18	**I am one that bear w of myself,**	*3140*
Jn	10:25	**Father's name, they bear w of me.**	*3140*
Jn	15:27	**ye also shall bear w, because ye.**	*3140*
Jn	18:37	**I should bear w unto the truth.**	*3140*
Ac	1:22	be a **w** with us of his resurrection.	*3144*
Ac	4:33	the apostles **w** of the resurrection	*3142*
Ac	7:44	tabernacle of **w** in the wilderness,	*3142*
Ac	10:43	To him give all the prophets **w**,	*3140*
Ac	14:17	he left not himself without **w**,	*267*
Ro	1:9	For God is my **w**, whom I serve	*3144*
Ro	2:15	their conscience also bearing **w**,	*4828*
Ro	8:16	itself beareth **w** with our spirit,	*4828*
Ro	9:1	not, my conscience bearing me **w**.	*4828*
Ro	13:9	Thou shalt not bear false **w**,	*5576*
Tit	1:13	This **w** is true. Wherefore rebuke	*3141*
Heb	11:4	obtained **w** that he was righteous.	*3140*
Jas	5:3	the rest of them shall be a **w**	*3142*

1Pe	5:1	a **w** of the sufferings of Christ,	*3144*
1Jn	1:2	we have seen it, and bear **w**,	*3140*
1Jn	5:6	And it is the Spirit that beareth **w**,	*3140*
1Jn	5:9	the **w** of God is greater:	*3141*
1Jn	5:10	Son of God hath the **w** in himself:	*3141*
3Jn	6	have borne **w** of thy charity	*3140*
Rev	1:5	Christ, who is the faithful **w**,	*3144*
Rev	3:14	**the faithful and true w, the**	*3144*
Rev	20:4	beheaded for the **w** of Jesus,	*3141*

WITNESSED

1Ki	21:13	the men of Belial **w** against him,	579
1Ti	6:13	Pontius Pilate **w** a good confession;	*3140*

WITNESSES See also EYEWITNESSES.

Nu	35:30	be put to death by the mouth of **w**.	5707
Dt	17:6	or three **w**, shall he that is worthy	5707
Dt	19:15	or at the mouth of three **w**, shall	5707
Jos	24:22	Ye are **w** against yourselves that	5707
Ru	4:9	Ye are **w** this day, that I have	5707
Ps	27:12	false **w** are risen up against me	5707
Isa	43:9	let them bring forth their **w**, that	5707
Isa	43:10	Ye are my **w**, saith the Lord, and	5707
Isa	44:8	declared it? ye are even my **w**.	5707
Jer	32:12	presence of the **w** that subscribed	5707
Jer	32:25	the field for money, and take **w**;	5707
Mt	18:16	**in the mouth of two or three w**	*3144*
Mt	23:31	**ye be w unto yourselves, that**	*3140*
Mt	26:60	though many false **w** came, yet	*5575*
Mt	26:60	At the last came two false **w**,	*5575*
Mt	26:65	what further need have we of **w**?	*3144*
Mk	14:63	What need we any farther **w**?	*3144*
Lk	24:48	**And ye are w of these things.**	*3144*
Ac	1:8	**and ye shall be w unto me both**	*3144*
Ac	2:32	raised up, whereof we all are **w**.	*3144*
Ac	3:15	from the dead; whereof we are **w**.	*3144*
Ac	5:32	And we are his **w** of these things;	*3144*
Ac	6:13	And set up false **w**, which said,	*3144*
Ac	7:58	and the **w** laid down their clothes	*3144*
Ac	10:39	we are **w** of all things which he did	*3144*
Ac	10:41	but unto **w** chosen before of God,	*3144*
Ac	13:31	who are his **w** unto the people	*3144*
1Co	15:15	and we are found false **w** of God;	*5575*
2Co	13:1	In the mouth of two or three **w**	*3144*
1Th	2:10	Ye are **w**, and God also, how holily	*3144*
1Ti	5:19	but before two or three **w**.	*3144*
1Ti	6:12	a good profession before many **w**.	*3144*
2Ti	2:2	hast heard of me among many **w**,	*3144*
Heb	10:28	mercy under two or three **w**	*3144*
Heb	12:1	about with so great a cloud of **w**.	*3144*
Rev	11:3	I will give power unto my two **w**,	*3144*

WITNESSETH

Jn	5:32	**witness which he w of me is true.**	*3140*
Ac	20:23	the Holy Ghost **w** in every city,	*1263*

WIT'S

Ps	107:27	man, and are at their **w** end.	2451

WIVES

Ge	6:2	them **w** of all which they chose	802
Ge	7:7	his sons' **w** with him, into the ark	802
Ge	30:26	Give me my **w** and my children	802
Ge	31:50	take other **w** beside my daughters	802
Ex	19:15	the third day: come not at your **w**.	802
Ex	22:24	your **w** shall be widows, and your	802
Nu	14:3	that our **w** and our children should	802
Dt	17:17	Neither shall he multiply **w** to	802
Dt	21:15	If a man have two **w**, one beloved	802
Jgs	3:6	took their daughters to be their **w**,	802
Jgs	8:30	body begotten: for he had many **w**.	802
Jgs	21:16	How shall we do for **w** for them that	802
1Sa	30:18	away: and David rescued his two **w**.	802
2Sa	5:13	took him more concubines and **w**	802
2Sa	12:11	he shall lie with thy **w** in the sight	802
2Sa	19:5	daughters, and the lives of thy **w**.	802
1Ki	11:3	And he had seven hundred **w**	802
1Ki	11:4	his **w** turned away his heart after	802
1Ki	11:8	did he for all his strange **w**, which	802
2Ch	11:21	of Absalom above all his **w** and	802
2Ch	29:9	and our **w** are in captivity for this	802
Ezr	10:2	have taken strange **w** of the people	802
Ne	13:27	our God in marrying strange **w**?	802
Est	1:20	**w** shall give to their husbands	802
Isa	13:16	be spoiled, and their **w** ravished.	802
Jer	8:10	will I give their **w** unto others	802
Jer	14:16	none to bury them, their **w**	802
Jer	18:21	let their **w** be bereaved of their	802
Jer	29:6	Take ye **w**, and begat sons and	802
Jer	29:23	adultery with their neighbours' **w**.	802
Jer	44:9	and the wickedness of your **w**	802
Jer	44:15	that their **w** had burned incense	802
Jer	44:25	Ye and your **w** have both spoken	802
Eze	44:22	shall they take for their **w** a widow	802
Da	5:23	thy **w**, and thy concubines, have	7695
Da	6:24	them, their children, and their **w**;	5389
Mt	19:8	**suffered you to put away your w:**	*1135*
Lk	17:27	**they drank, they married w, they**	
1Co	7:29	have **w** be as though they had none;	*1135*
Eph	5:22	**W**, submit yourselves unto your	*1135*
Eph	5:24	let the **w** be to their own husbands.	*1135*
Eph	5:25	Husbands, love your **w**, even as	*1135*
Eph	5:28	to love their **w** as their own bodies	*1135*
Col	3:18	**W**, submit yourselves unto your	*1135*
Col	3:19	Husbands, love your **w**, and be not	*1135*
1Ti	3:11	Even so must their **w** be grave,	*1135*
1Pe	3:1	ye **w**, be in subjection to your own	*1135*
1Pe	3:1	won by the conversation of the **w**;	*1135*

WIVES'

1Ti	4:7	refuse profane and old **w** fables,	*1126*

WIZARD

Le	20:27	or that is a **w**, shall surely be put	3049
Dt	18:11	spirits, or a **w**, or a necromancer.	3049

WIZARDS

Le	19:31	neither seek after **w**, to be defiled	3049
Le	20:6	and after **w**, to go a whoring after	3049
1Sa	28:3	spirits, and the **w**, out of the land	3049
1Sa	28:9	spirits, and the **w**, out of the land:	3049
2Ki	21:6	dealt with familiar spirits and **w**	3049
2Ki	23:24	with familiar spirits, and the **w**,	3049
2Ch	33:6	with a familiar spirit, and with **w**	3049
Isa	8:19	unto **w** that peep, and that mutter:	3049
Isa	19:3	have familiar spirits, and to the **w**.	3049

WOE

1Sa	4:7	**W** unto us! for there hath not	188
Pr	23:29	Who hath **w**? who hath sorrow?	188
Ecc	4:10	but **w** to him that is alone when	337
Ecc	10:16	**W** to thee, O land, when thy king	337
Isa	3:11	**W** unto the wicked! it shall be ill	188
Isa	5:8	**W** unto them that join house to	1945
Isa	5:11	**W** unto them that rise up early in	1945

Isa 5:18 **W** unto them that draw iniquity....... 1945
Isa 5:20 **W** unto them that call evil good....... 1945
Isa 5:21 **W** unto them that are wise in 1945
Isa 6:5 said I, **W** is me! for I am undone:....... 188
Isa 10:1 **W** unto them that decree............. 1945
Isa 33:1 **W** to thee that spoilest, and thou 1945
Isa 45:9 **W** unto him that striveth with his 1945
Isa 45:10 **W** unto him that saith unto his 1945
Jer 4:31 **W** is me now! for my soul is 188
Jer 10:19 **W** is me for my hurt! my wound 188
Jer 13:27 **W** unto thee, O Jerusalem! wilt......... 188
Jer 15:10 **W** is me, my mother, that thou......... 188
Jer 22:13 **W** unto him that buildeth his......... 1945
Jer 23:1 **W** be unto the pastors that 1945
La 5:16 **w** unto us, that we have sinned! 188
Eze 13:3 **W** unto the foolish prophets.......... 1945
Eze 16:23 (**w**, **w** unto thee! saith the Lord......... 188
Eze 24:6 **W** to the bloody city, to the pot 188
Eze 30:2 God; Howl ye, **W** worth the day! 1929
Eze 34:2 **W** be to the shepherds of Israel........ 1945
Hos 7:13 **W** unto them! for they have fled........ 188
Am 5:18 **W** unto you that desire the day of 1945
Am 6:1 **W** to them that are at ease in.......... 1945
Mic 2:1 **W** to them that devise iniquity........ 1945
Hab 2:9 **W** to him that coveteth an evil 1945
Hab 2:12 **W** to him that buildeth a town........ 1945
Hab 2:15 **W** unto him that giveth his........... 1945
Hab 2:19 **W** unto him that saith to the wood,.... 1945
Mt 11:21 **w unto thee, Bethsaida! for if** *3759*
Mt 18:7 **but w to that man by whom the**....... *3759*
Mt 23:13 **w unto you, scribes and**.............. *3759*
Mt 23:16 **W unto you, ye blind guides**.......... *3759*
Mt 23:27 **W unto you, scribes and** *3759*
Mt 24:19 **w unto them that are with child,** *3759*
Mt 26:24 **w unto that man by whom the**........ *3759*
Mk 14:21 **w to that man by whom the Son** *3759*
Lk 6:24 **But w unto you that are rich!** *3759*
Lk 6:25 **W unto you that are full! for ye** *3759*
Lk 6:25 **W unto you that laugh now! for**....... *3759*
Lk 6:26 **W unto you, when all men shall**....... *3759*
Lk 10:13 **w unto thee, Bethsaida! for if** *3759*
Lk 11:46 **W unto you also, ye lawyers!**.......... *3759*
Lk 11:47 **W unto you! for ye build the**.......... *3759*
Lk 11:52 **W unto you, lawyers! for ye have** *3759*
Lk 17:1 **w unto him, through whom they**...... *3759*
Lk 21:23 **w unto them that are with child,** *3759*
Lk 22:22 **w unto that man by whom he is**....... *3759*
1Co 9:16 **w** is unto me, if I preach not the....... *3759*
Jude 11 **W** unto them! for they have gone...... *3759*
Rev 8:13 **W**, **w**, **w**, to the inhabiters of the....... *3759*
Rev 9:12 One **w** is past; and, behold, there *3759*
Rev 11:14 The second **w** is past; and *3759*
Rev 11:14 behold, the third **w** cometh quickly *3759*
Rev 12:12 **W** to the inhabiters of the earth *3759*

WOEFUL

Jer 17:16 neither have I desired the **w** day; 605

WOES

Rev 9:12 there come two **w** more hereafter. *3759*

WOLF

Ge 49:27 Benjamin shall ravin as a **w**: 2061
Isa 11:6 **w** also shall dwell with the lamb, ... 2061
Isa 65:25 The **w** and the lamb shall feed 2061
Jn 10:12 **seeth the w coming, and leaveth**....... *3074*

WOLVES

Eze 22:27 are like **w** ravening the prey, ... 2061
Hab 1:8 more fierce than the evening **w**........ 2061
Zep 3:3 her judges are evening **w**; they 2061
Mt 7:15 **but inwardly they are ravening w.** *3074*
Mt 10:16 **forth as sheep in the midst of w**....... *3074*
Lk 10:3 **send you forth as lambs among w.**..... *3074*
Ac 20:29 grievous **w** enter in among you, ... *3074*

WOMAN

Ge 2:22 made he a **w**, and brought her 802
Ge 2:23 she shall be called **W**, because she 802
Ge 3:2 **w** said unto the serpent, We may 802
Ge 3:6 the **w** saw that the tree was good 802
Ge 3:12 The **w** whom thou gavest to be......... 802
Ge 3:13 **w** said, The serpent beguiled me........ 802
Ge 3:15 put enmity between thee and the **w**..... 802
Ge 3:16 Unto the **w** he said, I will greatly 802
Ge 20:3 for the **w** which thou hast taken; 802
Ex 2:9 **w** took the child, and nursed it......... 802
Ex 11:2 every **w** of her neighbour, jewels........ 802
Ex 21:22 men strive, and hurt a **w** with child 802
Ex 21:29 that he hath killed a man or a **w**........ 802
Le 12:2 If a **w** have conceived seed, and......... 802
Le 15:25 if a **w** have an issue of her blood........ 802
Le 19:20 whosoever lieth carnally with a **w**....... 802
Le 20:16 And if a **w** approach unto any beast, ... 802
Le 20:16 thou shalt kill the **w**, and the beast: 802
Le 20:27 or **w** that hath a familiar spirit 802
Le 21:7 neither shall they take a **w** put away..... 802
Nu 5:6 man or **w** shall commit any sin.......... 802
Nu 5:27 the **w** shall be a curse among her 802
Nu 5:28 And if the **w** be not defiled, but be...... 802
Nu 5:31 and this **w** shall bear her iniquity 802
Nu 6:2 either man or **w** shall separate.......... 802
Nu 25:6 a Midianitish **w** in the sight of Moses
Nu 30:3 a **w** also vow a vow unto the Lord 802
Nu 31:17 kill every **w** that hath known man 802
Dt 15:12 or an Hebrew **w**, be sold unto thee
Dt 17:5 bring forth that man or that **w**,......... 802
Dt 21:11 among the captives a beautiful **w** 802
Dt 22:5 The **w** shall not wear that which......... 802
Dt 22:22 found lying with a **w** married to an 802
Dt 28:56 The tender and delicate **w** among you
Jos 2:4 **w** took the two men, and hid them 802
Jos 6:22 house, and bring out thence the **w**...... 802
Jgs 9:53 And a certain **w** cast a piece of a........ 802
Jgs 9:54 men say not of me, A **w** slew him. 802
Jgs 13:9 angel of God came again unto the **w**.... 802
Jgs 14:3 never a **w** among the daughters 802
Jgs 14:10 So his father went down unto the **w**..... 802
Jgs 16:4 loved a **w** in the valley of Sorek, ... 802
Jgs 20:4 husband of the **w** that was slain,........ 802
Ru 3:8 and, behold, a **w** lay at his feet.......... 802
Ru 3:11 know that thou art a virtuous **w**........ 802
Ru 4:11 The Lord make the **w** that is come...... 802
1Sa 1:15 lord, I am a **w** of a sorrowful spirit: 802
1Sa 2:20 The Lord give thee seed of this **w**....... 802
1Sa 20:30 Thou son of the perverse rebellious **w**
1Sa 25:3 she was a **w** of good understanding, ... 802
1Sa 28:7 a **w** that hath a familiar spirit 802
1Sa 28:12 when the **w** saw Samuel, she cried 802
2Sa 11:2 roof he saw a **w** washing herself;........ 802
2Sa 11:2 **w** was very beautiful to look upon 802
2Sa 11:3 David sent and enquired after the **w** 802
2Sa 11:5 the **w** conceived, and sent and told...... 802

2Sa	11:21	did not a **w** cast a piece of a	802
2Sa	13:17	put now this **w** out from me, and bolt	
2Sa	14:9	**w** of Tekoah said unto the king	802
2Sa	14:19	the **w** answered and said, As thy	802
2Sa	14:27	she was a **w** of a fair countenance	802
2Sa	17:20	Absalom's servants came to the **w**	802
2Sa	20:16	Then cried a wise **w** out of the city	802
2Sa	20:21	And the **w** said unto Joab, Behold	802
1Ki	3:17	I and this **w** dwell in one house;	802
1Ki	3:26	Then spake the **w** whose the living	802
1Ki	14:5	shall feign herself to be another **w**	
1Ki	17:9	a widow **w** there to sustain thee	802
1Ki	17:24	the **w** said to Elijah, Now by this	802
2Ki	4:8	to Shunem, where was a great **w**;	802
2Ki	6:28	This **w** said unto me, Give thy son	802
2Ki	8:5	the **w**, whose son he had restored	802
2Ki	8:5	O king, this is the **w**, and this is	802
2Ki	9:34	see now this cursed **w**, and bury her:	
Job	14:1	Man that is born of a **w** is of few	802
Job	15:14	he which is born of a **w**, that he	802
Job	25:4	can he be clean that is born of a **w**?	802
Ps	48:6	and pain, as of a **w** in travail.	
Ps	113:9	maketh the barren **w** to keep house	
Pr	2:16	deliver thee from the strange **w**	802
Pr	5:20	why...be ravished with a strange **w**	
Pr	6:24	To keep thee from the evil **w**	802
Pr	6:26	by means of a whorish **w** a man is	802
Pr	6:32	committeth adultery with a **w**	802
Pr	7:10	met him a **w** with the attire of a	802
Pr	9:13	A foolish **w** is clamorous: she is	802
Pr	11:16	A gracious **w** retaineth honour	802
Pr	11:22	fair **w** which is without discretion	802
Pr	12:4	A virtuous **w** is a crown to her	802
Pr	14:1	Every wise **w** buildeth her house:	802
Pr	21:9	with a brawling **w** in a wide house	802
Pr	21:19	a contentious and an angry **w**	802
Pr	23:27	and a strange **w** is a narrow pit	
Pr	25:24	a brawling **w** in a wide house	802
Pr	27:13	a pledge of him for a strange **w**	
Pr	27:15	and a contentious **w** are alike	802
Pr	30:20	Such is the way of an adulterous **w**;	802
Pr	30:23	an odious **w** when she is married;	
Pr	31:10	Who can find a virtuous **w**? for	802
Pr	31:30	a **w** that feareth the Lord, she	802
Ecc	7:28	a **w** among all those have I not	802
Isa	13:8	be in pain as a **w** that travaileth:	
Isa	21:3	as the pangs of a **w** that travaileth:	
Isa	26:17	Like as a **w** with child, that draweth	
Isa	42:14	now will I cry like a travailing **w**;	
Isa	45:10	or to the **w**, What hast thou	802
Isa	49:15	Can a **w** forget her sucking child	802
Isa	54:6	as a **w** forsaken and grieved in	802
Jer	6:2	of Zion to a comely and delicate **w**	
Jer	13:21	take thee, as a **w** in travail?	802
Jer	22:23	thee, the pain as of a **w** in travail!	
Jer	30:6	hands on his loins, as a **w** in travail,	
Jer	31:22	earth, A **w** shall compass a man	5347
Jer	44:7	to cut off from you man and **w**	802
Jer	51:22	will I break in pieces man and **w**;	802
Eze	16:30	work of an imperious whorish **w**;	802
Eze	18:6	hath come near to a menstrous **w**,	802
Eze	23:44	unto a **w** that playeth the harlot:	802
Eze	36:17	as the uncleanness of a removed **w**	
Hos	3:1	love a **w** beloved of her friend	802
Hos	13:13	sorrows of a travailing **w** shall come	
Mic	4:9	have taken thee as a **w** in travail	
Mt	5:28	**whosoever looketh on a w to lust**	*1135*
Mt	9:20	a **w**, which was diseased with an	*1136*
Mt	15:28	unto her, **O w, great is thy faith:**	*1135*
Mt	22:27	And last of all the **w** died also	*1235*
Mt	26:7	him a **w** having an alabaster box of	*1135*
Mt	26:10	unto them, **Why trouble ye the w?**	*1135*
Mt	26:13	**this, that this w hath done, be told**	
Mk	5:25	certain **w**, which had an issue of	*1135*
Mk	5:33	But the **w** fearing and trembling,	*1135*
Mk	10:12	**a w shall put away her husband,**	*1135*
Mk	14:3	came a **w** having an alabaster box	*1135*
Lk	4:26	**unto a w that was a widow.**	*1135*
Lk	7:39	what manner of **w** this is that	*1135*
Lk	7:44	said unto Simon, **Seest thou this w?**	*1135*
Lk	7:45	**this w since the time I came in**	
Lk	7:46	**this w hath anointed my feet with**	
Lk	7:50	he said to the **w, Thy faith hath**	*1135*
Lk	8:43	a **w** having an issue of blood	*1135*
Lk	13:12	**W, thou art loosed from thine**	*1135*
Lk	13:16	**And ought not this w, being a**	*1135*
Lk	13:21	**which a w took and hid in three**	*1135*
Lk	15:8	**what w having ten pieces of silver,**	*1135*
Lk	20:32	Last of all the **w** died also	*1135*
Lk	22:57	him, saying, **W**, I know him not	*1135*
Jn	2:4	**W, what have I to do with thee?**	*1135*
Jn	4:7	a **w** of Samaria to draw water	*1135*
Jn	4:21	**W, believe me, the hour cometh,**	*1135*
Jn	8:10	**W, where are ... thine accusers?**	*1135*
Jn	16:21	**A w when she is in travail hath**	*1135*
Jn	19:26	his mother, **W, behold thy son!**	*1135*
Jn	20:13	**W, why weepest thou?**	
Jn	20:15	unto her, **W, why weepest thou?**	*1135*
Ac	9:36	this **w** was full of good works	
Ac	16:14	a certain **w** named Lydia, a seller	*1135*
Ro	1:27	leaving the natural use of the **w**	*2338*
Ro	7:2	**w** which hath an husband is bound	*1135*
1Co	7:1	good for a man not to touch a **w**	*1135*
1Co	7:2	every **w** have her own husband	*1135*
1Co	7:34	**w** careth for the things of the Lord	*1135*
1Co	11:3	the head of the **w** is the man:	*1135*
1Co	11:5	**w** that prayeth or prophesieth	*1135*
1Co	11:6	if the **w** be not covered, let her	*1135*
1Co	11:7	but the **w** is the glory of the man.	*1135*
1Co	11:8	For the man is not of the **w**;	*1135*
1Co	11:9	was the man created for the **w**;	*1135*
1Co	11:10	cause ought the **w** to have power	*1135*
1Co	11:12	For as the **w** is of the man, even so	*1135*
1Co	11:12	even so is the man also by the **w**;	*1135*
1Co	11:13	a **w** pray unto God uncovered?	*1135*
1Co	11:15	if a **w** have long hair, it is a glory	*1135*
Gal	4:4	sent forth his Son, made of a **w**	*1135*
1Th	5:3	as travail upon a **w** with child;	
1Ti	2:11	Let the **w** learn in silence with	*1135*
1Ti	2:12	I suffer not a **w** to teach, nor to	*1135*
1Ti	2:14	but the **w** being deceived was in	*1235*
Rev	2:20	**thou sufferest that w Jezebel.**	*1135*
Rev	12:1	a **w** clothed with the sun, and the	*1135*
Rev	12:6	**w** fled into the wilderness, where	*1135*
Rev	12:14	to the **w** were given two wings	*1135*
Rev	12:15	mouth water as a flood after the **w**,	*1135*
Rev	12:16	the earth helped the **w**, and the	*1135*
Rev	12:17	the dragon was wroth with the **w**	*1135*
Rev	17:4	**w** was arrayed in purple and	*1135*
Rev	17:6	I saw the **w** drunken with the blood	*1135*
Rev	17:7	tell thee the mystery of the **w**,	*1135*
Rev	17:18	**w** which thou sawest is that great	*1135*

WOMANKIND See also MANKIND.
Le 18:22 not lie with mankind, as with **w** 802

WOMAN'S See also MAN'S.
Ge 38:20 his pledge from the **w** hand: 802
Ex 21:22 according as the **w** husband will........ 802
Nu 5:25 jealousy offering out of the **w** hand 802
Dt 22:5 shall a man put on a **w** garment: 802
1Ki 3:19 And this **w** child died in the night;...... 802

WOMB
Ge 25:23 Two nations are in thy **w**, and two 990
Ge 25:24 behold, there were twins in her **w**....... 990
Ge 29:31 Leah was hated, he opened her **w**: 7358
Nu 8:16 instead of such as open every **w** 7358
Jgs 13:5 be a Nazarite unto God from the **w**:..... 990
Jgs 16:17 unto God from my mother's **w**: 990
1Sa 1:5 but the Lord had shut up her **w** 7358
Job 3:11 Why died I not from the **w**? why 7358
Job 10:19 carried from the **w** to the grave......... 990
Ps 22:10 I was cast upon thee from the **w**: 7358
Ps 58:3 wicked are estranged from the **w**:...... 7358
Ps 110:3 from the **w** of the morning:........... 7358
Ps 127:3 the fruit of the **w** is his reward 990
Pr 30:16 The grave; and the barren **w**;.......... 7356
Ecc 5:15 As he came forth of his mother's **w** 990
Ecc 11:5 the bones do grow in the **w** of her 990
Isa 13:18 have no pity on the fruit of the **w**; 990
Isa 44:24 he that formed thee from the **w** 990
Isa 48:8 called a transgressor from the **w**........ 990
Isa 49:1 Lord hath called me from the **w**; 990
Isa 49:5 formed me from the **w** to be his........ 990
Isa 49:15 compassion on the son of her **w**?....... 990
Jer 1:5 before thou camest forth out of the **w**.. 7358
Jer 20:18 I forth out of the **w** to see labour 7358
Eze 20:26 the fire all that openeth the **w**......... 7356
Hos 9:16 slay even the beloved fruit of their **w**.... 990
Hos 12:3 his brother by the heel in the **w** 990
Mt 19:12 **so born from their mother's w:** *2836*
Lk 1:15 Ghost, even from his mother's **w** *2836*
Lk 1:31 thou shalt conceive in thy **w**, and *1064*
Lk 1:41 the babe leaped in her **w**: and *2836*
Lk 1:42 and blessed is the fruit of thy **w** *2836*
Lk 2:23 Every male that openeth the **w** *3388*
Lk 11:27 Blessed is the **w** that bare thee......... *2836*
Jn 3:4 second time into his mother's **w**....... *2836*
Ac 14:8 a cripple from his mother's **w**,......... *2836*
Ro 4:19 yet the deadness of Sarah's **w**: *3388*
Gal 1:15 me from my mother's **w**, and *2836*

WOMBS
Ge 20:18 Lord had fast closed up all the **w** 7358
Lk 23:29 **and the w that never bare, and**........ *2836*

WOMEN
Ge 18:11 with Sarah after the manner of **w**....... 802
Ge 31:35 for the custom of **w** is upon me 802
Ex 2:7 call to thee a nurse of the Hebrew **w**,
Le 26:26 ten **w** shall bake your bread in one...... 802
Nu 31:18 all the **w** children, that have not 802
Jos 8:25 fell that day, both of men and **w**........ 802
Jgs 5:24 Blessed above **w** shall Jael the wife 802
Jgs 9:51 and thither fled all the men and **w**...... 802
Jgs 21:16 **w** are destroyed out of Benjamin? 802
Ru 1:4 took them wives of the **w** of Moab; 802
1Sa 2:22 how they lay with the **w** that........... 802
1Sa 4:20 time of her death the **w** that stood by
1Sa 15:33 thy sword hath made **w** childless 802
1Sa 21:4 kept themselves at least from **w**......... 802
2Sa 1:26 wonderful, passing the love of **w**........ 802
2Sa 20:3 and the king took the ten **w** his......... 802
1Ki 3:16 Then came there two **w**, that were 802
1Ki 11:1 Solomon loved many strange **w** 802
2Ki 8:12 and rip up their **w** with child.
2Ch 35:25 singing **w** spake of Josiah in their
Ne 8:2 congregation both of men and **w**....... 802
Ne 13:26 him did outlandish **w** cause to sin 802
Est 1:17 queen shall come abroad unto all **w**..... 802
Est 2:9 best place of the house of the **w** 802
Est 2:12 things for the purifying of the **w**; 802
Est 2:17 king loved Esther above all the **w** 802
Est 3:13 young and old, little children and **w**..... 802
Est 8:11 both little ones and **w**, and to take 802
Job 2:10 as one of the foolish **w** speaketh.
Job 42:15 all the land were no **w** found so fair..... 802
Ps 45:9 were among thy honourable **w**:
Pr 23:33 Thine eyes shall behold strange **w**
Pr 31:3 Give not thy strength unto **w**, nor 802
SS 5:9 beloved, O thou fairest among **w**? 802
Isa 3:12 oppressors, and **w** rule over them....... 802
Isa 4:1 seven **w** shall take hold of one man,..... 802
Isa 19:16 day shall Egypt be like unto **w**: 802
Isa 32:9 Rise up, ye **w** that are at ease; hear 802
Jer 9:20 hear the word of the Lord, O ye **w** 802
Jer 44:15 and all the **w** that stood by, a great...... 802
Jer 50:37 her; and they shall become as **w**:....... 802
Jer 51:30 hath failed; they became as **w**:......... 802
La 4:10 pitiful **w** have sodden their own 802
La 5:11 They ravished the **w** in Zion, and....... 802
Eze 9:6 maids, and little children, and **w**: 802
Eze 16:38 judge thee, as **w** that break wedlock
Eze 23:10 and she became famous among **w**:...... 802
Eze 23:48 that all **w** may be taught not to do 802
Da 11:17 shall give him the daughter of **w**, ... 802
Da 11:37 nor the desire of **w**, nor regard any 802
Hos 13:16 their **w** with child shall be ripped up
Am 1:13 they have ripped up the **w** with child
Mic 2:9 **w** of my people have ye cast out........ 802
Na 3:13 people in the midst of thee are **w**: 802
Zec 5:9 behold, there came out two **w**.......... 802
Zec 14:2 houses rifled, and the **w** ravished;....... 802
Mt 11:11 **Among them that are born of w**....... *1135*
Mt 14:21 five thousand men, beside **w** and *1135*
Mt 15:38 four thousand men, beside **w** and...... *1135*
Mt 24:41 **Two w shall be grinding at the** *1135*
Mt 27:55 many **w** were there beholding.......... *1135*
Mk 15:40 were also **w** looking on afar off: *1135*
Mk 15:41 other **w** which came up with him.
Lk 1:28 blessed art thou among **w** *1135*
Lk 1:42 said, Blessed art thou among **w**, ... *1135*
Lk 7:28 **Among those that are born of w** *1135*
Lk 8:2 certain **w**, which had been healed...... *1135*
Lk 17:35 **Two w shall be grinding together;**
Lk 23:49 **w** that followed him from Galilee, ... *1135*
Lk 23:55 the **w** also, which came with him *1135*
Lk 24:10 and other **w** that were with them,
Lk 24:22 and certain **w** also of our company *1135*
Lk 24:24 it even so as the **w** had said:........... *1135*
Ac 1:14 and supplication, with the **w**, ... *1135*
Ac 8:3 haling men and **w** committed them.... *1135*
Ac 9:2 whether they were men or **w**, he....... *1135*
Ac 13:50 the devout and honourable **w**......... *1135*
Ac 17:4 and of the chief **w** not a few *1135*

Ac 17:12 honourable **w** which were Greeks...... *1135*
Ac 22:4 into prisons both men and **w** *1135*
Ro 1:26 their **w** did change the natural use *2338*
1Co 14:34 **w** keep silence in the churches:........ *1135*
1Co 14:35 for **w** to speak in the church *1135*
1Ti 2:9 **w** adorn themselves in modest *1135*
1Ti 2:10 (which becometh **w** professing *1135*
1Ti 5:2 The elder **w** as mothers; the younger
1Ti 5:14 therefore that the younger **w** marry,
2Ti 3:6 captive silly **w** laden with sins,......... *1133*
Tit 2:3 The aged **w** likewise, that they be *4247*
Heb 11:35 **W** received their dead raised to........ *1135*
1Pe 3:5 in the old time the holy **w** also,........ *1135*
Rev 9:8 they had hair as the hair of **w** *1135*
Rev 14:4 which were not defiled with **w**;........ *1135*

WON
1Ch 26:27 Out of the spoils **w** in battles did they
Pr 18:19 brother offended is harder to be **w**
1Pe 3:1 may without the word be **w**........... *2770*

WONDER
Dt 13:2 the sign or the **w** come to pass,........ 4159
Dt 28:46 upon thee for a sign and for a **w**....... 4159
2Ch 32:31 enquire of the **w** that was done........ 4159
Ps 71:7 I am as a **w** unto many; but thou 4159
Isa 29:14 even a marvellous work and a **w**: 6382
Hab 1:5 and regard, and **w** marvellously:....... 8539
Ac 3:10 and they were filled with **w** and *2285*
Ac 13:41 Behold, ye despisers, and **w** *2296*
Rev 12:1 appeared a great **w** in heaven;......... *4592*
Rev 12:3 appeared another **w** in heaven;........ *4592*
Rev 17:8 that dwell on the earth shall **w** *2296*

WONDERED
Isa 59:16 **w** that there was no intercessor: 8074
Isa 63:5 **w** that there was none to uphold:...... 8074
Mt 15:31 Insomuch that the multitude **w** *2296*
Mk 6:51 beyond measure, and **w** *2296*
Lk 2:18 that heard it **w** at those things......... *2296*
Lk 4:22 and **w** at the gracious words which *2296*
Lk 8:25 they being afraid **w**, saying one to...... *2296*
Lk 9:43 they **w** every one at all things *2296*
Lk 11:14 dumb spake; and the people **w** *2296*
Lk 24:41 they yet believed not for joy, and **w**,.... *2296*
Ac 7:31 Moses saw it, he **w** at the sight:........ *2296*
Ac 8:13 and **w**, beholding the miracles......... *1839*
Rev 13:3 and all the world **w** after the beast...... *2296*
Rev 17:6 her, I **w** with great admiration......... *2296*

WONDERFUL
Dt 28:59 the Lord will make thy plagues **w**, ... 6381
2Sa 1:26 thy love to me was **w**, passing the...... 6381
Job 42:3 things too **w** for me, which I knew..... 6381
Ps 40:5 thy **w** works which thou hast done..... 6381
Ps 78:4 and his **w** works that he hath done..... 6381
Ps 111:4 his **w** works to be remembered: 6381
Ps 119:129 Thy testimonies are **w**:............... 6382
Ps 139:6 Such knowledge is too **w** for me; 6383
Pr 30:18 be three things which are too **w** 6381
Isa 9:6 and his name shall be called **W**, ... 6382
Isa 25:1 for thou hast done **w** things; thy....... 6382
Isa 28:29 which is **w** in counsel, and............ 6381
Mt 7:22 **name done many w works?**........... *1411*
Mt 21:15 saw the **w** things that he did,.......... *2297*
Ac 2:11 our tongues the **w** works of God *3167*

WONDERFULLY
1Sa 6:6 he had wrought **w** among them,....... 5953
Ps 139:14 for I am fearfully and **w** made: 6395
La 1:9 therefore she came down **w**: she....... 6382
Da 8:24 and he shall destroy **w**, and shall....... 6381

WONDERING
Ge 24:21 the man **w** at her held his peace,....... 7583
Lk 24:12 **w** in himself at that which was *2296*
Ac 3:11 is called Solomon's, greatly **w** *1569*

WONDERS
Ex 4:21 do all those **w** before Pharaoh, ... 4159
Dt 4:34 by signs, and by **w**, and by war 4159
Dt 7:19 and the **w**, and the mighty hand, ... 4159
Jos 3:5 the Lord will do **w** among you 6381
Ne 9:10 signs and **w** upon Pharaoh 4159
Ps 77:14 Thou art the God that doest **w**: 6382
Ps 78:11 his **w** that he had shewed them........ 6381
Ps 88:10 Wilt thou shew **w** to the dead? 6382
Ps 89:5 And the heavens shall praise thy **w**..... 6382
Ps 105:5 his **w**, and the judgments of his 4159
Ps 106:7 Our fathers understood not thy **w** 6381
Ps 107:24 the Lord, and his **w** in the deep........ 6381
Ps 136:4 To him who alone doeth great **w**:...... 6381
Da 4:3 and how mighty are his **w**! 8540
Da 6:27 he worketh signs and **w** in heaven 8540
Joel 2:30 And I will shew **w** in the heavens 4159
Mt 24:24 **and shall shew great signs and w;**...... *5059*
Mk 13:22 **rise, and shall shew signs and w,** *5059*
Jn 4:48 **Except ye see signs and w, ye**.......... *5059*
Ac 2:19 And I will shew **w** in heaven above,.... *5059*
Ac 2:22 you by miracles and **w** and signs,...... *5059*
Ac 4:30 and that signs and **w** may be done *5059*
Ac 5:12 were many signs and **w** wrought....... *5059*
Ac 6:8 did great **w** and miracles among....... *5059*
Ac 15:12 declaring what miracles and **w** God.... *5059*
Ro 15:19 Through mighty signs and **w**, by *5059*
2Co 12:12 signs, and **w**, and mighty deeds........ *5059*
2Th 2:9 all power and signs and lying **w**,....... *5059*
Heb 2:4 witness, both with signs and **w** *5059*
Rev 13:13 And he doeth great **w**, so that he *4592*

WONDROUS
Job 37:14 and consider the **w** works of God...... 6381
Job 37:16 **w** work of him which is perfect 4652
Ps 72:18 of Israel, who only doeth **w** things 6381
Ps 86:10 thou art great, and doest **w** things:..... 6381
Ps 105:2 him: talk ye of all his **w** works......... 6381
Ps 119:18 behold **w** things out of thy law 6381
Ps 145:5 of thy majesty, and of thy **w** works..... 6381
Jer 21:2 us according to all his **w** works, ... 6381

WONDROUSLY
Joel 2:26 God, that hath dealt **w** with you: 6381

WOOD
Ge 6:14 Make thee an ark of gopher **w**;........ 6086
Ge 22:9 laid him on the altar upon the **w** 6086
Ex 25:10 shall make an ark of shittim **w**:........ 6086
Ex 27:1 shalt make an altar of shittim **w**....... 6086
Le 1:12 order on the **w** that is on the fire 6086
Le 6:12 the priest shall burn **w** on it every 6086
Dt 4:28 work of men's hands, **w** and stone 6086
Dt 28:36 thou serve other gods, **w** and stone 6086
Jos 9:21 but let them be hewers of **w** and....... 6086
Jgs 6:26 sacrifice with the **w** of the grove....... 6086
1Sa 23:18 and David abode in the **w**, and........ 2793

2Sa 18:17 cast him into a great pit in the **w** 3293
1Ki 18:23 and lay it on **w**, and put no fire........ 6086
1Ki 18:38 the burnt sacrifice, and the **w**,......... 6086
2Ki 19:18 work of men's hands, **w** and stone:..... 6086
1Ch 16:33 shall the trees of the **w** sing out........ 3293
Ne 8:4 the scribe stood upon a pulpit of **w**.... 6086
Ne 10:34 and the people, for the **w** offering,..... 6086
Job 41:27 as straw, and brass as rotten **w** 6086
Ps 83:14 As the fire burneth a **w**, and as 3293
Ps 96:12 shall all the trees of the **w** rejoice 3293
Pr 26:21 to burning coals, and **w** to fire;........ 6086
SS 3:9 a chariot of the **w** of Lebanon......... 6086
Isa 7:2 as the trees of the **w** are moved........ 3293
Isa 37:19 work of men's hands, **w** and stone:..... 6086
Isa 45:20 set up the **w** of their graven image..... 6086
Jer 5:14 thy mouth fire, and this people **w**...... 6086
Jer 7:18 The children gather **w**, and the........ 6086
Jer 46:22 her with axes, as hewers of **w**.......... 6086
La 5:4 for money; our **w** is sold unto us 6086
Eze 15:3 **w** be taken thereof to do any work?.... 6086
Eze 20:32 countries, to serve **w** and stone........ 6086
Da 5:23 gold, of brass, iron, **w**, and stone,....... 636
Hab 2:19 him that saith to the **w**, Awake;........ 6086
Hag 1:8 up to the mountain, and bring **w**...... 6086
Zec 12:6 an hearth of fire among the **w**......... 6086
1Co 3:12 precious stones, **w**, hay, stubble; *3586*
2Ti 2:20 silver, but also of **w** and of earth; *3585*
Rev 9:20 and brass, and stone, and of **w**:........ *3585*
Rev 18:12 manner vessels of most precious **w**,.... *3586*

WOODS
Eze 34:25 wilderness, and sleep in the **w**. 3264

WOOL
Jgs 6:37 will put a fleece of **w** in the floor;...... 6785
Ps 147:16 He giveth snow like **w**: he 6785
Pr 31:13 She seeketh **w**, and flax, and 6785
Isa 1:18 red like crimson, they shall be as **w**..... 6785
Eze 34:3 fat, and ye clothe you with the **w** 6785
Eze 44:17 and no **w** shall come upon them 6785
Da 7:9 hair of his head like the pure **w**:........ 6015
Hos 2:9 will recover my **w** and my flax 6785
Heb 9:19 and scarlet **w** and hyssop, and......... *2053*
Rev 1:14 and his hairs were white like **w**........ *2053*

WOOLLEN
Le 19:19 garment mingled of linen and **w** 8162
Dt 22:11 sorts, as of **w** and linen together. 6785

WORD
Ge 15:1 **w** of the Lord came unto Abram 1697
Ex 8:10 he said, Be it according to thy **w**: 1697
Ex 8:31 Lord according to the **w** of Moses;..... 1697
Ex 9:20 He that feared the **w** of the Lord....... 1697
Nu 11:23 whether my **w** shall come to pass...... 1697
Nu 13:26 and brought back **w** unto them 1697
Nu 15:31 hath despised the **w** of the Lord....... 1697
Nu 20:24 rebelled against my **w** at the 6310
Nu 22:18 go beyond the **w** of the Lord.......... 6310
Nu 23:5 Lord put a **w** in Balaam's mouth....... 1697
Nu 27:21 Lord: at his **w** shall they go out........ 6310
Nu 30:2 he shall not break his **w**, he shall....... 1697
Dt 4:2 add unto the **w** which I command..... 1697
Dt 8:3 but by every **w** that proceedeth out
Dt 18:20 presume to speak a **w** in my name, ... 1697
Dt 21:5 by their **w** shall every controversy...... 6310
Jos 14:7 I brought him **w** again as it was 1697
1Sa 1:23 him; only the Lord establish his **w**..... 1697
1Sa 3:1 the **w** of the Lord was precious........ 1697
1Sa 3:7 neither was the **w** of the Lord yet...... 1697
1Sa 9:27 that I may shew thee the **w** of God..... 1697
1Sa 15:23 hast rejected the **w** of the Lord,........ 1697
2Sa 3:11 could not answer Abner a **w** again, ... 1697
2Sa 19:10 speak ye not a **w** of bringing the king
2Sa 22:31 perfect; the **w** of the Lord is tried: 565
2Sa 23:2 me, and his **w** was in my tongue....... 4405
1Ki 2:23 spoken this **w** against his own life 1697
1Ki 2:27 he might fulfil the **w** of the Lord,...... 1697
1Ki 8:56 hath not failed one **w** of all his 1697
1Ki 13:2 the altar in the **w** of the Lord,......... 1697
1Ki 13:26 disobedient unto the **w** of the......... 6310
1Ki 18:36 have done all these things at thy **w**..... 1697
1Ki 19:9 the **w** of the Lord came to him........ 1697
2Ki 1:16 God in Israel to enquire of his **w**?...... 1697
2Ki 10:10 earth nothing of the **w** of the Lord, ... 1697
2Ki 18:36 peace, and answered him not a **w**: 1697
2Ki 20:19 Good is the **w** of the Lord which 1697
1Ch 17:6 spake I a **w** to any of the judges of..... 1697
1Ch 21:6 king's **w** was abominable to Joab 1697
1Ch 21:12 what **w** I shall bring again to him...... 1697
2Ch 6:10 hath performed his **w** that he hath..... 1697
2Ch 36:21 To fulfil the **w** of the Lord by the 1697
Ezr 1:1 **w** of the lord by the mouth of......... 1697
Ezr 6:11 that whosoever shall alter this **w**....... 6600
Est 7:8 **w** went out of the king's mouth 1697
Ps 18:30 the **w** of the Lord is tried: he is a 565
Ps 33:4 For the **w** of the Lord is right;......... 1697
Ps 33:6 By the **w** of the Lord were the......... 1697
Ps 56:4 In God I will praise his **w**, in God I 1697
Ps 68:11 The Lord gave the **w**: great was......... 562
Ps 105:28 they rebelled not against his **w** 1697
Ps 106:24 land, they believed not his **w**: 1697
Ps 119:11 Thy **w** have I hid in mine heart......... 565
Ps 119:42 me: for I trust in thy **w**.............. 1697
Ps 119:67 astray: but now have I kept thy **w**....... 565
Ps 119:74 because I have hoped in thy **w** 1697
Ps 119:81 salvation: but I hope in thy **w**......... 1697
Ps 119:89 Lord, thy **w** is settled in heaven........ 1697
Ps 119:105 Thy **w** is a lamp unto my feet, and..... 1697
Ps 119:140 Thy **w** is very pure: therefore thy 565
Ps 119:148 that I might meditate in thy **w** 565
Ps 119:160 Thy **w** is true from the beginning: 1697
Ps 119:162 I rejoice at thy **w**, as one that........... 565
Ps 138:2 hast magnified thy **w** above all 565
Pr 12:25 but a good **w** maketh it glad 1697
Pr 13:13 despiseth the **w** shall be destroyed:..... 1697
Pr 15:23 and a **w** spoken in due season......... 1697
Pr 25:11 A **w** fitly spoken is like apples of....... 1697
Pr 30:5 Every **w** of God is pure: he is a 565
Ecc 8:4 Where the **w** of a king is, there is 1697
Isa 8:10 speak the **w**, and it shall not 1697
Isa 28:13 the **w** of the Lord was unto them...... 1697
Isa 30:21 ears shall hear a **w** behind thee, ... 1697
Isa 36:21 peace, and answered him not a **w**: 1697
Isa 40:8 **w** of our God shall stand for ever...... 1697
Isa 45:23 the **w** is gone out of my mouth in 1697
Isa 55:11 So shall my **w** be that goeth forth...... 1697
Isa 66:2 spirit, and trembleth at my **w**.......... 1697
Jer 1:12 I will hasten my **w** to perform it....... 1697
Jer 5:13 wind, and the **w** is not in them: 1699
Jer 6:10 the **w** of the Lord is unto them a 1697
Jer 8:9 have rejected the **w** of the Lord: 1697
Jer 15:16 and thy **w** was unto me the joy........ 1697

Jer	18:18	wise, nor the **w** from the prophet	1697
Jer	20:8	the **w** of the Lord was made a	1697
Jer	20:9	**w** was in mine heart as a burning	
Jer	23:18	who hath marked his **w**, and heard	1697
Jer	23:28	let him speak my **w** faithfully	1697
Jer	23:29	Is not my **w** like as a fire? saith the	1697
Jer	23:36	every man's **w** shall be his burden;	1697
Jer	27:18	if the **w** of the Lord be with them,	1697
Jer	28:9	the **w** of the prophet shall come to	1697
Jer	37:17	Is there any **w** from the Lord?	1697
Eze	12:25	**w** that I shall speak shall come to	1697
Eze	16:35	O harlot, hear the **w** of the Lord:	1697
Eze	21:2	drop thy **w** toward the holy places,	
Eze	33:7	shalt hear the **w** at my mouth,	1697
Eze	37:4	dry bones, hear the **w** of the Lord.	1697
Da	3:28	and have changed the king's **w**	4406
Da	4:17	demand by the **w** of the holy ones:	3983
Da	4:31	the **w** was in the king's mouth,	4406
Da	9:2	**w** of the Lord came to Jeremiah	1697
Joel	2:11	he is strong that executeth his **w**:	1697
Am	7:16	not thy **w** against the house of Isaac	
Am	8:12	and fro to seek the **w** of the Lord	1697
Hag	2:5	the **w** that I covenanted with you	1697
Zec	11:11	knew that it was the **w** of the Lord.	1697
Mt	2:8	bring me **w** again, that I may	*518*
Mt	4:4	**by every w that proceedeth out**	*4487*
Mt	8:8	but speak the **w** only, and my	*3056*
Mt	8:16	he cast out the spirits with his **w**,	*3056*
Mt	12:32	**speaketh a w against the Son of**	*3056*
Mt	12:36	**every idle w that men shall speak,**	*4487*
Mt	13:22	**choke the w, and he becometh**	*3056*
Mt	15:23	But he answered her not a **w**	*3056*
Mt	18:16	**every w may be established.**	*4487*
Mt	22:46	man was able to answer him a **w**,	*3056*
Mt	26:75	remembered the **w** of Jesus,	*4487*
Mt	27:14	he answered him to never a **w**:	*4487*
Mk	4:14	**The sower soweth the w.**	*3056*
Mk	4:20	**such as hear the w, and receive it,**	*3056*
Mk	7:13	**Making the w of God of none.**	*3056*
Mk	16:20	and confirming the **w** with signs	*3056*
Lk	1:2	and ministers of the **w**;	*3056*
Lk	1:38	be it unto me according to thy **w**	*4487*
Lk	2:29	in peace, according to thy **w**:	*4487*
Lk	4:4	**alone, but by every w of God.**	*4487*
Lk	4:32	for his **w** was with power	*3056*
Lk	5:5	at thy **w** I will let down the net	*4487*
Lk	8:12	**away the w out of their hearts.**	*3056*
Lk	8:15	**heart, having heard the w, keep it,**	*3056*
Lk	11:28	**hear the w of God, and keep it.**	*3056*
Lk	12:10	**speak a w against the Son of man,**	*3056*
Lk	22:61	remembered the **w** of the Lord	*3056*
Lk	24:19	mighty in deed and **w** before God	*3056*
Jn	1:1	In the beginning was the **W**,	*3056*
Jn	1:1	and the **W** was with God,	*3056*
Jn	1:1	and the **W** was God	*3056*
Jn	1:14	the **W** was made flesh, and dwelt	*3056*
Jn	5:38	**ye have not his w abiding in you:**	*3056*
Jn	8:31	**If ye continue in my w, then are**	*3056*
Jn	8:37	**my w hath no place in you.**	*3056*
Jn	8:43	**because ye cannot hear my w.**	*3056*
Jn	10:35	**unto whom the w of God came,**	*3056*
Jn	12:48	**w that I have spoken, the same**	*3056*
Jn	14:24	**the w which ye hear is not mine,**	*3056*
Jn	15:3	**w which I have spoken unto you**	*3056*
Jn	15:20	**Remember the w that I said**	*3056*
Jn	15:25	**that the w might be fulfilled**	*3056*
Jn	17:6	**me; and they have kept thy w.**	*3056*
Jn	17:14	**I have given them thy w; and**	*3056*
Jn	17:17	**through thy truth: thy w is truth.**	*3056*
Jn	17:20	**believe on me through their w;**	*3056*
Ac	4:31	spake the **w** of God with boldness	*3056*
Ac	6:4	and to the ministry of the **w**	*3056*
Ac	11:16	remembered I the **w** of the Lord.	*4487*
Ac	11:19	preaching the **w** to none but unto	*3056*
Ac	13:26	to you is the **w** of this salvation.	*3056*
Ac	13:46	It was necessary that the **w** of God	*3056*
Ac	14:3	which gave testimony unto the **w**	*3056*
Ac	17:11	received the **w** with all readiness	*3056*
Ro	9:6	Not as though the **w** of God hath	*3056*
Ro	9:9	For this is the **w** of promise	*3056*
Ro	10:8	**w** is nigh thee, even in thy mouth,	*4487*
1Co	4:20	the kingdom of God is not in **w**,	*3056*
1Co	12:8	given by the Spirit the **w** of wisdom;	*3056*
1Co	14:36	came the **w** of God out from you?	*3056*
2Co	2:17	many, which corrupt the **w** of God:	*3056*
2Co	4:2	the **w** of God deceitfully;	*3056*
2Co	5:19	unto us the **w** of reconciliation	*3056*
2Co	13:1	shall every **w** be established	*4487*
Gal	5:14	all the law is fulfilled in one **w**.	*4487*
Eph	5:26	the washing of water by the **w**.	*4487*
Eph	6:17	the Spirit, which is the **w** of God:	*4487*
Php	1:14	bold to speak the **w** without fear.	*3056*
Php	2:16	Holding forth the **w** of life; that I	*3056*
Col	3:16	Let the **w** of Christ dwell in you	*3056*
Col	3:17	whatsoever ye do in **w** or deed, do	*3056*
1Th	1:6	received the **w** in much affliction,	*3056*
1Th	2:13	ye received it not as the **w** of men,	*3056*
1Th	2:13	but as it is in truth, the **w** of God,	*3056*
2Th	2:2	neither by spirit, nor by **w**,	*3056*
2Th	3:1	the **w** of the Lord may have free	*3056*
1Ti	4:5	is sanctified by the **w** of God and	*3056*
1Ti	4:12	an example of the believers, in **w**	*3056*
1Ti	5:17	they who labour in the **w** and	*3056*
2Ti	2:9	but the **w** of God is not bound	*3056*
2Ti	2:15	rightly dividing the **w** of truth.	*3056*
2Ti	4:2	Preach the **w**; be instant in	*3056*
Tit	1:9	Holding fast the faithful **w** as he	*3056*
Tit	2:5	the **w** of God be not blasphemed	*3056*
Heb	1:3	all things by the **w** of his power	*4487*
Heb	2:2	For if the **w** spoken by angels was	*3056*
Heb	4:2	**w** preached did not profit them	*3056*
Heb	4:12	For the **w** of God is quick, and	*3056*
Heb	5:13	unskilful in the **w** of righteousness:	*3056*
Heb	6:5	have tasted the good **w** of God	*4487*
Heb	11:3	were framed by the **w** of God	*4487*
Heb	12:27	this **w**, Yet once more, signifieth	
Jas	1:18	begat he us with the **w** of truth	*3056*
Jas	1:22	But be ye doers of the **w**, and not	*3056*
Jas	3:2	If any man offend not in **w**, the	*3056*
1Pe	1:23	by the **w** of God, which liveth and	*3056*
1Pe	2:2	desire the sincere milk of the **w**,	*3050*
2Pe	1:19	also a more sure **w** of prophecy;	*3056*
2Pe	3:5	by the **w** of God the heavens were	*3056*
1Jn	1:1	have handled, of the **W** of life;	*3056*
1Jn	1:10	him a liar, and his **w** is not in us	*3056*
1Jn	2:5	But whoso keepeth his **w**, in him	*3056*
1Jn	2:14	and the **w** of God abideth in you	*3056*
1Jn	3:18	children, let us not love in **w**,	*3056*
1Jn	5:7	the Father, the **W**, and the Holy	*3056*
Rev	1:2	Who bare record of the **w** of God,	*3056*
Rev	1:9	for the **w** of God, and for the	*3056*
Rev	3:8	**and hast kept my w, and hast not.**	*3056*

Rev 3:10 **hast kept the w of my patience,** *3056*
Rev 6:9 that were slain for the **w** of God, ... *3056*
Rev 19:13 his name is called The **W** of God,....... *3056*
Rev 20:4 and for the **w** of God, and which *3056*

WORDS

Ge 27:34 Esau heard the **w** of his father, ... 1697
Ex 4:28 told Aaron all the **w** of the Lord 1697
Ex 5:9 and let them not regard vain **w**........ 1697
Ex 23:8 perverteth the **w** of the righteous...... 1697
Ex 34:1 the **w** that were in the first tables 1697
Ex 34:27 unto Moses, Write thou these **w**: 1697
Ex 34:28 the tables the **w** of the covenant 1697
Dt 1:34 the Lord heard the voice of your **w**,.... 1697
Dt 4:10 and I will make them hear my **w**,...... 1697
Dt 5:28 the voice of the **w** of this people, ... 1697
Dt 10:2 the **w** that were in the first tables 1697
Dt 11:18 lay up these my **w** in your heart 1697
Dt 16:19 and pervert the **w** of the righteous. 1697
Dt 17:19 to keep all the **w** of this law and 1697
Dt 18:18 and will put my **w** in his mouth; 1697
Dt 27:8 upon the stones all the **w** of this law ... 1697
Dt 29:9 therefore the **w** of this covenant 1697
Dt 31:12 observe to do all the **w** of this law:..... 1697
Dt 32:46 hearts unto all the **w** which I testify.... 1697
Jos 2:21 According unto your **w**, so be it 1697
Jos 8:34 he read all the **w** of the law,........... 1697
Jgs 2:4 angel of the Lord spake these **w** 1697
Jgs 13:12 said, Now let thy **w** come to pass 1697
1Sa 3:19 none of his **w** fall to the ground 1697
1Sa 8:10 Samuel told all the **w** of the Lord 1697
1Sa 21:12 And David laid up these **w** in his 1697
1Sa 28:20 afraid, because of the **w** of Samuel: 1697
2Sa 7:28 and thy **w** be true, and thou hast 1697
2Sa 14:3 So Joab put the **w** in her mouth 1697
2Sa 23:1 Now these be the last **w** of David 1697
1Ki 1:14 in after thee, and confirm thy **w** 1697
1Ki 3:12 I have done according to thy **w**: 1697
2Ki 6:12 the **w** that thou speakest in thy........ 1697
2Ki 22:11 king had heard the **w** of the book...... 1697
2Ki 22:13 the **w** of this book that is found:....... 1697
2Ki 23:3 to perform the **w** of this covenant 1697
1Ch 23:27 by the last **w** of David the Levites...... 1697
2Ch 9:6 I believed not their **w**, until I came,.... 1697
2Ch 11:4 they obeyed the **w** of the Lord,........ 1697
2Ch 34:21 the **w** of the book that is found: 1697
2Ch 34:31 to perform the **w** of the covenant...... 1697
2Ch 36:16 despised his **w**, and misused his 1697
Ezr 7:11 of the **w** of the commandments 1697
Ne 8:9 when they heard the **w** of the law...... 1697
Ne 8:12 the **w** that were declared unto......... 1697
Job 6:10 concealed the **w** of the Holy One 561
Job 12:11 Doth not the ear try **w**? and the 4405
Job 19:2 and break me in pieces with **w**? 4405
Job 19:23 Oh that my **w** were now written! 4405
Job 23:12 have esteemed the **w** of his mouth 561
Job 34:3 For the ear trieth **w**, as the mouth 4405
Job 35:16 he multiplieth **w** with knowledge...... 4405
Job 38:2 counsel by **w** without knowledge? 4405
Job 41:3 will he speak soft **w** unto thee?
Ps 12:6 The **w** of the Lord are pure **w** 565
Ps 19:4 their **w** to the end of the world........ 4405
Ps 19:14 Let the **w** of my mouth, and the 561
Ps 22:1 and from the **w** of my roaring?........ 1697
Ps 50:17 and castest my **w** behind thee. 1697
Ps 55:21 his **w** were softer than oil, yet were..... 1697
Ps 56:5 Every day they wrest my **w**: all 1697
Ps 107:11 rebelled against the **w** of God 561
Ps 109:3 me about also with **w** of hatred;....... 1697
Ps 119:103 sweet are thy **w** unto my taste! 565
Ps 119:130 entrance of thy **w** giveth light;......... 1697
Pr 1:2 to perceive the **w** of understanding;..... 561
Pr 1:6 the **w** of the wise, and their dark 1697
Pr 1:23 will make known my **w** unto you...... 1697
Pr 2:1 My son, if thou wilt receive my **w**, ... 561
Pr 2:16 which flattereth with her **w**;............ 561
Pr 4:20 My son, attend to my **w**; incline 1697
Pr 7:1 My son, keep my **w**, and lay up my 561
Pr 7:5 which flattereth with her **w** 561
Pr 10:19 multitude of **w** there wanteth not...... 1697
Pr 12:6 **w** of the wicked are to lie in wait 1697
Pr 15:1 but grievous **w** stir up anger 1697
Pr 15:26 the **w** of the pure are pleasant **w**
Pr 16:24 Pleasant **w** are as an honeycomb, ... 561
Pr 18:4 The **w** of the man's mouth are as 1697
Pr 18:8 **w** of a talebearer are as wounds 1697
Pr 19:7 he pursueth them with **w**, yet they...... 561
Pr 19:27 to err from the **w** of knowledge 561
Pr 22:21 the certainty of the **w** of truth; 561
Pr 22:21 mightest answer the **w** of truth......... 561
Pr 23:9 will despise the wisdom of thy **w** 4405
Pr 26:22 **w** of a talebearer are as wounds,........ 1697
Pr 29:20 thou a man that is hasty in his **w**? 1697
Pr 30:6 Add thou not unto his **w**, lest he....... 1697
Ecc 5:2 earth: therefore let thy **w** be few 1697
Ecc 5:3 voice is known by multitude of **w** 1697
Ecc 5:7 and many **w** there are also divers 1697
Ecc 10:14 A fool also is full of **w** a man.......... 1697
Ecc 12:10 sought to find out acceptable **w**:....... 1697
Ecc 12:11 The **w** of the wise are as goads,......... 1697
Isa 31:2 evil, and will not call back his **w**: 1697
Isa 32:7 to destroy the poor with lying **w**, ... 561
Isa 36:5 thou, (but they are but vain **w**) I 1697
Isa 36:22 and told him the **w** of Rabshakeh...... 1697
Isa 37:4 God will hear the **w** of Rabshakeh,..... 1697
Isa 37:4 will reprove the **w** which the Lord 1697
Isa 37:6 of the **w** that thou hast heard 1697
Isa 41:26 there is none that heareth your **w**....... 561
Isa 51:16 I have put my **w** in thy mouth,........ 1697
Jer 5:14 I will make my **w** in thy mouth fire,.... 1697
Jer 7:4 Trust ye not in lying **w**, saying, ... 1697
Jer 11:3 obeyeth not the **w** of this covenant,.... 1697
Jer 12:6 though they speak fair **w** unto thee
Jer 15:16 Thy **w** were found and I did eat 1697
Jer 23:9 because of the **w** of his holiness 1697
Jer 23:16 not unto the **w** of the prophets........ 1697
Jer 23:30 steal my **w** every one from his......... 1697
Jer 23:36 perverted the **w** of the living God...... 1697
Jer 26:5 hearken to the **w** of my servants....... 1697
Jer 26:15 to speak all these **w** in your ears 1697
Jer 29:23 have spoken lying **w** in my name,...... 1697
Jer 34:18 **w** of the covenant which they had 1697
Jer 36:16 surely tell the king of all these **w**....... 1697
Jer 36:28 the former **w** that were in the first 1697
Jer 39:16 bring my **w** upon this city for evil 1697
Jer 44:28 shall know whose **w** shall stand 1697
Jer 44:29 know that my **w** shall surely stand 1697
Eze 2:6 be not afraid of their **w**, nor be........ 1697
Eze 3:6 **w** thou canst not understand 1697
Eze 33:31 they hear thy **w**, but they will not...... 1697
Eze 35:13 have multiplied your **w** against me:.... 1697
Da 2:9 corrupt **w** to speak before me 4406

Da	6:14	the king, when he heard these **w**	4406
Da	7:25	great **w** against the most High	4406
Da	9:12	And he hath confirmed his **w**,	1697
Da	10:6	his **w** like the voice of a multitude	1697
Da	12:4	O Daniel, shut up the **w**, and seal	1697
Hos	6:5	slain them by the **w** of my mouth:	561
Am	7:10	land is not able to bear all his **w**.	1697
Am	8:11	but of hearing the **w** of the Lord:	1697
Zec	1:13	with good **w** and comfortable **w**	1697
Mal	2:17	wearied the Lord with your **w**	1697
Mal	3:13	Your **w** have been stout against	1697
Mt	12:37	**by thy w thou shalt be justified,**	*3056*
Mt	12:37	**thy w thou shalt be condemned.**	*3056*
Mt	24:35	**but my w shall not pass away.**	*3056*
Mt	26:44	third time, saying the same **w**	*3056*
Mk	8:38	**be ashamed of me and of my w**	*3056*
Mk	13:31	**but my w shall not pass away.**	*3056*
Lk	1:20	because thou believest not my **w**,	*3056*
Lk	9:26	**be ashamed of me and of my w,**	*3056*
Lk	20:26	they could not take hold of his **w**	*4487*
Lk	21:33	**but my w shall not pass away.**	*3056*
Lk	23:9	questioned with him in many **w**;	*3056*
Lk	24:8	And they remembered his **w**	*4487*
Lk	24:11	their **w** seemed to them as idle	*4487*
Jn	5:47	**how shall ye believe my w?**	*4487*
Jn	6:68	go? thou hast the **w** of eternal life	*4487*
Jn	8:47	**that is of God heareth God's w:**	*4487*
Jn	10:21	the **w** of him that hath a devil	*4487*
Jn	12:47	**And if any man hear my w, and**	*4487*
Jn	12:48	**and receiveth not my w, hath**	*4487*
Jn	14:23	**man love me, he will keep my w:**	*3056*
Jn	15:7	**my w abide in you, ye shall ask.**	*4487*
Jn	17:8	**them the w which thou gavest me;**	*4487*
Ac	5:5	Ananias hearing these **w** fell down	*3056*
Ac	5:20	to the people all the **w** of this life	*4487*
Ac	6:11	blasphemous **w** against Moses	*4487*
Ac	6:13	blasphemous **w** against this holy	*4487*
Ac	7:22	was mighty in **w** and in deeds	*3056*
Ac	10:44	While Peter yet spake these **w**	*4487*
Ac	15:15	this agree the **w** of the prophets:	*3056*
Ac	18:15	it be a question of **w** and names,	*3056*
Ac	20:35	remember the **w** of the Lord Jesus,	*3056*
Ac	20:38	most of all for the **w** which he spake	*3056*
Ac	26:25	but speak forth the **w** of truth	*4487*
Ro	10:18	**w** unto the ends of the world	*4487*
Ro	16:18	good **w** and fair speeches deceive	*5542*
1Co	2:4	with enticing **w** of man's wisdom	*3056*
1Co	2:13	**w** which man's wisdom teacheth,	*3056*
1Co	14:9	tongue **w** easy to be understood,	*3056*
1Co	14:19	five **w** with my understanding,	*3056*
1Co	14:19	thousand **w** in an unknown tongue	*3056*
2Co	12:4	and heard unspeakable **w**, which	*4487*
Eph	5:6	no man deceive you with vain **w**:	*3056*
Col	2:4	beguile you with enticing **w**	*4086*
1Th	2:5	any time used we flattering **w**,	*3056*
1Th	4:18	comfort one another with these **w**	*3056*
1Ti	4:6	nourished up in the **w** of faith and	*3056*
1Ti	6:3	and consent not to wholesome **w**	*3056*
1Ti	6:4	about questions and strifes of **w**,	*3055*
2Ti	1:13	Hold fast the form of sound **w**	*3056*
2Ti	2:14	strive not about **w** to no profit	*3054*
2Ti	4:15	he hath greatly withstood our **w**	*3056*
Heb	12:19	a trumpet, and the voice of **w**;	*4487*
2Pe	2:18	speak great swelling **w** of vanity,	
Rev	1:3	that hear the **w** of this prophecy	*3056*
Rev	17:17	the **w** of God shall be fulfilled	*4487*
Rev	21:5	for these **w** are true and faithful	*3056*
Rev	22:19	**w** of the book of this prophecy,	*3056*

WORK

Ge	2:2	the seventh day God ended his **w**	4399
Ex	5:11	of your **w** shall be diminished	5656
Ex	12:16	no manner of **w** shall be done in	4399
Ex	14:31	saw that great **w** which the Lord	3027
Ex	20:9	thou labour, and do all thy **w**:	4399
Ex	20:10	in it thou shalt not do any **w**, thou	4399
Ex	23:12	Six days thou shalt do thy **w**, and	4639
Ex	25:18	beaten **w** shalt thou make them,	4749
Ex	26:31	fine twined linen of cunning **w**:	4639
Ex	28:11	the **w** of an engraver in stone, like	4639
Ex	31:14	whosoever doeth any **w** therein	4399
Ex	31:15	Six days may **w** be done; but in	4399
Ex	32:16	the tables were the **w** of God, and	4639
Ex	35:21	offering to the **w** of the tabernacle	4399
Ex	36:4	wrought all the **w** of the sanctuary	4399
Ex	37:29	to the **w** of the apothecary	4639
Le	16:29	and do no **w** at all, whether it be	4399
Le	23:3	Six days shall **w** be done: but the	4399
Le	23:28	ye shall do no **w** in that same day:	4399
Nu	4:3	to do the **w** in the tabernacle of	4399
Nu	29:12	ye shall do no servile **w**, and ye	4399
Nu	29:35	ye shall do no servile **w** therein:	4399
Dt	4:28	serve gods, the **w** of men's hands	4639
Dt	5:14	in it thou shalt not do any **w**, thou,	4399
Dt	14:29	thee in all the **w** of thine hand	4639
Dt	15:19	shalt do no **w** with the firstling	5647
Dt	24:19	thee in all the **w** of thine hands	4639
Dt	28:12	to bless all the **w** of thine hand:	4639
Dt	31:29	through the **w** of your hands	4639
Dt	32:4	He is the Rock, his **w** is perfect:	6467
Ru	2:12	The Lord recompense thy **w**, and	6467
1Sa	14:6	may be that the Lord will **w** for us:	6213
1Ki	7:51	ended all the **w** that king Solomon	4399
1Ki	21:20	**w** evil in the sight of the Lord	6213
1Ki	21:25	did sell himself to **w** wickedness	6213
2Ki	19:18	no gods, but the **w** of men's hands,	4639
1Ch	6:49	all the **w** of the place most holy	4399
1Ch	23:28	the **w** of the service of the house	4639
1Ch	29:1	and tender, and the **w** is great:	4399
2Ch	8:9	make no servants for his **w**;	4399
2Ch	15:7	for your **w** shall be rewarded	6468
2Ch	24:13	and the **w** was perfected by them,	4399
2Ch	29:34	till the **w** was ended, and until the	4399
Ezr	4:24	ceased the **w** of the house of God	5673
Ezr	6:7	Let the **w** of this house of God	5673
Ezr	10:13	is this a **w** of one day or two:	4399
Ne	2:18	their hands for this good **w**	
Ne	4:6	for the people had a mind to **w**.	6213
Ne	4:17	one of his hands wrought in the **w**,	4399
Ne	6:3	why should the **w** cease, whilst I	4399
Ne	6:16	this **w** was wrought of our God	4399
Job	1:10	hast blessed the **w** of his hands	4639
Job	34:19	they all are the **w** of his hands	4639
Ps	8:3	thy heavens, the **w** of thy fingers	4639
Ps	58:2	Yea, in heart ye **w** wickedness;	6466
Ps	62:12	to every man according to his **w**	4639
Ps	64:9	and shall declare the **w** of God;	6467
Ps	90:17	establish thou the **w** of our hands	4639
Ps	102:25	heavens are the **w** of thy hands	4639
Ps	135:15	and gold, the **w** of men's hands	4639
Pr	11:18	wicked worketh a deceitful **w**:	6468
Pr	20:11	doings, whether his **w** be pure	6467

Pr	21:8	as for the pure, his **w** is right	6467
Pr	24:29	to the man according to his **w**.	6467
Ecc	2:17	**w** that is wrought under the sun.	4639
Ecc	3:11	find out the **w** that God maketh	4639
Ecc	3:17	every purpose and for every **w**	4639
Ecc	5:6	and destroy the **w** of thine hands?	4639
Ecc	7:13	Consider the **w** of God: for who	4639
Ecc	8:11	sentence against an evil **w** is not	4639
Ecc	8:17	Then I beheld all the **w** of God	4639
Ecc	12:14	bring every **w** into judgment	4639
Isa	2:8	worship the **w** of their own hands	4639
Isa	29:14	marvellous **w** among this people,	6381
Isa	29:16	shall the **w** say of him that made it,	4639
Isa	32:6	and his heart will **w** iniquity, to	6213
Isa	37:19	the **w** of men's hands, wood and	4639
Isa	40:10	with him, and his **w** before him	6468
Isa	45:9	What makest thou? or thy **w**,	6467
Isa	61:8	and I will direct their **w** in truth	6468
Isa	64:8	and we all are the **w** of thine hand	4639
Isa	65:22	long enjoy the **w** of their hands.	4639
Jer	10:15	are vanity, and the **w** of errors:	4639
Jer	17:22	neither do ye any **w**, but hallow	4399
Jer	18:3	he wrought a **w** on the wheels.	4399
Jer	31:16	for thy **w** shall be rewarded, saith	6468
Jer	48:10	the **w** of the Lord deceitfully	4399
Jer	51:18	They are vanity, the **w** of errors:	4639
La	3:64	according to the **w** of their hands	4639
La	4:2	the **w** of the hands of the potter!	4639
Eze	15:5	was whole, it was meet for no **w**:	4399
Eze	33:26	ye **w** abomination, and ye defile	6213
Da	11:23	with him he shall **w** deceitfully:	6213
Hos	13:2	all of it the **w** of the craftsman:	4639
Hos	14:3	any more to the **w** of our hands	4639
Mic	2:1	and **w** evil upon their beds!	6466
Mic	5:13	worship the **w** of thine hands	4639
Hab	1:5	a **w** in your days, which ye will	6467
Hab	2:18	maker of his **w** trusteth therein.	3336
Hab	3:2	revive thy **w** in the midst of the	6467
Hag	2:14	and so is every **w** of their hands;	4639
Mal	3:15	that **w** wickedness are set up;	6213
Mt	7:23	**from me, ye that w iniquity.**	*2038*
Mt	21:28	**Son, go w to day in my vineyard.**	*2038*
Mt	26:10	**hath wrought a good w upon me.**	*2041*
Mk	6:5	he could there do no mighty **w**,	*1411*
Mk	14:6	she hath wrought a good **w** on me	*2041*
Lk	13:14	days in which men ought to **w**:	*2038*
Jn	4:34	**that sent me, and to finish his w.**	*2041*
Jn	5:17	**worketh hitherto, and I w.**	*2038*
Jn	6:29	**This is the w of God, that ye**	*2041*
Jn	7:21	**I have done one w, and ye all**	*2041*
Jn	9:4	**I must w the works of him that**	*2038*
Jn	9:4	**cometh, when no man can w**	*2038*
Jn	17:4	**finished the w which thou gavest**	*2041*
Ac	13:41	a **w** which ye shall in no wise believe	*2041*
Ro	2:15	shew the **w** of the law written in	*2041*
Ro	7:5	did **w** in our members to bring.	*1754*
Ro	8:28	all things **w** together for good to	*4903*
Ro	11:6	otherwise **w** is no more **w**	*2041*
1Co	3:13	fire shall try every man's **w**.	*2041*
1Co	3:14	If any man's **w** abide which he	*2041*
1Co	3:15	If any man's **w** shall be burned, he	*2041*
1Co	9:1	are not ye my **w** in the Lord?	*2041*
1Co	15:58	abounding in the **w** of the Lord,	*2041*
2Co	9:8	may abound to every good **w**:	*2041*
Gal	6:4	But let every man prove his own **w**,	*2041*
Eph	4:12	for the **w** of the ministry, for the	*2041*
Php	1:6	which hath begun a good **w** in you	*2041*
Php	2:12	**w** out your own salvation with	*2716*
Php	2:30	for the **w** of Christ he was nigh	*2041*
Col	1:10	being fruitful in every good **w**, and	*2041*
2Th	2:7	mystery of iniquity doth already **w**:	*1754*
2Th	3:10	that if any would not **w**, neither	*2038*
2Th	3:12	that with quietness they **w**, and	*2038*
2Ti	2:21	and prepared unto every good **w**	*2041*
2Ti	4:5	do the **w** of an evangelist, make	*2041*
2Ti	4:18	shall deliver me from every evil **w**	*2041*
Tit	3:1	to be ready to every good **w**.	*2041*
Heb	6:10	forget your **w** and labour of love,	*2041*
Heb	13:21	Make you perfect in every good **w**	*2041*
Jas	1:4	let patience have her perfect **w**,	*2041*
Jas	1:25	but a doer of the **w**, this man shall	*2041*
1Pe	1:17	according to every man's **w**	*2041*
Rev	22:12	man according as his **w** shall be	*2041*

WORKERS

2Ki	23:24	Moreover the **w** with familiar spirits,	
Job	31:3	punishment to the **w** of iniquity?	6466
Job	34:22	where the **w** of iniquity may hide	6466
Ps	5:5	thou hatest all **w** of iniquity	6466
Ps	6:8	from me, all ye **w** of iniquity;	6466
Ps	14:4	the **w** of iniquity no knowledge?	6466
Ps	36:12	There are the **w** of iniquity fallen:	6466
Ps	94:4	**w** of iniquity boast themselves?	6466
Ps	94:16	for me against the **w** of iniquity?	6466
Pr	21:15	shall be to the **w** of iniquity.	6466
Lk	13:27	**from me, all ye w of iniquity.**	*2040*
1Co	12:29	teachers? are all **w** of miracles?	*1411*
2Co	11:13	as are false apostles, deceitful **w**.	*2040*
Php	3:2	Beware of dogs, beware of evil **w**,	*2040*

WORKETH

Ps	101:7	He that **w** deceit shall not dwell	6213
Pr	26:28	and a flattering mouth **w** ruin.	6213
Pr	31:13	and **w** willingly with her hands.	6213
Da	6:27	**w** signs and wonders in heaven.	5648
Jn	5:17	**Father w hitherto, and I work.**	*2038*
Ro	4:4	to him that **w** is the reward not.	*2038*
Ro	4:5	But to him that **w** not, but	*2038*
Ro	5:3	knowing … tribulation **w** patience;	*2716*
Ro	13:10	Love **w** no ill to his neighbour:	*2038*
1Co	12:6	the same God which **w** all in all	*1754*
1Co	12:11	**w** that one and the selfsame Spirit	*1754*
2Co	4:12	So then death **w** in us, but life in	*1754*
2Co	4:17	**w** for us a far more exceeding	*2716*
2Co	7:10	godly sorrow **w** repentance unto.	*2716*
2Co	7:10	the sorrow of the world **w** death.	*2716*
Gal	5:6	but faith which **w** by love.	*1754*
Eph	1:11	purpose of him who **w** all things	*1754*
Eph	2:2	spirit that now **w** in the children.	*1754*
Php	2:13	is God which **w** in you both to will	*1754*
Jas	1:3	trying of your faith **w** patience	*2716*
Jas	1:20	**w** not the righteousness of God	*2716*
Rev	21:27	whatsoever **w** abomination, or	*4160*

WORKING

Ps	52:2	like a sharp rasor, **w** deceitfully	6213
Ps	74:12	**w** salvation in the midst of the	6466
Ro	1:27	men **w** that which is unseemly	*2716*
Ro	7:13	**w** death in me by that which is	*2716*
1Co	4:12	labour, **w** with our own hands:	*2038*
1Co	12:10	To another the **w** of miracles;	*1755*
Eph	4:28	**w** with his hands the thing which	*2038*
Col	1:29	striving according to his **w**, which	*1753*

2Th 2:9 coming is after the **w** of Satan ... *1753*
2Th 3:11 **w** not at all, but are busybodies ... *2038*
Heb 13:21 his will, **w** in you that which is ... *4160*
Rev 16:14 the spirits of devils, **w** miracles, ... *4160*

WORKMAN
Isa 40:19 The **w** melteth a graven image, ... 2796
Hos 8:6 the **w** made it; therefore it is not ... 2796
Mt 10:10 for the **w** is worthy of his meat. ... *2040*
2Ti 2:15 a **w** that needeth not to be ... *2040*

WORKMANSHIP
Ex 31:3 and in all manner of **w**. ... 4399
Ex 35:31 and in all manner of **w**; ... 4399
Eph 2:10 For we are his **w**, created in ... *4161*

WORKMEN
2Ki 12:15 money to be bestowed on **w** ... 6213, 4399
1Ch 22:15 are **w** with thee in abundance ... 6213, 4399
Ac 19:25 with the **w** of like occupation, ... *2040*

WORK'S
1Th 5:13 highly in love for their **w** sake. ... *2041*

WORKS
Ex 5:13 Fulfil your **w**, your daily tasks, ... 4639
Dt 15:10 God shall bless thee in all thy **w** ... 4639
1Ki 13:11 **w** that the man of God had done ... 4639
2Ki 22:17 with all the **w** of their hands;. ... 4639
1Ch 16:9 talk ye of all his wondrous **w**
1Ch 28:19 even all the **w** of this pattern. ... 4399
Job 37:14 consider the wondrous **w** of God
Job 37:16 wondrous **w** of him which is perfect
Ps 8:6 dominion over the **w** of thy hands ... 4639
Ps 14:1 they have done abominable **w**. ... 5949
Ps 28:5 they regard not the **w** of the Lord, ... 6468
Ps 33:4 and all his **w** are done in truth ... 4640
Ps 40:5 wonderful **w** which thou hast done,
Ps 66:5 Come and see the **w** of God: he is ... 4659
Ps 73:28 God, that I may declare all thy **w** ... 4399
Ps 78:7 God, and not forget the **w** of God, ... 4611
Ps 92:5 O Lord, how great are thy **w**! ... 4639
Ps 104:13 is satisfied with the fruit of thy **w** ... 4639
Ps 107:8 for his wonderful **w** to the children
Ps 111:4 wonderful **w** to be remembered:
Ps 139:14 marvellous are thy **w**: and that ... 4639
Ps 145:4 shall praise thy **w** to another, ... 4639
Ps 145:9 tender mercies are over all his **w**. ... 4639
Ps 145:17 all his ways, and holy in all his **w** ... 4639
Pr 8:22 of his way, before his **w** of old. ... 4659
Pr 16:3 Commit thy **w** unto the Lord, ... 4639
Pr 31:31 her own **w** praise her in the gates ... 4639
Ecc 3:22 man should rejoice in his own **w**; ... 4639
Ecc 9:1 and their **w**, are in the hand of ... 5652
Ecc 9:7 for God now accepteth thy **w** ... 4639
Ecc 11:5 thou knowest not the **w** of God ... 4639
Isa 29:15 their **w** are in the dark, and they ... 4639
Isa 59:6 their **w** are **w** of iniquity, and the ... 4639
Isa 66:18 know their **w** and their thoughts: ... 4639
Jer 7:13 because ye have done all these **w** ... 4639
Jer 25:7 to anger with the **w** of your hands ... 4639
Da 4:37 heaven, all whose **w** are truth, ... 4567
Da 9:14 our God is righteous in all his **w**. ... 4639
Am 8:7 I will never forget any of their **w**. ... 4639
Jnh 3:10 And God saw their **w**, that they ... 4639
Mt 5:16 that they may see your good **w**, ... *2041*
Mt 7:22 name done many wonderful **w**?
Mt 11:21 if the mighty **w**, which were done
Mt 11:23 if the mighty **w**, which have been
Mt 16:27 every man according to his **w** ... *4234*
Mt 23:5 **w** they do for to be seen of men: ... *2041*
Lk 10:13 mighty **w**, had been done in Tyre
Jn 5:20 shew him greater **w** than these, ... *2041*
Jn 5:36 **w** which the Father hath given ... *2041*
Jn 7:7 of it, that the **w** thereof are evil. ... *2041*
Jn 8:39 ye would do the **w** of Abraham. ... *2041*
Jn 9:3 that the **w** of God should be made. ... *2041*
Jn 9:4 work the **w** of him that sent me. ... *2041*
Jn 10:32 which of those **w** do ye stone me? ... *2041*
Jn 10:38 ye believe not me, believe the **w**:. ... *2041*
Jn 14:12 greater **w** than these shall he do; ... *2041*
Ac 2:11 tongues the wonderful **w** of God.
Ac 9:36 this woman was full of good **w** and ... *2041*
Ac 15:18 Known unto God are all his **w** ... *2041*
Ac 26:20 and do **w** meet for repentance. ... *2041*
Ro 3:27 By what law? of **w**? Nay: but by. ... *2041*
Ro 4:6 imputeth righteousness without **w**, ... *2041*
Ro 9:11 not of **w**, but of him that calleth;) ... *2041*
Ro 9:32 but as it were by the **w** of the law. ... *2041*
Ro 11:6 by grace, then is it no more of **w**. ... *2041*
Ro 13:3 rulers are not a terror to good **w**. ... *2041*
2Co 11:15 end shall be according to their **w** ... *2041*
Gal 2:16 not justified by the **w** of the law, ... *2041*
Gal 2:16 by the **w** of the law shall no flesh ... *2041*
Gal 3:2 Received ye the Spirit by the **w** of ... *2041*
Gal 5:19 the **w** of the flesh are manifest, ... *2041*
Eph 2:9 Not of **w**, lest any man should. ... *2041*
Eph 2:10 in Christ Jesus unto good **w**, ... *2041*
Eph 5:11 with the unfruitful **w** of darkness, ... *2041*
1Ti 5:10 Well reported of for good **w**; if she ... *2041*
2Ti 1:9 calling, not according to our **w**, ... *2041*
2Ti 3:17 throughly furnished unto all good **w** ... *2041*
2Ti 4:14 reward him according to his **w** ... *2041*
Tit 1:16 but in **w** they deny him, being. ... *2041*
Tit 2:7 thyself a pattern of good **w** ... *2041*
Tit 3:5 Not by **w** of righteousness which ... *2041*
Tit 3:8 be careful to maintain good **w**. ... *2041*
Heb 1:10 heavens are the **w** of thine hands: ... *2041*
Heb 4:10 also hath ceased from his own **w** ... *2041*
Heb 6:1 of repentance from dead **w**, and of. ... *2041*
Heb 9:14 purge your conscience from dead **w**. ... *2041*
Heb 10:24 provoke unto love and to good **w**; ... *2041*
Jas 2:17 so faith, if it hath not **w**, is dead ... *2041*
Jas 2:18 shew me thy faith without thy **w**, ... *2041*
Jas 2:18 I will shew thee my faith by my **w**. ... *2041*
Jas 2:20 man, that faith without **w** is dead? ... *2041*
Jas 2:21 Abraham our father justified by **w** ... *2041*
Jas 2:22 and by **w** was faith made perfect? ... *2041*
Jas 2:24 how that by **w** a man is justified, ... *2041*
Jas 2:25 Rahab the harlot justified by **w**, ... *2041*
Jas 2:26 so faith without **w** is dead also ... *2041*
2Pe 3:10 **w** that are therein shall be burned ... *2041*
1Jn 3:8 might destroy the **w** of the devil ... *2041*
Rev 2:2 I know thy **w**, and thy labour, ... *2041*
Rev 2:5 and repent, and do the first **w**; ... *2041*
Rev 2:9 I know thy **w**, and tribulation, ... *2041*
Rev 2:13 I know thy **w**, and where thou ... *2041*
Rev 2:19 I know thy **w**, and charity, and ... *2041*
Rev 2:23 one of you according to your **w** ... *2041*
Rev 3:1 I know thy **w**, that thou hast a ... *2041*
Rev 3:8 I know thy **w**: behold, I have set ... *2041*
Rev 3:15 I know thy **w**, that thou art ... *2041*
Rev 9:20 yet repented not of the **w** of their ... *2041*
Rev 14:13 and their **w** do follow them ... *2041*

Rev	15:3	Great and marvellous are thy **w**	*2041*
Rev	18:6	her double according to her **w**:	*2041*
Rev	20:12	in the books, according to their **w**	*2041*
Rev	20:13	every man according to their **w**.	*2041*

WORKS'

Jn	14:11	believe me for the very **w** sake.	*2041*

WORLD

1Sa	2:8	and he hath set the **w** upon them	8398
2Sa	22:16	the foundations of the **w** were	8398
Ps	9:8	shall judge the **w** in righteousness,	8398
Ps	18:15	the foundations of the **w** were	8398
Ps	19:4	their words to the end of the **w**	8398
Ps	22:27	ends of the **w** shall remember	776
Ps	24:1	the **w**, and they that dwell therein	8398
Ps	50:12	for the **w** is mine, and the fulness	8398
Ps	89:11	for the **w** and the fulness thereof,	8398
Ps	90:2	hadst formed the earth and the **w**	8398
Ps	93:1	the **w** also is stablished, that it	8398
Ps	96:10	the **w** also shall be established that	8398
Ps	96:13	judge the **w** with righteousness	8398
Ps	98:7	the **w**, and they that dwell therein	8398
Ps	98:9	righteousness shall he judge the **w**	8398
Ecc	3:11	he hath set the **w** in their heart,	5769
Isa	13:11	I will punish the **w** for their evil,	8398
Isa	45:17	nor confounded **w** without end	5769
Isa	62:11	proclaimed unto the end of the **w**,	776
Isa	64:4	since the beginning of the **w** men	5769
Jer	51:15	established the **w** by his wisdom	8398
Na	1:5	the **w**, and all that dwell therein	8398
Mt	4:8	him all the kingdoms of the **w**,	*2889*
Mt	5:14	Ye are the light of the **w**. A city	*2889*
Mt	12:32	forgiven him, neither in this **w**,	*165*
Mt	13:35	from the foundation of the **w**	*2889*
Mt	13:38	The field is the **w**; the good seed	*2889*
Mt	13:39	the harvest is the end of the **w**;	*165*
Mt	13:40	so shall it be in the end of this **w**.	*165*
Mt	16:26	if he shall gain the whole **w**, and	*2889*
Mt	18:7	Woe unto the **w** because of	*2889*
Mt	24:3	coming, and of the end of the **w**?	*165*
Mt	24:14	shall be preached in all the **w** for	*3625*
Mt	24:21	not since the beginning of the **w**	*2889*
Mt	25:34	you from the foundation of the **w**:	*2889*
Mt	28:20	alway, even unto the end of the **w**.	*165*
Mk	4:19	And the cares of this **w**, and the	*165*
Mk	8:36	if he shall gain the whole **w**, and	*2889*
Mk	10:30	and in the **w** to come eternal life.	*165*
Mk	16:15	Go ye into all the **w**, and preach	*2889*
Lk	1:70	have been since the **w** began:	*165*
Lk	2:1	that all the **w** should be taxed	*3625*
Lk	4:5	unto him all the kingdoms of the **w**	*3625*
Lk	9:25	if he gain the whole **w**, and lose	*2889*
Lk	11:50	shed from the foundation of the **w**,	*2889*
Lk	12:30	do the nations of the **w** seek	*2889*
Lk	18:30	in the **w** to come life everlasting.	*165*
Lk	20:35	accounted worthy to obtain that **w**,	*165*
Jn	1:10	and the **w** was made by him,	*2889*
Jn	1:10	and the **w** knew him not.	*2889*
Jn	1:29	which taketh away the sin of the **w**.	*2889*
Jn	3:16	For God so loved the **w**, that he	*2889*
Jn	3:17	Son into the **w** to condemn the **w**;	*2889*
Jn	3:17	**w** through him might be saved.	*2889*
Jn	3:19	that light is come into the **w**,	*2889*
Jn	4:42	the Christ, the Saviour of the **w**	*2889*
Jn	6:33	and giveth light unto the **w**.	*2889*
Jn	6:51	I will give for the life of the **w**.	*2889*
Jn	7:7	The **w** cannot hate you; but me	*2889*
Jn	8:12	saying, I am the light of the **w**:	*2889*
Jn	8:23	I am not of this **w**.	*2889*
Jn	9:5	As long as I am in the **w**,	*2889*
Jn	9:5	I am the light of the **w**.	*2889*
Jn	9:39	judgment I am come into this **w**,	*2889*
Jn	11:9	he seeth the light of this **w**.	*2889*
Jn	12:19	behold, the **w** is gone after him	*2889*
Jn	12:25	that hateth his life in this **w**	*2889*
Jn	12:31	Now is the judgment of this **w**:	*2889*
Jn	12:31	the prince of this **w** be cast out.	*2889*
Jn	12:46	I am come a light into the **w**,	*2889*
Jn	12:47	to judge the **w**, but to save the **w**,	*2889*
Jn	13:1	loved his own which were in the **w**,	*2889*
Jn	14:17	whom the **w** cannot receive,	*2889*
Jn	14:27	not as the **w** giveth, give I unto you	*2889*
Jn	14:30	for the prince of this **w** cometh,	*2889*
Jn	14:31	**w** may know that I love the Father;	*2889*
Jn	15:18	If the **w** hate you, ye know that it	*2889*
Jn	15:19	of the **w**, the **w** would love his own:	*2889*
Jn	15:19	I have chosen you out of the **w**,	*2889*
Jn	16:8	he will reprove the **w** of sin, and of	*2889*
Jn	16:11	the prince of this **w** is judged.	*2889*
Jn	16:21	joy that a man is born into the **w**.	*2889*
Jn	16:28	I leave the **w**, and go to the Father.	*2889*
Jn	16:33	In the **w** ye shall have tribulation:	*2889*
Jn	16:33	cheer; I have overcome the **w**.	*2889*
Jn	17:5	I had with thee before the **w** was.	*2889*
Jn	17:9	I pray not for the **w**, but for them	*2889*
Jn	17:11	but these are in the **w**, and I come	*2889*
Jn	17:14	because they are not of the **w**,	*2889*
Jn	17:16	even as I am not of the **w**.	*2889*
Jn	17:18	so have I also sent them into the **w**.	*2889*
Jn	17:21	**w** may believe … thou hast sent me.	*2889*
Jn	17:23	**w** may know … thou hast sent me,	*2889*
Jn	17:24	me before the foundation of the **w**.	*2889*
Jn	17:25	the **w** hath not known thee: but I	*2889*
Jn	18:36	My kingdom is not of this **w**:	*2889*
Jn	18:36	if my kingdom were of this **w**, then	*2889*
Jn	18:37	for this cause came I into the **w**,	*2889*
Ac	3:21	holy prophets since the **w** began	*165*
Ac	17:6	have turned the **w** upside down	*3625*
Ac	17:31	will judge the **w** in righteousness	*3625*
Ro	1:20	from the creation of the **w** are	*2889*
Ro	3:19	all the **w** may become guilty before	*2889*
Ro	5:12	by one man sin entered into the **w**,	*2889*
Ro	5:13	(For until the law sin was in the **w**:	*2889*
Ro	10:18	words unto the ends of the **w**	*3625*
Ro	12:2	And be not conformed to this **w**.	*165*
1Co	1:20	foolish the wisdom of this **w**?	*2889*
1Co	1:21	the **w** by wisdom knew not God	*2889*
1Co	1:27	chosen the foolish things of the **w**	*2889*
1Co	1:27	chosen the weak things of the **w**	*2889*
1Co	1:28	And base things of the **w**, and	*2889*
1Co	2:7	God ordained before the **w** unto	*165*
1Co	3:19	wisdom of this **w** is foolishness	*2889*
1Co	4:9	are made a spectacle unto the **w**,	*2889*
1Co	6:2	that the saints shall judge the **w**?	*2889*
1Co	7:34	careth for the things of the **w**,	*2889*
1Co	8:4	that an idol is nothing in the **w**.	*2889*
2Co	4:4	the god of this **w** hath blinded the	*165*
2Co	5:19	reconciling the **w** unto himself,	*2889*
2Co	7:10	sorrow of the **w** worketh death.	*2889*
Gal	1:4	deliver us from the present evil **w**,	*165*
Gal	6:14	whom the **w** is crucified unto me,	*2889*
Eph	1:4	before the foundation of the **w**	*2889*

Eph	2:12	hope, and without God in the **w**	2889
Eph	3:21	throughout all ages, **w** without end	*165*
Eph	6:12	rulers of the darkness of this **w**	*165*
Php	2:15	whom ye shine as lights in the **w**;	2889
Col	2:8	after the rudiments of the **w**, and	2889
1Ti	1:15	came into the **w** to save sinners;	2889
1Ti	3:16	believed on in the **w**, received up	2889
1Ti	6:7	we brought nothing into this **w**,	2889
2Ti	1:9	Christ Jesus before the **w** began	*166*
2Ti	4:10	me, having loved this present **w**	*165*
Tit	1:2	promised before the **w** began;	*166*
Heb	1:6	in the firstbegotten into the **w**	*3625*
Heb	2:5	put in subjection the **w** to come,	*3625*
Heb	4:3	from the foundation of the **w**	2889
Heb	11:7	by the which he condemned the **w**	2889
Jas	1:27	himself unspotted from the **w**	2889
Jas	2:5	the poor of this **w** rich in faith,	2889
Jas	3:6	tongue is a fire, a **w** of iniquity:	2889
Jas	4:4	the friendship of the **w** is enmity	2889
1Pe	1:20	before the foundation of the **w**	2889
2Pe	1:4	the corruption that is in the **w**	2889
2Pe	2:5	And spared not the old **w**, but	2889
1Jn	2:2	also for the sins of the whole **w**	2889
1Jn	2:15	Love not the **w**, neither	2889
1Jn	2:15	If any man love the **w**, the love of	2889
1Jn	2:16	For all that is in the **w**, the lust of	2889
1Jn	2:17	And the **w** passeth away, and the	2889
1Jn	3:13	my brethren, if the **w** hate you	2889
1Jn	4:3	even now already is it in the **w**	2889
1Jn	4:4	is in you, than he that is in the **w**	2889
1Jn	4:9	his only begotten Son into the **w**	2889
1Jn	5:4	born of God overcometh the **w**:	2889
1Jn	5:5	Who is he that overcometh the **w**	2889
1Jn	5:19	the whole **w** lieth in wickedness	2889
Rev	3:10	**which shall come upon all the w,**	*3625*
Rev	11:15	kingdoms of this **w** are become	2889
Rev	12:9	which deceiveth the whole **w**:	*3625*
Rev	13:3	the **w** wondered after the beast	*1093*
Rev	13:8	from the foundation of the **w**	2889
Rev	17:8	from the foundation of the **w**,	2889

WORLDLY

Tit	2:12	denying ungodliness and **w** lusts,	2886
Heb	9:1	service, and a **w** sanctuary	2886

WORLDS

Heb	1:2	by whom also he made the **w**;	*165*
Heb	11:3	the **w** were framed by the word of	*165*

WORM

Ex	16:24	neither was there any **w** therein	7415
Job	25:6	How much less man, that is a **w**?	7415
Ps	22:6	But I am a **w**, and no man;	8438
Isa	51:8	the **w** shall eat them like wool:	5580
Isa	66:24	for their **w** shall not die, neither	8438
Jnh	4:7	But God prepared a **w** when the	8438
Mk	9:44	**Where their w dieth not,**	*4663*
Mk	9:48	**Where their w dieth not,**	*4663*

WORMS

Ex	16:20	and it bred **w**, and stank:	8438
Job	19:26	after my skin **w** shall destroy this	
Mic	7:17	of their holes like **w** of the earth:	2119
Ac	12:23	he was eaten of **w**, and gave up	*4662*

WORMWOOD

Pr	5:4	But her end is bitter as **w**, sharp	3939
La	3:15	hath made me drunken with **w**	3939
Rev	8:11	the name of the star is called **W**:	*894*
Rev	8:11	third part of the waters became **w**;	*894*

WORSE See also BAD.

Ge	19:9	now will we deal **w** with thee,	7489
2Sa	19:7	that will be **w** unto thee than all	7489
2Ch	6:24	thy people Israel be put to the **w**	5062
Jer	16:12	have done **w** than your fathers;	7489
Mt	9:16	**garment, and the rent is made w**	*5501*
Mt	12:45	**of that man is w than the first.**	*5501*
Mt	27:64	last error shall be **w** than the first	*5501*
Mk	2:21	**the old, and the rent is made w.**	*5501*
Mk	5:26	bettered, but rather grew **w**,	*5501*
Lk	11:26	**of that man is w than the first.**	*5501*
Jn	5:14	**lest a w thing come unto thee.**	*5501*
1Co	11:17	not for the better, but for the **w**	*2276*
1Ti	5:8	faith, and is **w** than an infidel	*5501*
2Pe	2:20	the latter end is **w** with them than	*5501*

WORSHIP

Ge	22:5	I and the lad will go yonder and **w**	7812
Ex	34:14	For thou shalt **w** no other god:	7812
Dt	11:16	and serve other gods, and **w** them;	7812
Jos	5:14	on his face to the earth, and did **w**	7812
1Sa	1:3	went up out of his city yearly to **w**	7812
1Sa	15:25	with me, that I may **w** the Lord,	7812
1Ch	16:29	**w** the Lord in the beauty of	7812
2Ch	7:19	and serve other gods, and **w** them;	7812
2Ch	32:12	Ye shall **w** before one altar, and	7812
Ps	29:2	**w** the Lord in the beauty of	7812
Ps	45:11	he is thy Lord; and **w** thou him	7812
Ps	95:6	O come, let us **w** and bow down:	7812
Ps	96:9	O **w** the Lord in the beauty of	7812
Ps	99:9	our God, and **w** at his holy hill;	7812
Isa	2:8	**w** the work of their own hands,	7812
Isa	46:6	a god: they fall down, yea, they **w**	7812
Isa	66:23	all flesh come to **w** before me,	7812
Jer	13:10	gods, to serve them, and to **w** them,	7812
Da	3:5	fall down and **w** the golden image	5457
Da	3:18	nor **w** the golden image which thou	5457
Mic	5:13	more **w** the work of thine hands	7812
Zec	14:16	from year to year to **w** the King,	7812
Mt	2:2	the east, and are come to **w** him	*4352*
Mt	2:8	that I may come and **w** him also	*4352*
Mt	4:9	if thou wilt fall down and **w** me	*4352*
Mt	4:10	**Thou shalt w the Lord thy God,**	*4352*
Mt	15:9	**But in vain do they w me,**	*4576*
Mk	7:7	**Howbeit in vain do they w me,**	*4576*
Lk	4:7	If thou therefore wilt **w** me	*4352, 1799*
Lk	4:8	**Thou shalt w the Lord thy God,**	*4352*
Jn	4:20	the place where men ought to **w**	*4352*
Jn	4:22	**Ye w ye know not what:**	*4352*
Jn	4:23	**the Father seeketh such to w him.**	*4352*
Jn	4:24	**is a Spirit: and they that w him**	*4352*
Jn	4:24	**w him in spirit and in truth.**	*4352*
Ac	7:42	them up to **w** the host of heaven;	*3000*
Ac	17:23	Whom therefore ye ignorantly **w**	*2151*
Php	3:3	which **w** God in the spirit, and	*3000*
Col	2:23	indeed a shew of wisdom in will **w**	*1479*
Heb	1:6	let all the angels of God **w** him	*4352*
Rev	4:10	and **w** him that liveth for ever and	*4352*
Rev	9:20	that they should not **w** devils, and	*4352*
Rev	13:8	dwell therein to **w** the first beast,	*4352*
Rev	13:15	not **w** the image of the beast	*4352*
Rev	14:7	and **w** him that made heaven, and	*4352*
Rev	14:11	who **w** the beast and his image,	*4352*
Rev	19:10	And I fell at his feet to **w** him	*4352*

Rev 19:10 **w** God: for the testimony of Jesus...... *4352*
Rev 22:8 I fell down to **w** before the feet of...... *4352*
Rev 22:9 the sayings of this book: **w** God *4352*

WORSHIPPED
Ex 12:27 the people bowed the head and **w** 7812
Ex 32:8 them a molten calf, and have **w** it...... 7812
2Sa 12:20 into the house of the Lord, and **w**:..... 7812
1Ki 9:9 upon other gods, and have **w** them,.... 7812
1Ki 16:31 went and served Baal, and **w** him. 7812
2Ki 21:21 that his father served, and **w** them: 7812
Ne 8:6 and **w** the Lord with their faces to 7812
Job 1:20 fell down upon the ground, and **w**, ... 7812
Jer 1:16 **w** the works of their own hands 7812
Eze 8:16 they **w** the sun toward the east......... 7812
Da 3:7 fell down and **w** the golden image 5457
Mt 2:11 mother, and fell down and **w** him:..... *4352*
Mt 28:9 held him by the feet, and **w** him. *4352*
Mt 28:17 they **w** him: but some doubted. *4352*
Mk 5:6 Jesus afar off, he ran and **w** him,....... *4352*
Mk 15:19 and bowing their knees **w** him......... *4352*
Jn 4:20 Our fathers **w** in this mountain;....... *4352*
Ac 17:25 Neither is **w** with men's hands *2323*
Ro 1:25 and **w** and served the creature......... *4573*
2Th 2:4 all that is called God, or that is **w**;...... *4574*
Rev 5:14 and **w** him that liveth for ever and..... *4352*
Rev 7:11 throne on their faces, and **w** God,...... *4352*
Rev 11:16 fell upon their faces, and **w** God, ... *4352*
Rev 13:4 and they **w** the beast, saying, Who *4352*
Rev 16:2 and upon them which **w** his image..... *4352*
Rev 19:4 four beasts fell down and **w** God *4352*
Rev 19:20 beast, and them that **w** his image *4352*
Rev 20:4 which had not **w** the beast, neither..... *4352*

WORSHIPPER
Jn 9:31 but if any man be a **w** of God, and..... *2318*

WORSHIPPERS
2Ki 10:19 He might destroy the **w** of Baal 5647
Jn 4:23 **true w shall worship the Father** *4353*
Heb 10:2 the **w** once purged should have........ *3000*

WORSHIPPETH
Ne 9:6 and the host of heaven **w** thee......... 7812
Isa 44:17 he falleth down unto it, and **w** it,...... 7812
Da 3:11 And whoso falleth not down and **w**, ... 5457
Ac 19:27 whom all Asia and the world **w**........ *4576*

WORST
Eze 7:24 I will bring the **w** of the heathen,...... 7451

WORTH
Le 27:23 unto him the **w** of thy estimation...... 4373
2Sa 18:3 thou art **w** ten thousand of us: 3644
Pr 10:20 the heart of the wicked is little **w**.
Eze 30:2 Howl ye, Woe **w** the day! 1929

WORTHY
Ge 32:10 I am not **w** of the least of all the....... 6994
1Sa 26:16 ye are **w** to die, because ye have 1121
2Sa 22:14 the Lord, who is **w** to be praised
1Ki 2:26 fields; for thou art **w** of death:.......... 376
Ps 18:3 the Lord, who is **w** to be praised:
Mt 3:11 whose shoes I am not **w** to bear:....... *2425*
Mt 10:10 **for the workman is w of his meat.** *514*
Mt 10:13 **if the house be w, let your peace.** *514*
Mt 10:13 **it be not w, let your peace return** *514*
Mt 10:37 **more than me is not w of me:** *514*
Mt 10:38 **followeth after me, is not w of** *514*
Mt 22:8 **which were bidden were not w** *514*
Mk 1:7 shoes I am not **w** to stoop down....... *2425*
Lk 3:8 therefore fruits **w** of repentance *514*
Lk 3:16 shoes I am not **w** to unloose:.......... *2425*
Lk 7:6 I am not **w** that thou shouldest........ *2425*
Lk 10:7 **for the labourer is w of his hire.** *514*
Lk 12:48 **did commit things w of stripes,** *514*
Lk 15:19 **no more w to be called thy son:** *514*
Lk 20:35 **accounted w to obtain that world,** *2661*
Lk 21:36 **accounted w to escape all these** *2661*
Lk 23:15 nothing **w** of death is done unto........ *514*
Jn 1:27 latchet I am not **w** to unloose *514*
Ac 5:41 were counted **w** to suffer shame *2661*
Ac 13:25 of his feet I am not **w** to loose.......... *514*
Ro 1:32 commit such things are **w** of death,..... *514*
Ro 8:18 time are not **w** to be compared......... *514*
Eph 4:1 that ye walk **w** of the vocation.......... *516*
Col 1:10 might walk **w** of the Lord unto......... *516*
1Th 2:12 That ye would walk **w** of God, who *516*
1Ti 4:9 saying and **w** of all acceptation. *514*
1Ti 5:17 be counted **w** of double honour,........ *515*
1Ti 5:18 The labourer is **w** of his reward......... *514*
1Ti 6:1 their own masters **w** of all honour,...... *514*
Heb 3:3 **w** of more glory than Moses *515*
Heb 11:38 (Of whom the world was not **w**:) *514*
Jas 2:7 they blaspheme that **w** name.......... *2570*
Rev 3:4 **with me in white: for they are w.** *514*
Rev 4:11 Thou art **w**, O Lord, to receive *514*
Rev 5:2 Who is **w** to open the book, and to *514*
Rev 5:12 **W** is the lamb that was slain to *514*
Rev 16:6 blood to drink; for they are **w** *514*

WOUND
Ex 21:25 burning, **w** for **w**, stripe for stripe 6482
Dt 32:39 I make alive; I **w**, and I heal: 4272
Pr 6:33 A **w** and dishonour shall he get;....... 5061
Pr 20:30 blueness of a **w** cleanseth … evil:...... 6482
Isa 30:26 and healeth the stroke of their **w** 4347
Jer 10:19 me for my hurt! my **w** is grievous:..... 4347
Jer 15:18 perpetual, and my **w** incurable, ... 4347
Jer 30:14 thee with the **w** of an enemy, ... 4347
Hos 5:13 heal you, nor cure you of your **w** 4205
Mic 1:9 her **w** is incurable; for it is come....... 4347
1Co 8:12 and **w** their weak conscience, ye *5180*
Rev 13:12 beast, whose deadly **w** was healed..... *4127*

WOUNDED
1Sa 31:3 Saul...was sore **w** of the archers........ 2342
1Ki 22:34 me out of the host; for I am **w** 2470
2Ch 18:33 out of the host; for I am **w**............ 2470
2Ch 35:23 Have me away; for I am sore **w**........ 2470
Ps 18:38 **w** them that they were not able........ 4272
Ps 109:22 and my heart is **w** within me.......... 2490
Pr 18:14 but a **w** spirit who can bear? 5218
Isa 53:5 he was **w** for our transgressions,....... 2490
Jer 30:14 I have **w** thee with the wound of 5221
Eze 28:23 the **w** shall be judged in the midst 2491
Eze 30:24 groanings of a deadly **w** man.......... 2491
Joel 2:8 the sword, they shall not be **w**......... 1214
Lk 10:30 **w him, and departed, leaving** *4127, 2007*
Lk 20:12 **and they w him also, and cast.** *5135*
Ac 19:16 fled out of that house naked and **w** *5135*
Rev 13:3 of his heads as it were **w** to death; *4969*

WOUNDING
Ge 4:23 for I have slain a man to my **w** 6482

WOUNDS
2Ki 9:15 to be healed in Jezreel of the **w** 4347
Ps 147:3 in heart, and bindeth up their **w**. 6094
Pr 18:8 words of a talebearer are as **w** 3859
Pr 26:22 words of a talebearer are as **w** 3859
Pr 27:6 Faithful are the **w** of a friend; 6482
Jer 30:17 and I will heal thee of thy **w**, saith 4347
Zec 13:6 What are these **w** in thine hands? 4347
Lk 10:34 **went to him, and bound up his w,** *5134*

WRAP
Isa 28:20 than that he can **w** himself in it 3664
Mic 7:3 desire: so they **w** it up. 5686

WRAPPED
1Ki 19:13 that he **w** his face in his mantle, ... 3874
Mt 27:59 he **w** it in a clean linen cloth,. *1794*
Mk 15:46 him down, and **w** him in the linen, ... *1750*
Lk 2:7 and **w** him in swaddling clothes *4683*
Lk 2:12 the babe **w** in swaddling clothes *4683*
Lk 23:53 it down, and **w** it in linen, ... *1794*
Jn 20:7 but **w** together in a place by itself *1794*

WRATH
Ge 39:19 to me; that his **w** was kindled. 639
Ex 22:24 And my **w** shall wax hot, and I 639
Le 10:6 lest **w** come upon all the people:. 7107
Nu 11:33 **w** of the Lord was kindled against 639
Nu 16:46 is **w** gone out from the Lord;. 7110
Dt 9:7 provokedst the Lord thy God to **w** 7107
Dt 11:17 Lord's **w** be kindled against you,. 639
Dt 29:23 in his anger, and in his **w**: 2534
Dt 32:27 that I feared the **w** of the enemy, ... 3708
Jos 9:20 let them live, lest **w** be upon us, ... 7110
2Sa 11:20 if so be that the king's **w** arise, ... 2534
2Ki 22:13 great is the **w** of the Lord that is 2534
1Ch 27:24 there fell **w** for it against Israel;. 7110
2Ch 12:7 my **w** shall not be poured out 2534
2Ch 19:2 therefore is **w** upon thee from. 7110
2Ch 24:18 **w** came upon Judah and Jerusalem 7110
2Ch 28:13 there is fierce **w** against Israel. 639
2Ch 32:26 the **w** of the Lord came not upon. 7110
2Ch 36:16 the **w** of the Lord arose against 2534
Ezr 5:12 the God of heaven unto **w**. 7265
Ezr 8:22 his power and his **w** is against all 639
Ezr 10:14 fierce **w** of our God for this matter 639
Est 2:1 the **w** of king Ahasuerus was. 2534
Est 3:5 then was Haman full of **w**.. 2534
Est 7:10 Then was the king's **w** pacified.. 2534
Job 5:2 For **w** killeth the foolish man,. 3708
Ps 2:12 when his **w** is kindled but a little. 639
Ps 21:9 shall swallow them up in his **w**, ... 639
Ps 37:8 Cease from anger, and forsake **w**: 2534
Ps 38:1 O Lord, rebuke me not in thy **w**: 7110
Ps 76:10 the **w** of man shall praise thee: 2534
Ps 76:10 remainder of **w** shalt thou restrain. 2534
Ps 78:38 and did not stir up all his **w**. 2534
Ps 89:46 ever? shall thy **w** burn like fire? 2534
Ps 90:11 according to thy fear, so is thy **w**. 5678
Ps 95:11 Unto whom I sware in my **w** that. 639
Ps 106:23 to turn away his **w**, lest he should. 2534
Pr 11:4 Riches profit not in the day of **w**: 5678
Pr 11:23 expectation of the wicked is **w** 5678
Pr 12:16 A fool's **w** is presently known:. 3708
Pr 14:29 He that is slow to **w** is of great 639
Pr 15:1 A soft answer turneth away **w**: 2534
Pr 16:14 The **w** of a king is as messengers 2534
Pr 19:12 The king's **w** is as the roaring of. 2197
Pr 19:19 A man of great **w** shall suffer. 2534
Pr 27:3 a fool's **w** is heavier than them 3708
Pr 29:8 snare: but wise men turn away **w** 639
Pr 30:33 forcing of **w** bringeth forth strife. 639
Isa 13:9 cruel both with **w** and fierce anger, ... 5678
Isa 54:8 In a little **w** I hid my face from 7110
Isa 60:10 in my **w** I smote thee, but in my. 7110
Jer 7:29 forsaken the generation of his **w**. 5678
Jer 10:10 at his **w** the earth shall tremble, ... 7110
Jer 48:30 I know his **w**, saith the Lord;. 5678
Jer 50:13 Because of the **w** of the Lord it 7110
La 3:1 seen affliction by the rod of his **w**. 5678
Eze 7:14 **w** is upon all the multitude 2740
Eze 7:19 in the day of the **w** of the Lord: 5678
Eze 38:19 in the fire of my **w** have I spoken, ... 5678
Hos 5:10 I will pour out my **w** upon them 5678
Hab 3:2 known; in **w** remember mercy. 7267
Hab 3:8 was thy **w** against the sea, that. 5678
Zep 1:15 That day is a day of **w**, a day of. 5678
Zep 1:18 them in the day of the Lord's **w**;. 5678
Zec 7:12 came a great **w** from the Lord of 7110
Mt 3:7 you to flee from the **w** to come? *3709*
Lk 3:7 you to flee from the **w** to come? *3709*
Lk 4:28 these things, were filled with **w**, ... *2372*
Lk 21:23 **the land, and w upon his people** *3709*
Jn 3:36 but the **w** of God abideth on him. *3709*
Ac 19:28 these sayings, they were full of **w**, ... *2372*
Ro 1:18 For the **w** of God is revealed from *3709*
Ro 2:5 heart treasurest up unto thyself **w** *3709*
Ro 4:15 Because the law worketh **w**: for. *3709*
Ro 5:9 be saved from **w** through him. *3709*
Ro 9:22 What if God, willing to shew his **w**, ... *3709*
Ro 9:22 vessels of **w** fitted to destruction: *3709*
Ro 12:19 but rather give place unto **w**:. *3709*
Ro 13:4 a revenger to execute **w** upon him *3709*
Eph 2:3 were by nature the children of **w**, ... *3709*
Eph 4:26 the sun go down upon your **w**:. *3950*
Eph 5:6 things cometh the **w** of God *3709*
Eph 6:4 provoke not your children to **w**: *3949*
Col 3:6 things' sake the **w** of God cometh. *3709*
1Th 1:10 delivered us from the **w** to come. *3709*
1Th 5:9 God hath not appointed us to **w**, ... *3709*
Heb 3:11 So I sware in my **w**, They shall *3709*
Jas 1:19 hear, slow to speak, slow to **w** *3709*
Jas 1:20 For the **w** of man worketh not the *3709*
Rev 6:16 and from the **w** of the Lamb: *3709*
Rev 6:17 the great day of his **w** has come; *3709*
Rev 12:12 having great **w**, because he knoweth . . . *2372*
Rev 14:19 great winepress of the **w** of God. *2372*
Rev 15:1 in them is filled up the **w** of God.. . . . . . *2372*
Rev 16:1 pour out the vials of the **w** of God *2372*
Rev 16:19 wine of the fierceness of his **w**. *3709*
Rev 19:15 fierceness and **w** of Almighty God.. . . . . *3709*

WRATHFUL See also WROTH.
Pr 15:18 A **w** man stirreth up strife: but 2534

WREST
Ex 23:6 shalt not **w** the judgment of thy 5186
Dt 16:19 Thou shalt not **w** judgment; thou 5186
Ps 56:5 Every day they **w** my words: 6087
2Pe 3:16 are unlearned and unstable **w**, ... *4761*

WRESTLE
Eph 6:12 For we **w** not against flesh *2076, 3823*

WRESTLED

Ge 32:24 there **w** a man with him until the........79
Ge 32:25 was out of joint, as he **w** with him.......79

WRETCHED

Ro 7:24 O **w** man that I am! who shall.........*5005*
Rev 3:17 **and knowest not that thou art w.**......*5005*

WRINGED See also WRUNG.

Jgs 6:38 and **w** the dew out of the fleece,.......4680

WRINGING

Pr 30:33 the **w** of the nose bringeth forth.......4330

WRITE

Ex 34:1 will **w** upon these tables the words.....3789
Ex 34:27 unto Moses, **W** thou these words: 3789
Nu 17:2 **w** thou every man's name upon.......3789
Dt 6:9 thou shalt **w** them upon the posts.....3789
Dt 10:2 I will **w** on the tables the words.......3789
Dt 24:3 **w** her a bill of divorcement,...........3789
Dt 27:8 **w** upon the stones all the words.......3789
Est 8:8 **W** ye also for the Jews, as it...........3789
Pr 3:3 **w** them upon the table of thine.......3789
Isa 10:19 be few, that a child may **w** them. 3789
Isa 30:8 go, **w** it before them in a table,........3789
Jer 22:30 **W** ye this man childless, a man........3789
Jer 31:33 parts, and **w** it in their hearts;.........3789
Jer 36:28 **w** in it all the former words that.......3789
Eze 24:2 man; **w** thee the name of the day,......3789
Hab 2:2 **W** the vision, and make it plain.......3789
Mk 10:4 to **w** a bill of divorcement,............*1125*
Lk 16:6 **and sit down quickly, and w fifty.**......*1125*
Lk 16:7 **Take thy bill, and w fourscore.**........*1125*
Jn 19:21 **W** not, The King of the Jews;..........*1125*
Heb 8:10 mind, and **w** them in their hearts: *1924*
1Jn 2:7 I **w** no new commandment unto......*1125*
1Jn 2:8 new commandment I **w** unto you,.....*1125*
1Jn 2:12 I **w** unto you, little children, ...*1125*
1Jn 2:13 I **w** unto you, fathers, because ye......*1125*
1Jn 2:13 I **w** unto you, young men, because.....*1125*
1Jn 2:13 I **w** unto you, little children, ...1125
Rev 1:11 **What thou seest, w in a book,**.........*1125*
Rev 1:19 **W the things which thou hast.**........*1125*
Rev 2:1 **angel of the church of Ephesus w;**.....*1125*
Rev 2:8 **angel of the church in Smyrna w;**.....*1125*
Rev 2:12 **of the church in Pergamos w;**.........*1125*
Rev 2:18 **angel of the church in Thyatira w;**.....*1125*
Rev 3:1 **angel of the church in Sardis w;**.......*1125*
Rev 3:7 **of the church in Philadelphia w;**......*1125*
Rev 3:12 **I will w upon him the name of my**....*1125*
Rev 3:12 **I will w upon him my new name.**
Rev 3:14 **the church of the Laodiceans w;**.......*1125*
Rev 10:4 thunders uttered, and **w** them not......*1125*
Rev 14:13 **W**, Blessed are the dead which die.....*1125*
Rev 19:9 **W**, Blessed are they which are.........*1125*
Rev 21:5 **W**: for these words are true...........*1125*

WRITER

Ps 45:1 my tongue is the pen of a ready **w**.....5608

WRITING See also HANDWRITING.

Ex 32:16 the **w** was the **w** of God, graven.......4385
Ex 39:30 pure gold, and wrote upon it a **w**, ...4385
Dt 10:4 according to the first **w**, the ten........4385
Ezr 4:7 **w** of the letter was written in the......3791
Est 3:12 every province according to the **w**.....3791
Est 8:9 to the Jews according to their **w**,.......3791
Est 9:27 two days according to their **w**, ...3791
Da 5:8 not read the **w**, nor make known......3792
Da 5:25 And this is the **w** that was written,.....3792
Da 6:8 establish the decree, and sign the **w**,........
Da 6:10 Daniel knew that the **w** was signed,....3792
Mt 5:31 **let him give her a w of divorcement:**
Mt 19:7 to give a **w** of divorcement, and to......*975*
Lk 1:63 And he asked for a **w** table, and.......*4098*
Jn 19:19 And the **w** was, Jesus Of Nazareth.....*1125*

WRITINGS

Jn 5:47 **if ye believe not his w, how shall**......*1121*

WRITTEN

Ex 24:12 commandments which I have **w**;......3789
Ex 31:18 stone, **w** with the finger of God.......3789
Dt 9:10 stone **w** with the finger of God;.......3789
Dt 28:58 this law that are **w** in this book, ...3789
Dt 29:20 the curses that are **w** in this book......3789
1Ki 21:11 as it was **w** in the letters which she.....3789
2Ch 30:18 passover otherwise than it was **w**......3789
2Ch 34:21 do after all that is **w** in this book......3789
Ezr 4:7 letter was **w** in the Syrian tongue,......3789
Ezr 5:7 was **w** thus; Unto Darius the..........3790
Ne 8:15 trees, to make booths, as it is **w**........3789
Ne 10:36 of our cattle, as it is **w** in the law,......3789
Ne 13:1 and therein was found **w**, that the.....3789
Est 3:9 it be **w** that they may be destroyed: 3789
Est 8:5 let it be **w** to reverse the letters........3789
Est 9:32 Purim; and it was **w** in the book.......3789
Job 19:23 Oh that my words were now **w**! 3789
Ps 69:28 and not be **w** with the righteous.......3789
Ps 139:16 thy book all my members were **w**, ...3789
Isa 4:3 one that is **w** among the living........3789
Jer 25:13 even all that is **w** in this book,.........3789
Jer 36:29 saying, Why hast thou **w** therein, ...3789
Eze 2:10 and it was **w** within and without:......3789
Eze 2:10 there was **w** therein lamentations, ...3789
Da 9:13 As it is **w** in the law of Moses, all......3789
Da 12:1 that shall be found **w** in the book......3789
Hos 8:12 I have **w** to him the great things.......3789
Mt 11:10 **For this is he, of whom it is w,**........*1125*
Mt 26:24 **Son of man goeth as it is w of.**........*1125*
Mt 27:37 up over his head his accusation **w**,.....*1125*
Mk 9:12 **how it is w of the Son of man,**........*1125*
Mk 14:21 **indeed goeth, as it is w of him:**........*1125*
Mk 15:26 of his accusation was **w** over,..........*1924*
Lk 4:17 he found the place where it was **w**,.....*1125*
Lk 10:20 **your names are w in heaven.**..........*1125*
Lk 18:31 **things that are w by the prophets.**.....*1125*
Lk 23:38 a superscription ... was **w** over him....*1125*
Lk 24:44 **which were w in the law of Moses,**.....*1125*
Lk 24:46 **is w, and thus it behoved Christ**.......*1125*
Jn 8:17 **It is also w in your law, that the**.......*1125*
Jn 15:25 **be fulfilled that is w in their law,**......*1125*
Jn 20:31 these are **w**, that ye might believe......*1125*
Jn 21:25 if they should be **w** every one, I.......*1125*
Ac 13:29 had fulfilled all that was **w** of him,.....*1125*
Ro 2:15 work of the law **w** in their hearts,......*1123*
Ro 15:4 were **w** for our learning, that we.......*4270*
1Co 4:6 think of men above that which is **w**, ...*1125*
1Co 5:11 **w** unto you not to keep company, ...*1125*
1Co 9:9 For it is **w** in the law of Moses,........*1125*
1Co 15:54 to pass the saying that is **w**,...........*1125*
2Co 3:2 Ye are our epistle **w** in our hearts,......*1449*
2Co 3:7 **w** and engraven in stones,.......*1722, 1121*
Heb 10:7 volume of the book it is **w** of me,).....*1125*

Heb	12:23	firstborn, which are **w** in heaven,	*583*
1Jn	2:26	These things have I **w** unto you	*1125*
1Jn	5:13	These things have I **w** unto you	*1125*
Rev	2:17	**and in the stone a new name w,**	*1125*
Rev	5:1	book **w** within and on the backside,.	*1125*
Rev	13:8	names are not **w** in the book of life	*1125*
Rev	14:1	Father's name **w** in their foreheads	*1125*
Rev	17:5	upon her forehead was a name **w**,	*1125*
Rev	17:8	names … not **w** in the book of life	*1125*
Rev	19:12	had a name **w**, that no man knew,	*1125*
Rev	19:16	and on his thigh a name **w**,	*1125*
Rev	20:12	things which were **w** in the books,	*1125*
Rev	20:15	was not found **w** in the book of life	*1125*
Rev	21:27	are **w** in the Lamb's book of life	*1125*
Rev	22:18	plagues that are **w** in this book:.	*1125*
Rev	22:19	things which are **w** in this book	*1125*

WRONG

Ge	16:5	unto Abram, My **w** be upon thee:.	2555
Ex	2:13	he said to him that did the **w**,	7563
Dt	19:16	against him that which is **w**;	5627
Jgs	11:27	doest me **w** to war against me:	7451
1Ch	12:17	there is no **w** in mine hands,	2555
Est	1:16	the queen hath not done **w** to the	5753
Ps	105:14	suffered no man to do them **w**	6231
Mt	20:13	**Friend, I do thee no w: didst not**	*91*
Ac	7:27	he that did his neighbour **w** thrust	*91*
2Co	7:12	for his cause that had done the **w**,	*91*
2Co	12:13	to you? forgive me this **w**	*93*
Col	3:25	But he that doeth **w** shall receive	*91*

WRONGED

2Co	7:2	we have **w** no man, we have	*91*
Phm	18	If he hath **w** thee, or oweth thee	*91*

WRONGFULLY

Job	21:27	which ye **w** imagine against me	2554
Ps	35:19	mine enemies **w** rejoice over me:	8267
Ps	119:86	they persecute me **w**; help thou	8267
Eze	22:29	oppressed the stranger **w**	3808, 4941
1Pe	2:19	God endure grief, suffering **w**	*95*

WROTE

Ex	34:28	he **w** upon the tables the words of	3789
Ex	39:30	pure gold, and **w** upon it a writing,	3789
Dt	5:22	he **w** them in two tables of stone,	3789
Dt	10:4	he **w** on the tables, according to	3789
Dt	31:9	Moses **w** this law, and delivered it.	3789
Jos	8:32	he **w** there upon the stones a copy	3789
1Ki	21:8	So she **w** letters in Ahab's name,	3789
Ezr	4:6	**w** they unto him an accusation	3789
Est	9:29	Mordecai … **w** with all authority,	3789
Jer	36:32	**w** … from the mouth of Jeremiah	3789
Da	5:5	saw the part of the hand that **w**	3790
Mk	10:5	**your heart he w you this precept.**	*1125*
Jn	5:46	**have believed me: for he w of me.**	*1125*
Jn	8:6	with his finger **w** on the ground	*1125*
Jn	8:8	down, and **w** on the ground	*1125*
Jn	19:19	And Pilate **w** a title, and put it on	*1125*
2Co	2:4	I **w** unto you with many tears;	*1125*

WROTH See also WRATHFUL.

Ge	4:6	said unto Cain, Why art thou **w**?	2734
Ge	34:7	and they were very **w**, because he	2734
Ge	40:2	Pharaoh was **w** against two of his	7107
Nu	16:15	And Moses was very **w**, and said.	2734
Nu	16:22	be **w** with all the congregation?.	7107
Dt	3:26	the Lord was **w** with me for your	5674
Dt	9:19	the Lord was **w** against you to.	7107
1Sa	20:7	but if he be very **w**, then be sure	2734
2Sa	13:21	all these things, he was very **w**.	2734
2Sa	22:8	and shook, because he was **w**	2734
2Ki	5:11	Naaman was **w**, and went away.	7107
2Ki	13:19	the man of God was **w** with him,	7107
2Ch	26:19	while he was **w** with the priests,	2196
Ne	4:1	we builded the wall, he was **w**,	2734
Est	1:12	therefore was the king very **w**,.	7107
Est	2:21	were **w**, and sought to lay hand on	7107
Ps	18:7	were shaken, because he was **w**	2734
Ps	78:21	the Lord heard this, and was **w**	5674
Ps	78:59	When God heard this, he was **w**,	5674
Isa	47:6	I was **w** with my people, I have	7107
Isa	54:9	that I would not be **w** with thee,	7107
Isa	57:17	I hid me, and was **w**, and he went	7107
Isa	64:5	thou art **w**; for we have sinned:.	7107
Jer	37:15	the princes were **w** with Jeremiah,	7107
Mt	2:16	was exceeding **w**, and sent forth,	*2373*
Mt	18:34	**his lord was w, and delivered**	*3710*
Mt	22:7	**the king heard thereof, he was w:**	*3710*
Rev	12:17	dragon was **w** with the woman	*3710*

WROUGHT

Ge	34:7	because he had **w** folly in Israel.	6213
Ex	10:2	what things I have **w** in Egypt,	5953
Ex	36:8	**w** the work of the tabernacle.	6213
Le	20:12	they have **w** confusion; their blood	6213
Dt	13:14	abomination is **w** among you;.	6213
Dt	22:21	she hath **w** folly in Israel, to play.	6213
Jos	7:15	because he hath **w** folly in Israel.	6213
1Sa	14:45	**w** this great salvation in Israel?	6213
1Sa	19:5	the Lord **w** a great salvation for all	6213
Ne	4:17	one of his hands **w** in the work,	6213
Ne	9:26	and they **w** great provocations.	6213
Ps	45:13	within: her clothing is of **w** gold	4865
Ps	139:15	curiously **w** in the lowest parts of	7551
Ecc	2:17	the work that is **w** under the sun is	6213
Isa	41:4	Who hath **w** and done it, calling	6466
Jer	18:3	he **w** a work on the wheels.	6213
Da	4:2	the high God hath **w** toward me.	5648
Jnh	1:13	sea **w**, and was tempestuous.	1980
Zep	2:3	which have **w** his judgment;	6466
Mt	20:12	**These last have w but one hour,**	*4160*
Mt	26:10	**she hath w a good work upon me.**	*2038*
Mk	14:6	**she hath w a good work on me.**	*2038*
Jn	3:21	**manifest, that they are w in God.**	*2038*
Ac	5:12	and wonders **w** among the people;	*1096*
Ac	15:12	God had **w** among the Gentiles.	*4160*
Ac	19:11	God **w** special miracles by the	*4160*
Ac	21:19	God had **w** among the Gentiles by	*4160*
Ro	7:8	**w** in me all manner of	*2716*
2Co	7:11	what carefulness it **w** in you, yea,	*2716*
2Co	12:12	signs of an apostle were **w** among	*2716*
Eph	1:20	Which he **w** in Christ, when he.	*1754*
Heb	11:33	**w** righteousness, obtained	*2038*
Jas	2:22	thou how faith **w** with his works,	*4903*
2Jn	8	not those things which we have **w**,	*2038*
Rev	19:20	the false prophet that **w** miracles	*4160*

WRUNG

Le	1:15	the blood thereof shall be **w** out	4680
Le	5:9	rest of the blood shall be **w** out.	4680
Isa	51:17	cup of trembling, and **w** them out	4680

YEA

Ge	3:1	**Y**, hath God said, Ye shall	637, 3588
Job	5:19	**y**, in seven there shall no evil touch	
Job	33:14	For God speaketh once, **y** twice, yet	
Job	40:5	not answer: **y**, twice; but I will	
Pr	6:16	**y**, seven are an abomination unto	
Pr	30:15	**y**, four things say not, It is enough:	
Pr	30:18	for me, **y**, four which I know not:	
Pr	30:29	go well, **y**, four are comely in going.	
Mt	5:37	let your communication be, **Y**, **y**;	*3483*
2Co	1:17	that with me there should be **y** **y**,	*3483*
Jas	5:12	your **y** be **y**, and your nay, nay;	*3483*

YEAR

Ex	23:17	Three times in the **y** all thy males	8141
Le	16:34	of Israel for all their sins once a **y**	8141
Le	19:25	the fifth **y** shall ye eat of the fruit	8141
Le	23:12	lamb without blemish of the first **y**	8141
Le	25:4	the seventh **y** shall be a sabbath	8141
Le	25:11	A jubile shall that fiftieth **y** be	8141
Nu	28:3	lambs of the first **y** without spot	8141
Dt	16:16	Three times in a **y** shall all thy	8141
Dt	24:5	but he shall be free at home one **y**,	8141
Dt	26:12	which is the **y** of tithing, and hast	8141
2Ch	24:5	the house of your God from **y** to **y**,	8141
Ne	10:34	at times appointed **y** by **y**, to burn	8141
Est	9:27	to their appointed time every **y**;	8141
Ps	65:11	crownest the **y** with thy goodness;	8141
Isa	61:2	the acceptable **y** of the Lord,	8141
Jer	28:16	this **y** thou shalt die, because thou	8141
Lk	4:19	**the acceptable y of the Lord**	*1763*
Lk	13:8	**Lord, let it alone this y also, till**	*2094*
Heb	9:7	the high priest alone once every **y**	*1763*
Heb	9:25	into the holy place every **y** with	*1763*
Heb	10:1	they offered **y** by **y** continually,	*1763*
Heb	10:3	again made of sins every **y**	*1763*
Rev	9:15	and a day, and a month, and a **y**,	*1763*

YEARLY

Jgs	11:40	of Israel went **y** to lament	3117
1Sa	1:3	up out of his city **y** to worship	3117
1Sa	1:21	offer unto the Lord the **y** sacrifice	3117
1Sa	20:6	there is a **y** sacrifice there for all	3117

YEARS

Ge	15:13	shall afflict them four hundred **y**;	8141
Ge	29:20	Jacob served seven **y** for Rachel;	8141
Ge	29:30	served with him yet seven other **y**	8141
Ge	47:9	the days of the **y** of my life been,	8141
Ex	12:41	of the four hundred and thirty **y**	8141
Ex	16:35	of Israel did eat manna forty **y**	8141
Dt	2:7	these forty **y** the Lord thy God	8141
Dt	8:2	thy God led thee these forty **y**	8141
2Sa	5:4	David was thirty **y** old when he	8141
2Sa	5:4	to reign, and he reigned forty **y**	8141
1Ki	6:38	so was he seven **y** in building it	8141
1Ki	7:1	building his own house thirteen **y**	8141
2Ki	20:6	will add unto thy days fifteen **y**;	8141
Ezr	3:8	from twenty **y** old and upward	8141
Job	15:20	the number of **y** is hidden to the	8141
Job	36:26	number of his **y** be searched out	8141
Ps	77:5	days of old, the **y** of ancient times	8141
Ps	78:33	in vanity, and their **y** in trouble	8141
Ps	90:4	For a thousand **y** in thy sight are	8141
Ps	90:9	we spend our **y** as a tale that is	8141
Ps	90:10	The days of our **y** are threescore **y**	8141
Ps	102:27	same, and thy **y** shall have no end	8141
Pr	4:10	and the **y** of thy life shall be many	8141
Pr	9:11	the **y** of thy life shall be increased	8141
Pr	10:27	**y** of the wicked shall be shortened	8141
Ecc	6:3	hundred children, and live many **y**	8141
Ecc	6:6	though he live a thousand **y** twice	8141
Ecc	11:8	But if a man live many **y**, and	8141
Ecc	12:1	nor the **y** draw nigh, when thou	8141
Jer	25:12	when seventy **y** are accomplished	8141
Da	9:2	by books the number of the **y**	8141
Joel	2:25	restore to you the **y** that the locust	8141
Mt	2:16	from two **y** old and under	*1332*
Lk	2:42	when he was twelve **y** old, they	*2094*
Lk	3:23	began to be about thirty **y** of age	*2094*
Lk	8:43	having an issue of blood twelve **y**,	*2094*
Lk	12:19	**much goods laid up for many y;**	*2094*
Lk	13:16	**hath bound, lo, these eighteen y,**	*2094*
Lk	15:29	**Lo, these many y do I serve thee,**	*2094*
Jn	2:20	Forty and six **y** was this temple in	*2094*
Ac	7:6	entreat them evil four hundred **y**	*2094*
Ac	13:20	space of four hundred and fifty **y**	*2094*
Ac	28:30	Paul dwelt two whole **y** in his own	*1333*
Heb	3:9	me, and saw my works forty **y**	*2094*
Heb	3:17	whom was he grieved forty **y**?	*2094*
Heb	11:24	Moses, when he was come to **y**	*1096, 3173*
2Pe	3:8	is with the Lord as a thousand **y**,	*2094*
2Pe	3:8	and a thousand **y** as one day	*2094*
Rev	20:2	and bound him a thousand **y**	*2094*
Rev	20:3	the thousand **y** should be fulfilled:	*2094*
Rev	20:4	reigned with Christ a thousand **y**	*2094*
Rev	20:5	until the thousand **y** were finished	*2094*
Rev	20:6	shall reign with him a thousand **y**	*2094*
Rev	20:7	when the thousand **y** are expired	*2094*

YESTERDAY

Job	8:9	(For we are but of **y**, and know	8543
Ps	90:4	years in thy sight are but as **y**	865
Heb	13:8	Jesus Christ the same **y**, and to day,	*5504*

YET

Ex	11:1	**Y** will I bring one plague more	5750
1Ki	19:18	**Y** I have left me seven thousand in	
Job	1:16	While he was **y** speaking,	
Job	1:17	While he was **y** speaking,	
Job	1:18	While he was **y** speaking,	
Job	3:26	neither was I quiet; **y** trouble came	
Job	5:7	**Y** man is born to trouble, as the	3588
Pr	6:10	**Y** a little sleep, a little slumber,	
Pr	24:33	**Y** a little sleep, a little slumber,	
Isa	53:10	**Y** it pleased the Lord to bruise him:	
Jer	48:47	**Y** will I bring again the captivity of	
Jnh	3:4	**Y** forty days, and Nineveh shall	5750
Lk	18:22	**him, Y lackest thou one thing:**	*2089*
Jn	7:33	**Y a little while am I with you,**	*2089*
Jn	7:39	the Holy Ghost was not **y** given;	*3768*
Jn	12:35	**Y a little while is the light with**	*2089*
Jn	13:33	**y a little while I am with you**	*2089*
Jn	14:19	**Y a little while, and the world**	*2089*
Jn	20:17	**am not y ascended to my Father:**	*3768*
Ro	5:8	while we were **y** sinners, Christ	*2089*
1Co	15:10	**y** not I, but the grace of God which	*1161*
2Co	8:9	**y** for your sakes he became poor	

Gal 2:20 **y** not I, but Christ liveth in me: *3765*
Heb 4:15 tempted like as we are, **y** without sin
Heb 5:8 **y** learned he obedience by the things
Heb 10:37 For **y** a little while, and he that *2089*
1Pe 4:16 **Y** if any man suffer as a Christian *1161*

YIELD
2Ch 30:8 **y** yourselves unto the Lord 5414, 3027
Pr 7:21 fair speech she caused him to **y** 5186
Mk 4:8 **and did y fruit that sprang up** *1325*
Ro 6:13 Neither **y** ye your members as *3936*
Ro 6:13 but **y** yourselves unto God, as *3936*
Ro 6:16 ye **y** yourselves servants to obey *3936*
Ro 6:19 so now **y** your members servants *3936*
Jas 3:12 no fountain both **y** salt water and *4160*

YIELDED
Ge 49:33 **y** up the ghost, and was gathered 1478
Mt 27:50 with a loud voice, **y** up the ghost *863*
Ac 5:10 at his feet, and **y** up the ghost: *1634*

YIELDING
Ge 1:11 fruit tree **y** fruit after his kind 6213
Ge 1:12 and herb **y** seed after his kind 2232
Ecc 10:4 for **y** pacifieth great offences 4832

YOKE
Le 26:13 I have broken the bands of your **y** 5923
Nu 19:2 and upon which never came **y**: 5923
1Ki 12:4 Thy father made our **y** grievous: 5928
1Ki 12:11 I will add to your **y**: my father 5928
Jer 28:11 I break the **y** of Nebuchadnezzar 5923
Mt 11:29 **Take my y upon you, and learn of** *2218*
Mt 11:30 **For my y is easy, and my burden** *2218*
Gal 5:1 again with the **y** of bondage, ... *2218*

YOKED
2Co 6:14 **y** together with unbelievers: *2086*

YONDER
Ge 22:5 lad will go **y** and worship 5704, 3541
Nu 23:15 offering, while I meet the Lord **y** 3541
Mt 17:20 **Remove hence to y place;** *1563*
Mt 26:36 **Sit ye here, while I go and pray y** *2563*

YOUNG
Ge 4:23 and a **y** man to my hurt 3206
Le 4:3 a **y** bullock without blemish 1121, 1241
Le 4:14 offer a **y** bullock for the sin 1121, 1241
Jgs 9:54 his **y** man thrust him through, and 5288
Jgs 14:10 feast; for so used the **y** men to do 970
1Sa 9:2 Saul, a choice **y** man, and a goodly: 970
2Ki 6:17 Lord opened the eyes of the **y** man; 5288
1Ch 22:5 Solomon my son is **y** and tender 5288
Job 1:19 it fell upon the **y** men, and they 5288
Ps 119:9 shall a **y** man cleanse his way? 5288
Ps 148:12 Both **y** men, and maidens; old 970
Pr 1:4 **y** man knowledge and discretion 5288
Pr 20:29 glory of **y** men is their strength: 970
Ecc 11:9 Rejoice, O **y** man, in thy youth; 970
Jer 11:22 the **y** men shall die by the sword; 970
La 1:18 my **y** men are gone into captivity 970
Joel 2:28 your **y** men shall see visions: 970
Am 4:10 your **y** men have I slain with the 970
Mt 2:8 search diligently for the **y** child; *3813*
Mt 2:11 the **y** child with Mary his mother *3813*
Mt 2:20 which sought the **y** child's life *3813*
Mk 10:13 they brought **y** children to him *3813*
Lk 7:14 **Y man, I say unto thee, Arise** *3495*
Jn 21:18 **When thou wast y, thou girdedst** *3501*
Ac 2:17 and your **y** men shall see visions, ... *3495*
Tit 2:4 teach the **y** women to be sober, ... *3501*
Tit 2:6 **Y** men likewise exhort to be *3501*
1Jn 2:13 I write unto you, **y** men, because *3495*

YOUNGER
Ge 19:38 And the **y**, she also bare a son, ... 6810
Ge 25:23 and the elder shall serve the **y** 6810
Ge 48:19 his **y** brother shall be greater 6996
Job 30:1 **y** than I have me in derision 6810, 3117
Lk 15:12 **the y of them said to his father,** *3501*
Ro 9:12 her, The elder shall serve the **y** *1640*
1Pe 5:5 ye **y**, submit yourselves unto the *3501*

YOURS
Ge 45:20 the good of all the land of Egypt is **y**
Dt 11:24 of your feet shall tread shall be **y**:
Jos 2:14 Our life for **y**, if ye utter not this our
2Ch 20:15 for the battle is not **y**, but God's
Jer 5:19 strangers in a land that is not **y**
Lk 6:20 **poor: for y is the kingdom of** *5212*

YOURSELVES See also SELVES.
Ex 32:29 Consecrate **y** to day to the Lord, ... 3027
Nu 16:21 Separate **y** from among this
Jos 7:13 say, Sanctify **y** against to morrow:
Jos 24:22 Ye are witnesses against **y** that ye
1Sa 4:9 Be strong, and quit **y** like men,
Job 19:3 that ye make **y** strange to me
Mt 6:20 **lay up for y treasures in heaven,** *5213*
Mt 23:31 **Wherefore ye be witnesses unto y,** *1438*
Lk 17:14 **Go shew y unto the priests** *1438*
Lk 23:28 **weep not for me, but weep for y,** *1438*
Ac 13:46 **y** unworthy of everlasting life, ... *1438*
Ro 6:16 whom ye yield **y** servants to obey *1438*
Ro 12:19 Dearly beloved, avenge not **y**, ... *1438*
2Co 13:5 Examine **y**, whether ye be in *1438*
Eph 5:19 Speaking to **y** in psalms and *1438*
Eph 5:21 Submitting **y** one to another
Eph 5:22 submit **y** unto your own husbands,
Col 3:18 submit **y** unto your own husbands,
Heb 13:17 the rule over you, and submit **y**: *5216*
Jas 4:7 Submit **y** therefore to God
Jas 4:10 Humble **y** in the sight of the Lord,
1Pe 2:13 Submit **y** to every ordinance
1Pe 5:6 Humble **y** therefore under the
1Jn 5:21 Little children, keep **y** from idols *1438*
Jude 20 building up **y** on your most holy *1438*
Jude 21 Keep **y** in the love of God, looking *1438*

YOUTH
Ge 8:21 of man's heart is evil from his **y**; 5271
Ps 25:7 Remember not the sins of my **y** 5271
Ps 103:5 thy youth is renewed like the eagle's. 5271
Pr 5:18 rejoice with the wife of thy **y** 5271
Ecc 11:9 Rejoice, O young man, in thy **y**; 3208
Ecc 11:10 for childhood and **y** are vanity 7839
Ecc 12:1 thy Creator in the days of thy **y**, ... 979
Jer 32:30 done evil before me from their **y** 5271
La 3:27 that he bear the yoke in his **y** 5271
Mk 10:20 these have I observed from my **y** *3503*
1Ti 4:12 Let no man despise thy **y**; but be *3503*

YOUTHFUL
2Ti 2:22 Flee also **y** lusts: but follow *3512*

Z

ZEAL

2Sa 21:2 slay them in his **z** to the children 7065
2Ki 10:16 and see my **z** for the Lord 7068
2Ki 19:31 **z** of the Lord of hosts shall do this 7068
Ps 69:9 **z** of thine house hath eaten me up; 7068
Ps 119:139 My **z** hath consumed me, because 7068
Isa 9:7 The **z** of the Lord of hosts will 7068
Isa 37:32 **z** of the Lord of hosts shall do this 7068
Isa 59:17 and was clad with **z** as a cloke. 7068
Isa 63:15 where is thy **z** and thy strength, ... 7068
Eze 5:13 I the Lord have spoken it in my **z**, ... 7068
Jn 2:17 **z** of thine house hath eaten me *2205*
Ro 10:2 record that they have a **z** of God, ... *2205*
2Co 7:11 yea, what **z**, yea, what revenge! *2205*
2Co 9:2 your **z** hath provoked very many *2205*
Php 3:6 Concerning **z**, persecuting the. *2205*
Col 4:13 that he hath a great **z** for you, ... *2205*

ZEALOUS

Nu 25:11 while he was **z** for my sake. 7065
Nu 25:13 because he was **z** for his God, and 7065
Ac 21:20 and they are all **z** of the law: *2207*
Ac 22:3 and was **z** toward God, as ye all. *2207*
1Co 14:12 as ye are **z** of spiritual gifts, ... *2207*
Gal 1:14 **z** of the traditions of my fathers *2207*
Tit 2:14 a peculiar people, **z** of good works *2207*
Rev 3:19 be **z** therefore, and repent.. . . . . *2206*

ZEALOUSLY

Gal 4:17 They **z** affect you, but not well; *2206*
Gal 4:18 good to be **z** affected always in a *2206*

ZION (**zi´-un**)

2Sa 5:7 David took the strong hold of **Z**; 6726
1Ki 8:1 of the city of David, which is **Z**. 6726
2Ki 19:21 daughter of **Z** hath despised thee 6726
2Ki 19:31 they that escape out of mount **Z**. 6726
1Ch 11:5 David took the castle of **Z** 6726
2Ch 5:2 of the city of David, which is **Z**. 6726
Ps 2:6 my king upon my holy hill of **Z**,. 6726
Ps 9:11 to the Lord, which dwelleth in **Z**: 6726
Ps 9:14 in the gates of the daughter of **Z**: 6726
Ps 14:7 of Israel were come out of **Z**! 6726
Ps 20:2 and strengthen thee out of **Z**; 6726
Ps 48:2 of the whole earth, is mount **Z** 6726
Ps 48:11 Let mount **Z** rejoice, let the 6726
Ps 48:12 Walk about **Z**, and go round 6726
Ps 50:2 Out of **Z** the perfection of beauty. 6726
Ps 51:18 good in thy good pleasure unto **Z** 6726
Ps 53:6 of Israel were come out of **Z**! 6726
Ps 69:35 For God will save **Z**, and will. 6726
Ps 74:2 this mount **Z**, wherein thou hast 6726
Ps 76:2 and his dwelling place in **Z** 6726
Ps 78:68 the mount **Z** which he loved 6726
Ps 84:7 every one of them in **Z** appeareth 6726
Ps 87:2 The Lord loveth the gates of **Z** 6726
Ps 87:5 And of **Z** it shall be said, This and 6726
Ps 97:8 **Z** heard, and was glad; and the 6726
Ps 99:2 The Lord is great in **Z**; and he is 6726
Ps 102:13 arise, and have mercy upon **Z**. 6726
Ps 102:16 when the Lord shall build up **Z**. 6726
Ps 102:21 declare the name of the Lord in **Z**,. 6726
Ps 110:2 the rod of thy strength out of **Z**:. 6726
Ps 125:1 in the Lord shall be as mount **Z** 6726
Ps 126:1 turned again the captivity of **Z**. 6726
Ps 128:5 The Lord shall bless thee out of **Z** 6726
Ps 129:5 and turned back that hate **Z** 6726
Ps 132:13 For the Lord hath chosen **Z**; 6726
Ps 133:3 upon the mountains of **Z**: 6726
Ps 134:3 and earth bless thee out of **Z**. 6726
Ps 135:21 Blessed be the Lord out of **Z**, ... 6726
Ps 137:1 we wept, when we remembered **Z** 6726
Ps 137:3 Sing us one of the songs of **Z** 6726
Ps 146:10 reign for ever, even thy God, O **Z**. 6726
Ps 147:12 O Jerusalem; praise thy God, O **Z**. 6726
Ps 149:2 let the children of **Z** be joyful in 6726
SS 3:11 Go forth, O ye daughters of **Z**, and 6726
Isa 1:8 daughter of **Z** if left as a cottage 6726
Isa 1:27 **Z** shall be redeemed with. 6726
Isa 2:3 for out of **Z** shall go forth the law, ... 6726
Isa 3:16 the daughters of **Z** are haughty, ... 6726
Isa 3:17 of the head of the daughters of **Z**. 6726
Isa 4:3 to pass, that he that is left in **Z** 6726
Isa 4:4 the filth of the daughters of **Z**. 6726
Isa 4:5 every dwelling place of mount **Z** 6726
Isa 8:18 hosts, which dwelleth in mount **Z** 6726
Isa 10:12 his whole work upon mount **Z**. 6726
Isa 10:24 O my people that dwellest in **Z**. 6726
Isa 10:32 the mount of the daughter of **Z** 6726
Isa 12:6 and shout, thou inhabitant of **Z**:. 6726
Isa 14:32 That the Lord hath founded **Z** 6726
Isa 16:1 the mount of the daughter of **Z**. 6726
Isa 18:7 of the Lord of hosts, the mount **Z**. 6726
Isa 24:23 of hosts shall reign in mount **Z**. 6726
Isa 28:16 I lay in **Z** for a foundation a stone,. 6726
Isa 29:8 be, that fight against mount **Z**. 6726
Isa 30:19 shall dwell in **Z** at Jerusalem:. 6726
Isa 31:4 come down to fight for mount **Z** 6726
Isa 31:9 the Lord, whose fire is in **Z** 6726
Isa 33:5 he hath filled **Z** with judgment 6726
Isa 33:14 The sinners in **Z** are afraid; 6726
Isa 33:20 Look upon **Z**, the city of our. 6726
Isa 34:8 for the controversy of **Z** 6726
Isa 35:10 and come to **Z** with songs and 6726
Isa 37:22 daughter of **Z**, hath despised thee, ... 6726
Isa 37:32 they that escape out of mount **Z**. 6726
Isa 40:9 O **Z**, that bringest good tidings. 6726
Isa 41:27 The first shall say to **Z**, Behold 6726
Isa 46:13 place salvation in **Z** for Israel my 6726
Isa 49:14 **Z** said, The Lord hath forsaken 6726
Isa 51:3 For the Lord shall comfort **Z**. 6726
Isa 51:11 and come with singing unto **Z**;. 6726
Isa 51:16 say unto **Z**, Thou art my people,. 6726
Isa 52:1 awake; put on thy strength, O **Z**;. 6726
Isa 52:2 thy neck, O captive daughter of **Z** 6726
Isa 52:7 saith unto **Z**, Thy God reigneth! 6726
Isa 52:8 the Lord shall bring again **Z** 6726
Isa 59:20 the Redeemer shall come to **Z**. 6726
Isa 60:14 The **Z** of the Holy One of Israel.. 6726
Isa 61:3 unto them that mourn in **Z**, ... 6726
Isa 62:11 Say ye to the daughter of **Z** 6726
Isa 64:10 **Z** is a wilderness, Jerusalem a 6726
Isa 66:8 for as soon as **Z** travailed, she 6726
Jer 3:14 family, and I will bring you to **Z**. 6726
Jer 4:6 Set up the standard toward **Z** 6726
Jer 4:31 the voice of the daughter of **Z**. 6726
Jer 6:2 have likened the daughter of **Z** to. 6726

Jer	6:23	war against thee, O daughter of **Z**	6726
Jer	8:19	Is not the Lord in **Z**? is not her	6726
Jer	9:19	voice of wailing is heard out of **Z**,	6726
Jer	14:19	Judah? hath thy soul lothed **Z**?	6726
Jer	26:18	**Z** shall be plowed like a field, and	6726
Jer	30:17	This is **Z**, whom no man seeketh	6726
Jer	31:6	let us go to up to **Z** unto the Lord	6726
Jer	31:12	come and sing in the height of **Z**	6726
Jer	50:5	They shall ask the way to **Z** with	6726
Jer	50:28	to declare in **Z** the vengeance of the	6726
Jer	51:10	declare in **Z** the work of the Lord	6726
Jer	51:24	evil that they have done in **Z**	6726
Jer	51:35	shall the inhabitant of **Z** say;	6726
La	1:4	The ways of **Z** do mourn, because	6726
La	1:6	from the daughter of **Z** all her	6726
La	1:17	**Z** spreadeth forth her hands, and	6726
La	2:1	covered the daughter of **Z** with a	6726
La	2:4	tabernacle of the daughter of **Z**	6726
La	2:6	and sabbaths to be forgotten in **Z**,	6726
La	2:8	the wall of the daughter of **Z**.	6726
La	2:10	The elders of the daughter of **Z** sit	6726
La	2:13	thee, O virgin daughter of **Z**?	6726
La	2:18	O wall of the daughter of **Z**, let	6726
La	4:2	The precious sons of **Z**,	6726
La	4:11	and hath kindled a fire in **Z**,	6726
La	4:22	is accomplished, O daughter of **Z**;	6726
La	5:11	They ravished the women in **Z**	6726
La	5:18	Because of the mountain of **Z**,	6726
Joel	2:1	Blow ye the trumpet in **Z**, and	6726
Joel	2:15	Blow the trumpet in **Z**, sanctify	6726
Joel	2:23	Be glad then, ye children of **Z**,	6726
Joel	2:32	for in mount **Z** and in Jerusalem	6726
Joel	3:16	Lord also shall roar out of **Z**	6726
Joel	3:17	the Lord your God dwelling in **Z**,	6726
Joel	3:21	for the Lord dwelleth in **Z**	6726
Am	1:2	The Lord will roar from **Z**, and	6726
Am	6:1	Woe to them that are at ease in **Z**	6726
Ob	17	upon mount **Z** shall be deliverance	6726
Ob	21	come up on mount **Z** to judge	6726
Mic	1:13	of the sin to the daughter of **Z**:	6726
Mic	3:10	They build up **Z** with blood, and	6726
Mic	3:12	shall **Z** for your sake be plowed	6726
Mic	4:2	for the law shall go forth of **Z**,	6726
Mic	4:7	shall reign over them in mount **Z**	6726
Mic	4:8	strong hold of the daughter of **Z**,	6726
Mic	4:10	to bring forth, O daughter of **Z**,	6726
Mic	4:11	and let our eye look upon **Z**.	6726
Mic	4:13	and thresh, O daughter of **Z**:	6726
Zep	3:14	Sing, O daughter of **Z**; shout	6726
Zep	3:16	and to **Z**, Let not thine hands be	6726
Zec	1:14	jealous for Jerusalem and for **Z**	6726
Zec	1:17	and the Lord shall yet comfort **Z**	6726
Zec	2:7	Deliver thyself, O **Z**, that dwellest	6726
Zec	2:10	and rejoice, O daughter of **Z**:	6726
Zec	8:2	jealous for **Z** with great jealousy	6726
Zec	8:3	I am returned unto **Z**, and will	6726
Zec	9:9	Rejoice greatly, O daughter of **Z**;	6726
Zec	9:13	and raised up thy sons, O **Z**,	6726

ZION'S (zi´-uns)

Isa	62:1	For **Z** sake will I not hold my	6726

INDEX OF PROPER NAMES

This index is a compilation of **proper names** found in Scripture. The **proper names** are followed by a pronunciation guide and defining or explanatory words or phrases. Definitions are denoted by italics. Words in all capital letters refer to words that occur elsewhere in this index. A few **key proper names** are followed by portions of Scripture, along with their references, designed to give an example of how the word is used in its context. These words are abbreviated to their first letter in the Scriptures portions (e.g., "Christ" is **"C"** [in boldface]).

A

AARON, a´-ron
light (s?) — Ex 4:14

AARONITES, a´-ron-ites
descendants of Aaron — 1Ch 12:27

ABADDON, a-bad´-don
destruction — Rev 9:11

ABAGTHA, a-bag´-thah
given by fortune — Est 1:10

ABANA, a´-ba-nah
stony — 2Ki 5:12

ABARIM, a´-ba-rim
regions beyond — Nu 27:12

ABBA, ab´-bah
father — Mk 14:36

ABDA, ab´-dah
servant — 1Ki 4:6

ABDEEL, ab´-de-el
same as ABDIEL — Jer 36:26

ABDI, ab´-di
servant of Jehovah — 1Ch 6:44

ABDIEL, ab´-di-el
servant of God — 1Ch 5:15

ABDON, ab´-don
servile — Jgs 12:13

ABED-NEGO, a-bed´-ne-go
servant (worshiper) of Nebo — Da 1:7

ABEL, a´-bel
1 *vanity* — Ge 4:2
2 *A meadow* — 2Sa 20:14

ABEL-BETH-MAACHAH, a-bel-beth-ma´-a-kah
meadow of the house of Maachah — 1Ki 15:20

ABEL-MAIM, a´-bel-ma´-im
meadow of the waters — 2Ch 16:4

ABEL-MEHOLAH, a´-bel-me-ho´-lah
meadow of dancing — Jgs 7:22

ABEL-MIZRAIM, a´-bel-miz-ra´-im
meadow of Egypt — Ge 50:11

ABEL-SHITTIM, a´-bel-shit´-im
meadow of Acacias — Nu 33:49

ABEZ, a´-bez
whiteness — Jos 19:20

ABI, a´-bi
short for ABIAH — 2Ki 18:2

ABIA, a-bi´-ah
Gr. for ABIJAH — Mt 1:7

ABIAH, a-bi´-ah
same as ABIJAH — 2Ki 18:2

ABI-ALBON, a-bi-al´-bon
father of strength — 2Sa 23:31

ABIASAPH, a-bi´-a-saf
father of gathering — Ex 6:24

ABIATHAR, a-bi´-a-thar
father of plenty — 1Sa 22:20

ABIB, a´-bib
an ear of corn, or green ear — Ex 13:4

ABIDAH, a-bi´-dah
father of knowledge — Ge 25:4

ABIDAN, a-bi´-dan
father of a judge — Nu 1:11

ABIEL, a´-bi-el
father of strength — 1Sa 9:1

ABIEZER, a´-bi-e´-zer
father of help — Jos 17:2

ABIEZRITE, a´-bi-ez´-rite
a descendant of Abiezer — Jgs 6:11

ABIGAIL, a´-bi-gale
father of exultation — 1Sa 25:14

ABIHAIL, a´-bi-hale
father of strength — Nu 3:35

ABIHU, a-bi´-hoo
He (God) is father — Ex 6:23

ABIHUD, a-bi´-hood
father of Judah — 1Ch 8:3

ABIJAH, a-bi´-jah
father of Jehovah — 1Ki 14:1

ABIJAM, a-bi´-jam
another spelling of ABIJAH — 1Ki 14:31

ABILENE, a´-bi-le´-ne
a grassy place (?) — Lk 3:1

ABIMAEL, a´-bi-ma´-el
father of Mael — Ge 10:28

ABIMELECH, a-bi´-me-lek
father of the king — Ge 20:2

ABINADAB, a-bi´-na-dab
father of nobility — 1Sa 7:1

ABINER, ab´-ner
same as ABNER — 1Sa 14:50

ABINOAM, a´-bi-no´-am
father of pleasantness — Jgs 4:6

ABIRAM, a-bi´-ram
father of loftiness — Nu 16:1

ABISHAG, a-bi´-shag
father of error (?) — 1Ki 1:3

ABISHAI, a´-bi-sha´-i
father of a gift — 1Sa 26:6

ABISHALOM, a-bi´-sha-lom
same as ABSALOM — 1Ki 15:2

ABISHUA, a´-bi-shoo´-ah
father of welfare — 1Ch 6:4

ABISHUR, a-bi´-shoor
of the wall — 1Ch 2:28

ABITAL, a-bi´-tal
father of dew — 2Sa 3:4

ABITUB, a-bi´-toob
father of goodness — 1Ch 8:11

ABIUD, a-bi´-ood
Gr. for ABIHUD — Mt 1:13

ABNER, ab´-ner
father of light — 1Sa 14:50

ABRAHAM, a´-bra-ham
father of a multitude — Ge 17:5

ABRAM, ab´-ram
high father — Ge 11:26

ABSALOM, ab´-sa-lom
father of peace — 2Sa 3:3

ACCAD, ak´-ad
fortress (?) — Ge 10:10

ACCHO, ak´-o
sand-heated — Jgs 1:31

ACELDAMA, a-kel´-da-mah
field of blood — Ac 1:19

ACHAIA, a-ka´-yah
Greece — Ac 18:12

ACHAICUS, a-ka´-ik-us
belonging to Achaia — 1Co 16:17

ACHAN, a´-kan
troubler — Jos 7:1

ACHAR, a´-kar
same as ACHAN — 1Ch. 2:7

ACHAZ, a´-kaz
Gr. for AHAZ — Mt 1:9

ACHBOR, ak´-bor
a mouse — Ge 36:38

ACHIM, a´-kim
short for JACHIN (?) — Mt 1:14

Names

ACHISH, a´-kish
angry (?) 1Sa 21:10

ACHMETHA, ak´-me-thah
fortress (?) Ezr 6:2

ACHOR, a´-kor
trouble Jos 7:24

ACHSA, ak´-sah
same as ACHSAH 1Ch 2:49

ACHSAH, ak´-sah
anklet Jos 15:16

ACHSHAPH, ak´-shaf
enchantment Jos 11:1

ACHZIB, ak´-zib
deceit Jos 15:44

ADADAH, a´-da-dah
festival (?) Jos 15:22

ADAH, a´-dah
ornament Ge 4:19

ADAIAH, a-da´-yah
whom Jehovah adorns 2Ki 22:1

ADALIA, a´-da-li´-ah
upright (?) Est 9:8

ADAM, a´-dam
red Ge 2:19

ADAMAH, a´-da-mah
red earth Jos 19:36

ADAMI, a´-da-mi
human Jos 19:33

ADAR, a´-dar
fire (?) Est 3:7

ADBEEL, ad´-be-el
miracle of God (?) Ge 25:13

ADDAN, ad´-an
humble (?) Ezr 2:59

ADDAR, ad´-ar
greatness (?) 1Ch 8:3

ADDI, ad´-i
ornament (?) Lk 3:28

ADDON, ad´-on
same as ADDAN Ne 7:61

ADER, a´-der
flock 1Ch 8:15

ADIEL, a´-di-el
ornament of God 1Ch 4:36

ADIN, a´-din
slender Ezr 2:15

ADINA, a´-di-nah
same as ADIN 1Ch 11:42

ADINO, a´-di-no
same as ADIN (?) 2Sa 23:8

ADITHAIM, a´-dith-a´-im
twofold ornament Jos 15:36

ADLAI, ad´-la-i
just (?) 1Ch 27:29

ADMAH, ad´-mah
same as ADAMAH Ge 10:19

ADMATHA, ad´-math-ah
earthly, dark-colored (?) Est 1:14

ADNA, ad´-nah
pleasure Ezr 10:30

ADNAH, ad´-nah
same as ADNA 2Ch 17:14

ADONI-BEZEK, a-do´-ni-be´-zek
lord of Bezek Jgs 1:5

ADONIJAH, a´-do-ni´-jah
Jehovah is my Lord 2Sa 3:4

ADONIKAM, a´-do-ni´-kam
lord of enemies Ezr 2:13

ADONIRAM, a´-do-ni´-ram
lord of height 1Ki 4:6

ADONI-ZEDEK, a-do´-ni-ze´-dek
lord of justice Jos 10:1

ADORAIM, a´-dor-a´-im
two chiefs (?) 2Ch 11:9

ADORAM, a-do´-ram
contracted from ADONIRAM 2Sa 20:24

ADRAMMELECH, ad-ram´-me-lek
Adar is king, or king of fire (?) 2Ki 17:31

ADRAMYTTIUM, ad´-ra-mit´-ti-um
the mansion of death Ac 27:2

ADRIEL, a´-dri-el
flock of God 1Sa 18:19

ADULLAM, a-dul´-am
justice of the people Jos 12:15

ADULLAMITE, a-dul´-am-ite
a native of Adullam Ge 38:1

ADUMMIM, a-dum´-im
the red (men?) Jos 15:7

AENEAS, e´-ne-as
praiseworthy (?) Ac 9:33

AENON, e´-non
springs Jn 3:23

AGABUS, ag´-ab-us
Gr. for HAGAB Ac 11:28

AGAG, a´-gag
flaming (?) Nu 24:7

AGAGITE, a´-gag-ite
member of house of Agag Est 3:1

AGAR, a´-gar
same as HAGAR Gal 4:24

AGEE, a´-gee
fugitive (?) 2Sa 23:11

AGRIPPA, a-grip´-ah
King Agrippa II
(A.D. 27–ca. A.D. 100)
Last of the Herods Ac 25:13

AGUR, a´-goor
an assembler Pr 30:1

AHAB, a´-hab
uncle 1Ki 16:29

AHARAH, a-har´-ah
after the brother 1Ch 8:1

AHARHEL, a-har´-hel
behind the breastwork 1Ch 4:8

AHASAI, a-haz´-a-i
same as JAHZERAH (?) Ne 11:13

AHASBAI, a-has´-ba-i
blooming 2Sa 23:34

AHASUERUS, a-haz´-u-e´-rus
king (?) Est 1:1

AHAVA, a´-ha-va
a place and a stream in Babylon Ezr 8:15

AHAZ, a´-haz
possessor 2Ki 15:38

AHAZIAH, a-haz-i´-ah
whom Jehovah upholds 1Ki 22:40

AHBAN, ah´-ban
brotherly 1Ch 2:29

AHER, a´-her
following 1Ch 7:12

AHI, a´-hi
brother 1Ch 5:15

AHIAH, a-hi´-ah
brother of Jehovah 1Sa 14:3

AHIAM, a-hi´-am
brother of the mother (?) 2Sa 23:33

AHIAN, a-hi´-an
brotherly 1Ch 7:19

AHIEZER, a´-hi-e´-zer
brother of help Nu 1:12

AHIHUD, a-hi´-hood
a brother is praiseworthy (?) Nu 34:27

AHIJAH, a-hi´-jah
same as AHIAH 1Ki 11:29

AHIKAM, a-hi´-kam
brother of the enemy 2Ki 22:12

AHILUD, a-hi´-lood
brother of one born 2Sa 8:16

AHIMAAZ, a´-hi-ma´-az
brother of anger 2Sa 15:27

AHIMAN, a-hi´-man
brother of a gift Nu 13:22

AHIMELECH, a-hi´-me-lek
brother of the king 1Sa 21:1

AHIMOTH, a-hi´-moth
brother of death 1Ch 6:25

AHINADAB, a-hi´-na-dab
brother of a nobleman 1Ki 4:14

AHINOAM, a´-hi-no´-am
brother of grace 1Sa 14:50

AHIO, a-hi´-o
brotherly 2Sa 6:3

AHIRA, a-hi´-rah
brother of a wicked man Nu 1:15

AHIRAM, a-hi´-ram
brother of a tall man Nu 26:38

AHIRAMITE, a-hi´-ram-ite
a descendant of Ahiram Nu 26:38
AHISAMACH, a-hi´-sa-mak
brother of aid Ex 31:6
AHISHAHAR, a-hi´-sha-har
brother of the dawn 1Ch 7:10
AHISHAR, a-hi´-shar
brother of the singer 1Ki 4:6
AHITHOPHEL, a-hi´-tho-fel
brother of impiety 2Sa 15:12
AHITUB, a-hi´-toob
brother of goodness 1Sa 14:3
AHLAB, ah´-lab
fertility Jgs 1:31
AHLAI, ah-la´-i
sweet (?) 1Ch 2:31
AHOAH, a-ho´-ah
same as AHIJAH (?) 1Ch 8:4
AHOHITE, a-hoh´-ite
a descendant of Ahoah 2Sa 23:9
AHOLAH, a-ho´-lah
(she has) her own tent Eze 23:4
AHOLIAB, a´-ho-li´-ab
father's tent Ex 31:6
AHOLIBAH, a´-ho-li´-bah
my tent is in her Eze 23:4
AHOLIBAMAH, a´-ho-li-ba´-mah
tent of the high place Ge 36:2
AHUMAI, a´-hoo-ma´-i
brother of (dweller near) water 1Ch 4:2
AHUZAM, a-hooz´-am
their possession 1Ch 4:6
AHUZZATH, a-hooz´-ath
possession Ge 26:26
AI, a´-i
a heap of ruins Jos 7:2
AIAH, ai´-ah
hawk 2Sa 3:7
AIATH, ai´-ath
ruins Isa 10:28
AIJA, ai´-jah
same as AI Ne 11:31
AIJALON, ai´-ja-lon
place of gazelles Jos 21:24
AIJELETH-SHAHAR, ai-je-leth-sha´-har
doe of the dawn Ps 22:title
AIN, a´-in
an eye, fountain Nu 34:11
AJAH, a´-jah
same as AIAH Ge 36:24
AJALON, ad´-jal-on
same as AIJALON Jos 19:42
AKAN, a´-kan
twisted Ge 36:27
AKKUB, ak´-oob
insidious 1Ch 3:24
AKRABBIM, ak-rab´-im
scorpions Nu 34:4
ALAMETH, a-lam´-eth
covering 1Ch 7:8
ALAMMELECH, al-am´-me-lek
king's oak Jos 19:26
ALEMETH, a-lem´-eth
same as ALAMETH 1Ch 8:36
ALEXANDER, al´-ex-an´-der
defending men Mk 15:21
ALEXANDRIA, al´-ex-an´-dri-a
city named after Alexander Ac 18:24
ALIAH, a-li´-ah
same as ALVAH 1Ch 1:51
ALIAN, a-li´-an
same as ALVAN 1Ch 1:40
ALLON, al´-on
an oak 1Ch 4:37
ALLON-BACHUTH, al-on-bak´-ooth
oak of weeping Ge 35:8
ALMODAD, al-mo´-dad
extension (?) Ge 10:26
ALMON, al´-mon
hidden Jos 21:18
ALMON-DIBLATHAIM, al´-mon-dib´-lath-a´-im
hiding of the two cakes (?) Nu 33:46
ALOTH, a´-loth
yielding milk (?) 1Ki 4:16
ALPHA, al´-fah
first letter of Gr. alphabet Rev 1:8
ALPHAEUS, al-fee´-us
successor Mt 10:3
ALUSH, a´-loosh
tumult of men Nu 33:13
ALVAH, al´-vah
high, tall, thick Ge 36:40
ALVAN, al´-van
tall Ge 36:23
AMAD, a´-mad
eternal people (?) Jos 19:26
AMAL, a´-mal
labor, sorrow 1Ch 7:35
AMALEK, am´-al-ek
grandson of Esau Ge 36:12
AMALEKITES, am-al´-ek-ites
descendants of Amalek Ge 14:7
AMAM, a´-mam
metropolis (?) Jos 15:26
AMANA, a-ma´-nah
fixed (?) SS 4:8
AMARIAH, a´-mar-i´-ah
Jehovah has said 1Ch 6:7
AMASA, a´-mas-a
burden 2Sa 17:25
AMASAI, a´-mas-a´-i
burdensome 1Ch 6:25
AMASHAI, a´-mash-a´-i
same as AMASAI Ne 11:13
AMASIAH, a´-mas-i´-ah
burden of Jehovah 2Ch 17:16
AMAZIAH, a´-maz-i´-ah
Jehovah strengthens 2Ki 14:1
AMI, a´-mi
same as AMON Ezr 2:57
AMINADAB, a-mi´-na-dab
same as AMMINADAB Mt 1:4
AMITTAI, a-mit´-a-i
true 2Ki 14:25
AMMAH, am´-ah
beginning, foundation 2Sa 2:24
AMMI, am´-i
my people Hos 2:1
AMMIEL, am´-i-el
people of God Nu 13:12
AMMIHUD, am-i´-hood
people of praise (?) Nu 1:10
AMMINADAB, am-i´-na-dab
people of the prince Ex 6:23
AMMINADIB, am-i´-na-dib
same as AMMINADAB SS 6:12
AMMISHADDAI, am´-i-shad´-a-i
people of the Almighty Nu 1:12
AMMIZABAD, am-i´-za-bad
people of the giver 1Ch 27:6
AMMON, am´-on
son of my people (?) Ge 19:38
AMMONITE, am´-on-ite
descendant of Ammon Dt 23:3
AMMONITESS, am´-on-ite-ess
fem. of AMMONITE 2Ch 12:13
AMNON, am´-non
faithful 2Sa 3:2
AMOK, a´-mok
deep Ne 12:7
AMON, a´-mon
faithful 2Ki 21:18
AMORITE, am´-or-ite
mountaineer Ge 10:16
AMOS, a´-mos
burden Am 1:1
AMOZ, a´-moz
strong Isa 1:1
AMPHIPOLIS, am-phi´-pol-is
around the city Ac 17:1
AMPLIAS, am´-pli-as
short for Ampliatus, *enlarged* Ro 16:8
AMRAM, am´-ram
people of the Highest Ex 6:18
AMRAMITES, am´-ram-ites
the descendants of Amram Nu 3:27

Names

AMRAPHEL, am´-ra-fel
one that divulges secrets (?) Ge 14:1

AMZI, am´-zi
strong 1Ch 6:46

ANAB, a´-nab
a place fertile in grapes Jos 11:21

ANAH, a´-nah
answer Ge 36:2

ANAHARATH, a-na´-har-ath
gorge Jos 19:19

ANAIAH, an-ai´-ah
Jehovah has answered Ne 8:4

ANAK, a´-nak
long-necked (?) Nu 13:22

ANAKIM, a´-nak-im
tribe named for Anak Dt 1:28

ANAMIM, a´-na-mim
a descendent of MIZRAIM Ge 10:13

ANAMMELECH, a-nam´-me-lek
idol of the king, or Anu is king (?) 2Ki 17:31

ANAN, a´-nan
a cloud Ne 10:26

ANANI, an-a´-ni
short for ANANIAH 1Ch 3:24

ANANIAH, an-an-i´-ah
whom Jehovah covers Ne 3:23

ANANIAS, an-an-i´-as
Gr. for HANANIAH Ac 5:1

ANATH, a´-nath
an answer to prayer Jgs 3:31

ANATHEMA, an-ath´-em-ah
accursed 1Co 16:22

ANATHOTH, a´-nath-oth
answers to prayer Jos 21:18

ANDREW, an´-droo
manly Mk 1:29

ANDRONICUS, an´-dro-ni´-kus
man-conquering Ro 16:7

ANEM, a´-nem
same as EN-GAN-NIM (?) 1Ch 6:73

ANER, a´-ner
a young man (?) Ge 14:13

ANETHOTHITE, a-neth´-oth-ite
a man of Anathoth 2Sa 23:27

ANETOTHITE, a-net´-oth-ite
same as ANETHOTHITE 1Ch 27:12

ANIAM, a-ni´-am
sighing of the people 1Ch 7:19

ANIM, a´-nim
fountains Jos 15:50

ANNA, an´-ah
grace Lk 2:36

ANNAS, an´-as
Gr. for HANANIAH Lk 3:2

ANTICHRIST, an´-ti-christ
instead of Christ 1Jn 2:18

ANTIOCH, an´-ti-ok
named for Antiochus, a general of Alexander the Great Ac 6:5

ANTIPAS, an´-tip-as
contraction of Antipater, *against the father* Rev 2:13

ANTIPATRIS, an´-tip-atr´-is
city named for Antipater, *against the father* Ac 23:31

ANTOTHIJAH, an´-to-thi´-jah
prayers answered by Jehovah (?) 1Ch 8:24

ANTOTHITE, an´-toth-ite
a man of Anathoth 1Ch 11:28

ANUB, a´-noob
bound together (?) 1Ch 4:8

APELLES, a-pel´-les
exclusion Ro 16:10

APHARSACHITES, a´-far-sa-kites
official Ezr 5:6

APHARSATHCHITES, a´-far-sath-kites
official Ezr 4:9

APHARSITES, a´-far-sa-kites
official Ezr 4:9

APHEK, a´-fek
strength Jos 12:18

APHEKAH, a´-fek-ah
same as APHEK Jos 15:53

APHIAH, af-i´-ah
refreshed (?) 1Sa 9:1

APHIK, a´-fik
same as APHEK Jgs 1:31

APHRAH, af´-rah
dust Mic 1:10

APHSES, af´-sees
dispersion 1Ch 24:15

APOLLONIA, ap´-ol-o´-ni-ah
belonging to Apollos Ac 17:1

APOLLOS, ap-ol´-os
abbr. of Apollonius Ac 18:24

APOLLYON, ap-ol´-yon
one that exterminates Rev 9:11

APPAIM, ap-a´-im
the nostrils 1Ch 2:30

APPHIA, af´-yah
Gr. for Appia Phm 2

APPII FORUM, ap´-py-i fo´-rum
marketplace of Appius Ac 28:15

AQUILA, ak´-wil-ah
an eagle Ac 18:2

AR, ar
city Nu 21:15

ARA, a´-ra
lion (?) 1Ch 7:38

ARAB, a´-rab
ambush Jos 15:52

ARABAH, a´-rab-ah
a plain Jos 18:18

ARABIA, a-ra´-bi-a
a desert 1Ki 10:15

ARABIAN, a-ra´-bi-an
a person from Arabia Ne 2:19

ARAD, a´-rad
wild ass 1Ch 8:15

ARAH, a´-rah
wandering 1Ch 7:39

ARAM, a´-ram
height Ge 10:22

ARAMITESS, a´-ram-ite-ess
female inhabitant of Aram 1Ch 7:14

ARAN, a´-ran
wild goat Ge 36:28

ARARAT, a-ra´-rat
the curse of trembling Ge 8:4

ARAUNAH, a-raw´-nah
calf (?) 2Sa 24:18

ARBA, ar´-bah
four Jos 14:15

ARBAH, ar´-bah
variant spelling of ARBA Ge 35:27

ARBATHITE, ar´-bath-ite
an inhabitant of Beth-arabah 1Ch 11:32

ARBEL, see BETH-ARBEL

ARBITE, arb´-ite
an inhabitant of Arab 2Sa 23:35

ARCHELAUS, ar´-ke-la´-us
prince of the people (?) Mt 2:22

ARCHEVITES, ar´-kev-ites
the men of Erech (?) Ezr 4:9

ARCHI, ar´-ki
an inhabitant of Erech Jos 16:2

ARCHIPPUS, ar-kip´-us
master of the horse Col 4:17

ARCHITE, ark´-ite
a native of Erech 2Sa 15:32

ARCTURUS, ark-tu´-rus
the Great Bear and Little Bear constellations Job 9:9

ARD, ard
fugitive (?) Ge 46:21

ARDITES, ard´-ites
descendants of Ard Nu 26:40

ARDON, ar´-don
fugitive 1Ch 2:18

ARELI, a-re´-li
heroic Ge 46:16

ARELITES, a´-rel-ites
descendants of Areli Nu 26:17

AREOPAGITE, a´-re-op´-ag-ite
a judge of the court of Areopagus Ac 17:34

AREOPAGUS, a´-re-op´-ag-us
hill of Mars Ac 17:19

ARETAS, ar´-e-tas
husbandman (?) 2Co 11:32

ARGOB, ar´-gobe
a rocky district Dt 3:4

ARIDAI, a-rid´-a-i
delight of Hari (?) Est 9:9

ARIDATHA, a-rid´-ath-ah
given by Hari (?) Est 9:8

ARIEH, a-ri´-eh
lion 2Ki 15:25

ARIEL, a´-ri-el
lion of God Ezr 8:16

ARIMATHAEA, a´-rim-ath-ee´-ah
same as RAMAH Mt 27:57

ARIOCH, a´-ri-ok
servant of the moon-god Ge 14:1

ARISTARCHUS, a-ris-tark´-us
best ruling Ac 19:29

ARISTOBULUS, a-ris´-to-bewl´-us
best counselor Ro 16:10

ARKITE, ark´-ite
fugitive (?) Ge 10:17

ARMAGEDDON, ar´-ma-ged´-on
height of Megiddo Rev 16:16

ARMENIA, ar-me´-ni-a
land of Aram 2Ki 19:37

ARMONI, ar-mo´-ni
belonging to a palace 2Sa 21:8

ARNAN, ar´-nan
active 1Ch 3:21

ARNON, ar´-non
swift Nu 21:13

AROD, a´-rod
wild ass Nu 26:17

ARODI, a´-rod-i
same as AROD Ge 46:16

ARODITES, a´-rod-ites
descendants of Arod Nu 26:17

AROER, ar´-o-er
ruins (?) Dt 2:36

AROERITE, ar-o´-er-ite
a man of Aroer 1Ch 11:44

ARPAD, ar´-pad
support 2Ki 18:34

ARPHAD, ar´-fad
same as ARPAD Isa 36:19

ARTAXERXES, ar´-ta-xerk´-ses
honored king (?) Ezr 4:7

ARTEMAS, ar´-te-mas
short for Artemidorus (?) Tit 3:12

ARUBOTH, a-roob´-oth
windows 1Ki 4:10

ARUMAH, a-room´-ah
elevated Jgs 9:41

ARVAD, ar´-vad
wandering Eze 27:8

ARVADITES, ar´-vad-ites
inhabitants of Arvad Ge 10:18

ARZA, ar´-zah
earth 1Ki 16:9

ASA, a´-sah
physician 1Ki 15:8

ASAHEL, a´-sa-hel
whom God made 2Sa 2:18

ASAHIAH, a´-sah-i´-ah
Jehovah has made 2Ki 22:12

ASAIAH, a-sai´-ah
same as ASAHIAH 1Ch 4:36

ASAPH, a´-saf
collector 2Ki 18:18

ASAREEL, a´-sar-e´-el
whom God has bound 1Ch 4:16

ASARELAH, a´-sar-el´-ah
same as JESHARELAH 1Ch 25:2

ASENATH, a´-se-nath
she who is of Neith (?),
a goddess of the Egyptians Ge 41:45

ASER, a´-ser
same as ASHER Lk 2:36

ASHAN, a´-shan
smoke Jos 15:42

ASHBEA, ash´-be-ah
I conjure 1Ch 4:21

ASHBEL, ash´-bel
blame (?) Ge 46:21

ASHBELITES, ash´-bel-ites
the descendants of Ashbel Nu 26:38

ASHCHENAZ, ash´-ke-naz
same as ASHKENAZ 1Ch 1:6

ASHDOD, ash´-dod
a strong place Jos 15:46

ASHDODITES, ash´-dod-ites
the inhabitants of Ashdod Ne 4:7

ASHDOTH-PISGAH, ash´-doth-piz´-gah
springs of Pisgah Jos 12:3

ASHDOTHITES, ash´-doth-ites
same as ASHDODITES Jos 13:3

ASHER, ash´-er
fortunate, happy Ge 30:13

ASHERAH, ash-er´-ah
same as ASHTORETH 2Ki 17:10

ASHERITES, a´-sher-ites
descendants of Asher Jgs 1:32

ASHIMA, ash´-im-a
an unknown deity 2Ki 17:30

ASHKELON, ash´-kel-on
migration Jgs 14:19

ASHKENAZ, ash´-ke-naz
a fire that spreads Ge 10:3

ASHNAH, ash´-nah
strong Jos 15:33

ASHRIEL, ash´-ri-el
same as ASRIEL 1Ch 7:14

ASHTAROTH, ash´-tar-oth
statues of Ashtoreth Jos 9:10

ASHTERATHITE, ash-ter´-ath-ite
a native of Ashteoth 1Ch 11:44

ASHTEROTH KARNAIM, ash´-ter-oth kar-na´-im
Ashteroth of the two horns Ge 14:5

ASHTORETH, ash-tor´-eth
she who enriches 1Ki 11:5

ASHUR, a´-shur
black 1Ch 2:24

ASHURITES, a´-sher-ites
1 a region of Israel 2Sa 2:9
2 an Arab tribe Eze 27:6

ASIA, a´-sia
a Roman province Ac 2:9

ASIEL, a´-si-el
created by God 1Ch 4:35

ASKELON, as´-kel-on
same as ASHKELON Jgs 1:18

ASNAH, as´-nah
bramble Ezr 2:50

ASNAPPER, as-nap´-er
same as ASSUR-BANI-PAL,
Assur has formed a son Ezr 4:10

ASRIEL, as´-ri-el
the prohibition of God Nu 26:31

ASRIELITES, as´-ri-el-ites
descendants of Asriel Nu 26:31

ASSHUR, ash´-oor
the gracious One (?) Ge 10:22

ASSHURIM, ash-oor´-im
Arabian tribe from Dedan Ge 25:3

ASSIR, as´-eer
captive Ex 6:24

ASSUR, as´-ser
1 the people of ASSHUR Eze 27:23
2 the land of ASSYRIA Ezr 4:2

ASSYRIA, as-ir´-ya
land named for Asshur Ge 2:14

ASSYRIANS, as-ir´-yans
inhabitants of Assyria Isa 10:5

ASTAROTH, as´-tar-oth
same as ASHTORETH Dt 1:4

ASUPPIM, a-soop´-im
collections 1Ch 26:15

ASYNCRITUS, a-sin´-krit-us
incomparable Ro 16:14

ATAD, a´-tad
buckthorn Ge 50:10

ATARAH, a´-tar-ah
a crown 1Ch 2:26

ATAROTH-ADAR, a´-tar-oth–ad-ar
same as ATAROTH-ADDAR Jos 18:13

ATAROTH-ADDAR, a´-tar-oth-ad-ar
crowns of power Jos 16:5
ATER, a´-ter
bound, shut up Ezr 2:16
ATHACH, a´-thak
lodging-place 1Sa 30:30
ATHAIAH, a-thai´-ah
whom Jehovah made (?) Ne 11:4
ATHALIAH, ath´-al-i´-ah
whom Jehovah has afflicted 2Ki 8:26
ATHENIANS, ath-e´-ni-ans
natives of Athens Ac 17:21
ATHLAI, ath´-la-i
short for ATHALIAH Ezr 10:28
ATROTH, at´-roth
same as ATAROTH Nu 32:35
ATTAI, at´-a-i
opportune 1Ch 2:35
ATTALIA, at´-ta-li´-a
named for Attalus, royal founder of the city Ac 14:25
AUGUSTUS, aw-gust´-us
venerable Lk 2:1
AVA, av´-va
iniquity, guilt 2Ki 17:24
AVEN, a´-ven
nothingness Eze 30:17
AVIM, av´-im
ruins Jos 18:23
AVITH, a´-vith
ruin Ge 36:35
AZAL, a´-zal
going away Zec 14:5
AZALIAH, a´-zal-i´-ah
whom Jehovah has reserved 2Ki 22:3
AZANIAH, a´-zan-i´-ah
whom Jehovah hears Ne 10:9
AZARAEL, a´-zar-a´-el
whom God helps Ne 12:36
AZAREEL, a´-zar-e´-el
same as AZAREEL 1Ch 12:6
AZARIAH, a´-zar-i´-ah
whom Jehovah aids 2Ch 22:6
AZAZ, a´-zaz
strong 1Ch 5:8
AZAZIAH, a´-zaz-i´-ah
whom Jehovah strengthened 1Ch 15:21
AZEKAH, az´-ek-ah
dug over Jos 10:10
AZEL, a´-zel
noble 1Ch 8:37
AZEM, a´-zem
strength, bone Jos 15:29
AZGAD, az´-gad
strong in fortune Ezr 2:12
AZIEL, az´-i-el
whom God strengthens 1Ch 15:20
AZIZA, a-zi´-zah
strong Ezr 10:27
AZMAVETH, az-ma´-veth
strength (?) 2Sa 23:31
AZMON, az´-mon
robust Nu 34:4
AZNOTH-TABOR, az´-noth-ta´-bor
ears (summits) of Tabor Jos 19:34
AZOR, a´-zor
helper Mt 1:13
AZOTUS, a-zo´-tus
Gr. for ASHDOD Ac 8:40
AZRIEL, az´-ri-el
help of God 1Ch 5:24
AZRIKAM, az-ri´-kam
help against an enemy 1Ch 3:23
AZUBAH, a-zoob´-ah
forsaken 1Ki 22:42
AZUR, a´-zoor
same as AZOR Jer 28:1
AZZAH, az´-ah
strong, fortified Dt 2:23
AZZAN, az´-an
strong Nu 34:26
AZZUR, az´-oor
same as AZOR Ne 10:17

B

BAAL, ba´-al
lord, master, possessor, Phoenician sun-god Nu 22:41
BAALAH, ba´-al-ah
mistress Jos 15:10
BAALATH, ba´-al-ath
same as BAALAH Jos 19:44
BAALATH-BEER, ba´-al-ath-be´-er
owner of a well Jos 19:8
BAAL-BERITH, ba´-al-be´-rith
lord of a covenant Jgs 8:33
BAALE, ba´-al-ay
pl. of BAAL 2Sa 6:2
BAAL-GAD, ba´-al-gad
lord of fortune Jos 11:17
BAAL-HAMON, ba´-al-ha´-mon
lord of a multitude SS 8:11
BAAL-HANAN, ba´-al-ha´-nan
lord of benignity Ge 36:38
BAAL-HAZOR, ba´-al-ha´-zor
lord of a village 2Sa 13:23
BAAL-HERMON, ba´-al-her´-mon
lord of Hermon Jgs 3:3
BAALI, ba´-al-i
my lord Hos 2:16
BAALIM, ba´-al-im
lords Jgs 2:11
BAALIS, ba´-al-is
exultation Jer 40:14
BAAL-MEON, ba´-al-me´-on
lord of habitation Nu 32:38
BAAL-PEOR, ba´-al-pe´-or
lord of the opening Nu 25:3
BAAL-PERAZIM, ba´-al-pe-raz´-im
lord of breaches 2Sa 5:20
BAAL-SHALISHA, ba´-al-sha-lish´-ah
lord of the third part 2Ki 4:42
BAAL-TAMAR, ba´-al-ta´-mar
lord of palm trees Jgs 20:33
BAAL-ZEBUB, ba´-al-ze´-boob
lord of flies 2Ki 1:2
BAAL-ZEPHON, ba´-al-zeph´-on
lord of winter Ex 14:2
BAANA, ba´-a-nah
Gr. for BAANAH 1Ki 4:12
BAANAH, ba´-a-nah
son of oppression 2Sa 4:2
BAARA, ba´-a-rah
foolish 1Ch 8:8
BAASEIAH, ba´-as-i´-ah
work of Jehovah 1Ch 6:40
BAASHA, ba´-ash-ah
wicked (?) 1Ki 15:16
BABEL, ba´-bel
confusion Ge 11:9
BABYLON, bab´-il-on
Gr. for BABEL 2Ki 20:12
BABYLONISH, bab´-il-one-ish
of, belonging to, Babylon Jos 7:21
BACA, ba´-kah
weeping Ps 84:6
BACHRITES, bak´-rites
descendants of Becher Nu 26:35
BAHARUMITE, ba-har´-oom-ite
an inhabitant of Bahurim 1Ch 11:33
BAHURIM, ba-hoor´-im
(town of) young men 2Sa 16:5
BAJITH, ba´-yith
a house Isa 15:2
BAKBAKKAR, bak-bak´-ar
searcher 1Ch 9:15
BAKBUK, bak´-book
a bottle Ezr 2:51
BAKBUKIAH, bak´-book-i´-ah
emptying (wasting) of Jehovah Ne 11:17
BALAAM, ba´-lam
destruction (?) Nu 22:5
BALAC, ba´-lac
same as BALAK Rev 2:14

BERI, be´-ri
man of the well 1Ch 7:36

BERIAH, be-ri´-ah
in evil (?) Ge 46:17

BERIITES, be-ri´-ites
descendants of Beriah Nu 26:44

BERITES, ber´-ites
descendants of Bichri 2Sa 20:14

BERITH, be´-rith
a covenant Jgs 9:46

BERNICE, ber-ni´-see
victorious Ac 25:13

BERODACH-BALADAN, be´-ro-dak-bal´-a-dan
Berodach (Merodach) has given a son 2Ki 20:12

BEROTHAH, be´-roth-ah
wells Eze 47:16

BEROTHAI, be´-roth-a-i
my wells 2Sa 8:8

BEROTHITE, be´-roth-ite
same as BEEROTHITE 1Ch 11:39

BESAI, be´-sa-i
sword, victory (?) Ezr 2:49

BESODEIAH, be´-sod-i´-ah
in the secret of the LORD Ne 3:6

BESOR, be´-sor
cool 1Sa 30:9

BETAH, be´-tah
confidence 2Sa 8:8

BETEN, be´-ten
belly, hollow Jos 19:25

BETHABARA, beth-ab´-ar-ah
house of passage Jn 1:28

BETH-ANATH, beth´-an-ath
echo Jos 19:38

BETH-ANOTH, beth´-an-oth
house of (the goddess) Anath Jos 15:59

BETHANY, beth´-an-y
house of dates Mt 21:17

BETH-ARABAH, beth-ar´-ab-ah
house of the desert Jos 15:6

BETH-ARAM, beth-a´-ram
house of the height Jos 13:27

BETH-ARBEL, beth-arb´-el
house of the ambush of God Hos 10:14

BETH-AVEN, beth-a´-ven
house of vanity (i.e. of idols) Jos 7:2

BETH-AZMAVETH, beth´-az-ma´-veth
house of strength Ne 7:28

BETH-BAAL-MEON, beth´-ba´-al-me-on
house of Baal-meon Jos 13:17

BETH-BARAH, beth-ba´-rah
same as BETH-ABARA Jgs 7:24

BETH-BIREI, beth-bir´-i
house of my creation 1Ch 4:31

BETH-CAR, beth´-kar
house of pasture 1Sa 7:11

BETH-DAGON, beth-da´-gon
house of Dagon Jos 15:41

BETH-DIBLATHAIM, beth´-dib-la-tha´-im
house of the two cakes Jer 48:22

BETH-EL, beth´-el
house of God Ge 12:8

BETHELITE, beth´-el-ite
a native of Beth-el 1Ki 16:34

BETH-EMEK, beth-e´-mek
house of the valley Jos 19:27

BETHER, be´-ther
separation SS 2:17

BETHESDA, beth-esd´-ah
house of mercy Jn 5:2

BETH-EZEL, beth-e´-zel
house of firmness (?) Mic 1:11

BETH-GADER, beth-ga´-der
house of the wall 1Ch 2:51

BETH-GAMUL, beth-ga´-mool
house of the weaned Jer 48:23

BETH-HACCEREM, beth´-hak-er´-em
house of the vineyard Ne 3:14

BETH-HARAN, beth-ha´-ran
same as BETH-ARAM Nu 32:36

BETH-HOGLA, beth-hog´-lah
same as BETH-HOGLAH Jos 15:6

BETH-HOGLAH, beth-hog´-lah
house of the partridge Jos 18:19

BETH-HORON, beth-ho´-ron
house of the hollow Jos 10:10

BETH-JESIMOTH, beth-je-shim´-oth
house of the deserts Nu 33:49

BETH-LEBAOTH, beth´-le-ba´-oth
house of lionesses Jos 19:6

BETH-LEHEM, beth´-le-hem
house of bread Ge 35:19

BETH-LEHEM EPHRATAH, beth´-le-hem ef´-ra-tah
Bethlehem the fruitful (?) Mic 5:2

BETH-LEHEM-JUDAH, beth´-le-hem-joo´-dah
Bethlehem of Judah Jgs 17:7

BETHLEHEMITE, beth´-le-hem-ite
a man of BETH-LEHEM 1Sa 16:1

BETH-MAACHAH, beth´-ma´-ak-ah
house of Maachah 2Sa 20:14

BETH-MARCABOTH, beth´-mar´-kab-oth
house of chariots Jos 19:5

BETH-MEON, beth´-me´-on
house of habitation Jer 48:23

BETH-NIMRAH, beth´-nim´-rah
house of sweet water Nu 32:36

BETH-PALET, beth´-pa´-let
house of escape, or of Pelet Jos 15:27

BETH-PAZZEZ, beth´-paz´-ez
house of dispersion Jos 19:21

BETH-PEOR, beth´-pe´-or
house (temple) of Peor Dt 3:29

BETHPHAGE, beth´-fa-jee
house of unripe figs Mt 21:1

BETH-PHELET, beth´-fe´-let
same as BETH-PALET Ne 11:26

BETH-RAPHA, beth´-ra´-fah
house of Rapha 1Ch 4:12

BETH-REHOB, beth´-re´-hob
house of Rehob Jgs 18:28

BETHSAIDA, beth´-sai´-dah
house of fishing Mt 11:21

BETH-SHAN, beth´-shan
house of rest 1Sa 31:10

BETH-SHEAN, beth´-she´-an
same as BETHSHAN Jos 17:11

BETH-SHEMESH, beth´-she´-mesh
house of the sun Jos 15:10

BETHSHEMITE, beth´-shem´-ite
a native of Bethshemesh 1Sa 6:14

BETH-SHITTAH, beth´-shit´-ah
house of acacias Jgs 7:22

BETH-TAPPUAH, beth´-tap-oo´-ah
house of apples Jos 15:53

BETHUEL, beth´-oo-el
house of God Ge 22:22

BETHUL, beth´-ool
same as BETH-EL (?) Jos 19:4

BETH-ZUR, beth´-zoor
house of the rock Jos 15:58

BETONIM, be-to´-nim
pistachio nuts Jos 13:26

BEULAH, be-ool´-ah
married Isa 62:4

BEZAI, be´-zai
short for BEZALEEL (?) Ezr 2:17

BEZALEEL, be-zal´-e-el
in the shadow of God (?) Ex 31:2

BEZEK, be´-zek
lightning (?) Jgs 1:4

BEZER, be´-zer
ore of precious metal Dt 4:43

BICHRI, bik´-ri
young 2Sa 20:1

BIDKAR, bid´-kar
cleaver (?) 2Ki 9:25

BIGTHAN, big´-than
given by God Est 2:21

BIGTHANA, big´-than-ah
same as BIGTHAN Est 6:2

BIGVAI, big´-va-i
happy, fortunate Ezr 2:2

BILDAD, bil´-dad
son of contention (?) Job 2:11

BILEAM, bil´-e-am
same as BALAAM (?) 1Ch 6:70

BILGAH, bil´-gah
cheerfulness 1Ch 24:14

BILGAI, bil´-ga-i
same as BILGAH Ne 10:8

BILHAH, bil´-hah
modesty Ge 29:29

BILHAN, bil´-han
modest Ge 36:27

BILSHAN, bil´-shan
seeker (?) Ezr 2:2

BIMHAL, bim´-hal
a descendant of Asher 1Ch 7:33

BINEA, bin´-ea
short for BAANA (?) 1Ch 8:37

BINNUI, bin´-oo-i
a building up Ezr 8:33

BIRSHA, bir´-shah
with wickedness Ge 14:2

BIRZAVITH, bir´-za-vith
wounds (?) 1Ch 7:31

BISHLAM, bish´-lam
in peace Ezr 4:7

BITHIAH, bith-i´-ah
daughter (worshiper) of Jehovah 1Ch 4:18

BITHRON, bith´-ron
a broken place 2Sa 2:29

BITHYNIA, bi-thin´-i-a
a province in Asia Minor Ac 16:7

BIZJOTHJAH, biz-joth´-jah
contempt of Jehovah Jos 15:28

BIZTHA, biz´-thah
double gift (?) Est 1:10

BLASTUS, blast´-us
a shoot Ac 12:20

BOANERGES, bo´-an-er´-jes
sons of thunder Mk 3:17

BOAZ, bo´-az
fleetness Ru 2:1

BOCHERU, bo´-ke-roo
firstborn (?) 1Ch 8:38

BOCHIM, bo´-kim
weepers Jgs 2:1

BOHAN, bo´-han
thumb (?) Jos 15:6

BOOZ, bo´-oz
same as BOAZ Mt 1:5

BOSCATH, bos´-kath
stony, elevated ground 2Ki 22:1

BOSOR, bo´-sor
Gr. and Aramaic for BEOR 2Pe 2:15

BOZEZ, bo´-zez
shining 1Sa 14:4

BOZKATH, boz´-kath
same as BOSCATH Jos 15:39

BOZRAH, boz´-rah
sheepfold Ge 36:33

BUKKI, book´-i
abbr. of BUKKIAH Nu 34:22

BUKKIAH, book-i´-ah
proved of the LORD 1Ch 25:4

BUL, bool
rain 1Ki 6:38

BUNAH, boon´-ah
prudence 1Ch 2:25

BUNNI, boon´-i
built Ne 9:4

BUZ, booz
contempt Ge 22:21

BUZI, booz´-i
descended from Buz Eze 1:3

BUZITE, booz´-ite
a descendant of Buz Job 32:2

C

CABBON, kab´-on
cake Jos 15:40

CABUL, kab´-ool
displeasing (?) Jos 19:27

CAESAREA, see´-zar-e´-a
named after Augustus Caesar Ac 8:40

CAESAREA PHILIPPI, see´-zar-e´-a fil-ip´-i
named after Philip the tetrarch Mt 16:13

CAIAPHAS, kai´-a-fas
depression (?) Mt 26:3

CAIN, kane
possession Ge 4:1

CAINAN, ka-i´-nan
possessor Ge 5:9

CALAH, ka´-lah
holy gate (?) Ge 10:11

CALCOL, kal´-kol
sustenance, maintenance 1Ch 2:6

CALEB, ka´-leb
a dog Nu 26:65

CALEB-EPHRATAH, ka´-leb-ef´-rat-ah
Caleb the fruitful 1Ch 2:24

CALNEH, kal´-nay
all of them Ge 10:10

CALNO, kal´-no
same as CALNEH Isa 10:9

CALVARY, kal´-va-ry
skull Lk 23:33

CAMON, ka´-mon
abounding in stalks Jgs 10:5

CANA, ka´-nah
place of reeds Jn 2:1

CANAAN, ka´-nan
low region Ge 9:18

CANAANITE, ka´-nan-ite
a zealot Mk 3:18

CANAANITES, ka´-nan-ites
inhabitants of Canaan Jgs 1:1

CANAANITESS, ka´-nan-ite-ess
fem. of CANAANITES 1Ch 2:3

CANDACE, kan´-da-see
title of queen-mother of Ethiopia Ac 8:27

CANNEH, kan´-ay
same as CALNEH (?) Eze 27:23

CAPERNAUM, ka-per´-na-um
city of consolation (?) Mt 4:13

CAPHTHORIM, kaf´-thor-im
same as CAPHTORIM 1Ch 1:12

CAPHTOR, kaf´-tor
a name for Crete (?) Dt 2:23

CAPHTORIM, kaf´-tor-im
inhabitants of Caphtor Ge 10:14

CAPPADOCIA, cap-pa-do´-shah
a province in Asia Minor Ac 2:9

CARCAS, car´-cas
an eagle (?) Est 1:10

CARCHEMISH, kar´-kem-ish
fortress of Chemosh Jer 46:2

CAREAH, ka-re´-ah
bald 2Ki 25:23

CARMEL, karm´-el
park Jos 12:22

CARMELITE, karm´-el-ite
a native of Carmel 1Sa 30:5

CARMELITESS, karm´-el-ite-ess
fem. of CARMELITE 1Sa 27:3

CARMI, karm´-i
a vine-dresser Ge 46:9

CARMITES, karm´-ites
descendants of Carmi Nu 26:6

CARPUS, karp´-us
fruit (?) 2Ti 4:13

CARSHENA, kar´-shen-ah
pillage of war (?) Est 1:14

CASIPHIA, ka-sif´-yah
silver (?) Ezr 8:17

CASLUHIM, kas´-loo-him
descendants from Egypt Ge 10:14

CASTOR, kas´-tor
A horseman, one of the sons of Zeus Ac 28:11

CEDRON, seed´-ron
same as KIDRON Jn 18:1

CENCHRAE, sen´-kre-ah
millet, small pulse Ac 18:18

CEPHAS, see´-fas
stone Jn 1:42

CHALCOL, kal´-kol
same as CALCOL 1Ki 4:31

CHALDEA, kal-de´-ah
synonym for Babylonia Jer 50:10

CHALDEANS, kal-de´-ans
inhabitants of Chaldea Job 1:17

CHALDEES, kal-dees´
same as CHALDEANS Ge 11:28

CHANAAN, ka´-nan
a form of CANAAN Ac 7:11

CHARASHIM, kar´-ash-im
craftsmen 1Ch 4:14

CHARCHEMISH, kar´-kem-ish
same as CARCHEMISH 2Ch 35:20

CHARRAN, kar´-an
same as HARAN Ac 7:2

CHEBAR, ke´-bar
great (?) Eze 1:1

CHEDORLAOMER, ke´-dor-la´-o-mer
servant of (the god) Lagamar Ge 14:1

CHELAL, ke´-lal
completion Ezr 10:30

CHELLUH, kel´-oo
completed Ezr 10:35

CHELUB, kel´-oob
bird-trap 1Ch 4:11

CHELUBAI, kel´-oob-a´-i
same as CALEB 1Ch 2:9

CHEMARIMS, kem´-ar-ims
persons dressed in black attire Zep 1:4

CHEMOSH, keem´-osh
subduer Nu 21:29

CHENAANAH, ke-na´-an-ah
fem. of Canaan 1Ki 22:11

CHENANI, ke´-nane´-i
same as CHENANIAH (?) Ne 9:4

CHENANIAH, ke´-nan-i´-ah
whom Jehovah supports 1Ch 15:22

CHEPHAR-HAAMMONAI, ke-far´-haam´-on-a´-i
village of the Ammonites Jos 18:24

CHEPHIRAH, ke-fi´-rah
same as CAPHAR Jos 9:17

CHERAN, ke´-ran
lute (?) Ge 36:26

CHERETHIMS, ke´-reth-ims
Cretans (?) Eze 25:16

CHERETHITES, ke´-reth-ites
same as CHERETHIMS (?) 2Sa 8:18

CHERITH, ke´-rith
gorge (?) 1Ki 17:3

CHERUB, cher´-ub
blessing, or *strong* (?) Ezr 2:59

CHERUBIM, cher´-oob-im
pl. of CHERUB Ge 3:24

CHESALON, kes´-al-on
hope Jos 15:10

CHESED, ke´-sed
conqueror (?) Ge 22:22

CHESIL, ke´-sil
a fool Jos 15:30

CHESULLOTH, ke-sool´-oth
confidences Jos 19:18

CHEZIB, ke´-zib
false Ge 38:5

CHIDON, ki´-don
javelin 1Ch 13:9

CHILEAB, kil´-e-ab
a form of CALEB (?) 2Sa 3:3

CHILION, kil´-yon
wasting away Ru 1:2

CHILMAD, kil´-mad
a city noted for trading with Tyre Eze 27:23

CHIMHAM, kim´-ham
longing 2Sa 19:37

CHINNERETH, kin´-er-eth
a lyre Jos 19:35

CHINNEROTH, kin´-er-oth
pl. of CHINNERETH Jos 11:2

CHIOS, ki´-os
an island in the Aegean Sea Ac 20:15

CHISLEU, kis´-lew
the ninth month Ne 1:1

CHISLON, kis´-lon
confidence, hope Nu 34:21

CHISLOTH-TABOR, kis´-loth-ta´-bor
flanks (?) *of Tabor* Jos 19:12

CHITTIM, kit´-tim
descendants of Javan Nu 24:24

CHIUN, ki´-oon
image Am 5:26

CHLOE, klo´-ee
the first shoot of green grass 1Co 1:11

CHOR-ASHAN, kor-ash´-an
smoking furnace 1Sa 30:30

CHORAZIN, ko-ra´-zin
a town in Galilee Mt 11:21

CHOZEBA, ko´-ze-bah
deceiver 1Ch 4:22

CHRIST, krist
Gr. for MESSIAH, *the anointed* Mt 1:1
Thou art the **C** Mt 16:16
saying, I am **C** Mt 24:5
the Messiah, which is called **C** Jn 4:25
is not this the **C**? Jn 4:29
sure that thou art that **C** Jn 6:69
preach **C** Php 1:15,16
the Spirit of **C** did signify 1Pe 1:11
denieth that Jesus is the **C** 1Jn 2:22
believeth that Jesus is the **C** 1Jn 5:1
reigned with **C** a thousand years Rev 20:4
priests of God and of **C** Rev 20:6

CHUSHAN-RISHATHAIM, koosh´-an-rish-a-tha´-im
blackness of the double crime Jgs 3:8

CHUN, choon
establishment 1Ch 18:8

CHUZA, koo´-za
modest, little Lk 8:3

CILICIA, si-lish´-ya
modest, jug (?) Ac 15:23

CINNEROTH, kin´-er-oth
same as CHINNEROTH 1Ki 15:20

CIS, sis
same as KISH Ac 13:21

CLAUDA, klawd´-ah
a small island near CRETE Ac 27:16

CLAUDIA, klawd´-yah
fem. of CLAUDIUS 2Ti 4:21

CLAUDIUS, klawd´-yus
Fourth of the Caesars (10 B.C.–A.D. 54) Ac 11:28

CLEMENT, klem´-ent
kind, merciful Php 4:3

CLEOPAS, kle´-op-as
short for Cleopatros Lk 24:18

CLEOPHAS, kle´-of-as
same as CLEOPAS Jn 19:25

CNIDUS, kni´-dus
nettle (?) Ac 27:7

COL-HOZEH, kol-ho´-zeh
every one that seeth Ne 3:15

COLOSSE, ko-los´-see
punishment, correction Col 1:2

CONANIAH, kon-an-i´-ah
same as CONONIAH 2Ch 35:9

CONIAH, ko-ni´-ah
contracted from JECONIAH Jer 22:24

CONONIAH, kon-on-i´-ah
whom Jehovah has set up 2Ch 31:12

COOS, ko´-os
summit Ac 21:1

CORE, ko´-re
Gr. for KORAH Jude 11

CORINTH, kor´-inth
decoration, ornament Ac 18:1

CORINTHIANS, kor-inth´-yans
inhabitants of Corinth Ac 18:8

CORNELIUS, kor-ne´-li-as
of a horn Ac 10:1

COSAM, ko´-sam
divining Lk 3:28

COZ, koz
thorn 1Ch 4:8

COZBI, kos´-bi
deceitful Nu 25:15

CRESCENS, kres´-ens
growing 2Ti 4:10

CRETE, kreet
carnal (?) Ac 27:7

CRETES, kreets
same as CRETIANS Ac 2:11

CRETIANS, kreet´-yans
inhabitants of Crete Tit 1:12

CRISPUS, krisp´-us
curled Ac 18:8

CUMI, koom´-i
arise Mk 5:41

CUSH, koosh
black Ge 10:6

CUSHAN, koosh´-an
a form of CUSH Hab 3:7

CUSHI, koosh´-i
the Cushites (Ethiopians) 2Sa 18:21

CUTH, kooth
same as CUTHAH 2Ki 17:30

CUTHAH, kooth´-ah
burning 2Ki 17:24

CYPRUS, si´-prus
copper Ac 4:36

CYRENE, si-reen´
a wall, the floor Mt 27:32

CYRENIAN, si-reen´-yan
a native of Cyrene Ac 6:9

CYRENIUS, si-reen´-yus
Gr. for the Ro. name Quirinus Lk 2:2

CYRUS, si´-rus
the sun 2Ch 36:22

D

DABAREH, da´-bar-ay
pasture Jos 21:28

DABBASHETH, dab-ash´-eth
hump of a camel Jos 19:11

DABERATH, da´-ber-ath
same as DABAREH Jos 19:12

DAGON, da´-gon
fish Jgs 16:23

DALAIAH, da-lai´-ah
whom Jehovah hath delivered 1Ch 3:24

DALMANUTHA, dal-ma-nu´-tha
a branch (?) Mk 8:10

DALPHON, dal´-fon
proud (?) Est 9:7

DAMARIS, dam´-ar-is
calf (?) Ac 17:34

DAMASCENES, dam´-as-eens
people of Damascus 2Co 11:32

DAMASCUS, dam-ask´-us
activity (?) Ge 14:15

DAN, dan
judge Ge 30:6

DAN-JAAN, dan´-ja´-an
woodland (?) 2Sa 24:6

DANIEL, dan´-yel
My God is judge Da 1:6

DANITES, dan´-ites
descendants of Dan Jgs 13:2

DANNAH, dan´-nah
judging Jos 15:49

DARA, da´-rah
contracted from DARDA 1Ch 2:6

DARDA, dar´-dah
pearl of wisdom (?) 1Ki 4:31

DARIUS, da-ri´-us
governor (?) Ezr 4:5

DARKON, dark´-on
scatterer (?) Ezr 2:56

DATHAN, da´-than
of a spring Nu 16:1

DAVID, da´-vid
beloved 1Sa 16:19

DEBIR, de´-ber
a recess Jos 10:3

DEBORAH, deb´-or-ah
bee Jgs 4:4

DECAPOLIS, de-ka´-pol-is
ten cities Mt 4:25

DEDAN, de´-dan
their breasts Ge 10:7

DEDANIM, de´-dan-im
inhabitants of Dedan Isa 21:13

DEHAVITES, de´-hav-ites
the Aryan Da,
a nomadic Persian tribe Ezr 4:9

DEKAR, de´-kar
piercing 1Ki 4:9

DELAIAH, de-lai´-ah
whom Jehovah has freed 1Ch 24:18

DELILAH, de-li´-lah
delicate Jgs 16:4

DEMAS, de´-mas
same as DEMETRIUS (?) Col 4:14

DEMETRIUS, de-me´-tri-us
belonging to Demeter Ac 19:24

DERBE, der´-bee
juniper (?) Ac 14:6

DEUEL, doo´-el
same as REUEL (?) Nu 1:14

DIANA, di-an´-ah
Lat. for Gr. goddess Artemis Ac 19:24

DIBLAIM, dib-la´-im
two cakes Hos 1:3

DIBLATH, dib´-lath
same as RIBLAH (?) Eze 6:14

DIBLATHAIM, dib-lath-a´-im
same as DIBLAIM Nu 33:46

DIBON, di´-bon
wasting Nu 21:30

DIBON-GAD, di´-bon-gad
wasting of Gad Nu 33:45

DIBRI, dib´-ri
eloquent Le 24:11

DIDYMUS, did´-im-us
twin Jn 11:16

DIKLAH, dik´-lah
a palm tree Ge 10:27

DILEAN, dil´-e-an
cucumber field (?) Jos 15:38

DIMNAH, dim´-nah
dunghill Jos 21:35

DIMON, di´-mon
same as DIBON Isa 15:9

DIMONAH, di-mo´-nah
same as DIBON (?) Jos 15:22

DINAH, di´-nah
vindicated Ge 30:21

DINAITES, di´-na-ites
the Armenian people Ezr 4:9

DINHABAH, din´-ha-bah
an Edomite city Ge 36:32

DIONYSIUS, di´-o-nis´-yus
belonging to Dionysus Ac 17:34

DIOTREPHES, di-ot´-ref-ees
nourished by Zeus 3Jn 9

DISHAN, di´-shan
antelope (?) Ge 36:21

DISHON, di´-shon
same as DISHAN Ge 36:21

DIZAHAB, di´-za-hab
a place abounding in gold (?) Dt 1:1

DODAI, do´-da-i
loving 1Ch 27:4

DODANIM, do´-dan-im
a tribe related to JAVAN Ge 10:4

DODAVAH, do´-dav-ah
love of Jehovah 2Ch 20:37

DODO, do´-do
same as DODAI 2Sa 23:9

DOEG, do´-eg
anxious 1Sa 21:7

DOPHKAH, dof´-kah
a knocking Nu 33:12

DOR, dor
dwelling Jos 11:2

DORCAS, dor´-kas
gazelle Ac 9:36

Names

ELIUD, el-i´-ood
God of Judah Mt 1:14

ELIZAPHAN, el-i´-za-fan
whom God protects Nu 3:30

ELIZUR, el-i´-zoor
God is a rock Nu 1:5

ELKANAH, el´-ka´-nah
whom God possessed Ex 6:24

ELKOSHITE, el´-kosh-ite
inhabitant of Elkosh Na 1:1

ELLASAR, el´-as-ar
a city of Mesopotamia Ge 14:1

ELMODAM, el-mo´-dam
same as ALMODAD Lk 3:28

ELNAAM, el´-na-am
whose pleasure God is 1Ch 11:46

ELNATHAN, el-na´-than
whom God gave 2Ki 24:8

ELON, e´-lon
oak Ge 26:34

ELON-BETH-HANAN, e´-lon-beth´-ha´-nan
oak of the house of grace 1Ki 4:9

ELONITES, e´-lon-ites
descendants of Elon Nu 26:26

ELOTH, e´-loth
same as ELATH 1Ki 9:26

ELPAAL, el´-pa-al
to whom God is the reward 1Ch 8:11

ELPALET, el´-pa-let
same as ELIPHALET 1Ch 14:5

ELTEKEH, el´-te-kay
whose fear is God Jos 19:44

ELTEKON, el´-te-kon
whose foundation is God Jos 15:59

ELTOLAD, el´-to-lad
whose posterity is from God Jos 15:30

ELUL, e´-lool
the sixth month of the year Ne 6:15

ELUZAI, el´-oo-za´-i
God is my praises 1Ch 12:5

ELYMAS, el´-im-as
a wise man Ac 13:8

ELZABAD, el´-za-bad
whom God gave 1Ch 12:12

ELZAPHAN, el´-za-fan
whom God protects Ex 6:22

EMIMS, eem´-ims
terrible men Ge 14:5

EMMANUEL, em-an´-u-el
same as IMMANUEL Mt 1:23

EMMAUS, em-a´-us
hot springs (?) Lk 24:13

EMMOR, em´-or
same as HAMOR Ac 7:16

ENAM, e´-nam
two fountains Jos 15:34

ENAN, e´-nan
having eyes Nu 1:15

ENDOR, en´-dor
fountain of Dor Jos 17:11

EN-EGLAIM, en´-eg-la´-im
fountain of two calves Eze 47:10

EN-GANNIM, en-gan´-im
fountain of gardens Jos 15:34

EN-GEDI, en´-ged-i
fountain of the kid Jos 15:62

EN-HADDAH, en-had´-ah
fountain of sharpness (swift) Jos 19:21

EN-HAKKORE, en´-hak-o´-ree
fountain of him that calleth Jgs 15:19

EN-HAZOR, en-ha´-zor
fountain of the village Jos 19:37

EN-MISHPAT, en-mish´-pat
fountain of judgment Ge 14:7

ENOCH, e´-nok
experienced (?) Ge 4:17

ENOS, e´-nos
man Ge 4:26

ENOSH, e´-nosh
same as ENOS 1Ch 1:1

EN-RIMMON, en´-rim´-on
fountain of the pomegranate Ne 11:29

EN-ROGEL, en´-ro´-gel
fountain of the fuller Jos 15:7

EN-SHEMESH, en´-she´-mesh
fountain of the sun Jos 15:7

EN-TAPPUAH, en´-tap-oo´-ah
fountain of the apple tree Jos 17:7

EPAENETUS, e-pe´-net-us
laudable Ro 16:5

EPAPHRAS, ep´-af-ras
a form of EPAPHRODITUS (?) Col 1:7

EPAPHRODITUS, ep-af´-ro-di´-tus
handsome Php 2:25

EPENETUS, e-pe´-net-us
same as EPAENETUS Ro 16:5

EPHAI, e´-fa´-i
languishing Jer 40:8

EPHER, e´-fer
calf Ge 25:4

EPHES-DAMMIM, e´-fez-dam´-im
boundary of blood 1Sa 17:1

EPHESIANS, e-fe´-zi-ans
inhabitants of Ephesus Ac 19:28

EPHESUS, ef´-es-us
desirable Ac 18:19

EPHLAL, ef´-lal
judgment 1Ch 2:37

EPHPHATHA, ef´-ath-ah
be opened Mk 7:34

EPHRAIM, ef´-ra-im
fruitful (?) Ge 41:52

EPHRAIMITES, ef´-ra-im-ites
inhabitants of Ephraim Jgs 12:4

EPHRAIN, ef-ra´-in
same as EPHRON 2Ch 13:19

EPHRATH, ef´-rath
short for EPHRATAH Ge 35:16

EPHRATAH, ef´-rat-ah
fruitful (?) Ru 4:11

EPHRATHITES, ef´-rath-ites
inhabitants of Ephrath Ru 1:2

EPHRON, ef´-ron
of, or belonging to a calf Ge 23:8

EPICUREANS, ep´-ik-u-re´-ans
followers of Epicurus Ac 17:18

ER, er
watchful Ge 38:3

ERAN, e´-ran
one who watches Nu 26:36

ERANITES, e´-ran-ites
descendants of Eran Nu 26:36

ERASTUS, e-rast´-us
beloved Ac 19:22

ERECH, e´-rek
length Ge 10:10

ERI, e´-ri
same as ER Ge 46:16

ERITES, er´-ites
descendants of Eri Nu 26:16

ESAIAS, e´-sai-as
same as ISAIAH Mt 3:3

ESARHADDON, e´-sar-had´-on
Ashur giveth a brother 2Ki 19:37

ESAU, e´-saw
hairy Ge 25:25

ESEK, e´-sek
strife Ge 26:20

ESH-BAAL, esh´-ba´-al
man of Baal 1Ch 8:33

ESHBAN, esh´-ban
reason, intelligence Ge 36:26

ESHCOL, esh´-kol
cluster Ge 14:13

ESHEAN, esh´-e-an
support (?) Jos 15:52

ESHEK, e´-shek
oppression 1Ch 8:39

ESHKALONITES, esh´-ka-lon-ites
men of Ashkalon Jos 13:3

ESHTAOL, esh´-ta-ol
petition (?) Jos 15:33

ESHTAULITES, esh-ta´-ool-ites
inhabitants of Eshtaol 1Ch 2:53

ESHTEMOA, esh´-tem-o´-ah
obedience Jos 21:14

ESHTEMOH, esh´-te-mo
same as ESHTEMOA Jos 15:50

Names

ESHTON, esht´-on
womanly 1Ch 4:11
ESLI, es´-li
same as AZALIAH (?) Lk 3:25
ESROM, es´-rom
same as HEZRON Mt 1:3
ESTHER, es´-ther
star Est 2:7
ETAM, e´-tam
a place of ravenous creatures Jgs 15:8
ETHAM, e´-tham
boundary of the sea (?) Ex 13:20
ETHAN, e´-than
firmness 1Ki 4:31
ETHANIM, eth´-an-im
incessant rains 1Ki 8:2
ETHBAAL, eth-ba´-al
living with Baal 1Ki 16:31
ETHER, e´-ther
plenty Jos 15:42
ETHIOPIA, e´-thi-ope´-yah
(region of) *burnt faces* Ge 2:13
ETHIOPIAN, e´-thi-ope´-yan
a native of Ethiopia Jer 13:23
ETHNAN, eth´-nan
a gift 1Ch 4:7
ETHNI, eth´-ni
bountiful 1Ch 6:41
EUBULUS, eu-bew´-lus
good counselor 2Ti 4:21
EUNICE, eu-ni´-see
blessed with victory 2Ti 1:5
EUODIAS, eu-ode´-yas
success Php 4:2
EUPHRATES, eu-fra´-tes
the fertile river (?) Ge 2:14
EUROCLYDON, eu-rok´-ly-don
strong wind from the northeast Ac 27:14
EUTYCHUS, eu´-tyk-us
fortunate Ac 20:9
EVE, ev
life Ge 3:20
EVI, e´-vi
desire Nu 31:8
EVIL-MERODACH, e´-vil-me´-ro-dak
man of Merodach 2Ki 25:27
EZAR, e´-zar
treasure 1Ch 1:38
EZBAI, ez´-ba-i
from ELIAM (?) 1Ch 11:37
EZBON, ez´-bon
1 son of Gad Ge 46:16
2 form of OZNI Nu 26:16
3 son of Bela 1Ch 7:7
EZEKIAS, ez´-ek-i´-as
same as HEZEKIAH Mt 1:9
EZEKIEL, ez-e´-ki-el
whom God will strengthen Eze 1:3
EZEL, e´-zel
departure 1Sa 20:19
EZEM, e´-zem
bone 1Ch 4:29
EZER, e´-zer
help 1Ch 4:4
EZION-GABER, e´-zi-on-ga´-ber
same as EZION-GEBER Nu 33:35
EZION-GEBER, e´-zi-on-ge´-ber
the backbone of a man 1Ki 9:26
EZRA, ez´-rah
help Ezr 7:1
EZRAHITE, ez´-rah-ite
a descendant of Zerah 1Ki 4:31
EZRI, ez´-ri
the help of Jehovah (?) 1Ch 27:26

F

FELIX, fe´-lix
happy Ac 23:24
FESTUS, fest´-us
joyful Ac 24:27
FORTUNATUS, for´-tu-na´-tus
prosperous 1Co 16:17

G

GAAL, ga´-al
loathing Jgs 9:26
GAASH, ga´-ash
shaking Jos 24:30
GABA, ga´-bah
hill Jos 18:24
GABBAI, gab´-a-i
a collector of tribute Ne 11:8
GABBATHA, gab´-ath-ah
height Jn 19:13
GABRIEL, ga´-bri-el
man of God Da 8:16
GAD, gad
a troop, good fortune Ge 30:11
GADARENES, gad´-ar-eens
inhabitants of Gadara Mk 5:1
GADDI, gad´-i
fortunate Nu 13:11
GADDIEL, gad´-i-el
fortune sent from God Nu 13:10
GADI, gad´-i
fortunate 2Ki 15:14
GADITES, gad´-ites
persons belonging to the tribe of Gad Dt 3:12
GAHAM, ga´-ham
sunburnt (?) Ge 22:24
GAHAR, ga´-har
hiding place Ezr 2:47
GAIUS, ga´-yus
Gr. for Caius Ac 19:29
GALAL, ga´-lal
worthy (?) 1Ch 9:15
GALATIA, ga-la´-shah
a place colonized by Gauls Ac 16:6
GALATIANS, ga-la´-shans
inhabitants of Galatia Gal 3:1
GALEED, gal´-e-ed
heap of witness Ge 31:47
GALILEE, gal´-il-ee
circuit Jos 20:7
GALLIM, gal´-im
heaps 1Sa 25:44
GALLIO, gal´-li-o
one who lives on milk Ac 18:12
GAMALIEL, ga-ma´-li-el
benefit of God Nu 1:10
GAMMADIMS, gam´-ad-ims
warriors (?) Eze 27:11
GAMUL, ga´-mool
weaned 1Ch 24:17
GAREB, ga´-reb
scabby 2Sa 23:38
GARMITE, garm´-ite
bony 1Ch 4:19
GASHMU, gash´-moo
same as GESHEM Ne 6:6
GATAM, ga´-tam
puny Ge 36:11
GATH, gath
winepress Jos 11:22
GATH-HEPHER, gath-he´-fer
winepress of the well 2Ki 14:25
GATH-RIMMON, gath-rim´-on
winepress of the pomegranate Jos 19:45
GAZA, ga´-zah
same as AZZAH Ge 10:19
GAZATHITES, ga´-zath-ites
inhabitants of Gaza Jos 13:3
GAZER, ga´-zer
place cut off 2Sa 5:25
GAZEZ, ga´-zez
shearer 1Ch 2:46
GAZITES, ga´-zites
inhabitants of Gaza Jgs 16:2
GAZZAM, gaz´-am
eating up Ezr 2:48
GEBA, ge´-bah
hill Jos 21:17
GEBAL, ge´-bal
mountain Ps 83:7

GEBER, ge´-ber
man 1Ki 4:13

GEBIM, ge´-bim
trenches Isa 10:31

GEDALIAH, ged´-al-i´-ah
whom Jehovah has made great 2Ki 25:22

GEDEON, ged´-e-on
same as GIDEON Heb 11:32

GEDER, ged´-er
wall Jos 12:13

GEDERAH, ged´-er-ah
enclosure, sheepfold Jos 15:36

GEDERATHITE, ged-er´-ath-ite
an inhabitant of Gederah 1Ch 12:4

GEDERITE, ged´-er-ite
native of Geder 1Ch 27:28

GEDEROTH, ged´-er-oth
sheepfolds Jos 15:41

GEDEROTHAIM, ged´-er-oth-a´-im
two sheepfolds Jos 15:36

GEDOR, ged´-or
wall Jos 15:58

GEHAZI, ge-ha´-zi
valley of vision 2Ki 4:12

GELILOTH, gel-il´-oth
regions Jos 18:17

GEMALLI, ge-mal´-i
possessor of camels Nu 13:12

GEMARIAH, gem´-ar-i´-ah
whom Jehovah has completed Jer 29:3

GENNESARET, gen-es´-a-ret
garden of Hazor (?) Mt 14:34

GENUBATH, je-noob´-ath
theft, robbery 1Ki 11:20

GERA, ge´-ra
a grain Ge 46:21

GERAR, ge´-rar
sojourning Ge 10:19

GERGESENES, ger´-ge-seens
inhabitants of Gerasa Mt 8:28

GERIZIM, ge-rize´-im
persons living in a desert Dt 11:29

GERSHOM, ger´-shom
expulsion Ex 2:22

GERSHON, ger´-shon
same as GERSHOM Ge 46:11

GERSHONITES, ger´-shon-ites
descendants of Gershon Nu 3:21

GESHAM, ge´-sham
rain 1Ch 2:47

GESHEM, ge´-shem
stout (?) Ne 2:19

GESHUR, ge´-shoor
bridge 2Sa 3:3

GESHURI, ge-shoor´-i
inhabitants of Geshur Dt 3:14

GESHURITES, ge-shoor´-ites
same as GESHURI Jos 12:5

GETHER, ge´-ther
dregs (?) Ge 10:23

GETHSEMANE, geth-sem´-an-e
oil press Mt 26:36

GEUEL, goo´-el
majesty of God Nu 13:15

GEZER, ge´-zer
precipice Jos 10:33

GEZRITES, gez´-rites
dwelling in a desert land 1Sa 27:8

GIAH, gi´-ah
gushing forth 2Sa 2:24

GIBBAR, gib´-ar
a hero Ezr 2:20

GIBBETHON, gib´-eth-on
a lofty place Jos 19:44

GIBEA, gib´-e-ah
hill 1Ch 2:49

GIBEAH, gib´-e-ah
hill Jos 15:57

GIBEATH, gib´-e-ath
hill Jos 18:28

GIBEON, gib´-e-on
pertaining to a hill Jos 9:3

GIBEONITES, gib´-e-on-ites
inhabitants of Gibeon 2Sa 21:1

GIBLITES, gib´-lites
inhabitants of Gebal Jos 13:5

GIDDALTI, gid-al´-ti
I have increased 1Ch 25:4

GIDDEL, gid´-el
gigantic Ezr 2:47

GIDEON, gid´-e-on
one who cuts down Jgs 6:11

GIDEONI, gid´-e-on-i
cutting down Nu 1:11

GIDOM, gi´-dom
a cutting off Jgs 20:45

GIHON, gi´-hon
a river Ge 2:13

GILALAI, gil´-al-a´-i
dungy (?) Ne 12:36

GILBOA, gil-bo´-ah
bubbling fountain 1Sa 28:4

GILEAD, gil´-e-ad
hill of witness Ge 31:21

GILEADITE, gil´-e-ad-ite
inhabitant of Gilead Jgs 10:3

GILGAL, gil´-gal
a circle Jos 4:19

GILOH, gi´-lo
exile Jos 15:51

GILONITE, gi´-lon-ite
an inhabitant of Giloh 2Sa 15:12

GIMZO, gim´-zo
a place abounding with sycamores 2Ch 28:18

GINATH, gi´-nath
garden 1Ki 16:21

GINNETHO, gin´-eth-o
garden Ne 12:4

GINNETHON, gin´-eth-on
same as GINNETHO Ne 10:6

GIRGASHITE, gir´-gash-ite
dwelling in a clayish soil 1Ch 1:14

GIRGASITE, gir´-gas-ite
same as GIRGASHITE Ge 10:16

GISPA, gis´-pah
flattery Ne 11:21

GITTAH-HEPHER, git´-tah-he´-fer
winepress of the well Jos 19:13

GITTAIM, git´-a-im
two winepresses 2Sa 4:3

GITTITES, git´-ites
inhabitants of Gath Jos 13:3

GIZONITE, gi´-zon-ite
same as GUNITES 1Ch 11:34

GOATH, go´-ath
lowing Jer 31:39

GOB, gobe
pit, cistern 2Sa 21:18

GOG, gog
1 descendant of Reuben 1Ch 5:4
2 prince of Meshech Eze 38:2

GOLAN, go´-lan
exile Dt 4:43

GOLGOTHA, gol´-goth-ah
a skull Mt 27:33

GOLIATH, go-li´-ath
exile (?) 1Sa 17:4

GOMER, go´-mer
complete Ge 10:2

GOMORRAH, go-mor´-ah
accumulation (?) Ge 10:19

GOMORRHA, go-mor´-ah
Same as GOMORRAH Mt 10:15

GOSHEN, go´-shen
drawing near (?) Ge 45:10

GOZAN, go´-zan
who nourishes the body 2Ki 17:6

GRECIA, greesh´-ah
same as GREECE Da 8:21

GRECIAN, greesh´-an
a Jew who speaks Gr. Ac 11:20

GREECE, grees
country of the Greeks Ac 20:2

GUDGODAH, gud´-god-ah
thunder (?) Dt 10:7

GUNI, goon´-i
painted with colors Ge 46:24

GUNITES, goon´-ites
descendants of Guni Nu 26:48

GUR, goor
a young lion 2Ki 9:27

GUR-BAAL, goor-ba´-al
dwelling of Baal 2Ch 26:7

H

HAAHASHTARI, ha´-a-hash´-tar-i
the muleteer (?) 1Ch 4:6

HABAIAH, hab´-a-i´-ah
whom Jehovah hides Ezr 2:61

HABAKKUK, ha-bak´-ook
embrace Hab 1:1

HABAZINIAH, hab´-az-in-i´-ah
lamp of Jehovah (?) Jer 35:3

HABOR, ha´-bor
joining together 2Ki 17:6

HACHALIAH, hak-al-i´-ah
whom Jehovah disturbs Ne 1:1

HACHILAH, hak´-i-lah
dark 1Sa 23:19

HACHMONI, hak´-mon-i
wise 1Ch 27:32

HACHMONITE, hak´-mon-ite
a descendant of Hachmoni 1Ch 11:11

HADAD, ha´-dad
fierce Ge 36:35

HADADEZER, had-ad-e´-zer
whose help is fierce 2Sa 8:3

HADADRIMMON, had-ad-rim´-mon
invocation to the god Rimmon Zec 12:11

HADAR, ha´-dar
enclosure Ge 25:15

HADAREZER, had´-ar-e´-zer
same as HADADEZER 1Ch 18:3

HADASHAH, had-ash´-ah
new Jos 15:37

HADASSAH, had-as´-ah
myrtle Est 2:7

HADATTAH, had-at´-ah
new Hazor Jos 15:25

HADID, ha´-did
sharp Ezr 2:33

HADLAI, had´-la-i
rest 2Ch 28:12

HADORAM, had-or´-am
noble honor Ge 10:27

HADRACH, had´-rak
dwelling Zec 9:1

HAGAB, ha´-gab
locust Ezr 2:46

HAGABA, ha´-gab-ah
same as HAGAB Ne 7:48

HAGABAH, ha´-gab-ah
same as HAGAB Ezr 2:45

HAGAR, ha´-gar
flight Ge 16:3

HAGARENES, hag´-ar-e´-nes
descendants of Hagar Ps 83:6

HAGARITES, hag´-ar-ites
same as HAGARENES 1Ch 5:10

HAGERITE, hag´-er-ite
same as HAGARENES 1Ch 27:31

HAGGAI, hag´-a-i
festive Hag 1:1

HAGGERI, hag´-er-i
wanderer 1Ch 11:38

HAGGI, hag´-i
same as HAGGERI Ge 46:16

HAGGIAH, hag-i´-ah
festival of Jehovah 1Ch 6:30

HAGGITES, hag´-ites
the posterity of Haggi Nu 26:15

HAGGITH, hag´-ith
festive 2Sa 3:4

HAI, ha´-i
same as AI Ge 12:8

HAKKATAN, hak´-at-an
the small Ezr 8:12

HAKKOZ, hak´-oz
the thorn 1Ch 24:10

HAKUPHA, ha-koo´-fah
bent Ezr 2:51

HALAH, ha´-lah
same as CALAH (?) 2Ki 17:6

HALAK, ha´-lak
smooth Jos 11:17

HALHUL, hal´-hool
opening (?) Jos 15:58

HALI, ha´-li
necklace Jos 19:25

HALLOHESH, hal-o´-hesh
same as HALOHESH Ne 10:24

HALOHESH, hal-o´-hesh
the enchanter Ne 3:12

HAM, ham
warm Ge 9:18

HAMAN, ha´-man
well-disposed Est 3:1

HAMATH, ha´-math
fortress Nu 34:8

HAMATH-ZOBAH, ha´-math-zo´-bah
fortress of Zobah 2Ch 8:3

HAMATHITE, ha´-math-ite
an inhabitant of Hamath Ge 10:18

HAMMATH, ham´-ath
warm springs Jos 19:35

HAMMEDATHA, ham-ed´-a-thah
given by the moon (?) Est 3:1

HAMMELECH, ham-me´-lek
the king Jer 36:26

HAMMOLEKETH, ham´-mo-le´-keth
the queen 1Ch 7:18

HAMMON, ham´-on
warm Jos 19:28

HAMMOTH-DOR, ham´-oth-dor
warm springs of Dor Jos 21:32

HAMON-GOG, ham´-on-gog
mother of Gog Eze 39:11

HAMONAH, ha-mo´-nah
multitude Eze 39:16

HAMOR, ha´-mor
ass Ge 33:19

HAMUEL, ham´-oo-el
heat (wrath) *of God* 1Ch 4:26

HAMUL, ha´-mool
who has experienced mercy Ge 46:12

HAMULITES, ha´-mool-ites
descendants of Hamul Nu 26:21

HAMUTAL, ha-moo´-tal
refreshing like dew 2Ki 23:31

HANAMEEL, han´-am-e´-el
a form of HANANEEL (?) Jer 32:7

HANAN, ha´-nan
merciful 1Ch 8:23

HANANEEL, han´-an-e´-el
whom God graciously gave Ne 3:1

HANANI, ha-na´-ni
same as HANANIAH (?) 1Ki 16:1

HANANIAH, han´-an-i´-ah
whom Jehovah graciously gave 1Ch 3:19

HANES, ha´-nes
a city in Egypt Isa 30:4

HANIEL, han´-i-el
favour of God 1Ch 7:39

HANNAH, han´-ah
gracious 1Sa 1:2

HANNATHON, han´-ath-on
gracious Jos 19:14

HANNIEL, han´-i-el
same as HANIEL Nu 34:23

HANOCH, ha´-nok
same as ENOCH Ge 25:4

HANOCHITES, ha´-nok-ites
descendants of Hanoch Nu 26:5

HANUN, ha´-noon
whom (God) pities 2Sa 10:1

HAPHRAIM, haf-ra´-im
two pits Jos 19:19

HARA, ha´-ra
mountainous 1Ch 5:26

HARADAH, ha´-ra-dah
fear Nu 33:24

HARAN, ha´-ran
mountaineer Ge 11:27

HARARITE, ha´-rar-ite
a mountaineer 2Sa 23:11

HARBONA, har-bo´-nah
same as HARBONAH — Est 1:10

HARBONAH, har-bo´-nah
donkey-driver — Est 7:9

HAREPH, ha´-ref
plucking — 1Ch 2:51

HARETH, ha´-reth
thicket — 1Sa 22:5

HARHAIAH, har-hai´-ah
dried up (?) — Ne 3:8

HARHAS, har´-has
same as HASRAH — 2Ki 22:14

HARHUR, har´-hoor
inflammation — Ezr 2:51

HARIM, ha´-rim
flat-nosed — 1Ch 24:8

HARIPH, ha´-rif
autumnal showers — Ne 7:24

HARNEPHER, har-ne´-fer
descendant of Ashur — 1Ch 7:36

HAROD, ha´-rod
terror — Jgs 7:1

HARODITE, har´-od-ite
inhabitant of Harod — 2Sa 23:25

HAROEH, ha-ro´-eh
the seer — 1Ch 2:52

HARORITE, har´-or-ite
a form of HARODITE (?) — 1Ch 11:27

HAROSHETH, ha-rosh´-eth
carving — Jgs 4:2

HARSHA, har´-shah
enchanter, magician — Ezr 2:52

HARUM, ha´-room
high (?) — 1Ch 4:8

HARUMAPH, ha-roo´-maf
flat-nosed — Ne 3:10

HARUPHITE, ha-roof´-ite
descendants of Hariph — 1Ch 12:5

HARUZ, ha´-rooz
active — 2Ki 21:19

HASADIAH, ha´-sad-i´-ah
whom Jehovah loves — 1Ch 3:20

HASENUAH, ha´-se-noo´-ah
she that is hated — 1Ch 9:7

HASHABIAH, ha´-shab-i´-ah
whom Jehovah esteems — 1Ch 6:45

HASHABNAH, ha-shab´-nah
same as HASHABIAH (?) — Ne 10:25

HASHABNIAH, ha´-shab-ni´-ah
same as HASHABIAH — Ne 3:10

HASHEM, ha´-shem
fat — 1Ch 11:34

HASHMONAH, hash-mo´-nah
fatness, fat soil — Nu 33:29

HASHUB, hash´-oob
thoughtful — Ne 3:11

HASHUBAH, hash-oob´-ah
same as HASHUB — 1Ch 3:20

HASHUM, hash´-oom
rich — Ezr 2:19

HASHUPHA, hash-oof´-ah
a form of HASUPHA — Ne 7:46

HASRAH, has´-rah
needy, lacking — 2Ch 34:22

HASSENAAH, has´-en-a´-ah
the thorny — Ne 3:3

HASSHUB, hash´-oob
same as HASHUB — 1Ch 9:14

HASUPHA, has-oof´-ah
made bare — Ezr 2:43

HATACH, ha´-tak
he that strikes (?) — Est 4:5

HATHATH, ha´-thath
terror — 1Ch 4:13

HATIPHA, ha´-ti-fah
seized — Ezr 2:54

HATITA, ha´-ti-tah
digging — Ezr 2:42

HATTIL, hat´-il
wavering — Ezr 2:57

HATTUSH, hat´-oosh
assembled (?) — 1Ch 3:22

HAURAN, how´-ran
hollow land — Eze 47:16

HAVILAH, ha-vil´-ah
sandy (?) — Ge 10:7

HAVOTH-JAIR, ha´-voth-ja´-ir
villages of Jair — Nu 32:41

HAZAEL, ha´-za-el
whom God watches over — 1Ki 19:15

HAZAIAH, ha-zai´-ah
whom Jehovah watches over — Ne 11:5

HAZAR-ADDAR, ha´-zar-ad´-ar
Addar-town — Nu 34:4

HAZAR-ENAN, ha´-zar-e´-nan
fountain-town — Nu 34:9

HAZAR-GADDAH, ha´-zar-gad´-ah
luck-town — Jos 15:27

HAZAR-HATTICON, ha´-zar-hat´-ik-on
middle-town — Eze 47:16

HAZARMAVETH, ha´-zar-ma´-veth
death-town — Ge 10:26

HAZAR-SHUAL, ha´-zar-shoo´-al
jackal-town — Jos 15:28

HAZAR-SUSAH, ha´-zar-soo´-sah
mare-town — Jos 19:5

HAZAR-SUSIM, ha´-zar-soo´-sim
horses-town — 1Ch 4:31

HAZAZON-TAMAR, ha´-za-zon-ta´-mar
same as HAZEZON-TAMAR — 2Ch 20:2

HAZELELPONI, haz´-lel-po´-ni
the shadow looking on me — 1Ch 4:3

HAZERIM, ha´-zer-im
villages — Dt 2:23

HAZEROTH, ha´-zer-oth
same as HAZERIM — Nu 11:35

HAZEZON-TAMAR, ha´-ze-zon-ta´-mar
pruning of the palm — Ge 14:7

HAZIEL, ha´-zi-el
the vision of God — 1Ch 23:9

HAZO, ha´-zo
vision — Ge 22:22

HAZOR, ha´-zor
castle — Jos 11:1

HEBER, he´-ber
1 same as EBER — 1Ch 5:13
2 *fellowship* — Ge 46:17

HEBERITES, he´-ber-ites
descendants of Heber — Nu 26:45

HEBREW, he´-broo
1 the language spoken by the Jews — Jn 19:20
2 a Jew — Jer 34:9

HEBREWESS, he´-broo-ess
a Jewess — Jer 34:9

HEBREWS, he´-broos
descendants of Eber — Ge 40:15

HEBRON, he´-bron
alliance — Ge 13:18

HEBRONITES, he´-bron-ites
the people of Hebron — Nu 3:27

HEGAI, he´-gai
meditation — Est 2:8

HEGE, he´-ge
same as HEGAI — Est 2:3

HELAH, he´-lah
rust — 1Ch 4:5

HELAM, he´-lam
stronghold — 2Sa 10:16

HELBAH, hel´-bah
fatness — Jgs 1:31

HELBON, hel´-bon
fertile — Eze 27:18

HELDAI, hel´-da-i
terrestrial — 1Ch 27:15

HELEB, he´-leb
fat, fatness — 2Sa 23:29

HELED, he´-led
the world — 1Ch 11:30

HELEK, he´-lek
portion — Nu 26:30

HELEKITES, he´-lek-ites
descendants of Helek — Nu 26:30

HELEM, he´-lem
a form of HELDAI 1Ch 7:35

HELEPH, he´-lef
exchange Jos 19:33

HELEZ, he´-lez
liberation 2Sa 23:26

HELI, he´-li
Gr. for ELI Lk 3:23

HELKAI, hel´-ka-i
a form of HILKIAH Ne 12:15

HELKATH, hel´-kath
a portion Jos 19:25

HELKATH-HAZZURIM, hel´-kath-haz´-oor-im
the field of swords (?) 2Sa 2:16

HELON, he´-lon
strong Nu 1:9

HEMAM, he´-mam
same as HOMAM Ge 36:22

HEMAN, he´-man
faithful 1Ki 4:31

HEMATH, he´-math
1 *fortress* 1Ch 2:55
2 same as HAMATH Am 6:14

HEMDAN, hem´-dan
pleasant Ge 36:26

HEN, hen
favour Zec 6:14

HENA, he´-na
troubling (?) 2Ki 18:34

HENADAD, hen´-a´-dad
favour of Hadad (?) Ezr 3:9

HENOCH, he´-nok
same as ENOCH 1Ch 1:3

HEPHER, he´-fer
pit Jos 12:17

HEPHERITES, he´-fer-ites
descendants of Hepher Nu 26:32

HEPHZI-BAH, hef-zi´-bah
in whom is my delight 2Ki 21:1

HERES, he´-res
the sun Jgs 1:35

HERESH, he´-resh
artificer 1Ch 9:15

HERMAS, her´-mas
same as HERMES Ro 16:14

HERMES, her´-mes
rock, refuge Ro 16:14

HERMOGENES, her-mog´-e-nes
begotten of Hermes [Mercury] 2Ti 1:15

HERMON, her´-mon
lofty Dt 3:8

HERMONITES, her´-mon-ites
inhabitants of Mount Hermon Ps 42:6

HEROD, he´-rod
name of several kings of the Jews Mt 2:1

HERODIANS, he-ro´-di-ans
partisans of the Herod family Mt 22:16

HERODIAS, he-ro´-di-as
sister of Herod Agrippa I Mt 14:3

HERODION, he-ro´-di-on
the song of Juno (?) Ro 16:11

HESED, he´-sed
mercy 1Ki 4:10

HESHBON, hesh´-bon
counting Nu 21:25

HESHMON, hesh´-mon
fatness Jos 15:27

HETH, heth
father of the HITTITES Ge 10:15

HETHLON, heth´-lon
hiding-place Eze 47:15

HEZEKI, hez´-ek-i
short for HIZKIAH 1Ch 8:17

HEZEKIAH, hez´-ek-i´-ah
the might of Jehovah 2Ki 18:1

HEZION, hez´-yon
vision 1Ki 15:18

HEZIR, he´-zir
swine 1Ch 24:15

HEZRAI, hez´-ra-i
enclosed wall 2Sa 23:35

HEZRO, hez´-ro
same as HEZRAI 1Ch 11:37

HEZRON, hez´-ron
same as HEZRAI Ge 46:12

HEZRONITES, hez´-ron-ites
descendants of Hezron Nu 26:6

HIDDAI, hid´-a-i
the rejoicing of Jehovah 2Sa 23:30

HIDDEKEL, hid-ek´-el
Gr. name for Tigris River Ge 2:14

HIEL, hi´-el
God liveth 1Ki 16:34

HIERAPOLIS, hi´-e-ra´-pol-is
a sacred or holy city Col 4:13

HIGGAION, hig-a´-yon
meditation Ps 9:16

HILEN, hi´-len
same as HOLON 1Ch 6:58

HILKIAH, hilk-i´-ah
portion of Jehovah 2Ki 18:18

HILLEL, hil´-el
praising Jgs 12:13

HINNOM, hin´-ome
wailing Jos 15:8

HIRAH, hi´-rah
nobility Ge 38:1

HIRAM, hi´-ram
noble (?) 2Sa 5:11

HITTITE, hit´-tite
descendant of Heth Jos 11:3

HITTITES, hit´-tites
plural of HITTITE Ge 15:20

HIVITES, hive´-ites
villagers Ex 3:8

HIZKIAH, hizk-i´-ah
might of Jehovah Zep 1:1

HIZKIJAH, hizk-i´-jah
same as HIZKIAH Ne 10:17

HOBAB, ho´-bab
beloved Nu 10:29

HOBAH, ho´-bah
a hiding-place Ge 14:15

HOD, hode
splendor 1Ch 7:37

HODAIAH, ho-dai´-ah
praise of Jehovah 1Ch 3:24

HODAVIAH, ho´-dav-i´-ah
Jehovah is his praise 1Ch 5:24

HODESH, ho´-desh
new moon 1Ch 8:9

HODEVAH, ho´-de-vah
same as HODAVIAH Ne 7:43

HODIAH, ho-di´-ah
same as HODAIAH 1Ch 4:19

HODIJAH, ho-di´-jah
same as HODIAH Ne 8:7

HOGLAH, hog´-lah
partridge Nu 26:33

HOHAM, ho´-ham
woe to them (?) Jos 10:3

HOLON, ho´-lon
sandy Jos 15:51

HOMAM, ho´-mam
destruction 1Ch 1:39

HOPHNI, hof´-ni
pugilist 1Sa 1:3

HOPHRA, hof´-rah
priest of the sun Jer 44:30

HOR, hore
mountain Nu 20:23

HORAM, ho´-ram
elevation Jos 10:33

HOREB, ho´-reb
desert Ex 3:1

HOREM, ho´-rem
enclosed, sacred Jos 19:38

HOR-HAGIDGAD, hor´-hag-gid´-gad
mountain of Gudgodah Nu 33:32

HORI, ho´-ri
cave-dweller Ge 36:22

HORIMS, hor´-ims
descendants of Hori Dt 2:12

HORITES, hor´-ites
same as HORIMS Ge 14:6

HORMAH, hor´-mah
a devoting, a place laid waste Nu 14:45

HORONAIM, hor´-o-na´-im
two caverns Isa 15:5

HORONITE, hor´-on-ite
native of Beth-horon Ne 2:10

HOSAH, ho´-sah
fleeing to Jehovah for refuge (?) Jos 19:29

HOSANNA, ho-san´-nah
save us we pray Mt 21:9

HOSEA, ho-ze´-ah
salvation Hos 1:1

HOSHAIAH, ho-shai´-ah
whom Jehovah has set free Ne 12:32

HOSHAMA, ho´-sha-mah
Jehovah hath heard (?) 1Ch 3:18

HOSHEA, ho-she´-ah
same as HOSEA Dt 32:44

HOTHAM, ho´-tham
signet ring 1Ch 7:32

HOTHAN, ho´-than
same as HOTHAM 1Ch 11:44

HOTHIR, ho´-thir
son of Heman 1Ch 25:4

HUKKOK, hook´-oke
decreed Jos 19:34

HUKOK, hook´-oke
same as HUKKOK 1Ch 6:75

HUL, hool
circle Ge 10:23

HULDAH, hool´-dah
weasel 2Ki 22:14

HUMTAH, hoom´-tah
fortress (?) Jos 15:54

HUPHAM, hoo´-fam
inhabitant of the shore (?) Nu 26:39

HUPHAMITES, hoo´-fam-ites
descendants of Hupham Nu 26:39

HUPPAH, hoop´-ah
covering 1Ch 24:13

HUPPIM, hoop´-im
same as HUPHAM (?) Ge 46:21

HUR, hoor
cavern Ex 17:10

HURAI, hoo´-ra-i
a linen weaver (?) 1Ch 11:32

HURAM, hoo´-ram
variant spelling of Hiram 2Ch 2:13

HURI, hoo´-ri
linen-worker (?) 1Ch 5:14

HUSHAH, hoo´-shah
haste 1Ch 4:4

HUSHAI, hoo´-sha-i
hasting 2Sa 15:32

HUSHAM, hoo´-sham
haste Ge 36:34

HUSHATHITE, hoo´-shath-ite
inhabitant of Hushah 2Sa 23:27

HUSHIM, hoosh´-im
those who make haste Ge 46:23

HUZ, hooz
same as UZ Ge 22:21

HUZZAB, hooz´-ab
it is decreed Na 2:7

HYMENAEUS, hi´-men-e´-us
belonging to Hymen 2Ti 2:17

I

ICHABOD, i´-ka-bod
inglorious 1Sa 4:21

IBHAR, ib´-har
whom God chooses 2Sa 5:15

IBLEAM, ib´-le-am
He destroys the people Jos 17:11

IBNEIAH, ib-ni´-ah
whom Jehovah will build up 1Ch 9:8

IBNIJAH, ib-ni´-jah
same as IBNEIAH 1Ch 9:8

IBRI, ib´-ri
Hebrew 1Ch 24:27

IBZAN, ib´-zan
active (?) Jgs 12:8

ICONIUM, i-kon´-yum
image-like Ac 13:51

IDALAH, id´-al-ah
snares (?) Jos 19:15

IDBASH, id´-bash
honeyed 1Ch 4:3

IDDO, id´-do
1 *loving* 1Ch 27:21
2 *seasonable* Zec 1:1

IDUMAEA, i-du-me´-ah
same as IDUMEA Mk 3:8

IDUMEA, i-du-me´-ah
same as EDOM Isa 34:5

IGAL, i´-gal
whom God will avenge Nu 13:7

IGDALIAH, ig´-dal-i´-ah
whom Jehovah shall make great Jer 35:4

IGEAL, i´-ge-al
same as IGAL 1Ch 3:22

IIM, i´-im
ruins Nu 33:45

IJE-ABARIM, i-je-ab´-ar-im
ruinous heaps of Abarim Nu 21:11

IJON, i´-jon
a ruin 1Ki 15:20

IKKESH, ik´-esh
perverseness of mouth 2Sa 23:26

ILAI, i´-la-i
most high 1Ch 11:29

ILLYRICUM, il-ir´-ik-um
province of Rome Ro 15:19

IMLA, im´-lah
same as IMLAH 2Ch 18:7

IMLAH, im´-lah
whom (God) will fill up 1Ki 22:8

IMMANUEL, im-an´-u-el
God with us Isa 7:14

IMMER, im´-er
talkative 1Ch 9:12

IMNA, im´-nah
whom (God) keeps back 1Ch 7:35

IMNAH, im´-nah
whom (God) assigns (?) 1Ch 7:30

IMRAH, im´-rah
stubborn 1Ch 7:36

IMRI, im´-ri
eloquent 1Ch 9:4

INDIA, in´-di-ah
1 *great river* (?),
2 Hebr. for Indus Est 1:1

IPHEDEIAH, if´-ed-i´-ah
whom Jehovah frees 1Ch 8:25

IR, eer
city 1Ch 7:12

IRA, i´-rah
watchful 2Sa 20:26

IRAD, i´-rad
descendant of Cain Ge 4:18

IRAM, i´-ram
belonging to a city Ge 36:43

IRI, i´-ri
same as IRAM 1Ch 7:7

IRIJAH, i-ri´-jah
whom Jehovah looks on Jer 37:13

IR-NAHASH, ir-na´-hash
snake-town 1Ch 4:12

IR-SHEMESH, ir´-she´-mesh
sun-town Jos 19:41

IRON, i´-ron
reverence Jos 19:38

IRPEEL, ir´-pe-el
which God heals Jos 18:27

IRU, i´-roo
same as IRAM 1Ch 4:15

ISAAC, i´-zak
laughter Ge 17:19

ISAIAH, i-zai´-ah
salvation of Jehovah Isa 1:1

ISCAH, is´-kah
discerning, expectant (?) Ge 11:29

ISCARIOT, is-kar´-i-ot
man of Kerioth Mt 10:4

ISHBAH, ish´-bah
praising 1Ch 4:17

ISHBAK, ish´-bak
he leaveth or relinquisheth (?) Ge 25:2

ISHBI-BENOB, ish´-bi-ben´-obe
one who dwells at Nob 2Sa 21:16

ISH-BOSHETH, ish-bo´-sheth
man of shame 2Sa 2:8

ISHI, yish´-i
salutary 1Ch 2:31

ISHIAH, ish-i´-ah
whom Jehovah lends 1Ch 7:3

ISHIJAH, ish-i´-jah
same as ISHIA Ezr 10:31

ISHMA, ish´-mah
desolation (?) 1Ch 4:3

ISHMAEL, ish´-ma-el
whom God hears Ge 16:15

ISHMAELITES, ish´-ma-el-ites
descendants of Ishmael Jgs 8:24

ISHMAIAH, ish-mai´-ah
whom Jehovah hears 1Ch 27:19

ISHMEELITES, ish´-me-el-ites
same as ISHMAELITES Ge 37:25

ISHMERAL, ish´-mer-a´-i
whom Jehovah keeps 1Ch 8:18

ISHOD, ish´-hode
man of glory 1Ch 7:18

ISHPAN, ish´-pan
cunning (?) 1Ch 8:22

ISH-TOB, ish´-tobe
men of Tob 2Sa 10:6

ISHI, eesh´-i
my husband Hos 2:16

ISHUAH, ish´-oo-ah
level Ge 46:17

ISHUAI, ish´-oo-a´-i
same as ISUI 1Ch 7:30

ISHUI, ish´-oo-i
same as ISHUAH 1Sa 14:49

ISMACHIAH, is-mak-i´-ah
whom Jehovah upholds 2Ch 31:13

ISMAIAH, is-mai´-ah
same as ISHMAIAH 1Ch 12:4

ISPAH, is´-pah
bald 1Ch 8:16

ISRAEL, iz´-ra-el
soldier of God Ge 32:28

ISRAELITES, iz´-ra-el-ites
descendants of Israel Ex 9:7

ISRAELITISH, iz´-ra-el-ite-ish
after the fashion of an Israelite Le 24:10

ISSACHAR, is´-ak-ar
he is hired (?) Ge 30:18

ISSHIAH, ish-hi´-ah
same as ISHIAH 1Ch 24:21

ISUAH, is´-oo-ah
same as ISHUAH 1Ch 7:30

ISUI, is´-oo-i
same as ISHUI Ge 46:17

ITALY, it´-a-ly
abounding with calves (?) Ac 18:2

ITHAI, ith´-a-i
ploughman 1Ch 11:31

ITHAMAR, i´-tha-mar
island of palms Ex 6:23

ITHIEL, ith´-i-el
God is with me Ne 11:7

ITHMAH, ith´-mah
bereavedness 1Ch 11:46

ITHNAN, ith´-nan
perennial (?) Jos 15:23

ITHRA, ith´-rah
excellence 2Sa 17:25

ITHRAN, ith´-ran
same as ITHRA Ge 36:26

ITHREAM, ith´-re-am
remainder of the people 2Sa 3:5

ITHRITE, ith´-rite
descendants of Jether (?) 2Sa 23:38

ITTAH-KAZIN, it´-ah-ka´-zin
time of the chief Jos 19:13

ITTAI, it´-a-i
same as ITHAI 2Sa 15:19

ITURAEA, i´-tu-re´-ah
a province, so named from Jetur Lk 3:1

IVAH, i´-vah
same as AVA 2Ki 18:34

IZEHAR, iz´-e-har
oil Nu 3:19

IZEHARITES, i´-ze-har´-ites
the descendants of Izehar Nu 3:27

IZHAR, iz-har
same as IZEHAR Ex 6:18

IZHARITES, iz´-har-ites
same as IZEHARITES 1Ch 26:23

IZRAHIAH, iz-rah-i´-ah
whom Jehovah brought to light 1Ch 7:3

IZRAHITE, iz´-rah-ite
same as ZARHITE (?) 1Ch 27:8

IZRI, iz´-ri
a descendant of Jezer 1Ch 25:11

J

JAAKAN, ja´-ak-an
one who turns Dt 10:6

JAAKOBAH, ja´-ak-o´-bah
same as JACOB 1Ch 4:36

JAALA, ja´-a-lah
wild she-goat Ne 7:58

JAALAH, ja´-a-lah
same as JAALA Ezr 2:56

JAALAM, ja´-a-lam
whom God hides Ge 36:5

JAANAI, ja´-an-a´-i
whom Jehovah answers 1Ch 5:12

JAARE-OREGIM, ja´-ar-e-or´-eg-im
forests of the weavers 2Sa 21:19

JAASAU, ja´-a-saw
Jehovah maketh (?) Ezr 10:37

JAASIEL, ja-as´-i-el
whom God created 1Ch 27:21

JAAZANIAH, ja´-az-an-i´-ah
whom Jehovah hears 2Ki 25:23

JAAZER, ja´-a-zer
whom (God) aids Nu 21:32

JAAZIAH, ja´-za-i´-ah
whom Jehovah strengthens 1Ch 24:26

JAAZIEL, ja´-az´-i-el
whom God strengthens 1Ch 15:18

JABAL, ja´-bal
a stream, river Ge 4:20

JABBOK, jab´-ok
pouring out Ge 32:22

JABESH, ja´-besh
dry 2Ki 15:10

JABESH-GILEAD, ja´-besh-gil´-e-ad
JABESH of Gilead Jgs 21:8

JABEZ, ja´-bez
causing pain 1Ch 4:9

JABIN, ja´-bin
whom He (God) considered Jgs 4:2

JABNEEL, jab´-ne-el
may God cause to be built Jos 15:11

JABNEH, jab´-nay
which (God) causes to be built 2Ch 26:6

JACHAN, ja´-kan
troubled 1Ch 5:13

JACHIN, ja´-kin
whom (God) strengthens 1Ki 7:21

JACHINITES, ja´-kin-ites
descendants of Jachin Nu 26:12

JACOB, ja´-kob
supplanter Ge 25:26

JADA, ja´-dah
wise 1Ch 2:28

JADAU, ja´-daw
same as IDDO Ezr 10:43

JADDUA, jad´-oo-ah
skilled Ne 10:21

JADON, ja´-don
a judge Ne 3:7

JAEL, ja´-el
same as JAALA Jgs 4:17

JAGUR, ja´-goor
a lodging Jos 15:21

JAH, ja
poetic form of JEHOVAH Ps 68:4

JAHATH, ja´-hath
grasping (?) 1Ch 6:20

JAHAZ, ja´-haz
a place trodden down Nu 21:23

JAHAZA, ja´-haz-ah
same as JAHAZ Jos 13:18

JAHAZAH, ja´-haz-ah
same as JAHAZ Jos 21:36

JAHAZIAH, ja´-haz-i´-ah
whom Jehovah watches over Ezr 10:15

JAHAZIEL, ja-haz´-i-el
whom God watches over 1Ch 16:6

JAHDAI, jah´-da-i
whom Jehovah directs 1Ch 2:47

JAHDIEL, jah´-di-el
whom God makes glad 1Ch 5:24

JAHDO, jah´-do
union 1Ch 5:14

JAHLEEL, jah´-le-el
hoping in God Nu 26:26

JAHLEELITES, jah´-le-el-ites
descendants of Jahleel Nu 26:26

JAHMAI, jah´-ma-i
lusty 1Ch 7:2

JAHZAH, ja´-zah
same as JAHAZ 1Ch 6:78

JAHZEEL, jah´-ze-el
whom God allots Ge 46:24

JAHZEELITES, jah´-ze-el-ites
descendants of Jahzeel Nu 26:48

JAHZERAH, jah´-zer-ah
may he bring back 1Ch 9:12

JAHZIEL, jah´-zi-el
same as JAHZEEL 1Ch 7:13

JAIR, ja´-er
(God) enlightens Nu 32:41

JAIRITE, ja´-er-ite
a descendant of Jair 2Sa 20:26

JAIRUS, ja-i´-rus
Gr. for JAIR Mk 5:22

JAKAN, ja´-kan
same as JAAKAN 1Ch 1:42

JAKEH, ja´-kay
pious (?) Pr 30:1

JAKIM, ja´-kim
(God) sets up 1Ch 8:19

JALON, ja´-lon
passing the night 1Ch 4:17

JAMBRES, jam´-brees
opposer (?) 2Ti 3:8

JAMES,
Eng. equivalent of JACOB Mt 4:21

JAMIN, ja´-min
right hand Ge 46:10

JAMINITES, ja´-min-ites
descendants of Jamin Nu 26:12

JAMLECH, jam´-lek
He makes to reign 1Ch 4:34

JANNA, jan´-nah
a form of John (?) Lk 3:24

JANNES, jan´-ees
an Egyptian Sorcerer 2Ti 3:8

JANOAH, ja-no´-ah
rest 2Ki 15:29

JANOHAH, ja-no´-hah
same as JANOAH Jos 16:6

JANUM, ja´-noom
sleep Jos 15:53

JAPHETH, ja´-feth
extension Ge 5:32

JAPHIA, ja-fi´-ah
splendid Jos 19:12

JAPHLET, jaf´-let
may he deliver 1Ch 7:32

JAPHLETI, jaf-le´-ti
descendants of Japhlet Jos 16:3

JAPHO, ja´-fo
beauty Jos 19:46

JARAH, ja´-rah
honey 1Ch 9:42

JAREB, ja´-reb
contentious Hos 5:13

JARED, ja´-red
descent Ge 5:15

JARESIAH, ja´-res-i´-ah
whom Jehovah nourishes 1Ch 8:27

JARIB, ja´-rib
adversary 1Ch 4:24

JARMUTH, jar´-mooth
height Jos 10:3

JAROAH, ja-ro´-ah
moon (?) 1Ch 5:14

JASHEN, ja´-shen
sleeping 2Sa 23:32

JASHER, ja´-sher
upright Jos 10:13

JASHOBEAM, ja-shob´-e-am
the people return 1Ch 11:11

JASHUB, ja´-shoob
he returns Nu 26:24

JASHUBI-LEHEM,
ja-shoob´-i-le´-hem
giving bread (?) 1Ch 4:22

JASHUBITES, ja´-shoob-ites
descendants of Jashub Nu 26:24

JASIEL, ja-si´-el
whom God made 1Ch 11:47

JASON, ja´-son
Graeco-Judaean
equivalent of JOSHUA Ac 17:5

JATHNIEL, jath´-ni-el
God gives 1Ch 26:2

JATTIR, jat´-yer
excelling Jos 15:48

JAVAN, ja´-van
wine (?) Ge 10:2

JAZER, ja´-zer
same as JAAZER Nu 32:1

JAZIZ, ja´-ziz
wanderer (?) 1Ch 27:31

JEARIM, je´-ar-im
forests Jos 15:10

JEATERAI, je-at´-er-a´-i
same as ETHNI 1Ch 6:21

JEBERECHIAH, je-ber´-ek-i´-ah
whom Jehovah blesses Isa 8:2

JEBUS, je´-boos
a place trodden down (?) Jgs 19:10

JEBUSI, je´-boos-i
same as JEBUS Jos 18:16

JEBUSITES, je´-boos-ites
the descendants of Jebus Nu 13:29

JECAMIAH, jek´-a-mi-ah
same as JEKAMIAH 1Ch 3:18

JECHOLIAH, jek´-ol-i´-ah
Jehovah is strong 2Ki 15:2

JECHONIAS, jek´-on-i´-as
Gr. for JECONIAH Mt 1:11

JECOLIAH, jek´-ol-i´-ah
same as JECHOLIAH 2Ch 26:3

JECONIAH, jek´-on-i´-ah
Jehovah establishes 1Ch 3:16

JEDAIAH, jed-ai´-ah
1 *Jehovah*—(?) 1Ch 4:37
2 *Jehovah knoweth* 1Ch 24:7

JEDIAEL, jed´-i-a´-el
known of God 1Ch 7:6

JEDIDAH, jed-i´-dah
beloved 2Ki 22:1

JEDIDIAH, jed´-id-i´-ah
beloved of Jehovah 2Sa 12:25

JEDUTHUN, jed-ooth´-oon
friendship (?) 1Ch 16:38

JEEZER, je-e´-zer
contracted from ABIEZER Nu 26:30

JEEZERITES, je-ez´-er-ites
descendants of Jeezer Nu 26:30

JEGAR-SAHADUTHA,
je´-gar-sa-ha-doo´-thah
the heap of testimony Ge 31:47

JEHALELEEL, je-hal´-el-e´-el
he praises God 1Ch 4:16

JEHALELEL, je-hal´-e-lel
same as JEHALELEEL 2Ch 29:12

JEHDEIAH, jed-i´-ah
whom Jehovah makes glad 1Ch 24:20

JEHEZEKEL, je-hez´-e-kel
same as EZEKIEL 1Ch 24:16

JEHIAH, je-hi´-ah
Jehovah lives 1Ch 15:24

JEHIEL, je-hi´-el
God liveth 1Ch 15:18

JEHIELI, je-hi´-el-i
my God liveth 1Ch 26:21

JEHIZKIAH, je´-hizk-i´-ah
same as HEZEKIAH 2Ch 28:12

JEHOADAH, je-ho´-a-dah
whom Jehovah adorns 1Ch 8:36

JEHOADDAN, je-ho´-ad-an
Jehovah is beauteous (?) 2Ki 14:2

JEHOAHAZ, je-ho´-a-haz
whom Jehovah holds fast 2Ki 10:35

JEHOASH, je-ho´-ash
Jehovah supports 2Ki 11:21

JEHOHANAN, je-ho´-han-an
Jehovah is gracious 1Ch 26:3

JEHOIACHIN, je-ho´-ya-kin
Jehovah has established 2Ki 24:6

JEHOIADA, je-ho´-ya-dah
Jehovah knoweth 2Sa 8:18

JEHOIAKIM, je-ho´-ya-kim
Jehovah has set up 2Ki 23:34

JEHOIARIB, je-ho´-ya-rib
Jehovah will contend 1Ch 9:10

JEHONADAB, je-ho´-na-dab
Jehovah is bounteous 2Ki 10:15

JEHONATHAN, je-ho´-na-than
same as JONATHAN 1Ch 27:25

JEHORAM, je-ho´-ram
Jehovah is high 1Ki 22:50

JEHOSHABEATH, je-ho´-shab´-e-ath
Jehovah is the oath 2Ch 22:11

JEHOSHAPHAT, je-hosh´-af-at
whom Jehovah judges 1Ki 15:24

JEHOSHEBA, je-ho´-she-bah
same as JEHOSHABEATH 2Ki 11:2

JEHOSHUA, je-hosh´-oo-ah
same as JOSHUA Nu 13:16

JEHOSHUAH, je-hosh´-oo-ah
same as JOSHUA 1Ch 7:27

JEHOVAH, je-ho´-vah
the Eternal One Ex 6:3

JEHOVAH-JIREH, je-ho´-vah-ji´-ray
Jehovah will provide Ge 22:14

JEHOVAH-NISSI, je-ho´-vah-nis´-i
Jehovah my banner Ex 17:15

JEHOVAH-SHALOM, je-ho´-vah-sha´-lom
Jehovah send peace Jgs 6:24

JEHOZABAD, je-ho´-za-bad
Jehovah gave 2Ki 12:21

JEHOZADAK, je-ho´-za-dak
Jehovah is just 1Ch 6:14

JEHU, je´-hu
Jehovah is He (?) 1Ki 19:16

JEHUBBAH, je-hoob´-ah
hidden 1Ch 7:34

JEHUCAL, je-hoo´-kal
Jehovah is mighty Jer 37:3

JEHUD, je´-hood
praise Jos 19:45

JEHUDI, je-hood´-i
a Jew Jer 36:14

JEHUDIJAH, je-hood-i´-jah
a Jewess 1Ch 4:18

JEHUSH, je´-hoosh
to whom God hastens 1Ch 8:39

JEIEL, ji´-el
treasure of God (?) 1Ch 5:7

JEKABZEEL, je-kab´-ze-el
God gathers Ne 11:25

JEKAMEAM, je´-ka-me´-am
he doth assemble the people 1Ch 23:19

JEKAMIAH, jek´-am-i´-ah
Jehovah gathers 1Ch 2:41

JEKUTHIEL, je-koo´-thi-el
the fear of God 1Ch 4:18

JEMIMA, je-mi´-mah
dove Job 42:14

JEMUEL, jem-oo´-el
day of God Ge 46:10

JEPHTHAH, jef´-tah
God opens Jgs 11:1

JEPHUNNEH, je´-foon´-eh
for whom it is prepared Nu 13:6

JERAH, je´-rah
the moon Ge 10:26

JERAHMEEL, je-rah´-me-el
whom God loves 1Ch 2:9

JERAHMEELITES, je-rah´-me-el-ites
descendants of Jerahmeel 1Sa 27:10

JERED, je´-red
descent 1Ch 1:2

JEREMAI, jer´-em-a´-i
dwelling in heights Ezr 10:33

JEREMIAH, jer-em-i´-ah
whom Jehovah has appointed Jer 1:1

JEREMIAS, jer-em-i´-as
same as JEREMIAH Mt 16:14

JEREMOTH, jer´-em-oth
high places 1Ch 8:14

JEREMY, jer´-em-ee
same as JEREMIAH Mt 2:17

JERIAH, jer-i´-ah
whom Jehovah regards (?) 1Ch 23:19

JERIBAI, jer´-ib-a´-i
contentious 1Ch 11:46

JERICHO, jer´-ik-o
a fragrant place Nu 22:1

JERIEL, je-ri´-el
founded by God 1Ch 7:2

JERIJAH, jer-i´-jah
same as JERIAH 1Ch 26:31

JERIMOTH, jer´-i-moth
same as JEREMOTH 1Ch 7:7

JERIOTH, je-ri´-oth
curtains 1Ch 2:18

JEROBOAM, jer´-ob-o´-am
whose people are many 1Ki 11:26

JEROHAM, je-ro´-ham
who is loved 1Sa 1:1

JERUBBAAL, je-roo´-ba-al
let Baal plead Jgs 6:32

JERUBBESHETH, je´-roo-be´-sheth
1 *let shame plead,*
2 another name for JERUBBAAL 2Sa 11:21

JERUEL, je-roo´-el
same as JERIEL 2Ch 20:16

JERUSALEM, je-roo´-sa-lem
founded in peace (?) Jos 10:1

JERUSHA, je-roo´-shah
possession 2Ki 15:33

JERUSHAH, je-roo´-shah
same as JERUSHA 2Ch 27:1

JESAIAH, je-sai´-ah
same as ISAIAH 1Ch 3:21

JESHAIAH, je-shai´-ah
same as ISAIAH 1Ch 25:3

JESHANAH, je-shan´-ah
old 2Ch 13:19

JESHARELAH, jesh´-ar-el´-ah
right before God (?) 1Ch 25:14

JESHEBEAB, je-sheb´-e-ab
father's seat 1Ch 24:13

JESHER, je´-sher
uprightness 1Ch 2:18

JESHIMON, je-shim´-on
the waste Nu 21:20

JESHISHAI, je-shi´-sha-i
like an old man 1Ch 5:14

JESHOHAIAH, je-sho´-ha-i´-ah
whom Jehovah humbles 1Ch 4:36

JESHUA, jesh´-oo-ah
Jehovah is salvation Ezr 2:2

JESHUAH, jesh´-oo-ah
help 1Ch 24:11

JESHURUN, jesh-oor´-oon
righteous Dt 32:15

JESIAH, je-si´-ah
Jehovah forgets 1Ch 12:6

JESIMIEL, je-sim´-i-el
whom God founds (?) 1Ch 4:36

JESSE, jes´-sy
gift (?) Ru 4:17

JESUI, je-soo´-i
same as ISHUA Nu 26:44

JESUITES, je´-soo-ites
descendants of Jesui Nu 26:44

JESURUN, je-soor´-oon
same as JESHURUN Isa 44:2

JESUS, je´-sus
Savior,

Names

K

KIRIOTH, kir´-i-oth
cities Am 2:2

KIRJATH, kir´-jath
city (?) Jos 18:28

KIRJATHAIM, kir´-jath-a´-im
double city Nu 32:37

KIRJATH-ARBA, kir´-jath-ar´-bah
city of Arba Ge 23:2

KIRJATH-ARIM, kir´-jath-ar´-im
contracted from KIRJATH-JEARIM Ezr 2:25

KIRJATH-BAAL, kir´-jath-ba´-al
city of Baal Jos 15:60

KIRJATH-HUZOTH, kir´-jath-hooz´-oth
city of streets Nu 22:39

KIRJATH-JEARIM, kir´-jath-je´-ar-im
city of woods Jos 9:17

KIRJATH-SANNAH, kir´-jath-san´-ah
city of thorns Jos 15:49

KIRJATH-SEPHER, kir´-jath-se´-fer
book-city Jos 15:15

KISH, kish
bow 1Sa 9:1

KISHI, kish´-i
short for KUSHAIAH 1Ch 6:44

KISHION, kish´-i-on
hardness Jos 19:20

KISHON, ki´-shon
tortuous Jgs 4:7

KISON, ki´-son
same as KISHON Ps 83:9

KITHLISH, kith´-lish
fortified Jos 15:40

KITRON, kit´-ron
burning Jgs 1:30

KITTIM, kit´-tim
same as CHITTIM Ge 10:4

KOA, ko´-ah
prince Eze 23:23

KOHATH, ko´-hath
assembly Ge 46:11

KOHATHITES, ko´-hath-ites
descendants of Kohath Nu 3:27

KOLAIAH, kol-ai´-ah
voice of Jehovah (?) Ne 11:7

KORAH, ko´-rah
bald Nu 16:1

KORAHITES, ko´-rah-ites
descendants of Korah 1Ch 9:19

KORATHITES, ko´-rath-ites
same as KORAHITES Nu 26:58

KORE, ko´-re
partridge 1Ch 9:19

KORHITE, kor´-ite
same as KORATHITE 2Ch 20:19

KOZ, koz
thorn Ezr 2:61

KUSHAIAH, kush-ai´-ah
bow of Jehovah 1Ch 15:17

L

LAADAH, la´-ad-ah
order (?) 1Ch 4:21

LAADAN, la´-ad-an
put in order (?) 1Ch 7:26

LABAN, la´-ban
white Ge 24:29

LACHISH, la´-kish
impregnable Jos 10:3

LAEL, la´-el
(devoted) to God Nu 3:24

LAHAD, la´-had
oppression 1Ch 4:2

LAHAI-ROI, la-hah´-i-ro´-i
to the living is sight Ge 24:62

LAHMAM, lah´-mam
their bread or *their war* Jos 15:40

LAHMI, lah´-mi
warrior 1Ch 20:5

LAISH, la´-ish
lion 1Sa 25:44

LAKUM, la´-koom
fort (?) Jos 19:33

LAMA, lam´-ah
why? Mt 27:46

LAMECH, la´-mek
destroyer Ge 4:18

LAODICEA, la-od-i-se´-ah
1 *people of justice*,
2 named after Laodice, wife of Antiochus II Col 2:1

LAODICEANS, la´-od-i-se´-ans
inhabitants of Laodicea Col 4:16

LAPIDOTH, la´-pid-oth
torches Jgs 4:4

LASEA, la-se´-ah
a city on the south side of Crete Ac 27:8

LASHA, la´-shah
fissure Ge 10:19

LASHARON, la-sha´-ron
of the plain Jos 12:18

LAZARUS, laz´-ar-us
Gr. for ELEAZAR Lk 16:20

LEAH, le´-ah
languid Ge 29:16

LEBANAH, leb´-an-ah
white Ezr 2:45

LEBANON, leb´-an-on
the white (mountain) Dt 1:7

LEBAOTH, leb´-a-oth
lionesses Jos 15:32

LEBBAEUS, leb-e´-us
same as THADDAEUS Mt 10:3

LEBONAH, leb-o´-nah
frankincense Jgs 21:19

LECAH, le´-kah
journey (?) 1Ch 4:21

LEHABIM, le´-hab-im
descendants of Mizraim Ge 10:13

LEHI, le´-hi
jaw-bone Jgs 15:9

LEMUEL, lem´-oo-el
(devoted) to God (?) Pr 31:1

LESHEM, le´-shem
precious stone Jos 19:47

LETUSHIM, le-toosh´-im
the hammered Ge 25:3

LEUMMIM, le-oom´-im
peoples Ge 25:3

LEVI, le´-vi
associate (?) Ge 29:34

LEVIATHAN, le-vi´-a-than
a water monster Ps 104:26

LEVITES, le´-vites
descendants of Levi Ex 6:25

LIBERTINES, lib´-ert-ines
freed-men Ac 6:9

LIBNAH, lib´-nah
whiteness Nu 33:20

LIBNI, lib´-ni
white Ex 6:17

LIBNITES, lib´-nites
descendants of Libni Nu 3:21

LIBYA, lib´-ee-ah
1 to the Jews, the western part of lower Egypt Eze 30:5
2 to the Romans, almost all of North Africa, west of Egypt Ac 2:10

LIKHI, lik´-hi
fond of learning (?) 1Ch 7:19

LINUS, li´-nus
flax 2Ti 4:21

LO-AMMI, lo-am´-i
not my people Hos 1:9

LOD, lode
strife (?) 1Ch 8:12

LO-DEBAR, lo´-de-bar
without pasture (?) 2Sa 9:4

LOIS, lo´-is
better 2Ti 1:5

LO-RUHAMAH, lo´-ru´-ham-ah
not having obtained mercy Hos 1:6

LOT, lot
veil Ge 11:27

LOTAN, lo´-tan
veiling Ge 36:20

LUBIM, loob´-im
the land or territory of the LUBIMS Na 3:9

LUBIMS, loob´-ims
same as LEHABIM 2Ch 12:3

LUCAS, loo´-cas
same as LUKE Phm 24

LUCIFER, loo´-sif-er
light-bearer Isa 14:12

LUCIUS, loosh´-yus
a noble (?) Ac 13:1

LUD, lood
strife (?) Ge 10:22

LUDIM, lood´-im
pl. for LUD Ge 10:13

LUHITH, loo´-hith
abounding in boards Isa 15:5

LUKE, luk
luminous, white Col 4:14

LUZ, looz
almond tree Ge 28:19

LYCAONIA, li´-ka-o´-ni-ah
abounding in werewolves Ac 14:6

LYDDA, lid´-ah
Gr. for LOD (?) Ac 9:32

LYDIA, lid´-ee-ah
a standing pool Eze 30:5

LYSANIAS, li-sa´-ni-as
ending sorrow Lk 3:1

LYSIAS, lis´-yas
a loosing Ac 23:26

LYSTRA, lis´-tra
that dissolves Ac 14:6

M

MAACAH, ma´-ak-ah
same as MAACHAH 2Sa 3:3

MAACHAH, ma´-ak-ah
royal (?) 1Ki 2:39

MAACHATHI, ma-ak´-a-thi
an inhabitant of Maachah Dt 3:14

MAACHATHITES, ma-ak´-ath-ites
pl. of MAACHATHI Jos 12:5

MAADAI, ma´-ad-a´-i
adorned Ezr 10:34

MAADIAH, ma´-ad-i´-ah
ornament of Jehovah Ne 12:5

MAAI, ma-a´-i
compassionate (?) Ne 12:36

MAALEH-ACRABBIM, ma´-al-eh-ak´-rab-im
ascent of scorpions Jos 15:3

MAARATH, ma´-ar-ath
a treeless place Jos 15:59

MAASEIAH, ma´-as-i´-ah
work of Jehovah Ezr 10:18

MAASIAI, ma´-as-i-a´-i
same as AMASHAI (?) 1Ch 9:12

MAATH, ma´-ath
small (?) Lk 3:26

MAAZ, ma´-az
wrath 1Ch 2:27

MAAZIAH, ma´-az-i´-ah
consolation of Jehovah 1Ch 24:18

MACEDONIA, mas-e-do´-nee-ah
a country north of Greece Ac 16:9

MACEDONIAN, mas-e-do´-nee-an
belonging to MACEDONIA Ac 27:2

MACHBANAI, mak´-ban-a-i
cloak 1Ch 12:13

MACHBENAH, mak´-be-nah
clad with a cloak (?) 1Ch 2:49

MACHI, ma´-ki
reduced, poor Nu 13:15

MACHIR, ma´-kir
sold Ge 50:23

MACHIRITES, ma´-kir-ites
descendants of Machir Nu 26:29

MACHNADEBAI, mak´-na-deb-a´-i
what is like the liberal (?) Ezr 10:40

MACHPELAH, mak-pe´-lah
a doubling Ge 23:9

MADAI, ma´-da-i
descendants of Japheth Ge 10:2

MADIAN, ma´-di-an
Gr. for MIDIAN Ac 7:29

MADMANNAH, mad´-man-ah
dunghill Jos 15:31

MADMEN, mad´-men
dungheap Jer 48:2

MADMENAH, mad´-men-ah
same as MADMEN Isa 10:31

MADON, ma´-don
place of contention Jos 11:1

MAGBISH, mag´-bish
congregating Ezr 2:30

MAGDALA, mag´-dal-ah
tower Mt 15:39

MAGDALENE, mag´-dal-e´-ne
inhabitant of Magdala Mt 27:56

MAGDIEL, mag´-di-el
praise of God Ge 36:43

MAGOG, ma´-gog
descendants of Japheth Ge 10:2

MAGOR-MISSABIB, ma´-gor-mis´-a-bib
fear round about Jer 20:3

MAGPIASH, mag´-pi-ash
moth slayer (?) Ne 10:20

MAHALAH, mah´-hal-ah
disease 1Ch 7:18

MAHALALEEL, ma-ha´-lal-e´-el
praise of God Ge 5:12

MAHALATH, mah´-al-ath
a musical instrument Ge 28:9

MAHALI, ma´-ha-li
weak Ex 6:19

MAHANAIM, ma´-han-a´-im
two camps Ge 32:2

MAHANEH-DAN, ma´-han-e-dan
camp of Dan Jgs 18:12

MAHARAI, ma´-har-a´-i
impetuous 2Sa 23:28

MAHATH, ma´-hath
taking hold (?) 1Ch 6:35

MAHAVITE, ma´-hav-ite
marrow (?) 1Ch 11:46

MAHAZIOTH, ma-haz´-i-oth
visions 1Ch 25:4

MAHER-SHALAL-HASH-BAZ, ma´-her-sha´-lal-hash´-baz
the spoil hastens, the prey speeds Isa 8:1

MAHLAH, mah´-lah
same as MAHALAH Nu 26:33

MAHLI, mah´-li
same as MAHALI 1Ch 6:19

MAHLITES, mah´-lites
descendants of Mahli Nu 3:33

MAHLON, mah´-lon
a sick person Ru 1:2

MAHOL, ma´-hol
a dance 1Ki 4:31

MAKAZ, ma´-kaz
end (?) 1Ki 4:9

MAKHELOTH, mak´-hel-oth
assemblies Nu 33:25

MAKKEDAH, mak´-ed-ah
place of shepherds (?) Jos 10:10

MAKTESH, mak´-tesh
a mortar Zep 1:11

MALACHI, mal´-ak-i
the messenger of Jehovah Mal 1:1

MALCHAM, mal´-kam
their king 1Ch 8:9

MALCHIAH, malk-i´-ah
Jehovah's king 1Ch 6:40

MALCHI-SHUA, malk´-i-shoo´-ah
king of aid 1Ch 8:33

MALCHIEL, malk´-i-el
God's king Ge 46:17

MALCHIELITES, malk´-i-el-ites
descendants of Malchiel Nu 26:45

MALCHIJAH, malk-i´-jah
same as MALCHIAH 1Ch 9:12

MALCHIRAM, malk-i´-ram
king of height (?) 1Ch 3:18

MALCHUS, mal´-kus
Gr. for MALLUCH Jn 18:10

MALELEEL, mal´-el-el
same as MAHALALEEL Lk 3:37

MALLOTHI, mal´-lo-thi
my utterance 1Ch 25:4

MALLUCH, mal´-ook
counselor 1Ch 6:44

MAMMON, mam´-on
fullness Mt 6:24

MAMRE, mam´-re
fatness Ge 14:13

MANAEN, ma-na´-en
Gr. for MENAHEM Ac 13:1

MANAHATH, ma-na´-hath
rest Ge 36:23

MANAHETHITES, ma-na´-heth-ites
inhabitants of Manahath (?) 1Ch 2:52

MANASSEH, ma-nas´-ay
one who causes to forget Ge 41:51

MANASSES, ma-nas´-es
Gr. for MANASSEH Mt 1:10

MANASSITES, ma-nas´-ites
members of the tribe of Manasseh Dt 4:43

MANOAH, ma-no´-ah
rest Jgs 13:2

MAOCH, ma´-ok
oppressed (?) 1Sa 27:2

MAON, ma´-on
habitation Jos 15:55

MAONITES, ma´-on-ites
same as MEUNIM Jgs 10:12

MARA, ma´-rah
sad Ru 1:20

MARAH, ma´-rah
bitter Ex 15:23

MARALAH, mar´-al-ah
trembling Jos 19:11

MARANATHA, ma´-ran-ah´-thah
our Lord cometh 1Co 16:22

MARCUS, mar´-kus
a large hammer Col 4:10

MARESHAH, ma-resh´-ah
capital Jos 15:44

MARK
a large hammer Ac 12:12

MAROTH, mar´-oth
bitterness Mic 1:12

MARS' HILL
Eng. for AREOPAGUS Ac 17:22

MARSENA, mar´-se-na
bitterness (?) Est 1:14

MARTHA, mar´-thah
lady Lk 10:38

MARY, ma´-ry
Gr. for MIRIAM Mt 1:16

MASH, mash
same as MESHECH Ge 10:23

MASHAL, ma´-shal
entreaty (?) 1Ch 6:74

MASREKAH, mas-rek´-ah
vineyard Ge 36:36

MASSA, mas´-ah
burden Ge 25:14

MASSAH, mas´-ah
temptation Ex 17:7

MATHUSALA, ma-thoo´-sa-lah
Gr. for METHUSELAH Lk 3:37

MATRED, ma´-tred
pushing forward Ge 36:39

MATRI, ma´-tri
rainy 1Sa 10:21

MATTAN, mat´-an
a gift 2Ki 11:18

MATTANAH, mat´-an-ah
same as MATTAN Nu 21:18

MATTANIAH, mat-an-i´-ah
gift of Jehovah 2Ki 24:17

MATTATHA, mat´-ath-ah
Gr. for MATTANIAH Lk 3:31

MATTATHAH, mat´-ath-ah
same as MATTANIAH Ezr 10:33

MATTATHIAS, mat´-ath-i´-as
Gr. for MATTATHAH Lk 3:26

MATTENAI, mat´-en-a´-i
liberal Ezr 10:33

MATTHAN, mat´-than
gift Mt 1:15

MATTHAT, mat´-that
same as MATTHAN Lk 3:24

MATTHEW, mat´-thew
Eng. for MATTATHIAH Mt 9:9

MATTHIAS, math-i´-as
Gr. for MATTATHAH Ac 1:23

MATTITHIAH, mat-ith-i´-ah
another form of MATTATHAH 1Ch 9:31

MAZZAROTH, maz´-ar-oth
the signs of the zodiac Job 38:32

MEAH, me´-ah
a hundred Ne 3:1

MEARAH, me´-ar-ah
cave Jos 13:4

MEBUNNAI, me-boon´-a´-i
built (?) 2Sa 23:27

MECHERATHITE, me-ker´-ath-ite
inhabitant of Mecherah (?) 1Ch 11:36

MEDAD, me´-dad
affectionate (?) Nu 11:26

MEDAN, me´-dan
contention Ge 25:2

MEDEBA, me´-deb-ah
flowing water (?) Nu 21:30

MEDES, medes
inhabitants of Media 2Ki 17:6

MEDIA, me´-di-ah
Gr. for MAADAI Est 1:3

MEGIDDO, me-gid´-o
place of troops Jos 12:21

MEGIDDON, me-gid´-on
same as MEGIDDO Zec 12:11

MEHETABEEL, me-het´-ab-e´-el
masc. of MEHETABEL Ne 6:10

MEHETABEL, me-het´-ab-el
God makes happy Ge 36:39

MEHIDA, me-hi´-dah
conjunction, union Ezr 2:52

MEHIR, me´-hir
price 1Ch 4:11

MEHOLATHITE, me-ho´-lath-ite
native of Meholah 1Sa 18:19

MEHUJAEL, me-hoo´-ja-el
struck by God Ge 4:18

MEHUMAN, me´-hoom-an
faithful (?) Est 1:10

MEHUNIM, me-hoon´-im
same as MEUNIM Ezr 2:50

MEHUNIMS, me-hoon´-ims
same as MEUNIM 2Ch 26:7

ME-JARKON, me´-jar´-kon
waters of yellowness Jos 19:46

MEJARKON, me-jar´-kon
yellow waters Jos 19:46

MEKONAH, me-ko´-nah
a base Ne 11:28

MELATIAH, mel´-at-i´-ah
whom Jehovah freed Ne 3:7

MELCHI, melk´-i
Gr. for MELCHIAH Lk 3:24

MELCHIAH, melk-i´-ah
Jehovah's king Jer 21:1

MELCHISEDEC, Melk-is´-ed-ec
same as MELCHIZEDEK Heb 5:6

MELCHI-SHUA, melk´-i-shoo´-ah
same as MALCHI-SHUA 1Sa 14:49

MELCHIZEDEK, melk-iz´-ed-ek
king of righteousness Ge 14:18

MELEA, mel´-e-ah
fullness (?) Lk 3:31

MELECH, mel´-ech
king 1Ch 8:35

MELICU, mel´-i-koo
same as MALLUCH Ne 12:14

MELITA, mel´-ee-tah
an island, now called Malta Ac 28:1

MELZAR, mel´-zar
steward Da 1:11

MEMPHIS, mem´-fis
the place of good Hos 9:6

MEMUCAN, me-mu´-can
certain, true (?) Est 1:14

MENAHEM, me-na´-hem
comforter 2Ki 15:14

MENAN, me´-nan
numbered Lk 3:31

MENE, me´-ne
numbered Da 5:25

MEONENIM, me-o´-nen-im
augurs Jgs 9:37

MEONOTHAI, me-o´-noth-a´-i
my habitations 1Ch 4:14

MEPHAATH, me-fa´-ath
beauty Jos 13:18

MEPHIBOSHETH, mef-ib´-osh-eth
destroying shame 2Sa 4:4

MERAB, me´-rab
increase 1Sa 14:49

MERAIAH, me-rai´-ah
rebellion Ne 12:12

MERAIOTH, me-rai´-oth
rebellions 1Ch 6:6

MERARI, mer´-a-ri
bitter Ge 46:11

MERATHAIM, mer´-ath-a´-im
rebellions Jer 50:21

MERCURIUS, mer-cu´-ri-us
pagan god of Rome (Gr. HERMES) Ac 14:12

MERED, me´-red
rebellion 1Ch 4:17

MEREMOTH, me´-rem-oth
elevations Ezr 8:33

MERES, me´-res
worthy (?) Est 1:14

MERIBAH, me´-reb-ah
water of strife Ex 17:7

MERIB-BAAL, me´-ri-ba´-al
contender against Baal (?) 1Ch 8:34

MERODACH, me´-ro-dak
Hebrew for proper name of BEL, *contention, death* Jer 50:2

MERODACH-BALADAN, me´-ro-dak-bal´-a-dan
Merodach gives a son Isa 39:1

MEROM, me´-rom
a high place Jos 11:5

MERONOTHITE, me-ro´-noth-ite
inhabitant of Meronoth 1Ch 27:30

MEROZ, me´-roz
refuge (?) Jgs 5:23

MESECH, me´-sech
same as MESHECH Ps 120:5

MESHA, me´-shah
deliverance 2Ki 3:4

MESHACH, me´-shak
who is what (the god) Aku is? Da 1:7

MESHECH, me´-shek
tall (?) Ge 10:2

MESHELEMIAH, me-shel´-em-i´-ah
Jehovah repays 1Ch 9:21

MESHEZABEEL, me-shez´-a-be´-el
God delivers Ne 3:4

MESHILLEMITH, me-shil´-em-ith
recompense 1Ch 9:12

MESHILLEMOTH, me-shil´-em-oth
retribution 2Ch 28:12

MESHOBAB, me-sho´-bab
brought back 1Ch 4:34

MESHULLAM, me-shool´-am
friend 2Ki 22:3

MESHULLEMETH, me-shool´-em-eth
fem. of MESHULLAM 2Ki 21:19

MESOBAITE, me-so´-ba-ite
inhabitant of Mesoba (?) 1Ch 11:47

MESOPOTAMIA, mes´-o-pot-a´-mi-ah
amidst the rivers Ge 24:10

MESSIAH, mes-i´-ah
anointed Da 9:25

MESSIAS, mes-i´-as
Gr. for MESSIAH Jn 1:41

METHEG-AMMAH, me´-theg-am´-ah
bridle of Ammah 2Sa 8:1

METHUSAEL, me-thoo´-sa-el
man of God Ge 4:18

METHUSELAH, me-thoo´-se-lah
man of the dart (?) Ge 5:21

MEUNIM, me-oon´-im
inhabitants of Maon (?) Ne 7:52

MEZAHAB, me´-za-hab
water of gold Ge 36:39

MIAMIN, mi´-ya-min
a form of MINIAMIN Ezr 10:25

MIBHAR, mib´-har
choicest 1Ch 11:38

MIBSAM, mib´-sam
sweet odor Ge 25:13

MIBZAR, mib´-zar
a fortress Ge 36:42

MICAH, mi´-kah
a form of MICHAIAH Jgs 17:1

MICAIAH, mi-kai´-ah
a form of MICHAIAH 1Ki 22:8

MICHA, mi´-kah
a form of MICHAIAH 2Sa 9:12

MICHAEL, mi´-ka-el
Who (is) like unto God? Da 10:13

MICHAH, mi´-kah
a form of MICHAIAH 1Ch 24:24

MICHAIAH, mi-kai´-ah
Who (is) like unto Jehovah? Ne 12:35

MICHAL, mi´-kal
brook 1Sa 14:49

MICHMAS, mik´-mas
form of MICHMASH Ezr 2:27

MICHMASH, mik´-mash
treasured 1Sa 13:2

MICHMETHAH, mik´-meth-ah
hiding place (?) Jos 16:6

MICHRI, mik´-ri
precious (?) 1Ch 9:8

MICHTAM, mik´-tam
writing (?) Ps 16:title

MIDDIN, mid´-in
extensions Jos 15:61

MIDIAN, mid´-yan
strife Ge 25:2

MIDIANITES, mid´-yan-ites
people of Midian Ge 37:28

MIGDAL-EL, mig´-dal-el
tower of God Jos 19:38

MIGDAL-GAD, mig´-dal-gad
tower of Gad Jos 15:37

MIGDOL, mig´-dol
fortress, tower Ex 14:2

MIGRON, mig´-ron
a precipice Isa 10:28

MIJAMIN, mi´-ja-min
same as MINIAMIN 1Ch 24:9

MIKLOTH, mik´-loth
staves, lots 1Ch 8:32

MIKNEIAH, mik-ni´-ah
possession of Jehovah 1Ch 15:18

MILALAI, mil-al-a´-i
eloquent (?) Ne 12:36

MILCAH, mil´-kah
counsel (?) Ge 11:29

MILCOM, mil´-kom
same as MOLOCH 1Ki 11:5

MILETUM, mi-le´-tum
same as MILETUS 2Ti 4:20

MILETUS, mi-le´-tus
red Ac 20:15

MILLO, mil´-o
a mound Jgs 9:6

MINIAMIN, min´-ya-min
on the right hand 2Ch 31:15

MINNI, min´-i
Armenia Jer 51:27

MINNITH, min´-ith
allotment Jgs 11:33

MIPHKAD, mif-kad
place of meeting Ne 3:31

MIRIAM, mir´-yam
rebellion (?) Ex 15:20

MIRMA, mir´-mah
fraud 1Ch 8:10

MISGAB, mis´-gab
height Jer 48:1

MISHAEL, mish´-a-el
Who is what God is? Ex 6:22

MISHAL, mi´-shal
prayer Jos 21:30

MISHAM, mi´-sham
cleansing 1Ch 8:12

MISHEAL, mi´-she-al
same as MISHAL Jos 19:26

MISHMA, mish´-mah
report Ge 25:14

MISHMANNAH, mish-man´-ah
fatness 1Ch 12:10

MISHRAITES, mish´-rah-ites
spread out (?) 1Ch 2:53

MISPERETH, mis-per´-eth
number Ne 7:7

MISREPHOTH-MAIM, mis´-re-foth-ma´-im
burning of waters Jos 11:8

MITHCAH, mith´-kah
place of sweetness Nu 33:28

MITHNITE, mith´-nite
gifts 1Ch 11:43

MITHREDATH, mith´-re-dath
given by Mithra Ezr 1:8

MITYLENE, mit-i-le´-ne
capital of the island of Lesbos Ac 20:14

MIZAR, mi´-zar
smallness Ps 42:6

MIZPAH, miz´-pah
a look out Ge 31:49

MIZPAR, miz´-par
number Ezr 2:2

MIZPEH, miz´-peh
watch-tower Jos 11:3

MIZRAIM, miz-ra´-im
fortresses Ge 10:6

MIZZAH, miz´-zah
fear Ge 36:13

MNASON, na´-son
reminding (?) Ac 21:16

MOAB, mo´-ab
progeny of a father Ge 19:37

MOABITES, mo´-ab-ites
people of Moab Dt 2:9

MOABITESS, mo´-ab-ite-ess
a lady of Moab Ru 4:5

MOADIAH, mo´-ad-i´-ah
festival of Jehovah Ne 12:17

MOLADAH, mo´-lad-ah
birth Jos 15:26

MOLECH, mo´-lek
Eng. for MOLOCH Le 18:21

MOLID, mo´-lid
begetter 1Ch 2:29

MOLOCH, mo´-lok
king Am 5:26

MORASTHITE, mo´-rasth-ite
native of Moresheth Jer 26:18

MORDECAI, mor´-dek-a´-i
worshiper of Merodach (?) Est 2:5

MOREH, mo´-reh
archer Ge 12:6

MORESHETH-GATH, mo-resh´-eth-gath
the possession of Gath Mic 1:14

MORIAH, mor-i´-ah
provided by Jehovah Ge 22:2

MOSERA, mo´-se-rah
bond Dt 10:6

MOSEROTH, mo´-se-roth
bonds Nu 33:30

MOSES, mo´-zes
saved from the water Ex 2:10

MOZA, mo´-za
fountain 1Ch 2:46

MOZAH, mo´-zah
same as MOZA Jos 18:26

MUPPIM, moop´-im
same as SHEPHUPHAN (?) Ge 46:21

MUSHI, moo´-shi
withdrawn Ex 6:19

MYRA, mi´-rah
balsam Ac 27:5

MYSIA, my´-si-ah
a province in NW Asia Minor Ac 16:7

N

NAAM, na´-am
pleasantness 1Ch 4:15

NAAMAH, na´-am-ah
pleasant Ge 4:22

NAAMAN, na´-am-an
same as NAAM 2Ki 5:1

NAAMATHITE, na-am´-ath-ite
inhabitant of Naamah Job 2:11

NAAMITES, na´-am-ites
descendants of Naaman Nu 26:40

NAARAH, na´-ar-ah
a girl 1Ch 4:5

NAARAI, na´-ar-a´-i
youthful 1Ch 11:37

NAARAN, na´-ar-an
same as NAARAH 1Ch 7:28

NAARATH, na´-ar-ath
same as NAARAH Jos 16:7

NAASHON, na-ash´-on
enchanter Ex 6:23

NAASSON, na-as´-on
Gr. for NAASHON Mt 1:4

NABAL, na´-bal
foolish 1Sa 25:3

NABOTH, na´-both
fruits (?) 1Ki 21:1

NACHON, na´-kon
prepared 2Sa 6:6

NACHOR, na´-kor
same as NAHOR Jos 24:2

NADAB, na´-dab
liberal Ex 6:23

NAGGE, nag´-e
Gr. for NOGAH Lk 3:25

NAHALAL, na´-hal-al
a pasture Jos 21:35

NAHALIEL, na-hal´-i-el
valley of God Nu 21:19

NAHALLAL, na´-hal-al
same as NAHALAL Jos 19:15

NAHALOL, na´-hal-ol
same as NAHALAL Jgs 1:30

NAHAM, na´-ham
consolation 1Ch 4:19

NAHAMANI, na´-ham-a´-ni
comforter Ne 7:7

NAHARAI, na´-har-a´-i
one who snores 1Ch 11:39

NAHARI, na´-har-i
same as NAHARAI 2Sa 23:37

NAHASH, na´-hash
serpent 1Sa 11:1

NAHATH, na´-hath
descent Ge 36:13

NAHBI, nah´-bi
hidden Nu 13:14

NAHOR, na´-hor
snorting Ge 11:22

NAHSHON, nah´-shon
same as NAASHON Nu 1:7

NAHUM, na´-hoom
comforter Na 1:1

NAIN, na´-in
pasture Lk 7:11

NAIOTH, nai´-oth
habitations 1Sa 19:18

NAOMI, na´-om-i
pleasant Ru 1:2

NAPHISH, na´-fish
cheerful Ge 25:15

NAPHTALI, naf´-tal-i
my wrestling Ge 30:8

NARCISSUS, nar-sis´-us
benumbing Ro 16:11

NATHAN, na´-than
gift 2Sa 7:2

NATHANAEL, na-than´-a-el
gift of God Jn 1:45

NATHAN-MELECH, na´-than-me´-lek
gift of the king 2Ki 23:11

NAUM, na´-oom
same as NAHUM Lk 3:25

NAZARENE, naz´-ar-een
a native of Nazareth Mt 2:23

NAZARETH, naz´-ar-eth
branch Lk 1:26

NAZARITE, naz´-ar-ite
one separated Nu 6:2

NEAH, ne´-ah
of a slope Jos 19:13

NEAPOLIS, ne-a´-po-lis
new city Ac 16:11

NEARIAH, ne´-ar-i´-ah
servant of Jehovah 1Ch 3:22

NEBAI, neb-a´-i
fruitful Ne 10:19

NEBAIOTH, ne-bai´-oth
high places 1Ch 1:29

NEBAJOTH, ne-ba´-joth
same as NEBAIOTH Ge 25:13

NEBALLAT, ne-bal´-lat
a town inhabited by the Benjamites Ne 11:34

NEBAT, ne´-bat
aspect 1Ki 11:26

NEBO, ne´-bo
a lofty place Dt 32:49

NEBUCHADNEZZAR, neb´-u-kad-nez´-ar
Nebo protect the crown 2Ki 24:1

NEBUCHADREZZAR, neb´-u-kad-rez´-ar
same as NEBUCHADNEZZAR Jer 21:2

NEBUSHASBAN, neb´-u-shas´-ban
Nebo will save me Jer 39:13

NEBUZAR-ADAN, neb´-u-zar´-a-dan
Nebo gives posterity 2Ki 25:8

NECHO, ne´-ko
conqueror (?) 2Ch 35:20

NECHOH, ne´-koh
same as NECHO 2Ki 23:29

NEDABIAH, ned´-ab-i´-ah
Jehovah is bountiful (?) 1Ch 3:18

NEGINAH, neg-een´-ah
a stringed instrument Ps 61:title

NEGINOTH, neg-een´-oth
stringed instruments Ps 4:title

NEGO, ne´-go
same as NEBO Da 1:7

NEHELAMITE, ne-hel´-am-ite
dreamed Jer 29:24

NEHEMIAH, ne´-hem-i´-ah
Jehovah comforts Ne 1:1

NEHILOTH, ne-hil´-oth
flutes Ps 5:title

NEHUM, ne´-hoom
consolation Ne 7:7

NEHUSHTA, ne-hoosh´-tah
bronze 2Ki 24:8

NEHUSHTAN, ne-hoosh´-tan
brazen 2Ki 18:4

NEIEL, ni´-el
moved by God Jos 19:27

NEKEB, ne´-keb
cavern Jos 19:33

NEKODA, ne´-ko-dah
a herdman Ezr 2:48

NEMUEL, nem´-oo-el
same as JEMUEL (?) Nu 26:9

NEMUELITES, nem-oo´-el-ites
descendants of Nemuel Nu 26:12

NEPHEG, ne´-feg
sprout Ex 6:21

NEPHISH, ne´-fish
same as NAPHISH 1Ch 5:19

NEPHISHESIM, ne-fish´-es-im
same as NEPHUSIM Ne 7:52

NEPHTHALIM, nef´-tha-lim
same as NAPHTALI Mt 4:13

NEPHTOAH, nef-to´-ah
opened Jos 15:9

NEPHUSIM, ne-foos´-im
expansions Ezr 2:50

NEPTHALIM, nep´-tha-lim
same as NAPHTALI Rev 7:6

NER, ner
light 1Sa 14:50

NEREUS, ne´-roos
liquid (?) Ro 16:15

NERGAL, ner´-gal
lion 2Ki 17:30

NERGAL-SHAREZER, ner´-gal-shar´-ez-er
Nergal protect the king Jer 39:3

NERI, ne´-ri
Gr. for NERIAH Lk 3:27

NERIAH, ner-i´-ah
lamp of Jehovah Jer 32:12

NETHANEEL, neth-an´-e-el
same as NATHANAEL Nu 1:8

NETHANIAH, neth´-an-i´-ah
whom Jehovah gave 2Ki 25:23

NETHINIMS, neth´-in-ims
the appointed Ne 10:28

NETOPHAH, net´-of-ah
dropping Ezr 2:22

NETOPHATHI, net-of´-ath-i
an inhabitant of Netophah Ne 12:28

NETOPHATHITE, net-of´-ath-ite
same as NETOPHATHI 2Sa 23:28

NEZIAH, ne-zi´-ah
illustrious Ezr 2:54

NEZIB, ne´-zib
garrison Jos 15:43

NIBHAZ, nib´-haz
a pagan god 2Ki 17:31

NIBSHAN, nib´-shan
level (?) Jos 15:62

NICANOR, ni-ka´-nor
victorious Ac 6:5

NICODEMUS, nik-o-de´-mus
victorious over the people Jn 3:1

NICOLAITANES, nik´-o-la´-it-ans
named after Nicolas Rev 2:6

NICOLAS, nik´-o-las
conqueror of the people Ac 6:5

NICOPOLIS, nik-o´-pol-is
city of victory Tit 3:12

NIGER, ni´-jer
black Ac 13:1

NIMRAH, nim´-rah
limpid (water) Nu 32:3

NIMRIM, nim´-rim
clear waters Isa 15:6

NIMROD, nim´-rod
rebellious (?) Ge 10:8

NIMSHI, nim´-shi
discloser (?) 1Ki 19:16

NINEVE, nin´-ev-eh
same as NINEVEH Lk 11:32

NINEVEH, nin´-ev-ay
dwelling (?) Ge 10:11

NINEVITES, nin´-ev-ites
inhabitants of Nineveh Lk 11:30

NISAN, ni´-san
beginning, opening Ne 2:1

NISROCH, nis´-rok
eagle (?) 2Ki 19:37

NO, no
abode (?) Na 3:8

NOADIAH, no´-ad-i´-ah
whom Jehovah meets Ne 6:14

NOAH, no´-ah
1 *rest* Ge 5:29
2 *wandering* Nu 26:33

NOB, nobe
high place 1Sa 21:1

NOBAH, no´-bah
a barking Nu 32:42

NOD, node
flight, wandering Ge 4:16

O

P

Names

PAU, pa´-oo
same as PAI Ge 36:39

PAUL, pawl
little Ac 13:9

PAULUS, pawl´-us
same as PAUL Ac 13:7

PEDAHEL, pe´-dah-el
God redeemed Nu 34:28

PEDAHZUR, pe-dah´-zoor
the Rock redeemed Nu 1:10

PEDAIAH, pe-dah-i´-ah
whom Jehovah redeemed 1Ch 27:20

PEKAH, pe´-kah
open-eyed 2Ki 15:25

PEKAHIAH, pe´-kah-i´-ah
whose eyes Jehovah opened 2Ki 15:22

PEKOD, pe´-kod
visitation Jer 50:21

PELAIAH, pe´-la-i´-ah
whom Jehovah made distinguished 1Ch 3:24

PELALIAH, pe´-lal-i´-ah
whom Jehovah judged Ne 11:12

PELATIAH, pe´-lat-i´-ah
whom Jehovah delivered Eze 11:1

PELEG, pe´-leg
division Ge 10:25

PELET, pe´-let
liberation 1Ch 2:47

PELETH, pe´-leth
swiftness Nu 16:1

PELETHITES, pel´-eth-ites
runners 2Sa 8:18

PELONITE, pel´-o-nite
used of one of David's mighty men 1Ch 11:27

PENIEL, pe´-ni-el
same as PENUEL Ge 32:30

PENINNAH, pe-nin´-ah
coral 1Sa 1:2

PENTECOST, pen´-te-kost
fiftieth Ac 2:1

PENUEL, pe´-noo-el
the face of God Ge 32:31

PEOR, pe´-or
point Nu 23:28

PERAZIM, pe-raz´-im
pl. of PEREZ Isa 28:21

PERES, pe´-res
divided Da 5:28

PERESH, pe´-resh
distinction 1Ch 7:16

PEREZ, pe´-rez
breach 1Ch 27:3

PEREZ-UZZA, pe´-rez-uz´-ah
same as PEREZ-UZZAH 1Ch 13:11

PEREZ-UZZAH, pe´-rez-uz´-ah
breach of Uzzah 2Sa 6:8

PERGA, per´-gah
citadel Ac 13:13

PERGAMOS, per´-ga-mos
same as PERGA (?) Rev 1:11

PERIDA, pe´-rid-ah
a recluse Ne 7:57

PERIZZITES, per´-iz-ites
belonging to a village Ge 34:30

PERSIA, per´-si-ah
a country of western Asia 2Ch 36:20

PERSIAN, per´-shan
belonging to Persia Da 6:28

PERSIS, per´-sis
a Persian woman Ro 16:12

PERUDA, per´-ood-ah
same as PERIDA Ezr 2:55

PETER, pe´-ter
a stone Mt 16:18

PETHAHIAH, pe´-thah-i´-ah
whom Jehovah looses 1Ch 24:16

PETHOR, pe´-thor
cleft, opening Nu 22:5

PETHUEL, peth´-oo-el
God's opening (?) Joel 1:1

PEULTHAI, pe´-ool-tha´-i
deed of Jehovah 1Ch 26:5

PHALEC, fa´-lek
Gr. for PELEG Lk 3:35

PHALLU, fal´-oo
Eng. for PALLU Ge 46:9

PHALTI, fal´-ti
deliverance of Jehovah 1Sa 25:44

PHALTIEL, fal´-ti-el
deliverance of God 2Sa 3:15

PHANUEL, fan-oo´-el
Gr. for PENUEL Lk 2:36

PHARAOH, fa´-roh
the sun Ge 12:15

PHARES, fa´-res
Gr. for PHAREZ Lk 3:33

PHAREZ, fa´-rez
breach Ge 38:29

PHARISEES, far´-is-ees
the separated Mt 5:20

PHAROSH, fa´-rosh
same as PAROSH Ezr 8:3

PHARPAR, far´-par
swift 2Ki 5:12

PHARZITES, farz´-ites
descendants of Pharez Nu 26:20

PHASEAH, fa-se´-ah
same as PASEAH Ne 7:51

PHEBE, fe´-be
moon Ro 16:1

PHENICE, fe-ni´-see
palm tree Ac 27:12

PHENICIA, fe-nish´-yah
land of palms Ac 21:2

PHICHOL, fi´-kol
attentive (?) Ge 21:22

PHILADELPHIA, fil´-a-delf´-yah
brotherly love Rev 1:11

PHILEMON, fil-e´-mon
affectionate Phm 1

PHILETUS, fil-e´-tus
beloved 2Ti 2:17

PHILIP, fil´-ip
lover of horses Mt 10:3

PHILIPPI, fil-ip´-i
a town named for Philip of Macedon Ac 16:12

PHILIPPIANS, fil-ip´-yans
inhabitants of Philippi Php 4:15

PHILISTIA, fil-ist´-yah
the land of the Philistines Ps 60:8

PHILISTIM, fil´-ist-im
wanderers Ge 10:14

PHILISTINES, fil´-ist-ines
same as PHILISTIM Ge 21:34

PHILOLOGUS, fil-o´-log-us
talkative Ro 16:15

PHINEHAS, fin´-e-as
serpent's mouth Nu 25:7

PHLEGON, fleg´-on
zealous, burning Ro 16:14

PHRYGIA, fridg´-i-ah
a large province of Asia Minor Ac 2:10

PHURAH, foor´-ah
branch (?) Jgs 7:10

PHUT, foot
a people related to the Egyptians Ge 10:6

PHUVAH, foo´-vah
mouth Ge 46:13

PHYGELLUS, fi-gel´-us
little fugitive 2Ti 1:15

PI-BESETH, pi-be´-seth
the city of (the goddess) Bast Eze 30:17

PI-HAHIROTH, pi´-ha-hi´-roth
where sedge grows Ex 14:2

PILATE, pi´-lat
armed with a javelin (?) Mt 27:2

PILDASH, pil´-dash
steel (?) Ge 22:22

PILEHA, pi´-le-hah
ploughman (?) Ne 10:24

PILTAI, pil´-ta-i
whom Jehovah delivers Ne 12:17

PINON, pi´-non
darkness Ge 36:41

PIRAM, pi´-ram
like a wild donkey Jos 10:3
PIRATHON, pi´-rath-on
leader Jgs 12:15
PIRATHONITE, pi´-rath-on-ite
an inhabitant of Pirathon Jgs 12:13
PISGAH, piz´-gah
a part, boundary Nu 21:20
PISIDIA, pi-sid´-i-ah
a district in the province of Galatia Ac 13:14
PISON, pi´-son
flowing stream (?) Ge 2:11
PISPAH, pis´-pah
expansion 1Ch 7:38
PITHOM, pi´-thom
abode of the setting sun (?) Ex 1:11
PITHON, pi´-thon
simple (?) 1Ch 8:35
PLEIADES, pli´-ad-ees
(coming at) the sailing season (?) Job 9:9
POCHERETH OF ZEBAIM, po-ke´-reth of Ze-ba´-im
offspring of gazelles (?) Ezr 2:57
POLLUX, pol´-ux
1 *a boxer*
2 one of the Dioscuri (sons of Zeus) Ac 28:11
PONTIUS, pon´-shus
belonging to the sea Mt 27:2
PONTUS, pont´-us
sea Ac 2:9
PORATHA, po´-rath-ah
having many chariots (?) Est 9:8
POTIPHAR, pot´-i-far
belonging to the sun Ge 37:36
POTI-PHERAH, pot´-i-fer´-ah
same as POTIPHAR Ge 41:45
PRISCA, pris´-kah
ancient 2Ti 4:19
PRISCILLA, pris-il´-ah
same as PRISCA Ac 18:2
PROCHORUS, prok´-or-us
he that presides over the choir Ac 6:5
PTOLEMAIS, tol-em-a´-is
city of Ptolemy Ac 21:7
PUA, poo´-ah
same as PHUVAH Nu 26:23
PUAH, poo´-ah
splendor Ex 1:15
PUBLIUS, pub´-li-as
governor of the island of Malta Ac 28:7
PUDENS, pu´-dens
shamefaced 2Ti 4:21
PUHITES, poo´-hites
descendants of Kirjath-Jearim 1Ch 2:53
PUL, pool
1 short for TIGLATH-PILESER (?) 2Ki 15:19
2 *son* (?) Isa 66:19
PUNITES, poon´-ites
descendants of Pua Nu 26:23
PUNON, poon´-on
same as PINON Nu 33:42
PUR, poor
a lot Est 3:7
PURIM, poor´-im
pl. of PUR Est 9:26
PUT, poot
same as PHUT 1Ch 1:8
PUTEOLI, poo-te´-o-li
wells Ac 28:13
PUTIEL, poot´-i-el
afflicted of God (?) Ex 6:25

Q

QUARTUS, kwart´-us
the fourth Ro 16:23

R

RAAMAH, ra´-am-ah
trembling Ge 10:7
RAAMIAH, ra´-am-i´-ah
trembling of Jehovah Ne 7:7
RAAMSES, ra-am´-ses
same as RAMESES Ex 1:11
RABBAH, rab´-ah
capital city Jos 13:25
RABBATH, rab´-ath
same as RABBAH Dt 3:11
RABBI, rab´-i
master Mt 23:7
RABBITH, rab´-ith
populous Jos 19:20
RABBONI, rab-o´-ni
my master Jn 20:16
RAB-MAG, rab´-mag
1 *most exalted,*
2 an officer under NEBUCHADNEZZAR Jer 39:3
RAB-SARIS, rab´-sar-is
chief eunuch 2Ki 18:17
RABSHAKEH, rab´-sha-kay
chief of the cupbearers 2Ki 18:17
RACA, ra´-cah
worthless Mt 5:22
RACHAB, ra´-kab
Gr. for RAHAB Mt 1:5
RACHAL, ra´-kal
traffic 1Sa 30:29
RACHEL, ra´-chel
ewe Ge 29:6
RADDAI, rad´-da-i
subduing 1Ch 2:14
RAGAU, ra´-gaw
Gr. for REU Lk 3:35
RAGUEL, ra´-goo-el
friend of God Nu 10:29
RAHAB, ra´-hab
1 *broad* Jos 2:1
2 *violence* Ps 87:4
RAHAM, ra´-ham
affection, tenderness 1Ch 2:44
RAHEL, ra´-hel
same as RACHEL Jer 31:15
RAKEM, ra´-kem
variegated 1Ch 7:16
RAKKATH, rak´-ath
shore Jos 19:35
RAKKON, rak´-on
same as RAKKATH Jos 19:46
RAM, ram
high Ru 4:19
RAMA, ra´-mah
Gr. for RAMAH Mt 2:18
RAMAH, ra´-mah
high place Jos 18:25
RAMATH, ra´-math
same as RAMAH Jos 19:8
RAMATHAIM-ZOPHIM, ra´-math-a´-im-zo´-phim
double high place of watchers 1Sa 1:1
RAMATHITE, ra´-math-ite
a native of Ramah 1Ch 27:27
RAMATH-LEHI, ra´-math-le´-hi
height of Lehi Jgs 15:17
RAMATH-MIZPEH, ra´-math-miz´-peh
height of Mizpeh Jos 13:26
RAMESES, ra´-me-sees
son of the sun Ge 47:11
RAMIAH, ram-i´-ah
Jehovah is high Ezr 10:25
RAMOTH, ra´-moth
pl. of RAMAH 1Ch 6:73
RAMOTH-GILEAD, ra´-moth-gil´-yad
heights of Gilead 1Ki 4:13
RAPHA, ra´-fah
giant (?) 1Ch 8:37
RAPHU, ra´-foo
healed Nu 13:9
REAIA, re-ai´-ah
a form of REAIAH 1Ch 5:5
REAIAH, re-ai´-ah
Jehovah has seen 1Ch 4:2
REBA, re´-bah
a fourth part Nu 31:8

REBECCA, re-bek´-ah
Gr. for REBEKAH Ro 9:10
REBEKAH, re-bek´-ah
a noose Ge 22:23
RECHAB, re´-kab
horseman 2Sa 4:2
RECHABITES, re´-kab-ites
descendants of Rechab Jer 35:2
RECHAH, re´-kah
side (?) 1Ch 4:12
REELAIAH, re´-el-ai´-ah
trembling caused by Jehovah Ezr 2:2
REGEM, re´-gem
friend 1Ch 2:47
REGEM-MELECH, re´-gem-me´-lek
friend of the king Zec 7:2
REHABIAH, re´-hab-i´-ah
Jehovah enlarges 1Ch 23:17
REHOB, re´-hob
street 2Sa 8:3
REHOBOAM, re´-hob-o´-am
who enlarges the people 1Ki 11:43
REHOBOTH, re-hob´-oth
roominess Ge 10:11
REHUM, re´-hoom
merciful Ezr 4:8
REI, re´-i
friendly 1Ki 1:8
REKEM, re´-kem
same as RAKEM Nu 31:8
REMALIAH, rem´-al-i´-ah
whom Jehovah adorned 2Ki 15:25
REMETH, re´-meth
a high place Jos 19:21
REMMON, rem´-on
another form of RIMMON Jos 19:7
REMMON-METHOAR, rem´-on-me´-tho-ar
stretching (to Neah) Jos 19:13
REMPHAN, rem´-fan
same as CHIUN Ac 7:43
REPHAEL, re´-fa-el
whom God healed 1Ch 26:7
REPHAH, re´-fah
riches 1Ch 7:25
REPHAIAH, ref-ai´-ah
whom Jehovah healed 1Ch 3:21
REPHAIM, re-fa´-im
giants 2Sa 5:18
REPHAIMS, re-fa´-ims
same as REPHAIM Ge 14:5
REPHIDIM, ref´-id-im
supports Ex 17:1
RESEN, re´-sen
bridle Ge 10:12
RESHEPH, re´-shef
flame 1Ch 7:25
REU, roo
same as RAGUEL Ge 11:18
REUBEN, roo´-ben
behold a son (?) Ge 29:32
REUBENITES, roo´-ben-ites
descendants of Reuben Nu 26:7
REUEL, roo´-el
friend of God 1Ch 9:8
REUMAH, room´-ah
exalted Ge 22:24
REZEPH, re´-zef
a stone 2Ki 19:12
REZIA, rez´-yah
delight 1Ch 7:39
REZIN, re´-zin
firm 2Ki 15:37
REZON, re´-zon
lean 1Ki 11:23
RHEGIUM, re´-ji-um
fracture, break Ac 28:13
RHESA, re´-sah
chieftain (?) Lk 3:27
RHODA, ro´-dah
a rose Ac 12:13
RHODES, rodes
a rose bush Ac 21:1
RIBAI, rib´-a-i
contentious 2Sa 23:29
RIBLAH, rib´-lah
fertility Nu 34:11
RIMMON, rim´-on
pomegranate 2Sa 4:2
RIMMON-PAREZ, rim´-on-pa´-rez
pomegranate of the breach Nu 33:19
RINNAH, rin´-ah
shout 1Ch 4:20
RIPHATH, ri´-fath
descendants of Gomer Ge 10:3
RISSAH, ris´-ah
ruin Nu 33:21
RITHMAH, rith´-mah
broom Nu 33:18
RIZPAH, riz´-pah
hot coal 2Sa 3:7
ROBOAM, rob-o´-am
Gr. for REHOBOAM Mt 1:7
ROGELIM, ro´-gel-im
fullers 2Sa 17:27
ROHGAH, ro´-gah
outcry 1Ch 7:34
ROMAMTI-EZER, ro-mam´-ti-e´-zer
I have exalted help 1Ch 25:4
ROME, rom
strength (?) Ac 2:10
ROSH, rosh
head Ge 46:21
RUFUS, roo´-fus
red Mk 15:21
RUHAMAH, roo´-ham-ah
obtained mercy Hos 2:1
RUMAH, roo´-mah
height 2Ki 23:36
RUTH, rooth
friendship (?) Ru 1:4

S

SABAOTH, sab-a´-oth
hosts Ro 9:29
SABEANS, sab-e´-ans
inhabitants of Seba Isa 45:14
SABTAH, sab´-tah
rest (?) Ge 10:7
SABTECHA, sab´-te-kah
descendants of Cush 1Ch 1:9
SABTECHAH, sab´-te-kah
same as SABTECHA Ge 10:7
SACAR, sa´-kar
hire, reward 1Ch 11:35
SADDUCEES, sad´-u-sees
named for Zadok, founder of the sect Mt 3:7
SADOC, sa´-dok
Gr. for ZADOK Mt 1:14
SALA, sa´-lah
Gr. for SALAH Lk 3:35
SALAH, sa´-lah
sprout (?) Ge 10:24
SALAMIS, sal´-a-mis
shaken, tossed Ac 13:5
SALATHIEL, sa-la´-thi-el
Gr. for SHEALTIEL 1Ch 3:17
SALCAH, sal´-kah
road Jos 12:5
SALCHAH, sal´-kah
same as SALCAH Dt 3:10
SALEM, sa´-lem
peace Ge 14:18
SALIM, sa´-lim
Gr. for SALEM Jn 3:23
SALLAI, sal-a´-i
exaltation Ne 11:8
SALLU, sal´-oo
same as SALLAI 1Ch 9:7
SALMA, sal´-mah
garment 1Ch 2:11
SALMON, sal´-mon
shady Ps 68:14
SALOME, sal-o´-me
peace Mk 15:40

SALU, sa´-loo
same as SALLU — Nu 25:14

SAMARIA, sa-ma´-ri-a
watch-mountain, watchtower — 1Ki 13:32

SAMARITAN, sa-mar´-i-tan
a native or inhabitant of Samaria — Lk 10:33

SAMGAR-NEBO, sam´-gar-ne´-bo
Be gracious, Nebo — Jer 39:3

SAMLAH, sam´-lah
garment — Ge 36:36

SAMOS, sa´-mos
a height (?) — Ac 20:15

SAMOTHRACIA, sa´-mo-thra´-shah
Samos of Thrace — Ac 16:11

SAMSON, sam´-son
like the sun — Jgs 13:24

SAMUEL, sam´-u-el
heard of God — 1Sa 1:20

SANBALLAT, san-bal´-at
Sin (the moon) giveth life (?) — Ne 2:10

SANSANNAH, san-san´-ah
palm branch — Jos 15:31

SAPH, saf
threshold — 2Sa 21:18

SAPHIR, saf´-ir
beautiful — Mic 1:11

SAPPHIRA, saf-i´-rah
Gr. for SAPHIR (fem.) — Ac 5:1

SARA, sa´-rah
same as SARAH — Ro 9:9

SARAH, sa´-rah
princess — Ge 17:15

SARAI, sa´-ra-i
contentious (?) — Ge 11:29

SARAPH, sa´-raf
burning — 1Ch 4:22

SARDIS, sar´-dis
prince of joy — Rev 1:11

SARDITES, sard´-ites
descendants of Sered — Nu 26:26

SAREPTA, sa-rep´-tah
Gr. for ZAREPHATH — Lk 4:26

SARGON, sar´-gon
(God) appoints the king — Isa 20:1

SARID, sa´-rid
survivor — Jos 19:10

SARON, sa´-ron
Gr. for SHARON — Ac 9:35

SARSECHIM, sar´-se-kim
prince of the wardrobe (?) — Jer 39:3

SARUCH, sa´-rook
Gr. for SERUG — Lk 3:35

SATAN, sa´-tan
adversary — 1Ch 21:1

SAUL, sawl
asked for — 1Sa 9:2

SCEVA, se´-vah
left-handed — Ac 19:14

SEBA, se´-bah
man (?) — Ge 10:7

SEBAT, se´-bat
rest (?) — Zec 1:7

SECACAH, sek´-ak-ah
enclosure — Jos 15:61

SECHU, se´-koo
watch-tower — 1Sa 19:22

SECUNDUS, se-cun´-dus
second — Ac 20:4

SEGUB, se´-goob
elevated — 1Ki 16:34

SEIR, se´-ir
hairy — Ge 14:6

SEIRATH, se´-ir-ath
well-wooded — Jgs 3:26

SELA, se´-lah
rock — Isa 16:1

SELAH, se´-lah
forte (?), a musical direction — Ps 3:2

SELA-HAMMAHLEKOTH, se´-lah-ham-ah´-lek-oth
rock of escapes — 1Sa 23:28

SELED, se´-led
exultation or burning — 1Ch 2:30

SELEUCIA, se-lu´-si-a
brightness (?) — Ac 13:4

SEM, sem
same as SHEM — Lk 3:36

SEMACHIAH, sem´-ak-i´-ah
whom Jehovah sustains — 1Ch 26:7

SEMEI, sem´-e-i
Gr. for SHIMEI — Lk 3:26

SENAAH, sen-a´-ah
thorny (?) — Ezr 2:35

SENEH, se´-nay
crag, thorn — 1Sa 14:4

SENIR, se´-nir
coat of mail — 1Ch 5:23

SENNACHERIB, sen-ak´-er-ib
Sin (the moon) multiplies brethren — 2Ki 18:13

SENUAH, se-noo´-ah
bristling (?) — Ne 11:9

SEORIM, se-or´-im
barley — 1Ch 24:8

SEPHAR, se´-far
a numbering — Ge 10:30

SEPHARAD, sef´-a-rad
1 *a descending book* (?),
2 *counting down* — Ob 20

SEPHARVAIM, se´-far-va´-im
twin Sipparas — 2Ki 17:24

SERAH, se´-rah
abundance — Ge 46:17

SERAIAH, ser-ai´-ah
soldier of Jehovah (?) — 2Sa 8:17

SERAPHIMS, ser´-af-ims
burning ones — Isa 6:2

SERED, se´-rad
fear — Ge 46:14

SERGIUS, sur´-ji-us
a Roman governor of Cyprus — Ac 13:17

SERUG, se´-roog
shoot — Ge 11:20

SETH, seth
substitute — Ge 4:25

SETHUR, se´-thoor
hidden — Nu 13:13

SHAALABBIN, sha´-al-ab´-in
earths of foxes — Jos 19:42

SHAALBIM, sha-alb´-im
same as SHAALABBIN — Jgs 1:35

SHAALBONITE, sha-alb´-on-ite
inhabitant of Shaalbim — 2Sa 23:32

SHAAPH, sha´-af
anger (?) — 1Ch 2:47

SHAARAIM, sha´-ar-a´-im
two gates — 1Sa 17:52

SHAASHGAZ, sha-ash´-gaz
beauty's servant (?) — Est 2:14

SHABBETHAI, shab´-eth-a´-i
born on the sabbath — Ezr 10:15

SHACHIA, sha´-ki-ah
lustful — 1Ch 8:10

SHADRACH, shad´-rak
decree of the moon-god (?) — Da 1:7

SHAGE, sha´-ge
wanderer — 1Ch 11:34

SHAHARAIM, sha´-har-a´-im
two dawns — 1Ch 8:8

SHAHAZIMAH, sha-haz´-i-mah
lofty places — Jos 19:22

SHALEM, sha´-lem
safe, perfect — Ge 33:18

SHALIM, sha´-lim
foxes — 1Sa 9:4

SHALISHA, sha´-lish-ah
a third part — 1Sa 9:4

SHALLECHETH, shal-e´-keth
felling — 1Ch 26:16

SHALLUM, shal´-oom
retribution — 2Ki 15:10

SHALLUN, shal´-oon
spoliation — Ne 3:15

SHALMAI, shal´-ma-i
peaceful (?) — Ezr 2:46

SHALMAN, shal´-man
short for SHALMANESER — Hos 10:14

SHALMANESER, shal´-man-e´-zer
be propitious 2Ki 17:3

SHAMA, sha´-mah
obedient 1Ch 11:44

SHAMARIAH, sha´-mar-i´-ah
whom Jehovah guards 2Ch 11:19

SHAMED, sha´-med
destroyer 1Ch 8:12

SHAMER, sha´-mer
keeper 1Ch 6:46

SHAMGAR, sham´-gar
destroyer (?) Jgs 3:31

SHAMHUTH, sham´-hooth
notoriety (?) 1Ch 27:8

SHAMIR, sha´-mir
a thorn 1Ch 24:24

SHAMMA, sham´-ah
desert 1Ch 7:37

SHAMMAH, sham´-ah
same as SHAMMA Ge 36:13

SHAMMAI, sham´-a-i
wasted 1Ch 2:28

SHAMMOTH, sham´-oth
deserts 1Ch 11:27

SHAMMUA, sham´-oo-ah
famous Nu 13:4

SHAMMUAH, sham´-oo-ah
same as SHAMMUA 2Sa 5:14

SHAMSHERAI, sham´-she-rai
conqueror 1Ch 8:26

SHAPHAM, sha´-fam
bald 1Ch 5:12

SHAPHAN, sha´-fan
coney 2Ki 22:3

SHAPHAT, sha´-fat
judge Nu 13:5

SHAPHER, sha´-fer
pleasantness Nu 33:23

SHARAI, shar´-a-i
free Ezr 10:40

SHARAIM, shar-a´-im
same as SHAARAIM Jos 15:36

SHARAR, shar´-ar
firm 2Sa 23:33

SHAREZER, shar-e´-zer
(God) protect the king 2Ki 19:37

SHARON, sha´-ron
plain 1Ch 27:29

SHARONITE, sha´-ron-ite
inhabitant of Sharon 1Ch 27:29

SHASHAI, shash-a´-i
pale Ezr 10:40

SHASHAK, sha´-shak
activity (?) 1Ch 8:14

SHAUL, sha´-ool
same as SAUL Ge 46:10

SHAULITES, sha´-ool-ites
family of Shaul Nu 26:13

SHAVEH, sha´-vah
plain Ge 14:17

SHAVEH KIRIATHAIM, sha´-vay kir-iath-a´-im
plain of Kiriathaim Ge 14:5

SHAVSHA, shav´-shah
same as SERAIAH 1Ch 18:16

SHEAL, she´-al
prayer Ezr 10:29

SHEALTIEL, she-al´-ti-el
I asked from God Ezr 3:2

SHEARIAH, she´-ar-i´-ah
gate of Jehovah 1Ch 8:38

SHEAR-JASHUB, she´-ar-ja´-shoob
the remnant shall return Isa 7:3

SHEBA, she´-bah
an oath 2Sa 20:1

SHEBAH, she´-bah
seven Ge 26:33

SHEBAM, she´-bam
fragrance Nu 32:3

SHEBANIAH, she´-ban-i´-ah
whom Jehovah hides 1Ch 15:24

SHEBARIM, she-bar´-im
breaches Jos 7:5

SHEBER, she´-ber
breaking 1Ch 2:48

SHEBNA, sheb´-nah
youth (?) 2Ki 18:18

SHEBUEL, she-boo´-el
captive of God 1Ch 23:16

SHECANIAH, she´-kan-i´-ah
same as SHECHANIAH 1Ch 24:11

SHECHANIAH, she´-kan-i´-ah
Jehovah dwells 1Ch 3:21

SHECHEM, she´-kem
back, shoulder Ge 34:2

SHECHEMITES, she´-kem-ites
inhabitants of Shechem Nu 26:31

SHEDEUR, she´-de-oor
giving forth of light Nu 1:5

SHEHARIAH, she-har-i´-ah
Jehovah seeks 1Ch 8:26

SHELAH, she´-lah
petition Ge 38:5

SHELANITES, she´-lan-ites
descendants of Shelah Nu 26:20

SHELEMIAH, she´-lem-i´-ah
whom Jehovah repays 1Ch 26:14

SHELEPH, she´-lef
drawing out Ge 10:26

SHELESH, she´-lesh
triad 1Ch 7:35

SHELOMI, she-lo´-mi
peaceful Nu 34:27

SHELOMITH, she-lo´-mith
peacefulness Le 24:11

SHELOMOTH, she-lo´-moth
same as SHELOMITH 1Ch 24:22

SHELUMIEL, she-loom´-i-el
friend of God Nu 1:6

SHEM, shem
name Ge 5:32

SHEMA, she´-mah
1 *echo* (?) Jos 15:26
2 *fame* 1Ch 2:43

SHEMAAH, she´-ma-ah
fame 1Ch 12:3

SHEMAIAH, she-mai´-ah
Jehovah has heard 1Ki 12:22

SHEMARIAH, she´-mar-i´-ah
Jehovah guards 1Ch 12:5

SHEMEBER, shem-e´-ber
soaring on high (?) Ge 14:2

SHEMER, she´-mer
guardian 1Ki 16:24

SHEMIDA, shem´-i-dah
fame of wisdom Nu 26:32

SHEMIDAH, shem´-i-dah
same as SHEMIDA 1Ch 7:19

SHEMIDAITES, shem-id´-a-ites
descendants of Shemida Nu 26:32

SHEMINITH, she-mi´-nith
eighth 1Ch 15:21

SHEMIRAMOTH, she-mi´-ram-oth
most high name 1Ch 15:18

SHEMUEL, she´-moo-el
same as SAMUEL Nu 34:20

SHEN, shen
tooth 1Sa 7:12

SHENAZAR, she-na´-zar
protect, O moon-god (?) 1Ch 3:18

SHENIR, she´-nir
same as SENIR Dt 3:9

SHEPHAM, she´-fam
nakedness Nu 34:10

SHEPHATHIAH, she´-fat-i´-ah
same as SHEPHATIAH 1Ch 9:8

SHEPHATIAH, she´-fat-i´-ah
whom Jehovah defends 2Sa 3:4

SHEPHI, she´-fi
baldness 1Ch 1:40

SHEPHO, she´-fo
same as SHEPHI Ge 36:23

SHEPHUPHAN, she´-foof-an
serpent (?) 1Ch 8:5

SHERAH, she´-rah
consanguinity 1Ch 7:24

SHEREBIAH, she´-reb-i´-ah
heat of Jehovah Ezr 8:18

SHERESH, she´-resh
root 1Ch 7:16

SHEREZER, sher-e´-zer
same as SHAREZER (?) Zec 7:2

SHESBAZZAR, shesh´-baz-zar
perhaps same as ZERUBBABEL Ezr 1:8

SHESHACH, she´-shak
same as BABEL Jer 25:26

SHESHAI, shesh´-a-i
clothed in white (?) Nu 13:22

SHESHAN, she´-shan
lily (?) 1Ch 2:31

SHETH, shayth
tumult Nu 24:17

SHETHAR, she´-thar
star Est 1:14

SHETHAR-BOZNAI, she´-thar-boz´-na´-i
bright star Ezr 5:3

SHEVA, she´-vah
vanity 2Sa 20:25

SHIBBOLETH, shib´-ol-eth
an ear of corn, or a flood Jgs 12:6

SHIBMAH, shib´-mah
fragrant Nu 32:38

SHICRON, shik´-ron
drunkenness Jos 15:11

SHIGGAION, shig-ga´-yon
a sorrowful song Ps 7:title

SHIGIONOTH, shig´-i-o´-noth
irregular Hab 3:1

SHIHON, shi´-hon
ruin Jos 19:19

SHIHOR, shi´-hor
black 1Ch 13:5

SHIHOR-LIBNATH, shi´-hor-lib´-nath
turbid stream of Libnath Jos 19:26

SHILHI, shil´-hi
darter 1Ki 22:42

SHILHIM, shil´-him
aqueducts Jos 15:32

SHILLEM, shil´-em
requital Ge 46:24

SHILOAH, shi-lo´-ah
outlet of water Isa 8:6

SHILOH, shi´-lo
rest Jos 18:1

SHILONI, shi´-lo-ni
inhabitant of Shiloh Ne 11:5

SHILONITE, shi´-lo-nite
same as SHILONI 1Ki 11:29

SHILSHAH, shil´-shah
triad 1Ch 7:37

SHIMEA, shim´-e-ah
famous 1Ch 3:5

SHIMEAH, shim´-e-ah
same as SHEMAAH 2Sa 13:3

SHIMEAM, shim´-e-am
same as SHIMEAH 1Ch 9:38

SHIMEATH, shim´-e-ath
rumor 2Ki 12:21

SHIMEATHITE, shi´-me-ath-ite
descendant of Shimeah 1Ch 2:55

SHIMEI, shim´-e-i
my fame Nu 3:18

SHIMEON, shim´-e-on
a hearkening Ezr 10:31

SHIMHI, shim´-hi
same as SHIMEI 1Ch 8:21

SHIMI, shim´-i
same as SHIMEI Ex 6:17

SHIMITES, shim´-ites
descendants of Shimei Nu 3:21

SHIMMA, shim´-ah
rumor 1Ch 2:13

SHIMON, shi´-mon
provision (?) 1Ch 4:20

SHIMRATH, shim´-rath
watchfulness 1Ch 8:21

SHIMRI, shim´-ri
watchful 1Ch 4:37

SHIMRITH, shim´-rith
vigilant 2Ch 24:26

SHIMROM, shim´-rome
same as SHIMRON 1Ch 7:1

SHIMRON, shim´-rone
watchful Ge 46:13

SHIMRONITES, shim´-ron-ites
descendants of Shimron Nu 26:24

SHIMSHAI, shim´-sha-i
sunny Ezr 4:8

SHINAB, shi´-nab
hostile (?) Ge 14:2

SHINAR, shi´-nar
same as BABYLON (?) Ge 10:10

SHIPHI, shi´-fi
abundant 1Ch 4:37

SHIPHMITE, shif´-mite
a native of Shephan 1Ch 27:27

SHIPHRAH, shif´-rah
beauty Ex 1:15

SHIPHTAN, shif´-tan
judicial Nu 34:24

SHISHA, shi´-shah
brightness 1Ki 4:3

SHISHAK, shi´-shak
illustrious 1Ki 11:40

SHITRAI, shit´-ra-i
official 1Ch 27:29

SHITTIM, shit´-im
acacias Nu 25:1

SHIZA, shi´-zah
cheerful (?) 1Ch 11:42

SHOA, sho´-ah
opulent Eze 23:23

SHOBAB, sho´-bab
apostate 2Sa 5:14

SHOBACH, sho´-bak
pouring 2Sa 10:16

SHOBAI, sho´-ba-i
bright (?) Ezr 2:42

SHOBAL, sho´-bal
stream Ge 36:20

SHOBEK, sho´-bek
forsaker Ne 10:24

SHOBI, sho´-bi
taking captive 2Sa 17:27

SHOCHO, sho´-ko
same as SHOCHOH 2Ch 28:18

SHOCHOH, sho´-ko
a hedge 1Sa 17:1

SHOCO, sho´-ko
same as SHOCHOH 2Ch 11:7

SHOHAM, sho´-ham
onyx 1Ch 24:27

SHOMER, sho´-mer
watchman 2Ki 12:21

SHOPHACH, sho´-fak
same as SHOBACH 1Ch 19:16

SHOPHAN, sho´-fan
baldness Nu 32:35

SHOSHANNIM, sho-shan´-nim
a musical instrument Ps 45:title

SHUA, shoo´-ah
wealth 1Ch 2:3

SHUAH, shoo´-ah
depression Ge 25:2

SHUAL, shoo´-al
jackal 1Ch 7:36

SHUBAEL, shoo´-ba-el
same as SHEBUEL (?) 1Ch 24:20

SHUHAM, shoo´-ham
pitman (?) Nu 26:42

SHUHAMITES, shoo´-ham-ites
descendants of Shuham Nu 26:42

SHUHITE, shoo´-hite
a descendant of Shua Job 8:1

SHULAMITE, shoo´-lam-ite
same as SHELOMITH SS 6:13

SHUMATHITES, shoo´-math-ites
people of Shumah 1Ch 2:53

SHUNAMMITE, shoon´-am-ite
an inhabitant of Shunem 1Ki 1:3

SHUNEM, shoon´-em
two resting places Jos 19:18

T

Names

TIKVATH, tik´-vath
same as TIKVAH 2Ch 34:22
TILGATH-PILNESER, til´-gath-pil-ne´-zer
same as TIGLATH-PILESER 1Ch 5:6
TILON, ti´-lon
gift (?) 1Ch 4:20
TIMAEUS, ti-me´-us
polluted (?) Mk 10:46
TIMNA, tim´-nah
unapproachable Ge 36:12
TIMNAH, tim´-nah
a portion Jos 15:10
TIMNATH, tim´-nath
same as TIMNAH Ge 38:12
TIMNATH-HERES, tim´-nath-he´-res
portion of the sun Jgs 2:9
TIMNATH-SERAH, tim´-nath-se´-rah
portion of the remainder Jos 19:50
TIMNITE, tim´-nite
a man of Timna Jgs 15:6
TIMON, ti´-mon
deeming worthy Ac 6:5
TIMOTHEUS, tim-o´-the-us
same as TIMOTHY Ro 16:21
TIMOTHY, tim´-oth-y
honoring God 2Co 1:1
TIPHSAH, tif´-sah
passage 1Ki 4:24
TIRAS, ti´-ras
crushing (?) Ge 10:2
TIRATHITES, ti´-rath-ites
descendants of Tirah 1Ch 2:55
TIRHAKAH, tir´-ha-kah
distance (?) 2Ki 19:9
TIRHANAH, tir´-han-ah
murmuring (?) 1Ch 2:48
TIRIA, tir´-i-ah
fear 1Ch 4:16
TIRSHATHA, tir-sha´-thah
the feared (?) Ezr 2:63
TIRZAH, tir´-zah
pleasantness Nu 26:33
TISHBITE, tish´-bite
inhabitant of Tishbe 1Ki 17:1
TITUS, ti´-tus
protected 2Co 2:13
TOAH, to´-ah
low 1Ch 6:34
TOB, tobe
good Jgs 11:3
TOB-ADONIJAH, tob´-a-do-ni´-jah
good is my Lord Jehovah 2Ch 17:8

TOBIAH, tob-i´-ah
Jehovah is good Ezr 2:60
TOBIJAH, tob-i´-jah
same as TOBIAH 2Ch 17:8
TOCHEN, to´-ken
a measure 1Ch 4:32
TOGARMAH, to-gar´-mah
rugged Ge 10:3
TOHU, to´-hoo
same as TOAH 1Sa 1:1
TOI, to´-i
wanderer 2Sa 8:9
TOLA, to´-lah
worm Ge 46:13
TOLAD, to´-lad
birth 1Ch 4:29
TOLAITES, to´-la-ites
descendants of Tola Nu 26:23
TOPHEL, to´-fel
lime Dt 1:1
TOPHET, to´-fet
burning Isa 30:33
TOPHETH, to´-feth
same as TOPHET 2Ki 23:10
TORMAH, torm´-ah
privily Jgs 9:31
TOU, to´-oo
same as TOI 1Ch 18:9
TRACHONITIS, tra-ko-ni´-tis
rugged Lk 3:1
TROAS, tro´-as
a region around Troy Ac 16:8
TROPHIMUS, trof´-im-us
master of the house (?) Ac 20:4
TRYPHENA, tri-fe´-nah
delicate Ro 16:12
TRYPHOSA, tri-fo´-sah
delicate Ro 16:12
TUBAL, too´-bal
production (?) Ge 10:2
TUBAL-CAIN, too´-bal-kane´
producer of weapons (?) Ge 4:22
TYCHICUS, tik´-ik-us
fortuitous Ac 20:4
TYRANNUS, ti-ran´-us
tyrant Ac 19:9
TYRE, tire
rock Jos 19:29
TYRUS, ti´-rus
Latin name of TYRE Jer 25:22

U

UCAL, oo´-kal
I shall prevail Pr 30:1
UEL, oo´-el
will of God (?) Ezr 10:34

ULAI, oo´-la-i
a river in Babylon Da 8:2
ULAM, oo´-lam
foremost 1Ch 7:16
ULLA, ool´-ah
yoke 1Ch 7:39
UMMAH, oom´-ah
community Jos 19:30
UNNI, oon´-i
depressed 1Ch 15:18
UPHARSIN, oo-far´-sin
and dividers Da 5:25
UPHAZ, oo-faz´
an unknown location known for its gold Jer 10:9
UR, oor
light Ge 11:28
URBANE, ur´-ban
pleasant Ro 16:9
URI, oo´-ri
fiery Ex 31:2
URIAH, oo-ri´-ah
light of Jehovah 2Sa 11:3
URIAS, oo-ri´-as
Gr. for URIAH Mt 1:6
URIEL, oo´-ri-el
light of God 1Ch 6:24
URIJAH, oo´-ri-jah
same as URIAH 2Ki 16:10
URIM, oo´-rim
light Ex 28:30
UTHAI, ooth´-a-i
helpful 1Ch 9:4
UZ, ooz
fertile Ge 10:23
UZAI, ooz´-a-i
hoped for (?) Ne 3:25
UZAL, ooz´-al
wanderer Ge 10:27
UZZA, ooz´-ah
strength 2Ki 21:18
UZZAH, ooz´-ah
form of UZZA 2Sa 6:3
UZZEN-SHERAH, ooz-zen-she´-rah
1 *little ear,*
2 named for the daughter of EPHRAIM 1Ch 7:24
UZZI, ooz´-i
short for UZZIAH 1Ch 6:5
UZZIA, ooz-i´-ah
form of UZZIAH 1Ch 11:44
UZZIAH, ooz-i´-ah
might of Jehovah 2Ki 15:13
UZZIEL, ooz´-i-el
power of God Ex 6:18

UZZIELITES, ooz´-i-el-ites
descendants of Uzziel — Nu 3:27

V

VAJEZATHA, va´-je-za´-thah
strong as the wind (?) — Est 9:9

VANIAH, va-ni´-ah
distress (?) — Ezr 10:36

VASHNI, vash´-ni
strong (?), but perhaps not a proper name — 1Ch 6:28

VASHTI, vash´-ti
beautiful — Est 1:9

VOPHSI, vof´-si
expansion (?) — Nu 13:14

Z

ZAANAIM, za´-an-a´-im
wanderings (?) — Jgs 4:11

ZAANAN, za´-a-nan
place of flocks — Mic 1:11

ZAANANNIM, za´-a-nan´-im
same as ZAANAIM — Jos 19:33

ZAAVAN, za´-av-an
disturbed — Ge 36:27

ZABAD, za´-bad
gift — 1Ch 2:36

ZABBAI, zab´-a-i
humming — Ezr 10:28

ZABBUD, zab´-ood
given — Ezr 8:14

ZABDI, zab´-di
short for ZEBADIAH — Jos 7:1

ZABDIEL, zab´-di-el
the gift of God — 1Ch 27:2

ZABUD, za´-bood
same as ZABBUD — 1Ki 4:5

ZACCAI, zak-a´-i
pure — Ezr 2:9

ZACCHAEUS, zak-e´-us
Gr. for ZACCAI — Lk 19:2

ZACCHUR, zak´-oor
mindful — 1Ch 4:26

ZACCUR, zak´-oor
same as ZACCHUR — Nu 13:4

ZACHARIAH, zak´-ar-i´-ah
whom Jehovah remembers — 2Ki 14:29

ZACHARIAS, zak´-ar-i´-as
Gr. for ZACHARIAH — Mt 23:35

ZACHER, za´-ker
memorial — 1Ch 8:31

ZADOK, za´-dok
just — 2Sa 8:17

ZAHAM, za´-ham
loathing — 2Ch 11:19

ZAIR, za´-ir
small — 2Ki 8:21

ZALAPH, za´-laf
wound (?) — Ne 3:30

ZALMON, zal´-mon
shady — 2Sa 23:28

ZALMONAH, zal-mo´-nah
same as ZALMON — Nu 33:41

ZALMUNNA, zal-moon´-ah
shelter denied — Jgs 8:5

ZAMZUMMIMS, zam-zoom´-ims
murmurmers — Dt 2:20

ZANOAH, za-no´-ah
marsh — Jos 15:34

ZAPHNATH-PAANEAH, zaf´-nath-pa´-a-ne´-ah
prince of the life of the age — Ge 41:45

ZAPHON, za´-fon
north — Jos 13:27

ZARA, za´-rah
Gr. for ZARAH — Mt 1:3

ZARAH, za´-rah
sunrise (?) — Ge 38:30

ZAREAH, za´-re-ah
hornet — Ne 11:29

ZAREATHITES, za´-re-ath-ites
inhabitants of Zareah — 1Ch 2:53

ZARED, za´-red
exuberant growth — Nu 21:12

ZAREPHATH, zar´-ef-ath
smelting furnace — 1Ki 17:9

ZARETAN, za´-ret-an
same as ZARTHAN — Jos 3:16

ZARETH-SHAHAR, za´-reth-sha´-har
the splendor of the morning — Jos 13:19

ZARHITES, zar´-hites
descendants of Zerah — Nu 26:13

ZARTANAH, zar´-ta-nah
same as ZARTHAN — 1Ki 4:12

ZARTHAN, zar´-than
same as ZARETAN — 1Ki 7:46

ZATTHU, zat´-thoo
same as ZATTU — Ne 10:14

ZATTU, zat´-oo
irascible (?) — Ezr 2:8

ZAVAN, za´-van
same as ZAAVAN — 1Ch 1:42

ZAZA, za´-zah
movement, abundance — 1Ch 2:33

ZEBADIAH, zeb´-ad-i´-ah
Jehovah hath given — 1Ch 8:15

ZEBAH, ze´-bah
sacrifice — Jgs 8:5

ZEBAIM, ze-ba´-im
same as ZEBOIM — Ezr 2:57

ZEBEDEE, zeb´-ed-ee
Gr. for ZEBADIAH — Mt 4:21

ZEBINA, ze-bi´-nah
bought — Ezr 10:43

ZEBOIIM, ze-boy´-im
gazelles — Ge 14:2

ZEBOIM, ze-bo´-im
1 same as ZEBOIIM — Ge 10:19
2 *hyenas* — 1Sa 13:18

ZEBUDAH, ze-boo´-dah
given — 2Ki 23:36

ZEBUL, ze´-bool
same as ZEBULUN — Jgs 9:28

ZEBULONITE, ze´-bool-on-ite
descendants of Zebulun — Jgs 12:11

ZEBULUN, ze´-bool-oon
habitation, dwelling — Ge 30:20

ZEBULUNITES, ze´-bool-on-ites
same as ZEBULONITES — Nu 26:27

ZECHARIAH, zek´-ar-i´-ah
same as ZACHARIAH — 2Ch 24:20

ZEDAD, ze´-dad
hunting (?) — Nu 34:8

ZEDEKIAH, zed´-ek-i´-ah
justice of Jehovah — 1Ki 22:11

ZEEB, ze´-eb
wolf — Jgs 7:25

ZELAH, ze´-lah
side — Jos 18:28

ZELEK, ze´-lek
fissure — 2Sa 23:37

ZELOPHEHAD, ze-lo´-fe-had
fracture — Nu 26:33

ZELOTES, ze-lo´-tees
1 *an emulator,*
2 Gr. for CANAAN — Lk 6:15

ZELZAH, zel´-zah
shade in the heat — 1Sa 10:2

ZEMARAIM, zem´-ar-a´-im
two fleeces — Jos 18:22

ZEMARITE, zem´-ar-ite
descendants of Canaan — Ge 10:18

ZEMIRA, ze-mi´-rah
melody, a song — 1Ch 7:8

ZENAN, ze´-nan
same as ZAANAN — Jos 15:37

ZENAS, ze´-nas
gift of Zeus — Tit 3:13

ZEPHANIAH, zef´-an-i´-ah
whom Jehovah hid — 2Ki 25:18

ZEPHATH, ze´-fath
watch-tower (?) — Jgs 1:17

ZEPHATHAH, ze´-fath-ah
same as ZEPHATH — 2Ch 14:10

ZEPHI, ze´-fi
same as ZEPHATH — 1Ch 1:36

Names

ZEPHO, ze´-fo
form of ZEPHI Ge 36:11

ZEPHON, ze´-fon
a looking out Nu 26:15

ZEPHONITES, ze´-fon-ites
descendants of Zephon Nu 26:15

ZER, zer
flint (?) Jos 19:35

ZERAH, ze´-rah
dawn 2Ch 14:9

ZERAHIAH, zer´-ah-i´-ah
whom Jehovah caused to rise 1Ch 6:6

ZERED, ze´-red
same as ZARED Dt 2:13

ZEREDA, ze´-re-dah
cool 1Ki 11:26

ZEREDATHAH, ze-red´-ath-ah
same as ZEREDA 2Ch 4:17

ZERESH, ze´-resh
gold (?) Est 5:10

ZERETH, ze´-reth
fissure, brightness (?) 1Ch 4:7

ZERI, ze´-ri
same as IZRI 1Ch 25:3

ZEROR, ze´-ror
bundle 1Sa 9:1

ZERUAH, ze´-roo-ah
leprous 1Ki 11:26

ZERUBBABEL, ze-roob´-ab-el
scattered in Babylon Hag 1:1

ZERUIAH, ze´-roo-i´-ah
cleft, divided 1Sa 26:6

ZETHAM, ze´-tham
olive 1Ch 23:8

ZETHAN, ze´-than
same as ZETHAM 1Ch 7:10

ZIA, zi´-ah
motion 1Ch 5:13

ZIBA, zi´-bah
planter 2Sa 9:2

ZIBEON, zib´-e-on
dyed Ge 36:2

ZIBIA, zib´-i-ah
gazelle (?) 1Ch 8:9

ZIBIAH, zib´-i-ah
same as ZIBIA 2Ki 12:1

ZICHRI, zik´-ri
famous 2Ch 23:1

ZIDDIM, zid´-im
sides Jos 19:35

ZIDKIJAH, zid-ki´-jah
justice of Jehovah Ne 10:1

ZIDON, zi´-don
fishing Ge 49:13

ZIDONIANS, zi-done´-yans
inhabitants of Zidon Jgs 10:12

ZIF, zif
blossom 1Ki 6:1

ZIHA, zi´-hah
drought Ezr 2:43

ZIKLAG, zik´-lag
a city in southern Judah Jos 15:31

ZILLAH, zil´-ah
shade Ge 4:19

ZILPAH, zil´-pah
dropping Ge 29:24

ZILTHAI, zil´-tha´-i
shady 1Ch 8:20

ZIMMAH, zim´-ah
planning 1Ch 6:20

ZIMRAN, zim´-ran
celebrated Ge 25:2

ZIMRI, zim´-ri
same as ZIMBAN 1Ki 16:9

ZIN, zin
thorn Nu 13:21

ZINA, zi´-nah
abundance (?) 1Ch 23:10

ZION, zi´-on
sunny 2Sa 5:7

ZIOR, zi´-or
smallness Jos 15:54

ZIPH, zif
flowing 1Ch 4:16

ZIPHAH, zi´-fah
fem. of ZIPH 1Ch 4:16

ZIPHIM, zif´-im
inhabitants of Ziph Ps 54:title

ZIPHION, zif´-yon
same as ZEPHON Ge 46:16

ZIPHITES, zif´-ites
same as ZIPHIM 1Sa 23:19

ZIPHRON, zif´-ron
sweet smell Nu 34:9

ZIPPOR, zip´-or
bird Nu 22:2

ZIPPORAH, zip´-or-ah
fem. of ZIPPOR Ex 2:21

ZITHRI, zith´-ri
protection of Jehovah (?) Ex 6:22

ZIZ, ziz
a flower 2Ch 20:16

ZIZA, zi´-zah
abundance 1Ch 4:37

ZIZAH, zi´-zah
fullness 1Ch 23:11

ZOAN, zo´-an
low region Nu 13:22

ZOAR, zo´-ar
smallness Ge 13:10

ZOBA, zo´-bah
a plantation 2Sa 10:6

ZOBAH, zo´-bah
same as ZOBA 1Sa 14:47

ZOBEBAH, zo´-beb-ah
walking slowly 1Ch 4:8

ZOHAR, zo´-har
light Ge 23:8

ZOHELETH, zo-he´-leth
serpentstone 1Ki 1:9

ZOHETH, zo´-heth
strong (?) 1Ch 4:20

ZOPHAH, zo´-fah
a cruse (?) 1Ch 7:35

ZOPHAI, zo´-fa-i
honeycomb 1Ch 6:26

ZOPHAR, zo´-far
chatterer Job 2:11

ZOPHIM, zo´-fim
watchers Nu 23:14

ZORAH, zo´-rah
a place of hornets Jos 19:41

ZORATHITES, zo´-rath-ites
inhabitants of Zorah 1Ch 4:2

ZOREAH, zo´-re-ah
same as ZORAH Jos 15:33

ZORITES, zor´-ites
same as ZORATHITES 1Ch 2:54

ZOROBABEL, zo-rob´-ab-el
Gr. for ZERUBBABEL Mt 1:12

ZUAR, zoo´-ar
same as ZOAR Nu 1:8

ZUPH, zoof
flag, sedge 1Sa 1:1

ZUR, zoor
rock Nu 25:15

ZURIEL, zoor´-i-el
God is the Rock Nu 3:35

ZURISHADDAI, zoor´-i-shad-a´-i
whose Almighty is the Rock Nu 1:6

ZUZIMS, zoo´-zims
1 *beauty,*
2 perhaps same as
ZAMZUMMIMS Ge 14:5